THE CHURCHILL DOCUMENTS

Books by Martin Gilbert

The Churchill Biography

Volume I: *Youth, 1874–1900* by Randolph S. Churchill
The Churchill Documents, Volume 1, *Youth, 1874–1896*
The Churchill Documents, Volume 2, *Young Soldier, 1896–1901*
Volume II: *Young Statesman, 1900–1914* by Randolph S. Churchill
The Churchill Documents, Volume 3, *Early Years in Politics, 1901–1907*
The Churchill Documents, Volume 4, *Minister of the Crown, 1907–1911*
The Churchill Documents, Volume 5, *At the Admiralty, 1911–1914*
Volume III: *The Challenge of War, 1914–1916* by Martin Gilbert
The Churchill Documents, Volume 6, *At the Admiralty, July 1914–April 1915*
The Churchill Documents, Volume 7, *"The Escaped Scapegoat", May 1915–December 1916*
Volume IV: *World in Torment, 1917–1922* by Martin Gilbert
The Churchill Documents, Volume 8, *War and Aftermath, December 1916–June 1919*
The Churchill Documents, Volume 9, *Disruption and Chaos, July 1919–March 1921*
The Churchill Documents, Volume 10, *Conciliation and Reconstruction, April 1921–November 1922*
Volume V: *The Prophet of Truth, 1922–1939* by Martin Gilbert
The Churchill Documents, Volume 11, *The Exchequer Years, 1922–1929*
The Churchill Documents, Volume 12, *The Wilderness Years, 1929–1935*
The Churchill Documents, Volume 13, *The Coming of War, 1936–1939*
Volume VI: *Finest Hour, 1939–1941* by Martin Gilbert
The Churchill Documents, Volume 14, *At the Admiralty, September 1939–May 1940*
The Churchill Documents, Volume 15, *Never Surrender, May 1940–December 1940*
The Churchill Documents, Volume 16, *The Ever-Widening War, 1941*
Volume VII: *Road to Victory, 1941–1945* by Martin Gilbert
The Churchill Documents, Volume 17, *Testing Times, 1942*
Volume VIII: *Never Despair, 1945–1965* by Martin Gilbert

Other Books

The Appeasers (with Richard Gott)
The European Powers, 1900–1945
The Roots of Appeasement
Winston Churchill (Clarendon edition)
Sir Horace Rumbold: Portrait of a Diplomat
Churchill: A Photographic Portrait
Exile and Return: The Struggle for Jewish Statehood
Final Journey: The Fate of the Jews of Nazi Europe
Churchill: An Illustrated Biography
Auschwitz and the Allies
Churchill's Political Philosophy
Winston Churchill: The Wilderness Years
Jews of Hope: The Plight of Soviet Jewry Today
Jerusalem: Rebirth of a City
The Holocaust: The Jewish Tragedy
Shcharansky: Hero of Our Time
The Second World War
In Search of Churchill
The First World War
The Day the War Ended: VE Day 1945
Jerusalem in the Twentieth Century
The Boys: Triumph over Adversity
Holocaust Diary: Travelling in Search of the Past
Israel: A History

History of the Twentieth Century, Volume I
Empires in Conflict, 1900–1933
History of the Twentieth Century, Volume II
Descent into Barbarism, 1934–1951
History of the Twentieth Century, Volume III
Challenge to Civilization, 1952–1999
'Never Again': A History of the Holocaust
The Jewish Century: An Illustrated History
Letters to Auntie Fori: The 5,000 Year History
of the Jewish People and Their Faith
The Righteous: The Unsung Heroes of the Holocaust
Churchill at War in Photographs
Churchill's War Leadership:
Continue to Pester, Nag and Bite
D-Day
Churchill and America
Kristallnacht: Prelude to Destruction
The Will of the People: Churchill and
Parliamentary Democracy
Somme: Heroism and Horror in the First World War
Churchill and the Jews
The Story of Israel
In Ishmael's House: A History of Jews in Muslim Lands
Churchill: The Power of Words

Historical Atlases

Atlas of American History
Atlas of the Arab–Israel Conflict
Atlas of British Charities
Atlas of British History
Atlas of the First World War

Atlas of the Holocaust
Historical Atlas of Jerusalem
Atlas of Jewish History
Atlas of Russian History
Atlas of the Second World War

Children's Illustrated Bible Atlas

Editions of Documents

Britain and Germany Between the Wars
Plough My Own Furrow: The Life of Lord Allen of Hurtwood
Servant of India: Diaries of the Viceroy's Private Secretary, 1905–1910
Churchill: Great Lives Observed
Lloyd George: Great Lives Observed
Surviving the Holocaust: The Kovno Ghetto Diary of Avraham Tory
Winston Churchill and Emery Reves: Correspondence, 1937–1964

THE CHURCHILL DOCUMENTS

EDITORS
MARTIN GILBERT
AND
LARRY P. ARNN

VOLUME 22
LEADER OF THE OPPOSITION
AUGUST 1945 TO OCTOBER 1951

Hillsdale College Press, Hillsdale, Michigan

Hillsdale College Press
33 East College Street
Hillsdale, Michigan 49242
www.hillsdale.edu

© 2019 Hillsdale College
portions © C & T Publications Limited
All rights reserved.

Printed in the United States of America

Printed and bound by Thomson-Shore, Dexter, Michigan

Cover design adapted from Hesseltine & DeMason, Ann Arbor, Michigan

THE CHURCHILL DOCUMENTS
Volume 22: *Leader of the Opposition, August 1945 to October 1951*

Library of Congress Control Number: 2006934101
ISBN: 978-0-916308-40-7
First printing 2019

Contents

Note	ix
Preface *by Larry P. Arnn*	xi
Acknowledgments	xxxvii
Sources and Bibliography	xxxix
AUGUST 1945	1
SEPTEMBER 1945	52
OCTOBER 1945	90
NOVEMBER 1945	116
DECEMBER 1945	158
JANUARY 1946	173
FEBRUARY 1946	193
MARCH 1946	222
APRIL 1946	278
MAY 1946	308
JUNE 1946	365
JULY 1946	393
AUGUST 1946	427
SEPTEMBER 1946	456
OCTOBER 1946	470
NOVEMBER 1946	518
DECEMBER 1946	563
JANUARY 1947	593
FEBRUARY 1947	611
MARCH 1947	629
APRIL 1947	678

Contents

MAY 1947	694
JUNE 1947	728
JULY 1947	735
AUGUST 1947	749
SEPTEMBER 1947	773
OCTOBER 1947	791
NOVEMBER 1947	840
DECEMBER 1947	880
JANUARY 1948	917
FEBRUARY 1948	947
MARCH 1948	985
APRIL 1948	1002
MAY 1948	1033
JUNE 1948	1072
JULY 1948	1097
AUGUST 1948	1140
SEPTEMBER 1948	1158
OCTOBER 1948	1176
NOVEMBER 1948	1221
DECEMBER 1948	1263
JANUARY 1949	1292
FEBRUARY 1949	1312
MARCH 1949	1341
APRIL 1949	1375
MAY 1949	1402
JUNE 1949	1432
JULY 1949	1444
AUGUST 1949	1466
SEPTEMBER 1949	1482
OCTOBER 1949	1516
NOVEMBER 1949	1558
DECEMBER 1949	1579
JANUARY 1950	1589
FEBRUARY 1950	1615

Contents

MARCH 1950	1664
APRIL 1950	1714
MAY 1950	1740
JUNE 1950	1761
JULY 1950	1777
AUGUST 1950	1819
SEPTEMBER 1950	1849
OCTOBER 1950	1882
NOVEMBER 1950	1919
DECEMBER 1950	1958
JANUARY 1951	1984
FEBRUARY 1951	1996
MARCH 1951	2011
APRIL 1951	2028
MAY 1951	2060
JUNE 1951	2093
JULY 1951	2103
AUGUST 1951	2139
SEPTEMBER 1951	2147
OCTOBER 1951	2160

APPENDICES

A: Ministerial Appointments, October 1951	2233
B: Code Names	2235
C: Abbreviations	2236
D: Churchill's Travels, September 1945 to December 1951	2243

INDEX	2249

Note

Winston Churchill's personal papers are among the most comprehensive ever assembled relating to the life and times of one man. They are so extensive that it was only possible to include in the narrative volumes of his biography a part of the relevant documents.

The Companion volumes, now titled *The Churchill Documents*, were planned to run parallel with the narrative volumes, and with them to form a whole. When an extract or quotation appears in a narrative volume, the complete document appears in an accompanying volume of *The Churchill Documents*. Where space prevented the inclusion of a contemporary letter in the narrative volume, it is included in the document volume.

This volume contains transcriptions of over 1,500 documents, each of which we have formatted to the style that has prevailed in all these document volumes. That style includes these features:

- For verbatim diary transcriptions, we use in the heading the author's name at the time of writing, e.g. General Sir Alan Brooke, not Lord Alanbrooke. For "recollections" (memoirs, reflections, etc.), we use the name of the author as it was at the time of publication of the document, e.g. Lord Avon, not Anthony Eden, for his writings published after he was elevated to the peerage.
- We use italicized text in diary entries to denote text not original to the diary. For example, italicized text in Sir Alexander Cadogan's diary entries was written by David Dilks, editor of Cadogan's diary, and italicized text in General Sir Alan Brooke's diary entries was written by himself at leisure in the 1950s. Footnotes have been added at appropriate points to make this clear.
- Reflections and memoirs occasionally include lengthy quotes from a primary document. These quotations are displayed with a further left indent within the document to keep the two types of text distinct.
- Ellipses not bracketed are original to the document reproduced. Bracketed ellipses denote our decisions to omit text.
- For documents taken from published sources, publication details are given in the 'Sources and Bibliography' below. This also contains publication details for works cited in the footnotes. Unsourced quotations in footnotes are in each case taken from the same source as the document to which the footnote is appended.

Preface

INTRODUCTION

This is the twenty-second volume of documents published in the official biography of Sir Winston S. Churchill, and we expect it to be the penultimate document volume in the series. It begins with Churchill and his party's loss of the 1945 election and his first and only service as Leader of the Opposition. It ends with the Conservative victory in 1951 that made him Prime Minister for the second time.

As this volume opens, Churchill has reached his seventy-first year. The end of the war and his exclusion from executive office reduced the pace of his life sharply, evident in the fact that this volume covers more than six years, whereas several of the earlier volumes cover about that many months. The documents included here have been chosen from a wide variety of sources and according to criteria consistent throughout the project.

The Churchill of these years was older and slower, but still a dynamo. He produced 266 speeches and eleven new articles. He gave 100 speeches in the House of Commons. He traveled over 50,000 miles.[1] Without a war to fight or a government to lead, he turned his energies especially to leadership of his party and to writing. During these years he produced the first five volumes of his best-selling work, *The Second World War*. The sixth and final volume would be published in 1953.

RESTING

One of the first things Churchill did after the election was rest. At the beginning of September, he traveled to Lake Como with his daughter Sarah. He called it "one of the most pleasant and delectable places I have ever struck";[2] later, "the last word in modern millionairism."[3] There was an air of "complete tranquillity and good humour" pervading these "beautiful lakes and valleys, which are unravaged by war."[4] He enjoyed being guarded by his old Regiment, the 4th Hussars, of which he remained the Colonel-in-Chief.

---

[1] See Appendix D: Churchill's Travels, September 1945 to October 1951.
[2] Winston to Clementine, 3 Sep. 1945, reproduced below (p. 55).
[3] Winston to Clementine, 5 Sep. 1945, reproduced below (p. 58).
[4] Ibid., p. 59.

In 1915, after the reverses of the Dardanelles, Churchill had found solace in painting. He returned to it now after this new defeat. He would complete 15 canvases while in Italy. This was "great fun," and he was "very much relieved to find that I had got no worse through not painting for six years."[1]

This time of rest was not the kind of working holiday typical to Churchill. While he painted, dined, and slept, he mostly kept to himself. He wrote to his wife in a letter that he did not want publicity or to see any strangers. He felt no "keen desire" to turn the pages of the newspapers, of which normally he was an inveterate reader. He wrote to Clementine that he was "much better in myself, and . . . not worrying about anything." He felt a "great sense of relief" at the closing of the Japanese war and that others have "to face the hideous problems of the aftermath. . . . It may all indeed be 'a blessing in disguise'."[2] A few weeks later he would write:

> I found it very odd being turned out of power just at the moment when I imagined I would be able to reap where I had sown, and perhaps bring about some lasting settlement in this troubled world. However it may all be for the best as there is no doubt that a Conservative Government would have been very roughly treated by the Left-Wing elements, and strikes and labour troubles would have made our path one of extreme difficulty. I found it none too easy to change over so quickly from a life of intense activity and responsibility to one of leisure in which there is nothing to be looked for but anticlimax.[3]

One does not find many instances of Churchill grateful to be relieved of power. He was resting not only from the war, but from the nine years of turbulence and strain that preceded it. Since 1931 he had lived with the Great Depression and his own financial challenges. He had waged an almost futile opposition to the Imperial and appeasement policies that dominated Parliament. He had seen and feared the Nazi peril even before Hitler became Chancellor in 1933, and the years of his relentless advances had been anxious and politically lonely for Churchill. Then came the war with its terrors and glories. This release from some of the pressures of public office did not come in the happiest way for Churchill, but he received it willingly.

Churchill had always believed that he was a great man. These years in opposition would demonstrate that much of the world thought so too. Sarah wrote him from Lake Como that children not more than 12 and 13 years old recognized him. Churchill himself wrote to his wife that he was everywhere "clapped and cheered, pressed with demands for autographs and so on."[4] His secretary reported to him that he had received almost 8000 letters and gifts

---

[1] Churchill to Birley, 13 Oct. 1945, reproduced below (p. 101).
[2] Winston to Clementine, 5 Sep. 1945, reproduced below (p. 60).
[3] Churchill to Tudor, 18 Jan. 1946, reproduced below (p. 184).
[4] Winston to Clementine, 5 Sep. 1945, reproduced below (p. 58).

from many countries since the election, the vast majority positive.[1] The staff could not answer them all.

EXPLAINING THE ELECTION

Churchill pondered and repined the election while he rested. For a time, he feared that the result marked a crippling change in Britain. Canadian Prime Minister Mackenzie King reported that Churchill told him over lunch that the election had been the "greatest surprise to him and quite a blow." Conditions were going to be "pretty serious in England as a consequence of the policy of destroying the rich to equalize incomes of all."[2]

He wrote most gravely to his friend Alfred Duff Cooper that there were some "unpleasant features in the election which indicate the rise of bad elements." He continued:

> Conscientious objectors were preferred to candidates of real military achievement and service. All the Members of Parliament who had done most to hamper and obstruct the war were returned by enormously increased majorities. None of the values of two years before were preserved. . . . The soldiers voted with mirthful irresponsibility. The General here says that the shortage of cigarettes and some questions of leave were the deciding factors. Also, there is the latent antagonism of the rank and file for the Officer class, and of course the hopes raised by the Socialists that a vote for Labour would get them out of the Army more quickly.[3]

These doubts about the judgment of the British people were rare in Churchill, and he soon had another explanation more charitable or just to them. In May 1946 he said in the House of Commons:

> We have been blood donors throughout the whole of the long six years of war. We have been tried to the last scrap of our strength. Nothing has been grudged, effort after effort has been made, not only physical but psychical, and it was natural in the moment of victory, when suddenly danger was removed, that there should be not expansion but collapse. That is a very fair, detached, broadminded explanation of the last General Election.[4]

This became Churchill's settled account of the election. The British people had "borne the brunt."[5] The election came at the moment of release from the strain, and if they wanted to try an experiment, it was their right. Churchill came to view his defeat with the "detachment" that he mentions in

---
[1] Dorothy Spencer: memorandum, 9 Oct. 1945, reproduced below (pp. 94–5).
[2] King: diary, 26 Oct. 1945, reproduced below (p. 110).
[3] Churchill to Cooper, 17 Sep. 1945, reproduced below (p. 76).
[4] Churchill: speech, 31 May 1946, reproduced below (p. 361).
[5] Ibid.

the quotation above. With that returned his sense of the heroism of the British people and his faith in their ultimate good judgement.

LEADER OF THE OPPOSITION

Churchill was an unlikely Leader of the Conservative Party. He had entered Parliament in 1900 as a Conservative, but in 1904 he left for the Liberals. He switched back to the Conservatives on his 50th birthday, November 30, 1924, when he brought several dozen Liberal MPs with him in opposition to the first Liberal–Labour coalition. The Conservatives gave Churchill a safe seat, Epping, which he would represent until the end of his retirement from politics.[1]

There had been much bad feeling between him and the Conservatives for the 20 years that he remained in the Liberal Party, and there would be again during his "wilderness years" from 1929 until 1939. Even in 1940, after he became Prime Minister, he recorded that initially the "Conservative Party had treated me with some reserve, and it was from the Labour benches that I received the warmest welcome when I entered the House or rose on serious occasions. But now[2] all joined in solemn stentorian accord."[3] Churchill arrived at the Leadership of the Conservative Party by a circuitous and bumpy road.

Churchill assumed the party leadership in October 1940, five months after he had become Prime Minister. Clementine Churchill had expressed reservations about this, as in wartime he would need to be more a national and less a party figure.[4] That is how he functioned. He was careful of the feelings and interests of his coalition partners, especially those from the Labour Party, despite his fundamental differences with them. This caused eruptions from Conservative backbenchers even during the war.[5]

When Churchill became Leader of the Opposition, some on the Conservative benches rumbled against him. Leo Amery wrote in a letter to Lord Beaverbrook that there was "indirect criticism" of Churchill at a candidate meeting for being an "autocrat and, as such, only consulting a few personal friends"; also, that the Central Office had concentrated on the "Winston placard and had not sufficiently publicized other conservative leaders."[6]

James Stuart, the Tory Chief Whip, complained that "Our leader did not often grace us with his presence but remained a law unto himself, taking part

---

[1] In 1945, the name of the constituency was changed to Woodford.
[2] That is, on 4 July 1940, when Churchill delivered a speech about the imminent danger of invasion.
[3] Churchill: recollection, 4 Jul. 1940, reproduced in *The Churchill Documents*, vol. 15, *Never Surrender, May 1940–December 1940*, p. 475.
[4] Martin Gilbert, Martin. *Churchill: A Life*, pp. 679–80.
[5] See e.g. Gilbert, *Winston S. Churchill*, vol. 6, *Finest Hour, 1939–1941*, p. 331; War Cabinet: Confidential Annex, *The Churchill Documents*, vol. 19, *Fateful Questions, September 1943 to April 1944*, p. 519; Harvie-Watt to Churchill, *The Churchill Documents*, vol. 20, *Normandy and Beyond, May–December 1944*, p. 2237; Churchill to Stuart, *The Churchill Documents*, vol. 21, *The Shadows of Victory, January–July 1945*, pp. 488–9.
[6] Amery to Beaverbrook, 11 Oct. 1945, reproduced below (p. 98).

Preface

in such debates as he wished to."[1] We cannot know precisely how much time Churchill spent in the House as Leader of the Opposition. We do know that he delivered an average of eight pages of speeches in the House of Commons per month, plus about six pages more out-of-doors. This compares to about eleven pages per month in the House the last time he was in opposition from 1929 to 1931 and almost five pages out-of-doors. In those years he was not Leader, but he was a member of the Shadow Cabinet. The weight of Churchill's speeches shifted while he was Leader of the Opposition to speeches out-of-doors. He was a national and world leader now, and he had much to say to the nation and to the world.

These criticisms from the Conservative Party did not result in the open revolt common against party leaders who take an electoral whipping. Amery states the reason: "Naturally no one wished to say anything in disparagement of Winston's immense services or of his future leadership."[2] The Conservatives who might have been his rivals had formed a bond with him through a terrible war, and they were aware that the public regarded him as a hero. When Churchill was encouraged by the *Times* to resign from the leadership of the party and become an elder statesman above party, he replied: "I stay till the pub closes, and I fight for my corner."[3]

Still he had his doubts. He wrote to the Duke of Windsor that he was not certain he would continue: "The difficulties of leading the Opposition are very great and I increasingly wonder whether the game is worth the candle."[4] And to his cousin Clare Sheridan: "My own life is confused with petty trivialities and ceremonies, and one is astonished how little time one has when one has nothing to do."[5]

He stayed, he said, "only from a sense of duty and of not leaving friends when they are in a lurch."[6] At the Conservative Party conference in Blackpool on 5 October 1946, he said: "It would be easy for me to retire gracefully in an odour of civic freedoms, and this plan crossed my mind frequently some months ago." He did not, however, because he felt "the situation is so serious and what may have to come so grave, that I am resolved to go forward carrying the flag as long as I have the necessary strength and energy, and have your confidence."[7]

LEADERSHIP STRATEGY

As Leader, Churchill counseled patience to his party. The Socialists would not be quickly stopped nor Conservative policies quickly welcomed. He wrote:

---

[1] Quoted in Andrew Roberts, *Churchill: Walking With Destiny*, p. 889.
[2] Amery to Beaverbrook, 11 Oct. 1945, reproduced below (p. 98).
[3] Quoted in H. A. Grunwald, *Churchill: The Life Triumphant*.
[4] Churchill to Duke of Windsor, 15 Dec. 1945, reproduced below (p. 168).
[5] Churchill to Sheridan, 7 May 1946, reproduced below (p. 311).
[6] Churchill to Duke of Windsor, 15 Dec. 1945, reproduced below (p. 168).
[7] Churchill: speech, 5 Oct. 1946, reproduced below (p. 478).

We must expect several more years of Socialist rule, and no one can tell what the condition of the country or the Empire will be at the end of it. It would not be wise for us at this stage, so soon after a smashing defeat, to press forward trying to outbid our opponents, who will very soon land the country in a formidable financial disaster. Events shape our affairs far more than programmes; they are now shaping them in a grievous fashion.[1]

Utterly opposed to the socialist agenda, still he bowed to the verdict of the people. Churchill said several times that the fact that Labour got only 48 percent of the vote impeached the radicalism of its policies, but he blamed the Labour Party, not the people, and not the Constitution. "I do not complain at all," he said, "of the workings of our constitutional democratic system. If the majority of the people of Britain on the morrow of our survival and victory felt as they did, it was right that they should have their way."[2] Contrast this to many candidates today who call for amending or ignoring the Constitution when they lose.

Churchill counseled his party to use its likely extended time in the minority to reformulate its appeal, build its strength, and make its case against socialism. He said that "great Parties are called upon to play their part, not by frantic biddings for office, but by firm adherence to the broad and general principles which they profess, and by the march of events which is a hard but effective education." Time was on their side: "Socialist mismanagement" will make itself felt "at home and abroad." Then "we shall be conscious of an ever-growing measure of public support. . . . For that time and call we must be ready."[3] On 4 September 1951, a month before the election that would bring him back into power, he kept up the same strategy: "It is not so much a programme we require as a theme. We are concerned with the lighthouse not a shop window."[4]

AGREEMENTS

Churchill's task as leader was to oppose, but he did not think it his job to oppose on all occasions or upon all issues. On 7 November 1945, as Prime Minister Attlee was about to make a trip to the United States, he explained that there are boundaries to the competition in a debate in the House of Commons:

> Although we are divided in domestic affairs by a considerable and widening gulf, we earnestly desire that in our foreign relations we shall still speak

---

[1] Churchill to Garnock, 26 May 1946, reproduced below (p. 353).
[2] Churchill: speech, 5 Oct. 1946, reproduced below (p. 472). In the election of 1945, Labour received 47.7% of the vote, Conservatives 36.2 %, the rest to other parties. Labour won 393 seats, 61.4% of the total; the Conservatives 30.8%.
[3] Churchill: speech, 18 Apr. 1947, reproduced below (p. 684).
[4] Churchill to Eccles, 4 Sep. 1951, reproduced below (p. 2148).

as the great united British nation, the British Commonwealth and Empire, which strove through all the perils and havoc of the war, unconquered and unconquerable.[1]

Throughout the Labour administration this cooperation held in the largest respects. The Labour government was committed to Churchill's own approach in foreign policy after the war: the special relationship with the United States; the United Nations; united Europe and other regional alliances;[2] "containment" (as it came to be called); reliance upon the atomic bomb for "deterrence" (as it came to be called) against Soviet aggression. Churchill had differences of degree in foreign policy with the government, but few of principle.

Churchill often celebrated the fact that Ernest Bevin, Labour Foreign Minister, opposed the expansion of communism and of the Soviet Union. Unlike many in his party, Bevin had opposed appeasement in the 1930s, and Churchill came to think highly of his energy and good sense. Churchill helped to bring him into Parliament in 1940 in order to make him Minister of Labour and National Service, a powerful post that gave him extensive control over the labor force. When Bevin retired in 1951, Churchill said in a radio broadcast:

> Although I differed from him in his handling of many questions, I feel bound to put on record that he takes his place among the great Foreign Secretaries of our country, and that, in his steadfast resistance to Communist aggression, in his strengthening of our ties with the United States and his share of building up the Atlantic Pact, he has rendered services to Britain and to the cause of peace that will long be remembered. As his war-time leader I take this opportunity to pay my tribute to him and to his devoted wife.[3]

The relations between Churchill and his wartime Deputy Prime Minister, now Prime Minister Clement Attlee, were always courteous in private, and sometimes sharp but often warm in public debate. Attlee consulted Churchill frequently, especially on the question of the atomic bomb. They settled amicably the question of broadcast time among the parties on the BBC. The Labour Cabinet agreed readily that Churchill could use documents from the official archives for his war memoirs. Churchill was paid over $1 million by Henry Luce of *Time* magazine for the rights to the book, and there were other bidders almost as high. The Cabinet voted that it would not claim for the government any share in these revenues.

These were times of fundamental difference in politics, but their civility contrasts sharply with contemporary experience. For example, in January 1949, union leader George Gibson and Labour MP John Belcher were found

---

[1] Churchill: speech, 7 Nov. 1945, reproduced below (p. 119).
[2] Although Churchill complained several times that the Labour government was behindhand in its support for European unity.
[3] Churchill: speech, 17 Mar. 1951, reproduced below (p. 2014).

to have conspired to peddle government influence for personal gain. They both resigned from their positions, Belcher from both his ministerial post and his parliamentary seat. Both were affiliated with the Labour Party. Here was a chance to make political hay.

Churchill did the opposite. On February 3, he made a statement on the scandal. He was sympathetic with both Belcher and Gibson, the latter of whom he knew. He was glad they were not subject to criminal prosecution, even though the record showed they had done wrong. He went on to say that the Labour Party had vindicated its honor and that of the House of Commons in this matter. He had stern words only for the phenomenon of political corruption:

> There is a gulf fixed between private conduct and that of persons in an office, and above all, in a Ministerial position. The abuse or misuse for personal gain of the special powers and privileges which attach to office under the State is rightly deemed most culpable, and, quite apart from any question of prosecution under the law, is decisive in respect of Ministers.[1]

In dismissing the idea that this episode should reflect badly on the Labour Party, Churchill quoted from a 1936 speech given by Clement Attlee. At that time the Conservatives were in power, Attlee was Leader of the Opposition, and Conservative MPs were implicated in a similar scandal. Attlee had said that "the Debate today does not raise in any way at all a party issue."[2] As Attlee in 1936, so Churchill in 1949.

WORLD LEADER

This agreement with Labour on foreign policy helped Churchill to serve as what he had become: a world leader. Having led the only victorious ally to fight in the war from first to last,[3] and having spoken words heard around the world, he had the standing to advance a strategy for the post-war world. If he had been at odds on foreign policy with his government at home, it would have undercut his message. As it was, he had a government behind him, and yet he was not of that government. This placed him in an unusual position to be helpful.

The first and most important invitation to use his unusual position came soon after the election on 3 October 1946. It came from the President of Westminster College, Frank McCluer, who invited Churchill to Missouri to speak about "problems of international concern." Harry Truman added a postscript to the letter in his own hand: "This is a wonderful school in my home state.

---

[1] Churchill: speech, 3 Feb. 1949, reproduced below (p. 1316).
[2] Ibid.
[3] Excepting the Soviet Union, which switched sides.

Hope you can do it. I'll introduce you."[1] This letter arrived not three months after Churchill had nursed his wounds at Lake Como.

The form of this letter presented useful ambiguities on the American side to match those on the British. It was not an invitation from the President of the United States to the opposition leader of a major American ally: it came from a college president. Inviting a speaker to be part of an annual lecture series was regular college business. On the other hand, such letters are not often sent with a postscript from the President of the United States. This was obviously an occasion of the first political significance, but neither Truman nor Churchill was obliged to say so.

Churchill would extend this ambiguity in the speech itself. He began by making it "clear that I have no official mission or status of any kind, and that I speak for myself." That is true: Churchill had no power to commit the British government to anything, still less the American. But he continued: "there is nothing here but what you see."[2] What did the audience see? A photograph of the dais during Churchill's speech shows him at the podium, Harry Truman sitting in plain sight to his right. In other words, there was nothing there to see but Winston Churchill and the head of state and government of the United States of America.

Churchill had arrived at the White House on the day before the speech, March 4. He rode down by train to Missouri with President Truman, and they spoke at length. Churchill reported to the Cabinet in London that Truman read the speech on the way to Fulton and called it "admirable," and that it would "do nothing but good, though it would make a stir."[3] Truman made no such comments in public.

This speech encapsulates Churchill's thinking about war, strategy, and their relation to politics. It sounds themes that had recurred in his speeches for decades, and it develops them into a general plan for the situation after World War II. His foreign policy would follow these themes for the rest of his career.

Commonly known as the "Iron Curtain speech," the title Churchill gave it was "The Sinews of Peace." In it he proposed a structure to hold the world in peace. The threats, he said, are the "two giant marauders, war and tyranny."[4] He called for a global and united effort to confront these marauders.

The most famous thing from the speech is its criticism of the Soviet Union: "From Stettin in the Baltic to Trieste in the Adriatic, an iron curtain has descended across the Continent."[5] This was not the first time that Churchill had used the vivid phrase "iron curtain," but by its use here it passed into the

---

[1] McCluer to Churchill, 3 Oct. 1945, reproduced below (pp. 90–1).
[2] Churchill: speech, 5 Mar. 1946, reproduced below (p. 227).
[3] Churchill to Attlee and Bevin, 7 Mar. 1946, reproduced below (p. 241).
[4] Churchill: speech, 5 Mar. 1946, reproduced below (p. 228).
[5] Ibid., p. 232.

parlance of international affairs. From it proceeded the international outcry against the speech, including from Stalin himself.[1] It became the most famous thing in the speech because it addressed the most urgent thing in the world situation. But most of the speech concerns what to do about that thing both in the immediate and in the long term.

Of the Soviets Churchill said, "There is nothing they admire so much as strength, and there is nothing for which they have less respect than for weakness, especially military weakness."[2] The Soviet military was potentially overwhelming against the forces that could be brought against it in Europe for the foreseeable future, even if the United States were to become involved. The obvious offset against that power was the atomic bomb. Churchill would keep that safeguard in place and not, for example, give its secrets to the United Nations: "It would be criminal madness to cast it adrift in the still agitated and un-united world." Also: "No one in any country has slept less well in their beds because this knowledge and the method and the raw materials to apply it, are at present largely retained in American hands. I do not believe we should all have slept so soundly had the positions been reversed and if some Communist or neo-Fascist State monopolized for the time being these dread agencies."[3]

In other words, it matters very much what *kind* of nation or nations dominate. Throughout the speech, Churchill called for world unity, but he sought to build that unity upon an alliance of the freedom-loving countries. They "must never cease to proclaim in fearless tones the great principles of freedom and the rights of man which are the joint inheritance of the English-speaking world and which through Magna Carta, the Bill of Rights, the Habeas Corpus, trial by jury, and the English common law find their most famous expression in the American Declaration of Independence."[4]

If the atomic bomb was the necessary condition of security, it was not sufficient. Eventually other powers less benign would achieve it. Churchill proposed a more durable solution, more important than any single weapon: a coalition of nations, as many as possible, to unite against aggression and tyranny. He favored such coalitions for most of his life. The title of volume three of his *The Second World War* is "The Grand Alliance." It was this alliance that made possible the victory in that greatest of wars.

This phrase points to what Churchill regarded as the key alliance and the key to all alliances: the "special relationship" between the British Empire and Commonwealth and the United States. This is the alliance of the "English-speaking peoples," peoples who can talk directly with each other, a community bound by its commitment to liberty. This, he said, was the "crux of what I have travelled here to say." This alliance was, Churchill argued, not only

---

[1] See Stalin: interview, 14 Mar. 1946, reproduced below (pp. 255–60).
[2] Churchill: speech, 5 Mar. 1946, reproduced below (p. 234).
[3] Ibid., p. 229.
[4] Ibid., pp. 229–30.

compatible with the United Nations, but "probably the only means by which that organization will achieve its full stature and strength."[1]

Churchill had made plain the priority of the special relationship among alliances in a letter to Foreign Minister Ernest Bevin on 13 November 1945. The special relationship was vital because the two countries must "stand or fall together." He did not agree with the "characteristic Halifax slant that we should melt it all down into a vague United Nations Trusteeship." The special relationship if maintained would help produce more friendly and trustful relations with the Soviet Union and would also strengthen the United Nations. Churchill wrote that he was "a strong friend of the Russian people" and he adhered to the Twenty Years' Treaty with the Soviet government, for which he was "responsible."[2] In his mind, everything began with the special relationship that would unite not just the United States and Britain, but also the British Empire and Commonwealth.

The English-speaking peoples used the same words to describe vital things. Their famous documents meant that the people of any country have "the right, and should have the power by constitutional action, by free unfettered elections, with secret ballot, to choose or change the character or form of government under which they dwell." Freedom of speech and thought should reign. Courts of justice should be independent of the executive, unbiased by any party. Laws should have received the broad assent of large majorities or be consecrated by time and custom. These are the "title deeds of freedom which should lie in every cottage home. Here is the message of the British and American peoples to mankind. Let us preach what we practise – let us practise what we preach."[3]

Churchill had spoken in these terms countless times, notably on 4 July 1918, American Independence Day, when the First World War was near its end. He spoke in honor of the Declaration of Independence under the title "The Third Great Title Deed of Anglo-American Liberties."[4] Churchill had been building the special relationship for a long time.

Upon this special relationship would be built a system of world alliances, with the United Nations at the top. But the United Nations must not be a "cockpit in a Tower of Babel."[5] A cockpit is where roosters fight. The Tower of Babel is where God deprived the peoples of a common language to prevent them speaking with each other. Without speaking the same language, that is, sharing freely principles that have a common meaning, the UN would be a place for fighting. Churchill would soon believe it had become just that.[6]

[1] Ibid., p. 231.
[2] Churchill to Bevin, 13 Nov. 1945, reproduced below (pp. 133–4).
[3] Churchill: speech, 5 Mar. 1946, reproduced below (p. 230).
[4] Robert Rhodes James, *Winston S. Churchill, His Complete Speeches*, vol. 3, p. 2613.
[5] Churchill: speech, 5 Mar. 1946, reproduced below (p. 228).
[6] For example, see Churchill: speech, 28 Oct. 1948, reproduced below (p. 1209); speech of 26 Feb. 1949, reproduced below (p. 1336); speech of 31 Mar. 1949, reproduced below (p. 1369); and speech of 15 Jul. 1950, reproduced below (p. 1794).

Churchill also sought to foster regional groupings to prevent wars inside them and to assemble common force to resist aggression. He calls for a "new unity in Europe, from which no nation should be permanently outcast." The world wars have proceeded from the "strong parent races in Europe," and therefore we should work for "a grand pacification of Europe, within the structure of the United Nations and in accordance with its Charter."[1] Churchill would add definition to this idea in a speech in Zürich on 19 September 1946, in which he would call for "a kind of United States of Europe."[2] He became one of the fathers of the European Union.

It is worth noting that Churchill did not propose that Britain would be a member of the European Union, only that it should be associated and friendly. Nor did he propose that the European Union be a government properly so called. He made this plain on 10 December 1948 in the House of Commons:

> We are not seeking in the European movement ... to usurp the functions of Government. I have tried to make this plain again and again to the heads of the Government. We ask for a European assembly without executive power. We hope that sentiment and culture, the forgetting of old feuds, the lowering and melting down of barriers of all kinds between countries, the growing sense of being "a good European" – we hope that all these will be the final, eventual and irresistible solvents of the difficulties which now condemn Europe to misery. The structure of constitutions, the settlement of economic problems, the military aspects – these belong to governments. We do not trespass upon their sphere.[3]

Nor did Churchill forget that the first object of the government of Britain was to protect the people of Britain. On 24 July 1949, Churchill wrote to Attlee after a gloomy briefing on the defense situation in Europe. He complained of selling jet airplanes to the Western allies and to other countries. This was "giving away of our actual means of life." It compares "with the struggle about the twenty-five squadrons which the French demanded in 1940. That we steadfastly refused." He called on Attlee to ensure that, "from now on, every jet-plane we make will be sent at once to the British fighter squadrons."[4]

Attlee replied to this on September 6. He said that the defense of Britain and the Commonwealth in his view "depends on building up what you used to call 'The Grand Alliance'." Churchill's line was "short term and, so to speak, isolationist."[5] Attlee appealed to the global strategy that Churchill and Attlee developed together during the war.

---

[1] Churchill: speech, 5 Mar. 1946, reproduced below (p. 233).
[2] Churchill: speech, 19 Sep. 1946, reproduced below (p. 459).
[3] I owe my knowledge of this quotation, and other things, to Andrew Roberts, who cites it in *Churchill: Walking with Destiny*, p. 900. The full speech is reproduced below, pp. 1270–85.
[4] Churchill to Attlee, 24 Jul. 1949, reproduced below (p. 1464).
[5] Attlee to Churchill, 6 Sep. 1949, reproduced below (p. 1485).

Churchill wrote back a significant letter on September 22. He said that "the question is not between short-term and long-term policies, or between isolation and a Grand Alliance. It concerns the physical life of Britain as a unit. A defenceless Britain can play no part in the defence of Europe. Her power to help in the past has arisen from an integral, insular security. If this falls, all falls. If it endures, all may be defended or regained."[1]

As a world statesman, Churchill was building a world structure to deter the Soviet Union, prevent war generally, and provide for trade and prosperity to grow and spread. But he thought that his first obligation was to Britain and that its safety must not be sacrificed.

Churchill did however wish all of these alliances to have teeth. The Soviet military forces were and would be for years much stronger than those in Western Europe. A combination of powers was necessary for the long-term object of preventing war, as well as for the immediate object of deterring the Soviet Union. On 11 August 1950, Churchill spoke in favor of a European army:

> There must be created and in the shortest possible time, a real defensive front in Europe. Great Britain and the United States must send large forces to the Continent. France must again revive her famous army. We welcome our Italian comrades. All – Greece, Turkey, Holland, Belgium, Luxembourg, the Scandinavian States – must bear their share and do their best. Courage and unity must not consider what they can get but what they can give. Let that be our rivalry in these years that lie before us.[2]

The alliance must not only settle the quarrel between France and Germany, but it should welcome the free or western part of Germany to join the alliance. On 13 August 1950, Churchill wrote to Truman of the "unexpected and fortunate fact that the view of the German Delegation, who represent all parties in the German Government, is that Germany should send a contingent to the European Army (say of five or six divisions), but should not have a National Army of her own."[3] By this arrangement the French could feel safe and the Germans could make a necessary contribution to the defense of all.

It is worth noting that Churchill repeatedly called for better relations with Russia. Acknowledging that Britain might "develop strong differences on many aspects of policy," and even if these differences were "moral," he urged that no "state of mind must be allowed to occur in this country which ruptures or withers those great associations between our two peoples." He saluted the "grand, simple, enduring effort" of the Soviets, and he acknowledged her "tragic load of suffering."[4]

---

[1] Churchill to Attlee, 22 Sep. 1949, reproduced below (p. 1495).
[2] Churchill: speech, 11 Aug. 1950, reproduced below (p. 1830).
[3] Churchill to Truman, 13 Aug. 1950, reproduced below (p. 1834).
[4] Churchill: speech, 7 Nov. 1945, reproduced below (p. 120).

Still Churchill was no friend of communism, and he thought the Soviet Union the chief danger. He told Mackenzie King that the Russians were "grabbing one country after another – one Capital after another." The Russian regime, he continued, was "very difficult" but "there was nothing to be gained by not letting them know that we were not afraid of them." They were "'realist lizards', all belonging to the crocodile family." They would be "as pleasant with you as they could be, although prepared to destroy you." They were "hard realists, out for themselves."[1] "Communism," he continued, "is a religion." "They were using any means to gain an end without that end being the end of Christianity, of Christian purposes.... They were realists to the extreme."[2]

Churchill would approach them as realists. At Fulton he said that he did "not believe that Soviet Russia desires war. What they desire is the fruits of war and the indefinite expansion of their power and doctrines."[3] Confronted with a world coalition led by the United States and Great Britain, he believed there would be no war. Also, he assured the Soviets repeatedly of the good faith and good will of Britain and her allies.

Churchill developed this strategy throughout his years in the Opposition. Most of it became the foreign policy of Great Britain, for which he was glad and grateful to the Labour Government, and of the United States, which he believed decisive.

Step-by-step the international coalition that Churchill favored was formed. The United States announced the Marshall Plan in 1948, and Secretary of State George Marshall said the growing United Europe movement had encouraged the decision. This justified Churchill taking partial credit.[4] In April 1949, twenty-two nations signed the North Atlantic Treaty Organization pact to create a common defense structure between Western Europe and the United States. Churchill gave it his "cordial welcome."[5]

The Western powers worked out these connections under constant pressure of events. On 24 June 1948, the Soviet Union began to obstruct passage of troops, equipment, and eventually food from the western zones of Germany to Berlin in the eastern or Russian zone. This would continue for almost a year, and West Berlin was kept alive by a massive airlift of supplies. In support of the firm policy of Ernest Bevin, Churchill said that the Soviet action raised "issues as grave as those which we now know were at stake at Munich ten years ago."[6]

---

[1] Mackenzie King: diary, 26 Oct. 1945, reproduced below (p. 111).
[2] Ibid., p. 112.
[3] Churchill: speech, 5 Mar. 1946, reproduced below (p. 234).
[4] See Baruch to Churchill, 22 Jul. 1947, reproduced below (pp. 743–4).
[5] Churchill: speech, 12 May 1949, reproduced below (p. 1411).
[6] Churchill: speech, 26 Jun. 1948, reproduced below (p. 1088).

Preface

On 25 June 1950, North Korean communist forces invaded South Korea after a series of border clashes. Fighting continued until an armistice was signed on 27 July 1953. Churchill would inherit this war when he resumed the premiership in October 1951. Again, in opposition he gave strong support to the Labour Government. He denounced the Soviet buildup of an "empire far beyond the dreams of the Tsars."[1]

However, Churchill continued, this "new menace" did not increase the dangers facing the Western powers, although it differed "in principle from the Berlin blockade, two years ago, which together we faced with composure and overcame by the Allied airlift, mainly carried by American planes but in which we bore an important share."[2] It differed because the Soviets now knew how to make the atomic bomb. He feared that Soviet policy was to involve the United States and its allies in lengthy wars against Russian proxies, which would prevent sufficient reinforcement in Europe and would allow Russia to build up her nuclear arsenal.[3] As in World War II, Churchill saw Europe as the decisive theater and urged concentration there. He also saw, as he had from his service as a young soldier, how to and how not to fight wars far from one's home. Nonetheless, Britain under both Attlee and Churchill maintained significant forces in the Korean War in support of the United States and the United Nations.

As his time in the Opposition grew to a close, Churchill became more optimistic that the Soviet Union would not attack Western Europe. The "men in the Kremlin were frightened and were conscious of the growing strength of the West and the ever-increasing superiority of the USA in the field of atomic warfare." Therefore, he believed, "it was possible to do business with them." He sketched out the lines of the deal. The Soviets would "have to retire from the countries in Eastern Europe which they had wrongfully over-run, but we could guarantee the gains both in Europe and Far East which we had recognised during the war and we should give them access to more ports by instituting international control of the Baltic entrances and the Dardanelles."[4]

This is an early instance of Churchill's oft repeated wish to hold a summit with the Soviets and the Americans. He would persist in this idea until his retirement in 1955, but it was never to be.

DOMESTIC OPPOSITION TO SOCIALISM

Churchill's relations with Labour took on an entirely different aspect in domestic policy. He was a lifelong anti-socialist, and his arguments against socialism were direct, strong, and well-developed. Now he took them further.

---

[1] Churchill: speech, 4 Jul. 1950, reproduced below (p. 1779).
[2] Ibid., 1779–80.
[3] Churchill: speech, 30 Nov. 1950, reproduced below (p. 1954).
[4] Harvey: record of a conversation, 11 Sep. 1951, reproduced below (p. 2152).

He had the dubious advantage of watching socialist policies implemented for the first time on a wide scale, and he was incessant in calling attention to what he regarded as its failures.

He used some of his most enduring phrases to condemn the whole idea of socialism:

- "Socialism is the philosophy of failure, the creed of ignorance and the gospel of envy."[1]
- Speaking of a proposal from a junior Minister to introduce a penalty of up to seven years penal servitude for building a house without a license, Churchill said: "in its revolt against the unequal sharing of blessings it glories in the equal sharing of miseries."[2]
- Of socialist debasement of the currency, he said, "every cloud has a *nickel* lining."[3]
- Socialists thought it "much better that everyone should have half-rations rather than that anyone should have double."[4]

Socialist principles produced, Churchill argued, disastrous practical effects. Socialism interfered with production, and therefore it raised prices and perpetuated rationing.[5] It did not permit money to "fructify in the pockets of the people," a phrase he had been using for decades, and for that reason it undermined the independence of the British people.[6] He quoted Attlee that "less and less are we depending on the incentive of individual profit." Churchill replied, "but may this not be an explanation of the apathy, paralysis, and lack of good housekeeping which has overspread all our affairs, big and small alike?"[7]

Socialism required a "horde of officials" that multiplied expense and diminished the scope of action of ordinary people. The Labour Government maintained "rates of war-time taxation" in order to maintain "700,000 more officials, all hard-working decent men and women but producing nothing themselves." They have "settled down upon us to administer 25,000 regulations never enforced before in time of peace."[8]

Churchill illustrated this point with delight in commenting on the statement of Labour Minister Douglas Jay, who had said:

> "Housewives as a whole cannot be trusted to buy all the right things, where nutrition and health are concerned. This is really no more than an extension of the principle according to which the housewife herself would

---

[1] Churchill: speech, 28 May 1948, reproduced below (p. 1068).
[2] Churchill: speech, 29 Apr. 1946, reproduced below (p. 307).
[3] Churchill: speech, 5 Oct. 1946, reproduced below (p. 476).
[4] Churchill: speech, 28 Nov. 1945, reproduced below (p. 152).
[5] See Churchill: speech, 18 Jul. 1946, reproduced below (pp. 250–4).
[6] See instances reproduced below (pp. 305, 608, 723, 1152 and 2086).
[7] Churchill: speech, 16 Aug. 1947, reproduced below (p. 767).
[8] Churchill: speech, 14 Feb. 1948, reproduced below (p. 965).

not trust a child of four to select the week's purchases. For in the case of nutrition and health, just as in the case of education, the gentleman in Whitehall really does know better what is good for people than the people know themselves."[1]

Effectively, Jay argued that as the child is to the mother, so the mother is to the "gentleman in Whitehall." This became a political catchphrase, made so in part by Churchill's repetition of it. Was there ever, he asked rhetorically, "a period in the history of this island when such a piece of impertinence could have been spread about by a Minister?"[2]

In arguing that this horde of officials could never do the job it set out to do, Churchill deployed arguments from the Nobel prize-winning book *The Road to Serfdom*, published in 1944 by the Austrian economist F. A. Hayek. For example, he said:

> I do not believe in the capacity of the State to plan and enforce an active high-grade economic productivity upon its members or subjects. No matter how numerous are the committees they set up, or the ever-growing hordes of officials they employ, or the severity of the punishments they inflict or threaten, they cannot approach the high level of internal economic production which, under free enterprise . . . constitutes the life of a free society.[3]

These arguments were not new to Churchill. He had been tutored in them at least as early as 1899 by the American statesman Bourke Cockran. Cockran would say that in war both sides lose, but the "transactions of trade, like the quality of mercy, are twice blessed, and confer a benefit on both parties."[4] During his Fulton speech 47 years later, Churchill named and quoted Cockran, "a friend of mine," as having said: "There is enough for all. The earth is a generous mother; she will provide in plentiful abundance food for all her children if they will but cultivate her soil in justice and peace."[5]

Instead of socialist management of economic resources, Churchill called for a "property-owning democracy, both independent and interdependent." This would include "profit-sharing schemes in suitable industries and intimate consultation between employers and wage-earners. In fact we seek so far as possible to make the status of the wage-earner that of a partner rather than of an irresponsible employee." The wage-earner should have "many other alternatives open to him than service under one all-powerful employer called the State."[6]

---

[1] Churchill: speech, 9 Feb. 1950, reproduced below (pp. 1637–8).
[2] Ibid., 1638.
[3] Churchill: speech, 28 Oct. 1947, reproduced below (p. 823).
[4] Quoted in McMenamin and Zoller, *Becoming Winston Churchill*, p. 14.
[5] Churchill: speech, 5 Mar. 1946, reproduced below (p. 230).
[6] Churchill: speech, 5 Oct. 1946, reproduced below (p. 480).

Churchill did not repudiate every domestic policy of the Labour Government. He had been a leader in building the social safety net since the first decade of his career, and he sought to improve and expand it. In January 1950, he broadcast to the nation on "The Conservative Point of View." In a passage redolent of his speeches from his Liberal days, he said:

> The scheme of society for which Conservatives and National Liberals stand is the establishment and maintenance of a basic standard of life and labour below which a man or a woman, however old or weak, shall not be allowed to fall. The food they receive, the prices they have to pay for basic necessities, the homes they live in, their employment, must be the first care of the State, and must have priority over all other peace-time needs. Once we have made that standard secure we propose to set the nation free as quickly as possible from the controls and restrictions which now beset our daily life.[1]

Churchill's strategy was what it had ever been: the provision of a floor, not the imposition of a ceiling. He believed that this strategy had worked since it was first implemented under his leadership, along with David Lloyd George, in the Liberal Government before World War I. Except for the intervention of two world wars and the Great Depression, he believed it would have continued to work without interruption. He did not agree that the extension of the franchise to include all over age 21 had led, or need lead, to socialism. Believing this, he argued that the only emergency was the emergency created by the socialist government, and if that were removed, the nation would be restored.

He did not propose any wrenching reversal of socialist innovations. He would put a stop to the nationalizing of industries, the hiring of bureaucratic managers, and the making of excessive regulations, and then there would be a gradual but certain revival of freedom and prosperity. Of the nationalized industries, he promised to denationalize only steel, which was nationalized after the 1950 election when Parliament was evenly divided and when Labour, Churchill believed, had no mandate. Of the nationalization of mining, Churchill said "we shall not repeal" it. He continued:

> That is not because we do not think those measures are wrong and foolish, but because no one can undo the harm that has been done. It is easier to break crockery than to mend it. It would be physically impossible to find out all the shareholders or owners and sell their properties back to them, in a damaged condition in most cases.[2]

Similarly, Churchill rejected the state ownership of all the land, saying the land would be better distributed among "two or three million.... Even rabbits are allowed to have warrens, and foxes have earths."[3] Confronted with the fact

---

[1] Churchill: speech, 21 Jan. 1950, reproduced below (pp. 1594–5).
[2] Churchill: speech, 21 Apr. 1948, reproduced below (p. 1016).
[3] Winston to Randolph, 10 Aug. 1946, reproduced below (p. 446).

that he had previously in his career supported nationalization of the railways, he replied that he did not "see anything immoral in the nationalisation of the railways provided fair compensation is paid to the present owners." But he did not support it now because it had been tried. All it produced in four years was "a very bad service for the public, heavy loss to the shareholders, and the worst railway strike ever known except the one preceding the General Strike."[1]

The chief engine of social improvement was nonetheless to be, Churchill argued, the liberated efforts of the British people. He would free them from being "hustled and harried this way and that, first by nationalistic or imperialistic ambitions or appetites, now by ideological doctrines and hatreds." The Conservatives would be the "guardians of the ordinary, humble, hard-working people, not only here at home, but in many lands. It is so little that they ask – only to get their daily bread by the sweat of their brow and enjoy the simple pleasures of life which were meant for all and should be denied to none."[2]

Churchill took his objection to the Labour Government to the level of the constitution. In the course of this he reiterated and refined arguments that he had been making since his youth.

An occasion for this came in November 1947, when the Labour Government introduced amendments to the Parliament Act of 1911, which removed the power of the House of Lords to veto legislation passed through the Commons, but still permitted the Lords to delay bills for up to two years. In 1947 the House of Lords was still in Tory hands, and it delayed many measures of the Labour Government, which otherwise with its large majority in the Commons would have passed them quickly into law. Labour proposed a new Parliament Act to lower the maximum delay from two years to one. In introducing the measure, Clement Attlee called it "a wise precautionary measure." Churchill interrupted to call it "a deliberate act of socialist aggression." Attlee pointed out that Churchill had helped to create the original Parliament Act of 1911.[3]

On November 11, Churchill relished the opportunity to compare his thinking of 1911 with that of 1947. He said that he still supported the Act of 1911, and he "well believed" the "mass of the nation" supported it. In "the evening of life" this gave him "gratifying sensations." He looked back upon the day when he used to address the "fathers and grandfathers of those who sit opposite and who fell away from the Liberal and Radical theme and lolloped into the slatternly trough of collectivism."[4] Churchill was enjoying his seniority.

Counter-intuitively, Churchill associated the British Constitution with the American. The American is a written Constitution with definite separations of the branches of government, definite and distinct sources of authority from

---

[1] Churchill: speech, 12 Nov. 1946, reproduced below (p. 541).
[2] Churchill: speech, 23 Jan. 1948, reproduced below (p. 937).
[3] Debate on the Address, 21 Oct. 1947, Hansard, vol. 443.
[4] Churchill: speech, 11 Nov. 1947, reproduced below (p. 859).

the people, and definite instructions for their relations. The British is unwritten, evolved over centuries, and seems to unite the executive and legislative branches: the executive, headed by the Cabinet, is selected by Parliament and leads its majority party. The very fact that it is the Cabinet means that it commands a majority to pass and implement legislation.

Despite these obvious differences, Churchill saw the British as the source or model for the American Constitution.

Of the apparent unity of the executive and the legislative in Britain, he said: "Of course, there must be proper executive power to any government." Nonetheless "our British, our English idea . . . has always been a system of balanced rights and divided authority." The "Government of the day and the officials they employ" must consider "many other persons and organised bodies."[1] "Democracy is not a caucus, obtaining a fixed term of office by promises, and then doing what it likes with the people."[2]

Churchill continued that "the whole history of this country shows a British instinct – and, I think I may say, a genius – for the division of power. The American Constitution, with its checks and counterchecks, combined with its frequent appeals to the people, embodied much of the ancient wisdom of this island." This "essential British wisdom" is never "so necessary as in a country which has no written Constitution."[3] In other words, separation of powers is more necessary (if that can be) in Britain than in America.

Due to the nature of the House of Commons and the delaying power of the Lords, Churchill thought that no government of the day could simply implement its will over years. A bill favored by the government might have trouble getting through the Commons and would surely be subjected to examination and debate. Even if it passed the Commons, it could be delayed for up to two years by the Lords.

Neither Churchill nor the Parliament Act of 1911 had intended to abandon bicameralism, another method of separation of powers. The Preamble to the Parliament Act announced that the House of Commons intended to substitute for the House of Lords "a Second Chamber constituted on a popular instead of a hereditary basis."[4] Churchill had, in 1925, proposed constitutional legislation to do precisely that. In his plan the House of Commons would appoint members of the House of Lords for staggered terms from a field of prominent citizens. This new House of Lords would have the power of "referendum," that is the power to compel an appeal to a vote of the people on controversial measures.[5]

[1] Ibid., p. 861.
[2] Ibid., p. 860.
[3] Ibid., p. 861.
[4] Churchill: speech, 28 Oct. 1947, reproduced below (p. 833).
[5] Cabinet: memorandum, 17 Nov. 1925, reproduced in *The Churchill Documents*, vol. 11, *The Exchequer Years, 1922–1929*, p. 577.

Preface

With its powers of debate, of voting, and of electing the executive, the House of Commons was not in Churchill's view the creature of the government of the day, but the author and controller of that government. It guaranteed that government policy would be made in plain sight, which meant that the people, the ultimate authority, would be informed at every stage and therefore ready, when elections came, to make judgments. Together with the House of Lords, the House of Commons guaranteed that policy would be made deliberately, with proper consideration of all the principles and interests affected. They operated together as a check upon the government and a bridge between the government and the people.

Churchill saw the House of Commons especially as the "champion of the people against executive oppression." It has ever been, he said, the "controller and, if need be, the changer of the rulers of the day and of the Ministers appointed by the Crown. It stands forever against oligarchy and one-man power."[1] It occupies this powerful position because it is closest to the people.

At the same time the House of Commons itself does not have unlimited power. It must act with and through a Cabinet, which will have its own ideas. Also, the bills it passes must go through the House of Lords and might be delayed past the next election. The reconstituted House of Lords that Churchill favored, could veto legislation that passed the Commons or refer that legislation to the people.

Separation of powers was in Churchill's mind closely related to the more fundamental principle of representation. Churchill had fought the power of the House of Lords to veto legislation because it was a hereditary body, and no one may rightly rule another because of the superiority of his lineage. He repudiated a claim by Herbert Morrison, Leader of the House of Commons, that he, Churchill, was "not a good democrat in those days, and not a good democrat now." "Just let me explain it to him," Churchill said. He continued:

> We hold that there ought to be a constant relationship between the rulers and the people. Government of the people, by the people, for the people, still remains the sovereign definition of democracy.[2]

In Churchill's understanding, representation of the people was to be performed not only during elections, but continuously. The spirit of the 1911 Parliament Act was "to secure the intimate, effective and continuous influence of the will of the people upon the conduct and progress of their affairs."[3]

Churchill had argued in regard to the 1911 Parliament Act that, because parliaments lasted about four years, the delaying power of the House of Lords was significant and beneficial. In its first two years a Parliament typically passed the legislation over which the election had been fought. In the second

---
[1] Churchill: speech, 24 Oct. 1950, reproduced below (p. 1913).
[2] Churchill: speech, 11 Nov. 1947, reproduced below (pp. 860–1).
[3] Ibid., p. 860.

two years it passed chiefly legislation upon which there was consensus, but also legislation that raised new controversies. The purpose of the delaying power of the House of Lords was to provide a check, on behalf of the people. If the House of Lords delayed these new and controversial measures, then an election was likely to intervene to give the people a chance to vote upon them. In that way the people would almost always have a chance to decide for itself the fate of any controversial measure.

To Churchill, members of Parliament had no standing to legislate except the authority of the people. Agreeing with Clement Davis, Leader of the Liberals, Churchill said that MPs must not become "whole-time professional politicians in this House. We are very experienced politicians, but we are not professional politicians. . . . We are representative British worthies, chosen by universal suffrage, and long may it be so that the House is a good representation of the wishes, the feelings, the character, and the diversity of the nation at large."[1]

In Churchill's view, the British and American constitutions are extensively harmonious in operation and perfectly harmonious in purpose. One can say that the authoritative statement of the purpose of the American Constitution is to "secure the rights" of the people, a principle Churchill continuously endorsed. Government "of the people, by the people, and for the people" is Lincoln's parsing of the principles of the Declaration of Independence in his Gettysburg Address.

Churchill protested strenuously against the revision of the Parliament Act, a losing cause. But he gave another warning that this was another step on the road to serfdom:

> I firmly believe that the liberty and the free life of Britain are in great danger at the present time at the hands of the party opposite. I quite agree that they cannot do it all at once, but the first step upon the road on which they have started is the effective strangulation of Parliamentary Debate and the substitution for it of legislation by Government decree.[2]

In these years of opposition, Churchill used his long-held constitutional ideas to attempt to slow the pace of nationalization and other socialist innovations.

These and many points like it laid the ground for Churchill's political strategy: to persuade the people that socialism was ultimately the enemy of their rights. He appealed for popular support not only against the Labour Government and its policies, but against the central principle of socialism itself:

> It seems impossible to escape the fact that events are moving and will move

---

[1] Churchill: speech, 12 Apr. 1946, reproduced below (p. 292).
[2] Churchill: speech, 3 Mar. 1947, reproduced below (pp. 632–3).

towards the issue – "The People versus the Socialists". On the one hand will be the spirit of our people, organised and unorganised, the ancient, glorious, British people. . . . On the other side will be the Socialist doctrinaires with all their pervasive propaganda, with all their bitter class hatred, with all their love of tyrannising, with all their Party machinery, with all their hordes of officials and bureaucracy.

He continued: "There lies the impending shock, and we must be ready to meet it as a true People's Party."[1] Churchill had always styled himself a "Tory Democrat." He had always believed that political authority must rest upon the people. Now he called upon them to join him in turning the country decisively away from its new course.

To build a lasting majority, Churchill needed to unite the party. Soon after the election he addressed complaints at the 1922 Committee[2] with a fighting speech against socialism and in favor of the watchwords "Freedom and Empire." Max Aitken wrote to his father Lord Beaverbrook that Churchill "rose and knocked them all flat one after the other" with these arguments.[3]

As often before, Churchill sought to build a coalition of the center that reached across parties. He referred to it as the "Union Party" to signify its standing "for the union of the Kingdom and the Empire and the union of men of good will of all classes against tyrannical and subversive elements."[4] He got nowhere with the main body of the Liberal Party despite many appeals. He pointed out to Clement Davies that it was not the Conservatives but Labour who had destroyed the Liberals. "Four out of every five Liberal seats have been devoured by the Socialists."[5] He remained close to his old friend Violet Bonham Carter, born Violet Asquith, daughter of the Liberal Prime Minister. In an unsent letter, he criticized her and other "leading Liberals" for "complete indifference and detachment to the vital interest of our country."[6] On the other hand he offered her one of the Conservative slots for political broadcasts, the Liberals having been offered none. She turned him down with gratitude.

Conservative efforts began to bear fruit as the decade drew to a close. Polls showed Labour losing favor, and by-elections went for the Tories in larger numbers. In the 1950 election the Tories picked up 90 seats. Labour won the popular vote narrowly by 700,000 out of almost 30 million votes cast. Attlee again formed a government, but this one with a tiny majority that was doomed to a short life.

---

[1] Churchill: speech, 28 Nov. 1945, reproduced below (pp. 155–6).
[2] The committee formed of the Conservative backbench Members of Parliament.
[3] Aitken to Beaverbrook, 2 Nov. 1946, reproduced below (p. 521).
[4] Churchill: speech, 5 Oct. 1946, reproduced below (p. 479).
[5] Churchill to Davies, 25 Jan. 1950, reproduced below (p. 1603).
[6] Churchill to Bonham Carter, Not Sent, 13 Nov. 1945, reproduced below (p. 132).

In the 1951 election the Conservative vote increased by 4.6 percent and the party gained an additional twenty-three seats for a majority of twenty seats over all parties. Labour also increased its vote and still held a majority of the popular vote by 0.8 percent. Churchill was returned to power as Prime Minister for the second and final time.

PERSONAL LIFE

Churchill's personal life for the most part flourished during these years. He got his rest after the election, and he soon set about writing, leading the Opposition, and functioning as a world figure. He and Clementine bought a house in London at Hyde Park Gate that they would own until Churchill's death. Churchill continued to love Chartwell, his home in Kent. In April 1950, he wrote to Clementine the first "Chartwell Bulletin" in many years. These were long reports of life at Chartwell when Clemmie was away. In this one he reported on the weather, the waterfalls, the fish, the farms, the herds, and many other things he adored. He also reported on the winnings of his racehorse, Colonist II, and his prospects in the "Winston Churchill" stakes, where the horse would meet "the best horses in the world."[1]

Churchill was paid handsomely for his writing, and he reached a state of financial comfort previously unknown to him. *The Second World War* became a project involving many workers. Clementine juggled space at Hyde Park Gate for the detectives and researchers. She considered asking Charles Wood to work at home so the detectives would have a place to sit.[2]

In addition to his war memoirs, Churchill wrote eleven new articles during this period. Their titles include: "One Way to Stop a New War," "The New American Policy," "Mr Churchill on Labour Programme," "The Tasks Ahead," and "Peace Would be Safe in Our Hands."

Now a vastly experienced author, Churchill said in 1949 his most famous thing about writing: "Writing a book is an adventure. To begin with it is a toy, an amusement; then it becomes a mistress, and then a master, and then a tyrant, and then the last phase is that, just as one is about to be reconciled to one's servitude, one kills the monster."[3] I have met many authors who think this description superior.

He took holidays at Lakes Como and Geneva, and in Paris, Havana, Marrakech, Venice, and Madeira. He holidayed most frequently at two villas on the French Riviera: La Capponcina and La Pausa, which were owned respectively by his friends Lord Beaverbrook and Emery and Wendy Reves.

Churchill's son Randolph, now father to his grandson Winston, divorced in

---

[1] Winston to Clementine, 18 Apr. 1950, reproduced below (p. 1719).
[2] Clementine to Wood, Not Sent, 5 Apr. 1951, reproduced below (p. 2030).
[3] Churchill: speech, 2 Nov. 1949, reproduced below (p. 1558).

1946. Grieving for this, Churchill wrote to Lady Digby, mother of Randolph's first wife Pamela, that the divorce "put an end to so many of my hopes. . . . The war strode in however through the lives of millions." Now "everything must be erected upon the well being and happiness of the boy."[1] Churchill would take a hand in raising the boy. In February 1949, he encouraged him to "learn all you can about the history of the past, for how else can one even make a guess at what is going to happen in the future?"[2] Words by which Churchill himself had lived.

Churchill also intervened with Randolph to encourage him to settle all the "minor points" of his divorce and avoid going to court. He and Clementine had written a letter to Pamela stating their confidence in her guardianship of grandson Winston. He told Randolph that he had "no doubt we could help a great deal in the interpretation of any agreement between you and P, and you could count on our help in this."[3]

BACK TO POWER

As this is expected to be the penultimate document volume in the great biography of Winston Churchill, it is fitting that it records his penultimate public service. In the immediate past, he had achieved his lifelong purpose of becoming Prime Minister and of leading his country in a struggle for survival. In the immediate future, he would reach the premiership one more time and then retire in glory.

As Leader of the Opposition he was guided by the same stars he had followed from his first days in politics. He had faith "that the universe is ruled by a Supreme Being and in fulfilment of a sublime moral purpose, according to which all our actions are judged."[4]

He had made a career out of the slogan "trust the people." They disappointed him many times, especially in 1945, or perhaps one would say he disappointed them. In any case, he kept his faith in them and his conviction that political authority must flow from and not to them. In his favored dichotomy, he wanted the people to own the government and not the government the people.

He still believed that ordinary people could grasp and hold the great questions of life and politics. He still believed that there should be no experts appointed to dominate those subjects. He still believed that education should tap and nurture that capacity in everyone. "We need a lot of engineers in

---

[1] Churchill to Digby, 6 Jan. 1946, reproduced below (pp. 176–7).
[2] Winston to grandson Winston, 9 Feb. 1949, reproduced below (p. 1322).
[3] Winston to Randolph, 9 Feb. 1949, reproduced below (pp. 1322–3).
[4] Churchill: speech, 21 May 1948, reproduced below (p. 1059).

the modern world, but we do not want a world of modern engineers;"[1] and "engines were made for men, not men for engines."[2]

On 24 October 1950 the House resumed its debates in its ancient chamber, now rebuilt after its destruction by German bombs. By Churchill's own intervention it was restored to its same dimensions, not big enough to provide a place for everyone to sit. In that first debate in the restored chamber, he said that the world wonders

> that we should build a Chamber, starting afresh, which can seat only two-thirds of its Members. It is difficult to explain this to those who do not know our ways. They cannot easily be made to understand why we consider that the intensity, passion, intimacy, informality and spontaneity of our Debates constitute the personality of the House of Commons and endow it at once with its focus and its strength.[3]

Churchill still believed that the House of Commons was the "workshop of democracy."[4] He had said when the planning began for restoration of the House of Commons during the war that "we shape our buildings, and then they shape us."[5] Certainly Churchill had helped to shape that particular building, and it had shaped him in return. "I am a child," he said, "of the House of Commons and have been here . . . I believe longer than anyone. I was much upset when I was violently thrown out of my collective cradle. I certainly wanted to get back to it as soon as possible."[6]

In his years as Leader of the Opposition, he was back, and happy.

Larry P. Arnn
Hillsdale College
Hillsdale, Michigan
February 2019

---

[1] Churchill: speech, 12 May 1948, reproduced below (p. 1049).
[2] Churchill: speech, 26 Feb. 1946, reproduced below (p. 220).
[3] Churchill: speech, 24 Oct. 1950, reproduced below (p. 1912).
[4] Ibid., p. 1913.
[5] Rhodes James, *His Complete Speeches*, vol. 7, p. 6869.
[6] Churchill: speech, 24 Oct. 1950, reproduced below (p. 1912).

Acknowledgments

I am grateful to many students who have assisted in every part of the work. They are: Bryce Asberg, Guenevere Balmes, Luke Barbrick, Rachael Behr, Morgan Brownfield, Adrienne Carrier, Johnathon Case, Nathanael Cheng, Colleen Coleman, Emma Cummins, Connor Daniels, Juan Davalos, Katherine Davenport, Jessica De Gree, Madison Estell, Stephen Goniprow, Luke Grzywacz, John Hancock, Ross Hatley, Adelaide Holmes, Clifford Humphrey, Annalyssa Lee, Josiah Leinbach, Jennifer Matthes, Evyn Melanson, Kristiana Mork, Ryan Murphy, Taryn Murphy, Stevi Nichols, Zachary Palmer, Anthony Pestritto, Lillian Quinones, Zack Reynolds, Tess Skehan, Genevieve Suchyta, Thomas Tacoma, Joseph Toates, Tara Ung, Keith Vrotsos, Julia Wacker, Joshua Waechter, Jonathan Walker, Doyle Wang, Jacob Weaver, Dominic Whalen, Christian Yiu, and Daniel Ziegler. All of these young people are students, graduate students, or alumni of Hillsdale College. This volume would not be possible without the skill, care, and understanding they have brought to their work.

Judson Alphin, Ronald Cohen, Aaron Kilgore, and Jack Shannon have ably provided research assistance as they did also for previous volumes. This volume contains some documents excavated decades ago in the Public Record Office, Kew Gardens, by me and by an old friend and colleague, Christopher Flannery. Acknowledging him puts me in mind of those fine days and makes me grateful that our friendship continues.

Sheila Ryan compiled the index. Ann Hart proofread the manuscript. Jennifer Omner set the type. They are intelligent and hard-working people, and they have made the volume as free of mistakes as a human thing of this type can be.

The meticulous Gillian Somerscales, who has been working with us since volume 17, has copy-edited this document volume. She is skilled in her craft. Sir Martin Gilbert told me once that she was the most careful proofreader he knew, a high distinction.

My colleague Richard Langworth has helped to clarify the foggier episodes and references in the volume and to track down some of the more elusive documents. This kind of thing is one of his specific excellences.

Doug Jeffrey, the best editor I know, has improved this volume in many places.

Acknowledgments

The excellent Soren Geiger, soon to leave the college for a time to attend law school, has overseen this project with diligence and success since the work fell to us at Hillsdale College with volume 17. He hopes to practice law in the employ of the college, but if another massive task such as this comes up, he will be conscripted.

The following foundations and individuals gave generous support for the publication of this volume: the Lynde and Harry Bradley Foundation, Milwaukee, Wisconsin; the Earhart Foundation, Ann Arbor, Michigan; the late George B. Ferguson, Peoria, Arizona; Mr and Mrs William L. Grewcock, Omaha, Nebraska; Mr and Mrs Thomas N. Jordan, Jr, Healdsburg, California; Mr and Mrs Robert S. Pettengill, Brighton, Michigan; the late Tim M. Roudebush and Mrs Ruth Roudebush, Lenexa, Kansas; the Saul N. Silbert Charitable Trust, Sun City, Arizona; and Mr and Mrs Emil A. Voelz, Jr, Akron, Ohio. They leave their mark and legacy in this work, impossible without them. We are deeply grateful.

I thank all these people above with affection and gratitude. They are a marvel.

LARRY P. ARNN
Hillsdale College
Hillsdale, Michigan
February 2019

Sources and Bibliography

The principal archival collection used in the course of compiling this volume is the Churchill papers, now permanently housed at Churchill College, Cambridge. Access has also been granted to material in the National Archives (Cabinet and Premier papers). In addition, the following collections of private papers have been used: Lord Beaverbrook papers, Lorraine Bonar papers, Lord Camrose papers, Arthur Chater papers, Lord Chelwood papers, Randolph Churchill papers, Sir John Colville papers, Lord Derby papers, Government of Israel Archives, Sir James Hawkey papers, Hillsdale College Archives, Lady Lytton papers, Sir Edward Marsh papers, Lord Quickswood papers, Lady Soames papers, Baroness Spencer-Churchill papers, Marian Walker Spicer papers, Harry S Truman papers.

The authors, editors and compilers of the following published works, from which documents, recollections and other quotations have been drawn, are gratefully acknowledged.

Atlantic Advocate, February 1965.
Birkenhead, *Halifax, The Life of Lord Halifax*, London, 1965.
Alan Campbell-Johnson, *Mission with Mountbatten*, London, 1953.
Sarah Churchill, *Keep on Dancing, An Autobiography*, New York, 1981.
Henry Channon, *Chips, The Diaries of Sir Henry Channon*, ed. Robert Rhodes James, London, 1967.
Randolph S. Churchill (editor), *The Churchill Documents*, vol. 2, *Young Soldier 1896–1901*, ed. Randolph S. Churchill, Hillsdale, MI, 2006.
Winston S. Churchill, *Europe Unite, Speeches 1947 and 1948*, ed. Randolph S. Churchill, New York, 1950.
Winston S. Churchill, *Great Contemporaries*, London, 1937.
Winston S. Churchill, *Winston S. Churchill, His Complete Speeches, 1897–1963*, ed. Robert Rhodes James, volumes 3, 7 and 8, London and New York, 1974.
Winston S. Churchill, *In the Balance, Speeches 1949 and 1950*, ed. Randolph S. Churchill, London, 1951.
Winston S. Churchill, *My Early Life*, New York, 1930.
Winston S. Churchill, *The Sinews of Peace*, ed. Randolph S. Churchill, London, 1948.

Winston S. Churchill, *Stemming the Tide, Speeches 1951 and 1952*, London, 1953.
Sir John Colville, *The Fringes of Power, Downing Street Diaries 1939–1955*, London, 1985.
Daily Telegraph, London, 30, 31 December 1946.
Robert T. Elson, *The World of Time Inc., The Intimate History of a Publishing Enterprise, 1941–1960*, New York, 1985.
Finest Hour, No. 55, Spring 1987.
Foreign Relations of the United States, 1948, Western Europe, volume 3, Washington, DC, 1974.
Martin Gilbert, *Churchill, A Life*, London, 1991.
Martin Gilbert, *Winston S. Churchill*, vol. 6, *Finest Hour, 1939–1941*, London, 1983.
Martin Gilbert, *Winston S. Churchill*, vol. 8, *Never Despair, 1945–1965*, London, 1988.
Martin Gilbert (editor), *The Churchill Documents*, vol. 11, *The Exchequer Years, 1922–1929*, Hillsdale, MI, 2009.
Martin Gilbert (editor), *The Churchill Documents*, vol. 15, *Never Surrender, May 1940–December 1940*, Hillsdale, MI, 2011.
Martin Gilbert (editor), *The Churchill Documents*, vol. 16, *The Ever-Widening War, 1941*, Hillsdale, MI, 2011.
Martin Gilbert (editor), *The Churchill Documents*, vol. 17, *Testing Times, 1942*, Hillsdale, MI, 2014.
Martin Gilbert and Larry P. Arnn (editors), *The Churchill Documents*, vol. 18, *One Continent Redeemed, January–August 1943*, Hillsdale, MI, 2015.
Martin Gilbert and Larry P. Arnn (editors), *The Churchill Documents*, vol. 19, *Fateful Questions, September 1943 to April 1944*, Hillsdale, MI, 2017.
Martin Gilbert and Larry P. Arnn (editors), *The Churchill Documents*, vol. 20, *Normandy and Beyond, May–December 1944*, Hillsdale, MI, 2018.
Martin Gilbert and Larry P. Arnn (editors), *The Churchill Documents*, vol. 21, *The Shadows of Victory, January–July 1945*, Hillsdale, MI, 2018.
Martin Gilbert and James Courter (editors), *Proceedings of the International Churchill Societies 1987*, Chicago, 1989.
Walter Graebner, *My Dear Mr Churchill*, London, 1965.
H. A. Grunwald, *Churchill, The Life Triumphant*, Rockville, MD, 1965.
Hansard (House of Commons Debates), London, various years.
Hastings Ismay, *The Memoirs of General The Lord Ismay*, London, 1960.
William Mackenzie King, *The Mackenzie King Record*, ed. John Whitney Pickersgill, volumes 3, 4, Toronto, 1970.
Hughe Knatchbull-Hugessen, Diplomat in Peace and War, London, 1949.
Harold Macmillan, *Tides of Fortune, 1945–1955*, London, 1969.
Michael McMenamin and Curt Zoller, *Becoming Winston Churchill, The Untold Story of Young Winston and his American Mentor*, Greenwood, CT, 2007.

Sources and Bibliography

Lord Moran, *Winston Churchill, The Struggle for Survival, 1940–1965*, Boston, 1966.
Nigel Nicolson (editor), *Harold Nicolson, Diaries and Letters 1939–1945*, New York, 1967.
Pravda, Moscow, 14 March 1946.
Andrew Roberts, *Churchill, Walking with Destiny*, New York, 2018.
Mary Soames, *Clementine Churchill*, London, 1979.
The Times, London, various issues.
Time magazine, 24 December 1948.
Vital Speeches of the Day, vol. 17, no. 20, August 1951.
Peter Willett, *Makers of the Modern Thoroughbred*, London, 1984.
Harold Wilson, *A Prime Minister on Prime Ministers*, London, 1977.

August 1945

Lord Halifax: reflections
(Lord Birkenhead, 'Halifax', pages 551–2)

1 August 1945

[. . .]

The invasion of Europe took place on 6 June 1944 and the day of victory came at last on 8 May 1945 while the San Francisco Conference was still pursuing its contentious way. Towards the end of July the Ambassador[1] went on leave to England, and he was at sea when he heard the news of the Labour landslide in the General Election. He had often been irritated by the Prime Minister in the past but now he was only conscious of a profound sympathy for him at the moment of his fall:

'I think it must be a cruel and bitter blow for him, and quite apart from every public consideration I feel more sorry for him than I can say. For one would suppose that this must be the effective end of his political life, and of his power, which has been food and drink to him for the last four years. It remains a terrible act of ingratitude.'

And later, when the ship was still bearing him across the Atlantic, the fallen Titan came into his thoughts again and he expressed them in a homely and typical analogy:

'The more I think about Winston's downfall the more I personally commiserate with him. It is rather like being carried by your best hunter over very stiff country without a fall, and when you get home instead of taking him into a nice stable with a good mash and making him comfortable, giving him a clip on the backside and turning him into a field full of thistles.'

On his first day in England he lost no time in visiting Churchill:

'He didn't disguise that it was a bitter blow to him but was large minded

---

[1] Edward Frederick Lindley Wood, 1881–1959. Educated at Eton and Christ Church, Oxford. MP (Cons.) for Ripon, 1910–25. Parliamentary Under-Secretary of State for the Colonies, 1921–2. President of the Board of Education, 1922–4. Minister of Agriculture, 1924–5. Baron Irwin, 1925. Viceroy of India, 1926–31. President of the Board of Education, 1931–4. Succeeded his father as 3rd Viscount Halifax, 1934. Secretary of State for War, 1935. Lord Privy Seal, 1935–7. Lord President of the Council, 1937–8. Foreign Secretary, 1938–40. Ambassador in Washington, 1941–6. OM, 1946.

about it all. He said that it was almost impossible to believe that a week ago he had been at Potsdam; the measurement of time seemed to have no relevance. He had for five years had everything through his hands day and night, and it was hard to realize that this had suddenly evaporated.' Churchill asked Edward what his intentions now were, and he told him that subject to his new Labour masters he would carry on with the plan he had arranged with him of returning to America for six months, and on 7 August he met Ernest Bevin[1] the new Foreign Secretary, who asked him to continue his work in Washington until 1 May 1946:

'To see Bevin at the Foreign Office who was very nice impressed me very favourably. I should be surprised if he doesn't do very well at the Foreign Office. I got in a word about not frightening the Americans with rough language of what might be in mind to do here. He seemed to take the point very readily.'

Harold Nicolson:[2] diary
('Harold Nicolson, Diaries and Letters', page 479)

1 August 1945

Robin Maugham[3] rings me up. He had been round to No. 10 on 26th July. Winston was in magnificent form and took his defeat with humour. He confessed that it was distressing after all these years to abandon the reins of power. Someone said, 'But at least, sir, while you held the reins, you managed to win the race.' 'Yes,' said Winston, 'I won the race – and now they have warned me off the turf.'

Somebody mentioned that I had lost the seat at West Leicester. Robin remembered the actual words which Winston used and memorised them. 'The House,' he said, 'will be a sadder place without him' – then he paused, and added, 'and smaller'. This pleases me more than anything.

---

[1] Ernest Bevin, 1881–1951. National Organiser, Dockers' Union, 1910–21. General Secretary, Transport and General Workers' Union, 1921–40. Member of TUC General Council, 1925–40. MP (Lab.) for Central Wandsworth, 1940–50; for East Woolwich, 1950–1. Minister of Labour and National Service in Churchill's Coalition Government, 1940–5. Secretary of State for Foreign Affairs, 1945–51. Lord Privy Seal, 1951.

[2] Harold George Nicolson, 1886–1968. Educated at Wellington and Balliol College, Oxford. Entered FO, 1909; Counsellor, 1925. Served at Paris Peace Conference, 1919; Teheran, 1925–7; Berlin, 1927–9. On editorial staff of *Evening Standard*, 1930. MP (Nat. Lab.) for West Leicester, 1935–45. Parliamentary Secretary, Ministry of Information, 1940–1. A Governor of the BBC, 1941–6. Joined Labour Party, 1947. Knighted, 1953.

[3] Robert Cecil Romer Maugham, 1916–81. Known as 'Robin'. Joined Inns of Court Rgt as a Trooper, 1939. Commissioned into County of London Yeomanry, 1940. Wounded in the head in desert tank warfare; despatches. Barrister, Lincoln's Inn, 1944. Wrote over 30 books and plays. Succeeded his father as 2nd Viscount, 1958.

August 1945

Henry Channon:[1] diary
('Chips', page 409)

1 August 1945

I went to Westminster to see the new Parliament assemble, and never have I seen such a dreary lot of people. I took my place on the Opposition side, the Chamber was packed and uncomfortable, and there was an atmosphere of tenseness and even bitterness. Winston staged his entry well, and was given the most rousing cheer of his career, and the Conservatives sang 'For He's a Jolly Good Fellow'. Perhaps this was an error in taste, though the Socialists went one further and burst into the 'Red Flag' singing it lustily; I thought that Herbert Morrison[2] and one or two others looked uncomfortable. We then proceeded to elect Mr Speaker and Clifton-Brown[3] made an excellent impression. It is a good sign that the Labour Party have decided to elect a Conservative Speaker unanimously.

Marian Holmes:[4] diary
(Marian Walker Spicer papers)

1 August 1945

Working for the new PM[5] is very different. He calls us in only when he wants to dictate something. No conversation or pleasantries, wit or capricious

---

[1] Henry Channon, 1897–1958. Known as 'Chips'. American by birth. Educated privately, and at Christ Church, Oxford. Married, 1933, Lady Honor Guinness, elder daughter of 2nd Earl of Iveagh. MP (Cons.) for Southend-on-Sea, 1935–50; for Southend-on-Sea (West), 1950–8. Parliamentary Private Secretary to Under-Secretary of State for Foreign Affairs (R. A. Butler), 1938–41. Knighted, 1957.

[2] Herbert Stanley Morrison, 1888–1965. Began work as an errand boy at age 14. Secretary to London Labour Party, 1915–40. MP (Lab.) for South Hackney, 1923–4, 1929–31, 1935–59. Minister of Transport, 1929–31. Minister of Supply, May–Oct. 1940. Home Secretary and Minister of Home Security, 1940–5 (Member of the War Cabinet, 1942–5). Lord President of the Council (responsible for economic planning and co-ordination) and Leader of the House of Commons, 1945–51. Foreign Secretary, 1951. Life Peer, 1959.

[3] Douglas Clifton Brown, 1879–1958. Educated at Trinity College, Cambridge. MP (Cons.) for Hexham, 1918–51. Deputy Speaker of the House of Commons, 1938–43. PC, 1941. Speaker of the House of Commons, 1943–51. Viscount Ruffside, 1951.

[4] Marian Holmes, 1921–2001. Secretarial staff of 10 Downing Street, 1938–57. Part of a small group doing dictation work for Churchill, 1943. Married, 1957, Steve Walker; 1979, James Spicer.

[5] Clement Richard Attlee, 1883–1967. Educated at Haileybury and University College, Oxford. Called to the Bar, 1906. Tutor and Lecturer, London School of Economics, 1913–23. On active service, Gallipoli, Mesopotamia (wounded) and France, 1914–19; Maj., 1917. First Lab. Mayor of Stepney, 1919, 1920; Alderman, 1920–7. MP (Lab.) for Limehouse, 1922–50; for West Walthamstow, 1950–5. Parliamentary Private Secretary to Ramsay MacDonald, 1922–4. Under-Secretary of State for War, 1924. Chancellor of the Duchy of Lancaster, 1930–1. Postmaster-General, 1931. Deputy Leader of the Labour Party in the House of Commons, 1931–45. Leader of the Opposition, 1935–40. Lord Privy Seal, 1940–2. Deputy PM, 1942–5. Secretary of State for Dominion Affairs, 1942–3. Lord President of the Council, 1943–5. PM, 1945–51 (Minister of Defence, 1945–6). Leader of the Opposition, 1951–5. Earl, 1955.

behaviour. Just staccato orders. Perfectly polite and I'm sure he is a good Christian gentleman. But it is the difference between champagne and water.
[. . .]

Winston S. Churchill to Sir Alan Lascelles[1]
(Churchill papers, 1/386)

1 August 1945
Most Private

My dear Lascelles,

I wish you would tell The King[2] how very greatly I appreciated his kindness to me in offering to confer upon me the Garter, and in so graciously allowing it to be made public that I had asked leave to decline. For me, I felt that the times were too sad for honours or rewards, but I am very proud that it should be known that the Sovereign I have served with my utmost strength should have regarded my efforts with so much approval. After all, my great reward is the kindness and intimacy with which The King has treated me during these hard and perilous years which we have endured and enjoyed in common.

I ought to let you know that I do not think it will be possible for me to continue Lord Warden of the Cinque Ports.[3] I am examining the whole position now, but I am pretty sure that I could not afford to keep up Walmer or to live there. When The King gave it to me in 1941, there was a very flattering parallel to what His Majesty's predecessor had done for the Younger Pitt,[4] and, in view of the enormous danger in which the Realm and in particular the south coast stood at that moment, the Office was particularly appropriate to the Minister of Defence. The Castle has been requisitioned by the military during the War, and they have been responsible for it. I have always returned such revenues as it yielded to the Exchequer, and I have only been able to

---

[1] Alan Frederick Lascelles, 1887–1981. Known as 'Tommy'. On active service in France, 1914–18. Capt., 1916; MC. ADC to Lord Lloyd (then Governor of Bombay), 1919–20. Asst Private Secretary to Prince of Wales, 1920–9. Secretary to Governor-General of Canada, 1931–5. Asst Private Secretary to King George V, 1935; to King Edward VIII, 1936; to King George VI, 1936–43. Knighted, 1939. PC, 1943. Private Secretary to King George VI, 1943–52; to Queen Elizabeth II, 1952–3.

[2] Albert Frederick Arthur George, 1895–1952. Second son of King George V. Educated at Royal Naval Colleges, Osborne and Dartmouth. Lt RN, 1918. Succeeded his brother as King, Dec. 1936. Crowned (as George VI), May 1937.

[3] The post of Lord Warden of the Cinque Ports, formerly known as Keeper of the Coast, dates from at least the twelfth century. Originally, the position oversaw the Cinque Ports – Dover, Sandwich, Rye, New Romney, Hastings, Hythe and Winchelsea – which supplied ships to the monarch before the creation of the Royal Navy. It was one of the most powerful positions in England. Today, it is one of the highest ceremonial offices. Churchill was appointed to this position in 1941 but was not installed until 1946. He held the position until his death in 1965. The Standard of the Cinque Ports, which Churchill received at his appointment, still hangs in his former study at Chartwell.

[4] William Pitt the Younger, 1759–1806. Second son of William Pitt, 1st Earl of Chatham. PM, 1783–1801, 1804–6, during the French Revolutionary and Napoleonic wars.

visit it on one single occasion for an hour. Now however with peace, the very considerable expense of the upkeep of the Castle and gardens would have to be met, and, in addition, I should be involved in a local public life to which I have neither the time nor the strength to do justice.

This is only to let you know that I may very shortly be writing to The King upon this subject, and I hope His Majesty will not mind if I ask to be released.

I am so much obliged to you for entering so fully into the matters we discussed together on Monday. After the weekend I hope to have the List completed. I fully agree that Mr Attlee should be consulted upon my proposal to submit the names of the three Chiefs of Staff[1] for Peerages, and of a CH for Ismay.[2] On the other hand, had I held my Office for four or five days longer, as precedents would have justified, instead of giving it up at once to facilitate the Conference, I should have been able to make my Submissions myself. I will, if you think it advisable, write to Mr Attlee myself upon the subject of these four proposed honours.

PS. Your charming letter[3] has just arrived. I am very grateful.

---

[1] Alan Francis Brooke, 1883–1963. Entered Army, 1902. On active service, 1914–18 (DSO and bar, despatches six times). GOC-in-C, Anti-Aircraft Command, 1939. Commanded II Army Corps, BEF, 1939–40. Knighted, 1940. GOC-in-C, Home Forces, 1940–1. CIGS, 1941–6. FM, 1944. Baron, 1945. Viscount Alanbrooke, 1946. OM, 1946. Master Gunner, St James's Park, 1946–56. His brother Victor, a fellow subaltern and close friend of Churchill in 1895–6, died from exhaustion on the retreat from Mons in 1914. Churchill was also a good friend of Brooke's brother Ronnie, whose Asst Adjutant he was in South Africa for some months, and with whom he galloped into Ladysmith on the night of its liberation in 1900.

Andrew Browne Cunningham, 1883–1963. On active service, RN, 1914–18 (DSO and two bars). VAdm. Commanding Battle Cruiser Sqn, 1937–8. DCNS, 1938–9. Knighted, 1939. C-in-C, Mediterranean, 1939–42. Head of British Admiralty Delegation, Washington DC, 1942. Naval C-in-C, Expeditionary Force, North Africa, 1942. C-in-C, Mediterranean, 1943. Adm. of the Fleet, 1943. 1st Sea Lord and CNS, Oct. 1943 to 1946. Baron, 1945; Viscount, 1946. Published his memoirs, *A Sailor's Odyssey*, 1951.

Charles Frederick Algernon Portal, 1893–1971. Known as 'Peter'. On active service, 1914–18 (despatches, DSO and bar, MC). Seconded to RFC, 1915. Maj. commanding 16 Sqn, 1917. Air Ministry (Directorate of Operations and Intelligence), 1923. Commanded British forces in Aden, 1934–5. Instructor, Imperial Defence College, 1936–7. Director of Organization, Air Ministry, 1937–8. Air Member for Personnel, Air Council, 1939–40. AOC-in-C, Bomber Command, Apr.–Oct. 1940. Knighted, July 1940. CAS, Oct. 1940 to Nov. 1945. Baron, 1945. Viscount, 1946. OM, 1946. KG, 1946. Controller, Atomic Energy, Ministry of Supply, 1946–51. Chairman, British Aircraft Corp., 1960–8.

[2] Hastings Lionel Ismay, 1887–1965. Known as 'Pug'. Educated at Charterhouse and Sandhurst. 2nd Lt, 1905; Capt., 1914. On active service in India, 1908, and Somaliland, 1914–20 (DSO). Staff College, Quetta, 1922. Asst Secretary, Committee of Imperial Defence, 1925–30. Military Secretary to Viceroy of India (Lord Willingdon), 1931–3. Col., 1932. Deputy Secretary, Committee of Imperial Defence, 1936–8; Secretary, 1938. Maj.-Gen., 1939. CoS to Minister of Defence (Churchill), 1940–5. Knighted, 1940. Deputy Secretary (Military) to War Cabinet, 1940–5. Lt-Gen., 1942. Gen., 1944. CoS to Viceroy of India (Lord Mountbatten), 1947. Baron, 1947. Secretary of State for Commonwealth Relations, 1951–2. Secretary-General of NATO, 1952–7. KG, 1957. Published *The Memoirs of Gen. the Lord Ismay*, 1960.

[3] Of 30 July 1945, reproduced in *The Churchill Documents*, vol. 21, *The Shadows of Victory, January–July 1945*, pp. 2027–8.

August 1945

Clement Attlee to Winston S. Churchill
(Churchill papers, 2/140)

1 August 1945   Berlin

My dear Churchill,
   When the surrender of the Japanese has been finally confirmed it is my proposal to broadcast a short, factual statement to the country. The King has intimated that he would honour me and certain other members of the Government by receiving us about one hour after I have made my broadcast. Those who would accompany me are Mr Morrison, Mr Bevin, Mr Greenwood,[1] Mr Alexander,[2] the three Chiefs of Staff, Sir Edward Bridges[3] and General Ismay.
   I suggested to the King that it would be appropriate that you should also come at the same time if you felt willing to do so, and His Majesty has indicated that this course would be most agreeable to him. I hope you will come and, if so, I will arrange for you to be informed of the time the King will receive us.

Clement Attlee to Winston S. Churchill
(Churchill papers, 2/3)

1 August 1945   Berlin

My dear Churchill,
   The Conference is ending tonight in a good atmosphere. I would like to let you know the broad results before the communiqué is issued.
   We have, of course, been building on the foundation laid by you, and there has been no change of policy.
   It was clear, when the Conference was suspended that the vital points were Reparations and the Polish Western Frontier. On the former the Russians were very insistent on their pound of flesh. We were firm on the need for supplies of food etc. from the Eastern zone for the rest of Germany and on

---

[1] Arthur Greenwood, 1880–1954. Asst Secretary, Ministry of Reconstruction, 1917–19. MP (Lab.) for Nelson and Colne, 1922–31; for Wakefield, 1932–54. Parliamentary Secretary, Ministry of Health, 1924. Minister of Health, 1929–31. PC, 1929. Deputy Leader of Labour Party, 1935. Member of War Cabinet, as Minister without Portfolio, 1940–2. Leader of the Opposition in the House of Commons, 1942–5. Lord Privy Seal, 1945–7. Labour Party Chairman, 1952.

[2] Albert Victor Alexander, 1885–1965. Educated at an elementary school, and technical classes, in Bristol. MP (Lab./Co-op.) for Hillsborough, 1922–31, 1935–50. Parliamentary Secretary, Board of Trade, 1924. 1st Lord of the Admiralty in Ramsay MacDonald's second Labour Government, 1929–31; in Churchill's wartime Coalition Government, 1940–5; in Attlee's Labour Government, 1945–6. Member of Cabinet Delegation to India, 1946. Minister of Defence, 1947–50. Viscount, 1950. Chancellor of the Duchy of Lancaster, 1950–1. Leader of the Labour Peers in the House of Lords, 1955–65. Earl, 1963. KG, 1964.

[3] Edward Bridges, 1892–1969. Son of the Poet Laureate Robert Bridges. On active service, 1914–18 (MC). Treasury, 1919–39. Secretary to the Cabinet, 1938–46. Knighted, 1939. Permanent Secretary, Treasury, 1945–56. Baron, 1957. KG, 1965.

not allowing reparations to have precedence of maintaining a reasonable economy in Germany. On Poland the Russians insisted on the Western Neisse and eventually the Americans accepted this. We were, of course, powerless to prevent the course of events in the Russian zone. We have tied the Poles down as closely as we can with specific pledges on elections, press facilities and repatriation of fighting Poles. We therefore agreed on the Western Neisse as the western boundary of Polish administration pending the Peace Conference decisions. Other questions proved soluble when these major matters were disposed of.

Uncle Joe was not in a good mood at the start caused I think by an indisposition which kept him in bed for two days. Thereafter he was in good form. The President was very co-operative. My having been present from the start was a great advantage, but Bevin picked up all the points extremely quickly and showed his quality as an experienced negotiator in playing his hand. I think that the results achieved are not unsatisfactory having regard to the way the course of the war had dealt the cards. I hope you have been able to get some rest. If you would care to come and see me to hear more details I should be delighted.

I was most grateful to you for sending me the statement on TA[1] and I have sent it to the President with certain minor changes which I am sure you will agree do not affect its general sense. The President has just told me that they have no comments and I enclose herewith a copy of my covering statement and of your draft in the form in which I sent it to the President. The President told me that Uncle Joe had not cross-examined him at all on this matter.

PS. We have reached a satisfactory agreement on the German Fleet, especially on U-Boats. Of these all are to be sunk except 30 which are to be divided equally between the Three Powers for experimental and technical purposes.

Brigadier-General Lord Croft[2] to Winston S. Churchill
(Churchill papers, 2/560)

1 August 1945

My dear Winston,

I hardly like to add to what I know must be a vast number of letters you

---

[1] TA: 'Tube Alloys', British work on what would become the atomic bomb, which from late 1941 had involved British and Canadian scientists working in collaboration with counterparts in the US.
[2] Henry Page Croft, 1881–1947. Educated at Eton, Shrewsbury and Trinity Hall, Cambridge. MP (Cons.) for Christchurch, 1910–18; for Bournemouth, 1918–40. Served in WWI, 1914–16 (despatches); Brig.-Gen., 1916. Bt, 1924. One of the Vice-Presidents, with Churchill, of the India Defence League, 1933–5. Member of Speaker's Conference on the Franchise, 1918; Civil List Committee, 1936; Committee of Privileges, 1939. Baron, 1940. Parliamentary Under-Secretary of State for War, 1940–5. PC, 1945.

have received, but I feel I must tell you how deeply I sympathise with you on the events of last week.

No one who loves this country can ever forget what we owe to you for rallying the nation in 1940 when there was so much excuse for dread and despair amongst men of little faith, and your ceaseless inspiration from that day until victory was won.

As a very humble member of your team, I feel that perhaps – apart from victory – the greatest gift you gave to the nation was the lives of our sons, for there can be no doubt that the strategy which you inspired and for which you were so largely responsible saved hundreds of thousands of our fighting men who must have perished in these great achievements but for your most brilliant guidance.

God moves in a mysterious way, and I have a feeling that during the next two or three years the spirit of our people may be so greatly tried that your successors may find it impossible to retain the confidence of the nation.

I go further and say that even your great reputation as the deliverer of our country might have suffered grievously in the aftermath of weariness, vexation and irritation which overwhelms so many millions of thoughtless people today.

As it is you are on the crest of your glory and just as you saved this fickle moving mass, which makes up our democracy, in 1940, so again they may turn to you to save them from those who so basely deserted at the moment when all owed you a debt we can never repay.

I have been very proud to fight under your banner and send you my affectionate hope that we may be privileged to do so again.

Clement Attlee to Winston S. Churchill
(Churchill papers, 2/3)

2 August 1945
Confidential

My dear Churchill,

I have just got back to England after a good flight, and I am sending at once an advance copy of the communiqué which will be released to the Press tonight at 10.30 p.m. I have not yet available a copy of the Protocol, but I will send you this as soon as possible.

These two documents will give you the main decisions, but I feel that you would also wish to see the Minutes and papers of the later proceedings. If so, I shall be very pleased to send them to you as soon as they are in print. I think this would be more convenient to you than to have them in typed form.

August 1945

President Harry S Truman to Winston S. Churchill
(Churchill papers, 2/142)[1]

2 August 1945
The White House

My dear Churchill,

Thank you so much for the beautiful pen. I shall use it constantly and always think of you.

We missed you very much at the conference. Glad you liked the picture. Please send me one of yours. The best of everything to you.

PS. I just opened the other package – and the picture is there! Thanks again. I appreciate the sentiment very much.

Winston S. Churchill to Lord Melchett[2]
(Churchill papers, 2/141)

2 August 1945

My dear Henry,

Thank you so much for the splendid Jeroboam which Randolph[3] brought over to Chequers on Sunday. I much appreciated your kind thought, and we drank the champagne with great delectation on what was my last night at Chequers.

I am so glad to hear from Randolph that you are recovering from your serious illness, and that you are now really on the mend.

Please give my regards to your Wife.[4]

---

[1] This letter was handwritten.

[2] Henry Ludwig Mond, 1898–1949. Educated at Winchester. On active service in France, 1915–18 (wounded, 1916). MP (Lib.) for Isle of Ely, 1923–4; for East Toxteth, 1929–30. Succeeded his father as 2nd Baron Melchett, 1930.

[3] Randolph Frederick Edward Spencer Churchill, 1911–68. Churchill's only son. Educated at Eton and Christ Church, Oxford. Left Oxford, 1932, without taking his degree. Worked briefly for Imperial Chemical Industries as Asst Editor of their house magazine. Joined *Sunday Graphic*, 1932. Wrote for many newspapers, including the *Evening Standard* (1937–9): reported during Hitler's election campaign of 1932, the Chaco War of 1935 and the Spanish Civil War. Accompanied Duke of Windsor on his tour of Germany, 1937. Unsuccessful Parliamentary candidate 1935 (twice), 1936, 1945, 1950 and 1951. Married, 1939, Pamela Hayward (div. 1946): one son; 1948, June Osborne (div. 1961): one daughter. MP (Cons.) for Preston, 1940–5. On active service, North Africa and Italy, 1941–3. Maj., British Mission to Yugoslav Army of National Liberation, 1943–4 (MBE Military, 1944). Unsuccessful Parliamentary candidate for Plymouth Devonport, 1950, 1951. Historian; editor of several volumes of his father's speeches, and author of the first two volumes of his biography and the first two sets of document volumes.

[4] Amy Gwen Wilson, 1899–1982. Daughter of Edward John Wilson, a businessman from South Africa. Married, 1920, Henry Ludwig Mond: three children.

August 1945

Winston S. Churchill to Clement Attlee
(Churchill papers, 2/3)

3 August 1945
Most Secret

My dear Attlee,

Thank you very much for your letters of August 1 and 2.[1] I am sorry about the Western Neisse, and I fear the Russians have laid an undue toll even on the Germany which is not in their zone. This was certainly not the fault of the British Delegation. I should be very glad to have the Minutes and papers on the later proceedings at Potsdam when they are in print.

It was kind of you to suggest to your Russian and American colleagues sending me such an extremely complimentary message, which I value greatly. I am going to have the original framed.

I have made a few verbal alterations in the latest copy of the Tube Alloys paper, which Rowan[2] will show you. Otherwise I am quite satisfied with it. You will see that the introduction which you will make was drafted originally by Anderson[3] as if it were a statement in Parliament, whereas probably the event will occur before Parliament assembles. This only means that instead of 'You will all have seen . . .', it should run 'Everyone will have seen . . .'; and later on, 'You will however expect' should perhaps begin 'Some account is now required of the part which this country has played.' My text requires a heading, which I suggest might be 'Mr Churchill's Statement'.

I shall not be in London much before the 15th, but I shall look forward to talking things over with you when the House opens. We have an immense amount of work to do in common, to which we are both agreed and pledged.

I enclose you a separate letter which I hope you will show to your new Secretary of State for War.[4]

---

[1] Reproduced above (pp. 6–7, 8).

[2] Thomas Leslie Rowan, 1908–72. Private Secretary to PM, 1941. Married, 1943, Catherine Patricia Love: two children. Principal Private Secretary to PM, 1945. KCB, 1949. Economic Minister, British Embassy, Washington DC, 1949–51. Head of Treasury Overseas Finance Div., 1951–8. Chair, British Council, 1971–2.

[3] John Anderson, 1882–1958. Educated at Edinburgh and Leipzig Universities. Secretary, Ministry of Shipping, 1917–19. Knighted, 1919. Chairman of the Board of Inland Revenue, 1919–20. Joint Under-Secretary of State in Government of Ireland, 1920. Permanent Under-Secretary of State, Home Office, 1922–32. Governor of Bengal, 1932–7. MP (Nat. Gov.) for the Scottish Universities, 1938–50. Lord Privy Seal, 1938–9. Home Secretary and Minister of Home Security, 1939–40. Lord President of the Council, 1940–3. Married, 1941, Ava Bodley Wigram, widow of Churchill's leading informant on German rearmament in the 1930s. Chancellor of the Exchequer, 1943–5. Chairman, Port of London Authority, 1946–58. Member, BBC Gen. Advisory Council, 1947–57. Viscount Waverley, 1952. OM, 1957.

[4] John James Lawson, 1881–1965. Known as 'Jack'. On active service with Royal Field Artillery during WWI. MP (Lab.) for Chester-le-Street, 1919–49. Parliamentary Private Secretary to Ramsay MacDonald; Financial Secretary, War Office, 1924–9. Parliamentary Secretary to Ministry of Labour, 1929–31. Vice-Chairman, British Council, 1944. PC, 1945. Secretary of State for War, 1945–6. Lord Lt of Durham, 1949–58. Baron, 1950.

August 1945

Winston S. Churchill to King George VI
(Churchill papers, 2/560)[1]

3 August 1945
Most Private

Chartwell

Sir,

I have read w emotion the letter[2] of farewell wh Yr Majesty has so graciously sent me. I shall treasure it all my life.

The kindness and intimacy with which Yr Majesty has treated me during these ever-glorious years of danger and of victory, greatly lightened the burden I had to bear. It was always a relief to me to lay before my Sovereign all the dread secrets and perils wh oppressed my mind, and the plans wh I was forming, and to receive on crucial occasions so much encouragement. Yr Majesty's grasp of all matters of State and war was always based upon the most thorough and attentive study of the whole mass of current documents, and this enabled me to view and measure everything in due proportion.

It is with feelings of the warmest personal gratitude to you, Sir, and devotion to the Crown that I have relinquished my Offices and my cares.

Yr Majesty has mentioned our friendship, and this is indeed a vy strong sentiment with me, and an honour which I cherish.

With my humble duty,
I remain Sir,
Yr Majesty's faithful servant and subject,

PS. I am much interested in Your Majesty's private note, and I consider the course which was adopted has averted a most unfortunate arrangement.
I was so glad to see how agreeably Your Majesty's meeting with President Truman went off.

Lord Halifax to Winston S. Churchill
(Churchill papers, 2/141)

3 August 1945

My dear Winston,

Truman particularly asked me to give you every message from himself, and to say how much he had valued meeting and working with you. He could not have been nicer.

He had had no come-back from UJ at all but felt that he was now right on the record. He and Jimmy Byrnes[3] had both liked Attlee, but hadn't taken

---

[1] This letter was handwritten.
[2] Reproduced in *The Churchill Documents*, vol. 21, *The Shadows of Victory, January–July 1945*, pp. 2029–30.
[3] James Francis Byrnes, 1879–1972. Admitted to Bar, 1903. Editor, *Journal and Review*, Aiken, 1903–7.

much to Ernie Bevin who they thought was graceless and rough! You will keep this no doubt to yourself.

It was nice seeing you.

Lady Soames:[1] recollection
(Mary Soames, 'Clementine Churchill', pages 388–9)

3 August 1945

While Clementine[2] addressed all her energy to moving out of the Annexe and No. 10, Winston divided his time between the penthouse suite at Claridges (while Diana[3] and Duncan[4] made haste to move into a furnished flat) and Chartwell. Orchard Cottage was once more a haven, and our devoted Cousin Moppet[5] took on the cooking. The gardens were a wilderness, the roses all a-tangle and the grass knee-high, but Winston roamed through them, and found them peaceful and beautiful.

The night before I left to rejoin my unit, my parents took me to see a revival

---

Official Court Reporter, 2nd Circuit, South Carolina, 1900–8; Solicitor, 1908–10. Married, 1906, Maude Busch. Member of Congress, 1911–25. Practising Attorney, Spartanburg, 1925–31. US Senator, 1931. Associate Justice, US Supreme Court, 1941–2. Director of Economic Stabilisation, 1942–3. Director, Office of War Mobilisation, 1943–5. Secretary of State, 1945–7. Governor, South Carolina, 1951–5.

[1] Mary Churchill, 1922–2014. Churchill's youngest child. Served in WWII in the Red Cross and WVS, 1939–41; in the ATS, 1941–6. MBE (Military), 1945. Married Capt. Christopher Soames, Coldstream Guards (later Baron Soames), 1947. DBE, 1980. Chairman, Royal National Theatre Board, 1989–95. Published *Clementine Churchill by her Daughter Mary Soames* (1979); an edition of her parents' private correspondence, *Speaking for Themselves, the Personal Letters of Winston and Clementine Churchill* (1998); and her own memoir, *A Daughter's Tale* (2011).

[2] Clementine Hozier, 1885–1977. Married Winston Churchill, 1908. They had five children: Diana (b. 1909), Randolph (b. 1911), Sarah (b. 1914), Marigold (b. 1918; d. 1921) and Mary (b. 1922). Active in WWI, through the YWCA, in providing canteens for munitions workers. In WWII, presided over the Red Cross Aid to Russia Fund and the Fulmer Chase Maternity Home. President, YWCA War and National Fund, 1951–7. Chairman, YWCA National Hostels Committee, 1949–51. As Baroness Spencer-Churchill, from 1965, took her seat on the cross-benches, and voted in favour of the abolition of the death penalty, 20 July 1965. A Trustee of Lord Attlee's Memorial Foundation, 1966.

[3] Diana Churchill, 1909–63. Churchill's eldest child. Married, 1932, Sir John Milner Bailey (div. 1935); 1935, Edwin Duncan Sandys (div. 1960). Officer in WRNS, 1939–41. Air Raid Warden, 1941–5; her parents were particularly anxious about her during flying bomb attacks. Began working as a volunteer for the Samaritans, 1962. Committed suicide, 1963.

[4] Edwin Duncan Sandys, 1908–87. Educated at Eton and Magdalen College, Oxford. MP (Cons.) for Norwood, 1935–45; for Streatham, 1950–74. Married Diana Churchill, 1935; div., 1960. On active service in Norway with BEF, 1939–41; wounded. Financial Secretary, War Office, 1941–3. Chairman of War Cabinet Committee for defence against German flying bombs and rockets, 1943. Joint Parliamentary Secretary, Ministry of Supply, 1943–4. Minister of Works, 1944–5. Minister of Supply, 1951–4. Minister of Housing and Local Government, 1954–7. Minister of Defence, 1957–9. Minister of Aviation, 1959–60. Secretary of State for Commonwealth Relations, 1960–4. Secretary of State for the Colonies, 1962–4. Life Peer, 1974.

[5] Maryott Whyte, 1895–1973. Known as 'Cousin Moppett' and 'Nana'. Clementine Churchill's first cousin. A 'Norland' nanny. Lived at Chartwell between the wars, and was Mary Churchill's nanny, as well as looking after Chartwell when Mrs Churchill was in London. During WWII, when Chartwell was closed, she lived in a cottage near the house to supervise the estate.

of Noel Coward's[1] *Private Lives*. It was a complete contrast to the events and emotions through which we were passing; my father simply loved it, and we all roared with laughter. To our moved amazement, on his entering and leaving the theatre, the whole audience cheered and clapped, and the principal actor, John Clements,[2] came forward and made a most charming speech. During the following days and weeks there were many such heart-warming incidents.

It was a beautiful, pearly morning on 3rd August, when my mother walked very early with me across the park to the assembly point from where I was to start my journey back to Germany, after a leave I was not likely to forget. Soon after my return to my battery we were inspected by Field Marshal Montgomery, and my first letter home described how

> . . . just before he climbed back into his minute 'plane he talked to me. He was charming and kind and wanted to know how Papa was, & he asked specially about you. He really was kind & said that should you need me it could be arranged for me to be flown back. So I thanked him and said I would remember what he said in case of need.

And then he flew off.

During these difficult weeks everyone they knew seemed to want to help Winston and Clementine. A warm-hearted friend, Audrey Pleydell-Bouverie,[3] who years before, in 1931 after Winston's serious accident in New York, had lent them her house over there, once more came forward with the generous offer of her house in the country, pending Chartwell's rehabilitation. Clementine's reply illustrates her feelings at this time:

> Now that again we have suffered another unexpected shock, once more you offer to take us in. It is sweet of you, dear Audrey, and I shall never forget it. But actually I think it is best to struggle into Chartwell and re-adjust our lives. . . .
> [. . .]

---

[1] Noël Pierce Coward, 1899–1973. Educated at Chapel Road School and privately. First appeared on stage, 1910. Rose to international fame as actor and playwright in the 1920s. On outbreak of war in 1939, served for a time in Bureau of Propaganda and then in the Secret Service, including intelligence gathering in the US. In 1941, prosecuted for contravening currency regulations. Produced the iconic wartime films *In Which We Serve* (1942), *This Happy Breed* (1943), and *Brief Encounter* (1945). Knighted, 1969.
[2] John Selby Clements, 1910–88. Educated at St John's College, Cambridge. Actor, Ben Greet's Shakespearean Company, 1930–5. Founder, Intimate Theatre at Palmers Green, 1935. Film actor, 1935–84. Artistic Director, Chichester Festival Theatre, 1966–73. CBE, 1956. Knighted, 1968.
[3] Audrey James, former wife of the American department store millionaire Marshall Field. In 1931, after Churchill had been knocked down by a car in New York, she had lent him and Mrs Churchill her New York house in which to recuperate. Married, 1938, Maj. Peter Pleydell-Bouverie, Chairman of the *Western Gazette* and Director of the *Bristol Evening Post*.

August 1945

Winston S. Churchill to Clement Attlee
(Churchill papers, 2/140)

3 August 1945
Confidential

Chartwell

Dear Prime Minister,

I wish to place on record the fact that when I heard from The King of Field Marshal Alexander's[1] appointment as Governor-General of Canada, of which I strongly approved, I invited Field Marshal Brooke to stay on for a year as CIGS.

I thought that it would be a pity to break the continuity of the Chiefs of Staff Committee, over which he presides, while there is so much movement going on, even if the Japanese war comes to an end. Moreover, in a year from now, Field Marshal Montgomery's[2] work in Germany may well be finished, and then he could succeed Brooke. I hope my invitation to the latter may be borne in mind, as it was actually made and accepted.

Clement Attlee to Winston S. Churchill
(Churchill papers, 2/3)

5 August 1945
Most Secret

My dear Churchill

Thank you for your letter of August 3.[3] I will see that the minutes and papers of the later proceedings at Potsdam are sent to you when they are in print.

I have seen the verbal alterations in the TA paper and they are all quite acceptable. I have also made the amendments in the covering statement as you suggest and headed your statement 'Mr Churchill's Statement'.

---

[1] Harold Rupert Leofric George Alexander, 1891–1969. Educated at Harrow and Sandhurst (as was Churchill). On active service, 1914–18 (wounded three times, despatches five times, DSO, MC). Lt-Gen. Commanding I Corps, 1940 (despatches). GOC Southern Command, 1940–2; Burma, 1942; Middle East, 1942–3. C-in-C, 18th Army Group, North Africa, 1943; Allied Armies in Italy (15th Army Group), 1943–4. Knighted, 1942. FM, 1944. Supreme Allied Cdr, Mediterranean Theatre, 1944–5. Viscount, 1946. KG, 1946. Governor-Gen. of Canada, 1946–52. Earl Alexander of Tunis, 1952. Minister of Defence (in Churchill's second premiership), 1952–4. OM, 1959. Published *The Alexander Memoirs*, 1962.

[2] Bernard Law Montgomery, 1887–1976. Educated at St Paul's School. On active service, 1914–18 (despatches, DSO). Maj.-Gen., 1938. Commanded 3rd Div. (retreat to Dunkirk), 1940; 8th Army (North Africa, Sicily, Italy), July 1942 to Jan. 1944. Knighted, 1942. C-in-C, British Group of Armies and Allied Armies, northern France, 6 June 1944 (Normandy landings). Commanded 21st Army Group, northern Europe, June 1944 to May 1945. FM, 1944. Commanded BAOR, 1945–6. Viscount, 1946. CIGS, 1946–8. Chairman, Western Union Defence Organization, 1948–51. Deputy Supreme Allied Cdr, Europe, 1951–8.

[3] Reproduced above (p. 10).

August 1945   15

I will certainly bring your letter about Field-Marshal Brooke to the notice of the new Secretary of State for War. Personally, as I think you know, I have the greatest confidence in the ability of the CIGS and I hope therefore that no difficulty will arise.

Winston S. Churchill to Sir James Grigg[1]
(Churchill papers, 2/149)

5 August 1945
Personal

My dear PJ,

Only now do I find the leisure and the life with which to write to you.

I must congratulate you on the very distinguished part you played at the head of the War Office in the last three years of the war against Germany. The administration of the Department was continuously perfected, enormous difficulties were overcome, and no serious breakdown occurred in the face of our various enemies abroad and at home. I took a great responsibility in drawing you from your comfortable and solid Civil Service post into the rough and tumble of politics. It has certainly been rough, and now there is the tumble! All the same, the efficiency of your work is recognized in many informed quarters, and, as a House of Commons connoisseur, I watched you with great pleasure getting stronger every day and more capable of dealing with political, apart from Departmental, issues.

There is one thing I must write to you about. As you know, I have stipulated in the strongest terms that your full Civil Service pension rates should be preserved from the date that you were willing to accept Ministerial office. I cannot believe that any Government, least of all the present one, would deny these. From the talks I have had with Bridges, I should imagine there would not be the slightest difficulty in your receiving the whole of your accrued pension rights up to the date when you were led astray by

Your sincere friend,

PS. Let me know how this matter goes.

---

[1] (Percy) James Grigg, 1890–1964. Educated at Bournemouth School and St John's College, Cambridge. Royal Garrison Artillery, 1915–18. Principal Private Secretary to successive Chancellors of the Exchequer, 1921–30. Knighted, 1932. Finance Member, Government of India, 1934–9. Elected to the Other Club (founded by Churchill and F. E. Smith), 1939. Permanent Under-Secretary of State for War, 1939–42. Secretary of State for War, 1942–5. PC, 1942. MP (Nat.), East Cardiff, 1942–5. British Executive Director, International Bank for Reconstruction and Development, 1946–7.

August 1945

Winston S. Churchill to Sir Alexander Cadogan[1]
(Churchill papers, 2/560)

5 August 1945

My dear Alec,

Thank you so much for all you say in your letter. A very formidable event has occurred in Britain, and I fear it will diminish our national stature at a time when we most need unity and strength.

All the work you have done in this War has been excellent. I rejoice to feel you will still be at your post during years when an even heavier burden will descend upon your strong shoulders. You have indeed played a man's part in this glorious struggle, which we got into in one muddle and have come out of in another. Nevertheless the lustrum will glitter in future times.

John Colville:[2] diary
(Sir John Colville papers)

6 August 1945

The first Atomic Bomb was dropped on Hiroshima and a new, terrifying era begins. I had known of the project since 1941 but had never fully realised its implications till now. The startling news was, at Winston's express request, broken to an unprepared England by W's Statement (drafted last weekend at Chequers) with a preface by Attlee.

---

[1] Alexander George Montagu Cadogan, 1884–1968. Seventh son of 5th Earl Cadogan. Educated at Eton and Balliol College, Oxford. British Minister to China, 1933–5; Ambassador, 1935–6. Knighted, 1934. Deputy Under-Secretary of State for Foreign Affairs, 1936–7; Permanent Under-Secretary, 1938–46. Permanent British Representative at the UN, 1946–50. Government Director, Suez Canal Co., 1951–7. Chairman, BBC, 1952–7.

[2] John Rupert Colville, 1915–87. Known as 'Jock'. Grandson of the Earl of Crewe. Page of Honour to King George V, 1927–31. Educated at Harrow and Trinity College, Cambridge. Entered Diplomatic Service, 1937. Asst Private Secretary to Neville Chamberlain, 1939–40; to Churchill, 1940–1. RAFVR, 1941–3. Asst Private Secretary to Churchill, 1943–5; to Clement Attlee, 1945. Private Secretary to Princess Elizabeth, 1947–9. CVO, 1949. Joint Principal Private Secretary to Churchill, 1951–5. CB, 1955. Active in the development of Churchill College, Cambridge. Knighted, 1974. Author of a number of volumes of recollections and history, as well as *The Fringes of Power, Downing Street Diaries* (1985).

Winston S. Churchill: statement
('Winston S. Churchill, His Complete Speeches', volume 7, pages 7206–8)

6 August 1945

THE ATOMIC BOMB

By the year 1939 it had become widely recognized among scientists of many nations that the release of energy by atomic fission was a possibility. The problems which remained to be solved before this possibility could be turned into practical achievement were, however, manifold and immense; and few scientists would at that time have ventured to predict that an atomic bomb could be ready for use by 1945. Nevertheless, the potentialities of the project were so great that His Majesty's Government thought it right that research should be carried on in spite of the many competing claims on our scientific man-power. At this stage the research was carried out mainly in our Universities, principally Oxford, Cambridge, London (Imperial College), Liverpool, and Birmingham. At the time of the formation of the Coalition Government, responsibility for co-ordinating the work and pressing it forward lay with the Ministry of Aircraft Production, advised by a committee of leading scientists presided over by Sir George Thomson.[1]

At the same time, under the general arrangements then in force for the pooling of scientific information, there was a full interchange of ideas between the scientists carrying out this work in the United Kingdom and those in the United States.

Such progress was made that by the summer of 1941 Sir George Thomson's committee was able to report that, in their view, there was a reasonable chance that an atomic bomb could be produced before the end of the war. At the end of August, 1941, Lord Cherwell,[2] whose duty it was to keep me informed on all these and other technical developments, reported the substantial progress which was being made. The general responsibility for the scientific research carried on under the various technical committees lay with the then Lord President of the Council, Sir John Anderson. In these circumstances (having

---

[1] George Paget Thomson, 1892–1975. Educated at Trinity College, Cambridge. Commissioned, Queen's Royal West Surrey Rgt, 1914. Prof., Imperial College London, 1930. Nobel Prize in Physics, 1937. Chairman, MAUD Committee (on the military potential of nuclear technology), 1940–1. Knighted, 1943. Master, Corpus Christi College, Cambridge 1952. President, British Science Association, 1959–60.

[2] Frederick Alexander Lindemann, 1886–1957. Known as 'the Prof'. Born at Baden Baden (where his mother was taking the cure). Educated in Scotland, Darmstadt and Berlin. PhD, Berlin University, 1910. Studied physical chemistry in Paris, 1912–14. Worked at the Physical Laboratory, RAF, 1915–18, when he helped organise the kite balloon barrage. Personally investigated the aerodynamic effects of aircraft spin. Prof. of Experimental Philosophy (physics), Oxford, 1919–56. Member, Expert Committee on Air Defence Research, Committee of Imperial Defence, 1935–9. Unsuccessful by-election candidate, Oxford University, 1937. Personal Assistant to the PM (Churchill), 1940–1. Baron Cherwell, 1941. Paymaster-General, 1942–5, 1951–3. PC, 1943. Viscount, 1956.

in mind also the effect of ordinary high explosive, which we had recently experienced), I referred the matter on August 30, 1941, to the Chiefs of Staff Committee in the following minute:

> General Ismay, for Chiefs of Staff Committee: Although personally I am quite content with the existing explosives, I feel we must not stand in the path of improvement, and I therefore think that action should be taken in the sense proposed by Lord Cherwell, and that the Cabinet Minister responsible should be Sir John Anderson. I shall be glad to know what the Chiefs of Staff Committee think.

The Chiefs of the Staff recommended immediate action with the maximum priority.

It was then decided to set up within the Department of Scientific and Industrial Research a special division to direct the work, and Imperial Chemical Industries Limited agreed to release Mr W. A. Akers[1] to take charge of this directorate, which we called for purposes of secrecy, the Directorate of 'Tube Alloys'. After Sir John Anderson had ceased to be Lord President and became Chancellor of the Exchequer I asked him to continue to supervise this work, for which he has special qualifications. To advise him, there was set up under his chairmanship a consultative council composed of the President of the Royal Society,[2] the Chairman of the Scientific Advisory Committee of the Cabinet,[3] the Secretary of the Department of Scientific and Industrial Research,[4] and Lord Cherwell. The Minister of Aircraft Production, at that time Lord Brabazon,[5] also served on this committee.

---

[1] Wallace Akers, 1888–1954. British physical chemist. Director of Tube Alloys project, 1941–5. CBE, 1944. Knighted, 1946. Director of Research, Imperial Chemical Industries, 1946–53. FRS.

[2] Henry Hallett Dale, 1875–1968. Graduated from University of Cambridge, 1903; medical degree, Cambridge, 1909. Knighted, 1932. Shared Nobel Prize in Physiology with German pharmacologist Otto Loewi, 1936. President of the Royal Society, 1940–5. OM, 1944. President of the British Association, 1947; of the Royal Society of Medicine, 1948–50. GBE, 1948. Wrote *Adventures in Physiology* (1953) and *An Autumn Gleaning* (1954).

[3] Maurice Pascal Alers Hankey, 1877–1963. Secretary to Committee of Imperial Defence, 1912–38. Knighted, Feb. 1916. Secretary to War Cabinet, 1916–18; to Cabinet, 1919–38. Director, Suez Canal Co., 1938–9, 1945–63. Baron, 1939. Minister without Portfolio, Sep. 1939 to May 1940. Chancellor of the Duchy of Lancaster, 1940–1. Paymaster-General, 1941–2. Chairman, Scientific Advisory Committee, 1941–2; Technical Personnel Committee, 1941–52. Advisory Council on Scientific Research and Technical Development to Minister of Supply, 1947–9.

[4] Edward Victor Appleton, 1892–1965. English physicist. Educated at St John's College, Cambridge. Served with the Royal Engineers during WWI. Asst Demonstrator in Experimental Physics, Cavendish Laboratory, 1920. Prof. of Physics, King's College London, 1924–36. Prof. of Natural Philosophy, Cambridge University, 1936–9. Secretary, Department of Scientific and Industrial Research, 1939–49. Knighted, 1941. Nobel Prize in Physics, 1947. Principal and Vice-Chancellor, University of Edinburgh, 1949–65.

[5] John Theodore Cuthbert Moore-Brabazon, 1884–1964. Educated at Harrow and Trinity College, Cambridge. Pioneer motorist and aviator; holder of Pilot's Certificate No. 1. Won the *Daily Mail* £1,000 prize for flying a circular mile, 1909. Lt (later Lt-Col.) in charge of RFC Photographic Section, 1914–18 (MC, despatches thrice). MP (Cons.) for Chatham, 1918–29; for Wallasey, 1931–42. Chairman, Air Mails Committee, 1923. Parliamentary Private Secretary to Lord Privy Seal, 1939–40. Minister of Transport, 1940–1. Minister of Aircraft Production, 1941–2. Resigned after expressing

August 1945

Under the chairmanship of Mr Akers there was also a technical committee, on which sat the scientists who were directing the different sections of the work and some others. This committee was originally composed of Sir James Chadwick,[1] Professor Peierls,[2] and Drs Halban,[3] Simon,[4] and Slade.[5] Later it was joined by Sir Charles Darwin[6] and Professors Cockcroft,[7] Oliphant[8] and Feather.[9] Full use was also made of university industrial laboratories.

---

the hope that Germany and the Soviet Union (then embattled at Stalingrad) would destroy each other. Baron, 1942. Wrote *The Brabazon Story* (1956).

[1] James Chadwick, 1891–1974. Educated at Universities of Manchester, Berlin and Cambridge. Lyon Jones Prof. of Physics, University of Liverpool, 1935–48. Nobel Prize in Physics, 1953. US Medal for Merit, 1946.

[2] Rudolph Ernst Peierls, 1907–95. German-born British nuclear physicist. Worked with Otto Robert Frisch and James Chadwick on atomic research during WWII. Worked on the Manhattan Project in New York and later in the Los Alamos Laboratory, 1943–5. CBE, 1945. Taught at University of Birmingham, 1945–63. Awarded Lorentz Medal, 1962. Knighted, 1968. Received Enrico Fermi Award, 1980. Building housing the sub-department of Theoretical Physics at University of Oxford named for him, 2004.

[3] Hans Heinrich von Halban, 1908–64. French physicist. Escaped to England, 1940; invited to continue his research at Cambridge. Sent to Montreal to head the research laboratories of the Manhattan Project, 1942. Removed from position in Montreal by Gen. Groves, Head of Manhattan Project, for visiting his former boss Frédéric Joliot-Curie in Paris, 1944. Invited by Lord Cherwell to lead atomic research team at Oxford University after the war. Retired, 1961.

[4] Franz Eugen Francis Simon, 1893–1956. Jewish German physical chemist and physicist responsible for separating the isotope uranium-235. Awarded Iron Cross 1st Class during WWI. Doctoral degree, University of Berlin, 1921. Invited by Lindemann to join Clarendon Laboratory, University of Oxford, 1933. Commissioned by Military Application of Uranium Detonation Committee to research separation of uranium-235, 1940. His successful research was transferred to the Manhattan Project. FRS, 1941. CBE, 1946. Rumford Medal of the Royal Society, 1948. Knighted, 1954.

[5] Roland Edgar Slade, 1886–1968. Served with Royal Engineers during WWI. Controller of Research, Imperial Chemical Industries, 1935–45. Member, Chemical Board, Ministry of Supply, 1939–46. Member, Technical Committee for Atomic Energy, 1942–6. Secretary, Chemical Council, 1944–5. Treasurer, Royal Institution, 1946–52. Royal Society of Arts Centenary Prize and Gold Medal, 1951.

[6] Charles Galton Darwin, 1887–1962. Grandson of Charles Darwin. Educated at Marlborough College, 1901–6; Trinity College, Cambridge, 1910. Commissioned, Royal Engineers, 1914. Tait Prof. of Natural Philosophy, University of Edinburgh, 1924. Master of Christ's College, Cambridge, 1936. Director, National Physical Laboratory, 1938. KBE, 1942.

[7] John Douglas Cockcroft, 1897–1967. Educated at St John's College, Cambridge. Worked under Ernest Rutherford at the Cavendish Laboratory. Completed doctorate under Rutherford, 1925. Fellow, St John's College, 1928; Supervisor, Mechanical Sciences, 1929; Supervisor, Physics, 1931; Jacksonian Prof. of Natural Philosophy, 1939. With Ernest Walton, first to split the atom, 1932. FRS, 1936. Hughes Medal, 1938. Asst Director, Scientific Research, Ministry of Supply, 1939. Member, Tizard Mission, 1940. Director, Canadian Atomic Energy Project, 1944–6. Nobel Prize in Physics, 1951. Scientific Research Member, UK Atomic Energy Authority, 1954–9. President, Institute of Physics, 1960–2; British Association for the Advancement of Science, 1961–3.

[8] Marcus Laurence Elwin Oliphant, 1901–2000. Educated at University of Adelaide. Exhibition scholar, Cavendish Laboratory, Cambridge University, 1927; member of first team to split the atom, 1932. Prof. of Physics, University of Birmingham, 1937. British delegate, Manhattan Project, 1943. Hughes Medal, 1943. Director, Research School of Physical Sciences, Australian University, Canberra, 1950. Founder and President, Australian Academy of Science, 1954–6. Knighted, 1959. State Governor, South Australia, 1971–6. Companion in the Order of Australia, 1977.

[9] Norman Feather, 1904–76. Educated at Trinity College, Cambridge. Received doctorate under Ernest Rutherford, 1931. Conducted first investigations of the neutron, 1932. Fellow, Trinity College, 1929–33; Lecturer in Natural Sciences, 1936–45. FRS, 1945; President, 1967–70. Prof. of Natural Philosophy, University of Edinburgh, 1945–75. Makdougall Brisbane Prize, 1970.

On October 11, 1941, President Roosevelt[1] sent me a letter suggesting that any extended efforts on this important matter might usefully be co-ordinated, or even jointly conducted. Accordingly, all British and American efforts were joined, and a number of British scientists concerned proceeded to the United States. Apart from these contacts, complete secrecy guarded all these activities, and no single person was informed whose work was not indispensable to progress.

By the summer of 1942 this expanded programme of research had confirmed with surer and broader foundations the promising forecasts which had been made a year earlier, and the time had come when a decision must be made whether or not to proceed with the construction of large-scale production plants. Meanwhile it had become apparent from the preliminary experiments that these plants would have to be on something like the vast scale described in the American statements which have been published today.

Great Britain at this period was fully extended in war production, and we could not afford grave interference with the current programmes on which our warlike operations depended. Moreover, Great Britain was within easy range of German bombers, and the risk of raiders from the sea or air could not be ignored. The United States, however, where parallel or similar progress had been made, was free from these dangers. The decision was therefore taken to build the full-scale production plants in America.

In the United States the erection of the immense plants was placed under the responsibility of Mr Stimson,[2] United States Secretary of War, and the American Army Administration, whose wonderful work and marvellous secrecy cannot be sufficiently admired. The main practical effort and virtually the whole of its prodigious cost now fell upon the United States authorities, who were assisted by a number of British scientists. The relationship of the British and American contributions was regulated by discussion between the late President Roosevelt and myself, and a combined policy committee was set up.

The Canadian Government, whose contribution was most valuable, provided both indispensable raw material for the project as a whole and also necessary facilities for the work on one section of the project, which has been carried out in Canada by the three Governments in partnership.

---

[1] Franklin Delano Roosevelt, 1882–1945. US Asst Secretary of the Navy, 1913–20. Governor of New York State, 1929–33. President of the US, 1933–45. Churchill's pre-war support for Roosevelt had been frequently repeated in his articles in both Britain and America. 'I am,' he wrote in *Colliers* magazine in the first year of Roosevelt's presidency, 'though a foreigner, an ardent admirer of the main drift and impulse which President Roosevelt has given to the economic and financial policy of the United States' (*Colliers*, 4 Nov. 1933).

[2] Henry Lewis Stimson, 1867–1950. Born in New York City. Admitted to the Bar, 1891. Secretary of War, 1911–13 (under President Taft). Col., American Expeditionary Force, France, 1917–18. Governor-General of the Philippines, 1927–9 (under Coolidge). Secretary of State, 1929–32 (under Hoover). Member of Panel, Permanent Court of Arbitration, The Hague, 1938–48. Secretary of War (under Roosevelt), 1940–5. First American politician to serve in the Cabinets of two Republican and two Democratic Presidents.

The smoothness with which the arrangements for co-operation which were made in 1943 have been carried into effect is a happy augury for our future relations, and reflects great credit on all concerned – on the members of the combined policy committee which we set up; on the enthusiasm with which our scientists and technicians gave of their best – particularly Sir James Chadwick, who gave up his work at Liverpool to serve as technical adviser to the United Kingdom members of the policy committee and spared no effort; and, not least, on the generous spirit with which the whole United States organization welcomed our men and made it possible for them to make their contribution.

By God's mercy British and American science outpaced all German efforts. These were on a considerable scale, but far behind. The possession of these powers by the Germans at any time might have altered the result of the war, and profound anxiety was felt by those who were informed. Every effort was made by our Intelligence Service and by the Air Force to locate in Germany anything resembling the plants which were being created in the United States. In the winter of 1942–43 most gallant attacks were made in Norway on two occasions by small parties of volunteers from the British Commandos and Norwegian forces, at very heavy loss of life, upon the stores of what is called 'heavy water', an element in one of the possible processes. The second of these two attacks was completely successful.

The whole burden of execution, including the setting-up of the plants and many technical processes connected therewith in the practical sphere, constitutes one of the greatest triumphs of American – or indeed human – genius of which there is record. Moreover, the decision to make these enormous expenditures upon a project which, however hopefully established by American and British research, remained nevertheless a heart-shaking risk, stands to the everlasting honour of President Roosevelt and his advisers.

It is now for Japan to realize, in the glare of the first atomic bomb which has smitten her, what the consequences will be of an indefinite continuance of this terrible means of maintaining a rule of law in the world.

This revelation of the secrets of nature, long mercifully withheld from man, should arouse the most solemn reflections in the mind and conscience of every human being capable of comprehension. We must indeed pray that these awful agencies will be made to conduce to peace among the nations, and that instead of wreaking measureless havoc upon the entire globe they may become a perennial fountain of world prosperity.

AUGUST 1945

Winston S. Churchill to Field Marshal Sir Alan Brooke
(Churchill papers, 2/140)

6 August 1945
Private

My dear Brookie,

You will remember that at Potsdam I asked you to stay on in your post for another year, after which Montgomery may perhaps be free from his work in Germany. After the result of the Election, I wrote to Mr Attlee putting on record my invitation to you and your acceptance of it, and asking him to put the matter before the new Secretary of State for War. I have had a reply from him this morning, saying that he thinks no difficulty will arise, adding that he has the greatest confidence in you.

I am sure you will like your new Secretary of State.[1] He is an absolutely true and decent fellow, but he will need all your help and that of the Department.

Winston S. Churchill to Lord Salisbury[2]
(Churchill papers, 2/560)

6 August 1945

My dear Jim,

I value so much your letter of July 29, which I have just read. In view of the long and varied political association of our families, I always accept with pleasure your commendation.

It must be a great joy to you to see how Bobbety[3] stood out in the storm, and the fine position which he has won for himself in the public life of our country.

The future outlook is not too bright. I have by no means lost faith in the British democracy, but ten years is too long between Elections.

Please give my regards to Alice.[4]

---

[1] Secretary of State for War, Jack Lawson.

[2] James Edward Hubert Gascoyne-Cecil, 1861–1947. Son of Cons. PM Lord Salisbury. Educated at Eton and University College, Oxford. MP (Cons.) for North East Lancashire, 1885–92; for Rochester, 1893–1903. Styled Viscount Cranborne until succeeding his father as 4th Marquess of Salisbury, 1903. President of the Board of Trade, 1905. Lord President of the Council, Oct. 1922 to Jan. 1924. Lord Privy Seal, 1924–9. Leader of the House of Lords, 1925–9.

[3] Robert Arthur James Gascoyne-Cecil, 1893–1972. Known as 'Bobbety'. As eldest son of 4th Marquess of Salisbury, styled Viscount Cranborne. MP (Cons.) for South Dorset, 1929–41. Parliamentary Secretary of State for Foreign Affairs, 1935–8; resigned with Anthony Eden, Feb. 1938. Paymaster-General, 1940. Baron Cecil of Essendon, 1941. Secretary of State for Dominion Affairs, 1940–2, 1943–5; for the Colonies, 1942. Lord Privy Seal, 1942–3, 1951–2. Leader of the House of Lords, 1942–5. KG, 1946. Succeeded his father as 5th Marquess, 1947. Leader of the House of Lords, 1951–7. Secretary of State for Commonwealth Relations, 1952. Lord President of the Council, 1952–7.

[4] Cicely Alice Gore, 1867–1955. Daughter of 5th Earl of Arran. Married, 1887, James Edward

Winston S. Churchill and Lord Camrose:[1] notes of an interview
(Camrose papers)

7 August 1945 *Daily Telegraph* offices

No details of the atomic bomb were communicated to Stalin[2] at Potsdam. He was informed by Truman that the Americans were about to launch the biggest bomb ever on Japan. It was anticipated that when he received this information Stalin would express congratulations and then ask if his people might be allowed to get particulars of the design and manufacture of the bomb. Churchill had decided that Stalin should then be told that as he had refused in the past to communicate any particulars of new discoveries made by Russian scientists and manufacturers, he would be refused particulars of the new bomb until he had come to a more reciprocal turn of mind. Churchill did not get Truman to say definitely that they would adopt this policy, but thought he would have been able to persuade him in the end. However, Stalin just expressed congratulations and, much to their surprise, did not ask for particulars.

Churchill is of the opinion that, with the manufacture of this bomb in their hands, American[3] can dominate the world for the next five years. If he had continued in office he is of the opinion that he could have persuaded the American Government to use this power to restrain the Russians. He would have had a show-down with Stalin and told him he had got to behave reasonably and decently in Europe, and would have gone so far as to be brusque and angry with him if needs be. If the President and his advisers had shown weakness in this policy he would have declared his position openly and feels certain that the American people would have backed the policy on the grounds that it would have been carrying out the Atlantic Charter.

Hubert Gascoyne-Cecil, 4th Marquess of Salisbury: four children. Extra Lady of the Bedchamber to HM Queen Alexandra, 1907–10. JP for Hertfordshire.

[1] William Ewart Berry, 1879–1954. Newspaper proprietor. Founded *Advertising World*, 1901. Editor-in-Chief, *Sunday Times*, 1915–36. Chairman, *Financial Times* Ltd, 1919–45; Allied Newspapers Ltd, 1924–36. Baron Camrose, 1929. Chief Proprietor and Editor-in-Chief, *Daily Telegraph* and *Morning Post*, 1936–54. Principal Adviser, Ministry of Information, 1939. Viscount, 1941. One of Churchill's close friends (elected to the Other Club in 1926), and from 1945 a principal financial adviser; in 1946, negotiated the sale of Churchill's war memoirs and also the purchase of Chartwell by a group of Churchill's friends and its conveyance to the National Trust (Camrose himself contributing £15,000 and 16 other friends £5,000 each).

[2] Josef Vissarionovich Djugashvili, 1879–1953. Born in Georgia. A Bolshevik revolutionary, he took the name Stalin (man of steel). In exile in the Siberian Arctic, 1913–16. Active in Petrograd during October Revolution, 1917. Commissar for Nationalities, 1917–18. General Secretary of Central Committee of Communist Party, 1922. Effective ruler of Russia from 1923. Purged his opponents with show trials, 1936–8, murdering without compunction opponents, critics and ordinary citizens who had committed no crime. Authorized Nazi–Soviet Pact, Aug. 1939. Succeeded Molotov as Head of Government, May 1941. Marshal of the Soviet Union, May 1943. Buried beside Lenin in the Lenin Mausoleum, 1953. 'Downgraded' to the Kremlin Wall, 1960. In 1989 Mikhail Gorbachev began the official process inside the Soviet Union of denouncing Stalin's crimes.

[3] America.

At the moment he has decided that he will not publish his account of the war direction in his lifetime. He has voluminous detail inasmuch as every month his own telegrams, decisions and instructions have been put into type by the Government printers, and he reckons that each month's printing is equal to, say, two issues of a weekly review like *The Spectator*.

Expressed some doubt as to whether he would continue to lead the Conservative Party for an indefinite period, but would do so for the immediate future.

His disappointment at not being one of those who would shape the future of the European peoples is very deep indeed and he found it difficult at various stages in the conversation to conceal his bitterness at the way the people of England had treated him.

Henry Morgenthau[1] to Winston S. Churchill
(Churchill papers, 2/3)

9 August 1945

Harper is publishing a book immediately on my plan for Germany. Mrs Roosevelt[2] has given her consent for me to use the plan for Germany that you and President Roosevelt agreed to and signed at Quebec. I would greatly appreciate receiving your consent as well. Please cable answer.[3]

Admiral of the Fleet Sir Andrew Cunningham to Winston S. Churchill
(Churchill papers, 20/208)

9 August 1945

My dear Mr Churchill,

I am very honoured to be included among your friends and I would be churlish indeed if I refused what you offer in such generous terms. I therefore gratefully accept.[4]

May I take this opportunity of saying how privileged and honoured I feel

---

[1] Henry Morgenthau, Jr, 1891–1967. A gentleman farmer in New York State before WWI. Lt, US Navy, 1918. A neighbour and early supporter of Governor (later President) Roosevelt. New York State Conservation Commissioner, 1931. Chairman, Federal Farm Board, 1933. Secretary of the Treasury, 1934–45. A strong supporter of active American defence preparations, and of Lend-Lease. His plan in 1944 to reduce post-war Germany to a pastoral condition, with almost no industry, was rejected by President Truman, who would not take him to the Potsdam Conference, whereupon he resigned.

[2] Anna Eleanor Roosevelt, 1884–1962. Married, 1905, Franklin D. Roosevelt. US Representative at UN General Assembly, 1945–52. Author of *This I Remember* (1950) and *The Autobiography of Eleanor Roosevelt* (1962).

[3] Churchill's office replied: 'Please inform Mr Morgenthau that Mr Churchill has received his telegram and would be very glad if he would suspend action until Mr Churchill has had time to consider his request further. Meanwhile, in order to prevent any confusion arising, perhaps Mr Morgenthau would provide Mr Churchill with exact text of statement which he wishes to publish.'

[4] Churchill had submitted to the King the names of the three Chiefs of Staff's for baronies.

to have worked under you and how very deeply I regret that circumstances have not permitted this, to me, most proud association to continue till the end of the war.

I shall never forget the kindness and consideration you showed to one who after all is but an indifferent staff officer.

Clement Attlee to Winston S. Churchill
(Churchill papers, 2/140)

10 August 1945

My dear Churchill,

We have as yet nothing more than the Tokyo broadcast, but are seeking confirmation. I will let you know as soon as I have news. Meanwhile in view of the probability of the Japanese surrender being effective in the next 48 hours, the Cabinet has been considering Parliamentary procedure and other matters.

I have asked Whitely[1] to inform Stark[2] of our conclusions.

I feel that the probability of the surrender of our last enemy is so great that I must, at once, offer to you, our leader from the darkest hours through so many anxious days my congratulations on this crowning result of your task.

Winston S. Churchill to Clement Attlee
(Churchill papers, 2/140)

10 August 1945

My dear Prime Minister,

I thank you for your letter of today's date. I was worried about the 14th Army, because at the time when I gave these directions to the Committee, they seemed destined not only for a further prolonged campaign but for immediate operations in Malaya. It may well be that events will now bring the Japanese War to an early close. Indeed I hope this may be so, for it means an immense lightening of the load we expected to carry.

I will certainly come to talk with you about these War Honours at any time you wish. I have taken a great interest in the schemes.

---

[1] William Whiteley, 1882–1955. MP (Lab.) for Blaydon, 1922–31, 1935–55. Opposition Whip, 1927. Lord Commissioner, Treasury, 1929–31. Comptroller of the Royal Household, 1940–2. Opposition Chief Whip, 1942–55. PC, 1943. Parliamentary Secretary to the Treasury, 1945–51.
[2] Harold Rainsford Stark, 1880–1972. Ensign, US Navy, 1905. Capt., USS *West Virginia*, 1933–4, Adm., 1939. Chief of Naval Operations, US Naval Forces in Europe, 1942–5. Present at the Atlantic Conference. Relieved of command following controversy regarding withheld information over Japanese movements leading up to the attack on Pearl Harbor.

August 1945

Winston S. Churchill to Brigadier-General Lord Croft
(Churchill papers, 2/560)

10 August 1945
Private

My dear Henry,

You have certainly written me one of the most moving letters[1] of the thousands I have received. I thank you most cordially for the kind and complimentary thoughts you have so well expressed. When we met the other day, I had not read your letter, or I would have thanked you personally.

I hope you will be able to help in Kensington and Bournemouth in getting the men I want back to the Front Bench. In the anxious days that lie ahead we shall need a strong and closely-knitted team.

Chiang Kai-shek[2] to Winston S. Churchill
(Churchill papers, 2/140)

12 August 1945

Dear Mr Churchill,

This letter which will be brought to you by the kindness of General Carton de Wiart[3] is written at a moment when the Battle of Asia has practically come to an end. The last Axis aggressor has announced his readiness to accept the terms of surrender which you helped to formulate at Potsdam, and we are now about to win a complete victory over the evil forces of tyranny and oppression.

At this glorious moment made possible only through the heavy costs which the Allies have paid for the cause of Freedom and Democracy, I wish again to pay a sincere tribute to the strength and wisdom with which you have led the

---

[1] Reproduced above (pp. 7–8).

[2] Chiang Kai-shek, 1887–1975. Joined Sun Yat-sen's revolutionary party in 1907. Member of the revolutionary army in Shanghai on the outbreak of the Chinese Revolution, 1911. Served at Chinese GHQ, 1918–20. Visited Soviet Union to study its military and social systems, 1923. Founder and Principal, Whampoa Military Academy, Canton, 1924. Member, General Executive Committee of the Kuomintang, 1926. C-in-C, Northern Expeditionary Forces, 1926–8. Chairman of State, and Generalissimo of all fighting services, 1928–31. Resigned, 1931. Director-General, Kuomintang Party, 1938. Chairman, Supreme National Defence Council, 1939–47. President of the Republic of China, 1948. Retired, 1948. Formed a Government on behalf of the Chinese Nationalists in Formosa (Taiwan), 1949.

[3] Adrian Carton de Wiart, 1880–1963. On active service with the Army in South Africa, 1901 (twice wounded), East Africa, 1914–15 (severely wounded, losing an eye). DSO, 1915. Served on the Western Front, 1916–18 (eight times wounded, losing his left hand); VC, 1916. Commanded British Mission to Poland, 1918–24. Retired, 1924. Recalled to service, 1939, to head British Military Mission with the Polish Army. Commanded Central Norwegian Expeditionary Force, 1940. Appointed to command British Military Expedition to Yugoslavia, 1941; captured by the Italians when his plane crash-landed in North Africa. Sent to London by the Italians when they wished to negotiate an armistice, 1943. Sent to China three weeks later as Special Military Representative with Gen. Chiang Kai-shek, 1943–6. Knighted, 1945.

British people to victory. Your inestimable contributions to our common cause will forever remain a source of inspiration to the Chinese people as well as to the peoples of the other Allied nations.

General Carton de Wiart has given me the best possible cooperation and I doubt if you could have chosen a better person for the mission which he has discharged in a most admirable manner. Please accept my warm regards and the renewed assurances of my highest esteem.

Leslie Rowan to Winston S. Churchill
(Churchill papers, 2/142)[1]

13 August 1945

My dear Winston – (if I may so call you this once),

I have today given out your retirement list and so, unhappily, done my last task for you. I hoped so much that I might have continued to work for you for many years as your PPS. In the event it was for less than a month. But whatever the future may hold it can hold nothing of which I shall be prouder than that short time.

While I have worked with you I have learnt and gained much, and I cannot find the words to thank you and indeed all your family, for all you have done for me.

Today for me marks the end of a glorious and memorable period, during which one man has brought hope and happiness to more people on the earth than anyone else in all its history. These same people expect the same from you in the future and *I* know they will not be disappointed.

Please call upon me if I can be of any help or service. You know I shall be proud to do it.

Clementine Churchill to Mary Churchill
(Mary Soames, 'Clementine Churchill', pages 389–90)

14 August 1945 Chartwell

My darling Mary,

Time crawls wearily along. It's impossible to realize that it is not yet three weeks since your Father was hurled from power. He is lion-hearted about it. . . .

We have settled into Westminster Gardens & I shall never forget Duncan & Diana's prompt & generous action in lending it to us. Now Nana & I are struggling to get the flat down here ready. Our 'married couple' on whom we

---

[1] This letter was handwritten.

pin great hopes arrive tomorrow, & all yesterday Nana, Miss Hamblin[1] & me scrubbed and polished their rooms – they are still not ready. But I must be truthful & say that I was not allowed to scrub & polish as it seems I am too old & inefficient – I merely heaved furniture about which you know is one of my favourite hobbies – And I opened hampers stuffed full of old curtains, rejoicing when I found some long-lost treasure & despairing when I discovered that mice (I repeat <u>mice</u>) have nibbled holes in some lovely old rose damask covers & made nests everywhere. As for the moth!!! 'Lay not up for yourselves treasures upon this earth.' . . .

But these are not treasures but necessities becos you can't buy 'nothink' [clothing and household fabrics were still rationed] . . .

I hope I shall be able to organise a comfortable & happy home for Papa; but the truth is that it is silly to have *two* homes just now (London & Country) because of the rations which get all eaten up in one place & becos' of servants – Rich people now-a-days have a *small* house in the country & when in London have permanent rooms in an hotel. . . . I blush to think that I who organised the Russian Fund, the kitchen in Fulmer Maternity Hospital & who complained about the organisation of the YWCA am stumped by my own private life. But I think I shall learn to do it. The difficulty is that Papa is unpredictable in his movements & altho' I'm used to that, I still find that very tiring to cope with. . . . Nana has been cooking for us & has been sweet to Papa, who feels her kindness very much just now.

'Now mind during these last months to keep your conduct & morale as high as it has been during the whole war,' says your old Mother who is dropping to pieces herself!

Your devoted Mummie[2]

Clement Attlee to Winston S. Churchill
(Churchill papers, 2/140)

14 August 1945

My dear Churchill,

It is the intention that if Japan's acceptance of our terms of surrender is received in time, there should be a National Service of Thanksgiving at

---

[1] Grace Ellen Hamblin, 1908–2002. Known as 'Hambone' to the Churchill children. Born in London. Educated at Crockham Hill Church of England school, near Chartwell, and at secretarial training college. Began secretarial work for Churchill in 1932. Worked as No. 2 to Mrs Pearman, 1932–8. Secretary to Mrs Churchill, 1939–66. In charge of secretarial and accounts work at Chartwell, 1945–65. OBE, 1955. Administrator at Chartwell for the National Trust, 1965–73. Secretary, Churchill Centenary Exhibition, 1974.

[2] Mary replied: '*Please*, on *no* account push/heave or lift grand pianos, thereby straining yourself. I am appalled by your account of the moth/mouse Fifth Column activities. It's too much to think humans have been rationed, while they have gorged themselves on our curtains. . . .' (Soames, *Clementine Churchill*, p. 390).

St Paul's on Sunday next at 3 p.m., at which the King and Queen[1] will be present. Should the surrender be delayed, the Service would take place on the following Sunday.

I very much hope that you and Mrs Churchill will be able to be present and I suggest that you and I should sit side by side in the Cathedral.

Winston S. Churchill to Clement Attlee
(Churchill papers, 2/140)

14 August 1945

My dear Prime Minister,

I appreciate the kindly thought which has prompted you to invite me to accompany you and your principal colleagues to The King on the occasion of the surrender of Japan to the Allies. Personally I should very much like to do so. I feel however that it might be misunderstood if I seemed to dissociate myself from my Conservative colleagues in the Coalition War Cabinet, namely, Mr Eden,[2] Sir John Anderson and Mr Lyttelton,[3] and might be interpreted as a slur on them. Therefore I would venture to suggest that they should come too.

Thank you also for your invitation to the Thanksgiving at St Paul's on Sunday next. I shall be very glad to come and I should like to sit by your side in the Cathedral. I presume our wives will be with us.

---

[1] Elizabeth Angela Marguerite Bowes-Lyon, 1900–2002. Married, 1923, Prince Albert Windsor, later King George VI. Duchess of York, 1923–36. Queen Consort of England, Wales, Scotland, Northern Ireland and the Commonwealth Dominions, and Empress of India, 1936–52. Queen Mother, 1952–2002.

[2] (Robert) Anthony Eden, 1897–1977. Educated at Eton and Christ Church, Oxford. Served on the Western Front, 1915–18 (MC). MP (Cons.) for Warwick and Leamington, 1923–57. Parliamentary Under-Secretary, FO, 1931–3. Lord Privy Seal, 1934–5. Minister for League of Nations Affairs, 1935. Foreign Secretary, 1935–8. Secretary of State for Dominion Affairs, Sep. 1939 to May 1940. Foreign Secretary, May 1940 to July 1945, Oct. 1951 to Apr. 1955. KG, 1954. PM, 1955–7. Earl of Avon, 1961. One of his brothers was killed near Ypres in October 1914; another in 1916 at the Battle of Jutland. His elder son was killed in action in Burma on 23 June 1945, aged 20.

[3] Oliver Lyttelton, 1893–1972. Educated at Eton and Trinity College, Cambridge. 2nd Lt, Grenadier Guards, Dec. 1914; on active service on the Western Front, 1915–18 (MC, DSO, despatches thrice, wounded Apr. 1918). Entered merchant banking, 1919. Joined British Metal Corp., 1920; later Managing Director. Controller of Non-Ferrous Metals, Sep. 1939. President of the Board of Trade, and PC, July 1940. MP (Cons.) for Aldershot, 1940–54. Minister of State, Middle East (based in Cairo), and Member of the War Cabinet, June 1941 to Mar. 1942. Minister of Production, Mar. 1942 to May 1945. Chairman, Associated Electrical Industries, 1945–51, 1954–63. Secretary of State for Colonial Affairs, 1951–4. Viscount Chandos, 1954. KG, 1970.

August 1945

Clement Attlee to Winston S. Churchill
(*Churchill papers, 2/140*)

14 August 1945

My dear Churchill,

Thank you for your letter of August 14. I am sorry that you feel the suggestion I made might be misunderstood and interpreted as a slur on your Conservative colleagues and the Coalition War Cabinet. I fear on the other hand that if you were accompanied by them it might be misunderstood for other reasons. For example, it might suggest the idea of a Coalition government. I had hoped that you might feel that this was an unorthodox and personal tribute to yourself as the main architect of victory, quite apart from any political considerations.

If however you still feel unable to accept unless you are accompanied by the others to whom you refer, I am assured that the King will receive you personally later in the day.[1]

As regards the Service at St Pauls, I am very glad that you will come. Certainly our wives will be with us.

General Sir Hastings Ismay to Winston S. Churchill
(*Churchill papers, 2/449*)

14 August 1945

My dear Prime Minister,

That I should be a Companion of Honour by your personal recommendation gives me a pride and a pleasure that words cannot express.

Nevertheless I believe you know what it has meant to me to be allowed to serve you during these last five years and more, and to watch you saving our beloved country. I hope that you also know how utterly desolate and unhappy I have been these last three weeks. Please let me come and see you sometimes.

When you told me that you had recommended me for a Companionship of Honour, I was too surprised to ever thank you properly. But now that I have joined you in this Companionship, I want to say that there is nothing in the world that I would rather have. I can still scarcely believe my luck. For this, and for countless other kindnesses during a 'wonderful gallop' – as you yourself described it, I thank you from the very bottom of my heart.

Your most devoted servant.

---

[1] Churchill wrote in the margin: 'I will of course attend if the King summons me.'

AUGUST 1945

John Colville: diary
(*Sir John Colville papers*)

15 August 1945

The Japanese, conquered by the Atomic bomb, accepted the Potsdam terms of surrender and, after several days' uncertainty, Mr Attlee announced the news at midnight. VJ Day.

The King and Queen opened Parliament in state. I drove to the House with Mr Attlee through exhuberant crowds. Winston received the greatest ovation of all.

Debate on the Address. Listened to Attlee and to Winston.

L. S. Amery[1] to Winston S. Churchill
(*Churchill papers, 20/208*)

15 August 1945
Private and Personal

My dear Winston,

I do hope that you did not think the other day that my declining of the GCB implied any lack of appreciation of your most generous intention, which I shall always remember as a sign of the real friendship which has always united us even when we have had our lesser differences. But, like yourself, I should like to remain a House of Commons man without any change in the designation which I have always borne for so many years. And I am well content to feel that the CH brings me into such goodly company as yourself and Smuts.[2]

With regard to the House of Commons, I fully realise that in the immediate future you will be most anxious to get back those younger members of your Front Bench team who can lead the attack day in day out – the picadors who will take the first exuberance of strength out of the bellowing and snorting bull. But I certainly should like to be back in good time to join you for the more serious work of swordsmanship to follow.

[1] Leopold Charles Maurice Stennett Amery, 1873–1955. Known as 'Leo'. A contemporary of Churchill at Harrow. Fellow of All Souls College, Oxford, 1897. *Manchester Guardian* correspondent in the Balkans and Turkey, 1897–9. Editorial staff of *The Times*, 1899–1909. MP (Cons.) for South Birmingham (later Birmingham Sparkbrook), 1911–45. Intelligence Officer in the Balkans and eastern Mediterranean, 1915–16. Asst Secretary, War Cabinet Secretariat, 1917–18. Parliamentary Under-Secretary, Colonial Office, 1919–21. 1st Lord of the Admiralty, 1922–4. Secretary of State for the Colonies, 1924–9. Secretary of State for India and Burma, 1940–5.

[2] Jan Christian Smuts, 1870–1950. Born in Cape Colony. Gen. commanding Boer Commando Forces, Cape Colony, 1901. Colonial Secretary, Transvaal, 1907. Minister of Defence, Union of South Africa, 1910–20. Second-in-Command of the South African forces that defeated the Germans in South-West Africa, July 1915. Hon. Member of the Other Club (founded by Churchill and F. E. Smith), 1917. South African Representative at Imperial War Cabinet, 1917 and 1918. PM of South Africa, 1919–24, 1939–48. Minister of Justice, 1933–9. FM, 1941. OM, 1947. One of Churchill's last public speeches was at the unveiling of Smuts' statue in Parliament Square in 1956.

As for my wife[1] she has been such a wonderful helper in all my work both at the Dominions and Colonial Offices and during these last few years in charge of the Indian Comforts Fund that it would please me more than anything to see that work recognised. I must tell you, however, that what I said to you was done without consulting her, and I have been right royally scolded since then!

Elizabeth Layton[2] to Winston S. Churchill
(Churchill papers, 2/140)

15 August 1945

With reference to cars and petrol:

The car which Sir William Rootes[3] has arranged to lend you for one month is a Humber Limousine, larger and heavier than the one we had understood you were to have. This will be here tomorrow, Thursday morning. Would you please try this for a few days (over the holiday period) and if you feel that a smaller car will suit you equally well, I have arranged that a change shall be made about Monday.

Hale[4] tells me that this month has been exceptionally heavy on the cars (with the move, etc.), and that usually at No. 10 60 or 70 gallons of petrol a month would be enough, including journeys to Chequers. I have arranged with the Fees Office, House of Commons that for the time being, until we see how much travelling is necessary, 50 gallons a month shall be allocated to you. This will include the 6 gallons allowance for an MP which is sent to Miss Whyte for her journeys to the station with vegetables, etc. I think 44 gallons a month should be enough for you, as a journey to and from Chartwell takes less than 5 gallons.

---

[1] Florence Greenwood, 1885–1975. Known as 'Brydde' after one of Chaucer's birds. Married, 1910, Leo Amery: two children. Her brother was 1st Viscount Greenwood, Chief Secretary for Ireland while Churchill was Colonial Secretary, 1921–2. CI, 1945.

[2] Elizabeth Layton, 1917–2007. One of Churchill's two personal secretaries, 1941–5. Accompanied Churchill on most of his overseas journeys, including Washington DC (1943), Cairo (1943), Moscow (1944), Athens (1944) and Yalta (1945). After the war, married Lt Frans Nel, a South African army officer who had been a POW in Germany from 1942 to 1945. In 1958 Elizabeth Nel published one of the most charming of all the books of reflections about Churchill, *Mr Churchill's Secretary*.

[3] William Edward Rootes, 1894–1964. Educated at Cranbrook School. Apprentice, Singer Car Co., 1909–13. Lt, RNVR, WWI. Founder, Rootes Group, 1913. Member, Board of Trade Advisory Council, 1931–4, 1939–40. Led industrial reconstruction of Coventry Cathedral after Luftwaffe bombing of Nov. 1940. KBE, 1942. Chairman, Dollar Exports Council, 1951–64. GBE, 1955. Baron, 1959.

[4] One of Churchill's personal chauffeurs, responsible for driving him during the daytime.

August 1945

General Sir Hastings Ismay to Winston S. Churchill
(Cabinet papers, 127/50)

15 August 1945

Now that we have come to journey's end, the Chiefs of Staff ask you to accept their warmest congratulations on the completion of the task that you undertook over five years ago, and their heartfelt thanks for the inspiration of your leadership and encouragement.

They wish you to know that you are much in their thoughts today.

John Colville to Elizabeth Layton
(Churchill papers, 2/3)

15 August 1945

Dear Miss Layton,

I enclose herewith a copy of Mr Morgenthau's 'Plan for Germany' which was initialled by Mr Churchill and President Roosevelt on September 15, 1944.[1]

The Embassy in Washington have been asked to inform Mr Morgenthau that Mr Churchill has received his telegram and would be very glad if he would suspend action until Mr Churchill has had time to consider his request further. We have asked Mr Morgenthau to provide the exact text of the statement which he wishes to publish, since there were a number of drafts of the original, and it seems a good thing to compare his text with our own.

On receiving Mrs Hill's[2] letter of August 9 containing Mr Morgenthau's telegram, I asked the Foreign Office for their advice urgently, and though I am afraid that the urgency may have been overtaken by the events of the last few days I am expecting a reply from them shortly. Perhaps, therefore, Mr Churchill would wait a few days before replying to Mr Morgenthau so that he may have available the Foreign Office views on the question of publication.

---

[1] See Morgenthau's telegram to Churchill of 9 Aug. 1945, reproduced above (p. 24).

[2] Rose Ethel Kathleen Hill, 1900–92. Chief Clerk, Automobile Association and Motor Union Insurance Company, Portsmouth, 1917–24, and a member of the Portsmouth Philharmonic Society (first violins), 1918–24. District Commissioner of Girl Guides, Bengal–Nagpur Railway, 1928–30. Secretary to the Chief Commissioner of Girl Guides for All-India, 1930–2. Broadcast as a solo violinist, Calcutta, Bombay and Delhi, 1935–6. Returned to England, 1937. Churchill's first Residential Secretary, July 1937; lived at Chartwell, July 1937 to Sep. 1939. Churchill's Personal Private Secretary, 1939–46. MBE, 1941. Curator of Chequers, 1946–69.

General George C. Marshall[1] to Winston S. Churchill
(*Cabinet papers, 127/50*)

16 August 1945
Restricted
Important
Personal

With the termination of hostilities my thoughts turn to you and the long hard pull up the heights to final triumph of your labour.

Clement Attlee: speech
(*Hansard*)

16 August 1945   House of Commons

[...]
I think it is fitting that today I should pay a tribute to one of the main architects of our victory. However we may be divided politically in this House I believe I shall be expressing the views of the whole House in making acknowledgment here of the transcendent services rendered by the right hon. Gentleman to this country, to the Commonwealth and Empire, and to the world during his tenure of office as Prime Minister. During those years he was the leader of the country in war. We have seen in Fascist countries a detestable cult of leadership which has only been a cover for dictatorship, but there is a true leadership which means the expression by one man of the soul of a nation, and the translation of the common will into action. In the darkest and most dangerous hour of our history this nation found in my right hon. Friend the man who expressed supremely the courage and determination never to yield which animated all the men and women of this country. In undying phrases he crystallised the unspoken feeling of all. 'Words only', it might be said, but words at great moments of history are deeds. We had more than words from the right hon. Gentleman. He radiated a stream of energy throughout the machinery of government, indeed throughout the life of the nation. Many others shared in the work of organising and inspiring the nation in its great effort, but he set the pace. He was able to bring into co-operation men of very different political views and to win from them loyal service. At critical times, by his personal relationship with the heads of Allied States, he

[1] George Catlett Marshall, 1880–1959. 2nd Lt, US Infantry, 1901. On active service in France, 1917–18; Chief of Operations, 1st Army; CoS, 8th Army Corps. ADC to Gen. Pershing, 1919–24. CoS, US Army, 1939–45. Chairman of the newly created JCS Committee to advise the President on strategy, 1941–5. Advocated the principle of 'Germany First' in Anglo-American military priorities. Representative of the President (Truman) to China with the rank of Ambassador, 1945–7. Secretary of State, 1947–9. Architect of the Marshall Plan to rebuild the shattered economies of Europe. Secretary of Defense, 1950–1. Nobel Peace Prize, 1953.

promoted the harmony and co-operation of all, and in the sphere of strategy his wide experience, grasp of essentials, his willingness to take necessary risks, were of the utmost value.

I had the honour to serve with the right hon. Gentleman in the War Cabinet throughout the whole of the Coalition Government from the days of Dunkirk to the surrender of Germany. There are many things on which we disagree, but I think it right to take this early occasion, before we turn to controversy, to express the gratitude and admiration for his leadership in war which we feel. His place in history is secure, and although he was no longer at the head of affairs when the Japanese surrendered and final victory came, this really was the outcome of plans made long before under his leadership.

Lady Soames: recollection
(Mary Soames, 'Clementine Churchill', page 391)

16 August 1945

Winston did not lurk long licking his wounds; when Parliament reassembled on 1st August, less than a week after the election results, he took his new place on the Opposition front bench. The Conservatives started singing 'For he's a jolly good fellow' as he walked to his place; the mass of the Socialist members rejoined by singing the 'Red Flag', which was on the whole thought to be ungracious, considering the magnitude of their victory. But not all parliamentary exchanges were to be on this level; Japan surrendered unconditionally on 14th August 1945, and two days later Mr Attlee, the new Prime Minister, paid a generous tribute to Churchill's leadership in the House of Commons:

> . . . In the darkest and most dangerous hour of our history this nation found in my Right Honourable friend the man who expressed supremely the courage and determination never to yield which animated all the men and women of this country. In undying phrases he crystallized the unspoken feeling of all. . . . His place in history is secure.

Winston also spoke in the same debate, and on 18th August my mother wrote to me from Westminster Gardens:

> Papa made a brilliant moving gallant speech on the opening of Parliament. He was right back in his 1940–1941 calibre. The new house full of rather awe-struck shy nervous members was rivetted & fascinated – On VJ Day many people gathered round this block of flats to see Papa & cheer him & he got mobbed in Whitehall by a frenzied crowd. These friendly manifestations have reassured & comforted him a little. He says all he misses is the Work & being able to give orders.
> The crowds shout 'Churchill for ever' & 'We want Churchill'. But all

the King's horses & all the King's men can't put Humpty Dumpty together again. . . .

John Colville to Kathleen Hill
(Churchill papers, 2/3)

17 August 1945

My dear Mrs Hill,

You will remember the telegram from Mr Morgenthau[1] asking Mr Churchill's permission to publish the text of the agreement between Mr Churchill and President Roosevelt initialled on the 15th September, of which I sent Miss Layton a copy under cover of my letter of the 15th August.

The Foreign Office have been thinking about Mr Morgenthau's request, and they very much hope that Mr Churchill will dissuade him from publication. In the first place, this is a confidential document which emerged from an International meeting, and it would be most regrettable if the principle became established that such documents should be published by one of the people who attended these meetings. Whatever the Americans do, it is greatly to be hoped that such a practice will not grow up in England and that we shall not encourage the Americans in their well known disregard of official secrets.

This is the major objection to publication; but there is also the fact that the plan which the President and the Prime Minister initialled at Quebec was not the plan finally adopted by the two Governments for the treatment of Germany after her surrender. It is not, for instance, now intended that the industries in the Ruhr and in the Saar should be put out of action and closed down, nor are these two districts to be placed under the World Organisation. The publication of this plan, therefore, would probably cause confusion in many people's minds, and in coming, as it would, shortly after the publication of the Potsdam communique, it might well be misconstrued.

The Prime Minister has not been consulted about all this, but if Mr Churchill wishes, we will of course do so. However, should he agree with the above, I do not think it is necessary that Mr Attlee should be brought into the matter, and I attach a draft telegram to Washington for Mr Churchill's consideration.

---

[1] Reproduced above (p. 24).

August 1945

Henry Channon: diary
('Chips', page 412)

21 August 1945

Winston, accompanied by Anthony Eden, addressed the 1922 Committee.[1] He seemed totally unprepared, indifferent and deaf, and failed to stir the crowded audience. I came away fearing that the Tory party was definitely dead.

An announcement in the evening newspapers staggered me. Wavell[2] is expected back at any moment.

Kathleen Hill: memorandum
(Churchill papers, 1/65)

21 August 1945

MR AND MRS CHURCHILL
Secretaries

Mr Churchill is the most important man in the country. He has the most varied and widespread interest and probably receives the largest post of any single individual. To give him adequate service for his political and literary work alone, I cannot conceive a plan whereby we could manage with less than 3 secretaries plus the assistance of Miss Hamblin at Chartwell on alternate weekends.

I submit the following plan on the assumption that Mr Churchill may in future work a long weekend at Chartwell, spending Tuesdays, Wednesdays and Thursdays in London, and part Mondays and Fridays:

London. (Say 3–4 days a week).
Hours: Mrs Hill   Miss Layton   Miss Sturdee[3]
          9.30 to 5.30   1–9 p.m.   9.30–5.30
          (Fridays 9.30–midnight)

---

[1] The 1922 Committee (formally the Backbench 1922 Committee), made up of all backbench Conservative Members of Parliament. Founded in 1923, after the Conservative victory in the 1922 general election, it meets every week when Parliament is in session, enabling Conservative backbenchers to have their views heard by frontbenchers. Frontbench MPs have a standing invitation to attend, but only backbenchers may vote.

[2] Archibald Percival Wavell, 1883–1950. On active service in South Africa, 1901, and on the Western Front, 1914–16 (wounded, MC). Military Attaché with Russian Army in the Caucasus, 1916–17, and with Egyptian Expeditionary Force, Palestine, 1917–18. CMG, 1919. Commanded British troops in Palestine and Transjordan, 1937–8. GOC-in-C, Southern Command, 1938–9. Knighted, 1939. C-in-C, Middle East, 1940–1; India, 1941–2; ABDACOM, 1942; India and Burma, 1942–3. FM, 1943. Viceroy of India, 1943–7. Earl, 1947. Biographer of FM Allenby, and author of an anthology of poetry, *Other Men's Flowers* (1944).

[3] Nina Edith 'Jo' Sturdee, 1922–2006. Secretary to Winston Churchill. Married, 1962, William Arthur Bampfylde Onslow.

While Miss Layton or I was in attendance upon Mr Churchill, Miss Sturdee could remain in the office to open and sort the post, <u>answer telephones and obtain calls</u>, receive callers, type letters and speeches, and help with filing, etc. Miss Layton, by coming on duty at 1 p.m., having had lunch, could relieve me for luncheon.

<u>Chartwell</u>. (Say 3–4 days a week, including Sundays)
 I would propose that Miss Hamblin and I, and Miss Layton and Miss Sturdee, work at Chartwell on alternate weekends, thus:

Hours.	<u>Miss Hamblin or Miss Sturdee</u>	<u>Mrs Hill or Miss Layton</u>
	9–5 p.m.	2 p.m.–midnight.

If we could work to this programme, it would allow the off-duty Secretary to answer telephones, prepare meals, wash dishes, make beds, etc.
 In my opinion, the weekend programme is barely adequate, but even so, the total number of working hours per secretary is 56 hours per week.
 There is sufficient extra work in the office and library, and in keeping records, at Chartwell to employ a full-time Secretary for at least 2–3 months.

Clement Attlee to Winston S. Churchill
(Churchill papers, 2/140)

21 August 1945

My dear Churchill,
 The Clerk of the House of Commons[1] has raised the question of the general publication of the Journals of the House of Commons for the war Sessions 1939–1945. He already has the full authority of the House to publish and has sought permission from His Majesty's Government. The sole reason for withholding the Journals until now has been the risks to security arising out of the references to the days, hours, and places of sitting. This of course no longer applies.
 The only other point is the Privilege case arising out of the alleged disclosure by a Member (Mr Granville)[2] of a statement made in Secret Session. This related to a statement about the Naval situation in the Mediterranean made by you on the 23rd April, 1942. Publication of the Journals would of

---

[1] Gilbert Francis Montriou Campion, 1882–1958. On active service with RASC, 1914–18. Clerk Assistant to the House of Commons, 1921–37. CB, 1932. KCB, 1937. GCB, 1948. Clerk of the House of Commons, 1937–48. Editor, *Erskine May: Parliamentary Practice*, 14th and 15th edns. Baron, 1950.

[2] Edgar Louis Granville, 1898–1998. Served with Australian Infantry Force, Gallipoli, Egypt and France, 1915–18. MP for Eye (Lib.), 1929–31; (Nat. Lib.), 1931–42; (Lib.), 1942–51. Parliamentary Private Secretary to Herbert Samuel, 1931; to Sir John Simon, 1931–6. Capt., RA, 1939–40. Baron, 1967. Sat in the Lords as an Independent.

course include the Report of the proceedings when the matter was referred to the Committee of Privileges and again when they presented their Report. The facts of the naval situation have been officially published by the Stationary Office in a pamphlet entitled 'The Mediterranean Fleet (Greece to Tripoli)' and the only new detail disclosed would be the name of the Member concerned.

I do not consider that there are any grounds for withholding the Journals from the public any longer and I propose to inform the Clerk of the House accordingly. Before doing so, however, I thought it right to inform you of my intention.[1]

Clementine Churchill to Colonel Frank Clarke[2]
(Churchill papers, 2/225)

21 August 1945

My dear Colonel Clarke,

We were delighted to get your letter, and I do want to thank you for the kind things you say about Winston.

We are thrilled by your invitation to stay with you. Alas, I do not think we can manage La Cabane and Snow Lake as we cannot cross the Atlantic so soon. We have to buy a little London house, try to open up our country home in Kent – which is much dilapidated by six years of unavoidable war neglect – and generally speaking readjust our lives. But your invitation to stay with you in Florida during some part of the Winter is most tempting. I think it would do Winston such a lot of good and I should enjoy it so much. May I write to you again?

Mary's Unit is in Germany with the Army of Occupation. I do long to get her back, but I have no idea when she will be demobilised.

---

[1] Churchill responded on Aug. 25: 'I do not consider that there is any reason why the Journals of the House during the war should not be published, as you propose' (*Churchill papers, 2/140*).

[2] Frank William Clarke, 1887–1967. Born in Toronto. Married, 1911, Julienne Lantier: four children. General Manager, Gulf Pulp and Paper Co., 1914; President, 1920. Director, Anglo-Newfoundland Development Co., 1921. Associate Founder, Clarke Steamship and Clarke Trading Co., 1921; President, 1922. President, Canadian Pulp and Paper Association, 1925. President, Quebec Logging Corp., 1926. Met Churchill while volunteering for the *British Gazette* during the General Strike, 1926. Vice-President, Canada Power and Paper Corp., 1928; Member of Board of Directors, 1930. President, Montmorency Paper Co. Ltd, 1933–50; Chairman, 1950. Hon. Col., Royal Rifles of Canada. Special Assistant to Adjutant-General, 1942. Churchill stayed at Clarke's winter home in Miami for six weeks in 1946; Clarke then accompanied Churchill to Fulton, Missouri on March 4–5. President, North American Marine Corp. Ltd, 1956–7.

Winston S. Churchill to Sir John Anderson
(*Churchill papers, 2/3*)

22 August 1945

My dear John,

I was distressed to see that the list of the Atomic Bomb Committee did not contain Lord Cherwell's name. I gathered from my talk with Attlee today that you had been consulted about the list and not only upon your presiding over the Committee. Lord Cherwell is, I believe, the only one of the former secret Committee who is not included. The great part of the work was done at the Oxford laboratory which is in his keeping. Finally, he is almost the only, if not the only, British expert authority who has been permitted to see the whole of the plants. Unless he had kept me well informed upon this matter, I should not have written my minute of August 30, 1941 which turned on the full power of the State to what was then a remote and speculative object. I feel it very much that he should have been slighted in this way.

Another feature in the list also disturbs me. I mean the appointment of Professor Blackett.[1] As you know, he had been kept carefully away from all this business, and I think it very likely that the inclusion of his name will have the effect of drying up those very contacts in the United States which it is hoped to maintain and develop through the fact of your taking the Chair.

I expressed my regret to Attlee on both these points, but I did not gather that he could or would do anything about it. I should be very glad to hear from you whether you were in any way consulted, and if so whether there is anything you can or will do. If nothing is done about Cherwell by the Government, I may be forced to make some public comment.

Clement Attlee to Winston S. Churchill
(*Churchill papers, 2/3*)

23 August 1945

My dear Churchill,

I know you will have appreciated the difficulty caused by the sudden decision of the American Government to shut down Lend-Lease. We are sending

---

[1] Patrick Maynard Stuart Blackett, 1897–1974. Educated at Royal Naval College, Osborne, 1910, and at Dartmouth, 1912. Active service with RN, WWI, including Battle of the Falklands, 1914. Educated at Magdalene College, Cambridge, 1921. FRS, 1933. Prof. of Physics at Birkbeck College, University of London, 1933–7; at University of Manchester, 1937–53; at Imperial College of Science and Technology, 1953–65. Royal Medal of the Royal Society, 1940. Director of Operational Research, Admiralty, 1942–5. His work there improved the survival odds of convoys and the armour-plating of aircraft. Nobel Prize in Physics, 1948. Wrote *Fear, War, and the Bomb, The Military and Political Consequences of Atomic Energy* (1948) and *Atomic Weapons and East/West Relations* (1956). CH, 1965. President of the Royal Society, 1965. OM, 1967. Baron, 1969.

Halifax with Keynes[1] and Sinclair[2] to Washington on Monday.

I gather that there is already some revulsion of feeling in our favour, and due to the crude statements by Crowley[3] and others it is thought that it would assist the work of the Mission if the statement enclosed were to be made tomorrow in the House by me. On the other hand, as we shall be on the Adjournment in the afternoon, there is the possibility of a ragged discussion in which things might be said by inexperienced Members which would defeat our purpose of creating a good atmosphere. I propose to suggest to the house the inadvisability of any Debate and it would be very helpful if you or Anthony could support me by stating your agreement.

Foreign Office to Washington DC
(*Churchill papers, 2/3*)

24 August 1945
Important
No. 8789

1. Please inform Mr Morgenthau that Mr Churchill, after giving the matter due consideration, much hopes that he will refrain from publishing the document about the future of Germany, which President and Mr Churchill initialled at Quebec last September. Mr Churchill feels that it would be a mistake to establish the principle that highly confidential agreements of this nature, drawn up at an International Conference, may be published in this way so soon after the event and before any agreement is reached between the two Governments about the publication of official records. Moreover, this agreement was initialled in circumstances very different from those at present prevailing, and since that time agreement about the future treatment of Germany has been reached at Potsdam between the Three Great Powers. Its publication might, therefore, be liable to misconstruction at the present time, and in Mr Churchill's opinion this would not conduce to the settlement of the German problem most favourable to the interests of all concerned.

---

[1] John Maynard Keynes, 1883–1946. Economist. Educated at Eton and King's College, Cambridge. Served in India Office, 1906–8; Treasury, 1915–19. Editor, *Economic Journal*, 1911–44. Principal Treasury Representative at Paris Peace Conference, 1919. Baron, 1942. Leader of British delegation to Washington DC to negotiate US loan, 1945. Publications include *The Economic Consequences of the Peace* (1919) and *The Economic Consequences of Mr Churchill* (July 1925).

[2] Archibald Henry Macdonald Sinclair, 1890–1970. Succeeded as 4th Bt, 1912. Second-in-Command (under Churchill) of 6th Royal Scots Fusiliers, Jan.–May 1916. Sqn Cdr, 2nd Life Guards, 1916–18. Maj., Guards Machine Gun Rgt, 1918. Private Secretary to Churchill, Ministry of Munitions, 1918–19. Churchill's Personal Military Secretary, War Office, 1919–21. Churchill's Private Secretary, Colonial Office, 1921–2. MP (Lib.) for Caithness and Sutherland, 1922–45. Secretary of State for Scotland, 1931–3. Leader, Parliamentary Liberal Party, 1935–45. Secretary of State for Air in Churchill's Coalition Government, 1940–5. Viscount Thurso, 1952.

[3] Leo Thomas Crowley, 1889–1972. Born in Milton Junction, Wisc. Head, Alien Property Office, 1942. Head, Office of Economic Warfare, 1943. Head, Foreign Economic Administration, 1943.

2. In addition, please convey to Mr Morgenthau following message from Mr Churchill: 'I think it would be wrong to publish the confidential document initialled last year by President Roosevelt and me. The situation has changed in many respects. New decisions have been taken by the three major Powers, and this publication of a secret aide-memoire would be harmful at the present time. I am sure you will respect my wishes, which are strongly shared by His Majesty's Government. Kind regards.'

Winston S. Churchill to Lord Cranborne
(Churchill papers, 2/1)

25 August 1945

My dear Bobbety,

Many thanks for your letter about the one I received from Lord Rankeillour.[1]

I have formed a Committee of the principal ex-ministers in Parliament to discuss as a 'shadow Cabinet' questions of policy from time to time. I have a very good room at the old House of Commons where we can meet. Our first meeting will be early in the new session. It will give me great pleasure if you will be one of our regular members. I am also asking Lord Woolton[2] and Lord Cherwell from the House of Lords. I hope this will be agreeable to you.

---

[1] James Fitzalan Hope, 1870–1949. Grandson of 14th Duke of Norfolk. Educated at Oratory School and Christ Church, Oxford. Unpaid Private Secretary to Postmaster-General, 1896–1901. MP (Cons.) for Sheffield Brightside, 1900–6; for Sheffield Central, 1908–29. Treasurer of His Majesty's Household, 1915–16. Junior Lord of the Treasury, 1916–19. Financial Secretary, Ministry of Munitions, 1919–21. Chairman of Committees and Deputy Speaker of the House of Commons, 1921–4, 1924–9. PC, 1922. Baron Rankeillour, 1932.

[2] Frederick James Marquis, 1883–1964. Knighted, 1935. Director-General of Equipment and Stores, Ministry of Supply, 1939–40. Baron Woolton, 1939. PC, 1940. Minister of Food, 1940–3. CH, 1942. Member of War Cabinet and Minister of Reconstruction, 1943–5. Chairman of Conservative and Unionist Central Office, 1946–55. Chancellor of the Duchy of Lancaster, 1952–5. Viscount, 1953; Earl, 1956.

AUGUST 1945

Maurice Ashley[1] to Winston S. Churchill
(Churchill papers, 2/140)

26 August 1945

Dear Mr Churchill,

I am extremely grateful to you for letting me have a testimonial which may well prove of great value to me – even if not for the purpose for which I originally sought it.

I am due to be demobilised in a few weeks time and intend to try to earn my living by writing rather than by returning immediately to day-to-day journalism. I am contemplating writing something on American history. I imagine that your great book on the English-speaking peoples will soon be appearing and will arouse wide interest in the relations between the two nations.

Now that the war is won, may I add my voice as that of an ordinary unimportant citizen to those of so many who have expressed their profound gratitude to you for all we owe you? I shall always take pride in the memory that I once served you in a humble capacity.

Clementine Churchill to Mary Churchill
(Mary Soames, 'Clementine Churchill', pages 390–1)

26 August 1945

But what really excited & relieved me was that you say you (my regiment)[2] may soon be disbanded & that you will apply for a post in England. Now my Darling please ask for a job at the War Office, so that you can live at home in your lovely bed-sitting room at Hyde Park Gate. Because I am very unhappy & need your help with Papa.

I cannot explain how it is but in our misery we seem, instead of clinging to each other to be always having scenes. I'm sure it's all my fault, but I'm finding life more than I can bear. He is so unhappy & that makes him very difficult. He hates his food, (hardly any meat) has taken it into his head that Nana tries to thwart him at every turn. He wants to have land girls[3] & chickens & cows

---

[1] Maurice Percy Ashley, 1907–. Educated at St Paul's School, London, and New College, Oxford (History Scholar). Historical Research Assistant to Churchill, 1929–33. On editorial staff of *Manchester Guardian*, 1933–7; *The Times*, 1937–9. Editor of *Britain Today*, 1939–40. Served in the Army, 1940–5 (Maj., Military Intelligence, becoming a specialist in the order of battle of the Japanese army). Deputy Editor of the *Listener*, 1946–58; Editor, 1958–67. Research Fellow, Loughborough University of Technology, 1968–70. Author of more than 25 historical works, many on Cromwellian and Stuart England, including biographies of Cromwell (1937), Marlborough (1939) and Charles II (1971). In 1968 published *Churchill as Historian*. CBE, 1978, for his historical writings; Doctorate of Letters at Oxford University, 1979.

[2] '(my regiment)' inserted by Lady Soames.

[3] The Women's Land Army was a volunteer organization of women, commonly known as 'Land Girls', who took up agricultural work to fill the void left by men who had been called to military service. Over 200,000 women worked as farm labourers during the two world wars.

here & she thinks it won't work & of course she *is* gruff & bearish. But look what she does for us. I can't see any future. But Papa is going to Italy & then perhaps Nana & I can get this place straight. It looks impossible & one doesn't know where to start. . . .

Then in a few days we shan't have a car. We are being lent one now. We are learning how rough & stony the World is.

I was much disturbed by this letter, for I realised that the adjustment from the wartime tension and tempo of their life was bound to be painful and difficult for both of them. For although they had lived for over five years on an exhaustingly heroic level, they had not suffered the physical shortages and domestic difficulties which had been the lot of ordinary people. Because they had to entertain so many people officially, they received 'Diplomatic Rations'; Chequers was staffed by the Women's Services, and civilian staff had been available for London; cars and petrol were always at hand. Now, of course, all these comforts and facilities disappeared. I understood how, in their emotionally and physically exhausted state, the combination of petty problems with the hurt and bewilderment of Winston's political downfall could produce tensions and flare-ups between them. Although I did not want to leave my unit before the regiment was actually disbanded, I felt a new priority had appeared and that, in the circumstances, I could ask for a home posting.[1]

General Dwight D. Eisenhower[2] to Winston S. Churchill
(Churchill papers, 2/141)

27 August 1945

Dear Mr Churchill,

It is difficult indeed for me to use any form of address to you other than 'Prime Minister'. Though I live to be a hundred I shall always think of you in that capacity and with that title.

When I learned through Colonel Gault[3] that you would find a visit to the Riviera most acceptable, I was naturally not only delighted but, on the spur of the moment, anticipated no difficulties of any kind. Unfortunately I

---

[1] The italicized text was written by Lady Soames.
[2] Dwight David Eisenhower, 1890–1969. Graduated from West Point Military Academy, 1915. Drafted the War Dept's study and plans for industrial mobilisation, 1929–33. Asst Military Adviser to Commonwealth of Philippine Islands, 1935–40. Asst CoS, in charge of Operations Div., War Dept, General Staff, Washington DC, 1941. OC US Forces in England (for European operations), 1942. C-in-C, Allied Forces in North Africa, Nov. 1942 to Jan. 1944. Hon. knighthood, 1943. Supreme Cdr, Allied Expeditionary Force in Western Europe, Jan. 1944 to May 1945. Hon. OM, 1945. Cdr, American Zone of Occupation, Germany, 1945. CoS, US Army, 1945–8. Supreme Cdr, NATO Forces in Europe, 1950–2. President of the US, 1953–61.
[3] Andrew Hamilton Gault, 1882–1958. Educated at Bishop's College School, Lennoxville. Consul-General for Sweden in Canada, 1909–11. Member, Council for the Montreal Board of Trade, 1911–13. Maj., Princess Patricia's Canadian Light Infantry, 1914–16. MP (Cons.) for Taunton, 1924–35. Col., Canadian Army, 1940–2; Brig., 1942–5.

encountered some. I have delayed writing you in the hopes that I might find these difficulties dissolving. I think I need scarcely tell you that, because of my unstinted admiration for you and your work, and because of the personal esteem in which I have always held you, nothing could give me greater pleasure than to make available to you any facility at any time that could possibly add to your recreation and enjoyment.

The first thing that bothers me is something that must necessarily be kept secret; it is that there exists a definite possibility that I might not be in this region at the time you would come to the Riviera. Whether or not this would result in any later embarrassment to yourself I do not know, but I would have the uneasy feeling that I would not be here to see that arrangements were carried out exactly as planned.

It is a second difficulty, however, that has really worried me. The only house that I know of on the Riviera that I would consider suitable for you and a part of your family is a villa named 'Sous les Vents', rented by the American forces and held for use by me and the other senior officers of this command. Some of these officers have been invited to use the house and are even entitled to be there on those rare and brief occasions when I myself can be present. Since I would want you, in the interests of your own privacy, to have exclusive possession during your tenure, my prior invitations to these officers would have to be cancelled, almost without explanation. The house is quite large and a number of people could be easily accommodated in it, but, while it would be an honor for any American general who might be there at the time to have you as his nominal guest, I fear this would be an unsatisfactory arrangement for you.

There are, of course, other Riviera accommodations under the control of the American Army; for example, the du Cap Hotel at Eden Roc. Suites could easily be made available with no embarrassment, but this would have the disadvantage of exposing you to curiosity seekers and deny you, partially at least, the peace and quiet you seek.

Because you know so well of my deep and lasting appreciation for the staunch and unwavering support you accorded me all during the war, and of the great satisfaction I have taken in your friendly and always hospitable attitude toward me, you must sense how much embarrassment it causes me to write you of these annoying difficulties. There is no one living to whom I have a greater desire to show, in some concrete way, the depth of my admiration and affection, and so I have recited the facts to you in laborious detail in order that you might understand exactly. If you can suggest some solution in a letter I will do my utmost to work it out.

With assurances of my continued respect and affection,

August 1945

Winston S. Churchill to John Peck[1]
(Churchill papers, 2/2)

27 August 1945

1. You should assure the Prime Minister that there is no foundation so far as I am aware of either of these two statements. The idea of a quadripartite occupation of Korea was never mentioned in any conversation which I had with President Roosevelt.

2. The question of the administration of Japan by the American Supreme Commander[2] without any Allied Control Commission was never discussed between me and President Truman. I should strongly have opposed such a suggestion.

Winston S. Churchill to Charles Montag[3]
(Churchill papers, 2/141)

29 August 1945

Thank you so much for your very kind telegram. I am going to paint at Lake Como for a few weeks in the near future. Please let me know your address in Switzerland in case we can make a contact, and write to me at 67 Westminster Gardens, London, SW1, saying whether any good supplies of paints & brushes can be obtained in France or Switzerland. My stock is somewhat depleted. Kindly keep this communication entirely private.

The Owner of the Bulldog.
(or: Churchill)

---

[1] John Howard Peck, 1913–95. Asst Private Secretary to 1st Lord of the Admiralty (Lord Stanhope), 1937–9; to Minister for Co-ordination of Defence (Lord Chatfield), 1939–40; to 1st Lord of the Admiralty (Churchill), Apr.–May 1940; to PM (Churchill), 1940–5. Transferred to Foreign Service, 1946. Ambassador to Senegal, 1962–6; to Mauritania, 1962–5. Under-Secretary of State, 1966–70. Ambassador to Republic of Ireland, 1970–3. Knighted, 1971. Published his memoirs, *Dublin from Downing Street*, in 1978.

[2] Douglas MacArthur, 1880–1964. On active service, 1917–18 (twice wounded). CoS, US Army, 1930–5. FM, Philippine Army, 1936. Retired, 1936. Returned to active duty, 1942. Supreme Allied Cdr, South-West Pacific Area, 1942–5. Hon. knighthood, 1943. C-in-C, US forces, Far East Command, 1943–51. Supreme Cdr, Allied Powers in Japan, 1945–51. C-in-C, UN forces in Korea, 1950–1.

[3] Charles Montag, 1880–1956. Born in Winterthur, Switzerland. Went to Paris, 1903. Studied painting in Brittany and Provence. Painted mostly landscapes and still life. Exhibited his paintings in Zurich, 1917. Died in Paris.

AUGUST 1945 47

Field Marshal Sir Harold Alexander to Winston S. Churchill
(Churchill papers, 2/140)[1]

30 August 1945

My dear PM,

This is just a note to welcome you on your arrival in Italy. I hope you will forgive me for not being here to meet you in person, but I am attending a big Polish ceremony at Monte Cassino which I have promised for a long time to attend. But I shall come up on the 6th and if I may I should like to spend a couple of minutes with you and then go on to Trieste where the XIII Corps are holding a Tattoo from 9th–11th. If that would amuse you, they would love to see you – however, we can discern this when we meet.

I hope you had an agreeable journey from England and I hope you will be comfortable and happy in this villa – you must ask for anything you want.

With best wishes for you and your party.

John Colville: diary
(Sir John Colville papers)

31 August 1945

I dined with Mr and Mrs Churchill in their flat at Westminster Gardens. Jack[2] and Sarah[3] were there. W spoke sourly of Herbert Morrison. He said that the Administration were making a muddle of demobilization and that Mr George Isaacs,[4] 'like Pharaoh, has hardened his heart and has told the people they may not go'.

[1] This letter was handwritten.
[2] John Strange Spencer-Churchill, 1880–1947. Known as 'Jack'. Churchill's younger brother. Educated at Harrow. On active service in South Africa, 1900 (wounded). Maj., Queen's Own Oxfordshire Hussars, 1914–18. Served at Dunkirk, 1914; on Sir John French's staff, Flanders, 1914–15; on Sir Ian Hamilton's staff at the Dardanelles, 1915; on Gen. Birdwood's staff, France, 1916–18. Stockbroker; partner with the City firm of Vickers da Costa, 1918–40. In 1931 he was elected to the Other Club, founded by his brother and F. E. Smith in 1911. Asked once why he so enjoyed his brother's company, Churchill is said to have replied: 'Jack is unborable.' When his London home was made uninhabitable by bombing in WWII, 'Uncle Jack' stayed at 10 Downing Street with his brother's household.
[3] Sarah Millicent Hermione Spencer Churchill, 1914–83. Dancer and actor. Born while her father was returning from the siege of Antwerp, 7 Oct. 1914. Married, 1936, Vic Oliver (div., 1945). Appeared on stage in Birmingham, Southampton, Weston-super-Mare and London, 1937–9; on tour with Vic Oliver in the play *Idiot's Delight*, 1938; in London in *Quiet Wedding*, 1939, and in J. M. Barrie's *Mary Rose*, 1940. Appeared in the film *Spring Meeting*, 1940. Entered WAAF, Oct. 1941. Asst Section Officer, later Section Officer, Photographic Interpretation Unit, Medmenham, 1941–5. Accompanied her father (as ADC) to the conferences at Teheran (Nov. 1943) and Yalta (Feb. 1945). Married, 1949, Anthony Beauchamp (d. 1957); 1962, 23rd Baron Audley, MBE (d. July 1963). In 1951, appeared on the US stage in *Gramercy Ghost*. Published *The Empty Spaces* (poems) in 1966, *A Thread in the Tapestry* (recollections) in 1967, *Collected Poems* in 1974 and *Keep on Dancing* (further recollections) in 1981.
[4] George Alfred Isaacs, 1883–1979. General Secretary, National Society of Operative Printers and Assistants, 1909–49. Mayor, Borough of Southwark, 1919–21. MP (Lab.) for Gravesend, 1923–4; for Southwark, 1929–50. Minister of Labour and National Service, 1945–51. Minister of Pensions, 1951.

August 1945

Randolph S. Churchill to Winston S. Churchill
(Churchill papers, 1/42)[1]

31 August 1945
Personal

My dearest Papa,

I am more sorry than I can say that I should have provoked you so much tonight. Knowing your prejudice against literary agents I was most careful in all I said to make no mention of them. What I said was that in view of the immense complexity of the whole situation what was wanted was that it should be studied and reported on by one expert. I was not even thinking of a literary agent but of a lawyer. When therefore you started to answer me as if I had suggested a literary agent I tried to explain what it was I had really said. I'm afraid my interruptions must have been very clumsy because I made you extremely angry.

I went away because I cannot bear to have you talk to me like that in front of other people – particularly in front of Brendan[2] on whose account I have already been so grievously wounded.

But I beg you to forgive me and to believe that I was solely concerned to avoid an argument on a subject which I knew to be sterile.

I so hope that the sun will shine at Como and that you will paint some lovely pictures.

Lady Soames: recollection
(Mary Soames, 'Clementine Churchill', page 392)

31 August 1945

A short time later, on 31st August 1945, I was able to write with some good news:

My Darling Mummie,

I was so grieved to read in your letter, which arrived yesterday, of all your worries and desolations. I feel for you and Papa more deeply than I can say; and I know only too well, how much of the burden weighs on you.

I asked at once for an interview with the 'Queen AT' over here, and today I drove down to Headquarters . . . (we are about 120 miles away from

---

[1] This letter was handwritten.
[2] Brendan Bracken, 1901–58. Journalist and financier. Educated in Australia and at Sedbergh School. Chairman of the *Financial News*, 1928. MP (Cons.) for North Paddington, 1929–45; for Bournemouth, 1945–50; for East Bournemouth and Christchurch, 1950–1. Elected to the Other Club, 1932. Parliamentary Private Secretary to PM (Churchill), 1940–1. PC, 1940. Managing Director, *The Economist*, 1940, 1941. Minister of Information, 1941–5. 1st Lord of the Admiralty, May–July, 1945. Chairman, *Financial Times*, 1945. Viscount, 1952.

them) and saw her . . . and explained everything. She was kind and very helpful. A posting to England (London) is going to be arranged for me. So darling Mummie, I hope so much to be with you perhaps within a month.

True to their word, the Army authorities arranged for me to be posted as an Administrative Officer to a War Office Holding Unit in London, in Radnor Place. I did not live at home, but as my parents' new house was just the other side of Hyde Park from my billet, even a few hours off meant I could visit them easily and often.

Sir John Anderson to Winston S. Churchill
(Churchill papers, 2/3)

31 August 1945

My dear Winston,

I am much concerned to think that Cherwell may feel slighted by his omission from the atomic energy Committee. Throughout this business my relations with him have been, as I think you know of the closest and most cordial character; and I should be very happy to be able still to consult him freely.

Ministers are of course solely responsible for the composition of the Committee; but it is right to say that I was consulted as to its general constitution though not as to names. I recommended representatives of the Services and the Departments (on the Chiefs of Staff and Heads of Dept. level with an equal number of representative scientists to be selected after consultation with the President of the Royal Society).

Cherwell's name did not come up at the only interview I had with Attlee; but, if it had, I should certainly have deprecated his inclusion, for, though I could not have given this as my reason to Attlee, it seems to me very important that someone who knows the subject thoroughly should be available, free and untrammelled, to advise you and other opposition leaders on any proposals that may be made. Cherwell and myself are I think the only two people who could play that part and I should regard it as very unfortunate if we were both to some extent sterilised by membership of a Committee appointed to advise the Government confidentially.

As regards Blackett I had reason to think that Dale would recommend his inclusion and I warned Attlee about his reputed political views. As a matter of fact, however, having regard to the amount of information now made public, on which any competent scientist can work, I think he is probably safer on the Committee than off it.

I would have replied sooner but have been laid up for a couple of days.

Winston S. Churchill: notes
(Churchill papers, 1/30)

31 August 1945

MR CHURCHILL'S INSTRUCTIONS

1. Find out from Mr Cox,[1] the Executive Officer of the Kent War Agricultural Committee, who is arranging it, when the German prisoners are coming to Chartwell. An arrangement is being made with the War Office authorities.

The prisoners are to clear the camouflage from the lakes. Care must be taken to pull the stakes out properly, and not break them off below the surface.

It is important that Mrs Churchill should see what the prisoners do. They should not be allowed to tear up a lot of things roughly. They can cut nettles and thistles, fill in trenches and rifle pits that were made by the Army.

If the War Office wish to make a charge for the square stones, the number in front of the Studio must be counted in. If the charge is reasonable, I should like to keep the lot, and leave them all where they are for the present.

2. Mrs Churchill does not wish to keep the two Nissen huts. However, it would be as well to find out how much the War Office want for them. If nothing, then we might find some use for the material. If a serious charge is demanded, they should be told to remove the huts.

3. Explain to Major Marnham[2] that I am not pressing him to assist in the cultivation of the 6 acres. Stevens said he would do it.

4. There is a certain amount of Major Marnham's agricultural implements in the shed at the back of the loose-box, and also in the little yard near the chicken-house. Inquiry might be made tactfully about these, because it would be as well to get these places clear, as they will be useful.

5. Horse and cart. Mr Stevens is ready to sell a horse and cart and harness for about £90, viz: £40 horse, £40 cart, and £10 harness. I do not mind his having a good price, provided it is not altogether out of relation to the market. Our old cart has rotted away.

6. All the boxes of books in store are to come down to Chartwell, and I will sort them out in the pantry. They need not be taken out of their boxes. I will select the books intended for the London house.

---

[1] P. W. Cox. Labour Officer, Kent War Agricultural Executive Committee, 1919; Chief Executive Officer and Secretary, 1920–45.

[2] Reginald John Marnham. MC, 1918. Parliamentary candidate (Lib.) for Chertsey, 1923. Owner of Chartwell Farm, 1941–6.

August 1945

Work for Whitbread[1]

1. Finish clearing up the nettles etc. below the new chicken-house.

2. Cut the remainder of the nettles at the bottom of the lowest lake and clear the overflow gully. Do not let out anymore water than is now in the lake, but clear behind the sill.

3. Finish cutting the nettles in the dump next to the loose-boxes. Clear the little rock stream from where it flows out of the pool of the 40 golden orfes down the meadow to the swimming pool. Do not attempt any making good, so far as making it hold water is concerned. I will attend to the water when I come back. Do not touch any of the pools.

4. The path from the house to the cottage does not follow the line of the small stepping-stones. I explained this to Whitbread, and he will make it right in due course.

It is fairly urgent to put the first 4 or 5 steps in order from near the lavender bushes down the path. They are slippery and uneven, and may cause an accident. The stones need placing flat or replacing with halves of the big ones like those in front of the Studio. Very likely a new piece of oak is required. The steps running down by the side of the wall can be left for the present.

5. The nettles and thistles in the enclosure around the top pool in the field which is full of rushes, next to the concrete catchment basin, should be cut.

6. More general work to be undertaken as and when convenient, as, for instance, the inspection and putting in order of the fox-proof fence. Probably some wire netting will be required for this, but not much, as it is only patching and filling in places where the fox has scratched underneath.

7. When the horse and cart come, fallen wood should be collected from the park and from the belts and brought to the saw-bench. It is not necessary to cut the wood up at the present time.

8. On a wet day, Whitbread will clean out the Studio.

9. The additional fruit-garden, which is wired in, underneath Miss Seymour's[2] cottage, should be cleared of weeds and thistles. Mrs Churchill should arrange with Harris what it is best to do with this. Should we try to grow more fruit there as originally intended, or should we put down potatoes or (?) sunflowers. The first thing is to clear it of weeds.

---

[1] Henry Whitbread (1892–?). Worked for Churchill at Chartwell for 18 years before, during and after the war. One of those who taught Churchill bricklaying. A former company sergeant-major and an outspoken Socialist, he was much liked and depended upon by Churchill.

[2] Horatia Seymour, 1881–1966. Clementine Churchill's friend. Daughter of Horace Seymour, Gladstone's Private Secretary, 1880–5, and Deputy Master and Comptroller of the Royal Mint from 1894 until his death in 1902. In 1908 she was a bridesmaid at Churchill's wedding.

September 1945

Winston S. Churchill to Sir William Rootes
(Churchill papers, 2/140)

1 September 1945

My dear Sir William Rootes,

As I am going abroad for two or three weeks to stay with Field Marshal Alexander in Italy, I am returning to you this day the car which you so very kindly lent me. It has been a great comfort to me to have the use of this car, and to be able to hire the most excellent driver you have supplied.

I should be most grateful if you could extend this privilege to me for about ten days on my return, as I have not yet had time to make permanent arrangements. I should not like you to be put to any expense on this account.

I must thank you also for lending me the open car on VJ Day. It was a great pleasure to me to use it driving through the delighted crowds.

Once more thanking you for your courtesy,

Lord Moran:[1] diary
('The Struggle for Survival', pages 313–14)

2 September 1945

We left Northolt this morning in Alex's Dakota and arrived at Milan after a flight of five and a half hours. All the time Winston remained buried in a printed copy of the minutes which for five years he had sent out month by month to the Chiefs of Staff and the Cabinet. Even during luncheon he went on reading, only taking his eyes from the script to light a cigar. I drove with him to the house on Lake Como that had been prepared for him.

'People say my speeches after Dunkirk were the thing. That was only a part,

---

[1] Charles McMoran Wilson, 1882–1977. Physician. On active service as Medical Officer, 1914–18; Maj., RAMC (MC, despatches twice). Dean, St Mary's Hospital Medical School, 1920–45. Knighted, 1938. Churchill's doctor, 1940–55. President, Royal College of Physicians, 1941–50. Baron Moran, 1943. In 1965, immediately after Churchill's death, published *Winston Churchill, the Struggle for Survival*.

not the chief part,' he complained. 'They forgot I made all the main military decisions. You'd like to read my minutes, Charles.'

I asked him had they worn well. He smiled comfortably.

'They are mine. I can publish them.'

[. . .]

Sarah Churchill to Clementine Churchill
('Keep on Dancing, An Autobiography', pages 78–9)

3 September 1945   Lake Como

I wish you were here with us. I was so distressed to see you so unhappy and tired when we left, and so was he. We never see a lovely sight that he doesn't say: 'I wish your mother were here.' Wow! You know, I expect you will feel a little low and tired and oppressed by the million domesticities that will now sink down upon you, for a bit. Six years is a long time to live at such a high tempo, knowing as fully as you did all the moments of anxiety and worry, and decisions. You are bound to feel a reaction – as he does, and will for some time.

I'm quite anxious in case time lies heavy here. He has said he does not wish to see anybody but Alex (Field Marshal Alexander in whose house we were staying) and Admiral John Cunningham,[1] who are coming in a few days – of course I think that is wonderful! But wonder how long he will really find Charles[2] and me and a youthful ADC company at dinner. For the first time, for a long time, I felt nervous and selfconscious the first night at dinner. We sat at an enormous green glass table, with a cool impersonal yard or two of green glass between us, in an oval pale green room, with 4 white-coated 4th Hussar batmen attending to us. I felt like a goldfish in a bowl. I looked across the green stretch at a slightly perspiring ADC in an agony of nerves, in case something should go wrong, at Charles lost in a coma of philosophical meditation with himself about how many bugs the Italian water he was about to drink contained and whether they would prove fatal or not, and then to Papa looking pink in his white suit, and rather aggressively at some soup. 'Is this hot or cold?' he asked suddenly – 'Oh dear,' I thought. 'Very hot, sir,' replied the white-coated attendant. Papa drank his soup – I felt the next few weeks depended entirely on whether they could make consommé or not.

---

[1] John Henry Dacres Cunningham, 1885–1962. Entered RN as a Cadet, 1900. Cdr, 1917; Navigator on HMS *Renown*, 1917, and HMS *Lion*, 1918. ACNS (Air), 1937; 5th Sea Lord and CNAS, 1938. Commanded 1st Cruiser Sqn, 1938–41. Took part in the Norwegian campaign (evacuation of Namsos), May 1940. Naval Cdr, Dakar expedition, Sep. 1940. 4th Sea Lord and Chief of Supplies and Transport, 1940–2. Knighted, 1941. C-in-C, Levant, 1943. C-in-C, Mediterranean, and Allied Naval Commander, 1943–5 (including the Anzio and South of France landings). 1st Sea Lord, 1946–8. One of his two sons, a submariner, was killed in action in 1941.

[2] Lord Moran.

They could! Very good. The tension in the goldfish bowl eased – all was well! As a matter of fact, I think all is very well.

Firstly the ADC (Captain Ozier[1]) is a tremendous success. He is a big husky young man who has been through the entire war, and seen much action. I thought him about 30, but he is only 25 – Dunkirk to the Gothic line via Alamein, has physically matured him – but he is extremely youthful to talk to, intelligent, kind and considerate to Papa. They get on like a house on fire. Charles and I sit back comfortably while the two boys fight the battles from Omdurman to Alamein!

Next the painting – the first picture was a success – a luminous lake and boats, backed by a beetling crag, with a miniature toy village caught in the sunlight at its foot.

Thirdly – of course the villa. It is a Hollywood palace with mirrors and mirrors – I never know whether I'm coming or going as I converge on myself from 100 angles – and my bathroom! It is cream and apricot marble. The bath is in the middle of the room like a throne – right in front of long French windows – so that one can see out over the lake to the mountains, and again more mirrors – so about six of me step into the apricot throne. It's fun – but I never feel I'm alone, and the first evening I was convulsed with giggles as a chorus of Sarahs completed her ablutions!

The weather is perfect, by no means too hot as yet – a cool breeze runs round the lake as though to order in the early morning – and then again in the late afternoon. The nights are cool and the crickets sing under the windows.

We should be very happy here – now at last one can sit in the sun without the thought of war sitting just beside one.

As for the Italians – I search their faces – they are all gay, brown and smiling, and seemingly quite untouched by the war. War to them is obviously like everything else in their lives, something physical – a physical catastrophe that happens, is unpleasant, is over, and forgotten, like an earthquake; not a moral or emotional upheaval to be pondered on, a bitter lesson from which something must be learnt. Oh no – the tooth has stopped aching – the sun shines again. Who won it? Who lost it? Who cares? That was last week – this is today. Look! Churchill – Churchill – Hurrah – Hurrah! Both the young and old know him. I was astonished at a bunch of children – the eldest not more than 12 or 13 – looked at us calmly and the eldest said, 'Churchill'. They can't do enough for us, they bring out chairs for us to sit on, towels to dry our hands with, and then retire about 20 yards and sit and watch for hours. Our ADC has the hearty contempt that all the soldiers who have fought them, or been long in Italy have for them. I think he thinks we are too polite with them. In front of a barrage of smiles, it is difficult to be other than cordial – but then suddenly the picture of Mussolini and his mistress[2] in the market square flash

---

[1] John Ogier, 1921–77. Maj., 4th Queen's Own Hussars, 1944. ADC to Churchill, 1945.
[2] Clara Petacci, 1912–45. Mussolini's principal mistress, 1936–45. Executed with Mussolini in Mezzegra, 1945.

into one's mind – and one remembers that there is no stability, no reserve in this crowd. They smile as the sun shines – and the sun shines brightly today.

He is going to start a new picture today. I really think he is settling down – he said last night: 'I've had a happy day.' I haven't heard that for I don't know how long!

Winston S. Churchill to Clementine Churchill
(Baroness Spencer-Churchill papers)

3 September 1945   Lake Como

My darling Clementine,

This is really one of the most pleasant and delectable places I have ever struck. It is a small palace almost entirely constructed of marble inside. It abuts on the lake, with bathing steps reached by a lift. It is of course completely modernized, and must have been finished just before the War, by one of Mussolini's rich commercants who has fled, whither it is not known. The villa is officially called the Headquarters of the 2nd Division but no one else is here except our party and a very agreeable young officer from the 4th Hussars who has been told off as my aide-de-camp. Every conceivable arrangement has been made for our pleasure and convenience. Sarah and I have magnificent rooms covering a whole floor, with large marble baths and floods of hot and cold water.

Alex is coming here on the 6th for a few days and has suggested I go on with him to Trieste, where there is to be a Tattoo. I am rather doubtful about this, as I do not want publicity or to see strangers. Moreover, here the weather is delightful, being bright and warm with cool breezes. Yesterday we motored over the mountains to Lake Lugano, where I found quite a good subject for a picture. I made a good beginning and hope to go back there tomorrow, missing one day. I have spotted another place for this afternoon. These lake-shore subjects run a great risk of degenerating into 'chocolate box', even if successfully executed.

I have been thinking a lot about you. I so hope you will not let the work of moving in to these 2 houses wear you down. Please take plenty of rest. With fondest love

Your devoted husband,[1]

                                                             [Drawing of a pig]

---

[1] The last paragraph and valediction were handwritten.

Clementine Churchill to Winston S. Churchill
(*Churchill papers, 1/41*)[1]

4 September 1945

My darling Winston,

On Saturday the day you flew away, I went to Woodford to open a Vegetable Show held by the local Allotment Holders. It was a gray uncertain afternoon and I thought of you and Sarah in the windy rainy misty skies. Driving along the road so familiar for more than twenty years, I thought how the War had changed it. Many of the humble but neat little homes were shattered, all were battered and squalid. In every space, where before had been only shops and houses, huge menacing Venereal Disease posters were erected. After passing half a dozen of these – suddenly I saw a new design – the picture of an insect (upside down so that you could see his mandibles and count his crawling feet) magnified to 12 feet and across it written 'Beware the Common Bed Bug'.

Mary's Birthday is on Saturday the 15th – I enclose her address, but perhaps if you and Sarah send me the letters they will reach her faster than posting in Italy. (The post varies 4 days to a week.)

I have visited my Maternity Hospital. Mr and Mrs Attlee[2] visited it last week from Chequers. They have a niece, the wife of a young Naval Officer who has had her baby there. She has now gone on to 'Fir Croft', the Convalescent Home nearby. (You may remember Lord Portal gave me this hope).

The doctor came to me and said 'do you think Mr Churchill would visit us once, before we close in December? It would give us all such joy.' I said I could not promise but would tell you.

My love to Sarah. I do hope her nettle rash has not only subsided, but has really vanished so that she can enjoy everything. And I do hope your painting is fine and does not give you indigestion. I expect you are bathing too?

When you see Alex pray give him my respects and admiration.

---

[1] This letter was handwritten.
[2] Violet Helen Millar, 1895–1964. Married, 1922, Clement Attlee: four children. Styled Countess Attlee, 1955.

Admiral Sir Bruce Fraser[1] to Winston S. Churchill
(Churchill papers, 2/141)

5 September 1945

My dear Prime Minister (if I may still call you this),

I thought you would like a line written with the pen with which the surrender was signed and in an envelope stamped on the day aboard *Missouri* and *Duke of York*. The Americans did it very well and MacArthur impressed us all beyond measure with his dignity and bearing.

Opposite stood Shigemetou[2] completely impassive and before the war I had dined with him many times in London when he was ambassador. A strange sight.

Yesterday landed at Yokohama, saw MacArthur and then drove to Tokyo rather pushing my way through American barriers.

The 17 mile drive shows every house razed to the ground by fire, but on arrival by the Emperor's Palace many of the main buildings are standing as HE bombs had not yet been used.

The Japanese impassive but friendly and I think all the kick has now gone out of them. It was quite a pleasure to see the British Embassy untouched and well cared for, and what a thrill to be the first to sign my name in the visitors' book since the war started, lying as it was in almost the original place.

Also, the King and Queen's portraits on the wall.

None of the Japs looked unfed; I think the main cause of the sudden end was
  (a) The blockade (sea power supported by the land and air still dominates).
  (b) The bombing when once the bombers and their supplies had been carried by the Navy within range.

They apparently had a great system of a lathe or a little machinery in every house. Once this started to break up, their production was gone.

Our prisoners rather better than I had expected; a good deal of malnutrition and some of the longer ones rather weary. T/B seems the most prevalent.

The one bad place was a hospital camp where there was much ill treatment.

May I again thank you for all your kindness to me and may I send my very best wishes to all your family.

---

[1] Bruce Austin Fraser, 1888–1981. OBE, 1919. CB, 1939. 3rd Sea Lord and Controller of the Navy, 1939–42. VAdm., 1940. KBE, 1941. Second-in-Command, Home Fleet, 1942. KCB, 1943. C-in-C, Home Fleet, 1943–4; Eastern Fleet, 1944; British Pacific Fleet, 1944–5. GCB, 1944. Adm., 1944. Baron Fraser of North Cape, 1946. 1st and Principal Naval ADC to the King, 1946–8. Adm. of the Fleet, 1948. 1st Sea Lord and CNS, 1948–51.

[2] Mamoru Shigemitsu, 1881–1957. Japanese Minister to China, 1930–6 (when he lost a leg to a Korean terrorist's bomb, an injury that caused him pain for the rest of his life). Ambassador to the Soviet Union, 1936–8; to Britain, 1938–41. Appointed Ambassador to the Nanking (puppet) Government two days after Pearl Harbor. Ambassador to France, 1942. Foreign Minister, 1943–5. One of the two Japanese who participated in the Japanese surrender on board USS *Missouri*, 1945. Imprisoned for war crimes. Subsequently Deputy PM and Foreign Minister, 1954–6.

September 1945

Winston S. Churchill to Clementine Churchill
(Baroness Spencer-Churchill papers)

5 September 1945   Lake Como

My darling,

We have had three lovely sunshine days, and I have two large canvasses under way, one of a scene on the Lake of Lugano and the other here at Como. The design is I think good in both cases, and it has been great fun painting them. Today I was going to finish the second of the two, but last night we had a heavy and prolonged thunderstorm and now there are clouds and no sunlight effects.

I cannot describe to you the luxury of this small palace. It is the last word in modern millionairism. It must not be judged as a work of art but simply as a most convenient, up-to-date residence adapted to the lake situation. Doors, windows and shutters all slide or shut with the utmost smoothness and precision. It is nice walking barefoot on the large marble floors or soft carpets. I have a portico at either end of my rooms. The dining room is a striking creation of marble and mirrors, not unduly decorated. There is a large cage with a beautiful parrot of doubtful temper, and another in which twenty canaries chirrup or at night sleep in a long row on their perch. There is a small bathing-pool in the garden which is full of very clear water, but also the lake is only a few yards away. A lift carries you up the 70 or 80 feet from the water to the successive floors of the house. I bathed yesterday for a few minutes after painting at Lake Lugano, but I have not been in the water here.

Alex arrives tomorrow, and I am looking forward very much to seeing him. I cannot say too much for the care and authority which he has bestowed on making my visit pleasant. For instance, I am guarded by the 4th Hussars. 24 men and two officers travelled 400 miles (I blush to say) from Austria to be my personal protectors here, and the Colonel, Barne,[1] arrived also yesterday, a most agreeable man, who, again, has come this enormous distance. On the road he had a motor accident of a most dangerous character which might easily have killed him and the two others on board. The car was gradually forced off the road by a lorry, struck the embankment, went over a 12-foot prop turning twice in the air, to be smashed out of all recognition. The Colonel, his servant and the driver were all unhurt. Fancy what I should have felt if they or any of them had been killed!

However, thank God we are now safely assembled, and I have three 4th Hussar Officers. The men are all picked men, but were very keen to come and are particularly smart and intelligent. My aide-de-camp Major Ogier – he

---

[1] Anthony Miles Barne, 1906–96. Commissioned 2nd Lt, Royal Dragoons, 1927. Movement Control Officer, Haifa, 1939–40; Staff Capt., 1940. GHQ, Middle East, 1940–1. CO, Royals, 1942–3; Second-in-Command, 1943. Second-in-Command, 4th Queen's Own Hussars, 1943–4; CO, 1944–6. OBE, 1945. CO, 62 Training Rgt, 1947–8. Asst Commandant, Army Apprentice School, Harrogate, 1948. Commandant, RAC Depot, 1948–51. Retired with hon. rank of Lt-Col., 1953.

is only 24 – is most attentive and tireless in planning painting and bathing expeditions with picnic lunches. Last night General Heydemann,[1] who commands the 2nd Military District, came and dined. This house is nominally his Headquarters, though he has never used it and keeps it for the Field Marshal. He brought with him his Staff Officer, Sir Nigel Mordaunt,[2] who has distinguished himself in the war and is now delighted to return in a few days to the Stock Exchange whence he sprung. He is a friend of Randolph's and spoke very appreciatively of him. He seems quite young to have reached the position of GSOI. The General lunched with us after the last war at Sussex Square. He was employed in Palestine, and evidently it was on this subject that I made contact with him. He is a very able man and has managed all the difficult problems of the military occupation, the displaced persons and the relations with the Italians and foreign contingents, Poles, etc., in his area with great success. He is, like his Staff officer, a dyed-in-the-wool Tory, and says the soldiers all voted wrong for two reasons, first, the shortage of cigarettes, and secondly, their belief that a Labour Government would get them out of the Army quicker. Although his name is Heydemann and his extraction German and his appearance Semitic, he served for many years in the Queen's Bays and rose to command that regiment.

An air of complete tranquillity and good humour pervades these beautiful lakes and valleys, which are unravaged by war. There is not a sign to be seen in the countryside, the dwellings or the demeanour or appearance of the inhabitants which would suggest that any violent events have been happening in the world. I am, of course, immediately recognised, even by a small party of young girls right out in the mountains, and everywhere am clapped and cheered, pressed with demands for autographs and so on. The feeling of the population towards the British Army seems very good, and I understand everything works most smoothly. Of course, however, the Italians are very good at making themselves agreeable. They are a handsome race in these mountains, with a great many fair-haired people, both men and women. The children are well nourished, and nobody seems to have suffered in any way. The Partisans are frequently to be seen in their half-uniform carrying their weapons. I am told that in this part of the country they were very strong and ardent, and that there were hardly any Germans, so that they were also successful. The people have the air of having won the war (if there was a war), and make the V-sign to me with gusto. All they want is a large influx of tourists to make their happiness and prosperity complete. Meanwhile the place of these is supplied by large British, American, New Zealand and South African leave resorts established in all the hotels for officers and men. On the road near this house is painted a large sign 'American Bar – English spoken.'

[1] Cecil Albert Heydeman, 1889–1967. Educated at Temple Grove. Bde Cdr, 2nd Cavalry Bde, 1935. Cdr Presidency, Assam District, Calcutta, 1939–41. Div. Cdr, 1941–3.
[2] Nigel John Mordaunt, 1907–79. Educated at Christ Church, Oxford. Married, 1938, Anne Tritton: four children. Succeeded as 13th Bt, 1939. On active service during WWII (despatches). MBE, 1954.

September 1945

It has done me no end of good to come out here and resume my painting. I am much better in myself, and am not worrying about anything. We have had no newspapers since I left England, and I no longer feel any keen desire to turn their pages. This is the first time for very many years that I have been completely out of the world. The Japanese War being finished and complete peace and victory achieved, I feel a great sense of relief which grows steadily, others having to face the hideous problems of the aftermath. On their shoulders and consciences weighs the responsibility for what is happening in Germany and Central Europe. It may all indeed be 'a blessing in disguise'.

I imagine to stay here for another fortnight from now, as I have ascertained that this would be welcomed, and thereafter I may stay with Duff[1] and Diana[2] in Paris for two or three days. He has sent me a cordial invitation.

I long to hear from you how you are progressing on your two fronts, and whether Whitbread is continuing to give you satisfaction, and when the German prisoners are going to come. I expect to find when I return that all the barbed wire they have collected from the grounds will have been made into an impenetrable defence around the property in order to prevent the premature arrival of milch cows. How are the Beaverbrook chickens? Have they laid any eggs yet? Is there any particular flavour about the eggs that you do not like? I fear you must be very near the end of the lemon-scented magnolias.

The sun is beginning to gleam fitfully through the clouds, so perhaps we are going to have a painting afternoon.

Darling a tiresome thing has happened to me. When I was very young I ruptured myself & had to wear a truss. I left if off before I went to Harrow & have managed 60 years of rough & tumble. Now however in the last 10 days it has come back. There is no pain, but I have had to be fitted w a truss wh I shall have to wear when not in bed for the rest of my life.

Charles got a military surgeon from Rome who flew & has been in for the last 3 days.

I do hope you are having a good rest & not taking things too seriously. I have still had no letters or papers & have not the slightest idea what is going on.

Always yr loving husband
[Sketch of a pig]

Sarah is a joy to all.

---

[1] Alfred Duff Cooper, 1890–1954. Known as 'Duff'. Educated at Eton and New College, Oxford. Entered FO as a clerk, 1913. On active service, Grenadier Guards, 1917–18 (DSO, despatches). MP (Cons.) for Oldham, 1924–9; for St George's, Westminster, 1931–45. Financial Secretary, War Office, 1928–9, 1931–4; Treasury, 1934–5. PC, 1935. Secretary of State for War, 1935–7. 1st Lord of the Admiralty, 1937–8. Minister of Information, 1940–1. British Representative, Singapore, 1941. Chancellor of the Duchy of Lancaster, 1941–3. British Representative to French Committee of National Liberation in Algiers, Jan.–Aug.1944. Ambassador to France, 1944–7. Knighted, 1948. Viscount Norwich, 1952.

[2] Diana Olivia Winifred Maud Manners, 1892–1986. Daughter of 8th Duke of Rutland. Married, 1919, Alfred Duff Cooper (later Viscount Norwich). After her husband's death in 1954, known as Lady Diana Cooper.

Lord Moran: diary
('The Struggle for Survival', pages 320–1)

5 September 1945

[. . .]

When I went to his room to settle him for the night he was reading his minutes. The war was over, he was out of it all, but as he read his mind went back to the great crises when everything was at stake. He lived again the Battle of Britain. Though it was after midnight he made me sit down. 'You see, Charles, it was very nearly the end of everything.'

I have heard him tell this story many times. He always picked the same day, September 15, when he went to Fighter Command at Uxbridge. Winston sees everything in pictures. I could feel the tension in the operation room, fifty feet underground. I could see Park[1] walking up and down giving his orders. And then, as more of our fighting squadrons were put in, more of the little electric bulbs on the great blackboard glowed red. All the bulbs were red now, all our squadrons were in the air. Park was standing still. At last, unable to control himself, the PM turned to him: 'How many more have you got?' 'I am putting in my last,' Park replied. The two men waited, but nothing happened. The Germans, too, had put in their last. As the PM climbed the stairway the All Clear sounded.

[. . .]

Harold Nicolson to Winston S. Churchill
(Churchill papers, 2/142)

6 September 1945

Dear Mr Churchill,

Randolph (whom I met yesterday) encouraged me to give you two very different comments which I have recently received. I should not have the impertinence to write these to you were it not that Randolph assured me that you liked getting these perfectly authentic expressions of opinion.

The first comes from a young friend of mine who, owing to his having a bad stammer has not been able to get a Commission and is serving as a Corporal with the British Army of the Rhine. He is therefore able to give me a picture of barrack-room opinion. He writes as follows:

'In their futile political arguments they speak of Labour collectively, but when they wish to say Conservative they say Churchill. And yet when the

---

[1] Keith Rodney Park, 1892–1975. New Zealand Expeditionary Force, 1914. Royal Field Artillery, 1915 (on active service at Gallipoli and in France). Capt., RAF, 1918 (MC and bar; DFC). Commanded No. 2 Fighter Group, Apr.–Dec. 1940. AOC No. 23 Group, Training Command, 1941. Commanded RAF Egypt, 1942. Knighted, 1942. AOC Malta, 1942–3; Middle East, 1944. Allied Air C-in-C, South East Asia, 1945–6.

election results came out there was no rejoicing or even satisfaction. Men who had spent the past weeks with their voices perpetually raised in heated and fantastic obloquy of Mr Churchill sat down and said, half ashamedly – "poor old Basket. Best bloody Prime Minister we ever 'ad. He'd know how to get us out of this mess. Wonder how he feels now. This 'ere Attlee – 'e aint got the touch the same as the old man had. Bugger me, wish I'd known."'

The second comment comes from a more educated source. I was dining with Arthur Salter[1] last night and he told me about the new House of Commons. He said that seldom can any election have returned so large a number of eager, intelligent and somewhat bewildered young Members. 'The whole thing' he said,

> 'might have got out of hand had it not been for Churchill. It was not only the speeches that he made on the Address, but his general attitude and the patience with which he has sat in the House and listened to many maiden speeches. He has succeeded in making all these young impatient people realize what centuries of tradition lie behind the House of Commons and has shown to them that when one of the greatest Statesmen in our history can accept electoral defeat without bitterness, and display the utmost deference to the working of the Constitution and the authority of the House itself, then younger Members, however gifted and impatient they may feel, must adopt a similar attitude of discipline and reverence.'

He then added the following sentence which I am glad to say much impressed the Americans who were present:

'One is apt' he said 'to take the word "magnanimity" as some academic expression. Churchill, since July 26, has given it a concrete splendour.'

I only send you these since Randolph told me it might please you.

---

[1] James Arthur Salter, 1881–1975. Transport Dept, Admiralty, 1904. Chairman, Allied Maritime Transport Executive, 1918. Knighted, 1922. Director, Economic and Finance Section, League of Nations, 1919–20, 1922–31. Prof. of Political Theory and Institutions, Oxford University, 1934–44. MP (Ind.) for Oxford University, 1937–50; (Cons.) for Ormskirk, 1951–3. Parliamentary Secretary, Ministry of Shipping, 1939–41; Ministry of War Transport, 1941. Head of British Merchant Shipping Mission, Washington DC, 1941–3. PC, 1941. Deputy Director-General, UNRRA, 1944. Chancellor of the Duchy of Lancaster, 1945. Minister of State for Economic Affairs, 1951–2. Minister of Materials, 1952–3. Baron, 1953. Head of Special Economic Mission to Iraq, 1954.

September 1945

Clementine Churchill to Winston S. Churchill
(Churchill papers, 1/41)[1]

6 September 1945

My darling Winston & Sarah,

No letters yet from either of you, & I expect mine take as long to reach you. But I am kept informed by the Press that you have painted 2 pictures from the shore of the lake near your 'three storied villa', & that you sometimes go out in a motor boat & that you drive about in a yellow car, & that your privacy is being respected, & that there are guards round the villa, & that you have had secret meetings with Italian royalists, & that there is no truth in these rumours, & that you sometimes sit on a terrace & talk to your 'Physician Lord Moran' & to your 'daughter Sarah'!

The workmen have begun mending the roof etc of the new house & the Press (*Evening Standard*) forced their way in & photographed the rooms & threatened to reveal what you had paid for it;[2] but I telephoned and asked them not to publish anything & they desisted.

People seem disappointed but resigned over the slow demobilization. But Mary will be out in February & she has applied for a London 'posting' so we shall have her living with us this Autumn & Winter which will be a joy & a comfort.

Winston S. Churchill to Sir John Anderson
(Churchill papers, 2/3)

7 September 1945   Lake Como, Italy

My dear John,

Thank you for your letter, but I am very sorry that Cherwell was not included. I did not know that membership of this Committee prevented consultation with the responsible leaders of the Opposition; I am sure that in practice it will not do so. With regard to Blackett, the point is not so much what he will do as what the Americans will do. I apprehend that they will be increasingly shy of imparting the further developments, and that the presence of Blackett will undo some of the advantages that may be gained by your membership.

PS. Lovely here in these sunlit, unravaged valleys. I paint all day. My regards to Ava.[3]

---

[1] This letter was handwritten.
[2] In margin: 'I can't think how they found out!'
[3] Ava Bodley, 1896–1974. Married, 1925, Ralph Follet Wigram (d. 1936): one son; 1941, John Anderson.

September 1945

Clementine Churchill to Winston S. Churchill
(Churchill papers, 1/41)[1]

7 September 1945

My darling Winston,

   I was so much pleased to get your telegraph saying that you had achieved some victories in the field of painting What Fun! Please don't impose on them but leave well alone! I'm just off to Chartwell after not being there for more than a week. There has been so much to do here in connection with the land or house. So now, I am expecting to find not a single nettle, the new trees nicely compressed into shape and I'm going to be introduced to Max's hens – I wrote to Horatia, explaining that presently we should need her cottage and she is very upset and wrote me a curt letter which I enclose. My handwriting is worse than usual because I have packed my two fountain pens and this is the Office pen!

Alfred Duff Cooper to Winston S. Churchill
(Churchill papers, 2/140)[2]

7 September 1945   Paris

My dear Winston,

   I have not bothered you before with a letter because I was sure that you were overwhelmed with correspondence, nor could I easily express my feelings with respect to the result of the election. The more I think of it however the more I am convinced that the true interpretation of that event is that the Conservative party were paying for the sins of the past – sins of which you were guiltless – and I only partly guilty. They were paying for Munich and for Hoare–Laval, for having failed in those two branches of affairs in which it was believed they could be trusted, the conduct of foreign affairs and the maintenance of defence. After 20 years of hardly interrupted power they landed the country into a war for which they had failed to make the proper preparations. A fearful indictment. The normal swing to the left had been restrained during the period because the middle classes distrusted the socialists but after they had seen Socialist Ministers working successfully under your direction and control for five years they lost that distrust and have now definitely adopted the Labour party as the best alternative, and the party itself has ceased to be a class party.

   However I had not meant to bore you with a political lecture. I am really writing to say how much I was looking forward to seeing you in Paris and how

---

[1] This letter was handwritten.
[2] This letter was handwritten.

I now fear that I may be deprived of that pleasure. I have been summoned to London to be there during the conference of Foreign Ministers which begins on the 10th and can hardly last less than a fortnight. Diane however will be in Paris and will be most delighted to receive you at the embassy and will make you, I hope, very comfortable. Blum[1] is now in London. He wrote to me before he left to ask whether it was true, as he had read in the papers, that you were in Italy. He hoped not for, he said, 'England will not seem to me like England without Winston Churchill.' For the moment his prestige stands higher than that of any many in France. The General[2] has lost and continues to lose ground. He commits one folly after another – the crowning one being his refusal to receive a deputation on which all the most important political parties were represented. Herriot[3] has lost a little ground and Reynaud[4] a lot as the result of the Pétain[5] trial. The Radical–Socialist party conference did further harm to Herriot and still more to Daladier.[6] The political future of France is very obscure.

So, incidentally, is my own. Bevin has not been able so far to give me any assurances that I shall not be withdrawn. My own belief is that he wishes to

---

[1] Léon Blum, 1872–1950. Born in Paris, of Jewish parents. Chef de Cabinet to Minister of Public Works, 1914. Deputy for Paris, 1919. A leader of the 'Front Populaire', 1936. PM, June 1936 to June 1937. Vice-President of the Cabinet, 1937–8. PM and Finance Minister, Mar.–Apr. 1938. Interned in Germany, 1941–5. PM and Foreign Minister, Dec. 1946 to Jan. 1947. President of the French Socialist Party.

[2] Charles de Gaulle, 1890–1970. On active service on the Western Front, 1914–16 (thrice wounded; despatches). POW, 1916–18 (five attempts to escape). Commanded 4th Armoured Bde, 5th Army, Sep. 1939; 4th Armoured Div., May 1940. Under-Secretary for War and National Defence, 6 June 1940. Chief of the Free French (later President of the French National Committee), London and Brazzaville, 1940–2. President, French Committee of National Liberation, Algiers, 1943. President of the Provisional Government of the French Republic, and head of its armed forces, Nov. 1943 to Jan. 1946. PM, June 1958 to Jan. 1959. President, Dec. 1958 to June 1969.

[3] Édouard Herriot, 1872–1957. French writer and politician. Mayor of Lyons, 1905. Minister of Supplies, 1916. A Socialist–Radical deputy from 1919. PM and Foreign Minister, June 1924 to Apr. 1925, July 1926 (for one day), and June–Dec. 1932. Minister of Education, 1926–8. Wrote *The Well-Springs of Liberty* (1940). Interned by the Germans, 1943–5. On VE Day, 8 May 1945, he was at the British Embassy in Moscow, having recently been liberated by the Soviet Army. President of the Socialist–Radical Party, 1945. President of the National Assembly, 1947–54.

[4] Paul Reynaud, 1878–1966. On active service, 1914–18 (twice decorated). Entered Chamber of Deputies, 1919. Minister of Colonies, 1931–2. Minister of Justice, Apr.–Nov. 1938. Minister of Finance, 1930, Nov. 1938 to Mar. 1940. PM, 21 Mar. to 17 June 1940 (Foreign Minister, 21 Mar. to 18 May, 6–17 June 1940). Arrested by the Vichy Government, Sep. 1940. Deported to Germany, 1943–5. Released, 1945. Minister of Finance, 1948. Deputy PM, 1953. President of Finance Committee of the National Assembly, 1958.

[5] Henri Philippe Benoni Orner Joseph Pétain, 1856–1951. Commanded an infantry regiment, Aug. 1914; an army corps, Oct. 1914; 2nd Army, June 1915. In charge at siege of Verdun, 1916. CGS, April 1917. C-in-C, May 1917 to Nov. 1918. Vice-President, Supreme War Council, 1920–30. War Minister, 1934. Ambassador in Madrid, 1939–40. PM, 16 June 1940; negotiated the armistice with Germany, 22 June 1940. Chief of State, 1940–4. Condemned to death after the liberation of France, 1945; sentence commuted to life imprisonment.

[6] Edouard Daladier, 1884–1970. Entered Chamber of Deputies, 1919. Minister for Colonies, 1924. PM, 1933 and again in 1934 (for two months). Minister of War and Defence, 1932–4, June 1936 to 18 May 1940. PM, Apr. 1938 to Mar. 1940. An opponent of Vichy, he was held in custody in Germany from 1943 to 1945, including some months at Buchenwald concentration camp.

keep me on but is being subjected to pressure in the other direction. It would look a little cold if they kept on Edward Halifax with his Munich record and sacked me with mine. I should be sorry to leave Paris but not heart-broken. If I could find a constituency I am sure that I should thoroughly enjoy helping you in the House of Commons. I have never been in opposition except for a few months in 1931 and I believe I should enjoy it. I am delighted to see that Brendan has got Bournemouth. You will soon have a pretty powerful staff around you – and ought to have a lot of fun.

I hope that if I miss you in Paris I shall see you here in London.

Winston S. Churchill to Clementine Churchill
(Baroness Spencer-Churchill papers)

8 September 1945　　　　　　　　　　　　　　　　　　　　　　　Lake Como

My dearest one,

Alex and his aide-de-camp,[1] who is the son of Lord Templemore,[2] have left us after staying two nights. I hope Alex will come back again next weekend. He certainly enjoyed himself painting, and produced a very good picture considering it is the first time that he has handled a brush for six years. I have now four pictures, three of them large, in an advanced state, and I honestly think they are better than any I have painted so far. I gave Alex your message and he was very pleased.

The painting has been a great pleasure to me, and I have really forgotten all my vexations. It is a wonderful cure, because you really cannot think of anything else. This is Saturday, and it is a week since we started. We have had newspapers up till Wednesday. I have skimmed through them, and it certainly seems we are going to have a pretty hard time. I cannot feel the Government are doing enough about demobilization, still less about getting our trade on the move again. I do not know how we are ever to pay our debts, and it is even difficult to see how we shall pay our way. Even if we were all united in a Coalition, gathering all the strength of the nation, our task might well be beyond our powers. However, all this seems already quite remote from me on

---

[1] Desmond Clive Chichester, 1920–2000. Son of 4th Baron Templemore. Educated at Harrow and Christ Church, Oxford. Married, 1946, Lorna Althea Ravenhill (d. 1948) : one son; 1951, Felicity Stella Harrison: one son. On active service during WWII, 1939–45. Commissioned, Coldstream Guards, 1940. MC, 1944. ADC to FM Sir Harold (later Lord) Alexander, 1945, 1948–50; to Gen. Sir William Duthie Morgan, 1945–6.

[2] Arthur Claud Spencer Chichester, 1880–1953. Educated at Harrow and Royal Military Academy, Sandhurst. Married, 1911, Clare Meriel Wingfield: three children. 2nd Lt, Royal Fusiliers, 1900. On active service during 2nd Boer War (1902) and WWI (1914–18). DSO, 1918. OBE, 1919. Succeeded as 4th Baron Templemore, 1924. Parliamentary Private Secretary to Under-Secretary of State for War, 1927–9. Lord-in-Waiting to King George V, 1929, 1931–4. Capt., Yeomen of the Guard, 1934–45. KCVO, 1938. Cons. Chief Whip in House of Lords, 1940–5. PC, 1943.

this lovely lake, where nearly all the days are full of sunshine and the weather bright and cool.

Much better than the newspapers was your letter, with its amusing but rather macabre account of the journey to Woodford. I am longing to hear how our affairs are progressing. I do hope you are not overtaxing yourself with all the business that there is to do. We shall certainly not forget about Mary's birthday; but let me know what you have done about a present.

Considering how pleasant and delightful the days have been, I cannot say they have passed quickly. It seems quite a long time since I arrived, although every day has been full of interest and occupation. I have converted my enormous bathroom into a studio with makeshift easels, and there all this morning Alex and I tried to put the finishing touches on our pictures of yesterday. He has set his heart on buying a villa here on a promontory. I have not seen it inside, but from the outside it looks the most beautiful abode one can possibly imagine, and I understand that inside it is even more romantic, going back to the fifteenth century. He was a little startled when I pointed out to him that no one will be allowed to buy a property across the exchange perhaps for many years.

He begged me to stay on here as long as I like, but I think I shall come back the 18th or 19th. I am doubtful whether I shall stop in Paris. I expect in another ten or eleven days I shall be very keen to get home again. Sarah has been a great joy, and gets on with everybody. She and I both drive the speed-boats. They are a wonderful way of getting about this lake, and far safer than the awful winding roads around which the Italians career with motorcars and lorries at all sorts of speeds and angles.

Charles plays golf most days. There is a very pretty links here, and he has fierce contests with himself or against Bogey.[1] His devoted care of me is deeply touching.

You may be amused to see the elaborate form in which your telegram, which I rejoiced to receive today, was sent.

My Darling I think a gt deal of you & last night when I was driving the speed-boat back there came into my mind your singing to me 'In the Gloaming' years ago. What a sweet song & tune & how beautifully you sang it in all its pathos. My heart thrills w love to feel you near me in thought. I feel so tenderly towards you my darling & the more pleasant & agreeable the scenes and days, the more I wish you were here to share them & give me a kiss.

You see I have nearly forgotten how to write with a pen. Isn't awful my scribbles?

Miss Layton has heard from her 'boy-friend'[2] in S Africa that she is to go

---

[1] Possibly John Ogier.

[2] Frans Nel, 1917–2000. South African. Member, Corps of Signals, 1936–40. POW, 1942–5. Married Elizabeth Layton, 1946.

out there (not Canada) immediately if possible to marry him. So she is vy happy. Yesterday the South African officers came from their hotel & took her out to 'water-plane' behind their speed boat. She looked vy handsome whirling along in the water & made three large circles in front of the villa before she tumbles in. Sarah is writing you now. The DB[1] is starting. Always yr loving husband.[2]

[Sketch of pig]

Winston S. Churchill to James Byrnes
(Churchill papers, 2/140)

8 September 1945

My dear Mr Byrnes,

I have not till this moment found opportunity to answer your most kind letter of July 31, which it was a pleasure to receive. Although our official contacts did not last long, they were sufficient to show me your great grasp of affairs and power of getting things done. I also felt that we should be able to develop those close personal relations of friendship and confidence which are of such great value.

I have come here to Como at the invitation of Field Marshal Alexander, and am passing the days most pleasantly in painting. I fear therefore I shall not be in London during the meeting of the Foreign Ministers, unless that is protracted beyond about the 25th. I look forward so much, however, to seeing you again.

Winston S. Churchill to Mary Churchill
(Lady Soames papers)[3]

10 September 1945   Lake Como

My darling Mary,

'Many Happy Returns of the Day!' This shd reach you on yr Birthday the 15th; but if it comes earlier or later it carries with it the fondest love of yr Father. I have watched with admiration & respect the career of distinction and duty wh you have made for yourself during the hard years of the war. I look forward in the days that may be left me to see you happy & glorious in peace. You are a gt joy to yr mother & me & we are hoping that vy soon you will be living w us at Chartwell and in our new house in London. It will be lovely having you w us.

[1] Dinner bell.
[2] The last three paragraphs were handwritten.
[3] This letter was handwritten.

Here it is sunshine & calm. I paint all day & every day & have banished care & disillusionment to the Shades. Alex came & painted too. He is vy good. Monsieur Montag is coming to comment & guide me in a few days. I have three nice pictures so far, & am now off to seek for another. Sarah is writing you herself.

With all my affection
Your loving Father

PS. We will choose a present for you together when you come home.

Winston S. Churchill to Robert Graves[1]
(Churchill papers, 2/141)

11 September 1945   Lake Como

My dear Graves,

I have finished 'The Golden Fleece'. It is the stiffest of all your books, but once it gets hold of you, you cannot put it down. I am astonished at the tremendous amount of study and knowledge you have amassed, and how once again you are able to illumine the darkness, in this case profound, and so enable modern eyes to see these old mysteries. For this I am indeed grateful.

Some say that the present day Greeks are only Levantines, or at best the descendants of the slaves of the Ancient Greeks. But your book shows that their ancestors behaved in exactly the same way as they do now, and that Greek mythology is as tangled as Greek politics.

Once more thanking you for sending me much an interesting book,

---

[1] Robert von Ranke Graves, 1895–1985. Writer. Educated at Charterhouse and St John's College, Oxford (Hon. Fellow, 1971). Though a pacifist, he served in France during WWI with the Royal Welch Fusiliers. Bronze Medal for Poetry, Olympic Games, Paris, 1924. Prof. of English Literature, Egyptian University, 1926. Clark Lecturer, Trinity College Cambridge, 1954. Gold Medal of National Poetry Society of America, 1960. Prof. of Poetry, University of Oxford, 1961–6. Arthur Dehon Little Memorial Lecturer, MIT, 1963. Gold Medal for Poetry, Cultural Olympics, Mexico, 1968. Queen's Gold Medal for Poetry, 1968. His books (over 137) and manuscripts are on permanent exhibition at Lockwood Memorial Library, Buffalo, NY. In 1968 the village of Deya, Mallorca, where he had lived since 1929, recognised him as an adoptive son.

September 1945

Winston S. Churchill to Field Marshal Sir Harold Alexander
(Churchill papers, 2/140)

11 September 1945
Personal
No. 11

Montag comes Thursday 13th. I hope for heavy concentration on the pigmentorial front, preliminary bombardment beginning 14th and general assault 15th–16th. Essential you should be present on the battlefield and encourage troops to further victories. Weather conditions favourable and supplies of all kinds ample, especially now that Swiss communications can be opened.

Dorothy Spencer[1] to Kathleen Hill
(Churchill papers, 2/1)

11 September 1945

LETTERS ADDRESSED TO MR CHURCHILL

I thought you would like to have an idea how things stand now that the contents of the big box have been gone through and sorted.
I. <u>Letters of thanks from Party organisations.</u>
II. <u>Letters of thanks from other organisations. British. Empire and Foreign.</u>
We are sending Mr Churchill's facsimile acknowledgment to these (I and II) and are now up to date with them.
III. <u>Letters of thanks from individuals.</u>
    (a) <u>British</u>. There are some 5,600 of these and so far nothing has been done about them.
    (b) <u>Empire</u>. There are just about 250 of these and we are proposing to send the facsimile acknowledgment.
    (c) <u>Foreign</u>. There are over 900 of these and so far nothing has been done about them.
IV. <u>Gifts of various kinds.</u>
There have been several of these which have all been answered and the gifts passed on to you.
V. <u>Periodicals and other miscellaneous publications.</u>
    (a) Where these were accompanied by a letter and/or an acknowledgment seemed called for, they have had a letter of thanks. We are up to date with these.
    (b) In other cases where not accompanied by a letter, no letter of thanks has been sent.

[1] Dorothy Spencer, 1916–69. Educated at Somerville College, Oxford. Official, HQ of Conservative and Unionist Party Organization, 1923–56.

<u>NB.</u> We have the periodicals etc. here.

   VI. <u>Requests for autographs, photographs etc.</u>

We are trying to answer all these (by individual refusals) and have dealt with a considerable number, but there are about 100 still to do.

   VII. <u>Miscellaneous requests for help or advice: suggestions, proposals put forward, invitations etc.</u>

There are a considerable number of these, the majority of which need no answer.

In some cases, however, a reply is advisable, e.g. the writer is advised to pursue the matter with his own MP and we have now more or less caught up with those requiring an answer.

   VIII. <u>Demobilisation queries, complaints, etc.</u>

There is quite a batch of these which so far are unanswered. I have asked advice about the desirability of answering them. It may be, however, that we shall have to advise the writers to refer to their own MPs.

   IX. <u>Disapproving and critical letters.</u>

There are just a few of these which we are not answering.

   X. <u>Cranks, etc.</u>

There is the usual quota of these which we are not answering.

FURTHER ACTION

I now have about 2,500 left of Mr Churchill's facsimile acknowledgment. About 250 of these will be used on 'Empire individuals' (Group IIIb). What do you consider the next best use to make of the remainder? Do we want to acknowledge the foreign ones (Group IIIc)?

So far as British individuals are concerned (Group IIIa) they are impossible to cope with, with existing staff, and of course we have not enough acknowledgments to cover them. If it were thought desirable we could arrange in time for them to be gone through and to pick out about 1 in 3 for the facsimile acknowledgment but this might be rather invidious.

Alternatively we could make a special effort to mobilise some voluntary workers to address envelopes and send every (British) one a facsimile acknowledgment. This would mean ordering about 4,000 ~~or 5,000~~ more copies as a few more letters may come in.

What do you think?

September 1945

Winston S. Churchill to Clementine Churchill
(Baroness Spencer-Churchill papers)

13 September 1945   Lake Como

My Darling,

The days pass very pleasantly. It takes an hour to an hour and a half by motor-car through winding roads, or speed-boat across the lake, to reach the painting grounds, so we take our lunch with us and have picnics nearly every day. I have six pictures in all, but some are not quite complete. Yesterday evening there was a lovely scene at the far end of the lake and I thought the first go-off was not at all bad. Montag arrives today from Switzerland, and he will be a great help. I am hoping that Alexander will return for the weekend. He enjoyed himself very much when he was here on the 6th. However I expect he has a great deal of work to do.

The country people are most friendly and in the smallest villages press up clamouring for autographs, which I rarely give. There are masses of children, many very pretty and not at all ill-nourished. Yesterday where I was painting I witnessed the extraordinary spectacle of a tiny tot of about four who pushed a great heavy boat off the shore, and jumped in and punted it about. The strength of this little being in pink cotton seemed a prodigy. Evidently she was a personality in local Italian affairs. She was armed with a small switch, with which she kept her two brothers in order. She declined to come up and make friends with us, but gave me an arch smile from a distance and was finally placated by a piece of chocolate. The beauty and richness of the country makes a great impression upon me.

I have not definitely settled on my plans. The weather is appreciably cooler than when we arrived. There is an autumn nip in the wind. Yesterday was one of the most lovely days we have had, but today is greyish and clouds keep out the sun. I have done absolutely nothing but painting, and have hardly time to read the newspapers when they arrive. I have had a long, charming letter from Duffie, which I will send you. I do not think I will go to Paris on the way home, as he will not be there owing to the Conference of Foreign Ministers, and though he says Diana would welcome me, I think I will choose some other time. I rather plan to leave here between the 18th and 20th. It is possible that I may motor along the Riviera with Major Ogier. There is no difficulty about motor-cars, petrol, food, etc. I could take three or four days from Genoa to Cannes and paint by the way. In this case Sarah, Charles[1] and Miss Layton will come back on the 18th, but you may expect to see me turn up at the Biggin Hill airfield any time after the 22nd or 23rd. I will of course let you know beforehand.

Your letter last night enclosed Horatia's note. It certainly was curt. She is

---
[1] Lord Moran.

very unreasonable. It was very good of you to write about the cottage. I am so anxious to get it back.

Always my dearest one
with all my heart
your loving husband
W
[Sketch of pig]

PS. We think it will be better to send Mary her letter direct from here through General Nares,[1] who is now deputy in Berlin but was going to entertain me at this villa. He will forward it from Berlin, and there is a daily direct Air courier service from AFHQ to Berlin by which our letter will be sent. Major Ogier will report on it all today. He is a most agreeable and good-looking young man, and takes infinite pains to amuse us and make us comfortable. He has made up his mind to enter politics and fight Driberg[2] in Essex. He is going to become a farmer and set to work for five years to fling him out of the seat. This seems to be a very good idea.

Winston S. Churchill to Chiang Kai-shek
(Churchill papers, 2/140)

14 September 1945
No. 1103

I was pleased to receive your letter of August 12th[3] by the hand of General Carton de Wiart.

The Battle of Asia is indeed won, and the first of the aggressors has at last been laid low. I am proud to have led the people of this country to victory over Italy and Germany and to the threshold of victory over Japan, and especially I am proud to have been associated with Your Excellency in the long struggle. To the much-enduring people of China the world owes a great debt, and to no one more than Your Excellency, who has been to so many millions inside and outside China a symbol of Chinese resistance and courage.

I much appreciate your kind remarks about General Carton de Wiart. I am glad that the manner in which he performed his duties as my personal representative at Chungking has merited your approbation.

---

[1] Eric Paytherus Nares, 1892–1947. Educated at Marlborough College. Served in France and Belgium in WWI. Maj., 1927. Lt-Col., 1936. Col., 1938. Maj.-Gen., 1943.

[2] Thomas Edward Neil Driberg, 1905–76. Educated at Lancing College and Christ Church, Oxford. Joined the Communist Party aged 15. From 1928, worked on the *Daily Express*, where he became the widely read columnist 'William Hickey'. MP (Lab.) for Maldon, 1942–59; for Barking, 1959–74. Expelled from Communist Party, 1941. Took Labour Whip, 1945. Chairman of Labour Party, 1957. Baron Bradwell shortly before his death.

[3] Reproduced above (pp. 26–7).

September 1945

Clement Attlee to Winston S. Churchill
(Churchill papers, 2/3)

15 September 1945
Secret and Private

My dear Churchill,

In conjunction with my colleagues and with the Policy Committee under John Anderson, of which you are aware, I have recently been considering what we should now do about the future of the atomic bomb and its reactions on international relations and policy. It seems to me that the first step should be to open up the matter with the President of the United States, to give him our tentative views and to ascertain which way his mind is moving. This might be followed later by a personal discussion.

In view both of your position as Leader of the Opposition and of the close connection you have had with this matter since its very inception I should value your comments on the enclosed draft letter which it is my intention to address to President Truman.

I am sorry to worry you while you are out of the country but the matter is one of some urgency and I trust therefore that you will find it possible to let me have a reply as soon as you conveniently can.

Winston S. Churchill to General Dwight D. Eisenhower
(Churchill papers, 2/141)

16 September 1945   Lake Como, Italy

My dear Ike,

By some strange mischance your letter of August 27[1] only reached me here yesterday. I perfectly understand the whole position, and am only sorry that you should have been put to so much trouble.

I have had a very pleasant three weeks here on Lake Como, whither Alex invited me. I have not had a thought for anything but painting.

I hope we shall meet again soon.

---

[1] Reproduced above (pp. 44–5).

Winston S. Churchill to Lord Cholmondeley[1]
(Churchill papers, 2/140)

16 September 1945

My dear Rock,

I have read your charming letter with great pleasure, and I think it particularly kind of you to have written to me.

It has been very pleasant here, and I have not given a thought to anything but painting.

Give my regards to Sybil.[2]

I feel so much sympathy with what you say. But there is no gulf in England (as in France) between the Old world and the New.[3]

Winston S. Churchill to Harold Nicolson
(Churchill papers, 2/142)

16 September 1945   Lake Como, Italy

My dear Harold,

Thank you so much for your kindness in passing to me two such contrasting but agreeable comments.[4]

It has been very pleasant here, and I have not given a thought to anything but painting.

PS. I am so sorry you are not in Parliament where you were one of the best first-class debaters.[5]

Winston S. Churchill to Alfred Duff Cooper
(Churchill papers, 2/140)

17 September 1945   Lake Como, Italy

My dear Duffie,

I thought it most kind of you to write me so long and weighty a letter in

---

[1] George Horatio Charles Cholmondeley, Earl of Rocksavage, 1883–1968. On active service in South Africa, 1901–2. Married, 1913, Sybil, sister of Sir Philip Sassoon. On active service in France and Flanders, 1914–18. Maj., RAF, 1920. Succeeded his father, 1923, as 5th Marquess of Cholmondeley. Joint Hereditary Lord Great Chamberlain; bore the Royal Standard at the coronation of King George VI.

[2] Sybil Rachel Betty Cecile Sassoon, 1894–1989. Married, 1913, George Horatio Charles Cholmondeley: three children. Styled Marchioness of Cholmondeley, 1923. Superintendent, WRNS, 1939–46. CBE, 1946.

[3] The last two sentences were handwritten.

[4] See Nicolson to Churchill, 6 Sept. 1945, reproduced above (pp. 61–2).

[5] Churchill handwrote the postscript.

your own hand,[1] and I shall always keep it as one of the souvenirs of our friendship. I agree very largely with the conclusions which you have formed. Nevertheless there are some unpleasant features in this election which indicate the rise of bad elements. Conscientious objectors were preferred to candidates of real military achievement and service. All the Members of Parliament who had done most to hamper and obstruct the war were returned by enormously increased majorities. None of the values of two years before were preserved. The voters have swung back to the mood of the Fulham by-election.[2] The soldiers voted with mirthful irresponsibility. The General here says that the shortage of cigarettes and some questions of leave were the deciding factors. Also, there is the latent antagonism of the rank and file for the Officer class, and of course the hopes raised by the Socialists that a vote for Labour would get them out of the Army more quickly.

A period not only of great difficulty and hardship but of disillusionment and frustration awaits the country. The new Ministers will not have time or strength for revolutionary measures. They will be dominated by the daily pressure of administration and finance, in both of which they will fail to give satisfaction. We are back at the two-Party system, and must await in a patriotic state of mind the inevitable revulsion.

It was very kind of you and Diana to be willing to have me in Paris for a few days. I think however I would prefer to propose myself, if I may, later in the year, all being well. I shall be back in London on the 24th, weather permitting. Perhaps we may meet there. If things go wrong about the Paris Embassy, I will certainly help you in any way I can to get a seat, and of course once elected you would be welcome to our 'shadow' meetings. We shall have very interesting and responsible work to do in Opposition.

It has been very pleasant here, and I have hardly given a thought to anything but painting.

Winston S. Churchill to Clementine Churchill
(Baroness Spencer-Churchill papers)

18 September 1945   Lake Como

My darling one,

I hope you will not mind my change of plans. The weather has been so good and the prospects seem so favourable that the opportunity of having another four or five days in the sunshine was too tempting to miss. Alexander was delighted that his plane should carry Moran and Sarah home and return

[1] Reproduced above (pp. 64–6).
[2] Referring to the Fulham East by-election of 1933, in which the heavily favoured Conservative candidate William Waldron lost to Labour candidate John Wilmot. Known as the 'peace by-election' because of the signal it sent of the nation's drift toward pacifism.

for me. Thus it was not necessary for me to curtail my holiday on account of Sarah having to return to her unit and Moran to his business. I did not want to send them home in the ordinary transport plane with perhaps 20 other passengers. All this is now avoided. I plan to go to Genoa tomorrow, and stay two nights there, so as to get two afternoons at a picture, and then on via Nice or Cannes to Marseilles, hoping to get another picture by the way. I am arranging to fly home on the 24th, so as to give plenty of time for the plane to return to bring Alex to England on October 1.

I really have enjoyed these 18 days enormously. I have been completely absorbed by the painting, and have thrown myself into it till I was quite tired. I have therefore not had time to fret or worry, and it has been good to view things from a distance. I think you will be pleased with the series of pictures, eight in all (now nine!) which I have painted. I am sending them home by Sarah, who will give you all our news. I hope you will be able to keep them in their packet till I come, for I am so much looking forward to showing them to you and Mary one by one myself. If of course you cannot bear it, I shall forgive you. I am sure you will consider they are a great advance, particularly the later ones. I am confident that with a few more months of regular practice, I shall be able to paint far better than I have ever painted before. This new interest is very necessary in my life.

Montag has just left, having been with us four days. He was most helpful in his comments. I do not entirely agree with his style, and when he paints himself it is disappointing, but he has a vast knowledge and one cannot paint in his presence without learning. I am quite embarrassed by the magnificent outfit of colours and brushes which he brought with him. They must have cost him £50 at least, and he is not at all a rich man. However, we made much of him here and Sarah got up to take him to the station at 7.30 this morning. He was very full of an invitation from 'The Swiss family' for me to go on into Switzerland and paint for a few weeks there. On being pressed, he said it was the Federal Government & the Municipality of Zurich, where he lives. However the Government is shy of making a formal invitation as they cannot measure the political situation in England. This plan was too difficult altogether, because as you realize one cannot take any money abroad, and it is absolutely necessary for one to know at whose cost one is living. It is possible that the Federal Government may send a friendly message inviting us to be their guests at some time in the future. However, the year is getting late now and as I do not return till the 24th we shall have Parliament upon us quite soon. I will however cast about for future expeditions. Sunshine is my quest.

I have made great friends with these two young officers of the 4th Hussars. The Lieutenant, Tim,[1] is a great character, a Southern Irishman and devoted to horses. He will scout on ahead of us on each stage of our journey and

---

[1] A. D. D. Rogers (?–1984). Known as 'Tim'. Founder of the Airlie Stud in Ireland.

find a sleeping-place. We shall come along behind, and stop off at any scene that catches my fancy. My party is now very small. I only have Sawyers[1] and Sergeant Davies.[2] We are all men, so it will not be difficult for us to fend for ourselves along the route. We have every facility in the way of cars.

I send you herewith some nice letters I have received and answered. Duffie's[3] is well worth thinking about. I wonder whether on getting this, if you have decided to entertain Blum yourself, you would not ask him to lunch too. Rock[4] writes a charming letter; alas for his poor old vanished world! However, I am content to vanish with it. Harold Nicolson was prompted by Randolph to send me these very civil remarks.[5] I have signed the cheque for Southon,[6] and enclose it herewith. I am most anxious to see how much progress you have been able to make. But it really does not matter about being ready at any particular date, either Chartwell or the house in London.

Sarah has been a joy. She is so thoughtful, tactful amusing & gay. The stay here wd have been wrecked without her.[7]

[Drawing of a pig]

Captain A. D. D. Rogers: recollection
(Peter Willett, 'Makers of the Modern Thoroughbred', pages 248–9)

21 September 1945

They moved to Monte Carlo the next day and settled down to a pleasant and leisurely routine in the Hôtel de Paris. Churchill would work at his correspondence in bed until 11.30, when he would get up, have an early lunch, and spend the rest of the day painting. He and Tim would have dinner together, and Churchill would retire to bed early, leaving Tim with the not insoluble problem of amusing himself in Monte Carlo for the rest of the evening. Early in their stay Tim received an urgent message from Clementine Churchill enjoining him at all costs to prevent Churchill gambling in the casino. The subject was not raised until four days before their departure, when Churchill remarked that it would be fun to have a flutter. Tim told him that he had

---

[1] Frank Sawyers, 1903–72. Churchill's valet throughout the war years. Awarded the new Defence Medal in Churchill's Resignation Honours List, 14 Aug. 1945. On leaving Churchill in 1947, he was valet to the Asst Governor-General of Rhodesia, then to Lord Astor at Hever Castle in Kent, then to a Colonel in Chicago. When Churchill died, Sawyers was flown to the funeral in the same plane as Gen. Eisenhower. A letter of recommendation penned in 1946 is reproduced below (pp. 380–1).

[2] Cyril Noel Davies, 1906–95. Joined Metropolitan Police, 1929. Churchill's bodyguard during and after WWII. Retired, 1954.

[3] Reproduced above (pp. 64–6).

[4] Lord Cholmondeley.

[5] See Nicolson to Churchill, 6 Sept. 1945, reproduced above (pp. 61–2).

[6] Robert Southon, a local builder frequently employed on work at Chartwell between the 1920s and the 1940s.

[7] Churchill handwrote the last paragraph.

instructions from Clemmie to scotch any such idea. 'Then you shall go and gamble for me,' was Churchill's rejoinder.

Tim played with great circumspection the whole evening and ended up £250 to the good. He returned to the hotel and reported to Churchill, who told him scornfully, 'That's not the way to gamble; I shall have to go down myself tomorrow and show you how to do it.' Churchill had taken the bit between his teeth, and Tim knew that further remonstrance would be useless. The next night Churchill won £3000, but the night after he lost it all; and on the final night he lost £7000 and instructed Tim to hand it to the casino manager with a request that it should not be presented until Churchill sent word, because foreign exchange controls made immediate payment awkward. Tim delivered the cheque and the message. Flourishing the cheque above his head, the manager answered in theatrical tones, 'Pray tell Mr Churchill that this cheque will never be presented.'

Tim hurried back to the hotel and, as he came into the room, Churchill asked anxiously, 'Well, what did he say?' 'He said that the cheque will never be presented.' 'That's much more agreeable,' said Churchill. 'We'll have a bottle of champagne.'

So, over glasses of champagne, the last link in the friendship between these two strangely assorted men was forged – a friendship which, like the family friendship with the Barnetts, was to give a powerful impetus to Tim's career as a breeder years later.

Winston S. Churchill to James Stuart[1]
(Churchill papers, 2/1)

23 September 1945

John Anderson is reported to have spoken in London to the effect that no reduction in taxation was justified at present. If true this would hamper the action of the Opposition, and I do not agree with it. I propose to have a meeting of the Shadows early in October to discuss these sort of large issues. You should ask our former colleagues to be so kind as to defer pronouncements till we have met.

---

[1] James Gray Stuart, 1897–1971. 3rd son of 17th Earl of Moray. Educated at Eton. On active service, 1914–18 (MC and bar). MP (Cons.) for Moray and Nairn, 1923–59. Entered Whips' Office, 1935. Deputy Chief Whip, 1938–41. PC, 1939. Government Chief Whip, 1941–5. Opposition Chief Whip, 1945–8. Secretary of State for Scotland, 1951–7. Viscount, 1959.

September 1945

Winston S. Churchill to Clementine Churchill
(Baroness Spencer-Churchill papers)

24 September 1945   Villa Sous le Vent, Antibes, France

My darling,
 Here is some account of my doings.
 We motored in four hours to Genoa through lovely country with a particularly striking view of Pavia over the Ticino River and arrived after dark to find the local British colonel in charge of the district installed in the marble palace which belonged to Pirelli.[1] You remember that little man who makes the tyres and was sometimes helpful in public business in long ago days when I was at the Exchequer. His dwelling, which is reputed to have cost one-hundred-thousand pounds before the war is half a marble palace and half a Swiss chalet and seems an utterly incongruous structure such as would be built by a prosperous Fascist manufacturer. There it stands on a rocky bluff overlooking the sea and the bathing place where I got a beautiful clear water of the palest green to try to paint. I worked hard for two days at the illusion of transparency and you shall judge when you see the result how far I have succeeded.
 The weather was delightful and it seemed to me very foolish to go home on the 24th. We, therefore, sent Tim Rogers (lt.) and Major John Ogier on ahead to reconnoitre the neutral State of Monaco. Their report was highly pleasing and the manager at the hotel which is only half full was delighted to receive us on reasonable terms. We motored there on the 21st along the coast road which you will remember we traversed together on our return from the Cairo conference in 1921 and where I had the row at Ventineigla[2] with the French customs officer. Every important bridge over the valleys leading down to the sea has been smashed to pieces by bombing or naval artillery and all kinds of deviations had to be made. Nevertheless in five hours we came through and arrived in the lap of luxury at Monte Carlo. The square in front of the hotel and the Casino is very empty and dead looking but the Monagesques gathered in crowds and welcomed me on every occasion with the greatest fervor. We had our meals on the veranda facing the Casino but I did not transgress the 80 paces which separated me from that unsinkable institution. Instead we sent Tim in with 2 milles to try his luck on strict instructions how to play and after he had prepared himself by two days of intense thought. After a half hour he returned bringing 2 other milles with him. He left the town the next day.
 General Eisenhower sent his aide-de-camp[3] to see me on arrival, asking me to come on to his villa at Antibes which was vacant and fully staffed. I

---

[1] Giovanni Battista Pirelli, 1848–1932. Italian engineer and entrepreneur. Senator of the Kingdom of Italy, 1909.
[2] Ventimiglia.
[3] Craig D. Campbell, 1917–?. ADC to Gen. Eisenhower, 1941–5. POW, Mar. 1943. Escaped, Feb. 1945.

therefore moved in here after two days at Monte Carlo. My two young officers and I are now in this beautiful place surrounded by every comfort and assistance. In four or five days I propose to return to Monte Carlo and to stay there until the 5th or 6th of October when I shall be back to have a few shadow cabinet meetings and settle the policy of the opposition before Parliament meets. I wonder whether we shall be able to hold these in the new house even if the residence is not complete in other respects. The dining room will be most convenient for that.

I went back to Cap Martin, where I painted a picture which you will remember and had another go at olive trees with a brightly colored background gleaming in the sun, but I must return there a third time as yesterday afternoon there was no sunlight – only warmth and brightness but not enough to cast a shadow which I need for my effect. A relative of Lord Rothermere[1] has acquired his villa where you remember we stayed for a while and his small children who are very nice came out and brought the picture which I painted eight years ago. It is not a patch on what I can do now, although, as you know, I have hardly touched a brush in the interval. Apparently they had been brought up on the picture and were tremendously excited to see the painter.

I have sent you various telegrams all of which I suppose took two or more days to get through. Your telegram saying you could not come out here took 48 hours to reach me and I suppose that mine equally miscarried. Therefore, Alex's airplane came out without the various things I have asked for and hence Major Ogier's visit. He will collect what is wanted and bring it back here. I am sure you will like him very much. I really don't know when you will get this letter although I hope it may go by airplane tomorrow to the military assistant of the CIGS.[2] He should send it to you expeditiously. I am writing full directions otherwise he may direct it to 10 Downing Street where it may be overwhelmed in the enormous post which afflicts a Prime Minister.

When Alex returns home at the end of this month he and Margaret[3] should be invited to lunch with us in the new house. After lunch we will show him the Como pictures together with the new series now developing on the Riviera. He is most anxious to see them. I had his own picture varnished and framed and sent to GHQ. It is quite good and he thoroughly enjoyed the hours spent upon it.

I have all this batch of newspapers now up to the 21st and am wading

---

[1] Esmond Cecil Harmsworth, 1898–1978. Capt., Royal Marine Artillery, 1918; his two older brothers had already been killed in action on the Western Front. ADC to Lloyd George at Paris Peace Conference, 1919. MP (Cons.) for Isle of Thanet, 1919–29. Chairman, Newspaper Proprietors' Association, 1934–61. Member of Advisory Council, Ministry of Information, 1939. Succeeded his father as 2nd Viscount Rothermere, 1940.

[2] Arthur Brian Boyle, 1913–65. Military Assistant to CIGS, 1943–5. HM Counsel Learned in the Law, 1958. Recorder of the Borough of Sunderland, 1960; of the City of Newcastle upon Tyne, 1961. CBE, 1945.

[3] Margaret Diana Bingham, 1905–77. Married, 1931, Harold Alexander: four children. Viceregal Consort of Canada, 1946–52. GBE, 1952.

through them. Also the pilot brought out Sunday's *Observer* of the 23rd with him. I was sure there would be a complete deadlock at the Foreign Ministers' conference, but I hardly expected the Russians to come out so boldly with a demand for one or more of the African colonies of the Italians in the Mediterranean for naval and air bases. Their wish is a strange one and belongs to a very crude and out of date form of Czarist imperialism. In these matters they are about forty years behind the times, and I do not myself see any serious objections to their having these places if they will be reasonable in other directions. All navies, seaborne commerce and overseas naval and air bases are merely hostages to the stronger sea and air power. However, I have no doubt that these demands will cause a great stir. The Bolshevization of the Balkans proceeds apace and all the cabinets of Central, Eastern and Southern Europe are in Soviet control, excepting only Athens. This brand I snatched from the burning on Christmas day. The failure of the conference will, of course, have bad results. The Russians have no need of agreement and time is on their side, because they simply consolidate themselves in all these countries they now have in their grasp. I regard the future as full of darkness and menace. Horrible things must be happening to millions of Germans hunted out of Poland and Czecho-Slovakia into the British and American occupied zones. Very little is known as to what is happening behind the Russian iron curtain but evidently the Poles and Czecho-Slovakians are being as badly treated as one could have expected.

We shall have to have a two day debate on demobilization and if it be true that the Labour government have thrown over their Zionist policy and mean to adhere to Chamberlain's[1] White Paper there will be a row about that. Curiously enough, in this matter the government will be against their own party and I equally differ from the Tories.

There will be no lack of topics to discuss when we all come together again. Meanwhile this rest and change of interest is doing me no end of good and I never sleep now in the middle of the day. Even when the nights are no longer than 5, 6 or 7 hours, I do not seem to require it. This shows more than anything else what a load has been lifted off my shoulders.

Since I dictated this (to an American stenographer) yr 2nd telegram has come in. I am so glad you think me right to stay.[2]

With tender love
Your devoted
W

---

[1] (Arthur) Neville Chamberlain, 1869–1940. Educated at Rugby and Mason College, Birmingham. Lord Mayor of Birmingham, 1915–16. Director-General of National Service, 1916–17. MP (Cons.) for Ladywood, 1918–29; for Edgbaston, 1929–40. Postmaster-General, 1922–3. Paymaster-General, 1923. Minister of Health, 1923, 1924–9, 1931. Chancellor of the Exchequer, 1923–4, 1931–7. Leader of the Conservative Party, 1937. PM, 1937–40. Lord President of the Council, May–Nov. 1940.

[2] Churchill handwrote this last paragraph.

September 1945

Winston S. Churchill to Clementine Churchill
(Baroness Spencer-Churchill papers)[1]

24 September 1945   Gen Eisenhower's Villa, Antibes

My Darling,

As communications are so bad Major Ogier (who brings this) decided to fly home today & come back Wednesday. I hope you will meet him & if possible give him luncheon Tuesday. He is a charming man & I have taken a gt liking to him. He will tell you all about our doings & needs.

Naturally I am vy sorry you cd not come out by Alex's plane – It wd have done you good to bask in this mellow sunshine for a spell.

I made a good arrangement w the Manager of the Hotel de Paris Monte Carlo to put my party (3) up at £4.4.0 a head a day all included. I cannot describe the kindness & attentiveness w wh we were treated. The food scrumptious – the wines the best. It was like the old days.

We moved in here last night at Ike's request & repeated invitation – this was arranged by a General sent specially from Germany. It is a palatial villa with every comfort & more. I shall stay here about one week & then go back to Monte Carlo Hotel for a few days. I may not be home till the 5th or 6th October. But why shd I not stay here in the sunlight & have a little rest & detachment after all these years of unrequited struggle.

Do make the most of John Ogier. He is a grand man & contemplates farming in Essex with his father and turning Mr Driberg out at the Gen Election. He has an MC mention in desp & 2 wounds. He has only been in the army 4 years & is already the trusted sq. leader of the 4th Hussars. He has not been home for 4 years & will be seeing his family. He is just off.

                                                        Your ever loving
                                                        W

Winston S. Churchill to Clement Attlee
(Churchill papers, 2/3)

[24 September 1945]
Personal and Secret
Show again on return
Keep for Tuesday meeting

1. I thank you for consulting me about the draft message. I am in general agreement with the sentiments you express and feel with you the appalling gravity of the matter. However the message does not seem to me to make clear what in fact you want the Americans to do. Do you want them to lay their

---

[1] This letter was handwritten.

processes before a conference of the United Nations? It would not be easy for them to convene a conference themselves unless they were prepared to share their knowledge and the uranium etc. Do you wish them to tell the Russians? Is this what is meant by (quote) 'An act of faith' (unquote). If so I do not believe they will agree, and I personally should deem them right not to, and will certainly have to say so, if and when the issue is raised in public.

2. The responsibility for propounding a world policy clearly rests with the USA. I imagine they have two or three years lead, and will have got still further on in that time. I am sure they will not use their advantage for wrong purposes of national aggrandisement and domination. In this short interval they and we must try to reach some form of security based upon a solemn covenant backed by force, viz. the force of the Atomic bomb. I therefore am in favour, after we and the USA have reached agreement, of a new United Nations Conference on the subject. I do not however consider that we should at this stage at any rate talk about (quote) 'Acts of Faith' (Unquote). This will in the existing circumstances raise immediate suspicion in American breasts.

3. Moreover we have a special relationship with them in this matter as defined in my agreement with President Roosevelt. This almost amounts to a military understanding between us and the mightiest power in the world. I should greatly regret if we seemed not to value this and pressed them to melt our dual agreement down into a general international arrangement consisting, I fear, of pious empty phrases and undertakings which will not be carried out. (See what happened about the submarines.)

4. Nothing will give a foundation except the supreme resolve of all nations who possess or may possess the weapon to use it at once unitedly against any nation that uses it in war. For this purpose the greater the power of the US and GB in the next few years the better are the hopes. The US therefore should not share their knowledge and advantage except in return for a system of inspection of this and all other weapon-preparations in every country, which they are satisfied after trial is genuine. Evidently we all have to hasten.

5. These are of course only my immediate reactions to your proposed message. I sympathise deeply in your anxieties.

Clement Attlee to President Harry S Truman
(Churchill papers, 2/3)

25 September 1945
Top Secret

Dear Mr President,

Ever since the USA demonstrated to the world the terrible effectiveness of the atomic bomb I have been increasingly aware of the fact that the world is now facing entirely new conditions. Never before has there been a weapon which can suddenly and without warning be employed to destroy utterly the nerve centre of a great nation. The destruction wrought by the Germans through their air fleet on Warsaw and Rotterdam was startling enough, but subsequent attempts to do the same to London were defeated though without much to spare. Our own attacks on Berlin and the Ruhr resulted in the virtual destruction of great centres of industry. In Europe the accumulated material wealth of decades has been dissipated in a year or two, but all this is not different in kind from what was done in previous wars in Europe during the Dark Ages and the Thirty Years War, in America by your own civil war. Despite these losses civilisation continued and the general framework of human society and of relations between peoples remained. The emergence of this new weapon has meant, taking account of its potentialities, not a quantitative but a qualitative change in the nature of warfare.

Before its advent military experts still thought and planned on assumptions not essentially different from those of their predecessors. It is true that the conservative (with a small c!) mentality tended to maintain some of these although they were already out of date. For instance we found at Potsdam that we had to discuss a decision taken at the Crimea Conference as to the boundaries of Poland. These were delineated by rivers although the idea of a river as a strategic frontier has been out of date ever since the advent of air warfare. Nevertheless it was before the coming of the atomic bomb not unreasonable to think in terms of strategic areas and bases although here again it has seemed to me that too little account has been taken of the air weapon.

Now, however, there is in existence a weapon of small bulk capable of being conveyed on to a distant target with inevitable catastrophic results. We can set no bounds to the possibilities of airplanes flying through the stratosphere dropping atomic bombs on great cities. There are possible developments of the rocket for a similar purpose. I understand that the power of the bombs delivered on Nagasaki may be multiplied many times as the invention develops. I have so far heard no suggestion of any possible means of defence. The only deterrent is the possibility of the victim of such an attack being able to retort on the victor. In many discussions on bombing in the days before the war it was demonstrated that the only answer to the bomber was the bomber. The war proved this to be correct. This obvious fact did not prevent bombing but resulted in the destruction of many great centres of civilisation. Similarly if mankind continues to make the atomic bomb without changing the political relationships of States sooner or later these bombs will be used for mutual annihilation.

The present position is that whilst the fundamental scientific discoveries which made possible the production of the atomic bomb are now common knowledge, the experience of the actual processes of manufacture and knowledge of the solutions which were found to the many technical problems which arose, are confined to our two countries and the actual capacity for production exists only in the United States. But the very speed and completeness of our joint achievement seems to indicate that any other country possessing the necessary scientific and industrial resources could also produce atomic bombs within a few years if it decided now to make the effort. Again, our two Governments have gone a long way in securing control of all the main known sources of uranium and thorium, the two materials at present believed to be of importance for the process. But new sources are continually coming to light and it would not be surprising if it were found that large deposits existed in parts of the world outside our direct or indirect control. Nor may it be altogether easy to defend the measures which we have already taken in this matter when they become known and are considered in the light of such principles as that of the freedom of access to raw materials.

It would thus appear that the lead which has been gained as a result of the past effort put forth in the United States may only be temporary and that we have not much time in which to decide what use is to be made of that lead. It is true that other countries, even if they succeed in producing atomic bombs, may not, at any rate at first, be able to produce them on the same scale. I am told, however, that, in future, it may be possible for the process to be developed at a far smaller cost in industrial resources than has inevitably been demanded by your pioneer production enterprise, carried through in time of war when speed was the first essential; and in any case, with a weapon of such tremendous destructive power, it is perhaps doubtful whether the advantage would lie with the possessor of the greatest number of bombs rather than with the most unscrupulous.

A further consideration which I have had in mind is that the successful manufacture of bombs from plutonium shows that the harnessing of atomic energy as a source of power cannot be achieved without the simultaneous production of material capable of being used in a bomb. This means that the possible industrial uses of atomic energy cannot be considered separately from its military and security implications.

It is clear to me, therefore, that, as never before, the responsible statesmen of the great Powers are faced with decisions vital not merely to the increase of human happiness but to the very survival of civilisation. Until decisions are taken on this vital matter, it is very difficult for any of us to plan for the future. Take the case of this country. During the war we had to shift much of our industry to the less exposed parts of our island. We had to provide shelters for our people. Now we have to restart our industries and rebuild our wrecked homes. Am I to plan for a peaceful or a warlike world? If the latter I ought to direct all our people to live like troglodytes underground as being the only hope of survival, and that by no means certain. I have to consider the defence forces required in the future in the light of San Francisco, but San Francisco did not envisage the atomic bomb. Its conceptions of security are based on appreciations of a situation existing in June of this year. We considered regional security and a policing of the world by the Powers with the greatest resources in the interests of all so that there should be available the forces to prevent aggression.

I have only mentioned Great Britain as an example; for every Head of Government must, in varying degree, find himself confronted with the same problems.

In these circumstances while realizing to the full the importance of devising means to prevent as far as possible the power to produce this new weapon getting into other hands, my mind is increasingly directed to considering the kind of relationship between nations which the existence of such an instrument of destruction demands. In your country and ours resort is not had to violence not just because we have efficient police forces but because the vast majority of our citizens are law abiding and conditions are such that men are not driven to have recourse to desperate measures. Our constitutions allow of peaceful change.

We have it seems to me if we are to rid ourselves of this menace to make very far reaching changes in the relationship between States. We have in fact in the light of this revolutionary development to make a fresh review of world policy and a new valuation of what are called national interests. We are ourselves attempting to undertake a review. What was done on American initiative at San Francisco was a first step at erecting the framework of a new world society, but necessarily it could have regard only to the requirements imposed by the technical advances in methods of warfare then known. Now it seems to us that the building, the framework of which was erected at San Francisco, must be carried much further if it is to be an effective shelter for humanity. We have to secure that these new developments are turned to the benefit rather than to the destruction of mankind. We must bend our utmost energies to secure that better ordering of human affairs which so great a revolution at once renders necessary and should make possible.

I am therefore most anxious, before we proceed much further with our own deliberations, to know how your mind is moving; and it is primarily for this reason that I have set before you at such length my tentative views before they have really begun to crystallise.

Mr Byrnes has had a preliminary talk with Mr Bevin here on the matter but, later on, I think it may be essential that you and I should discuss this momentous problem together so that we may agree what the next step should be and be in a position to take it before the fears and suspicions which may be developing elsewhere have got such a firm hold as to make even more difficult any solution we may decide to aim at.

September 1945

Clementine Churchill to Winston S. Churchill
(Churchill papers, 1/41)[1]

27 September 1945

My darling,

I'm sitting waiting for Major Ogier who, in a few minutes is coming to luncheon with me. He appeared last Tuesday afternoon having been delayed by stormy weather.

He certainly is a most delightful young man and I'm looking forward to seeing him again and getting to know him. Mary is coming in to luncheon to meet him.

We have, I hope collected all the things you need, minus bathing suits, which seem unobtainable.

Your own are in store so deep they cannot be fished out without Sawyers' expert hand. Last night <u>Mary</u> and I went to see Henry IV Part I. A magnificent performance. You must see it when you come back. There are a batch of new plays which will be fun to go to.

Duff came to see me. Mr Bevin wants him to stay on in Paris which is a comfort to him as he felt insecure.

Everybody is worried about the Council of Foreign Monsters! (Ministers) I think Molotov's conduct over Hungary is meant to be fit for the long tat of the Atomic bomb. Some of the soldiers are (Maitland Wilson and now Patton[2]) being indiscreet and being rapped over the knuckles.

It's very cold here. I hope you are having warmth and sunshine.

Your Jack has been to Weymouth and is looking better. Randolph is in Ireland staying with Lord Fitzwilliam.[3]

---

[1] This letter was handwritten.

[2] George Smith Patton, Jr, 1885–1945. Executive Officer, 3rd Cavalry Rgt, 1932–5. Asst CoS (G2), Hawaiian Dept, 1935–7. Director of Instruction, Cavalry School, 1937–8. CO, 9th Cavalry Rgt, 1938; 5th Cavalry Rgt, 1938; 3rd Cavalry Rgt, 1938–40; 2nd Armored Div., 1940–2. Commanding Gen., I Armored Corps, 1942; London Base Command, 1942; Western Task Force, North Africa, 1942–3; I Armored Corps, North Africa, 1942; II Armored Corps, North Africa, 1943; 7th Army, North Africa, 1943; 7th Army, Sicily, 1943–4; 3rd Army, North West Europe, 1944–5. Military Governor of Bavaria, 1945. Commanding Gen., 15th Army, Germany, 1945. Died from injuries sustained in a car accident, 1945.

[3] William Henry Lawrence Peter Wentworth-Fitzwilliam, 1910–48. 8th Earl Fitzwilliam. Married, 1933, Olive Dorothea Plunket. Capt., Grenadier Guards. Succeeded as 8th Earl, 1943.

September 1945

Clement Attlee to Winston S. Churchill
(Churchill papers, 2/3)

28 September 1945
Personal and Top Secret

My dear Churchill,

I have been considering the problem of Questions in Parliament on the subject of raw materials for atomic energy which might involve reference to secret agreements with Belgium, Holland and Brazil of which you may be aware.

Sir John Anderson as Chairman of the Advisory Committee agrees with the Foreign Office view that if possible the best course would be to get the Speaker to rule that Questions on this subject endanger vital interests and should not be allowed on the Order Paper. The Foreign Office point out that if we inadvertently refer publicly to the agreements we should get into trouble with the three countries concerned, in some of which only individual Ministers are aware of the agreements, and we should of course also get into trouble with the United States Government. It would be necessary to make similar arrangements in the Lords.

I am proposing to see the Speaker about this matter personally but before proceeding further, I should be glad to know if I may tell him that this proposal has your support.

October 1945

Frank McCluer[1] to Winston S. Churchill
(Churchill papers, 2/230)

3 October 1945   Westminster College, Fulton, Missouri

My dear Mr Churchill,

In 1936 an English-born woman, Mrs John Findley Green,[2] established at Westminster College[3] a memorial lectureship to be known as the John Findley Green[4] Foundation. The lectureship was established to bring to the college campus each year a man of international reputation who would discuss economic, social, or political problems of international concern in a series of three or four lectures. After the lectures are delivered, the lecturer leaves the manuscript with the college in order that they may be published in book form.

This letter is to invite you to deliver the Green Lectures in the winter of 1945–1946, or in the spring of 1946. We should be glad to arrange the dates to suit your convenience.

The arrangement for the scheduling of the lectures may be made to suit your convenience. It had been our thought to have one lecture at the college one evening and to have another lecture delivered in St Louis, Missouri (USA) on the evening of the following day. The college is located one hundred miles from this metropolitan center and we should like to arrange for your appearance under the auspices of the Green Foundation before the great audience which would assemble in St Louis to hear you. We know that any discussions coming from you and delivered from this forum here in the heart of the United States will be of immense and enduring significance, and will promote the international understanding requisite to the maintenance of peace. We earnestly hope that you will do us the honor of accepting this invitation.

A suitable honorarium will be provided. In this instance, we shall also be glad to allow you to arrange for the publication of the lectures, or we shall make the arrangement and allow you to share in the royalties.

[1] Frank Lewis McCluer, 1896–1979. President, Westminster College, Mo., 1933–47.
[2] Eleanor Essie Green, 1868–?. Wife of John Findley Green.
[3] In Fulton, Mo.
[4] John Findley Green, 1864–1932. Educated at Westminster College, Mo., 1884.

Enclosed you will find excerpt from the Instrument of Gift, establishing the John Findley Green Foundation Lectureship at Westminster College.[1]

Clement Attlee to Winston S. Churchill
(Churchill papers, 2/3)

4 October 1945
Secret and Private

My dear Churchill,

I have waited until your return to this country to thank you for your telegram in reply to my letter of 15th September[2] about the atomic bomb. I send you herewith a copy of my letter to the President in its final form. As you will see, the beginning of the penultimate paragraph of the original draft has been omitted.

I am also sending a copy of this correspondence to Eden as you requested.

I had hoped that you would be back in time to come with Mrs Churchill to dinner here on 2nd October in honour of the Bruces[3] before their retirement. It was a most pleasant function and we all enjoyed seeing Mrs Churchill again.

I hope that you have had a thorough rest. At home we have been having a very heavy time indeed, although I have managed to have one or two fairly quiet days at Chequers.

Winston S. Churchill to Clement Attlee
(Churchill papers, 2/3)

6 October 1945
Personal and Top Secret

My dear Prime Minister,

I thank you for your three letters of September 28,[4] and 29, and October 4.

I am much obliged to you for sending me a copy of your letter to the President. I fully recognize the fearful gravity of the problem with which it deals.

---

[1] President Truman wrote a personal note on the original letter: 'This is a wonderful school in my home state. Hope you can do it. I'll introduce you. Best regards, Harry S Truman.'

[2] Reproduced above (p. 74).

[3] Stanley Melbourne Bruce, 1883–1967. Born in Melbourne, Australia. On active service, Europe, 1914–17 (twice wounded, despatches, MC). PM and Minister for External Affairs, Australia, 1923–9. Minister without Portfolio, 1932–3. Australian Representative at the League of Nations, 1932–8. President, Council of the League of Nations, 1936. High Commissioner for Australia in London, 1933–45. Representative of Australia, British War Cabinet, 1942–5; Pacific War Council, 1942 to May 1944. Minister for Australia to Netherlands Government-in-Exile, London, 1942–5. Viscount, 1947. Chairman, World Food Council, 1947–51.

Ethel Dunlop, 1879–1967. Married, 1913, Stanley Bruce.

[4] Reproduced above (p. 89).

I am sorry I was not able to come with my wife to your dinner to the Bruces. She has told me how very agreeable it was.

I shall be seeing my political friends on Tuesday at the House of Commons, and should like to have a talk to you about Business after that. You may certainly tell the Speaker that I agree with you that 'Questions in Parliament on the subject of raw materials for atomic energy which might involve reference to secret agreements with Belgium, Holland and Brazil'[1] should not be put on the Paper, at any rate for the present.

I had a very pleasant holiday, and painted a lot of daubs. I have returned to this country much refreshed but, unhappily, with a cold which I am nursing attentively.

Winston S. Churchill to Duke of Westminster[2]
(Churchill papers, 2/142)

7 October 1945

My dear Bennie,

How kind of you and the Naval Cadets to want me to give away their prizes in December. Alas, I have a great reluctance to making these kind of engagements, and wish to keep as much as possible of my time and strength for the responsible work I have to do in leading the Opposition.

I am sorry not to have answered before, but I have been away on my holiday. I stayed at the Hotel de Paris in Monte Carlo, where all was most agreeable and everything possible done by the Management for my comfort. I have brought back fifteen paintings as the result of those thirty-five days of sunshine. I do not find things very good here.

Let me know when you come to London. It would be very nice to have a talk.[3]

---

[1] Quotation from Attlee's letter to Churchill of Sep. 28.

[2] Hugh Richard Arthur Grosvenor, 1879–1953. Known as 'Bendor'. One of Churchill's closest friends. Educated at Eton. Succeeded his grandfather as 2nd Duke of Westminster, 1899. ADC to Lord Roberts, South Africa, 1900–2. Commanded an armoured car detachment, Royal Naval Div., 1914–15. DSO, 1916. Personal Assistant to the Controller, Mechanical Dept, Ministry of Munitions, 1917. A Member of the Other Club from 1917. A Vice-President (with Churchill) of the India Defence League, 1933–5.

[3] The last sentence was handwritten.

October 1945

Clement Attlee to Winston S. Churchill
(Churchill papers, 2/3)

8 October 1945
Top Secret

My dear Churchill,

Many thanks for your letter of October 6 and for your agreement with the proposal which I am putting to the Speaker about certain Parliamentary Questions on raw materials for atomic energy. This will be a great help to me.

I shall be very glad to have a talk with you about Business after you have seen your political friends on Tuesday.

I am so glad that you had a pleasant holiday and I hope you will soon be fully recovered from your cold.

Field Marshal Sir Bernard Montgomery to Winston S. Churchill
(Churchill papers, 2/143)[1]

8 October 1945

Dear Mr Churchill,

I have arrived in England today for conferences, and other matters. I would much like to see you some time to discuss the arrangements for your coming to the Alamein Dinner; I will give you a copy of the speech I shall make. We shall expect a terrific speech from you!

I will be in London on Monday next 15 October. Would there be any chance of seeing you that day. With kind regards to Mrs Churchill.

Sir George Franckenstein[2] *to Winston S. Churchill*
(Churchill papers, 2/1)[3]

8 October 1945

Dear Mr Churchill,

Will you allow me to send you, the champion of freedom and justice and a friend of Austria, the enclosed appeal for the reunion of the South-Tyrol to the North-Tyrol, as well as a copy of a letter I addressed to Sir Alexander

---

[1] This letter was handwritten.
[2] Georg Freiherr von und zu Franckenstein, 1878–1953. Austro-Hungarian diplomat (serving in Washington, St Petersburg, Rome, Tokyo, India, London, Belgium and the Caucasus). Austrian Envoy Extraordinary and Minister Plenipotentiary, London, 1920–38. Following the German annexation of Austria in 1938, he was knighted by King George VI. Wrote *Facts and Features of My Life* (1939).
[3] This letter was handwritten.

Cadogan dealing with this question which is both morally and economically of the greatest importance for Austria.

According to reliable news the Italian authorities and troops in the South Tyrol are continuing the fascists' policy of oppression. They use every means to intimidate the German speaking population and to make it impossible for them to express their fervent wish for the liberation and the reunion of the South Tyrol with Austria. The Italians are thus endeavouring to distort the real facts and to influence the judgement of the Council of the Foreign Ministers to the detriment of justice and fair play.

May I express the hope that you will give your powerful support to the rights and wishes of a people who for many years have so undeservedly suffered injustice and persecution.

If you could find time to see me for a few minutes so that I may put our cause before you I should be extremely grateful.

With kindest regards

Field Marshal Sir Bernard Montgomery to Winston S. Churchill
(Churchill papers, 2/143)[1]

9 October 1945

Dear Mr Churchill,

I would like to present to you a map showing the exact sites of my Tactical HQ from Alamein to the Baltic. You have yourself visited a good many of them.

The map may be of considerable historical interest in years to come.

Dorothy Spencer: memorandum
(Churchill papers, 2/1)

9 October 1945

LETTERS ADDRESSED TO MR CHURCHILL SINCE 26TH JULY
POSITION UP TO 9TH OCTOBER, 1945

<u>Received facsimile letter.</u>

1.	Letters of thanks from Party Organisations	63
2.	Letters of thanks from other Organisations	
	British	30
	Empire	42
	Foreign	7

[1] This letter was handwritten.

3. Letters of thanks from individuals

British	about	6,000
Empire		445
USA	about	600
Other foreign		330*

* To receive facsimile reply via Foreign Office.

(NB. There are 36 untranslated foreign letters not yet acknowledged.)
<u>Received individual replies:</u>
4. Gifts of various kinds   24
5. Requests for autographs, photographs etc.   320
6. Miscellaneous requests for help or advice   275

<u>No reply.</u>
7. Periodicals and miscellaneous publications
(Acknowledgements sent only to those with covering letter)   Scores
8. Letters from people with 'axes to grind'   268
9. Critical or hortatory   76
10. Cranks or lunatics   217
11. Anonymous   Hundreds

<u>Note:</u> 50 people have written thanking Mr Churchill for the facsimile letter.

This statement does <u>not</u> include a number of letters received immediately after the Election results were declared (which were dealt with at 24 Old Queen Street) nor a considerable number of letters which, after acknowledgment, were passed on to Mr Churchill's private secretary with a suggestion that he should see them or that further action should be taken.

Lord Cherwell to Winston S. Churchill
(*Churchill papers, 2/3*)

11 October 1945   Christ Church, Oxford

My dear Winston,

You said you wished to know the line I intended to take if I spoke next Tuesday. Broadly the points I would emphasise are:

(1) Relieve Darnley[1] of his anxiety lest the whole world should blow up.
(2) Say we must not exaggerate the benefits to be expected from nuclear power since the production of power only costs a minute fraction of the national effort.
(3) Explain how nonsensical it is to talk about the 'secret' or the

---

[1] Esme Ivo Bligh, 1886–1955. Painter, musician and flower-breeder. Married, 1912, Daphne Rachel Mulholland (div. 1920): two children; 1923, Nancy Ellinor Kidston (div. 1936): one child; 1940, Rosemary Potter: three children. Maj., RAF. Succeeded as 9th Earl of Darnley, 1927; 18th Lord Clifton, of Leighton Bromswold, 1937. In later life a pacifist.

'formula'. Make it plain that hundreds of engineers would have to be taken over to America and carefully instructed in all the refinements and improvements of the various processes, if other nations were to be given equal opportunities to make bombs. Ask whether this equal facility in making bombs would conduce to world-peace.

(4) Emphasise the danger of slogans like 'hand over control to the United Nations' without realising that this means nothing unless:
   (a) concrete schemes have been worked out for universal world-wide inspection to prevent secret production,
   (b) manufacture and storage of the weapon is begun by the United Nations in some out of the way spot,
   (c) those in power are prepared and able to use these bombs ruthlessly against any nation found to be illegally manufacturing them.

(5) Say everyone must desire an effective form of control if it can be put into force but reiterate that some concrete scheme should be worked out before and not after everybody was taught to make the bombs.

I am not finally committed to speak, but various people, especially Addison,[1] said they thought I ought to in view of the line I took when this subject was raised in June.

It would be most kind if you could possibly let me know quickly whether you think it desirable that I should take part in the Debate. If I do not it would probably be best to stay away.

I hope you slept well in your new house and remain, as ever, yours, C.

Clement Attlee to Winston S. Churchill
(Churchill papers, 2/3)

11 October 1945
Confidential

My dear Churchill,

I feel sure you will be interested to have the latest report of the Committee on the Grant of Honours, Decorations and Medals and I am therefore sending you one herewith confidentially for your own information. As you will

---

[1] Christopher Addison, 1869–1951. Hunterian Prof. of Anatomy, Cambridge, 1901. MP (Lib.) for Hoxton, 1910–22. Parliamentary Secretary to Board of Education, 1914–15; to Ministry of Munitions, 1915–16. Minister of Munitions, 1916–17. Minister in Charge of Reconstruction, 1917. President of Local Government Board, 1919. Minister of Health, 1919–21. Minister without Portfolio, 1921. Published a volume of *Memoirs* in 1924 and his war-time diary, *Four-and-a-half-Years*, in 1934. Joined the Labour Party before the general election of 1929. MP (Lab.) for Swindon, 1929–31, 1934–5. Minister of Agriculture and Fisheries, 1930–1. Baron, 1937. Viscount, 1945. Secretary of State for Dominion Affairs in Clement Attlee's Labour Government, 1945–7. Paymaster-General, 1948–9. Lord Privy Seal, 1949–51. KG, 1946.

see, it proposes the institution of a War Medal and radical changes in the time qualification for the Campaign Stars. I feel sure that this is the best solution of a difficult problem and the scheme has accordingly been submitted to The King prior to consultation with the Dominions.

You may recall that when we discussed the question of the grant of an Emblem to the Fourteenth Army you mentioned the question of Clasps. I have been considering this carefully and I have come to the conclusion that it would not be wise to recommend the institution of Clasps to the War Medal. A large number would be necessary, and the difficulties which would be encountered in endeavouring to settle what Clasps should be instituted would be great. Were they instituted, the settlement of questions of entitlement in individual cases and the machinery of issue would require a substantial amount of time and labour. The manufacture and distribution of the Stars themselves will take a considerable time, and, moreover, it is to be doubted whether, in present conditions, recipients of the Medal will expect any Clasps in addition. I am therefore not proposing to make any recommendation on this matter.

L. S. Amery to Lord Beaverbrook[1]
(Beaverbrook papers)

11 October 1945

All I did say the other morning at the Candidates' meeting was something to the effect that with one exception the Conservative Press had shown so little instinct for Conservative policies that they had said practically nothing about the danger to Empire Preference. The papers I referred to were of course yours, but I did not in so many words say the *Express*, and therefore you must not give me any more credit than is my due!

The attack on you only came in the afternoon after I had said my say, and the next speaker who got up after Summers[2] was Gluckstein,[3] who commented humorously 'So we have succeeded in finding a scapegoat!' If you want to know the substance of the criticism against you, it was in part, as you

---

[1] William Maxwell Aitken, 1879–1964. Known as 'Max'. Canadian financier and newspaper proprietor. MP (Cons.) for Ashton under Lyne, 1910–16. Knighted, 1911. Canadian Expeditionary Force Eye-Witness in France, May–Aug. 1915; Canadian Government Representative at the Front, Sep. 1915 to 1916. Bought the *Daily Express*, his largest-circulation newspaper, Dec. 1916. Baron Beaverbrook, 1917. Chancellor of the Duchy of Lancaster and Minister of Information, 1918. Minister for Aircraft Production, 1940–1. Minister of State, 1941. Minister of Supply, 1941–2. Lord Privy Seal, 1943–5.

[2] Gerard Spencer Summers, 1902–76. Chairman, Sheet Makers Conference, 1936–9. MP (Cons.) for Northampton, 1940–5; for Aylesbury, 1950–70. Director-General of Regional Organisation, Ministry of Supply, 1941–4. Secretary, Dept of Overseas Trade, 1945. Knighted, 1956.

[3] Louis Halle Gluckstein, 1897–1979. Educated at Lincoln College, Oxford. MP (Cons.) for Nottingham East, 1929–45. Knighted, 1953. CBE, 1964. Conservative Councillor, Greater London Council for the Cities of London and Westminster, 1964–7. Alderman, 1967–73.

suggest, for having Left Wingers as editors and more particularly Low[1] as your cartoonist. But it was even more an indirect criticism of Winston for being an autocrat and, as such, only consulting a few personal friends, whose influence upon his election policy was no doubt largely exaggerated by rumour. The same indirect criticism was also made by other speakers who suggested that the Central Office had made a mistake in concentrating on the Winston placard and had not sufficiently publicised other Conservative leaders and the Conservative team as a whole, arguing that this country does not like one-man leadership. Naturally no one wished to say anything in disparagement of Winston's immense services or of his future leadership, but this particular undercurrent of dissatisfaction was very conveniently vented on you.

President Harry S Truman to Winston S. Churchill
(*Churchill papers, 2/230*)

11 October 1945 The White House

My dear Mr Churchill

One of President Roosevelt's fondest desires was to have a painting of you, Premier Stalin and himself placed in the Capitol here in Washington as a testimony of the historical importance of the meetings at Teheran and Yalta.

He had hoped that the work could be done by Mr Douglas Chandor[2] whose peculiar kind of artistic gift he admired and who, he felt, was better fitted than anyone else for doing this particular painting.

Knowing how strongly President Roosevelt felt that such a painting would be a worthy addition to the historical mementos of this country, I should like to ask if you would be willing to sacrifice some of your valued time to allow Mr Chandor to come over to do this painting.

I have also written to Premier Stalin asking if he, too, could spare sufficient time to permit Mr Chandor to paint his picture in order to complete this historic work symbolizing the unity of our three nations.

You may be sure that your acquiescence in helping to consummate this cherished desire of President Roosevelt would be greatly appreciated by me.

---

[1] David Low, 1891–1963. Political cartoonist. Born in New Zealand. Came to London, where he was cartoonist on the *Star* from 1919, the *Evening Standard* from 1927 and the *Daily Herald* from 1950. Knighted, 1962. Author of more than 25 volumes of cartoons.

[2] Douglas Chandor, 1897–1953. Educated at Radley College, 1914, and Slade School, London. Painted portraits of Franklin and Eleanor Roosevelt, Winston Churchill and Queen Elizabeth II.

Clement Attlee to Winston S. Churchill
(Churchill papers, 2/3)

12 October 1945

My dear Churchill,

I saw Mr Speaker with regard to Questions in Parliament on the subject of raw materials for atomic energy, and he will do his best to see that Questions of this nature are kept off the Paper. Should they be raised by a Supplementary, I shall state that it is contrary to the national interest to make any statement. He understands the position fully. Thank you so much for your help.

Winston S. Churchill to Field Marshal Sir Bernard Montgomery
(Churchill papers, 2/143)

13 October 1945

My dear Monty,

Thank you so much for your letter of October 9[1] and for sending me the map showing the sites of your Tactical Headquarters from Alamein to the Baltic. It is a most interesting record of your famous advance and I greatly value your kind thought in presenting me with this historic memento.

Winston S. Churchill to Admiral Sir Bruce Fraser
(Churchill papers, 2/141)

13 October 1945

I am most grateful to you for your very kind letter of September 5,[2] written on the date and with the pen of the unconditional surrender of Japan. Your work during the war has always commanded my highest respect and admiration. Not once nor twice in our rough island story the path of duty was the path of glory.

---

[1] Reproduced above (p. 94).
[2] Reproduced above (p. 57).

OCTOBER 1945

Winston S. Churchill to Clement Attlee
(Churchill papers, 2/3)

13 October 1945
Confidential

My dear Prime Minister,

I thank you for sending me the latest report of the Committee on the Grant of Honours, Decorations and Medals. I had been led to the conclusion that the institution of the Defence Medal would satisfy the over-weighted demands of the Air ground staff and, for this sake, I faced the issue of Defence Medals to over six million persons. I never thought, after this, that a War Medal would be introduced to cover everybody who had done twenty-eight days' service in uniform from the beginning to the end of the War. There must easily be twelve million people who will thus be decorated. Whether the satisfaction afforded by so universal a decoration will be worth the expense is very problematical and the addition of this extra Ribbon and Medal is of course a further dilution of the currency of Honours.

I see on page 4, para. 7, that the Commanders-in-Chief are not to be awarded the Stars but instead would be gratified by sharing, with the twelve million above mentioned, inclusion in the War Medal. This would apply, I presume (if I have read the paragraph right), to people like the three Chiefs of the Staff and to men like Harris[1] and Sholto Douglas,[2] who have all the time, as Commanders-in-Chief, been discharging great acts of military decision with the dire responsibility attached to sending men out on perilous quests. If this is what is settled, I think it most unjust; but perhaps I have read the paper wrong.

This invidious distinction is still further emphasized by the reduction of the qualification period for the various Stars, in many cases to a single day. This also greatly reduces the value of the Stars to those who have gained them under present conditions.

Broadly speaking, I deprecate both these relaxations, *i.e.* the additional War Medal and the one-day Stars, which constitute a dilution at once costly and

---

[1] Arthur Travers Harris, 1892–1984. Known as 'Bomber Harris'. On active service, 1914–18 with the RFC (later RAF); AFC. Served in India, 1921–2; Iraq, 1922–4; Egypt, 1930–2. OBE, 1927. Director of Plans, Air Ministry, 1934–7. AOC 4 Bomber Group, 1937. Head of RAF Mission to US and Canada, 1938. Married, 1938, Thérèse Hearne: one daughter. AOC, Palestine and Transjordan, 1938–9. AVM, 1939. CB, 1940. DCAS, 1940–1. Head of RAF Delegation to US, 1941. Air Mshl, 1941. KCB, 1942. C-in-C, Bomber Command, 1942–5. Air Chf Mshl, 1943. Mshl of the RAF, 1945. GCB, 1946. Manager of South African Marine Corp., 1946–53. Bt, 1953.

[2] William Sholto Douglas, 1893–1969. On active service, 1914–18 (despatches thrice, MC, DFC). Commanded 43 and 85 (Fighter) Sqns, 1917–18. ACAS, 1938–40. DCAS, 1940. AOC-in-C, Fighter Command, 1940–2; Middle East Command, 1943–4; Coastal Command, 1944–5. Knighted, 1941. Air Chf Mshl, July 1942. AOC British Air Forces of Occupation, Germany, 1945–6. Governor, British Zone of Germany, 1946–7. Baron Douglas of Kirtleside, 1948. Chairman, British European Airways, 1949–64.

unwholesome, and I much regret the exclusion of the really responsible great officers of the three Services from the Ribbons of the various Theatres upon which their influence and policy have been decisive. As to the 'Clasps', I can quite understand the task might prove insuperable.

Pray excuse the critical character of these comments, but it would not be much use my disguising my opinion. It may of course be that I have read the paper wrong. If so, I would be glad to be corrected.

Winston S. Churchill to Captain Oswald Birley[1]
(Churchill papers, 2/146)

13 October 1945
Private

My dear Oswald Birley,

You have lain heavy on my conscience for the last year, but I hope that as soon as I am thoroughly installed here it will be possible for me to give you some sittings. I told the Speaker, who wrote to me, that I would do so. Will you let me know whether November would be a convenient month.

I had great fun painting in Italy and the south of France, and was very much relieved to find that I had got no worse through not painting for six years.

With renewed apologies and excuses for my past shortcomings, believe me

Winston S. Churchill to L. S. Amery
(Churchill papers, 2/1)

15 October 1945

My dear Leo,

Thank you very much for your kind letter. I will attend to the Swiss Publisher's proposal. I will also get the two books you mention, as soon as they are in England.

I hope you have had a good rest. I had a lovely holiday in Italy and on the Riviera but, alas, have been plagued by a cold and a sore throat, which I brought back with me.

I have fixed to go to Harrow for the songs on October 31.

[1] Oswald Hornby Joseph Birley, 1880–1952. Portrait painter and royal portraitist. Born in New Zealand. Educated at Harrow and Trinity College, Cambridge. On active service in France with the Royal Fusiliers, 1914–16; Intelligence Corps, 1916–18. Capt., 1916. MC, 1919. Married, 1921, Rhoda Vava Mary Lecky Pike: two children. Maj., Sussex Home Guard, 1940–3. Knighted, 1949. Known for his portraits of Winston Churchill, King George V, Queen Mary, King George VI, Queen Elizabeth the Queen Mother, and Queen Elizabeth II. Also painted such notable figures as Gens Eisenhower and Montgomery, Adm. Mountbatten, Air Mshl Trenchard, J. P. Morgan and Andrew Mellon.

October 1945

Winston S. Churchill to Sir George Franckenstein
(*Churchill papers, 2/1*)

15 October 1945

My dear Franckenstein,

Thank you so much for your letter[1] about the Southern Tyrol, which I will certainly reflect upon.

It is nice to hear from you again, but I shudder to read the accounts that come to me of the Russian maltreatment of Vienna and the paralysis of Allied assistance.

Lady Violet Bonham Carter[2] to Winston S. Churchill
(*Churchill papers, 2/146*)

15 October 1945

My dearest Winston,

First – it is lovely to know that you are back again, and Cys[3] tells me that you were looking literally 'in the pink' at the Other Club last week. I am sorry to read that you have since developed a sore throat – and do hope it will clear up quickly.

I am writing because I hear that Duncan Sandys has forwarded on to you a letter from Dr Mallon[4] which was not meant for your eyes – but as you have seen it, here is the full story.

I had the idea to reassemble the remains – or the cream of the remains – of our old pre-war 'Focus' (Freedom and Peace) to entertain you at a little 'tributary' luncheon or dinner – *if* you fancied the idea. With this end in view I confided in Dr Mallon (who is my colleague on the BBC Board) and asked

---

[1] Reproduced above (pp. 93–4).

[2] Helen Violet Asquith, 1887–1969. Elder daughter of H. H. Asquith, Lib. PM 1908–16. Educated in Dresden and Paris. Married, 1915, Sir Maurice Bonham Carter (d. 1960). President, Women's Liberal Federation, 1923–5, 1939–45; Liberal Party Organization, 1945–7. A Governor of the BBC, 1941–6. Member of the Royal Commission on the Press, 1947–9. Unsuccessful Parliamentary candidate (Lib.), 1945, 1951. DBE, 1953. Baroness Asquith of Yarnbury, 1964. Wrote *Winston Churchill as I Knew Him*, 1965.

[3] Cyril Asquith, 1890–1954. Barrister, judge, and Law Lord. Fourth son of H. H. Asquith, Lib. PM 1908–16. Educated at Winchester and Balliol College, Oxford: Hertford, Craven and Ireland Scholarships, 1911; Eldon Scholar and Fellow of Magdalen College, 1913. Capt., Queen's Westminster Rifles, 1914–19. Married, 1918, Anne Stephanie Pollock. Judge of High Court of Justice, King's Bench Div., 1938–46. Lord of Justice of Appeal, 1946–51. Baron Asquith of Bishopstone, 1951. Member of Lord Chancellor's Law Reform Committee, 1952. Member of the Other Club.

[4] James Joseph Mallon, 1875–1961. Secretary of the National League to establish a Minimum Wage, 1906. Member of the first 13 Trade Boards (established by Churchill under the Trade Boards Act), 1909. Warden of Toynbee Hall, 1919–54. A Governor of the BBC, 1937–9, 1941–6. CH, 1939. Adviser to the Ministry of Food on Feeding in Air Raid Shelters, 1940–5. Member of the National Assistance Board, 1948.

him to try and find Richards[1] (who acted as Secretary of the 'Focus') and get a list of the names of its members. When I read them and considered how many of them you would still enjoy meeting, I was going to consult you and proceed accordingly. Mallon failed to trace Richards, and consulted Duncan Sandys, who, not realizing that the whole thing was in the nature of a 'surprise', (and in a very embryonic stage) mistakenly forwarded the letter on to you.

So the gaff is blown. The 'surprise' (for what it is worth!) is 'off', and it only remains for me to write to you now and ask whether such a meal in such company would be a pleasure to you or not? Say yes or no quite frankly. (Incidentally, it looks as though both 'freedom' and 'peace' will still need vigilant, and militant, guardians!)

My love to you and Clemmie – and get well quick.

Clement Attlee to Winston S. Churchill
(Churchill papers, 2/140)

16 October 1945

My dear Churchill,

I hope you are bearing it in mind that a photograph of yourself is required to complete the gallery on the staircase at No 10. It ought to be a really good one; and I hope you will make the selection yourself.

I hope that your throat is better.

Winston S. Churchill to Lady Violet Bonham Carter
(Churchill papers, 2/146)

18 October 1945

My dear Violet,

I thank you very much for your letter[2] and its hospitable intention.

I think it would be better to leave a meeting of this kind for some more distant date. It would be a pity if we became involved in tiresome arguments, as might well occur while differences are so sharp. Perhaps later on we shall all be able to take easier views.

Yours very sincerely,

---

[1] Arthur Harold Richards, 1889–1943. Publicity Manager, *Daily News* (from 1930, *News Chronicle*) and *Star*, 1924–35. In June 1930, organized a special feature on Churchill's life story to launch the new title. Manager, Junior Team, Chelsea Football Club, 1935–6. Organizing Secretary, Anti-Nazi Council 'Focus', to combat Nazi propaganda and to help its victims, 1936–9. Adviser to Lady Rhondda on *Time and Tide*, 1939. Worked in Ministry of Information, 1940–1. Active in charitable work for British and Allied forces.

[2] Reproduced above (pp. 102–3).

OCTOBER 1945

Winston S. Churchill to Sir James Hawkey[1]
(*Sir James Hawkey papers*)

18 October 1945

My dear Sir James,

Thank you so much for your letter, and I realize deeply what a splendid occasion[2] this will be for me and Mrs Churchill.

I have not made the progress I had hoped. My throat is still inflamed and my voice quite incapable of any effort. However I hope the next forty-eight hours will show an improvement and that my vocal cords can be touched up before I start. If I am voiceless on the day, I will, none the less, come and have my speech read out in my presence. I shall only speak for ten or twelve minutes.

I will certainly visit the guests in both the Halls after the Ceremony, but this must not involve any more speechmaking.

At present I can hardly croak. I am all right in myself, as long as I do not get a fresh cold.

Winston S. Churchill: speech
('*Winston S. Churchill, His Complete Speeches*', volume 7, page 7225)

21 October 1945   Bancroft School, Woodford Green

TASKS AHEAD

It is a pleasure for me to know that after 20 years' association with the division, a period of many political vicissitudes and marked by the perilous war years, we are better friends now than ever before. My wife and I rejoice that after these experiences you are still animated by such kindly feelings to us.

I freely avow to you, my friends, that it was not without a pang that I found myself dismissed at the General Election from the honourable task of guiding our country. I had hoped that the position I had gained in the world, the experience and knowledge which I had acquired, and the links

---

[1] Alfred James Hawkey, 1877–1952. Educated at Woodford Collegiate School. A baker. Chairman of Clark's Bread Co. Vice-Chairman, Aerated Bread Co. Married, 1904, Vera Kathleen Price (1883–1949): one son (Roger), one daughter (Dinah). Elected to Woodford UDC, 1909; Chairman, 1916–34. Chairman of Wanstead and Woodford UDC, 1934–7. Organized Food Control in Woodford, 1914–18. Deputy Chairman, Epping Conservative Association, 1922–6; Chairman, 1927–52. Knighted, 1926. A member of the Executive Committee of the India Defence League, 1933–5. Mayor of Wanstead and Woodford, 1937–8, 1943–5; responsible for emergency feeding and information services in the Borough during the Blitz, 1940–1. Member of the Essex County Council. Bt, 1945. In his war memoirs Churchill described Hawkey as 'my ever-faithful and tireless champion' (*The Gathering Storm*, p. 258).

[2] Accepting the Freedom of the City of Bancroft School in his Woodford constituency, which took place on Oct. 21.

which had been forged in the fires of war with other lands and leaders might have been of service in this critical time of transition and in the fateful work of trying to revive the life and glory of Europe within the circle of assured world peace.

I had looked forward also to throwing all my personal strength and that of my friends and colleagues into the demobilization of the forces, into the rebuilding of our homes, in the switch-over of our industries to peace-time production, and into the liberation of British genius and energy from the long thraldom of war conditions.

I shall not waste your time or my own with vain repinings, but on the contrary you may be sure that I shall devote myself unwearyingly to whatever duties may come my way and strive always to preserve those causes of British honour and human freedom in which we have all been so closely bound together in the great days that are past. (Cheers.)

I share with many people deep anxiety about the future and it seems to me that these next few years might well decide our own place in the world. It is a place which, if lost, may never be regained. The break-up of the famous Coalition Government inevitably has led to a division of our people into opposing parties, such as we have not seen since the days before the first great world war. It would be grievous if the rift deepened and widened until it became a gulf, while all the time the problems and dangers which beset us would tax to the full our united fraternal strength.

Although I may have expressed serious thoughts for an occasion of rejoicing I will not end without reaffirming my invincible belief that the future of Britain, and of the vast Commonwealth and Empire around her, is in our own hands, and that the qualities which have carried our island race to the vanguard of mankind will not desert us now.

Damaskinos Papandreou[1] to Winston S. Churchill
(*Churchill papers, 2/1*)

22 October 1945 Athens

Your Excellency,

I have the honour to forward you an open letter sent today to the Ambassadors of our Great Allies in Athens.

The Greek People will never forget that you were always a true friend to them and that during one of the most critical moments of Greek history you

---

[1] Damaskinos Papandreou, 1891–1949. Born George Papandreou in Dorvitsa, Greece. Ordained priest in Greek Orthodox Church, 1917. Bishop of Corinth, 1922. Elected Archbishop of Athens, 1938; exiled when Greek PM John Metaxas voided the election. Recalled and appointed Archbishop of Athens, 1941. Aided escape of Greek Jews from the country during German occupation and publicly protested against their persecution. Regent of Greece, 1944–6.

were their saviour. And for this reason, they always speak of you with admiration, gratitude and devotion and turn to you when they are in danger.

Unluckily the present state of affairs in our Country is again critical. Movements along our frontiers are causing us anxiety, and at home <u>EAM–Communism is re-organising for a new revolutionary action</u>. I do not know whether this is effected by internal initiative or following orders. All the same the well-known policy repeats itself, inspired by defeatism and shutting its eyes to the truth, its hopes that by continuous concessions to the 'Trotkist' Left, it will manage to appease it in such a way as to obtain its consent for a normal political life and the undisturbed functioning of democratic institutions! . . .

In my opinion, only the rapid formation of a free, strong and valid Greek State can constitute a decisive means to confront the numerous dangers and defend Greece. For this reason, <u>rapid</u> genuine elections with the majority system is the only possible solution; any continuation of this unsettled state of affairs <u>increases the opportunities of EAM–Communism and endangers the Country still more</u>.

For the adoption and application of this sole solution, the huge majority of the Greek People plead to Your Excellency for help. You know and can judge the situation much better than any of us.

Winston S. Churchill: speech
('Winston S. Churchill, His Complete Speeches', volume 7, pages 7235–6)

23 October 1945   Albert Hall, London

ALAMEIN REUNION DINNER

This is indeed a memorable occasion, for it is the first of the Eighth Army Alamein Dinners held since the War was won, and I hope it will be the precursor of a long line of annual celebrations. The Battle of Alamein takes its place with the most famous victories in British history. It was the turning point in British military fortunes during the World War. Up till Alamein we survived. After Alamein we conquered. It coincided also with the turn of the tide on the immense Russian Front and was the herald of the great Anglo-American invasion of North-West Africa.

When I arrived in Cairo at the beginning of August, 1942, I found a grave and critical situation. I found also a British and Imperial Army that did not know why it had been forced to retreat 400 miles with the loss of 80,000 men. It was an Army in no wise daunted, but an Army bewildered and enraged. My visit synchronised with the arrival of very powerful reinforcements, including the very latest weapons and tanks, which had been set in motion some months before. It was only after most careful consideration, aided by the advice of General Brooke and Field Marshal Smuts, that I proposed to the Cabinet the changes of command which were necessary. General Alexander became the Commander-in-Chief in the Middle East, with a definite Directive to concentrate all his efforts against Rommel[1] and, after the death in action of General Gott,[2] the illustrious Field Marshal who has just spoken, took the command of the Eighth Army into his strong and skilful hands. The appointment of these two great officers, whose names at the time were little known outside professional circles, will be acclaimed by history. Neither of these two men was ever defeated or long checked in the intense and bloody fighting which was before us all in so many different lands in the thirty-three months which lay before us and our goal. 'Alex' and 'Monty' are now household words. They are beloved by the people of the Empire, as they were by their soldiers, and their fame will long be cherished by their fellow countrymen and honoured by the free nations of the world.

It is of Monty, as I have been for some time allowed to call him, that I speak especially tonight. The advances of the Eighth Army under his command will ever be a glittering episode in the martial annals of Britain, and, not only of Britain but, as the Field Marshal has said, of the mighty array of Commonwealth and Empire which gathered around this small island and found its representation in all the desert battles. Field Marshal Montgomery is one of the greatest living masters of the art of war. Like Stonewall Jackson,[3] he was a professor and teacher of the military science before he became an actor on the world stage. It has been my fortune and great pleasure often to be with him at important moments in the long march from Mersa Matruh to the Rhine. Either on the eve of great battles, or while the struggle was actually in progress, always I have found the same buoyant, vigorous, efficient personality with every aspect of the vast operation in his mind, and every unity of mighty armies in his grip.

He is now discharging a task of enormous responsibility and difficulty in the administration of shattered and ruined Germany and we look to him to help those misguided and now terribly smitten people through the sombre winter which is approaching. I cannot doubt that after that he has further first-rate contributions to make to the future structure of the British Army. I

---

[1] Erwin Rommel, 1891–1944. Entered German Army, 1910. On active service in WWI in France, Italy and Romania; awarded Germany's highest decoration for bravery, *Pour le Mérite*, Battle of Caporetto, 1917. Col. commanding Hitler's HQ Guard, 1939–40. Commanded Afrika Korps, Feb. 1941 to Mar. 1943. Inspector of Coastal Defences, 1944, with responsibility for preparing France against an Allied assault; wounded by an Allied attack, 17 July 1944 (three days before the anti-Hitler bomb plot). Under suspicion of implication in the bomb plot, he accepted the option of suicide and was given a state funeral.

[2] William Henry Ewart Gott, 1897–1942. Known as 'Strafer'. Educated at Harrow. Entered KRRC, 1915. Capt., 1921. Maj., 1934. Lt-Col., 1st Battalion, KRRC, 1938. Acting Lt-Gen., XIII Corps, 1942.

[3] Thomas 'Stonewall' Jackson, 1824–65. Educated at US Military Academy, West Point. Lt, 1st US Artillery, 1846–8. Prof. of Artillery Tactics and Natural Philosophy, 1851–61. Maj.-Gen., Confederate States of America, 1861; Lt -Gen., 1862–3. Orchestrated Confederate victory at Chancellorsville, 1863.

therefore feel it an honour that he should have proposed my health and that he should have wished to associate me here with the Eighth Army and its glorious victory.

Long may old comradeship continue between those who fought side by side at Alamein. May it also continue among all who fought in the desert and by their unflinching courage and unwearying vitality and fidelity raised the reputation of the British Armies.

Winston S. Churchill to Ralph Assheton[1]
(Churchill papers, 2/1)

24 October 1945

My dear Assheton,

I heartily commend you to the electors of the City of London. You started your career in the City and your relations with it have been intimate and unbroken for more than twenty years. As Financial Secretary to the Treasury in the National Government you worked in day-to-day association with the leading bankers and merchants. No one knows better than you how great a part they played during the war in helping to carry out the financial policy of Sir Kingsley Wood[2] and Sir John Anderson, under both of whom you served.

The war has left our country beset with a multitude of unprecedented embarrassments almost every one of which resolves itself ultimately into a question of how to make both ends meet. Upon the rehabilitation and revival of its industries – and in particular of its vital export trade – depends the nation's ability, not only to pay for all those great projects of social betterment which were set in train by the National Government, but even to attain to a tolerable standard of peacetime existence.

The City of London is the nerve-centre of British trade and commerce. It is proper that its representatives in Parliament should be men who, like you and my friend Sir Andrew Duncan,[3] have a specialized knowledge of its widely-ramified interests and activities.

[1] Ralph Assheton, 1901–84. MP (Cons.) for Rushcliffe, Nottinghamshire, 1934–45; for the City of London, 1945–50; for Blackburn West, 1950–5. Parliamentary Secretary, Ministry of Labour and Ministry of National Service, 1939–42; Ministry of Supply, 1942–3. Financial Secretary, Treasury, 1943–4. Chairman of Conservative Party Organization, 1944–6. Bt, 1945. Baron Clitheroe, 1955.

[2] Kingsley Wood, 1881–1943. Member of London County Council, 1911–19. Chairman, London Insurance Committee, 1917–18. MP (Cons.) for Woolwich West, 1918–43. Knighted, 1918. Parliamentary Private Secretary to Minister of Health, 1919–22. Parliamentary Secretary, Ministry of Health, 1924–9 (when Neville Chamberlain was Minister). PC, 1928. Chairman, Executive Committee of the National Conservative and Unionist Association, 1930–2. Board of Education, 1931. Postmaster-General, 1931–5. Minister of Health, 1935–8. Secretary of State for Air, 1938–40. Lord Privy Seal, Apr.–May 1940. Chancellor of the Exchequer from May 1940 until his death.

[3] Andrew Rae Duncan, 1884–1952. Coal Controller, 1919–20. Chairman, Advisory Committee, Mines Dept, 1920–9. Knighted, 1921. A Director of the Bank of England, 1929–40. MP (Nat.) for City of London, 1940–50. President of the Board of Trade, 1940, 1941. Minister of Supply, 1940–1, 1942–5.

As Chairman of the Conservative Party it is eminently desirable that you should resume your place in Parliament at the earliest possible moment, and I hope next week will see you back again beside your colleagues, reinforcing the team of constructive critics on the Opposition Front Bench.

William Mackenzie King:[1] diary
('The Mackenzie King Record', volume 3, pages 83–8)

26 October 1945

Mackenzie King lunched with Winston Churchill on October 26. As he drove up to Churchill's new home on Hyde Park Gate,[2]

who should appear on the sidewalk but Randolph without any hat on, looking very well and strong, and Mary. They both gave me a very warm welcome. When the front door was opened Winston came along from the front of the hall to the steps to meet me. He could not have given me a warmer or more friendly greeting.

After the butler had taken my overcoat, hat and umbrella he opened the door into the drawing room where Mrs Churchill was waiting and came forward. She also greeted me in the warmest way, saying Dear Mr King, how glad we are to have you with us again. Glasses of sherry were passed around and we all had a little talk together. There was a question as to whether Randolph would wait for luncheon. Churchill told him they had only so many snipe for luncheon but that he could arrange a seat for him. Randolph said, however, he had just come up with Mary but he was not staying for lunch. He left almost immediately, and after we had had a few words in what would be Winston's library, the shelves are in but books are not there yet, we went downstairs to luncheon – a lovely room looking out onto a little garden at the back with a brick wall covered with vines – a crystal globe on the little statue.

Mrs Churchill told me that she had gone to pick out the snipe herself. There was another delicious dish and there was some debate whether it should come first or last. The first dish was caviar which I think he said Randolph had procured somewhere. Churchill persisted in adding more to the dish. This, when I was helping myself modestly.

A little wine was served, also some vodka, and port. The vodka had been brought from Russia. Mrs Churchill told the waiter not to use it but to throw it out. She said brandy was a better substitute. It was clear that the vodka had been brought on with a view to discussing Russian conditions.

---

[1] William Mackenzie King, 1874–1950. Born in Ontario. First entered Canadian Government as Minister of Labour, 1909. Leader of Liberal Party of Canada, 1919. Leader of the Opposition, 1919–21, 1930–5. PM of Canada, 1921–30, 1935–48. Secretary of State for External Affairs, 1935–46. OM, 1947.

[2] The passages in italic are written by the editor of the diaries, John 'Jack' Pickersgill.

OCTOBER 1945

In the course of the conversation Mrs Churchill told me of the reception she had in Russia. With what meticulous care they did everything to make a guest feel much at home. She spoke of Stalin keeping Mrs Stalin[1] in the background but of Molotov[2] having Madame Molotov[3] taking a most important part as a hostess. She evidently had been quite beautiful and was a person of strong personality. When she, Mrs Churchill, had gone in they had asked her if she would like a little music before luncheon. Music was played just sufficiently long to make the atmosphere pleasant and harmonious. Attentions were also paid in other ways. For example, when she acquiesced in the music, servants came in with their hair powdered, etc., brought the piano in and moved furniture to one side. Everything was done in the style that would have taught Buckingham Palace lessons in how to delight guests. She spoke of the courses that were served as being no end in number and delicious in the dishes served, etc. The whole business had been to impress her with the refinement and culture and high quality of living which was the order of things for the Russians.

During lunch, Mackenzie King reported, Churchill

did most of the talking in an exceedingly nice way. He has a marvellous mind, ranges from one subject to another with perfect ease and adequate expression.

Winston spoke quite frankly about the elections. He said it had been the greatest surprise to him and quite a blow. That he feared conditions were going to be pretty serious in England as a consequence of the policy of destroying the rich to equalize incomes of all. That he himself would have been prepared to take three quarters of the income of wealthy men but he would have left them enough to have an incentive to work. He was afraid lawyers who would take great cases would simply take a limited number and not bother with the rest. Same would govern the actions of men generally and the wealth of the country would be lessened. He spoke particularly about Cripps[4] as being the one mostly responsible. . . .

[1] Nadezhda Sergeevna Alliluyeva, 1901–32. Married, 1919, Josef Stalin. Died by suicide, 1932.
[2] Vyacheslav Mikhailovich Scriabin, 1890–1986. Used the underground name 'Molotov'. Took part in the first Russian Revolution of 1905 as a student; arrested and deported to Siberia. Secretary of *Pravda*, 1911. Exiled for a second time, 1915. Member of the Executive of the Petrograd Soviet, 1917. Chairman, Council of People's Commissars, 1930–41. People's Commissar for Foreign Affairs, 1939–46. Deputy Chairman of State Defence Committee, 1941–5. Took part in the Teheran, Yalta and Potsdam Conferences, 1943–5. Foreign Minister, 1946–9, 1953–6. 1st Deputy Chairman, Council of Ministers, 1953–7. Soviet Ambassador to Mongolia, 1957–60; to the International Atomic Energy Agency, Vienna, 1960–2.
[3] Polina Semyonovna Zhemchuzhina, 1897–70. Joined Bolshevik Social Democratic Labour Party, 1918. Married, 1921, Vyacheslav Molotov. Narkom of Fishing Industry, 1939. Candidate member, Central Committee of the Soviet Communist Party, 1939–40. Arrested for treason in 1948 and sentenced to five years' exile; acquitted following Stalin's death.
[4] Richard Stafford Cripps, 1889–1952. Educated at Winchester. Barrister-at-law, 1913. Served with the Red Cross, France, 1914. Asst Superintendent, Queen's Ferry Munitions Factory, 1915–18 (when

I spoke to Churchill about enjoying the debate. He told me that his action from the benches in waving to me had been quite spontaneous. He asked me if I had been there while he was speaking. He said you have not heard me speak impromptu before. I said to him I thought his words were so well chosen that he must have given thought to them in advance. He said, no, he had no intent to say more than just a word. That the whole speech was spontaneous. He seemed anxious to know that it was along the right lines. I told him I liked the moderation of it, the courtesy extended, etc. He said that was traditional. He did intend some day soon to go very hard after the Government. To move a vote of censure, in fact, for the length of time they were taking to demobilize men. He thought these men should not be doing nothing all round England and far too many of them on the Continent. They should be employed in industry and helping to get on with the work of production.

Churchill then got onto the question of Russia. He said that Russia was grabbing one country after another – one Capital after another. He said that all these different countries, naming the lot of the Balkans, including Berlin, would be under their control. He thought they should have been stood up to more than they were. I asked him if it was true that Stalin had told them at one time that if need be settlements would have to be made by force. He said no, that was not true, though he had had some pretty stiff talks with Stalin. He did not know what was the truth about Stalin's position. Whether he was sick or well. The Government had told him nothing.

He spoke about the Russian regime as being very difficult but said there was nothing to be gained by not letting them know that we were not afraid of them. That they would not thank us for lying down before them at any stage. He said that he had strongly pressed before the war to make no settlements or awards until the armies were holding all the positions they had taken. He stressed very strongly what realists they were. He called them 'realist lizards', all belonging to the crocodile family. He said they would be as pleasant with you as they could be, although prepared to destroy you. That sentiment meant nothing to them – morals meant nothing. They were hard realists, out for themselves and for no one else and would be governed only in that way. I asked him how they got the money to develop the power they have. He said to me that they had quantities of gold and platinum in Russia. That was one source and they had paid for nothing that had been given to them. He then spoke of the difference between the people and the militarist regime. He said that the militarist regime were a class by themselves and were the controlling factor.

---

his work much impressed Churchill, then Minister of Munitions). KC, 1927. Knighted, 1930. MP (Lab.) for East Bristol, 1931–50; for South-East Bristol, 1950. Solicitor-General, 1930–1. Ambassador to Russia, 1940–2. Lord Privy Seal and Leader of the House of Commons, 1942. Minister of Aircraft Production, 1942–5. President of the Board of Trade, 1945–7. Minister of Economic Affairs, 1947. Chancellor of the Exchequer, 1947–50.

Mackenzie King noted that

as Churchill and I talked I felt I would like to get his views on the situation with which we are faced. I said to him; would you think it disloyalty to the Government if I were to tell you of a situation which I had come over about which was one that concerned us all. (We were both Privy Councillors.) It was not a party matter but something that I felt he ought to know about. I would be glad to have his view on it. He said certainly he would keep in strict confidence anything I might say to him. I then told him about the happening at Ottawa[1] and one or two aspects of it. He said this is indeed interesting and most important. It did not, however, seem to take him by surprise. He said you must remember that with the Communists, Communism is a religion. One could say if one were using an expression that should not be misunderstood that some men would call them Jesuits without Jesus in the relationship. What he meant was that they were using any means to gain an end without that end being the end of Christianity, of Christian purposes. He said that it was impossible to view them in any other than a most realistic way. They were realists to the extreme. He said to me he thought that where men had done what was wrong the wrong should be exposed but he agreed that it would be better not to do anything without exploring the situation very carefully at first. He strongly approved of the President, Britain and Canada all acting together in the matter. He thought it would be as well to delay action until a careful plan had been worked out but that it should not be allowed to go by default. He felt it was right to talk to the Ambassador but to leave it there would be a mistake. That the world ought to know where there was espionage and that the Russians would not mind that; they had been exposed time and again. He felt that the Communist movement was spreading everywhere and that those who were Communists would do anything for their cause, deceive everybody. They had no religion or religious belief beyond that of what they were seeking in their cause.

He then went on to speak about the US and the UK. He said to me he hoped I would do all I could to keep the two together. I said to him I did not think the British Commonwealth of Nations could compete with the Russian situation itself nor did I think the US could. That I believed that it would require the two and they must be kept together. He said to me, that is the thing you must work for above everything else if you can pull off a continued alliance between the US and Britain. It must not be written, it must be understood. But if you can get them to preserve the Joint Chiefs of Staff arrangement and have plans made to keep the two together you will be doing the greatest service that can be done the world and that is your particular mission. I asked him if he did not think there should be uniformity of arms used in time of war. He said he

---

[1] Igor Gouzenko, a Soviet cipher clerk working in Ottawa, defected to Canada in September 1945. While there he revealed the extensive Soviet espionage going on in Canada at that time.

was altogether of that view and that in all particulars we must keep together as one people against the rest of the world. He stressed this again when I was leaving, stating to me that my mission was to get that alliance between the UK and the US. He asked me if I had spoken to the Government here on those lines. I told him it was precisely the line I was emphasizing to everyone. He said you have the key position and you can do more than any other man toward bringing this about.

Churchill told the Prime Minister that he had received several invitations to visit North America, one from the University of Missouri[1]

to give a course of lectures on European conditions.... Truman had scribbled in his own hand across the letter that he would like very much to see him come and deliver the course. He mentioned a large honorarium, etc. He said that he thought he might go and deliver one lecture on the conditions of the world. He would not wish any honorarium but this might give him a chance to talk with Truman and he might be helpful to British and American relations in that way.

As he was leaving, Mackenzie King again asked Churchill

to keep to himself what I had said about Russia until the Government spoke to him of it. He assured me that he would not mention it to another person. I feel quite justified at having spoken to him as this is something much apart from any party affair. He stressed how anti-Communist he knew Bevin was and also said he was glad Bevin had got the Foreign Office rather than Dalton.[2]

When I was coming away he spoke to me about the elections in Canada. Earlier I had told him about the results in three provincial elections and of the Conservative party being completely wiped out in each provincial seat. I said the truth was that the word Conservative did not suit this present age. That Liberal had come to mean what Liberal-Conservatives really stood for. That the CCF or Socialist party represented the other extreme....

When I was leaving he said to me, in reference to the elections, other men are as children in the leadership of the party as compared to yourself. You have shown understanding and capacity to lead that other men have not got, or words to this effect. He used the expression that he hoped that God would

---

[1] In fact Westminster College in Fulton, Mo.
[2] Edward Hugh John Neale Dalton, 1887–1962. Educated at Eton and King's College, Cambridge. Called to the Bar, 1914. On active service in France and Italy, 1914–18. Reader in Commerce, University of London, 1920–5; Reader in Economics, 1925–6. MP (Lab.) for Camberwell, 1924–9; for Bishop Auckland, 1929–31, 1935–59. Parliamentary Under-Secretary, FO, 1929–31. Chairman, National Executive of the Labour Party, 1936–7. Minister of Economic Warfare, 1940–2. President of the Board of Trade, 1942–5. Chancellor of the Exchequer, 1945–7; resigned over a Budget leak, 1947. Chancellor of the Duchy of Lancaster, 1948. Minister of Town and Country Planning, 1950–1. Baron, 1960.

bless me. No words could have been kinder than his as we parted. It was the sweetest side of his nature throughout – a really beautiful side. One cannot help loving him when that side of his nature is to the fore.

Harold Macmillan[1] to Winston S. Churchill
(Churchill papers, 2/2)

30 October 1945
Personal

My dear Winston,

I hope you are willing to send me a message. Since you are <u>very</u> popular in this Constituency, it would be well if the message was of a personal kind referring to our association in good and bad times, and particularly to whatever work I may have been able to do in the Mediterranean war.

We have made a good start but it is not going to be an easy fight. The tide of slop and sentiment is still flowing and the people seem not to realise the serious condition of affairs.

For practical purposes, the message should be short and concentrated.

President Harry S Truman:[2] press conference[3]
(Churchill papers, 2/28)

31 October 1945

Question: Mr President, it was said in the House of Commons yesterday that President Roosevelt and former Prime Minister Churchill reached a secret agreement at Quebec on the peace-time use of the atom bomb. Do you –

The President: (Interposing) I don't think that is true. As nearly as I can find out on the Atom Energy Release Program, Great Britain, Canada and the United States are in equal partnership on its development. And Mister Attlee

---

[1] (Maurice) Harold Macmillan, 1894–1986. Educated at Eton and Balliol College, Oxford. On active service, Grenadier Guards, 1914–18 (wounded three times). MP (Cons.) for Stockton-on-Tees, 1924–9, 1931–45; for Bromley, 1945–64. Author of *Reconstruction: A Plea for a National Policy* (1933); *Planning for Employment* (1935); *The Next Five Years* (1935); *The Middle Way* (1938); and *Economic Aspects of Defence* (1939). Parliamentary Secretary, Ministry of Supply, 1940–2. PC, 1942. Minister Resident, Allied HQ, North-West Africa, 1942–5. Secretary for Air, 1945. Minister of Housing and Local Government, 1951–4. Minister of Defence, 1954–5. Secretary of State for Foreign Affairs, 1955. Chancellor of the Exchequer, 1955–7. PM, 1957–63. Chancellor of the University of Oxford, 1960. Earl of Stockton, 1984.

[2] Harry S Truman, 1884–1972. Educated at Kansas City School of Law, 1923–5. Married, 1919, Bess Wallace. 1st Lt, 129th Field Artillery, 1918–19. Judge, Jackson County Court, Mo., 1922–4; Presiding Judge, 1926–34. US Senator, 1934–44. Vice-President, 1945. President, 1945–53.

[3] Churchill saw a transcript of this press conference on Nov. 6.

is coming over here to discuss that phase of the situation with the President of the United States.

Question: Well, Mr President, are these three countries in equal possession of the knowledge of how we produced that bomb?

The President: They are.

Question: Great Britain knows as much about how we produce that as we do?

The President: They do.

November
1945

Winston S. Churchill to Harold Macmillan
(*Churchill papers, 2/2*)

1 November 1945

My dear Harold Macmillan,

I wish you all possible success in your fight. The work which you did as British Resident Minister in the Central Mediterranean and, afterwards, as Acting President of the Allied Commission for Italy during the war, was important, difficult and delicate. It required qualities of an exceptional order and it must have given you an acquaintance with the affairs of the Mediterranean States and of the Middle East which few can rival.

Moreover in the social field at home, you are distinguished for your constructive and progressive outlook. We need you very much on the Front Opposition Bench in the House of Commons and the electors of Bromley, Beckenham and Penge will render good service to the Nation at this juncture, by returning you with an ample majority.

Winston S. Churchill to Sir Hughe Knatchbull-Hugessen[1]
(*Churchill papers, 2/222*)

1 November 1945

My dear Ambassador,

Thank you for your letters of October 27 and 30. I am afraid you are getting the programme very crowded, and if there is delay in one place, great inconvenience will be caused. I had not contemplated speaking so long at the Joint Session of the Legislature, but I will certainly allow myself the time if I

---

[1] Hughe Montgomery Knatchbull-Hugessen, 1886–1971. Known, after secret documents in his possession had been stolen by the German spy 'Cicero' in Turkey, as 'Snatch'. Entered FO, 1908. British Minister to the Baltic States, 1930–4; in Teheran, 1934–6. Knighted, 1936. Ambassador to China, 1936–7; to Turkey, 1939–44; to Belgium, 1944–7. In 1949 published his memoirs, *Diplomat in Peace and War*.

can think of enough suitable to say while I am in Paris from November 11–14. I should be very much obliged if you would let me have suggested speeches for all the places. You alone know the conditions and it is a great help to me to have a text to work on. Meanwhile I am looking forward to a statement from you on the basis of a 25-minute speech.

I enclose a copy of an extract from a statement to the Italian people[1] which I made when leaving Italy in August 1944. Pray let me know how such sentiments and ideas, repeated in a very different form, would go down in Belgium. These are, in my view, the characteristics of true democracy.

I will endeavour to borrow some Doctor's robes from Oxford, of which I am an LL.D. Part of the time I shall wear my khaki uniform as Lord Warden of the Cinque Ports. This will probably be at the dinners.

I will certainly speak a few sentences in French to the Hotel de Ville crowd, but it would be a great mistake to assume that I am bilingual.

Winston S. Churchill to Brendan Bracken
(*Churchill papers, 2/1*)

2 November 1945

My dear Bracken,

I do not need to recall to the electors of the Bournemouth Division the excellent services you rendered as Minister of Information in the Coalition Government. Still less need I remind them of your gifts of speech, your wide knowledge of affairs, or your keen political insight. But I would emphasize to them the value of these qualities in the present House of Commons, where your vigorous personality and advocacy of Conservative principles will be a great help on the Opposition Front Bench.

The Opposition has a vital duty in this Parliament. The Socialist Government claim to have a mandate from the nation to revolutionize the structure of our society. They have a Parliamentary majority out of all proportion to the numbers who voted for them. This they gained by promises of immediate action which, their leaders now admit, are impossible to fulfil. It will be the function of the Opposition to support any measures of the Government that will promote peace among the nations and hasten the return of prosperity at home. At the same time, however, we shall endeavour to open the eyes of the public to the waste and danger inherent in the textbook policies to which the Government are committed.

An awakened public opinion made articulate by a vigilant Opposition will enforce upon Ministers the need to face their primary tasks of demobilizing

---

[1] Winston S. Churchill: message to the Italian people, 28 Aug. 1944, in *The Churchill Documents*, vol. 20, *Normandy and Beyond, May–December 1944*, page 000.

the Forces, of reducing the war-time restrictions and of restoring the normal life and industry of the country.

Parliament is the poorer today for your absence, and I hope that the electors of Bournemouth will return you as their Member by an emphatic majority.

Winston S. Churchill to Queen Wilhelmina[1]
(*Churchill papers, 2/142*)

2 November 1945

Madam,

I have been deeply moved by the extraordinary compliment which Your Majesty and the Royal Netherlands Government have paid me. The Casket of letters written by John, Duke of Marlborough[2] to the Grand Pensionary Heinsius[3] is a unique treasure and will ever be guarded with reverence by me and my family. It is a great honour to me to be thus associated in Your Majesty's mind with the great deeds of yore, when our two nations stood together in the cause of freedom against the Continental tyrant.[4]

I am grateful indeed that it should be thought that any services which I have been able to render in these last terrible years, entitle me to such a mark of kindness from Your Majesty and from the Government and people of the Netherlands.

---

[1] Wilhelmina, 1880–1962. Became Queen of the Netherlands at the age of ten, on the death of her father. A fluent speaker of English, French and German. Maintained the neutrality of Holland, 1914–18. Following the outbreak of war in September 1939, she reiterated the call for neutrality. Announced her willingness (with King Leopold of the Belgians) to use her good offices to negotiate a peaceful settlement, November 1939. Issued a 'flaming protest' at the German violation of Dutch neutrality, 10 May 1940. Brought to Britain by a British destroyer, 13 May 1940. Lived in London, 1940–5, narrowly escaping death in 1943 when a bomb fell near her home, killing two members of her household. Returned to Holland, 1945. Abdicated in favour of her daughter Juliana, 1948.

[2] John Churchill, 1650–1722. Ancestor of Winston S. Churchill. Son of Sir Winston Churchill (c.1620–88). Commissioned, Foot Guards, 1667. Served at Tangier, 1668–70; in Third Dutch War, 1672–4. Sent with English troops to assist Louis XIV against the Dutch, 1672. Promoted Col. of English Rgt by Louis XIV, 1674. Married, c.1677, Sarah Jennings. Lt.-Gen,, serving as C-in-C and Peer of the Realm, 1685. Earl of Marlborough and PC, 1688. Commander of English forces during Nine Years War. 1st Duke of Marlborough, 1702.

[3] Anthonie Heinsius, 1641–1720. Dutch statesman. Pensionary for Delft in the States of Holland, 1679. Special negotiator to France, 1682. Grand Pensionary of the Estates-General of the Netherlands, 1689–1720.

[4] Louis XIV, King of France 1643–1715.

November 1945

Winston S. Churchill to Brigadier Harold Edwards[1]
(Churchill papers, 2/141)

2 November 1945

Dear Brigadier Edwards,

Thank you so much for your letter of September 15. It seems a long time ago that I was basking in the sunshine of the Riviera, but I am toiling on with the treatment.

It was good of you to write.

Winston S. Churchill to Field Marshal Sir Bernard Montgomery
(Churchill papers, 2/143)

3 November 1945

My dear Monty,

Thank you so much for your letter of October 27 and for sending me the first pamphlet you issued on the 'Conduct of Battle' to complete my set.

I <u>did</u> enjoy our reunion at the Alamein Dinner the other evening. It was indeed an honour and a happy occasion for me.

Winston S. Churchill: speech
(Hansard)

7 November 1945   House of Commons

FOREIGN POLICY (PRESIDENT TRUMAN'S DECLARATION)

Mr Churchill: The departure of the Prime Minister for the United States in all the present circumstances is so important, that we thought it right there should be a Debate in this House beforehand. Although we are divided in domestic affairs by a considerable and widening gulf, we earnestly desire that in our foreign relations we shall still speak as the great united British nation, the British Commonwealth and Empire, which strove through all the perils and havoc of the war, unconquered and unconquerable. It is our wish, on this side of the House, so far as we can give effect to it, and as long as we can give effect to it, that the Prime Minister shall represent abroad, not only the Socialist majority in the present, and we trust, transient House of Commons, but all parties in the State. What I am anxious to submit to the House this afternoon has no other object than that.

---

[1] Harold Clifford Edwards, 1899–1989. Educated at National University of Wales. Consultant surgeon to Southern Command, 1942–4; to Central Mediterranean Forces, 1944–6. CBE, 1945.

From the conversations I have had with the Prime Minister and the Foreign Secretary, I have formed the opinion that His Majesty's Government would think it inopportune today for our Debate to range over the whole European scene, or to deviate either into the tangled problems of particular European countries, or into the troubles of the Middle East, for example, Greece, Syria, Palestine, Egypt. It would seem wise to concentrate, therefore, as much as possible, on the eve of a mission of this character, upon the supreme matter of our relations with the United States, and, in particular, as it seems to me, upon the momentous declaration to the world made by President Truman in his Navy Day address in New York on Saturday, 27th October.

It would not, however, be possible to speak on this subject of the United States without referring to the other great partner in our victory over the terrible foe. To proceed otherwise would be to derange the balance which must always be preserved, if the harmony and poise of world affairs is to be maintained. I must, therefore, begin by expressing what I am sure is in everybody's heart, namely, the deep sense of gratitude we owe to the noble Russian people and valiant Soviet Armies, who, when they were attacked by Hitler, poured out their blood and suffered immeasurable torments until absolute victory was gained. Therefore, I say that it is the profound desire of this House – and the House speaks in the name of the British nation – that these feelings of comradeship and friendship, which have developed between the British and Russian peoples, should be not only preserved but rapidly expanded. Here I wish to say how glad we all are to know and feel that Generalissimo Stalin is still strongly holding the helm and steering his tremendous ship. Personally, I cannot feel anything but the most lively admiration for this truly great man, the father of his country, the ruler of its destinies in times of peace, and the victorious defender of its life in time of war.

Even if as, alas, is possible – or not impossible – we should develop strong differences on many aspects of policy, political, social, even, as we think, moral, with the Soviet Government, no state of mind must be allowed to occur in this country which ruptures or withers those great associations between our two peoples which were our glory and our safety, in the late frightful convulsion. I am already trespassing a little beyond those limits within which I have agreed with the Government it would be useful that this Debate should lie, but I feel it necessary to pay this tribute to Soviet Russia with all her tragic load of suffering, all her awful losses and devastation, all her grand, simple, enduring effort. Any idea of Britain pursuing an anti-Russian policy, or making elaborate combinations to the detriment of Russia, is utterly opposed to British thought and conscience. Nothing but a long period of very marked injuries and antagonisms, which we all hope may be averted, could develop any such mood again in this land.

I must tell the House, speaking with my own knowledge, that the world outlook is, in several respects, today less promising than it seemed after the

German capitulation of 1918, or after the Treaty of Versailles in 1919. I remember well the period immediately after the last war, when I was a Minister in high office and very close to the Prime Minister of the day. Then, there were much higher hopes of the world's future than there are now. Many things, no doubt, have been done better this time, though we have not yet felt the effects of them, but certainly there is today none of that confidence among men that they or their children will never see another world war, which there undoubtedly was in 1919. In 1919 there was the same sense of hope and belief as there is now that we were moving into a new world and that easements and ameliorations awaited the masses of our people. But added to that, there was the buoyant and comforting conviction that all the wars were ended. Personally, I did not share that conviction even at that enthusiastic moment, but one felt it all round one in a degree that is lacking today.

It is our first duty to supply the solid grounds on which this hope may arise again and live. I think the speech of the President of the United States on 27th October is the dominant factor in the present world situation. This was the speech of the head of a State and nation, which has proved its ability to maintain armies of millions, in constant victorious battle in both hemispheres at the same time. If I read him and understand him correctly, President Truman said, in effect, that the United States would maintain its vast military power and potentialities, and would join with any like-minded nations, not only to resist but to prevent aggression, no matter from what quarter it came, or in what form it presented itself. Further, he made it plain that in regions which have come under the control of the Allies, unfair tyrannical Governments not in accordance with the broad principles of democracy as we understand them would not receive recognition from the Government of the United States. Finally, he made it clear that the United States must prepare to abandon old-fashioned isolation and accept the duty of joining with other friendly and well-disposed nations, to prevent war, and to carry out those high purposes, if necessary, by the use of force carried to its extreme limits.

It is, of course, true that all these propositions and purposes have been set forth in the Declaration of the United Nations at San Francisco in May. None the less, this reaffirmation by the President of the United States on 27th October is of transcendent importance. If such a statement had been made in the summer of 1914, the Kaiser[1] would never have launched an aggressive war over a Balkan incident. All would have come to a great parley, between the most powerful Governments of those days. In the face of such a declaration, the world war of 1914 would not have occurred. Such a declaration in 1919 would have led to a real Treaty of Peace and a real armed League

[1] Wilhelm, 1859–1941. First cousin of King George V. Succeeded his father as German Emperor, 1888. Churchill first saw him in 1891, at the Crystal Palace fire brigade display, and in 1909 was his guest at German Army manoeuvres at Würzburg. Abdicated, Nov. 1918. In exile at Doorn in Holland from 1918 until his death.

of Nations. Such a declaration at any time between the two wars would have prevented the second. It would have made the League of Nations, or a world League strong enough to prevent that re-arming of Germany, which has led all of us through so much tribulation and danger, and Germany herself to punishment and ruin which may well shock the soul of man. Therefore, I feel it is our duty today, in the most definite manner, to welcome and salute the noble declaration made by the President of the United States and to make it plain that upon the principles set forth in the 12 Articles, which follow so closely upon those of the Atlantic Charter, we stand by the United States with a conviction which overrides all other considerations. I cannot bring myself to visualise, in its frightful character, another world war, but none of us knows what would happen if such a thing occurred. It is a sombre thought that, so long as the new world organisation is so loosely formed, such possibilities and their consequences are practically beyond human control.

There is a general opinion which I have noticed, that it would be a serious disaster if the particular minor planet which we inhabit blew itself to pieces, or if all human life were extinguished upon its surface, apart, that is to say, from fierce beings, armed with obsolescent firearms, dwelling in the caverns of the Stone Age. There is a general feeling that that would be a regrettable event. Perhaps, however, we flatter ourselves. Perhaps we are biased but everyone realises how far scientific knowledge has outstripped human virtue. We all hope that men are better, wiser, more merciful than they were 10,000 years ago. There is certainly a great atmosphere of comprehension. There is a growing factor which one may call world public opinion, most powerful, most persuasive, most valuable. We understand our unhappy lot, even if we have no power to control it.

Those same deep, uncontrollable anxieties which some of us felt in the years before the war recur, but we have also a hope that we had not got then. That hope is the strength and resolve of the United States to play a leading part in world affairs. There is this mighty State and nation, which offers power and sacrifice in order to bring mankind out of the dark valley through which we have been travelling. The valley is indeed dark, and the dangers most menacing, but we know that not so far away are the broad uplands of assured peace. Can we reach them? We must reach them. This is our sole duty.

I am sure we should now make it clear to the United States that we will march at their side in the cause that President Truman has devised, that we add our strength to their strength, and that their stern sober effort shall be matched by our own. After all, if everything else fails – which we must not assume – here is the best chance of survival. Personally, I feel that it is more than survival. It may even be safety, and, with safety, a vast expansion of prosperity. Having regard to all these facts of which many of us here are aware at the present time, we may confidently believe that with the British Empire and Commonwealth standing at the side of the United States, we shall together be strong enough to prevent another world catastrophe. As long as our peoples act in absolute faith and honour to each other, and to all other nations, they need fear none and they need fear nothing. The British and American peoples come together naturally, and without the need of policy or design. That is because they speak the same language, were brought up on the same common law, and have similar institutions and an equal love of individual liberty. There is often no need for policy or statecraft to make British and Americans agree together at an international council table. They can hardly help agreeing on three out of four things. They look at things in the same way. No policies, no pacts, no secret understandings are needed between them. On many of the main issues affecting our conduct and our existence, the English-speaking peoples of the world are in general agreement. It would be a mistake to suppose that increasingly close and friendly relations between Great Britain and the United States, imply an adverse outlook towards any other Power. Our friendship may be special, but it is not exclusive. On the contrary, every problem dealing with other Powers is simplified by Anglo-American agreement and harmony. That is a fact which I do not think the Foreign Secretary, or any one who took part in the recent Conference, would doubt. It is not as if it were necessary to work out some arrangement between British and Americans at a conference. In nearly every case where there is not some special difficulty between them, they take the same view of the same set of circumstances, and the fact that that is so, makes it all the more hopeful that other Powers gathered at the Conference will be drawn into the circle of agreement which must precede action.

It is on this basis I come – and I do not want to detain the House very long – to the atomic bomb. According to our present understanding with the United States, neither country is entitled to disclose its secrets to a third country without the approval of the other. A great deal has already been disclosed by the United States in agreement with us. An elaborate document giving an immense amount of information on the scientific and theoretical aspects was published by the Americans several weeks ago. A great deal of information is also common property all over the world. We are told by those who advocate immediate public disclosure, that the Soviet Government are already possessed of the scientific knowledge, and that they will be able to make atomic bombs in a very short time. This, I may point out, is somewhat inconsistent with the argument that they have a grievance, and also with the argument, for what it is worth, that we and the United States have at this moment any great gift to bestow, such as would induce a complete melting of hearts and create some entirely new relationship.

What the United States do not wish to disclose is the practical production method which they have developed, at enormous expense and on a gigantic scale. This would not be an affair of scientists or diplomatists handing over envelopes containing formulæ. If effective, any such disclosure would have to take the form of a considerable number of Soviet specialists, engineers and scientists visiting the United States arsenals, for that is what the manufacturing centres of the atomic bomb really are. They would have to visit them, and they would have to dwell there amid the plant, so that it could all be explained to them at length and at leisure. These specialists would then return to their own country, carrying with them the blueprints and all the information which they had obtained, together, no doubt, with any further improvements which might have occurred to them. I trust that we are not going to put pressure on the United States to adopt such a course. I am sure that if the circumstances were reversed, and we or the Americans asked for similar access to the Russian arsenals, it would not be granted. During the war we imparted many secrets to the Russians, especially in connection with Radar, but we were not conscious of any adequate reciprocity. Even in the heat of the war both countries acted under considerable reserve.

Therefore, I hope that Great Britain, Canada and the United States will adhere to the policy proclaimed by President Truman, and will treat their knowledge and processes as a sacred trust to be guarded for the benefit of all nations and as a deterrent against aggressive war. I myself, as a British subject, cannot feel the slightest anxiety that these great powers should at the present moment be in the hands of the United States. I am sure they will not use them in any aggressive sense, or in the indulgence of territorial or commercial appetites. They, like Great Britain, have no need or desire for territorial gains. To my mind, it is a matter for rejoicing – (*Interruption.*) Is this an argument or a duet?

Mr Logan:[1] I said that if the bomb went off there would be no working class.

Mr Churchill: I am not sufficiently familiar with the vernacular to follow the exact purpose and intensity of that joke. I am sure they will not use those powers in any aggressive way. Like Great Britain, they have no need for territorial gain. Personally, I feel it must be in most men's minds here today that it is a matter for rejoicing that these powers of manufacture are in such good hands. The possession of these powers will help the United States and our Allies to build up the structure of world security. It may be the necessary lever which is required to build up that great structure of world security.

How long, we may ask, is it likely that this advantage will rest with the United States? In the Debate on the Address I hazarded the estimate that it would be three or four years. According to the best information I have been able to obtain, I see no reason to alter that estimate, and certainly none to diminish it, but even when that period is over, whatever it may prove to be, the progress made by the United States' scientists and, I trust, by our own, both in experiment and manufacture, may well leave us and them with the prime power and responsibility for the use of these dire superhuman weapons. I also

---

[1] David Gilbert Logan, 1871–1964. JP, Liverpool, 1924. City Alderman, 1929–35. MP (Lab.) for the Scotland Div. of Liverpool from 1929 until his death.

agree with President Truman when he says that those who argue that, because of the atomic bomb, there is no need for armies, navies and air forces, are at present 100 per cent wrong. I should be glad to hear, in whatever terms His Majesty's Ministers care to express themselves, that this is also the view of His Majesty's Government.

I cannot leave this subject without referring to another aspect which is forced upon me by speeches made in a recent Debate on the Adjournment. It was said that unless all knowledge of atomic energy, whether of theory or production, were shared among all the nations of the world, some of the British and American scientists would act independently, by which, I suppose, is meant that they would betray to foreign countries whatever secrets remained. In that case, I hope the law would be used against those men with the utmost rigour. Whatever may be decided on these matters should surely be decided by Parliaments and responsible Governments, and not by scientists, however eminent and however ardent they may be. Mr Gladstone[1] said that expert knowledge is limited knowledge. On many occasions in the past we have seen attempts to rule the world by experts of one kind and another. There have been theocratic Governments, military Governments and aristocratic Governments. It is now suggested that we should have scientistic – not scientific – Governments. It is the duty of scientists, like all other people, to serve the State and not to rule it because they are scientists. If they want to rule the State they must get elected to Parliament or win distinction in the Upper House and so gain access to some of the various administrations which are formed from time to time. Most people in the English-speaking world will, I believe, think it much better that great decisions should rest with Governments lawfully elected on democratic lines. I associate myself with the majority in that opinion.

The hon. and gallant Gentleman the Member for the King's Norton Division of Birmingham (Captain Blackburn)[2] showed the other night that some breach of trust had already occurred, when he referred to the secret agreement signed by President Roosevelt and myself at Quebec in 1943, and endeavoured to give some account of it. Let me say that, so far as I am concerned, I have no objection to the publication of any document or any agreement which I have signed on this subject with the late President. Surely, however, this is a matter for both the British and United States Governments to settle together in full agreement. Neither of them has the right to publish without the consent of the other, and it would be very wrong for anyone to try to force their hands or press them unduly.

Captain Blackburn: May I point out that I did not make the suggestion that

---

[1] William Ewart Gladstone, 1809–98. PM, 1868–74, 1880–5, 1886, 1892–4.
[2] Albert Raymond Blackburn, 1915–91. Educated at Independent Rugby School and University of London. Married, 1939, Barbara Mary Robinson (div. 1954); 1956, Marianne Ferguson (div. 1959); 1959, Tessa Hume. 2nd Lt, East Yorkshire Rgt, 1940. Capt., 1940. Transferred to Royal Rgt of Artillery, 1942. Maj., 1944. MP (Lab.) for Birmingham King's Norton, 1945–50; for Northfield, 1950–1.

I knew of any secret agreement or that a leakage had occurred? I said that it was apparent from the Smyth Report, to which the right hon. Gentleman has referred, and from the White Paper and other circumstances, that some such agreement must, in fact, have been entered into.

Mr Churchill: I took great pains to read carefully what the hon. and gallant Gentleman said in his very eloquent and able speech, and I think the references which I have made today, and which also were carefully considered, will be found appropriate and not unjust. I am not making any attack. I only say that it occurred to me to be quite clear from what he said that there has been somewhere a breach of confidence, which he published and brought to the notice of the House in the exercise of his responsibilities as a Member of Parliament. This, of course, was immediately telegraphed to the United States, and at the Press Conference the next day President Truman was questioned about it. A truncated report appeared in some of the newspapers here, with the answers which he gave, but not setting forth the exact question which elicited the answer. I have taken pains to verify the actual text of the answers which President Truman gave at his Press Conference on 31st October. He was asked by correspondents the following question: 'Mr President, it was said in the House of Commons yesterday that President Roosevelt and former Prime Minister Churchill reached a secret agreement at Quebec on the peacetime use of the atom bomb. Do you – ' The President interposed: 'I do not think that is true.' Those were the exact words, where he interposed. 'As nearly as I can find out, on the atom energy release programme, Great Britain, Canada and the United States are in equal partnership on its development, and Mr Attlee is coming over here to discuss that phase of the situation with the President of the United States. Question: Well, Mr President, are these three countries in equal possession of the knowledge of how we produce the bomb? The President: They are. Question: Great Britain knows as much about how we produced that as we do? The President: They do.' It seems to me that that is a satisfactory statement of the whole position, and it affords an exceedingly good basis upon which the Prime Minister may begin any discussion he may wish to have with the President. Subject to anything that the Foreign Secretary may say, I strongly advise the House for the present to leave the question where it now lies.

May I in conclusion submit to the House a few simple points which, it seems to me, should gain their approval? First, we should fortify in every way our special and friendly connections with the United States, aiming always at a fraternal association for the purpose of common protection and world peace. Secondly, this association should in no way have a point against any other country, great or small, in the world, but should, on the contrary, be used to draw the leading victorious Powers ever more closely together on equal terms and in all good faith and good will. Thirdly, we should not abandon our special relationship with the United States and Canada about the atomic bomb, and we should aid the United States to guard this weapon as a sacred trust for the maintenance of peace. Fourthly, we should seek constantly to promote and strengthen the world organisation of the United Nations, so that, in due course, it may eventually be fitted to become the safe and trusted repository of these great agents. Fifthly, and this, I take it, is already agreed, we should make atomic bombs, and have them here, even if manufactured elsewhere, in suitable safe storage with the least possible delay. Finally, let me say on behalf of the whole House that we wish the Prime Minister the utmost success in his forthcoming highly important visit to Washington.

Winston S. Churchill to President Harry S Truman
(Churchill papers, 2/230)

8 November 1945
Private and Personal

My dear Mr President,

I have had the pleasure and honour to receive several agreeable notes from you, for which I thank you.

I have had it in my mind to visit the United States of America about the end of January. Colonel Frank Clarke, a Canadian, who gave me and the British Chiefs of Staff some wonderful trout fishing after the first Quebec Conference, has often desired me and Mrs Churchill to stay with him at his house in Florida. My doctor thinks that four or five weeks of rest and recuperation in the sunshine and with sea-bathing, would be good for me, and the prospect is certainly most attractive.

I have also had an invitation from the President[1] and Government of Mexico to pay them a visit should I come across the Atlantic. I have never seen Mexico and I thought a week there might be most interesting. I am however making further inquiries about the height, which might not be particularly good for me.

Finally I have had informal suggestions that I should pay a visit to Brazil, and if I were to cross the Atlantic I would certainly do so.

I have consulted HM Government about such a tour and they inform me they view it with favour.

Therefore all these projects have gone some distance in my mind and in preparation, but I have not so far taken any final decision. This would depend on the political situation here. As Leader of the Opposition I have duties which are capable of being devolved but which are, none the less, important in certain circumstances. I shall however, in the next fortnight or three weeks, make up my mind.

[1] Manuel Ávila Camacho, 1897–1955. Secretary of National Defense, Mexico, 1937–39. President of Mexico, 1940–6.

Should I come to the United States, I would travel by one of the Queen liners, leaving about January 16 or 17, land in New York and travel immediately south to Florida, where I would remain in the utmost seclusion possible. I should not be able to contemplate the effort involved in composing and delivering the four lectures for the Green Foundation of the Westminster University of Missouri. Of course however, if you, as you suggest in your postscript, would like me to visit your home state and would introduce me, I should feel it my duty – and it would also be a great pleasure – to deliver an Address to the Westminster University on the world situation, under your aegis. This might possibly be advantageous from several points of view. At any rate it is the only public-speaking engagement which I have in mind and the explanation for it would be my respect for you and your wishes.

I have also your kind letter about the picture for the Capitol. Naturally I should be quite ready to give Mr Douglas Chandor the opportunities which you desire, to paint his portrait of me. I should greatly appreciate the honour of figuring in the picture and of having it hung in Washington, as is suggested. If however I should decide to come to the United States, it would perhaps be more convenient for Mr Chandor to come down and paint me in Florida, and I have no doubt this could be easily arranged with my host. Should I not come, I should be very glad to see him over here any time after January next, if that is sufficiently soon.

I dare say you will have seen from the speech I made yesterday how very much I admire your recent declarations and my great desire to carry forward the policy which you have announced by every means in the power of the Conservative Party.

I send this letter by the Prime Minister's private secretary, Leslie Rowan, who was formerly my own private secretary, and whose friendship I preserve. Perhaps you will let me know, at your earliest convenience, either by his hand or through the American Ambassador in London,[1] what you feel about my tentative plans.

Lady Violet Bonham Carter to Winston S. Churchill
(Churchill papers, 2/146)

8 November 1946

Dearest Winston,

Many thanks for your letter[2] and for telling me so frankly that you do not

---

[1] John Gilbert Winant, 1889–1947. Known as 'Gil'. On active service in France, 1917–18. Governor of New Hampshire, 1925–7, 1931–5. Chairman of Social Security Board (an integral part of Roosevelt's New Deal), 1935–7. US Ambassador in London, 1941–6. OM, 1946. Author of *A Letter from Grosvenor Square* (1947) and his wartime speeches, *Our Greatest Harvest* (published posthumously, 1950).

[2] Reproduced above (p. 103).

feel inclined to meet your old friends and supporters at the present time. Their intention in asking you to luncheon was not to 'involve you in tiresome arguments' (that would indeed be a strange and perverse conception of hospitality!) but to give you pleasure.

You say in your letter that 'perhaps later on we shall be able to take easier views'. My own views could not be 'easier' than they are. But even if they were otherwise, I should not find any difficulty in meeting and eating with those who do not happen to share them. If all my life I had been obliged to eat only with those I voted with, and to vote only with those I ate with, both my politics and my meals would have been much duller than (thank Heaven!) they have been.

Ever yours (not the <u>least</u> 'sincerely'),

General Dwight D. Eisenhower to Winston S. Churchill
(Churchill papers, 2/141)

9 November 1945
Important
Eyes Only
Top Secret

Dear Mr Churchill,

It was typical of your kindness and consideration to send me your message which I received this morning.[1] As far as I am concerned you need make no statement whatsoever because many interesting incidents of the war have been more distorted in the telling than has that one. The facts were, of course, that on that occasion you, with your usual support and expression of confidence, left the decision entirely to me, but De Gaulle's representations of the extraordinary political developments that would follow upon partial withdrawal from Alsace convinced me that there would be deterioration in the military situation in the rear far over-balancing the saving of one or two divisions. I repeat that so far as I am concerned there need be no statement issued. On the other hand, if for any reason you consider it desirable, I have no objection to your making public any statement of the facts that you may think proper.

With warm and respectful regards and in the hope of seeing you late in the month when I hope to be making a trip to see your country. I would be grateful if you would remember me kindly to Mrs Churchill and your family.

---

[1] On Nov. 7, Churchill wrote: 'With regard to statements published here on October 31 about my visit to you about this time last year, I am of course quite ready to issue a contradiction if you think it worth while. Best of luck.'

November 1945

Winston S. Churchill to Sir James Grigg
(Churchill papers, 2/149)

10 November 1945
Personal
Secret

My dear PJ,

I am most grateful to you for the charming letter[1] which I have just received. I am not however at all content with the position and am asking Bridges for a copy of the letter or minute which I left behind me at the Treasury, by which I consider His Majesty's present Government is bound morally, if not legally.

2. On another subject altogether, you will have seen my efforts to get at the facts about the distribution of the Army at the present time. The Government have stated that there are about 2,300,000 officers and men in the three Services overseas and about 2,160,000 serving at home, making a total of 4,460,000, nearly six months after the war is over. Now they are trying to put the blame for the slow demobilization upon the Generals and, in particular upon Monty. This is the reverse of the truth. I am anxious to split up the above figures for the numbers abroad into <u>west of Suez</u> and east of Suez. This will show how very few men in the East and the Far East are used as a means of stopping the demobilization of great numbers at home and in Germany. You must have a very clear idea of what the lay-out was at the time you left, and I can easily find out from Leathers[2] what the shipping movements have been. Thus it will be easy to arrive at an approximate figure of the present position. The reason which Attlee gave me in confidence for not disclosing exactly the numbers east of the Suez was that they did not want to show how much part the Indian personnel were playing in the Indonesian troubles, on account of Indian Congress opinion. I thought this a very inadequate pretext, and, so far as it goes, it points to the comparatively small numbers of United Kingdom personnel involved in these far theatres.

3. I should be very glad if you would give me the best information you can on the subject as I propose to have the matter raised again in Parliament, possibly on a Vote of Censure in the next fortnight or so. I shall of course in no way bring you into the matter, but make my own estimates on my responsibility as I did in my recent speech.

4. I look forward to seeing you and your wife[3] again. As soon as we have got over our house-moving troubles, we hope you will both come to luncheon here.

5. I agree with you that things are going very badly.

---

[1] Regarding Grigg's pension rights.
[2] Frederick James Leathers, 1883–1965. Managing director of Steamship Owners Coal Association, 1916. Adviser to Ministry of Shipping, 1914–18, 1940–1. Baron, 1941. Minister of War Transport, 1941–5. CH, 1943. Viscount, 1954.
[3] Gertrude Charlotte Hough, 1885–?. Married, 1919, James Grigg.

NOVEMBER 1945

Kathleen Hill to Harold Wilson[1]
(*Churchill papers, 2/2*)

10 November 1945

Dear Mr Wilson,

Mr Churchill finds that the present table in his room at the House of Commons is not large enough to accommodate 14 or 15 members of the Consultative Committee of the Opposition – its maximum seating capacity in comfort is, I should think, only about 8 or 9. Mr Churchill would therefore be glad if a larger table could be provided for him.

Winston S. Churchill to Mr Whitbread
(*Churchill papers, 1/30*)

10 November 1945

THE FISH POOL

1. The water will remain at its present level in the two lakes. There should be room for the fish in the upper pool. Every care should be taken to close, by means of wire netting, the penstock. It does not matter the water going to and fro but I do not want the big fish to escape from the upper pool.

2. I am afraid of people coming by night and netting the fish crowded in here. Therefore no further efforts should be made to pull any more stakes or brushwood out of the part which is still filled with water.

3. The Germans should clear all the exposed parts thoroughly of brushwood and debris. Then they should go to the swimming pool, the bottom of which should be quite cleared of debris and camouflage. Next they should go up the sunken trench between the swimming pool and the meadows and clear all the barbed wire from there and cut away the weeds and briars that have grown among it. They should continue to work upwards on the barbed wire till it cuts the road and then take out the barbed wire near Harris's cottage and opposite the tennis ground.

4. While the fish are crowded together in this narrow space, it would be as well to give them a few handfuls of food each day.

5. The pulling out of the last stakes and brushwood in this inundated part of the upper pool could be started on Friday. As soon as I get back I will supervise the pulling out of the fish with the net, which I am trying to procure, and the carrying of them in the tins to the garden pool where, of

---

[1] (James) Harold Wilson, 1916–95. Educated at Jesus College, Oxford, 1934. Lecturer in Economic History, New College, 1937. Research Fellow, University College, 1938. Director of Economics and Statistics, Ministry of Fuel and Power, 1943–4. MP (Lab.) for Ormskirk, 1945–50; for Huyton, 1950–83. Parliamentary Secretary, Ministry of Works, 1945–7. President of the Board of Trade, 1947–51. Leader of the Labour Party, 1963–76. PM, 1964–70, 1974–6. Baron, 1983.

course, as there is no mud, they will have to be fed till they go to sleep for the winter.

6. When the fish are moved into the garden pool, a sharp eye should be kept to drive away herons. Also when they are in the lake and here there is no harm in the water being made and kept muddy.

Winston S. Churchill: speech
('Winston S. Churchill, His Complete Speeches', volume 7, page 7248)

12 November 1945   French Institute, Paris

A NEW EUROPE

[. . .] Everywhere I have been I have received proofs of affection and hospitality that have profoundly touched me.

I can recall that a year ago I witnessed Paris in the joy of liberation.

After the terrible tests we have passed through we cannot expect everything to be settled immediately. But from what I have seen I feel that I can congratulate France on the progress made.

My hope, as you know, is that a new and happier Europe may one day raise its glory from the ruins we now see about us. And in this noble effort the genius, the culture and especially the power of France should play its true and incontestable role.

Winston S. Churchill to Lady Violet Bonham Carter
(Churchill papers, 2/146)

13 November 1945   Chartwell
Private
Mrs C to see
Hold
NOT SENT

My dear Violet,

Thank you for your letter of November 8.[1] As you return to the charge, I am forced to say that, in my view, you and other leading Liberals, have behaved with a complete indifference and detachment to the vital interests of our country, and have sought Party advantage in a reckless and wanton manner. Animal hatred of the Conservative Party, which appears to be the sole remaining theme of Liberalism, certainly did the Tory Party an immense amount of harm at the late General Election without doing the slightest good

---

[1] Reproduced above (pp. 128–9).

to Liberal interests. You may well find that the future will bring great dangers and privations upon us all, for which certainly you will bear a small but quite recognizable responsibility.

In writing the above I am not animated by any sense of personal soreness at having been dismissed.

Winston S. Churchill to Ernest Bevin
(Churchill papers, 2/2)

13 November 1945
Most Secret

Dear Ernest,

Thank you for sending me the telegrams, which I have duly burnt.

1. The long-term advantage to Britain and the Commonwealth is to have our affairs so interwoven with those of the United States in external and strategic matters, that any idea of war between the two countries is utterly impossible, and that in fact, however the matter may be worded, we stand or fall together. It does not seem likely that we should have to fall. In a world of measureless perils and anxieties, here is the rock of safety.

2. From this point of view, the more strategic points we hold in Joint occupation, the better. I have not studied particular islands and bases in detail on the map, but in principle there is no doubt that the Joint occupation greatly strengthens the power of the United States and the safety of Britain. Although the United States is far more powerful than the British Commonwealth, we must always insist upon coming in on equal terms. We should press for Joint occupation at all points in question rather than accept the exclusive possession by the United States. We have so much to give that I have little doubt that, for the sake of a general settlement, they would agree to Joint occupation throughout.

3. I do not agree with the characteristic Halifax slant that we should melt it all down into a vague United Nations Trusteeship. This ignores the vital fact that a special and privileged relationship between Great Britain and the United States makes us both safe for ourselves and more influential as regards building up the safety of others through the international machine. The fact that the British Commonwealth and the United States were for strategic purposes one organism, would mean:

    (a) that we should be able to achieve more friendly and trustful relations with Soviet Russia, and

    (b) that we could build up the United Nations organization around us and above us with greater speed and success. 'Whom God hath joined together, let no man put asunder.' Our duties to mankind and all States and nations remain paramount, and we shall discharge them all the better hand in hand.

4. As you know, I write as a strong friend of the Russian people, and as one of those responsible for the Twenty Years' Treaty with the Soviet Government, to which Treaty I most strongly adhere. The future of the world depends upon the fraternal association of Great Britain and the Commonwealth of the United States. With that, there can be no war. Without it, there can be no peace. The fact that strategically the English-speaking world is bound together, will enable us to be all the better friends with Soviet Russia, and will win us the respect of that realistic State. Strategically united, we need have no fear of letting them come out into the great waters and have the fullest efflorescence as their numbers and their bravery deserve.

5. The Joint Association of the Great British Commonwealth and the United States in the large number of islands and bases, will make it indispensable to preserve indefinitely the organization of the Combined Chiefs of Staff Committee. From this should flow the continued interchange of military and scientific information and Intelligence, and also, similarity and interchangeability of weapons, common manuals of instruction for the Armed Forces, inter-related plans for the war mobilization of civil industry, and finally, interchange of officers at schools and colleges.

6. What we may now be able to achieve is, in fact, Salvation for ourselves, and the means of procuring Salvation for the world.

You are indeed fortunate that this sublime opportunity has fallen to you, and I trust the seizing of it will ever be associated with your name. In all necessary action you should count on me, if I can be of any use.

Winston S. Churchill to Pierre Flandin[1]
(*Churchill papers, 2/149*)

14 November 1945

Dear Monsieur Flandin,

For many years I regarded you as a strong friend of the Franco-British Entente, and you were the French statesman with whom I had the closest personal contacts before the War. I well remember your visit to me when, as Foreign Secretary, you came early in the morning to my flat in London after the German invasion of the Rhineland in 1936. Although I was at that

---

[1] Pierre-Étienne Flandin, 1889–1958. Chef de Cabinet to PM (Millerand), 1913–14. Entered Chamber of Deputies, 1914. Director, Allied Aeronautical Service, 1917. Under-Secretary for Air, 1920. President, First International Conference on Aerial Navigation, 1921. Minister for Commerce for five days, June 1924; Nov. 1929 to Mar, 1930. Minister for Finance, 1931 and 1932. Leader of the centre-right group of Deputies, 1932. PM, Nov. 1934 to June 1935. Minister for Foreign Affairs, Jan.–June 1936. Foreign Minister and Vice Premier until ousted by François Darlan, 1940–1. Arrested by the Allies in North Africa, 1943. Tried by the French Government, 1946, but acquitted on the charge of collaboration with the Germans (Randolph Churchill spoke in Flandin's defence at the trial, on his father's behalf).

time out of Office, it was to me that you came first, asking my help, which I gladly promised, in your endeavours to bring about a more decisive joint action between the two countries in view of the gross outrage which Hitler had committed.

In those days, His Majesty's Government were still hoping against hope that the Hitler menace would not materialize in war, and in this hope and wish they were undoubtedly supported by very large majorities of the British and, as far as I could see, the French people. I very much regret that the ideas we had in common at that time could not have been brought into effect, and that a solid front or circle of nations, including those of the Little Entente, was not built up against the ever-growing encroachments of Germany.

Afterwards, when the Munich Agreement was made, you sent a telegram to Hitler congratulating him on the peaceful settlement. I did not agree with this for reasons which I gave abundantly in public, but I must admit that the Munich Settlement was supported by very large majorities on both sides of the Channel, not only in the Parliaments but in the countries at large. I did not consider that the differences between us at this time in any way altered our personal relations, or weakened my confidence in you as a French friend of England.

Presently terrible things happened and France, under the overwhelming fury of the German irruption, asked for an Armistice. As an Englishman, I have never reproached the French nation on account of this yielding to dire necessity. My grief was that, although we had done all that we had promised, we had not been able to do more. However we made up for this later on, and in the end, all came right.

When, in the middle of December 1940, I learned that you had joined the Vichy Government, I was glad. I thought to myself, 'here is a friend of England in a high position in the Vichy Government, and I am sure that this will lessen the danger of that Government declaring formal war upon us'. I also thought it only too probable that you would not last long, and that the Germans would have you out. This is exactly what happened, at the beginning of February.

I have heard that in your period of Office, you managed to stop an expedition being sent from Dakar against the Free French centre at Tchad. If this is true, it would seem to me important that the facts should be elicited, because any such expedition from Dakar would have added greatly to the troubles which General de Gaulle and I were facing together at that rather forlorn and desperate time before the corner had been turned.

Accordingly when later in 1942 and 1943 you were in Algiers, I did not hesitate to enter into friendly relations with you through the medium of my son, Randolph, and I always regarded you as on our side and against the common foe and his collaborators.

Now of course in all this that I have written, I am judging these matters as an Englishman, and not presuming to do so as if I were a Frenchman. You have however asked me, in your danger, to put down what our personal relations have been, and I feel I should be failing in a duty of friendship, which I always try to do, if I did not set forth the facts as I saw them and felt them at the time. It is for you and your legal advisers to judge whether the reading of this letter will be serviceable to you, or not. So far as I am concerned, I leave the decision entirely in your hands.

Winston S. Churchill: speech
('Winston S. Churchill, His Complete Speeches', volume 7, pages 7249–50)

15 November 1945   Brussels University

THE FOUNDATIONS OF FREEDOM

It is a real pleasure for me to visit this great seat of learning and an honour, which I deeply appreciate, to receive, on the occasion of my visit, the degree of Doctor in the Faculty of Law. If there is one word which men associate with the name of Brussels University it is Freedom. Founded in an atmosphere of newly-won freedom for the purpose of defending freedom of thought against all encroachments, the University can proudly claim to have fulfilled its mission.

It was right that it should close its doors during the German occupation; for there was no place for it in a Nazified Europe. Only when the armies of our deadly enemy had been swept away from Belgium soil could professors and students meet again to resume their normal tasks.

This did not mean that they were idle while the University was closed. Many of them entered the ranks of the resistance movement. Some of the University's choicest sons have suffered death at the hands of Hitler's executioners or in his loathsome concentration camps. Their example will, I am sure, shine like a beacon for those who follow the path they once trod.

You said, in the course of your address, for which I thank you, Monsieur le Recteur,[1] that one of the principles for which this University stands was 'the free examination of thought and ideas'. How little then is it to be wondered at that this institution should have been one of the first targets of the German invader in Belgium. For while the Nazis affected to despise thought and criticism, actually they feared and hated it even more than the physical weapons of their adversaries. How often used Hitler to sneer at the virtues of objectivity and toleration! How zealously did his army of brownshirts set about stamping them out wherever they were to be found in Germany itself during the early days of his regime! That people, always so docile in the face of a

[1] Jacques Cox, 1898–1972. Belgian astronomer and mathematician. Rector, University of Brussels, 1944–7.

tyrant, watched one puny bastion of freedom after another go down before the Nazi onslaught without stirring a finger to protect them.

Yet when the Nazis overran the occupied countries, they found to their cost that here freedom was built on firmer foundations. They used every kind of method to achieve their ends. More subtle than the Kaiser's Huns they sought at first to conceal their brutal aims behind a screen of correct behaviour and specious promises. It was a gilded cage into which they tried to entice the unwary.

The concessions which they at first demanded seemed even reasonable. Some there were in the occupied countries who in the early days found themselves caught behind the glittering bars. Let us be thankful that there were institutions like Brussels, like Leyden, like Prague, where the traditions of liberty were so firmly rooted that no thoughts of compromise could be entertained. The wave of totalitarianism beat against them in vain. The example they set was soon followed by the rest of their fellow-countrymen. Many who had been dismayed by the German victories took fresh courage: many who had been for a moment deceived by the enemy's specious promises, recovered themselves and became men again. The movements of active resistance were born and played a worthy part in their countries' liberation. So the evil dream passed and the chance to renew their lives in an atmosphere of freedom was restored to the sorely-stricken countries of Europe.

Yet the champions can never afford to sleep. Intolerance and persecution are no sooner overcome than they return in new shapes. Institutions like Brussels University, which have so manfully withstood the assaults of Nazidom, have special importance in a Europe which is emerging from its long sickness. This is my message to those whom I am so happy to call my new associates. Always be on guard against tyranny whatever shape it may assume. Remember the cause of Freedom for which heroes died. Thus, and thus alone, will you be worthy sons and daughters of the honoured University to which you belong.

Winston S. Churchill: speech
('Winston S. Churchill, His Complete Speeches', volume 7, pages 7250–1)

15 November 1945   British Embassy, Brussels

HONORARY DEGREE CONFERMENT

The Catholic University of Louvain has a long and noble history; for there the Christian virtues have been taught ever since the fifteenth century. Among the names of its Rectors, your own[1] will be remembered in its annals as one of

[1] Honoré Marie Louis Van Waeyenbergh, 1891–1971. Educated at Catholic University of Leuven and Institute of Philosophy, 1909–12. Injured while serving Belgian Army as stretcher-bearer, 1914.

the most distinguished of all. Therefore, I am greatly honoured by the decision of this seat of learning to confer on me the degree of Doctor of Law. It is a source of regret to me that the shortness of my stay in Belgium has prevented me from receiving this honour in the University itself, and I must thank you and your colleagues for your courtesy in coming here for the purpose of holding this ceremony.

I have just returned from your sister University of Brussels where a similar honour has been conferred upon me, and where I had occasion to congratulate professors and students for their worthy attitude during the German occupation of your country. I know well that when the members of its Council reached their resolve to close their doors sooner than yield to the demands of the Nazi oppressors, they were fortified by the knowledge that they could count on a hospitable welcome for their students at Louvain. More fortunate for the moment than they, thanks to the powerful protection of the Vatican, you were able to set their minds at rest on the one score which might have caused them anxiety – the future of their charges. Thus, forgetting old rivalries, the Universities of Belgium – for Liège and Ghent did the same – presented a united front to the Germans, thereby laying the foundations for that future resistance which was to prove so effective an element in victory.

When, as was inevitable, the Nazis turned their attention to Louvain and demanded from you, Monseigneur, the lists of your students with a view to conscripting them for slave labour in their war factories, they met with a firm refusal. Threats were of no avail: nor when they imprisoned you in a common gaol, did you flinch for a moment. Let me assure you that when the news of actions such as yours reached the shores of Britain from the occupied countries, they provided no small encouragement to us in our struggle, for they showed us that in Europe there were still men and women who had faith in our ultimate victory and who were prepared to risk imprisonment and death in the same cause for which we ourselves were fighting.

Thirty years ago all the world heard of the destruction of the Library of Louvain University. A wanton deed, a horrid scene, lit – as Mr Asquith[1] called it – by the 'flames of barbarian vengeance'. Much was done by American generosity to repair the losses after that war. Now this time you again fell a victim to the same ruthless foe. Many of your treasured possessions have again been burnt or destroyed. The lustre which the University has was won must be your

---

Ordained priest, 1919. Doctorate in Classical Philology, 1924. Teacher and Director of St Gummaruscollege (Lier), 1924–7; St John Berchmans College, Antwerp, 1927–36. Vice Rector, Catholic University of Leuven, 1936; Rector, 1940–62.

[1] Herbert Henry Asquith, 1852–1928. Married, 1877, Helen Melland (d. 1891); 1894, Emma Alice Margaret (Margot) Tennant. MP (Lib.) for East Fife, 1886–1918; for Paisley, 1920–4. Home Secretary, 1892–5. Liberal Imperialist during Boer War. Chancellor of Exchequer, 1905–8. PM, 1908–16. Resigned Liberal leadership, 1926. Earl of Oxford and Asquith, 1925. Churchill served under Asquith as President of the Board of Trade (1908–10), Home Secretary (1910–11) and 1st Lord of the Admiralty (1911–15).

consolation. I beg you to convey my sincere regrets to all teachers and students that I have been prevented from expressing my thanks and good wishes to them in Louvain itself. I wish you all success in your work of reconstruction and in the larger purposes that lie before you.

Winston S. Churchill: speech
('Winston S. Churchill, His Complete Speeches', volume 7, pages 7251–3)

16 November 1945   Joint Meeting of the Senate and Chamber, Brussels

THE FUTURE OF EUROPE

The ties between Great Britain and Belgium found their culmination in the great struggle from 1914–1918. It was hoped that the wars were over. Yet we have witnessed an even more destructive world-wide struggle. Need we have done so? I have no doubt whatever that firm guidance and united action on the part of the Victorious Powers would have prevented this last catastrophe. President Roosevelt one day asked what this War should be called. My answer was, 'The Unnecessary War'. If the United States had taken an active part in the League of Nations, and if the League of Nations had been prepared to use concerted force, even had it only been European force, to prevent the re-armament of Germany, there was no need for further serious bloodshed. If the Allies had resisted Hitler strongly in his early stages, even up to his seizure of the Rhineland in 1936, he would have been forced to recoil, and a chance would have been given to the sane elements in German life which were very powerful especially in the High Command, to free Germany of the maniacal Government and system into the grip of which she was falling.

Do not forget that twice the German people, by a majority, voted against Hitler, but the Allies and the League of Nations acted with such feebleness and lack of clairvoyance, that each of Hitler's encroachments became a triumph for him over all moderate and restraining forces until, finally, we resigned ourselves without further protest to the vast process of German re-armament and war preparation which ended in a renewed outbreak of destructive war. Let us profit at least by this terrible lesson. In vain did I attempt to teach it before the war.

The tragedy of Europe shocks mankind. It darkens the pages of human history. It will excite the amazement and horror of future generations. Here in these beautiful, fertile and temperate lands, where so many of the noblest races of mankind, the heirs of Roman civilisation, the champions of Christian chivalry, have developed their character, their arts, and their literature, we have twice in our lifetime seen all rent asunder and torn to pieces in frightful convulsions which have left their mark in blackened devastation throughout many ancient States and famous cities. And had not Europe's children of earlier times come back across the Atlantic Ocean with strong and rescuing arms, all the peoples of Europe might have fallen into the long night of Nazi totalitarian despotism.

In this work of rescue our British island, which has repeatedly in the last 400 years headed victorious Coalitions against European tyrants, has also now played a decisive part. Upon Britain fell the proud but awful responsibility of keeping the Flag of Freedom flying in the Old World till the forces of the New World could arrive. But now the tornado has passed away. The thunder of the cannons has ceased, the terror from the skies is over, the oppressors are cast out and broken, and we find ourselves breathless but still alive, exhausted but free. The future stands before us, to make or mar. Two supreme tasks confront us. We have to revive the prosperity of Europe: and European civilisation must rise again from the chaos and carnage into which it has been plunged: and at the same time we have to devise those measures of world security which will prevent disaster descending upon us again.

In both these tasks, Belgium and the Belgian people must play an honourable part. The restoration and rebuilding of Europe, both physical and moral, is animated and guided by the kindred themes of Liberty and Democracy. These words are on every lip. They have cheered us and helped to unify us in the struggle. They inspire our rejoicings in the hour of victory. Now that the fighting is over, it is necessary to define these glorious war cries with more fullness and precision.

You will pardon me if I come a little closer to the conception of free democracy based upon the people's will and expressing itself through representative assemblies under generally accepted constitutional forms. There are certain simple, practical tests by which the virtue and reality of any political democracy may be measured. Does the Government in any country rest upon a free, constitutional basis, assuring the people the right to vote according to their will? Is there the right of free expression of opinion, free opposition, free advocacy, and free criticism of the Government of the day? Are there Courts of Justice free from interference by the Executive or from threats of mob violence, and free from all association with particular political parties? Will these Courts administer open and well established laws associated in the human mind with the broad principles of decency and justice? Will there be fair play for the poor as well as for the rich, and for private persons as well as for Government officials? Will the rights of the individual, subject to his duties to the State, be maintained, asserted, and exalted? In short, do the Government own the people, or do the people own the Government? Here are some of the more obvious tests by which the political health and soundness of any community may be ascertained.

Above all, there must be tolerance, the recognition of the charm of variety, and the respect for the rights of minorities. There was a time when the Age of Faith endeavoured to prevent the Age of Reason, and another time when the

Age of Freedom endeavoured to destroy the Age of Faith. Tolerance was one of the chief features of the great liberalising movements which were the glory of the latter part of the nineteenth century, by which states of society were reached where the most fervent devotion to religion subsisted side by side with the fullest exercise of free thought. We may well recur to those bygone days, from whose standards of enlightenment, compassion and hopeful progress, the terrible twentieth century has fallen so far.

Now let us think of our other supreme task, the building of a world-instrument of security, in which all peoples, great and small, have a vital interest, and assuredly none more than those who dwell in the famous 'cockpit of Europe'. I do not take the view which was fashionable some time ago that the day of small States is ended, and that the modern world can only adapt itself to great Empires. I trust that the new world-instrument of the United Nations, upon which so many of our hopes are centred, will be strong and comprehensive enough to afford security and justice to large and small States alike. For this purpose however the help and guidance of the greatest Powers, as they now stand forth in the world, cannot be set aside. The more closely these Great Powers are bound together in bonds of faith and friendship, the more effective will be the safeguards against war and the higher the security of all other States and nations.

It is evident of course that the affairs of Great Britain and the British Commonwealth and Empire are becoming ever more closely interwoven with those of the United States, and that an underlying unity of thought and conviction increasingly pervades the English-speaking world. There can be nothing but advantage to the whole world from such a vast and benevolent synthesis. But we also in Britain have our Twenty Years' Treaty with Soviet Russia which in no way conflicts with other associations, but is none the less cherished by us as one of the sure anchors of world peace. We hope that in due course the natural unity and alliance between Great Britain and France may find reaffirmation in a new treaty. Then there are our well-known ancient links with Belgium and other countries, which in past years have stood such formidable trials.

Special associations within the circle of the United Nations, such as those of which I have been speaking, or the great unity of the British Empire, or the association which prevails throughout the Americas, far from weakening the structure of the supreme body, should all be capable of being fused together in such a way as to make it indivisible and invincible. I see no reason why, under the guardianship of a world organisation, there should not arise the United States of Europe, which will unify this Continent in a manner never known since the fall of the Roman Empire, and within which all its peoples may dwell together in prosperity, in justice, and in peace.

November 1945

Sir Hughe Knatchbull-Hugessen: recollection
('Diplomat in Peace and War', pages 238–9)

16 November 1945

[. . .] He came to the Embassy[1] in November 1945, with his daughter Mary. The weather up to the eve of his arrival had been abominable. But the night before he was expected there was a thick mist which I knew promised fine weather. The sun shone for the three days of the visit; the rain returned the moment he had left.

I have never seen such excitement or such enthusiasm. Presents of all kinds began to pour into the Embassy long before his arrival – cigars, flowers, books, paintings; there was a large work of art in marzipan representing Snow White and the Dwarfs. Crowds assembled and waited for hours. Even in more select gatherings, such as the Palais des Académies where he was made an Associate, people stretched out their hands to touch him as he passed up the hall. In the streets stray remarks were overheard – 'Shall I say "Hurrah" in English or French, which do you think he would like best?' and from an old lady who had placed her camp-stool at a street corner – 'Now I have seen Mr Churchill, I can die.'

It was the season of those large double chrysanthemums. Suggestive of fair-sized bath-sponges, they rained on us from house-tops and windows as we drove through the streets. The car was half full of flowers each time we returned from a drive. People broke through the police-cordon, dodged the motorcycle escort which surrounded the car and threw their bouquets into the car if they were not actually successful in handing them to Mr Churchill. One girl leapt on to the running-board, threw her arms around his neck and kissed him fervently. This was all right, but what was more alarming was the number of mothers, each holding a baby, each baby clutching a few flowers, who broke through and urged their bewildered offspring to give the flowers to Mr Churchill. It was a risky performance and I was in considerable fear more than once that we should return to the Embassy with a car-load of unidentified babies.

The scenes in the Grand' Place must have equalled if they did not surpass anything ever witnessed before. On both occasions, when the Field-Marshal[2] and Mr Churchill came out on to the balcony, the crowd of upturned faces in the square below and the colossal cheer which broke out showed that when Brussels honoured such guests she really meant it. The same scene was repeated the following summer when Mr Churchill visited Luxembourg. Some said, in fact, that the enthusiasm was if possible even more vividly expressed.

---

[1] The British Embassy in Brussels.
[2] Montgomery.

November 1945

Ernest Bevin to Winston S. Churchill
(Churchill papers, 2/2)

17 November 1945
Top Secret and Personal

Dear Winston,

I am grateful to you for your letter of November 13th[1] and for giving me so fully your views.

I agree with you about joint bases. But the difficulty is that we have committed ourselves to the United Nations, and I must keep this aspect in mind.

Winston S. Churchill to King George VI
(Churchill papers, 2/178)

18 November 1945

Sir,

I had a long conversation with your Brother[2] and the Duchess[3] in Paris on Wednesday last, and I think I ought to set before Your Majesty the position as I understood it.

Of course the dearest wish of the Duke and Duchess would be that their marriage should be recognized, and the Duchess received by Queen Mary[4] or by The Queen herself. This they have accepted as finally refused, and I do not think any further request will be made.

The next wish that the Duke had was to live in England with his Wife, as he has a perfect right to do. I have talked this over with Your Majesty, and I fully share the view that this would lead at the present time and in the next few years to many inconveniences. The Duke asked Your Majesty for a statement on this point, and was told that his residence in England would be embarrassing. As I told Your Majesty on my return from America just over a year ago, when I was your Minister, the Duke assured me that he would never be a cause of distress and vexation to you and your Family in England. The Duke and Duchess therefore both resign altogether this idea. In fact they said, 'We are The King's most loyal subjects.'

---

[1] Reproduced above (pp. 133–4).

[2] Edward Albert Christian George Andrew Patrick David, 1894–1972. Entered RN as a Cadet, 1907. Prince of Wales, 1910–36. 2nd Lt, Grenadier Guards, Aug. 1914. Attached to Sir John French's Staff, Nov. 1914. Served in France and Italy, 1914–18. Maj., 1918. Succeeded his father as King Edward VIII, Jan. 1936. Abdicated, Dec. 1936. Duke of Windsor, 1936. Married, 1937, Wallace Warfield Simpson. Governor of the Bahamas, 1940–5.

[3] Wallis Warfield, 1896–1986. Daughter of Teakle Wallis Warfield of Baltimore, Md. Married, 1937, Edward, Duke of Windsor (as her third husband). Duchess of Windsor, 1937. Resident in the Bahamas, where the Duke was Governor, 1940–5; in France from 1945.

[4] Victoria Mary, 1867–1953. Only daughter of Mary Adelaide, Duchess of Teck (a granddaughter of King George III, and Queen Victoria's first cousin), and Francis, 1st Duke of Teck. Married, 1893, George, Duke of York, later King George V.

For some time past I have understood that it was Your Majesty's wish and that of The Queen that the Duke should find a residence in the United States permanently or, at least, for some years to come. It is likely to be very difficult for them to live in France, at any rate in the immediate future, and I gather that in default of any special employment, such as an Embassy or a Governorship under suitable conditions, they would be willing to live in the United States. Therefore it seems to me that in all these great matters, they are entirely considerate to Your Majesty's wishes and willing to be guided by the interests of the Crown, although of course there is no power to prevent them living where they like, saying what they like, or acting as they choose. I certainly feel that this attitude should win some small recognition not only from you, Sir, but from His Majesty's Government.

The Duke of Windsor strongly desires not to be completely separated from his country, and to have some status which expresses, however remotely and modestly, his connection with Great Britain and with the Royal Family. He wishes to be of service to his fellow-countrymen, and he believes that living his life in the United States he may have opportunities of promoting the good relations between the two countries. All he asks is that he should have some official status. When Sir Alan Lascelles and Sir Walter Monckton[1] talked to me on this subject, I suggested a form of words which seemed to me to cover the position, namely, that the Duke's activities would be 'within the ambit of the British Embassage to the United States, without especial assignment of duties'. It is of course for Your Majesty's Ministers to advise you on a point like this. Writing as an old Servant of the Crown, I should have thought that not only did it present no difficulty – for the case of the former King is unique – but that it was very definitely for the public interest that the Duke and Duchess, dwelling in the United States, should be of their own free will under some general control, that the Duke should have constant official contacts with the British Ambassador at Washington, and that he should have a good adviser at hand or at his side.

I would even go so far as to say that there might be serious disadvantages in utterly casting off the Duke of Windsor and his Wife from all official contact with Great Britain, and leaving him in a disturbed and distressed state of mind to make his own life in the United States. I thought it very becoming in them both to wish to be guided and helped through the official contact which has been suggested, and far better for the interests of Great Britain and the Monarchy than that there should be bitterness and reproaches, and all kinds of free comments, quite possibly ill-advised, on events as they occur.

---

[1] Walter Turner Monckton, 1891–1965. Educated at Harrow and Balliol College, Oxford. President of the Oxford Union, 1913. On active service, 1915–19 (MC). Called to the Bar, 1919. KC, 1930. Attorney-General to the Prince of Wales, 1932–6. Knighted, 1937. Director-General, Press Censorship Bureau, 1939–40. Director-General, Ministry of Information, 1940–1; British Propaganda and Information Services, Cairo, 1941–2. Solicitor-General, 1945. MP (Cons.) for Bristol West, 1951–7. Minister of Labour and National Service, 1951–5. Minister of Defence, 1955–6. Paymaster-General, 1956–7. Viscount, 1957.

In short, Sir, when I consider all that they have so readily acceded to in the limitations of their personal life, I think it is a very small thing that they now ask, to have some kind of unpaid official position with the British Embassy in America, from which nothing but benefit can come to the State, and I think the opposite course might not be free from much vexation to all concerned. It would seem to me far the best course for the Duke and Duchess to settle down in the United States with dignity and goodwill, and have good advice in respect of their utterances and activities.

If Your Majesty should think it worth while to show this letter to the Prime Minister or the Foreign Secretary, I have no objection.

Winston S. Churchill to Sir Hughe Knatchbull-Hugessen
(Churchill papers, 2/222)

20 November 1945

My dear Ambassador,

I am most grateful to you for the wonderful visit which you arranged for me to Belgium. But for your initiative and the confidence I had in your judgment, I should not have undertaken it. It was all a success of the very highest order and has, I am sure, done much good to Anglo-Belgian relations. It provided the Belgian people with an opportunity of letting off their explosive feelings of enthusiasm for the British nation, and I was fortunate enough to be the recipient of these sentiments.

All the speeches which were prepared by you or your staff were admirable and, though I did not in every case use them wholly, they formed the foundation upon which it was easy for me to compose the various remarks I made. Will you please thank Mr de Sausmarez[1] for the work he did upon them. It must have been a great labour preparing all these drafts.

Finally, please thank your wife[2] from me and give her my kindest regards, for her great share in making our visit so happy and successful.

I should be very glad to know what the future reactions are. My only regret is that my wife could not be with me to see for herself all that happened.

PS. I am sending you a Photo as you desired.

---

[1] Cecil Havilland de Sausmarez, 1907–86. MBE, 1946. Representative of British Council in Belgium, 1946–8. Tutor, Wilton Park, 1951–8. People's Deputy, States of Guernsey, 1961.
[2] Mary Gilmour Wolrige Gordon, 1890–1978. Married, 1912, Hughe Knatchbull-Hugessen.

NOVEMBER 1945

I. C. Fletcher[1] to Kathleen Hill
(Churchill papers, 2/2)

20 November 1945

Dear Miss Hill,

Mr Wilson has asked me to write to you to say that before your letter of the 10th November[2] was received a larger table had already been put in Mr Churchill's room at the House of Commons. It is understood that Mr James Stuart considers the new table to be large enough for Mr Churchill's needs, but Mr Wilson has asked me to let you know that if Mr Churchill would desire a yet larger table, instructions will be given for one to be provided.

Sir Stafford Cripps to Winston S. Churchill
(Churchill papers, 2/140)[3]

21 November 1945

My Dear Winston,

May I as an old colleague still imbued with gratitude for all you did for us during the war send to you and Clementine my very best wishes for a happy Christmas and a good New Year.

I hope you both enjoy your trip to USA and the sunshine that you will meet there both in the sky and in the hearts of the American people.

Winston S. Churchill to Colonel Frank Clarke
(Churchill papers, 2/225)

22 November 1945
Personal and Confidential

My wife and I have been considering most carefully your very kind invitation[4] to Florida and if it is still convenient to you to have us we would gladly accept it. In this case we should start in one of the *Queens* reported to sail about mid-January reaching New York five days later, say twentieth–twenty-first. There may be a desire to welcome me at New York in which case I should be willing to spend a day there, coming on southwards by train and

[1] Harold Wilson's secretary at the Ministry of Works.
[2] Reproduced above (p. 131).
[3] This letter was handwritten.
[4] On 18 Oct., Col. Clarke had written to Churchill: '[. . .] There is a report in the paper today that you are laid up with a sore throat and I trust it is not serious. I do hope that you will decide to come out to Florida with Mrs. Churchill and the two girls this winter and avoid the rigors of London's winter. I asked Peter and Joan Portal to tell you how delighted and honored I would be to have you whenever you can come for a good long visit and rest' (*Churchill papers, 2/225*).

probably reaching you in Florida about January twenty-third. Both my wife and I stand in need of some rest and sunshine and we hope it would be possible for us to live very quietly indeed with you for some few weeks.

The President has asked me to visit Westminster University, Missouri, which is his home state, and deliver an address. He proposes himself to be present and introduce me. This will obviously be a public appearance of considerable importance. The President wishes me to name a date and I should propose to offer him any convenient day in the fortnight after February twenty-third. This is the only engagement which I propose to make at the present time. Other plans can be discussed between us all when we are together.

I should bring my valet but in accordance with your suggestion no secretary though I shall need one on the spot. May my wife please bring her maid as she is not very strong now. If you have room and it is in no way inconvenient we should like to bring our daughter Sarah.

Now my dear Colonel Clarke, if this plan appears burdensome to you, I do beg of you to let me know for I should most readily understand. If on the other hand you find it agreeable, will you kindly let me know as soon as possible so that I can telegraph to the President and he can fix the exact date of the Missouri meeting. Meanwhile all should be kept secret. Kindest regards.

Winston S. Churchill to Ernest Bevin
(Churchill papers, 2/141)

27 November 1945
Secret and Personal

My dear Ernest,

I am distressed about the position in Greece and I attach a couple of telegrams to show you the kind of messages I am getting from Athens.

I did not follow you in Debate the other day, because I did not wish to emphasize differences, but I am sure you will understand that I am not free from personal responsibility in this business.

At the time you made your very courageous speech to the TUC, the question of whether the plebiscite should be held before or after the Election was not one of special significance. I had not myself, at that time, any view upon it. We were fully engaged in fighting against the Communists for the life of Athens. However, when I considered the matter later on, I came to the conclusion that it would be better for the plebiscite to precede the Election for the very reason which you adduced in your speech – to try to take the Greek Monarchy out of Party politics. A plebiscite on the constitutional issue of Republic or Monarchy could take place without any of the Greek Parties being involved as Parties. Individuals would vote and thereafter Elections would follow, in which they could all express themselves freely. By reversing this process, as has been done, the Elections to be held in March are bound to be dominated by the Monarchical issue. If a substantial majority is returned to the Greek Parliament which favours the return of the King, or an early plebiscite on the subject, it would be very difficult for us to prevent this. In fact I fear that the course adopted may lead to the very conclusion you so rightly wish to avoid.

Of course anyone can see why the Communists and other Parties of the Left do not want to have a plebiscite now. They fear it would result in an overwhelming vote in favour of a Monarchy as against a Republic. But this very fact offends the other side who feel that England is interfering and using the financial lever in order to procure the success of Left-Wing views. The Report of our Trade Unions Delegation shows how terrible were the crimes committed by the Communists, and of course, especially in Athens, there is a tremendous reaction against the wholesale butcheries and treacheries which were perpetrated. I doubt whether these deep impressions will fade, and I consider it would be very dangerous and also wrong for Great Britain to interfere heavily, using the economic weapon, in order to bring about a Communist–Left-Wing triumph in Greece. I could not myself remain silent in the face of a policy of that kind. I expect that the Monarchists will gain as well as lose by British Left-Wing interference. At any rate, their front will be the rallying point of a large majority of the Greek people.

You may be sure that it is my earnest desire to help you wherever I can in the difficulties of our foreign affairs, which you are conducting with so much firmness and with disdain for cheap applause. Nevertheless I fear I may have to raise this Greek issue in detail on the Christmas Adjournment. Perhaps, if an opportunity occurs, we might have a few words together beforehand.

Winston S. Churchill: speech
('*Winston S. Churchill, His Complete Speeches*', volume 7, pages 7254–9)

28 November 1945　　　　　　Conservative Party Central Council Meeting
　　　　　　　　　　　　　　　　　　　　Friends House, London

THE PERILS OF SOCIALIST CONTROL

You give a generous welcome to one who has led you through one of the greatest political defeats in the history of the Tory Party. It may perhaps be that you give me some indulgence for leading you in some other matters which have not turned out so badly.

In October 1940, at your desire I accepted the Leadership of the Conservative Party because I felt it absolutely necessary for the sustained, vigorous direction of the War to be political chief of this great, strong Party with whom I have so many ties of sentiment and conviction. With the solid, unflinching, unwavering support of the Conservative Party, with its large majority over all other Parties in the House of Commons, I was able to impart those elements of stability and authority to the Coalition Government which carried us safely through the long years of war. On my decisive dismissal from power by the electors when the victory was won, I deemed it my duty to remain at the head of the Conservative Party until better arrangements could be made. But I am sure you will all realise that I hold the Leadership you have conferred upon me, not from any motives of personal ambition – for what could I possibly want? – but only because of the strong convictions which I hold about the future of our country, and my desire to serve you as long as you may think me of any use, or I feel that I have anything worthy of your acceptance to give.

I have used such facilities as remain to me to organise an opposition Front Bench in the House of Commons of really able, competent, modern-minded men, and we have at least a score of trained and experienced politicians, including new and younger figures, all of whom are united in their resolve to carry forward the cause of the greatness of Britain, her Commonwealth and Empire, and her place in the world. Behind us the new Parliament has brought a large accession of ability by which we shall be steadily supported and reinforced as the work of the present Parliament proceeds. It is well that this should be so, because the plight into which our country has fallen on the morrow of its wonderful victory, requires the utmost persistent endeavours of all who believe in the strength, the continuity, and the grandeur of the British name.

I hope you will believe that it is with no personal bias, soreness or conceit that I declare that the vote of the nation at the General Election was one of the greatest disasters that has smitten us in our long and chequered history. We need not waste time in examining the reasons which led to that event. As I said in the House of Commons in June, 1940 – that breathless moment in our existence: 'If we open a quarrel between the past and the present we shall find that we have lost the future.' Let us advance then into the future with the same confidence and dogged determination which all the world admired in those days when our national life and, may we not say, the freedom and glory of the world were at stake. If every measure is taken, as it should be taken, if every effort is made, as it must be made, if every act of comradeship and audacity is performed, as it will be performed, there is no reason why we should not lead our country out of its hideous lapse and error in domestic affairs, just as we in Britain did in the great world struggle, of which for a whole year we bore the brunt alone. Here, happily, we have not got to fight the terrible foreign foe, but only to regain the goodwill and revive the morale of our fellow-countrymen who came such a melancholy cropper at a moment when the opportunities of Britain were so great and our tasks so hard.

We have no longer to face the mortal perils of foreign conquest and subjugation. There are however other dangers which lie about us on every side which, if not overcome and defeated, will cramp and press the British nation down to levels we have never contemplated, and rob us not only of our place in the world which we won by superb achievement, but also of that reasonable prosperity for all classes on which we have hitherto erected our English and British way of life. Therefore so long as you care to maintain me in my present position, I shall call upon every man and woman who values the true greatness of our country and the noble Commonwealth and Empire spread around it, to do their utmost to revive the powerful heart-beat of our race and nation, and to make headway against the morbid and reactionary Socialist sectarians who, in an unguarded moment, led our people so far astray and got their stranglehold upon Britain. The struggle, I can assure you, will be hard and long, but I am as certain as I ever was in the darkest days that, provided we do not fail or falter or flag, we shall once again have the honour of guiding the destiny of Britain.

Let me now survey some of the aspects of this new conflict, far above Party or class interests, on which we must embark. Only four months have passed since, for the first time in our history, we became hag-ridden by the Socialist doctrinaires. I had hoped that however the new Government might feel, or whatever their difficulties might be with their own extremists, they would at least have devoted themselves to the task of reviving and ultimately liberating these islands after the inevitable thraldom and sacrifices of the war. Surely this practical duty, so vital, so urgent to every home, should have had overriding priority above Party fads and slogans and over long-term visionary roads to Utopia.

We are at a point in our history where the choice which Oliver Cromwell[1] placed before his victorious soldiers is again before us. It is the choice between 'Being and Wellbeing'. But as you know well from the daily and hourly experiences of your lives, we are being harassed, hampered, tied down and stifled for the sake of vain, ill-thought-out and physically unattainable plans for a Socialist future. If we look across the Channel to a small country like Belgium, which I visited a few days ago, we see a Socialist Government in power with Communists included in it. But what are they working at for the moment? Their whole idea is to get their country's head above water, to get the industries to work, get the ravages of war repaired, and make trade thrive and prosper. As we look across the broad Atlantic, we see the mighty evolution of the United States from war to peace proceeding in a violent, convulsive, passionate manner, which causes no doubt great commotion and disturbance, but which has already led to an enormous increase of output of all necessary things for the home market, with an immense, ever-growing overspill for foreign export.

Now these are very vital months for our island. We are cruelly burdened and smitten by the sacrifices and supreme exertions which we made in the

[1] Oliver Cromwell, 1599–1658. Led Parliament against King Charles I and the Royalists in the English Civil Wars.

war. We do not seek to live on the charity of other nations. Whatever is the standard of living we can maintain and develop in this island, we are resolved to achieve it by our own exertions. But what is Mr Attlee's Government doing? I say they are hampering and delaying the practical recovery of Britain for the sake of their Party fads and bitter, cast-iron Socialist dogmas. From every quarter the same tale comes to hand. All enterprise, all initiative, is baffled and fettered. The queues are longer, the shelves barer, the shops are emptier. The interference of Government Departments with daily life is more severe and more galling. More forms have to be filled up, more officials have to be consulted. Whole spheres of potential activity are frozen, rigid and numb, because this Government has to prove its Socialistic sincerity instead of showing how they can get the country alive and on the move again.

Let me set before you several major facts which are already affecting nearly every family in this island. First, the demobilisation of the Services is proceeding at a rate far below what any efficient administration would have achieved. Vast masses of men are being held under military discipline, kept not only from their homes but from the industries and jobs which are clamouring for them. No military reason justifies keeping over 4 millions of men under compulsory military service at the present moment. Many Service men were deluded into voting for the Socialists by the prospects held out to them of a far more speedy release. What has happened is that at least a million and a half are being kept doing nothing, or at invented tasks, by a pedantic adherence to the Bevin Plan. This Plan, of which in many respects I entirely approve, was prepared for a situation when the war with Germany would be over, and the war with Japan would continue for at least eighteen months thereafter. It is wholly inapplicable to the present and actual position.

Then there is Housing. Mr Aneurin Bevan,[1] who distinguished himself so much during the war by his bitter taunts at every moment of difficulty and exceptional danger, is in charge of Housing. But he cannot find time to rebuild our shattered houses. He is too busy chasing landlords and profiteers around the ruins. The building trades throughout the country are hampered and paralysed. The necessary builders are not being got out of the Services in order to begin the work. The whole vast, intricate building apparatus of our private enterprise, which built 250,000 houses every year before the War, has been deliberately cast under a cloud as if it were something indecent and improper and, at any rate, to be sharply discouraged. But even the local authorities,

---

[1] Aneurin Bevan, 1897–1960. Known as 'Nye'. A coal miner from the age of 13. Miners' Disputes Agent, 1926. MP (Lab.) for Ebbw Vale from 1929 until his death. Forced in 1944 to give the Labour Party a written assurance of loyalty or be expelled (he gave the assurance). As Minister of Health, 1945–51, introduced the National Health Service. Minister of Labour and National Service, 1951; resigned in protest against defence spending and National Health Service charges. Treasurer of the Labour Party, and Deputy Leader of the Opposition, from 1956 until his death. His often acerbic manner (he was reported to have called the Conservatives 'lower than vermin') caused Churchill to dub him a 'merchant of discourtesy'.

which are Mr Bevan's chosen instrument, are themselves hampered and baffled by needless labyrinths of controls and particular conditions.

The gloomy State vultures of nationalisation hover above our basic industries. It may well be that some of these experiments in nationalisation will have to be tried. There are great numbers of our fellow-countrymen who only learn, as indeed we all do, by the process of trial and error. It is only, I fear, by suffering that the British people will learn the best course to take. The profit-motive, we are told, must be eliminated from these basic industries. Instead there will be the loss motive which, after various permutations will emerge as a heavy and additional charge either upon the public in higher costs of fuel and travel, or, as is more probable, in heavy additional charges upon the national Exchequer.

We are told that everything must be concentrated upon the export trade. But whoever supposed that a fertile and healthy export trade could be maintained except on the overspill of a very much larger internal and domestic trade? A healthy export is the cream upon the far greater volume in the milk-pail. Whoever thought of starving the home trade as a peacetime measure of stimulating exports?

Sir Stafford Cripps is under the profound delusion that he can build up an immense, profitable export trade while keeping everything at the minimum here at home. Look what he is doing to the motor car industry. It is astonishing so clever a lawyer should not have got his case up better. He is a great advocate of 'Strength through Misery'. He tried this theme on the public when he entered the Government in February, 1942. I did not like it. I preferred 'Strength through Victory', and that is what we got. And that is what we have got to get now.

Every effort is made by the Socialist Government to restrain, diminish and, if possible, destroy the purchasing or consuming power of the public. They assure us that if this purchasing power, which used to be considered the foundation of prosperity is not damped down and choked, we shall have a rise in prices which means a continuance and aggravation of inflation, or, in other words, a fall in the purchasing power of money. But surely the remedy for this is not scarcity but abundance? The remedy is to fill the shops with the simple goods and utensils which every household and home in the country needs. Then we shall have a beneficial cycle instead of the dismal vicious circle in which at present we are forced to rotate.

All these things fit together. If we get the workers out of the Forces, and get the factories moving and get the goods into the shops, then the more purchasing power the better. The Socialists put the emphasis the wrong way round. They begin with restriction, they prolong the scarcity, and they found on this scarcity an argument for further restriction. Their root principle is that it is much better that everyone should have half-rations rather than that anyone should have double. But why not try to get whole rations for everyone even if some get more? If they began by production and the release of national energy, they would soon produce the volume of consumer goods which would enable the mass of the people to buy with their hard-won savings some of the things they need so much.

Over all this hangs the vast problem of our finance, external and internal. When Sir John Anderson, Chancellor of the Exchequer in the Coalition Government, over which I presided, framed the Budget for the year 1945-6, ending on March 31st, 1946, he planned to obtain for our war needs alone by taxation and by borrowing four thousand five hundred million pounds. That was on the basis of twelve months of war in its culminating intensity against both Germany and Japan. But Victory crowned our efforts far sooner than we dared to hope. When March 31st, next year is reached, there will only have been the equivalent of three months of war out of the twelve months for which the Budget was provided. Of course there are great winding-up expenses, but is it not a staggering fact that the new Chancellor of the Exchequer only expects to save by this nine months shortening of the war out of twelve about £200 million from a total of £4,500 million – about one fortnight of war expenditures? I say without any hesitation that at least eight hundred million could have been saved by sensible, vigorous administration of the finances, and of course by setting free on earlier dates some of the millions of men and women who are now kept in camouflaged unemployment apart from any military need, not by the Generals – that is a falsehood – but by the Socialist politicians.

All the gravely disquieting facts dominate, paralyse and starve the recovery to which the British people are entitled after their long struggle. Unless the Government can be compelled by public opinion and Parliamentary pressure to amend their courses, we shall be left far behind in the race for export markets, on which it is universally agreed we depend for half the food we eat and most of our raw materials.

In time of war when national survival is at stake, everyone expects restrictions, privations and hardships. In addition to bombing, many of the sufferings of the front are endured by the civil population at home. In wartime you have had a great deal of Socialism in our own time. Most people hoped that when the war was over and all our enemies were forced into unconditional surrender, there would be easement, improvement and liberation of national energy for peacetime production. But the Socialists as a definite part of their policy condemn us to endure the restrictions and rigours of war as a part of our normal life in time of peace. Sir Stafford Cripps appeals to us to endure austerity with fortitude. I say without a moment's hesitation we are quite ready to endure any amount of necessary, unavoidable hardship. We do not shrink from austerity if that is the only road to salvation. But surely at the same time it lies with those who inculcate these sombre courses to prove that they themselves are, by every form of human wit and contrivance, trying their best to get the country on its legs again, to bring it through and out of this hard period, and so regain our place as a living and active community in the tremendous world that is growing up around us.

The attempt to socialise Great Britain is fraught with mortal danger. There has never been a community in the world like ours. Here in this small island we maintain forty-six millions of people, who played a greater part per head in winning the world-war than any other people, and who, before the war, had developed a standard of living and social services above that of any country in Europe and in many respects above that of the United States. These forty-six millions differ from every other community that has ever existed in the world by the fact that they are perched upon the completely artificial foundation of not providing even one half of their food, and being dependent for the purchase of the bulk of their food and raw materials on persuading foreign customers, to accept the wares and the services they offer. Vast, intricate, delicate, innumerable, are the methods of acquiring external wealth which the British nation has developed in recent generations, and the population has grown step by step upon the livelihood produced. This is no country of vast spaces and simple forms of mass production. We have important and substantial basic industries. We have an agriculture which, out of self-preservation, we are expanding to the utmost. But it is by many thousands of small individual enterprises and activities that the margin by which alone we can maintain ourselves has been procured.

Here is where the application of Socialist doctrines can destroy Great Britain far more surely than the magnetic mine, or the air-raid, or the U-boat warfare. They will choke and dry up, and they are choking and drying up, all these multitudinous processes and giving up in return nothing but promises and formulas. The Socialists are planning to make the Thames flow; there is to be a grand opening ceremony; after long preparation the sluices will be opened, and the ancient river will roll forward amid loud cheers – but meanwhile they are cutting off and drying up all those countless rills by which alone the flood of waters of our prosperity and life can be provided. A catastrophe is approaching this country of a different character but just as serious as occurred in 1939. Happily it is more easily to be avoided by sensible action while time remains. Will that action be taken or not? I am astounded that the principal Ministers in the Government do not see what is coming towards them.

I learn from the newspapers that we have borrowed or are to borrow about one thousand million pounds from the United States: how long is that going to keep us going? And what are the remedies or comforts which the Socialist Ministers offer? Fortitude – austerity – 'tighten your belts' – 'prepare yourselves to suffer, we are at the helm'. For the rest, cheap and bitter abuse of every form of property, of every kind of enterprise except those which are owned by the State, and, above all, rigid, universal, overlapping controls throughout the whole of the infinitely varied impulses of our natural British life. I warned the nation before the war, and my advice was not taken. I warn them now that nothing but a genuine wholehearted effort not only to liberate but to stimulate the entire life-energies of our people will carry us through the crisis in our national economy into which we are already plunged and which will intensify with every month that passes.

Some have said to me: 'Let us have a new policy for the Tory Party.' The Four Year Plan, the greatest Social Reform Programme ever put forward by any British Government, has not even been passed into law, let alone into administration. Never mind, they say: 'We want something fresh. Formulate, please, a new programme with novel counter-attractions of baits and bribes and promises to win back a majority from our large well-meaning electorate.' At the same time and sometimes the same people, complain: 'Why do we not oppose more strongly many of the Government's Bills?' I will tell you why. Because in many cases for some time to come they are in great measure our own Bills – like the vast Insurance Bill – which we advocated and prepared in the Coalition, and which we are determined by conviction to place upon the Statute Book for the good of the British people. But legislation will not suffice at this moment in our national fortunes. The Socialists, in their pamphlet at the election, said: 'Let us face the future.' Surely now we have a more immediate task when all is so grim: 'Let us face the present.'

It is the duty of everyone to do their utmost for the country; night and day they should be thinking about it and its anxious problems. It is incredible to me that any patriotic man or woman could be guilty of apathy at a time like this. If we do our duty this is no reason to be downhearted, whether we succeed or not in saving the country from a grievous ordeal we shall have done our best. And why should we not succeed? Even under the adverse and unique conditions of the recent election we are half the nation. When the Socialist Government, in their clumsy arrogance, imposed upon us war-time controls for five more long years, they had not got a majority of the electorate behind them. Together with the Liberals and Independents who voted we represented a larger total of votes against the five-years' restriction than those who voted for it. The Socialists have no majority in the nation; even with all the adventitious aid they got at the last election, they are a minority. They have a right to govern and administer the country but they have no right to ride rough-shod over the majority of their fellow country-men.

All this which I have been gathering together and laying before you this morning – and it is but a small part of what could be said – leads me to a conclusion, which I beg you most gravely to ponder over in your hearts. I foresee with sorrow but without fear in the next few years we shall come to fundamental quarrels in this country. It seems impossible to escape the fact that events are moving and will move towards the issue – 'The People versus the Socialists'. On the one hand will be the spirit of our people, organised and unorganised, the ancient, glorious, British people, who carried our name so high and our arms so far in this formidable world. On the other side will be the Socialist doctrinaires with all their pervasive propaganda, with all their bitter class hatred, with all their love of tyrannising, with all their Party machinery, with all their hordes of officials and bureaucracy. There lies the impending shock, and we must be ready to meet it as a true People's Party, gathering together all that is vital and healthy in our island life and caring for nothing except the glory, strength, and freedom of Britain.

Winston S. Churchill to Sir Alan Lascelles
(Churchill papers, 2/178)

29 November 1945
Private and Personal

My dear Alan,

I am entirely against this Irish plan,[1] which I think is full of danger. It should not merely be discouraged but effectively prevented. Neither HRH nor Shane Leslie[2] has said a word to me. This only illustrates the importance of having at the Duke of Windsor's side, or close at hand, a competent, responsible advisor. Therefore I hope the other matter will go through. Should you be communicating with the Duke on the subject you may certainly quote me as being against the Irish plan in general terms.

Winston S. Churchill to President Harry S Truman
(Churchill papers, 2/230)

29 November 1945

My dear Mr President,

I duly received your most kind letter of November 16. My wife and I and our daughter Sarah plan to leave England about the middle of January in one of the *Queens* and would reach New York on the 21st or 22nd. We would then go South by train to Miami and rest there for a few weeks in the most complete seclusion possible. I should be very happy to come to Westminster University,

---

[1] Lascelles had written to Churchill that day to tell him that the Duke of Windsor had asked to be accommodated in Ireland so he could study 'the Irish background to the general question of Anglo-American relations'. Lascelles expressed his scepticism about this plan and asked Churchill's opinion.

[2] John Randolph Shane Leslie, 1885–1971. Author and lecturer. Churchill's first cousin. Son of Sir John Leslie and Leonie Jerome. Educated at Eton and King's College, Cambridge. Received into the Catholic Church, 1908. Contested Derry City as an Irish Nationalist, 1910, but defeated. Served in British Intelligence in the US, 1915–16. Editor of the *Dublin Review*, 1916–25. Succeeded his father as 3rd Bt, 1944.

Missouri, at any date convenient to you in the fortnight after February 23. If this period is not convenient I could come a week earlier or a week later. Naturally I would let you know beforehand the line which I propose to take in my address on World Affairs, so that nothing should be said by me on this occasion which would cause you embarrassment. I do not however think this is likely to happen, as we are so much agreed in our general outlook. Perhaps you will now fix the date and let me know. I will then announce the date of my departure and my engagement at Missouri in terms agreeable to you. I will arrange this through Winant. I do not contemplate making any other public speaking engagements during my visit to the United States, certainly not before we meet at Missouri. I have had so many colds and sore throats already this winter that Lord Moran, my doctor, is very anxious for me to have a month in the warmth and sunshine, and I shall therefore be under medical protection from the many kindnesses which I feel sure will be offered me by my American friends when they hear of my plans.

I think you are quite right about Mexico, and I have abandoned that project altogether. It would not be good for me to live at such a height even for a week or ten days. I shall indeed look forward very much to some talks with you. The United States has reached a pinnacle of glory and power not exceeded by any nation in the whole history of the world, and with that come not only opportunities literally for saving misguided humanity but also terrible responsibilities if those opportunities cannot be seized. Often and often I think of you and your problems as I did of those of our dear friend FDR. I am most thankful you are there to fill his place.

Lady Soames: recollection
('Clementine Churchill', page 399)

30 November 1945

This year saw the first of Winston's peace-time birthday parties, one of many such for us all, glowing and glorious occasions. And in order to gather as many of the family together as possible, Winston and Clementine decided to spend Christmas in London. It was quietish, but very pleasant, with Diana and Duncan, Sarah, myself, Uncle Jack and Aunt Nellie,[1] all mustered. It made a quiet and peaceful ending to a year that had seen such cataclysmic events for the world, and had been full of drama in our own personal lives as well.

---

[1] Nellie Hozier, 1888–1957. Clementine Churchill's sister. Served as a nurse in Belgium, 1914. Captured by the Germans, Aug. 1914, but released almost immediately. Married, 1915, Col. Bertram Romilly (1878–1940: Egyptian Camel Corps, 1914–17; Chief Instructor, Cairo Military School, 1925–8).

December 1945

Sir Hughe Knatchbull-Hugessen to Winston S. Churchill
(Churchill papers, 2/222)

1 December 1945   Brussels

Dear Mr Churchill,
    Many thanks for your letter[1] and for the photograph which I am delighted to have.
    I am glad you were pleased with the visit. It certainly was the most outstanding success. I don't think I have ever seen anything go so perfectly from beginning to end. People here still continue to talk about it with enthusiasm and I am certain it has done a lot of good. I hope that some of the things you said may have had the effect of inducing people here to pull themselves together and realise that there are more important issues for their country than squabbling about whether the King is to come back or not. Of course this is of great importance but I don't think it is important enough to justify the country splitting itself up altogether. But one may have a hope that, rather than let that happen, common sense will prevail.
    Your speech[2] in the Chamber has been the subject of running comment in the Press. People have also mentioned to me with enthusiasm what you said about the United States of Europe. I only wish we were nearer to that consummation than we seem to be at present.
    Many thanks for your kind message to my wife. I have also given your message to de Sausmarez. I am glad the draft speeches were of use.
    I hope you were not too exhausted with the whole thing. It must have been a considerable strain, not only from the point of view of what you had to give out but also of what you had to take in in the way of the popular demonstrations which I thought were extremely moving.
    I hope you found Mrs Churchill better when you got back.

---

[1] Reproduced above (p. 145).
[2] Reproduced above (pp. 139–41).

DECEMBER 1945

Field Marshal Sir Bernard Montgomery to Winston S. Churchill
(Churchill papers, 2/143)

3 December 1945

Dear Mr Churchill,

These photos taken at the Alamein dinner are so good that I feel you would like a set. I hope you keep well these days. 71 is a good age and you do not want to overdo it.

Lord Halifax to Winston S. Churchill
(Churchill papers, 2/227)

3 December 1945
Private and Personal
Washington DC

My dear Winston,

I meant to have sent you our birthday greetings but I guessed you would have plenty of these anyway and we thought of you on the day which I expect did you as much good and gave you a shade less trouble than a telegram.

I was delighted to hear that you contemplate a visit over here in the New Year and we shall look forward to seeing you both some time. Let us know as and when your plans take any shape. You will get a very warm welcome from all your American friends, who are still frankly puzzled at what seemed to them the great ingratitude of the British people! We have been ploughing along with all our financial and trade negotiations and have now pretty well reached the end. What this end will be the next forty-eight hours will, I imagine, decide. We have not got what I had hoped but from their point of view the Americans have not been unreasonable. The trouble has been that they imagined, and having imagined magnified, their own political difficulties to a greater extent than I believe a more courageous leadership would have accepted, and they could I believe by taking perhaps a slightly greater risk with their public opinion have got away with something that would have smelled very much sweeter on the British side, and proved itself in the long run a very much larger act of statesmanship than what they have in fact achieved. I have no doubt that if and when it all comes before Parliament there will be many critical voices raised, but I hope yours will not be among them for you will see more clearly than most how disagreeably wide in its implications and grim is the alternative.

I am afraid there isn't at all a good account of Harry.[1] Dorothy[2] saw Louise[3] in New York a few days ago and learned from her that something of the old trouble has reasserted itself in the sense that he does not get proper benefit from his food and is consequently weak. Nor can one suppose that there is much hope for any more in the way of operations after all he has been through. Louise professed to be cheerful but left Dorothy with some doubt as to whether she really believed it. There could be no better tonic for him than seeing you.

I have just written to Ernie Bevin to tie up with him the date that I discussed with him when I was in London about my giving up this job, which we have now settled should be May 1st next.

Give my love to Clemmie. I hope you are well. It looked as if you must have had a pretty exhausting time on your continental trip.

President Harry S Truman to Winston S. Churchill
(Churchill papers, 2/230)

6 December 1945

Referring to your letter of 29 November,[4] en route by air mail, which Winant has telegraphed to me and to which I will reply by mail upon its receipt, it is believed you should have the following information without delay.

The Westminster University has tentatively set Tuesday, 5 March, as the date for your address.

The university would like to know if this date is entirely satisfactory to you and when it can make a public announcement of your forthcoming address.

I can provide air transportation from here to the college in my plane or from Florida if you prefer to go that way.

I am looking forward with great pleasure to seeing you.

---

[1] Harry Hopkins, 1890–1946. Director of the (New Deal) Works Progress Administration, 1935–8. Secretary of Commerce, 1938–40. Administrator of Lend-Lease, 1941–5. President Roosevelt's closest aide; lived at the White House when he was not on wartime missions to London or Moscow, or in hospital (in 1937 he underwent surgery for cancer of the stomach). Travelled to Moscow on a mission for President Truman, May 1945.

[2] Dorothy Evelyn Augusta Onslow, 1885–1976. Married, 1909, Edward Frederick Lindley Wood, later Earl of Halifax. Vicereine of India, 1926–31. An Extra Lady of the Bedchamber to Queen Elizabeth the Queen Mother, 1937–1946. JP, East and West Ridings of York, 1935. Hon. Doctor of Laws, Leeds University, 1939. After the Earl's death, styled Dowager Countess of Halifax, Dame of Grace in the Order of St John of Jerusalem.

[3] Louise Gill Macy, 1906–63. Married, 30 July 1942, Harry Hopkins (his third wife). A New York fashion authority and former Paris editor of *Harper's Bazaar*.

[4] Reproduced above (pp. 156–7).

Winston S. Churchill to Frederick Crowder[1]
(Churchill papers, 2/1)

7 December 1945

Dear Mr Crowder,

I send you my best wishes for success in your first election contest. The electors of North Tottenham have good reason to support a young candidate whose active service with the famous Eighth Army has given him an understanding of the needs of the Service man. That understanding seems deplorably lacking in the Socialist Government, which has already shown itself unequal to the vital human problems that are crying out for solution at this moment.

Five months ago the nation, bemused by unscrupulous propaganda and deluded by promises that pandered to their own hopes, hoisted a Socialist Government into the saddle. Some people are already beginning to recognise the blunder they made. It is to be hoped that irreparable harm will not have been wrought before there is a general awakening to the sterility of Socialist doctrine. Every vote polled for you in North Tottenham will be a vote for a return to sanity and to the sure paths of progress along which Conservatives march. It will also signalise the growing resistance to all forms of totalitarian control.

---

[1] Frederick Petre Crowder, 1919–99. Educated at Eton and Christ Church, Oxford. On active service with 2nd Battalion Coldstream Guards, 1939–45. MP (Cons.) for Ruislip-Northwood, 1950–79. QC, 1964.

December 1945

Winston S. Churchill to Clement Attlee
(Churchill papers, 2/2)

7 December 1945
Private

My dear Prime Minister,

The following note of our talk last night about Thanks to Commanders, may be of convenience to you.

There might be three Resolutions. The first to the Americans, which should contain the three Commanders-in-Chief under whom our Forces served at different times, namely, Eisenhower, Nimitz[1] and MacArthur, and the three American Chiefs of Staff, Marshall, King[2] and Arnold.[3]

The second would be to our own people represented by the three outstanding men in each of the three Services, namely, Army, Brooke, Alexander and Montgomery; Navy, Pound,[4] Andrew Cunningham and Fraser; Air, Portal, Tedder[5] and Dowding.[6] These are really the great figures of the War and, in my opinion, they have no equals.

[1] Chester William Nimitz, 1885–1966. Educated at US Naval Academy, 1901–5; Naval War College, 1922. Active service in WWI, 1917–18. Cdr, Battleship Div. 1, 1938. Chief of Bureau of Navigation, 1939–41. C-in-C, US Pacific Fleet, 1941; Pacific Ocean Areas, 1942–5. Special Asst to the Secretary of the Navy in Western Sea Frontier, 1948–9. Raised funds to restore the Japanese battleship *Mikasa*, Adm. Togo's 1905 flagship.

[2] Ernest Joseph King, 1878–1956. Highest-ranking cadet at US Naval Academy, 1901. While still at the Academy, served during the Spanish–American War of 1898. On active service at sea during WWI. A submariner, 1923–5. Cdr, Aircraft Carriers, 1926–32. C-in-C, US Fleet, from 30 Dec. 1941; Chief of Naval Operations, Mar. 1942 to the end of the war. Fleet Adm., 1944. Hon. knighthood, 1945.

[3] Henry Harley Arnold, 1886–1950. Born in Pennsylvania. Pioneer airman: learned to fly with Orville Wright. Chief of US Army Air Corps, 1938. Member of US JCS, 1941–5. Commanding Gen., USAAF, 1942.

[4] Alfred Dudley Pickman Rogers Pound, 1877–1943. Entered RN, 1891. Torpedo Lt, 1902. Capt., 1914. 2nd Naval Assistant to Lord Fisher, Dec. 1914 to May 1915. Flag Capt., HMS *Colossus*, 1915–17. Took part in Battle of Jutland, 1916. Served on the Admiralty Staff, 1917–19. Director of Plans Div., 1922. Commanded Battle Cruiser Sqn, 1929–32. 2nd Sea Lord, 1932–5. Knighted, 1933. C-in-C, Mediterranean, 1936–9. Adm. of the Fleet, 1939. 1st Sea Lord and CNS, 1939–43. Declined a peerage, 1943. OM, 1943, bestowed by the King's Private Secretary in hospital, Oct. 6. Pound died on 21 Oct. 1943; after his funeral at Westminster Abbey, his ashes were scattered at sea.

[5] Arthur William Tedder, 1890–1967. Educated at Whitgift and Magdalene College, Cambridge. Colonial Service (Fiji), 1914. On active service, RFC, France, 1915–17, and Egypt, 1918–19 (despatches thrice). Commanded 207 Sqn, Constantinople, 1922–3; Royal Navy Staff College, 1923–4; No. 2 Flying Training School, 1924–6. Director, RAF Staff College, 1921–9. Director of Training, Air Ministry, 1934–6. AOC RAF Singapore, 1936–8. Director-General, Research and Development, Air Ministry, 1938–40. Deputy AOC-in-C, RAF, Middle East, 1940–1; AOC-in-C, RAF, Middle East, 1941–3. Knighted, 1942. Air Chf Mshl, 1942. AOC-in-C, Mediterranean Air Command, 1943. Deputy Supreme Commander (under Gen. Eisenhower), 1943–5. Baron, 1946. CAS, and 1st and Senior Air Member, Air Council, 1946–50. Chairman, JSM, 1950–1. Chancellor of the University of Cambridge from 1950 until his death.

[6] Hugh Caswall Tremenheere Dowding, 1882–1970. Educated at Winchester. Joined RA, 1900; RFC, 1914. On active service, 1914–19 (despatches). CGM, 1919. Director of Training, Air Ministry, 1926–9. CB, 1928. AOC, Fighting Area, Air Defence of Great Britain, 1929–30. Air Member for Research and Development, 1930–6. KCB, 1933. AOC- in-C, Fighter Command, 1936–40. GCVO, 1937. GCB, 1940. Mission to the US for the Ministry of Aircraft Production, 1940–2. Baron, 1943.

The third Resolution might be for the Dominions. We could perfectly well thank Dominions Commanders on a different scale from our own. The Dominions Office could no doubt find out from the different Dominions which men they would like us most to thank, and we could then insert four names, which I suppose would probably be Crerar,[1] Blamey,[2] Poole[3] and Freyberg.[4]

I am postponing putting anything down at all next week, hoping to hear from you. It would be a good thing if we could have unanimity on this subject.

Winston S. Churchill to President Harry S Truman
(Churchill papers, 2/230)

8 December 1945
Personal and Confidential

Very many thanks for your telegram.[5] March fifth for Westminster University is quite agreeable to me. I suggest the following form of announcement subject to any changes you may think desirable:

BEGINS. Mr Churchill has accepted the invitation of Westminster College, Missouri, to deliver an address on 'World Affairs' on March 5, 1946. This invitation was endorsed by the President of the United States who will himself introduce Mr Churchill to the members of the college. (Stop)

NP – Mr Churchill will leave England by sea for New York about the middle of January. He has been recommended by Lord Moran, his medical adviser, to spend a month or more in a warm climate and to have a complete rest. He has accepted the invitation of Colonel Frank Clarke of

---

[1] Henry Duncan Graham Crerar, 1888–1965. Capt., Canadian Field Artillery, 1914. On active service, Western Front, 1914–18 (DSO, 1917). Director of Military Operations and Intelligence, Canada, 1935–8. Col. Commandant, RMC, Canada, 1938. Senior Officer, Canadian Military Headquarters, London, 1939–40, with rank of Brigadier. CGS, Canada, 1940–1. Commanded Canadian Corps in Italy, 1943. GOC 1st Canadian Army, Northern Europe, 1944–5.

[2] Thomas Albert Blamey, 1884–1951. Born in New South Wales. On active service, 1914–18 (despatches seven times, DSO). CoS, Australian Corps, 1918; Australian Imperial Force, 1919. Chief Commissioner of Police, Victoria, 1925–37. Knighted, 1935. Chairman of Australian Man Power Committee, 1939–40. GOC 6th Australian Div., Australian Imperial Force, 1939–40; I Australian Corps, 1940–1; Australian Imperial Force, Middle East, 1941. Deputy CoS, Middle East, 1941. C-in-C, Allied Land Forces, South-West Pacific Area, 1942–5. FM, 1950.

[3] William Henry Evered Poole, 1902–69. Born in Caledon, Cape Colony. Commandant, South African Military College, Robert Heights, 1938–40. GSO I, 1st and 2nd South African Divs, 1940–1. CO, 2nd South African Bde, 1941–2, 1942–3. Cape Fortress Cdr, 1942. GOC 6th South African Armoured Div., Italy, 1943–5. General Officer Administration, Union Defence Forces Administrative HQ, Italy, 1945–6. Deputy CGS, Union Defence Forces, 1946–198. Head of South African Military Mission to Germany, 1948–51. Ambassador to Greece, 1960. Order of King George I, 1964. Retired, 1966.

[4] Bernard Cyril Freyberg, 1889–1963. Sub-Lt, Royal Naval Div., 1914. Lt Cdr, 1915. VC, 1916. Brig., 29th Div. in France, 1917–18. GOC, New Zealand forces, 1939–45. Commanded Allied forces in Crete, 1941. Knighted, 1942. Governor-General of New Zealand, 1946–52. Baron, 1951. Deputy Constable and Lieutenant-Governor of Windsor Castle, 1952–63.

[5] Reproduced above (p. 160).

Quebec to stay at his house in Florida during February. Mr Churchill does not contemplate any other public engagement in the United States at the present time. He will be accompanied on his visit by Mrs Churchill and his daughter Mrs Sarah Oliver. ENDS.

Winston S. Churchill to General George C. Marshall
(Churchill papers, 2/144)

9 December 1945
Private and Secret

You are reported to have stated to the Senate Committee that President Roosevelt and I had telephone conversations which were tapped by the enemy. I should be very much obliged to you if you would let me know exactly what it is you have said on this subject. Of course the late President and I were both aware from the beginning, even before Argentia, that anything we said on the open cable might be listened into by the enemy. For this reason we always spoke in cryptic terms and about matters which could be of no use to the enemy, and we never on any occasion referred directly or indirectly to military matters on these open lines. It will probably be necessary for me to make a statement on this subject in the future, and I should be very glad to know how the matter stands.

Leslie Rowan to Private Office
(Churchill papers, 2/144)

[December] 1945

In reply to his[1] queries.

A. Had they any record of a warning by General Marshall re Transatlantic telephones.

The reply is No.

B. Had they the date and or text of his conversation with President Roosevelt before Pearl Harbour.

The reply is that this was taken for Censorship purposes, but has been destroyed.

---

[1] Churchill's.

DECEMBER 1945

Winston S. Churchill to Colonel Frank Clarke
(Churchill papers, 2/225)

10 December 1945 Chartwell
Secret

Most grateful for your telegram and letter. Number 1[1] has now fixed March 5 for Missouri and has expressed a cordial desire for me to come. It will be a great relief to have a little sunshine and repose under your hospitable shield.[2]

Winston S. Churchill to Lord Halifax
(Churchill papers, 2/227)

12 December 1945
Dedip
No. 12427

1. Some time ago I received an invitation to address the Westminster University of Missouri. This was endorsed by the President who said it was his home State and that he would himself introduce me. Learning from the Foreign Office that this would be agreeable to them and from President Truman, that March 5th would be a suitable date, I have agreed to deliver an address on 'World Affairs' under his auspices on that date.

2. For some time Colonel Frank Clarke, of Quebec, Canada, whom you surely know, has invited me to stay with him at Miami, where he has a villa. Lord Moran is very anxious that I should have four or five weeks in the sunshine on account of the many colds and sore throats I have had this year. Accordingly I leave England by one of the *Queens* about the middle of January, arriving at New York around the 21st. Winant tells me it is quite likely they will wish to give me some sort of reception in New York but nothing is arranged about this at present. I propose to travel direct from New York to Miami, and to live there in the utmost possible seclusion till I go to Missouri. I do not contemplate at the present time any other public engagements, as I really stand in need of rest. I have made no plans of any kind after Missouri, but I thought I would probably pass through Washington and perhaps you could shelter me for a day or two on my way home, again in one of the *Queens*. I shall be very grateful for any advice you can give me on my plans.

3. Clemmie and Sarah are coming with me though Sarah will probably have to return to England before the end of the visit.

4. I am very glad you have been able to reach an arrangement about the loan. You must have had very difficult and protracted negotiations.

---

[1] President Truman.
[2] Churchill originally wrote 'umbrella' instead of 'shield'.

Clement Attlee to Winston S. Churchill
(Churchill papers, 2/2)

13 December 1945
Private

My dear Churchill,

I have considered again with my colleagues the question of Parliament passing Votes of Thanks to Commanders. As you know, we consider that the general Vote of Thanks, not particularising individuals, was the wisest way of dealing with the matter and I do not find much criticism of this decision. Nevertheless, we looked at the proposal for naming certain Commanders as representatives in order to avoid the difficult task of selection. We found, however, that there was not any unanimity as to individuals to be named. I am quite sure that it is impossible to get a list which would not offend large bodies of servicemen who would resent the omission of a particular leader as under-valuing the contribution made to victory by a particular Operation or by a particular Force. You will, I am sure agree, that a public wrangle as to the merits or demerits of particular Officers would be most unfortunate. The Speaker, and those sponsoring the Resolution, would be put in a difficult positions if amendments were placed on the Paper.

As regards the Dominions, the selection of certain Dominion Commanders would, first of all, have to be agreed with their respective Governments – a matter of some difficulty – and even if this was effected there would inevitably be comment at the omission of United Kingdom Commanders of comparable rank and service. I had considered whether I could get over the difficulty of mentioning the names of Dominion officers by using the terms Armies, Navies and Air Forces in a general Motion covering all British Commanders. It has, however, been represented to me that this would cause dissatisfaction overseas.

While there is of course a strong case for the inclusion of the American Officers, because we had in the War a Combined Chiefs of Staff and Americans commanding British troops, I fear that the putting down of this Motion might lead to Members proposing Votes of Thanks to Russian Commanders, perhaps also the Chinese, or even leaders of resistance movements. I am sure that the Debate would be inevitably confused, undignified, and unlikely to improve international relations. Hereditary Honours have been, and will be, awarded to all the distinguished leaders of the fighting forces mentioned in your letter who are still alive. There is, therefore, no reason whatever for the suggestion that they have been in any way slighted. I have no reason to believe that there is any desire on the part of the Officers concerned for the action proposed. I would therefore strongly urge you not to proceed further in the matter.

December 1945

Admiral Lord Louis Mountbatten[1] to Winston S. Churchill
(Churchill papers, 2/141)

14 December 1945

My dear Mr Churchill,

I am sending this letter home by my Flag Commander, Arthur Leveson,[2] who you met at Chequers and Quebec. He is also bringing with him a surrendered Samurai sword, which I ask you to accept since it was surrendered as a result of the overall victory against Japan of which you were the principal architect.

Please accept my best wishes for Christmas and the New Year for yourself and your whole family.

General George C. Marshall to Winston S. Churchill
(Churchill papers, 2/144)

14 December 1945

I testified in connection with the security phase of the use of the telephone to Hawaii and the Philippines and the Panama Canal Zone in the following words:

> I say again I am not at all clear as to what my reasons were regarding the telephone because four years later it is very difficult for me to tell what went on in my mind at the time. I will say this, though, it was in my mind regarding the use of transocean telephone.
>
> Mr Roosevelt, The President, had been in the frequent habit of talking to the Prime Minister by telephone. He also used to talk to Mr Bullitt[3] when he was Ambassador in Paris and my recollection is that that (meaning the talks with Bullitt) was intercepted by the Germans.
>
> I had a test made of induction from telephone conversations on the

---

[1] Prince Louis Francis Albert Victor Nicholas of Battenberg (His Serene Highness Prince Louis of Battenberg), 1900–79. Known as 'Dickie'. Second son of Prince Louis of Battenberg (Churchill's 1st Sea Lord, 1911–14), who in 1917 was created Marquess of Milford Haven and assumed the surname of Mountbatten. Naval Cadet, 1913–15. Midshipman, 1916. Cdr, 1932. Naval Air Div., Admiralty, 1936. Capt., 1937. Commanded HMS *Kelly*, 1939 (despatches twice). Chief of Combined Operations, 1942–3. Acting Adm., 1943. SACSEA, 1943–6. Viscount Mountbatten of Burma, 1946. Viceroy of India, 1947. Earl, 1947. Governor-General of India, 1947–8. 1st Sea Lord, 1955–9. Adm. of the Fleet, 1956. CDS, 1959–65. Murdered by IRA terrorists, 27 Aug. 1979, while fishing in a boat on a lake in the Irish Republic.

[2] Arthur Edmund Leveson, 1908–81. Married, 1934, Olivia Campbell (div. 1940); 1944, Margaret Ruth Maude. Lt, Naval War Staff, Admiralty, 1939–42. Flag Lt to Adm. Lord Louis Mountbatten. Flag Cdr to SACSEA. OBE, 1946.

[3] William Christian Bullitt, 1891–1967. Entered State Dept, 1917. President Wilson's special emissary to Russia, 1919. US Ambassador to the Soviet Union, 1933–6; to France, 1936–41. President Roosevelt's Special Representative in the Far East, 1941. Special Asst Secretary of the Navy, 1942–3. Served as a Major in the French armed forces, 1944.

Atlantic cable near Gardner's Island. I found that that could be picked up by the induction. I talked to the President not once but several times. I also later, after we were in the war, talked with the Prime Minister in the endeavor to have them be more careful in the use of the scrambler.

I trust my statement will not prove of any embarrassment to you.

Winston S. Churchill to Duke of Windsor
(*Churchill papers, 2/178*)

15 December 1945
Private

Sir,

I have read with great interest your letter to me of December 11 and the Aide Memoire which was enclosed. I have at present little influence and no power. You may rest assured however that I will do my best to remove the obstacles which exist at the Foreign Office. I suppose they are worrying about a new Ambassador, who will be appointed in May, and how he would feel towards the whole business. I certainly think it would be a good thing if you came over to see Mr Bevin when he returns from his mission to Moscow. I am going over myself with Lord Halifax. It is a very great advantage that The King and Your Royal Highness have reached such a good understanding.

I had great difficulties with the Tory Party about the American loan. In order to avoid a split in the Division, the Shadow Cabinet agreed upon the policy of abstention. This is not very heroic and I personally should have preferred 'Go as you please,' and in this case Anthony and I would of course have voted with the Government. However it was feared that, although 'Go as you please' in the House of Commons made no difference at all, having regard to the Government's immense majority, it might in the House of Lords have led to a heavy vote against the whole policy. Cranborne was emphatic that his task would be much eased if we adopted abstention as a policy, and that is what we did.

The difficulties of leading the Opposition are very great and I increasingly wonder whether the game is worth the candle. It is only from a sense of duty and of not leaving friends when they are in a lurch, that I continue to persevere.

December 1945

Winston S. Churchill to President Harry S Truman
(Churchill papers, 2/230)

16 December 1945
Personal

It is now settled that I leave in the *Queen Elizabeth* on January 10th, arriving at New York on the 15th. I confirm the date of March 5th for Missouri.

Winston S. Churchill to Lord Halifax
(Churchill papers, 2/227)

18 December 1945
Important
Personal
No. 12661

Thank you so much for your letter of December 3rd[1] and your telegram. I leave on January 10th in the *Queen Elizabeth*, arriving at New York on January 15th. We shall be staying with Colonel Frank Clarke at the Waldorf-Astoria and plan to go south by train or 'plane on the 16th or 17th.

In case they should wish to give me a public reception in New York, I should be glad to know whether the weather is not much too cold for driving in an open car through the streets, largely bare-headed, and whether it might not be better to put it off till the middle of March, when I shall be going home and the season will be less severe. Please advise me about this.

Whatever happens in New York, I propose to go into purdah completely till March 5th at Missouri, after which I should be delighted to spend a few days in Washington, especially if you have room at the Embassy. Sarah will probably have returned home separately by then.

Of course I would address Congress if they paid me the compliment of inviting me. I do not contemplate visiting any other cities.

I am expecting to hear from the President the form of the announcement.

Winston S. Churchill to Colonel Frank Clarke
(Churchill papers, 2/225)

20 December 1945   Chartwell

Thank you for your telegram. Please make statement on the line you propose. In view of the winter cold my doctor thinks I had better not have a public reception in New York on arrival, as this would entail long drives

---

[1] Reproduced above (pp. 159–60).

through the streets in an open car. It would be better to do this after leaving Washington on the way back in the second or third week of March. We should like therefore either to leave the ship at Sandy Hook or some convenient point and proceed to the train or alternatively remain on board the ship and then proceed to the train. We think it much better to travel by train than by air as it is only two nights with one intervening day. This is what the doctors advise. I am informing New York authorities of my willingness to pay them a visit on my departure, should they so desire but byepass them this time. I should hope therefore to travel south evening of 15th and not spend even one night in New York. It will be noble of you to meet us on arrival but this puts you to a very long journey and much trouble and it would be quite easy for us to find our way down to your hospitable abode, where I need and seek sunshine and rest. I do hope my coming five days earlier will cause you no inconvenience. My daughter Sarah cannot come till a fortnight later, so that our party will be myself, and wife with a maid and valet and one Scotland Yard officer.

Thank you so much for your Christmas wishes, which we cordially return.

I cannot tell you how much I am looking forward to this bright and quiet holiday, but I earnestly hope I shall be no undue care or burden to you.

Frank McCluer to Winston S. Churchill
(Churchill papers, 2/230)

20 December 1945   Fulton, Missouri

My dear Mr Churchill,

We are gratified and honored that you have accepted the invitation of Westminster College to deliver the Green Foundation Lecture on March 5. You will be introduced, as you know, by the President of the United States and arrangements are being made for the broadcasting of your address.

Mr J. Raeburn Green,[1] son of the donor of the Green Foundation and one time Secretariat of the League of Nations, called me this morning to say that he could not imagine any program under the auspices of the Green Foundation which would bring to the family of the donor of the Foundation so much happiness and pride.

It will be an honor to welcome you to this campus and to have the college offer the forum for an address, which we know will be of significance to the world.

---

[1] John Raeburn Green, 1894–1973. Educated at Westminster College (1914) and Harvard Law School (1917). Married, 1917, Elisabeth Haskell Cox. Member, Legal Section, Secretariat of the League of Nations, 1920–1. Democratic nominee for Congress, 1928. Wrote *Liberty under the Fourteenth Amendment* (1942). President, Board of Trustees, Westminster College, 1953.

December 1945

Winston S. Churchill to King George VI
(Churchill papers, 2/141)

22 December 1945   Chartwell

Sir,

It is most kind of Your Majesty to send me the splendid signed copy of the photograph of our famous 'balcony scene'. I am most grateful to the Queen and the Princesses for signing their names too. This is indeed a magnificent Christmas Card for me, and it will ever be preserved in my family as a memorial of a great and joyous day, and also as another instance of the kindness and honour with wh Your Majesty has always treated Yr Faithful and devoted servant and subject, Winston S. Churchill.

PS. May I add my most sincere wishes for Your Majesty's Happy Christmas and Bright New Year.

Winston S. Churchill to Field Marshal Sir Harold Alexander
(Churchill papers, 2/140)

22 December 1945

My dear Alex,

I hope that these tubes will beguile some of your leisure hours. Most of them were given to me by Charles Montag when he came to Como, but I have added a few of my own favourites, particularly Garance rose doré and Veronese green.

All my very best wishes for a Merry Christmas and a Happy New Year.

General Dwight D. Eisenhower to Winston S. Churchill
(Churchill papers, 2/226)

26 December 1945

Dear Mr Churchill,

Today I received word from my little home town in Kansas that you have been extended an invitation to visit that place upon leaving Fulton, Missouri, where I understand you are to be in early March.

My home town is one of only a few thousand souls but it is rather typical of the locality in the great central farming region of the United States, a region that fifty years ago was the center of the cattle industry.

I imagine that there is little chance that you can accept the invitation but I assure you that if you could do so you would be certain of a very warm welcome among people who would very much like to pay to you a tribute of admiration and affection.

If, during your tour in the United States, there occurs to you anything in which I might be helpful in making your visit more enjoyable, I hope you will let me know instantly. I would consider it a great honor to be of even the slightest assistance in making your trip a memorable and happy one.

Please remember me kindly to Mrs Churchill and to the children, and as always, with warm and respectful regards to yourself.

Josef Stalin to Winston S. Churchill
(Churchill papers, 2/142)

26 December 1945

I thank you for your good wishes on my birthday.

I was on leave and I regret that I am only now sending you belatedly my best wishes on your birthday.

General Sir Hastings Ismay to Winston S. Churchill
(Churchill papers, 2/142)

31 December 1945
Private

My dear Mr Churchill,

Thank you very much for your letter of December 28th on the subject of the minute which you wrote last April criticizing Tedder's work at Eisenhower's Headquarters.

I have, in accordance with your instructions, destroyed my copy of the minute in question and also my copies of the minutes which the Chiefs of Staff addressed to you on the subject.

I will tell the Chiefs of Staff of your wishes, at the very first opportunity, and see to it that any copies that they may have kept of the minutes in question are duly destroyed.

The whole Defence Office joins me in sending you respectful good wishes for the New Year.

January 1946

Winston S. Churchill to Colonel Frank Clarke
(Churchill papers, 2/225)

1 January 1946

1. I feel that I could not possibly get on without one of my trained lady secretaries who alone know all my affairs and contacts over here and how to make the notes of such speeches as I shall be forced to deliver. It would not be necessary for her to sleep in the villa and perhaps you would kindly book for her a room in the local hotel in my name, but I must have someone at hand to manage my affairs or I should have no peace or leisure. This does not mean I should not welcome the assistance of one of your Secretaries and it may well be there will be need for both. May I therefore bring Miss Sturdee who is about to become the head of my private office. Remember I have continuous responsibilities as Leader of the Opposition and am sure to have a heavy mail and constant telegrams from England. I deeply regret to be such a weighty burden.

2. Thank you so much for your telegram about Sarah. She hopes to follow about a fortnight later but as she is returning to the stage she may be detained here by her professional work.

3. The President has evidently explained to the New York authorities about my by-passing the City on arrival and visiting them on departure. Mayor La Guardia[1] has told me he will pass to his successor the advices he has received. Lord Halifax tells me I am to be met by the Senior General and Senior Admiral[2] in New York and I have welcomed this compliment. I do not know how you plan we spend the time between our being taken off the ship and leaving by the Florida train. If convenient I should much like to see Harry Hopkins if his health is good enough but we must not press him.

[1] Fiorello Henry La Guardia, 1882–1947. Born in New York of Jewish Italian parentage. On active service in Italy with USAAF, commanding a bomber squadron, 1917–18. Republican member of the House of Representatives for New York, 1919–21, 1923–33. Mayor of New York, 1933–45. Director, UNRRA, 1946.

[2] These arrangements were changed when Churchill was advised against travelling in an open car through the New York streets in midwinter; in consequence there is insufficient information to identify these two individuals.

January 1946

Winston S. Churchill to Sir Edward Bridges
(Churchill papers, 4/5)

3 January 1946

My dear Edward,

I am greatly indebted to you for the trouble you have taken,[1] which I fear may have made an inroad upon your scanty and well-earned leisure.

I am adopting all your suggestions. I agree that the whole passage about de Gaulle should be omitted at the present time. There is however a difficulty which cannot be overlooked. Michael Foot, MP[2] and Tom Driberg, MP have both availed themselves of the House of Commons Resolution lifting the Ban to make statements giving the idea that I made a very serious attack upon General de Gaulle on this occasion. In fact, what I said was both moderate and true. If the passage is omitted without explanation, these two gentlemen (sic) will no doubt make hostile comment and say that the account is defective. I therefore propose to insert the following statement:

> Begins. The Prime Minister then referred to General de Gaulle's attitude in terms which, though courteous and friendly, were critical. As General de Gaulle is now the Head of a friendly State, the publication of this passage would be premature. Ends.

I have also omitted the following on page 31:

> 'There might be a considerable danger to the Allied Cause which I am most anxious to avoid. It would be a pernicious nuisance if we here had our particular set of French favourites and the United States had another lot whom they ran. To avoid this . . .'

I should be greatly obliged if you would make inquiry by the Cabinet Office about the telegrams which are quoted from the President and General Eisenhower, and Darlan's[3] letter to General Clark. I do not doubt that the

---

[1] Churchill sought to publish his war-time speeches given in Parliamentary Secret Session. Sir Edward Bridges sent him three pages of notes, including the suggestion that a number of passages from Churchill's speech of 10 Dec. 1942 (reproduced in *The Churchill Documents*, vol. 17, *Testing Times, 1942*, pp. 1499–1517) would give offence both to the Americans and to the French.

[2] Michael Mackintosh Foot, 1913–2010. Born in Plymouth, Devon, brother of Sir Dingle Foot. Educated at Wadham College, Oxford. Editor, *Evening Standard*, 1942 to July 1943; *Tribune*, 1948–52, 1955–60. MP (Lab.) for Plymouth Devonport, 1945–55; for Ebbw Vale, 1960–83; for Blaenau Gwent, 1983–92. Secretary of State for Employment, 1974–6. Leader of the House of Commons, 1976–9. Lord President of the Council, 1976–9. Deputy Leader of the Labour Party, 1976–80. Leader of the Opposition (Labour), 1980–3. Oldest sitting member of the House of Commons, 1987–92.

[3] Jean Louis Xavier François Darlan, 1881–1942. Entered French Navy, 1899. On active service, 1914–18 (three citations). Adm., 1933. C-in-C of French Navy, Apr. 1939 to June 1940. Minister of Marine (under the Vichy Government), June 1940 to Apr. 1942. Distrusted by the Germans. He was in North Africa visiting his sick son when the Allies landed on 8 Nov. 1942. Chief of State in French North Africa (with Gen. Eisenhower's approval) from 11 Nov. 1942 until his assassination on 24 Dec. 1942.

President's office will give permission in the same way that I the other day assented to two of my private telegrams to the President being published in connection with the Congressional investigation of the Pearl Harbour episode.

It is hoped that the delay will not be too long, as I am thinking of publishing about the end of January or the early part of February.

Winston S. Churchill to James Stuart
(Churchill papers, 2/2)

4 January 1946
Confidential

Thank you for your minute of December 21 and the enclosure. The remedy for this evil[1] is of course publicity. I am quite sure that the Government would disclaim all intentions of prejudicing particular concerns on account of their owners or managers exercising their political rights freely and that if challenged they will make this clear. No doubt many of our people are timid and easily cowed. For this they should be put to shame.

I think of referring to this matter when I speak in Edinburgh on April 29, in order to encourage our weaklings and elicit from the Government the necessary assurances. In case there is any more evidence of this, I should be glad if you would let me know.

2. Thank you for your charming letter. The OM comes from the King alone and is not given on the advice of ministers. This renders it more attractive to me.

Lord Beaverbrook to Winston S. Churchill
(Churchill papers, 2/450)[2]

4 January 1946

My dear Winston,

The Order of Merit is the highest distinction – but in this case it is too low. Your deeds can never be acknowledged in letters of honours and decorations.

There is a reward. You know too little of it. That reward is in the hearts of a great population, here and in the Empire. The affection and devotion of the race grows stronger, and as the years go by you will come to understand it.

When the full story of the war is revealed your fame will increase if any increase is possible.

Yours affectionately,

---

[1] That Conservatives in the coal-mining industry might feel intimidated by the Labour Government's nationalization of the industry and as a result sever public ties with the Conservative Party.
[2] This letter was handwritten.

176 January 1946

Sir Alan Lascelles to Winston S. Churchill
(Churchill papers, 2/171)[1]

5 January 1946
Private

Dear Mr Churchill,

On Wednesday night, The King will address the assembled delegates of UNO after the State Banquet. This, I suppose, is about the most important speech that HM will be called upon to make during his reign.

After a month's rumination, the FO sent me yesterday what, after a life-time spent sitting among bad drafts, I have no hesitation in saying is the worst draft I ever read. It does not even translate; there are passages in it of an obscurity unrivalled in the worst unrelated palimpsest.

To the best of my ability, I have re-written it, and tried to put some juice into its jejune body. Here is the result.

Would you very kindly look through it, and, when you come to Buck Palace at 3.45 on Tuesday give me any suggestions you can for its improvement?

I am – of course with The King's approval – asking your help not as Leader of HM's Opposition, but as one who (in your own words to me at our last interview) has written 'some not altogether bad books'.

PS. Perhaps you could manage to get to BP a little before 3.45 and see me before you go up to The King?

Winston S. Churchill to Lady Digby[2]
(Churchill papers, 1/41)[3]

6 January 1946

My dear Pamela,

I grieve very much for what has happened which put an end to so many of my hopes for the future of Randolph and Pamela.[4] The war strode in however through the lives of millions. We must make the best of what is left among the ruins. Everything must be erected upon the well being and happiness of

---

[1] This letter was handwritten.
[2] (Constance) Pamela Alice Bruce, 1895–1978. Daughter of Maj. Henry Campbell Bruce, 2nd Baron Aberdare of Duffryn, and Constance Mary Beckett. Married, 1919, Edward Kenelm Digby, 11th Baron Digby of Geashill. JP, 1934. Senior Commandant, ATS, Dorset, 1938–40. Chief Commandant, ATS, 1940–4. Member, Dorset County Council, 1943–52. OBE, 1944. County Alderman, 1957. President, Dorset Branch, British Red Cross Society, 1964–78.
[3] This letter was handwritten.
[4] Pamela Digby, 1920–97. Daughter of 11th Baron Digby. Married, 1939, Randolph Churchill (div., 1946); their son Winston was born at Chequers in 1940. Subsequently married Leyland Hayward, and then Averell Harriman. Took US citizenship, 1971. US Ambassador to Paris from 1993 until her death.

the boy.[1] Pamela has brought him up splendidly. There must be friendship to shield him from the defects of a broken home.

It is a comfort that the relations between our families remain indestructible.

PS. My warmest regards to Kennie.[2]

Winston S. Churchill to Sir Alan Lascelles
(Churchill papers 2/171)

8 January 1946
Private

My dear Alan,

I send you herewith a few suggestions I have made on the text which you sent me of the Speech. May I say it is a good Speech and covers the ground effectively?

In case there is anything you wish to ask me about it, I shall be available a little before 3.45 p.m. this afternoon, when I have an Audience.

Winston S. Churchill to Field Marshal Lord Montgomery
(Churchill papers, 2/143)

8 January 1946

I am most deeply obliged to you for sending me a copy of the story of your Campaign from Alamein to the Sangro River, and particularly touched by the all too kind and complimentary inscription which you have written in it. This is indeed a most generous tribute from a great Commander to his Political Chief. Certainly the relations which I had with you, with Alexander, and with the High Command of the three Services generally, were of a most friendly and intimate character in spite of the great stresses through which we went. How different from the rows of the 'frocks' and 'Brass hats' which

[1] Winston Spencer-Churchill, 1940–2010. Son of Randolph and Pamela Churchill; grandson of Winston Churchill. Born at Chequers. Educated at Eton and Christ Church, Oxford. A newspaper correspondent from 1963 (Yemen, Congo, Angola). MP (Cons.) for Stretford, 1970–83; for Davyhulme, 1983–97. Parliamentary Private Secretary to Minister of Housing and Construction, 1970–2; to Minister of State, Foreign and Commonwealth Office, 1972–3. Conservative Party front-bench spokesman on defence, 1976–8. Member of Select Committee on Defence, 1983–97. A Governor of the English-Speaking Union, 1975–80. Executive Member of 1922 Committee, 1979–85. Among his published books are *First Journey* (1964); *The Six Day War*, written with his father (1967); *Defending the West* (1981); *Memories and Adventures* (1989); and a biography of his father, *His Father's Son* (1996). Married, 1964, Mary Caroline 'Minnie' d'Erlanger (div. 1997); 1997, Luce Engelen.

[2] Edward Kenelm Digby, 1894–1964. On active service 1914–18 (DSO, MC and bar). Married, 1920, Hon. Pamela Bruce. Succeeded his father as 11th Baron Digby, 1920. Military Secretary to Governor-General of Australia, 1921–3. Asst Inspector of Infantry, War Office, 1940–2. Inspector of Infantry Training Establishments, 1942–4.

characterized the last War. I am proud that you feel that the contribution of the Minister of Defence made your great task easier of accomplishment.

I hope one day that your book,[1] in which I wrote so many entries, will be published in facsimile to a wide public. There is set out, milestone by milestone, the glorious advance of the Eighth Army and of the British Army of the Rhine, and almost all the forecasts of the Political Chief were vindicated superbly by the sword of the Commander.

I am so glad we had that day on the Rhine together and saw a few shells playing about.

Clement Attlee to Winston S. Churchill
(*Churchill papers, 2/150*)

9 January 1946
Private

My dear Churchill,

Thank you for your letter of January 6th about Marshal of the Royal Air Force Sir Arthur Harris. I hope you do not think that I in any way underestimate the value of the services which Sir Arthur Harris rendered to the country. His claims were very carefully considered, and I reached the conclusion after much thought that it would not be possible to include his name for a peerage in the list without either on the one hand increasing the List considerably beyond its present size or, on the other hand, omitting names whose exclusion, if his had been included, would have given rise to dissatisfaction and criticism which in my view would have been justifiable. I may add that the list of peerages had the complete approval of The King.

I am sorry that we find ourselves in disagreement on this matter, for I can hold out no hope that the decision which has been taken in this case will be revised. But whatever view you may take, I beg you not to think that we underestimate the services of Sir Arthur Harris. When you were Prime Minister he received the GCB, and now he has been promoted Marshal of the Royal Air Force. I should not have thought that a promotion to this high rank, which was so rarely accorded during the war, could be regarded as an inadequate recognition of his great services.

---

[1] *Ten Chapters.*

January 1946

Winston S. Churchill to D. W. Brogan[1]
(Churchill papers, 4/443)

10 January 1946
Private

RMS *Queen Elizabeth*

My dear Professor Brogan,

I return you herewith the medieval section[2], together with Professor Galbraith's[3] notes, which I have dealt with or inserted.

You will see that I have marked a good many 'discuss' or 'suggest'. It would be a great convenience if you would talk these over with him and make (in blue ink this time) the amendments which you think necessary in the text. Any about which there is doubt or difference I should like to discuss with you both on my return.

The two salient points not dealt with seem to be the long note by Professor Galbraith, which I have retyped and marked XYZ, about the state of affairs at the death of Edward the Confessor[4] and, secondly, the presentment which I have made of the Magna Carta. I am very much pleased with the idea of Professor Galbraith that a vindication of this Charter against some forms of criticism should be undertaken, so as to show how much more it was than a mere assertion of feudal privileges by the barons against the King.[5] The rest of Professor Galbraith's notes in green (with my comments in red) will apprize you of the position.

I have arranged with Messrs. Cassell & Company that they will put into galley proofs, in the near future, the amended version. I should be very glad therefore if you and Professor Galbraith could make the necessary amendments (apart from the Magna Carta story) on this existing proof which I now send you and then, without referring to me, send the proof to my secretary at 28, Hyde Park Gate, who will forward it to Cassells for setting up in proof. We shall thus have nice clean galleys to work upon for the final reading.

I am greatly impressed with the precision and learning of Professor Galbraith's work, as I am also with your own. The only service this book of mine can render is to excite the interest of large numbers of people who, once they have escaped from school, might not otherwise read about these periods at

---

[1] Denis William Brogan, 1900–74. Educated at Glasgow University, Balliol College, Oxford, and Harvard University. Prof. of Political Science, Cambridge University, 1939–1968. Knighted, 1963. Published 14 books on political systems and numerous articles.

[2] Of Churchill's *A History of the English Speaking Peoples* (1956–8).

[3] John Kenneth Galbraith, 1908–2006. Educated at University of Toronto. Tutor, Harvard University, 1934–9; Lecturer, 1948–9; Paul M. Warburg Prof. of Economics, 1949–75. Research Fellow, Cambridge University, 1937. Asst Prof. of Economics, Princeton University, 1939–42. Director, State Department Office of Economic Security Policy, 1945. US Ambassador to India, 1961–3. Chairman, Americans for Democratic Action, 1967–9. Published 48 books and more than 1,000 articles and essays on different subjects.

[4] Edward the Confessor, 1003–66.

[5] King John 'Lackland', 1166–1216. King of England, 1199. Signed Magna Carta, 1215.

all. It is therefore most necessary that I should not make any mistakes which would allow critics to discredit the general accuracy of the work.

I return you also herewith the notes you wrote on Scotland and Ireland. I have inserted that marked 'ABC' after the end of the reign of Henry VII,[1] so that they can thus be incorporated in the new proofs which are to be printed. I have kept a copy for myself.

I have also inserted my latest revise of the Joan of Arc[2] episode which comes after p. 248. I have corrected it after reading Anatole France's[3] highly documented study. Perhaps you will think my praise excessive. Nevertheless it can go into the reprint and we can discuss it later on.

Winston S. Churchill to Andrew Rothstein[4]
(Churchill papers, 4/28)

10 January 1946   RMS *Queen Elizabeth*

Dear Mr Rothstein,

I am deeply interested in what you have been good enough to write to me about John, Duke of Marlborough. I had no idea of the document you mention and should be much obliged if you could put me on its track.

It is certainly probable on the face of it that Peter I[5] would have desired to deflect Charles XII[6] to the western scene and that Marlborough's acquisitive nature would have suggested the lure. On the other hand there is no doubt that Marlborough did his utmost to cushion Charles XII off into Russia and, in his talks with him in 1707, he was certainly successful. If my memory serves me right (I have not got my book with me) there was considerable anxiety lest Charles XII should be drawn into intervening on the side of France through his quarrels with some of the German princes of the Grand Alliance.

I await with much interest any further information you can give me or any further work you may do upon the subject.

---

[1] Henry Tudor, 1457–1509. King Henry VII of England, 1485–1509. Married, 1486, Elizabeth of York, uniting the houses of York and Lancaster to end the Wars of the Roses and establish the Tudor dynasty.

[2] Jeanne d'Arc, 1412–31. Known as 'The Maid of Orleans'. Rallied and led French forces of Charles VII against English occupying force, 1429. Excommunicated and burned at the stake, 1431; excommunication later nullified. Declared martyr. Beatified, 1909; canonized, 1920.

[3] Jacques-Anatole-François Thibault, 1844–1924. Wrote under the pseudonym 'Anatole France'. A sceptical, ironic and urbane writer and critic, considered the ideal French man of letters in his time.

[4] Andrew Rothstein, 1898–1994. On active service with Oxfordshire and Buckinghamshire Light Infantry, 1917–19. Refused orders to assist Tsarist forces against the Bolsheviks during the Russian Civil War. Founding member, Communist Party of Great Britain, 1920. Correspondent, Soviet Press Agency, 1921–45. President, Foreign Press Association, 1943–50. Author, *Peter the Great and Marlborough, Politics and Diplomacy in Converging Wars* (1986).

[5] Pyotr Alekseyevich, 1672–1725. Known as 'Peter the Great'. Co-Tsar of Russia with Ivan V, 1682–96; sole Tsar, 1696–1725. Emperor of Russia, 1721–5.

[6] Charles XII, 1682–1718. Prince of Sweden, 1682–97. King of Sweden, 1697–1718.

January 1946

Winston S. Churchill to Henry Whitbread
(Churchill papers, 1/30)

11 January 1946

The chalk pool is to continue to run out through the middle opening and not to be filled to the brim in my absence. You should look at the swamp below the chestnut trees in the meadow and see if it dries up. Do not do anything else to the chalk pool in my absence.

2. It is most important to make sure that the fish pool is water-tight in its top six inches, and I hope you will be able to find the leak which flows into the sump pit and stop it.

3. The rocky channel from the water garden to the filter must be made absolutely water-tight and the boggy part on the right-hand side looking down-hill, should be drained.

4. The filter above the swimming pool should be completely emptied, cleaned and new sand put in. The leak which now shows itself below the stop-cock from this pool should be found, so that everything goes through the pipe and is controlled by the stop-cock. There is no need to use any company's water in the water garden in my absence.

5. Both the swimming pool and the catchment area on the side of the hill should be emptied in order to fill the two lakes. It is necessary, first of all, to make the dam between the two lakes water-tight, both by cementing the cracks and filling in with puddled clay along the base where necessary.

6. The swimming pool itself wants a thorough washing and cleaning and a careful search for all leaks or cracks which should be stopped. When I return I will have it painted.

7. The overflow rock work from the swimming pool requires a thorough re-cementing. The bottom of the catchment area on the hill certainly leaks and all the cracks should be well chiselled out and re-cemented, wire netting being put in with the cement wherever it is required.

8. The fox-proof fence should be repaired with wire netting around its whole circumference. You should ask Mr Cox[1] and/or Miss Whyte[2] for any additional wire netting that is required at my expense.

9. All the fire wood cut down should be carried to the saw bench and sawn into logs and stored in the wood shed. If the German prisoners have gone before this work is completed, you should ask Miss Whyte, to get you the help of one of the gardeners for a morning or afternoon from time to time. As long as the German prisoners are there, they will help you in these various tasks. Should you have finished them all, you should inform Miss Whyte and give help in the garden from time to time.

Let me know how you get on.

---

[1] Percy Cox, 1888–1975. Estate manager of Chartwell in the 1940s and 1950s.
[2] Maryott Whyte, Clementine Churchill's cousin, who lived in a cottage near Chartwell.

General Assembly of Virginia: resolution
(Churchill papers, 2/230)

16 January 1946

STATE JOINT RESOLUTION NO. 6
INVITING THE HONORABLE WINSTON SPENCER CHURCHILL
TO ADDRESS THE GENERAL ASSEMBLY OF VIRGINIA

WHEREAS, during England's darkest hours in World War II her great Prime Minister, the Honorable Winston Spencer Churchill, with matchless eloquence and indomitable will, inspired his bomb-scarred nation to fight on until the resources and weight of the democratic nations could be mustered to overthrow the ruthless conqueror; and

WHEREAS, by his patience and understanding, and his ability to work with other great leaders in the cause of freedom, Winston Churchill helped weld together in an invincible military union the British Empire, the Soviet Union, and the United States of America, and thereby insured the destruction of the Axis powers, the liberation of prostrate Europe, and the survival of civilization itself; and

WHEREAS, because of his American mother the beautiful and accomplished Jenny Jerome, and his many personal ties with our own country, the presence of Winston Churchill in the United States is a source of satisfaction, not only to the few who know him as an intimate and well-loved friend, but to the many who look upon him as one of history's immortals; now therefore,

BE IT RESOLVED by the Senate of Virginia, the House of Delegates concurring, that the General Assembly of Virginia, the oldest law-making body in the western hemisphere, hereby invites the Honorable Winston Spencer Churchill to appear before it at such time as may suit his convenience, and to address it upon such subject as he may deem appropriate; and

BE IT FURTHER RESOLVED, that the Clerk of the Senate transmit a copy of this resolution to the Honorable Winston Spencer Churchill upon his arrival in the State of Florida.

Randolph S. Churchill to Winston S. Churchill
(*Churchill papers, 1/42*)[1]

18 January 1946
Personal

Chicago

My dearest Papa,

I sent a challenge to Henry Wallace;[2] but, as I feared, he declined – on the scarcely convincing grounds that he was 'too busy'.

The tour continues to go well and I expect to clear a profit of about £1,500. But some of the fees are slow in coming in and meanwhile I have a lot of money locked up in my car which I shall sell for a profit at the end.

As a result I have not been able yet to remit as much money as I had hoped to England. Consequently my affairs there are somewhat embarrassed and I have need of £500. I wonder if you could be so very kind as to lend me this sum? I could repay when I return at the beginning of April.

If you would do this for me I should indeed be grateful. I hate asking you to do this but the emergency, though temporary, is rather acute. If you can help me in this way, the most convenient thing would be if you would pay it into my account at Lloyds Bank. Could you please let me know?

I have followed with great interest your movement for a United Europe. I do hope it has got off to a good start.

With fondest love to you all
Your loving Son,
Randolph

---

[1] This letter was handwritten.

[2] Henry Agard Wallace, 1888–1965. US Secretary of Agriculture, 1933–40 (his father had held the same post, 1921–4). US Vice-President, Jan. 1941 to Jan. 1945. Chairman, Board of Economic Warfare and Supply Priorities and Allocations Board, 1941–4. On 8 May 1942, delivered his 'Century of the Common Man' speech, with its positive vision of a post-war world beyond the defeat of the Nazis. Toured Latin America, 1943, helping to persuade 12 countries to declare war on Germany. Secretary of Commerce, 1945–6. Progressive Party Nominee, 1948 Presidential election, advocating friendly relations with the Soviet Union and an end to the Cold War; gained 2.4% of the popular vote.

January 1946

Winston S. Churchill to Major-General Sir Hugh Tudor[1]
(Churchill papers, 2/230)

18 January 1946   Florida

My dear Hugh,

I am most grateful to Mr Barr[2] for letting me have news of you and for coming round to see me. We had a very pleasant talk and he told me about your health and how you were getting on. He seems to have made a good recovery from his serious operation.

I have come down here for a holiday and some sunshine. I do not propose to undertake any political work until March 5, when I meet the President in his home State, Missouri, to deliver a speech under his auspices. I hope to find sunshine and painting here, but today it is grey and cold.

I am very much concerned to hear of the trouble you have with your eyesight and hope you have got good medical advice. I have always understood that an operation for cataract was simple and not severe. It grieves me indeed to learn that at present you cannot read. I have heard, further, of how you have learned to use the type-writer. I hope you will let me know how things are going.

I have seen a good deal of the 4th Hussars from time to time during the war. I am their Colonel and I inspected them four times in different theatres during the war. When I went to Como a few months ago, Alexander paid me the compliment of sending a detachment all across Italy to look after me with two very good young officers – quite up to the standard of the old days.

I found it very odd being turned out of power just at the moment when I imagined I would be able to reap where I had sown, and perhaps bring about some lasting settlement in this troubled world. However it may all be for the best as there is no doubt that a Conservative Government would have been very roughly treated by the Left-Wing elements, and strikes and labour troubles would have made our path one of extreme difficulty. I found it none too easy to change over so quickly from a life of intense activity and responsibility to one of leisure in which there is nothing to be looked for but anticlimax. However luckily I have my painting, into which I have plunged with great vigour, and many other amusements, so that the time passes away pleasantly and rapidly.

What a wonderful thing it is, looking back, to see all we have survived. All the follies that England commits in time of peace did not prevent her

---

[1] Henry Hugh Tudor, 1871–1965. On active service in South Africa, 1899–1902. Brig.-Gen. commanding the artillery of 9th (Scottish) Div., 1916–18. Maj.-Gen. commanding 9th Div., 21–24 March 1918; commanding the Irregular Forces in Ireland (the 'Black and Tans'), 1920–1. GOC special gendarmerie in Palestine (known as 'Tudor's lambs'), 1922, with rank of AVM. Knighted, 1923. Published his WWI diaries *The Fog of War* (1959).

[2] George M. Barr. A major figure in the Newfoundland lobster export industry, with whom Sir Hugh Tudor lived for several decades in St John's, Newfoundland.

true greatness from shining forth in the hour of need. And now, although other perils can be discerned, we may at least say that the German danger is behind us.

I heard from Reggie Barnes[1] the other day. He has not been at all well, but is now about again. Reggie Hoare[2] also is recovered from a serious operation. I also think of Albert Savory,[3] our Number 2. It is forty-five years since he was killed in action, and yet so vivid are the memories and friendships of early youth that I can remember him as if it was but yesterday we were all planning to win the Cavalry Cup. So strong and lasting also, my dear friend, are my feelings towards you, not only of far-off Bangalore days, but of the great moments of Plug Street[4] and March 21.[5]

Willie Y. Darling[6] is now one of my supporters in the House of Commons. He is a grand fellow, well worthy of the 'Black and Tans'.

Wishing you the best of fortune

---

[1] Reginald Walter Ralph Barnes, 1871–1946. Entered Army, 1890. Lt, 4th Hussars, 1894; one of Churchill's close Army friends. Went with Churchill to Cuba, 1895. Capt., 1901. Lt-Col. commanding 10th Hussars, 1911–15. Col., 1914. Brig.-Gen., commanding 116th Infantry Bde and 14th Infantry Bde, 1915–16. Commanded 32nd Div., 1916–17; 57th Div., 1917–19. Maj.-Gen., 1918. Knighted, 1919.

[2] Reginald Hoare, 1865–1947. An officer in the 4th Hussars, which he later commanded. In 1897, served in India with Churchill; both were members of the regimental polo team. On active service in South Africa, 1899–1901, and in WWI, 1914–18 (wounded, despatches, DSO, CMG).

[3] Albert Savory, 1870–1900. Lt, 4th Hussars, 1898. A member, with Churchill, of the polo team that won the Inter-Regimental Tournament at Bangalore, 1899. In *My Early Life* Churchill recalled: 'Prolonged rejoicings, intense inward satisfaction, and nocturnal festivities from which the use of wine was not excluded, celebrated the victory. Do not grudge these young soldiers gathered from so many regiments their joy and sport. Few of that merry throng were destined to see old age. Our own team was never to play again. A year later Albert Savory was killed in the Transvaal, Barnes was grievously wounded in Natal, and I became a sedentary politician increasingly crippled by my wretched shoulder. It was then or never for us . . .'

[4] Ploegsteert in Belgium, where Churchill was stationed in early 1916 after resigning from the Government and going to the front. He wrote an article titled 'Plugstreet' that is published in *Thoughts and Adventures* (1932).

[5] The date refers to the German offensive launched on 21 Mar. 1918, which led Churchill to return to Ploegsteert and witness the destruction that had occurred there.

[6] William Young Darling, 1885–1962. Educated at James Gillespie's School, Daniel Stewart's College and Heriot-Watt College, Edinburgh University. Trained for business in Edinburgh and London; held various appointments in Ceylon and Australia up to 1913. Enlisted in the ranks of the Black Watch, 1914. Commissioned in the Royal Scots. Served 1915–17 in France, Salonika, Gallipoli (evacuation), Egypt (MC and bar, despatches). ADC, 1918–19, in France, Belgium, and Germany. Served in Ireland, 1920–2. Resumed business career, 1922. Member, Edinburgh Town Council, 1933; City Treasurer, 1937–40. Nat. Government Candidate, West Lothian, 1937. Chief ARW, 1938–9. District Commissioner, South Eastern Scotland, 1939–41. Lord Provost of Edinburgh, 1941–4. Chairman, Scottish Council on Industry, 1942–6. Director, Royal Bank of Scotland, 1942–57. MP (Cons.) for South Edinburgh, 1945–57.

Cecil F. Elmes[1] to Winston S. Churchill
(Churchill papers, 2/226)

21 January 1946   New York

Dear Mr Churchill,

When Mrs W. Bourke Cockran[2] died a year ago, most of the former property of my uncle, Bourke Cockran,[3] passed to her sister Marjorie[4] – Shane Leslie's wife – but his personal effects and papers were willed to me. Browsing through them I ran across this letter[5] written by you in 1899 when you were a prisoner of President Oom Paul Kreuger[6] in the Second Boer War and before you made your memorable escape to the British lines. I thought it might interest and entertain you.

You will note that you were writing Bourke on your twenty fifth birthday and were terribly worried over the passing years and 'how little time remains' for further achievement. Shades of Rabbi Ben Ezra![7] Bourke and I often talked about you and his deep feeling for you. He seemed always to sense that Destiny had you in her keeping.

I thought you would be interested particularly to reread this postscript with its fine youthful impatience and urgency.[8] What PPS would you add to it today, now that, under Providence, the long years were granted you and even days for the calm of retrospect – with Britain brought victorious through her direst ordeal?

General Dwight D. Eisenhower to Winston S. Churchill
(Churchill papers, 2/226)

22 January 1946

Dear Mr Churchill,

From a personal viewpoint I regarded it as scarcely short of calamitous when I found that your passing through Washington coincided with my appearance before an informal joint session of Congress. From the moment I learned that

---

[1] Cecil Frederick Elmes, 1881–1976. Nephew and legal consultant to William Bourke Cockran.

[2] Anne Louisa Ide, 1876–1945. Married, 1906, William Bourke Cockran.

[3] William Bourke Cockran, 1854–1923. Born in Ireland; emigrated to US, 1871. A noted orator. Member of Congress for New York (Dem.), 1891–5, 1904–9, 1920–3. Befriended Churchill in 1895.

[4] Marjorie Ide, 1886–1951. Married, 1912, Shane Leslie.

[5] Reproduced in *The Churchill Documents*, vol. 2, *Young Soldier, 1896–1901*, pp. 1082–4.

[6] Stephanus Johannes Paulus Kruger, 1825–1904. Member, Commission for Constitution of the New Republic (Transvaal), 1855–6. Commandant Gen., 1861–4. President, South African Republic, 1883–1902.

[7] Abraham ibn Ezra, 1102–67. Poet, mathematician, and scholar. Made famous by Robert Browning's poem 'Rabbi ben Ezra' (1864), which begins 'Grow old along with me!/ The best is yet to be . . .'.

[8] 'I am 25 today – it is terrible to think how little time remains!' Reproduced in *The Churchill Documents*, vol. 2, *Young Soldier 1896–1901*, pp. 1082–4.

you were coming to this country for a visit I have been looking forward to a long chat with you. There are a number of details that have cropped up since the war, which, so far as I am concerned, were entirely unforeseen. Many of these have to do with the slant that a number of our ambitious and amateur writers are taking in recording what they seem to want to call 'The History of the War'.

My hope of seeing you, therefore, springs not only from an earnest desire to renew the warmest and most satisfying contact I had in all Europe, but to discuss with you what, if anything, you and I might do either individually or any other way, to help keep the record straight. In looking over some of these so-called factual accounts I find that in many instances details reported are inaccurate but this is not nearly so important as the clear indication that each self-alleged writer has some preconceived notion or idea that colors the whole picture.

Certainly, from my viewpoint, the outstanding characteristic of British–American associations in Europe was – quite aside from the brilliant military successes achieved – the warmth and generosity of cooperation displayed by the governments and by the individuals involved. The accounts, however, seem to like to emphasize those occasional instances when there was honest difference of opinion and give to these an entirely false value when measured against the day-by-day cooperation and mutual support that together constituted the key to victory.

My own schedule for the next few weeks will apparently offer me little opportunity to seek you out but if I do not have a chance to see you any other place I do hope that your own itinerary contemplates some little time in Washington. I suppose it is too much to hope that you would stay for a period in my house. Within a few days my wife[1] and I are moving into a very commodious set of quarters at Fort Myer and if it would be possible at all for you and Mrs Churchill to stay with us we would not only be overjoyed personally but the mere fact that you would consent to be my guest would do much to impress upon everybody in America the true nature of an association (from my viewpoint a treasured friendship) that characterized our common effort throughout my service in Europe. The climate here is rather vile and of course many people would make insistent demands upon you but at my house at Fort Myer you could have complete independence and every ounce of protection and security from social or other contacts that you might desire.

Failing any chance to see you here, I will still look for an opportunity for contacting you elsewhere in the United States, but I am frank to say that such an opportunity would have to present itself almost on a moment's notice.

With my very best wishes to you and to Mrs Churchill.

---

[1] Mamie Geneva Doud, 1896–1979. Married, 1916, Dwight D. Eisenhower. First Lady, 1953–61.

Winston S. Churchill to James Wootton-Davies[1]
(Churchill papers, 2/8)

24 January 1946   Miami Beach, Florida

I hope you will allow me to make a personal appeal to you not to split the vote in the bye-election. It is of the very greatest importance to the Party to win a bye-election and the results have effects over the whole field of public affairs. I should regard it as a great act of loyalty and magnanimity on your part to stand aside or even to give your full support to the candidate chosen by the Association. This would be in full harmony with the service you have rendered to the Party in the past. These very serious times require hard sacrifices from all. I much regret that being abroad I cannot see you personally to talk the whole thing over.

Winston S. Churchill to General Dwight D. Eisenhower
(Churchill papers, 2/226)

26 January 1946
Private

My dear Ike,

Thank you so much for your letter of January 22[2] and also for the telegram you kindly sent to England, congratulating me on receiving the Order of Merit. This telegram has at length reached me.

Thank you also for your letter of December 26.[3] It is indeed kind of your home town to invite me to visit them, but I fear my plans will not allow me to meet their wishes. I should greatly have liked to visit the town in which you were born. Pray convey my warm thanks to the authorities for their thought of me.

With regard to your offer of hospitality while we are at Washington, I have made all my arrangements to stay at the Embassy during the few days we shall be there, after we leave the White House where I understand my wife will remain during the President's journey with me to Missouri. I do hope you will invite me and my wife to dine with you, and also that we can have some good long talks together.

I was not able, at our wartime conference to go with the British Chiefs of Staff to Williamsburg at the invitation of General Marshall. I should greatly like to see this place and I wonder if we could plan a day's expedition there

---

[1] James Henry Wootton-Davies, 1884–1964. Educated at Technical School, Chester. Chemist. Married, 1937, Shirley G. M. Wootton. MP (Union.) for Heywood and Radcliff Div., Lancaster, 1940–5. JP, County of Lancaster.

[2] Reproduced above (p. 186–7).

[3] Reproduced above (pp. 171–2).

together. I should be free between March 7 and 10. I talked to Bedell[1] about this idea and perhaps he has mentioned it to you.

I have skimmed over the Butcher[2] articles and I must say I think you have been ill-used by your confidential aide. The articles are, in my opinion, altogether below the level upon which such matters should be treated. Great events and personalities are all made small when passed through the medium of this small mind. Few people have played about with so much dynamite and made so little of it. I am not vexed myself at anything he has said, though I really do feel very sorry to have kept you up so late on various occasions. It is a fault I have and my host here, Colonel Clarke, has already felt the weight of it. It is rather late at my age to reform, but I will try my best.

With every good wish and looking forward much to seeing you.

Winston S. Churchill to President Harry S Truman
(Churchill papers, 2/158)

29 January 1946   Miami Beach, Florida

My dear Mr President,

I avail myself of the fact that your personal pilot[3] is going from here tomorrow to Washington to send you these few lines.

It is very kind of you to place a powerful plane at my disposal and I am going to Cuba in it on Friday for a week. I have abandoned my plan of going to Trinidad as it is too long a hop for pleasure-time, but I am examining the possibilities of going to Veracruz, which is on the sea level and where I hear the scenery is very fine for painting. I shall be back here on February 10.

I am very glad to know you are coming along this coast. I will certainly come out and see you on your ship if you would wish it. I need a talk with you a good while before our Fulton date. I have a Message to deliver to your

---

[1] Walter Bedell Smith, 1895–1961. Known as 'Beetle'. Served during WWI with 4th Infantry Div. (US) in France; commissioned 1st Lt in the Regular Army. Adjutant, 12th Infantry Bde, 1922. At the outbreak of WWII, appointed Secretary of the US JCS and American Secretary of the Anglo-American CCS. Went to England in 1942 as CoS to Gen. Eisenhower, with whom he remained to the war's end. Smith laid the basis for the negotiation of the Italian armistice of 1943 and arranged the surrender of the German forces in the west in May 1945. US Ambassador to the Soviet Union, 1946–9. Director of Central Intelligence (head of the CIA), 1950. Retired from Army and as DCI, 1953. Under-Secretary of State, 1953–4; involved in creation of the National Security Agency.

[2] Harry C. Butcher, 1901–85. Educated at Iowa State College. Manager of CBS Radio Network's station in Washington DC, 1932. Coined the term 'fireside chat' referring to Roosevelt's radio broadcasts, 1933. Commissioned Lt Cdr, US Naval Reserves, 1939. Served as Naval Aide to Gen. Dwight D. Eisenhower, 1942–5. Cdr, 1943. Capt., 1944. Published a diary of his and Eisenhower's wartime activities called *My Three Years with Eisenhower*, 1946. Owned a radio station in Santa Barbara, Calif., 1946–80.

[3] Henry Tift Myers, 1907–68. Known as 'Hank'. Co-Pilot, American Airlines, 1930s. Entered Army Air Transport Command, 1941. First Presidential Pilot, 1944–50. DFC, 1943. Air Medal, five Oak Leaf Clusters.

country and to the world and I think it very likely that we shall be in full agreement about it. Under your auspices anything I say will command some attention and there is an opportunity for doing some good to this bewildered, baffled and breathless world.

I have just received a telegram from Harry Hopkins' wife saying that he is failing rapidly. I have a great regard for that man, who always went to the root of the matter and scanned our great affairs with piercing eye.

Let me congratulate you in what seems to be an improvement in the strike situation. My feeling, as an outsider, has been that there is so much good work and good wages going about at this time that the common interest of the State and the workers is enormous and will prevail, after the inevitable, convulsive movements of post-war readjustment have had their hour.

Lord Derby[1] to Sir Percy Loraine[2]
(Derby papers)

29 January 1946

... Personally I think it is quite wrong of Winston to have gone abroad at such a time as this and for so long. I admit he wanted a holiday. Still that he could have taken, but really to be left as we are now without any controlling power in our Party is to my mind bad statesmanship though I think Eden is doing very well and I admit much better than I expected. Still it is not the same as having Winston and I think he will find it difficult to get back his old power when he does come back.

Ralph Assheton to Winston S. Churchill
(Churchill papers, 2/8)

29 January 1946

Your personal appeal[3] to Wootton Davies couched in such persuasive language has been entirely successful. We are all exceedingly grateful to you for your powerful intervention.

---

[1] Edward George Villiers Stanley, 1865–1948. Educated at Wellington College. Lt, Grenadier Guards, 1885–95. MP (Cons.) for West Houghton, 1892–1906. Postmaster-General, 1903–5. 17th Earl of Derby, 1908. Director-General of Recruiting, Oct. 1915. Under-Secretary of State at the War Office, July–Dec. 1916. Secretary of State for War, Dec. 1916 to 1918. Ambassador to France, 1918–20. Secretary of State for War, 1922–4. Member, Joint Select Committee on the Indian Constitution, 1933–4. Subject of Randolph Churchill's book *Lord Derby, 'King of Lancashire'* (1960).

[2] Percy Lyham Loraine, 1880–1961. Served as 2nd Lt in South African War, 1900–1. Entered Diplomatic Service as an Attaché at Constantinople, 1904. 12th Bt, 1917. 1st Secretary, Warsaw, Oct. 1919. Minister in Teheran, 1921–6; in Athens, 1926–9. High Commissioner for Egypt and the Sudan, 1929–33. PC, 1933. Ambassador in Ankara, 1933–9; in Rome, 1939–40.

[3] Of Jan. 24, reproduced above (p. 188).

Winston S. Churchill to Frank McCluer
(Churchill papers, 2/230)

30 January 1946
Private

Dear Mr McCluer,

Thank you very much for your letter of January 26. I hope to see the President when he comes here in the middle of February and I will discuss with him the arrangements for the time and the subject matter of my address. In all the circumstances, it will be a political pronouncement of considerable importance. As it is going to be broadcast, I doubt whether the proceedings could be so long as an hour and a half. I was thinking myself that the President would be about twenty minutes and I about forty, but I will discuss this all with him.

I do not know when there will be any text ready. Probably I shall not compose it till the very end of February. However I hope it may be possible to give the Press an advance copy before it is actually delivered on the broadcast.

I have received from you a box of very fine apples. Thank you so much for sending me this welcome and delicious gift, which we are enjoying.

General Dwight D. Eisenhower to Winston S. Churchill
(Churchill papers, 2/226)

30 January 1946

Dear Mr Churchill,

I am immediately making tentative arrangements for you and me to go to Williamsburg for a day during the period of March 7 to 10.[1] I will try to get a real guide so that we may see and understand the most in the least time. I have not been there myself since its restoration as a Colonial town was undertaken.

Your comments on the 'Diary' echo my sentiments. Incidentally, I assure you that I never complained about staying up late. I didn't do it often and certainly I always came away from one of those conferences with a feeling that all of us had gotten some measure of rededication to our common task.

Actually, the only concern I had about the publication of those diary notes (which I had no idea were being kept in such a detailed and personal way) was that you might get the impression that I had anything to do with the whole matter either in the preparation of the notes or in their publication. As long as you understand the situation I will give the matter no further thought.

The morning papers carried the news of Harry Hopkins' death. He is one man whose real contribution to the victory will never really be understood

---

[1] See Churchill to Eisenhower, Jan. 26, reproduced above (pp. 188–9).

because he was too much of a controversial figure in this country. Anyone who writes about him very favorably will be accused of bias and playing politics. Nevertheless there are many of us who will always feel for him a debt of appreciation.

My wife and I will be looking forward with real pleasure to having you and Mrs Churchill for dinner.

February 1946

Summary of a press conference
(Churchill papers, 2/231)

1 February 1946   Havana, Cuba

Press reaction to Mr Churchill's visit and press conference was enthusiastic, as it has been since the days previous when news of his possible visit broke. The press strongly criticized the Cuban Ministry of State for the poor handling of the Conference at which a minor official allowed unknown reporters assigned to the State Department to obstruct the work of the more serious and well-informed correspondents and specialists in international affairs. However, the final product of these correspondents and specialists with the assistance of the Office of the Press Attaché and the kindness of Reuters correspondent was of a uniform high quality. The order of the questions were inverted in different newspapers and there were variations in the translation of different phrases, but in general it appears that a great effort was made to achieve a faithful interpretation, with, of course, the more exact version appearing in the more reputable newspapers.

HEADLINES

El Mundo (Right Centre): CHURCHILL DEEMS UNITY OF BIG POWERS INDISPENSABLE

Hoy (Communist): 'OF COURSE THE NAZI CRIMINALS SHOULD BE PUNISHED' – Winston Churchill

Diario de la Marina (Extreme Right): MR CHURCHILL RECOGNIZES CERTAIN RIGHTS OF SMALL COUNTRIES ON THE VETO OF THE FIVE POWERS

Informacion (Right Centre): TWOULD BE A MISTAKE FOR UNO TO INTERFERE IN SPAIN, SAYS CHURCHILL – REFUSED TO COMMENT ON LABOUR GOVERNMENT

El Pais (Right Centre): 'THE ALLIANCE OF THE BIG THREE IS ESSENTIAL FOR THE PEACE' – Winston Churchill

EL MUNDO

First quotation was that in which Mr Churchill stated: 'I do not discuss the government of my country when I am away from there.'

The second quotation was on the subject of Spain. Mr Churchill said 'I believe it would be a mistake to intervene in the internal affairs of Spain.'

The third quotation: when queried about Greece and the Soviet protest 'Our troops are in Greece at the request of the Greek Government. If they had not been there, that nation would be under the Communist masses and under the terror of tyranny. They have prevented a Communist massacre.'

On the problem of Java the *Mundo* reporter continues remarking that Mr Churchill did not wish to answer the question and notes that he showed confidence in the ability of Sir Archibald Clark-Kerr[1] to improve the difficulties.

On the Argentine question note is made that Mr Churchill stated he was not up to date on information but that he hoped conditions would improve.

Questioned on General MacArthur, Mr Churchill replied: 'He is a great man and a great soldier and has managed with notable ability the disarmament of 2½ million Japanese troops etc. At the same time he has shown himself an able diplomat in achieving the cooperation of the Emperor.'

What can you say on the statement made by Mr Bevin with regard to Russian accusations? To this Mr Churchill replied: 'Never comment on something that you haven't read in the papers yourself.'

The British statesman considers essential to the peace that the unity of the Great Powers be maintained. He proclaimed that the UNO should be helped in the problems of the post-war.

On the question of Greece the reporter did not get the answer quite right, quoting Mr Churchill in this wise: 'I believe bringing it out in the open would help.'

On the Far East: 'England, United States and India should cooperate shoulder to shoulder in the post-war restoration of these nations.'

The question on the trial of the war criminals is answered in paraphrase: The distinguished politician explains the great horrors for which justice must be exacted.

From thence to the end the interview becomes lighter, says *El Mundo*'s correspondent.

---

[1] Archibald Clark Kerr, 1882–1951. Entered Diplomatic Service, 1906. Envoy Extraordinary and Minister Plenipotentiary to Central American Republics, 1925–8; to Chile, 1928–30; to Sweden, 1931–4. Knighted, 1935. Ambassador to Iraq, 1935–8. Ambassador to China, 1938–42; after the British Consulate in Chungking was almost completely destroyed by Japanese bombing in 1940, and other diplomatic missions left the city, Clark Kerr kept the Union Flag flying on the Embassy building, close to Chinese Government buildings. Ambassador to the Soviet Union, Feb. 1942 to Feb. 1946. PC, 1944. Special British Envoy to Java, 1946. Baron Inverchapel, 1946. Ambassador to US, 1946–8.

FEBRUARY 1946

HOY

Starts right off by quoting Mr Churchill to the effect that while not at present very well informed on the matter, he hoped that the situation in the Argentine would 'improve'.

Mentions that another reporter asked the distinguished visitor his impression on D Day and says: Churchill replied: 'What I thought was that we had a lot of trouble ahead.'

On the question of the Nuremberg trials *HOY* quotes Mr Churchill to the effect that: 'Terrible evidence has been presented against the accused, and there is no doubt that the trials are just. The guilty have been allowed defence. But I would never have believed in the atrocities committed by them, if I had not seen the evidence which revealed their terrible crimes. . . .'

Commenting on a question with regard to Mr Bevin's statement on Russia, the Communist organ stresses Mr Churchill's evading an answer and highlights his expressions of hope that friendship between the United Nations would prevail.

Returning to the question of the Argentine, which was formulated by the *HOY* reporter, the reply is again quoted. The remark on Spain is also paraphrased.

The interview ends with comment on the difficulties of the reporters at the conference, and mentions that Mr Churchill expressed himself as aware of Cuba's efforts in the war against the Axis.

DIARIO DE LA MARINA

Begins with a paragraph in which it evokes the days of 'blood, sweat and tears' and goes on to call to mind the equally loved President Roosevelt. Regrets that the circumstances of the Press Conference were not conducive to more constructive questions etc. Goes on to state that the blame lies either with the Office of the Protocol or with the members of the Ministry of State entrusted with the organization of the Press Conference.

Starts off mentioning that the first question was on the subject of General MacArthur and stresses (in heavy type) that Mr Churchill stated he was the man for the job.

Mentions that an American correspondent inquired as to the reported coming meeting with President Truman and quotes: 'I'm not sure yet that I will see President Truman but I understand that he wishes to arrange this meeting to take place during his coming vacation on the Presidential yacht in Florida.'

Mentions that a United Press representative asked the distinguished visitor if the international policy of Russia continues in agreement with the ideals held by the Big Three during the war. 'This is a difficult question' answered Mr Churchill, after hesitating a second, and continued predicting 'the continuation of unity among the Allies.'

Diario de la Marina continues with questions as to the tobacco industry and the British market. Mr Churchill declared, the newspaper says, that he did not propose to carry on conversations neither official nor semi-official on this matter while in Cuba and stated 'I am on a holiday and I have no official mission.'

Questioned on the veto right of the Big Powers: 'I believe he added that it is a matter of right for them, although I understand that the small countries should also have their rights.'

On atomic energy the reporter stressed Mr Churchill's hope that it would never be used for destructive purposes.

On the Anglo-American Loan quotes Mr Churchill's reply 'I cannot discuss that. Congress is discussing it.'

Questioned on whether he deemed that his visit to the United States would improve Anglo-American relations, 'I don't know but I certainly hope that that will be the result.'

States that the guest was informed of the contributions made by Cuba to the United Nations, and says that Cuba's contribution had been 'very good'.

Ends saying he told the newspapermen in leaving that he was delighted to be in this wonderful, tropical country.

INFORMACIÓN

The reporter stated he could capture only a few of Mr Churchill's phrases: 'It would be a great mistake for the United Nations to intervene in the problems of Spain.'

With regard to the trial of war criminals at Nuremberg: stated 'It is necessary to give them an opportunity to defend themselves in spite of the terrible accusations against them.'

With regard to the Labour Party and to Mr Bevin's statement, quoted: 'I cannot make any comments as I have not read his declarations.'

On his early recollections he said when he was a youth he remembered being very much impressed by the reading of the Home Rule Bill in the House of Commons by Mr Gladstone.

On a Super State, he went on to say that 'undoubtedly there was a progressive movement towards unity (meaning continental unity) but 'we must preserve liberty. The world is always moving forward both in space and in thought. . . . I do not fear the future as long as we maintain the prerogatives of freedom'.

With reference to the recent elections which brought the Labour Party to power Mr Churchill expressed the opinion that the people had chosen the Labour Programme supporting the nationalisation of basic industries 'and in my country' he said 'the people can do as they like although it often happens later that they don't like what they have done. . . .'

The former Prime Minister of Great Britain stated that 'in his opinion the unity which existed between the United Nations during the war against Totalitarianism will continue in the post-war period'.

The British War Leader stated that he was delighted to be in this tropical country and that he was well informed of Cuba's contribution to the war effort which had been good.

On being asked whether his present visit to the United States would help to improve the relations between the United States and Great Britain, he said he didn't know but hoped that such might be the result.

Churchill also said that during his stay in Cuba he would not hold any official or unofficial conversations with regard to the purchase by Great Britain of Cuban tobacco, saying he was on a vacation and had no official mission.

Referring to Japan, the statesman paid tribute to the part played by the United States Forces in occupying Japanese territory and thought that General Douglas MacArthur's administration was good.

On the subject of Spain, Mr Churchill stated that in his opinion there should be no interference, thereby reiterating his previous declarations in the House of Commons.

Asked about his announced interview with Mr Truman in Florida, Mr Churchill said that he did not yet know anything about the circumstances of the meeting but only that Mr Truman wished to see him in Florida waters and that he would be very pleased to go to the rendez-vous.

On being questioned about the alliance between the United States, Great Britain and Russia, he said that this was essential for the maintenance of peace in the world, adding: 'The UNO should be given every facility to solve post-war problems.'

In answer to questions on the atomic bomb and its far reaching effects, Mr Churchill said that in reality very little is yet known about nuclear energy and therefore nobody can estimate what its possibilities may be.

Replying to the question about the presence of British troops in Greece Mr Churchill responded quickly that had it not been for the presence of British troops, Greece would have succumbed to a general massacre.

Comments on the difficulties of the interview due to the excessive number of persons around Mr Churchill.

EL PAIS

Begins explaining the difficulties of the reporters, but continues with the questions and answers appearing in the papers already reviewed to some length. Ends speaking of Mr Churchill's kindness to the press despite the difficulties.

FEBRUARY 1946

President Harry S Truman to Winston S. Churchill
(*Churchill papers, 2/158*)

2 February 1946																			The White House

My dear Mr Churchill,

It was a pleasure to furnish you with a pilot and I hope you had the use of him as long as you needed him.

I shall probably be in Florida on the eleventh of February and will immediately get in touch with you. I hope you find it convenient to visit me on the yacht. I know you have a real message to deliver at Fulton and, of course, I shall be most happy to talk with you about it.

It certainly was too bad about Mr Harry Hopkins, but I had been expecting it for almost a week. He is a great loss to the country and especially to me, because he was familiar with all the meetings which Mr Roosevelt attended during the war.

I sincerely hope you are having a good rest and enjoying your visit in Florida. Veracruz is a lovely city at this time of the year and has some very beautiful scenery. One of the most beautiful mountains in the world is just a short distance from Veracruz — seeming to rise right out of the Gulf of Mexico when you are coming into the harbour, to a height of over 18,000 feet. That mountain, Mount Rainier in the State of Washington and Popocatepetl at Mexico City, I think, are our most beautiful peaks, principally because they stand alone and are not surrounded by other mountains.

I am looking forward to a pleasant visit with you.

James Stuart to Winston S. Churchill
(*Churchill papers, 2/8*)

2 February 1946

My dear ex-Prime Minister,

I enclose an account of our activities for the first two weeks of Parliament, which we have just completed, and an outline of Business for the immediate future. I did not write before this, as I did not want to worry you with unnecessary letters and there was nothing of importance during the first week apart from the Civil Aviation Debate.

Anthony asks me to say that, as I am writing now, he will write a few days later.

I hope you are enjoying good weather and health. I miss your robust presence very much.

PS. Marlowe[1] (of Brighton) referred to H. Morrison as 'the Rt. Hon: a

---

[1] Anthony Marlowe, 1904–65. Educated at Trinity College, Cambridge. Army, 1939–45. On staff

totalitarian gentleman' the other day: he had to withdraw, but it was quite effective.

The result of the Preston Bye-election was rather disappointing. I do not think any serious blunders were made and our speakers, including Anthony Eden and Macmillan, who went up there were very pleased with their meetings. The candidate had, however, stated throughout that he saw no sign of any swing away from Labour and this proved to be the case.

During the two weeks since the meeting of the House on January 22nd I feel that the Opposition has worked together better as a team and, with the help of the work done by the Party Committees assisted by the Secretariat (which is now operating quite efficiently), the debates have been satisfactory with many speeches of a high standard.

On the 24th January we voted against the Government Motion approving the White Paper on Civil Aviation. Harold Macmillan and Galbraith[1] spoke from our Front Bench and we had three good maiden speeches from Air-Commodore Harvey,[2] George Ward[3] and John Foster.[4]

The main debate has been on the second reading of the Coal Bill. Anthony Eden followed Shinwell[5] and J. S. C. Reid[6] spoke at night before Chancellor.[7] On the second day our reasoned amendment was moved from the Back

---

of Judge Advocate General of the Forces. Lt.-Col., 1942. MP (Cons.) for Brighton, 1941–50; for Hove, 1950–65.

[1] Thomas Dunlop Galbraith, 1891–1985. Educated at Glasgow Academy, RN College Osborne and Dartmouth. Married, 1915, Ida Galloway. Staff, C-in-C Scotland Coast, 1919–20, 1939–40. Deputy British Admiralty Supply Representative in US, 1940–2. MP (Nat. Cons.) for Pollock Div., Glasgow, 1940–55. Joint Parliamentary Under-Secretary of State for Scotland, 1945, 1951–5. A Governor, Wellington College, 1948–61. PC, 1953. Baron Strathclyde, 1955. Minister of State, Scottish Office, 1955–8. Freedom of Dingwall, 1965; of Aberdeen, 1966.

[2] Arthur Vere Harvey, 1906–94. Educated at Framingham College. RAF, 1925–30. Director, Far East Aviation Co. Ltd, 1930–5. Adviser, Southern Chinese Air Forces, 1932–5. Sqn Ldr, Surrey Sqn, 1937–44. MP (Cons.) for Macclesfield Div. of Cheshire, 1945–71. Baron, 1971.

[3] George Reginald Ward, 1907–88. Educated at Christ Church, Oxford. RAF, 1932–7, 1939–45. MP (Cons.) for Worcester City, 1945–60. Parliamentary Under-Secretary of State, Air Ministry, 1952–5. Parliamentary and Financial Secretary, Admiralty, 1955–7. Secretary of State for Air, 1957–60. Viscount, 1960.

[4] John Galway Foster, 1904–82. Educated at New College, Oxford. Fellow of All Souls, 1924. Lecturer, Private International Law, 1934–9. Recorder, Dudley, 1936–8; Oxford, 1938–51, 1956–64. First Secretary, British Embassy, Washington DC, 1939. Brig., 1944. MP (Cons.) for Northwich, Cheshire, 1945–74. QC, 1950. Parliamentary Under-Secretary of State, 1951–4. KBE, 1964.

[5] Emanuel Shinwell, 1884–1986. Unsuccessful Parliamentary candidate (Lab.) for Linlithgowshire, 1918; elected, 1922; re-elected, 1923; defeated, 1924; re-elected at a by-election in April 1928 and again at the general election of 1929; defeated, 1931. Re-elected for Seaham, 1935. Parliamentary Secretary, Mines Dept, 1924, 1931. Minister of Fuel and Power, 1945–7. Secretary of State for War, 1947–50. Minister of Defence, 1950–1. Labour Party Chairman, 1964–7.

[6] James Scott Cumberland Reid, 1890–1975. Educated at Jesus College, Cambridge. Admitted to Scottish Bar, 1914. Served in WWI, 1915–19. MP (Union.) for Stirling and Falkirk Burghs, 1931–5; for Glasgow Hillhead, 1937–48. QC, 1932. Solicitor-General, Scotland, 1936–41. PC, 1941. Lord Advocate, 1941–5; Dean, Faculty of Advocates, 1945–8. Baron Reid of Drem, 1948. Chairman, Malaya Constitutional Commission, 1956–7. CH, 1967.

[7] Hugh Dalton, Chancellor of the Exchequer.

Benches by Raikes[1] and David Eccles;[2] Harold Macmillan wound up for us before Herbert Morrison. We then kept the House sitting until 3 a.m. on the Committee Stage of the Money Resolution; having asked for three days for the debate, we felt that we were justified in carrying this on and proving to the Leader of the House that he could not have his own way all the time.

There were several speeches of a high order in this debate, especially by David Eccles. Our opposition has been managed very efficiently by Harold Macmillan, Crookshank[3] and JSC Reid, all of whom took an active part in criticising the Money Resolution.

I have been very worried by the manner in which the Leader of the House (Morrison) has been forcing the pace and not offering reasonable time for the preliminary consideration of Bills – e.g., the National Insurance Bill presented on Thursday of last week and to be debated next week – and we have made several protests. As a result of Anthony's renewed protests on the Business announcement this week, the Government have for the first time made some concession and given us an extra day on National Insurance. I have a feeling that the late sitting on Coal this week had a salutary effect. It certainly involved me in a number of arguments with Back Bench Socialists, who took the view that it was a waste of time. I replied to them all that, if their Leader of the House would treat us in a more reasonable spirit, a succession of late nights might be avoided and that they had better make their complaints to him; but I assured them that, as things are going, they would get plenty more of them in the course of time.

Next week the main Business will be the Control of Investment Bill, against which we have tabled a reasoned amendment which will be handled by Ralph Assheton and Brendan Bracken. Following this Wednesday and Thursday will be devoted to the second reading of the National Insurance Bill, which will be

---

[1] Henry Victor Alpin MacKinnon Raikes, 1901–86. Educated at Westminster School and Trinity College, Cambridge. Called to the Bar, 1924. MP (Cons.) for Ilkeston, 1931–45; for Wavertree, 1945–50; for Garston, 1950–7. Flt Lt, RAFVR, 1940–2. Knighted, 1953.

[2] David McAdam Eccles, 1904–99. Married, 1928, Sybil Dawson; 1984, Mary Hyde. Educated at Winchester and Oxford. Ministry of Economic Warfare, 1939–42. Coordinator, Anglo-American Munitions Programme, Ministry of Production, 1942–3. Economic Adviser, HM Ambassadors at Madrid and Lisbon, 1940–2. MP (Cons.) for Chippenham Div. of Wilts, 1943–62. PC, 1951. Minister of Works, 1951–4; of Education, 1954–7, 1959–62. KCVO, 1953. President of the Board of Trade, 1957–9. Baron, 1962. Trustee, British Museum, 1963–99; Chairman of Trustees, 1968–70. Viscount, 1964. Chairman, Anglo-Hellenic League, 1967–70. Paymaster-General, 1970–3. President, World Crafts Council, 1974–8. CH, 1984.

[3] Harry Frederick Comfort Crookshank, 1893–1961. On active service, 1914–18. Capt., 1919. FO, 1919–24 (Constantinople and Washington). MP (Cons.) for Gainsborough, 1924–56. Secretary for Mines, 1936–9. Financial Secretary, Treasury, 1939–43. Postmaster-General, 1943–5. Minister of Health, 1951–2. Lord Privy Seal, 1952–5 (Churchill's second premiership). In 1954 and 1955, one of the Conservative Cabinet Ministers most determined that Churchill should retire. Viscount (under Eden), 1956.

handled by R. A. Butler[1] assisted by R. K. Law[2] and probably John Anderson. They are also giving us Monday in the following week (11th February) to complete the second reading and the Money Resolution.

On February 12th and 13th we shall probably have the second reading of the Trades Disputes Bill, which is a one-clause affair repealing our Act and reinstating the law as it was before the General Strike. They hope by this means to avoid a lot of amendments, but it has yet to be decided whether, in fact, they have been as clever as all that. We hope to be able to deal with the pre-1927 law clause by clause and move to reinstate such sections of it as may seem desirable.

On the 14th and 15th February we shall probably have a Foreign Affairs debate.

I should have mentioned that we had a very good division against the second reading of the Coal Bill – 184 in our Lobby against 361; the total Conservative strength is 195 and we had the assistance of seven Liberal Nationals but no other Liberals, apart from Gwilym Lloyd George,[3] who opened the second day's debate and made a very effective speech.

I should also have mentioned that Thorneycroft[4] spoke very well on the Coal Bill from the Back Benches and seems to be a man who cannot be ignored. Oliver Lyttelton's Trade and Industry Committee has elected him as Chairman of the Transport Sub-committee to fight nationalisation of road haulage, in spite of the fact that he is no longer on the Front Bench.

John Anderson and Andrew Duncan voted with us against the Coal Bill.

---

[1] Richard Austen Butler, 1902–82. Known as 'Rab'. MP (Cons.) for Saffron Walden, 1929–65. Under-Secretary of State, for India, 1932–7; for Foreign Affairs, 1938–41. Parliamentary Secretary to the Ministry of Labour, 1937–8. President of the Board of Education, 1941–5. Minister of Labour, 1945. Chancellor of the Exchequer, 1951–5. Lord Privy Seal, 1955–9. Leader, House of Commons, 1955–61. Rector, University of Glasgow, 1956–61. Home Secretary, 1957–62. Chairman, Conservative Party, 1959–65. Chancellor, University of Sheffield, 1959–77. Deputy PM, 1962–3. First Secretary of State, 1962–3. Foreign Secretary, 1963–4. Father of the House, 1964–5. Master of Trinity College, Cambridge, 1965–78. Chancellor, University of Essex, 1966–82.

[2] Richard Kidston Law, 1901–80. Youngest son of Andrew Bonar Law. Editorial Staff, *Morning Post*, 1927; *New York Herald-Tribune*, 1928. MP (Cons.) for Hull South-West, 1931–45; for South Kensington, 1945–50; for Haltemprice, 1950–4. Member, Medical Research Council, 1936–40. Financial Secretary, War Office, 1940–1. Parliamentary Under-Secretary of State, FO, 1941–3. PC, 1943. Minister of State, 1943–5. Minister of Education, 1945. Baron Coleraine, 1954. Chairman, National Youth Employment Council, 1955–62.

[3] Gwilym Lloyd George, 1894–1967. Second son of David Lloyd George. Educated at Eastbourne College and Jesus College, Cambridge. On active service in France, 1914–19 (Maj., RA; despatches). MP (Lib.) for Pembrokeshire, 1922–4, 1929–50; for Newcastle North, 1951–7. Parliamentary Secretary, Ministry of Food, 1941–2. Minister of Fuel and Power, 1942–5; of Food, 1951–4. Home Secretary and Minister for Welsh Affairs, 1954–7. Viscount Tenby, 1957.

[4] Peter Thorneycroft, 1909–94. MP (Cons.) for Stafford, 1938–45; for Monmouth, 1945–66. Parliamentary Secretary, Ministry of War Transport, 1945. President of the Board of Trade, 1951–7. Chancellor of the Exchequer, 1957–8. Minister of Aviation, 1960–2. Minister of Defence, 1962–4. Secretary of State for Defence, 1964. Baron, 1967.

February 1946

Anthony Eden to Winston S. Churchill
(*Churchill papers, 2/6*)

4 February 1946
Immediate
Personal and Top Secret
Deyou
No. 9

Bevin has written to me that owing to statements by Byrnes[1] about the Yalta agreement on Far East signed by Roosevelt Stalin and yourself British Government have to make this public on February 11th. I do not think we can object to this hoping Stokes[2] may (?not) attack us for not admitting its existence when questioned about secret agreement last year. On June 7th 1945 you told him in a supplementary answer that there was no secret engagement at Yalta at all except the addition of two Russian Republics to the United Nations. Best view is I think that Stokes's original question referred to relations with other European repeat European powers.

All well here. Usual routine rolls drearily on.

Winston S. Churchill to Anthony Eden
(*Churchill papers, 2/6*)

5 February 1946
Foreign Secretary to be informed

Before I agree to publication of Yalta Agreement on Far East, I wish to see the text. In my recollection its object was to bring Russia into the war against Japan as soon as possible. It was therefore primarily military in its character and in view of the peaceful relations subsisting between Russia and Japan, no mention of it could of course be made. I do not recall any reference to the Kuriles.

2. I ought also to see the text of Stokes' Question of June 7 1945 and my Supplementary, as the context is decisive. I should in no case have considered a military agreement as coming within the category of undisclosed secret arrangements as obviously there were, throughout the war, repeated secret military agreements, which could never form the subject of Question and Answer in the House of Commons.

[1] Byrnes alleged ignorance of the secret protocol signed at Yalta promising the transfer of strategic territory to Russia in exchange for Russia's guarantee to enter the war against Japan following the fall of Nazi Germany. The text of this protocol is reproduced in Eden to Churchill, 8 Feb., reproduced below (pp. 203–4).

[2] Richard Rapier Stokes, 1897–1957. On active service, RA, 1915–18 (MC and bar). Unsuccessful Parliamentary candidate (Lab.), 1935. MP (Lab.) for Ipswich from 1938 until his death. A persistent critic of the conduct of the war, 1940–5. Minister of Works, 1950–1; Minister of Materials, 1951.

3. I shall be back at Miami on 8th. It should be easy to furnish me with the texts in question. I should protest strongly against HMG so handling the matter in my absence that it appeared I had made an untrue statement. When the text reaches me I will myself furnish a suitable reply, for the consideration of the Government or for use by you if no agreement is reached upon it.

Winston S. Churchill to General Dwight D. Eisenhower
(Churchill papers, 2/226)

6 February 1946   The British Legation, Havana
Private

My dear Ike,

I received your telephone message yesterday.[1] March 8 would be a very good day to go to Williamsburg, and I am accordingly marking it on my card. Mrs Churchill has already seen Williamsburg but she would like very much to come again, and also Sarah has not seen it at all. Will you let me know whether it is men only, or whether the ladies can be fitted in conveniently. Colonel Clarke will accompany me, so our party would total four.

I have been sent a very gratifying Resolution from the Virginia General Assembly,[2] requesting me to address them, and I wondered whether I could not fit this in with the Williamsburg expedition. I shall not decide whether to accept the Virginia invitation until I have talked it over with the President. There is another one in similar very kindly terms from Kentucky. Obviously I could not do both. (And now another from South Carolina.) I am dining with the President on February 11 and will write to you the upshot of our talks. I am worried about the way things are going. There is only one safe anchor; wh both you & I know.

Anthony Eden to Winston S. Churchill
(Churchill papers, 2/6)

8 February 1946
Most Immediate
Top Secret

Text of Yalta agreement is as follows.

AGREEMENT

The leaders of the three Great Powers – Soviet Union, the USA, and Great Britain – have agreed that in two or three months after Germany has

---
[1] See letter of Jan. 30 reproduced above (pp. 191–2).
[2] Reproduced above (p. 182).

surrendered and the war in Europe has terminated the Soviet Union shall enter into the war against Japan on the side of the Allies on condition:

(1) The status quo in outer-Mongolia (Mongolian Peoples' Republic) shall be preserved.

(2) The former rights of Russia violated by treacherous attack of Japan in 1904 shall be restored viz:

    (a) Southern part of Sakhalin as well as all islands adjacent to it shall be returned to the Soviet Union.

    (b) Commercial port of Dairen shall be internationalised, pre-eminent interests of the Soviet Union in this port being safeguarded and lease of Port Arthur as a naval base of USSR restored.

    (c) Chinese–Eastern railroad and South-Manchurian railroad which provides an outlet to Dairen shall be jointly operated by establishment of a joint Soviet-Chinese company it being understood pre-eminent interests of Soviet Union shall be safeguarded and that China shall retain full sovereignty in Manchuria.

(3) Kuril Islands shall be handed over to the Soviet Union. It is understood that agreement concerning Outer Mongolia and ports and railroads referred to above will require concurrence of Generalissimo Chiang Kai-shek. President will take measures in order to obtain this concurrence on advice from Marshal Stalin.

Heads of the three Great Powers have agreed that these claims of the Soviet Union shall be unquestionable (?only) after Japan has been defeated.

For its part the Soviet Union expressed its readiness to conclude with National Government of China a pact of substantiation and alliance between the USSR and China in order to render assistance to China with its armed forces for the purpose of liberating China from the Japanese yoke.

(Signed) JV Stalin
Franklin R. Roosevelt
Winston S. Churchill
February 11th, 1945

2. Following is text of question which Stokes asked you in the House of Commons on June 7th, 1945, and of your reply together with supplementaries.

Extract from Hansard, Thursday, June 7th, 1945.

TEHRAN AND YALTA DECISIONS (PUBLICATION)

Mr Stokes asked the Prime Minister what agreements were arrived at Tehran or Yalta with regard to (? relation with) other European powers not so far disclosed to British public.

FEBRUARY 1946

The Prime Minister: I have nothing to add to Saturday's statements which have already been made on results of these conferences.

Mr Stokes: Will the Prime Minister please repeat assurance given by the Foreign Secretary that no secret engagements of any kind whatever were entered into either at Yalta or Tehran.

The Prime Minister: I cannot give a guarantee that newspaper reporters were there all the time.

Mr Price:[1] If it is a fact that there are no undisclosed conditions to Yalta decisions, why is it that the Russian Government have acted in the matter of broadening of Polish Government in a way totally in conflict with declared decisions of Yalta Conference?

The Prime Minister: Certainly there were no secret engagements entered into there at all except that we kept secret the addition of two members to (?Russia) Byelo-Russia and the Ukraine. Those were kept secret at the desire of the US so that the President could get home and make necessary arrangements on the spot. Otherwise there were no secret engagements but conversations of course proceeded in a very intimate manner and I am not prepared to say everything discussed at Yalta could be made subject of a verbatim report.

Mr Stokes: With great respect to the Prime Minister, his answer was quite irrelevant. I was not talking about newspapers. Will he repeat assurance given to the House by the Foreign Secretary that no secret engagements were entered into at either of those conferences?

The Prime Minister: Yes, Sir. I have, but I do not accept the view that is absolutely necessary that there should never be on any occasion a secret clause in some arrangement provided it is reported to a wide cabinet. It may very often be necessary to do so. It would hamper very much the whole proceedings if no understandings could be made which had not to be immediately published. I should not approve that myself although I know a lot of claptrap is talked about it.

3. In point of fact in spite of what Stokes said in his first supplementary the Foreign Office confirmed no evidence that I ever gave any assurance that no secret agreements of any kind whatever were entered into at Yalta. Only assurance I gave was in course of a debate on foreign affairs on May 25th, 1944, which could not of course have referred to Yalta Conference which took place in February, 1945. Assurance that I gave was as follows: 'Despite all those difficulties, and I may say temptations in this respect in wartime, we have not on any occasion in these four years entered into any secret engagement

---

[1] Morgan Philips Price, 1885–1973. Educated at Harrow and Trinity College, Cambridge. Landowner and farmer. MP (Lab.) for Whitehaven, 1929–31; for Forest of Dean, 1935–50; for West Gloucestershire, 1950–9. Author of several books on Russia both before and after the revolution of 1917 (which he witnessed).

of any kind with anybody.' Stokes' statements of June, 1945, are therefore misleading.

4. Present intention of Foreign Secretary is to publish White Paper containing text of Far Eastern Agreement on February 11th next. This is being done at the request of the US Government and Soviet Government (former originally proposed an earlier date for publication) and it is very unlikely that they would agree to further postponement. As regards protecting your position you are surely covered by the fact that Stokes' question refers to agreements 'with regard to relations with other European Powers'. Moreover, as you say Far Eastern Agreement was an agreement covering future military operations such as could never form the subject of question and answer in the House. It is intended to give the Press guidance on these lines when the time comes for publication. I feel, and I think you will agree, that any reference in the White Paper to your replies to Stokes would in the circumstances be undesirable but Foreign Secretary and I would welcome your views.

Anthony Eden to Winston S. Churchill
(*Churchill papers, 2/6*)[1]

8 February 1946　　　　　　　　　　　　　Binderton House, Chichester

My dear Winston,

Well; well; the food, or rather the lack of it. The govt have handled the situation very clumsily. Even admitting that they could do little to meet their shortages – of which I am unconvinced, why not maize from the Argentine – they did less to prepare the unhappy public. Ben Smith[2] comes back beaming from the US, speaks of maintenance and even possible improvement of rationing, and then we have this. It is hard to judge how angry the people are, for they are so weary, and it is easy to exaggerate. But I guess that they are pretty angry all the same, and my post-bag is enormous.

We are to have a debate on Thursday & Woolton, with whom I have had several discussions, will follow this up in the Lords the following week. I gather that Arthur was much peeved that his colleagues had told us nothing and there has been some hand washing. But this won't feed our people, and some are going to be really hungry if we don't work it out. Woolton says the cut in the fat ration is by far the most serious. You will remember he was

---

[1] This letter was handwritten.

[2] Ben Smith, 1879–1964. Joined Merchant Navy as a boy. Later served in RN for seven years. Left the Navy to become a hansom-cab, and then a taxi-cab, driver. An active member of the London Cab Drivers' Union. Organizer, Transport and General Workers' Union. MP (Lab.) for Rotherhithe, 1923–31, 1935–46. A junior Labour Whip, 1925. Parliamentary Secretary, Ministry of Aircraft Production, 1942. Minister Resident in Washington DC for Supply, 1943–5. Knighted, 1945. Minister of Food, 1945–6.

always preaching to us in the bad days that it must be maintained & that bread must not be rationed.

This food business dominates all politics. It has had no reaction on party fortunes so far and is probably too recent to do so yet. Apart from food, the govt is holding its own comfortably & the solid phalanxes in this House & in this country are quite unshaken. The cry is still 'give them a chance', and it was found to be so. But should the food business become even worse, as is, I gather, unhappily only too likely, we may see a revulsion.

We all miss you very much. The party seem reasonably content, now that they have something to criticize. Our former colleagues have been loyal & helpful to Max quiescent about my shortcomings! So all that is not too bad.

Beatrice[1] is off to the Barbados early next week via New York. The trip will do her good I hope, and she is increasingly excited about it.

Here after a week of gales the sun has suddenly come out and I am writing this in the garden. Snowdrifts, aconites, and crocuses all trying to pretend that it is spring. But a poor sun to Yours, & no warm sea to splash in. All the same England is a good land, or would be if there weren't so many socialists in it.

Beatrice joins me in love to you & Clemmie & Sarah.

<p align="center">Winston S. Churchill to Anthony Eden
(<i>Churchill papers, 2/6</i>)</p>

9 February 1946 Miami Beach, Florida
Top Secret

Your telegram of February 8. There is no need to refer to Stokes in the White Paper. Should he raise the matter I hope you and the Government will make it clear firstly, that my Supplementary Answer was governed, 'with regard to relations with other European Powers,' secondly, that an Agreement about Russia coming into the war against Japan was a military secret of the most deadly character which, had it leaked out, might have led to a forestalling Japanese attack on Russia in the Far East. It is not conceivable that such an Agreement should have been in any way akin to the matters about which the Supplementary Question was asked which in fact, as the context suggests were about Poland.

Many thanks for the trouble you have taken and for the Foreign Office facilities.

---

[1] Beatrice Helen Beckett, 1905–57. Married, 1923, Anthony Eden; the eldest of their three sons, Simon, was posted Missing in Action, 1945. Left Eden to live in US, 1946; div., 1950.

February 1946

Winston S. Churchill to Cecil F. Elmes
(Churchill papers, 2/226)

9 February 1946   Miami Beach, Florida

My dear Mr Elmes,

I have received with much pleasure your letter of January 21.[1] It is interesting and amusing to me to see what I wrote in 1899, and your kindness in sending me a copy of my letter has revived many a vivid memory of those far-off days.

The observations written in the zeal of my youth is now all too true. Perhaps, however, with the wisdom of years, I am a little more philosophical in my outlook and conceptions of what the passing of time means.

Thank you so much for writing to me.

Winston S. Churchill to James Wootton-Davies
(Churchill papers, 2/8)

10 February 1946

Dear Wootton-Davies,

Thank you so much for your long and most interesting letter and for the public-spirited course which you adopted. I will have everything that you have written carefully studied on my return, and I hope I shall have an opportunity of thanking you personally for your services.

Like you, I am full of anxiety for the future of the country and of its position in the world.

Major-General Sir Hugh Tudor to Winston S. Churchill
(Churchill papers, 2/230)

12 February 1946   Newfoundland

My dear Winston,

Thank you so much for your very interesting and welcome letter.[2] George Barr gave it to me when he arrived back yesterday. I intended to write to you, but waited because I gathered you wanted as complete a rest as possible; and so the fewer letters the better. It was to congratulate you on the King having given you the Order of Merit, that I wished to write. It is, I believe, the highest honour the King can bestow, that does not carry with it a title.

---

[1] Reproduced above (p. 186).
[2] Of Jan. 18, reproduced above (p. pp. 184–5).

FEBRUARY 1946   209

I have just had a letter from Darling. He says he voted against the Loan. He thinks that American business would be obliged, in their own interests to invest in British concerns, which would do as well as a loan. He has a suspicion that the Government is afraid to tell the Country the financial straits we are in; and so want the loan to tide things over. I believe Darling will do well in Parliament, and will give you valuable support.

The overwhelming victory of the Labour Party must have been a great surprise to you. Even before the election, I had heard the view expressed by Conservatives that it would be as well if Labour got in; as any government was bound to become unpopular in tackling the job of clearing up the mess left by so many years of war. But they did not, I am sure, bargain for such a huge Labour majority. It must indeed have seemed very strange to be a man of leisure again, after six years of all-engrossing toil.

One advantage of having a Labour Government in power at the present time is that it can be sure of loyal support in dealing with foreign affairs. In view of Russia's strange behaviour, this is of great importance at the present time. Unless Russia changes her behaviour, the UNO will become a farce.

You asked Barr what my views are regarding Palestine. I am inclined to sympathize with Ibn Saoud[1] when he said 'England had no more right to declare a National Home for Jews in Palestine, than I, Ibn Saoud, would have to declare a National Home for Arabs in Devonshire'. Palestine, both in Hebrew and in Arabic, is called Philistine, the land of the Philistines. So the descendants of the Philistines, though Arabicised and mixed with the Arabs, have an even older historic claim on the country than the Jews, who I suppose, strictly speaking, can only lay a historic claim to that small part of Palestine that was occupied by the tribe of Judah. Something must be done to settle the Jewish problem. It is unfortunate, that, although one may have good friends among the Jews, as a race they are not liked, and no country seems to want them. They are wonderful people, but so are the Arabs, who kept civilization alive through the Dark Ages. Even in English we use many Arabic words – tarif, admiral, chemist, algebra – to mention a few. The constellations are mostly named by the Arabs.

I have always thought the Balfour declaration a mistake; and I think without it Jews could have come into the Country to the same extent as they now have, without exciting the fear and animosity of the Arabs. As things are I fear a solution, satisfactory to both Jews and Arabs is hardly possible. America has plenty of room. If she would open her doors to Jewish Immigration, it would go far towards settling the problem of the Jews of Europe.
[. . .]

[1] Ibn Saud, 1880–1953. Born in Riyadh, a member of the Wahhabi dynasty. Exiled as a child by the Turks. Led a Bedouin revolt to regain Riyadh, 1902. King of Hejaz and Nejd, 1926–32; of Saudi Arabia, 1932–53.

I am so glad to hear from Barr that you look very fit and well. For the sake of the Empire I wish you were still guiding our destinies. I rather think too, that we lost some prestige abroad, because of the British electors' seeming ingratitude to you.

Do please remember me to Mrs Churchill.

Winston S. Churchill to General Dwight D. Eisenhower
(Churchill papers, 2/226)

13 February 1946   Miami Beach, Florida
Private

My dear Ike,

I am looking forward very much to paying a visit to Williamsburg under your auspices on March 8, and you are going to tell me what are the best arrangements for transportation there and back.

Lord Halifax will be able to inform you what is settled about my addressing the Virginia Legislature and whether that can be arranged at Williamsburg or at Richmond. It may be that, if only Richmond is open, there will not be time on the same day. I hope however that both may be combined. Mrs Churchill, my daughter, Mrs Oliver and Colonel Clarke are pleased that they may come with me and also that they are to dine with you and Mrs Eisenhower on March 9.

With regard to my visit to the Pentagon on March 9, might I ask you not to make any final arrangements about that at the present moment, as I must be careful not to undertake too much in the way of considered speeches. When I have made a little more progress with what I am to say at Fulton and also at Williamsburg (or Richmond), I should like to write to you again. I gather there is no particular hurry in concluding these arrangements, which would be of a simple nature.

Once more thanking you for all your kindness.

Winston S. Churchill to President Harry S Truman
(Churchill papers, 2/158)

14 February 1946   Miami Beach, Florida

It seems to me that starting for Fulton at 7 a.m. on March 5 by Air, with a motor drive at the end will be a very tiring prelude at my age for a most important speech and other ceremonies. Moreover the weather imposes a considerable element of uncertainty upon flying and if the day were bad we might have to come down somewhere or perhaps not start at all, with great disappointment at Fulton, where every kind of plan is being made. Will you not very kindly consider instead taking me by train? If we started around 10 or 10.30 a.m. on the 4th, we should arrive at St Louis fresh as paint and in ample time for everything.

If you decided to adopt this plan I, with my wife and daughter, would fly to you on the 3rd and spend the night with you and you and I would start off the next morning.

Will you please wire me whether this change commends itself to you.

Winston S. Churchill to Clement Attlee
(Churchill papers, 2/210)

17 February 1946   Miami Beach, Florida
Private and Personal

At the suggestion of Lord Halifax it was arranged that Secretary Byrnes should bring Baruch[1] to see me here, in order that I could have a talk with him about the Loan. I was surprised that so much importance should be attached to Mr Baruch's attitude as to make the Secretary of State travel 1,000 miles one day and go back the same distance the next, merely for this purpose. However all passed off very pleasantly. I have been ill for the last three days but was able to receive them both in my bedroom, where we had a two hours talk on the Loan and on affairs in general.

2. Part of this time was occupied in considerable argument between Baruch and Byrnes. They are good friends but obviously hold totally different views. Baruch has a great dislike for Keynes and complained of his mismanagement of the negotiations. He is also vexed at not having been consulted himself, although on this point Byrnes said Mr Clayton[2] had kept him informed. Baruch thought it a mistake that interest should be charged for the Loan, that Imperial preference should be brought into it at all and that we should not be able to convert as soon as was proposed. On the other hand he considered that we should specify precisely the object for which we required the Loan. If it was for food or raw material he would gladly have them supplied. He made

---

[1] Bernard Mannes Baruch, 1870–1965. Born in South Carolina, the son of a Jewish doctor who had emigrated from East Prussia in the 1850s. A self-made financier, he became a millionaire before he was 30. As Chairman of the US War Industries Board from 3 March 1918 until the end of the war he was in almost daily communication with Churchill (then Minister of Munitions). Accompanied President Wilson to the Paris Peace Conference, 1919. In 1929 and 1931 he was one of Churchill's hosts on the latter's visits to the US. From 1946 to 1951 he was US Representative on the Atomic Energy Commission. When he presented his private archive to Princeton University in 1964 it contained 1,200 letters from nine Presidents, and 700 communications from Churchill.

[2] William Lockhart Clayton, 1880–1966. Married, 1902, Susan Vaughan. Member, Committee on Cotton Distribution of War Industries Board, 1918. Entered Government Service, 1940. Coordinator of Inter-American Affairs, 1940. Administrator of Surplus War Property Administration, 1944. Asst Secretary of State in Charge of Economic Affairs, 1944–6.

no objection to machine tools but said that Mr Brand[1] had assured him that we did not require equipment. He repeated continually that there would be no question but that the United States would supply Great Britain with all the food she needed in the transition period. On the other hand, he considered no case had been made out for so large an amount as four billion dollars, and commented adversely upon our heavy dollar credits.

I explained to him that these were more than balanced by the indebtedness we had incurred to India, Egypt, etc. for the war effort. He was opposed to the American Loan being used for repaying or otherwise providing for such debts saying that we had both defended these countries from invasion and ruin, that it was an American interest to see that Britain did not collapse but not an American interest to have her pay her debts to those we had defended. You know well my views on this part of the story. I was not able to supply particulars of exactly what we wanted the Loan for, but if you like to let me have them in a compendious form, I shall have a further opportunity of showing them to Baruch when I am in New York, who will certainly be mollified by being consulted. He is of course very much opposed to American money being used to make Socialism and the nationalization of industry a success in Britain.

I rejoined that the failure of the Loan at this stage would bring about such distress and call for such privation in our island as to play into the hands of extremists of all kinds and lead to a campaign of extreme austerity, detrimental alike to our speedy recovery and to our good relations. I also explained to him the deficit between export and import and the inevitable delay in building up our export trade which we had completely sacrificed for the common cause. He did not seem convinced but undoubtedly he is most anxious not to be unfriendly to our country, for which he expressed the most ardent admiration.

3. In a further talk with Byrnes, I learned that Baruch is regarded in financial matters as an oracle and that heavy opposition by him to the Loan and adverse pronouncements would be injurious. Byrnes advised that I should tell him I would have further talks with him and that meanwhile he should keep closely in touch with Secretary Byrnes himself, who would keep him informed.

4. I am thinking now about my speech at Fulton, which will be in the same direction as the one I made at Harvard two years ago, namely fraternal association in the build-up and maintenance of UNO, and intermingling of necessary arrangements for mutual safety in case of danger, in full loyalty to the Charter. I tried this on both the President and Byrnes, who seemed to like it very well. Byrnes said that he could not object to a special friendship within the Organization, as the United States had already made similar friendships

---

[1] Robert Henry Brand, 1878–1963. Educated at New College, Oxford, 1901–5. Secretary, International Colonial Council of South Africa, 1902–9. CMG, 1910. Vice-President of International Conference of Brussels, 1920. DCL, Oxford University, 1937. Head, British Food Mission to US, 1941–4. British Member of Combined Food Board, 1942–4. British Treasury Representative to US, 1944–6. Baron, 1946.

with the South American States. There is much fear of Russia here as a cause of future trouble and Bevin's general attitude at UNO has done us a great deal of good.

5. I should be glad if you keep this telegram very private but of course Bevin and the Chancellor should see it if you think it worthwhile, and I should like you to give Anthony a copy.

6. I ought to let you know that there is a great deal of feeling here among the high officers of the American Air Force about what is thought to be the slighting treatment of Bomber Harris. This will no doubt find expression when he comes here to receive the American Distinguished Service Medal on his way to make his home in South Africa. I am sorry about all this. Honours are made to give pleasure and not to cause anger. Surely you might consider a Baronetcy.

Clement Attlee to Winston S. Churchill
(*Churchill papers, 2/210*)

25 February 1946
Top Secret, Private and Personal

Thank you very much for your telegram which I have circulated only to Bevin, Dalton and Eden.

I am so sorry to hear that you have been unwell. I hope you are now recovered. I am most grateful to you for talking with Baruch. I am sure that you will have done much good. I gathered when I was in Washington that he was apt to regard himself as slighted if not fully consulted as the oracle of finance. Halifax should have full information on our requirements for dollars but I am asking Chancellor to send you a compendious note. In our view the four billion is a bare minimum. I am sure your Fulton speech will do good. I am sorry for any feeling about Harris but you know better than I do the difficulty of keeping a balance both within a service and between services.

I hope remainder of your visit will be entirely pleasant.

Winston S. Churchill: speech notes
(*Lorraine Bonar papers*)

26 February 1946 University of Miami

> I have enjoyed my stay in your genial sunshine
> and it has done me a lot of good.
>
> I am grateful for all the kindness and
> consideration

w wh you hv treated
a servant of the Allied cause
in the fearful war we hv won.

The accounts I read
Of the severity of life in England
and the darkening scene at home

make me and my wife naturally anxious
to return there as soon as possible.

I am very glad therefore to have an opportunity
of expressing my thanks to Miami Beach,
Miami and to Florida
and to all this shining coast

for so easy and agreeable a wayside halt
on the road we all have to tread.

This opportunity is afforded me
in a manner most gratifying

by the resolve of the University of Miami
to give me a degree as Doctor of Law.

I regard this as a vy high compliment indeed,
and that I should receive the degree
in the presence of this vast
and gracious concourse

makes the occasion memorable in my life.

I wish also, on behalf of my country,
to thank the University of Miami

for the wonderful help wh they gave us
in the late war
by training cadets for the RAF
before the US became a belligerent.

Upwards of 12 hundred cadets of the RAF
received here a very high quality
of technical, navigational
and meteorological training.

They flew 5 ½ million miles, I am told, over
    Florida upon instructional courses,

    and the majority, indeed a very large
        majority gave their lives shortly
        afterwards
    for their country and our common cause.

It is a consolation to learn
    tt they left so many pleasant memories
        behind them

    among the 2 thousand Miami households
        who received them
            with true American hospitality

    and afterwards followed their fortunes
        and their fate

    almost as if they were the sons of the soil.

Kindred hearts will beat in Britain
    on this account

    when they read of our ceremony here today.

I return, Mr President, to the Degree which you
    have just conferred upon me.

I am especially honoured by the presence here
    of Dr Snavely[1] the Executive Director of
    The Association of American Colleges

    and I thank him for all the far too flattering
        things which he has said about me.
I am surprised that in my later life
    I should have become so experienced
        in taking degrees,

---

[1] Guy Everett Snavely, 1881–1974. Educated at Johns Hopkins University. Prof. of French, Allegheny College, 1907–10; Registrar, 1908–19. Director, Southern Div., American Red Cross, 1918–19. President, Birmingham-Southern College, 1921–37. 1955–7. Executive Director, Association of American Colleges and Universities, 1937–55.

when, as a school-boy
>I was so bad at passing examinations.

In fact one might also say
>that no one ever passed so few examinations
>>and received so many degrees,

From this a superficial thinker might argue
>that the way to get the most degrees
>>is to fail in the most examinations.

This would however, ladies and gentlemen, be a conclusion
>unedifying in the academic atmosphere
>>in which I now preen myself,

and I therefore hasten to draw another moral
>w wh I am sure we shall all be in accord:

namely, that no boy or girl
>should ever be disheartened
>>by lack of success in their youth

but should diligently and faithfully
>continue to persevere
>>and make up for lost time.

There at least is a sentiment
>which I am sure the faculty and the Public,
>>the scholars and the dunces

will all be cordially united upon.

This raises the interesting question
>of the age at which knowledge and learning
>>may be most fruitfully imparted and acquired.

Owing to the pressure of life
>and everyone having to earn their living

>>a University education of the great majority
>>>of those who enjoy that high privilege
>is usually acquired after 20.

February 1946

These are great years for young people.

The world of thought and history
        and the treasures of learning

            are laid open to them.

They have the chance of broadening their minds,
        elevating their view
               and arming their moral convictions

            by all the resources
                that free and wealthy communities
                    can bestow.

It is the glory of the US
        that her graduates of universities
            are numbered not by the million
                but by the 10 million

            and certainly any young man or woman
                who has these measureless advantages
                laid before them

            and has not the mother wit
                to profit by them to the full

            has no right to complain
                if he or she makes only a mediocre
                    success of life.

Still, Mr President, I am going to put in a plea
        for the late starters.

Not only is the saying true,
        'It is never too late to mend',

            but university education
                may be even better appreciated
                    by those in the early twenties
                          than by those in the later teens.

The attention which a mature mind can bring
> to a study of the philosophies,
>> humanities, and the great literary monuments
>>> of the past

> is stronger and more intense
>> than at an earlier age.

The power of concentration,
> the retentiveness of the memory,
>> the earnestness and zeal
>>> with which conclusions are sought

> should, in most cases,
>> be greater in the older students.

This, ladies and gentlemen has a practical
> and a supreme application
>> at the present time.

Millions of young men have had their education
> interrupted by the war.

Their lives have been slashed across
> by its flaming sword.

We must make sure that, in both our countries,
> they do not suffer needlessly

>> for this particular form
>>> of the sacrifice which they have made.

I have been cheered
> and also, so far as my own country
>> is concerned,

> spurred,

>> by the tremendous efforts which are being made
>>> by all the educational bodies of the US
>>>> and by the American people generally

  to make up to these young men
    by all kinds of special arrangements
     and facilities

  what they may have lost
    by their services at the Front.

I have read that it is proposed
  to provide facilities almost immediately
    for upwards of 15 hundred thousand
     young men most of whom are
      coming home from the fighting lines

  and that in 5 years
    it is hoped that 4 millions
     may be provided for.

This is indeed a splendid aim and effort.

I suppose Mr President and Dr Snavely
  that you are making appropriate arrangements
    on a great scale

  to adapt conditions of university life
    to these veterans, as you call them,

  though they are still pretty young
    to earn such a title,

  or warriors anyhow,

  who come back,
    after fighting their country's battles
     in the Air, on the oceans and on
      the land
  from Okinawa and Iwo-Jima to Normandy,
    the Siegfried Line and the Rhine.

Men who have fought in action
  and led others
    or, by their example, inspired others,

have had an education invaluable
    to the formation of character

and to the development of those qualities
    by which freedom and justice
        are preserved in strong nations,

and by nations for weak nations.

They must also be given the wider view,
    in outline at any rate,

    of the treasures which mankind has gathered
        in its long, checkered pilgrimage
            across the centuries.

You do well to provide, as you are doing,
    on this prodigious scale

    for the baptism of such as are of riper years.

This is an age of machinery and specialization
    but I hope, none the less
        – indeed all the more –

    that the purely vocational aspect
        of university study

    will not be allowed to dominate or monopolize
        all the attention
            of the returned Service men.

Engines were made for men,
    not men for engines.

Mr Gladstone said many years ago
    that it ought to be part
        of a man's religion

to see that his country is well governed.

Knowledge of the past
    is the only foundation we have

    from which to peer into

    and try to measure the future.

Expert knowledge, however indispensable,
    is no substitute for
        a generous and comprehending outlook
            upon the human story

    with all its sadness
        and with all its unquenchable hope.

March 1946

Clark Clifford:[1] *recollection*
(*'Finest Hour'*, No. 55, Spring 1987, pages 22–3)

4 March 1946

The president had a private car, called The Magellan.[2] It had an observation platform on the back and it was equipped so that in the rear portion you walked into a very attractive living room, furnished as you might furnish a men's club. The reason they went by train was to give Churchill and Truman an ample opportunity to talk. Mr Truman wanted the opportunity to visit with Churchill, and Churchill, who had been very close to Franklin Roosevelt, felt he had no relationship with Truman and wanted to develop one.

My recollection is that we left Washington around noon, and we all came in and sat down in the living room. Mr Churchill said, 'Mr President, we're going to be together now for a week or so. I would like to dispense with formality, and I would like to have the privilege of calling you Harry.' Truman said, 'Mr Churchill, I would be honored if you would call me Harry.' Then Mr Churchill said, 'Well, if I am going to call you Harry, then you must call me Winston.' Mr Truman, as you know, was a very modest fellow, so he said, 'That would be very difficult for me to do, Mr Churchill. I have such a high regard and enormous respect for you.' But Churchill said, 'You must do it, or I can't call you Harry.' And Mr Truman said, 'All right, then. It's Harry and Winston.'

The next thing Truman said was, 'About six weeks ago, Clement Attlee came over to see me.' There was a very chill silence. Then Churchill said, 'There is less there than meets the eye.' Mr Truman, knowing that he'd kind of put his foot in it, just bravely felt he had to go on. So he said, 'Well, he seems

---

[1] Clark McAdams Clifford, 1906–98. Officer, US Navy, 1944–6. White House Counsel, 1946–50. Chair, President's Advisory Board, 1963–8. US Secretary of Defense, 1968–9. Political adviser to Presidents Truman, Kennedy, Johnson and Carter.

[2] *Ferdinand Magellan*, built 1929 by the Pullman Co., modified and armoured for presidential use as 'United States Railcar No. 1' in 1941, which made it the heaviest railcar ever built in the US. After its official retirement in 1954, acquired by the Gold Coast Railroad Museum near Miami, Fla. On 12 Oct. 1984 it returned to life briefly when President Reagan used it for a one-day whistle-stop campaign tour in Ohio.

to be a very modest fellow.' 'Yes,' Churchill said, 'He has much to be modest about.' Then Churchill said, 'Harry, I've read in the press over a period of years that you play poker.' And Truman said, 'Yes, I guess I've played poker for a good many years, Winston.' Churchill proudly said, 'I first learned to play poker in the Boer War. I love the game.' Well, my God, that was very impressive; none of us could remember when the hell the Boer War was.

Winston asked, 'Do you think we might have the chance of playing poker on this trip?' Harry said, 'I will guarantee that we'll play some poker.' Then we all had lunch and Churchill retired. He took a nap after lunch each day. While he was gone, the President called us all in together. 'Men, I know this man is very smart, and he's probably a very good poker player. I want to impress upon you the fact that the reputation of American poker is at stake. I expect every man to do his duty.'

After dinner that night there were seven of us. The Filipino mess boys put a green felt cover on the dining-room table and we began. Now, this group played a reasonably stiff game. The President liked to play a game that was really poker, with a decent element of skill in it. So Mr Churchill was carefully acquainted with the stakes. You got your first stack of $500, and if you lost that, you got a second stack of $500. But after you went through your second stack, you went 'on poverty'. Each pot was pinched of a few chips, which were put into a silver bowl, so that by the time anyone went broke, why, that silver bowl was almost full of chips, and you'd get $100 to start again. Not a loan, an outright grant.

The group used to play regularly. I've seen any number of fellows end up winners at the end of a game, or the end of a weekend, after having been 'on poverty' two or three times. The most you could lose was $900 because if you lost the last pot, you still got your $100 grant from the silver bowl. We played dealer's choice: stud, draw, seven-card stud and high-low, which is a great gambling game because it keeps everybody in the pot.

We played about an hour and a half, and Mr Churchill excused himself to go to the men's room. The President looked over to his staff and counselors and said, 'Men, Mr Churchill has lost $850. Now, remember, he is our guest. We certainly are not treating him very well.' Charlie Ross[1] (former *Post-Dispatch* Washington correspondent, then Truman's press secretary) spoke up: 'Boss, you can't have it both ways. Which do you want us to do, play poker or carry this fellow along?'

The President said, 'Boys, I want Mr Churchill to have a good time. I recognize the standards of poker as played in Great Britain aren't nearly up to the standards in the United States. But I want him to have a lovely time.' So he was nursed along, and he won some wonderful big pots. I saw some people

---

[1] Charles Griffith Ross, 1885–1950. Educated at University of Missouri. Prof., Missouri School of Journalism, 1908. Chief Washington Correspondent, *St Louis Post-Dispatch*; winner, Pulitzer Prize, 1932; Editorial Editor, 1934–9; Contributing Editor, 1939–45. White House Press Secretary, 1945–50.

drop out with three aces, and he'd win with a pair of kings. He had a marvelous time, and yet he couldn't go back and say he'd beaten this group playing poker. When the last game was over he'd lost about $80.

We played going out and coming back, and it was a great deal of fun because it would be interspersed with comments by Churchill, philosophical musings mostly. There's only one that I remember. One evening, we stayed up late. Everybody else went to bed, and Charlie Ross and I stayed up and talked to him afterwards. He was kind of mellow by that time. He had the reputation of being a fairly formidable drinker, and I think I know the reason why. It was because he always had a Scotch highball in front of him, but he would nurse the highball, and it would take him about an hour and a half to drink it. I did not find him to be a heavy drinker at all.

This evening, he said, 'If I were to be born again, I would wish to be born in the United States. At one time it was said that the sun never sets on the British Empire. Those days are gone. The United States has the natural resources; they have an energetic, resilient people. The United States is the hope of the future. Even though I deplore some of your customs. You stop drinking with your meals.'

Max Lincoln Schuster[1] to Winston S. Churchill
(Churchill papers, 4/5)

4 March 1946　　　　　　　　　　　　　　　　　　　　　　　Rockefeller Center
New York City

Dear Mr Churchill,

We have just this morning received the letter and manuscript of 'The Secret Session Speeches', which you sent to Mr Marshall Field[2] from Miami on March 1st.

We deem it a high honor and a privilege of the first order to be entrusted with the publication of these historic addresses. We shall be happy to do all in our power to obtain speedy and wide distribution and will send you galley-proofs for your approval as soon as it is physically possible to do so.

In view of our most friendly cooperation with Messrs Cassells, we shall fully respect the fact that they will distribute their British edition in Canada as well.

Enclosed you will find our check for the American currency equivalent of £1000, in accordance with your understanding with Mr Field.

Enclosure check $4035.00.

---

[1] Max Lincoln Schuster, 1897–1970. Educated at Pulitzer Graduate School of Journalism, Columbia University. Copywriter, *New York Evening World*, 1913. Correspondent, *Boston Evening Transcript*, United Press, 1913–17. Chief of Publicity, Bureau of War Risk Insurance, 1917–21. Founder and President, Simon & Schuster Publishers, 1921–66.

[2] Marshall Field III, 1893–1956. Educated at Cambridge University. 122nd Field Artillery, 1917–21. Investment Banker, Field, Gloare, Ward & Co., 1926. Owner, Simon & Schuster, 1944–56. Owner, *Chicago-Sun Newspaper*, 1948. *Secret Sessions Speeches* was published in Canada by McClelland & Stewart.

March 1946

Programme for trip to Fulton, Missouri
(Churchill papers, 2/230)

4–7 March 1946

March 4 – 1.15 p.m. Leave British Embassy in President Truman's car, to call at The White House for President Truman.
    Proceed to train.
    2.0 p.m. Leave Washington on Special Train.

March 5 – 8.45 a.m. (central time) Arrive St Louis, Missouri.
    9.0 a.m. Leave St Louis, Missouri
    11.30 a.m. Arrive Jefferson City, Missouri
    President Truman and Mr Churchill to drive in open car through Jefferson City and on to Fulton, a distance of 20 miles. If the weather is bad, a closed car will be used for the latter party of the journey.
    Lunch with Dr McCluer, President of Westminster College.
    3.15 p.m. Academic procession moves to gymnasium.
    3.30 p.m. Invocation, Moderator of the General Assembly of the Presbyterian Church (2 minutes).
    3.32 p.m. Statement of purpose of the John Findley Green Memorial Lectureship – President of the College (2 minutes).
    3.34 p.m. Introduction of Mr Winston Churchill by President Truman.
    THE GREEN FOUNDATION LECTURE – MR WINSTON CHURCHILL.
    Conferring of Honorary Degrees (takes little time).
        Citation of the President of the US.
        Citation of Mr Winston Churchill.
    Return to Dr McCluer's house for buffet supper.
    Travel by car to Jefferson City.
    6.45 p.m. Entrain at Jefferson City.
    9.15 p.m. Arrive St Louis.
    9.30 p.m. Leave St Louis.

March 6 – 10.30 a.m. Arrive Columbus, Ohio.
    President leaves train. Mr Churchill proceeds in same coach, with his personal staff and party to Pittsburgh, where coach is attached to public service train.

March 7 – 7.45 a.m. Arrive Washington.

Private Office: memorandum[1]
(Churchill papers, 2/230)[2]

4 March 1946

To Fulton with President	Return from Columbus without President
D General Vaughan[3] Mr Connelley[4]	D Mr Campbell[5] Mr Moarman[6]
C President	C Dr Harris[7] Col. Clarke
Bath	Bath
B Mr Churchill	B Mr Churchill
A Admiral Leahy[8]	A Sergeant Williams Sawyers

[1] This diagram reflects the hand-drawn original showing the allocation of accommodation in the VIP carriage of the President's train.

[2] This memo was handwritten.

[3] Harry Briggs Vaughan, 1888–1964. District Engineer, Philadelphia, 1940–3. Commanding Gen., UK Base Section, 1944–5; Bremen Post Command, 1945.

[4] Matthew J. Connelley, 1907–76. Civil servant. Appointments Secretary to the President, 1945–53.

[5] Ronald Ian Campbell, 1890–1983. Entered Diplomatic Service, 1914. Minister Plenipotentiary, Paris, 1938–9. Minister at Belgrade, 1939–41. Knighted, 1941. Minister in Washington DC, 1941–5. Ambassador to Egypt, 1946–50. Director, Royal Bank of Scotland, 1950–65.

[6] Daniel J. Moorman.

[7] E. G. Harris, 1903–77. On staff of Appointments Secretary Matthew Connelley, 1946. Prof., Journalism Dept, UCLA, 1950–70. Speechwriter for President Truman during a leave of absence, 1952.

[8] William D. Leahy, 1875–1959. Commissioned in US Navy, 1899. Adm., 1936. Chief of Naval Operations, 1937. Governor of Puerto Rico, 1939. American Ambassador to Vichy France, 1940–1. CoS to the President and to JCS, 1942–9. Hon. knighthood, 1945. Published his memoirs, *I Was There* (1950).

Winston S. Churchill: speech
('Winston S. Churchill, His Complete Speeches', volume 7, pages 7285–93)

5 March 1946 Fulton, Missouri

THE SINEWS OF PEACE

I am glad to come to Westminster College this afternoon, and am complimented that you should give me a degree. The name 'Westminster' is somehow familiar to me. I seem to have heard of it before. Indeed, it was at Westminster that I received a very large part of my education in politics, dialectic, rhetoric, and one or two other things. In fact we have both been educated at the same, or similar, or, at any rate, kindred establishments.

It is also an honour, perhaps almost unique, for a private visitor to be introduced to an academic audience by the President of the United States. Amid his heavy burdens, duties, and responsibilities – unsought but not recoiled from – the President has travelled a thousand miles to dignify and magnify our meeting here today and to give me an opportunity of addressing this kindred nation, as well as my own countrymen across the ocean, and perhaps some other countries too. The President has told you that it is his wish, as I am sure it is yours, that I should have full liberty to give my true and faithful counsel in these anxious and baffling times. I shall certainly avail myself of this freedom, and feel the more right to do so because any private ambitions I may have cherished in my younger days have been satisfied beyond my wildest dreams. Let me, however, make it clear that I have no official mission or status of any kind, and that I speak only for myself. There is nothing here but what you see.

I can therefore allow my mind, with the experience of a lifetime, to play over the problems which beset us on the morrow of our absolute victory in arms, and to try to make sure with what strength I have that what has been gained with so much sacrifice and suffering shall be preserved for the future glory and safety of mankind.

The United States stands at this time at the pinnacle of world power. It is a solemn moment for the American Democracy. For with primacy in power is also joined an awe-inspiring accountability to the future. If you look around you, you must feel not only the sense of duty done but also you must feel anxiety lest you fall below the level of achievement. Opportunity is here now, clear and shining for both our countries. To reject it or ignore it or fritter it away will bring upon us all the long reproaches of the aftertime. It is necessary that constancy of mind, persistency of purpose, and the grand simplicity of decision shall guide and rule the conduct of the English-speaking peoples in peace as they did in war. We must, and I believe we shall, prove ourselves equal to this severe requirement.

When American military men approach some serious situation they are wont to write at the head of their directive the words 'overall strategic concept.' There is wisdom in this, as it leads to clarity of thought. What then is the overall strategic concept which we should inscribe today? It is nothing less than the safety and welfare, the freedom and progress, of all the homes and families of all the men and women in all the lands. And here I speak particularly of the myriad cottage or apartment homes where the wage-earner strives amid the accidents and difficulties of life to guard his wife and children from privation and bring the family up in the fear of the Lord, or upon ethical conceptions which often play their potent part.

To give security to these countless homes, they must be shielded from the two giant marauders, war and tyranny. We all know the frightful disturbances in which the ordinary family is plunged when the curse of war swoops down upon the breadwinner and those for whom he works and contrives. The awful ruin of Europe, with all its vanished glories, and of large parts of Asia glares us in the eyes. When the designs of wicked men or the aggressive urge of mighty States dissolve over large areas the frame of civilized society, humble folk are confronted with difficulties with which they cannot cope. For them all is distorted, all is broken, even ground to pulp.

When I stand here this quiet afternoon I shudder to visualize what is actually happening to millions now and what is going to happen in this period when famine stalks the earth. None can compute what has been called 'the unestimated sum of human pain'. Our supreme task and duty is to guard the homes of the common people from the horrors and miseries of another war. We are all agreed on that.

Our American military colleagues, after having proclaimed their 'overall strategic concept' and computed available resources, always proceed to the next step – namely, the method. Here again there is widespread agreement. A world organization has already been erected for the prime purpose of preventing war, UNO, the successor of the League of Nations, with the decisive addition of the United States and all that that means, is already at work. We must make sure that its work is fruitful, that it is a reality and not a sham, that it is a force for action, and not merely a frothing of words, that it is a true temple of peace in which the shields of many nations can some day be hung up, and not merely a cockpit in a Tower of Babel. Before we cast away the solid assurances of national armaments for self-preservation we must be certain that our temple is built, not upon shifting sands or quagmires, but upon the rock. Anyone can see with his eyes open that our path will be difficult and also long, but if we persevere together as we did in the two world wars – though not, alas, in the interval between them – I cannot doubt that we shall achieve our common purpose in the end.

I have, however, a definite and practical proposal to make for action. Courts and magistrates may be set up but they cannot function without sheriffs and constables. The United Nations Organization must immediately begin to be equipped with an international armed force. In such a matter we can only go step by step, but we must begin now. I propose that each of the Powers and States should be invited to delegate a certain number of air squadrons to the service of the world organization. These squadrons would be trained and prepared in their own countries, but would move around in rotation from one country to another. They would wear the uniform of their own countries but with different badges. They would not be required to act against their own nation, but in other respects they would be directed by the world organization. This might be started on a modest scale and would grow as confidence grew. I wished to see this done after the first world war, and I devoutly trust it may be done forthwith.

It would nevertheless be wrong and imprudent to entrust the secret knowledge or experience of the atomic bomb, which the United States, Great Britain, and Canada now share, to the world organization, while it is still in its infancy. It would be criminal madness to cast it adrift in this still agitated and ununited world. No one in any country has slept less well in their beds because this knowledge and the method and the raw materials to apply it, are at present largely retained in American hands. I do not believe we should all have slept so soundly had the positions been reversed and if some Communist or neoFascist State monopolized for the time being these dread agencies. The fear of them alone might easily have been used to enforce totalitarian systems upon the free democratic world, with consequences appalling to human imagination. God has willed that this shall not be and we have at least a breathing space to set our house in order before this peril has to be encountered: and even then, if no effort is spared, we should still possess so formidable a superiority as to impose effective deterrents upon its employment, or threat of employment, by others. Ultimately, when the essential brotherhood of man is truly embodied and expressed in a world organization with all the necessary practical safeguards to make it effective, these powers would naturally be confided to that world organization.

Now I come to the second danger of these two marauders which threatens the cottage, the home, and the ordinary people − namely, tyranny. We cannot be blind to the fact that the liberties enjoyed by individual citizens throughout the British Empire are not valid in a considerable number of countries, some of which are very powerful. In these States control is enforced upon the common people by various kinds of allembracing police governments. The power of the State is exercised without restraint, either by dictators or by compact oligarchies operating through a privileged party and a political police. It is not our duty at this time when difficulties are so numerous to interfere forcibly in the internal affairs of countries which we have not conquered in war. But we must never cease to proclaim in fearless tones the great principles of freedom and the rights of man which are the joint inheritance of the Englishspeaking world and which through Magna Carta, the Bill of Rights, the Habeas Corpus, trial by jury, and the English common law find their most famous expression in the American Declaration of Independence.

All this means that the people of any country have the right, and should have the power by constitutional action, by free unfettered elections, with secret ballot, to choose or change the character or form of government under which they dwell; that freedom of speech and thought should reign; that courts of justice, independent of the executive, unbiased by any party, should administer laws which have received the broad assent of large majorities or are consecrated by time and custom. Here are the title deeds of freedom which should lie in every cottage home. Here is the message of the British and American peoples to mankind. Let us preach what we practise – let us practise what we preach.

I have now stated the two great dangers which menace the homes of the people: War and Tyranny. I have not yet spoken of poverty and privation which are in many cases the prevailing anxiety. But if the dangers of war and tyranny are removed, there is no doubt that science and cooperation can bring in the next few years to the world, certainly in the next few decades newly taught in the sharpening school of war, an expansion of material well-being beyond anything that has yet occurred in human experience. Now, at this sad and breathless moment, we are plunged in the hunger and distress which are the aftermath of our stupendous struggle; but this will pass and may pass quickly, and there is no reason except human folly or subhuman crime which should deny to all the nations the inauguration and enjoyment of an age of plenty. I have often used words which I learned fifty years ago from a great Irish–American orator, a friend of mine, Mr Bourke Cockran. 'There is enough for all. The earth is a generous mother; she will provide in plentiful abundance food for all her children if they will but cultivate her soil in justice and peace.' So far I feel that we are in full agreement.

Now, while still pursuing the method of realizing our overall strategic concept, I come to the crux of what I have travelled here to say. Neither the sure prevention of war, nor the continuous rise of world organization will be gained without what I have called the fraternal association of the English-speaking peoples. This means a special relationship between the British Commonwealth and Empire and the United States. This is no time for generalities, and I will venture to be precise. Fraternal association requires not only the growing friendship and mutual understanding between our two vast but kindred systems of society, but the continuance of the intimate relationship between our military advisers, leading to common study of potential dangers, the similarity of weapons and manuals of instructions, and to the interchange of officers and cadets at technical colleges. It should carry with it the continuance of the present facilities for mutual security by the joint use of all Naval and Air Force bases in the possession of either country all over the world. This would perhaps double the mobility of the American Navy and Air Force. It would greatly expand that of the British Empire Forces and it might well lead, if and as the world calms down, to important financial savings. Already we use together a large number of islands; more may well be entrusted to our joint care in the near future.

The United States has already a Permanent Defence Agreement with the Dominion of Canada, which is so devotedly attached to the British Commonwealth and Empire. This Agreement is more effective than many of those which have often been made under formal alliances. This principle should be extended to all British Commonwealths with full reciprocity. Thus, whatever happens, and thus only, shall we be secure ourselves and able to work together for the high and simple causes that are dear to us and bode no ill to any. Eventually there may come – I feel eventually there will come – the principle of common citizenship, but that we may be content to leave to destiny, whose outstretched arm many of us can already clearly see.

There is however an important question which we must ask ourselves. Would a special relationship between the United States and the British Commonwealth be inconsistent with our overriding loyalties to the World Organization? I reply that, on the contrary, it is probably the only means by which that organization will achieve its full stature and strength. There are already the special United States relations with Canada which I have just mentioned, and there are the special relations between the United States and the South American Republics. We British have our twenty years Treaty of Collaboration and Mutual Assistance with Soviet Russia. I agree with Mr Bevin, the Foreign Secretary of Great Britain, that it might well be a fifty years Treaty so far as we are concerned. We aim at nothing but mutual assistance and collaboration. The British have an alliance with Portugal unbroken since 1384, and which produced fruitful results at critical moments in the late war. None of these clash with the general interest of a world agreement, or a world organization; on the contrary they help it. 'In my father's house are many mansions.' Special associations between members of the United Nations which have no aggressive point against any other country, which harbour no design incompatible with the Charter of the United Nations, far from being harmful, are beneficial and, as I believe, indispensable.

I spoke earlier of the Temple of Peace. Workmen from all countries must build that temple. If two of the workmen know each other particularly well and are old friends, if their families are intermingled, and if they have 'faith in each other's purpose, hope in each other's future and charity towards each other's shortcomings' – to quote some good words I read here the other day – why cannot they work together at the common task as friends and partners? Why cannot they share their tools and thus increase each other's working powers? Indeed they must do so or else the temple may not be built, or, being built, it may collapse, and we shall all be proved again unteachable and have to go and try to learn again for a third time in a school of war, incomparably more rigorous than that from which we have just been released. The dark ages may return, the Stone Age may return on the gleaming wings of science, and what might now shower immeasurable material blessings upon mankind, may even bring about its total destruction. Beware, I say; time may be short. Do not let us take the course of allowing events to drift along until it is too late. If there is to be a fraternal association of the kind I have described, with all the extra strength and security which both our countries can derive from it, let us make sure that that great fact is known to the world, and that it plays its part in steadying and stabilizing the foundations of peace. There is the path of wisdom. Prevention is better than cure.

A shadow has fallen upon the scenes so lately lighted by the Allied victory. Nobody knows what Soviet Russia and its Communist international organization intends to do in the immediate future, or what are the limits, if any, to their expansive and proselytizing tendencies. I have a strong admiration and regard for the valiant Russian people and for my wartime comrade, Marshal Stalin. There is deep sympathy and goodwill in Britain – and I doubt not here also – towards the peoples of all the Russias and a resolve to persevere through many differences and rebuffs in establishing lasting friendships. We understand the Russian need to be secure on her western frontiers by the removal of all possibility of German aggression. We welcome Russia to her rightful place among the leading nations of the world. We welcome her flag upon the seas. Above all, we welcome constant, frequent and growing contacts between the Russian people and our own people on both sides of the Atlantic. It is my duty however, for I am sure you would wish me to state the facts as I see them to you, to place before you certain facts about the present position in Europe.

From Stettin in the Baltic to Trieste in the Adriatic, an iron curtain has descended across the Continent. Behind that line lie all the capitals of the ancient states of Central and Eastern Europe. Warsaw, Berlin, Prague, Vienna, Budapest, Belgrade, Bucharest and Sofia, all these famous cities and the populations around them lie in what I must call the Soviet sphere, and all are subject in one form or another, not only to Soviet influence but to a very high and, in many cases, increasing measure of control from Moscow. Athens alone – Greece with its immortal glories – is free to decide its future at an election under British, American and French observation. The Russian-dominated Polish Government has been encouraged to make enormous and wrongful inroads upon Germany, and mass expulsions of millions of Germans on a scale grievous and undreamed-of are now taking place. The Communist parties, which were very small in all these Eastern States of Europe, have been raised to pre-eminence and power far beyond their numbers and are seeking everywhere to obtain totalitarian control. Police governments are prevailing in nearly every case, and so far, except in Czechoslovakia, there is no true democracy.

Turkey and Persia are both profoundly alarmed and disturbed at the claims which are being made upon them and at the pressure exerted by the Moscow Government. An attempt is being made by the Russians in Berlin to build up a quasiCommunist party in their zone of Occupied Germany by showing special favours to groups of leftwing German leaders. At the end of the fighting last June, the American and British Armies withdrew westwards, in accordance with an earlier agreement, to a depth at some points of 150 miles upon a front of nearly four hundred miles, in order to allow our Russian allies to occupy this vast expanse of territory which the Western Democracies had conquered.

If now the Soviet Government tries, by separate action, to build up a proCommunist Germany in their areas, this will cause new serious difficulties in the British and American zones, and will give the defeated Germans the power of putting themselves up to auction between the Soviets and the Western Democracies. Whatever conclusions may be drawn from these facts – and facts they are – this is certainly not the Liberated Europe we fought to build up. Nor is it one which contains the essentials of permanent peace.

The safety of the world requires a new unity in Europe, from which no nation should be permanently outcast. It is from the quarrels of the strong parent races in Europe that the world wars we have witnessed, or which occurred in former times, have sprung. Twice in our own lifetime we have seen the United States, against their wishes and their traditions, against arguments, the force of which it is impossible not to comprehend, drawn by irresistible forces, into these wars in time to secure the victory of the good cause, but only after frightful slaughter and devastation had occurred. Twice the United States has had to send several millions of its young men across the Atlantic to find the war; but now war can find any nation, wherever it may dwell between dusk and dawn. Surely we should work with conscious purpose for a grand pacification of Europe, within the structure of the United Nations and in accordance with its Charter. That I feel is an open cause of policy of very great importance.

In front of the iron curtain which lies across Europe are other causes for anxiety. In Italy the Communist Party is seriously hampered by having to support the Communisttrained Marshal Tito's claims to former Italian territory at the head of the Adriatic. Nevertheless the future of Italy hangs in the balance. Again one cannot imagine a regenerated Europe without a strong France. All my public life I have worked for a strong France and I never lost faith in her destiny, even in the darkest hours. I will not lose faith now. However, in a great number of countries, far from the Russian frontiers and throughout the world, Communist fifth columns are established and work in complete unity and absolute obedience to the directions they receive from the Communist centre. Except in the British Commonwealth and in the United States where Communism is in its infancy, the Communist parties or fifth columns constitute a growing challenge and peril to Christian civilization. These are sombre facts for anyone to have to recite on the morrow of a victory gained by so much splendid comradeship in arms and in the cause of freedom and democracy; but we should be most unwise not to face them squarely while time remains.

The outlook is also anxious in the Far East and especially in Manchuria. The Agreement which was made at Yalta, to which I was a party, was extremely favourable to Soviet Russia, but it was made at a time when no one could say that the German war might not extend all through the summer and autumn of 1945 and when the Japanese war was expected to last for a further 18 months from the end of the German war. In this country you are all so well-informed about the Far East, and such devoted friends of China, that I do not need to expatiate on the situation there.

I have felt bound to portray the shadow which, alike in the west and in the east, falls upon the world. I was a high minister at the time of the Versailles Treaty and a close friend of Mr Lloyd-George, who was the head of the British delegation at Versailles. I did not myself agree with many things that were done, but I have a very strong impression in my mind of that situation, and I find it painful to contrast it with that which prevails now. In those days there were high hopes and unbounded confidence that the wars were over, and that the League of Nations would become allpowerful. I do not see or feel that same confidence or even the same hopes in the haggard world at the present time.

On the other hand I repulse the idea that a new war is inevitable; still more that it is imminent. It is because I am sure that our fortunes are still in our own hands and that we hold the power to save the future, that I feel the duty to speak out now that I have the occasion and the opportunity to do so. I do not believe that Soviet Russia desires war. What they desire is the fruits of war and the indefinite expansion of their power and doctrines. But what we have to consider here today while time remains, is the permanent prevention of war and the establishment of conditions of freedom and democracy as rapidly as possible in all countries. Our difficulties and dangers will not be removed by closing our eyes to them. They will not be removed by mere waiting to see what happens; nor will they be removed by a policy of appeasement. What is needed is a settlement, and the longer this is delayed, the more difficult it will be and the greater our dangers will become.

From what I have seen of our Russian friends and Allies during the war, I am convinced that there is nothing they admire so much as strength, and there is nothing for which they have less respect than for weakness, especially military weakness. For that reason the old doctrine of a balance of power is unsound. We cannot afford, if we can help it, to work on narrow margins, offering temptations to a trial of strength. If the Western Democracies stand together in strict adherence to the principles of the United Nations Charter, their influence for furthering those principles will be immense and no one is likely to molest them. If however they become divided or falter in their duty and if these all-important years are allowed to slip away then indeed catastrophe may overwhelm us all.

Last time I saw it all coming and cried aloud to my own fellow-countrymen and to the world, but no one paid any attention. Up till the year 1933 or even 1935, Germany might have been saved from the awful fate which has overtaken her and we might all have been spared the miseries Hitler let loose upon mankind. There never was a war in all history easier to prevent by timely action than the one which has just desolated such great areas of the globe. It could have been prevented in my belief without the firing of a single shot, and Germany might be powerful, prosperous and honoured today; but no one would listen and one by one we were all sucked into the awful whirlpool. We surely must not let that happen again. This can only be achieved by reaching now, in 1946, a good understanding on all points with Russia under the general authority of the United Nations Organization and by the maintenance of that good understanding through many peaceful years, by the world instrument, supported by the whole strength of the Englishspeaking world and all its connections. There is the solution which I respectfully offer to you in this Address to which I have given the title 'The Sinews of Peace.'

Let no man underrate the abiding power of the British Empire and the Commonwealth. Because you see the 46 millions in our island harassed about their food supply, of which they only grow one half, even in wartime, or because we have difficulty in restarting our industries and export trade after six years of passionate war effort, do not suppose that we shall not come through these dark years of privation as we have come through the glorious years of agony, or that half a century from now, you will not see 70 or 80 millions of Britons spread about the world and united in defence of our traditions, our way of life, and of the world causes which you and we espouse. If the population of the Englishspeaking Commonwealths be added to that of the United States with all that such cooperation implies in the air, on the sea, all over the globe and in science and in industry, and in moral force, there will be no quivering, precarious balance of power to offer its temptation to ambition or adventure. On the contrary, there will be an overwhelming assurance of security. If we adhere faithfully to the Charter of the United Nations and walk forward in sedate and sober strength seeking no one's land or treasure, seeking to lay no arbitrary control upon the thoughts of men; if all British moral and material forces and convictions are joined with your own in fraternal association, the highroads of the future will be clear, not only for us but for all, not only for our time, but for a century to come.

The Times: article
(The Times)

6 March 1946

MR CHURCHILL'S SPEECH

Mr Churchill's speech at Fulton, Missouri, yesterday was primarily an American occasion. None of the war leaders – not even President Roosevelt himself – had a stronger appeal to the American imagination than Mr Churchill, and the fact that he was speaking as a private citizen on a well-earned holiday did nothing to detract from the interest evoked by his appearance on an American platform. It is a sign of the times that he could commend to an enthusiastic American audience the advantages of common international action and should have made it clear that these advantages would only be reaped if Uno were equipped with an 'international armed force'. Mr Churchill has never been one of those who believed that words could supply the place of action, and it was appropriate that he would have been insistent on the need for clothing international cooperation in the concrete forms of power.

It was within this framework that Mr Churchill reiterated his eloquent plea for 'the fraternal association of the English-speaking peoples'. What he called 'the special relationship between the British Commonwealth and Empire and the United States' rests on the unshakable natural foundation of a common language and a large common stock of ideas. Mr Churchill proposed to give form to this natural community of outlook by an agreement for 'the joint use of all naval and air force bases in the possession of either country all over the world'. It will be interesting to watch American reactions to this proposal. The difficulties in Anglo-American relations have traditionally arisen at the point where the call comes to translate common sentiment into common political commitments. What Mr Churchill said of the Russians in another part of this speech is equally true of Americans: they admire strength, and have no respect for weakness. Tradition may have been modified under stress of war by a growing American realization that the integrity of the British Isles is an element, and perhaps an indispensable element, in American security. But there is no reason at all to expect American action, or even universal support from American opinion, for the defence of essential British strategic and economic positions in the Middle East, in Asia, or in Africa. To most of his fellow countrymen there will seem to be logic and good sense in Mr Churchill's plan. But it is still understandably easy to excite prejudice in the United States against specific commitments oversea; and nothing would be more dangerous, or more calculated to put American friendship in jeopardy, than an attempt to frame British foreign policy on a presumption of assured American backing. Anglo-American friendship is an essential element in British policy. It can never be its sole and all-sufficient foundation or an excuse for failing to pursue independent action along the lines which British interests and British prosperity require.

In the light of these considerations particular interest attached to the passages of Mr Churchill's speech, which had been the subject of a good deal of unauthorized speculation in advance, on relations with the Soviet Union. The general tone of most of these passages was a refutation of the prophets. Mr Churchill cited the Anglo-Soviet treaty of 1942, which he too would like to see extended from twenty to fifty years, among the special ties between nations which would give strength to world organization, and he expressed the determination of the British people to 'persevere through many difficulties and rebuffs in establishing lasting friendship'. Nor did he suggest that it would be anything but hazardous to ignore the point of view of the vigorous and masterful Power which bestrides eastern Europe and a large part of Asia, even when that point of view seems clumsily and rudely expressed and difficult for minds reared in a different tradition to understand. Relations between Great Britain and the Soviet Union provide at this time a cardinal test for British statesmanship. They require to be based, as Mr Churchill said, not on 'appeasement' but on 'settlement'. That settlement must take account both of the effective interest and of the effective power of both parties. So far as Britain is concerned, favourable results will not be achieved by a policy of words unaccompanied by action, and still less by reliance on American support as a substitute for a balanced and carefully weighed British policy. Nothing that Mr Churchill said at Fulton yesterday was incompatible with full recognition of these underlying realities.

Mr Churchill was perhaps less happy in the passages in his speech in which he appeared to contrast 'western democracy' and 'Communism' as irreconcilable opposites dividing, or attempting to divide, the world between them today. Yet it would be an assumption of despair to hold that they are doomed to fatal contest. Indeed, a clearer recognition of two points might well serve to mitigate on both sides some of the asperities of recent exchanges. The first is that there are many forms of government intermediate between western democracy and Communism, and some of them may be better adapted at the present stage of development to the requirements of eastern Europe or of the Middle or Far East. The second is that, while western democracy and Communism are in many respects opposed, they have much to learn from each other – Communism in the working of political institutions and in the establishment of individual rights, western democracy in the development of economic and social planning.

The ideological warfare between western democracy and Communism cannot result in an out-and-out victory for either side. The issue will be determined neither by clashes of eloquence nor by clashes of arms, but by the success of the great nations in dealing with the problems of social organization in the broadest sense which the war has left behind it. Meanwhile the realistic settlement of outstanding issues – in Persia, in Germany, in Manchuria, in Turkey, and elsewhere – which Mr Churchill rightly demands stands first on the agenda; and no settlement can be durable which fails to provide a basis of mutual security and respect for obligation without which there can be no hope of lasting peace.

Chicago Sun: article
(Churchill papers, 4/5)

6 March 1946

CHURCHILL'S CALL FOR WORLD DOMINATION

Winston Churchill at Fulton was fighting for his world. It is a world which no longer exists in reality. It cannot be reconstituted. It ought not to be reconstituted. To follow the standard raised by this great but blinded aristocrat would be to march to the world's most ghastly war.

We say that Churchill is great, and so he is, for strength and genius to which tribute has many times been paid on this page, and to which the world owes much. But – quite aside from the lethal wrongness of his goal – his greatness was heavily marred in the Fulton speech by a sanctimoniousness unworthy of any great man.

His boast of the happy freedom of prostrate Greece; his picture of the world's God-fearing cottages as the beneficiary of his strategy of world domination; his failure – while denouncing Russian expansion – to utter a syllable concerning British guns which fell colonial peoples struggling for freedom and dignity; his recourse to Scripture, 'In my Father's house there are many mansions,' to justify a world system of alliances dominated by a master alliance of Anglo-Saxon *herrenvolk* – such sanctimony is not what one ought to be able to expect of Winston Churchill.

But Churchill's personality is not the issue. The Churchill objective is. And that objective is world domination, through arms, by the United States and the British Empire.

Gone, he says, is the balance of power. And gone it is. If he could reconstitute it, to permit Britain's holding the balance again, he would do so. He knows that this is impossible. Russia and America are the two great powers. So, paying scornful lip service to the United Nations, heaping denunciation on the Soviet Union, he appeals to the United States for an alliance – even an eventual union of nations – to save the privileged imperial world which he cannot believe is dead.

If the American people accepted his plan – thus belying the principles of emancipation and equality which lie deep in their consciences – the plan might, indeed, bring a somewhat longer twilight of the old imperial order than otherwise will be witnessed. Churchill would have us maintain not only 'fraternal association' of our military advisers, similarity of weapons and military methods, and exchange of officers and cadets. Britain and America would mutually use each other's naval and air bases 'all over the world'. That, he hopes, will be strong allurement to our military nationalists: [. . .]

For the sake of maintaining these bases in a world which then would be careening to war, the Churchill alliance would tie America to maintaining the outposts of the British Empire around the world, against subject peoples struggling to escape the yoke.

With blind disregard of the warnings of the atomic scientists, he assumes that the Anglo-Saxon peoples can long keep the 'secrets' of the atomic bomb. In a world where more nations than Russia live in fear from our atomic monopoly, he quips that 'no one in any country' has slept less well because of the monopoly. When he says it would be 'madness' to entrust secret atomic knowledge to the United Nations in its infancy, he is saying that we must have no world control, no inspections. For these mean nothing unless control and inspection function with the requisite knowledge.

And what does he offer us for safety from atomic destruction? A 'breathing spell' through monopoly – then 'superiority' after 'Communist or neo-Fascist' states get the bombs. The scientists will not bear him out in the contention that there is any safety that way. How many consciences will bear him out in a contention that it is morally tenable?

Russian acts of aggressive expansionism indeed cause grave alarm. We want a settlement too; but a settlement of just agreement – not an attempted freezing of the *status quo* which was won by power and aggressions in the past. Western civil liberties are precious to us, as to Mr Churchill. We want them extended through Europe, Russia, Asia. But that will only be if the gap is bridged between Russia and the West. It will never be bridged in Mr Churchill's way.

To be sure, he speaks again of his regard for Russia, and Stalin. But such words are hollow in an address of threat and menace which would pose the British and American peoples against Russia to win 'peace' for a 'century' through an alliance of the fortunate of the earth.

We hope that no syllable of official American encouragement was given Mr Churchill for this speech. But there is an arresting sequence of events. The putting up of the 'atom spy scare'; the Vandenberg[1] speech against Russia; the Byrnes speech against Russia; the report that Mr Churchill conferred at the White House in advance on his address; Mr Truman's presence with him on the platform 'to dignify and magnify' the meeting [. . .]

---

[1] Arthur Hendrick Vandenberg, 1884–1951. Married, 1918, Hazel Harper Whittaker. Educated at University of Michigan. Editor, *Grand Rapids Herald*, 1906–28. US Senator from Michigan, 1928–51. US Representative to UN General Assembly, 1945. Rep. Senate Conference Chairman, 1945–7. Chairman, Senate Committee on Foreign Relations, 1947–9. President pro tempore, Senate, 1947–9.

March 1946

Winston S. Churchill to Marshall Field
(Churchill papers, 4/5)

7 March 1946 British Embassy
Washington DC

Dear Mr Marshall Field,

It was a great surprise to me to read in the *Chicago Sun* the enclosed leading article of March 6. I seem to have been under a complete misapprehension about the *Chicago Sun*. I had understood it was an attempt to counter the vicious McCormick[1] propaganda and I greatly admired the public spirit which had led you to make exertions to that end. As the views expressed here are the stock Communist output, I feel it might be an embarrassment to you if your publications were in any way connected with me. I feel this the more because I was about to suggest to you that the 'poisonous' speech I delivered at Fulton should be added to the little volume we have under consideration, and this will be done in the English edition. I should be much obliged therefore if you would send me back the copy which I sent to you, and which you may have forwarded to your staff.

I must apologize to you for not having followed sufficiently closely the line taken by your newspapers, and for having misled myself so foolishly about them.

I trust our personal relations may remain unaffected.

Winston S. Churchill to President Harry S Truman
(Truman papers)[2]

7 March 1946

My dear Harry, (You see I am obeying yr commands)

I send you a set of my war time books which you may care to put in your library. They cover a long and stormy period. There are two other volumes which will come to you when they are published in the next few months, namely 'Victory' and 'Secret Session Speeches'. To these last I shall add the Fulton address.[3]

---

[1] Robert Rutherford McCormick, 1880–1955. Known as 'Col.'. Born in Chicago. Cousin of James Medill Patterson. Educated partly in England. Member of Chicago City Council, 1904–6. President, *Chicago Tribune*, 1911. War Correspondent with British, French and Russian forces, 1915. Maj., 1st Illinois Cavalry, US–Mexican border, 1916. On active service in France, 1918. Col., General Staff, 1918. Editor and publisher of the bitterly anti-British *Chicago Tribune* from 1919 until his death. Chairman of the Board of the *New York Daily News*, 1919–25. President, *Washington Times Herald*, 1949–54.

[2] This letter was handwritten.

[3] In fact, the Fulton speech was not published in book form until 1948, when it was included in – and provided the title for – Churchill's first volume of post-war speeches, *The Sinews of Peace*.

MARCH 1946 241

I enjoyed my journey with you so much and am most grateful for all the kindness you have shown me during my visit to your well-loved country.

Winston S. Churchill to Clement Attlee and Ernest Bevin
(Churchill papers, 2/4)

7 March 1946
Most Secret and Personal

The President told me, as we started on our journey from Washington to Fulton, Missouri, that the United States is sending the body of the Turkish Ambassador,[1] who died here some days ago, back to Turkey in the American battleship *Missouri*, which is the vessel on which the Japanese surrender was signed and is probably the strongest battleship afloat. He added that the *Missouri* would be accompanied by a strong task force which would remain in the Marmara for an unspecified period. Admiral Leahy told me that the task force would consist of another battleship of the greatest power, two of the latest and strongest aircraft carriers, several cruisers and about a dozen destroyers, with the necessary ancillary ships. Both mentioned the fact that the *Missouri* class carry over 140 anti-aircraft guns. I asked about the secrecy of this movement and was told that it was known that the body of the late Ambassador was being returned in a warship but that the details of the task force would not become known before March 15. I feel it my duty to report these facts to you, though it is quite possible you may have already been informed through other channels. At any rate, please on no account make use of the information until you have received it from channels, other than my personal contact with the President.

2. The above strikes me as a very important act of state and one calculated to make Russia understand that she must come to reasonable terms of discussion with the Western Democracies. From our point of view, I am sure that the arrival and stay of such a powerful American Fleet in the Straits must be entirely beneficial, both as reassuring Turkey and Greece and as placing a demurrer on what Bevin called cutting our life-line through the Mediterranean by the establishment of a Russian naval base at Tripoli.

3. I did not consult the President on the exact text of my speech at Fulton before I finished it, but he read a mimiographed reproduction which was made on the train in its final form, several hours before I delivered it. He told me he thought it was admirable and would do nothing but good, though it would make a stir. He seemed equally pleased during and after. I also showed

---

[1] Munir Ertegun, 1883–1944. Educated at Istanbul University. Turkish Ambassador to Switzerland, 1925–30; to France, 1930–2; to UK, 1932–4; to US, 1934–44. Body sent back to Turkey for burial owing to there being no mosque in Washington DC.

it to Mr Byrnes the night before leaving Washington, making it clear that this was quite private and informal. He was excited about it and did not suggest any alterations. Admiral Leahy, to whom I showed it first of all, was enthusiastic. Naturally I take complete and sole personal responsibility for what I said, for I altered nothing as the result of my contacts with these high American authorities. I think you ought to know exactly what the position is and hope you will observe the very strong and precise terms in which I disclaim any official mission or status of any kind and that I spoke only for myself. If necessary these words of mine could be quoted.

4. Having spent nearly three days in the most intimate, friendly contact with the President and his immediate circle, and also having had a long talk with Mr Byrnes, I have no doubt that the Executive forces here are deeply distressed at the way they are being treated by Russia and that they do not intend to put up with treaty breaches in Persia or encroachments in Manchuria and Korea, or pressure for the Russian expansion at the expense of Turkey or in the Mediterranean. I am convinced that some show of strength and resisting power is necessary to a good settlement with Russia. I predict that this will be the prevailing opinion in the United States in the near future.

Winston S. Churchill: speech
('Winston S. Churchill, His Complete Speeches', volume 7, pages 7293–6)

8 March 1946   General Assembly of Virginia

THE ENGLISH-SPEAKING PEOPLES

I was deeply moved by the glowing terms of the Joint Resolution of both branches of the Legislature inviting me here to address the General Assembly of Virginia. I take it as a high honour to be present here this morning to discharge that task. I always value being asked to address a Parliament. I have already on two occasions in the war addressed the Congress of the United States. I have addressed the Canadian Parliament. I have addressed a Joint Session of the Belgian Legislature, more recently, and there is a place of which you may have heard across the ocean called the House of Commons, to which, invited or uninvited, I have, from time to time, had things to say. I have also had invitations, couched in terms for which I am most grateful, from the State Legislatures of South Carolina, Kentucky and Mississippi. It would have given me the greatest pleasure to accept and fulfil all of these. But as I have not the life and strength to repay all the kindness which is offered me, I felt that these other States would be willing to accept the primacy of the Virginia Assembly, as the most ancient, law-making body on the mainland of the western hemisphere. And thus I find myself here before you this morning in Richmond in the historic capital of world-famous Virginia.

I am also about to visit Williamsburg. During the war, at one of our Conferences, General Marshall arranged to take the British Chiefs of Staff for a visit to Williamsburg and I had planned to go with them, but the work I had to do made it necessary for me to remain in Washington; and so, on this visit to the United States, I had promised myself the treat of seeing Williamsburg, and my friend, General Eisenhower, who is with us today, undertook to pilot me around. I have great satisfaction in meeting him over here. We had a lot of business to do together during what I believe has been called, in another connection, 'the late unpleasantness' and I have formed impressions that will last me all my days of his single-hearted purpose, wide and profound views on military science and his great power of making the soldiers and officers of our two countries work together under all the shocks and strains of war as if they were the soldiers of one single nation.

I hope I shall acquit myself to your satisfaction but the responsibility for what may happen is yours. Do you not think you are running some risk in inviting me to give you my faithful counsel on this occasion? You have not asked to see beforehand what I am going to say. I might easily, for instance, blurt out a lot of things, which people know in their hearts are true, but are a bit shy of saying in public, and this might cause a regular commotion and get you all into trouble. However, the people of Virginia and, above all, the people of Richmond have proved in the past that they have strong nerves and that they can face not only facts but fate with fortitude and pride. Of course my mind goes back into the past so much of which we have in common. The light of the Elizabethan age, which Shakespeare, Raleigh[1] and Grenville[2] adorned, casts its unfading lustre upon our scene here in Williamsburg nearby. This was a cradle of the Great Republic in which more than 150 years afterwards the strong champions of freedom and independence were found to have been nursed. With what care did these early Fathers of our modern inspiration preserve the title deeds of freedom in Parliamentary privilege, in trial by jury, in the Habeas Corpus, in Magna Carta, and in English Common Law! With what vigilance did Thomas Jefferson,[3] Patrick Henry[4] and Robert

---

[1] Walter Raleigh, 1554–1618. Poet and explorer. Educated at Oxford and Middle Temple. Fought in France, 1569; Ireland, 1580. Capt., King's Guard, 1587. Explored Guinea in search of El Dorado, 1595. Landed at Roanoke in present-day North Carolina, 1589.

[2] Richard Grenville, 1542–91. Educated at Cambridge and the Inner Temple. Sheriff of Cornwall, 1577. Knighted, 1577. Voyaged to Roanoke Island, 1585–6.

[3] Thomas Jefferson, 1743–1826. Author of the Declaration of Independence, 1774. Virginia Delegate, Second Continental Congress, 1775–6. Governor, Virginia, 1779–81. Virginia Delegate, Congress of the Confederation, 1783–4. US Minister to France, 1785–9. Secretary of State, 1790–3. US Vice-President, 1797–1801. President, 1801–9.

[4] Patrick Henry, 1736–99. Signatory of the Declaration of Independence, 1776. Governor, Virginia, 1776–9, 1784–6.

Henry Lee,[1] and even George Washington,[2] the Father of his country, defend these title deeds in later, unhappy but pregnant times! The theme of individual liberty and of the rights of citizens so painfully evolved across the centuries in England was upheld through every stress and confusion by Virginia and that theme lights the English-speaking world today. It lights our world and it is also a beacon shining through the mists and storms to many lands, where the rights of man – his honour, his happiness, his freedom – are yearned for or are so far enjoyed only precariously. I salute you here in this General Assembly as the guardians of the sacred flame.

Another century passes across our minds and we see Virginia and Richmond the centre of a tragedy which, however agonising at that time, is now forever illuminated by drama and romance. I have visited most of your battlefields on the peninsula, on the Happahannock, in the Wilderness, and I was guided there some years ago by your distinguished historian Mr Freeman,[3] who is, I believe, here today, and whose works are a solid contribution, not only to the fame of the south but to the whole strength of the indissoluble Union. Yet it is in the words of an English General Officer that I shall express myself to you this morning. General Henderson,[4] the author of *The Life of Stonewall Jackson* and of *The Campaign of Fredericksburg*, was a man I knew nearly 40 years ago, and this is what he wrote:

> Far and Wide, between the mountains and the sea stretches the fair Virginia for which Lee[5] and Jackson and their soldiers,
> 'One equal temper of heroic hearts',
> fought so well and unavailingly; . . . yet her brows are bound with glory, the legacy of her lost children; and her spotless name, uplifted by their victories and manhood, is high among the nations. Surely she may rest

---

[1] Richard Henry Lee, 1732–94. Virginia Delegate, First Continental Congress, 1774; Second Continental Congress, 1775. Signatory of the Declaration of Independence, 1776; of the Articles of Confederation, 1778. President of the Confederation Congress, 1784–5. US Senator from Virginia, 1789–92. President *pro tempore*, US Senate, 1792.

[2] George Washington, 1732–99. Virginia Delegate, First Continental Congress, 1774; Second Continental Congress, 1775. C-in-C, Continental Army, 1775–83. Senior Officer, US Army, 1789–99. US President, 1789–97.

[3] Douglas Southall Freeman, 1886–1953. Born at Lynchburg, Va. Educated at Richmond College, 1904; Johns Hopkins College, 1918. Lectured widely, including at the Universities of California, Columbia, Pennsylvania, Richmond and Rochester, and Northwestern University. Employed by the *Times Dispatch* of Richmond, 1928, and associated with the paper until his death. Rector and President of the Board of Trustees of Richmond College, from 1936 until his death. Author of several books, including a four-volume life of Robert E. Lee, for which he won the Pulitzer Prize in 1934.

[4] George Francis Robert Henderson, 1854–1903. Educated at St John's College, Oxford. Instructor in Tactics, Military Law and Administration, Sandhurst, 1892–9. Author of *Stonewall Jackson and the American Civil War* (1898) and *The Campaign of Fredericksburg* (1899).

[5] Robert E. Lee, 1807–70. Graduated from West Point, 1829. 2nd Lt, 1829. Capt., 1836. Maj., 1847. Superintendent, Military Academy at West Point, 1852–5. Resigned his commission, April 1861. Commissioned Maj.-Gen. in the Army of the Confederate States, May 1861. Confederate General in the American Civil War. Surrendered to Gen. Ulysses S. Grant at Appomattox Court House, 1865. President of Washington University, Lexington, Va., 1865.

content, knowing that so long as men turn to the records of history will their deeds live, giving to all time one of the noblest examples of unyielding courage and devotion the world has known.

My grandfather (Mr Leonard Jerome)[1] was a Northerner in the state of New York, and you would not expect me to believe the cause for which he strove. We have moved on into a broader age and larger combinations. Old battles are remembered not as sources of bitterness but to celebrate the martial virtues and civic fidelity of both sides in that immortal struggle. Out of this story have also come examples of high character in which Americans have shown themselves in no wise wanting in the new trials and tribulations through which we have just passed.

Today the American Union is the most powerful champion of national and individual freedom and it carries with it a large portion of the hopes of men. There was about General Robert E. Lee a quality of selflessness which raises him to the very highest rank of men, whether soldiers or statesmen, who have been concerned with the fortunes of nations. And in General Marshall and in General Eisenhower, and others of the Army and Navy of the United States whom I could mention, that character, that quality of selflessness has been a bond uniting all Allied Armies and the key to the victory which we have gained together.

It has been said that the dominant lesson of history is that mankind is unteachable. You will remember how my dear friend, the late President Roosevelt, had to argue only a few years ago, that Americans were not what is called 'soft' and how he asserted that this was 'The land of unending challenge', and I myself have read in secret documents German reports which spoke before they met them of 'these ridiculous American troops'. Surely these European countries should not have forgotten or ignored so soon the example of tenacity, willpower and self-devotion which shines through all the records of the great war between the American States. We, too, in our British islands and in our great self-governing Empire spread about the world, have proved that our race when stirred to its depth has qualities deserving of respect.

In fact, in proportion to our numbers, our efforts, our sacrifices and our losses have not been surpassed. Moreover, it fell to us to have the honour of standing alone for a whole year against the main strength of the mighty Axis and the time for preparation which was thus gained was, as I am sure General Eisenhower will agree, a vital service to the United States and to the common cause.

---

[1] Leonard Walter Jerome, 1817–91. A lawyer and small-town newspaper proprietor. Married, 1849, Clarissa Hall. Came to New York in 1855, becoming a successful stockbroker and financier. Principal proprietor of the *New York Times*. US Consul in Trieste, 1851–2. A keen yachtsman, a patron of opera, and founder of the American Jockey Club. Father of Jennie (Lady Randolph Churchill), Clara (Mrs Moreton Frewen) and Leonie (Lady Leslie).

But it is upon the future rather than upon the past that I wish to rest this morning. In these last years of my life there is a message of which I conceive myself to be a bearer. It is a very simple message which can be well understood by the people of both our countries. It is that we should stand together. We should stand together in malice to none, in greed for nothing but in defence of those causes which we hold dear not only for our own benefit, but because we believe they mean the honour and happiness of long generations of men. We ought, as I said to the Congress of the United States in a dark hour in 1941, to walk together in majesty and peace. That I am sure is the wish of the overwhelming majority of the 200 million Britons and Americans who are spread about the globe. That this is our destiny, or, as most of us would put it, the Will of God, seems sure and certain. How it is to be expressed, in what way and in what hour it is to be achieved I cannot tell.

I read the other day that an English nobleman, whose name is new to me, has stated that England would have to become the 49th state of the American Union. I read yesterday that an able American editor had written that the United States ought not to be asked to re-enter the British Empire. It seems to me and I dare say it seems to you, that the path of wisdom lies somewhere between these scarecrow extremes. We must find the means and the method of working together not only in times of war and mortal anguish but in times of peace with all its bewilderments and clamour and clatter of tongues. It is in the years of peace that wars are prevented and that those foundations are laid upon which the noble structures of the future can be built. But peace will not be preserved without the virtues that make victory possible in war. Peace will not be preserved by pious sentiments expressed in terms of platitudes or by official grimaces and diplomatic correctitude, however desirable this may be from time to time. It will not be preserved by casting aside in dangerous years the panoply of warlike strength. There must be earnest thought. There must also be faithful perseverance and foresight. Greatheart must have his sword and armour to guard the pilgrims on their way. Above all, among the English-speaking peoples, there must be the union of hearts based upon conviction and common ideals. That is what I offer. That is what I seek.

MARCH 1946

James Forrestal[1] to Winston S. Churchill
(*Churchill papers, 2/226*)

8 March 1946   Washington DC

My dear Mr Churchill,

I telephoned Lady Halifax today to ask her to say to you that in case you felt like coming to my house for a meal any time during your stay I would be delighted. She tells me you are booked solid. If your plans should alter, the invitation stands.

I probably have been remiss in not sending you this message earlier but I assumed there were so many pressures on you that you might be grateful if some were withheld.

Averell[2] is back and in good form. I do not think you would find him in any profound disagreement with your observations of last Tuesday.[3]

Winston S. Churchill: record of a speech
(*Churchill papers, 2/226*)

9 March 1946   The Pentagon
                                                                                                              Washington DC

At the invitation of Secretary of War Robert P. Patterson[4] and General of the Army Dwight D. Eisenhower, Mr Winston Churchill met informally today several Army and Navy officers with whom he was associated in the Mediterranean and European campaigns and also a number of Army and Navy officers and War and Navy Department officials whom he had not met previously.

---

[1] James V. Forrestal, 1892–1949. Under-Secretary, US Navy Dept (the position held by Franklin D. Roosevelt in WWI), 1940–4. Established a Controlled Materials Plan, to establish priorities with regard to materials. Sent to London to negotiate Lend-Lease arrangements, 1941. Acting Secretary of the Navy, 1944. An eye-witness of the Allied landings in the South of France 1944 (as was Churchill). Recommended unification of all three services into a Department of Defense. Opposed too rapid a demobilization, 1945.

[2] William Averell Harriman, 1891–1986.Chairman of the Board, Merchant Shipping Corporation, 1917–25; Union Pacific Railroad, 1932–46. Member, Business Advisory Council, Dept of Commerce, 1933–40. Roosevelt's emissary (Special Representative) in London, to negotiate Lend-Lease arrangements, March 1941. Accompanied Lord Beaverbrook on his mission to Moscow, with the rank of Ambassador, Sep. 1941. Served on Combined Production and Resources Board, London, 1942. US Ambassador to Moscow, 1943–6; to Britain, 1946. US Secretary of Commerce, 1946–8. Special Assistant to President Truman, 1950–1. Chairman, NATO Commission on Defence Plans, 1951. Asst Secretary of State, Far Eastern Affairs, 1961–3. US negotiator, Limited Test Ban Treaty, 1963; Vietnam peace talks, Paris, 1968–9. Married, 1971, Pamela Leland Hayward (Pamela Digby), Randolph Churchill's former wife.

[3] Reproduced above (pp. 227–35).

[4] Robert Porter Patterson, 1891–1952. Born in Glens Falls, NY. Educated at Harvard University, 1915. On active service, WWI. 2nd Lt, 1917. DSC, 1918. Married, 1920, Margaret Winchester. Appointed Judge, Southern District Court of New York, 1930; Second Circuit Court of Appeals, 1939. Asst Secretary of War, 1940. Under-Secretary of War, 1940–5. Secretary of War, 1945–7. Died in a plane crash in Elizabeth, NJ.

The meeting was held in the Office of the Secretary of War at 5 p.m. today (March 9, 1946).

Mr Churchill was introduced by General Eisenhower who expressed his pleasure at having been closely associated with the former British Prime Minister during the campaign in North Africa and Europe. In a brief speech, Mr Churchill expressed his personal appreciation and that of the British Government to the American officers who organized and led the United States forces in the war.

In introducing Mr Churchill, General Eisenhower said:

'Gentlemen, I am not going to consume time by needless introduction of our distinguished visitor today, but there is one personal quality in our friendship and association during the war to which I should like to bring your attention. Because of his position as Defense Minister in addition to that as Prime Minister, he was associated more closely with the operation of the British Chiefs of Staff than was the case of our own President. Because of that and because he was kind enough to invite me often to those meetings, there developed a very close association between the Defense Minister of Great Britain and myself with respect to the operations both in the Mediterranean and later in Europe.

The only thing that I wanted to say was this: In the course of that association there never was a single instance when the full might of the British Empire, and I mean 'scraping the bottom of the barrel' was not available to an Allied operation once it had been agreed upon. That was due to the force, the determination and the leadership of the Prime Minister of Great Britain. Because most of you have not been privileged to have the close association that I did, I was very happy when at the request of the Secretary of War, Mr Churchill consented to come today in order to renew World War contacts he made with many of us, and, in addition, to come a little closer to some of those that were affected by his decisions, but who did not have that privilege of his close association. So he has consented to be with us today and have a handshake with all of you.'

Mr Churchill said:

'General of the Army Eisenhower, Fleet Admiral Leahy, Fleet Admiral Nimitz and General of the Air – am I right – General of the Air Spaatz?[1] It is indeed a very great pleasure and honor to me that the Secretary of War and General Eisenhower should have asked me here today and have given

[1] Carl Spaatz, 1891–1974. Entered West Point Military Academy, 1910. Served with American Expeditionary Force, France, 1917–18. US observer in Britain during Battle of Britain, 1940. OC US 8th Air Force and Commanding Gen., USAAF, European Theatre, 1942; North-West African Air Force, 1943. Commanding Gen., Strategic Bombing Force, operating against Germany, 1944. Hon. knighthood, 1944. Commanding Gen., US Strategic Air Forces in Pacific, supervising final strategic bombing of Japan, 1945. Commanding Gen., USAAF, 1946–7. CoS, USAAF, 1947–8.

me an opportunity, before going home, to meet the high officers of the United States services and to express to them on behalf of my own country and of the British services our admiration and gratitude for all they have done in this great common struggle carried to absolute victory in arms.

The prevailing feature of our work together was the intimacy of association. Language is a great bridge. There are many, many ideas we have in common and also practice: but there was a spirit of loyalty, of good will, of comradeship which never has been seen in all the history of war between Allied Armies, Navies, Air Forces fighting together side by side.

On General Eisenhower's staff, which I saw often and closely in Africa, in France and in Germany, it was carried to extreme perfection. And, as you know, the best people were picked for the various posts, and they gave orders and took orders without regard to which country their next neighbour or opposite number belonged to. I used the word 'opposite number' by mistake, because there were no 'opposite numbers' – there was absolute intermingling of staff work, and the same was true in the commands in the field. Many British and American troops served with perfect confidence under the commanders of the other country. And speaking for our own people, we always had more than fair treatment and felt absolute confidence in those to whom we confided the lives of our soldiers.

I am certain that our effective unity saved scores of thousands of lives, perhaps far more, and abridged the course of the struggle, as nothing else could have done. That must be regarded as a precious possession which we have in common and which whenever circumstances may require it – I cannot think they will do so in our lifetime – will be available to strengthen any joint efforts our Governments may order in some future period. No one was more the champion and embodiment of this unity than General Eisenhower. I never had a chance to visit the Pacific but I am told the same conditions prevailed there as were established by him at SHAEF Headquarters and in the field. Of course, when people are on different ships they don't come so closely together as they do in the camps and billets. But it was one great force that overthrew the mighty powers with which we were confronted and which were dashed to ruin and helplessness by our exertions.

I have been thinking a great deal about the work of the United States' services. I will speak a little more of the Army than of the others because I saw more of it. I greatly admired the manner in which the American Army was formed. I think it was a prodigy of organization, of improvisation. There have been many occasions when a powerful state has wished to raise great armies, and with money and time, and discipline and loyalty that can be accomplished. Nevertheless the rate at which the small American Army of only a few hundred thousand men, not long before the war, created the mighty force of millions of soldiers, is a wonder in military history.

I was here 2 or 3 years ago and visited with General Marshall from whom I received a most delightful telegram just now – an Army Corps being trained in South Carolina, and we saw there the spectacle of what you may call the mass production of divisions.

In great and rapid rotation they were forged, and moved on to further stages of their perfection. I saw the creation of this mighty force – this mighty Army, victorious in every theatre against the enemy in so short a time and from such a very small parent stock. This is an achievement which the soldiers of every country will always study with admiration and with envy.

But that is not the whole story, nor even the greatest part of the story. To create great Armies is one thing; to lead them and to handle them is another. It remains to me a mystery as yet unexplained how the very small staffs which the United States kept during the years of peace were able not only to build up the Armies and Air Force units, but also to find the leaders and vast staffs capable of handling enormous masses and of moving them faster and farther than masses have ever been moved in war before.

The United States owes a debt to its officer corps. In time of peace in this country, as in my own, the military profession is very often required to pass a considerable number of years in the cool shade. One of Marlborough's veterans[1] wrote the lines, now nearly 250 years ago,

God and the soldier we adore
In time of danger, not before;
The danger passed and all things righted,
God is forgotten and the soldier slighted.

Undoubtedly the military profession in the great Western democracies, which wholeheartedly desire peace, is one which has required great sacrifices from those who devote themselves to it. All around them goes the busy exciting world of business and politics with all its varieties, but the officers frugally, modestly, industriously, faithfully pursue their professional studies and duties, very often for long periods at a time, without the public notice. That you should have been able to preserve the art not only of creating mighty armies almost at the stroke of a wand, – but of leading and guiding those armies upon a scale incomparably greater than anything that was prepared for or even dreamed of, constitutes a gift made by the Officer Corps of the United States to their nation in time of trouble, which I earnestly hope will never be forgotten here, and it certainly never will be forgotten in the Island from which I come. You will, I am sure permit me to associate with this amazing feat, the name of General Marshall the creator of this Instrument of Victory.

---

[1] Francis Quarles, 1592–1664. Educated at Christ's College, Cambridge, and Oriel College, Oxford. Chronologer of the City of London, 1639. Published books of paraphrased Bible verse and poetry; his most famous was *The Emblems*.

I offer you gentlemen my most earnest congratulations on the manner in which, when the danger came, you were not found wanting. We talk a great deal about the future of armies and we are studying this matter across the ocean ourselves, and the relation between the officers and the other ranks. I speak not entirely as an amateur. I went through 5 years of professional training at the beginning of my life, in those impressionable years, and I have had the good fortune to be in all the wars that Great Britain has been engaged in in one capacity or another during my lifetime. We now have to choose very carefully the line of division between the officers and other ranks upon which authority should stand. There is only one line in my view, and that is professional attainment. The men have a right to feel that their officers know far better than they do how to bring them safely and victoriously through terrible difficult decisions which arise in war. And for my part as far as Great Britain is concerned, I shall always urge that the tendency in the future should be to prolong the courses of instruction at the colleges rather than to abridge them. And to equip our young officers with that special technical professional knowledge which soldiers have a right to expect from those who can give them orders if necessary to go to their deaths. It is quite clear that class or wealth or favour will not be allowed in the modern world to afford dividing lines. Professional attainment, based upon prolonged study, and collective study at colleges, rank by rank, and age by age – those are the title needs of the commanders of the future armies, and the secret of future victories.

I venture to use these few words to you this afternoon because I have had a very varied experience in peace and war, and have met so many men who have played great parts, and I felt it a high honor to be invited to meet you again this afternoon, and to revive old acquaintances and shake hands with new ones. I thought these few observations I ventured to make might not be thought unfitting or unacceptable.

Leader of the Opposition Office: note
(*Churchill papers, 2/82*)

11 March 1946

THE FULTON SPEECH
Socialist MPs who signed Warbey Motion

Mr Churchill spoke at Fulton, Missouri, USA, on March 5th, 1946. On March 11th, 1946, Mr Driberg (Soc), and Mr Warbey[1] (Soc), made a

[1] William Noble Warbey, 1903–80. Educated at King's College London and London School of Economics. Language teacher and interpreter, France and Germany, 1925–6. Master, Derby

request to the Prime Minister that he should repudiate the tone and temper of Mr Churchill's speech. In reply Mr Attlee made it clear that Mr Churchill had spoken in an individual capacity in a foreign country and that neither he (Mr Attlee), nor the British Ambassador in Washington were under any obligation to approve or disapprove the Fulton speech.

A motion of censure against Mr Churchill was put down in the House of Commons, in the name of Mr Warbey, in the following terms –

'<u>World Peace and Security</u> – That this House considers that proposals for a military alliance between the British Commonwealth and the USA for the purpose of combatting the spread of Communism, such as were put forward in a speech at Fulton, Missouri, USA by the right honourable gentleman the Member for Woodford, are calculated to do injury to good relations between Great Britain, USA and the USSR, and are inimical to the cause of world peace; and affirms its view that world peace and security can be maintained, not by sectional alliances, but by progressively strengthening the power and authority of UNO to the point where it becomes capable of exercising, in respect to world law, order and justice, the functions of a world government.'

The list of Socialist MPs who supported the motion was as follows: [. . .][1]

President Harry S Truman to Winston S. Churchill
(*Churchill papers, 2/158*)

12 March 1946 The White House
Washington DC

My Dear Winston,

I can't thank you enough for the autographed volumes on the war period. I am going to read them with a great deal of interest.

I can't tell you how very much we all enjoyed your visit to this country and I hope it will not be the last one. The people in Missouri were highly pleased with your visit and enjoyed what you had to say.

Please express my best wishes to Mrs Churchill and Mrs Oliver. I regret exceedingly I did not have the privilege of meeting them.

I know you will have a grand reception in New York and I hope you will have a most pleasant voyage to England.

Municipal Secondary School, 1927–8. Secretary and Tutor, University Tutorial College, London, 1929–37. Married, 1931, Audrey Grace Wicks. Tutor–organiser, National Council of Labour Colleges, 1937–40. Chief English Press Officer to Norwegian Government in London, 1941–5. MP (Lab.) for Luton Div. of Bedfordshire, 1945–50; for Broxtowe Div. of Nottinghamshire, 1953–5; for Ashfield Div. of Nottinghamshire, 1955–66. Travel organiser, 1950–1. Editor, *Look and Listen*, 1952–5. Executive Director, Organisation for World Political and Social Studies, 1965–80.

[1] The list names 105 Socialist MPs. The motion was never debated.

Clarence K. Streit:[1] article[2]
(Churchill papers, 2/226)

13 March 1946

UNION INSTEAD OF ALLIANCE

The general American reaction to Mr Churchill's proposal at Fulton is understandable and ominous. It is much the same as the British reaction to similar proffers the French made to them after World War I. We know now where that led.

Why did the British reject the French alliance until it was too late to prevent war? They said they put their faith in the League of Nations and feared an alliance would undermine confidence in it and hopelessly divide it. They said the alliance would be against another great power, Germany, and would kill their hope of peaceful understanding with it and of freedom evolving there. They often said there was no need for a formal alliance with France against German aggression for in that event Britain would back France anyway.

The British were the ones who argued then that their best service to peace would be to keep in a middle position – be the 'honest broker', as they put it, between France and Germany. They carried this balance-of-power policy to new heights and achieved that masterpiece of plausible folly – the Locarno Treaty.

We Americans are not yet proposing to safeguard the United States, Britain, Russia and the UN by our taking Britain's role in a new Locarno. But the philosophy behind our general reaction to the Churchill proposal leads straight in this direction.

Behind the British reluctance to ally themselves with France lay this decisive consideration: They knew that such an alliance meant, in effect, giving the French government a blank check, underwriting its foreign policy, while having no control over it. They felt that this might well encourage the French government to continue rather than abandon certain of its policies which they considered only less dangerous to peace than German aggressiveness.

The British should understand that this reasonable fear now weighs heavily in American minds against alliance with them. It weighs the more because many Americans feel there is no direct danger of our becoming involved in war with Soviet Russia. They conveniently ignore Manchuria, China, and the fact that no conception is so sharply opposed to communism as our political and economic individualism. They see British policy in Europe, the

---

[1] Clarence Kirshman Streit, 1896–1986. American journalist. Volunteer in American Expeditionary Force, France, 1917–19. Correspondent, *Philadelphia Public Ledger*, 1920–4; *New York Times*, 1925–39. President, Association to Unite the Democracies (formerly Federal Union, Inc.), 1939–86. Editor, *Freedom & Union*, 1946–86. President, International Movement for Atlantic Union, 1958–86.

[2] This article was published in the *Washington Post*.

Mediterranean, southern Asia and the empire in general as the only thing liable to entangle us in war with Russia. There is no gainsaying the soundness of Walter Lippmann's[1] shrewd objection that the Churchill proposal would leave the initiative to the British government in this vast and explosive area.

When one has found American objections to alliance with Britain as valid as former British objections to alliance with France, Mr Churchill can still reply that British acceptance of the French alliance in 1919 could not possibly have had worse results than their long refusal had for Britain, France, Germany, the league and world peace.

But the choice is not between alliance now or no alliance until it is too late to prevent war. There is a much better way to meet the grave problem which Mr Churchill tackled with his customary courage. It is the way of union – full federal union – of the free, which he himself proposed for Britain and France when their alliance crashed in 1940.

A basic flaw in any alliance is the cult of nationalism responsible for it. Why is alliance suggested instead of federal union? Either because of a desire to preserve the possibility of independent national action at the showdown, or because of a belief that public opinion is too nationalistic to accept anything stronger. But if national feeling prevents a real federal union, it will also prevent the alliance from being sufficiently firm to deter war effectively.

Those who urge an alliance pay homage thereby to the national philosophy that is the heart of the trouble. They advocate the very system which is most certain to keep it strong . . . and the alliance fragile. Those who urge union strike at this philosophy from the start. They show why the maintenance of national sovereignty as regards foreign policy, defense and a few other things is not a blessing but a danger to liberty. And they set up a system, a common government in those fields where it is conducive to liberty, which unites its citizens more and more as time goes on.

An alliance requires us to give the British government a blank check on its foreign and colonial policy; a union involves no blank checks. An alliance requires us to have not merely blind confidence in our own Executive, but even blinder confidence in a British government which is not responsible to us at all. We avoid this by union.

An Alliance – and obviously an agreement to share bases and standardize weapons – is limited to military and diplomatic affairs; it is therefore bound to be against another power and lead to counter-alliances. A union is not thus limited; it is made not merely to lessen the burden of defense but to free and develop trade and communications among its members and to advance the liberty of its citizens generally.

---

[1] Walter Lippmann, 1889–1974. Educated at Harvard University. Associate Editor, *New Republic*, 1914–17. Assistant to Secretary of War, 1917. Capt., US Military Intelligence, 1918. Editor, *New York World*, 1919–31. Special writer to *New York Herald Tribune* syndicate, 1931–62. Married, as his second wife, Helen Byrne Armstrong, 1938. Pulitzer Prize for International Reporting, 1962.

No means of uniting states or of increasing armed strength runs less danger of hostile reaction than a union of the freest people made expressly to preserve civil liberty. Russia's celebrated realists, whatever line they may lay down for bargaining purposes, know as well as we do that the more individual liberty a government provides, the slower and more publicly it must act and the less it is capable of surprise aggression.

Mr Churchill is right in urging us to scrap the balance-of-power policy we are now pursuing and put overwhelming power behind freedom as the safest way to peace. But a union, both by its philosophy and structure, gives far more power than the tightest alliance. And this power is not only military, but economic, productive and moral.

For my part, I believe that nothing less than union of the American, British and French people behind the world's strongest bill of rights can suffice to secure their liberty and prevent World War III. Indecision and half-measures in the 1920s and 1930s cost the British fearfully. They will cost us even more in a few years. We have no time to waste on dangerous illusions.

Josef Stalin: interview[1]
(Pravda)

14 March 1946

Question: How do you appraise Mr Churchill's latest speech in the United States of America?

Answer: I appraise it as a dangerous act, calculated to sow the seeds of dissension among the Allied States and impede their collaboration.

Question: Can it be considered that Mr Churchill's speech is prejudicial to the cause of peace and security?

Answer: Yes, unquestionably. As a matter of fact, Mr Churchill now takes the stand of the warmongers, and in this Mr Churchill is not alone. He has friends not only in Britain but in the United States of America as well.

A point to be noted is that in this respect Mr Churchill and his friends bear a striking resemblance to Hitler and his friends. Hitler began his work of unleashing war by proclaiming a race theory, declaring that only German-speaking people constituted a superior nation. Mr Churchill sets out to unleash war with a race theory, asserting that only English-speaking nations are superior nations, who are called upon to decide the destinies of the entire world. The German race theory led Hitler and his friends to the conclusion that the Germans, as the only superior nation, should rule over other nations. The English race theory leads Mr Churchill and his friends to the conclusion that the English-speaking nations, as the only superior nations, should rule over the rest of the nations of the world.

[1] Conducted by a correspondent of the Soviet newspaper *Pravda*.

Actually, Mr Churchill, and his friends in Britain and the United States, present to the non-English speaking nations something in the nature of an ultimatum: 'Accept our rule voluntarily, and then all will be well; otherwise war is inevitable.'

But the nations shed their blood in the course of five years' fierce war for the sake of the liberty and independence of their countries, and not in order to exchange the domination of the Hitlers for the domination of the Churchills. It is quite probable, accordingly, that the non-English-speaking nations, which constitute the vast majority of the population of the world, will not agree to submit to a new slavery.

It is Mr Churchill's tragedy that, inveterate Tory that he is, he does not understand this simple and obvious truth.

There can be no doubt that Mr Churchill's position is a war position, a call for war on the USSR. It is also clear that this position of Mr Churchill's is incompatible with the Treaty of Alliance existing between Britain and the USSR. True, Mr Churchill does say, in passing, in order to confuse his readers, that the term of the Anglo-Soviet Treaty of Mutual Assistance and collaboration might quite well be extended to 50 years. But how is such a statement on Mr Churchill's part to be reconciled with his position of war on the USSR, with his preaching of War against the USSR? Obviously, these things cannot be reconciled by any means whatever. And if Mr Churchill, who calls for war on the Soviet Union, at the same time considers it possible to extend the term of the Anglo-Soviet Treaty to 50 years, that means that he regards this Treaty as a mere scrap of paper, which he only needs in order to disguise and camouflage his anti-Soviet position. For this reason, the false statements of Mr Churchill's friends in Britain, regarding the extension of the term of the Anglo-Soviet treaty to 50 years or more, cannot be taken seriously. Extension of the Treaty term has no point if one of the parties violates the Treaty and converts it into a mere scrap of paper.

Question: How do you appraise the part of Mr Churchill's speech in which he attacks the democratic systems in the European States bordering upon us, and criticises the good-neighbourly relations established between these States and the Soviet Union?

Answer: This part of Mr Churchill's speech is compounded of elements of slander and elements of discourtesy and tactlessness. Mr Churchill asserts that 'Warsaw, Berlin, Prague, Vienna, Budapest, Belgrade, Bucharest, Sofia – all these famous cities and the populations around them lie within the Soviet sphere and all are subject in one form or another not only to Soviet influence, but to a very high and increasing measure of control from Moscow'. Mr Churchill describes all this as 'unlimited expansionist tendencies' on the part of the Soviet Union.

It needs no particular effort to show that in this Mr Churchill grossly and unceremoniously slanders both Moscow, and the above-named States bordering on the USSR.

In the first place it is quite absurd to speak of exclusive control by the USSR in Vienna and Berlin, where there are Allied Control Councils made up of the representatives of four States and where the USSR has only one-quarter of the votes. It does happen that some people cannot help in engaging in slander. But still, there is a limit to everything.

Secondly, the following circumstance should not be forgotten. The Germans made their invasion of the USSR through Finland, Poland, Rumania, Bulgaria, and Hungary. The Germans were able to make their invasion through these countries because, at the time, governments hostile to the Soviet Union existed in these countries. As a result of the German invasion the Soviet Union has lost irretrievably in the fighting against the Germans, and also through the German occupation and the deportation of Soviet citizens to German servitude, a total of about seven million people. In other words, the Soviet Union's loss of life has been several times greater than that of Britain and the United States of America put together. Possibly in some quarters an inclination is felt to forget about these colossal sacrifices of the Soviet people which secured the liberation of Europe from the Hitlerite yoke. But the Soviet Union cannot forget about them. And so what can there be surprising about the fact that the Soviet Union, anxious for its future safety, is trying to see to it that governments loyal in their attitude to the Soviet Union should exist in these countries? How can anyone, who has not taken leave of his wits, describe these peaceful aspirations of the Soviet Union as expansionist tendencies on the part of our State?

Mr Churchill claims further that the 'Russian-dominated Polish Government has been encouraged to make enormous, wrongful inroads on Germany'.

Every word of this is a gross and insulting calumny. Outstanding men are at the helm in present democratic Poland. They have proved by their deeds that they are capable of upholding the interests and dignity of their country as their predecessors were not. What grounds has Mr Churchill to assert that the leaders of present-day Poland can countenance in their country the domination of representatives of any foreign State whatever? Is it not because Mr Churchill means to sow the seeds of dissension in the relations between Poland and the Soviet Union that he slanders 'the Russians' here?

Mr Churchill is displeased that Poland has faced about in her policy in the direction of friendship and alliance with the USSR. There was a time when elements of conflict and antagonism predominated in the relations between Poland and the USSR. This circumstance enabled statesmen like Mr Churchill to play on these antagonisms, to get control over Poland on the pretext of protecting her from the Russians, to try to scare Russia with the spectre of war between her and Poland, and retain the position of arbiter for themselves. But that time is past and gone, for the enmity between Poland and Russia has given place to friendship between them, and Poland – present-day democratic Poland – does not choose to be a play-ball in foreign hands any longer. It seems to me that it is this fact that irritates Mr Churchill and makes him indulge in discourteous, tactless sallies against Poland. Just imagine – he is not being allowed to play his game at the expense of others!

As to Mr Churchill's attack upon the Soviet Union in connection with the extension of Poland's Western frontier to include Polish territories which the Germans had seized in the past – here it seems to me he is plainly cheating. As is known, the decision on the Western frontier of Poland was adopted at the Berlin Three-Power Conference on the basis of Poland's demands. The Soviet Union has repeatedly stated that it considers Poland's demands to be proper and just. It is quite probable that Mr Churchill is displeased with this decision. But why does Mr Churchill, while sparing no shots against the Russian position in this matter, conceal from his readers the fact that this decision was passed at the Berlin Conference by unanimous vote – that it was not only the Russians, but the British and Americans as well, that voted for the decision? Why did Mr Churchill think it necessary to mislead the public?

Further, Mr Churchill asserts that Communist Parties, which were previously very small in all these Eastern States of Europe, have been raised to prominence and power far beyond their numbers and seek everywhere to obtain totalitarian control. Police governments prevail in nearly every case, and 'thus far, except in Czechoslovakia, there is no true democracy'.

As is known, the Government of the State in Britain at the present time is in the hands of one party, the Labour Party, and the opposition parties are deprived of the right to participate in the Government of Britain. That Mr Churchill calls true democracy. Poland, Rumania, Yugoslavia, Bulgaria and Hungary are administered by blocs of several parties – from four to six parties – and the opposition, if it is more or less loyal, is secured the right of participation in the Government. That Mr Churchill describes as totalitarianism, tyranny and police rule. Why? On what grounds? Don't expect a reply from Mr Churchill. Mr Churchill does not understand in what a ridiculous position he puts himself by his outcry about 'totalitarianism, tyranny and police rule'.

Mr Churchill would like Poland to be administered by Sosnkowski[1] and Anders,[2] Yugoslavia by Mihailovich[3] and Pavelich,[4] Rumania by Prince

[1] Kazimierz Sosnkowski, 1885–1969. GOC Warsaw Military District, 1918–19. Vice-Minister of War, 1919–20. C-in-C, Reserve Army, 1920; Southern Front, 1920. Minister of War, 1920–3, 1923–4. GOC VII Corps Area, 1925–7. Inspector of the Army, 1927–8, 1928–39. GOC Operational Group Sosnkowski, 1939. Vice-President, Polish Government-in-Exile, 1939–41. Deputy C-in-C, Polish Armed Forces, 1939–43; C-in-C, 1943–4.

[2] Władysław Anders, 1892–1970. CoS to Inspector-General of Cavalry, 1925–6. CO, Cavalry Bde Samodzielnej, 1926–37; Cavalry Bde Nowogrodzkiej, 1937–9. GOC Operational Cavalry Group, 1939. POW, Soviet Union, 1939–41. GOC Forces in Soviet Union, 1941–2; 5th Div., 1941–2; Army of the East, 1942–3; II Corps (Italy), 1943–6. Inspector-General of Polish Forces in the West, 1945–54.

[3] Draža Mihailović, 1893–1946. Leader of the Chetniks, a Serbian nationalist guerrilla force formed to resist the Axis and Croatian collaborators, 1941–3. Minister of the Army and Navy, Yugoslav Government-in-Exile, 1942–4. C-in-C, Royal Yugoslav Army of the Interior, 1943–6.

[4] Ante Pavelich, 1889–1959. Member of the Parliament of Yugoslavia, 1927–9. Founder of the fascist organization Ustaše, 1929. Exiled to Germany, 1929. Travelled to Italy under a false passport and lived under assumed names, 1929–41. Leader (Poglavnik) of the Independent State of Croatia,

Stirbey[1] and Radescu,[2] Hungary and Austria by some King of the House of Hapsburg, and so on. Mr Churchill wants to assure us that these gentlemen from the Fascist backyard can ensure true democracy.

Such is the 'democracy' of Mr Churchill.

Mr Churchill comes somewhere near the truth when he speaks of the increasing influence of the Communist Parties in Eastern Europe. It must be remarked, however, that he is not quite accurate. The influence of the Communist Parties has grown not only in Eastern Europe, but in nearly all the countries of Europe which were previously under Fascist rule – Italy, Germany, Hungary, Bulgaria, Rumania, and Finland – or which experienced German, Italian or Hungarian occupation – France, Belgium, Holland, Norway, Denmark, Poland, Czechoslovakia, Yugoslavia, Greece, the Soviet Union and so on.

The increased influence of the Communists cannot be considered fortuitous. It is a perfectly logical thing. The influence of the Communists has grown because, in the years of the rule of Fascism in Europe, the Communists showed themselves trusty, fearless, self-sacrificing fighters against the Fascist regime for the liberty of the peoples. Mr Churchill in his speeches sometimes recalls the plain people from little homes, slapping them patronisingly on the back and parading as their friend. But these people are not so simple as may at first sight appear. These plain people have views of their own, a policy of their own, and they know how to stand up for themselves. It was they, the millions of these 'plain people,' who isolated their reactionaries and advocates of collaboration with Fascism in Europe, and gave their preference to the Left democratic parties. It was they, the millions of these 'plain people', who after testing the Communists in the fires of struggle and resistance to Fascism, came to the conclusion that the Communists were fully deserving of the people's confidence. That was how the influence of the Communists grew in Europe.

Of course Mr Churchill does not like this course of development and he sounds the alarm and appeals to force. But neither did he like the birth of the Soviet regime in Russia after the First World War. At that time, too, he sounded the alarm and organised an armed campaign of 14 States against

---

1941–5. Escaped to Argentina after the end of the war through Operation ODESSA. Died of wounds from an assassination attempt in Madrid.

[1] Barbu Alexandru Stirbey, 1872–1946. Son of Prince Alexander Dimitri Stirbey. Married, 1895, Princess Nadeje Bibescu. PM of Romania, 4–20 June 1927. Exiled following the collapse of his government. Returned to Romania on the invitation of King Michael I following the royal coup of 23 Aug. 1944. Member of the Romanian delegation that signed the Armistice Agreement with the Soviet Union, 12 Sep. 1944. Opposed the formation of a Communist government in Romania. Died 24 March 1946; probable cause of death was liver cancer, but it was rumoured that he was poisoned by NKVD agents on the orders of Josef Stalin.

[2] Nicolae Radescu, 1876–1953. Born in Bucharest. CoS, 2nd Cavalry Div., 1917–18; Gendarmerie Corps, 1919–20. General Staff, 1920–6. Military Attaché to London, 1926–8. Inspectorate-General of Calvary, 1929–31. GOC 1st Cavalry Div., 1931–3. Retired, 1933. Recalled after successful anti-Fascist coup, Aug. 1944. CGS, 1944. PM and Minister of the Interior, 1944–5. Dismissed from office under Soviet pressure, 3 Mar. 1945. Fled to Cyprus and later (1947) New York City.

Russia, setting himself the goal of turning back the wheel of history. But history proved stronger than the Churchill intervention, and Mr Churchill's quixotry led to his unmitigated defeat at that time. I don't know whether Mr Churchill and his friends will succeed in organising a new armed campaign against Eastern Europe after the Second World War; but if they do succeed – which is not very probable because millions of plain people stand guard over the cause of peace – it may confidently be said that they will be thrashed, just as they were thrashed once before, 26 years ago.

Charles Murphy:[1] recollection
(Robert T. Elson, 'The World of Time Inc.', pages 158–61)

14 March 1946

In Time Inc.'s archives is an account of the dinner written by Charles J. V. Murphy. Cocktails were served in a reception room, during which ritual, according to Murphy,

> Mr Churchill's eyes lighted upon an imposing portrait on the wall. Striding across the room, he halted before the solemn, haughty countenance of what appeared to be an eighteenth century personage. He squinted at it fiercely, then asked bluntly: 'Who is that blighter?' The question caught the host between wind and water.... For a moment the painfully contrived structure of Mr Churchill's beloved Anglo-American community based upon a common cultural heritage hung in the balance; then Harry,[2] after a hasty glance at the little brass nameplate on the frame, announced with something less than his customary aplomb that it was William IV.[3] 'William IV?' answered Mr Churchill in obvious surprise. 'Hrumph ... Looks more like Lord Rosebery[4] to me.... Same heavy jowls....' 'Ah', Harry said, waving gaily at the brooding portrait, 'but there the resemblance ends.' This learned sally into the characters of England's inept and blundering

---

[1] Charles J. V. Murphy, 1904–87. Born in Newton, Massachusetts. Attended Harvard College, but did not graduate. Joined the Associated Press in 1925. Also worked for the United Press, *New York Evening Post* and *New York World*. Became a freelance writer in 1930. Joined with Time Inc., 1936, with which he was a writer and reporter. Co-author of *The Windsor Story*, (1979) a biography of the Duke and Duchess of Windsor, and co-author of *The Lives of Winston Churchill*, (1945).

[2] Henry Robinson Luce, 1898–1967. Born in China, the son of an American missionary there. On active service with US Army in France, 1917–18. Founder (1923), Editor and Publisher of *Time*, of *Fortune* (1928) and (1936) of *Life*, becoming a multi-millionaire. Evolved the cinema programme *The March of Time* (1935). Organized United China Relief, 1940. His wife Clare Boothe Luce, a pre-war friend of Randolph Churchill, was later US Ambassador to Italy.

[3] William IV, 1765–1837. RN, 1778–1811. Duke of Clarence, 1789. King of Great Britain and Ireland, 1830–7.

[4] Archibald Philip Primrose, 1847–1929. Succeeded his grandfather as 5th Earl of Rosebery, 1868. Lord Privy Seal, 1885. Secretary of State for Foreign Affairs, 1886, 1892–4. PM, 1894–5. In 1906, he published a short memorial volume, *Lord Randolph Churchill*. His younger son Neil Primrose was killed in action in Palestine, 18 Nov. 1917.

monarch and the erudite and devoted biographer of our guest's father, Lord Randolph Churchill,[1] caught the rest of the company off guard. However, the conversation was almost immediately restored to a less demanding altitude as Harry took the guest by the arm and wheeled him around to view a monumental creation of the Union Club's hors d'oeuvres department.

As a centerpiece the club chefs had prepared a huge American eagle carved from ice, holding mounds of caviar. The eagle was slowly melting, and as Churchill accepted a martini he eyed the sculptured bird and remarked, 'The eagle seems to have a cold.' He then asked if he might be seated, and, according to Murphy,

> Harry himself brought up a chair and the old man sat down in front of the dissolving ice eagle and contemplated the caviar with satisfaction. On seeing a *Time* editor spread the caviar on dry toast, the gourmet was galvanized into registering a sharp warning: 'This stuff needs no reinforcement.' To set the example, he spooned himself a whopping helping which he transferred with scant interruption from his plate to his mouth, occasionally emitting an appreciative belch. 'I hope, gentlemen,' he announced, 'you don't find me too explosive an animal.' Thinking that Churchill was referring to the controversial Fulton speech, Harry at once started to protest, saying that on the contrary Mr Churchill had only put into words what was gravely in the minds of many Americans. But the guest . . . cut off the compliment, saying, 'I am happy to hear that, sir, but the explosions I had in mind were those given off by my internal pleasure.' As he downed another spoonful, he added reflectively, 'You know, Uncle Joe used to send me a lot of this, but I don't suppose I'll ever be getting any more.'

> The Soviet onslaught had certainly shaken him. One moment the situation was 'a crisis of the most urgent nature, holding real danger for my country'. But on second thought he was inclined to regard the Russian reaction as an ill-tempered, crude and typical Communist trick. He pointed out how Moscow, before uttering a word, had waited eight days to judge world reaction and prepare its line; how then the whole apparatus of propaganda had opened up on him, with Stalin himself joining the historians and editorial writers in an orchestra of abuse and vilification. 'This in itself,' he concluded, 'is flattering.' He could not resist making fun of the clumsiness of the process and even at Stalin's heavy-handed attack on him personally. 'You know,' he suggested half-seriously, 'if *I* had been turned loose on Winston Churchill, I would have done a much better job of denunciation.' The thought gave him pleasure. Brightening perceptibly, he went on to

---

[1] Randolph Henry Spencer Churchill, 1849–95. 3rd son of 7th Duke of Marlborough. Secretary of State for India, 1885–6. Leader of the House of Commons and Chancellor of the Exchequer, June 1886. Resigned in Dec. 1886 and held no further political office.

tell how Hitler had attacked him in almost identical terms: 'Warmonger, métier of wars, imperialist, reactionary, has-been – why, it is beginning to sound almost like old times.'. . . It nettled him to be told that many Americans could not fathom his hostility toward Russia and a suggestion that his attacks were taken by some earnest citizens as Red-baiting brought the almost fierce retort: 'I won't change on that account.'

Among those present, Murphy recalled, were some who felt that Churchill had indeed been Red-baiting. But on the whole Luce's associates, obeying their host's pre-dinner injunction, were happy to keep the honored guest in his 'groove of discussion'. One moment of tension occurred when *Fortune's* John Davenport[1] asked:*

> 'How did it happen, Mr Churchill, that you and Mr Roosevelt were so misled at Yalta as to offer such a high price to the Russians in order to lure them into the Pacific war – a war that was already won?'
>
> The host sat up as if stabbed. Waggling an ecclesiastical forefinger at Editor Davenport, he said sternly: 'Mr Churchill, it is hardly necessary to answer that question. Foremost among the subjects on which Mr Davenport certainly is not an expert is the Far East and the Japanese war.' It is doubtful that Mr Churchill even fully appreciated the submerged differences that accounted for the flurry which, as seen from his chair, whirled up out of nothing. How could he have known of the schism inside Time Inc. which during the war had divided its editors among those who subscribed to the doctrine that the Pacific war was *the really tough war* (Murphy's emphasis), the consequences of which would have the most decisive effect on the American destiny, and others who held, with Editor Davenport, that Europe was *the* important war. . . . Mr Churchill, having fought out this very question with the American Chiefs of Staff and indirectly with the American public, must have been surprised by the intensity of feeling lingering among Time Inc. editors. On the other hand, his political judgment had been challenged and, refusing to be sheltered by Harry's intervention, he gallantly seized the nettle.

Churchill's answer was the predictable and stock answer: the prospect of long and bloody conflict if the Japanese islands had to be invaded; and then he lapsed into his own version of Yalta. The 'flurry' did not mar a 'famous' evening. Gruntled but still not hooked to a contract, Churchill departed for England, where *Life* would continue to pursue him.*

* Davenport was co-author, with Murphy, of *The Lives of Winston Churchill*, which appeared in *Life* in 1945 and later that year as a book (Charles Scribner's Sons).

[1] John Davenport, 1905–87. Educated at Yale University. Editor, *Barron's Financial*, 1949–54. Asst Managing Editor, *Fortune* magazine, 1954–69. Author of *The Lives of Winston Churchill* (1946) and *The US Economy* (1964).

Clement Attlee to Winston S. Churchill
(Churchill papers, 2/4)

14 March 1946
Immediate
Personal
No. 514

I have just heard from Ben Smith of the very helpful remarks which you made at the National Press Club luncheon about the American Loan and I should like to send my warm thanks and appreciation for the friendly line you took.

2. Thank you also for the long and interesting telegram[1] which you sent to Bevin and me on March 7th – I hope we may have a talk on your return. I have shown the telegram to Eden.

3. I trust that the remainder of your stay will be pleasant and that you are keeping well. Best wishes to Mrs Churchill and yourself.

Winston S. Churchill: speech
(Churchill papers, 5/4C)

15 March 1946 　　　　　　　　　　　　　　　　　Waldorf Astoria Hotel
New York

THE DARKENING INTERNATIONAL SCENE

When I spoke at Fulton ten days ago I felt it was necessary for someone in an unofficial position to speak in arresting terms about the present plight of the world. I do not wish to withdraw or modify a single word. I was invited to give my counsel freely in this free country and I am sure that the hope which I expressed for the increasing association of our two countries will come to pass, not because of any speech which may be made, but because of the tides that flow in human affairs and in the course of the unfolding destiny of the world. The only question which in my opinion is open is whether the necessary harmony of thought and action between the American and British peoples will be reached in a sufficiently plain and clear manner and in good time to prevent a new world struggle or whether it will come about, as it has done before, only in the course of that struggle.

I remain convinced that this question will win a favourable answer. I do not believe that war is inevitable or imminent. I do not believe that the rulers of Russia wish for war at the present time. I am sure that if we stand together calmly and resolutely in defence of those ideals and principles embodied in

---
[1] Reproduced above (pp. 241–2).

the Charter of the United Nations, we shall find ourselves sustained by the overwhelming assent of the peoples of the world, and that, fortified by this ever-growing moral authority, the cause of peace and freedom will come safely through and we shall be able to go on with the noble work – in which the United States has a glorious primacy – of averting famine, of healing the awful wounds of Hitler's war and rebuilding the scarred and shattered structure of human civilisation. Let me declare, however, that the progress and freedom of all the peoples of the world under a reign of law enforced by a World Organisation, will not come to pass, nor will the age of plenty begin, without the persistent, faithful, and above all fearless exertions of the British and American systems of society.

In the last ten days the situation has greatly changed as the result of decisions which must have been taken some time ago. Instead of a calm discussion of broad and long-term tendencies we now find ourselves in the presence of swiftly moving events which no one can measure at the moment. I may be called upon to speak about the new situation when I get back home.

There are however a few things I am bound to say tonight lest a good cause should suffer by default. If any words that I have spoken have commanded attention that is only because they find an echo in the breasts of those of every land and race who love freedom and are the foes of tyranny. I certainly will not allow anything said by others to weaken my regard and admiration for the Russian people or my earnest desire that Russia should be safe and prosperous and should take an honoured place in the van of the World Organisation. Whether she will do so or not depends only on the decisions taken by the handful of able men who, under their renowned chief, hold all the 180 million Russians, and many more millions outside Russia, in their grip. We all remember what frightful losses Russia suffered in the Hitlerite invasion and how she survived and emerged triumphant from injuries greater than have ever been inflicted on any other community. There is deep and widespread sympathy throughout the English-speaking world for the people of Russia and an absolute readiness to work with them on fair and even terms to repair the ruin of the war in every country. If the Soviet Government does not take advantage of this sentiment, if on the contrary they discourage it, the responsibility will be entirely theirs.

There is for instance a very good way in which they could brush aside any speeches which they dislike. It is a way which is open to them now in the next fortnight. The British Government of which I was the head, signed a treaty with Russia and with Persia solemnly undertaking to respect the integrity and sovereignty of Persia and to evacuate that country by a certain date. This treaty was reaffirmed at Teheran by the Tri-partite Agreement signed by the Head of the Soviet Government, by the late President Roosevelt and by me. In fulfilment of this Agreement the United States and the British have already left that country. But we are told that the Soviet Government instead of leaving, are actually sending in more troops. Now this is one of those cases for which the United Nations Security Council was especially devised, and I am very glad to read in the newspapers that the Soviet representatives will attend the meeting of the Security Council which is to take place in New York on 25 March. By all means let the matter be thrashed out there and let respect be shown even by the greatest or more deeply-interested powers, to the conclusions of the Security Council. In this way the reign of world law and the international foundations of enduring peace would be immeasurably consolidated.

There is no reason why Soviet Russia should feel ill-rewarded for her efforts in the war. If her losses have been grievous, her gains have been magnificent. Her two tremendous antagonists, Germany and Japan, have been laid low. Japan was overthrown almost entirely by American arms. Russia recovered almost without striking a blow all that she lost to Japan forty years ago. In the west the Baltic states and a large part of Finland have been reincorporated in Russia. The Curzon Line is no longer questioned. Then we come to the Straits of the Dardanelles. I welcome the Russian flag on Russian ships on the high seas and oceans. I have always told our Soviet allies that Great Britain would support the revision of the Montreux Convention about the Straits. At Potsdam the Americans and British offered to Russia a joint guarantee of the complete freedom of the Straits in peace and war, whether for merchant ships or ships of war. To this guarantee Turkey would gladly have subscribed. But we were told that that was not enough. Russia must have a fortress inside the Straits, from which she could dominate Constantinople. But this is not to keep the Straits open but to give the power of closing them to a single nation. This is out of harmony with the principle urged by the United States representatives of the freedom of the great waterways of Europe, the Danube, the Rhine and other rivers, which run through many countries. At any rate, there was the offer and I have no doubt it is still open, and if Soviet Russia still persists in putting pressure on Turkey, the matter must in the first instance be pronounced upon by the United Nations Security Council. Thus early will come a very great test for the World Organisation on which so many hopes are founded.

It has been frequently observed in the last few days that there is a great measure of misunderstanding. I entirely agree with that. Could you have a greater example of misunderstanding than when we are told that the present British Government is not a free democratic government because it consists only of the representatives of a single party, whereas Poland, Rumania, Bulgaria and other countries have the representatives of several parties in their governments. But this also applies to the United States, where one party is in office and wields the executive power. All this argument overlooks the fact that democratic governments are based on free elections. The people choose freely and fairly the party they wish to have in office. They have every right to criticise that party, or the government based upon it and can change it by constitutional processes at any time they like or at frequent intervals. It can hardly be called a democratic election where the candidates of only one party are allowed to appear and where the voter has not even the secrecy of the ballot to protect him. These misunderstandings will be swept away if we get through the present difficult period safely and if the British, American and Russian peoples are allowed to mingle freely with one another and see how things are done in their respective countries. No doubt we all have much to learn from one another. I rejoice to read in the newspapers that there never were more Russian ships in New York harbour than there are tonight. I am sure you will give the Russian sailors a hearty welcome to the land of the free and the home of the brave.

Now I turn to the other part of my message – the relations between Great Britain and the United States. On these the life and freedom of the world depend. Unless they work together, in full loyalty to the Charter, the organisation of the United Nations will cease to have any reality. No one will be able to put his trust in it and the world will be left to the clash of nationalisms which have led us to two frightful wars. I have never asked for an Anglo-American military alliance or a treaty. I asked for something different and in a sense I asked for something more. I asked for fraternal association, free, voluntary, fraternal association. I have no doubt that it will come to pass, as surely as the sun will rise tomorrow. But you do not need a treaty to express the natural affinities and friendships which arise in a fraternal association. On the other hand, it would be wrong that the fact should be concealed or ignored. Nothing can prevent our nations drawing ever closer to one another and nothing can obscure the fact that, in their harmonious companionship, lies the main hope of the world instrument for maintaining peace on earth and goodwill to all men.

I thank you all profoundly for all your gracious kindness and hospitality to me during this visit I have paid to your shores. Mine is not the first voice raised within your spacious bounds in this cause of freedom and of peace. Nor will it be the last that will be encouraged by the broad tolerance of the American people. I come to you at a time when the United States stands at the highest point of majesty and power ever attained by any community since the fall of the Roman Empire. This imposes upon the American people a duty which cannot be rejected. With opportunities comes responsibility. Strength is granted to us all when we are needed to serve great causes. We in the British Commonwealth will stand at your side in powerful and faithful friendship, and in accordance with the World Charter, and together I am sure we shall succeed in lifting from the face of man the curse of war and the darker curse of tyranny. Thus will be opened even more broadly to the anxious toiling millions the gateways of happiness and freedom.

Winston S. Churchill: speech
('Winston S. Churchill, His Complete Speeches', volume 7, pages 7302–3)

18 March 1946   Columbia University, New York

A BROADER AND FAIRER WORLD

In my heart there is no abiding hatred for any great race on the surface of the globe. I earnestly hope that there will be no pariah nations after the guilty are fully punished. We have to look forward to a broader, fairer world, richer and fuller in every way under the aegis and authority of the world organization, to guard the humble toiler, the small homes of all nations, from renewed horrors and tyranny.

In that task you will be upheld to the utmost by all the moral and material resources which the British Commonwealth and Empire can supply. Thus walking forward together, with no aim of subjugation or material profit or sordid interest, marching forward together we may render at this juncture a service to humanity which no countries before have ever had the honour to do.

. . . One thing the GIs and British soldiers returning home have got is a good grounding in Anglo-American slang. I suggest without any prejudice, that they now require full knowledge and facilities of the majesty and power of their own mother tongue. I see in some newspapers and books undue reliance upon slang.

In its right place slang has its virtues, but let us keep a tight hold on our own mother tongue, because that is the key to the treasure house of the past and the great works of the future.

The study of history is also essential. Even our Communist friends should study this. They should study the admirable modern works on the life and soul and that will show them not only a great deal about their past but will give a very fair indication of their future.

Efforts should be made to maintain actual facts that occurred. I hope Anglo-American history may be studied from that point of view so that we may at any rate understand how it is we are all here in the world.

I have great sympathy with the ordinary, humble common toiler. What chance has he when the institutions in which he was brought up vanish in the night or are liquidated? How can the one individual confront scores of problems and adjust himself to the position into which he is forced by tyrants who from time to time seize upon the Governments of great States? . . .

March 1946

Povilas Zadeikis[1] to Winston S. Churchill
(Churchill papers, 2/8)

18 March 1946   Lithuanian Legation
No. 536   Washington DC

Sir,

On March 15, 1946, in your Waldorf–Astoria address[2] reference was made to Baltic–Soviet relations: 'There is no reason why Soviet Russia should feel ill-rewarded for her efforts in the war. . . . In the west the Baltic States . . . have been reincorporated in Russia.'

It sounds like implied appeasement whether or not it was meant to be so.

Hoping that you may be interested to know the Lithuanian attitude to the above referred to part of your speech, I beg your indulgence to bring to your attention the following:

Lithuania fell under Russian rule in 1795. After one hundred twenty years of Russian domination, Lithuania, toward the end of World War I, re-emerged as an independent democratic Republic. 'Russia without any prejudice recognizes the self-rule and the independence of the State of Lithuania with all juridical consequences resulting from such recognition' (Lithuanian–Soviet Peace Treaty of 1920). The Lithuanian Republic had been recognized by every nation of the world, and had become a member of the League of Nations. In addition to the Peace Treaty of 1920, Lithuania and Soviet Russia, as equal partners, had signed the Non-Aggression Pact, the multilateral agreement on the definition of aggression, the Mutual Assistance Pact of 1939. However, on June 15, 1940, Soviet Russia in violation of all treaties, committed an act of unprovoked aggression, brutally interfered in Lithuania's internal affairs, imposed a puppet government, and after staging mock elections of the communistic type, unilaterally annexed Lithuania on August 3 of the same year. This ignominious act of self-aggrandizement at the expense of a small neighbor, and in violation of the will of the Lithuanian people, is a crime against both Divine and man-made laws. Such an act hardly merits to be termed as 'reincorporation', but it must be called by its proper name: imperialistic grab that endangers not only the existence of one nation, but undermines the advent of peace everywhere. The annexation of the Baltic States by Russia cannot be classed among the rewards 'for her efforts in the war', for it would mean the surrender of moral principles and the triumph of brutal force over right and justice.

---

[1] Povilas Zadeikis, 1887–1957. Educated at University of St Petersburg. Lithuanian Minister of Defence, 1919. Member, Lithuanian financial mission to the United States, 1920–1. First Lithuanian Consul in Chicago, 1924–35; in New York, 1935–57.

[2] Reproduced above, pp. 263–6.

March 1946

Winston S. Churchill to Clement Attlee
(*Churchill papers, 2/210*)

19 March 1946
Personal and Secret

I have had long talks with Mr Baruch and you can tell the Chancellor of the Exchequer that I do not think that he will take any action against the Loan. This does not mean that his view about it has changed, but he considers that the Russian situation makes it essential that our countries should stand together. He is of course in very full agreement with me on that. Indeed he spoke last night to me in the sense that he might urge that the loan should be interest-free as a gesture of unity. I do not suppose this would have any result on the event.

2. Baruch's appointment on the UNO Atomic Committee is of the utmost importance and it is my opinion an effective assurance that these matters will be handled in a way friendly to us. There is no doubt that the Soviet aggressiveness has helped us in many directions.

3. I am starting home tomorrow and look forward to a talk with you on my return.

Elisha Friedman[1] to Winston S. Churchill
(*Churchill papers, 2/6*)

19 March 1946   New York

Your discussion at Bernard Baruch's dinner last night was brilliant without peer. You covered a vast range of topics with the assured touch of a master.

I was particularly interested in your comparison of the British cabinet system and the American presidential system. Our system seems to be stuck at the eighteenth-century stage of British political evolution. The royally appointed governor, the executive, was opposed by the popularly elected legislature in the thirteen American colonies. Yet we now artificially perpetuate an opposition even though the people now elect both the legislature and the executive.

Some years ago I wrote on a comparison of one hundred years of British Premiers and American Presidents. In that comparison the Cabinet system comes off with credit. Copies are enclosed. True, we had great men in war

---

[1] Elisha Michael Friedman, 1899–?. Educated at City College of New York. Statistician to Advisory Committee, Council of National Defense, 1917–18. Economic Liaison, Foreign Trade Adviser's Office, 1919–20. Lecturer in Finance, New York University, 1920. Author of *American Problems of Reconstruction* (1918); *Labor and Reconstruction in Europe* (1919); *International Commerce and Reconstruction* (1920).

crises, – Abraham Lincoln,[1] Woodrow Wilson,[2] and Franklin Roosevelt. But they arose not essentially because of our system, but as an accident of history. The lines of the Psalmist apply here, – 'The Lord preserveth the simple'. And the Lord has preserved us through no merit of our own.

With your stand on Russia, as revealed in your public statements and in your answers to questions at the Baruch dinner last night, I found myself so much in agreement that I take the liberty of sending you a copy of my book, 'Russia in Transition'. Though it was published over a decade ago, the appraisal of the merits and defects of the Soviet system still seems valid, as indicated in the enclosed letter from my good friend, the late Lord Stamp.[3] May I hope it will help to support your statements on Soviet Russia, and the need for it to join in international cooperation to maintain peace.

But you moved me most deeply, when you said that you were a Zionist. Had I not already asked you too many questions, I should have liked to hear you amplify your statement, because BMB[4] told me that you were trying to convert him to Zionism. This was heartening to me, for I have not succeeded in doing so, after thirty years of effort, though he did make a handsome contribution through the late Justice Brandeis[5] to the Zionist Organization of America.

I take the liberty of sending you also a copy of my book, 'Survival or Extinction', a sociological study of the Jewish problem. This was written many years ago. Since then the justification for Zionism has unfortunately grown more tragically urgent. The book is now out of print and this, one of my library copies, can have no greater value than to be kept and read by a creator of opinion now and, I hope, soon again a maker of policy.

May I enclose also a copy of my brief to the Anglo-American Committee on Palestine at the Washington sessions, the reprints of two letters to the *New York Times*, covering Mr Hoover's[6] proposal for Iraq, on which I have been working with him until he left on his food mission Sunday.

[1] Abraham Lincoln, 1809–65. Representative, Illinois House of Representatives, 1834–42. US Representative (Whig) for Illinois's 7th district, 1847–9. US President, 1861–5.
[2] Thomas Woodrow Wilson, 1856–1924. US President, 1912–21. In December 1916, sought to persuade the belligerents of WWI to negotiate peace, but in April 1917, following repeated German sinkings of US ships, obtained a declaration from Congress that a state of war existed with Germany.
[3] Josiah Charles Stamp, 1880–1941. Economist and statistician. Entered Inland Revenue, 1896; Board of Trade, 1898. Resigned from Civil Service, 1919. Secretary and Director, Nobel Industries Ltd, 1919–26. Knighted, 1920. Joint Secretary, Royal Statistical Society, 1920–30; President, 1930–2. British Representative on the Reparations Commissions Committees of 1924 (Dawes) and 1929 (Young). Member of the Court of Enquiry, coal mining industry dispute, 1925. Director of Imperial Chemical Industries, 1927–8. Baron, 1930.
[4] Bernard Mannes Baruch.
[5] Louis Dembitz Brandeis, 1856–1941. Born in Kentucky, to Jewish immigrant parents. Educated at Dresden and Harvard Law School. Associate Justice, US Supreme Court, 1916–39.
[6] Herbert Hoover, 1874–1964. Chairman, American Relief Committee, London, 1914–15; Commission for Relief in Belgium, 1915–19. Food Administrator for US, 1917–19. US Secretary of Commerce, 1921–8. US President, 1929–33. In Aug. 1940, proposed a relaxation of the British naval blockade of Germany to enable food supplies to go to France, Belgium and Holland. In March 1946, at the request of President Truman, undertook the co-ordination of world food supplies for 38 countries.

Were you to stay here longer, I should esteem it a great honor to be permitted to talk to you again. Otherwise, I shall content myself with the hope that I may have the privilege of seeing you either on your next voyage to the United States, or when I resume my trips to Britain to visit many friends in public life and in the academic world.

In appreciation of your courageous efforts for a free world, not only for the Anglo-American countries, but for men everywhere, and with best wishes for many years distinguished service,

I am, with high esteem and warm regard

Winston S. Churchill: press release
(*Churchill papers, 2/225*)

20 March 1946

Mr Churchill was asked how he had enjoyed his trip to America and whether he had benefitted by it in health. He said, 'I have enjoyed it very much. I came here for a rest cure and now I am going home to have a rest after the rest cure.'

Q. Was the Reception accorded to your Fulton Speech a surprise to you?

Reply: The Fulton speech was addressed to long-term policies and broad and general themes. Since then, as a result of Soviet troop movements in Persia ordered some time ago, a more difficult and sharper situation has developed. I do not think that this should be beyond the capacity of UNO. Obviously however this is a very important test for the United Nations Organization at the beginning of its career. If it should show itself helpless and futile a most grievous blow will be struck at the ~~structure~~ instrument upon which the hopes of the world are founded. I share these hopes. A resolute effort must be made by all concerned to prevent the outbreak of future wars. This can only be done by dealing with disputes at an early stage and before the parties concerned have got themselves into positions from which they cannot withdraw.

Q. What have you to say to the Soviet proposals to defer consideration of the matter till April 10?

Reply: It would be very dangerous to let matters go from bad to worse in Persia and on the frontiers of Turkey and Iraq. It is very easy to raise disorder in those countries. With money, force and inflammatory propaganda, lawful governments may be overthrown, a state of disorder created and a Quisling government installed. But the Security Council of the United Nations must show that it is a reality and not a pretence; that it deals with facts and truth. I trust that we shall not find that the World Organization allows itself to be confronted with a fait accompli. That would greatly add to the difficulties with which we are confronted.

March 1946

Q. What do you think of the United Nations' efforts to get Franco[1] out of Spain?

Reply: I hold no brief for Franco.[2] If I were a Spaniard I would not wish to live under his government. But it seems to me that he must be very grateful to the French Government in particular for having given him a new lease of life. The Spaniards are proud, morose people with long memories. Their memories even go back to the Peninsular War against Napoleon.[3] They do not like to have their affairs dictated to them by a foreign power. I am sorry the French Government should have yielded to Communist pressure and picked a quarrel with Spain. There is more freedom in Spain than in any Communist governed country. Left to themselves the Spaniards will develop increasingly liberal regimes. Moreover it must not be forgotten that Spain has recently had a most deadly and devastating Civil War. Even the extreme left-wing elements in Spain do not wish to renew the carnage which has stricken almost every home in Spain. The underlying feeling in Spain is that too much blood has been shed already in internal quarrels and that it would be better to try and have a little peace and life and happiness and even prosperity. The Spaniards will not thank foreigners for telling them that they ought to revolt again, especially when the foreigners assure them that they do not mean to interfere themselves.

Q. What do you think about the gift of 600 thousand tons of grain by Soviet Russia to France? Reply: I understand the bulk of this grain came from the United States and was meant to nourish the Russian people. It appears it will be transported by American ships to France and Monsieur Thorez[4] has expressed his thanks to Russia for this great help. I hope the French people, with their accustomed wit and shrewdness, will realize the exact character and purpose of this remarkable transaction.

Q. I suppose we may take it, Mr Churchill, that you are still an opponent of International Communism? Reply: I have never been able to get to like it very much. We must never not forget that all the Communists in the world would have seen England sunk for ever beneath the waves by Hitler's Germany, and that it was only when Soviet Russia was attacked that they put themselves in line with the modern world. I always admire the bravery and patriotism of the

---

[1] Francisco Franco Bahamonde, 1892–1975. Entered Spanish Army, 1907. Second-in-Command, Spanish Foreign Legion, 1920. During the Republican regime he served abroad, in the Balearic Islands, Morocco and the Canary Islands. One of the leaders of the Nationalist revolt, July 1936. Head of State, 1939–75. Sent Spanish volunteers to fight with Germany against Russia, June 1941.

[2] The struck-through portions reflect Churchill's edits to the transcript of the interview.

[3] Napoléon Bonaparte, 1769–1821. Born in Ajaccio, Corsica. 1st Consul of France, 1799–1804. Emperor of France, 1804–15.

[4] Maurice Thorez, 1900–64. Born in Noyelles-Godault. Became a coal miner at the age of 12. Joined French Socialist Party, 1919; French Communist Party, 1920. Party Secretary, French Communist Party, 1923–30; Secretary General, 1930–64. Member of Chamber of Deputies, 1932–40, 1946–58. After the occupation of France in WWII, went into exile in Soviet Union, 1943; returned to France, Nov. 1944. Deputy PM, 1946–7.

Russian Armies in defending their own soil, when it was invaded by Hitler's legions. I have the greatest regard for the Russian people with all their virtues, courage and ~~generosity~~ comradeship. But I made it clear ~~to Mr Stalin~~ in my broadcast of June 22, 1941,[1] that my support of Russia in no way weakened my opposition to Communism which means in fact the death of the soul of man.

Q. How would the fraternal association you suggest between the United States and Great Britain differ from the relationships now existing between those two nations?

Reply: Only by becoming stronger, more intimate more effective and more mutually conscious.

Q. Have you any message to give the United States on your departure?

Reply: The United States must realize its power and its virtue. It must pursue consistently the great themes and principles which have made it the land of the free. All the world is looking to the American democracy for resolute guidance. If I could sum it up in a phrase I would say, 'Dread nought, America'.

Q. What do you say about Great Britain and the British Commonwealth and Empire?

Reply: The underlying unities which prevail among us are such as to make us unconquerable.

Jack Bisco[2] to Winston S. Churchill
(Churchill papers, 2/230)

22 March 1946   New York

My dear Mr Churchill,

I want to express to you my sincere appreciation for your splendid courtesy in granting me the privilege of transmitting your interview over the world-wide facilities of the United States.

From every quarter of the globe we have reports today that the story got smash play.

And may I add, Sir, that I now fully understand why Randolph is such a good newspaperman. He is just a chip off the old block, as we say here in America.

---

[1] Reproduced in *The Churchill Documents*, vol. 16, *The Ever-Widening War, 1941*, pp. 835–8.
[2] Jack Bisco, 1908–91. Vice-president and general business manager, United Press International, 1946.

March 1946

Clement Attlee to Winston S. Churchill
(*Churchill papers, 2/29*)

27 March 1946
Personal and Confidential

My dear Churchill

I hope you and your family have come back refreshed and well after your stay in the United States. I am very much looking forward to a talk with you as soon as you can manage it.

In the meantime, there are two documents which I should like you to see.

1. An outline of a possible scheme for Post War Higher Defence Organisation. This is not yet in its final form, and we are still collecting evidence from those who have had experience of our Defence Organisation in the past. I hope very much that when you have read this we may have a talk as I should greatly value your views. Eden, Lyttelton, PJ[1] and various others have been good enough to give us their views.

2. We have made further progress with the scheme about the War Medal and the time qualification for Campaign Stars, about which I last wrote to you on the 19th October last, when I sent you an HW Paper.[2] For convenience I am enclosing another copy. We have now got to the stage of drawing up a White Paper, which I hope may be published fairly soon. We are awaiting the final views of the Dominions. A copy of the White Paper is enclosed, and it may be helpful if I mention to you the changes which have been made since you last wrote to me.

   (a) The War Medal. Service up to the 2nd September 1945 will now qualify wherever rendered instead of having the previous differentiation between service in the European and Atlantic theatres and in the Pacific and Burma theatres (paragraph 2 III of the White Paper and paragraph 3 II of HW 2383).

   (b) The India Service Medal. This is a new proposal which it has been felt right to adopt in view of the exceptional circumstances which are mentioned in paragraph 3 of the White Paper.

   (c) The Defence Medal. The time qualification for military service overseas from or outside the country of residence in territories subject to enemy air attack or closely threatened has been reduced from twelve to six months (paragraph 9 of the White Paper). I must confess that I have found this a most difficult and complicated subject, but I feel that although the awards of the various Medals and Stars will be on a fairly wide scale, any other scheme would inevitably omit a large number of deserving cases. I very much hope that you will find it

---

[1] Sir (Percy) James Grigg.
[2] 'HW': a catalogue code referring to records created or inherited by Government Communications Headquarters.

MARCH 1946

possible to give the scheme your blessing. As you will see, the White Paper contains an Appendix which summarises the conditions of award of all the Stars and Medals.

Lady Violet Bonham Carter to Winston S. Churchill
(Churchill papers, 2/146)[1]

29 March 1946

Dearest Winston,

Welcome home and congratulations on the truth you spoke at Fulton. It is the root of the matter whether people wish to recognize it or not. Events have powerfully reinforced your words. I am delighted that the Americans are shaping up a bit 'pourvu que ça dure'[2] (as Napoleon's mother always said!). Love to you and Clemmie

PS. International Air Force – yes you and I and some others have always favoured that. But who the devil should we be allowed to use it against under UNO's peculiar constitution, Portugal and Switzerland perhaps? The veto would protect the rest.

Winston S. Churchill to Clement Attlee
(Churchill papers, 2/29)

31 March 1946

My dear Prime Minister,

Thank you for letting me see your memorandum on Higher Organisation for Defence. I am in general agreement with it, subject to the following observations, which I hope you will consider:

(1) The 'Defence Committee' of war time should surely become a revived 'Committee of Imperial Defence' in time of peace. The convenience and flexibility of this administration are very great, and leave all the highest matters of defence in the hands of the Prime Minister, who presides when he chooses, delegates to his deputy, and summons whom he thinks fit. Moreover the title of the Committee is well known, embraces the Dominions, and all are familiar with its working.

(2) I should prefer 'Secretary of State and Treasurer of the Armed Forces of the Crown' to the title 'Minister of the Armed Forces'. There are so many 'Ministers', and this one should certainly have the rank and title of Secretary of State. The word 'Treasurer' emphasizes clearly his association with the

---

[1] This letter was handwritten.
[2] If only it could last.

financial and administrative side rather than with the technical and strategic aspect of his responsibilities. This latter should be vested clearly in the Prime Minister, as Chairman of the Committee of Imperial Defence, who will, through whatever channels or by whatever processes he may choose, be the final arbiter on the broad questions of strategy. It is to him that the Committee of the three Chiefs of Staff, whose continuance together is vital, should look directly.

(3) You will find it interesting to read my father's memorandum on Army and Navy administration, included in the report of Lord Hartington's[1] Commission of March 21, 1890. It is surprising how much was foreseen in this pregnant document, although the machinery therein proposed would not now be suitable. For instance, there we find the idea of combination between the Services; the primacy of the fighting chiefs of the Services in formulation of war plans, subject to Cabinet approval; the institution of the new Minister, which you are now about to propose; the assignment to that Minister of the business of supply – 'He would as it were set up and carry on a great shop from which the military and naval head could procure most of the supplies they needed' (here we have a clear forecast of the Ministry of Munitions); and lastly the presentation of a joint Defence Budget by the new Minister, both to the Cabinet in the first instance and afterwards to Parliament – a project to which I have always attached great importance and which the advent of the Air has made indispensable.

(4) Even after the strategic issues have been decisively assigned to the Chiefs of Staff communicating directly with the Prime Minister and Minister of Defence, an enormous sphere remains for the new Minister, whatever be his title. Especially there is this keeping 'a great shop' which is virtually the Minister of Supply and Minister of Aircraft Production in combination. The new Minister would supply the three Services with all they require, except only that warship-building would remain with the Admiralty. The military departments would thus be freed from the making of contracts work, in which they have so often failed. A great deal of coordination has already been achieved and this should now be finally settled. In making contracts for the three Services the new Minister would be responsible also for using his patronage and power to make sure that expansive capacity was maintained and developed, not only in Government arsenals but in private firms, which would enable the transition to war conditions, or the danger of war, to be smooth and rapid.

I see you have assigned military research to this new Minister, under whom should also surely be the Imperial War College, where the three Services are

---

[1] Spencer Compton Cavendish, 1833–1908. Marquess of Hartington, 1858, on his father's succession as 7th Duke of Devonshire. Educated at Trinity College, Cambridge. Lord of the Admiralty, 1863. Secretary of State for War, 1866, 1882–5; for India, 1880–2. Postmaster-General, 1868–71. Chief Secretary for Ireland, 1871–4. MP (Lib.) for North Lancashire, 1857–68; New Radnor, 1869–80; Northeast Lancashire, 1880–5; Rossendale Div. of Lancashire, 1885–91. Succeeded his father as 8th Duke of Devonshire, 1891.

taught to work together. I trust that this College, in the founding of which I was concerned after the last war, will not only be maintained but encouraged. There should be a junior course instituted in some way or other for officers of from seven to ten years' service, in order to facilitate what will ultimately arise, namely fusion. If these processes were hurried it would cause all manner of friction, but we should now begin to breed the generation which will achieve it.

(5) Finally, although I know how difficult it is to telescope offices, I am of opinion that there should be a peace time contraction in the machinery at the top. It is hard to reduce the status of the Secretaries of State for War and Air and of the First Lord from their present positions, and I do not suggest it now. But surely the Ministry of Aircraft Production and the Ministry of Supply could be headed as soon as a convenient opportunity offers by Under-Secretaries of the rank of the Financial Secretary to the Treasury, at £2,000 a year, who should be effectively subordinated to the new Secretary of State and Treasurer of the Armed Forces of the Crown, or whatever he is called?

The Lord Randolph Churchill memorandum is found in my Life of him, in the Appendix to the second volume. I am almost sure I presented a copy of this book to the Cabinet Room Library, but if this is not so Rowan should telephone and let me know and I will send you one.

I hope to read the paper on Medals in a few days.

April
1946

Sarah Churchill to Winston S. Churchill
(Churchill papers, 1/42)[1]

1 April 1946

My darling Papa,
    This is just to thank you very inadequately for taking me with you – this time in the civilian capacity – on another trip. I know it was far from perfect for you, but you contributed much to the world cause, quite apart from what you did for poor Old England. As for me – you know it is a joy to be with you both. I have a private account to settle with Miss Sturdee. Apart from all the lovely dresses you gave me, which I will do as soon as I have put my house in order here. I can't thank you enough for the lovely – and as always the thrilling time I had.
    Ever your devoted and loving (in or out of uniform) ADC.

Alfred Duff Cooper to Winston S. Churchill
(Churchill papers, 2/5)

2 April 1946

My dear Winston,
    [. . .]
    Your speech at Fulton, while it was very well received in Conservative circles, created – no doubt wrongly – the impression that your hopes were centred solely on the United States and that you had given up France as a lost country which could no longer be of assistance to anyone. There is, I am afraid, a great deal of pessimism with regard to politics throughout the country, and the people are very sensitive to anything that seems to confirm their pessimistic outlook. They know that the Communists are being helped

---

[1] This letter was handwritten.

with advice, and possibly with money and weapons, by the Soviets, and they cannot understand why we and the Americans refuse to help the parties who are trying to defeat the Communists.

That, I am afraid, is the case all over Europe. There is not one purely European country where there is a Communist majority; and yet there are many Communist Governments and everywhere the Communists seem to be gaining power and importance. There are probably more Communists in France than in most countries, and, even so, they have a far larger share of newspapers than they are entitled to by their numbers.

I hope if there are any other points on which you would like information, you will let me know.

[. . .]

Clement Attlee to Winston S. Churchill
(Churchill papers, 2/29)

3 April 1946

My dear Churchill,

Thank you very much for your letter of March 31st[1] about the memorandum on Higher Organization for Defence. I am very greatly obliged to you for sending me your observations in such detail, and I am glad to know that you think the draft proposals are generally on the right lines. I am considering the various points which you have made and I hope to send you a reply in the course of a few days.

I have read your father's memorandum with the greatest interest; he was certainly far ahead of his time.

James Gerard[2] to Winston S. Churchill
(Churchill papers, 2/226)

4 April 1946   New York

My dear Sage,

Not since the visit after the War of the Revolution of LaFayette[3] to the United States has any guest had the reception given you here.

---

[1] Reproduced above (pp. 275–7).

[2] James Watson Gerard, 1867–1951. Lawyer. Judge, US Supreme Court, State of New York, 1907. US Ambassador to Berlin, 1913–17; acted as an intermediary between the British and German Governments on all matters concerning British POWs in Germany, 1914–17. Honorary knighthood, 1917. Returned to practise law in the US, 1917.

[3] Marie Joseph Paul Yves Roche Gilbert du Motier, 1757–1834. Marquis de Lafayette. Officer, Musketeers, 1771. Capt., Dragoons, 1775. Maj.-Gen., US Army, American War of Independence.

And, in addition, your winged words have contributed in no small degree to the settlement of the affairs of the world and the supremacy of the United Nations.

To my great regret I did not have a chance to have five minutes' talk with you.[1]

Winston S. Churchill to Sir Orme Sargent[2]
(Churchill papers, 2/8)

4 April 1946
Private

My dear Orme Sargent,

I should be much obliged if I could be given a note of the statements I made about Tito[3] and Mihailovich. I have of course some of them, but I want to make sure of the position I took on behalf of His Majesty's government as I may have to refer to the matter in the near future. I trust that Mihailovich will receive a fair and full public trial and that our influence is used to that end.

I should also be glad for advice as to what answer, if any, to send to the Lithuanian Minister to the United States of America whose letter to me of March 18[4] I enclose herewith.

Finally I send you a document on Roumania which you may be interested to read. I do not know whether there is anything to be said about it.

Winston S. Churchill to Ernest Bevin
(Churchill papers, 2/5)

5 April 1946
Private and Personal

My dear Bevin,

I read in the newspapers various statements about our proposed alliance with France. I need scarcely say that I am strongly attached to the idea, having been for so many years in the closest touch with France in all her vicissitudes.

---

[1] Churchill responded on Apr. 9: 'I am deeply grateful to you for your kind letter.'

[2] Orme Garton Sargent, 1884–1962. Known in FO as 'Moley'. Educated at Radley. Entered FO, 1906. Second Secretary, Berne, 1917; First Secretary, 1919. Attended Paris Peace Conference, 1919. Counsellor, FO, 1926. Head of Central Dept, FO, 1928–33. Asst Under-Secretary of State for Foreign Affairs, 1933. Knighted, 1937. Deputy Under-Secretary of State, 1939; Permanent Under-Secretary, 1946–9.

[3] Josip Broz Tito, 1892–1980. President of League of Communists of Yugoslavia, 1937–80. President of Federal Executive Council, 1943–63. Federal Secretary of People's Defence, 1943–53. Marshal of Yugoslavia, 1943–80. Federal Secretary of National Defence, 1945–53. President of Yugoslavia, 1953–80. Secretary-General of Non-Aligned Movement, 1961–4.

[4] Reproduced above (p. 268).

However, I ask myself the question whether we should not be well advised to allow the elections in France to take place before this matter is carried through. We shall then have a much more representative Government to deal with and it could not be said that we are doing anything to influence the course of the elections. As these are likely to be held, I understand, in June there is not long to wait, and I do not suppose that your plans in any case would come to a head before then. Perhaps you are able to reassure me.

Whatever else may or may not be said about the Greek elections, they are surely a great vindication of our policy, both in the Coalition and since, of not allowing Greece to fall into the hands of the Communist Party as the result of an unconstitutional seizure of power. It is quite clear that the Greeks did not wish to be governed by the Communists, who would undoubtedly have seized the Central Government in December 1944 if we had not intervened in full force. I hope it will be feasible to bring the British troops home as soon as possible as this will put an end to the suspicion that we are trying to gain some advantage for ourselves in Greek territory.

I do not propose to ask for a Debate on Foreign Affairs till after the Easter holidays, but I thought you would not mind my writing these few lines to let you know where I stand.[1]

Clement Attlee to Winston S. Churchill
(Churchill papers, 2/29)

5 April 1946

My dear Churchill,

In my letter of yesterday,[2] I promised to write to you further about the points you made on the proposals on Higher Organisation for Defence.

I will take them in order –

(1) This is largely a question of nomenclature. The constitutional developments with the Dominions since the Committee of Imperial Defence was formed, have I think, made the title inapplicable. The proposals under discussion deal particularly with the organisation of the Defence Forces for which the United Kingdom is responsible. I propose to consider with the Dominion Prime Ministers the kind of organisation which would best ensure cooperation between the units of the British Commonwealth. You are aware of the susceptibilities of some of the Dominions, particularly Canada on this matter. I shall try to get the substance rather than the outward form. The use of the word 'Imperial' in this connection is I am advised likely to create unnecessary friction. In other respects our idea is that

[1] The last paragraph was handwritten.
[2] Reproduced above, dated Apr. 3 (p. 279).

the Post-War Defence Committee will be closely modelled on the pre-war Committee of Imperial Defence.

(2) I share your dislike for the multiplication of 'Ministers'. I prefer historical titles. I do not think the new Minister should be a Secretary of State as although he will have some administrative function, his position is not quite that of a Departmental Minister. I agree with you that the Prime Minister must remain Chairman of the Defence Committee.

(3) Your father saw the need for a Minister of Munitions or as we call it today a Minister of Supply. I gather that you conceive of the new Minister being also the Minister of Supply. The general conception of the draft scheme is that of a Minister of Supply serving the three fighting Services and the Minister of the Armed Forces acting in respect to them as the instrument of the Prime Minister.

The co-ordination of the fighting Services and their Supply Minister on the one hand and the civilian Ministers in respect of the activities in the field of Defence – would be effected by the Prime Minister. I think with you that in due course the status of these four Ministers will have to fall relatively to that of the new Minister.

I entirely agree with you as to the need for the continuance of the Imperial Defence College. This has already been provided for and the first post-war course, which includes three American officers, commenced on the 2nd of April. It is hoped to double the pre-war numbers of students going through the next course. Plans for the junior staff course on an inter-Service basis are going forward.

I need hardly say that should you care to discuss these points further, I should be delighted to do so.

Walter Graebner:[1] recollection
('My Dear Mr Churchill', pages 43–7)

6 April 1946

Late in life Churchill for a while considered dispensing with his team of secretaries, at least for night work, and using machinery to record his thoughts. He allowed the SoundScriber company of America to install, free of charge, the most advanced machine its engineers could design, equipped with microphones that could pick up his voice wherever he was – whether in his bed, his bath or his study. It went for hours without requiring new disks and it started and stopped from the action of the sound waves.

---

[1] Walter Graebner, 1909–76. Chief of *Time* magazine's Chicago bureau, 1935–7; of London bureau, 1937–46. European area director, Life–Time, 1946–53. Chairman, Erwin Wasey Ltd, 1953–63. Director, Interpublic Ltd, 1963–6.

Churchill was fascinated by the wonderful equipment, and derived a good deal of pleasure from trying it out. But he never thought seriously of using it. 'I'm too old for that kind of thing,' he said. 'I think I'll go on using secretaries as long as I can afford them. Anyway I rather like having them around when I work.'

The installation of the SoundScriber, however, did give Mr Churchill a chance to state in his own words his recipe for combining a full working day with the good life. I was with the head of the SoundScriber Company, a Mr Gfroerer,[1] when he went down to Chartwell to supervise the installation of the machine, and listened in on the following conversation:

> Churchill: What is your day in America like (looking Mr Gfroerer straight in the eye)? What time do you get to your office and when do you stop working?
>
> Gfroerer: I'm at my desk every morning at eight and leave at five-thirty. At noon I have a short break for lunch. We do that five days a week, and sometimes I go around to the office Saturday mornings to read the mail.
>
> Churchill: My dear man, you don't mean it. That is the most perfect prescription for a short life that I've ever heard.
>
> Mr Gfroerer, a little frightened and somewhat staggered by Churchill's sudden probing into his private life, then confessed that his wife[2] also did not approve of his hours at all, and would certainly be delighted to hear the views of Mr Churchill.
>
> Gfroerer: Mrs Gfroerer hates to get up at six forty-five and have breakfast so early. Then she doesn't see me until six in the evening. We have dinner early, and by ten I'm so tired that I fall into bed and am asleep in two minutes. I know I've got to slow down. That's what Mrs Gfroerer is always telling me.
>
> Churchill: You must sleep sometime between lunch and dinner, and no halfway measures. Take off your clothes and get into bed. That's what I always do. Don't think you will be doing less work because you sleep during the day. That's a foolish notion held by people who have no imagination. You will be able to accomplish more. You get two days in one – well, at least one and a half, I'm sure. When the war started, I *had* to sleep during the day because that was the only way I could cope with my responsibilities. Later, when I became Prime Minister, my burdens were of course even greater. Often I was obliged to work far into the night. I had to see reports, take decisions and issue instructions that could not wait until the next day. And at night I'd also dictate minutes requesting information which my staff could assemble for me in the morning – and place before me when I woke up.

---

[1] Herbert Gfroerer, 1894–1970. Chairman of the board and chief executive, SoundScriber Corp.
[2] Fannie Palmer, 1899–1987.

Churchill relighted his cigar, poured himself a little more brandy, passed the bottle and continued:

But a man should sleep during the day for another reason. Sleep enables you to be at your best in the evening when you join your wife, family and friends for dinner. That is the time to be at your best – a good dinner, with good wines . . . champagne is *very* good . . . then some brandy – that is the great moment of the day. Man is ruler then – perhaps only for fifteen minutes, but for that time at least he is master – and the ladies must not leave the table too soon.

Gfroerer: I must slow down. My wife has been telling me that for years, but something is always happening at the office. Mrs Gfroerer will agree with everything you've said when I tell her.
Churchill: Do you always get up for breakfast?
Gfroerer: But, of course.
Churchill: Your wife, too?
Gfroerer: Why, yes.
Churchill: My, my. My wife and I tried two or three times in the last forty years to have breakfast together, but it didn't work. Breakfast should be had in bed, alone. Not downstairs, after one has dressed.

His eyes twinkling, Churchill added:

I don't think our married life would have been nearly so happy if we both had dressed and come down for breakfast all these years.

In his old age, as the continuing responsibilities of high office drained his strength, Churchill's longing for a good sleep became almost an obsession, and when he failed to get one, he acted a little as if he had been cheated. One summer's day at Chartwell, when he told me rather grumpily that he had awakened two mornings in succession at six o'clock, I asked him whether he was still taking sleeping pills. 'One every night for the last ten years,' he said proudly. Since it was nearly time for his afternoon nap, I ventured the suggestion that he have a pill then and there, adding that he was only taking a half dose anyway. Churchill quickly sent for his pills, and rather revengefully popped one into his mouth. About twenty minutes later he happily announced that he was off to bed.

Winston S. Churchill to Alfred Duff Cooper
(*Churchill papers, 2/5*)

7 April 1946
Personal and Private

My dear Duffie,

Thank you so much for your most interesting letter.[1] I am naturally most grieved to see France fall again into political fatuity and, of course, if they became definitely Communist, I should consider them ruined for ever. I am hoping that no Anglo-French Alliance will be made until after the Elections. I certainly think we should do all we can to make it clear that we have no sympathy with Communists.

Have you by any chance read the extraordinary, vigorous refusal which the Labour Executive sent to the Communist appeal for affiliation? I could have a photostat made of it if you like, as I think you might certainly find it of value to have it by you. I still nurse the hope that France will shape her destiny in harmony with the two great western democracies.

It will be a gloomy outlook, even if the three-party compromise continues, because the Communists, who give nothing, will not only carry a great number of points, but will infiltrate steadily through their organization and persistency into the Socialist party, already so weak in spirit and character.

The folly of the French action about Franco is patent to the world. They have given Franco a new lease of life and, quite apart from this, it is a great danger when foreign policy, taking the form of closing frontiers and threats of blockade, is decided not on merits but to meet political balances at a Cabinet table.

I am sending you, by Foreign Office Bag, my Breguet watch and a letter to the firm, and I shall be much obliged if you will have these sent round to them.

I shall not come to France until after the Elections. I hope that even a Communist France will not debar me from Monte Carlo.

Things are pretty grim here.

Winston S. Churchill to Anthony Eden
(*Churchill papers, 2/6*)

7 April 1946
Personal and Private

My dear Anthony,

I have been thinking over the matter which I broached to you on my return, and have come to the conclusion that it would be better not to make a formal

[1] Of 2 Apr., reproduced above (pp. 278–9).

change at the present time. My health is a good deal better since I returned and Moran and a specialist he called in assure me that my dizziness will pass in four or five weeks. It is already definitely better. Also I seem to have more strength. I wish therefore to try to carry on for a while, and I feel sure I can count on your help in an ever-increasing measure and that, when I am not at the House and you are, you will feel that you have perfect freedom of action. Broadly speaking our policy will be regulated by the weekly meetings of the Shadows. I am most anxious to handle matters so as to make the formal transference, when it occurs, smooth and effectual.

I look forward to working in all the old confidence and intimacy which has marked our march through the years of storm.

Apart from the improvement in my health, a minor point has influenced me, namely, my hearing from James Stuart that you would not in any case draw the £2,000 a year salary as Leader of the Opposition, on account of the interest you take in the Bank. I have been worried to think of your doing the work while I was away and my drawing the salary. I quite appreciate the sense of delicacy which has moved you, although there is nothing in the Statute which affects the matter.

One of the things I have to settle in the near future is the wish of Ralph Assheton to retire from the Chairmanship of the Party. My own feeling at present is for Harold Macmillan to take his place, who would bring a great deal of force and zeal into the business and who is certainly one of our brightest rising lights. Let me know what you think of this.

By the way, I heard that you were vexed that I had asked Swinton[1] to come to our meeting the other day. I think whoever is acting Leader of the House of Lords must come to these meetings and it was in that temporary capacity that I invited him. I am sure he did not mean to reflect on your Anglo-Egyptian Treaty.

I hope you will make a good debating speech on Tuesday in reply to the Chancellor. I am sure he will be glad to pay his way with his own sorry crowd by some features of hate and spite.

---

[1] Philip Cunliffe-Lister, 1884–1972. On active service, 1914–17 (MC). Joint Secretary, Ministry of National Service, 1917–18. MP (Cons.) for Hendon, 1918–35. President of the Board of Trade, 1922–3, 1924–9, 1931. Secretary of State for the Colonies, 1931–5. Viscount Swinton, 1935. Secretary of State for Air, 1935–8 (when he advocated a larger Air Force expansion than the Government was prepared to accept). Brought back into Government on the outbreak of war as Chairman of UK Commercial Corporation, responsible for pre-empting purchases of supplies and materials overseas that were needed by the German war machine. Appointed by Churchill in May 1940 as Chairman of the Security Executive, concerned with measures against sabotage in Britain and overseas. Organized supply route to the Soviet Union through the Persian Gulf, 1941–2. Cabinet Minister Resident in West Africa, 1942–4. Minister for Civil Aviation, 1944–5. Minister of Materials, 1951–2. Deputy Leader, House of Lords, 1951–5. Secretary of State for Commonwealth Relations, 1952–5. Earl of Swinton, 1955.

Winston S. Churchill to Ernest Bevin
(Churchill papers, 2/145)

9 April 1946

My dear Foreign Secretary,

You will no doubt remember the case of General Mihailovitch from the days when we were colleagues in the War Cabinet. I think it would be fair to say that in the period before Tito became active General Mihailovitch was effective in organising Serbian resistance. Later, all attempts to bring him and Tito together failed, and they became increasingly hostile to each other. We made repeated attempts in this latter period to induce Mihailovitch to take some action against the enemy, but on one pretext or another he put us off, so that we had to give our main support to Tito. Subsequent to this there was also, I think, evidence to show that at least Mihailovitch's subordinate commanders had been collaborating actively with the enemy.

Despite all this I do not feel it right that Mihailovitch should be summarily tried and convicted by Tito without an effort being made by His Majesty's Government to secure a fair trial for him. There is surely no reason why he should be treated worse than Goering.[1] I know that Anthony Eden has been in touch with the Foreign Office about this and that you are trying to ascertain what the actual position is, and whether Mihailovitch is in fact in Tito's hands. I should hope that if this proves to be true you might feel it possible to intervene on behalf of His Majesty's Government and ask for a fair trial before the world.

Anthony Eden to Winston S. Churchill
(Churchill papers, 2/6)[2]

10 April 1946
Personal and Private

My dear Winston,

Thank you so much for your letter[3] in which you tell me that you have reconsidered the position since our talk, and would now like to carry on with

---

[1] Hermann Goering, 1893–1946. Served as a Lt in the German Infantry, 1914. Cdr, Richthofen Fighter Sqn, 1918. A follower of Hitler from 1923. Wounded during the unsuccessful Munich putsch of Nov. 1923, after which he lived in Austria, Italy and Sweden. Air Adviser in Denmark and Sweden, 1924–8. Returned to Germany, and elected to the Reichstag, 1928. President of the Reichstag, 1932–3. PM of Prussia, 1933. C-in-C, GAF, 1933–45. Air Chf Mshl, 1935. Commissioner for the Four-Year Plan, 1936. FM, 1938. President of the General Council for the War Economy, 1940. Sentenced to death at Nuremberg, Oct. 1946; committed suicide the night before his intended execution.
[2] This letter was handwritten.
[3] Reproduced above (pp. 285–6).

the leadership of the opposition in the House. As I told you the other day, this is entirely agreeable to me, and I am delighted at the doctors' good report.

I am very ready to try to give you any help I can, just as I feel sure all our other colleagues are, and you can count on me to play my part with you and them.

When, however, you write of help 'in an ever-increasing measure' I am bound to reply that I cannot see how this can be worked. It is only the leader of the opposition who can guide and father the party in the House, and take the day to day decisions. To do this he must be constantly in the House and in touch with the rank and file of the party. The position is quite different from that when a leader of the House, with a majority behind him, can act for the Prime Minister. In short there is, I am sure, no room for anything in the nature of a Deputy Leader of the opposition in the House of Commons.

I do not imagine, after our talk the other night, that this is in your mind; but I think that I ought to let you know what is on mine.

PS. Thank you for letting me know your idea about Assheton's successor. I have a suggestion to make, and perhaps we could have a word about it some time. Woolton?

Jo Sturdee to John Peck
(Churchill papers, 2/228)

10 April 1946
Personal

Dear Mr Peck,

Thank you for your letter of yesterday's date. It was nice to hear from you again and even the sight of your handwriting brought back many happy memories of No. 10 and all that. I had heard some vague sort of rumour that you were at the British Embassy in Lisbon or some other such place, which sounded very exciting. I do hope you are enjoying it all at the Foreign Office.

Mr Churchill had signed the photograph you sent for Mr Charles E. Maxwell[1] – after the usual questions, 'What?', 'Who' and 'Why' – and I return it to you herewith, as requested, for you to cope with. He was very interested to learn that you had left No. 10 and said 'What is he doing there?' I'm afraid all he got was my usual blank look and 'I don't know.'

He is in very fine form these days and very tolerant. He keeps us all dancing about and amused. I don't know that his holiday in America was much of a

---

[1] Former Lt, US Navy. Radio announcer for Joe Mitchell Chappel, an American author and radio show host.

rest for him, but he seems to have come back refreshed and just as vigorous as ever.

Needless to say I thoroughly enjoyed it all over there. It was hectic, in more ways than one.

We miss Mrs Hill very much. Lizzie Layton is now a happy, married woman and seems to be settling down to bliss with her handsome South African in Pretoria. And so life goes on.

Winston S. Churchill to Anthony Eden
(Churchill papers, 2/6)

11 April 1946

My dear Anthony,

Thank you for your letter.[1]

With regard to what you say about there being 'no room for anything in the nature of a Deputy Leader of the Opposition in the House of Commons', I hope this does not mean that you will not continue to act for me when I am away or that you wish to give up presiding over the meetings of the Chairmen of the Party committees. There ought surely to be room for a second-in-command such as you certainly were before I went abroad. I hope to be able to be at the House every sitting day, except perhaps an occasional Monday, but I should like to have someone who would be willing to act for me should I be called away for any reason. The only engagement I have which will take me out of the country is to visit Holland on Wednesday, May 8. This will mean my absence from the House on Wednesday, Thursday and Friday of that week: I hope, however, to be back on Monday or Tuesday, May 14, at the latest. May I presume that you will take charge on this occasion?

I am much interested in your suggestion of Woolton. James Stuart also mentioned him to me, and, oddly enough, yesterday Sir James Hawkey, my local Chairman, put forward quite independently the same idea.

There is a rumour that a statement on iron and steel is to be made on Monday. If so, I shall be there and some remarks will have to be made. Oliver Lyttelton is preparing a note for me. Should the Government postpone the announcement until Tuesday, I shall stay in the country on Monday as the business is not important and will ask Oliver Stanley[2] to watch the proceedings, as I imagine you do not wish to interrupt your well-earned holiday.

[1] Reproduced above (pp. 287–8).
[2] Oliver Frederick George Stanley, 1896–1950. Son of 17th Earl of Derby. Educated at Eton. On active service, France, 1914–18 (MC, despatches). Maj., 1918. Called to the Bar, 1919. MP (Cons.) for Westmorland, 1924–45; for Bristol West, 1945–50. Parliamentary Under-Secretary, Home Office, 1931–3. Minister of Transport, 1933–4; of Labour, 1934–5. PC, 1934. President of the Board of Education, 1935–7; of the Board of Trade, 1937–40. Secretary of State for War, Jan.–May 1940; for the Colonies, 1942–5.

April 1946

Anthony Eden to Winston S. Churchill
(Churchill papers, 2/6)[1]

11 April 1946

My dear Winston,

Thank you for your letter of today. As I told you on the bench this evening I shall be very ready to deputise for you when you are out of the country. I shall also be glad to continue to preside over the meetings of the Chairmen of the party committees. Please, therefore, don't worry about these things.

My only point (which I stick to!) is that when you are here there is no room for a deputy leader in the House.

Winston S. Churchill to Ernest Bevin
(Churchill papers, 2/145)

11 April 1946

My dear Ernie,

Following upon the letter which I wrote to you on April 9,[2] after consultation with Anthony, about General Mihailovitch, I send you the enclosed statements,[3] which have just reached me.

I feel it my duty to send these things on because they affect a man's life, & he ought to have a fair public trial.

Ernest Bevin to Winston S. Churchill
(Churchill papers, 2/5)

11 April 1946
Private and Personal

Dear Winston,

Thank you for your letter of April 5th.[4]

I was interested by what you write about France. I have not been advocating the immediate conclusion of an alliance. When Gouin[5] made his statement, I

---

[1] This letter was handwritten.
[2] Reproduced above (p. 287).
[3] Made by Churchill in the House of Commons about Mihailovic and Tito between Sep. 1943 and Dec. 1945.
[4] Reproduced above (pp. 280–1).
[5] Félix Gouin, 1884–1977. Born in Bouches-du-Rhône. Educated at Aix-en-Provence. Voted against Pétain, 1940. President, Provisional Consultative Assembly, 1943–5. Chairman, Provisional Government of France, 1946. Vice-President, Council of Ministers, June–Dec. 1946. Minister in Charge of Planning Commission in Cabinet of Léon Blum, 1946–7. Minister and President of the Council for Planning in Cabinet of Paul Ramadier, 1947.

took soundings in Paris in order to find out whether the French Government wished to proceed to the conclusion of an alliance, or whether they wished first to reach a settlement of the problem of Germany's western frontier, which had been their attitude hitherto. I found that in making his statement Gouin had in fact been speaking only for his own party and was not speaking for the French Government as a whole. So the matter rests there.

I am having the papers referred to in the *New York Times* cutting looked up. I will also have Vyshinsky's[1] statement looked up, and if it was made in a public session I will send you a copy of it.

I hope that you have come back refreshed from your visit to the United States.

With every good wish.

Winston S. Churchill to Lord Halifax
(Churchill papers, 2/6)

12 April 1946
Private

My dear Edward,

I received today the enclosed letter from the Foreign Office, so that at long last the message from our 'Shadow' Cabinet has reached me. I never received the telegram in America, which is the reason why this letter has been written by the Foreign Office. I should have been much comforted if I had had it at the time. I do not know whether you have heard at all about it not being sent on to me after it reached the Embassy, but, if not, it might be of interest to you to inquire because at the time it was quite important to me, and it is possible that messages of real importance may come through in future and be held up in this way. James Stuart has been making inquiries of the cable companies and others and has obtained receipts of its delivery in Washington, and the Foreign Office were also asked to assist. Forgive my bothering you with this but I felt you ought to know.

It is not so bad over here as one thought it would be from the reports reaching America. The Government seem to me to be learning a good deal from responsibility and contact with events. The Budget is, of course, a 'mark time' affair, but people seem to rejoice at anything now and are even thankful if things get no worse. The Chancellor, who has inherited the mighty revenue gained by the Coalition Government on the impulse of the struggle

---

[1] Andrei Yanuarevich Vyshinsky, 1883–1954. Born in Odessa. Prof. of Criminal Law, Moscow, 1923. Deputy State Prosecutor, 1933; State Prosecutor, 1935. Principal public figure conducting the 'purge trials'. First Deputy Minister for Foreign Affairs, 1940. Soviet Representative to Allied Commissions for the Mediterranean and Italy during WWII. Foreign Minister, 1949–53. Principal Soviet Delegate at the UN, 1953–4.

for life, proposes to lead a lush life upon it and finds a little small change in his pocket for local charities, designed to give him a good name in the neighbourhood. I am very glad the indications of the Loan getting through are so much improved.

I do hope you have fully recovered from your really serious attack, and have had a proper convalescence and rest. We all look forward to your return, and I hope you will be a regular attendant at our weekly meetings. It will be very uphill work for the Party for some years to come.

Clemmie and I send our warmest regards to Dorothy and thanks for all her hospitality and kindness.

Winston S. Churchill: speech
(Hansard)

12 April 1946

I am very glad that an agreement has been confirmed between the Government and the Opposition parties on this matter.[1] The discussions which take place through the usual channels are of very great importance to the smooth working of the House, and it would be a great pity if such discussions took place and afterwards the conclusions reached had to be thrown over. That would vitiate and obstruct to a certain extent that admirable method of working, which has done so much to keep the course of public business smooth and, in a way, to promote the corporate sense here. I am glad that the Government have discussed the matter very fully with their supporters, and have adhered to the view which they expressed last week through the Leader of the House. Of course, this is a matter in which everybody has striven to aim at the greatest good of the greatest number, and to fit in as far as possible all the different obligations which we have to discharge. I certainly agree with the Leader of the Liberal Party that it would be a disaster if we became whole-time professional politicians in this House. We are very experienced politicians but we are not professional politicians, in the sense in which that phrase is used in some other countries. We are representative British worthies, chosen by universal suffrage, and long may it be so that the House is a good representation of the wishes, the feelings, the character, and the diversity of the nation at large.

The business of the House of Commons and the business of the executive Government are matters of the utmost consequence. As far as the executive Government are concerned, the hon. Member who spoke last[2] has long

---

[1] A proposed change in convening time for the House of Commons. The proposal was to convene at 2.30 p.m., but Herbert Morrison moved to amend this to 2.45 p.m. in order to give more time for committee meetings earlier in the day.

[2] Samuel Viant, 1882–1964. Educated at Davenport Higher School. Asst Postmaster-General,

experience of this House and his opinion is mature and wide in these matters, but it is a long time since he was a Minister and things have got much more severe since then. I am quite sure that the burden of pressure on Ministers is all that they can possibly carry. It was so in the days of the Coalition Government during the war, and I have not the slightest doubt that now, with this immense pressure of legislation, from which Ministers do not seem anxious to relieve themselves in any way – though we would be pleased to enter into some discussions on that through the usual channels – the work must be enormous. Ministers have to deal with Questions and often the Questions go back to Departments for further information so that answers can be given.

I understand that, except in cases of emergency, the Cabinet meetings are now held in the morning. The Government work through committees whose meetings are not chronicled, but without which it would be impossible to carry on the infinitely complex work of the modern State. I do not think that the mere urging of Ministers to get up early in the morning, to have their Cabinets a quarter of an hour earlier or anything like that, would be useful at the present time, because I am sure that they are busy from the time they wake until the time they go to sleep and that sometimes used to be very late in time of war. I think that the process of the executive Government must be carefully secured, but how about the House of Commons? We have an immense mass of legislation which can only be dealt with by the fullest use of the Standing or Grand Committees upstairs, and I am anxious that the Standing Committees should have their full chance, should be fully interwoven with the life of the House, so that the House can judge after a little more experience in another year, what changes, if any, are required in its procedure.

I have always believed that the work of the Standing Committees would greatly accelerate the business of the House, but we must give the Committees a chance. If they sit all the morning and disperse at 1 o'clock, there ought to be some interval before hon. Members are expected to be back at their places to take part in what is, after all, the most lively part of the Parliamentary day and one most characteristic of the House of Commons, namely, Question time. An hour and a quarter is not very long in which to get lunch, and surely hon. Members ought to have a little rest before immediately addressing themselves to new tasks. You cannot get good, patient consideration of grave public matters by men who are hustled and rushed around on a closely cut schedule from one point to another in the course of the day. Tempers are apt to get frayed, digestions may well be affected, and the course of public business is neither satisfactory or agreeable.

Therefore, I think that, although this is a very small change, it is a very helpful change. We gain half an hour a day of Parliamentary time; we get a quarter of an hour more interlude in the middle of the day. There are many

1929–31. Member, Committee of Privileges, 1953–7. Chairman, Trustees of the Members' Fund, 1955–7. Mayor, Willesden, 1960–1.

countries where the middle of the day is a time of repose, and it may well be that the human race would consult its health and advantage if it lived more in the natural manner, breaking the day by short intervals for repose, reflection and refreshment, instead of working from morning to night. I think it is not really very much to ask that a Member of Parliament, who has important questions to ask and business to carry on in the afternoon, and who has sat till one o'clock on a Committee upstairs, following it with great attention, should now have an hour and a half in which to prepare himself, before he is again called upon to discharge his important tasks.

The hon. Gentleman who spoke last said that he never knew of any good business being done after 9.30, and that was his experience in the House. I certainly remember that the great Debates of former days took place between 10 and 12 at night. On those occasions the Leader of the Opposition spoke for an hour and the Leader of the Government wound up, in speeches every word of which was studied with the greatest attention by the very keen political classes who followed their affairs. In those days politics largely took the place of football. Public men had their attendant troops of fans and backers who knew their form to a turn. Consequently these Debates created great interest and were a fine exposition of what had occurred sometimes in a two days' or three days' Debate. This again led to crowded Houses, a great deal of excitement and, as I have several times pointed out, this House of Commons lived upon its vivid moments and often even upon its scenes. So we should never get too mealy mouthed or frightened about little tiffs that occur in the course of our affairs.

I saw very good work done then in educating the country and in forming opinion in the House. When the Budget Debate was wound up last night by my right hon. Friend the Member for West Bristol (Mr Stanley) in a most witty speech, and when it was replied to by the Chancellor of the Exchequer in a speech of his usual lucidity and rather less than his usual party asperity, and both speeches were most informing and instructive and formed a very vivid close to the Debate, where were the Members? The House was nearly empty, or at least much less full than it is now for long periods of the day.

Mr Bowles (Nuneaton):[1] It would be less full an hour later.

Mr Churchill: I do not think that is so at all, and I am sure that the choosing of the time for winding up speeches between 7.30 and 9.15 does not give a chance for the case to be stated on both sides as it ought to be stated at the end of a long Debate. I believe this extra half hour, which is fully justified by the improvements of communication which have already occurred, and which will increasingly come back to us, will be very beneficial in that way. I am glad the Government have been able to take this course. I think there is a great deal

---

[1] Francis George Bowles, 1902–70. Educated at University College London and London School of Economics. Solicitor, Pearl Assurance Co., 1925–47. MP (Lab.) for Nuneaton, 1942–64. Deputy Chairman of Ways and Means, 1948–50. Capt. of the Yeomen of the Guard, 1964–70. Baron, 1964.

of advantage in trying to work in the House as a whole. I know quite naturally there will be differences of opinion on these matters of personal habit and convenience but, broadly speaking, I am sure the course that is proposed by the Leader of the House is one that will commend itself to the great majority of the House on both sides, and that it is one which will conduce to the continued efficiency and swift progress of our vast affairs at home and abroad.

Sir Orme Sargent to Winston S. Churchill
(Churchill papers, 2/8)

15 April 1946

Dear Mr Churchill,

As I promised in my letter of 9th April, I enclose a list of the statements you made about Tito and Mihailovich. I hope this will meet your requirements.

You also asked me for advice on what answer, if any, it would be desirable to return to a letter[1] from the Lithuanian Minister to the USA.

His Majesty's Government recognize that Lithuania has been incorporated into the USSR *de facto*, but this incorporation has not been recognized *de jure*. I suggest, therefore, that if you consider a reply to Mr Zadeikis is required, it should be to the effect that your statement was simply one of incontrovertible fact, and that you were not purporting to pronounce on the legal or moral aspects of the situation.

I return herewith the documents enclosed in your letter.

Ernest Bevin to Winston S. Churchill
(Churchill papers, 2/7)

17 April 1946

Dear Winston,

Thank you for your two letters of the 9th April and the 11th April about General Mihailovic.[2]

I need hardly say that I share your desire that General Mihailovic should be given a fair trial and I think I made this clear in answer to questions in the House on the 3rd April. At present I am still without information whether he is to be charged with collaboration with the enemy or with action against the National Liberation Movement – which you will, I am sure agree, is very material.

The United States Government recently requested the Yugoslav Government to make arrangements whereby United States Officers who might have

---

[1] Reproduced above (p. 268).
[2] Reproduced above (pp. 287 and 290).

information bearing on charges against General Mihailovic of collaboration with the enemy should be permitted to give evidence in connexion with the trial. The Yugoslav reply to these representations of which you will doubtless have seen reports in the Press, amounted to a flat refusal and does not encourage the hope that the Yugoslav Government will pay much heed to representations from outside.

Winston S. Churchill to Clare Sheridan[1]
(*Churchill papers, 1/42*)

19 April 1946
Private

My dear Clare,

Thank you so much for your letter.

I consulted Bernie[2] about the carving tools. He insisted on paying for them, and so all is well. You will receive them in due course, either directly or through me.

I don't see anything shattering in the circular you enclose. This statement was made in 1940, and, if the Germans had overthrown Hitler then and sought an honourable peace, the power of Great Britain and of the whole world to help them would have been much greater than after more than four years of destructive war. I am afraid your former Russian friends have got all the feeding districts on which Germany lived, and, with the aid of the Poles, have driven vast masses of helpless Germans into the British and American Zones where there is great scarcity of food.

Winston S. Churchill to Najeeb al Armanazi[3]
(*Churchill papers, 2/8*)

19 April 1946

Your Excellency,

Thank you for your letter of April 11.

I do not think it is very appropriate to make the National Day of Syria correspond to 'The withdrawal of foreign troops'. This does far less than justice to the British troops who were there to protect your independence and have eventually achieved it.

[1] Clare Consuelo Sheridan, 1885–1970. Churchill's cousin. Daughter of Moreton Frewen and Clara Jerome. Educated in Paris and Germany. Sculptress and writer. Sculpted busts of Churchill, Lenin, Trotsky and Gandhi. European correspondent, *New York World*, 1922.

[2] Bernard Baruch.

[3] Najeeb al Armanazi, 1897–1968. Secretary, Syrian National Congress, 1920. Director, Presidential Office, 1932–42. Secretary-General, Syria, 1942–50. Syrian Ambassador to India, 1950–6; to UK, 1956–61.

A far better date would be that on which the British, French and Syrian authorities signed the Agreement for the independence of Syria before the advance into Syria in the summer of 1941.

I certainly should not wish to participate in such a Celebration as you have in mind. It seems to me to be based on prejudice rather than on the gratification which should attend the reassertion of Syrian independence.

Winston S. Churchill to General Sir Hastings Ismay
(*Churchill papers, 2/144*)

23 April 1946

My dear P,

In view of some very malicious and utterly untruthful articles and publications that have appeared in the United States, I think it right to set out simply what happened about the Supreme Commands in the war as these matters were settled mainly between me and the President in personal conversation. I thought that my broadcast at Westminster on May 7, when I receive the Freedom would be a good occasion. I have therefore put down on the enclosed a note from memory. I should be much obliged if you would check this for me and also show it to Brookie who can supply the dates, or approximate dates, which concern himself. I think the public ought to know that he was offered this great command, that the President accepted his name, and how splendid he was when the plan had to be changed.

> I think it right to put on record the facts about the various appointments of the principal British and American commanders, as there seems to be misunderstanding and even misrepresentation about them.
>
> From the beginning it was agreed by President Roosevelt and me that the expedition to North Africa in 1942 should be under an American commander and that it should be primarily an American operation. Accordingly, the President selected General Eisenhower, and he took up his Headquarters in London in the summer of 1942. Thereafter he became the Supreme Commander in Africa, and we made no suggestion for altering this arrangement, even when General Alexander arrived with General Montgomery's Eighth Army in Tunisia, and when, in consequence, the British had, with the British First Army, about fourteen divisions to three United States divisions engaged in the fighting. The operations were conducted by General Alexander, as deputy to General Eisenhower, and the relations between these two officers were of the most loyal, friendly and intimate character.
>
> As the United States had the African command, it had also been agreed between the President and me that the commander of the cross-Channel invasion of France – 'Overlord' as it was called – should be British, and I

suggested for this purpose, with the President's agreement, General Brooke who, it may be remembered, had commanded in the decisive battle on the road to Dunkirk, with both Alexander and Montgomery as his subordinates. I informed General Brooke of this intention early in 1942. This great operation was to begin with equal British and American forces, and as it was to be based on Great Britain it seemed right to make such an arrangement. However, as the year advanced and the immense plan of the invasion began to take shape, I became increasingly impressed with the very great preponderance of American troops that would be employed after the original landing with equal numbers had been successful, and I, myself, took the initiative of proposing to the President that an American commander should be appointed for the expedition to France. He was gratified at this suggestion, and I daresay his mind had been moving that way. We therefore agreed in the summer of 1943 that an American commander should command 'Overlord' and that the Mediterranean should be entrusted to a British commander, the actual date of the change being dependent upon the progress of the war. I informed General Brooke of this change, which he accepted, and he bore the great disappointment with soldierly dignity.

During the whole of 1943, I understood that the President would choose General Marshall for 'Overlord'. At the conference at Teheran in November, Stalin asked the name of the American commander and the President said he would reserve his decision on the appointment until further Anglo-American conversations had taken place on the way back in Cairo. I understood that General Marshall was still his choice, and that General Eisenhower would take General Marshall's place as Chief of the Army Staff in Washington.

This was how matters stood when we returned to Cairo in the middle of December, 1943. I had the greatest confidence in General Marshall and his appointment would have been welcome to all of us. However, the President now informed me that he could not spare General Marshall, whose great influence at the head of military affairs and of the war direction, under the President, was invaluable and indispensable to the successful conduct of the war. He therefore told me that he proposed to nominate Eisenhower to 'Overlord' and asked me for my opinion. I said it was for him to decide but that we had also the warmest regard for General Eisenhower and would trust our fortunes to his direction with hearty goodwill.

It fell to me then, as British Minister of Defence responsible to the War Cabinet, to propose the British Commander-in-Chief in the Mediterranean. This we confided to General Wilson,[1] it being also settled that

---

[1] Henry Maitland Wilson, 1881–1964. Known as 'Jumbo'. On active service in South Africa, 1899–1902; on Western Front, 1914–17 (despatches, DSO). GOC-in-C, Egypt, 1939; Cyrenaica, 1940; Greece, 1941; Palestine and Transjordan, 1941. Knighted, 1940. C-in-C, Allied forces in Syria, 1941; Persia–Iraq Command, 1942–3; Middle East, 1943. Supreme Allied Cdr, Mediterranean Theatre, 1944. FM, 29 Dec. 1944. Head of British Joint Staff Mission, Washington DC, 1945–7. Baron, 1946.

General Alexander should command the whole campaign in Italy, as he had done under General Eisenhower in Tunisia. It was also arranged that General Devers[1] of the US Service should become General Wilson's deputy in the Mediterranean, and Air Chief Marshal Tedder General Eisenhower's deputy in 'Overlord', and that General Montgomery should actually command the cross-channel invasion force until such time as the Supreme Commander could transfer his Headquarters to France and assume the direct operational control. All this was carried out with the utmost smoothness in perfect agreement by the President and by me, with Cabinet approval, and worked in all good comradeship and friendship by all concerned.

I should add that when General Alexander succeeded General Wilson in October, 1944, as Supreme Commander in the Mediterranean, I myself, proposed, on behalf of His Majesty's Government, that General Mark Clark[2] should take command of the whole of the forces in Italy, which he did with great distinction and success. All these arrangements were in accord with the view of the combined Anglo-American Chiefs of Staff and were not unaccompanied by success in every sphere.[3]

General Sir Hastings Ismay to Winston S. Churchill
(Churchill papers, 2/144)

25 April 1946

My dear Mr Churchill,

I return herewith the notes for your broadcast on 7th May.

Brookie has confirmed that you told him of your original intention that he should command 'Overlord' early in 1943, and says that you told him of

---

[1] Jacob Loucks Devers, 1887–1979. Graduated from US Military Academy at West Point, 1909. CoS, Panama Canal Dept, 1939–40. Cdr, 9th Infantry Div., 1940–1; US Armored Forces, 1941; US Forces in Europe, 1943. Deputy Supreme Cdr, Mediterranean Theater, 1944. Cdr, 6th Army Group, 1944. Chief of Army Ground Forces, 1945–9. Retired from US Army, 1949.

[2] Mark (Wayne) Clark, 1896–1984. On active service with US Army, 1917–18. CoS for US ground forces in England (for European operations), 1941–2. Made secret visit by submarine to North Africa in preparation for Nov. 1942 landings (Operation 'Torch'). Cdr, 5th Army, Anglo-American invasion of Italy, 1943, and capture of Rome, June 1944. Hon. knighthood, 1944. Apr. 1945, received the surrender of 230,000 German troops in Italy, Tyrol and Salzburg. US High Commissioner and Commanding Gen., Austria, 1945–7. Deputy Secretary of State, 1947.

[3] A second version Churchill wrote ended: '. . . I myself, proposed on behalf of His Majesty's Government, that United States Gen. Mark Clark should take command under him of the whole of the forces in Italy, three-quarters of which were British, Imperial or British-controlled. This he did with marked distinction and success. All these arrangements were at each stage agreeable to the view of the Combined Anglo-American Chiefs of Staff and were accompanied by decisive success in every sphere. There really is not much for anyone to make mischief in this simple and honourable tale.' Elizabeth Gilliatt, Churchill's Private Secretary, asked him if he would like to see her suggested amendments, to which he responded: 'Do what you like with it. I never want to see it again.'

the change at Quebec in August, 1943. His only other comment was that it was the bitterest pill that he ever had to swallow, and he wonders whether you could revise the passage which I have sidelined 'A' to bring out this point; and also to emphasise that the change was due solely to international considerations and not to any unfitness on Brookie's part.

I may add that I showed him your letter to me and that he was very touched and pleased with your concluding sentence.

I have also made a few amendments to the draft. The only one of substance is in paragraph 2 and the reason for it is that Eisenhower had already come to England as Commander of the United States Forces in the European Theatre before the North African venture was even decided upon.

Najeeb al Armanazi to Winston S. Churchill
(Churchill papers, 2/8)

25 April 1946

Sir,

I was very much distressed by your letter of April 19th.[1] There is evidently a most unfortunate misunderstanding which I am anxious to dissipate.

The Syrian people and the Syrian Government will never forget that they owe their independence, principally, to the policy of the British Government, first proclaimed by you when in 1941 you stated 'Syria must come into her own', and to the subsequent action of British troops. To us, April 17th is the day which marks the fulfilment of this policy and on which Syria became really free and independent. It would have been a great pleasure to me to have been able to express to you, personally, the feelings of all Syrians on that day.

In the view of the Syrian people, the withdrawal of British troops who entered our country in 1941 as liberators, is the outward and visible confirmation that the task set themselves by the British has been accomplished,

The services rendered by Great Britain to Syria during the events of last summer under your Premiership, has magnified the debt my country owes to yours, which we shall always be proud to acknowledge.

All those who were present in Damascus, Aleppo, and the other Syrian towns during the recent ceremonies there, can bear witness to the fact that no opportunity was lost by the Government and people of Syria of showing their gratitude and affection for the British troops, who have won the esteem and admiration of every Syrian.

May I be permitted to add that when I addressed myself, recently to the present Secretary of State for Foreign Affairs regarding the withdrawal of foreign troops I expressed to him our deep thanks and profound gratitude

---

[1] Reproduced above (pp. 296–7).

towards Great Britain, to which he wrote in reply: 'I much appreciate your Excellency's expressions of gratitude, on behalf of the Government and People of Syria, for the help and assistance extended to them by His Majesty's Government, and I heartily reciprocate the hope that the cordial relations so happily existing between our two countries will continue to be strengthened and developed.'

In choosing April 17th as Syria's National Day, I need hardly say that it was the fact of the withdrawal of French troops, marking the achievement of our independence, which the Syrian Government had in mind, but in framing the invitation we were anxious not to draw any embarrassing distinction between British and French troops, and I am glad to say that the French Ambassador attended the celebration in London.

Winston S. Churchill: speech
('Winston S. Churchill, His Complete Speeches', volume 7, pages 7306–8)

27 April 1946   Aberdeen, Scotland

THE NEEDS OF A SICK WORLD

The qualities of firmness of character for which the Scottish race is renowned are thought to reach their fullest and most precise manifestation in the granite city of Aberdeen. But Aberdeen is also famed for warm hearts, keen affection and bright eyes. I am deeply moved by your welcome. I regard it as a special compliment to an Englishmen to be invited to receive the Freedom of this City and a Degree from its eminent University, and the generosity and kindness which you show me are a joy indeed.

Scotland has a splendid record in the war and at no moment was there the slightest weakening of her national purpose or energy. The Clyde was one of our great productive arsenals and an invaluable outlet to our ocean life-lines. Scapa, the Clyde, Rosyth were the bases of the Home Fleet. Scottish fishermen fed us faithfully. They drew the red herring across Hitler's path. They feed us now and I hope they will feed us more, and perhaps others as well. Thousands of Scotsmen joined the Minesweepers and the Royal Air Force. The Merchant Fleets never daunted in their grim task of braving the U-boats and the hostile aircraft drew heavily upon the skill and daring of the Scottish sea-faring and engineering classes. Many rose to distinction in these widely-varying spheres of action. Many new hero names are celebrated. Scores of thousands of Scotsmen served in famous British regiments. The Scots Guards preserved and adorned their long-established reputation. The three Scottish Divisions, the Fifteenth Scottish Division, the Fifty-Second Lowland Division and the Fifty-First Highland Division, were all in at the death and all had fought their way across the Rhine to the Elbe. It happened, however, that the Division of which I saw the most was your own Division, the Fifty-First Highland Division.

We all remember with poignant feelings the destruction or capture of this Division in June 1940, after the desperate fighting at St Valery, but that disaster was repaired and avenged in full measure. Four times at different stages in our eventful journey I visited or inspected the reconstituted Highland Division in the field. I saw them in Egypt, when they had just landed as timely reinforcement in those anxious days before the tide of our military fortune turned once and for all at Alamein. I spent two days with their Brigades just after they had disembarked. The next time I saw them was in February 1943. They had marched a long way from Cairo and the Delta, leaving their mark upon the enemy in every battle in which they were engaged. Now through the wide streets of the fine Italian-African city of Tripoli they marched in faultless array to the skirl of the pipes. I have never seen men march with more conscious pride. None would have believed they had toiled through a thousand miles of desert when one saw their spotless turnout and attire.

More than a year passed before I met them again. I visited their Headquarters' ship at Portsmouth on the day before the Division sailed for the liberation of France. And finally I reviewed the whole Division in Germany on the eve of their forcing the Rhine among the vanguards of the British and Canadian attack, and there I told them what swiftly proved true, 'One good heave now will finish the job.'

It gives me keen pleasure to revive these vivid memories which we share in common.

The record of the Highland Division stands on the Scroll of Honour among the most famous of all formations of the British and Imperial Armies. We may today recall that it was the Great Pitt[1] who in the seventeen-fifties drew the Highlanders from their glens where romance had given them European fame, and brought them hence-forward into the forefront of all the battles by which the British Empire – about which our intellectual nitwits are so bashful – was built up and by which the broadening freedom of the western world was steadfastly maintained. Scotsmen in Scotland and all over the world may cheer their hearts and let their pulses stir as they tell the tales of Highland valour, deathless in the songs and annals of the Northern Kingdom.

Although I do not claim any very traceable Scottish ancestry, I have many links with Scotland. I took the precaution of being born on St Andrew's Day. I found my wife in Scotland. I commanded the 5th Battalions of the Royal Scots Fusiliers in the first Great War and am its Colonel today. I represented in Parliament for fifteen years the home of the Black Watch on the banks of the Tay. And now here today you give me the Freedom of Aberdeen. You will excuse me on this very personal occasion if I dwell upon the contacts and ties

---

[1] William Pitt, 1708–78. Known as 'Pitt the Elder'. Earl of Chatham, 1766. PM, 1766–8. A great and classically erudite orator.

which I cherish with the grand race of men bred in the North and respected in every clime.

What of the future?

This is a time when hatred is rife in the world, and when many mighty branches of the human family, victors or vanquished, innocent or guilty, are plunged in bewilderment, distress or ruin. The world is very ill. Two fearful wars in our lifetime have torn the heart out of its grace and culture. Measureless injury has been done to much that the 19th Century would have called 'Christian civilisation'. All the leading nations have been racked by stresses which have blunted their sensibilities and have destroyed their agreeable modes of social intercourse. Only science has rolled forward, whipped by the fierce winds of mortal war, and science has placed in the hands of men agencies of destruction far beyond any development of their common sense or virtue. In a world where over-production of food was formerly from time to time a problem, famine has laid its gaunt fingers upon the peoples of many lands and scarcity upon all. The psychic energies of mankind have been exhausted by the tribulations through which they have passed and are still passing. It is not only blood-letting that has weakened and whitened us. The vital springs of human inspiration are, for the moment, drained. There must be a period of recovery. Mankind cannot in its present light bear new shocks and quarrels without descending to altogether cruder and primordial forms. Yet we do not know that the hatreds and confusion which abound will not confront us with even harder trials than those we have so narrowly and painfully survived. In many countries where even united efforts would fall far short of what is needed, party strife and faction is fomented or machine made and skeleton fanatics rave at each other about their rival ideologies. All the while the ordinary folk of every country show themselves kindly and brave and serviceable to their fellow men. Yet they are driven against one another by forces and organisations and doctrines as wantonly and as remorselessly as they ever were in the ages of absolute Emperors and Kings. There never was a time when a breathing space was more needed, a blessed convalescence, a truce of God and man.

Aberdeen is a focus of virile thought and activity, and I have heard of no part of the world, where freedom reigns, in which Aberdonians have not been able to hold their own and make their way. I should be deeply interested to know what the people of Aberdeen really think about the world position and the course which the British Islanders should take in this present anxious period. I am sure that, if our country were committed to your guidance, measures would be proposed and enforced which would conduce to the enduring greatness of Scotland and of all Britain, and that these measures would at no point be tinctured or tainted by moods of helplessness, fatalism or despair.

There was a time when the hatreds of the Scots and the English were as bitter as any passions ever known among men. Those days are long gone by for us. So may it be for all. The underlying unities which animate the British Isles, the British Commonwealth of Nations, nay the English-speaking world, are such as to make us unconquerable and to make us sure that we can deliver our message to the human pilgrimage generation after generation in sunlight or in storm, however the winds may blow.

Winston S. Churchill: speech
('*Winston S. Churchill, His Complete Speeches*', volume 7, pages 7308–11)

29 April 1946   Scottish Unionist Rally, Edinburgh

FAILURES OF THE GOVERNMENT'S 'DOCTRINAIRE SOCIALISM'

... A mighty population has grown up in this island, based upon all these far-reaching intricate, and delicate operations, and if they are not restored and revived in full and growing activity, we shall not be engaged in a fight to improve our standard of living but in a struggle to live at all. ...

There never was in all human history a community so numerous in a position at once so magnificent and so precarious. There never was so great a people who could less afford to make mistakes or indulge in folly or faction as are we in this British island to-night. The results of serious mistakes at this time would not be the misfortune of this class or that, or the humiliation of one party or the other but the dissipation of the means by which more than half our population live, ending in an abridgement of about one-third to half our population and the final extinction of Britain as the centre of the widest, the most experienced, and most tolerant association of races and nations that has existed since the fall of the ancient Roman Empire. ...

The first of all the Government errors and the one which will cost us most dear and retard in the most painful way, or even prevent, our recovery and return to normal conditions of prosperity and freedom is of course the attempt to establish doctrinaire Socialism in this critical period, and the unprincipled use of war-time measures and extra-Parliamentary powers, not for the purpose of winning the war, for that is won, and not for the purpose of bridging the transition period, but in order to give satisfaction to Socialist theories and fads, and in the hopes of gathering low-grade party advantages. It is this deliberate and increasing tendency which is hampering and poisoning our national life at the present time, and which will, if not arrested, inflict needless hardship and suffering upon all classes, and particularly upon the mass of the wage-earners.

It astonishes me that a body of men, charged with such awful responsibility, and coming into so grand and noble an estate as our country, shining with all the glories of its victory, should fall so far short alike of their duty and of their opportunity in so many fields and on so many occasions. I shall now give you some examples of wrong treatment of the nation and administrative failures which have already darkened the path we have trodden since the General Election.

Firstly, tardy demobilization, and delay in fixing and reaching the standards of defence which we must for the present maintain, and much consequent uncertainty for our young men. Secondly, increased lush and lavish expenditure resulting from this tardy demobilization, and also from the desire to hold and create a vast horde of officials of all kinds as a burden upon the general public. Thirdly, the failure to allow the production of consumer goods in sufficient quantities which arises from the misuse or waste of man-power and the maintenance of war-time taxation and restriction in time of peace. Fourthly, the failure of the rehousing programme both in repairs and in new building.

Fifthly, the disturbance and enfeeblement of industry and enterprise through the launching of vague, ill-thought-out schemes of nationalization and by the ceaseless outpouring of threats and abuse on all employers of labour and on all forms of wealth, however honourably acquired, and upon every form of private enterprise, upon which even the Socialist Ministers admit we must depend for our livelihood to the extent of 80 percent for many years to come. And sixthly, the campaign of hatred and vilification carried out on the part of one half of the nation against the other half at the very time when, above all others, the unity of the nation is vital not only to our prosperity but even to our existence. . . .

Our financial situation is difficult and causes grievous anxiety. The Chancellor of the Exchequer is the heir to all the enormous revenues produced by the crushing taxation imposed in our struggle for life, and cheerfully agreed to for that purpose, by every class in the community. He considers himself entitled to lead a riotous life of national expenditure without one thought of economy, and even expects applause if he gives away a few trifles from Budget to Budget. . . . By the end of March, 1947, Mr Dalton will have got rid of over £9,000,000,000 in 24 months, of which only four months have been spent in war. I say without hesitation that a thrifty and forward-looking Government could have saved an additional £700,000,000 or £800,000,000 sterling without any administrative failure and could have given this money back in tax relief to fructify in the pockets of the people of all classes, including those classes which have been burdened most heavily by war.

We are living now on the basis that the Government are spending one-half of the entire national income, nineteen-twentieths of which is provided not by surtax or estate duties, which have already reached confiscatory levels, but by the taxation of the wage and small salary earning masses. A continuance of the present scale of taxes can only have one result, and that is the result which the Socialist Government always profess themselves most eager to avoid – namely, inflation. . . . The remedy is plain. . . . It is the diminution of public expenditure and the lightening of national burdens carrying with it a restriction in the powers now exercised and sought to be exercised by a party majority, and secondly, by the consequential multiplication of consumer goods and services, which is the sovereign cure and preventive of inflation.

Now we have to go cap in hand to the United States for a loan of about £1,000,000,000 to balance our necessary imports for the next two or three years. I am in favour of this loan, not because I like it but because we cannot do without it; and I do not blame the Government for seeking it.

But surely at a time like this, when we have to go to the United States for a vital loan to tide over this hard period of transition and recovery from a struggle in which we kept nothing back, gave all we had and more, when everybody is urged to save as I urge them to save and to contribute to national savings, the Government and the Chancellor of the Exchequer and the President of the Board of Trade, above all other men, should show themselves careful of every shilling that is raised or borrowed or spent. . . .

Of all the problems which press for good, strong and quick handling the rebuilding of our shattered homes and the building of new homes is the most urgent. One would have thought that Mr Aneurin Bevan, who has been placed in charge of housing on account, I suppose, of the prominent part he played in criticizing the national war effort, would at least have tried to do the best he could for all the hundreds of thousands of families who wish to have a roof of their own over their heads. I really cannot understand how anyone of intelligence and vigour of mind, entrusted with such a duty, should not have been moved by the impulses alike of glory and of mercy to try to do the best for all.

But the housing of the people in this crisis takes only second place in the mind of the responsible Minister. The first is occupied by the need of proving that he is a sound, thorough-going Socialist and puts the class and party war in the forefront of his thoughts. . . .

What are the causes of this grievous breakdown, this horrible shortage? . . . The first cause is the pedantic, irrational enforcement of Socialistic prejudice. Whereas four out of five of the homes completed since the war have been built by private enterprise, the Minister of Health's policy has been to license only one house built by private enterprise for every four by local authorities. In order to carry out this unnatural ruling and to show what a good Socialist the Minister is, the people have to endure not only needless delays and restrictions of building effort but even unemployment of available labour in this sphere to which above all others it is called.

The second cause, which has not yet operated to the full, is due to a blunder of the first magnitude. The Socialist Ministers concerned with house repair and house building forgot the bricks. They were so busy hunting harassed, hard-hit landlords round the ruins of the old houses that they forgot the bricks to build the new. They brought home the bricklayers from the Army, but they forgot the brickmakers, without whom the bricklayers' work cannot proceed. . . .

The other night a junior Minister came down to the House of Commons with a regulation to impose severe penalties upon builders and others who might be found guilty of building or repairing houses without a licence. Seven years' penal servitude was the maximum prescribed for this crime, till war-time unknown to the law. Almost the same day I read that 1,000 prefabricated houses, every one of which would have housed a family in independence and privacy for a few years till we got round the corner, had been exported to Holland. A few months earlier we learned that 5,000 prefabricated houses which the Coalition Government had ordered in America had been diverted to France. They talk of seven years' penal servitude! What sort of sentence should be passed on Ministers of the Crown who are so much more nice than wise that they did not hesitate to inflict hardship and disappointment on so many thousands of families who want to have a hearth and home of their own? But Socialism is like that: in its revolt against the unequal sharing of blessings it glories in the equal sharing of miseries. I am told of the popular slogan, 'Labour gets things done.' But surely, in housing at any rate, we can already see that it should run, 'Socialism gets things done in.'

Even now I would appeal to the Ministers concerned: let them declare that neither vested interest nor party prejudice shall stand in the way of the most homes for the most families in the shortest time by any method that the resources and ingenuity of Britain can contrive, and we will join them at once in a new all-out national heave. . . .

Indeed there never was a country nor a people whose way of getting a livelihood was more unsuited to the crude application of the Socialist system. Nor was there ever a moment in our long history – just as we are emerging in a distracted world from an exhausting struggle – which was less suitable for such an experiment. The more harshly the attempt is persisted in, the worse will be the condition of the mass of the people and the less chance will the British nation have, not only of holding its place in the world but even of gaining its daily bread. . . .

If the normal, active, well-established processes of enterprise and production are bent and burred by the violent impingement of a Utopian Socialist scheme, we are on the road, and a direct and short road, to financial bankruptcy and economic collapse, the inexorable effect of which will be an immense decline in our present standard of living and the final and fatal loss of our world position, by which alone we can keep ourselves alive.

May 1946

Lord Halifax to Winston S. Churchill
(*Churchill papers, 2/6*)

1 May 1946   Washington DC
Urgent
Top Secret

    UJ's speech is pretty insolent but I suppose he would say that you began it. Any public argument between you will get the world nowhere except into a worse temper. I would like to see you say publicly tomorrow something on these lines:

    (A) UJ has completely misunderstood what I said at Fulton;
    (B) UJ does not appear to appreciate any of the causes that are responsible for the present anxiety about Russian policy;
    (C) I attach too much importance to my war comradeship with UJ to be willing to allow it to be frosted over if this can be avoided; and therefore,
    (D) With the permission of His Majesty's government I have sent a message to UJ suggesting that after my return to England I should pay a visit to him for the purpose of full and frank discussion.

    2. I believe that something of this kind would have a profound effect both in the US and at home and that it might do something that neither Attlee nor Truman could do.

    3. If you agree with the suggestion in (D) and will let me know what you would wish said to the government, I will pass on the message by most immediate telegram.

May 1946

Winston S. Churchill to Najeeb al Armanazi
(Churchill papers, 2/8)

2 May 1946

Your Excellency,

I thank you for your letter of April 25[1] which is quite satisfactory to me. As, however, the public form of the celebration of 'the withdrawal of the foreign troops' in no way recognises the part played by Great Britain in the establishment of Syrian independence, I still feel that the occasion is not well chosen or clearly explained.

Lord Halifax to Winston S. Churchill
(Churchill papers, 2/6)

3 May 1946   Washington DC

My dear Winston,

I had a talk to Sumner Welles[2] yesterday, who led off by saying that he thought that the service you had rendered to the cause of Democracy in the world by your speeches here was a greater service than anyone had rendered during the last years. He sorrowfully said that there was no one in the United States Administration who could have done what you did in the way of arousing the American people to the necessity of facing facts.

I know that this general thought will be no surprise to you after your own talks with him, but I thought none-the-less you might like to hear his considered judgement.

I look forward to seeing you.

Duke of Windsor to Winston S. Churchill
(Churchill papers, 2/178)

5 May 1946

Dear Winston,

The Duchess and I followed your activities in America with great interest, and only hope you and Mrs Churchill got some rest and relaxation in Florida despite your heavy schedule of public engagements.

I welcomed your bold speech at Fulton, Mo., the frankness of which

---

[1] Reproduced above (pp. 300–1).
[2] Benjamin Sumner Welles, 1892–1961. A relative by marriage of Franklin D. Roosevelt. US Foreign Service, 1914–25. During Roosevelt's Presidential election campaign in 1932, provided foreign policy expertise and was a major financial contributor. Special Envoy to Cuba, 1933. Under-Secretary of State, 1937–43. Visited Italy, Germany and England to discuss peacemaking proposals, Feb.–March 1940.

impressed me profoundly. No one but you has the experience to tell the world the true implications of Soviet foreign policy and, being out of office, you were free to do so. That part of your speech, I am glad to say, received overwhelming applause, and even if your reference to an Anglo-American Military Alliance offended in certain quarters of America, I can see no hope of avoiding a third global war in our time unless our two countries can think and act in closer harmony than they used to.

Since you were good enough to interest yourself in a plan for my future employment which offered the best and most dignified solution to the always difficult position in which my brother and I are placed vis-à-vis each other, I now have to report that the plan whereby the British Government was to employ me in connection with Anglo-American relations in America has been entirely abandoned.

My brother wrote that he had discussed the matter again with both Attlee and Bevin on more than one occasion and they are both adamant in thinking that at this moment it would not be a good thing for a near relative of his to be attached to the British Embassy in Washington in an official position there. He adds that he has used all his persuasive powers with both of these two Ministers to make them see his point of view.

I am not in the least surprised over the negative outcome of the consideration of this project concerning my future for, far from discovering any eagerness to conclude what would have been the best solution to a difficult situation for all concerned, during my two visits to London I could sense definite reluctance to the scheme in Downing Street and the delay of a decision one way or another for so many months further confirmed this impression.

However, as it is now evident that the British Government has no need of my services and as I have no intention of remaining idle, I must look for a job in whatever sphere and country I can find one suitable to my qualifications. This I well realize is not going to be all that simple, but I have sufficient confidence in myself to feel that I can still make some contribution towards the solution of some of the complex problems which beset the world today.

The Duchess and I moved here[1] the end of March after packing up our rented house in Paris which you will recall was sold. This was no easy undertaking under existing conditions in France, and we shall eventually terminate the lease of this one as well as it is far too large for postwar living. However, we are planning to spend the summer here, but we will probably go to Paris for a few days the latter part of this month. I need not say in behalf of both of us how welcome you and Mrs Churchill would be at La Cröe if you felt the need for sunshine and could get away from your Parliamentary commitments. At any rate, we shall go to Great Britain sometime in August, and hope there will be an opportunity of meeting then if not before.

---

[1] Château La Cröe, Antibes.

Winston S. Churchill to Clare Sheridan
(*Churchill papers, 1/42*)

7 May 1946
Private

My dear Clare,

I was very sorry you were disappointed about the tools. This, I am sure, is no fault of those who wish to meet your need. You should now draw out, as you can well do, on six, eight or ten sheets of foolscap paper in exact full size the tools you have in mind. Then I will send these diagrams to your friend, Bernie Baruch, and I am sure that, if the United States of America has not sunk beneath the surface of the ocean, you will receive what you want.

Dear Clare, I am worried about your plans. My own life is confused with petty trivialities and ceremonies, and one is astonished how little time one has when one has nothing to do. It would be very nice if you could come to Chartwell to lunch with me one day. I am almost always there at weekends; we could then have a talk.

The following advice is given without any careful study of the facts, and is for your private eye alone. The purchasing power of money is falling every day. There are other general troubles, but the value of the land and house of Brede will rise proportionately. This is not the time to get rid of real estate. It is wiser to hang on and live on one's capital or selling power of one's tail for a year or two. This is my serious advice. If you have anything solid hold on to it now. We have a very bad time to go through, but England will survive. It would be wrong to take any hasty final decision now.

Please write in answer to this, sending the particulars of your tools; and do not try to be a Bolshevik and complain of Bolshevism at the same time.

Winston S. Churchill: speech
('*Winston S. Churchill, His Complete Speeches*', volume 7, pages 7311–14)

7 May 1946 House of Commons

BRITISH TROOPS IN EGYPT

Mr Speaker, I feel we were right and even bound to invoke the somewhat unused procedure of the House and move the Adjournment, with your permission, under Standing Order No. 8. (Editor's Note: Under this procedure, the Speaker may accept a motion for the Adjournment on a matter of urgent importance and give it precedence over the business arranged for that day. The motion had been moved by Churchill after a statement by Mr Attlee which implied that the withdrawal of British forces from Egypt had been proposed by the Government. A heated debate ensued.) These great questions which are suddenly opened up before Business without any power or facility or opportunity of debate being offered, place us all in a difficulty, and very often during the war the Opposition – or those who sat on this side, because they hardly called themselves the Opposition – used to say that they would very much appreciate if a Motion were put down at the time such a statement was made. The right hon. Gentleman the Prime Minister did not take that course. I am not criticizing him for it. He made the statement, and I am bound to say that it caused me a most painful shock, and I think that was the general feeling on this side of the House when he informed us that the Government were proposing, or were intending, or had, in fact, actually proposed to the Egyptian Government the evacuation of all British naval, military and air forces from Egypt. We have, therefore, used our Parliamentary rights. We have been very chary of showing any differences with the Government upon external matters. We are not consulted in any way, but none the less we have given every help we could, often by keeping silent and often by not saying how much we approve of their conduct, because that might be no help to them at all. But here was a point where I feel that a very serious division – I did feel, and to some extent still do feel that a really serious division – of purpose and of method divides us.

It is a very serious thing to begin a negotiation of this character with the statement that you are proposing to give away the main point. I cannot conceive that that is good diplomacy. The Government will say, 'Oh, it must be judged by the results whether it is good diplomacy or not,' but still that remains: you begin by proposing not merely to move the troops from Cairo – on that we could have easily agreed – but to remove them altogether out of Egypt. Then His Majesty's Government propose to have a long negotiation to see what effective measures can be taken for the defence of the Canal zone, and the Prime Minister – if I understood him rightly because I have not seen the text of his speech, I only heard it – said that if the Canal zone is not effectively protected as a result of the negotiations, we shall revert to the Treaty of 1936. Is that so? Have I rightly interpreted him in that matter?

The Prime Minister: What I said was that obviously if negotiations break down, the original Treaty still stands.

Mr Churchill: Yes, I see. Then the negotiations are for the purpose of securing a satisfactory defence of the Canal zone in a matter most agreeable to Egyptian sentiment. If they break down, then we revert to the 1936 Treaty. That is a very important admission, and I am bound to say it relieves my anxiety to some extent, but it in no way improves the view which we take of the method by which the Government intend to handle this matter. They begin by saying, 'We will withdraw the troops.' They go on to say, 'If the Canal zone is not properly defended, we revert to the 1936 Treaty with the troops on the Canal zone.' But who has ever suggested that there is any method of safeguarding the Canal except by troops in the Canal zone? You will not get any military man of eminence and responsibility to say that the Canal can be kept open – because that is the whole point; it is to keep the Canal open. Anyone can close the Canal from hundreds of miles away; it is to keep it open that we require troops on the spot, not only when danger has come but in the months before the storm has burst.

Look at the position we are now in. We begin by saying, 'We are willing to evacuate all our forces from Egypt.' We then say, 'Unless satisfactory methods are devised for safeguarding the Canal zone, we revert to 1936 with our troops there.' And all the time we know that there is no satisfactory method of keeping the Canal open, and making sure that it is kept open, except by keeping troops there. How, then, is it likely to make a good atmosphere, to remove suspicion, to go and promise at the outset what you know in your heart you will have to take back, or hope will be given back to you during the course of the negotiations?

I think the negotiations are proposed on a most curious basis. I am greatly relieved to hear the Prime Minister's statement that if you do not get effective defence of the Canal zone, the 1936 Treaty operates again. I do not know that the Egyptians will be so relieved to hear that statement. It seems to me that we have suffered very much indeed from this curious method of what is called 'approach'. The word 'approach' really means 'departure' – a good way of expressing it.

We, therefore, find ourselves forced to part company in this external matter. There are only two other points to which I wish to refer, because the whole case was admirably epitomized by my right hon. Friend the Member for Warwick and Leamington (Mr Eden). There is the question of the Chiefs of Staff and their opinion. The right hon. Gentleman said that they entirely agreed with the approach. Naturally we do not know what took place in these discussions, but I can quite see that it was a very foolish question to put to the Chiefs of Staff. They are not the judges of the diplomatic methods of approach. If the right hon. Gentleman the Leader of the House, who is to reply, were to say that the Chiefs of Staff expressed the opinion that it was possible to keep the Canal open without having troops in the Canal zone, I am bound to say it would have a very decisive effect on my mind. But one can always put questions to military men which are of a political character and to which they find it difficult to give an answer.

If we look back on the history of the Irish ports, I think it was in 1937, the Chiefs of Staff were consulted but the form of question put to them was one to which they could only give an affirmative answer. I hope the Leader of the House will tell us definitely if the Chiefs of Staff believed that there is a method of keeping the Canal open without having British soldiers in the Canal zone. If he can say that, I must say I bow – under the reserves – to the opinion of the Chiefs of Staff.

Then there is the question of the Dominion Prime Ministers. Egypt owes us a great debt. Since the days of Cromer[1] we have done our best to shield her from all the storms which beat about the world. We have done a great deal, though not nearly as much as we ought to have done, to force forward the lot of the fellaheen and the masses of the people. We have been hampered by our respect for the authority of the Egyptian potentates and assemblies and by not wanting to interfere too much in the affairs of the country. But it is a shocking thing how little progress there has been among the great masses of Egyptian fellaheen. I have been mixed up in this Egyptian affair in one way or another for 50 years, and I felt it a most painful blow when the right hon. Gentleman tossed out in five sentences of admirable terseness that all the Forces were to be withdrawn from Egypt. It was most painful. The debt we owe to Egypt is £400 million and that, I suppose, will be the most tangible link between the two countries, the payment of that debt. But the debt which Egypt owes to us is that in two world convulsions she has been effectively defended by Great Britain and not only by this island. The Australians and New Zealanders and South Africans have shed their blood freely to prevent Cairo and Alexandria being looted and ravished, ground down and subjugated, by Italian and German hordes.

When the Government say that the Dominions are consulted, I wonder very much whether the word 'consulted' has been defined with sufficient accuracy for us to base ourselves upon it. Dominion Premiers, or their representatives, are in London. The Prime Minister says they have been consulted. I agree with him in saying that he is responsible. He says, 'I take the responsibility.' That is quite true, but as to the degree of consultation, I do not know. The Chiefs of Staff, in my view, were asked a question which was a political question and gave an answer which did not touch reality. The Dominion Prime Ministers were not consulted in the sense of participating in a discussion which would shape the policy of the Government. They were told what the policy of the Government was after His Majesty's Ministers have, in the proper exercise of their responsibility, arrived at their own conclusion. I am only putting that issue. But if ever there was a question on which the Ministers of South Africa, of Australia, of Canada and of New Zealand should be taken right into the councils of His Majesty's Government it was this question of the handling of the position in Egypt.

I fear that we cannot leave the matter in mere Debate. We are bound to mark our protest and misgivings at this early stage by a vote. I earnestly hope that this effort of ours to give significance to our proceedings, to make people realize the deadly slope on to which we are getting, not only in Egypt, but in many other countries at the present time, this effort to call a halt, to enlist the

---

[1] Evelyn Baring, 1841–1917. Entered Army, 1858. Private Secretary to Viceroy of India, 1872–6. British Agent and Consul-General, Egypt, 1883–1907. Baron Cromer, 1899; Earl, 1901. Chairman of the Dardanelles Commission, 1916–17 (died 29 Jan. 1917, before the Commission had completed its work).

keen, patriotic, energetic spirit of men I know on that Bench – this can only be done if, at this stage, and much to our regret, we record, by vote, a definite disagreement on an external matter with His Majesty's Government.

Winston S. Churchill: speech
('The Sinews of Peace', pages 121–7)

7 May 1946

THE BRITISH COMMONWEALTH

Mr Mayor,[1] your Excellencies, Mr Speaker, my lords, ladies and gentlemen, it is an honour to me, which I shall always remember as long as I live, that I should become the first Freeman of Westminster, and that this should be accorded to me in terms of kindness and of compliment far beyond my merits, in the presence of a gathering so distinguished, so varied, so representative of the country as a whole and of all parties in the State. But the very quality and character of this assembly imposes upon me an extremely difficult task: I have to walk the tight-rope of truth, between unseemly controversy on the one hand and vacuous platitudes on the other. You will, I am sure, be indulgent judges of how I perform this feat. Here also there is the additional complication of striking the happy mean between saying what we all think and what we all think had better be left unsaid. Mr Mayor, if this is what is called receiving the Freedom, it will I am sure be realised that freedom is expressed not only by its assertions but its limitations. As a matter of fact, I am sure the Mayor will not mind my observing that I shall exercise very much less freedom in this part of Westminster than that which I am accustomed to enjoy in that other part of Westminster which has been the centre of my life for forty-seven years – the House of Commons; and perhaps I shall even exercise less freedom here than I did in another Westminster across the Atlantic Ocean in the State of Missouri a couple of months ago.

I was glad that you mentioned to the audience, Mr Mayor, the uses to which this building has been put, because when I came into this hall I had a sort of feeling that I had been here before.

Let me begin my remarks by reminding you of the Westminster by-election of 1923. I have fought more contested elections than any one else, and of all of them the Westminster election was the most exciting and dramatic. Yet I shall offend no party, Conservative, Labour or Liberal, in referring to it. It was a non-party election in the true sense because at that election all parties were

---

[1] Greville Reginald Howard, 1909–87. Educated at RMC, Sandhurst. Councillor, Westminster City Council, 1937–9, 1945–6. RN, 1939–45. Mayor, Westminster, 1946–7. Chairman, Public Cleansing, Transport, Baths and Contracts Committee, 1945, 1947–9. MP (Nat. Lib.) for St Ives Div. of Cornwall, 1950–66.

agreed in opposing me. It was only by 43 votes in an electorate of 22,000 that I was defeated. Happily the hostile operations of the three historic parties against me were not combined; the Big Three were not working together in perfect harmony on that occasion – so different from what we have now; and a few months after the conflict I found myself Chancellor of the Exchequer in a government formed by the party of my narrowly victorious opponent.

Such is life with its astonishing twists and turns. You never can tell what is going to happen next, nor can you tell what will be the consequences of any action you may take. The principle of the boomerang, a weapon which we owe to the genius of the Australian aboriginals, is, it would seem, increasingly operative in human affairs. Thus, Mr Mayor, we may note how some of the actions of our Russian friends have helped to cement Anglo-American friendship and co-operation, and how the activities of the French Communist Party have given General Franco a new lease of life.

The relation of cause to effect which these incidents illustrate cannot always be judged with precision. The human story does not always unfold like an arithmetical calculation on the principle that two and two make four. Sometimes in life they make five or minus three; and sometimes the black-board topples down in the middle of the sum and leaves the class in disorder and the pedagogue with a black eye. The element of the unexpected and the unforeseeable is what gives some of its relish to life and saves us from falling into the mechanical thraldom of the logicians. Now it is astonishing how often the calculators in this world are proved wrong. It is impressive how sternly is borne in upon us the simple truth that honest action from day to day, in accordance with the best promptings of our hearts, is the surest path even to worldly success.

Last week, Mr Mayor, when I was in Aberdeen, I spoke about the state of the world. I said the world was very ill. But this is not surprising when you consider the frightful operations which have been performed upon its inhabitants and the vast injury to all its means of food and transport and the dissipation of so much of its psychic energies and resilience, which follow the intense and overstrained exertions which have been made by so many branches of the human family. But, here in Westminster, in the Abbey Division, which claims, not without reason, to be the heart of the British Empire and Commonwealth of Nations, here, under the shadow of Big Ben and the Abbey, I should like to speak a little about our own affairs in their relation to world affairs.

We must all be deeply conscious of the gravity of the times in which we live, and that our place in the world will perhaps be finally decided by what may happen in the next few years. It would, I am sure, be a profound shock to the great mass of the British people if they woke up one morning and found that our Empire and position in the East and Middle East had vanished overnight and if the mission we have faithfully discharged in so many lands came to an abrupt end and incontinent collapse. If such a disaster occurred we should certainly have the right to reproach before history all public men in any way responsible, at the present time or in previous years, for such a failure of duty on the morrow of our victory, won by what seemed to many to be against desperate odds, which was nevertheless in the end complete and unconditional.

We are the only unbroken nation that fought against Hitler's tyranny in the war from start to finish. We declared war upon Germany when Hitler invaded Poland. We sought no material gains; we coveted no man's land or treasure. We, and with us the whole Empire and Commonwealth, all unprepared as we were, or partly prepared, drew the sword against the mighty antagonist at the call of honour and in defence of the rights of weaker nations, according to our plighted word, according to the fair play of the world. We did not fight only in the sacred cause of self-defence, like the Russian patriots who defended their native soil with sublime devotion and glorious success. No one attacked *us*. We fought for a higher and broader theme. We fought against tyranny, aggression and broken faith, and in order to establish that rule of law among the nations which alone can be the shield of freedom and progress.

Wherein did we fail? We did not fail when we were all alone. Neither did we fail, when mighty nations joined us, in giving all we had to what we from the beginning had proclaimed was the cause of mankind.

But let us look back a little upon the past. From Trafalgar and Waterloo to the first German War the British Navy was supreme upon the seas. Our sea power during the greater part of the nineteenth century equalled that of all other nations put together. Did we misuse that power? On the contrary, there never were so few warships afloat. History, which has been my guide and inspiration, will show to future ages that the control of the seas which the British held so long was used not for the exercise of warlike ambition but to keep the peace, to suppress the slave trade and to make the seas safe for the commerce of all nations. All our ports, even our own coastwise trade, were opened to the entry and competition of men and goods from every land. For at least two generations we were, as the American writer Walter Lippmann has reminded us, a guardian, and almost a guarantor of the Monroe doctrine[1] upon which, as Canning's[2] eye foresaw, the free development of South America was founded. We and the civilised world owe many blessings to the

---

[1] Statement made to the European powers by President James Monroe in 1823. He pledged that the US would not interfere in the affairs of already existing European colonies in the Western Hemisphere. Nevertheless, should any European nation attempt to expand its influence in the New World through the establishment of new colonies, such an act would be held by the American Government as an act of aggression against the US.

[2] George Canning, 1770–1827. Commissioner of the Board of Control, 1799–1800. Paymaster-General, 1800–1. Treasurer of the Navy, 1801, 1804–6. Foreign Secretary, 1807–9, 1822–7. Leader of the House of Commons, 1822–7. Chancellor of the Exchequer and PM, 1827. As Foreign Secretary, Canning devoted considerable effort to gaining recognition for the newly independent Latin American countries. In his 1826 address on the King's Message respecting Portugal, he declared: 'I called the New World into existence, to redress the balance of the Old' (*Hansard*, ser. 2, vol. 16, cols 390–8).

United States, but we have also in later generations made our contribution to their security and splendour.

What of our Empire? What of our Commonwealth of Nations? Taught by the hard necessary lessons of the American Revolution, we found the way, unique in history, to build and hold together a free association of self-governing dominions by voluntary ties and spontaneous forces, and these, like our vast Eastern and Colonial Empire, rose superior even to the awful stresses of 1940. There is not, and there never has been, and perhaps there never will be again, so widespread, so truly united a gathering of nations and races as was then and is today comprised within the circle of the ancient British Crown.

Will it continue or will it pass away; and if it passes away what coherent theme will take its place? What would fill the void, for void there would certainly be? These are the questions which we must ask ourselves. I grieve that it should be necessary to do so. We are bound to ask ourselves these questions. Not only are we bound to ask them of ourselves but of the world, and not only for our own sake but in the far broader interests of mankind.

I read last week an interesting and challenging report by an Anglo-American Commission on Palestine. This report declared that the British must remain in Palestine in pursuance of their mandate from the former League of Nations, and must remain there until the Jews and Arabs were content to live together as friends and fellow workers. It will evidently be a long time, Mr Mayor, before the quarrel between Jacob and Esau has faded away from the life of the Middle East. Are we not entitled to ask our friends whose judgment is the same as ours to give us a helping hand?

But I will look further East. I must look to India. India is a continent as large as and more populous than Europe, and not less deeply divided by racial and religious differences than Europe. India has no more unity than Europe, except that superficial unity which has been created by our rule and guidance in the last 150 years. India, protected by the British nation and parliament, has not in modern times been torn to pieces by hideous internal warfare; nor has it been invaded from over the sea. The anxieties felt by the Anglo-American Commission about Palestine arise in India on a far greater scale. It would be easy for Great Britain to cast away these cares. Some voices bid us quit Palestine; others bid us quit India. But surely not only Britain but all the world should consider deeply what the consequences would be and what other arrangements can be made to safeguard millions of men and women – and in India four hundred millions – from the cruel fate which has laid Europe with all its glories in dust and ashes and now threatens China with a protraction of her torment.

Naturally, amid the perplexities which beset so many governments, our hearts and our hopes go out to a world organisation, to the new United Nations structure and its Charter, to which all true-hearted men should give their allegiance. I pray that this may prosper. But what happens if the United Nations themselves are sundered by an awful schism and clash of ideologies, interests, policies and passions? What happens if, with all our loyal endeavours, we can build no more than a Tower of Babel? What is to happen if the United Nations, victorious in their grand conflict against Nazism and Fascism, give place, as they may do, to a vast confrontation of two parts of the world and two irreconcilably opposed conceptions of human society?

It is right to pose these questions. It is even impossible not to pose them. But what are the answers going to be? You will, I am sure, feel that these are problems which should dominate the minds of all the men in all the lands. They should dominate their minds because failure to find the answers may lead the whole human race into a new period of misery, slaughter and abasement more agonising and more fatal than those which we have twice endured in the lifetime of most of us here.

I should not like to raise these tremendous issues which lie about us and beset us on every side, and which rightly preoccupy the thoughts not only of statesmen and leaders but of vast masses in many countries, without offering some guidance, such as I have sometimes done in bygone years.

The supreme hope and the prime endeavour is to reach a good and faithful understanding with Soviet Russia through the agency and organism of the United Nations. In this patient, persevering, resolute endeavour the English-speaking world and the western democracies of Europe must play their part and move together. Only in this way can catastrophe be averted; only in this way can the salvation of all nations and races be gained. I hope that in this world organisation there will be a strong France and a revived Italy, and that many smaller but ancient and famous states will make their weight tell in the noble task of building and maintaining an all-powerful world-governing instrument to preserve freedom and to prevent war. Of France particularly I would say that without a full revival of the true greatness and culture of France there can be little prospect of restoring Europe to its former fame. In the darkest days I have never lost faith in France, and I feel confident that she has now a splendid part to play in the peaceful establishment of progressive western civilisation and democracy, and that France, after all her troubles, may yet lead Europe into the peace and plenty of a free and happy age.

But let me conclude upon our own task. No state or nation is worthy to take part in this sacred, august duty of rebuilding the world under the protection of a world instrument whose men and women are not prepared to give their lives if need be, and to make whatever preparations are required to ensure that they and their country are not found impotent and unready in the world cause. The future, Mr Mayor, is to be saved only by the generous and the strong. We here in Britain and in the Commonwealth and Empire must never fear or fail to take our place among them.

May 1946

Winston S. Churchill to Bernard Baruch
(Churchill papers, 2/153)

8 May 1946
Private and Confidential

My dear Bernie,

You have I think already met Charles Portal, who has just ceased to be the Chief of our Air Force, and will be for the next two years or more responsible for advising the Government on all technical matters with atomic energy. Portal is one of my greatest friends and we worked together during almost the whole five years of the war in the closest intimacy. He is a man of commanding ability, and true as a bell. It is my great desire that you and he shall establish close and confident contact, and I am sure that you will make friends with him. Any courtesy or kindness which you can show him will be deeply valued by

Yours ever

Winston S. Churchill to Lord Alanbrooke
(Churchill papers, 2/5)

8 May 1946
Strictly Private and Personal

My dear Brookie,

I am profoundly concerned that you should be associated, as I am told, with the Government's policy of evacuating all British forces, naval, military and Air, from Egypt and that your name and technical reputation should be quoted in support of this deadly policy.

There is no way whatever of guarding the Canal, in the sense of keeping it open, except by the permanent presence of British personnel in the Nile Valley. An attempt to bring them in at the last moment would be countered by a Russian threat of bombing Cairo or of precipitating war, and no British Government working for peace, as they always will until the last moment, would dare to take that step. Nor would any Egyptian Government refuse a Russian guarantee that if they remained completely neutral and allowed no foreign troops within their bounds, they would not be in any way molested. A demand upon the Egyptians to sabotage any installations and facilities that may be prepared would no doubt be a part of the hostile procedure previous to a declaration of war or to a showdown leading to a British submission.

All idea of America being brought into Palestine to help, on account of their Jewish interests seems to me also to be destroyed by the Government's policy. How can the United States be expected to send troops or aid to an establishment which will in future be represented as the British place d'armes in Palestine, in order to dominate or terrorize Egypt.

I fear you have been sadly misled and that unfair questions have been put to you. You should read carefully what were the questions put to Chatfield[1] and the other Chiefs of the Staff, which resulted in the loss of the ports of Southern Ireland, and brought us to within an ace of destruction.

Winston S. Churchill: speech
(Churchill papers, 5/5)

9 May 1946

The Hague

THE UNITED STATES OF EUROPE

Mr Speaker,[2]

You do me a great honour in inviting me to speak to the States-General today. I see in all this the regard which you have for my dear country and the relief which you had especially in gaining liberty against the invader. I thank you. Personally I have always worked for the cause of liberty standing against tyranny and for the steady advances of the causes of the weak and poor. This is not, as you know, the first time I have had the opportunity of addressing august or famous Assemblies. I have already addressed the Congress of the United States, the Parliaments of Canada and Belgium, the General Assembly of Virginia and besides these there is always the House of Commons at home, where from time to time, I venture still to speak a word or two. Let me in my turn present you my compliments upon the progress made in this country since the expulsion of the German invaders. Holland has regained stability and strength in Europe with great rapidity. I offer my respectful congratulations to all public men who, without regard to Party or interests, have contributed to this achievement. The stability of the Constitution of the Netherlands, centering upon the union of the Crown and people, is an example to many countries. I trust that your affairs abroad will prosper equally with those at home.

---

[1] Alfred Ernle Montacute Chatfield, 1873–1967. Entered RN, 1886. Served at the battles of Heligoland (1914), Dogger Bank (1915) and Jutland (1916). 4th Sea Lord, 1919–20. Knighted, 1919. RAdm., 1920. ACNS, 1920–2. 3rd Sea Lord, 1925–8. C-in-C, Atlantic Fleet, 1929–31. VAdm., 1930. C-in-C, Mediterranean, 1931–2. 1st Sea Lord, Jan. 1933 to Sep. 1938. Adm. of the Fleet, 1935. Baron, 1937. PC, 1939. Minister for Co-ordination of Defence, 1939–40 (with a seat in the War Cabinet). Chairman, Civil Defence Honours Committee, 1940–6. Author of *The Navy and Defence* (1942), and *It Might Happen Again* (1947).

[2] Josef van Schaik, 1882–1962. Speaker, Dutch House of Representatives, 1929–33, 1937–48. Minister of Justice, 1933–5; of Transport and Water Management, 1948; of Internal Affairs, 1948–51. Deputy PM, 1948–51. Member, Council of State, 1951–7.

In Britain we know and value the services which Holland has rendered to European freedom in ancient and in recent times. The Four Freedoms which the great President Roosevelt proclaimed have always been cherished in Holland and were carried by his forebears in their blood to the New World. Even in the days of the Roman Empire the Batavian Republic had established a unique position. In the long, fierce convulsions in Europe which followed the Reformation, Holland and England were united as the foremost champions of Freedom. In those struggles after that change in the human mind which followed the Reformation long after the collapse of the Roman Empire, Holland and England were left as the foremost upholders of freedom. Our ancestors stood together on the bloody dykes, and there are few cities in the Netherlands which do not enshrine the memories of brave resolves and famous feats of arms. Bitter were the struggles of those old days and desperate were the odds you had to face. Looking across the generations I like to feel how Britain's stand in 1940 and 1941 resembled the glorious hour when William the Silent[1] declared that rather than surrender, the Dutch would die on the last dyke. Holland gave us King William the Third,[2] who led both our countries against the overweening tyranny of Louis XIV.[3] And after him John Churchill was Commander-in-Chief not only of the British but of the far larger armies maintained by the Dutch Republic, when she had risen through freedom and independence to power and greatness 250 years ago.

Her Majesty the Queen and the Government of the Netherlands have made me a gift which will be for me for ever an honour and a treasure. They have presented me with the 613 letters which John Churchill wrote to the Grand Pensionary during the long 10 years of the Grand Alliance, which alliance he directed, largely formed, and finally crowned with victory. I express again to this meeting of both of your Houses my gratitude and that of my family for this extraordinary mark of your kindness to me.

Since the bygone struggles between Protestants and Catholics of the sixteenth and seventeenth centuries, there is at least one profound and beneficent new fact of which all should take account. The Church of Rome has ranged itself with those who defend the rights and dignity of the individual, and the

---

[1] William de Zwijger, 1533–84. Prince of Orange, 1544–84. Stadholder of Holland, Zeeland and Utrecht, 1559–84; of Friesland, 1580–4.

[2] William III, 1650–1702. Son of William II, Prince of Orange, and Mary, daughter of Charles I of England. Married, 1677, Mary, daughter of James, Duke of York (later King James II of England). Stadholder, United Provinces of the Netherlands, 1672–1702. After James II had a son, Protestants in England invited William to drive James from England and claim the throne. King of England, Scotland, and Ireland, 1689–1702. Declaration of Right of Accession, 1689. Directed European opposition to Louis XIV of France during Nine Years War (1688–97).

[3] Louis Dieudonné, 1638–1715. Son of Louis XIII of France and Queen Anne of Austria. King of France, 1643–1715. Invaded Spanish Netherlands, 1667. Conquered land in Flanders during Franco-Dutch War, 1672–8. Fought Nine Years War against the Grand Alliance (Spain, England and Holy Roman Empire). Fought for his grandson, Philip V, to inherit the Spanish Empire in the War of the Spanish Succession, 1701–14.

cause of personal freedom throughout the world. I speak of course as one born of a Protestant and Episcopalian family, and I rejoice to see the new and ever-growing unity in lay matters, and not perhaps in lay matters only, between those liberalising forces which must ever light the onward march of man.

Let me pay my tribute to the part borne by Holland in the overthrow of Hitler's hideous tyranny. After your troops and water defences had been overwhelmed by the sudden, treacherous onslaught, which happened six years ago tomorrow, the Dutch people had no longer the means to maintain organised armies in the field, but the will power and firmness of character shown during the grim years of foreign oppression and occupation were definite factors in the ultimate downfall of Naziism, and the Resistance Movement, for which so many thousands of patriots gave their lives, played an even more important part. In Britain we understand how you must have suffered in these years of torment of soul and mind to which starvation and bombardment were lesser afflictions. All honour to those who perished for the cause. May their memory cement the unity of all true Dutchmen. I thank you on behalf of Great Britain for your work. I am glad to meet here my friend, Professor Gerbrandy,[1] the former Prime Minister, who was in Britain with us in all the dark days and who was so vigilant and faithful a champion of the rights and interests of the Netherlands.

Speaking here today, where my words may carry far and wide, it is my first duty to affirm the sanctity of the rights of smaller States. In affirming these rights, I base myself upon that grand figure of Victorian Liberalism, Mr Gladstone. Mr Gladstone, in his third Midlothian speech, said on 27 November 1879:

> The sound and the sacred principle that Christendom is formed of a band of nations who are united to one another in the bonds of right; that they are without distinction of great and small; there is an absolute equality between them – the same sacredness defends the narrow limits of Belgium (and of course Holland) as attaches to the extended frontiers of Russia, or Germany, or France. I hold that he who by act or word brings that principle into peril or disparagement is endangering the peace and all the most fundamental interests of Christian society.

The duty, Mr Speaker, of the large powers of the modern world is to see that those rights of every nation are jealously and strictly protected. The purpose of the United Nations Organisation is to give them the sanction of

---

[1] Pieter Sjoerds Gerbrandy, 1885–1961. Netherlands Minister of Justice, 1939. Joined Dutch Government-in-Exile in London, 1940. Appointed PM in place of Dirk Jan de Geer, seen as defeatist by Queen Wilhelmina. PM, 3 Sep. 1940 to 24 June 1945, serving also in turn as Minister of Justice, Minister for the Colonies and Minister of the Conduct of the War. Opposed separatist movement in Indonesia, 1946–50. Frequently referred to by WSC as 'Mr Cherry Brandy'.

international law, for which Holland and Grotius[1] are so justly famous, and also to make sure that the force of right will, in the ultimate issue, be protected by the right of force.

I will now, Mr Speaker, if you will permit me, if I do not trespass too long upon your courtesy and goodwill, speak of nationalism. Is it an evil or is it a virtue? Where nationalism means the lust for pride and power, the craze for supreme domination by weight or force; where it is the senseless urge to be the biggest in the world, it is a danger and a vice. Where it means love of country and readiness to die for country; where it means love of tradition and culture and the gradual building up across the centuries of a social entity dignified by nationhood, then it is the first of virtues. It is indeed the foundation of a progressive and happy family of nations. Some of our shallow thinkers and false guides – and there are many today – do not distinguish between these two separate and opposing conceptions. They mix them together and use all arguments according as their fancy or their interest prompts them. They condemn nationalism as an old-world obsession and seek to reduce us all, both countries and individuals to one uniform pattern with nothing but material satisfactions as our goal. Or again, sometimes with almost the same breath, they pervert the noble sentiments of patriotism to the hideous, aggressive expansion of old-world imperialism, and to the obliteration by force or by wrongful teaching of all the varieties and special cultures, all those dear thoughts of home and country without which existence, however logically planned, would be dreary and barren beyond thought or imagination.

After the end of the great conflict from 1914 to 1918 it was hoped that the wars were over. Yet we have witnessed an even more destructive world-wide struggle. Need we have done so? I have no doubt whatever that firm guidance and united action on the part of the Victorious Powers could have prevented this last catastrophe. If the United States had taken an active part in the League of Nations, and if the League of Nations had been prepared to use concerted force, even had it only been European force, in order to prevent the rearmament of Germany, there was no need for further serious bloodshed. Let us, Sir, profit at least by this terrible lesson. In vain did I try to teach it before the War.

Mr Speaker, the tragedy of Europe shocks mankind. Well, as you said in your Address, 'Europe is totally ravaged'. The tragedy darkens the pages of human history. It will excite the amazement and horror of future generations. Here in these beautiful, fertile and temperate lands, where so many of the noblest parent races of mankind have developed their character, their arts and their literature, we have twice in our own lifetime seen all rent asunder and torn to pieces in frightful convulsions which have left their mark in blackened

---

[1] Huig de Groot, 1583–1645. Known as 'Grotius'. Jurist and scholar. Educated at University of Leiden. Author of *Adam in Exile* (1601) and *De Indus* (1605). Leading figure in Dutch Protestant reform. Published over 20 works of literature and philosophy.

devastation through the entire continent. And had not Europe's children of earlier times come back across the Atlantic Ocean with strong and rescuing arms, all the peoples of Europe might have fallen into the long night of Nazi totalitarian despotism. Upon Britain fell the proud but awful responsibility of keeping the Flag of Freedom flying in the old world till the forces of the new world could arrive. But now the tornado has passed away. The thunder of the cannons has ceased, the terror from the skies is over, the oppressors are cast out and broken. We may be wounded and impoverished. But we are still alive and free. The future stands before us, to make or mar.

Two supreme tasks confront us. We have to revive the prosperity of Europe; and European civilisation must rise again from the chaos and carnage into which it had been plunged; and at the same time we have to devise those measures of world security which will prevent disaster descending upon us again. In both these tasks Holland has an important part to play. The restoration and rebuilding of Europe, both physical and moral, as you have pointed out in your Address, Mr Speaker, is animated and guided by the kindred themes of Liberty and Democracy. These words are on every lip. They have cheered us and helped to unify us in the struggle. They inspire our rejoicings in the hour of victory. But now that the fighting is over, it is necessary to define these glorious war cries with a little more fullness and precision.

You will pardon me, I trust, if I come a little closer to the conception of free democracy based upon the people's will and expressing itself through representative assemblies under generally accepted constitutional forms. There are certain simple, practical tests by which the virtue and reality of any political democracy may be measured. Does the Government in any country rest upon a free constitutional basis, assuring the people the right to vote according to their will, for whatever candidates they choose? Is there the right of free expression of opinion, free support, free opposition, free advocacy and free criticism of the Government of the day?

Are there Courts of Justice free from interference by the Executive or from threats of mob violence, and free from all association with particular political parties? Will these courts administer public and well-established laws associated in the human mind with the broad principles of fair play and justice? Will there be fair play for the poor as well as the rich? Will there be fair play for private persons as well as for Government officials? Will the rights of the individual, subject to his duties to the State, be maintained, asserted and exalted? In short, do the Government own the people, or do the people own the Government? There is the test. Here are some of the more obvious tests by which the political health and soundness of any community may be ascertained.

Now let us think of our other supreme task, the building of a world instrument of security, in which all peoples have a vital interest, and assuredly none more than those in these sorely-tried Low Countries, which have sometimes been called the cockpit of Europe.

The more closely the largest Powers of today are bound together in bonds of faith and friendship the more effective will be the safeguards against war and the higher the security of all other states and nations. It is evident of course that the affairs of Great Britain and the British Commonwealth and Empire, are becoming ever more closely interwoven with those of the United States, and that an underlying unity of thought and conviction increasingly pervades the English-speaking world. There can be nothing but advantage to the whole world from such a vast and benevolent synthesis. But we also in Britain have our Twenty Years' Treaty with Soviet Russia, which in no way conflicts with other associations, but which we hope may prove one of the sure anchors of world peace. We trust that in due course the natural unity and alliance between Great Britain and France will find reaffirmation in a new instrument. We welcome every step towards strength and freedom taken by the French people. We rejoice to see France moving forward to her old place in which if there were a void, Europe would be vitally wounded. We hope that the Western democracies of Europe may draw together in ever closer amity and ever closer association. This is a matter which should be very carefully considered and if found wise should be pressed from many angles with the utmost perseverance.

Special associations within the circle of the United Nations, such as those of which I have been speaking, or like the great unity of the British Empire and Commonwealth, or like the association which prevails throughout the Americas, North and South, far from weakening the structure of the supreme body of UNO, should all be capable of being fused together in such a way as to make UNO indivisible and invincible; above all there must be a tolerance, the recognition of the charm of variety, and the respect for the rights of minorities. There was a time when the Age of Faith endeavoured to prevent the Age of Reason, and another time when the Age of Reason endeavoured to destroy the Age of Faith. Tolerance was one of the chief features of the great liberalising movements which were the glory of the latter part of the nineteenth century, by which states of society were reached where the most fervent devotion to religion subsisted side by side with the fullest exercise of free thought. We may well recur to those bygone days, from whose standards of enlightenment, compassion and hopeful progress, the terrible twentieth century has fallen so far. I say here as I said at Brussels last year that I see no reason why under the guardianship of the world organisation, there should not ultimately arise the United States of Europe, both those of the East and those of the West which will unify this Continent in a manner never known since the fall of the Roman Empire, and within which all its peoples may dwell together in prosperity, in justice and in peace.

Winston S. Churchill: speech
('Winston S. Churchill, His Complete Speeches', volume 7, pages 7323–4)

10 May 1946   University of Leyden

'LET FREEDOM REIGN'

. . . The decision to make me a Doctor of Laws is deeply valued by me. The Rector[1] has explained how rarely this distinction is given, and especially in cases like mine. It has to be proved that the recipient, by his moral qualities, his attitude, and character has influenced the course of history in a favourable sense.

I felt this might be a rather difficult task for the promoter to prove, but the promoter's reasoning with his logic and deduction seems to be very good. As he proceeded my natural modesty was undermined, and I will confess to this august assembly that I allowed myself to be convinced by him. . . .

Six years ago on this very day of the week the treacherous onslaught was made on Holland. In the morning this onslaught was made. In our country I became Prime Minister that evening.

I think of all we have gone through in our different ways since then – our trial in Britain and yours over here. Yours was to be restrained and dominated for those long five years by vile and brutal tyranny, to have all the evils of oppression, and to find solace only in the glories of revolt and secret association and preparation. The nightmare has ended. The land is clear, the tyrant is overthrown.

The victors have overthrown the arbiters. The great wheel has swung full circle. One can see the awful finger of destiny or providence working here in this sphere of transient life, where generations so swiftly succeed one another, carrying forward their message and bearing their tribulation as they can.

Rector Magnificus, a great responsibility is felt by you and those associated with you in guiding this torch to young men and women at universities. You have indeed at this time a special measure of responsibility. We must make sure that one form of tyranny is not succeeded by another.

I am opposed, and always have been, to tyranny in every guise. It makes no difference to me what dress it wears, what slogans it mouths. I consider it a supreme duty of the individual subject or citizen to do his utmost to guard not only the liberty of his country, but the liberty of the individuals dwelling under the constitution of his native land. The motto of your university, which is among the most ancient and most democratic of the universities, is: 'Let freedom reign.' That is the motto I will accept for myself with the diploma you have so kindly just given me.

---

[1] Rudolph Pabus Cleveringa, 1894–1980. Educated at University of Leiden; Prof., Commercial and Civil Law, 1927–40, 1945–58. Defended Jewish scholars during Nazi persecution. Imprisoned by Germans, 1941–4. Member, Council of State, 1958–63.

Field Marshal Lord Montgomery to Winston S. Churchill
(Churchill papers, 2/143)[1]

12 May 1946
Private

Dear Mr Churchill,

You must be feeling upset at what is happening in Egypt and the way it has been handled. We lack your strong hand on the helm at these times.

As one who has gained much inspiration from you during the late war, I felt I would like to tell you this: before I move on to our official appointment in which it will be unsuitable for me to say such things.

Winston S. Churchill to Clement Attlee
(Churchill papers, 2/42)

14 May 1946
Private and Personal

My dear Prime Minister,

I feel I ought to let you know the position which I take up myself about India.

First, I consider myself committed up to the Cripps Mission in 1942, though you know what a grief this was to me. However, the imminence of Japanese invasion of India and the hope, which failed, of rallying all forces possible to Indian national defence compelled me to take the line I did. But everything stood on the basis of an Agreement between the great forces composing Indian life. If that Agreement is not forthcoming, I must resume my full freedom to point out the dangers and evils of the abandonment by Great Britain of her mission in India.

Secondly, we had always contemplated that a Constitution would be framed of Dominion status and only when that was definitely established should the latent right of a Dominion to quit the Empire or Commonwealth become operative. If, at the present time, you reach immediately a solution of independence, I should not be able to support this. I may add that the dangers of civil war breaking out in India on our departure are at least as great as those which are held by the Anglo-American Commission on Palestine to make a continuance of British or Anglo-American Mandate necessary.

I earnestly hope that we shall not find ourselves suddenly confronted with far-reaching and irrevocable decisions in these fields, for it will be a great shock to the British nation to find themselves, all of a sudden, stripped of their Empire and position in the East on the morrow of their victory in the War.

[1] This letter was handwritten.

MAY 1946

Winston S. Churchill to Field Marshal Lord Montgomery
(*Churchill papers, 2/143*)

14 May 1946

My dear Monty,

It is very kind of you to write me your letter of May 12[1] in your brief interval of freedom from official duties. I hope however that you will give the whole of this subject your careful and unprejudiced thought. Danger arises when military and political questions are mixed up together and put before Staffs in a confusing way in order to obtain their assent to policies with which on purely technical grounds they would have disagreed. The Irish Ports is a case in point, and you should certainly make yourself acquainted with what took place there at that time, and what was the form in which the issue was put before Lord Chatfield and others. Something of the kind has I fear happened now.

I am delighted that you are going to publish *Ten Chapters*. I am sure it will make a fine stir. Let me know when you take over, as I should like to have a talk with you before you are enmeshed.

PS. It would be good to let a Press reproduce <u>in facsimile</u> – one or two of these chapters.

Winston S. Churchill: speech
('*The Sinews of Peace*', pages 135–8)

16 May 1946   House of Commons

INDIA CABINET MISSION – STATEMENT ON THE ADJOURNMENT

I think the right hon Gentleman (The Prime Minister) was right to read to the House the able but melancholy document to which we have listened, and it was appropriate that he should read it, instead of merely circulating it with the Votes. Certainly I have heard nothing for a long time which so deeply deserves the attention of Parliament and of the British nation, and the respectful attention which the House gave to every word uttered by the Prime Minister is a proof that this opinion is well founded. It would, of course, be most unwise this afternoon for any of us to attempt detailed comment upon the long and complicated proposals which have now been laid before us. I am bound to make clear without delay what is the position of the official Opposition. I, as the head of the Coalition Government and my colleagues of those days, are committed to the offer made to the people of India at the time of the Cripps mission in 1942, by which we offered Dominion Status as expressed by the

---
[1] Reproduced above (p. 328).

Statute of Westminster, including, as it does, the latent right of secession. We offered this to the many peoples of India, subject to certain provisions.

The first of those provisions was that there should be broad, real, sincere agreement between the main Indian parties. The second was that in the Constitution we should have provision for the honourable discharge of the obligations we have contracted in India towards the minorities who, added together, are themselves a majority, and, also, for the discharge of those obligations embodied in our treaties with the India States. These proposals were made by us at a moment when the danger of Japanese invasion threatened India in a terrible manner, and I, personally, was induced to agree to them by the all-compelling war interest, as it seemed, of trying to rally all the forces in India to the defence of their soil against Japanese aggression and all the horrors that would follow therefrom.

The Cripps mission failed. The answer which Mr Gandhi[1] gave to the British Government at that moment of mortal peril was 'Quit India'; and he and the Congress proceeded to raise or encourage a revolt, or widespread disturbances, affecting, principally, the communications on which the British and Indian Forces relied for holding the threatened fronts. These disorders, although seriously fomented, were suppressed with surprising ease and very little loss of life, and the incitement to revolt found practically no response, outside the political classes, from the great masses of the Indian people. We persevered with the war; we toiled on; and presently the tide turned. India was successfully defended, and it emerged from this second world convulsion of our lifetime protected from external violence by the arms, sea power and diplomacy at the disposal of the British Empire, including, of course, the valiant contribution of the India Forces themselves and the Gurkhas from Nepal. Nevertheless, we still persisted in our offer which had been rejected in 1942, and the late Secretary of State for India, Mr Amery, on June 14 last, when the Government had ceased to be a Coalition and was a Conservative Government, used the following words, which were quoted by my right hon Friend the Member for Saffron Walden (Mr R. A. Butler) when the proposal was made to send the Cabinet Mission in India in February. This is what Mr Amery said:

> As the statement makes clear, the offer of March 1942, stands in its entirety. That offer was based on two main principles. The first is that no limit is set to India's freedom to decide for herself her own destiny, whether as a free member and partner in the British Commonwealth or even without it. The second is that this can only be achieved under a constitution or constitu-

---

[1] Mohandas Karamchand Gandhi, 1869–1948. Known as Mahatma Gandhi. Educated at University of Bombay, 1887. Led civil disobedience and non-violent protests in South Africa and India. Leader of movement for Indian independence.

tions framed by Indians to which the main elements in India's national life are consenting parties.

By that statement we were and we are bound. Now, however, a new situation has arisen. We are confronted with the fact, reiterated in the Prime Minister's statement, that there is no agreement. The main elements in India's national life are not at the present time 'consenting parties' – I am quoting the words of Mr Amery's speech. No one will doubt the sincerity and the earnestness with which the Cabinet Ministers concerned and the Viceroy (Lord Wavell) have laboured to bring about the solution of Indian disagreement. They have worked for that solution with the zeal that would be natural if it were to gain an empire and not to cast one away. But they have failed, and the fact that they have failed, through no fault of their own, in spite of all their efforts, devotion and ingenuity, is a fact which should, in itself, be an education in Indian matters, not only throughout this country, but throughout the world. During these negotiations it has been increasingly clear that the object sought for was not Dominion Status, with the subsequent and consequent right of secession, but direct and immediate independence. I am not sure that the results of this short circuit have been fully realised by the House. It certainly came as a surprise to me.

Thirdly, the new proposals which we have heard seem, at first sight, to shift the onus of deciding the future constitution of India from the Indian parties to His Majesty's Government, who have themselves come forward no doubt from the best of motives, with an elaborate and detailed scheme. In so far as this shifting of the onus may prove to be the case, it certainly seems to have been an unfortunate step. It goes beyond what we understand was the purpose of the Ministers' mission, the mandate which they received, which was – it was so defined by the Prime Minister, I think – to set up machinery for Indians to decide the form of government. It will, I hope, be common ground between us that we cannot enforce by British arms a British-made Constitution upon India against the wishes of any of the main elements in Indian life. That is a very important fact to establish.

There remains the discharge of our obligations to the Indian minorities and to the Indian States. We must study the document with prolonged and searching attention in order to see that these duties have been faithfully safeguarded. It would seem, at first sight, that attention should be particularly directed to the position of the Muslim community of nearly 80 million, who are the most warlike and formidable of all the races and creeds in the Indian sub-continent, and whose interest and culture are a matter of great consequence to India as a whole, and vital to the peace of India. Secondly, we must examine the provisions made for the depressed classes, or 'untouchables' as they are called, who number nearly 60 million, and for whose status and future repeated assurances have been given and pledges made by many British Governments, in ancient and in more recent times.

Finally, there are the relations which the Indian States, which comprise a quarter of the population and a third of the territory of the Indian sub-continent, are to have to the Crown and to the new Government. At present, those relations are defined by solemn treaties dependent upon the paramountcy of the Crown. Apparently, this is to be abolished, in a sentence which was obscure: it may be neither one thing nor the other. It would be relegated to a kind of 'no man's land', this question of paramountcy; and if that be so, it would seem – I do not attempt to probe the legal issues – that all foundation for these treaties would be swept away.

All these matters and many others will occur to hon. Members as they study the able White Paper. It will require several weeks of profound and earnest consideration, and certainly it would not, in my view, be desirable to bring this whole matter to Debate in the House of Commons, with all that a Debate in these circumstances might entail, in any precipitate manner. We do not even know at the present time, although we may elucidate that by question and answer, what are the legislative steps which would be required in the setting up of an interim government, or, in the event of an agreement being reached, for the creation of a new Constitution, or for the abrogation of the King's title as Emperor of India. Therefore, I say, in the name of the Opposition, that a new situation has been created, that we are bound to review it in light of the existing facts, and that we reserve our entire freedom of action as to the future course we shall take.

B. R. Ambedkar[1] to Winston S. Churchill
(Churchill papers, 2/42)

17 May 1946   New Delhi

Cabinet missions proposals are a shameful betrayal of the cause of 60 millions of untouchables. No representation in constituent assembly no representation in the advisory committee no protection by treaty. Handing over untouchables bound hand and foot. Untouchables all over India are grateful to you for your speech in Parliament. Future of untouchables very dark. Entirely depend upon you for safeguarding their interest.

[1] Bhimrao Ramji Ambedkar, 1893–1956. 'Untouchable' by caste. Educated at Elphinstone College, Bombay; Columbia University, NY; London School of Economics. Minister for Law, India, 1947–51.

May 1946

Winston S. Churchill to George Trevelyan[1]
(Churchill papers, 2/157)

18 May 1946

My dear George Trevelyan,

I am touched by the kindness of your letter, and gratefully accept the noble gift[2] you offer. I shall always treasure it among my records of Marlborough. These are now becoming considerable, and I am taking special measures to preserve them.

This gives me the opportunity of reminding you of the inspiring letter you wrote me in 1941 or 1942. In this you referred to the ill-success which attended Lord Chatham's first two years of war direction, but how nevertheless later on everything worked out well. I was much cheered by this letter when it came, after so many disappointments and reverses, and I have several times wished to lay my hands on it again. Perhaps you could give me the quotation you used in it. You must not however suppose I am so conceited as to place myself with the great men of the past. It was only the crisis which stood at an equal or even higher level. Those were the days of great men and small events. We have endured an age in which the reverse proportions apply.

I wonder also whether your knowledge of Macaulay's[3] writings can give me the passage in which he describes the agony of the Dutch when they prepared to sail across the Atlantic and beyond the ocean 'to find the exchange of a wealthier Amsterdam and the schools of a more learned Leyden'. I tried to verify this before I went to Holland the other day to receive a Degree from the University of Leyden, but as I could not get in touch with you I had to go into action on memory alone.

Once more thanking you for your kindness, and expressing my gratitude at your superb contribution to the historical knowledge of these sad times.

---

[1] George Macaulay Trevelyan, 1876–1962. A great-nephew of the historian Lord Macaulay. Educated at Harrow and Trinity College, Cambridge. Historian; author of seven books before 1914, including a trilogy about Garibaldi. Commandant, 1st British Ambulance Unit for Italy, 1915–18. Regius Prof. of Modern History, Cambridge University, 1927–40. OM, 1930. Master of Trinity College, Cambridge, 1940. Chancellor of Durham University, 1949–57. Among his later books were *Blenheim* (1930) and a biography of Sir Edward Grey (1937). In 1944 he published his *English Social History, A Survey of Six Centuries*.
[2] A letter of 4 Aug. 1688 from the 1st Duke of Marlborough to William of Orange. The text of the letter is included in book I of *Marlborough, His Life and Times* (1933).
[3] Thomas Babington Macaulay, 1800–59. Whig politician, essayist, poet, and historian. MP (Whig) for Calne, 1830–2; for Leeds, 1832–4; for Edinburgh, 1839–47, 1852–6. Secretary to the Board of Control, 1832. Secretary at War, 1839–41. Paymaster-General of the Forces, 1846–8. Baron, 1857. Published *Lays of Ancient Rome* (1842), *Critical and Historical Essays* (1843) and *History of England from the Accession of James the Second* (1848).

Winston S. Churchill to Clement Attlee
(Churchill papers, 2/145)

18 May 1946

My dear Prime Minister,

I think it would be very good if all ex-servicemen possessing medals were asked to wear them on the day of the Victory celebrations. Those who have fought in former wars hardly ever have a chance to wear their medals on their plain clothes. I hope you will consider this, because these medals are often won with very severe service and their owners do not frequently have an opportunity of putting them on. Both you and I might like to wear ours, although we could not compete with the rank and file in deserts or suffering. Will you kindly think this over? I have several times in the past suggested to the King that his birthday and other occasions should be marked in this way. It might well be that the proposal would be agreeable to his Majesty. Anyhow, I hope you will make it, for I am sure it would be gratefully received.

Winston S. Churchill to Queen Wilhelmina
(Churchill papers, 2/234)

18 May 1946

Madam,

I shall always preserve the most delightful memories of my visit to Holland and of Yr Majesty's gracious and charming hospitality at Amsterdam to me and to my wife and Mary. When I look back on these five days they seem to have been a pageant of kindness and honour, and I shall never forget the seas of upturned joyous faces wh welcomed me in the streets of Amsterdam, Rotterdam and Leyden. To address the States General, to receive the degree of so famous a University, and the gold medal of Amsterdam, and also my visit to Rotterdam where the crowds were enormous and the enthusiasm beyond description – all these are events in my life which I rejoice to have experienced.

But Yr Majesty's personal kindness touched me most deeply and I shall recall it every time I wear the Dutch Lion. I saw and admired during the long years of war and exile Yr Majesty's dignity, fortitude and inherent authority amid all the misfortunes and disappointments. Now I have seen the Beloved Sovereign restored to her people and surrounded by the truest men and women of the stubborn, valiant Dutch race. I saw stability, comradeship, industry and moral strength on every side. I feel high confidence in the future of the Netherlands under the guidance and inspiration of Yr Majesty's commanding personality. May all our hopes come true.

May 1946

Sir Walter Monckton to Winston S. Churchill
(Churchill papers, 2/42)

18 May 1946 New Delhi

My dear Mr Churchill,

Your speech on the Government Statement on India gave great satisfaction to such of the Princes and the Muslim Leaguers as I came across yesterday. Mr Jinnah[1] has not yet come down from Simla but I hope to see him before I leave India on the 26th May.[2]

The difficulty of our position with a huge Labour majority in the House is clearly recognised, as is the fact that a head-on collision would in any event be impossible after all that has been said about giving India freedom.

To my mind, the most important point is that we should do all we can to persuade and encourage the principal elements in India to remain attached to the British Empire. I see little prospect of inducing Congress to take such a line but Congress, as such, has a very uncertain future once India is free. Nothing else but the struggle for independence holds together the discordant elements of the party. On ordinary political issues it is hard to see how great industrialists like Birla[3] and the Communists will pull together. And a man like Narain[4] who hates us and calls himself a Congress Socialist, is likely to disrupt the party. Even in the Conferences with the Cabinet Mission the four Congress representatives had great difficulty, and did not always succeed, in maintaining a united front. In addition, there is little in the records of the present Congress leaders to suggest that they will show the capacity to undertake the responsibilities of office.

The Muslim League, on the other hand, are naturally ready – though they will not be anxious to express their readiness publicly – to see the British connection retained. They know that India won't be able to stand alone in the world. (Even Congress leaders feel the weight of this and are not inclined to prefer Russia or the USA as the big partner.) They know too that they will have

---

[1] Mohammed Ali Jinnah, 1876–1948. Member of Imperial Legislative Council in India from 1910. President, all-India Muslim League 1916, 1920 and from 1934. Known as the 'Founder of Pakistan'; served as its first Governor-General, 1948.

[2] Monckton had been employed as a Constitutional Adviser by the Nizam of Hyderabad since the 1930s. At this point he was assisting the Hyderabad delegation in its negotiations with the Cabinet mission sent out by the UK Labour Government to make arrangements for the transfer of power in India.

[3] Ghanshyam Das Birla, 1894–1983. Industrialist; member of a family of wealthy financiers. President, Indian Chamber of Commerce, 1924. Member, Bengal Legislative Council Fiscal Committee. Member, Indian Legislative Assembly (resigned in protest against legislation favouring Imperial Preference, 1930). Unofficial adviser to Government of India on Indo-British trade negotiations, 1936–7. Personal friend of Gandhi; throughout the 1930s, paid monthly allowances to many leading members of the Indian National Congress. Subsequently one of the principal financiers of the Congress Party, and a donor of large sums for charitable and educational purposes.

[4] Jayaprakash Narayan, 1902–79. Educated at University of Iowa. Member, Indian National Congress, 1929. Founding member, Praja Socialist Party, 1952.

the sympathy of the British in their efforts to get a fair deal as a minority. If we can show this sympathy and gradually help them to a more secure position as the constitutional changes develop, I believe they will respond.

The Princes' interests run side by side with those of the Muslim League, though both parties will refrain from saying so; the Hindu Rulers are in a majority and would not like to identify themselves with the League. Nevertheless, the Muslim Princes are likely to take the lead in the forthcoming negotiations. Kashmir and other large Hindu States will watch to see what line Hyderabad takes: and HH of Bhopal,[1] the Chancellor of the Chamber of Princes, is both in ambition and ability outstanding among the Rulers and will probably be head (as he is already provisionally) of the Negotiating Committee mentioned in the Cabinet Delegation's paper. I have been in close and constant touch with him. He has made speeches in favour of India's independence and has said that after such independence it will be worth considering whether the mutual interests of Great Britain and India might not best be served by either joining the British Commonwealth or by alliance with it. He has taken this independent line because he and his brother Princes have got to live in India and, therefore, want to make the best terms they can with British Indian Leaders unless (which they have come to doubt) there is real hope of help for the Princes from England. But I know that he would prefer the British connection and feels that he could play for a draw for 3 or 4 years if there was some assurance of less separatist policy in Great Britain thereafter and a friendlier attitude towards the Native States. It was here that your words were specially welcome.

As to the reception of the Cabinet scheme – Congress are plainly delighted; the Muslim League (no doubt disappointed about Pakistan) are keeping silent: my bet is that they will protest but take a part eventually in the interim Government. The States are on the whole satisfied that, so far as it goes, the scheme does not embarrass them as much as they feared. But they know that in the next stage, when they actually negotiate, they may get help from the Viceroy, but are not likely to get it from HMG where they fear Stafford's influence.

I am seeing the Viceroy tonight and the C-in-C tomorrow and then go to see the Nizam[2] in Hyderabad for a couple of days. I expect to be in England by the 30th May and may come back here in August or September.

[. . .]

---

[1] Hamidullah Khan, 1894–1960. Chief Secretary to Government of Bhopal headed by his mother (Begum of Bhopal), 1916–22; Member for Law, Justice and Finance, 1922–6. Succeeded his mother as ruler of Bhopal, 1926. Knighted, 1929. Chancellor, Muslim University, Aligarh, 1930–5; Indian Chamber of Princes, 1931–2, 1944–7.

[2] Osman Ali Khan, 1886–1967. Diamond magnate and philanthropist. Ruler of Hyderabad, 1911–48. Introduced electricity, railways, roads and airways to the state. Built Osmania University. Dubbed the world's richest man by *Time* magazine, 1937.

Winston S. Churchill to Duke of Windsor
(Churchill papers, 2/178)

19 May 1946
Confidential

Sir,

I have received with great pleasure your most kind letter of May 8.[1]

In the train on the way to Fulton I spoke to the President about your intention to reside for a while in the United States and he expressed pleasure at this. I then mentioned to him the idea that you should be associated with the British Embassy, and he thought that this would be a good plan. I reported this conversation to the King when I went to Windsor towards the end of last month. He asked me whether I had informed you, and I said that I was informing him first.

I am very sorry about this foolish obstruction by Bevin and Attlee, and I wish I had it in my power to overcome it. But we are all under the harrow, and our position in the East is clattering down in full conformity with our financial situation at home.

I am very much tied by the leg to my work as Leader of the Opposition in the House of Commons, and have to turn up there at least three days a week as long as I choose to keep the position. I am very glad that you will both be coming over here in August, and I shall look forward to coming to see you whenever you find it convenient. In this confused aftermath of a second world convulsion in our short spans, it is a grand thing that you and your wife should have found such true happiness. I beg you to convey to the Duchess my respects and kindest regards. Please accept all my best wishes. I am sure better days will dawn.

Winston S. Churchill to Lord Cherwell
(Churchill papers, 2/147)

19 May 1946

My dear Prof,

I cannot visit the English Speaking Union between 4.30 p.m. and 6.30 p.m. on Friday June 21. I am at what poor Keynes called in the last few weeks of his life 'saturation point'. It is so easy to put these things down on the card, and so bloody when the day comes round.

About your letter.[2] You should begin by saying: 'Everyone wishes that our country should do its utmost, even at the most heavy sacrifices, to alleviate famine in other lands, and we are indeed willing to give from our own scarcity.'

---

[1] Reproduced above, dated May 5 (pp. 309–10).
[2] To Churchill, of May 16. Churchill's following statement refers to a note Cherwell was considering writing to the *Daily Telegraph*.

'The facts of the situation should however be kept constantly in view.' After the word 'tons' in the third line of your draft, insert: '. . . on the assumption, which is certainly untrue, that there is no other food in the distressed areas but that brought in as famine relief. This . . .'

At the end of your first paragraph, after the word 'Portugal', add (not as a fresh paragraph): 'Everyone knows that there is no risk of absolute starvation in the country districts. It is only in the towns that the worst is to be expected. It is clear therefore that the numbers to be provided for are very much less than the aforesaid 136,000,000.'

Pray think this over and if you agree redraft accordingly. I should like to see the final version. There is no hurry because it would be well to let the Morrison mission, and the decisions upon it, be completed before you say anything. With this timing no-one can accuse you of hampering the negotiations.

Winston S. Churchill to Sir Nevile Bland[1]
(Churchill papers, 2/234)

19 May 1946

My dear Ambassador,

I send enclosed herewith a letter[2] which I have written to the Queen thanking her for her gracious courtesy to me. But let me also thank you and Lady Bland[3] for all your kindness and the care which you took in arranging the details of what was a most memorable and, though strenuous, thoroughly enjoyable experience to me and to us all.

I am so glad to see that the elections have gone exactly as we expected – or even better – and that a great measure of stability is present in the affairs of the Netherlands. The difference between the Dutch and the British at the present moment is that the Dutch were compressed by the war and are now erect and expanding, whereas we, who were blood donors throughout, are now exhausted psychically, economically, and above all, financially, and find victory bleak and disappointing.

My wife and Mary tell me of the lovely time they had after I left. Owing to the gifts I have received I shall evidently have to learn to drink gin. I believe it is quite good once you have the knack of it, provided you keep in practice. At present I remain faithful to whiskey.

PS. Pray be so kind as to deliver the enclosure to Her Majesty by whatever means you think best.

---

[1] (George) Nevile Maltby Bland, 1886–1972. Entered FO, 1911. Counsellor, Brussels, 1930–5. Head of Treaty and Protocol Dept, 1935–8. Knighted, 1937. Minister to the Netherlands, 1938–42; Ambassador, 1942–8.

[2] Reproduced above (p. 334).

[3] Portia Ottely, 1893–1968. Married, 1919, Nevile Bland; two sons (one killed in action, 1943) and one daughter.

May 1946

General Sir Hastings Ismay to Winston S. Churchill
(Churchill papers, 4/44)

20 May 1946

My dear Mr Churchill,

I have now been twice through the notes you gave me last week. What absorbing reading they make and what prodigious moments they recall.

In accordance with your wishes, I have not attempted to check the exact military dispositions or plans at any given moment, nor our discussions with the French, the Dutch and the Belgians both before and after the outbreak of war, nor the precise sequence of events. In fact all that I have done is to dictate my recollections of those acts in the drama at which I was present. My notes are attached. I have also made a few pencil amendments as regards dates, times, personalities, etc. on your own notes.

The only papers that I have consulted are the official records of the meetings of the Supreme War Council. I had these printed last year and sent you a bound copy, which I expect that you have taken away with you. I believe that you would wish to re-read them some time.

If my notes are not the sort of thing that you wanted, please let me know, and I will have another shot.

Clement Attlee to Winston S. Churchill
(Churchill papers, 2/145)

21 May 1946

My dear Churchill

Many thanks for your letter of May 18th[1] suggesting that all ex-servicemen possessing medals should be asked to wear them on the day of the Victory celebrations. I think this an admirable suggestion and I am immediately taking it up. I will let you know the outcome as soon as possible.

Winston S. Churchill to Lieutenant Charles Heron Mullan[2]
(Churchill papers, 2/5)[3]

21 May 1946

Dear Lieutenant Mullan,

I write to wish you the decisive success in your election campaign which

---

[1] Reproduced above (p. 334).
[2] Charles Heron Mullan, 1912–96. Educated at Castle Park. MP (Union.) for Co. Down, 1946–50. Parliamentary Member, Ulster Unionist Council, 1945–60. VRD, 1950. Chairman, Belfast Juvenile Courts, 1964–79. CBE, 1979. Vice-President, Juvenile Courts Association, 1980–93.
[3] This letter was handwritten.

your political qualifications and distinguished service in the Royal Navy throughout the war have earned for you.

Ulster Unionists will assuredly recognise the urgent need at the present moment of reinforcing the one Party in the British Parliament that places the maintenance of the Commonwealth and Empire in the forefront of its programme.

A year ago our world-wide Empire of self-governing nations stood at the pinnacle of its fame and prestige among the peoples of the world. In the months that have elapsed since the reins of Government passed into the hands of the Socialist Party our position and our influence upon world affairs have grievously declined.

This Government of timid yet dangerous zealots, not content with making wild experiments with the future of British Industry, has now begun to liquidate our interests and our prestige all over the world. Only by a watchful, persistent, and unflinching Opposition can the worst excesses of this minority Socialist Government be checked or abated. After all even under the peculiar conditions of the General Election we Conservatives polled nearly half the nation.

Ulster has never failed to keep the Flag flying. I earnestly hope that the electors of County Down will give you their votes for the sound and progressive principles for which the Conservative Unionist Party stands, and indeed – far above Party – for all that makes Britain great.

George Trevelyan to Winston S. Churchill
(Churchill papers, 2/157)[1]

21 May 1946

Dear Winston Churchill

I was rejoiced to get your letter[2] this morning. Your ancestor's letter shall go first to Harraps for reproduction for your book, and they will send it on to you. I am pasting some words on the back of the frame, but of course you are not bound to keep it in the frame unless you wish.

If you may not compare yourself to the elder Pitt, everyone else does and historians will always delight to work out the parallel with its differences.

I send you one of the two passages for which you asked. The other I can't find. No answer, till you get the letter from Harraps.

---

[1] This letter was handwritten.
[2] Reproduced above (p. 333).

May 1946

Lord Garnock[1] and Ivo Geikie-Cobb[2] to Winston S. Churchill
(Churchill papers, 2/6)

22 May 1946
Cambridge
Magdalene College

My Dear Sir,

We hope you will not mind our troubling you, but we venture to write jointly to ask you about a matter which, as young Conservatives, troubles us not a little – namely the lack of a concrete published party policy. We realise that it is far easier for the Socialists to promise 'Utopia' for everyone, than it is for our party to put out a comprehensive and attractive programme for the future; but at the same time, we do feel that a policy, couched in such a way that it is attractive for the man-in-the-street and easy for everyone to understand, ought to be brought out by the party.

We are not alone in feeling this; scores of people of our age and older have told us that their views are in conflict with those of the Government, but that they are not really Conservatives because they cannot find out whether their views and the party's are similar.

If a programme to enlist the support of the electorate is being put out daily, then there is far too little of it to be seen in the Daily Press, fifty per cent of which, surely, is anti-Labour?

We have both seen plenty of encouraging signs among the workers that they are dubious as to this Government's intentions; for example, when working on the railways during vacations, we found many railwaymen, who had voted Labour, to be not at all keen on the prospect of nationalisation. They were all, however, quick to add that they were equally opposed to the Conservative Party. Surely if a popular campaign was undertaken by the party, and given the nation-wide publicity which Labour gets for its campaigns, many of these lukewarm people might be won over to our way of thinking. It seems to us that the sole reason for many people not being active Conservatives is that they lack official guidance and help from the party itself.

We are therefore approaching you, as leader of the party, hoping that you will be able to give consideration to our plea that the Conservative policy should be overhauled and a campaign which will appeal to the mass of the people be promptly inaugurated.

---

[1] William Tuckder Lindesay-Bethune, 1901–85. Married, 1925, Marjory Cross. Succeeded his father as 13th Viscount of Garnock, 23rd Lord Lindsay of the Byres, 14th Lord Parbroath, and 14th Earl of Lindsay, 1943. Representative Peer, 1947–59. Honorary Col., Fife and Forfar Yeomanry, Scottish Horse, 1957–62. Zone Commander, Northern Civil Defence Zone, Scotland, 1963–9. Member, Fife City Council, 1956–64. President, Shipwrecked Fishermen and Mariners Royal Benevolent Society, 1966–76.

[2] Ivo Geikie-Cobb, 1887–1953. Physician, author and neurologist. Educated at St Thomas's Hospital, London. Married, 1913, Audrey de Poix: three children. Worked in Overseas Service Dept of the BBC, 1940–5.

We hasten to add, that while we are both members of the university Conservative Association, we are writing to you in a purely private capacity.

Winston S. Churchill to James Maxton[1]
(Churchill papers, 2/7)[2]

22 May 1946

My dear James,

I have been thinking a lot about you lately, & today David Kirkwood[3] told me you had sent me a charming message saying we were both good House of Commons men. But I always say of you 'The greatest gentleman in the House of Commons'. I hope you are regaining yr strength, because we all miss you vy much down here, and no one more than yr sincere friend.

Winston S. Churchill to B. R. Ambedkar
(Churchill papers, 2/42)

22 May 1946
Priority

You may be sure that the Conservative party will do its utmost to protect the future of the sixty million untouchables whose melancholy depression by their co-religionists constitutes one of the gravest features in the problem of the Indian sub continent. We shall take our stand on the broad principle set forth in the American Declaration of Independence that all men are born free and equal and entitled to life liberty and the pursuit of happiness.

---

[1] James Maxton, 1885–1946. Organiser in Scotland for Glasgow Federation of Independent Labour Party, 1919–22. MP (Lab.) for Bridgeton Div. of Glasgow from 1922 until his death. Chairman, Independent Labour Party, 1926–31, 1934–9. Biographer of Lenin.

[2] This letter was handwritten.

[3] David Kirkwood, 1872–1955. Trained as an engineer on the Clyde, Scotland. Active in Clydeside trade union movement. Deported from the Clyde, 1916, for organizing a protest against an increase in house rents. Member of Glasgow Town Council, 1918–22. MP (Lab.) for Clydebank Dumbarton Burghs, 1922–50; for Dumbartonshire, 1950–1. PC, 1948. Baron, 1951. Wrote *My Life of Revolt* (1935, with a foreword by Churchill).

May 1946

Winston S. Churchill: speech
(*'The Sinews of Peace'*, pages 139–50)

24 May 1946   House of Commons

EGYPT
(Treaty Negotiations)

Motion on the Civil Estimates

    Although we have not yet had the privilege of hearing his voice, I am sure I express the general sense of the House when I say that we are very glad to see the Foreign Secretary (Mr Ernest Bevin) back in his place. I earnestly hope that his health has not been affected by the very hard work he has had to do and the amount of worry inseparable from the discharge of all his functions. I quite sympathise with his preoccupation. He was at Paris, and I regret very much that he was not able to give his full mind to the subject we are discussing today. He was announced as the head of the delegation, but it was understood that he could not go himself, and Lord Stansgate[1] went. We have to be very careful not in any way to trespass on the conventions of the Chamber that nothing must be said dis-respectful to a Member of the other House, but I think I may go as far as to say that the substitution of Lord Stansgate for the Foreign Secretary involves the employment of an altogether lighter weight.

    I come to the timetable of the recent Egyptian story. We must get the timetable right. Chronology is the secret of the matter. In 1936 a Treaty was made by which the British were to withdraw from Cairo and Alexandria to the Canal. The Egyptian Government were to build the barracks and installations in the Canal zone, and when they were built the British were to leave Cairo and Alexandria and repair to them. We should certainly have carried out that undertaking as and when it fell due, but later, long before the barracks were built or our time for removal to the Canal zone arrived, war burst on the world, and Egypt was soon threatened by an Italian invasion for which an army of nearly a quarter of a million troops had been moved steadily forward on the North African coast towards the Egyptian frontier. As we now know, it was to be included in Mussolini's African Empire. Naturally, it was not possible for the Egyptian Government to build the barracks and installations during the war, nor could anybody expect that the British troops would voluntarily withdraw to the Canal zone in the years of war. If they had done

---

[1] William Wedgwood Benn, 1877–1960. MP (Lib.) for Tower Hamlets St George, 1906–18; for Leith, 1918–27; (Lab.) for Aberdeen North, 1928–31; for Manchester Gorton, 1937–42. Junior Lord of the Treasury, 1910–15. On active service during WWI with RFC, 1915–19 (despatches twice). Secretary of State for India, 1929–31. Viscount Stansgate, 1941. Secretary of State for Air, 1945–6. The eldest of his three sons was killed on air operations in 1944. His second son, Anthony Wedgwood Benn (Tony Benn) later renounced the peerage, having instigated the Act passed in 1963 that made disclaimer possible.

so, Cairo would have been sacked by the Germans and the Italians, and the Delta would have been subjugated.

No one can suggest for a moment that we have not kept our word. No one can reproach the Egyptian Government with not having built the barracks. There is no ground whatever for what the Prime Minister the other night, I am sorry to say, called 'suspicion' on the part of the Egyptians. The only sentiment that the Egyptians should permit themselves upon this war interlude is not suspicion but gratitude. However, the war has ended. Nearly all the Italians and Germans who ventured into Africa were destroyed or captured at a medium stage in the struggle. Egypt remained intact, enriched, securely defended. None of her troops were involved except in keeping internal order and for anti-aircraft defence. She was saved by the Armies of the British Empire from all the horrors which have racked the whole of Europe and large parts of Asia. And at the end we are assured that a large money debt is due from this country to Egypt for the supplies we purchased locally to feed the armies which were successfully defending the soil of the Delta. No, I repeat, gratitude, not suspicion, is the only sentiment becoming to the Government of Egypt.

There is however one practical step which should have been taken by us. It was mentioned today by my right hon. Friend the Member for Warwick and Leamington (Mr Eden). The withdrawal of the troops from Cairo and Alexandria ought to have been completed many months ago. It would have been a wise act of policy, and of efficient administration. It would have been entirely in the spirit, and going far beyond the letter, of the Treaty of 1936, to withdraw the British troops and to withdraw the enormous swollen staff from Cairo and from Alexandria even though the barracks in the Canal zone had not been erected by the Egyptian Government. Camps could have been put up, new telegraph communications could have been arranged, or rearranged, and the necessary forces could have been moved as a gesture of good will away from the Egyptian capital. That this was not done, is the responsibility of His Majesty's Government. I have no doubt that there were many difficulties, but that it was not done is their responsibility. The fault certainly does not lie on the 1936 Treaty, or anything in connection with the carrying out of that Treaty. The fault lies on the Treasury Bench. It may not be a very grievous fault; it may be one for which there are many explanations, but when we are told that the Egyptians have suspicions of our attitude at a time when an altogether different sentiment would be natural, then I think I am bound to point out that one way in which confidence in our desire not to interfere with their independence or sovereignty could have been sustained or stimulated would have been by a very considerable exodus – I think that is a very good local word – from Cairo and Alexandria of the enormous masses of staff officers and motor cars and so forth, which have been a prevailing feature of the streets of these cities during these years of war.

I would first examine the military aspect on which many speakers have delivered themselves. His Majesty's Government have made it clear after considering any military advice they have received, that they regard it as vitally important that the Suez Canal should be defended. When we talk about defending the Suez Canal, I presume the Government mean that it should be kept open. What reason could there be for a naval Power like Britain to fear it being kept open? If the warships or transports of another nation with a weaker navy obtained passage through the Suez Canal in time of war we should encounter them in the Indian Ocean basing ourselves either on Aden or the East African harbours. We do not suffer if the Canal is kept open. We can only suffer if it is closed. I assert that it is impossible to keep it open, unless British personnel are permanently stationed in the Canal zone. There may be doubts about our ability to keep it open in the air age, even if we have garrisons and fighter aircraft in that zone. But at any rate without that personnel there is no chance of keeping it open whatever. I do not believe that any military advice by the responsible Chiefs of Staff would challenge this assertion. If I am to be told that the Chiefs of Staff say that the canal can be kept open without any permanent garrison and air forces in the Canal zone, I treat their opinions with the utmost respect, but put on record that I am utterly unconvinced. But we do not know what questions were put to the Chiefs of Staff or on what political data they were called upon to report.

In the case of the Irish ports, in the Spring of 1938, absolutely wrong political data in my opinion, were put before the Chiefs of Staff – another set of Chiefs of Staff – and they gave advice which nearly brought us to our ruin. (*Laughter*) I have heard all this mocking laughter before in the time of a former Government. I remember being once alone in the House, protesting against the cession of the Southern Irish ports. I remember the looks of incredulity, the mockery, derision and laughter I had to encounter on every side, when I said that Mr de Valera[1] might declare Ireland neutral. We are seeing exactly the same sort of thing happening today, although I am not so much alone as I used to be. I would hardly have believed it possible that such things could happen twice in a lifetime.

Let me make it perfectly clear that our position is that His Majesty's Government have no right to claim the approval of the Chiefs of the Staff for any policy without informing the House of the precise questions upon which their advice was obtained. I am astonished that people should talk continuously

---

[1] Eamon de Valera, 1882–1975. Born in New York. A leading figure in the Irish Easter Rising, 1916. Sentenced to death; sentence commuted to life penal servitude on account of his American birth. Released under general amnesty, June 1917. President of Sinn Féin, 1917–26. Elected to Parliament as a Sinn Féin MP, 1918. Imprisoned with other Sinn Féin leaders, 1918; escaped from Lincoln gaol, Feb. 1919. President of the Irish Republic, 1919–22. Rejected the Irish Treaty and fought with the Irregulars against the Free State Army, 1922–3. President of Fianna Fáil, 1926–59. Leader of the Opposition in the Free State Parliament, 1927–32. PM and Minister for External Affairs, 1932–48. PM again, 1951–4, 1957–9. President of the Republic of Ireland, 1959–73.

about the Suez Canal and say nothing about the Isthmus of Suez. Until my right hon. Friend (Mr Eden) mentioned the matter this morning, and reminded us that this extraordinary region is the junction between three Continents, I have not heard the Isthmus mentioned, or read of it in any of the newspapers. Even if the Canal were blocked by aerial bombardment, as it might be if our fighter air force were overcome, or if a lucky shot or several lucky shots fell home, there is always the means of transhipment across the Isthmus of Suez. With our fleet and air power properly disposed, this can be assured. Under proper air protection in the Suez Canal zone, and with naval command of the Eastern Mediterranean, our troops could be disembarked at Suez and could re-embark at Red Sea ports. But if the overland route across the Isthmus is to be available, with the necessary installations and air bases, it is necessary to have British, and we hope, of course, Egyptian air and ground forces in effective control of the Canal zone. Without that failure is inevitable.

Let me now examine the other alternatives which are suggested. I have, of course, no official information on these matters. I rely upon the public organs and the general discussion that goes on in this country, and upon my own knowledge which I have acquired of these subjects in the not too distant past. It is widely said that we should establish ourselves in Palestine. The British troops who will in time of war defend the Canal, and the Isthmus of Suez, will be maintained, on this hypothesis, in camps or barracks in Southern Palestine. From there they will be able to fly in or will move in by motorised transport as soon as a state of emergency is reached. Here I have to speak of Palestine as a place of arms outside Egyptian territory, for British Forces which have to re-enter Egypt, at or before the moment of crisis. It is even said that our troops are already moving off in this direction, or that plans have been made to move them as fast as possible.

The consequence on the Palestine position of such a decision must not be overlooked. I am in entire agreement with the policy of the Government in trying to enlist American aid and co-operation in solving, or at any rate in dealing with the Jewish–Arab quarrel in Palestine. My views on this question are well known. I am for a Jewish national home in Palestine, with immigration up to the full absorptive capacity. I am also convinced that we cannot carry this out unless we have the help and active collaboration of the United States. Only by the action of our two Powers together can the objects to which we are pledged, and which the President of the United States evidently desires, be attained. I admire the Report of the Anglo-American Commission; but I think it is too much to put on Britain alone, single-handed, weakened as she is by her efforts in the war. It is too much for her alone to have to carry out this policy to which we are pledged and which the United States desire. I was most hopeful that the report of the Anglo-American Commission, and the manifest interest of the United States and the declaration of President Truman about the acceptance of 100,000 Jews immediately in Palestine, would lead to co-operation between the two countries.

I have no difference with His Majesty's Government on that. I agree with them entirely. But from the moment when Britain is going to use Palestine as a jumping-off ground to re-enter Egypt, and defend the Canal and the Isthmus, it seems to me that quite a different question is raised, and I fear that the hope of gaining the aid of the United States on the Palestine question, the Arab–Jew question in Palestine, will be seriously prejudiced. If they refuse, far and away the best hope of a solution being reached by the two great English-speaking Powers on the Palestine difficulty – in a manner which would be respected both by Jews and Arabs – all that vanishes and we shall find ourselves left alone in Palestine, from which we derive no advantage of any kind other than that of keeping our pledged word, and we shall have to carry on alone a wearing dispute either with the Jews or with the Arabs, or possibly with both. In any case we shall incur the increasing hostility and criticism of both these powerful forces, and, of course, of all the sideline spectators in all the various countries. It seems that by using Palestine as a jumping-off ground for the re-occupation of the Canal zone in time of an emergency we will impair the prospects of American aid, and will leave ourselves with the most thankless, profitless, and unfortunate task that can be imagined. That is my first conclusion.

I turn Westward. It is also said, and here again I rely upon nothing but what I read in the different public prints, we may obtain the trusteeship of Cyrenaica, where powerful air bases can be established, so that another jumping-off ground may be established there. This also seems to me a dangerous and unwise alternative. First, we throw away our grand position of seeking nothing for ourselves except honour, nothing out of the late war, after all our prodigious exertions, except to see that our duty is done as best we can, and is thoroughly and consistently maintained. We become immediately an interested party, seeking new bases in lands which were not ours, and in which we had no treaty rights before the war began, and we shall be immediately represented – and I do not need to indicate some of the quarters from which we shall be immediately represented – as a greedy, grasping nation, playing at power politics and demanding territories formerly owned by others for the sake of our own designs upon Egypt. We may be quite sure that, if we seek to build a new strategic position in Cyrenaica, in relation to the Suez Canal and Isthmus, Russia will renew or reinforce her demand for bases in the Eastern Mediterranean. Upon this argument, we should enter under every disadvantage, and I do not believe that we should succeed in gaining our desires without paying an inordinate price. Therefore, I say that, both to the East and to the West of the Canal, these alternatives for jumping-off grounds would involve us in endless difficulty and vexation, that we shall come down from our high position as a Power not seeking any advantage from the war, that we shall encourage or condone all the appetites of other countries, and pay very dearly for any accommodation that we might obtain.

I go further and submit to the Committee, in extension of this argument, that, whether we establish our jumping-off grounds in Palestine or Cyrenaica, or both, and whatever price we pay for them, they will not be of any effective use in time of emergency for the purpose of defending the Canal or the Isthmus of Suez and keeping them open. Let us try to foresee what will happen if tension grows at any time in the future and an emergency arises. My right hon. Friend (Mr A. Eden) very fittingly referred to this matter this morning. We shall then be in dispute with some other Great Power. That makes the emergency, and the moment will come when the military advisers will say, 'We ought to re-occupy the military installations, camps and airfields in the Canal zone. We ought immediately to move in from our bases to the East or to the West of Egypt.' What might be the behaviour of the Egyptian Government at such a juncture? We all know of the great sympathy there is when a small country is in so terrible a situation as that. No doubt we shall be told that there would be a treaty of alliance, but I cannot feel that, under such dire pressures, it would be of any avail. The great Power with whom we shall be in dispute would, of course, say to the Egyptian Government: 'We should regard any movement into the Canal zone of British Forces as an unfriendly act.' Can anyone suppose that the Egyptian Government, confronted with this situation and not desiring anyhow to have British troops or Air Forces in the Canal zone, will not refuse permission for us to re-enter. And what then? They will say, 'We do not agree that a state of international emergency has arisen, and we deny your right to decide upon the fact contrary to us.'

Meanwhile, the days will be slipping very quickly by. If such an attitude were adopted and there were no British personnel in the Canal zone, the Egyptians, or any ill-disposed persons, would be able to put out of action all the installations, radar equipment, airfields and so on, long before we could get there and the mere threat that they would do so, and had perhaps prepared the necessary measures to do so, would render our attempt to enter futile even before it was made. Can one imagine the British Government in such a situation, when the dread issue of peace or war in a renewed world struggle may be hanging in the balance, forcing the issue, whether Egypt agreed or not? My right hon. Friend the Member for Warwick and Leamington reminded us of the difficulties of staff conversation. I have seen two great wars break out, and I know what a difficulty it was in the first, even to obtain the mobilisation of the British Fleet, which, in fact, I had to order in 1914 without the consent of the Cabinet, and only upon the personal assent of the Prime Minister (Mr Asquith) and the Foreign Secretary (Sir Edward Grey).[1] This is not a question

---

[1] Edward Grey, 1862–1933. 3rd Bt, 1882. Educated at Winchester and Balliol College, Oxford. MP (Lib.) for Berwick-on-Tweed, 1885–1916. Foreign Secretary, 1905–16. Viscount, 1916. Ambassador on special mission to the US, 1919.

of the mobilisation of our own forces; it is a positive act, an act which will be widely regarded and denounced as an act of aggression, as an act destroying the last hopes of peace. There are always hopes of peace which it is a terrible thing to trample on and extinguish. Therefore, I say, we shall purchase our jumping-off grounds, either in Palestine or Cyrenaica, or both, only at the greatest detriment to our political position and policy among the nations. And when we have lavished our money upon them, they will prove useless in the hour of need.

The United Nations Organisation might well be called upon to prohibit the incursion of the British into Egypt. This would certainly be the case if the Egyptian Government stated that, in their view, the emergency did not warrant the action. Therefore, both alternatives, costly as they will be, will be utterly futile. Now it appears that the Egyptian Government already say: 'There must be no return until Egypt declares war.'

That is what I read only yesterday in the newspapers from Cairo. We have yet to learn what answer His Majesty's Government will make to this. The other night the Prime Minister said:

'We can only carry out our obligations if we have been put in a position by the Egyptian Government to bring our Forces into action in the area without loss of time in an emergency – '

I intervened to say: 'Before fighting begins.'

The Prime Minister answered: 'Yes, certainly'. That is a very solid, serious, resolute statement and the Prime Minister further said:

'If the whole matter breaks down, there is still, of course, the 1936 Treaty.'

The more I think of these alternative devices, the more I feel that the surest resting place at this time would be the 1936 Treaty and that we should rest there for the next five or six years in the hope that UNO, meanwhile, will grow up, and gather a great world army which will put so many of these strategic dangers, nightmares and calculations back into the limbo of the vanished past. So much for the military aspect; I hope it may be carefully considered by the House.

I now come to the diplomatic procedure. The right hon. Gentleman the Foreign Secretary has been working night and day in Paris. The position which has been adopted by the Government is that, first, they will evacuate Egypt, and, secondly, they will defend the Canal. This is a complete and total contradiction in terms. Then we are told that, in order to start on the negotiations in goodwill, we had, 'reluctantly', to say – that was the Lord President's (Mr Herbert Morrison's) remark – we will evacuate Egypt and that the second stage will be to examine how the Canal and Isthmus can be defended without British troops, and if it is clearly proved that anyone can see that anything of this kind is possible, the negotiations will break down and we shall revert to the Treaty of 1936.

I cannot imagine a more lamentable and, indeed, disingenuous procedure.

We promise something as a prelude to the negotiations in order to give them a good start, but, in fact, we concede the whole point at issue, subject to conditions which cannot be obtained and, then, a little later on as the discussions proceed, we shall either have to accept some pure sham, or the negotiations will break down. Then, indeed, we shall be reproached with having excited hopes which could never be realised and with having endeavoured to procure Egypt's goodwill at the outset, when all along we knew we could not possibly give them what we had promised. That is not the way to deal with any people, least of all is it the way to deal with an Oriental people. I do not believe in tantalising diplomacy, holding out hopes which fail because of the inherent difficulties in the path of the negotiators.

The course which the Government have been pursuing seems to me to be marked with the utmost unwisdom. A perfectly sensible and straightforward course was open. The Government of Egypt had the right to raise the question of revision of the Treaty at the tenth year. They have done so. His Majesty's Government could then have replied, 'We will certainly discuss the matter with you, but you should first of all tell us exactly what it is that you propose and how the essential matters of the defence of the Canal and Isthmus of Suez are to be provided for.' The Egyptian Government would next, in due course, have put forward their plan. We could then have said, 'We will discuss this plan with the Dominions, and especially with those Dominions who have in two wars exerted themselves in your defence, and the graves of whose soldiers in scores of thousands lie in the desert.' We ought to have approached this grave issue as a united Commonwealth and Empire.

There is another important point which the late Foreign Secretary has mentioned. We ought to have made sure that the Egyptian Government speak for the other great parties in Egypt besides the Court party which is now in power. There are the Wafd who lately had a considerable majority. What has happened now? The Egyptian Government make their proposals, and if they were all accepted that would not settle our relations with Egypt. The Wafd opposition would simply go on better. As it is, they are already denouncing this offer of the evacuation of Egypt as wholly insufficient because the question of the Sudan has not been settled in a similar manner. We ought to have approached this matter with much fuller knowledge of what the Egyptians of the leading parties would agree as a settlement, and we ought to have met in council beforehand with our Dominions and presented a united delegation to take part in the discussion. That would have been a reasonable and sensible procedure.

Let me, however, say this. Great departures of this character ought not to be influenced by threats of mob violence and by threats of attacks on British troops and installations. There have always been such threats. It is the responsibility of the Egyptian Government to keep the Treaty which we have signed with them, until another one is signed, and meanwhile to maintain order in their country. I have not the slightest doubt that they have full capacity to do so. The Government have taken an entirely wrong course while there was a perfectly right and proper course open to them, and further, if this wrong course is persisted in it will ruin our interests in the Middle East, destroy our communications with our possessions and fellow Dominions in the Indian and Pacific Oceans, and will in the Foreign Secretary's own expressive phrase, 'Sever the lifeline of the British Empire'.

In our brief Debate on the Adjournment Motion a fortnight ago, I said that the Dominions had not been consulted. I said they had been told. I asked the Prime Minister this question pointedly, and when I shook my head at his reply, he rejoined amid a roar of cheers that I was not there. It appears, however, that I was right. The Prime Minister has withdrawn from the position which he took up. He has not only withdrawn but he has apologised – a manly and, I may also add, the only thing to do. We now know that instead of an agreement with the Dominions upon this policy of Egypt, and abandoning the defence of the Suez canal, as I have declared, all that the Governments of the Dominions have agreed, is that we should shoulder the responsibility alone. Is it our responsibility alone? Have we any moral right to assume the entire burden of dealing with the fate of our communications through the Mediterranean, and of the defence of the Canal and the Isthmus of Suez? It seems to me that this is a very dangerous right for us to claim, and a very onerous responsibility to assume. After all, in the 1914–1918 war and in this last war – the defence of these large interests has been very largely entrusted to the Australians, New Zealanders and South Africans. Without their aid we would not have succeeded in protecting Egypt. It is a strange thing to call upon brave soldiers to travel thousands of miles across the ocean to fight for great strategic objectives, all well-defined and fully declared, and then to turn around immediately afterwards, and discredit altogether those strategic objectives – or apparently do so – for which so many men, at our request and under our leadership, have come so far to give their lives. Apart from the interests of Britain, apart from the danger to Imperial communications in the Eastern Mediterranean, I say a shock has been given to the British self-governing Commonwealth, and their confidence in the guidance and leadership of the mother country has been painfully and injuriously affected by the apparent casting away of those interests which we have hitherto declared to them were vital.

It always looks so easy to solve problems by taking the line of least resistance. Again and again in my life I have seen this course lead to the most unexpected result, and what looks like being the easy road turns out to be the hardest and most cruel. No nation is so remarkable as ours for the different moods through which it passes, moments of great dejection, moments of sublime triumph, heroism, fortitude and then exhaustion. What has been gained with enormous effort and sacrifice, prodigious and superb acts of valour, slips away almost unnoticed when the struggle is over. I earnestly hope that the Government

– with whom I do not attempt to pick a quarrel, but to whom I am giving a serious warning on this matter at this moment – will realise that there is only one safe resting place for this country, and that is the firm maintenance of the Treaty of 1936.

Winston S. Churchill to George Trevelyan
(Churchill papers, 2/157)

24 May 1946

My dear George Trevelyan,

Thank you so much for your letter[1] and for the quotation. My memory is tenacious and somewhere I have gathered the phrase which I am sure I did not imagine 'the exchange of a wealthier Amsterdam and the schools of a more learned Leyden'. This does not appear in your quotation. If this cannot be traced or does not exist in Macaulay's writings I have been guilty of a misquotation to the University of Leyden which I will confess by sending them the extract which you have been good enough to enclose. This will give them great pleasure, though I would rather have a quotation which contained the word 'Leyden'. I am sure I am right that the passage exists but please do not put yourself to any trouble about it. I will look further in my correspondence for the very nice letter you wrote me in the war. The parallel certainly came off in this respect. After two years of almost unbroken misfortune redeemed by survival we entered from Alamein onwards upon two and a half years of unbroken victory. Your letter came a few months before the turn of the tide.

All that you propose in your letter about the *Marlborough* Document is most agreeable to me, and I shall carefully preserve the words which you are good enough to write on the back of the frame which add so much value to your gift.

Winston S. Churchill to General Sir Hastings Ismay
(Cabinet papers, 127/50)

26 May 1946   Chartwell

My dear P,

Please look at the marked passage in the Hansard of the debate on May 7, 1940, which shows what Mr Chamberlain said about the devolving of increasing measures of control upon me during the month of April 1940. You will remember I became Chairman of the Service Ministers' Committee and

[1] Reproduced above (p. 340).

had the right to prepare directives for the Chiefs of Staff, and that you were appointed my representative on the Chiefs of Staff Committee.

I should be very much obliged if I could have the texts and the dates of these changes. I have forgotten all about them except, of course, that I succeeded Chatfield at this time in the co-ordinating work. However, I certainly bore an exceptional measure of responsibility for the brief and disastrous Norwegian Campaign – if campaign it can be called.

Winston S. Churchill to Lord Garnock
(Churchill papers, 2/6)

26 May 1946
Private and Confidential

Dear Lord Garnock,

I am much obliged to you for your letter of May 22.[1]

Of course all these matters are making their impression on the public mind and are constantly considered by the Conservative ~~Party~~ Leaders. We must expect several more years of Socialist rule, and no one can tell what the condition of the country or the Empire will be at the end of it. It would not be wise for us at this stage, so soon after a smashing defeat, to press forward trying to outbid our opponents, who will very soon land the country in a formidable financial disaster. Events shape our affairs far more than programmes; they are now shaping them in a grievous fashion.

The whole idea of co-partnership is agreeable provided it does not develop into syndicalism, but co-partnership alone would not be a commanding policy. An excellent letter was written by Lord Cranborne on this subject to *The Daily Telegraph* some months ago.

You may be sure I give my mind to all these matters. In the meanwhile, if you have any constructive ideas, pray write them to me. It is very easy to talk about having a great constructive campaign and a new policy, but not nearly so easy to put it down. There are always the Ten Commandments, the greatness of Britain and its Empire, freedom, decency, the well-being of the cottage home, and fair play in our own land and to all the world.

---

[1] Reproduced above (pp. 341–2).

May 1946

Lady Lloyd George[1] to Winston S. Churchill
(Churchill papers, 2/152)

28 May 1946

My dear Mr Churchill,

I am most sincerely grateful to you for your kindness in connection with my papers, and the position *vis-à-vis* the Cabinet Office.

I should certainly be willing to execute a Deed similar to the one you mention in order to safe-guard the papers. I have heard from Sir Edward Bridges, suggesting that I should see him and talk with him on the matter, and I am arranging to do so when I return to London from here after Whitsun. I very much hope that he will agree to this solution of the difficulty. I will let you know the result of the interview.

I cannot express fully to you how much I appreciate your help and advice, especially in view of the immense amount of work with which you still have to cope. I was so delighted to read of the wonderful ovations you received during your visit to Holland. It must have been very gratifying, and a real tonic.

Winston S. Churchill to Clement Attlee
(Churchill papers, 2/4)

29 May 1946

My dear Prime Minister,

Many thanks for your letter of May 27. I am in general agreement with CP(46)188 which you enclosed.

My father, Lord Randolph Churchill, had a clause in his will enjoining upon his literary executors that no document or State paper relating to the official work of the Offices he had held should be made public without the consent of the Departmental Minister concerned and of the Prime Minister of the day. I have myself incorporated this provision in my own Trust. However, permission ought not to be unreasonably withheld, especially as time goes on, and it seems to me that the principles set forth in paragraphs 7 and 8 of CP(46)188 form a good guide as to future practice.

It would seem to me that a Prime Minister, as responsible head of a British Government, should be free if he wishes to explain and defend his conduct of affairs, and that for this purpose he should be accorded exceptional consideration by the Government of the day. During my tenure Lord Baldwin[2] asked

---

[1] Frances Louise Stevenson, 1888–1972. Schoolteacher. Private Secretary to Lloyd George, 1913–43. Married Lloyd George, 1943. Countess Lloyd-George of Dwyfor, 1945. Published her memoirs, *The Years That Are Past*, in 1967.

[2] Stanley Baldwin, 1867–1947. Educated at Harrow and Trinity College, Cambridge. MP (Cons.) for Bewdley, 1908–37. Financial Secretary, Treasury, 1917–21. President of the Board of Trade, 1921–2. Chancellor of the Exchequer, 1922–3. PM, 1923–4, 1924–9, 1935–7. Lord President of the Council, 1931–5. Earl, and KG, 1937.

for such facilities, and I thought it no more than common justice to have them given to him.

In my own case an unusually large proportion of my work was done in writing, i.e. by shorthand dictation, and there is therefore in existence an unbroken series of minutes, memoranda, telegrams, etc., covering the whole period of my Administration, all of which were my own personal composition, subject to Staff or Departmental checking. I certainly hope that in accordance with the principles laid down these, or many of them, may some time see the light of day in their textual form. These pieces, written at the moment and under the impact of events, with all their imperfections and fallacies of judgment, show far better than anything composed in subsequent years could do the hopes and fears and difficulties through which we made our way. I am by no means certain that I should wish to publish these documents in my life time, but I think they would certainly win sympathy for our country, particularly in the United States, and make them understand the awful character of the trials through which we passed especially when we were fighting alone, and the moral debt owed to us by other countries.

I am impressed by the references in paragraph 6 of CP(46)188 to the position in the United States, where there is no Official Secrets Act and where at any time partial and misleading disclosures or versions of what took place may be made public. Two recent books by Captain Butcher, USN, and Mr Ingersoll[1] are very offensive and disparaging to this country and to my own personal conduct of the war, and many statements are made which are quite untrue and in some cases malicious. I must of course consider my position from time to time in relation to American revelations, but I will naturally consult His Majesty's Government as proposed.

Winston S. Churchill: speech
('Winston S. Churchill, His Complete Speeches', volume 7, pages 7334–41)

31 May 1946 House of Commons

WORLD FOOD SITUATION

Let me begin by relieving any anxiety in the mind of the Lord President of the Council (Mr Herbert Morrison) that I am going to berate him about the slip that occurred in the announcement of the results of his mission. I think myself he was somewhat ill used by the statements of the public relations officer in the United States. I am very glad that that matter has been agreeably cleared up by Mr Clayton's expression of regret. There is, I am sure, irony of fate in the right hon. Gentleman being ill used by a public relations

[1] Ralph Ingersoll, 1900–85. Educated at Yale University's Sheffield Scientific School. Reporter, *New York American*, 1923–5. Managing editor, *New Yorker*, 1925–30; *Life–Time*, 1930. Wrote *Top Secret* (1946). Founded Ingersoll Publications, 1957.

officer. It is rather the case of the engineer being hoisted with his own petard. The only criticism that I would pass upon this episode is that it is very easy to clear these matters of announcements between the two sides of the Atlantic Ocean. We had scores of them in the war and I do not remember any case – there may have been some – where there was any dispute or complaint. I hope that course of carefully checking up agreed statements will be followed in the future.

There is one other observation which I will address to the right hon. Gentleman, and thereafter I will leave him entirely to gather his forces for any statement he wishes to make to us. I hope he is not going to lecture us today on bringing party matters and party feeling into discussions of large public issues. There is no man I can think of from whom such rebukes and admonitions come less well. I would not go so far as to describe him in the words used by the Minister of Health (Mr Bevan) a year ago when he was in an independent position, as a third-class Tammany boss. I believe that was the expression his colleague used about him, which I resented very much at the time. I thought it was very much to be deprecated using disparaging expressions about important institutions of friendly countries. Also we must, after all, admit that third class is perhaps too low a valuation to put upon the right hon. Gentleman's qualities as a party man and a party manager. I hope that he will not, therefore, attempt to asperse our character and motives in bringing these matters before Parliament and bringing party politics into discussions of world issues. I am bound to say I do not see why world issues discredit upon the Administration of the day. The duty of the Opposition is to probe and analyse these situations. It is the duty of the Opposition to expose Ministerial failures and incompetence, and if, as a result of this necessary process of the discharge of public obligations, a number of people in the country take a less favourable view of Ministers than they had hitherto done, that is certainly no reason for any reproach being levelled at the Opposition.

I come to what is one of the really important points before us today – what we have to get for the 200,000 tons of wheat. I listened to the original statement of the Lord President of the Council and I have taken the trouble to read it again. (An Hon. Member: 'Rigmarole'.) I did not apply rigmarole to the statement but to the subsequent one which he made, which should be studied; it will be found to correspond exactly with that description. The right hon. Gentleman certainly gave the impression to the House that in consideration – and I put it to all those who heard it – of our making this sacrifice of 200,000 additional tons of wheat we were going to receive very remarkable and special measures of help, as would first appear, from the United States in respect to India and in respect of the British zone in Germany. Certainly, I derived that impression, and I, therefore, asked for the exact dimensions of that help. Perhaps the right hon. Gentleman will be so good as to give it now. He has this opportunity, and I really think he should clear it up, because the matter is one of the very first magnitude. The Prime Minister, on 4th April, said in the Debate on food:

> We have, as I believe the people of this country would have wished us to do, reduced our margin of safety to the very limit to help others, but further we cannot go. – (Official Report, 4th April, 1946; Vol. 421; c. 1413.)

That was only on 4th April and now before the end of May 200,000 tons are given.

Everyone knows that the consequences of giving those 200,000 tons are likely to be very serious. I will not enter upon the reactions, for they will be thoroughly dealt with later on, because my right hon. Friend the Member for Southport (Mr R. S. Hudson)[1] *(Interruption)* – I always like to check up on these points – who has always been associated in my mind with a highly successful record as Minister of Agriculture, will be speaking later in the Debate. I am assured that very grave consequences will follow from this new departure from the Prime Minister's statement of 4th April in going beyond the limitations which he then thought were the utmost that could be imposed on the people of this country. I say I hope that the right hon. Gentleman will tell us what exactly has been gained. It ought to be given to us today. There is no military secret involved and no diplomatic offence can be given. Why cannot he tell us? Why not emulate the very wise declaration of the new Minister of Food[2] that frankness would be the leading element in his policy? I ask pointedly and explicitly for an explanation of what advantages we have got from this very heavy sacrifice, with the injurious consequences which it entails, and which the right hon. Gentleman – I do not say wrongly; I do not prejudge the general issue – has found it necessary to impose upon us, and of which he has convinced his colleagues. That is the crux of the matter which we want to have established today.

But there is also another important issue, namely, the resignation of the Minister of Food, of which we have had no explanation of any kind whatever. This affects the status of Ministers as a whole. We are told that we ought to trust them and respect them; the country is adjured to give them its confidence and put its trust in their knowledge and comprehension of the affairs of the Departments. A Minister holds a position in the public eye for nearly a year,

---

[1] Robert Spear Hudson, 1886–1957. Educated at Eton and Magdalen College, Oxford. Attaché, Diplomatic Service, 1911; First Secretary, 1920–3. MP (Cons.) for Whitehaven, 1924–9; for Southport, 1931–52. Parliamentary Secretary, Ministry of Labour, 1931–5. Minister of Pensions, 1935–6. Secretary, Dept of Overseas Trade, 1937–40. PC, 1938. Minister of Shipping, Apr.–May 1940. Minister of Agriculture and Fisheries, 1940–5. Viscount, 1952.

[2] John Strachey, 1901–63. Educated at Eton and Magdalen College, Oxford. Married, 1928, Esther Murphy (div. 1933); 1933, Celia Simpson. Wg Cdr, RAFVR. MP (Lab.) for West Dundee, 1945–50. Parliamentary Under-Secretary of State, Air Ministry, 1945–6. PC, 1946. Minister of Food, 1946–50. Secretary of State for War, 1950–1. Wrote *The Coming Struggle for Power* (1932), *The Menace of Fascism* (1933), *The Nature of Capitalist Crisis* (1935), *The Theory and Practice of Socialism* (1936), *Arise to Conquer* (1944), *The End of the Empire* (1959).

he is criticised and complained of by some and ardently defended by others. Suddenly, he vanishes, not a trace remains, not a bubble is noticeable upon the surface of the waters. That is an extraordinary way to manage affairs. The precedent regarding the resignation of Ministers must be taken upon a peacetime basis. Very often, in wartime, when considerable reconstruction of the Administration has taken place Ministers have not found it necessary to come forward and make individual statements.

Mr Sydney Silverman (Nelson and Colne):[1] They did not in the right hon. Gentleman's time.

Mr Churchill: I said that in wartime, when there was a general or partial reconstruction, it was not thought necessary for Ministers to make statements. But this is surely a matter to cheer the hon. Member whose pacifist tendencies are so well known. We are now at peace, and we are about to celebrate its joys –

Mr Silverman: I do not know what the right hon. Gentleman intended to convey by his remark about my pacifist tendencies being well known. If he intended to mean by that that I was known to prefer peace to war I hope we all do, but if he intended in any way to mean that I was opposed to the active prosecution of the war he knows that he is mistaken, and I hope he will withdraw it.

Mr Churchill: I accept with pleasure the hon. Gentleman's statement that he prefers peace to war, and that his preference is remarkably pronounced and manifested on a great many occasions. But peacetime is what we are supposed to be dwelling in now, and I submit that all the precedents of peacetime oblige a Minister to make a statement when he retires from office. I cannot, in my long experience, remember many cases to the contrary. If we look back before the war there were three most recent cases. There was the resignation of my right hon. Friend the Member of Warwick and Leamington (Mr Eden) – that will cheer up Members opposite; they clutch at straws – in 1937, accompanied by that of Lord Cranborne, a member of the Government, both of whose explanations were received in a most grave and attentive spirit by the House. Then there was the resignation of Mr Duff Cooper, now Ambassador in Paris, after the Munich crisis. Again, a very full and moving explanation was given to the House. This is the first case, in peacetime, of the resignation of a Cabinet Minister, and I say that those are precedents which should be followed. Not only should they be followed on this occasion, but they should be followed in the future. I thought it my duty to give full notice to the ex-Minister of Food, and I wrote to him this letter two days ago:

---

[1] Samuel Sydney Silverman, 1895–1968. MP (Lab.) for Nelson and Colne from 1935 until his death. Member of Parliamentary delegation to Buchenwald Concentration Camp, 1945. Chairman of World Jewish Congress.

My Dear Ben Smith: I feel that I ought to let you know that we have decided to meet the general wish of the House by asking for a Debate on the Ministry of Food on Friday. Naturally, the House will expect a statement from you as to the reasons for your resignation, and if this is not forthcoming I shall be forced to comment unfavourably on the departure from the peacetime usage involved when a Minister who has held an important Ministry disappears without any explanation being offered to Parliament.

I have searched the benches opposite with my eyes, but I cannot see any sign of the burly and engaging form of the right hon. Gentleman. He has departed '*spurlos versengkt*', as the German expression says – sunk without leaving a trace behind. I must say that I am surprised that he does not wish to defend himself or his administration, which has been so much under fire. We are told, or it is rumoured, that he went on difference with his colleagues. Surely some explanation of those differences should be given. It is very unusual for Ministers to leave any Government on difference, and not offer any explanation. He may, of course, have been dismissed for incompetence, but even in that case one would imagine that he would wish to say some word in his own defence.

I have a regard for the right hon. Gentleman. He served in my administration and at Washington, and we gained golden reports on his work there. He was most popular, and had access to and influence in American circles. I am very much distressed that misfortune should have overtaken him, but I must say that his flight from the scene is ignominious and unbecoming, and not at all in accordance with what one would have expected from him. What is the strange power which strikes a resigning Minister down? Perhaps the Leader of the House can tell us a little about that. I ask him pointedly, did the Minister go on a difference of policy and, if so, what was that difference, or was he removed because he was not thought equal to this particular task? I am sure that we can have an answer to that. At any rate, I hope it will be pressed for persistently during this discussion.

Those are the two main points which have led me to bring this matter forward today. But no one can doubt that the postwar history of the Ministry of Food and the policy which the Government have pursued have been extremely disappointing. Warnings were given last autumn. We had, in December, a fatuous remark by the representative of the India Office. On 10 December, the Under-Secretary of State for India[1] said:

> The food situation in India will continue to require constant watching but

---

[1] Arthur Henderson, 1893–1968. Son of the Labour leader Arthur Henderson. On active service in WWI, 1914–18. MP (Lab.) for Cardiff South, 1923–4, 1929–31; for Kingswinford, 1935–50; for Rowley Regis and Tipton, 1950–66. QC, 1939. Joint Parliamentary Secretary of State for War, 1942–3. Financial Secretary, War Office, 1943–5. Parliamentary Under-Secretary of State, India Office and Burma Office, 1945–7. PC, 1947. Minister of State for Commonwealth Relations, 1947. Secretary of State for Air, 1947–51. Baron Rowley, 1966.

my noble Friend,[1] who is in continuous touch with the Government of India on this subject, sees no cause for apprehension of famine whether in Bengal or elsewhere in India. – (Official Report, 10th Dec., 1945; Vol. 417, c. 26.)

That was in December. In this House we had Debates in November, in February and in April which culminated with the Prime Minister's pledge. My right hon. Friend the Member for Warwick and Leamington and my right hon. Friend the Member for Southport were very prominent in those Debates. My right hon. Friend the Member for Southport drew attention to divergencies which he said existed between the statements made by the Food Ministry and the statements issued by the Prime Minister from No. 10, Downing Street. We should like to know what, in fact, was the truth of those differences which existed then. At any rate, the Indian quotation which I have read is sufficient to convict the administration of an extraordinary lack of foresight in the matter.

Mr Bowles (Nuneaton): Can one foresee a monsoon failing?

Mr Churchill: The failure of the wheat supply of the world is not due to a shortage in any one particular country. It is due to a shortage in particular countries, but it is not due to any general failure of the world crop. That is a very essential point. The conditions in the British zone in Germany should have been foreseen beforehand. The story is indeed a tragic one. At the end of the Potsdam Conference, the Russians and Poles were allowed to occupy up to the Western Neisse, and not the Eastern Neisse, and another great influx of hungry and homeless people, numbered by millions, was driven into the British zone. The British zone is the least favourably circumstanced from a food point of view. There is the least agriculture and the most manufacture. There you have the great population of the ruined Ruhr. We have a more difficult task in our zone even than the United States in theirs. The great feeding grounds which nourished Germany as a whole lie to the East of the iron curtain, and food supplies have not been sent from there to the population of Germany as a whole, to whom they belong, and which should have been reserved for their nourishment. On top of this has come this incursion of a very large additional number of hungry, suffering people. This had all been foreseen, because it arose out of decisions which were reached at Potsdam. I am not making this a matter of serious complaint; personally, I would not have agreed to it, although I might not have been able to prevent the establishment of the Western Neisse as the frontier between Poland and Germany.

[1] Frederick William Pethick-Lawrence, 1871–1961. Educated at Eton and Trinity College, Cambridge. Opposed South African War. Editor, *The Echo*, 1902–5; *Labour Record and Review*, 1906–7. Joint Editor, *Votes for Women*, 1907–14. Sentenced to nine months in prison for conspiracy in connection with a militant suffragette demonstration, 1912. Unsuccessful Peace Negotiation Parliamentary candidate for South Aberdeen, 1917. MP (Lab.) for West Leicester, 1923–31; for East Edinburgh, 1935–45. Financial Secretary, Treasury, 1929–31. Secretary of State for India and Burma, 1945–7. Baron, 1945. Member, Political Honours Scrutiny Committee, 1949–61.

Therefore, I say that the Government have been guilty throughout of a lack of foresight. Hard as it is to pierce the future, they have been singularly unsuccessful, and this casts its light upon the general question of planning, which is their great hope and in which they repose unbounded confidence. This food shortage, as far as wheat is concerned, is not the result of a failure of world harvests; it is failure of distribution. That is all it is. The fixing of price controls, though very beneficial and necessary in many ways, has restrictions which are unforeseeable. For instance, we are told that because the price of wheat was controlled below the normal level which would have been reached by free markets, great quantities in the United States have been fed to cattle, or used for purposes other than human consumption, and that that is the prime cause of the difficulty. It is very dangerous when planners get to work upon matters which are so intricate and vast that they must escape from designed control and can really only be harmoniously discharged by what is called the higgling of the market. I consider that greater liberty to private enterprise in these matters would have resulted in a more harmonious and normal supply. If that had been attended by undue rises of price, I personally would support, and have always supported in those cases, the Government of the country affected taking funds from the Exchequer to mitigate the increase of price to the people, which is what we are doing now.

The hard conditions of this country have continued for a very long time. More than any other country we have borne the brunt. When I was in Holland the other day, I felt myself in a community which had been gripped and compressed in the enemy's clutch. The grip is released, and once food has flowed in, the people spring forth, strengthened by the compression they have endured. We have been blood donors throughout the whole of the long six years of war. We have been tried to the last scrap of our strength. Nothing has been grudged, effort after effort has been made, not only physical but psychical, and it was natural in the moment of victory, when suddenly danger was removed, that there should be not expansion but collapse. That is a very fair, detached, broadminded explanation of the last General Election. I feel that that will excite controversy in no part of the Committee. We have had a very hard time, but owing to the great skill with which the wartime food administration was discharged, associated very much with the comprehending and sympathetic handling of this problem by Lord Woolton, it is true to say, as the new Minister of Food said, I think, that the actual health of the people has not been prejudicially affected. But the hard manual workers have been greatly weakened in their energy. It is impossible for hard manual work to be carried on with full efficiency upon these present scales of rationing. I have no doubt this is affecting the miners, the blast furnace men and all those whose work is of the heaviest physical character. Then there is this monotony of diet, which I am very glad to hear the new Minister intends to remedy and rectify.

It is on top of all this, however, that the 200,000 extra tons are to be diverted.

Our margins are woefully reduced. They have declined more than half – even, I think, to something like ⅓ of what was considered necessary. We are a unique community: 48,000,000 in an island that grows only half its food. I shudder to think our fortunes might perhaps be confided to some Food Board in which we should be only one in 20, and I trust that it will be borne in mind that there is no other country in a position even remotely approaching this vast energetic community in these islands perched up so precariously on the basis of foreign imports, foreign trade and foreign exchange.

I noticed in a Debate in another place that my noble Friend Lord Cherwell was sceptical about the figures which have been recently given, and to some extent he was not contradicted in this by the Leader of the Government in the House of Lords, Lord Addison. I must say I rather share the scepticism. The figure of 8.39 million tons was given as being needed in Europe in the next few months, and it is shown that that would suffice to give 136 million of people, which is the population concerned, a diet of 1,600 calories per day – not very great but sufficient to avert the worst grip of famine. This 8,390,000 tons makes it sufficient to give that diet to the whole of the population affected, but it does not start on the assumption – because we have not heard how these calculations have been made – that there is absolutely no food there at all. As a matter of fact, there is a great deal of food in every country. Does this American calculation proceed on the assumption that the country is no better off than the towns? If so, these are both most fallacious foundations.

Everybody knows that there is a great deal of food grown – agricultural produce – and food they have saved and perhaps concealed. A great deal of food exists, and to start on the basis of a tabular margin that there is nothing at all is a very foolish way to approach the problem – or, I will put it differently, it is not the wisest way to tackle a problem of this importance. Not to discriminate between town and country populations is a matter very likely to lead to altogether wrong calculations. I ask the right hon. Gentleman if he could perhaps tell us whether one is right in thinking that these figures, Mr Hoover's figures, are the ones we accepted, whether they are the operative figures on which all our present calculations are based, and whether, in fact, they are the figures on which we are asked to give up an additional 200,000 tons of wheat, with all the evil consequences which that entails.

I have now completed what I had to say but I will not sit down without wishing the new Food Minister all success in his most difficult task, which brings him to every fireside in the land and makes all the people follow his words and his actions with the very deepest anxiety and attention. I hope he may bring back to the Food Ministry some at least of the Woolton traditions where confidence was felt in the cottage homes in the Minister of State who regulated, often with severity, the daily fare which was at their disposal. I say that the hon. Gentleman brings to his part a brief but bright reputation in charge of difficult affairs and of presenting them to the House of Commons, and there will be no disposition to wish him other than good fortune in his work. But I say that the resignation of the late Food Minister registers beyond doubt or challenge a grave failure on the part of His Majesty's Government in a vital branch of policy. It cannot be denied that after all the criticisms, discussions, and arguments on this side and that, the Minister has gone and that that registers a breakdown and a failure in the great question of food, and that food now takes its place with housing as examples of the aggravation of the public privations which arise from Socialist incapacity.

The Lord President of the Council (Mr Herbert Morrison): The coming about of this Debate has, I must say, taken a varied and somewhat tortuous course. When I reported on my visit to Washington there were some rather strong interchanges between the right hon. Gentleman and myself, initiated in their strength by the right hon. Gentleman. His lead was followed by the newspapers which support him in the country and, generally speaking, there was a heavy barrage against me by the whole of the Conservative Press, both in lettering and in pictures. I make no complaint about that; I am used to it, and indeed I should be embarrassed if I had too much support from the Conservative newspapers, but the right hon. Gentleman promises to protect me against that menace.

Then there were the activities of the public relations officer of the State Department at Washington, and that set things going again. Here, indeed, was hope that the Lord President had been thrown over by the United States Government, and I admit that if that had been so I should have been in a position of some interest and would have had something to say about it. But here again the public relations officer was elevated in the Conservative Press and I was correspondingly 'pushed down the drain'. I am bound to say that I was interested to note that for once – as far as I know, for the first time – a public relations officer had commended himself to the Conservative Party and the Conservative Press.

Mr Churchill: The right hon. Gentleman should do me the justice of noting that I personally declared that he was ill-used in the matter.

Winston S. Churchill: speech
('*Winston S. Churchill, His Complete Speeches*', volume 7, pages 7341–2)

31 May 1946 House of Commons

RATIONING OF BREAD

I would like to congratulate the hon. Gentleman (Mr John Strachey, the new Minister of Food) upon the eloquence with which he moved us during the latter part of his speech, and although I think his views of the outlook were exaggerated, it is certainly better for a Minister to begin in a difficult office of this character in a spirit of facing, and even magnifying, difficulties, rather than in a lighthearted spirit, expressing hopes which may not afterwards be fulfilled. I always find, myself, that the British nation will never forgive optimism that is not borne out, but that if pessimism is not borne out one's previous inaccuracies are forgiven.

I had intended to move a reduction of £5 in the token Vote in order to show our disagreement with the policy which the Government have followed, and in order to mark our censure of their administration of food, which has culminated in the departure of a Minister who, until only the other day, we were told to admire, and in whom we were told to confide. I am not satisfied with the answers given by the Lord President. The information he gave us was very vague, and rather muddled. We still do not know if we start in the calculation of what is to be given to India, and to the British zone in Germany. It appears that the sacrifice of the 200,000 tons, which was represented as a great moral contribution to the solution of human difficulties, is also belittled by the right hon. Gentleman. So, both sides of the argument seem to have vanished. But in the last part of the Lord President's speech or, rather, in the ante-penultimate part, he made a declaration of immense and formidable importance with regard to the rationing of bread. I do not feel that it would be proper at all to give a vote this afternoon which might be taken as opposing that policy. If the Government feel compelled, at a later date, to introduce it I should like much more consideration of that matter.

There is, as I indicated, in the rationing of bread, one very great difficulty, namely, that it is consumed in immense quantities by the poorer people, and that the shortage of other foods or a rise in prices of other foods, increases the eating of bread. All this is elementary, of course, but it touches profound issues, and I, personally, would not be prepared to go into the Lobby to vote, dissatisfied as we are with the statements which have been made, when the vote would appear to mean that this grave issue had been, without due consideration, resisted by us. Therefore, I shall not move a reduction of the Vote.

June 1946

Winston S. Churchill: speech
('*Winston S. Churchill, His Complete Speeches*', volume 7, pages 7342–54)

5 June 1946   House of Commons

FOREIGN AFFAIRS

The year that has passed since the end of the German war has been darkened by a virtual breakdown or stalemate in the concert and collaboration of the three Great Powers, as well as by a painful decline in British influence and prestige. It would be wrong to cast the blame of these misfortunes upon the Foreign Secretary, to whose sombre patient speech we listened yesterday. We feel he has done his best to resist the sad and dangerous tendencies with which we are oppressed before the world, and he has stood forth as the representative of much that is wise and courageous in the British character. No criticism which I may make on particular aspects of his administration is intended to obscure the outstanding services which he has rendered in this period of disappointment and perplexity.

The problems of the aftermath, the moral and physical exhaustion of the victorious nations, the miserable fate of the conquered, the vast confusion of Europe and Asia, combine to make a sum total of difficulty, which, even if the Allies had preserved their wartime comradeship, would have taxed their resources to the full. Even if we in this island had remained united, as we were in the years of peril, we should have found much to baffle our judgment, and many tasks that were beyond our strength. I am an opponent of the Socialist Party but I readily admit that they have made an important contribution to the cause of world peace. They have made this contribution by their resolute denunciation of Communism and by their refusal to allow the Communist Party to enter and permeate their ranks. The Communist Party in this island is not at present a serious danger. Everyone remembers how they urged us into the late war and how, when we were already irrevocably committed, they immediately turned about, on orders from Moscow, and after some –

Mr Gallacher:[1] That is a lie.

Hon. Members: Withdraw.

Mr Churchill: I leave it to you, Mr Speaker, I really do not mind. I thought, as I remarked on a previous occasion, that the hon. Member was well broken to the House, and not likely to make this kind of observation.

Mr Gallacher: It is necessary occasionally.

Mr Churchill: I see, I do not think that I need trouble myself very much with the hon. Member's opinion, but I quite understand that he will not like what I am going to say. I certainly will not be deterred from saying it by the prospect of any further insults from him. Everyone remembers how they immediately turned about, on orders from Moscow, and after some abject and grovelling retractions on the part of their leaders, they denounced our life struggle as a capitalist, Imperialist war. We also remember how thereafter, they did their best, their utmost – which was very little – to hamper our national defence. Nor can we forget that, as far as they were concerned, we might have sunk in 1940 and 1941 beneath the ocean and been blotted out for ever, except as Hitler's serfs, from among the nations of mankind –

Mr Gallacher: That is not true. On a point of Order, Mr Speaker, I challenge the Leader of the Opposition that if he goes to the Home Office he will find that the first report made on the blitz and on the means that should be taken to care for the people, was written by the hon. Member for West Fife (Hon. Members: 'Speech') It is a fact.

Mr Speaker: That is not quite a point of Order.

Mr Gallacher: It is all wrong to say what the right hon. Gentleman has said.

Mr Churchill: We might have been blotted out for ever, as far as they were concerned, and I say it will take them many years to live that down in the British Isles. But it is not at home that the Communists are important. The significance of the action of the Labour Party lies in its effects abroad. There is no doubt that it has brought strength to Great Britain at a time when other causes were weakening us, and there is no doubt that it has produced beneficial consequences on both sides of the Atlantic Ocean. The Foreign Secretary has been a leader in all this and he deserves a full share of the credit.

I shall now permit myself to make a few comments upon various aspects of our affairs in this vast and gloomy field. I must make it clear at the outset that I have no official information. Since I laid down my office at the end of July last, I have not seen any of the Foreign Office telegrams. I form my opinion

---

[1] William Gallacher, 1881–1965. Chairman, Clyde Workers' Committee, 1914–18. Imprisoned four times for political activities, 1917, 1918, 1921 and 1925. Attended 2nd Congress of Communist International, Moscow, 1920 (where he met Lenin). Member, Executive Committee of Communist International, 1924, 1935. Stood as Parliamentary candidate, unsuccessfully, against Churchill in Dundee, 1922. MP (Communist) for West Fife, 1935–50 (the only Communist MP 1935–45, then one of two). President of the Communist Party of Great Britain, 1953–63.

from my knowledge of the past, from the newspapers, and from distinguished people from abroad who sometimes when they visit this country come to see me. His Majesty's Ministers have decided to deal with the Parliamentary Opposition on strict party lines. No doubt we have our own personal relationship arising out of the long comradeship of the war – there is always that background – but there is absolutely no official contract of any kind between the government and the Opposition in foreign affairs, except occasional acts of courtesy like handing me a copy of an announcement of great importance half an hour before it is read –

The Prime Minister (Mr Attlee): It is quite true that the actual text of that announcement was only handed over a short time before the meeting, but I must point out that I did bring to the notice of the right hon. Gentleman, and also of the right hon. Gentleman the Member for Warwick and Leamington (Mr Eden) and of the right hon. Gentleman and Member for West Bristol (Mr O. Stanley) our intentions with regard to Egypt in the week before.

Mr Churchill: I was only using this as an illustration. It is quite true, as the Prime Minister has said, that he asked me and my two colleagues to go to Downing Street about ten days before; but that was not on Egypt, that was on Palestine. He then told us of the White Paper, the report about Palestine. He was not even in a position to hand us a copy at that moment. Conversation ran on and Egypt was mentioned, it is perfectly true. It is also true, if we are to go into these matters, that a few days later I met the Prime Minister in the Lobby and we had a few words in private in my room in which he mentioned – if I may say so – the word 'evacuation', and I said straight away we could not agree to that. These were not matters of important consultation. We have not been consulted in any way. (An Hon. Member: 'Why object?') I am not objecting at all. The French have hitherto dealt, since the war, with their foreign affairs on a national basis. The United States of America, taught by Mr Wilson's disastrous mistake in 1919, are careful to include in their delegation leading representatives of the Republican Party; but his Majesty's Government have followed the Russian principle in foreign affairs of one-party Government. I am not complaining. I do not suggest that the practice should be altered at this late stage, when domestic divergencies grow wider and deeper month by month.

We do our utmost on this side of the House to support His Majesty's Government in the foreign sphere, and to impart as far as possible a national character to British foreign policy, but if I should be misinformed on any point in what I am going to say, and the Government have reasons for their action which they have not disclosed, the House, I hope, will make allowance for any error into which I, as a member of the general public, may fall.

Let me begin with Greece. It was not mentioned yesterday. In Greece the course of events has vindicated the policy of the National Coalition Government. This policy in the main has been followed by the present Government.

For all purposes of controversy, it rests upon two documents, either of which it is very hard to challenge. The first is the report of the trade union delegation which, under Sir Walter Citrine,[1] at my invitation visited Athens in January, 1945, and revealed the atrocities committed by the Communists in the city. The second is, of course, the report of the British, American and French Commission which supervised the elections in March, 1946. There is no doubt whatever that these elections were the fairest ever conducted in Greece, or in any Balkan State. They have proved conclusively that the Greek people did not wish to have dictatorial power in Greece seized by a Communist minority through a process of revolution, treachery, terrorism and murder, and that we were right to intervene by force of arms to prevent such a disaster.

We have never intended or desired to interfere in the affairs of Greece, except in so far as was necessary to enable the Greek people to decide freely the form and character of their own Government after the confusion of the war and of the German occupation. I thought, and I still think, that it would have been better to hold the plebiscite before the election and that is how it was originally planned. The Foreign Secretary told us some months ago that, while he was not opposed to monarchy in Greece if the Greek people desire it, he did not want a 'party Monarchy'. I am very much afraid that the reversal in procedure which he has adopted runs a risk of bringing about the very thing which he wishes to avoid. Nevertheless, I hope that, should the Greek people vote for a Monarchy, the King will have the wisdom and the virtue to make it clear that he is the servant of the State, on a level above all parties and equally accessible to all parties. I hope our troops in Greece will be able to come home as soon as the plebiscite has been taken. They deserve, and I believe they will receive, the heartfelt gratitude of the Greek people.

His Majesty's Government have shown, it seems to me, a wise restraint, or, at least, a marked lack of enthusiasm, in not interfering in the internal affairs of Spain. None of us likes the Franco régime, and, personally, I like it as little as I like the present British Administration, but, between not liking a Government and trying to stir up civil war in a country, there is a very wide interval. It is said that every nation gets the government that it deserves. Obviously, this does not apply in the case of Great Britain, but I have a sort of feeling that the Spanish people had better be left alone to work out their own salvation, just as we hope to be left alone by foreigners in order to work out ours. It seemed to me very unwise of the late French Government, under Communist impulsion, to take such an aggressive line against Spain. It is a very shocking thing for the Cabinet of any State to try to solve its own political problems by beating up

---

[1] Walter McLennan Citrine, 1887–1981. Secretary, Electrical Trades Union, 1914–20; Asst General Secretary, 1920–3. Asst Secretary, TUC, 1924–5; General Secretary, 1926–46. Director, *Daily Herald*, 1929–46. Knighted, 1935. Visited Russia, 1936, 1938. PC, 1940. Member of National Production Advisory Council, 1942–6, 1949–57. Baron, 1946. Member, National Coal Board, 1946–7. Chairman, Central Electricity Authority, 1947–57. CBE, 1958.

another country. In this case, French intervention has only had the result of giving Franco a new lease of life.

The Spaniards are a proud and morose people, and they have long memories. They have not forgotten Napoleon and the attempted French subjugation of Spain 130 years ago. Besides this, they have had a civil war which has cost them a million lives. Even the Communists in Spain will not thank foreign Governments for trying to start another civil war, and anything more silly than to tell the Spaniards that they ought to overthrow Franco, while, at the same time, assuring them that there will be no military intervention by the Allies, can hardly be imagined. Still more ill-placed is the Polish intervention before UNO. Everyone knows where their impulse comes from. Let us discard cant and humbug. I believe it is a fact, to put it mildly, that there is as much freedom in Spain under General Franco's reactionary régime – and actually a good deal more security and happiness for ordinary folk – than there is in Poland at the present time.

We are now confronted with a proposal that all the nations of UNO should break off relations with Spain. Before I examine that project in detail, there are some general propositions now in vogue which deserve scrutiny. Let me state them in terms of precision: 'All oppression from the Left is progress. All resistance from the Right is reactionary. All forward steps are good, and all backward steps are bad. When you are getting into a horrible quagmire, the only remedy is to plunge in deeper and deeper.' These rules, it seems to me, from time to time require review by the intelligentsia. They require review in the light of experience and of the circumstances we see around us. I was in favour of not admitting the present Spanish Government to UNO. It would have given general offence in the new Assembly, upon which so much depends. But this idea of all our countries withdrawing their ambassadors, will only have the effect of preventing us worrying and admonishing General Franco with diplomatic representations and gradually smoothing the way for better times in Spain. It will also affront Spanish national pride to such an extent that there will be a general rally of Spaniards to the Government of their country, and its sovereign independence.

What is to happen when the ambassadors have been withdrawn? Our trade with Spain is very valuable. We get all sorts of things from Spain, from iron ore to oranges. We shall have to go on trading with Spain. We have an important market there, and I suppose that when we have withdrawn our ambassadors, we shall require to have commercial counsellors, or some other arrangement, in order to remain in fruitful contact with one of the oldest and now least aggressive of the nations of Europe. I suppose there would be instituted a kind of diplomatic black market, with its agents going in through the back door, instead of through the front. We may be quite sure that 28 million people living on that great peninsula, would be in some contact with the outer world, even without the ambassadors now accredited to them. I should have thought that we had enough troubles on our hands without getting into such futile and fatuous entanglements, and I do not at all credit the Government with any such unwisdom.

We all hope that the conference of the Foreign Secretaries, this Big Four or Big Three – or Big Two-and-a-Half, as the anti-British American newspapers sometimes describe them – will soon make some progress in settling European affairs. (*Interruption.*) I think it applied to nations, not to individuals. I could not feel any satisfaction when I read in the newspapers that one of the first points upon which they had all been able to come to a unanimous decision in Paris was to confirm the assignment of the Austrian Tyrol to Italy. This was always held by liberal-minded folk in many lands to be one of the worst blots on the Treaty of Trianon which was not, in itself, a model in European annals. It is, of course, quite true – I do not wish to conceal anything – that Hitler and Mussolini, after the most careful consideration of the problem, agreed to confirm and enforce the decision. But, surely, those two miscreants are rather out of the picture today. The sentence I myself contributed to the Atlantic Charter, about no transference of territory apart from the will of the local inhabitants, has proved, in many cases, to be an unattainable ideal and, in any case, did not, in my experience, apply to enemy countries. But I know of no case in the whole of Europe, more than that of the Austrian Tyrol, where the Atlantic Charter, and the subsequent Charter of UNO, might have been extended to the people who dwell in this small, but well-defined, region which is now involved in the general war settlement.

Why cannot the natives of this mountainous and beautiful land, the land of the patriot Hofer,[1] be allowed to say a word about their destiny on their own behalf? Why cannot they have a fair and free plebiscite there under the supervision of the Great Powers? Let me put this question. Is it not illogical to have one standard of ethnic criteria for Trieste and Venezia Giulia, and another for the Southern Tyrol? The Soviet Government are quite logical; they are willing to override the ethnic criteria in both cases. I think that we might try, in this case, to emulate their symmetry of thought. There are no grounds for suggesting that any decisions adverse to the restoration of the Southern Tyrol to Austria were taken by the Government of which I was the head. We made positive declarations, in agreement with our Allies, about the independence of Austria, and by that was meant pre-Anschluss Austria. But this is in no way inconsistent with the addition to Anschluss Austria, or pre-Anschluss Austria, of the Southern Tyrol, if it is the wish of the people of that country.

No quarrel remains between us and Austria. Every liberal principle which we proclaim – and the application of liberal principles is the main hope of Europe – will be impugned by the assignment of the Austrian Tyrol to Italy

---

[1] Andreas Hofer, 1767–1810. Tirolese patriot, popular and military hero who fought for Austrian independence against Napoleonic France and Bavaria, 1809–10. Led the people to victory in the Battle of Berg Isle against the Bavarians, 1809. Executed by order of Napoleon, 1810.

against the wishes of its inhabitants. I have every desire that we should live on the most friendly terms with Italy. I look forward to seeing that historic country take its place in the concert of Europe. As Ministers opposite will remember, I made the utmost exertions, as Minister of Defence, to prevent Italy from being robbed of her fleet, and I was supported by my colleagues in the War Cabinet in the loan to Russia of 13 British warships to prevent the immediate distribution of the Italian fleet, which was fighting with us, between the three great Powers. We have not been told what happens to these 13 vessels now that the Italian fleet is to be divided up among the three great Powers. It might be a graceful gesture to Russia to convert the loan into a gift. We certainly wish to welcome Russia and her navy and her merchant commerce freely to the oceans; we recognize the importance to Russia of access to warm water ports, and I should like to hear from the Government what their intentions are about these 13 vessels. I mention them now, only to show our great care for Italy, and our desire that she should draw a line between the miserable past and what I trust will be a brighter future.

We were glad to hear the important declaration of the Foreign Secretary about the port and city of Trieste. The concessions already made by Great Britain and the United States in accepting the French compromise, or via media, go very far, and the three leading Western democracies ought now to stand firmly together on this point. The internationalisation of the port of Trieste is, as the Foreign Secretary said, vitally important to the whole of Central Europe and, particularly, to the Danubian Basin. I welcome the firm language he has used upon the subject. From all this tangle, some salient points emerge which the House ought to recognise: the sovereignty of nations, the equal rights of States, both great and small, under world law and, in regard to borderland or disputed territory, the wishes of the people concerned to be ascertained by free and fair elections. We shall be pretty safe if we stick to those simple, broad, well-tried principles.

I turn to another quarter. I have been struck in my visits to Belgium in November and to Holland recently, with the enormous recovery made by those countries since the war, and the vigour with which all parties there are unitedly plunging into the whole process of national recovery. The close relations which are growing up between those two countries, the association of the Catholic Church with extremely advanced liberal and social policies, the general aversion from Communism, all these are evident. But what impressed me even more, was the deep affection of these countries for Great Britain. Rightly or wrongly, they have it in their hearts that Britain, by her resistance when she was all alone, saved the world and enabled their liberties to be regained. Why are we not to be close friends with the Dutch and the Belgians? Has any other nation in the world a right to object to that?

We have all watched with deep satisfaction the steady recovery and rise of France, and the strength and stability increasingly shown by her people. The wounds which France suffered in the war were frightful. They were not only physical wounds; there were times when the soul of France seemed in jeopardy. I never lost faith in the greatness of the French people or the grandeur of France, and we all rejoice today to see her increasingly take her place in the forefront of the free democracies of the world. The Foreign Secretary did not make any reference to an Anglo-French treaty. Perhaps it has been wise to wait until the shape which the immediate post-war Governments of France will take has become manifest. But, of course, our relations with France do not depend on signatures attached to formal documents. Our friendship has sprung out of our comradeship, out of our former victory, out of our agony and out of our final triumph. I can only say here, as I said to the States-General at The Hague, that there can be no revival of European dignity and splendour without a strong France. I trust we shall endeavour to establish intimate and cordial relations with all our nearest neighbours on the Continent, in order that all the populations concerned can have the best standard of living possible in these hard times, and also that common regional security shall not be ignored.

Here let me deal with two expressions of prejudice which are now used in an endeavour to prevent friendly peoples coming together to mutual advantage without hostility to anyone else in the world. The first is the word 'bloc'. To be on good, easy, sympathetic terms with your neighbours is to form a bloc. To form a bloc is a crime, according to every Communist in every land, unless it be a Communist bloc. So much for the word 'bloc'. It happens also that we are closely associated with the United States. We think very much alike on great world problems on the morrow of our victory – because the British and Americans did have something to do with the victory. The Foreign Secretary often finds himself at these conferences in agreement with Mr Byrnes, just as my right hon. Friend the Member for Warwick and Leamington (Mr Eden) was often in agreement with Mr Hull,[1] and just as I was often in agreement with President Roosevelt and, after him, with President Truman. Now all this process, without which I can assure hon. Members we should not be sitting here this afternoon, is to be condemned and ruled out by the expression 'ganging up'. If two countries who are great friends agree on something which is right, they are 'ganging up,' so they must not do it. We should brush aside these terms of prejudice, which are used only to darken counsel and which replace, in certain minds, the ordinary processes of thought and human feeling. If the liberal nations of the world – the Western democracies, as they are called – are to be turned from their natural associations and true affinities by bugbear and scarecrow expressions like 'bloc' and 'ganging up,' they will only have themselves to thank when once again they fall into misfortune.

[1] Cordell Hull, 1871–1955. Member of US Congress for Tennessee, 1907–21, 1922–31. Senator, 1931–3. Secretary of State, 1933–44. Nobel Peace Prize, 1945. Published *The Memoirs of Cordell Hull* in 1948.

The House could not but be impressed by the measured and formidable complaint which the Foreign Secretary unfolded yesterday, step by step and theatre by theatre, about the treatment which the Western Allies have been receiving from the Soviet Government. Deep and widespread sorrow has been caused in Britain by the decline of contact and goodwill between our country and Russia. There was, and there still is, an earnest desire to dwell in friendly co-operation with the Soviet Government and the Russian people. On the other hand, the Foreign Secretary received the approval of the vast majority of the people when he protested against the prolonged, systematic campaign of vilification which has been, and is being daily pumped out upon us by the Soviet propaganda machine. Apart from the Communists and the 'cryptos' – that is to say, the Communists without the pluck to call themselves by their proper name – very few people were shocked by the homely language he chose to employ at the London Conference in January, nor indeed, do the vast majority of the House of Commons dissent from the argument he unfolded in the speech with which he opened this Debate.

Nevertheless, I am sure that it is the general wish of the British and Russian peoples that they should have warm and friendly feelings towards each other. We seek nothing from them except their goodwill, and we could play our part, with other nations, in coming to their aid with such resources as we may have if their just rights or safety were assailed. We were all glad to hear the Foreign Secretary say that he was still in favour of the 50-years treaty or 20 years treaty with Russia. Personally, I attach great importance to the existing Treaty, I have never made a speech on European questions without referring to it. It may go through bad times – lots of treaties do – but it would be a great misfortune if it were incontinently discarded. But surely, talking of treaties, this Four Power 25 year treaty between America, Britain, Russia, and France, which the United States have proposed to deal with Germany, is a tremendous project. The Foreign Secretary was right to say how much more valuable such a guarantee of the United States to be in the forefront of European affairs for 25 years would be to Soviet Russia for her own security, than the harnessing – 'harnessing' was the word – of a number of reluctant or rebellious border or satellite States. I am very glad to know that we are to support the United States proposal, and I thought the words which the Foreign Secretary used about it were singularly well chosen.

However, there is no use in concealing the fact that the Soviet propaganda and their general attitude have made a profound impression upon this country since the war, and all kinds of people in great numbers are wondering very much whether the Soviet Government really wish to be friends with Britain or to work wholeheartedly for the speedy re-establishment of peace, freedom and plenty throughout the world. Across the ocean, in Canada and the United States, the unfriendly Soviet propaganda has also been very effective in the reverse direction to what was intended. The handful of very able men who hold 180 million Soviet citizens in their grasp ought to be able to get better advice about the Western democracies. For instance, it cannot be in the interest of Russia to go on irritating the United States. There are no people in the world who are so slow to develop hostile feeling against a foreign country as the Americans, and there are no people who, once estranged, are more difficult to win back. The American eagle sits on his perch, a large, strong bird with formidable beak and claws. There he sits motionless, and M Gromyko[1] is sent day after day to prod him with a sharp pointed stick – now his neck, now under his wings, now his tail feathers. All the time the eagle keeps quite still. But it would be a great mistake to suppose that nothing is going on inside the breast of the eagle. I venture to give this friendly hint to my old wartime comrade, Marshal Stalin. Even here, in our patient community, Soviet propaganda has been steadily making headway backwards. I would not have believed it possible that in a year, the Soviets would have been able to do themselves so much harm, and chill so many friendships in the English-speaking world.

Let us also remember that the Soviet Government is greatly hampered in its relations with many foreign countries by the existence of Communist fifth columns. There are some States which hang in the balance, where these Communists organisms are aspiring, or conspiring, to seize the control of the Governments, although they are in a small majority in the population. Of course, if they succeed, the State is overturned and becomes harnessed as a satellite, but everywhere else the activities of Communist fifth columns only do Russia harm. In fact, they are an active process in bringing about the very thing which the Soviets most dislike, namely, a general consensus of opinion against them and their ways. I earnestly hope that when this present technique and these methods have been fully tried and found not helpful to the interest and the greatness of Soviet Russia, they will be discarded, and that a more reasonable and neighbourly spirit will prevail, in which case I am sure we would all be very ready, so far as words are concerned, to let bygones be bygones.

Then there is the Communist spy system, the exposure of which is at present confined to Canada. It has made a deep mark on Transatlantic opinion. These revelations, by no means complete, have stirred the whole Dominion of Canada. Of course, many countries have sought and seek information about the designs of other countries. But the difference between that and the Soviet system is that they do not have to hire their agents in the ordinary way. In the Communist sect it is a matter of religion to sacrifice one's native land for the sake of the Communist Utopia. People who, in ordinary life, would

---

[1] Andrei Andreyevich Gromyko, 1909–89. Known during the Cold War as 'Mr No'. Senior Instructor at Institute of Economics, Moscow, 1936–9. Counsellor, Soviet Embassy, Washington DC, 1939–43. Ambassador to the US, 22 Aug. 1943 to 1946. Permanent Representative of the Soviet Union to the UN, 1946–8. 1st Deputy Minister of Foreign Affairs, 1949–57. Ambassador to UK, 1952–3. Minister of Foreign Affairs, 1957–85. 1st Deputy Chairman of the Council of Ministers, 1983–5. Member of Supreme Soviet, 1985–8.

behave in a quite honourable manner, if they are infected with this disease of the mind will not hesitate a moment to betray their country or its secrets. There are many instances of that. It is this peculiarity which renders Soviet Communist espionage as dangerous as their propaganda is futile and often childish. The Canadian Government and its Prime Minister, Mr Mackenzie King, have only done their duty with courage and justice in exposing what has been brought up in the Dominion of Canada.

Far more serious than anything in the sphere of propaganda or espionage are the facts of the European situation. I have been censured for wrongly championing the Russian claims to the Curzon Line. So far as the Curzon Line is concerned, I hold strongly that this was a rightful Russian frontier, and that a free Poland should receive compensation at the expense of Germany both in the Baltic and in the West, going even to the line of the Oder and the Eastern Neisse. If I and my colleagues erred in these decisions we must be judged in relation to the circumstances of the awful conflict in which we were engaged. We are not now in the presence of the Curzon Line as the Western frontier of Soviet authority. It is no longer a question of the line of the Oder. So long as Poland is held in control the Soviet domination in one form or another, runs from Stettin in the Baltic to the outskirts of Trieste in the Adriatic, and far South of that. The Russified frontier in the North is not the Curzon Line; it is not on the Oder; it is on the Elbe. That is a tremendous fact in European history, and one which it would be the height of unwisdom to ignore. Not only has a curtain descended, from the Baltic to the Adriatic, but behind that, is a broad band of territory containing all the capitals of Eastern and Central Europe and many ancient States and nations, in which dwell nearly one-third of the population of Europe, apart from Russia. At the present moment all this is ruled or actively directed by the same group of very able men, the Commissars in the Kremlin, which already disposes with despotic power of the fortunes of their own mighty Empire. It is here in this great band or belt, if anywhere, that the seeds of a new world war are being sown.

We may be absolutely sure that the Sovietising and, in many cases, the Communising of this gigantic slice of Europe, against the wishes of the overwhelming majority of the people of many of these regions, will not be achieved in any permanent manner without giving rise to evils and conflicts which are horrible to contemplate. Meanwhile, it was clear from the speech of the Foreign Secretary that the policy of the Soviet Government seems, up to the present, to be to delay all final settlements of peace and to prevent the peoples of Western and Eastern Europe from getting together in friendly, social and economic association, as many of them would like to do. On a short-term view, time is on the side of the Soviets, because the longer a free and peaceful settlement of Europe is delayed, the more time the Russian forces and Communist organisations have at their disposal in order to liquidate whatever elements obnoxious to their ambitions venture to show themselves in these wide lands. The populations of the Baltic States are no longer recognisable as those which existed before the war. They have suffered a double liquidation, both at German hands and Russian hands. The population of Pomerania is said to be but a third of what it was before the war. There was a very interesting article in the *Manchester Guardian* on that point the other day. Every effort is being made to Communise and Russify the whole of the Soviet-occupied zone of Germany.

Poland is denied all free expression of her national will. Her worst appetites of expansion are encouraged. At the same time, she is held in strict control by a Soviet-dominated government who do not dare have a free election under the observation of representatives of the three or four Great Powers. The fate of Poland seems to be an unending tragedy, and we, who went to war, all ill-prepared, on her behalf, watch with sorrow the strange outcome of our endeavours. I deeply regret that none of the Polish troops – and I must say this – who fought with us on a score of battlefields, who poured out their blood in the common cause, are to be allowed to march in the Victory Parade. They will be in our thoughts on that day. We shall never forget their bravery and martial skill, associated with our own glories at Tobruk, at Cassino and at Arnhem. Austria and Hungary are stifled, starved and weighed down by masses of Russian troops. We agree with the Foreign Secretary in all he said on this point yesterday. I do not speak of Czechoslovakia, which is a special case. For the time being I accept President Benes's[1] statement that it is the duty of Czechoslovakia to interpret Russia to Western Europe and Western Europe to Russia. But for the rest – I do not want to go into more detail – the position is gravely and woefully disquieting.

All this brings us to the problem of Germany. Seventy or eighty millions of Germans still exist in the centre of Europe, constituting its largest racial block. Two-fifths of the German population lie East of the 'iron curtain', and three-fifths to the Westward. Together with the Americans and to some extent the French, the responsibility for the control of this vast mass of three-fifths of one of the most powerful nations in the world lies upon us. It lies upon the three Allied Western Powers. The Soviet Government are organising their own zone through the establishment in the power of German Communist elements with Soviet support and control. Different methods are being adopted in the British and American zones. We have to face the fact that, as we are going on at present, two Germanys are coming into being, one organised more or less on the Russian model, or in the Russian interest, and the other on that of the Western democracies, and that the line of demarcation is not fixed

---

[1] Edvard Beneš, 1884–1948. Born in Bohemia, the son of a farmer. Educated in Prague, Berlin and London. A leading member of the Czechoslovakia National Council, Paris, 1917–18. Czech Minister for Foreign Affairs, 1918–35; PM, 1921–2. President of the Czechoslovak Republic, 1935–8. In exile as President of the Czechoslovak National Committee in London, 1939–45. Re-elected as President of the Republic, Prague, 1945. Resigned, 1948. Author of many books and pamphlets on the Czech question.

with regard to any historical or economic conditions, but simply runs along the line agreed to when the whole future of the war was highly speculative, and nobody knew to what points armies would be likely to go or what would become of the struggle. It runs along the line to which, a year ago, the British and American Armies voluntarily retired – a 150 mile retreat in some cases, on a 400 mile front – after the Germans had surrendered.

Thus, the bulk of the German population and their manufacturing resources are in Anglo-American hands and the bulk of their food grounds in Soviet hands. It would not be contrary to the decision reached at Potsdam if His Majesty's Government followed the United States in not allowing any further transference to Russia of German factories and plants under their control except in return for proportionate deliveries of food for the German people, whose livelihood and, indeed, whose lives, depend in some cases upon those factories and upon the productivity of their area. In this way alone, will the burden upon us be lessened. Either we shall get the food for the Germans for whom we are responsible, or we shall be able to take the best measures possible to enable them to earn their own living. The first thing is that the Germans should earn their own living. It would seem very foolish to deprive them of the means of doing so, and then have to take the bread out of our own children's mouths in order to keep them alive in a miserable condition.

We should be very glad, and, I am sure, the Americans also would be very glad, to reach the condition of a general peace with the German nation, however truncated or compartmented it might be, in agreement with our Russian Allies. I cannot feel, from what we read and from what we heard yesterday, that this is likely to be the position for some time, and in the meantime the only course open will be to discuss matters with the Soviets upon a realistic basis. We cannot afford, and the United States cannot afford, to let chaos and misery continue indefinitely in the zones of Germany which we occupy. I was deeply impressed by the broadcast address of Field-Marshal Smuts last week. No more than Field Marshal Smuts have I any need to court popularity or win applause by saying fashionable things. I give my faithful counsel, as I did in bygone years, when I was always in a minority and sometimes almost alone. I must speak of Germany. Indescribable crimes have been committed by Germany under the Nazi rule. Justice must take its course, the guilty must be punished, but once that is over – and I trust it will soon be over – I fall back on the declaration of Edmund Burke,[1] 'I cannot frame an indictment against an entire people.' We cannot plan or even dream of a new world or a new Europe which contains pariah nations, that is to say, nations permanently

---

[1] Edmund Burke, 1729–97. Anglo-Irish statesman, author, orator, political theorist and philosopher. Served for many years in the House of Commons as a member of the Whig Party. Prominent opponent of the French Revolution. Living before the terms 'conservative' and 'liberal' were used to describe political ideologies, Burke was prized by both conservatives and liberals in the nineteenth century. From the twentieth century he has generally been viewed as the philosophical founder of modern conservatism.

or for prolonged periods outcast from the human family. Our ultimate hopes must be founded – can only be founded – on the harmony of the human family. So far as it remains in the power of this island people to influence the course of events, we must strive over a period of years to redeem and to reincorporate the German and the Japanese peoples in a world system of free and civilised democracy. The idea of keeping scores of millions of people hanging about in a sub-human state between earth and hell, until they are worn down to a slave condition or embrace Communism, or die off from hunger, will only, if it is pursued, breed at least a moral pestilence and probably an actual war.

There are obvious limits to our powers, but so far as we have power, and in agreement with the United States great power may be exercised, we must do our best for the German people, and after the guilty have been punished for their horrible crimes we must banish revenge against an entire race from our minds. We must make sure they do not rearm, and that their industries are not capable of rapid transition to war production, but the danger to European peace and to the future of free democratic civilisation is not, at this moment, Germany – that menace belongs to the first and second acts of the world tragedy. The danger is the confusion and degeneration into which all Europe, or a very large part of it, is rapidly sinking. Moreover, we need not fear that our position will be worsened, or that its dangers will be brought more near, by the adoption of clear and firm policies.

Above all, we should not again let the years slip by while we are pushed and slide down the slippery slope. We still have a breathing space. Let us not waste it, as we did last time. The last great war could have been prevented with the utmost ease by prudent, firm and righteous action, five, four or even three years before it occurred. (*Interruption.*) No right to lay flattering unction to their souls resides upon the benches opposite in this matter. (An Hon. Member: 'Or behind you.') I am dealing with this great matter which belongs to history, and from which no British party can draw particular credit. Other countries were concerned in that period, and I have no doubt whatever in saying that even up to 1939 it was possible, if we had utilised the full powers of the League of Nations – (*Interruption.*) – I travelled all round the country on that campaign, which amounted to what is now called 'ganging up' the League of Nations against Hitler, but did not succeed.

We are not in dispute about this. We agree with His Majesty's Government that Britain cannot delay indefinitely making a peace with all those countries with whom we have been at war and with whom we have no further quarrel. They have yielded themselves unconditionally to our arms and to those of our Allies; nothing is more costly, nothing is more sterile, than vengeance. We should make a peace with Germany or with whatever parts of Germany are still in our control. We should make peace with Italy who has been our Ally for the last two years of the war. If this peace cannot be achieved by inter-Allied discussion in Paris or elsewhere, then I agree with the Foreign Secretary, and with the Government of the United States, that we should carry the matter to UNO, and to the 21 nations who were actively engaged in the fighting – I quote the words used from the Front Bench opposite yesterday – and make the best solution possible. But it must be a quick one.

It is in this world organisation that we must put our final hopes. If we are to be told that such a procedure as this would rend the world organisation, and that a line of division, and even of separation, might grow up between Soviet Russia and the countries she controls on the one hand, and the rest of the world on the other, then I say – and I say it with much regret, but without any hesitancy – that it would be better to face that, when all has been tried and tried in vain, than tamely to accept a continued degeneration of the whole world position. It is better to have a world united than a world divided; but it is also better to have a world divided, than a world destroyed. Nor does it follow that even in a world divided there should not be equilibrium from which a further advance to unity might be attempted as the years pass by. Anything is better than this ceaseless degeneration of the heart of Europe. Europe will die of that.

I have no direct responsibility for the peace settlement after the last war. I was in the Government, but not in the War Cabinet, nor in the main delegations which representatives of all parties comprised, and which met in Paris. Indeed, I vehemently criticised many features of the Treaties of Versailles and Trianon, and what I said is on record. But now we have no peace. President Wilson, Mr Lloyd George[1] and M Clemenceau[2] were criticised for their long drawn out and hard treatment of the conquered. But what is happening now? After the last war, peace was made with Germany and Austria seven months after the fighting stopped. Ten months have passed already, and no one can predict when a peace will be made, or even when relations will be established with the conquered Powers that will be in practice equivalent to peace. Rumania, Bulgaria, Austria, Hungary – they have no peace. Even Italy, which fought at our side after Mussolini's tyranny was broken, has no peace. This cannot go on.

The Foreign Secretary said he would make another effort to bring about an agreed solution of European affairs. That is, of course, for him and for His Majesty's Government to decide. I do not say he is wrong. We all hope

---

[1] David Lloyd George, 1863–1945. Educated at a Welsh Church school. Solicitor, 1884. MP for Caernarvon, (Lib.) 1890–1931, (Ind. Lib.) 1931–45. President of the Board of Trade, 1905–8. PC, 1905. Chancellor of the Exchequer, 1908–15. An original member of the Other Club, 1911. Minister of Munitions, May 1915 to July 1916. Secretary of State for War, July–Dec. 1916. PM, Dec. 1916 to Oct. 1922. OM, 1919. Earl, 1945.

[2] Georges Clemenceau, 1841–1929. Mayor of Montmartre, 1870. Member of the Chamber of Deputies, 1876–93, 1902–29. Radical journalist; editor of *Justice*. Minister of the Interior, 1906. PM, 1906–8. PM and Minister of War, Nov. 1917 to Jan. 1920. Known during the war as 'the Tiger'. In *Great Contemporaries* (1937), Churchill wrote of him: 'Happy the nation which when its fate quivers in the balance can find such a tyrant and such a champion.'

earnestly for a successful conclusion to the approaching or, shall I say, impending, conference in Paris. We must certainly await its results. But it is surely necessary for people to begin asking themselves what course we ought to take supposing, as is not impossible, no sort of agreement is reached which would command the moral conscience and approval of the world at large. What are we to do? I am not asking the Foreign Secretary to answer the question now but, of course, his speech remains incomplete without some effective conclusion. It is no use producing a dozen points of difference with one of the greatest Powers in the world and then breaking off with a mere denial of a pessimistic state of mind.

I well understand the difficulties of His Majesty's Government, but never again will the parties of the Left be able to reproach the men of Versailles. Europe is far worse off in every respect than she was at the end of the last war. Her miseries, confusion and hatreds far exceed anything that was known in those bygone days. More than once the formidable truth has been stated that great nations are indestructible. Let us beware of delay and further degeneration. With all their virtues, democracies are changeable. After the hot fit, comes the cold. Are we to see again, as we saw the last time, the utmost severities inflicted upon the vanquished, to be followed by a period in which we let them arm anew, and in which we then seek to appease their wrath? We cannot impose our will on our Allies, but we can, at least, proclaim our own convictions. Let us proclaim them fearlessly. Let Germany live. Let Austria and Hungary be freed. Let Italy resume her place in the European system. Let Europe arise again in glory, and by her strength and unity ensure the peace of the world.

Winston S. Churchill to Sir Strati Ralli[1]
(Churchill papers, 1/65)

7 June 1946

Dear Sir Strati Ralli,

Your letter of June 4 to Miss Sturdee.

Sawyers came everywhere with me in these six and a half tempestuous years, and showed many excellent qualities. He is absolutely honest, capable of attending to a great many personal details as a valet, and always rises to the occasion. In my illnesses he has been very attentive, and he stood up to the bombardment well. He was particularly good in the air journeys which at first had to be made in uncomfortable machines. He waits well at table, and also has an admirable manner with visitors. He has a good memory and always

---

[1] Eustratio Lucas Ralli, 1876–1964. Educated at Eton and New College, Oxford. Fought in the Boer War, 1900–1. Partner at Ralli Brothers, 1911; Chairman, 1931. Name legally changed to Strati Ralli by deed poll, 1931.

knows where everything is. He is leaving me at his own wish, and I am sorry to lose him.

If there is anything else you want to talk over with me, I should be very glad to see you myself, if you would propose some time to call upon me here. I shall be out of town until June 18, so it would have to be a day after that.

L. S. Amery to Winston S. Churchill
(Churchill papers, 2/145)

7 June 1946

My Dear Winston,

May I be allowed to congratulate you most sincerely on your speech in Wednesday's debate?[1] You and Smuts have struck the only note which can save us from a worse disaster even than this last war. Somehow or other we must help to rebuild this old home of civilisation which we call Europe, first of all up to the present iron curtain, and eventually, I hope, up to the Curzon Line which is the real frontier between Europe and Asia. However that latter stage may be left mainly to the countries concerned and will not be in the picture for a good many years.

It seems to me that we are back at the natural and inevitable policy of this country, which is the so-called balance of power, or rather the building up of resistance to aggressive domination. The field of our operations used to be Europe, and the key was the Low Countries. Today that field is what Mackinder[2] called the World Island, namely the great bloc of the Old World, and the area or immediate neighbourhood whose independence we must preserve is the whole of Europe, including Greece and Turkey. Spatial dimensions have changed, but the underlying principles are the same.

In that policy we shall have to rely on the United States as the steadying factor in the Far East. But so far as Europe and the Middle East are concerned we must make our own policy and go ahead with it, even if on a short-sighted view the Americans don't altogether like it. For instance, we can never hope to build up an effective Western Europe unless its various nations are allowed and encouraged to co-operate in the economic field as well as in the political. That is to say they must be allowed to give each other every kind of economic preference. My own opposition to the American Loan conditions has been influenced throughout, not only by my conviction that we must at all costs

---

[1] Reproduced above (pp. 365–80).
[2] Halford John Mackinder, 1861–1947. Reader in Geography, Oxford University, 1887–1905. Principal of University College Reading, 1892–1903. Made the first ascent of Mount Kenya, 1899. Director, London School of Economics, 1903–8. MP (Cons.) for Glasgow Camlachie, 1910–22. Active in organizing recruiting in Scotland, 1914–18. Head, British Mission to Denikin, 1919. British High Commissioner for South Russia, 1919–20. Knighted, 1920. Chairman, Imperial Shipping Committee, 1920–45.

retain Empire Preference, but by my equally strong conviction that we must encourage the nations of Western Europe to give preference to each other and build up a European Commonwealth. You haven't much time, I know, but I hope you may be able to look into the little book on the Washington Loan Agreements which I sent you.

I know you are anxious and unhappy about India. But there are some tides in the world which one cannot fight against directly, but which one can only try to direct into the right channels. I have felt throughout that the one thing to do was to get the Indian political leaders into an interim government and once there to feel that India is in effect as independent as any Dominion. In that case they may continue to carry on under the existing constitution and realise increasingly the advantages of at any rate staying within the Commonwealth. Also such a government is one with which reasonable short-term agreements can be made about defence and trade. What I have never liked is the idea that everything should be held back for a constitutional convention which is bound to be unpractical and extremist. My only hope now is that an interim government will somehow be formed and that the Government here will declare its intention of treating it as independent under the existing constitution; in other words that the Viceroy's reserve powers under that constitution will be exercised on his own authority and not on any instructions from here. Given that situation the discovery of a constitution for all India may take years, and the whole Indian atmosphere become more reasonable.[1]

Winston S. Churchill to T. M. Snow[2]
(*Churchill papers, 2/238*)

8 June 1946
Private

Dear Mr Snow,

When I was staying with Field Marshal Alexander at Como last September, Charles Montag, who is an old friend of mine, came along to help me in my painting efforts. He begged me to go to Switzerland where he said were many attractive subjects. However, the exchange difficulties seemed to be serious there, and nothing came of it. He may have talked in this sense to people in Switzerland, with the result that an invitation has been sent me, which, as you will see from the enclosed letter, is sponsored by a number of leading firms in Switzerland, who wish to remain anonymous, to stay for a month in August/September in a villa in the Engadine. I should be greatly obliged if you would

---

[1] Churchill responded on June 10: 'Thank you very much for your letter.'
[2] Thomas Maitland Snow, 1890–1997. Educated at Winchester and New College, Oxford. Secretary, HM Diplomatic Service, 1923; Counsellor, 1930. Minister to Cuba, 1935–7; to Finland, 1937–40; to Colombia, 1941–4 (Ambassador, 1944–5); to Switzerland, 1946–9. Retired, 1950.

look at the list of people and consider the matter. Of course, I would much rather pay all my expenses myself, but the exchange regulations impose serious difficulties. I should like to go to Switzerland for a month, and I hear that there is a widespread desire among their people for me to go there. It might be that I would give one day to pay my respects to the Government at Berne, or perhaps at Zurich University, but otherwise I should live quite privately. Of course my sole object is to be able to rest and paint in freedom, and this very agreeable villa seems a good place.

I should like to know your opinion about the whole project. Pray do not hesitate to express it with the utmost freedom, for I have not yet finally committed myself and could easily make alternative plans. From a purely painting point of view, the district round Avignon is more attractive. Still, I am told one is no burden in Switzerland and everyone has good rations there. Pray forgive me for worrying you in this way.

Winston S. Churchill to Alfred Duff Cooper
(Churchill papers, 2/237)

8 June 1946
Private

My dear Duffie,

I am on the whole definitely much relieved and comforted by the results of the French elections as well as by the referendum. I have a feeling of increasing stability in France, and indeed throughout Western Europe. It looks as if the Communist virus is being decidedly corrected. I should have been very hard hit in my feelings to France if the Communist deserter from the French Army in time of war had definitely appeared at the head of the French Government. That would indeed have been a blow.

I think of coming to France, once the new Government has been formed, for a long weekend, probably about the middle of July. Of course, if the peace conference is on, I should not wish to come at the same time. I wonder, however, whether you and Diana would care to have me and Clemmie for a few days? If it is in the least inconvenient we can easily stay at the Ritz, I have no doubt, and come to see you from there.

I am anxious to renew my contacts with some of the old crowd who have now, I am glad to see, returned, as well as with Bidault,[1] Heriot[2] and Co. I have not made up my mind about the Ruhr, etc., and should like to understand

---

[1] Georges-Augustin Bidault, 1899–1983. Founded the Catholic Association of French Youth and the anti-Fascist newspaper *L'Aube*, 1932. Joined French Army, 1939. Joined French Resistance and organised an underground newspaper *Combat*, 1941. Foreign Minister in French Provisional Government, 1944, 1946. Head of French Delegation to the San Francisco Conference, 1945. President of France, 1946.

[2] Herriot.

the French point of view. I am thinking about the invitation from the Mayor of Metz,[1] but if I came over at all on July 14 it would be the procession in the Champs Elysées I should like to see.

Let me know what would be convenient to you and what you advise.

Winston S. Churchill to Lord Cecil[2]
(Churchill papers, 2/19)

9 June 1946

My dear Bob,

For a great many years past I have been in touch with Count Coudenhove-Kalergi[3] on the question of 'The United States of Europe'. Requests have been made to me to take Briand's[4] place at the organization. As you know, the Hitler irruption shattered all these ideas. I am still being pressed upon the same subject, either to take the Presidency, which lapsed with Briand's death, or to take the Honorary Chairmanship of the meeting of the Pan-European Council which they are planning to hold some time in the next two or three months.

I am far from being disinclined to this project, but I should like your advice, and to know what you think about it. I have a feeling that an immense amount of pro-British sentiment in Western Europe at any rate could be evoked by my working in this association, and also that I personally could save it from rivalry with the United States of America, and might prevent its having at the outset a needlessly anti-Soviet bias.

Perhaps you would talk to Lionel Curtis[5] and let me know how you feel

---

[1] Gabriel Hocquard, 1892–1974. Mayor of Metz, 1938–40, 1944–7. Councillor of the Republic, 1946–8.

[2] Edgar Algernon Robert Cecil, 1864–1958. Known as 'Bob'. Third son of 3rd Marquess of Salisbury. Educated at Eton and University College, Oxford. MP (Cons.) for East Marylebone, 1906–10; for Hitchin, 1911–23. Under-Secretary of State for Foreign Affairs, 1915–18. Minister of Blockade, 1916–18. Asst Secretary of State for Foreign Affairs, 1918. Viscount Cecil of Chelwood, 1923. Lord Privy Seal, 1923–4. President of the League of Nations Union, 1923–45. Chancellor of the Duchy of Lancaster, 1924–7. Nobel Peace Prize, 1937.

[3] Richard Nikolaus 'Ejiro' Coudenhove-Kalergi, 1894–1972. Born in Tokyo. Son of Heinrich Johann Marie Coudenhove-Kalergi and Mitsuko Aoyama. Married, 1915, Ida Klausner (div.); 1952, Alexandra Bally (d.); 1969, Melanie Hoffman. Founded Pan-European Movement, 1922. Published his manifesto *Pan-Europa*, 1923. Editor, *Paneuropa*, 1925–38. Author of *Europe Must Unite* (1939). Advocated the concentration of national power into a small number of blocs: Pan-Europe, Pan-America, Japan and China, the British Empire and Russia.

[4] Aristide Briand, 1862–1932. PM of France, 1909–10, Jan.–Mar. 1913, Oct. 1915 to Mar. 1917, Nov. 1925 to July 1926, July–Oct. 1929. Minister of Justice, 1912–13, 1914. PM and Minister of Foreign Affairs, Jan. 1921 to Jan. 1922. Minister of Foreign Affairs, April–July 1925, 1926–32. Awarded the Nobel Peace Prize for his part in the Locarno Agreements, 1926.

[5] Lionel George Curtis, 1872–1955. Served in South African War as a Private, 1899. Secretary to Sir Alfred Milner in South Africa, 1900. Town Clerk, Johannesburg, 1902–3. Asst Colonial Secretary, Transvaal, 1903–9. Editor, *Round Table*, 1909. Prof. of Colonial History at Oxford University, 1912. Member, British League of Nations Section, Paris Peace Conference, 1919. Secretary to British

about this. It might become very big indeed, and a potent factor for world peace. After all, Europe is the foundation of almost all the glories and tragedies of mankind.

Winston S. Churchill to Lieutenant-Colonel John Astor[1]
(Churchill papers, 2/145)

12 June 1946
Personal and Private

My dear John,
Thank you for your letter. I am very glad to be of any service to you.

I never forget being at St Margaret's Bay, where some of our children were sheltering in 1918, when the news of your terrible wounding came in. This was a great sacrifice exacted from you for our country and, as half American, it appeals to me very much.

I make this the occasion of writing a letter which has been in my mind for a long time. I have been a life-long constant reader of *The Times* and, while I greatly admire all the rest of the paper, I have deeply regretted the policy of its leading articles. Only yesterday Laski's[2] criticisms of Bevin's foreign policy are emphasized and even commended by the remark that they will find an echo in both Parties and even beyond them. Apart from this, the whole tendency of *The Times* is to lay stress upon the swing to the Left which has already, as you well know, caused very great injury to the structure and prosperity of our country and is going to cause much more as the next three or four years unfold. We are told that the policy of the newspaper is largely settled by several very advanced Socialists, one of whom writes the leading article, and that Barrington-Ward[3] himself has not much to say to it. I am assured you do not interfere at all in policy and certainly that policy seems to be, on many occasions, contrary to your views and convictions as a member of the Conservative Party.

Delegation at Irish Conference in London, 1921. Colonial Office Adviser on Irish Affairs, 1921–4. Author of several books and numerous pamphlets on Commonwealth affairs and theory. CH, 1949.

[1] John Jacob Astor, 1886–1971. ADC to Viceroy of India, 1911–14. On active service, 1914–18 (severely wounded); Maj., 1920. MP (Cons.) for Dover, 1922–45. Chairman of *The Times*, 1922–59. Lt-Col., 5th Battalion, City of London Home Guard, 1940–4. Baron, 1956.

[2] Harold Joseph Laski, 1893–1950. Son of Nathan Laski (an influential member of the Jewish community in North-West Manchester, Churchill's former constituency). Lecturer in History, McGill University, Montreal, 1914–16, and Harvard University, 1916–20; in Political Science, Magdalene College, Cambridge, 1922–5. Prof. of Political Science, London School of Economics and Political Science, 1926–50. Member of Executive Committee of Labour Party, 1936–49.

[3] Robert McGowan Barrington-Ward, 1891–1948. Joined staff of *The Times*, 1913. Bde Maj., 1914–18 (MC, DSO, despatches thrice). Asst Editor, *Observer*, 1919–27. Asst Editor and Chief Leader Writer, *The Times*, 1927–34; Deputy Editor, 1934–41. Supported Neville Chamberlain and appeasement, writing in his diary at the time of Munich: 'Most of this office is against Dawson and me!' Succeeded Geoffrey Dawson as Editor of *The Times*, 1 Oct. 1941. Retired owing to ill-health, 1947.

I feel that at my age I am justified in writing to you, my friend and neighbour, to assure you that you cannot disclaim responsibility for the direction of *The Times* when you are proprietor, and it may well become a reflection upon your life and service that you stood by and did nothing. I earnestly hope therefore that you will assert your authority and make sure that your great newspaper conforms to the convictions which you hold.

I hope this letter will not give you offence, but anyhow I felt it my duty in the public interest to write it.

Winston S. Churchill to Clement Attlee
(*Churchill papers, 2/4*)

12 June 1946
Private and Confidential

My dear Prime Minister,

Some months ago, before Christmas, when we had an informal talk about the BBC, I gathered that it was your view that, if there were any political broadcasts of a controversial nature, there should always be an answer made. With this I agree and I see no reason why the proportion of votes cast at the General Election should not be a guide in the according of facilities to the various Parties, provided they have a minimum of say, a million votes reported.

I have now come to the conclusion that political broadcasting should be resumed by responsible leaders of Parties and figures outside the Party, and I am proposing to write formally to the BBC and request facilities in the course of the next month for myself.

In view of the paper shortage it is not possible for speeches of leading men to be widely reported and consequently the nation is not receiving normal guidance on controversial matters. You have yourself on numerous occasions emphasized your reliance on free discussion, and I should like to know what your attitude would be before I write my letter to the BBC.

Winston S. Churchill to Ralph Assheton
(*Churchill papers, 2/7*)

12 June 1946

My dear Ralph,

I see all over the country posters which date back from the General Election which are defaced and in a bad and dirty condition. They show a photograph of me and the words, 'Help him finish the job – Vote National'. I consider that this kind of advertisement is now quite out of date and indeed harmful.

I should like you therefore to arrange to have all these posters cleaned right away and the cost of the work charged to the Party.

Jo Sturdee to Winston S. Churchill
(Churchill papers, 1/30)

14 June 1946   Chartwell

Mr Churchill,

Mr Newman[1] says that the life of butterflies is not very long – probably about ten days – so it is not surprising that some them are already dying. He sent off six dozen more Tortoiseshells for you yesterday, so they should be arriving here soon. Mr Newman also says that you had told him that you intended to leave the cage door open on nice days and let them go out among the flowers, and he thinks this would be a very good thing. He points out that perhaps some of the butterflies will be laying their eggs which perhaps may hatch out in due course.[2]

Winston S. Churchill to Clement Attlee
(Churchill papers, 2/4)

22 June 1946

My dear Prime Minister,

I must now acknowledge the two letters you sent me on June 15.

1. I had thought myself that it would be more appropriate for the House of Commons to vote a sum of money to erect a statue to President Roosevelt, opposite the Government buildings in the Parliament Square, near to where the statue of Abraham Lincoln now stands – or rather sits. However events have taken a different course and I quite see that it is impossible to reverse them.

---

[1] George Newman, 1870–1948. Bacteriologist. Demonstrator at King's College, London, 1896–1900. Chief Medical Officer, Board of Education, 1907–35. Knighted, 1911. Chairman, Health of Munitions Workers Committee, 1915–18. Medical Member, Central Control Board (Liquor Traffic), 1915–19. Chief Medical Officer, Ministry of Health, 1919–35. Author of several medical works, including *Hygiene and Public Health* (1917).

[2] Churchill wrote on June 17: 'Ask whether a little pot of honey wd be any good to them.' In 1987, Grace Hamblin recalled: 'A nearby butterfly farm sent him chrysalises which he liked to see develop. One morning, I was with him spreading out the chrysalises, and he left the door of the little hut open. I said, "Did you want to leave the door open, or should I close it?" He said, "I can't bear this captivity any longer!" Thus we no longer kept butterflies, but they are supposed to remain in the garden once you start. It's a lovely occupation. When he knew that Chartwell would eventually go to the National Trust and be open to the public he said, "I hope the National Trust will grow plenty of buddleia for my butterflies"' (*Proceedings of the International Churchill Societies 1987*, pp. 43–4).

I therefore shall be very glad to second any Bill you may introduce to carry through the erection of a Memorial in Grosvenor Square to this great man and saviour of Europe. I shall consider it a privilege to support you on this occasion.

2. I hope also that you will be successful in your scheme for erecting a Memorial Tablet to him in Westminster Abbey. All my colleagues are in agreement with this.

2.[1] With regard to the extension of the Government Hospitality Fund, I feel this is a matter on which the Government must make whatever proposals it wishes to Parliament. My colleagues and I are clear that we must reserve our full freedom to comment upon the matter.

[. . .]PS. I am so glad you liked the medallion. It will make an excellent paperweight.

Winston S. Churchill: speech
('Winston S. Churchill, His Complete Speeches', volume 7, pages 7355–6)

25 June 1946   House of Commons

FINANCE BILL

I should not like the speech of the Chancellor of the Exchequer (Mr Dalton) to pass without a word of comment, early in the morning though it may be. I think it is a great pity that so much time has been taken up by reading extracts and counter-extracts from Lord Beaverbrook's newspapers. We all wish to see a free Press, and to see opinions expressed with the utmost frankness and contrary to the ordinary party lines, but it would be a great infliction upon us, if we were to have all this read over to us again at this time, and have to undergo as it were a repeat of what we had perhaps already noticed when we opened our morning newspapers. The question raised by my right hon. Friend the ex-Chancellor of the Exchequer, the Member for the Scottish Universities (Sir J. Anderson), is a very serious and complicated question. It raises this issue of whether it is a good thing to eliminate very rich people and whether in a country wealth should be abolished. That is arguable. I am not interested in the matter, because I have never been a very rich person. The right hon. Gentleman's party have set out to abolish poverty, though they have not been successful in doing so, but the abolition of wealth is well within their power. They can eliminate large fortunes by legislation, in Budget after Budget, together with prolonging, in times of peace, taxation induced by the extreme needs of war. That is what they will quickly achieve.

---

[1] Paragraph numbering error in original.

Whether the country will be the better or the worse for it is a question which runs into all kinds of ethical and philosophical aspects, as well as into those which are economic. The duty of the Chancellor of the Exchequer is to think of revenue and I am of opinion that, from the point of view of the revenue, the elimination of what I might call the most obvious and fruitful taxpayers will be a source of decline. Here are people who pay these excessive, high rates. Soon they will vanish. Very soon they will disappear. You may say that it is a good thing. I am not deciding in my own mind whether or not it is a good thing. But from the point of view of the revenue it is a bad thing. It is better to have one man who leaves £2 million than ten men who leave £200,000, because of the much larger yield to the Exchequer. Because of the accepted principle in this country of scaling up the Death Duty and Income Tax there is no doubt of that. Also it applies that if you have an estate of £2 million a year the person who owns it will conserve a great part of it which will be amenable to future taxation. It does not follow then that the elimination of the larger taxpayer will be more fruitful to the revenue. It will be less fruitful. It is also true to say that the existence of a number of very considerable fortunes will lead to greater expenditure. These are facts, and if only the right hon. Gentleman would consult his statisticians at the Treasury he would ascertain that they are facts. That is on the question of the revenue. The right hon. Gentleman has made a most courteous and careful answer to statements made in the Debate. All the same I think he is animated by spite. He said the other day that he would not offer his sympathy, that he had no sympathy, with the very rich. I am sure they would not want his sympathy. It would be very unpleasant. But the question is not one of sympathy; it is revenue with which the right hon. Gentleman is concerned. The whole course of his finance is towards the elimination of great fortunes and destroying large revenues. It is also calculated to produce many other minor deterrents to enterprise and production with which we need not trouble ourselves at present. But that is the consequence of the course which the Chancellor pursues – a deep injury to the revenue.

Then there is the question of inflation. Undoubtedly the effect on an estate, three-quarters of which is to be confiscated on death, is to encourage the expenditure of money during lifetime, contrary to all our desires for saving and so forth. These matters are not important from one point of view because you could count on the fingers of your hands and on your toes as well, probably, all the persons who will be affected by this legislation. You can sweep them away. I see that there are only thirty-two persons who pay tax above a certain scale. In his career the Chancellor will undoubtedly eliminate them, and while he is doing so, he will be diminishing the various productive and provident processes, and when he has done that, he will have a taxpayer population which will yield a less fruitful revenue than that which he now enjoys. But that the process is popular no one can deny. You can get loud cheers by advocating it. But the question we are concerned with is whether it is a fruitful, thrifty method of fostering the revenues of the Exchequer, and a healthy, harmonious and enriching process for developing the wealth of the State and of the country. That has not been answered. Neither from the point of view of the revenue nor in respect of the danger of inflation, have the arguments of my right hon. Friend the ex-Chancellor been in any way met. This country now marches on into very different financial scenes, and its fortunes will not be altered by whether or not you abolish all property above a certain amount. It will not be affected by that in a decisive fashion, but in so far as this kind of taxation has any influence at all, it is detrimental to the general wealth and undoubtedly it is detrimental to the broad, free, progressive, natural development of our country and its economic life.

The right hon. Gentleman has an extraordinary responsibility cast upon him. He is the inheritor of all the taxation voted by the Conservative Party – voted by the vast Conservative majority in the late House of Commons, in order to win the war. He has that immense revenue confided to him. He ought not to let his desire to win a cheap cheer, he ought not to let the advantage of wreaking some petty feeling of jealousy or spite, to lead him into courses which are detrimental to the revenue, and although I do not say they are large enough to affect the general course of our affairs they are, at the same time, injurious to our general wealth-producing capacity. After all, what are you dealing with? You are dealing with a trifling portion of the population in order to sweep it away. In war time all was offered, all was given. You can sweep them away, but remember where we have got to now. We have reached a point at which there is no more taxing the rich in order to give social advantages to the rest of the community. The parish is on the parish. You have put the whole community on itself. In the future, as you advance further upon the path of social reform, you will no longer be taking away the rich man's money amid loud cheers. All you will be doing will be showing the working man that the political parties can spend his wages for him better than he can himself.

Lieutenant-Colonel John Astor to Winston S. Churchill
(Churchill papers, 2/145)[1]

26 June 1946
Personal and Private

My dear Winston,

I greatly appreciate your letter of June 12.[2] This is the first opportunity I have had of answering, as I am on tour with our Empire Press Party. Please

---

[1] This letter was handwritten.
[2] Reproduced above (pp. 385–6).

forgive me if I write briefly, as we are carrying out a very full programme from a special train.

First, I do assure you you have been given inaccurate information, and I cannot recognize the picture you have painted. I protest that Barrington Ward does exercise the full authority that as Editor he should. Whatever Socialists there may be in the office, I am quite sure they do not attempt to settle policy. The leader writer you refer to I assume to be E. H. Carr.[1] I have often heard him criticized for leaders for which he was in no way responsible. In recent years he has written few leaders, and I am convinced that he has no undue influence with Barrington Ward. I have never disclaimed ultimate responsibility for policy. I do not interfere in day-to-day editing. But I took it on myself to 'accept the resignation' of Geoffrey Dawson[2] – for reasons I need not go into. He was anxious to stay on.

I do keep in close touch with BW. He is most ready to discuss any point of policy, staff, or office business, and I am sure he does not keep anything from me. I cannot remember any occasion on which the policy of *The Times* has been contrary to my views or convictions. I certainly claim to be a member of the Conservative Party but have often been out of sympathy with its right wing.

I submit that, especially recently, current issues have tended to divide the respective Parties within themselves. Time may show that *The Times* has not infrequently been right.

I am only too well aware of my many shortcomings. Whether I have been able to do anything useful in *The Times*, or indeed in any direction, it is for others to say. I can only hope for the best.

I apologize for the abrupt terms of this letter, assure you I have not taken offence at any of your statements, and have written in all sincerity. I deeply appreciate the spirit of your letter, and only hope you will some day give me an opportunity for a talk.

---

[1] Edward Hallett Carr, 1892–1982. FO, 1916; attached to British Delegation, Paris Peace Conference, 1919. Asst Adviser on League of Nations Affairs, 1930–3. Prof. of International Politics, University of Wales, 1936–46. Director of Foreign Publicity, Ministry of Information, 1939–40. Asst Editor, *The Times*, 1941–6. Historian; biographer of Dostoevsky, Marx and Bakunin.

[2] George Geoffrey Robinson, 1874–1944. Educated at Eton and Magdalen College, Oxford. Fellow of All Souls, 1896. Private Secretary to Milner in South Africa, 1901–5. Editor, *Johannesburg Star*, 1905–10; *The Times*, 1912–19, 1923–41. Took the surname Dawson, 1917.

Winston S. Churchill to Duncan Sandys
(Churchill papers, 2/23)

29 June 1946

My dear Duncan,

I sent on to you on June 27 a letter I have received from Bob Cecil, to whom I referred on the subject of Count CK[1] and the United States of Europe. I think it would be a pity for me to join an organization which had such a markedly anti-Russian bent, and I was not aware that this was Count CK's conception. His book was written in very different circumstances from those which now prevail, and I think it would be a very good thing to find out exactly where he stands, and to put the points to him explicitly before I mix myself up with the matter or even approach it formally. If you found it convenient to visit him in Switzerland (at Gstaad) on your way back from Germany I think it would be very useful. You could then discuss and explore the whole subject and we could talk it over together when you come back. I hope you are enjoying yourself. I look forward to having a very full account from you of all you must have seen.

Our plans still hold for Switzerland. Clemmie and Mary are coming too, and we start on August 23. However, as the height was thought too much for me, they are offering us a villa on the Lake of Geneva instead of at St Moritz. This will be much warmer, and very likely there will be bathing.

Winston S. Churchill to D. W. Brogan
(Churchill papers, 4/443)

30 June 1946 Chartwell
Private

My dear Professor Brogan,

I have made you up the best sheaf I can of the proofs that I have with me, keeping my own copy. Nothing here is finally fixed. Chronology should rule. The subject was first treated from the point of view of an account of the politics of George III's reign and later on about the quarrel with America. But these are inseparably intermingled and cannot be handled in compartments. I have therefore made some attempt to put them in their proper order. I have put a few spares and duplicates and repetitions in the file. This is the best I can do with the short notice you gave me. I do not want to be left without my parent copy. I have put in the bulk of the corrections, most of which were due to your revise. I am sorry that there is so much disorder. When you return we will have a reprint.

---

[1] Coudenhove-Kalergi.

July 1946

L. S. Amery to Winston S. Churchill
(Churchill papers, 2/145)

1 July 1946

My dear Winston,

Attlee will no doubt make out some sort of case for what they have done in Palestine and you may not feel it possible to do more than express your misgivings on the immediate issue. But I do hope you will press him as to what is his policy for the future and how he means not only to settle Palestine, but to bridge the gulf of bitterness between us and the people on whom, in the long run, we shall have to look to to support our military position in the Middle East, now we are clearing out of Egypt.

The whole of this sorry business is the bitter fruit of irresolution and postponement ever since the Government of 1936, after endorsing the Peel Report, ran away from it. Looking round for some excuse for postponing a decision they then summoned the Arab States into conference with the result, which any child could have foretold, of making things worse. Then came the White Paper which reversed twenty years of policy and was so unworkable that having broken faith with the Jews we were bound, sooner or later, to break faith with the Arabs as well. During the Coalition we did find a policy, clear cut and definite, which could have been put through with far less force than we shall have to employ now and with far less bitterness. That was dropped and the whole thrown back on an amiable but entirely ignorant and unpractical Anglo-American Commission – the situation inevitably getting worse all the time. Even that might have been all right if Attlee had given a straight endorsement of its proposals on our responsibility. But his threats about disarmament and his whole attitude were bound to make things worse. On top of that comes Bevin's irresponsible outburst at Bournemouth – throwing a match into a barrel of gunpowder with a vengeance. Now we have committed ourselves to taking the high hand with the Jews, rightly or wrongly. But what next? Are we never to have a policy? That is the real question and I hope you may be able to pin Attlee down on that.

I only wish I were in the House to back you up.

Winston S. Churchill to Clement Attlee
(Churchill papers, 2/237)

2 July 1946
Private

My dear Prime Minister,

I was glad to hear that you have decided that my visit to Metz is of an exceptional and public character. This enables me to fulfil the engagement which I made with General Giraud[1] in 1942 when, in the course of his intervention in 'Torch',[2] I said to him, 'I give you rendezvous at Metz.' I imagine the telegram I sent him then, referring to my pre-war visit to Metz, and subsequent events have led to this invitation, which I should have been sorry not to be able to accept.

I also think it may do good to Anglo-French relations as I have a very long association with France, even before the last war began.

Let me assure you that my motives are entirely public and that pleasure forms no part in them. In fact it is a great exertion to travel all this way. Still, I think it may be an opportunity of saying a few words of friendship and encouragement to the French, which will reach many homes in France. Therefore, while thanking you for your courtesy, I hope my visit will not be looked upon as a personal favour to me but as a means of furthering the general interest.

2. With regard to the copy of the telegram to the President about Palestine which you sent me, I talked to Stanley and Eden on the telephone yesterday and they have no doubt by now supported you in the Adjournment moved last evening. I should however like to make my position clear to you. Terrorism is no solution for the Palestine problem. Yielding to terrorism would be a disaster. At the same time I hold myself bound by our national pledges, into which I personally and you also and your Party have entered, namely the establishment of a Jewish National Home in Palestine, with immigration up to the limit of 'absorptive capacity', of which the Mandatory Power is the judge. I might hope we should agree upon this.

Several of my friends are far from abandoning Partition, and I am very much inclined to think this may be the sole solution.

---

[1] Henri-Honoré Giraud, 1879–1949. Military Governor of Metz and Cdr, 6th Military Region, 1936–40. Commanded French 7th Army, based on Dunkirk, 1940; advanced into Holland, 10 May 1940. Taken prisoner May 1940; escaped, 1942; brought out of Vichy France by a British submarine. C-in-C, United French Armed Forces, 1943–4.

[2] 'Torch': Allied invasion of North Africa, 1942.

B. R. Ambedkar to Winston S. Churchill
(Churchill papers, 2/42)

2 July 1946   Bombay

Dear Mr Churchill,

I saw in the Papers that you demanded a date to raise a debate in the House of Commons on India in order to allow the Conservative Party to express its opinion on the proposals of the Cabinet Mission. I have no doubt you will refer to the grave injustice done to the 60 millions of Untouchables by the Cabinet Mission. I have written a letter to Major Attlee to explain to him how the pledges given by HMG to the Untouchables have been flagrantly broken by the Cabinet Mission and how the Mission handed over the Untouchables to the tender mercies of the Caste Hindus who have reduced them to the status of animals. I am sending you herewith a copy of that letter with its accompaniments. It will serve you as a brief on behalf of the Untouchables. I know you are a very busy person. But for the sake of saving 60 millions of Untouchables, I do hope that you will find time to go through the papers and make a powerful plea on their behalf requiring Government to change their proposals so as to assure the Untouchables political safeguards which would be fool proof and knave proof. I need hardly say how eagerly the Untouchables of India are looking forward to your speech in Parliament on this question which is to them of the greatest importance.

Clare Sheridan to Winston S. Churchill
(Churchill papers, 1/42)[1]

2 July 1946

My dear Winston,

I have seen Oswald Birley's portrait, & find it very interesting. It is more than just a portrait – he has got something into it that is extremely puzzling – one can look at it for a long time, & come back to it, & still try to understand. I cannot make out if you are just going to smile, or have just smiled, & whether it is the eyes or the mouth that smile – or whether you have just said something rather important or are listening – or whether you are just a wee bit hurt –? Like the Gioconda,[2] we shall look & look at it & never know – That clenched hand on the table is magnificent – [. . .]

---

[1] This letter was handwritten.
[2] Leonardo da Vinci's *Mona Lisa*.

Lord Camrose: memorandum of a conversation with Winston S. Churchill
(Camrose papers)

3 July 1946

Has now decided on a scheme drawn up by Fladgates (Solicitors to Lloyds Bank) whereby the Lord Randolph Churchill MSS, the Duke of Marlborough's papers given to him recently by the Queen of the Netherlands, his own personal papers relating to his life since his entry into Parliament up to September 1939 and all his war papers are transferred to a trust for the benefit of his children. The Trustees are to be Clemmie, Prof. and Brendan.

The Trustees will offer for sale the access to, and right to use, the War papers; the others are just owned by the Trust but, so far as his papers up to 1939 are concerned, these will probably be given to Randolph to write his life, but not until five or ten years after his death.

In due course I will be asked to make an offer for the use of the War papers and, at the same time, if I so elect, an offer to him to edit them. The idea would be a lump sum to the Trust and an annual payment to him of £10,000 or £15,000 for three or four years.

Estimates that the War papers and his editing of them should be worth about £500,000 and cites Hearst's[1] offer of $1,000,000 for the American rights alone, although he realized that there might be difficult points about the offer if he attempted to accept it.

Expects the Trust Deed to be ready in the next ten days and will then get Fladgates to explain the objects to me. Is advised that the scheme behind the Trust protects the assets against Death Duties but confessed he did not know how.

Feels much better than when he returned from America and full of energy. Had intended to retire then but hates 'the enemy' so much that he will stay on to put them out. Would like Anthony to take on the leadership of the Opposition on condition that he, Winston, has the right to 'barge in' on any occasion he wants to. Difficulty of making the arrangement at the moment is that Anthony feels he cannot take the salary while he is a director of public companies, an idea at which Winston scoffs.

Quite happy about his financial affairs. Has about £90,000 in 'equities' and some War Loan. Will live on his capital and all will be well unless he lives 'to an inordinate age'.

Was disappointed at the opinion I had expressed over the telephone,

---

[1] William Randolph Hearst, 1863–1951. Born in San Francisco; son of a US Senator. Editor and Proprietor, *New York American, New York Evening Journal, Boston American, Boston Advertiser, Chicago Herald and Examiner, Chicago American, San Francisco Examiner* and *Los Angeles Examiner*. Married, 1903, Millicent Wilson: five sons. Unsuccessful candidate for Mayor, New York, 1905. Congressman. Lived at his self-designed castle, the Hearst Ranch, San Simeon, a treasure-house of medieval and Renaissance European art and furniture which Churchill had visited in 1929 as Hearst's guest. During the 1930s Churchill wrote a number of articles for Hearst's newspapers.

concerning the appointment of Woolton as Chairman of the Conservative Party Central Office. Said the appointment met with unanimous approval in the Party but went on to say he hoped Woolton would not be too social or too fond of making after-dinner speeches. Did not seem excited about W himself and said (with a grin) some people did not care for him personally. At any rate his experience ought to make him a good man for the routine work and that was what was wanted in such a position.

Very delighted at a recent purchase from Berry Bros. of 10 dozen Pol Roger 1928 (his favourite wine) at 35/- per bottle and 12 dozen half bottles. Excellent wine 'At that price' to drink for lunch and he intends to do so!

Offered to subscribe £10,000 to the Endowment Fund for Chartwell which I declined. Arranged to go down there first week in August to survey the situation.

Winston S. Churchill to Brendan Bracken
(Churchill papers, 2/6)

3 July 1946

As a regular reader of *The Economist* I am disturbed by the strong Left-wing bias of all its comments on foreign affairs. As you know, I think very highly of Crowther[1] and all his work on economic matters seems to me of the very first order. At the same time he is a wet pink and, when not confronted with the business facts of *The Economist*, yields himself to a point of view in foreign affairs even more to the Left than that of the present Socialist Government.

It is distressing to read the weekly papers. *The Tribune* and *The New Statesman* are violent anti-Tory productions. *The Spectator* is a stuffy, genteel Left-centre production. Now there is *The Economist* over which you have so great a measure of control. Surely this might confine itself more to financial, economic and business aspects, in which it is the leading authority. As it is, in foreign affairs, it marches side by side with *The Times*, except that it is written with more ability.

Do consider this and talk to me about it when we meet.

Clement Attlee to Winston S. Churchill
(Churchill papers, 2/4)

4 July 1946

My dear Churchill,

I have been in discussion with my colleagues on the subject of the

---

[1] Geoffrey Crowther, 1907–72. Educated at Clare College, Cambridge, 1928–9; Yale University, 1929–30. Married, 1932, Margaret Worth: six children. Joined *The Economist* on recommendation of J. M. Keynes, 1932; Asst Editor, 1935; Editor, 1938–56. Baron, 1968.

resumption of political broadcasting which you raised with me in your letter of the 12th June.[1]

I presume that you were writing officially on behalf of the Opposition.

I have also been informed of your request to the BBC to reply to the Lord President's broadcast of Sunday night last.

The Government are in agreement with you as to the desirability of resuming political broadcasting and would welcome discussions with representatives of the Opposition and with the BBC in order to clear up any points not covered in previous conversations.

You will, I know, have in your mind the distinction between broadcasts addressed to the nation by the Government, such as you made yourself during the War and expositions of policy made from the political angle. In the view of the Government the broadcast of the Lord President of the Council falls into the former category.

I enclose a letter which the Postmaster General[2] has sent to the Director General of the BBC[3] setting out the views of the Government.

Clement Attlee to Winston S. Churchill
(Churchill papers, 2/237)

4 July 1946

My dear Churchill,

Thank you very much for your letter of July 2.[4] I was glad that it was possible to decide that your visit to Metz is of an exceptional and public character that consequently the Government can make available air transport to take you there and back. I am sure that what you say there will further the general interest and if you feel that it would be a help to have a word before you go with the Foreign Secretary, he will, I am sure, be glad to give you any information which might be of help to you in drawing up your speech.

2. I am grateful to you for making clear your position about Palestine.

I knew I could rely on your support in the view that it would be disastrous

---

[1] Reproduced above (p. 386).

[2] William Francis Hare, 1906–97. Educated at Eton and Oxford. Married, 1933, Judith de Marffy-Mantuano (div. 1945); 1958, Stephanie Sandra Yvone Wise (div. 1963); 1963, Pamela Read. Succeeded his father as 5th Earl of Listowel, 1931. London City Council Member (Lab.) for East Lewisham, 1937–46; for Battersea North, 1952–7. Labour Party Whip, House of Lords, 1941–4. Parliamentary Under-Secretary of State, India Office, 1944–5. Deputy Leader, House of Lords, 1944–5; Chairman of Committees, 1965–76. Postmaster-General, 1945–7. Secretary of State for India, 1947; for Burma, 1947–8. Minister of State, Colonial Affairs, 1948–50. Joint Parliamentary Secretary, Ministry of Agriculture and Fisheries, 1950–1. Governor-General, Ghana, 1957–60.

[3] William John Haley, 1901–87. Educated at Victoria College. Sub-editor, *Manchester Evening News*, 1922; Director, 1930. Director-General, BBC, 1944–52. KCMG, 1946. Editor, *The Times*, 1952–66. Editor-in-chief, *Encyclopaedia Britannica*, 1968–9.

[4] Reproduced above (p. 394).

to yield to terrorism. The information in our possession regarding the activities of the Jewish organizations and their connection with terrorism left us no alternative but to approve the action the military authorities have now taken. Stanley was most helpful in this matter in the debate on the Adjournment.

I and my Party are in complete agreement with you in standing by the national pledges relating to the establishment of a Jewish National Home. We are still engaged in examining the recommendations of the Anglo-American Committee, though we are delayed at the moment while awaiting the arrival of President Truman's representatives. We are of course by no means committed to these recommendations, which seem clearly to involve a burden beyond our resources to carry alone.

We shall not accept any solution which represents abandonment of our pledges to the Jews or our obligations to the Arabs or which jeopardises [. . .][1]

Clement Attlee to Winston S. Churchill
(*Churchill papers, 2/42*)

5 July 1946

My dear Churchill,

I should be very glad to have a meeting with you, as Leader of the Opposition, about the handling of the Indian question in Parliament. I would propose to have with me the members of the Indian Delegation and Addison, and I expect you would wish to be accompanied by three or four of your colleagues. It would be useful to have representatives from both Houses. I am also proposing to invite Clem Davies[2] and Samuel.[3]

I hope this will be agreeable to you, and if so I suggest that we might meet after Questions at about 3.30 p.m. next Wednesday, July 10, in my room at the House of Commons.[4]

---

[1] Remainder of letter is missing.

[2] Clement Davies, 1884–1962. An expert on agricultural law. MP (Lib.) for Montgomeryshire, 1929–62. Leader of the Liberal Party, 1945–56. President, Welsh Liberal Federation, 1945–8; Parliamentary Association for World Government, 1951. One of his two sons and his only daughter were killed in action in the WWII.

[3] Herbert Louis Samuel, 1870–1963. Educated at University College School and Balliol College, Oxford. MP (Lib.) for Cleveland, 1902–18; for Darwen, 1929–35. Chancellor of the Duchy of Lancaster, 1909–10. Postmaster-General, 1910–14. President, Local Government Board, 1914–15. Home Secretary, 1916, 1931–2. Chairman, Select Committee on National Expenditure, 1917–18. Knighted, 1920. High Commissioner, Palestine, 1920–5. Chairman, Royal Commission on the Coal Industry, 1925–6. Leader, Parliamentary Liberal Party, 1931–5. Viscount, 1937. OM, 1968.

[4] Concerning the attendees of this meeting, Churchill wrote: 'Self, Eden, Rab Butler, Simon'.

Mohammed Ali Jinnah to Winston S. Churchill
(Churchill papers, 2/42)

6 July 1946   New Delhi

Dear Mr Churchill,

    It is not without deep regret that I have to say that the Cabinet Delegation and the Viceroy have, by handling the negotiations in the manner in which they did, impaired the honour of the British Government and have shaken the confidence of Muslim India and shattered their hopes for an honourable and peaceful settlement. They allowed themselves to play in the hands of Congress, who all along held out the threat of non-cooperation and civil disobedience, if they were not satisfied; and virtually, from the very beginning, adopted an aggressive and dictatorial attitude, pistol in their hand. They are determined to seize power and try to establish Caste-Hindu domination over Muslim India and the other communities inhabiting this vast sub-Continent. I hope when you go through all the relevant correspondence and hear the Mission, you will come to the same conclusion as I have indicated above. I think you will agree with me that it is not only an obsession but has become a disease with the Congress, and it is an impossibility. Even now, having wrecked the formation of the Interim Government as proposed by the Cabinet Delegation and the Viceroy in their final Statement of 16th June, they have accepted the long-term plan, not in the spirit of cooperation and to construct but to wreck it. This will be clear to you from the reservations and interpretations that they have put upon the long-term plan and which are contrary to those embodied in the Statement of the Cabinet Delegation and the Viceroy dated 16th May and their further statement of May 25th (particularly grouping of provinces).

    I therefore trust that the British Government will still avoid compelling the Mussalmans to shed their blood, for, their surrender to the Congress at the sacrifice of the Muslims can only result in that direction. If power politics are going to be the deciding factor in total disregard for fairplay and justice, we shall have no other course open to us except to forge our sanctions to meet the situation which, in that case, is bound to arise. Its consequences, I need not say, will be most disastrous and a peaceful settlement will then become impossible.

    I am writing this letter to you in confidence and to one whom I have known for a long time. Today you happen to be the Leader of the Opposition and, I hope, you will give your most earnest and careful consideration to what I have urged not without painfulness, which is apparent from my letter and you will maintain the honour of the British nation for fairplay.

    I am enclosing herewith for your information and consideration my two Statements that I have issued, in case you have not come across them; and also two editorials from the only British paper now left in India.

    I am sending a similar letter to Mr Attlee, the Prime Minister.

    This letter is strictly private, personal and confidential.

Winston S. Churchill to Sir Edward Bridges
(*Churchill papers, 2/146*)

6 July 1946

My dear Edward,

I have been looking through the despatches on the Anzio operation, of which a copy has been sent me. I consider that General Maitland-Wilson's dispatch requires a correction.

1. In the first paragraph, on page 7, he states:

'The Prime Minister said that in view of our air superiority it was unlikely that the Germans would be able to reinforce from the North. . . .'

You will see from the record which General Hollis[1] kept of this conference, No. 13 in Hist. (G) 5, that this should run:

'Some discussion then ensued on the question of whether the Germans would be able to reinforce quickly from the North. There was general agreement that this was unlikely, particularly in view of our air superiority.'

I should not therefore be called upon to accept the responsibility for pronouncing on this point.

2. Page 8, third paragraph. I think I should be more fully quoted, see my Frozen No. 892 on Page 10 of Hist. (G) 5, the relevant extracts of which read as follows:

'(1) We cannot leave the Rome situation to stagnate and fester for three months without crippling amalgamation of "Anvil"[2] and thus hampering "Overlord". We cannot go to other tasks and leave this unfinished job behind us.

(2) Today we decided in conference with General Eisenhower and Smith that orders should be prepared for two divisions for 'Shingle' with target 20 January. . . .

(4) Everything therefore turns on delaying return to the United Kingdom of remaining 56 LSTs for three weeks. How foolish it would be after having kept 75 so long to take them away at the very moment which they can render supreme service. Every effort of ingenuity must be made to fill the gap. Admiral John Cunningham says that if 56 start leaving Bizerta by 5 February convoy there will be time enough to bring them for May

---

[1] Leslie Chasemore Hollis, 1897–1963. Known as 'Jo'. Joined Royal Marine Light Infantry, 1914. Served with Grand Fleet and Harwich Force, 1915–18, including the Battle of Jutland. Asst Secretary, Committee of Imperial Defence, 1936–9. Lt-Col., 1937. Senior Asst Secretary in the Office of the War Cabinet, 1939–46. Brig., 1939. CBE, 1942. Maj.-Gen., 1943. Sole representative of the Defence Office with Churchill during the PM's illness at Carthage and recuperation at Marrakech, 1943–4. Knighted, 1946. Chief Staff Officer to the Minister of Defence, 1947–9. Commandant General, Royal Marines, 1949–52. Author of *One Marine's Tale* (1956) and *War at the Top* (1959).

[2] 'Anvil': Allied operation against the South of France, originally planned to take place simultaneously with 'Overlord', the Allied invasion across the English Channel.

"Overlord" and Captain Power[1] has furnished me with proposals, endorsed by the naval Commander-in-Chief, to achieve that end, and the only point unprovided which I can see is reconstructing these craft on reaching the United Kingdom which must be at a minimum rate of 25 a month. This should have priority over all the Admiralty construction, whether merchant ships or anti-submarine craft. I am confident dockyards can achieve this and I ask directions to be given to that effect.'

I suggest that this longer quotation should be added as a footnote, if it is not convenient to insert in the text of General Wilson's despatch.

I hope I may hear that these amendments can be made.

Winston S. Churchill to L. S. Amery
(Churchill papers, 2/145)

7 July 1946

My dear Leo,

Thank you for your letter of July 1.[2] These people cannot make up their minds about anything which moves quickly or has deep roots. I will bear what you say in mind in case I have an opportunity of making a speech on the subject.

The position in Palestine has been rendered more difficult by the scuttle from Egypt. We can no longer claim to be disinterested in view of the strategic importance of a base somewhere near the Suez Canal.

Winston S. Churchill to Clement Attlee
(Churchill papers, 2/4)

8 July 1946
Private

My dear Prime Minister,

Your letter of July 4 in regard to broadcasting. I understand there is to be a meeting on this subject between the Parties and the BBC, and I shall be

---

[1] Arthur John Power, 1889–1960. Entered RN, 1904. On active service during WWI. Married, 1918, Amy Bingham (d. 1945): three children; 1947, Margaret Joyce Watson. CVO, 1936. CO, HMS *Ark Royal*, 1938–40. Flag Capt. and Chief Staff Officer to RAdm. of Aircraft Carriers, Home Fleet, 1938–40. A Lord Commissioner of the Admiralty and ACNS, 1940–2. CB, 1941. RAdm. Commanding 15th Cruiser Sqn, 1942–3. Flag Officer-in-Charge, Malta, 1943. KCB, 1944. C-in-C, East Indies Station, 1944–5. GBE, 1946. A Lord Commissioner of the Admiralty and Chief of Naval Personnel (2nd Sea Lord), 1946–8. C-in-C, Mediterranean Station, 1948–50; Portsmouth, 1950–2. GCB, 1950. Naval C-in-C, 1951–2. First and Principal Naval ADC to King George VI, 1951–2. Allied C-in-C, Channel and Southern North Sea Command, 1952–3.

[2] Reproduced above (p. 393).

very glad to nominate two or three of my friends to meet an equal number of yours. The exact scope of the discussion had better be arranged through 'the usual channels'.

I am glad you agree with me as to the desirability of resuming political broadcasting. I must, however, make it clear that the position in which we now stand is entirely different from the days of the Coalition. Then there was a National Government based on the official representation of the three larger or historic Parties. Now we have a purely Party Government interpreted in the strictest manner. Also, in those days we were engaged in a war of potentially mortal character. Now there is no fighting going on any more. These two points of difference between the present and former position are fundamental.

We cannot admit that Mr Morrison's broadcast was uncontroversial. It was no doubt a very good statement of the Government case. We request opportunities for putting forward our own point of view.

Of course, there may be topics on which there would be no controversy, and we should welcome statements from the chosen representatives of His Majesty's Government. These ought to be agreed upon beforehand. It would be a very wrong thing if this modern and potent instrument of propaganda were used unfairly and one-sidedly between the two halves of the nation.

Pray excuse me for putting these points to you, because I am sure you will feel they ought to be discussed between us in order to see if there is any chance of agreement.

Anthony Eden to Winston S. Churchill
(Churchill papers, 2/495)[1]

9 July 1946

My dear Winston,

On my return home I found the lovely medallion you have designed and given to the colleagues who served under you in the great coalition. Thank you so much for it; and for the thought that prompted such a memorable gift.

I cannot suppose that any of us, even were we to live for more than a hundred years, can ever again know such stupendous times. For all their suffering I am glad to have lived through them, and proud to have done so much under your leadership. Thank you for this enduring memory of them.

---

[1] This letter was handwritten.

July 1946

Winston S. Churchill to Lieutenant-Colonel John Astor
(Churchill papers, 2/145)

13 July 1946
Personal and Private

My dear John,

I thank you for yours of June 26,[1] and I am very glad you were not offended at my outspoken letter on a subject about which I feel deeply.

I should like very much to talk things over one of these days. I have a high respect for you and the work you do. I know your love of the Country, and I am very conscious of the fallibility of judgment.

Winston S. Churchill to Leslie Rowan
(Churchill papers, 2/6)

13 July 1946

My dear Leslie,

What is the position about the motor car that was to be presented to Ibn Saud by me? Considering he gave various presents to me and to the Foreign Secretary, one would like the personal contact to be maintained. How does the matter stand? Of course, the bulk of the expense must be found by the British Government, nevertheless we handed over to them the valuable presents we received.

I should be sorry not to be able to pay a personal courtesy to Ibn Saud, though of course it should be stated that the gift was also on behalf of His Majesty's Government.[2]

Winston S. Churchill: speech
(Churchill papers, 5/7)

14 July 1946   Metz, France

FRANCE AND EUROPE

Many memories are stirred in my mind by this visit to Metz and your joyous welcome. Sixty-three years ago my father took me on my first visit to France. It was in the summer of 1883. We drove along together through the Place de

[1] Reproduced above (pp. 390–1).
[2] Attlee wrote to Ibn Saud on July 10: 'Your Majesty, The Rolls-Royce car which is now being delivered to Your Majesty was first offered by Mr Churchill as a gift from His Majesty's Government. It now falls to me to associate myself and my colleagues with this gift and to express the hope that this British car will serve you well and testify in some small degree to the very close and cordial relations between our two countries.'

la Concorde. Being an observant child I noticed that one of the monuments was covered with wreaths and crepe and I at once asked him why. He replied, 'These are monuments of the Provinces of France. Two of them, Alsace and Lorraine, have been taken from France by the Germans at war. The French are very unhappy about it and hope some day to get them back.' I remember quite distinctly thinking to myself, 'I hope they will get them back.' This hope at least has not been disappointed.

Many years passed before I attended the manoeuvres of the French Army in 1907. The Entente Cordiale had been established between Great Britain and France. I was already a youthful Minister of the Crown. In those days the soldiers wore blue tunics and red trousers and many of the movements were still in close order. When I saw, at the climax of the manoeuvres, the great masses of French infantry storming the position, while the bands played *Marseillaise*, I felt that by those valiant bayonets the rights of man had been gained and then by them these rights and also the liberties of Europe would be faithfully guarded. That was nearly 40 years ago, but from that moment I have always worked with you not only out of friendship for France but because of the great causes for which our two countries have suffered so much and risked all. The road has been long and terrible. I am astonished to find myself here at the end of it. In all that ordeal of two generations our countries have marched and struggled side by side and I, your guest here today, have never neglected anything that could preserve and fortify our united action. Therefore I speak to you not only as a friend but as a lifelong comrade. In all the frightful experiences we have undergone in our resistance to German aggression and tyranny our two countries have struggled along together to keep the flag of freedom flying and at an awful and hideous cost we have accomplished our duty. Never let us part.

I come now to the 20 years between the two Great Wars. The manpower and much of the physical and moral strength of France was exhausted by the sacrifices she had made for the victory in 1918. The world must never forget that two million Frenchmen gave their lives. With the British Empire it was a million but from a far larger population. The injury inflicted by the First Great War upon the life-energies of France was profound. Crowned with victory, lighted by glory she was drained of blood. Britain, in one of those strange reactions which have so often baffled our friends and foes alike, sank into pacifism and the US, with all her might and power, sought a vain refuge in isolation. These were all disasters of the first magnitude.

There never was a war more easy to prevent than this last horror through which we have passed. All that was needed was to enforce the disarmament clauses of the Treaty of Versailles and to make sure that Germany did not rearm. All that was needed was to assert the principle that solemn treaties, exacted from a beaten enemy, can only be altered by mutual agreement. In the League of Nations there was erected a noble instrument which, even without the aid of the United States, if it had been given a fair chance, could have maintained the disarmament of Germany and preserved the peace of Europe. But the Allies drifted amicably but helplessly like froth upon the ebb and flow of the tide. There is no need to apportion the blame. We have all endured the punishment, and at the end we are still alive with the future in our hands to make or mar. We have many troubles and privations to endure. There are many trials before us. But our hearts should be full of thankfulness to God that we have been preserved from the most hideous forms of destruction.

Now I come to the Second World War; not so bloody, as measured by men killed in the open field, but far more frightful and desperate. I was called upon to play some part in its events and every stage and crisis is burnt into my mind. Never have I allowed the slightest recrimination between Britain and France and never must you allow the slightest recrimination between France and Britain. History will tell its tale, for us both, of tragedy, of triumph and of honour.

It has woven our two peoples together in a manner indissoluble and inviolable. We fought each other for many centuries. And now we must help each other all we can. Shame be to any who deny this vital fact. There may be pity for those who let the ordinary worries and divergences of the daily and yearly life of nations destroy their sense of proportion and of historical continuity, but we must make sure these weaklings do not rule the future. We cannot afford to be misled or to indulge in short-term policies. Vision, courage, self-denial, faith and faithful service must animate us. And when the light does not shine clearly on our path, we must not lose heart, for I am sure – as sure as I was in 1940 – that we shall steadfastly and preservingly make our way through.

When President Roosevelt and I decided (with the support of our Governments and military men) upon the Anglo-American liberation of French North-West Africa in 1942 and in the early stages of that vast operation, General Giraud and I gave each other *rendezvous at Metz*. Well here we are. The General – he is a deputy now – and I have this in common; we shall both find a chapter in the future editions of memorable escapes. I have escaped as a prisoner-of-war and no prison has ever been able to hold him. It gives me great pleasure to salute him here in his native city where he has exercised high command and enjoys the highest esteem. When my comrade, General de Gaulle – that unconquerable French spirit – received me so splendidly in Paris in November 1944, I told him about this rendezvous at Metz and he said it must take place. I do not pretend we have never had any disagreements but we were thoroughly agreed on this. Yes, and also we have neither of us ever lost hope in the greatness of France, of the conviction that victory would be won.

There are two issues which are specially appropriate to this occasion. The first is Europe. What will be the fate of Europe? Here in this continent of superior climates dwell the parent breeds of western and modern civilization. Here is the story, descending from the ancient Roman Empire, of Christendom, of the Renaissance, and of the French Revolution. It is from the hatreds and quarrels of Europe that the catastrophes of the whole world have sprung. Shall we reestablish again the glory of Europe and thus consolidate the foundations of Peace? Why should the quarrels of Europe wreck the gigantic modern world? Twice in our lifetimes we have seen the brave and generous people of the US spend their treasure and their blood to procure harmony in Europe and to rescue Europe from itself. Twice has the British Empire and the Commonwealth of Nations plunged into the Continental struggle to prevent the overlordship of Germany. Twice has our heroic ally, Russia, poured out its blood in European battles. This time we must reach finality. Europe must arise from her ruin and spare the world a third and possibly fatal holocaust.

We victors have set up together the United Nations Organisation to which we give our loyalty and in which we found our hopes. At the head of this stands the United States of America in all her power and virtue. But without the aid of a united Europe the great new world organization may easily be rent asunder or evaporate in futility because of the explosions which originate in Europe and may once again bring all mankind into strife and misery. Therefore the first word I give you here today is 'Europe'. May she regain her happiness and may her small, as well as her great, nations dwell together in security and peace. May there be a decent life achieved and set up for Europeans. May they all be faithful servants and guardians of the World Organisation on which the dearest hopes of tortured humanity are centred. My second word is 'France'. There can be no revival of Europe with its culture, its charm, its tradition and its mighty power, without a strong France. Many nations in the past have wished and tried to be strong. But never before has there been such a clear need for one country to be strong as there is now for France. When I think of the young Frenchmen growing into manhood in this shattered and bewildered world, I cannot recall any generation in any country before whose eyes duty is written more plainly or in more gleaming characters. Two hundred years ago in England the Elder and the greater Pitt addressed the invocation to his fellow-countrymen, torn, divided and confused by fraction as they then were. 'Be one people.' That was his famous invocation. And in our island, for all its fogs and muddles, we are one people today and dangers if they threaten will only bind us more firmly together. Using my privilege as your old and faithful friend, I do not hesitate to urge upon all Frenchmen, worn or worried though they may be, to unite in the task of leading Europe back in peace and freedom to broader and better days. By saving yourselves you will save Europe and by saving Europe you will save yourselves.

408　July 1946

Lord Cherwell to Winston S. Churchill
(Churchill papers, 5/7)[1]

17 July 1946

Is the decision to ration bread based upon long-term or upon short-term considerations? If short-term, we shall save at most 35,000 in five weeks, surely a trivial amount.

If long-term, it implies the decision today without awaiting the outcome of harvests in the exporting countries to cut bread consumption in this country. Indeed it might almost be held to forgo claims we have on the wheat pool in advance. Or is there perhaps some graver argument, such as shortage of foreign exchange, which makes the Government determine in advance that they will be unable to purchase the wheat required to give us unlimited bread in the coming year?

Sarah Churchill to Winston S. Churchill
(Churchill papers, 1/42)[2]

18 July 1946

Darling Papa,

I am afraid I could not wait as I have a luncheon engagement. I only came to kiss you and say, 'Wow'. Mary told me Metz was most thrilling. Hope to see you soon. Good luck for this afternoon. Wow – rewow and my love.

Winston S. Churchill: speech
('The Sinews of Peace', pages 176–84)

18 July 1946　　　　　　　　　　　　　　　　　　　　　House of Commons

INDIA (CABINET MISSION)

Everyone is glad to see that the right hon. and learned Gentleman's (Sir Stafford Cripps's) health is restored. We were anxious about him when he was in India because naturally these long, intense, soul-stirring conferences with the Mahatma Gandhi and Mr Nehru,[3] accompanied by the exceptionally hot

---

[1] Lord Cherwell dictated this note for Churchill after having read a draft of Churchill's speech on bread rationing (reproduced below, pp. 415–22).

[2] This letter was handwritten.

[3] Jawaharlal Nehru, 1889–1964. Educated (as was Churchill) at Harrow. Barrister-at-law, Inner Temple, 1912. Member, All-India Congress Committee, 1918–47. President, Indian National Congress, 1929. Imprisoned by the British several times, for his political activities and calls for non-co-operation. Vice-President, Interim Government of India, 1946. PM of India from 1947 until his death. Both his daughter, Indira Gandhi, and his grandson, Rajiv Gandhi, were subsequently Prime Ministers of India; both were assassinated.

weather of the Indian summer, might well have imposed a very severe strain upon him, but we are glad to see today that his health is restored. He has certainly given us a very long and categorical statement of the Mission on which he has been engaged with two other Members of the Government. I shall not attempt to follow him in any proportionate length. I hope he will not think it disrespectful on my part if I do not attempt to make a reply covering the entire ground, because I thought we were all agreed that it is better to put off the general Debate upon this tremendous event in the history of India, and in our history, until we meet again in the autumn. If everyone were to do full justice to all the aspects upon which the right hon. and learned Gentleman has touched, it is perfectly certain that we should only reach our other attractive topic of bread rationing at a very late hour tonight.

We shall see more clearly, I think, in the autumn how matters stand, and we shall see the outlines, at any rate, of the decisions which have to be taken. The Government have promised a full dress Debate at a convenient moment, and the Mission recommends, by implication, the postponement of the discussion until then. When we return after the recess, we shall have that Debate, and all I wish to do now is to put on record some of the principal divergencies which separate us, as well as recognizing the points to which we are all committed.

For good or ill, we are all committed to the offer made at the time of what I may call the Cripps Mission in the spring of 1942. That offer was made at the moment when the Japanese held full naval command of the Bay of Bengal, and it seemed that India might be invaded and ravaged by a large Japanese army. I, as Prime Minister, took my full share of responsibility in those circumstances for making the offer of 1942. Those days of peril are gone. Although we received no assistance from the Congress Party in India, whose attitude throughout the war was one of non-co-operation, in spite of that, 2,000,000 or more Indians volunteered to fight for the cause of freedom. The Congress Party gave us no assistance; on the contrary, they did us the greatest injury in their power, but the disorders were easily suppressed and the danger of foreign invasion was warded off.

Mr Cove[1] (Aberavon): What did the Muslim League do?

Mr Churchill: The Muslim League did not give active co-operation as a League, but the Punjab State alone produced upwards of 800,000 volunteers. The remarkable thing, since I am drawn into this by this interruption, is that the political parties did not at all sway the influence and actions of the Indian millions. Millions of men volunteered, without conscription, to fight, and great numbers gave their aid in war work, and the political parties, who are the only parties with whom the government are dealing, had no means of controlling the enthusiasm and loyalty of their people.

Nevertheless, although, as I say, we got no assistance, we declared that the offer which we had made should stand. The present Government had,

[1] William George Cove, 1888–1963. MP (Lab.) for Wellingborough, 1923–9; for Aberavon, 1929–49.

therefore, a right to our agreement and support in sending out the Mission of Cabinet Ministers, who have just returned after arduous experiences. The directions given to the Mission, however, went beyond, and, as I hold, needlessly beyond, those which governed the wartime Cripps Mission of 1942. The Coalition offer was, as the right hon. and learned Gentleman has just reminded us, of Dominion status, which includes, of course, the Clause in the Statute of Westminster, what we might call the escalator Clause, which affirmed the right of secession, in the last resort, from the British Commonwealth of Nations by any Dominion. The Coalition offer was also conditional upon agreement being reached between the principal parties in India, so that the offer of full Dominion status including the right to secede, would not lead to disastrous, and possibly devastating civil war.

His Majesty's present Government went beyond the offer of 1942. They instructed their delegates to offer full independence directly, instead of Dominion status, which left the final decision open to a fully-constituted Dominion of India, after seeing how they were getting on and how the general situation lay. So far as I can see, the result which is now put before us – and nothing in the speech of the right hon. and learned Gentleman in any way detracts from it – is the immediate independence of India and the severance of all constitutional ties uniting the former Indian Empire to the British Commonwealth of Nations. I wish to register my dissent from this extension and short-circuiting of the original offer. The responsibility for making the further advance and for pressing full and immediate independence upon India, without giving Indians a chance to get into the saddle and look around to see where their broad interests lie – the responsibility for that is the responsibility of the present Government, and I, for my part, can share no part of that responsibility. I consider that this short-circuiting or telescoping of the normal and reasonable constitutional processes upon which both parties were agreed does not give the best chance of a happy or peaceful solution of the Indian problem, and that, having regard to the elements in India to whom the Government mainly addressed themselves, it prejudges, in an adverse sense, the case of whether the vast sub-continent of India, with its population of 400,000,000, should remain, of its own free will, within the circle of the association of the British Commonwealth. The Government had the power to make this change and theirs is the responsibility for making it. That is all I am concerned to establish today. I am not going to trespass, if I can avoid it, upon merits. I am merely showing where we lie in the relationship to this formidable and enormous topic.

Secondly, the offer of 1942 was conditional upon agreement being reached among the principal forces and parties in the life of India. This has certainly not been achieved. The Mission proceeded themselves to shape the outlines of the settlement, and to endeavour, as far as possible, to induce all the elements concerned to agree to it as a working basis. Again, I do not challenge the right of the Government to take this action, for which, no doubt, they have a large Parliamentary majority. I am only trying to make it clear that, in this respect also – the question of agreement – the Government have gone beyond any position to which I and my colleagues in the National Coalition Government were committed by the offer of 1942. I do not think that the right hon. and learned Gentleman denies that.

Sir S. Cripps: Will the right hon. Gentleman allow me? Surely, the right hon. Gentleman will agree that I had precisely the same job to do in 1942? I took a scheme which was got out by the Government and I tried to get both parties to agree to it. That is exactly what has happened in this case.

Mr Churchill: My point was that the right hon. and learned Gentleman took out a different scheme. As a great precision man, and a man of the highest legalistic attainments, a small point like that ought not to have escaped his notice.

Sir S. Cripps: The right hon. Gentleman is very amusing, but not quite accurate. What he was saying was that we ought not to have imposed some settlement, but that it should be a condition that both parties agreed to it, and that, in this case, they had not agreed to it and it was something which we had imposed upon them. I was pointing out that, in 1942, under the right hon. Gentleman's Government, a scheme was got out by the Cabinet in London and was sent out, and my object was to try to get both parties to agree to a scheme which was sent out from London. The right hon. Gentleman cannot complain that what we have done now is to get two parties to agree to a scheme.

Mr Churchill: In the first place, the right hon. and learned Gentleman has not got the two parties to agree; they are in the most violent disagreement, and their passion is mounting day by day. In the second place, the scheme which he took out was a different one. In the third place, when that scheme did not commend itself to those to whom he addressed himself, he took the positive action – and I do not say he was wrong from his point of view to do it – of trying to solve the Indian problem for the Indians instead of leaving it to the Indians to solve, or not to solve. He took the positive course of trying to solve it, and proposed a basis on which he hoped they would come together.

Sir S. Cripps: As in 1942.

Mr Churchill: In 1942, the right hon. Gentleman had no authorisation to attempt to make a separate declaration apart from any view built up between Indians, as he has done now. I am not making this a complaint against the right hon. and learned Gentleman; I can quite see that when they were there and nobody would agree to anything, the third party came in and said, 'Let us have a try. Won't you agree to this?' All I say is, that it is quite different from the proposals to which we agreed.

There is a third point of great importance, namely, the faithful discharge of our obligations, contracted over so many years and affirmed by so many British Governments, to the various minorities in India. I was sorry that in his speech of, I think, 15 March, the Prime Minister should have spoken in a somewhat adverse, or at least uncertain sense, about the rights of minorities, because the protection of those fundamental rights affects our duty to discharge the pledges which we have so often given. These minorities in India are very considerable. The right hon. and learned Gentleman has mentioned several of them today. There are, for instance, the 40 to 60 million of the depressed classes who are consternated by the lack of representation which they are to receive in the future Constituent Assembly. I have received most vehement and painful appeals from the leaders of these great communities, and I discussed them with my colleagues on this side of the House.

When one speaks of a community as large as 60 million, the word 'minority' loses much of its significance. Such immense masses of human beings deserve to be treated with respect and consideration, positively and not relatively, even if there are other and still larger masses who take a different view. After all, in these islands we have only 46 million, a much smaller number than the depressed classes of India. We should be sorry just to be called a minority by Europe and to have our way of life ordered for us by a mass vote of all the other countries. In fact, I think that we should very likely recur, with satisfaction, to our insular position. When the issue affecting minorities numbered by scores of millions is also one which concerns the fundamental rights of those minorities, all pledges with regard to them require most scrupulous attention by the ruling authority at the moment it hands over these masses, with their fate and their fortunes, to another system of Government. That is a point which, I trust, will not be found to be one of difference in principle, although there may be difference in emphasis.

Then there are the Muslims – who number over 80 million – and make up so large a majority of the martial races of India. There is no doubt that there is a complete lack of agreement at the present time between the two principal communities. The Mission have laboured hard, and they have dealt particularly with these two communities, allowing many other valuable and important forces, who have a right to live also, to fall back into the background. As between these two communities, the difficulties were never more acute and the gulf never more wide than at the present moment. The outlook is very grave. The acceptance by the martial races of the final settlement which we shall make before we leave India is indispensable to future peace.

Thirdly, among the elements which go to make up India, are the Indian States which, together, comprise nearly 95 million. The position of these States has been fixed by solemn treaties made with their rulers. It is proposed to abrogate those treaties and to abolish the principle of paramountcy which, at present, alone defines the relationship of these States – in some cases almost nations, in some cases models of good government in India – to whatever new Central Government is set up in India. If all the minorities are added together, they constitute much more than half the inhabitants of India. I am glad to say that, as far as I understand the position, His Majesty's Government have not abandoned the principle of the discharge of their responsibilities towards the minorities in India which aggregate at least 225 million out of 400 million. I hope we shall hear from the First Lord of the Admiralty that they have not abandoned their responsibilities in that matter.

The attitude of the Mission, and of the Government whom they represented, is expressed on this point in a single sentence of the plan which they put before the representatives of Indian life with whom they dealt. This is the sentence:

> 'When the constituent Assembly has completed its labours, His Majesty's Government will recommend to Parliament such action as may be necessary for the cession of sovereignty to the Indian people subject only to two provisos which are mentioned in the statement and which are not, we believe, controversial, namely, adequate provision for the protection of minorities, and willingness to conclude a treaty to cover matters arising out of the transfer of power.'

This seems to me to be a somewhat light, optimistic and almost casual manner of treating responsibilities extending to an appreciable part of a human race and touching those fundamental rights – life, liberty and the pursuit of happiness – which we have regarded as the birthright of every human being. It makes it clear, however, and all I desire to do is to emphasise this by putting on record that all arrangements to be made by the Constituent Assembly, and any treaties which may subsequently be brought into existence between the Crown and Parliament of Great Britain and the new sovereign independent Government of India, must be subject to the fulfilment of the honourable discharge of our obligations. I hope we are agreeable on that. I hope we are not going to hear a contradiction from the First Lord on that. A Bill, or perhaps several Bills, will have to be presented to Parliament and will have to pass through all their stages, and that is the time when the final decision will have to be taken. Nothing must be agreed to by us at the moment of the transference of sovereignty which will be in derogation of our solemn undertaking.

I cannot conclude without referring to the question of the interim Government, in respect of which the right hon. and learned Gentleman gave us a full exposition. A great part of the Mission's work in India was devoted to the vain attempt to form a coalition cabinet acceptable alike to the Muslims and to the caste Hindus, and this Cabinet was to replace the Viceroy's Executive Council which was dismissed in order to clear the decks and make room for the new government. There was to be no change for the time being in the constitutional position. What it has led to is a temporary reversion in so far as personnel is concerned, to a government of well-tried and experienced officials. In fact, for the moment, but only for the moment, Indian affairs have gone full circle, and we are back again at the system of 40 years ago before the Morley–Minto reforms. Everyone can see that this cannot last very long. Moreover, from the reports which I have received from India, the Muslim community feel themselves deeply aggrieved by what they regard as a departure from the terms of Paragraph 8 of the statement of 16 June made by the Cabinet delegation and the Viceroy. This statement runs as follows:

> 'In the event of the two major parties or either of them proving unwilling to join in the setting up of a coalition government on the above lines, it is the intention of the Viceroy to proceed with the formation of an interim government which will be as representative as possible of those willing to accept the statement of 16 May.'

The Muslim League agreed to enter this, and when the Hindu Congress members refused, or it broke down on this point of procedure, I understand that the Muslim League made a violent complaint. I see the force of the right hon. and learned Gentleman's argument that it is very difficult to form a coalition with only one party, or even to form a coalition and fill it up with civil servants and non-party figures. I believe that would be a difficulty. At the same time, there is the feeling among the Muslims of India that faith has been broken with them. I am not making that charge. On the contrary, I can see that it is a misunderstanding, but there is no doubt that there is a serious misunderstanding.

Sir S. Cripps: I would like to correct one point as regards the timing. The right hon. Gentleman said that the Muslims accepted and then Congress refused. But Congress had refused before the Muslims arrived at any decision, and they knew before they arrived at a decision that it was useless for them to arrive at a decision because already the scheme had gone.

Mr Churchill: I am not making an accusation against the Government in the matter. I am sure the right hon. and learned Gentleman does not deal with people in bad faith, and those gentlemen who were there may have been misunderstood. There has been a serious misunderstanding, but the consequences of the misunderstanding carry us forward into the future The General Secretary of the Muslim League has gone so far as to say that unless the situation is clarified, it would be suicidal for the League to enter into a Constituent Assembly. All this appears to raise the most formidable issues, because I can assure the Government – and those who have been to India know well – that the agreement of the Muslims to the new system affects the whole foundation of the problem. One cannot contemplate that British troops should be used to crush the Muslims in the interests of the caste Hindus. Whatever our responsibilities may be, whatever may be the day appointed on which we quit India, we must not make ourselves the agents of a caste Government, or a particular sectional Government in order to crush by armed force and modern weapons, another community which, although not so numerous, is numbered at 90 millions.

July 1946

Winston S. Churchill: speech
('Winston S. Churchill, His Complete Speeches', volume 7, pages 7365–72)

18 July 1946   House of Commons

BREAD RATIONING

I beg to move,

That the Bread (Rationing) Order, 1946, dated 12 July, 1946 (S. R. & O., 1946, No. 1100), a copy of which was presented on 15 July, be annulled.

We have given the most careful consideration to, and we have had long discussions among ourselves upon, all the statements and figures which have been given to us on this subject by His Majesty's Government, and as the result we cannot feel convinced that the imposition of bread rationing is necessary on 21 July. Unless some new fact is disclosed which we do not now know, we shall be bound to vote against the imposition of this heavy, awkward, galling burden at this time. I will now proceed to examine *seriatim* the reasons which have so far been vouchsafed to us. The Minister of Food (An Hon. Member: 'Here is your man.') I am glad to see him safely out of the oven. The Minister's case has rested upon the state of the pipeline of 31 August, 1946. The 'pipeline' is his own expression, a very good expression, and it is on the state of that chain of moving supplies on 31 August that he rests his case. We are told that the pipeline will contain only eight weeks' supply, and that we use 100,000 tons a week – actually, I think we use a little more, 112,000 tons – whereas we have worked in the war to ten and a half weeks' supply and made that a necessary precautionary essential. We are told that less than eight weeks' supply in the pipeline will endanger distribution, at any rate in particular localities.

Somewhere below the figure of 800,000 tons – these are the words of the right hon. Gentleman the Minister of Food – there would come a point where the distribution system of the country, first of the wheat, and then of the flour after it had been milled, would begin to creak and groan, and finally break down. We cannot, he argues, run that risk. But by 31 August we reap the new home harvest. At least between 200,000 and 300,000 tons of this harvest will be garnered in September – and perhaps more may be accelerated by special measures – and the rest, amounting in the end to over 1,700,000 tons, can be garnered and delivered to the millers, as may be needed from October onwards, by arrangements which can easily be made now. We have not been told what other supplies will reach us from abroad in August and September. In September, the Minister is counting on 250,000 tons from our own harvest. So we need import only about 150,000 tons to maintain the pipeline above the danger point.

Why should this be so difficult? In September, 1944, a bad year, with the war going on, we imported 292,000 tons of wheat across the U-boat blockade.

In September last year, we imported 318,000 tons of wheat. Why should we not be able to import 150,000 tons of wheat in September? Have we left it too late? If so, tell us so. In matters of this kind it is much better to tell the truth. This country is not afraid of facing ugly facts. We would not be here now if we had shrunk from that. I must say that, so far as I am aware – I have endeavoured to get all the information possible from those who know about the state of this trade – there is no difficulty in importing 150,000 tons, and indeed, far more than that, in September. After September we have the whole of the home harvest within our reach to draw on as we think fit, and although the problem of our bread supply may remain, its urgency will have vanished. Spring may bring other troubles, but the urgency will have vanished. The latest published harvest estimates of the four great exporting countries – Canada, the United States of America, the Argentine and Australia – are now declared to be 10,000,000 tons in excess of the statistics given in the April White Paper. Therefore, on the facts now before us – I emphasise 'now before us' because it is the crux on which I rest my argument – it is clear that any imminent danger will have passed by 31 August. Why, then, is there this need of bread rationing on 21 July? That is the point we have to settle tonight.

There could hardly have been selected a more inconvenient date for the introduction of bread rationing, because so many people are away from their homes, or about to go away, on their annual and hard-won holidays. I will speak of the difficulties and confusion of this scheme, so hurriedly conceived, in a few minutes. But I return to the point which I am making – What is the reason for bringing this scheme into operation on 21 July? It cannot, certainly, be on account of the valuable savings which are to be made in bread consumption by the declared scale of rationing during the five weeks involved. What are those savings? They are estimated by the Government now as a maximum – I am taking the best figure for them – of seven per cent of consumption in a whole year. In the five weeks concerned, the saving amounts only to about 40,000 tons, or 1/5 of the 200,000 tons that the Lord President of the Council agreed to forgo when he visited the United States of America. The Lord President agreed to forgo two weeks' supply – the critical two weeks' supply. Now, to save less than three days' supply, we are to take upon ourselves all the inconveniences and friction of the present scheme of bread rationing beginning on Sunday next. I cannot believe that this petty saving is the true reason of the Government's serious decision.

Let us, then, continue our search for that reason. The next explanation which presents itself for the Government's anxiety to start rationing is that they anticipate a serious long-term shortage of wheat, and desire to prepare for it. The proposed ration scale, yielding a saving of only seven per cent per annum, would certainly be no remedy for a serious long-term shortage of world wheat. It was for that reason that, when nearly one month ago the Minister of Food announced his intention to ration bread, I immediately formed the impression that cuts far more formidable than would be enforced at the beginning would be imposed upon us later on, once the rationing scheme was in working order.

I do not think that the Minister of Food was entitled to be vexed with me or surprised that I came to that conclusion, because I remember that the Lord President had said on 31st May that, of course, if it should become necessary for him – that is, the Minister of Food – to economise in consumption then this machinery would be there ready for the purpose. I thought that meant that it would be put up on a certain scale and, if serious economies were necessary, it would be turned on, as it would have to be turned on. I have been given a quotation, which I did not hear with my own ears, but which I have verified, in which he said on the same day:

> The purpose is, as my right hon. Friend –
> The Lord President of the Council –
> has said already, above all, to give us control of the situation . . . we are sailing . . . into a storm area . . . but we are determined to go into that storm area with the capacity and the ability to shorten sail –

in this connection 'shorten sail' means to cut the ration –

> at the shortest notice if that proves necessary. – (Official Report, 31 May, 1946; Vol. 423, c. 1575.)

The right hon. Gentleman, who has had so many burdens come upon him at the beginning of his career as a Minister of Cabinet rank, resented what I said, and since then he has given repeated assurances that the scales contained in the Order now before us – which we are praying this House now to annul – are the worst we have to expect. I have certainly understood, and I think there are repeated quotations to confirm, that he has said that they are the worst we have to expect, but if I am wrong by all means let us be told. Ought we to reach this point in this long discussion and not know a thing like that?

The Minister of Food (Mr Strachey) indicated dissent.

Mr Churchill: We have an uncertain shake of the head from the Minister. The assurances have been given all over the country, and repeated everywhere, that this is the maximum scale of cuts that is to be imposed – those contained in the Schedule to this Order. Where do we stand? I was very much struck with that uncertain lateral movement of the Minister's head. Does the right hon. Gentleman know where he is? (Hon. Members: 'Yes'.) Then, rejoicing in that happy position, let him tell us where we are. Where do we stand on this question of future reductions of the present bread ration scale? Why be afraid to tell the British public the truth? If we have to take it, we can take it, but a Government that is afraid to tell people what they are going to be up against will not get the confidence of those people in enduring the hardships. I am glad to see the hon. Lady the Member for West Fulham (Dr Edith Summerskill)[1] taking her place and hope that she has completely recovered from the distressing accident about which we were all much concerned.

The Minister has told us in the House that there is no question of the ration being reduced. Moreover, far from threatening further cuts, he has hinted and more than hinted at the early removal of bread rationing altogether. Where do we stand? Some doubt was thrown, I admit, on these assurances by the speech of the Minister of Agriculture last Saturday when he said:

> If there should be any possibility of the United States defaulting on the 467,000 tons of wheat we are expecting from them, or of the British farmers failing to deliver the 570,000 tons for which they have been asked –

I suppose within a certain time –

> our bread rationing would not only be necessary but the allocation, which is bare enough, would have to be reduced.

What is the position of the Government? I ask the Minister of Food, or the Prime Minister, specifically here and now across the Table, whether they adhere to their statement that the scale of bread rations in this Order now before us will not be further reduced? Is that true or is it not true? (Hon. Members: 'Answer'.) I ask the Prime Minister, Is it true or is it not true that what he is proposing now is a final ration scale so far as the immediate year to which we are concerned is involved? Is it or is it not? The Prime Minister cannot answer; he may think it very wily tactics at the head of a great majority to take refuge in the obscure recesses of silence, but out of doors people want to know what are the facts and what is the true position. Right hon. Gentlemen have no right to reproach us with opposing them upon this matter, when they cannot answer and when they think it better to sit glum and mum, in the hope that the storm will blow over. I call the attention of the House to the fact that no answer has been given as to whether these ration scales are to be decreased or not. (Hon. Members: 'Wait'.) After all, this has all been talked about for a month, and so many pledges have been given to us that one would have thought that the Minister could say, 'I stick to what I have said; there will be no increased cuts and, more than that, I hope to take off rationing.' Does the Minister run away from that now or can he say 'Yes' or 'No'? Already these triumphant leaders of victorious democracy along the bench opposite are far on the road to becoming a line of extinct volcanoes. There is not even a little geyser to show that they are alive.

---

[1] Edith Clara Summerskill, 1901–80. Earned an MRCS and LRCP, 1924. Married, 1925, Edward Jeffrey Samuel, but did not take his name. MP (Lab.) for West Fulham, 1938–55; for Warrington, 1955–61. Member, Labour Party National Executive Committee, 1944–58; Chairman, 1954–5. Parliamentary Secretary, Ministry of Food, 1945–50. Minister of National Insurance, 1950–1. Parliamentary Member, Political Honours Scrutiny Committee, 1967–76.

After saying that, I draw attention of the House to the fact that the right hon. Gentleman has thrown a great deal of doubt upon the statement which he made that there will be no additional cut in the ration. Of course, if the right hon. Gentleman, as soon as he gets this system into operation, is going to turn the screw sharp and hard, and put on very much more serious rationing, with much more severe cuts, then that at least is an explanation. It is a sad and sombre explanation, but at least it is something one can understand. If it is not true that rations are to be cut more severely, we are irresistibly driven to the conclusion that no case has been made for the institution of bread rationing. If we are to be told that this is the prelude to further cuts, and that this is to give facilities for shortening sail, to any extent that may be necessary, the Government may be greatly censured, but nevertheless, the measures that they put forward may be the only ones possible for us in our unfortunate position. That is the second point I make. Do the Government stand by their statement that this Order contains the worst we have to expect in the next six months or so? I suppose we shall get an answer when the right hon. Gentleman speaks.

Mr Strachey indicated assent.

Mr Churchill: Why it should be kept a secret till then I do not know. I only asked the right hon. Gentleman whether he was going to keep his word or not, but if he likes to reserve himself on that point, very well. We contrast the smallness of the saving with the immense amount of hardship, and we are left wondering what is the reason for this violent act, unless there is to be a big increase in the cut. On the statements which have been made to us, the need is not apparent, and if the need be proved, the remedy appears wholly ineffective. It is like using a steamhammer to crack a nut when there is nothing in the nut. That is the impression we have so far derived from all we have been told.

Since the bread shortage was first bruited abroad, the season has progressed. It is now possible to estimate with good assurance the harvests of the great food-exporting countries. We may base ourselves on the promise of bumper harvests in 1946. Whereas in the five years 1935–39 the average total of 37 million tons of wheat was reaped, in the four great wheat-exporting countries, last year's harvest was 46 million tons, and the comparable figure for this year is estimated at 55 million tons, or 17 million tons above the prewar average. Moreover, British home production has made a very considerable increase – 30 per cent or 40 per cent – over what it was before the war. Is that not so? Therefore it would seem that the Minister is on safe ground in promising not to make further cuts in the ration scale and also in holding out hopes of the speedy removal of bread rationing.

Where is his case for making this Order operative on 21 July? It is indeed a strange chain of circumstances which the right hon. Gentleman, and those with whom he acts, have to explain – bumper harvests, peaceful and open seas, Socialist planning, and yet, with all these blessings, bread rationing on 21 July. I drew a distinction between drawing up a system of bread rationing and actually bringing it into force. His Majesty's Government have made so many miscalculations in the past on these subjects, that it would no doubt be no more than prudent for them to set up the whole machinery of bread rationing. Indeed, if they fear there may be a breakdown in supplies in particular localities, through the pipeline getting unduly drained and beginning to creak and groan – about which we have had no information – if they fear that, they are bound to take this action, however wasteful, cumbrous and unpopular it may be.

I put it to the House, for careful consideration, that it would be better, in the public interest, in the next few weeks, to prepare a rationing scheme on better lines, in full consultation with the trade and the bakers, so as to make it as little onerous as possible, but not to enforce it until the necessity is proved. I have a word to say to the bakers and the traders who are concerned. They have been ill-treated. They have not been consulted, nor have they been given a chance to aid the Government in solving the problem with all the expert and practical knowledge which they alone possess. Nevertheless, I strongly advise them to do their best to make whatever scheme is thrust upon them by the Government, and on the authority of Parliament, work as well as possible. If the scheme breaks down in operation, let it be clear to the country that it is because of its own inherent defects and not that the breakdown has been brought about by any lack of honest effort on the part of the trade concerned. This is the advice which I and my Friends on this bench feel it our duty to give them. (*Interruption.*) Does not the hon. Member approve of my giving that advice? We will play the game by you if you play the game by us. You have made us feel that we have hardly a right to live in our own country.

That all this friction, disturbance, inconvenience and hardship will be imposed upon the public, and all the vast process of handling and clipping scores of millions of coupons will be imposed upon the traders, the roundsmen and the housewives for such small results – seven per-cent – only deepens the mystery of why the Government feel impelled to take this step, and why they feel impelled to take it now, without giving the scheme a chance to be properly prepared and arranged, or trying to carry people with them in their management of affairs. There would be an obvious advantage in taking more time to prepare the best possible scheme, in having friendly consultation with all the bakers and others, and putting the machinery in good order, in case an emergency – which has been in no way disclosed to us, let alone proved – should arise. That would be a sensible thing to do. What is the reason why it is not done? . . .

. . . The only intelligible reason for imposing bread rationing 21 July is so shocking as to seem incredible. I certainly am not adopting it until it is forced upon me. It is that we shall shortly reach, or perhaps have already practically reached, the distributional minimum of 800,000 tons in the pipeline, and that we are now condemned to live from hand to mouth for the five weeks between 21 July and 31 August. Can the Government really have allowed this to come to pass? Can I have an answer to the question now? Why was this date 31 August chosen to give us an account of the state of the pipeline, the only account we have been told we are to receive of the state of the pipeline? Naturally, I thought, it will be running down from the figure of 1,500,000 tons or whatever it was, and by 31 August it will get to 800,000 tons, somewhere below which the danger of breakdown in distribution, which must at all costs be avoided, might occur. Why was this particular date chosen? What is the intermediate position? How much is there in the pipeline now? How much will there be in the pipeline a fortnight hence? Is the position of the Government that the stocks in the pipeline may fall gradually to the danger level by 31 August, or is there something else which is grave, and of which we have not been told, between now and 31 August?

I have nearly finished the few remarks I have to make. Naturally, if the right hon. Gentleman will not answer my perfectly plain question by an interjection, I will wait until he makes his statement, but I feel sure that everyone in the House – not only on one side – will consider that answers to these plain questions of fact should be given and that the House should not have to vote without knowing what the answers are. We have found it difficult to understand the reasons which have led the Government to propose bread rationing now, and a fear has arisen that we have not been told the facts. I ask the right hon. Gentleman for a definite assurance. I hope to be reassured, and I believe I can be reassured, that we are not already at the danger point of 31 August. I gather that we are not –

Mr Strachey indicated assent.

Mr Churchill: . . . Never will I have any emotion but joy and relief at anything which helps our country. If there had been a great breakdown, or something terrible going to break out upon us now, some skeleton in the right hon. Gentleman's cupboard going to leap out, I would still have counselled him to let it out at once, and not be frightened about it. But as I understand that he will give an answer which is reassuring on this point, namely, that the pipeline will not fall below 800,000 tons before 31 August, I can only tell him that, so far as I am able to obtain any information on the subject, that was the answer I expected him to give. If that is so, where is the case for imposing this rationing scheme on 21 July? If it is said that there is a great saving, that is an argument. If one says that some terrible thing is about to happen and that we must have the scheme now, that is an argument. If it is said that we are putting it into operation and will have to make it more severe in the future, that is an argument. But all these arguments are demolished. What then is the argument for bread rationing on 21 July?

To sum up, if the Government were to tell us that a grave crisis had arisen or would arise in the course of the present month before the British harvest is reached and that its extent could be measured in terms of days of breakdown of distribution before 31 August, that would be a new fact of the first magnitude, which we should have to take into consideration. We should condemn the Government for their earlier mismanagement, but proceed to judge their new proposal on its merit. Moreover, besides all this, if the Government say that the present scales of rationing, which are practically no saving in consumption, are only the forerunners of much more drastic action which they apprehend will be needed, then we are willing to recognise that they have substance in the case which they make, no matter who was responsible for the mismanagement. If, however, His Majesty's Government cannot say one thing or the other, neither a crisis before 31 August, nor an increase in the severity of rationing after 31 August, it is plain that they have made no case which could justify any responsible Member of Parliament in agreeing to an ill thought out scheme involving a great measure of hardship on the people, for all its cost and trouble and worry, appears at once panic-stricken in motive, and futile in action.

Winston S. Churchill to Field Marshal Lord Montgomery
(Churchill papers, 2/238)

23 July 1946

My dear Monty,

I have no doubt I could buy from the paint shop at Zurich any supplies I may need. I am therefore bringing with me only about one tube of each of the many colours I use, and a moderate outfit of brushes. I sent you an advance note of a few of the colours of which I am short. I should also be very much obliged to you if you would kindly order for me at my expense the canvasses (toiles) on the attached list.

I am going to try a new method, namely to make a vivid note on the scene in a single afternoon and then try to reproduce on a very much larger canvas. I am at this moment making an enlarged replica of a sketch which I made in Egypt twenty-five years ago, and I find it very interesting. My canvas is about six feet by four and a half feet. What do you think of this idea? It certainly is great fun.

PS. I enclose a copy of a letter which I have written to the F. Office which explains itself and my plans.

July 1946

Winston S. Churchill to Sir Alan Lascelles
(Churchill papers, 2/495)

23 July 1946

My dear Alan,

You may have noticed that I have had a medallion struck which I have given as a souvenir to each of the 122 Ministers who served under me in the National Coalition Government. I wonder whether The King would care to have one of these as a curiosity. It would make an excellent paper weight. After all, His Majesty saw a great deal of his principal Ministers in those days. I should be honoured if he would allow me to send him one of them.

L. S. Amery to Winston S. Churchill
(Churchill papers, 2/18)

24 July 1946

My dear Winston,

I have just got back from three weeks in Switzerland most of it spent in Zermatt. The people there, more particularly Joseph Seiler[1] who runs all the leading hotels and whom you may remember as manager of the King David in Jerusalem, though quite understanding why the Engadine would suit you better, still ask me to convey to you their hopes that you might be tempted just to come to Zermatt for a day or two to renew your memories of many years ago.

Speaking of the King David[2] it looks as if we were paying more and more dearly for irresolution and procrastination in Palestine. I hope, when you have a chance, that you will lift up your voice for the only practical solution which is the one adopted by the Cabinet now two years ago. I believe public opinion here and everywhere else, including Palestine is ripe for it.

While in Switzerland I met Coudenhove-Kalergi, who is busy reviving his Paneuropean organisation and is most anxious that you should accept now the Presidency of Honour of the conference which he is proposing to convene in the spring. I myself can see no other solution of the European problem than the spread of the conception of a European Commonwealth. I believe you could do a very big thing if you made that your particular work, and should be only too willing to enrol myself under your banner in that cause.

---

[1] Joseph Seiler, 1896–1948. Swiss hotel owner and manager. Managed the King David Hotel in Jerusalem in 1946. His family operated hotels throughout Switzerland and continues to do so, including the Mont Cervin Palace in Zermatt.

[2] The King David Hotel, an international hotel in Jerusalem, was bombed by Zionist terrorists on 22 July 1946; 91 people were killed and 46 injured.

I expect to be spending most of August with Simon[1] and Sadie[2] Rodney at Oakfield and could always come over for a talk.

Winston S. Churchill to L. S. Amery
(Churchill papers, 2/18)

25 July 1946

My dear Leo,

Thank you very much for your letter of July 24. I am going to a villa on the Lake of Geneva instead of to the Engadine as I feared that the altitude might be trouble for me.

I have thought a good deal about Coudenhove-Kalergi. His conceptions have a strong anti-Russian tendency, but I am still pondering upon the matter and have interested Duncan Sandys in it.

Government and Opposition meeting: minutes
(Churchill papers, 2/4)

30 July 1946   Prime Minister's Room
Confidential   House of Commons

POLITICAL BROADCASTING

The Lord President of the Council said that the Government welcomed these talks with the Opposition. They agreed with Mr Churchill that political broadcasting should be resumed. The ultimate responsibility, of course, rested with the BBC, but the Government thought that it would help the BBC, if an attempt could be made in the first instance to reach agreement through the usual channels on proposals which could subsequently be discussed with them.

The Government's broad views were:

(a) Any Government must be free from time to time to use the wireless for Ministerial broadcasts which, for example are purely factual, or explanations of legislation or administrative policies approved by Parliament; or in the nature of appeals to the nation to co-operate in national policies, such as fuel economy or recruiting, which require the active participation of the public. Broadcasts on State occasions also came in the same category.

In making such broadcasts, the Ministers should be as impartial

---

[1] Charles Christian Simon Rodney, 1895–1980. Educated at Repton. Capt., Grenadier Guards. Fought in WWI (POW) and WWII, gaining the rank of Major.

[2] Gladys Greenwood, ?–1966. Known as 'Sadie'. Married Simon Rodney.

July 1946

as they could, and in the ordinary way there would be no question of a reply by the Opposition.
(b) 'Outside' broadcasts, e.g. of speeches at Labour or Conservative Party Conferences, which were in the nature of news items, should carry no right of reply by the other side.
(c) The Parties had been able to agree amicably on arrangements for broadcasts before the General election, and the Government hoped that it might be possible to secure agreement now on a proposal to the BBC for a limited number of controversial broadcasts to be allocated to the various Parties in accordance with their polls at the last General Election. The Opposition would have the right, subject to discussion through the usual channels, to choose the subjects for their own broadcasts.
(d) Where any dispute arose, an effort should be made to settle it through the usual channels. Where this was not possible the BBC would, of course, have to decide the matter on its own.

Mr Churchill said that he did not think that there was much between the Government and the Opposition. They were united in wanting fair play, and, for good or ill, they both firmly believed in a Party System. A fair arrangement had been made at the General Election, and the Opposition would be prepared to accept an allocation based on the number of votes cast. Strictly, as between the Government and the Opposition, this would work out at a proportion of about 12 to 10.5, but the Government might be prepared to concede equality, having regard to the constitutional responsibilities of the Opposition.

The Lord President took note of this point and indicated that it could be further considered.

Mr Churchill suggested that the number of controversial broadcasts to be given be discussed with the BBC.

Points dealt with in the discussion were:

Ministerial Broadcasts

Mr Churchill said that he fully recognised that the Government had responsibilities beyond those of the Opposition. They had the care of the nation and account must be taken of their special position. There were some subjects, too, on which there was general agreement. National savings and recruiting were examples of questions on which the Government had the complete support of the Opposition. On the other hand, there might well be broadcasts which the Government regarded as non-controversial, but which seemed controversial to the Opposition. A factual statement might present a rosier picture than the situation really justified; and the Opposition, for example, thought that this title of the Lord President's recent broadcast – 'Britain gets going again'

– was controversial. Nobody should be a judge in his own cause, and where the Opposition considered that a Government broadcast was controversial, there ought to be provision for discussions, through the usual channels, with a view to a reply. Electioneering must not be done under the guise of national broadcast.

Mr Eden said that it was conceivable that, in some cases, the Opposition could help by making an appeal to the nation from a rather different angle.

The Lord President said that he had tried hard not to be controversial in his recent broadcast, and, if only from reference to it in two Conservative newspapers, he thought he had succeeded. This broadcast was part of the Production Drive, which had been initiated by a similar broadcast by the Prime Minister, and in the Government's view it was non-controversial. He thought himself that this was also true of the title; his only motive in choosing it had been to find a title which would stimulate the interest of listeners.

The Lord President agreed with Mr Churchill that, when the Opposition considered that a Ministerial broadcast overstepped the mark, the matter should be discussed through the usual channels.

Arrangements for Controversial Broadcasts

(a) Number of Broadcasts

It was agreed that this would be a question for discussion with the BBC, with whom the decision rested. They would, no doubt, have views on the amount of political broadcasting which would be acceptable to the public, and it was important not to exhaust the interest and patience of the latter, nor to rival Parliament. If quotas were fixed for the different parties, there would, of course, be no obligation on them to use their whole quota.

(b) Choice of Subjects

It was agreed that either side would be free if it wished to use one of its quota of broadcasts for the purpose of replying to a previous broadcast, but it would be under no necessity to do so.

(c) Other Parties

It was agreed that General Election polls formed the best basis for calculating the allocation to the other political parties, and that the allocation should be made yearly. It was reasonable that only parties with a substantial electoral strength should have the right to a quota. This would mean the exclusion of eminent Independents and other distinguished individuals not nominated by any Party, but it was impracticable to provide for them.

Further Meeting

It was decided that there should be a further meeting after the Recess at which the BBC should be invited to be represented.

August 1946

Winston S. Churchill: speech
('Winston S. Churchill, His Complete Speeches', volume 7, pages 7324–9)

1 August 1946   House of Commons

PALESTINE

The House is, naturally, obliged to the President of the Board of Trade (Sir Stafford Cripps) for the painstaking speech which he has delivered to us, and which supplements, in many points, the interesting and detailed statement delivered by the Lord President of the Council (Mr Herbert Morrison) yesterday. We are also much obliged to my right hon. Friend the Member for West Bristol (Mr Stanley), whose speech, I think, furnished the House with a wealth of carefully thought, judiciously selected and rightly produced facts, and represents a very large body of our opinion at the present time upon this most difficult question. In the short time which I will venture to occupy the House, I am going to touch a little on some of the grave realities which lie outside the peaceful tones of the oration of the President of the Board of Trade, and the quiet circumstances of this House, because the situation in which we are placed is a very grievous one, and one which is not improving at all. I must also go back a little into the past, because on this question we have got to look to the past.

The position which I, personally, have adopted and maintained, dates from 1919 and 1921, when as Dominions and Colonial Secretary, it fell to me to define, with the approval of the then Cabinet and Parliament, the interpretation that was placed upon our obligations to the Zionists under the Mandate for Palestine entrusted to us by the League of Nations. This was the declaration of 1922, which I, personally, drafted for the approval of the authorities of the day. Palestine was not to be a Jewish National Home, but there was to be set up a Jewish National Home in Palestine. Jewish immigration would be allowed up to the limit of the economic absorptive capacity – that was the phrase which I coined in those days and which seems to remain convenient – the Mandatory Power being, it was presumed, the final judge of what that capacity was. During the greater part of a quarter of a century which has passed, this policy was carefully carried out by us. The Jewish population multiplied, from about 80,000 to nearly 600,000. Tel-Aviv expanded into the great city it is, a city which, I may say, during this war and before it, welcomed and nourished waifs and orphans flying from Nazi persecution. Many refugees found a shelter and a sanctuary there, so that this land, not largely productive of the means of life, became a fountain of charity and hospitality to people in great distress. Land reclamation and cultivation and great electrical enterprises progressed. Trade made notable progress, and not only did the Jewish population increase but the Arab population, dwelling in the areas colonised and enriched by the Jews, also increased in almost equal numbers. The Jews multiplied six-fold and the Arabs developed 500,000, thus showing that both races gained a marked advantage from the Zionist policy which we pursued and which we were developing over this period.

The right hon. and learned Gentleman, the President of the Board of Trade, spoke of the past 25 years as being the most unkind or unhappy Palestine has known. I imagine that it would hardly be possible to state the opposite of the truth more compendiously. The years during which we have accepted the Mandate have been the brightest that Palestine has known and were full of hope. Of course, there was always friction, because the Jew was, in many cases, allowed to go far beyond the strict limits of the interpretation which was placed upon the Mandate. Disturbances occurred in 1937 and in 1938; in 1939 Mr Chamberlain's Government produced the White Paper, which limited immigration on grounds other than the economic absorptive capacity of the country. That after a five-year interval, would have brought immigration to an end except by agreement with the Arab majority, which certainly would not have been obtained. This was in my view a failure to fulfil the obligations we had accepted, and I immediately protested against this departure. I found myself in full agreement with the Labour and Liberal Parties of those days.

I see that yesterday the leader of the Liberal Party (Mr Clement Davies) who is not here today, in paying a tribute to my speech on that occasion deplored the fact that I had not the courage to vote against the Government. As to the courage that is required for one to give a vote against the Government one is elected to support, we no doubt shall have many examples today. I did take the trouble to look up the Divisions on that occasion, and I have for greater security brought this bulky volume to the Table. I find that I did vote against the Government of the day in support of the reasoned Amendment moved by the right hon. Gentleman who is now the Lord President of the council (Mr Herbert Morrison) and that was the subject on which I spoke. However, I think that, on the whole, Members can always speak and not vote, though it is better to let the vote follow the speech. In this case, I conformed to the strictest tenets, and I trust that when the Leader of the Liberal Party rejoins his flock, they may acquaint him of the fact that his great responsibilities and multifarious duties have, no doubt, led him to an oversight, and a complete misstatement of a matter of fact.

I have never altered my opinion that the White Paper constituted a negation of Zionist policy which, the House must remember, was an integral and indispensable condition of the Mandate. That is the view which I hold today. It was violently resented by the Jews in Palestine, and by world Jewry, a large majority of whom – although there are notable exceptions – regard Zionism as a great ideal, and as the cherished hope of their race, scattered throughout the world. Then came the war. After the fall of France, and the attack upon us by Italy, when we stood utterly alone, we had great need to concentrate our troops against the enemy, and economise in our outlying garrisons and commitments. At my desire the Jewish community in Palestine was armed, encouraged to organize and, in fact, to play a part in the defence of the Holy Land, in order to liberate British units there. The horrible persecutions by the Nazis left no doubt as to which side they were on, or could be on. The possibility of a German invasion, striking through Turkey, Syria and Palestine to the Suez Canal, as well as through Persia, towards the Persian Gulf, and at what were then deemed to be our vital communications, at what was then considered to be an important element in our affairs – our Eastern Empire and possessions, as well as Australia and New Zealand – was a very real anxiety in 1941–2. At a most critical time in 1941, it was aggravated by the revolt of the pro-German Arab elements in Iraq. No doubt our Zionist policy may have led, in part, to the divergence of Arab sentiment. But the revolt was quelled. Syria was liberated, and Persia was occupied. Immense preparations and fortifications were made against German penetration of the Caucasus, and this danger complicated the whole defence of Europe from the West. But this menace was removed, at once and for ever, by the victories of Stalingrad and El Alamein.

Meanwhile, the Jewish community had developed strong, well-armed forces, and the highest military authorities reported to the Cabinet during 1941–2 that if the continued bickerings between Jews and Arabs grew into serious conflict, the Jews could not only defend themselves, but would beat the Arabs in Palestine, though that was, of course, the very opposite position from that which existed at the time of the Mandate in 1919. At that time, the Jews were a defenceless minority, and it was a great part of our duty to protect them from the hostility of the very much stronger Arab forces who emerged with so much distinction and credit from the struggle against the Turks. Thus, there are two facts to be borne in mind. First, that Zionists and the Palestine Jews were vehemently and undividedly on our side in the struggle and, secondly, that they no longer need our assistance to maintain themselves in their national home against local Arab hostility. A general attack upon them by all surrounding Arab States would be a different matter, and that would clearly be one which would have to be settled by the United Nations Organization. But the position is different from what it was when the Mandate was granted.

Meanwhile how did we treat the Arabs? We have treated them very well. The House of Hussein reigns in Iraq. Feisal[1] was placed on the throne, his grandson[2] is there today. The Emir Abdullah, whom I remember appointing at Jerusalem, in 1921, to be in charge of Transjordania, is there today. He has survived the shocks, strains and stresses which have altered almost every institution in the world. He has never broken his faith and loyalty to this country. Syria and the Lebanon owe their independence to the great exertions made by the British Government to make sure that the pledges made at the time when we were weak, but, nevertheless, were forced to take action by entering the country to drive out the Vichy French, were honoured. We have insisted on those pledges being made good. I cannot touch on the Arabs without paying my tribute to this splendid King, Ibn Saud, of Saudi Arabia, who in the darkest hours never failed to send messages and encouragement of his unshakable faith that we should win and gain through. I cannot admit that we have not done our utmost to treat the Arabs in a way which so great a race deserves and requires. There was no greater champion of Arab rights than the late Colonel Lawrence.[3] He was a valued friend of mine, and of my right hon. Friend the Member for Horsham (Earl Winterton)[4] who served with him in the Desert. With him I always kept in very close touch. When Lawrence gave me his book, *The Seven Pillars of Wisdom*, he wrote in it that I had made a happy end to this show. I will not have it that the way we treated this matter was inconsiderate to the Arabs. On the contrary, I think that they have had a

---

[1] Faisal I bin Hussein Ali al-Hashemi, 1885–1933. Son of Amīr Husayn ibn Alī. Met Lawrence of Arabia, 1917. Led Northern Army in Arab Revolt, 1916–18. Led delegation to Paris Peace Conference on behalf of Arab independence, 1919. King of Syria, 1920; of Iraq, 1921–33.

[2] Abd al-Ilāh, 1913–58. Also known as 'Abdullah'. Son of King Ali ibn Hussein of Hejaz. Regent of Iraq, 1939–53; Crown Prince, 1943–58. In March 1941, the pro-German Rashi Ali al-Gaylani, a former PM of Iraq, seized power in Baghdad, forcing Emir Abdullah to flee; he returned with British aid in May. Assassinated in the 14 July Revolution.

[3] Thomas Edward Lawrence, 1888–1935. Born in North Wales. Educated at Jesus College, Oxford. Travelled in Syria and Palestine while still an undergraduate. Obtained a first-class degree in History, 1910. On archaeological work at Carchemish, 1911–14. Explored, with Leonard Woolley, the Negev desert south of Beersheba, 1914. Served in Geographical Section, General Staff, War Office, 1914–15; Military Intelligence, Egypt, 1915–16. Accompanied Ronald Storrs to Jedda, 1916, at the inauguration of the Arab Revolt against the Turks. Liaison officer and adviser to Emir Feisal, 1917–18. Took part in the capture of Akaba from the Turks, July 1917, and the capture of Damascus, Oct. 1918. Accompanied Feisal to the Paris Peace Conference, 1919. Fellow of All Souls, Oxford, 1919. At Churchill's request, joined Middle East Dept of Colonial Office, Jan. 1921; resigned, 1922. Enlisted in RAF (as J. H. Ross), 1922, and again (as T. E. Shaw) in 1923. Served in India, 1926–8. Retired from RAF, 1935. Killed in a motorcycle accident. Wrote *Seven Pillars of Wisdom* (1926).

[4] Edward Turnour, 1883–1962. Educated at Eton and New College, Oxford. MP (Cons.) for Horsham, 1904–51. Succeeded his father as 6th Earl Winterton, 1907; as an Irish peer, continued to sit in the House of Commons. Served at Gallipoli, in Palestine and in Arabia, 1915–18. Under-Secretary of State for India, 1922–4, 1924–9. Chancellor of the Duchy of Lancaster, 1937–9. Paymaster-General, 1939. Chairman, Inter-Governmental Committee for Refugees, 1938–45. Father of the House of Commons, 1945–51.

very fair deal from Great Britain. With all those countries which are given to their power and control, in every way they have had a very fair deal. It was little enough, indeed, that we had asked for the Jews – a natural home in their historic Holy Land, on which they have the power and virtue to confer many blessings for enjoyment, both of Jew and Arab.

It is quite true that the claims and desires of the Zionists latterly went beyond anything which were agreed to by the Mandatory Power. This caused alarm and unrest among the Arabs, but the limits of the policy which I explained to the House have never been exceeded by any British Government, and if they are discharged they constitute the faithful fulfilment of our pledges, on which the Mandate hangs. At the General Election which followed the victorious ending of the German war, the Labour Party, which was believed to champion the Zionist cause in the terms I have defined, and not only in these terms, but going, in many cases, far beyond – to set up a Jewish State in Palestine, and so forth – this Labour Party, some of whom we see here today, gained a large majority in the House of Commons. During the Election, they made most strenuous pro-Zionist speeches and declarations. Many of their most important leaders were known to be ardent supporters of the Zionist cause, and their success was, naturally, regarded by the Jewish community in Palestine as a prelude to the fulfilment of the pledges which had been made to them, and indeed opening the way to further ambitions. This was certainly the least which everybody expected.

In fact, all sorts of hopes were raised among the Jews of Palestine, just as other hopes were raised elsewhere. However, when the months slipped by and no decided policy or declaration was made by the present Government, a deep and bitter resentment spread throughout the Palestine Jewish community, and violent protests were made by the Zionist supporters in the United States. The disappointment and disillusionment of the Jews at the procrastination and indecision of the British Labour Government are no excuse, as we have repeatedly affirmed here, for the dark and deadly crimes which have been committed by the fanatical extremists, and these miscreants and murderers should be rooted out, and punished with the full severity of the law. We are all agreed about that, and I was glad to hear the right hon. and learned Gentleman the President of the Board of Trade affirm the intention of the Government not to be coerced by terrorism. But the expectations which had been aroused by the Party opposite and the resultant revulsion of feeling, are facts, none the less, to be held constantly before our minds. They cannot say all these things, and then let a whole year pass away and do nothing about it, and then be surprised if these pledges come home to roost in a most unpleasant manner.

Had I had the opportunity of guiding the course of events after the war was won a year ago, I should have faithfully pursued the Zionist cause as I have defined it; and I have not abandoned it today, although this is not a very popular moment to espouse it; but there are two things to say about it. First, I agree entirely with what the President of the Board of Trade said on this point – no one can imagine that there is room in Palestine for the great masses of Jews who wish to leave Europe, or that they could be absorbed in any period which it is now useful to contemplate. The idea that the Jewish problem could be solved or even helped by a vast dumping of the Jews of Europe into Palestine is really too silly to consume our time in the House this afternoon. I am not absolutely sure that we should be in too great a hurry to give up the idea that European Jews may live in the countries where they belong. I must say that I had no idea, when the war came to an end, of the horrible massacres which had occurred; the millions and millions that have been slaughtered. That dawned on us gradually after the struggle was over. But if all these immense millions have been killed and slaughtered, there must be a certain amount of living room for the survivors, and there must be inheritances and properties to which they can lay claim. Are we not to hope that some tolerance will be established in racial matters in Europe, and that there will be some law reigning by which, at any rate, a portion of the property of these great numbers will not be taken away from them? It is quite clear, however, that this crude idea of letting all the Jews of Europe go into Palestine has no relation either to the problem of Europe or to the problem which arises in Palestine.

Mr S. Silverman: The right hon. Gentleman is not suggesting, is he, that any Jew who regarded a country in Europe as nothing but the graveyard and cemetery of all his relatives, friends and hopes should be compelled to stay there if he did not want to do so?

Mr Churchill: I am against preventing Jews from doing anything which other people are allowed to do. I am against that, and I have the strongest abhorrence of the idea of anti-Semitic lines of prejudice. Secondly, I have for some years past – this is really the crux of the argument I am venturing to submit to the House – felt that an unfair burden was being thrown upon Great Britain by our having to bear the whole weight of the Zionist policy, while Arabs and Moslems, then so important to our Empire, were alarmed and estranged, and while the United States, for the Government and people of which I have the greatest regard and friendship, and other countries, sat on the sidelines and criticized our shortcomings with all the freedom of perfect detachment and irresponsibility. Therefore, I had always intended to put it to our friends in America, from the very beginning of the post-war discussions, that either they should come in and help us in this Zionist problem, about which they feel so strongly, and as I think rightly, on even terms, share and share alike, or that we should resign our Mandate, as we have, of course, a perfect right to do.

Indeed, I am convinced that from the moment when we feel ourselves unable to carry out properly and honestly the Zionist policy as we have all these years defined it and accepted it, and which is the condition on which we received the Mandate for Palestine, it is our duty at any rate to offer to lay down the Mandate. We should therefore, as soon as the war stopped, have made it clear to the United States that, unless they came in and bore their share, we would lay the whole care and burden at the feet of the United Nations organisation; and we should have fixed a date by which all our troops and forces would be withdrawn from the country. At that time we had no interest in Palestine. We have never sought or got anything out of Palestine. We have discharged a thankless, painful, costly, laborious, inconvenient task for more than a quarter of a century with a very great measure of success. Many people have made fine speeches about the Zionist question. Many have subscribed generously in money, but it is Great Britain, and Great Britain alone, which has steadfastly carried that cause forward across a whole generation to its present actual position, and the Jews all over the world ought not to be in a hurry to forget that. If in the Jewish movement or in the Jewish Agency there are elements of murder and outrage which they cannot control, and if these strike not only at their best but at their only effective friends, they and the Zionist cause must inevitably suffer from the grave and lasting reproach of the atrocious crimes which have been committed. It is perfectly clear that Jewish warfare directed against the British in Palestine will, if protracted, automatically release us from all obligations to persevere as well as destroy the inclination to make further efforts in British hearts. Indeed, there are many people who are very near that now. We must not be in a hurry to turn aside from large causes we have carried far.

There is the figure of Dr Weizmann,[1] that dynamic Jew whom I have known so long, the ablest and wisest leader of the cause of Zionism, his whole life devoted to the cause, his son killed in the battle for our common freedom. I ardently hope his authority will be respected by Zionists in this dark hour, and that the Government will keep in touch with him, and make every one of his compatriots feel how much he is respected here. It is perfectly clear that in that case we shall have the best opportunities of carrying this matter further forward.

I am sorry to weary the House with these reminiscences and 'might have beens' but it was my intention when the war was over to place this position before our American friends in the plainest words – the plainest words, which, spoken in good will and good faith are the words to which Americans are most likely to respond. I am in full accord with every effort the Government have made to obtain American support in sharing the burden of the Zionist policy. The Anglo-American Commission was a step in the right direction. The negotiations which have taken place since are another favourable step,

[1] Chaim Weizmann, 1874–1952. Born in Russia. Educated in Germany. Reader in Bio-chemistry, University of Manchester, 1906. Naturalised as a British subject, 1910. Director, Admiralty Laboratories, 1916–19. President of the World Zionist Organisation, and of the Jewish Agency for Palestine, 1921–31, 1935–46. Chairman, Board of Governors, Hebrew University of Jerusalem, 1932–50. Adviser to the Ministry of Supply, London, 1939–45. First President of the State of Israel from 1949 until his death. His eldest son, Flight Lt Michael Weizmann, RAF, was killed in action in 1942.

as was this scheme which has been read out as agreed to by the expert bodies joined on the Commission. It is far more important that there should be agreement than that there should be this or that variant of the scheme. I fully agree that the Government were right to labour with the United States. I will not try to examine the various schemes of partition or cantonisation which have been put forward, nor would I dwell on that idea, which I always championed, of a wider union – an Arab–Jew federal system of four or five States in the Middle East, which would have been one of the great Powers, with Jew and Arab combined together to share the glory and mutually protect and help each other. As I say, almost any solution in which the United States will join us could be made to work.

All these processes of inquiry, negotiation and discussion have been the occasion, so frequently referred to in this Debate, of prolonged and very dangerous delays and if at the end of all these delays success is not attained, namely Anglo-American co-operation on equal terms to carry out a Zionist policy within the limits defined or as we may agree – if that is not attained then we are confronted with a deplorable failure in the conduct of our affairs in Palestine since the end of the second great war. It was with very great regret that I read this morning of the non-agreement of the United States, and the right hon. and learned Gentleman who has just sat down, quite bluntly and bleakly told us that there was no agreement at the present time. I hope it is not the final word. This agreement was the one great goal to which we were invited to aspire; here was the one excuse the Government could put forward for the long delays and indecisions which have involved us in so much cost and serious bloodshed. If this Anglo-American co-operation fails, as it seems so far to have failed, then I must say that the record of the Administration during this year – and a Government must be judged by results – in the handling of Palestinian affairs will stand forth as a monument of incapacity.

It may be that they have had difficulties; but Governments are judged by results. I turned up with a number of defeats during the war and I was very much criticised about it. I had several times to come down with reports of defeats, but when afterward there were successes we were entitled to be praised. Up to this particular minute, this has been a complete failure; it has gone from bad to worse and one does not feel that there is any grip of the matter which is going to succeed. The one rightful, reasonable, simple, and compulsive lever which we held and, if you will, still hold, was and is sincere readiness to resign the mission, to lay our Mandate at the feet of the United Nations Organization and thereafter to evacuate the country with which we have no connection or tradition and where we have no sovereignty as in India and no treaty as in Egypt. Such was the position we could have adopted until a few months ago, and I am sure it would have procured a good result. The cogency of such a statement once it was believed would, I am sure, make the solution much more possible and if no solution was obtained, then our responsibilities would have been honourably discharged. Once make it clear that the British have no interests in remaining in Palestine and no wish to do so, and that they decline to carry forward single-handed this harsh, invidious burden, then you will get attention paid to what you say and what you ask and all kinds of good solutions for the Jew and Arab alike, based on the co-operation and resources of the English-speaking world, will immediately come into the field of possibility.

However, His Majesty's Government, by their precipitate abandonment of their treaty rights in Egypt, and, in particular, the Suez Canal zone, are now forced to look for a strong place of arms, for a jumping-off ground in Palestine in order to protect the Canal from outside Egypt. By this unwisdom they have vitiated disinterestedness and we can now be accused of having a national strategic motive for retaining our hold on Palestine. I must regard this as a very grave disaster and an immense weakening of our positon. What the Government have done in Egypt – though no doubt from very good motives – has greatly weakened our moral position in Palestine by stripping us of our disinterestedness in that country. I pointed out in the Debate on Egyptian policy a few weeks ago, that the moment we were dependent upon Palestine for a base from which to defend the Suez Canal, we should greatly hamper all possibility of obtaining American co-operation. Well, look at the position to which we have now been brought.

Take stock round the world at the present moment; after all we are entitled to survey the whole field. We declare ourselves ready to abandon the mighty Empire and Continent of India with all the work we have done in the last 200 years, territory over which we possess unimpeachable sovereignty. The Government are, apparently, ready to leave the 400 million Indians to fall into all the horrors of sanguinary civil war – civil war compared to which anything that could happen in Palestine would be microscopic; wars of elephants compared with wars of mice. Indeed we place the independence of India in hostile and feeble hands, heedless of the dark carnage and confusion which will follow. We scuttle from Egypt which we twice successfully defended from foreign massacre and pillage. We scuttle from it, we abandon the Canal zone about which our treaty rights were and still are indefeasible; but now, apparently, the one place where we are at all costs and at all inconveniences to hold on and fight it out to the death is Palestine, and we are to be at war with the Jews of Palestine, and, if necessary, with the Arabs of Palestine. For what reason? Not, all the world will say, for the faithful discharge of our long mission but because we have need, having been driven out of Egypt, to secure a satisfactory strategic base from which to pursue our Imperial aims.

I thank the House for listening. I have trespassed on their time at some length, but I wish to look forward before I conclude and not to look back. I will not go so far in criticizing and in censuring without proposing positive action, with all the responsibility and the exposure to counter-attack which one incurs when one proposes definite and serious action. Here is the action

– action this day. I think the Government should say that if the United States will not come and share the burden of the Zionist cause, as defined or as agreed, we should now give notice that we will return our Mandate to UNO and that we will evacuate Palestine within a specific period. At the same time, we should inform Egypt that we stand by our treaty rights and will, by all means, maintain our position in the Canal zone. Those are the two positive proposals which I submit, most respectfully, to the House. In so far as the Government may have hampered themselves in any way from adopting these simple policies, they are culpable in the last degree, and the whole Empire and the Commonwealth will be the sufferers from their mismanagement.

Winston S. Churchill to Lord Cecil
(Chelwood papers, 92/481)

2 August 1946

My dear Bob,

I have an instinct that the right of the Austrian Tyrol to decide its destiny by plebiscite is a Touchstone which may unite many comprehending and generous hearts. I should like to know what you and your friends and Chatham House feel about it. Pray consult with Lionel,[1] if you are inclined, and let me know how you feel.

Dr Chaim Weizmann to Winston S. Churchill
(Churchill papers, 2/8)

2 August 1946

My dear Mr Churchill,

Please accept my deep gratitude and appreciation of your speech in the House of Commons yesterday, and my warm personal thanks for your most kind and generous references to me: they will always be a source of pride to me, and come as some compensation for the travails and tribulations through which I have had to pass of late. I wish indeed that Fate had allowed you to handle our problem; by now it would probably all have been settled, and we would all have been spared a great deal of misery.

The present situation in Palestine, and indeed throughout the Middle East, bristles with difficulties and stresses. It is about this that I wanted to talk to you – I have been out there for the last five months. If the present trouble is not settled quickly, and the tension reduced, I tremble to think of the consequences – not only in the Middle East, but also to relations with the United States.

[1] Curtis.

I am still anxious to have a word with you about all this at your convenience. I shall be in Town from Tuesday morning (the 6th) until the following Tuesday; then I am afraid I have to go into a nursing-home for another operation on my eyes.

With renewed thanks, and many kinds regards from us both to you and Mrs Churchill.[1]

Senators of the Polish Republic[2] to Winston S. Churchill
(Churchill papers, 2/7)

3 August 1946

Sir,

We write this letter not with a view to pretending to reveal anything new to you but to point out certain contradictions between words and deeds which have occurred in this policy of the Main Powers during recent years. Our main object is to make known to you that we, the signatories, together with practically all our countrymen, and probably millions of other Europeans, look to you as the one and only man capable of changing the present shameful current of events and of bringing to the world the realization that humanity is tottering on the edge of a precipice in which evil reigns.

The fate, not only of Poland, but of Europe is bound with the Eastern frontier as drawn in the Treaty of Riga. On that frontier depended Europe's peace. Because of it, the Balkan States could remain independent and the Basin of the Danube and its Estuary, together with the Balkan States, belonged to Europe. Ten years before the war you wrote the following about the frontiers set in the Treaty of Riga: 'A Peace Treaty was signed on October 12th at Riga which secured the independence of Poland and her means of defence against Russian invasion or subversion. . . . The frontier of Asia and the conditions of the Dark Ages had advanced from the Urals to the Pripet Marshes. But there it was written – so far and no farther!' (*The Aftermath* page 272).

The frontier of the Treaty of Riga could and should have been maintained but Great Britain and America were forced, because of the prevailing conditions, to accept the unfair claims of Russia thus allowing the 'conditions of the Dark Ages' to become law in half of Europe – from Hamburg down to Trieste.

The Atlantic Charter states: 'We desire to see no territorial changes that do not accord with the freely expressed wishes of the people concerned and we wish to see sovereign rights and self-government restored to those who have been forcibly deprived of them.' And yet, irrespective of their creeds and nationalities, the people of Eastern Poland, the Estonians, Latvians

[1] Churchill replied by telegram on Aug. 4: 'So glad to hear from you' (*Churchill papers, 2/8*).
[2] These men were exiles from their homeland.

and Lithuanians were incorporated into the Soviet Union by force. Political persecution, intolerance of Religion, concentration camps, dispersal by resettlement and even wholesale extermination – those are the methods applied in these countries today. The result? An economic, political, cultural, and demographic exhaustion.

This is the truth about territories engulfed by the Soviet Union. As for the rest of Poland and all the other Central European countries left to Russia's control by the agreements at Teheran and Yalta – they also, under Communist rule, slowly succumb to the Soviet pattern.

It is an attribute of greatness to own up to mistakes and try to remedy them. You were inclined to admit that Great Britain and America had made certain mistakes during the war in 1944 and 1945. And yet it was maintained more than once that if the Polish Government had willingly agreed to the 'Curzon Line', the independence of Poland would have been saved.

You stated recently in a speech in the House that Russia's boundaries have moved up the river Elbe, and you spoke of the 'Iron Curtain'. We are convinced that you do not now believe that behind this 'Iron Curtain' Poland could be independent, even if governed by Mr Mikolajczyk.[1]

Today, as you admitted yourself in your last speech on May 27th, when Poland's lot is so hard; when international relations, built upon the wrong done to our country and upon the slavery of so many European Nations, become more and more complicated and disconcerting – today we turn to you, privately and confidentially, with the plea to take up our cause and to induce a return to the only principles which can restore true freedom to Europe and secure it for England. We still remember the great speech you made on the 22nd March 1943 in which you spoke of the bygone glory of Europe and from which you did not exclude us 'The Inspiration of Nations'.

This war has proved once more that, apart from Poland, at least half of Europe is threatened with slavery. And this is but the beginning. Can any Englishman's mind be at peace when there is the possibility that the 'Union Jack of Freedom flying over the White Cliffs of Dover with only a moat of silver sea defensive to your houses against the barbarism of the Dark Ages reigning in the less happier lands' which sooner or later will share the fate of Eastern Europe (Speech of Gaunt, Duke of Lancaster – Shakespeare's *Richard II*).

Because we stood by you in the darkest hours that ever befell your country

---

[1] Stanisław Mikołajczyk, 1901–67. Joined Polish Peasants' Party (PSL), 1922. Co-founded Wielkopolska Union of Rural Youth, 1927. Elected to Polish Parliament as member of PSL, 1933. Vice-Chairman of PSL, 1935; President, 1937. Escaped to London with Władysław Sikorski and Władysław Raczkiewicz, forming the Polish Government-in-Exile, 1939. Deputy PM of Polish Government-in-Exile, 1941–3; PM, 1943–4. Deputy PM of Poland, 1945–7. Tried to accommodate Churchill's hoped-for compromise with Stalin over post-war Poland by joining the so-called Unity Government after the war. Initially commanded a majority; thwarted through rigged elections and resigned. Exiled, 1947; fled to England and the US. Chairman, International Peasant Union, 1948–64. Author of *The Pattern of Soviet Domination* (1948).

and because your name will be always linked with the liberation of the world from German totalitarianism, we appeal to you once again to take up our cause, which is the cause of millions of Europeans who, with us, wish fervently for release from this new tyranny.

Senators of the Polish Republic

Ignacy Balinski[1]	Prof Wojciech Jastrzebowski[2]	Adam Koc[3]
Jozef Godlewski[4]	Tadeusz Katelbach[5]	Wanda Norwid Neugebauer[6]
Karol Niezabytowski[7]	Konstanty Rdultowski[8]	Stefan Rosada[9]

---

[1] Ignacy Baliński, 1862–1961. Married, 1894, Lisa Marie Chomętowska. Supreme Court Judge, Poland, 1918–?. Chairman, City Council of the Capital, Warsaw, 1918–27. Senator (Nat. Dem.) Poland, 1922–7. Moved to UK, 1939.

[2] Wojciech Jastrzebowski, 1884–1963. Polish artist. Senator, Republic of Poland, 1935–8.

[3] Adam Koc, 1891–1969. Led a pro-coup faction against Polish Government (Koc Group), 1924–5. Supported successful coup against Polish Government, 1926. Head of Staff, Commandant VI Military District in Lwów, 1926–8. MP (Nonpartisan Bloc), Poland, 1928–38. Vice-Minister, Treasury, 1930–5, 1939. State Commissioner, Bank of Poland, 1932–6; Head, 1936. Senator, 1938–9. Fled to France with the Polish gold reserves, 1939. Minister, Treasury, 1939; 2nd Vice-Minister, 1939–40. Settled in the US to try to preserve Polish bank accounts, 1940.

[4] Józef Godlewski, 1890–1968. Married, 1924, Fabianna hr. Hutten-Czapska: two children. President, National Unification Camp, Poland, 1937. Senator, 1938. Fled Poland, 1939. Stationed in Scotland, 1940. President, North-East Association of the Republic of Poland, UK, 1942–9. Published *Lviv and Vilnius*, 1946–9. Founder, Eastern Association of the Republic of Poland, 1955; President, 1966–8. Vice-President, Council of the Republic, 1958–63. Commander Cross of the Order of Polonia Restituta, Poland, 1968.

[5] Tadeusz Katelbach, 1897–1977. Studied Law, Warsaw University. Fought in Polish–Ukrainian War, Lwów, 1918–19. Editor-in-Chief, *Gazeta Wileńska* newspaper. Polish spy, Geneva, 1925–6. Senator (Camp of National Unity) Lublin, Poland, 1938–9. Fled to Romania, 1939. Joined political group of Ambassador Roger Raczyński, 1939. Moved to Paris, 1939; to Portugal, 1940; to London, 1940. Chairman, German Dept, Office of Documentation, 1940. Employee, Radio Free Europe, Polish section, 1955–65. Moved to US, 1965.

[6] Wanda Norwid Neguebauer. Co-founder in Poland of Women's League; Family Taxpayer Family; Care Society. Chairwoman, Women's Provincial Committee; 'Military Family' Sports Club, 1932. Vice-President, Board of Association, 1933. Vice-Chairwoman, Polish Woman's Council. Senator (Obóz Zjednoczenia Narodowego: National Unity Camp), Lodz, Poland, 1935.

[7] Karol Niezabytowski, 1865–1952. Member, Russian State Council, 1911–12. Member, Polish Council, Minsk, 1918. Minister of Agriculture, 1926. Senator (Bezpartyjny Blok Współpracy z Rządem: Nonpartisan Bloc for Cooperation with the Government), Polesie, 1928–30. Fled to France, 1939.

[8] Konstanty Rdultowski, 1880–1953. President, Polish Motherland School, Minsk; Agricultural Society, Baranavich; Chamber of Agriculture, Nowogródzka and Vilna; Polish Legionary Association, Turka. MP (BBWR) Nowogródzka, 1928–30. Senator, Cracow, 1930–5; Mayor, 1934. Senator, Lviv, 1935–8. Sentenced to a labour camp at Karabas in the Soviet Union, 1940–8.

[9] Stefan Rosada, 1897–1974. Senator, Poland, 1938–9. Deputy Chairman, military court, Krzemieniec, 1939. Held in several Soviet labour camps. Joined Anders Army, 1942. Moved to UK, 1942; to US, 1951.

Winston S. Churchill to Lord Woolton
(Churchill papers, 2/8)

3 August 1946
Private

1. This memorandum is deeply interesting and raises questions which are urgent and will cause us all trouble.

I have no doubt that it would be a great error for us at this juncture to shut doors on any friends, and that our policy should be to take the broadest ground possible. Therefore I hope that everything will be done to obstruct and delay splits with the National Liberals in the various critical constituencies. We must treat them properly, for they have been loyal allies. A Party is not a club, becoming more and more eclectic. It ought to be a 'snowball starting an avalanche'. I feel sure you will be in sympathy with this view.

2. I am increasingly drawn to the idea of 'The Union Party', the members of which would be called Unionists and could call themselves at pleasure 'Conservative Unionists', 'Liberal Unionists', 'Trade Unionists', 'Democratic Unionists', 'Progressive Unionists', etc. I feel this is the broad high road by which alone the greatness of our Country and Empire can be maintained. 'The Union Party' would stand for the union of the Empire and Commonwealth, the union of men of goodwill, and of every class, opposed to the Socialist doctrinaires, and also to the union or fraternal association of the English-speaking peoples all over the world. 'We all go the same way home.'

Pray consider these matters, which are of the utmost consequence.

[. . .]

Winston S. Churchill to Mohammed Ali Jinnah
(Churchill papers, 2/42)

3 August 1946
Private and Confidential

Dear Mr Jinnah

1. I received your letter of July 6[1] and, together with my colleagues, have given it most careful consideration.

2. As you know, from my public statements, I am very much opposed to the handing over of India to Hindu caste rule, as seems very largely to be intended, and I have always strongly espoused the rights of the Moslems and the Depressed Classes to their fair share of life and power. I feel that it is most important that British arms should not be used to dominate the Moslems,

---

[1] Reproduced above (p. 400).

even though the caste Hindus might claim a numerical majority in a constituent assembly.

3. I was, however, surprised to read all the insulting things that were said about Britain at the Moslem Congress in Bombay, and how the Moslems of India were described as 'undergoing British slavery'. All this is quite untrue and very ungrateful. It also seems to be an act of great unwisdom on the part of the Moslems. The tendencies here to support the Congress are very strong in the Government party, and you are driving away your friend. I am sorry to see you taking up an attitude towards Great Britain which cannot be reconciled with your letter to me asking for help.

4. Having got out of the British Commonwealth of Nations, India will be thrown into great confusion, and will have no means of defence against infiltration or invasion from the North.

5. I shall be glad to hear from you.

Winston S. Churchill to W. A. J. Lawrence[1]
(Churchill papers, 2/150)

3 August 1946
Most Private and Confidential

Dear Mr Lawrence,

I have made a few comments on these extracts which are, of course, most complimentary to me, and I have no objection to their being published, I hope with my small amendments.

Our friend should be very careful in all that he writes not to admit that we ever did anything not justified by the circumstances and the actions of the enemy in the measures we took to bomb Germany. We gave them full notice to clear out their munition-making cities. In fact, they had very good shelters and protection, and the position of the civilian population was very different from that of London, Coventry, Liverpool, etc. when they were bombed in the second year of the war. I am not quite clear about Dresden. It may be we were asked to do this as part of some large military combination, but I am afraid the civilian losses there were unduly heavy. All these affairs anyhow are overshadowed by what we did to Japan with the atomic bomb, yet this in a way gave the Japanese a reason for surrender, which in their eyes saved their military honour, and saved Britain and the US several hundred thousand lives.

Perhaps you would convey these remarks to Air Marshal Sir Arthur Harris at the same time that you let him know that I have no objection to the publication of the extracts he has sent me. You should, moreover, thank him on my behalf for his kindness and give him my warmest regards.

[1] Wg Cdr Lawrence, assistant to Mshl of the RAF Sir Arthur Harris.

442 AUGUST 1946

Winston S. Churchill to Anthony Eden
(<i>Churchill papers, 2/7</i>)

8 August 1946

My dear Anthony,

1. I should be so much obliged if you would look at the letter[1] from a Senator of the Polish Republic, and return it to me with your comments. This letter has distressed me.

2. I send you herewith a copy of the Report of a discussion by the National Union Executive Committee on the change of name of the Party, which Woolton has sent me, and a copy of my letter to him on the subject. I think you should see these.

Winston S. Churchill to Lord Woolton
(<i>Churchill papers, 2/8</i>)

8 August 1946

I am of the opinion that the enclosed* might be made into a very valuable piece of propaganda. It shows so clearly the division between the free world and of a property-owning democracy and the Socialist conception of State employees living in Council Houses, and no doubt ultimately removable from them if they do not vote the Party ticket.

Will you consider whether it would not be possible to put small placards, about two feet by eighteen inches, up in various places with the original poster and the repudiation of it by the Socialist Government. There are many parts where it would be most effective. It might play a part at bye-elections in Constituencies where there is on the whole a Conservative bias. Pray let me have your views about his.

Both I and my wife were struck by the cancellation of the poster. Could we reprint it without infringement of copyright? We should first have to find out about this.

* Cutting from *Sunday Express* of 4 August 1946: 'Savings Poster withdrawn. It embarrassed the Socialists.'

[1] Reproduced above (pp. 437–9).

Winston S. Churchill to Alfred Duff Cooper
(Churchill papers, 2/238)

8 August 1946
Private

My dear Duffie,

I am going to stay in Switzerland from August 23 to the middle of September at the Villa Choisie, near Rolle, on the Lake of Geneva. This is opposite Evian les Bains and other French territory. I should like to be able to go across, with any members of my party (which is purely family), at some time or other in a private capacity. I hear that the neighbourhood of Evian is very good for painting. I wonder if you would be so kind as to make sure I have the necessary facilities to cross the frontier without too much formality. I daresay the French would be willing to let me have some consideration in this.

I was much impressed by the results of the Flandin trial. Randolph's evidence, as read in the procès verbal, was very effective. I hope this will mark the turning point in the heresy-hunting which the Communists have stimulated as part of their fraud of monopolizing 'le capital de la Résistance'.

You seem to be having a jolly time at the Conference.[1]

Winston S. Churchill to Lord Winterton
(Churchill papers, 2/42)

9 August 1946   Chartwell

My dear Eddie,

I do not think I can do better than send you the enclosed file, which speaks for itself. Will you let me have it back with your answer as soon as possible. I should be very glad if you felt able to propose the Resolution, which would place us in full accord.

RESOLUTION

That this Conference, while faithfully pursuing the achievement by the Indian peoples of Self-Government within the British Commonwealth of nations, with all the rights and freedoms enjoyed by other British Dominions, views with grave concern the present deteriorating situation, and affirms that it is the duty of Parliament whatever happens to make sure that in any settlement which may be proposed the rights of minorities and of the Indian States shall be effectively safeguarded and the mission of Britain in India be honourably discharged.

---

[1] The Paris Peace Conference, 29 July–15 Oct. 1946.

Winston S. Churchill to Lord Woolton
(Churchill papers, 2/8)

9 August 1946
Important
Private

My dear Woolton,

Thank you very much for your letter and for the report of the National Union Executive Committee discussion.

I do not think it will be possible to make a bargain with the Liberal Party at this stage. Many of their leaders are malignant. However, there is a certain amount of movement in the Constituencies for the reunion of the anti-Socialist Liberals, and this will grow. If the Liberal Party could be induced to come out as a united Party against Socialism a fruitful field would be opened for mutual help between Allies. At present the intention of the leaders, like Samuel, Lady Violet, and of course Clem Davies, is to run amok again with hundreds of candidates.

I am of the opinion that we should go forward with the proposal to make 'The Union Party', whose members would be called Unionists, but who might be Conservative Unionists, Liberal Unionists, Trade Unionists, or Labour Unionists. I should like to discuss this when the Shadows meet on September 23, and if there were general agreement I would myself open the matter at Blackpool on October 5.

It is not for the National Union of Conservative and Unionist Associations to change the name of the Party. That can only be done by a Party meeting held afterwards for this express purpose. I see great dangers in delay, but on the other hand I agree about timing. Of course if I opened at Blackpool it would give a strong lead and many who are now undecided would be favourable. However there would have to be an interval of a month or so before it was necessary to decide on calling a Party meeting, and we should see how opinion shaped itself, and whether we were carrying the broad masses along. Personally I have very little doubt that it ought to be done and done on this occasion. Still, to use time is not to waste it.

I am sending a copy of this letter to Anthony, together with the report.

PS. Herbert Williams[1] did not behave well during the War, and evidently intends to be consistent in his conduct.

---

[1] Herbert Geraint Williams, 1884–1954. Electrical and marine engineer. Educated at University of Liverpool. Secretary, Machine Tool Trades Association, 1911–28. Secretary, Machine Tool Dept, Ministry of Munitions, 1917–18. MP (Cons.) for Reading, 1924–9; for South Croydon, 1932–45; for Croydon East, 1950–4. Parliamentary Secretary, Board of Trade, 1928–9. Knighted, 1939. Member of House of Commons Select Committee on Expenditure, 1939–44. Chairman, London Conservative Union, 1939–48; National Union of Conservative and Unionist Associations, 1948. Bt, 1953.

Winston S. Churchill to Guy Lambert[1]
(Churchill papers, 2/8)

10 August 1946

Sir,

I have to acknowledge the receipt of War Office letter No. 20/Misc/2750(SD1) of July 29 which has been sent to me by the Essex TA & AF Association.

In my view it is a mistaken policy to place Territorial Army Original Units, particularly those with a strong local connection, in suspended animation in preference to disbanding war-formed units, which have no historical background and small facilities for gathering recruits.

The policy apparently to be pursued will sap the strength of the Territorial Army. A regiment like the Queen's Own Oxfordshire Hussars, of which I am at present Colonel, has a history of over 200 years. It drew continually upon farmers' and small tradesmen's sons in the Woodstock, Banbury, Henley and Whitney districts. These provided a steady stream of high-class volunteer recruits in times when military affairs were at a low ebb, as they often are between wars.

I consider it is very improvident and shortsighted of the Army Council to dispense with such units. I am personally in favour of compulsory national service but I doubt very much indeed whether it will be adopted as a permanent system by His Majesty's Government and maintained in view of all the talk about scientific development, etc. You will then find you have cut off that which has stood you in good stead on previous occasions when, through our usual follies, we are unexpectedly overtaken by war.

The Queen's Own Oxfordshire Hussars have accommodated themselves to all the changes required by the War Office in weapons, having become successively Territorial Field Artillery, an Anti-Tank Regiment and finally an Armoured Car or Light Tank Regiment. In fact, you are exchanging a growing plant for a cut flower.

---

[1] Guy Williams Lambert, 1889–1983. Educated at Oxford. Higher Div. Clerk, War Office, 1913. Private Secretary to H. W. Forster, Financial Secretary, 1916. Married, 1917, Nadine Noble. Chevalier, Légion d'Honneur, 1920. Principal Private Secretary to Secretaries of State for War (Sir L. Worthington-Evans and T. Shaw), 1926–9. Asst Under-Secretary of State for War, 1938–51. President, Society for Psychical Research, 1955–8. CB, 1942.

Winston S. Churchill to Randolph S. Churchill
(Churchill papers, 1/42)

10 August 1946
Private

My dear Randolph,

Your article has no doubt already gone out but I have just inserted a few comments which occurred to me as I read it.

I am opposed to State-ownership of all the land but we must not conceal from ourselves that we should be much stronger if the soil of our country were divided up among two or three million people, instead of twenty or thirty thousand. Man is a land animal. Even rabbits are allowed to have warrens, and foxes have earths.

George Bernard Shaw[1] to Winston S. Churchill
(Churchill papers, 2/165)

12 August 1946

My dear Churchill,

I was very glad to receive your friendly birthday message. This in your case is a cordial personal feeling; but it also tickles me as the only other message from anyone of your political eminence was from Eamon de Valera!

No man of action has any chance of being a British Prime Minister until a war frightens the electorate out of chronic dread of government interference and preference for guaranteed faineants like Ramsay[2] and Baldwin. But the worst of military glory is that the electorate, understanding only the glory and the fear of defeat, forces their leader either to keep feeding them with glory and go from Austerlitz to Moscow, Leipsic, Waterloo and St Helena, or, like the first Churchill and Wellington,[3] chuck soldiering and become political nobodies like Lloyd George.

The alternative is to keep the electorate excited about social programs so popular that the Blimps and reactionaries-in-general cannot withstand them.

---

[1] George Bernard Shaw, 1856–1950. Playwright, author and Fabian socialist, a friend of Churchill's mother, and an irrepressible wit. Nobel Prize in Literature, 1925. Churchill wrote of him: 'Mr Bernard Shaw was one of my earliest antipathies. Indeed, almost my first literary effusion, written when I was serving as a subaltern in India in 1897 (it never saw the light of day), was a ferocious onslaught upon him, and upon an article which he had written disparaging and deriding the British Army in some minor war' (*Pall Mall* magazine, Aug. 1929, reprinted in *Great Contemporaries*).

[2] (James) Ramsay MacDonald, 1866–1937. MP (Lab.) for Leicester, 1906–18; for Aberavon, 1922–9; for Seaham, 1929–31, (Nat. Lab.) 1931–5. Leader of the Labour Party, 1911–14. PM and Secretary of State for Foreign Affairs, Jan.–Nov. 1924. PM, 1929–35. Lord President of the Council, 1935–7.

[3] Arthur Wellesley, 1769–1852. Maj.-Gen., 1802. MP (Tory) for Rye, 1806; for Mitchell, 1807; for Tralee, 1807. Commanded British Army in Peninsular War, 1808–14. Duke of Wellington, 1814. Master-General of the Ordnance, 1818–27. PM, 1828–30. Leader of the House of Lords, 1828–30, 1834–5, 1841–6. Foreign Secretary, 1834–5.

In short, Disraeli's[1] invention of your father's creed of Tory Democracy; for Socialism killed Laissez-faire Liberalism (Cobdenism) stone dead, and the ~~Socialists have~~ Labour Party failed to carry out the Fabian program worked out for it by Webb[2] and Shaw, partly through incompetence (Ramsay's Cabinet could not meet because none of the members were on speaking terms, and Snowden[3] hated Ramsay above all men) and partly because the Socialists, having a program but no money, had put themselves under the thumb of the Trade Unionists, who had money but no program except to exploit the Cobdenist system exactly as the financiers and employers were doing, believing that Trade Unionism could beat them at that game. The effective Trade Union leaders, from Broadhurst[4] to Citrine, have been, and still are, thorough-going Tories (Broadhurst hated and dreaded John Burns)[5] and no collaboration was possible between Citrine and Maxton.

Observe that these toughest of Tories are not democrats: the Trade Union Secretary is the most absolute dictator left on earth; and the card vote reduces the TUC to utter absurdity democratically.

What, then, is the situation you are confronted with? Socialism became Fabian when Lenin announced his NEP a quarter of a century ago. The NEP, forced on the Bolsheviks by bitter experience, proved that I was right when I warned the young Socialists against their notion of Capitalism in full swing on Monday, revolution on Tuesday, and Communism in full swing on Wednesday, and established Webb's inevitability of gradualness as an alternative to civil war. There is no longer any issue between Cobdenism and Socialism: Cobden[6] as a world architect is as dead as a door nail; but he will come to

---

[1] Benjamin Disraeli, 1804–81. Son of Isaac D'Israeli, author and literary critic. Entered Parliament, 1837; MP (Tory) for Maidstone, for Shrewsbury and for Buckinghamshire, 1837–76. Became Leader of the Party in the Commons, 1848. PM, 1868, 1874–80. Wrote more than a dozen novels, the last, *Endymion*, published in 1880. Earl of Beaconsfield, 1876. KG, 1878.

[2] Sidney James Webb, 1859–1947. Joined Fabian Society, 1885. Married, 1892, Beatrice Potter. Member, London County Council, 1892–1910. Prof. of Public Administration, University of London, 1912–27. Member, Labour Party National Executive, 1915; Chairman, 1922. MP (Lab.) for Seaham, 1922–9. President of Board of Trade, 1924. Secretary of State for Dominion Affairs, 1929–30; for the Colonies, 1929–31. 1st Baron Passfield, 1929. PC, 1924. OM, 1944.

[3] Philip Snowden, 1864–1937. Educated at Board School. Entered Civil Service, 1886; retired, 1893. Chairman, Independent Labour Party, 1903–6, 1917–20. MP (Lab.) for Blackburn, 1906–18; for Colne Valley, 1922–31. PC, 1924. Chancellor of the Exchequer, 1924, 1929–31. Viscount, 1931. Lord Privy Seal, 1931–2. One of Churchill's principal critics while Churchill himself was Chancellor of the Exchequer (1924–9).

[4] Harry Broadhurst, 1905–95. Known as 'Broady'. Served with RA; transferred to RAF, 1926. Congratulated by King Edward VIII for his acrobatic performance in the Gloster Gauntlet, 1936. AFC, 1937. DSO, 1941. DFC, 1942. AOC, Air HQ Western Desert, 1943–4; 83 Group, 1944–5. Officer of the Legion of Merit (US), 1944. KBE, 1945. Despatches, 1946. Grand Officer of the Order of Orange-Nassau (Netherlands), 1947. C-in-C Second Tactical Air Force, 1953–6. AOC-in-C Bomber Command, 1956–9. C-in-C Allied Air Forces Central Europe, 1959–61. GCB, 1960.

[5] John Burns Hynd, 1902–71. Trade Union Clerk of National Union of Railwaymen, 1925–44. MP (Lab.) for Sheffield Attercliffe, 1944–70. Chancellor of the Duchy of Lancaster, 1945–7. Grand Cross of Merit with Star, Chevalier of the Legion of Honour and Great Golden Cross of Honour with Star, 1958.

[6] Richard Cobden, 1804–65. British manufacturer and statesman. Alderman of Manchester, 1838.

life again when Socialism has gone far enough to raise the question of individual freedom during leisure. Meanwhile the Communist basis of all possible civilization must be accepted by all parties and leaders who know what they are talking about. From the police station in the next street to the Cabinet, the Treasury, the War Office, the Admiralty, the Air Force, the Bench and the Crown, the rock foundation of all possible systems is pure Communism; and the man who questions this is no gentleman. You have been a soldier and a Commissar all your life: your books will belong to the Commonwealth 50 years after your death, like mine. The controversies of the future will be between the people who want to work twelve hours a day and be free for private enterprise or private leisure at forty and those who want to work four hours a day in a five day week, and retire at seventy. (All the would-be artists and philosophers will grow out of this party.)

I do not suggest that you should revive the cry of Tory-Democracy. But what about Democratic Aristocracy, fiercely critical not of Communism, but of Labour Legislation. The National Health Act imposes crude Trade Unionism on the doctors, who will impose the forty inoculations, now imposed on soldiers and travelers, on everybody at half a crown a dose. Your fellows had a first rate chance of taking the lead from Col. Elliott,[1] shewing up the Labour Party as a Trade Union dictatorship and enlisting the dread of doctors that is now rife in all classes. On rationing they had better have proposed the communization of bread and milk than come out second to the Labour back benchers in criticism. Listowel and Dalton on the Budget should have been attacked fiercely for not giving us back the penny letter and halfpenny postcard instead of overcharging us scandalously for postage and giving the plunder to lighten the supertax. There is no end to the games that Democratic Aristocracy might play and get in front as the popular party and keep there.

You have never been a real Tory: a foundation of American democracy, with a very considerable dash of author and artist, and the training of a soldier, has made you a phenomenon that the Blimps and Philistines and Stick-in-the-muds have never understood and always dreaded.

Your beautiful mother[2] crossed the breed at the right moment just as De Valera's father[3] did. You two are the only statesmen I am presuming to write to.

Founding member of the Anti-Corn Law League, 1838. Married, 1840, Catherine Anne Williams: six children. MP (Ind.) for Stockport, 1841–7; for Yorkshire (West Riding), 1847–57; (Lib.) for Rochdale, 1859–65. Signatory of the Cobden–Chevalier Treaty, 1860.

[1] Walter Elliot, 1888–1958. MP (Cons.) for Lanark, 1918–23; for Kelvingrove 1924–45, 1950–8; for the Scottish Universities, 1946–50. Minister of Agriculture and Fisheries, 1932–6. Secretary of State for Scotland, 1936–8. Minister of Health, 1938–40. Director of Public Relations, War Office, 1941–2.

[2] Jeanette Jerome, 1854–1921. Known as 'Jennie'. Daughter of Leonard Jerome and Clarissa Hall of New York. Married, 1874, Lord Randolph Churchill (d. 1895): two children, Winston and Jack; 1900, George Cornwallis-West (div. 1913); 1928, Montagu Porch. Editor, *Anglo-Saxon Review*, 1899–1901.

[3] Juan Vivion de Valera, 1854–85. Born in Cuba. Married, 1881 (in New Jersey), Catherine Coll.

This letter is, I hope, readable; but it is purposefully unanswerable. I know too well the burden of letters that must be answered. So here's Aristotle to your Alexander and Hobbes to your Charles. <u>alias</u>.

Anthony Eden to Winston S. Churchill
(Churchill papers, 2/7)

13 August 1946

My dear Winston,

1. Thank you for letting me see the letter[1] from the Polish Senators. I cannot remember having met any of them personally. Their main thesis is that we should have upheld the frontier of the Treaty of Riga, but I do not think that you felt at any time during our discussions with the Russians that this was a fair frontier. Certainly the British Government did not think so at the time, and, as you know, delayed its recognition in consequence.

I share all your feelings of distress about this Polish business. It may be that nothing we could have done would have provided a happier outcome. All the same I think that if Mikolajczyk could have gone into Poland as Prime Minister at the time when you and I worked so hard to bring about an agreement in Moscow, the position might have been better. Certainly, Mikolajczyk, Romer,[2] Grabski,[3] all held that view at the time, and so I believe did Raczynski,[4] the Polish Ambassador in London. Unhappily Mikolajczyk had to wait many months while the Polish Government in London wrangled, and the situation in Poland got steadily worse from every point of view.

I am quite ready to talk over the question of a reply to this letter when we meet, if you so wish.

2. Thank you for letting me see the report of the discussions of the National Union Executive Committee on the change of name of the Party. Perhaps we can speak of this also.

Hope you have a good day at Dover.

---

[1] Reproduced above (pp. 437–9).
[2] Tadeusz Romer, 1894–1978. Secretary, Polish War Victims Relief Fund, WWI. First Secretary of Polish diplomatic mission to Paris, 1919. Polish envoy to Portugal, 1935–7. Polish Ambassador to Japan, 1937–41. Polish Ambassador to Soviet Union, 1942–3. Commissioner for Polish Affairs, Middle East, 1943. Polish Minister of Foreign Affairs, 1943–4.
[3] Stanisław Grabski, 1871–1949. Leader, National Democratic Party, Galicia, 1907; Polish National Committee, 1917; Constituent Assembly, 1919. Minister of Education and Religious Affairs, 1923, 1925–6. Chairman, National Council, 1942–4. Deputy President, Homeland National Council, 1945.
[4] Edward Bernard André Maria Raczyński, 1891–1993. Educated at Kraków and Leipzig Universities, and at London School of Economics. Entered Polish Ministry of Foreign Affairs, 1919. Polish Minister to League of Nations and Polish Delegate to Disarmament Conference, 1932–4. Ambassador to London, 1934–45. Acting Polish Minister for Foreign Affairs (in London), 1941–2. Minister of State for Foreign Affairs in Gen. Sikorski's Cabinet, London, 1942–3. Chairman of Polish Research Centre, London, 1940–67. President of Polish Government-in-Exile, 1979–86.

Lord Winterton to Winston S. Churchill
(Churchill papers, 2/42)

13 August 1946
Confidential

My dear Winston,

I shall be delighted to move the resolution on India at Blackpool and I am grateful to Rab for suggesting that I should do so and to you for accepting his proposal.

I shall, of course, consult you and Rab in advance in regard to what I say.

I am in deep spiritual accord with you over the Indian question; you, to my mind, see clearly, in all its naked grimness, the shape of things to come in the sub-continent if the British Government continues its present attitude.

I hope you are having a real holiday; I am going to Sweden with my wife[1] next week for three weeks' rest.

PS. I'm greatly disturbed at Wavell's action in asking Nehru to form an Interim Congress Government because of the effect upon the Moslem league and Ambedkar's depressed [. . .] organisation. I'm going to write vigorously about the matter in my Weekly Article in the *Sunday Chronicle*. The Press in general has been far too timid and hesitant in its discussion [. . .]; the dangers have not been adequately exposed.

Jo Sturdee to Winston S. Churchill
(Churchill papers, 5/1 A)

16 August 1946

You wanted to see a list of all the speeches you have made since the General Election.

Attached is also a list of the speeches you made in 1945 before the General Election, which not been gathered together for a book.

Do you wish to take them all away to Switzerland with you?[2]

---

[1] Cecilia Monica Wilson, 1902–74. Married, 1924, Edward Turnour, 6th Earl Winterton.
[2] Churchill replied: 'No. How many words do they make so far?'

Winston S. Churchill to Major Reginald Marnham
(*Churchill papers, 1/30*)

17 August 1946

My dear Marnham,

I am very much obliged to your for undertaking to cut my corn. I do hope you will bill me properly for it as I am already so much in your debt for all your many courtesies and aids.

Cox, who is so able and helpful, will I am sure make all the necessary arrangements and has my full authority while I am away.

I must particularly thank you for having kept us supplied with milk, from which we have extracted cream, for a whole year; and now that we shall soon become self-supporting in this matter is a fitting moment to express our gratitude.

I hope you will let me look in upon you some time next week and inspect your Constabulary.

I do not think you need be troubled immediately about the future of Chartwell as a national possession affecting the amenities at Chartwell Farm. Of course I cannot tell how long I shall live but the actuarial tables afford a reasonable working basis.

Pray look in upon me at any time or send for me if any difficulty arises.

PS. I am glad about the licence to repair the road.

Winston S. Churchill to Lord Cecil
(*Chelwood papers, 92/462*)

17 August 1946
Chartwell

My dear Bob,

I am so glad we are in agreement about the Austrian Tyrol. Boothby,[1] who is very active in this matter, is in touch with Chatham House. I am quite ready to join in any association which may be formed. I am telling Bob Boothby to work at it and that I will come along. In the vast confusion of Europe it is indeed a Touchstone.

Such baffling situations as those which now confront us can only be dealt

---

[1] Robert John Graham Boothby, 1900–86. Educated at Eton and Magdalen College, Oxford. MP (Cons.) for East Aberdeenshire, 1924–58. Parliamentary Private Secretary to Chancellor of the Exchequer (Churchill), 1926–9. Parliamentary Secretary, Ministry of Food, 1940–1. A British Delegate to the Consultative Assembly, Council of Europe, 1949–57. Knighted, on Churchill's recommendation, 1953. Baron, 1958. Chairman, Royal Philharmonic Orchestra, 1961–3. Published *The New Economy* (1943), *I Fight to Live* (1947), *My Yesterday, Your Tomorrow* (1962) and *Recollections of a Rebel* (1978).

with selectively. One way is to make up one's mind which is the true point of attack on the long front of evil and bewilderment.

Winston S. Churchill to Robert Boothby
(Churchill papers, 2/47)

17 August 1946
Private

My dear Bob,

Thank you for your letter of August 13.

I send you the correspondence I have had with Bob Cecil. I like your list so far as it goes and hope you have some Labour men among them. By all means invite Cranborne, Vansittart[1] and Beveridge[2] and the two you mentioned from the House of Commons.[3] You should also write to Archie (Sinclair), telling him I am in it. I must leave the development of the campaign to you, but pray keep me informed, especially in regard to any public announcement. The 'fact-finding Committee' is a very good one.

---

[1] Robert Gilbert Vansittart, 1881–1957. Educated at Eton. Entered Diplomatic Service, 1902. Asst Clerk, FO, 1914; 1st Secretary, 1918; Counsellor, 1920. Secretary to Lord Curzon, 1920–4. Principal Private Secretary to Ramsay MacDonald, 1928–30. Knighted, 1929. Permanent Under-Secretary of State for Foreign Affairs, 1930–8. Elected to the Other Club, 1933. Chief Diplomatic Adviser to the Foreign Secretary, 1938–41. PC, 1940. Baron, 1941. His autobiography, *The Mist Procession*, was published posthumously in 1958. His brother Arnold was killed in action in 1915.

[2] William Henry Beveridge, 1879–1963. Civil servant at the Board of Trade, 1908–16, when first Lloyd George and then Churchill gave him considerable responsibilities in connection with the creation of a scheme of compulsory state-aided national insurance. Ministry of Munitions, 1915–16; Ministry of Food, 1917–18 (Permanent Secretary, 1919). Knighted, 1919. Director, London School of Economics and Political Science, 1919–37. Member, Royal Commission on the Coal Industry, 1925. Master, University College, Oxford, 1937–45. Chairman, at Churchill's suggestion, of the Interdepartmental Committee on Social Insurance and Allied Services, 1941–2, and author of its report, *Social Insurance and Allied Services* (1942; the 'Beveridge Report'). MP (Lib.) for Berwick upon Tweed, 1944–5. Baron, 1946. Author of more than 20 books on politics and political science.

[3] Oliver Crosthwaite-Eyre, 1913–78. Educated at Downside and Trinity College, Cambridge. Col., Royal Marines, 1945. MP (Cons.) for New Forest and Christchurch, 1945–50; for New Forest, 1950–68.

John Paton, 1886–1976. General Secretary, Independent Labour Party, 1927–33. MP (Lab.) for Norwich, 1945–50; for Norwich North, 1950–64.

Winston S. Churchill to George Bernard Shaw
(Churchill papers, 2/165)

18 August 1946
Private

My dear Bernard Shaw,

How very kind of you to write me such a stimulating and indeed provocative letter.[1] I shall treasure it among my extending archives and I hope they will be enriched by several more as time passes.

I have always been much stirred by Joan. Anatole France is pretty good about her. She is indeed a gleaming star. I am taking your play about her away with me to read on my 'holiday'. Like you, my work and my holidays are the same.

It must be agreeable to enjoy such a prolonged view of the dissolving human scene and to be perennially rejuvenated by the resilience and permanence of what you have written.

We do not agree about Communism. The impending division or collision will be Communism v The Rest. I read with some sympathy Maeterlinck's[2] 'Life of the Bee'. At any rate the bees have preserved the monarchical principle!

I am not attracted by 'The soul of the white ant'. To hell with all static ideals of human society. What matters is the behaviour of individuals under an infinitely varying and, we must hope, on the whole improving atmosphere and surroundings.

Do you think that the atomic bomb means that the architect of the universe has got tired of writing his non-stop scenario? There was a lot to be said for his stopping with the Panda. The release of the bomb seems to be his next turning point.

The following is serious. Ought we not to try and settle the Irish question. Could we not call it quits in the long tragedy? We succeeded in exercising remarkable forbearance about the Irish ports.

---

[1] Reproduced above (pp. 446–9).
[2] Maurice Maeterlinck, 1862–1949. Belgian playwright, poet and essayist. His 1892 play *Pelléas et Mélisande* is regarded as one of the masterpieces of French Symbolist drama. Nobel Prize in Literature, 1911. Count of Belgium, 1932.

August 1946

Mohammed Ali Jinnah to Winston S. Churchill
(Churchill papers, 2/42)

22 August 1946 Bombay
Personal, Private and Confidential

Dear Mr Churchill,

I thank you for your cablegram, acknowledging my letter, and your reply of 3rd August 1946.[1]

I am rather surprised to read paragraph 3 of your letter. It shows that even you have not got a full grasp of the situation in India and it seems that your press is not very helpful in that direction while the Congress propaganda of misrepresentation is so widely spread and their press so powerfully organised by the capitalist patrons of the Congress.

What do you expect the Mussalmans to do? You admit the tendencies in England to support the Congress are very strong in the Government party. We have had a bitter taste of it – perhaps the bitterest. The Muslim League was progressively betrayed by the Cabinet Delegation and the Viceroy and was being gradually steam-rolled. When the Secretary of State for India and his colleagues and the Viceroy finally disclosed their hands, undoubtedly, there could be only one result and that is a general revolt against the British. For else, who is responsible to force down and thrust upon 100 million Muslims of India terms which the Congress alone will be pleased to accept? Even the final proposals of the Cabinet Mission both with regard to the long-term and short-term, with which I was far from satisfied, were rejected by the Congress and the Muslim League alone accepted them; and now the Viceroy is making efforts to propitiate the Congress.

The situation is very serious and dangerous; and it is very difficult for me to make you understand the details, but, since you have expressed a desire to hear from me I am enclosing herewith copies of my recent statements to the Press.

---

[1] Reproduced above (pp. 440–1).

Winston S. Churchill to Mohammed Ali Jinnah
(Churchill papers, 2/42)

22 August 1946
Draft
NOT SENT

Dear Mr Jinnah,

Thank you for your letter of August 22 and its enclosures which I am studying.

With regard to what you say about paragraph 3 of my previous letter, it seems to me that your friends should have been careful to distinguish between complaints against the British Party Government of the day and abuse of the British Nation as a whole. Britain has played a noble part in India, and has given India not only effective protection from external attack for many generations, but the British raj is the only form in which the unity of India can possibly be maintained. There is no nation in the world that would voluntarily, in the moment of world victory, quit and cast away so great an Empire. Personally, I hope that wiser counsels will prevail and that India will not put itself outside the shelter of the British Commonwealth of Nations and all the world influence we can command. That is, however, a matter for the Indian elected bodies to settle under Dominion status.

I do not think we shall lose very much by leaving India at the present time, and that feeling is undoubtedly widespread here. There is a feeling it is a great burden and danger and that we are continually abused by the political classes who, irrespective of race or religion, vie with one another in scolding us. What would happen to India when we have gone is another matter. Having thought much about these matters, I foresee a period of civil war and anarchy, not only as a result of a struggle between religions, but also, as in China, between Communists and anti-Communists.

September 1946

Sarah Churchill to Winston S. Churchill
(Churchill papers, 1/42)[1]

6 September 1946

Darling Papa,

How very very sweet of you in the rush of your departure to have remembered the two pictures I asked for. My darling Marrakech, and the best of lemon-scented magnolias. I will take great care of them, and before I leave the country will see them safely restored to 28 Hyde Park Gate – I do hope you are having a wonderful time – I think of you all often – and know the fun I'm missing. What a lovely weekend we had before you left! Please think about my Italian picture. I would not be happy doing it – if you were not happy about it. It is called 'Daniele Cortis' by Fogazzaro. All the rest of my news is in Mummie's letter – I have no blotting paper – hence the 3 unnecessary pages.[2]

Robert Boothby to Winston S. Churchill
(Churchill papers, 2/47)[3]

7 September 1946

Dear Mr Churchill,

I had called a meeting of the 'fact-finding' committee on the Tyrol for next week; but, in view of this morning's good news,[4] we have decided not to go on at present.

---

[1] This letter was handwritten.

[2] Churchill responded on Sep. 10: 'Can see no objection to your film plan but am much distressed at your health. Please kindly see Moran before leaving. Wire me you will do so and I will apprise him. No need return pictures yet. Much love – Papa.' Sarah replied on Sep. 11: 'Thank you for both your sweet telegrams. Am really much better but promise I will see Moran before I leave. Will let you know my plans much love to you all – Sarah.'

[3] This letter was handwritten.

[4] Agreement between Italians and Austrians at the Paris Peace Conference on the question of the German population in South Tyrol.

Of course things may take a turn for the worse, and the Russians are capable of trying to put a spoke in the wheel.

But on the face of it, the Tyrolese have got what they wanted, plus the chance of genuine economic cooperation with Italy.

It is perhaps the only encouraging development in the darkening European scene.

It may interest you to know that the Austrians have ascribed this happy turn of events entirely to our debate in the House of Commons, which apparently made a great impression on de Gasperi.[1]

So I am more than ever indebted to you for making it possible.

Winston S. Churchill to Field Marshal Lord Alanbrooke
(Churchill papers, 4/196)

9 September 1946 Villa Choisi
Private Switzerland

My dear Brookie,

I have been putting together a few notes about the first battle in France before Dunkirk, and for this purpose have had available, besides my own documents, a very full diary prepared by the Historical Section and also Gort's[2] despatch. I do not gather from either of these exactly when and how your action was fought near the Ypres–Menin road. I always understood this was a most important feature of the successful withdrawal into the Dunkirk perimeter, that you commanded the divisions of Alex and Monty and I think a third division, that you repulsed the enemy on the whole corps front with heavy loss, and that at the same time the four British divisions we were withdrawing from Lille were streaming homewards along the road only a few miles behind your front line. I should be so much obliged if you could give me a note on this, as it has always figured in my mind.

We have had horrible weather here; indeed, they say it has never been so bad at this season. However, the villa is very comfortable. I have been playing at 'still life' and experimenting in Tempera which is a most amusing medium for preliminary work.

Things do not seem to be very good anywhere. Indeed I could easily find stronger terms in which to describe them.

---

[1] Alcide de Gasperi, 1881–1954. Italian statesman and founder of the Christian Democracy party. PM, 1945–53.

[2] John Standish Surtees Prendergast Vereker, 1886–1946. Educated at Harrow and Sandhurst. Succeeded his father as 6th Viscount Gort, 1902. 2nd Lt, 1905. Capt., 1914. On active service, 1914–18 (despatches nine times, VC, MC, DSO and two bars). Gen., 1937. CIGS, 1937–9. Elected a member of the Other Club, 1938. C-in-C, British Field Force, 1939–40. Inspector-General to the Forces for Training, 1940. Governor and C-in-C, Gibraltar, 1941–2; Malta, 1942–4. High Commissioner and C-in-C, Palestine, 1944–5.

September 1946

Duncan Sandys to Winston S. Churchill
(Churchill papers, 1/42)[1]

15 September 1946

My dear Winston,

Diana & I enjoyed every moment of our stay with you & Clemmie in Switzerland. It was a wonderful holiday & reminded us so much of the happy time we all had together in Marrakech ten years ago.

I am waiting impatiently to hear your Zurich speech. It is coming at a very good moment. The allied governments have had plenty of time to hammer out some solution to the European problem and have quite obviously failed. I am sure that in these present circumstances the public in all countries is very much in the mood to listen to what the late pilot has got to say.

We shall look forward to seeing you all when you get back at the end of the week.

Winston S. Churchill: speech
('Winston S. Churchill, His Complete Speeches', volume 7, pages 7379–82)

19 September 1946   Zurich University

THE TRAGEDY OF EUROPE

I wish to speak to you today about the tragedy of Europe. This noble continent, comprising on the whole the fairest and the most cultivated regions of the earth, enjoying a temperate and equable climate, is the home of all the great parent races of the western world. It is the fountain of Christian faith and Christian ethics. It is the origin of most of the culture, arts, philosophy and science both of ancient and modern times. If Europe were once united in the sharing of its common inheritance, there would be no limit to the happiness, to the prosperity and glory which its three or four hundred million people would enjoy. Yet it is from Europe that have sprung that series of frightful nationalistic quarrels, originated by the Teutonic nations, which we have seen even in this twentieth century and in our own lifetime, wreck the peace and mar the prospects of all mankind.

And what is the plight to which Europe has been reduced? Some of the smaller States have indeed made a good recovery, but over wide areas a vast quivering mass of tormented, hungry, care-worn and bewildered human beings gape at the ruins of their cities and homes, and scan the dark horizons for the approach of some new peril, tyranny or terror. Among the victors there is a babel of jarring voices; among the vanquished the sullen silence of

---

[1] This letter was handwritten.

despair. That is all that Europeans, grouped in so many ancient States and nations, that is all that the Germanic Powers have got by tearing each other to pieces and spreading havoc far and wide. Indeed, but for the fact that the great Republic across the Atlantic Ocean has at length realised that the ruin or enslavement of Europe would involve their own fate as well, and has stretched out hands of succour and guidance, the Dark Ages would have returned in all their cruelty and squalor. They may still return.

Yet all the while there is a remedy which, if it were generally and spontaneously adopted, would as if by a miracle transform the whole scene, and would in a few years make all Europe, or the greater part of it, as free and as happy as Switzerland is today. What is this sovereign remedy? It is to re-create the European Family, or as much of it as we can, and provide it with a structure under which it can dwell in peace, in safety and in freedom. We must build a kind of United States of Europe. In this way only will hundreds of millions of toilers be able to regain the simple joys and hopes which make life worth living. The process is simple. All that is needed is the resolve of hundreds of millions of men and women to do right instead of wrong and gain as their reward blessing instead of cursing.

Much work has been done upon this task by the exertions of the Pan-European Union which owes so much to the Count Coudenhove-Kalergi and which commanded the services of the famous French patriot and statesman, Aristide Briand. There is also that immense body of doctrine and procedure, which was brought into being amid high hopes after the first world war, as the League of Nations. The League of Nations did not fail because of its principles or conceptions. It failed because the Governments of those days feared to face the facts, and act while time remained. This disaster must not be repeated. There is therefore much knowledge and material with which to build; and also bitter dear-bought experience.

I was very glad to read in the newspapers two days ago that my friend President Truman had expressed his interest and sympathy with this great design. There is no reason why a regional organization of Europe should in any way conflict with the world organization of the United Nations. On the contrary, I believe that the larger synthesis will only survive if it is founded upon coherent natural groupings. There is already a natural grouping in the Western Hemisphere. We British have our own Commonwealth of Nations. These do not weaken, on the contrary they strengthen, the world organization. They are in fact its main support. And why should there not be a European group which could give a sense of enlarged patriotism and common citizenship to the distracted peoples of this turbulent and mighty continent and why should it not take its rightful place with other great groupings in shaping the destinies of men? In order that this should be accomplished there must be an act of faith in which millions of families speaking many languages must consciously take part.

We all know that the two world wars through which we have passed arose out of the vain passion of a newly-united Germany to play the dominating part in the world. In this last struggle crimes and massacres have been committed for which there is no parallel since the invasions of the Mongols in the fourteenth century and no equal at any time in human history. The guilty must be punished. Germany must be deprived of the power to rearm and make another aggressive war. But when all this has been done, as it will be done, as it is being done, there must be an end to retribution. There must be what Mr Gladstone many years ago called 'a blessed act of oblivion'. We must all turn our backs upon the horrors of the past. We must look to the future. We cannot afford to drag forward across the years that are to come the hatreds and revenges which have sprung from the injuries of the past. If Europe is to be saved from infinite misery, and indeed from final doom, there must be an act of faith in the European family and an act of oblivion against all the crimes and follies of the past.

Can the free peoples of Europe rise to the height of these resolves of the soul and instincts of the spirit of man? If they can, the wrongs and injuries which have been inflicted will have been washed away on all sides by the miseries which have been endured. Is there any need for further floods of agony? Is it the only lesson of history that mankind is unteachable? Let there be justice, mercy and freedom. The peoples have only to will it, and all will achieve their hearts' desire.

I am now going to say something that will astonish you. The first step in the re-creation of the European family must be a partnership between France and Germany. In this way only can France recover the moral leadership of Europe. There can be no revival of Europe without a spiritually great France and a spiritually great Germany. The structure of the United States of Europe, if well and truly built, will be such as to make the material strength of a single state less important. Small nations will count as much as large ones and gain their honour by their contribution to the common cause. The ancient states and principalities of Germany, freely joined together for mutual convenience in a federal system, might each take their individual place among the United States of Europe. I shall not try to make a detailed programme for hundreds of millions of people who want to be happy and free, prosperous and safe, who wish to enjoy the four freedoms of which the great President Roosevelt spoke, and live in accordance with the principles embodied in the Atlantic Charter. If this is their wish, they have only to say so, and means can certainly be found, and machinery erected, to carry that wish into full fruition.

But I must give you a warning. Time may be short. At present there is a breathing-space. The cannon have ceased firing. The fighting has stopped; but the dangers have not stopped. If we are to form the United States of Europe or whatever name or form it may take, we must begin now.

In these present days we dwell strangely and precariously under the shield and protection of the atomic bomb. The atomic bomb is still only in the hands of a State and nation which we know will never use it except in the cause of right and freedom. But it may well be that in a few years this awful agency of destruction will be widespread and the catastrophe following from its use by several warring nations will not only bring to an end all that we call civilisation, but may possibly disintegrate the globe itself.

I must now sum up the propositions which are before you. Our constant aim must be to build and fortify the strength of UNO. Under and within that world concept we must re-create the European family in a regional structure called, it may be, the United States of Europe. The first step is to form a Council of Europe. If at first all the States of Europe are not willing or able to join the Union, we must nevertheless proceed to assemble and combine those who will and those who can. The salvation of the common people of every race and of every land from war or servitude must be established on solid foundations and must be guarded by the readiness of all men and women to die rather than submit to tyranny. In all this urgent work, France and Germany must take the lead together. Great Britain, the British Commonwealth of Nations, mighty America, and I trust Soviet Russia – for then indeed all would be well – must be the friends and sponsors of the new Europe and must champion its right to live and shine.

L. S. Amery to Winston S. Churchill
(Churchill papers, 2/18)

20 September 1946

My dear Winston,

You have indeed lit a torch to give its message of hope to shattered Europe. The French are startled, and they were bound to be, but the idea will sink in all the same. As for the Germans your speech may have been just in time to save them from going Bolshevist. You have done few bigger things, even in the great years behind us.

Only you cannot leave the matter with one speech. This morning's silly leader in *The Times* shows how much more is needed in the way of follow up and amplification. Have you thought of the opportunity Blackpool will give you for that? Naturally you will have to give some of your speech to kicking this incompetent Government in the pants. But I believe you could rouse our people to great enthusiasm with the conception of a world organised in groups of partner nations, each with its own distinctive history and characteristics, as a preferable alternative to a mere black and white ideological fight between American mid-Victorian individualism and Russian State slavery. In doing so you will appeal at once both to pride in our own Empire and to the desire that we should stand for a policy of our own. By that I mean our own as a nation, but with a definite lead in that policy of our own as the Conservative Party.

I am profoundly convinced that, if we are to recapture the working classes of this country, we have got to interest them both in our vision and in our ideas of how to attain it. Mere fusion on anti-Socialist lines will not create that interest and will not prevent further erosion by aggressive Socialist doctrine of both Conservative and Liberal rank and file.

If there is anything you think I can do usefully in connection with the European movement you will let me know.

The Times: article
(*The Times*)

20 September 1946

A VOICE FROM ZURICH

Mr Churchill chose his platform well. In a double sense, Switzerland was peculiarly appropriate for the launching of a call for a United States of Europe. The history of Switzerland as a confederation speaks for itself. Common interests, a common culture overriding diversities of language, and common dangers in this case too, were able to make out of the cantons of Switzerland a confederation, a single State. In that State many diversities of language, custom, religion, and race were overcome, and yet survived their overcoming, so that Switzerland today is a State united yet multiple, homogeneous yet diverse, and, moreover, with a record of peace, progress, and prosperity unique in Europe. But if the history of Switzerland as a confederation offers this example, her history as a State among the other States of Europe also proclaims the difficulties. Clinging ever more firmly, since its extinction during the Napoleonic wars, to her neutrality as her best protection, Switzerland has proved herself least ready of all the States of Europe – and the record justifies her wisdom hitherto – to unite with her neighbours in common enterprises. If Mr Churchill's United States of Europe ever comes into being, Switzerland will hardly be a founding member.

Mr Churchill's speech at Zurich yesterday showed once again his familiar characteristics. There was courage; he was not afraid to startle the world with new and even, as many must find them, outrageous propositions. There was imagination, ready to overleap caution and convention, to meet a new situation with a bold conception rather than with pedestrian prudence. Many will be reminded of his offer of union to France in 1940. There was a sense of history, encouraging him to view the present 'tragedy of Europe' as a stage in a developing drama, and to diagnose the ills of a continent in terms of its past and its probable future. But is the remedy Mr Churchill prescribes one to which Europe, in its present situation, will submit? It must be admitted that there are few signs of it. Even in western Europe there is little to suggest that the unity so much spoken of, and indeed so much desired, is on the way.

Mr Churchill in fact, no doubt deliberately, left many things unsaid. He could also be accused, and no doubt will be, of saying more than he meant. As he himself declared, the conception of a United States of Europe is not new. But the version of it he recommends seems novel, at least under that name, and to many dangerous under any name. Many will see in his speech a call not for a United States of Europe but for a United States of Western Europe. That indeed is what takes the speech out of the realm of truisms into that of controversy. If Russia came into his projected Council of Europe, said Mr Churchill, then all indeed would be well. If there was any chance of Russia coming in on Mr Churchill's terms, it might be retorted, then all would be unnecessary. Though he did not say so in so many words, Mr Churchill's speech was in fact based on the assumption that Europe is already irrevocably divided between East and West. This is the peril of his argument and of its enunciation at this moment. Europe, he argues, is divided and menaced, preserved from earlier ruin only by the 'protection' of the atomic bomb. No one knows better than Mr Churchill that a common menace is the best stimulant to common action, and it is because he believes that a common menace to western Europe already exists that he calls for unity now. His call is given a still more challenging turn by the inclusion of Germany within the unity he postulates.

Mr Churchill speaks as a man of unique experience, uniquely respected, as his reception in Switzerland, and earlier in Belgium and Holland, has amply shown. But for all that he speaks as a man without responsibility for his country's policy. Those who now bear that responsibility are not behind him in idealism – witness Mr Bevin's speech of last November in which he spoke of his hopes for a 'World Assembly' directly elected by the peoples of all countries. That was a hope for a far distant future. Meanwhile British policy has not yet despaired, and cannot yet afford to despair, of averting the division of Europe and the world into two. It has not yet despaired of making Germany, not a factor in the balance of East against West or of West against East, or a pawn divided between the two, but a united State which, under joint control, will strengthen and embody the unity of the controlling Powers, and they cannot be assisted in their patient labours by the implications that will be read into yesterday's speech at Zurich. So long as the purposes of unity and conciliation can be maintained, British policy, while always preserving the unity of Europe as a conception and even looking for a United States of Europe as the eventual ideal, cannot work for such a United States of Europe as Mr Churchill must be taken to have meant. 'The first practical step,' said Mr Churchill, 'will be to form a Council of Europe.' But the first practical steps of British policy must necessarily be more humdrum, and they may prove to be best directed along the path of economics rather than of politics. The most practical steps which

Europe is taking today towards greater unity may well be represented by such developments as the recent Franco-British economic agreement, the progress that is being made towards economic union between Holland and Belgium, and the project, soon to be discussed by the United Nations Economic and Social Council, for setting up an Economic Commission for Europe. The most effective next steps will be, wherever possible, the opening of exchange and intercourse with eastern Europe and, above all, the Soviet Union itself in the urgent tasks of reconstruction.

If the British Government's hopes of maintaining a wider unity in Europe were to prove ultimately and unmistakably vain, then many minds in western Europe would no doubt revert to Mr Churchill's project for a lesser but closer unity. In that event the plan would have the spur of menace more sharply behind it than it has in truth today, and might be correspondingly closer to realization. Mr Churchill has proved that, private citizen though he be, he can still utter words which no one can afford to ignore. His plea that the world should not 'drag forward, across the years that are to come, hatreds and revenges which have sprung from the issues of the past' is one that will be widely and fervently echoed. But it remains to be seen whether French opinion will be prepared to tolerate, even from Mr Churchill, the suggestion that 'the first step in the recreation of the European family must be a partnership between France and Germany', and Germany today is in no position to offer partnership to anyone, still less a partnership that acknowledged and ratified her own division between East and West. Mr Churchill has shown again his special skill in dropping into the waters of international relations stones whose ripples last long and travel far.

Winston S. Churchill to Robert Boothby
(Churchill papers, 2/47)

22 September 1946
Private

My dear Bob,

I am very glad things have taken a more satisfactory turn about the Austrian Tyrol. I have no doubt that our debate in the House of Commons had a definite effect, and the credit of it belongs to you.

[. . .]

Winston S. Churchill to Sir Edward Bridges
(Camrose papers)

23 September 1946

My dear Edward,

I am pressed from many quarters to give my account of the British war story and, without at present making any definite plans, I have been getting my papers in order and considering the project. I should like to tell the story so far as possible in my own words written at the time. As you know a great part of my work was done in writing (dictated transcript) and I should scarcely need to publish any documents other than those I have composed myself. I should of course not wish to publish any paper which was not considered in the public interest by the Government of the day, and I should be quite ready to discuss the omission of any particular phrase, sentence or passage in memoranda otherwise unobjectionable. Moreover I do not expect that any publication can take place for two or three years and I may not live so long. I should agree to a final revision of the text in detail by HMG before publication, in case the foreign situation might be such as to make what is now harmless injurious. This can only be judged in the future.

2. I should like to know, without necessarily accepting the view as final, whether in principle there would be any objection to the publication of the kind of memoranda which are attached to this note. I feel I have a right, if I so decide, to tell my tale and I am convinced that it would be to the advantage of our country to have it told, as perhaps I alone can tell it. There are three classes of documents composed by myself which must be considered:

(a) Papers written by me as Minister of Defence or Prime Minister (or as First Lord of the Admiralty in the early months). Specimens of these will be found attached. I might not wish to quote these papers in full. That would depend on the course of the narrative. But, subject to the public interest being safeguarded on particular points (as judged by the Government of the day before publication), I should like to know that I am free to use them as I may think fitting to the narrative.

(b) There is an immense series of my Minutes which I had printed for convenience of reference in a series of monthly records. In using these I should naturally consider my own obligation to all those who served with or under me. You have copies of all these in your possession and I should be very ready to consult with the Government of the day on any particular point which they might question. Some day undoubtedly they will all be published. However in telling a tale the words written in the circumstances of the moment are of far greater significance than any paraphrase of them or subsequent composition.

(c) Finally there is the 'Personal' correspondence. This consists of about 1,000 telegrams to President Roosevelt and his successor and probably as many more to other Heads of Government within and without the British Empire. These telegrams will certainly become public one day but, subject to review before eventual publication, they constitute a very favourable explanation of the course and conduct of the National Coalition Government of which I was the head.

The answers which were received to these telegrams from President Roosevelt and from other Heads of Governments including especially Dominions, could not of course be published without the agreement of the Parties concerned, nor indeed is their textual publication necessary to the course of the narrative. They could easily be summarized in so far as it is necessary, and of course I know all that happened.

3. What I should like to know now is that the kind of use I propose to make of papers, Minutes and Telegrams which I wrote myself, as the responsible Head of the Government, would be agreeable in principle to His Majesty's present advisers, subject of course to a final review on particular points and passages by the Government of the day before any publication is made.

4. I should be glad to receive the Prime Minister's view upon this matter at his convenience in order that I may consider what course to take.

Count Richard Coudenhove-Kalergi to Winston S. Churchill
(Churchill papers, 2/19)[1]

23 September 1946

My dear Winston Churchill,

Your speech made me one of the happiest men on earth. I cannot express my feelings of gratitude for all it meant for Europe, for the Pan European Movement and for me.

Your help is incalculable in its [. . .] consequences: now that you have raised the European question the governments can no longer ignore it while the people of Europe are with us!

I fully agree with your basic idea that the French and German people must constitute the core of Europe – but their reconciliation will be the consequence, not the condition of European Union. Like after the Civil War in the USA and the South African War reconciliation will slowly follow federation.

It is, therefore, up to France to take up the ball you threw from Zurich – France, Europe's Piedmont. But who will be its Caucus?

Thank you again for all you did for all you do and for all you are.

---

[1] This letter was handwritten.

T. M. Snow to Ernest Bevin
(Churchill papers, 2/245)

25 September 1946
No. 494

British Legation
Berne

Sir,

I have the honour to report that Mr Winston Churchill, accompanied by his family, arrived at the Villa Choisi near Nyon on the Lake of Geneva on the 23rd ultimo. A group of Swiss sponsors had arranged to be the hosts of Mr Churchill and his family during their visit, and it was they who obtained the loan of the Villa Choisi for the use of the party. The villa is a pleasant 18th century house with tree-shaded lawns extending to the lake. The staff of the villa were provided by the Swiss sponsors, other Swiss lent *objets d'art* to adorn it. General Guisan[1] (Officer Commanding the Swiss Army during the war) lent his military cook and his campaigning tent, in which Mr Churchill could paint in the garden in wet weather. The approaches to the villa were permanently guarded by Swiss troops and police, and everything possible was done to allow him to have a quiet time during his stay at the villa, and he received a few guests only – among them General Guisan and General Smuts. M Montag, a Swiss art dealer[2] long resident in Paris where he knew Mr Churchill, was the prime mover in planning the visit, and accompanied Mr Churchill during the whole of it.

2. Miss Mary Churchill won most flattering notice from the Swiss press by her presence of mind and courage in administering first aid to a man who had just been badly injured in a road accident not far from the Villa Choisi. Towards the end of the stay at the Villa Choisi, Mrs Churchill unhappily damaged her rib through a fall in a motor boat and was unable to join in the public part of Mr Churchill's visit to Switzerland.

3. Mr Churchill left the Villa on September 16th and, accompanied by Miss Mary Churchill, went to Geneva, where he was received by an enthusiastic crowd and lunched with the President[3] and Committee of the International Red Cross. The same afternoon he and Miss Churchill left Geneva for Berne, where his party were put up at the Chateau de Lohn (the Swiss Chequers)

---

[1] Henri Guisan, 1874–1960. Joined Swiss Army as an artillery officer, 1894. Commanded Swiss Armed Forces, 1939–45. According to his obituary in *The Times:* 'In 1940, after the collapse of France when many Swiss were discouraged and a defeatist spirit showed signs of developing, his resolute attitude and his expressed determination to defend Switzerland against any invader did much to rally the national morale. He modified the defence plan so that resistance on several fronts could be made and built the so-called Swiss redoubt in the Alps, where ammunition and stores were accumulated in a highly fortified system, and strong-points, storehouses, and barracks, were hewn in the rock' (*The Times*, 9 April 1960).

[2] Charles Montag.

[3] Carl Jacob Burckhardt, 1891–1974. Educated at University of Zurich, 1922; Prof. of Modern History, 1927–9; Prof., Institute of Higher International Studies, 1932–7, 1939–45. High Commissioner of the League of Nations in the Free City of Danzig, 1937–9. Worked for International Red Cross 1923–7; President, 1945–8. Swiss Ambassador to France, 1945–9. Peace Prize of the German Book Trade, 1954.

about four miles outside Berne. On the following day the Federal Council entertained Mr Churchill and Miss Churchill at a luncheon party, at which the Federal Councillors and their wives and various Swiss personalities were present, at the Chateau d'Allmendingen, a charming Swiss country house lent by its owners to the Federal Council for the occasion. After luncheon, four open carriages with outriders in 18th century costume drove Mr Churchill and party in procession to Berne. The four miles of the road to Berne were lined by delighted, cheering and enthusiastic crowds, and Berne itself was beflagged and beflowered. After passing in procession through the main streets of Berne, the cavalcade drew up at the Town Hall, where there was a civic reception and Mr Churchill addressed the crowd from the balcony in English. It was noticeable that the majority of those present seemed readily able to follow what he said. In the evening my wife[1] and I gave a reception and supper at the Legation in Mr Churchill's honour and some 280 guests were present and included many prominent Swiss personalities from various parts of Switzerland. On the following day Mr Churchill and Miss Churchill left for Zurich after attending a luncheon party at the French Embassy.

4. The enthusiasm evoked by Mr Churchill's visit to Berne eclipsed, so I was assured by those who should know, any reception received by any other figure in living memory in Berne.

5. Similar scenes were also witnessed in Zurich, where Mr Churchill spent from the evening of September 18th to the morning of September 20th. On September 19th he was entertained to luncheon by the Cantonal Government of Zurich. At this luncheon Mr Churchill made a speech which was broadcast both by the British and Swiss broadcasting services and received wide publicity in the press. Mr Churchill appealed for a federated Europe as the only means of avoiding the disasters which loomed ahead.

Winston S. Churchill to Prince Charles, Count of Flanders[2]
(Churchill papers, 2/249)

29 September 1946   Airborne!

Sir,

We enjoyed our visit to[3] much and it was great pleasure to meet Your Royal Highness and to have such long and interesting talks. I shall often think about all your problems as Regent under these extraordinary conditions and earnestly hope that you will solve them. I am sure the key is duty.

[1] Phyllis Annette Malcolmson. Married, 1927, Thomas Maitland Snow: three children.
[2] Prince Charles-Theodore Henry Antoine Meinrad, 1903–83. Educated at Royal Naval College, Osborne. Count of Flanders, 1910. Returned to Belgium, 1926, to serve in Belgian Army as 2nd Lt. Appointed Prince Regent by Belgian Parliament, serving from 1944 to 1950, when King Leopold III returned.
[3] so.

I was painfully affected by all you told me about your brother's[1] singular attitude and behaviour to you in these long tragic years. I have a brother who is five years younger than me and whom I dearly love and have always cherished. I grieve indeed that you have never found the same kindness and protection which Nature decrees.

My visit to Paris was successful. I had long talks at the British Embassy with Byrnes, Bedell Smith and General Smuts. How much we all agree! There has been no publicity to cause embarrassment to Mr Bevin and I have brought my knowledge of the general position up-to-date, and renewed my very intimate American contacts.

I write this in your beautiful and silent aeroplane. It was indeed kind of you to let it take me home by a triangular route. We carry with us very pleasant memories and send you back our warmest wishes for yourself and your country.

Winston S. Churchill to General Sir Hastings Ismay
(Churchill papers, 4/19)

30 September 1946

My dear P,

I am having a few of these early chapters about the battle in France in 1940 printed by Messrs Eyre and Spottiswoode's confidential section, and I will send them to you as they come through. They are of course only very provisional notes and are derived mainly, though possibly incorrectly, from the Staff Diary which you so kindly sent me. It may interest you to read them, and make any notes you like in correction or improvement. However, it will probably be several years before they see the light, and of course they must undergo organised examination by the young gentlemen I am going to employ.

---

[1] Leopold, 1901–83. Married, 1926, Princess Astrid of Sweden (d. 1935): two children; 1941, Mary-Lilian Baels: three children. King Leopold III of Belgium, 1934–50. Surrendered his army to the Germans, 1940. Confined by the Germans to his royal château, 1940–4; in Austria, 1945. Forbidden to return to Belgium, 1945–50. Abdicated in favour of his son, 1950.

October
1946

Syed Waris Ameer Ali[1] to Winston S. Churchill
(Churchill papers, 2/5)

2 October 1946

Dear Mr Winston Churchill,
   You have doubtless forgotten that I was one who supported your opposition to many aspects of the India Act of 1935.
   Your approach to the Indian problem has been amply justified by recent events. In fact the Prime Minister of an Indian Province said to me quite lately in reference to the present situation 'This would never have happened if Mr Churchill had been in office.' No one contests the ultimate aim of granting Indians of all races as much scope as possible in the Government of their own country. The response of India during the war has been magnificent, save for the Congress Party which represents the quintessence of caste Hindu privilege & Hindu Big Business. This Party sponsored a dangerous outbreak on the lines of communication of the 14th Army before the battle of El Alamein, when it was thought that we had lost the war. During this revolt, Moslem officials & the Moslem public, along with many Hindus, stood loyal. The leaders of the Congress met with lenient treatment & were, as often before, interned. After the Labour Government came to power, they were released last autumn to conduct an election campaign. Helped by the prestige gained by unchecked abuse of the existing Government & by unlimited funds, they naturally carried away the Hindu electorate. Matters were complicated by the treatment of certain captured traitors amongst Indian officers & men who joined the Japanese. Many were either released wholesale, or some were put on trial in places accessible to hysterical agitation & were then pardoned.
   The attitude of the loyal ranks of the Indian Army to these men is shown

[1] Syed Waris Ameer Ali, 1886–1975. Son of Syed Amir Ali of Oudh (the first Indian PC) and Isabella Konstam. Educated at Wellington and Balliol College, Oxford. Married, 1918, Anne Radford (d. 1943); 1951, Lady Eleanor Dawson. Entered Indian Civil Service, 1908. Served in United Provinces; District and Sessions judge in Oudh. Retired, 1929. Resident in London from 1929. Member of the Council, Indian Empire Society, 1930–2. Adviser to High Commissioner for India in London, 1939–45. CIE, 1942.

by a Punjabi regiment which gave no quarter to a company of its own Sepoys who had joined the Japanese, when it met them in action in Burma. The Congress lauded these traitors to the skies, whilst no equivalent praise was lavished on the loyalists who had suffered so much in captivity. This, added to the natural unrest amongst young Indians in the Forces awaiting demobilisation & deprived of an expected career, caused much anxiety, & doubtless intensified the Cabinet's desire for a constitutional solution. As a result of the Cabinet mission, the Viceroy has called upon the erstwhile opponents of the war effort to form a Ministry from the Congress. The Moslem League which is supported by at least 90 per cent of the 90 million Moslems, and offered cooperation with the Cabinet Mission, feels now that it has been thrust aside & is affronted by the Congress nomination of Quisling Moslems, as well as their statement that they will brook no future interference on behalf of minorities. The upshot has been widespread disorder & bloodshed, & perforce the use of British troops to restore order & even to bury the dead. There is every prospect of further carnage. The Congress is said to be organising the Sikhs as its spearhead. It is no slur on many gallant & loyal Sikhs to say that their nation provided a large proportion of the men who joined the Japanese.

The greater Princes are looking to their armies, & the smaller Princes are combining, in the face of Congress threats.

It is idle therefore for the *Times* to say that the new central Government commands the support of three quarters of the people. At most it commands that of little more than half of British India. The Depressed classes have been shamefully byepassed, whatever the *Times* may say. The Moslems will never willingly be ruled by a Government representing Hindu idolaters, priests, & money-lenders, & there are 120 million within the British Empire. Moslems in all the Allied Force have not proved unworthy in the late war, & provided a large proportion of the front line troops of the Indian Army.

There is a curious black out of important news from India. We have not heard in the English Press of the Congress majority in the United Provinces legislature voting to abolish the old established landholding system, thereby proposing to expropriate with what compensation is not known, some seven million people, hitherto known for political stability. Nor have we heard of the tribal intrigues culminating in the murder of the Political Agent at Bannu last month, nor whether Hindus or Moslems began the rioting at Calcutta.

Is all this a part of the most pitiful abandonment of helpless masses that the British Empire has yet seen?[1]

---

[1] Churchill replied on Oct. 14: 'Thank you for your letter of October 2. I am very glad to hear from you. You and I have certainly no need to revise the opinions we formed ten and fifteen years ago.'

Winston S. Churchill: speech
('*Winston S. Churchill, His Complete Speeches*', volume 7, pages 7382–90)

5 October 1946   Conservative Party Conference
Blackpool

'EVERY DOG HIS DAY'

We have certainly had a depressing year since the General Election. I do not blame the Socialist Government – for the weather. We must also make allowances for all the difficulties which mark the aftermath of war. These difficulties would have taxed to the utmost the whole moral and physical resources of a united nation, marshalled and guided by a National Government. The Socialists broke up the national unity for the sake of their political interests, and the nation decided at the polls for a Socialist Party Government. This was their right under our well-tried Constitution. The electors, based on universal suffrage, may do what they like. And afterwards they have to like what they do. There is a saying in England, 'Experience bought is better than taught.' We have bought the experience. I do not complain at all of the workings of our constitutional democratic system. If the majority of the people of Britain on the morrow of our survival and victory felt as they did, it was right that they should have their way. In consequence a Party Government has come into office which has shown itself markedly unequal to holding our place in the world or making the best of Britain on the morrow of its prolonged, intense exertions and immortal services to mankind.

The Socialist Party have only done their duty in accepting the responsibility so unexpectedly cast upon them by the electors. If they cannot do their job, that is our misfortune, but it was their duty to try. Also it was the duty of everyone to help them to overcome the national and world problems with which they were confronted. That still remains the settled policy of His Majesty's Opposition.

As Leader of the Conservative and Unionist Party, at our annual Conference it is my duty to take a long and broad view. At present we are not, like some of our neighbours on the Continent, plunged in fundamental discussions about our Constitution. Government as well as Opposition – Socialists, Conservatives, and Liberals – are united against Communism and the Communist Party. The declared hostility of the Socialists towards Communism, although it is not at present important in this country, has exercised a significant and salutary influence abroad. There is also a considerable measure of agreement upon the main lines of foreign policy. This is especially true of our close association with the United States, whose firm and unchanging policy in Europe and abandonment of the doctrines of Isolation constitute the main bulwark of the peace of the world. We should all like also to preserve our wartime friendship with the Russian people and with the Soviet Government if they will allow us to do so, and will stop what Mr Bevin calls 'the war of nerves'.

Even at home, as I stated when the new Parliament first came together, there is an immense body of social legislation upon which, apart from details, there is general agreement. All that part which carries benefits to the cottage-home and seeks to give social security to the individual wage-earner was in fact devised, shaped, resolved and proclaimed by the National Coalition Government with its overwhelming Conservative majority. It is our most earnest desire to see our country successfully emerge from the confusion and exhaustion of war and take its part in building or rebuilding an unshakable structure and system of European and world peace. There was therefore and there still is a very great body of major issues on which the British nation is united, and if only the Socialist Government would devote themselves to national rather than Party aims, and make us feel that they are trying to find the best way out of our grievous difficulties, many benefits would come to the whole of our people and to the British Empire and Commonwealth of Nations.

We certainly do not grudge the King's Ministers their offices. It is a sign of national political health and maturity when each of the great constitutional Parties can shoulder the responsibilities of administration, when all sorts and conditions of men and women can have their turn in the high functions of State, and every dog his day. What rouses our regret and growing resentment is first, that the Socialist Ministers are so much wrapped up in their Party doctrines that they cannot give a fair chance to our national interests and prosperity. Secondly, that they pour upon us an endless drizzle of insult and abuse. To hear their speeches and to read their newspapers one would suppose that Mr Attlee and his Socialist colleagues were the only people who had anything to do with winning the war. The Conservative Party is, according to them, a mere jumble of outworn interests and privileges which has now been swept away forever from any share in our national life. The leader of the ten Liberals in the House of Commons (Mr Clement Davies) re-echoes these bitter taunts. The historic theme of Liberalism – expressed by Gladstone, by John Stuart Mill[1] – the Liberalism of John Bright[2] and John Morley[3] – all that great

[1] John Stuart Mill, 1806–73. Son of the economist James Mill. Learned Greek at the age of three and Latin at eight. Worked for the East India Company, 1823–58. Married, 1951, Harriet Taylor. MP (Lib.) for Westminster, 1865–8. Developed the economic ideas of opportunity cost, comparative advantage in trade and economies of scale. Author of *System of Logic* (1843), *Principles of Political Economy* (1848), *On Liberty* (1859) and *The Subjection of Women* (1869).

[2] John Bright, 1811–89. MP (Lib.) for Durham, 1843–7, for Birmingham, 1857–89. Most well-known for his staunch support of free trade, particularly in his battle against the Corn Laws.

[3] John Morley, 1838–1923. Editor, *Fortnightly Review*, 1867–82, strongly supporting Liberalism and Liberal policies. Editor, *Pall Mall Gazette*, 1880–3, changing the paper's outlook from conservatism to radicalism. Biographer of Burke (1867), Voltaire (1872), Rousseau (1873), Cobden (1881), Cromwell (1899) and Gladstone (in three volumes, 1903). MP (Lib.) for Newcastle, 1883–95, 1896–1908. Irish Secretary, 1892–5. Secretary of State for India, 1905–10. Viscount, 1908. Lord Privy Seal, 1910–14. Resigned from Cabinet on outbreak of war, 1914. A 15-volume edition of his historical and political writings was published in 1921.

conception of a free, humane, generous and progressive civilisation is now reduced in the mind of this unfortunate person – the leader of the ten – to an animal hatred of Toryism.

But after all we are entitled to be treated with respect. We embody many of the strongest elements in the nation. We stand for high causes. Even under the confused conditions of the General Election ten and a half million people voted for us. Today we are half, or more than half, the country.

The Socialist Government itself did not represent a majority of the nation.[1] Under our present electoral system they have a majority of two to one in Parliament, and as on every occasion they seem to set Party before country, they can certainly vote us down in the House of Commons and carry through their fads and fancies and, regardless of the national interests, wreak their Party spite upon the other half of their fellow-countrymen. In little more than a year they have diminished British influence abroad and very largely paralysed our revival at home. Surely after all we have gone through we have enough to bear and dangers enough to face without the obtrusion upon us of this aggressive partisanship. One would have hoped that victors of the election would rise to the level of their task, that they would have due regard for our common inheritance, that they would think for the country as a whole, and do their best for their native land. But, alas, they feel differently. They have to ram Socialist dogmas, which only a small minority of them even comprehend, down the throats of the British people in order to show what good Party men they are, no matter what it costs the ordinary working-class family in common everyday prosperity, convenience and freedom of life.

To all this they add quite exceptional ineptitude and inefficiency and many silly blunders in the conduct of our affairs. Do you seek for proofs? Look around you. Look at the taxes. Look at the unbridled expenditure which is leading us daily into inflation, with all its bitter consequences. Look at the queues as you walk about our streets. Look at the restrictions and repressions on every form of enterprise and recovery. Look at the ever-growing bureaucracy of officials quartered permanently on the public. Let us look at Food. The German U-boats in their worst endeavour never made bread-rationing necessary in war. It took a Socialist Government and Socialist planners to fasten it on us in time of peace when the seas are open and the world harvests good. At no time in the two world wars have our people had so little bread, meat, butter, cheese and fruit to eat.

Look at the housing of the people. At the end of 13 months of his housing performance, Mr Aneurin Bevan points proudly to 22,000 new permanent houses completed. Before the war between 25,000 and 30,000 permanent houses were erected in Great Britain every *month*. But now, in August, only 4,566 permanent houses were completed, that is to say only about one-sixth

---

[1] In the 1945 general election, the Conservatives won 49.7% of the popular vote (13,310,891 votes), Labour 46.4% (12,405,254) and the Liberals 2.7% (722,402).

of the number built mainly by private enterprise without any fuss or bother every month before the war.

How shall we stigmatise the incompetence which left large numbers of buildings, camps, and habitations vacant under Government control while hundreds of thousands of families yearn for any kind of roof over their heads and privacy at their hearths till something better can be provided? I have before expressed my astonishment that any man responsible for housing, like Mr Aneurin Bevan, should not have tried to deal with his problem on the merits and make as many homes as possible in the shortest time by every means available, even if he had to lay aside during these years of emergency some of his doctrinaire malice. The amount of needless suffering, vexation and frustration his prejudices have caused cannot be measured. There is however a poetic justice in the fact that the most mischievous political mouth in wartime has also become, in peace, the most remarkable administrative failure.

Let us look at Coal. The foundation of Britain's industry, commerce and life has hitherto depended on cheap and abundant coal. Yet Mr Shinwell boasts that the era of cheap coal is gone forever. But the question which now concerns us is not one of cheap coal, but of an actual shortage. All the strains and pressures of the war did not prevent us from getting through the difficulties with which each winter confronted us. The Socialists assured us that the nationalisation of the coal mines would give a renewed surge of energy and time-keeping to the miners. Their work below ground – away from the light of day – is hard and exceptional and I am glad they have received an extra ration of meat. The coal position is, however, grim. The Government only just scraped through last year. We seem likely to begin this winter with stocks about five million tons below the last year's figure. It seems certain therefore that we shall be forced to reduce the consumption of coal this winter and the only question open is whether house-holders will shiver or factories go on short time. As for our export of coal, which used to bring us in something like £30,000,000 a year of fertile foreign exchange, that has of course departed at the moment when we need it most. So much for the new spirit which we were assured the nationalisation of the coal mines would create among the miners.

The Socialist Minister of Agriculture[1] recently announced – I take his own words – 'very tragic and almost disastrous cuts in the supplies of animal feeding stuffs'. When we learn that these cuts involve a reduction of 40 per cent of the feeding stuffs of our dairy herds and from 40 to 60 per cent of the feedings stuffs of our pigs and poultry, it is no wonder that Ministers should confess that our food will become worse than in the worst days of the war. The supply of labour for the land is precarious. Next year the acreage under corn must be largely increased. The 200,000 German prisoners of war who helped

---

[1] Thomas Williams, 1888–1967. MP (Lab.) for Don Valley, 1922–59. Parliamentary Secretary, Ministry of Agriculture and Fisheries, 1940–5. Minister of Agriculture, Fisheries, and Food, 1945–51. Baron, 1961.

the harvesting this year will be gone, and as the Housing Rural Workers Act has been deliberately let die by the Government the shortage of houses in the country is worse even than in the towns. In fact, less than half of the agricultural workers who served in the forces are returning to the land. The long-term agricultural programme, evolved by my colleague, Mr Hudson, in consultation with all the farming experts, has been abandoned, and nothing worthy of the name of an agricultural policy has been put in its place.

I have on other occasions set before you the immense injury which has been done to our process of recovery by the ill-considered schemes and threats of nationalisation which have cast their shadows over so many of our leading industries. The attempt to nationalise the steel industry, which was so effective in war and so buoyant in its plans for the future, is the most foolish of all the experiments in Socialism from which we have yet suffered. The wanton destruction by Sir Stafford Cripps of the Liverpool Cotton Exchange has inflicted a deep lasting injury upon the Lancashire cotton trade and upon the City of Liverpool. The nationalisation of Cables and Wireless, although agreeable to Australian Socialist conceptions, has been a dead loss to this Island, not only in foreign exchange but in facilities of communication which private enterprise had patiently built up to the national advantage. The shortage of all necessary articles for ordinary domestic consumption persists. We are complacently assured that the number of people employed on manufacture for home consumption is getting back to pre-war level, but what of the maldistribution of effort? In June we had 515,000 more people working in the metal and chemical industries than pre-war, but 456,000 less in the textile and clothing industries. Again, we had nearly 300,000 more non-industrial civil servants, but 677,000 less workers in the distributive trades. And now the British housewife, as she stands in the queue to buy her bread ration, will fumble in her pocket in vain for a silver sixpence. Under the Socialist Government *nickel* will have to be good enough for her. In future we shall still be able to say 'Every cloud has a *nickel* lining.'

Look where you will, we are suffering a needless decline and contraction at a time when we had the right to brighter days. I have visited many of the smaller countries on the Continent. All are making much more of themselves and of their chances than we are. Nowhere is there the drab disheartenment and frustration which the Socialist Party have fastened on Britain.

But now I turn abroad. I wish to speak of India. I am very glad you passed the Resolution about India at the Conference yesterday. You all know my views about India and how we have desired to give full Dominion Status to India, including the right embodied in the Statute of Westminster for the Indian peoples, like other Dominions, to quit the British Commonwealth of Nations altogether. The way in which the Socialist Government have handled this problem has been such as to give the vast masses of the people of India hardly any choice but to become separated from the British Crown which has so long shielded them from internal convulsions or foreign invasion. The Government of India has been placed – or should I rather say thrust – into the hands of men who have good reason to be bitterly hostile to the British connection, but who in no way represent the enormous mass of nearly 400 millions of all the races, States, and peoples of India who have dwelt so long in peace with one another. I fear that calamity impends upon this sub-Continent, which is almost as big as Europe, more populous, and even more harshly divided. It seems that in quite a short time India will become a separate, a foreign and a none too friendly country to the British Commonwealth of Nations. Indian unity created by British rule will swiftly perish, and no one can measure the misery and bloodshed which will overtake these enormous masses of humble helpless millions, or under what new power their future and destiny will lie. All this is happening every day, every hour. The great ship is sinking in the calm sea. Those who should have devoted their utmost effort to keep her afloat have instead opened the sea-cocks. The event will long leave its mark in history. It may well be that Burma will soon suffer the same fate. I am grieved to have to state these sombre tidings to you. Most of you will certainly live to see whether I am right or wrong. Sometimes in the past I have not been wrong. I pray that I may be wrong now.

What has been the effect of our immense act of surrender in India? On the morrow of our victory and of our services, without which human freedom would not have survived, we are divesting ourselves of the mighty and wonderful empire which had been built up in India by two hundred years of effort and sacrifice, and the number of the King's subjects is being reduced to barely a quarter of what it has been for generations. Yet at this very moment and in the presence of this unparalleled act of voluntary abdication, we are still ceaselessly abused by the Soviet wireless and by certain unfriendly elements in the United States for being a land-grabbing Imperialist power seeking expansion and aggrandisement. While Soviet Russia is expanding or seeking to expand in every direction, and has already brought many extra scores of millions of people directly or indirectly under the despotic control of the Kremlin and the rigours of Communist discipline, we, who sought nothing from this war but to do our duty and are in fact reducing ourselves to a fraction of our former size and population, are successfully held up to world censure. It is astonishing that no effective reply should be made by His Majesty's Government and that it should be left to Field Marshal Smuts, the great South African, our former valiant enemy of Boer War days, to raise his voice in vindication of British magnanimity, tolerance and good faith.

What are we to say of the handling of the Palestine problem by the Socialist Government? At the election they made lavish promises to the Zionists and their success at the polls excited passionate expectations throughout the Jewish world. These promises were no sooner made than they were discarded, and now all through this year the Government stand vacillating without any plan or policy, holding on to a mandate in which we have no vital interest, gaining the distrust and hostility both of Arab and Jew, and exposing us to worldwide reprobation for their manifest incapacity. Thus both at home and abroad the British nation and Empire have been deprived of the rewards their conduct deserves.

I have naturally considered very carefully what is my own duty in these times. It would be easy for me to retire gracefully in an odour of civic freedoms, and this plan crossed my mind frequently some months ago. I feel now however that the situation is so serious and what may have to come so grave, that I am resolved to go forward carrying the flag as long as I have the necessary strength and energy, and have your confidence. It is of the highest importance to our name and endurance as a great power and to the cohesion of our national and imperial life that there should be re-established at the earliest moment some poise and balance between the political forces in our island, and that those who were so unexpectedly clad with overwhelming Parliamentary power should be made to realise that they are the servants, and not the masters, of the British nation. When I think of what has already happened, what is happening, and what is going to happen in the next year or two, I feel, as you feel, profoundly stirred. Our reaction must not be despair, because that is an emotion which we do not allow. It must be wrath – not despair but wrath – and wrath must translate itself not in vain expletives but in earnest action and well-conceived measures and organisation.

The Government have informed us that there will not be a General Election till the 1st of May, 1950. I have no doubt that they will cling to office and exploit their Parliamentary advantage to the last possible moment. But there are many things uncertain in this world, and as soon as it is apparent, as it may soon be apparent, that the movement of the national mind and the people's will is with us, we shall be living in quite a different climate from that which we now endure. The whole tribe of highly intellectual left-wing scribblers assure us that the Socialist Administration will rule for 20 years. All the strong forces gathered at this Conference they declare are moribund or dead. They will sing quite a different tune once they realise, and are made to realise, that they have a growing majority of the nation against them. This change can be effected in three ways. First by a continuance of wise and efficient action in the House of Commons and also in the House of Lords. Secondly, at the by-elections in the country. Thirdly, and all the time, by the gathering together of those virile, vital forces in our race which keep Britain alive. Even though the present House of Commons draws out its weary term to the dregs, once we are on the move in earnest we shall feel the soil of Britain firm again under our feet.

In order to achieve a position of moral ascendancy every sacrifice and effort should be made by those to whom our country's greatness is dear. For such a purpose we must lay aside every impediment and every prejudice and marshal every scrap of strength we can. Never must we underrate the immense resources of patriotism which can be gathered for our cause, which today is no ordinary Party cause but carries with it, as I am sure, the life and future of Britain.

I am glad that there has been a discussion upon the name of our Party. Of course the policy for which we stand is infinitely more important than the name we bear, but we ought to make sure that the mere name is in no way a stumbling block to the great mass of voters without political affiliations who are affronted and disgusted by the Socialist mismanagement of our affairs. A new generation of electors is at hand. Great latitude in this matter has always been customary among us. At present we call ourselves, according to our liking, Unionists, Conservatives, Tories or Tory Democrats. We also have with us our faithful allies, the Liberal Nationals. But whatever name we use this party is in fact already and has been for sixty years 'The Union Party', standing for the union of the Kingdom and the Empire and the union of men of good will of all classes against tyrannical and subversive elements.

We need not pay any attention to the mockery of our opponents. The Liberal Party has so mishandled its affairs and has been so mauled by the Socialists that it has very little left besides its famous name. The Labour Party have identified themselves with the fallacious, narrowing doctrines of Socialism. We can afford to disdain their taunts. Neither of these Parties is in any posture to give us advice.

The principles of our Party are not up for auction. We propose no bargain to any section of public opinion. If however there are others who, in growing numbers, are marching along the path which Duty marks out for us, no memories of past differences or outworn quarrels should be allowed to stand in the way of these natural unities which spring from a common policy and a single aim.

I do not believe in looking about for some panacea or cure-all on which we should stake our credit and fortunes trying to sell it like a patent medicine to all and sundry. It is easy to win applause by talking in an airy way about great new departures in policy, especially if all detailed proposals are avoided. We ought not to seek after some rigid, symmetrical form of doctrine, such as delights the minds of Socialists and Communists. Our own feelings and the British temperament are quite different. So are our aims. We seek a free and varied society, where there is room for many kinds of men and women to lead happy, honourable and useful lives. We are fundamentally opposed to all systems of rigid uniformity in our national life and we have grown great as a nation by indulging tolerance, rather than logic.

It certainly would be an error of the first order for us to plunge out into a programme of promises and bribes in the hopes of winning the public favour. But if you say to me: 'What account are we to give of the policy of the Conservative Party? What are we to say of our theme and our cause of the faith that is in us?' That is a question to which immediate answer can always be given.

Our main objectives are: To uphold the Christian religion and resist all attacks upon it. To defend our Monarchical and Parliamentary Constitution. To provide adequate security against external aggression and safety to our seaborne trade. To uphold law and order, and impartial justice administered by Courts free from interference or pressure on the part of the executive. To regain a sound finance and strict supervision of national income and expenditure. To defend and develop our Empire trade, without which Great Britain would perish. To promote all measures to improve the health and social conditions of the people. To support as a general rule free enterprise and initiative against State trading and nationalisation of industries.

To this I will add some further conceptions. We oppose the establishment of a Socialist State, controlling the means of production, distribution and exchange. We are asked, 'What is your alternative?' Our Conservative aim is to build a property-owning democracy, both independent and interdependent. In this I include profit-sharing schemes in suitable industries and intimate consultation between employers and wage-earners. In fact we seek so far as possible to make the status of the wage-earner that of a partner rather than of an irresponsible employee. It is in the interest of the wage-earner to have many other alternatives open to him than service under one all-powerful employer called the State. He will be in a better position to bargain collectively and production will be more abundant; there will be more for all and more freedom for all when the wage-earner is able, in the large majority of cases, to choose and change his work, and to deal with a private employer who, like himself, is subject to the ordinary pressures of life and, like himself, is dependent upon his personal thrift, ingenuity and good-housekeeping. In this way alone can the traditional virtues of the British character be preserved. We do not wish the people of this ancient island reduced to a mass of State-directed proletarians, thrown hither and thither, housed here and there, by an aristocracy of privileged officials or privileged Party, sectarian or Trade Union bosses. We are opposed to the tyranny and victimisation of the closed shop. Our ideal is the consenting union of millions of free, independent families and homes to gain their livelihood and to serve true British glory and world peace.

Freedom of enterprise and freedom of service are not possible without elaborate systems of safeguards against failure, accident or misfortune. We do not seek to pull down improvidently the structures of society, but to erect balustrades upon the stairway of life, which will prevent helpless or foolish people from falling into the abyss. Both the Conservative and Liberal Parties have made notable contributions to secure minimum standards of life and labour. I too have borne my part in this. It is 38 years ago since I introduced the first Unemployment Insurance Scheme, and 22 years ago since, as Conservative Chancellor of the Exchequer, I shaped and carried the Widows' Pensions and reduction of the Old Age Pensions from 70 to 65. We are now moving forward into another vast scheme of national insurance, which arose, even in the stress of war, from a Parliament with a great Conservative majority. It is an essential principle of Conservative, Unionist, and Tory policy – call it what you will – to defend the general public against abuses by monopolies and against restraints on trade and enterprise, whether these evils come from private corporations, from the mischievous plans of doctrinaire Governments, or from the incompetence and arbitrariness of departments of State. Finally, we declare ourselves the unsleeping opponents of all class, all official or all Party privilege, which denies the genius of our island race, whose sparks fly upwards unceasingly from the whole people, its rightful career, reward and pre-eminence alike in peace and war.

How then do we draw the lines of political battle? The British race is not actuated mainly by the hope of material gain. Otherwise we should long ago have sunk in the ocean of the past. It is stirred on almost all occasions by sentiment and instinct, rather than by programmes or worldly calculation. When this new Parliament first met, all the Socialist Members stood up and sang 'The Red Flag' in their triumph. Peering ahead through the mists and mysteries of the future so far as I can see, I see the division at the next election will be between those who wholeheartedly sing 'The Red Flag' and those who rejoice to sing 'Land of Hope and Glory'. There is the noble hymn which will rally the wise, the soberminded and the good to the salvation of our native land.

Winston S. Churchill to Clement Attlee
(Churchill papers, 2/4)

6 October 1946
Private

Dear Prime Minister,

I may find it necessary to publish in the near future the letter which I addressed to you on 31 May, 1945,[1] in the enclosed correspondence. My colleagues feel that it should be known how very different is the treatment we receive from that which was offered to you and your Party at a time when we had a large majority in the House of Commons and had expectations of securing the majority in the new Parliament. I should therefore be glad to know how you wish your letter in reply to be treated. It would be best to publish it in full, but I can of course summarize it if you wish the actual text to remain private. Pray let me know your wishes at your convenience.
Secret

The European situation has deteriorated gravely. I am informed that the Soviet Government have over 225 divisions on a war footing beyond the Russian frontiers in the occupied territories of Europe. This compares with

---

[1] Reproduced in *The Churchill Documents*, vol. 21, *The Shadows of Victory, January–July 1945*, p. 1558.

about 25 British and American divisions, of which some are only Police divisions without artillery. This seems a serious position, and I may have to put questions to you upon it or raise the point in debate in the new Session.

We have no knowledge of what has happened about the Atomic bomb. By my agreements with the President, of which the originals are in your possession, we are certainly entitled to a share of the information during the period of the war, which presumably means until peace is signed. We are also entitled, in my view, to have a share of these bombs as they are produced, and this might well be an economical alternative to our making them ourselves with the utmost rapidity and with all our existing knowledge. No information of any kind has been vouchsafed to us on these subjects, and I may shortly press for a debate upon them in public or in secret session.

In bringing these matters and our previous correspondence to your notice, I am not making any formal request to you to keep us informed, or asking for any political or party favour. It is however essential, in my view, that the public should be fully aware of the fact that, on the morrow of the war gained by our combined exertions, there is no kind of consultation or contact between His Majesty's Government and the official Opposition on foreign policy, peace negotiations or national defence.

Your courtesy in sending me a copy of your paper on the Central Organisation for Defence a few hours before it was published – for which I thank you – in no way touches the main issue.

Winston S. Churchill to Herbert Swope[1]
(Churchill papers, 2/210)

6 October 1946

I am very glad to have the opportunity of paying tribute to my old and honoured friend Bernard Baruch on the occasion of this memorable dinner of Freedom House. We became friends by many months of cabled correspondence in the first Great War when we were striving together for the same world causes as we have all had to carry once again to victory this time. I salute the leading elder statesman of America knowing well his wisdom and virtue.

I turn to what is in all our minds. We have entered the atomic age. At one of their most disorganized moments men have been gifted with supernatural

[1] Herbert Bayard Swope, 1882–1958. Born in St Louis, Mo. War Correspondent with the German armies, New York *World*, 1914–16; Chief Correspondent, Paris Peace Conference, 1919; Executive Editor, 1920–9. Pulitzer Prize for best reporting, 1917. Commissioned Lt-Cdr, US Navy, 1918. Assistant to Bernard Baruch, War Industries Board, 1919. Member, International Press Commission, 1919, and a leading advocate of greater publicity for the Conference. First journalist to publish both the terms of the League of Nations Covenant and the full text of the reparations agreement. In retirement, 1929–42. Consultant to Secretary of War, 1942–6. Author of several books, including *Inside the German Empire* (1917).

powers. No one knows whether they will use them for prosperity or damnation. We British have our rights recorded in solemn form but the prime responsibility rests with the United States. There is no man in whose hands I would rather see these awful problems placed than Bernard Baruch. All God's children may sleep comfortably in their beds for the next few years; and during this merciful breathing space there must be worked out an august design which will make mankind master of its destiny and will secure to every humble cottage home in every country life, liberty, and the pursuit of happiness.

I trust he may long be spared to raise this fearful agency above the level of national or material conflict and make it the servant and not the destroyer or the enslaver of the human race.

Winston S. Churchill to William Chenery[1]
(Churchill papers, 4/31)

6 October 1946

I am willing to write an article on the United States of Europe on the lines and in expansion of the Zurich Address. This is what you suggested in your telegram. It has of course a close bearing upon the question 'Is a third war unavoidable?' But I am disinclined to write under so sensational a title. I suggest as title for your consideration 'One way to stop a third war'. I should think three or four thousand words would be required and could probably complete it in the course of the present month. I should not like you to make a long and dangerous flight on my account. Let us first talk on the telephone. I will ring you at two p.m. your time tomorrow seventh.[2]

---

[1] William Ludlow Chenery, 1884–1949. Born in Virginia. Educated at University of Chicago. Reporter for *Chicago Evening Post*, 1910–14. Leader Page Editor, *Rocky Mountain News*, 1914. Editorial writer, *Chicago Herald*, 1914–18; *New York Herald*, 1923. Associate Editor, *The Survey*, 1919; *New York Globe*, 1921–3. Managing Editor, *New York Sun*, 1923. Editor, *New York Telegram-Mail*, 1924; *Collier's Weekly*, 1925–43. President, Pelham (New York) Board of Education, 1937. Publisher, *Collier's Weekly*, 1943–9.

[2] Churchill duly wrote 'The Highroad of the Future', published in *Collier's*, 4 Jan. 1947, and in the *Daily Telegraph* on 30 and 31 Dec. 1946 under the headlines 'One Way to Stop a New War' and 'The Grand Design of a United Europe', reproduced below (pp. 489–92). Chenery paid $25,000 for this article. For more on this, see Martin Gilbert (ed.), *Winston Churchill and Emery Reves: Correspondence, 1937–1964* (1997), p. 268.

Winston S. Churchill to Major-General Sir Edward Spears[1]
(Churchill papers, 2/156)

8 October 1946

My dear Louis,

Thank you so much for sending me your article for the *New Universal Encyclopedia*. I cannot pretend to have studied it in detail because I find it difficult to read so much typescript. I feel quite sure that my reputation will not suffer in your hands.

I often think of all our affairs together, especially the walk round the Vimy Ridge and your spirited encounter with Petain on our visit to Paris. Life slips away, but one fights with what strength remains for the things one cares about. I expect that is your position too.

If you care to send me the proof of your article in print, I should be obliged.

Clement Attlee to Winston S. Churchill
(Churchill papers, 2/4)

9 October 1946
Private

My dear Churchill,

I have received your letter of October 6[2] and note what you say as to the necessity which you anticipate you may feel to publish your letter of May 31, 1945.

You will recall from the correspondence that I was quite willing for it be published at the time. I do not know why this was not done and I am unable to appreciate the reasons which impel you to a belated publication.

The facilities referred to in your letter were offered by you and accepted by me in view of the exceptional circumstances existing at the time. A wartime coalition had just been broken up and in accordance with your wishes a General Election was about to take place. Parliament was ten years old. No one knew what the result would be. You had as you say expectations of a majority, but others thought differently.

I also accepted your offer made in your letter of June 2[3] to accompany you to the Potsdam Conference as Leader of the Party which might during its

---

[1] Edward Louis Spears, 1886–1974. Capt., 11th Hussars, 1914. Four times wounded, 1914–15 (MC). Liaison Officer with French 10th Army, 1915–16. Head of British Military Mission to Paris, 1917–20. Brig.-Gen., 1918. MP (Nat. Lib.) for Loughborough, 1922–4; (Cons.) for Carlisle, 1931–45. Churchill's Personal Representative with the French PM, May–June 1940. Head of British Mission to de Gaulle, 1940. Head of Mission to Syria and the Lebanon, 1941. First Minister to Syria and the Lebanon, 1942–4. Knighted, 1942. Bt, 1953.

[2] Reproduced above (pp. 481–2).

[3] Reproduced in *The Churchill Documents*, vol. 21, *The Shadows of Victory, January–July 1945*, p. 1566.

progress be returned to power. This naturally made it essential that I should be kept fully informed of the international and war position.

If you will refer to my reply you will see that I was mindful of the constitutional position in this country and expressly stated that I should not base any claim in the future on this exceptional concession having been made. This was, of course, on the assumption that I should continue in opposition. I had thought that you would take the same line, if our positions were reversed.

However, although you state that you are not making any formal request for information you appear to be endeavouring to formulate some charge that you have not been fairly treated. In support of this you desire to adduce what happened in 1945 as a precedent, although as far as I know you have never made any suggestions that these facilities should be extended to you.

I have repeatedly said that Bevin and I are always willing to see you or Eden or both of you if there were matters you wished to raise. And if you now desire more frequent meetings between us for the discussion of matters of foreign policy and defence, I should be very willing and would give you as much information as possible.

Let me add that I have had quite a considerable experience of the practice in these matters as from 1931 to 1935 I was deputy to Mr George Lansbury[1] and from 1935 to 1940 I was Leader of the Opposition. I know, therefore, what was the practice of your three immediate predecessors in office. It was as follows.

From time to time the Prime Minister of the day would ask the Leader of the Opposition to see him to explain some particular situation in order that he might come to an informed conclusion on his course of action in the House.

On occasions the Leader of the Opposition would seek an interview with the Prime Minister or sometimes the Foreign Secretary for a similar purpose. There was, however, in my experience never the kind of continuous consultation and access to papers which you seem to think you should obtain.

In this matter I have followed precedent. When you have been in this country, I or the Foreign Secretary have from time to time informed you of particular points in the Foreign situation. In your absence we have made contact with Eden. We have both, as I have said above, always been willing to see either or both of you if there were matters which you wished to raise. In my experience it would be inadvisable from the point of view of the Opposition to go further than this, without placing on the Opposition Leader a responsibility that must remain with the Government.

You are, I am sure, aware of the tendency of certain Foreign Powers to

---

[1] George Lansbury, 1859–1940. Left school at the age of 14. Was employed unloading coal trucks for the Great Eastern Railway. First attempted to enter Parliament, 1895. MP (Lab.) for Bow and Bromley, 1910–12. Resigned to fight the seat as a supporter of women's suffrage. Not re-elected until 1922. Mayor of Poplar, 1919–20; 1936–7. Editor, *Daily Herald*, 1919–25. First Commissioner of Works in the second Labour Government, 1929–31. Leader of the Labour Party, 1931–5.

believe that speeches by eminent persons like yourself must have been concerted with the Government. This has been an embarrassment to us and doubtless to you. If it were known that the Opposition were consulted to the extent to which you seem to suggest, it would become almost impossible to convince them to the contrary. The knowledge of this being so would, I am sure, cause you to impose upon yourself a most unwelcome restraint.

I note your anxiety as to the balance of armed forces in the world today. You will recall, I am sure, your demands last year for more rapid demobilisation.

I cannot recall that you have ever asked me for information on the Atomic Bomb, but of course I should be glad to give it to you.[1]

I am sorry that the White Paper on Central Organisation for Defence could not be sent earlier. It was despatched to you as soon as it was printed. You had of course been informed of the general principles some months ago. I am grateful to you and your colleagues for having given me the benefit of your experience.

If on consideration you desire to publish your letter of May 31, I think it would be desirable to publish also the full text of my reply of June 8,[2] and this correspondence with the omission of the passages marked secret.

Please let me know if you want to talk about this. It is not an easy matter, and like you I am anxious that we should not have avoidable differences about matters of foreign affairs and defence.

Bernard Baruch to Winston S. Churchill
(Churchill papers, 2/210)

9 October 1946   New York

Dear Winston

I was touched deeply by the telegram you sent to the dinner given me by Freedom House – touched by the sentiments it expressed – and touched, even more, that you should have taken time from your pressingly busy life to do such a thoughtful and considerate act. When it was read, your name was greeted by great applause which supported my view, as expressed by the Toastmaster – our friend Herbert Swope – who read the wire, saying it was from the greatest Englishman who ever lived.

I hope our paths may cross soon again.

I have seen Randolph several times recently and I find him looking well.

With respect and affection born of years.

PS. I am deeply concerned. The people are awakened internationally but not economically. What are your winter plans.

[1] This and the immediately preceding paragraph were marked 'Secret'.
[2] Reproduced in *The Churchill Documents*, vol. 21, *The Shadows of Victory, January–July 1945*, pp. 1637–8.

OCTOBER 1946

Cabinet: minutes
(Premier papers, 8/1321)

10 October 1946
Cabinet Meeting No. 85 of 1946

[. . .]

7. The Cabinet had before them a memorandum by the Prime Minister (CP (46) 369) covering a copy of a letter from Mr Churchill seeking agreement in principle to the inclusion of certain official documents in an account which he proposed to write of the war of 1939–45.

The Prime Minister explained that the documents in question included: (i) memoranda circulated by Mr Churchill to the War Cabinet on strategic issues, (ii) minutes addressed by him to the Chiefs of Staff or to his colleagues; and (iii) telegrams addressed by him to President Roosevelt and other heads of Governments, together with summaries of the replies received by him.

Mr Churchill had made it clear that he would agree to submit the text for revision on behalf of the Government before publication, and would be ready to discuss the omission of any portion of it to which objection might be taken. This would enable the Government to ensure that nothing was included which would injure us in our relations with other nations, or be contrary to the public interest, or impair the confidential relations between Ministers or between Ministers and their advisers. When Mr Churchill submitted the text of his book it might be found desirable to consult other Governments, including the Dominion Governments, with regard to the publication of particular telegrams addressed to heads of Governments and of summaries of the replies to these telegrams; but it seemed clear that there was no need to consult these Governments at the present stage. It was understood that there would be no question of the publication of any part of Mr Churchill's book for about two or three years.

The Cabinet –

(1) Agreed that Mr Churchill should be informed that His Majesty's Government were ready to give their agreement in principle to the proposal that he should include in his account of the 1939–45 war memoranda and minutes written by himself as Prime Minister or as First Lord of the Admiralty, together with telegrams from himself to President Roosevelt and other heads of Governments, on the understanding that before any part of his book was published the text would be submitted for final revision on behalf of the Government, in the light of the situation existing at the time.

OCTOBER 1946

Sir Edward Bridges to Winston S. Churchill
(*Camrose papers*)

10 October 1946
Personal

Dear Mr Churchill,

Here is the official reply to your letter of 23rd September.[1] As you will see, it is 100 per cent acceptance; with no provisoes, other than those which you yourself suggested.

You know, I hope, that I and my colleagues in the Cabinet Office will always be ready to give you any help we can over these questions of documents and so forth. It will be our endeavour to be as helpful to you as you have been to us. We are most grateful to you.

I am sending off the letter at once, as I know that you are anxious for the answer. I will return the enclosures later, by special messenger.

Sir Edward Bridges to Winston S. Churchill
(*Camrose papers*)

10 October 1946

Dear Mr Churchill,

I have submitted to the Prime Minister your letter of the 23rd September, 1946,[2] saying that you are considering giving your own account of the British war story, and asking whether it can be agreed <u>in principle</u> that this account should include the publication of memoranda and minutes written by yourself as Prime Minister (or as First Lord of the Admiralty in the first months of the war) and also telegrams from yourself to President Roosevelt and other heads of governments.

In reply I am authorised by the Prime Minister to say that HM Government are very ready to give their agreement in principle to this proposal on the understandings set out in your letter. Thus, they note that you would be ready to discuss the omission of any particular phrase, sentence or passage; and also that there should be final review on any particular points and passages by the Government of the day before publication. They note, also, that you do not expect that the publication of any part of the material would take place for two or three years.

I mentioned to you that HM Government also consider that it would be necessary to consult the United States' Government before publication of any messages to (or from) President Roosevelt. The Foreign Office would be happy to make the necessary communication on your behalf to the US Government

---

[1] Reproduced above (pp. 465–6).
[2] Reproduced above (pp. 465–6).

should you so desire. Similar arrangements could also be made for consulting other governments.

There is also the question of publishing a suitable acknowledgement of Crown copyright in respect of what must be regarded as official documents. But this is a matter which can well be settled later on.

Winston S. Churchill to Clement Attlee
(*Churchill papers, 2/4*)

10 October 1946
Personal and Private

My dear Prime Minister,

1. I thank you for your letter of October 9 enclosing the first draft of your speech on the Roosevelt Memorial Bill, which I am very glad to support. I am much obliged to you for your references to the personal friendship which developed between me and the President. I do not expect to speak for more than five or six minutes.

2. Let me also acknowledge your other letter of October 9 in reply to mine of the 6th.[1] I will discuss what you say about the publication with some of my colleagues, and will write to you next week on the subject and also about the form of publication.

3. There is, however, one point with which I must deal now. It is upon the first of your 'Secret' paragraphs about 'my demands last year for more rapid demobilisation'. I also gave the figures for the three services to which, in my view, reductions should be made. These figures were:

Royal Navy	150,000
Army	1,000,000
Royal Air Force	400,000
Total men	1,550,000

The figures which His Majesty's Government have announced they are working to are considerably less than this total, especially in respect of the Army and the Air Force, viz., the figures to be attained by 31 December, 1946:

Royal Navy	175,000
Army	650,000
Royal Air Force	275,000
Total men	1,100,000

I also added (Hansard 22 October, 1945, column 1696):

'I must, however, make one very serious reservation. In my calculations and estimates I have definitely excluded the possibility of a major war in the next few years. If His Majesty's Government consider that this is wrong,

---

[1] Reproduced above (pp. 481–2).

then it would not be a case of demobilisation at all but of remobilisation, because what has taken place and is going on has already woefully impaired the immediate fighting efficiency of the enormous Forces we still retain. I believe, however, it may be common ground that this possibility of a major war may rightly be excluded, and that we have an interlude of grace in which mankind may be able to make better arrangements for this tortured world than we have hitherto achieved. Still I make that reservation.'

Since those days the situation has gravely deteriorated, but I do not suggest that it is in the power of the United States and Great Britain to match the enormous deployment of Russian armies outside Russia, in Europe, to which I referred. It is clear to me that only two reasons prevent the westward movement of the Russian armies to the North Sea and the Atlantic. The first is their virtue and self-restraint. The second, the possession by the United States of the Atomic bomb.

I thought it right to convey to you the information which I have obtained, as I used to do to the Governments before the war.

Winston S. Churchill: speech
('The Sinews of Peace', pages 216–17)

11 October 1946   House of Commons

THE ROOSEVELT MEMORIAL BILL

I rise to support the Second Reading of the Measure which the Prime Minister has proposed to us in felicitous terms and with so much feeling. It was my duty, eighteen months ago, to address the House on the sad occasion of President Roosevelt's death, and I am sure I did not go beyond historical fact and general conviction in describing him as the greatest American friend we have ever known, and the greatest champion of freedom who had ever brought help and comfort from the new world to the old. It is indeed fitting that a memorial should be raised to him in this island, and that old, mighty, war-scarred London should be the chosen place. I could have wished that the House had taken upon it the charges to erect this monument, as I am sure it would have been most willing to do, but the method chosen of raising money by a great number of small subscriptions has the important advantage that it permits so many people to give effect, by an individual act, to their heartfelt feelings, and it is, I think, in accordance with what President Roosevelt himself would have wished.

I am obliged to the Prime Minister for the reference which he made to the comradeship which grew between the late President and me during the war, and to the fact that this was of service to the interests of the people of our countries and to the cause for which all the Allies fought so hard and so long. This comradeship in great affairs was founded upon friendship, and roused in my heart a sentiment of sincere affection for this noble, august and charming personality. I received from him so many marks of kindness and good will that I felt buoyed up in the ordeal of the war by the fact of walking hand in hand with this outstanding chief of the American people.

The Prime Minister has spoken of Washington and Lincoln, and who can doubt that Franklin Roosevelt will take his place with them in the history, not only of the United States, but of the world? We are so much nearer to him in point of time that we cannot see his life's work in the perspective and setting which belong to the famous figures of the past, but already none can doubt his rank and stature. There are many tests by which we may try to measure the greatness of the men who have served high causes, but I shall select only one of them this morning, namely, the favourable influence exerted upon the fortunes of mankind. In this, Roosevelt's name gains pre-eminence even over those of the illustrious figures we have mentioned. Reflecting on the past, one has the feeling that the changes associated with Washington would probably have come to pass in due course by the irresistible movement and evolution of events. Nor can we doubt that slavery would have been abolished, even apart from Abraham Lincoln, in the vast spread of the humanities which lighted the nineteenth century. Of Roosevelt, however, it must be said that had he not acted when he did, in the way he did, had he not felt the generous surge of freedom in his heart, had he not resolved to give aid to Britain and to Europe in the supreme crisis though which we have passed, a hideous fate might well have overwhelmed mankind and made its whole future for centuries sink into shame and ruin. It may well be that the man whom we honour today not only anticipated history but altered its course, and altered it in a manner which has saved the freedom and earned the gratitude of the human race for generations to come. On this side of the House we give our cordial support to the Measure which the Prime Minister has just introduced.

Winston S. Churchill to Lord Camrose
(<i>Churchill papers, 4/5</i>)</center>

15 October 1946

My dear Camrose,

1. Lately I have been putting my papers on the War in order, and for convenience have had a few of them, with my notes, printed by Messrs Eyre and Spottiswoode who are the confidential printers for the Government. I have sent you copies of what has so far come to hand, and a further instalment should reach you in America by the next Air Mail. This would cover some aspects of the years 1941, 1942 and 1943.

2. I thought it right to enquire of His Majesty's Government as to their views about my use of these documents, and submitted to them, through Sir Edward Bridges, a number of samples about which I desired a ruling in principle.

I enclose you a copy of the official answer I have received, and of Sir Edward Bridges' covering note. These are entirely satisfactory.

3. Should I eventually undertake the very serious work of giving my account of the British share in the War, I shall use these documents and many others like them as I think fit, both from the historical and literary point of view; and of course in strict accordance with the conditions I proposed to the Government, which they accepted.

The proofs which you have and others which will be sent to you must be regarded as samples of a very much larger body of documents which I could at my discretion and taste make public. They are only furnished to you now as an illustration of the material available. It may well be that many of them would not be interesting to the general public, and an author must consider the balance and presentation of his work as a whole. I am not therefore committing myself to use (should I undertake the work) all these documents or their full text. The wealth of material is, however, so great that there will be no difficulty in telling the tale, which is a good one.

4. I should propose to follow the method I used in *The World Crisis* which itself is modelled on the lines of Defoe's *Memories of a Scottish Cavalier*, namely a thread of personal narrative amusing to the reader, on which are hung the great situations and the necessary documentations.

5. The work would seem to divide itself into four or five books, each with heavy appendices comprising one hundred and fifty to two hundred thousand words – a total wordage of over eight hundred thousand. It would probably be convenient that these books should be produced in the following succession, namely: Book one and Book two to be brought out and serialised together. These cover, as the rough draft indicates: Book I, the Introduction, dealing with the period between the Wars, up to the outbreak, and thereafter with my period as First Lord of the Admiralty ending May 10, 1940. Book II would cover the period from May 10, when I became Prime Minister, to the end of the year 1940.

I should think 1941 to 1942 would fill Book III, and 1943, 1944 and 1945 might be one or two books as the work develops.[1]

6. I should hope, should I undertake the work, that Books I and II would be available at the end of 1947 for serialisation in the early part of 1948. I cannot give any guarantee on account of political work which I may have to do. I am certainly not going to be hurried. On the other hand, the amount of original composition already available in the documents which I wrote at the time, is

---

[1] *The Second World War* spanned six volumes and 1.6 million words of text, not including appendices.

very substantial and of course commands the highest historic interest. This also applies to the documentation of the succeeding books which, if there were four, might come out at yearly intervals. Should I undertake the task I shall immediately assemble the documentation and have the facts necessary for its setting carefully prepared so that in the event of my being unable to complete the task, the whole corpus and documentation design will be available, and it would be for another author to finish it.

7. Finally I must emphasise that the sample material and treatment of the topics are purely provisional, and far more work is required upon them, and that the author must remain the sole judge. Secondly that my connection with the work is purely hypothetical, and dependent entirely upon the arrangements made between you and the Chartwell Library Trust.

Brendan Bracken to Lord Beaverbrook
(Beaverbrook papers)

16 October 1946

Winston is in very good fettle and is determined to continue to lead the Tory Party until he becomes Prime Minister on earth or Minister of Defence in Heaven.

Winston S. Churchill to Willy Sax[1]
(Churchill papers, 1/17)

16 October 1946
Private

Dear Mr Sax,

I am very much obliged to you for your two kind letters, and for sending me a press filled with white colour. I look forward to receiving the other colours of which I left you specimens, as they are unprocurable in England now.

Since I came home I have been amusing myself with painting in Tempera, which I find a most delightful medium offering great possibilities both in the ground-work and the finish of pictures, and working in so happily with oil colours in the final stages. I should be much obliged if you could send me in a letter the exact description of the glycerine which you said could be spread upon the colours on the palette to prevent their drying up, and thus avoid needless waste.

As I told you, I am sure that the use of these colours will give pleasure to very large numbers of people. Finally, let me thank you for all your courtesy.

[1] Willy Sax, 1898–1964. Swiss paint manufacturer and supplier. Personal friend of Churchill from 1946. Author of *Paints for Churchill's Canvas* (1995).

Air Marshal Sir Keith Park to Winston S. Churchill
(Churchill papers, 4/198)

19 October 1946
Private

My dear Mr Churchill,

I have taken quite literally the injunction contained in the last paragraph of your letter of the 16th October asking me to go through your note recording your visit to my Group Headquarters at Uxbridge on that memorable day, the 15th September in 1940.

Your book on the last war will be more widely read than any other on this side also on the other side of the Atlantic. Moreover your words will carry more authority than the recordings of others. It is therefore of some importance that your note on the 15th September should be correct technically as well as in its more general sense.

I have done as you suggested by writing my comments and amendments in pencil into the enclosed draft document. If my remarks are not clear or are not all you require I shall be very willing to supplement them in writing or to make a journey up to London to explain in person to you.

I look forward greatly to reading your book or books on the last war and shall at all times be glad to give any small help within my powers. Please do not hesitate to state your demands.

The last time we met was at poor Moyne's[1] charming desert house near Mena house in Egypt before I went out to join Dickie Mountbatten in SE Asia. He was a grand fellow to work with and did a great job in the Far East.[2]

Winston S. Churchill to Lord Cranborne
(Churchill papers, 2/23)

19 October 1946
Private

My dear Bobbety,

Thank you very much for your letter of October 14. I am indeed sorry to have put you to so much trouble. I am not attracted to a Western bloc as a

---

[1] Walter Edward Guinness, 1880–1944. 3rd son of 1st Earl of Iveagh. Educated at Eton. On active service in South Africa, 1900–1 (wounded). MP (Cons.) for Bury St Edmunds, 1907–31. On active service, 1914–18 (despatches thrice). Under-Secretary of State for War, 1922–3. Financial Secretary, Treasury, 1923–4, 1924–5. Minister of Agriculture and Fisheries, 1925–9. Baron Moyne, 1932. A director of Arthur Guinness, Son & Co., brewers. Elected to the Other Club, 1934. Secretary of State for the Colonies, 1941–2. Deputy Minister Resident, Cairo, 1942–4; Minister Resident, 1944: murdered there by Jewish terrorists.

[2] Churchill responded on Oct. 22: 'Thank you so much for all the trouble you have taken in correcting my notes. It has so greatly helped me in telling this story' (*Churchill papers, 4/198*).

final solution. The ideal should be EUROPE. The Western bloc as an instalment of the United States of Europe would be an important step, but the case should be put on the broadest lines of a unity of Europe and Christendom as a whole. This conception is free from the vice of dividing Europe into an Eastern Russian-controlled bloc and a Western Anglo-American-influenced bloc, as Mr Wallace recommends in the present unhappy situation. Moreover, without Germany, however sub-divided or expressed, there is no force of nationhood in the West which could hold the balance with the Soviet power.

I do not believe that in striving for the larger synthesis we should hinder such practical and partial steps as are possible. I am sure that in going for the limited Western bloc of weak or shattered States we should be reducing our policy from a grand design to mere diplomatic manipulation. If we succeed in forming the Western bloc, as at present envisaged, we should only increase our responsibilities without adding to our strength.

Winston S. Churchill: memorandum
(Churchill papers, 2/19)

20 October 1946

THE UNITED STATES OF EUROPE
STATEMENT OF AIMS

The anarchy of Europe has already brought about two world-wars in our time. Its continuance must lead to an even more terrible catastrophe. In the mechanised world of today the small nation States of the past can scarcely hope for political or economic survival as isolated units. The peoples of Europe, or as many of them as are willing to make a start, should come together in order to create an effective European union, not aimed against any other nations but designed to maintain their common peace, to restore their common prosperity and above all to preserve their common heritage of freedom.

Our first loyalty in this country is to the British Empire and Commonwealth, but we are convinced that the freedom and welfare of its peoples are intimately bound up with the freedom and welfare of the peoples of Europe. Our sacrifices give us the right, our victory imposes on us the duty and our interests confirm the wisdom of giving a lead to the European nations and assuring them of our fullest support in whatever effort they are willing to make towards a United Europe.

The aim must be to unite all Europe from the Atlantic to the Black Sea. If, however, the countries of Eastern Europe are for the present unable to join the proposed European Federation, then the countries of western Europe should make a start on their own, always leaving it open to the other States to join later as and when they can.

The United States of Europe would be neither dependent on, nor opposed to, the Soviet Union or the USA. With its associated Dominions and dependencies it would command resources at least as great as those of the two existing Federations in the East and in the West. Like USA and USSR, the United States of Europe would be fitted into the structure of the United Nations Organization and subject to the authority of the Security Council.

It would be wrong for us to commit ourselves at the outset to any precise project for a European Constitution. The United States of Europe must grow from free consultation between the representatives of all its peoples and from practical experience of concerted action.

The task now is to urge men of good will of all parties and in all countries to take counsel together that Europe may arise.

* * *

To promote these objects it is proposed to form an international movement with sections in every European country. It is proposed to hold a conference of representative Europeans to start the movement, next February or March. A small British handling group, composed of members of all parties, has been formed under Mr Churchill's Chairmanship to make the necessary arrangements.

Winston S. Churchill to Major Reginald Marnham
(Churchill papers, 1/32)

20 October 1946

Dear Major Marnham,

1. I am prepared, subject to contract, to accept your offer to sell me the whole property, with possession, from 1 January, 1947, for the sum of twenty-five thousand pounds (£25,000). I shall be glad if you will instruct your solicitors to prepare the draft contract and enter into communication with Messrs. Nicholl, Manisty, Few & Company, who will act for me. As far as any valuations may be required for the tenant right, etc., Messrs. Knight, Frank & Rutley will act for me.

2. I think the plan you have proposed for leaving the herd on the farm until, say, Michaelmas, 1947, is a sensible and convenient method of ensuring the continuity of production, and again, subject to details being adjusted between us by correspondence, I should like to adopt it.

3. I should propose that, for the time being, there should be no disturbance with regard to your present employees, including your foreman, Page, and I should be obliged if you would reassure them on this point. I understand from Mr Cox that one of them is about to leave. I should be glad if you would let

me have a statement as to the wages you pay, and the families who live in the cottages.

4. Mr Cox tells me that you would be willing to continue with all the necessary cultivations until the purchase is completed with effect from 1 January, 1947, and he will make these arrangements with you on my behalf.

Let me thank you again for your courtesy in giving me the first refusal.

Winston S. Churchill: speech
('Winston S. Churchill, His Complete Speeches', volume 7, pages 7391–8)

23 October 1946   House of Commons

FOREIGN AFFAIRS

The right hon. Gentleman the Foreign Secretary wished to open this Debate and I may say, merely to safeguard future practice, that it is not quite usual for a two days' Debate to be opened from the Government benches. However, I willingly agreed to the right hon. Gentleman making his statement, and we all have been greatly interested in the speech which he has made. Indeed, I think there was a very general measure of agreement in the House with everything, or nearly everything, he said. Where there may be differences, they are not differences on what he said so much as on what, for no doubt very good reasons, the right hon. Gentleman left unsaid. As to the value of what are called the 'open discussions' which have been proceeding in Paris, I can only comment that they seem to be bad diplomacy, but, none the less, valuable education. As to the veto, that is a very serious matter. It is well known that Soviet Russia would not have joined the original San Francisco Conference unless they had had what they regard as the essential security of the veto. I quite agree with the right hon. Gentleman that it was never contemplated at any time that the veto should be used in the abrupt, arbitrary and almost continuous manner that we have seen it used, but that it should be reserved as a last assurance to a great Power that they would not be voted down on a matter about which they were prepared to fight. There is, certainly, a great departure from that tradition, and the Foreign Secretary will be supported on this side of the House in endeavouring to secure a modification in the uses of the veto, even if he is not at this time able to secure a very considerable restriction of its employment.

We all wish the Foreign Secretary a successful mission to the United States. No one complains of his having to be out of the country. It is his duty to go over and, indeed, I, myself, believe very much that advantage comes from that. Even in the days of the National Coalition, Ministers sometimes left the country for considerable periods, and I, having left the right hon. Gentleman the Prime Minister to carry on affairs, allowed myself all the necessary latitude in this respect. We all, as I say, wish that the right hon. Gentleman may have a successful mission in the United States, and we are confident that, in many respects, he will be upholding, not Party but national, and indeed not national, but world issues.

In the Debate yesterday the right hon. Gentleman made considerable references to Germany, and perhaps the most important part of his speech consisted of declarations of policy about Germany, and about the Anglo-American occupied zones in Germany. Agreement on this was expressed by my right hon. Friend the Member for Saffron Walden (Mr R. A. Butler). We are in full agreement with the modifications and the mitigations of the severity of German life under present conditions, so far as these are physically and economically possible. It is only common sense that the Germans should earn their own living, and I think it is only common sense that they should manage their own affairs, provided, and always provided, that effective disarmament is enforced and maintained over a prolonged period of years. We do not want to have the burden of teaching the Germans how to manage their own affairs, and we do not want to have the burden of earning their living for them. The remarks of the Chancellor of the Exchequer on this subject might be held by captious critics to be a criticism of the policy so far pursued by His Majesty's Government. (Dr Hugh Dalton speaking to the Bankers & Merchants of the City of London, Mansion House, on 16 October 1946, said: 'The British taxpayer is being called upon to find more than eighty million a year to feed and to supply the Germans in the British zone, many millions of whom for many years followed their leaders with intense and unashamed ardour until their wicked plans were finally frustrated.')[1]

However, there is just one point I should like to make on the subject of Germany managing her own affairs. The right hon. Gentleman announced that he was proceeding to nationalise the various great German industries and place them under the Commander-in-Chief. All I can tell the House is that experience shows that one may be quite sure that when the Germans have the power of managing their own affairs, they will not be attracted to a policy, whatever it may be, by the fact that it has been imposed upon them by foreigners. It was exactly what happened after the first world war when we imposed upon Germany, by force, all the blessings of a liberal constitution. All the blessings of freedom from the tyranny of conscription and many benefits fought for by generations of effort in this country were enforced by the victors upon the defeated Germans and were, for that reason, odious in their eyes. But, as I say, it may be that it will work differently this time.

I must comment first this afternoon upon two or three special questions which are likely to cause trouble and are, indeed, already causes of disquiet. I have nothing to add today to the statements which I have made on previous

[1] This parenthetical commentary, and that on p. 504 below, were written by Robert Rhodes James, editor of *His Complete Speeches*.

occasions about Egypt and Palestine. No one can say that His Majesty's Government have not done their best to meet Egyptian wishes. Indeed, many of us thought that they had gone too far and had adopted the wrong methods in stating, at the outset of their negotiations, that they were willing to evacuate the Canal zone, which zone is secured to us for the next few critical years to come by the Anglo-Egyptian treaty of 1936. The result has been what was then predicted, namely, that their maximum offer was taken as the starting point for new discussions, and these discussions now even involve the whole sovereignty and future of the Sudan. I remind the right hon. Gentleman the Prime Minister of his statement on 7 May, when he said that, obviously, if negotiations break down the original treaty still stands. I hope that His Majesty's Government will act in this sense.

Before we separated for the Autumn Recess, I spoke about Palestine. I must refer to that subject, linked as it is with all other questions of the Middle East. If we are not able to fulfil our pledge to the Jews to create a national home for the Jewish people in Palestine – which is our undoubted pledge – we are entitled and, indeed, bound in my view – because it is our duty, to lay our Mandate at the feet of the United Nations Organisation. The burden may yet be too heavy for one single country to bear. It is not right that the United States, who are so very keen on Jewish immigration into Palestine, should take no share in the task, and should reproach us for our obvious incapacity to cope with the difficulties of the problem.

At present, we have no policy as far as I can make out, nor have we had one for more than a year. The amount of suffering which this indecision in regard to a question which, I admit, may well be called the 'riddle of the Sphinx', is causing to all concerned, simply cannot be measured. From the moment when we declare that we will give up the Mandate – giving proper notice, of course – all our difficulties will be considerably lessened, and if other interested Powers wish us to continue, it is for them to make proposals and help us in our work. We have at this moment a large proportion of our overseas Army in Palestine engaged in a horrible, squalid conflict with the Zionist community there. This is a disproportionate exertion for us, a wrong distribution of our limited forces, and the most thankless task ever undertaken by any country. If we stand on the treaty of Egypt about the Canal zone, we have no need to seek a new strategic base of very doubtful usefulness in Palestine, and we can present ourselves to the world organisation as a totally disinterested party. Superior solutions may then, for the first time, become open. I strongly commend this course of action to His Majesty's Government and to the House.

I was very glad yesterday to hear what the Foreign Secretary said about Greece. The result of the Greek plebiscite upon the return of the King fully vindicates the course pursued by the National Coalition Government, by the interim Government of which I was the head, and by His Majesty's present advisers. We have always said it was a question for the Greek people to decide freely for themselves. This they have done under conditions which impartial foreign observers have pronounced not unfair, and which are incomparably more free and valid than anything that has been seen in that part of the world for a very long time. That pronouncement ought to be the end of our special wartime responsibilities towards Greece. I was glad to hear that our troops will be brought home as soon as possible. (*An Hon. Member: 'When will that be?'*) I am not pressing for details. There is a kind of guerrilla warfare on the Northern frontier of Greece which does not arise out of internal Greek affairs. It arises out of very much larger complications. But still I am most anxious that our troops should come home. I am tired of hearing it said that we are in Greece for something which we wish to get out of the country, or for some advantage. I know of no advantage that we gain or seek in Greece except those ordinary advantages enjoyed by all nations, of trade and friendship, which we ourselves enjoyed before the war.

The future safety and independence of Greece, like many other vital matters, lie in the hands of UNO. Our ancient friendship with Greece will never flag or die, but here, as elsewhere, we seek no gain or benefit of a selfish character for ourselves and, as I have just said, we have no desire for any advantages which we did not possess before the war. I hope that all Greeks who wish for the survival of their country will help the new regime and Government, and that the Government will be continually broadened to include all who prefer the life and freedom of Greece to its ruin and absorption in a Communist Balkan *bloc*. I hope fair play will be given to the new regime and the new Government of Greece, and that every step taken will not be the target for sharp arrows of carefully barbed, poisoned propaganda. It is very easy for foreign observers in a position of perfect detachment, to abuse a Government which is struggling against a Communist conspiracy, fomented and supported by outside intrigues. An armed Communist advances upon you, you react against him; therefore, you are a reactionary.

I must now speak about Poland. Here, indeed, an unhappy scene is unfolded to our eyes. In my opinion, the Soviet Government have departed, I am sorry to say, in the spirit and in the letter from many of the agreements and understandings into which we entered with them before Yalta, and at Yalta. It was my firm belief that Marshal Stalin would rest content with the Curzon line, and with a Poland friendly to Russia, and permanently divorced from Germany. On that, I offered on many occasions my counsel to the House. It was agreed that, on this basis, there should be free elections in Poland and that the Polish Republic should be an independent Power. What has happened now? A Government has been set up in Poland which in no way represents the Polish nation. That Government is incapable of holding free or fair elections. The Peasant Party are to be given no full and free opportunity of voting in accordance with their convictions, and of having their votes counted in accordance with their numbers. We must be very careful to distinguish in our minds between the present Polish Government, and the heart of the Polish nation to whose sorrows and sufferings there seems never to be an end.

I presume that the most delicate and difficult situation at the moment is that which exists around Trieste, where British and American divisions confront the very much larger forces which Marshal Tito has kept under arms and assembled there. Gratitude does not seem to be the outstanding feature of Marshal Tito's character. I am sure every one here was shocked at the brutal and callous manner in which American aeroplanes and their passengers were shot down by the air force of a country whose liberation and independence would never have been achieved but for British and American aid and exertion, or without the victorious campaigns fought in Italy and Germany by the Western Allies. The whole attitude of the Yugoslav Communist Government towards this country, and even more towards the United States, is far from friendly. Considering that the United States is the main contributor to UNRRA, and that scores of millions of pounds of supplies have been poured into Yugoslavia since the end of the German war, the murder of the American airmen and passengers presents itself in a singularly repulsive light.

Conditions in Yugoslavia are sinister and melancholy. The whole country is being converted, as far as possible, into a Communist area. Communism is being taught in the schools, and every effort is being made to create a Soviet Socialist Republic in the closest association with Moscow. It is not for us to interfere in the internal affairs of another country. (*Laughter.*) Well, I am afraid I make my principle of general application. The Catholic Church and clergy in Croatia are being persecuted with the greatest severity, and the strictest measures of police government are applied to political dissentients. The circumstances of the trial and condemnation of the Archbishop of Zagreb[1] have created widespread regret. There is growing discontent in Serbia, to whose peasant proprietors Communist doctrines are unwelcome.

The course followed by His Majesty's Government has, throughout, been wise and correct, and I am glad to see it has been taken in the closest harmony with that of the United States. I earnestly trust that this policy towards Yugoslavia will be pursued by His Majesty's Government with perseverance, and that the great city of Trieste will be preserved as an international port, an outlet upon salt water for the commerce of all the States and peoples in the Danube Basin. I trust, also, that large Italian populations will not be transferred against their own will to Communist rule, contrary to the whole principle of the Atlantic Charter. I was very glad to hear from the Prime Minister today, when he referred to the speech made by my right hon. Friend the Member for

[1] Aloysius Stepinac, 1898–1960. Born in Brezani, Croatia. Studied Architecture, University of Zagreb. Conscripted, Austro-Hungarian Army, 1916–19. Attended seminary, Rome, 1924–30. Ordained priest, 1930. Catholic Archbishop of Zagreb, 1937. Tried and convicted for Nazi collaboration, 1946; sentenced to 17 years' hard labour. Released, 1951. The trial was later admitted to have been framed as punishment for refusing to sever ties with Catholic Church. Cardinal, 1953. Beatified, 1998.

Saffron Walden, that the British troops would not leave the Trieste area until the treaty has been fully signed and accepted by all States who are likely to be party to it.

Now I am going to look back a little, in fact, I am going to look back for a year almost to the day, when on 22 October, 1945, I pressed for more rapid demobilisation. I made the following statement, which, I venture to think the House will permit me to read, as I copied it from *Hansard*:

> I must, however, make one very serious reservation. In my calculations and estimates I have definitely excluded the possibility of a major war in the next few years. If His Majesty's Government consider that this is wrong, then it would not be a case of demobilisation at all but of remobilisation, because what has taken place and is going on has already woefully impaired the immediate fighting efficiency of the enormous Forces we still retain. I believe, however, it may be common ground that this possibility of a major war may rightly be excluded, and that we may have an interlude of grace in which mankind may be able to make better arrangements for this tortured world than we have hitherto achieved. Still, I make that reservation.

On this basis, I also gave the minimum figures to which in my judgment – a judgment without official information – the reduction should be made, and I stated the figures. Those figures were: Royal Navy, 150,000; Army, 1,000,000; Royal Air Force, 400,000; total men, 1,550,000. The figures to which His Majesty's Government announced in February they were working are considerably less than this total, especially in respect of the Army and Air Force; the Navy is a little larger. These are the Government's figures to be obtained by 31 December this year, in the next 10 weeks: Royal Navy, 175,000; Army, 650,000, instead of 1,000,000; Royal Air Force, 275,000, instead of 400,000; total in the Services, taking only the published figures, 1,100,000 as against 1,550,000. I believe there are 100,000 recruits additional in training. The Government, therefore, have gone much further in reducing our military strength, notably in the Army and Air Force, than the figures I put forward on the basis of getting down to our minimum figure, whatever it was, as quickly as possible. I am not today treating this issue as controversial, as a matter of quarrel between the Government and the Opposition. The Government have the power and responsibility, and they ought to have the knowledge. I am, however, forced to examine the question whether the situation has deteriorated in the year that has passed.

Eight months ago, I made a speech at Fulton in the United States. It had a mixed reception on both sides of the Atlantic, and quite a number of hon. Members of this House put their names to a Motion condemning me for having made it. As events have moved, what I said at Fulton has been outpaced and overpassed by this movement of events, and by the movement of American opinion. If I were to make that speech at the present time and in the same place, it would attract no particular attention. At that time, I said that I did not believe the Soviet Government wanted war. I said that what they wanted were the fruits of war. I fervently hope and pray that the view which I then expressed is still correct, and on the whole I believe it is still correct. However, we are dealing with the unknowable. Like everyone else, I welcome the recent declarations of Marshal Stalin, and I always welcome any signs of affability which M Molotov may display. I know him quite well, and, as the right hon. Gentleman the Foreign Secretary will corroborate, he is not nearly so spiky in private relationship as he appears in his public declarations. In these matters, it is not words that count, it is deeds and facts.

This afternoon I am not going to examine the likelihood of another war, which would, of course, be total war. In the Foreign Secretary's calm, assured and measured review of the world situation yesterday, it was evident that various differences of policy exist between the Soviet Government and what are called, for want of a better name – and it is not a bad name – the Western democracies. There are differences in the Far East; there are disputes about Persia; there are various grave and serious questions connected with the Dardanelles; above all, there is the situation at Trieste, there is Poland and its elections, and there are others. The right hon. Gentleman found it necessary – and he was quite right – to survey the whole far from cheering panorama, and touch upon all those points of view; and though his language was diplomatically correct in every respect, one could not help seeing those points of direct difference emerging as between the great Powers which are involved. It would be most unwise to ignore those differences, and every effort should be made to adjust them. I am sure every effort will be made by patient, friendly and, I hope, occasionally secret discussions between the principal Powers and personalities involved.

It was easier in Hitler's day to feel and forecast the general movement of events than it is now. Now we have to deal not with Hitler and his crude Nazi gang, with anti-Semitism as its principal theme; we are in the presence of something very much more difficult to measure than what was set out so plainly in the pages of *Mein Kampf*. We are in the presence of the collective mind, whose springs of action we cannot define. There are 13 or 14 very able men in the Kremlin who hold all Russia and more than a third of Europe in their control. Many stresses and pressures, internal as well as external, are working upon them, as upon all human beings. I cannot presume to forecast what decisions they will take, or to observe what decisions they may have already have taken; still less can I attempt to foresee the time factor in their affairs. One of our main difficulties in judging all these matters is that real intercourse and intimacy between our peoples are, to all intents and purposes, very much discouraged and prevented by the Soviet Government. There is none of that free comradely life and mixing which very soon would bring immense changes in the relationships of these vast communities, and might sweep away suspicion, without relaxing vigilance.

The Prime Minister referred just now in his speech – he used the expression and I noted it down at the time – to 'the total mobilised forces which may constitute a positive danger to peace'. That is certainly a serious remark, coming as it does from the head of His Majesty's Government. Now, I am going to ask a question – it is all I have to say before I sit down – on which, I feel, the House, the nation and, indeed, the world should be told the truth as far as it is known to His Majesty's Government, and should be reassured, if it is possible, and as far as possible. To make it easier for the Government to give a brief and general answer, to make it possible for them to give an almost monosyllabic answer, I will put my question in a constructive form. Here is the question: Is it or is it not true that there are today more than 200 Soviet divisions on a war footing in the occupied territories of Europe from the Baltic to Vienna, and from Vienna to the Black Sea? There is the question which I am asking, and it acquires particular significance in view of the Prime Minister's reference, which I heard only this afternoon in the House, to 'total mobilised forces which may constitute a positive danger to peace'. I am not referring to the armies of satellite Powers which, in Poland, are numerous but reluctant, and in Yugoslavia and Bulgaria are less numerous but more ardent.

I shall be very much relieved if I can be told in the course of today's Debate that the figures I have given – which I have not given without prolonged consideration and heart-searching, or without discussion with colleagues – are altogether excessive, and if His Majesty's Government can relieve our anxieties in the matter I am quite ready to accept their statement, but I feel bound to put the question. (Later in the Debate Mr Hector McNeil,[1] Under-Secretary for Foreign Affairs, said 'I am unable to say whether the information of the right hon. Gentleman about the number of Russian divisions in occupied countries between the Baltic and the Black Sea is correct, or what proportion of these divisions is on a war footing; but it is, of course, well known that there are very considerable Russian forces in these countries.') When we think of all the helpless millions and hundreds of millions struggling to earn their living, toiling along the uphill path, hoping for the future, doing their best, one cannot but feel that they ought to know the main outlines, at least, of what is going on around them, which may so vitally affect them. That is all I wish to say today. We shall have further opportunities of discussing the whole position in the new Session and, of course, during the Debate on the Address.

---

[1] Hector McNeil, 1907–55. Labour member of Glasgow Town Council, 1933–6, 1937–8. Stood unsuccessfully for Parliament, 1935, 1936. MP (Lab.) for Greenock, 1941–55. Parliamentary Private Secretary to Parliamentary Secretary to Minister of War Transport, 1942–5. Parliamentary Under-Secretary of State, FO, 1945–6. PC, 1946. Minister of State for Foreign Affairs, 1946–50. Led British delegation to Economic and Social Council of the UN in New York, 1946, 1947. Secretary of State for Scotland, 1950–1.

Winston S. Churchill: speech
('*Winston S. Churchill, His Complete Speeches*', volume 7, page 7398)

24 October 1946 Loughton

COMMUNISM

... The British Government have rendered a very considerable service in breaking with the Communist Party. I agree with every word Mr Attlee has said. Indeed I could have added a few more words of my own. In this country the Communist Party does not bulk so largely in our minds. It is there, a venomous thing – crawling and creeping around, but it is not immediately one of the main objectives of politics.

The fact that the British Government had decisively broken with the Communists, and were fronted against them, although it did not immediately affect the course of affairs in this island, had an important and beneficial result abroad, because there were countries on the Continent of Europe, like France, quivering under the Communist attack. The fact that the Government took this stand and put its foot down on the Communists, not in any unfair way, but resisting them by argument, the fact that the Communists were banned and barred by the Labour Party and the TUC was something which added greatly to the stability of Europe. It set an example in many lands where lives and freedom hung in the balance.

In fairness he must recognize that the Government to which he was strongly opposed in so many matters had not impeded freedom of speech. They might like to but they had not; some had not wished to, others had not dared to ...

Mr Bevin, a sort of working-class John Bull, had maintained a continuity of policy in foreign affairs to a very considerable extent. Greece has had a fair and free plebiscite and election and had been rescued from the danger of being involved in the Communist Balkan *bloc* which was being actively fomented by the trained Communist agents who came out from the Mecca of Communism in Moscow ...

I had yesterday to give a serious warning in the House of Commons. I had to ask whether it was not true that there were more than 200 Soviet divisions on a war footing in the occupied territories of Europe. I did not ask that question without weighing very carefully the whole matter, and without consulting others, my friends and colleagues, and laying before them the evidence upon which I proceeded. I did not ask the question without informing the Government beforehand of my intention. The answer was neither one thing nor the other, but you may take it from me that the facts I adduced are correct.

Winston S. Churchill to Clement Attlee
(Churchill papers, 2/29)

27 October 1946

My dear Prime Minister,

Following on my remarks in Debate the other day I wish to bring a delegation from the Conservative Party to meet you and any of your Ministers you care to have with you in the next week or ten days. Our delegation will be four in number, including myself and Mr Eden.

It is my duty to impart to you certain information which I have received which causes me deep concern, and involves the safety of the country. In submitting this information to you I in no way inhibit myself or my colleagues from making it public if we consider this accords with our responsibility. On the other hand, of course, any conversations which may occur or any information which you may think fit to give us would be treated on the principles set out in our correspondence of June 1945.

I cannot think any difficulty would arise. Pray let me hear from you at your convenience.

Winston S. Churchill: speech
('Winston S. Churchill, His Complete Speeches', volume 7, page 7399)

28 October 1946   Chartwell

PAST MISTAKES IN FOREIGN AFFAIRS

. . . We have passed through a great struggle – it was not necessary that that struggle should have ever taken place. There was no need whatsoever for Germany to have been allowed to rearm.

I was very much in favour of friendly treatment of Germany after the last war, but was not in favour of allowing those very dangerous people to get the deadly weapons of war in their hands again. Lassitude, weakness, putting off until tomorrow what ought to be settled today, lack of decision, fear of running against the strong currents of public opinion, which I am glad to say in this country are prevailingly pacifist – all prevented measures being taken by the League of Nations, of which America was not then a member, and enabled a monster to spring on to the summit of power and lead the German nation once more upon the road of havoc for Europe and the world and ruin and misery for themselves.

Now there was a new scene. We had emerged successfully from the deadliest crisis and the whole world had a new chance.

What will they do with it? That is one of those mysteries of the future which I shall not attempt to plumb. On the first day that I am a freeman of the

Borough of Beckenham I shall certainly not attempt the role of prophet, but will be content with the honour which you have conferred upon me, which, I can assure you, I most profoundly appreciate.

Lord Simon[1] to Winston S. Churchill
(Churchill papers)

28 October 1946

My dear Winston,

Thank you so much for sending me a copy of your 'secret session speeches'. Some day I shall intercept you and ask you to write in the fly leaf as from you to me. I had, in fact, already bought a copy and read them all through again.

Demosthenes' speeches against Philip of Macedon — I say this with some knowledge of the originals — are in some respects very like yours, the same conviction that nothing mattered except freedom, and that the intelligence of his own people was equal to overthrowing even the most powerful enemy if all pulled together, and all in most compelling language. But Demosthenes did not see the achievement for which he acted and spoke. That is the great difference and whatever troubles come I shall always think of you as having that priceless consolation.

Oliver Lyttelton to Winston S. Churchill
(Churchill papers, 2/29)

28 October 1946

Dear Winston,

This is what I dictated this morning. I hope the general line meets with your approval. I am tidying it up in the meanwhile.

On the subject of research and development, and the pressure you put upon scientists and others, I would much like to tell the anecdote about the Schnortzel submarines and the wrecks. Do you remember saying 'Why don't we have a radar device fixed to the wrecks which keeps on saying "I'm a wreck, I'm a wreck"?', or do you think this is a mistake on security or other grounds.

---

[1] John Allsebrook Simon, 1873–1954. Educated at Fettes and Wadham College, Oxford. MP (Lib.) for Walthamstow, 1906–18; for Spen Valley, 1922–31. Knighted, 1910. Attorney-General, with a seat in the Cabinet, 1913–15. Home Secretary, 1915–16; resigned in opposition to conscription. Maj., RAF, serving in France, 1917–18. MP (Nat. Lib.) for Spen Valley, 1931–40. Foreign Secretary, 1931–5. Home Secretary, 1935–7. Chancellor of the Exchequer, 1937–40. Viscount, 1940. Lord Chancellor, 1940–5.

Clement Attlee to Winston S. Churchill
(*Churchill papers, 2/29*)

28 October 1946

My dear Churchill,

I shall be very pleased to meet you and your colleagues on the matter you mention. The time you suggest would not be very convenient, as I should wish to have Alexander with me and we could not both leave the Debate on the White Paper. It would suit me if you could make it convenient to come to my room on Tuesday afternoon, November 5, after questions.

I have some points germane to, though not immediately arising from the subject which I should like to mention to you.

Edward Roberts[1] to Winston S. Churchill
(*Churchill papers, 2/116*)

29 October 1946

Dear Sir,

Enclosed is the complete text of the Stalin questions and answers, to which Mr Baillie[2] referred in his telegram to you of last night.

Stalin refers to you in his answer to Question No. 6, on Page 2. The answer to Question No. 7 appears to be a further indirect reference. The answer to Question No. 20 also may be of especial interest to you in view of your recent question in the House concerning Soviet troops in Eastern Europe.

As Mr Baillie stated in his telegram, the United Press will be extremely pleased to afford full distribution to any comment you may care to make. I have been assigned to deliver this text to you and await any reply, verbal or written.

Complete text of questions submitted to Generalissimo J. V. Stalin by Hugh Baillie, President of the United Press of America; and Stalin's replies thereto:

Question No. 1 – Do you agree with Secretary Byrnes feeling, as expressed in his radio address last Friday (these questions were sent Monday, Oct. 21) that there is growing tension between the USSR and the United States.

Answer – No.

---

[1] Edward V. Roberts, 1912–89. Reporter for Florida newspapers, 1930s. Correspondent, United Press, 1945–50. Joined State Department, 1951. Worked for US Information Agency, 1953–71; Inspector General, 1970.

[2] Hugh Baillie, 1890–1966. American journalist. Head of United Press Association, 1935–55. Interviewed European leaders including Hitler, Mussolini and Chamberlain. Covered US invasion of Sicily, 1943, and Belgian campaign, 1944. Continued to cover world famous events and leaders after WWII.

Question No. 2 – If such increasing tension exists could you tell me the reason or reasons for it, and what are the most essential bases for its removal?
Answer – The question becomes obsolete in connection with answer to previous question.

Question No. 3 – Do you foresee that present negotiations will result in peace treaties which will establish cordial relations among the nations which were allied in the war against fascism, and eliminate the danger of war from these former axis sources?
Answer – I hope it will be so.

Question No. 4 – If not, what would be the principal obstacles to the creation of such cordial relationships among the nations which were allies in the great war?
Answer – The question becomes obsolete in connection with answer to previous question.

Question No. 5 – What is Russia's attitude with regard to the decision of Yugoslavia not to sign the peace treaty with Italy?
Answer – Yugoslavia has grounds to be dissatisfied.

Question No. 6 – What constitutes today, in your judgment, the worst threat to world peace?
Answer – Instigators of a new war, in the first place Churchill, and those who think like him in Great Britain and the United States. (His partisans)

Question No. 7 – If such threat should arise, what would be the best steps to be taken by the nations of the world to avoid a new war?
Answer – Instigators of a new war have to be unmasked and kept in check.

Question No. 8 – Is the United Nations Organization a guarantee of the integrity of small countries?
Answer – It is difficult to say yet.

Question No. 9 – Do you think that the four zones of occupation in Germany should, in the near future, be thrown together insofar as economic administration is concerned with a view to restoring Germany as a peaceful economic unit, and thus lessening the burden of occupation to the four powers?
Answer – It is necessary to re-establish not only the economic but the political unity of Germany as well.

Question No. 10 – Do you feel that it is feasible at this time to create some sort of general administration to be placed in the hands of the Germans themselves, but under allied control, which will make it possible for the Council of Foreign Ministers to draft a peace treaty for Germany?
Answer – Yes, I think so.

Question No. 11 – Do you feel confident in the light of the elections which have been held in the various zones this summer and fall, that Germany is developing politically along democratic lines which give hope for its future as a peaceful nation?
Answer – I am not sure of it for the time being.

Question No. 12 – Do you feel that, as has been suggested in some quarters, the level of permitted industry should be raised above the agreed level to permit Germany to pay her own way more fully?
Answer – Yes, I do.

Question No. 13 – What should be done beyond the present four-power program to prevent Germany from again becoming a world military menace?
Answer – It is necessary to extirpate in practice the remnants of fascism in Germany and to democratize her most thoroughly.

Question No. 14 – Should the German people be allowed to reconstruct their industry and trade and become self-supporting?
Answer – Yes, they should.

Question No. 15 – Have the provisions of Potsdam in your opinion been adhered to; if not, what is needed to make the Potsdam declaration an effective instrument?
Answer – They are not always adhered to, especially in the field of democratization of Germany.

Question No. 16 – Do you feel that the veto power has been used to excess during the discussions among the four foreign ministers, and in the meetings of the United Nations Security Council?
Answer – No, I do not.

Question No. 17 – How far does the Kremlin feel the allied powers should go in hunting down and trying minor war criminals in Germany; does it feel that the Nuremberg decisions created a sufficiently strong basis for such action?
Answer – The farther it will go the better.

Question No. 18 – Does Russia consider the western frontiers of Poland as permanent?
Answer – Yes, she does.

Question No. 19 – How does the USSR regard the presence of British troops in Greece; does it feel that Britain should supply more arms to the present Greek government?
Answer – As unnecessary.

Question No. 20 – What is the extent of the Russian military contingents in Poland, Hungary, Bulgaria, Yugoslavia and Austria, and how long do you feel that in the interests of securing the peace these contingents must be maintained?
Answer – In the west, that is in Germany, Austria, Hungary, Bulgaria, Romania and Poland, the Soviet Union has at the present time, sixty divisions altogether – rifle and armored – the majority of them not in full strength. There are no Soviet troops in Yugoslavia. In two months time, when the decree of the presidium of the Supreme Soviet of 22 October of this year concerning the last demobilization classes will be implemented, forty Soviet divisions will remain in the said countries.

Question No. 21 – What is the attitude of the government of the USSR toward the presence of American warships in the Mediterranean?
Answer – Indifferent.

Question No. 22 – What is the present outlook for a commercial agreement between Russia and Norway?
Answer – Difficult to say for the time being.

Question No. 23 – Is it possible for Finland to again become a self-sufficient nation after the reparations have been paid, and is there any idea in contemplation of revising the reparations program so as to expedite Finland's recovery?
Answer – The question is put wrongly. Finland was and remains a fully self-sufficient nation.

Question No. 24 – What will the trade agreements with Sweden and other countries mean with regard to reconstruction in the USSR; what outside aid do you consider desirable for the accomplishment of this great task?
Answer – An agreement with Sweden constitutes a contribution to the cause of economic cooperation between the nations.

Question No. 25 – Is Russia still interested in obtaining a loan from the United States?
Answer – She is interested.

Question No. 26 – Has Russia yet developed its own atom bomb or any similar weapon?
Answer – No.

Question No. 27 – What is your opinion of the atom bomb or similar weapon as an instrument of warfare?
Answer – I gave already my valuation of the atom bomb in the known answer to Mister Werth.[1]

Question No. 28 – How in your opinion can atomic power best be controlled; should this control be created on an international basis, and to what extent should the powers sacrifice their sovereignty in the interest of making the control effective?
Answer – A strong international control is needed.

Question No. 29 – How long will it require to rebuild the devastated areas of western Russia?
Answer – Six or seven years, if not more.

Question No. 30 – Will Russia permit commercial airlines to operate across the Soviet Union; does Russia intend to extend her own airlines to other continents on a reciprocal basis?
Answer – Under certain conditions this is not excluded.

Question No. 31 – How does your government view the occupation of Japan; do you feel it has been a success on the present basis?
Answer – There are successes, but it would be possible to attain better successes.

---

[1] Alexander Werth, 1901–69. Born in St Petersburg. Fled with his father from Russia before the Revolution of 1917. Educated at University of Glasgow, 1922. Sub-editor, *Glasgow Herald*, 1927–8. Moscow correspondent for several British newspapers, 1941–8; for the BBC, 1941–6; for the *Guardian*, 1946–9. Senior Simon Research Fellow, Manchester University, 1953–5. Visiting Prof. of History, Ohio State University, 1957. Wrote numerous books on Russia and France, including *France, 1940–1955* (1956) and *Russia at War 1941 to 1945* (1964).

Winston S. Churchill: press statement
(Churchill papers, 2/116)

29 October 1946

Mr Churchill issued the following statement from Chartwell, Westerham, this afternoon:

I have a regard and respect for Premier Stalin, and always remember all we went through together. I also wish to see the Russian people who fought so bravely for their native land, safe, prosperous and happy. It was always my desire that once the War was won the Soviet Government should play one of the leading parts in the rebuilding of our shattered world.

By the Anglo-Russian Treaty made when I was Prime Minister in 1941, we are bound not to interfere in each other's internal affairs or system of society. Therefore I do not see why we cannot all be friends and help each other, and thus advance the whole basic standard of livelihood of the broad masses of people in every land.

I am glad to see Premier Stalin's statement about Russian forces in the occupied territories he mentions. But even sixty divisions on a war footing would of course greatly exceed the British and American forces in enemy occupied territory in Europe. Moreover, Premier Stalin's figures do not include Roumania. Nor of course do they include the heavy Soviet concentrations in the Leningrad and Odessa regions.

I asked His Majesty's Government whether my estimate of 200 divisions applied to the West was excessive, and I asked the question in such a form that it could be answered 'Yes' or 'No'. Considering the difference between 200 divisions and 60 divisions, it ought to have been possible, if I was in error, for a contradiction to be given. None was forthcoming. On the contrary the statement of the Prime Minister and the Under Secretary of State for Foreign Affairs showed only anxiety at the strength of the Soviet mobilized forces.

No one would have been more pleased than I to be told that I was misinformed. No one will be more pleased if this proves to be the case. It is clearly most important that the facts should be made known. It is difficult to believe that Allies occupying together enemy territory recently gained with their blood, should not know about the strength of each other's garrisons. Indeed, one would have thought they would have interchanged and shared this information between themselves as a matter of course, and that there reciprocal inspection of the forces mobilized in their respective zones. We hear a great deal about suspicions. Nothing sweeps away suspicions like facts, and I consider it my duty to continue to press for the facts.

I should add that my information, which of course is not official information, contemplated a strength of ten thousand men per Soviet division.

However, during the last war, American and British divisions sometimes ran as high as forty or fifty thousand men, and thirty thousand would be a fairly good average figure including of course auxiliary services, corps troops and lines of communication. It is not possible to judge the strength of an army unless not only the number of organized divisions are known, but also and at the same time, the total ration strength.

It seems to me that a clearing up of this matter would be highly beneficial from every point of view, and surely the present meeting of UNO should be the occasion for the fullest and fairest possible disclosure of all the many military forces that cause anxiety to any of those who fought and won the great victory together.

Jo Sturdee to Winston S. Churchill
(*Churchill papers, 2/116*)

29 October 1946

Mr Hopkinson[1] telephoned. He wishes to point out that, with regard to Premier Stalin's replies to the questions put, Rumania is excluded. Rumania is very rich and he thinks it is probable that there are a great many Russian forces there as that country has the most natural resources on which their men could live. At one time, some time ago, there were a million men there, but Mr Hopkinson has not been able to ascertain any figures of the forces there now. Finland and Albania were also left out, but Mr Hopkinson does not think there are any Russian forces in either of those countries to speak of.

---

[1] Henry Lennox D'Aubigne Hopkinson, 1902–96. 3rd Secretary, Washington DC, 1924–9. 2nd Secretary, FO, 1929–31; Stockholm, 1931–2; Cairo, 1934–8. Asst Private Secretary to Foreign Secretary, 1932–4. 1st Secretary, Athens, 1938–9; War Cabinet Secretariat, 1939–40. Private Secretary to Permanent Under-Secretary, FO, 1940–1. Diplomatic Adviser to Minister of State, Middle East, 1941–3. Minister Plenipotentiary to Portugal, 1943–4. CMG, 1944. Deputy High Commissioner to Rome and Political Adviser to Allied Commission, Italy, 1946–50. MP (Cons.) for Taunton, 1950–6. Secretary of Overseas Trade, 1951–2. PC, 1952. Minister of State, Colonial Affairs, 1952–5. Baron Colyton, 1956. Chairman, Anglo-Egyptian Resettlement Board, 1957–60.

Report for Winston S. Churchill[1]
(*Churchill papers, 2/30*)

30 October 1946
Confidential

RUSSIAN TROOPS IN RUMANIA

1. According to information received and collected from different reliable resources the strength of the Red Army stationed in Rumania at the end of July 1946 was:
    23 Infantry Divisions (1 of NKVD type)
    2 Cavalry Divisions
    1 Motorised Division
    1 Artillery Division (on the Bulgarian–Rumanian frontier)
    5 Armoured Brigades
    1 Marines Brigade
    1 Air Corps
The stationement of these units on Rumanian territory is shown in the annexed map.

2. These units are kept in constant move in order to avoid the possible friendly relations between the Russian soldiers and the Rumanian population, as well as to keep the secret about the strength of this Army of occupation.

3. According to the same information the number of the Russian soldiers in Rumania amounts to nearly 750,000.

4. The airdromes occupied by the Red Air Forces are:
    Baneasa, Pipera and Otopeni (around Bucharest)
    Mizil
    Zilistea (near Buzua, with great capacity)
    Craiova
    Turnu-Severin
    Arad
    Targsor (near Ploesti)
    Timisoara
    Constantza
    Carol I (near Silistra)
    Rosiori de Vede
    Sibiu
    Ghimbev

5. The Red Army in Rumania is living on the country. Nevertheless, big depots for this Army have been already constituted in Southern Bessarabia.

6. The Red Air Forces in Rumania are under intense combat training.

---

[1] The author of this report cannot be identified.

7. The Red Army is Rumania is completing the armaments, or even receiving new armaments.

Winston S. Churchill to General Sir Hastings Ismay
(Churchill papers, 4/19)

30 October 1946
Private

I cannot trace two papers which I wrote in 1941 or 1942. The first was a hostile analysis of the operation called, I think, 'Sledgehammer', for the incursion of an armoured division into France on a 'butcher and bolt' raid. The second was an essay on a larger-scale combined descent upon occupied France, in which violence, scale, rapidity and variety of points of impact were to be the main features.

I am sure you could easily find duplicates for me.

Winston S. Churchill to Lord Woolton
(Churchill papers, 2/306)

30 October 1946

My dear Woolton,

I am very much inclined to address the Primrose League. We must not be ashamed of ourselves. My father's League number is Number One. The League commemorates the life work of the great Benjamin Disraeli whose government gave the first of the Charters to the Trade Unions of this country, and who was the inspirator of Tory Democracy. Lord Randolph Churchill raised this flag again with great success in 1885 and, although the extension of the franchise of the agricultural labourers lost us a certain number of the county seats, he carried the great cities of England with a vehement new figure called 'the Tory working man'.

However if you feel misgivings upon the subject let us talk it over when we meet.

Field Marshal Lord Alanbrooke to Winston S. Churchill
(*Churchill papers, 4/196*)[1]

31 October 1946

My dear Winston,

I am at last sending you the notes you asked me for, concerning the operation of the II Corps during the retreat from Brussels to Dunkirk. I am so sorry to have been so long about it, but had to check up one or two points. I think the account is fairly correct and is based on a diary I kept at that time.

If there are any points that are not clear, or in which you require more information I could come around and clear the matter up.

If you could let me have this map back when you have finished I would be very grateful as I have no copies of them.

I am afraid I am not much of a historian, and hope you will not have too much difficulty in following these notes![2]

Winston S. Churchill: speech
(*'Winston S. Churchill, His Complete Speeches', volume 7, pages 7399–400*)

31 October 1946 London

SUSPICION BETWEEN NATIONS

... It is always possible when great achievements have been made, that they are found less sweet and gratifying in the realization than they were while they were being struggled for. Though I do not consider that our dangers are past – and everyone can see for himself that our troubles have by no means entirely fallen away – all Britons must move forward with confidence into the future sure that they will be able to grapple with the situations which will present themselves if they remain worthy of their name and tradition as they have always done in the past.

We are told that one of the great evils from which we suffer is international suspicion. There is a very good remedy for suspicions. It is full disclosure of the facts, and that simple remedy of hope will be applied to the world situation by the United Nations Organization now meeting in the United States. What is called war talk will be swept away by an interchange of actual military facts, supported by adequate reciprocal inspections on terms of honourable equality between all the Powers, great and small, which are involved.

---

[1] This letter was handwritten.
[2] Churchill wrote on the original letter: 'Reread. Keep handy. Book III, Ch. III'.

November 1946

R. A. Butler to Winston S. Churchill
(Churchill papers, 2/42)

1 November 1946

Mr Churchill,

I had a long talk with Dr Ambedkar last night. As a result I consider that you ought, if you possibly can, to spare him time for an interview. I doubt whether you need trouble to spare more than half an hour since his contributions, though sincere and valuable, are not sparkling. I summarise below some of the points he made.

1. The Scheduled Castes,[1] who provided between 50 and 60 thousand men for the Imperial Forces in the late war, have been thrown over by the Viceroy and the Cabinet Mission. There is great bitterness among them.

2. The two Scheduled Caste representatives in the Cabinet are the pawns of Mr Gandhi and Mr Jinnah respectively. They are not chosen by the Scheduled Castes Federation. Mr Jinnah's nominee is one of Dr Ambedkar's Party. So far so good, but this method of choosing representatives is insulting to the Scheduled Castes.

3. There is still some doubt whether the Scheduled Castes will be treated as a minority within the Constituent Assembly, so ready were Sir Stafford Cripps and the Cabinet Mission to accept Mr Gandhi's view that they formed part of the Hindu community.

4. Were Mr Gandhi's view to be accepted, it would mean that the Scheduled Castes are thrown back into the control of their age-long exploiters.

5. Dr Ambedkar wishes to be sure that any proposed safeguards, which emerge from the proposals of the Advisory Committee, recommended in the Cabinet's White Paper, really are safeguards calculated to protect the minorities.

[1] Also referred to as 'Depressed Classes' or 'Untouchables'.

Winston S. Churchill to General Charles de Gaulle
(Churchill papers, 2/30)

1 November 1946
Private and Confidential

My dear de Gaulle,

I have received from various quarters disquieting information about the Soviet mobilized strength in the occupied territories of Europe and of the immense disproportion which exists between the Soviet forces and those of their satellite states, on the one hand, and those of the other Allies, on the other hand. There is very little doubt in my mind that it is in the power of the Soviet armies to advance westward with considerable rapidity. This does not of course prejudge the question of whether they would wish to do so.

I have also heard, though this is mere rumour, that you are anxious about the position. In these circumstances I should like to know whether you would agree to send some trusted friend of yours to meet my son-in-law, Duncan Sandys, who was a Minister and a Member of Parliament during my administration. He could come to Paris almost any time.

It seems to me that an interchange of views in strict privacy might be advantageous to both our countries. The method I am suggesting would have the advantage of attracting no attention. However, I shall quite understand and shall not be in the least offended if you think such a contact inadvisable, or perhaps it would be better to wait until after November 10.[1]

Randolph S. Churchill to Winston S. Churchill
(Churchill papers, 1/42)

2 November 1946

Many thanks your cable.[2] All goes well. In last ten days have motored two fifty miles made one lecture written one column per day and have never felt better. American public opinion seems very robust and increasingly anticommunist particularly middle west where we quote incendiaries unquote seem very popular. Am visiting Fulton Sunday to write column Fulton revisited. Then returning via Chicago New York where will be Ambassador Hotel November fifteen for one week. Please let me know if you would like me see anyone New York in connection your libel action. Fondest love to you and all family.

---

[1] Date of the first French legislative election for the National Assembly of the Fourth Republic.
[2] Churchill had telegraphed Randolph on Oct. 31: 'How are you getting on? Please send long cable.'

Max Aitken[1] to Lord Beaverbrook
(*Churchill papers, 2/146*)

2 November 1946

My dear Boss,

We had a good debate on the Press last Tuesday, but by now you will have seen Hansard. The outstanding speakers in my opinion were Wilson Harris[2] of the *Spectator*, and W. J. Brown.[3]

The Notes are going pretty well. We manage to get in a scoop or two each week, which brightens it up from a news point of view.

Churchill came to the 1922 Committee for complaints about (1) No young fellows being brought forward. (2) No policy. (3) Lack of satisfactory committees before debates.

The Chairman, Sir Arnold Gridley[4] came to his feet and said now is the time for everybody to speak out against Mr Churchill, as they had been speaking in the Smoke room. This put a good many on the spot, and brought to their feet (1) Lord Hinchingbrooke,[5] (2) Col. Erroll[6] (3) Beverley Baxter[7] (4) Peter Thorneycroft. Next speech was by Harry Strauss[8] who spoke very

[1] John William Maxwell Aitken, 1910–85. Known as 'Max'. Educated at Westminster School. Married, 1939, Cynthia Monteith (div. 1944); 1946, Ursula Kenyon-Slaney (div. 1950); 1951, Violet de Trafford. Flying Officer, RAF, 1939–45. DFC, 1940. DSO, 1942. MP (Cons.) for Holborn, 1945–50. Chairman of Beaverbrook Newspapers Ltd. 2nd Baron Beaverbrook, 1964. 2nd Bt Aitken, 1964. Disclaimed his peerage, 1964.

[2] Henry Wilson Harris, 1883–1955. Editor, *The Spectator*, 1932–53. MP (Ind.) for Cambridge University, 1945–50.

[3] William John Brown, 1894–1960. General Secretary of the Civil Service Clerical Association, 1921–42. MP (Lab.) for Wolverhampton West, 1929–31. MP (Ind.) for Rugby, 1942–50.

[4] Arnold Babb Gridley, 1878–1965. Controller of Electric Power Supply, Ministry of Munitions, 1916–19. KBE, 1920. MP (Cons.) for Stockport, 1935–50; for Stockport South, 1950–5. Baron, 1955.

[5] Alexander Victor Edward Paulet Montagu, 1906–95. Known as 'Hinch'. Styled Viscount Hinchingbrooke, 1916–62. MP (Cons.) for South Dorset, 1941–62. On active service in France, 1940. Founded Tory Reform Committee, 1943. President, Anti-Common Market League, 1962–84. Succeeded his father as 10th Earl of Sandwich, 1962; disclaimed the title, 1964. Joined Conservative Monday Club, 1964. Wrote *Essays in Tory Reform* (1944); *The Conservative Dilemma* (1970).

[6] Frederick James Erroll, 1914–2000. Educated at Trinity College, Cambridge. Engineer, 1936–8. Commissioned, 4th County of London Yeomanry (Sharpshooters), Territorial Army, 1939. Involved in tank construction and testing, 1940–3. Served in India and Burma, 1944–5. MP (Cons.) for Altrincham and Sale, 1945–64. Parliamentary Secretary, Ministry of Supply, 1955–6; Board of Trade, 1956–8. Economic Secretary to the Treasury, 1958–9. Minister of State for Trade, 1959–61; for Power, 1963–4. President of the Board of Trade, 1961–3. Baron Erroll of Hale, 1964; of Kilmun, 1999.

[7] Arthur Beverley Baxter, 1891–1964. Educated in Canada. Canadian Engineers, 1918. Joined London *Daily Express*, 1920; Managing Editor, 1924; Editor-in-Chief and Director, 1929–33. Managing Editor, *Sunday Express*, 1922. Editor-in-Chief, Inveresk publications, 1929. Public Relations Counsel, Gaumont British Picture Corporation Ltd, 1933–5. Editorial Adviser, Allied Newspapers, 1938. MP (Cons.) for Wood Green, 1939–45, 1945–50; for Southgate,1950–64. Fellow, Royal Society of Literature. Knighted, 1954. Wrote *The Parts Men Play* (novel); *The Blower of Bubbles* (short stories); *Strange Street* (autobiography); *Men Martyrs and Mountebanks; First Nights – and Noises Off* (critical articles); *First Nights and Footlights* (critical articles); *It Happened in September* (play).

[8] Henry George Strauss, 1892–1974. Educated at Christ Church, Oxford, 1915. Called to the Bar, Inner Temple, 1919. MP (Cons.) for Norwich, 1935–45; for Combined English Universities, 1946–50;

well on the impracticability of a policy.

Churchill then rose and knocked them all flat one after the other. The cheers for him at the end of his speech could be heard right down the corridor.

His points were that you could not throw old men off the Front Bench if they were entitled to sit there through being ex-Ministers or Privy Councillors, only one young fellow had been invited to sit on the Front Bench, and that was F. E. Smith,[1] and in that case he had been given a Privy Councillorship.

The policy was Freedom and Empire, and our duty to oppose, and to agree only with a kick. On the committee situation he agreed to tighten up, and left it to James Stuart.

The Party is getting much more active. I think Blackpool put new heart into them. The Whips are more aggressive and there is quite a different spirit from before the Recess.

The Socialists on the other hand, although full of confidence have lost their gaiety. I think there are some doubters among them on the freedom issue.

Our figure this week is 871 copies down. This is chiefly due to the end of the seaside season, together with curtailment of flat racing.

The weather is cold, rainy, and foggy; otherwise all goes well.

Winston S. Churchill to General Sir Hastings Ismay
(Churchill papers, 2/151)

4 November 1946

My dear P,

Thank you very much for your letter of October 31. Please send me any notes on your recollections of the incidents in which we were involved. I have incorporated your Tobruk amendments in my revise. I am also composing a passage on the lines of your lecture to the Foreign Policy Association in New York.

Please remind me of things that occur to you. It is a great help to have one's memory jogged.

---

for Norwich South, 1950–55. Parliamentary Private Secretary to the Attorney-General, 1936–42. Parliamentary Secretary, Ministry of Town and Country Planning, 1942–45; Board of Trade, 1951–55. KC, 1946. Bencher, Inner Temple, 1969. Baron Conesford of Chelsea, 1955.

[1] Frederick Edwin Smith, 1872–1930. Known as 'FE'. MP (Cons.) for Walton, 1906–19. With Churchill, founded the Other Club, 1911. Head of Press Bureau, Aug. 1914; resigned, Oct. 1914. Lt-Col., attached to the Indian Corps in France, 1914–15. Solicitor-General, May 1915. Knighted, 1915. Attorney-General, Nov. 1915 to 1919. Baron Birkenhead, 1919. Lord Chancellor, 1920–2. Viscount, 1921. Earl, 1922. Secretary of State for India, 1924–8.

Government and Opposition meeting: minutes
(Churchill papers, 2/38)

5 November 1946
Confidential

Prime Minister's Room

POLITICAL BROADCASTING

The meeting had before them a note of proposals prepared after the discussion between representatives of the Government and the Opposition (Annexed to these Minutes).

The Lord President of the Council referred to paragraph 24 of the White Paper on Broadcasting Policy which stated that the Government did not think it desirable to attempt to reduce to written rules the principles which should govern the Corporation in regard to political broadcasting. It was not a matter which could easily be dealt with by hard and fast rules, but a note on the lines of that circulated might be useful as an aide memoire. He suggested that any arrangements which were made, should be the subject of periodical discussions between the BBC and representatives of the Government and the Opposition.

Controversial Political Broadcasts

Sir Allan Powell[1] said that the Governors of the BBC were not clear whether, taken together, paragraphs 2 and 4 of the note which had been circulated meant that the BBC would not be free to arrange for anybody to give a controversial political broadcast unless he was nominated by one of the major political parties, and except on a subject chosen by them. He recalled correspondence between Mr Churchill, Mr Lloyd-George, Sir Austen Chamberlain,[2] and the BBC before the war, in which they had protested on principle against the exclusion from the wireless of Members of Parliament not chosen by the Party organisations. The Governors were anxious to avoid a situation similar to that which had occurred when, for a number of years, Mr Churchill was deprived of the use of the wireless in this country.

The Lord President said that the intention of the document was broadly as stated by Sir Allan Powell, though it was not, of course, intended to prevent the BBC from arranging for Members of Parliament to make broadcasts

---

[1] Allan Powell, 1878–1948. In charge of 4,000 soldier and civilian war refugees at the War Refugees Camp, Earl's Court, London, 1914–18. CBE, 1920. Clerk, Metropolitan Asylums Board (Public Assistance), 1922–30. Knighted, 1927. Mayor of Kensington, 1937–9. Chairman of the BBC, 1939–46.

[2] (Joseph) Austen Chamberlain, 1863–1937. Half-brother of Neville Chamberlain. Educated at Rugby and Trinity College, Cambridge. MP (Cons.) for East Worcestershire, 1892–1937. Chancellor of the Exchequer, 1903–5. Unsuccessful candidate for leadership of Conservative Party, 1911. Secretary of State for India, 1915–17. Minister without Portfolio, 1918–19. Chancellor of the Exchequer, 1919–21. Lord Privy Seal, 1921–2. Foreign Secretary, 1924–9. KG, 1925. 1st Lord of the Admiralty, 1931.

which did not come into the politically controversial category, or to participate in round table discussions, brains trusts and similar programmes, even though there was a political element. The proposals put forward dealt with major broadcasts, and he thought that participation in these must be confined to spokesmen nominated by the great political parties which were represented in the House of Commons. Otherwise, he would not wish to be too rigid, though he thought that in cases of doubt, the BBC would be wise to consult the Party leaders through the usual channels.

Mr Churchill said that it was important that the BBC should not usurp the functions of the great political parties. The party system was fundamental in our political life. It would not be right that the BBC should have the power to disturb the balance which resulted from the working of the Party system, or that they should be able, by the choice of the speakers, to single out particular Members of Parliament for preferment. It was not for the BBC to make the political leaders of the nation. He agreed that there might be special cases where an opportunity of making a political broadcast should be given to a person of outstanding national eminence, who was outside the official hierarchy of one of the political parties. He thought, however, that such cases could be raised ad hoc by the BBC as they occurred, and he favoured periodical discussions about the working of the arrangements generally.

The Lord Privy Seal said that the proposal was for a limited number of broadcasts, and for this reason alone, he did not see how, in the ordinary way, it would be possible to go beyond the major political parties.

Mr Eden suggested that the Governors' difficulty might be met if they reserved their position as regards persons of outstanding eminence.

Sir William Haley asked how the proposals could be reconciled with the responsibility of the Corporation to the nation as the custodians of the wireless. In due course, they would have to account for the way in which they discharged their trust. Would it be enough for them to say that they had handed over their responsibility in this important field to the Party organisations? Would the back bench Member of Parliament be content with an arrangement under which broadcasts were confined to nominees of the Party leaders?

Mr Churchill thought that the proposals would commend themselves to back bench Opposition Members more than an arrangement under which the selection of Members of Parliament for this purpose rested with the BBC. It should not be assumed that the Party leaders would not wish to give back benchers the opportunity of taking part in the broadcasts. It seemed to him that the Governors of the BBC would have an entirely satisfactory answer to any criticisms of the kind envisaged by Sir William Haley if they explained that, in their opinion, it was not for them to disturb the political balance, and that they had consulted the leaders of the major Parties. As a result they had come to the conclusion that the responsibility for choosing the speakers and the subjects for broadcasts of this character properly rested with the Party leaders and not with the BBC.

The Lord President pointed out that, under their Charter, the BBC were precluded from expressing opinions of their own. It seemed to him that if the BBC chose speakers for these broadcasts, it would be extremely difficult for them to avoid weighting the scales in favour of particular political points of view. He agreed with Mr Churchill that back bench Members of Parliament would be likely to prefer the selection of speakers by their Party leaders to selection by the BBC and said that the BBC should refer any critics in Parliament to the Party leaders, who would have to shoulder the responsibility for the advice which they had given to the Governors.

The Meeting

(1) Agreed that the arrangements for controversial political broadcasting should be reviewed after a year and that it should be open to the political parties or the BBC to ask for earlier discussions if any question arose which made this desirable.

(2) Asked the Chairman and the Director-General of the BBC to report to the Governors the views which had been expressed by the Government and Opposition representatives, and to invite the Governors to consider, in light of the discussion, whether they wished to suggest any amendments in the aide memoire. The representatives of the Government and the Opposition were agreed on the following points, which they hoped would dispose of the difficulties felt by the Governors:

(a) Controversial political broadcasting in the sense of the aide memoire referred primarily to formal broadcasts on behalf of the great political parties.

(b) Below this level, there might be other broadcasts with a controversial political element, e.g. of the nature of discussion groups, brains trusts, news items, or debates in which there was an immediate reply by a representative of the other side, for which the BBC should be free to continue to select Members of Parliament as speakers. It was desirable, however, that in any case of doubt, the BBC should consult the political parties.

(c) Should the BBC wish to arrange for a controversial political broadcast by a Member of Parliament of outstanding eminence not nominated by one of the political parties, they should consult the leaders of the parties. In the event of disagreement between the parties or between them and the BBC, the ultimate decision would rest with the Governors.

Number of Broadcasts

Sir Allan Powell said that from the point of view of maintaining the interest of the public, it was desirable that there should not be too many broadcasts of this kind.

The Meeting agreed –
    (3) That a start might be made with an allocation of twelve broadcasts in the first year, to be divided amongst the political parties in accordance with their Polls at the last General Election. This would give six broadcasts to the Government, five to the Opposition and one to the Liberals. It was suggested that the Budget broadcasts should be included in the allocation. Each party, in consultation with the BBC, should be free to draw upon its quota when it chose, and the annual allocation should be reviewed in the discussion which it was proposed should take place in a year's time.

Ministerial Broadcasts

Sir Allan Powell asked what was the view of the meeting on the number of Ministerial broadcasts, which, since the General Election had greatly exceeded the number of Opposition broadcasts.

Mr Churchill said that the King's Government must be carried on, and the Opposition recognised the primacy of the Government's claims in this respect. It was quite right, that, as stated in the aide memoire, the Government – in view of their responsibilities – for the care of the nation – should be able to use the wireless from time to time for Ministerial broadcasts which are purely factual, or explanatory, or in the nature of appeals to the nation to cooperate in national policies. It was, however, incumbent on Ministers making such broadcasts to be as impartial as possible, and the Opposition must have the right of raising through the usual channels, the question of a reply in any case where it seemed to them that a Minister had exceeded the limit.

The Lord President agreed with Mr Churchill that Ministers must do their utmost to avoid controversy in broadcasts of this character, and that the Opposition should have the right to raise the matter through the usual channels if they did not think that the Minister had been as impartial as was possible in the circumstances.

ANNEX
Note of Proposals

1. It is desirable that political broadcasts of a controversial character should be resumed.

2. In view of their responsibilities for the care of the nation the Government should be able to use the wireless from time to time for ministerial broadcasts

which, for example, are purely factual, or explanatory of legislation or administrative policies approved by Parliament; or in the nature of appeal to the nation to cooperate in national policies, such as fuel economy or recruiting, which require the active participation of the public. Broadcasts on state occasions also come in the same category.

It would be incumbent on Ministers making such broadcasts to be as impartial as possible, and in the ordinary way there would be no question of a reply by the Opposition. Where, however, the Opposition thought that a Government broadcast was controversial it should be open to them to take the matter up through the usual channels with a view to a reply.

3. 'Outside' broadcasts, e.g. of speeches at Party Conferences, which are in the nature of news items, should carry no right of reply by the other side.

4. A limited number of controversial broadcasts should be allocated to the various parties in accordance with their polls at the last General Election. The allocation should be calculated on a yearly basis and the total number of such broadcasts should be a matter for discussion between the parties and the BBC.

5. The Opposition parties should have the right, subject to discussion through the usual channels, to choose the subjects for their own broadcasts. Either side would be free, if it wished, to use one of its quota for the purpose of replying to a previous broadcast, but it would be under no necessity to do so. There would, of course be no obligation on a party to use its whole quota.

6. Where any dispute arose an effort should be made to settle it through the usual channels. Where this was not possible, the BBC would have to decide the matter on its own.

Winston S. Churchill to George Hicks[1]
(Churchill papers, 2/21)

7 November 1946

My dear George Hicks,

Do you take an interest in the United States of Europe? I propose to form an All-Party Handling-Group of seven or eight people to get a move on here. To one with all your experience I do not need to argue the matter. I have no doubt you are thinking deeply and anxiously about the future and of the part which a United Europe might play in it. I therefore send you first, a provisional draft of a Manifesto and secondly, a list of the Handling-Group, as complete to date.

[1] Ernest George Hicks, 1879–1954. National Organizer for Bricklayers' Society, 1912. President, National Federation of Building Trade Operatives, 1919, 1936–7. First General Secretary, Amalgamated Union of Building Trade Workers, 1921–41. President, TUC, 1926–7. MP (Lab.) for East Woolwich, 1931–50. Member, Central Housing Advisory Committee (leading to Housing Act 1935); Holidays with Pay Committee; Anglo-Russian Parliamentary Committee; Empire Parliamentary Association. Parliamentary Secretary, Ministry of Works, 1940–5. CBE, 1946.

Without the resurrection and reconciliation of Europe there is no hope for the world.

I shall be glad to hear from you.

Winston S. Churchill to King George VI
(Churchill papers, 2/171)[1]

7 November 1946

Sir,

Some weeks ago on my inquiry Yr Majesty vy graciously said that I might send you one of the Medallions I issued as a souvenir to all the Ministers who served in the National Administration wh I formed and led by Yr Majesty's command.

I now have received it from the makers & trust Yr Majesty will care to keep it in memory of all the hard days we went through together, as I offer it in feeble recognition of all the help & kindness I enjoyed from Yr Majesty & the Queen during my discharge of the task confided to me.

A. V. Alexander to Winston S. Churchill
(Churchill papers, 2/29)

11 November 1946
Top Secret

Dear Mr Churchill,

At your meeting with Attlee and myself on the 5th of November, you asked whether it was true that the railways in Czechoslovakia were being widened to the Russian gauge and we promised to make enquiries. Now I send you a note by the Joint Intelligence Staff on the matter.

CZECHOSLOVAK RAILWAYS

(a) All main lines East of COP[2] have been converted to Russian broad gauge. (COP was originally in Czechoslovakia, but is now Russian territory).

(b) There have been unconfirmed reports of conversions to broad gauge West of COP. One of these states that the line running North-East from Bratislava to the Northern Czech frontier has been converted to Russian broad gauge, but this may refer only to one of the two parallel tracks. Further unconfirmed reports also state that in one or two places lines crossing the Polish Czech frontier have been converted to broad gauge for a short distance into Czechoslovakia.

---

[1] This letter was handwritten.
[2] Ukrainian city of Chop. Called 'Cop' when it was part of Czechoslovakia (until 1938). Significant railway terminus.

(c) In general, it appears that West of COP, normal standard gauge is still in operation, and that there is no material change in the Czechoslovak rail network.

Winston S. Churchill to Lord Beaverbrook
(Beaverbrook papers)

11 November 1946

Alan Moorehead[1] in the *Sunday Express* is making a series of untruthful and offensive statements about me and Montgomery. Today is very bad. I hope you will call for a report. I may have to make a public statement.[2]

General Sir Hastings Ismay to Winston S. Churchill
(Churchill papers, 4/351A)

11 November 1946

My dear Mr Churchill,

I have now read through Alan Moorehead's article in yesterday's *Sunday Express* and I am sure that there is no truth in the statement that you went to Montgomery's Headquarters 'barely a week before D-Day' in order to 'address the General Staff upon the subject of vehicles and loading priorities'.

The only meeting at Montgomery's Headquarters that I can recall is the one which took place at St Paul's School on the 15th of May, i.e. three weeks before the invasion, when the King, you and Field Marshal Smuts were present. On that occasion, Sir Humfrey Gale[3] and Sir Miles Graham[4] unfolded the Q Plans[5] and you expressed some doubt as to whether there were not too many vehicles in the initial assault. You did not, however, press the point very far, and I myself certainly left the meeting with the feeling that the plans presented had received your full approval.

---

[1] Alan McCrae Moorehead, 1910–83. Educated at Scotch College, Melbourne, and Melbourne University. Travelled to England, 1937. War Correspondent, Mediterranean and North African fronts, London *Daily Express*, 1939–43.

[2] Lord Beaverbrook responded: 'Very sorry to hear it and I am telephoning to Christiansen this evening.' Arthur Christiansen was Editor of the *Daily Express*, 1933–57.

[3] Humfrey Myddelton Gale, 1890–1971. Deputy Asst QMG, War Office, 1930–2. Instructor at Staff College Camberley, 1935–7. Asst Director of Transport and Supplies, War Office, 1937–9. Deputy Director of Transport and Supplies, War Office, 1939. Deputy Adjutant and QMG, BEF, 1939–40. Chief Administration Officer, Home Forces, 1940, 1941–3; Scottish Command, 1940; SHAEF, 1943–5. VCS, SHAEF, 1944–5. Representative of Director-General of UNRRA in Europe, 1945–7.

[4] Miles William Arthur Peel Graham, 1895–1976. On active service during WWI (twice wounded, despatches twice, MC), 1914–18. Chief Administrative Officer to Gen. Bernard Montgomery, 1942–6. CBE, 1943. KBE, 1945.

[5] Quartermaster plans.

I must, however, add that after the meeting was over, you went off to Field Marshal Montgomery's office with him alone, while I talked to some of the Staff outside. I do not know what passed at this private meeting, but I distinctly remember leaving St Paul's building with you and that you did not express any satisfaction with the arrangements on the drive home.

I have asked the Secretaries at No. 10 to look up your diary and see whether you paid any visits other than the above to Montgomery's Headquarters. They tell me that you attended an exercise called 'Thunderclap' there on 7th April, i.e. two months before D-Day. I did not accompany you on that occasion, but it seems extremely unlikely that any Q plans came under discussion.

If you wish me to pursue the matter further, I could get in touch with Miles Graham, who was Montgomery's Chief Administrative Officer, and find out his version of the story: but I will not, of course, do so unless you authorise it.

General Sir Hastings Ismay to Winston S. Churchill
(*Churchill papers, 4/351A*)

11 November 1946

My dear Mr Churchill,

In your letter of the 4th of November,[1] you asked me to let you have notes on my recollections on any incidents in which we were involved. I therefore send you the following local colour about the minute which you addressed to me on April 20th 1941 on the subject of the despatch of tanks to the Middle East (See Book III – Directives, page 50).

At about 11 a.m. on April 20th, you summoned me to Ditchley and read out the minute in question, which you had only just dictated. You told me to take it straight up to London and summon the Chiefs of Staff to discuss it at once. As it was a Sunday, the Chiefs of Staff had to be collected from their country residences, and it was not until 6 p.m. that we got round the table.

Although it is not recorded in the minutes of the meeting, I distinctly remember that the first reactions were –

(a) That the tanks were not available in this country: and
(b) That, even if they were available, the chances of their getting through the Mediterranean were remote, since on the day before entering the Narrows and on the morning after passing Malta they would be liable to dive bombing attack out of range of our shore-based fighters.

However, after a very long meeting, opposition petered out, and the Chiefs of Staff were able to report to you at 12 noon the following day the ways and

---

[1] Reproduced above (p. 521).

means by which Operation 'Tiger'[1] could be carried out. So far as I remember, they got through unscathed, but this will have to be checked.

Later: I have now found out that one ship out of the five, *The Empire Song*, was mined and sunk just this side of Malta.[2]

Winston S. Churchill: speech
(Hansard)

12 November 1946   House of Commons

DEBATE ON THE ADDRESS

The extensive armoury of the English language has frequently been ransacked on these occasions, in order to find new and unhackneyed terms of compliment and congratulation which can be applied by the Leader of the Opposition to the hon. Members who have been chosen by the Government to move and second the Address. I confess that I should have found myself baffled, in the selection of any new terms or any new feature, but for the remarkable fact that neither of the two hon. Gentlemen[3] is wearing uniform or Court dress. Here, at any rate, is one of the really broad advances of democracy, and it may be some comfort to hon. Gentlemen below the Gangway, if their thirst for blood is not slaked in other ways. But here I must utter a word of warning to Ministers opposite. They must remember that, in this direction, they are moving contrary to the general tendencies of the Soviet Government, which has distinguished itself throughout the world by the gold-laced glory of its official uniforms, and by the punctilio which it observes on all occasions. We may, therefore, possibly regard this innovation either as an advance of democracy, or as a demonstration on the part of the Government of their differences with the Communist regime.

But I do wholeheartedly congratulate both hon. Gentlemen on their speeches, on the unexceptionable character of the sentiments to which they have given vent, and on the form in which they have cast their arguments, I was particularly pleased to hear the mover of the Address, the hon. Member for the Acock's Green division of Birmingham (Mr Usborne[4]), speak with favour of the United States of Europe, and I trust that if ever we are able to come to practical action in that field, he will not fail to enrol himself as a servant of that cause, for a regional consciousness of Europe, while certainly vital in itself, is an essential and fundamental part of the policy of the world

---

[1] 'Tiger': British merchant convoy carrying tanks and aircraft from Gibraltar to Egypt, 5–12 May 1941.

[2] This sentence was handwritten in the margin of the letter.

[3] Henry Usborne and James Hoy.

[4] Henry Charles Usborne, 1909–96. Educated at Bradfield College. MP (Lab.) for Acocks Green, 1945–50; for Birmingham Yardley, 1950–9.

organisation of the United Nations. I also give my compliments to the hon. Member for Leith (Mr Hoy[1]), and thank him for his very kind references to me. He commanded the universal assent of the House in his tribute to Scotland, and to the work done at Leith in pursuance of the war. The efforts of Scotland and the contribution of Scotland are entitled to world-wide fame; and I must remind the House that they also voted extremely sensibly at the General Election.

This is the second King's Speech of the Socialist Government. They have been 16 months in office. We have had one of the most laborious and protracted Sessions – fruitful, hon. Members may say, but at any rate productive of something which is on record. At this moment, in reply to the second King's Speech, we may profitably attempt to take stock of the position. The world situation has not improved. The Prime Minister, at the Mansion House, drew a sombre picture from which I cannot dissent. At the General Election, we were assured that a Socialist or Left-Wing Government 'would get on especially well with the Soviet Government of Russia, but relations have steadily deteriorated.' The British and American Forces in Europe have melted away, as was inevitable – I am not making it an accusation – in the case of governments resting upon the popular will, after a great victory. The Russian Armies, based on the despotic form of government, have been maintained in Europe in vast strength, and mostly on a war footing. More than one-third of Europe is held under the Russian Soviet control. The Soviet military frontier is on the Elbe, and it is impossible to forecast what the future and the fate of France will be. No fruition has yet attended the peace negotiations even about the smaller satellite enemy Powers – perhaps the Prime Minister will be able to make some statement on this point today.

The United Nations organisation, as he has so forcibly pointed out at the Mansion House, has not, so far, fulfilled our hopes; it remains however – and in this I agree with the mover of the Address – our citadel, and we are in full accord with His Majesty's Government in their loyal and faithful support of this institution, whose reign and ascendancy are an earnest of the desire of the overwhelming majority of mankind. To record these melancholy facts which we see around us, is not necessarily to blame His Majesty's Government. The difficulties have been enormous, and the forces which confront them are intractable. British influence abroad has greatly diminished since wartime days. It is not to attack the Government that I mention these facts, but in order to survey our own position. The Foreign Secretary has done his best, and we on this side have given him whatever support was in our power – we have even sometimes supported him to an extent which caused him embarrassment in

---

[1] James Hutchison Hoy, 1909–76. Educated at Causewayside and Sciennes public schools. MP (Lab.) for Leith, 1945–50; for Edinburgh Leith, 1950–70. Parliamentary Private Secretary to Secretary of State for Scotland, 1947–50. Joint Parliamentary Secretary, Ministry of Agriculture, Fisheries and Food, 1964–70. Vice-President, Trustee Savings Bank Association, 1957. PC, 1969. Baron, 1970.

other quarters. We cannot charge the Government with being responsible for all the evils of the situation abroad. They have certainly not been guilty of any wrongful or provocative action. We readily believe that their motives are as innocent and virtuous as those which are set out in the mellifluous language of the Gracious Speech, with large parts of which we are in full agreement. It was the duty of the Socialist Government to take office when called upon to do so so decidedly by the electors. It is not their fault if they are not equal to the job, though it may be our misfortune.

It cannot be claimed, however, that even a National Coalition Government would have successfully surmounted all the adverse tides which have been flowing. The Conservative Party cannot of course accept any responsibility for Potsdam, as matters were taken out of our hands in the vital phase of those discussions. (Hon. Members: 'Oh.') These are facts, but I am sure, whoever had conducted Potsdam, it would have left behind it many grievous legacies for the future of Europe. Nevertheless, the fact remains that 18 months after the surrender of Germany, and more than a year after that of Japan, and in spite of the firm, helpful attitude of the United States based on the joint action – what they call 'bi-partisan' – of their two historic parties, the world scene is still dark, anxious and confused. No decisive improvement can be recorded, except, of course, that in the mercy of God the cannons have ceased to fire.

In the forefront of any survey of the world stands Germany, a vanquished nation. 'Stands', I said – no, prostrate, shattered. Seventy or 80 millions of men and women of an ancient, capable and terribly efficient race are in a ruined and famished condition in the heart of Europe. This confronts us with problems which at present are quite unsolved by the victors. We and the Americans continue to rule and administer the German people in our zones at extravagant and almost unbearable cost – I think in this I carry the Chancellor of the Exchequer with me – to ourselves, and with increasing dissatisfaction to the Germans. We have not been told, and I will not attempt to discuss what is happening in the Russian zone. We are all agreed that the proper course is, as I said before we separated, to make the Germans earn their own living, and make them manage their own affairs as soon as possible, and to give them all possible aid while preventing every form of rearmament. If we are agreed on that, let us enforce it. Let us stick to it and enforce it on every occasion as opportunity serves. Though we have not been informed of any attempt which has been made to forecast the form of the peace treaty with Germany, surely it is urgent to make a peace with the German people, or as many of them as lie within our spheres of responsibility. There must be an end to vengeance and retribution.

I am told that Germany must be punished. I ask: When did punishment begin? It certainly seems to have been going on for a long time. It began in 1943, and continued during 1944 and 1945, when the most frightful air bombardments were cast upon German cities, and when the general exhaustion of their life under the cruel Nazi regime had drained the last ounces of strength from the German race and nation. The Nuremberg trials are over, and the guilty leaders of the Nazi regime have been hanged by the conquerors. We are told that thousands yet remain to be tried, and that vast categories of Germans are classed as potentially guilty because of their association with the Nazi regime. After all, in a country which is handled as Germany was, the ordinary people have very little choice about what to do. I think some consideration should always be given to ordinary people. Everyone is not a Pastor Niemoller[1] or a martyr, and when ordinary people are hurled this way and that, when the cruel hands of tyrants are laid upon them and vile systems of regimentation are imposed and enforced by espionage and other forms of cruelty, there are great numbers of people who will succumb. I thank God that in this island home of ours, we have never been put to the test which many of the peoples of Europe have had to undergo. It is my hope that we shall presently reach the end of the executions, penalties, and punishments, and that without forgetting the hard lessons of the past, we shall turn our faces resolutely towards the future. There is much to be said not only on the general problem of Germany, but on the character of our administration in the zone confided to us since Germany surrendered. My right hon. Friend the former Foreign Secretary will deal more at length with the whole German question, and also with British administration of the zone, in the course of the general Debate on the Address. He will speak either tomorrow or the day afterwards, according to what the course of our affairs may render convenient and necessary.

Coming now to the affairs of the British Empire, or former British Empire, with its Commonwealth possessions and mandated territories, I was struck by a statement which was reported to have been made by Mr Clayton, an official of the United States Government, about Imperial Preference. The statement was made at the end of last week. This subject has often been thrashed out and the facts are common knowledge to every Member who studies our affairs with due attention. Everything is on record. We were repeatedly assured by His Majesty's Government, notably at the time of the acceptance of the American Loan – for which we must not be ungrateful – that no commitments to the prejudice of Imperial Preference had been entered into by His Majesty's Government, and that we are entirely free in any discussions which may take place on the future of world trade or world economy. I ask the Prime Minister to say, when he replies in due course, if he is in a position to renew these assurances on the present occasion in order that we may consider, on this

---

[1] Friedrich Gustav Emil Martin Niemöller, 1892–1984. Officer, German Imperial Navy, 1915–18. Married, 1919, Else Bremer. Educated at William's University in Münster, 1923. Ordained, Evangelical Church of Old Prussian Union, 1924. Founded Pfarrennotbund to resist Nazi discrimination against Christians of Jewish background, 1933; Confessional Church, 1934. Arrested, 1937. Interned at Sachsenhausen and Dachau concentration camps, 1938–45. President, Protestant Church, Hesse and Nassau, 1947–61; World Council of Churches, 1961. Awarded Lenin Peace Prize, 1966.

side of the House, what action we should take. I thought it right to give the right hon. Gentleman, whose official position alone prevents me from describing him as 'my right hon. Friend', due notice of the question which I have asked on this point.

I may, however, hazard, for my own assurance and that of some of my hon. Friends on these benches, the personal opinion that it would be a great surprise to me, at least, if a Republican Congress were to embrace Free Trade so wholeheartedly, completely, and passionately, and to promote such a casting down of tariff walls of all kinds as to call in question, even as a matter of discussion, the comparatively small, modest Preference duties which have been built up in the British Commonwealth of Nations, which have become part of our supreme common life and which are even more important to us as symbols of our indissoluble union than for their commercial advantages, which are, none the less, considerable. However, I await the declarations of the Prime Minister upon this point.

There is a paragraph in the Gracious Speech about India. This paragraph has the advantage that the Government accept and take upon themselves, as is their duty – it is no more than their duty – the responsibility for what is happening in India, and base their policy upon the statement made by them and the Ministers of the Crown who were recently employed on the mission to India. This is not the time to debate the character and consequences of the British abandonment of India. We have been promised two days' Debate on this subject. I do not consider that anything has been lost by its postponement up to the present. It may well be, however, that before Christmas we shall ask for a formal Debate. We may be forced to ask for it on account of the increasing degeneration in the life of the Indian peoples, and the bloodstains which are already appearing, in wide and numerous areas, on the Indian map.

I will content myself today with one remark, one passage, designed to illustrate the gravity of the events which are now in progress in India. Suppose Europe had been ruled – and this may appeal to the mover of the Address – for several generations, I may even say many generations, by a European Council, and had dwelt in internal peace and safety from external aggression, without any wars, with hardly anybody killed during all that time by steel or lead, except common criminals in the course of common crime. Suppose peace and order had been maintained by an impartial organisation seated, let us say, at Geneva, and that it had required to maintain its authority only fifty to sixty thousand armed council or international troops, and had carried on all its work with little more than 1,200 officials. Suppose this long reign of peace had endured, that nearly a century had passed, and immense increases of population had taken place meanwhile, and that equal laws and justice had been given to all and observed by all the many nations, races, and religions of Europe, so that the Russians and Poles, French and Germans, Austrians and Italians, Protestants and Catholics, Communists and Conservatives, had managed to get along for 60 to 70 years without flying at each other's throats, without killing each other.

That certainly would have been regarded as a blessed era, a kind of Age of the Antonines in Roman history. And that impression would not have been destroyed even though there were admittedly many shortcomings, and also, admittedly, boundless need and hope and means for further improvement. Supposing now that, in the name of progress, it were decided to remove the elements of stability and impartiality which had rendered an all-European organisation possible and had conferred such inestimable blessings upon the masses of the European peoples, that would be a most serious step; it would be a milestone in the history of Europe, and, not only of Europe, but of the world, because we must remember how everything is connected with everything else, especially nowadays. Suppose, moreover, the preparations for the withdrawal of the central power and guiding hand had already released many of the disruptive and rival forces which lurk in every continent and that these were stirring again with age-old animosities, long buried, so long held in neutrality; and suppose, in particular, that the wars of religion in Europe between Catholic and Protestant, which formerly ravaged Europe and which were the cause of the Thirty Years War, again threatened to break out; suppose that already in the last few months in Europe 10,000 Protestants and Catholics had murdered one another. I think that the situation would be one which would justifiably cause widespread anxiety, and which would, when the proper time comes, afford justification for a full and deliberate Debate. We shall hold the Government to their promise to give us this opportunity, but we are quite ready to fix the time in accordance with their convenience, and also with the situation as it exists in India.

I have spoken on recent occasions at length on the proposed abrogation of the Anglo-Egyptian Treaty and the abandonment by British Forces of the Canal zone. I do not know whether the Prime Minister has any further information for us on the negotiations which have been lately conducted in Cairo and the conversations which have taken place over here, but if he feels that the moment is not suitable, we should not demur to his view, or press him in any way.

About Palestine, however, it is impossible to avoid expressing deep regret at the many changes of tactics and method, at the needless disappointment created throughout world Jewry by the failure to fulfil the hopes which the party opposite excited by their promises and convictions at the General Election, and above all, at the lack of any policy worthy of the name. This absence of any policy or decision on these matters, which have become more complicated as they proceed, has allowed havoc and hatred to flare and run rife throughout Palestine for more than a year – and no one knows where we are today. I have nothing to add to what I have previously advised. Here, perhaps, I may speak for myself, because I have always supported the Zionist movement, and many of my friends here took a different view of it at the time, before the war. I cannot, in any way, recede from the advice which I have ventured to give, namely, that if we cannot fulfil our promises to the Zionists, we should without delay place our mandate for Palestine at the feet of the United Nations, and give due notice of our impending evacuation of that country. If this offer is accepted, a burden, which has become too heavy and too invidious for us to bear alone, will have been lifted from our shoulders and placed in international safekeeping.

If, however, the United States, which is so keenly interested in Jewish immigration, would deprecate such a course on our part, it would be for them to help us in the most effective way, not only with money but with men, and with all that flows from a concerted policy advanced by two great English-speaking Powers. I am not at all deterred in recommending this course by the fact that it has been demanded by the Soviet Government. I was rather glad to find that our minds are flowing in the same direction in one aspect of international affairs. I am convinced that this procedure would either relieve us from the most thankless of all human tasks, from the reproach which attends our ill success and infirmity of purpose, and from the physical and practical difficulties of the task, or, on the other hand, that it would secure us the support necessary from Jewish and American sources by which alone our work can be accomplished and our mission fulfilled. To abandon India, with all the dire consequences that would follow there from, but to have a war with the Jews in order to give Palestine to the Arabs amid the execration of the world, appears to carry incongruity of thought and policy to levels which have rarely been attained in human history.

I leave these external issues in which, in spite of their melancholy features, there is much common ground between the two main parties – after all, we are all in the same boat in the result of many of these things – and I come to the administration and political topics which are open at home. Some of these are referred to in the Gracious Speech. The hon. Gentleman who moved the Address spoke of his great desire to demobilise all the Armed Forces after proper conditions had been established, and I am sure that is a widespread desire – but not yet; like the cynical saying, 'We all want to get to Heaven but not immediately.' The decision of His Majesty's Government to continue compulsory national service for the Armed Forces for an indefinite period after 1949 is one which they would certainly not have reached without good and grave reasons. In a matter like this, which affects in a vital manner the safety of our country, by avoiding one-sided disarmament, and the maintenance of peace, it will be the duty of the Opposition to support the Government, and we shall certainly do so not only in this House but out of doors.

No one can say there is anything undemocratic about national service for the defence of the country and for the preservation of our free island life, and I assume, of course, that it will be imposed equally and universally upon all

British subjects in Great Britain, without any distinction being drawn between rich and poor. There is a question of some difficulty about Northern Ireland. That must be discussed in a temperate spirit, in view of all the past history of that question. I hope, however, that with the least possible delay we shall be placed in possession of the Government's scheme, especially in regard to the Army, so that we may know the part in our future system which the Territorial Army and voluntary enlistment of all kinds will play, and how these features will be reconciled with permanent national compulsory military service. I hope we can also be assured that there is no question of extending compulsory national service in the Armed Forces, which defend the life of the State, to compulsory service in the industries of the country. In time of war, this sacrifice may be made, and was freely and voluntarily made, by the trade unions and by the people of the nation, but anything in the nature of industrial conscription in time of peace would be intolerable, and all tendency in that direction must be resisted by all who wish to avoid the serfdom of totalitarian regimes.

I do not wish to trespass unduly upon the time of the House, but the King's Speech covers many topics, and one may be accused of underrating the value of some particular topic if it is not given customary mention in despatches. I reminded the House recently that I suggested last November that a total of 1,550,000 men should be maintained for the three Services for some time to come. The Government informed us in February that they hoped to reduce the figure to a total of 1,100,000 by 31st December next. I now understand that this process has been stopped – I only read it from the newspapers – and that the 1,100,000 is to be increased by 200,000, 300,000 or 400,000 men. It is no part of my duty to search for points of agreement with the present Government, but it does seem that a figure of 1,100,000, plus 300,000 or 400,000 more, if that is adopted, will bring them very near the 1,550,000 which I put forward a year ago.

Here I must frankly deplore the mismanagement and maladministration of the Armed Forces during the last year. All of the three Ministers responsible have been removed, promoted or dismissed, and new men have been appointed. The former First Lord[1] has now become Minister of Defence. I would like to take the occasion of offering him my hearty congratulations and of saying that we look forward with confidence to his discharge of these duties. The right hon. Gentleman has a very special ability and experience, and I, personally, have always felt the warmest regard for him on account of the very rough times we went through together during the war. But what with his long journey to India and his protracted work on the Paris Conference, which was also quite good – I much preferred it to his work on his previous excursion – he cannot have given much thought to Admiralty business. We are

[1] A. V. Alexander.

told the Admiralty runs itself. I am not so sure. Today we are told the Navy is undermanned. I saw placarded in the newspapers about recent Fleet exercises that the Navy was undermanned; one battleship, or something like that, was all they could manage. Yet the figures presented to us in February gave them no fewer than 175,000 men on Vote A, or far more than were required for the very large Fleets which were fully manned before the Second World War began. There must be some mismanagement here, and although partial explanations may be forthcoming, I should particularly like to know what is the proportion of men in Vote A of the Navy who are seaborne tonight, and how many of them are employed on shore, and to have comparisons between that and the Navy in previous phases of its administration. A very searching and severe review of naval establishments is undoubtedly required, and I trust this will be undertaken during the Estimates Debates of this year. I recognise, of course, that the Fleet Air Arm is an addition to the prewar Navy, and also may be counted as part of our air power.

The former Secretary of State for Air, Lord Stansgate, also has been so much abroad, negotiating for our evacuation of Egypt and the Canal zone, that he has not been able to bring his commanding talents to bear upon the intricate problems and clamant problems of postwar military aviation. Lord Stansgate has gone, and we now have a new Secretary of State for Air,[1] but he has gone, too, to the United States.

Finally, there is the War Office. The former Secretary of State for War[2] – I do not know whether my right hon. Friend is here today – is deservedly popular and respected in all sections of the House. His many good and charming qualities, high patriotism and public spirit, are admired by all. That, however, does not in any way efface the fact that he was not qualified to discharge, or capable of discharging, the extraordinary and complicated tasks with which the War Office is cumbered and pressed in the transition period at the end of a great war. There is great importance in having a political Minister constantly making his influence felt in each of the Service Departments. It is one of the cases where that much abused class, the politicians, is indispensable. Left to themselves, the Service chiefs will not be able to produce solutions of many of the difficulties which occur, and they would be the first to say how much they stand in need of political guidance. This guidance they have not had, I think,

---

[1] Philip John Noel-Baker, 1889–1982. First Commandant, Friends Ambulance Unit, France, 1914–15. League of Nations Secretariat, 1919–22. MP (Lab.) for Coventry, 1929–31; for Derby, 1936–70. Parliamentary Secretary, Ministry of War Transport, 1942–5. Secretary of State for Air, 1946–7; for Commonwealth Relations, 1947–50. Delegate, United Nations Preparatory Commission, 1945; Member, British Delegation, UN General Assembly, 1946–7. Minister of Fuel and Power, 1950–1. Nobel Peace Prize, 1959. Baron, 1977.

[2] Frederick John Bellenger, 1894–1968. Started work as a tea-packer at the age of 14. Later a boy messenger in the Post Office. Enlisted, Aug. 1914. On active service, RA, 1914–18 (twice wounded). 2nd Lt, 1916. Cons. member, Fulham Borough Council, 1922–8. MP (Lab.) for Bassetlaw from 1935 until his death. Capt., RA, 1939–40 (including the retreat to Dunkirk). Financial Secretary, War Office, 1945–6. Secretary of State for War, 1946–7.

in any effective form – in any form worth speaking of – for more than a year, and we have paid pretty dearly in all sorts of directions for the lack of this essential element in our organisation.

Take the Kluang court martial, and all that business there.[1] With my immense Army experience, with all the Secretaries of State for War I have seen, criticised or applauded, I cannot understand how any Secretary of State for War, coming into his office one morning and, presumably, reading some of the newspapers, would not have said to the Army Council, or whatever it may be, 'Here you are going to try 240 men – since when has there been a mass court martial like that? Look up the precedents. The Cabinet would have to settle a question of that kind.' Nothing of this sort seemed to occur, and so we got into an extremely tiresome and vexatious muddle which did not reflect very well upon the smooth and imperturbable administration of our military law and justice, although I take this occasion to say that I thought the first entrance of the new Secretary of State[2] to the House and his remarks upon this subject were by no means unbecoming.

I am sure that if he feels that he has to stand between the Army and criticism and see that justice is done, there will be many opportunities for him to make his tenure of the office praiseworthy and possibly even memorable. Far more serious is the total failure to produce a policy or scheme in respect of the Army which can be explained to Parliament and which, once understood by the country, can become a powerful aid to voluntary recruitment. Failure, and failure worthy of censure, is applied to the Government administration of the three Service Departments since they came into power, and this failure has been demonstrated beyond contradiction by the dismissal of two out of the three Ministers involved.

I have only a few more topics which I must touch upon, and these leave the military, foreign, Colonial, and Imperial spheres and come a little nearer to our home affairs. We are relieved to hear that Ministers will prosecute with the utmost vigour the task of providing suitable homes for My people. This is a day of rejoicing. Is this really true? Have they made up their minds to turn over a new leaf?

Mr Shurmer[3] (Birmingham, Sparkbrook): Which is more than ever you did.

Mr Churchill: I have passed more social legislation in this House than any man before. I guarantee that it would have been possible to give a far greater impetus and movement to the house building programme. I have more than

---

[1] On 14 May 1946, some 250 privates of the 13th Paratroop Battalion stationed at the Muar Camp in Malaya refused to obey orders and were later charged with mutiny. Three were acquitted; eight were sentenced to five years' penal servitude and the rest to two years' imprisonment. When news reached the UK two days after sentencing, the Judge Advocate-General quashed the sentences owing to irregularities that made the trial unsatisfactory.

[2] Emanuel Shinwell.

[3] Percy Lionel Edward Shurmer, 1888–1959. MP (Lab.) for Birmingham Sparkbrook, 1945–59.

once appealed publicly to the Minister of Health, and I am sure that if he chose from now henceforth to be animated by the instruction and statement in the Gracious Speech and let nothing stand in the way of the largest number of homes of all kinds in the shortest possible time by all methods for the largest number of people, he could even now regain a great deal of the position and the hopes which were founded upon his accession to office with his many undoubted abilities. Instead of that we did not get the homes. We got insults every time. Every kind of insult was flung out, not that we seasoned politicians mind what was said about us by people for whom we entertain no respect. It is maddening for the people who need the homes and houses merely to see the right hon. Gentleman working out his little party spites, as well as personal and class spites which in the great position he now occupies he ought to have outlived. I have heard him described as a new Lloyd George. Good gracious me, it was certainly not by this kind of contribution that this former great Welshman made his name a household word, which will long endure and be remembered in the homes of Britain.

We are also told that it will be the constant endeavour of His Majesty's Ministers to alleviate the hardships and inconveniences of the housewives. This again will certainly be a welcome change. Let me repeat the old adage, 'It is never too late to mend.' There may still be a moment, 'Betwixt the stirrup and the ground,' 'He mercy sought, and mercy found.' So far during their tenure of power, in spite of the great power which they wield and of the very severe measures that they are able to force upon the working people, who have just voted for them in large numbers, and, therefore, give loyal obedience to much which they would otherwise not have sustained and endured, they have in many ways made things actually worse than they were in the war years. There have been arguments about food. In the first year of peace it is worse than it was in the last year of war. I am told that that will bear statistical and searching examination. By all means let it be examined, and let us see what the figures are. I will even put a Question on the Paper if desired to elicit a written answer. It is very gratifying to hear the Ministers in the King's Speech admitting their intention to break with their evil past and to go forward and endeavour to alleviate the lot of the housewife. But what is the substance behind these declarations? The change of heart is very good, but what are the acts and deeds by which they are to be accompanied? What is the first remedy for all these misfortunes and for all these difficulties? What is the first step of alleviation which we are promised in the Gracious Speech? It is the nationalisation of the railways and of inland transport.

Mr Shurmer: You said that 20 years ago.

Mr Churchill: I am not going to pretend I see anything immoral in the nationalisation of the railways provided fair compensation is paid to the present owners. I profess myself, as the hon. Gentleman has reminded the House, in favour of this policy in 1919, but what happened? (*Interruption.*)

Mr W. J. Brown (Rugby): Hon. Members on the Government benches must not get so rattled.

Mr Churchill: Sir Eric Geddes[1] was placed in complete charge of the railways with all the facilities and power which would have accrued to a State aided nationalised system. What happened? All that he produced in four years was a very bad service for the public, heavy loss to the shareholders, and the worst railway strike ever known except the one preceding the General Strike.

I must admit that this practical experience of nationalisation – and we do learn by trial and error provided we profit by our experience – damped – I cannot say my youthful – my early enthusiasm for this project. But the railways are only part of the problem. They were a very clearly marked out public service, and one finds it difficult to see why the arguments which have been applied to the Post Office could not equally be applied to the railways, but now the whole problem is changed. (Hon. Members: 'Why?') It is changed by the enormous developments in road transport and haulage. Here is a field of complications of the most extraordinary variety. Why the Government should choose this particular moment to throw all this new sphere into confusion and disturbance and make a large addition to the National Debt in order to thrust the clumsy butter-fingers of the State into all this intricate apparatus cannot be imagined, still less explained. And that it should be represented as a measure for alleviating the inconveniences and hardships of the housewife – that at any rate is a preposterous fraud. The same is true of their projects for electricity and gas. We can assure the Government that we shall meet the proposals for the nationalisation both of inland transport and of electricity with strenuous and uncompromising opposition.

Winston S. Churchill to John Gordon[2]
(Churchill papers, 4/351A)

12 November 1946

Dear Sir,

My attention has been drawn to the series of articles appearing in the *Sunday Express* by Mr Alan Moorehead. I am very much surprised to read such untruthful statements. For instance, in the article of November 3 a most

---

[1] Eric Campbell Geddes, 1875–1937. An engineer on Indian railways before 1914. Deputy Director-General, Munitions Supply, 1915–16. Director-General, Transportation, BEF, France, 1916–17; Military Railways and Inspector-General, Transportation, all theatres of war, 1916–17. Knighted, 1916. PC, 1917. Hon. Maj.-Gen., and Hon VAdm., 1917. MP (Cons.) for Cambridge, 1917–22. 1st Lord of the Admiralty, 1917–18. Minister without Portfolio, 1919. Minister of Transport, 1919–21. President, Federation of British Industries, 1923, 1924.

[2] John Rutherford Gordon, 1890–1974. Reporter, *Dundee Advertiser*, 1904; *People's Journal* and *Glasgow Herald*, 1911. Served with King's Rifle Corps, WWI. Chief Sub-editor, *Daily Express*, 1922. Editor, *Sunday Express*, 1928–52.

offensive statement about Field-Marshal Montgomery is attributed to me which I never made. Then the edition of November 10 on page 2, beginning with the words, 'By the time the invasion was ready Churchill', down to the words in the next column, in the paragraph entitled 'The bombshell', 'Then he walked out', is pure invention of a mischievous and offensive character. Nothing like these incidents which are described ever occurred. I have therefore cabled to Lord Beaverbrook asking him to look into the matter.

Winston S. Churchill: press notice
(Churchill papers, 2/143)

12 November 1946

Mr Churchill issued the following statement from No. 28, Hyde Park Gate, last night:

My attention has been drawn to the book entitled *Montgomery* written by Alan Moorehead. This contains a number of mis-statements reflecting upon my conduct of the war, which it may be well to correct. I select only two:

First, on page 114 the following occurs:

'Churchill had been a rigid and somewhat erratic ruler. Twelve months before, he had forced Wavell against his will to go Greece instead of continuing on to Tripoli. And when the Greek invasion failed, as it inevitably had to fail, Wavell was dismissed. In the Army there had been some bitterness about this, not so much because the soldiers had been compelled by the politicians to go to Greece, but because Mr Eden, the Foreign Minister, had grossly misjudged the Balkan situation. Mr Eden had visited Turkey and had conducted a further meeting with the Turkish Foreign Minister in Cyprus. On his return to Cairo, Mr Eden had given the warmest encouragement to the idea that Turkey would support us if we carried out the Greek invasion – which, of course, was untrue. And in the end Eden had stayed and Wavell had been dismissed.'

This of course is quite untrue. General Dill,[1] the Chief of the Imperial General Staff, was with Mr Eden in the Middle East at this time, and the decision to send an Army to Greece was taken by me and the War Cabinet upon the formal advice of General Wavell, approved and endorsed by General Dill, after the fullest discussions had taken place with the principal Commanders in Cairo.

The following is the final operative telegram:

---

[1] John Greer Dill, 1881–1944. Born in Northern Ireland. Entered Army, 1901. On active service, 1914–18 (DSO). Commanded British forces in Palestine, 1936–7. Knighted, 1937. GOC Aldershot Command, 1937–9. Commanded I Army Corps, France, 1939–40. CIGS, 1940–1. FM, 1941. Head of the British Joint Staff Mission, Washington DC, from 1941 until his death.

'Mr Eden, Cairo.

Cabinet this morning considered project in light of telegrams exchanged between us. Chiefs of Staff advised that, in view of steadfastly-express opinion of Commanders-in-Chief on the spot, of CIGS and Commanders of the Forces to be employed, it would be right to go on. Cabinet decided to authorize you to proceed with the operation, and by so doing Cabinet accepts for itself the fullest responsibility. We will communicate with Australian and New Zealand Governments accordingly.'

Secondly, on page 194, about the landing in Normandy and the number of vehicles required:

'By the time the invasion was ready, Churchill, most of the British Cabinet, and a great part of the Allied Command were ardent admirers of Montgomery's skill, his confidence and his toughness of moral character.'

. . .

'Churchill queried the loading programme. There were too many vehicles on the boats.'

. . .

'It so often happens in a crisis when one is exposed to a thousand anxieties the mind will fix on one and make it the sounding-board for all the rest. So Churchill fixed on this matter of the vehicles and the loading priorities. Barely a week before D-day he decided to go down to Montgomery's headquarters and address the General's staff upon the subject. Montgomery was waiting to receive him, but first led the way into a study. And there Montgomery put down his cards on the table.

It was unwise, he said, for the Prime Minister to speak to the staff at that moment. Even if he, Montgomery, was wrong it was too late now to alter things. The loaded trains were running to the ports. The boats were loading. The whole vast invasion machine was turning over and to alter things now would hopelessly dislocate the whole operation. He was absolutely confident that the loading programme was sound, that every single vehicle was necessary. If the Prime Minister could not accept his word on this – if he insisted on an alteration at this eleventh hour – then someone else must be found to lead the expedition.

Someone else must lead the expedition! The bombshell fell quietly in the room. Suddenly Churchill gave way. He had had something more than a tolerable or a human burden on his mind in the past few months; and now this was too much. Possibly he saw, and with a sense of overwhelming relief, that events ha~~ now had reached the point where they were beyond the control of any one man, where inevitably this monstrous project was sweeping upwards to its final crisis, that everyone was reacting in a certain way because he <u>had</u> to react in that way and that there was no longer any turning back or turning aside for anyone. And he gave way. The resignation of Montgomery was unthinkable and they both knew it. The two men remained a little longer in the room while the tension slid away. Then Montgomery reminded him that the staff was waiting outside.

Churchill got up and went out. The generals, the brigadiers and the colonels were drawn up in a line. One by one Montgomery introduced them. Everyone there sensed there had been a crisis. Most of them guessed what had taken place in the study.

Churchill got to the head of the line and surveyed them for a moment without speaking. Then the old lion had his final roar. Some sly imp of genius made him say, and with dignity: 'I'm not allowed to talk to you, gentlemen.' Then he walked out. The scene was all his.'

***

The following is the true story: On May 17, General Ismay was instructed by me to write in the following sense to General Montgomery:

'The Prime Minister has asked me to tell you that he was much concerned by some of the statements made at last Monday's Conference on the subject of administrative arrangements for "Overlord". He was told, for example, that 2000 officers and clerks were to be taken over to keep records, and he was given a statement (copy attached) which shows that at D plus 20 there will be one vehicle to every 4.84 men.

The Prime Minister would like to have a discussion with you and your staff on the whole question of the British tail, and he wonders whether it would be convenient to you to have this before dinner at you Headquarters next Friday, May 19.

	US Vehicles	Personnel	British Vehicles	Personnel	Total Vehicles	Personnel
D + 20	96,000	452,000	93,000	450,000	189,000	902,000
D + 60	197,000	903,000	168,000	800,000	365,000	1,703,000

Plus replacement of casualties.'

***

When I arrived for dinner General Montgomery asked to speak to me alone and I went into his room. I do not remember the actual course of the conversation, but no doubt he explained the difficulties of altering the loading scale at this stage, 17 days before D-day. I am sure however that at no time either in this conversation or in any other of the scores I had with him during the war did General Montgomery threaten to tender his resignation, and that nothing in the nature of a confrontation such as is described took place. After our talk we went to dinner, at which only eight or nine persons, mostly the General's personal staff, were present. All our proceedings were of a most friendly character, and nothing resembling the scene described by Mr Moorehead took place.

It is true, as the author states, that when that night General Montgomery asked me to put something for him in his private book, as I had done before other great battles, I wrote the following, which has already been published elsewhere:

'On the verge of the greatest adventure with which these pages have dealt, I record my confidence that all will be well, and that the organization and equipment of the Army will be worthy of the valour of the soldiers and the genius of their chief.'

I may add, however, I still consider that the proportion of the transport vehicles to fighting men in the early phase of the cross-Channel invasion was too high and that the operation suffered both in risk and execution from this fact.

Publicity is given in this book to the statement that I said at an earlier period about General Montgomery: 'In defeat unthinkable; in victory insufferable.' This is quite untrue and is an unworthy attempt on the part of the author to make mischief by sensational journalism between those who worked together in friendship through many strains and stresses.

George Hicks to Winston S. Churchill
(Churchill papers, 2/21)[1]

13 November 1946

My dear Winston Churchill,

Following my short note of acknowledgment to you yesterday in regard to becoming a member of the 'Handling Group' for the advocacy of the United States of Europe, and that I should have to take certain soundings that has been done, and I am definitely advised that as the Labour Party stands for the same principle then I should refrain from associating myself with any other group, and should pursue the advocacy of the same idea within the framework of the Labour Party.

Please allow me to express appreciation for the invite extended to me and may I wish you and the group best results in the advocacy of this most praiseworthy effort.

I shall continue to give support for this excellent work.

---

[1] This letter was handwritten.

But I am sure you will in all the circumstances appreciate the position that I am unable in any representative way to accept your kind invitation.

Joint Intelligence Committee: report
(*Churchill papers, 2/29*)

14 November 1946

[. . .]

Naval Factors

6. The naval paragraphs on page 5 of the paper are very broad, and do not call for any detailed comment. We consider, however, that the overwhelming Anglo-US naval strength would not necessarily deter Russia from embarking on a major land campaign in Europe should she so desire.

FURTHER COMMENTS
Re-organisation and Re-equipment of the Soviet Army

7. It is noteworthy that, in the paper under review, no mention is made of the re-organisation and re-equipment of the Soviet Army, in particular as regards the mechanisation of infantry formations. These are important current features of Russian military activity, although in July information on this subject was scanty.

Command and Grouping of Soviet Forces

8. We agree with the paper under review, except that we do not believe that Marshal Voroshilov[1] was ever appointed Commander-in-Chief, Transcaucasus.

Delivery of Winter Clothing to the Yugoslav Army

9. We consider this to be a routine matter, and we have no evidence to support the suggestion that the delivery of winter clothing indicates preparation for a winter campaign.

---

[1] Klimenti Yefrimovitch Voroshilov (Voroshiloff), 1881–1969. An underground mineworker at the age of 7. Organised the first ever strike in his district at the age of 18. Worked under Stalin in Baku before WWI. Chairman of the Committee for the Defence of Petrograd, Nov. 1917. C-in-C, defence of Tsaritsyn, 1918. People's Commissar for the Military Region of Kharkov, 1919. Defeated Gen. Wrangel's White Russian Army in Crimea, 1920. Quelled Kronstadt uprising, 1921. Cdr, Moscow Region, 1924 (following death of Lenin). People's Commissar for Naval and Military Affairs, 1925–34. Marshal, 1935. People's Commissar for Defence, 1935–40. For a short while after the German invasion in June 1941, commanded Leningrad Front; then sent to the Urals to organise the reserves. C-in-C, Soviet Forces in Hungary, 1944–7. Head, Control Commission in Hungary, 1947. Following Stalin's death in 1953, became Chairman of the Praesidium of the Supreme Soviet (in effect, President of the USSR). Confessed to 'anti-Party sins', 1957. Published memoirs of his early struggles, *Life Stories*, in 1968.

Russian Forces in the Far East

10. We note that the estimate of Russian forces in the Far East given in the paper under review is much greater than similar US estimates. We consider these latter estimates are likely to be more accurate than those made by any other authorities.

(Signed) W. E. Parry[1]
G. W. R. Templer[2]
T. W. Elmhirst[3]

Field Marshal Lord Montgomery to Winston S. Churchill
(Churchill papers, 4/335)[4]

15 November 1946

My dear Mr Churchill,

Pug Ismay has been telling me of your conversations with him about the articles in the *Sunday Express* by Moorehead. He gave me the impression that you considered the articles, and in fact the whole of Moorehead's forthcoming book, had been read and approved by me before publication: and that you have been told this by someone.

Whoever told you this is telling a definite lie and is trying to make mischief.

I have never seen the book; I read the articles for the first time in the *Sunday Express*. I do hope you will understand this.

These newspaper men are a great trouble to one. They seize hold of stories, mess gossip, and so on; they twist it about with a view to getting something

---

[1] William Edward Parry, 1893–1972. Entered RN, 1905. On active service in WWI. Married, 1922, Maude Mary Phillips: two children. Capt., 1934. In charge of Anti-Submarine Establishment, HMS *Osprey*, Portland, 1936–7. CO, HMS *Achilles*, 1939; HMS *Renown*, 1943. Naval Member, New Zealand Naval Board, 1940–2. Naval ADC to the King, 1943–4. RAdm., 1944. Naval Cdr, Force L (Normandy invasion), 1944. Staff, Allied Naval C-in-C, Expeditionary Force, 1945–6. Director, Naval Intelligence, 1946–8. VAdm., 1948. C-in-C, Indian Navy, 1948–51. CB, 1939. KCB, 1950. Adm., 1951.

[2] Gerald Walter Robert Templer, 1898–1979. Educated at Wellington College and Sandhurst, 1912–15; Staff College, Camberley, 1928–9. Commissioned 2nd Lt, Royal Irish Fusiliers, 1916; 7th/8th (Service) Battalion, Western Front, 1917. Lt, 1918. Capt., 1928. GSO III, 1931. DSO, 1936. Maj., 1938. Acting Col., 1941. Acting Maj.- Gen., 1942. Acting Lt-Gen., 1942. Field Cdr, Italy, 1943–4. Maj.-Gen., April 1945. Despatches, Nov. 1945. KMG, 1946. Director, Military Intelligence, 1946–8. VCIGS, 1948–50. KBE, 1949. GOC-in-C, Eastern Command, 1950–2. GCB, 1951. Col., Royal Horse Guards, 1951–62. British High Commissioner, Malaya, 1952–4. GCMG, 1955. CIGS, 1955–8. FM, 1956.

[3] Thomas Walker Elmhirst, 1895–1982. Educated at Royal Naval College, Osborne, 1908. RN, 1912–15. RNAS, 1915–18; RAF, 1919 (AFC). Deputy Director of Intelligence, Air Ministry, 1940; operations room at RAF Uxbridge during Battle of Britain. Second-in-Command, British Air Forces, North West Europe, 1943–5. CB, 1945. ACAS (Intelligence), 1945–7. KBE, 1946. C-in-C, Air Forces, India, 1947–8; Royal Indian Air Force, 1948–50; Indian Air Force, 1950. Lt-Governor, Guernsey, 1953–8. Knight, Order of St John.

[4] This letter was handwritten.

sensational; they think only of their own interests and take no thought that their actions may endanger warm friendships formed in the war period.

Max Aitken to Winston S. Churchill
(Churchill papers, 4/335)[1]

15 November 1946

Dear Mr Churchill,

The Alan Moorehead book on Montgomery does not come out until the 25th of this month. We will be reviewing the book in our issue of *The Sunday Express* of the 24th.

The review will be written by Antony Head and will of course be submitted to you beforehand.

Moorehead is most anxious to make any alterations in his second edition that you would like and has asked me if it would be possible for you to see him. I have explained to the Editor of *The Sunday Express* that you will not expect an answer to your original letter.[2]

Christopher Soames[3] to Winston S. Churchill
(Churchill papers, 1/42)[4]

16 November 1946   Paris

Dear Mr Churchill,

I have so much to thank you for. I am, alas, well aware of my incapacity to express to you in words my gratitude – for many – for the kindness and understanding with which you received and accepted me – for the patience and sympathy with which you permitted me to offload to you my petty worries and troubles – for the friendship which I felt I was offered.

Lunch at Chartwell was, for me, such a great awakening. Please believe me when I say that I had the impression of living for an all-too-short period of

---

[1] This letter was handwritten.
[2] Reproduced above (pp. 541–2).
[3] Arthur Christopher John Soames, 1920–87. Educated at Eton, Royal Military College and Sandhurst. 2nd Lt, Coldstream Guards, 1939; Capt., 1942. Asst Military Attaché, British Embassy, Paris, 1946–7. Married, 1947, Mary Churchill; five children. MP (Cons.) for Bedford Div. of Bedfordshire, 1950–66. Parliamentary Private Secretary to PM, 1952–5. Parliamentary Under-Secretary of State, Air Ministry, 1955–7. Parliamentary and Financial Secretary, Admiralty, 1957–8. Secretary of State for War, 1958–60. Minister of Agriculture, Fisheries and Food, 1960–4. Director, Decca Ltd, 1964–8; James Hole & Co. Ltd, 1964–8. British Ambassador to France, 1968–72. Grand Officier de la Légion d'honneur, 1972. Medal of the City of Paris, 1972. European Commissioner for Trade and for External Relations, 1973–7. Grand Cross of St Olav, Norway, 1974. Hon. LLD St Andrews, 1974. Governor of Southern Rhodesia, 1979–80. Lord President of the Council, 1979–81. Leader of the House of Lords, 1979–81. Hon. DCL Oxon, 1981.
[4] This letter was handwritten.

time in another world – a world of greatness such as I never believed existed. I took away with me such wonderful memories.

I am afraid it is most difficult for me to get over to England again yet-awhile. Pressure of work is severe, and I am now suffering the just consequences of allowing my work to amass itself during the past month. However, I am confident that the moment will come when I will be able to arrange a weekend in England, and I do so hope that I will be able to see you then.

Winston S. Churchill to Field Marshal Lord Montgomery
(Churchill papers, 4/335)

17 November 1946

My dear Monty

I was very glad to get your letter of November 15. I did not believe the statements made to me that you had read this book beforehand, although this was asserted by the publisher, Hamish Hamilton,[1] to Brendan Bracken, and by Moorehead to the editor of the *Sunday Express*. It seems probably that the good natured help you gave him has been grossly misrepresented by the author. None the less I am happy to have your repudiation.

I hope if you have time you will read pages 194, 195 and 196, which are certainly offensive to me. I must say I had forgotten about this particular dinner, but Pug has unearthed the letter he wrote you, at my direction, on May 17, 1944, a copy of which is enclosed. I am quite sure that at no time in our long and arduous comradeship did you ever treat me in this way, and in particular that you never threatened me with the resignation of your Command. It would be quite natural I should raise with you the point mentioned in Pug's letter, and that we should discuss it privately as we discussed so many other difficult problems. If, however, you had treated me in the way described in these pages I should certainly not have stayed to dinner with you. If I remember rightly, we were only a very small party, eight or nine, mostly your personal staff. It is probable that I shall have to put these facts on record, but I cannot think this will lead to any disagreement between us. I am in full accord with the last paragraph of your letter.

PS. See also the offensive passage on the top of page 158. Nothing like this was ever said or thought by me.

---

[1] British publishing house founded in 1931 by James Hamish Hamilton (1900–88).

Winston S. Churchill: broadcast
('The Sinews of Peace', pages 243–4)

18 November 1946

ROOSEVELT MEMORIAL FUND

I am very glad to be invited to support the Prime Minister in calling for subscriptions to the British memorial to President Roosevelt. The House of Commons would gladly have voted all the money needed but it was thought better that the Fund should be made up by small subscriptions so that very large numbers of people could have a chance to take their share. In the great republic across the Atlantic the head of the State is also the head of a Party, in the midst of all the controversies of partisan politics. But over here, in Britain, we only knew him as a world-statesman who was a friend in need and a friend indeed to our country and to the causes of freedom and civilisation which were our cause and which were his cause. For more than five years I worked with him in true comradeship. We sent each other, on each side, nearly a thousand long telegrams and so kept commanding unity of purpose and policy amid the innumerable perplexing problems of war, which in its intimacy and in its practical effectiveness surpassed any tale which history tells of the alliances of great nations with common aims and in equal peril.

I conceived an admiration for President Roosevelt as a statesman, a man of affairs and a war leader. I felt the utmost confidence in his upright and inspiring character and outlook and these ripened in my breast a personal regard and affection for him which will dwell with me as long as I live. His love of his own country, his respect for its constitution, his power of gauging the tides and currents of its free, mobile, public opinion were manifest. But added to these were the beatings of that generous heart which was always stirred to anger and to action by spectacles of aggression and oppression by the strong against the weak. His physical affliction lay heavily upon him. It was a marvel that he bore up against it through all the years of Party controversy in his own country and through the years of world storm. As I said to the House of Commons not one man in ten millions, stricken and crippled as he was, would have attempted to plunge into a life of physical and mental exertion, of hard and ceaseless political strife. Not one in a generation would have succeeded in becoming undisputed master of the vast and tragic scene.

There is no doubt that the late President foresaw the dangers closing in upon the pre-war world with far more prescience than most well-informed people on either side of the Atlantic. There never was a moment's doubt on which side his sympathies lay. The bearing of the British nation in that time of stress when we were all alone filled him and vast numbers of his countrymen with the warmest sentiments towards our people. Even while the United States was nominally neutral he advised the extraordinary measure of assistance called 'Lend-Lease', which will stand forth as the most unselfish and unsordid financial act of any country in all known history. He was one of those men about whom one could feel that the worse things got, the better he would be. It is not for us in this island to appraise his position in American history, but we have a right to proclaim that he played a decisive part in the fortunes and the future of mankind, that he was the greatest American friend Britain has ever known and the most powerful champion of freedom who has ever brought help and comfort from the new world to the old.

Now in war-scarred London we raise a monument to his memory and to his fame. It is the heartfelt tribute of British gratitude. To the pleasant ceremonial garden, with its fountains and trees and flowers, of which the Prime Minister has spoken, in which this monument will stand, all sorts and conditions of men and women will resort and if Franklin Roosevelt's inspiration lingers there none will take away any thought which does not arouse fearless resistance to tyranny in all its forms and which does not harmonise with the broadening hopes and higher humanities which may someday reign over all the land and sea.

Winston S. Churchill to Sir Edward Bridges
(Churchill papers, 2/5)

18 November 1946

My dear Edward,

Will you tell the Prime Minister that I am going to ask him to lay as a Parliamentary paper the Canadian report of Russian espionage. Apparently it is extant and accessible to newspapers, and two or three lengthy instalments were published some weeks ago in the *Sunday Dispatch*. It seems to me therefore that Members of Parliament ought to be in possession of it. Pray let me know when it would be convenient for me, or someone, to ask a Private Notice Question or if desired an ordinary Question.

General Sir Hastings Ismay to Winston S. Churchill
(Churchill papers, 4/351A)

20 November 1946

My dear Mr Churchill,

I send herewith two of the documents for which you asked in your letter of November 17th, namely –

    (i) The print of the Dakar incident that was prepared as a result of your minute of 6th October.

(ii) The print of telegrams received from the Secretary of State for War during October 1940.[1]

The list of operation code names used in 1940 is a much more difficult matter, as no such list has ever been compiled. I am, however, having our records searched and should be able to give you the information before the end of this week.

Winston S. Churchill to General Sir Hastings Ismay
(Churchill papers, 4/19)

20 November 1946

My dear P,

Could you find out for me who wrote the admirable pamphlet about the Air battle of Britain called, 'Air Ministry Pamphlet 156'.

This man might be very helpful to me in constructing the short but accurate condensation which I must make of this episode.

Directors of Plans: report
(Churchill papers, 2/29)

23 November 1946
Top Secret

We have examined a certain appreciation concerning Russian strengths and intentions, which also comments on the measures which the Anglo-American staffs are purported, in consequence, to have put in hand.

2. We attach at Annex a report by the Service Directors of Intelligence commenting on the appreciation of Russian strengths and intentions.

3. The forces with which the Americans and ourselves are credited are greatly in excess of those available and it would, therefore, be impossible to give effect to the plans which are supposed to have been made for the Anglo-American forces.

4. We agree in general with the conclusions of the Service Directors of Intelligence, that –

    (a) Just as British and American capabilities are exaggerated, so also estimates of Russian strengths are excessive.

    (b) Nevertheless, the appreciation under examination reaches a correct conclusion in regard to relative Russian superiority and the practical possibility of a Russian conquest of Western Europe.

5. In general, our view of the appreciation under examination is that, while the anxiety over the international situation which it reflects is justified, it is

---

[1] Anthony Eden.

over pessimistic, particularly in view of the military inaccuracies which are revealed and the undue weight or credence given to certain reports and contributory factors.

J. F. Stevens[1]
J. H. N. Poett[2]
G. H. Mills[3]

Winston S. Churchill to Lord Woolton
(*Churchill papers, 2/14*)

24 November 1946
Private

My dear Woolton,

Thank you very much for you letter of November 23 about the two by-elections.[4] In the future we might consider where a capable Liberal candidate is standing for a hopeless seat, giving him a chance. If this were done once or twice it might breed a fellow-feeling and secure us Liberal support in other places. We might talk this over at one of our meetings. Lady Rhys-Williams[5] made a strong appeal to me to give Martell[6] a chance, but I did not feel like it, so did not make the proposal.

You are quite right in all you say about Paddington.

Time will tell.

---

[1] John Felgate Stevens, 1900–89. Educated at King's College, Cambridge. RN, 1918. Capt., HMS *Cleopatra*, 1942–3. CBE, 1945. Cdr, HMS *Implacable*, 1948. KBE, 1955. Director of Plans, Admiralty, 1946–8. Director, Naval Training, 1949. CoS to Head of British Joint Services Mission, Washington DC, 1950–1. CB, 1951. Flag Officer, Home Fleet Training Squadron, 1952. C-in-C, America and West Indies Station and Deputy Supreme Allied Commander, Atlantic, 1953–5.

[2] Joseph Howard Nigel Poett, 1907–91. Educated at Sandhurst. Joined Durham Light Infantry, 1927. Posted in Egypt, 1927; in Waziristan, 1929; in India, 1930. Maj., 1939. Lt-Col., 1941. CO, 5th Parachute Div., 1943. DSO and Bar, 1945. Director of Plans, War Office, 1946. CB, 1952. GOC, 3rd Div., 1952–4. Commandant, Staff College Camberley, 1957–8. GOC-in-C Southern Command, 1958–61. KCB, 1959. C-in-C, Far East Land Forces, 1961–3.

[3] George Holroyd Mills, 1902–71. Educated at RAF College, Cranwell, 1920; RAF Staff College, 1935. Cdr, No. 115 Air Sqn, 1939–41. DFC, 1940. Station Cdr, RAF Watton, 1941–2. Director of Policy, Air Ministry, 1943–5; of Plans, 1946–9. CB, 1945. AOC, Balkan Air Force, 1945; No. 1 Group, 1949–50; Air HQ Malaya, 1952–3. AOC-in-C, Bomber Command, 1953–5. KCB, 1954. Cdr, Allied Air Forces, Central Europe, 1956–9. GCB, 1959.

[4] In Rotherhithe (won by Bob Mellish, Lab.) and Paddington North (won by William Field, Lab.).

[5] Juliet Glyn, 1898–1961. Private Secretary to Parliamentary Secretary, Ministry of Transport, 1919–20. Married, 1921, Rhys Rhys-Williams, 1st Bt. Contested (Lib.) Pontypridd by-election, 1938; Ilford North, 1945. Hon. Secretary, Women's Liberal Federation, 1943. Chairman, Publications and Publicity Committee, Liberal Party, 1944–6.

[6] Edward Drewett Martell, 1909–89. Educated at St George's School, Harpenden. Married, 1932, Ethel Maud Beverley. Royal Army Corps, 1939–45. Member (Lib.), London County Council, 1946–9. Contested (Lib.) Rotherhithe by-election, 1946; Hendon North, 1950; (Ind.) East Ham, 1957; (Cons.) Bristol South East by-election, 1963. Formed People's League for the Defence of Freedom, 1956. Joined Conservative Party, 1962. Chairman, Hastings Conservative Association, 1963.

554 NOVEMBER 1946

Lord Camrose to Winston S. Churchill
(Churchill papers, 4/57)

24 November 1946

Henry Luce offers 1,250,000 dollars for all serialization book rights in United States. Is working in conjunction with *New York Times*. *New York Times* will serialize daily and Luce weekly in *Time*. Book would probably be published by Simon and Schuster. *New York Times* has made me an independent offer of 300,000 dollars for serialization in his paper in event of Luce's combined offer not being acceptable. *Herald Tribune* offers 1,100,000 dollars but not yet definitely confirmed for serial rights United States and rest of world excluding British Empire. Chenery offers 500,000 dollars for serial rights having withdrawn previous offer of larger figure. Offers for American book rights from three firms all in neighbourhood of 200,000 dollars but possibly final offer could be increased to 225,000 dollars. All offers are subject to work being completed by (Mr Churchill) and to appropriate re-arrangement if otherwise. General understanding regarding payment is a sum down on signing of contract and rest proportionately on delivery of manuscript. Possibly Luce and *Herald Tribune* might be improved in final show-down but not very materially. Reves[1] believes that, with basis of 300,000 dollars from *New York Times* and individual nation-wide canvassing by him of all newspapers outside New York he could bring total for serial to much larger figure. This would require two or three months time and substantial commission. Would also necessitate considerable advance publicity. My talks here have convinced me that early completion of contract is desirable for many reasons and should like to have your reactions offers named above.

For your information Wheeler[2] made offer today of 675,000 dollars for serial rights North and South America.

General Sir Hastings Ismay to Winston S. Churchill
(Churchill papers, 4/19)

25 November 1946

My dear Mr Churchill,
I am told that the Officer nominally responsible for Air Ministry Pamphlet

---

[1] Emery Reves, 1904–81. Founded Cooperation Publishing Service, 1933. Winston Churchill's literary agent, 1937. Naturalised as British subject, 1940. Married, 1964, Wendy Russell.

[2] John Neville Wheeler, 1886–1973. Born in New York. Educated at Columbia University, 1908. Reporter, *New York Herald*, 1908–12. President, Wheeler Syndicate, 1912–16; Bell Newspaper Syndicate, 1916. Married, 1918, Elizabeth W. Thompson. On active service with American Expeditionary Force in France, 1917–19. General Manager, North American Newspaper Association and Associated Newspapers, 1930–5; President and Director from 1935. Director, Consolidated News Features; Wheeler Development Corporation.

156 was Air Chief Marshal Sir Robert Brooke-Popham,[1] but I have found out, through private channels, that the man who did most of the work was Flight-Lieut. Goodwin,[2] who is now a Professor of History at Jesus College, Oxford.

Will you let me know if you wish me to do anything about getting in touch with him? – or perhaps you would prefer to do so direct?

Winston S. Churchill to General Charles de Gaulle
(Churchill papers, 2/30)

26 November 1946

My dear General de Gaulle,

Duncan Sandys brings this to you at Colombey. I am anxious to know for my own personal guidance, and of course in strict confidence, your own views upon the following two points.

First, what do you think about the danger of a Soviet advance westward to the sea? It is evident that they have the power to do it at any time. On the other hand the end might not be so agreeable as the beginning. This was certainly Hitler's experience and it may be a deterrent. Sandys will give you various information which I have received from Continental sources. My own view is that there are over two million Soviet troops in the occupied territories of Europe or in immediate reserve in the Leningrad and Odessa regions. Their exact organization, mobility and efficiency cannot be accurately measured.

The second point is about the United States of Europe. You will have seen my speech at Zürich and it is my conviction that if France could take Germany by the hand, and with full English cooperation, rally her to the west and to European civilization, this would indeed be a glorious victory and make amends for all we have gone through and perhaps save us having to go through a lot more.

I have watched with the closest attention the course of French politics, as you no doubt are watching ours. The main characteristic of the present Socialist-Labour Government in England is its hatred of Communism and Communists. In this they will of course be supported by the Conservative Party.

[1] Henry Robert Moore Brooke-Popham, 1878–1953. Entered Army, 1898; RFC, 1912. On active service, 1914–18. Director of Research, Air Ministry, 1919–21. Commandant, RAF Staff College, 1921–6. Knighted, 1927. AOC Fighting Area Air Defences of Great Britain, 1926–8; Iraq Command, 1928–30. AOC-in-C, Air Defence of Great Britain, 1933–5. Air Chf Mshl, 1935. Inspector-General, RAF, 1935–6. Retired list, 1937. Governor and C-in-C, Kenya, 1937–9. Recalled to RAF as C-in-C, Far East, 1941. Reverted to the retired list, 1944.

[2] Albert Goodwin, 1906–95. Educated at Jesus College, Oxford. Asst Lecturer, European History, Liverpool University, 1929–31. Fellow, Jesus College, Oxford, 1931–9. Married, 1935, Ethelwyn Millner. Staff Officer, War Room, Air Ministry, 1940–3; Historical Branch, 1944–5. Prof. of Modern History, University of Manchester, 1953–69.

Winston S. Churchill to Clement Attlee
(*Churchill papers, 2/18*)

27 November 1946
Private

My dear Prime Minister,

This is about the United States of Europe. 'Europe must federate or perish!' You very kindly wrote favouring Citrine joining our small Handling-Group with which to make a start. With much regret he has come to the conclusion that he ought not to undertake any activities which would cut across the Coal Board. I followed up your advice about Gibson[1] and had an acceptance from him, a copy of which I enclose. I thought I might ask George Hicks, who is not engaged at present, and he expressed a sincere desire to take part. However he said he would have to take 'a few soundings'. As the result of these he felt he ought to decline.

Since then the project has been bruited about in *Reynolds News*, of which I enclose you a cutting. I cannot think it is contrary to Party interests of any kind that such an all-Party movement should be started. I certainly thought that this was your feeling. I hope therefore that no general directions will be given preventing any Members of the Parliamentary Party from taking part in it.

Anyhow, I should be very much obliged if you would let me know how the matter stands, because if there were to be a veto on Socialist members joining this organization, which is an important out-work of your main policy, I should have to make another plan. Personally I should have thought it would have been reasonable to let it stand on the same sort of basis as the New Commonwealth, of which I am British Honorary President. If this is not to be, pray let me know.

I could come to see you after or during Questions on Thursday if that were convenient.

Winston S. Churchill to Lord Camrose
(*Churchill papers, 4/57*)[2]

28 November 1946

After careful consultation I am sure that it would be best for there to be no publicity and for you to discuss whole position and form of statement if any when you get back here. Meanwhile no authorized statement should be issued. If there are rumours, leakages and much publicity this does not commit us in

---

[1] Charles William Gibson, 1889–1977. MP (Lab.) for Kennington, 1945–50; for Clapham, 1950–9.
[2] Letter written in response to Camrose's of Nov. 24, reproduced above (p. 554).

any way. If questioned by the Press I shall reply I have no statement to make and I hope Mr Luce will do the same should he be rung up. It cannot do him much harm to wait a few weeks.

Winston S. Churchill to General Sir Hastings Ismay
(Churchill papers, 4/19)

28 November 1946

My dear P,

Thank you for your letter of November 25.[1] I think it would be well if you got in touch with Professor Goodwin and told him how much interested I was in his account. If you think well of him I should like to see him myself in the course of the next month.

Winston S. Churchill: speech
(Churchill papers, 2/336)

28 November 1946   Harrow School

My dear Head Master,[2] Ladies and Gentlemen,

As you expressed, this is the seventh time I have been here, and that is quite a long time. But I do so much enjoy hearing our old songs and you sing them so beautifully and with so much feeling that I cannot help feeling refreshed and in a sense rejuvenated every time I make one of these excursions. Of course if one has to make a speech on every occasion the problem of variety presents itself in a more direct and serious form as the tally lengthens and I have been casting about this morning for some subject to which particularly to draw your attention, some precept to be of advantage to commend to you in suitable terms so that you can carry away some real moral or lesson. So I thought to myself I would speak on the subject of punctuality. Unfortunately I have to offer you my apologies for being several minutes late, and I will therefore alter my topic – but only a slight alteration – and call it unpunctuality.

I could have offered you many excuses for coming a few minutes late. I could have dwelt upon one of those interchanges which take place sometimes in the House of Commons between me and Mr Herbert Morrison. This certainly would have been a very solid and acceptable excuse. I could of course

---

[1] Reproduced above (pp. 554–5).

[2] Ralph Westwood Moore, 1906–53. Educated at Wolverhampton Grammar School and Christ Church, Oxford (Scholar). Asst Master, Rossall School, 1928–31. Sixth Form Master, Shrewsbury School, 1931–8. Head Master, Bristol Grammar School, 1938–42. Headmaster, Harrow School, 1942–53. Member, BBC General Advisory Council, 1952. Member of the Hispanic Council. Member of the Councils of St Mary's and of Charing Cross Hospital Medical Schools.

have dwelt upon the state of the traffic and congestion of the road, which also would have been valid and solid. I should have mentioned to you that my wife, who had hoped to be with me today, is in France, and she usually keeps me up to the mark. But I am not going to use any of these. I am going to offer you my apologies and say that the only excuse I can give is one which has very often occurred to me in my long life – I did not start quite soon enough. If any little incident occurs which makes you a little late on any occasion you should try this excuse upon your form-master and very likely it will be received with such consideration as it deserves.

I enjoy very much coming here. Indeed I feel that my Harrow life is, as it were, beginning. I am a seven-yearer now. I always find old Jacker[1] here, whom I remember as the great idol of all cricketers, not only at Harrow but throughout the country, and with whom I have served in Governments, and who is a great friend of this School and one of its principal guardian angels.

I am delighted to hear from the Head Master of the growing strength in the numbers of the School, though there was a time when the bombs of the enemy were a deterrent, a considerable deterrent upon your parents from sending their sons to so exposed a station. But you carried on and got through and now, after the war, as you say – and I am delighted to hear it – Harrow emerges stronger than ever.

We must however also think of our country and we must think of the world. You young gentlemen will be going forth into the world, to the Universities, to military service – which I am sure you all cheerfully accept as a duty to the nation, for it is the duty of all to do what is considered necessary by the Government of the day for the safety of the country. You will be going forth into the world and you may find it, if I may say so, full of problems, more baffling problems than it has ever been before. It has been said that from every version of success, however great, comes forward something to make a greater struggle necessary. That is why the words of the American poet, Walt Whitman,[2] have always deeply impressed themselves upon me. Victory gives liberty and liberty presents problems more difficult than those that have already been overcome. But it also presents means of dealing with those problems and offers superior solutions to them all. And so there is no limit to the effort and to the achievements which men may make.

I was much moved when you sang that wartime verse – and it is indeed to me a dear and cherished compliment that here in this School where fifty years ago, fifty years ago – forty years on is no good to me – where fifty years

---

[1] Francis Stanley Jackson, 1870–1947. Educated at Harrow and Trinity College, Cambridge. Cricketer for Cambridge, Yorkshire and England. Wisden Cricketer of the Year, 1894. English national cricket captain, 1905. Lt., Harrow Volunteers, 1900; Capt., 1900; Lt-Col., 1914. MP (Cons.) for Howdenshire, 1915–26. Financial Secretary, War Office, 1922–3. PC, 1926. Governor of Bengal, 1927–32. GCIE, 1927; GCSI, 1932. Chairman, Governors of Harrow School, 1942–7.

[2] Walter Whitman, 1819–92. American poet. Works included *Leaves of Grass* and 'O Capt.! My Capt.!'

ago I lived and struggled and toiled and got along one way or another. Well, I was not very successful. I was not particularly attracted by Latin or Greek or Mathematics. I liked them, but they are awfully difficult to bring out the way the masters want them to come. And I was not very keen on Footer, and I never played Cricket, except under compulsion. I remember I had to go and call on Jacker one morning because it had been alleged that I was not present when I should have been, fielding the ball for some of the big boys. However, instead of giving me a whopping he gave me an extra breakfast. I hope I am not giving him away. But we have always been very good friends and would have been whatever course of action he had decided to take.

However, as I say, my visit here today brings back to me all those memories of the past and I value very much the kindness with which you renew these invitations.

When you go forward into the world, always keep in touch with the old School. Do not be ashamed of the sneer and mockery which some people cast upon the Old School Tie. For my part I think it would be a scandal if the old school tie were ever to be a bar to others having an equal and fair chance. There is a free and open society in our country, ever becoming a more classless society, and those who have inspiration in their hearts from the traditions of the past can consider themselves happy to have an advantage which is denied to others.

Therefore, I say brace yourselves to the tasks which are before you. Ever cherish in your bosoms as your dearest treasure the greatness, the glory and the true revival of our dear island home.

Duncan Sandys: report to Winston S. Churchill
(Churchill papers, 2/20)

29 November 1946

On Friday, November 29th, 1946, I motored from Paris to Colombey to see General de Gaulle. I arrived about midday, stayed to lunch and left again about half past four.

RUSSIAN INTENTIONS

I had about an hour's talk with the General before lunch, during which we discussed the question of Russia's intentions in Europe. I showed him the secret report on Soviet troop dispositions. He did not appear to have any detailed information of his own, but was inclined to think that the Russians had appreciably less than 200 Divisions in the Western theatre and were in the process of demobilising a considerable number of their more seasoned troops.

He felt sure that the Russians were, for the present, not ready for war. Their policy was one of opportunism. They were out for anything they could get in the way of additional territory or influence, but they would not, in his opinion, be prepared to go to the lengths of fighting for it. There would doubtless be a succession of diplomatic clashes. The Russians might on occasions overreach themselves. But even so, he did not think this would result in war. Having no public opinion to consider, the Soviet Government would, if they found resistance too great, be quite prepared to retract their demands. In such an eventuality, the Western allies would, in order to avoid war, do everything possible to save the Soviet face.

For these reasons, General de Gaulle considered that until such time as she developed the atom bomb, Russia would be most unlikely to provoke war. However, taking a longer view, he was of opinion that war between the Western Democracies and Soviet Russia was sooner or later a virtual certainty.

FRENCH INTERNAL SITUATION

During lunch we discussed current French politics and the stalemate which had resulted from the recent General Election. De Gaulle seemed to be out of sympathy with all parties and spoke contemptuously about many of the political leaders, including Monsieur Bidault.

He considered that nothing but the most drastic measures could prevent a serious monetary collapse. In his opinion, the Assembly, as now constituted, is too weak and divided to enact the unpopular measures which the situation demands.

From what he said, it was clear that General de Gaulle expects that when the crisis comes, France will turn to him to save her and all his thoughts and actions are influenced by this idea. This also accounts for his decision, for the present, to hold himself aloof from all current political controversy.

EUROPEAN FEDERATION

After lunch we went out for a walk for about an hour and later returned to the General's study. We talked principally about the idea of European federation. De Gaulle undoubtedly believes firmly in this project but his support is hedged around with numerous qualifications.

He said that the reference in Mr Churchill's Zurich speech to a Franco-German partnership had been badly received in France. Germany, as a state, no longer existed. All Frenchmen were violently opposed to recreating any kind of unified, centralised Reich, and were gravely suspicious of the policy of the American and British Governments. Unless steps were taken to prevent a resuscitation of German power, there was the danger that a United Europe would become nothing else than an enlarged Germany.

He stressed that if French support was to be won for the idea of European union, France must come in as a founder partner with Britain. Moreover, the two countries must reach a precise understanding with one-another upon the attitude to be adopted towards Germany before any approaches were made to the latter.

De Gaulle further thought that France should make her support for the policy of European federation conditional upon the settlement of outstanding differences between herself and Britain. A permanent allocation of coal from the Ruhr; consent to the continuance of French military occupation in Germany over a long period and possibly the incorporation of the Northern Rhineland in the French Zone; the establishment of a regime of international control of the Ruhr industries satisfactory to France; a fuller recognition of French interests in Syria; an Anglo-French agreement to adopt a common line towards the Arab countries. '*Voilà mes conditions*,' he said.

I replied that it would be most unfortunate if France's support for the cause of closer European co-operation were to be made dependent upon the settlement of all kinds of extraneous issues. Great as was Britain's interest in the consolidation of Europe, it was a matter of even more vital importance to France. I found it, therefore, difficult to believe that any French Government would attempt to make this matter a subject for bargaining.

General de Gaulle stuck to his point. He felt that the success of any scheme of European federation would depend upon the existence of complete confidence between France and Britain and that this would not be achieved until all the various differences which were at present impairing Anglo-French relations were settled to the satisfaction of France.

I found General de Gaulle a friendly and agreeable host, but it was evident that he still felt very bitter about the events in Syria and what he regarded as the slighting attitude of the Big Three towards France during the last years of the war. '*On nous a chassé de la Syrie. . . . A Yalta et à Potsdam on nous a mis à la porte.*'[1] These and similar remarks recurred on and off throughout our talk.

At the end of the day, the general impression left with me was that de Gaulle was fully convinced of the desirability of European Union and would from time to time, when he thought fit, express his qualified agreement with the idea. However, he is far too much of an individualist to consider working together with any group of people, either in France or abroad, on any project which he had not himself initiated. In any case, his attention is at present exclusively concentrated upon internal French politics. He hopes and expects, sooner or later, to be recalled to power in some moment of crisis. Meanwhile he will be reluctant to involve himself in any controversy which might, in his opinion, prejudice his prospects.

On 29 November 1946 Winston S. Churchill sold Chartwell to the National Trust for £50,000.

---

[1] 'We were chased out of Syria . . . At Yalta and at Potsdam we were thrown out.'

Winston S. Churchill to Tom Driberg
(Churchill papers, 2/50)

30 November 1946
Private

Dear Mr Driberg,

Thank you for your letter of November 28. I am very glad to know that more than a hundred Members are supporting your Motion.[1] I will certainly try to help get a proper discussion of the matter. Parliament is involved and there ought to have been more consideration about the statue, and possibly alternative models. On every ground I am sure that the sitting position is right.

My remark about your being a 'quasi-Member' of the Labour party was not intended to be a precise definition or to formulate doctrinal charges.

B. R. Ambedkar to Winston S. Churchill
(Churchill papers, 2/42)

30 November 1946 · Bombay

Dear Mr Churchill,

As suggested by you I have prepared a short brief in support of the case of the Untouchables for your use in the forthcoming debate in Parliament on India. I hope you will find it useful.

We are relying on you as our greatest supporter for securing to the Untouchables the right to separate recognition and separate representation.

In the new situation that has developed and in the new confabulations that are taking place in London between HMG, the Congress and the League there is a possibility of that new India Policy may be outlined promptly by HMG and the opposition. In that case I am sure you will fight for our independence from the Hindus.

---

[1] Concerning controversy surrounding a statue in tribute to Roosevelt being sculpted by Reid Dick.

December 1946

Winston S. Churchill to Ben Chifley[1]
(Churchill papers, 2/145)

[December] 1946

Am honoured and deeply touched by your splendid invitation and I hope indeed some day I may have the time accorded to me to visit Australia and New Zealand as I have long desired to do. Alas, it is impossible for me to come in the spring of 1947. My work here in leading the Opposition is very heavy and I am not sure that my strength is equal to so long a journey by air. Let me repeat how much I value your invitation and how sorry I was we did not meet when you were over here.

Elizabeth Gilliatt[2] *to Burke Trend*[3]
(Churchill papers, 1/41)

3 December 1946

Dear Mr Trend,

Thank you for your letter of the 28th November, which I have now shown to Mr Churchill.

Mr Churchill desires me to say that he certainly does not seek any personal favours from His Majesty's Government. He thought, however, that his family associations with the United States had been of public advantage in the war, and might still be of public advantage; and it was on public even more than on private grounds that he wished to make this small symbolic contribution to the rebuilding of the Church of Pompey, in which his American forebears are

---

[1] Joseph Benedict Chifley, 1885–1951. Born in Bathurst, New South Wales, Australia. Married, 1917, Elizabeth McKenzie. Minister of Defence, 1931–2. Treasurer, 1941–9. Minister for Postwar Reconstruction, 1942–5. PM, 1945–9. Leader of Australian Labor Party, 1945–51.

[2] Elizabeth Gilliatt, Private Secretary to Winston S. Churchill, 1946–55.

[3] Burke Frederick St John Trend, 1914–87. Educated at Merton College, Oxford. Joined HM Treasury, 1937; Under-Secretary, 1949–5; 3rd Secretary, 1959–60; 2nd Secretary, 1960–2. CVO, 1953. KCB, 1962. Cabinet Secretary, 1963–73. Rector, Lincoln College, Oxford, 1973–83. Baron, 1974.

buried. However, if the Chancellor feels that it is not possible to allow this personal token of twenty-five pounds to be given by him, he will write to Syracuse body and explain the circumstances.

Mr Churchill presumes he will be permitted to publish or refer to the Treasury letter.[1]

Winston S. Churchill to Harold Macmillan
(Churchill papers, 2/55)

3 December 1946
Private

My dear Harold,

I return to you the letter which you had thought of sending to *The Times*. It is just the sort of letter they would like to print as indicating that the criticisms by the British Socialist Left Wing against the present Greek Government have support on the Conservative side. I personally do not think we ought to add to the difficulties of this Greek Government which is based upon the fairest election that has ever been held in the Balkans and which is struggling against murderous Communist rebellion, aided by weapons and supplies pushed over the Yugoslavian and Bulgarian borders, no doubt with the encouragement of the Russians. I am anxious, as I told you, that the British troops should be withdrawn as soon as possible and I am sure it would be fatal for us to try to manage the internal affairs of Greece, which has always been tormented by the egotism and ambition of quite a large number of rival politicians of mediocre quality.

Thank you very much for consulting me.

---

[1] Churchill had requested permission to send money to Syracuse, New York, for the restoration of the Church of Pompey, but this was denied by the Bank of England and the Treasury. He then asked permission of the Chancellor of the Exchequer, Hugh Dalton, who also declined to give it.

Winston S. Churchill to Leslie Charles Graham-Dixon[1]
(Churchill papers, 2/149)

3 December 1946

My dear Graham-Dixon

My wife and I would be so pleased if you and Mrs Graham-Dixon[2] could come over and lunch with us next Sunday. I should very much like to show you Chartwell.

We shall probably be meeting before then.

Come <u>please</u> if you can spare the Sunday, at about 12.30 p.m. so that we can have a walk around before luncheon.

Winston S. Churchill to Clement Attlee
(Churchill papers, 2/29)

4 December 1946

My dear Prime Minister,

Thank you very much for your letter of yesterday, and its enclosure, which I will study most carefully. I presume I may show this in strict confidence to the other two members of the delegation which I brought, Mr Eden and Colonel Stanley.

Cd I also be told the numbers of men estimated for the divisions on the table. My Swiss figures were given on a basis of 10,000. I understood you were estimating 15,000.

Clement Attlee to Winston S. Churchill
(Churchill papers, 2/18)

4 December 1946

My dear Churchill,

I have been considering with my colleagues the question of the United States of Europe and the position of our members. While, of course, our members are free to take whatever course seems good to them in respect of joining an organization, it has been suggested that the objects aimed at by the organization would be better achieved through the United Nations Association rather than through a separate society, the aims of which might be misunderstood and misrepresented.

---

[1] Leslie Charles Graham-Dixon, 1901–86. Educated at St John's College, Oxford. Called to the Bar, Inner Temple, 1925. Married, 1925, Dorothy Rivett. Acted as one of Churchill's barristers. QC, 1950.
[2] Dorothy Rivett. Married, 1925, Leslie Graham-Dixon.

Winston S. Churchill to Thomas Dewey[1]
(Churchill papers, 2/148)

4 December 1946

My dear Mr Dewey

I was delighted to get your letter of November 9 and think it is most kind of you, amid your heavy executive cares, to have written it.

Between our two countries things are happily in such a posture that no matter which Party is responsible for the time being, our two Vast organizations will move harmoniously forward together.

It was a great encouragement to me that you should come to the dinner given me by the City of New York, in all the squawl that arose after Fulton. If I made the Fulton speech today, it would be criticized as consisting of platitudes.

I always felt you would be re-elected to your great office because the American people, as do their Allies, respect you for the forebearance and restraint which you exercised in the Presidential election of 1944 placing, without question, the public war interest above all personal or Party consideration.

I should very much like to have another long talk with you. I have made no plans but it may be that, in the late Spring, I may find it possible to come over to Canada, whither Alex has given me cordial invitations. In that case I should have to go to Toronto and I had even an idea of visiting Chicago. Anyhow I will let you know, because it would give me great pleasure to see you again.

Pray commend me to your wife,[2] who showed me such charming hospitality.

Duncan Sandys to Winston S. Churchill
(Churchill papers, 2/21)

5 December 1946

As you know, certain British newspapers reported recently that the Dutch Government had rejected your plan for European union.

I have obtained fuller particulars from the Dutch Embassy. It seems that this statement is based on two sentences in a Government memorandum dealing generally with foreign affairs, which I attach.

The passage in question reads as follows:

> The Government does not think the time ripe for developing the idea of a European federation. It is not possible, politically speaking, to see Europe without the Soviet Union or the United Kingdom.

---

[1] Thomas Edmund Dewey, 1902–71. Born in Owosso, Mich. Asst US Attorney, Southern District of New York, 1931; Acting US Attorney, 1933. Special Prosecutor, New York City, 1935–7. District Attorney, New York County, 1937–43. Governor (Rep.) of New York, 1943–54. Candidate (Rep.) for US Presidency, 1944, 1948. Delegate from New York to Republican National Convention, 1952, 1956. Private attorney, 1955–71.

[2] Frances Eileen Hutt, 1903–70. Married, 1928, Thomas Dewey.

The impression I get from this passage, particularly from the last sentence, is that the Dutch Government, like most other Governments, is merely sitting on the fence.

Clement Attlee to Winston S. Churchill
(*Churchill papers, 2/29*)

6 December 1946
Secret

My dear Churchill,

Thank you for your letter of December 4. I have no objection to your showing the copy of a Report by the Directors of Plans enclosed in my letter of December 3, to Mr Eden and Colonel Stanley.

The number of men estimated per Division for the table attached to the Directors of Plans' Paper was 15,400. This was arrived at as follows:

Average war establishment of a Division	10,000
Average overheads per division (i.e. Corps Troops, line of communication troops, etc.)	12,000
This brings the total war establishment of the divisional slice to	22,000
It is, however, estimated that the average <u>Strength</u> of a divisional slice is 70% of Establishment, i.e.	<u>15,400</u>

Winston S. Churchill to Colonel Frank Clarke
(*Churchill papers, 2/161*)

7 December 1946

My dear Frank,

I now send you with my very best wishes for Christmas the following books, which I have bound for you:

> *The Story of the Malakand Field Force*
> *The River War*
> *Ian Hamilton's March*
> *My African Journey*
> *Liberalism and the Social Problem*
> *My Early Life – A Roving Commission*
> *Thoughts and Adventures*
> *Arms and the Covenant*
> *Step by Step*
> *Great Contemporaries*
> *India*

Into Battle
The Unrelenting Struggle
The End of the Beginning   ⎫
The Dawn of Liberation   ⎬ Wartime Speeches
Onwards to Victory   ⎭
Victory

You have I understand got *Marlborough* similarly bound. It is now out of print and practically unobtainable, but about Easter a new edition will be coming out, so if you have not got it let me know. Have you got an edition of the *World Crisis* with its two pendant volumes *The Aftermath* and *The Eastern Front?* There are five volumes in all. If not I will have these put in hand. There is also my *Life of Lord Randolph Churchill*. Have you got this? It again is out of print, but I am hoping it will appear presently. Then there is *London to Ladysmith via Pretoria*. Finally there is the book of Secret Session Speeches which I am having bound for you and will follow. It takes such a very long time to get things done over here, that I am afraid you must have thought me very dilatory.

I do hope however this series will form an agreeable part of your library.

PS. I am still hoping to improve the picture of Miami. Fulton still holds its own!

PPS. The Secret Session Speeches have just arrived, so I am sending them now.

Winston S. Churchill to Captain Arthur Granville Soames[1]
(*Churchill papers, 2/156*)

8 December 1946
Private

I am sorry to say that Clemmie has been ordered by her doctor to take at least three weeks rest-cure. She has found life vy strenuous of late, & I want her to be fit for the joyous event to wh we all look forward.[2]

---

[1] Arthur Granville Soames, 1886–1962. 2nd Lt, Coldstream Guards, 1905, Lt, 1907. Married, 1913, Hope Mary Woodbine Parish (div. 1934): three children, including Christopher (married Mary Churchill, 1947); 1934, Annette Constance Jardine, née Fraser (div.); 1948, Audrey Alma Humphreys. Sheriff of Buckinghamshire, 1926–7.

[2] Mary Churchill's marriage to Christopher Soames, which took place on 11 Feb. 1947.

Winston S. Churchill to Clement Attlee
(Churchill papers, 2/29)

10 December 1946
Secret

My dear Prime Minister,

Thank you very much for your letter. I said 200 divisions of 10,000 men each; i.e. 2,000,000 men. In this I included the Russian concentrations around Leningrad and Odessa. The American figure of 106 divisions at 15,400 each equals 1,632,400 men, so there is not much between us.

I earnestly hope the Russians will now begin to reduce to the figure of 200,000 asked for by Byrnes, which seems to me admirably conceived, and which we should be right to support. I shall be most grateful if you will let me know when it is achieved, and will make you my public congratulations.

Winston S. Churchill to Mohammed Ali Jinnah
(Churchill papers, 2/42)

11 December 1946
Private

My dear Mr Jinnah

I should greatly like to accept your kind invitation to luncheon on December 12. I feel, however, that it would perhaps be wiser for us not to be associated publicly at this juncture.

I greatly valued our talk the other day, and I now enclose the address to which any telegrams you may wish to send me can be sent without attracting attention in India. I will always sign myself 'Gilliatt'. Perhaps you will let me know to what address I should telegraph to you and how you will sign yourself.

Winston S. Churchill: speech
('Winston S. Churchill, His Complete Speeches', volume 7, pages 7410–17)

12 December 1946   House of Commons

INDIA

The House is indebted to the President of the Board of Trade (Sir Stafford Cripps) for the careful, lucid and comprehensive statement which he has made, and we all associate ourselves with him in his appeal to the leaders of the various parties in India to abstain from violent propaganda or invective against each other, which may have the effect of bringing about a recrudescence or intensification of the grave disorders which have occurred. The right hon. Gentleman deplored, in moderate terms the fact that we were having a Debate on this subject today. But it would be a pity if the British Empire in India passed out of life into history, without the House of Commons seeming to take any interest in the affair, and without any record, even in *Hansard*, of the transaction.

It is several months since we have even discussed the Indian drama which is unfolding itself remorselessly. So far, in the Parliament, we have never voted in a Division on these issues, momentous though they be to Britain, to the British Commonwealth of Nations, to the world at large and even more, to the 400 million who dwell in the India Continent. Words are almost inadequate to describe their vastness. But memorable as these issues may be, we have never divided the House on them, nor shall we do so on this occasion. We must still indulge the hope that agreement will be reached between the two great Indian religions and between the political parties which give modern expression to their age-long antagonisms. We should, however, be failing in duty if we in this House gave the impression to India that we were inattentive, or even indifferent, to what is happening, and what is going to happen out there. For many generations, Parliament has been responsible for the government of India, and we can only relieve ourselves, or be relieved, from that burden by the passing of a solemn Act. While we are responsible, it would, in my opinion, be disastrous and be discreditable to the House if the whole Session passed away, with nothing but a casual reference being made to these tremendous and immeasurable events which are taking place.

There is another aspect. If we remained silent after all these months, it might be thought that we were in agreement with His Majesty's Government, and that the policy which they were pursuing was a national policy and not a party policy of the forces which they represent. It might be thought that this was a policy of Britain as a whole, and that the execution of it was endorsed by the British people as a whole, whereas, for good or ill, the responsibility rests with His Majesty's Government. On their heads lies the responsibility, not only for the execution of the policy, but for the powerful impulse they have given to a great many tendencies which are dominant in this matter today. I say nothing to derogate from any utterances or statements which have been made by the Members of other parties. They are all excellent, but I should be very sorry indeed, to feel that, as matters unfold in India, there is any question of our being held accountable at the present moment, for the course of events. Therefore, we are bound to take an opportunity to challenge the Government on this matter by bringing the affair to the light of day.

The newspapers, with their alluring headlines, do not do justice to the proportion of current events. Everyone is busy, or is oppressed by the constant cares and difficulties of daily life. Headlines flicker each day before them. Any disorder or confusion in any part of the world, every kind of argument, trouble, dispute, friction or riot all flicker across the scene. People go tired to bed, at the end of their long, bleak, worrying days, or else they cast care aside, and live for the moment. But, all this time, a tremendous event in Asia is moving towards its culmination, and we should be unworthy of the times in which we live, or of the deeds which we have done if, through unduly careful restraint, we appeared to others unconscious of the gravity, or careless of the upshot of events which affect the lives of vast numbers of human beings who, up to the present, have dwelt for well or ill beneath our protecting shield. My colleagues and I were convinced that if we put off all notice of Indian affairs until the end of January – because that is what it would have come to – or, possibly, February of next year after all these months of silence, the immense accountability of the House of Commons and of the British nation might slip, with so much else, uncared for, away. For these reasons, I am sure that we ought not to separate without making at least a passing comment, to put it mildly, upon the main new features of the Indian problem which have presented themselves to us so prominently in the last few weeks.

There are three main new features to which I would direct the attention of the House this afternoon. There was, and there still is, a general measure of consent here and throughout the island to the final transference of power from the House of Commons to Indian hands, but also it is agreed that that transference, if it is to take place, must be based upon the agreement and the co-operation of the principal masses and forces among the inhabitants of India. Only in this way could that transference take place without measureless bloodshed out there, and lasting discredit to our name in the world. Those who are content with the general movement of our relations with India over the last 20 years have hoped that the desire of many Indians to be rid for ever of British rule and guidance would have brought about a melting of hearts among the vast populations inhabiting the Indian continent, and that they would have joined together to maintain the peace and the unity of India, and stride forth boldly into their independent future, on which we impose no bar.

Those are not my views; they are the views of a very great number of people. But it is necessary to place on record the undoubted fact that no such melting of hearts has, so far, occurred. I think that that would be considered in harmony with the habit of understatement which has often received acceptance in this House. On the contrary, all the facts and all the omens point to a revival, in an acute and violent form, of the internal hatreds and quarrels which have long lain dormant under the mild incompetence of liberal-minded British control. This is the dominating fact which stares us in the face today. The House will probably be of the opinion that it is too soon for us to accent this melancholy conclusion, or to regulate our conduct by it. To me, however, it would be no surprise if there were a complete failure to agree. I warned the House as long ago as 1931, when I said that if we were to wash our hands of all responsibility, ferocious civil war would speedily break out between the

Muslims and Hindus. But this, like other warnings, fell upon deaf and unregarding ears.

I have always borne in mind the words my father used when he was Secretary of State for India 60 years ago. He said:

> Our rule in India is, as it were, a sheet of oil spread out over a surface of, and keeping calm and quiet and unruffled by storms, an immense and profound ocean of humanity. Underneath that rule lie hidden all the memories of fallen dynasties, all the traditions of vanquished races, all the pride of insulted creeds, and it is our task, our most difficult business to give peace, individual security and general prosperity to the 250 millions of people –

there are now 400 millions –

> who are affected by those powerful forces, to bind them and to weld them by the influence of our knowledge, our law and our higher civilization, in process of time into one great united people and to offer to all the nations of the West the advantages of tranquillity and progress in the East.

There is the task which, with all our shortcomings and through all our ordeals, we have faithfully and loyally pursued since Queen Victoria assumed the Imperial Crown. That is the task which we have now declared ourselves willing to abandon completely, provided that we have such assurance of agreement between the Indian races, religions, parties and forces as will clear us from the responsibility of bringing about a hideous collapse and catastrophe. We have no such assurance at the present time. Agreement in India, which was the basis of all our policy and declarations, was the indispensable condition. It was the foundation of the Cripps Mission in 1942; it was the keynote of the Cabinet Mission sent out this year, but there is no agreement before us yet; I stress 'yet'. There is only strife and bloodshed, and the prospect of more and worse. That is the first point of which we must take note – the absence of agreement which, it was common ground between us, should stand as the foundation of the future transference of power in India.

The second point to which I would like to draw the attention of the House is the cardinal error of His Majesty's Government when, on 12 August, they invited one single Indian party, the Congress Party, having made other efforts, to nominate all the members of the Viceroy's Council. Thereby they precipitated a series of massacres over wide regions, unparalleled in India since the Indian Mutiny of 1857. Indeed, it is certain that more people have lost their lives or have been wounded in India by violence since the interim Government under Mr Nehru was installed in office four months ago by the Viceroy, than in the previous 90 years, of four generations of men, covering a large part of the reigns of five Sovereigns. This is only a foretaste of what may come. It may be only the first few heavy drops before the thunderstorm breaks upon us. These frightful slaughters over wide regions and in obscure uncounted villages have, in the main, fallen upon Muslim minorities. I have received from high and credible witnesses, accounts of what has taken place, for instance, in Bihar. The right hon. and learned Gentleman gave us his report. What happened in Bihar casts into the shade the Armenian atrocities with which Mr Gladstone once stirred the moral sense of Liberal Britain. We are, of course, cauterized by all that we ourselves have passed through. Our faculty for wonder is ruptured, our faculty for horror is numbed; the world is full of misery and hatred. What Mr Gollancz,[1] in a remarkable book – which, I may say, shows an evident lack of peace of mind – has called 'our threatened values', do not stir us as they would have done our fathers or our predecessors in the House; nor, perhaps, after all our exertions and in our present eclipse, have we the physical and psychic strength to react against these shocking tidings, as former generations and earlier Parliaments, who have not suffered like us, would certainly have done.

The official figure of the lives lost since the Government of India was handed over to the Interim Administration of Mr Nehru is stated at 10,000. I doubt very much whether that figure represents half the total racial and religious murders which have occurred up to date. An outbreak of animal fury had ravaged many large districts, and may at any time resume or spread its devastation through teeming cities and Provinces as big as England or the main British island. It is some comfort to recall, and I was glad the right hon. and learned Gentleman reminded us of it, that both Muslim and Hindu leaders have joined together to arrest, or at least mitigate this appalling degeneration. I have been informed that it was Mr Nehru himself who gave the order which the Provincial Government of Bihar had been afraid to give, for the police and troops to fire upon Hindu mobs who were exterminating the Muslim minorities within their midst. That was certainly to his credit and may be taken, so far as it goes, as an encouraging sign.

Nevertheless, I must record my own belief, which I have long held and often expressed, that any attempt to establish the reign of a Hindu numerical majority in India will never be achieved without a civil war, proceeding, not perhaps at first on the fronts of armies or organized forces, but in thousands of separate and isolated places. This war will, before it is decided, lead through unaccountable agonies to an awful abridgement of the Indian population. Besides and in addition to this, I am sure that any attempt by the Congress Party to establish a Hindu Raj on the basis of majorities measured by the standards of Western civilisation – or what is left of it – and proceeding by the forms and formulas of governments with which we are familiar

---

[1] Victor Gollancz, 1893–1967. Educated at New College, Oxford. Publisher, Benn Brothers, 1920–8. Founder, Gollancz Ltd, 1928; National Committee for Rescue from Nazi Terror, 1941. Governor, Hebrew University of Jerusalem, 1944–52; Alternate Governor, 1952–64. Chairman, National Campaign for the Abolition of Capital Punishment, 1955–6, 1964–7; Joint Chairman, 1960–4. Knighted, 1965.

over here, will, at a very early stage, be fatal to any conception of the unity of India.

The right hon. Gentleman gave us some account of the differences that had arisen about the declaration of 15 May, as between the two parties and so forth. But the technical and procedural points now in dispute in Delhi are not the issue at stake; they are only the tactical and argumentative counters; they are only the symbols of passions and hatreds deep in the soil of India, and measured by the standard of a thousand years. The unity of India is of superficial appearance, imposed by many generations of British rule, upon a mighty continent. It will pass away for long periods of time, once the impartial element of guidance from outside is withdrawn. Whatever may be thought of these conclusions – and I have no doubt there is great difference of opinion about attempts to draw conclusions in regard to matters of such vast, vague and obscure a character – the facts upon which they are based should, I am sure, at this stage not pass without occasional mention in the House of Commons, which, as I have said, until other arrangements are made bears a lawful, legal and inescapable responsibility for what happens in India.

The third new and important fact, of which we must this afternoon take notice, is the declaration by His Majesty's Government – made, I think, by the Prime Minister last week. Let me read the last paragraph of the declaration:

> There has never been any prospect of success for the Constituent Assembly except upon the basis of an agreed procedure. Should a Constitution come to be framed by a Constituent Assembly in which a large section of the Indian population has not been represented, His Majesty's Government could not of course contemplate – as the Congress have stated they would not contemplate – forcing such a Constitution upon any unwilling parts of the country.

If this is at last the settled policy of His Majesty's Government it will carry them far. It comprises within its scope, it means to me, the discharge of our obligations, both to the inhabitants of India and to those who are called the Scheduled, or Depressed classes, or the Untouchables as they are regarded by their fellow Hindus, to which obligation we have long been pledged in honour. How this policy will be carried into effect is not possible to foresee, and still less to foretell, at this moment. It is indeed a formidable programme after so many slowly-grown loyalties have been repudiated, and so many bulwarks cast away. I take note of that declaration, because it seems to me to be a most important milestone in this long journey, which combines the pangs of uphill progress with the evils which beset us upon downhill progression.

The Muslims, numbering 90 million, some separate States and the rest intermingled in an extraordinary manner with the Hindus, comprise the majority of the fighting elements in India. The Untouchables, for whom Dr Ambedkar has the right to speak, number, as I contend, anything from

40 to 60 millions. It is to them that His Majesty's Government owe a special duty of protection. At present in these negotiations they are not regarded, in a technical sense, as a minority, so I understand. There is a technical sense. If you are a minority, certain treatment is open to you; but if you are not a minority, then you are denied that treatment. They have been outwitted and outmanoeuvred in various ways, through the Poona Pact form of the elections, as the right hon. Gentleman admitted with candour and sincerity, and the affection or pretence it put forward that they are merely a part of the vast Hindu community, and are not entitled to be considered as a minority entity in India's life. I must particularly ask the Prime Minister, or whoever is to speak for the Government, to state the Government's view and intentions upon this point. Are the 60 million Untouchables to be considered as an entity by themselves, entitled to the consideration which is to be given to entities, or are they merely to be used to swell the numerical size of those whom they regard as their oppressors? I should be very glad if a clearer pronouncement could be made upon that point. I do not anticipate that it will be an unfavourable one.

I have already remarked, earlier in the Session, that the word 'minority' has no relevance or sense when applied to masses of human beings numbered in many scores of millions. When there are many scores of millions the word 'minority' really does not apply. We are only 46 million in this island, but we do not consider ourselves a minority: we consider ourselves an entity – at least so far. Ninety million Muslims and sixty million people of the Depressed Classes are not relative facts, but actual and absolute facts. The Depressed Classes are fully entitled to be considered as an entity, and I repeat my request to the right hon. Gentleman that a very clear statement should be made on this point.

I must now draw the attention of the House to the character of the Constituent Assembly, which apparently is to proceed to make a republic for India, and engage upon it at once. I have not today the intention of scrutinizing the electoral foundation upon which this rests – 30 millions out of 400 millions –

The Prime Minister (Mr Attlee): Not 400 millions in British India.

Mr Churchill: They are dealing with the fortunes of all India. Large parts of it are not represented at all. There are 30 million electors, who have not much experience with modern political methods, and that is the foundation. I say that is not necessarily capable of giving a complete democratic verdict such as would be required in other more advanced communities.

Mr Cove (Aberavon): Is the right hon. Gentleman in favour of extending the franchise?

Mr Churchill: Yes, certainly, I have always been in favour of extending the franchise. I believe in the will of the people. I do not believe in the perversion of the will of the people by actively organized and engineered minorities, who, having seized upon power by force or fraud or chicane, come forward and then use that power in the name of vast masses with whom they have long lost all effective connection. I say that as to the general foundation. A decision is to be taken, as a result of which the British connection with India will come to an end. I am not at all admitting that that decision represents the wish or expression of the people of India; nor do I admit that the minorities who are going to utter that expression can claim the democratic title which, in modern days, attaches to those who speak for the large majorities of universal suffrage elections. The Cabinet Mission's proposal of 15 May for the setting up a Constituent Assembly was essentially a proposal that the main political parties of India should meet, and through their representatives – 70 Muslims, 220 Hindus, in which were absorbed the unfortunate Untouchables, and 4 Sikhs – endeavour to work out the proposed Constitution. Do His Majesty's Government consider that the meeting now taking place in New Delhi, which the Muslim League are not so far attending at all, is in any sense the meeting of a valid Constituent Assembly? The fact that the Muslims are refusing to attend remains a fact, whoever is to blame for it, and a meeting of one side without the other is not a conference. Indeed, the text of the proposals of the Government and the right hon. and learned Gentleman, whose ability has been devoted with such disastrous effects to furthering this policy –

Mr Sorensen[1] (Leyton, West): Shame.

Mr Churchill: I remember well when the right hon. and learned Gentleman went out as representative of the Government of which I was the head, and how we had to pull him up because – (*Interruption.*) I do not want to say anything –

Sir S. Cripps: If the right hon. Gentleman intends to disclose what passed between me and the Cabinet on that occasion, I hope he will disclose it all.

Mr Churchill: The right hon. and learned Gentleman is quite right in what he says, and I shall not pursue the point. (*Laughter.*) What is all this laughter? No one impugns the conscientious integrity and virtue of the right hon. and learned Gentleman, but I must say that in the Cabinet Mission, of which we have the results published, which has taken place under the present Government, his influence has, I have every reason to believe, been used for an altogether undue emphasis being placed upon the advantages being given to the Hindus. At any rate, the right hon. and learned Gentleman can defend himself. No one more than he has taken responsibility in this matter, because neither of his colleagues could compare with him in the acuteness and energy of mind with which he devotes himself to so many topics injurious to the strength and welfare of the State.

To return to the validity of the present Constituent Assembly, on which I trust we shall have some statement, the document of 15 May states that if the President of the Assembly should decide that a matter raised is not 'a major communal issue', the party which objects and maintains that it is a major

---

[1] Reginald Sorensen, 1891–1971. Unitarian Minister and politician. MP (Lab.) for Leyton West, 1929–31, 1935–50; Leyton, 1950–64. Baron, 1964. Lord-in-Waiting for House of Lords, 1964–8.

communal issue, may claim that the matter is referred for the opinion of the Federal Court. How is it possible that this procedure can work if the party which objects is not there at all? The meeting in Delhi is not, therefore – I wish to hear a statement from the Government on this – the proposed Constituent Assembly which they put forward. Let me take a more homely analogy. If the bride or bridegroom fails to turn up at church, the result is not what, to use an overworked word, is called a 'unilateral' wedding. The absolute essence of the matter is that both parties should be there. While we hope that this may still be the case, it is still pertinent to inquire if His Majesty's Government consider that their conference of a Constituent Assembly has begun.

I am grateful to the House for listening to me after we have had so full an account from the responsible Minister of the Crown. I feel bound, however, to end upon a positive conclusion, although I will express it rather in terms of negation. In all this confusion, uncertainty and gathering storm, which those who have studied the Indian problem over long years might well have foreseen, there appear at the present time to be three choices – the proverbial three choices – before the British Parliament. The first is to proceed with ruthless logic to quit India regardless of what may happen there. This we can certainly do. Nothing can prevent us, if it be the will of Parliament, from gathering together our women and children and unarmed civilians, and marching under strong rearguards to the sea. That is one choice. The second is to assert the principle, so often proclaimed, that the King needs no unwilling subjects and that the British Commonwealth of Nations contemplates no compulsory partnership, that, in default of real agreement, the partition of India between the two different races and religions, widely differing entities, must be faced; that those who wish to make their own lives in their own way may do so, and the gods be with them; and that those who desire to find, in a variety of systems, a means of association with our great free Commonwealth may also be permitted to take the course which, ultimately, they may show themselves ready to take.

It follows, of course, from this second alternative, that anarchy and massacre must be prevented and that, failing a measure of agreement not now in sight, an impartial Administration responsible to Parliament, shall be set up to maintain the fundamental guarantees of 'life, liberty and the pursuit of happiness' to the millions, nay, the hundreds of millions, of humble folk who now stand in jeopardy, bewilderment and fear. Whether that can be achieved or not by any apparatus of British controlled government that we can form from our dissipated resources, is, again, a matter upon which it is now impossible to form a final judgment.

One thing there is, however, that, whatever happens, we must not do. We must not allow British troops or British officers in the Indian Army to become the agencies and instruments of enforcing caste Hindu domination upon the 90 million Muslims and the 60 million Untouchables; nor must the prestige or authority of the British power in India, even in its sunset, be used in partisanship on either side of these profound and awful cleavages. Such a course, to enforce religious and party victory upon minorities of scores of millions, would seem to combine the disadvantages of all policies and lead us ever deeper into tragedy, without giving us relief from our burdens, or liberation, however sadly purchased, from moral and factual responsibility. It is because we feel that these issues should be placed bluntly and plainly before the British and Indian peoples, even amid their present distresses and perplexities, that we thought it our bounden duty to ask for this Debate.

Field Marshal Lord Montgomery to Winston S. Churchill
(Churchill papers, 2/495)

13 December 1946

Dear Mr Churchill,

Thank you so very much for the medallion. I had indeed heard of it, but I did not for a moment expect that I would be included in the list of those to receive it from you. Under your leadership we went through some very dark days; without your leadership I feel we might have gone under.

Thank you so much.

Winston S. Churchill to William DeWitt Wallace[1]
(Churchill papers, 4/7)

14 December 1946
Most Private and Personal

My dear Mr Wallace,

I had a talk the other night with Field Marshal Smuts about his impressions of the American Press which he had studied during his recent visit. He expressed astonishment upon the lack of focus upon the great issues affecting the world. I mentioned to him *The Reader's Digest*, with its immense circulation, as the great corrective of the voluminous daily organs. To my surprise he had never heard of it and was greatly interested.

I wonder whether you would care to send him a copy every month for a short while? I have no doubt he would gladly pay for it, but I thought perhaps you would like to make him an Honorary Member of your vast circle.

Some months ago I talked in this sense to the Queen and she expressed

---

[1] William Roy DeWitt Wallace, 1889–1981. Educated at Macalester College and University of California, Berkeley, 1911. Married, 1921, Lila Bell Acheson. Founded *Reader's Digest*, 1922. Presidential Medal of Freedom, 1972.

great interest. It occurred to me that you might like to send her a series in the future as they come out.

I can of course easily take out two subscriptions for myself and transfer them, but I have so much respect for your organization and the good work you are doing in concentrating American minds upon the serious side of world affairs, at a time when the United States is the centre of so many homes and the bearer of so many burdens, that I thought you would like to do this yourself.

Pray let me know how you feel about this idea of mine, which I hope you will find agreeable.

Jo Sturdee to Commander Charles Thompson[1]
(Churchill papers, 2/157)

15 December 1946

Dear Commander Thompson,

Thank you for your letter of December 10.

1. I am terribly sorry about the books. On hearing from you of the mistake, I wrote to Captain Harding apologizing and asking him to forward his wrong enclosures to you, but have heard nothing since. I hope he hasn't died on us. I will write to him again.

2. Mr Churchill was pleased to sign the photograph you enclosed for your nephew. He seemed to feel complimented by the story around it. I returned it to you herewith.

3. I send you herewith a letter from Pat Kinna.[2] I have had a look through all the photograph albums in Mr Churchill's possession, but alas cannot find one of the Mena Conference[3] round the table. I hate to be beaten but I'm afraid this one is too much for me. Can you think of any way in which we could help? Sorry I'm always such a bore.

Mrs Churchill's engagements are still in a state of cancellation. Miss Mary

---

[1] Charles Ralfe Thompson, 1894–1966. Known as 'Tommy'. Midshipman, 1911. Served mainly in submarines, 1915–31. Flag Lt and Flag Cdr, Board of Admiralty, 1936–40. OBE, 1938. Retired with rank of Cdr, 1939. Personal Assistant to Minister of Defence (Churchill), 1940–5. CMG, 1945.

[2] Patrick Francis Kinna, 1913–2009. His father, Capt. Thomas Kinna, had been decorated for his part in the relief of Ladysmith (28 Feb.1900), in which Churchill had also taken part. An accomplished shorthand typist, after eight years at Barclays Bank he won the All-England Championship for Secretarial Speeds. Joined Intelligence Corps, 1939; posted to Paris as clerk to Maj.-Gen. HRH the Duke of Windsor. Recommended by the Duke's staff to Churchill. Churchill's shorthand clerk, 1941–5. In addition to his Pitman shorthand speed of 150 words per minute, Kinna could take dictation straight on to a manual typewriter at 90 words per minute. In 1945 he turned down the opportunity to stay with Churchill after the war, and from 1945 to 1951 he worked for the Foreign Secretary, Ernest Bevin. Joined the timber firm Montague Meyer, 1951, rising to become personnel director.

[3] Cairo Conference, 22–6 Nov. 1943. Code name 'Sextant'.

is getting all ready for her marriage, although no date has been fixed yet. Mr Churchill got caught in the fog the other night. He walked all the way from Hyde Park Corner to Knightsbridge, got fed up I suppose, and so spent the night at Hyde Park Hotel. But with all these things the world goes on.

PS. Thank you very much. We are all overworked but very well.

Winston S. Churchill to Lord Beaverbrook
(Churchill papers, 2/146)

[December] 1946

Low's *Evening Standard* cartoon yesterday is for the second time in ten days grossly insulting to General Marshall. Ought you not to consider the main questions? Nothing but harm is being done to the *Evening Standard*, to you and to most of the things we both care about. The *Daily Herald* would not print such stuff.

Winston S. Churchill: speech
('Winston S. Churchill, His Complete Speeches', volume 7, pages 7417–19)

20 December 1946   House of Commons

BURMA

I was not proposing to embark upon a formal or full-dress Debate upon the evacuation or abandonment of Burma. This, it seems to me, must be a subject for discussion upon another occasion. All that I was intending to do was to mark, for the nation and the country at large, the significance of the statement which the Prime Minister rattled off so quickly and so smoothly as if it were an ordinary matter of routine. It should be realized that a very important and far-reaching declaration has now been made by the Prime Minister, and we should consider what its consequences will be.

As I said on another occasion, it is less than a year since the Japanese were expelled or destroyed. There have been no adequate elections, no representative assembly formed, and nothing that could be said to be a representative or settled view of the people there. Those people are only now returning, with great difficulty, as the Government have pointed out, and as was pointed out in the White Paper issued last year, to their ruined homes in many parts of that country, which were ravaged by the Japanese. Yet we are told that we must accelerate the process of our departure as much as possible, that special measures must be taken, and these gentlemen invited from Burma to come over here and discuss with the Government the peaceful transference of power and the rapid departure of the British. Before they come, before they would even condescend to come, a declaration has to be made in terms which place this matter in the same state as what is happening now in India.

This must be realized. We have held Burma since 1885. We have followed its affairs with attention. My father was the Minister responsible for the annexation of Burma. During that time, great progress has been made in that small country. There are 17 million people, mostly, or a very large proportion of them, primitive people. Good progress has been made. We defended them as well as we could against the Japanese invasion, but we were not successful. It was only after the tremendous campaign of three years of heavy fighting that the Japanese were driven out, and the country was liberated from the invaders' hands. In those circumstances it would have been reasonable to allow law and order to be established, and the people to settle down on their farms and in their habitations. Then we could have resumed consideration of the question of self-government, to which we had definitely pledged ourselves, but all in due course, and in due time. Again, by the unfortunate form of the Prime Minister's declaration to which the right hon. Gentleman has now given vent, and which has taken its place as an operative declaration, the intermediate state of Dominion status is, to all intents and purposes, eliminated, just as it was in India. In eliminating that interim stage of India it was said: 'This makes no difference, because Dominion status implies the right to contract out of the British Empire.'

The proper stages are of the utmost consequence. If, in India, we had proceeded under Dominion status, and had established a Government based upon Dominion status, that Government could then have addressed itself to the question whether to use what I call the escalator Clause or not. A very different situation would then have arisen. There would have been an opportunity for the friends of this country who desire that we should stay, and who appreciate the blessings which British rule has conferred upon these regions, to rally. They would have had a chance to decide whether, upon a basis of full Dominion status, they would be partners in the British Commonwealth of Nations or not. The elimination of that stage, the short circuiting of that process, has the effect, and could only have the effect, of repulsing all loyalties, the abandoning of friends, and compelling everyone in India to face the fact that the British were going. The result is that no fair chance has been given to the people of India to express themselves, in a calm atmosphere and under proper conditions, upon the questions whether, having obtained full self-government, they would wish to leave the British Commonwealth of Nations or not.

This evil process, which has been attended by disasters of which at present we are only on the threshold, and which will to a large extent occupy or dominate the mind and attention of the present Parliament in the months and years to come, is now quite needlessly extended to Burma. I cannot see why this should be done, unless it is to try to induce the Burmese representatives to come over here and discuss this matter with us. This haste is appalling. 'Scuttle' is the only word that can be applied. What, spread over a number of years, would be a healthy and constitutional process and might easily have given the Burmese people an opportunity of continuing their association with our congregation of nations, has been cast aside. We are seeing in home affairs the unseemly rush of legislation, disorganizing our national life and impeding our recovery, legislation thrust upon Parliament at break-neck speed, hon. Members debarred from taking part in Debates by matters being transferred from the Floor of this House to other parts of the building. We see the same haste which, I suppose, will be praised as vigour. 'Labour gets things done!'

As regards divesting ourselves of these great possessions of the British Crown, and freeing ourselves from all responsibility for the populations – primitive and often divided – who have hitherto looked to British justice and administration for the means of lending their ordinary lives in peace, I thought it necessary at the earliest moment to dissociate myself and those who sit on this side from the course of action which the Government are taking. I said the other day about India that we take no responsibility for the course the Government take; they must bear the responsibility. I see it was said in another place that I was suggesting that should the Conservative Party be returned to power, we would reverse this process. I think it would be utterly impossible to reverse it. The words that have come from the lips of the right hon. Gentleman today, supported as they are by the overwhelming majority of this House – unrepresentative of the balance of forces in the country – are irrevocable. He has in fact shorn Burma away from the British Crown by what is being done. That, at least, is a matter of which notice should be taken, if it be only passing notice, even in this period when we are getting so accustomed and indurated to the process of the decline and fall of the British Empire.

Winston S. Churchill to Lady Gunilla Barnes[1]
(Churchill papers, 2/146)[2]

23 December 1946

My dear friend,

I was deeply grieved to hear of the death of my old and cherished comrade. I feel for you in yr irreparable loss. It was an effort but also a satisfaction to Reggie to come to the 4th Hussars dinner, when he spoke with so much emotion of our long and faithful partnership. I fear you will be vy lonely now; but one can always dwell on past happiness and have faith in the future.

We send you our heartfelt sympathy.

---

[1] Widow of Sir Reginald Barnes, whom she had married in 1919, and earlier of C. D. Wijk.
[2] This letter was handwritten.

Winston S. Churchill to Clement Attlee
(*Churchill papers, 2/145*)

28 December 1946
Private

My dear Prime Minister,

I think it very kind of you to send me these intelligence reports on information collected from the Germans. It is very interesting to me to check our own ideas and estimates at particular points – when all was unknown – by reference to the facts now available from enemy sources.

I am worrying a good deal about this book. It is a colossal undertaking and I may well collapse before the load is carried to the top of the hill. However, it is a good thing to get a certain amount of material together which, if not history, will at least be a contribution thereto.

Thank you also very much for your Christmas wishes to me and Clemmie. These cordially reciprocate.

Winston S. Churchill to Frank Ballard[1]
(*Churchill papers, 2/20*)

28 December 1946
Private

My dear Mr Ballard,

It is my deep conviction, as I think you know, that if we are to avoid the catastrophe of a third World War we must somehow contrive to bring order out of the chaos in Europe, break down national hatreds and suspicions and foster by every means in our power the essentials of unity and the practice of co-operation.

To attain this end we must arouse the fervour of a crusade. We shall need all our resources of statesmanship and our propaganda. But I believe that if properly presented, there will be a tremendous response from the war-wracked millions of the Continent of which we form a part.

I have therefore brought together a few people drawn from all political parties as well as from non-political walks of life who are anxious to get the ball rolling in this country. I have called this small group a 'Steering Committee', for its purpose is not necessarily to set up a new organisation but rather to stimulate those which already exist, as well as individual leaders of opinion who are in sympathy with our aims, into action for the furthering of this specific idea. It is also our intention to encourage the formation of similar groups in as many countries of Europe as possible.

---

[1] Frank Hewett Ballard, 1885–1959. Christian pastor and apologist. Moderator, National Free Church Federal Council.

The statement of aims attached to this letter (which is still open to minor amendments) will be published about the middle of January.

The impact of this initiative on public opinion will largely depend on the representative character of those who sponsor it. The sentiments to which we must appeal and the forces which we seek to stir are rooted in the spiritual depths of our fellow men and women. It is therefore essential that from the outset we should have the support of the Churches throughout Europe.

It is in this connection that I venture to bring this matter to your attention. All the signatories of our first declaration will sign in their individual capacities and not as representatives of parties or organisations. I should be deeply grateful if you would consent to add your name.

But if you should feel that as chief representative of the Free Churches your doing so would give too official an endorsement to our campaign perhaps you would suggest some prominent churchman whom I could approach and whose name would carry the necessary weight.

I am asking Mr Ernest Brown[1] to bring you this letter in order that he may tell you all that is in our mind.

Winston S. Churchill to Victor Gollancz
(Churchill papers, 2/20)

28 December 1946

Dear Mr Gollancz,

Thank you very much for your letter of December 23. I have told Duncan Sandys that I am in no way opposing Earl Russell's[2] joining our small band. I am looking forward to seeing you on January 15.

I read your book which Randolph sent me with the greatest interest. I hope to have a talk with you about it one day. I am not responsible for Potsdam after I left. I would never have agreed to the Western Niesse and was saving it up for a final 'show-down'.

---

[1] Ernest Brown, 1881–1962. A Baptist lay preacher. On active service in Italy, 1916–18 (MC). MP (Lib.) for Leith, 1927–31; (Nat. Lib.) 1931–45. Parliamentary Secretary, Ministry of Health, 1931–2. Secretary to the Mines Dept, 1932–5. PC, 1935. Minister of Labour, 1935–40 (and National Service, May 1939 to May 1940). Secretary for Scotland, 1940–1. Minister of Health, 1941–3. Chancellor of the Duchy of Lancaster, 1943–5. Minister of Aircraft Production, 1945. CH, 1945.

[2] Bertrand Arthur William Russell, 1872–1970. Educated at Trinity College, Cambridge, 1893; Fellow, 1895–1916, 1919–20, 1944–9. Founder, Beacon Hill School, 1927. 3rd Earl Russell, 1931. Lecturer, London School of Economics, 1937. OM, 1949. Nobel Prize in Literature, 1950.

Winston S. Churchill: article
(Daily Telegraph)

30 December 1946

ONE WAY TO STOP A NEW WAR

Eight years have passed since I wrote about 'The United States of Europe',[1] and several things have happened meanwhile. I described the unhappy and dangerous plight of the Continent, torn by ancient quarrels, stirred by modern Nationalism, divided and hampered by a maze of tariff-walls, overshadowed by the Hitler–Mussolini Axis, exhausted and drained by one Great War, and oppressed by fear of another. Now here tonight in my same old room at Chartwell I am writing on the same subject, and I plead the same cause.

Eight years ago I thought the argument was unanswerable. But it proved utterly vain. Within eighteen months Europe was plunged in a war more awful in its devastation than any ever waged by man, and – more than that – once more the European Quarrel dragged America from its isolation, once more it involved the whole world. It almost seems an evil omen.

Certainly the scene we survey in the autumn of 1946 bears many uncomfortable resemblances to that of 1938. Indeed, in some respects, it is even darker. The peoples of Europe have fallen immeasurably deeper into the pit of misery and confusion. Many of their cities are in ruins. Millions of their homes have been destroyed. They have torn each other into pieces with more ferocity on a larger scale and with more deadly weapons than ever before.

But have they found stable and lasting peace? Is the brotherhood of mankind any nearer? Has the Reign of Law returned? Alas, although the resources and vitality of nearly all the European countries are woefully diminished, many of their old hatreds burn on with undying flame. Skeletons with gleaming eyes and poisoned javelins glare at each other across the ashes and rubble-heaps of what was once the august Roman Empire and later a Christian civilisation.

Is there never to be an end? Is there no salvation here below? Are we to sink through gradations of infinite suffering to primordial levels:

> A discord. Dragons of the prime,
> That tare each other in the slime;[2]

or can we avoid our doom?

There is the old story of the Spanish prisoner pining for years in his dungeon and planning to escape. One day he pushes the door. It is open, it has always been open. He walks out free. Something like this opportunity lies

---

[1] Article published in *Saturday Evening Post* and *News of the World* 9 May 1938 under the heading 'Why Not "The United States of Europe"?'.
[2] The quotation is from *In Memoriam: A.H.H.* by Alfred Tennyson (1850).

before the peoples of Europe today. Will they grasp it? Will they be allowed to grasp it? Will they have time?

The heart of an old man goes out to all these poor ordinary folk. How good, how kindly they are; how helpful and generous to one another in their village life; how capable of ceaseless progress and improvement. And here on their cottage thresholds stand Science, Invention, Organisation, Knowledge – aye, and Power, too. Not only are they offered the simple joys which, or the hopes of which, have cheered the pilgrimage of Man – food, warmth, courtship, love, marriage, a home, little children playing by the fire, the fair fruits of honest toil, rest and serenity when life's work is done. They are offered far more; a wider, more agreeable form of existence, conscious and responsible citizenship, the career open to talent, a richer and more varied dietary, fun, amusements, happy, genial intercourse with one another.

President Roosevelt declared the Four Freedoms. Of these the chief is 'Freedom from fear'. This does not mean only fear of war or fear of the foreign invader. Even more poignant is the fear of the policeman's knock; the intrusion upon the humble dwelling; the breadwinner, the son, the faithful friend, marched away into the night with no redress, no *Habeas Corpus*, no trial by jury, no rights of man, no justice from the State.

Such are the conditions which prevail today over the greater part of Europe. A horrible retrogression! Back to the Dark Ages, without their chivalry, without their faith.

Yet all this could be ended at a single stroke. Two or three hundred millions of people in Europe have only got to wake up one morning and resolve to be happy and free by becoming one family of nations, banded together from the Atlantic to the Black Sea for mutual aid and protection. One spasm of resolve! One single gesture! The prison doors clang open. Out walk, or totter, the captives into the sunshine of a joyous world.

I do not conceal from the reader that an act of the sublime is required. It is a very simple act, not even a forward bound. Just stand erect, but all together.

I selected France as the land from which the signal should come; first because it involved a finer self-conquest for the French than for any other great people to take the lead, and secondly because in no other way can France regain her true glory and place in the world. Such are conditions which comprise the elements of the sublime. It is now for France to take the Germans by the hand and lead them back into the brotherhood of man and the family of nations.

I am encouraged by a famous voice from the past. At the National French Assembly in Bordeaux on 1 March 1871, while the French Republic and Germany were still at war, Victor Hugo said:

> And no one will hear France cry, 'It is my turn, am I your enemy? No! I am your sister. I have retaken all, and I give it all back on one condition: that is that we shall be but one united people, but one single family, but

one Republic. I will demolish my fortresses. You will demolish yours. My vengeance, it is fraternity. No more frontiers, the Rhine for all! Let us be the same Republic. Let us have the United States of Europe, let us have Continental federation, let us have European freedom!'

It was difficult then. The prophetic message was rejected. The poet's inspiration died. Events took a different course. Germany flaunted the laurels of victory and France for more than forty years brooded upon revenge. We had two world wars, in the first of which France was bled white, and in the second laid low and conquered; and in both of which Europe and the whole world were convulsed and shattered. And now they talk of a third world war to finish off what is left of our civilisation and humanity.

The only worthwhile prize of victory is the power to forgive and to guide; and this is the prize which glitters and shines before the French people at this solemn moment in their long history.

The Cause or Question points itself at the United States in a remarkable manner. Isolationism is no more. The Atlantic Ocean is no longer a shield. The Pilgrim Fathers could now cross it in a day; but the troubles from which they fled and the tyrannies against which they revolted can follow just as quick. Not content with tearing their own continent into shreds, the quarrels and hatreds of Europe have now laid their claws upon the New World.

Americans should realise that they must seek the root of these evils. Prevention is better than cure. Why be ravaged every twenty-five years with pestilences bred in Europe? Would it not be reasonable prudence to use the power which has come to the New World to sterilise the infection-centres of the Old? Prolonged and careful study of Europe and courageous, tireless action to prevent the recurrence of war-pestilence would not seem to be a prime interest of every thoughtful American, enjoined upon him by prudence as well as virtue.

The peace and safety of the United States of America requires the institution of a United States of Europe. It is better to face, in an orderly fashion and on high, the remote potential antagonism of two continental groupings than to be dragged for certain into one toil and horror after another by chronic degeneration and the blind convulsions of chance.

The United Nations Organisation is the hope of mankind and the expression in American minds of these ideas and arguments. Regional organisms or federations under the supreme world organisation are foreseen and encouraged in the San Francisco Charter. It is agreed that they are not detrimental to the main structure. It has now to be realised as a fundamental practical truth that without them the central structure cannot stand or function.

Let me use the military modes and terminology with which our sad experience has made us only too familiar. When a great army is formed by a nation or band of allies it has its General Headquarters: who would pretend, with our experience, that any General Headquarters could deal directly with a mob of brigades and divisions, each headed by their own colourful commander, each vaunting the prowess of their own recruiting district or home State, each pleading the particular stresses of their own task and station?

After what we have been through everyone knows that within the Army there must be Groups of Armies and also Army Corps, all with their properly integrated staffs and authority, and that by these alone can the will of the Supreme Command be made effective upon the course of events. Otherwise the great enterprises of war could not be conducted with the slightest hope of success.

In the same way and for the same reasons, unless the intermediate organisms are provided, the World Peace Organisation will either clatter down in ruin or evaporate in empty words. What could be more vain and futile than a crowd of little States, with a few big ones pushing about among them, all chattering about world unity, all working for their separate interests, and all trying to sum up their decisions by votes.

In fact, however, great progress has been made to the creation of these mighty, secondary organisms, and the main pillars of the world-structure are already towering up as realities before our eyes.

There is the United States of America within its larger association of the Western Hemisphere. There is the Soviet Union, with its Slavonic fraternities. There is the British Empire and Commonwealth of Nations spread all over the globe and united by sentimental loyalties which flow to the flame and emerge stronger every time the furnace becomes incandescent.

We must undoubtedly contemplate an Asiatic grouping cherishing the spirit of Asia. The enormous populations of the Far Eastern world, now plunged in defeat or internal confusion, will some day find a coherent expression.

Why then should there not be a place, and perhaps the first place – if she can win it by her merits – for Europe, the Mother Continent and fountain source not only of the woes but of most of the glories of modern civilisation?

Here is an aspect which must be observed. Not only do three at least of the pillars of the world Peace Temple stand forth in all their massive strength. But they are already woven together by many ties of affinity, custom and interest.

The United States of America, as the most powerful country in the modern age, is the guardian of the Western Hemisphere and has connections which are growing everywhere. The vast mass of Soviet Russia in Europe and Asia, with its Slavonic attachments, can only give an improved life to its many peoples through the vivifying but no doubt disturbing tonic of worldwide trade and contracts.

The British nation, lying in the centre of so many healthy and beneficent networks, is not only the heart of the British Empire and Commonwealth of Nations, and an equal partner in the English-speaking world, but it is also a part of Europe and intimately and inseparably mingled with its fortunes. All this interlacement strengthens the foundations and binds together the World Temple.

Winston S. Churchill: article
(*Daily Telegraph*)

31 December 1946

THE GRAND DESIGN OF A UNITED EUROPE

Let me now set forth tersely what it is we have to do. All the people living in the continent called Europe have to learn to call themselves Europeans, and act as such so far as they have political power, influence or freedom. If we cannot get all countries, we must get all we can; and there may be many. Once the conception of being European becomes dominant among those concerned, a whole series of positive and practical steps will be open.

First there must be a Council of Europe. This Council must look always forward rather than back. Secondly it must seek the most free and fertile trade between all its members, and must work steadily for the abolition or at least the diminution of tariff and customs barriers between member-States of the Council on the broad principle of the American Inter-State Commerce Act. Thirdly, it must strive for economic harmony as a stepping-stone for economic unity.

Next, the Council of Europe must reach out towards some common form of defence which will preserve order among and give mutual security to its members, and enable Europe to take an effective part in the decisions of the Supreme United Nations Organisation.

Inseparably woven with this is the approach to a uniform currency. As we have to build from chaos this can only be achieved by stages. Luckily coins have two sides, so that one can bear the national and the other the European superscription. Postage stamps, passports, trading facilities, European social reunions for cultural, fraternal and philanthropic objects will all flow out naturally along the main channel soon to be opened.

If at the beginning the Governments of the various countries involved are not able to take official action, strong societies and organisations must be formed of a private and popular character. There is no reason to suppose that existing Governments, although they may not immediately feel able to take the initiative, will be adverse.

Mr Attlee has declared, 'Europe must federate or perish', and he does not readily change his opinions. Prominent names could be cited of men in office and power in many countries in and out of Europe who hold the same view. General Smuts, the South African soldier-statesman-philosopher, has proclaimed himself a champion of the idea. Belgium, Holland and Luxembourg have already begun naturally and unostentatiously to put it into practice.

There is much talk of a 'Western bloc'; but that by itself is too narrow a scheme. Nothing less than Europe and Europeanism will generate the vital force to survive. It may well be that everybody cannot generate the vital force to survive. It may well be that everybody cannot join the club at once. The beginning must be made. The nucleus must be formed in relation to the structure as a whole, so that others can join easily as soon as they feel inclined or feel able. The ideal is so commanding that it can afford a gradual realisation.

But we are told this conception of a free reviving, regenerated Europe is anti-Russian or, to speak more exactly, anti-Soviet in its character, intention and effect.

This is not true. The many peoples of Russia and Asia who are comprised in the Union of Socialist Soviet Republics, and who occupy one-sixth of the land surface of the globe, have nothing to fear and much to gain from the creation of a United States of Europe, more especially as both these groupings must be comprised within the World Organisation and be faithful to its decisions.

We are also told that International Communism will be hostile; and it may well be that the devotees of this anti-God religion in every country will be enjoined to raise their voices in favour of keeping Europe divided, helpless, impoverished and starving. Such conditions, they may argue cogently, are an essential preliminary to world Communist domination. All this may be so.

But Europe and the great world around it must find their own way through their troubles and perplexity. They must not let themselves be deterred from what is right and beneficial for their own policy and interests by any arbitrary veto.

We must have the four great entities and contributors to world Government all playing their part and bearing their proper weight in the World Organisation. We must hope, indeed, that China will make a fifth. No one party or section of mankind must bar the grand design of a United Europe. It must roll forward, and within its proper limits it will roll forward, righteous and strong.

On my return from Zurich I read in an English newspaper, the *Southern Daily Echo*, the following commentary on what I had said:

> 'Geographers point out that the Continent of Europe is really the peninsula of the Asiatic land mass. The real demarcation between Europe and Asia is no chain of mountains, no natural frontier, but a system of beliefs and ideas which we call Western Civilisation.
>
> In the rich pattern of this culture there are many strands: the Hebrew belief in God; the Christian message of compassion and redemption; the Greek love of truth, beauty and goodness; the Roman genius for law. Europe is a spiritual conception, but if men cease to hold that conception in their minds, cease to feel its worth in their hearts, it will die.'

These sentiments are so beautiful, and their expression so fine an example of English prose, that I venture to quote them with due acknowledgements, and I trust they may resound far and wide and waken their response in every generous heart. Well may it be said, 'Let Europe arise.'

It seems a shocking thing to say that the atomic bomb in the guardianship of the United States is the main safeguard of humanity against a third world war. In the twentieth century of the Christian era, with all the march of science and the spread of knowledge, with all the hideous experiences through which we have passed, can it be that only this dread super-sanction stands between us and further measureless misery and slaughter? Those of us who were born in the broad liberalism of the nineteenth century recoil from such a mockery of all our dreams, of all our defined conceptions.

Nevertheless, I believe that the fact is true. Greater divergencies have opened among men than those of the religious wars of the Reformation, or of the political and social conflicts of the French Revolution, or of the power-struggle just concluded with Hitler's Germany. The schism between Communism on the one hand and Christian ethics and Western Civilisation on the other is the most deadly, far-reaching and rending that the human race has known.

Behind Communism lies the military power of Soviet Russia, which, so far as the continent of Europe is concerned, is at the present time overwhelming. This power is in the firm grasp of thirteen or fourteen extremely able men in the Kremlin. We cannot measure the internal pressure to which they are subjected, on the morrow of Russia's sufferings and sacrifices, nor can we tell how far they may be swayed by crude ambitions of world-conquest.

We are confronted at once by a Theme and a Sword. If the issues now afoot in the world were capable of being decided by the strength of ground armies, the outlook for the Western democracies and for modern civilisation would be indeed forlorn.

The atomic bomb is the new balancing factor. Everyone knows it will not be used except in self-defence against mortal injury and provocation. No one can be sure whether it is a final and decisive method of war. Air power, however manifested and armed, may decide a war; but alone it cannot hold a front on land. Still, of all the deterrents against war now acting upon the minds of men, nothing is comparable to this frightful agency of indiscriminate destruction.

While this supreme weapon rests in the hands of the United States alone, it is probable, though we cannot say it is certain, that a breathing-space will be accorded to the world. We cannot tell how long this breathing-space will last. Let us make sure that it is not cast away.

If, in this interval, we can revive the life and unity of Europe and Christendom, and with this new reinforcement build high and commanding a world structure of peace which no one dare challenge, the most awful crisis of history will have passed away and the high road of the future will again become open.

There is no reason why all questions between State socialism and individual enterprise should not be settled gradually and peacefully by the normal workings of democratic and parliamentary machinery. The pyramid of society may become more solid and stable when its top is melted down to broaden its base. If during the next five years we can build a world structure of irresistible force and inviolable authority, there are no limits to the blessings which all men may enjoy and share.

For this purpose few things are more important and potentially decisive than that Europe should cease to be a volcano of hatred and strife and should instead become one of those broad upland regions upon which the joy, the peace and glory of millions may repose.[1]

---

[1] With one exception, this is substantially the same text as the second part of Churchill's 'Highroad of the Future' article for *Collier's*, 4 Jan. 1947. See Churchill to Chenery, 6 Oct. 1946, reproduced above (p. 483). The exception is the penultimate paragraph, in which the last sentence in *Collier's* reads: 'If during the next five years we can build a world structure of irresistible force and inviolable authority <u>for the purpose of ensuring peace</u>, there are no limits to the blessings which all men may enjoy and share.'

January
1947

Jo Sturdee to Major George Furness[1]
(Churchill papers, 2/55)

4 January 1947

Dear Sir,

I am desired by Mr Churchill to thank you for your letter of January 1, in which you inform him that you will be defence counsel for Mamoru Shigemitsu in the International Military Tribunal for the Far East sitting in Tokyo.

Mr Churchill asks me to say that he does not feel able to intervene in this matter. He thinks you may however be interested to note what he said in a speech he made to the House of Commons in Secret Session on June 25, 1941.[2] You will find this reference on page 44 of the book, *Secret Session Speeches*, by Mr Churchill, a copy of which I sent you yesterday.

Winston S. Churchill to Winston Churchill
(Churchill papers, 1/42)

5 January 1947

Darling Winston,

Thank you for your charming card.

I now send you a box of very lovely paints, and some brushes. These paints must only be squeezed out a drop at a time, not more than the size of a pea. You can mix them with water freely, using plenty of water; but

---

[1] George Abbot Furness, 1896–1985. Born in Elizabeth, NJ. Educated at Harvard University and Harvard Law School. Enlisted, US Army, 1918. Served with US Army Air Corps during WWII. Moved to Japan in 1946 as one of the lawyers from the West to defend Japanese war criminals. Served as counsel for Mamoru Shigemitsu and Adm. Soemu Toyoda. While living in Japan, he acted in many Japanese movies, usually as a minor character from the West.
[2] Reproduced in *The Churchill Documents*, vol. 16, *The Ever-Widening War, 1941*, pp. 857–8.

they dry and become no good any more in about half an hour. You may use about three times as much of the white tubes; that is to say a blob about equal to three peas, each time you paint a picture.

Do not waste these paints for they are very hard to get and come from abroad.

After you have tried them by yourself I hope you will come down one afternoon so that I can show you myself how to use them.

With much love,
Your affectionate grandfather

PS. You do not need to squeeze out all the colours at once, only two or three at a time as you need them.

Winston S. Churchill to Lord Camrose
(Churchill papers, 4/57)

8 January 1947

My dear Lord Camrose,

I am willing to write my Memoirs of The World War if The Daily Telegraph Limited can arrange for me to have access to and full use of the documents to which you refer. These, as you know, I placed in trust some time ago in order that they might be effectually safeguarded in the public interest in the event of my death.

You will appreciate the magnitude of such a task at my age and with my various commitments but I offer the following proposals:

(a) The work will comprise five volumes of some 150,000 to 200,000 words each.

(b) Delivery of the volumes will be spread over approximately four years from now.

(c) I should receive £175,000 (subject to your stipulations as to taxation as to which I agree) for writing these Memoirs to be paid by instalments on delivery of the volumes with the proviso that I would ask for £15,000 as an advance payment generally on account of the total consideration which I am to receive and which last mentioned sum would be repayable by me or my personal representative in the event of my not completing the contract.

The terms of my contract must necessarily be reduced to writing by our respective Solicitors but pray let me know if, subject to this, you agree my proposals in principle.

Winston S. Churchill to George Heaton Nicholls[1]
(Churchill papers, 4/7)

8 January 1947

My dear High Commissioner,

At my suggestion Mr and Mrs DeWitt Wallace, the proprietors of *Reader's Digest*, propose to send Field Marshal Smuts a copy of their monthly publication as long as he lives. This arose out of a conversation I had with him.

I shall be much obliged if you will let him know beforehand so that, when the copy arrives, he may be reminded of our talk and make the necessary acknowledgment.

Eleven millions of these 'Digests' are sold in the United States and it is calculated that forty million people read it. It is also translated into fourteen foreign languages and represents a pretty high-grade focus of thought upon our extremely muddled human affairs.

Dorothy Bodycote[2] to Jo Sturdee
(Churchill papers, 4/57)

9 January 1947

Dear Private Secretary,

Lord Camrose would like you to inform interested parties that he has now definitely closed with Sir Keith Murdoch[3] for a sum of £20,000 in payment of the Australian and New Zealand general rights.

He has also closed with the Argus Newspapers in South Africa for the sum of £10,500, which is £2,500 more than appeared in the list supplied to Mr Moir.[4]

Mr Emery Reves' offer of £45,000 for the Foreign book[5] and serial rights has been confirmed in writing.

---

[1] George Heaton Nicholls, 1876–1959. Married, 1912, Ruby Hitchins. Elected to Union Parliament for Zululand, 1920. Representative of opposition party for South African delegation at Second Round Table Conference between the Governments of India and South Africa, Cape Town, 1933. Member, Indian Colonisation Enquiry Committee (Young Committee), 1933. Senator, 1939, 1948–59. Administrator, Natal, 1942–4. High Commissioner, Union of South Africa in London, 1944–7. Delegate, UN Assembly, New York. PC, 1948.

[2] Secretary to Lord Camrose.

[3] Keith Arthur Murdoch, 1886–1952. Journalist. Born in Melbourne, Australia. Went to Gallipoli as War Correspondent, 1915. War Correspondent with the Australian forces, and Manager of the United Cable Service, 1915–18. Knighted, 1933. Director-General of Information, Commonwealth of Australia, 1939–40. Owner of several Australian newspapers.

[4] Anthony Forbes Moir, 1903–67. Solicitor and legal adviser for Winston Churchill. Married, 1939, Bettine Ethel Read Hardy. Senior Partner, Fladgate & Co., solicitors, ?–1957; Stephenson Harwood & Tatham, solicitors, 1958–67.

[5] Foreign-language editions.

Winston S. Churchill to Lord Woolton
(Churchill papers, 2/53)

12 January 1947
Private

My dear Woolton,

Many thanks for your minute, enclosing the letter from Colonel Blair[1] of January 8. I am sure it would be better not to run a candidate against Sir Archibald Sinclair in Caithness on this occasion and not to attempt to extract him from any such pledge as is indicated by Colonel Blair. I may add that I have received several letters from MPs and have been visited by Captain Peter Thorneycroft, all strongly deprecating our opposing Sinclair at this bye-election.

There is no need to hurry in bringing the representatives of the Caithness Association to London and the meeting can take place on the 15th without them as you suggest. I should be glad however if you would show my letter to Sir Arthur Young[2] and Colonel Blair beforehand.

Later.

Since writing this I have received your further letter of January 9. It does not affect my opinion but it is evident that first we must meet together as you propose on the 15th and in addition to that, we shall have to put the matter to the Shadow Cabinet, who must finally decide on a point of this kind.

Winston S. Churchill to Hugh Dalton
(Churchill papers, 2/54)

13 January 1947

My dear Chancellor of the Exchequer,

I have received your letter of January 8. I am of the opinion that what you propose[3] is right and I shall support it myself, and I have little doubt this line will be followed by my friends.

The intention of Parliament in according the Prime Minister a salary of £10,000 was not primarily concerned with his personal convenience, but to

---

[1] Patrick James Blair, 1891–1972. Educated at Edinburgh Academy and Balliol College, Oxford. Lt-Col., 1st Scottish Horse Bde, 1918; 9th Royal Scots, 1920–7. DSO, 1919. Political Secretary to Scotland Unionist Party Chairman, 1922–60. Col., Territorial Army, 1924. CBE, 1943; KBE, 1958. Hon. Col., 7th/9th Royal Scots, 1945–55.

[2] Arthur Stewart Leslie Young, 1889–1950. Served with Scottish Rifles in WWI. MP (Cons.) for Partick, 1935–50. Scottish Unionist Whip, 1941. Lord Commissioner of the Treasury, 1942–4. Vice-Chamberlain of HM Household, 1944–5. Bt, 1945.

[3] Concerning the PM's expenses in entertainment of domestic and international visitors. The Speaker was allowed to treat £4,000 of his £10,000 salary as non-taxable income in recognition of these expenses. Dalton's proposal was that the PM should be 'on the same footing as the Speaker', i.e. should be allowed the same £4,000 as non-taxable income.

enable him to discharge the public duties indispensable to his office and to his residence at Number 10. The principle must be affirmed in our public life that all persons called upon to hold the office of Prime Minister, and possibly some other offices, should be able to discharge their duties with dignity and efficiency irrespective of any private means that they possess.

I certainly think the matter should be announced to Parliament and as, at my age, I may fairly be considered a disinterested witness, I shall certainly speak in this sense.

Winston S. Churchill to Lieutenant-General Sir Frederick Browning[1]
(Churchill papers, 2/58)

14 January 1947
Private

My dear Browning,

I am very sorry to receive your letter (100/Inf/5288 (MS3T)) of January 10, which completely obliterates the names of all the famous Calvary Regiments (everyone of which is presumably modernised with the latest armoured fighting vehicles) and merges them in the Royal Armoured Corps with many other units which have no history before the last war. The tendency to eliminate tradition and esprit de corps is one most harmful to the Army especially in its voluntary aspect. I shall feel it my duty to raise this, among other matters, when the Army Estimates are presented, and I shall be obliged, therefore, if you would let the Secretary of State know this. I cannot see why it is necessary to treat the Royal Scots Greys as an unmentionable unit or the 12th Lancers who had such a wonderful record. The whole policy is directly contrary to the promises I received from the late Secretary of State for War, promises which it would cost nothing in money to fulfil. I do not think political prejudices ought to hamper the efficiency of the Service, nor ought we to be forced into prolongation or extension of conscription by the needless diminution of the stimuli to voluntary recruitment.[2]

Perhaps you will also mention to the Secretary of State the fact that I shall be putting down a question to the Prime Minister about the numbers and cost of the Garrison now maintained in Palestine, as a Private Notice Question the week after Parliament reassembles.

Thank you also for your letter about the reduction of the 4th Queen's Own Hussars to cadre strength. I will write to you upon this point later.

[1] Frederick Browning, 1896–1965. Educated at Eton College and RMC, Sandhurst. Entered Army, 1915. GOC, 1st Airborne Div., 1941–3. Maj.-Gen., Airborne Forces, 1943. Cdr, Airborne Troops, 1943. Lt-Gen. 1943. CB, 1943. CoS to SACSEA, 1944–6. KBE, 1946. Military Secretary, War Office, 1946–8. KCVO, 1953. GCVO, 1959.

[2] On Jan. 23, Churchill sent an additional sentence to be inserted here: 'I am of course in favour of the continuance of compulsory national service for the Armed Forces.'

Field Marshal Lord Montgomery to Winston S. Churchill
(Churchill papers, 2/143)[1]

21 January 1947

Dear Mr Churchill,
  When in Moscow, Stalin asked if I ever saw you and made enquiries as to your health. I said you were in first class form.
  He then said that you disagreed with him now on political matters, but he would always have the happiest memories of his work with you as the great war leader of Britain; he added that he had the greatest respect and admiration for what you had done during the war years.
  I told him that I would tell you of what he had said; he said he would be delighted if I would do so.
  I hope you keep well.
  I much regret I cannot attend Mary's wedding; I leave for Switzerland on 3 Feb for a much-needed holiday.

General Sir Hastings Ismay to Winston S. Churchill
(Churchill papers, 2/144)

22 January 1947

My dear Mr Churchill,
  I send you herewith my recollection of the events leading up to the appointment of General Eisenhower as Supreme Commander of 'Overlord'.
  I am as sure as I can be that our refusal to unify the 'Overlord' and Mediterranean Commands and put them under one Supreme Commander was the reason that led the President to give up the idea of Marshall and substitute Eisenhower.

Winston S. Churchill to Field Marshal Lord Montgomery
(Churchill papers, 2/143)

23 January 1947

My dear Monty,
  Thank you very much indeed for the message which you have brought me from Stalin. I shall venture to write to him in a similar spirit.
  I hope I may see you before you leave for Switzerland on February 3. Mary always remembers the kindness and distinction with which you treated her when her Battery was under your Command.

---
[1] This letter was handwritten.

John Henderson[1] to Elizabeth Gilliatt
(*Churchill papers, 2/144*)

23 January 1947

Dear Miss Gilliatt,

Mr Churchill may already be aware that the appointment of General Marshall to the State Department has revived a rumour in the United States that if it had not been for Mr Churchill's antagonism General Marshall would have been appointed Commander of the European Invasion Forces. Lord Inverchapel[2] has reported that this rumour, which could easily have an exacerbating effect on day to day Anglo-American relations, is so widely believed that he considers that no unilateral repudiation by His Majesty's Government, any more than a mere undocumented statement by General Marshall at a press conference, would kill it successfully.

We are now proposing to tell Lord Inverchapel that it was Mr Churchill himself, in view of the great preponderance of American troops to be employed in the French campaign, who took the initiative of proposing to President Roosevelt that an American Commander, and not General Brooke as had been previously agreed, should have command of the European Invasion Forces; that from the summer of 1943 onwards Mr Churchill understood that the President intended to select for this appointment General Marshall in whom Mr Churchill and his staff had the greatest confidence; and that it was only in December 1943 at Cairo that President Roosevelt told Mr Churchill that he could not spare General Marshall and that he proposed to nominate General Eisenhower to the post.

At the same time we are proposing to authorise the Ambassador to suggest to General Marshall that the only really satisfactory way of killing the story once and for all would be for an official statement to be issued from the American side – possibly by the White House. When speaking to General Marshall we feel that Lord Inverchapel might wish to quote the following two extracts from messages addressed by Mr Churchill to President Roosevelt and General Marshall.

(1) Message to President Roosevelt of the 23rd October, 1943.

'I repeat I have the greatest confidence in General Marshall and that if he

---

[1] John Nicholas Henderson, 1919–2009. Educated at Stowe School and Hertford College, Oxford. Minister of State's Office, Cairo, 1942–3. Asst Private Secretary to Foreign Secretary, 1944–7; Private Secretary, 1963–5. Staff, HM Embassy, Washington DC, 1947–9; Athens, 1949–50; Vienna, 1953–6; Santiago, 1956–9. Permanent Under-Secretary's Dept, FO, 1950–3, 1962–3. Married, 1951, Mary Xenia Cawadias Barber. Northern Dept, FO, 1959–62; Head, 1963. CMG, 1965. Minister in Madrid, 1965–9. Ambassador to Poland, 1969–72; to West Germany, 1972–5; to France, 1975–9; to US, 1979–82. KCMG, 1972. GCMG, 1977. Member, BBC General Advisory Council, 1983–7. Lord Warden of the Stannaries, Keeper of the Privy Seal of Duke of Cornwall, and member of Prince's Council, 1985–90. KCVO, 1991.

[2] British Ambassador to the US; formerly Sir Archibald Clark Kerr.

is in charge of "Overlord" we British will aid him with every scrap of life and strength we have.'

(2) Message to General Marshall of the 24th October, 1943.

'I do hope to hear of your appointment (to command "Overlord") soon. You know I will back you through thick and thin and make your path here smooth.'

We should, of course, not wish the Ambassador to use these extracts, which might subsequently be published in an official United States statement, without our having received Mr Churchill's prior agreement to this course. Would you please therefore let us know Mr Churchill's views in the matter.

Winston S. Churchill to Léon Blum
(Churchill papers, 2/18)

24 January 1947

My dear Monsieur Blum

You will perhaps have heard of the steps we have taken and the Group we have formed in order to promote the idea of United Europe. I send you enclosed our statement of aims and a list of the members of the Provisional Launching Group. You will see that this is comprised of all political Parties and men and women otherwise deeply opposed in politics. I greatly hope that a French Group may be formed on parallel lines, so that Britain and France can keep in touch with each other on the further steps that may be taken. I was delighted to hear that there was a possibility of your associating yourself with such a French movement. I earnestly hope this is true, since nothing could be more advantageous to this great cause than that you should be associated with it.

A member of our Committee, Commander King-Hall,[1] who sat as an Independent in the late Parliament and is a man of singular ability, is going over to Paris on Monday and will be there for two or three days. He will be able to explain to you in greater detail what we are doing, and give you any further information you may require.

It was a great pleasure to me to see you the other day, and I heartily congratulate you on the brilliant success of your short administration, which tends to prove that the day of the septuagenarians is not past.

---

[1] William Stephen Richard King-Hall, 1893–1966. On active service, RN, 1914–18. Admiralty Naval Staff, 1919–20. China Sqn, 1921–3. Intelligence Officer, Mediterranean Fleet, 1925–6; Atlantic Fleet, 1927–8. Admiralty War Staff, 1928–9. Founded K. H. News Letter Service, 1936. MP (Ind.) for Ormskirk Div. of Lancashire, 1939–44. Ministry of Aircraft Production, 1940–2. Ministry of Fuel and Power, 1943–5. Founded Hansard Society for Parliamentary Government, 1944; Chairman of Council, 1944–62. Radio and television commentator on public events. Author of more than 20 historical and political books. Knighted, 1954. Baron (Life Peer), 1966.

Elizabeth Gilliatt to John Henderson
(*Churchill papers, 2/144*)

24 January 1947

Dear Mr Henderson,

Thank you for your letter of yesterday, which Mr Churchill has now seen.

Mr Churchill has been thinking about this matter himself on account of reports that have reached him of the tales being told in the United States. He does not consider it is quite so simple as would appear from your letter. He asked General Ismay to let him have a full account of the facts, and this I now send you with the request that you will let us have it back as soon as you have read it and identified the documents cited. It is possible that Mr Churchill may himself make a statement upon the subject.

Meanwhile he would be glad to see the text in draft of any communication which the Foreign Office propose to send to Lord Inverchapel.

The salient facts are that Mr Churchill himself proposed to the President that there should be an American Commander for the cross-Channel operation. He understood from the President that it would certainly be General Marshall, and he cordially welcomed this choice. The appointment of an American Commander for the cross-Channel operation eventually called 'Overlord' was of course contingent upon a British Commander in the Mediterranean, but in November 1943 the President proposed that General Marshall should command both theatres. Mr Churchill could not agree to this for the reasons stated in his telegram to Field-Marshal Dill of 6th November, 1943.[1] The matter then remained in abeyance until the Teheran Conference. At this time Mr Churchill still believed that General Marshall would command 'Overlord' and told Marshal Stalin that he thought this was the President's wish. When they got back to Cairo the whole question of a Supreme Commander for the two theatres was discussed by the Combined Chiefs of Staff and the arguments set out by the British Chiefs of Staff were found overwhelming and were accepted. While these discussions were proceeding on the Staff level Mr Churchill still remained under the impression that General Marshall would command 'Overlord' and that Eisenhower would take his place at Washington; and that a British Commander would be nominated by him (Mr Churchill) for the Mediterranean. However, a few days before they left Cairo the President told him that he could not spare Marshall for 'Overlord' and proposed Eisenhower. Mr Churchill immediately accepted this suggestion, having complete confidence in the military attainments of both these officers. It was then his idea that General Alexander should command the Mediterranean and this was quite agreeable to the President. However, on further consideration of the matter at a later date, he felt that General

[1] T.1899/3, dated 8 Nov. 1943, reproduced in *The Churchill Documents*, vol. 19, *Fateful Questions, September 1943–April 1944*, pp. 829–30.

Alexander should command directly the armies fighting in Italy, and that the Supreme Command of the Mediterranean should go to General Wilson. In all these matters Mr Churchill was in full accord with the British Chiefs of Staff and of course enjoyed the approval of the War Cabinet.

It is Mr Churchill's personal belief that the British refusal to agree to Marshall being Supreme Commander over both theatres made the President feel he could not part with him at Washington, but Mr Churchill did not realise this at the time, and has no proof of it now.

In the above circumstances Mr Churchill thinks it might be imprudent to rest only on the first part of the story and have the second part brought out by way of rejoinder from the American side. He would be glad to hear from you, and he thinks the Secretary of State ought to be informed.

Leslie Rowan to Winston S. Churchill
(Churchill papers, 2/144)

27 January 1947
Secret

My dear Winston,

The Prime Minister has seen your correspondence with the Foreign Office about the tale being told in the United States regarding your opposition to the appointment of General Marshall and has asked me to send you the enclosed draft telegram which it is proposed to send to Lord Inverchapel. The Prime Minister would be glad to have any comments on this as soon as convenient.

CLEMENT ATTLEE TO LORD INVERCHAPEL

Draft

Your telegram No. 219 (of the 11th January; Mr Churchill's rumoured opposition to General Marshall's appointment as Commander-in-Chief, European Invasion Forces).

Full investigation of the facts shows that this matter is more complicated than at first appeared and it would be difficult to issue a statement which would remove all misapprehensions from the mind of the US public.

2. I should therefore be against this course unless you feel that the matter is still of such general public interest that it is essential we should do so. I should be glad of your views.

3. I will send you as soon as possible a full statement of the facts which may be of use to you as confidential background for any discussion of the subject you may wish to have with General Marshall.

4. There is however a possibility that Mr Churchill may himself issue a

statement which would make some corroborative announcement from an official American source desirable. I will keep you informed of developments; but in the meantime you will no doubt wish to tell General Marshall of Mr Churchill's possible statement.

Winston S. Churchill to Leslie Rowan
(*Churchill papers, 2/144*)

29 January 1947
Secret

My dear Leslie,

Thank you for your letter of January 27, and for sending me a copy of the proposed telegram to Lord Inverchapel. I suggest the following amendments to this:

(1) Paragraph 1 should read: '. . . from the mind of the US public. Mr Churchill was strongly in favour of General Marshall's appointment to the Command of "Overlord" and thought this was settled. He was however opposed to a suggestion made in November 1943 that General Marshall should be Supreme Commander both of the Mediterranean and "Overlord". This would have destroyed the whole working of the Combined Chiefs of Staff Committee, and the difficulties were so strongly urged at Cairo by the British Chiefs of Staff that the American Chiefs of Staff were apparently convinced. However, this is probably the cause of the President feeling that he could not spare General Marshall from Washington. General Eisenhower was therefore proposed instead, and was immediately welcomed.'

(2) Paragraph 2, first line. Omit the words 'this course' and amend this paragraph to read: 'I should therefore be against immediate publication without more consideration unless you feel. . . .'

I am also sending you herewith a newspaper cutting which Averell Harriman has sent me, and which I suggest the Prime Minister ought to see. It may be that the matter has died down.

Jo Sturdee to Winston S. Churchill
(*Churchill papers, 2/171*)

29 January 1947

Sir Alan Lascelles telephoned. The King would much like you to go and see him before his departure for South Africa. The time he would like is 12 noon on Wednesday, January 29.[1]

---

[1] Churchill wrote in the margin: 'Yes'.

He explained you may wear any clothes. It would be entirely informal – His Majesty would just like to shake you by the hand before he goes.

Lord Inverchapel to Clement Attlee
(Churchill papers, 2/144)

31 January 1947
Secret
No. 643

Your telegram No. 928.

Mr Harriman's statement (see my telegram No. 351) has certainly done much to convince more responsible opinion here. Public interest is now dormant, and I agree that there is no advantage in immediate publication.

2. Nevertheless I shall be glad to receive the full statement of the facts as soon as possible.

Winston S. Churchill: speech
(Hansard)

31 January 1947   House of Commons

PALESTINE

The House has listened to two speeches from opposite sides of the Chamber, both of which have been characterised by a great deal of knowledge and thought, and distinguished if I may say so, by grace of delivery. Both these Members have evidently acquainted themselves closely with the problems of maintaining law and order in Palestine. We should all agree with my hon. and gallant Friend the Member for Macclesfield (Air-Commodore Harvey) in the tribute which he paid, and which other speakers have also paid, to the behaviour and restraint which our troops have observed. None of us underestimates the prolonged trial, not only physical but moral, to which they have been subjected by this series of detestable outrages.

The hon. Member for Grimsby (Mr Younger)[1] said that it was impossible for us to imitate the mass extermination methods of the Germans. There, again, we would all be in agreement. The idea that general reprisals upon the

[1] Kenneth Gilmour Younger, 1908–76. Son of James Younger, 2nd Viscount Younger of Leckie. Barrister, Inner Temple, 1932. MP (Lab.) for Grimsby, 1945–59. Chairman, UNRRA Committee of the Council on Europe, 1946–7. Parliamentary Under-Secretary, Home Office, 1947–50. Minister of State, 1950–1. PC, 1951. Joint Vice-Chairman, Royal Institute of International Affairs, 1953–5, 1958–9; Director, 1959–71. Chairman, Howard League for Penal Reform, 1960–73; Advisory Council on Penal System, 1966–76; Committee of Inquiry on Privacy, 1970–2; Data Protection Committee, 1976. KBE, 1972.

civil population and vicarious examples would be consonant with our whole outlook upon the world and with our name, reputation and principles, is, of course, one which should never be accepted in any way. We have, therefore, very great difficulties in conducting squalid warfare with terrorists. That is why I would venture to submit to the House that every effort should be made to avoid getting into warfare with terrorists; and if a warfare with terrorists has broken out, every effort should be made – I exclude no reasonable proposal – to bring it to an end.

It is quite certain that what is going on now in Palestine is doing us a great deal of harm in every way. Whatever view is taken by the partisans of the Jews or the partisans of the Arabs it is doing us harm in our reputation all over the world. I deplore very much this struggle that we have got into. I do not think we ought to have got into it. I think it could have been avoided. It could have been avoided if promises had not been made by hon. Members opposite at the Election, on a very wide scale, and if those promises had not been woefully disappointed. I must say that. All my hon. Friends on this side of the House do not agree with the views which I have held for so many years about the Zionist cause. But promises were made far beyond those to which responsible Governments should have committed themselves. What has been the performance? The performance has been a vacuum, a gaping void, a senseless, dumb abyss – nothing.

I remember so well nine or ten months ago my right hon. Friend (Mr Oliver Stanley), now sitting beside me here, talking to all of us in our councils and saying that whatever happens this delay and vacillation shall not go on. But certainly a year has gone by, and we have not advanced one single step. We have not advanced one single step either in making good our pledges to those to whom we have given them, or in reaching some broader solution, or in disembarrassing ourselves of burdens and obligations – burdens which we cannot bear, and obligations which we have shown ourselves unable or unwilling to discharge.

My right hon. Friend dealt particularly with one aspect, and one aspect only. This is a conflict with the terrorists, and no country in the world is less fit for a conflict with terrorists than Great Britain. That is not because of her weakness or cowardice; it is because of her restraint and virtues, and the way of life which we have lived so long in this sheltered island. But, sir, if you should be thrown into a quarrel, you should bear yourself so that the opponent may be aware of it. I deprecate this quarrel, and I will deal a little further with its costs. I deprecate this quarrel very much indeed, and I do not consider it was necessary. Great responsibilities rest on those who have fallen short of their opportunities. Once you are thrown into a quarrel, then in these matters pugnacity and will-power cannot be dispensed with.

It is a terrible thing to be drawn into a quarrel and be cowed out of doing your duty. My right hon. Friend (Mr Oliver Stanley) gave instances. There was another some four or five months ago where death sentences were revoked because of threats. He gave two other instances, one which I will look into in a little more detail because it rather affects the answer the right hon. Gentleman gave me across the Floor the other day. He gave the instance of the caning. I am not discussing the merits or demerits of that punishment or the age at which it should be inflicted, but when sentences of caning are inflicted upon people who have committed offences against the law, to commute and abolish further sentences because one British major and three British sergeants were taken off and flogged is to show all the vices of overcaution and to show that we have not the willpower to face up to this small, fanatical, desperate minority who are committing these outrageous acts.

You may remit a sentence of caning because you do not like that form of punishment, you may remit it because you have a tender heart, you may remit it because some new circumstance has arisen since the magistrate or tribunal gave the decision, but you do not remit it because a British major is fished out of his apartment and three British sergeants are caught and subjected to that punishment, and because you are afraid it may happen to some more. How should we have got through the late struggle if we had allowed our willpower to relax in that way? What would have been said if, when the Germans were bombing London, we had sent them a message, saying, 'If only you will leave off we will guarantee never to touch Berlin.' This is the road of abject defeat, and though I hate this quarrel with the Jews, and I hate their methods of outrage, if you are engaged in the matter, at least bear yourselves like men.

Now, I come to the particular case of Mr Dov Gruner,[1] the man under sentence of death. He was going to hang, I think the next morning, and the terrorists seized a judge off the bench and an officer in the street and took them off, saying they would kill them if the sentence was carried out. And sentence was not carried out. We were immediately told that the prisoner had appealed to the Privy Council. That was not true. It was an excuse, and a procedure vamped up; the Jewish Agency were brought in to make some suggestions and, as far as I can gather from the accounts, he was persuaded only with great difficulty to make an appeal. The fortitude of this man, criminal though he be, must not escape the notice of the House. He made his appeal and now he has withdrawn it. I shall come in a minute to the question of how this works, but what are we to say about altering the course of justice because criminals threaten to add to their crimes?

Let us suppose that there was a murder gang at work in England and that one member was caught and was going to be executed after due process of law. If it were then said by his associates that if sentence were carried out they

---

[1] Dov Bela Grüner, 1912–47. Born to religious Jewish family in Hungary. Studied engineering, Brno. Joined Zionist youth movement Betar, 1938. Emigrated to Palestine, 1940. Enlisted, British Army, 1941. Took part in Irgun arms raids against British army depot in Netanya and Ramat Gan police station, 1946; arrested. Sentenced to death and hanged, 1947.

would kill the Home Secretary, does anybody imagine that a British Minister would not go forward with the process of law? As F. E. Smith said many years ago, he would make his will and do his duty. Does anybody imagine that the path of justice would be turned aside by a hair's breadth because of a threat of that nature? It may be replied that here there were hostages, which made it a harder case, but let me again put it in terms we can all understand. Suppose the friends of this criminal, members of a gang, decide that they will catch some Member of this House, some Minister, or the son or the relative of a Minister, and say 'We have him in hiding; you hang So-and-So, and we will kill him.' Is there a Member in this House who would tolerate the slightest movement of the course of justice from its path, whatever happened, even if it were his own flesh and blood affected? I think not.

Here, we are giving this exhibition on the wide stage of the Middle East, with the United States looking on and following this matter with the closest attention, here we are giving this spectacle and exhibition of the fact that under the threat of the killing of these hostages, the Government are unable to carry forward the course of justice. Was it true – let us look at the details – that the course of justice was not interrupted in any way? I should like to know. I am sorry that we have not had an answer to the question which was put by my right hon. Friend earlier in the day. I am sorry that we have not had an answer from the Minister, because naturally one would be influenced by it. Three days ago the right hon. Gentleman said:

> 'Yesterday afternoon information was received that an application for special leave to appeal to the Privy Council on behalf of Dov Gruner was being lodged. The General Officer Commanding[1] accordingly was obliged to grant a delay.'

Is it a fact, or is it not a fact, that it is the criminal himself who has to make the appeal? If it can be done by some outside agency, it is another matter, but if it is a fact in law – and I cannot pretend to be informed on the matter – that the criminal himself has to initiate the proceedings, then the statement which was made was not in accordance with the facts. I should just like that to be cleared up. The right hon. Gentleman said in reply to a question I asked:

> 'There has been no turning aside from the normal process of justice.'

---

[1] Evelyn Hugh Barker, 1894–1983. Educated at Wellington College and RMC, Sandhurst. Joined KRRC, 1913. Served in European War, 1914–18, in France, Salonica and South Russia (despatches; MC). Capt., 1916. Bde-Maj., 1917. DSO, 1918. GSO III, War Office, 1919. Married, 1923, Violet Eleanor Thornton. Maj., 1930. CO, 8th Infantry Bde, 1931–3; 2nd Bde, KRRC, 1936–8. Lt-Col., 1936. Col., 1938. CO, 10th Infantry Bde, 1938–40. CBE, 1940. Maj.-Gen., 1941. CO, 54th Div., 1941–2; 49th Div., 1943–4; VIII Corps, 1944–6. Lt-Gen., 1944. CB, 1944. KBE, 1945. CO, British Troops in Palestine and Transjordan, 1946. Hon. Col., Loyal Suffolk Hussars, 1946–50. Col. Commandant, KRRC, 1946–56. GOC-in-C, Eastern Command, 1947–50. Gen., 1948. ADC General to the King, 1949–50. KCB, 1950. Hon. Col., Beds Yeomanry, 1951–60; Herts and Beds Yeomanry, 1961–2.

If the Jewish Agency were invoked, and if they brought pressure to bear on this man against his inclinations – for he was ready to be killed for the crimes of which he had been convicted – on what grounds was the statement made that an appeal had been lodged? I should like that to be explained. I do not think that the right hon. Gentleman's answers, according to the facts as now known, correspond to the actual facts. We have seen it stated that he did not want to ask any favours of the British Government. The appeal at that moment – he was going to be executed the next day – could only have been made by some outside body. Is that valid? Then we are told that he gave way two days afterwards, and after the surrender of hostages he said he would appeal, but now we are told that he has withdrawn even this application. You cannot wonder that you will be defeated and humiliated, if you allow threats of maltreatment of hostages to turn you from the administration of law as it would otherwise have been carried out. I should like the right hon. Gentleman to speak upon this subject and give very precise answers. If he would like to give the answers now I will gladly give way to him, but he may prefer to include them in his speech.

This is a lamentable situation. However we may differ, it is one of the most unhappy, unpleasant situations into which we have got, even in these troublous years. Here, we are expending hard-earned money at an enormous rate in Palestine. Everyone knows what our financial difficulties are – how heavy the weight of taxation. We are spending a vast sum of money on this business. For 18 months we have been pouring out our wealth on this unhappy, unfortunate and discreditable business. Then there is the manpower of at least 100,000 men in Palestine, who might well be at home strengthening our defeated industry. What are they doing there? What good are we getting out of it?

We are told that there are a handful of terrorists on one side and 100,000 British troops on the other. How much does it cost? No doubt it is £300 a year per soldier in Palestine. That is apart from what I call a slice of the overheads, which is enormous, of the War Office and other Services. That is £30 million a year. It may be much more – between £30 million and £40 million a year – which is being poured out and which would do much to help to find employment in these islands, or could be allowed to return to fructify in the pockets of the people – to use a phrase which has dropped out of the discussion now, but which was much in vogue at one time in Liberal circles, together with all sorts of antiquated ideas about the laws of supply and demand by people like Adam Smith,[1] John Stuart Mill, and other worthies of that kind. One hundred thousand men is a very definite proportion of our Army for one and a half

---

[1] Adam Smith, 1723–90. Philosopher and economist. Educated at University of Glasgow and Balliol College, Oxford. Lecturer, University of Glasgow, 1748–50; Prof., 1751–64. Chair of Logic, 1751; of Moral Philosophy, 1752. Tutor to Duke of Buccleuch, 1794–7. Commissioner of Customs, 1778. Author of *The Wealth of Nations* (1778).

years. How much longer are they to stay there? And stay for what? In order that on a threat to kill hostages we show ourselves unable to execute a sentence duly pronounced by a competent tribunal. It is not good enough. I never saw anything less recompensive for the efforts now employed than what is going on in Palestine.

Then we are told, 'Oh, well, we must stay there because we have evacuated Egypt, and we need a place for strategic purposes in order to guard the Canal.' I should have thought that was a very wrong idea. At any rate, you have an easement in this respect, because the negotiations already clumsily begun with Egypt have ended in a reversion, as the Prime Minister promised, to the 1936 Treaty, which has another 10 years to run. Let us then stay in the Canal Zone and have no further interest in the strategic aspects of Palestine. At any rate, there is that argument, but I have never thought that we had a strategic interest there. I have always believed that in other ways we should maintain our interests. But then one may say, 'We have to stay there because of our faith and honour.' Good gracious, sir, we cannot say that. We have broken our pledges to the Jews. We have not fulfilled the promise made at the Election, and, having found ourselves incapable of carrying out our policy, we have no right to say, 'Oh, we have to stay there from motives of honour.' Then others say, 'You must stay, because, if you go, Jew and Arab will be at each other's throats.' It is said there will be a civil war. I think it is very likely indeed, but is that a reason why we should stay? We do not propose to stay in India, even if a civil war of gigantic character were to follow our departure. No, that is all brushed aside. We are not going to allow such things to make us stay. We are told to leave the Indians to settle their own affairs by getting a verdict from a body which is unrepresentative and then march out. In Palestine we are told we cannot go, because it would lead to a terrible quarrel between Jews and Arabs and there would be civil war as to who would have the land.

I do not feel myself at all convinced by such arguments. If it be the case, first, that there is no British interest – which I declare with a long experience that there is not – then the responsibility for stopping a civil war in Palestine between Jew and Arab ought to be borne by the United Nations, and not by this poor, overburdened and heavily injured country. I think it is too much to allow this heavy burden to be put on our shoulders costing £30 million a year and keeping 100,000 men from their homes. I see absolutely no reason why we should undergo all this pain, toil, injury and suffering because of this suggested advantage.

I urge the House as I did six months ago before we went for our summer holidays in August – (An Hon. Member: 'There is a Conference going on now.') – I quite agree that there is a Conference going on now, but when that Conference is over, unless it produces a solution which it is in our power to enforce effectively, then in my view we should definitely give notice that, unless the United States come in with us shoulder to shoulder on a fifty-fifty basis on an agreed policy, to take a half-and-half share of the bloodshed, odium, trouble, expense and worry, we will lay our Mandate at the feet of UNO. Whereas, six months ago, I suggested that we should do that in 12 months I suggest now that the period should be shortened to six months. One is more and more worried and one's anxiety deepens and grows as hopes are falsified and the difficulties of the aftermath of war, which I do not underrate, lie still heavily upon us in a divided nation, cutting deeply across our lives and feelings. In these conditions we really cannot go on, in all directions, taking on burdens which use up and drain out the remaining strength of Britain and which are beyond any duty we have undertaken in the international field. I earnestly trust that the Government will, if they have to fight this squalid war, make perfectly certain that the willpower of the British State is not conquered by brigands and bandits and that unless we are to have the aid of the United States, they will at the earliest possible moment, give due notice to divest us of a responsibility which we are failing to discharge and which in the process is covering us with blood and shame.

February 1947

Sir Edward Bridges to Winston S. Churchill
(Churchill papers, 2/146)

3 February 1947

Dear Mr Churchill,
    On Saturday you asked me these three questions:
1. Is there any objection to your ceasing to draw your salary as Leader of the Opposition and drawing in lieu your pension as a former Prime Minister?
2. Can this arrangement be made retrospective to 1st January 1947?
3. If you drop your salary as Leader of Opposition, but decide for the present not to draw your pension as a former Prime Minister, can you at a later date ask that payment of the pension should start?

I have looked into the matter, and the answers to your questions are as follows:
1. There is no objection.
2. The arrangement can be made retrospective to 1st January 1947. (I understand that a cheque for your salary as Leader of the Opposition for the month of January was sent to you on Friday. If you have not cashed it, the simplest plan would be that you should return the cheque for cancellation. If you have cashed it, it would be open to you, if you wish, to send a cheque payable to the Accountant, HM Treasury, of corresponding amount.)
3. If you decide for the present not to draw your pension as a former Prime Minister, you can ask for the pension to be issued at any time in the future. But in that event the presumption would be that the issue of pension would run from a current date.

    I hope that this gives you all the information you require.
    I should add that I have mentioned this matter of the Chancellor of the Exchequer, who authorizes me to say that he agrees with the answers set out above.

Albert Goodwin to Winston S. Churchill
(*Churchill papers, 4/198*)

4 February 1947

Dear Mr Churchill,

I must apologise for the delay in returning your chapters on the 'Blitz' and the Battle of Britain. I must plead, in part excuse, that pressure of work in term-time is extremely heavy and also most of my family have been ill during the past week. I have only then[1] few comments to make on your extremely interesting account of 1940.

Chapter entitled 'Personal Notes on the Blitz'

P. 7. You appear to have omitted the third point which caused you anxiety during the Blitz. I suppose this may be on other sheets which I do not possess.

P. 10 footnote. According to HMSO publication 'Front-line, 1940–1' (p. 118) the incident relating to the old lady occurred on Clydeside after the raid of 14 March, 1941.

Chapter entitled 'Battle of Britain'.

P. 2. First sentence. I think it is clear from the evidence that the Germans did in fact realize the disadvantages of fighting over the Channel for they soon organized an efficient sea-rescue service to pick up their pilots who baled out.

P. 3. You speak of 'ME Nines' and 'ME Tens'. Strictly speaking these should be 'Me. 109' and 'Me. 110' – but I know you have a certain distaste for accuracy in the case of German technical jargon.

It is, however, a mistake to refer to 'Heinkel Threes'. These machines were Heinkel 111's (one hundred and eleven).

Chapter entitled 'The Wizard War'.

P. 2. I wonder whether it would be worth checking your statement that IFF[2] was available before the war. I have a vague recollection that it wasn't available then, but in this I'm sure you are probably correct.

General Ismay's Notes

Bristol Visit. This university ceremony occurred on 12 April, 1941. The recipients of degrees were Winant and R. G. Menzies[3] – not Bruce.

[. . .]

PS. I also wondered whether you might consider adding (in brackets) the

---

[1] these.

[2] IFF: Identification Friend or Foe – radar apparatus (using long-wave frequency) to distinguish British aircraft from enemy aircraft.

[3] Robert Gordon Menzies, 1894–1978. Born in Jeparit, Victoria, Australia. Established himself as leading constitutional lawyer prior to entering Victorian Parliament in 1928. MP (United Aus.) for Kooyong, 1934–66. Attorney-General, 1934–8. Minister for Industry, 1934–9. PM of Australia, 1939–41, 1949–66. Minister for Coordination of Defence, 1939–42. Minister for Information and Minister for Munitions, 1940. Leader of the Opposition, 1943–9. KG, 1963.

explanation of such technical abbreviations as 'CHL':[1] 'GCI'[2] etc. as a help to the General public?

Winston S. Churchill to Lieutenant-General Sir Frederick Browning
(Churchill papers, 2/58)

5 February 1947

My dear Browning,

Thank you very much for your letter of January 31. I am very glad to have your assurance that there is no intention to do away with the individuality of the Cavalry regiments. It seems to me most important that the names should be mentioned in correspondence, and I was glad to hear from Field Marshal Montgomery that the badges on the shoulders would in no circumstances be abolished.

Winston S. Churchill to Josef Stalin
(Churchill papers, 2/57)

6 February 1947

My dear Marshal Stalin,

I was very glad to receive your kind and cordial message from Field Marshal Montgomery.[3] I always look back to our comradeship together in years when all was at stake.

I was also delighted to hear from Montgomery of your good health. Your life is not only precious to your country, which you saved, but for the friendship between Soviet Russia and Great Britain and indeed the whole English-speaking world, on which the future happiness of mankind depends.

---

[1] CHL: Chain Stations Home Service Low Cover: the short-wave frequency version of IFF (see note above), which was more accurate than IFF but had a shorter range.
[2] GCI: Ground-Controlled Interception: air defence tactic which guides interceptor aircrafts to an airborne target (first used in WWI).
[3] See Churchill to Montgomery, 23 Jan. 1947, reproduced above (p. 598).

February 1947

Randolph S. Churchill to Winston S. Churchill
(Churchill papers, 1/42)[1]

7 February 1947   Salt Lake City, Utah

My dearest Papa,

I was greatly touched by your letter of January 29 which reached us here today. I am overjoyed to learn that you have acquired the Chartwell Farm, and am more grateful than I can say that you are leaving it to me in your will. I long ago decided that I would like eventually to live in the country – and to be able to do so so close to Chartwell, with all its happy memories and associations, fills me with gratitude and joy.

I have read all you wrote about my present occupations and future plans with careful attention. I am deeply moved by this latest example of the deep interest you have always taken in my welfare. Though I always try and put a brave face on it to the world, and indeed to you, I must own that I am myself far from pleased with my present situation. At the same time I do not take quite so gloomy a view of it as you do.

As you know the only career in which I am seriously interested is politics. For this career I believe I have aptitude and eligibilities which are granted to few. This may seem a little arrogant, but I know that if I am ultimately proved right in my belief then all the credit will be due to yourself for the upbringing and inspiration you have given me. So far my political life has not been a great success. While fully realizing that I have made my full share of mistakes I believe also that circumstances have not so far been propitious. But I am still young and fortune may yet come my way.

I have of course long regretted that I did not 15 years ago take your excellent advice and adopt a legal career. Sloth – as my besetting sin – was mainly responsible. Also overconfidence, for I always expected that political life would suddenly open up for me. When I came home after the war I was 34. It was too late to think of a career that would require a lengthy preparation. I had a 5 year old son and felt the need to earn my living as best I could. Of course I have been improvident, but on the whole I do not think the last 18 months of my life have been wasted. I have travelled a great deal and established connections – particularly in the US – which will be valuable to me all my life. My column has taught me habits of industry I never knew before. And my lecturing has given me invaluable practice in public speaking. I agree that it would be more satisfactory at my age if I had a fitted career and position in life. But considering all the circumstances (including the war) I still regard those as the formative years of my life. And I think I have learned more in the last year than in the previous ten!

I am the last person to try to pretend that my life has been as successful as

---

[1] This letter was handwritten.

I had hoped it would be by this time. But looking around among my contemporaries I do not feel entirely discouraged. I have long agreed with you that the friendship of England and America is the hope of the future. Against this background I feel I have some credentials that justify a little optimism. There is no Englishman of my age who knows this country as well as I do or who has so many influential American friends. There is no other Englishman of my age who can get his articles regularly printed in the American Press; and there is no one else alive of any age (except yourself) who could have had the amazing oratorical success I have had on this present tour. This last I would say to no one but you, whose name I bear and who has made this possible. But I promise you it is the sober truth.

Of course I know how much you would like me to achieve solid success in your lifetime. But you must notice how improbable that is; even harder for me than for Duncan.

It happens that I have matured (after a premature blossoming) much later than you did. But though I am far from self-satisfied I have confidence I will eventually make my mark and carry on the tradition. It's very hard however for two sensations to carry the same flag simultaneously!

I know how often I have offended you by my clumsy attempts to stand on my own feet, develop my own personality and make my own way in life. I can only hope that I shall later be a worthier and more satisfactory son than I have been in your lifetime.

Please don't expect too much of me now. Believe instead, I beg you, that I have no other ambition than to be ultimately judged a knowable and faithful son. No day passes but that you are constantly in my thoughts and I am grateful that you think so often of me. Give me your confidence and I shall not fail you. Your devoted son.

Winston S. Churchill: speech
(Hansard)

10 February 1947 House of Commons

FUEL AND POWER CRISIS

[. . .]
Presently in this Session we will ask for a further opportunity of discussing the coal problem, but today we have nothing before us except the speech of the Minister of Fuel and Power (Mr Emanuel Shinwell). I listened to this speech with attention and I felt sure he was going to reach a thoroughly complacent conclusion. It reminded me of what I think Burke said of the Governments he was attacking in a former century:

We have a very good Government, but we have a very bad people.

As a subsection of this argument, we were told of all the achievements with which the right hon. Gentleman had adorned his Ministerial career. That part really amounted to saying, 'How Bill Adams did not win the Battle of Waterloo.'[1] I have followed very closely the right hon. Gentleman in war and in peace. He was a bitter critic of any errors we made in the times that are gone, in the years of struggle, but he was infinitely glad whenever we won. In that respect his attitude was differentiated markedly from that of some other colleagues who sit with him now upon that Front Bench. I, for my part, will follow his example, and, though critical, I would like to say how very glad I am whenever I read of an upsurge at the mines as a result of better work and more regular timekeeping by the miners. Whatever one may think about political considerations, one must always rejoice at anything which helps our country in its perils and harsh times. There is very little doubt in my mind that things are going to get worse. I do not mean that this particular emergency is going to lay us low, but the country is going to suffer. It is going to suffer increasingly, and it will learn by its sufferings. We hope and pray that this period of tribulation may be abridged and mitigated as far as possible.

We have a long way to look back in this coal problem, and the right hon. Gentleman, foreseeing perhaps that he might be deprived of his igloo of bad weather by some of his critics below the Gangway, went right back to 1940. [. . .]

I do not – and here I share the feelings which have been expressed on the other side – I do not blame the Government for the weather. Still, there is always a weather danger in the winter in this country, and this is the first winter, as was well said, which has brought us to disaster. Every year from 1940 onwards I had to look forward, until I was relieved of my responsibilities, to this fear of a coal shortage in the winter, and two or three times, with the advice on which I relied, I discounted some of the gloomy prophecies which were made; but this is the first time, in time of peace, when we have come to such a collapse as we have at the present time. Again, I say we need not exaggerate the degree of the disaster, but neither must we underestimate its very serious nature, in view of our financial position and our economic position. It is very serious to our country. This is not a week's loss of production. It will dislocate industry for at least a month one way and another, with serious financial results, and this at a time when the Chancellor of the Exchequer, in his finely chosen language, tells the world that we are living 'on tick'. I say that we are in the presence of an inexcusable breakdown, and it is not to be escaped by a general academic discussion upon the coal position and upon the difficulties of finding sufficient manpower.

---

[1] *How Bill Adams won the Battle of Waterloo* was a comic monologue of 1890, written and performed by George H. Snazelle and based on his imagined conversations with Waterloo veterans in the pub. The story was advertised as 'A yarn founded on fact' and the character Bill Adams is meant to represent the average British soldier.

What I wish to do this evening – and this is the purpose of this specific Debate which we should otherwise have asked for on the Adjournment as relating to a matter of definite and urgent importance – is to focus on the statement of the Minister of Fuel and Power. He has given no explanation of his tactics on Friday. He ought to have seen the danger long ago, and he ought to have provided against it, or at least he ought to have told us what was coming, or what might come. Is that very much to ask? He ought to have had an emergency plan made months ago, for regulating electricity supplies on the basis of the known coal shortage and of the danger which is ever present of a hard winter spell. In war, many misfortunes happened which could not be prevented, and, God knows, we went through some frightful disappointments and miscalculations in the war.

[. . .] I was wishing to get to the point that, if it had not been for that Debate, I do not know how the House would have been informed of these cuts. At the end of the Debate or when it was well advanced, in the last part of his speech, to the astonishment of everybody the right hon. Gentleman made this formidable announcement.

We have been told by the Prime Minister today that we could hardly have been told earlier because the Decision was taken only that morning. Is there to be no foresight? Is there to be no preparation for emergencies of this kind? The decision is taken in the morning, and the Minister, at the end of his speech, tells us of these grave and far-reaching measures of administration, which now have to be forced, not only upon the domestic consumers, but upon all the industries of the country. Why was this decision only taken that morning? I say that there could have been a thoroughly well worked out plan. Was the plan which was announced a good one? Here I cannot pronounce, because I have not access to the resources of the right hon. Gentleman, but was it a good plan for regulating electricity?

Is it workable and useful scheme? Many great electrical supply centres and authorities assure us that it is impossible to enforce this particular plan. And that if enforced it would be ineffectual. I was hoping that the right hon. Gentleman would have dealt with this matter in the course of his speech. I am told – and perhaps the Chancellor will deal with this point if he is to reply – that cutting domestic consumers for three hours and for two hours, will not result in saving much coal because the furnaces have to be kept going all the time. They are very hot when the cut begins, and, in view of the banking up and the accumulated demand which will come upon them the moment the supply is resumed, they cannot be let down, so that the saving of coal is not actually appreciable. Whether this is true or not, I cannot tell, but I should be glad to hear. If foresight had been used it seems to me that a system of staggered use by consumers might have been devised and drilled into them with all the facilities of modern government, and if the Government had convinced us, the Opposition, of the necessity for these measures we would have aided them in the same ways as we have aided them in the National Savings Movement.

[. . .] Apart from the distribution of electricity, if the industry had been consulted earlier this plan of allocation of coal, or whatever was the best plan, would have been operative long before the weather crisis was likely to arise. It would have been operative and not just ready in January – when just as it was going to come into operation down came the shocking blizzard. It could perfectly well have been operated two or three months before, and there would have been no shock such as has been administered to our industry. We should have had the best allocation of coal, if it is the best allocation – and I cannot see that the right hon. Gentleman the President of the Board of Trade had any doctrinaire motive for not making it the best allocation of coal. It seems to me one of the cases where his theories and his duties flowed into one channel. In addition, we should have had an exactly worked out scheme for curtailing electricity supplies and administering them in a period of emergency should it come.

Here are two grave faults and administrative collapses by the Socialist planning Government. First, they did not adopt the right allocation plan in good time. That is admitted. Secondly, they did not draw up a carefully worked out scheme, which could be put into operation by a simple order for the effective rationing of electric current throughout the 24 hours. I must tell you the truth, Mr Deputy-Speaker.[1] They are all so busy with doctrinaire nationalization, and so ardently involved in the class war, that they have no time, or strengths or brains for making the ordinary administrative arrangements which common prudence demands. This is characteristic of our affairs at this time at home and abroad. What we are experiencing now is a sample of Socialism or, if you will, of half-baked Socialism.

I notice that the Attorney-General[2] is not here. He is probably busy making some speech for which he will afterwards have to apologise. I am not attacking the right hon. and learned Gentleman because, as a matter of fact, I welcome his admission, with great frankness, as rightly linking this breakdown with the fortunes of the Socialist experiment. He made a remarkable admission. The whole fortunes of Socialism apparently depend on whether we can get out of this crisis or not. He should have a little more confidence in the theoretical foundations of a great movement, or – I notice that the right hon. and learned

---

[1] James Milner, 1889–1967. On active service, 1914–18 (wounded, despatches, MC and bar). MP (Lab.) for Leeds South East, 1929–51. Chairman, Fire Committee (Civil Defence of the Houses of Parliament), 1943–5; Ways and Means, 1943–51. Deputy Speaker of the House of Commons, 1943–51. Baron, 1951.

[2] Hartley William Shawcross, 1902–2003. Educated at Dulwich College. Married, 1924, Rosita Alberta Shyvers (div. 1943); 1944, Joan Winifred Mather (div. 1974); 1997, Monique Huiskamp. Called to Bar, Gray's Inn, 1925; Bencher, 1939. Senior Law Lecturer, Liverpool University, 1927–34. QC, 1939. Chairman, Enemy Aliens Tribunal, 1939–40. Recorder, Salford, 1941–5; Kingston-upon-Thames, 1946–61. Knighted, 1945. MP (Lab.) for St Helens, 1945–58. Attorney-General, 1945–51. PC, 1946. UK Member, Permanent Court of Arbitration, The Hague, 1950–67. President of the Board of Trade, 1951. Life Peer, 1959. GBE, 1974.

Gentleman has just come in and I will finish with him – a more careful study of Karl Marx,[1] if he can spare the time from his many activities, will perhaps refresh his flagging fortitude and faith.

The brute fact is that Socialism means mismanagement. It means mismanagement, bad housekeeping, incompetence in high places and progressive degeneration of our island life. We now have a vast increase of civil servants looking after our affairs, I have some figures here. In June 1939, there were 539,000 civil servants engaged in national government; in November, 1946, there were 1,007,000, or almost double. In local government there was a rise from 846,000 to 1,025,000 – a great increase.

[. . .] Here we have almost doubled the staff required to manage the country. This increase of those who do not add directly to the production of the country is an enormous one, and yet with all the assistance of this 400,000 or 500,000 additional civil servants, we have not even got the capacity or the organizing force to work out this simple plan for the distribution of electricity or find the best means of allocating coal to the industries until it is admittedly too late. All this burden is cast upon us through the increase of the civil servants looking after our affairs – hundreds of thousands living on the sweat of the toilers, hampering energy, enterprise and ingenuity at every stage. Yet, with this vast increase, they are not even capable of taking the simplest administrative precautions against dangers which must have been, or ought to have been, apprehended as very likely to occur in the present season of the year. I have spoken about these matters, and I shall take other opportunities of speaking in the country upon them. There is no need for us on this side of the House to hesitate to point the moral. There is the Chancellor of the Exchequer. I believe he will reply. (Hon. Members: 'Hear, hear'.) Tributes will be more welcome when they are the result of a fine performance, but not when they are merely the ebullition of perfervid loyalty.

I am astonished at the levity with which the Chancellor of the Exchequer deals with his tremendous task. The other day he made a speech at Gateshead which I can only characterize as odious and disgraceful. It was most unsuited to the position which he holds where from time to time some feeling of being a national trustee ought to break in upon his party factions. This is what he said, speaking of the coal shortage:

> The wretched private coalowners before they flitted –

not a particularly accurate word to describe the transaction –

> left us with stocks of coal lower than ever before in our history. This winter we have had coal cuts and sheddings of electricity loads. That is entirely the responsibility of private enterprise . . .

---

[1] Karl Heinrich Marx, 1818–83. Educated at Universities of Bonn and Berlin, 1835–6. Philosopher, sociologist and economist. Author of *The Communist Manifesto* and *Das Kapital*.

It is perfectly vain to suppose that by unthinking cheers, however warmly they may express partisanship, any change was made in the basic facts as known to the bulk of the nation. For at least seven years, the entire control of the coal industry, the regulation of its staffs and the provision against winter shortages have been regulated by the Government of the country, first of all for five years under the national Coalition, and since then by those who now have the power. And yet although everything has been directed under this control to the necessary stocks to get us through the winter and to tide over the year, and although this control has been absolute and complete throughout the industry for seven years, it is considered a clever thing to say:

The wretched coalowners flitted . . .

Is it worth cheering that statement that this was 'one of the great breakdowns of private enterprise'? Time alone will show whether this country will submit indefinitely to arguments so fallacious and absurd. It has well been said that one can fool all the people some of the time and some of the people all the time, but not all the people all the time. I have every hope, under the mercy of Providence, of living to see a very great awakening in our country, and that false arguments animated by harsh malicious jealousies and spites will be condemned in England, as they have been condemned in the past. I hope, indeed, that the crisis will soon pass, but the marks will remain for a long time in our economy and finance. We should all do our best to comply with such Government instructions as reach us, and let us hope that the nation will realize, from this flagrant example, the downward stairway upon which they are now thrust, and of which they have only descended the first few steps.

Geoffrey Geoffrey-Lloyd[1] to Winston S. Churchill
(*Churchill papers, 2/55*)

12 February 1947

Dear Mr Churchill,

You may find a brief note on conditions in Birmingham useful as background.

Your speech in Monday's Debate has been very well received. Feeling is

---

[1] Geoffrey William Geoffrey-Lloyd, 1902–84. Educated at Harrow School and Trinity College, Cambridge. Private Secretary to Sir Samuel Hoare (Secretary of State for Air), 1926–9; to Stanley Baldwin (PM, then Leader of the Opposition), 1929–31. MP (Cons.) for Birmingham Ladywood, 1931–45; for Birmingham King's Norton, 1950–5; for Sutton Coldfield, 1966–74. Parliamentary Private Secretary to Stanley Baldwin (Lord President of the Council, then PM), 1931–5. Parliamentary Under-Secretary, Home Office, 1935–9. Chairman, Oil Control Board, 1935–45. Secretary for Mines, 1939–40. Secretary for Petroleum, 1940–2. Minister in Charge of Petroleum Warfare, 1940–5. Parliamentary Secretary (Petroleum), Ministry of Fuel and Power, 1942–5, 1951–5. PC, 1943. Minister of Information, 1945. A Governor of the BBC, 1946–9. Minister of Education, 1957–9. Baron, 1974.

running very high throughout the City and comment in the queues is very bitter about the Government. A point of some psychological importance is that the working class women are particularly angry. The men are now hanging about the house during the day and have to be given a mid-day meal which they normally take in the factory canteens. This creates great difficulties and, for example, the queues outside Marsh & Baxters, the big pork and sausage merchants, are said to be longer than at any time during the war.

Domestic coal supplies are also very scarce. There are long queues for coke at the Gas Works and there have been one or two ugly scenes. Many working class homes have been without any coal in the house for two or three weeks. A reliable doctor in a working class district informs me that the old people, lacking stamina to resist these conditions, have been 'shrivelling up' and that he knows cases where death has resulted. This doctor is in and out of working class homes all the time and he tells me that there is a great deal of real misery and wretchedness. The people are saying that things are worse than during the Blitz. He finds only about one in ten who say that the crisis is not the Government's fault.

Clementine Churchill to Mary Soames
(Mary Soames, 'Clementine Churchill', pages 416–17)

16 February 1947

My Darling and beloved Mary,

I addressed the envelope first, and writing your new name for the first time[1] gave me a sensation of anguish and satisfaction – anguish that your life at home is ended, satisfaction that you are founding with the man you love your young own home with all its hopes & joys and experiences.

Your jubilant telegram thrilled us all & we are in imagination sharing the blue sky & dazzling sunshine & reality your blissful happiness. It is agonisingly cold here & in this completely electric house we are feeling the 5 hour daily switch off. But I got a doctor's certificate for Papa's bedroom as he can really not work in the icy cold. We have pulled his bed near the window so he can see without a lamp. . . .

My darling Mary. I am quite numb & I have not begun to miss you yet. I went once into your deserted bed-room, but not again. But what sun-lit vistas open before me in the future – of you and your children & you & Christopher both so young battling victoriously and happily through this grave new world . . .

Diana has just been in. She sends you her love. She was very sweet & relaxed & I enjoyed her visit. . . .

---

[1] Mary Churchill and Christopher Soames were married on 11 Feb. 1947.

Papa did not go to Chartwell this weekend because of the biting cold & I think he has been quite happy here. He sends you his dear love & messages to Christopher.

Jock (Colville) came to luncheon & I thanked him for all the trouble he took. He really is the King Pin of Ushers.

. . . Goodbye Darling for now. Give Christopher one kiss from me if you can spare it from yourself!

Winston S. Churchill to Clement Attlee
(*Churchill papers, 2/4*)

18 February 1947
Private and Confidential

My dear Prime Minister,

I have been reflecting on what you told me about your India policy, though I have not discussed it with anyone except, as you agreed, Anthony Eden. Until I know what is the policy and the directive, I cannot form any opinion about it nor give you any undertaking of support. As I told you the other day, when we had a short talk, I must hold myself entirely free.

Winston S. Churchill to Henry Luce
(*Churchill papers, 4/25*)

19 February 1947

My dear Mr Luce,

Thank you so much for your letter of February 8. It seems to me all the legal matters are moving to a satisfactory conclusion. We have received very definite advices that the United States Withholding Tax will not apply. Meanwhile, I am devoting all my leisure, such as it is, upon the book, and I have already more than 600,000 words in print.

I am concentrating first of all upon the period ending December 31, 1940. This constitutes two volumes, or a double volume, and will certainly not be less than 350,000 words. It may well be more. I will presently select from the proofs ten or a dozen of the chapters which are most matured and will send them to you. Of course I cannot tell what form they will finally take. In the first instance I have aimed at getting the line through from the Atlantic to the Pacific, and I shall work up the accommodation as the traffic develops. Many things that are put in now may appear redundant or too technical for the reader. Other passages will be improved upon, and all must be fitted into the balance of the work. It is always wise in an undertaking of this kind to have plenty of ballast to jettison.

I have so far divided this first double volume into three books – 'Between the Wars'; 'The Twilight War'; and 'Total War' – respectively, and I am now inclining somewhat to divide it into two volumes, the first of which will carry us down to my assumption of power on May 10, 1940, and the second to the end of that year. I keep on changing as I view the scene as a whole. I hope by the Summer or Autumn of this year to have everything in good shape up to the end of 1940, but thereafter there is a great work to be done of refinement and proportion, and the more time I get, the better it will be.

I am much amused to see the rubbish that has been published so far in the United States about our affairs, how easily the documents will blow it all away.

1941 is also a good tale, for after 1941 the main American interest opens, when we are allies in such close harmony. Whether I shall live to complete these projects, I cannot tell, but at any rate I am getting so much material together, even beyond the double-volume to the end of 1940, that you may feel a good confidence.

On all these matters I will keep in touch with Walter Graebner with whom I have established most agreeable relations.

I repainted the picture I sent you so often, in trying to make it pass muster, that I almost despaired of it. However, I hope you will admire the sheep. They are certainly a great improvement upon the two miserable quadrupeds which first figured in the landscape.

Pray give my regards to Clare,[1] and let me know if at any time you are likely to be over here.

Winston S. Churchill to Dino Grandi[2]
(Churchill papers, 2/54)

23 February 1947

Dear Signor Grandi,

You have my full permission to use and publish my letter of October 1939 in any way you think fit.[3]

---

[1] (Anne) Clare Boothe, 1903–87. Born in New York City. Married, 1923, George Tuttle Brokaw: one child (div. 1929); 1935, Henry R. Luce. Writer, Associate Editor and Managing Editor, *Vanity Fair*, 1929–34. US House of Representatives (Rep.) for New York, 1943–7. US Ambassador to Italy, 1953–7. Member, President's Foreign Intelligence Advisory Board, 1973–7, 1982–7. A pre-war friend of Randolph Churchill. Author of *Europe in the Spring* (1940).

[2] Dino Grandi, 1895–1988. Born at Mordano (Bologna). On active service, 1915–18 (three MCs for valour). Educated at Bologna University. Journalist and political organiser; led the Fascist movement in the north of Italy, 1920–1. Chief of the Fascist General Staff, 1921. Elected to the Chamber of Deputies, 1921. Deputy President of the Chamber, 1924. Under-Secretary of State for Foreign Affairs, 1925–9. Foreign Minister, 1929–32. Italian Ambassador in London, 1932–9. A member of several London clubs, including the St James's, the Athenaeum and the Travellers'. Member of the Fascist Grand Council. Count, 1937. President of the Chamber of Fasci and Corporazioni, Italy, 1939–43. Minister of Justice, Rome, 1939–43.

[3] In his letter to Grandi of Oct. 1939, Churchill wrote: 'It was a grief to me that events, against

I consider your action in July 1943[1] was of great assistance to the progress of the Allied cause.

Winston S. Churchill to Lord Cranborne
(Churchill papers, 2/67)

23 February 1947
Private and Confidential

Thank you for your letter of February 20. The point to which I attach importance is the futility and bankruptcy of the Government after all these costly delays in arriving at no positive conclusion. The question of whether, if they had arrived at such a conclusion, it would be well to submit it formally to UNO is altogether different. It would be a pity to cut out from our criticisms the damning fact that they have achieved absolutely nothing – not even an opinion – as the result of all the waste and bloodshed. I shall be speaking on Tuesday, which is nearly a week before you do, so that you will be able to see what is the best course to take. Of course you have a perfect right to say anything you like but I see no need to give the Government unnecessary bouquets.

I am delighted to see the Motion which you have put down for Tuesday about India and I earnestly hope it will be pressed to a Division. It might well be thought wise for us thereafter to move the same Motion in our House. The terms could certainly not be bettered.

Winston S. Churchill to Leslie Rowan
(Churchill papers, 2/45)

23 February 1947
Private and Confidential

My dear Leslie,

There is a matter connected with my tenure as Prime Minister, quite apart from anything connected with my War Memoirs, about which I wish to have information.

It is the discussion which took place I think in 1942 or 1943 in the War Cabinet about the growing indebtedness to India, when the Cabinet agreed that we should notify the Viceroy that we reserved our right to put in a

---

which you and I both strove, clouded a period in your memorable mission to this country. I rejoice that the forward path now seems brighter for Anglo-Italian friendship, and you may be sure I am continually working to that end. I feel a solid confidence that we shall be victorious in this war, which we are resolved to pursue at all costs until Europe is freed from the German menace; and I do not feel convinced that it will take so long as it did last time.'

[1] On 24 July 1943 the Grand Council of Italy passed Grandi's resolution to remove Mussolini from the premiership.

counter-claim for the defence of India when the time came. Later on it was agreed, at the request of the Viceroy, that this should not be made public.

I should be much obliged if these papers could be made available to me. In the event of my requiring to disclose these proceedings in public which is not impossible, I should ask formally, through the Prime Minister, for the King's permission.

Sir Edward Marsh[1] to Winston S. Churchill
(Churchill papers, 1/43)

24 February 1947

My dear Winston,

I am most deeply grieved at the thought of your loss in dear Jack.[2] There couldn't have been a more perfect relation between two brothers than yours with him, and I know what he was in your life.

I was very fond of him – and he will be badly missed at the Alton Club.

I'm so glad he lived to take part in Mary's wedding.

PS. Of course don't dream of answering.

Sir Archibald Sinclair to Winston S. Churchill
(Churchill papers, 1/43)[3]

24 February 1947　　　　　　　　　　　　　　　　　　　　　Thurso Castle

Dear Winston,

I have just heard about Jack on the wireless – a black day for Marigold[4] and me – a cruel blow for you and Clemmie.

He looked terribly ill when I was last in London – but happy in his new flat with Clarissa[5] not far from him and happy, as always, in his devotion to you and yours to him.

---

[1] Edward Howard Marsh, 1872–1953. Educated at Cambridge University: 1st Class, Classical Tripos, 1893; Senior Chancellor's Medal for Classics, 1895. Clerk, Colonial Office, 1896. Asst Private Secretary to Neville Chamberlain, 1900–3; to Oliver Lyttelton, 1903–5; to Winston Churchill, 1905–15, 1917–22, 1924–9; to H. H. Asquith, 1915–16; to the Duke of Devonshire, 1922–4; to J. H. Thomas, 1924, 1929–36; to Malcolm MacDonald, 1936–7. KCVO, 1937. Trustee, Tate Gallery, 1937–44. Chairman, Contemporary Art Society, 1937–52.
[2] John Churchill died on 23 Feb. 1947 of cardiac arrest.
[3] This letter was handwritten.
[4] Marigold Forbes, 1897–1975. Daughter of Col. J. S. Forbes, DSO, and Lady Angela St Clair Erskine. Married, 1918, Archibald Henry Macdonald Sinclair (later 1st Viscount Thurso): four children. Styled Viscountess Thurso, 1952.
[5] Clarissa Churchill, 1920–. Daughter of Winston Churchill's brother Jack. Married, 1952, Anthony Eden (as his second wife).

The loss of Jack must be almost the worst thing that has ever happened to you, dear Winston. Jack's friendship was precious and all who held it must share your grief – and Clemmie's – as we do.

John Martin[1] to Winston S. Churchill
(Churchill papers, 1/43)[2]

24 February 1947

Dear Mr Churchill,

I hesitate to intrude, yet cannot forbear from sending you a line of sympathy.

It will never be possible to think of our strangely happy life in the Private Office mess at the Annexe without remembering Jack – his unfailing courage and good humour and the overflowing cheerfulness of a gayer and more genial age.

I feel doubly sorry that this bereavement should have fallen on you at a time already darkened by so many shadows and anxieties.

Yours, constantly and proudly encouraged by the memory of service behind you in those great days,

Sarah Churchill to Winston S. Churchill
(Churchill papers, 1/42)[3]

26 February 1947   Rome

My darling Papa,

What a very very sweet telegram. How very very remiss I have been. It is not that I have not thought. As I told you, each night when my cup of hot consommé arrives, it is no effort to shut out the hotel room and conjure up vividly the lovely dining room of 28 Hyde Park, and hear your voice and see both you and Mama clearly. Always I am seized with nostalgia and a great desire to write; there and then; more speedily than thought even, to tell you how much you are with me; always (for the hours and work have been exacting) I have ben overpowered by sleep! Forgive me.

Darling darling Papa. The news of Uncle Jack's death grieves me terribly. Not so much for him, as I feel; indeed he so often said to me, it would be but a blessed relief for him when it came, but for you. I know what it will

---

[1] John Miller Martin, 1904–91. Entered Dominions Office, 1927. Seconded to Malayan Civil Service, 1931–4. Secretary, Palestine Royal Commission, 1936–7. Private Secretary to the PM (Churchill), 1940–1; Principal Private Secretary, 1941–5. Asst Under-Secretary of State, Colonial Office, 1945–56; Deputy Under-Secretary, 1956–65. Knighted, 1952. High Commissioner, Malta, 1965–7. His memoir, *Downing Street, The War Years*, was published shortly after his death in 1991.
[2] This letter was handwritten.
[3] This letter was handwritten.

mean for you – how suddenly terribly lonely you will feel. What a large part of your life. What a host of memories he takes with him. I know you loved him dearly, and he adored you, with a love untinged by any hint of envy of the triumphs, excitement and high destiny of your life. Humorous, gentle & patient – and how we loved him as children! 'God save the King' & the 'British Grenadiers' played on his teeth – seemed to me as a child, the height of artistic achievement!

During the war – when I was ill for a bit – I spent some sick leave with him in Weymouth. It was there I really got to know him. Please do not be too sad – well if that is impossible – not too lonely. Wow.

The film[1] is virtually over – but I shall still be here another 3 weeks – for any re-shooting that may have to be done – but which is not always easy to decide upon till the cutting and linking of the film are a little more advanced. It has been a great adventure & experience, and I hope when you see it – you will say, worthwhile. I will bring a copy of the film in my pocket, and perhaps we could see it together at Chartwell.

I have had a happy letter from Mary. What a beautiful wedding it was. How beautifully you both walked up the aisle, both so proud of each other.

I can't wait to get back and see Chartwell and all the new farms! It sounds too thrilling.

The enclosed picture is to give you an idea of the conditions your mule chose to work in, about a month ago for some 20 days. I sat in the little canvass hut huddled over a brazier of smouldering ashes, and whenever there was a glint of sun, I was dragged out and photographed! Our breath vaporized in the air, and my tears (theatrical ones!) froze on my cheeks, and I enjoyed every minute of it!

Wow my darling Papa – all my thoughts and love are with you.

John Colville to Winston S. Churchill
(*Churchill papers, 1/43*)[2]

27 February 1947

Dear Mr Churchill,

I know how bitterly you will miss Jack and I feel I must write and say how miserable I am, both on your account and my own. Nobody who knew him could have anything but real affection for him; indeed, I never remember hearing an unpleasant word spoken of him, which is a great deal more than I can say of anybody else I know.

---

[1] The film was *Daniele Cortis*, directed by Mario Soldati and starring Sarah Churchill and Gino Cervi. It depicts the breakdown of an unhappy marriage, something Sarah herself had experienced two years earlier.

[2] This letter was handwritten.

I am so glad that I had the opportunity of getting to know him so well during the war and, lately, of seeing a good deal of him in his club. I feel the richer for having known him and the memory of his attraction, good manners and generous character will always remain with me.

March 1947

Harold Macmillan to Winston S. Churchill
(Churchill papers, 1/43)[1]

1 March 1947

My dear Winston,

I would like just to send a line of condolence with you. I know what a sorrow your brother's sudden death must have been.

Please do not acknowledge this, but I should like you to know how much anything which saddens you causes the sympathy of all your friends and colleagues.

Winston S. Churchill: speech
(Hansard)

3 March 1947   House of Commons

THE TOWN AND COUNTRY PLANNING BILL
AND PARLIAMENTARY DEMOCRACY

I do not intend to take up much of the time of the House today, but, as a very old Member, I should like to give my support to my right hon. Friend the Member for Warwick and Leamington (Mr Eden), in the protest which he has made against this Guillotine Motion. I have never seen anything like it on the Order Paper of the House of Commons; I do not think that there is any case of the occupation and domination of the House by the Executive similar to this. It always has been thought an advantage to Governments to have their Measures put through the Parliamentary mill. I have sat in a lot of Governments, and I do not think that any of them would not have been rather afraid of just having their own ideas, shaped by their officials, driven through on to the Statute Book.

[1] This letter was handwritten.

When you are dealing with matters of great principle where one side of the House thinks this and another side of the House thinks that then we come to a clash where no kind of parley is possible, and it can only be settled by voting. But with Bills of this kind, like Town and Country Planning, Transport, Electricity – all these Bills which affect vast numbers of people, and vast numbers of local authorities, and small and intricate interests that have grown up throughout the country – it surely would be an advantage to the Government to have these Measures a little shaped and a little fitted to the shoulders of the public who are to obey them.

I should have thought that it was not at all wise to proceed on this naked line of saying, 'We have a majority; we are going to get our Measures through, and we will not give time for them to be discussed – we will vote you down.' That, I should have thought, was an attitude inconsistent with the kind of view of national affairs, of the way in which peoples and State ought to be governed, that we have taken in the world successfully during the last few years. That is reducing legislative Assemblies to mere registration machines of Government will. The whole aspect of the British Constitution has been to the contrary. It has been the shaping of legislation by the action of Parliament, by the influence of minorities from day to day; and even the time factor has had a modifying effect. That is why, in this island, there is a very great respect for the law, because the laws have been shaped by Government and Opposition.

As was pointed out by an hon. Member on this side of the House below the Gangway,[1] there is a feeling that the laws that come down to the people from Parliament and the Crown are laws which Parliament, as a whole, has had a hand in shaping. That is particularly important in regard to all these very complicated matters. It is quite true that in foreign countries they have followed other methods. They have admired our Parliamentary system, but they have not liked it, because of the corresponding inconvenience. They have liked to have assemblies filled with members so long as the Executive will was in no way affected. They have even allowed free criticism from time to time in order that an appearance might be given that anyone could blow off steam and that they were free Parliamentary countries, but they have not allowed any interference with the will of the Executive by Parliamentary Debate or by the length of time involved in full discussion. I could mention a good many countries where this has been the case, and we have certainly set ourselves very much against that kind of thing. We have always had the idea that, for good or for ill, the Measures which go out, and which the nation has to obey, should carry with them the sanction of Parliament and should have been shaped by Parliamentary fingers.

[. . .] We had wondered whether the party opposite would uphold

---

[1] Rhys Hopkin Morris, 1888–1956. Educated at Universities of Wales and London. On active service, 1914–18 (despatches). MP (Lib.) for Cardiganshire, 1923–32; for Carmarthen, 1945–56. Metropolitan Police Magistrate, 1932–6. Regional Director for Wales, BBC, 1936–45. OBE, 1942.

Parliament. They owe a great debt to Parliament. Parliament has enabled them, by peaceful and constitutional methods, to advance by the will of the people to the discharge of the great offices and functions of the British nation, with the assent even of those who have voted against them − to discharge the high functions of the State and to settle our fate and fortune. Can they complain of the Constitution which has led them on to power? Believe me, it is not democracy only, it is Parliamentary democracy, that we uphold. Parliamentary democracy is absolutely opposed to this idea of legislation by ukase, as it used to be called in Russia a long time ago − legislation by decree − this idea of government of the people by the officials for the party bosses. It has always been odious here. I am really astonished that some of those whom I see opposite, or who sit on that Bench, have been ready to press their advantage at the Election in this harsh manner to the detriment of Parliament.

As I said, it is an advantage to them to have the hands of Parliament mixed up in their legislation. Of course, if we are simply to have these Measures proclaimed, flung at us with very little notice, and then carried through, our old system has undoubtedly passed away. Whatever mandates the Government may claim they had at the last Election, they had no mandates to mutilate and hamper the control of Parliament over the legislation which it passes. There is the Home Secretary,[1] a Minister for whom I entertain much respect; I cannot believe that in his heart he considers, any more than I can believe that the Prime Minister in his heart considers, that three days' discussion on the Floor of the House is all that should be permitted for the shaping of this mighty and complicated Transport Bill. Of course, the Government have the advantage of a Parliamentary majority, and within certain limits it can be used with great effect. It may be it would be to our advantage that the Government should use it in the way they are now proposing to use it. It may well be that legislation which goes from this House to the country, which it is known that Parliament had not had a chance to shape, which is full of all the mistakes and errors made by overworked draftsmen and officials, and which has not gone through the Parliamentary mill, would do the Government more harm than if they carried the considerable reforms which they have in mind by the recognised processes of Parliamentary discussion.

I profoundly regret the course which is being taken. And what is the reason that this course should be taken? We are told by the Government, 'We have our mandate which was given us at the election and we shall carry our Bills,' but the mandate, whatever it may be, prescribed no time limit. There was no Guillotine upon the mandate. The life of Parliament is a reasonable time

---

[1] James Chuter Chuter-Ede, 1882–1965. Educated at Christ's College, Cambridge. Married, 1917, Lilian Mary Williams. MP (Lab.) for Mitcham, 1923; for South Shields, 1935–64. Parliamentary Secretary, Ministry of Education, 1940–5. Home Secretary, 1945–51. Deputy Leader, House of Commons, 1947; Leader of the House 9 Mar.–26 Oct. 1951. Deputy Chairman, BBC General Advisory Council, 1952–9. Life Peer, 1964.

for the execution of any programme which is put before the people. There is really no reason why some of these bills should not have gone through to the next Session of this Parliament, with the full advantage of discussion on the Floor of the House. That would be of great benefit to the public and would not be any detriment to the Government. But no, the Bills are ordered to be put through this Session and through they must go. They were in the King's Speech – the Speech which Ministers place in the mouth of the King at the beginning of the Session – not the mandate, and that has to be carried through in this Session. That is the end of it, we are told. I am inclined to think that this course of affairs is most deeply detrimental to all concerned. Here is a resolve to carry through these Measures irrespective of whether they are properly or fairly discussed, because there is no accusation of obstruction.

Then we are told, 'Oh well, we have another reason for getting them through. It is not merely that they were in the King's Speech, and, therefore, we are going to put them through however complex they may be, but we do not want to have an autumn Session.' Can anyone imagine such a state of degradation for a Parliament to fall into to say that it will pour out a flood of machine-made legislation upon the country and will not allow proper discussion, because the Government cannot be forced to the inconvenience of an autumn Session? If Parliament had to choose between having a prolonged Session on the one hand, or not having Bills properly discussed on the other, I have not the slightest doubt what they would choose. Even now I feel that one might appeal to the Government. I wish the Prime Minister were here. I know he has a lot to do. I know him well, for we worked together side by side and I know his fine qualities. I did not think he would ride roughshod over the House in this way, and I do not think that it will reflect well upon his name and repute that Measures should be driven through without plenty of time and latitude available for discussion and consideration.

[. . .]

It is only by suffering that the people of this country have learned. They will have plenty of suffering and further experience of Socialist rule, beginning by the strangulation of Parliamentary Debate, enforcing ill-considered legislation through the snoopers of 17 different Departments, and finally no doubt, as the ideals are further realised, being assisted by a police Gestapo. There is the path on which we are embarked under the impulse of hon. Members opposite. The first step has been taken. (*Interruption.*) The hon. Gentleman should contain himself. The first step in endangering our National liberties is the – (*Interruption.*)

Mr Speaker: I should like to suggest that hon. Gentlemen should not generate more indignation than they can contain.

Mr Churchill: I firmly believe that the liberty and the free life of Britain are in great danger at the present time at the hands of the party opposite. I quite agree that they cannot do it all at once, but the first step upon the road on which they have started is the effective strangulation of Parliamentary Debate and the substitution for it of legislation by Government decree.

Enoch Powell[1] to Winston S. Churchill
(*Churchill papers, 2/43*)

4 March 1947

Dear Mr Churchill,

The following are the data for which you asked me this morning.

1) <u>Statute of Westminster 1931</u>. The text of this Statute is on pages 303 to 307 of the enclosed 'Speeches and documents'. Remarks by A. B. Keith[2] on the legality of secession, on the lines of those which you read to me from Mr Amery's letter, will be found on pages xxxiv to xxxv of the introduction.

2) Date of Round Table Conferences – December 1930 to December 1932.

3) <u>Cripps proposals</u>. A copy of the text is appended to this letter at Annexure I. The offer was announced on 11th March, 1942.

In fact, on his return from India, Sir Stafford Cripps declared: 'I stated when I left India that in default of acceptance the draft declaration must be considered as being withdrawn.'

On the other hand, Mr Amery on 30th July 1942 (Hansard, Commons, col: 674) stated: 'It proved impossible to secure the support of the principal elements of India's national life for the specific proposals in that declaration, and the draft was accordingly withdrawn. Nevertheless, HMG stand firmly by the broad intention of their offer;' and you yourself on the 10th September 1942, (Hansard, Commons, col: 302) made the following statement: 'The broad principles of the declaration made by His Majesty's Government which formed the basis of the Mission of the Lord Privy Seal to India, must be taken as representing the settled policy of the British Crown and Parliament. These principles stand in their full scope and integrity.'

4) The arrest of the Congress leaders occurred on 9th August, 1942.

I shall be in the box under the gallery throughout the debate tomorrow.

---

[1] John Enoch Powell, 1912–98. Educated at Trinity College, Cambridge. Prof. of Greek, University of Sydney, 1937–9. Capt., General Staff, 1940–1. Maj., 1941. Lt-Col., 1942. Col., 1944; Brig., 1944. Voted Labour, 1945, but joined Conservative Party, 1946. Member of Conservative Research Department under R. A. Butler, 1946–7. MP (Cons.) for Wolverhampton South West, 1950–74; (Union.) for South Down, 1974–87. Married, 1952, Margaret Pamela Winston. Financial Secretary, Treasury, 1957–8. Minister for Health, 1960–3. Shadow Secretary of State for Defence, 1965–8.

[2] Arthur Berridale Keith, 1879–1944. Educated at Balliol College, Oxford. Called to Bar, Inner Temple, 1904. Deputy Boden Prof. of Sanskrit, Oxford University, 1907–8. Private Secretary, Under-Secretary of State for Colonies, 1912. Married, 1912, Margaret Balfour. Regius Prof., Sanskrit and Comparative Philology, Edinburgh University, 1914–44; Lecturer, British Constitution, 1927–44. Crown Member, Governing Body, School of Oriental Studies, 1916–35. Member, Committee on Home Administration of Indian Affairs, 1919. Examiner, British Constitution and Public Administration and Finance, University of London, 1923–32. Author of numerous books on Constitutional Law and Asian Studies.

Lieutenant-General Charles Gairdner[1] to Winston S. Churchill
(Churchill papers, 2/153)

5 March 1947

Dear Mr Churchill

Before leaving Japan, General MacArthur asked me to give you the following message:

'My warmest admiration for one who, though no longer in power, is still as indomitable as ever in adhering to the principles in which he believes.'

I expect to return to Tokyo about <u>16th March</u>. I wonder if you would care to send General MacArthur a message?

Winston S. Churchill: speech
(Hansard)

6 March 1947   House of Commons

INDIA (GOVERNMENT POLICY)

When great parties in this country have for many years pursued a combined and united policy on some large issue, and when for what seemed to them to be good reasons, they decide to separate, not only in Debate but by Division, it is desirable and even necessary, that the causes of such separation and the limitations of the differences which exist, should be placed on record. This afternoon we begin a new chapter in our relations across the Floor of the House in regard to the Indian problem. We on this side of the House have, for some time, made it clear that the sole responsibility for the control of India's affairs rests, of course, with His Majesty's Government. We have criticised their action in various ways but this is the first time we have felt it our duty as the official Opposition to express our dissent and difference by a formal vote.

Let us first place on record the measure of agreement which lies between us, and separate that from the differences that now lead us into opposite Lobbies. Both sides of the House are bound by the declaration made at the time of the British Mission to India in March 1942. It is not true to suggest, as was done lately, that this decision marked a decisive change in the policy of the British Parliament towards India. There was a long story before we got

[1] Charles Henry Gairdner, 1898–1983. CO, 10th Royal Hussars, 1937–40. GSO I, 7th Armoured Div., North Africa, 1940–1. Brig., Armoured Fighting Vehicles, Middle East Command, 1941. Deputy Director of Plans, 1941. CBE, 1941. GOC 6th Armoured Div., North Africa, 1941–2; 8th Armoured Div., 1942–3. Commandant, Staff School Haifa, Palestine, 1942. CoS, 15th Army Group, Italy, Feb.–Aug. 1943. Director, Armoured Fighting Vehicles, Army HQ India, 1943–5. Head of British Liaison Mission to Japan, 1945–6. British Representative to Gen. MacArthur, 1945–8. CB, 1946. KCMG, 1948. Governor, Western Australia, 1951–63; Tasmania, 1963–8. GBE, 1969.

to that. Great Britain had for many years been committed to handing over responsibility for the government of India to the representatives of the Indian people. There was the promise of Dominion status implicit in the declaration of August 1917. There was the expansion and definition of Dominion status by the Statute of Westminster. There was the Simon Commission Report of 1930, followed by the Hoare[1]–Linlithgow[2] Reforms of 1935. There was the Linlithgow offer of 1940, for which, as head of the Government in those days, I took my share of responsibility. By this, the Viceroy undertook that, as soon as possible after the war, Indians themselves should frame a fully self-governing Constitution. All this constituted the preliminary basis on which the proposals of the Cripps Mission of 1942 were set. The proposals of this Mission were not, in fact, a departure in principle from what had long been growing up, but they constituted a definite, decisive and urgent project for action. Let us consider the circumstances in which this offer was made.

The violent irruption of Japan upon East Asia, the withdrawal of the United States Fleet to the American coast, the sinking of the *Prince of Wales* and the *Repulse*, the loss of Malaya and the surrender of Singapore, and many other circumstances of that time left us for the moment without any assured means of defending India from invasion by Japan. We had lost the command of the Bay of Bengal, and, indeed, to a large extent, of the Indian Ocean. Whether the Provinces of Madras and Bengal would be pillaged and ravaged by the Japanese at that time seemed to hang in the balance, and the question naturally arose with poignant force how best to rally all Indian elements to the defence of their native land.

The offer of the Cripps Mission, I would remind the House, was substantially this: His Majesty's Government undertook to accept and implement an agreed Constitution for an Indian Union, which should be a Dominion, framed by an elected Constituent Assembly and affording representation to the Princes. This undertaking was subject only to the right of non-acceding Provinces to receive separate treatment, and to the conclusion of a treaty guaranteeing the protection of religious and racial minorities. The offer of the Cripps Mission was not accepted by the political classes in India who alone are vocal and to whom it was addressed. On the contrary, the Congress, led

[1] Samuel John Gurney Hoare, 1880–1959. Educated at Harrow and New College, Oxford. MP (Cons.) for Chelsea, 1910–44. Succeeded his father as 2nd Bt, 1915. Lt-Col., British Military Mission to Russia, 1916–17, and to Italy, 1917–18. Secretary of State for Air, Oct. 1922 to Jan. 1924, 1924–9. Secretary of State for India, 1931–5; for Foreign Affairs, 1935. 1st Lord of the Admiralty, 1936–7. Home Secretary, 1937–9. Lord Privy Seal, 1939–40. Secretary of State for Air, Apr.–May 1940. Ambassador to Spain, 1940–4. Viscount Templewood, 1944.

[2] Victor Alexander John Hope, 1887–1952. Known as 'Hopie'. Educated at Eton. Succeeded his father as 5th Baron Niddry of Niddry, 8th Lord Hope, 8th Viscount of Aithrie, 8th Earl of Hopetoun, and 2nd Marquess of Linlithgow, 1908. On active service, 1914–18 (despatches). Civil Lord, Admiralty, 1922–4. Deputy Chairman, Conservative Party Organisation, 1924–6. Chairman, Royal Commission on Indian Agriculture, 1926–8; Joint Select Committee on Indian Constitutional Reform, 1933–4; Medical Research Council, 1934–6. PC, 1935. Viceroy of India, 1936–43. KG, 1943.

by Mr Gandhi and Mr Nehru, did their utmost to make a revolt intended to paralyse the perilous communications of our Army in Burma and to help the fortunes of Japan. Therefore, the National Coalition Government of those days made a large series of mass arrests of Indian Congress leaders, and the bulk were kept in prison until the end of the war. I was not myself present in the Cabinet when these decisions were taken. I was at Cairo preparing for the operations which opened at Alamein, but I highly approved of the action which was taken in my absence by the then Deputy Prime Minister, the present Prime Minister, who sits opposite, and which I think was the only one possible on that occasion.

Therefore, it is quite clear that, whatever was the offer of the Cripps Mission, it was not accepted. On the contrary, it was repudiated by the parties to whom it was addressed. In fact, on his return from India, the President of the Board of Trade – the right hon. and learned Gentleman (Sir Stafford Cripps) who made such a careful statement yesterday – said:

> I stated when I left India that, in default of acceptance, the draft Declaration must be considered as being withdrawn.

I have taken the trouble to verify the quotation. I, for my part, have never bowed – nor do I make any reflection upon him – to the dictum 'ease would recant vows made in pain as violent and void'. Returning to this country later in the year, I stated on 10 September 1942, with the full assent of my colleagues:

> The broad principles of the declaration made by His Majesty's Government, which formed the basis of the Mission of the Lord Privy Seal to India, must be taken as representing the settled policy of the British Crown and Parliament. These principles stand in their full scope and integrity.

That is where I stand now. Both sides of this House are bound by this offer, and bound by all of it, and it is on the basis of this offer being an agreed matter between the parties, and on that basis alone, that our present and future controversies arise. If I am bound by the offer of Dominion status and all that it implies, the Prime Minister is equally bound, or was equally bound, to the conditions about agreement between the principal communities, about the proper discharge of our pledges about the protection of minorities and the like. The right hon. Gentleman has a perfect right to change his mind. He may cast away all these stipulations which we jointly made, and proceed only with the positive side of the offer. He has the right to claim the support of his Parliamentary majority for any action he takes, but he has no right to claim our support beyond the limits to which we are engaged by the Cripps declaration.

A statement was made during the period of what is called the Caretaker Government, of which I was the head, by the then Secretary of State, Mr Amery, to which frequent reference has been made as if it implied some further advance, but that is not true. I was not consulted on the exact terms of his statement, as I certainly should have been if the Secretary of State had intended to make a further advance upon the position established by the Cripps Mission in 1942. It was Mr Amery who said:

> The offer of March 1942 stands in its entirety. That offer was based on two main principles. The first is that no limit is set to India's freedom to decide for herself her own destiny, whether as a free member and partner in the British Commonwealth or even without it. The second is that this can only be achieved by a Constitution or Constitutions framed by Indians to which the main elements in Indian national life are consenting parties. . . . That, I may say, is an affirmation, not only of our own loyal purpose, but of the inescapable fact of the Indian situation. We can only transfer our ultimate control over India to a Government or Governments capable of exercising it. . . .[1] Our responsibilities to the people of India themselves forbid that course, and, indeed, our responsibilities to the peace of the world forbid it.

I have ventured to ask Mr Amery whether his statement was intended to make any new declaration beyond the limits of that of the Cripps Mission, and he wrote to me:

> I cannot see anything in it which affects, one way or another, the argument which you have used with regard to the sequence in which the Indian Constituent Assembly or an Indian Dominion might declare in favour of separation. In my statement, I simply recalled the two main principles on which the 1942 offer was based, one of which was that no limit is set to India's freedom to decide for herself her own destiny, whether as a free member and partner in the British Commonwealth, or even without it. At that time, none of us had considered the possibility of an Indian Constituent Assembly being invited to declare for or against separation before the Constitution had been accepted by Parliament here, and I cannot imagine that my definition of the principle could have been taken at the time as suggesting or inviting a different sequence to that which we had always contemplated.

The Minister of Defence (Mr A. V. Alexander): What is the date of that?

Mr Churchill: That was written to me two days ago, because the point was made against me that some new declaration had been made during the time of the interim Government while the election was going on, and I am anxious to show that there is nothing which has been said by us, consciously, which in any way carries the matter – (*Interruption.*) There is nothing controversial about it; I am only trying to lay down the basis on which we can agree to differ – the basis of 1942 and the present time. Before this latest pronouncement of theirs,

---

[1] The sentence omitted here reads: 'We cannot hand India over to anarchy or to civil war.'

His Majesty's Government had already departed from the Cripps Mission declaration of 1942, and they had departed from it in three major aspects. First, they had eliminated the stage of Dominion status. The Cripps Mission expressly said that the objective was the creation of a new Indian Union which would constitute a Dominion associated with the United Kingdom and the other Dominions by common allegiance to the Crown, but equal to them in every respect, in no way subordinated in any aspect of domestic or external affairs.

That stage was entirely cut out by the Prime Minister in his speech sending out the Cabinet Mission a year ago. I was not in the country at the time, or I would have drawn attention to the serious change, but it may well be that all my hon. Friends on this side of the House do not regard that particular change as so serious as I do. I am laying out the facts that justify the Division that is to take place tonight on what has been an actually pursued policy. If the Dominion Status procedure had been involved, in my view, the new Indian Dominion would have been perfectly free to leave the Commonwealth if it chose, but full opportunity would have been given for all the dangers and disadvantages to be surveyed by responsible Indian Ministers beforehand, and also for the wishes of the great mass of the Indian people to be expressed, as they cannot be expressed now. It would have been possible to insert in the Dominion Constitution the necessary safeguards for minorities, and for the fulfilment of the British pledges to the various elements of Indian life, notably the Depressed Classes. This would have been a part of the agreement between the Indian Union and Great Britain, and would have been embodied in the necessary British legislation on the lines of the British North America Act, to which the great free Dominion of Canada has always attached importance, and still does. So the second departure from the Cripps Mission declaration was the total abandonment by His Majesty's Government, of all responsibility for carrying out its pledges to minorities and the Depressed Classes, as well as for fulfilling their treaties with the Indian States. All these are to be left to fend for themselves, or to fight for themselves as best they can. That is a grave major departure.

The third departure was no less grave. The essence of the Cripps Mission declaration was that there should be agreement between the principal Indian communities, namely, the Muslims and the Hindus. That, also, has been thrown overboard. But I state, as it is my duty to do when we take a step such as we are going to take tonight, of great formality and solemness, that it is the Government who have broken away from the agreement which has been reached between parties, and has so long subsisted between parties, and that it is not we in the Conservative Party who have, in any way, gone back on our faithful undertaking. To these departures from our principle, there must be added a formidable list of practical mistakes in handling the problem during that past year since the Cabinet Mission was sent out. Some of these mistakes may have been made by the Government, and some of them by the Viceroy, but they are both jointly responsible for all.

First there was the attempt to formulate a Constitution and press it upon the Indians, instead of leaving the Indians, as had been promised, the duty of framing their own proposals. That action, however well intended, has proved to be devoid of advantage, and must be rated as a mistake. Secondly, there was the summoning of a so-called Constituent Assembly upon the altogether inadequate and unrepresentative franchise, an Assembly which was called into being, but which had absolutely no claim or right to decide the fate of India, or any claim to express the opinion of the great masses of the Indians. That is the second mistake. The third mistake was the dismissal of the eminent Indians composing the Viceroy's Council, and the handing over of the government of India to Mr Nehru.

This government of Mr Nehru has been a complete disaster, and a great degeneration and demoralisation in the already weakened departmental machinery of the Government of India has followed from it. Thirty or forty thousand people have been slaughtered in the warfare between the two principal religions. Corruption is growing apace. They talk of giving India freedom. But freedom has been restricted since this interim Nehru Government has come to power. Communism is growing so fast that it has been found necessary to raid and suppress Communist establishments and centres which, in our broad British tolerance we do not do here, and have never done in India. (*Interruption.*) I am illustrating the steps to freedom which, so far, have been marked by every degree in which British control is relaxed, by the restriction of the ordinary individual, whatever his political view. It was a cardinal mistake to entrust the government of India to the caste Hindu, Mr Nehru. He has good reason to be the most bitter enemy of any connection between India and the British Commonwealth.

I consider that that must be regarded as the third practical administrative mistake, apart from those large departures in principle which may be charged against the present British Government in this Indian sphere. Such was the situation before the latest plunge which the Government have taken, was made, and it is this plunge which, added to all that has gone before, makes it our duty to sever ourselves altogether from the Indian policy of His Majesty's Government, and to disclaim all responsibility for the consequences which will darken – aye, and redden the coming years.

I am offering the House an argument concerning the steps we are going to take, which I and my friends have regarded as most serious and most anxious steps. I have stated where we agree, and I am now proceeding to show the differences of principle and mistakes of administration due to Government action. The Viceroy, Lord Wavell, has been dismissed. I hold no brief for Lord Wavell. He has been the willing or unwilling agent of the Government in all the errors and mistakes into which they have been led, and which I have just described, but I have no idea why he has been cast aside at this juncture. The Prime Minister has refused to give the slightest indication of the differences which must have arisen between the Government and the Viceroy. It is not possible for us to form an opinion on many aspects of the Indian controversy while this concealment is maintained. It is most unusual for great political severances of this kind to take place in time of peace without statements being made both by the Government and the dismissed functionary, to justify their respective positions. I had some argument the other day with the Prime Minister about this. It is quite true that in war many Ministers were removed from their offices without their wishing to make any explanation to Parliament, but if they had wished to do so, or if there had been any demand in Parliament for an explanation, such as we have made in this case, I should certainly have felt it my duty, as Prime Minister, to facilitate such a process – I am not in the least afraid to defend any action in my public life, here in this House, if it is challenged in due course – provided, of course, that military plans were not exposed or compromised.

Before the war, statements for the reasons justifying the resignations of Ministers or functionaries were a commonplace. My right hon. Friend the Member for Warwick and Leamington (Mr Eden) resigned in 1938. We all approved his action – (Hon. Members: 'Oh'.) I content myself by saying that opinions were divided on that question, as upon so many others. He and Lord Cranborne resigned; they both made full explanations and were answered by the Prime Minister of the day. Going back over the years in English history, we know all the great statements that have been made on the resignations of Ministers and important persons upon great public differences, and this is what they owe to themselves today. When Sir Ben Smith resigned the other day, I was astonished that he did not make a statement about differences which were known to exist, although I am not quite so astonished about it now. It is an unwholesome way of conducting public affairs in time of peace that Ministers or Viceroys should be dismissed or should resign, and should not feel it necessary to their self-respect to explain to the nation the reasons for their departure. However, I understand that Lord Wavell will be free as soon as he returns to this country. Is that so?

The Prime Minister (Mr Attlee) indicated assent.

Mr Churchill: That is so. Certainly it will be expected of him to make a statement. There is one point, however, on which we ought to have some information today, because it is material to the issues before us. Was the Viceroy in favour of the time limit, or was he not? I hoped that we should have some information on that point, at least.

Let me now turn from the dismissed Viceroy to the new Viceroy.[1] I do not think that the 14 months' time limit gives the new Viceroy a fair chance. We do

---

[1] Adm. Lord Louis Mountbatten was sworn in as Viceroy on 24 Mar. 1947 and given 14 months to achieve Indian independence.

not know what directives have been given to him. No explanation of that has been provided. Indeed, we are told very little. Looking on this Indian problem and having to address the House upon it, I am surprised how many great gaps there are in information which should be in the full possession of the House. We are told very little. What is the policy and purpose for which he is to be sent out, and how is he to employ these 14 months? Is he to make a new effort to restore the situation, or is it merely Operation Scuttle on which he and other distinguished officers have been despatched? The Prime Minister should deal with this and should tell us something of the purpose behind all these movements. Parliament has its powers, but it may use them wrongly and unwisely if it is not given information which, in all other periods that I have known, would have been placed at its disposal – except, of course, in time of war when we must not tell the enemy what we intend to do.

Everyone knows that the 14 months' time limit is fatal to any orderly transference of power, and I am bound to say that the whole thing wears the aspect of an attempt by the Government to make use of brilliant war figures in order to cover up a melancholy and disastrous transaction. One thing seems to me absolutely certain. The Government, by their 14 months' time limit, have put an end to all prospect of Indian unity. I myself have never believed that that could be preserved after the departure of the British Raj, but the last chance has been extinguished by the Government's action. How can one suppose that the thousand-year gulf which yawns between Muslim and Hindu will be bridged in 14 months? Here are these people, in many cases, of the same race, charming people, lightly clad, crowded together in all the streets and bazaars and so forth, and yet there is no intermarriage. It is astounding. Religion has raised a bar which not even the strongest impulse of nature can overleap. It is an astounding thing. Yet the Government expect in 14 months that there will be an agreement on these subjects between these races.

I speak in all consciousness of the fallibility of human judgment in regard to future events, of which we are all conscious. Sometimes I have not always been wrong in giving forecasts, though I have often failed to get the support I required at the time when it would have been advantageous. Henceforward in India, in my view, everyone will start staking out their claims and preparing to defend them; and they have the assurance of the British Government that they will recognise them and treat with them if they only make enough noise and establish themselves. They have only to make enough demonstration of their identity and right to separate existence and consideration. That will not lead to a melting of hearts, which will throw them all together and sweep away this centuries-old, this millennium-old division. On the contrary, it is inviting them to take advantage of the time that is left to peg out their claims, and to take up strong ground to defend their rights, which they value more than life itself.

No arrangement has been made about all the great common Services. My right hon. Friend the Member for the Scottish Universities (Sir J. Anderson) yesterday, in a speech instinct with deep and slowly acquired knowledge of the problem, dealt with the question of the common Services. There are very many: Defence, foreign affairs, communications by road, rail and air, water, the waterways, with great rivers that flow from one territory into another, some greater than the Danube and the Rhine in Europe. All these manifest themselves, and come into vast populations and the broad territories of Hindustan. There are the so-called Imperial Services; that is to say, the Indian Civil Service, the Indian Police, the Customs and Tariffs; there are subsidies for many Provincial activities like education and development, both industrial and agricultural, the finding for the above purposes of reserve powers for Provinces in case of some emergency; provision for paying pensions, earned in many parts of India by Indians, by some of the bravest fighting men in the world for their loyalty to successive emperors and the British Crown, and for their bravery in the war. What guarantee have they, when divisions are to be made in this manner?

India is to be subjected not merely to partition, but to fragmentation, and to haphazard fragmentation. A time limit is imposed – a kind of guillotine – which will certainly prevent the full, fair and reasonable discussion of the great complicated issues that are involved. These 14 months will not be used for the melting of hearts and the union of Muslim and Hindu all over India. They will be used in preparation for civil war; and they will be marked continually by disorders and disturbances such as are now going on in the great city of Lahore. In spite of the great efforts which have been made by the leaders on both sides to allay them, out of sheer alarm and fear of what would happen, still these troubles break out, and they are sinking profoundly into India, in the heart of the Indian problem – (*Laughter.*) – the right hon. and learned Gentleman (Sir Stafford Cripps) ought not to laugh. Although of fanatical disposition, he has a tender heart. I am sure that the horrors that have been going on since he put the Nehru Government in power, the spectacle we have seen in viewing these horrors, with the corpses of men, women and children littering the ground in thousands, have wrung his heart. I wonder that even his imagination does not guide him to review these matters searchingly in his own conscience.

Let the House remember this. The Indian political parties and political classes do not represent the Indian masses. It is a delusion to believe that they do. I wish they did. They are not as representative of them as the movements in Britain represent the surges and impulses of the British nation. This has been proved in the war, and I can show the House how it was proved. The Congress Party declared non-co-operation with Great Britain and the Allies. The other great political party, to whom all main power is to be given, the Muslim League, sought to make a bargain about it, but no bargain was made. So both great political parties in India, the only forces that have been dealt with so far, stood aside. Nevertheless, the only great volunteer army in the world that fought on either side in that struggle was formed in India. More than three and a half million men came forward to support the King Emperor and the cause of Britain; they came forward not by conscription or compulsion, but out of their loyalty to Britain and to all that Britain stood for in their lives. In handing over the Government of India to these so-called political classes we are handing over to men of straw, of whom, in a few years, no trace will remain.

This Government, by their latest action, this 14 months' limitation – which is what I am coming to – cripple the new Viceroy and destroy the prospect of even going through the business on the agenda which has to be settled. This can only be explained as the complete adoption of one of Mr Gandhi's most scatterbrained observations, which I will read to the House. It was made on 24 May 1942, after the Mission. He said:

> Leave India in God's hands, in modern parlance, to anarchy; and that anarchy may lead to internecine warfare for a time, or to unrestricted dacoities. From these a true India will arise in place of the false one we see.

There, as far as I can see, is a statement indistinguishable from the policy His Majesty's Government are determined to pursue.

I wish to pursue this matter and, with the great respect, indulgence and kindness I always receive from the House, to unfold a connected argument to them in all its stages. I must compare, with bewilderment, the attitude of His Majesty's Government towards India and towards Palestine. There is a time limit for India, but no time limit for Palestine. I must say, that astonished me. Two bottles of powerful medicine have been prepared, but they are sent to the wrong patients. The policy in these two places taken together is incomprehensible. I do not understand how they can have originated from any coherent human brain; and even from a Cabinet which, no doubt, has many incoherencies in it, it is incomprehensible. Can the House believe there are three or four times as many British troops in little petty Palestine as in mighty India at the present time? What is the idea behind such a thing? What is the point and sense of this distribution of our forces, which we are told are so limited? I do not know where the sustained effort we are making in Palestine comes from, or what element of obstinacy has forced this peculiar assertion in the midst of general surrender and scuttle of British will power in Palestine. I do not know where it comes from; but evidently some very powerful Minister has said he is going to have his way in it, and nobody has dared to withstand him. I cannot tell who it is. I have only my surmise.

The sustained effort we are making in Palestine, if applied in India, would have enabled the plan of the Cripps Mission to be carried out, fully discussed with full deliberation and firmness; and we should have kept all our pledges, and we should have gone steadily forward through this crisis. It is indeed a paradox that the opposite course should be taken, and that here, in India, where such vast consequences are at stake, we are told we must be off in 14 months; whereas, in this small Palestine, with which we have been connected but 25 years, and hold only on Mandate, we are to make all these exertions, and pour out our treasure, and keep 100,000 men or more marching around in circumstances most vexatious and painful to them.

Well, I have made the case of the reasons and grounds why the Opposition, the Conservative Opposition, feel it necessary to dissociate themselves from the further progress of the Government on this road to ruin. I have given, I think, good grounds for the step which we now take, and which we are not taking without a great deal of heart-searching and consideration. But before I sit down, I should like to touch upon another aspect. I read this morning in the Official Report the speech of the hon. Member for Gateshead (Mr Zilliacus).[1] I do not know whether he is in the House.

Mr Zilliacus (Gateshead): Here.

Mr Churchill: We do not often find ourselves thinking on similar lines.

Mr Kirkwood (Dumbarton Burghs): The right hon. Gentleman will have to watch himself.

Mr Churchill: David, keep quiet. (*Laughter.*) We are old allies, and do not interfere with each other when we are in action. As I say, I read the speech of the hon. Member for Gateshead. We do not often find ourselves in agreement or thinking along similar lines. Nor am I in agreement with much that he said last night. But it is a fact that I had already intended myself to strike the note of the United Nations being brought into the Indian problem. I have for some time pressed upon His Majesty's Government that, if they are unable to carry out their pledges in Palestine or keep order there, they should return their Mandate, or, at any rate, invoke the aid of UNO to help them in their work; and that, after six or seven months' delay – a needless delay – they have actually done. Now, is it not difficult to resist the feeling that the same train of reasoning applies on a far greater scale and with much stronger force to India? We are told that we cannot walk out of Palestine because we should leave behind us a war between 600,000 Jews and 200,000 Arabs. How, then, can we walk out of India in 14 months and leave behind us a war between 90 million Muslims and 200 million caste Hindus, and all the other tribulations which will fall upon the helpless population of 400 million? Will it not be a terrible disgrace to our name and record if, after our 14 months' time limit, we allow one fifth of the population of the globe, occupying a region nearly as large as Europe, to fall into chaos and into carnage? Would it not be a world crime that we should be committing, a crime that would stain – not merely strip us, as we are being stripped, in the material position – but would stain our good name for ever?

[1] Konni Zilliacus, 1894–1967. Served in European war, 1914–18. Member of Information Section, League of Nations, 1919–39. Ministry of Information, 1939–45. MP (Lab.) for Gateshead, 1945–50; for Manchester Gorton, 1955–67. Expelled from Labour Party, 1949. Readmitted, 1952.

Yesterday, the President of the Board of Trade and other speakers brought into great prominence our physical and military weakness. How can we keep a large Army in India for 15 or 20 years? He and other speakers stressed that point; and, certainly, it is a very grave point. But he might as well have urged that in our present forlorn condition we have not only not the physical strength, but not the moral strength and willpower. If we, through lack of physical and moral strength, cannot wind up our affairs in a responsible and humane and honourable fashion, ought we not to consider invoking the aid or, at least, the advice of the world international organisation, which is now clothed with reality, and on which so many of us, in all parts of the House, base our hopes for the peaceful progress, freedom, and, indeed, the salvation of all mankind?

I say to His Majesty's Government that, if they feel it right in the case of little Palestine to lay their difficulties before UNO, what conceivable reason can there be for not following a similar course in the case of this vast subcontinent of India? Granted the position to which they have carried affairs by their actions, if they cannot, through their weakness and moral prostration, fulfil their pledges to vast, helpless communities numbered by scores of millions, are they not bound in honour, in decency, and, indeed, in common sense to seek the aid of the wider instruments and authorities? I say that if all practical hopes of Britain's discharging her task have vanished – it is not my view, but it is the prevailing mood: it is the mood of those who are all powerful today – if they have all vanished, then, at least, there is this new world organisation, brought into being by the agonies of two devastating wars, which should certainly not be overlooked or ignored.

The hon. Member for Gateshead spoke of the precedent of the multinational membership of the United Nations, he instanced the Soviet Union and spoke of the possibility of affording those safeguards for minorities which, we are assured by His Majesty's Government, Britain has lost the strength and willpower to provide. He spoke of the right of minorities to appear before the Permanent Court of International Justice. I must say that I do not think such aspects should be overlooked in this position, in this period of British depression and eclipse.

I thank the House for listening so long and so attentively to what I have said. I have spoken with a lifetime of thought and contact with these topics. It is with deep grief I watch the clattering down of the British Empire with all its glories, and all the services it has rendered to mankind. I am sure that in the hour of our victory now not so long ago, we had the power to make a solution of our difficulties which would have been honourable and lasting. Many have defended Britain against her foes. None can defend her against herself. We must face the evils that are coming upon us and that we are powerless to avert. We must do our best in all these circumstances and not exclude any expedient that may help to mitigate the ruin and disaster that will follow the disappearance of Britain from the East. But, at least, let us not add – by shameful flight, by a premature hurried scuttle – at least, let us not add to the pangs of sorrow so many of us feel, the taint and smear of shame.

Clement Attlee to Winston S. Churchill
(Churchill papers, 2/46)

10 March 1947
Confidential

My dear Churchill,

After the Colonial Secretary's statement on the 4th March you asked whether there would be anything further to say about the possibility of expediting the reference of the Palestine question to UNO if you asked a Question in about a week's time; and I understand that you have now asked whether a statement could be made tomorrow.

The position is that we have suggested the immediate setting up of an ad hoc Commission of Enquiry, which would get to work at once and report to the General Assembly. I understand that this proposal is acceptable to the Secretary-General of UNO and to the French, the Chinese and the Russian representatives. Unfortunately, however, the Americans have raised certain difficulties. The Foreign Secretary hopes that he will be able to dispose of these by discussion with General Marshall in Moscow and it may therefore be possible to make a further statement in a few days, but I think you will understand that anything said now might well increase the difficulties. I hope that in these circumstances you will be willing to defer your request for a statement. I will, of course communicate with you again as soon as there is anything further to report.

Winston S. Churchill: speech
(Hansard)

12 March 1947   House of Commons

ECONOMIC SITUATION

Order read for resuming Adjourned Debate on Question.

That this House welcomes the laying before Parliament of a survey of the nation's requirements and resources for the year 1947, is concerned at the seriousness of the situation disclosed, and will support the Government in all practical measures taken in co-operation with all sections of the people of the country to overcome the difficulties and to make secure the foundations of our industry so as to provide a high standard of living for our people. – (Sir Stafford Cripps.)

Question again proposed.
Mr Churchill: I beg to move in line 2 to leave out from '1947' to the end, and to add:

> and while recognising the ever-increasing gravity of the economic crisis and willing to give its support to any practical measures to meet it, regrets that the full facts of the situation have for so long been withheld from the country; and has no confidence in a Government whose actions hitherto have served only to aggravate the national difficulties and whose proposals for the future are either inadequate or injurious.

The problems which confronted the British nation on the morrow of their victory required the strength of a united people to solve and overcome. Instead of that, the Socialist Government, in their hour of unexpected success, set themselves to establish the rule of a party, and of a sect within a party. Having even then, as my right hon. Friend the Member for the Scottish Universities (Sir J. Anderson) reminded us, polled only 37 per cent. of the total electorate, they nevertheless deemed it their mission to impose their particular ideological formulas and theories upon all the rest of their fellow countrymen, regardless of the peril in which we all stood, regardless of the urgency of the work to be done, most of all, regardless of the comradeship by which alone we had survived the war.

This was a crime against the British State and people, the consequences of which have hampered our recovery, darkened our future and now endanger our very life. In our immense administrative difficulty, the Prime Minister and his colleagues should have concentrated upon their immediate practical tasks, and left the fulfilment of party ambition and the satisfaction of party appetites, at least until we, and the rest of the world with us, stood on firmer and safer ground. Before they nationalised our industries they should have nationalised themselves. They should have set country before party, and shown that they were Britons first, and Socialists only second. They should have set the day-to-day well-being of the whole mass of the nation before and above the gratification of party passions. In this they would have found an honourable and worthy mission, from which lasting honour for themselves and their party might have been reached.

On the contrary, mouthing slogans of envy, hatred and malice, they have spread class warfare throughout the land and all sections of society, and they have divided this nation, in its hour of serious need, as it has never been divided, in a different way from that in which it has ever been divided, in the many party conflicts I have witnessed in the past. In less than two years our country, under their control, has fallen from its proud and glorious position in the world, to the plight in which it lies this afternoon, and with even more alarming prospects opening upon us in the future. That is their offence, from which we shall suffer much, and with the guilt and discredit of which their name and the doctrines of their party will long be identified in British homes.

For our part, when this Government first took office, although profoundly distressed by the vote of the electorate – (*Laughter*) – no one more than me – we immediately offered any services which we could render to the national cause, not only at home, but in the United States. I, and my leading colleagues did our utmost, against a good many of our friends here, in our party, to help the Government to obtain the American loan of £1,000 million, in spite of the disadvantageous conditions under which it was offered. I used such personal influence as I had in the United States, as the Chancellor of the Exchequer knows, to clear away American misunderstandings, so far as it is in the power of any private citizen to do any such thing. On every occasion hitherto, my colleagues and I have emphasised the importance of national savings, and we shall continue to do so, but I have an increasing feeling, in view of inflation, that at any rate the smallest class of savings might be linked to some permanent standard of values. We have voted with the Government in everything they have done for the sake of our country, but what has been the return? An aggressive party attack has been made upon us.

I am sorry to see, from the newspapers, though I am glad I was not here, that the Minister of Defence distinguished himself by showing that aggressive spirit last night. An unbroken stream of scorn and hatred has been poured out upon us, not only by Government speakers in all parts of the country, but from the official Government newspaper, the *Daily Herald*. One would have thought that the ten million people, who voted for us, or with us, at the Election, were hardly fit to live in the land of their birth, although most of them were folks who had given a lot for the national victory.

The first and the gravest injury which our country has sustained is psychological. It is the injury to the spirit. I was the Prime Minister responsible, as head of the Government, for the present crushing weight of direct taxation including the almost confiscatory taxation of wealth. All this was done with a great Conservative majority by a Prime Minister of the Conservative Party and by a Chancellor of the Exchequer of the Conservative Party. I was also responsible, as head of the Government, for the controls and regulations of all kinds that were in force at the end of the war. We must not forget that afternoon in May, 1940 – I was not here; I had to go to Paris – when the enormous Tory majorities in both Houses of Parliament voted into the hands of the Government, for the sake of our country's survival, practically all the rights of property and, more precious still, of liberty on which what we have called civilisation is built. That ought not to be forgotten when hon. Members opposite mock at us as exploiters, rack renters and profiteers. It ought not to be forgotten, nor grinned at, that Conservative majorities in both Houses of

Parliament, in one single afternoon, offered all they had and all that they were worth.

Britain saved herself at that time. Perhaps it may be argued, in the light of history, that she saved the world. But what is so particularly odious and mean, and what has caused this deep schism in our island life, is that this sacrifice so nobly made for victory – not only for our own survival and self-preservation but for the victory of the world cause of freedom – should be used and exploited for party purposes and for the institution of a system of Socialism abhorrent to the mass of the nation, destructive of the free life we have known here so long, and paralysing to our native enterprise and energy. Advantage has been taken of the generous impulses of the nation and they have been used for the opposite purpose for which they were given. Rarely has there been such a distortion of trust or breach of ordinary British fair play. It is that malversation of wartime sacrifices, that 'fraud on the power' which has riven the nation in twain and rendered it incapable, while the abuse continues, of overcoming and surmounting its many problems and difficulties.

I have hitherto dealt with what I call the psychological aspect. I now come to the material things by which we live – a lower level, but still essential for the continuance of existence. I will first deal with bread and coal. I shall be told, 'You complained of too much regulation. You, Mr Churchill, complained of too much regulation about bread, and you also complained of too little regulation about coal. Where do you stand upon control of these two fundamental supplies?' It may be asked – it is a perfectly fair question and I give hon. Members opposite an opportunity to cheer it – 'Have you any central theme of thought in these matters, or are you merely taking points off a harassed Government as difficulties arise?' I will answer that question as bluntly as I have put it, but it will take a little while. There was no need for a bread shortage and there was no need for the breakdown in coal. I assert that the shortages which have caused us so much trouble and misfortune, both in bread and coal, are merely marginal and could have been provided against by reasonable foresight and prudence.

Of course, now that the crisis has come, all kinds of emergency measures may be necessary, but if we look back to a year ago, it would have been possible though not easy – many things are not easy nowadays – to maintain sufficient supplies to avoid the disasters which have come upon us. First, take bread. The whole of this process of costly and vexatious rationing, to which even in the crisis of the U-boat war we never had to resort, has only saved so far 290,000 tons of wheat out of a total consumption of perhaps 2,500,000 tons since bread rationing began. Why, then, did Sir Ben Smith give away 200,000 tons of our agreed allocation in April, 1946? Why did the Lord President, in May, waive our claims to another 250,000 tons of foreign wheat which His Majesty's Government had been convinced, and the Food Ministry had been convinced, our people needed? Here were 450,000 tons that we could have had for our under-nourished people which were whistled down the wind last year for reasons which have never been properly explained to Parliament.

Compassion, charity and generosity are noble virtues, but the Government should be just before they are generous. There is no virtue or wisdom in so far undermining the physical strength of our population that we ourselves have to join the ranks of those who were broken by the war and cease to have the power to help the world even to make the British wheels go round. There are international bodies of great power and force nowadays, and undoubtedly they will continue. We do not get very well treated on these international bodies, anyhow. We do not seem to be able to stand up for ourselves, for our own rights and our needs. Of course, when the new British Food Minister[1] says that we are on the whole better nourished than ever before, not much sympathy can be expected from international bodies dealing with a number of countries who are not at all backward in making their claims and dilating upon their woes. Let me repeat what the Chancellor of the Duchy of Lancaster (Mr J. B. Hynd) is reported to have said the other day:

> Already in this country the people are probably enjoying the highest standard of living in the world. We are not even suffering from as many shortages as people would imagine.

What chance have we got before these international committees of making our case for the hard-working people of this island, when it is given away beforehand by the Minister? I affirm here this afternoon that the British people today are under-nourished. They are less well fed – (*Interruption*.) I have never heard much anger expressed, in my long experience, from the Left Wing and Radical quarters about anything which got more food to the people. It has always been a point they championed. But now the Government's Socialist policy comes first and the welfare of the people comes second. I say that our people are less well fed in this victorious but precariously balanced island, with its magnificent but at the same time delicate and ramshackle structure of wealth producing apparatus, than are the populations of Holland, Belgium and Denmark. They are three countries which have just emerged from long years of Prussian German Nazi rule.

I say there was no need for bread rationing with all its inconveniences and the additions to our clerical staffs and paper forms so dear to the hearts of the party opposite. I say there was no need for all this inconvenience if we had not needlessly and wrongfully given up the basic share to which our condition entitled us, which our ships could carry, and which our money, albeit borrowed, could last year and this year at any rate buy.

I challenge the Government directly and in detail, on this food issue. We are frequently informed that 2,400 calories is the minimum daily amount to

---

[1] John Strachey.

maintain a human being in a state of health. It was only a few weeks ago that we were told in this House by the Parliamentary Secretary to the Ministry of Food[1] – who is in her place and whose authoritarian demeanour would inspire all, if her agreeable personality did not somewhat discourage it – that our rations gave us less than 1,400 calories, and that from food bought on points, another 200 calories could be derived, 1,600 calories in all. Yet the Chancellor of the Duchy – he has gone – I did not mean to knock him out so quickly. The Chancellor of the Duchy was challenged because the Germans only got, as was said, 1,550 calories. He explained that this was merely the basic ration, and that two-thirds of the Germans were getting rations varying from 2,550 calories to 3,990 calories. I hope it is true. I would not begrudge anybody the food they can get, but how do the statements correspond with the arguments which are used to make us content with the diet which, without having committed great crimes in the world, our nation has now to receive?

We are told, of course, that our people get another 1,300 calories from foods outside the rationed types. Well, I should like to know where. To get 1,300 calories each, persons would have to eat 5 lb. of potatoes or 8 lb. of cabbage every day, and which of us, I should like to know, except perhaps the President of the Board of Trade, would do that even if we could buy such quantities of vegetables and could afford to pay the price which is being charged for them? I am quite prepared to take my share of whatever the British nation subjects itself to, but not necessarily to contemplate receiving with composure the consequences of the mismanagement of the right hon. Gentleman and his colleagues. I repeat that the British people are under-nourished today. This lethargy in work and falling-off in individual output to which attention has been drawn from every quarter of the House, is only partly due to Socialist teachings. It is mainly due to a shortfall in the necessary calories in respect especially of the heavy manual workers. All this is quite apart from the dreary, dull monotony of diet which directly affects incentive. Let us put up a fight for John Bull's food anyhow – (Hon. Members: 'Hear, hear'.) He will make the sacrifices if he is called upon to do so, but to run him down as low as this, is a scandal and a shame.

In the whole business of purchasing food and other commodities the State, that is to say the Government officials and Ministers involved, have already shown a lack of foresight and judgment which plainly reveals their incapacity as compared with private traders competing with one another, animated by the profit motive, and corrected constantly by the fear of loss and by the continual elimination of the inefficient. That is a general principle. I say that the wanton and partisan – this is only an incident, but I cannot omit it here – destruction of the Liverpool Cotton Exchange will be for ever held against the

---

[1] Edith Summerskill.

distinguished record of the President of the Board of Trade as an act of folly and of pedantry, amounting to little less than bad citizenship.

Now I turn from bread to coal – (Hon. Members: 'Where is the Minister?') I am sorry that the Minister of Fuel and Power (Mr E. Shinwell) is not here. I intend to devote an important section of argument to the matter for which he is responsible. I cannot, however, consider that the Business of the House should be frustrated by the evidently calculated absence of the Minister concerned in any particular matter which it is necessary to raise. I will address myself to the Prime Minister as far as possible in this matter.

Here in the case of coal the argument is much clearer than in that of bread. The saving produced by all this stoppage of industry, with its measureless reactions upon our means of earning our livelihood in future years, and averting financial catastrophe, has been very small. What does it amount to? The only figure we had was given to us by the Prime Minister. He said there was a saving of 550,000 tons at the electrical generating stations. That is much less than a single day's output of the mines. How much should I add for the other direct saving: two, three, four days' output? The Government have not told us. Perhaps I should say it is four days – five at the very most. That is all we have saved by the whole of the inconveniences and hardship inflicted on the domestic consumer and the stoppage of industry, leading, mind you, to a rise in unemployment only just short of the previous high peak of unemployment, the last time a Socialist Government was in office in 1930. It is no pleasure to me to hit the Minister of Fuel and Power now that he is down – I do not know whether he is out or not, but he is certainly not here. I must, however, mark his total lack of foresight. The misleading statements which he made repeatedly are so notorious that I will not trouble the House by quoting them, though I have them here. They have certainly robbed him – I say this seriously to the Prime Minister – of the credence and confidence of the public. Everyone knows he is a very straight, honourable man in private life, but no one will believe his statements about the coal situation in future, and no statement that he makes will receive the slightest attention. It is a matter which certainly should be considered, and which perhaps explains his absence from our Debate this afternoon. He failed to persuade the Cabinet in good time or else they failed to persuade him – I cannot tell, naturally – but he failed to persuade the Cabinet of the calamities which would come upon us, if we ran short of the few odd millions of marginal coal which should be kept as a sacred reserve, as what is called the distributional minimum or, in the *Digest*, distributive stock.

There were produced in the year 1946, 189 million tons of coal. If we had had only 4 million or 5 million tons more, we could have got through without this disaster, and with something in hand. Five million tons extra, and we should have come through this hard, hazardous winter without a breakdown. The plainest warnings were given. It is remarkable, looking back, how often the figure of 5 million tons of coal was mentioned. Belatedly, the Minister of Fuel and Power himself realised it:

> What stands between us and success this winter?

he asked on 26th September of last year.

> A matter of 5,000,000 tons of coal.

On that coal, he said, depended the salvation of this country. And Mr Horner[1] – Comrade Horner – speaking at a coal-production conference at Edinburgh on 6 October, said:

> For each 5 million tons of coal of which the industry might be short, there will be a consequential loss of employment to more than 1,000,000 people.

There was certainly not any lack of warning from that quarter. Five million tons of coal. Why, the Government allowed its Minister of Fuel or its President of the Board of Trade to export 9 million tons, no doubt with very good reason, in this same year. No doubt the reasons were good but, nevertheless, 9 million tons of coal were exported in bunkering or otherwise during the year, and 5 of these 9 millions kept at home, or 5 millions imported in good time, would have saved us from a breakdown in the whole of our productive industry which will cost us directly tens of millions and, indirectly, hundreds of millions in the productive energies of our people.

It is no new topic. We watched the coal position vigilantly every year of the war. We took the necessary difficult decisions each year in good time. In January or February you must always make sure that you will be able, by the winter, to build up your stocks to the normal 18 million tons of coal or thereabouts, so that you do not drop below the distributional minimum on account of any extra winter consumption. All through the war, we succeeded in keeping this reserve intact. The President of the Board of Trade stated in his comprehensive speech two days ago that during the war we had steadily reduced our stocks. That is quite untrue.

The President of the Board of Trade (Sir Stafford Cripps) indicated dissent.

Mr Churchill: It is no good the right hon. and learned Gentleman shaking his head; he cannot alter his own *Statistical Digest*, or what he calls his own *Statistical Digest*, by shaking his head. Our so-called distributive stocks, parcelled out throughout the whole country for the daily consumption, in the winter of 1944, were larger than those in 1939. In the intervening years between 1939 and 1944 they were larger still. Why, then, did he say to the House that we had eaten into, or worn down, our reserve of coal during the war? It is quite inaccurate. The right hon. and learned Gentleman two days ago, with a great deal

---

[1] Arthur Lewis Horner, 1894–1968. Educated at Merthyr Elementary Schools. Miner's agent, 1933. Resident, South Wales Miners, 1936–46. General Secretary, National Union of Mine Workers, 1946–59.

of emphasis, lifted up this book which I hold in my hand, and charged hon. Members that they had probably never read it or would not recognise it. He took it as a book for which he should have the credit – 'Socialism gets things done' – as if he had published this book, brought it out. Why, this very return, this *Digest*, was brought into being at my wish, in the autumn of 1940, but, of course, in the war the figures could not be published. What the right hon. and learned Gentleman has done is to claim the parentage and the credit – if credit there be for such an obvious act, as to make it public.

However, while he has made it public, and lectured hon. Members of this House on not studying it with more attention, there are some facts in it which have at any rate escaped his omniscient eye. The first one is that there was no inroading of stocks under all the cruel, hard necessities of the war. The figures can be found on page 20. For the first time, in the dawn of 1945, the National Government of those days saw the red light. We have a record of what happened at the turn of that year. The usual coal scrutiny was made, as it ought to be made, by the responsible Ministers at the head of the Government, 10 months before the event. It was reported to me that we should have in April – April is the key month, because then we turn from the winter expenditure to the summer scale in the coal year – only 10 million tons instead of the normal 12 million tons which we had always considered the minimum, and therefore it would be difficult to build up to more than 16 million tons by the end of October. Look at that – January, 1945. Those were very rough days. The Von Rundstedt[1] offensive which had been launched in the Ardennes was still in progress. We were preparing to cross the Rhine. Everything was being strained for that. Nevertheless, at that moment, rather than fall below the minimum precautionary coal reserve, I sent a minute, being well advised, to the Minister of Fuel and Power – my right hon. and gallant Friend the Member for Pembroke (Major Lloyd-George), the bearer of a famous name – stopping all further commitments to export coal, even to the Armies, without my express permission.

It is a very serious thing to run short of coal in this island when a matter of five million tons can save it. It can ruin the whole of one's war making capacity. What happened after I left office I do not know. By the winter of 1945 the Socialist Government had only built up our distributive stock to 13.8 million tons. Fortunately for them, industry was changing over and had not got fully into its stride. The winter was mild, so we got through to the spring without any major dislocation. That was a period for which we were jointly responsible. There was the National Government, followed by the Conservative Government at the beginning, and the right hon. Gentlemen opposite at

[1] Karl Rudolf Gerd von Rundstedt, 1875–1953. Cdr, Army Group South, in Polish campaign; Army Group A during German invasion of France, 1939–40. FM, 1940. Dismissed by Hitler following German retreat form Rostov. Recalled and appointed C-in-C in the West, 1942. Dismissed after German defeat in Normandy, July 1944. Recalled as C-in-C in the West, Sep. 1944. POW, 1945–9.

the end. What happened then? In April, 1946, the so-called distributive stocks were down to less than seven million tons – smaller than they had ever been in this century. Surely, then the danger must have been glaring.

The National Government had taken extraordinary measures when our stocks dropped to 10 million tons; it was a very strong measure to check the supply of fuel to the Army when we were pushing a great operation. It is true we can always rely on them having a little up their sleeves. The quartermaster spirit is not lacking in the ranks of the British Army, but still the position was very serious. We took these extraordinary measures when the stocks dropped to 10 million tons. The present Government, however, who have been so busy with so many important intellectual exercises, do not seem to have taken any care, although the stocks dropped to 7 million tons. For a year it must have been obvious that, without exceptional measures, we should never reach the desired 18 million tons by the autumn. That was the time when the Government should have realised what impended. That is the time when they should have taken steps to meet the otherwise inevitable catastrophe – a catastrophe which would have happened, whatever the weather. The weather has added to the misery and discomfort of all our people, but it has not altered the march of economic events in a decisive fashion.

Why did not the Government do anything? I ask the Prime Minister to let us know tonight. We were not at war then. All our enemies were conquered. The seas were opened. I am told there is more tonnage afloat now than there ever has been. A little ordinary forethought and a little planning would have made sure that the necessary minimum of stocks in reserve was not lacking. I cannot understand the answer to this question. Why did the Government not buy more coal? If they could not get it in any other way, why did they not buy it? I am assured that it could have been bought. Five million tons would have done it, and more than done it. It might have cost £8 million or £9 million, but if we did not want it, we could have sold it again. We should have wanted it as it turned out, and we should not have sold it again.

Here are these gentlemen who are all so clever and eager to make an earthly Paradise, where all the work does itself, where all we have to do is to soak the rich – if any can be found – and hire more officials for control, if there are any unemployed. They had forgotten this elementary precaution. They were so busy planning Utopia, so ardent to score off their party opponents, that they forgot their duty, they gave away our bread, and forgot our coal. If 5 million tons of coal had been bought in the last 12 months, in America or South Africa, it would not have stopped this hard winter but, at least, we would have had the means to come through it without a collapse. It is not a very good advertisement for Socialist planning. In fact, a frightful injury, easily avoidable, has been inflicted upon the wage-earning masses and the unhappy middle class, which will lead to worse privation in the future. That is one of the justifications for the Amendment which I am moving.

Before I leave the subject of coal, there is one other fact upon which I must correct the President of the Board of Trade. On Monday I asked whether the rise in the consumption of electricity had not been offset by the corresponding reduction in the domestic consumption of coal. The right hon. and learned Gentleman's answer was:

> No, Sir. The right hon. Gentleman is quite wrong. There has not been a corresponding reduction at all.

According to this *Statistical Digest*, of which we share the parentage, in 1938, the last prewar year, the domestic consumers got 45,500,000 tons of coal. In 1946, they got only 31 million tons of coal – a drop of nearly a third. In the same period the consumption of coal for electricity works increased by about 11 million tons, from 15 million to 26 million tons. But of this, as the Secretary of State for the Dominions[1] informed us in another place, only about one-third is to be reckoned against the domestic consumer. Thus, whereas the domestic consumer was cut by 14,500,000 tons of coal, and as his or her – the housewives come into this – increased use of electricity corresponded to less than 4 million tons, there was a net reduction of 10 million tons in 1946 as compared with 1938, which is the last prewar year. The population has not diminished. The ordinary people still feel the difference between heat and cold. They still have to use fuel sometimes to cook their dinner. Why, then, should there be this severe reduction in the supply of coal? I venture to think that the right hon. and learned Gentleman should study more carefully than he evidently has found time to do, with so much on his hands, this *Digest* which he commended so ceremoniously to us the other day.

So much for bread and coal. I think I have answered that question – that the Government could have avoided both these shortages by taking reasonable precautions, and that any other Government which has ever sat on the benches opposite would, in the normal working of its affairs, have had the foresight to take these quite manageable measures in good time and not lead us where we are today.

I must say a word about housing. I am sorry that the Minister of Health[2] is not here, and still more sorry for the cause. We are glad to know he is improving in health. We shall all be very glad to have him back here, in order to bring home to him the position in which we stand. The destruction wrought by the enemy by the bombing of our homes raised the building and repair of our houses to the very first urgency after food and fuel. In nearly two years, in spite of all the regulations, penalties and paper forms, we built fewer permanent houses than were built every two months under private enterprise and Tory government before the war. Remarkable. In those two years, when it was really

---

[1] Christopher Addison, 1st Viscount Addison.
[2] Aneurin Bevan.

Operation No. 1, fewer permanent houses were built than were built in the ordinary course of affairs, under private enterprise and a Tory Government before the war. (Hon. Members: 'What about after the last war?') I thought it was coming. We shall, no doubt, be reminded of Dr Addison, now Lord Addison, KG. We must, no doubt, be reminded of his failure after the previous war. It is quite true that he was a great failure; and he was dismissed by Mr Lloyd George, with lively Labour approbation. It is no part of my duty to defend Lord Addison today. But the need of rehousing then, was not comparable with what it is at the present time, because the cessation of building was not so complete and prolonged, and millions of houses had not been damaged or destroyed by bombing. Besides, everyone should live and learn.

We improved a lot of things in the war which has just finished, from the mistakes made in the 1914–18 war. Certainly we ought to have rectified a lot of the mistakes made in the last peace, in the one which has now come to us. I am sure it would have been possible, with energy, ingenuity and good will, for the Minister responsible to set in motion again the vast, flexible, complete system of house building, both by private enterprise and by local authorities, which in the years before the recent war was producing houses of a good kind for letting or sale, at a rate four times as rapid as that of which the Government can boast today, after two years of peace and nearly 20 months of office. Socialist propaganda and trade union prejudice have attained a remarkable result in Lord Quibell's[1] case. Here was a Socialist peer, a former and much respected colleague of ours, who tried to stimulate house building by a system of bonuses for the builders, through the number of bricks laid per hour. The builders liked this system, and responded to it. Up went the production rate. Well, we all know what happened to Lord Quibell's scheme. And this is typical of what is happening all over the country.

I turn to the national expenditure of money and manpower. I will mention only a certain number of items which might demand the attention of the House of Commons. First of all, instead of leaving the Germans to manage their own affairs and helping them as much as we could, as Christian men, while stopping rearmament, we are spending £20 million a year on trying to solve their problems when we cannot solve our own, in trying to teach them all to hate the Nazis and only succeeding in teaching them to hate us. Then there is Palestine: £82 million since the Socialist Government came into power squandered in Palestine, and 100,000 Englishmen now kept away from their homes and work, for the sake of a senseless, squalid war with the Jews in order to give Palestine to the Arabs, or God knows who. 'Scuttle', everywhere, is the order of the day – Egypt, India, Burma. One thing at all costs we must preserve: the right to get ourselves world-mocked and world-hated over Palestine,

---

[1] David John Kinsley Quibell, 1879–1962. MP (Lab.) for Brigg in Lincolnshire, 1929–31, 1935–45. Signatory to Post-War Forest Policy, 1943. Baron, 1945. Mayor of Scunthorpe, 1953.

at a cost of £82 million. Then there is all this silliness, amounting almost to lunacy, about the spending of the American loan. I must say, I thought it was to be used to re-equip our factories and plants, and to give us the essential food while we got on our feet again. But apparently far less than one-tenth – I am not going into smaller fractions – was spent on re-equipment and all the rest is subject to further decision.

Then there is the story about the dried eggs. Half the foreign exchange spent on dried eggs last year, if devoted to bringing in maize, would have given twice as much real nourishment to the British people, and there would have been the chickens as well. But no. The maize must go to the delightful people in Yugoslavia and Albania, who murdered 44 of our sailors a few weeks ago. Indeed, some of it may have gone to the Poles and Czechs who, I understand, are offering to export eggs and poultry to us. Then there are the Poles in this country. I would have had them all parked out suitably in Germany, far from the Russian or Polish lines, within six months of the end of the German war. It never occurred to me that anything else but that would have been done. Now they are with us here, eating I am told, in many cases, better rations than we are allowed to have ourselves. I am sorry for these men; they are brave men who have defended their country's cause. But presently the Government will have a bitter quarrel with them, a quarrel which has begun already. Surely, it would have been wiser, in principle at any rate, to have 180,000 Poles in Germany and 180,000 more Englishmen at home. Then, of course, we are told it might have offended Russia. His Majesty's Government have been very successful in not offending Russia. Perhaps they will allow me to offer my congratulations on that.

At the present time we have the pleasure of being administered by 460,000 more civil servants – double the size of the prewar Army – than we had before the war began, at a cost calculated at £150 million a year. The Socialist ideal is to reduce us to one vast Wormwood Scrubbery. I do not wish to exaggerate it, because it is quite true that at Wormwood Scrubs there is only one official to every four prisoners, whereas up to the present we have the advantage of only one official to look after every eight wage earners or producers. There is nothing like getting the facts accurately. I am looking at the expenditure of the year. I hope the Chancellor of the Exchequer will be following this discussion, for I am sure he cannot be entirely blind to some of the tendencies which I am indicating.

We come now to the Minister of Defence. As I say, I was glad not to have heard his quite unexpected performance yesterday. I have a regard for him, and I also think that a Minister of Defence should stand a little aloof from party and Parliamentary disputes. (Hon. Members: Why?) Because he is supposed to run the Services, in which all parties take an interest from one point of view or another. Of course, I doubt whether he has improved his prestige and authority by the exhibition he made of himself last night.

I am bound to say, I hope the Service Estimates will be examined by the House with great care. Quite apart from the fighting strengths which have to be maintained – which I am not arguing today – I fear a very great degree of non-effective padding has been introduced into all three Services under a lax and incompetent political control. I should like to know, as the result of a searching inquiry, whether, for instance, in the Navy there is not a much smaller proportion of men afloat to men ashore, or of men afloat to the money we pay, than has ever been known before. I should like to see some figures on that. I should like to know whether, in the case of the Air Force, there is not an ever-increasing ground-staff compared with those who fly; and in the case of the Army, whether the proportion of fighting men – which is, after all, the end and object of military forces – is not getting continually smaller. It is the old story I have often told of the teeth and the tail. At the moment, I believe, the teeth are falling out and the tail is growing ever longer and fatter. Surely, the Chancellor of the Exchequer and the House of Commons as a whole should take some interest in this aspect.

I suspect, moreover, that the military, naval, and the Air Force chiefs, for whom I have the greatest regard, are not sufficiently controlled in these financial aspects by the present Government. The control by Parliamentary Ministers of the Services is more important in time of peace than in time of war, when military views necessarily predominate. We have weak or absentee Ministers in all three Service Departments. All three heads have been changed in a year. There are new Ministers now. There is a new Minister of Defence, if he would not absorb himself entirely in politics. Nevertheless, it is the duty of the House of Commons to make sure that strict Parliamentary and financial control should prevent waste, and overcharge to the public. It is doubly important now to reduce redundant non-effectives – quite apart from strategic issues – when so many of our troops are abroad and, consequently, affect our limited foreign exchange.

There are two great topics with which I ought, certainly, to deal – agriculture and finance; but I cannot trespass too long upon the indulgence of the House. (Hon. Members: 'Go on.') The first of these topics was dealt with last night by my right hon. Friend the Member for Saffron Walden (Mr R. A. Butler); and we shall explore, or ask to be allowed to explore, most thoroughly in the near future, the very grave situation in home-grown foods, and future plans for growing them. As to finance, I shall follow the example of the Chancellor of the Exchequer, and reserve what I have to say on that dominating subject until the Budget, which is now not far distant.

The French have a saying, 'Drive Nature away, and she will return at the gallop.' Destroy the free market, and you create a black market; you overwhelm the people with laws and regulations, and you induce a general disrespect of law; you guillotine legislation in the House of Commons, and pass masses of Orders in Council. You may decree that a builder who builds a house without a licence is liable to seven years' penal servitude, but you will find that juries will not convict him. You may try to destroy wealth, and find that all you have done is to increase poverty. In their class warfare, the Government have no right to appeal to the spirit of Dunkirk.

We were all touched and deeply moved at the gifts made by Australia and New Zealand in reducing their sterling balances by £30 million or £40 million for the sake of the dear old Motherland, now in the mess and muddle into which she seems to them to have been thrown. But it was unpleasant to feel that this aid from our children from across the ocean was little more than half of the money racketed away by the post-war Army in Germany – £58 million in what the Secretary of State for War[1] complacently called a 'merry game' with NAAFI cigarettes, marks and sterling. That is the simplest test, and to some extent the measure, of the demoralisation which 'Socialism in our own time', for all the honourable wishes and intentions of its votaries, and for all their Pharisaical sneers at an honest profit motive – that is the measure of the kind of degeneration it has brought upon our decent people.

Are there not other needless squanderings and leakages of our life's strength? Is it true that, throughout this winter, nearly one-third of the total capacity of the electric generating production industry has been engaged on export orders? Is it wise, when our whole export programme is cramped through the shortage of generating equipment and of coal, that we should try to boost the export figures in this way? What is the truth about the export of this electric generating equipment and mining machinery at this time above all others? What was the quantity of this vital apparatus exported last year? What was its value? Where did it go? And what did we receive in exchange? The President of the Board of Trade told us that it was particularly for Russia. What then did we receive in exchange? (*Interruption.*) I took the trouble to look it up.

Sir S. Cripps: Will the right hon. Gentleman allow me? I said that in the early stages during the war, we were having to manufacture a lot for Russia.

Mr Churchill: None went to Russia last year? Is that so?

Sir S. Cripps indicated assent.

Mr Churchill: I shall, then, not press my inquiry. But a very proper inquiry to make is, what did we get back in return for what was sent? Or when are we going to get it back? Are we going to get back any of the railway sleepers of which Russia has so many? The right hon. and learned Gentleman referred to the early days of the war. Have we been repaid anything, or have we given it?

Sir S. Cripps: The right hon. Gentleman asks questions about current manufacture. That is being paid for in the ordinary way. He knows all about these things.

Mr Churchill: What I feel is this – and I shall look at it from this point and that point, and hon. Members ought to do the same. The 45 million who live

---

[1] Frederick Bellenger.

in these islands cannot bear everything on their threadbare shoulders. None gave so freely from the beginning to the end of the war as we did. Now, in our exhaustion, we cannot be blood donors to every part of the world. Surely, there ought to be some sense of national self-preservation in the hearts of our rulers.

I read with interest, and not without surprise, paragraph 9 of the White Paper. The House, no doubt, has it in mind. The point that struck me was this:

> Our methods of economic planning must have regard to our special economic conditions. Our present industrial system is the result of well over a century's steady growth, and is of a very complex nature. The decisions which determine production are dispersed among thousands of organisations and individuals. The public is accustomed to a wide range of choice and quality in what it buys. Above all, our national existence depends upon imports, which means that the goods we export in return must compete with the rest of the world in price, quality and design, and that our industry must adapt itself rapidly to changes in world markets.

The Leader of the Liberal Party[1] must have been very pleased at this. It carries us back to the old days of Adam Smith and John Stuart Mill. It carries us back to the periods when the laws of supply and demand had some validity, and when the qualities of free enterprise, hard work, thrift, contrivance, and good housekeeping were said to be the sources of national wealth. This paragraph 9 of the Government White Paper might have been conceived by Mr Gladstone or Mr Bright. It might have been in the clear-cut language of Herbert Henry Asquith, in the days when the calm lamp of Liberal wisdom shed its refulgent gleam upon a happier world. I wonder who was the civil servant who wrote this for his Socialist masters. Out of the 2,000,000 we have at present, he should be the last one to be sacked. What is the meaning of this death-bed confession? It is the recognition that the life of this island people of 47 million cannot be maintained under the Socialist system. It is a confession that not only have we been deeply injured by all the Government's neglects and mismanagement of our ordinary daily affairs, but that the Socialist dream or the Socialist nightmare – which you will – for which so much of our great prosperity has been sacrificed, is false and foolish, and that it would not enable our present numbers of people to inhabit this island or maintain the standard of life to which we have hitherto attained. Why, then, with a situation so complex, throw a series of nationalising spanners into this indispensable system, which is the 'steady growth of well over a century'? Why do it wantonly at a time when external facts are so adverse, and all the resources so scarce?

Let me put this case in more general terms. In most cases, management

[1] Clement Davies.

by private enterprise is not only more efficient, but far less costly to the wage-earners, than management by the huge official staffs now quartered upon the producers. Let every man now ask himself this: Is it the interest of the wage-earners to serve an all-powerful employer – the State – or to deal with private employers, who, though more efficient in business, are in a far weaker position as masters? Is it the interest of the housewife to queue up before officials at public distribution centres, as Socialism logically involves, or to go as a customer to a private shopkeeper, whose livelihood depends on giving good and friendly service to his customers? Of course, the State must have its plan and its policy. The first object of this plan should be to liberate and encourage the natural, native energies, genius and contrivance of our race, which, by a prodigy, have built up this vast population in our small island, and built up a standard of living which, before the war, was the envy of every country in Europe. The first object, then, is to liberate these energies; the second stage is to guide and aid all the forces that these native energies generate into the right channels. The Government have begun the wrong way round. They have started with control for control's sake on the theory of levelling down to the weakest and least productive types, and thus they have cramped and fettered the life-thrust of British society. I have assembled and cited all these examples of the foolish misdeeds of the Government as an explanation and justification of why we have no confidence in them, and why we regard their continuance in office as a growing national disaster.

If I turn to the future, it is only for a moment. In considering the future, one is on much less certain ground, first of all, because we do not know all the facts, and it is foolish to prophesy unless they are known, and, secondly, because it is always difficult to strike the true note between giving a necessary warning and spreading despondency and alarm. I do not wish to emphasise unduly the various degrees and forms in which the crisis will present itself to us in the next 12 months. In the White Paper, the Government have certainly gone a long way in indicating some of our principal dangers and have not shrunk from confessing that much of what they have been teaching all these years to the wage-earning masses is false, or that the great hopes they encouraged and the promises they made at the General Election are falser still.

One thing appears to me to be perfectly clear. The Government cannot save the country and carry on the class warfare and a Socialist programme of nationalisation at the same time. They must choose between the two. Either they must go down in a measureless crash with their party flags nailed stoutly to the mast, and carry our country down too, or they must make an effort by dropping their Socialist legislation, by freeing industry and enterprise from the trammels in which they have entangled them, and by restoring, at the earliest date, the outraged sense of national unity, to get out of the troubles in which we are. That is their choice, and their only choice. We have not the power to control their decision. The choice is theirs, but on it our fate depends.

Whatever they decide, we shall do our best to minimise the evils they have wrought. We shall inculcate obedience to their decrees wherever these affect the national safety or well-being, even though we dissociate ourselves from all responsibility for the ruin now facing the land.

We do not desire a Coalition. We do not grudge the Ministers their offices, and certainly not their cares. Nevertheless, we must earnestly hope that the Prime Minister and his principal colleagues will take the right turning at this grave moment in British history. The speech which the right hon. Gentleman[1] made at Hanley to win party cheers on 15th February was ominous. It was not up to the level of events, nor was it worthy of the hour. I trust that tonight he will have the courage to strike a truer note of national leadership, and one more worthy of his wartime record in both the wars.

I have two convictions in my heart. One is that, somehow or other, we shall survive, though for a time at a lower level than hitherto. The late Lord Fisher[2] used to say 'Britain never succumbs'. The second is that things are going to get worse before they are better. Before the glowing promises, by which the wearied and unthinking people were seduced at the General Election, have been atoned for, all of us, wherever we sit, will have much to endure. We are bound to give the warning while the time remains. It is right to arouse our people to the peril in which they stand. Only when they realise fully the decline and descent, psychological, social, financial and economic, into which we have fallen, and, in part, been thrust, since our glorious victory, will those forces arise in the land in which redemption and recovery can be found.

Winston S. Churchill: speech
('Winston S. Churchill, His Complete Speeches', volume 7, pages 7462–3)

14 March 1947 Meeting of the Central Council of the National Union of Conservative and Unionist Associations

CONSERVATIVE POLICY ON HOME AFFAIRS

. . . I am sure the delegates feel that Parliamentary Opposition in the Standing Committee on the Transport Bill should be congratulated on the Government's withdrawal of their oppressive measures against licence holders. These men in office, who have muddled our food, muddled our coal, whistled a great part of our Empire down the wind, and lowered our position among

---

[1] Clement Attlee.

[2] John Arbuthnot Fisher, 1841–1920. Known both as 'Jackie' and, because of his somewhat oriental appearance, 'the old Malay'. 1st Sea Lord, 1904–10. Adm. of the Fleet, 1905. Baron, 1909. Retired, 1911. Head of the Royal Commission on Fuel and Engines, 1912–14. Re-appointed 1st Sea Lord at Churchill's urging, 1914. Resigned, in protest at Churchill's Dardanelles plans, 1915. Successfully encouraged Churchill to call for his reinstatement, 1916, but in vain. His memoirs were published in 1919.

the nations of the world in a manner indescribable and astonishing in so short a time, these men are not sure of themselves when they feel, and will increasingly feel, the draught, the wind; the cyclone from the country. Even though we have not got half their number in the House of Commons, nevertheless, we should be able to play our part in withholding some of the worst maltreatment which they had contemplated for their fellow countrymen.

It is the vital duty of every man and woman who care about the greatness and survival – let alone the prosperity – of the country to do the utmost to turn the Government out of office at the earliest possible moment. There was never such an opportunity offered to the Conservative Party of serving the nation as a whole and the cause of freedom in every land.

Our policy can be stated in a nutshell. We accept and affirm the principles of minimum standards of life and labour and the building up of those standards continuously as our resources allow. But above these minimum standards the British people must not be fettered or trammelled. There must be competition upwards – not downwards. When minimum standards are achieved everyone should do their best to make the best of themselves and of the land they love and live in. Above all, never despair, never give in.

Winston S. Churchill to Lord Beaverbrook
(Churchill papers, 2/146)

15 March 1947

Low's *Evening Standard* cartoon yesterday is for the second time in ten days grossly insulting to General Marshall. Ought you not to consider the main question? Nothing but harm is being done to the *Evening Standard*, to you and to most of the things we both care about. The *Daily Herald* would not print such stuff.

Winston S. Churchill to Lord Quickswood[1]
(Quickswood papers)

16 March 1947 Chartwell

My dear Linky,

It was comforting to hear from you about Jack. I feel lonely now that he is not here, after 67 years of brotherly love. I remember my father coming in to my bedroom at the Vice Regal Lodge in Dublin & telling me (aged 5) 'You

---

[1] Hugh Richard Heathcote Gascoyne-Cecil, 1869–1956. Known as 'Linky'. Fifth son of 3rd Marquess of Salisbury (and so uncle to Cranborne). Educated at Eton and University College, Oxford. MP (Cons.) for Greenwich, 1895–1906; for Oxford University, 1910–37. Provost of Eton, 1936–44. Baron Quickswood, 1941. In 1908 he was 'best man' at Churchill's wedding.

have a little brother.' We have always been attached to one another, & after his house was blown up in the war he lived w me at No. 10 or the Annexe.

He had no fear & little pain. Death seems vy easy at the end of the road.

Do you think we shall be allowed to sleep a long time. I hope so. (Ready to serve if really required).

The only thing Jack worried about was England. I told him it wd be all right.

Thank you for all you taught me in my youth. I hope we may meet. Let me know when you are in London.

Anthony Eden to Winston S. Churchill
(*Churchill papers, 4/52*)

19 March 1947
Confidential

My dear Winston,

I ought to have sent you some papers about my resignation[1] earlier, but it has been difficult to collect them. I now enclose:

A. The diary kept at the time by Oliver Harvey[2] who was then my Principal Private Secretary. He is, as you know, still a Civil Servant and Deputy Under Secretary. He is in Moscow at the moment and I have not therefore been able to ask him whether I may show it to you, but I feel sure he would not object. I think you may find it sufficiently interesting to glance through as background.

You will not agree with all of it, nor would I, and it suffers from the disadvantages of a day to day diary, but none the less the account in particular of President Roosevelt's offer and its rejection by Neville Chamberlain may be useful.

B. I enclose a memorandum by Cranborne which is a good short summary of our differences. When he originally showed it to me I suggested that the following paragraph should be added:

'Eden would have considered going to Rome if Austria could be included in the conversations. This, however, was not accepted by Italy, and there was evidence to show that Mussolini had already come to an agreement with Germany about Austria in return for support in Spain.'

---

[1] From the position of Foreign Secretary in 1938.
[2] Oliver Charles Harvey, 1893–1968. Educated at Malvern and Trinity College, Cambridge. On active service in France, Egypt and Palestine (despatches), 1914–18. Entered FO, 1919. First Secretary, Paris, 1931–6. Counsellor, and Principal Private Secretary to successive Secretaries of State for Foreign Affairs, 1936–9, 1941–3. Minister to Paris, 1940. Asst Under-Secretary of State, 1943–6. Knighted, 1946. Deputy Under-Secretary of State (Political), 1946–7. Ambassador to France, 1948–54. Baron, 1954.

C. A note by myself on the American issue. I cannot recall for what purpose this was written but it reads like the Cabinet paper. I also enclose a copy of *Time and Tide* which contains an article by Dick Law on Chamberlain which is I think well done. I have marked a passage in it. He also refers to the American differences.

Finally Sumner Welles also deals with this Roosevelt initiative in his book *A Time for Decision*. Unfortunately my copy is in the country, but if you have not got one I will look up the passage next time I am at home and send it to you. It is good supporting evidence of the line we took.

Could your Secretary let me have the documents back sometime.

Winston S. Churchill to Lewis Douglas[1]
(Churchill papers, 2/54)

19 March 1947

My dear Ambassador,

A thousand welcomes to our battered shores, to which we know you bring a strong breeze of friendship based on knowledge.

I belong to a small dining club, called The Other Club, and I am taking the chair there on the night of Thursday, March 27. Brendan and some of your friends are members. Bernie[2] has several times dined with us on his visits. It would give me great pleasure if you could come as my guest. We shall be about twenty-five people. Dinner is 8.15 for 8.30 p.m., but I could call for you in Grosvenor Square and conduct you to the Savoy where we dine.

I do hope you will be able to come.

Winston S. Churchill to Lord Simon
(Churchill papers, 2/43)

19 March 1947

My dear John,

I thought some confusion might arise over the talk now going on about Dominion status, which as you know was the constitutional course I have advocated.

---

[1] Lewis Williams Douglas, 1894–1974. Born in Bisbee, Arizona. Educated at Massachusetts Institute of Technology, 1916. On active service in WWI. 2nd Lt, 1917. Instructor, Amherst College, 1920. Representative (Dem.) in Arizona House of Representatives, 1923–5; in US House of Representatives, 1927–33. Director of the Budget, 1933–4. Principal and Vice-Chancellor, McGill University, Montreal, Canada, 1938–9. Deputy Administrator, War Shipping Administration, 1942–4. US Ambassador to Great Britain, 1947–50. Director, General Motors Corp., 1944–65. Head of Government Study of Foreign Economic Problems, 1953. Member, President's Task Force on American Indians, 1966–7.

[2] Bernard Baruch.

I therefore send you this short note which I shall be obliged if you will check and improve.

There is some talk about India having Dominion status now as an interim stop to independence. This would mean that the new Viceroy could in fact cease to discharge his statutory duties and act on the advice of Nehru. Such a course would not be legal without legislation, and I presume, before the House of Commons parted with its own responsibilities, it would require to know the authorities to whom powers should be transferred and the constitution under which they should be exercised.

Francis Graham-Harrison[1] to Elizabeth Gilliatt
(Churchill papers, 2/4)

20 March 1947

Dear Miss Gilliatt,

I enclose, as arranged on the telephone, the printed record of the proceedings of the Yalta Conference and the file of telegrams dealing with reparations. I hope that this will give Mr Churchill what he requires, but if there is anything more that is wanted, please let me know.

I shall be grateful if you will let me have these documents back in due course.

Winston S. Churchill to Sir Edward Marsh
(Sir Edward Marsh papers)

24 March 1947 Chartwell

My dear Eddie,

... I am at the present time on the brink of a trip to the Riviera and indulging in all my customary vacillation where alternative forms of pleasure are concerned.

---

[1] Francis Laurence Theodore Graham-Harrison, 1914–2001. Educated at Magdalen College, Oxford. Married, 1941, Carol Mary St John Stewart. Private Secretary to Parliamentary Under-Secretary of State, Home Office, 1941–3; Asst Secretary, 1953–7; Asst Under-Secretary of State, 1957–63; Deputy Under-Secretary of State, 1963–74. Asst Private Secretary to PM, 1946–9. Secretary, Royal Commission on Capital Punishment, 1949–53. CB, 1962.

March 1947

Winston S. Churchill to Clement Attlee
(Churchill papers, 2/4)

25 March 1947

My dear Prime Minister,

I am returning you the papers about Yalta. I see no objection to the Protocol flagged on p. 112 being published as it stands. You, I think, and not I were responsible for the Potsdam Protocols. About the Yalta telegrams, His Majesty's Government have just published the telegram they sent to Eden and me, which might be read as indicating some difference between the 1945 War Cabinet and its delegation at Yalta.

I think therefore that you should publish also Eden's Jason No. 226, the last paragraph of which makes the position of the delegation clear.

Clement Attlee to Winston S. Churchill
(Churchill papers, 2/4)

27 March 1947

My dear Churchill,

I send you herewith the texts of the Yalta, Potsdam and Tehran documents which I would like to lay as White Papers over the weekend. I am glad to note from your letter of the 25th that you have no objection as regards the Yalta document, and I agree that I am responsible as regards the Potsdam Protocol.

Since I spoke to you on the telephone the Americans have forced our hand by publishing, without consulting us, the Tehran Agreement which I also enclose. This is the reason why I feel we must now publish this document as well as the other two. I take it that you will see no objection. I understand that Sargent has already discussed the matter with Eden.

You mention in your letter that the Foreign Secretary quoted at the Moscow Conference an extract from one of the Fleece telegrams from the War Cabinet to the British Delegation at Yalta. Having read it I cannot see that it suggests any difference between you and the Cabinet in London. But if you feel that this should be put beyond all doubt, I would suggest that a semi-official notice might be issued to the Press from No. 10 saying that the instructions sent by the Cabinet to you and Eden at Yalta which Mr Bevin referred to the other day in Moscow, were intended to confirm the view you had already expressed to the Cabinet and in no way represented any difference of opinion. I think this is a safer way of achieving what you want than to publish, as you suggest, Jason No. 226. It would be hardly possible to publish this telegram without publishing at the same time at least Fleece No. 330 and 331 (and maybe others), and to do this would I am sure be most undesirable, for these telegrams contain a lot of stuff which clearly ought still to be kept secret. Besides, once we begin publishing telegrams of this sort we should be pressed to publish yet more and thus easily get into very deep water.

I hope you will agree.

Lewis Douglas to Winston S. Churchill
(Churchill papers, 2/54)

29 March 1947

My Dear Mr Churchill,

Thank you very much for giving me a preview of the paper you have prepared. It would be if not impertinent at least very audacious to suggest that any word be added or any phrase subtracted. I hope you will pardon me for returning it this morning instead of yesterday, and that this delay has not inconvenienced you.

The evening at The Other Club was good fun and I am eternally grateful to you for giving me a glimpse of the delights and gaieties so carefully guarded and fostered by the powers of 'Impenetrable Mystery'. Will you extend to them my gratitude?

I hope that during the week following I will have the pleasure of seeing you and Mrs Churchill. On Monday I will try to settle the matter to suit your convenience.

PS. I find that you have fled to Chartwell for the weekend, and I am therefore further delaying the return of the paper until you arrive Monday morning.

Winston S. Churchill to Clement Attlee
(Churchill papers, 2/4)

30 March 1947

My dear Prime Minister,

Thank you for your letter of March 27. As my Secretary informed your Office on the telephone, I agree to the proposal you make for the publication of the specified Yalta, Potsdam and Teheran Conference papers.

In view of what you say in the second part of your letter, I do not at this moment request the further publication of telegrams exchanged between the War Cabinet at home and Mr Eden and myself when we were at Yalta.

Winston S. Churchill: speech
(Hansard)

31 March 1947 House of Commons

NATIONAL SERVICE BILL

I think the House is indebted to the Minister of Labour (Mr Isaacs) for his extremely lucid and careful description of the Bill, and particularly for the attention he has given to points which cause anxiety here or there. He has evidently carefully mastered the details of the Measure and was able compendiously to give to the House a very full account of it.

On this occasion we support His Majesty's Government. We shall try to do so when they stand for national as apart from party interests and sectarian themes. We even go so far as to compliment them on the courage they have shown in resisting the subversive and degenerate elements in their midst – and elsewhere. Below the Gangway opposite, we see representatives of those conceptions and ideas which nearly brought us to ruin in the late war, and have gone far and are going farther to pull us down after our victory. Therefore I congratulate the Government on standing up to them. It is always difficult for Ministers in contact with reality to resist those feckless and crack-pate elements to which they have pandered in their thirst for power, and on which they largely depend as a Government for their life and office. We shall vote with the Government on the Bill, on all occasions when they are challenged by the crypto-Communists and pacifists and other trends of Left-wing opinion which they have exploited to the full in bygone days, and which they now very naturally resent.

The Minister of Defence (Mr A. V. Alexander) has not made things easier by his aggressive speech the other night when he went out of his way to attack us on this side of the House. Old and experienced politicians will understand his difficulties. We realise that he was trying to gather up in advance a little credit for his own party, for the work which he had to do for the country by showing how well he could be rude to the Tories. After all, that cost him nothing. On an issue of this kind he can be sure that he will get our support any way and at any time when he is doing his duty. To my friends here who were angered the other night I would say that small petty episodes must not be allowed to deter convinced and determined men from their path of duty. I say also to the Minister of Defence – quite appreciating the state of mind he was in – that it is sometimes better, on the whole, to do things not quite so nakedly. *Ars est celare artem.* For the benefit of the Etonians on the other side I will translate that as 'Art is to conceal art.'

We shall support the Bill in all its stages, but that does not mean that we shall not try to shape and modify it as well as we can, to fit it to what we conceive to be the national need. Here I may say that the Bill has evidently been very carefully shaped and considered. We shall do nothing to endanger its passage into law. We shall be careful to be present in good strength to support the Government. Moreover, we shall take no points off them in the constituencies, on the ground that they have gone forward and done this thing. We have quite enough to pick on without that. I will, however, permit myself to make some comments on the past.

The Prime Minister is not here. I have no doubt that he has many other things to do. But it is certainly an irony of fate that the Prime Minister and the Minister of Defence should be the men to bring a conscription Bill before the House now, after two years of peace, when all our enemies have surrendered unconditionally. Why, these were the very politicians who, four months before the outbreak of the war, led their followers into the Lobby against the principle of compulsory military service, and then had the face to accuse the Conservative Party of being 'guilty men'. I and a handful of others have a right to criticise and censor the lack of preparation for the late war, but the Prime Minister and his friends have no right to do so; the whole effort of their party was designed to make every preparation for defence of the country and resistance to Hitler so unpopular, that it was politically impossible. Now, in the long swing of events, the Prime Minister and the Minister of Defence, who refused in May 1939 to vote for conscription against Hitler and Nazism, when that was proposed by Mr Hore-Belisha[1] in Mr Chamberlain's Government, come forward in a time of peace and victory, to ask us to support conscription against some other danger, some other dictatorship, which I do not propose this afternoon precisely to define. This performance this afternoon encourages me. I do not despair of the party opposite. It is never too late to mend; we all may live and learn, and they may live and learn, but the question is whether, when they have learned, we shall still be alive.

I turn now to the Liberal Party. They, at least, are consistent and they are united, but they have not the task of organising and disciplining such large forces as those which occupy the hourly attention of the Government Whips. I remember well the day when my right hon. Friend, Sir Archibald Sinclair, who is not with us at the moment, marched his followers into the Lobby, with the Prime Minister and with the Minister of Defence, to vote 'No' to conscription against Hitler and Nazism in the spring of 1939. In this world of human error and constant variations, usually of an unexpected character, the Liberal Party can range themselves in party doctrine, few but impeccable. They have no need to recur for safety or vindication to that well-known maxim, or dictum,

---

[1] Leslie Hore-Belisha, 1893–1957. Known, on account of his Jewish origins, as 'Horeb Elisha'. His father, an Army officer, died when he was nine months old. Educated at Clifton and St John's College, Oxford. On active service in France, 1915–16; Salonika, 1916–18. President, Oxford Union, 1919. MP (Lib.) for Plymouth Devonport, 1923–31; (Nat. Lib) 1931–42; (Ind.), 1942–5. Parliamentary Secretary, Board of Trade, 1931–2. Financial Secretary, Treasury, 1932–4. Minister of Transport, 1934–7 (with seat in Cabinet from Oct. 1936). PC, 1935. Secretary of State for War, 1937–40 (Member of War Cabinet, 1939–40). Minister of National Insurance, 1945. Baron, 1954.

that 'Consistency is the last resort of feeble and narrow minds.' They are quite entitled to say that they have always been against compulsory service. They were against it before the first world war, and, in spite of some considerable pressure from Mr Lloyd George, they were against it after the first world war. In the interval many things have changed, but here today the Liberal Party are ready to sacrifice themselves in the constituencies, and face any amount of unpopularity, fearless of by-elections, however they may come, and ready at this juncture to stand firm by the old theme and the old flag. It is no part of my policy to pick unnecessary quarrels with the right hon. and learned Gentlemen the Member for Montgomery (Mr Clement Davies) and those whom he leads, and I shall, therefore, content myself with paying this well-deserved tribute to their rigid and inflexible consistency.

I shall venture to present to the House some of the reasons which lead the Conservative Party to give their support to this Socialist Government on the Second Reading of the National Service Bill. First, let me refer to one or two points of detail. Since the war stopped, the mismanagement of our Armed Forces has been remarkable. For a whole year there were three Service Ministers who have since been dismissed or moved because they were either incompetent or absentees. One was promoted. He was not promoted because he was incompetent, but because he was an absentee. At any rate, the three great Service Departments have had to drift and flop along as they might. I criticised the demobilisation policy of the Government early in November 1945, at the very beginning. I still think that it was not carried out with proper speed, down to the limits which were required by the public safety. We know that the Government were forced by a wave of public opinion to change the plans they had prepared, but still they kept hundreds of thousands of men and women waiting about needlessly doing nothing, when they were urgently needed in civil life. In these matters, time passes and draws a sponge across the past, but I should have been ashamed not to have demobilised down to the necessary figure at a very much greater speed than was attained. But the past is no more. I must register the point that perhaps a year was lost in the case of many men who could have been giving our country the necessary fillip at that time, in getting industry to work, but were retained in the Services doing what we now conceive to be perfectly useless tasks, not only abroad, but, in very large numbers in England.

We have next the White Paper by the Minister of Defence. I must again remind the House that the right hon. Gentlemen used very hard language about the arguments of his political opponents the other night, and about their style. No more barren, dismal, flatulent, platitudinous document than his White Paper – if you can call it 'his' White Paper – has ever been laid before the House of Commons. His friends – and I am certainly a wartime friend – hope that it is to his credit that he had nothing to do with writing it. It was one of those rigmaroles and grimaces produced by the modern bureaucracy into whose hands we have fallen – a kind of vague palimpsest of jargon and officialese, with no breadth, no theme and, above all, no facts.

I think I shall be speaking for everyone in all parts of the House when I say there is a broadly-spread feeling that our manpower in the Forces is being wasted, muddled and mismanaged. There has been no administrative thrift, and there has been insufficient good housekeeping. This applies to all three Services. There never was a time when the effective fighting strength of the Army, Navy and Air Force bore a smaller proportion to the total number of men taken by compulsion. The Estimates, which have been presented to the House and debated fully in the recent weeks, gave us no clue to the fighting strength of our Armed Forces. The Navy Estimates, for instance, do not dare to specify the ships and fleets the Navy have in commission. That was invariably done before the war, and I see no reason why it should not be done at the present time. Nor have we the slightest idea from the Estimates, of the numbers in the Navy afloat, and the numbers ashore.

I believe that the Minister of Defence is to wind up this Debate, and perhaps he will be so good as to answer this particular question. The Navy have around 200,000 men today – maybe a little less – and according to the Estimate they are reducing the numbers to 182,000 by this time next year. Out of these 200,000 men, I want to ask how many are sleeping afloat tonight, and how many are sleeping ashore. I think we might be told that. I do not think it would endanger the safety of the country, although it may stir people up a little at the Admiralty. I should like to know the answer, because after all, the Navy is a thing which is in various ways associated and often connected with the sea, and a sailor is always supposed to have something to do, at some time or other, with salt water. Perhaps I may have an answer to that question when the time comes. Nor do the Royal Air Force venture to state the number of fighting squadrons they have. Finally, the War Office give us no indication of the number of divisions or mobile brigades which are formed out of a total establishment of about 750,000.

We are told by the Government, 'Oh, we cannot do it, because foreign powers will gain an advantage,' but I thought that all our enemies had surrendered unconditionally, and the House may remember that we went in procession to St Margaret's to return thanks for the victory. It appears now that we cannot do what we did in 1939, and in 1914, namely, state in broad terms, what foreign powers know perfectly well, the broad outline of our naval and military organisations. Apart from your war against the Jews in Palestine, I thought there was peace. At any rate, the House may be sure that the Soviet Government know perfectly well what we have got in the Navy and in the forces in Europe, and that they have got a lot of good friends moving freely about in this country, who will not hesitate to tell them about any little points on which they may be short.

Perhaps in the air there may be a little more mystery, because the air is a 'kittle cattle' kind of service. Whether a squadron is in the first line, or the second line, or in training or in preparation, and what is the exact grading of the various machines and pilots – all that affords an infinite field in which confusion may be created and statistics multiplied and spawned in vast quantities and varieties. Therefore, I am not pressing so much in regard to the air, but believe me, nothing is gained by refusing to tell the House what ships we have in commission, and how many broad organisations of troops we have in the field. What we have to keep secret is not that, but our mobilisation plans, and equipment, and the potential rate at which our Forces can be manned.

I hope we shall not have this humbug of saying, 'We cannot say how many ships there are in commission, because we do not want foreign nations to know.' I have never heard such a pretence presented to the House before. The reason why the facts are not disclosed in the Estimates is because the Government do not dare to expose themselves to criticism for the little they have to show, compared with the great numbers they have and the vast sums of money they are spending. We reserve to ourselves the fullest right to examine and criticise the policy and the Bill which is now brought before us, from the standpoint both of its quantitative and qualitative results. Nevertheless, when all is said and done, even if we do not get satisfactory answers, we shall unfailingly support the principle of national service for the Armed Forces of our country.

I and my Friends, after careful thought, feel bound to give it loyal support. That does not at all deprive us of the full right to point out how very badly other things have been managed, and how much one is in agreement with the feeling the hon. Gentlemen has just expressed. Compulsory military service is not necessarily a problem for a regular standing army; but the only way of making us a nation of fighting men in time of war is by national service in time of peace. As all our habits in the past have been to live in a peaceable manner, we have entered all our wars unprepared or ill-prepared, and the delay before we are able to place an army in the field at the side of our Allies has been a very serious weakness, not only in the physical but in the moral sphere.

There is nothing contrary to the spirit of democracy in the principle of compulsory national defence, provided it is universal, provided that rich and poor men of every class and party have to pay their due at the same time. On the contrary –

Mr Cove (Aberavon): All in the ranks, not in the officer class?

Mr Churchill: Certainly. I am much in favour of national service being on a basis of absolute equality. There used to be a period when it was possible to hire substitutes – it was so in the American Civil War – but these practices have long passed away. There is nothing contrary to the principles of democracy. On the contrary, it emphasises the principle of equality of sacrifice, and by mingling all the classes together, in common duty and honourable service, it is a favourable agent for diminishing class differences which exist in a free and varied society. It has been defended and practised by all the most advanced democratic countries in Europe since the French Revolution. Reliance for the defence of the soil on national armies rather than on long-service professionals, or mercenaries as they were called, was, in the nineteenth century, at any rate, a strong barrier against reaction in a rapidly-changing and, upon the whole, advancing and progressing world.

It is quite true that conscription for prolonged foreign service presents itself in a different light, and cannot be maintained as a permanency. The maintenance of garrisons abroad raises problems and requires qualities and conditions which are not reconcilable with the short-term service characteristic of national compulsory armies. That is found by every country where the army is raised by conscription and yet requires a certain proportion to be provided for foreign garrisons. Now, at this time, after a war in which the whole people took part has been waged and extraordinary confusion reigns in the world, it is necessary to have compulsion for service overseas – a hard thing for any government to maintain. But that is not a basis on which our Army or any other army can indefinitely be maintained. The loss of India and Burma are lamentable and melancholy events, and they signalise in striking manner, the rapid decline in British power and prestige. But living at a more humble level does, in fact, relieve us of some strain in this military sphere. The maintenance of an Army in India has been a great burden. To keep 50,000 to 60,000 men permanently in the Service has entailed the maintenance of a professional Army, based upon long service. It is like holding the dumbbell at arm's length – quite tiring, very different from if it is held here. For several generations that has prevented the development of an effective national Army in this country, which for much the same expense could have been made far stronger than was possible.

I do not intend to go into the Cardwell system. Every one knows that foreign service required seven years with the Colours, five with the Reserve, or even eight with the Colours and four with the Reserve, which leaves a very small reserve to be built up; whereas, if we had not had to maintain this large force abroad, we could have developed two years with the Colours and ten with the Reserve, or one and half with the Colours and ten and a half with the Reserve, or, as the Government are doing, one and half with the Colours, and five and a half with the Reserve. Had such a system been possible before the war, we could have had, at the outset, three or four times as many divisions ready to go, with results that cannot be measured; because we now know from the German figures, very different conditions prevailed at Munich time, and even at the outbreak of war, from those which prevailed in May 1940, when Hitler had reached the moment when he could strike.

Certainly, our power to keep the peace in the twentieth century has been greatly hampered by the fact that we did not possess a national Army. We were in a position which laid us open to reproach from European countries, not only potential foes, but Allies and neutrals, that we would use everybody else's blood – every one has heard the taunt – to pursue our policy and gain our ends, and would content ourselves with implementing their efforts by sea power and money, and latterly, of course, by air power. It is arguable even that we tried to play too large a part in European affairs between the wars and before the first war, while not being able or willing to accept the same conditions of service, or put up the same manpower as our Allies or potential Allies were forced to do. We should have carried far more weight in the councils of peace if we had had national service.

There is no doubt that the passage of this Bill now, in this hour of dark depression, will help to sustain our otherwise failing influence in world affairs, and particularly in the United Nations Organisation. That influence is being steadily reduced by the policy of the Government, both at home and abroad. It is remarkable that this curious Administration should step aside from its broad downward path to take this single solitary step towards a more hopeful national policy. We welcome the step all the more because of the contrast in which it throws so much else they have done.

'So shines a good deed in a naughty world.'

It has long been recognised in this and other countries that there is a great gulf fixed between national service for military purposes and what is called industrial conscription, or the direction of labour, in time of peace. There is a great gulf. In the war we leapt that gulf, but never before has it been, and we earnestly trust it will not be, dreamed of in time of peace. There is no need to confuse the two.

Service to save the country has always, from ancient times, been considered the first duty of the citizen. It is however questionable, in my mind, whether any exemptions of young men from military service should be made in time of peace for particular industries. I was glad to hear the Minister of Labour say that it would be only for underground coalmining. Yes, away from the light of the sun, that is a different kind of sacrifice which is made. But even this seems, in a way, to reflect both upon the character of military service and the character of mining. It is one thing in wartime to stop miners from going to fight as soldiers, sailors and airmen, as they frequently wanted to do, and quite another to encourage a particular kind of young man to go into mining as a means of avoiding military service. It may be necessary in this crisis, but it is not a healthy basis for the State or society as a whole. Both service – the Armed Forces and mining – are honourable, and nothing should be done which seems to reflect upon either. It would certainly be a most unfortunate expedient to have, as a permanent matter, to try to increase the manpower in the mines by a class of youths who dislike military service. I should be sorry to see that develop over a long period of time.

The fact that we support the Government on the broad principle of national service for the Armed Forces in no way weakens our intention to censure the waste of manpower by those Forces. On the contrary, it should strengthen us in our duty to do so. I say without hesitation that the present condition of all three Services, as a result of Ministerial incompetence since the war, is disgraceful. I hope that the Chief of the Imperial General Staff is to be at his desk giving his whole mind to this matter, and that he will be able on all occasions to give the fullest possible assistance to the Minister of Defence, in order that the matter may be viewed from a central point of view. General Montgomery is a very gifted man, and I hope that he will be close to the Minister of Defence in all the months that are to come.

I am very grateful to the House for giving me so much of their attention. (*Interruption.*) As we are all going to work and vote together, we may as well be on friendly terms, so that the House may be responsible for insisting on the proper use being made in the Forces of young men taken from so many important industries and walks of life, and upon a proper proportion of fighting strength being developed as a result of so much sacrifice and expense. It seems to me that all parties and sections of parties might join in this with equal earnestness. If Parliament did its duty, and if the Government allowed Parliament to do its duty, there would be set up a Parliamentary committee of all parties, similar to the National Expenditure Committee, which did such useful work during the war; or even a joint committee of both Houses to investigate, with full power to call for persons and papers, the use of manpower in the three Forces, and with power, by leave of the House, to sit in secret from time to time. Such a body would be of the greatest value, not only to the country as a whole, but to the Service Ministers, and to the Minister of Defence, none of whom is able, apparently, to cope with the problem himself.

I believe that there are many scores of millions which could be saved from the present immense total of £900 million demanded this year on the Estimates of the three Services. I would very much like to have had a chance to get loose upon them with my red pencil. I am perfectly certain that we could have had a very considerable saving, and I am perfectly certain that this could be achieved simultaneously with a positive increase in the fighting power of the Services. Therefore, we shall support His Majesty's Government in the Lobby tomorrow night, and on other occasions, when necessary, throughout this Bill; but let no Minister imagine that we do not regard their wasteful, inefficient and incompetent administration of the fighting Services as a scandal of the first order.

April
1947

Winston S. Churchill: press notice
(Churchill papers, 2/55)

5 April 1947 Chartwell
6 p.m.

The decision of the Socialist Government to alter fundamentally the plan of National Service, which they submitted last Monday to the House of Commons, raises far-reaching issues. The Conservative and National Liberal Parties voted with the Government because they were assured by the public declarations of Ministers and had every reason to believe that the plan submitted to Parliament was the result of long, careful and deliberate study by the responsible Ministers of the Crown and was based upon the advice of the military experts. We believed that the proposals represented the minimum defence arrangements which would meet our needs and our commitments in the next few years. On this basis the Bill passed its second reading by a majority of over 300, of whom 132 were members of the Opposition.

Now it appears that this ~~grave matter~~ elaborate scheme for which we were asked to vote had no foundation, that it was not related to our national needs, that the Ministers who brought it forward had no conviction, and that rather than have trouble with the 'tail' of their Party they have cast their policy aside. The effect of this naked confession will be injurious to the reputation of our Country at this critical time all over the world. It makes it plain beyond doubt that while the Government come forward with great demands upon the patriotism of the people and goodwill of the House of Commons, they are not basing themselves upon a true and considered view of what we really need. The want of decision reflects directly upon the Prime Minister, and in the second place upon the Minister of Defence. Why did they call upon us on national grounds to vote for proposals last Monday which now they admit were not necessary in the public interest? This is another example of the policy of 'scuttle' before anything that looks difficult or fierce which has characterised the Socialist Government administration, and which in less than two years has reduced us from our Victory Day to our present confusion and disrepute. It exposes for all to see the weakness and incompetence of the Socialist Government in all matters affecting the life of the Nation, great or small, at home or abroad.

Last Monday I declared in the House of Commons the intention of the Conservative Party to sustain the Government not only on the Second Reading but throughout all the stages of this Bill. We must now reconsider our position and course of action in the light of the national interest.

Winston S. Churchill to Winston Churchill
(Churchill papers, 1/42)

15 April 1947

Darling Winston

Thank you very much for your picture, which I am going to show to your Papa tonight. I am so sorry that the weather prevented your coming down here to have a lesson in painting from your Grandpapa, but I hope in a few weeks that this will be arranged, and we will play about together with those nice paints. I hope you have not used them all yet, but if you have I have plenty more here.

Duncan Sandys to Winston S. Churchill
(Churchill papers, 2/22)

17 April 1947

My dear Winston,

I hear that there is a certain amount of feeling among Conservative back-benchers that they have not been taken sufficiently into your confidence about your United Europe movement that there is, in consequence, a danger that they may become hostile to it.

I think, therefore, that it would be very wise if you could on some occasion in the near future, tell the Conservative 1922 Committee something about our movement and endeavour to secure their goodwill and support.

Winston S. Churchill: speech
('Winston S. Churchill, His Complete Speeches', volume 7, pages 7470–5)

18 April 1947

Primrose League Meeting
Albert Hall
London

EMPIRE AND FREEDOM

We are met here today to consider an important question. Here is the question. How can we help our country in this hour of disappointment and need, and even danger? Our country is being driven into ruin, and our Empire scattered and squandered. We are falling fast in the estimation of the world. What plans can we make, what steps can we take, to raise ourselves again, as we can if we all try, to the glorious level which we reached and held only a few years ago? That is the issue which I put before the Primrose League this afternoon.

Let us first take counsel of the past, and draw wisdom and courage from the memory of the great men who have gone before us. I am very glad to address the Primrose League today. I am proud of the fact that my father's League number is No. 1. When he, with a group of friends, founded the League in 1883, it was intended to cherish the memory and revive the inspiration of Lord Beaconsfield, who knew so well how to maintain the honour and the interests of our country abroad and at the same time open new paths in social advance at home. He it was who gave in 1875 the British Trade Union movement the Charter which has made it so often a responsible and stabilising force in British industry. He it was whose policy in 1876 placed upon the brow of Queen Victoria the Imperial Crown of India – now being so shamefully cast away. When the League was founded, it was intended by my father to be the vanguard of Tory democracy, and that is what we are determined to make it today. The association of the greatness of Britain with the ceaseless advance in the comfort, happiness and security of the British people must still remain our guide, and Disraeli's motto 'Empire and Freedom', which is our watch word, is as true today as when it was spoken 70 years ago. Indeed it never was more needful that we should labour body and soul to preserve and unify whatever is left of our Empire and Commonwealth, which we have just carried safely and victoriously through the deadliest of all wars. And who can doubt that individual freedom, on which alone a cultured civilisation can survive, is challenged and assailed today as it has not been for many centuries of our long history. With this famous call to duty and service uplifting our hearts we may turn invigorated to face the difficulties and perils which surround us.

Everyone is conscious of the approaching crisis in our financial and economic affairs. The Socialist Government is living upon the American dole and squandering with profligate rapidity this loan, which could only be justified as a means of re-equipping our industries after the war in which we had made supreme exertions. But although the Government is receiving large external aid, the general conditions of the country are, in almost every respect, worse than they were even in some of the wartime years and of course incomparably worse than before the war. There are three times as many people employed by the Government to manage our affairs as were used by the Conservative Governments before the war. A mighty army of 450,000 additional civil servants have been taken from production and added, at a prodigious cost and waste, to the oppressive machinery of Government and control. Instead of helping national recovery this is a positive hindrance. The bulk of this new and heavy burden is borne mainly on the shoulders of the wage-earning masses, and has the effect of frustrating individual initiative and enterprise in every sphere of our daily life, our trade and our industry. At the same time a hideous waste and extravagance prevails in every department of the State.

Dr Dalton (Chancellor of the Exchequer), as he calls himself, though I have not heard of any patients he has cured, is now asking for three thousand million pounds to cover the next twelve months; that is three times the cost of the State in the years before the war, even when heavy rearmament was in progress. Although this doctor has spent, or proposes to spend, about 11 thousand million pounds in the 32 months from the end of the war till the end of the new financial year in April 1948, what has he to show for it? One would imagine that with all these vast sums of money being spent there would have been at least a fictitious and fleeting sense of prosperity. On the contrary, a harder, more curtailed, more restricted way of life and standard of living has been imposed upon every class of the community, and we are assured by the Government themselves that a worse time lies ahead and may continue for years. It is the Rake's Progress, but with this remarkable difference, that the progress is not accompanied by dear-bought if questionable pleasures, but by dear-bought unquestionable miseries. The usual reply which the Government make to such accusations is that, at any rate they will do their best to ensure that the miseries are equally shared. They are to be equally shared by the thrifty and the improvident, by the successes and by the failures of our complicated society, by the strong, active workers and the Tired Tims and Weary Willies, by the buoyant, creative, productive genius of our island, as well as by the weaker and feebler elements which exist in every nation and should be the proper objects of rescue and compassion, but which should never be allowed to set the pace for the forward-march of society. Certain it is that a prolongation of this system of denying rewards and sharing miseries would break the mainspring of the British island and that it would be only a question of time, and not a very long time, when Great Britain would be unable to support the immense population of 47 millions which have been assembled here, and that millions would have to emigrate or starve, or, at the best, subsist on the charity of capitalist America, at whose free enterprise our Socialists mock, and whose wealth they envy.

Dr Dalton is boasting that he has balanced the Budget. My friends in the House of Commons have pointed out the curious statistical calculations, by which he has arrived at this result. If any private company were to present its balance sheet by practising such methods, they would come within the scope of the Criminal Law. But what is the balanced Budget, even when thus produced? It is a balance between three thousand millions of extravagant expenditure on the one hand, and three thousand millions of crushing, paralysing taxation on the other. One set of evils are balanced against another set of evils, and we are invited to admire a perfect equilibrium. I have no doubt whatever, and I do not speak without knowledge of experience, that the Budget this year should have taken 500 million pounds off the expenditure and another 500 millions off the taxation. This could certainly have been done by vigorous, efficient administration and by an abatement of class hatred and class warfare; and the result would have been an immediate expansion of activity in every aspect of our life at home, as well as an improvement in our vital export trade.

We have had here lately a visitor from the United States (Mr Henry Wallace) who has foregathered with that happily small minority of crypto-Communists who are making a dead set at the foreign policy which Mr Ernest Bevin, our Foreign Secretary, has patiently and steadfastly pursued with the support of nine-tenths of the House of Commons. The object of these demonstrations has been to separate Great Britain from the United States and weave her into the vast system of Communist intrigue which radiates from Moscow. Now I travel about a certain amount myself, and am received with much kindness by all classes, both in Europe and America. But when I am abroad I always make it a rule never to criticise or attack the Government of my own country. I make up for lost time when I come home. But when I am abroad and speaking to foreigners I have even defended our present Socialist rulers, and always I have spoken with confidence of the future destiny of our country. Here at home we must do our duty, point out the dangers, and endeavour so to guide the nation as to avoid an overwhelming collapse. But I have no patience with Englishmen who use the hospitality of a friendly nation to decry their own. I think this is a very good principle, and one which deserves general attention.

This is a great advantage to the United States. It enhances the strength of the nation, and by preserving continuity of foreign policy in spite of changes of Party Government it makes it easier for other countries to work with the United States or at least know where they are. You will remember that when I was Prime Minister of a Conservative Government two years ago I took Mr Attlee with me to Potsdam for the very purposes I have described. The present Socialist Government follow a different method. They do not consult His Majesty's Opposition, and give us no material information. Nevertheless, whenever they are doing what we consider their national duty, we give them our support, and do our best to make their policy successful. We always endeavour to support the Government when the public interest is involved.

Take the case of National Service. We all went into the Lobby with them and voted with them on this unpopular but necessary measure. And what happened? They assured us that 18 months was absolutely indispensable to meet our needs, that all our military advisers had worked it out with them for a long time past. Vehement appeals were made and positive assurances were given that this 18 months' scheme alone would meet our needs. So we voted with the Government and even complimented them on their courage. But what happened? Forty-eight hours later, because some of their own people had voted against them and they were afraid of their own tail, the Minister of Defence (Mr A. V. Alexander) turned round and ran like a hare, and informed us that the requirement of 18 months was abandoned, and that 12 months would do all that was necessary. This of course is quite untrue, and makes nonsense of all the arguments he had laid before us with so much apparent conviction. This is a typical example of the infirmity of purpose and lack of moral courage which degrades the character of the Socialist Government.

There is, I believe, a considerable measure of agreement in this country on the fundamental principles which would guide our foreign policy. In the first place we base our hopes upon, and give our loyalties to, a World Organisation to prevent war. Our desire is that all the nations of the world shall work together faithfully for that supreme object. We must not allow ourselves to be discouraged by the difficulties. Nor must we become impatient at the shortcomings of the United Nations conception in these early days. We must persevere upon our course and not be turned from it by every unfavourable gust or even by adverse winds and baffling currents. If, after earnest and prolonged trial, it is found that some members of the World Organisation wish to bring it to nought or to break away from it, then those nations which remain must band themselves together even the more strongly, and must carry forward the banners of Freedom and Justice, and uphold the ideals of true democracy with strong hands and fearless hearts. Within the bounds and under the authority of the World Organisation, we have first and foremost in our hearts our own British Commonwealth and Empire, which must ever draw closer together and be the faithful servant of the high causes for which we have fought so long and given so much. We also wish, as good Europeans who share and express the civilisation of Western Europe, and are closely linked with our nearest neighbours, above all with France and the Low Countries, to see the noble Continent of Europe rise from its agony and ruin, and, united by the interchange of friendly services between all its peoples, become, in the course of time, one of the main examples of peace-loving human society. When next I speak in this hall, a month hence, to an audience representative of all Parties, I shall commend the cause of United Europe to my fellow-countrymen and to the world. Meanwhile I ask my friends in the Conservative Party, which I have the honour to lead, to give the whole question their earnest consideration, so that all of us may join the invocation and indeed in the prayer 'Let Europe Arise'.

Here then are the first principles of our foreign and world policy. Faithful allegiance to the United Nations Organisation, and tireless exertions to create and strengthen the underpillars upon which alone it can stand. What is our policy towards Soviet Russia – that mighty mass of the earth's surface, whose vast population fought so valiantly against the cruel invasion which Hitler, in his wickedness and folly, so launched upon them? I say with all sincerity that our policy towards Russia must be one of honourable friendship from strength. It cannot be cowardly appeasement from weakness. We earnestly hope that all the peoples of Russia may be safe, prosperous and happy under whatever form of Government they may choose or may accept. We wish them well and will welcome every possibility of increasing trade and intercourse between our countries in order to give us each a better understanding of the other. If that should fail, we shall at any rate have done our duty and done our best. Finally it must be made absolutely clear that we shall allow no wedge to be driven between Great Britain and the United States of America, or be led into any course which would mar the growing unity in thought and action, in ideals and purpose, of the English-speaking nations, spread so widely about the globe, but joined together by history and by destiny.

Let me end where I began, at home. On the morrow of our defeat at the General Election, which cost our country and Empire so dear, there was naturally much talk about our putting forward a new Programme of Conservative and Unionist policy in order to counter the promises and baits which our opponents had so lavishly used. But I and my principal colleagues adhered to the view that great Parties are called upon to play their part, not by frantic biddings for office, but by firm adherence to the broad and general principles which they profess, and by the march of events which is a hard but effective education, even to the most feckless and unthinking. The wisdom and propriety of this course have been proved more quickly than I imagined, and the careful studies we have made into industrial conditions will presently be the subject of a statement in detail. Every one of us can feel that the heart of the British nation is returning to the Conservative and Liberal principles of society, which, though often opposed, have been so wantonly assailed by the advocates of half-baked Socialism and by a Government whose spirit of class warfare and spate of mischievous laws are only matched by the waste and incapacity of their administration.

As Socialist mismanagement makes itself felt at home and abroad in every field of our national life, we shall be conscious of an ever-growing measure of public support, and be borne upwards upon a tide of wrath and disillusion against Socialist doctrinaires and still more upon the resolve of the nation not to despair of Britain and her fortunes, but to act while time remains. For that time and call we must be ready. We shall not be found unequal to the scale of events. We shall confront squalid Socialist schemes of scarcity, restriction, and the equal sharing of the miseries which they create, with a policy which will appeal not only to Conservatives and our Liberal allies, but to that wide union of Britons who mean to save their island home while time remains. Our Social policy can be stated almost in a sentence. We seek to establish minimum standards of life and labour below which no one shall be allowed to sink or fall. Then there must be free competition upwards – upwards but not downwards. Thus we shall liberate once again the strength and genius of the nation and make all the vast process of energy, invention, thrift and good housekeeping, play its part in restoring the common weal.

Winston S. Churchill to Christopher Soames
(Churchill papers, 1/32)

22 April 1947

It is most important to get the water for the walled garden settled. One or two of the German prisoners should help Whitbread unscrew the pipes which we saw yesterday, and the other Germans can work at your drain in the field. There are about 50 good land drains close up to where the new boiler has been dumped in the front of the house, so a beginning could be made at getting some.

After that I want all the Prisoners to quit wood cutting and concentrate on opening up the old lead pipe we walked over yesterday, so that new pipes can be laid alongside, then at the last moment disconnect and pull out the lead. (It would not do for the extension for carrying oil to the swimming-pool – it is not big enough.)

I do not know how long it will take the Germans to open up the trench. I fear it will not be possible to do it by Friday as I had hoped. Therefore let us aim at Monday for the change-over. Southon should be asked to send his plumbers then. One, or at the outside two days should see the whole of the pipes laid, and the Germans filling in as they go.

I wonder whether the bothy roof could not be made water-tight by putting a thatch over the present roof. Thus, all the wet would be kept out by the thatch, and the slates would be an added protection and would not have to be broken up. There must be good thatchers about now and I think it would all look very picturesque. Stevens would, I am sure, tell you where to get a good thatcher.

Harold Macmillan to Winston S. Churchill
(Churchill papers, 2/53)

23 April 1947
Private and Confidential

My dear Winston,

I feel that I must tell you that I was very concerned at the announcement on the BBC last Friday, that the Conservative Party had decided to vote for eighteen months, when the period of national service comes under discussion.

As I understood the conclusion of the Consultative Committee, it was that this matter remained open for final decision, after the Party had been consulted.

It is true that the Defence Committee took your view: but, if I may say so, this was largely under the influence of the very strong lead which you gave from the Chair. Moreover, that Committee is naturally very much swayed by professional considerations.

I feel strongly that it would be a very grave error for the Party to be definitely committed by its leaders to the eighteen months. If some members force a division, that will not hurt us. What matters is that we should place all the responsibility on the Government and keep our position open for the election.

The Conservative Private Members Committee is to discuss this question on Thursday. It may be that you will decide to listen to their views, without taking part yourself. But, if you think it right to express your own opinion, I hope you will not think it disloyal, if I and others of your colleagues do the same.

I understand that the final decision will be made at the Shadow Cabinet, after the meeting of the 1922 Committee.

Robert Hudson to Winston S. Churchill
(Churchill papers, 2/53)

23 April 1947

My dear Winston,

I am worried at the position that is developing on the eighteen versus twelve months conscription issue.

At the meeting of the Consultative Committee last week I was under the impression that the balance of opinion was, if anything, against voting in favour of eighteen months; that no decision was, however, reached, and that a final decision would be taken this week after hearing the views of Back Benchers on the various Party Committees.

I had rather assumed that members of the Consultative Committee would refrain from trying to influence the discussions on these Committees. It seems, however, that I was wrong.

As I said last week, I feel that the conscription issue is bound to play an important part at the next Election, and I think, therefore, it is imperative that the Party as a whole should not incur any avoidable unpopularity. It is not as though, by voting for eighteen months now, we should in fact be able to secure the adoption of that term.

As I feel very strongly on this point, I hope in the circumstances you will not think it disloyal if I take an active part in the discussion at the 1922 Committee tomorrow.

Winston S. Churchill: speech
('Winston S. Churchill, His Complete Speeches', volume 7, pages 7475-6)

23 April 1947 Wanstead

NATIONAL SERVICE

... The Government's decision to reduce the period of compulsory national service from 18 to 12 months is disquieting because it is not recommended by our experts. They yielded to the dictation of the extreme Left Wing members of their party. This shows that our affairs are not being conducted in this respect at least on their merits, but in a loose and nervous manner, not for the safety of the country but for the party considerations which have always dominated them.

Sir Stafford Cripps, one of the ablest men in the Government and also one of the most alarmed, made a stirring appeal to the nation for a great effort of work and thrift, and austerity in every direction. The Opposition joins in those appeals, but could do so with much more confidence if Sir Stafford Cripps devoted himself to national causes instead of to doctrinaire and foolish fads and issues.

Vast expenditure is of a wasteful character and cannot fail to do the greatest harm to our whole recovery, because the taxes must be raised to pay for it.

Mr Dalton (Chancellor of the Exchequer) boasts that he has balanced his Budget, but he has balanced on the one side absolutely unnecessary and ruinous extravagance, and on the other side crushing, blinding, paralysing taxation. At present we are living to a large extent upon the American loan, and I am shocked to see the rate at which it is flowing out because a great part of it is being spent on tobacco and films. I have no doubt that a great deal is being used to pay debts which we owe to sterling countries by means of dollar receipts, but this is coming to an end very quickly.

When it comes to an end – and it will in a short time – we shall be in a very grave position. How are we to escape our difficulties except by some prodigious wisdom and genius, national unification, and devotion such as was shown in the terrible days of the war?

We have had a most serious decline in the esteem and respect in which we are held by the United States and Russia. The Government, always ready to scuttle from any difficulty, have evidently cast away our mighty Indian Empire. In Palestine a different process is at work in the minds of the Government. There we have to go on fighting at all costs. There are four times as many troops in Palestine as in India. We must carry on this 'squalid war of terrorism'. We are fighting the Jews in order to give the country to the Arabs.

But Palestine is not a twentieth part of the importance of India to us, and is an immense source of expense and worry, and is bringing upon us a great deal of disapprobation from many countries.

Finally, I am sure we can find some means of coming through our perils. This is St George's Day, when England may well be proud of her history. Where is the dragon? . . . The dragon is the Socialist Government.

President Harry S Truman to Winston S. Churchill
(Churchill papers, 2/158)[1]

24 April 1947   The White House

My dear Winston,

To follow instructions as you have I make the same style of address. I appreciate very much your addressing me as 'My dear Harry'.[2]

You are exceedingly kind in your statement that I have made a contribution to world peace. I hope I have.

You have not been idle yourself. Eventually, I am sure we shall attain our goal.

May God bless and keep you in good health.

Field Marshal Lord Montgomery to Sir John Anderson
(Churchill papers, 2/53)

25 April 1947

My dear Anderson,

With reference to our conversation on Wednesday evening.

If the National Service Bill gets delayed or hung up, we are completely sunk. Regular recruiting has not yet reached the figure we need, nor is it likely to for some time.

From my angle, as a soldier, I consider it is vital to get the Bill through the

[1] This letter was handwritten.
[2] See letter of Mar. 7, reproduced above (pp. 240–1).

House quickly, and smoothly. I also consider it is necessary to get it through the House without a lot of argument and trouble: which would impair confidence throughout the nation on the matter. Times are not too good as you know; we must be certain that our defence services will stand firm and will not be subject to buffeting by political wrangles.

For the good of the show as a whole, we need the Bill on the Statute Book as soon as possible so that we can plan ahead constructively.

I do hope that the Conservative Party will lend a hand and will not be too troublesome. I also hope that they will not ask awkward questions about the Chiefs of Staff. Perhaps you could use your influence to help the show.

Grace Hamblin to Winston S. Churchill
(Churchill papers, 2/4)

25 April 1947

Miss Marston[1] has telephoned to say that the *Daily Graphic* have given her the following message:

In a speech to the Scottish TUC at St Andrews Mr Attlee has attacked you by saying that you were the worst Chancellor of the Exchequer of the century and that our troubles today should really be attributed to the mess you have made over things in the past. This speech is to be released at 12.15 today and the *Daily Graphic* would like to print your reply on the same page in their tomorrow's issue.

The Times: article
(The Times)

26 April 1947

MR ATTLEE REPLIES TO MR CHURCHILL
'MISERY' ALLEGATIONS

The Prime Minister, addressing the Scottish TUC at St Andrews yesterday, replied to Mr Churchill's Primrose League speech with the allegation that the Conservative leader had brought untold misery on the people of Britain and that much of the present troubles could be traced to 'his error of ignorance'. In his speech Mr Attlee said:

> I remember very well when Mr Churchill was Chancellor of the century. It was he that brought us back on the gold standard, which led to the crisis in the coal industry from which we are suffering today. He inflicted untold

---

[1] Lettice Marston, 1927–. One of Churchill's secretaries, 1946–53. Later married Robert Shillingford.

misery on the people of this country. Of course he did not intend this, but he accepted the advice he got from the Bank of England. He sinned, no doubt in all ignorance, but much of our troubles today can be traced back to that error of ignorance and to his simple trust of others in a field where he had little knowledge.

It is not my habit to sit down under attacks. I am prepared to defend and also counter-attack. I have observed that Mr Churchill has been addressing the Grand Habitation of the Primrose League. It was a speech only too characteristic of the leader of the Conservative Party. There was not a drop of policy in the torrent of abuse in which he indulged.

He started off with a wail about the scattering and squandering of the Empire. He talked of India being shamelessly cast away. This is the kind of language he has been using for years about India. He seems to imagine that in India we can go back 50 years. He ignores the great movement for self-government which has been spreading throughout Asia for decades. He abandons the democratic principle for which we fought in the war. It is significant that when I announced in the House of Commons that Indians had the right to choose the future of their country, whether to stay in the British Commonwealth or go out, there was not a single speech in opposition. Mr Churchill was away. The fact is that on this subject Mr Churchill never thinks; he only gives way to his emotions.

Birmingham Post: article
(*Churchill papers, 2/4*)

28 April 1947

MR CHURCHILL REPLIES
'LIVING COST DOWN, WAGES UP WHILE I WAS CHANCELLOR'
PREMIER ACCUSED
DELIBERATE DISTORTION IN HIS SPEECH

Mr Churchill, in a reply last night to the Prime Minister's attack on him at the Scottish Trades Union Congress on Friday, refuted the suggestion that he caused 'untold misery' when he was Chancellor of the Exchequer.

He pointed out that during his five years' service in that office the cost of living, unemployment and income-tax were reduced, and the real wages of the nation's workers were steadily and substantially increased.

He recalled that Mr Attlee was a member of Lord Snowden's committee which recommended the return to the Gold Standard, and described the Prime Minister's accusation that he attacked the Civil Service in his recent Primrose League speech as 'deliberate distortion' and 'unworthy misrepresentation'.

Mr Attlee, he concluded, must have found himself very hard pressed to have to go back nearly twenty-five years to find excuses for the present Government's mismanagement and blunders.

Mr Churchill's statement said:

Mr Attlee described me as the 'most disastrous Chancellor of the century'. Yet, during my tenure of that office in the Conservative Government, the cost of living declined by at least eighteen points, while money wages remained stable. This represented a great benefit to the working people of this country. At the same time, the number of men and women employed in the insured trades rose by nearly 600,000. Within two years, under a Socialist Government, the rate of unemployment had more than doubled.

Under Socialist rule

Mr Attlee made much play with the figure of 2,000,000 unemployed. I must point out that it was under the Socialist Administration of 1929, which followed the Conservative Government, that the number of unemployed first passed 2,000,000.

Mr Attlee referred to my action in bringing this country back to the Gold Standard in 1925. He says that I acted on advice. Indeed, I did – on the advice of a Committee appointed by Lord Snowden, the Chancellor in the Socialist Government in 1924, of which Mr Attlee was himself a member.

What did Lord Snowden say about our return to the Gold Standard? On the Second Reading of the Gold Standard Bill he said that while the Government had acted with undue precipitancy he and his Socialist colleagues were in favour of a return to the Gold Standard at the earliest possible moment. Later on, in December, 1926, Lord Snowden wrote an article in the *Financial Times* in which he said: 'All the facts therefore do not support the impression that the return to gold has been detrimental to industry. The Bank Rate has not been raised, unemployment has not risen, real wages have not fallen, and the price level has been fairly well maintained.'

So far from causing what Mr Attlee calls 'untold misery', the facts, as I have said, show that while I was the Conservative Chancellor of the Exchequer the real wages of our workpeople steadily and substantially increased.

Legislative landmarks

The return to the Gold Standard was not the only act of my five years' administration of the Exchequer. Old Age Pensions were brought down from the remote age of seventy to sixty-five, and the Widows' and Orphans' Pensions scheme, which was an entirely new departure, was introduced. A great de-rating Act was passed, enabling factories to be set up without being deterred by heavy rates in districts where unemployment was rife. A very large sum of money for those days was provided by me for the establishment of the electric grid.

A succession of reductions in the rate of income-tax on earned income to married income-tax payers with children were secured. And, finally, the tax on tea, which is a heavy burden to the old, the weak and the poor, was repealed.

Mr Attlee accuses me of attacking the Civil Service. This is utterly untrue and must be a deliberate distortion. What I said, and what I repeat is that we have now too many officials compared with the number of wage-earners engaged in productive industry.

Futile tasks

I have the highest regard for our Civil Servants, with whom I have worked in many offices and for many years. It is no fault of theirs if they are now made too numerous: it is the fault of this Government that is constantly heaping upon them fresh tasks, many of which are needless and futile.

The overburdening of our administrative machine is one of the greatest mistakes this Government is making. To describe criticism of this mistake as an attack on the Civil Service is an unworthy misrepresentation.

Mr Attlee must feel himself very hard pressed to have to go back nearly a quarter of a century to find excuses for the mismanagement and blunders of which he evidently feels his Government guilty.

Winston S. Churchill to Sir John Anderson
(Churchill papers, 2/53)

28 April 1947

My dear John,

Thank you for sending me Montgomery's letter.[1] I think he would do much better to keep clear of politics, of which he knows little, and do his duty as a faithful adviser of the government. We do not require to be lectured by him, especially when so much of his recent conduct is unexplained.

I have, as you may have heard, carried the Conservative 1922 Committee to the support of the advice which I gave our Shadow Cabinet. It really might be wise for you to hint to Montgomery that he had much better mind his own business and leave politicians to mind theirs. Reading it again, I think his letter most impudent. Thank you for showing it to me all the same.

---

[1] Reproduced above (pp. 688–9).

April 1947

Winston S. Churchill to Clement Attlee
(Churchill papers, 2/53)

28 April 1947   Chartwell

My dear Prime Minister,

In view of the fact that neither you nor the Leader of the House[1] will in future serve upon the Committee of Privileges and of the alteration in the status of that body which will necessarily ensue, I feel that as the Leader of the Opposition I ought myself to withdraw. We shall nominate an experienced member of the Conservative Party to fill the vacancy. As I have already begun consideration of the W. J. Brown case, I am willing to continue until that is concluded.

You will allow me to place on record my regret that the character of the Committee should have been altered in a way which cannot fail to derogate from its authority. This can only lead to its reports becoming far more frequently the subject of Debate in the House than was previously the case.

Clement Attlee to Winston S. Churchill
(Churchill papers, 2/53)

30 April 1947

My dear Churchill,

Thank you for notifying me of your intention of withdrawing from the Committee of Privileges.

Having been a member of the Committee for fifteen years and Chairman for five, I cannot agree that the mere fact of neither the Prime Minister nor the Leader of the House being members alters the status of the Committee or derogates from its authority. This indeed was the position in 1942 and I am unaware of any ill effects.

I note that you will nominate an experienced member of your Party in your place.

I shall in accordance with the usual practice recommend the House to accept without question anyone whom the responsible leader of a Party considers to be a respected Member of the House.

---

[1] Herbert Morrison.

May 1947

Winston S. Churchill to Henry Luce
(Churchill papers, 4/57)

2 May 1947

I have been distressed by the text of the 'blurb' which is to be used as background for the official announcement[1] next week. I have reluctantly consented to an amended draft of this background stuff which Graebner has telegraphed to you. Considering that no publication will be made for nearly a year from now I wonder whether all this advertisement and proclamation will not be forgotten. After all what matters is the interest and value of the story. Can you not therefore be content with the official announcement agreed upon between our lawyers? I should greatly prefer this. We cannot prevent unofficial comment and discussion such as has already taken place several times in the press and if anything very foolish is said it is always possible to correct it. Of course we shall all be rung up and asked a number of questions to which it is quite easy to reply 'we have nothing to add to the official announcement that has been made. No comment' etc. I should be much obliged if you will think this over and cable me. If you feel that the 'blurb' must be issued as background I will supply you with a further amended version as it is essential to me to state that nothing will be published by me without the consent of HMG in regard to the public interest.[2]

---

[1] Of the forthcoming serialization in *Life* of the first volume of Churchill's *The Second World War*.

[2] Luce responded: 'Your message about the blurb has been received and I can assure you that we wish to avoid anything which might be distasteful to you or prejudicial to your labours. Furthermore we very much hope that we shall have your advice and help in all phases of this operation. That is why we sent Graebner to you with the tentative draft of the proclamation. Our problem lies in the fact that this is a very sizeable operation, and unless it is conducted with wit and energy on all fronts it may suffer by comparison with other journalistic operations which are merely second – or third – class ventures. As this is the first broadside in substance we will abide by the material which you have approved but because of local circumstances and customs I hope you will allow us a degree of freedom in our dealings with the American channels and publicity.'

Winston S. Churchill to Clement Attlee
(Churchill papers, 2/53)

5 May 1947

My dear Prime Minister,
I thank you for your letter of April 30.[1]
The position in 1942 under the stress of the war affords no precedent. You yourself, as Deputy Prime Minister and the second personage in a Government representing all Parties, presided. There was no official Opposition and no Leader of the Opposition.

Winston S. Churchill to Field Marshal Lord Alexander
(Churchill papers, 2/83)

6 May 1947

Am concerned about Kesselring's[2] death sentence and propose to raise question in Parliament. Can you do anything?

Lettice Marston to Winston S. Churchill
(Churchill papers, 2/55)

6 May 1947

The *Daily Telegraph* and other newspapers have telephoned to say that Mr A. V. Alexander has replied to your statement on the Conscription Bill, speaking to a meeting of the Cooperative Party at Llandudno this morning on a resolution asking the Government to suspend progress on the National Conscription Bill until the question of disarmament is settled by UNO.
In his speech Mr Alexander says:

'Mr Churchill seems to have overlooked the fact that the National Liberals put on paper on Thursday morning an amendment to reduce the period of conscription from 18 to 9 months, so that he and his allies do not seem to be very united on this particular issue. . . . In the light of the debate in the House of Commons, we have taken the decision to reduce the period from 18 to 12 months having once again consulted the Chiefs of Staff. How Mr Churchill can then proceed to argue that apparently that is altering the principle of the whole Bill, I fail to understand.'

---

[1] Reproduced above (p. 693).
[2] Albert Kesselring, 1885–1960. Active service with Bavarian Foot Artillery, 1914–16 (Iron Cross). Posted to General Staff, 1917. Chief of the Luftwaffe General Staff, 1936–7. Cdr, Luftflotte 1, 1939–40; Luftflotte 2, 1940–3. Oberbefehlshaber Süd, 1941–5. Oberbefehlshaber West, 1945. Sentenced at Nuremberg to death by firing squad. The death verdict was received by many in the UK as too harsh. His sentence was commuted to life imprisonment, but he was released in 1952.

Mr Alexander went on to say that he would reserve his remarks on that point until that clause was debated in the House of Commons in Committee. By 1954 the numbers of men who had been called up and had done their training would have passed into the Reserve and the Government would have achieved its objective in getting their numbers into the Reserve. . . .

The Press are asking for your comments, which I said you would not wish to make until you have read the whole speech, if then.

Winston S. Churchill: speech
(Hansard)

7 May 1947   House of Commons

NATIONAL SERVICE

I have been looking around for something upon which to congratulate the right hon. Gentleman (Mr A. V. Alexander, Defence Minister). After some difficulty, I have found at least one point on which I can offer him my compliments, and that is the control of his facial expression, which enabled him to deliver the ridiculous and deplorable harangue to which we have listened, and yet keep an unsmiling face. Indeed, there were moments when I was not quite sure whether he was not taking his revenge on the forces which compelled him to his present course of action, by showing them how ridiculous their case was, and how absurd their position would be when it was presented to the House of Commons. I spoke yesterday of the care and thought given to the social and industrial side of the Bill as explained by the Minister of Labour, and I am willing to believe that equal attention was given to the military side. That is the foundation of the complaint which we make. Let me read what the right hon. Gentleman said, not in the autumn of last year, but on March 20th of this year of grace, 1947. I must read to the House what the right hon. Gentleman said, because I was naturally greatly impressed by it:

> At the direction of the Prime Minister, the Chiefs of Staff in the autumn prepared their considered appreciation of the defence requirements of this country. They put forward their detailed Estimates of the manpower requirements of the three Services as the minimum necessary to implement the defence commitments. The Chiefs of Staff — I want to emphasise this point strongly — did not produce their considered proposals without relation to considerations of the available manpower resources of the country and of all the realities of the manpower situation. They presented to the Government a severely practical statement from their point of view of the manpower requirements of the Services, not based on the numbers ideally required to carry out those commitments satisfactorily, but upon an

appreciably lower scale on which they thought they could manage. . . . To put the matter in a sentence, I would say that the numbers required by the Armed Forces to carry out the defence commitments of this country have been very carefully screened by the Chiefs of Staff in their report to the Government.

That is a curious phrase which has crept in. 'Sifted' would have been a more natural word, and would avoid any ambiguity with the word 'concealed'. 'Screened' is a modern vulgarism. I continue the quotation:

> Those proposals were, in turn, considered in relation to the realities of the economic position. The report of the Chiefs of Staff was scrutinised with extreme care and in great detail. So were the initial sketch estimates prepared by the Service Departments on the basis of that report, and of the production programmes put forward by the joint War Production staff. The main burden of that examination fell on myself and my Service colleagues assisted on the production aspect by the Minister of Supply. Discussions subsequently took place in the defence committee and in the Cabinet. As a result very substantial reductions of the original proposals were achieved, with the full cooperation of the Service Ministers and of the Chiefs of Staff. The Estimate, in its first form, as submitted to me, envisaged a total expenditure of £1,064,000,000 and that figure was eventually cut to £899,000,000, involving a reduction of £165,000,000, or more than 15 per cent of the original proposal. Substantial reductions were also achieved in the manpower figure for the Services themselves and for their production. In particular, the size of the Forces, already put by the Chiefs of Staff below what they regarded as necessary for our commitments, was fixed at a still lower level.

I think I am justified in saying that great and close attention was also given to the military side. This I repeat was said not in the autumn of last year, but on 20 March, 1947, and it was the right hon. Gentleman who was speaking. He will not deny that it was he who said that. I have *Hansard* here – a real copy of the *Official Report*. Only five or six weeks ago the right hon. Gentleman used those heavy, serious, arguments, showing the care with which everything had been examined, and the refinements and judgments at each stage by the natural and normal processes of Parliamentary government, and showing at every point, how the Chiefs of Staff had produced what they thought necessary, until finally an agreement was reached on which all could unite in saying that it was the minimum. I do not think any one can fail to be impressed by the powerful character of the statement made to the House, and we on this side of the Committee were impressed by it. But, now the right hon. Gentleman comes down and tells us in elegant language that what he said on 20 March was all 'piffle and poppycock'. (An Hon. Member: '*Touché*'.) I would not dream of using terms like that unless they were quoted on the high authority of a Minister of the Crown.

How can the right hon. Gentleman now bear with composure, the fact that he used those words, which we thought were used in good faith, which we thought were based on a real solid decision, and conviction, and study of the question on its merits? How can the Prime Minister sit at his side, with all his great responsibility, and now pretend that, owing to a study of the economic position achieved in 48 hours – after 70 or 80 hon. Members below the Gangway had voted against him – the whole scene is transformed? One can only leave these matters to the broad judgment of the country as a whole, and I am quite sure that nothing could have more weakened confidence in the present Administration than the light-hearted way in which they immediately respond to the pressure of their tail below the Gangway. This is a scorpion organisation, with a sting in its tail. How can it be pretended that the new 12 months' system has been thought out carefully, in proportion to our needs? On March 20th the right hon. Gentleman was speaking in the words which I have read to the Committee. He then based himself on the elaborate schemes so carefully prepared in the autumn. Two days later than the Division, he has prepared an entirely different scheme, based on 12 months' service. He must have worked very hard during those 48 hours to make all the tremendous changes and recasting of the immediate and intricate Service problems, in all three Services – all in 48 hours. It is wonderful what great strides can be made when there is a resolute purpose behind them.

The right hon. Gentleman has not concealed the fact that he still thinks that the 18 months was most highly desirable and necessary, but in his statement he made explaining this somersault, or tergiversation – however one likes to express it – he admitted, nakedly and squalidly, that the reason was political. He said nothing about this wonderful revelation of economic difficulties in which our country stood, which came to him on the morrow of the Division in the House. What he said was in the light of the Debate in the House of Commons – (Hon. Members: 'Why not?') Certainly, but one had hoped that the arguments he put before us for 18 months were based on a long and careful study. That they should have been cast aside and thrown overboard as a result of 70 or 80 Members voting against the Government is, if I may say so, a degradation and disreputability of government which has rarely been seen in this House.

I am glad that the right hon. Gentleman – I do him justice for this – did not pretend that the Chiefs of the Staff were in agreement with what had been done. He used the word 'consulted'. Well, one can always consult a man and ask him 'Would you like to have your head cut off tomorrow?' and after he has said, 'I would rather not,' cut it off. 'Consultation' is a vague and elastic term. I am glad that the right hon. Gentleman made no pretence that he was acting on expert advice in this matter, or that he had behind him the authority of the

Chiefs of Staff. It is not the business of the Chiefs of the Staff to decide these matters. I am a Parliamentarian myself, I have always been one. I think that a Minister is entitled to disregard expert advice. What he is not entitled to do is to pretend he is acting upon it, when in fact he is acting contrary to it. I am not accusing the right hon. Gentleman of violating that canon. He has made it perfectly clear that this is a political manoeuvre for a political purpose, and founded on political arguments and political arguments solely.

I must say I am very sorry for the Minister of Defence. His naked, squalid confession that all design, planning and expert advice were thrown aside, although he had received a 300 majority from the House, of which we contributed 132, lowers his position as Minister of Defence, and I am afraid that he will never be able to retrieve what he has lost. What confidence can we place in his future statements about the defence of the country when it is quite clear that if 70 or 80 pacifists or 'cryptos', or that breed of degenerate intellectuals who have done so much harm, vote against him he is prepared to run away, abandon all his prepared plans, worked out over months, and produce, in 48 hours, anything that can be rushed out to placate his critics.

I have here a quotation from Burke which he used about a Government in bygone days. It does not quite apply; I will show afterwards why it does not. It reads:

> They never had any kind of system, right or wrong, but only invented occasionally some miserable tale for the day in order meanly to sneak out of difficulties into which they had proudly strutted.

The reason why that quotation does not wholly apply is that, in this case, the Government did have a careful system and argument and scheme prepared, and they have cast it away in order to avoid their Parliamentary difficulties. At any rate, the right hon. Gentleman may be quite sure that people will no more, in the future, believe what he says about national defence than they believe what the Minister of Fuel and Power says about the state of our fuel stocks. It is quite certain that all the Army plans, based on 18 months' service, must be completely altered for 12 months' service. This would apply even more to the Naval and Air Force plans.

I am rather distressed by the problem which will now be put to many young men. Although a 12 months' period looks easier, there might be an advantage to be gained both by the State and the individual by having an 18 months' period, which will not be gained from the 12 months' period. There is the case of a young man I know, who was an apprentice electrical artificer, a clever lad, who was called up to the Navy the other day. I asked him how he felt about going. He was rather sorry to leave his job for 18 months but he was very ready to go. In 18 months he could have been bent into the electrical work of a ship of war, whereas to attempt to do that in 12 months would be a sheer loss and waste to the Service, without even getting to the point where he would be able to bring his specialised technical acquirements to the handing of the ever-increasing electrical complications of a warship. The effect of this upon the Navy and upon the Air Force, neither of which have stood in very great need of conscription –

Mr Paget[1] (Northampton): How long in war did it take to bend an electrical artificer into the working of a ship – six weeks.

Mr Churchill: There is rather an argumentative point about that – what does 'bend' mean? I submit to the Committee that there was a chance of making these young men who are called up, and who have to make a considerable sacrifice, much more effective in the technical aspects than they can possibly be in the period of a year's training, the great bulk of which will be used for the more primitive forms of training. Anyhow, it is quite certain that no plan for the 12 months could have been made in 48 hours. Surely, the right hon. Gentleman and the Prime Minister will admit that. When, I would like to know, did he make up his mind? How long after the Division figures had been published, did he take to decide that it must be 12 months instead of 18 months? How was he able to pass this whole vast scheme and system through his head, and make all the consequential changes that were necessary? What happened was simply sheer panic in the face of pressure from a minority, and a minority which had been decisively outvoted by the House of Commons.

The party on this side of the House have suffered a great deal from the taunt of 'guilty men', which was made great use of at the Election, and which hon. Gentlemen think they can jeer about today. But nothing I have seen in my Parliamentary experience, and I have a right to speak on this matter, has been equal, in abjectness, in failure of duty to the country, and in failure to stand up for convictions and belief, to this sudden *volte-face*, change and scuttle of which the Prime Minister and his Minister of Defence were guilty. They may never be called to account in the future for what they are doing now, but it is perfectly certain that, henceforward, we have no foundation to rest upon in respect of defence. The title of the Minister of Defence should be changed. He should be called the 'Minister of Defence unless Attacked'. What a lamentable exhibition he has made of himself – one which must be deeply injurious to the reputation which he built up for himself during the war, when he had different leadership.

I am not going to keep the Committee any longer, because many hon. Gentlemen on this side will go more into the details of this matter. As soon as I heard of the change – it was astonishing, considering we supported the Government in the Lobby with all our strength, that not even a word was said

---

[1] Reginald Thomas Paget, 1908–90. Educated at Eton and Trinity College, Cambridge. Barrister, 1934. Lt, RNVR, 1940–3 (invalided out). Unsuccessful Parliamentary candidate (Lab.) for Northampton, 1935. MP (Lab.) for Northampton, 1945–74. Hon. Secretary, UK Council of European Movement, 1954. Master, Pytchley Hounds, 1968–71. Life Peer, 1974.

to us on a matter of this kind – as soon as I heard it on the telephone I issued a statement saying that we must consult together to reconsider our position. We have done so. (An Hon. Member: 'The boys had told you off.') The hon. Member, no doubt, has been snooping around to try to collect information from the meetings of the Conservative Party. I can assure him that I have not changed my view one-eighth of an inch since this business started. We have come to the conclusion that in spite of this change – (*Interruption*.) The hon. Member for East Coventry (Mr Crossman)[1] is very hilarious. He is entitled to be. He is the one who has forced this change on the Government. As a matter of fact, for the purpose of our national defence he ought to be sitting in the place of the Prime Minister or the Minister of Defence.

Mr Crossman (Coventry, East): I supported the Government.

Mr Churchill: In spite of the change, I say, we shall continue to support this Bill.

Mr Mikardo (Reading):[2] Then what is all the fuss about?

Mr Churchill: When the Question is put, 'That the word "eighteen" stand part of the Clause,' we shall vote for it, in exactly the same way as we did on the Second Reading when we were appealed to so strongly by the Government and the Minister of Defence to support this period of 18 months. Then we relied on the assurances of the Government that the 18 months' period was absolutely necessary for our security and the discharge of our obligations. Nothing having been said to relieve us of that argument, we shall continue to vote as they urged us to vote on the last occasion. We are sorry that His Majesty's Ministers and the 250 Socialists who voted for 18 months' service a month ago, will not have the courage to come into the Lobby with us. They have this consolation, for what it is worth. They will be able to say to their constituents, 'We voted for 18 months because we thought it was right. But please remember – credit us with this – that we ran away as soon as we heard it was unpopular.' When this matter is discussed in constituencies I doubt if the principle will be much a matter of controversy, but if it is, it is not credit that hon. Members will gain by their 'right about turn' but widespread and deeply felt contempt.

---

[1] Richard Howard Stafford Crossman, 1907–74. Educated at Winchester School and New College, Oxford. Fellow and Tutor, New College, 1930–7. Leader, Labour Group, Oxford City Council, 1934–40. Married, 1937, Inezita Hilda Baker (div. 1952); 1954, Anne Patricia McDougall. Asst Editor, *New Statesman and Nation*, 1938–55; Editor, 1970–2. Deputy Director, Psychological Warfare, AFHQ Algiers, 1943; Asst Chief, SHAEF, 1944–5. OBE, 1945. MP (Lab.) for Coventry East, 1945–74. Member, Labour Party Executive Committee, 1952–67. PC, 1964. Minister of Housing and Local Government, 1964–6. Leader of the House and Lord President of the Council, 1966–8. Secretary of State for Social Services, 1968–70.

[2] Ian Mikardo, 1908–93. Married, 1932, Mary Rosette. MP (Lab.) for Reading, 1945–50, 1955–9; for South Div. of Reading, 1950–5; for Poplar, 1964–74; for Tower Hamlets, Bethnal Green and Bow, 1974–83; for Bow and Poplar, 1983–7. Member, National Executive Committee, Labour Party, 1950–9, 1960–78; Chairman, 1970–1. Chairman, International Committee, Labour Party, 1973–8; Parliamentary Labour Party, 1974; Select Committee on Nationalized Industries, 1966–70.

No one has ever suggested that the Liberal Party have acted with inconsistency in this matter. I was, however, very glad to see that the Parliamentary group in the House had been decisively overruled by the Liberal Conference, who considered that the national interest should prevail, and were quite ready to cut themselves off from the chance of picking up a few stray Labour votes at by-elections or on other occasions.

Mr Byers:[1] Before the right hon. Gentleman makes charges of that nature, he might have the decency to read the resolution which was passed.

Mr Churchill: I was paying compliments. I was complimenting, first of all, the consistency of the Liberal Parliamentary party in what has long been a tradition of Liberalism. I was complimenting also the larger body outside with whom they are in relation for the courageous and firm steps they have taken. I hope the presentation of these bouquets will not be attended by such violent reactions as seem to animate my hon. Friend the Member for North Dorset (Mr Byers).

If Ministers should succeed in defeating their own original proposal of 18 months, we then come to the insertion of the word 'twelve'. If we were looking at this question from a narrow view of party interests, we could have said 'As this Bill no longer represents a considered scheme or the conviction of the Government or of their experts, we will no longer support the Measure, and give the Government an awkward Division.' But we think that this matter is above party and above Parliamentary tactics. We support the principle of national service because it sustains the moral health and safety of the nation. We shall, therefore, vote with the Government for the insertion of the word 'twelve' while entering the strongest protest against the levity, opportunism and panic-stricken cowardice which they have shown.

Winston S. Churchill: speech
(Hansard)

12 May 1947   House of Commons

HIS MAJESTY'S RETURN FROM SOUTH AFRICA

I wish to associate myself and the Conservative Opposition with the Motion which the Prime Minister has moved. We are all cordially ranged with the right hon. Gentleman on this question and his happily-worded speech leaves little need for addition. We all sympathise with the feelings of the King and

---

[1] Charles Frank Byers, 1915–84. Educated at Westminster and Christ Church, Oxford. President, Oxford Liberal Club, 1937. Married, 1939, Joan Elizabeth Oliver. Enlisted, RA, 1939. Commissioned, 1940. Served with Middle Eastern Forces and Central Mediterranean Force, 1940–4. Lt-Col., 1943. GSO I, 21 Army Group HQ, 1944–5. OBE, 1944. MP (Lib.) for North Dorset, 1945–50. Liberal Chief Whip, 1946–50. Chairman, Liberal Party, 1950–2, 1965–7; Vice-President, 1954–65. Life Peer, 1964. Liberal Leader, House of Lords, 1967–84. PC, 1972.

Queen when they were in South African sunshine, while the rigours of the winter descended upon us here. It must have been, we know, a great worry and preoccupation to them not to be with us, as the King and Queen always have been with us in all the dark, unpleasant moments through which we have passed. It appears to me, and, I believe, to my friends on this side, that the constitutional advice, tendered by the Prime Minister and by the Government to the Crown, that the tour should continue, was entirely in the national, Commonwealth and Imperial interest, and was in every respect wise and correct. We have read in the papers of the festivities which have taken place, of the many picturesque receptions held, of the welcome given by varied races, of the journeys that have been made and of the survey made by Their Majesties of the wide panorama of South Africa. One must not forget, although each of these ceremonies in itself is a matter of great pleasure to the principal personages concerned, nevertheless, taken in a long unending routine, they become a very serious strain upon physical, mental and moral strength. To be continually presented with these demonstrations of affection and loyalty, and to receive them with such unfailing graciousness and untiring good will is, indeed, a great achievement, but it must not be supposed that it does not involve heavy toil, nor must it be supposed that it has not brought with it great advantages, as the Prime Minister has said, both to South Africa, and to the larger organism of which South Africa forms so romantic and interesting a part.

The Prime Minister reminds us also that the homecoming of Their Majesties and the Princesses corresponds with the anniversary of the tenth year of the King's reign. What a period of peril and torment we have had to live through. Yet all the strains and stresses which we have all undergone, and in which the King and Queen and the Royal Family have shared to the utmost of their power, never failing in their duty – all these stresses have only resulted in making more secure and solid the foundation of our institutions in this country, and increasing the loyalty and love formed by all parties to the King and Queen, in the discharge of the great constitutional office entrusted to them.

Winston S. Churchill to President Harry S Truman
(Churchill papers, 2/158)

12 May 1947 Chartwell
Private

My dear Harry,

(To mark the informality of this letter, I follow your injunction, in the style of address). I cannot resist after the year that has passed and all that has happened writing to tell you how much I admire what you have done for the peace and freedom of the world, since we were together.

Winston S. Churchill to Clement Attlee
(*Churchill papers, 2/83*)

13 May 1947

My dear Prime Minister,

Thank you for your letter of May 12.

About Kesselring, I should of course be quite willing to leave the matter in abeyance while the case is *sub judice*, provided that there is a suitable interval between an adverse decision and the execution of the sentence. It is in my opinion a matter of public policy whether the process of killing the leaders of the defeated enemy has not now exhausted any usefulness it may have had. I shall be obliged if you will let me know whether there will be an interval of sufficient length between the confirmation and execution to enable the matter to be raised in Parliament. Otherwise I shall put you a Question, as an urgent matter, at the usual time tomorrow, Wednesday, May 14.

Perhaps you will have noted Sir Oliver Leese's[1] view.[2]

Winston S. Churchill: speech
('*Winston S. Churchill, His Complete Speeches*', *volume 7, pages 7483–8*)

14 May 1947   Albert Hall, London

UNITED EUROPE

All the greatest things are simple, and many can be expressed in a single word: Freedom; Justice; Honour; Duty; Mercy; Hope. We who have come together here tonight, representing almost all the political parties in our British national life and nearly all the creeds and churches of the Western world – this large audience filling a famous hall – *we also* can express our purpose in a single word – 'Europe'. At school we learned from the maps hung on the walls, and the advice of our teachers that there is a continent called Europe. I remember quite well being taught this as a child, and after living a long time, I still believe it is true. However, professional geographers now tell us that the Continent of Europe is really only the peninsula of the Asiatic land mass. I must tell you in all faith that I feel that this would be an arid and uninspiring conclusion, and for myself, I distinctly prefer what I was taught when I was a boy.

---

[1] Oliver William Hargreaves Leese, 1894–1978. Educated at Eton College. Commissioned into British Army, 1914. On active service during WWI (wounded thrice, DSO, despatches). CO, 29th Independent Bde Group, 1940–1. GOC, West Sussex County Div., 1940–1; 15th Scottish Div., 1941; Guards Armoured Div., 1941–2; XXX Corps, North Africa, 1942–3; 8th Army, Italy, 1943–4. KCB, 1943. C-in-C, Allied Land Forces, South-East Asia, 1944–5; Eastern Command, 1945–6. American LOM, 1945. French Légion d'Honneur, 1946. Retired, 1946.

[2] Leese was opposed to the execution of Kesselring, and had said so in an interview published in the *Sunday Pictorial* of 11 May 1947.

It has been finely said by a young English writer, Mr Sewell,[1] that the real demarcation between Europe and Asia is no chain of mountains, no natural frontier, but a system of beliefs and ideas which we call Western Civilisation. 'In the rich pattern of this culture', says Mr Sewell,

> there are many strands; the Hebrew belief in God; the Christian message of compassion and redemption; the Greek love of truth, beauty and goodness; the Roman genius for law. Europe is a spiritual conception. But if men cease to hold that conception in their minds, cease to feel its worth in their hearts, it will die.

These are not my words, but they are my faith; and we are here to proclaim our resolve that the spiritual conception of Europe shall not die. We declare, on the contrary, that it shall live and shine, and cast a redeeming illumination upon a world of confusion and woe. That is what has brought us all together here this evening, and that is what is going to keep us all together – however sharply or even deeply we may be divided – until our goal is reached and our hopes are realised.

In our task of reviving the glories and happiness of Europe, and her prosperity, it can certainly be said that we start at the bottom of her fortunes. Here is the fairest, most temperate, most fertile area of the globe. The influence and the power of Europe and of Christendom have for centuries shaped and dominated the course of history. The sons and daughters of Europe have gone forth and carried their message to every part of the world. Religion, law, learning, art, science, industry, throughout the world all bear, in so many lands, under every sky and in every clime, the stamp of European origin, or the trace of European influence.

But what is Europe now? It is a rubble-heap, a charnel-house, a breeding-ground of pestilence and hate. Ancient nationalistic feuds and modern ideological factions distract and infuriate the unhappy, hungry populations. Evil teachers urge the paying-off old scores with mathematical precision, and false guides point to unsparing retribution as the pathway to prosperity. Is there then to be no respite? Has Europe's mission come to an end? Has she nothing to give to the world but the contagion of the Black Death? Are her people to go on harrying and tormenting one another by war and vengeance until all that invests human life with dignity and comfort has been obliterated? Are the States of Europe to continue for ever to squander the first fruits of their toil upon the erection of new barriers, military fortifications and tariff walls and passport networks against one another? Are we Europeans to become incapable, with all our tropical and colonial dependencies, with all our long-created trading connections, with all that modern production and transportation can do, of even averting famine from the mass of our peoples? Are we all, through

---

[1] Gordon Sewell, ?–1978. Columnist, *Southern Daily Echo*.

our poverty and our quarrels, for ever to be a burden and a danger to the rest of the world? Do we imagine that we can be carried forward indefinitely upon the shoulders – broad though they may be – of the United States of America?

The time has come when these questions must be answered. This is the hour of choice and surely the choice is plain. If the people of Europe resolve to come together and work together for mutual advantage, to exchange blessings instead of curses, they still have it in their power to sweep away the horrors and miseries which surround them, and to allow the streams of freedom, happiness and abundance to begin again their healing flow. This is the supreme opportunity, and if it can be cast away, no one can predict that it will ever return or what the resulting catastrophe will be.

In my experience of large enterprises, I have found it is often a mistake to try to settle everything at once. Far off, on the skyline, we can see the peaks of the Delectable Mountains. But we cannot tell what lies between us and them. We know where we want to go; but we cannot foresee all the stages of the journey, nor can we plan our marches as in a military operation. We are not acting in the field of force, but in the domain of opinion. We cannot give orders. We can only persuade. We must go forward, step by step, and I will therefore explain in general terms where we are and what are the first things we have to do. We have now at once to set on foot an organization in Great Britain to promote the cause of United Europe, and to give this idea the prominence and vitality necessary for it to lay hold of the minds of our fellow countrymen, to such an extent that it will affect their actions and influence the course of national policy.

We accept without question the world supremacy of the United Nations Organisation. In the Constitution agreed at San Francisco direct provision was made for regional organisations to be formed. United Europe will form one major Regional entity. There is the United States with all its dependencies; there is the Soviet Union; there is the British Empire and Commonwealth; and there is Europe, with which Great Britain is profoundly blended. Here are the four main pillars of the world Temple of Peace. Let us make sure that they will all bear the weight which will be imposed and reposed upon them.

There are several important bodies which are working directly for the federation of the European States and for the creation of a Federal Constitution for Europe. I hope that may eventually be achieved. There is also the movement associated with Mr Van Zeeland[1] for the economic integration of Europe. With all these movements we have the most friendly relations. We shall all help each other all we can because we all go the same way home. It is not for us at this stage to attempt to define or prescribe the structure of constitutions. We ourselves are content, in the first instance, to present the idea

---

[1] Paul van Zeeland, 1893–1973. A Director of the Belgian National Bank, 1926; Deputy Governor, 1934. PM of Belgium, 1935–7 (when he devalued the franc by 28%). President, Co-ordinating Foundation for Refugees, 1939. In exile in England, 1940. Belgian Minister of Foreign Affairs, 1949–54.

of United Europe, in which our country will play a decisive part, as a moral, cultural and spiritual conception to which all can rally without being disturbed by divergencies about structure. It is for the responsible statesmen, who have the conduct of affairs in their hands and the power of executive action, to shape and fashion the structure. It is for us to lay the foundation, to create the atmosphere and give the driving impulsion.

First I turn to France. For 40 years I have marched with France. I have shared her joys and sufferings. I rejoice in her reviving national strength. I will never abandon this long comradeship. But we have a proposal to make to France which will give all Frenchmen a cause for serious thought and valiant decision. If European unity is to be made an effective reality before it is too late, the wholehearted efforts both of France and Britain will be needed from the outset. They must go forward hand in hand. They must in fact be founder-partners in this movement.

The central and almost the most serious problem which glares upon the Europe of today is the future of Germany. Without a solution of this problem there can be no United Europe. Except within the framework and against the background of a United Europe this problem is incapable of solution. In a continent of divided national States, Germany and her hard-working people will not find the means or scope to employ their energies. Economic suffocation will inevitably turn their thoughts to revolt and revenge. Germany will once again become a menace to her neighbours and to the whole world; and the fruits of victory and liberation will once more be cast away. But on the wider stage of a United Europe German industry and German genius would be able to find constructive and peaceful outlets. Instead of being a centre of poverty and a source of danger, the German people would be enabled to bring back prosperity in no small measure, not only to themselves, but to the whole continent.

Germany today lies prostrate, famishing among ruins. Obviously no initiative can be expected from her. It is for France and Britain to take the lead. Together they must, in a friendly manner, bring the German people back into the European circle. No one can say, and we need not attempt to forecast, the future constitution of Germany. Various individual German States are at present being recreated. There are the old States and Principalities of the Germany of former days to which the culture of the world owed much. But without prejudice to any future question of German federation, these individual States might well be invited to take their place in the Council of Europe. Thus, in looking back to happier days we should hope to mark the end of that long trail of hatred and retaliation which has already led us all, victors and vanquished alike, into the pit of squalor, slaughter and ruin.

The prime duty and opportunity of bringing about this essential reunion belongs to us and to our French friends across the Channel. Strong bonds of affection, mutual confidence, common interest and similar outlook link France and Britain together. The Treaty of Alliance which has lately been signed only gives formal expression to the community of sentiment that already exists as an indisputable and indestructible fact. It is true that this task of reconciliation requires on the part of France, which has suffered so cruelly, an act of faith, sublime in character; but it is by this act of faith and by this act of faith alone that France will regain her historic position in the leadership of Europe.

There is also another leading member of our family of nations to be held in mind. There is Italy. Everything that I have said about the imperative need of reaching a reconciliation with the German race and the ending of the fearful quarrels that have ruined them, and almost ruined us, applies in a less difficult degree to the Italian people, who wish to dwell happily and industriously within their beautiful country, and who were hurled by a dictator into the hideous struggles of the North. I am told that this idea of a United Europe makes an intense appeal to Italians, who look back across the centuries of confusion and disorder to the glories of the classic age, when a dozen legions were sufficient to preserve peace and law throughout vast territories and when free men could travel freely under the sanction of common citizenship. We hope to reach again a Europe purged of the slavery of ancient days in which men will be as proud to say 'I am a European' as once they were to say '*Civis Romanus sum*'. We hope to see a Europe where men of every country will think as much of being a European as belonging to their native land, and wherever they go in this wide domain will truly feel 'Here I am at home'. How simple it would all be, and how crowned with glory, if that should ever arise.

It will of course be asked: 'What are the political and physical boundaries of the United Europe you are trying to create? Which countries will be in and which out?' It is not our task or wish to draw frontier lines, but rather to smooth them away. Our aim is to bring about the unity of all nations of all Europe. We seek to exclude no State whose territory lies in Europe and which assures to its people those fundamental personal rights and liberties on which our democratic European civilization has been created. Some countries will feel able to come into our circle sooner, and others later, according to the circumstances in which they are placed. But they can all be sure that whenever they are able to join, a place and a welcome will be waiting for them at the European council table.

When I first began writing about the United States of Europe some 15 years ago, I wondered whether the USA would regard such a development as antagonistic to their interest, or even contrary to their safety. But all that has passed away. The whole movement of American opinion is favourable to the revival and re-creation of Europe. This is surely not unnatural when we remember how the manhood of the United States has twice in a lifetime been forced to re-cross the Atlantic Ocean and give their lives and shed their blood and pour out their treasure as the result of wars originating from ancient European feuds. One cannot be surprised that they would like to see a peaceful and united Europe taking its place among the foundations of the World Organisation to which they are devoted. I have no doubt that, far from encountering any opposition or prejudice from the Great Republic of the New World, our Movement will have their blessing and their aid.

We here in Great Britain have always to think of the British self-governing Dominions – Canada, Australia, New Zealand, South Africa. We are joined together by ties of free will and affection which have stood unyielding against all the ups and downs of fortune. We are the centre and summit of a world-wide commonwealth of nations. It is necessary that any policy this island may adopt towards Europe and in Europe should enjoy the full sympathy and approval of the peoples of the Dominions. But why should we suppose that they will not be with us in this cause? They feel with us that Britain is geographically and historically a part of Europe, and that they also have their inheritance in Europe. If Europe united is to be a living force, Britain will know that their youth, like that of the United States, has twice in living memory traversed the immense ocean spaces to fight and die in wars brought about by European discord in the prevention of which they have been powerless. We may be sure that the cause of United Europe, in which the mother country must be a prime mover, will in no way be contrary to the sentiments which join us all together with our Dominions in the august circle of the British Crown.

It is of course alleged that all advocacy of the ideal of United Europe is nothing but a manoeuvre in the game of power politics, and that it is a sinister plot against Soviet Russia. There is no truth in this. The whole purpose of a united democratic Europe is to give decisive guarantee against aggression. Looking out from the ruins of some of their most famous cities and from amid the cruel devastation of their fairest lands, the Russian people should surely realize how much they stand to gain by the elimination of the causes of war and the fear of war on the European Continent. The creation of a healthy and contented Europe is the first and truest interest of the Soviet Union. We had therefore hoped that all sincere efforts to promote European agreement and stability would receive, as they deserve, the sympathy and support of Russia. Instead, alas, all this beneficent design has been denounced and viewed with suspicion by the propaganda of the Soviet Press and radio. We have made no retort and I do not propose to do so tonight. But neither could we accept the claim that the veto of a single power, however respected, should bar and prevent a movement necessary to the peace, amity and well-being of so many hundreds of millions of toiling and striving men and women.

And here I will invoke the interest of the broad, proletarian masses. We see before our eyes hundreds of millions of humble homes in Europe and in lands outside which have been affected by the war. Are they never to have a chance to thrive and flourish? Is the honest, faithful, breadwinner never to be able to reap the fruits of his labour? Can he never bring up his children in health and joy and with the hopes of better days? Can he never be free from the fear of foreign invasion, the crash of the bomb or the shell, the tramp of the hostile patrol, or what is even worse, the knock upon his door of the political police to take the loved one far from the protection of law and justice, when all the time by one spontaneous effort of his will he could wake from all these nightmare horrors and stand forth in his manhood, free in the broad light of day? The conception of European unity already commands strong sympathy among the leading statesmen in almost all countries. 'Europe must federate or perish,' said the present Prime Minister Mr Attlee, before the late terrible war. He said that, and I have no reason to suppose that he will abandon the prescient declaration at a time when the vindication of his words is at hand. Of course we understand that until public opinion expresses itself more definitely, Governments hesitate to take positive action. It is for us to provide the proof of solid popular support, both here and abroad, which will give the Governments of Europe confidence to go forward and give practical effect to their beliefs. We cannot say how long it will be before this stage is reached. We ask, however, that in the meantime His Majesty's Government, together with other Governments, should approach the various pressing Continental problems from a European rather than from a restricted national angle. In the discussions on the German and Austrian peace settlements, and indeed throughout the whole diplomatic field the ultimate ideal should be held in view. Every new arrangement that is made should be designed in such a manner as to be capable of later being fitted into the pattern of a United Europe.

We do not of course pretend that United Europe provides the final and complete solution to all the problems of international relationships. The creation of an authoritative, all-powerful world order is the ultimate aim towards which we must strive. Unless some effective World Super-Government can be set up and brought quickly into action, the prospects for peace and human progress are dark and doubtful.

But let there be no mistake upon the main issue. Without a United Europe there is no sure prospect of world government. It is the urgent and indispensable step towards the realization of that ideal. After the first Great War the League of Nations tried to build, without the aid of the USA, an international order upon a weak, divided Europe. Its failure cost us dear.

Today, after the Second World War, Europe is far weaker and still more distracted. One of the four main pillars of the Temple of Peace lies before us in shattered fragments. It must be assembled and reconstructed before there can be any real progress in building a spacious superstructure of our desires. If, during the next five years, it is found possible to build a world organization of irresistible force and inviolable authority for the purpose of securing peace, there are no limits to the blessings which all men may enjoy and share. Nothing will help forward the building of that world organisation so much as unity and stability in a Europe that is conscious of her collective personality and resolved to assume her rightful part in guiding the unfolding destinies of man.

In the ordinary day-today affairs of life, men and women expect rewards for successful exertion, and this is often right and reasonable. But those who serve causes as majestic and high as ours need no reward; nor are our aims limited by the span of human life. If success comes to us soon, we shall be happy. If our purpose is delayed, if we are confronted by obstacles and inertia, we may still be of good cheer, because in a cause, the righteousness of which will be proclaimed by the march of future events and the judgment of happier ages, we shall have done our duty, we shall have done our best.

Winston S. Churchill to General Lord Ismay
(Churchill papers, 4/25)

15 May 1947

THE DIEPPE RAID[1]

I can see nothing in the papers I now have from you and Allen[2] and my own records which explains who took the decision to revive the attack after it had been abandoned and Montgomery had cleared out. This is the crux of the story. Surely this decision could not have been taken without the Chiefs of Staff being informed. If so, why did they not bring it to my attention, observing I did not leave England till July 30 or 31? It was a major decision of policy to renew it after the men had been put on board the ships, briefed, and dispersed with the secret. If the decision was taken after I left the country, was the Defence Committee or the War Cabinet informed? How did this all go? It is left a blank in these accounts.

[. . .]

---

[1] On 19 Aug. 1942 a force of some 6,000 troops (mainly Canadian, with RAF and RN support) mounted a raid on the German-held port of Dieppe (Operation 'Jubilee'). The heavily entrenched German defenders inflicted severe casualties. Churchill considered the raid 'costly but fruitful' (*The Hinge of Fate*, p. 459), yielding valuable lessons that would inform planning for operations in North Africa later in 1942 and Normandy in 1944.

[2] George Rolland Gordon Allen, 1891–1980. Known as 'Peter'. Educated at United Services College, 1901–3. Lt, 1912. OBE, 1919. Lt-Cdr, 1920. Cdr, 1926. Married, 1928, Alicia Lilian Griffin Eady. Deputy Director, Trade Div., Admiralty, 1939–42. Capt., 1941. Special Service, HMS *Quebec*, 1942–3; HMS *President*, 1944–7. DSO, 1943. CSO to RAdm., Force 'G', HMS *Odyssey*, 1943–4 (despatches). CBE, 1944. Commodore, 1945. Author of *Victory in the West*, vol. 1: *The Battle of Normandy* (1962).

Winston S. Churchill: speech
(*Churchill papers, 2/52*)

16 May 1947   Ayr, Scotland

TRUST THE PEOPLE

The year that has passed since I last had the honour to address the Unionist Associations of Scotland has been marked by a steady improvement in the strength of our Party throughout the United Kingdom. The Municipal Elections in England have shown a decided recovery, in spite of the fact, which is often overlooked, that the assimilation of the national and municipal franchise by the Conservative majority in the late Parliament added upwards of seven million non-rate-paying voters to the electorates involved. This is a remarkable vindication of the maxim 'Trust the people', which has guided the Conservative Party ever since the days of Lord Beaconsfield and later of Lord Randolph Churchill. I look forward with confidence to the autumn Municipal Elections and I hope they will be fought with due regard to national as well as to local affairs.

We have had recently – I do not know whether you noticed it or not – we have had recently a Parliamentary bye-election at Jarrow. Now there could hardly have been a more unfavourable spot than this Socialist stronghold. The Conservatives and Liberals were disappointed that they did not do better, and the Socialists were greatly relieved they did not do worse. I made some enquiries and I am informed that if you apply the turnover of votes at Jarrow to the figures of the last General Election, it would imply a loss of 60 seats, or 120 reduction in the majority of the Socialist Government. If these results in the most unfavourable locality in the country for us should give relief to the Socialist Party, and even excite their jubilation, it only shows what misgivings and guilty consciences they have as they approach the next appeal to the nation.

I read with pleasure, Mr Chairman, your remarks yesterday in your opening speech about the progress made in Scotland in bringing into closer accord the Conservative and Liberal National forces in the Northern Kingdom. I am glad this process has also taken place in England, and that the Socialist menace to the life and freedom of the British nation, for it is nothing less, will be increasingly resisted by all independent and Liberal-minded men and women. The once great Liberal Party has been worn down not by Conservatives but by the Socialist movement, and also by our present electoral system. It would be indeed a national misfortune if Liberalism as a political entity should not continue to assert itself in our Island. I think it is a mistake for Liberals to waste their time in abusing Conservatives, or Unionists. They should concentrate their fire upon the common opponent. We do not seek alliances with those who do not wish to work with us, but there is no reason why the Liberal

Party should not assume the kind of position which was called in the war 'co-belligerent' – not an ally, but a 'co-belligerent' – or why reciprocal services of goodwill, courtesy and mutual aid should not be interchanged between us, wherever, but only wherever, there is an honourable and sincere agreement on fundamental principles. It is not by unnatural deals and political bargains that the political interests of the nation or any Party in it will be advanced, but rather by a frequent recurrence to first principles, and, to quote the famous words of the American constitution, 'the faithful expression of true thought and agreement, and natural behaviour by all concerned for the public benefit'.

NATIONAL FORTUNES HAVE WORSENED

While our Conservative Party position – Unionist Party position – has solidly improved, I regret to tell you that our national fortunes at home and abroad, have, as I predicted to you last year, steadily worsened. There is no part of the world in which our affairs have not been mismanaged and in which our influence and prestige have not painfully declined. At home our finance has followed the spendthrift's ruinous path, and Dr Dalton is spending three thousand pounds in the current year in order to give us far worse services and harder conditions than were obtained in the last pre-war year under a Conservative Government for only one thousand pounds a year. Allowance must be made for the necessary increased military forces we have to keep, and also for the decline in the purchasing power of money, which is a very serious factor in our affairs. But when all has been taken into account, there is no doubt whatever that we are having a far poorer and more restricted national life than we had before the war, and that we are paying far more for it and far more than we can afford to pay for it. This is why we decided to vote against the Finance Bill on the double ground of its wasteful extravagance and faulty accounting.

I am glad that the sudden rise of unemployment to two millions which resulted from the Government's want of foresight in maintaining our coal reserves at the indispensable and well-known minimum, has now come down to below half-a-million. But when we compare this figure with pre-war times, it must be remembered that our conditions are different. A far larger number of our people are today employed on non-productive work. We have to keep 700,000 or 800,000 more men in the military forces than before the war. Most of this is necessary but much of it is wasted, and certainly we are making fools of ourselves by keeping 100,000 soldiers in Palestine in the most dismal of all the quarrels into which any British Government has ever blundered. Then there are no fewer than 650,000 additional non-productive civil servants, local and national, added to our pre-war total. The whole of this unproductive employment of our manpower has to be paid for by taxes, which can only be levied upon the productive energies of our people, and which are also a direct and devastating burden on the consuming power of the whole community. If conditions before the war were related to those prevailing today, the total of the unemployed and of the unprofitably-employed would be nearer two millions than one.

PROPAGANDA FALSEHOOD

This leads me to a wider field. An extraordinary myth, or large scale propaganda of falsehood, has been spread in all directions by the Socialist Government about the lamentable conditions in Great Britain mainly under Conservative Parliaments between the wars, and a lot of young people are being taught to believe that this was a sad period of stagnation in our national and social life. The Socialist Party hope that by creating this impression they will find some excuse for their own failure, which has brought such needless hardship on the masses of our people at the present time. In fact however the years between the two wars, although scarred by a general strike and a prolonged coal stoppage, and although scarred by the economic and financial collapse of Mr Ramsay MacDonald's Second Socialist administration in 1931 – these years were a period of almost unequalled expansion and progress in the life of the wage-earning masses throughout this Island.

Between 1919 and 1939 four million new houses were built in England and Wales alone, or half as many houses as already existed before the first world war. By 1939 the normal hours of work were 47 or 48 in most industries, and in those which are covered by the Factories Act maximum hours were on an average of 44, and this compared with an average week of 54 hours in the majority of industries before 1914. The expectation of life of a new-born baby had risen by nine years – a very important fact to be borne in mind not only by the baby but by the parents – and the new entrants to the elementary schools in London had gained an average of two inches in height and five pounds in weight, since the days before the first world war – all under the blighting influence of Tory misrule. There had also been a steady improvement in the food of the people, and a marked increase in the consumption of milk, cheese, butter and eggs, and of fruit and vegetables. In the 15 years from the formation of Mr Baldwin's Second Administration in 1924, in which I had the honour to be Chancellor of the Exchequer, down to the outbreak of war in 1939, in these 15 years, a period during which, for more than 12 years there were controlling Tory majorities in the House of Commons, wage rates increased by nearly six per cent and the cost of living fell by nine per cent making the increase of real wages by 15 per cent. In this period also production of steel increased by 60 per cent, the output of the engineering and shipbuilding industries by 50 per cent, the electricity consumption was quadrupled, the new and important rayon industry was developed from nothing, and the consumption of sugar rose by one-third. In fact industrial production as a whole reached new levels of expansion and output.

Far-reaching social legislation, for some of which I was personally responsible, was devised and carried by the Conservative Government. Old Age

Pensions, which had been doubled in 1919, were placed on a contributory basis and were brought down from 70 to 65 by me in 1925, and all Means Tests swept away. Widows and children were provided for in a manner never achieved in any previous age or other country in the whole world by the provision I made in the Tory Budget of 1925. It is quite true that unemployment caused deep anxiety. This was mitigated by the development of the Unemployment Insurance Scheme, which, if you will forgive me for being so egotistical as to mention it, I first started nearly 40 years ago under Mr Asquith, that eminent Liberal statesman; and in 1930 an unemployed man with a wife and three children received more subsistence allowance in purchasing power than a railway porter in full employment had received in 1914. This was before the Labour Party had begun to contribute its beneficent assistance to our affairs.

UNEMPLOYMENT BOUNDED UP

During the course of 1929, 1930, and 1931, the 2¼ years of the Socialist Government, unemployment bounded up, bounded up, I must admit, from the impact of the American collapse, from 1,100,000 which it was when I left the Exchequer, to 2,800,000 under the Socialist Administration of Mr MacDonald and Mr Snowden, of which the present Prime Minister, Mr Attlee, was a member. Nevertheless when the Conservatives regained power it was reduced again to nearly the million level; that is to say lower than it is today when allowance is made for what I have explained to you as unprofitable employment. I could give you innumerable examples of the constant, ceaseless, progress that was made in the social life of the people between the two wars under Parliaments with large Tory – because I am not afraid of that word – or Unionist majorities. And so, far from the period between the two wars being a dark miserable age, it was in almost every respect far better for all classes than what we are going through now, and what we are told by the Socialist Ministers themselves we shall have to endure for an indefinite number of years to come.

There is, of course, no reason why a continuance and unlimited improvement in the standard of living of our people, like those of other countries, should not take place, in these modern times with all these modern resources, and I do not quote to you the substantial achievements of the Tory Administration between the wars, except for the purpose of showing what a lie it is for the Socialists to pretend that this was a kind of 'Hungry Forties' epoch in British history, whereas it was a steady, patient, careful advance in every direction and on every front in the improved life of the whole people.

A GREAT SET-BACK

What we have to ask now is why this advance has been interrupted and why it has not only been stopped but set back. No-one can doubt that a great set-back has occurred and that life is worse and harder in every respect than it was before the war, and even, except for the bloodshed, than it was when we were fighting, through all those long years, for our lives against the terrible enemy, with his bombs and his U-boats. Here is the question which from this platform I invite the British nation to ask themselves: Why are we worse off now, in so many ways than we were in the toughest days of the war? Now I have not asked this question without being ready to give you the answer to it. The answer is that at our moment of weakness and exhaustion, after the victory had been won, the Socialist Party fell on us and got us down and, for the sake of their fads and fallacies, are ready to sacrifice all the practical measures which would have led to our speedy revival. Mr Attlee, the Prime Minister, made a long speech abusing me – I value compliments from any quarter! – praising all that he and his Government has done to make a new Britain. He and the vehement partisans who use him have done nothing to build a new Britain. All they have done is to knock out the old. That, I must admit, they have done very effectively.

Mr Attlee boasts of the many Bills which his Government have passed into law, without, he might have added, troubling very much about whether they were discussed in Parliament or not. There is not one of these measures which confers any benefit upon the wage-earning masses of the nation, or makes any improvement in the social conditions of the people, except those measures which were all prepared, shaped and drafted by the National Coalition, on the basis of large Conservative majorities, and proclaimed by me in the Four Years' Plan of 1943. National insurance, education, health services – every one of these was agreed to and arranged by the National Government, with the approval of a House of Commons possessing a Tory and Liberal National majority 225 over all others put together. These National Coalition measures which this new Parliament has carried are the only measures yet brought before us which can bring any real benefit to the life of the people.

A SHOCKING MISFORTUNE

What then is this Socialist contribution? Let us look at it more closely, for it is that which has denied us our recovery from the horrors of war, and while almost every other victorious country has been going ahead with energy and vigour, has cast us into the pit of privation and frustration to an extent which – here I speak with extreme seriousness – if it be prolonged, may well be fatal. It was a shocking misfortune that on the morrow of our victory, after we had rendered services for which the whole world should be grateful, we were suddenly struck down and laid low by the arrival in power of a narrow, bigoted, incapable Socialist faction, who, instead of trying to help the country out of its perils and solve its problems, cared above all for the gratification of their Party dogmas and did not scruple to divide our nation as I have never seen it divided before. This is their offence against the State and people, namely that they have used the power that a misguided electorate gave them – an electorate which for ten years had not had a chance to use the franchise – in an unthinking moment, not to forward the national recovery and revival, but to prove what good Party men they are, and thrust their Socialist doctrines upon our Island in its hour of exhaustion.

Do not underrate I warn you – and I have given some warnings before – in any degree the gravity of the economic and financial circumstances and distresses into which we are moving. They will be of a greater intensity and severity than we have known before. There is no victorious country in the world that is being racketted to pieces in the way we are, and there is no country, because of its complicated artificial structure, less capable of surviving such maltreatment.

I set before you last year in Edinburgh – perhaps there are some here who remember – the artificial and precarious character of Great Britain, how her majestic world power and standard of living, which was the envy of Europe, had been built up in this Island by free enterprise, by adventurous trading abroad, and careful and thrifty administration at home. There never was a community so large as ours, 47 million souls, that stood in so dangerous an economic position. We have to import nearly half our food and most of our raw material. We have to pay for this by rendering services or selling goods to foreigners in return for which they sell us what we require. In the last century we grew industrially great upon cheap and abundant coal, and our population grew from 20 to 47 millions upon free imports of food from all the world. The consequence is that without developing our own agriculture, we have gathered in this Island a population far greater than it could naturally support.

In addition we had accumulated under the capitalist system a great mass of foreign investments, from which we received a substantial income every year, and this income, which was the subject of graduated taxation, paid a great part of the social services in which it was admitted by Mr Ramsay MacDonald himself, when Socialist Prime Minister, that we were ahead of all other countries. But the bulk of that asset beyond the seas, our foreign investments, we gave freely to the common cause. It is gone, and with it many of the promises by which the Socialists gained their majority at the last election, of easier times, larger meals, better housing, shorter hours, less work, higher wages – many of these promises are seriously affected. Mr Attlee was angry with me the other day because I censured the folly and improvidence with which the American Loan was being spent. I did the best I could to help the Government to get that loan because I thought they were going to try their best to help us get on our feet after the supreme exertions we had made. But after all, it is a very strange, uncomfortable position for us to get into that we cannot pay our way or earn our livelihood without a large annual payment given us by friends from abroad. What is to happen when this payment comes to an end, as it will do soon? Are the Socialist Ministers going again to the capitalist, free-enterprise Government of the United States to ask for another Loan while at the same time they boast of all the easements and blessings they are promising to the wage-earning masses here by the introduction of Socialism, and of all the fine schemes they are planning for the improvement of our daily life? How can they go and ask for this further loan while all the time they continue to deride and condemn the American way of life and industry and freely prophesy its early collapse?

PARTY FANATICS

What then is the situation with which they confront us? Every country is free to choose its own form of Government, but surely it should justify its sovereignty by being self-supporting. But how can we ever become self-supporting while the present discord continues and while more than half the energies of the Government are devoted, not to rescuing the country from its hard and dangerous situation but in giving satisfaction to their own Party fanatics and doctrinaires, and beating up their political opponents, and the classes they dislike.

What is the system, if you can call it a system, on which the Socialist Government is now planning the future economy of Britain? They have disturbed or paralysed a large portion of our staple industries by nationalisation or threats of nationalisation and disquieted many others by preparations for the same. At the same time they tell us that four-fifths of our production will, for a good many years to come, remain in the hands of private enterprise seeking private profits. One-fifth of our industry is to be nationalised and four-fifths are to remain as we knew it before. Meanwhile they attack, without ceasing, the four-fifths on which, never forget, our export trade almost entirely depends, and denounce and scorn the business men and employers, on whom they admit they depend, as being mere selfish profit-seekers and exploiters of people; and yet for four-fifths of our economy they themselves declare we must depend on them. Can you imagine a surer way of conducting our country to the abyss than to nationalise a fifth of its industry, and live on the other four-fifths while abusing and maltreating them in an ever-increasing measure? There cannot be a shorter road to ruin than the one I have described. I ask anyone to consider – there is something to be said for the logic of Communism, there is something to be said for the freedom of Capitalism.

HOUSING FAILURE

I warned you last year about the Socialist Housing policy. It has turned out even worse than we feared. Under the much abused Tory rule before the war we were able to build one thousand permanent houses a day in this Island, two-thirds by private enterprise. In the last two years of the Socialist new world and new impulse and revelation we have built barely one hundred permanent houses a day, and in Scotland, I am told, we have built less than ten a day – less than ten!

We could not expect immediately after the fighting stopped to resume the pre-war rate of house construction. That could not happen after the last war. The National Coalition Government therefore planned to have 220,000 new permanent houses finished by now, May 1947. That was our promise, renewed by the Conservative, or so-called 'Caretaker Government' which I formed after we were deserted in the National Coalition by the Socialists. Mr Arthur Greenwood derided this programme as 'chicken food'. But his colleague responsible, Mr Bevan – I wish to be fair to old Ernie – (*laughter*) has only built one-third of this number. He has only given us one-third of the ration of chicken food which Mr Arthur Greenwood ridiculed as hopelessly inadequate compared with what the Socialists would do. This tragic fiasco, which causes severe and needless distress to hundreds of thousands of over-crowded people, is mainly due to Mr Bevan's pedantic irrational indulgence in Socialist prejudice. In his spiteful desire to wipe out the private builder by ordering that only one house in five should be built by private enterprise, he has thrust a burden upon the local authorities which in many cases they were quite unable or unsuited to bear. Moreover, whereas private builders who go bankrupt if they fail do not begin to build houses until they can be pretty sure of finishing them within a reasonable time, local authorities without any personal incentive or corrective are now left with large numbers of half-finished houses upon their hands which for months, and even in some cases years will be idle and useless.

Nowhere has the chaos produced in the building industry by Socialist Party spite been better illustrated than here in Scotland. In the two years following upon the war, less than 7,000 new permanent houses have been built. But at the beginning of this year there were 35,000 unfinished houses all dawdling by the way. The Government never hoped to finish more than two-thirds of this number by the end of 1947. Now they have to confess that their actual achievement will be even below that meagre figure, how far below they cannot and they dare not say. As for Scottish Rural Housing, and the reconditioning of homes – that has been brought to a complete standstill, with needless consequences of suffering and inconvenience of which many of you in this hall must be well aware.

The Socialist Government have failed in almost everything they have touched. In this case, in the field of housing, their failure is not so much due to incompetence as to an arbitrary assertion of their Party doctrines, regardless of the suffering entailed. They have got to learn some simple facts. Houses are built of bricks, mortar and goodwill; in Scotland of stone, lime and also of goodwill. But on neither side of the Border are they built of politics, prejudice and spite.

Frequently in their growing fear the leading Ministers make appeals for a united national effort, and this is certainly needed for all our sakes. But what right have these men to invoke the energies of the nation? They only represent less than half the nation, even on the sorry showing of the last election; and yet they lose no opportunity for injuring and insulting the other half, or more than half.

MINISTER DEEPLY ALARMED

Take Sir Stafford Cripps, the President of the Board of Trade, a Minister who is evidently deeply alarmed. A few weeks ago he made an earnest appeal to the producers of this country for greater exertions, and to them and all others to reduce their consumption by every possible means. He spoke of the vital consequences to the export trade, and we all agree with him in that. But this is the very Minister who a year ago, as I told you at Edinburgh, destroyed the Liverpool Cotton Exchange which earned at least a million pounds a year in foreign currency, mainly American dollars. And then there was his colleague,[1] who gave away our cables and wireless system, and lost us another 2½ millions of foreign exchange. So here are 3½ millions of foreign exchange – I take this only as an example – with which we could have bought our own food and raw materials, deliberately cast away to give satisfaction to Socialist doctrines. When Sir Stafford Cripps asks his hard-pressed fellow-citizens to do their best and try their utmost, he should, I think, remember that he and his colleagues have on these two counts alone annihilated an output for export purposes that 5,000 to 7,000 Britons could not produce by working their hardest for a whole year.

Sir Stafford Cripps is an able and upright man, tortured and obsessed by his Socialist tenets. He should ask himself whether with a blot like this upon his record, he is the man to call for further efforts and exertions from others. No one has a right to ask for loyalties which they are not prepared to match in their own heart and conscience.

And what of Mr Shinwell, who is appealing to us all and ordering us all to submit to every discomfort and inconvenience in the matter of warmth, light and electric power? (And we most certainly do all we can to obey the instructions we receive!) But surely a Minister in such a position should be national minded (and while he is nationalising everything he might nationalise himself), surely he, above all, should think of our anxious harassed community as a whole, and not simply of that section to whose support he owes his continuance in His Majesty's Government. Some of these Ministers talk of 'the Dunkirk spirit'. We all remember Dunkirk. But what would have been the position at Dunkirk, and the fate of our Army, if the controller of the ships and boats who went to take our men away had said:

'Bring off the Trade Unionists and Labour men only. The rest are not worth a tinker's curse'?

[1] Hugh Dalton.

THE NATIONAL INTEREST

I have said repeatedly that we do not grudge the Government their offices. Many of us have held office for so many years that we are by no means dazzled or attracted by the prospects of resuming it. It is a good thing that everyone should have the chance to hold office under the Crown. We recognise the difficulties of the situation after the war. We were and we are, as we have shown in the voting on the National Service Bill, ready to support them in anything that is for the national interest; but in return all we have received is acrid partisanship and frantic class and Party strife. Even the other day, when we went into the Lobby to support the Government on the 18 months' service, we were alone. Because the Prime Minister and the Minister of Defence, Mr Alexander, had fled, cowed by 70 or 80 votes against them from their own tail.

After nearly 50 years of political life, I understand, even when I do not share, the feelings of organised labour and of the great Trade Unions, with whom I have so often worked in peace and war, and whose part in our national life is invaluable – invaluable, though I am sorry that at this moment when they have more influence than they ever had before over the Government of the country they have less influence than they ever had before over their own members. The British working man, especially the radical element, has a deep-seated and natural love of fair-play and resents the idea of being exploited by the rake-off of monopolies or other rackets. Where such abuses lead to a living industry being hampered we are all agreed the law should provide effective redress, correction and control.

THE INDUSTRIAL CHARTER

In our Conservative Industrial Charter we have made it clear that we will march with the Trade Unions in all this. But there is another aspect I should like organised, and above all, nationalised labour to consider. It is this. Will not the daily toil of the actual producing worker have a heavier burden thrust upon it by enormous hordes of disinterested and largely uninterested officials than would be the case under private management? And will not these officials be less efficient, more costly and far more dictatorial than the private employers? We have reached a period in the history of our country when all classes have got to think and think very hard. In such industries as have up to the present been nationalised the former shareholders are being paid off often on unfair terms, but nevertheless paid off, so that the rentier charge still lies upon the industry and upon the original producer. In addition to this we now have imposed the whole structure of bureaucratic control in most cumbrous forms. I mentioned the 650,000 more officials who are employed to look after us than we needed before the last war. That is an enormous burden to cast upon the productive energies of the country. If the costs of running an industry by a State bureaucracy are shown to be much greater than they were in the days of private management, and if the efficiency of management is largely reduced, that can only mean that the prime producer will get less for his work than he formerly did.

This can be made up to him by a subsidy to his particular industry from the national exchequer. If the mines and the railways are run at a loss which the taxpayer makes good out of his weekly income tax and taxation of the things he has to buy, this additional burden or bureaucratic management can be spread to the fellow-workers throughout the country. But this last process is only possible while a small proportion of our industries are nationalised. As the State control extends and bureaucracy supersedes the private employer, so will it become more difficult to quarter these industries which have ceased to pay upon the hard-pressed exchequer. We can easily reach a point where the whole industry of the country, or the greater part of it, will be run at a loss, to be made good by the general taxpayer who is, after all, in 90 cases out of 100, a part of the national productive forces himself. This is a very serious consideration. We shall in fact have substituted a far less fertile and fruitful process of production and a far more arbitrary official control for the kind of steadily improving life which has hitherto kept our country in the van of the nations and far ahead of the general conditions prevailing in Europe. Coal, transport and electricity have been or will soon be nationalised. While I deplore the disturbance of our life which these experiments cause, I am by no means sure that the making of them may not be a good lesson which may convince large numbers of our fellow-countrymen, in a way that no verbal argument would ever have done.

It is imperative, however, that we should know all the facts about these experiments. No doubt the Government will wish to conceal the accounts and to prevent the cost from being known. But when we come into power, as we shall do at the first opportunity, we shall unfailingly expose these accounts to the nation in order that the real consequences of the Socialist experiments shall be made plain. I am sure myself after a long life of public affairs that you will find that the regimenting of industries under the State involves management charges far greater than ever were incurred by private enterprise and private profits, and I believe it will be found that this management will be less skilful than private proprietors, and certainly far less dependent upon the goodwill of their workpeople.

CONSERVATIVE POLICY

Now I have a word to say especially in regard to Scotland. When Scotland is increasingly confronted by hard applications of Socialist fallacy, with all its resulting centralisation in London, it will become more and more necessary for the Scottish people to assert their right to manage this class of their affairs under conditions which do not leave them entirely controlled by Departments of Whitehall, for that is the faith of the Unionist Party in Scotland, and of all gathered in this great hall. The Unionist Party in Scotland will have all our aid in looking after that extremely important aspect of our present affairs.

After the Blackpool Conference last year I appointed an Industrial Policy Committee under Mr Butler, the author of the great Education Act, about which Mr Attlee is boasting. The Committee travelled up and down the country to seek the advice of those who were managing or working in our industries. Their report has been published this week. It is a broad statement of policy, to which those who are opposed to the spread of rigid Socialism can now rally. It has been written in a spirit of honest and progressive realism. We call it 'The Industrial Charter', because without drawing hard and fast lines, it explains the new development of the relationship of the State and the citizen and it seems to us to fit the needs of our time. Britain, like any other country, is always changing – like any other, never draws a line without smudging it. We have not the sharp logic of Continental countries. We seek to benefit private enterprise with the knowledge and guiding power of modern Governments, without sacrificing the initiative and drive of individual effort under free, competitive conditions. Our policy is based on the two main principles of fair play and adequate opportunity. We seek to establish a minimum standard of life and labour, below which no one who is prepared to meet the obligations of good citizenship should be allowed to fall. Above that minimum standard, we wish to give the fullest possible play for competitive individual enterprise and every chance for the native genius of our Island race, springing perennially from every class, to win its full and fair reward. As I said in my Four-Year Plan broadcast of 1943, I believe there is a broadening field for State enterprise in modern conditions. But instead of this being designed to repress and constrict individual exertion, we consider that the function of Government guidance is to give the broadest possible chance for everyone to make the best of himself or of herself in the true service of the nation. For this purpose, we believe that competition rather than State monopoly will be the best safeguard of the consumer, and a good spur to the efficiency of the producer.

Finally we believe that it should not be the aim of the State to engross all the money earned by the people and spend it for them, but rather that this money should be allowed to 'fructify in the pockets of the people' – to use an old phrase of Gladstonian times – so that the incentives to industry, ingenuity and audacity shall ceaselessly fertilise the springs of national life.

The last time I spoke to you a year ago, you gave me in your Resolution the great phrase, 'A property-owning democracy'; and this year, at the Conference yesterday, you passed a motion containing an equally pregnant expression, 'The avoidance of over-government'. It is by the interplay of these ideas within the scope of a free, patriotic and democratic State that we resolve to find the means to restore and preserve the true and enduring splendour of our Island home.

Winston S. Churchill to Sir Orme Sargent
(Churchill papers, 2/57)

20 May 1947
Private

My dear Sargent,

The enclosed was given me in Paris as extracts from a Soviet government film, no doubt intended for widespread propaganda purposes. It seems very offensive and of course completely mendacious.

I should be glad if you will ask the Secretary of State what he thinks of it and whether it is worthwhile doing anything about it. I wonder if it is wise to let such lies go unchallenged? The fact that they are trying to spread this hatred gives one rather a bad impression of the future.

Winston S. Churchill: press statement
(Churchill papers, 2/58)

20 May 1947

Mr Churchill made the following statement in reply to Mr Wallace's speech in Oslo:

'I did not describe Mr Wallace as a crypto-Communist. This misstatement was given publicity by the BBC who made an immediate correction on their misrepresentation being pointed out. What I said was –

> "We have had here lately a visitor from the United States who has fore-gathered with that happily small minority of the crypto-Communists who are making a dead set at the foreign policy which Mr Ernest Bevin, our Foreign Secretary, has patiently and steadfastly pursued with the support of nine-tenths of the House of Commons."

Mr Wallace says that "I dare not confess publicly or privately the convictions of my Group that war is inevitable." My view is as follows: War is not inevitable, but it would be inevitable if Britain and the United States were to follow the policy of appeasement and one sided disarmament which brought about the last war.'

Winston S. Churchill to Clement Attlee
(Churchill papers, 2/43)

21 May 1947
Secret

My dear Prime Minister,
 I have now had an opportunity of consulting my colleagues upon the terms of a possible settlement in India which you and the Viceroy put before us last night.
 As a result I am in a position to assure you that if those terms are made good, so that there is an effective acceptance of Dominion status for the several parts of a divided India, the Conservative Party will agree to facilitate the passage this Session of the legislation necessary to confer Dominion status upon such several parts of India.

Thomas Boggs[1] to Winston S. Churchill
(Churchill papers, 2/18)

21 May 1947   Washington DC

Dear Mr Churchill,
 Greetings from a fellow legislator.
 I don't know whether or not you have been following the efforts of Senator Fulbright of Arkansas[2] and I to secure the passage in the Congress of the United States a resolution reading as follows:

> 'That the Congress hereby favors the creation of a United States of Europe within the framework of the United Nations.'

 This resolution has met with the unanimous support of the press of America, and we are very hopeful that we will secure its passage. I am enclosing herewith excerpts from the Congressional Record of March 21, May 9 and May 13, including remarks made by Senator Fulbright and myself.
 Any comments that you might like to make will be highly appreciated. Incidentally, I am including in the Congressional Record within the next few

---

[1] Thomas Hale Boggs Sr, 1914–72. Educated at Tulane University. Admitted to the Bar, Louisiana, 1937. Married, 1938, Lindy Boggs. Representative (Dem.) for Louisiana, US House of Representatives, 1941–3, 1947–73; Majority Whip, 1962–71; Majority Leader, 1971–2. Disappeared in Alaska after a presumed plane crash in 1972.

[2] James William Fulbright, 1905–95. Educated at University of Arkansas, 1925; Rhodes Scholar, Oxford, 1928; Law Dept, George Washington University, 1934. Admitted to the Bar, DC, 1934. Attorney, Antitrust Div., US Dept of Justice, 1934–5. Law Instructor, University of Arkansas, 1936–9; President, 1939–41. Representative (Dem.) for Arkansas, US House of Representatives, 1943–5. US Senator for Arkansas, 1945–74. Presidential Medal of Freedom, 1993.

days the full text of the magnificent address which you delivered in London last week.[1]

Winston S. Churchill to Clement Attlee
(Churchill papers, 2/43)

22 May 1947 Chartwell

My dear Prime Minister,

I had a talk with the Viceroy this morning and I suggested to him that, if you approved, he might meet Eden, John Anderson and Harold Macmillan (who is acting in Rab Butler's place as head of our India Committee) and possibly John Simon. There were a good many questions asked at our luncheon meeting yesterday which I was not able to answer in detail, and I would like my friends to clarify these matters. None of them, so far as I can judge, will affect, in any way, the decision to which we came, which I communicated to you yesterday. Perhaps you will let the Viceroy know if he might have this talk with them. Mountbatten had received a request from Godfrey Nicholson[2] to see him, on behalf of our House of Commons Conservative India Committee. I think it would be a pity if these matters were discussed with any but Privy Councillors, and I have most carefully enjoined secrecy upon all my colleagues. I hope therefore that private Members in my Party will not be consulted at this stage. This advice was very agreeable to Mountbatten.

I hope you will give us timely notice before any legislation is introduced so we can consider how things stand. We are at your service if you should wish, at any time, to see us on this matter, which I hope may go forward on a bipartisan basis.

Sir Orme Sargent to Winston S. Churchill
(Churchill papers, 2/57)

27 May 1947
Confidential

Dear Mr Churchill,

Thank you for your letter of the 21st May[3] about the scenario of the Soviet film *Battle of Stalingrad*.

Our Embassy in Moscow had already brought this scenario to our attention,

---

[1] Reproduced above (pp. 704–11).
[2] Godfrey Nicholson, 1901–91. A distiller. MP (Cons.) for Morpeth, 1931–5; for Farnham Div. of Surrey, 1937–66. Bt, 1958. His daughter, Emma Nicholson, was elected to the House of Commons, as a Conservative, in 1978, later joining the Liberal Democrats.
[3] Reproduced above, dated May 20 (p. 724).

and on the same day that you wrote to me, but before I received your letter, I sent a telegram to Peterson[1] asking him whether he thought we should take this up, and if so, in what way. When we have considered his reply, I shall put the matter to the Secretary of State, and let you know what he decides.

Have you considered issuing a personal protest against this gross misrepresentation? It seems to me that the scenario is insulting to you personally no less than to the country as a whole, and that you would be quite justified in doing so. If you wish to take private action, we shall be glad to let you have a copy of the full text of the scene. But you will probably agree with me that it would be better to synchronize action in the matter, so I suggest that you wait until I have consulted the Secretary of State.

I shall not fail to let you know his decision at once.

---

[1] Maurice Drummond Peterson, 1889–1952. Educated at Oxford University. Entered Foreign Service, 1913. British Counsellor in Spain, 1929–31. Head of Egyptian Dept, FO, 1931–5; League of Nations and Western Dept, 1935; Abyssinian Dept, 1935–6. Acting High Commissioner in Cairo, 1934. Minister to Bulgaria, 1936–8. KCMG, 1938. Ambassador to Iraq, 1938–9; to Spain, 1939–40; to Turkey, 1944–6; to Soviet Union, 1946–9. Controller, Overseas Publicity, Ministry of Information, 1940–1. Under-Secretary of State, FO, 1942–4. GCMG, 1947.

June 1947

Winston S. Churchill: speech
(Hansard)

3 June 1947   House of Commons

INDIA (TRANSFER OF POWER)

It is, of course, impossible for the House to weigh and measure the full meaning of the most important statement which has just been made to us by the Prime Minister. I am bound to say that it seemed difficult to understand, but the White Paper which is in the Vote Office will have to be studied with attention and will probably carry the largest measure of proof to those who are best instructed. No doubt we shall have a Debate at a suitable moment on this question. I am not asking for any particular date to be fixed at the present moment. I am bound to say, however, that the two conditions foreseen at the time of the Cripps Mission, which was set up under my Administration – namely, first, agreement between the Indian parties and, secondly, a period of Dominion Status in which India or any part of it may freely decide whether or not to remain within the association of the British Commonwealth of Nations – seem to be fulfilled.

Mr Stokes: On a point of Order, Mr Speaker. May I ask whether there is any Motion before the House? Surely, this is developing into a Debate and is out of Order.

Mr Churchill: May I respectfully say that this is a matter of considerable importance? Surely, the Opposition party should be permitted to make some passing and brief comments.

Mr Speaker: I was watching the matter. Of course, it is perfectly true that there is no Motion before the House, but I do think that at this moment, there should be a slight amount of latitude. I feel sure hon. Members will not abuse it and I think it is only right.

Mr Churchill: As I was saying, the two principles on which the Cripps Mission stood – namely, agreement and a period of Dominion Status with perfect freedom to choose – appear to be fulfilled, as far as I can see from the copy of the White Paper which is now in the Vote Office which, through the courtesy of the Prime Minister, I received an hour ago.

Mr Gallacher: Why have we not all had a copy?

Mr Churchill: Even in Russia there are distinctions between grades which different people occupy. If it should prove to be the case that these two conditions have been maintained in fact and in form, then I say that all parties in this House are equally pledged by the offer and the declaration that we have made, and on these points we can only be well assured by the course of events in the next few weeks and months. It is quite true that the agreement of the various parties in India has only been achieved on the basis of partition. I gather that is the foundation. Nevertheless, after a reasonable period of deliberation and responsibility, should all these parties decide to remain within the British Commonwealth of Nations, the theme of the unity of India will be preserved, and the many nations and States of India may find their unity within the mysterious circle of the British Crown, just as the self-governing Dominions have done for so many years after all other links with the mother country, save those of sentiment, have been dissolved. It may, therefore, be that through a form of partition, the unity of India may, none the less, be preserved.

I do not wish to trespass upon the indulgence of the House but, finally, we must ask ourselves even at this early moment whether, after matters have proceeded thus far – and my opinions about them are well known – any better way can be found of saving India from the blood bath which may stand so near. I cannot doubt that, at first sight, and subject to the unknown factors working out in a favourable manner, it would seem that a settlement on these lines may offer to India some prospect of escape from one of the most hideous calamities which has ever ravaged the vast expanses of Asia. Naturally, we cannot form opinions upon the very great outlines and the complicated details that have been given; nor can we form decided opinions without knowing what will be the correspondence of the actual facts with what is hoped for from them, by the Government, the Viceroy and others responsible for India.

However, I will say at once with regard to the right hon. Gentleman's statement about impending legislation, that if the facts correspond to the outlines with which we have been presented this afternoon, and if it is necessary, as I gather it is, that legislation should be introduced to implement speedily the transference of power on Dominion Status terms, to the various parts of India so that they can decide their future for themselves at leisure, it would not be right that such legislation should be deemed contentious, or that any long delays should elapse after it is introduced before it is passed into law. Therefore, while reserving our full freedom to discuss points of detail, we shall not oppose any Bills to confer Dominion Status on the various parts of India, which may be presented to us on the basis of the statement made this afternoon by the Prime Minister. The Prime Minister said that great credit was due to the Viceroy. These are matters about which it is extremely difficult to form decided opinions on now, but if the hopes which are enshrined in this Declaration should be borne out, great credit will indeed be due, not only to the Viceroy but to the Prime Minister who advised His Majesty to appoint him.

Lady Anderson[1] to Winston S. Churchill
(Churchill papers, 2/145)[2]

4 June 1947

My Dear Winston,

I wonder if you would like some more maple syrup — perhaps it is too warming?

I am indeed distressed to hear from John that you are to have an operation.[3]

I have had six, I can feel for you. I am very very sorry indeed.

The horribleness of our cooks during the last 14 months has prevented me from begging you to come and have luncheon or dinner here.

I know you like a good omelette and excellent soup — and neither of these things have our miserable cooks been able to make at all.

Dinner without soup seems to me incomplete.

I am worn out with their incompetence.

Dear dear Winston, you are very much in my thoughts —

Do my darling Ralph Wigram's[4] days with you come into your book, or was his anxious Calvary over —

Do you remember how in the beautiful letter you wrote me at the time of his death, you spoke of him as the 'Light in the broken lamp'.

It is the most wonderful letter I've ever had in my life.

With love dear Winston

Let me know about the maple syrup.

---

[1] Ava Bodley Wigram, who had married John Anderson in 1941.
[2] This letter was handwritten.
[3] Churchill was operated on for a hernia on 11 June 1947.
[4] Ralph Follett Wigram, 1890–1936. Educated at Eton and University College, Oxford. Married, 1925, Ava Bodley. Temporary Secretary, British Embassy, Washington DC, 1916–19. Third Secretary, FO, 1919; Second Secretary, 1920. First Secretary, British Embassy, Paris, 1924–33. CMG, 1933. Counsellor and Head of Central Dept, FO, 1934.

Elizabeth Gilliatt to John Colville
(Churchill papers, 2/57A)

12 June 1947
Private and Personal

Dear Mr Colville,
Thank you for your letter of 30th May (R 5997/5085/19, signed by Mr Williams[1] on your behalf). I have shown this to Mr Churchill and he minuted on it as follows (he wishes you to know that this is for your private information):

> 'Undoubtedly he (Stalin) said it to me in conversation on our last night together at Potsdam – as an alternative to a base in the Straits. But I cannot think the matter of any consequence.[2]
> WSC   10 June 1947'

Ernest Bevin to Winston S. Churchill
(Churchill papers, 2/57)

16 June 1947
Confidential

Dear Winston,
Sargent has shown me his correspondence with you about the scenario of the Soviet film 'Battle of Stalingrad'. Since he wrote to you on the 27th May,[3] we have received Sir Maurice Peterson's comments on the manner in which we should approach the Soviet Government regarding this falsification of history. Peterson thinks, and I agree with him, that if we content ourselves with representations to the Soviet Ambassador in London,[4] we cannot be sure that the latter's report to Moscow will not take the edge off our protest. I accordingly propose to instruct Sir Maurice Peterson to speak personally to Stalin and hand him an aide memoire.[5] I enclose the draft of

---

[1] Michael Sanigear Williams, 1911–84. Entered FO, 1935; served at HM Embassy, Spain, 1938–9; at FO, 1939–47, 1952–6; in Rome, 1947–50; in Rio de Janeiro, 1950–2. Married, 1942, Joy Hunt (d. 1964); 1965, Mary Harding. CMG, 1954. Minister at Bonn, 1956–60; in Guatemala, 1960–2. Ambassador to Guatemala, 1962–3. Asst Under-Secretary, FO, 1963–5. Minister to the Holy See, 1965–70. KCMG, 1968.
[2] Churchill had written an article for the *Daily Telegraph* on Apr. 29 in which he mentioned Stalin's request for a base on the Aegean Sea.
[3] Letter reproduced above (pp. 726–7).
[4] Georgiy Nikolaevich Zarubin, 1900–58. Soviet Ambassador to Canada, 1944–6; to UK, 1946–52; to US, 1952–8.
[5] The five-page aide-memoire rebutted the accusation made in the film 'that the invasion of France was deliberately delayed by His Majesty's Government until 1944 in order to prolong Russian sacrifices in the war against Germany and that this delay was moreover contrary to a promise alleged to have been given by Mr Churchill in 1942 that the invasion of France would take place in that year' (*Churchill papers, 2/57*).

this document and I shall give careful consideration to any emendations that you may care to suggest.

I should be entirely in favour of your sending a private letter of protest if you feel so inclined. I should of course be very happy for you to use the bag if you wish to address it personally to Generalissimo Stalin or Monsieur Molotov.

Elizabeth Gilliatt to Winston S. Churchill
(*Churchill papers, 2/53*)

18 June 1947

Mr Stuart[1] would like your approval of the following announcement, dealing with the changes in the Committee of Privileges:

'Mr Churchill has already announced his intention to withdraw from the Committee of Privileges, and his place will be taken by Captain Crookshank. It is also intended that for the next Session, 1947/1948, Sir David Maxwell Fyfe's[2] place shall be taken by Mr J. S. C. Reid. For the remainder of the present Session, however, Captain Crookshank is unable to undertake this work owing to previous engagements, and Mr Reid is being added to the Committee now until the new arrangements for next Session have been completed. These proposals must of course come before the house for approval.'

May Mr Stuart please go ahead with the Motion announcing these changes? It should be, he thinks put on the Paper tonight.[3]

---

[1] James Stuart, Opposition Chief Whip.

[2] David Patrick Maxwell Fyfe, 1900–67. Educated at George Watson's College, Edinburgh and Balliol College, Oxford (Hon. Fellow, 1954). Scots Guards, 1918–19. Staff, British Commonwealth Union, 1921–2. Called to Bar, Gray's Inn, 1922. Practised on Northern Circuit, Liverpool, 1922–34. QC, 1934. Bencher, 1936. Treasurer, Gray's Inn, 1949. Unsuccessful Parliamentary candidate (Cons.) for Wigan, 1924. Married, 1925, Sylvia Harrison. MP (Cons.) for West Derby Div., Liverpool, 1935–54. Member, General Council of the Bar, 1936. Recorder, Oldham, 1936–42. Knighted, 1942. Solicitor-General, 1942–5. Attorney-General, 1945. PC, 1945. Deputy Chief Prosecutor, Nuremberg Trials, 1945–6. Member (Cons.), Council of Europe, Strasbourg, 1949. Home Secretary and Minister for Welsh Affairs, 1951–4. GCVO, 1953. Viscount Kilmuir, 1954. Lord High Chancellor, 1954–62. Hon. Fellow, Royal College of Arts, 1955. Baron, 1962. 1st Earl of Kilmuir, 1962.

[3] Churchill wrote at the bottom of this message: 'Yes'.

Winston S. Churchill to Ernest Bevin
(Churchill papers, 2/57)

21 June 1947
Confidential

My dear Ernest,

Thank you very much for your answer about the Soviet film 'Battle of Stalingrad'. I am obliged to you for the instructions which you have given to our Ambassador in Moscow and for the aide memoire which is to be handed to the Marshal. I do not think I will write myself, especially as His Majesty's Government have taken the appropriate action.

Clement Attlee to Winston S. Churchill
(Churchill papers, 2/145B)[1]

27 June 1947

My dear Churchill,

I was glad to see you looking so well when I saw you this week. When I was recovering from an operation in 1939, you kindly sent me a volume of your speeches which I read with much appreciation. As a very minor practitioner of an art of which you are acknowledged master, I am sending you this volume, not for reading, but only as a tangible expression of my wishes for your speedy and complete restoration to health.

---

[1] This letter was handwritten.

June 1947

Clement Attlee to Winston S. Churchill
(Churchill papers, 2/83)

30 June 1947

My dear Churchill,

You will remember that we have had some correspondence[1] about the sentence on Kesselring, and I think you may wish to know for your personal information how this stands.

The proceedings of the Court Martial have been examined by the Judge Advocate General,[2] who has advised that they were legally in order and has so informed General Harding, the GOC in C in Italy.[3]

General Harding has now reported that he has decided to confirm the findings of 'Guilty' in the case of Kesselring and also in the cases of von Mackensen[4] and Maeltzer[5] who were connected with Kesselring in the same series of incidents. He has however decided to commute the sentences in all three cases to imprisonment for life. This sentence will be promulgated as soon as possible.

---

[1] Reproduced above (p. 704).

[2] Henry Davies Foster MacGeagh, 1883–1962. Educated at Oxford. Married, 1917, Rita Kiddle. Called to Bar, Middle Temple, 1906: Bencher, 1931; Reader, 1943; Deputy Treasurer, 1949; Treasurer, 1950. Commissioned, London Rifle Bde, TA, 1909–23; Col., 1923–34. Military Assistant, Judge Advocate General, 1916–23. Deputy Asst Adjutant-General, War Office, 1917. Asst Adjutant-General, 1918–23. CBE, 1919. Military Deputy, Judge Advocate General, 1923–34. QC, 1924. Deputy Judge Advocate General, British Forces, China, 1927. KBE, 1930. Judge Advocate General, Army and RAF, 1934–54. Silver Jubilee Medal, 1935. Coronation Medal, 1937, 1953. KCB, 1946. Medal of Freedom, Gold Palm, 1947. GCVO, 1950.

[3] Allan Francis Harding, 1896–1989. Known as 'John'. Educated at King's College, London. On active service, WWI, 1914–18 (MC). CO, 1st Battalion Somerset Light Infantry, 1939–40. GSO, Middle East Command, 1940. Brig. General Staff, Western Desert Force, 1940–1 (DSO, CBE); XIII Corps, 1941–2. Deputy Director of Military Training, Middle East Command, 1942. Deputy CoS, Middle East Command, 1942. GOC 7th Armoured Div., North Africa, 1942–3 (wounded, Jan. 1943); VIII Corps, 1943. CoS, 15th Allied Army Group, Italy, 1943–4. GCB, 1944. GOC, XIII Corps, Italy, 1944–5; Central Mediterranean Force, 1946–7. GOC-in-C, Southern Command, 1947–9. C-in-C, Far East Land Forces, 1949–51; British Army of the Rhine, 1951–2. ADC-General to the King, 1950–2. CIGS, 1952–5. Governor and C-in-C, Cyprus, 1955–7. Baron, 1958.

[4] Friedrich August Eberhard von Mackensen, 1889–1969. CoS, German 14th Army, 1939–40. Col. Gen., 1943–4. Convicted of war crimes, Rome, 1947; death sentence commuted. Released, 1952.

[5] Kurt Malzer, 1894–1952. Staff Officer, Luftwaffe, 1939; Air District Cdr, 1940; General Major, 1941. Military Cdr, Rome, 1939. Responsible for Ardeatine Massacre, 24 Mar. 1944. Convicted of war crimes, Rome, 1946; death sentence commuted.

July
1947

Denis Kelly[1] to Winston S. Churchill
(*Churchill papers, 4/57*)

1 July 1947

Mr Churchill,

The smaller Muniment Room, which I propose to call Muniment Room A, contains documents up to 1918; the larger room, which I propose to call Muniment Room B, contains the remainder. Each room will be subdivided into political, literary and personal sections. Boxes will be numbered serially – 1–50 for Muniment Room No. 1, and 51 onwards for Muniment Room No. 2. (I hope shortly to obtain an estimate from Chubbs for renumbering and re-engraving the existing boxes and keys.)

Each box will contain a list of contents. A second copy of each such list will be bound, together with lists from other boxes, into separate volumes for each room. From these volumes a subject index will be compiled to cover both rooms.

This achievement of cataloguing and indexing, even under fairly broad headings, all the documents in each room, will, however, be wrecked within two months if the process known as 'rummaging' is allowed to continue. At the same time I realise that you and your staff's freedom of access to the documents must be unfettered, and I have given some thought as to how these apparently conflicting aims can be reconciled. I propose that the following system be instituted: a small pool of deed boxes should be maintained for your personal use in the study at Chartwell and elsewhere and these boxes should on no account be placed in either of the Muniment Rooms. They should be marked with the letter 'P' (standing for 'pool' or 'personal') and in

---

[1] Richard Denis Lucien Kelly, 1916–90. Educated at Marlborough College and Balliol College, Oxford. Surrey and Sussex Yeomanry, 1939–40. Indian Mountain Artillery, India and Burma, 1941–5. Called to the Bar, *in absentia*, Middle Temple, 1942; Bencher, 1976; Emeritus, 1987. Married, 1945, Anne Marie Anderson (div. 1954). Archival and literary assistant to Churchill during preparation for publication of *The Second World War* and *A History of the English Speaking Peoples*, 1947–57. Published an abridgement of Churchill's *The Second World War* (1959); *The Ironside Diaries, 1939–40* (1962). Recorder, Crown Court, 1972–80.

them can be kept the documents which are in use. After having been perused, pruned or destroyed as the case may be, they should be put into one of the pool boxes which will be clearly marked 'documents for return to Muniment Room'. Whoever is appointed in charge of the Muniment Rooms will then be responsible for ensuring that the document, or what is left of it, is returned to the appropriate box under which it has been catalogued and indexed. There would thus be two distinct series of boxes with separate serial numbers – the boxes in the Muniment Rooms and the pool boxes – and when any new boxes are ordered from Chubbs it should be made clear for which series they are required in order that they may be numbered accordingly.

So far I have only dealt with the problem of returning documents after they have been used. In order to avoid a recrudescence of rummaging when documents are taken <u>out</u> of the Muniment Rooms, I would suggest that one of your staff be appointed 'Custodian of the Archives'. This person would be responsible for acquainting fellow members with the method of finding specific documents and of keeping a register of withdrawals and returns.

I should be grateful for your criticisms and comments on these proposals at as early a date as may be convenient to you, so that I may start the task of detailed cataloguing and indexing as soon as possible. At present the boxes have merely been sorted out in chronological order, and roughly according to subject matter.

Winston S. Churchill to Clement Attlee
(Churchill papers, 2/43)

1 July 1947

My dear Prime Minister,

I am much concerned to hear from my colleagues whom you consulted yesterday that you propose to call the India Bill, 'The Indian Independence Bill'. This, I am assured, is entirely contrary to the text, which corresponds to what we have previously been told were your intentions. The essence of the Mountbatten proposals and the only reason why I gave support to them is because they establish the phase of Dominion status. Dominion status is not the same as Independence, although it may be freely used to establish Independence. It is not true that a community is independent when its Ministers have in fact taken the Oath of Allegiance to the King. This is a measure of grave constitutional importance and a correct and formal procedure and nomenclature should be observed. The correct title would be, as it seems to me, 'The Indian Dominions Bill'. I should however be quite willing to support it if it were called, 'The India Bill, 1947' or 'The India Self-Government Bill'.

I am glad to hear you are considering such alterations.

Clement Attlee to Winston S. Churchill
(Churchill papers, 2/145)

3 July 1947

My dear Churchill,

During the war you kindly invited me, and many others, to Dinners in the Rooms overlooking the Garden at No. 10, to meet the King. You have, I think, expressed the view that it would be a good idea to have some small plaque set up in these Rooms in order to commemorate these Dinners. I think this would be an excellent idea, and I wondered whether you would like to suggest wording. I have had a list drawn up of the Dinners and the Guests, and copies are attached. As you will see, there were fourteen Dinners in all.

Clement Attlee to Winston S. Churchill
(Churchill papers, 2/43)

4 July 1947

My dear Churchill,

I have delayed replying to your letter[1] while awaiting any further communication from the Viceroy on the point raised by your colleagues as to the title of the Bill. Owing to the time factor, it was impossible to make a change even if it was desirable.

I do not agree with the point which you make. Dominion Prime Ministers constantly stress the point that they are independent States within the British Commonwealth. They bear allegiance to The King who is The King of all Dominions. The insistence on independence does not touch the point of allegiance, but emphasizes the complete freedom of every member of the Commonwealth from control by any other member.

I think this is a most valuable counter to the demand for independence outside the Commonwealth as it shows that this demand can be satisfied within it. This is, in fact, the meaning of Dominion Status.

---

[1] Of 1 July, reproduced above (p. 736).

Sir Alan Lascelles to Winston S. Churchill
(Churchill papers, 2/148)[1]

7 July 1947
Private

Buckingham Palace

Dear Mr Churchill,

The King thinks you would like to know, for your strictly private information that he has given his consent to the betrothal of Princess Elizabeth[2] to Philip Mountbatten.[3] A formal announcement will be made on Thursday morning next – till then it is a profound secret.

Alan Campbell-Johnson:[4] diary
('Mission with Mountbatten', pages 132–3)

8 July 1947

London

After dinner yesterday Ismay attended a meeting at 10 Downing Street which lasted beyond midnight. Although there were some doubts expressed about Mountbatten's personal position arising from the change from an arbitral to a partisan status, particularly in the event of disputes between the two Dominions, Ministers were generally in favour of Mountbatten accepting the Indian offer. Attlee, it seems, went so far as to say that Mountbatten could see this thing through, and no one else could do so. The Government were deeply impressed by the Moslem League's support for the proposition which Ismay was able to convey to them in writing from Liaquat. The position is, in fact, that both sides have now requested Mountbatten to remain on with one side.

This morning the Prime Minister called in the following Opposition leaders: Salisbury,[5] Macmillan, Butler, Samuel and Clem Davies. Ismay put the problem before them. Lord Samuel was rather anxious to revive the idea which he had originally expressed to Mountbatten in my flat, a Viceroy presiding over the two Governors-General. But the general sense of the meeting was that such a suggestion was now too late to put into practice, and in any case likely to be unacceptable to the Congress. The Liberals were whole-heartedly in favour of Mountbatten remaining as Governor-General of India. But while

---

[1] This letter was handwritten.
[2] Elizabeth Alexandra Mary Windsor, 1926–. Married, 1947, Philip Mountbatten. Succeeded her father as Queen Elizabeth II, 1952.
[3] Philip Mountbatten, 1921–. Educated at Royal Naval College. Married, 1947, Elizabeth Windsor. Prince Consort, Duke of Edinburgh, Earl of Merioneth and Baron Greenwich, 1952.
[4] Alan Campbell-Johnson, 1913–98. Educated at Oxford. Married, 1938, Imogen Fay de la Tour Dunlap. Political Secretary to Sir Archibald Sinclair, Leader of Liberal Party, 1937–40. Wg Cdr, Inter-Allied Records Section, SACSEA HQ, 1943–6. OBE, 1946. CIE, 1947. Officer, US LOM, 1947. Press Attaché to Viceroy and Governor-General, India (Earl Mountbatten of Burma), 1947–8. Chairman, Campbell-Johnson Ltd, 1953–78. Director, Hill & Knowlton Ltd, 1976–85.
[5] The 5th Marquess, formerly Lord Cranborne.

the Conservative leaders were personally in full accord with the proposal, they felt that they could not commit themselves officially until they had had a chance to consult Churchill, who was down at Chartwell convalescing from recent illness, and Eden, who was also unable to be present at the meeting.

Attlee accordingly suggested to Ismay that he should go down to Chartwell himself, which he did forthwith. Any expectations Ismay may have had of a difficult interview with the great man were quickly dispelled. He did not think the position had been in any way altered by Jinnah's action, and dictated a message for Ismay to send by cable to the Viceroy, the substance of which was that a constitutional Governor-General retained an unlimited right to receive information and to give advice, and that on this basis Mountbatten could give the new Government aid which he should not withhold. While leaving it with Mountbatten's conscience and judgement to decide when his usefulness was exhausted, Churchill stressed in particular the political value of his role in mitigating the communal tension, preserving the interests of the Princes and strengthening the ties of sentiment between India and the rest of the Commonwealth.

Ismay, much relieved, came back to London post-haste and told Churchill's Conservative colleagues of the interview and message which was relayed to Delhi immediately. This decisive expression of opinion, combining as it did the great man's breadth of view and immediate grasp of essentials with his ability to relate his exact ideas to perfect logic, set everybody's mind at rest.

With every day that passes the virtues of diplomacy by informal discussion are increasingly borne in on me. It has certainly been possible for Ismay to dispel doubts both from the view-point of Mountbatten in Delhi and of the Government and Opposition in London with a speed and certainty which no amount of long-distance letters, *aides-memoire* or telegrams could have done.

King George VI to Winston S. Churchill
(Churchill papers, 2/171)[1]

12 July 1947   Buckingham Palace

My dear Winston,

Thank you so very much for your kind message of congratulation on my daughter's engagement. I was sure you would have liked to have a warning of the announcement. The Queen and I are so happy that the news has been so well received everywhere. The young people have known each other for some years now, & it is their happiness which we hope for in their married life.

I am so glad to hear from Mrs Churchill that you are progressing well & that you are about again. I hope to have a special Privy Council meeting at the

---

[1] This letter was handwritten.

end of July at which I wish to give my assent to my daughter's marriage, & to which meeting I hope you will be able to attend as Leader of the Opposition. I hope also to have a Privy Counsellor from each of the Dominions. There will be no other business of course.

With renewed thanks

Princess Elizabeth to Winston S. Churchill
(Churchill papers, 2/171)[1]

13 July 1947   Buckingham Palace

Dear Mr Churchill,

I write to send you my sincere thanks for your kind letter of congratulations on my engagement, which has touched me deeply.

We are both extremely happy, and Philip and I are quite overwhelmed by the kindness of people who have written sending us their good wishes. It is so nice to know that friends are thinking of one at this important moment in one's life, and I would like to thank you once again for being one of the first who have sent their good wishes.

Winston S. Churchill to Clement Attlee
(Churchill papers, 2/43)

14 July 1947   Chartwell
NOT SENT

My dear Prime Minister,

I was sorry to receive your letter of July 4[2] about the title of the India Bill. Our discussions when you invited us to meet the Viceroy turned upon the new fact that both the main Indian Parties were prepared to accept Dominion Status at the present time, and that this was to be embodied in the forthcoming legislation about which you asked us to give assurances. The use of the word 'Independence' in the title of the Bill is contrary to what we were led to believe was its purpose. It is not true that Dominion Status and Independence are identical terms. Dominion Status is defined by the Statute of Westminster, which sets out the position of the Dominions or Commonwealths of the British Empire. The introduction of the term 'Independence' is therefore a misnomer and a loose and inaccurate description. I consider we should have been informed of this unexpected departure beforehand.

As the Bill in its substance confirms exactly to the account you gave us of it, I am content to leave my protest on record in this correspondence.

[1] This letter was handwritten.
[2] Reproduced above (p. 737).

July 1947

Winston S. Churchill to King George VI
(*Churchill papers, 2/171*)

16 July 1947 — Chartwell

Sir,
 I am grateful for Your Majesty's most kind letter.[1] The news has certainly given the keenest pleasure to all classes and the marriage will be an occasion of national rejoicing, standing out all the more against the sombre background of our lives.
 I look forward to attending the Privy Council to which Your Majesty intends to bid me, and am very glad that my recovery will allow me to be there. I thank you sir for the inquiries you have made and with my humble duty remain
 Your Majesty's devoted and faithful servant

Winston S. Churchill to Leslie Rowan
(*Churchill papers, 2/154*)

19 July 1947
Private

My dear Leslie,
 Your letter about Mr Baldwin's eightieth birthday: I have been reading so much about the past lately that I could not bring myself to send a salutation. I do not know how your present chief would feel. I wish Stanley Baldwin no ill, but it would have been much better for our country if he had never lived.
 Let us keep in touch.

Helen Blake[2] to Winston S. Churchill
(*Churchill papers, 2/146*)[3]

20 July 1947

Dear Mr Churchill,
 I am afraid I was so overcome saying goodbye to you yesterday, that I didn't thank you properly for all those wonderful presents – the photo & books I shall always treasure very dearly & as for the cheque – I have never had such a big one. Thank you very, very much.
 I really did enjoy looking after you & above all seeing you so well at the end. I hope for your sake you won't need the 'bullying' nurse for many a long day.

---

[1] Reproduced above (pp. 739–40).
[2] Nurse who cared for Churchill at Chartwell following his hernia operation of June 11.
[3] This letter was handwritten.

Everyone was so kind to me at Hyde Park Gate and Chartwell – I was very happy & shall miss you all.

Now please take great care of yourself & don't work too hard.

Bernard Baruch to Winston S. Churchill
(Churchill papers, 2/210)

22 July 1947   New York

My Dear Winston,

It made me very happy to know that you came through your operation in such fine shape and to learn that you will be better than ever. 'Better than ever' means something with you because you have always been mighty good.

I have been wondering for some time how you were going to treat certain subjects in your book. It will be difficult to ignore them or to gloss them over. For instance, what are you going to do about Harry Hopkins? Harry was all out for war, but he certainly interfered with its progress here, i.e., from the industrial mobilization side. He, together with Sidney Hillman,[1] said, 'We don't want any more old world war stuff,' and that 'this was a different kind of war'. He delayed production very much by improvising and by insistence upon appointing his inexperienced men.

Harry was jealous of everyone who touched the President and did much to stop the progress of events here. The best thing about him was that he was all out for war, but he wanted to run the whole war himself. Many times Roosevelt agreed to certain changes, but then Harry would stop him in the interests of his own friends. You know what his attitude – and that of his friends – was toward anyone who touched or might touch the President. He was more jealous than any woman I have ever seen.

Just as in previous years, in 1938 when I was in London you and I talked over the coming conflict. The night before I left for America you said: 'Well, the big show will be on very soon. You will be running it in America and I (Winston) will be on the sidelines here.' It was just the opposite. In fact, I had to take the most humiliating experiences and frustrations in order to help in any way.

You remember, undoubtedly, how I told Purvis[2] and his successor[3] not to be

---

[1] Sidney Hillman, 1887–1946. Founded Amalgamated Clothing Workers of America, 1914. Member, Labor Advisory Board, 1933. Vice-President, Congress of Industrial Organizations, 1937–42. Chair, CIO Political Action Committee, 1942–6.

[2] Arthur Blaikie Purvis, 1890–1941. Born in London. Worked for Nobel Explosives Co., Glasgow, 1910–24. Moved to Canada, becoming President of Canadian Industries Ltd (manufacturers of chemicals). A leading industrialist in Canada between the wars. Chairman, National Employment Commission, 1936–8. Director-General, British Purchasing Commission (New York and Washington), 1939–40. Chairman, Anglo-French Purchasing Board, Washington DC, Dec. 1939 to June 1940. PC, 1940. Chairman, British Supply Council in North America, 1941. Killed in an air crash, 14 Aug. 1941.

[3] Clive Latham Baillieu, 1889–1967. Educated at Trinity College, Melbourne University, and Magdalen College, Oxford, 1913. Called to the Bar, Inner Temple, 1914. Served in WWI (despatches).

too great friends with me, as it might interfere with his White House relationships. I impressed that continually upon you. I was always fearful our mutual affection and admiration might interfere with the war effort.

I know that Hopkins' interference with the mobilization and bringing in new men to do what already had failed caused the slowing of victory, with much loss of lives and treasure.

I must say that toward the very end, Hopkins and Stettinius[1] asked the President to send me abroad to see you. I recall most distinctly our talks and your fear as to what would happen when the war ended, and Stalin found himself in great power.

Now when the peace is on, I see Messrs Attlee and Bevin saying what I said sometime ago in my speech before the South Carolina Legislature – that the whole world must get back to work. We must have uninterrupted, steady production or we, America, cannot do for ourselves or the world what we would want to do.

I think in England they are too parsimonious with their dollars and resources. They ought to give the English people a little more or a greater diversified diet and some better clothes. It looks from here as though the dominant party in England is pursuing the policy that Hitler and Mussolini did with their people, telling them how badly off they were and how they must suffer in order to win.

We were all greatly disappointed here because the English miners were not willing to dig enough coal to keep their own people from freezing.

I think that if you had been reelected and Roosevelt had lived, we could have carried out what we discussed and what I recommended to our people. Less would have been required from us, for you could have done more for yourselves. The English people, who took so much in the war under your guidance, I still believe, can take anything when peace is in front of us. They are just too severe with your people. Some additional or varied food and clothing for the men and women will increase their confidence and help their morale. They will then do better for themselves.

OBE, 1918. KBE, 1938. CMG, 1929. Australian Representative, Imperial Economic Committee, 1930–47. Director-General, British Purchasing Commission, Washington DC, 1941–2. Member, British Supply Council, North America, 1941–3. Head, Raw Materials Mission, Washington DC, 1942–3. British Representative, Combined Raw Materials Board, 1942–3. President, Federation of British Industries, 1945–7. Vice-Chairman, Dunlop Rubber Company, 1945–9; Chairman, 1949–57; President, 1957–67. Chairman, English Speaking Union, 1951–65. Baron, 1953. First President, British Institute of Management, 1959.

[1] Edward Reilly Stettinius, Jr, 1900–49. Born in Chicago. Married, 1926, Virginia Gordon Wallace: three children. Chairman, Finance Committee, US Steel, 1934; of the Board, 1938. Chairman, War Resources Board, 1939. Chairman, National Defense Advisory Commission, 1940. Director, Priorities Board and Priorities Div., Office of Production Management, 1941. Supervised Lend-Lease programme. Special Assistant to the President, 1941–3. Under-Secretary of State, 1943–4. Secretary of State, Dec. 1944 to 1945. Accompanied Roosevelt to Yalta Conference, 1945. Led US delegation to San Francisco Conference, 1945. First US delegate to the UN, 1946. Published *Roosevelt and the Russians: The Yalta Conference* (1949).

I do not agree with those who think the English people are finished. They have vast resources at their command in their citizenry at home and their possessions and dominions overseas. If the English, French and ourselves show half as much courage as the Russians show bluster, there would not be so much trouble in the world.

I have been plugging for the so-called 'Marshall Plan', which is another version of the United States of Europe. It is rather hard to convince people who have been hammered so hard politically, economically and spiritually – as the Germans hammered the rest of the world – to regain faith in themselves.

I am advocating that we send a very strong man to Paris, who will raise the hopes and increase the confidence of the French. The same ought to be done with the Dutch and the Belgians. As you said, the combination of Western Europe would be greater than the manpower and resources of those behind the Iron Curtain. Certainly, the Citizens of Western Europe are superior to those of Eastern Europe. After all, in our citizens we have our greatest assets.

You may recall how I felt about the Ruhr coal and how I thought that was the key to the situation and the English ought to endeavour to get some 20,000,000 tons a year as their reparations. That together with what you produce at home would put you in a strong position.

I have been advocating here that instead of making loans direct to governments, in many instances there should be trades between industries or syndicates in different countries. For instance, if the English cotton industry wanted to buy machinery and raw materials in this country, the syndicate of producers here could sell to the producers of the cotton industry there, with the loan to be repaid commencing three years after the original loan and to be finally repaid or refinanced in seven annual payments. The whole loan would be repaid in ten years from the beginning.

If British industry has control of spending the money and ordering machinery, they will spend it much more wisely than would the Bureaucrats. British industry will know how to conduct itself so as to get the proper valuta to transfer the means of payment back to the American syndicates. The American syndicates, carrying out the requests of the English syndicates, would be guaranteed repayment by the Reconstruction Finance Corporation. But it would not be a trade between governments; instead, it would be between industries.

Any industry in England can get all it wants from American industry, but I doubt whether the British government will be able to obtain further loans, gifts or subsidies from the American government. I do not believe that England needs it.

I think France needs it less than England. But what France needs is courage after the German occupation.

After hearing all that the Europeans have had to say, I am in hopes that America will take a position in aiding Europe, similar to the one on the atom bomb – that we will agree to stand upon certain things if we have to stand alone. But that position will depend upon the facts brought out and the necessities of the occasion. Our people have no desire to destroy anyone. We want to help and live in peace.

The problem of the displaced peoples is a very sore one with all of us. We must find a haven for the 1,365,000 people who do not want to return to terror or death. I look upon the Palestinian question as bad enough. But here is something of greater importance. If there could be established some place in the world where people could go to escape from terror and mistreatment, I believe, there would be enormous desertions from the Russian Armies in occupied countries. It would be of such large proportions that the Russians would be afraid to send their younger troops. Once it were definitely known that a Russian who left the army would not be deported and could remain in another country – from what I hear – I believe the exodus would be so great it would become dangerous to the Russian government. How about our African scheme?

When the Balts, Letts, Poles, Jews and other displaced peoples can be sent to some country where they can work themselves out and a way is left open for the Russians and those behind the Iron Curtain to escape, you will find the power of those countries slipping very fast.

I am very anxious for the American government to stop being so neutral and to take a stronger economic position. I want them to buy the rubber, sugar and all non-perishable raw materials for sale in the world, rather than to lend money.

I dislike seeing great England in a position of asking for loans, when I think she really does not need the loans. There was too much Keynes about this last trade. If you remember, Anderson and Keynes both agreed that they did not need any such sum of money as they finally did obtain from us.

I am not afraid of a German restoration, for surely if we accept a system of international inspection, control and punishment for the atom bomb – the most dangerous of all weapons – we could have the same thing for German industry. We had it all right after World War I, but the system broke down. I remember so well your warning to me about a reviving Germany. I believe it was somewhere around 1935 or earlier that you said France had a hundred divisions while Germany had only thirty-two, but you did not know how long it would be before Germany had as many or more divisions than France. An effective system of inspection, control and punishment would have prevented the revival of Germany for the second World War. It will do so for any other war.

The great difficulty is Russia, as it is in every direction. But here I would proceed as I stated on the atom bomb. I feel as you do – give them an opportunity to come along, and if they do not, let us do it if we stand alone.

Russia has the longest border to defend of any country. It runs from the Bering Strait, clear across to Turkey and up to Western Europe to Sweden.

She has swallowed many countries and their peoples but has not conquered their spirit. If war ever comes between Russia and a first-class power or combination of powers, there will be a revolt on every border. They have no lines of communication such as Germany had to shift from East to West or North to South. No one in his senses would invade Russia. All one need to do would be to bombard her from every direction from the air, destroying her cities and crops. Then those on the borders or a small mobile force could move in any direction they wished. No war against Russia now would be conducted like Napoleon or Hitler did.

I remember when we talked about the war in Italy, you said, 'Well we can go over the roof.' That is what we can do with Russia.

However, I do not think it is absolutely necessary that we war with Russia, but we must stand and stand somewhere. She will surely wear civilization out if we do not. I showed all possible patience when dealing with them on the atom bomb. Many of our people here (that did not include Truman or Byrnes but some others in the State Department) wanted me to compromise. But there was no compromising with Russia any more than with Germany under Hitler. They wanted the destruction of our position without anything from them except a Niagara of words.

I had my sailing for July second, but I decided not to go to England because of what was happening in Europe. It would have been difficult for me to be a private citizen and keep quiet – and I did not want to be another Henry Wallace. My friends there are you, Brendan and the Beaver. I know you and Brendan are opposed to the present Government. I could say nothing that might not possibly be offensive to the British Government as constituted. Their problems already are too great for an outsider to make them any more difficult. The American belief is that the English lost their head about Greece and Turkey.

Everyone here says – what I guess you hear over there – that the English have no more dollars. Of course, the English have a lot more dollars which their people can get through the sale of commodities or securities. But naturally, like everyone else, they want to have their cake and eat it. If we have no war, soon there will be too much or at least enough stuff, and then it will be a buyers' market.

Evidently, you are having trouble that was anticipated, that is, of not being able to adjust your exports and still give the English people something more to go on with.

We have the problem of demands for our people and yet they want to go on with continued aid to the rest of the world. We can accomplish all that if we get back to uninterrupted work – say a forty-four hour work week.

If I could run over to England just to spend a week with you and come right back, I would do so. I did not go abroad, also, because I knew you were not well at the time. Further, I knew that you had much work to do.

Is there anything in this story printed here that *Life* has sent over a battery of men to help you? The writing of the book is a tremendous undertaking. I hope you will not strain your energies too much.

Always remember that if you want to escape by coming to America, you need only to tell me when you are coming, and I shall have a place for you and yours.

There are many other thoughts that run through my mind.

Winston S. Churchill to Charles Mills[1]
(Churchill papers, 2/57)

29 July 1947

My dear Mr Mills,

We have great need in the House of Commons of experienced men versed in public business. I have therefore been trying to gather as much strength as possible for our Party by encouraging the return to Parliament of former Ministers of proved capacity.

As Parliamentary Under-Secretary to the Ministry of Supply Mr Sandys was a great help to the Government in the difficult and much disputed business of tank production. This work won him the confidence of the Chiefs of Staff, and in the spring of 1943 they asked him to take the responsibility for investigating the rumours about German rockets and flying bombs and for recommending countermeasures. For more than a year he was in the very centre of this most anxious and complicated affair, and there is no doubt of the quality of his services or of his foresight. The bombing attack on Peenemunde which so markedly delayed the onfall of this new peril and saved so many lives in London, was undertaken almost entirely as the result of his recommendation.

When the war came near its end I deliberately chose him for the Housing business because his pertinacity, his precision of mind and remarkable energy were needed for this formidable and inevitably thankless task. The elections supervened before he had a chance to carry out the plans which had been largely made and would, if executed, have left us in a far better Housing position than we are today.

I am very sorry that he was not on the Front Opposition Bench to tackle Mr Aneurin Bevan from day to day, because I am confident he could have exposed that fraudulent boaster in the most effective manner.

I therefore hope that your Committee will carefully consider his qualifications to be your candidate at the next General Election, which may not be so far distant, and I am sure you will believe that no other thought but the public interest actuates me in making such a recommendation to you.

[1] Charles Mills. Alderman and JP. Chairman of Wandsworth Council Highways Committee 1939–51.

Clement Attlee to Winston S. Churchill
(Churchill papers, 2/43)[1]

31 July 1947

My dear Churchill,

We are proposing to put down the following resolution regarding the appreciation of the country of the services of the Indian Civil and Military Services, in both Houses.

'That this House on the occasion of the transfer to Indian hands of the responsibility for the affairs of India wishes to place upon record its profound appreciation of the ability and devotion with which, during the long period of British rule, the Civil and Military Services of the Crown in India have served India and its peoples.'

It appears to me that this would be an appropriate occasion for the motion to receive an all-Party backing, and I wonder whether this idea would commend itself to you? If so, perhaps you and John Anderson might like to add your names to the resolution when we put it down.

We had it in mind for the motion to be taken on Friday next, the 5th August.[2]

Perhaps you would let me know whether you and John Anderson would feel inclined to be associated with us in this matter.

---

[1] Churchill wrote on this letter: 'Read to Mr Stuart. I hope Mr Eden will act for me. I shall not be able to be there.'

[2] Actually Friday 8 Aug.

August 1947

Winston S. Churchill: speech
('Winston S. Churchill, His Complete Speeches', volume 7, pages 7500–9)

4 August 1947   West Country Conservative Rally
Blenheim Palace

A 'DOCTOR'S MANDATE'

Although we are gathered in these pleasant surroundings our minds are oppressed by the evil plight into which our country has fallen. Cabinet Ministers tell us every weekend how bad our position is and that the twelfth hour will strike before the end of the year. The main facts are obvious to every thinking man or woman. Under the capitalist system of free enterprise, we had bred in Great Britain nearly 47 millions of people, half of whose food came from beyond the seas, but whose progress was constant and whose standard of living before the war was already the highest in Europe. Since then two disasters have come upon us: the second World War and the first Socialist Government – with a majority. By supreme exertions we surmounted the first disaster. The question which glares upon us today is: 'How shall we free ourselves from the second?'

It is almost exactly two years since we emerged victorious from the mortal struggle with the German Nazi Power and all our enemies surrendered unconditionally. Then we stood high in the world, and our name and fame were celebrated in many lands. I could not have believed on the morrow of the German and Japanese surrenders that so short a period of time could bring us all so low. Nearby on the continent of Europe we see countries which were conquered, ravaged and stripped by the enemy, and were liberated by our strong arms, which already have restored a thriving, active life to their people. But we, proud Britain, who stood alone against the mighty tyrant, who kept the flag of freedom flying unaided for more than a whole year, are now forced to live on foreign aid and also to subject ourselves to privations worse than those of the war; and if these hardships fail, there lies before us not only bankruptcy but starvation. Such are the facts laid before us by the Ministers of the Socialist Government and confirmed by all that we can learn for ourselves.

We are told that on Wednesday next the Prime Minister is to unfold another catalogue of pains and penalties which everyone must endure. In spite of all our warnings, he has left action so late that I fear that his measures will not be equal to the emergency, and will only be another instalment of privation, frustration, and restriction along our downward path. I do not know what Mr Attlee is going to do. I can however tell you beforehand what our Conservative attitude will be towards any Government scheme that is put before us. We shall accept, support and endure any and all sensible proposals, however severe, that are truly made in the national interest. We shall support them not only in Parliament but in our daily lives and work. On the other hand, we shall oppose any proposals which we deem unwise or unnecessary, or which are inserted for the purpose of pandering to class jealousy and Party spite.

When Mr Attlee's Government came into power we did not underrate the difficulties with which they would have to contend. These difficulties would have strained to the utmost all the resources of a National Government and a united nation. We did not grudge the new Ministers their offices, nor envy them their responsibilities. We have steadfastly supported them in every step they have taken sincerely in the public interest. In that spirit we supported their policy of seeking a large American Loan to tide us over the transition from war to peace and to re-equip our industry, our agriculture and our mines. I was alarmed at some of the conditions that were imposed in this Loan. I drew particular attention in the House of Commons to the proposal to make sterling convertible into dollars within so short a time as fifteen months, whereas at Bretton Woods as much as five years was contemplated. I said that this proposal appeared so doubtful and perilous that the best hope was that in practice it would defeat itself. We also objected to the proposal that if we were incapable of finding dollars to pay for American imports of tobacco or other commodities, we must reduce also in equal proportions all similar imports from our Dominions and Colonies or any other alternative source. But the Socialist Government gave way on both these points. However, I relied, and rely now, on the wisdom of the fair-minded American people, to make the necessary easements, without which a policy for which they have made heavy sacrifices will certainly fail in its effect. There is no shame in one brave and faithful Ally, deeply injured in the common struggle, asking another to help him recover and stand upon his feet. Had the positions been reversed, we should have done the same for them.

Therefore I supported the American Loan and I will still support and justify further appeals to the United States provided that we are doing our best, that we are making the most of our resources, that we are determined to become a self-supporting nation and system at the earliest moment and will put aside every impediment, and labour long and hard. It is when we are not trying our best, not making the most of ourselves and our resources, not pursuing a wise or practical policy, not coming forward as a united nation, not trying to deal with the problems on their merits – it is then that there is humiliation in asking and receiving aid from a mighty and friendly Ally.

The object of the American Loan, and its only possible justification, was to enable us to get our industry and agriculture working with the fullest activity, and to bring in the necessary food – for we grow barely half we need – to keep us alive till conditions of world trade were restored. It was thought that this would take between three and four years of good administration, strict economy, and united effort by all parties and classes under conditions of growing freedom from war-time restrictions. Alas, these hopes have not been fulfilled. The first misfortune of rising prices was not wholly the fault of the Socialist Government. It was no doubt aggravated by the bad bargains in bulk-buying made by government officials: but the main fact is that prices rose in the United States so that the Loan became much less valuable in goods and in breathing-space than was expected. That is an aspect which I am sure the United States ought to and will take into consideration in relaxing the conditions which hamper our purchases in sterling from our Dominions and Colonies, or which enable our foreign creditors – for we have become a debtor nation – to exact payment from our limited supply of dollars, saved, earned, or borrowed, all of which and more are required for our period of recovery.

But there are other reasons why the Loan has been ineffective. Owing to the follies and indecision of the Socialist Government a great part of the Loan has been spent, not on the re-equipment of our industry nor upon the import of basic foodstuffs. Instead much has been frittered away in American films and tobacco and in large quantities of foods and fruits, which however desirable as indulgences, were not indispensable to our actual recovery. When you borrow money from another country for the sacred purpose of national rehabilitation, it is wrong to squander it upon indulgences. If now sharp changes and curtailments are to be made in the Loan expenditure on non-essentials it will be everyone's duty to accept them. But what can be thought of a Government which has drifted on from day to day until the Loan is nearly exhausted? There is not one proposal that Mr Attlee can make on Wednesday next that would not have been far more effective if made a year or six months ago. That is my first main charge against the Socialist Ministers. Why wait till the twelfth hour is near before taking the measures which every prudent housewife would have taken in her own home as soon as she understood what was happening? The Government had the knowledge; but they had neither the sense nor the decision to act.

No. They were too busy planning and making their brave new world of controls and queues, of hordes of officials and multitudes of regulations. They exhausted what energies they had, and consumed their time and thought in carrying out their party fads, in choking the House of Commons with partisan legislation, in disturbing, discouraging and even paralysing business enterprise by nationalisation schemes of no productive value, but which cast their threatening shadows and interferences far and wide over the whole field of British industry. That is how they wasted the time we could have gained by the American Loan, just as they wasted so large a portion of the Loan itself.

But let me press my indictment further. The expansion of British industry and population in the nineteenth century was largely achieved upon the basis of cheap and abundant coal. The Minister who has impeded our house-building, Mr Aneurin Bevan, described us as an island made of coal and surrounded by fish. This, like most of his statements, is a grotesque exaggeration. But how has the coal industry fared under the Socialists? They assured us that the miners would give a far greater production if the pits were national property than if they felt they were working for private owners. Not only we, but all Europe, desperately needs coal, and no part of Europe needs it more than Britain. Yet now that the coal mines are nationalised, the cost of producing coal, which affects every industry, is much higher. With more miners at work and more machinery, we are producing 15 million tons less a year than came out of the pits in 1914. I have always held that special inducements may fairly be offered to the miners because they work below the ground, far from the light of the sun. It is many years ago since I moved the Second Reading of the Mines Eight Hours Bill. But now that the mines are working directly for the nation, they are producing less at a far heavier cost than when they were working for the private capitalist owner, with his far more intimate and flexible management.

The extraordinary carelessness of the Government and of their egregious Mr Emanuel Shinwell, Minister of Fuel and Power, which led to the breakdown in fuel, light and power at the beginning of this year, inflicted severe, avoidable hardships on our whole people and struck another heavy blow both at domestic production and at our vital export trade. Today every form of appeal and flattery is addressed to the miners by the frightened and disillusioned Socialist Ministers. They are even compared to the air pilots who won the Battle of Britain. I do not believe the miners, who are thoughtful members of the community, will have their heads turned by that. They have got to face the facts of our position, as we all have. They have got to realise that a five-day week, founded upon an American dole in the shape of imports produced by the exertions of American workingmen, is not likely to last very long unless it results in improved production. Coal is the second of the major failures of the Socialist Party who promised us all so much.

Their third major fault is the wild financial extravagance in which the Government have indulged. Nothing like this has ever been seen before. The Chancellor of the Exchequer (Dr Dalton) has taken from us 3,000 million pounds to cover Socialist administration for the current 12 months. That is more than three times the cost of the State in the years before the war. Altogether he has spent, or proposes to spend, about 11,000 million pounds in the 21 months from the end of the war until the end of the new financial year in April 1948. But what has he to show for it? One could imagine that with all these vast sums of money being spent and while the American Loan is still flowing in, there would have been at least a fleeting sense of prosperity. On the contrary, a harder, more curtailed, more restricted way of life and standard of living has been imposed upon every class of the community, and now a worse time lies ahead which the Government assures us may continue for years.

I will give you some instances of this appalling waste of the limited resources of our hard-pressed people. The whole expenditure on the armed forces requires searching examination. There never was a time when so much money was given to the service departments for such meagre results in fighting power.

Look next at the mismanagement of the British Zone of Germany. Immense sums of the money, largely in dollars, of which we are so short, have been and are being poured out in the British Zone of Germany, and the only result is an ever-increasing discontent. Instead of placing upon the Germans the responsibilities of managing their own affairs and giving them all the help we could from time to time, we have used our victory to impose upon them a highly incompetent administration. This enables them to cast upon us the blame of all the miseries they have brought upon themselves. The respect and even admiration with which we were regarded in Germany in the hour of our victory is changing fast into a sullen hatred, not unmingled with contempt, when they read how millions were lost in illicit gains by trafficking in currency and cigarettes. Hundreds of millions of pounds have been needlessly squandered on an administration of Germany which has brought nothing but misery to the German people and nothing but discredit to the British occupation.

Then there is Palestine. While we have blithely cast away India and Burma, regardless of what may happen in the near future after our slowly-built-up Empire has passed away, the Socialist Government have at all costs clung on to Palestine. Nearly 100,000 British soldiers have been kept in Palestine, and 30 or 40 millions a year of our hard-earned money has been cast away there. Our sympathies go out to the British soldiers who have endured these unspeakable outrages with so much fortitude and discipline and who are just kept marking time month after month under the most false and painful conditions, waiting for the Government to think of some sort of plan or policy. No British interest is involved in our retention of the Palestine Mandate. For nearly 30 years we have done our best to carry out an honourable and self-imposed task. A year ago I urged the Government to give notice to the UNO that we could and would bear the burden of insult and injury no longer. But the Ministers only gaped in shameful indecision, and they are only gaping still.

It is a surprising fact that since the war we have spent or loaned abroad, without any return, over 740 million pounds more than the total we have so far spent from the American Loan. We have in fact simply passed the benefit on to others, while incurring a grave obligation ourselves. It is necessary for us to realise that there are limits to our hard-pressed strength, and that while we are unable to support ourselves at home, in spite of all our sacrifices, we can no longer bear all the burdens which in better days we allowed to be cast upon us.

But it is here at home that our worst waste and extravagance is found. There are two or three times as many people employed by the Government to manage our affairs as were used by the Conservative Government before the war. A mighty army of 450,000 additional officials has been taken from production and added, at a prodigious cost and waste, to the oppressive machinery of government and control. Instead of helping national recovery, this is a positive hindrance. The bulk of this new and heavy burden is borne mainly on the shoulders of the wage-earners, from whom the main mass of taxation is drawn. And all that we get from it is an increasing frustration and waste of time and paper in every sphere of our trade and industry.

It has only been possible for 47 millions to live in Great Britain by the utmost exercise of all those qualities of individual initiative and enterprise which have been in former times the outstanding distinction of the British character. The Socialist belief is that nothing matters much so long as miseries are equally shared, and certainly they have acted in accordance with their faith. I remember in Victorian days anxious talk about 'the submerged tenth' – that part of our people who had not shared in the progress of the age, and then later on in the old Liberal period we spoke of going back to bring the rearguard in. The main army we saw had reached the camping ground in all its strength and victory, and we should now, in duty and compassion, go back to pick up the stragglers and those who had fallen by the way and bring them in. That was the Liberal solution, and as a Minister under Mr Asquith, and also under Mr Baldwin, in a Conservative Government, I have personally carried great legislation for that purpose. But now, under the Socialists, it is no longer a question of bringing the rearguard in, but of bringing the whole army back. It is no longer the plan of helping the submerged tenth, but of submerging the other nine-tenths down to their level. This is what in fact is taking place day by day, as you can see in your own lives and homes as you look around you. There lies the road to ruin.

I am frequently asked, 'What is the alternative to Socialism proposed by the Conservative Party?' And we are invited to put forward a programme in the utmost detail of what we would do. We have already, in our Industrial Charter, shown the broad lines on which our economic policy would be shaped. But it would be very foolish for us, without the machinery of Government at our disposal or the power to give effect to our plans, to commit ourselves to an elaborate programme which would be eagerly pounced upon by our opponents, if only as a means of distracting attention from their own misdeeds and failures. Anyone can see however that the vigorous production of food on the largest possible scale in this island holds the first place. Let us be under no error in this matter. The prosperity of agriculture and food production depends on larger supplies of labour, and to have the labour we must have the rural houses in which they can dwell and rear their families. These the Socialists have refused. It also depends upon a full supply of the agricultural machinery which the Government has so recklessly exported to foreign countries. This was indeed devouring the seed-corn.

But while, to quote a famous expression, we do not intend to prescribe before we are called in, and while we shall ask for a 'doctor's mandate' to deal with the situation, whatever it may be, when that time comes, there are two things I will tell you that we will not do.

The first is, we shall not allow the advance of society and economic well-being of the nation to be regulated and curtailed by the pace of the weakest brethren among us. Proper incentives must be offered and full freedom given to the strong to use their strength in the commonweal. Initiative, enterprise, thrift, domestic foresight, contrivance, good housekeeping and natural ability must reap their just reward. On any other plan the population of this island will sink by disastrous and agonising stages to a far lower standard of life and to two-thirds of its present numbers.

I will tell you another thing we will not do. We will not attempt to gain popularity or votes by a plethora of wild, lying promises and bribes and the creation of false illusions, such as those with which the Socialists misled the electorate two years ago.

I will now look back for a moment into the past. There is a legend or large-scale propaganda of falsehoods which has been spread in all directions by the Socialist Government about the lamentable conditions in Great Britain, mainly under Conservative Parliaments, between the wars, and a lot of young people are being taught to believe that this was a sad period of stagnation in our national and social life. The Socialist Party hope that they will thus create a dark background to relieve their own manifest failures. In fact however the years between the wars, although scarred by the economic and financial collapse under Mr Ramsay MacDonald's minority Socialist Administration in 1931, formed a period of almost unequalled expansion and progress in the life of the wage-earning masses throughout this island. Between 1919 and 1939 four million new houses were built in England and Wales alone, or half as many houses as already existed before the first world war. The normal hours of work were substantially reduced in all industries, particularly those covered by the Factories Act. The expectation of life of a new-born baby rose by nine years, and the new entrants to the elementary schools in London gained an average of two inches in height and five pounds in weight since the days before the first world war. All this happened under Tory rule. There was also a steady improvement in the food of the people, and a marked increase in the consumption of milk, cheese, butter and eggs, and of fruit and vegetables. In the 15 years from the formation of Mr Baldwin's second Administration in 1924, in which I had the honour to be Chancellor of the Exchequer, down to the outbreak of war in 1939, in these 15 years, a period during which, for more than 12 years there were controlling Tory majorities in the House of Commons, wage rates increased by nearly six per cent and the cost of living fell by nine per cent, making the increase of real wages 15 per cent. Industrial production as a whole reached new levels of expansion and output.

Far-reaching social legislation, for some of which I was personally responsible, was devised and carried by the Conservative Government. Old Age Pensions, which had been doubled in 1919, were placed on a contributory basis and were brought down from 70 to 65 by me in 1925, and all Means Tests swept away. Widows and children were provided for in a manner never achieved in any previous age or other country in the whole world by the provision I made in the Tory Budget of 1925. It is quite true that unemployment caused deep anxiety, especially when, under the Socialist Government of Mr Ramsay MacDonald, it rose to its terrible peak in 1930. This was mitigated by the development of the Unemployment Insurance Scheme, which I first started nearly 40 years ago under that eminent Liberal statesman, Mr Asquith.

After the Socialists were dismissed by the people in 1931, unemployment fell steadily to a million. No one was satisfied with that, and it still remained our worst problem at home. But so far from the period between the two wars being a dark and miserable age, it was in almost every respect far better for all classes than what we are going through now, and what we are told by the Socialist Ministers themselves we shall have to endure for an indefinite number of years to come. There is of course no reason why a continuous and unlimited improvement in the standard of living of our people, like those of other countries, should not take place in these modern times with all the resources of science in our hands.

There has been a lot of talk by Socialist Ministers against a Coalition. They need not waste their breath. No suggestion of that kind has ever been made by the Conservative Party. What could be more wrong than for the Conservative Party to pass a sponge over all the mismanagement and incompetence of the last two years, and to share the responsibilities of the men who have led us into so much needless misfortune. Such an act of folly would destroy the only hope of national recovery, namely the dismissal from office by the British electorate of those who have so obviously failed in their task. The duty of all Conservatives and Unionists at this time is first to do their daily work with all their strength and to set an example of zeal and diligence in every walk of life; but at the same time it is our duty to convince the people of the fallacies of Socialism and of the incapacity and bad citizenship of many of its supporters. Called upon to become the trustees of the nation, they have cared only for the exploitation of their partisan doctrines. At a time when they should have sought to unite all the strong forces which have made our country great, they have cared only for the class warfare on which they have thrived. And of which they are the expression. The first step in regaining national solvency and presently of recreating national unity is to have a Parliament which truly represents the majority of the nation. There has been lately some talk about a General Election. We do not fear a General Election, and everyone should be ready. Mr Attlee and his followers gained their disproportionate Party majority under an electoral system which is largely obsolete, with an electorate for ten years unversed in the normal workings of our political life, and at a time when the organisation of the Conservative Party had been completely sacrificed to the war effort. By the energy of Lord Woolton and of our workers in all the constituencies our organisation has been greatly improved. The hard teachings of experience have come home, and will come home month by month, to millions of voters who were deceived by idle dreams. I say without hesitation that there will be no recovery from our present misfortunes until the guilty men whose crazy theories and personal incompetence have brought us down, have been driven from power by the vote of the nation. Then, indeed, there would be a bound forward in Britain's credit and repute in every land. Then, indeed we should set our feet again upon the high road which, though it is hard and stony and uphill all the way, leads out of the quagmires in which we are now floundering and sinking.

I will turn before I close to wider fields which deeply influence our island fortunes. The foundation of British policy must be an ever-closer association with the United States. I have never asked at any time for an alliance. I want something much more than that. We must seek something less precise and far more potent. The whole English-speaking world must move forward together in fraternal association along the lines of destiny. This will be the greatest hope of peace among nations and of the freedom and dignity of ordinary men and women over the largest portion of the globe.

The conception of United Europe joined together in amity and fact, though not perhaps as yet in form, in no way conflicts with the fraternal association of the English-speaking Commonwealth and States. On the contrary, both these natural and vital affiliations are drawn together in their due subordination to the supreme UNO, and can only be contributory parts of the world system.

It is on this basis and within these limits that I commend the cause of United Europe to the Conservative and Unionist Party in Great Britain. This is not a Party theme. It is one to which all parties in our island should and will subscribe. I was very glad that Mr Bevin said in the House of Commons that he had supported the idea many years ago. Let him support it now, for now is the appointed time. It is less than a year since I revived this cause in Zurich, and I look back with deep comfort on the immense forward strides it has taken since then. Mr Marshall, the famous general and organiser in the war, and now, under President Truman, the director of the Foreign Affairs of the

USA, had stated publicly that his plan for aiding Europe to recover from the trough of misery into which it has fallen, was directly linked with the declarations and proposals for the Union of Europe which I have made in the name of the all-Party Committee which we have formed. Sixteen countries on the Continent have been gathered by Mr Bevin and M Bidault into a conference to plan with the authority of Governments their own individual and collective economic recovery.

This has solved many of the difficulties which were beyond the scope of an unofficial all-Party of British men and women such as we have formed. It has answered many of the questions about which we might have disagreed among ourselves. Our task is now simple and plain. Beneath the European organisation for economic purposes, fostered by the United States, we shall pursue with all our strength the moral, cultural and political unities which will enable a distracted Continent to stand erect upon its feet again, and cherish a brotherhood which will gradually, as the years pass by, efface old feuds and revive departed glories. Our plan for United Europe is no menace or challenge to any state outside it. All our doors are open. Anyone can join the Club if they are sincerely attracted by its principles and wish to share in the advantages it can surely bestow. If there be some countries that have not the liberty to join us at the present time, let them be sure that they will always be welcome.

We are told that it is wrong to divide Europe into two parts and into two systems; but this is not our aim and certainly not our fault. It is true that an Iron Curtain has descended across Europe, from Stettin on the Baltic to Trieste on the Adriatic. We do not wish the slightest ill to those who dwell on the east of that Iron Curtain, which was never of our making. On the contrary, our prosperity and happiness would rise with theirs. Let there be sunshine on both sides of the Iron Curtain; and if ever the sunshine should be equal on both sides, the Curtain will be no more. It will vanish away like the mists of morning and melt in the warm light of happy days and cheerful friendship. I trust these thoughts will become facts and not merely dreams. Here is the path at home and abroad along which we should persevere with malice to none and with hope for all.

Winston S. Churchill to Count Richard Coudenhove-Kalergi
(Churchill papers, 2/19)

5 August 1947

My dear Coudenhove-Kalergi,

Thank you for your letter of July 21 enclosing a copy of your questionnaire on the subject of European federation. I do not, as a general practice, sign questionnaires, nor have I so far committed myself to any precise form of constitution such as implied in the word 'federation'. However my warm support for the general idea of European unity is, I think, already sufficiently well known.

I much appreciate your invitation to become Joint Honorary President of the proposed European Parliamentary Union together with Monsieur Blum. I am giving the matter most sympathetic consideration. However, before sending you a definite answer, I should like to be certain that the conference is going to be a really representative gathering, and in particular that there will be adequate delegations from the British and French Parliaments. Such information as I have been able to obtain from Mr Gordon Lang,[1] the Chairman of the British Parliamentary Group, has not yet been altogether reassuring. Perhaps however you can let me have further information on this point.

Winston S. Churchill: speech
(Hansard)

7 August 1947 House of Commons

TRANSITIONAL POWERS BILL (SUPPLIES AND SERVICES)

This seems to be a somewhat complicated and obscure matter. I gather that the Government had in mind that they would accelerate our departure for the country by this more compendious procedure, and that they thought that the Measure which they are introducing was one which would be passed without any discussion or after very brief discussion at the tail-end of this part of the Session. For that reason they are quite ready to take very exceptional steps – for instance, to sweep away all the ideas of financial precautions and control by the House of Commons which are the foundation of our existence as a legislative body. The Money Resolution would be left out, and it does seem rather serious to sweep away these long-established customs to which we all owe our rights to be here and which are the milestones of democracy in its path to power as against the security of a despotic Crown in the old days. All that is to be swept away, and we are told by the right hon Gentleman,[2] as far as I understand it – which seems to be very odd – that the fact that a Minister signified that he had the Royal Assent to sweeping away these financial precautions was sufficient to settle the matter once and for all. The whole of these financial arrangements emerged from quarrels between Parliament and the Crown, and why we should now be told that we are safeguarded because a Minister says that he has the Royal Assent to dispense with these provisions

---

[1] Gordon Lang, 1893–1981. Married, 1916, Emilie Anne Evans. MP (Lab.) for Oldham, 1929–35; for Stalybridge and Hyde, 1937–51. Chairman, Parliamentary Federal Group, 1947–51. Member, Council of Hansard Society, 1948–54.
[2] Herbert Morrison.

invented for our protection puzzles me exceedingly. I should be delighted to hear any further discussion.

Mr H. Morrison: I only want to say that in his last observations the right hon Gentleman is absolutely and completely wrong.

Hon Members: Why?

Mr Churchill: It is very easy for the right hon Gentleman to rise from his place and say that his opponent is absolutely and utterly wrong. As one most anxious to sit at his feet in the matter, might I ask him whether he would vouchsafe any reason for this sweeping contradiction. Why is it utterly and totally wrong? What is the point of bringing the King's Recommendation into this matter when it clearly is a House of Commons insistence upon the financial provisions being observed? Of course, the King's Assent has been required and is invariably required to the proposing of a money charge, but that was simply to prevent everybody getting up in all parts of the House and bidding for popularity by proposing to give away large sums from the Exchequer to their constituents or other people in whom they had an interest. There is no relation at all.

I do not think the right hon Gentleman has made out any case for this procedure except that it would have accelerated our proceedings if the Bill had been noncontroversial, and would have enabled us to depart from these scenes a day earlier. But, unhappily, we shall have to face the fact that this Bill involves very considerable discussion, and I do not see why we should be stripped of the Money Resolution, deemed essential by our ancestors to protect the rights of this House in matters of finance. What is the argument that there is not much expense to this Bill? I have never heard such a suggestion. Here is a Bill which, so far as I can make out, invests the Government with totalitarian powers. There is nothing they cannot do under the Bill. They can spend all the money they can ever filch from the pockets of hard-working people of this country. Then we are told that it has no financial implication. Surely, that is a matter which should be examined in due course, and at the proper time. I do not feel that I have listened to any argument tonight which would justify me in agreeing, without protest, to the elimination of one of the most historic, traditional, and essential safeguards of the power of Parliament over the expenditure of public money.

Winston S. Churchill to Lord Woolton
(*Churchill papers, 2/64*)

11 August 1947
Private and Confidential

My dear Fred,
    Your note of August 7.
    Most of these extracts were published some months ago and the situation is continually changing. The Liberal Party are whole-heartedly with us in our defence of the liberties of the working classes from Socialist serfdom. The *News Chronicle* leading article today shows clearly that they will oppose the nationalization of steel. In my opinion all this will come to an issue in 1948, and it is my belief that we shall all be together in one line against this vile faction. I hope therefore you will continue to do everything in your power to promote unity of action with the Liberals on the basis of an Independent Liberal Party. On this being achieved depends the future revival of Britain.
    I am so glad you are having a well-earned holiday. Pray talk to me as soon as you come back; and meanwhile let nothing be done to rebuff the growing association.

Winston S. Churchill to Lord Camrose
(*Churchill papers, 4/57*)

11 August 1947
Private

My dear Bill,
    Thank you very much for the J. B. Atkins[1] book.[2] I have read the chapter which concerns me, and I may say it is most agreeable.
    I think it would be quite right to close with the £1,000 for Rhodesia. Mr Longwell[3] and Mr Graebner came to lunch with me yesterday. I gave Longwell a set of the proofs of Books I and II and also showed him the great mass of official photographs of which I have about twenty albums. There are also my own scrap books and many detached photographs. Would it not be best for me to send all this to you and for your people to talk it over with Longwell? He assured me that they had every wish to treat Reves and his clientele with all fairness and consideration. If that is agreeable to you, I will transport the packages to wherever you wish.

---

[1] John Black Atkins, 1871–1954. Journalist. Special Correspondent for *Manchester Guardian* in Greco-Turkish war, 1897; Spanish–American war, 1898; South Africa, 1899–1900; London Editor, 1901–5. Asst Editor, *Spectator*, 1907–26. Editor, *A Monthly Bulletin*, which he founded for the improvement of public houses, 1931–48; vigorous advocate of poetry and play readings in public houses.

[2] *Incidents and Reflections* (1947).

[3] Daniel Longwell, 1916–74. Editor, Doubleday, ?–1934. Founding Editor, *Life* Magazine, 1934–54; Chairman, Board of Editors, 1946–54.

Winston S. Churchill to Clementine Churchill
(Baroness Spencer-Churchill papers)[1]

11 August 1947

My darling one,

The debate on the Special Powers bill is important & will be resumed today. It is likely that the Lords will amend it & possibly a crisis may arise. I have to go up to London today (Alas) & I fear this week will be much mauled. I send you a cutting from the *Times* in case you have not got a copy.

When I got back from the House on Friday I found a field being cut & so joined Christopher with my gun. In one minute I shot 1 rabbit with one shot – the first I have fired for nine years! I am off now to supervise the tidying up of Bardogs. Never did so small a farm harbour such masses of manure. The weather is lovely & I hate to be drawn to town.

Yesterday Raymond Blackburn MP came to luncheon bringing with him his father 73 & a high Tory. He amused me vy much. His medical advice for long life is plenty of Champagne & cigars. He is delighted to see his son quarrelling with the Socialists & hopes he will be flung out of their ranks. This may happen. The son is up in arms against this Special Powers bill, & declares that the Socialists could never face an Election if the Lords throws it out. Their Lordships too are on the war path & the whole matter requires most cool & careful handling especially as we stand to gain by delay. But I think this crisis or its prolongation will bring about an appeal to the country next year at latest. The liberals are all out with us in full cry, & today Victor Gollancz joins the fray. Even the *Times* is hostile to HMG. Attlee's broadcast was an awful flop.

I got the children to dinner last night & am seeing a good deal of them – in spite of the poor little dog, who makes me vy sore. It is wrong & silly to let little things vex me – yet they do.

Mr Graebner & Mr Longwell of *Life* & *Time* were here for hours yesterday (Sunday). They brought as goodwill offerings Cigars, Brandy a Meisner ham & lots of chocolate for you. We did a great deal of business. I work all day & night at the book with Bill D.[2] and it is bounding ahead. I must get the decks cleared for the ensuing battle.

My darling I do hope you are enjoying yrself in sunshine & are bathing & basking. Cast care aside. What we may have to face cannot be worse than all

[1] This letter was handwritten.
[2] Frederick William Dampier Deakin, 1913–2005. Known as 'Bill'. Educated at Westminster School, 1926–30. Studied for six months at the Sorbonne, 1931, then at Christ Church, Oxford, 1931–4: BA Hons, 1st class, Modern History. Taught in Germany, 1934–5. Fellow and Lecturer at Wadham College, Oxford, 1936–49. Research Assistant to Churchill, 1936–9. 2nd Lt, RA (TA), 8 July 1939. Served with Queen's Own Oxfordshire Hussars, 1939–41. Special Operations, War Office, 1941. British Military Mission to Tito, 1943. DSO, 1943. Lt-Col., 1943. First Secretary, British Embassy, Belgrade, 1945–6. Director of Researches for Churchill, 1946–9. Warden of St Antony's College, Oxford, 1950–68. Author of *The Brutal Friendship*, a study of the relationship between Hitler and Mussolini (1962). Knighted, 1975. Published an account of his wartime experiences in Yugoslavia, *The Embattled Mountain* (1971).

we have crashed through together. I send you my fondest love. You are ever in my thoughts.

Yr devoted loving

Clementine Churchill to Winston S. Churchill
(Churchill papers, 1/41)[1]

12 August 1947 [Brittany]

My darling Winston,

The weather is too lovely here & my travelling companions are very agreeable – Sylvia Henley[2] you know, tho' not so well as Venetia[3] – Her daughter Rosalind[4] is now a charming woman of 40 – She married her distant cousin (and mine) Pitt-Rivers[5] from whom she is separated. He was interned during the war for doing Nazi propaganda. The party is completed by her son Anthony,[6] a nice boy of 15 for whose birthday I have given *My Early Life* which you inscribed for him before I left.

Rosalind is a Doctor of Science & is with a team of other learned birds (mostly male) employed by the Privy Council on Research Work. They are now trying to find the cure for 'the Common Cold' so far without result. She works in a big Laboratory at Hampstead and lives next door to it. She knows a good deal about Doctor Nunn May,[7] the Communist who is serving ten years for giving 'Atom' secrets to the Russians. She says he never should have been employed by the Government as he made no secret of his views that all scientific secrets should be shared – even in war time! – by all mankind.

We are now off to Quiberon Bay. I feel stronger. A month of this would set me up for the rest of my life.

Tender Love
From your poor old Clemmie

[1] This letter was handwritten.
[2] Sylvia Laura Stanley, 1882–1980. Clementine Churchill's cousin; daughter of Edward Stanley, 4th Baron Sheffield. Married, 1906, Brig.-Gen. Anthony Morton Henley: four children. OBE, 1962.
[3] Beatrice Venetia Stanley, 1887–1948. Daughter of Edward Stanley, 4th Baron Sheffield, and Mary Bell. Married, 1915, Edwin Samuel Montagu. Known for her close connections with PM H. H. Asquith and his daughter, Violet.
[4] Rosalind Venetia Henley, 1907–90. Married, 1931, George Henry Lane Fox Pitt-Rivers. Educated at University of London: MSc, 1931; PhD, 1939. Head, Chemistry Div., National Institute for Medical Research, 1969–72.
[5] George Henry Lane Pitt-Rivers, 1890–1966. A second cousin by marriage of Clementine Churchill. On active service, 1914–18 (severely wounded). An anthropologist, he opposed mixed marriages between races and creeds; published *Weeds in the Garden of Marriage* (1931). On his release from prison, inaugurated the Wessex Music Festival.
[6] George Anthony Lane-Fox Pitt-Rivers, 1932–. Married Valerie Scott. Director, Dorset Natural History and Archaeological Society, 1997–2004.
[7] Alan Nunn May, 1911–2003. Educated at Trinity Hall, Cambridge. Member, Communist Party, 1930–40. Convicted of espionage, 1946.

Winston S. Churchill to Clementine Churchill
(Baroness Spencer-Churchill papers)

13 August 1947

My darling one,

We had a flare-up about the Government's demanding a blank cheque. I send you a few cuttings in case you are not receiving the English papers. I propose to broadcast Saturday night, in a tone of which you will, I think, approve.

It is delicious here. I have just been bathing with Mary and Christopher and Julian.[1] Six new cows have arrived which Christopher bought. They look very fine and will replace the Marnham contingent when it leaves at the end of next month.

Bennie[2] and his new wife[3] came down here yesterday and spent the whole afternoon going round the farm. She is charming and he as sunlit as ever. They were very disappointed you were not here, but he just rang up in the morning and was off to Ireland the next day.

The Marlborough medal has arrived from General Whitaker.[4] It was presented by Queen Anne[5] to him and is probably the only one struck. It is a most magnificent and valuable treasure. I am wearing it at present at the other end of my watch chain.

Everything here is pretty grim and poor little Attlee is hard-pressed. I have no feelings of unfriendliness towards him. Aneurin Bevan is making the running to gain power by extreme left-wing politics. If this proves true, we must certainly expect a political crisis, in addition to the economic collapse, which is worse than ever, and for which the Government have no plan. We had vehement Liberal support against the 'Dictator Bill', including even Samuel, and from the Socialist side, Raymond Blackburn, who I think is going to leave them, and Victor Gollancz. Perhaps you saw his letter in *The Times*. However the House of Lords have decided to meet every three weeks and they have the power to annul any Regulation which the Government decree. Moreover Regulations are not protected, as is Legislation, by the Parliament Act. Of

---

[1] Julian George Winston Sandys, 1936–97. Son of Edwin Duncan Sandys and Diana Spencer-Churchill, Churchill's eldest daughter. Educated at Eton, Salem and Melbourne. 2nd Lt, 4th Hussars, 1955. Capt., Queen's Royal Irish Hussars, 1964. Called to the Bar, Inner Temple, 1959. Member, Midland Circuit, 1960–76; Western Circuit, 1982–9; Gray's Inn, 1970–97. Married, 1970, Elizabeth Jane Martin. QC, 1983.

[2] Hugh 'Bendor' Grosvenor, Duke of Westminster.

[3] Anne Winifred Sullivan, 1915–2003. Married, Feb. 1947, Hugh Grosvenor. Styled Duchess of Westminster.

[4] Robert Frederick Edward Whitaker, 1894–1967. Educated at Ardingly College. RA, 1914–38. Married, 1919, Minnie Miles (div. 1953); 1956, Brenda Johnson. Col., 1938; Brig.-Gen., 1939; Maj.-Gen., 1945. General Manager, Lloyds Bank, 1952–7.

[5] Anne Stuart, 1665–1714. Married, 1683, Prince George of Denmark. Ascended to the throne, 1702. Last monarch of the Stuart dynasty.

course these powers will not be used by us except in extreme cases, but it is a satisfaction to feel that we are not at their mercy.

The harvest is proceeding with tremendous vigour and in perfect weather. Most of the fields are already cut and stooked and some have been put up on tripods. Christopher is very good at it all day long. The lettuces in the walled garden were sold for £200, though they cost only £50 to grow. Thus it may be that the garden will pay its expenses and even be a contributor to the farm. The Smiths seem very pleased. The hot-houses are dripping with long cucumbers. The grapes are turning black and a continuous stream of peaches and nectarines go to London. I have one a day myself − '*le droit du seigneur*'.

The book advances rapidly and I do not doubt I shall be free of the first portion, namely till December 31, 1940, by the end of October. It is very necessary to clear the decks as I am sure considerable events impend.

The Mule has promised to come and stay with me for a day or two. I expect her Hollywood plans will have come to an end through the Government tax on American films. It seems to have been done in the worst possible way − so as to cause the utmost irritation in America and procure a minimum dollar relief for the British nation. They really are awful fools.

Juliet[1] is coming to luncheon on Saturday. Christopher has heard from Lord de L'Isle[2] − very civil but in a negative sense. He has been philosophical about it. After all one cannot expect plums to drop absolutely ripe into one's mouth and I dare say there are half a dozen people with long, local attachments, in this highly developed constituency.

Darling, I have just heard that you are returning 17th instead of 25th. How lovely! I send this to Reims on the chance of catching you. You will find everything bright & happy here.

Always yr devoted[3]

---

[1] Juliet Duff, 1881–1965. Only child of 4th Earl of Lonsdale. Married, 1903, Sir Robert Duff (killed in action, 1914); 1919, Maj. Keith Trevor, MC (div., 1926, at which time she resumed her former name).

[2] William Philip Sydney, 1909–91. Educated at Eton and Magdalene College, Cambridge. Married, 1940, Jacqueline Corrine Yvonne Vereker (div. 1962); 1966, Lady Glanusk. VC, 1944. MP (Cons.) for Chelsea, 1944–5. Ministry of Pensions, 1945. Succeeded his father as Baron De L'Isle and Dudley, 1945. PC, 1951. Secretary of State for Air, 1951–5. 1st Viscount De L'Isle, 1956. CMG, 1961. Governor-General, Australia, 1961–5. KG, 1968. Chancellor, Order of St Michael and St George, 1968–84.

[3] Last paragraph added later by hand.

Winston S. Churchill: broadcast
('*Winston S. Churchill, His Complete Speeches*', volume 7, pages 7517–21)

16 August 1947   London

NO EASY PASSAGE

My grief at the plight into which our country is falling forces me to speak to you to-night, as you sit in your homes at the end of the day – and I am sure that many of you will listen. In my position I have no interest but to tell you what I believe is the truth, so far as I can discern it. After what we went through in the war, everything to me is anti-climax, and I only have to say and do what I conceive to be the best in the national interest.

When the war was won, the electors voted a majority to the Socialist Party. It fell to Mr Attlee to form the first Socialist Government with a Parliamentary majority in the whole of our history. Under our free and tolerant constitution, such great changes happen smoothly, however unexpected they may be. It was the duty of the Socialist Party, or the Labour Party, whichever they like to call themselves, to take over the guidance of our affairs. It was not a small estate to which they succeeded. All our enemies had been conquered and our name and fame stood high in the world, not only with our allies but among our defeated foes. It was widely recognised that we had saved the cause of freedom by standing alone against triumphant tyranny for more than a whole year, and fighting for the common cause from start to finish. The very efficiency of the National Government and of our united effort enabled us to draw upon our vitality and resources to the last ounce and the last inch of the strength we had gathered through so many generations of island life. It was inevitable that there should be a reaction, caused partly by our exertions in years of peril, and partly by our relief at having survived.

No one underrates the difficulties which the Socialist Ministers had to face when they came into office. Nor should they in their turn undervalue the inheritance they received from the long centuries of the past. It is a high honour to serve in the forefront of this ancient state with all its traditions and customs, its complex civilisation, and ways of life and thought. Mr Attlee and his party had not only a severe ordeal, but also a glorious opportunity before them. The National Government, of which I was the head, had won the war. It was for the Socialist Government to win the peace. And it was for them to make the most of the remaining resources of the nation – to heal the wounds of war, to maintain our position in the world, and to give some measure of happiness and reviving prosperity to the men and women who had fought so well. Surely this was a noble aim. Surely this was a task which might well have commanded their whole loyalty and strength. It was, and it still is, the bounden duty of everyone to help them in any truly national policy which they pursue.

Unhappily these men, called to the august task of setting the country on its feet again, were obsessed, and dominated by a party faction and class prejudice, and they cared far more for pleasing their own extremists than for solving the grim problems of the aftermath which beset us all. I do not blame them so much for the mistakes they have made, many and grievous though they be; I blame them for their wrongful choice in caring more for their party theories and dogma than about the revival of our strength, and the giving of comfort and hope to so many millions of cottages and apartment homes.

Of course, it is easy to say that others would have done better when that cannot be proved, but there can be no dispute about the Socialist failure or its gravity when we remember that there are four hundred thousand more people at work than in 1939; that food can be grown at home much more easily with the improved agricultural machinery; that there is more machinery in our coalmines; that the seas are open and that there never were so many ships afloat upon the seas; and that we have had all this time the easement of the American loan. With all this in mind, it is hard to believe there has not been gross mismanagement, or that we have not been put to avoidable hardship and privation. Moreover, the remedies now proposed are deemed on all sides far below what is necessary to bridge the gap between imports and exports; and finally, the loan itself has been unwisely and improvidently spent, thus shortening the breathing space which we hoped it would provide.

The Prime Minister is reported to have said at Barnsley on 21 June:

> We're moving into a new social and economic system of society in which the incentive of fear is being removed – fear of unemployment and fear of destruction.

That is what he said. Why then are our walls placarded with the grisly warning: 'We work or we want'? What is that but the fear of destitution? 'Less and less', said Mr Attlee,

> are we depending on the incentive of the individual profit.

But may this not be an explanation of the apathy, paralysis, and lack of good housekeeping which has overspread all our affairs, big and small alike? 'The more then', said the Prime Minister,

> must we develop, especially in the younger generation, the incentive for service to others, and service to community.

But how do the Government propose to develop these admirable qualities? I'm sorry to have to tell you that it is by compulsion – the direction of labour, the restriction of the right to free engagement, the denial of the right, during many centuries deemed fundamental in a free society, especially in a democracy, except in times of mortal war when the invader threatens to come upon you, the right for every man to choose or change his employment as he thinks fit. All these rights are now assailed or threatened. Ordinary incentives having been destroyed, war-time compulsion has to be substituted. Does this not show the fallacy of these high-sounding Socialist pretensions? Everyone, according to Mr Attlee, ought to give his services to the community. If not, he will be made to. It may well be that large numbers of persons before they move from one situation to another will have to have their private affairs examined by the officials of the local Labour Exchange who will decide upon their fate, and send them where they please. We are not told what punishment they will suffer if they refuse to obey. What was the Means Test we used to hear so much about compared with such an inquisition? Yet this is clearly the necessary foundation for Socialism. I do not believe that any of these methods will aid us in our economic crisis. The arrival of unwilling workers in industries to which they are strangers may well do more harm than good. Efficient arrangements for the steady and selective supply of raw materials would give far more fruitful results in a great many industries and over the whole field. Rarely if ever in history have the noble and altruistic qualities to which Mr Attlee appealed been developed in the human race by compulsion. On the contrary, it is from resistance to tyranny in all its various forms that the qualities which dignify and glorify mankind have sprung to life – aye, to eternal life, in the human breast.

I am shocked that two years after all fighting has stopped the Socialist Government tell us we must have these various forms of industrial conscription. 'War is hell', said the American General Sherman,[1] many years ago, but surely peace is supposed to be somewhat different? I am astounded that the trade unions with whom I have often worked in great matters, in peace and war, should be willing to countenance such a degradation of the fundamental rights and status of the labouring man or woman. I must make it absolutely clear that I will not support it as a part of our peace-time system, nor I believe will the great party I have the honour to lead – nor will liberal-minded men and women – Conservative, Liberal, or Labour – accept this altogether un-British conception. Before such a departure from our British standards could be made in time of peace, not only Parliament but the people must be consulted. Was not this the very kind of thing we fought against in the war, and thought we had beaten down for ever with our strong right arm?

There is something else that has shocked me. I read and am told that after two years of Socialist rule, more than half a million of our people have applied to emigrate from this island to Canada, South Africa, Australia, New Zealand, and several hundred thousand more want to go to the United States or South America. These must be among our most lively and active citizens in the prime of life who wish to go to some place where they can make the best

---

[1] William Tecumseh Sherman, 1820–91. Educated at US Military Academy. Married, 1850, Ellen Boyle Ewing. Superintendent, Louisiana Military Academy, 1859–61. Col., US Infantry, 1861; Brig.-Gen., 1861; Maj.-Gen., 1862–5; Gen., 1865–9. Gen.-in-Chief of the Army, 1869–83. Enacted total war in Georgia in his famous march to the sea during the American Civil War.

of themselves and their children. And this is happening at a time when we are scouring Europe for twenty or thirty thousand or more of the unfortunate displaced persons of the great war to come in and swell our labour force. I say to those who wish to leave this country – I am not speaking to individuals, I am speaking generally – individuals may have special reasons – I say to the general mass of those who wish to leave this country, 'Stay here and fight it out.' If we work together with brains and courage as we did in the days not long ago, we can make this country fit for all our people. Do not desert the old land. We cannot spare you. This Socialist attempt at the conscription of labour as a condition of our country in time of peace is only a passing phase. Britain will rise again in all her strength and freedom. Be sure of that.

But then, I am asked: 'What would you do, Mr Churchill, if you had the responsibility and the power which you had in the days of Dunkirk?' If I had that power, with a Cabinet of the best ability and experience in the country, which I certainly would gather, I would give you promptly and in good time the decisions which are necessary, and I have no doubt Britain would survive. We should come through now as we did then. Have I always told you wrong before?

I have but a few more minutes. But even now in this crisis, I will outline to you the broad principles which should guide us. The choice which lies before the British nation about the form of its society is between a system of competitive selection and a system of compulsion. Both these forms of society are hard. The struggle for life is unceasing. There is no easy or pleasant road. It will be uphill all the way. But I am sure that it is only by personal effort, free enterprise and ingenuity, with all its risks and failures, with all its unequal prizes and rewards, that anything like forty-seven millions of people can keep themselves alive in this small island, dependent as it is for half of its food on selling high-quality goods and rendering necessary services to the rest of mankind. I am sure that industrial compulsion and all that follows from it adopted as a peace-time system will result in an ever-diminishing standard of production, standard of living and respect for law; and of an ever-increasing army of officials fastened on the top, of us all. The only path to safety is to liberate the energies and genius of the nation, and let them have their full fruition.

It is forty-one years since, as a young Liberal Minister in Mr Asquith's Government, arguing against this same Socialist fallacy, I said:

> The existing organisation of society is driven by one mainspring – competitive selection. It may be a very imperfect organisation or society, but it is all that we have got between us and barbarism.

I should now have to add, totalitarianism, which indeed is only state-organised barbarism. 'It is all we have been able to create', I said in days before most of you were born.

through unnumbered centuries of effort and sacrifice. It is a whole treasure which past generations have been able to secure and to bequeath. Moreover, this system is one which offers an almost indefinite capacity for improvement. We may progressively eliminate the evils – we may progressively augment the good which it contains. I do not want to see impaired the vigour of competition, but we can do much to mitigate the consequences of failure. We want to draw a line below which we will not allow persons to live and labour yet above which they may compete with all the strength of their manhood. We want to have free competition upwards – we decline to allow free competition to run downwards.

That was my faith as I expressed it more than forty years ago in the same words, and it is my faith to-night. And if there were any country in the world to which these truths apply, it would be to our British Island. I warn you solemnly, if you submit yourselves to the totalitarian compulsion and regimentation of our national life and labour, there lies before you an almost measureless prospect of misery and tribulation of which a lower standard of living will be the first result, hunger the second, and a dispersal or death of a large proportion of our population the third.

You have not always listened to my warnings. Before the war, you did not. Please pay good attention to this now. On the other hand, I offer you no easy passage. An intense struggle for life will have to be made by all. Many will be wounded and faint or fall in our supreme effort to keep our national body and soul together. These we will succour from our growing and victorious strength. The strong will go back to help the weak. Instead of attacking capital, we will attack monopoly. Instead of imposing restrictions and control, we will attack restrictive practices of all kinds. It is only by marching along the path of freedom that Britain can win salvation, and when we win, as we shall surely do, we will make this ancient, glorious land honoured again among the nations; and a free and decent home for all its people who love it well.

Field Marshal Lord Montgomery to Winston S. Churchill
(Churchill papers, 2/143)[1]

17 August 1947

Dear Mr Churchill,

I thought your broadcast last night was quite excellent: balanced, fair, and putting the issue very squarely.

I felt I would like to tell this to my old war time chief.

---

[1] This letter was handwritten.

Lord Altrincham[1] to Winston S. Churchill
(*Churchill papers, 2/145*)[2]

17 August 1947

My dear Winston,

God bless you – your broadcast last night gave us all a sense of deliverance.

After months in a rudderless plane, losing altitude at a rapidly increasing rate with nothing certain ahead but a crash, to feel the old pilot at hand again is manna in the wilderness. The spontaneous opinions of our very mixed household, ancient & modern, make me feel that this whole country will have been cheered like us. Love to Clemmie.

Winston S. Churchill to General Douglas MacArthur
(*Churchill papers, 2/153*)

23 August 1947
Private and Confidential

My dear General MacArthur,

This letter is to introduce to you my son, Randolph who has my entire confidence.

I have been meaning for a long time to tell you with what interest and sympathy I have followed your policy and administration in Japan. In spite of what happened in the war, I have a regard for the Japanese nation and have pondered upon their long, romantic history. To visit Japan is one of my remaining ambitions; but I can hardly hope it will be fulfilled. I am so glad you have been able to raise them up from the pit into which they had been thrown by the military castes, who only had a part of the facts before them. They ought to be our friends in the future, and I feel this wish has been a key to many of your important decisions.

I often think of Lumsden,[3] my Lieutenant-General whom I sent to you, and

---

[1] Edward William Macleay Grigg, 1879–1955. Known as 'Ned'. Educated at Winchester and New College, Oxford. Editorial staff, *The Times*, 1903–5, 1908–13. Served in the Grenadier Guards, 1914–18 (Churchill shared his front-line dugout in Nov. 1915). Military Secretary to Prince of Wales, 1919. Knighted, 1920. Private Secretary to Lloyd George, 1921–2. MP (Nat. Lib.) for Oldham, 1922–5; (Nat. Cons.) for Altrincham, 1933–5. Governor of Kenya, 1925–31. Elected to the Other Club, 1932. Parliamentary Secretary, Ministry of Information, 1939–40. Financial Secretary, War Office, 1940. Joint Parliamentary Under-Secretary of State for War, May 1940 to March 1942. Minister Resident, Middle East, 1944–5. PC, 1944. Baron Altrincham, 1945. Editor, *National Review*, 1948–55. His son, the journalist and historian John Grigg, was one of four peers to disclaim their titles in 1963, as permitted by the Peerage Act of that year.

[2] This letter was handwritten.

[3] Herbert Lumsden, 1897–1945. Educated at Royal Military Academy, Woolwich. Served in WWI, 1915–18 (MC); 2nd Lt, RA, 1915. Served in WWII, 1939–45 (despatches twice; DSO and bar; wounded). GOC 1st Armoured Div., North Africa, 1941–2; XXX Corps, North Africa, 1942. Temp. Maj.-Gen., 1942. Temp. Lt-Gen., 1943. Commanded X Corps, 8th Army, 1942–3; VIII Army

who lost his life while on your staff. As Colonel of the 13th Lancers he brought the Armoured Car into fashion in the disastrous battle we had to fight on the French left before Dunkirk.

It would have been very easy to prevent the last war but it is not so easy to cope with in the future. The peace and freedom-loving nations must not make exactly the same mistakes again. That would be too hard.

With every good wish and my sincere congratulations on your masterly achievements as a general and statesman.

Corps, Jan.–July 1943; II Army Corps, July–Oct. 1943. British Liaison Officer with Gen. MacArthur, South-West Pacific, 1943–5. Maj.-Gen., 1944. Killed by a kamikaze Japanese attack aboard USS *New Mexico*, Okinawa, Jan. 1945.

September 1947

Harold Macmillan to Winston S. Churchill
(*Churchill papers, 2/57*)

1 September 1947

My dear Winston,

I have a rather remarkable friend, or perhaps I should say acquaintance. His name is H. I. Swainston.

He came to see me in 1937, and after a talk with me gave up his own salaried position and started a business of his own which has proved very successful. During the second war, he took the lead in organising a movement for officers called the Administrative Staff College, of which you may have heard. It looks like being a success.

He now tells me that he feels very strongly about the state of the Nation and wishes to abandon the management of his business, taking the position of Chairman of the Company. This will, of course, entail a very considerable financial sacrifice, but he is an enthusiast. He wants to devote himself solely to unpaid work for the Conservative Party. He is really a remarkable character, for he has one of those personalities which makes him able to persuade people to do what they do not want to. Now I can easily send him to see Woolton – which of course, he will do – but he has asked if you will see him for ten minutes, or at most a quarter of an hour. For it is the story of your life, and your personality, that is the true reason for his taking this decision. If you could do so, it would be an act of kindness and might help to bring us a valuable recruit. Armed with the inspiration of a talk with you, he will offer his services to Woolton who I am sure will be able to use him.

If you are agreeable to seeing him, could you let me know what place and time would suit you? I asked him to send me an account of himself. It might interest you to glance through it and I accordingly send it herewith.

PS. I much enjoyed my visit to you yesterday. At present we can only 'watch and pray'. But I feel sure that we shall have our chance soon. I hope not too soon.[1]

---

[1] Churchill wrote on the letter: 'I am so sorry. I can't see him. If I saw individuals there is no knowing where it might end.' Churchill replied formally to Macmillan on Sep. 5: 'Thank you so much for

Winston Churchill to Winston S. Churchill and Clementine Churchill
(Churchill papers, 1/42)[1]

3 September 1947

Dear Grandma and Grandpa,
　Thank you for having me to stay. I had a lovely time. We took the boat back to Hamley's and had a new one in exchange. I hope Rufus leg is better.

　　　　　　　　　　　　　　　　　　　　　　　　　　Love
　　　　　　　　　　　　　　　　　　　　　　　　　　Winston[2]

Christopher Soames to Winston S. Churchill
(Churchill papers, 2/54)

9 September 1947

　Thank you so much for showing me this letter.
　Colonel Wise[3] states that critics of our Occupational force in Germany allege that they are:
　　(a)　Incompetent.
　　(b)　Over-staffed.
He agrees with these allegations – indeed it would be hard to disagree with them. Personally I would add that they are over-housed and that, from private soldiers upwards, they live in an unnecessarily luxurious manner, thus placing an increased load on the taxpayer. There is no doubt that efficient control could eliminate many of these faults.
　Colonel Wise goes on to say that in spite of the weakness of the Control Commission it would be fatal if we were to withdraw from Western Germany. He infers that the Russians would enter it close on our heels. We have spoken on this subject before, and I know that you are not of this opinion. Personally, I agree with Colonel Wise. Though the Russians may not have the will or the determination forcibly to occupy Western Germany, they certainly have the capacity, gained through experience, to infiltrate their agents in order to inseminate Communist propaganda and gradually take over key positions.
　I am myself convinced that were we, at this juncture to withdraw our troops from Western Germany, it would become, through the German Communist Party, a potential enemy instead of a much-needed friend. Furthermore our actions in Germany are closely linked with our relationship with France. Were

---

sending me the papers about Mr Swainston. Alas, much as I should have liked to see him, I fear this is impossible; I am hard pressed from all sides, and cannot see many whom I would wish.'

[1] This letter was handwritten.

[2] The Churchills replied to their grandson on Sep. 13: 'Thank you so much for your letter – Grandpapa and Grandmama.'

[3] Alfred Roy Wise, 1901–74. Educated at Repton and Oriel College, Oxford. Asst District Commissioner, Kenya Colony, 1923–6. MP (Cons.) for Smethwick, 1931–45; for Rugby, 1959–66. Served with British Intelligence Organization, Germany, 1946–54. Lt-Col.

we to 'scuttle' it would be handing a powerful weapon to the French Communist Party.

Winston S. Churchill: speech
('Europe Unite', pages 135–9)

10 September 1947   Guildhall, London

INTERNATIONAL CONGRESS OF PHYSICIANS

My Lord President,[1] My Lord Mayor,[2] Your Excellencies, My Lords, Ladies and Gentlemen:

A third of a century has passed since the last International Congress of Physicians was held in London. I was reading a few days ago the reports of that meeting in 1913 and the speeches which were delivered then by my two great friends and political colleagues of those days, Lord Morley and Sir Edward Grey. Reading them again, it was impossible to resist the impression of the sedate, orderly, progressive, and liberal-minded world in which they dwelt, or of the splendour of Europe growing in culture and wealth and also, alas! in pride, on the eve of the great catastrophe which has over-whelmed the human race and in the aftermath of which we are still involved. I say to our foreign friends from so many countries now, thirty-four years later, how warmly we welcome you back to the banks of the Thames, and how proud we are to do our best to entertain you in the City of London, amid the ruins we have not yet been able to repair, and in this ancient Hall which bears in every aspect the scars of honourable and victorious conflict. What a fearful journey we have all made since the meeting of the Congress of Physicians in London in 1913, and what a contrast is the shadowed world of today to the hopeful, though already anxious, society of men and of nations which then represented our national and international life. And what a change we have, in all the doubts and confusion of the present time, from the glittering structure of society which in so many lands had been built up across the centuries by so much toil and skill.

I noted, in reading those speeches, that both John Morley and Edward Grey spoke in 1913 of the advance in science, with unquestioning faith in its wholly beneficent mission. Now, however, when mankind without having improved at all, in fact having lost the sense of many of its most precious values, has got control of the most terrible agencies of destruction, and when many of its ablest and most brilliant minds are working night and day on the means for the annihilation of the human race – or such portions of it as they may be

---

[1] Herbert Morrison.
[2] Bracewell Smith, 1884–1966. Councillor and Alderman, Holborn Borough Council, 1922–37. Mayor, Holborn, 1931–2. Sheriff, 1943–4. Knighted, 1945. Lord Mayor of London, 1946–7. Bt, 1947. KCVO, 1948.

temporarily opposed to at any time – working on these methods of annihilation both by the devastation of explosions and by the organised spreading of disease among men, cattle, and crops, it is evident that a certain amount of discrimination must be mingled with our satisfaction at our triumph over nature and of our piercing of her secrets.

But tonight all our thoughts are turned to healing and not to destruction, and we can unfeignedly and unreservedly rejoice at the progress of medicine and – if I am allowed to mention it here – of its close and friendly companion, surgery. Fanned by the fierce winds of war, medical science and surgical art have advanced unceasingly, hand in hand. There has certainly been no lack of subjects for treatment. The medical profession at least cannot complain of unemployment through lack of raw material. The inventive genius of mankind is stirred and spurred by suffering and emergency, and the long succession of noble discoveries in the application of the healing art stand forth with all the greater brilliance against the dark and hideous background of hatred and chaos. The miseries of the population have given opportunities to the medical profession of rendering service to their fellow mortals on an unexampled scale. Science, in many spheres so baleful, offers an ever-broadening and brightening outlook for the toil and devotion of those who follow the practice of medicine. There is no profession or calling whose members can feel a greater or deeper conviction of duty of lasting value to be done. There is no profession in which they can feel a surer confidence in an expanding future in their fight against pain and disease. This, my Lords and Gentlemen, must be at once an intense and lively inspiration to those who devote their lives to the study and practice of medicine, and I am very glad to offer those who are gathered here in this most distinguished assembly my respectful congratulations on the path they have chosen in life.

I have been inclined to feel from time to time that there ought to be a hagiology of medical science and that we ought to have saints' days to commemorate the great discoveries which have been made for all mankind, and perhaps for all time – or for whatever time may be left to us. Nature, like many of our modern statesmen, is prodigal of pain. I should like to find a day when we can take a holiday, a day of jubilation when we can fête good Saint Anæsthesia and chaste and pure Saint Antiseptic. I would not venture in a company so distinguished as this to pretend to any qualifications to judge who should figure in this list, but if I had a vote I should be bound to celebrate, among others, Saint Penicillin, whom I see represented here, and Saint M&B, both invaluable figures, to whom I was introduced during the war in good time by Lord Moran, and but for whose benediction I might be regarding your present troubles, if not otherwise preoccupied, from a more serene sphere.

It seems to me that the medical profession had endless worlds to conquer. An eminent American freethinker was once asked how he would have made the world different, if he had been God. 'I should have made health infectious instead of disease,' he answered. I throw this out as a constructive suggestion. We are all out nowadays for constructive suggestions, and here is something for your programme of future activities. At any rate, it would be a great reform in politics if wisdom could be made to spread as easily and as rapidly as folly.

I asked Lord Moran to tell me what to say in this discourse. He suggested I might compare the professions of medicine and politics, but I was bound to reject this suggestion. It is quite impossible to make such a comparison, because medicine requires the study and experience of a life-time, while everyone in a free country, as part of his birthright, knows all about politics after leaving the infant school and on every occasion when he is released from the asylum.

Go forward then, Gentlemen, members of this great vocation, upon your upward path and strive with ever brighter prospects and more powerful weapons against the sufferings and weakness which afflict us here below. I wish you all success in your noble endeavours, and it is with the greatest sense of honour that I propose to you the health of the Medical Profession and couple the toast with the name of Lord Moran.

Randolph S. Churchill to Winston S. Churchill
(Churchill papers, 1/42)

13 September 1947　　　　　　　　　　　　　　　The Australia Hotel, Sydney

My dearest Papa,

I am sending you under separate cover some corrected proofs of the speeches.[1] You will see there are one or two passages that I have marked for your attention.

I have now been here ten days and am beginning to get the feel of the country. So far I have had two lectures in Melbourne. Casey[2] very kindly took the chair at the first one. Tonight I am speaking in Sydney and the Lord Mayor[3] is taking the chair and I am to be introduced by your old friend, Billy Hughes.[4]

[1] The collection published as *The Sinews of Peace* (1948). Randolph had resumed his pre-war role as editor of his father's speeches, the previous volume being *Arms and the Covenant* (1938).
[2] Richard Gardiner Casey, 1890–1976. Born in Australia. Educated in Australia and at Trinity College, Cambridge. On active service at Gallipoli and in France (DSO, MC), 1915–18. Active in Australian politics between the wars. Australian Minister for Supply and Development, 1939–40. Australian Minister to the US, 1940–2. British Minister of State Resident in the Middle East (based in Cairo) and Member of the British War Cabinet, 1942–3. Governor of Bengal, 1944–6. Minister of External Affairs, Australia, 1951–60. Baron, 1960. Governor-General of Australia, 1965–9.
[3] Reginald James Bartley, 1899–1982. Married, 1928, Florence Teresa. Alderman, City of Sydney Council, 1941–59; Lord Mayor, 1943–4, 1946–8.
[4] William Morris Hughes, 1864–1952. Educated in Wales and London. Emigrated to Australia, 1884. MP (Lab.) 1st Federal Australian Parliament. Minister for External Affairs, 1904, 1921–3, 1937–9. Prime Minister of Australia, 1915–23. Australian Delegate to the Paris Peace Conference, 1919. Minister for Health and Repatriation, 1934–5. Minister for Industry, 1939–40. Attorney-General, 1939–40. Minister for the Navy, 1940–1. Member, Australian Advisory War Council, 1941–5.

Everyone out here is much concerned at all the news from England. There is a really warm-hearted feeling towards Britain and nearly everyone seems anxious to do whatever they can to help. The Australian Government, however, seems to lag somewhat behind public opinion. The atavistic memories of the Irish Catholics who dominate the administration are stronger than the natural affinity which socialists might be expected to feel for a fellow-socialist Government in distress.

The burning topic of the hour is the nationalization of the private banks. I am repeatedly being questioned about it. I have found a formula for dealing with this question which avoids the Scylla of interfering in Australian politics and the Charybdis of criticizing HMG when overseas. I decline to comment on the situation here, but add that Britain's socialists, despite all their other follies, have not yet done anything so silly as that. This goes down very much.

Casey has recently been elected President of the Liberal Party, which is, in effect, the Conservative Party under another name. Menzies is still the leader of the Liberal Party and is far and away the ablest man in the country. He is hated by everyone. I have not seen him yet, but expect to when I go to Canberra. I saw Evatt[1] just before he left for New York. Like everyone else, he spoke with great affection and admiration about you. He asked me to send you 'his affectionate homage'.

In Melbourne I met a Colonel Brading, who rode in your troop in the 21st Lancers at Omdurman. This country has much to commend it. Many people in England seem to think that Australia is a sort of poor man's America. In fact, it is in every way much more civilised. Despite the lack of servants the well-to-do classes live much better than in America. They plant trees, shrubs and flowers. The clubs are as good as the best in London, the women gay and attractive, the oysters the best in the world and the climate, at any rate at this time of the year, delicious.

I have seen a lot of Streety[2] who has rallied around and is generally attentive to my welfare.

Miss Elgie is coming to dine with me tonight before the lecture.

I had a most frustrated journey out here, and was delayed in Basra. I thus arrived in Delhi three days late and missed the Mountbattens by half an hour.

Pug, too, was away in Kashmir recovering from dysentery. However, I stayed in his house and was most comfortable. Dickie left a charming letter for me containing many affectionate references to yourself.

---

[1] Herbert Vere Evatt, 1894–1965. Born in Australia. Member (Lab.) New South Wales Legislative Assembly, 1925–9. KC, 1929. Justice of the High Court of Australia, 1930–40. Attorney-General and Minister for External Affairs, 1941–9. Member, Australian Advisory War Council, 1941–5; Australian War Cabinet, 1941–6. Australian Representative, UK War Cabinet, 1942, 1943. Australian Member, Pacific War Council, 1942–3. Freedom of the City of Athens, 1945. Deputy PM of Australia, 1946–9. Leader, Australian Delegation, UN General Assembly, 1946, 1947. Chairman, UN Palestine Commission, 1947. Leader, Parliamentary Labour Party, Australia, 1951–60.

[2] Margery Street. Known as 'Streetie'. Private Secretary to Clementine Churchill, 1921–33. Returned to Australia, 1933.

In Calcutta I had a long talk with Gandhi, who spoke in terms of high admiration for yourself. He would not commit himself precisely, but I think his influence will be cast on the side of keeping India at least nominally inside the Empire.

I only had three quarters of an hour in Singapore, but had a talk with the Killearns[1] who very civilly came down to the airport and met me. They are most anxious to find fresh employment when their present job ends in March. Both wish to be remembered to you.

W. S. Robinson's[2] friends in the Zinc Corporation flew me up last Monday to Broken Hill, where they have the great zinc and lead mines. It is an amazing undertaking; the miners work thirty-five hours a week and many of them earn as much as twenty-five pounds.

All goes well here. I do hope you and Mamma are flourishing and that all in well with you all. Please give my love to you Mamma and all the family.[3]

Lord Cherwell to Winston S. Churchill
(Churchill papers, 2/53)

14 September 1947

My dear Winston,

You asked us at luncheon on Wednesday to write concerning the suggested committee to consider the economic situation.

As you know, I have long advocated that the Conservative Party should study and decide what steps are required to deal with the present economic circumstances. This is essential primarily because a policy could not be improvised if you were suddenly called upon to take office. But it is also important to ensure that the Party is not pledged to accept or oppose any particular proposals which it might be compelled, if it came into power, either to repudiate or to put into effect as the case might be.

I do not think that such a large committee as was adumbrated at luncheon on Wednesday could hammer out any effective plan. It would, of course, be

---

[1] Miles Wedderburn Lampson, 1880–1964. British Minister to China, 1926–33. Knighted, 1927. High Commissioner for Egypt and the Sudan, 1934–6. Ambassador to Egypt and High Commissioner for the Sudan, 1936–46. PC, 1941. Baron Killearn, 1943. Special Commissioner in South-East Asia, 1946–8.
Jacqueline Aldine Leslie Castellani, 1910–2015. Married, 1934, Miles Wedderburn Lampson; three children. Styled Lady Killearn, 1943.

[2] William Sydney Robinson, 1876–1963. Born in Melbourne. Financial Editor, *Age*, 1899–1907. Adviser to Australian PM on non-ferrous metals, WWI; on metals and concentrates, WWII. Managing Director, Broken Hill Associated Smelters, 1915–35; National Smelting Corp., 1923–9; Burma Corp., 1924; Imperial Smelting Corp., 1929–49. Member, British Board of Trade, 1917–18. Director, Zinc Corp., 1920–35; Managing Director, 1925–47; President, 1947–51. His memoirs, *If I Remember Rightly*, were published posthumously in 1967.

[3] Churchill replied on Sep. 25: 'Delighted to receive your letter of September 13. Hope all is going well. Best love from us all.'

useful to consult or to be able to consult the 20 or 30 people mentioned. But the real work and the drafting would have to be done by not more than half a dozen men. Otherwise we should only get a long screed on Civil Service lines written by the Secretary of the Committee.

I am strongly against publication of the fact that such a committee has been formed and still more so against publication of its conclusions. It might be that certain of the conclusions could be stated publicly in a general form with advantage, but that would be for you and the Consultative Committee to decide at a later date.

But although the fact that there was some official body of doctrine should not be published, familiarity with certain broad conclusions, which had been accepted by the Consultative Committee, would ensure some sort of uniformity in the public utterances of its members; and their speeches no doubt would provide a line for other Conservative speakers and prevent pronouncements which would later on have to be repudiated.

I must admit frankly that I have an uneasy feeling that all these considerations may be somewhat academic. I fear that the country cannot return to a healthy state unless and until there has been a showdown, like the General Strike or worse, with the shop-stewards and perhaps the TUC. With labour in its present mood no government, least of all a Conservative government can ensure lasting prosperity.

With *souvenirs affectueux* to you all, believe me, as ever.

Alan Lascelles to Winston S Churchill
(*Churchill papers, 2/171*)[1]

16 September 1947   Balmoral Castle

Dear Mr Churchill,

The king has told me to ask you if you would be so kind as to have a look at the enclosed draft for HM's speech when he unveils the statue to his father in Westminster on Oct. 22nd, and suggest any improvements in it that may occur to you.

It could quite well be compressed a bit and in several places the phraseology seems to me rather stilted – though nothing like as stilted as was the speech made by King George V (which you doubtless heard) when he unveiled the statue of King Ed. VII at the bottom of Waterloo Place.

It is not easy, of course, to make a speech of this kind about one's own father.

[1] This letter was handwritten.

Winston S. Churchill to Ernest Bevin
(*Churchill papers, 2/55*)

19 September 1947
Private and Personal

My dear Bevin,

I have received the enclosed letter from Mr Romer about the dangerous position of M Mikolajczyk in Poland. As you will see by consulting the records, I put the utmost pressure on him to return there and had, at the time, every reason to believe that this was agreeable to Stalin. If now he is going to be victimized in the Soviet manner, I shall certainly feel it necessary to speak in good time about the matter and also to refer particularly to Stalin's agreeable relations with Mikolajczyk at the time Eden and I were in Moscow in October 1944. I consider that the execution, but even the persecution, of Mikolajczyk is a matter of the very first magnitude.

I have no doubt you share my views, but I feel it my duty to write you this letter in order that everything possible may be done to stop this increasing villainy.

Winston S. Churchill to President Harry S Truman
(*Churchill papers, 2/158*)[1]

24 September 1947

My dear Harry,

As our friend Lou Douglas is going home for a spell I cannot resist sending by his hand a few lines to tell you how much I admire the policy into which you have guided your great country; and to thank you from the bottom of my heart for all you are doing to save the world from famine and war. I wish indeed I could come over and see you and many other friends in the Great Republic. The political situation here requires my constant presence. I think there is no doubt that if there were a General Election, the Conservatives would be returned by a majority. That is however the reason why an Election is unlikely.

You have my warmest good wishes in your memorable discharge of your tremendous office, and you can be sure that all the strongest forces in Britain are, and will be, at your side if trouble comes.

---

[1] This letter was handwritten.

Reginald Maudling[1] to Winston S. Churchill
(*Churchill papers, 2/59*)

25 September 1947

Dear Mr Churchill,

I enclose some notes on one or two points which may be of some use to you for your speech in Woodford on Saturday.

I am trying to find the quotation from John Morley.

I have had a word with the television experts. They tell me that in fact no bright light will shine into your face. The strong light will be directly above. They also tell me that all the men employed in working the lighting system have been responsible for the lighting at previous meetings which you have addressed and are well aware of your requirements. There will be no flashes of any kind and the light will be steady.

I think that in the circumstances you should not find it too strong. It might perhaps be wise to have your notes typed on paper that is matt, as you might get a reflection from the lights from a very smooth surface.

If you like, I will gladly make further enquiries and go along myself to somewhere where they can show me the type of lighting in practice.

Winston S. Churchill to Sir Orme Sargent
(*Churchill papers, 2/53*)

26 September 1947
Private

My dear Sargent,

Thank you very much for your letter of September 15, and for all the information you send me. I am indeed obliged to you for the trouble you have taken in this matter.

In view of what you say I think it would be better if I told Dr Brod that I do not wish to make any statement at the present time, and I am accordingly doing so.

---

[1] Reginald Maudling, 1917–79. Educated at Merton College, Oxford. Married, 1939, Beryl Laverick. Called to the Bar, Middle Temple, 1940. MP (Cons.) for Herts, Barnet, 1950–74; for Barnet, Chipping Barnet, 1974–9. Parliamentary Secretary to Minister of Civil Aviation, 1952. Economic Secretary to Treasury, 1952–5. PC, 1955. Minister of Supply, 1955–7. Paymaster-General, 1957–9. President of the Board of Trade, 1959–61. Secretary of State for the Colonies, 1961–2. Chancellor of the Exchequer, 1962–4. Home Secretary, 1970–2.

September 1947

Lord Beaverbrook to Winston S. Churchill
(Churchill papers, 2/146)[1]

26 September 1947

My dear Winston,

I have a house on the border of Monte Carlo. It is known as 'Capponcina'.

Will you and Clemmie visit this place during the Autumn or Winter? You know I have control of Canadian funds. I can provide staff and food and drink too and motor. So if you will accept my invitation you might let me know the convenient times.

There is plenty of room for secretaries and any servants you may require. I am leaving in an hour for Canada where I stay until the end of October. But you can notify Millan when you will go to the South and he will inform Madame Franco who is my housekeeper.

Luce is asking me to do a short story for his paper when your great work is serialized. I propose to write – about your meeting at the Admiralty with Ironside[2] and Dill.

Jo Sturdee to Winston S. Churchill
(Churchill papers, 1/42)

26 September 1947

The *Daily Mirror* of Australia telephoned. They wonder if you would comment upon Mr Randolph's pronouncement about Australia which he has made at a Press Conference in that country today. He has said:
1. That Australia is not taking her full share in Imperial Defence.
2. That Australia is trying to lure away the best of Britain's manhood.
3. That another War is inevitable.
4. That Russia clearly aims at the infiltration and domination of Trades Unions in British countries.

They are most concerned about this criticism of their country and are interested to know if you would let them know your views.[3]

---

[1] This letter was handwritten.
[2] William Edmund Ironside, 1880–1959. 2nd Lt, RA, 1899. On active service in South Africa, 1899–1902. Maj., 1914. Staff Officer, 4th Canadian Div., 1916–17. Commandant, Machine Gun Corps School, France, 1918. Brig.-Gen. commanding 99th Infantry Bde, 1918. Maj.-Gen. Commanding Allied Troops, Archangel, Oct. 1918 to Oct. 1919. Knighted, 1919. Head, British Military Mission to Hungary, 1920; to Poland, Aug. 1939. CO Ismid Force, Turkey, 1920; North Persian Force, 1920–1. Lt-Gen., 1931. QMG, India, 1933–6. Gen., 1935. GOC-in-C, Eastern Command, 1936–8. Governor and C-in-C, Gibraltar, 1938–9. CIGS, 1939–40. C-in-C, Home Forces, May–July 1940. FM, 1940. Baron, 1941. On 4 July 1938 Churchill wrote of Ironside to Sir Abe Bailey: 'He is the finest military brain in the Army at the present time.'
[3] Churchill wrote on this note: 'No answer'.

Winston S. Churchill: speech
('Winston S. Churchill, His Complete Speeches', volume 7, pages 7523–7)

27 September 1947 Constituency Meeting
Royal Wanstead Schools

A CIVIC AND PATRIOTIC DUTY

I congratulate you on the very great success which has attended the Autumn campaign in our constituency. The well-attended meetings, the excellent speeches made by the distinguished members of both Houses of Parliament who have been so kind as to come, the large increase of our Party membership and in particular the general atmosphere of activity and vigour reflect great credit on all concerned and in particular upon the young Conservative Organisation which has given its powerful and invaluable impulse. This is indeed a time when every man or woman who cares about the greatness of Britain, and its survival as a leading power – and indeed about the grim process of winning our daily bread – should feel bound to use to the full political rights and liberties which have been so painfully won by our forebears and which up to the present we are still allowed to enjoy. I cannot understand any Conservative or Liberal-minded elector remaining inert and idle at a time like this. Everyone can help in some way or other. No one knows till he tries how much influence one convinced and well-informed person can exert upon those with whom he comes in contact in the ordinary round of daily life.

This is no time for ordinary Party politics, the warfare of the Ins and the Outs. It is a civic and patriotic duty of the first order to take an active part in political work. Mr Gladstone said many years ago that it ought to be part of a man's religion to see that his country is well-governed. When I recall where we stood at the victorious end of the war and compare it with where we now lie at home and abroad, I can hardly believe it possible that such a vast decline and fall in our world status and in our home standard of living, economy and finance should have taken place so quickly. When two years ago I said that the General Election of 1945 was a national disaster, I did not think that this would be proved true in so short a time. There is not one single aspect or sphere of British national life that has not undergone a marked deterioration. We are living worse than we did in the full stress of the war. What the German U-boats could never do to us has been achieved by our own misguided fellow-countrymen through their incompetence, their arrogance, their hordes of officials, their thousands of regulations and their gross mismanagement of our affairs, large and small. Moreover, the longer this continues the worse things will get and the harder will be the work of national revival. All the world is staggered by the sudden fall of Britain from the high position at the summit of freedom-loving nations which she had won in the finest hour of her history.

But what has happened so far is only a foretaste of what is to come. Under Socialism, with all its malice and class jealousy, with all its hobbling and crippling of diligence, initiative and enterprise, it will not be possible for more than two-thirds of our present population to live in this island. That is why there is all this talk of emigration. That is why young men and women, and people in their prime, the flower of our race – of our ancient unconquerable race – are turning their eyes overseas and hope to find in broader lands a chance to make their way, to make the best of themselves, to found a home and family, which is denied them there. On the other hand the Socialist Government is trying to fill their places with the poor flotsam and jetsam of war-stricken Europe called 'displaced persons'. I will not speak of these people without sympathy; but how terrible is our situation in the vast modern world that has grown up around us when so many of our best and most active people wish to leave our shores and we have to become the repository of the unhappy wreckage of Europe.

Is it not time that everyone, old or young, who sees the truth, should labour to convince all those with whom he comes in contact, of the peril in which we stand? They should join the Unionist and Conservative Party Association, they should subscribe to the fullness of their means towards keeping up the necessary national organisation which, under Lord Woolton, is steadily improving, and above all they should not lose faith in the recovery of our country when the years of Socialist incompetence and squalor have passed from us like a hateful dream. Here, in this constituency we must not only think of ourselves. We must be ready to help our neighbours, especially our neighbours in the Epping Division in their efforts to throw off the Socialist yoke.

An extraordinary myth, or large-scale propaganda of falsehood, has been spread in all directions by the Socialist Government about the lamentable conditions in Great Britain mainly under Conservative Parliaments between the wars, and a lot of young people are being taught to believe that this was a sad period of stagnation in our national and social life. The Socialist Party hope that by creating this impression they will find some excuse for their own failure, which has brought such needless hardship on the masses of our people at the present time.

The many differences we have with the Government do not extend to foreign policy, which has, under Mr Bevin, preserved a stability and continuity which contrasts very favourably with what his colleagues have done at home. We have given our Party support in the House of Commons to the main lines of his foreign policy, which is so bitterly attacked by the Communist Party and by the crypto-Communists and other Left-Wing elements in the House of Commons. When I spoke at Fulton in the United States nearly two years ago, at the invitation of President Truman, I gave my warnings about the Iron Curtain that the Russians had drawn across Europe and the many ancient and famous European capital cities which had fallen into the Soviet Communist power. American opinion, at first startled and much divided, has since those days flowed along the lines I indicated to such an extent that if I repeated the Fulton speech in America today, it would be regarded as a stream of tepid platitudes. This great confrontation by the United States of militant Communism backed by the Soviet military power, has been brought about almost entirely by the aggressions and the intrigues of the Soviet Government in all the countries on their borders, and by their attempts to paralyse the working of the United Nations Organisation, on which all our hopes were founded, by the brutal use of their veto.

I am very glad we are able to give our full support to the United States in the efforts she is making to preserve Freedom and Democracy in Europe, and to send food to its distressed and distracted countries. We hear a great deal of the 'Dollar Shortage'. What are dollars? Dollars represent the toil and skill and self-denial of scores of millions of American wage-earners, which they are contributing of their own free will, in most cases without any hope of repayment, to help their fellow-men in misfortune across the ocean. Such a process should be treated on all occasions with the respect which is its due. No country in the world has ever done anything like it on such a scale before.

The unity of policy that exists throughout the English-speaking world does not arise from any bargainings or treaties, but from the fact that there is a natural agreement between Great Britain and the United States on almost all questions which arise. That is because we pursue the same ideals and have a common inheritance of literature and law. I was glad to see another example of this spontaneous unity of thought in the stern diplomatic protests handed to the Bulgarian Government by the American and British Governments against the shameful judicial murder of the Bulgarian patriot and anti-Nazi, M Petkov.[1] This crime gives a measure of the ruthless cruelty with which Communist minorities once they have captured the Government machinery, treat their political opponents. There can be no doubt that the prime responsibility for this murder lies with the Soviet Government. It is no doubt intended to give a lesson to the various countries of Eastern Europe which have fallen into the Soviet grip of what will be the fate of any public figures, however popular or honourable they are, who venture to oppose by constitutional means the Puppet Governments the Soviet Governments have erected.

Let me look farther afield. The fearful massacres[2] which are occurring in

[1] Nikola Petkov, 1893–1947. Born in Sofia, Bulgaria. Studied Law in Paris, 1922. Secretary, Bulgarian legation, Paris, 1922–3. Joined Bulgarian Agrarian National Union, 1923; Member, Standing Committee, 1932–3, 1944; Secretary General, 1945. Editor, *Zemya*, 1931–2. Elected to National Assembly, 1938. Arrested for opposition to Tsar Borris III, 1938. Prisoner, Gonda Voda concentration camp, 1940–1, 1943–4. Co-founder, Fatherland Front (FF), 1943. Member, FF National Committee, 1945. Minister without Portfolio, 1944, following FF coup. Left government and founded opposition party, BANU-Petkov, 1945. Editor, *Naronno zemedelsko znam* (opposition newspaper), 1945–7. Sentenced to death and hanged, 1947. Rehabilitated, 1990.

[2] Starting in August 1946 and escalating during and after the Partition of India in 1947, Hindu and Muslim refugees migrating to the sovereign nation friendly to their religion, India and Pakistan

India are no surprise to me. It is heartrending to read the brief accounts all the newspapers contain. I shall always remember with gratitude how my constituents here supported me and the group of 70 or 80 Conservative Members, when, for four years between 1931 and 1935, we fought against the India Constitution Bill. And only four months ago I explained to the House of Commons the reasons why I believed that the abandonment of our responsibilities in India would be followed by a hideous bloodbath. Perhaps I may quote to you what I said on this point:

> How can you suppose that the thousand-year gulf which yawns between Moslem and Hindu will be bridged in 14 months?
>
> The Indian parties and political classes do not represent the Indian masses.
>
> No arrangement can be made about all the great common services.
>
> All will be the preparation for the ensuing Civil War.
>
> In handing over the government of India to the so-called political classes you are handing over to men of straw of whom in a few years, no trace will remain.

We are of course only at the beginning of these horrors and butcheries, perpetrated upon one another, men, women and children, with the ferocity of cannibals, by races gifted with capacities for the highest culture and who had for generations dwelt side by side in general peace under the broad, tolerant and impartial rule of the British Crown and Parliament. I cannot doubt but that the future will witness a vast abridgement of the population throughout what has, for 60 or 70 years, been the most peaceful part of the world, and that, at the same time, will come a retrogression of civilisation throughout these enormous regions, constituting one of the most melancholy tragedies Asia has ever known.

The Government have now at last decided to evacuate Palestine and transfer their mandate to the hands of the United Nations Organisation. In this case they are fulfilling exactly the advice which I gave them in August 1946. It is strange to reflect that probably half the exertions which they made to maintain our rule in Palestine, would, if they had been applied to India, have maintained an orderly and peaceful development and transition. Five times as many British troops were actually concentrated in this tiny Palestine, which had never been British territory, as were assigned to our task and trusteeship in our mighty and famous Indian Empire of 400 millions. Such a lack of sense of proportion has rarely been exposed. Now that we have announced our decision to quit Palestine I trust it will be carried out as quickly as possible. In the last two years the Government have wasted 100 or 150 millions of pounds and the services of a hundred thousand of our finest troops in Palestine, gaining

---

respectively, were massacred by bands of violent mobs of adherents to the other religion. Estimates of the numbers killed vary from 200,000 to 2 million; a further 14 million people were displaced.

us nothing but ill-will and discredit, there and in every quarter of the world. During these two years they were unable to come to any decision or produce any policy, and the incapacity of the Ministers concerned has made a heavy, and now shown to be a useless, inroad upon our limited resources. Such is the tale of the Socialist Government abroad.

I end where I began – here at home. There lies before us at home here in our island a period of increasing restriction and privation. Everyone must do his best to produce and to save as much as possible. But I fear that whatever our efforts and sacrifices should be, they will not, under present conditions, avoid an economic and financial situation the gravity of which no one can measure. What is needed is a new spirit in the hearts of our people and a new unity in our common action. This will not be achieved until there is a new House of Commons, representative of all the strength and wisdom of the nation. That is why you are right to take every step to spread political truth among all you meet and to make sure that, should an Election be sprung upon us at any moment next year, you will be able to say, with solid confidence 'We are Ready.'

Tadeusz Romer to Winston S. Churchill
(*Churchill papers, 2/55*)

28 September 1947

Dear Mr Churchill,

Thank you for your kind letter of 25th September.[1] I deeply appreciate your thoughtfulness in keeping me informed of your action on behalf of M Mikolajczyk. I note with gratitude that your firm intervention has already produced results.

I strongly support your contention that to mention the name of M Mikolajczyk while he is still at liberty would do more harm than good. However, it might serve to some useful purpose if details of the recent trial in Cracow were made public in this country, and condemned as severely as the Petkov and other trials. I enclose some particulars in this respect which you may care to utilize.

I am always at your disposal, and a message by telephone or letter will reach me at any time.

Thanking you again for your support of M Mikolajczyk's case.

---

[1] Churchill had written to Romer: 'I have received a letter from the Foreign Secretary, of which I am sending you a copy. Before I make any reference to M Mikolajczyk I hope you will give me your advice. It might well be that my speaking in public about him would do more harm than good' (*Churchill papers, 2/55*).

Sir James Grigg to Winston S. Churchill
(*Churchill papers, 2/54*)[1]

28 September 1947

My dear Winston,

Thank you very much indeed for your letter.

I liked your speech at Snaresbrook a lot. You told me two years ago things were going to get 'perfectly bloody'. How bloody I doubt if even you foresaw. And I don't see how we can ever recover morally from what we have done in India.

Ernest Bevin to Winston S. Churchill
(*Churchill papers, 2/55*)

30 September 1947
Private and Personal

Dear Winston,

I have now given detailed consideration to your letter of the 19th September about the dangerous position of Mikolajczyk.

I fully appreciate how you feel, and I am very conscious of our moral obligation in the matter of his personal safety. I also share your fear that Mikolajczyk may be arrested and tried on a trumped-up charge.

I have been considering what we can do to avert this. For your own entirely personal and secret information, I have sent a personal message to the Polish Prime Minister, M Cyrankiewicz,[2] whom I met when I was in Warsaw, and who is a member of the Socialist Party. I have emphasized to him how much relations between the two countries would suffer if action were to be taken against Mikolajczyk. I have not yet had any reply, but I hope that my message may have some effect.

Count Romer, whose letter you enclose, suggests that we should expose publicly the farcical nature of these treason trials in Eastern Europe. This we have of course already been doing and there has been a great deal of publicity on this subject, particularly in the case of Archbishop Stepinac and the recent case of Petkov. But all our representations about Petkov have not prevented his trial and execution, and the elimination of his Party. This confirms my view that if we raise the case of a man like Petkov or Mikolajczyk here publicly, as an issue between ourselves and those in power in the country concerned, the latter's reaction is to accept it as a challenge, to represent the man in question

---

[1] This letter was handwritten.

[2] Józef Cyrankiewicz, 1911–89. Educated at Jagiellonian University, Kraków. Captured by Germans and interned at Auschwitz, 1941–5. Secretary-General, Polish Socialist Party, Central Executive Committee, 1945. Polish PM, 1947–52, 1954–70. Chairman, Polish Peace Committee, 1973–86.

as a tool of the Western powers, and to take steps to eliminate him. So I think it would be a mistake and dangerous for Mikolajczyk that there should be publicity at the present time about his possible danger. I therefore regret the recent reference to him in the *Daily Telegraph*. Count Romer's letter to Sargent has been answered in this sense.

If action is taken against Mikolajczyk, there no doubt will be a great deal of publicity, and you may be sure that I shall take any steps likely to help. For the present I feel sure that my personal message to the Polish Prime Minister was the best action to take, and if he has any real influence, I hope it may be effective.

October 1947

Winston S. Churchill to Paul Reynaud
(*Churchill papers, 2/57*)

1 October 1947

My dear Reynaud,

Thank you so much for your letter giving me valuable supplementary information on the events at Bordeaux in June 1940.

I am very anxious to consider the story of these tragic days in light of all available and reliable evidence, and your responsible and concrete comments are most valuable to me.

PS. I hope we may meet soon.

Winston S. Churchill: speech
(*'Winston S. Churchill, His Complete Speeches', volume 7, pages 7527–8*)

3 October 1947   Town Hall, Brighton

PEACETIME DIFFICULTIES

... I was nearly three years at school here. It was at 29 and 30, Brunswick Place, under two charming and gifted ladies, the Misses Thompson,[1] I began to take some of those early steps in knowledge which, if not always the most agreeable, could hardly be dispensed with. (*Laughter.*) At any rate I learned some important things at Brighton in those days. I learned to ride and I learned to swim, and I learned to dance, and I began to learn by heart many of those passages of poetry which have been a great treasure and comfort to

---

[1] Charlotte (b. 1843) and Catharine (b. 1845) Thomson were sisters who ran a preparatory school in Brighton. Neither ever married. The Misses Thomson's Preparatory Academy left Hove in 1898, moved to Oathall Road, Haywards Heath, and was renamed the Brunswick Preparatory School. Winston Churchill attended the school from 1884 to 1888. Charlotte Thomson and Winston had a close relationship. He often wrote to his mother about her. Charlotte took Winston to Harrow School for his entrance exam in 1888.

me during my life – heroic poetry and famous tales and legends of the past. The committing of passages to heart, and the recording of them, is the most valuable part of education, and sinks more deeply into the composition of the child than a lot of chatter-patter that is hurriedly spread over him in order to pass some examination.

. . . I came to see the then General Montgomery, who commanded the famous 3rd Division, which was at the time spread along more than 30 miles of coast. This was the invasion front. Invasion was said to be imminent. We dined alone – a small party of four or five of us in the Royal Albion Hotel, which was otherwise almost deserted. I looked out of the window at the pier and saw Grenadier Guards sandbagging a kiosk at the end and making loopholes to repel a landing. And this was – perhaps my memory was at fault – the kiosk which in my young days I had always known as devoted to the performing fleas. (*Laughter.*) Well, the particular performing fleas which we were concerned with at the time did not perform.

For that fact we are entitled to rejoice in a great deliverance. We now know the large armies that were massed by the enemy across the narrow strip of sea to invade our islands and we now know how horrible were the plans they had formed for the treatment of our population. The great bulk of the adult males were to be shipped across into Europe and there toiled to death as slaves. The whole country was to be ruined and subjugated to a vile and wicked despotism and tyranny. However, various precautions were vouchsafed us, and the salt water on which our flotillas ruled tireless night and day was not the kind of ditch that could be easily crossed.

The enemy for their venture across the Channel had gathered a great quantity of shipping and had made most elaborate preparations, but the war went back again to the airmen who gave all and to the needy and who, as we have shown last week, are remembered, and who, by their valour and devotion, by their extraordinary skill, by the good preparations that had been made in their training, and the quality of their machines – long before I was responsible – achieved a crowning victory which will ever stand in the annals of these islands.

We then saw the threat of invasion roll away and found ourselves in a position to force upon Hitler that long war which, like all despots, he dreaded and which step by step led to a deserved and frightful conclusion of his life.

Very different is the scene today with people freed from the immediate menace of invasion. On the other hand it is said that peace has her victories no less renowned than war. She certainly has her troubles no less wearisome and burdensome than war. We find ourselves, having fought with all our enemies abroad, confronted now with very hard times and very difficult times. It is quite certain that we shall need all our endurance, fortitude, all our civic knowledge and social discipline and initiative in order to escape from the difficulties which now surround us.

It has often been said that victory may be less pleasing when possessed, but for my part I believe firmly that we shall succeed after periods of hard searching and strenuous effort in bringing our country back again to a full enjoyment of the great inheritance it had won for itself and hoped it had won for all the nations of the world. . . .

Winston S. Churchill: speech
('Winston S. Churchill, His Complete Speeches', volume 7, pages 7528–37)

4 October 1947　　　　　　　　　　　　　　　　　　　　　　Brighton, England

CONSERVATIVE PARTY ANNUAL CONFERENCE ADDRESS

The year that has passed since we last met together at Blackpool has been one of steady and unbroken advance for our Party in every field of political life. Judged by every test that we can apply, judged by the by-elections and the municipal elections, judged by the great increase in our membership, by the strong and robust growth of the Conservative Youth Movement, by the immense improvement achieved by our Party organisation, both local and national, our Party is far stronger than it was this time last year. Much of this is due to the skilful and fostering care of the Party Chairman, Lord Woolton, whose appeal for adequate funds by voluntary subscription, to offset the arbitrary Socialist political levy, I most cordially endorse. I trust he will receive the full support which he needs if he is to discharge the great responsibility we have placed upon him. We have every reason to believe, from all the political indications that we can obtain, that the Socialist Government which, even in the hour of its triumph, did not represent a majority of the electors, is now in a substantial minority, and is ruling without the support and against the wishes of the larger part of the nation. Experience shows that when Governments or Parties turn on the downgrade, they very rarely recover by clinging to office. In the present circumstances, when the consequences of Socialist spite, folly and blundering are about to fall upon every home and business in ever-sharper forms, we can safely say that time is on our side. It does not rest with us when a General Election will take place; but it is quite certain that we should be most imprudent not to be ready for one at any time this year or next. It is therefore my duty to enjoin the utmost activity and exertion upon all our friends and throughout our organisation. Carelessness, levity, sloth, apathy among Conservatives and Liberal-minded men and women constitute, at this time, a failure in service to the country, whose life both as a free community and as a great State is in jeopardy at the present juncture.

This afternoon I shall be speaking mainly of our home problems, but I must register before your eyes the tragedy which has already begun to engulf India. A year ago almost to the day I said to you:

I fear, and I must express my forebodings, that calamity impends upon India. Indian unity created by British rule will swiftly perish, and no one can measure the misery and bloodshed which will overtake these enormous masses of humble, helpless millions, or under what new power their future and destiny will lie. The event will long leave its mark in history. It may well be that Burma will soon suffer the same fate. Most of you will certainly live to see whether I am right or wrong. Sometimes in the past I have not been wrong. I pray that I may be wrong now.

Alas, I was not wrong! You can judge for yourselves how far this forecast has already been fulfilled. In this melancholy tale of the casting away of the British Empire in India and of the misfortunes and slaughter which are falling upon its peoples, all the blame cannot be thrown on one Party. But the Socialist Government on gaining power threw themselves into the task of destroying our long built-up and splendid structure in the East with zeal and gusto, and they certainly have brought widespread ruin, misery and bloodshed upon the Indian masses to an extent no man can measure, by the methods with which they have handled the problem. It is not possible at this moment, I regret to say, for us to do anything to stop the avalanche which has been unloosed. Things are what they are, and their consequences will be what they will be.

Let us return to our own anxieties at home. The Socialists complain that we take every advantage of national misfortune to win popularity for our Party at their expense. When these misfortunes have been brought upon us by their mistakes and incompetence, it is our duty as an Opposition to mark them with censure. But whenever and wherever the Government acts in what we believe is the national interest, we give them our support without any thought of our Party. We have given a steady support to Mr Bevin in his conduct of foreign affairs, and especially in maintaining that close and fraternal association with the United States upon which the peace and safety of the modern world depends. We supported the Government on conscription even when they ran away from the term of service they believed was necessary. We criticised their flight – we even mocked at it – but we did not withdraw our votes from their Bill. We give them our aid in the National Savings Movement because that is an important corrective against the evil of inflation. But where the Government in this grave hour pursue partisan, unhealthy and even pernicious policies, we are bound to attack them and to arouse the people to a sense of their danger.

The last Election, the one of 1945, was fought under conditions the like of which we have never seen before. Ten whole years had passed, of which nearly six were spent in mortal war, since there had been an appeal to the people. There had been no political education going on in the meanwhile. A large proportion of our organisers had gone away to the wars. There was complete neglect of Party education, so far as we were concerned. All was concentrated upon gaining the victory against the common foe. The consequence was that this ancient country, at the height of its fame, was turned bottom upwards – at any rate turned upside down – and is only now recovering its position and its poise. Because of the abnormal and unprecedented conditions prevailing in 1945, I state here to you that the Government have no moral right to deny the electorate a free expression of their opinion at an early date, upon an entirely different situation. I am sure that these problems now crowding upon us, and the economic crisis which is imminent, will not be mastered except by the election of a new House of Commons, representative of the strength and wisdom of the nation. The first step to a national recovery is to get rid of these men, and for that reason on public and patriotic grounds, far above Party, it is our duty to attack the Government by every means in our power, and enable the people at the earliest moment to take a hand in their own affairs.

There is a legend which is spread about – that the Conservative Party are not concerned about the sufferings arising from unemployment, that they are callous about the problems and agony of a man who wishes to work and cannot find a job. In his speech at Southport last week, Mr Ernest Bevin spoke with enthusiasm and admiration about the White Paper on Employment. Here was the great policy which he and his colleagues proclaimed. I was very much interested in these remarks and we looked into the matter. We did not have to look very far because it was in our minds. Now this White Paper was produced under the Government of which I was the head, a Government which, I may remind you, rested upon a Conservative majority in the House of Commons of 150 over all other Parties put together, and it represents our considered view of this problem. If Mr Bevin praises this document he and his friends have no right to criticise us on the grounds that we have no employment policy, because we have far more right than the Socialist Party to claim this proposal as our own. And who do you think prepared this paper which Mr Bevin extols? You have not far to look. It was Lord Woolton who presided over the Cabinet Committee who prepared this White Paper, and he has every right to be considered its original author. To this document, which Lord Woolton drafted and I approved as Prime Minister, and of which Mr Bevin boasts so loudly, the Socialists have not yet added one single coherent idea. There is the answer which you should make to the lying legend which is so laboriously being propagated in all parts of the country. And, mind you, the Russian Bolsheviks have discovered that truth does not matter as long as there is reiteration. They have no difficulty whatever in countering a fact by a lie which, if repeated often enough and loudly enough, becomes accepted by the people. I think it very important that such legends should be dealt with by all speakers in our country until they are swept away and play no part in influencing people who have not followed closely the course of public affairs.

There is another aspect of our affairs to which I must direct your attention. The inroads which are increasingly made upon the customary liberties of the British nation in time of peace become every month more serious. Many of them wear the aspect of the Totalitarian State – Nazi or Communist or Fascist, they are all the same, there is no difference between them at all. Any of them would be fatal to all we care about in the world. The kinds of restrictions of liberties which are now being developed wear the aspect of that Totalitarian State against which we have warred and from which we thought we had saved the world. Every effort is being made to prevent people from going abroad – which is always a sure sign of bad government at home. Every effort is taken to cut down the full reporting of events by the newspapers through manipulation of the paper shortage. The Government have now begun opening letters in the post on the pretext that people may send their valuables out of the country. They have asserted their power by wartime regulations, newly emphasized by a Parliamentary Statute, to deprive the British people in full time of peace, of their right to choose or change their occupation as they see fit. The Labour Exchanges, which I founded nearly forty years ago to help people find employment and move from one job to another – if the Socialist policy is capable of effective enforcement, which I greatly doubt – may now become the instrument of industrial coercion for all classes, even for those people who could easily find employment for themselves at work in which they are proficient.

Confiscatory taxation has been applied to wealth to an extent only practised in Communist countries. All our daily life is increasingly subjected to ten thousand Regulations and Controls, in the enforcement of which a multitude of officials, larger than any army we have ever maintained in time of peace, is continually employed. Hundreds of new crimes have been invented for which imprisonment or penal servitude may be inflicted. In fact, on every side and by every means the machinery for the totalitarian grip upon British society is being built upon and perfected. One could almost wonder whether the Government do not reconcile themselves to the economic misfortunes of our country, to which their mismanagement has so notably contributed, because these misfortunes give the pretext of establishing even more controls and an even larger bureaucracy. They make mistakes which make things worse. As things get worse they claim more power to set them right. Thus they move ever nearer to the scheme of the All-powerful State, in which the individual is a helpless serf or pawn.

And here I come to the remark of the Prime Minister last Saturday when he said, 'Some do not understand the amount of Freedom which we rightly *give* to an Opposition to criticise.' The word that struck me in this sentence is the word 'give'. So it is Mr Attlee who *gives* us our rights to freedom of speech and political action, and we are invited to be grateful for his magnanimity. But I thought these same rights had been won for the British people beyond dispute or challenge by our forebears in bygone generations. These were the rights for which, to quote a famous Whig phrase, 'Hampden[1] died in the field and Sydney[2] on the scaffold.' And now it is Mr Attlee who thinks he has given them to us. Let him cherish these illusions, but let him not be so foolish as to try to take them away. Well was it said, 'the price of freedom is eternal vigilance'. Small steps and graduated stages are the means by which, in the history of many countries, the freedom of great and noble races has been slowly frittered and whittled away.

In the deepening trough into which we are falling the Government have handed over the solution of our economic problems to Sir Stafford Cripps. Well he is certainly the ablest brain in the Administration – at least we have one first-class intelligence now brooding upon our affairs. He starts on his new task, I am sorry to say, with an unfortunate record. When he appeals for a supreme national effort to improve the export trade, we cannot forget that in his Socialist prejudice he destroyed the Liverpool Cotton Exchange which, apart from its services to the cotton industry, gained us between one and two millions sterlings'-worth a year of dollars or of hard foreign currency, and that if perhaps five thousand men laboured to their utmost strength in the export business year after year, they could hardly repair this annual loss, inflicted by Sir Stafford Cripps's personal intervention. Nevertheless if Sir Stafford will devote his keen intellect to the revival of British economic life, and will rise superior to the strange quirks of mind to which he has so long been a slave – it is never too late to mend – he will receive all possible help from us and may even leave his name upon a worthy page in the story of the British people.

I must make it clear that we Conservatives do not believe there is a quack cure-all for the trouble and tribulations of human life. We are quite sure the nationalization of our industries will not make them profitable to the country or satisfactory for their workers. This is already being proved by the hard teachings of experience. It is not the interest of the ordinary wage-earner to be the Servant of the State, to be the servant, that is, of an all-powerful employer centralizing the whole management of nationalized industries in the public Departments of Whitehall. It is far better for the workers to be able to deal with private employers through their Trade Unions Organisations. It was the Trade Unions whom Benjamin Disraeli and the Conservative Party gave strong support to in 1875 by the Acts which in the words of Sidney and Beatrice Webb – great philosophers whom I knew in my younger days – 'finally recognized collective bargaining with all its necessary accompaniments by the law of the land'. The Trade Unions are a long-established and

---

[1] John Hampden, 1595–1643. Educated at Thame School, Oxfordshire; Magdalen College, Oxford; Inner Temple. Married, 1619, Elizabeth Symeon. MP for Grampound, Cornwall, 1621–5; for Wendover, Buckinghamshire, 1625–43. Challenged authority of King Charles I. Killed in the First Civil War.

[2] Algernon Sidney, 1622–83. Cavalry Officer, Parliamentary forces, 1644. MP (Whig) for Cardiff, 1645–53. Delegate to Sweden and Denmark, 1659–60. Exiled from England, 1660–77. Implicated in the Rye House Plot to assassinate King Charles and Prince James, 1683; convicted of treason and beheaded. Author of several works of political philosophy.

essential part of our national life. Like other human institutions they have their faults and weaknesses. At the present time they have more influence upon the Government of the country, and less control over their own members, than ever before. But we take our stand by these pillars of our British society as it has gradually been developed and evolved itself, of the right of individual labouring men or women to adjust their wages and conditions by collective bargaining, including the right to strike; and the right of everyone, with due notice and consideration for others, to choose or change his occupation if he thinks he can better himself and his family. I welcome the growing number of Trade Unionists who are openly declaring their adherence to our Conservative faith. I trust that they will take a full part in the activities of their branches and lodges, not as Party men but as good Trade Unionists, determined to keep their movement free of domination by any Party, creed, sect or faction.

Let me speak now of our own Party course of action. I have followed with great attention all that has taken place in this Conference and have most carefully considered what I have been told. In a long and varied life I have constantly watched and tried to measure the moods and the inspirations of our British people. There is no foe they will not face. There is no hardship they cannot endure. Whether the test be sharp and short or long and wearisome, they can take it. What they do not forgive is false promises and vain boastings. It is far better for a candidate to say to a British constituency: 'If you vote for me, a hard time lies before you, I will be your faithful champion' – far better to say that than to promise Utopia with the moon thrown in. The people are very alert and intelligent nowadays. They know perfectly well whether a Party or a candidate is simply angling for their votes or whether he is an honest man, ready to give loyal service in a period of stress and difficulty which cannot be precisely measured. The times in which we live are much too serious for politicians to make audacious bids for votes. Our liberties, our honour, the revival of our status in the world, the everyday freedom and welfare of the broad masses of our people, the whole varied and free structure of British social life, our very sustenance – our daily bread – all these are in peril. A distinction must be drawn between an electioneering programme and the broad principles of the Party policy. I am sure it would not be wise for us to bind ourselves to a rigid programme of what exactly we should do if the responsibility for facing the crises into which we have been led devolved upon the Conservative party. In this world of sin and woe one has frequently to be on guard against traps laid by the enemy or by doubtful friends. We cannot tell what misfortunes are going to fall upon our country. We cannot tell when a new House of Commons will be chosen or what its composition will be. I cannot think of anything more foolish than that, without the power to act, or the machinery of Government at our disposal, we should commit ourselves to a detailed programme of executive action. Certainly, while I lead the Party, we shall not attempt to bribe our way into office by promises we know we could never fulfil, or try to outbid a Socialist party in their levelling policies. We shall never tell the British people that if they vote for us all they will have to do is enjoy a good and easy time.

I do not envy the man, whoever he is, who has to face the problems of British survival in the next few years. But I am sure that his power to help the nation in its dire need would be crippled, if not destroyed, if he were committed beforehand to a programme of pledges and promises which he would be no more able to redeem than the unfortunate Mr Attlee and Mr Morrison. Look at these unhappy men. Two years ago they romped into office as if it were part of our Victory joy-day. Now they are found out, with all their vain assurances. They are exposed. They are in the grim and disagreeable position of having promised blessings and given burdens, of having promised prosperity and given misery, of having promised to abolish poverty and only abolished wealth, of having vaunted their new world and only wrecked the old.

For all these reasons and many others, I have refused altogether, in full agreement with my colleagues, to commit our Party to a definite and detailed programme. In our Industrial Charter, which is the official policy of the Party, we have shown quite plainly the broad democratic view we take of current affairs and the many forms of social activity which we espouse and encourage in our free, tolerant, and progressive Party association. This able document was prepared over many weeks by a Committee of experienced Conservative former Ministers, who kept closely in touch with Conservative Members of the House of Commons, and, after many discussions and amendments, it was officially approved by me at what we call a Consultative Committee, six months ago. It must be a great satisfaction to Mr Butler, who presided over the Committee, that proposals so varied, and in many cases controversial, should have received the overwhelming, indeed unanimous, approval of this, the greatest of all our Conferences we have ever held. You have also heard from my trusted friend and comrade of so many years – and such years – Mr Eden, a description with which I cordially agree, of the seven main objectives towards which, whether in office or opposition we shall strive to make our way. I am in full agreement and I will now myself put the case before you, in my own way and in my own words.

The scheme of society for which we stand is the establishment and maintenance of a basic minimum standard of life and labour below which a man or woman of goodwill, however old and weak, will not be allowed to fall. The food they receive, the prices they have to pay for basic necessities, the homes they live in, must be the first care of the State, and must have priority over all other peace-time requirements. Once that standard is being faithfully and even rigorously worked for by all concerned, and without prejudice to it, we propose (if and when we have the power) to set the people free as quickly as possible from the controls and restrictions which now beset their daily life. We propose to sweep away with sturdy strokes the vast encumbrance of regulations and penalties which are today preventing our people from making a good living in their island home. Once the basic standard has been established we shall liberate the energies, the genius, the contrivance of the British nation from the paralysing and humiliating thraldom in which they are now plunged. Above the minimum basic standard there will be free competition. Everyone will be free to make the best of himself without jealousy or spite by all the means that honour, and the long-respected laws and customs of our country allow. Where it is still possible for monopolistic abuses of any kind to restrain the flow of trade or to injure the living standards of our people, the Law should provide adequate remedy and redress, and we should take steps to see that this was the case. In our Industrial Charter we have set out clearly the lines upon which action to prevent such abuses should proceed. But our main objects will be the liberation and energizing of all wealth-producing enterprises without clogging the efforts or grudging the prizes of those who are successful in what must ever be the battle of life. There on the Home Front is our theme and our cause.

Once the basic standard below which we will not allow our people to fall has been established, and the supply of basic necessities assured to the least fortunate of our fellow-countrymen, the price mechanism must be allowed to work again in accordance with the well-understood principle of the laws of supply and demand. For this purpose certain basic steps, which I will state to you in general terms, and looking at the problem from the present date, are obviously needed. First of all, the distortion of our finances, for which the war and, after that curse, the Chancellor of the Exchequer, is responsible, must be corrected. It must be corrected in a simple manner. It is astounding how simple some of these things are. The wasteful and needless expenditure by the Government which we see on all sides must be reduced by several hundred million pounds a year, and a large part of this, when saved, must be immediately given in relief of taxation in such a way as to increase the incentives to diligence, thrift, ingenuity and profit-making. I use that last word advisedly. How do you think are forty-seven millions, or fifty, as I am told by the actuaries we shall be in thirty years time at the present rate, to live in this small island unless there is good and thrifty housekeeping at every stage, and unless our industries and businesses are run at a profit and not at a loss?

To effect the necessary reductions in expenditure it will be necessary to curtail our wasteful expenditure abroad. Once the Zionist cause was deserted by the Socialists, I did not shrink from advocating our laying the responsibility for Palestine at the feet of the United Nations. This alone would have saved, if done at the time – I recommended it at the time – and when it is carried into force it will save us – nearly a hundred million pounds a year. This mismanagement of Germany and the vast sums of money squandered thereupon since our victory, is a disgrace to those Ministers responsible. Our policy should be to make the Germans keep themselves, and earn their own living in domestic freedom with whatever help we can give them, and in accordance with a treaty of peace which will make sure they are permanently kept disarmed. The method of large-scale State-buying of food and raw materials which in so many instances has led to grievous waste must be closely reviewed, searchingly scrutinised, and due recourse should be had once again to the flexible trade channels and market processes upon the basis of which our crowded population had reached before the war a higher standard of living than existed anywhere in Europe.

The restoration of our finances must carry with it the maintenance of the buying power of the pound sterling in terms of goods and services. Far from reducing Family Allowances, we must safeguard them by preventing the pounds, shillings and pence in which they are paid from becoming what Mr Arthur Greenwood (whose departure I regret on personal grounds) so revealingly described as 'meaningless symbols'. The workplace should have real wages and not sham wages. All social reform, whether by insurance or State grants and subsidies, which is not founded upon a stable medium of internal exchange, becomes swindle and a fraud. This is particularly cruel and unjust when applied to old people, pensioners of all kinds, and those who have practised self-denial and thrift all through their lives in order to provide for their declining years. Along all these paths the Conservative or Tory Party, aided by their ever-growing Liberal and Liberal-minded allies, will cut their way back inch by inch and mile by mile to the main highroad of public sanity, which will lead after long and hard marches to freedom, prosperity and abundance.

Naturally, in the position in which we now stand, and I trust as a settled and permanent policy, we must develop our own agriculture on a very large scale. We must grow a much larger proportion of our food in this island. By this means we can, not only reduce our need for foreign imports, but make a more healthy and balanced life for our whole community by adding to commercial activity a flourishing and fertile countryside. Even the Socialist Ministers now recognise the mistakes they made in denying the houses for agricultural labourers to live in; in exporting so much precious agricultural machinery and spare parts; and in their haphazard, zig-zag changes of policy in food production. Is it not a scandalous confession that they should now be planning to reach only in four years time the level of agricultural production that ruled in 1945 under war conditions and the administration of Mr Hudson who is on the platform here? An active and expanding agriculture is vital to the recovery and even to the survival of our country.

Why should we suppose these problems are insoluble? The productive capacity of the human race is greater this afternoon than it ever was before. The improvement and multiplication of agricultural machinery of all kinds and the use of chemical manures and improved methods of cultivation have thrown open to the whole world surer methods of obtaining its daily bread than ever existed before. There are more ships afloat on the sea this afternoon than there have ever been at any previous time. Why then should we be told that we must face for long and indefinite periods a shrinking and contracting dietary and standard of living? The shortage from which we and some other nations are suffering and are going to suffer is not the result of any failure by nature or science. It is the result of ignorant, clumsy, malicious hands being laid upon the free, flexible means of production, distribution, and exchange, upon which the present populations of various countries have come into existence.

Why, in the same way, should it be suggested that we, in this island, cannot have at least as good a life all round as we had before the war, and the means of making constant progressive improvement upon it? It is quite true that we exerted ourselves to the point of exhaustion in the war. The very efficiency of the National Government, as I mentioned the other day, threw the last reserves of our strength into action. But actually, when we get up each morning, what, I ask, has happened to curtail our resources, provided, of course that we all work hard as we did before? What is it that we have lost? I am aware of only two reasons. We have given to the common cause half of our foreign investments. They are gone. But that is a loss which could certainly be made up by reasonable thrift and self-denial, and by the progress of science, which is unceasing; and it in no way explains the stagnation into which we are sinking.

The second reason is this. We are told we have to pay many millions a year across the exchange in order to pay back countries, like Egypt and India and some others, for the debts we incurred wilfully for defending them from Japanese, German or Italian invasion. There, assuredly, I consider we should present our counter-claim. We should say: Here is our bill for the services we rendered them; because there is no doubt that on any fair accounting, it is they and not we who are the debtors. If allowance is made for these two factors and they are dealt with in a resolute manner, there is not the slightest reason why we should not regain both the standard of living and the liberties of trade and enterprise which were so long our pride and our means of national greatness. Do not, therefore, believe these fantastic tales that the modern world with all its science, is broke and ruined. Crazy doctrines, clumsy fingers, Meddlesome Matties, vicious and morbid trends of policy are manufacturing shortages and misery by their vice and folly. It is not nature which has failed, but bad policies and foolish men who stand between the masses of the people and that full fruition of their toil which is their right and which is their due.

I have now reached the culmination to the lengthy argument I have ventured to submit to you in these grave times which I felt deserved most serious statement; and I give to you what the Conservative Party will ever regard as the first of all its objectives – the enduring unity of the British Empire and of those free Commonwealths which we alone have known how to found, and whose devotion to the old Motherland is our chief abiding glory. We are not prepared to barter away the Imperial Preferences which play an essential part in the integrity of our world-wide system. Nor do we believe that such action will be necessary. Even in the stress of war, even at the time – the grim time – of the Atlantic Charter, and on every subsequent occasion with President Roosevelt, I always carefully safeguarded the principle of Imperial Preference and this in no way prevented the growth of an ever-warmer and more intimate friendship between us and between our two countries, as has also been mentioned at the Conference, as is well known.

I am also an earnest advocate of a United Europe and of the important part which Britain must play in its achievement. Unless we were tied down to the alternative of a choice between two rigid customs unions in the full technical sense of the word, there is nothing incompatible in these aims, even in the purely economic field. I was very glad to hear how Lord Winterton was speaking to the Conference yesterday upon this subject. I am convinced, and I do not speak without some knowledge both of Europe and of the United States, that it is possible to reconcile our position as the centre of the British Empire with full development of close economic relations with all the friendly countries of Europe. Canada's participation in the policy of Empire Preferences has never stood in the way of those special economic relations with her great neighbour which geography and the structure of her economy have encouraged. This was pointed out to you by Mr Amery, so long a devoted pioneer in this field. Nor need either our Empire or our European economic policy conflict with that of the United States. On any broad interpretation of the generous policy set in motion by Mr Marshall, the Secretary of State, agreement can certainly be reached. The Republic of the United States, with whom we stand shoulder to shoulder on all the fundamental issues of human freedom, is as much concerned with the recovery of our Commonwealth and Empire as she is with that of Europe and I doubt not that a harmonious adjustment of the whole problem can be achieved, if it is handled in the right way and on the right occasion.

For my own part I will be content with nothing less. I strive for all three great systems – the British Commonwealth of Nations, the European Union and the fraternal association with the United States. I believe that all are possible and that our island, at the centre of the sea-ways with all the vast resources of sea-borne and air-borne communications at its disposal, with all the services it has rendered to the onerous causes of mankind, this island will become the vital link between them all.

October 1947

Sarah Churchill to Winston S. Churchill and Clementine Churchill
(Churchill papers, 1/42)[1]

5 October 1947   Rome

Darling Mamma and Papa,

Mary M. will bring you this letter. It is lovely here, for it is not too hot, and I find it as lovely and enchanting as ever. The work goes slowly – not my side of it!! I have done the monologue and rough adaption and we have cut 300 yards out of the film!! That is an enormous amount and the picture will gain enormously I'm sure – beyond recognition when it is in English, of course we cannot cut or alter the hero but anyway I hope one day you will see an English version just to be surprised how fast moving and simplified we have made it. But all the organisation crawls – the film belays to too many people and it is impossible to contact them all at the same time and get a decision out of them. Still I plod on. Every other day I abandon it – and every other take heart again. An air of oppression hangs over life here. Whether it means anything – I do not know – but wherever you go now the walls and pavements and streets are marked with the hammer and sickle. The other night I went for a walk – near the Forum – through all the sunken ruins of Rome. In the moonlight and shadow it was mysterious and beautiful – and odd effects of the moonlight gave the ruins substance, I had been reading 'Graziella' by Lamartine.[2] In describing Rome he finishes by saying '*Je ne sentais aucun besoin de société. Je jouissais même de mon isolement. Rome et mon âme me suffisaient!*'[3] Well I was feeling like that!! Very elated and completely happy – I had to cross the large empty space of Piazza Veolia – There like a big black hideous spider drawn right in the middle of the square was an ever more menacing hammer and sickle – a stone's throw away – overlooking it – was Mussolini's balcony. How can I describe suddenly how sinister and ominous the whole scene became – I had been walking in a dream world of sunken cities and gardens – but here was the world of fact – unhappiness hunger and violence. You will say they were not hungry under Mussolini – no – but there was oppression and ultimate discord and his medieval palace looked cruel and forbidding. Everyone here is resigned to war – they will believe nothing but that our restrictions are necessary only in as much as we are preparing for war.

There have been one or two communist demonstrations – but I must say – they are completely quiet. The Romans appear quite apathetic and it's hard to know what they are thinking.

---

[1] This letter was handwritten and ends with a drawing of a donkey.
[2] Alphonse de Lamartine, 1790–1869. Bodyguard to King Louis XVIII, 1814. Married, 1820, Maria Ann Birch. Member, National Assembly, Second Republic of France, 1848. Author and poet. Works include *Méditations poétiques* (1820); *Histoire des Girondins* (1847).
[3] 'I have no need for society. I have enjoyed my isolation. Rome and my soul are enough for me.'

They do not appear hungry – I have looked long and hard – under a brown skin of course you could hide galloping consumption I suppose – but the children and the women and men all look well fed – yet they talk of winter starvation – and everyday strikes are threatened and all because of one thing – the cost of food and houses. I eat in small restaurants. Even a simple meal for one person is 8 shillings – I don't understand it. The shops are full of everything butter, oil, sugar – things the poor English have almost forgotten. Perhaps the genius of Communist propaganda is creating discontent. I am very sad to have to report that the film world is very bad – any picture with the slightest inclination or anything even that could be interpreted as left tendency is snapped up at once and framed by them. It's sad because it makes of an art – that should be free to relate fact – good or bad – a tool of propagandists. Incidentally the communist party's banner is a portrait of Garibaldi.[1] At night to scare us they chalk up the hammer and sickle – but in daylight for election purposes they prefer using the portrait of a patriot to mislead the masses.

A band of small children have just passed by singing the International!!

Well forgive these hurried scribbled impressions, but you will get this letter quicker – and this time a little before I arrive myself! I think I will be here at least another fortnight. Anyway I will let you know. Wow wow wow darlings. Much love all.

Winston S. Churchill to Ernest Bevin
(*Churchill papers, 2/55*)

6 October 1947

My dear Ernest,

Thank you very much for your letter of September 30[2] about Mikolajczyk. I do not see how anything better can be done at this moment than what you propose. I shall certainly take your advice about publicity. At the same time, if this man is murdered I think we should go far to mark our horror of such an act.

I have sent a copy of your letter to Anthony.

---

[1] Giuseppe Garibaldi, 1807–1882. Italian nationalist, general and radical politician. Born in Nice, France. Merchant captain, 1832. Participated in a mutiny, 1834; escaped to France and lived in exile in South America, 1836–48. Led Uruguayan Navy against Juan Manuel de Rosas, dictator of Argentina, 1842. Married, 1842, Anna 'Anita' Maria Ribeiro da Silva: three children. Elected Deputy, Roman Assembly, 1849. Conquered Sicily and Naples on behalf of King Victor Emmanuel II, 1860; Venice, 1866. Famously wrote: 'If ever England, your native country, should be so circumstanced as to require the help of an ally, cursed be that Italian who would not step forward with me in her defence' (letter to Joseph Cowen, later MP for Newcastle-on-Tyne, 12 April 1854).

[2] Reproduced above (pp. 789–90).

Paul Reynaud to Winston S. Churchill
(Churchill papers, 2/57)

7 October 1947

Mon cher et éminent ami,

L'article que le Président Herriot vient de publier dans la *Revue de Paris*, dans lequel il dépeint avec beaucoup de noblesse quelle fut mon attitude à Bordeaux, au sujet de l'armistice, répond péremptoirement aux attaques publiées contre moi en Amérique, sur l'inspiration de Léger. Je ne crois pas inutile cependant de vous communiquer une addition qui figurera dans l'édition définitive de mon livre, à la page 390 du tome II.

Je tiens, par ailleurs, à vous signaler que n'ayant pas le procès-verbal français de la réunion du Conseil suprême tenu à Tours le 13 juin 1940, je me suis adressé au Foreign Office qui a bien voulu me communiquer le procès-verbal établi par votre collaborateur en me demandant seulement de ne pas publier le texte intégral. C'est ce que j'ai fait, en me tenant aussi près du texte et en ajoutant seulement les quelques phrases nécessaires pour expliquer mon attitude.

J'ai pensé que ces indications pouvaient avoir quel qu'intérêt pour les Mémoires que vous allez publier.

Veuillez agréer, mon cher et éminent ami, l'expression de mes sentiments dévoués.[1]

Winston S. Churchill to Sir Alan Lascelles
(Churchill papers, 2/171)

7 October 1947

My dear Alan,

I send you herewith a few suggestions about the King's Speech on the unveiling of King George V's Memorial. I also return the first draft which you sent me, on which I made a few recommendations.

I thought the original draft excellent in every way, and as you will see my suggestions are, with one exception, only verbal. The exception is with

---

[1] 'My dear and distinguished friend,
  The article that President Herriot has just published in *La Revue de Paris*, in which he depicted my attitude on the subject of the armistice in Bordeaux with great nobility, decisively answers the attacks on me published in America, inspired by [Alexis] Léger. I do not, however, think it worthless to bring to your attention an addition included in the final edition of my book, on page 390 of Volume II.
  I also want to tell you that because I did not have the French minutes of the Supreme Council held in Tours on 13 June 1940, I contacted the Foreign Office, who kindly sent me the minutes taken by your adviser, asking only that I would not publish the full text. So that is what I did, keeping close to the text and adding only the few phrases necessary to explain my view.
  I thought this information might be of some interest for the Memoirs that you are going to publish.
  Please accept, my dear and distinguished friend, the expression of my devoted sentiments.'

reference to the multiple kingship, which I consider to have been a great and historical event, and an enormous addition to the prestige of the Crown. It would be well, I think, to consult a Minister on it as it is a point of substance.

I am much honoured that the King should have let me see the draft.

Princess Elizabeth to Winston S. Churchill
(Churchill papers, 2/148)[1]

13 October 1947   Buckingham Palace

Dear Mr Churchill,

I have today received the beautifully bound volumes of your book, for which I would like to thank you very much indeed.

I am so delighted to have them, and I really cannot thank you enough for giving me such a lovely wedding present.

I am most touched by your very kind thought and by your good wishes, which I very much appreciate.

President Harry S Truman to Winston S. Churchill
(Churchill papers, 2/158)[2]

14 October 1947   The White House
Washington DC

My dear Winston,

It was kind and thoughtful to send me the message by Mr Douglas.[3]

The world is facing serious problems and it has been my lot to have to make decisions on a great many of them. Our Russian friends seem most ungrateful for the contribution which your great country and mine made to save them. I sometimes think perhaps we made a mistake – and then I remember Hitler. He had no heart at all. I believe that Joe Stalin has one but the Polit bureau won't let him use it.

Vyshinski has assured my re-election I think, although the voters would do me a very great favor if they retired me. No one man can carry the burden of the Presidency and do it right. But I have a good team now.

Your Fulton speech becomes more nearly a prophecy every day. I hope conditions will warrant your paying us another visit. I certainly enjoyed your stay here immensely.

You are very kind to me, and I think, give me too much credit. But I like it – particularly from you.

[1] This letter was handwritten.
[2] This letter was handwritten.
[3] Reproduced above (p. 781).

May you continue to enjoy health and happiness and a long life – the world needs you now as badly as ever.

Winston S. Churchill: speech
('Winston S. Churchill, His Complete Speeches', volume 7, pages 7538–40)

14 October 1947   Broadcast to New York

THE AL SMITH[1] MEMORIAL

This gathering has for its purpose a salutation to the memory of Al Smith by those who knew him or who have carefully studied his character and life's work. I had the pleasure to meet him several times and enjoyed long talks with him on men and things. In those days he had been four times Governor of the State of New York and had been defeated as candidate for the Presidency. He spoke to me, not without feeling, of the lack of continuity in American public life for party leaders. The unsuccessful candidate for the Presidency, although he commands the hopes and esteem of nearly half the nation, often has no public sphere in which he can carry forward all the prestige and allegiances he has gathered in a nationwide campaign. With us, over here, it is different, and in many cases a Prime Minister falls from power only to walk four or five yards across the floor of the House of Commons and carry forward his work as Leader of the Opposition. I have a great respect for the American Constitution, but in this instance, I must confess that I definitely prefer the British system, or perhaps I should say custom, for we have no system.

I had followed Al Smith's contest for the Presidency with keen interest and sympathy. I was in the fullest agreement with his attitude on Prohibition. I even suggested to him a slogan – 'All for Al and Al for All'. He certainly was a man of the highest quality of brain and heart, who rose under the free institutions of America, as anyone has a right to do, from humble beginnings to high, long, and successful executive office. To be chosen four times Governor remains a record for the Empire State. His devotion to the religion he had learned as a child was perhaps a hindrance to him in a political appeal to the vast and varied American democracy, but it was the comfort and aspiration of his life, and his many private virtues and gaiety of nature and personal charm hung on this golden thread. He loved his fellow men and was capable of giving them the noblest forms of service and sacrifice. Long may his memory be cherished in the mighty city of which he is a shining and faithful son.

Let me turn from this great American to the Causes which I am sure, were

---

[1] Alfred Emanuel Smith, 1873–1944. Married, 1900, Catherine Ann Dunn. Member (Dem.), New York State Assembly, 1903–15. Sheriff, New York County, 1915. President, Board of Aldermen, Greater New York, 1917. Governor, New York, 1918–20, 1923–8. US Presidential candidate (Dem.), 1928.

he with us now, he would have made his own. We have travelled a long way in opinion since I spoke at Fulton under the auspices of the President eighteen months ago, and many things which were startling or disputable then have now become the foundation of dominant Anglo-American thought. During all this time the Soviet Government have poured out, through their radio in twenty-six languages, and in all the speeches made on their behalf, an unceasing stream of abuse upon the Western World, and they have accompanied this virulent propaganda by every action which could prevent the world settling down into a durable peace or the United Nations Organisation playing its part as a great world instrument to prevent war. Indeed the Conferences at Lake Success[1] – perhaps prematurely named – have become a forum in which reproaches and insults are hurled at each other by the greatest States, hurled at each other for all mankind to hear if they care to listen. But some of them are getting tired.

I have been much puzzled to know why it is that the Soviet Government have taken this violently aggressive line. From an external point of view it seems so foolish that we wonder what is the real motive behind it. I cannot believe that it is the prelude to war. These fourteen men in the Kremlin, who rule with despotic power the vast populations and territories of which they are the masters, are very capable and well-informed. If their minds were set on war, I cannot believe that they would not lull the easy-going democracies into a false sense of security. Hitler was a master of this and always, before or during some act of aggression, he uttered soothing words or made non-aggression pacts. Therefore, while I cannot exclude the danger of war, I do not think the violent abuse which the Soviet Government and their Communist adherents all over the world lavish on all existing forms of civilization, is necessarily a sign of danger. It is more likely, in my opinion, being used for internal purposes. If there are only fourteen men, all eyeing one another and deeply conscious of the enormous populations they hold in chains of mind and spirit enforced by terror, it may well be that they think it pays them and helps them to perpetrate their rule by representing to the otherwise blind-folded masses of the brave and good-hearted Russian people, that the Soviet Government stands between them and a repetition of the horror of invasion which they withstood when it came, so manfully. I devoutly hope that this view of mine may prove to be correct.

But the United States and the western democracies of Europe would fail to profit by the hard experiences they have undergone if they did not take every measure of prudent, defensive preparation which is open to them. While taking all necessary steps and above all, maintaining a solid front, we should not however be hasty in abandoning our hope in the United Nations Organisation. It may be that the Soviet Government and their Communist Fifth

---

[1] Lake Success, NY, location of UN HQ, 1947–52.

Columns in so many countries will, at some moment or other, quit the United Nations Organisation. Then there would be what is called 'Two Worlds'. We should all be sorry to see that, but if one of these worlds is far more powerful than the other, and is equally vigilant and is also sincerely desirous of maintaining peace, there is no reason why a two-world system should lead to war. Great wars come when both sides believe they are more or less equal, when each thinks it has a good chance of victory. No such conditions of equality would be established if the Soviet Government and their Communist devotees were to make a separate organisation of their own. Indeed the two great systems might even begin to be polite to one another and speak again the measured language of diplomacy. Therefore it seems to me we should not be unduly depressed if the Soviet–Communist forces should decide to part company with the World Organization. Certainly we ought not to give away anything which is essential to our security in order to persuade them to linger with us for the purpose of paralysing the joint harmonious action of three-quarters of mankind.

I must now say a word about my own country and yours. First of all I ask you to pay no attention to the many insulting things which are said about the United States by the Communists and crypto-Communists and fellow-travellers in our Island. Their interest and their instructions naturally lead them to say everything in their power to make division between us. You should completely ignore their taunts and jeers. For instance, I noticed in the newspapers bitter words from a Mr Priestley[1] (Editor's note:[2] Mr J. B. Priestley, the author and dramatist, had written in an American magazine: 'The most powerful Government on earth seems to have no continuing policy, no tradition to guide it, and is clearly swayed by what is largely an irresponsible sensation-loving Press and an electorate that can be stampeded like cattle. Imagine our feelings. It is like being locked in a house with a whimsical drunken giant.'), who gained some acceptance in the war from the fact that we used him for broadcasting purposes. He has no influence. No American should allow himself to be irritated or offended by such diatribes. They do not represent in the slightest degree the feeling of the British nation or, I may say, of His Majesty's Government. We have a Socialist Government – you may have heard of that – and I am the Leader of the Conservative Party in opposition to it – perhaps you have heard of that, too. But I can tell you that there is no country in Europe which makes a firmer or more solid front against Soviet and Communist encroachments than Great Britain. There is no doubt whatever that the Government and the overwhelming mass of British people, at home and throughout our Commonwealth, if any great issue should arise affecting human freedom, would

---

[1] John Boynton Priestley, 1894–1984. Educated at Trinity Hall, Cambridge. Devon Rgt, 1914–19. UK delegate to UNESCO conferences, 1946–7. Freeman, City of Bradford, 1973. OM, 1977. Author of 27 novels and numerous plays, political works, essays and television scripts.

[2] The parenthetical note was added by Robert Rhodes James, editor of *His Complete Speeches*.

act with the United States in the same solidarity and fraternal intimacy which has, so lately given us victory against the combined dictatorships of Germany, Italy and Japan.

I believe that Britain will rise again with even higher influence in the world than she now exercises. I work for the revival of a United Europe. I am sure that the English-speaking world can weather all the storms that blow, and that above all these a world instrument, in Al Smith's words 'to weld the democracies together', can be erected, which will be all powerful, so long as it is founded on freedom, justice and mercy – and is well armed.

Lady Rhys-Williams to Winston S. Churchill
(Churchill papers, 2/64)

14 October 1947
Confidential

Dear Mr Churchill,

Mr Harrod[1] came to see me yesterday, and we had a full discussion about the political situation. He has made up his mind that the Liberal Party should collaborate with the Conservatives, and proposes to write a memorandum setting out his views, and insist upon its consideration by the Party Committee, of which he is a member. If he can get no support, he told me that he would resign. I urged him not to resign, but rather to fight hard to carry his point, and to give them no peace about it.

He told me, which is quite amazing, that the Party Committee has not met for three months! When I was on it we used to meet every fortnight or oftener. It seems then the work of the Liberal 'Shadow Cabinet' is becoming as shadowy as everything else about the Party.

I also discussed the possibility of his standing at Stoke Newington, with Conservative support, should the bye-election materialise. He did not definitely commit himself, but I felt sure that he would agree.

I am also enclosing a report from Mr Huntley Sinclair, the Liberal Candidate for the Western Isles, who has just been to Glasgow to a dinner given by a group of Liberals, Liberal Nationals and Conservatives, who are trying to arrange for pacts in the Scottish constituencies. Mr Sinclair (who is Hon Treasurer of the Liberal International, and a member of the 'Design for Freedom' Committee) is evidently hoping that he will not be opposed by a Conservative; but I have written to tell him that he can hardly expect that no Conservative should stand against him unless he declares himself as your supporter.

[1] (Henry) Roy Forbes Harrod, 1900–78. Educated at New College, Oxford. Fellow, Modern History and Economics, Christ Church, Oxford, 1922–67. Married, 1938, Wilhelmine Cresswell. Wrote biographies of John Maynard Keynes (1951) and Lord Cherwell (1959), as well as many works of economic theory.

Winston S. Churchill to Lady Rhys-Williams
(Churchill papers, 2/64)

15 October 1947

Dear Lady Rhys-Williams,
Thank you very much for your various letters, which I have most carefully considered. In order to prevent misunderstanding I ought to make it clear to you that I am not in any position at the present time to offer Conservative support to Mr Roy Harrod, should he stand as a Liberal for Stoke Newington. I have no idea what the Conservative Party decision would be there. I shall be very glad to hear further from you. You know how much I sympathize with your general attitude.

Sir Alan Lascelles to Winston S. Churchill
(Churchill papers, 2/171)

17 October 1947   Buckingham Palace

My dear Mr Churchill,
The King wishes me to tell you how particularly grateful he is for the help which you so kindly gave him over the draft of His Majesty's speech at the Unveiling of the King George V Statue next Wednesday. His Majesty has adopted all the excellent suggestions which you made, though after, as you suggested, taking Ministerial advice, he has re-cast the 'golden circle' paragraph, though he retains, I am glad to say, these two words.[1]

Randolph S. Churchill to Winston S. Churchill
(Churchill papers, 1/45)

20 October 1947   New Zealand

My dearest Papa
Miss Buck telegraphed me yesterday that you had been enquiring for details about my controversy with the Waterside Workers in New Zealand. I gather she has already sent you a copy of the article which occasioned the dispute. I enclose copies of the letters which passed between me and Mr Hill, the Union Secretary.

This controversy and still more numerous attacks made on me by local

---

[1] The relevant portion of the speech reads: 'Throughout his reign my father served the Constitution with an unswerving loyalty. It is fitting that his statue should stand here in the heart of London between the Abbey, where he was crowned, and the Houses of Parliament, where the business of the State was conducted in his name, and where by the Statute of Westminster the Crown became the golden circle within which all the free Dominions of the British Commonwealth were united.'

Communists for being a 'war monger' and a 'Spiv' have stirred up a lot of interest; as a result of which, my lectures have been better attended here than in Australia. It was only planned that I should do six in New Zealand, but as a result of the general interest evoked, I am doing thirteen in all.

Of a more serious character is my Libel Action against the *Southern Cross* which is the only Labour paper in New Zealand. Hardly had I set foot in the country when they published a very libelous attack upon me, which, I felt, could not afford to be overlooked.

I enclose a copy of their article, together with my solicitor's letter to them and a copy of our Statement of Claim.

As a result of these proceedings, I have had to cancel my trip to Tokyo and shall leave here tomorrow week directed to San Francisco. There I am doing a month's lecturing and will probably then have to return here about December 10 for the Libel Action, which is set down in the Courts in Wellington for that day.

I am very disappointed to miss the visit to Japan and particularly to General MacArthur. What would you like me to do with your letter to him? I could send it by Military Bag from Washington, with a covering note regretting that I could not deliver it in person. I will take no action in this till I hear from you.

The Freybergs have been extremely kind to me and I spent four very agreeable days with them at Government House in Wellington. I shall be seeing them again next weekend. I told him how much you and Mamma do appreciate the parcels he has been sending. It will be nice if you could drop him a line some time.

Major Sir Desmond Morton[1] to Winston S. Churchill
(Churchill papers, 4/141)

21 October 1947 Brussels
Private

My dear Winston

To be mentioned in any way in your new book is an honour far greater than I deserve. To be mentioned in the very kind terms you propose to use leaves me overwhelmed.

In your letter you are good enough to say that you think I helped our country. It certainly was my hope and desire, but unfortunately those in power

[1] Desmond John Falkiner Morton, 1891–1971. On active service, WWI. Met Churchill in the field while Churchill was painting, 1916. Shot through the heart while commanding a field battery at the Battle of Arras, April 1917, but survived. MC. ADC to Sir Douglas Haig, 1917–18. Head of Committee of Imperial Defence's Industrial Intelligence Centre, 1929–39. Member of Imperial Defence Sub-Committee on Economic Warfare, 1930–9. CMG, 1937. Personal Assistant to Churchill throughout the Second World War. CB, 1941. KCB, 1945.

then would not listen to me. Nevertheless I am more than happy to feel that the little I could do for you, either in those pre-war days or during the war, was of any service to you.

In what you wish to say there is nothing to which I could object save on the grounds of modesty. On a small point of accuracy, the Industrial Intelligence Centre which you mention did not work under the Foreign Office but under the Committee of Imperial Defence. My hierarchical Chief was in practice Maurice Hankey, and at a later stage when he was appointed, the Minister of Defence Coordination. I suggest therefore that you should change the words 'Foreign Office' into 'Committee of Imperial Defence'.

You might also like to make some slight alteration in the words 'unique distinction of having been shot through the heart'. I have been told by doctors that that is what occurred, but still remain somewhat dubious about it. Even if it is true it is not unique, since Arthur Sloggett,[1] Director General of Medial Services in the war of 1914 had a similar experience at Omdurman, and came to see me in hospital in consequence.

It is certainly true that Ramsay MacDonald gave me personal permission to talk freely to you, as you state.

I was so sorry not to be able to see you during the short time between my leaving hospital and going back to Brussels, but through purely personal difficulties, I could not get down to Earlylands, and unfortunately it could not be arranged on one or two days when you were in London. I do hope that after your own operation you are now as well as I am, which can be described as fitter than I have been for a very long time. I am back in Brussels now, wrestling with reparations which do not come from Germany, and trying to divide up 350 tons of solid gold amongst nations to whom it is due. Unfortunately the United Kingdom is not one of them. The job is not unamusing, since it is a minor UNO, for which the Agency acts as a sounding board. It is far more political than financial. My fellow Delegates from the 18 Allied nations gathered there are, in many cases, political rather than official figures; so much so that I felt bound to invite the Government to appoint in my room a Junior Minister if they so desired. They were good enough to say that they felt confidence in my abilities to represent them, since it was a matter of foreign rather than home affairs. After this I have received no instructions other than copies of the Foreign Secretary's speeches. Since Ernie dislikes the Bolsheviks as much as I do, and sees the necessity both of playing in with the Americans and stimulating an economic unity in Western Europe, I have found not the slightest difficulty so far in saying what I think he would wish me to say with heart as well as mind.

---

[1] Arthur Thomas Sloggett, 1857–1929. Entered RAMC, 1881. Medical Officer, Indian Frontier, 1884; Dongola, 1896; Sudan, 1897–8 (gravely wounded); South Africa, 1899–1902. Director of Army Medical Services, India, 1911–14. Hon. Surgeon to the King, 1911–29. Knighted, 1914. Lt-Gen., 1914. Director-General, Army Medical Service, 1914–18. Col. Commandant, RAMC, 1921–8.

My only regret is that as a result of this appointment I have no private life or home consolations in my old age. My beloved garden at Earlylands sees me not, though I am gradually being ruined financially through having to pay for two homes in England which I cannot use, as well as for life in Brussels which is not cheap.

Please convey my deepest affection to Mrs Churchill, and if you will accept it too, as always for yourself.

Winston S. Churchill to Sir Edward Bridges
(Churchill papers, 1/68)

21 October 1947
Private and Confidential

My dear Edward,

I should be much obliged if you could tell me about the regulations affecting foreign travel. The doctors advise that I should spend a portion of the winter in a warmer climate, and certificates will be provided. I have received an invitation from American friends to stay for six or seven weeks at their expense at Marrakech. They would also provide air transportation there and back. All I should require is a little pocket money; what is the maximum that could be permitted? Is there any regulation forbidding a person to leave the country, even though no exchange expense is involved? I do not wish to ask any favour of His Majesty's Government, but only to be informed.

I should be accompanied by Mrs Churchill and by two lady secretaries for any literary work. They would also be guests of the American hosts, but presumably some small allowance for personal expenses would be required.

It would be very kind of you to let me know about the rules.

Winston S. Churchill to Christopher Soames
(Churchill papers, 1/32)

21 October 1947

CHARTWELL JOBS

1. The bath should be taken up to Miles' cottage, Mr Southon should be asked to send up a plumber to arrange for a cold water supply.

2. Whitbread and the German prisoners to finish the small yard for the calves at Bardogs, and other minor tasks mentioned including cementing the floor of the big barn where it has broken away. The Chestnut fencing to stop the children falling into the deep road, now newly finished, should be completed.

3. If time permits the Germans should trench the garden at Bardogs between the concrete paths, and also the path which will be the third chicken run when needed. If possible the wall foundation at right angles to the white wall newly built at Bardogs should be finished so that I can build it. Whitbread should take away whatever of the existing wooden structure and boarding is necessary.

4. <u>Painting</u>. Whitbread and Kurn,[1] should time permit, should paint that green chicken house, and also make good and paint any concrete mending or crack in the swimming pool. The gate posts and the post near the middle lake should be removed if time permits. All this can be fitted in at convenience.

5. Friday, we aim at cutting down the big dangerous tree. A fifty yard rope should be provided as otherwise in falling it will destroy two other good trees. It must fall inwards of course. The electric saw will be used. No attempts should be made to remove stone from Bardogs till this is provided for. It may be possible to combine the two operations on Friday, for which Whitbread and one German prisoner will be needed to throw the tree. Hazledon and the other three prisoners would be available to move stone.

6. In the event of running short of work please be so kind as to ring me up.

Winston S. Churchill: speech
(Hansard)

22 October 1947   House of Commons

ADDRESS OF CONGRATULATIONS TO THEIR MAJESTIES AND
PRINCESS ELIZABETH ON THE FORTHCOMING ROYAL MARRIAGE

I am very glad to second the Motion which the Prime Minister has moved in felicitous terms, and to associate the Conservative Party and the Opposition with it in the most cordial manner. I welcome the novel suggestion which the Prime Minister has made, that this Address should be presented by Privy Councillors representing all parties. There is no doubt that the approaching marriage gives keen and widespread pleasure in British homes and that it stirs most warm and lively sympathies in the hearts of the British nation. Our constitutional monarchy and the Royal Family play a vital part in the tradition, dignity and romance of our island life. We congratulate the King and Queen upon the happiness which the betrothal of a beloved daughter in such auspicious circumstances has given them.

I am in entire accord with what the Prime Minister has said about Princess Elizabeth and about the qualities which she has already shown, to use his

---

[1] A retired bricklayer from Westerham who helped to teach Churchill bricklaying.

words, 'of unerring graciousness and understanding and of human simplicity'. He is indeed right in declaring that these are among the characteristics of the Royal House. I trust that everything that is appropriate will be done by His Majesty's Government to mark this occasion of national rejoicing.

'One touch of nature makes the whole world kin,'

and millions will welcome this joyous event as a flash of colour on the hard road we have to travel. From the bottom of our hearts, the good wishes and good will of the British nation flow out to the Princess and to the young sailor who are so soon to be united in the bonds of holy matrimony. That they may find true happiness together and be guided on the paths of duty and honour is the prayer of all.

Lady Rhys-Williams to Winston S. Churchill
(Churchill papers, 2/64)

24 October 1947
Strictly confidential

Dear Mr Churchill,

I had lunch with Lord Layton[1] yesterday, and think I should report to you about what he told me concerning Liberal–Conservative relations.

He said that the new Gallup poll, which has not yet been published, shows a heavy drift away from Labour, and is almost equally discouraging to the Liberals. He was in a difficulty to know how to present the bad news in the *News Chronicle*, but intended to do so as he felt it ought to be known. He admitted that he himself was now convinced that you ought to be returned to power, but believed that there was no chance of this before the full five years were up, as, particularly after seeing these bad figures, it would be very odd if Mr Attlee took the risk of an election; he would be likely to do all in his power to postpone one until the last moment, hoping that the worst of the hardships would be over in two years time, and the electorate less likely to blame him then. He said that he himself did not think this would be wise tactics on the part of Attlee, as it would end in a landslide against him, as against Balfour in 1906, but he was certain he would play for time.

I asked him what he felt about the Liberal position in all this, and expressed my own views. Instead of reacting against them as he has before, he said 'We

[1] Walter Thomas Layton, 1884–1966. Educated at University College, London, and Trinity College, Cambridge. Married, 1910, Eleanor Dorothea Osmaston. Director, National Mutual Assurance, 1921–64. Editor, *The Economist*, 1922–38; Deputy Chairman, 1945–53. Knighted, 1930. Chairman, *News Chronicle*, 1930–40, 1944–50. Baron, 1947. Deputy Leader, Liberal Party, House of Lords, 1952–5. Member, Reuters Trust, 1953–63.

are many of us thinking very seriously on these lines; but the trouble is, if we are to come to an agreement with the Conservatives now, and there is no election for two years, by the time the election comes, the Liberals will have become completely identified with the Conservatives, as the Liberal Nationals have done; and that will be the end of an independent Liberal Party.'

I put to him the view that, if no arrangement was come to, and the tide continued to turn against Liberals, by the time the election came there would be no effective Liberal Party in any case; a few more Edgehills would expose their weakness to such an extent that no one would take them seriously. In any case the quality of the candidates now being put up was much too poor.

He said he was very much agreed with me about this, especially about the poor quality of the bulk of the candidates, and he agreed that it would be very much better for the prestige of Liberalism in the world if the Liberal Party were represented in the next House by a reasonable number – say 36 – members, drawn from our best and most experienced people, who would get in owing to an agreement with you, than to try for a full scale fight and get in only a handful, and those not the best. He was also very much in favour of trying to get some promise with regard to electoral reform in the towns. He said that, however poor the outlook for Liberalism might seem, he was confident – and indeed the figures showed – that there were at least 3,000,000 Liberal voters in the country, and he was most anxious not to divide them. A too hasty, or unprepared alliance with the Conservatives might alienate a lot of them, and in fact defeat the object of getting the whole vote to turn in your favour.

I pointed out that, whatever might be decided about the date of an announcement of alliance, it was vital that an approach should be made to you at an early date. The right moment to announce the change might occur at any moment, as a result of some fresh crisis, and the newspapers such as the *News Chronicle* could be preparing the ground, instead of pounding away with anti-Tory propaganda which might be thrown up against them in the event of a later alliance. I think he felt the truth of this.

As an upshot of the talk I felt absolutely sure that there is no real intention of going through with the plan to fight every seat. If a General Election were to be announced, approaches would be made to you at once. Even if it seemed probable that one would occur by next year, immediate negotiations would be attempted. But the prospect of two years' wait, with the Independent Liberal flag, in effect, hauled down, makes them afraid that it would never be raised once more. The situation is really rather sad, though, as I think, completely dishonest, since in reality they mean to support you, and ought to say so <u>now</u>.

The face-saver to which they would cling would be, I believe, some form of electoral reform, as I reported before.

I got the impression that at the present time, the real opponent of any form of alliance is Lord Samuel, who has immense prestige in the party.

Mr Fothergill[1] is merely trying with great energy, to keep his end up, and would be glad to lay down the burden if only the rest would agree.[2]

Winston S. Churchill: press statement
(Churchill papers, 2/55)

24 October 1947

Mr Churchill has issued the following statement to all electors in the forthcoming Municipal Elections:

All over the country men and women are asking today, 'What can we do about a Government which, by its failures has forfeited our trust and by its folly is endangering our future, and yet, under our constitution, has still nearly three years of office to run?' On the first of November and the following days all friends of Britain and her life and glory have one clear opportunity. It was the Socialists and not the Conservatives who decided that these elections should be fought not on local issues but on nation-wide Party lines. Now you can let them have what they wanted. Every vote you cast against a Socialist candidate in your city or town will be a warning to the Socialist Government in Whitehall that they are losing the support which the people gave them two years ago. Here is one of the rare chances you will have of saving your country from the dangers and misfortunes into which it is now being led.

Here is your duty – vote against the Socialist candidate on November the first.

Sir Edward Bridges to Winston S. Churchill
(Churchill papers, 1/68)

24 October 1947

Dear Mr Churchill,

Thank you for your letter of the 21st October[3] in which you asked about the regulations affecting foreign travel.

Briefly, they are as follows.
(1) Anybody may leave this country for any destination.
(2) Anybody may buy return tickets in this country to any destination,

---

[1] Charles Philip Fothergill, 1906–59. Educated at Bootham School. Deputy Transport Commissioner for Scotland, 1943–5. Chairman, Liberal Party, 1946–9, 1952–4; President, 1949–52; Vice-President, 1952–5.
[2] Churchill responded on Nov. 1: 'Thank you so much for your most interesting letter of October 24. I am sure it is much better to let things develop in a natural way.'
[3] Reproduced above (p. 815).

whether the means of transport are British or foreign, and take with them £5 in sterling for the sole purpose of spending on a British ship or aircraft or on return to this country.

(3) No foreign exchange is provided, even as pocket money, unless very severe health criteria are satisfied. I attach a copy of the medical certificate which has to be completed, and you will see that the applicant for foreign exchange has to be suffering from a specific disease and that, in the doctor's opinion, life would be endangered unless the patient went abroad.

Members of Parliament get special privileges only when they are travelling in a representative capacity, and when their expenses are paid we allow approximately £1 a day for pocket money and odds and ends, but nothing for wives or secretaries.

I hope that this gives you the information which you require.

Winston S. Churchill to Alfred Duff Cooper
(*Churchill papers, 4/141*)

25 October 1947
Private

My dear Duffie,

First let me say how sorry I was to learn of the approaching end of your mission, which I confided to you four years ago. I must offer to you my sincere congratulations and thanks upon its success, and for all you have done. You could not have rendered this fine public service without Diana. Bevin told me that you would not be leaving Paris until the New Year or later, but I hope that after that we shall be working together in politics.

Meanwhile I have been toiling at my book about the War. So far I have only completed the story of the interval between the wars; but the rest is far advanced up to the end of 1940. There are several chapters in which you are involved, and in which you will certainly be interested. I should be most grateful if you would read them for me, and say if there is anything referring to yourself which you would like omitted. I have quoted a letter or two, but if you prefer it they can be left out. Anything that you care to add by way of enrichment, and any marginal comments you may feel inclined to make, will be welcomed by me.

I am planning to go to Marrakech on December 12 for six or seven weeks, and to stay at the Mamounia Hotel. Because of currency restrictions I shall be the guest of my American publishers. The doctors have recommended a sojourn in warmer climes, and the publishers are very anxious to make it possible for me to work under the most favourable conditions. All questions of currency and finance are settled. Perhaps, however, you would let the French

Government know that I may wish to visit Morocco with Clemmie and Sarah; for I daresay they would be inclined to show me their usual kindness and courtesy. I hope to do a good deal of painting as well as writing, and to have a complete break with the melancholy drama which is developing over here and will reach its climax in the coming year.

Winston S. Churchill: speech
('Winston S. Churchill, His Complete Speeches', volume 7, pages 7391–8)

28 October 1947　　　　　　　　　　　　　　　　　　　　House of Commons

DEBATE ON THE ADDRESS

Order read for resuming Adjourned Debate on Question of 21st October: That an humble Address be presented to His Majesty as followeth:

Most Gracious Sovereign,
　　We, Your Majesty's most dutiful and loyal subjects, the Commons of the United Kingdom of Great Britain and Northern Ireland, in Parliament assembled, beg leave to offer our humble thanks to Your Majesty for the Gracious Speech which Your Majesty has addressed to both Houses of Parliament. – (Mr Blyton.)[1]

Question again proposed.
Mr Churchill: I beg to move, at the end of the Question, to add:

But humbly regret that the Gracious Speech, while clearly revealing the intention of Your Majesty's Government to continue their partisan policies, gives no assurance of the national leadership, the administrative competence, or the measures necessary to meet the economic crisis and so give relief to Your people from their ever increasing hardships.

Last week the Minister for Economic Affairs (Sir Stafford Cripps) made an important and courageous speech. In it he proclaimed the complete failure of the whole policy of State planning and management of industry in time of peace, of which he has long been the leading exponent and, lately, an important executive Minister. He also confessed to some of the grave miscalculations and wrong estimates made by himself and by the Government of which he is still a member. He revealed with more precision than any of his colleagues has yet done the depth of misfortune into which we have been led since this new Parliament was elected two and a quarter years ago upon a flood of high hopes and promises. He called for perseverance in his policy of restrictions, controls and arbitrary direction from Whitehall. He read out a further list

---

[1] William Reid Blyton, 1899–1987. Educated at Dean Road Secondary Modern School. MP (Cons.) for Houghton-le-Spring, 1945–64.

of pains and penalties to be inflicted upon the British public, and he called for a spirit of unity from the whole nation in bearing these new sacrifices so that he could continue with ever greater vigour the experiments in Socialism which have already made what he described as 'our economic survival' a matter of uncertainty. In the same week the Prime Minister announced the Government's intention to nationalise the iron and steel industry as a contribution to our industrial recovery, and his intention to establish what is virtually single-chamber Government as a stimulus to national unity.

These various declarations taken together constitute in themselves, apart from all other facts and arguments, the fullest justification for the Amendment to the Address in reply to the King's Speech which we have placed on the Paper. Let us, therefore, examine these issues with attention. The need to increase our export trade is, of course, paramount. We shall do our best to help the Minister for Economic Affairs to reach the targets for export at which he is aiming. It is the duty of all parties to promote by every means in their power the productivity of our country. However, it is most important that the people should not be misled. Nationalisation has proved a failure. Dear coal and, soon, dearer transport gravely weaken our competitive powers in foreign markets. It is more in the interests of the wage earners to work for private employers than to be the servants of an all-powerful but ill-instructed State machine. This they are finding out for themselves. Nationalisation, so far as it has proceeded, has had at any rate a definite though limited educative value.

The speech of the Minister for Economic Affairs, with its long series of damaging admissions, was in fact a confession of fundamental error. Confession is good for the soul, but after confession should come penance, not praise. I would not therefore attempt to occupy the time of the House with eulogies of the right hon. and learned Gentleman. While giving full support to the export drive, I cannot bring myself to believe that the course upon which the Minister for Economic Affairs urged the country to embark for a voyage of several years – even if no other industry is to be nationalised – I cannot believe that this voyage can bring us out of our misfortunes and difficulties, and the right hon. and learned Gentleman certainly gave no undertakings that it would do so. No one can say he encouraged false hopes in his speech the other day. I feel myself a strong conviction that he is leading us down the wrong road and that at the end of all his efforts and our privations we shall in a year or two be worse off than we are now.

I will venture to give two main reasons for my anxiety. The first is that I do not believe that a successful export trade can be founded upon a starved home market. I pointed this out two years ago when I asked how we could suppose that a fertile and healthy export trade could be maintained, except on the overspill of a very much larger internal and domestic trade. The President of the Board of Trade, which was the position the right hon. and learned Gentleman then occupied, I said, was under the profound delusion that he could build up an immense and profitable trade while keeping everything on a minimum here at home. No doubt it is right to put all possible emphasis upon the export trade, and, as I have said, we shall assist him in every way possible, but exports are only the steam over the boiling water in the kettle. They are only that part of the iceberg that glitters above the surface of the ocean. No long-term scheme for keeping a vast community alive can be based on an export trade alone. Down this path we shall only get into ever-narrowing situations. At any moment foreign price movements or our own rising costs of production may vitiate and overthrow all our carefully-worked-out calculations.

The United States, from an immense volume of home production, throws down its surplus of exports. How can we compete with that in any neutral market? The conception that any community can make its living without a healthy and vigorous home market and strong domestic consuming power is a fallacy condemned by every one of the great economists of the past. There was indeed an interval after the victory when there was what is called a 'sellers' market', of which a temporary advantage could be taken and was to some extent taken. I supported the American Loan because I hoped that with this external aid and the sellers' market we might revive our normal peacetime fertile activities here. But the sellers' market is departing, and the American Loan has gone. Meanwhile we have not been able to create free thriving business and productive activity at home. The right hon. and learned Gentleman and the Government are now inviting us to follow them further into a dark and narrowing tunnel at the end of which there may be no daylight.

My second reason for differing from the Minister for Economic Affairs lies even deeper. I do not believe in the capacity of the State to plan and enforce an active high-grade economic productivity upon its members or subjects. No matter how numerous are the committees they set up, or the ever-growing hordes of officials they employ, or the severity of the punishments they inflict or threaten, they cannot approach the high level of internal economic production which, under free enterprise, personal initiative, competitive selection, the profit motive corrected by failure, and the infinite processes of good housekeeping and personal ingenuity, constitutes the life of a free society. It is no doubt true that the State can always present large projects to the public gaze; large projects can be unfolded. The difference between what is seen and what is not seen was often noticed by the old economists. What is not seen is the infinite variety of individual transactions and decisions which, in a civilised society, within the framework of just and well-known laws, insure the advantage not only of the individual concerned, but of the community, and provide that general body of wellbeing constituting the wealth of nations. All this is blotted out by an overriding State control, however imposing some of its manifestations may be. It is this vital creative impulse that I deeply fear the doctrines and policy of the Socialist Government have destroyed, or are rapidly destroying, in our national life. Nothing that they can plan and order and rush around enforcing will take its place. They have broken the mainspring, and until we get a new one the watch will not go.

If these general ideas applied to any country in the world, they would apply to this island, where we cannot grow much more than half the food we need, and where we have to purchase the rest of it and many raw materials by selling goods or rendering services to foreign countries. We have never been unable to do this before. A vast population grew up here under free enterprise and the capitalist system. Immense investments were made in foreign countries which refreshed and stimulated our home market with imports. Half of these have now gone in the war in the common cause, but half remain. The loss of half of our foreign investments is no sufficient explanation of our plight. We could certainly by a united effort fill that gap.

Why is it then that suddenly we should have to be told that the system by which we lived at a higher standard than any other country in Europe has come to an end? This is an important question for the House coldly and deliberately to consider. What is the new factor that has intervened to ruin our affairs, and to prevent us from holding our place in the world? I would only attempt to answer such a question after many heart-searchings and with many misgivings about my power to do so, having regard to the fallibility of human judgment. All the same, I will venture to give to the House my opinion for what it is worth. The reason why we are not able to earn our living and make our way in the world as a vast, complex, civilised community is because we are not allowed to do so. The whole enterprise, initiative, contrivance, and genius, of the British nation is being increasingly paralysed by the restrictions which are imposed upon it in the name of a mistaken political philosophy and a largely obsolete mode of thought. I am sure that if Parliament set the nation free it would be able to earn its own living in the world. I am sure that this policy of equalising misery and organising scarcity, instead of allowing diligence, self-interest and ingenuity to produce abundance, has only to be prolonged to kill this British Island stone dead.

We are told, and I am told, that we Conservatives have no policy. Hon. Members say that we complain of the hard times, we criticise the Government, who are doing their best according to their lights, but that we have no positive policy of our own. Here is the policy: Establish a basic standard for life and labour and provide the necessary basic foods for all. Once that is done, set the people free – get out of the way, and let them all make the best of themselves, and win whatever prizes they can for their families and for their country. Only in this way will Britain be able to keep alive and feed its disproportionate population, who were all brought into existence here upon the tides of freedom, and will all be left stranded and gasping by the Socialist ebb. Only in this way will an active, independent, property-owning democracy be established. I repeat, therefore, that our policy is an adequate basic standard, and above that, within just and well-known laws, let the best man win – (*Laughter.*) The crackling of thorns under a pot does not deter me. Ministers may not agree with this, and their followers still cling to the shibboleths which they have learned to substitute for any other more ameliorative mental process, but at least they must admit that here is a policy, a theme, a proposition, a method which reaches into every sphere of human thought and action, and constitutes the division between us, which will be brought one day to the decision of a country far better instructed upon these matters than it was on the last occasion.

It is not nature which has failed us. It is not nature which has failed mankind. It is Governments, which, misled and steeped in folly or perversity, have rejected and squandered the fruits of nature, endeavouring to prevent the normal working of its processes, even though those fruits are presented by the ever-more efficient servitors of an ever-widening science. The true path is still open if we could only have the wisdom and the courage to enter it. But we shall never enter it by substituting Whitehall planning on anything but the highest and most general level for the native genius and infinitely varied capabilities of our race.

At this point I must turn to the United States with whom our fortunes and interests are intertwined. I was sorry that the hon. Member for Nelson and Colne (Mr S. Silverman), whom I see in his place, said some weeks ago that they were 'shabby moneylenders'. That is no service to our country nor is it true. The Americans took but little when they emigrated from Europe except what they stood up in and what they had in their souls. They came through, they tamed the wilderness, they became what old John Bright called 'A refuge for the oppressed from every land and clime'. They have become today the greatest State and power in the world, speaking our own language, cherishing our common law, and pursuing, like our great Dominions, in broad principle, the same ideals. And the hon. Member for Nelson and Colne calls them 'shabby moneylenders'. It is true that they have lent us a great deal of money. They lent us £1,000 million in the first World War, a debt which we solemnly confirmed after the war, in time of peace. But all that they let drop. Then there was Lend-Lease, before they came into the second war, in all about £7,000 million.

Mr Sydney Silverman (Nelson and Colne): What about cash-and-carry before that?

Mr Churchill: Two years ago we borrowed another £1,000 million sterling from them, or nearly four billion dollars. I asked the other day a rhetorical question, 'What are dollars?' Dollars are the result of the toil and the skill of the American working man, and he is willing to give them on a very large scale to the cause of rebuilding our broken world. In many cases he gives them without much prospect of repayment. Shabby moneylenders!

For the purposes of my argument this afternoon, I wish to refer chiefly to the economic policy of the United States. Their high tariff and buoyant internal production make it difficult for them to receive imports. (Hon. Members: 'Hear, hear'.) That is what we are endeavouring to achieve here by the method of prohibition of consumption. It is regrettable, because there can for no long time be a fertile importation or exportation without the corresponding operation. I like to hear these old Free Trade principles come forth. On the other hand, their capitalistic competitive system gives them an enormous home productivity far greater than ours per head, even with nationalisation in the wind. During the war we have seen them perform astonishing feats of mass production, like building all the Liberty ships, a prodigy of creative force and the salvation of Britain and her Allies.

Very strict controls were imposed in the United States during the war, as they were over here during the war, by general consent. Strong men pushed about in America, and under a free Constitution gave orders which the nation was eager to obey. What happened when the war was over? Advantage was not taken of the wartime measures in order to enforce the particular conceptions and doctrines of any political party. What happened when the war was over? In the summer of 1946 the major step was taken of making a clean sweep of almost all controls; and all legislation supporting the Office of Price Administration fell to the ground. And, of course, the cost of living bounded up. It is now 60 per cent above 1939. But what is the corrective of price rising? It is production. American production is now 80 per cent above 1939. Where prices rise through scarcity, there is evil. That evil can always be corrected by production.

Mr S. Silverman rose –

Hon. Members: Give way.

Mr Churchill: I am capable of deciding for myself. That evil can always be corrected by production. Where prices rise in spite of abundance, it is not a sign of evil, but often of strength. It must have been a heart-shaking decision of the American Government and of the President, who has great executive power, to abandon price controls and, as it were, throw the reins upon the horse's neck. The strong horse is pulling the wagon out of the mire. I know what many hopes are on the opposite side of the House, but they will not be cheered by the results. We have a strong horse too. He is not so large but he is strong. Alas, he is bitted and bridled and hobbled and haltered till he can hardly move.

The American cost-of-living index after the total casting away of controls is, as I said, 60 per cent above 1939. The British cost-of-living index has been held down by the immense food subsidies, but our wholesale price index, which is the nearest comparative figure, in spite of our controls and, as I hold, largely because of them, is 90 per cent above 1939. The United States, therefore, have high prices in spite of abundance, and we have high prices as well as scarcity. According to all the economists I have ever studied, high prices in spite of abundance is good, and low prices because of scarcity is bad. I do not say that in our peculiar island economy, with all the complications of our artificial life for so crowded a population, with the position created by the last two years of wartime controls maintained in peace. I do not say that we could afford to act with the drastic, sweeping gestures which have characterised the policy of the United States. We must preserve our basic standards. All the same, I feel fortified by what has happened in the United States, in the view which I expressed a few minutes ago, that the sovereign remedy for our present ills and darkening misfortunes is to set the people free. In principle, and subject to all necessary adjustments, that is the counter-policy with which the Conservative, Unionist, National Liberal and, I hope and believe, Liberal Parties, confront the Socialist Government.

The first count in the indictment of His Majesty's Ministers I have been describing is the fundamental difference between free enterprise with its rewards and forfeits directed by social legislation, on the one hand, and State planning and meticulous governessing on the other. That is the first count which remains and it is very necessary that we should put these matters out plainly. After all, we have an educated democracy in this island. One would not think it from some of their temporary aberrations. It is very necessary that it should be realised how great is the moral and intellectual division of thought and of argument between the two sides of the House in these matters. That is the first count against the Government for leading the nation into an ever-darkening alley.

The second count is their incompetence in administration and executive action. Of this I will give some instances. The first that confronts us at home is, of course, the collapse of the housing schemes. This is a perfect example of the evil consequences of crippling private enterprise. All conceivable agencies should have been employed to repair the havoc of the war and make up for the cessation of cottage building during its course. The local authorities, the large private building companies and, above all, the small men throughout the country, should have been given a fair and equal chance and generous encouragement to build the vast number of small houses which the people so urgently need. Instead of this, a bitter campaign has been waged by the Minister of Health against the small private builder and against private enterprise in building. What is the result? A quarter of a million houses are now in the present stage unfinished, half finished or quarter finished. Enormous numbers of people are crowded together in circumstances most painful to them, producing unfavourable reactions in family life in many cases – a great hampering and impediment to them all. These buildings all stand unfinished, as it were in ruins amid the older houses of the war and all around there is an immense mass of grandiose capital expenditure projects now cut short by the right hon. and learned Gentleman the Minister for Economic Affairs. He told us the other day that the housing target for 1949, in the fifth year after the war was over, is to be no more than 140,000 houses.

If, on the other hand, the Government would only set the building trade free and give it a fair chance, we would find tens of thousands of cottages growing up – (*Interruption.*) Try it and see. We should find tens of thousands of cottages growing up all over the country additional to the local authority programme and without requiring any materials – (*Laughter*) – which have to be imported from hard currency countries. There are all kinds of devices that can be used to construct habitations suitable for people to live in and all ought to be tried before our people are condemned to live under the present conditions. We are delighted that hon. Members opposite are able to show hilarity and keep up their spirits amid their grievous responsibilities and the unpleasant exposure which it is my duty to make of them. One hundred and forty thousand houses in 1949, in spite of our bitter need, under the Socialist Government. That compares with 350,000 houses built in the year before the war – and now laugh – by private enterprise under a Tory Government and without any agitation and with half the present need. (An Hon. Member: 'Nonsense'.) Why does the hon. Member say, 'Nonsense'? The figure told us by the right hon. and learned Gentleman for 1949 was 140,000. Let anyone dispute the fact that we were building at the rate of 1,000 houses a day or 350,000 houses a year before the war began. That is a practical proof not only of the fallacy of Socialist theories, but of the ineptitude which defaces their administration.

I will conclude my strictures in the social and domestic field – I have a large field to cover and will endeavour to distribute them evenly – by reading the latest economies proposed by the new Minister of Fuel and Power,[1] who represents, I believe, Socialist intellectualism and the old school tie. He advocated – according to what I read in the public Press and I have made some inquiries about its authenticity – he advocated a policy of fewer baths. I really must read the words which he is reported to have used, as I think they constitute almost a record:

> Personally, I have never had a great many baths myself, and I can assure those who are in the habit of having a great many that it does not make a great difference to their health if they have less. As for your appearance –

said this representative of His Majesty's Government –

> most of that is underneath and nobody sees it.

When Ministers of the Crown speak like this on behalf of His Majesty's Government, the Prime Minister and his friends have no need to wonder why they are getting increasingly into bad odour. I had even asked myself, when

---

[1] Hugh Todd Naylor Gaitskell, 1906–63. Educated at New College, Oxford. Married, 1937, Anna Dora Creditor. MP (Lab.) for Leeds South, 1945–63. Ministry of Fuel and Power, 1946–7. Minister of Fuel and Power, 1947–50. Chancellor of the Exchequer, 1950–1. Shadow Chancellor of the Exchequer, 1951–5. Leader, Labour Party, and Leader of the Opposition, 1955–63.

meditating upon these points whether you, Mr Speaker, would admit the word 'lousy' as a Parliamentary expression in referring to the Administration, provided, of course, it was not intended in a contemptuous sense but purely as one of factual narration.

Now I turn from this vision of the new Utopia to wider and far more tragic scenes. Since we separated for the Recess, the consequences of the Government's policy in India and in Burma have become apparent. Burma has been cast away, and India plunged into the first of the long series of sanguinary convulsions which I have, through the last 20 years, repeatedly predicted would follow our departure. At least half-a-million Indians have already perished at each other's hands by violent means, and now some seven or eight million are homeless fugitives. All the racial and religious hatred, all the dynastic feuds held in suspense under the *Pax Britannica* are now in full and devastating career. We have not, on this side of the House, obstructed Socialist policy in regard to India, but we have repeatedly disclaimed all responsibility for the measures and methods followed by the present Government, and the Prime Minister has always accepted this responsibility both for his party and Government and in an exceptional degree for himself.

The Secretary of State for Burma, or whatever is or was his title, has spoken of the butchery in India as a trifle compared with what any other course would have entailed. The slaughter of 500,000 human beings, and the misery of so many millions more is not an event which even the most callous and the most brutalised of beings should describe as a trifle or which should be compared to some hypothetical alternative. It is not a trifle; it is a horror, which should raise grief and heart-searchings in all concerned. I will only quote the words which I heard John Morley speak in this House nearly 40 years ago as the apostle of Irish self-government. That great leader of uncompromising Radical opinion said:

> There is I know, a school of thought who say that we might wisely walk out of India, and that Indians can manage their own affairs better than we can. Anyone who pictures for himself the anarchy, the bloody chaos which would follow might shrink from that sinister decision. . . . When across the dark distances you hear the sullen roar and scream of carnage and confusion, your hearts will reproach you with what you have done.

Let the Prime Minister reflect on that.

The Government have at last adopted the policy which I urged upon them in the summer of 1946 of laying the Palestine Mandate at the feet of UNO and giving a time limit for our evacuation of the country. It is a measure of their inadequacy and of their embarrassment in taking decisions, and of the curious balance of forces in their Cabinet, that more than a year and a half of expense and discredit and waste of our limited military Forces, has been allowed to flow out since then. Yet they came to the same conclusion which should have been taken, with all its consequent saving, nearly 18 months ago. There is no dispute between us as to policy; we support them in their policy. It is the delay to which I am drawing attention, and the strange impotence of will and lack of control and leadership which renders these fatal and ghastly compromises, prolonged for month after month, at the present time. Whoever was responsible for our staying in Palestine with five times the Army we were keeping in India, at a cost of at least £80 million a year, to say nothing of the torturing ordeal of our troops and officers, and a world-wide prejudice excited against us, whoever that Minister was, he bears a guilty load.

I now come to the astonishing maladministration and mismanagement of the Armed Forces, on which we are now spending the huge sum of £800 million a year. I believe in the civilian control of the Armed Forces by political Ministers of the Crown. They have most important functions to discharge, which cannot be discharged by the professional experts. The chief of these is to secure good value for the men and money voted by Parliament. Since the war, there has not been, to all intents and purposes, any Air Minister. Lord Stansgate, better known as Mr Wedgwood Benn, was hardly ever at his office. He was absent for long periods in the Egyptian negotiations, and a year ago he was replaced by the right hon. Member for Derby (Mr P. Noel-Baker), who has a new place now. He was replaced by him, but before this capable Minister could possibly master the complicated details of the Air Force and, just, perhaps, as he was about to make his personal influence effective on his day to day administration, he is moved elsewhere and someone else put in. I declare that there has been no competent Parliamentary control over the Air Force since this Government was formed, and that tens of millions of pounds – to say nothing of manpower – have been lost to this country by this negligence.[1]

Then there is the War Office. I will say nothing harsh about the two Secretaries of State who have, in two years, successively been dismissed from that most important post. It cannot be pretended that during their short tenures they were capable of making any effective contribution to the strict economical administration of the Army. And now the War Office, which is spending nearly £400 million in the present financial year, and has 600,000 men as its disposal, most of them of only indirect military value, has been turned into a receptacle for the most flagrant, though not the most penitent, of Ministerial failures.[2]

Lastly, I come to the Navy. I said two years ago this very month that 150,000 men was quite sufficient for the Navy, having regard to the general

[1] Arthur Henderson served as Secretary of State for Air from 7 Oct. 1947 to 26 Oct. 1951; he replaced Philip Noel-Baker (4 Oct. 1946 to 7 Oct. 1947), who had replaced Viscount Stansgate (3 Aug. 1945 to 4 Oct. 1946).

[2] Emanuel Shinwell (former Minister of Fuel and Power) served as Secretary of State for War from 7 Oct. 1947 to 28 Feb. 1950; he replaced Frederick Bellenger (4 Oct. 1946 to 7 Oct. 1947), who had replaced Jack Lawson (3 Aug. 1945 to 4 Oct. 1946).

situation in the world and the size of other navies. But the Government persisted on squandering our money on an additional 40,000 or 50,000 men borne on Vote A, by far the greater part of whom lived ashore. It is, perhaps, not necessary that the Navy should require to avail itself of the Conscription Act. Certainly, once the time of service was reduced from 18 months to 12 it was very little use to the Navy. But, having gone on this bloated, enlarged scale, it became cumbered up with large numbers of conscripts and great numbers of people to teach the conscripts and to manage the food, and so forth. And now, suddenly without the slightest relation to foreign affairs or military considerations, the Navy is reduced to 147,000 men, and in consequence of violent change of policy, for reasons as I have said, entirely unconnected with national safety or any coherent scheme of defence, the Home Fleet is reduced to one cruiser and four destroyers, and the Minister of Defence has to call them 'battle' destroyers in order to deceive the ignorant.

We have no battleships and no battle cruisers. It does not cost anything to call a destroyer a 'battle' destroyer. That is what we are reduced to. And this naked statement is flung all over the world as another proof to foreigners of our decline and weakness. We are paying in the Estimates of this year no less than £196 million for the Navy – a figure altogether unprecedented and unheard of in time of peace, even on the eve of the Great War. And even when the present cut has been effected we shall have a far larger manpower than we had at the outset of the late war; we shall have 147,000 to 133,000. Yet, owing to the incompetence and lack of political grip, we cannot man a quarter of the ships that were in commission in 1939.

The Foreign Secretary said the other night that as Foreign Secretary he would be no party to 'taking the chances the Chamberlain Government took, which landed us in a mess in 1939'. The fact remains that there is a far larger sum of money, and with larger manpower, actually producing barely a quarter of the ships which were in commission, armed and on the high seas at the time when the war broke out. I have not the slightest doubt that with 147,000 men on Vote A, and with a money Vote two-thirds of the present amount, a perfectly adequate fleet could be maintained by any competent Administration. I am sorry that the Minister of Defence, Mr A. V. Alexander, should so soon have frittered and cast away the credit which he gained in the National Government of which I was the head. The first count in the indictment is the wrong choice of all policy and thought. The second is the ineptitude and inefficiency of administration.

The third count in our Amendment is the indictment of the reckless and malignant partisanship of the Government, and the inconsistency of that partisanship with the appeals made for national unity, the Dunkirk spirit, and all that. We consider that this Government, except in the field of foreign affairs, have forfeited all claim to be the faithful guardians of the national interest, and that they are just playing a low down party game from start to finish. Nothing could prove this more clearly than the behaviour of the Prime Minister about steel nationalisation and the Parliament Act. According to common report, widespread division arose in the Cabinet about the nationalisation of steel. Those Ministers who are opposed to it at this juncture, on the ground that it will hamper production, claimed that there should be a year's delay. As the purchase price of this year's delay in doing a wrong and foolish thing, the extremists in the Cabinet were offered a corresponding diminution of one year in the powers left to the Second Chamber by the Parliament Act. On this petty and unworthy ground, the Prime Minister thought it right to reopen the Constitutional settlement which was reached in the Parliament Act of 1911, and which has formed the basis of our Constitution for the last 36 years.

The Prime Minister has admitted that he has no complaint against the conduct and behaviour of the House of Lords. All this disturbance is to be raised for the sake of some political deal inside the Cabinet to enable them to carry on from month to month. The levity of these proceedings, which even in quiet times would be grossly culpable, is at this moment, when frantic appeals are made simultaneously to us for national unity for the sake of the economic survival of our country, base and shameful to the last degree. I had as much to do with the Parliament Act of 1911 as anybody. For nearly a fortnight, in the absence of Mr Asquith, that great Prime Minister of former times, I conducted the Bill through the House of Commons. They were stormy days and nights, and early mornings. I shall always be proud of my association with that Measure. I was in favour of it then, and I am in favour of it now. It resulted from fierce political battles and two General Elections in a single year. The second General Election was necessary because the Crown refused an extraordinary creation of peers without a renewed appeal to the electorate. On this subject I presume this is the ruling precedent.

The Lord President of the Council (Mr Herbert Morrison): Would the right hon. Gentleman forgive me? He has made a reference to the Crown, and said that this was the ruling precedent. I wonder if he would develop that point, because we ought to be clear what he means.

Mr Churchill: I merely recited the history of those days, and that is the latest precedent which is available upon the subject.

Mr Morrison: Why drag the Crown in?

Mr Churchill: It must be clear – almost clear enough for the right hon. Gentleman, even in his most comprehending moments. The object and spirit of the Parliament Act was not to enable the House of Lords to veto the will of the people, but to make sure that the will of the people was, in fact, made effective. For this purpose the life of a House of Commons was reduced from seven to five years, and a provision was inserted to enable a Bill to be carried forward under the Parliament Act procedure across a General Election. The dissolution of Parliament in no way affects the efficacy of the Parliament Act. No Government are hampered by it in carrying through their legislation unless they are afraid that the people will not support them at the polls. The fact that the Government now wish to shorten the term of the suspensory powers of the second Chamber proves conclusively that they fear they would be defeated at a General Election. What they are, therefore, trying to do is not to give effect to the will of the people, but to carry through their party legislation irrespective of the will of the people. This is not democracy. It is authoritarianism. (An Hon. Member: 'What an incredible muddle.') I quite understand that may be the hon. Member's condition. Total powers are to be given to any Government obtaining power at a General Election, no matter how abnormal the conditions of that election, to carry whatever legislation they choose during their five years spell, irrespective of whether the people wish for that legislation, and irrespective of whether the Government still have their confidence or not.

Mr George Hicks (Woolwich, East): Hereditary powers.

Mr Churchill: We will come to that in a minute. What is now proposed is virtually single Chamber Government, and the granting to the Cabinet, which already has taken it in time of peace – the whole of the arbitrary wartime powers and regulations – a monstrous invasion of our liberties and a vile breach of faith between man and man who have to work together. What they are now proposing to do is to obtain for the Cabinet irresistible power to pass any Measures they may wish to bring forward, without regard to the will of the people or to their own foundation in public confidence. This is a formidable issue to fling out at this time of economic crisis – at this time when, in full peace, despotic wartime powers are ruling – and to be flung out, not as a result of grave historic and prolonged constitutional controversies, but as a cheap, paltry, disreputable deal between jarring nonentities in a divided Administration.

Since the matter has been raised, it is my duty to point to the Preamble of the Parliament Act. This makes it perfectly clear that its authors contemplated the abolition of the hereditary principle. Let me read the paragraph:

> And whereas it is intended to substitute for the House of Lords as it at present exists a Second Chamber constituted on a popular instead of a hereditary basis, but such substitution cannot be immediately brought into operation. . . .

On this we have lived for 36 years. In the face of this unprovoked aggression against the constitutional settlement of 1911, the House of Lords is evidently free to propose any alterations in its own composition which it may consider necessary for the stability of the State, and to use the powers reserved to them by the Parliament Act, which is a modern Parliamentary title as they may think fit.

Now let us take the case of steel, for the sake of which this further assumption of dictatorial power is demanded by the present Cabinet. There is no doubt that the ruling forces for the time being in the Cabinet have lost faith in the nationalisation of the steel industry as one of the remedies for our immediate troubles. By a handful of votes, freely published in the Press, the Prime Minister and the Leader of the House managed to obtain from their party meeting permission to put this Measure off until a more opportune season. Anyone can see from the speech of the Minister for Economic Affairs – and, after all, he is the man at the labouring oar – what his opinion is. He said:

> The main raw material with which we are concerned is steel, and those engaged in the steel industry are doing a magnificent job of production. Many of them are working seven days a week . . . and they are already well on the road to their optimum target of 14 million tons.

He might also have added that the British steel industry had never had a strike for 40 years, except the General Strike which was for political purposes and was forced upon them, and that this 'magnificent job of production', to use his own words, has been carried out under the shadow and uncertainty of Ministerial threats and vacillations. Yet this is the moment when the Prime Minister declared that he intends to nationalise steel within the lifetime of the present Parliament. In order to placate those who complain of the delay he throws this serious constitutional issue of the House of Lords as a sop into the political stewpan. It was just in order to prevent such discreditable party and Ministerial manoeuvres gravely affecting the life of our country that the authors of the Parliament Act made provision for the people being consulted and for their will to prevail.

I have now, I think, covered the ground set forth in the Amendment placed upon the Order Paper and on which we shall vote tomorrow. People sometimes say to me, 'How lucky you were to be dismissed from power at the moment of victory. If you had been the head of a Conservative Government the Labour Party would have arranged and fomented a series of strikes, or even a general strike, in order to regain by industrial strife what they have lost at the polls.' There may be some truth in that; it cannot be proved; but I should not have been afraid to do my duty had I been supported by the will of the people constitutionally expressed. I am sure that this Parliament has exhausted its usefulness, and that every month it continues the deeper will be the divisions and the harsher the discords of our national life. Of course, Ministers and their supporters may cling to office till the last dregs of their self-respect are gone – and the last remnant of our financial resources has been scattered. But the longer they wait the worse it will be for their party fortunes and their personal reputations – and the worse it will be for our unhappy country, torn by feud and faction, and strangled by incompetence and folly.

It is with deep anxiety about our affairs and our country that I move this Amendment to the Address. It seems hard that we should have come to this melancholy pass. Of course, nations who are beaten in war, who fail at the moment of supreme national trial, must expect, and nations who embark on wrong and wicked courses of tyranny and aggression deserve, the chastisement of fortune. But we have won all our wars. In this most terrible war of all, we not only saved ourselves but kept the flag of freedom flying in the world alone for more than a year. We gave all we had to the common cause. We gave it freely: we coveted no territory; we had no racial hatreds to gratify; we had no vengeance to slake. We were always, being a peaceful nation, backward in preparation. But we always won. In all the long wars I have seen in my life we have always won; and in the last of them our glory and our virtue have been admired by friend and foe. And yet, after all this, we now find ourselves reduced to the grim – that is the word I see in the newspapers – the grim and meagre plight exposed to us last Thursday by the Minister for Economic Affairs. I am astonished and stricken that we should have reached this pitch after all our victories, after all the services we have rendered to the common weal of mankind. Only by true regeneration of theme and spirit, carrying with us the whole force of the nation, shall we save our souls alive.

Winston S. Churchill to Lord Beaverbrook
(Beaverbrook papers)

28 October 1947
Private

My dear Max,

I must thank you for yr vy kind letter & invitation sent to me on yr departure. I am planning to go to Marrakesh (as the guest of *Life*) from December 11 to the end of January, as this gives the best hopes of warmth sunshine & paintable subjects. This will be I fear my only excursion this year, as the political siren draws me more closely to her ugly talons. Perhaps in the spring & <u>especially if you were there</u> I might fly out to yr villa. Anyhow I value yr hospitable offer.

We are struggling along here and making steady progress as a party, tho' not alas as a country.

My operation has proved a complete success & it is a gt relief to be free from all that nuisance.

PS. The book advances like an elephant. I am glad you are going to write about the incident you mention. Let me hear from you about yr fortunes & yr plans.

Winston S. Churchill: speech
(Hansard)

29 October 1947 — House of Commons

PETROL RATIONING

I do not rise for the purpose of plunging into the grave and serious Debate upon the merits of the question of basic petrol ration and its abolition. I do not rise, either, for the purpose of increasing the excitement and indignation which obviously exists in many parts of the House. I rise to suggest that we ought not to bring this matter to a conclusion tonight. It is quite evident that there are a great many points of view which should be set forth. Many have been put forward from the benches opposite. The answers to these many views and to the individual complaints and explanations of difficulty, should all be put forward. The Minister has made a broad statement of the economic situation to which we are reduced, and endeavours to contrast this evil with the evils which would follow other economies. These are very large questions, and the House ought not to be forced to resolve them tonight. It would be much better to allow this to go forward and to allow opinion to develop, because I cannot feel that the statement of the Minister, however glib, however logical it may appear, is the answer to the difficulties with which we are faced on this practical question of how best to meet the problem of our dollar situation.

I ask the Government not to press this matter to a Division tonight. I am assured that there is plenty of time for this Prayer to be resolved at a later period in the month of November. There is evidently very great interest; look at the condition of the House at this time – this late hour – after all the exciting Debate we have had during the day. Surely this is a domestic matter of ordinary practical housekeeping and management of our internal and small, but very important, affairs in which the opinion of the House ought really to have reasonable fair play and the opportunity to express itself through its channels. The decision which is come to should be worked out by the full instrument of Parliament and not merely by that slick chart drawn by Ministers or by officials. Surely we should take it up when we have a little more time. It would conduce to the public and general interests, irrespective of the many differences which exist between us as political opponents.

Henry Channon: diary
('Chips', pages 415–16)

29 October 1947

Big day at the H of C. Winston opened the debate – it was on an amendment to the Gracious Speech, and he was magnificent, but there were touches of sadness in his patriotic eloquence, and at times I found him almost inaudible. He is ageing. But he impressed and moved the House, and Morrison's reply was, in comparison, weak and cheap. Later the atmosphere grew stormy over the Government's decision to abolish the basic petrol ration; the Socialists themselves sounded full of misgivings and several of them pleaded with their Front Bench to relent; but never has an administration been so blind, so bewildered and so unrelenting. When the closure was moved, their majority had dropped to 20; and on the actual issue – basic petrol or not – they won by only 27 votes. . . .

Tonight *The Winslow Boy* by Terence Rattigan[1] opens in New York; the play was dedicated to my son Paul,[2] and I shall always be interested in how it fares.

Winston S. Churchill: speech
(Hansard)

30 October 1947   House of Commons

COMMITTEE ON PRIVILEGES REPORT

I must confess that I had some doubt about which way to vote in the last Division. I think the arguments were exceedingly complex and difficult, and it was only after considerable heart-searching that I came to the conclusion that it was right to vote against the Government's Motion. But now we have a new situation; all that is past. This is not a complicated or difficult situation; in my opinion, it is an extremely simple one. The House has now decided that the member for Gravesend (Mr Allighan)[3] has been guilty of dishonourable

---

[1] Terence Rattigan, 1911–77. Educated at Trinity College, Oxford. Author of 27 plays and numerous screenplays.

[2] Henry Paul Guinness Channon, 1935–2007. Educated at Eton and Oxford. 2nd Lt, Royal Horse Guards (The Blues), 1955–6. President, Oxford University Conservative Association, 1958. MP (Cons.) for Southend West, 1959–97. Personal Private Secretary to Minister of Power, 1959–60; to Home Secretary, 1960–2; to First Secretary of State, 1962–3; to Foreign Secretary, 1963–4. Married, 1963, Ingrid Olivia Georgia Wyndham Guinness. Opposition Spokesman on Arts and Amenities, 1967–70. Parliamentary Under-Secretary of State, Dept of Energy, 1970–2. Minister for Housing and Construction, 1972–4. Minister of State, 1979–81; for the Arts, 1981–3; for Trade, 1983–6. Secretary of State for Trade and Industry, 1986–7; for Transport, 1987–9. Chairman, House of Commons Finance and Services Committee, 1992–7. Baron Kelvedon, 1997.

[3] Ernest George Allighan, 1895–1977. Known as 'Garry'. MP (Lab.) for Gravesend, 1945–7. Expelled from the House of Commons for divulging confidential information about Parliament and then lying during the investigation. Author of books on the politics of South Africa and Rhodesia.

conduct, and that is the formal decision of Parliament and of the House of Commons, to be entered in the Journal and published throughout the length and breadth of the land. He is guilty of dishonourable conduct. The Home Secretary, speaking just now, dwelt strongly upon this. He spoke of how we were all accustomed to call each other, as a very essential element in our proceedings, 'honourable Members'. How can you stigmatise a Member as dishonourable by the most formal and solemn vote, and then, after an interval, long or short, immediately resume calling him an honourable Member? I do not see how that is possible. I do not think that to bring about a situation of that kind has a grain of logic in it.

The hon. Member has now been called by the House 'dishonourable'. What is the punishment that the Leader of the House proposes? He proposes that the Member shall be suspended for six months without salary, but is that going to touch the question of whether he is an honourable Member or a dishonourable Member? How can it do so? It simply means that, after an interval, the Member will return here, without in the slightest degree having lifted from himself the terrible stain, the indelible stigma the House has inflicted upon him, and then make such show as he can in going about his public business. Is it really in the interests of the House and the country that that situation should arise?

Moreover, I should like to call the Lord President's attention to this, though I know he has it in his mind, as his speech showed – we are now attempting to prescribe the punishment of the hon. Member, but the punishment we are inflicting falls upon the constituency. Here is a constituency – Gravesend – with a lot of people with great anxieties and so on, and they are to have no representation for six months. They have no power to force this hon. Gentlemen to resign. If he is a person with the honour this House has found him to have, he will pay no attention to them, and there is no power in the Constitution for the constituency or party organization to compel him to resign. He can sit very comfortably until the end of this Parliament, and after the six months is over, he can draw the salary of Parliament. That he can do. Considering how very unattractive and limited will be the opportunities open to him in this House, one can easily see that he may not be a very regular attendant. We shall be punishing the constituency.

After all, we are the representatives of the people, and it is the people who are the important factors in these matters. We have been dealing with matters within our knowledge and our own methods of conducting business, and with our own values of conduct in these matters of morals, but this is a question of the rights of electors and the rights of democracy. The people have a right to express their opinion. Is the House of Commons to pass a Motion saying that their Member of Parliament is dishonourable, and they are to have no means whatever for two or three years of obtaining any relief from his presence as their representative? Are they to be virtually disfranchised for six months when all kinds of matters affecting their interests occur?

No, sir. Really, on every ground of logic and democracy, we should allow the electors to have their opportunity. Therefore, it seems to me that there can be only one result of the Motion which the Government have carried in the House, namely, that the hon. Member should be expelled from the House. If he is expelled, he can go to his constituents and tell them his tale. If they choose to return him, he returns with the full authority of their vote, and, whatever our opinions are on the matter, in my view, no one will be entitled to refer to his past again. It is a rough and ready decision. A constituency is sometimes inclined to sustain a Member, and that is the remedy, but by this method the constituency has no power either to vindicate its Member or secure for itself other representation. Therefore, it seems to me that the course which the Government have now proposed is one which cannot be defended or justified on any ground whatever. I will certainly move, or support, at the right and proper moment in our proceedings an Amendment, which follows inevitably and logically on the one which the Leader of the House[1] moved earlier, that the Member should be expelled from the House and should have a chance of defending himself before his constituents, and the constituency should have a chance of saying whether they want another Member or not.

Winston S. Churchill to Sir Orme Sargent
(Churchill papers, 2/54)

31 October 1947
Confidential

My dear Sargent,

I was rather shocked by the enclosed picture,[2] and in view of the part I played three years ago I should like to be better informed upon the subject. We have not of course the same responsibility as we had in those days, but when we remember how many islands there are in which people can be put until things blow over, it seems to me very unwise for the present Greek Government to carry out mass executions of this character and almost reduces us to the Communist level.

---

[1] Herbert Morrison.
[2] Enclosed with this letter was a a cutting from the *Daily Worker* showing pictures of executions at Salonica under the caption 'British Bullets Killed these Greeks'.

November 1947

Bernard Baruch to Winston S. Churchill
(Churchill papers, 2/210)

2 November 1947   New York

Dear Winston,

Considering the grave shortages which either exist or are supposed to exist in England, it would be the height of folly to take off controls. Here in America, we made the mistake of taking off controls too soon. We did not know the extent of our demands nor the extent of our supply. So we now find ourselves in the present predicament, with prices soaring and everybody wanting more for what he has to sell – whether it be goods or services – and constant illegal strikes or threats of total strikes.

The England that we know whose possessions you said you would not liquidate is an entirely different England now. For the choicest jewels in her diadem have been cast away. India and Burma are 'freed'. That is what they say. You are withdrawing from Greece, Turkey, Egypt and Palestine, and have threatened to withdraw even from Germany. The England that I had hoped would grasp the opportunities before her, on the defeat of the Germans and the Japs, is not now the England that can grasp them.

Unless England can get back her cheap fuel which enabled her – by assembling raw materials from all over the world – to make the best goods at the lowest prices, it looks from here that she will no longer be able to do so. If you turn to oil, you will always have the fear of having the supply cut off. So, it seems to me, you must modernize your coal industry, get a certain amount of reparations from the Ruhr which you can mix in with your present supply, and, above all, do what Replogle[1] and I suggested to you after World War I, and that was to bring in better methods of production.

---

[1] Jacob Leonard Replogle, 1876–1948. Steel magnate. Married, 1905, Blanche Kenley McMillen. Named by Forbes as one of the wealthiest individuals in the US, 1918. Steel Director, War Industries Board, WWI. DSM, US Army (as civilian), 1918. Presidential Elector, Pennsylvania, 1920. Delegate from Florida, Republican National Convention, 1928, 1932, 1936, 1940, 1944. Member, Republican National Committee, 1940.

I believe that by bringing in your scientists and engineers that you can almost remake British industry. You still have that great spirit which made the English nation feared and respected all over the world and the leader in policing civilization.

We are told here that the average Briton has more food than he ever had but the Park Lane people have less. I am inclined to believe that your Government is too austere with your population. However, concerning that, you are a better judge than I.

Taking off controls now would be a mistake. What people, in general, fear – and I should think the Britishers fear – would be a continuance of controls that would never let them be free again. There is only one thing that will put the world aright, whether it is in Britain, here or elsewhere, and that is for men to work longer and produce more per man, per hour or per machine.

This ferment of all classes all over the world is nothing new, for we had it after World War I. It is accentuated and fomented, doubtless, by the Communists. But we shall have to look into their complaints and determine whether we can better their conditions from the standpoint of earnings, education, medical care and as great a share in what they produce and still keep the Capitalistic system going.

There is one thing that everybody steers away from – we here as you do there – and that is you must settle the three and a half billion of frozen sterling. That is a debt which hangs over Britain and must be funded or cleared away. I never understood why the people dealing with the debt on your side and ours did not make that a *sine qua non* of any help from here. That, and the proper revaluation of the pound will have to take place before Britain gets on a solid basis.

I am sure that Socialization has not done any good. The banking was practically regulated beforehand. The railroads were critically watched and the coal business was run at a loss. I am wondering whether you have ever considered having any engineers outside of England look into your methods of production, which I am told have not improved in the last thirty years.

What I warned Randolph about was the question of removing the controls. For then the one with the longest purse would get what there was. Then there would be an enormous demand for an increase in wages or services or strikes that would paralyze the government itself.

I would keep these controls on until it was demonstrated that supply was very close to the demand. Then the controls would die by themselves. That was the position which I took in an appearance before the Congress, a copy of which I am sending to you. I know you won't read it, but if you do, you will know all there is to know about what has to be done, the mistakes that were made and what you will have to avoid.

I am also enclosing a page from one of my speeches, regarding England, that might interest you.

I congratulate you upon the forerunner of what appears to be sanity in Britain and, I hope, here.

Winston S. Churchill: speech
('Winston S. Churchill, His Complete Speeches', volume 7, pages 7577–8)

2 November 1947 London

LOCAL ELECTION VICTORIES

I wish to express my warm thanks and congratulations to all voters who took part in the nation-wide protest against Socialist mismanagement of our affairs. This splendid victory of Conservative and Liberal-minded men and women over the inept and wrong-headed forces which have already led us far along the road to ruin at home and abroad is the best thing that has happened to our country since the electoral disaster of 1945.

I rejoice to see the industrial areas with Lancashire in the forefront returning to their old faith in Tory democracy and its modern development. For years the Socialists have fought the local elections with all the strength of their party machine. We were therefore bound at this grave time also to fight on national party lines.

The result deprives the Socialist Government of any mandate they obtained at the General Election. Henceforward they will govern without the moral support and against the will of the people.

The war-time Parliament with its large Conservative majority took the far-reaching decision to make the Parliamentary and local franchises the same. We added 7,000,000 voters to the local registers. This was a fine example of rising above a short view of party interests, and of proclaiming once again our watchword, 'Trust the people.'

Once again that faith has been rewarded, and we may move forward with renewed confidence in Britain's destiny, sure that the nation will not allow itself to be fettered and frustrated or proved unequal to the exertions and sacrifices that lie before us.

Winston S. Churchill: speech
(Churchill papers, 2/336)

4 November 1947 Harrow School

Mr Moore, Ladies and Gentlemen,

I never was much good at music, though I think for a time I underwent some lessons here on that topic – that art, I beg pardon. But I always had the feeling that if I really went in for a functional part of the orchestra the part which I felt I would most particularly like was that of conductor. There is something about the conductor which gives full satisfaction to any wishes you may have to make order reign over chaos and harmony from independent discords. And of course it always seemed to me that if you did not quite know it all yourself the orchestra would help you out, as long as you moved the baton this way and that with a genuine feeling of authority.

Now you have referred, Mr Moore, to the fact that this is the eighth year in succession that I have come down here and been refreshed and cheered by hearing Harrow boys sing all their lovely songs to me. The first time I came none of you were here. In fact another complete generation was here. Eight years ago things were very grim. I congratulated many of those who were here, young gentlemen, of having the honour so early in life to be under the fire of the enemy. The School had been bombed and much lay ahead we could not measure – immeasurable but certainly hard. However, that has all passed, rolled away, and we have a new generation and most of you have come here since the war was over. That great event has rolled back into the past but the institution which we celebrate in our reunion here continues.

You spoke, Mr Moore, of the background of history. I certainly feel that Harrow and its sons give a tremendous background to history. I am sure that without a knowledge of history, a reflection upon the past, it will never be possible to plan and march in the right direction through all difficulties of the future. You should all study history, all kinds of history, and have a picture of the long succession of events which have brought us to our present position across the centuries of strife. We are far and away the oldest Parliamentary democracy in the world and far and away the most experienced people in the world, and it is a mercy of providence that has given and preserved for us our island heritage. We have not been marched upon or ravaged for over four hundred years, and one ought to have that as a background before one embarks on one's own effort to contribute to the welfare of our country and to carry on the work of those who have stood so well by us in the past.

I always enjoy listening to all your songs. I know a great many of them by heart. I know 'Boy' and could pass a stiff examination in it. Yes, I know that one. I rose very high, I got to be head of the fags; but I never had the opportunity of calling it out myself. That was a pleasure reserved in a different form for subsequent stages of my career. It gives me the greatest pleasure to come down here and I always feel buoyed up – inspired I had better say – by a visit. I was not gifted in scholarship; and cricket and football were not to me sources of joy and certainly not of distinction. But in coming down here one has the feeling of a great institution continuing, growing and living through the generations and animating endless successions of faithful servants with inspiration and with hope.

Our country has hard times before her and no one should flinch from his duty. We have different kinds of perils and problems to face. There are those of blaring and crashing war. There are those of grinding and gnawing peace. But whatever they are they are the same in essence in the tests that they apply to the human soul. You here will be going out into the world. You must never despair of your country's glory; you must never cease to labour for its enduring fame. Do not be daunted by dark signs. Do not be daunted by the long monotony of wearying toil. But go forward unflinchingly, whether it be to cast away lives at the call of honour in the day of battle or whether it be in the faithful routine of toil day after day in the years of peace. Whatever it be, remember that the reward is the same in that you pass on to another generation the glories, the happiness and the virtues of your island home.

Alfred Duff Cooper to Winston S. Churchill
(Churchill papers, 4/141)[1]

4 November 1947   Paris

My dear Winston,

Thank you very much for sending me the proof of chapters XVII–XXII. I have read them almost at a sitting with breathless interest and my appetite is painfully whetted for the remainder. Not since Caesar[2] wrote the history of his own campaigns has such a narrative been told with equal art and authority. I am proud to find my own name graven there in contexts that are generous and flattering. I have no criticism, only admiration.

You say that Blomberg[3] married an actress. I was told she was a licensed prostitute – a fact which only Himmler[4] knew before and he allowed the marriage to proceed in order to ruin Blomberg afterwards – which he accomplished. The story may be gossip but no obloquy would have been incurred by marrying an actress. Goering did the same.

Thank you also for what you are kind enough to say about my mission. It

[1] This letter was handwritten.
[2] Julius Caesar, 100–44 bc. Governor of Roman Spain, 61–60; of Roman Gaul, 58. Added the area that makes up modern France and Belgium to Roman Empire. Expeditions to Britain, 55 and 54. Consul of Rome, 44.
[3] Werner von Blomberg, 1878–1946. Born in Pomerania, son of an officer. Decorated for bravery in action, 1914–18. Minister of Defence, 1932–8. In March 1936, urged Hitler to withdraw German troops from the Rhineland. Dismissed after the scandal which followed his second marriage (on 12 Jan. 1938) to a typist/secretary in the War Ministry with what was subsequently discovered to be an 'all too incontrovertibly established police record' as a prostitute. In exile for a year; returned to Germany, Jan. 1939, and lived in complete retreat in Wiessee, Bavaria, throughout the war.
[4] Heinrich Luitpold Himmler, 1900–45. Joined SS, 1925. SS-Oberführer, 1927; Obergruppenführer, 1933. Established first official concentration camp at Dachau, 1933. Head, Gestapo, 1934. Chief, German Police, 1936. Ordered construction of extermination camps as part of the 'Final Solution', 1942. Head, Reserve Army, 1944. C-in-C, Army Group Upper Rhine, 1944. Cdr, Army Group Vistula, 1945. Stripped of all command positions and Nazi Party membership, April 1945. Captured and committed suicide, May 1945.

has, I think been successful and I owe that success, as I owe so much, to you. I don't intend to take much part in politics during the next twelve months. I can't start biting the hand that has been feeding me for the last two and a half years until the last crumbs have been digested – unless, of course, unforeseen events accelerate the digestive process.

We look forward to seeing you and Clemmie and Sarah here on December 10th. We are hoping to give a small farewell party that night so it is a happy coincidence. I wanted to give a big ball for the Princess' wedding but the Government wouldn't let me. I think they were wrong.

Winston S. Churchill to Christopher Soames
(<i>Churchill papers, 1/32</i>)</div>

4 November 1947

NEEDED WORK

1. After the tree has been tidied up and cleared away and the fences repaired, Whitbread and Kurn should attend to the gates, so that they swing and shut properly. There may also be some new ones to put up. The first are those on the road from the Home Farm to the seven-children house. Only one gate is needed at the end of the bottom lake. This should be the wooden one on the road. The iron gate should be removed, as it and the iron gate near the bathing pool are needed for Bardogs. I wish to have iron gates and not wooden gates at each side of the wooden yard (with the dolls), so as to obstruct the view as little as possible. The gates of course swing on their uprights. On Monday next Southon is sending the builder Sales, who will help me site the dolls properly, and that is the time when I hope to mount the gates.

2. Moving the stones from Bardogs can wait this week. As soon as the paint comes of the right colour, Whitbread and Kurn can paint the cracks and repairs they have made in the swimming pool. They will need a blow-lamp for this.

3. I should very much like the Belties[1] to come as soon as possible. Could they be accommodated in the Park, including the bulldozed part, by the end of the week?

4. If there is a rainy day, Whitbread, Kurn, and the German prisoners should all cut up the wood and refill the woodshed. What is left of the dry wood at the back should be brought forward near the entrance for first consumption. The greenwood of the tree that was uprooted at the 10-acres should go right at the back, overlooking the little calf-yard, and the tree we have just cut down, which is dead, should be put between the green wood and the dry.

---

[1] Black cattle of Dutch origin with a broad band of white round the middle.

This will be the best arrangement for us. I do not want to cut another tree until we have got the yard clear and the woodshed filled.

5. Another urgent job is of course the wire netting round the second chicken run at Bardogs. What has happened about the wire netting? If it has arrived by Friday Whitbread and Kurn could put it up at once.

6. Let me know on the telephone what other jobs you want the German prisoners to do this week.

BONFIRES

I see some bonfires in the four cottage gardens. I hope care will be taken not to burn the houses down. A word of caution would be wise.

Winston S. Churchill: speech
(Hansard)

5 November 1947   House of Commons

BURMA INDEPENDENCE BILL

[. . .]

The position which was occupied by the National Government, of which I was the head, is set out in the White Paper of May, 1945, and the substance is contained in the first paragraph:

> It is and has consistently been our aim to assist her political development till she can sustain the responsibilities of complete self-government within the British Commonwealth and consequently attain a status equal to that of the Dominions and of this country.

That was conditional upon a three years' breathing space for rehabilitation, and also to give time for the wishes of the people to manifest themselves calmly and deliberately, and under conditions of peace and order.

A return to the constitution of 1935 was the objective in the interval. The framing of a new constitution for full 'self-government within the British Commonwealth' subject to special protection for the frontier tribes – and particularly mentioned in the White Paper are the Shan States – from all of whom we received much loyalty and aid in freeing the country from Japanese invasion was to follow. There would have been no difficulty in carrying out this programme in an orderly and careful manner. Half, perhaps one-third, or one-quarter, of the British troops squandered in Palestine on a policy now abandoned, the fatuity of which is now recognised, would have sufficed to enable the transfer of power to a Burmese Government, on the basis of Dominion status, to be carried out by regular and measured steps, and with due consideration for all interests, opinions and feelings involved in that population of many various strains. Instead, the whole business has been conducted by the British Government from weakness and not from strength. The breathing space has been curtailed and we are now confronted, not with Dominion status, which, as in the case of India, we considered an indispensable stage in any policy to which we on this side of the House were committed: instead Burma has been plunged at once into full independence.

This Bill is to cut Burma out of the Empire altogether and to make her a foreign power. At the earliest moment when these intentions to hustle the whole process through were known – although at that time the right hon. Gentleman did not mention independence, and seemed to indicate that a decision in that sense was not probable – I protested. The right hon. Gentleman made a statement, and on December 20th, 1946, I made an immediate protest. I said:

> It was said, in the days of the great Administration of Lord Chatham, that one had to get up very early in the morning in order not to miss some of the gains and accessions of territory which were then characteristic of our fortunes. The no less memorable Administration of the right hon. Gentleman opposite is distinguished for the opposite set of experiences. The British Empire seems to be running off almost as fast as the American Loan. The steady and remorseless process of divesting ourselves of what has been gained by so many generations of toil, administration and sacrifice continues. In the case of Burma, it is hardly a year since, by the superb exertions of the Fourteenth Army and enormous sacrifices in life and treasure – sacrifices in British blood and in Indian blood – the Japanese were forced to surrender, destroyed, or driven out, and the country was liberated. And yet, although barely a year has passed away, there is this extra-ordinary haste that we should take the necessary measures to get out of Burma finally and for ever. The same formula the right hon. Gentleman says will be used as was used in the case of India, with the same extensions he put on to that formula when the Indian Mission was sent out, eliminating the –

at this moment, as there had been no question before the House, you, Mr Speaker, did me the honour to interrupt me, so that I was not able to conclude my sentence, which would have finished –

eliminating the stage of Dominion status.

There is great importance in the stage of Dominion status, in that it does give a definite period in which, with all the advantages of Dominion Government and the full authority attaching thereto, all matters can be considered without heat or prejudice; in which those who feel that they would wish to adhere to and enjoy the great advantages and protection afforded by the British Commonwealth of Nations to all its members, would have an opportunity of making their weight felt, without any question intervening of direct interference by British administrators in their local affairs.

[...]

Today we are confronted with the result of complete independence and the cutting of Burma out of the British Empire and out of the protection of the British Empire. There is to be no interval stage of Dominion status where with calm and with deliberation all parties, all interests, all sections of the community and all creeds would see where their final fortunes would best lie. There are grave doubts as to whether the assent of the frontier tribes has been honestly and genuinely given. I do not consider that we have any guarantee that there has been a fulfilment of our duties towards those who fought valiantly at our side. Indeed, I am told that through these mountainous regions, this half circle of mountains and hills about which the Prime Minister spoke, there is a condition of armed preparation and incipient revolt prevailing. About 12,000 murders and dacoities or armed robberies are reported to have taken place in the first seven months of this year and this is only a prelude –

The Prime Minister: Which is below the average.

Mr Churchill: The average must have been upset by the extraordinary events of the last five or six years but even if it were only an average of 12,000 murders and dacoities amongst a population of 15 million, it would hardly be convincing proof of their fitness for full self-government.

This is only a prelude, in my view to a bloody welter which I fear will presently begin, as it has in India, with which the right hon. Gentleman the Minister for Economic Affairs has been so intimately concerned. No effective provision has been made for the protection of, or fair compensation to, important British commercial interests, built up over many years to the mutual benefit of the Burmese and British peoples. The constitution provides that private property may be expropriated – that is British private property – under a law which leaves it to the Burmese Government to prescribe if and what compensation should be payable. There is to be national treatment of public utilities and national treatment of all natural resources and other measures which are fashionable in Socialist States. The Burmese Government are also like our own, a Socialist Government aiming at the nationalization of all important industries, but 60 per cent of the British businesses and installations, according to the statement by a Burmese Minister last month, will be in the hands of the Burmese nation. Independent Burma is, we are told, to be a Socialist State. No effective provisions have been made for compensation such as has been practised here even by hon. and right hon. Gentlemen who sit opposite. It rests with the Burmese Government, whose country is far from rehabilitation, and whose finances are in a disorder rivalling our own, to decide in the case of any dispute what, if any, compensation has to be given to their great industries which have been growing up for generations and from which this country has received an external source of wealth, and in which the people of Burma have themselves found great employment and increases of local wealth, which are the foundations of the revenue of Government.

This is what we are invited to assent to and to become responsible for in the Bill which is now before Parliament. We on this side of the House have no power to prevent what the Government intend to do, but we have to consider what our own attitude must be on an occasion of this kind. I say that we can accept no responsibility for this Bill, and I do not think it should be settled merely on questions of oil companies or vested interests. It raises whole issues affecting the British Commonwealth of Nations and our actions must be based on Imperial and moral grounds. We accept no responsibility for this Bill. We wish to dissociate ourselves from the policy and the methods pursued by the Government. They must bear the burden and it falls with peculiar weight upon the Prime Minister himself. I interrupted him the other night and said that I did not mean to charge him with personal blood guilt. There is a difference. He individually is a humane man, but he is in the position of the signalman who has made a fatal mistake rather than that of the murderer, who has placed an obstruction on the line. The responsibility rests upon him in a broad political manner, and I am bound to say I would be very sorry to go down to history bearing upon me the name and the burden which will rest on him. The Government must bear the burden.

Burma is a pendant of India and is likely to reproduce, though, of course, on a far smaller scale, the horrors and disasters which have overspread her great neighbour and which should ever haunt the consciences of the principal actors in this tragedy. All loyalties have been discarded and rebuffed; all faithful service has been forgotten and brushed aside. There is no assurance that the power of the new Government will be sufficient to maintain internal order, or, I might add, national independence against far larger and far more powerful neighbours. We stand on the threshold of another scene of misery and ruin, marking and illustrating the fearful retrogression of civilisation which the abandonment by Great Britain of her responsibilities in the East have brought and are bringing upon Asia and the world. I say this to the Government: You shall bear that burden. By your fruits you will be judged. We shall have no part or lot in it. We have not obstructed your policies or Measures and they must now take their own course. We, at least, will not be compromised or disgraced by taking part in them, or denied the opportunity of pointing the moral to the British nation as and when occasion may occur. On those grounds we shall, at the close of the Debate, move the rejection of the Bill.

Firoz Khan Noon[1] to Edward Keeling[2]
(Churchill papers, 2/43)[3]

5 November 1947
Confidential

Ankara

Dear Mr Keeling,

Here is a note which I have recorded for you and Mr Churchill. It is secret and not to be shown to any one else here.

We in Pakistan shall be more grateful if you can persuade your govt to sell us sufficient arms to save our freedom. We are being attacked by the Hindus of Pakistan may go under if not helped now. If the labour govt won't, can Mr Churchill please use his influence with USA and persuade them to sell us arms. Any assistance given at this time will not be forgotten. The labour govt seem not to realize the duty they owe to a new dominion. Perhaps they do not know the critical position into which Pakistan is being reduced.

Edward Keeling to Winston S. Churchill
(Churchill papers, 2/43)[4]

6 November 1947

Dear Mr Churchill,

I am here as a member of a parliamentary delegation to Turkey, and have encountered my old friend Firoz Khan Noon, who is on a short visit here as personal representative of Jinnah.

He has given me the enclosed note[5] which I pass on to you.

I understand he has not had much success in enlisting the sympathy of Turks for Pakistan. The fact is that the Turks are absorbed in one thing only – the fear of Russia.

---

[1] Firoz Khan Noon, 1893–1970. Educated in Lahore and Oxford. Advocate, Lahore High Court, 1917–26. Minister for Education and Medical and Public Health, Punjab, 1931–6. Knighted, 1933. High Commissioner for India in the UK, 1936–41. Member, Viceroy's Executive Council for Labour Affairs, 1941–2; for Defence, 1942–5. Indian Envoy to the British War Cabinet, 1944–5. Member of All-Pakistan Legislature, 1947–50. Governor of East Pakistan, 1950–3. Chief Minister of West Punjab, 1953–5. Foreign Minister of Pakistan, 1956–7. PM, Foreign Minister and Minister of the Interior, 1957–8.

[2] Edward Keeling, 1888–1954. Officer in Indian Army Reserves during WWI (MC, 1918). MP (Cons.) for Twickenham, 1935–54.

[3] This letter was handwritten.

[4] This letter was handwritten.

[5] Reproduced immediately above.

Sir Alan Lascelles to Winston S. Churchill
(*Churchill papers, 2/148*)

7 November 1947　　　　　　　　　　　　　　　　　　　Buckingham Palace
Strictly Personal and Private

Dear Mr Churchill,

PRINCESS ELIZABETH'S ANNUITIES

What I hoped to avoid has now happened – The King is now involved in a wrangle with Dr Dalton over figures.

As a result of yesterday's meeting, Dalton has now proposed that The King should hand over £200,000; in return, the sum of £15,000 a year should be voted to Princess Elizabeth and Philip Mountbatten jointly, over and above the £15,000 a year to which the Princess is already legally entitled under the Civil List Act of 1937; no mention is made of any children.

If The King approved this arrangement, and the annuity of £15,000 once got on to the Statute book, as a result of the Select Committee's report (even supposing that they do not dock it), the odds against any future Government amending the Act to increase the annuity are heavy. We should then be faced with the Heiress Presumptive, her husband, and children, having to make do on £30,000 a year (some of which would be subject to taxation) until the Princess becomes Queen – which may not be for another thirty years. This seems to me a result not at all compatible with the principle which you upheld to me in our talk on Wednesday evening, that the future Queen must be given the wherewithal to live in a manner fitting her position – a principle to which nobody subscribes more emphatically than I do.

But, though we have not yet mentioned Dr Dalton's proposal to the King (hoping that he may yet realize that, like the Dutch, he is 'giving too little and asking too much') both Alexander[1] and I are quite certain that nothing will induce His Majesty to accept it.

Dalton asks The King to surrender £200,000, with which sum, plus the interest on each year's balance, The King himself could allow Princess Elizabeth just as much for the next fifteen years as is now proposed. Moreover, parting with so large a sum would seriously cripple the Privy Purse, and exhaust all the reserves, carefully accumulated to meet the rising cost of wages, etc. and so avoid a repetition of the quasi-bankruptcy of the Privy Purse which occurred in 1921.

I believe Dalton told you that the accumulated savings from the Civil List

---

[1] Alexander Henry Louis Hardinge, 1894–1960. Educated at Harrow and Trinity College, Cambridge. On active service, 1915–18 (wounded, MC). Adjutant, Grenadier Guards, 1919–20. Asst Private Secretary to King George V, 1920–36. Private Secretary to King Edward VIII, 1936; to King George VI, 1936–43. PC, 1936. Knighted, 1937. Succeeded his father as 2nd Baron Hardinge of Penshurst, 1944 (his elder brother having died of wounds received in action, 18 Dec. 1914).

amount to £379,000. That is a misleading figure, for it represents the accumulated savings from the beginning of the reign. It is just as if Dalton were to tell you or me that we have still got intact any legacies or windfalls that we may have had during our lifetimes. We know well that they are not intact. Moreover, there are now no longer likely to be any Civil List balances and I understand this year the Civil List expenditure will end up about £17,000 on the wrong side, with the prospect of a possible further rise in wages and prices to meet.

The present situation is that Dalton has been asked to re-consider his figures. I am not very hopeful that he will come back with any offer that The King would accept; we shall then reach that familiar position – deadlock. It may be that the only solution will be a reversion to the original plan.

When I spoke to A. Eden on the telephone this morning, I told him that I was apprehensive that the figures which Dalton might propose would be inadequate, and my forebodings were only too well grounded. Eden generously said that, since the present plan had been put forward by yourself and himself, he would certainly give us any help he could in any financial dog-fight that might result.

I know well that you too will be no less helpful, if we should be obliged to call upon you. The object of the present letter is merely to put you in the picture of things as they are at present.

Our main object now is not to be hurried into any final decision. I understand that the delivery of any message from The King could be deferred until Tuesday, 18th, if necessary. Meanwhile, I will do my best to keep you in touch with developments.

Sir Alan Lascelles to Winston S. Churchill
(Churchill papers, 2/148)[1]

7 November 1947 Buckingham Palace
Private

Dear Mr Churchill,

Since I wrote this letter, I have heard that you will probably be asked to attend a further meeting with the PM and Dalton early next week, at which the figures which I have noted to you will be officially revealed to you.

Probably I have no business to quote them to you; you know, I am very sure that I only do so because of my great anxiety that the King's position should be fully understood by you and any other members of the opposition involved in this matter.

Probably Ministers would be constitutionally justified in demanding that

---

[1] This letter was handwritten.

the King should get a new private secretary if they knew that I had sent you this communication.

Therefore although it seems almost impertinent in me to do this – I ask you most earnestly to give no indication whatever when the meeting takes place, that you have any foreknowledge of the proposal which Dalton will then communicate to you.

Winston S. Churchill to William Sydney Robinson
(Churchill papers, 1/69)

7 November 1947
Private

My dear WS,

I have just heard, through Messrs Thomas Cook & Son, Ltd., that you and your co-Directors have offered to put your 8-seater VIP Lancastrian aircraft at my disposal to fly me and my party to Marrakech on December 17, entirely free of charge. I had greatly hoped to get away by December 11 and therefore I should very much like to examine the question of the twin-engined Dakota, which could go on or about the day I was aiming at. Before making up my mind I should like to discuss the journey in the Dakota, and for this purpose Air-Commodore Powell[1] and Wing-Commander Arthur are coming to see me this morning.

I need scarcely say how grateful I am for this princely offer and how much it facilitates my wish and need for a short holiday in the sunshine, which the doctors recommend.

Jo Sturdee: note of a conversation between Mr Churchill,
Air Commodore George Powell and Wing Commander Arthur
(Churchill papers, 1/69)

7 November 1947   28 Hyde Park Gate

It was arranged that:
1. The party to fly in their VIP Dakota to consist of:
   Mr Churchill.

---

[1] Anthony George Powell, 1913–2001. Entered RAF College, 1931. Pilot, No. 26 Sqn, 1932; No. 208 Sqn, 1933. Signals Officer, No. 208 Sqn, 1937. Maintenance Liaison Officer, HQ No. 202 Group, 1939. Transferred to Technical Branch, 1940. Staff Officer, Directorate of Telecommunications, 1942; Deputy Director, 1943. Group Capt., Plans, HQ Technical Training Command, 1948. Head, Electronics Branch, SHAPE, 1955. Senior Air Staff Officer, HQ No. 90 (Signals) Group, 1958. Senior Air Staff Officer, HQ Signals Command, 1958. Director, Technical Policy, 1962. Director of Signals (Air), 1966.

Scotland Yard Detective.[1]
Mr Greenshields.[2]
Two Secretaries, if necessary one secretary to go by sea.

2. The plane to take off from Croydon at 11 a.m. on Wednesday, December 10, to arrive in Paris in time for luncheon at British Embassy. Mr Churchill would then attend Mr Duff Cooper's Farewell Party, sleep the night there and leave for Marrakech early the next morning.

3. The plane should take off from a Paris airfield at 9 a.m. on Thursday, December 11, arriving in Marrakech about 5 p.m.

4. Luggage. There would be room for about 20 suitcases as well as painting materials and a certain amount of Book papers. (I think this should be gone into further).

5. Mrs Churchill, Mrs Oliver, Maid and perhaps one secretary should go by sea.

General George C. Marshall to Winston S. Churchill
(Churchill papers, 2/144)

8 November 1947

Dear Mr Churchill,

Though I will see you soon, I send in advance my congratulations on your birthday.

Your continued vigor and youthful spirits discount the pessimism that such anniversaries seem to engender in so many of us after fifty.

The years do fly by, but for you each year seems to offer more and greater opportunities to serve your people and the world.[3]

Sir Orme Sargent to Winston S. Churchill
(Churchill papers, 2/54)

8 November 1947
Confidential

Dear Mr Churchill

Many thanks for your confidential letter of 31st October[4] enclosing a cutting from the *Daily Worker* showing pictures of executions at Salonica under the caption 'British Bullets Killed these Greeks'.

I agree that these pictures, to which our attention had already been drawn

---

[1] C. S. Price.
[2] Churchill's valet, 1948–53.
[3] Churchill replied: 'Thank you so much for your charming message.'
[4] Reproduced above (p. 839).

by His Majesty's Consul-General at Salonica[1] on the 24th October, are the worst possible form of propaganda for the Greek Government in its present struggle and a gift to Communist propaganda. We have been following the trial of these people with considerable interest and His Majesty's Consul-General at Salonica has provided a series of detailed reports from which it is clear that these persons were members of a widespread criminal organisation which had been responsible for a number of deaths, including throwing a hand-grenade into a bus filled with Greek Air Force personnel near Salonica. This terrorist organisation was, on the evidence heard at the trial, openly linked with the Communist Party of Greece (KKE) and was known to have been in existence since at least April 1946. This organisation is made up of what, in Communist jargon, are described as 'Communist Self-Defence Units' which are in fact the lineal descendants to the former notorious 'OPLA' units which, you will remember as the Communist execution squads of the 1944 rebellion. Indeed their purpose is much the same, aiming as they do, at the assassination of prominent Right-wingers and officers in the security forces.

In the course of June of this year sixty-seven persons, including three women, were arrested and their trial by Court Martial opened at Salonica on 28th August, the charges being those of 'murder, attempted murder, espionage at Sedhes airfield on behalf of armed bands, illegal possession of arms and explosives, conspiracy to commit illegal and subversive acts, and recruitment of civilians for KKE bands'. The following extract from a report by His Majesty's Consul-General at Salonica dated 18th September gives a convenient summary of the case:

'The OPLA organisation, to which sixty-four of the defendants belonged (the remaining three were Military and Air Force personnel whose trial was linked with that of the others for convenience) is known to have existed in Salonica following the speech made by Zachariades[2] at the White Tower in May, 1946, when he urged the proper organisation of the communist movement in this city. With the entry into force of the Public Order Act in June, 1946, instituting deportations and Special Courts Martial, the OPLA group, which consisted principally of young communist enthusiasts, was formed to take an active part in the struggle against the 'fascist' government. The existence of the organisation became well known to the Police,

---

[1] Thomas Cecil Rapp, 1893–1984. Educated at Cambridge University. Served in WWI, 1914–18. Acting Vice-Consul, Port Said, 1920. Married, 1922, Dorothy Clarke. Vice-Consul, Cairo, 1922; Rabat, 1927. Consul, Sofia, 1931; Moscow, 1932; Zagreb, 1936. Consul-General, Zagreb, 1939–41; Tabriz, 1943–4; Salonika, 1944–5. Captured and interned in Germany, 1941–3. Head of British Economic Mission to Greece, 1946–7. Ambassador to Mexico, 1947–50. Head of British Middle East Office, Cairo, 1950–3.

[2] Nikos Zachariadis, 1903–73. General Secretary, Communist Party of Greece (KKE), 1931–56. Arrested by Metaxas dictatorship, 1936. Held in captivity by Nazis when they invaded Greece, 1941. Liberated by US Army, 1945. Served in KKE Democratic Army of Greece (DSE) during Greek Civil War, 1946–9. Expelled from KKE, 1957. Committed suicide, 1973.

who learned in the course of investigations that a number of prominent persons were scheduled for execution by it during August, 1946.

It was not until October 1946, however, that the first murder was committed, when a gendarme of the National Security Section covering the Toumba quarter, the communist Stronghold of Salonica, was shot dead. This was followed by the murder, two days later, of Captain Kofitsas,[1] Acting Public Prosecutor of the Salonica Special Court Martial. A number of other crimes followed, culminating in the murderous attack on the RHAF bus on the 30th April of this year. As a result of this last outrage, the leader and organiser, Papageorgiou,[2] was traced and arrested and on the basis of documents and depositions not only were the other defendants arrested, but the KKE was definitely linked with this OPLA organisation.'

The trial, according to the same report was conducted in a 'scrupulously fair manner' and 'full latitude was given the prisoners to speak on their own behalf, and all were legally represented'. Our Consul-General ends his report as follows:

'A well-known lawyer of Republican sentiments has stated to His Majesty's Consul that the local legal world is well satisfied with the manner in which the whole affair was conducted, and that any suspicion of torture or even undue pressure must be completely ruled out.'

The court awarded fifty-two death sentences, six sentences of life imprisonment, one sentence of fifteen years while six persons were acquitted. The trial ended on the 15th September, the day on which the new Greek Government declared an amnesty for bandits who surrendered to the authorities; as an ancillary measure executions were suspended for the period of one month. The amnesty was prolonged for a further month from 15th October but according to the reports we have received from Athens, public opinion was not in favour of the continued suspension of death sentences which were consequently put into effect and forty-seven out of the fifty-two persons condemned to death in this trial were executed on 17th, 21st and 23rd October.

We are not actually aware of the circumstances in which press photographers were allowed to be present at these executions but, as you know only too well, the Greeks are their own worst propagandists and it is quite likely that they allowed press photographers from Liberal and Right Wing papers to be present at these executions in the expectation that the publication of

---

[1] Dimitrios Kofitsas, 1902–46. Educated at Officers' School, Greek Gendarmerie. 2nd Lt, 1933. Head, Special Security Services, Thessaloniki. Refused to provide information to the Germans during Nazi occupation. Imprisoned twice by the Germans. Assassinated, 1946.

[2] Andreas Papageorgiou. Leader of Greek self-defence unit connected to Greek Communist Party, 1947.

photographs would act as a deterrent. The Communists, who no doubt were aware of this, were naturally able to turn the situation to their advantage by seeing that their members made a good show when facing the execution squad and the result, deplorable though it may be, is these unfortunate photographs.

I think you will agree that the detailed accounts of the trial which we have received show that these people for the most part deserved their fate and that detention on Islands, which is only intended as a preventive measure for persons suspected of being in contact with armed bands, would have been completely unsuitable for these potential and actual assassins.

Since the above was drafted, our attention has been called to the atrocity story carried on the front page of the *Daily Mirror* for November 10th, in which reference is made to the display of decapitated heads. We are instructing our Ambassador in Athens[1] to investigate this report, which, however, dates from June of this year, and to point out to the Greek Government the publicity which reports of such alleged atrocities is receiving in this country and the harm which is caused thereby.

Winston S. Churchill to Bernard Baruch
(Churchill papers, 2/210)

9 November 1947

My dear Bernie,

Thank you so much for your letter.[2]

I am very glad to be informed about the American position. It is difficult to judge from over here. I have never advocated the abandonment of all controls. On the contrary, my policy stands on the foundation of basic minimum ration, at a controlled price, for the masses of the people, and it is only after that standard has been secured that free competition would be permitted. I was speaking on general aims. Our aim is freedom, but that does not exclude controls. The Socialists' aim is controls which will exclude British freedom.

Please keep in touch with me.

---

[1] Clifford John Norton, 1891–1990. Educated at Rugby and Queen's College, Oxford. On active service at Gallipoli, 1915, and in Palestine, 1916–18. Political Officer, Damascus, Deraa and Haifa, 1919–20. Entered Diplomatic Service, 1921. Private Secretary to Sir Robert Vansittart, 1930–7. CMG, 1933. CVO, 1937. Counsellor, British Embassy, Warsaw, 1937–9. Minister to Switzerland in Berne, 1942–6. KCMG, 1946. Ambassador to Greece, 1946–51.

[2] Reproduced above (pp. 840–2).

Sir Alan Lascelles to Winston S. Churchill
(Churchill papers, 2/148)[1]

10 November 1947
Personal and Secret

Dear Mr Churchill,

Many thanks for your letter of yesterday.

I said I would let you know further developments: Alexander[2] and I saw the Doctor this afternoon; he said that he was not at all surprised that the King had rejected his last proposal – he had never expected otherwise.

After much discussion, we prepared a new draft Royal Message, in which no figures are mentioned and in which the King's offer to make a refund is made contingent on the report of the Select Committee – i.e. the King is not committed to handing over any sum until HM knows what provision the Select Committee is prepared to make.

This revised draft will, I understand, be shown to you when you meet the PM and Chancellor.

Meanwhile, the King has authorised me to write to the Chancellor that 'HM would have no objection to this draft being used if it is eventually thought desirable to do so' – i.e. the King has not given his final approval of the draft, and the door is left open for any further changes in it which might be recommended after your coming meeting.

Jo Sturdee to Winston S. Churchill
(Churchill papers, 1/68)

10 November 1947

I have worked it out and the cost of board and food for you and your party at the Mamounia Hotel will amount to $6,000. This sum excludes all drinks, car and chauffeur expenses, laundry and telephones and postage and other petty expenses. The figure you suggested to Mr Graebner is $10,000.

Could you enquire if, in case of need, you could have any more money sent out to you, as I think the procedure in this event would be a little more difficult?

---

[1] This letter was handwritten.
[2] Hardinge.

Winston S. Churchill: speech
(Hansard)

11 November 1947   House of Commons

PARLIAMENT BILL

Order read for resuming Adjourned Debate on Amendment to Question (10th November), 'That the Bill be now read a Second time'. – (Mr H. Morrison.)

Which Amendment was, to leave out from 'That' to the end of the Question, and to add instead thereof:

> this House declines to give a Second Reading to a Bill which, without mandate, justification or public demand, seeks to destroy the constitutional safeguards embodied in the Parliament Act, 1911, when no complaint has been put forward of the use by the House of Lords of its existing powers; when no attempt has been made to deal with the composition of the Second Chamber which that Act laid down as an essential consequence can only be to distract attention from the economic perils with which the country is confronted. – (Sir D. Maxwell Fyfe.)

Question again proposed, 'That the words proposed to be left out stand part of the Question.'

Mr Churchill: Yesterday, after several courtesies which I acknowledge, the Leader of the House and Lord President of the Council cited me as a witness in this case. Therefore, I thought it my duty to come here and testify, although I must admit under some protest from my medical advisor. I frankly admit that I like this old controversy. I like to feel that what I thought right 36 years ago, the great party which I now lead, and the famous party which I then served, and also what I well believe the mass of the nation, think right now. It is in the evening of life that these are gratifying sensations. I am glad to look back upon the days when I used to address the fathers and grandfathers of those who sit opposite and who fell away from the Liberal and Radical theme and lolloped into the slatternly trough of collectivism. Therefore, I in no way resent the references which the Lord President has made to my previous convictions, speeches, and records, and I am particularly obliged to the right hon. Gentleman for the quotation which he made from my explanation of the Parliament Act 36 years ago. I am sorry I could not hear him, but I read the report, and for greater security I have a copy with me. He said:

> The present Leader of the Opposition, in the 1910 Debates which led up to the consideration of the Parliament Bill, which became the Parliament Act, 1911, expounded what he conceived at that time to be the policy underlying the proposals which were passed into law in the Parliament Act,

1911. He assumed that Parliaments would on the average last for about four years, and he said that in the first two years of a Parliament the controversial questions upon which the Election had been fought would normally have been disposed of. Then, the argument continues, in the second two years of the Parliament there would be two classes of Bills – Bills upon which there was a broad measure of agreement between parties, and fresh controversial measures, which the Government might bring forward, but which, if rejected by the House of Lords, would await what he called 'the ratification of a new decision of the electorate'.

Well, Sir, I had forgotten this speech. When this Debate was advertised, I asked that my past speeches should be looked up, and I intended to read them all; but there were about 30, so I did not find the time to do it. But this speech exactly represents where we stand today, and what the Parliament Act was intended to establish.

In these confused and baffling times, it is right to recur to broad general principles. The spirit of the Parliament Act, and the purpose of that Act, were to secure the intimate, effective and continuous influence of the will of the people upon the conduct and progress of their affairs. That was the purpose – not the will of the governors of the governesses of the people, but the will of the people. The right hon. Gentleman, after quoting this passage, which I must say was an odd selection on his part – a little act of personal friendship, I think, because nothing can be more helpful to me – said that he doubted whether even in my Liberal days I was a very good democrat. I certainly spoke for a united Government and party, of which Mr Lloyd George and I were supposed to be the Radical spear-point, and I spoke at a time when political controversy was very keen – more sharply followed by the mass of the people from day to day than it is now, when newspapers were able to report every word, and every word was minutely scanned by friend as well as foe. I am sure that if I had diverged at that time from the general line of the Liberal Radical Party, and had, so to speak, made what the hon. Member for West Fife (Mr Gallacher) would call 'a diversionary error', it would most certainly have been pointed out. In those days Ministers left office because of some slight diversion, not too serious a diversion, from what was settled, cleancut policy of the party. Therefore, I think that I was speaking with full authority.

I do not feel that the Leader of the House has any right to suggest that I was not a good democrat in those days, and not a good democrat now. How does the right hon. Gentleman conceive democracy? Just let me explain it to him, Mr Speaker, or explain some of the more rudimentary elements of it to him. Democracy is not a caucus, obtaining a fixed term of office by promises, and then doing what it likes with the people. We hold that there ought to be a constant relationship between the rulers and the people. Government of the people, by the people, for the people, still remains the sovereign definition of democracy. There is no correspondence between this broad conception and the outlook of His Majesty's Government. Democracy, I must explain to the Lord President, does not mean, 'We have got our majority, never mind how, and we have our lease of office for five years, so what are you going to do about it?' That is not democracy, that is only small party patter, which will not go down with the mass of the people of this country. Presently, we shall convince the party opposite that the will of the people will prevail. We accept that tribunal, and all their plans will be to shirk it.

The right hon. Gentleman has an obvious, unconcealable, well-known relish for petty dictatorship. He has many good qualities, but he should always be on guard against his propensity and love to cat-and-mouse the people from morning until night. Look at all the power he is enjoying today. No Government has ever failed more completely to meet their daily practical needs. Yet the right hon. Gentleman and his colleagues are avid for more power. No Government has ever combined so passionate a lust for power which such incurable impotence in its exercise. The whole history of this country shows a British instinct – and, I think I may say, a genius – for the division of power. The American Constitution, with its checks and counterchecks, combined with its frequent appeals to the people, embodied much of the ancient wisdom of this island. Of course, there must be proper executive power to any Government, but our British, our English idea, in a special sense, has always been a system of balanced rights and divided authority, with many other persons and organised bodies having to be considered besides the Government of the day and the officials they employ. This essential British wisdom is expressed in many foreign Constitutions which followed our Parliamentary system, outside the totalitarian zone, but never was it so necessary as in a country which has no written Constitution.

The right hon. Gentleman spoke about Parliament, about the rights of Parliament, which I shall certainly not fail to defend. But it is not Parliament that should rule; it is the people who should rule through Parliament. That is the mistake he made, an important omission. All this was comprehended by those who shaped the Parliament Act and the settlement which developed upon that Act, so that it was never mentioned again for 36 years until now. That is what the Government are seeking to mutilate, if not to destroy. The object of the Parliament Act, and the spirit of that Act, were to give effect, not to spasmodic emotions of the electorate, but to the settled, persistent will of the people. What they wanted to do they could do, and what they did not want to do they could stop. All this idea of a handful of men getting hold of the State machine, having the right to make the people do what suits their party and personal interests or doctrines, is completely contrary to every conception of surviving Western democracy.

'Some reverence for the laws ourselves have made,
Some patient force to change them when we will.'[1]

We accept in the fullest sense of the word the settled and persistent will of the people. All this idea of a group of supermen and super-planners, such as we see before us, 'playing the angel', as the French call it, and making the masses of the people do what they think is good for them, without any check or correction, is a violation of democracy. Many forms of Government have been tried, and will be tried in this world of sin and woe. No one pretends that democracy is perfect or all-wise. Indeed, it has been said that democracy is the worst form of Government except all those other forms that have been tried from time to time; but there is the broad feeling in our country that the people should rule, continuously rule, and that public opinion, expressed by all constitutional means, should shape, guide, and control the actions of Ministers who are their servants and not their masters.

I remember, many years ago, old John Morley talking to me about βουλή, a Greek word, born in the classical cradle of democracy, meaning the wish, the will, and the determination, with special reference to the gods, or to destiny, or, as it was adapted, to the desire of the mass, the inward desire of the mass of the people. This implies that there should be frequent recurrence, direct or indirect, to the popular will, and that the wish – the βουλή – should prevail. That is what the party opposite is afraid of, and that is what this Act is devised to prevent. (Hon. Members: 'Rubbish'.) That is the first broad submission which I make to the House upon this important Measure. I do not expect to convert hon. Members opposite in a few minutes, but I am going to show them the language which can be used against their policy and which will be used on every platform in this country.

However, it is argued that the present Second Chamber is a biased and unrepresentative body; that it does not act evenly between the two sides or parties in the State. Let me just look into that dispassionately. There is, of course, a difference between the two sides in our political life. Temperament, conditions, upbringing, fortunes, interests, environment decide for every individual in a free country which side he will take. One side claims to be the party of progress, as if progress was bound to be right, no matter in what direction. The other side emphasises stability, which is also very important in this changing world. But no one would rest content with that. This is an unreal and far too narrow a dichotomy. I heard that word 40 years ago as a debating rejoinder from Mr Asquith. I went home and looked it up in the dictionary, and I do not think that it has been used in this House until now. Both progress and stability are needed to make a happy country. But the right hon. Gentleman

---

[1] From Alfred Lord Tennyson, *The Princess* (1847).

complains that the present Second Chamber has, from its composition, an undue bias in favour of stability.

Well, Mr Speaker, if you have a motorcar – and I believe some are still allowed – you have to have a brake. There ought to be a brake. A brake, in essence, is one-sided; it prevents an accident through going too fast. It was not intended to prevent accidents through going too slow. For that you must look elsewhere, to another part of the vehicle; you must look to the engine and, of course, to the petrol supply. For that there is the renewed impulse. To prevent your going too slow you must look to the renewed impulse of the people's will; but it is by force of the engine, occasionally regulated by the brake, that the steady progress of the nation and of society is maintained, and tens of millions of humble people are given steady conditions in which they can live their lives and make all their plans for their homes, their families and for bringing up their children, and have a chance of bettering themselves, and, at the same time, forwarding the cause of the whole community. (An Hon. Member: 'Two million unemployed'.) Two million unemployed under a Socialist Government. Never has that figure of two million unemployed occurred under any but a Socialist administration. (*Interruption.*) It is really a matter of history and arithmetic. Never has there been a substantial rise above two million except under a Government headed by the Socialist Party.

The Prime Minister (Mr Attlee): I think that the right hon. Gentleman must have made a mistake in the date. The peak date for unemployment was in the Coalition Government of 1931.

Mr Churchill: It was the Coalition Government of 1931 that reduced the unemployed figure the figure of nearly three million to just above one million, and it was the right hon. Gentleman, even in these days of full employment and shortage of labour, who managed to raise unemployment to over two million at the beginning of the present year by gross mismanagement of the fuel problem. All this myth about the tragedy of unemployment between the wars – (Hon. Members: 'Myth?') The myth is that it was due to the Conservative Party, yet all the peaks and heights were reached and all the most serious causes occurred during the brief terms when the Socialists were in office.

I have been drawn from the general thread of my argument, which I am most anxious should be comprehended by hon. Members opposite, if not for their conversion, at least, for educative purposes. I was speaking just now about the 'brake'. If the Socialist Government do not like the character of this particular brake, certainly we are not defending it.

Mr Kirkwood (Dumbarton Burghs): What has that to do with the Bill?

Mr Churchill: Certainly we are not defending it. I must say that the Government themselves seem to be a little more reconciled to it than they used to be, judging by the number of Socialist hereditary nobles who are being created. If they do not like the character of the brake, why do they not propose the reform of the Second Chamber? We are quite ready to confer with them and to help them in such a task. As the Socialist Government now stand, they maintain hereditary principle. The hereditary Chamber is to have one year's suspensory veto but not two. One year's suspensory veto by a hereditary assembly is the true blue of Socialist democracy; two years is class tyranny.

One is astonished that the human mind can be constrained into such silly postures. But then the explanation is furnished and backed by ever-accumulating evidence that this Bill does not arise out of any consideration of general principles, or of the needs of the State, or of the practical requirements of the day, but only out of a deal between Cabinet Ministers quarrelling about the nationalisation of steel. There is no doubt, however, that what His Majesty's Government seek and intend is virtually what is called single-Chamber Government. On this issue there are wide and world-famous arguments. No free country enjoying democratic institutions that I know of has adopted single-Chamber Government.

Mr Ronald Mackay[1] (Hull, North West): The State of Queensland has single-Chamber Government.

Mr Churchill: It is the exception which proves the rule. No free country —

Mr Warbey (Luton) rose —

Mr Speaker: I think it is a mistake for hon. Gentlemen to interrupt continuously. It would be much better if each one waited and heard the arguments whether they like them or not, and then they could listen to the arguments in reply by the Home Secretary.

Mr Churchill: I am glad to be reminded because I asked this morning for a check up to be made over the British Empire, and I was not aware that there was a single-Chamber Government in Queensland, but that State is only part of a federal system.

Mr Warbey: What about Norway?

Mr Churchill: No free country of which I have heard up to the present — I quite agree that there might be some countries throughout the world — which is enjoying democratic institutions has adopted single-Chamber Government. The United States, the Swiss, the Dutch, the Belgians, the French even in their latest constitution have a Second Chamber. Eire has created its own Senate. Our Dominions, the most democratic countries in the world, all have, with the exception of Queensland I am reminded, sought and preserved two-Chamber Government — what clever people would call bi-cameral Government. All feel that between the chance vote of an election on universal suffrage and the permanent alteration of the whole slowly-built structure of the State and nation there ought to be some modifying process.

---

[1] Ronald William Gordon Mackay, 1902–60. Known as 'Kim Mackay'. Educated at Sydney University. Admitted solicitor, Sydney, 1926. Relocated to England, 1934. Admitted solicitor, England, 1934. Unsuccessful Parliamentary candidate (Lab.) for Somerset, 1935; (Ind. Soc.) for Llandaff and Barry, 1942. MP (Lab.) for Hull North-West, 1945–50; for North Div. of Reading, 1950–1.

Show me a powerful, successful, free democratic constitution on the principle of single-Chamber Government.

Mr Warbey: I have told the right hon. Gentleman of one.

Mr Churchill: Norway is not a very powerful state and would not have been a state at all but for our exertions. I am speaking of the general experience of the world and I say that the overwhelming majority that I know of have a Second Chamber, mostly with lesser powers than the popular assembly and with a different outlook and function. By the way, all this insistence on Norway or Queensland by the other side of the House illustrates and proves my point that is single-Chamber Government which hon. Gentlemen opposite seek.

Mr Sydney Silverman (Nelson and Colne) *rose –*

Mr Churchill: The hon. Gentlemen the Member for Nelson and Colne (Mr S. Silverman) is not in this matter at all. There are quite a lot of matters in which he takes an interest but this is not one of them.

Mr Warbey rose –

Mr Churchill: I do not mind in the least being interrupted. It does not worry me –

Mr Warbey rose –

Mr Churchill: I do not give way unless I think it worthwhile. Some of the foreign countries arrive at the two-chamber system by a proportion of members retiring every two years or every year; some by a franchise based on a higher age limit; some by the influence of local authorities standing on a different foundation; and some, like the Canadian Senate, are nominated for life and retire gradually by the effluxion of time. In some there are joint sessions where a majority decision decides in case of deadlock. I remember in 1910 we worked in the hectic interval between the two elections of that year in conference with the Opposition, but it broke down as so many other things do, on figures.

But all these constitutions have the same object in view, namely, that the persistent resolve of the people shall prevail without throwing the community into convulsion and disorder by rash or violent, irreparable action and to restrain and prevent a group or sect or faction assuming dictatorial power. Single-Chamber Government, as I have said, is especially dangerous in a country which has no written Constitution and where parliaments are elected for as long as five years. When there is an ancient community built up across the generations, where freedom broadens slowly down from precedent to precedent, it is not right that all should be liable to be swept away by the desperate measures of a small set of discredited men. 'A thousand years scarce serve to form a State. An hour may lay it in dust.'[1] This is the argument against Second-Chamber Government, which is evidently so espoused on that side of the House. In this field the outlook of His Majesty's Ministers is marked by

[1] Lord Byron, *Childe Harold's Pilgrimage* (1812).

the same meanness of thought and spirit which characterise so much of their action and which destroy their power to help or unite and save our suffering country. They wish to keep the present Second Chamber on the hereditary basis so that they can abuse it, insult it and attack it and yet to cripple its powers, although these powers stand on 36 years of modern Parliamentary title so that, in effect, it is both vulnerable and powerless. That is their tactical method. By this artful, and insincere scheme they hope to substitute for the will of the people the decisions of the Government. This sinister intrigue will be exposed by us without fear to the electorate resting upon a universal suffrage.

The Government say – let us look closer into the point – 'We have the right to pass into law everything we mentioned or even hinted at in our election pamphlet, "Let us Face the Future".' It is arguable whether a Government, which is losing daily the real support of the nation, has the right to claim that such a bill must be paid even within the limits of what they call their mandate. At any rate no one should be under any delusions on this matter. There is no constitutional or legal bar upon the right of a Government possessing a majority in the House of Commons to propose any legislation they think fit whether it has figured in their pre-election promises or programmes or not. The people have no guarantee, except the suspensory power of the House of Lords or Second Chamber, nor can they be given any other guarantee that Measures never thought of at the Election and to which they object will not be imposed upon them.

Look around at what is happening every day. The idea of a mandate is only a convention. A band of men who have got hold of the machine and have a Parliamentary majority undoubtedly have the power to propose anything they choose without the slightest regard to whether the people like it or not, or the slightest reference to whether or not it was included in their Election literature. I will not expatiate upon the kind of laws they could pass if all is to be settled by a party majority in the House of Commons, under the discipline of the Whips and the caucus. But anyone can see for himself, and it is now frankly admitted on the opposite side of the House, that what is aimed at now is single-Chamber Government at the dictation of Ministers, without regard to the wishes of the people and without giving them any chance to express their opinion. There is, in fact, only one thing that they cannot do under the Parliament Act, 1911, and that is to prolong the life of Parliament beyond the five years' span to which we reduced it in those old days. I must say I am very glad we thought of it.

As a free-born Englishman, what I hate is the sense of being at anybody's mercy or in anybody's power, be he Hitler or Attlee. We are approaching very near to dictatorship in this country, dictatorship that is to say – I will be quite candid with the House – without either its criminality or its efficiency. But let the party opposite not imagine they will rule our famous land and lead our group of Commonwealths and our Empire – or what is left of it – by party dodges and Cabinet intrigues. Lots of people have tried to break the British nation and some were foreign. They all came a cropper. Do not imagine, I say to right hon. Gentlemen opposite, that you have got this country in pawn. The British are a proud people and, more than any other country in Europe, they have known how to control their rulers. (*Interruption.*) You are our rulers now and we are going to show you that there are limits to your control.

Let hon. Members opposite not delude themselves by supposing that by raising this issue they will draw an ancient red herring across the fundamental economic and imperial issues now at stake which involve the life of Britain as a great Power. Why are they devising dodges to keep themselves in office, and to get the last scrunch out of their freak majority and legal term? Is it not ignoble, is it not indeed most imprudent, for these incompetent Ministers, amid all the miseries they have brought upon us, to adopt the attitude, the arrogant attitude, 'We have got our ration of time. Let us exploit it to the utmost. To Hell with the will of the people. We will teach them from our superior knowledge what they ought to want.' Is it not much better to recur to the simple process of keeping in touch with the people, and of not being afraid to consult them, or even to take a dismissal at their hands?

Why are the Government so afraid of appealing to the people for what they tell us is their great, democratic, philanthropic policy of Socialistic progress into the brave new world? Why are they so afraid? No one has obstructed their will. They have carried all the Measures they wished. They have brought us low and they are bringing us to ruin. What more can they want? Yet – and the Bill brings it before us effectively at the moment – when the Government may be the most execrated of all Administrations, they will claim the right, against the will of the people and, if they choose, without any consultation with the people, to exercise unlimited legislative power.

This is a dictatorship that we are facing, a timid, incompetent dictatorship, but a dictatorship no less, and one that at any time in the lifetime of this Parliament may be replaced by a determined, totalitarian oligarchy. Is the party opposite really to be entitled to pass laws affecting the whole character of the country in the closing years of this Parliament without any appeal to the people who have the vote and who placed them where they are? No, Sir, democracy says, 'No, a thousand times No. You have no right to pass legislation in the closing phase of a Parliament which is not accepted or desired by the mass of the people.' It may well be that Ministers on that Bench are going to be more hated than any Government which has held office since the franchise was extended in the great Reform Bill of 1832. It may well be that not only bankruptcy but actual starvation will come upon this island, largely from their mismanagement.

How do we know that, in the next 18 months, we shall see the same feeble despots in office? They may be replaced at any time by a convulsion in this

House or at Transport House, or in the complicated party structure of the Government majority, by other men, no less mischievous but more malignant, more ruthless. These may hoist themselves into power, men who have never presented themselves to the electors as leaders of the nation. Are they to have the full, unbridled authority to pass any laws they choose irrespective of the views and feelings of the whole nation regarding the Government or the Bills proposed? These are issues which are before us now on the Second Reading of the Bill on which we shall give our vote.

There are, I must admit, moments when I am sorry for the Lord President of the Council (Mr Herbert Morrison), a man outpassed at the moment by his competitors, outdated even by his prejudices, scrambling along trying to regain popularity on an obsolete issue and on an ever-ebbing tide. I hope he will not mind my quoting or adapting some lines, although they are of a martial character, about his position:

> 'Crippses to right of him, Daltons to left of him,
> Bevans behind him, volleyd and thundered.'

It must have been very harassing.
Then there is another line:

> 'What tho' the soldiers knew
> Someone had blunder'd.'

There is even one more line a little further back on in the poem which may not be irrelevant:

> 'Then they came back, but not the four hundred.'[1]

Mr Kirkwood: The wish is father to the thought.

Mr Churchill: I see that the Home Secretary (Mr Ede) is going to follow me. I am sorry for him, too. He always wears the air of injured innocence which we might expect to find on the face of a virtuous and respectable mayor or alderman who has been caught in a somewhat disreputable and compromising situation. I ask him: does he really think he can cling to office for two and a half years more until this Bill has passed into law under the workings of a Parliament Act?

The last election was abnormal. There had not been one for 10 years. There had been a total cessation of ordinary party warfare, on our side at least. A large portion of our voters, our men, were abroad – several millions – and out of touch with any of the party associations with which they would have been ranged had they been at home. It was abnormal. I have no doubt that in party circles it is calculated that the majority gained at the last Election, whatever may be said about it, will be able to run on for its full legal term and

---

[1] From (first quotation adapted from) Alfred, Lord Tennyson, 'The Charge of the Light Brigade' (1855).

make the British people drain their cup to the last dregs. No doubt it will be helpful – here I see the hand of the master craftsman, the Lord President –

The Lord President of the Council (Mr Herbert Morrison): The right hon. Gentleman has promoted me.

Mr Churchill: Craft is common both to skill and deceit. No doubt it will be helpful to party discipline to be able to say to an unhappy, disillusioned party, 'We must hold together until we get the Parliament Bill through and thus carry our glorious nationalisation of steel which will put the country right once and for all. Hold on, boys, for another year. Let us have a full run for our money. Let us get all out of it we can.' I do not think it will happen this way. If there was a General Election tomorrow the Socialist majority would vanish. If they wait another year, they themselves will vanish for a considerable period, 'unwept, unhonoured, and unsung'[1] – and unhung. They have paralysed and stifled the whole native life-effort of our people. Do not let them delude themselves by supposing that they will escape on the issue of 'the Peers versus the People'. The electors are going to vote on their mismanagement and on their partisanship in this grave crisis in our history. Their calculations will not succeed. They will not escape, even by this partial Measure, the will of the people, and the longer they try to do so, the more decisive will be the condemnation they will receive at the national hands.

House of Commons: Oral Answers
(Hansard)

13 November 1947

BUDGET PROPOSALS (NEWSPAPER PUBLICATION)

Mr Raikes (by Private Notice) asked the Chancellor of the Exchequer whether he has considered the accurate forecast of the Budget proposals in a newspaper on sale at 3.45 p.m. yesterday, a copy of which has been sent to him, and if he will institute an inquiry into the source of the information.

The Chancellor of the Exchequer (Mr Dalton): I very much regret to tell the House that the publication to which the hon. Member refers arose out of an incident which occurred as I was entering the Chamber to make my speech yesterday. In reply to questions put to me by the Lobby correspondent of the *Star* newspaper, I indicated to him the subject matter contained in the publication in question. I appreciate that this was a grave indiscretion on my part, for which I offer my deep apologies to the House.

Mr Raikes: Will the Chancellor of the Exchequer convey to that newspaper, apart from any indiscretion on his part, the very grave breach of journalistic

---

[1] From Sir Walter Scott, *The Lay of the Last Minstrel* (1805).

honour on the part of a newspaper receiving such information to publish it in advance before it could properly appear?

Mr Churchill: May I acknowledge on the part of the Opposition, the very frank manner in which the right hon. Gentleman has expressed himself to the House and our sympathy with him at the misuse of his confidence which has occurred?

Mr Beverley Baxter: May I ask the Chancellor, since this involves the professional honour of journalists in general, did the Lobby correspondent in question know that it was a friendly and private if, perhaps, ill-judged statement, or did he think it was for immediate publication?

Mr Dalton: I do not think that I should add to what I have said to the House. I take the blame for having committed an indiscretion in my relationship with this Lobby correspondent whom I have known, as we have known so many of the Lobby correspondents over a period of years, and I do not think that it would be suitable for me to pass any judgment on him. I have apologised for my part in the matter, and I would prefer to leave it there.

Winston S. Churchill to Hugh Dalton
(Churchill papers, 2/53)

13 November 1947

My dear Chancellor of the Exchequer,

Since question-time today, when I intervened on the subject of the disclosure of Budget secrets, I have received further information. I have now seen the very precise and comprehensive form of the announcement. I am also told that no obligation of secrecy was imposed upon the journalist, though that certainly seems to me to have been implicit. There could have been dealings as the result of this premature disclosure.

In these circumstances, while I acknowledge the frankness of your apology to the House, and my sympathy with you in the breach of confidence which may have been committed, I feel it is necessary that the incident should be the subject of an enquiry by a Select Committee. Such is the view of my Conservative colleagues and, I also know of the Liberal Party. It seems to me very likely this would be your own wish too. We are therefore putting a Motion on the Paper in this sense.

I am sending a copy of this letter to the Press.

Anthony Eden to Winston S. Churchill
(Churchill papers, 2/210)[1]

13 November 1947

My dear Winston,

Thank you for letting me see Bernie B's letter.[2] There is much force in what he writes, but, of course, the Americans have never been over-controlled in the sense that we now are. We have to keep some controls, but we can surely simplify them or reduce their number.

Winston S. Churchill to Prince Charles, Count of Flanders
(Churchill papers, 2/146)

17 November 1947

Sir,

I regret to say that Mary's doctor does not wish her to make another journey to town this week, on account of her condition.[3] They begged me to say how sorry they both were not to be able to come. On consulting my Engagements Card, I find, as I suggested to Your Royal Highness, that I have political work that night, and my wife and I are therefore not able to accept the very kind invitation with which you honoured us. For this reason, I have not proceeded with trying to get the theatre tickets, but I will do so at once if Your Royal Highness wishes to make another party. We shall no doubt meet tomorrow night at the Palace.

I look forward greatly to my expedition next summer, and really think I might make something of these two very attractive subjects.

Henry Luce to Winston S. Churchill
(Churchill papers, 4/141)

18 November 1947   New York

Dear Mr Churchill,

This weekend I read the opening book of your magnum opus. It was a great pleasure to do so and, for a reason you will understand better than anyone, a pleasure profoundly mixed with pain. The pain of reviewing the tale of human folly and weakness which you unfold is at times almost unendurable. In producing this effect you have wonderfully succeeded in your mission to history.

---

[1] This letter was handwritten.
[2] Reproduced above (pp. 840–2).
[3] Mary was pregnant with her first child, Nicholas Soames, born 12 Feb. 1948.

In your introductory remarks on the proof, you say that this semi-final manuscript is being sent to a number of people for their critical comments. I do not assume that it was intended that I should be included in this distinguished category but anyhow I am going to 'include myself in' and offer you a few points for your consideration. Some of these points I will make as one of your 'American editors' and some simply as a reader.

Firstly then, I can see that this first book presents to the Editors of *Life* very special problems in excerpting. This is mainly because so much of the book has a meaning for any British reader, who is more or less acquainted with the course of British politics over the last twenty-five years, which it cannot have for any except a very few American readers. It is not merely that your story is tied so closely to British socio-political history in general; it is also that as a true British politician (and, in my opinion, of course, the greatest) your story is tied so closely to the House of Commons. I make this point without suggesting that there is anything which you either can or should do about it; it is a problem, however, which we will have to face and, facing, will, I am sure, achieve a good solution.

As an editor, there is only one major criticism which I wish to submit. It seems to me that the architectural proportions of this book are not as well worked out as they might be. The structural problem with which you were presented is, I suppose, obvious enough, – namely to unfold a general panorama of, mainly, European history and, at the same time, to do it, as far as possible, in terms of your own immediate knowledge and of your own (as it turned out) providential connection with the various stages of the drama.

There are many places in the book – e.g. the opening paragraphs of many of the chapters – where the sense of the surge of events is given in a most masterly manner. But the onward movement is not consistently maintained. The principal reason for the slackening of pace is, probably, the inclusion of so many passages from your speeches, articles, and memoranda. Very often, indeed nearly always, these passages give the correct interpretation of events; what you saw at the time is the truth which history must confirm. Nevertheless this technique slows up the present re-narration of events.

I remember years ago reading Monypenny[1] and Buckle's[2] life of Disraeli – a fine piece of work (though lacking entirely your vigor of language) but

---

[1] William Flavelle Monypenny, 1866–1912. Educated at Trinity College, Dublin and Balliol College, Oxford. Assistant to the Editor (George Earle Buckle), *The Times*, 1893. Editor, Johannesburg *Star*, 1899. Served in Imperial Light Horse, Second Boer War. Director of Supplies for the rehabilitation of refugees in Lord Milner's administration. Began definitive biography of Benjamin Disraeli, 1910; completed two volumes before his death (George Earle Buckle completed the biography by writing four more volumes).

[2] George Earle Buckle, 1854–1935. Educated at New College, Oxford (Scholar); Fellow of All Souls College, 1877–85. Called to the Bar, Lincoln's Inn, 1880. Asst Editor, *The Times*, 1880; Editor, 1884–1912. Married, 1898, Alicia Isobel Payn (div. 1898); 1905, Beatrice Anne Earle. Published *The Life of Disraeli* (1920), completing work begun by W. F. Monypenny; *The Letters of Queen Victoria* (1926).

marred, I thought, by too many and too lengthy quotations from the protagonist, antagonist and other characters.

In itself, each and every one of your quoted passages is thoroughly interesting but taken together I think they mar the architectural sense which has characterized every speech and book of yours that I remember reading.

May I put the matter another way? During the years that led on to disaster you were engaged in a continuous debate against the drift of things. The fact that you and a few others <u>were</u> conducting this debate and never flagged from it, is (it is hardly an exaggeration to say) the one redeeming feature of the scene. Had you and your friends not been there with the words of truth, one would be bound to feel on looking back that human affairs had come to such a point of folly and dishonor that they really weren't worth bothering about; that the human drama had simply disintegrated into such a cacaphony of raucous cries and meaningless good will that one had just better ignore the whole period and wait for some wholly fresh chapter of human history to begin in some distant century. But you <u>were</u> there! Human judgment, founded on the courage of conviction, could still be right as well as wrong. And for that reason there is a moral in the tale and the pain of it is purgative and edifying. Therefore, all the things you said at all the various moments in those years of the locusts is of the essence of Western European history. You must, with no false modesty, get your record on the record over against the drift of things. Can you do this with quicker, sharper strokes so that the whole story achieves a greater dramatic unity?

You may not think this is a valid or useful criticism – but anyway there it is, the only important one, which it seems to me, I have to offer.

Thirdly, as a reader rather than as an editor, I would like to raise the question as to whether your implicit analysis of the course of European history goes deep enough. You interpret the drift to catastrophe mainly in terms of unnecessary folly and unnecessary weakness. All history may indeed be so interpreted. And to repeat, your own record is the clear proof that if leaders and the led had thought and acted in a different way, as was continuously and actually proposed to them by you among others, mankind could have been spared unspeakable sorrows. Nevertheless, the question still remains: <u>why</u> were leaders so stupid and weak? Why did the nations and peoples of Europe throw up such bad leadership?

In one very striking passage you give a clue. You say that tremendous scientific and technological power had been opened up to an insufficiently 'mature' civilization. As another has put it, Western Civilization had failed to achieve moral strength to match the physical power it disposed of. And another would say that there had been an actual decay in moral fibre. And yet others would say that we had simply failed to learn how to establish adequate principles and practices for 'industrial civilization'.

As a reader reading your account of the years between the war, I accept and am carried along by all that you say about folly and weakness but even if now and then I get clues as to your analytical insight (e.g. the suggestion about monarchy) still as a reader I would also like to know more explicitly what you, my chief guide through purgatory, has to say about why the human race in this period was doomed or doomed itself to so much folly.

* * *

It is surely almost superfluous for me to say that I am overjoyed that the great work has already been carried so far forward. This first book is in itself an achievement of capital importance, fulfilling, as I have ventured to say, a unique mission to history. We, for our part, will make the magazine presentation of it a labor of love as well as, we hope, one of profit to our readers and ourselves and of satisfaction to you.

Meanwhile we watch contemporary events in Britain with keenest interest and would even be willing, if we had the choice, to risk delay in your literary production if an awakened British people would turn to you to lead them, and Europe, away from stagnation. We could make no greater personal sacrifice!

Let us hope that we may still win that peace that was thrown away, or not deserved, a decade and more ago.

With gratitude and admiration for all that you have done and are doing.

Lady Violet Bonham Carter to Winston S. Churchill
(Churchill papers, 2/146)[1]

19 November 1947

Dearest Winston,

It was a joy to see you yesterday – in such brilliant health and youth – and I came away endowed with that 'shot of life' which you have never failed to give me. [. . .]

What a quicksand of <u>horror</u> Europe has become – and our small island a tiny foothold of solid earth – where human beings may still find sanctuary. How lucky you and I are to have so much life <u>behind</u> us – lived in a world which was free and civilized – and seemed secure.

All my love and blessings always,

---

[1] This letter was handwritten.

Winston S. Churchill to Admiral Lord Louis Mountbatten
(Churchill papers, 2/43)

21 November 1947
Private

My dear Dickie,

I send you herewith a copy of the note of which I spoke.[1] No doubt it is one-sided. I have your promise that the writer will suffer no ill on this account.

It was very kind of you to come and have a talk the other morning. You know I have a high regard for you, as I had for your father.[2]

I am too much grieved with what is happening in India to write more.

But you always have my good wishes, & my admiration for your achievements.

Winston S. Churchill to Henry Luce
(Churchill papers, 4/141)

22 November 1947

Am most interested by your letter[3] and in considerable agreement with your view. I have not yet tried to read book at a run. I hope to do this in the seclusion of Marrakech and in the light of the commentaries for which I have asked. I hope you have recovered. Writing.

Winston S. Churchill to Henry Luce
(Churchill papers, 4/141)

22 November 1947
Private

My dear Mr Luce

I have read your letter with great attention, and am in much agreement with what you say. You must remember that so far I have been assembling the material and arranging it in chronological order. I work chapter by chapter and, as I cabled you, have not up to the present attempted to read Book I through at a run. This I shall hope to do in the seclusion of Marrakesh and in the light of the commentaries which I have invited from various people. I certainly contemplate the excision of ten to fifteen thousand words, and probably more.

[1] From Firoz Khan Noon to Edward Keeling, reproduced above (p. 850).
[2] Prince Louis Alexander of Battenberg, 1854–1921. Cousin of King George V. Naturalized as a British subject in 1868, when he entered the RN. 1st Sea Lord, 1912–14. At the King's request, discontinued the title of Prince and assumed surname Mountbatten, 1917. Marquess of Milford Haven, 1917. Adm. of the Fleet, 1921. Father of Lord Louis Mountbatten, later Earl Mountbatten of Burma.
[3] Reproduced above (pp. 871–4).

Coming to your first special point; the tale is necessarily told not only from the British, but from my personal, stand-point. It is presented only as a contribution to history. It may well be that Chapters II and III will be compressed into one, and also that Chapter X (Air Defence Research) and Chapter XV (The Rebuilding of the Fleet), which are altogether too technical, will be shortened and redistributed between other chapters and the Appendix. I have carefully kept my eye fresh for the final shaping of the work, although I now have its structure complete in my mind.

The above deals to some extent with your second point, and I have no doubt the quotations will be greatly reduced or melded in the narrative. I had not intended Book I to be so lengthy, but the task expanded as I went along.

The third question which you raise, namely why were the leaders so stupid and weak, and why did the nations and peoples of Europe throw up such bad leadership, shall certainly receive an answer. The reason is because in those years there happened exactly what is happening today, namely no coherent or persistent policy, even in fundamental matters, among the good peoples, but deadly planning among the bad. The good peoples, as now, drifted hither and thither, to and fro, according to the changing winds of public opinion and the desire of public men of medium stature to gain majorities and office at party elections from electorates, who were absorbed in earning their daily bread, whose memories were short and whose moods changed every few years.

There was, of course, also the lack of a world instrument of government for the prevention of war. This was largely because the United States abandoned the League of Nations at its birth. The League of Nations made a far better start than the present UNO, and the prospects of peace were brighter ten years after the First World War than they are now, only two-and-a-half years after the Second. But the lack of will-power and conscious purpose among the leading states and former allies drew us upon these slippery slopes of weak compromises, seeking the line of least resistance, which led surely to the abyss. The same thing is happening now, only with greater speed, and unless there is some moral revival and conscious guidance of the good forces, while time remains, a prolonged eclipse of our civilization approaches.

The above is the conclusion to be drawn from all this assembly of facts in Book I, and I shall make this abundantly plain before this part of the work leaves my hands.

I must warn you that I am increasingly convinced that I cannot finish Book I before the end of January, a month later than I had hoped. I am relying on my seven weeks at Marrakech, free from all distractions, except a little painting, to enable me to present a final picture. I do not think that this delay need affect the making of excerpts for the serials. It will, however, prevent the book publishers beginning pagination before the beginning of February.

I am sending a copy of your letter and of this reply to Camrose.

I am afraid your operation was both serious and painful, and I hope you are recovering. I will not cumber paper by repeating to you all the wise advice which the doctors gave me in similar circumstances a few months ago, but I have no doubt it applies with full force and will be accepted by the patient with the usual modifications.

Sir Crisp English[1] to Winston S. Churchill
(Churchill papers, 2/148)[2]

24 November 1947

Dear Mr Winston Churchill,

It is now just 25 years ago, since I operated upon you for appendicitis at 4 Dorset Square, and since then I have followed up all your splendid activities with much pleasure, and send you <u>all the best of good wishes</u> and <u>good luck</u> for many more years to come. Personally, I am still 'carrying on' at this same address.

PS. Yesterday was 22 years since I operated upon Miss Churchill: All good wishes to her.

William Mackenzie King: diary
('The Mackenzie King Record', volume 4, pages 112–13)

24 November 1947

I had better add here immediately what I heard Churchill say, on the day following, which answered the question that I asked as to just how America could meet a situation against Europe, at this time, against Russia.[3] Churchill had been speaking of the possibility of war along lines very similar to those followed by Bevin. So much so that Smuts who was sitting at the same table, looking over at me, said that is very like what we heard yesterday or words to that effect. I turned to Churchill and asked him how America could possibly mobilize forces at this time for another war. He turned to me sharply, his eyes bulging out of his head, and said: they would, of course, begin the attack in Russia itself. You must know they have had plans all laid for this, for over a year. What the Russians should be told at the present conference, if they are unwilling to co-operate, is that the nations that have fought the last war for

---

[1] Crisp English, 1878–1949. Educated at Westminster School and St George's Hospital (William Brown Scholar). Hunterian Prof. of Surgery, Royal College of Surgeons, 1903–4. FRCS, 1903. Married, 1905, Annie Gaunt McLeod. Served in European War, 1914–18; despatches four times. CMG, 1917; KCMG, 1918. Member, War Office Medical Board, 1918–19. Prime Warden, Worshipful Company of Goldsmiths, 1937–8.

[2] This letter was handwritten.

[3] Mackenzie King was at this point in London to meet members of the Government.

freedom, have had enough of this war of nerves and intimidation. We do not intend to have this sort of thing continue indefinitely. No progress could be made and life is not worth living. We fought for liberty and are determined to maintain it. We will give you what you want and is reasonable in the matter of boundaries. We will give you ports in the North. We will meet you in regard to conditions generally. What we will not allow you to do is to destroy Western Europe; to extend your regime further there. If you do not agree to that here and now, within so many days, we will attack Moscow and your other cities and destroy them with atomic bombs from the air. We will not allow tyranny to be continued.

This came as a revelation to me. I had not thought of plans being already in existence for war against Russia by bombing from the air. I know of course how America has continued to stock piles of atomic bombs and that her supply is very great. That she has also planes for the purpose and men trained. But from Churchill's words, it would seem as if his inside information was to the effect that America was expecting that she might have to act in a short time and had made her plans accordingly. Churchill said he believed if Molotov and Stalin and others were told that this is what would happen, they would yield and put an end to their bluff. He really believed they were hoping to increase their territories as Hitler had sought to increase his by bluff, etc. He sat back and said that war can be saved if we stand up to them now. I can see as clearly as can be, that if that stand is not taken within the next few weeks, that within five years or a much shorter time, there would be another world war in which we shall all be finished. His whole face and eyes were like those of a man whose whole being was filled with the belief which he had. He turned to me and he said: I told you many, many years before this last war, . . . that England would be at war within five years, and that she ran the risk of not possessing our own island at the end of that time. You remember this? I told him that I indeed remember it, and had made a memo of it at the time. He said: I am telling you now what I see in the future. . . . I confess that while he was talking, I myself had a sort of vision of a welter of the world. It might just be the effect of his own words but they were strong and powerful and deeply felt. This statement gave me what seemed to supply what had been left out in the statements at Downing Street. I could see that of necessity, it would be so with the Indian delegates present; also I cannot see the wisdom of entrusting matters of this kind to types of men that some of the High Commissioners are and may be from time to time.

So much for the meeting at Downing Street.

Winston S. Churchill to Sir Crisp English
(*Churchill papers, 2/148*)

25 November 1947

My dear Crisp English,

How nice of you to write to me. I have never had the slightest trouble all these twenty-five years. Of course we went over the old ground again the other day when I had my operation for hernia. The two cuts are pretty well merged into one, so it looks much bigger.

Thank you so much for all you say in your letter and for your kind thoughts.

I do not know whether you can find time to look through this little book of Secret Session Speeches, which I send you. They differ from ordinary speeches as they give the vitals of the story.

December 1947

Winston S. Churchill to Alfred Duff Cooper
(Churchill papers, 2/161)

1 December 1947

My dear Duffie,

You very kindly asked me to come to your Farewell Party. I am sorry that Clemmie does not feel up to the Marrakech expedition and is going to stay at home. My party will be Sarah and Colonel Bill Deakin, whom I think you know. He is an Oxford don who distinguished himself in the war, rising from Second Lieutenant in the Oxfordshire Hussars to Colonel and, in the Foreign Office, to the Chargé d'Affaires at Belgrade. He helps me in my book. It would be very nice if you could put him up, but I could easily arrange for him to go to the Ritz, though I hope you will ask him to your Party. In addition there are two secretaries, a valet and a detective, but if you are at all crowded, these can be accommodated elsewhere. We should propose to arrive in time for luncheon on the 10th, and we have to leave early the next morning.

I wonder whether you would be so kind as to ask the French Government to let the authorities in Morocco know that I am proposing to stay there from December 11 until the last week in January, and staying at the Mamounia Hotel. The British Government are sending with me an experienced Scotland Yard detective,[1] who has been abroad with me before, and who will contact their Sûreté. My visit is quite private but they would like to be informed beforehand.

---

[1] Sgt Williams.

Winston S. Churchill to Lord Hall[1]
(Churchill papers, 2/149)

2 December 1947
Private

My dear First Lord,

I think it is my duty to inform you that when a vacancy occurred in the office of First Sea Lord on the death of Admiral Pound in 1943 I offered that post to Admiral Fraser, then Commander-in-Chief of the Home Fleet. He, in a very becoming manner, asked to be excused from accepting it, as he thought that Sir Andrew Cunningham had a greater hold upon the goodwill of the Navy. I therefore did not press him unduly, and he went back to the Fleet, where he had the good fortune to encounter in his Flagship the *Scharnhorst*, which he sank. I feel that the fact of his refusing the office of First Sea Lord, to which he was most highly recommended by the Chiefs of Staff and others, should find its place among the considerations which will be before you should another vacancy occur.

Walter Graebner to Jo Sturdee
(Churchill papers, 1/68)

3 December 1947

Dear Miss Sturdee,

I am sending you a copy of a letter from the National City Bank which confirms that 5,000 dollars have been deposited in Marrakech to the account of Mr Churchill. You will also note the name of the Bank which we are using. I have underlined it.

I explained to you over the telephone why we were depositing 5,000 dollars only and not more. Our bankers tell us that once currency is purchased in another country it cannot be withdrawn. As we do not wish to leave a balance in Marrakech after the holiday is over, we have limited the first deposit to 5,000 dollars. As more is required we will make the necessary deposits.

Please let me know if there is anything more I can do in connection with the holiday.

---

[1] George Henry Hall, 1881–1965. MP (Lab.) for Aberdare, 1922–46. Civil Lord of the Admiralty, 1929–31. Under-Secretary of State for the Colonies, 1940–2. PC, 1942. Financial Secretary to the Admiralty, 1942–3. Parliamentary Under-Secretary of State for Foreign Affairs, 1943–5. Secretary of State for the Colonies, 1945–6. Viscount, 1946. 1st Lord of the Admiralty, 1946–51. Deputy Leader of the House of Lords, 1947–51.

Winston S. Churchill: note
(Churchill papers, 2/60)

[December] 1947

IDEAS FOR MANCHESTER

Artificial Britain.

Our Precarious position.

Compare USA and France with Britain's tradition – if all the rest of the world sank beneath the ocean.

Russia. Impossibility of getting our living under Socialism. Nothing but thrift, ingenuity, enterprise, good-housekeeping can support this population of 48 million rising to 50, though altering unfavourably among those in the prime of life.

The Lancashire Cotton Trade. How we used to boast in the old days. A mighty industry, built up on a crop grown one end of the world and markets at the other, anchored here by British skill and craftsmanship. The cost of production under State Socialism imposes greater burdens than private industry, running for profits, which profits are in turn corrected by graduated taxation.

Coal. Very glad about improvement in output. I have always considered that the miners have a special claim on account of working 'away from the light of the sun'. Coal problem cannot be considered apart from cost. Look at the increase in the cost of coal which affects every industry, especially transport, which also will now have to support the State management. At the same time interest is paid to the railway shareholders. All this is a tax on national production. Expense for management of the coalmines from centralized departments, Whitehall. How many collieries have added greatly to their cost of management? There can be no question of denationalizing coal. Should some part of the burden of management not be borne by the Exchequer, so as to secure cheaper fuel for our harassed industries?

Fallacy of an export trade without corresponding importation. Read the petition of the Merchants of London 1838 – a stock Free Trade quotation (Mr Maudling to supply).

India.

Manchester Guardian.

Winston S. Churchill: speech
('*Winston S. Churchill, His Complete Speeches*', volume 7, pages 7572–9)

6 December 1947   Manchester

BRITAIN IN PERIL

It is almost 40 years since I spoke in Belle Vue. Then there was an open-air meeting, at which Lloyd George, John Burns and I appeared together, and championed many of the great social reforms which have since been carried into law by Liberal or Conservative Governments in which I have served. It is curious that, while in the days of my youth I was much reproached with inconsistency and being changeable, I am now scolded for adhering to the same views I had in early life and even for repeating passages from speeches which I made long before most of you were born. Of course the world moves on and we dwell in a constantly changing climate of opinion. But the broad principles and truths of wise and sane political action do not necessarily alter with the changing moods of a democratic electorate. Not everything changes. Two and two still make four, and I could give you many other instances which go to prove that all wisdom is not new wisdom.

In Lancashire, and especially in this City, there has always been a keen interest in economic and trade issues, and Lancashire Folk are renowned for the patient and persistent manner in which they follow and judge such arguments. This is not surprising considering that your prosperity, nay, your continued survival, depends upon the right solution being found and the right policy adopted. It is therefore about economic and social matters that I shall speak to you tonight in order to set forth some broad, plain truths irrespective of whether they are immediately popular or not. But here I must point out that it is not possible in an hour to deal with the whole of this vast and tangled field, but only to strike the notes which one feels ring true, so that I hope those who criticize – and in a free country there should always be criticism – will not find fault with me that some large issues have not been dealt with. The speeches I have made since the General Election cover the whole field of our affairs, and it is only by taking them together that any fair or complete picture can be obtained.

I regret that it is a sad and anxious tale that I must tell this afternoon. Our country, the heart of our Empire with its Commonwealth and possessions under every sky and climate, is in peril to a degree which I have hardly ever known before. Government and Opposition, Socialists, Tories and Liberals, however else they may be divided are all agreed on that. I am deeply anxious about our survival in this island as a free, prosperous, civilized community. I am quite sure that Socialism, that is to say the substitution of State control by officials for private enterprise, will make it impossible for 48 millions to live in this island, and that at least a quarter of all who are alive today will have to disappear in one way or another after enduring a lowering of standards of food and comfort inconceivable in the last 50 years. Emigration, even if practised on a scale never before dreamed of, could not operate in time to prevent this melancholy decline.

I believe that the monopoly by the State of all the means of production, distribution and exchange would be fatal both to our material well-being and to our personal freedom, as we have long enjoyed them. The cost of State Management takes more from the workers than will ever be taken by the profits of private enterprise. It is not the interest of the wage-earners to have to deal with the all-powerful State employer rather than with the flexibility of private business. When losses are made, under the present system these losses are borne by the individuals who sustained them and took the risk and judged things wrongly, whereas under State management all losses are quartered upon the tax-payers and the community as a whole. The elimination of the profit motive and of self-interest as a practical guide in the myriad transactions of daily life will restrict, paralyse and destroy British ingenuity, thrift, contrivance and good housekeeping at every stage in our life and production, and will reduce all our industries from a profit-making to a loss-making process.

You cannot compare the conditions in this crowded island with those which prevail in vast expanses like Russia, and even there the standards of living and conditions of serfdom which exist would be intolerable to free-born British men and women. For all these reasons, and many others which could be adduced, I invite you while time remains to condemn and turn away from the morbid fallacy of Socialism, and work toward the double system of building up and maintaining a basic standard of life and labour, with proper care for the children and the aged, for the weak and unfortunate, and once that has been achieved to allow the freest play of British genius and enterprise and fair and free competition upwards, with all its rewards and penalties operating in free and healthy society. It is that choice which is open to the British people today, and it is because I am sure that they will choose rightly that, far from despairing of our future, I regard it with confidence and hope. It was certain that we should be faced with formidable difficulties after the war in which the very efficiency of our national Government had drawn to the utmost limits upon the life energies of the people. All our united strength applied with wisdom would be required to bring about our recovery. The Socialist Government is responsible for aggravating our difficulties, not only by a series of grievous blunders and miscalculations, of which I will presently give you some examples, but also by wantonly dividing the nation through class warfare, and by preferring their rigid and mistaken doctrines to the practical measures by which the greatest good of the greatest number can alone be achieved. Everyone can see that in the transition from war to peace and in the maintenance of basic standards of life and labour there would have to be, during a period of stress and scarcity, many controls. But the Government, in their zeal to establish a Socialist Utopia, have made unfair and abusive use of wartime controls, and today aim at nothing less than despotic authority over the whole population – as incompetent as it is complete.

I will now recount to you some of the major glaring errors into which the Socialist Government have been drawn by the ineptitude of their Ministers and by their class and Party bias. The first is of course the mismanagement of our finances by the late Chancellor of the Exchequer, Dr Dalton who has escaped from his post at a time when his mistakes were coming home to roost, with wild and vain expenditure which, even in the present year amounts to 3,000 millions. He has made it impossible to reduce wartime taxation to a point where normal incentives could be restored to all classes engaged in production; and by his monetary policy he has continually lowered the purchasing power of the £ sterling, thus undermining the whole basis of wages, savings, pensions, family allowances, and health and invalidity insurance. Two years ago, I stated in the House the figures to which I believed our Armed Forces should be reduced. The figures are now more or less accepted by the Government. If they are safe now they were certainly safe two years ago when the world outlook was less dangerous; but thousands of millions of pounds were lost in the tardy demobilisation of the wartime forces.

Eighteen months ago I urged that we should return our Mandate for Palestine to the UNO. That is now being done, but probably 200 millions have been wasted in the interval by obstinate adherence to a policy which the Government themselves have now abandoned. Half the British soldiers kept in Palestine under conditions of intolerable provocation would, if they had been stationed in India, have enabled the transference of power and responsibility from British to Indian hands to have been made in a gradual and orderly manner, and would have averted the slaughter of at least a quarter of a million Hindus and Moslems in series of hideous massacres, the like of which have never stained the British Empire in all its history. The blame for these various blunders and calamities rests upon the Government as a whole. Mr Herbert Morrison said on November 24th that the reason potatoes were scarce was that people were able to eat much more of them than they could in the days of (Tory) unemployment. It is hardly possible to cram more untruth into a single sentence. It is quite true that people are eating nearly twice as many potatoes as they did before the war in the bad days of Tory rule, but that is because they have been driven off other more attractive foods; and now this last resource to which many housewives had looked is being itself cut off. As to unemployment before the war the worst period occurred under, and as a result of the MacDonald Socialist Government.

As soon as the measures introduced by the Conservative Party when they regained office in 1931 began to work, that is to say in a few months, this figure of 2,813,000 unemployed was steadily reduced to little more than 1,000,000 and even so, the calories of the food of an unemployed man on the dole, as it was called, were better than those of a fully-employed wage-earner today. But this, I assure you, is only the beginning of what we have to face if we allow our affairs to continue in the hands of these incompetent Ministers, and if we allow our country to be rent and torn by their class warfare and destructive doctrines.

Now I must draw your attention to a most astonishing utterance this week by the Minister of Labour. Defending an Order giving him absolute power over the livelihood and employment of men and women between the ages of 18 and 50, of women between 18 and 40, 'We are not prepared', he said,

> to recognise that anyone has a right to conscientious objection to going to work unless that person is prepared at the same time to say that he will not eat.

Never did I expect to hear the doctrine of 'Work or Starve' proclaimed so brutally in the House of Commons, and above all from the lips of a Socialist Minister. Why, this has been the greatest taunt that the Socialist Party have levelled against the Capitalist system, and only the other day Mr Bevin was deriding my advocacy of competitive selection (once the basic standard has been achieved) as compulsion by starvation, work or starve. Now we get it from the Treasury Bench, from the Socialist Minister of Labour himself. As a matter of fact it was never true to say that our system of society before the war was based on Work or Starve. Nobody starved. There is an annual report to the House of Commons which records exactly all deaths attributable to privation. The figures are less than 20 a year and under the Tory Government before the war we now know that the diet of a workman on the dole exceeded that which Sir Stafford Cripps has lately prescribed for the nation as a whole. The calories of an unemployed man at Stockton (for instance) were 2910 under the Conservatives and Sir Stafford Cripps now tells us that we must be content with 2700 for regularly employed ordinary wage earners, and even that may, indeed almost certainly will, undergo a sharp reduction in the future, No, the doctrine Work or Starve is a new doctrine which the Socialist Party are putting out and even that does not express the full consequences of their action which will be Work *and* Starve – not Work or Starve but Work *and* Starve.

Let me give you some more examples. Having borrowed this money from the US and having to live on foreign aid, was it not most imprudent to give it all away again to foreign countries or to allow it to be written off against debts which we contracted to India and to Egypt for defending them from invasion by Japan or Germany? Mr Bevin told us in May last that by then we had given or loaned abroad no less than £740 million – more than three-quarters of the American Loan. We borrowed it with one hand and gave it away with the other. One ought to be just before one is generous.

The greatest service that Britain can now render to the world is to recreate her exhausted strength. Yet it is a fact that we gave away all we had borrowed from America to foreign countries and played the 'Lady Bountiful' with American money which we vitally needed to give us the time to get going again. Mr Bevin rightly pointed out that the loans we made imposed just as big a strain on our exports as our outright gifts in this crucial transitional period. Surely it was madness when we had to borrow all this money from the US to go and hand over three-quarters of it and more to other European nations, in addition to India and Egypt whom we had saved from being pillaged by Japan and Germany? The fact is there has been no grip from the summit in the management of our affairs; no leadership to find the way through our difficulties. Ministerial personalities have jostled against each other for their own schemes and departments. A very small measure of the controls lavished upon the ordinary people of the country would have co-ordinated and harmonized the policy of the Government, and would have brought that policy into some relation with the needs and difficulties which two years ago anyone could see were coming upon us.

Naturally now we must export everything we can, and I earnestly hope that the targets given to the various industries will be achieved. But to make goods is not always to sell them. It is a well-known fallacy to suppose that any prolonged exportation can take place without reciprocal importation, and the same is true the other way round. Trade is exchange and the foundation of trade is barter. You will find that foreign countries will increasingly refuse to take your exports if you will not in return receive proportionable imports from them and from other countries to whom they have already sent their goods. There is no escape from these homely truths so widely realized in Lancashire and as old as the petition of the Merchants of the City of London in 1820. But there is another cause that will hamper our exports as well as stint our home consumption. The foundation of this island's commerce was cheap and abundant coal. Upon this the brains, inventiveness, good business management and enterprise of our people enabled our population to double itself in a century. Now here, living, breathing, toiling, suffering, what is to happen if the foundation fails?

I rejoice indeed that there has been in the last few weeks some improvement in the output from the coal mines, and I earnestly hope that the target of 200 millions set by the Government may be realized. But that target itself is far too small for our vital needs. Moreover the 200 millions is not a true figure. It takes no account of the 7 to 10 per cent reduction in the quality of the coal by the inclusion of slate, dirt and rubbish. It takes no account of the fact that, compared to 1941 we are getting 10 millions tons a year from surface coal. The output per miner is below 270 tons this year compared to 295 in 1941 and over 300 in 1937. Surely in two years of peace we should have been able to improve upon our wartime figure? On the contrary, we have fallen far behind it. Then comes the question of price. Coal is now well over double what it costs before the war. Now on the top of this far more highly priced coal and more costly management, we have the nationalization of railways and transport, which will certainly mean a deterioration in the services rendered to the public, and an increased burden to be borne by the taxpayer. The Government are refusing to answer questions about the working of the nationalized industries, because they wish to conceal from the public during these critical years the wasteful character of State management as compared with private ownership. Therefore, you have two platforms of additional burden upon trade and industry – coal and transport – one erected on top of the other, and both creating conditions of extreme difficulty for the conduct of our business, industry and enterprise. How, with this double handicap imposed upon us, can we expect, over any long period of time, to sell our goods abroad in the open competition of the world, even if that competition were not restricted and distorted, as it is by the action of many foreign States? We should find it increasingly difficult to export our produce without which we cannot purchase the food and raw materials indispensable to our daily life.

I was very glad to see in this morning's newspapers that the United States Government have agreed to release immediately the remaining 100 million pounds of the Loan, although we have declared our inability to carry out the Convertibility Clause, to which the Government unanimously agreed. No doubt we shall be told by the Socialist Government's supporters that this is only another case of 'shabby money-lending'. This action will however bring a temporary respite of a few months to the country and to the Government. At the rate at which we have been spending our gold and our dollar reserves lately this 100 million will last less than two months, after which, while continuing in our present austerity, we shall be again forced to use up our last resources, which we hold not only for ourselves but for the sterling area. I helped the Government as much as possible to obtain the original American Loan, and when Mr Snyder,[1] the American Chancellor of the Exchequer, was over here a little while ago, I appealed to him to give every possible aid to the Socialist Government. In all dealings with foreign powers His Majesty's Opposition have consistently set country before party.

All the more is it obligatory on our present rulers to use any aid they may obtain from other countries to gain as much time as possible for the restoration of our finances and the revival of our trade, both at home and overseas. At such a time as this and in the conditions we now have to face the Socialist Government have no right to inflame the differences which divide us in this country by such acts of Party spite as breaking up the constitutional settlement

[1] John Wesley Snyder, 1895–1985. Educated at Vanderbilt University. Married, 1920, Evelyn Cook. National Bank Receiver, Office of Comptroller of the Currency, Washington DC, 1930–7. Head, St Louis Loan Agency, Reconstruction Finance Corp., 1937–43. Executive Vice-President, First National Bank of St Louis, 1943–5. Director, Office of War Mobilization and Reconversion, 1945–6. US Secretary of the Treasury, 1946–53. US Governor, International Monetary Fund, 1946–53. Advisor, US Treasury, 1955–69.

of the Parliament Act of 1911 for the purpose, openly avowed by the Home Secretary, of nationalizing the steel industry, which, under private ownership is making such a gallant effort to beat all previous records of steel production. It is a disgraceful deed for Ministers responsible for the affairs of the whole nation, while they are living on foreign money or on the last reserve of our own treasure, to divide the country even more bitterly for the sake of their Party doctrines, and to refuse to deal with our grave problems on their merits and on national rather than on Party lines.

While Mr Attlee and Sir Stafford Cripps follow this path of faction they strip themselves of all moral authority to lead the nation in its time of adversity and danger; they prove themselves unworthy of public confidence, and it becomes the bounden duty of every patriotic elector to drive them from office at the first opportunity. The reason why I supported the American Loan and have done all I can to make it fully effective was, of course, to gain time for this great country to get into its stride again. I hoped that with careful management it would give us four years nor did I care if this made the path of the Socialist Government easier. They have made every imaginable miscalculation and mistake. Instead of building up our trade and agriculture they launched out into a great programme of capital expenditure which they have now to abandon or slash ruthlessly after all the effort expended on it. Yet on the other hand they have failed to keep our agricultural production at the level which it reached in the war. It has fallen this year far below what was produced under my Administration in the height of the war, when we had vast numbers of workers in the Armed Forces and no German prisoners, and we are told that next year there will be practically no improvement. It is not a question of weather; it is a question of the number of acres ploughed and the amount of stocks maintained. We complained rightly of the fuel shortage last year, which caused a spasm of unemployment, and a loss of over 2000 million pounds to our export trade. But Mr Shinwell's failure in fuel supplies is nothing like so glaring as that of the Minister of Agriculture in producing home-grown food. The Government even hampered agricultural production by stopping the building and repair of cottages for the extra agricultural workers who are so sorely needed. I repeat without qualification that such gross lack of foresight and incompetence has never been shown by any British Government.

To sum up, I say that we are in a position similar to that in the crisis of the U-boat war – a cold, long-drawn crisis, of facts and figures, of graphs and curves, – but that no effectual measures are being taken, as we took in the war, to cope with our danger, and that we are a divided and not a united nation. Why I have thought it right to lay the hard and unchallengeable facts before you as I did in the emergencies of the war is that I have never found the British nation afraid of being told the ugly truth; I have never found them disheartened by it if they were sure that everything that was helpful and wise was being done by their leaders. I am sure that the first step we should take is to demand a new Parliament. This present House of Commons, elected under the abnormal conditions of 1945, and under the delusion of the fantastic promises made by the Socialists in their thirst for power, will not afford a foundation upon which a Government can be created capable of meeting the people's needs. This present Parliament does not represent the nation. While they claim absolute powers over our rights and liberties they have no right to speak in the name of a majority of the electors.

This has been proved by the results of the last 4 by-elections. In the last 4 by-elections which occurred fortuitously the Conservative vote was 91,400 and the Socialist vote 68,200. If you add the Liberal and Scottish National votes the total of the anti-Socialist votes is 103,000 against 68,000 Socialist votes, or more than 6 to 4 against the Government. These figures should be contrasted with those of the present House of Commons, where the Socialists have a majority obtained under abnormal conditions and false pretences of more than two to one against all other parties. No more convincing proof could be presented that Parliament does not represent the nation. Its mandate is withdrawn and its mission is repudiated, and it is to a new Parliament that we should look. No Government which could be formed in this Parliament would have a right to speak in the name of the people, nor have the present Government the right or the power to conjure up again those unconquerable forces which bore us through perils and stresses no other community in the world could have surmounted. All our strength is here. The difficulties are different but our power to overcome them remains. The longer the election of a new Parliament is delayed, the worse it will be for the country, the harder our conditions and the more baffling our problems will become.

Should another opportunity be given to the nation to take a hand in its own affairs, the Conservative Party will go into action upon the Policy laid down at the Brighton Conference. First, we will strive to maintain the basic standard of life and labour, and will not hesitate to keep whatever controls are necessary for that primary purpose. Secondly, once that purpose has been clearly achieved our aim will be to set the people free in the widest possible sense so that they may use their native genius in the fullest degree. The Conservative Party will follow the policy laid down at the Brighton Conference, including what is called the Industrial Charter. This policy comprises the reduction of our National expenditure by £500,000,000 and the use of the bulk of that money to give greater incentive to all forms of production. We will strive to maintain the basic standard of life and labour which we shall not allow accident or misfortune to endanger. Our aim will be to set the people free. Thirdly, we will do our utmost to maintain the purchasing power of the pound sterling, without which all our social services and savings will be destroyed. Fourthly, we will maintain and invigorate our fraternal association with the USA. And last of all, but most honoured of all, we will labour to unite and combine our Commonwealth of Nations and Empire beyond the seas, without which the safety of this Island cannot endure nor its prosperity return. To this I must add: We shall not make any promises of lush and easy times. Whatever Government might result from a new Parliament it must be resolved to do its best for the nation as a whole, without fear, favour or affection and without class bias or Party spite.

Alfred Duff Cooper to Winston S. Churchill
(Churchill papers, 2/161)[1]

6 December 1947

My dear Winston,
Your letter of December 1st[2] has only reached me this afternoon. We are delighted that you are coming and eagerly look forward to your arrival. I know and like Bill Deakin very much. If there is no room for him in the house we will bed him out.

Our party is on and I don't think there will be a revolution, so bring your ball dress and tiara.

I pray that the weather will permit of your flying.

Winston S. Churchill: press statement
(Churchill papers, 2/55)

7 December 1947

The Socialist newspapers, almost without exception, represent me as saying yesterday at Manchester, 'I am quite sure that . . . at least one quarter of all who are alive today will have to disappear in one way or another after enduring a lowering of standards of food and comfort inconceivable in the last fifty years.' What I actually said was, 'I am quite sure that Socialism, that is to say the substitution of State control by officials instead of by private enterprise, will make it impossible for 48 millions to live in this island, and that at least a quarter of all who are alive today will have to disappear in one way or another after enduring a lowering of standards of food and comfort inconceivably in the last 50 years.' The omission of the first part of the sentence alters its entire meaning.

---

[1] This letter was handwritten.
[2] Reproduced above (p. 880).

Winston S. Churchill to Chas Butler[1]
(Churchill papers, 2/58)

8 December 1947

It would be almost a mockery in these dreary times to wish *Tory Challenge* and its readers the traditional New Year wish. The tribulations which we are enduring call for courage, patience, grim resolution and unflagging exertions on the part of all who love their country and hope to see it rise again from the lowly state to which it has been brought by the unwisdom of its rulers. Our task as Tories is to rouse the people of Britain once again to a sense of greatness and a passion for freedom. So long as they are willing to barter their liberties, one by one, for the promise of material benefits which in fact will never materialize, this dear land of ours will never recover either its former prosperity or the proud position that it once occupied among the nations of the world.

Winston S. Churchill to Christopher Soames
(Lady Soames papers)

8 December 1947
To be taken as a guide only

1. When do the German prisoners go home to Germany? However this may be, it would be well to dispense with them for the time being as soon as possible. Before they go, they should cut the stone needed for the roads, finding a new quarry if the present one is exhausted. They could also help in sawing wood and, if convenient, in bringing in the big tree in the Ten Acre field which wants more splitting on the spot and possibly further sawing. We want to have the woodshed full, after providing a thousand suitable billets for No. 28.

2. I have talked to Whitbread about a 'Jacob's Ladder'. Sufficient stones for building the small extra balustrade are available in the stable yard. Whitbread says he can find stone coping sufficient to cover the top of the new wall and replace the damaged coping stone on the old bit. There are a lot of good stones bedded in places where they are not noticeable, like the end of the bottom lake and the approaches to my studio, which could easily be cut in half with a hammer and chisel and replaced by some of the ragged concrete slabs, of which there are many at Bardogs. Mrs Churchill says she will explain to Whitbread exactly how she wants it done.

3. Mrs Churchill also wants the garden door and the little iron gates in the kitchen garden re-hung, and it would be well to paint them.

---

[1] Managing editor of *Tory Challenge*, a political periodical in print 1947–53.

4. Whitbread and Kurn should work at getting in the wood, as may be convenient, and particularly in using the circular saw in the stable yard on wet days. The overall strategic objective is a full woodshed.

5. Probably after Christmas the gang contracted for from the local authority will arrive to do hedging and ditching. When they do, they will be at least a month on this, and there is no need to begin the fencing of Puddledock Lane on the Ten Acres side until I come back. However, if the hedging and ditching is completed sooner, let me know.

6. I am writing to Lord Dudley[1] about Tihes Wood which I think is at least five acres and is in a dreadful state of disorder after Mrs Livingston's woodmen have done their work. I should like to be back when this is done, even if that means that there can be no new planting this year. The first thing I shall do when I come back is to burn all the rubbish and collect all burnable wood, both for ourselves and the cottagers. However, for this or for any major scheme a special plan would be necessary, and if the German prisoners are still in England we might apply for some of them, minus the foreman. I hope all this can stand over until I return.

7. I wrote a few small points today for Kurn and Whitbread which could be fitted in, as convenient. These are attached.

8. I should be sorry to see the peach house (i.e. the third from the gateway) stripped of its trees. Apart from them which are unsuitable and come to Chartwell. I admire the shape of this house and it is beautiful in the spring to see it in blossom. I do not therefore wish to convert it to lettuces and tomatoes, at any rate for another year.

9. Whitbread should make sure that the dynamo in the main pump house below the bottom lake is not endangered by frost. It may not be necessary to bring it into the house, as is done with the other pumps, but then it must be carefully wrapped up in the case of a cold spell.

10. I am in favour of getting rid of the 'Pelties',[2] but this should be done gradually, so as not to be ungraceful to Mr Timberlake.

11. Great care must be taken in ploughing the meadows in front of the house not to damage the aqueduct. No tractor vehicle should go within 4 yards of this. Whitbread knows exactly how it runs.

12. The only thing that presses at Bardogs is the laying on of wires between the dolls. The object is to obstruct the view as little as possible. Is it necessary to have an instrument for making holes in the dolls? If so, 8 to 10 inches of one inch pipe should be inserted in sockets in their tops and the top wire run through a hole bored in these. As to the second wire, the best way to do it is to

---

[1] William Humble Eric Ward, 1894–1969. On active service 1914–18 (wounded, MC). MP (Cons.) for Hornsey, 1921–4, 1931–2. President, Society of British Gas Industry, 1926–7; British Iron and Steel Federation, 1935–36; Birmingham Chamber of Commerce, 1937–9. Succeeded his father as 3rd Earl of Dudley, 1932. Regional Commissioner for Civil Defence, No. 9 (Midland) Region, 1940–5.

[2] 'Belties' (a type of cattle).

bore a hole on the sides of the dolls and insert a link or a steel peg from which the intermediate wire can be drawn.

13. I am not worrying about the Bardogs kitchen garden at the present time. I should like to be there when the tidying up of this is done, and I hope it will be done before the spring.

CHARTWELL WORK

1. Three balls to be put on the red brick wall at the side of the gardener's house.

2. Mend the top part of the brick work at the farm entrance gate.

3. Put a hook on the gate opposite to the Seven Children house.

4. Put a new gate on the way up to the Tihes Wood, and also rebuild a new passage way across the ditch beyond it.

5. Whitbread should point in the east house at Bardogs, with cement, where the earth has been taken away.

6. Tidy up the roots of the old tree by the east house at Bardogs. Just level them off, there is no need to dig up the roots, or alter the upright stump at the end.

Winston S. Churchill: press notice
(*Churchill papers, 1/69*)

10 December 1947

Mr Churchill has left by air for Marrakech in Morocco where he proposes to spend the next six weeks. He will be working at his War Memoirs, the earlier portions of which it is hoped may be published in the spring of 1948. He will be the guest while there of *Time* and *Life* and the *New York Times*, who have undertaken the publication of his book in serial form in America.

He is accompanied by his daughter, Mrs Oliver, and Colonel F. W. Deakin of Wadham College, Oxford.

Mr Churchill plans to return for the re-assembly of Parliament.

Sarah Churchill to Clementine Churchill
(*'Keep on Dancing, An Autobiography', pages 164–6*)

11 December 1947

It was the most perfect flight. We were transported as carefully as a crate of eggs and deposited gently on the pink airfield in about eight and a half hours. We flew across the Bay (of Biscay) and down the border of Spain and Portugal and only had to fly at 8,000' for about an hour. We had a most delicious luncheon – eggs in aspic, cold chicken and champagne – prepared for us by the Embassy. Papa thoughtfully wanted to spare them this trouble and had asked the manager of the Ritz Hotel to prepare lunch for us. Equally alert and thoughtful was Rufus Clarke,[1] who called up to inquire: apart from the honour they no doubt felt at being given the order, just how much did they think of charging? £30 was the modest minimum. At this, Rufus took it upon himself to ask the chef at the Embassy to oblige!

Our day in Paris was enormous fun and well worthwhile. Anne[2] and Esmond Rothermere gave us lunch. Diana and Duff (Cooper – the British Ambassador) had to go to a farewell press lunch – which they spared Papa from – and from which Diana bolted at the last minute!

The party in the evening was scintillating. 'La crème de la crème' even la crème fouettée floated about in Christian Dior, Jacques Faths, Schiaparelli and Lanvin.[3]

We dined with the Comte and Comtesse de Chambord first – the Comtesse is an amiable and large lady – who for this occasion was dressed in black and green horizontal stripes! The star of the ball of course was Odette[4] [. . .] She wore a Schiaparelli dress of vermilion satin, hour glass and bustle which was caught with a bow just below the 'Topsy' as Papa remarked – and which made the men's eyes linger in the far distance long after she had passed! Diana (Cooper) of course looked lovely – pale aquamarine satin, covered with aquamarine tulle, her fair hair crowned with gardenias; she went through the whole evening unchanged – even at 5 o'clock in the morning. The star couple were Odette and Papa – Papa looked pink and smiling and shy and sweet. He stood irresolute in the middle of the ballroom aglow with his medals and stars – 'I would like to dance with you,' he said to Odette, 'but really I am not very good. Won't you sit down and talk to me for a moment?'. . .

Do not be unhappy about your decision – though it would be a crown of enjoyment to have you here. As you are not feeling very well, I'm sure you are wise: Paris was exhausting and followed by the flight, I would have been more worried about you than him, for he is the toughest of the lot of us and his powers of recuperation rapid. Only of course I am worried about the cold. It is much colder than last time. Bright sun but really cold after 4. Bill (Deakin) and I will really have to get him indoors by 4.30. The hotel is warmer than the villa, though – which is a good thing.

I hope everything goes all right. Of course I am a little anxious – I hope he is going to be happy and content. It is impossible to know yet.

[1] Christopher Soames's best man at his marriage to Mary Churchill.
[2] Ann Charteris, 1913–81. Married, 1932, Shane Edward Robert O'Neill, 3rd Baron O'Neill (d. 1944); 1945, Esmond Cecil Rothermere, 2nd Viscount of Rothermere (div. 1952); 1952, Ian Fleming (d. 1964).
[3] Christian Dior, Jacques Fath, Elsa Schiaparelli and Jeanne Lanvin: four of the top fashion designers of the period.
[4] Mistakenly identified by the editor of *Keep on Dancing* as Odette Pol Roger, of the champagne-producing family; in fact it was the wartime intelligence officer Odette Samson, 1912–95.

December 1947

Winston S. Churchill to Clementine Churchill
(Baroness Spencer-Churchill papers)

12 December 1947   Marrakech

My darling One,

Sarah will have told you of our festivities in Paris. There is genuine sorrow at Duff's departure and certainly there will be a sense of inadequacy in his successor.

I read the *Daily Telegraph*'s account of your communiqué and thought it extremely good. I do not propose to say anything more, whatever comments are made, I can't think they will be at all disagreeable.

The flight was perfect in every way and we have been welcomed here in a suitable fashion by the French authorities. The weather is cold out of the sun, but the sunlight is brilliant and warm. I shall have to take much care about not catching cold. The hotel is well-heated and there is a very distinct change going out of the doors in the evening. During the day one can fling the wide windows open, but when darkness falls everything must be shut.

I painted this afternoon for a couple of hours from the roof of the hotel where there are two or three lovely views and I do not expect to move beyond the precincts for several days. Sarah and Bill have made excursions in the town and in the Arab quarters. The food is excellent and I have made an arrangement with the hotel which will enable me and my party to stay here for 42 days at about two-thirds of the money provided. This leaves a margin for contingencies. Judging from the first start I have made today, I think I am going to paint better than I have done before. The days are very short however, for the effect does not come on till 2.30 and it is dusk and chilly at 5. Next week we will try some picnics to places you have seen when I was convalescing here four years ago. 'Flower Villa' has been bought from Mrs Taylor[1] by the nephew of the Marquis de Breteuil.[2] He has invited me to go and paint in his garden but I looked at this very thoroughly when we were there last and did not think much of it and there is just as good a view from the top of this hotel as from his tower. The Atlas are magnificent and as glorious as ever in the evening light.

The Moroccans are enjoying the experience of voting for the first time, but it is clearly understood that the military government is supreme.

England and politics seem very distant here. I continue to be depressed

---

[1] Edith Bishop, 1874–1959. Married, 1896, Moses Taylor (d.): five children; 1938, G. J. Guthrie Nicholson. Owned properties in Marrakech, Morocco; Portsmouth, Rhode Island; Charleston, South Carolina; France; and Mount Kisco, New York.

[2] Suydam Gaston Le Tonnelier, 1905–60. CoS, Colonial Exhibition for Governor General Marcel Olivier, 1931. Founded African Society of Advertising and Publishing. Created and published newspapers in Marrakech, Casablanca, Tangier, Dakar, Senegal and Paris, 1933–58. Marquis de Breteuil, 1937. Served with French Army during WWII. Commander of the Legion of Honour; Military Medal; Croix de Guerre. Owner of Villa Taylor, 1947–60. Elected member of the Academy of Sciences Overseas, 1960.

about the future. I really do not see how our poor island is going to earn its living when there are so many difficulties around us and so much ill-will and division at home. However I hope to blot this all out of my mind for a few weeks.

I worked hard all the morning on the book and shall begin again after dinner. I did not get my sleep today because we had to entertain to cocktails the four officers of the aeroplane who brought us here so well. They will bring this letter back when they start on Sunday morning.

Tender love my dearest Clemmie. I do hope you will be peaceful and happy, and will often think of your ever loving.

W

Winston S. Churchill to Clementine Churchill
(Churchill papers, 1/44)

14 December 1947

Your lovely letter arrived. Have so far not left building. Am painting from the tower and working night and day. Have sent heavy batch of proofs home by our returning plane. Weather lovely am planning picnic. Hope you will like mandarins. Mule in great form. Much love.

Sarah Churchill to Winston S. Churchill
(Churchill papers, 1/45)

December 1947

Darling Papa,

Forgive me butting in. I understand that perhaps you are a little depressed by the criticism of Reves? This may or may not be true. In any case – don't listen to too many critics – each critic criticises from a personal angle. The work is yours – from deep within you – and its success depends on it flowing from you in an uninterrupted stream.

I have made the mistake up to now (you have not I know!) of listening to too many people in my work. The only peace I find faintly creditable was when I stopped up my ears and listened to myself.

Now of course – one must have critics – particularly those who can criticise the whole sincerely – not from a small window – A journalist will criticise it as being, say, a little ponderous – seeing newspaper headlines and excerpts for weeklies etc. – A technical man – for the technicalities – a soldier from the army view etc. It is your story, as you moved through, what will one day be history. You are the best historian – You are the best journalist – the best poet – shut yourself up and only listen to a very few, and even there, write this book from the heart of yourself – from the knowledge you have – and let it stand or fall by that. It will stand – everyone will listen to your story – I hate to see you pale and no longer happily preoccupied – wow wow wow darling –

Your loving Mule,
Sarah
[Drawing of 'mule thinking']

Sarah Churchill to Clementine Churchill
('Keep on Dancing, An Autobiography', pages 166–8)

16 December 1947

It's getting much warmer! It is quite different to when we arrived. We have settled down into a pleasantly monotonous routine which varies very little. So far he has not left the hotel, he paints from a high balcony of the new wing of the hotel – and as it has till now been cold, I am glad. But today a sortie is planned – just a small one – to the pink walls. He is inclined to work a little too late. Bill is an enormous help to him – but also a temptation to work too late at night.

Bill planned to leave December 22nd and meet his wife[1] in Paris for Christmas but now great telegrams have been sent to persuade her to come out here for five days so that Bill can stay longer. The 'girls' and Sergeant Williams and Greenshields are all very good and devoted, and seem happy and thrilled with the place – as indeed they might be, for it is really a terrestrial paradise. The people in the hotel are very nice and do not stare or bother one – with an exception of one man who tried to take photographs of Papa. We ignored several attempts, then Sergeant Williams appeared from behind a palm tree and delivered a little lecture about the rules of a private hotel being respected and the man, crestfallen, packed up his Brownie camera and fled down an olive grove. Sergeant Williams retired majestically behind his palm tree again!

Colonel and Madame Hauteville[2] are lunching tomorrow. The Colonel is the Commander of the area. On our arrival he drew Bill aside and said: 'I want you to understand this is *not* a democratic area – this is a military area. If there is anything – or anyone – you do not like, just give me a telephone call – I will be right over!' The Glowie[3] himself met us – and we are shortly to eat a sheep's eye or two with him.

---

[1] Livia Stela Nasta, 1916–2001. Known as 'Pussy'. Secretary, Ministry of Cooperation, Bucharest, 1939. Fled Romania, 1941. Secretary, Sqn Ldr, RAF 2nd Photographic Reconnaissance Unit, Heliopolis, Egypt, 1941. Joined SOE, 1942. Married, 1943, William Deakin.

[2] Roger Marie Antoine Benoît d'Hauteville, 1895–1970. Married, 1929, Kathleen Reagh. Chef de la Région de Marrakech, Sep. 1944. Gen., 1949.

Kathleen Marie Eglé Hélène Mac Carthy Reagh, 1903–91. Married, 1929, Roger d'Hauteville.

[3] Thami El Glaoui, 1879–1956. Appointed Pasha of Marrakech, 1912–56. Deposed Sultan of Morocco, 1953; pardoned by the Sultan in 1955. (Sarah corrects her mistake in her letter to Clementine on 19 Dec. 1947, reproduced below, pp. 902–4.)

The 'Souks' are deserted of tourists, and the poor Arabs look forlorn sitting in their little shops surrounded by their bright but cheap wares. Though the hotel is full, I feel they are rich French from other parts of Morocco rather than France, who are used to the life and do not buy souvenirs. They must miss the 'sooveneer' hunting GIs of the War. So, accordingly, Miss Gilliatt and Miss Sturdee (secretaries) were given a great welcome when Bill and I escorted them down to the Souks. They fell for a big Moroccan bag each and were delighted, and people hurried from all neighbouring shops to see the now rare birds 'tourists', buying.

It took us an hour to buy the bags, for we looked at everything else – and bags and belts and silks were sent from the other shops for our inspection; they were still nice to us when they saw we were not really buying anything. Miss Gilliatt declared it was the most wonderful afternoon of her life – so it was really a successful afternoon.

I do hope your oranges and lemons got through the customs all right. Large quantities will not be easy to send now the plane has gone back but we are going to try and send small amounts regularly. There is a limit to the amount you may send us.

The British Consuls at Casablanca have been wonderful in organising whisky – for there is none here. . . .

Clementine Churchill to Winston S. Churchill
(Churchill papers, 1/44)[1]

16 December 1947

My darling Winston,

I am happy that the sun is shining with you. Here we are muffled in drizzle and mist, <u>but</u> it is quite warm and muggy. Whereas I am nervous about the sharp cold that comes down from the Atlas. I remember the delicious air (like champagne) and I feel it will do you good <u>if only</u> you don't catch cold. Please take great pains not to. The only part of your time table which matters is the time you come in – ought not that to be about four o' clock? I suppose you lunch about 12? to get the most sun. I hope you will have gay picnics.

I dined with the young? Birkenheads[2] to meet Mr Marshall. It was a really delightful party. I sat between 'General' Marshall and Lord Camrose

---

[1] This letter was handwritten.
[2] Frederick Winston Furneaux Smith, 1907–75. Churchill's godson. Succeeded his father as 2nd Earl of Birkenhead, 1930. Joined 53rd Anti-Tank Rgt, 1938. Capt., 1940. Maj., 1942. Political Intelligence Dept, FO, 1942. British Military Mission to Yugoslav Partisans, 1944–5. Biographer of his father (1933), of Lord Halifax (1965) and of Churchill (this work was completed by his son, the 3rd Earl; publ. 1989).
Sheila Berry, 1913–92. Daughter of 1st Viscount Camrose. Married, 1935, Frederick Winston Furneaux Smith, 2nd Earl of Birkenhead. Author of *Against Oblivion* (1943), *Peace in Piccadilly* (1958) and *Illustrious Friends* (1965). Temporary Lady-in-Waiting to Duchess of Kent, 1949–53.

and the others were Lady Camrose,[1] Oliver Stanley, Bob Laycock[2] and his lovely 'Angie'[3] and Patricia Sherwood,[4] another daughter of Lord and Lady Camrose. The Conference had ended in dismal failure half-an-hour before but Mr Marshall did not refer to it once. He talked much about you and President Roosevelt with whom it seems he often disagreed & whom he sometimes did not consult. He said that he (the President) would direct his mind like a shaft of light over one section of the whole subject to be considered, leaving everything else in outer darkness. He did not like his attention being called to aspects which he had not mastered or which from lack of time or indolence or disinclination he had disregarded. Mind you he did not actually use these words, but the gist, and I thought much more were implied.

The House of Commons was thoughtful, sad and respectful about Mr Baldwin.[5] Gallacher showed real feeling. It would seem that even Communists have bowels of compassion. I will try & arrange with Duncan or failing him Tommy to attend the Memorial Service. This one is meant only for the men in the Baldwin iron works. Yesterday I went to have tea with little Winston. He is charming with his Mama & I spent a happy hour in Pamela's flat. She has had a horrid hunting accident but has nearly recovered. In the New Year I am taking Winston to see 'Treasure Island' and next Monday which is Edwina's[6] Birthday, she & I & Diana & Julian are betaking ourselves to the Big Circus at Olympia.

Mary & Christopher have invited me to stay with them for Christmas and on the Saturday we are inviting all the children on the Chartwell Estate (there are 23 children) and their Mothers to tea and a conjuror. I fear you will not be able to toil through this long letter in my not always clear handwriting but let Sarah read it aloud to you.

[Drawing of a cat]

---

[1] Mary Agnes Corns, 1873–1962. Married, 1929, William Berry; eight children. Styled Baroness Camrose, 1929; Viscountess Camrose, 1941.

[2] Robert Edward Laycock, 1907–68. Joined Royal Horse Guards, 1927. Leader of Commando group known as Layforce which operated behind the lines in North Africa from 1940 (disbanded after high casualties during attack on Crete, 1941). Led Commando attempt to assassinate Rommel in the Western Desert. Active behind the lines in Sicily and Italy, 1942–3. Trained Commando groups in Britain, 1943. Maj.-Gen., 1943. Chief of Combined Operations, 1943–7 (including planning of the D-Day landings). Governor and C-in-C, Malta, 1954–9.

[3] Angela Clare Louise Ward, 1916–99. Married, 1935, Sir Robert Edward Laycock.

[4] Molly Patricia Berry, 1915–95. Daughter of William Ewart Berry, 1st Viscount Camrose, and Mary Agnes Corns. Married, 1936, Roger Charles George Chetwode; 1942, Hugh Michael Seely, 1st Baron Sherwood (div.); 1958, Lt-Col. Sir Richard Charles Geers Cotterell, 5th Bt.

[5] The former Conservative PM Stanley Baldwin died on 13 Dec. 1947.

[6] Edwina Sandys, 1938– . Daughter of Duncan and Diana Sandys; Churchill's first granddaughter. Married, 1960, Piers Dixon, son of the diplomat Sir Pierson Dixon (div., 1973); two sons, Mark (b. 1962) and Hugo (b. 1963).

Winston S. Churchill to Clementine Churchill
(Baroness Spencer-Churchill papers)

18 December 1947   Marrakech

My darling Clemmie,

We have been here a week today. The weather is lovely and increasingly warm. It is always supposed to rain for two or three days at Christmas, but at present the skies are cloudless. At 10 o'clock in the morning it is possible to lie in bed, as I am doing now, with the French Windows wide open on to the balcony. I have been working very hard, rather too hard, in fact. My routine is: Wake up about 8 a.m., work at Book till 12.30, lunch at one, paint from 2.30 till 5, when it is cold and dusk, sleep from 6 p.m. till 7.30, dine at 8, Oklahoma[1] with the Mule – who was given a credit of £28 and has been completely stripped (I have given her another credit, but she says she will not accept it). At 10 or 11 p.m. again work on Book. Here I have been rather naughty; the hours of going to bed have been one o' clock, two, three, three, three, three, two, but an immense amount has been done and Book II is practically finished. I am not going to sit up so late in the future.

The painting has not gone badly but I only have these two and a half short hours of good light. Three daubs are on the way.

We have followed exactly the same routine each day, but I think we shall go for a picnic on Saturday. Yesterday the Comte d'Hauteville and his wife (he is the Colonel commanding the whole of this district with both military and civil powers) came to luncheon with us. They are persons of quality. She looks like a more gracious Eva Keyes.[2] We are going to lunch with them on Sunday. Tonight we dine with the Glaoui. He is the same age as me. He has sent large crates of grapefruit, oranges, and mandarins, and enormous jars of butter, jam, and honey, and a basket of dates. Monsieur Majorel[3] will be away for another fortnight, but I will then get into contact with him. I have invited Mrs Deakin to come on here for Christmas as this will enable me to keep Bill till at least the New Year.

Comte d'Hauteville is planning a 3 days' excursion for me and Sarah, and the Prof if he comes, after the Deakins leave in the New Year. It is much more ambitious than Taroudant, which he says is only a 'petit Marrakech'. We are to go right through the Atlas Mountains into what he calls wonderful country beyond, in the Sahara Desert, or half desert as it is there. I shall know more about this plan before I decide on it, but certainly it sounds attractive and by then a change of routine may be necessary.

[1] The card game 'Oklahoma gin rummy'.
[2] Eva Mary Salvin Bowlby, 1882–1973. Married, 1906, Roger Keyes. Their elder son was killed in action in Libya in 1941.
[3] Jacques Majorelle, 1886–1962. Architect and painter. Born in Nancy, France. Travelled to Marrakech for health reasons in 1917, settling there in 1919. Married, 1919, Andrée Longueville (div. 1947); 1956, Marie-Thérèse Hamann, known as 'Maïthé' or 'Maïté'. Designed the Majorelle Garden in Marrakech, 1924.

They are very attentive in the Hotel; the only fault has been the bathwater not being hot, but this is being attended to. The food and wine are beyond criticism. Generally I am much settled down and very glad to be here, and to feel that I have a good long spell ahead of me, away from the distractions of British politics, and the sense of gathering gloom in our affairs which oppresses me.

Yes I like to rest here where I combine rest & continual occupation. Sarah & Bill find lots to talk about. Do tell me about Chartwell. Dictate me a Chartwell Bulletin, with a supplement by Christopher. I hope you are getting all that you want done (Have mercy!) & that Whitbread and Kurn are making progress with Jacob's ladder.

Tender love my dearest Clemmie & every wish that my heart can signal for your health & happiness.
Always your devoted husband

Sarah Churchill to Clementine Churchill
('Keep on Dancing, An Autobiography', pages 168–72)

19 December 1947

I have been commanded by Papa to write to you all, a full description of the dinner we had with SE the Glaoui (not, I understand, Glowie!)

It really was a most superb and sumptuous evening. Bill and I and Papa all enjoyed ourselves enormously. The more so, because we were alone with him and his son (not the yellow knickerbocker motorcycle one).[1] The evening therefore was quite informal and despite the Glaoui's bad French, really at times incomprehensible, not a bit stiff.

His son met us at the door and acted as interpreter, often springing to his feet during the course of the evening to serve both his Father and Papa in a most humble, filial, and Papa said, absolutely proper manner! It was certainly an evening conducted in the *ancien régime* style to put it mildly. The Glaoui and Papa basked in a positively navy-blue reactionary mood, while colossal negresses and eunuchs (?) (Papa says NO! not these) padded about, carrying to and fro great copper and earthenware bowls and plates of food.

We sat round a low table. The juniors on pouffes, and Papa and the Glaoui on a low sofa. They padded and propped Papa up with cushions till he was tightly wedged on his sofa, so he couldn't fall off – and dinner began.

We had been warned it would be strictly Arab style, but still there were many things to learn.

At first a red copper intricately worked bowl was brought, also a large copper kettle. 'You are to wash your hands,' murmured Papa. I held out both,

---

[1] El Glaoui had eight sons.

and warm rose water was poured over them. I was handed a small towel, the size of a sheet, to wipe them with. I noticed the Glaoui only washed one hand, the right. Then we started.

I wonder if I can remember all we ate, because eat is all we did! A sort of second wind came to us round about the sixth platter of food, and, by then, all shyness of eating with one's fingers having gone, we were plunging merrily ahead as to the manner born. However, we were to learn that all courses are not eaten with fingers, and Papa committed one small social error by plunging his fingers in to the centre of a great bowl of what looked like stewed and mashed apples and semolina, only to be handed a spoon! How could one know? The Glaoui gallantly waved away his spoon and plunged too! Later, somewhere round the tenth course, an ice cream turned up. I am sorry to say that though it was quite clear that this was one of the courses to be eaten with a spoon, Papa was enjoying himself so much that, muttering, 'I simply must,' he plunged his fingers into the ice cream. The Glaoui and son luckily were highly amused.

Now, back to the menu. First, soup in bowls with spoon. Then I think a whole sheep, yes, a whole roast sheep. Fingers. We were definitely at this stage still a little restrained. I could hardly believe I was expected to claw quite viciously at any part of the animal I thought looked tempting. I gave a nervous tug, but nothing much happened. I then found out that the son, in intervals of eating heartily himself dislodged delicate morsels and left them lying about in my segment of the lamb.

I was very grateful. Presently, Glaoui himself passed me a trifle he had dislodged. Then I think, yes, then a thing that looked like an enormous mille-feuille appeared. We boldly dug our fingers in! It was indeed a kind of mille-feuille, but not sweet. It was a vegetable one, full of sage and strange sweet herbs, and dripping in butter and flaky pastries. Then, came the most wonderful almond paste pastry wheel, made in widening circles. Oh! 'how I wished I hadn't eaten so much.' This, for me, was *the* dish.

First it was easy to eat – you just broke off a piece quite neatly like a biscuit, and munched and crunched merrily. Delicious almond paste, slightly reminiscent of mince-pie, but crispier and more nutty. I made my side of the wheel look pretty silly. By this time I felt I was very nearly grease up to my elbows, so I discreetly had a good tidy up. My table napkin and Papa's began to look like a baby's bib after a disagreement as to where the rusk and milk should go. The Glaoui's napkin and that of his son remained snowy white. When I looked up the almond wheel had gone and there, to our amazement and slight misgivings, was a bowl containing pigeons in lemon sauce.

'Crickey!' said Papa.

After the briefest pause, we forged ahead dipping our bread in the yellow sauce, and plucking at the half-submerged pigeons. Then came another with dry semolina! the one Papa inadvertently plunged his fingers into, only to discover it was a spoon course. But by now we had our second wind and nothing could daunt us. Papa looked up with a seraphic smile, and said sotto voce: 'This goes on for hours, you know.'

Now memory blurs a bit, I think a final meat course. But who knows? Some little time after, the ice cream turned up. Spoons *please* in future! Then tangerines heaped in a pyramid, but we said no. Then came the intricately-worked bowl again. I remembered. I held out one hand only, a little water, a little soap, a little water the vast towel! The Glaoui this time however washed both his hands; I mean a real scrub! practically behind the ears! Then they cleared the table away, and I am so sorry to say this revealed a little circle of food at my feet that had unfortunately fallen during the battle. The whole thing was very difficult but by then we had warmed and after Papa had plunged his fingers into the wrong bowl no one looked back!

Brandy, cigars in another room. All the rooms were rather cold, for they had no doors just great hangings like carpets, so that you can imagine yourself in a tent, if you want to. Luckily Papa kept his coat on the whole time.

We talked of this and that. The Glaoui nodded and began to get a little somnolent.

'You're so right,' said Papa suddenly – 'quite right. Clothes for instance – very sensible. *Toutes voilées ou toutes nues*. Quite right!'

The Glaoui awoke with a start. '*Ce sont des topiques philosophiques*,' continued Papa. The Glaoui agreed vigorously!

Coffee good. Mint tea delicious. Papa drank two cups. He signed some of his books for him. They saw us to the door. It was a lovely evening, they saw we had really enjoyed ourselves, which was better than all our thanks could be. The Glaoui's Guard of Honour saluted. . . . We discovered that Sgt Williams had eaten the same, in the same fashion, in an adjoining room. He was delighted, and Miss Sturdee and Miss Gilliatt could hardly believe their ears. An Arabian night, to be sure!

PS. In point of fact – in retrospect we discovered we didn't eat very much! It's just the confusion of dishes and manner of eating – if we were asked again, I would do much better. Wow, darling – I will write soon to you again. He is happy and well, loves his routine. Today we are off for the first picnic. Mrs Deakin has arrived safely.

Winston S. Churchill to Air Commodore George Powell
(Churchill papers, 1/69)

19 December 1947

Dear Air Commodore Powell,

I am writing to let you know how much I enjoyed the flight in your luxurious and most comfortable plane to Paris and then to Marrakech. The whole crew were attentive, proficient and agreeable. Pray accept, and convey to all concerned my warm thanks for the care and attention with which the flight was planned and executed. It was indeed kind of you and your co-Directors to think of showing me this courtesy, which has been of so much practical assistance to me.

You were good enough to say, when I saw you, that when the time came I could approach you and see whether it would be possible for you to arrange to have me and my party flown home. I plan to be here for about six weeks altogether. If you are able to carry us home I should be glad to hear from you how much extra weight (if any) the plane could take, bearing in mind of course a wide margin for safety.

Christopher Soames to Winston S. Churchill
(Churchill papers, 1/45)[1]

22 December 1947　　　　　　　　　　　　　　　　　　　　Chartwell Farm

My dear Mr Churchill,

Firstly, about the horse and brougham. I think it is quite out of the question to buy one. The horse, brougham, and harness would cost in the region of £300. Over and above that you would have to engage a coachman to look after the horse and drive it. He would be £5.10 a week less lodging. It would also be difficult to feed the horse without carting oats and hay up from here. Alternatively, he could be lodged & fed at some stable, but that would cost £4.10 a week.

Alternatively, one could be hired. But to have a clean and smart turn-out with an efficient coachman would cost about £15 a week and that only on the assumption that you took it with a 6 month contract.

I would really advise against it for the following reasons.

Firstly, Mrs Churchill's bill for a hired car from Godfrey Davies is no more than £15 a week, and

Secondly, the advantages of a car over a brougham do not have to be stressed.

Thirdly, she has only to apply and she will certainly be granted permission to drive her own car for a limited number of miles a week in London. I have already spoken to her about this.

Now for the farm. Whitbread is working on the Jacob's Ladder. He is having to make concrete oblongs in moulds to go on the top of the balustrade. When that is completed he is going on sawing up wood. The prisoners are still here. They have not yet finished quarrying the stone for the road – 60 tons are

---

[1] This letter was handwritten.

needed, and they have quarried about 40. After Christmas, Hagledon[1] goes on a week's holiday. The prisoners leave off for their Christmas holiday mid-day on Wednesday 24th. They do not return until Monday 29th. I am arranging for them to be sent over daily from the camp without a foreman, and we will keep them until Saturday 3rd when they leave for good. By then they will have completed the quarrying and done one or two more odd jobs.

Southon is sending a man over after Christmas to drill the necessary holes in the dolls at Bardogs to set up the fence. All goes well on the farm. We are producing nearly twice as much milk as was produced on this farm in December '46.

I have put out feelers again to find out whether Obriss will be in the market. I have heard rumours that it may be – but not yet awhile. The next-door farm to Obriss, on the same side of the road, is for sale. I don't think it would suit you as it is laid out as a stud farm with only twenty acres of land and extensive stabling which has fallen into disrepair, inasmuch as it was occupied by the Army during the war.

I do hope the weather is being kind to you and that you are having a good rest. It has been very mild here – no frost and very little rain.

Mary & I both send our best love to you and the Mule, and wish you a very happy Christmas.

Winston S. Churchill to Clementine Churchill
(Baroness Spencer-Churchill papers)

24 December 1947   Marrakech

My darling Clemmie,

The weather continues to be cloudless and lovely. The air is cold and in the shade or when the sun goes down it is biting. I am very careful to wrap up warmly and never paint after 5 o' clock. I have five (six now)[2] pictures on the stocks. They are really much better, easier, looser, and more accomplished than those I painted twelve years ago (which I also have with me). I think you will be interested in them. They look much more like the real thing, though none as yet are finished, and there is many a slip.

Yesterday we went for a picnic at Ouriki, where we had three picnics together in 1943/44. Do you remember it? It is an opening of a beautiful gorge in the hills, with great snowy mountains in front and red buildings on either side of the enclosing foothills, and quite a river flowing out of the mountain chain. The whole party went, and I think everybody enjoyed themselves. We are going again in two or three days to the same place so that I can finish my picture.

[1] Probably Hazledon.
[2] This parenthetical addition was handwritten.

Bill's wife has arrived and makes herself most agreeable. He has not been quite well with a slight temperature. I sent him to bed early last night, and today he is normal again.

I continue to be extremely fit, and my existence is strictly divided into sleeping, eating, painting, and the Book, with a nightly game of Oklahoma with the Mule. We have been here a fortnight tomorrow and so far hardly any letters and not all the bags have come through. I am greatly relieved that the copy I have sent home is all now safely received. Of some parts I have not kept a copy here, and loss would have been a terrible vexation. The progress I have made is immense. Book I is practically finished and so is Book II. I believe they will cease to be burdens on me except for minor corrections by the end of the year. It would have been quite impossible for me to do this work if I had not buried myself here, where every prospect pleases, and only the twenty-four hours are too short. As I have often told you, I do not need rest, but change is a great refreshment. I am so glad you had such an interesting dinner to meet General Marshall. I think we have made good friends with him. I have long had a great respect for his really outstanding qualities, if not as a strategist, as an organiser of armies, a statesman, and above all a man. Cripps seems to me to be taking a far more responsible view of his duties than his predecessor, the dirty Doctor, did, and his speech about the Royal Grants was courageous and dignified. I do not think the Debate has done any harm. All will be forgotten, and they will get their £5000 a year extra.

I am also glad that neither the fire nor the burglar did you any harm, and I am delighted to hear of the putting away of the valuables, etc. The great danger is an unoccupied house or an unoccupied part of a house. It is essential there should be a man and wife at Chartwell. Also the local Police might help. Never mind the expense – a stitch in time saves nine. Lights could be shown here and there after dark. The moment they know the house is empty they have it at their mercy, and in three or four hours there is no ordinary safe or strong room into which they cannot break.

The only incident we have had here has been a crazy French Colonel, who had fought bravely in the war and is now retired and quite dotty. He is also said to have undesirable political connections and was forbidden by the Colonel commanding the 'Region' to deliver an address in Marrakech. He came here nevertheless and stayed in the Mamounia, and presented himself a little before midnight to thank me for having given him the Victoria Cross (which is a delusion) and asked for my advice on his various grievances. I received him because I thought he had come from Rabat with some of my proofs which I was expecting to get. When I saw he was a mental case I dismissed him courteously. However, in the meanwhile the French Police had sent on his dossier stating that he was quite mad and queer. On searching his suitcase, which they and Sgt Williams very promptly did, they found a loaded automatic pistol of which they deprived him. He made no complaint. Great vigilance was practised by the French Police, and he was carefully watched during the weekend he stayed here. He prowled about the hotel till 5 a.m., and the Colonel-Governor got very excited and he was ordered back to Rabat on Monday. I took a friendly farewell of him in the restaurant, and hope I may never see his face again. (No, he turned up at the dance last night.)

I have not given up hopes that Prof may be able to come. The Deakins will probably leave in the early days of January. Montag arrives on the 9th for a week, and Mr Graebner on the 10th. I am hoping the Mule will stick it out with me. Her Jewish friend has arrived at Casablanca and I think they plan a tour of Fez together. I am sending you the telegrams I have received from Randolph.

Here is a paragraph for your expert mind. The expense for the first week for seven of us was £300, which is a little more than a fiver a day per head. Considering the excellent food, and service of the highest class, and that we have an office and a studio besides our bedrooms, this is not excessive, taking into account the state of the world. They give you enormous helpings, at least four times what one could eat. I have remonstrated about this, but I gather it is not wasted, any more than Glaoui's banquet, of which Sarah has given you a very full description. I do not eat very much myself, even at lunch, but it is nice to see beef again. £300 for six weeks = £1800. £2500 in dollars are being supplied, and Miss Sturdee has had a message from Mr Graebner saying that there is plenty more if necessary. I think myself the original figure I mentioned will cover everything.

When you recollect how much it means to all these publishers to get delivery of Volume I by the end of February, and that they would perhaps lose many thousands of pounds and suffer immense inconvenience if I failed them, I feel fully justified in the course I have taken, which results only from the fact of our currency regulations which prevent my using my own money. Moreover, considering that all here is concentrated on the Book, I have no doubt our American hosts can make a perfectly valid case for the money to be treated as expenses from the point of view of American Income Tax. If this be so, it will not cost them much.

It is practically certain that I shall not go to America, but come back straight from here on the 19th or 20th. I have telegraphed to Bernie saying I will try to come in the early Spring. It is important for me to go there, not only for large political reasons, but also on the Book. There will be no difficulty in obtaining expenses from the Government for an American visit on an adequate scale. However, I have made no plans.

With fondest love, my sweet & darling Clemmie,
Your ever devoted husband,
W [Drawing of a pig]

Winston S. Churchill to Isaiah Berlin[1]
(Churchill papers, 4/57)

25 December 1947   Marrakech

Dear Mr Berlin,

Thank you so much for all the work you have done which is of much use to me. I do not agree with all your comments and will presently send you back my various rejoinders. In a great many cases I am accepting your suggestions.

I now send you the first six chapters which, as you will see, have been completely remoulded. I have not yet decided to leave out the political stuff, though I agree it is a little off the track. I should like to know how you think the new first six chapters run. Personally I feel they fit together much better than they did before. However please state exactly what your view is upon them and to what extent your first impressions have been affected by the drastic changes I have made.

Sarah Churchill to Clementine Churchill
('Keep on Dancing, An Autobiography', pages 172–4)

26 December 1947

... Papa is really well – working terribly hard – but no longer so late. One or two of us, me included, have suffered from a peculiar migraine these last days – I think it is the strong air and bright sunlight. I sent for my medicine and since two days it has disappeared. Christmas Eve was a gala evening. Papa invited the girls and Sergeant Williams and Greenshields who generally sit in the opposite corner to join us for the evening! We all put on evening dress and Greenshields in a great flutter borrowed a black tie from Bill and we all met in the sitting room for a cocktail, and then we went down in force to the dining room at 10.30. A glittering scene met our eyes. In the short space of the afternoon, they had transformed the large dining room. A gigantic Christmas tree 25–30 feet high had been installed and decorated. The windows were hung with branches laden with oranges, and daubs of white paint on the window panes made it seem that a blizzard was blowing outside – clever idea.

Everyone was 'dolled up'. It was a very international atmosphere – Danes, Swiss, Portuguese, Spanish, American – the smattering of English us, French, and an Italian waiter. When midnight struck, they lowered the lights, and with

---

[1] Isaiah Berlin, 1909–97. Born in Riga, Russia (now Latvia). Emigrated to Britain, 1921. Educated at Corpus Christi College, Oxford. Lecturer, New College, 1932. Elected to Prize Fellowship, All Souls, 1932. Worked for British Information Services, New York City, 1940–2; for British Embassy, Washington DC, 1942–6. Visited Soviet Union, 1945–6. Married, 1956, Aline Halban. Knighted, 1957. Chichele Prof. of Social and Political Theory, Oxford, 1957–67. Visiting Prof., Humanities, City University of New York, 1966–71. Founding President, Wolfson College, Oxford, 1966–75. OM, 1971. President, British Academy, 1974–8. Published the essay *Two Concepts of Liberty* (1958).

one accord the International melee rose as a man to their feet just on the spur of the moment and looked to Papa. They raised their glasses, and clapped – and 'Vive Churchill' and 'Bravo' echoed round the room. The band who had practised hard all afternoon English surprises for us, played 'It's a long way to Tipperary' as the Christmas pudding was brought in. Renewed clappings and murmurs, and Papa stood up very moved and bowed to them all, and received the Christmas pudding as he does a casket on being given the freedom of a city. Then he got up – and I thought he was going to – but no,

'Whirl me round the floor once, Mule – I think I can manage it.'

This was too much for them – like a famous dance team we took the floor amidst a roar of applause – we were very good – it was a waltz. Then he danced during the evening with Miss Sturdee, Miss Gilliatt and Mrs Deakin – and I was whirled off my feet by Sergeant Williams – who is pretty hot on a rumba (Scotland Yard training is most extensive). I was also whirled by Greenshields, who was too shy at first but ended up the strongest. Papa stayed till two!

One event I did not relate in letters home. At the party, I had noticed that my father had been attracted by a good-looking fair lady who had sat against the wall with a gentleman; but now that the festivities were in progress she was alone, profiled against the snow-screened window.

My father said, 'Why is she alone?'

'The gentleman had to go back to his family,' I said.

'How do you know that?'

'Don't gentleman usually go home to their families?'

Immediately he rose to his feet and said, 'Dance me around the floor.'

He danced me around the floor and stopped at the forlorn but proud lady. Looking at her he said, 'You are the Christmas fairy, may I have a dance?'

My job once again ended, I returned to my seat and he took the lady in his arms. I have no idea what he said, but I can imagine. He never liked to see a beautiful woman alone. When their turn at dancing was done, he left her at her place. Meanwhile, the detectives were wondering if she had been imported as a spy. We never discovered her name but later received a telegram: YOU WILL NEVER KNOW MY NAME BUT I AM PROUD TO HAVE DANCED WITH WINSTON CHURCHILL.

When the party was over, we left the room accompanied by our detectives. We were seen upstairs and ensconced in our beds, dreaming of the happy evening. Sometime during the night, I felt a tap on my shoulder.

Immediately all my senses were alert: 'Is my father all right?'

'Non, je suis votre protecteur.'

So I said what I hoped was a Churchillian phrase: 'So keep protecting us!'

The gallant Frenchman removed himself from my room and was later removed from his duty.

Winston S. Churchill to Lettice Marston
(Churchill papers, 4/57)

26 December 1947

I now send you the first six Chapters of Book I, and the 'ALMOST FINAL' Contents Table, which have reached what is nearly a Final form. The other Chapters will follow soon. Twenty-four copies should be printed of these as they arrive, and also of Chapter VII – 'THE DARKENING SCENE' – which you already have. Of these 24 copies, two should come out here for me, and one to Mr Deakin, who will be in Paris; one each to General Pownall[1] and Commodore Allen for themselves; and one to Mr Isaiah Berlin, with my covering letter attached. All these should be sent as the revised proofs come back from the Printer. On the other hand the following should have copies only when the whole book is complete, which will not be long: Mr Graebner one; Mr Henry Luce, one (through Mr Graebner); General Pownall, one (to show to the Secretary of the Cabinet); and Lord Camrose, twelve. The remaining three should be kept by you for office purposes and emergencies.

Mr Deakin is returning to Paris on December 30 or 31. He will bring with him the whole of the rest of Book I. He will make arrangements for a trustworthy messenger from the British Embassy to travel at my expense by air to London with it. You should of course telegraph all receipts of proofs from me, including the arrival of the final lot.

Clementine Churchill to Winston S. Churchill
(Churchill papers, 1/44)[2]

26 December 1947   Chartwell Farm

My Darling,

Here I am most hospitably entertained by Mary and Christopher in their comfortable & pleasant farm house. We spent a happy & peaceful Christmas Day & we drank – your health & Sarah's before we fell to on the fat turkey. Today Mary has been put to bed by Doctor Ward[3] because she has got a very

---

[1] Henry Royds Pownall, 1887–1961. Entered Army, 1906. On active service, 1914–18 (DSO, MC). Director, Military Operations and Intelligence, War Office, 1938–9. CGS, BEF, 1939–40. Knighted, 1940. Inspector-General, Home Guard, 1940. GOC, British Forces, Northern Ireland, 1940–1; in Ceylon, 1942–3. VCIGS, 1941. C-in-C, Far East, 1941–2. GOC-in-C, Persia, 1943. CoS, SACSEA (Lord Mountbatten), 1943–4. Churchill's principal helper on the military aspects of his war memoirs, 1945–55. Chief Commissioner, St John's Ambulance Bde, 1947–9. Chancellor, Order of St John, 1951.

[2] This letter was handwritten.

[3] Kenneth Langhorne Stanley Ward. Son of Dr Stanley Edward Ward. Received his medical degree at Edinburgh, 1917. Former RN Surgeon. Resident Medical Officer at St Mary's Hospital for Women and Children, Plaistow. Medical Officer, Infant Welfare Centre, Sandridge, near St Albans. Asst Medical Officer, Edenbridge Cottage Hospital, four miles from Chartwell.

bad cough. When I arrived on Christmas Eve it had already got a grip on her & now it is worse. It is not down on her lungs & Doctor Ward says it won't go down there if she stays in an even temperature. It has suddenly turned very cold but the winter sun is streaming in on me as I write. Tomorrow Saturday is the Children's Party for the 23 children & their Mothers on the Chartwell Estate. I have got a conjuror for them & nice food – only it's sad Mary won't be there to help. Last Tuesday I took Edwina and Julian to the Big Circus at Olympia & they loved it. It was Edwina's 9th birthday. She is a very pretty little girl & maybe a 'beauty' one day I think. Diana came too & we really had a delightful afternoon. Your second letter came two days ago & it makes me happy to feel that your paws are buttered. Everybody here is sneezing & coughing & I am indeed glad you are having these few weeks' respite from the English Winter.

The ramp of the Jacob's ladder has been topped with concrete slabs because Whitbread could not find enough stone. I don't think I will like it although it is very neatly done. The concrete should I think have been mixed with soot to make it a soft grey colour. Perhaps we could plant a hedge below which would hide it in time. From the far side of the orchard it looks hard & rigid.

Your loving Clemmie [Drawing of a cat]

Anthony Eden to Winston S. Churchill
(Churchill papers, 2/68)[1]

26 December 1947

My dear Winston,

All good wishes for 1948. May it bring you much happiness and the gov't some salutary lessons!

Nicholas[2] and I are off on our Persian & Arabian travels on Sunday. Our old friend Ibn Saud has asked me to stay with him in Riyadh, & I shall try to fit that in, even though it means drinking water again. Unless you instruct me otherwise, I will convey your good wishes to any friendly potentates we have met before, in Teheran or Bagdad and to Ibn Saud himself.

I hope that Marrakech is all that you hoped for in sunshine & enjoyment and that the book & the painting go well.

The last days in the House after you left were not momentous. I saw the 22[3] executives with Oliver Stanley & R. A. Butler and told them of the work that was being done, & of the help they could give. They seemed well pleased.

[1] This letter was handwritten.
[2] Valentine G. Lawford, 1911–91. Known as 'Nicholas'. Asst Private Secretary to Anthony Eden at the FO, 1940–5. Friend of Douglas Fairbanks, Duff Cooper, the Rothschilds, Gertrude Stein and the Mendls. Served as interpreter between Churchill and de Gaulle during Operation 'Overlord' in June 1944. Moved to New York in 1950 and remained there until his death.
[3] The 1922 Committee of Conservative backbench MPs.

Ernie Bevin gave us a Foreign Affairs survey related almost entirely to the record of the conference's failure. He doesn't look at all well, nor am I told, is he.

All being well, I should reach London again about 19 Jan, so please do just as suits you best about your return. The Foreign Affairs debate is booked for Thursday & Friday in that week, & I hope will record govt's determination to go ahead with all the friends we can find, American & western European to rebuild that half of Europe that is still free.

The communist electoral challenge to the gov't is interesting, though I hardly think they will poll at all heavily in Wigan. Camlachie would have been more helpful for them I should have thought.

[. . .]

Colin Coote[1] to Arthur Watson[2]
(Camrose papers)

28 December 1947

I have read the draft of Winston's book. It is, as you say, scrappy in places and, though it contains some very fine passages, I received the definite impression that the writer feels rather tired and hurried. It must, of course, be remembered that it is not merely a narrative, but a record and, therefore, large extracts from official documents, which have little interest to the general reader, have had to be included. But I do think that the whole book falls rather between the two stools of a narrative and a record. It does not reach the level of absorbing interest maintained throughout by Winston's book on the First World War.

The two portions included in this parcel stop short of the really vital part of the war, and I should imagine that this will be at once more novel, and of more sustained interest. Even so far as it has gone, the book is, of course, the most devastating exposure of Baldwin, Chamberlain and Lloyd George, the latter in his later years.

From our point of view, I fancy that the books will not suffer from compression, and that extracts from it could be made which would be better in effect than the complete work.

---

[1] Colin Reith Coote, 1893–1979. On active service during WWI (DSO). Member of Gloucestershire Rgt, 1914–17. Married, 1916, Marguerite Doris Wellstead: two children (div. 1925). MP (Lib.) for Wisbech, 1917–18; for Isle of Ely, 1918–22. Correspondent, *The Times*, Rome, 1922–6. Writer, *Daily Telegraph*, 1942–79; Deputy Editor, 1945–50; Editor, 1950–64. Knighted, 1962.

[2] Arthur E. Watson, 1880–1969. Educated at Rutherford College of Technology, Newcastle, and Armstrong College, University of Durham. Married, 1904, Lily Waugh. Joined *Daily Telegraph*, 1902. On active service during WWI, 1914–18. Maj., RFA, 1918. Asst Editor, *Daily Telegraph*, 1923; Editor, 1924–50.

Isaiah Berlin to Winston S. Churchill
(Churchill papers, 4/141)

28 December 1947

    The narrative when it gets into its stride seems to me wonderfully rapid and absorbing, but it seems to me to take some time to get going properly. The main theme is the Rise of Hitler, and the blindness of England and the Western World. If the story is to start with the earlier 'peaceful years', 1924–1929, it may be felt to lack something unless the central events which linger in the popular memory – the General Strike, relations with Russia (the Zinoviev Letter, the Arcos Raid), etc. are placed in proper focus; alternatively all this could be condensed into a general prelude to the real story – with not too rigid a skeleton of chronology – a kind of commentary on the moods and acts of these remote deluded years, not overweighted with specific detail, a background to the awful things to come. It seems to me that at present neither of these effects is altogether achieved. The account of Locarno is, if you will allow me to say so, very masterly. But after the splendid premium of Chapter I, which sets the stage nobly for a procession of great events, Chapters II and III are something of an anti-climax: the play of personalities, e.g. the Chamberlains, Mr Baldwin, etc., while it is both unfamiliar and interesting, and while it could appropriately embroider the big events of the period, scarcely seems weighty enough to occupy the centre of the picture. In fact the story told in these two chapters seems to me too episodic and insubstantial to act as an adequate scaffolding to the more tremendous story of the Rise of Hitler, with which the book really gets into a wonderful stride. I should like to suggest that either:

    (a) Chapters II and III be left out altogether – since Chapters I and IV seem to me to follow one another without a break; or

    (b) That these chapters be shortened drastically and take the form of a general commentary on the lull between two violent periods, with personal and political details lightly sketched in, and no attempt to concentrate a specific issue, e.g. neither on Locarno nor the return to the Gold Standard; or

    (c) If you prefer to take up the story where the Aftermath left off, that more be done about the General Strike, Russia, Anglo-American relations or absence of relations, etc., although I quite see that there may be strong political reasons against doing this.

Sarah Churchill to Clementine Churchill
('Keep on Dancing, An Autobiography', pages 174–6)

30 December 1947

Well of course he caught a cold – he was really very good but I feared it was inevitable. It is much colder here this year – and we have none of us except him felt too terribly well. I have worried and worried – even in the mid-day the contrast between sun and shadow is very sharp. This morning however he is very much better – and has survived the whole thing without a degree of temperature – and went straight to bed the moment he caught it – and wasn't a bit difficult – because he knew you would worry. This morning I have a terrible sore throat too, we are all slightly *congestionné*. This is not a good Marrakech year – although the sun shines brightly, it is too cold and although everything is lovely, I have worried and will worry about this. He must and will now cut an hour off the afternoon – but it is sad we have caught this really exceptionally cold year. I have thought seriously about moving 500 miles further south to Agadir – where Villiers[1] who has arrived says it is warmer – a sea breeze – but less exceptional change between Midday and Sundown – and Sunlight and Shadow – but of course it is a formidable *déménagement*, and we do not know if the hotel could accommodate us and of course he does not want to go. The Doctor has just been and says he has now the *'légère bronchite;! 'Savez – c'est Marrakech'*, he continued – it is an exceptional year:

'It is too cold and too hot – it is too perfect this year'!

Next morning – not very good news from Agadir and Taroudant this morning – we will probably have to stick it out here. It sounds funny to say 'stick it out' in this lovely place and with this sunshine, but of course the anxiety of the cold has cast a gloom on us all. However, we read that you are all having terrible weather including blizzards so perhaps we are worrying unnecessarily, and all our spirits will perk up again in a few days.

Papa is depressed by events – he thinks it is very serious and hopes the Americans take decisive action in Greece, and (will) not fall between two stools.

Mrs Deakin is upset about her Rumania. 1947 comes to an end on a disquieting moment – perhaps we shall all feel much better when our colds are gone!

---

[1] David Villiers, 1906–85. British painter, poet and aesthete. Close friend of Sarah Churchill and Clementine Churchill.

Christopher Soames to Winston S. Churchill
(Churchill papers, 1/45)[1]

31 December 1947   Chartwell Farm

My dear Mr Churchill,

What a lovely present you gave me for Christmas. It was more than ever acceptable as we were almost out of whisky and unable to get any more. It was so generous of you. Thank you so much.

We were all miserable to hear you had been kept indoors with a cold. I do hope you have beaten it off and are able to go out and enjoy the scenery and pleasures of Marrakech. Mary has had an awful cough but is now nearly recovered. We are going to stay with Diana & Duncan for the weekend, which will be our last sortie until Mary has her kitten.[2]

The farm progresses not unsuccessfully. Last month's milk cheque was £312 (Marnham's milk cheque for last November was roughly £120). The prisoners (less Hazledon) are here till the end of this week. They then depart. The men have been over about the hedging and ditching. I am now awaiting their estimate.

Whitbread has completed the Jacob's ladder and has been sawing up wood like mad. Three heifer calves were born over Christmas; one on Christmas Eve, one on Christmas day and one on Boxing Day. We have massacred a pig, and have sent him off to be cured; so you will have delicious peach and milk fed bacon and ham for your breakfasts when you return.

Mary sends you her best love, as indeed do I.

---

[1] This letter was handwritten.
[2] i.e. the child she was expecting. There is a hand-drawn kitten next to this sentence.

January
1948

Winston S. Churchill to Lord Moran[1]
(Churchill papers, 1/45)

1 January 1948

A bad cough in the tubes but not in the lungs has now lasted for six days without temperature or improvement. Neither Dr Diot[2] nor I could say condition is serious enough to warrant your journey. On the other hand he would be very glad if you were here. Weather is brilliant but rather treacherous as the air is exceptionally cold this year. There is a good deal of pneumonia about in the town. It would be a great comfort if you and Dorothy[3] would come out and I am sure that you would find it very pleasant. I should be most grateful if you feel you can come. Arrange journey through Miss Marston. Blood count follows.

Sarah Churchill to Clementine Churchill
(Churchill papers, 1/45)

1 January 1948

Darling Mummie I feel incoherent telephone messages will have upset you. Apart from the cough he seems well in himself and his colour and appetite are good and temperature normal. But feel that presence of Moran is essential to guide and relieve anxiety else all benefits of holiday will be spoiled.

Much love.

---

[1] This letter was copied to Clementine Churchill.
[2] Physician who worked in Marrakesh, Morocco. Treated Churchill when he had bronchitis following a visit to France in 1948.
[3] Dorothy Dufton, 1895–1983. Married, 1919, Charles McMoran Wilson, later Lord Moran: two children. MBE, 1918.

Denis Kelly to Winston S Churchill
(*Churchill papers, 4/143*)

3 January 1948

Mr Churchill
    Here are some Press extracts about the East Fulham by-election: (Chapter 8. Page 1)
    Polling day was on October 25th 1933: result:

John Wilmot[1] (Lab)	17,700
Alderman W. J. Waldron[2] (Con.)	12,950
Labour majority	4,840

The Times said on Oct. 10th:

'(Mr Wilmot) is challenging the record of the National Government on such matters as unemployment, slum clearance and disarmament.'

On October 17th:

'Mr Wilmot declares that the action of the German Government in leaving the Disarmament Conference has increased the determination of the working classes to support the "peace men".'

In his letter to the Conservative candidate,
Mr MacDonald (then PM) said:

'The issue before the electors is an unusually simple one. Two years ago they placed the National Government in power in a time of great danger to the country. Its first task was to avert the immediate peril; to restore budgetary solvency, to see that the national currency did not suffer a panicky collapse, and to create conditions in which industry and agriculture could be carried on with some degree of confidence despite the state of confusion and depression which existed in the outside world. . . .'

. . . 'Now the electors of East Fulham have to decide whether to support a Government consisting of men who have put party politics on one side in order to cooperate to bring the country safely through a very difficult period; or an Opposition whose only contribution from beginning to end of the crisis has been an attempt to exploit every difficulty and every unavoidable hardship for partisan ends.'

Comment: No word of disarmament or international affairs.

[1] John Wilmot, 1895–1964. MP (Lab.) for East Fulham, 1933–5; for Kennington, 1939–45; for Deptford, 1945–50. Parliamentary Private Secretary to Minister of Economic Warfare, 1940–2; to President of the Board of Trade, 1942–4. Joint Parliamentary Secretary, Ministry of Supply, 1944–5. PC, 1945. Minister of Supply, 1945–7. Baron, 1950.
[2] William James Waldron, 1876–1957. Sheriff, City of London, 1935–6. Col., 1st Anti-Aircraft Div. RASC, 1934–9. Knighted, 1936.

On October 19th it reported Mr Baldwin's letter to the Conservative candidate as follows:

'... Notwithstanding the great improvement in our industrial and financial situation during the past two years while the National Government has been in office, we cannot fail to recognise the difficulties which still surround us, especially in the international sphere. ...' (my italics)

The Times also reported as follows:

'The following statement was made to the Press by the East Fulham Liberal Association last night:

'The replies of the two candidates having been received, the association, regarding the question of disarmament as of vital importance (my italics) recommend all Liberal voters to give Mr John Wilmot their support, if on no other grounds on the question of disarmament alone.'

The Manchester Guardian of October 26th reports Wilmot as saying after the result of the poll was declared:

'My victory is a message of hope to all who are working for peace in every country. The British people demand that there shall be no more war, and that the British Government shall give a lead to the whole world by initiating immediately a policy of general disarmament ...' (my italics)

Mr Lansbury said:

'... the verdict is also a direct message to the Government that our people will not tolerate a new race in armaments which the rearming of Germany must inevitably create. It is, in fact, a clear and unmistakeable demand that the nations shall unite in themselves, disarming to the level of Germany as a preliminary to total disarmament. ...'

The Manchester Guardian's leader of Oct. 28th commented:

'... If the choice is between a Conservative who is content with the Government's confused efforts for disarmament and would follow it blindly in a new race of arms, and a Labour candidate who puts the active maintenance of a collective peace system even above British nationalism and Imperialism or exclusive alliances, it is the latter who should be supported. ...'

The Fulham Chronicle of Oct. 20th reports that the East Fulham Liberal Association sent a questionnaire to both candidates in which the second question was as follows:

'Will you press the Government to make further and more strenuous efforts to achieve Disarmament?'

Wilmot's answer was:

'Certainly. I regard the necessity for Disarmament and unceasing work for peace by international cooperation through the League of Nations, as of urgent and paramount importance.'

The Conservative candidate said we had gone far enough.

I spent Friday afternoon reading the back files of the local newspapers in the Fulham public library. My personal impression was that international affairs did not bulk very large and that the by-election was fought mainly on local and domestic issues.

So far, the local Labour Party have not been able to find a copy of Wilmot's election address.

Winston S. Churchill to King George VI
(*Churchill papers, 2/171*[1])

3 January 1948　　　　　　　　　　　　　　　　　　　　　　　　　　Marrakech

Sir,

I am most grateful to Yr Majesty and to the Queen for sending the Christmas Card with the picture of Table Bay from the deck of the *Vanguard*. My wife and I will keep this with other tokens of Yr Majesty's kindness among our most valued possessions.

I am vy glad that the Debate & the Select Cte[2] on the Royal grants had such a satisfactory conclusion. There are always a number of venomous people in a free country who write spiteful letters & say poisonous things. In the days of Queen Victoria[3] the most violent Republicanism was thought fashionable among those who then constituted the 'Left'. But these never represented the British nation wh is devoted to our Ancient Constitutional Monarchy the form of which has been enhanced by the ten years glorious reign of Yr Majesty, & who finds its sure foundation in the people's heart.

Yr Majesty's Ministers, if I may venture to say so, as Leader of the Opposition, behaved in a most becoming manner & all is now settled in accordance with the dignity of the Crown & in its lasting interests.

In signing my Christmas Card I observed that Yr Majesty wrote R instead of RI. I found this vy painful, but I still hope that much will one day return. May God Bless Your Reign is the prayer of Yr Majesty's devoted humble servant & subject.

---

[1] This letter was handwritten.
[2] Committee.
[3] Alexandrina Victoria, 1819–1901. Daughter of Edward, Duke of Kent; granddaughter of King George III. Queen of the United Kingdom of Great Britain and Ireland, 1837–1901; Empress of India, 1876–1901. Married, 1840, Albert of Saxe-Coburg-Gotha (d. 1861): nine children.

January 1948

Winston S. Churchill to Lord Camrose
(*Churchill papers, 4/141*)

4 January 1948 Marrakech
Private

My dear Bill,

A friend of mind, Mr Isaiah Berlin, read Book I at my request and, apart from many points of detail, made the following comment (Enclosure 'A').[1] Thereafter Sir Norman Brook,[2] the Secretary to the Cabinet who was reading the Book by my desire, made independently a similar comment.

Of course it would be quite easy to cut out and abridge the domestic–political material and throw Chapters 2 and 3 into one.

You will also see that I have reshaped these chapters in the 'Almost Final' edition and I think to some extent have met the criticisms. Before I make up my mind finally I should like to have your opinion after you have read the first five chapters in the latest edition. I am asking one or two other friends to give me their individual opinion also on this specific point.

It may be said that Book I will be 135,000 words with 10,000 or 12,000 in the Appendices. Book II now shows 80,000 words with, it may be 20,000 words in the Appendices. These latter can of course be reduced.

Will you very kindly let me know your opinion so that I may take my own decision.

It is lovely out here and I hope you will come. I am getting better quickly but thought it wise to ask Moran to come out in case of trouble.

---

[1] 'Isaiah Berlin felt that two at least of the early chapters were "too episodic and insubstantial to act as an adequate scaffolding to the more tremendous story of the Rise of Hitler, with which the book really gets into a wonderful stride"' (Martin Gilbert, *Winston S. Churchill*, vol. 8, *Never Despair, 1945–1965* (1988), p. 393).

[2] Norman Craven Brook, 1902–67. Educated at Wadham College, Oxford. Principal Private Secretary to Sir John Anderson, 1938–42. CB, 1942. Deputy Secretary of the Cabinet, 1942–5. KCB, 1946. Secretary of the Cabinet, 1947–56. GCB, 1951. PC, 1953. Secretary to the Treasury, 1956–62. Baron, 1963. Chairman of the Governors, BBC, 1964–7. Suggested the title *The Hinge of Fate* for vol. 4 of Churchill's war memoirs.

Winston S. Churchill: press notice
(Churchill papers, 1/69)

4 January 1948

Mr Churchill said:

'I am much better and I am going painting this afternoon. The sunshine will do me good. You will find this one of the most beautiful places in the world especially as we have much warmer air with the sunshine now than we had a short while ago. I called Lord Moran out here because at my age everyone has to be careful.'

Winston S. Churchill to Emery Reves
(Churchill papers, 4/141)

4 January 1948 Marrakech

Many thanks for your factual corrections which I am carefully considering. The quote Almost Final unquote text of Book I should reach you soon. Pray give me your suggestions for cutting documents and speeches. Much has already been done in new text. My method is to tell the tale from current authentic documents where possible. Please reread the whole from the beginning. Shall be back in London January 22 and would gladly run through text with you thereafter. Have every hope now of delivering Books I and II for page proofs by end January. Have made immense progress out here as you will see. Every good wish.

Emery Reves to Winston S. Churchill
(Churchill papers, 4/141)

5 January 1948 New York

Dear Mr Churchill,

I was very happy indeed to receive your cable this morning and to see that you agree with my suggestions.

Together with Houghton Mifflin we have been discussing the publication of the first volume with the Book-of-the-Month Club, as their cooperation would be of immense help in the distribution. They always make their decisions many months ahead of publication, and they are unable to decide without their independent judges having read the books. In view of the serialisation scheme, it will be impossible to postpone book publication, therefore as time is very short, we have decided with Houghton Mifflin to let the judges look into the Provisional Final text of Book I.

JANUARY 1948   923

I refused to part with the copy I have, so the judges came to my office, one by one, and read the text here. These five people, considered to be the highest literary authorities in the United States (Henry Seidel Canby,[1] Dorothy Canfield Fisher,[2] Christopher Morley,[3] John P. Marquand,[4] and Clifton Fadiman)[5] are naturally bound to secrecy.

They were all tremendously impressed and the examination of this unfinished text will be sufficient basis for further negotiations.

I watched them reading while they were sitting in my room. They were completely absorbed, but they all skipped the documents and speeches, and said exactly what I indicated to you in my last letter. Encouraged by this unanimous view of the most influential American literary experts, I should now like to make the following suggestions:

1) All speeches, documents should be integrated into the narrative. You can very well refer to documents and speeches and make lengthy quotations from them whenever necessary, but this should be an organic part of the text, to be continued – in quotes – in the same paragraph, even in the same phrase.

2) Quotations should be reduced to a minimum. If you would refer to your past speeches, statements, etc. in a way like: 'In 1937 I said in a speech in the House of Commons that . . .', nobody would doubt what you say, and reading would be greatly facilitated.

3) There should be no differentiation of type in the text. Narrative and quotes should be in the same type to avoid interruptions in the reading of one organic text.

4) All documents you wish to use should be printed in full in an appendix, which could be set in smaller type. Documents in the appendix should be classified according to the chapters to which they refer, so as to avoid interruption of the text even by footnotes.

5) I feel that almost all the documents you use are interesting and

---

[1] Henry Seidel Canby, 1878–1951. Born in Wilmington, Del. Educated at Yale University. Married, 1907, Marion Ponsonby Gause: two children. Instructor, Yale University, 1900–22; Prof. of English, 1922. Editor, *The Saturday Review*, 1902–4. Asst Editor, *Yale Review*, 1911, 1920. US Liaison to British Ministry of Information, 1918. US Office of Information, Australia and New Zealand, 1945.

[2] Dorothy Frances Canfield, 1879–1958. Born in Lawrence, Kan. Educated at Columbia University. Married, 1907, John Redwood Fisher. American educator. Author of *A Montessori Mother* (1916).

[3] Christopher Morley, 1890–1957. Born in Bryn Mawr, Pa. Educated at Haverford College and New College, Oxford. Married, 1914, Helen Booth Fairchild: four children. Staff, *Evening Public Ledger*, 1918–20; *New York Evening Post*, 1920–4. Contributing Editor, *Saturday Review of Literature*, 1924–39. Author of *Thunder on the Left* (1925), *Kitty Foyle* (1939), and over 100 other novels and essays.

[4] John P. Marquand, 1893–1960. Born in Wilmington, Del. Educated at Harvard University. Married, 1922, Christina Sedgwick (d. 1935); 1937, Adelaide Hooker: three children. Author of *Thank You, Mr Moto* (1936), *Think Fast, Mr Moto* (1937) and 25 other works.

[5] Clifton Paul Fadiman, 1904–99. Born in Brooklyn, NY, son of Russian Jewish immigrants. Educated at Columbia University, 1925. Editor, Simon & Schuster, 1925; *The New Yorker*, 1933–43. Master of Ceremonies, *Information Please* (radio programme), 1938–48. Member, Editorial Board, Book of the Month Club, 1944–93.

should be integrated into the text, with very few exceptions. I have found one section that I would suggest be eliminated, viz. your lengthy exchange of letters with the Admiralty about 14" or 16" guns on battleships. This is a technical problem which would interest a few readers and would seem to be a side-track off the main road. When battleship guns are treated in detail, one wonders why not also bombers, flamethrowers, torpedoes and other weapons. If you wanted to explain the technical problems of weapons, the work might be tremendously inflated and might change its character. I feel that you should concentrate on telling the human drama of the past years and not deviate into technicalities. There may be a few other short passages which might be omitted, but nothing struck me as much as the memoranda on the gun calibre on battleships. This passage should be reduced to less than a page.

I note that an 'almost final' text of Book I is on the way. As soon as I receive it, I shall carefully re-read the whole text again.

I also hope very much that I shall be able to come over to London for a short stay after your return, if you think my suggestions and assistance might be of some use. It is hardly possible to handle the details by correspondence.

PS. Do you plan to come over to America in the near future? I would naturally keep all information confidential, but would like to coordinate my plans with yours.

Winston S. Churchill to Emery Reves
(Churchill papers, 4/141)

6 January 1948 Marrakech

There is no question of altering the whole character of work in manner you suggest.

Emery Reves to Winston S. Churchill
(Churchill papers, 4/141)

6 January 1948 New York

Regret misunderstanding there is no question altering character work which is superb and unparalleled. As explained my letter January fifth integration documents purely technical editorial matter which would be accomplished few days with minimum alteration in text and documents. Of course I may be altogether wrong.

January 1948

Winston S. Churchill to Emery Reves
(Churchill papers, 4/141)

7 January 1948   Marrakech

Thank you for telegram You have not yet seen 'Almost Final' copy. As these chapters reach you by all means make your suggestions in writing on the copy. We will discuss them in London.

Emery Reves to Winston S. Churchill
(Churchill papers, 4/141)

7 January 1948   New York

Houghton Mifflin and other publishers would like to know final title first volume for catalogue they feel 'Downward Path' sounds somewhat discouraging would prefer more challenging title indicating crescendo events How do you like 'Gathering Clouds' 'The Gathering Storm' or 'The Brooding Storm' But you probably have better Regards

Winston S. Churchill to Sir Stafford Cripps
(Churchill papers, 4/19)

8 January 1948   Marrakech

My dear Stafford,

I am so much obliged to you for your letter, and for sending me the extracts from your Diary. It is most kind of you to take this trouble on my behalf.

Thank you both very much for your good wishes which we warmly reciprocate.

It was good of you amid your many toils to write it all out like that.

I have done an immense amount of work here, & the weather though treacherous is lovely.

Sarah Churchill to Lieutenant-Colonel Bill Deakin
(Churchill papers, 1/68)

9 January 1948

Papa said last night the Deakins left a very pleasant memory. Thought you would like to know we miss you and hope you are safely back in London. Love to both.

King George VI to Winston S. Churchill
(Churchill papers, 2/171)[1]

11 January 1948   Buckingham Palace

My dear Winston,

It was indeed kind of you to have written[2] to me as you did for our Christmas card, & over the satisfactory ending of the debate of the Civil List Act. I must thank you gratefully for all your help & understanding way in which you placed the matter before the members of the Select Committee, some of whom who had doubts as to the need of the grant. At first it looked as if nothing was to be done about it, but the change of Chan[3] of the Exchequer made all the difference.

I am so glad that you are well again now, & I hope you will benefit from the change in Marrakesh.

All good wishes to you in 1948.

Winston S. Churchill to Emery Reves
(Churchill papers, 4/141)

12 January 1948   Marrakech

Your letter of January 5 I do not agree with your suggestions but only that you may make them. There is no question of changing the book in manner you suggest.

Emery Reves to Winston S. Churchill
(Churchill papers, 4/141)

14 January 1948   New York

Five Almost Final chapters absolutely perfect. You have reshaped everything as I would have suggested. If other chapters edited likewise our sole criticism fully met. Strongly feel excellent chapters II and III should stay unabridged domestic picture serial for understanding coming events. Relegating documents to Appendix whenever possible making narrative more dramatic just like first five chapters is sole desire Houghton Mifflin and Book of Month Club who approved all my suggestions before I submitted them. Would gladly take *Queen Mary* Saturday but understand Graebner bringing final text. Please advise when you expect releasing complete First Volume and whether you think I could be any use London before that date. Must come over near future

---

[1] This letter was handwritten.
[2] Letter reproduced above (p. 920).
[3] Chancellor.

anyway but am endeavouring solve problem of being simultaneously London and New York during February.

Lady Violet Bonham Carter to Winston S. Churchill
(Churchill papers, 2/146)[1]

19 January 1948

Dearest Winston,

Only a line of welcome & joy that you are back – safe & sound. What a fright you gave us & what a relief it was to hear that you are better. You are badly needed here. My love to Clemmie and you.

Sarah Churchill to Winston S. Churchill
(Churchill papers, 1/45)[2]

21 January 1948

My darling darling Papa,

It isn't possible to thank you enough, or begin to tell you how much I have loved being with you at Marrakech.

It was the most lovely holiday for me.

I love Marrakech. The valley of Ourika holds a very strong place in my affections, almost as strong as Rome!

You know I would come with you anywhere in the world, for the joy I have in just watching you paint or work and being happy.

Dorothy and Charles and Lord Camrose and Prof – everyone enjoyed themselves. I know Mummie did greatly at moments – only naturally the anxiety and hurry are bound to upset her a little, but deep inside she was glad to come I know. And you gave the Deakins a second honeymoon! Wow – darling Papa.

Please never hesitate to ask me (though I have already had more than my fair share of travels with you) to come anywhere with you – or just sit around. If I am not working, I will always come.

The valley of Ourika – Christmas night – our drive back together just before you caught the cold – the Blonde – the lunatic – the moments of 'Bliss' are all firmly imprinted in my heart and mind.

Darling Papa. Thank you. Wow!

Much much love
Your loving Sarah

---

[1] This letter was handwritten.
[2] This letter was handwritten.

PS. I hope to send you shortly my two stories, perhaps three that I wrote while there, and a small book of Poems called 'Moans of a Mule'.

Winston S. Churchill to Lord Salisbury
(Churchill papers, 2/66)

22 January 1948

My dear Bobbetty,

Am I right in thinking that your line will be to say 'the Government have committed an act of aggression upon us by proposing, for Party reasons, to upset the Constitutional settlement reached nearly forty years ago. To that we are definitely opposed. Now Addison comes forward and makes a number of proposals reforming the composition of the House of Lords, some of which have received considerable support from the Conservative Party in bygone years. Clearly a new situation has been created. It is not one which affects in any way our opposition to the Bill now before us, but it would only be in accordance with respectful Parliamentary procedure in matters of grave import that we should examine carefully the new proposals that are made, and as I gather that the Government would welcome an adjournment of the debate on their Bill we, for our part, are very glad to support this. Indeed, if necessary, I will move the adjournment myself. However it must be clearly understood that the fact that we have an adjournment to enable us to examine the new proposals of the Government in no way diminishes our opposition to the Bill now before us. We shall look forward with much interest to a further fuller and more precise statement of their constructive proposals by His Majesty's Government, and we will address our minds to them with the utmost attention, it being clearly understood that our opposition to the present partisan and factious measure is in no way prejudiced or diminished,' or words to this effect. If so I agree with you.

It may be noted that an improvement in composition, character and weight in the Second Chamber should be accompanied by an increase and not a decrease in power.[1]

Winston S. Churchill: speech
(Hansard)

23 January 1948   House of Commons

FOREIGN AFFAIRS

I think I may say that this is the first time in my experience I have ever been called upon to follow the hon. Lady the Member for Epping (Mrs Manning).[2] I hope she will forgive me if I do not attempt to reproduce from memory the intricate discussions which took place at Yalta and afterwards at Potsdam. Broadly speaking, at Yalta we reached an agreement about the Eastern Frontiers of Poland on the basis of full Polish independence. We did not reach the point of deciding what compensation should be given to Poland for the changes on her Eastern Frontiers in favour of Russia – what compensation should be given her at the expense of Germany – but there had been some talk, even during the days of Teheran, about the line of the Oder.

As the hon. Lady knows, the Oder forks into the Eastern Neisse and the Western Neisse and we had always thought that up to the Eastern Neisse was fair compensation for Poland at the expense of Germany, having regard to her gains on the Baltic shore, and of fair compensation for the concessions she had made of districts which, though large in territory, consisted mainly of the Pripet Marshes, to Russia in the East, and which were an essential part of the strategic defence of the Soviet Union. When we got to Poland everything was in flux. Great masses of people were being driven about by the advancing Soviet Armies. The Poles pressed on accordingly and not only the Eastern Neisse was occupied, driving millions of refugees before them, but

---

[1] In 1947, fearing the House of Lords would block nationalization of the iron and steel industry, the Labour Party introduced a Parliament Bill. Finally passed in 1949, it reduced the time the House of Lords could delay financial bills from two years to one. As Conservative leader in the Lords (1945–57), Salisbury proposed a statement of principles, the Salisbury Convention, under which the Lords would not oppose the second or third reading of any government's legislation promised in its election manifesto. Salisbury believed that since the electorate had given Labour a decisive mandate, it would be incorrect for the Lords to frustrate such legislation.

[2] Elizabeth Leah Perrett, 1886–1977. Educated at St John's School and Homerton College, Cambridge. Married, 1914, William Henry Manning. MP (Lab.) for East Islington, 1931; for Epping, 1945–50. Author of *What I Saw in Spain* (1933) and *A Life for Education* (1970). DBE, 1966.

the other tracts between the Eastern and Western were occupied. These two added together comprise a very large part of the arable land of Germany. The feeding grounds of Germany were thus, in a marked manner, separated from the mouths of Germany, and millions of people were driven from the frontiers into the British zone, in the main, where they now are under conditions which no one can contemplate without growing anxiety. The hon. Lady says that we must recognise the *fait accompli* that they have been driven out and that the newcomers have settled themselves down there. All I can say is, we have not agreed to that; and it was only agreed to by the United States on the basis that it would be provisional until a peace treaty was made. Well, that is how the matter stands, and no one can possibly doubt that it remains a complication and a dark cloud over the map of Europe.

I am sorry, and a little surprised, that the depressing declaration about the destruction of so large a part of our material reserve of battleships should have been announced at the very time that the Foreign Secretary was about to make so serious and important a pronouncement,[1] because I have no doubt this unwise and improvident step will have its effect upon our influence and authority in international discussions. I do not, of course, intend to discuss the merits here. We shall ask for formal debate in due course, upon this and other aspects of our naval administration at the present time, particularly directed to the point of what value we are getting for the unprecedented peacetime sums of money which are being voted, and for the very large assignments under Vote A.

There is, however, another question of a Foreign Office character, connected with old battleships and warships, on which I must say a word. At the time the Italian Fleet surrendered I had a great desire personally to give Italy the feeling that they would be welcomed into the Allied ranks, and to show respect, as far as possible, for their national sentiment and pride. My colleagues in the National Coalition agreed to try to avert the proposed division of the Italian Fleet between Russia, Britain and America, and we were successful in this so far as the United States was concerned. We also persuaded Russia – by a very considerable sacrifice on our part, namely, the loan of a battleship and fourteen other vessels – to forgo any claim she might have on the Italian Navy. The Americans gave one ship, and we gave fourteen out of the fifteen that were used. They were a timely reinforcement to our Soviet Ally. I hope this arrangement will stand, and that the Soviets will keep our British ships, which they have adapted to their own uses, rather than insist upon having a proportion of the reduced Italian Navy handed over to them. It is very important that Italy should feel we have a regard for her feelings and sentiments in a matter like this, in which they can be so much more easily

---

[1] On the previous day, Bevin had given a long and wide-ranging speech on foreign affairs, emphasizing the danger of Soviet expansion over Eastern Europe, the threat of it over Western Europe, and the need for some kind of European Union.

satisfied than, for instance, on the question of Colonial possessions. We should do our best in that direction, and if we fail we shall not have lost any good will in that part of the world.

There is another point I should like the Prime Minister to mention, if he will, when he replies. It is only a very small point. I beg your pardon; it is only a very precise point, and not a small point at all. It is: What has happened to the negotiations with Albania by which we were to have some satisfaction given to us for the murder of forty British naval men and the grievous injury to many more by a State we had helped and nourished to the best of our ability?[1] That is not a matter which can be ignored or forgotten, because it occurred in time of peace, and cannot be, as it were, swept into the vast, confused catalogue of human injuries and wrong deeds which were done on both sides in the course of the great war. This was a very special matter. I think the representative of the Admiralty, the Parliamentary and Financial Secretary,[2] used very direct language upon the subject, which I believe was supported by the Foreign Office in their diplomatic negotiations. We trust that some statement may be made upon this, and that we shall certainly not allow the matter to rest in its present state of deadlock and stalemate. On the whole, the Government have maintained a continuity in foreign policy with that pursued under the National Coalition Government of which I was the head, and of which my right hon. Friend the Member for Warwick and Leamington (Mr Eden) was Foreign Secretary. We have, therefore tried to give them all possible help, and thus keep the foreign policy of Britain outside the area of party controversy. In Greece, the Government have pursued exactly the same policy as my right hon. Friend and I went to Athens that Christmas –

Mr Piratin[3] (Mile End): Shame.

Mr Churchill: The hon. Member is perhaps a good judge of shame.

Mr Piratin: From these benches we have to judge of it every day.

Mr Churchill: We tried to give all possible help. In Greece, the Government have pursued exactly the same policy which my right hon. Friend and I flew to Athens that stormy Christmas time in order to assert; and which at the

---

[1] On 22 Oct. 1946, while passing through the Corfu Channel near the coast of Albania, the British destroyer *Saumarez* hit an underwater mine and was severely damaged. Another British destroyer, the *Volage*, began towing the *Saumarez* to Corfu but also struck a mine. In all, 42 men died in this episode, and 32 were never accounted for. Despite objections by the Communist Government of Albania, British minesweepers were sent into the channel and discovered that the mines had been laid after the end of the war, in violation of international law. The British Government claimed that Albania was liable for the incident and submitted the matter to the UN Security Council.

[2] John Dugdale, 1905–63. Private Secretary to Clement Attlee, 1931–9. On active service, RASC, 1940–5; MC (as Temp. Capt.), 1942. MP (Lab.) for West Bromwich, 1941–63. Parliamentary Private Secretary to Attlee (Deputy PM), 1945. Parliamentary and Financial Secretary, Admiralty, 1945–50. PC, 1949. Minister of State for Colonial Affairs, 1950–1.

[3] Philip Piratin, 1907–95. Married, 1929, Beatrice Silver (diss.); 1944, Cecilia Gresser. Member (Communist), Stepney Borough Council, 1937–49. London Organizer, British Communist Party, 1939. MP (Communist) for Mile End, 1945–50. Author of *Our Flag Stays Red* (1948). Circulation manager, *Daily Worker*, 1954–6.

time the present Foreign Secretary so loyally and courageously defended at the Trade Union Congress with great success, and for which he achieved acceptance by that body at that time. Not only has this policy been carried through with persistence and perseverance by this country, but it has now also received the active and growing support of the United States, who have relieved us of a large part of the burden and responsibility which we were finding it hard to bear.

When I look back at the attacks made upon our Greek policy three years ago by *The Times* and *Manchester Guardian*, and by hon. Members, some of whom are important Ministers today, at the bitter prejudice that existed, and still exists in some quarters of the House, and at the violent attacks which were made upon it by men who now fill the important offices of Minister of Health[1] and Secretary of State for War,[2] who are now leading Ministers of the Crown, I must congratulate the Foreign Secretary on having been able to make his will effective and to procure the support and acquiescence of the Socialist Government and Party, including these Ministers, for a clear, steady policy – for what? For preventing the vast majority of the Greek people from being conquered and enslaved by a Communist minority, steeped in bloodshed and crime, and aided and tormented by Communist intrigues and incursions from Albania and Bulgaria, inspired and directed by Soviet Russia.

Mr Cocks (Broxtowe):[3] The right hon. Member did not say that in 1944. It was not the position then.

Mr Churchill: It is quite true that in 1944 Mr Stalin did not oppose the action which we took. *Izvestia* and *Pravda* were silent, while *The Times* and *Manchester Guardian* were vocal in their attacks. But then, it must be remembered that we had with the leaders of the Russian State very intimate relations, which had grown up in the comradeship of the long, bloody and terrible war which we thought was reaching a happy and final conclusion. Those agreements were kept when they were made, even though they were hard sometimes. I am so very glad to see the great change that has taken place in American opinion on this subject. Four years ago, the views we held so strongly about Greece, and the action we took in consequence, were the subject of widespread disapproval throughout the United States. Not only the large majority of the Press, but the State Department also, were highly critical of what was then held to be an Imperialist and reactionary policy on the part of Great Britain. However, in the interval the United States Government have entirely come round to our view, and are acting in exactly the same upright and disinterested spirit and intention as that which animated the National Coalition Government, in

[1] Aneurin Bevan.
[2] Emanuel Shinwell.
[3] Frederick Seymour Cocks, 1882–1953. Author of *The Secret Treaties* (1918), denouncing British policy during WWI. MP (Lab.) for Broxtowe, 1929–53. Member, Joint Select Committee on Indian Constitutional Reform, 1933–4; All-Party Committee on Parliamentary Procedure, 1945–6. Leader, All-Party Parliamentary Delegation to Greece, 1946. CBE, 1950.

which I was associated so cordially with both the present and former Foreign Secretaries. My hope is that having put their hand to the plough the United States will not look back, and Greece will be allowed and enabled to settle its affairs in accordance with the freely-expressed wishes of the majority of the people, and that it will not be reduced to one of the Communist-ridden Police States, such as have been set up against the will of their peoples behind what has come to be called 'The Iron Curtain'. I cannot help also feeling content to see that not only the British, but the American Government, have adopted to a very large extent the views which I expressed at Fulton nearly two years ago, and have, indeed, gone in many ways far beyond them.

Mr Gallacher (Fife, West): That is where the trouble started.

Mr Churchill: I am only reporting facts, which are naturally a source of satisfaction to me. I was much criticised on both sides of the Atlantic for the Fulton speech, but in almost every detail, and certainly in the spirit and in its moderation, what I there urged has now become the accepted policy of the English-speaking world. The language used by the Prime Minister and the Lord President of the Council about Soviet Russia, and about the dangers of a new war, far exceeds in gravity and menace anything which I said at that time, or, indeed, have ever said on this subject since the war. The joint use of bases, the maintenance of the common staff arrangements between Great Britain and the United States, and the close integration of our foreign policies, are being pursued throughout the English-speaking world without any prejudice to the overriding and supreme status of the world instrument of the United Nations, which it is our solemn duty to sustain to the best of our ability, and ultimately to bring into effective reality as the sovereign instrument of world government.

In another sphere, events are also moving along the lines which I have earnestly desired. It is a year ago since I spoke at Zurich. There I pleaded for the ideal and objective of a United Europe, and later we formed a Committee of all parties in this country to promote that cause.

Mr Gallacher: Not all parties.

Mr Churchill: On work of gathering together the strength and friendship of Europe, trying to weave it into one body, and forgetting some of the feuds and quarrels of the past, we should certainly not have asked for the assistance of those whose declared purpose it is to rupture all that happy programme. As I say, we formed this all-party Committee, with the exception of the Communists, whom we did not invite, and whom we do not now invite to join us in that or in any other form of social and political activity. The essence of my conception at that time, which was certainly not a new one – and the right hon. Gentleman said that it was twelve years ago since he had this idea –

The Secretary of State for Foreign Affairs (Mr Ernest Bevin): Twenty years ago.

Mr Churchill: It shows how durable is truth. The essence of my conception was that France should forgo her thousand year quarrel with Germany, and rise again to a leading position in Europe by bringing the German people back, with all our aid and goodwill, into the comity of nations. That implied a sublime act of faith on the part of France, but we are now in a region where such acts are perhaps the only ones which will be decisive.

I must say a word about our unofficial Committee for a United Europe, and also about its limitations. I am most anxious to reassure the Government and the Foreign Secretary on this subject. We do not aspire to compete with Governments in the executive sphere. What we seek to do is to build up moral, cultural, sentimental and social unities and affinities throughout all Europe, or all those parts of Europe where freedom still reigns. We are anxious to spread the idea of the men and women of many countries being good Europeans, as well as patriotic citizens of their native lands, ready and eager to meet and work with one another on terms of honour and amity, to forget past tragedies as far as possible, to recognise that what has happened in the past is unpayable by mortal man and that to exact its payment would wreck the world, and to build for a future which may one day make amends for all.

I was very glad to observe that six months ago Mr Marshall spoke of our movement as a link in the chain of thought which had led him to his memorable decision. Of course, we are watching with the greatest sympathy all the steps which are being taken under the Marshall Plan by the Governments of 16 countries to bring about economic unity and wellbeing over these wide areas, in which I have heard it said 270 million people dwell. But that is primarily the business of the responsible executive Governments in every country. There is also the question of measures of common defence which is now coming to the fore. That again is a matter for the executive Governments. The relationship of this committee to the executive responsible Governments is very similar to that of UNA to the United Nations, or the old League of Nations Union to the League of Nations. It is an unofficial body of private persons engaged in carrying forward the ideas on which these institutions are founded.

We welcome everything that was said by the Foreign Secretary about the more intimate relations we are to seek with France and with what are called the Benelux countries, and I presume with Switzerland, if she would wish it, and also, I am glad to hear, with Italy. On this side of the House we give our full support to this policy. We are sure that, as my right hon. Friend said last night and as the hon. Member for Epping said just now, this European policy of unity can perfectly well be reconciled with and adjusted to our obligations to the Commonwealth and Empire of which we are the heart and centre. I cannot believe that those difficulties will not be settled by patience and care. It is no help to draw sharp lines of contradiction between them. We need both as pillars in a world of reviving prosperity.

Nothing in the activities of our unofficial movement and committee can hamper the progress of the policy of His Majesty's Government. On the contrary, we hope to provide at least the atmosphere and even contribute to the foundation of that scheme for a united Europe of all free countries who, without giving up their customs and traditions, will come to regard themselves as parts of that great entity of Europe from which the civilisation of the modern world has sprung and without whose coherent existence it cannot be preserved. I hope that the Prime Minister and the Foreign Secretary will not commit the great mistake and failure of duty of trying to divert this movement of European unity into Party channels. For instance, we are told that there should be a European association of Socialist Parties. This has been brought forward as a reason for opposing the all-Party movement which some of us have tried to set on foot and which has many connections in Europe, but surely nothing could be more unwise and more reactionary than that. Once we try to make a united Socialist Europe we put ourselves on the same level as those who are trying to make a united Communist Europe. It is simply the ideas of the Cominform with another label, and there would no doubt come into being on this strange theory a united Liberal Europe, a united Roman Catholic Europe and a united Right Wing Europe and so on, all quarrelling with each other.

That is not the way to recreate the new historical continental entity, the structure of which is now recognised as vital to the modern world. On the contrary, it would only be a means of introducing strife and disorder in a scene already wracked by hideous stresses. Let us try to keep the idea of a united Europe above the Party divisions which are inevitable, permissible and even tolerable in all free countries. Let us try on a basis above Party to bring the collective personalities of the anxious States and nations as a whole into the larger harmony on which their future prosperity – aye, and indeed their life – may well depend.

Mr Scollan[1] (Renfrew, Western): We cannot do that in this country, never mind Europe.

Mr Churchill: We have very great unities in this country. The vast majority of the people of this country are united on fundamentals both in regard to constitution and freedom. They are also united in resistance to continental forms of totalitarianism and also united in their pride of their past and will I trust become united in their hopes for their future.

It is evident to anyone who listened to the Debate – I am afraid I was not in my place last night, though I gather that there were some very interesting speeches and some very interesting reactions to those speeches – that there are differences in foreign policy in the party opposite and that not all are agreed with the line which Ministers in His Majesty's Government are taking. At the same time I had the feeling yesterday while the Foreign Secretary was speaking

---

[1] Thomas Scollan, 1882–1974. President, Scottish TUC, 1934. MP (Lab.) for Western Renfrewshire, 1945–50.

that he was the toiler, the man on the labouring oar, and deserved the effective support of the House of Commons without consideration of party. Moreover, I am quite sure that at least 75 per cent of the people of this country and an equal majority of this House will support him and sustain him in the painful, wearisome and anxious task to which he has been called owing to the free and accepted workings of our Constitution. I have the feeling that the British people as a whole will recognise him as representing important elements in their decent ways of life and also as one who possesses strong and brave qualities above personal interest or factional clatter. Therefore, I do not intend in anything I say willingly to add to the burden that he bears. When we on this side of the House give our support to a Minister and to the general trend of his policy, we shall take care that it is not only a fair weather gift.

I read while I was abroad the speech which was delivered by the Lord President of the Council (Mr Herbert Morrison) on foreign affairs on 12th January. I am sorry that he is not in his place. I must say that it was a very serious speech, especially coming from him. I was sorry that he should have tried to inject into this pronouncement on foreign affairs ordinary party jibes and controversy. He was reported in the *Daily Telegraph* as saying:

> We must avoid the Tory drift and class prejudice in the conduct of foreign policy between the wars.
>
> The greatest fault the Conservative Party committed between the wars was in being too much influenced by the pacifist views which prevailed on that side of the House.

He went on to say:

> The Conservative Party carries a terrible load of responsibility for the muddle which led to the war.

That speech was referred to last night by the Minister of State (Mr Hector L. MacNeil), whom I am glad to see back in his place after having acquitted himself in a buoyant and distinguished manner on the other side of the Atlantic. When I read this speech of the Lord President of the Council I thought it necessary to ask the Conservative Central Office to produce for me a list of his previous convictions. Let me reassure the House that I will not burden it by reciting all of them – (An Hon. Member: 'Why not?') – because after a bit one might even have too much of a good thing with such an ample list. This however, I will say, that if we are to go into the conduct and opinions of individuals between the two wars, as we are quite prepared to do – I am very ready to do so – it would be quite possible to distribute the blame for the many mistakes made in such a way as to give the Lord President of the Council no particular cause for personal self-satisfaction.

In case at any forthcoming General Election there may be an attempt to revive these former controversies, we are taking steps to have little booklets prepared recording the utterances at different moments, of all the principal figures involved in those baffling times. For my part, I consider that it will be found much better by all Parties to leave the past to history, especially as I propose to write that history myself.

After the various grave things that have been said by the Foreign Secretary, and, out of doors, by other Ministers, it would be wrong to let this Debate evaporate in benevolent and optimistic platitudes. We are, after all, the guardians of the ordinary, humble, hard-working people, not only here at home, but in many lands. It is so little that they ask – only to get their daily bread by the sweat of their brow and enjoy the simple pleasures of life which were meant for all and should be denied to none.

> 'To make a happy fire-side clime
> For weans and wife
> There's the true pathos and sublime
> Of human life'.[1]

But now all these millions of humble humans are hustled and harried this way and that, first by nationalistic or imperialistic ambitions or appetites, now by ideological doctrines and hatreds, and all their small lives may be shattered and convulsed, millions at a time, and they may be only regimented up to suffering wounds and unrewarded toil. We, their representatives in this world-famous assembly, have a great responsibility, and we cannot always discharge it by treading easy paths and saying smooth things.

I am often asked, 'Will there be war?' and this is a question I have often asked myself. Can you wonder, Sir, that this question obtrudes itself upon us when the Lord President of the Council speaks, as he did ten days ago, of the 'risk of war' with Russia – twice, I think he used that phrase – and speaks of:

> The availability and, if necessary, the readiness of armed force to prevent the outbreak of violence –

and when the Prime Minister says – and I agree with him when he says:

> Soviet Communism pursues a policy of Imperialism in a new form – ideological, economic, and strategic – which threatens the welfare and way of life of the other nations of Europe.

These are statements from men whose whole lives have been spent in denouncing the dangers of militarism, when they have not been actively engaged in fighting for their lives against tyranny. These are the speeches of Socialists. It is not a question of Jingoism. These are the speeches of Socialists and the Ministers responsible.

Can you doubt that times are grave when the word 'sabotage' is used in

---

[1] Robert Burns, 'Epistle to Dr Blacklock' (1789).

accusation of one of the greatest Powers of the world, both by Mr Marshall in the United States and by the Foreign Secretary in this House? Such language in any previous period would have been incompatible with the maintenance of any form of diplomatic relations between the countries affected. I think it quite right to say the things said, but when they are said it is certainly not odd that we should have to ask ourselves this grim and hateful question, 'Will there be war?' When I last spoke on these questions in the House in October, 1946, 15 months ago – I venture, by the way, to refer to what I have said in the past, because I do not speak on these matters on the spur of the moment, but from a steady stream of thought which I have followed and pursued with a study and experience of these matters over many years – I said:

> I am not going to attempt to examine this afternoon whether war, which would, of course, be total war, is imminent or not. I cannot tell at all what the men at the head of the different Governments will do. There are too many of what Bismarck[1] called, *Imponderabilia*. It was easier in Hitler's day to feel and forecast the general movement of events. But now we have not to deal with Hitler and his crude Nazi gang. We are in the presence of something very much more difficult to measure. We are in the presence of a collective mind whose springs of actions we cannot judge. Thirteen men in the Kremlin hold all Russia and more than a third of Europe in their grip. Many stresses and pressures are working on them. These stresses and pressures are internal as well as external. I cannot presume to forecast what decisions they will take. Even less can I attempt to foresee the time-factor in their affairs. Still, it is certain that these 13, or it may be 14, men have it in their power to loose on the world horrors and devastations, compared with which all we have gone through would be but a prelude. We are told that they would never do such a thing, and I earnestly hope this may be true. They are certainly calculating, ruthless men, officially divorced from Christian ethics in any form, and with Asiatic views of the value of human life and liberty. On the other hand, they have a vast expanse of the land surface of the globe and all its populations to guide and develop as they choose, with arbitrary power and with all that science – if not perverted – can bestow upon future generations of mankind. Eight months ago I made a speech at Fulton in the United States. It had a mixed reception and quite a number of Members of this House put their names to a Motion condemning me for having made it; but what I said at Fulton in the presence

[1] Otto Eduard Leopold von Bismarck, 1815–98. Born into an aristocratic family in Schönhausen, Germany. Married, 1847, Johanna von Puttkamer: three children. Prussian representative to the German Confederation, 1851–7. Ambassador to Russia, 1857–62; to France, 1862. As PM (1862–73), pursued unification of German states around Prussia. His success in the Franco-Prussian War of 1870–1 persuaded the previously recalcitrant southern German states to join a German empire, making King Wilhelm I of Prussia an Emperor. Chancellor of Germany, 1871–90. Negotiated alliance with Austria-Hungary, later including Italy, 1879. Resigned and retired to his estate near Hamburg, 1890.

of the President of the United States has been outpaced and overpassed by the movements of events and of American opinion. At that time, I said that I did not believe that the Soviet Government wanted war. I said that what they wanted were the fruits of war, and I pointed to the heavy impact of Soviet Russia upon Eastern and Central Europe – the Iron Curtain and so forth – their demands in the Dardanelles and Persia, and their aspirations in the Far East. I fervently hope and pray that this view, which I then expressed, is still correct. But now I cannot tell. I should not blame His Majesty's Government if, even with all the information at their disposal, they also were not able to come to a definite conclusion. For all these reasons therefore, I expressed no opinion tonight upon the future, upon what the Soviet Government intend, or upon whether war is imminent or not.

Certainly, in the interval that has passed, the Soviet Government have not used their overwhelming military power in Europe to march westward to the North Sea, the Channel and the Atlantic Ocean. Nevertheless, it is common ground between all parties that the situation has deteriorated, especially in the last six months. No, indeed, it is not odd that this ugly question should still be put, and force itself upon us: 'Will there be war?' I will only venture now to say that there seems to me to be very real danger in going on drifting too long. I believe that the best chance of preventing a war is to bring matters to a head and come to a settlement with the Soviet Government before it is too late. This would imply that the Western democracies, who should, of course, seek unity among themselves at the earliest moment, would take the initiative in asking the Soviet for a settlement.

It is idle to reason or argue with the Communists. It is, however, possible to deal with them on a fair, realistic basis, and, in my experience, they will keep their bargains as long as it is in their interest to do so, which might, in this grave matter, be a long time, once things were settled. When this Parliament first assembled, I said that the possession of the atomic bomb would give three or four years' breathing space. Perhaps it may be more than that. But more than two of those years have already gone. I cannot think that any serious discussion which it may be necessary to have with the Soviet Government would be more likely to reach a favourable conclusion if we wait till they have got it too.

We may be absolutely sure that the present situation cannot last. The Foreign Secretary spoke yesterday of the Russian frontier line which runs from Stettin to Trieste. This was exactly the line which I mentioned in my speech at Fulton – Stettin to Trieste. He also mentioned the Elbe, and who can ever believe that there will be a permanent peace in Europe, or in the world, while the frontiers of Asia rest upon the Elbe? But now this line runs farther south along the Adriatic shore, and there is actual fighting now going on in Greece to decide whether it shall not curl round Athens, and so to the Dardanelles and

Turkey. Surely, there can be doubt in our minds that this is highly dangerous, and cannot endure. It is not only here in Europe that there are these iron curtains, and points of actual collision. In China and in Korea there are all kinds of dangers which we here in England find it baffling to measure. There is also much to be considered in the Middle East. There are very grave dangers – that is all I am going to say today – in letting everything run on and pile up until something happens, and it passes, all of a sudden, out of your control.

With all consideration of the facts, I believe it right to say today that the best chance of avoiding war is, in accord with the other Western democracies, to bring matters to a head with the Soviet Government, and by formal diplomatic processes, with all their privacy and gravity, to arrive at a lasting settlement. There is certainly enough for the interests of all if such a settlement could be reached. Even this method, I must say, however, would not guarantee that war would not come. But I believe it would give the best chance of preventing it, and that, if it came, we should have the best chance of coming out of it alive.

Sir Norman Brook to Clement Attlee
(Premier papers, 8/1321)

23 January 1948

Mr Churchill has sent to me, in instalments, printed proofs of the first volume of his book on the Second World War.

This is in two parts. Book I covers the period from 1919 to the outbreak of the war in 1939. For the greater part of this time Mr Churchill was out of office; and his account of this period involves no disclosure of information which he obtained as a Minister of the Crown. His work as Chancellor of the Exchequer in Mr Baldwin's Government from 1924 to 1929 has little bearing on the main war theme of his book, and he touches only very lightly upon it. These passages raise no questions with which I need trouble you.

2. Book II, however, covers the period when Mr Churchill was First Lord of the Admiralty, from the outbreak of the war to the fall of the Chamberlain Government. Here Mr Churchill begins to use the method of writing which he adopted in 'The World Crisis': he reproduces textually personal Minutes which he wrote as a Minister of the Crown and, to a somewhat lesser extent, memoranda which he submitted to his colleagues in the War Cabinet.

3. The Cabinet have already agreed in principle (on 10th October, 1946) to Mr Churchill's proposal that he should reproduce such documents in his book – on the understanding that, before publication, the text would be submitted 'for final revision on behalf of the Government in the light of the situation existing at the time'.[1] These concluding words reflect the Cabinet's impression

---

[1] See Cabinet minutes, 10 Oct. 1946, reproduced above (p. 487).

JANUARY 1948 941

that no part of Mr Churchill's book would be ready for publication until the end of 1948 or 1949. The Foreign Secretary, who was at the Paris Conference at the time, had some idea that earlier publication of some of these documents might be embarrassing to him in his conduct of foreign policy. It is true that Mr Churchill has made faster progress than we then expected. But (i) since the Foreign Secretary expressed these doubts, the international situation has changed in a direction which presumably reduces the risk of embarrassment being caused by the publication of Mr Churchill's wartime papers; and (ii) the events described in this particular volume are already eight years old, and the volumes dealing with the later war years will not be published for some months at any rate. The Cabinet's decision of principle does not, therefore, seem to be affected by the fact that publication will begin rather earlier than had previously been expected.

4. The point of principle being thus agreed, the question for decision now is whether objection need to be taken on their merits to the publication of any of the particular documents which Mr Churchill wishes to reproduce in their volume.

No objection need be raised to the Minutes which he wishes to print in this volume. And, in general, I doubt whether any question will arise about his personal Minutes – unless in later volumes he should wish to print Minutes reflecting strong divergences of view among Ministers.

I should, however, draw your attention to the following War Cabinet memoranda which he proposes to reproduce in the present volume:

WP (39) 52	Notes on the General Situation	25th September, 1939
WP (39) 57	Norway and Sweden	29th September, 1939
WP (39) 125	Australian Naval Defence	17th November, 1939
WP (39) 126	The Northern Barrage	19th November, 1939
WP (G) (39) 110	The Black Out	20th November, 1939
WP (39) 162	Norway – Iron Ore Traffic	16th December, 1939
WP (40) 54	Degaussing of Merchant Ships	15th March, 1940
WP (40) 96	Effect of Russian–Finnish Treaty on our Naval Situation	14th March, 1940

Copies of all these papers are attached. Of the paper on the Northern Barrage Mr Churchill proposes to print only the first paragraph of the covering note. The rest he proposes to reproduce in full – subject, in some cases, to the omission of the introductory paragraph.

5. One of the general principles approved by the Cabinet on 23rd May, 1946 was – 'To the extent that questions (e.g. of defence) have to be treated at the time they arise with exceptional secrecy, there is a case for permitting a correspondingly greater measure of relaxation with regard to them when the considerations (e.g. of military security) which formerly kept them secret no longer apply.' All save the first of these papers relate to military matters of

this kind; and, on that principle, I would say that Mr Churchill may properly be given permission to disclose now the views which he expressed, and the reports which he made, to his War Cabinet colleagues on these matters. The first paper discusses issues of foreign policy as well as strategy; but after this lapse of time I doubt whether its publication would affect our relations which foreign Governments and Sir Orme Sargent agrees that no objection need to be raised to its inclusion in the book.

I therefore submit that Mr Churchill may be given permission to publish all the Cabinet papers listed in paragraph 4 above.

6. It is, however, desirable that he should make suitable acknowledgement of the Crown copyright in these documents. This was mentioned to him in 1946 in general terms. I now propose to secure from him a formal undertaking to include, among any other acknowledgements which he prints in the preface to his book, a statement to the following effect: 'I also acknowledge my obligation to His Majesty's Government for permission to reproduce the text of certain official documents of which the Crown copyright is legally vested in the Controller of His Majesty's Stationery Office.'

7. The questions covered in the preceding paragraphs of this minute are, in my opinion, matters for your personal decision. The Cabinet, having approved the general principle, need not be asked to consider its application to particular documents. You may, however, think it wise to tell the Cabinet that in pursuance of their earlier decision Mr Churchill has been given permission to reproduce eight War Cabinet papers in Volume I of his book. As regards the Palace, it will suffice if I keep Sir Alan Lascelles generally informed of the extent of Mr Churchill's proposed disclosure of War Cabinet business.

8. There is one further question which Sir Edward Bridges and I would wish to bring to your attention at this stage. Mr Churchill's receipts from this book will be very large; and the Government may well be asked whether some part of them should not accrue to the State. Mr McKinlay, MP,[1] put a Question in the House of Commons in February, 1946 with Mr Churchill in mind, asking whether the Government would introduce legislation enabling the State to claim 50 per cent of all earnings of former Ministers of the Crown derived from the publication of books or newspaper articles based on official documents collected during their term of office (see attached extract from Hansard); and similar suggestions are likely to be put forward in future. We have, therefore, considered whether it would be appropriate to suggest to Mr Churchill that he should offer to surrender some part of his royalties to the Exchequer.

There is no precedent for making such a suggestion to a former Minister; and the Stationery Office doubt whether such a suggestion could fairly be based on grounds of Crown copyright. It is their practice to charge reproduction fees

[1] Adam Storey McKinlay, 1887–1950. Born in Govan. MP (Lab.) for Glasgow Partick, 1929–31; for Dumbartonshire, 1941–50; for Dumbartonshire West, 1950.

(i) where a book is likely to be in commercial competition with official publications on sale; or (ii) where the Crown copyright material reproduced, whether or not it has been published previously, makes a substantial contribution by volume to the commercial value of the book; or (iii) where the Crown copyright material has saved the author or his publisher alternative expense (e.g. where official maps are used as an alternative to maps specially drawn). Even when the bulk of a book consists of copyright official documents, reproduction fees are not normally charged if the commercial value of the book derives intrinsically from the original work in it – as, for example, in a substantial work of commentary or criticism on an official text. In these circumstances we are satisfied that it would be contrary to Stationery Office practice, and would involve an entirely new departure in policy, to suggest that Mr Churchill should make over some of his royalties to the State because his book is based on knowledge which he acquired when in office and reproduces a substantial number of documents which he wrote as a Minister of the Crown.

It is true that Viscount Montgomery was asked to accept an arrangement by which he shares with the Stationery Office the royalties on his book 'Normandy to the Baltic'. But that book was in effect a rather more personal version of the Official Dispatch which all Commanders-in-Chief write. It was written while Viscount Montgomery was himself a serving officer and he had substantial assistance from serving officers in writing it – the work being based wholly on official documents and carried out in official time and at official expense. This book is not, therefore, comparable in this respect with Mr Churchill's.

In our judgment there are no sufficient grounds for suggesting to Mr Churchill that he should pay over to the Exchequer any part of his receipts from his book. As, however, this question may be raised in Parliament, we think it right to bring it to your notice and to suggest that a decision on it should be taken at this stage.

Laurence Helsby[1] to Sir Norman Brook
(Premier papers, 8/1321)

24 January 1948

Sir Norman Brook

The Prime Minister has asked me to let you know that he agrees with the recommendations in your minute of 23rd January about the first volume of Mr Churchill's book on the Second World War; and that he will mention the matter at Cabinet on some convenient occasion.[2]

---

[1] Laurence Norman Helsby, 1908–78. Educated at Keble College, Oxford. Principal Private Secretary to PM, 1947–50. GCB, 1950. KBE, 1955.

[2] Helsby wrote to Brook on Jan. 26: 'The PM mentioned this at Cabinet and his conclusions were endorsed.'

Winston S. Churchill to Hamish Hamilton[1]
(*Churchill papers, 2/276*)

24 January 1948
Private

Dear Mr Hamish Hamilton

Thank you very much for the most interesting 'Von Hassell[2] Diaries'. Pray tell your correspondent that I am very carefully studying the efforts made by the German champions of civilization to save their country. All will be understood by history.

I am so sorry to learn of the disastrous fire at your offices. Please accept my sympathy in what must be, to say the least of it, a most inconvenient situation.

Winston S. Churchill to Anthony Eden
(*Churchill papers, 4/19*)

25 January 1948

My dear Anthony

I send you a final revise of the chapter you have kindly read several times about your resignation. You should note the reference to Vansittart which have been introduced since you saw it last.

Cabinet: conclusions
(*Premier papers, 8/1321*)

26 January 1948
Secret
Cabinet Meeting No. 7 of 1948

[...]
4. The Prime Minister recalled that the Cabinet had agreed in principle, on 10th October, 1946, that Mr Churchill should be at liberty to include in his forthcoming book on the Second World War memoranda and minutes which he had written when in office, and telegrams from himself to President Roosevelt and other heads of Governments, on the understanding that the text of the book would be submitted, before publication, for final

---

[1] James Hamish Hamilton, 1900–88. Born in Indiana. Educated at Caius College, Cambridge. Founded publishing co. Hamish Hamilton Ltd., 1931.

[2] Ulrich von Hassell, 1881–1944. Born in Ankalam, Germany. Entered German FO, 1908. Married, 1911, Ilse von Tirpitz: four children. Consul-General, Barcelona, 1921–6. Ambassador in Copenhagen, 1926–30; in Belgrade, 1930–2; in Rome, 1932–8 (sacked in 1938 for criticism of Hitler's regime). Became an active opponent of the Nazi regime and was secretly involved in the attempted military coup against Adolf Hitler of July 1944. Arrested and executed for high treason, 8 Sep. 1944. His diaries were posthumously published as *The Von Hassell Diaries: 1938–1944*.

January 1948

revision on behalf of the Government.[1] In accordance with this arrangement Mr Churchill has now submitted the first volume of his book in which he proposed to reproduce, in addition to other original documents, a number of papers which he had circulated to the War Cabinet when First Lord of the Admiralty. The Prime Minister said that he had satisfied himself that the publication of these papers was consistent with the general principles which the Cabinet had approved on 23rd May, 1946 (CM (46) 51st Conclusions, Minute 5); and he had decided that Mr Churchill might properly be given permission to publish these documents in his book.

The suggestion had been made in Parliament (Hansard: 14th February 1946: Columns 521–522) that former Ministers should pay to the Exchequer some part of their earnings from the publication of books based on official documents collected during their term of office; and it was possible that this suggestion might be repeated in relation to Mr Churchill's book. The Prime Minister was satisfied, however, that there were no sufficient grounds for suggesting to Mr Churchill that he should pay over to the Exchequer any part of his receipts from his book by reason of the fact that it was based largely on information which he had acquired as a Minister and included a number of official documents in respect of which the Crown copyright could be claimed.

The Cabinet –

Took note with approval of the Prime Minister's statements.

Jo Sturdee to Winston S. Churchill
(Churchill papers, 2/70)

27 January 1948

This letter, written to you by Baronne Pessonne de Sennevoy of Toulon, draws your attention to the belief, which is strong in France, that there was an understanding between you and Marshal Pétain. This 'understanding' is brought to light in a book written by Professor Rougier,[2] who was present at the talks of agreement.

If this is true this lady appeals to you to make it known publicly that there was this understanding between you and the Marshal, as this would then justify the actions with the Germans of the Marshal, who is now serving a life sentence like a criminal. If this is not true we can reply that the agreement did not take place and that her hopes are unfounded.

---

[1] See Cabinet minutes, 10 Oct. 1946, reproduced above (p. 487).
[2] Louis Auguste Paul Rougier, 1889–1982. French philosopher in the classical liberal tradition of Montesquieu. Educated at University of Lyon; doctorate, Sorbonne, 1920. Taught in Algiers, 1917–20; in Rome, 1920–4; in Cairo, 1931–6. Instructor, University of Besançon, 1925–48; New School for Social Research, 1941–3; Université de Montreal, 1945; Université de Caen, 1954–5.

Winston S. Churchill to Monsieur Singla
(Churchill papers, 1/69)

28 January 1948

Dear Monsieur Singla,

On my return to England I feel I should like to write to let you know how very much I enjoyed my stay at the Hotel de la Mamounia. The five weeks in these most comfortable and agreeable surroundings and in the sunshine of Marrakech did much to invigorate me and give me the rest and change I needed.

I should like you to accept and to convey to all the members of your staff my warm thanks for the courtesy and attention which you all showed to me and my party. We have lasting and lively memories of the many acts of kindness and consideration towards us in your hotel. I hope indeed I may one day be able to take advantage once again of another holiday in the calm and care of the Mamounia.

Winston S. Churchill to Air Commodore George Powell
(Churchill papers, 1/69)

29 January 1948

Dear Air-Commodore Powell

Now that I am back safely in this country, thanks to you, your co-Directors and those members of your organization concerned, I should like you to know how much I have appreciated all the care and goodwill which the various flights on my behalf have entailed. I have, as you know, a very high opinion of the crew of the *Hollywood* and indeed of all your personnel, and I could not have felt more confident of being in good hands.

I am particularly conscious also of your timely and comforting help in flying Mrs Churchill and Lord and Lady Moran out to Marrakech when I was ill so quickly and at such short notice. It made so much difference to know they would be safe and with me early in case of danger – of which at my age I must always be careful! In this instance I hope your company will allow me to pay the proper charges, as this was something altogether outside your original gift, which I was only too glad to accept, and of which I am warmly appreciative.

Please thank once again all those members of your staff concerned on my behalf for their work and consideration for our safety and comfort.

I am sending you herewith copies of some of my books which I have inscribed for you and which I hope you will accept as a token of my appreciation for all your help and thought for my wellbeing.

PS. Since dictating the above I have received your account for which I enclose a cheque.

February
1948

Winston S. Churchill to Clement Attlee
(Churchill papers, 2/21)

1 February 1948 Chartwell

My dear Prime Minister,

I am writing to you about the Hague Conference which is being organized jointly by a number of societies in Britain and other countries to further European unity, a cause which has been espoused so warmly by Mr Bevin on behalf of His Majesty's Government. I enclose an explanatory note from which you will see that considerable progress has been made with the arrangements for this Conference and that a wide measure of political support has already been obtained for it on the Continent. You will notice that prominent Socialist leaders in other countries have accepted invitations to attend.

The cause of European unity is one which we both have at heart, and I trust it may be kept above the level of our domestic party politics.

I ask you to make it clear that the efforts of the promoters of this Conference which in no way conflicts with the policy of his Majesty's Government enjoy your goodwill and that members of the Labour Party need have no hesitation in attending.

Winston S. Churchill to Christopher Soames
(Churchill papers, 1/32)

1 February 1948
Private

My dear Christopher,

You will recall that Mr Wood,[1] after his visit to Chartwell regarding the arrangements for audit of the Farm Accounts, raised the point that, while your salary had been fixed at £400.00 per annum when you took charge of

[1] James Wood, 1886–1972. Founded Wood, Willey & Co., accountants, 1934. Served as Churchill's farm accountant.

the Farm, no arrangement had been made with regard to the occupation by you of the Farm House and other matters.

It was suggested that your emoluments should include such perquisites and refunds as are normally available to Farm Managers in similar circumstances including the provision by me of the Farm House free of rent, the payment by me of the rates, lighting and heating of the same, and of the cost of a reasonable amount of farm labour necessary to maintain the Farm House garden. In addition, the cost of running your motor car on farm business and all incidental expenses which you incur in your farm management should of course be refunded to you.

Accordingly I desire to place on record my agreement to these arrangements with effect from the date on which you took over and from January 1, 1948, in view of the considerable increase in acreage now under your supervision, your salary will be at the rate of £600.00 per annum and similar arrangements regarding perquisites and refunds will apply.

Either party may ask for revision of these terms at any time by giving one month's notice in writing.

Oliver Stanley to Winston S. Churchill
(Churchill papers, 4/19)

2 February 1948

My dear Winston,

First of all, many thanks indeed for your kind enquiries. I am feeling a good deal better, but as I am still running a temperature the doctor won't let me come back to London, at any rate this week.

It was very good of you to send me the new draft to have a look at. From my point of view the new Chapter 8 is a great improvement and spreads the blame more evenly between all parties.

I have also had a look at the bit on Anthony's resignation. I don't know how far you will consider it right to describe the exact happenings at the Cabinet Meeting, but the present description is not quite accurate, and I'm afraid I must have misled you. Both the Prime Minister and Anthony stated their own cases, and it was only then that each Minister was asked to express his opinion. My complaint was that only after that did Anthony reveal the difference to be so great that it was a matter for resignation: He had certainly not given that impression in his first statement of the case. The statement by the Prime Minister to which you refer, followed this announcement of Anthony's, and it was only then that we realised that our choice was not between two different methods and tempos on an agreed negotiation, but between Chamberlain and Eden.

I naturally tell you exactly what occurred, but I confess I am a little anxious as to how far such a detailed statement of the events at a Cabinet is fit for publication.

Elizabeth Gilliatt to Winston S. Churchill
(*Churchill papers, 2/63*)

3 February 1948

There are <u>191</u> Unionist Members of Parliament.
Up to and including last week's luncheon you have had:
    3 peers (2 Shadow Cabinet, 1 Constituency Speaker)
    2 other 'Shadows'
    11 Old Members
    19 New Members
        35 in all

By the end of this Session, assuming you have 2 Old and 4 New each week, you will have 14 more Old and 27 more New Members; this will make a grand total of 76.

Christopher Soames to Winston S. Churchill
(*Churchill papers, 1/32*)[1]

3 February 1948   Chartwell Farm

My dear Mr Churchill,
Thank you so much for your letter[2] laying out details of my salary and perquisites. It is indeed kind of you to give me such a generous wage.

I am only too conscious of my lack of experience as a farmer; but I assure you that I will safeguard your interests in this farm to the very best of my ability – and indeed in any other sphere in which I might be able to render you some small service.

L. S. Amery to Winston S. Churchill
(*Churchill papers, 2/145*)

4 February 1948

My dear Winston,
You have refrained, wisely if I may say so, for some time past from saying anything about Palestine. But I wonder whether the time has not come for you,

---
[1] This letter was handwritten.
[2] Of 1 Feb., reproduced above (pp. 947–8).

possibly in your next broadcast, to sound a note of warning as to the appalling situation into which the Government is resolutely and inflexibly drifting?

It is now more than eleven years since the Peel Commission urged partition as the only solution which would fulfil both the pledges in the Mandate viz a national home for the Jews and Arabs, and would also relieve us of an ever more unpleasant and costly task of administration. That was again the conclusion of the Cabinet Committee under Morrison which you appointed. The only objectors on that committee were Archie Sinclair, who thought our conclusion unfair to the Jews and only agreed very reluctantly, and Dick Law who objected that it gave too much to the Jews. In Cabinet no one except Anthony spoke against it. Bevin never even whispered that he had his own alternative solution on which he would stake his reputation!

After the war partition became not only the best solution but the inevitable solution. We, for our part, were not prepared to carry the burden any longer. There was no possibility of either Jews or Arabs agreeing on any solution and the Jews were far too well armed and far too determined to accept subjection to Arab Government. The only question was whether partition should be backed and if necessary for a short time enforced by an impartial authority, or whether the matter should be left to a free fight for all, resulting after infinite havoc and destruction in such frontiers as the fighting eventually determined.

I still think myself that the right thing would have been for us to announce our scheme and declare that the whole of our authority and force would be put behind it in order to get it started. At the same time, we could have asked the Americans, or UNO, to give their blessing and such moral or material support as they wished to give to what we believed to be the only way of avoiding chaos in the Middle East.

We did however, after infinite havering and procrastination, while the situation got steadily worse, throw the thing at the head of UNO. To the surprise of the whole world UNO came to a definite conclusion, incidentally to all intents and purposes identical with that of your own Cabinet Committee. If UNO meant anything to us, and involved any loyalty on our part, the least we could have done was to have given such help as we could to the implementing of the decision which we had invited. We could have made it clear that we wished to withdraw our forces and our administration as quickly as possible, but that we should do everything in our power to assist UNO in supplementing those forces and making arrangements to take their place. The very least we could have done would have been to invite the UNO Commission to come out as soon as possible in order to discuss future arrangements and see how far steps could be taken to carry out the transfer as smoothly as possible. There was at any rate one item of the UNO programme on which there was no disagreement, namely that there should be an International Administration to maintain the security of the Holy Places. There could have been no possible objection to our allowing the Commission at any rate to get together a Gendarmerie for that purpose.

As it is we have made it quite clear that we disapprove of the conclusion which we invited without suggesting any alternative conclusion which we would assist in carrying out, and that we are determined to clear out under conditions which must involve the very maximum of bloodshed and of the destruction of much of the splendid administrative work done by British officials and of the no less wonderful economic achievements of the Jewish settlers.

What do we get out of it? Certainly not Arab gratitude, Egypt and Iraq have both let us know that. We might at least have got Abdullah's gratitude for giving him more than two thirds of Palestine if partition had been our policy. As for the Jews, poor Weizmann's efforts to show that we are still their real friends are becoming increasingly hopeless, and even moderate Jews are beginning to think that the detestable Irgun ruffians were really right in saying that we are the enemy.

That is so far as the free fight is confined to Palestine alone. But suppose it spreads? The Americans are bound to give help and encouragement to the Jews, even if the Administration remains officially neutral. The Russians are consequently bound to throw themselves on the Arab side. If that situation develops and becomes increasingly serious, how can we, in view of the general world position, go on being in the wrong camp in the Middle East?

The British public have been so bored with the whole business, and above all with the Irgun terrorists that they have shrugged their shoulders and acquiesced in the Government policy so far. But there may be a tremendous revulsion when they realise what is really going to happen. That revulsion will be perhaps keenest on the part of the Government's own supporters, for there is no part of Bevin's policy which has caused more widespread resentment throughout the whole Labour Party, and not merely among the fellow travellers, than his Palestine policy. From the purely partisan point of view there is no weaker joint in their harness or, shall I say, no more obvious Achilles heel. The question is one which might well bring the Government down and, if so, save us from much irrevocable harm that might be done by them in the next two years.

However I will not put it on that ground. What I do feel is that thirty years ago we undertook, on our own responsibility, a policy which we believed would not only relieve the Jewish problem, but would help towards the regeneration of the decayed Middle East in the interests of Arabs quite as much as of Jews, and would offer us a friendly military base if we required it, in defence of the Suez Canal and as a link in our air communications with the East. The League accepted from us a Mandate substantially of our own drafting and one which we interpreted in our own spirit, beginning with your own White Paper of 1922, as we thought best in the interest of Palestine and as a reasonable fulfilment of our pledges. We have every right to say that we wish to reduce our commitments and to take practical steps to do so in an orderly manner. But it is nonsense to talk of our surrendering an impossible task which was wished and pushed on to us by the League of Nations and criminal to scuttle under conditions which must involve civil war in its worst shape and without giving UNO even a chance of setting up some framework or control before the free fight for all has begun.

Clement Attlee to Winston S. Churchill
(Churchill papers, 2/21)

4 February 1948

My dear Churchill,

Thank you for your letter about the Hague Conference on Western Union.[1] As I think you realise, it would be undesirable for the Government to take any official action in regard to this Conference.

Any advice to members of the Labour Party as to their participation in the Conference is a matter for the Executive of the Labour Party.

Anthony Eden to Winston S. Churchill
(Churchill papers, 4/19)

4 February 1948

My dear Winston,

I have looked further into the records and I find that my recollection is correct.[2]

The first full discussion in Cabinet took place on Saturday afternoon, and it was on that day that I made it clear that I could not carry out the policy which the majority of my colleagues approved, and I therefore offered to resign.

The Cabinet then adjourned till Sunday afternoon when the whole issue was again discussed at very considerable length.

Afterwards a meeting of a number of Ministers was held in a further attempt to reach agreement. It was then that I made it plain finally that I could not agree to the course that the Government wanted to pursue.

It is clear therefore that even though some of my colleagues may originally have been surprised, there was ample consideration of the issues before the final break on Sunday evening. There does not seem to me to be much in Oliver Stanley's point that I should have warned the Cabinet that I was going to resign at the end of my first statement instead of later in the meeting.

---

[1] Reproduced above (p. 947).
[2] Concerning Chapter 15 of *The Gathering Storm* (Chapter 14 in the final published text).

I enclose herewith, <u>most private</u>, a copy of a letter which Maurice Hankey sent to me on the night of my resignation which will show you that he at least, as Secretary of the Cabinet, had no doubt of the reality of the difference between the Prime Minister and myself. I am sure that Neville himself had no doubt from what he himself said to me on more than one occasion. I am equally sure that I have no doubt.

I also attach a copy of the actual letter which I sent to Neville Chamberlain at the time of my resignation. This has, of course, already been made public, but I stand by every word I wrote then.

I have not of course attempted any amendment at all of Page 12 myself, but if there is anything more you think I can do to help, I am at your disposal.

Winston S. Churchill to Lieutenant-General Sir Henry Pownall
(Churchill papers, 4/140)

4 February 1948

Please see passage marked in red on the enclosed letter from Vansittart. This does not affect my opinion. The forming-up of Russia in the line against Hitler would have been a terrific event to him. Moreover the Russians proposed to obtain, and thought they could do so – the agreement of Rumania to the passage of their troops into Czechoslovakia. A whole plan was prepared to this effect, and in the event of a War I have no doubt it could have been carried through by all the pressures and guarantees of a Grand Alliance. However, will you kindly look into the military aspect? What was the exact route through Rumania, which the Russians had in mind, and what sort of force could they have developed if they had tried their best? I can't see why they should not have tried their best considering their own danger.

Winston S. Churchill to Clement Attlee
(Churchill papers, 2/21)

5 February 1948
NOT SENT

My dear Prime Minister,

Your letter of February 4.[1] If the Executive of the Labour Party advise their members to boycott the proposed Conference at The Hague on European Unity, this may well have very far-reaching and harmful effects upon the Cause. It will certainly give rise to serious controversy. At least we ought to know as soon as possible what their decision is. Although it is of an unofficial character, all sorts of arrangements have to be made, among others by

---

[1] Reproduced above (p. 952).

the Dutch Government, for an international conference of this kind. I trust therefore that a public announcement will be made.

I am broadcasting on February 14, and in the event of a complete breakdown of Party co-operation I should propose to deal with this subject at some length. I hope therefore that you may be able to let me know in the course of the next few days what the decision is.

Winston S. Churchill to Walter Graebner
(Churchill papers, 2/161)

5 February 1948 Chartwell
Private and Personal
NOT SENT

My dear Graebner,

I should be very much obliged if, when you come back at the end of February, you would bring with you a thousand 'Winston Churchill' cigars from Tabacalera Cubana of Agramonte 106, Havana, Cuba. The Treasury gave me permission early in 1946 to keep a few hundred dollars in the First National Bank of New York. I can therefore enclose a cheque for $340, which is what the last account for the same order was.

I am very sorry to say that Rufus the Second[1] has been afflicted by St Vitus' Dance as a result of his inoculation against distemper. Miss Lobban[2] is trying to have him cured, but I think I would like to look a little further afield before I affiance myself. Thank you so much for all you have done in this matter. I have got a lovely little model of Rufus the First which I will show you when you come back.

I was so glad you were able to come out to Marrakech, and you were very kind to Sarah and Lady Moran in your adventurous journey home. What a shocking accident this is with the Tudor aeroplane![3]

I am weighed down by the book. I have delivered to the printer the whole of Book I, but there are a certain number of overtakes. Lord Camrose is having a fair copy made which will be ready I hope in a week or so and will be sent to all concerned at the earliest moment. Book II is also finished bar the final re-reading, and I am sending that to the printer in a few days' time. I have taken Luce's advice about remelding Chapters II and III of Book I. This has involved a slight further delay. Book III is also finished, and Book IV far advanced.

---

[1] Churchill's poodle, a gift from Walter Graebner to replace the original Rufus, who had been run over and killed during the Conservative Party Conference at Brighton in October 1947.

[2] Caretaker to Churchill's poodle, Rufus II, during the dog's illness in 1948. Worked at Duke Street Kennels in London. Churchill presented her with a copy of *The Second World War*, inscribing and signing each volume, and adding in two volumes a drawing by himself of his dog.

[3] The Tudor IV aircraft *Star Tiger* disappeared while carrying passengers on a BSAA flight from Lisbon to Bermuda on 30 Jan. 1948.

Douglas Clifton Brown to Winston S. Churchill
(Churchill papers, 2/78)

5 February 1948

My dear Churchill,
　The Table[1] is a little worried over a remark of yours yesterday, doubtless due to the way I answered the point of order and gave thereby a false impression.
　Hansard, Col. 1823, reports you as having said that Questions were ruled out 'because it is thought that Ministers do not wish to have these questions answered'.
　I do not think that you meant that the Chair ruled out a question merely because it was inconvenient to a Minister to answer it.
　Of course, in matters of doubt as I explained, enquiries go on between the Table Clerks and the Ministry concerned, to ascertain the facts and responsibility, but the last word must rest with me as to whether or not the question is in order, and the convenience of a Minister does not affect the issue one way or the other. I do not mind for myself, but I think the Table Clerks think that a reflection has indirectly been cast on them when they refuse to accept questions, so I wonder if this could be cleared up when the debate on nationalized industries takes place, as I am sure that you did not mean to cast reflections on their integrity.

Sir Norman Brook to Winston S. Churchill
(Churchill papers, 4/57)

6 February 1948

Dear Mr Churchill,
　When I saw you last week I said that I had no further comments to offer on Books I and II. I must therefore apologise for raising now, at this late state, a point on Chapter XIII of Book II. My excuse is that this particular Chapter reached me much later than the others.
　On pages 5–7 of Chapter XIII you reproduce in full an aide-memoire by the Chiefs of Staff on Operation 'Hammer'.[2] The Prime Minister is apprehensive about the consequences of your reproducing textually memoranda submitted to Ministers by the Chiefs of Staff. He fears that, if controversy arises about the division of responsibility between Ministers and the Chiefs of Staff for critical decisions taken during the war, the Government may be pressed to publish the relevant papers submitted at the time by the Chiefs of Staff. And he thinks that the Government would have difficulty in resisting such pressure if interested parties were able to say that you had been allowed

---
[1] The Table Office, where Parliamentary questions and motions for debate are tabled (submitted) for inclusion in upcoming business.
[2] 'Hammer': planned assault on Trondheim.

to publish certain of these papers, of your own selection, in your book. He is not so much concerned about this particular paper, or the reasons which led the Chiefs of Staff to change their minds about the frontal assault on Trondheim: what he has in mind is a demand for the publication of all the relevant papers on more controversial topics such as the fall of Singapore or Tobruk.

The general authority which the Cabinet gave did not extend beyond documents which you had written yourself; and the Prime Minister thinks it would be inexpedient to extend this to documents written by persons other than yourself. He sees special danger in your reproducing Staff studies and other papers by the Chiefs of Staff. In these circumstances he asks that, instead of quoting this particular report on Operation 'Hammer', you will paraphrase it.

In the hope that I may save you some trouble, I have myself made a paraphrase and submit the enclosed draft for your consideration.

Strictly speaking, the same arguments of principle apply to your reproduction, on pages 10–11 of Chapter XIII, of a paper written by Ismay for the Military Coordination Committee. The Prime Minister has not asked that this should be paraphrased. I suggest, however, that it would be preferable if the introductory words, on page 10, were so altered as to avoid implying that the paper was formally submitted to a Committee of the War Cabinet. I suggest that these introductory words should be altered so as to read – 'The actual position as we saw it at this moment cannot be better stated than in the following paper written by General Ismay on April 21.'

Anthony Eden to Winston S. Churchill
(Churchill papers, 4/19)

6 February 1948

My dear Winston,

I am sorry to bother you further about chapter 15[1] of your book, but I think perhaps I ought to say that I have since spoken to Norman Brook and asked him to look up the detailed minutes of the discussions concerning my resignation. He confirms that Chamberlain at the outset of these meetings made plain his point of view and that it diverged from mine. He then called upon me to express my point of view. Brook also confirms that the discussions took place over two days over a number of meetings.

There cannot therefore have been any real doubt in the mind of any member of his Cabinet of the reality of our difference. No answer, please.

---

[1] Chapter 14 in the published text.

Winston S. Churchill to Harold Macmillan
(Churchill papers, 2/67)

9 February 1948

My dear Harold,

I hoped to see you at the House last Thursday, but we could not make contact. I do not agree with what you propose,[1] and I do not think our colleagues would do so either. It would be a great mistake to formalise the loose and unsubstantial association which governs the work of an Opposition. I propose to continue the present system as long as I am in charge. I do not think things are going so badly. Thank you very much for writing.

Winston S. Churchill to Douglas Clifton Brown
(Churchill papers, 2/78)

9 February 1948

My dear Mr Speaker,

I certainly had no intention on reflecting on the integrity of the Table Clerks;[2] but I object very much to their turning the statements of Ministers into cast-iron rules, and cutting out hundreds of questions dealing with vital matters now of great importance to the Members and their constituents.

I am very glad to know that the last word about whether a Question should be asked or not rests with the Speaker of the House of Commons. We have entered a new period where whole spheres of business are being forbidden to the House of Commons. This cannot be accepted. Ministers with their majority may decide for any particular Parliament what is to happen, and what answers shall be given in such cases; but Members ought not to be denied the right to ask Questions about matters they are sent to Parliament to look after.

I will certainly deal with this fully when I take part in the Debate.

---

[1] Macmillan had sent Churchill a memorandum on 4 Feb. 1948 proposing that the Opposition should create a small managing committee to meet frequently in order to better organize their efforts. He proposed that the managing committee operate in relation to the Shadow Cabinet similarly to how the War Cabinet had operated in relation to the full Cabinet during the war.

[2] See Clifton Brown to Churchill, Feb. 5, reproduced above (p. 955).

Emanuel Shinwell to Winston S. Churchill
(*Churchill papers, 2/21*)

10 February 1948

My dear Churchill,

The submission you made to me on the subject of the United Europe Committee was considered by members of the National Executive Committee of the Labour Party today. The matter was discussed at some length but eventually it was decided to re-affirm the decision to discourage members of the Labour Party from participating in the proposed congress. It is felt that the subject of European unity is much too important to be entrusted to unrepresentative interests and the proposed composition of the congress seems to us open to objection, in particular because the number of private individuals selected by an unknown process robs the congress of any real representative character. My Executive feel that such a congress can scarcely hope to make any practical contribution towards the furtherance of European unity and may, on the contrary, discredit the idea.

Sir Norman Brook to Winston S. Churchill
(*Churchill papers, 4/57*)

11 February 1948
Private and Personal

Dear Mr Churchill,

In view of what you told me in our telephone conversation this morning, I should like you to know how it came about that Ministers discussed the question of the royalties on your book.

It was Bridges and I who raised this question. We did so because we thought it possible that some suggestion might be made in Parliament that you should surrender some part of your royalties to the State. On 14th February, 1946, Mr McKinlay, MP, put a Question in the House of Commons asking whether the Government would introduce legislation enabling the State to claim 50 percent of all earnings of former Ministers derived from the publication of books or newspaper articles based on official documents; and it was clear from the supplementaries that it was your writings which he had in mind. A negative answer was returned to that Question; but it seemed likely that the matter might be raised again and we thought it advisable to obtain a definite ruling from Ministers. We therefore submitted the point to the Prime Minister, with a recommendation that there were no grounds for suggesting that any part of the royalties of your book should be paid over to the State. Mr Attlee accepted our view. When he told the Cabinet that he had given you permission to reproduce certain War Cabinet papers in Volume I of the book, he mentioned Mr McKinlay's Question and said that it was possible that this suggestion might be repeated in Parliament in relation to your book. But, he said, he was quite satisfied that there were no grounds for suggesting that any part of the royalties on your book should be paid over to the State. This conclusion was endorsed by the Cabinet – no one expressing any contrary view.[1]

I am sure you will realise that, in raising this, Bridges and I had no other motive than to get settled once and for all a question which, if it had been brought up in Parliament at short notice, might have proved embarrassing to all concerned.

I have thought it right to send you privately this statement of the true facts in view of the misleading account which reached you. I should be very sorry if the question of Crown copyright – on which I will write to you separately in the course of the next day or so – were clouded by any misunderstandings about Ministers' views on the question of royalties.

Harold Macmillan to Winston S. Churchill
(Churchill papers, 2/67)

12 February 1948

My dear Winston,

Many thanks for your letter of the 9th February.[2] Certainly things are not going badly. But I think you underestimate the need for some permanent and effective instrument for giving policy guidance to all concerned. If this is not forthcoming from the top, it is in fact given by the young men of the Secretariat or Central Office who have to turn out the answers to the questions which are asked. There are a number of important matters on which we have given no official view; for example, the Russian Commercial Treaty; a more precise policy on controls; conscription. Even on the over-riding problem of the economic and financial crisis, we are in danger of losing the initiative.

This is partly because we tend to postpone decisions until they are made necessary by a Parliamentary situation – the introduction of a Bill and the occasion of a Debate. But if the Party is to work effectively throughout the whole machine which we have now available, I think something more is required.

However, I leave it in your hands, having discharged what seemed to me my duty.

---

[1] See Cabinet minutes of Jan. 26, reproduced above (pp. 944–5).
[2] Reproduced above (p. 957).

Winston S. Churchill to Clement Attlee
(Churchill papers, 2/21)

12 February 1948

My dear Prime Minister,

In your letter to me of February 4[1] you referred me to the Executive of the Labour Party for information about their attitude towards participation in the Hague Conference. Accordingly I visited Mr Shinwell at the War Office and explained the case to him. I have now received from him the letter which I append.[2]

I can only hope that this is not the last word the British Labour Party and yourself, as its Leader and the Prime Minister of Great Britain, have to say upon this issue.

Whatever your decision the International Organizing Committee will, I am sure, go forward with the Conference, and we hope that Party differences in various countries will not be allowed to impede the policy to which Mr Bevin, in the name of your administration, has so rightly committed himself.

Winston S. Churchill to Lord Beaverbrook
(Churchill papers, 1/78)

12 February 1948

Leading article *Evening Standard* February 11 is so obviously intended to injure Tory chances in impending by-elections that alas I cannot while remaining Leader accept your most kind and attractive invitation to be so publicly your guest in Jamaica. Am making arrangements at hotel. I do not exaggerate importance of your newspaper action on our affairs nor of course is our friendship affected. Trust you will be able to give me good news of your health and that we shall meet when I arrive 8th or 9th. It is a sad world.

Lord Beaverbrook to Winston S. Churchill
(Churchill papers, 1/78)

12 February 1948

I hope you will propose no such change. Every arrangement made for your stay. I will not be here so you will not be embarrassed by me. Separate telegram on newspapers policy.

---

[1] Reproduced above (p. 952).
[2] Reproduced above (p. 958).

Sir Norman Brook to Winston S. Churchill
(*Churchill papers, 4/57*)

13 February 1948

Dear Mr Churchill.

As promised, I have gone into the question whether Crown copyright covers the personal minutes which you wrote while in the office and I have consulted both the Treasury Solicitor[1] and the Controller of the Stationery Office[2] on the point.

It is clear beyond doubt that under Section 18 of the copyright Act, 1911 (copy enclosed) the Crown has copyright in any documents written by a Minister in the discharge of his official duties. I am advised that the Minutes which you wrote as a Minister of the Crown are clearly 'work . . . prepared by or under the direction or control of His Majesty'; and that the law would make no distinction between a paper which you wrote for the Cabinet and one of your personal minutes.

This doctrine has been confirmed on more than one occasion by the Law Officers of various Governments over a number of years. Thus, in 1933 the Lord Chancellor[3] and the Law Officers held that section 18 applies to 'letters written by any one of His Majesty's Servants on affairs in connection with which the writer has some responsibility, direct or indirect, in virtue of the office which he holds'.

The Government have, however, no desire to make difficulties for you by reason of the fact that the copyright in these documents belongs to the Crown. There is no question of asking for fees in respect of their publication, or of asking you to pay over to the State any part of the royalties on your book. I can also assure you that we shall not, solely on the ground of the Crown copyright, ask you to refrain from reproducing your personal minutes in your book, though we may occasionally have to ask on general grounds (e.g. the desirability of not impairing the relations between ministers and officials) that you should consider omitting some particular minute.

The law being as it is, the acknowledgement of Crown copyright which

---

[1] Thomas James Barnes, 1888–1964. Asst Solicitor, Board of Inland Revenue, 1919. Legal Adviser, Ministry of Shipping, 1918–20. Solicitor, Board of Trade, 1920–33. Knighted, 1927. Procurator-General and Treasury Solicitor, 1934–53.

[2] Norman Gibb Scorgie, 1884–1956. Educated at Cambridge University. First Class in Law Tripos, 1907. Whewell Scholar, International Law, 1908. Married, 1912, Iza Donnan (d. 1945). Served during WWI, 1915–19 (despatches thrice). OBE, 1919. CBE 1927. Deputy Controller, HMSO, 1919–40; Controller and King's Printer, 1942–9. MVO, 1931. CVO, 1935. Deputy Director-General, Ministry of Information, 1940–1. Principal Asst Secretary, Mines Dept, 1941–2. Knighted, 1945. Chairman, B. Winstone & Sons, Ltd, 1949–55.

[3] John Sankey, 1866–1948 Read History at Oxford. Admitted to the Bar, 1892. KC, 1909. Judge, 1914. Knighted, 1914. GBE, 1917. PC, 1928. Lord Justice of Appeal, 1928. Baron. 1929. Viscount, 1932. Lord Chancellor, 1929–35. Well known for his work on the Declaration of the Rights of Man in 1940.

you have undertaken to make in the preface to your book cannot prejudice you in any way. Indeed, it seems to me that it is to your advantage to make this acknowledgement; for if, after your book has come out, any unauthorised person should seek to publish some of your personal minutes, or any other matter covered by your acknowledgment, only the Crown would have a legal right to take action against him, and, having acknowledged Crown copyright, you would have a strong case for calling on the Crown to take such action.

COPYRIGHT ACT, 1911

18. Without prejudice to any rights or privileges of the Crown, where any work has, whether before or after the commencement of this Act, been prepared or published by or under the direction or control of His Majesty or any Government department, the copyright in the work shall, subject to any agreement with the author, belong to His Majesty, and in such case shall continue for a period of fifty years from the date of the first publication of the work.

Winston S. Churchill: broadcast
('Winston S. Churchill, His Complete Speeches', volume 7, pages 7590–3)

14 February 1948

A NEW PARLIAMENT

The Chancellor of the Exchequer, Sir Stafford Cripps, has laid before us in terms of the utmost candour the lamentable and critical plight to which our country has been reduced in finance and economics after two-and-a-half years of Socialist mismanagement and misrule. Although these declarations by so important a Minister must injure our credit throughout the world, he was right to tell the truth as he sincerely believed it. It must have been a melancholy task for him, because so few men were more optimistic about our Utopian future or lavish in their promises at the time of the General Election. There was no foundation for the fantastic hopes which he encouraged of a brighter and easier life for Britain in his eager bidding for votes and power. A hard time lay before us. He had been for four years an important Minister in the National Government, of which I was the head, and had the fullest information of the state of our affairs. The path of confession and repentance is always painful and for that reason it commands a measure of public respect. Let me say at once that it is the duty of every one of us without distinction of party to do our utmost to rescue our native land from the dangers, privations and misfortunes in which she is now plunged. We must try our utmost to combat inflation and to increase our productive capacity and exporting power by every possible means. I think it, therefore, right to dwell for a moment, upon some of the great things we, most of us, have in common – Socialists, Conservatives, Liberals – and enjoy in common, even in this period of party strife into which we have been thrust. However, as this is Valentine's Day, I had better make it clear that I am not making any proposal for a coalition government.

Let me come to those large matters on which we are in agreement. First of all, there are in our island none of those fundamental, constitutional cleavages such as rack so many other states and nations. The overwhelming mass of the British people upholds our free democratic, parliamentary institutions and our ancient monarchy under which across the centuries these institutions have come into being. Secondly, the Government and the Opposition are united in their resistance to the Communist conspiracy – it is nothing less – and to the hateful doctrines of Communism which have proved fatal in many parts of Europe to human rights – to ordinary simple fundamental human rights as we understand and cherish them here. Thirdly, there is a general agreement between all parties except, of course, the small but venomous Communist faction, upon the broad lines of our foreign policy. We are working ever more closely with the United States and we are all trying our best to create a United Europe in which Great Britain will play her part. I have been very glad to see the Foreign Secretary, Mr Bevin moving so steadily along these paths which I urged him to follow nearly two years ago.

I am sorry, however, that certain elements in the Socialist ranks are trying to make the cause of United Europe a monopoly of the Socialist Party. An important conference of supporters of the European cause is to be held at The Hague next May. This event has been welcomed by all parties except, of course, the Communists. It has been welcomed by all parties throughout the countries of Western Europe. Alone, the British Labour Party has decided to discourage its members from attending. When I proclaimed this idea at Zurich in September 1946, I earnestly hoped that it might be at once all-party and above party, but through their petty jealousies and internal divisions, the Government is being drawn into the grave and anti-social error of trying to form an exclusive union of the Socialists of Europe. By forming in this wide sphere a kind of 'closed shop' they seem to want to repel the aid and support of all other parties and influences in this country and on the Continent. In this behaviour they are only imitating the Communists whom they so loudly condemn. If Europe is to be united it can only be through the growing sense of brotherhood among all the states and nations acting as living entities. In this way alone can the well-being of the vast mass of ordinary simple families and homes be revived and maintained.

The Socialists will never have the strength by themselves to weave Europe together as they and we desire. They will need all the help and goodwill of all the men in all the lands. It is a wanton and reckless act for the British Socialist Party to try to paralyse all other efforts but their own, and if they succeed in sabotaging this conference at the The Hague it will involve them in the lasting discredit of having, by their narrowness and bitterness, inflicted injury upon the whole free and civilised world and its future. How can Mr Bevin hope to unite the nations of Europe when his party are not even able to unite with those who agree with them on this policy here at home; and are not able to agree with them, not because of any grave injuries in the past, but just because they are Conservatives or Liberals? We are asking nations on the Continent, between whom rivers of blood have flowed, to forget the feuds of a thousand years and work for the larger harmonies on which the future depends: and yet we in this island, who have so much in common, who have no serious grievances or vendettas to repay, are unable to lay aside even for the sake of such a cause, even for the sake of a cause on which we are all agreed, party strife and party prejudices. I earnestly trust that the Prime Minister – and we have a Prime Minister, or ought to have – whose devotion to the cause of European Union is well known, will not ignore his own responsibilities in so large a question.

We find this same spirit of Socialist Party rancour – this is a point to which I must particularly draw your attention – we find this same spirit infecting the whole of our economic and financial affairs, and it is one of the most serious factors which has brought us into our present misfortune and danger here at home. I shall not try to rival Sir Stafford Cripps and other leading Ministers in painting the picture in dark colours. One may be sure they would not have said these things if they were not forced to do so by their knowledge of the facts. The Government, who themselves at this moment represent only a minority of the electors, make frantic appeals for a renewed effort by the nation as a whole. We shall all do our best, but ought they not themselves to set an example by laying aside for the time being party fads and prejudices which are an obstacle to national unity? They urge us to increase production; yet what is the British industry which stands forth above all others as a model, beating all previous records as a great producer? It is the steel trade, in which there has never been an industrial strike for forty years, which is beating all records at this very moment in spite of the uncertainty by which it has been disturbed and hampered. Yet it is this industry that the Socialist Government has selected as the next victim for nationalisation. The steel industry is to be transferred from the list of our British profit-makers under private enterprise to the loss-makers' account, and under the mismanagement of officials or left-wing politicians and pensioners, to become a charge upon our overburdened taxpayers. The lifebuoy to which we were clinging in our distress is to be turned into another millstone to drag us into the depths. And all for the sake of the Socialist programme alone. How unworthy of our country in its dire need! If the Prime Minister, Sir Stafford Cripps, Mr Bevin and other leading Ministers are sincere in their appeals to the nation, let them announce that they will, as a sacrifice to national unity and prosperity, abandon the nationalisation of steel. If they refuse, they will strip themselves of all the title-deeds of national leadership.

Look now to another sphere. Look now how they have squandered our money. I did my best to help them get the American loan. I hoped it would give us four years' breathing space after the exhaustion of the war in which we made unequalled efforts, but it has all been slushed away in less than two years. While we ourselves are hard put to it to get our daily bread, we have given or lent £750,000,000 or nearly as much as the whole of the American loan to other countries in the last two years. 'Be just before you are generous' is an old saying. 'Charity begins at home' is another. But what did they care? A rate of war-time taxation has been maintained in a manner which has hampered and baffled enterprise and recovery in every walk of life: 700,000 more officials, all hard-working decent men and women but producing nothing themselves, have settled down upon us to administer 25,000 regulations never enforced before in time of peace. I am told that 300 officials have the power to make new regulations, apart altogether from Parliament, carrying with them the penalty of imprisonment for crimes hitherto unknown to the law. Dr Dalton, the practitioner who never cured anyone, in his 'rake's progress' at the Exchequer, spent in his Budgets for three years over £10,000,000,000. Enormous sums, too, have been poured out on new projects, many of them good in themselves, which have now to be abandoned or hung up because too much was started all at once. The money we earn buys less every day and thus endangers not only wages, but our savings and social services.

The unhappy Sir Stafford Cripps is the heir to all this improvidence and folly. Whatever mistakes he has made in the past, he is paying for them now and so are we. Already he talks about dangers of impending totalitarianism. Totalitarianism: I think I must look up some of my speeches of the late General Election when I see the way he thinks we are drifting. We must all do our best to help him in any measures which are honestly conceived in the national interest. But I must tell you frankly that this island, the heart of a once mighty Empire, and still at the centre of world affairs, will never regain its strength, its vigour or its health, unless it allows its native energy and genius, under all proper safeguards, to work naturally and freely again.

What are we doing now? We are in much discomfort. The austerity campaign is to have a further stimulus. There is privation even and insufficient food for important classes of manual workers. People with small fixed incomes are very hard pressed. What are we living on? That is the point. How are we keeping going from day to day? Let me tell you. We are living on the last remaining assets and overseas investments accumulated under the capitalist system – this is what we are living on: we are living on them in the hope that we may bridge the gap before the new American grant-in-aid under the Marshall plan comes in. Our last reserves will then be nearly gone, and even with the American help there will be a heavy deficit to be met each year on all our overseas purchases.

Why have all these misfortunes come upon us? The fact that we have sacrificed half our foreign investments in the late war is no sufficient explanation.

Why is it that we find ourselves unable to earn our living as we have done in the long years that are gone, in the years when our great population was built up and our standards of living, although by no means satisfactory or final, were at least superior to those in any part of Europe and even in many parts of the United States? Making allowances for all the new officials, our labour force is greater today than in 1938. We have far better machinery and great improvements in industrial science. Why then can we not earn our living, pay our way, and stand on our own feet? We are assured that our total output is greater than before the war. Why then is there a shortage in shops and why do people have to queue for every kind of household equipment and often for necessities? It is because our whole life is being handled the wrong way round. The Socialist planners have miscalculated and mismanaged everything they have touched. They have tried to substitute government control and direction for individual enterprise and skill. By their restrictions they make scarcity; and when scarcity comes they call for more restrictions to cure it. They keep the British bulldog running round after his own tail till he is dizzy and then wonder that he cannot keep the wolf from the door.

The first step to national recovery and indeed survival is to have a new Parliament, a new Parliament which can start fair in the light of present circumstances as we now know them and with no other aim but to try to solve our problems on their merits. We need a Parliament which, instead of trying to cram the whole infinitely complex life of this vast artificial community into the prejudiced and partial conceptions and limited outlook of narrow minds and party formulas, will allow the laws of supply and demand to play their part. We need a Parliament which will restore the natural and normal incentives to every form of honourable, personal effort and thrift, a Parliament which, while helping failure and weakness to catch up, will not grudge diligence, self-denial, and invention their just rewards; and finally, having established decent basic standards and food prices for our society, will, for the welfare and salvation of all, set the people free.

Isaiah Berlin to Winston S. Churchill
(Churchill papers, 4/141)

14 February 1948

Dear Mr Churchill,

I must apologize for taking so long to acknowledge your letter from Marrakesh, but as Bill Deakin can testify, the monstrous overcrowding of post-war Oxford – and in particular of my own teeming College has, at any rate for the present, destroyed the civilised habits of a more leisurely time, with the result that one does what one can when one can. I have read the latest batch of proofs with close attention and greatly welcome the result – particularly such changes and rearrangements as I have noticed. I had returned the earlier lot of proofs when I sent my original letters to you, and didn't therefore have them by me for the purpose of a detailed page by page comparison, but I feel sure that I remembered all the passages on which I have sent you comments. The transpopulation of the long memoranda to appendices is, I am convinced a very great improvement; it lightens the text and gives the whole added balance, momentum and coherence. There are one or two points of minor detail concerned with dates and trivial facts – the fate of Radek[1] for example – which I have mentioned to Deakin and with which I will not burden you. I add 2 points of greater importance at the end of this letter. In general, the architecture of the whole of Book I now strikes me as being far more symmetrical and impressive: the opening chapters particularly, which before seemed to me (I hope you did not mind my telling you that – you did, I recollect, order me to be quite candid) to get off to a slow start, now set the tempo and the rhythm for the entire work: the awful descent to the abyss, liberated from technical digressions, is a magnificently cumulative rapid and continuous narrative. I admired the earlier version greatly and now more than ever think it a literary and political masterpiece. I long for the rejoinders which you were kind enough to say that you might send – but I have no doubt that you are immensely busy and shall not repine. While I accept your verdict on disputed – or at least disputable – passages as your considered judgement, and, as such, final, there are 2 points which I venture to bring up again. The first is this: the story told, I imagine, for the first time in print of the events behind Mr Eden's resignation in 1938 reminded me of an account I had heard of this during the War, and I remember being told by someone at the Foreign Office that after Mr Eden came back post haste from Grasse he forced through a formal reversal of the Cabinet decision rather in the teeth of Neville Chamberlain – although by that time it was all too late. The President felt he had been snubbed and bad consequences followed. If this is true and I expect you will have had the benefit of Mr Eden's advice on this incident, the details of what occurred in the Cabinet may be worth greater detail and emphasis. But perhaps my memory has played me false, or the facts are confidential and in any case I should not wish to make too much of this suggestion. The second point is the information given by Benes to Stalin about the conversations between the Soviet soldiers and the Germans in the middle thirties: the footnote in the text which notes the conjecture about the part played by the GPU to which I drew your attention originally suggests that it is a well substantiated hypothesis. Perhaps I overstated the case in my account of it, and if so I must

---

[1] Karl Bernhardovich Radek, 1885–1939. Russian (Bolshevik) agent, Sweden, 1917. Moved to Petrograd after the October Revolution, 1917. Accompanied Trotsky to Brest-Litovsk, March 1918. Head, Central European Dept, Foreign Ministry, 1918. Sent to Germany on a secret revolutionary mission, Nov. 1918; arrested, Feb. 1919; released, Dec. 1919. Member, Bolshevik Central Committee, 1919–24. Supported Trotsky, 1924. Expelled from Communist Party, 1927. Banished to Urals, 1928. Recanted, 1929. Readmitted to Party, 1930. Tried, and sentenced to ten years in prison, 1937.

plead guilty: while I believe that the story is very plausible, the evidence for it rests on gossip and information collected by anti-Soviet Russian emigres, and is therefore easily challenged. Hence it will perhaps be best to say no more than something like 'there are those who hold that' rather than 'there is some evidence that', otherwise the Czechs may make a fuss as well as the Russians. I think that I drew Deakin's attention to this and he probably has already offered a suitable emendation. It only remains to say once more how greatly I appreciate the opportunity of seeing this great work in progress, and what an honour and source of fascination it has been to me. I sincerely hope that you have now fully recovered and need not add that if there is anything further that you would like me to do, I should be only too ready to do it.

Lady Violet Bonham Carter to Winston S. Churchill
(*Churchill papers, 2/146*)[1]

16 February 1948
Personal

Dearest Winston,

I listened with delight to your broadcast on Sat. night.[2] It was magnificent – and I hope it made them (the Labour Executive, Shinwell and Co.) feel as uncomfortable as they deserve to. I shall be seeing Archie tonight and shall press him to enter our fold.

I had to broadcast on my father last night – a difficult task to compress into 14 minutes. Some quotations from yourself were a great help – but few things have cost me more 'toil, sweat & tears' – for it was not my reputation but his which was at stake. By a coincidence it was the 20th anniversary of his death.

PS. I hear rumours that you may be going to support our Electoral Reform Amendment.

Winston S. Churchill: speech
(*Hansard*)

16 February 1948   House of Commons

REPRESENTATION OF THE PEOPLE BILL

I am sure that those who know the Home Secretary (Mr Ede) best will be the first to sympathise with him in the task that has fallen to his lot today. One cannot help admiring the strategy, if not the actual tactical execution,

[1] This letter was handwritten. Churchill replied on Feb. 17: 'Thank you so much for your letter.'
[2] Reproduced above (pp. 962–6).

of his speech, which consisted in devoting more than 50 minutes to reading out this bulky Bill, and for the rest of the time taking refuge in the 'Dictionary of National Biography' and giving extremely sketchy and partial accounts of various eminent men who have been connected with the universities. That was a very shrewd – I would not say crafty, but very shrewd – and well-conceived method of dissociating himself, or at any rate standing clear, from all the live and vital issues which this Bill contains. I am bound to say that he surprised me by the manner in which he managed to fill an hour and a quarter of the time of the House without really approaching in a vital or direct manner any of the burning issues which this Bill arouses in all parts of the House.

In discussing constitutional questions of this character, it is desirable to emphasize at the outset the points upon which we are in general agreement. We all value and cherish our broad free Parliamentary system, and it is our duty to submit ourselves with all the grace we can to whatever may be the will of the people from time to time, subject to the procedure of Parliament and to the inalienable rights of the minority.

In regard to the representation of the House of Commons, there are two principles which have come into general acceptance. The first is: 'One man, one vote' – there was an old joke about 'man embracing woman except where the contrary appears in the text'. The first one is: 'One man, one vote': and the second is: 'One vote, one value'. The first has been almost entirely achieved. There are only barely a quarter of a million votes out of 34 million which are not at present governed by the principle of 'one man, one vote'. With regard to 'one vote, one value', nothing like so much progress has been made. That has, for many years, been asserted by the Conservative Party. I well remember in my youth seeing the placards, 'One man, one vote', to which the answer was put up, 'One vote, one value, too'. Of course, in regard to 'one vote, one value', there can only be an approximation. It can only arise out of the process of gradual improvement, because of the rights of Scotland, and Northern Ireland and Wales, because of the sparsely-inhabited districts, and because of the need not to cut needlessly by redistribution Bills across the entities and historic continuity or boundaries of particular constituencies. But we are all agreed that this process should be constant and active.

Redistribution is particularly necessary now because of the present over-representation of the Socialist Party. Only 30,000 votes are needed to return a Member who is willing to upset and sweep away all that we have been able to build up across the centuries. 45,000 votes are required to return a Conservative, and 185,000 to return a Liberal. Making all allowances for the advantage which often goes to the winning side at a general election, this is an evil and a disproportion which has become a great abuse and cannot be neglected by any supporter of democracy. Therefore, we may say that there is a broad general acceptance of the principle of 'one man, one vote', and also of making a steady approximation to 'one vote, one value', and that both those principles, especially, of course the second, are subject to certain exceptions. That, at any rate, is the position in which we have hitherto stood and in which we still stand.

It would not be possible for us on this side of the House to oppose a Measure which, whatever its blemishes, conforms to the wide and well-established convictions and foundations of our British Parliamentary life. Everyone agrees that the redistribution of constituencies at frequent intervals should conform to the movements of the population, and that the Parliaments resulting from a general election should be a fair representation of the wish of the people throughout the land. We, therefore, support the main principles of this Bill on grounds which are agreeable to the true representation of the people and to our Parliamentary and democratic system to which we all adhere. However, there is another custom which has come into being in the last 60 years, and which has been accepted by all parties as a valuable and wholesome method of procedure in our public and political life. It has become a well-established custom that matters affecting the interests of rival parties should not be settled by the imposition of the will of one side over the other, but by an agreement reached either between the leaders of the main parties or by conferences under the impartial guidance of Mr Speaker. [. . .]

Of course, in dealing with the conflicting interests and natural divergent desires a considerable measure of compromise and goodwill and, may I add, good faith were necessary. These have often played their part in the adjustment of our political difficulties and have not prevented the active processes of political controversy. I must, however, admit that when I read for the first time in Mr Speaker's letter to me in May, 1944, the account of the agreement which had been reached, I was astonished to find that the Conservative representatives had agreed to the extra-ordinary step of assimilating the Parliamentary and Local Government franchise, so that both elections were to be polled on the same register. This step involved the addition of no fewer than seven million non-ratepaying electors to the municipal franchise. This would evidently be of enormous advantage, or so it appeared to be, to the Socialist Party, who always fought these local elections on party lines, and who might expect to receive from this mass of non-ratepaying electors a very considerable accession of strength.

I asked some of my Friends who had served on the Speaker's Conference about this. Some of them were very high-and-dry Tories, like the former Chief Whip, Lord Margesson.[1] I was told that the kind of answer I received was that after all it was a bargain and an agreement, that they knew very well that this would be deeply detrimental to what are called the Centre and Right-wing interests, but that the Report of the Conference must be taken as a whole.

---

[1] Henry David Reginald Margesson, 1890–1965. Educated at Harrow and Magdalene College, Cambridge. On active service, 1914–18 (MC). Capt., 1918. MP (Cons.) for Upton, 1922–3; for Rugby, 1924–42. Asst Government Whip, 1924. Junior Lord of the Treasury, 1926–9, 1931. Chief Government Whip, 1931–40. PC, 1933. Secretary of State for War, 1940–2. Viscount, 1942.

It was further pointed out to me that the University representation and the representation of the City of London, with one or two Members – that was not entirely settled – were accepted by the Socialist leaders, and, of course, the process of redistribution in accordance with the movements of the population was a necessary step in the normal political progress of the country.

I and my Conservative colleagues, therefore, accepted the Report, which Mr Speaker sent to me in May, 1944. We accepted this agreement between all parties as a whole. We subjected ourselves to the very great disadvantages, as it seemed to us at that time and as it proved at the first municipal elections which were held, of the addition of seven million non-ratepaying electors upon the municipal register. (*Interruption.*) I am only reciting the facts. They may be rather painful to hon. Members opposite, but they will get more painful as I continue. It is a sort of British idea that when you reach an agreement you take the rough with the smooth. A decent, honourable agreement between both parties about the basis of their elections is the foundation, and has been for many years the foundation, of our Parliamentary government, which amid all its stresses is the model for, as it was the cradle of, democratic institutions throughout the world.

It would have been possible for us in 1944 to have resisted our Labour colleagues in this matter of the local franchise and ask for its reconsideration, but we accepted the recommendations of this Conference as a whole and took every step punctually and in good time to make them effective. A Bill was introduced at the end of 1944 for the resumption of municipal elections, it established the new basis which added seven million non-ratepaying electors to the register. This Bill was introduced by the present Lord President of the Council in the days of the National Coalition, and he said that:

> 'Time did not permit of us dealing in this Bill with all the recommendations of Mr Speaker's Conference.'

Of course, at that time I personally was very busy with the conduct of the war, and the question of electioneering did not play a large part in my thoughts, nor, may I add, during those years, in the thoughts of the Conservative Party throughout the country.

The Lord President of the Council (Mr Herbert Morrison): The right hon. Gentleman has raised a point –

Mr Churchill: I have said that in those years of the war I did not pay much attention to electioneering. Of course, when there was a general election naturally I had to, but not in those years of the war; nor indeed was such great attention concentrated upon them by the Conservative Party who completely ignored many matters which afterwards proved of great importance to them.

Mr Morrison: I only wanted to make the point that the right hon. Gentleman has implied that he was preoccupied with the war and did not take a personal interest in these matters or in the result of the Speaker's Conference. I think that would be misleading, because it would imply that the rest of us took advantage of his preoccupations with the war. I ask the right hon. Gentleman to tell the House whether, in fact, he did not take a very lively interest in those proposals.

Mr Churchill: The right hon. Gentleman has given a paraphrase of what I said, and anyone can see what a trustworthy witness he is by listening to and comparing the grotesque travesty which he has uttered with what I have actually said. It is quite true that I did not accuse the right hon. Gentleman of not having taken an interest in the war. Of course, he did. He took an interest in some other matters, too – very much more, if I may say so, than any man in this House. We have accepted – (Hon. Members: 'Answer'.) There is nothing to answer. (*Laughter.*) I always notice that the party opposite indulge in laughter which resembles a crackling of thorns under a pot whenever they are confronted with any mental proposition which their intelligence forces them to resent or reject.

We had accepted the Speaker's Conference settlement, and we were quite ready that it should be carried into effect, for better or for worse, for richer or for poorer, in the most convenient manner. However, by introducing this Measure, for which the Lord President obtained the sanction of the Cabinet, the right hon. Gentleman got the one great outstanding gain for his party in the bargain or settlement. Time alone, he said, prevented the carrying out of the other provisions.

We were, of course, defeated in the July elections. Everybody here and in the country can feel their own way about that. We were also most heavily defeated in the municipal elections by the arrival of the additional seven million non-ratepaying voters. However, there was the settlement reached by the Speaker's Conference; there was the agreement to which both sides were parties. The Labour Party had taken their full advantage of their side of the bargain, and it was left to them, with indisputable power to carry it out in its entirety, and in its integrity. This, we were assured, would be done. The Boundary Commission was sent upon its work, and we now have its report before us.

[. . .]

It is quite true that nothing can bind a Parliament. Every Parliament is entirely free to behave like a gentleman or like a cad; every Parliament is entirely free to behave honestly or like a crook. Such are the sovereign rights of this august assembly. Every Parliament is entirely free, for instance, to repudiate the pledges in regard to Savings Certificates given to all who lent money to the Government, although it would not be advisable to do so. Their sovereign right is unimpaired. Every Parliament is entirely free to repudiate the treaties made by its predecessors, even if foreign countries make complaint that they have been treacherously dealt with. Every Parliament has these rights, but what relation has that to the problem before us?

It was the Lord President of the Council who made the statement – which, when I mentioned it, was cheered below the Gangway – that future Parliaments could not be bound. Parliament is omnipotent; nothing can bind a future Parliament. But there is such a thing as good faith and fair dealing between man and man, and especially between those who have long been colleagues in a dreadful struggle. There is also good faith and fair dealing which should exist apart from ordinary party fighting – the kind of laws of war, as it were, the Geneva Convention of politics – which have grown up between the principal parties in the State, and which play a daily part in our relations and business.

It is quite true that Parliament is free, but the eminent Labour men and Socialist leaders who agreed to the Speaker's Conference Report, many of them high Ministers in the present Government, are not free to take out of an agreement those points which suited them and to break the corresponding counter-balancing agreements to which they had simultaneously consented.

The Secretary of State for Scotland (Mr Woodburn):[1] As one of the members of that Conference, I would point out that the right hon. Gentleman has made several statements about a bargain. One of the reasons why the University vote was retained was because it was returning to this House distinguished persons of a non-political character. But, since the election, the Conservatives have broken that agreement by using the University vote to send back to this House Conservatives whom, at the General Election, the electors rejected at the polls. In addition to that, so far as the come-and-go was concerned, there were –

Mr Churchill: The right hon. Gentleman may make his speech tomorrow.

Mr Woodburn: The right hon. Gentleman will not be here tomorrow to hear it, so I will make it now. Twenty-five extra seats were given to Parliament, and it was recognised by the right hon. Gentleman and his colleagues –

Mr Deputy-Speaker (Major Milner): I do not think the right hon. Gentleman is entitled to make a speech.

Mr Woodburn rose –

Mr Churchill: I have regained possession of the House. I had resolved to be present tomorrow when the right hon. Gentleman made his speech, because he himself has on record a number of quite remarkable quotations, which I have seen and which he used at the time, but I do not think it would be wise for him to anticipate, in the course of an interruption, the oration which he will

---

[1] Arthur Woodburn, 1890–1978. An engineer, (iron foundry) administrator, author and economist. MP (Lab.) for Clackmannan and East Stirling, 1939–70. Member, Select Committee on National Expenditure, 1939–45. Parliamentary Private Secretary to Secretary of State for Scotland, 1941–5. Secretary of State for Scotland, 1947–50.

then deliver. I am sure I am very glad, however, to see that he feels the force of the point which I am putting to him. To his colleagues who sit upon the opposite Front Bench, I say that the honour of a great party is involved, and also, I must say, the self-respect of several important Ministers, particularly the Prime minister and the Lord President of the Council.

The Prime Minister (Mr Attlee): If the right hon. Gentleman is challenging me, I must point out that I made no bargain on this matter. The matter was adopted for the Bill which was brought before the last Parliament. No pledge whatever was given on this matter.

Hon. Members: Withdraw.

Mr Churchill: On the contrary, I shall reiterate. The right hon. Gentleman occupied a certain position in that Government. We accepted the report of the Speaker's Conference as a whole, and he knows that that was so.

The Prime Minister: The right hon. Gentleman might take my point. We were dealing with legislation to be introduced in that Parliament. The proposals came from the Speaker's Conference; they were agreed by that Government, and the Bill was introduced. There was no pledge whatever with regard to future legislation.

Mr Churchill: But the Lord President of the Council, who sits at the side of the Prime Minister, said on that occasion that time alone prevented the other provisions of the agreement being brought into effect.

Mr H. Morrison: If the right hon. Gentleman makes these provocative statements he must expect interruption. Certainly it was the case that time did not allow that Parliament to deal with every one of the issues which were raised at the Speaker's Conference, but to imply by that that any party which was returned was obligated to carry out every one of those recommendations in the next Parliament is sheer nonsense. There was no bargain, either at the Speaker's Conference or in the Government.

Mr Churchill: There was a definite agreement which has been grossly falsified.

Mr Lever[1] (Manchester, Exchange) rose –

Mr Churchill: I must reserve the concession I make to interruptions to right hon. Members on the Front Bench who feel their position acutely.

The Home Secretary spent 50 minutes reading the contents of this lengthy Bill, but there was one word on the front page of the Bill to which he did not refer. I will draw attention to it. It is a small point, but I think it illustrates the level of the technique to which the leaders of an all-powerful Government have thought it worth while to descend. The sentence on the first page says that the Bill 'gives effect to most of the recommendations of the Final Report of the Speaker's Conference of 1944 (Cmd. 6543) . . .' I should like the House

---

[1] Harold Lever, 1914–95. Educated at University of Manchester. MP (Lab.) for Manchester Exchange, 1945–50; for Manchester Cheetham, 1950–74; for Manchester Central, 1974–9. Chancellor of the Duchy of Lancaster, 1974. Baron, 1979.

to look with some attention at the word 'Final'. I am sure that anyone reading that would have supposed, in the ordinary way, that this was the final and complete digest of the recommendations of the Speaker's Conference which formed the subject of this Bill.

When I looked at Command Paper 6543, I found that it deals only with minor matters of electoral reform on which there was a very large measure of agreement. It was contained in the second letter addressed to me by the Speaker on 20th July, 1944. I found that this was not the Final Report of the Speaker's Conference, and it dealt with none of the great matters decided then. It was only an addendum which dealt with election expenses, the costs of Parliamentary elections, etc., and had nothing whatever to do with the great issues upon which this Bill is founded. It is simply intended to mislead, at first sight, the press and the public. I am not suggesting that the Lord President or the Prime Minister or the Home Secretary put it in – I do not know who did – but I think it shows the technique and the spirit that animates the Government in their discharge of these grave constitutional matters. They knew that it would not be true to say that they were giving effect to most of the recommendations of the Speaker's Conference, and by inserting the word 'final' they switched the argument on to another document and so let it all run quite smoothly. I should have thought the Government would have been ashamed to play such petty tricks as that and to be so simple as to suppose that they would escape detection or exposure.

> 'O, what a tangled web we weave,
> When first we practice to deceive.'

[. . .] We hold ourselves bound, subject to minor exceptions of long established use and custom, to support the principle of one man one vote, and to work steadily towards one vote one value. We shall not stand between the working masses of the nation and the necessary changes in their representation which the Boundary Commission have recommended. But we cannot accept as a permanent settlement the treatment of the City of London, with all its world-wide reputation, or the abolition of the University franchise. As the right hon. Gentleman has said, no one can bind future Parliaments. We are certainly freed, personally, by the action the Government have taken, and as a party by the treatment we are now receiving, and no question of breach of faith can be involved if a future Parliament reverses these unfair and one-sided decisions. In general, we hold ourselves entirely bound to the position reached in the Speaker's Conference of 1944, and we are content with the words in which these decisions were expressed by the lips of many of the prominent members of the present Socialist Party.

I must say a word about the City of London, with its unique and wonderful record. It is now to be submerged by the constituencies of Shoreditch and Finsbury. There are a lot of very good people in Shoreditch and Finsbury, but

I really do not think they will wish to walk about under the false pretence of being the City of London. I certainly hope that whatever may be the electoral shuffle, no one will use the expression 'City of London' when referring to the new constituency which, it is rumoured, is being prepared for the Prime Minister after the next election – if Prime Minister he still should be. This is an act of pure party spite, introduced for the purpose of reconciling the supporters of the Government to the ordinary and necessary processes of redistribution, designed to give more equal representation to all parts of the country, by which they may well suffer some correction of the disproportionate, undemocratic advantage and privilege which they now enjoy.

There will, of course, be a specific Amendment on the subject of the abolition of University representation and, therefore, I will not anticipate the objections and arguments which will be used on that occasion, but I may say this: under the educational reforms which were devised in the National Coalition Government, of which I was the head, very great extension has been made of access to the universities. They are no longer, as they were in bygone generations, the close preserve of wealth and rank. They are no longer a later stage in career of public-school education. On the contrary, three-quarters of the universities are now filled by young men from the public elementary schools, and I rejoice that this is so. Probably much more than three-quarters in the future will be drawn from the public elementary schools and from the broad mass of our population from whom the sparks of genius fly upwards, constantly and ceaselessly, in a glittering stream.

There are others who will remind us of the many famous men who have come to this House from the universities, many of them as independent Members able to speak with freedom on a lot of topics, such as, for example, divorce and gambling, which might prove embarrassing to what are called territorial Members. The present representation of the universities adds to the distinction of the House. There are only 12 out of 615 Members, but they dignify and widen the whole course of our democratic proceedings. The right and custom has come down to us for nearly 350 years. Now it is to be swept away, in breach of the agreements reached at the Speaker's Conference, for the sake of some small, fleeting electioneering advantage to a party already so markedly over-represented in accordance with their voting strength. The other night the Prime Minister made a rhetorical allusion to the casket of Socialist democracy in which the treasure which we have inherited can alone be safely preserved. The character of this Bill gives us some idea of the nature of the contents of this casket. I have thought of the inscription which he might write upon the casket. Here it is: 'Intellect and education need not apply.'

I wonder that anyone, looking forward to a great future expansion of the Socialist Party, should be in such a hurry to believe, and even to proclaim, that they will never win the educated intelligentsia of this country, represented by those who are graduates of our universities, although drawn in overwhelming majority from the public elementary schools. A worse advertisement could hardly be given to those who claim to know the secrets of the future and who assure us that they, alone, have the key to our social development. 'No brains wanted' – this is the declaration of the Socialist Party. If there were any real faith in their party doctrines or their party future, they would have been ashamed of this. And all for the sake of eliminating a dozen seats which they do not hold in their great majority at the present moment. The whole of this particular gesture wears a totalitarian aspect. It constitutes a breach of faith with the agreements of the past and is a measure of the degradation into which Socialist arrogance and self-sufficiency intend to plunge the free, varied, tolerant life of this island, unless they are arrested – as they will be – by the good sense and reviving mental vigour of the British nation.

Winston S. Churchill to Anthony Eden
(Churchill papers, 4/19)

18 February 1948

My dear Anthony,

Thank you so much for your comments on the chapter[1] and for sending me Hankey's letter, which I now return.

Considering that you were giving up everything and going out into the wilderness and Chamberlain, who was wrong, on the merits, was gaining complete control of the Foreign Office, I can only describe his letter as the caress of a worm. That is what I found him in the latter part of his life, when he was lamentably falling short of the magnificent performance of his prime.

Winston S. Churchill to General Lord Ismay
(Churchill papers, 4/19)

22 February 1948

<u>Book 3. Ch. 7. Page 3.</u>

I remember so well reading in an aeroplane coming back from France in 1944 the record of my harangue at Tours, which you preserved. The Provisional French Government, when established in Paris, asked for some information on what I said at the proceedings, and this was actually sent them by HMG. I remember reading it in transit, therefore it must be extant and well worth reviving, or at least looking at.

---

[1] See Eden's letters of Feb. 4 and 6, reproduced above (pp. 952–3, 956).

Winston S. Churchill to General Lord Ismay
(Churchill papers, 4/19)

22 February 1948

Conversations in Paris, May 1940

You have your record of this which preserves the remark, 'Shoot the strikers.' You have seen that this has not been reproduced by me. There is however a French procès verbal. How it was kept I do not know, because we all stood up; there was no meeting round a table and the conversation was general and informal. Have you read this and compared it with your own notes? You may be challenged on my version in which you have concurred.

Winston S. Churchill to Colonel Frank Clarke
(Churchill papers, 2/161)

23 February 1948

My dear Frank,

Graebner will tell you about the matter on which I telegraphed. As he was flying over, I gave the details to him and he will contact you. Sir Stafford Cripps was good enough to say that I could have whatever I wanted, but I do not wish to receive favours in small matters from a Government which I am strongly criticizing. Life is increasingly difficult here and it is going to be much worse.

I still meditate a lightning descent on the United States, perhaps around Easter. Baruch wishes to look after me, but I hope of course you will come up or down and join us in New York. I should travel both ways in the 'Queens' and spend only five or six days in what is still 'the land of the free'. I only think of coming to renew any contacts and hope to avoid all public pronouncements.

Pray keep this entirely secret as everything is uncertain here and my work is very heavy.

Winston S. Churchill to General Lord Ismay, Lieutenant-General Sir Henry Pownall, Commodore G. R. G. Allen and Lieutenant-Colonel Bill Deakin
(Churchill papers, 4/19)

24 February 1948

1. Volume I is now with the publishers. They have to submit to me the galleys for final proof reading. This should happen in about a month from now, after which a fortnight might be allowed. This then is the time to put in anything which we have left out, or to delete anything which we should not have put in.

Will you very kindly look at it all from this point of view in this interval. I am making my own reconnaissance to the rear at the same time. This applies both to *Between the Wars* and *Twilight War*. The Appendices should be carefully studied.

2. I hope to complete Volume II, Books III and IV, in the next fortnight and this should have priority over Volume I. I am bound to deliver Volume II by May 1, 1948. It will not however be published till January 1, 1949. There is therefore plenty of time to work it up. The naval part comes in mainly in Book IV but important notes by Commodore Allen affect the Dunkirk Deliverance tale.

I am now working on Book IV. Nearly a year will be available for revising all Volume II, i.e. both Books III and IV, and no doubt it can be greatly improved. As soon as I have got Book IV off my hands I am going to leave all this behind me and concentrate on Volume III, 1941, the prospect of which I find refreshing.

Government and Opposition meeting: minutes
(Churchill papers, 2/38)

25 February 1948   Lord President's Room
Confidential   House of Commons
3.45 p.m.
DRAFT

POLITICAL BROADCASTING

1. Mr Churchill said that on the whole the Conservative Opposition were satisfied with the existing arrangements for Ministerial broadcasts and were content that they should continue on the same lines for another year. He fully recognised that the Government who were carrying the burden of the day must have access to the BBC, which was perhaps the greatest of all instruments of publicity, and one which acquired increased importance and effect in a time of restriction of newsprint. There had been, however, one particular case, namely, that of the Minister of Fuel and Power's broadcast on 15th January 1948 on petrol rationing, in which they felt that the political emphasis had been rather too pronounced and the broadcast had approached the border-line of controversy; and although the Opposition had not in this case claimed a right of reply, they wished to emphasise their right to put the other side, if a Ministerial broadcast proved to be controversial.

Mr Bracken said there were some subjects which were so controversial that, with the best will in the world, it was impossible for a Minister to broadcast about them without exciting controversy.

The Lord President said he appreciated the point made by the Opposition.

He had himself been watching it and would continue to do so. The Prime Minister and he had enjoined upon his Ministerial colleagues the importance of objectivity in Ministerial broadcasts, and he was sure that his colleague, the Minister of Fuel and Power, had worded his broadcast on basic petrol with this aspect well in mind. It was not in the interests of the Government that Ministerial broadcasts should arouse controversy, in a case where the Opposition demanded and obtained a right of reply, even if, subsequently, the Government had the last word. One of the difficulties was that in time of stress, the number of both Ministerial and Party broadcasts tended to increase simultaneously as had recently been the case. He would do his best to achieve a better spread of Party broadcasts in the coming year, which he thought would also help to meet the Opposition's point.

2. Mr Churchill complained that undue prominence had been given to the Communist point of view in news and features on the BBC. The Communists were not a party but a conspiracy. It was a mistake, in his view, to treat them on an equality with other Parties, but he would have had no complaint if the Communist point of view had received attention in exact proportion to the voting strength of its party membership in the country. As it was, it was given an importance and prominence far beyond its deserts. Mr Churchill then gave instances in support of his claim, that with the exception of Sir Stafford Cripps, Messrs Pollitt[1] and Horner had received more prominence on the BBC than any other politician. He also warned the BBC to be on the lookout for Communist penetration inside their own organisation.

In reply, Sir William Haley asked for time to ascertain the facts. He said the impression easily got about that increased attention was being given to a particular point of view, but this was a question of fact which he would like to check. As regards the reporting of the recent Communist Party Conference, he denied that the BBC had treated this as if it had been of equal importance with a Labour or Conservative Party Conference, to which the BBC were accustomed to send special recording gear. The Corporation's difficulty was that while newspapers had the means of grading the emphasis given to a particular piece of news, i.e. by giving it physically less space or putting it on a back page, the BBC had no such means at their disposal. Anything that went into the 9 o'clock news received practically equal emphasis. The choice was between putting in and leaving out a particular item. The BBC had to be careful to be fair to minorities. He thought a greater danger than the one Mr Churchill had raised was the belief sometimes held that in every discussion the Marxist point of view should be given, whether relevant or not.

As regards the question of BBC personnel, he did not himself think that

---

[1] Harry Pollitt, 1890–1960. Secretary, Hands Off Russia Movement, 1919; National Minority Movement, 1924–9; Communist Party of Great Britain, 1929–56.

there were many Communists on the staff of the Corporation, but if the question arose, the BBC were up against the doctrine that no man should be penalised for his political convictions. Mr Churchill dissented from this doctrine, and added that it was not the rights of individuals, but the security of the country that was at stake.

The meeting invited Lord Simon, on behalf of the Governors, to review the facts and consider the points which had been raised, with a view to further discussion with the parties.

3. In the course of the discussion on Communism, it was pointed out that both Communist Members of Parliament, Mr Gallacher and Mr Piratin had been given the chance (though not in the same year) of reporting on the week's proceedings in Parliament in the 'Week in Westminster'. Mr Bracken asked why it was necessary for MPs to give this report at all when the BBC themselves had an excellent Parliamentary correspondent. Would it not be better to leave this straightforward piece of Parliamentary reporting in the hands of the correspondent like 'Today in Parliament'? The Lord President thought that nine out of ten MPs of all Parties, who gave this report, succeeded in being substantially impartial, although there had been rare exceptions on both sides. His own view was that this weekly report was better done by a Member of Parliament than a Lobby correspondent, and MPs valued the facility. The Director-General said that the terms of the invitation to the MPs stressed the importance of impartial treatment.

The BBC representatives took note of the views expressed.

4. The BBC proposed a new clause in substitution of clause 6 (iv) of the Aide Memoire, as follows:

> While legislation on any question is before either House of Parliament the BBC will confine its broadcasting on that question to factual statements, or explanatory and impartial surveys of the issues, and to the normal reporting of Parliament.

The Director-General said that the BBC found the present total restriction on the mention of current legislation in the course of its passage into law unduly restrictive, and the Corporation would be grateful for some relaxation so that it might be possible to explain in a factual and objective way the issues at stake.

Mr Churchill said the word 'confine' in the third line was misleading. He had read the amendment as a restriction, not as a relaxation of existing powers. Mr Bracken thought the proposed relaxation a little dangerous. The BBC were seeking powers which they might regret having taken when they had got them. He was not clear that any useful purpose would be served by the amendment which the BBC proposed.

It was agreed that the BBC should prepare an explanatory memorandum explaining with examples the way in which they would propose to make use of the new powers. Meanwhile, consideration of the amendment should be deferred.

5. The Director-General said that the broadcasts on the Budget were indisputably controversial in that the Opposition were accorded a right of reply to the Government's case. If as it happened last year, there were two Budgets within the year, the two extra broadcasts given by the Government and the Conservative party upset the ratio between the Parties, making it 8–7–1 instead of 6–5–1, which seemed unfair to the Liberals. The BBC asked, therefore, that, should there be more than one Budget in the year, consideration should be given to including the broadcasts on the supplementary Budget within the Party quota. The general view of the meeting was, however, that the Budget broadcasts were of a different order from Party political broadcasts, both in their general appeal to the public and in the way in which the public received them.

It was agreed that the Budget broadcasts should remain outside the Party quota.

6. The Director-General reported that there had been some demand that the political parties in Scotland, Wales and other regions should have the same facilities on the regional services as the political parties on the national Home Service. The Governors had reached no conclusion on the matter, but wished to report it for the information of the Parties. The general view of the meeting was that there was no satisfactory basis on which Party broadcasts could be organised on a limited regional basis, and that such broadcasts would be likely to cause confusion among the Parties.

It was agreed that the suggestion should be resisted.

7. It was agreed that, subject to further consideration of the point raised at (4) above, the agreement should be renewed on the same conditions as before for the year ending 28th February 1949.

Winston S. Churchill to Admiral Lord Fraser
(Churchill papers, 2/149)

25 February 1948

My dear Fraser,

I have been meaning to write for some days to send you my congratulations on your appointment as First Sea Lord. I am very glad indeed that the choice has fallen upon you. I thought it right to bring to the notice of the First Lord the fact that I offered you this great position in the war and that you declined it in so becoming a manner.

I look forward to your arrival at the Admiralty where I am quite sure you are greatly needed. I am far from satisfied with the manner in which the very large funds and manpower, hitherto at the disposal of the Navy, have been employed. Never was there so little to show in fighting value for the men and money Parliament has voted. Moreover this condition has been accompanied by what I feel sure is a deliberate writing down of our real strength which has already produced damage to our prestige over all the world, and especially, as we have seen, in South America. I am also shocked at the manner in which old battleships, two of which were practically rebuilt in 1939/40, are being scrapped. I believe this policy is also applied to destroyers. When we look back through our experiences in the last war, when the fifty aged American destroyers became one of our main objects of desire, and remember how even the old *Centurion* was ready to play her part in the invasion crisis, it is I am sure a very great mistake to cast all this latent and undefined strength away. My experience, which is unique, is that the moment war is declared every ship in the basins is a factor of value. To describe the Home Fleet as consisting of one cruiser and four 'battle' (!) destroyers seemed to me most unwise to publish, and also untrue in fact. It would be easy to arrange emergency complements which would enable the battleships we are using for training or target purposes to be recorded as available, if need be, at short notice.

I only trouble you with all this because I shall be making very serious criticism of the Admiralty when the vote comes on in the near future. I am glad you have no responsibility for all this, and of course I wish you all success when you take over, I believe, in August.

Sir Norman Brook to Clement Attlee
(*Premier papers, 8/1321*)

26 February 1948

I conveyed to Mr Churchill your request that he should not reproduce in his book the text of the Aide Memoire prepared by the Chiefs of Staff about the change of plan for the assault on Trondheim. Mr Churchill readily agreed that the text of this paper should not be published in his book, and has inserted in its place a shorter paraphrase which I prepared for him. He has asked me to let you know that he fully appreciates the force of the considerations which prompted you to ask him not to publish this paper.

I take it, however, that you do not wish to lay down an absolute rule that Mr Churchill should not include in his book *any* official document not written by himself. In a further instalment of the book which I am now examining he reproduces an extract from a minute by General Hollis conveying to him the comments of the Chiefs of Staff on a Minute which he had addressed to them, about the invasion risk. You will find this extract on page 12 of the attached Chapter XIII on The Invasion Problem. I hope you will agree that we need not raise objection to this quotation from General Hollis' minute. It is a purely factual statement; but it does have the advantage of showing that the Chiefs of Staff had considered these problems, and made their dispositions, before they received Mr Churchill's Minute. Mr Churchill quotes so many of his own documents that there is some danger of his creating the impression that no-one but he ever took an initiative. This chapter as it stands comes near to creating that impression; and the quotation of General Hollis' minute, which gives the views of the Chiefs of Staff at first hand, is a valuable corrective.

Subject to your views, therefore, I do not propose to raise any objection to the inclusion of this extract.

(I have already asked Mr Churchill to paraphrase the quotations from a paper by the Naval Staff which appears on pages 7–8 of this Chapter).[1]

---

[1] Attlee wrote on Brook's message: 'I agree.'

March 1948

Clement Attlee to William Mackenzie King
(*Premier papers, 8/1321*)

3 March 1948

My dear Prime Minister,

In his book on the *Second World War* Mr Churchill is following the method which he employed in *The World Crisis* and including a number of papers which he wrote himself at the time. Some of these are in the nature of State documents, and for these he is asking our formal permission to publish. The volume on which he is now engaged covers the first part of 1940 and in this he wishes to publish the texts of certain messages which he sent to Heads of Governments. I have agreed with Mr Churchill that you should be informed in advance of any messages sent to you which he proposed to publish, and I am therefore sending you the enclosed texts of three messages which he wishes to include in this volume. These are messages sent to you on the 5th and 24th June, 1940, and a message sent to you and to the Prime Ministers of Australia, New Zealand and South Africa on 16th June, 1940.[1]

From the point of view of His Majesty's Government in the United Kingdom, I see no objection to the publication of these messages. Unless you see objection, I propose to tell Mr Churchill that he is at liberty to reproduce these documents in his book. May I ask you to be so good as to send me a telegram in reply?

As regards the telegram of 16th June, 1940, I am writing similarly to the other Prime Ministers concerned.

---

[1] Reproduced in *The Churchill Documents*, vol. 15, *Never Surrender, May 1940–December 1940*, pp. 254, 339, 409.

March 1948

Winston S. Churchill: speech
(Hansard)

8 March 1948   House of Commons

NAVY ESTIMATES

I think the House will have formed a favourable impression of the speech delivered by the Parliamentary Secretary to the Admiralty (Mr Dugdale). His father[1] was for many years a brother officer of mine in the Oxfordshire Yeomanry, and I am glad, on personal grounds, to see him acquit himself with distinction in the House of Commons. Let me say at the outset of my remarks this afternoon that I have not sought any information from the Government or the Admiralty – who might well have been willing to supply it if I had asked them – about the naval matters which are under discussion. I prefer to depend entirely on statements which have already been made to the public, and upon my own knowledge, which enables me to interpret those statements. It is customary on these occasions to compare the strength of the Navy with that of other fleets, built and building. Today that is impossible because there is no enemy, no enemy at sea. All our former enemy navies are sunk beneath the waves, or distributed among the victors. The Soviet Navy has not yet taken shape, except, perhaps, for submarines, about which there should be serious consideration. But for the rest, the United States and France are in the closest harmony with us, and the German, Italian and Japanese Fleets do not exist. So there is no enemy against which to match the strength of the British Fleet, and this has been true since 'VJ Day' in August, 1945.

Therefore, the strength, or non-existence, of other Fleets at this time affords us no measure of the force which we should maintain. On the surface of the waters there is no enemy. But the Navy has a dual function. In war it is our means of safety; in peace it sustains the prestige, repute, and influence of this small island; and it is a major factor in the cohesion of the British Empire and Commonwealth. The tasks which the Navy has performed in peacetime are hardly less magnificent than those they have achieved in war. From Trafalgar onwards, for more than 100 years Britannia ruled the waves. There was a great measure of peace, the freedom of the seas was maintained, the slave trade was extirpated, the Monroe Doctrine of the United States found its sanction in British naval power – and that has been pretty well recognised on the other side of the Atlantic – and in those happy days the cost was about £10 million a year.

I wonder, therefore, as there are no enemies, no enemy battle fleets to be taken into consideration, why the Socialist Government should be so anxious to conceal the facts about the Navy and our naval power. Why, if there are no

---

[1] Arthur Dugdale, 1868–1941. Cloth manufacturer. Lt, Queen's Own Oxfordshire Hussars, 1892; Lt-Col. Commanding, 1914–19.

immediate enemies, should exceptional secrecy be preserved about our naval strength? Such secrecy was not thought necessary by men quite as capable as the present Minister of Defence in bygone years. Why, then, in these days, when there is no enemy possessing a naval power, should returns be refused like the Dilke Return, which was freely given to Parliament up to the eve of the wars on 1914 and 1939? The Dilke Return has been suspended and I am told there is but one copy of the Navy List in the Library. In 1914 our ratio to the German Fleet was only 16 to 10 in battleships. On mobilization, we had 64 battleships, and the enemy about two-thirds of that. A Fleet action which might upset the whole future of the world at the very outset was our main pre-occupation. But that did not prevent the Government of those days from presenting to Parliament a fair and full statement of our naval strength. Why, then, does the Government shrink from doing it now?

All through the year 1939 there was great anxiety, rather like there is now, but all the full returns to which the House of Commons had been accustomed were presented, and I do not think we suffered at all from telling the truth to Parliament and to the world. There is something to be said for telling the truth to Parliament. We are a country governed by Parliament and finance and control of expenditure have always been the traditional and effective means by which the House of Commons has brought its authority to bear upon policy and shape its course. But, now the Socialist Government say that their naval plans are so secret that they cannot practise the frankness shown by the Liberal Government on the eve of the war in 1914, or by the Conservative administration in 1939.

The whole of this policy of concealment is silly. It only makes people ask themselves 'What have the Government got to hide? If there are no enemies it must be their own shortcomings and administrative failures that they wish to hide.' There is no doubt a lot in this, but when I come to examine these matters more closely I cannot find an altogether convincing explanation, because the real strength of the Royal Navy is far above what the Government has lately made it out to be. This argument of secrecy is fraudulent, but it arises not from malice, but from stupidity. Nothing that the Government could conceal about the Navy, its strength or its weakness, could be so bad as what they have themselves proclaimed to the world. Nothing they could tell to foreigners would be so disparaging to British interests as what they have already said themselves about the strength of the Fleet.

My criticism today of Socialist Admiralty policy is twofold. First, the Admiralty never gave so little fighting value for so much money or so many men, and secondly never was such value as there is so ill-presented to the world. I am always shy of criticising Governments about their mistakes in this changing scene – (*Laughter.*) – this is a test I commend to hon. Members – unless I am on record as having warned them and advised them beforehand. Therefore, I have no compunction in reading what I said three years ago about the naval strengths we should maintain. In the Autumn of 1945, not quite three years ago, I said:

> I take the Navy first. On existing plans, allowing for intake, on 31st December, this year, the strength of the Navy would be 665,000 of whom 55,000 are women, so that the navy would retain 448,000 at the end of June 1946. I am astounded that such figures should be accepted by His Majesty's Government. I know no reason why Vote 'A' of the Navy should exceed the figure at which it stood in the Estimates of 1939, namely, 133,000. We had a fine Navy at the outbreak of war. I was sent to the Admiralty, at a few hours notice, on 3rd September 1939, and that is what I found, relatively to the forces of other countries against whom we were matched, or likely to be matched. I have yet to hear any argument which justifies our planning to maintain, or maintaining, at the present time – unless it be in connection with the Fleet Air Arm – a larger naval force in personnel than we had at the beginning of the late war. I remember that at the height of the Nelson period, in the war against Napoleon, we reached a Vote A of 148,000, and that, oddly enough, was the figure that I was responsible for reaching in August 1914. Let us take, as a working figure, 150,000.

That is where I was then, and that is where I stand now, although getting on for three years have passed. Then the Government tossed their heads in scorn, and the present Minister of Defence – this was before he had reached the 'piffle and poppycock' stage – pawed the ground, sniffed and snorted in a manner of complete disdain that a figure such as that could possibly be mentioned in connection with the Royal Navy.

I prescribed 150,000 as a general figure. Now the Minister of Defence tells us that 145,000 is to be the permanent strength of the Navy. Why not have done it then? Yes, let the Government ask themselves. Why had they not the wit and prescience and knowledge of the subject to take the proper steps then? Now, when 30 months have passed, much has been lost. Hundreds of thousands of men, costing scores of millions of money, were kept in the naval service on our Navy Estimates without any need or without any reason except the incapacity of Ministers to understand the problems with which they were confronted.

Now the Government accept my figures of 30 months ago. They took two years to clear out of Palestine after they were told to do so. Now they accept these figures of 30 months ago. They are to regulate, so they tell us, the permanent future of the Navy. Was it not a pity not to take these decisions in 1945? Think of all that would have been saved, think of all that would have been gained, by the release of men to build up our country's industries in the short intervening time before the American Loan ran out. I have not made the calculation of how many scores of millions of pounds and hundreds of millions of man-hours would have been saved if the Government and the right hon. Gentlemen opposite had done then what I advised them to do, and what they are now doing.

But there has been no policy, no control, no guidance, just jostling along, living from hand to mouth and from day to day. It has just been drift and mental inertia, and this is not only typical but an extremely precise instance which illustrates this point. It is typical of the degeneration of our affairs and administration throughout our whole country and in every branch of our national life. And how ill-timed is this new conversion of the Government to what I told them three years ago. They could hardly have hit it off worse. In fact, it is the record of misfits. When the world was safe on the morrow of our victory the Government and the Admiralty squandered our money on keeping up a vast strength against nothing. Now that danger revives, according to the speeches of almost every important Minister, they are found in the process of casting away the numbers and strength of our Forces.

Contrast the European scene of 1945 with what we see today. Contrast the problems of our foreign policy with the naval armaments policy presented on these two dates. Then there was no danger, but the Government had not the enlightenment to make the necessary reductions to ensure an adequate foundation for the Fleet. Now, when fears and dangers grow, they make, last year and this year, immense reductions. It is a strange inversion of thought for which there is, as far as I can see, no explanation except muddle and drift. If his Majesty's Government had done what I advised them to do in 1945 they would today have their Navy growing in strength and integral cohesion; they would be approaching that period of which the Financial Secretary[1] spoke just now when we should, in fact, have something like a Home Fleet in commission again.

Mr James Glanville[2] (Consett): The electors did not accept the right hon. Gentlemen's advice.

Mr Churchill: I am afraid that that is a shaft too deadly for me to reply to.

Now, at the moment when the world is so wrongly discounting what we are worth, and when it is so important for us to make the best of ourselves, we have the least possible to show, and we are caught at the worst possible moment, having wasted such vast sums and so much precious manpower meanwhile. It is a story for which the right hon. Gentlemen opposite (Mr A. V. Alexander) has a continuing responsibility, whether as First Lord of the Admiralty or as Minister of Defence. I say that all the Government ought to be ashamed, and that those responsible for this mishandling of our affairs ought to be punished by every suitable means known to the British Constitution. One of the most appropriate and usually employed punishments is a prolonged holiday. We are not bloodthirsty in this country, but that, I trust, may be meted out in due course.

[1] John Dugdale.
[2] James Edward Glanville, 1891–1958. MP (Lab.) for Consett, 1943–55.

I do not know which of their errors is more to be censured – the one of keeping all these men two and three years ago when they were not needed, or the folly of featuring the process of naval reduction at the present anxious time. But we have had both. We have had the worst of all worlds. Our strength was wasted and consumed when we were strong and safe; our weakness is now advertised when we are hard-pressed and in danger in so many parts of the world. The Government have brought off a double event which I can only describe as the quintessence of asininity.

I said a little while ago that there was no enemy on the surface of the sea. May be, however, there is a new enemy under the seas, but of that I will not speak this afternoon, because I am keeping myself to the general public statements which we have before us. The fact that there is no enemy on the seas, that none is drawn up in line of battle is no reason for breaking down the prestige of the Royal Navy, but every step that the Government and the Admiralty have taken has been in this direction in the last two months. The Financial Secretary was complaining of criticism. He complained of speeches made about the Government's maladministration prejudicing the reputation of our country. I agree with him, that we ought to try to count for as much as we can among the nations at the present time, although one of the ways is by trying to rectify through criticism the many errors that are committed. No one has disparaged our naval strength like the Government for which the Financial Secretary has spoken.

The Financial Secretary complained of gloomy speeches that are made, while the Government pour them out themselves, but I am not talking of speeches, I am talking of deeds. Actions speak louder than words. The deeds of a powerful though blundering Government count much more than any speeches which can be made by persons in a private station. What could there be more foolish in itself or more injurious to the country than the official announcement that was made that the British Home Fleet consisted only of one cruiser and four 'battle' destroyers? I was astonished at this new naval term. I have heard of battleships and battle cruisers, but the Minister of Defence must be getting hard up when he has to speak about 'battle' destroyers. It appears, however, that he had an excuse to shelter himself behind, because these are destroyers not significant because they are ones that go into battle, but significant because they are ones which are named after famous naval battles. The right hon. Gentleman saw a way of carrying and cloaking his powers by using the word 'battle' so that it gave a more bracing and inspiriting feeling to the uninstructed public who might read his announcement. I am sorry for the right hon. Gentleman. When he left my care and supervision he had a fine reputation. Now he will have to work very hard to retrieve it.

I say what a folly and what a libel this announcement was upon the Fleet. I agree with the Financial Secretary that next to the United States the British Navy is incomparably the strongest on the seas and, even compared to the

United States it has immense latent but easily mobilized resources, especially at the present time. Why then declare that our principal Fleet consisted of only one cruiser and four battle destroyers? After all, we have the four *King George V* battleships, and the *Vanguard*, which is in many ways the strongest and latest battleship afloat. We have a number of modern aircraft carriers. We have immense reserves of trained veteran sea-faring men. Why should the Admiralty and the Government write themselves down in this idiotic way, and why should they have done it at this time above all others? Surely, these are fair questions to ask in the conduct of our affairs?

It would have been quite easy for an intelligent Admiralty administration, political and professional, to have arranged the complements of the ships of the Home Fleet in such a way as to convey to the world its true power and value. All these fine modern ships could have been included in our Home Fleet in perfect truth and candour. The fact that some of them are being used for training purposes should in no way have prevented their inclusion in any statement of our national Fleet strength. The Minister of Defence tried to repair this error of statement to some extent in his speech the other night, and, of course, that was the theme of the Financial Secretary's speech this afternoon, but what a ghastly folly it was.

I come now to the word 'operational', which I notice figures on page 5 of the White Paper. This is a new term to me, and in time of peace a grossly misleading term. I think it comes from the Air Ministry and they apply it to certain tank-landing-craft or air-servicing-craft, but it is a new importation into the Navy. I am glad to see the Lord President of the Council in his place today. He spoke the other day about Socialist simpletons. There must have been Socialist simpletons in charge of the Navy when the term 'operational' was slid into our Naval terminology in time of peace. What is 'operational'? Everyone knows the increased complexity of the equipment and crews of warships. Once the term 'operational' is introduced the Socialist simpletons have little more to say. Here is a man short from manning an anti-aircraft gun. Obviously, only a portion of the anti-aircraft guns can be manned at one time. Here is a technician missing from the radar department. Here are shortages in the ammunition supply services, which are not fully manned. They are not operational if one chooses to call it so.

Complements are prescribed in the office of the Second Sea Lord, so it is quite easy to classify a ship as nonoperational because it has not got the precise complement approved by the Board of Admiralty which might be necessary in time of war or danger. I would never tolerate such a classification in time of peace. In time of war it is known whether the ships are operational or not by whether, in fact, the emergency is sufficient to make a Government send them to sea and whether they can steam and fire their guns. In time of peace it is altogether a misleading definition, and one which Ministers should be very careful not to be entrapped by.

I have never been a slave to professional opinion. 'Expert knowledge,' said Mr Gladstone, 'is limited knowledge.' I have several times seen the Admiralty make grave mistakes when deprived of competent political guidance. There was the folly of building a Dreadnought, which made obsolete all the immense reserve of ships we then possessed and enabled all newcomers in Naval competition to start from scratch. There was the Anglo-German Naval Treaty of 1935. There was the failure to build destroyers in the programme of 1937. There was the amazing surrender of the Irish Ports in 1938. All these were errors strongly supported by professional Admiralty opinion on the highest and most disinterested grounds. I must say the introduction of this word 'operational' as a means of proclaiming British Naval weakness to the world takes its place with the other misfortunes and errors which I have mentioned.

A competent administration of the Admiralty could, in one week, have made arrangements through the Department of the Second Sea Lord, for all these good ships which are used for training or in immediate reserve, to be manned effectively for action within a single month. All these could have been counted as living entities within the Home Fleet with perfect propriety and truth. Are we so rich and prosperous that we can afford to cast away and to squander our remaining assets and credit? Why did the Government do such a thing? Not assuredly because of their malice – their interest was the other way – but because of the ineptitude which characterises so many branches of their administration. The Minister of Defence may say, 'Only the facts matter. We may have stated them badly, but it is the facts that count.'

Sir, it is not only the facts that count. When this declaration was made that the British Home Fleet consisted of one cruiser and four battle destroyers, a great shock went through the whole free, democratic world. Britain has always floated upon her Navy. Her great Indian Empire has gone down one drain, and now the Admiralty proclaims that the British Home Fleet has gone down another. Can you wonder, with these weapons, that you are cheeked by Chile, abused by the Argentine and girded at by Guatemala? If anybody had set himself to work to downcry our country and all who depend on it, he could not have acted more shrewdly than by this senseless and, I must add, lying declaration of the strength of our Home Fleet.

But there was an even worse effect upon what is left of the British Empire and Commonwealth, still a great association with a high mission to mankind. My right hon. Friend the Member for Bournemouth (Mr Bracken) told me that he was in South Africa when this lamentable, and untruthful, exposure of our weakness occurred. Instantly, the anti-British parties and Press out there derided General Smuts. 'All these years,' they said, 'he has been telling us that we must hold on to Britain because of the naval defence and security which she gives us. Where is it now,' they asked, 'where is that security now?' One cruiser and four destroyers! Why, Sir, they said that it was less than the Chilean Navy. I believe this was a fact. A battleship, one cruiser, and six destroyers was the Chilean Navy. And the Chileans noted this point too, hence these alarums and excursions. All our friends in South Africa, Boer and Briton alike, who held to the great association of the Commonwealth, were embarrassed in the face of the Admiralty statement. They did not know what to say.

Let me tell them now – I found myself upon the Financial Secretary – that it was all rubbish, and that there never was, in time of peace, a British Navy which had so few possible naval foes and so many powerful naval friends. There never was a British Navy, in time of peace, which had more ample resources and power. Let them not be misled by this passing phase of mismanagement and disorganization. A period of wise, vigorous and careful administration, making the best and most thrifty use of our resources, could soon restore our naval strength and repute throughout the world.

On top of this declaration of the weakness of the Home Fleet, and the very great reduction in our squadrons in various quarters of the globe – the Government do not like to publish figures of that, but, of course, foreigners have no difficulty in finding out what British ships are on the various stations; the British public is the only public which does not know these facts: but on top of this, we come to the scrapping, announced with so much gusto, of the older ships on the Fleet. The Financial Secretary spoke of the scrapping after the last war and used the figure 39 for several years. In those days battleships were counted by tens whereas they are counted now by units, by ones. There were 60 or 70 battleships and cruisers, and so forth, in existence then, and all had been kept for a very lengthy time. When all had been scrapped, a very large reserve remained. What the Government have done is to scrap the whole reserve of capital ships. The hon. Gentlemen was perhaps not entitled to go beyond the statement that only five of the *Queen Elizabeth* class capital ships were to be scrapped, but I understand that the *Malaya*, the *Ramillies* – I have forgotten all their names – are to be scrapped as well.

We would be very foolish to get rid of ships like the *Nelson* and the *Valiant*, on which a lot of money has been spent, and to keep the ships on which no repairs have been done of a great character for a great many years. But I take it that they are all to go, the whole 10 of them, including the *Renown*. That leaves no material reserve at all. The *Queen Elizabeth*, the two *Nelsons*, the *Renown*, and the *Royal Sovereign* are all consigned to the scrap heap.

I suppose that the Minister of Defence will reply to this Debate. One may first ask, and I should like to have some answer to this precise point, whether if such a measure were necessary, this was the right moment for it. Was it the right moment to announce this wholesale clearance and destruction, when we really ought to make the most of all we have got? Was it right to proclaim such a decision to the world? I wonder how the Foreign Office felt about it, or whether they were consulted. I wonder how the Colonial Office felt about it – because all people keep their eyes on the British Navy. Why was it necessary to blurt it out at this time? There was no hurry. Many of the ships would not go to the knacker's yard for nearly two years. There was not the least hurry to bring out this wholesale destruction of these historic units at this juncture. The Government perfectly well could have let that question rest, whatever decision they had reached in their own minds. Nothing effective could be done, in many cases, for at least two years. I, therefore, hope that some of them may yet be saved.

I have some experience in these matters because twice on the first night of two great wars I have sat in the First Lord's chair at the Admiralty, and well I know how in the hour of crisis one looks around for every single item of strength that can be scraped together. A set of short-term half-wits in time of peace may brush away old vessels with all kinds of penny-wise, pound-foolish arguments and, if they have the political power, I have no doubt that they will find many experts to testify that these vessels are useless, especially if the experts have a hope that they are going to get new ones built in their place, which they are not.

But when war comes, that is not what you feel. Before the second Great War, I think I prevented by speeches in this House the destruction of several ships which a year or two later we found most useful. I remember that very old vessel the *Centurion*, battered by target practice for many years, playing an important part in our plans for resisting cross-Channel invasion, and she was moved to Plymouth for that very purpose. There are such things as 'expendables'. There are occasions on which an old ship structure can perform a great feat of arms, and where it would be wrong to risk an up-to-date capital unit of the Fleet, of which there are nowadays so few that they can be counted on the fingers. I am also told that these old battleships might conceivably become strongly armoured launching platforms for guided missiles to be discharged from. There are many uses to which they could be put. There is plenty of room in the bases. Why could they not rest there for a while? Why, anyhow, did the Government want to blurt it out now?

Then, there were the 50 American destroyers, which were bought at high cost in 1940. They had lain for a quarter of a century in the shipyards and bases of the United States. The United States put them by for a rainy day, as they might come in handy, and now they have become what everyone realised what they would be – an important factor in our fortunes, and a very useful counter in the hands of the United States. If the United States had followed the purblind policy now proposed by the British Admiralty under the direction of the Socialist Ministers, these 50 destroyers would have been scrapped 25 years before as mere junk. My experience has been that it is always better to keep the old ships or, at any rate, the best of them – I will not say that we should keep them all, and we did not do that last time – but to keep the old ships, because the cost of maintaining them in the various degrees of care and maintenance is nothing as compared with their insurance value, and still less to the part they may play in some grievous emergency.

With these preliminaries, let me now come to the particular vessels, or some of the particular vessels. *Nelson* and *Rodney* are only 25 years old, and they were the strongest ships of their kind when they were built. The *Queen Elizabeth* and the *Valiant* were virtually rebuilt barely eight years ago at a cost almost equal to what I asked the House of Commons to vote for them when they were first laid down in 1912. It was a case of building a new cast round the old bung-hole but they cost between £2 million and £3 million, I think, only a few years ago. I remember how eagerly we awaited their return to the Fleet in 1940, and we all know what a part they played in the war. I do not recommend complete reconstruction now, but it is very wrong to throw them away. These battleships are only symbols of power now, but they count as invaluable resources, and they are considered in every country, friendly or hostile, throughout the world. There is an indefinite and unknowable value, in old ships. No foreigner can tell you what part they play, what part they could play after a year or 18 months of reconstruction, or find out accurately what is being done to them at home.

But now the Government have proclaimed a clean cut; they have gloried in stripping themselves to the bone. All that sense of a latent, indefinable strength in the background is precipitately and incontinently swept away. This has been greatly to the detriment of British influence in the world in time of peace and it would certainly be deeply injurious in any naval war. Even in this plan of cutting us down to the bone and rigidly and starkly exposing the limits of our strength the Government have no policy. The *Valiant* is now ordered to the scrap-heap, but it is only a year or two ago that the Admiralty demanded and obtained from this house £250,000 to give her far-reaching repairs and modernization, which were carried out. That £250,000 has been taken from the taxpayers, earned by the toil and skill of the working people and squandered in repairs by the present Government on this one ship alone. Think of all those workmen refitting this ship, working upon hard steel, so many hours, days and months, only to find at the end of their toil that the result is immediately consigned contemptuously to the scrap-heap. This particular episode of the repair and refitting of the *Valiant* is exactly like using 1,000 skilled men to dig a hole in the ground, and then, when they have dug it, using them again to fill it up. Why, even in the convict prisons, the idea of useless labour has been rightly condemned and abolished. In the convict prisons, yes; but not in the Admiralty under the present administration. They are welcome to their slogan 'Scrap the lot'; for my part, I prefer, when I look at that Front Bench, Lord Fisher's famous dictum, 'Sack the lot.'

I return to the question of manpower. Three years ago, I mentioned a figure of 150,000 as the rough, overall measure for the Navy and its Air Arm. The Government now tell us that they are aiming at a permanent strength of 145,000 men, including the Fleet Air Arm, or whatever they call it now. There is nothing between us in numbers, and I am content with that figure. I have said that I thought, three years ago, that that should be the figure, and now, at last, they have come down to it. I hope that, with this apportionment of men – and, after all, it is the men whose numbers govern the money Vote at a time when there is no large new construction programme – it should be possible to maintain an adequate Navy under present conditions and having regard to the whole world situation.

How are these men being used? We had some figures, which I had not heard before, from the Parliamentary Secretary this afternoon. I see that, three years ago, I hazarded a guess that at that time there were nearly as many men of the Navy ashore as afloat. That was brushed aside; but it was admitted by the Parliamentary Secretary on 1st March, only a week or so ago, that, out of 143,500 men, 84,700 were ashore, which is more than half the total numbers now demanded in Vote A. All this cannot be covered up by talk of the importance of research, which nobody denies, and the development of social services and amenities, by the need of training and retraining men ashore rather than afloat, or by the Air Arm of the Fleet.

All these count, but most careful examination should be made. The prime purpose of the Navy is its war strength, the safety of the country and its power and fame. The House of Commons should go into these matters with rigour and persistence. Something was told us about some committee. I was not quite clear about it. Some committee has been set up by the Government in order to give them a bouquet. Some of the very nice things which the committee said about them were read out to us. I had not heard about this committee; I would like to see a committee of the House of Commons have a look at these matters themselves, as they would have done in almost any other Parliament than this. It is not a popular part of our duties to pare and prune, but there ought to be ceaseless pruning and paring of the non-combatant Departments, not only in the Navy, but in the Army, and, believe me – although I am not dealing with it here – in the Air Service, which is producing the very minimum of results for the enormous sums entrusted to it.

In these last three years, instead of cutting down to a necessary permanent peace level as soon as possible after the victory, and thus letting the Navy work up efficiency on that basis, year by year, there was no policy or plan. The Navy was cut down by successive steps, each of which was announced as permanent at the time. As soon as one basic manning figure was fixed, it was found impracticable to adhere to it, and another was announced. The unfortunate Board of Admiralty have been driven from pillar to post, and have really had no chance of making well-thought-out and thrifty schemes. Planning has been made quite impossible. This reaches its extreme in the Fleet Air Arm, which has had to devote its time to making one plan after another with great labour and then tearing them up, without ever being able to implement any particular scheme, because a further Cabinet decision had been reached.

The efficiency of British administration in the Fighting Services has sunk to its very lowest level at the present time, and no one in the Government has the mental grip and vitality to reform and restore it. Although there is no enemy on the seas – this is a matter to which the Parliamentary Secretary did not refer, though it might have come under his attention at any moment – there are nearly three times as many officials, naval and civil, at the Admiralty and its ancillary establishments as there were on the outbreak of war in 1939. Here are the figures: 4,950 before the outbreak of the war, and 12,650 today. All that these three times as many officials can produce is a pitiful admission – and an untruthful admission – there is not one single battleship 'operational' at the present time. There are nearly 8,000 additional clerks and officials employed on managing the Navy compared with what there were at the outbreak of the war, when for less men and less money a far larger Fleet was made efficient. I must say that the number of naval officers has not increased; that is creditable to the profession. But what has happened has been this enormous growth of civilian officials of all kinds who have been superimposed, and who make work for themselves and their descendants every day they sit in their office chairs. The whole presentation of the Admiralty staff is a scandal, which any House of Commons worthy of its financial responsibilities should probe, scrub and cleanse. I have been shown unofficial calculations, which anybody can make for himself, that an equivalent number of men to these 8,000 differently trained and employed – and, no doubt, much less well remunerated – could man two battleships, four cruisers and ten destroyers, now all laid up. It is the duty of the House to cut into this abuse and excessive tophamper.

To sum up – I am obliged to the House for listening to me for so long; I had not thought I should be so long – I accuse the Socialist Government and Admiralty administration, for which they are responsible, of giving altogether inadequate value in fighting power for the men and money provided by Parliament. Secondly, I accuse them of disparaging our naval strength in a time of increasing danger by their public pronouncements and by their wholesale and precipitate destruction of our material reserves and resources. Thirdly, I censure their misuse – uneconomical and wasteful misuse, lush indulgence in misuse – of the manpower provided. And finally, running through it all, I censure the lack of policy and comprehension which in this as in other spheres has led our country down to levels of insufficiency which we have never plumbed before.

March 1948

Winston S. Churchill: statement
(Hansard)

10 March 1948   House of Commons

I should like to associate my hon. Friends on this side of the House with the expressions that have been used about Jan Masaryk[1] by the Secretary of State for Foreign Affairs. Like him, we knew Masaryk over here during the dark years of the war, and very often my right hon. Friend and I saw him and were able to appreciate the working of that competent mind and resolute, unflinching soul. We mourn his loss – it is a heavy loss – but one cannot help rejoicing, as the right hon. Gentleman has done, that the famous name he bore will continue to be an inspiration to the peoples of Czechoslovakia.

Christopher Soames to Winston S. Churchill
(Lady Soames papers)

19 March 1948

May I draw your attention to two passages in Book I?

The first is in the 2nd and 3rd paragraphs on the first page of Chapter XVIII. In my humble opinion it is a harsh attack on the Polish people. To quote: 'It is a mystery and tragedy of European history that a people capable of every heroic virtue, gifted, valiant, charming as individuals, should repeatedly show such inveterate baseness[2] in almost every aspect of their collective[3] life.' Was the gallant defence of Warsaw not an aspect of their collective life?

I am sure that in future chapters, the Polish armed forces will be shown to have played a most active and effective part in the war. But could some mention of that not be made here in order a little to balance the picture you paint of the Polish people?

The seizure of Teschen was a vile act perpetuated by the Polish government. Munich was a despicable act perpetrated[4] by the British government. But nobody blames the British people for it.

The other point I would like to mention refers to the third paragraph on page 11 of Chapter 19. Referring to the Opposition voting against conscription you say: 'I understood fully their difficulties especially when confronted with a government they did not trust and had good reasons for not trusting.' Does this not infer that in your opinion the government was untrustworthy?

---

[1] Jan Garrigue Masaryk, 1886–1948. Minister of Foreign Affairs, Czechoslovak Government-in-Exile in London, 1940–5; in Prague, 1945–8 (Deputy PM, 1941–5). Died after falling from a high window in Prague; whether he took his own life, or was murdered by the Communist authorities, is a much-disputed question.

[2] Churchill crossed out 'baseness' and wrote 'faults'.

[3] Churchill crossed out 'collective' and wrote 'Governmental'.

[4] Churchill crossed out 'despicable act perpetrated' and wrote 'gross case of weakness'.

After reading these chapters it is evident that there were all too many weaknesses in the higher ranks of the Conservative Party at that time. But were they untrustworthy in the fuller sense of the word? I must say that is how I construed the passage.

I do hope you do not mind my raising these two points. I enjoy reading the book so much. It is a thrilling story.[1]

Winston S. Churchill to Lord Beaverbrook
(Churchill papers, 2/146)[2]

23 March 1948

Thank you for sending me the article from the *Reader's Digest*.[3] I am always glad to see the independence of Canada asserted, but I think it a pity and also dangerous to do it in a way that breeds bad blood inside the English-speaking world.

I see the *Express* has taken a rather anti-American line since you returned to the helm, and I have heard some comments in the House about bias for the Communists and the Russians. All these differences are going to become acute and deadly in the future, and of course as a Party we are supporting the Government against their extreme-Leftists and 'cryptos', because these are matters of life and death of the same order and character as those which developed before the last war. I have not heard of any differences in the Party about the line which we have taken.

As you have been away so long I venture to write this to you.

When are we going to meet again?

Winston S. Churchill to Isaiah Berlin
(Churchill papers, 4/17)

27 March 1948

My dear Isaiah Berlin,

At last I send you the honorarium, with my thanks for your work and the help you have given me in connection with the book.

(With 200 guineas)

---

[1] Churchill wrote on the letter: 'Good'.
[2] Sir Martin Gilbert notes that it is not clear whether this letter was ever sent.
[3] The article referred to is 'A Canadian's Memo to Uncle Sam' by Leslie Roberts, published in the Feb. 1948 edition of *Reader's Digest*; it suggested that the US lacked humility in dealing with its friendly neighbours and allies.

Winston S. Churchill to Colonel Frank Clarke
(Churchill papers, 2/161)

28 March 1948

My dear Frank,

Thank you so much for sending me the cigars. I am sorry to hear from Graebner that you will not allow me to reimburse you, as I could have done within my small currency limits.

Everything is very hard and difficult over here, and the only certainty is that it will get a great deal worse. Only disaster will teach, and that, I fear, is coming.

Randolph is with me now and gives very pleasing accounts of his visit to Miama.[1] He says you have hung the little picture I did in your sitting-room. I do not see how I can get across the Atlantic at the present time. I am greatly pressed by my book, and by the other self-exacting work I have to do. In fact I am working as hard as I did during the war though not, alas, with the same results. I am altogether much stronger and in better health than when I was with you, and I am sure I could swim further from the Surf Club beach. I have very agreeable memories of those days; and after all Fulton has turned out to be a signpost which hundreds of millions of people have followed.

Reverting to the question of cigars, Graebner brought me the enclosed, from which you will see that they are using my name as a trade mark. They would be very welcome to do so but I think they should pay a royalty in kind. If you have a spare moment you might suggest it to them.

I am very anxious about things, both here at home and abroad.

---

[1] Miami.

Winston S. Churchill to Sir Shane Leslie
(Churchill papers, 1/44)

30 March 1948

My dear Shane,

I have now received from your publishers an uncorrected proof of your book. I have not been able to do more than peer into it, as I have much pressing work of my own to do. Let me say however that I am greatly shocked by some things I have seen. I very much resent charges made against my Father of purloining letters, on page 176, and the whole story of the Aylesford divorce is intolerable. There are many other references to my Father and Mother which I have noticed and resent. The letters of King Milan[1] and Count Kinsky[2] to Clara[3] and my Mother should certainly be excluded.

In addition I have been upset by the tone of many passages. Randolph, who has read the book, knows how I feel, and if it were convenient to you he would be very glad to see you and discuss with you what changes should be made so as to make the book less unacceptable to my family.

I very much hope that you will see your way to making the necessary alterations; but in any case I could not allow any of my letters, of which I hold the copyright, to be made public at this time. Many such requests reach me from different sources, and I have had to make a rule to refuse them all.

---

[1] Milan Obrenović, 1854–1901. Born in Marasesti, Moldavia. Prince of Serbia, 1868–82; King, 1882–9. Married, 1975, Natalie Petrovna Keshko (div. 1888). Abdicated the throne in favour of his son, 1889, thereby becoming Count of Takovo. Renounced Serbian nationality, 1892. Exiled, 1900.

[2] Charles Kinsky, 1858–1919. Served in Austro-Hungarian diplomatic service. Lady Randolph Churchill had hoped to marry him after Lord Randolph's death.

[3] Clara Jerome, 1850–1935. Lady Randolph Churchill's sister. Married, 1881, Moreton Frewen: three children.

April
1948

Anthony Eden to Winston S. Churchill
(Churchill papers, 4/144)

1 April 1948
Private and Confidential

My dear Winston,
　Thank you so much for letting me see the book, and I am still absorbing it. The sweep of the Munich chapters is tremendous and, I think, unchallengeable.
　I enclose herewith a few random comments on the two earlier chapters.[1] These are merely my reflections and not of course meant for publication. Some day I may be able to write something about all this myself.
　I am getting on pretty well but still feel a bit shaky on my legs when I walk much.

Bernard Baruch to Winston S. Churchill
(Churchill papers, 2/210)

2 April 1948

My dear Winston,
　Admiral E. E. Stone[2] of the United States will be staying with Admiral Robert[3] L. Conolly,[4] at 20 Grosvenor Square, from April 8th to the 12th. If,

---

[1] Eden sent this letter with 13 pages of comments and notes.

[2] Earl Everett Stone, 1895–1989. Born in Milwaukee, Wisc. Educated at US Naval Academy; Naval Postgraduate School; Harvard University. Entered Navy as an Ensign, 1917. Aide and Radio Officer, Cdr Base Force, Pacific Fleet, 1919–23. Office of Naval Communications, US Navy Dept, 1928–30, 1933–5; Director, 1946–9. Executive Officer, USS *California*, 1941. CO, USS *Wisconsin*, 1944. RAdm., 1946. Director, Armed Forces Security Agency, 1949–51.

[3] Probably an error for 'Richard'.

[4] Richard Lansing Conolly, 1892–1962. Born in Waukegan, Ill. Educated at US Naval Academy; Naval Postgraduate School; Columbia University. Ensign, US Navy, 1914. Navy Cross, 1918. Executive Officer, USS *Foote*, 1918. Asst Engineer Officer, USS *New York*, 1924. Engineer Officer, USS *Concord*, 1927. Cdr, USS *Du Pont*, 1929. RAdm., 1942. Staff, Chief of Naval Operations, 1942. President, Naval War College, Newport, 1950–3; Long Island University, 1953–62.

some time when you are in the city, you can arrange to have him go around and meet you, it would please him and me. He is over there on some duty, the nature of which I do not know.

Everybody wants me to get you to make a speech at some college and get a degree. Whenever you get ready to come, let me know and I will make all the arrangements but not to speak.

I am expecting to sail on July 1st, spend about one week in England to see as much of you as I can, then go to Vichy and then return for a few days to say Good-bye to you. I shall sail on August 14th for home.

I am looking forward with great joy to seeing you once again.

Winston S. Churchill to Major Vyvyan Adams[1]
(Churchill papers, 2/67)

2 April 1948

My dear Vyvyan Adams,

Thank you for your letter. I take the opposite view. I cannot imagine a worse time to abolish the Death Penalty than now in the height of the outburst of criminality from which we are suffering. I may even speak against it if the opportunity occurs. I am sorry not to find myself in agreement with you. They have, of course, abolished the Death Penalty in Russia because they prefer to toil them to death in slavery.

Winston S. Churchill to General George C. Marshall
(Churchill papers, 2/20)

4 April 1948

Mr Victor Gollancz is a well-known publisher of Left-Wing literature and of books against the Conservative Party. He is also a prominent Socialist who has been working cordially with me in our All-Party Organization of the United Europe Movement, of which he is a Vice President, and he has vigorously championed its cause. He puts these questions far above our serious Party differences. In this, as in the treatment of Germany, he has the root of the matter in him.

I should be very glad if you could spare him a little of your precious time.

---

[1] Samuel Vyvyan Trerice Adams, 1900–51. Educated at Haileybury and King's College, Cambridge. Called to the Bar, 1927. MP (Cons.) for West Leeds, 1931–45. Member, Executive of the League of Nations Union, 1933–46. On active service, 1939–45 (Maj., Duke of Cornwall's Light Infantry). In 1940, under the pen name 'Watchman', he published *Churchill: Architect of Victory*. Political researcher, 1946–51.

April 1948

Winston S. Churchill to Léon Blum
(Churchill papers, 2/18)

7 April 1948

My dear Monsieur Blum,

I have read what you have written in *Le Populaire* and I feel it my duty to apprise you and your friends of some facts about the Movement for United Europe of which you may not be aware. You say, 'Mr Churchill has a character too original and too powerful for him not to leave his mark on everything he touches. . . . He continues to play a part of the first importance in the internal politics of his country and in international politics. The stamp of his approval brought with it the danger that the European federation could have a character too narrowly Churchillian. Thus is explained the embarrassment, circumspection and hesitation of the Labour Party, and, in consequence, of international Socialism. The Federalist movement would have great difficulty in emerging from the shadow of a too illustrious name.'

When at Zurich in September 1946 I revived the ancient and glorious conception of a United Europe, associated before the war with the names of M Briand and Count Coudenhove-Kalergi, which I had supported for many years, I had no idea it would become a Party question. I thought it would become a movement and an inspiration on a level far above Party politics in any country. Indeed if we cannot rise above Party differences in a common cause on which we all agreed, how can we hope to bridge the fearful gulfs of reciprocal injuries between nations great and small, and thus repair the ruin of Europe? This was I believe your view too, until you became aware of the adverse decision of Mr Shinwell and the Executive of the British Socialist Party. It would be a disaster to a supreme and vital cause if ordinary party politics in Britain were to obstruct this great international movement.

Nothing could be more wrong and foolish than for the Socialist Parties of Europe to try and create and maintain a monopoly of a cause and policy which belongs not to local Parties, but to whole States and nations. The Socialist Parties are not in a majority in any European country and they have no excuse to try and warn off and drive away all the other Parties of the Left, the Centre and the Right, without whose aid the results at which we all aim could not be achieved. To do this would be to imitate the Communist technique of the one-Party System. The idea that Europe could be united on a one-Party Socialist basis, fighting the Communists on the one hand and all the other Parties on the other, is of course absurd. You will need all the help you can get and we shall need all the comradeship of which we are worthy, if we are to win this great prize for all the peoples, for all the Parties 'for all the men in all the lands'.

For these reasons the Conservative Party in Britain have given their full support to Mr Bevin in the policy of a Western European Union, which he has adopted. No-one is seeking to deprive him or the British Socialist Government of any credit which is theirs. The position of a Minister, holding the high executive Office of Foreign Secretary, is quite different from that of a private person, even if he has the misfortune to be, to quote your flattering words, 'too illustrious'. The Minister has executive responsibility and has to act as well as to speak. There will be great credit for Mr Bevin, and indeed for all, if a good result is gained and Europe stands aloft once more in splendour. Those will be unworthy of the occasion and fall below the level of events, who allow Party feelings or personal likes and dislikes to hinder the way to the main result.

When we decided many months ago to attempt a Conference at the Hague, it was the best step open to private people to further the cause that has now been espoused by sixteen Governments and would be joined by many more if they were free. The British All-Party Committee, Conservatives, Liberals and Socialists alike, have always had the aim of keeping the whole movement above Party politics in England or in any other country. At the present time I understand that an important delegation of British Socialists will be present at the Hague in May. I do not believe that my particularist or sectarian differences will prevent a memorable demonstration in favour of the general purpose which we all share. This will be an aid to all the executive governments concerned in carrying out the policy upon which they have recently agreed. We seek to create a helpful atmosphere and to gather and focus opinion and support from every quarter. We act in the same way and we play exactly the same part in relation to the declared policy of the British Government as the United Nations Association does to the hard-pressed World Organization of the United Nations, and the same part as was played before the war by the League of Nations Union to the League of Nations. These are the great hopes of mankind and it is the duty of all to cherish them and bring them to success.

I cannot feel that my own initiative has been harmful. You may remember that Mr Marshall at his News Conference on June 12, 1947, disclosed that my advocacy of the United States of Europe had influenced his development of the idea that Europeans should work out their own economic recovery and that the United States should extend financial help.

I feel greatly honoured to have been a link in setting in train the Marshall Plan upon which all our Governments are united and all our hopes depend.

The British Socialist Party have not threatened with disciplinary measures or victimization any of their members who may come to the Hague as individuals, and I trust that the French Socialist Party will allow full freedom to its own members; for I am sure that all who fall out of the line in those grave and melancholy times will still expose themselves to the reproach of history. I hope therefore for all our sakes that the position may be made plain in a manner conducive to the dignity and independence of all Parties and to the causes and principles which Parties exist to serve.

I address this letter to you, my dear Monsieur Blum, because of our association in the struggles of the past and my hope that our closing years may see us united in the march towards what is noble and true.

Sir Shane Leslie to Winston S. Churchill
(Churchill papers, 1/44)[1]

7 April 1948

My dear Winston,

I only wish to say that I never regretted anything so much in my life as the offense this book has given you. All excuses are lies, so I make none, but I wish you to have no further worry on the matter. I entirely accept all omissions or corrections which Randolph cares to make. I will change my plans and come over before the end of the month to discuss with him as you suggest. I am afraid my error has lost me your affection. Do not trouble to answer as I am writing fully to Randolph by this post.[2]

Winston S. Churchill: speech
('Winston S. Churchill, His Complete Speeches', volume 7, pages 7624–5)

12 April 1948   Savoy Hotel, London

PILGRIMS' DINNER TO MRS ROOSEVELT

I have little to add, except my heartfelt agreement, to what the Prime Minister has said. I am asked to sustain and support what he has said and to respond to the appeal he has made to us all to cherish the memory of our great friend. Obviously we are divided in this island on practical and doctrinal issues, but we are all united here tonight in paying our tribute to the memory of Franklin Roosevelt, and I am glad to be invited to testify to this, and to support what the Prime Minister has said.

We sedulously avoid all special associations with one Party or the other in the United States. Republicans and Democrats are the same to us. Our sympathies are with the American nation and with those whom it chooses by the processes of democratic election to guide its vast affairs. Indeed any other course would imply a bias or even interference with internal American politics. When we come to speak of Franklin Roosevelt, however, we enter the sphere of British history and of world history, far above the ebb and flow of Party politics on either side of the Atlantic. And I shall not hesitate to

---

[1] This letter was written, by hand, in response to Churchill's letter of March 30, reproduced above (p. 1001).

[2] Churchill responded on Apr. 10: 'Thank you so much for your letter and I am most grateful to you. Affectionately Winston' (*Churchill papers, 1/44*).

affirm, and indeed to repeat, that he was the greatest American friend that Britain ever found, and the foremost champion of freedom and justice who has ever stretched strong hands across the oceans to rescue Europe and Asia from tyranny or destruction. The longer his life and times are studied the more unchallengeable these affirmations which I have made to you tonight will become.

But I will go further, and place on record my conviction, shared I believe by the whole British Empire and its Commonwealths, that in his life and by his action he changed, he altered, decisively and permanently the social axis, the moral axis of mankind by involving the New World inexorably and irrevocably in the fortunes of the Old. His life must therefore be regarded as one of the commanding events in human destiny. As a result of his personal influence and exertions, the principle of 'one world,' as his opponent Mr Wendell Willkie[1] called it, the principle of 'one world' in which all the men in all lands must play their part and do their duty, has been finally proclaimed and comprehended. In all this he was unswervingly supported – twice indeed during the continuance of the struggle – by the spirit and genius of the American people who, apart from all internal differences or administrative incidents, found in him during the war the full expression of their mission, their power, and, as it has proved, their glory.

Here tonight we do more than honour to his memory. We have the good fortune to have among us Mrs Roosevelt. Many of us know what we owe to our wives in life's varied journeys. Mrs Roosevelt has made her own distinctive contribution to the generous thought of modern society. In her speech tonight she has given us a measure of the individual bearing and influence and comprehension which she has brought into the field of world affairs. But at this moment when we are celebrating the setting-up of the Roosevelt monument and fine statue in London, which recalls to me the figure which I loved and honoured, we must ascribe to Mrs Roosevelt the marvellous fact that a crippled man, victim of a cruel affliction, was able for more than ten years to ride the storms of peace and war at the summit of the United States. The debt we owe to President Roosevelt is owed also to her. I am sure she feels around her tonight, in this old parent land, and in this great company, the esteem and affection of the whole British people.

The ancients spoke of personages who were happy in the occasion of their death. Certainly President Roosevelt died in full career and undisputed control at the moment when certain victory was in view. He did not live to endure the quarrels of allies, hitherto united by common perils; nor to endure the

---

[1] Wendell Lewis Willkie, 1892–1944. Born in Indiana. A lawyer and initially a Democrat. Became a Republican in opposition to Roosevelt's New Deal. Unlike many Republicans, not an isolationist. Republican Presidential candidate, 1940. Lost to Roosevelt, but gained a larger Republican popular vote than any previous contender (later exceeded by Eisenhower, 1952). Visited Britain, the Soviet Union and China as Roosevelt's personal emissary, 1940–1.

exhaustion of the spiritual forces which, during a life-and-death struggle for a noble cause, had lifted men and whole nations far above their normal level. He did not have to face the grave economic aftermath of splendid sacrifices and deeds. He was spared all this. In my sombre moments, when I have them, as I sometimes do, I remember the lines of Lindsay Gordon[1] –

> 'We tarry on; we are toiling still
> He is gone and he fares best.
> He fought against odds; he struggled uphill.
> He has fairly earned his season of rest.'

But I do not think that could be the epitaph of the famous man whose memory we honour tonight. First because the troubles we now encounter are less than those he overcame. Next because the United States which sustained him has risen, as the result of his direction and Presidency, to the foremost place among the nations. And above all that, having this solemn and awful responsibility and burden cast upon her, the Great Republic has neither bowed nor flinched before her task and duty. She has found from her free democracy and federal system a wealth of gifted men and a unity of national purpose equal to all the tasks which may be set. These tasks will be hard, the burdens heavy, the decisions difficult and grave. But they will not be too much for us to bear; and in the championship of all the world causes with which the name of Franklin Roosevelt is bound up, the British Empire and Commonwealth of nations will prove itself a valiant and faithful friend and ally of the United States, in peace as it was in war, in the future as in the past. Thus, as Mrs Roosevelt has bade us believe, thus all will come right.

Duncan Sandys to Winston S. Churchill
(Churchill papers, 2/21)

13 April 1948

My dear Winston,

This is a line to confirm what I told you about the arrangements for the Hague Congress.

I suggest that you should arrive in time for dinner on Thursday, May 6th, or alternatively, during the morning of Friday, May 7th.

The Congress opens at 2.30 on Friday, May 7th. There will be two short speeches of welcome by the Burgomaster of the Hague[2] and the Chairman[3]

---

[1] Adam Lindsay Gordon, 1833–70. Born in Fayal, Azores, Portugal. Educated at Cheltenham College; Royal Military Academy Woolwich; Royal Worcester Grammar School. Married, 1862, Margaret Park. Author of *The Feud* (1864), *Ashtaroth* (1867), *Sea Spray and Smoke Drift* (1867) and *Bush Ballads and Galloping Rhymes* (1870).

[2] Willem Visser, 1904–75. Burgomaster, the Hague, 1947–9.

[3] Pieter Adriaan Kerstens, 1896–1958. Married, 1921, Sybilla van Straaten. Chairman, IKP,

of the Dutch Reception Committee who will ask you to take the chair and deliver your opening presidential address, which we suggest should be about half an hour. After your speech there will be an interval, followed by a further plenary session which will be presided over by Ramadier.[1] Speeches will be made by two or three of the most prominent foreign delegates and I hope that you will feel able to attend. Before dinner, the Dutch Prime Minister[2] and other members of the Dutch Government are giving an official reception to all the delegates and would, of course, feel slighted if you did not come to it.

Saturday will be devoted entirely to discussions, in which you presumably will not wish to take any part. During Sunday morning there will be a plenary session in which the report of the Cultural Committee will be adopted. It will not be necessary for you to be present. There will be a mass meeting on Sunday afternoon in the main square of Amsterdam, which will be addressed by a few of the leading personalities of the Congress. We are counting on you to make a ten minute speech to the crowd which is expected to be at least 25,000.

There will be three plenary sessions on Monday; the first two will be devoted to the adoption of the reports of the Political and Economic Committees and the last will be a closing session at which two or three winding-up speeches will be made. You should, I think, be present at the final session and I hope also that you will look in on and off during the other two.

On the evening of the last day (Monday, May 10th) it is possible that the Queen will give a dinner to about forty people followed by a reception to all the delegates by Princess Juliana[3] and Prince Bernhard.[4] These two events are not officially confirmed.

PS. We have held up the invitation to Anthony Eden, because we thought it should come from you. Would you send him a line?

1933–41. Member, Dutch-India House of Assembly, 1935–42. Dutch Minister of Commerce, Industry and Shipping, 1942–4; of Agriculture and Fisheries, 1942–4. Member, First Chamber, States-General, 1946–52. Vice-Chairman, KVP, 1946–52. Chairman, Dutch Organizing Committee, European Congress, The Hague, 1948. Member, Advisory Assembly, Council of Europe, 1949–51. Member, European Economic Committee, 1951–8.

[1] Paul Ramadier, 1888–1967. Member for Villefranche-de-Rouergue, Chamber of Deputies, 1928–40. French Minister of Labour, 1938–40. PM, 1946–7. President, International Labour Bureau, 1952–5. French Minister of Finance, 1956.

[2] Louis Beel, 1902–77. Educated at Radboud University, Nijmegen; Bisschoppelijk College of Roermond. Secretary to the Educational Religious Inspector, Roermond diocese, 1922. Minister of the Interior, 1945, 1951–6. High Commissioner of the Crown, Dutch East Indies, 1948. Minister of Social Work and Deputy PM, 1952. PM and Vice President of the Council of State, 1958–9.

[3] Juliana Louise Emma Marie Wilhelmina, 1909–2004. Born in The Hague. Educated at Leiden University. Married, 1937, Bernhard of Lippe-Biesterfeld. Queen Regent, 1947–8. Queen of the Netherlands, 1948–80.

[4] Bernhard Graf von Biesterfeld, 1911–2004. Educated at University of Lausanne, Switzerland; Friedrich-Wilhelm University, Berlin. Married, 1937, Princess Juliana Wilhelmina. Prince Consort, 1954–76. Founder and First President, World Wildlife Fund, 1962–76.

Winston S. Churchill to Cassell & Co.
(*Churchill papers, 4/351*)

14 April 1948

Pray print the following, with First Priority:
Volume III. Books 5 and 6.

At this stage in the work I am only assembling the personal documents around which the story will build itself. Many of these will be omitted and all will be severely edited in the public interest. This applies equally to the minutes and the telegrams. Only a few copies have been printed, and it is not intended that they shall go outside our own secret circle.

(2) We now need to find many of the answers to the telegrams and results of the minutes. These again, not being dictated by me, will be summarized or woven into the narrative. Narrative must be provided to fill in the spaces and it is important to find out anything which conflicts with or stultifies my telegrams and minutes. Full justice must be done to the other side. We cannot however print an equal flood of documents. For good or ill these are the ruling documents, and the ones which constitute the corpus of the Volume. It is only after these papers have gone through a severe process of criticism and refinement that I shall ask the approval of the Cabinet Office to their publication. In two or three months we ought to be able to submit a fairly matured text.

Sir Orme Sargent to Winston S. Churchill
(*Churchill papers, 2/69*)

16 April 1948
Confidential

Dear Mr Churchill,

You wrote to me on March 28th while I was away on leave about Mr Morgenthau's request to publish an agreement made at Quebec in 1944 between yourself and President Roosevelt. I have now got together the relevant papers and the facts seem to be as follows.

Mr Morgenthau telegraphed to you in August 1945 asking for permission to reproduce in his book *Germany is our Problem* the plan for Germany which you and President Roosevelt 'agreed and signed at Quebec'. At that time, you yourself had no clear recollection of this document and asked us to make a search. The document in question turned out to be that contained in telegram No. 169 of September 15th, 1944, in the Gunfire series,[1] of which I now enclose a copy for your information. For various reasons we considered it would be undesirable to publish this document and we so informed Mr Morgenthau through our Embassy in Washington. Mr Morgenthau replied on

---

[1] Reproduced in *The Churchill Documents*, vol. 20, *Normandy and Beyond, May–December 1944*, p. 1386.

September 13th, 1945, undertaking not to publish 'the confidential document initialled by Mr Churchill and President Roosevelt at Quebec'.

Mr Morgenthau's book appeared in due course and contained as a sort of preface a reproduction of a photographic copy of the memorandum summarising the 'Morgenthau Plan' which President Roosevelt took with him to Quebec. In his foreword Mr Morgenthau says 'In September 1944 President Franklin D. Roosevelt asked me to outline for him a programme for the direction of Germany after her defeat. He wished to take such a document to the Quebec Conference which was to be held in a few weeks and he knew that I had devoted a good deal of thought and study to the subject. . . . No part of that plan has ever been made public by me until now. This book is an elaboration of the programme which I then submitted to the President for his use. It is essentially the same framework, but with additional research and documentation to supplement the much slimmer document which Mr Roosevelt took to Quebec.' I cannot find that Mr Morgenthau claims anywhere in this book that you endorsed his memorandum or even that Mr Roosevelt did, although he does claim that the basic principles of the programme have since represented the official position of the United States Government and that the objectives of his policy were also those set out in the Potsdam Agreement.

While therefore it is true that Gunfire 169 is on the lines of Section 4 of Mr Morgenthau's brief for the President, there seems to be no doubt that Mr Morgenthau did not publish any document initialled by yourself or even claim any support from yourself personally for his ideas.

As regards the question of consulting yourself whenever questions affecting your period of responsibility come up in the House, I will try and arrange that the Office shall get into touch with you whenever time and circumstances permit.[1]

Christopher Soames to Winston S. Churchill
(*Churchill papers, 1/32*)

16 April 1948

I would like, if I may, to give you a short appreciation of the economic condition of the farm.

1. The weekly milk cheque should pay for the wages (less those from the Market Garden, which is a separate unit, and Whitbread and Kurn who are non-productive) and all running expenses, including the purchase of seeds and fertilisers but excluding, of course, any capital expenditure. This would mean that the money derived from the sale of cash crops and livestock would be available to make further capital improvements.

---

[1] Churchill replied the same day: 'Thank you for your letter of April 16 and for what you tell me about Mr Morgenthau's publication of the agreement made at Quebec in 1944.'

2. Our present position is as follows. The monthly wage bill (again excluding the Market Garden, Whitbread and Kurn) amounts to approximately £270. I estimate running expenses to be about £200 a month, making a total expenditure of £470. With the number of cows which you now have the average monthly milk yield throughout the year is 2,400 gallons. This brings in £300 a month. Therefore quite apart from any capital improvements I am forced at present to ask you to pay about £170 a month, or over £2,000 a year, out of your private account to meet the wage bill and current expenditure.

3. In order to find this extra £170 a month from the farm, we must produce a further 44 gallons of milk a day. This we could do if we had sufficient cows to keep both the Chartwell and the Bardogs cowsheds full. This would mean a further capital outlay of about £6,000, but I am convinced that this would be an economically sound policy.

4. I fully understand that you are farming for fun and not for profit. But nevertheless it would, I submit, be more advisable for you to expend £6,000 this year to purchase stock rather than to pay the same amount out in small sums over a period of three years at the end of which there would be nothing to show for it.

Lewis Douglas to Robert Lovett[1]

('Foreign Relations of the United States, 1948, Western Europe', volume 3, pages 90–1)

17 April 1948
Personal and Top Secret

Dear Bob,

I have had several visits with Churchill since my return, the last being on Thursday when he discussed the possibility of war with the Soviet.

You probably know his view, that when and if the Soviet develop the atomic bomb, war will become a certainty, even though by then Western Europe may have become again the seat of authority and a stable political part of the world. He believes that now is the time, promptly, to tell the Soviet that if they do not retire from Berlin and abandon Eastern Germany, withdrawing to the Polish frontier, we will raze their cities. It is further his view that we cannot appease, conciliate, or provoke the Soviet; that the only vocabulary they understand is the vocabulary of force; and that if, therefore, we took this position, they would yield.

You know better than I the practical infirmities in the suggestion. They cover quite a wide range, including the political.

Churchill believes also that if the Soviet try to inconvenience us in Berlin

---

[1] Robert Abercrombie Lovett, 1895–1986. Born in Huntsville, Tex. Educated at Yale University, 1918. Special Assistant to Secretary of War, 1940–1. Asst Secretary of War for Air, 1941–5. Under-Secretary of State, 1947–9. Deputy Secretary of Defense, 1950–1. Secretary of Defense, 1951–3.

(as they are doing), we should retaliate by insisting upon a careful examination of the crews of every one of their ships putting into our ports, by annoying their shipping and their use of the Suez and Panama Canals, and by any other method which appears to be appropriate.

I, myself, doubt very much the wisdom of this policy, principally because it won't cause enough inconvenience. It seems to me to wave the strand of straw, disguised as a club, would have no effect. On every score the other measures about which we have been talking, if taken reasonably soon, may present to our friends to the east such a demonstration of solidity and irresistible force that we may be able to deter the Soviet and to quash any ideas that they may have. I am inclined to think that such a demonstration, even though the Soviet may ultimately develop – if they have not already developed – the atomic bomb, may deter them.

I think there is much in what Churchill says; that we cannot appease, conciliate, or provoke the Soviet; that we can only arrest and deter them by a real show of resolution. Such a demonstration of determination combined with the reestablishment of Western Europe as a center of power, may lead to a satisfactory settlement.

Winston S. Churchill: speech
('Winston S. Churchill, His Complete Speeches', volume 7, pages 7625–32)

21 April 1948　　　　　　　　　　　　　　　　　　　　　　　　　　Albert Hall

CENTRAL COUNCIL OF THE WOMEN'S ADVISORY COMMITTEE
OF THE CONSERVATIVE PARTY

When I last spoke in this famous hall a year ago, it was in the cause of United Europe, which you so cordially appraised at your big meeting yesterday. Today men of all Parties rejoice at the progress which has been made, and many problems which seemed a year ago baffling and inscrutable, have solved themselves. Many ancient and powerful States have rallied to the theme. Our own Government has adopted the policy. The United States have lent their all-powerful aid. We have had the Marshall Plan of aid to Europe, and especially as we now learn from the newspapers, aid to Britain. Our Foreign Secretary, Mr Bevin, has played an active and distinguished part. Solemn covenants have been agreed. Britain, France and the countries of Western Europe who call themselves Benelux have joined together in an association of mutual help which may soon become an organisation for common defence, in which the might and authority of the US will be the decisive factor.

I have always tried to keep this Movement outside and above Party politics, and I shall continue to strive to do so. There can be no hope for the world unless the peoples of Europe unite together to preserve their freedom, their culture and their civilisation founded upon Christian ethics. There can be no return of prosperity unless they help each other to the utmost, and unless they turn to the best advantage the life-giving stream of succour which is flowing towards us across the Atlantic Ocean. It would indeed be a shame if Party difference or personal jealousies in this country were allowed to confuse or quench this growing light in a period when so much is at stake.

Good news, Ladies and Gentlemen, has come in this morning; the defeat of the Communists in the Italian elections is an historic event. Italy, liberated by the Allies from the Fascist dictatorship of Mussolini, has saved herself for the time being from the Bolshevik dictatorship of Stalin. We have always wished for friendship with the Italian people. Now they have chosen to range themselves with Western and Christian civilisation. We may all (all, that is to say, except Communists, the crypto-Communists, fellow-telegraphers and fellow-travellers), we may all be thankful for this. Italy now regains her place in the ranks of the principal Powers of Europe, instead of being like so many unhappy countries, made to live in the cage with the bear. Personally, I rejoice to see Italy resume her full contacts with Britain and the US, and I feel as if we were now welcoming home an old friend after a tragic interlude.

We have all been deeply shocked and grieved at the fate of Czechoslovakia. Here was a people who wished to be free, who longed for association with the Western World, who had got contributions to make to the European circle both in culture and in politics. Their lot has been indeed hard. No sooner were they freed from the tyranny of Hitler's Gauleiters than, like Poland, they were dragged down into subjugation by the Soviet Quislings. I am sure we all especially those who knew him closely, feel a deep respect for Masaryk who has, by his supreme sacrifice, cast a new lustre on an already-famous name.

I hear people say of the Soviet aggressions and intrigues, 'Thus far and no farther'. That is no doubt a widely-held resolve. But, we must not delude ourselves. There will never be a settled peace in Europe while Asiatic Imperialism and Communist domination rule over the whole of Central and Eastern Europe. It is a relief amid our many anxieties to feel that, whatever our domestic Party differences may be, and after all it is a principle of our ideas that they should be freely expressed, the British nation and British Empire are overwhelmingly united against the Communist menace, and we of the Conservative Party will certainly give our full support to any well-considered measures which even the present Socialist Government may deem necessary against it.

I have touched upon these wider questions in a period which I cannot feel is wholly devoid of anxiety. I wish we could find a similar unity of purpose in our life at home. When we contrast the position we gained three years ago by outstanding exertions and achievements in the life and death struggle of the world with what we see around us now, it is hard to believe that one day's thoughtless voting could have brought so much evil and misfortune into our island life, or so dismal a retrogression in our world position. One would have thought at least that when the Socialists stepped into power, with their great majority, they would have tried to serve national rather than Party interests after the war in this period of strain and after what we had gone through and done together.

Instead, it has been their principal aim from start to finish to assert and enforce their Party doctrines and dogmas upon the whole of their fellow-countrymen, and to spread class-warfare, with all its injury to national effort, far and wide throughout the land. Even if we had all been pulling together with the comradeship and loyalties of the wartime years we should have had a hard task to overcome. That task has been made insuperable by the attempt of a Parliamentary majority, which in no way represents the strength and character of the British people, to impose their fads and their fancies upon the whole great mass of people, whose recovery and welfare should have been their supreme and indeed their sole aim.

To this wrong and evil deed, they have added a record of administrative blunders and mismanagement at home and overseas, which cannot be matched in our history. This combination, the combination of partisanship and incompetence has brought us, three years after our victory, to the humiliating and painful position of not being able to earn our daily bread, or seeing any prospect of doing so under Socialist rule for many years to come. I can assure you that a continuance of Socialist experiments in theory, and of their ineptitude and incompetence in practice, will bring upon us not only worse privations and restrictions than those we now bear, but economic ruin and not only economic ruin but the depopulation of the British Isles on a scale which no one has ever imagined or predicted.

Take another example. As I listened the other night in the House to the crazy cheers with which the Socialist backbenchers, in defiance of the advice of the majority of their leading Ministers, swept away the Death Penalty for the wickedest forms of murder at a time when crimes of robbery and violence by armed men have so grievously increased, I could not but wonder if these hysterical, emotional Members could be the same men who regarded the slaughter, as a result of their mistakes and mismanagement, of at least half a million Indians in the Punjab alone, as a mere incident in the progress of oriental self-government. What a confession of impotence it was that the Prime Minister and the Cabinet, who did not dare to stand by their declared convictions of what they thought was right and necessary in the present circumstances, should have cast their duty to the wind and left this grave decision on Capital Punishment to the casual vote of the most unrepresentative and irresponsible House of Commons that ever sat at Westminster.

Look next at what they have condemned us to in Palestine. It is nearly two years since I realised that they were incapable of solving the Jewish–Arab problem there, and still less of keeping the promises they had made to the Zionists. I advised them in these circumstances to lay their mandate at the feet of the United Nations Organisation and bring our sorely-tried troops out of a country which offered us nothing but suffering, discredit and expense. This advice they have at length adopted. But think of the long and weary months in which we have been tramping fruitlessly on this blood-stained treadmill in Palestine, because Ministers could not make up their minds either to act or to go. With every week that has passed the situation has become worse and more anguished. Solutions that were possible two years ago have been swept away. A vast sum of money and many precious lives have been wasted through infirmity of purpose, lack of conviction and lack of ordinary common sense. And here on a great scale overseas you see what I see in the House, a total absence, a total vacuity of leadership of any kind.

What of their policy on nationalising industry? So far as we can judge at present it has simply meant the transference of industries which were profitable and holding their own, to be new burdens on the shoulders of the hard-pressed taxpayer. The shareholders have been and are being swindled (according to the term I read in the evening paper which was used at the meeting of the Standing Committee on the Nationalisation of Gas by my friend, Mr Brendan Bracken) by the terms of compensation and also in being paid in already-depreciated Government Stock. The workers in these industries are finding out that the State is at once a clumsy and all-powerful employer, and the other shareholders, the public, for their part, will have a less efficient service than before the war, and will also have to foot the bill. It may be that as these facts become obvious (and the British people are always buying their experience hard), as they become obvious even to the most bigoted or ignorant, a healthy educative process will set in. But we are certainly buying our experience at a very high cost, and we are paying this high cost and at the time of all others when we can least afford to squander our diminished resources.

In our Industrial Charter, which we brought into being as a means of showing how we would grapple with industrial problems, we have said that we shall not repeal the nationalisation of the mines. That is not because we do not think those measures are wrong and foolish, but because no one can undo the harm that has been done. It is easier to break crockery than to mend it. It would be physically impossible to find out all the shareholders or owners and sell their properties back to them, in a damaged condition in most cases. We shall have to do the best we can in the face of the blunder which has been made and which we endeavoured to prevent at every stage.

The climax will be reached in this nationalisation sphere if the Government have the hardihood to nationalise the steel industry which is vital to our whole economic life, particularly to our export trade, and is, at the present moment, a record-breaking model of efficiency under private enterprise. We are assured by Ministers, themselves bitterly divided on the issue, that this wanton blow at British industrial revival will be struck next year. If so, I think you will agree that it should be resisted by every constitutional means at our disposal.

When we turn to the field of social legislation, we are confronted with a fanfare of ridiculous boastings. The Socialists dilate upon the National Insurance Scheme, Family Allowances, improved education, welfare foods, food subsidies and so forth. They point to the benefits flowing to the people from these schemes and particularly to the housewives and children. But there are two facts which, up till quite recently, they have tried to hide. The first is that all these schemes were devised and set in motion in days before the Socialists came into office. They all date from the National Coalition Government of which I was the head. I have worked at national insurance schemes almost all my life and am responsible for several of the largest measures ever passed. The main principles of the new Health Schemes were hammered out in the days of the Coalition Government, before the party and personal malignancy of Mr Bevan plunged health policy into its present confusion.

The Family Allowance Act was passed by the Conservative Caretaker Government. School milk was started in 1934 by a Conservative Parliament. The idea of welfare foods was largely developed by Lord Woolton. The Education Act was the work of Mr Butler. Thus, the only benevolent social policies of which the present Government vaunt themselves were not conceived by them, but were only the legacy which they grasped from a Conservative House of Commons which had a majority of 150 over all other Parties. These facts should be repeated on every occasion by those who wish the truth to be known.

It is of the utmost importance that people should not be misled by reiteration over and over again until it becomes a kind of conviction; and the simple facts have to be brought into place in this busy life we now lead with the facts of the events of all kinds recorded in the newspapers. But listen to Dr Dalton. 'We have mounted', he said in the House of Commons the other night, 'we have mounted without halt or hesitation the great social programme which the electors voted for when our majority was returned. We are entitled to say that the new Britain, represented by this House of Commons, has taken the cost of social security proudly in its stride.' I must admit that Mr Attlee has had a stroke of luck in being able to get rid of Dr Dalton just at the moment when the follies and misfortunes of his financial administration were coming home to roost. But is it not an astonishing fact that a man who has been for nearly three years Chancellor of the Exchequer should say that 'this House of Commons has taken the cost of social service proudly in its stride.'

Does he suppose we do not all know that without the American Loan of a thousand millions, which was largely frittered away by him, without the promise of further munificent American aid, we now read in the newspapers, amounting to over 330 million pounds of sterling a year, it would be quite impossible to maintain our present standards, even of consumption, and equally impossible to avoid large-scale unemployment? As Lord Woolton reminded us yesterday, it was only last week that Mr Herbert Morrison, in a momentary lapse into candour, told us at Liverpool, I think it was, that without American aid we should have to face one or two millions unemployed. And the new Chancellor of the Exchequer has made no secret of our dependence on American dollars, not only for this year but for several years to come.

Now, Ladies and Gentlemen, I greatly admire what the Americans have done and are doing for Europe, and what they are doing for Britain above all other countries, but I cannot feel that we should take their money '*proudly* in our stride', without an effort to free ourselves from the Socialist fallacies, which have deprived us, for the time being, of the power to earn an independent living for ourselves. The effect of the generous help which is given and promised may make us thankful, but surely it should not make us proud. Least of all do I see how any Socialist can be proud of living on the charity of the greatest capitalist, free-enterprise state in the world, whose system of wealth production they deride and denounce on every occasion.

We may indeed ask ourselves how it is that capitalism and free enterprise enable the US not only to support its own vast and varied life and needs, but also to supply these enormous sums to lighten the burdens of others in distress. Nor should it be supposed as you would imagine, to read some of the Left-Wing newspapers, that all Americans are multi-millionaires of Wall Street. If they were all multi-millionaires that would be no reason for condemning a system which has produced such material results. The struggle for life is hard in the US. If prices are high there that is largely because of the immense exportations they are making without return, in relief of other countries, without any corresponding importation. To all this must be added the strong provision they are making for the armed defence of freedom all over the world. We must not be in any doubt as to what is preserving the peace and security of the world at the present time. It is the power and strength of the United States.

All this money which comes to us has to be earned by a mass of ordinary people in America who, by their free choice, for the sake of world causes, voluntarily deny themselves many things they might otherwise consume; and accept the responsibilities of world leadership at heavy cost to themselves. *There* may be found a true reason for national pride. We, too, Ladies and Gentlemen, have a right to be proud of what we did in the war, but not, I think, very proud of what we have done since. We shall be proud once again, when we are earning our own keep and paying our own way.

I now come to the scandal of the present Budget. I have no doubt that Sir Stafford Cripps is trying his best to bring home some sense of reality to the scatter-brained crowd by whom he is surrounded and on whose support he depends. But nothing can excuse the exaction of 3,500 millions in taxes in the third year after the war has been won – three years, three years, three years. When I spoke here 14 months ago – a little more than a year ago, when I spoke here to the Primrose League – I censured an expenditure of 3,000 millions and urged that it should be cut by 500 millions, which should be used as far as possible in relief of taxation to increase incentives for all classes of producers. Actually, the taxation is higher now than at any time in the war. The idea that a nation can tax itself into prosperity is one of the crudest delusions which has ever fuddled the human mind. Taxes will not restore our prosperity, not even if hundreds of thousands of extra officials are added to the Government. There was no reason whatever why such small reliefs as have been given in the present Budget could not have been found by careful economies in the vast flood of money the Socialists pour out. The Conservative Opposition in the House of Commons therefore voted against all the extra taxes which have been imposed, and we shall continue to do so at every stage.

The vast expenditure and consequent burden of taxation is not only a hindrance to national revival, but is one of the main reasons for what is called 'inflation'. This word is freely used, or heard, or listened to by lots of people who do not understand its meaning. It simply means that you get less goods for the money you earn. This carries with it a reduction in the real value of social services, of fixed incomes, savings, and pensions, and is a subtle and insidious way of depriving the people with one hand of what the Socialists pretend they have given them with the other. We do not take the Socialist view, expressed by Mr Greenwood, that money is a meaningless symbol. It is the only practicable way of regulating all the myriad relations and transactions of daily life, and to maintain the stability of money over considerable periods of time is one of the first principles of the Conservative Party.

However we may regard Sir Stafford Cripps' record there is no doubt he has shouldered the main weight of the Government's task. He has a brain which, at any rate, is something to begin with. He has also a conscience which, like the curate's egg, is good in parts. It must have been a pang to him to have to introduce into his first Budget a measure of class hatred like the Capital Levy, which he knows only too well is the sop he had to throw to Cerberus in order to gratify the evil instincts of his supporters, and that he had to do this against his true convictions as I believe, regardless of the effect upon the whole principle of thrift and national saving.

I congratulate you on the success of your Conference. On every side I have heard there has never been a Women's Conservative Conference like this, with such a high standard of speeches. It brings confirmation, if any be needed, both of the vigour and power of our Conservative Party and of the steadily-growing part that women are playing in our counsels.

In many different capacities, whether as candidates for Parliamentary or Municipal Elections, or as agents and organisers in the field, more and more women are ardently rendering service to the Conservative Party and thereby to the country. It is right that this should be so, for women are carrying an ever-heavier share of the burden of our social economic life. Indeed I often feel, and in this I hope to have your agreement, that under the Socialist Government that share has become heavy enough.

I confess that the Socialist attitude to women's labour appears to be the reverse of gallant. We are told that over 5 million labourers, nearly all or mostly men, were last year given reductions of 3½ hours. It would be very difficult to find 5 million women who have had the same experience. While the men are given shorter hours their womenfolk are expected to work even longer hours. They have the queues thrown in. There is a great and necessary part that women must play in many forms of industry, particularly the textile industry. But this should be an addition to our national earning power and not a mere shifting of the burden from the men to the housewives. We have set up a Conservative Committee under the chairmanship of Mr McCorquodale,[1] who won a resounding victory at Epsom, to study the difficulties which face women today and, after hearing evidence and taking advice from all quarters, to guide us on the general policy which our Party should pursue. I am sure you will agree that it is right that this Committee should contain both men and women.

You have, no doubt, often heard the question, 'What can we do to get rid of this Government?' There is one thing that we can all do now, and that is strive to increase the Membership of the Conservative Party by every means in our power. Lord Woolton has told us how numerous were the people who subscribed to his Fund. Thanks to that we now have a Fighting Fund. Not indeed so large as those which the Socialists are able to gather through their political levy, largely from Conservative and Liberal working men, but still it is something to go on, and we hope to increase it. We are now calling for another million. Lord Woolton, and Mr Eden in his speech on Monday night, have opened the Recruiting Campaign for another million – this time not of money but of men and women. We need a million new subscribing members. We must not forget that however good our policy may be we cannot hope to win an Election unless that policy is made known to every voter in the land, and unless there exists a mass of convinced and instructed canvassers who can counter the dreary fallacies which form so much a part of the paraphernalia of the socialist Utopia.

To do this we must have a live and active organisation in every Constituency. In our political struggle nothing is more important than canvassing. There is no way so sure or certain of bringing our message right into the homes of the people as the pleasant, friendly contact, man to man, or woman to woman. So I appeal to you to develop your canvassing organisations, both

---

[1] Malcolm Stewart McCorquodale, 1901–71. MP (Nat. Cons.) for Yorkshire, Sowerby Div., 1931–45; (Cons.) for Epsom, 1947–55. Parliamentary Private Secretary to President of the Board of Trade, 1939; to Minister of Labour, 1942–5. Baron, 1955.

as a means of recruiting new members in this campaign that has just begun, and as the most effective weapon to ensure the success of our candidates when the momentous election comes and when the Conservative Party will have the opportunity of saving the country. The time has come – indeed it is overdue – when this country needs a new Parliament and a new approach to solve our national problems. The Conservative Party, if called on by the electors, will form a Government devoid of Party prejudices and working with single-minded purpose to restore our national prosperity and the true greatness of our country. Let all be ready when the hour strikes; let all work tirelessly till the hour strikes and thus render true service not to a Party but to the island home we love so well.

Government and Opposition meeting: minutes
(Churchill papers, 2/38)

22 April 1948　　　　　　　　　　　　　　　　　　　Lord President's Room
Confidential　　　　　　　　　　　　　　　　　　　　House of Commons
5.20 p.m.

COMMUNIST VIEWS ON THE BBC

1. At the previous meeting on 25th February,[1] Lord Simon had been invited to review the facts and consider the points which had been raised with a view to further discussion with the Parties.

Lord Simon began by thanking the Parties for the criticisms they had made and assuring them that the Governors would at all times be ready carefully to investigate reasonable criticisms. They had given full consideration to the points raised as regards Communism and recognised that it was a legitimate point of criticism that Communist views had perhaps in some cases been given undo prominence, though clearly the Governors could not rule out all reference to Communism. At the request of the Governors the Director-General had had talks with leading members of the BBC staff and had brought to their notice the need for keeping a careful check in this matter. The Governors had arranged for the Director-General to report to them on this matter once a month.

Mr Churchill stressed that an unfair and undue proportion of broadcasting time had, in the past, been taken up by reports of Communist activities. As an example, he mentioned a news item concerning Mr Pollitt's comment on certain Parliamentary matters when Mr Pollitt himself had not even been present in the House. He pointed out that the Communists were enemies of the country and that they were an unconstitutional party; and he thought that

[1] See minutes reproduced above (pp. 979–82).

the BBC's desire for tolerance of their views rested on a misunderstanding of the nature of the Communist creed. It was not to be expected, if the Communists themselves were in control, that any kind of freedom of expression would be tolerated. His fear was that a nest of Communist sympathisers within the BBC were seeking to organise the propagation of these views.

The Lord President agreed with Mr Churchill that care should be taken to ensure that no disproportionate time on the air was given to the reporting of Communist views, and that, in deciding what was 'proportionate', the numerical weakness of the Communists in the country and in Parliament should be remembered. He agreed, however, that in so far as there was a genuine feeling to be expressed, the BBC would be wrong in suppressing it entirely.

It was agreed that the BBC, in the light of this discussion, would continue to maintain a careful check on the amount of publicity which Communist views obtained on the air.

COMMUNISTS WITHIN THE BBC

2. Mr Churchill asked what action had been taken to discover and prevent Communist infiltration into the staff of the BBC.

Lord Simon explained that for ten years the Corporation had taken great care in the selection of its staff, with this danger in mind, and he was satisfied that no one was at present employed who could justifiably be dismissed by the use of a similar procedure to that which had recently been instituted in the Civil Service. To justify dismissal, there had to be evidence of a person's actual influence on talks or other broadcast features, and where this had been discovered, action had, in fact, been taken. He would be glad to know if any other lines of action could be suggested.

The Director-General added that if persons who, on admission to the staff, had been acceptable, later adopted undesirable political views, that generally became known. He emphasised that the Corporation attached such importance to complete impartiality that if it became apparent that an employee's political views would urge him to prejudice this standard, suitable action would be taken, even though no actual offence had, in fact, been committed. He confirmed that 'partiality' in this respect would apply to the favouring of the views of any party whatsoever, in relation, of course, to the job which the individual concerned was doing. A recent investigation into references to Communists which had been made on the air had shown that at least one reference had been made by every member of the news staff – a proof that there was no suspicious concentration on one or two individuals.

Mr Churchill reiterated the danger of Communism being given a publicity which only the BBC could give, and which it would never obtain through the representative institutions of the State. He was glad to note the counter-measures which Lord Simon and the Director General had described, but he warned the meeting to remember that the Communists had no respect for the truth or tolerance of any kind. He hoped that the Director General would be willing to see four Czechs[1] whom he had met, who had recently escaped from Czechoslovakia and who ought to be given a chance of putting forward their views on the recent events in their country, particularly as similar views about the Communist danger were widely held here.

Sir William Haley agreed to do this.

BROADCASTS ON CURRENT LEGISLATION

3. The Lord President said that at the last meeting the BBC had asked for a modification of the rules regarding broadcast references to matters which were the subject of current legislation. There were now two points for decision:
  (i) Should the proposed new clause be agreed; and
  (ii) If so, should it run for an experimental period of, say, six months or until the next annual review.

He read the following extract from a letter which had been received from the Director-General explaining the reasons which had led the Corporation to suggest the new clause:

> Our aim is not in any way to be controversial or to seek to be an alternative debating forum to Parliament when a Bill is before the House. From the time it is tabled until it finally reaches the Statute Book there is a very long period, and we do feel that it should be possible for explanatory and impartial surveys of the issues involved in such Bills to be broadcast. Quite apart from the more controversial Bills, there is a considerable body of legislation such as the Children's Bill, the Criminal Justice Bill, the Matrimonial Causes Bill, in which discussion is not along Party lines.
>
> In broadcasting factual statements and explanatory and impartial surveys of the issues of legislation, we would in no way be seeking to persuade but merely to inform our listeners. No MPs would be used. It is perhaps worth pointing out that it was the BBC itself that proposed the original clause. The intention then was merely to avoid broadcast controversy over legislation

---

[1] Julius Firt, 1897–1979. Born in Sedlčany, Austria-Hungary. Member (Nat. Soc.), Provisional National Assembly, 1945–6; Member (Nat. Soc.), Constituent National Assembly, 1946–8.

Vladimir Josef Krajina, 1905–93. Born in Slavonice, Austria-Hungary. Educated at Charles University, Prague. Leader of Czech underground resistance. Member (Dem. Soc.) Czech Parliament, 1945–9. Migrated to Canada when the Czech Government was taken over by Communists in 1949.

Sergej Ingr, 1894–1956. CO, 16th Bde, Czechoslovakian Army, 1933–5. Deputy GOC, III Corps, 1936–8; GOC, 1937. C-in-C, Czechoslovakian Forces, France, 1939; Armed Forces, 1944–5. Minister, National Defence, 1940–4.

Jaroslav Stransky, 1884–1973. Born in Brno, Austria-Hungary. Educated at Charles University, Prague. Member (Nat. Dem.), Revolutionary National Assembly, 1918–20; Member (Nat. Dem.), National Assembly of Czechoslovak Republic, 1920–1; Member (Nat. Soc.), National Assembly of the Czechoslovak Republic, 1929–38. Minister of Justice, Czechoslovak Government-in-Exile, 1941–5. Member (Nat. Soc.), Provisional National Assembly, 1945–6; Member (Nat. Soc.), Constituent National Assembly, 1946–8. Minister of Justice, 1945. Deputy PM, 1945–6. Minister of Education, 1946–8.

simultaneously with its being debated in Parliament. It was never intended to exclude factual, objective statements. As a matter of fact we have all along included such explanatory and impartial surveys both in our Schools programmes and in talks, and it was merely because we realised that such a practice was against the strict interpretation of the clause as it stands that we raised the matter.

The Lord President said he was a little worried about what seemed to be the suggestion that under the proposed new arrangement straight talks should be given on subjects which were being currently debated in Parliament, as distinct from incidental broadcast references to them.

Mr Brendan Bracken sympathised with the BBC's request, since if all reference to these subjects on the air were to be forbidden, the BBC would be at an unfair disadvantage compared with the newspapers.

Mr Churchill demurred from this view on the grounds that it was wrong to compare the BBC, which was a monopoly and reached almost everybody, with individual newspapers which had a more limited public, were subject to competition and often had known party affiliations. It was, moreover, impossible to give even 'factual' statements without at the same time propagating a certain view. The selection of certain facts from among the large number available was the most effective method of propaganda.

The Director-General explained that the original rule governing the BBC's activities in this field had been laid down during the war by the Corporation itself. It had been thought necessary in order to protect the BBC after they had been asked to put on a Ministerial broadcast on a Bill then before Parliament. The wording agreed in the existing Aide-Memoire had, however, proved to be unduly restrictive and if strictly interpreted might perhaps be regarded as inconsistent with some broadcasts which were already being given e.g. during talks to schools. He agreed that it was necessary at all costs to avoid the danger of the BBC becoming a second forum for debate on matters currently before Parliament, but he pointed out that, if no discussion at all on a Bill was to be allowed until it became law, this might involve two years' silence.

Mr Churchill thought this particular disadvantage was being overrated since once the main initial debate in Parliament was over some relaxation of the rule could be allowed. He suggested that it would be preferable to let the existing arrangements stand, particularly as there had been, so far, no complaint against the BBC on this score. He would like to have the opportunity of hearing certain of the broadcasts concerned, before agreeing to any alteration.

The Lord President agreed that it was difficult to tell, without specific examples, whether broadcasts on matters before Parliament were, in fact, in danger of being controversial.

Lord Simon undertook to report the views of the meeting to the Governors and to take a later opportunity, if necessary, of making further representations to the Government and the Opposition, if that was thought necessary.

'THE WEEK IN WESTMINSTER'

4. Mr Churchill asked what method of selection was used for speakers in 'The Week in Westminster', and suggested that the recent trouble which had arisen between Mr Emrys Hughes,[1] MP, and Mr Shinwell, as a result of statements made in one of these broadcasts, was an indication that the speakers were not always chosen on the best advice.

The Director-General explained that speakers for the 'Week in Westminster' were chosen from the political parties on the same ratio as political broadcasts were allocated, and that the BBC consulted with senior people in the Parties, including officials, about the choice of speakers.

Mr Churchill suggested that it would be as well for the BBC to take the views of the Party Whips on the names which were put forward. They were in the best position to know whether the speakers suggested could be relied on to give a reasonable account.

The Lord President reminded the meeting that the criticism used to be made when the Whips had had a say in the choice of speakers that only 'yes men' were allowed on the air, and the Director-General confirmed this, with reference to the experience of 1943–44.

Mr Churchill pointed out that war conditions made some restrictions essential; and it was not, in any case, suggested that the Whips should do more than give their advice.

Lord Simon thought that there was something to be said for a venturesome attitude in this matter, but he agreed that there was no harm in taking the advice of the Whips about new candidates for this series of broadcasts.

General Lord Ismay to Winston S. Churchill
(Churchill papers, 4/208)

22 April 1948

My dear Mr Churchill,

I send you herewith the first instalment of notes on our intervention in Greece. Their purpose is:

    (a) To remind you of the general background: and
    (b) To link up your minutes and telegrams on the subject.

Would you let me know whether this is in any way helpful and the sort of

---

[1] Emrys Hughes, 1894–1969. Educated at City of Leeds Training College. Married, 1924, Nan Hardie (d. 1947). Editor, *Forward*, 1931–46. MP (Lab.) for South Ayrshire, 1946–69. Publications include *Winston Churchill in War and Peace* (1950).

thing you want. If so, I will press on with the rest of the story: but I am anxious not to waste your time by presenting my material in the wrong form.

Winston S. Churchill to General Lord Ismay
(Churchill papers, 4/208)

23 April 1948

My dear Pug,

Thank you so much for your note on intervention in Greece. Have you read the relevant parts of De Guingand's[1] book, and Professor Falls',[2] which contain many challenges to our work based on ignorance or impudence, or both? There is also a dull book about Wavell.[3]

Where your note stops there come a very important series of questionings by me and the War Cabinet before the final plunge was taken to go to Greece. I have not got with me at present the reassuring telegrams which were sent from Eden, Dill, and Wavell.

It is also important to establish the facts about the left flank in the Desert at Benghazi and towards the south of Agheils. We have, I am sure, a telegram from Wavell detailing the measures he had taken to make it secure. In addition Eden tells me that Wavell and Dill went up there personally and spent two days on the spot going into the matter with the Commanders (I presume O'Connor[4] and Neame[5]). Eden offered to go with them but they said it was purely a military affair and he would be fully occupied in Cairo.

---

[1] Francis Wilfred de Guingand, 1900–79. Known as 'Freddie'. Educated at Ampleforth College and RMC, Sandhurst. Military Assistant to Secretaries of State for War, 1933–6, 1939–40. Joint Planning Staff, GHQ Middle East, Cairo, 1940–2. Director, Military Intelligence, Middle East, 1942. Brig. General Staff (Operations), 8th Army, 1942–4. CoS to Gen. Bernard Montgomery, 1942–5; 21st Army Group, 1944–5. KBE, 1944. LOM, 1945. Retired, 1946. Author of *Operation Victory* (1947), *African Assignment* (1953), *Generals at War* (1964) and *From Brass Hat to Bowler Hat: Sir Francis de Guingand* (1979).

[2] Cyril Bentham Falls, 1888–1971. Wrote several volumes of the British Official *History of the Great War*, 1923–39. Military Correspondent, *The Times*, 1939–45. Chichele Prof. of the History of War, Oxford University, 1946–53. Author of *The Nature of Modern Warfare* (1941), *Ordeal by Battle* (1943) and *The Second World War: A Short History* (1948).

[3] Probably Robert John Collins, *Lord Wavell, 1883–1941, A Military Biography* (London, 1948).

[4] Richard Nugent O'Connor, 1889–1981. On active service in France and Italy, 1914–18 (despatches nine times, MC, DSO and bar). Military Governor of Jerusalem, 1938–9 (despatches). GOC 7th Div., 1939; 6th Div., 1939–40; Western Desert Force, 1940; XIII Corps, 1940–1; British troops in Egypt, 1941. CB, 1940. KCB, 1941. POW (Italy), 1941–3 (escaped). Cdr, VIII Corps, France, 1944 (despatches). Adjutant-General to the Forces, 1946–7. ADC-General to the King, 1946–8. GCB, 1947. KT, 1971.

[5] Philip Neame, 1888–1978. On active service, Royal Engineers, 1914–18 (VC, DSO, despatches five times). Published *German Strategy in the Great War* (1923). Instructor, Staff College Camberley, 1919–23. Gold Medal, British Olympic Sporting Rifle Team, France, 1924. Brig. General Staff, Eastern Command, 1934–8. Commandant, Royal Military Academy Woolwich, 1938–9. CB, 1939. Deputy CoS BEF, 1939 to Feb. 1940. GOC 4th Indian Infantry Div., 1940; Palestine and Trans-Jordan, 1940–1; Cyrenaica, 1941; Channel Islands, 1945–7. Military Governor, Cyrenaica, 1941. POW (Italy), Apr. 1941–3 (escaped). Lt-Governor, Guernsey, 1945–53. KBE, 1946. Retired, 1947.

The next thing that happened was that Wavell withdrew the experienced Australian Division and replaced it by a newly-trained Division. He sent back the remaining brigade of the 7th Armoured Division, wearing out its tanks by a 400-mile trek back to Cairo. He could easily have left these tanks in situ and refreshed their tired crews from his large surplus of tank men at the base. The 7th Armoured Division wore out its tanks in going home to be refitted, and did not come into action for nearly five months. Its tanks had enough kick in them to have beaten Rommel instead of trekking home. It was replaced by the 2nd Armoured Division, which was new to the game. These are explanations of why our left flank in the Desert was bashed in, with immense resulting disaster.

Another matter which has to be thrashed out is the port of Benghazi. It was always urged by me and agreed by the Chiefs of Staff that Benghazi should be made a main base, with full air protection, and that the 400-mile route to Cairo, which wore out all our transport, should be dropped. But quite soon in the Minutes you will see that Benghazi Port is considered to be unusable because of the destruction wrought by the enemy. However, only a few weeks later, you notice that when the Germans got it back it began to function as a most important naval base. This certainly requires examination.

You must understand that it is no part of my plan to be needlessly unkind to the men we chose at the time, who no doubt did their best.

Winston S. Churchill to Major-General Sir Ian Jacob[1]
(Churchill papers, 2/67)

25 April 1948

My dear Jacob,

I was visited the other day by some Czechs – Mr Firt, Mr Krajina, General Ingr and Mr Stransky. I enclose a note of their particulars. They impressed me very much and they spoke to me, amongst other things, about the question of the Czechoslovak broadcasts by the BBC. They told me that the BBC is listened to now in Czechoslovakia even more than during the war, but that there is a feeling that the best use of this great opportunity is not being made.

I spoke to Sir William Haley about this matter at the Conference between Parties which he attended last Thursday and he said he saw no reason why a delegation of these Czechs should not be received at the BBC. This would please and satisfy them very much. I thought I would let you know about all this.[2]

[1] Edward Ian Claud Jacob, 1899–1993. 2nd Lt, Royal Engineers, 1918. Military Asst Secretary, Committee of Imperial Defence, 1938. Lt-Col., 1939; Col., 1943. Military Asst Secretary to the War Cabinet, 1939–45. CBE, 1942. Retired with rank of Lt-Gen., 1946. Knighted, 1946. Controller, European Services, BBC, 1946–7; Director of Overseas Services, 1947–51; Director-General, 1952–60. Chief Staff Officer to Minister of Defence, and Deputy Secretary to Cabinet, 1952.

[2] Jacob replied on Apr. 27: 'Thank you very much for your letter of April 25th telling me of your talk

Winston S. Churchill to Ernest Bevin
(*Churchill papers, 2/67*)

25 April 1948

My dear Foreign Secretary,

I was visited the other day by four Czechs, Mr Firt, Mr Krajina, General Ingr and Mr Stransky. I enclose a note of their particulars. I think it might be well if they had a chance to put their case to an all-Party meeting in the House of Commons, as was done in the case of M Mikolajczyk.

If you think this would be a good thing I will ask our Whips to talk to yours about it.[1]

Winston S. Churchill to Lewis Douglas
(*Churchill papers, 2/67*)

25 April 1948

My dear Lew,

I was visited the other day by some Czechs – Mr Firt, Mr Krajina, General Ingr and Mr Stransky. I enclose a note of their particulars.

They wonder whether you would be good enough to receive a delegation of Czechs, who would raise with you various points about the condition of Czech refugees in the American zone of Germany, the facilitating of contacts between Czechs abroad (apparently it is very difficult for them to communicate with those in the American zone and vice versa), the possibilities of radio propaganda to Czechoslovakia, and matters of that kind.

I was much impressed with these four Czech refugees and by their story, and I said I would approach you on their behalf.[2]

---

with Mr Firt, and Mr Krajina, General Ingr and Mr Stransky. We have already been in touch with two of these men, and I will pursue your suggestion. We are doing our utmost to take full advantage of the opportunity presented to our Czech Service by the present situation, and I am always ready to hear suggestions which may lead to an improvement.'

[1] Bevin replied on Apr. 26: 'Thank you for your letter of the 25th April, suggesting that four Czechs, Mr Firt, Mr Krajina, General Ingr and Mr Stransky, might be given an opportunity of addressing an all-Party meeting in the House of Commons. I agree that this is a good idea, and I have warned our Whips that yours will be getting into touch with them to make the necessary arrangements.'

[2] Douglas replied on Apr. 26: 'Thank you so much for your note of April 25. I shall be delighted to receive the delegation of Czechs and to discuss any points which they might like to raise. My secretary will call yours to find out how we may reach the members of the delegation so as to arrange for an appointment.'

Winston S. Churchill: speech
('Winston S. Churchill, His Complete Speeches', volume 7, pages 7632–3)

26 April 1948 House of Commons

MOTION OF CONGRATULATIONS TO THEIR MAJESTIES ON THEIR SILVER WEDDING

I rise to associate most cordially with the Motion of the Prime Minister the Conservative Party, and those who constitute what is called His Majesty's Opposition. I feel sure that we, in all parts of the House, have appreciated the dignity and choice of terms in which the Prime Minister has commended this Motion to the House – how many points he has rested on which command the assent not only of all minds, but of all hearts. There is little which I wish to add to what he has said. Certainly, in these days, it has been a great help and inspiration to the whole people to see another example of a happy British home, of family life maintained, in the full glare of publicity which falls upon exalted personages, for a quarter of a century in such a manner as to warm all decent hearts and to give us all a feeling of the great, enduring strength of human relationships and of the institutions of civilised and Christian societies.

This silver wedding celebration has given an opportunity for spontaneous, generous emotions by millions of our people from all parts of the country. They have crowded the streets and have cheered the figures of the Sovereign and his Consort. It has all been a spontaneous and, indeed, an irresistible impulse of a wholly unselfish character springing from the hearts of our people. The reign of the King and Queen is less than ten years, but in that period they have had a hard time. They have had to pass through convulsions and ordeals unequalled even in the whole sixty years of the Imperial splendour of Queen Victoria, and equal stresses of mind have fallen upon them. In an unassuming and simple manner they have shared the perils, sorrows and anxieties of the whole people and of all the Commonwealth beyond the sea, and now at least they have found that the great perils of the late war are over and we have entered a period of peace.

The Prime Minister has been right to dwell upon these matters and he has also been right in proposing that Privy Councillors representative of all parties should present an Address to the Crown. There is only one point in his speech which I would venture to mention. He spoke of the Golden Wedding which he hoped would be celebrated when the dark fear and horror of war will be for ever banished from the world. Although all of us will not see it, that is a hope which we all cherish and share.

April 1948

Winston S. Churchill to Sir Stafford Cripps
(Churchill papers, 2/376)

26 April 1948

My dear Stafford,

Thank you very much for your letter and courtesy. I will certainly write to the Turkish firm and accept their gift, which will avoid hurting their feelings. I have no intention of selling the watch — indeed it may well rest here with a number of others when this place[1] is handed over to the National Trust.

I am sure the concession you have made is right and fair. There are several more trifling gifts pending, of which I attach a separate note; and of course I may be given something in Oslo when I receive my degree. In that case I will write to you.

I am so sorry you are not coming to the Hague. I should have liked to lift this whole business above our Party politics and try to make a real brotherhood of Europe, overriding all national, class and Party frontiers. But I quite understand your difficulties, especially when you have already such a heavy burden to carry.

Lord Camrose to Winston S. Churchill
(Churchill papers, 4/57)

29 April 1948

Dear Winston,

The Printer's account is not worth dividing, and we are sending the full amount direct to the Chiswick Press.

We are sending you today cheque for £35,000, being payment due to you on the delivery of Volume II. The payment to the Trustees is due on the 1st June, but we shall probably anticipate this date.

The proofs have been delivered to all the people concerned and we now await their remittance.

---

[1] Chartwell.

Winston S. Churchill: speech
('Winston S. Churchill, His Complete Speeches', volume 7, pages 7633–5)

30 April 1948 Albert Hall, London
Primrose League

TOWARDS A NEW PARLIAMENT

We live in grave and anxious times, and there can be no one here who does not feel his responsibility towards the State at this juncture. The Primrose League is not necessarily a party organisation. It has principles to which it expects parties to conform and which it holds to whatever parties may do. The League supports them in their friendship with the United States, in their attitude towards Soviet aggression, and in their policy for a United Europe or Western Europe, in regard to which an important conference is taking place in London. We are not going to quarrel with them about where these ideas originated; we are committed to give them support when they move forward upon lines which we believe are in the main interests of our island.

We also follow with the Socialist Government in their resistance to Communism and Communists in all their varieties – and there are many different species and shades, from pale pink to darkest carmine – and we have very little doubt that nothing but overwhelming external force would impose that odious system upon this country. On the other hand, I hope you will not mind my saying that we regret that the Socialists have thrown away the great opportunity, and even the sacred trust, which was confided to them at the time of the General Election in 1945. They have thrown away their opportunity and failed in their duty because, first of all, they set party before country. They provoked and embittered the class war, they squandered the resources of the nation, and they have restricted and hampered its energies and initiative. In all this they have deserved ill of our generation. They have made a quite definite contribution to the loss by Great Britain of her place in the world, which will only be regained by long and hard efforts. While these Socialist Ministers are boasting of their achievements and of all the benefits they have given to the public – of which the public are not always conscious from day to day – they seem to forget that they live on the charity of the greatest capitalist free enterprise State in the world, the United States. I have often spoken to you in the country upon these subjects, and so have many of my colleagues who maintain the fight in the House of Commons and House of Lords. One must never be afraid or ashamed of ramming home a point. It is reiteration which is important. One must never be shy of pressing home the great points of public controversy which make their appeal to the common sense and conscience of the nation.

Now our first and most vital need is a new Parliament. The result of the Southwark by-election today[1] alone indicates that the nation is definitely transferring its allegiance to the Conservative Party. Similar results spread all over the country would show that a heavy burden of responsibility will fall upon us. The consequences of the approaching General Election, whenever it may come – and it cannot be indefinitely delayed – are momentous. I do not remember in my long life any political occasion which has been so fraught with momentous consequences. If we are not able on that occasion to produce a substantial definite Conservative majority, it is not merely our place in the world or our local or individual prosperity which will be affected, but the actual power of this island to maintain its population on anything like the existing scale.

Great responsibility rests upon the Conservative Party not to fail the country, and they can only face that responsibility if at all times they put general and national interests first in their thoughts and allow no sectional issues of class or purely party interests to deflect them from their main duty. It is no exaggeration to say that at the present time the Conservative interest harmonises completely with the need of the nation, and it is high time that a Government was installed in power which had behind it a Parliament, not based on the principles of class war and party bitterness, but seeking to deal with the difficult problems of the time in accordance with truth and good faith. There is the need of intense exertion by everyone in the political field. No one should waste a day. No one should allow a day to pass without endeavouring to bring his or her personal influence to bear upon some other British citizen in order that we may be worthy of the burden that may come to us in order that the new Parliament may arm us with the necessary support.

[. . .]

---

[1] Roy Jenkins (Lab.) won with 65% of the vote, defeating the Conservative candidate J. M. Greenward.

May
1948

John Colville: diary
('The Fringes of Power', pages 623–4)

2 May 1948

Six weeks of warmth and sunshine have given way to cold and rain. Christopher had tummy trouble; Mary a vile carbuncle which gave her great pain. In the evening we went to Winston's private cinema, saw an exceptionally good film called *To Be Or Not To Be*, and dined most agreeably. Winston, who had been busy all day painting a red lily against the background of a black buddha, switched from art to Operation 'Tiger'* and rather to my embarrassment told in great detail the story of my trouble with Monty when he took me out to Germany for the crossing of the Rhine in March 1945. He was scathing about Monty's self-advertising stunts and said he presumed British soldiers would soon have to be called 'Monties' instead of 'Tommies'. Speaking of the Anglo-American disputes over the question of a Second Front in the Cotentin in 1942, Winston said, 'No lover ever studied every whim of his mistress as I did those of President Roosevelt.'

* Transport of tanks for Wavell's army through the Mediterranean in 1941.

European conference at The Hague: notes on planning
(Churchill papers, 2/21)

4 May 1948

COMPOSITION

It is proposed to invite leading European personalities of all shades of democratic political opinion and representative figures from the Churches, the Trade Unions, Industry, the Universities, Art, Literature, the Professions, etc.

PURPOSE

The object of the Conference will be:
- (a) To affirm the urgent need for close and effective unity among the peoples of Europe,
- (b) To demonstrate the wide-spread support which already exists for this idea,
- (c) To discuss the first practical steps which could be taken towards the realization of this aim,
- (d) To launch an international educational campaign to popularize the idea.

It will be emphasized that the ultimate aim is the unity of all Europe. However, owing to present political conditions in Eastern Europe and Spain, it will doubtless only be possible to obtain a representative attendance from the 'Marshall' countries, with the possible addition of Czechoslovakia and Finland.

COMMITTEES

The discussions of the Conference will, for the most part, be conducted in three Committees:
- (a) Political,
- (b) Economic and Social, and
- (c) Cultural and Moral.

Reports to be submitted to these Committees are in the course of preparation by groups in different countries, under the direction of all-Party Committees in Britain, France, Belgium, Holland, Italy and Switzerland.

AGREEMENTS IN HOLLAND

The Conference has the full support of the Netherlands Government which proposes to give an official Reception on the opening night to all persons attending the Conference. In addition the Netherlands Government has made available for the Conference the historic Ridderzaal in the Parliament Buildings, which is normally reserved for Joint Sessions of the two Houses of Parliament. Princess Juliana and Prince Bernhardt have indicated their desire to give a Reception at the Royal Palace on the closing night of the Conference.

During the course of the Conference it is proposed to hold a Mass Meeting in the Stadium at Amsterdam.

The expenses of the Conference will be met from a Fund which is being raised among supporters of the cause in Holland. £10,000 has already been subscribed and up to a further £10,000 is assured.

May 1948

INITIAL ACCEPTANCES

In order to assure a wide basis of political support, advance invitations have been addressed to leading political figures in the principal countries of Western Europe. The list of those who have so far accepted to attend includes:

Dr Beel (Prime Minister of the Netherlands).
M Leon Blum.
M Joyaux[1] (President of the French CGT – Force Ouvrière).
Signor La Malfa[2] (Chairman of the Finance Commission of the Italian Chamber of Deputies).
M Motz[3] (Leader of the Belgian Liberal Party).
M Paul Reynaud.
Professor Rivet[4] (Socialist Deputy and Chairman of the large all-Party European group in the French Parliament).
Signor Ruini[5] (Chairman of the Parliamentary Commission responsible for drawing up the new Italian Constitution).
Count Sforza.[6]
Signor Silone[7] (Prominent Member of the Italian Socialist Party).

---

[1] Léon Jouhaux, 1879–1954. Union Representative to the French General Confederation of Labour, 1906; Interim Treasurer, 1909; Secretary-General, 1909–47. Signatory, Matignon Agreement, 1936. Founding Member and President, General Confederation of Labour – Workers' Force, 1948. Nobel Peace Prize, 1951.

[2] Ugo la Malfa, 1903–79. Educated at Ca' Foscari University of Venice. Italian Minister of Transport, 1945. Minister of Reconstruction, 1945. Member, Constituent Assembly of the Italian Republic, 1946–8. Minister of Foreign Trade, 1946. Member, Legislature of the Italian Republic, 1948–79. Minister without Portfolio, 1950–1. Minister of Foreign Trade, 1951–3. Minister of the Budget, 1962–3. Vice-President, Council of Ministers, 1974–6, 1979. Minister of Budget and Economic Planning, 1979.

[3] Roger Jean Henri Motz, 1904–64. Born in Schaarbeek. Senator (Lib.) for Brabant, 1946. Minister of Information, Belgian Government-in-Exile, WWII; of Economics, 1958; of State, 1958–64. Honorary President, Belgian Liberal Party, 1945–53, 1958–61. President, Liberal International, 1952–8.

[4] Paul Rivet, 1876–1958. Educated at Military Medical School, Lyon. Founding member, Watchfulness Committee of Antifascist Intellectuals, 1934. Founded Musée de l'Homme, Paris, 1937. Member (French Section of the Workers' International: SFIO), National Constituent Assembly, 1945–6; Member (SFIO), National Assembly, 1946–51. Wrote *Les Origines de l'homme Américain* (1943).

[5] Bartolomeo Ruini, 1877–1970. Also known as 'Meuccio'. Educated at University of Bologna. Under-Secretary, Italian Ministry of Industry, Trade, and Labour, 1919–20. Member, XXV Legislature of the Kingdom of Italy, 1920–1. Minister of the Colonies, 1920. Minister of Reconstruction of Lands Freed by the Enemy, 1945. Member, Constituent Assembly of the Italian Republic, 1946–8. President, Commission for the Constitution, 1946–8. President, Senate of the Italian Republic, 1953. Senator of the Italian Republic, 1963–70.

[6] Carlo Sforza, 1873–1952. Italian Count and anti-Fascist politician who fled to France in 1927, then moved to the US in 1940. In 1943 he returned to Italy, refusing to join the Badoglio Government unless King Victor Emmanuel (whom he called the 'Pétain of Italy') abdicated. Joined Cabinet, April 1944. President of Italy's preliminary parliamentary assembly, Sep. 1945.

[7] Ignazio Silone, 1900–78. Born in Pescina dei Marsi, Italy. Member, Central Committee, Italian Communist Party, 1921–9. Left Communist Party, 1930. Member, Executive Committee, Italian Socialist Party, 1941–7. Married, 1944, Darina Laracy. President, Italian Pen Club, 1945–59. Member, Italian Constituent Assembly, 1946–8. Publications include *Fascism: Its Origins and Growth* (1934), *Mr Aristotle* (1935), *The School for Dictators* (1938), and several novels and plays.

M Spaak.[1]
M Teitgen[2] (French Minister of Defence).
M Van Zeeland.
A representative of the Vatican (whom the Pope proposes to designate).
Leading figures in Britain from the Conservative and Liberal Parties, the Churches, the Universities, etc.

EUROPEAN YOUTH RALLY

The Conference is to be followed by a European Youth Rally in Belgium, to be attended by several thousand young people from as many European countries as possible. This project has the strong support of M Spaak and the Belgian Government, which has agreed to provide free railway transport inside Belgium, the necessary camping facilities and to meet the entire cost of the feeding and living expenses of those attending the Rally.

ORGANIZING COMMITTEE

The Hague Conference and the European Youth Rally are being organized by the Joint International Committee of the Movements for European Unity. This Committee was formed last December and is composed of representatives of the Conseil Français pour L'Europe Unie (an all-Party French Committee under the chairmanship of M Herriot), the European Economic League (an international organization composed of prominent European economists under the chairmanship of M Van Zeeland), the Union Européenne des Federalistes (an international movement to which federalist societies in most European countries are affiliated, under the chairmanship of Dr Brugmans[3]) and the United Europe Movement (Chairman, Mr Churchill). Conversations are in progress with a view to including also representatives of the United Socialist States of Europe Society, the European Parliamentary Union, and the Italian European Coordinating Committee.

---

[1] Paul-Henri Spaak, 1899–1972. Belgian Minister of Foreign Affairs and Trade, 1936–8. PM, May 1938 to Feb. 1939. Minister of Foreign Affairs, Sep. 1939 to Aug. 1949 (in London, 1940–5), 1954–7. PM, 1947–9. Deputy PM, Minister of Foreign Affairs and African Affairs, 1961–6.

[2] Pierre-Henri Teitgen, 1908-97. French Minister of Information, 1944; of Justice, 1945–6; of Defence, 1947–8; of Overseas Territories, 1950. Member, National Assembly, 1945–58. Deputy PM, 1947–8, 1953–4. President, Christian Democratic Party, 1952–6. Member, European Court of Human Rights, 1976.

[3] Hendrik Brugmans, 1906–97. Born in Amsterdam. Educated at University of Amsterdam and Sorbonne, Paris. Founding Member and President, Union of European Federalists, 1947–9. Rector, College of Europe, Bruges, 1950–72. Charlemagne Prize, 1951.

May 1948   1037

Winston S. Churchill: speech
('Winston S. Churchill, His Complete Speeches', volume 7, pages 7635–9)

7 May 1948   The Hague

THE CONGRESS OF EUROPE

Since I spoke on this subject at Zürich in 1946, and since our British United Europe Movement was launched in January 1947, events have carried our affairs beyond our expectations. This cause was obviously either vital or merely academic. If it was academic, it would wither by the wayside; but if it was the vital need of Europe and the world in this dark hour, then the spark would start a fire which would glow brighter and stronger in the hearts and the minds of men and women in many lands. This is what has actually happened. Great governments have banded themselves together with all their executive power. The mighty republic of the United States has espoused the Marshall Plan. Sixteen European States are now associated for economic purposes; five have entered into close economic and military relationship. We hope that this nucleus will in due course be joined by the peoples of Scandinavia, and of the Iberian peninsula, as well as by Italy, who should now resume her full place in the comity of nations. All who have worked and tried their best and especially Ministers in responsible office – we must not forget what their difficulties are – like Mr Bevin, M Bidault, M Spaak, and General Marshall and others, have a right to feel content with the progress made and proud of what they have done.

This is not a movement of parties but a movement of peoples. There is no room for jealousies. If there is rivalry of parties, let it be to see which one will distinguish itself the most for the common cause. No one can suppose that Europe can be united on any party or sectional basis, any more than any one nation can assert an overweening predominance. It must be all for all. Europe can only be united by the heart-felt wish and vehement expression of the great majority of all the peoples in all the parties in all the freedom-loving countries, no matter where they dwell or how they vote.

We need not waste our time in disputes about who originated this idea of United Europe. There are many valid modern patents. There are many famous names associated with the revival and presentation of this idea, but we may all, I think, yield our pretensions to Henry of Navarre,[1] King of France, who, with his great Minister Sully,[2] between the years 1600 and 1607, laboured

---

[1] Henry of Bourbon, 1553–1610. Prince de Bearn, 1555–72. King (Henry III) of Navarre, 1572–89; (Henry IV) of France, 1589–1610. Renounced Protestantism and converted to Roman Catholicism, 1593.

[2] Maximilien de Béthune, 1560–1641. Close friend and counsellor of King Henry IV of France. Grand Master of Artillery, 1601–10. Duke of Sully, 1606. Famous for his 'Great Design' for a European confederation, or 'Christian Republic', published in his Économies royales (1638).

to set up a permanent committee representing the fifteen – now we are sixteen – leading Christian States of Europe. This body was to act as an arbitrator on all questions concerning religious conflict, national frontiers, internal disturbance, and common action against any danger from the East, which in those days meant the Turks. This he called 'The Grand Design'. After this long passage of time we are the servants of the Grand Design.

This Congress has brought together leaders of thought and action from all the free countries of Europe. Statesmen of all political parties, leading figures from all the Churches, eminent writers, leaders of the professions, lawyers, chiefs of industry and prominent trade-unionists are gathered here. In fact a representative grouping of the most essential elements in the political, industrial, cultural and spiritual life of Europe is now assembled in this ancient hall. And although everyone has been invited in his individual capacity, nevertheless this Congress, and any conclusions it may reach, may fairly claim to be the voice of Europe. It is time indeed that that voice should be raised upon the scene of chaos and prostration, caused by the wrongs and hatreds of the past, and amid the dangers which lie about us in the present and cloud the future. We shall only save ourselves from the perils which draw near by forgetting the hatreds of the past, by letting national rancours and revenges die, by progressively effacing frontiers and barriers which aggravate and congeal our divisions, and by rejoicing together in that glorious treasure of literature, of romance, of ethics, of thought and toleration belonging to all, which is the true inheritance of Europe, the expression of its genius and honour, but which by our quarrels, our follies, by our fearful wars and the cruel and awful deeds that spring from war and tyrants, we have almost cast away. It is indeed fitting that this first Congress of Europe should meet in Holland, which, with her neighbours of the Benelux group, is already leading the way by her example, and for whose hospitality and countenance we express our gratitude. And may I here say with what especial significance and warmth we greet the presence here of Princess Juliana and Prince Bernhardt who have so graciously come to join us in our opening session. Indeed Benelux, that happy novel term, is at once a model and a pioneer for our immediate advance.

The Movement for European Unity must be a positive force, deriving its strength from our sense of common spiritual values. It is a dynamic expression of democratic faith based upon moral conceptions and inspired by a sense of mission. In the centre of our movement stands the idea of a Charter of Human Rights, guarded by freedom and sustained by law. It is impossible to separate economics and defence from the general political structure. Mutual aid in the economic field and joint military defence must inevitably be accompanied step by step with a parallel policy of closer political unity. It is said with truth that this involves some sacrifice or merger of national sovereignty. But it is also possible and not less agreeable to regard it as the gradual assumption by all the nations concerned of that larger sovereignty which can alone protect their diverse and distinctive customs and characteristics and their national traditions all of which under totalitarian systems, whether Nazi, Fascist, or Communist, would certainly be blotted out for ever.

Some time ago I stated that it was the proud mission of the victor nations to take the Germans by the hand and lead them back into the European family, and I rejoice that some of the most eminent and powerful Frenchmen have spoken in this sense. To rebuild Europe from its ruins and make its light shine forth again upon the world, we must first of all conquer ourselves. It is in this way only that the sublime, with its marvellous transmutations of material things, can be brought into our daily life. Europe requires all that Frenchmen, all that Germans, and all that every one of us can give. I therefore welcome here the German delegation, whom we have invited into our midst. For us the German problem is to restore the economic life of Germany and revive the ancient fame of the German race without thereby exposing their neighbours and ourselves to any rebuilding or reassertion of their military power of which we still bear the scars. United Europe provides the only solution to this two-sided problem and it is also a solution which can be implemented without delay.

It is necessary for the executive governments of the sixteen countries, associated for the purposes of the Marshall Plan, to make precise arrangements. These can apply at present only to what is called Western Europe. In this we wish them well and will give them all loyal support; but our aim here is not confined to Western Europe. We seek nothing less than all Europe. Distinguished exiles from Czechoslovakia, and almost all the Eastern European nations, and also from Spain, are present among us. We aim at the eventual participation of all European peoples whose society and way of life, making all allowances for the different points of view in various countries, are not in disaccord with a Charter of Human Rights and with the sincere expression of free democracy. We welcome any country where the people own the Government, and not the Government the people. It is not the fault of those who are gathered here today, nor of the Governments involved in the Marshall Plan or in the Western Union, and least of all is it the fault of the United States, that the unity of Europe cannot be at present complete. All the States of the East and South-East of Europe, except Greece, are constrained to hold aloof from us and most of them are not allowed to express themselves by free democratic electoral processes. We must aim at nothing less than the union of Europe as a whole, and we look forward with confidence to the day when that union will be achieved.

I was anxious at first lest the United States of America should view with hostility the idea of a United States of Europe. But I rejoice that the great Republic in its era of world-leadership has risen far above such moods. We must all be thankful as we sit here that the nation called to the summit of the world by its mass, its energies and its power, has not been found lacking in those qualities of greatness and nobility upon which the record of famous States depends. Far from resenting the creation of United Europe, the American people welcome and ardently sustain the resurrection of what was called the Old World, now found in full partnership with the New.

Nothing that we do or plan here conflicts with the paramount authority of a world organisation of the United Nations. On the contrary I have always believed, as I declared in the war, that a Council of Europe was a subordinate but necessary part of the world organisation. I thought at that time, when I had great responsibility, that there should be several regional councils, august but subordinate, that these should form the massive pillars upon which the world organisation would be founded in majesty and calm. This was the direction in which my hopes and thought lay three or four years ago. To take an example from the military sphere, with which our hard experiences have made us all familiar, the design for world government might have followed the system of three or more groups of armies – in this case armies of peace – under one supreme headquarters. Thus I saw the vast Soviet Union forming one of these great groups. The Council of Europe, including Great Britain linked with her Empire and Commonwealth, would be another. Thirdly, there was the United States and her sister republics in the Western Hemisphere with all their great spheres of interest and influence.

In the mind picture which it was possible to form as victory in the war became certain, there was the hope that each of these three splendid groupings of states and nations whose affairs of course would sometimes overlap, might have settled within themselves a great number of differences and difficulties, which are now dragged up to the supreme world organisation, and that far fewer, but also far more potent figures would represent them at the summit. There was also the hope that they would meet not in an overcrowded Tower of Babel, but, as it were, upon a mountain top where all was cool and quiet and calm, and from which the wide vision of the world would be presented with all things in their due proportion. As the poet Blake[1] wrote:

> Above Time's troubled fountains
> On the great Atlantic mountains
> In my golden house on high.

To some extent events have moved in this direction, but not in the spirit or the shape that was needed. The western hemisphere already presents itself as a unit. Here at The Hague we are met to help our various Governments to create the new Europe. But we are all grieved and perplexed and imperilled by

---

[1] William Blake, 1757–1827. Born in London. Married, 1782, Catherine Boucher. Worked as an artist, poet and engraver. Poems include (among many others) *Songs of Innocence* (1789), *Songs of Experience* (1794), *Visions of the Daughters of Albion* (1793), *Milton* (1804). Regarded as one of the earliest Romantic poets. The lines here quoted are from his poem 'The Caverns of the Grave I've Seen', a dedicatory verse accompanying his watercolour painting of *The Last Judgment* (1810).

the discordant attitude and policy of the third great and equal partner, without whose active aid the world organisation cannot function, nor the shadow of war be lifted from the hearts and minds of men and nations. We must do our best to create and combine the great regional unities which it is in our power to influence, and we must endeavour by patient and faithful service, to prepare for the day when there will be an effective world government resting upon the main groupings of mankind. Thus for us and for all who share our civilisation and our desire for peace and world government, there is only one duty and watchword: Persevere. That is the command which should rule us at this Congress. Persevere along all the main lines that have been made clear and imprinted upon us by the bitter experiences through which we have passed. Persevere towards those objectives which are lighted for us by all the wisdom and inspiration of the past.

I have the feeling that after the second Thirty Years' War, for that is what it is, through which we have just passed, mankind needs and seeks a period of rest. After all, how little it is that the millions of homes in Europe represented here today are asking. What is it that all these wage-earners, skilled artisans, soldiers and tillers of the soil require, deserve, and may be led to demand? Is it not a fair chance to make a home, to reap the fruits of their toil, to cherish their wives, to bring up their children in a decent manner and to dwell in peace and safety, without fear or bullying or monstrous burdens or exploitations, however this may be imposed upon them? That is their heart's desire. That is what we mean to win for them.

President Roosevelt spoke of the Four Freedoms, but the one that matters most today is Freedom from Fear. Why should all these hard-working families be harassed, first in bygone times, by dynastic and religious quarrels, next by nationalistic ambitions, and finally by ideological fanaticism? Why should they now have to be regimented and hurled against each other by variously labelled forms of totalitarian tyranny, all fomented by wicked men, building their own predominance upon the misery and the subjugation of their fellow human beings? Why should so many millions of humble homes in Europe, aye, and much of its enlightenment and culture, sit quaking in dread of the policeman's knock? That is the question we have to answer here. That is the question which perhaps we have the power to answer here. After all, Europe has only to arise and stand in her own majesty, faithfulness and virtue, to confront all forms of tyranny, ancient or modern, Nazi or Communist, with forces which are unconquerable, and which if asserted in good time may never be challenged again.

I take a proud view of this Congress. We cannot rest upon benevolent platitudes and generalities. Our powers may be limited but we know and we must affirm what we mean and what we want. On the other hand it would not be wise in this critical time to be drawn into laboured attempts to draw rigid structures of constitutions. That is a later stage, and it is one in which the leadership must be taken by the ruling governments in response no doubt to our impulse, and in many cases to their own conceptions.

We are here to lay the foundations upon which the statesmen of the western democracies may stand, and to create an atmosphere favourable to the decisions to which they may be led. It is not for us who do not wield the authority of Governments to confront each other or the world with sharply-cut formulas or detailed arrangements. There are many different points of view which have to find their focus. We in Britain must move in harmony with our great partners in the Commonwealth, who, I do not doubt, though separated from us by the ocean spaces, share our aspirations and follow with deep attention our trend of thought. But undue precipitancy, like too much refinement, would hinder and not help the immediate mission we have to fulfil. Nevertheless we must not separate without a positive step forward. The task before us at this Congress is not only to raise the voice of United Europe during these few days we are together. We must here and now resolve that in one form or another a European Assembly shall be constituted which will enable that voice to make itself continuously heard and we trust with ever-growing acceptance through all the free countries of this Continent.

A high and a solemn responsibility rests upon us here this afternoon in this Congress of a Europe striving to be reborn. If we allow ourselves to be rent and disordered by pettiness and small disputes, if we fail in clarity of view or courage in action, a priceless occasion may be cast away for ever. But if we all pull together and pool the luck and the comradeship – and we shall need all the comradeship and not a little luck if we are to move together in this way – and firmly grasp the larger hopes of humanity, then it may be that we shall move into a happier sunlit age, when all the little children who are now growing up in this tormented world may find themselves not the victors nor the vanquished in the fleeting triumphs of one country over another in the bloody turmoil of destructive war, but the heirs of all the treasures of the past and the masters of all the science, the abundance and the glories of the future.

Winston S. Churchill: speech
('Winston S. Churchill, His Complete Speeches', volume 7, pages 7640–1)

9 May 1948　　　　　　　　　　　　　　　　　　　Public square, Amsterdam

UNITED EUROPE

As I look out upon this great concourse of the people of Amsterdam this fine Sunday afternoon, in days which are associated in all our minds with the joys of liberation from foul and cruel foreign tyranny, I cannot help feeling how much our two peoples of Great Britain, for whom I speak, and the Netherlands have in common. And when I look back upon the past to the days when King William III ruled England as well as Holland, and after him, when the Duke of Marlborough commanded the Dutch and British Armies through so many years of victory, I feel sure that this long and famous comradeship will be preserved and that we who share the same way of life, the same conceptions of Christian civilization, should walk forward together hand in hand and, if need be, shoulder to shoulder to face the problems of the future. I drive about this pleasant, beautiful country, so fertile, so tidy and up-to-date, with its canals and electricity, the home of a free people who have the right to choose and change their government, whose Ministers and whose revered sovereign are the servants and not the masters of the people, and as I drive I have the strong conviction that the kind of life and laws and liberty you and we, on the other side of the Channel, have established ought not to be brushed or flattened out by any form of totalitarian tyranny, either the hated Nazi domination which we have cast out or by any other form of similar despotism.

For myself I am not the enemy of any race or nation in the world. Russians, Germans, Japanese, we all understand their toils and their sufferings. It is not against any race or nation that we range ourselves. It is against tyranny, in all its forms, ancient or modern, new or old, that we take our stand. Tyranny presents itself in various forms but it is always the same, whatever slogans it utters, whatever name it calls itself by, whatever liveries it wears. It is always the same and makes a demand on all free men to risk and do all in their power to withstand it. Here also we find ourselves in harmony with the great Republic of the United States, whose services to mankind in this period of tension and strain demand our gratitude and also command our faithful cooperation. Any alliance which the British, the Dutch and other free governments may make between themselves is not directed against any particular country or people but only against the powers of evil, whoever they may be and wherever they may be. You have heard it said no doubt about extremes resembling one another. Certainly the North Pole and the South Pole are very far apart. But if you woke up to-morrow morning at one or the other you would not know which it was. There might be more penguins at one end of the world, and more polar bears at the other. But all around you would be ice and snow and the blast of freezing winds over vast dreary spaces.

Our idea is something different. We make another picture in our minds. We think that United Europe might be a better place to live in than either the Arctic or Antarctic. And that is why we, your visitors and guests, have come here from so many lands, speaking so many languages to accept the generous hospitalities of the Hague and Amsterdam and to try to take a step forward together in harmony with the policy of our freely-elected governments towards reviving the old glories of Europe and enabling this famous Continent to resume its place as an independent and self-supporting member of a World Organization. As a part in this World Organization we hope that there will soon be formed a Council of Europe which will comprise the governments and peoples of as many European states as hold our convictions and accept the broad freedoms of democratic life established on the freely-expressed will of the people in many places, though we make great allowances for difficulties in great populations acting through Parliamentary institutions. This is the Europe which we wish to see arise in so great a strength as to be safe from internal disruption or foreign inroads. We hope to reach again a Europe united but purged of the slavery of ancient, classical times, a Europe in which men will be proud to say, 'I am a European.'

We hope to see a Europe where men of every country will think as much of being a European as of belonging to their native land, and that without losing any of their love and loyalty of their birthplace. We hope wherever they go in this wide domain, to which we set no limits in the European Continent, they will truly feel 'Here I am at home. I am a citizen of this country too.' Let us meet together. Let us work together. Let us do our utmost – all that is in us – for the good of all. How simple it would all be, how crowned with blessings for all of us if that could ever come, especially for the children and young men and women now growing up in this tortured world. How proud we should all be if we had played any useful part in bringing that great day to come. And here I invoke the interest of the broad, proletarian masses. We see before our eyes scores of millions of humble homes in Europe and in lands outside which have been afflicted by war. Are they never to have a chance to thrive and flourish? Is the honest, faithful, breadwinner never to be able to reap the fruits of his labour? Can he never bring up his children in health and joy and with the hopes of better days? Can he never be free from the fear of foreign invasion, the crash of the bomb and the shell, the tramp of the hostile patrol, or what is even worse, the knock upon his door by the political police to take the loved one from the protection of law and justice, when all the time by one spontaneous effort of his will he could wake from all these nightmare horrors and stand forth in his manhood, free in the broad light of day?

But if we are to achieve this supreme reward we must lay aside every impediment; we must conquer ourselves. We must rise to a level higher than the grievous injuries we have suffered or the deep hatreds they have caused. Old feuds must die. Territorial ambitions must be set aside. National rivalries must be confined to the question as to who can render the most distinguished service to the common cause. Moreover we must take all necessary steps and particular precautions to make sure that we have the power and the time to carry out this transformation of the western world. Much of this of course belongs to the responsibilities of the chosen governments responsible in so many countries. But we have gathered together at The Hague, to proclaim here and to all the world the mission, the aim and the design of a United Europe, whose moral conceptions will win the respect and gratitude of mankind and whose physical strength will be such that none will dare molest her tranquil sway.

Eric Seal[1] to Winston S. Churchill
(Churchill papers, 2/155)

10 May 1948

Your speech at The Hague touches the same high level of vision as those you made in 1940.

You were the chief architect of Victory by force of arms over the Nazi tyranny. May you be given life and energy to add to these great feats of arms the crowning achievement of the final liberation of Europe by the force of a great idea.

Colonel Frank Clarke to Winston S. Churchill
(Churchill papers, 2/161)

11 May 1948   New York

My dear Winston,

I listened with great interest and enthusiasm to your speech at The Hague and have since read the text of your speech at Amsterdam. A number of people who listened in on your broadcast which, with one or two slight interruptions, came through very clearly, have spoken to me about it most enthusiastically, and I am sure that the public reaction will be very good in this country. Bernie told me he had sent you a cable of congratulations.

The political situation on this side in the Republican primaries is getting more and more complicated and there is a growing feeling that Stassen[2] may be the choice. I fear that if Pennsylvania throws in for Stassen he may get the nomination. On the other hand, it looks as though Taft cannot possibly be nominated, in which case there may be a reshuffling of the delegates and then your friend Dewey would have a very good chance at being nominated on the third or fourth ballot. I will continue to keep you posted on what I hear from the inside on this at present kaleidoscopic picture, as I feel sure that you must be keenly interested.

[1] Eric Arthur Seal, 1898–1972. Served in RAF, 1918. Entered Patent Office, 1921; Admiralty, 1925. Principal Private Secretary to 1st Lord (Lord Stanhope, then Churchill), 1938–40; to PM (Churchill), 1940–1. Deputy Secretary of the Admiralty (North America), 1941–3; Under-Secretary (London), 1943–5. Member, British Supply Council, Washington DC, 1943. Director-General, Building Materials, Ministry of Works, 1947–8; Deputy Secretary, 1951–9. Deputy Under-Secretary of State, FO (German Section), 1948–51. Knighted, 1955. When he was in office, Churchill would say: 'The Seal is on his ice floe.'

[2] Harold Stassen, 1907–2001. Born in West St Paul, Minn. Married, 1929, Esther Gladys Glewwe: two children. Governor (Rep.) of Minnesota, 1939–43. Enlisted in US Navy, 1943–5, serving as Asst CoS to Adm. William Halsey. One of eight US signatories of the UN Charter, 1945. Defeated by Thomas Dewey for nomination as Republican Presidential candidate, 1948; by Dwight D. Eisenhower, 1952. President, University of Pennsylvania, 1948–52. Member of Eisenhower's Cabinet and the National Security Council, 1953. Director, Mutual Security Agency and Foreign Operations Administration, 1953–8. Special Asst to the President for Disarmament Policy, 1955.

I might add that the general feeling is that Truman cannot possibly win unless there is a complete change in the world picture between now and November.

Bernie appears to be all set to leave for Europe on the first of July, and I think he will definitely make the trip provided there are no urgent developments here that will cause him to cancel at the last moment.

My kindest regards to all the family.

Winston S. Churchill: speech
('*Winston S. Churchill, His Complete Speeches*', volume 7, pages 7642–3)

11 May 1948   Royal Palace, Oslo

ROYAL DINNER ADDRESS

Your Majesty,[1] Your Royal Highness, Ladies and Gentlemen:

It is a great pleasure for me to visit Norway, and I feel myself deeply honoured by the words which Your Majesty has addressed to me at this brilliant gathering. I have also been deeply moved by the great friendliness which you have revealed for me, as manifested by the people of Oslo without regard to class or party or age – for I have noticed that the most enthusiastic appear to be found among the young. You have spoken of the hard days of war, which we have now left behind us. You mentioned the speeches which I then delivered – but I must say to you that I was not then speaking for myself. I was only a voice for the conviction and resolution with which the whole British nation was animated wherever it might find itself on the globe's surface. I was expressing the feelings which were shared by all my colleagues in the War Cabinet during those dark days – by Socialists, Liberals and Tories. All shared the common opinion, that we must fight to the end, whatever happened, even if it should lead to total destruction. But the miracle happened – thanks to the silver strip of sea which has protected us throughout the centuries. Thanks to it we managed to come through; but we did not come through alone, we came through in the company of great allies, mighty forces which advanced shoulder to shoulder and swept from the surface of the earth yet one more tyranny.

Your Majesty, you have said in the course of your gracious speech that we, at that time, after the fall of France, that we were all alone. Well, I am very glad to be able to say that at that time we had the Norwegian Merchant Navy, and that great enormous fleet of tankers, of other vessels too – but above all of tankers – carrying from all parts of the world that vital essence of war-making

---

[1] Haakon VII, 1872–1957. Born Christian Frederik Carl Georg Valdemar Axel. Married, 1896, Princess Maud, daughter of Edward VII: one son. King of Norway, 1905–57. Established Norwegian Government-in-Exile in England, 1940.

capacity. We did not feel entirely alone because we had that invaluable help from Norway, given at great cost for many. Many a good ship was sunk, and I remember how your Prime Minister[1] of those days said 'We feel as if they are our own children.' We are very grateful for the sacrifices which were then made. Many of your children were lost at that time. But the Merchant Navy of the allies was an extremely important factor, and the help which came from Norway was a very important factor in the victory over the U-boats at a time when we had a very tiny margin to work on and our existence depended on the lifeline across the Atlantic being maintained, which united us with the land of the free, the home of the brave, which is so dear in all our hearts. It was this lifeline which we had to maintain, and the addition of many millions of tons of merchant shipping, manned by hardy and courageous men from Norway, played a very definite part in our existence. Your Majesty, it has been a great joy to me to receive so many proofs of your friendship, and to have received this high order which I am now wearing for the first time here in Oslo.[2] May I express the deepest gratitude of myself and my wife for the reception which has been accorded us?

There is only one more thing which I would say. We have gone through a terrible war with great sufferings. The people in this country had to sustain the burdens and humiliations of an occupation. But that is now over. It is over, and I do not believe that we shall again be exposed to the same danger. We must sincerely hope that our own victory, won as it was with the help of so many things in the course of time, will carry the world forward and into a better and brighter time. And we must also hope that we have not removed one danger only to evoke another, but that one day – perhaps many of those who are present here will experience it – perhaps one day we shall attain the summits, attain the mountain tops where peace and security reign, where freedom for the whole people, men and women, will prove a reality and where everyone may enjoy the freedoms which President Roosevelt held up before humanity – and above all, that the peoples may enjoy freedom from fear, so that they may be in a position to reap the fruits of their labours. Your Majesty, I would again thank you for the friendly words which you have addressed to me, and I shall always look back on this evening in Oslo as one of the most memorable of my life, one which I will hold in high honour so long as I live.

---

[1] Johan Nygaardsvold, 1879–1952. Norwegian MP, 1916–49. PM of Norway, 1935–45.
[2] Churchill had been awarded the Grand Cross with Chain of the Royal Norwegian Order of St Olav.

Winston S. Churchill: speech
('Winston S. Churchill, His Complete Speeches', volume 7, pages 7643–5)

12 May 1948   University of Oslo

THE FLAME OF CHRISTIAN ETHICS

Your Majesty, Your Royal Highnesses, Mr Rector,[1] ladies and gentlemen:

I attach the highest value to the honour which you have shown me today by creating me a 'Doctor Philosophiae' at this famous University of Oslo. I have also been deeply moved by all the heartfelt kindness which has surrounded me both in this hall and outside. The Rector has mentioned the trials and tribulations through which we have passed, and he has referred to my contribution to our efforts during that time in a manner which no man should hear until he is dead. I shall long remember the eloquent words which he has used, and I hope that I shall do nothing in the span of life which still remains to me to cause him to alter his opinion. He has also reminded us of the tragic events which have taken place in this fine hall, of the bitterness which so many brave Norwegians felt in their breasts, and of the contribution which Norwegian sailors made to victory and the common cause. I would like to associate myself unreservedly with all that he has said.

Norway, which never attacked anyone, and which adhered strictly – yes, almost too strictly – to her neutrality, was the object of vile and dishonest aggression. She was beaten to the ground. But although you may strike down a man's body, his soul will nevertheless go marching on. And so it was with us. We passed through these years of tribulation and emerged from them together, shoulder to shoulder. And for the rest of the way we will go hand in hand in peace and friendship.

One might assume from my many university degrees that I am a very erudite man. When I was young, nobody believed that I should become so learned. I have never had the advantage of a university training, and I must say I was never any use at the examination desk. From that I learnt that one must never be discouraged by defeats in one's youth, but continue to learn throughout one's whole life. It is a great privilege to have received a university training, and the more comprehensive such university studies may have been, the better. In that great and friendly country on the other side of the Atlantic, students are numbered by the million. And the greater the opportunities of receiving university training in any country, and the more those opportunities are used, the securer and cleaner will be the life of that country.

But one must not look on education as something which ends with one's youth. A university training is the key to many doors, doors both of knowledge and wisdom. A man's education should be the guiding line for the reading of

---

[1] Otto Lous Mohr, 1886–1967. Chairman, Norwegian Students' Society, 1917. Prof. of Anatomy, University of Oslo, 1919–52; Rector, 1946–52.

his whole life, and I am certain that those who have made good use of their university studies will be convinced of the importance of reading the world's great books and the literature of their own land. They will know what to read and how to understand it. He who has received a university training possesses a rich choice. He need never be inactive or bored, there is no reason for him to seek refuge in the clack and clatter of our modern life. He need not be dependent on headlines which give him something new every day. He has the wisdom of all time to drink from, to enjoy so long as he lives.

There is a good saying to the effect that when a new book appears one should read an old one. As an author I would not recommend too strict an adherence to this saying. But I must admit that I have altered my views about the study of classical literature as I have grown older. At school I never liked it. I entirely failed to respond to the many pressing and sometimes painful exhortations which I received to understand the full charm and precision of the classic languages. But it seems to me that should the classic studies die out in Europe and in the modern world, a unifying influence of importance would disappear. As a doctor philosophiae and as the chancellor of a university in my own country, I would like to pass a few remarks on the views which I have reached concerning education.

Gradually, as I have passed through life, I have developed a strong feeling that a university training should not be too practical in its aims. Young people study at universities to achieve knowledge, and not to learn a trade. We must all learn how to support ourselves, but we must also learn how to live. We need a lot of engineers in the modern world, but we do not want a world of modern engineers. Great events have come to pass during our lifetime. Our generation has to a great extent parted company with the horse. Instead, we have been blessed with the internal combustion engine. I can say nothing about the future, which is unknown to us, but I wonder whether the generation to which I belong has won or lost by this change.

We all speak with great respect of science. Indeed, we have to. One of my great friends, Lord Hugh Cecil, has recently defined science as organised curiosity. We must be careful not to discover too much, not to discover things of such wide implication that our immature civilisation is incapable of manipulating and employing them. The development of communications has made the world smaller; and so it has reduced the heritage of mankind. But in Norway, with its vast extensions, I do not think that you will suffer any difficulties through lack of 'living space'. No technical knowledge can outweigh knowledge of the humanities. And at this point I would like to emphasise that philosophy and history are bracketed together by the faculty which has given me my doctorate. I myself have paid tribute to the study of history, and I have read a great deal about England's history in the days of antiquity, and even written upon themes therefrom.

I thus learnt about the Vikings, who played a very disturbing and inspiring role in the thoughts of my earliest youth. How splendid were these men who travelled freely over the wide world! Indeed, if I must add one word of criticism to the Vikings, it must be on the score that they were entirely lacking in any conception of neutrality. But in any case, they have left their mark upon history. I am looking forward greatly to seeing the Viking ships which King Haakon has promised to show me tomorrow. As remarkably well preserved as they are, they have carried down to us through the centuries a picture of their own heroic age.

I was born in the nineteenth century, and I shared in its hope and confident faith that a liberal period was dawning and that the ever-widening civilisation of mankind would triumph. But the hopes of the nineteenth century have stranded. And now we live in this terrible twentieth century, with its thirty years war. All the strongest and ablest peoples in the world have been thrown against each other – with the help of machines – to destroy each other with the most dreadful weapons. And we are emerging from this period in a condition of confusion and exhaustion of which we are all aware, and which demands of us a special effort, a particularly strict self-discipline and self-confidence. We talk in England about the values of life which are now threatened, but we know well that there is much in civilisation today which cannot be compared with the things which were regarded as fundamental verities in the century which has passed. The Greek and Latin philosophers often seem to have been unaware that the society in which they lived was founded upon slavery. They spoke of freedom and political institutions, but they were quite unaware that their culture was built upon detestable foundations. We are all aware that we can seek encouragement from the great progress which we have made. We all enjoy freedom, freedom for all. The flame of Christian ethics is still our best guide. Its animation and accomplishment is a practical necessity, both spiritually and materially. This is the most vital question of the future. The accomplishment of Christian ethics in our daily life is the final and greatest word which has ever been said. Only on this basis can we reconcile the rights of the individual with the demands of society in a manner which alone can bring happiness and peace to humanity.

Winston S. Churchill: speech
('Winston S. Churchill, His Complete Speeches', volume 7, pages 7645–7)

12 May 1948   Hotel Bristol, Oslo

TO END BITTERNESS

Rector of the University, Ladies and Gentlemen:

It is rather difficult for me to speak now, – after having listened to the orators of tonight. You would not like it if I became conceited. But I must tell you that the more kindness and appreciation I meet, the more humble I become. I do not take all this to myself. I know very well how vain it is for individuals to try to gather to themselves the credit which really belongs to the great countries and the great nations whose virtues they have had the opportunity of crediting to themselves in world history. I have often been praised for things I said at the beginning of the War, when England was fighting alone. That was only expressions of my people, it was their courage and great qualities I put into words. And it was what my colleagues wanted me to say, – if I had not, they would have pulled me to pieces, as I certainly would have pulled them to pieces the other way round.

I thank the Professor very much for all he said. It is very gratifying for me to meet all this kindness. Things have been referred here which I have said during the years far back, right back to the First World War. But what I then said and have been saying all the time, was the opinion of the British people, no matter which class or political party. The welcome you have given my wife and me and your kindness by calling us up here overwhelms us. During the War we saw in our imagination the terrible events which happened here in your country. But I am happy to see now so few traces of that terrible time. We only see kind and smiling faces all round us and you show me your gratitude in every possible way.

Ladies and Gentlemen, we have emerged from the most terrible of all wars, the most terrible which has yet been fought in the world. We fought then for principles which are very dear to the overwhelming majority of the human race. I cannot see why it is that we should now be anxious lest we lose what our victory has brought us. We ask only the right to live in peace, without fear, to bring up our children by the toil of our minds and of our bodies, to give them a fair chance in the world, to have our homes to ourselves. We do not wish to harm anyone. Neither you here in Norway nor we would deprive anyone of their personal freedom. There are certain fundamental facts, certain great principles and causes for which we must always fight and make the supreme sacrifice, as we did in the last war. We must always be ready to make sacrifices for the great causes; only in that way shall we live to keep our souls alive. I am one of those who hope and believe in a favourable outcome of the difficulties which are confronting us now. I believe that we must gradually get away from the hysteria which is a symptom of the aftermaths of every great war. I pray that it may be so and that a way may be open which we will clear of the remnants of the past. I said it in Holland, and I say it here again, that we must abandon all bitterness and all wish for revenge. That is hard for those who suffered very much, who have for instance lost their dear ones. But we must not let such feelings go on into the future. Unless we remove the shackles from our feet we will drag behind us long trails of old grievances. We must now justify the principles we have fought for; we must pay our debts to one another.

There is another fact which comes before me in my new capacity of 'Doctor

Philosophiae': the vanity of human calculation. It is well to look ahead and plan ahead, but cold egotistical calculation may bring evil results. Take for instance Count Ciano[1] who started the attack on France and England in the moment when France was beaten. 'France will not come again in five thousand years,' he said. But in two years the situation was changed. That does show how even seemingly clever calculations very often do not come off at all.

Human judgment may fail. You may act very wisely, you think, but it may turn out a great failure. On the other hand, one may do a foolish thing which may turn out well. I have seen many things happen, but the fact remains that human life is presented to us as a simple choice between right and wrong. If you obey that law you will find that that way is far safer in the long run than all calculation which can ever be made.

I want to say this to you because that is something my experience has taught me. But I certainly do not want you to understand me to say that I have always done the right thing – I should be ashamed to claim that. But I do have the feeling that one must act in accordance with what one feels and believes, and that we must now keep up old relations in freedom and in peace and move together to establish that happy world which surely the toilers, the hard-toiling masses, have a right to enjoy after all they have suffered.

I thank you most cordially for your kindness and for all you have done for me. I wear the ring of the Oslo University on my finger and will consider it as a kind of marriage ring. I must confess that I have quite a selection of University Degrees and their insignias at home, but I have never received a ring with any degree before. I wish you all good luck and a happy future for the people of Norway, and prosperity and fame for the University of Oslo.

Winston S. Churchill: speech
('Winston S. Churchill, His Complete Speeches', volume 7, pages 7647–8)

13 May 1948   City Hall, Oslo

WHY MUST WE ALWAYS FIGHT?

Mr Deputy, Your Majesty, your Royal Highness, citizens of Oslo who are gathered here:

It is a great pleasure for me to receive your so very hearty welcome. And I feel, or ought to feel, overwhelmed by all this homage, if it were not for the fact

---

[1] Gian Galeazzo Ciano, 1903–44. Son of Adm. Constanzo Ciano, Count of Cortellazzo. Studied Law at University of Rome, 1922. Entered Italian Diplomatic Service, 1925. Married, 1930, Benito Mussolini's daughter, Edda. Chief of Press Bureau and Under-Secretary of State for Press and Propaganda, 1933–4. Minister of Foreign Affairs, 1936–43. Influential in bringing about Italy's entry into the war after the fall of France, 1940. Appointed Ambassador to the Vatican after Mussolini dismissed his entire Cabinet, 1943. Captured by pro-Mussolini partisans, charged with treason, found guilty and executed, 1944. His diaries were published in English in 1946.

that I know this welcome and this homage is not shown to me for my own sake, but because I faithfully have tried throughout the years to serve a great cause, faithfully tried, to the best of my ability, to defend freedom and the cause of democracy. In this, I have had the constant and faithful support of my country and the British people. All our life's honour and dignity are dependent upon these basic principles. I owe a great debt to His Majesty King Haakon for the great hospitality and honour that he has shown me.

At home, in our island kingdom, we have not had an invasion for about a thousand years – not since that gentleman[1] whose statue is being erected inside here came over to us – a thousand years! Well, we won't quarrel about that. I was on the other side then. In my country we have a monarchist democracy. The king is the servant of the people. In both our lands, it is the people who control the government, not the government the people. That is the great dividing line between the states of the present day and it is just this point that is the cause of so much trouble in the world today. But I am convinced that the Norwegian people will always be on the side that defends the right to be free, the right to free thought, to free speech and to representation of the people. Only in such conditions can a people live in freedom and choose their own leaders, men who have experience and ability to lead development in tune with the times, but at the same time with full regard to the old traditions, with all the toil and all the conflict that lies behind them in the past.

Citizens of Oslo! The war was a hard time for you, when your country was attacked in a shameful, a traitorous manner. You did everything you could – and when you could do no more in Norway than maintain a stubborn silent front against your attackers, your ships still sailed the seas, and carried the vital supplies, right under the noses of the U-boats – and this was one of the great contributions to final victory.

I am happy to be able to come here this afternoon to thank you all for what you did during the war – but also to urge you never to forget that life is one continuous struggle, and I would ask you also in the future to hold high the banner for those values which have most significance in the lives of free men and women – and for which they are willing to sacrifice their lives. That is the foundation for a safe society, for a free life for the individual, irrespective of which sky they live under, or in which climate they live. That is the message I have wanted to bring you from my own country, but I know that you already have it in your hearts, for in thought and inspiration I feel here the harmony that exists between us.

Why must we always fight? Why must the world's countless poor, hard-working millions constantly be tormented by one kind of oppression after another? Why should they be forced into a meaningless fight against peoples

---

[1] Harald Hardrada, 1015–66. King of Norway, 1046–66. Killed in Battle of Stamford Bridge prior to the Norman Conquest, 1066.

of another land, people who are just as well-meaning and ordinary as themselves, when the whole quarrel could probably be put right if only they could talk things over.

Let us have the principles clear! Freedom, democracy, and rule by the people themselves, subject only to the changes and adjustments which the times and developments carry with them. I am proud to have been able to come here, and of the invitation to speak here to this mighty audience – thousands and thousands of people. I can assure you that the friendship you have shown me does not make me vain and conceited, because I know that it is not because of my own personality – such as it may be – but because, by God's grace. I have had the opportunity to fight for some of the causes which are most dear to humanity, and which will always find a faithful servant and champion in the Norwegian people.

Winston S. Churchill: speech
('Winston S. Churchill, His Complete Speeches', volume 7, pages 7648–9)

13 May 1948   Norwegian Parliament, Oslo

PARLIAMENTARY DEMOCRACY

Mr President, honourable members,

I have, in the last few years, spoken in a large number of Parliaments in the free countries of the world – the American Congress, the Canadian Parliament, in Switzerland, the Netherlands and Belgium. And it is a very great pleasure to me to come here this morning for a short time and be greeted and allowed to say a few words here. I am an old parliamentarian myself, and I have served 45 of the last 48 years in the House of Commons, which we pride ourselves is the cradle of parliamentarianism and a pattern for all nations.

In our parliamentary system we can be assured that the will of the people will always find open and free expression. With us, the government is the servant of the people and not its master. Any violation of this principle would lead to protests from all sides. I have great faith in the parliamentary system. It is through it that we have won all the freedoms and rights that we have in Great Britain. It has given us great pleasure to experience, as I have experienced in the course of the years, that Norwegians value so highly and have such great respect for their representatives who are chosen by the people, and that they are so convinced that the parliamentary system and constitutional monarchy is so well suited to their disposition.

It has made a deep impression on me to read the accounts of the terror perpetrated by the Germans here in Oslo, when they took Oslo by a traitorous coup. I was struck by the fact that the first thought of the Norwegian King, when he learned what had happened, was not only that the King and

Government, but also the people's chosen parliament, must escape to the free areas where they could arouse the people and inspire them to resistance against the oppressors. In our own country, we had the same unbreakable spirit to fight on, even in the darkest days.

The other day, in London, a memorial plaque was unveiled to remind us of the days when we had to move from one place to another when Parliament was destroyed by a bomb, after having been damaged several times previously. Fortunately, the members were not present on that occasion. But in spite of the hard pressure of war, we managed to carry on with our parliamentary life, and the elected representatives of the people were not in any way scared away from carrying out their parliamentary duties in the usual way and all the decisions that were made – some of them exceptionally serious – were made with the assent of representatives of the people, who themselves rose as one above the party boundaries in the fight for freedom.

I congratulate Norway on having such strong parliamentary institutions. As I said, I speak from long experience and I believe in parliamentary debates as the only way in which progress for the country, and the changes which are unavoidable from time to time as the spirit of humanity develops, either forwards, or sometimes in another direction, can be solved in free debate. And in the House of Commons I have always made myself the spokesman for the greatest possible freedom of debate even if it should lead to sharp encounters and hard words. Therefore, Mr President, I thank you for giving me this opportunity to come here today and receive this honour – which I regard very highly – in addition to all the honour with which I have been almost overwhelmed since I came to Oslo.

I think we should have faith in the institutions which have for so long borne the stress and strain of war and peace and that we should improve them and bring them into line with the times, so that we may be ready to take our share of good and evil that may come in the future. But at the same time we must preserve the traditions of the past and the customs which lie close to the hearts of the peoples of all lands. I wish Norway all luck in the future, I wish her security, I wish her peace, I wish her freedom. And I am sure that the Storting[1] will prove itself to be the most effective instrument of humanity that can be found.

---

[1] The Norwegian Parliament.

Winston S. Churchill to Clementine Churchill
(Baroness Spencer-Churchill papers)[1]

14 May 1948   Slottet, Oslo

My Darling,

It was most interesting, & I made a fourth speech without repeating myself. The dinner was a remarkable display of wealth, plenty & elegance. The table was about <u>5 yards across</u> & 20 yards long.

I will come along later & tell you more.

I hope you had a pleasant dinner.

                                                                                             Your devoted

Winston S. Churchill to King Haakon VII
(Churchill papers, 2/174)[2]

18 May 1948   Chartwell

Sir,

My wife and I were thrilled by our visit to Norway and we are both most grateful for all Yr Majesty's personal kindness and hospitality. I was deeply moved by the goodwill and welcome given to me by the great masses of people of every class who thronged the streets during the whole four days. We carry away with us a gleaming memory wh we shall preserve all our lives.

                                            Your Majesty's obedient and devoted servant

Winston S. Churchill to Major Reginald Marnham
(Churchill papers, 2/153)

19 May 1948

My dear Marnham,

Thank you so much for your letter of May 14. I should very much like to see the portrait[3] and would be much obliged if you would send it over to me at your convenience.

I hope we are going to meet again soon, as I should like to take you round the farm which, with Bardogs and French Street, has now become quite extensive. I have been much hunted lately, but am hoping to get a little freedom in June. Perhaps you will let me suggest a rendezvous.

I am anxious about the trend of events.

---

[1] This letter was handwritten.
[2] This letter was handwritten.
[3] Of the Duke of Wellington, painted by an Irish artist named Heaphy. A Mrs Fiddian gave the portrait to Marnham to give to 'our greatest living Statesman and Leader, who is also a Soldier and an Artist' (letter to Churchill from Marnham, 14 May 1948, *Churchill papers, 2/153*).

Winton S. Churchill to General Lord Ismay, Lieutenant-General Sir Henry Pownall, Commodore G. R. G. Allen and Lieutenant-Colonel Bill Deakin
(Churchill papers, 4/19)

19 May 1948

These chapters are merely a provisional build-up. Please do everything you can to fill them up. We are, however, very limited for space, and it is utterly impossible to publish a tithe of the material available. I will very soon send a note about the necessary lines that have to be supplied. Meanwhile I welcome any aid.

Randolph S. Churchill to Winston S. Churchill
(Churchill papers, 1/45)

21 May 1948

My dear Papa,

I think you ought to read the enclosed article in this week's *Economist*.[1] It is of a negative character, but it brings out some of the snags inherent in the present situation.

Your loving son
Randolph

PS. John Marriott,[2] who returned from Palestine two weeks ago, tells me that all the local British commanders believe the Arabs will win unless they make incredibly foolish mistakes. This is his own view. On the other hand, Wavell told a friend of mine last night that he is convinced the Jews can hold their own.

---

[1] 'Whose War in Palestine?', *The Economist*, 22 May 1948, on the current state of the Arab–Israeli war. On 29 Nov. 1947, the UN had passed Resolution 181, the 'Partition Resolution', to split Palestine into an Arab and an Israeli state. Fighting between the two parties began within hours of its passage, intensifying with the invasion of forces from neighbouring Arab states on 14 May 1948 after the British withdrew from Palestine and Israel's independence was declared.

[2] John Charles Oaks Marriott, 1895–1978. Served in the European War, 1915–18 (despatches; MC; Croix de Guerre; DSO, 1917). Married, 1920, Maud Kahn (d. 1960). Deputy Asst Adjutant and QMG, London District, 1933–7. MVO, 1935. CVO, 1937. KCVO, 1950. CO, 2nd Battalion, Scots Guards, 1938; 29 Indian Infantry and 201 Guards Bdes, 1942–5. Served in the Middle East, 1940–2 (bar to DSO). Cdr, Guards Div., 1945–7. GOC, London District, 1947–50. CB, 1947.

Winston S. Churchill: speech
('*Winston S. Churchill, His Complete Speeches*', volume 7, pages 7649–51)

21 May 1948   Westminster Abbey

UNVEILING OF THE COMMANDO MEMORIAL

Today we unveil a memorial to the brave who gave their lives for what we believe future generations of the world will pronounce a righteous and a noble cause. In this ancient Abbey, so deeply wrought into the record, the life and the message of the British race and nation – here where every inch of space is devoted to the monuments of the past and to the inspiration of the future – there will remain this cloister now consecrated to those who gave their lives in what they hoped would be a final war against the grosser forms of tyranny. These symbolic images of heroes, set up by their fellow-countrymen in honour and remembrance, will proclaim, as long as faithful testimony endures, the sacrifices of youth resolutely made at the call of duty and for the love of our island home and all it stands for among men.

This memorial with all its grace and distinction does not claim any monopoly of prowess or devotion for those to whom it is dedicated. We all know the innumerable varieties of dauntless service which were performed by His Majesty's soldiers and servants at home and abroad in the prolonged ordeals of the Second World War for right and freedom. Those whose memory is here saluted would have been the first to repulse any exclusive priority in the Roll of Honour. It is in all humility which matches their grandeur that we here today testify to the valour and devotion of the Submarine Service of the Royal Navy, in both wars, to the Commandos, the Airborne Forces and the Special Air Service. All were volunteers. Most were highly skilled and intensely-trained. Losses were heavy and constant, but great numbers pressed forward to fill the gaps. Selection could be most strict where the task was forlorn. No units were so easy to recruit as those over whom Death ruled with daily attention. We think of the 40 British submarines, more than half our total submarine losses, sunk amid the Mediterranean minefields alone, of the heroic deaths of the submarine commanders and crews who vanished forever in the North Sea or in the Atlantic Approaches to our nearly-strangled island. We think of the Commandos, as they came to be called – a Boer word become ever-glorious in the annals of Britain and her Empire – and of their gleaming deeds under every sky and clime. We think of the Airborne Forces and Special Air Service men who hurled themselves unflinching into the void – when we recall *all* this, we may feel sure that nothing of which we have any knowledge or record has ever been done by mortal men which surpasses the splendour and daring of their feats of arms.

Truly we may say of them as of the Light Brigade at Balaclava, 'When shall their glory fade?' But there were characteristics in the exploits of the

Submarines, the Commandos and the Airborne Forces which, in different degrees, distinguished their work from any single episode, however famous and romantic. First there was the quality of precision and the exact discharge of delicate and complex functions which required the utmost coolness of mind and steadiness of hand and eye. The excitement and the hot gallop of a cavalry charge did not demand the ice-cold efficiency in mortal peril of the submarine crews and, on many occasions, of the Airborne Force and the Commandos. There was also that constant repetition, time after time, of desperate adventures which marked the work of the Commandos, as of the submarines, requiring not only hearts of fire but nerves of tempered steel. To say this is not to dim the lustre of the past but to enhance, by modern lights, the deeds of their successors whom we honour here today.

The solemn and beautiful service in which we are taking part uplifts our hearts and gives balm and comfort to those living people, and there are many here, who have suffered immeasurable loss. Sorrow may be assuaged even at the moment when the dearest memories are revived and brightened. Above all, we have our faith that the universe is ruled by a Supreme Being and in fulfilment of a sublime moral purpose, according to which all our actions are judged. This faith enshrines, not only in bronze but forever the impulse of these young men, when they gave all they had in order that Britain's honour might still shine forth and that justice and decency might dwell among men in this troubled world. Of them and in presence of their memorial, we may repeat as their requiem as it was their theme and as the spur for those who follow in their footsteps, the well-known lines:

> 'Heard are the voices.
> Heard are the sages
> The worlds and the ages.
> Choose well; your choice is
> Brief and yet endless.
> Here eyes do regard you
> In eternity's stillness.
> Here is all fullness
> You brave to reward you.
> Work and despair not.'[1]

---

[1] Johann Wolfgang von Goethe (1749–1832), 'Masonic Lodge' (1827).

Major-General Robert Laycock to Winston S. Churchill
(Churchill papers, 2/303)[1]

23 May 1948

Dear Mr Churchill,
   Everyone concerned is most grateful to you for having unveiled the Memorial on Friday.
   It seemed to me and to all to whom I have spoken since, that the whole service, and particularly the words which only you could have composed and spoken, were of exceptional beauty.
   Instead of the mournful gloom of so many Memorial Services, the whole atmosphere in the Abbey on Friday was one of grandeur and triumph.
   All of us are grateful to you and, particularly, I think, the mothers and widows whose sorrow you have made easier to bear.

Winston S. Churchill to Captain Oswald Birley
(Churchill papers, 2/146)

24 May 1948

   Thank you so much for your letter. How very kind of you to go and look at my pictures in the Academy. I am glad you chose the 'Blenheim Tapestries' when you went to tea with Mary. I myself had not thought the picture was good enough, but the judge at the Academy immediately and independently took your view, and certainly I did not feel ashamed of it when I saw it hanging on the line. I was most grateful for the help and encouragement you gave me.
   When you have a spare quarter of an hour, will you put down a little note about the Chartwell in snow picture, 'Winter Sunshine', and how you came to award it a prize. I think it would be amusing to paste it on the back.

Winston S. Churchill: speech
('Winston S. Churchill, His Complete Speeches', volume 7, page 51)

26 May 1948   Houses of Parliament, London

PRESERVING CONTINUITY

   ... I gladly associate myself with what the Prime Minister said about the former Chamber, and I feel that they owe my colleagues and I a debt for having adhered in spite of some temptation, to the form of the Chamber

---

[1] This letter was handwritten.

which we agreed to in the war-time Government. I am quite sure that in this way greater continuity can be maintained in our Parliamentary institution.

I could not easily say what was the great age of Parliament, but the Victorian era, with its great figures of debate like Gladstone and Disraeli, will always hold its own in British history as a great Parliamentary period in which the ideas of constitutional government we had evolved in this island spread to many other countries where in many cases and in different degrees they still flourish. I look forward to the completion of this Chamber and I am sure that it will be with feelings of the deepest satisfaction that all members who sat in the former Chamber will find themselves back in surroundings which, though less magnificent, will be more familiar. (*Laughter*.)

The House of Commons is a living and deathless entity which survived unflinchingly the tests and hazards of war. It preserved our constitutional liberties under our ancient monarchy in a manner which has given a sense of stability not only in this island but as an example to nations in many lands. From the stone that is now laid may there rise a new House of Commons which, however events and our fortunes may go, will still preserve the rights and privileges of free debate and permit the free development of our national life under the guidance of an institution which all the world recognizes as one of the great features of the modern civilized world.

Winston S. Churchill to Lewis Douglas
(*Churchill papers, 4/57*)

26 May 1948

My dear Lew,

I am sorry that your letter of May 7 has remained unanswered until now. This is because it was forwarded to me in Oslo, missed me there and has only today caught up with me.

All the radio rights are involved in various contracts I have made and I fear it would not be possible for me to grant the permission which is sought by the State Department. I will however consult with Lord Camrose on his return from the United States.

I am deeply disturbed about the situation which has arisen in Palestine and at the policy of His Majesty's Government and am proposing to raise the matter in the House of Commons.

Winston S. Churchill: speech
('Winston S. Churchill, His Complete Speeches', volume 7, pages 7652–60)

28 May 1948 Perth, Scotland

THE EVILS OF SOCIALIST GOVERNMENT
SCOTTISH UNIONIST MEETING

Before I attempt to deal with the issues raised by the Conference I should like to say a word upon the news which has reached us today from South Africa. A great world statesman has fallen[1] and with him his country will undergo a period of anxiety and perhaps a temporary eclipse. It is our duty to avoid being drawn into the Party disputes of our self-governing Dominions and to work in goodwill and helpfully with any Government which may be returned by the free and fair elections which are characteristic of the British Commonwealth but I could not let this memorable event pass without paying my tribute to the famous world figure who has been cast aside by the country he led through so many perils and for whose independence he fought with such valour in bygone days and for whose revival he worked with so much perseverance over long years, raising South Africa to a level of repute and influence in the world never known before. General Smuts crowned with a seal of lasting triumph the act of magnanimity of the British Government which followed the South African War. His name and that of Louis Botha[2] will ever be respected not only in Great Britain but in all the free nations of the world. These men, by their courage in the field, by their dauntless patriotism, by their faithful execution of all honourable agreements entered into, by their wise far-seeing outlook and unflinching adherence to the greatest of human causes, have contributed not only to the fame of South Africa but to the permanent enduring glories of mankind. As one who has been my trusted friend for nearly 50 years, with whom I have found myself in agreement on so many grave and hazardous decisions, General Smuts ever claims my admiration and regard and I am glad to have this opportunity at this gathering of Unionist representatives of all Scotland of giving him our salute of admiration and respect.

I congratulate you on the success of the Conference at political treatise. I rejoice to see and feel the vitality and activity of the Unionist Party in Scotland. I draw from it the best auguries for the future and I feel sure that if we pursue the same course and the same methods that have manifested themselves in this Conference Scotland will play a most important part in the great

---

[1] FM Jan Smuts, whose Government was defeated in the general election of 26 May 1948. Smuts had supported a policy of racial reconciliation; his loss ushered in the Apartheid era.
[2] Louis Botha, 1862–1919. Member, Volksraad (Parliament of the Transvaal), 1897–9. In Nov. 1899, led the ambush during the Boer War that captured the British armoured train on which Winston Churchill was a passenger. PM of the Transvaal, 1907–10; of Union of South Africa, 1910–19.

and anxious decisions which impend upon us in the future. This is the third time I have addressed the Scottish Unionist Association. The years pass very quickly away, but I could tonight repeat the speeches I made on both previous occasions without wishing to alter a word. Much that I foretold, with your agreement, has already come true. Every year has become worse. Every year we have squandered more of our painfully gathered assets. Every year more industries have been crippled or hampered. Every year we have become more dependent on the financial aid of the United States. How long can it go on? Never, I say, was so lamentable a fall so swiftly accomplished as that of Great Britain when she emerged victorious from a war in which she had borne the brunt; a fall from that triumphant hour to that of a pensioner of a friendly country whose economic system the Government abuses and insults.

Let us look first abroad. One of the least creditable actions of the Socialist Government and Party was their attempt, their vain attempt, to sabotage the Congress of Europe at The Hague three weeks ago. Although this was entirely in harmony with their own policy of Western Union and of General Marshall's plan of aid for Europe they could not get over the feelings of jealousy at the fact that in a speech I made at Zurich in September, 1946, I had revived this great scheme so long in the minds of European thinkers and that General Marshall had publicly linked my name and our all-party movement for a United Europe with the institution of the Marshall Plan. This is very small-minded behaviour and unworthy of the gravity of the issues at stake. It is also rather ungrateful, because the Marshall Plan of Aid for Europe is what the Socialist Government is hoping to live on for the rest of the Parliament. What could be more absurd than this Socialist idea of a Union of Europe to be confined only to the members of the Socialist Party who are nearly everywhere in a minority in Europe and are losing votes to the moderate and central parties, just as they are in this country and who in many others have shown themselves truly incapable of withstanding Communist penetration. The most serious of all the reasons to excuse their conduct was given by Dr Dalton. This ex-Minister, embittered by his loss of office, said that the Socialist Party could not attend gatherings where they might meet people whom they disliked. This seemed a very dangerous thing for him to say, for if everybody followed his precept the Doctor would certainly have a very lonely pilgrimage through life.

However, we should not allow the insincere and unworthy behaviour of the Socialist Government and Party to affect the steadfastness of our support not only for United Europe but for the foreign policy the Government have hitherto pursued. Nor must we in any way weaken our support of any steps they may take which are sincerely made for the well-being and safety of our country as a whole. Mr Bevin has shown both courage and steadfastness in resisting and defeating the attacks made upon him by the Communists, crypto-Communists and 'fellow-travellers' or, as a member said the other day 'fellow telegraphists', of his own Party, and as long as he continues to carry out the policy which I laid down in my speech at Fulton in the United States two years ago and outlined in Zurich 18 months ago the Conservative Party will do their utmost to invest our foreign policy with national rather than Party sanction. With this we shall only be following the fine example of the United States where, in spite of the stresses of an approaching Presidential election they maintain what they call a bipartisan attitude towards the conduct of foreign affairs. This attitude causes them as far as possible, to work in direct consultation with the leading figures of the state, whereas in this country our government are so entirely self-sufficient and self-satisfied that they treat us with the most complete indifference. But the fact that we give them our support in all that is national in no way deprives us of the right to criticise instances of ineptitude or gross errors when these are plainly harmful to the national interest.

The outstanding case of mis-management is, of course, the Socialist handling of Palestine. I will recall to you the main features of this unhappy tale. At the General Election of 1945 the Socialists stated the pledges given to the Zionists in a more extreme form than ever before. No sooner were they in office than they turned their backs upon all the pledges and caused thereby deep disappointment and anger among the Jews in Palestine. It would, I believe, have been possible to have made and enforced an equitable partition of Palestine on the morrow of our victory using the forces in hand. But there was no policy or resolute action and everything was allowed to drift month after month from bad to worse. When I saw how ill things were going and saw the incapacity of the Government to remedy them I advised the Government to return the Mandate – for after all Palestine was only a mandated country – and leave a country where we could no longer play a useful or an honourable part. They were solid and determined in futility for nearly 18 months before they acted, as they sometimes do, upon the advice which I had given them. During this time many horrible murders were perpetrated upon our troops who were exposed to the hardest of all tests and all this while in Palestine both the Jews and the Arabs were preparing for war, inflicting meanwhile reciprocal injuries and outrages upon one another. If the Government had laid down the Mandate when I first advised them to do it, it would have been a melancholy event but the results would have been immeasurably less damaging and destructive than what has happened now. Meanwhile the Government has squandered two or three hundred millions of hard-earned money and limited overseas assets in Palestine. They have kept nearly 100,000 British soldiers idle and tormented in that small country, half of whom retained in India to cover an orderly transference of power from the Imperial to the Indian Governments might well have prevented the massacre of half a million people in the Punjab alone. We have gained nothing in Palestine but the hatred of both sides, Jew and Arab alike, and the reproaches and censures of all the world and we have now reached a point where the long and faithful work of nearly 30 years has been ended in ignominy and when our affairs have been handled with so much clumsiness and lack of mental grip that we might well be involved in a dispute with the United States at a time when good relations are indispensable to us, and when no one can gain from any divergence or differences except the Soviet Government and the Communist 5th Columns in every part of the world. I am glad that the British officers in the Arab Legion have now been withdrawn from all active participation in the struggle which is proceeding in Palestine and particularly from the attack upon Jerusalem. It would be amazing in any Government but this that the danger of allowing British officers to be compromised in this way was not seen beforehand. If this step, which everyone agrees is necessary, is taken now why was it not taken as part of the preparations for leaving the country? I mourn with sorrow and anxiety the useless waste of life and worldwide discredit which we have incurred and I regard the three years of Socialist mis-management of Palestine as a typical but outstanding example of mal-administration and incapacity which, at home and abroad, is largely accountable for our present misfortunes and for the decline of our reputation over all the world and for the casting-away of our hard-won victory.

The complete failure of nationalisation is already apparent. The experiment has cost us dear. It was made at a time when, above all others, we should have concentrated upon practical aims and increased efficiency of production and management. Some may think that it was necessary that the experiment should be tried on one of the basic industries or services, if only in order to convince the people that private enterprise and management within the well-conceived laws of a modern State are the only fertile forms in which production can be conducted. We have already seen that the experiment has failed. One great industry after another has been transferred from the profit-making to the loss-making side of the account, from the credit to the debit of our national balance. The cost of management and the number of officials employed has laid a heavy burden on the nationalised industries, which burden the nationalised industries are laying on the Exchequer. Already the wage-earning classes in these industries are beginning to realise that they will receive a far less instructed and flexible direction from the State as a supreme and all powerful agency than they would get by making their bargains through the Trade Union machinery with a variety of private employers. All this will become more obvious every day. Bureaucratic management cannot compare in efficiency with that of well-organised private firms. We are told that the management by officials is disinterested management. That may be true. The bureaucrats suffer no penalties for wrong judgments; so long as they attend their offices punctually and do their work honestly and behave in a polite manner towards their political masters they are sure of their jobs and their pensions. They are completely disinterested in the directness of their judgement. But the ordinary private trader, as you know in your own lives, faces impoverishment or perhaps bankruptcy if he cannot measure things right from day to day and those who show themselves unable to do this are replaced by more capable men and organisers. Those key industries now nationalised are to be ruled by people who have no interest in being right and suffer no consequences for being wrong. The settling of the complicated trade problems of the nation by committees or boards – all disinterested – cannot possibly enable Britain to live and maintain her present population. Nothing less than the complete discrediting and abandoning of the Socialist conceptions about industry can save the country. The old Radical campaign against exploitation, monopolies, unfair rake-offs and the like, in which I took a part in my young days, was a healthy and necessary corrective to the system of free enterprise. But this grotesque idea of managing vast enterprises by centralised direction from London can only lead to bankruptcy and ruin and, mind you, the loss in these industries is confined not only to those that are nationalised, it is not only a question of transferring the deficit to the shoulders of the taxpayer. The basic industries – coal, transport, gas, electricity – affect all other industries by which we earn our national livelihood. It seems a mad way to try to govern a country by picking out one-fifth of its industries, which is what they have done, nationalising them and changing their profit-making capacity to charging a loss to the Exchequer, at the same time hampering the other four-fifths by higher basic charges, innumerable regulations imposed without Parliamentary control and accompanied by every form of spiteful and carping propaganda.

The over-centralisation in Whitehall or other English headquarters affects Scotland in a serious manner and alters the conditions which have hitherto prevailed since the happy union of the two countries. Scottish enterprise, contrivance and thrifty management has been increasingly baffled by the intrusion of an English Parliamentary majority into whole fields of Scottish national life until now left entirely free. This subordination of a mass of Scottish businesses to the dictates of an English Socialist majority is one which Scotsmen of all Parties should gravely consider. The remedy is not in any weakening of the ties which join our two countries but in the effective stopping of the evil before it has gone too far.

The increasing proof of the failure of nationalisation has caused misgivings and division in the Socialist ranks. At the Scarborough Conference we had the old spectacle of those behind crying 'Forward' and those before crying 'Back'. Dr Dalton again presented arguments for nationalisation which none but he would use. He told us in fact that if private firms made undue profits they would be punished by being nationalised. He said 'If it appears that certain monopolies are ignoring the Chancellor's request, then that would be an argument for putting them in the next list of industries for socialisation. Our programme will depend on the conduct of private enterprise in this period.' Here indeed is a strange admission from a recent Chancellor of the Exchequer.

First, compensation paid to the shareholders has been penal and unfair in its character; and secondly, nationalisation, instead of being the boon and blessing and refreshment to our energies which it was represented to be, has now become a method of threatening and chastising firms and businesses which do not comply with Socialist admonitions. 'Abandon making profits,' cries this leader of left-wing Socialism 'or we will maltreat you as we have done the basic industries.' It is certainly quite easy for private businesses exposed to these menaces to avoid making profits in the same way as the nationalised industries have done. They have only to allow the cost of management to rise and desist from enforcing a high standard of economy in administration to avoid committing the offence of making profits. Considering that all profits which take the form of dividends are already taxed up to perhaps 12/- in the £ it is easy to see how the revenue will suffer, and this no doubt will be used as an argument for increasing still further the rates of taxation, already at a point where it is crushing the life and prosperity of the whole nation. Spinning like a teetotum in a vicious circle the Socialists make every error and misfortune they inflict upon us the argument for further controls and exactions. The crucial test will be steel. If the Government pursue their alleged intention to strike down the most efficient breadwinning, export-conquering industry in Britain, they will strip themselves of all title to a national position and show themselves ready to injure their country and fellow men by setting their Party fads and Cabinet intrigues far above maintaining the livelihood and independent existence of our island home.

You will remember that when in November I said 'set the people free,' and that 'America has flung the reins on the horse's neck and the strong horse is pulling the cart out of the mire,' and that when shortly afterwards President Truman made a statement on the need for all kinds of controls in American life, Ministers said how wrong I was. That is six months ago, and there is no change whatever in the American system. The President has made various statements to the American Congress, democratically chosen, but they are still holding along their path, and still throwing the reins on the strong horse's neck, and the strong horse is still drawing not *only* the American wagon but our own as well up the steep hill. But we are told 'See how prices have risen in America.' I don't know about you, but they seem to me to have risen here as well! But look how many peoples are being aided by America! If the United States were producing only for her own consumption, there would be a great fall in the cost of living there; but having attained the leadership of the world of which in the hour of victory we proved ourselves incapable, they are making these vast exportations without any return, and on a part of these exportations we are living. It may be necessary for us to seek and accept American aid in the plight into which we have fallen, but it should be the first aim of every Briton to free ourselves from that condition at the earliest moment, not only by hard work but by laying aside every impediment and above all by not allowing party doctrines and party fads to impede the national effort and rob the people of the fruits of their exertions and sacrifices. How Socialist Ministers can go about bragging of their social programme and of the nationalisation of industry on Party grounds, how they can deride the system of free enterprise and capitalism which makes America so great and wealthy, and then at the same time eagerly seek the aid which has hitherto been so generously granted from across the Atlantic, is a position which baffles the limitations of our language to explain.

We are oppressed by a deadly fallacy. Socialism is the philosophy of failure, the creed of ignorance and the gospel of envy. Unless we free our country while time remains from the perverse doctrines of Socialism, there can be no hope for recovery. This island cannot maintain its population as a great power. The most energetic and the nimblest will emigrate, and we shall be left here with a board of safe officials brooding over a vast mass of worried, hungry and broken human beings. Our place in the world will be lost forever, and not only our individual self-respect but our national independence will be gone. These hard-won privileges have been dear to us in the past. But all this structure of obstinacy and unwisdom erected for Party and not national aims must be viewed in the light of the supreme and dominating fact of our present position. The Socialist Government in London has become dependent upon the generosity of the capitalist system of the United States. We are not earning our own living or paying our way, nor do the Government hold out any prospect of our doing so in the immediate future. It is this terrible fact which glares upon us all.

I had hoped that the thousand million loan we borrowed from the United States in 1945 would be used to tide us over the transition from war to peace and that it would give us at least 4 years' breathing-space to adjust our affairs after the exhaustions of the war. It was spent and largely squandered in 2 years and we are now dependent upon further American generosity and also eating up from hand to mouth the remaining overseas investments and assets accumulated under the capitalist system of former years. As my friend in the corner[1] so naively said in the House of Commons the other day, 'We are eating the Argentine Railways this year, what are we going to eat next year?'

Boasting of everything they have done Mr Attlee's Cabinet – because I must mention his name sometimes; I do not want to put any slight on him – Mr Attlee's Cabinet have in fact reduced this country to a position in which it has never stood before and in which it cannot continue. All their social legislation was conceived by the National Coalition Government with a great Conservative parliamentary majority and is now being paid for by a friendly but foreign country whose economic and social system they abhor. A little while ago we were told, 'See how few are unemployed.' But now

---

[1] James Reid.

Mr Morrison and Mr Bevin alike are forced to admit that, but for the American loans and doles, there would be unemployment on a great scale. Under the old system followed by society, by which our improving civilisation has been built up by free enterprise, we were at any rate able to live independently. You cannot have independence unless you pay your own way. The very word 'independence' means that you do not depend on anybody, but by your own strong right arm and the sweat of your brow earn your daily bread and bring up your own family. But that for the time being has gone from us as a nation, and here is Socialism, strutting around like some silly peacock spreading its plumes while all the time it has to be hand-fed and spoon-fed by capitalist America.

We are asked what we should do. You may be sure that if we had the responsibility we should act with single regard to national interests and deal with the difficulties of the time by practical measures without regard to the interests of any class or party but as we did in the war, solely with the overwhelming hope of national salvation. I have consistently warned you against the folly of trying to outbid the Socialist Party in their efforts to win votes at any cost to the national welfare. It is a great mistake for a party in opposition and without executive power to try to furnish precise, elaborate programmes of what they would do. By so doing we should only fall into the trap that is set for us by our political opponents. But it is only right that we should even now give in broad outline what with our present knowledge we believe to be some of the right and necessary steps.

We have published our Industrial Charter which has been carefully studied, and we will certainly meet the wishes expressed at the Conference to make sure that a shorter, more compendious version is available in the near future. In this Charter, which does great credit to those concerned in its preparation, we are trying to mitigate in industry the effects of years of Socialist teaching. We are trying to get away from the idea that there is an unavoidable conflict between the interests of employers and employed. This can never be done by Socialism, which simply makes the employer more powerful, more impersonal and more remote from the worker. It can only be done in the way which we have described. We must encourage payment by results so that the good worker can earn more. Not only earn more but take more home. We must be very careful to preserve a fixed, stable value for our money. We must provide greater facilities for education and training in industry. We must get the best equipment we can. We should encourage joint consultation and co-partnership between employers and employed. They must share the knowledge of their common problems and their common achievements. While the authority of management must be maintained, for you need leadership in industry as in any other occupation, there is much to be gained if management and workers can develop the greatest possible understanding and respect for the functions and the responsibilities of the other. Much that we have advocated in our

Industrial Charter is already the practice of many of the best firms in this country. Our aim will be to bring all firms up to the standards of the best.

Then we have approved and are about to publish an Agricultural Charter. It deals with the greatest industry and one on which we are inevitably dependent for survival. In framing this Agricultural Charter the greatest pains have been taken to ascertain the true interests of Scottish farmers and many persons of knowledge and experience have been consulted and I shall be very glad to know, from all the channels which are open to me, what the impression is when these important proposals are made public as they will be in the course of the month of June.

The other day I had the pleasure of presiding at a meeting in the Albert Hall which was addressed by our friend Lord Woolton, who has done so much excellent work in furnishing us once again with an organisation for the Conservative Party in England. Lord Woolton proposed the removal of certain controls and, after all, no one knows more about this than he, for he looked after us in the war, at a time when everything had to be brought here through the U-boat strangle hold. Here are some of the controls which he mentioned might be removed. Bread rationing, leather controls – he advocated only a month ago the removal of the rationing of children's shoes. He would remove the controls which impede the private house-builders. He would do away with the present system of direction of labour. What right has anyone to say that we have no positive and constructive proposals? Although we are in opposition and have not the executive power, what right has anyone to say that we have not got carefully thought-out plans for handling this complicated and worsening situation should we at any time be called upon by the nation to be responsible for it?

When I was here two years ago I got from the Scottish Unionist Association a pregnant phrase which struck me deeply: 'a property-owning democracy'. That is a broad and helpful theme for us to pursue. Owning one's own house is not a crime. Saving up to secure and maintain independence is a virtue. Why should we not make it clear that not only houses built by private enterprise – when that is again allowed – may be purchased and obtained by instalments by their tenants who will become the owners of the freehold, but that also there should be a right to purchase council houses by instalments. Here is a positive step which should be taken. It will be most bitterly opposed by the Socialist Party who want everyone to be the tenants of the State. Your Chairman[1] used another phrase which I wish to associate with this meeting. He spoke of the strong movement of youth which we feel in the Universities and in all parts of the countries in favour of the Unionists and Tory Party, and he said 'We are

---

[1] Charles Gibson Connell, 1899–1985. Born in Edinburgh. Educated at Edinburgh University. On active service during WW1, 1914–18. 2nd Lt, Royal Field Artillery, 1917–19. Writer to the Signet, 1923. Married, 1927, Constance Margaret Weir: two children. Joint Hon. Secretary, Scottish Unionist Association, 1938–54; President, 1944–5. Knighted, 1952. Fellow, Royal Society of Edinburgh, 1965.

a Party of opportunity.' That is a good title for us to take. An opportunity for us all to serve together to regain for our dear country the place she lost a short time ago and which we ardently desire to see her regain.

The recovery will not be swift or easy. I am making you no extravagant promises. I think it would be a terrible thing to buy power in this time by making promises which will be impossible to fulfil. Every day our remaining resources are disappearing, every day that class and party warfare sinks more deeply into our national life may mean many weeks of loss in the process of recovery. How easy to fall, how hard to rise! But it does not rest with us. So long as these Socialist Ministers can beg or borrow a dollar from capitalist America you may be sure they will continue in their courses. The British nation always likes to buy its experience afresh every time. It looks as if they will have every opportunity of doing so at the highest cost.

We all see the great advantages that could be derived from a national unity which saved us in the war, but as I have repeatedly said, there can be no coalition in the life of the present Parliament. We require a new Parliament which alone can be the foundation of a Government which truly sets the welfare of the people as a whole before any other consideration in the world and which would be representative of all the strongest forces in the country. One thing is certain, that this Parliament elected under conditions which were altogether abnormal, is the most unrepresentative and incapable that has ruled Britain in modern times. If you want to see public opinion, look at what happened about the death penalty. 75 per cent at least of the population is against the opinion expressed by a majority of 25 incapable and irresponsible members of Parliament in the recent division in the House upon this subject. If ever there were a case for a referendum, this is one on which the people should be allowed to express their own views and not irresponsible votes in the House of Commons.

I have been calling continually for a new Parliament. Some say the longer it is delayed, the better it will be for our electoral prospects; that people will have to suffer much more before they will be convinced. But I feel that we shall all be running a grievous risk if the life of the present Government is prolonged. The need of the nation is a new Parliament and the end of the most unrepresentative, inadequate and undistinguished House of Commons which has ever sat at Westminster in modern times. Make sure that you are all ready when the call comes.

June
1948

Henry Channon: diary
('Chips', page 426)

2 June 1948

Went with Alan[1] to the Savoy, where we attended the Conservative lunch for Winston Churchill. 'The boss' was in the gentlest of moods and made a mild, almost apologetic speech, which was yet not devoid of point and wit. I was very near to him and watched his easy smile and wet blue eyes that always look as if he had been crying. During his speech he made it clear that he expects to win the Election 'next year', or early in 1950, with a 'three-figure' majority. His reception was tepid, but not in the least unfriendly – though gone is the rapture of yester year. I think that the Party resents both his unimpaired criticism of Munich, recently published, and his alleged pro-Zionist leanings.

Winston S. Churchill to Field Marshal Lord Montgomery
(Churchill papers, 2/143)

4 June 1948

My dear Monty,

I am sorry not to have answered your first letter of May 15 before, but I have been much pressed lately. I will certainly write a brief foreword[2] as you desire, and I thank you for the kind expressions in your letters.

I feel I ought to let you know that I am anxious about the world situation and about the state of the British Services, especially the showing we make for the money and men provided. Should trouble come it will, I fear, be proved

---

[1] Alan Tindal Lennox-Boyd, 1904–83. Educated at Christ Church, Oxford. MP (Cons.) for Mid Bedfordshire, 1931–60. Lt, RNVR, 1940–3. Secretary, Ministry of Aircraft Production, 1943–5. Minister of State for Colonial Affairs, 1951–2. Secretary of State for the Colonies, 1954–9. Viscount, 1960. Director, Royal Exchange, 1962–70.

[2] To the book of speeches *Forward from Victory*, published Oct. 1948. See Churchill to Montgomery, 18 July 1948, reproduced below (p. 1127).

that we are even less well-prepared than we were at the beginning of the late war.

There are some things I cannot understand. When I was at The Hague I was told that it had been decided at the Conference in London to give 50,000 rifles to the Netherlands Government. The War Office however said they could not spare them and the matter, at that time, was held in suspense. At the end of the war we must have had four or five million rifles in the hands of the Army and the Home Guard. In addition large numbers of German rifles must have been captured, considering that nearly three million Germans surrendered to you and Alex in the course of a few days. Compared with this, 50,000 is a very small item for a country so exposed as Holland.

I had intended to write to the Prime Minister on the subject and then, possibly, to ask him to see a deputation from the Opposition leaders asking for information about our material reserves, which were and ought still to be enormous. As we are in correspondence I mention this to you beforehand. It may be that I have been misinformed or perhaps that the matter has already been settled.

It would seem a great pity if the whole of the Low Countries had to go over to American patterns, leading to confusion of equipment, considering how close we are to them.

Field Marshal Lord Montgomery to Winston S. Churchill
(Churchill papers, 2/143)[1]

7 June 1948

My dear Mr Churchill

Thank you for your letter and for saying you will write a brief foreword. You could not be more anxious about the general situation than I am, and in particular about the measures being taken to deal with it. The progress made towards the coordinated development of our Post-war Defence Services: is NIL. I am doing the best I can to produce a good Army; I enclose you the two addresses I gave at Cambridge to the General Officers of the Army.

Unless a firm grip is taken from the top, we shall drift to disaster. I would like to come and tell you about it, and give you the whole story; I consider it very necessary I should do so.

I am free on
Wednesday night 16 June
Thursday night 17 June

I could come and dine quietly with you one of those days. Or would you like to dine with me here, at my flat?[2]

[1] This letter was handwritten.
[2] Churchill asked his secretary to propose instead lunching at Chartwell the following Sunday, June 13.

JUNE 1948

Field Marshal Lord Montgomery to Winston S. Churchill
(Churchill papers, 2/143)[1]

10 June 1948

Dear Mr Churchill,

I will come and lunch with you at Chartwell on Sunday and will tell you all you want to know. I will come alone.

My book of speeches is to be called

Forward from Victory

This makes a good title as the last one published was my personal messages to the troops during the war: which I called

Forward to Victory.

If you could write a brief foreword I would collect it on Sunday. They[2] want to go ahead with the book.

Winston S. Churchill to Lieutenant-Colonel John Astor
(Churchill papers, 2/145)

10 June 1948
Private

My dear John,

Thank you so much for such a very pleasant and interesting evening, which I hope will be productive of good results to our harassed and hobbled country.

I was greatly impressed with your pictures, which show accomplishment and technique carrying them altogether out of the amateur field in which I disport myself. The only comment I would venture to make with great diffidence is that you might try in the near future, just as an experiment, a more brilliant and intense colorization with sharper contrasts and greater depth. This might amuse you as a variant upon your very clearly-marked style.

I also thought that the portraits were very good. I wish indeed I had your facility; though I have strong views my technique is faulty. I wonder you do not have a little private and anonymous exhibition, perhaps in Paris. I have Mr Charles Montag coming over here sometime in the next month or so who is a great connoisseur, and whom I have talked painting with for the last twenty-five years. If you like the idea he might come and look at your pictures, because I think you would find it rather amusing winning public approbation anonymously.

The times ahead of us are serious, and the issue at the next Election, if not forestalled by graver events, may be decisive upon the British survival as a great power by the side of the United States.

[1] This letter was handwritten.
[2] The publisher, Hutchinson & Co.

Pray give my regards to Violet.[1] Clemmie hopes to come over and see her very soon.

Winston S. Churchill to Sir Alan Lascelles
(Churchill papers, 2/171)

10 June 1948
Private

My dear Alan,

During my visit to Norway recently I received from the hands of King Haakon the Grand Cross and Chain of the Royal Order of St Olav. I am writing to ask if I may have the King's permission to wear this Order on appropriate occasions.

If necessary I wd of course write to the King direct. But I do not wish to trouble him.

PS. I was concerned about the Trooping of the Colours incident. These awkward things shd not be put on the King. A minister should be made to advise.

Herbert Morrison to Winston S. Churchill
(Churchill papers, 2/69)

14 June 1948

My dear Churchill,

I have seen in the Press your reference to my comments at Cardiff with regard to the discharge of your duties as Leader of the Opposition.

I at once accept your statement that you do not draw the £2,000 salary as Leader of the Opposition, nor that you draw the ex-Prime Minister pension of £2,000. I, therefore, withdraw the financial references I made at Cardiff and express my regret at having made them.

I would add that my observations arose out of your own references on Saturday[2] to Weary Willies and Tired Tims and – as my Parliamentary colleagues present would I feel sure agree – my comments were made in a bantering and in no way spiteful spirit.

In view of the publicity in tonight's evening papers I have thought it right to send a copy of this letter to the Press.

---

[1] Violet Mary Elliot, 1889–1965. Third daughter of 4th Earl of Minto. Married, 1909, Lord Charles Mercer Nairne, younger son of 5th Marquess of Lansdowne (killed in action, 1914); 1916, John Jacob Astor, later 1st Baron Astor. Styled Lady Astor of Hever, 1956.

[2] Actually on Sunday, 13 June, in a speech at the Royal Albert Hall in London.

June 1948

Winston S. Churchill to Clementine Churchill
(Baroness Spencer-Churchill papers)

15 June 1948

Darling,
   You did promise Sept 12 1908 'To Love, Honour & <u>Obey</u>'. Now herewith are <u>Orders</u>.

   3.15   You come up here to <u>rest</u>. EYH[1] will bring you & is waiting
   7.30   Dinner
   8.30   Journey to 28
   9.40   Bed and a <u>read</u>
   Given at Chartwell GHQ

The Tyrant
[Drawing of a pig]

Sir Alan Lascelles to Winston S. Churchill
(Churchill papers, 2/171)

15 June 1948   Windsor Castle
Private and Personal

My dear Mr Churchill,
   The King gladly gives permission for you to wear your Grand Cross and Chain of the Royal Order of St Olav and does not wish to trouble you to write to him personally about it.
   As regards the postponement of the Trooping of the Colour: The King feels, as did his father[2] and grandfather[3] before him, that the Birthday Parade is essentially a function personal to the Sovereign, with which the Secretary of State for War has no direct concern. In the present instance The King himself took the responsibility for ordering the cancellation, having of course consulted the GOC, London District, and having acquainted himself with the latest meteorological news. If The King were going to carry out, at Plymouth for example, a programme entailing his going out to visit certain units of the Navy, and if the C-in-C, Plymouth, reported to The King that the weather was unsuitable for such a visit, His Majesty would himself order its cancellation, without any reference to the First Lord of the Admiralty. I think The King regards the Birthday Parade as being in the same category.

---

[1] EYH: the registration mark of a small car (a Morris) in which Churchill used to be driven around the fields at Chartwell.

[2] George Frederick Ernest Albert of Saxe-Coburg and Gotha, 1865–1936. Second son of King Edward VII and Queen Alexandra. Naval Cadet, 1877. Midshipman, 1880. Married, 1893, Mary of Teck (later Queen Mary). Prince of Wales, 1901. Ascended throne on his father's death as King George V, 1910. Crowned, 1911. Assumed surname of Windsor, 1917.

[3] Albert Edward, 1841–1910. Eldest son of Queen Victoria. Succeeded his mother as King Edward VII, 1901. Married, 1863, Princess Alexandra.

Winston S. Churchill to Sir Alan Lascelles
(*Churchill papers, 2/171*)

16 June 1948
Private

My dear Alan,

Will you thank The King for his gracious permission for me to receive and wear the Order of St Olav.

About the Parade; as an old and devoted servant of the Crown I do not feel this was a fair responsibility to put upon the King. It is the business of Ministers to shield the Sovereign from all kinds of decisions which may arouse public controversy and feeling. The Secretary of State for War is equally responsible for advising or for not advising on a matter affecting the movement of troops, or the cost and difficulty of the replacement of uniforms if damaged. The occasion of the inspection of a dockyard, if you will allow me to say so, is not similar. On this particular day more than a quarter of a million people had been waiting for hours in the streets, and their disappointment was natural. The incident is now closed; but I remain of the opinion that steps should be taken to relieve the Sovereign of the invidious responsibility of deciding such a difficult matter, and that in future it should be borne by Ministers, who can defend their actions, whether right or wrong, in Parliament.

Thank you for your letter.

Brendan Bracken to Lord Beaverbrook
(*Beaverbrook papers*)

16 June 1948

Herbert Morrison has just made a damn fool of himself. He attacked Churchill for drawing his salary as Leader of the Opposition and failing to attend regularly at the House of Commons. For reasons you will know Churchill would, indeed, be silly to draw his salary as Leader of the Opposition. It would all dissolve in income-tax. Morrison has now been forced to apologise and as he is not very popular in his Party he cannot afford the sort of snub that Churchill has given him.

I dined with Lew Douglas last night. Smuts was the other guest. The old man declared that looking back on a long life of politics from 1895 when he was Minister of Justice in Kruger's Government he regarded the defeat of Churchill in 1945 as one of the great landslides in human history. Douglas argued that it was better for Churchill that he was deprived of office after the war. He would have been confronted by a series of General Strikes, coal strikes and every other sort of strike. Smuts replied that Churchill could have coped with such developments and they were of little account when weighed against the fact that the present Government have destroyed a large part of the British Empire and Churchill would have saved it.

Winston S. Churchill to Reginald Maudling
(Churchill papers, 2/69)

17 June 1948
Private

My dear Maudling,

It would be very kind of you to get something ready for me for the Luton Hoo meeting. Of course, the Agricultural Charter will be out in the morning papers, and that will require ten minutes or so. Generally speaking, I should take the Brighton Conference speech as a foundation and make a restatement of our position a year later, which has so much improved from a Party standpoint. I think the broad principles should be reaffirmed. I should like very much to have something of yours to work on.

I am trying to fit in a five minute stop at your house on my way to Hatfield on Saturday, and will let you know in good time.

I send you herewith a memorandum which I received from David Stelling,[1] and which you may like to see. Of course, one of the best ways of helping us would be for American capital to be invested in British industries. This would redress the trade balance, and also replenish plant. We should have of course to maintain conditions which do not threaten all property with confiscation. Pray let me know what you think.

Winston S. Churchill: speech
('Winston S. Churchill, His Complete Speeches', volume 7, pages 7662–9)

23 June 1948 House of Commons

POLITICAL GERRYMANDERING

I beg to move, to leave out from 'That' to the end of the Question, and to add:

> This House, while recognising the necessity for an equitable scheme of redistribution, declines to give a Third Reading to a Bill which repudiates agreed recommendations of Mr Speaker's Conference 1944, and disregards for the purpose of Party advantage the findings of the Boundary Commission, thereby bringing discredit on Ministers of the Crown and lowering the traditional standards of our public life.

---

[1] C. David Stelling. Editor of *Yea and Nay, A Series of Lectures and Counter-lectures Given at the London School of Economics in Aid of the Hospitals of London* (1923). Author of *Why I am a Conservative* (1943).

I rise to move the rejection of this Bill by a reasoned Amendment. Whatever may be thought of the harangue or oration to which we have just listened, no one will suggest that it was calculated to raise either the level or the temperature of our Debate. We have heard several speeches of this kind from the right hon. Gentleman (Mr Morrison), the greater part of which consists in reading out long extracts from the non-controversial passages of the Bill, which is already fully before us, with a few party gibes thrown in to ingratiate himself with his supporters. I shall not myself attempt this afternoon to inject undue heat into the discussion. (Hon. Members: 'Get on.') How do you mean, get on? I have only just begun. I propose on the Third Reading to make a calm, general survey in order to present the episode in which we are now concerned to the House in its plain and simple light.

In our Parliamentary system, to which the Socialist Party pay frequent lip-service, and from which they have derived their power to rule the State, it is necessary from time to time to have a redistribution of the constituencies in accordance with the movements of population. This is particularly true after the disturbances of great wars. We, therefore, in the National Coalition Government, took the appropriate measures, by mutual agreement between the parties concerned, and by agreement between the individual Ministers concerned. The basis on which we acted was broad and plain; it was ordinary British fair play as between parties; and we thought that this should be achieved and ensured by a Speaker's Conference and an impartial Boundary Commission. Accordingly, all the proper steps were taken; each side gave up some of its party claims and interests, and a definite agreement was reached between parties and Ministers, involving, I say, the personal good faith of those directly concerned. We had a great majority – 150 over all parties – in that Parliament, but we accepted the broad agreement.

No one knew then how the impending General Election would go. No one knew then what would be the report and plan of the Boundary Commission when they had examined the whole matter according to the principles laid down. We could not have had anything more simple or more straightforward than the plan that was made by the National Coalition Government for bringing our electoral system up to date in view of the many changes that had occurred. However, as hon. Members are well aware, the Socialists won the election by a great majority, and our colleagues in the War Cabinet – including particularly the Prime Minister and the Lord President of the Council, then Home Secretary, who were bound by the previous agreement – decided eventually to break that agreement and see if they could get some additional party advantage to themselves, although this did not become immediately apparent. The Home Secretary now claims that nothing that happens in one Parliament should affect or bind the decisions of another. But in those circumstances, when it was a National Coalition Government, those arguments are even less effective than they would be in other circumstances. I contend that both persons and parties were bound by what was then decided.

But the matter does not rest here. It does not rest at all in the atmosphere of the last Parliament. When the assent of the new Parliament was required for the preliminaries of electoral reform, and so forth, for which there had to be temporary legislation, the Socialist Ministers concerned all spoke of the matter as one that had been settled by agreement between parties, and as if all that remained was to carry out the agreement. A great many quotations have been flung from one side of the House to the other in the course of these Debates, but let me give these, which I do not think have been quoted before. For example, on the Second Reading of the Elections and Jurors Act, 1945, the present Home Secretary said on 21st November, 1945:

> . . . as soon as we get the report of the Committee, whose names I hope to be able to announce in the course of the next three or four days, we shall be able to proceed with a permanent Measure of legislation which will bring us back, I hope to the compilation of the register by canvass, publication, claim and objection and –

these are the words to which I wish to draw the attention of the House –

> will enable us to implement the remaining recommendations of the Speaker's Conference.

Could anything be more clear than that the Speaker's Conference decisions were carried forward by the Government, after its victory, armed with its great majority, from the last Parliament to this? Again, the Joint Under-Secretary of State for Scotland[1] – who distinguished himself in this Bill almost as much as his chief – said when winding up:

> But, as had already been stated, this temporary Measure –

that is the Elections and Jurors Act –

> and, as far as I can see, when the present Government introduce legislation implementing all the recommendations of the Speaker's Conference that are found practicable –

(Hon. Members: 'Ah!') I suppose by 'practicable' he meant 'All that we can get our people to vote for'; but it was not understood in that way by the House at the time –

> there is no likelihood of any opposition in the House whatever. Members from all parts of the House have been pleading with the right hon.

---

[1] Thomas Fraser, 1911–88. Married, 1935, Janet Scanlon. Secretary, Lanark Constituency Labour Party, 1939–43. MP (Lab.) for Hamilton Div. of Lanarkshire, 1943–67. Joint Parliamentary Under-Secretary of State for Scotland, 1945–51. PC, 1964. Freeman of Hamilton, 1964. Minister of Transport, 1964–5. Chairman, North of Scotland Hydro-Electric Board, 1967. Member, Royal Commission on Local Government in Scotland, 1966–9. Chairman, Scottish Local Government Staff Commission, 1973–7.

Gentleman this afternoon to implement the recommendations of the Speaker's Conference. – (Official Report, 21st November, 1945; Vol. 416, c. 503)

That was how the matter was opened to the House in November, 1945, after the General Election. Clearly, when the Government spokesman said there was no likelihood of any opposition in the House, he cannot have been contemplating the abolition of the university seats, or even of the business premises vote. The one minor qualification he made referred to people being registered for only one residence and one business qualification. Taken together, these quotations which I have read, which have escaped the searching examination of these Debates, make it perfectly clear that the Government felt themselves bound after the General Election – I emphasise, after the General Election – to implement the recommendations of the Speaker's Conference; and further, that after the General Election it was in their minds to retain university representation.

After some months it appeared that the report of the Boundary Commissioners, on what they thought was a fair redistribution, might cost the Socialist Party as much as 35 seats of its enormous majority, already so disproportionate to the votes cast by the electors. For a Socialist majority to carry a Bill conceived on democratic principles for the representation of the people which might cost them 35 seats, was more than their virtue could stand. They wanted to be fair; they wanted to keep their agreements; they wanted to submit to the decision of the impartial umpires; they wanted to respect the Speaker's Conference and maintain Parliamentary redistribution upon a higher plan than the mere decision of majorities in the House of Commons; but the loss of these 35 seats was driving them too far.

The Socialists had about 20 seats in London which returned some of their leading Ministers, including the Prime Minister, which seats averaged only about 20,000 electors. These obviously must be liquidated by any redistribution Bill. They are, indeed, a good example of the unequal and unrepresentative character of the majority which gained the election of 1945. Obviously, these seats were going to be lost to the party opposite anyhow. Although the principles on which the Boundary Commission operated over the whole country sometimes hit one party and sometimes another, these very small London boroughs certainly represented a dead loss to the Socialists. Also the reports of the Boundary Commission did not give them any compensation for this because they were also found to be over-represented in other parts of the United Kingdom as well.

We must admit it was an awkward situation for well-meaning men to find themselves in. They wished to do what was straightforward and fair, and in accordance with what had been agreed upon between both parties and also personally agreed upon between the Ministers in the Coalition Government and between me and the present Prime Minister as leaders of the two parties. They had the natural British instincts of good faith and fair play. If it had been a matter of a half a dozen seats the Lord President of the Council might have taken it, but 35, however equitably and fairly awarded, was too much for his political fibre to bear. In these matters the right hon. Gentleman is like those road vehicles which have a label on their back, 'Load not to exceed five tons.' We quite understand his attitude; those who know him best and his intense interest in party electioneering understand it best. As Oscar Wilde[1] said, 'I can resist anything except temptation.'

And so, with great reluctance, long hesitations and with a natural repugnance, it was decided to cheat. I am sorry to have to use that word, but it is the only one which fits exactly the process which we have witnessed in the last few months. I must admit that the fall from grace was accomplished by gradations. At the Speaker's Conference it had been agreed that the university representation and that of the City of London should be maintained. Here were 13 seats held, as it happened, by Conservative, Liberal or Independent Members. The Labour Party had not got one of them – I wish to do full justice to their difficulty. The Secretary of State for Scotland – I do not think he is in his place today – I dare say precautions have been taken to keep him out of the Debate – was very frank about this. As none of the universities had returned any Labour Members but only Conservatives, Liberals or Independents, they had, in his opinion shown themselves unfitted to exercise the franchise and therefore should be deprived of it. Let me quote his actual words. In a really remarkable intervention in a speech I was making on 16th February,[2] he said:

> As one of the members of that Conference, I would point out that the right hon. Gentleman has made several statements about a bargain. One of the reasons why the university vote was retained was because it was returning to this House distinguished persons of non-political character. But, since the Election, the Conservatives have broken that agreement by using the universities to vote to send back to this House Conservatives whom, at the General Election, the electors rejected at the polls. – (Official Report, 16th February, 1948; Vol. 447, c. 865.)

Clearly this quotation shows that the Secretary of State for Scotland admitted that the bargain continued after 1945. How otherwise could the bargain be broken by the Conservatives 18 months after the election? How do the Conservatives break a bargain when universities or other constituencies choose to return the people for whom the great majority wish to vote? The proposition advanced by the Secretary of State for Scotland is, of course, absurd. If, as is probable, he had particularly in mind the result of the by-election in the

---

[1] Oscar Wilde, 1854–1900. Educated at Oxford. Author and playwright. Publications include *Poems* (1881), *The Picture of Dorian Gray* (1891) and *The Importance of Being Earnest* (1895).

[2] Reproduced above (pp. 968–77).

Scottish Universities when my right hon. and gallant Friend the Member for those universities (Lieut.-Colonel Elliot) was returned – (An Hon. Member: Where is he?') Well, he is a Scotsman, and they often think of their native land. There is nothing wrong with that. I wish there was more of it. His proposition is absurd, because if he had in mind this Scottish business, his complaint appears to be that my right hon. and gallant Friend was a Conservative.

But there were five candidates at this election – a Conservative, Socialist, Liberal, Liberal National and Independent – and all except the Independent were party men, and, with the exception of my right hon. and gallant Friend, all lost their deposits. The Socialist candidate was Dr Joad – (An Hon. Member: 'He lost his ticket.') – an avowed adherent of the Socialist Party. If the objection is to party men, it would have been equally wrong for the university electorate to have returned Dr Joad. Therefore, the only candidate for whom they could have voted was the Independent. Such was the perverted logic of the Secretary of State for Scotland, but it constitutes a clear admission that 18 months after the General Election his opinion was that there still had been an electoral bargain, and that the university franchise stood; if it had not been upset by the fact that the Scottish universities quite freely chose to return by an overwhelming majority a gentleman who supported the Conservative Party.

So it was decided, because they returned a Conservative Member, to abolish the university representation, and one of the City seats has also been wiped out. That was 13 out of the 35, and it may well be that the Ministers whose honour and good faith is specially concerned in this matter wished to stand on these 13. But the party opposite could not rise to their level. They could not see how a Redistribution Bill which still left them with a loss of 20 seats according to the basis of population and the principles applied by the Boundary Commission, could possibly be considered democratic.

It is my belief, from what I gathered in the earlier stages of this discussion, that the Home Secretary was genuinely shocked at the suggestion of making alterations in the ordinary constituencies of the country contrary to the recommendations of the Boundary Commission, and that he resisted these proposals in his own characteristic way – that is to say he resisted them on conscientious grounds until the party feeling got too hot. Then of course he had to bow to the storm. What is an honourable Socialist to do when asked to do a dishonourable thing? It is a dilemma and an extremely difficult problem. Obviously he must resist it as long as he can, but the party feels that there must be reason and a sense of proportion in all these matters. A Socialist Minister cannot push these questions of good faith, fair dealing and settled agreement beyond a certain point. If there is enough pressure below the Gangway, the Minister must give way. Are they not all pledged to toe the party line?

We saw the same process with the Home Secretary over the death penalty. We shall come to that later in this Session. I am sorry for the Home Secretary, because I still believe he feels his various humiliations acutely. It would be to his credit if he did, and my sincere advice to the right hon. Gentleman would be to retire from an office for which he is plainly unfitted by his qualities, as well as by his defects, and to return to private life, where he had previously shown himself quite a decent sort of fellow.

In this case, I must admit that the party pressure was severe. It was expressed by the former Chancellor of the Exchequer, now the Chancellor of the Duchy, whom, I believe some persons have been glad to see back on the Front Bench. I have no wish to overstate the case. Party pressure was expressed by the former Chancellor of the Exchequer in his brief interlude of potential opposition. He demanded that another group of constituencies should be so handled as to give the Socialist Party, according to their calculations, an additional 17 seats. Another 17 seats added to the 13 already secured, would very nearly make the Redistribution Bill harmless from a Socialist Party point of view. That is to say, the readjustment of the representation in proportion to the movements of population would take place without inflicting any injury upon them. It was near enough, 30 as against 35.

It only remained to throw in the Amendment about limiting the use of motor cars in elections so as to hit the Tories in the rural areas and make them walk – which, I can assure hon. Members opposite, they certainly will do, and walk with their boots on – to enable the whole process of redistribution to be accomplished without prejudice to the party interests of the Socialist Government and of their majority. Thus the broad principle would be established that redistribution in accordance with the movements of the population may be effected from time to time, provided that the Socialists are no losers by it.

That is where we are now. Indeed, I suppose we ought to think ourselves fortunate and even favoured that the process has stopped there and that the gerrymandering of the constituencies has not been carried further than merely maintaining existing balances. In Communist or satellite countries they go much further, and hold that the will of the people can only be expressed in the way in which the party which have got hold of the offices desire and resolve. In Czechoslovakia, they manage it all in a much more thorough-going fashion. This is also true of Yugoslavia. In Soviet Russia, 95 per cent vote for Stalin and the Communist Government and the other 5 per cent are given the tip to vote the other way, to show how fair and free the election has been. I quite agree that His Majesty's Government have not gone as far as that. They believe in free democracy, fair play and good faith, so long as you do not try them too high.

Let me repeat that I am not comparing conditions in Czechoslovakia with any that the Government are establishing by this Redistribution Bill. I wish to give them full credit for their moderation. They have not sought, and they have not dared, to deprive the British people of its free representation. They have only executed this small, minor, pinching, piece of chicanery which they call the Representation of the People Bill. They have not committed a crime, but only a small mean shabby trick. On the whole, I think they will lose in reputation more than they will gain in seats by what they have done. I wonder if it was worth it, having regard to the scale on which they are doing business? They are rather like a wealthy man who travels on the railway and ingeniously avoids paying for his ticket for part of the journey. It shows a lack of sense of proportion, but we for our part must not rate the matter too seriously.

If there is a strong popular tide flowing against the Socialists at the next election, the petty swindles the Government have perpetrated will be all swept away. What will not be so easily washed away, however, is the stain on the character of Ministers, who were definitely bound by agreements entered into in good will and in good faith by its responsible leaders – and who, because they could not bear to suffer the comparatively small disadvantage which normal redistribution would have inflicted upon them, have revealed their moral limitations to their fellow countrymen.

I leave the past and come to the future. It is quite certain that the conduct of the Socialist Government in this matter has deeply impaired the principle of settling necessary redistribution measures by a Speaker's Conference and an impartial Boundary Commission. The precedent has been established that a Socialist Party may break all previous engagements if they obtain a majority in the new Parliament. The continuity and decorum of our national life as far as the representation of the people goes, has been broken, and it may take a generation to build it up again. Nevertheless, we on this side of the House will do our best to labour for that end. The compromise settlement of the Speaker's Conference was disadvantageous to us in some points. But, in protest at the conduct of Ministers we have decided to vote against this Bill. We do not regard it as an honest Measure of redistribution. Should we obtain a majority at the next General Election, we shall not, however, hold ourselves free to make any changes in the representation of the people so far as concerns constituencies which are not comprised within the ambit of the Speaker's Conference of 1944. I have the strong view that voting should be compulsory as it is in Australia and Holland and that there should be a small fine for people who do not choose to exercise their civic duty.

Let me say why I introduced the words 'so far as it concerns constituencies'. We have no intention of acting outside the limits of what was agreed between the two parties at your Conference, Mr Speaker. Some things in that Conference hurt us very much or we thought that they would hurt us very much. Others were advantageous, but in the future we shall take the rough with the smooth and make no departure from the general basis there reached. Up to that limit, however, we hold ourselves perfectly free so far as the next Parliament is concerned to repair and redress the injuries and breaches of agreement which this present Bill now contains.

For example, as the right hon. Gentleman apprehends, should we gain a majority we shall immediately introduce a Bill to restore university representation. We say that it was agreed upon by all parties at the Speaker's Conference. The 12 university seats, should our Bill become law, will be re-established and the elections for them will be held at once with results which will become effective in the next Parliament. There is nothing like putting it plainly, and we shall be judged in the country by our decision to take that step. Future Parliaments may see other Redistribution Bills, but I can only hope that by that time our standard of public life in this country will have been so far restored as to lift the whole process of redistribution to levels above the electioneering interests of rival parties and direct it solely with the desire of basing our ancient Parliament upon the broadest, freest and truest expression of the people's will.

Winston S. Churchill: speech
('Winston S. Churchill, His Complete Speeches', volume 7, pages 7669–77)

26 June 1948   Conservative Fete, Luton Hoo

BRITAIN 'FLOUNDERING AND SINKING'

When we look back on the years that have passed since the General Election of 1945 we may indeed rejoice at the continued regathering of the strength of the Conservative Party in every part of the country and in every aspect of its work. This can be seen in our local organisations, in our finances (they must not be forgotten), in our membership which, although the recruiting campaign was started only a short time ago, is now over 2 millions, in our great successes at the local elections, in our youth movement so strongly marked in the Young Conservative Associations throughout the land, in the quality and fervour of our meetings, which I have never seen surpassed, or in this vast gathering, the largest I have ever addressed in my life. You will remember how in their hour of triumph the Socialists declared that never again would a Conservative Government be seen in Britain. Now by every test that can be applied we have a substantial majority in the country, and we have good reason to hope that, if every man and woman who is a convinced supporter of the Conservative cause will work continuously to spread the light of truth among the people, that majority which now exists in the country will be reproduced in a new Parliament whenever the opportunity is accorded to us.

We are ready at any time to meet the Socialists in the constituencies should this mischievous and incompetent House of Commons be dissolved, but we also have the feeling that time is on our side, and that with every month that passes the spirit of the Nation will revive more strongly and the sense of having been mismanaged and misled by the Socialist sectarian doctrinaires, and also the sense of the vital need for a more capable administration will impress itself upon the public mind. There is no part of the country where a stronger and more concentrated blow can be struck for the salvation and revival of Britain than here in the Eastern Area. In 1945 at the General Election Conservatives and Liberal Nationals, who are now working so cordially with us in this region and elsewhere (and I am very glad to see Lord Teviot[1] on the platform here today) lost 15 seats out of the 24 which we held previously. Of these 15 seats 7 were lost by majorities of under a thousand votes. You have therefore a great opportunity. The Target for Tonight, the target you should set before yourselves is nothing less than the gaining of the whole 24 seats we previously held. I am sure this can be done if everyone continues to work with the utmost ardour and does not tire, either through fatigue or through that insidious foe, over-confidence.

But though these are inspiring days for our party our minds are oppressed by the evil plight into which our country has fallen at home and abroad. Because in the moment of victory, in one foolish afternoon, the British electorate voted into power a Government and a Party which was in no way worthy of our victories or equal to our strength, we have had to suffer evils and humiliations almost as bad as those undergone by defeated nations. The decline of British influence abroad and the general retrogression of our imperial fortunes and power is alas the common theme of world discussion and in every country our eclipse is attributed to the land-slide into Socialism of 1945 and the incapacity of our present rulers.

It is painful to contrast today the position of Socialist Britain and that of the capitalist United States. The Americans are actually involved in a Presidential Election and yet in the midst of all that struggle and party strife they preserve what is called bi-partisan conduct of foreign affairs far above party. The Government and the Opposition work together and are represented by their leading men in all matters of foreign policy. Both sides in the midst of the electoral struggle are prepared to vote generous subsidies to Europe and especially to Britain. Both sides are supporting the strong and effective defence without which the peace of the world cannot be maintained, and all this in the middle of vehement and bitter party electioneering. We are dependent, I am sorry to say, upon the great Republic for our safety and our daily bread, and I rejoice to see a wealth of talent and ability in the leading men of both parties of the United States, which is indeed fortunate for a country which has taken over from Great Britain the first position in world leadership.

Meanwhile here at home Mr Attlee and his administration in spite of their tremendous national responsibilities have not yet shown themselves able to rise above party interest and intrigue. Their idea of United Europe is a United Europe of Socialists, although the Socialist Parties throughout Europe are in a condition of decline, and nowhere except in this unlucky island can they

---

[1] Charles Iain Kerr, 1874–1968. DSO, 1919. Married, 1930, Florence Angela Villiers. MP (Lib. Nat.) for Montrose Burghs, 1932–40. Lord Commissioner, Treasury, 1937–9. Lib. Nat. Chief Whip, 1937–9; Chairman, 1940–56. Comptroller, Royal Household, 1939–40. Baron, 1940.

form a purely Socialist Government. At home our Government are intensely occupied not in trying to make things better for the country but first of all in giving satisfaction to their own party machine and to what I can only call their outworn doctrines. They are engaged in an elaborate system of calculations and manoeuvres in order to be able to establish what is virtually a Single Chamber Government, and to pass the Bill to nationalize our steel industry before the people can be consulted on that important matter.

Nowhere have they fallen so far below the level of events and in the standards of our public life as in the Redistribution Bill they have just carried through the House of Commons. They have violated the agreed recommendations of the Speaker's Conference to which they were bound as men and as a Party. They have largely disregarded the Report of the impartial Boundary Commission. They have sought to preserve the disproportionate advantages they used at the General Election without regard to the fair and proper representation of the people for which a Redistribution Bill was already overdue. Finally they have swept away our long established representation of our Universities because, as they openly avow, these centres of light and learning, to which all classes have ever-increasing access, do not at this moment return any Socialist members to Parliament. I have thought it right to declare in the name of the Conservative Party that should we obtain a majority in the forthcoming General Election we shall reverse this last act of spite and partisanship and will restore the representation of the 12 University seats. We shall do this in accordance with the proposals and agreements of the Speaker's Conference and we shall do it in such a way as to make it effective during the life of the new House of Commons. In fact there will be a restoration of the franchise of the Universities immediately after we shall have gained victory at the Polls. I am sure that this decision will command the wholehearted assent and agreement of this magnificent audience. We must now extend our view beyond this island to Foreign and Imperial Affairs.

We are all naturally anxious about what is happening in Berlin. Last month, on May 4, our Foreign Secretary, Mr Bevin, said in Parliament: 'We are in Berlin as of right. It is our intention to stay there.' It is certain he would not have said that without having made sure that the United States were equally resolved. On the other hand, there can be no doubt that the Communist Government of Russia has made up its mind to drive us and France and all the other Allies out, and to turn the Russian zone of Germany into one of the satellite States under the rule of totalitarian terrorism. This situation raises issues as grave as those which we now know were at stake at Munich ten years ago. It is our hearts' desire that peace may be preserved, but we should all have learned by now that there is no safety in yielding to dictators, whether Nazi or Communist. The only hope of peace is to be strong, to act with other great freedom-loving nations, and to make it plain to the aggressor, while time remains, that we shall rally the free men of the world and defend ourselves and our cause by every means should the aggressor strike a felon's blow. I cannot guarantee that even a firm and resolute course will ward off the dangers which now threaten us; but I am sure that such a course is not merely the best but the only chance of preventing a third war in which the most fearful agencies of destruction yet known to man will be used to the fullest extent. The Conservative Party will therefore support His Majesty's Government in the stand which, with all their devotion to the cause of peace, which we too share, they have felt bound to make. I trust that our defences have not been neglected and that the immense sums of money we have voted for the Armed Forces will have been turned to good account by those who are responsible for them. It is our duty to show, whatever our Party differences may be, that in resistance to foreign tyranny we are a united nation. And I still believe that by this means peace may be preserved.

I must dwell a little longer upon Imperial and Foreign Affairs. This week you will have seen the King's renunciation of his title as Emperor of India. This melancholy event, which ends Lord Beaconsfield's dream and fine conception of eighty years ago, is only typical of what is happening to our Empire and Commonwealth in so many parts of the world. Nearly two years have passed since I said at our Annual Conservative Conference:

> I fear, and I must express my forebodings, that calamity impends upon India. Indian unity created by British rule will swiftly perish, and no one can measure the misery and bloodshed which will overtake these enormous masses of humble helpless millions, or under what new power their future and destiny will lie. The event will long leave its mark in history. It may well be that Burma will soon suffer the same fate. Most of you will certainly live to see whether I am right or wrong. Sometimes in the past I have not been wrong. I pray that I may be wrong now.

Alas, I was not wrong. You can judge for yourselves how far this forecast has already been fulfilled. Nearly half a million Indians have already paid the forfeit with their lives. In this fateful tale of the casting away of the British Empire in India and of the misfortunes and slaughter which have fallen or are falling upon its peoples all the blame cannot be thrown on one Party. But the Socialist Government on gaining power threw themselves into the task of demolishing our long-built-up and splendid structure in the East with a zeal and gusto most remarkable, and they certainly have brought widespread ruin, misery and bloodshed upon the Indian masses to an extent which no one can measure. Power has been recklessly confided to Indian political parties which in no way represent the needs or feelings of the 400 million people who had dwelt so long under the protection of the British Crown and Parliament. Already there has been something very like a collapse in the process of internal administration, and we must now expect an indefinite epoch of internecine and religious strife. We have witnessed the violent action of

Mr Nehru's Hindu Government against Kashmir, four-fifths of whose people are Moslems. It may be that quite soon this same Nehru Government, using the modern weapons we left behind us, will attack the ancient State of Hyderabad, with its 17 millions of people, and overthrow the Government of the Nizam, who has earned the title 'our faithful Ally'. It was the declared intention of the Prime Minister and others concerned in this Indian tragedy that Hyderabad, like other Indian States, should be free to join either the Moslem or the Hindu Dominion now set up in India. In this case the word of Britain has been broken in a manner which would have been judged shameful in any other period of our history; and now it seems that the only course for Hyderabad to take is to lay its case before the United Nations Organisation.

In Burma also my solemn warnings have been fulfilled. Burma has been cast away and is now a foreign country. It is already descending rapidly into a welter of murder and anarchy, the outcome of which will probably be a Communist Republic, affording most dangerous strategic advantages to Soviet Russia in this important part of the world on which we depend for vital supplies of tropical produce, and which lies on one of our sea roads to Australia and New Zealand. In Malaya the long arm of Communism, unchecked by feeble British Administration, had begun a campaign of murdering British planters and their wives as part of the general process of our ejection.

I am not going to repeat what I have said about the disasters and muddles in Palestine. It does not matter where you look in the world, you will see how grievously the name and prestige of Britain have suffered since the British Nation fell flat upon its face in the moment of its great victory. Nearly two years have passed since Albania, which we helped and nourished during the war, murdered over 40 British sailors by mining our ships in the Corfu channel. Not the slightest satisfaction has been obtained for this outrage of ingratitude and treachery. I could give you many other instances which prove how British rights and British lives are being disregarded by minor foreign states to a degree never known before in the history of our country. But I will select only one more example of Socialist performance. I choose it because, though on a smaller scale, it is symbolic.

When the Admiralty made their misleading announcement some months ago that the British Home Fleet was reduced to one cruiser and 4 'battle' destroyers, the government of Chile and Argentine thought we were so completely finished that they occupied some of our possessions in the Antarctic near the famous Falkland Islands. Mr Bevin told us in the House last week that the invading parties are still there. But His Majesty's Government seem to be unable to do anything to assert our rights. And it is at this juncture, of all others, that the Board of Admiralty, whose political members seem strangely infected by the Socialist mood, have offered to sell the cruiser *Ajax* to the Chilian Government so that she can help protect this wrongful intrusion upon British territory. The *Ajax* is, of course, the most famous warship in the South

Atlantic because of the part she played in sinking the *Von Spee* in the Battle of the River Plate, nine years ago. Nothing could do more at this moment to humiliate Britain throughout South America than the sale of this ship to Chile. I suppose the Admiralty thought they could get a few more dollars out of the Chilians on that account. It is like selling the shirt that Nelson[1] wore at Trafalgar to General Franco and getting a little extra for the blood stains. We are all in favour of economy in a Government which is spending 3000 millions this year and in an Admiralty which never before took so much money from the taxpayer with so little to show for it except masses of officials; but this seems to me to be carrying thriftiness too far, especially when you consider all the other facts I have mentioned. Poor though we may be, unable to pay our own way as we are under Socialism, I did not think we had sunk so low as to have to market our national and naval dignity in so squalid a fashion.

It is almost exactly three years ago since we emerged victorious from the mortal struggle with the Nazi German power, and all our enemies surrendered unconditionally. Then we stood high in the world; and our name and fame were celebrated in many lands. I could not have believed on the morrow of the German and Japanese surrenders, that so short a period of time could bring us all so low. Nearby on the continent of Europe we see countries which were conquered, ravaged and stripped by the enemy, and were liberated by our strong arms, which have already restored a thriving, active life to their people. Belgium is a case in point where some progress has been made and where, whatever party the Ministers belong to, 'Making the best of it' has been their maxim. But we, proud Britain, who stood alone against the mighty tyrant, who kept the flag of freedom flying unaided for more than a whole year, we are now forced to live on foreign aid and also to subject ourselves to privations almost worse than those of the war.

One would have thought that when the Socialists leaped into power, with their great majority they would have tried to serve national interest rather than Party interests after what we had all gone through together, and for the sake of the great inheritance of which they had become the Trustees. When Mr Attlee's Government came into power we did not underrate the difficulties which they would have to contend. These difficulties would have strained to the utmost all the resources of a National Government and a united nation. We did not grudge the new Ministers their offices, nor envy them their burdens. We have steadfastly supported them in every step they have taken sincerely in the public interest. In that spirit we supported their policy of seeking a large American loan to tide us over the transition from war to peace and to re-equip our industry, our agriculture and our mines. Instead, however, it has been their principal aim from start to finish to assert and enforce their Party doctrines and dogmas upon the whole of their fellow countrymen, and to spread

---

[1] Horatio Nelson, 1758–1805. Capt., RN, 1779. C-in-C, Mediterranean Fleet, 1803–5. Led RN to victory against Napoleon's navy in the Battle of Trafalgar, in which he was killed.

class-warfare, with all its injury to national effort, far and wide, throughout the land. Even if we had all been pulling together we should have had a hard task to overcome. The combination of partisanship and incompetence has brought us, three years after our victory, to the humiliating and painful position of not being able to earn our daily bread, or seeing any prospect of doing so, according to Ministerial statement, under Socialist rule for many years to come. I can, for my part, assure you that a continuance of experiments in socialist theory, and of their ineptitude and incompetence in practical administration will bring upon us not only worse privations and restrictions but economic ruin prolonged indefinitely; and not only economic ruin but the depopulation of the British Isles on a scale which no one has ever imagined or predicted.

When we turn to the field of social legislation, we are confronted with ridiculous boastings. The Socialists dilate upon the National Insurance Scheme, Family Allowances, improved education, welfare foods, food subsidies, and so forth. They point to the benefits flowing to the people and particularly to the housewives and children from these schemes. But there are two facts which, up till quite recently, they have tried to hide. The first is that all these schemes were devised and set in motion in days before the Socialists came into power. They all date from the National Coalition Government of which I was the head. I have worked at National Insurance schemes almost all my life and am responsible for some of the largest measures ever passed, both under Mr Asquith as Prime Minister, and under Mr Baldwin. The main principles of the new Health Schemes were hammered out in the Coalition days before the Party and personal malignancy of Mr Bevan plunged health policy into its present confusion. The Family Allowance Act was passed by the Conservative Caretaker Government. School milk was started in 1934 by the Conservative Parliament. The idea of welfare foods was largely developed by Lord Woolton, to whom we owe so much in other directions. The Education Act was the work of Mr Butler, who has also distinguished himself with the Industrial Charter and in another sphere I shall mention later. Thus the only benevolent social policies of which the present Government vaunt themselves were not conceived by them but were in fact the legacy which they received from a Conservative House of Commons which had a majority of 150 over all other Parties.

But there is a second fact. Listen to Dr Dalton. 'We have mounted,' he said in the House of Commons, 'without halt or hesitation, the great social programme which the electors voted for when our majority was returned. We are entitled to say that the new Britain, represented by this House of Commons, has taken the cost of social security proudly in its stride.' Is it not an astonishing fact that a man who was for nearly 3 years Chancellor of the Exchequer should say that this House of Commons has taken the cost of social security in its stride! Does he suppose that we do not all know that without the American Loan of a thousand millions, which was largely frittered away by him, and without the promise of further munificent American aid, amounting to something like 330 million pounds of sterling a year, it would be quite impossible to maintain our present standards even of consumption, and equally impossible to avoid large-scale employment. Mr Herbert Morrison, in a momentary lapse into candour, and also, I may say, into accuracy, told us at Liverpool last month that without American aid we should be facing one or two millions unemployed. Least of all do I see how any Socialist can be proud of living on the charity of the greatest capitalist free-enterprise state in the world, whose system of wealth production they deride and denounce on every occasion. We may indeed ask ourselves how it is that capitalism and free enterprise, if they are so wrong and out of date, enable the United States not only to support its own vast and varied life and needs, but also to supply these enormous sums to lighten the burdens of other countries in distress.

The climax will be reached if the Government have the hardihood to nationalize the steel industry which is vital to our whole economic life, particularly to our export trade, and is at the present time a record-breaking model of efficiency under private enterprise. We are assured by Ministers that this wanton blow at British industrial revival will be struck next year. And that it is for this that the Socialists are making the wholly unprovoked attack upon the House of Lords, which has rendered us great service in rejecting the ill-considered policy of the Death Penalty and which, under Lord Salisbury's able leadership, is gaining strength and public repute far outside the bounds of the Conservative Party with every week, almost, that passes. So much for their social programme.

Another major fault is the wild financial extravagance into which this Government have plunged. Nothing like it has ever been seen before. The new Chancellor of the Exchequer has taken from us 3,000 million pounds to cover Socialist administration for the current 12 months. That is at a rate of more than 3 times the cost of the State in the years before the war, though some deduction should be made for the decline in the purchasing power of money. Altogether the Socialists spent about 11,000 million pounds, in addition to the figure I have mentioned in the 32 months from the end of the war until the end of the financial year in April 1948. And what have they to show for it? One could imagine that with all these vast sums of money being spent and while the American Loan was still flowing in, there would at least have been a fleeting sense of prosperity. On the contrary, a harder, more curtailed, more restricted way of life and standard of living has been imposed upon every class of the community, and now a worse time lies ahead which the Government assures us may continue for many years.

I have on other occasions spoken of the Government's extravagance abroad. But it is here at home that our worst waste and extravagance is found. There are two or three times as many people employed by the Government to manage our affairs as were needed by the Conservative Government before the war. A mighty army, larger than our pre-war army, of 450,000 additional officials has been taken from production and added, at a prodigious cost and waste. Instead of helping the national recovery this is a positive hindrance. The bulk of this new and heavy burden, let me remind you, is borne mainly on the shoulders of the wage-earners, from whom the great mass of taxation is drawn. And all that we get from it is an increasing frustration and waste of time and paper in every sphere of our trade and industry.

I am frequently asked, 'What is the alternative to Socialism proposed by the Conservative Party?' And we are invited to put forward a programme in the utmost detail of what we should do. We have already, in our Industrial Charter, shown the broad lines on which our economic policy would be based. We reject entirely the Socialist doctrine that the State should own and manage all the industry and commerce of the country. The state has a part to play. The White Paper on Employment Policy, drawn up under the war-time Coalition and since ignored by the Socialists, shows for example how the State might in future strive to maintain a high and stable level of employment. But we hold that the mainspring of our industrial life must still be that free competitive enterprise upon which our commercial greatness has been founded. In particular, we will spare no effort to eradicate the effects of years of Socialist teaching that there is an inevitable conflict in industry between the worker and the employer. Here there is much to be done and much that can only be done by the wisdom and example of those engaged in the management of industry who share our views. By producing proper incentives to increased output and higher efficiency, by clearing the way of promotion from the factory floor to the board room table, by encouraging joint consultation and co-partnership in the widest sense, we can and we shall re-establish the harmony in industrial relations, jeopardized by Socialist teachings. That harmony must be restored if our economic life is to regain its full health and vigour.

It would be very foolish for us, without the machinery of Government at our disposal or the power to give effect to our plans, to commit ourselves to an elaborate programme which would be eagerly pounced upon by our opponents, if only as a means of diverting attention from their own misdeeds and failures. But while we do not intend to prescribe before we are called in, and while we shall ask for a 'doctor's mandate' to deal with the situation, whatever it may be, when that time comes, there are two things I will tell you now that we will not do. The first is, we shall not allow the advance of society and the economic well-being of the nation to be regulated and curtailed by the pace of the weakest brethren among us. Proper incentives must be offered and full freedom given to the strong to use their strength to the utmost in the commonwealth. Initiative, enterprise, thrift, domestic foresight, contrivance, good housekeeping and natural ability must reap their just rewards. That will guide us. I will tell you another thing we will not do. We will not attempt to gain popularity or votes by a plethora of wild, lying promises and bribes and the creation of false illusions, such as those with which the Socialists misled the electorate three years ago.

Anyone can see however that the vigorous production of food on the largest possible scale in this island holds the first place. Let us be under no error in this matter. The prosperity of agriculture and food production depends on larger supplies of labour, and to have the labour we must have the rural houses in which they can dwell and rear families. These the Socialists have refused. Our food supply also depends upon a full supply of the agriculture machinery which the Government has on occasion so recklessly exported to foreign countries. That was indeed devouring the seed-corn. In our Agricultural Charter published this morning, we have declared that the proper level of agricultural production in this country must be half as much again, as pre-war. That is our aim. The Agricultural Charter shows how it can be won by the well-tried principles of Conservative policy.

We repulse the Socialist doctrine of land nationalization. British farming should be carried on in the future as in the past by private enterprise and management. We give the farmer confidence in the future of his industry by guaranteeing prices and markets for all the food he can produce up to the level we have stated as our objective. Half as much again, and we can see what happens then. The British farmer should be given first place in the British market, and we shall certainly protect the British horticulturist against the casual dumping of foreign surpluses. Next to the home farmer comes the Empire producer. We shall do all in our power to develop and stimulate the production and the importation of food, not only from our great Dominions but from the colonies which we have in many parts of the world.

In all this we must reduce to a minimum the interference of the State in the production or the marketing of food. We are opposed to the extensions of bureaucracy suggested by the Lucas Committee on Marketing. If the public are to provide important guarantees to the farming community, there must be proper security for the consumer. The State is entitled to give guidance, and, if necessary, to see that this guidance is enforced, to ensure that farmers and landowners do not flout the rules of good husbandry and good estate management. In this Agricultural Charter, which is the companion work to the Industrial Charter, we explain how we would provide for the agricultural industry the new financial capital that is needed, and the due proportions of steel and other capital equipment.

Finally, we seek to apply to the agricultural industry the principles that underlie the Industrial Charter, namely a keen incentive to a greater effort, and a reorganized status for the individual worker. In this way, and in this way only, can our British agricultural meet the claims the nation will be forced to make upon it in the coming years. I commend the Agricultural Charter to your consideration, for it is a document of the utmost importance to all, producer and consumer alike, who live in, live on, or live by our native land.

There has been a lot of talk by Socialist Ministers against a Coalition. They need not waste their breath. No suggestion of that kind has ever been made by the Conservative Party. What could be more wrong than for the Conservative Party in time of peace to pass a sponge over all the mismanagement and incompetence of the last 3 years, and to share the responsibilities of the men who have led us into so much needless misfortune? Such an act of folly would destroy the only hope of national recovery, namely the dismissal from office by the British electorate of those who have so obviously failed in their task.

Let me sum up. Under the capitalist system of free enterprise, we had bred in Great Britain nearly 47 millions of people, half of whose food came from beyond the seas but whose progress was constant and whose standard of living before the war was already the highest in Europe. It has only been possible for our 47 millions to live in Great Britain by the utmost exercise of all these qualities of individual initiative and enterprise which have been in former times the outstanding distinction of the British character. I say without hesitation that there will be no recovery from our present misfortunes until the politicians whose crazy theories and personal incompetence have brought us down, have been driven from power by the vote of the Nation. Then indeed there would be a bound forward in British credit and repute in every land. Then, indeed, we should set our feet again upon the high road which, though it is hard and stony and uphill all the way, leads out of the quagmires in which we are now floundering and sinking. There, in a new Parliament, lies the only way to make England herself again, the heart of the British Empire and a home for all her peoples.

Winston S. Churchill to John Strachey
(*Churchill papers, 2/68*)

29 June 1948

Dear Strachey,

Thank you for the copy of the speech you made at Nairobi. I expect it is a much bigger place than when I was there forty years ago. In those days you could see a rhinoceros from time to time from the windows of the Nairobi Club, and new arrivals were invited go out and win their spurs.

July 1948

Winston S. Churchill to Sir Shane Leslie
(Churchill papers, 1/44)

1 July 1948

My dear Shane,

I have begun to read your book and want to tell you at once I do not like the Introduction which suggests that I only took the trouble to find out about our Grandfather when I had to do a broadcast for America. Can you not manage to leave me out of this?

It is a pity to make out that the family were engaged in 'unending bewailment' at the loss of their fortunes. They were left much better off than most people.

I have no objection to your quoting, on page 8 of the Introduction, what I actually said on July 15, 1941.

I think the expression on page 14 – 'the maternal pit from which he was digged' – most unpleasant.

The story attributed to me on page 15 about my Father being remembered as 'Winston's father' is utterly untrue. I never spoke in such disrespectful terms of him. I should have thought the biography I have written proved the reverence with which I regarded him.

I should leave out the second paragraph on page 18 especially the last four lines.

I doubt whether there is any need to talk about 'the corrosion of luxury' on p. 22.

Winston S. Churchill to General Dwight D. Eisenhower
(Churchill papers, 2/148)

1 July 1948
Private

My dear Ike,

Thank you so much for your charming letter. I am very glad you are not leaving it to history to write the account of your conduct of these great events, and I look forward to reading your story. I do not myself expect to reach the period of 'Torch' until Volume IV, which I have not yet begun. I hope therefore to have the advantage of reading your account beforehand. We were so often in full agreement that the tale of our relations should be easy and agreeable for each of us to tell. The only point about which I was unhappy at the time was your inability to give me the help I needed to take Rhodes in the autumn of 1943. I still hold to the view I took then, but I quite understand your difficulties. As you know, I did not agree with 'Anvil', which ws launched in 1944, as I thought it too far to assist you in your Normandy struggle. As things turned out it was you who helped 'Anvil' and not 'Anvil' which helped you. However these are matters on which only another generation can pronounce.

It is a great joy to me to see our two countries working together ever more closely. In this alone lies the salvation of the world. I feel we shall always be marching together along that road.

I am very proud of the Degree I received from Columbia University, and feel sure that its high mission is being fulfilled under your guidance and inspiration.

With every good wish to you and Mrs Eisenhower,

Winston S. Churchill to Patrick Buchan-Hepburn[1]
(Churchill papers, 2/67)[2]

5 July 1948   Chartwell

My dear Patrick,

It gives me pleasure to ask if you will fill James's[3] place (as you have already done so long and well) in a formal manner. We have been friends ever since 1929 when you volunteered to be my private secretary in the cool shades of Opposition. Now in times at once darker for the nation and more hopeful to our party, I look forward to our close association. It is my earnest belief

---

[1] Patrick George Thomas Buchan-Hepburn, 1901–74. Private Secretary to Churchill, 1929–30. MP (Cons.) for East Toxteth, 1931–50; for Beckenham, 1950–7. Served in RA, 1940–3. Cons. Deputy Chief Whip, 1945–8; Chief Whip, 1948–51. PC, 1951. Government Chief Whip, 1951–5. Minister of Works, 1955–7. Baron Hailes, 1957. Governor-General of the West Indies, 1958–62. CH, 1962.
[2] This letter was handwritten.
[3] James Stuart, former Cons. Chief Whip.

that we may together take part in a restoration to power of the Conservative and Tory Progressive force on whom our survival as a great State so largely depends.

What will happen outside I cannot predict. But let us make sure we do our best on the Home Front.

You have my full confidence and that of the party in the House of Commons.

Brendan Bracken to Winston S. Churchill
(Churchill papers, 4/144)

6 July 1948

My dear Winston,

You will remember our talk at the Other Club about your references to Poland in the American edition of your book.

Count Raczynski, the former Polish Ambassador, sent me the enclosed note in which he has underlined the passages which deeply offended the Poles in Britain,[1] but they remain deeply devoted to you.

I know that their sense of obligation to you will be deepened if you can tone down the references to Poland to which they object.

Winston S. Churchill to Lieutenant-General Sir Henry Pownall
(Churchill papers, 4/220)

6 July 1948

Thank you so much for your various notes. Could you at your leisure give me one on 'Battle Axe',[2] June 16–18, 1941. I exerted myself a great deal to bring about this battle which was the hope I had set before myself all the time in Operation 'Tiger'.[3] Alas, I could not pull it off. Wavell did his very best, but the delays in getting the Tiger Cubs into action were heartrending, and due to petty causes like air coolers etc. I had hoped to fight this battle before the end of May. Rommel was then at his last impetuous gasp. Every round he had to fire, every can of petrol he had to use were his last heart beats. There he lay at Sollum with a thousand miles of communications behind him and all his hitherto successful bluff remaining to be called. In front of him was an army with road, rail and sea communications, three or four times as strong and with more than three hundred brand new tanks. Tobruk lay behind him to menace

---

[1] These contained phrases such as: 'ingratitude over the centuries has led them through measureless suffering', 'squalid and shameful in triumph', 'too often led by the vilest of the vile' and 'two Polands: one struggling to proclaim the truth and the other grovelling in villainy'.

[2] Operation 'Battleaxe': the failed Allied invasion of Cyrenaica.

[3] 'Tiger': British merchant convoy carrying tanks and aircraft from Gibraltar to Egypt, 5–12 May 1941.

his life-line and it is incredible to me why this was not achieved. An extensive battle towards Sollum and a grab on his tail from Tobruk would have spelt his utter ruin. I cannot conceive why this could not be done. Rommel's glory was built up on our incompetence just as his armies were sustained by his captures of our petrol and ammunition.

Presently comes the battle of June 18. Wavell tried a great deal. He not only flew up but flew out to the Desert Flank, where our Armoured Division had gone astray, in order to bring it back. Meanwhile General Messervy[1] (I think anyhow there was a Mess in it) retired before he could get back to him. The battle was broken off. Losses were about equal, and thereafter from June 18 to October 15, about four months, nothing was done on this front. This proves how weak Rommel was and how he hung on by his eyelids. All that was necessary, even if the battle was muddled, was to go on fighting him and forcing him to fire his ammunition and use up his petrol. But no. For my sins I appointed the great General Auchinleck,[2] who naturally wanted to play for a sitter no matter what was lost in every other direction.

These notes may be of some help to you. The moral is that war consists of fighting, gnawing and tearing, and that the weaker or more frail gets life clawed out of him by this method. Manoeuvre is a mere establishment, very agreeable when it comes off. But fighting is the key to victory.

I had meant this only to be a note. I now find I am beginning to write the book. Please forgive me.

---

[1] Frank Walter Messervy, 1893–1974. Educated at Eton and Sandhurst. 2nd Lt, Indian Army, 1913. On active service, 1914–18 (France, Palestine, Syria); 1919 (Kurdistan). CO, Gazelle Force, Sudan, 1941; 9th Indian Infantry Bde, Keren, 1941; 4th Indian Div., Western Desert, and Cyrenaica, 1941–2; 1st Armoured Div., Cyrenaica, 1942; 7th Armoured Div., Western Desert, 1942; 43rd Indian Armoured Div., 1942–3; 7th Indian Div., Arakan, and at Kohima, 1944; IV Corps, Burma (Tamu to Rangoon), 1944–5. DSO, 1941. Taken prisoner, but escaped, 1942. Col., 1941; Maj.-Gen., 1941; Lt-Gen., 1945. Bar to DSO, 1944. Knighted, 1945. GOC-in-C, Malaya Command, 1945–6; Northern Command, India, 1946–7. C-in-C, Pakistan Army, 1947.

[2] Claude John Eyre Auchinleck, 1884–1981. Known as 'The Auk'. Entered Indian Army, 1903. On active service in Egypt and Aden, 1914–15; Mesopotamia, 1916–19 (DSO, 1917); North-West Frontier of India, 1933, 1935. Deputy CGS, Army HQ, India, 1936. Member, Expert Committee on the Defence of India, 1938. Commanded Anglo-French ground forces, Norway, May 1940. Knighted, 1940. C-in-C, Southern Command, 1940; India, 1941 (sent troops to Iraq to crush the pro-German Rashid Ali revolt), 1943–7; Middle East, 1941–2. FM, 1946. Lived in retirement in Marrakech. After death at age 96, buried in Commonwealth War Graves Commission plot in European cemetery in Casablanca.

Winston S. Churchill to Lieutenant-General Sir Henry Pownall
(Churchill papers, 4/19)

7 July 1948

Napoleon 'Boney' Bonaparte Fuller[1] was a friend of mine in the first world war, and is a man of great ability. He was however so much mixed up with the Nazis before the second war that he was unsuitable for employment. This was decided under Mr Hore Belisha, but no doubt explains his bitterness. It would be worth while to reflect upon his military criticism.

Field Marshal Lord Alexander to Winston S. Churchill
(Churchill papers, 2/160)[2]

9 July 1948

My dear Winston,

I am so grateful for your book *The Gathering Storm* which you so kindly sent me – and I am going to enjoy reading it at my leisure which I shall do on my holiday in Prince Edward Island where we go for a month next Sunday. Of course I have read what has appeared in the paper, but the real thing is going to be a rare treat which I am much looking forward to. When I was in London in April, Munnings[3] took me round the RA for a pre-view just before I left and I must congratulate you on your Academy exhibits. I had already seen and admired 'Chartwell in the Snow' and the 'Pool' – but the interior of Blenheim I had not seen before – and they are exquisite – that is not my opinion only – but what Munnings, Brundrit[4] and many others of the pros said. Do you remember our painting excursion on Lake Como in 1945? What fun it was! & what world changes since then. My old pal Tito is at last running true to form – I think I told you then that in spite of being a 100% Communist, he was going to run his Yugoslavia as he wished – and not take orders. I still have hopes that we shall see you out here one day – when you can get away. Love to all your family.

[1] John Frederick Charles Fuller, 1878–1966. Known as 'Boney'. Educated at RMC, Sandhurst, 1897–8. Served in South African War, 1899–1902. Staff Officer, European war, 1914–18. Maj.-Gen., 1930. Chief Instructor, Camberley Staff College, 1923–6. Military Asst CIGS, 1926–30. Retired, 1930. Wrote 32 books on warfare and mechanized warfare.
[2] This letter was handwritten.
[3] Alfred James Munnings, 1878–1959. Educated at Norwich School of Art, 1892–8. Associate, Royal Academy, 1919; Member, 1925; President, 1944–9. Associate, Royal Society of Painters in Water-Colours, 1921; Member, 1929. Knighted, 1944. Hon. LLD, Sheffield University, 1946. KCVO, 1947.
[4] Reginald Grange Brundrit, 1883–1960. British painter. Educated at Bradford School of Art and Slade School of Fine Art, London. Studied under the British painter and sculptor John Macallan Swan. Associate Member, Royal Academy, 1931. Royal Academician, 1938. Paintings include *English Landscape* (1937), *Nightfall* (1940), *Below the Sluice* (1942) and *Above the Falls* (1945).

July 1948

President Harry S Truman to Winston S. Churchill
(Churchill papers, 2/158)[1]

10 July 1948   Washington DC

My dear Winston,

I was deeply touched by your good letter of June 7. I am going through a terrible political 'trial by fire'. Too bad it must happen at this time.

Your great country and mine are founded on the fact that the <u>people</u> have the right to express themselves on their leaders, no matter what the crisis.

Your note accompanying *The Gathering Storm* is highly appreciated, and I have made it a part of the book.

We are in the midst of grave and trying times. You can look with satisfaction upon your great contribution to the overthrow of Nazism & Fascism in the World.

'Communism' – so called is our next great problem. I hope we can solve it without the 'blood and tears' the other two cost.

May God bless and protect you.

                 Ever sincerely your friend.

Winston S. Churchill: speech
('Winston S. Churchill, His Complete Speeches', volume 7, pages 7678–84)

10 July 1948   Woodford Green

A NEW PARLIAMENT

I am grateful to you, Mr Chairman, for all the very gracious expressions you have used about my work while I have been the Member first for Epping and now for Woodford. One always measures friendships by how they show up in bad weather. In Sir James Hawkey I have found a supporter, a champion and a loyal friend in most difficult times, and it may well be that if his influence, hard work and resolute conviction had not prevailed after Munich in this constituency, I might not have had the opportunity of rendering you any of those services which he has mentioned.

Well, we meet here this afternoon – flaming July – but nowadays they get the months shuffled; April becomes July and the other months are put in corresponding disorder. However the British people have always been superior to the British climate. They have shown themselves capable of rising above it, and certainly they have derived from it many of those strong enduring principles and ways of life which make their existence in our island home different from any other community in the world. We meet here at a time which

---

[1] This letter was handwritten.

is very encouraging to our Party. In the three years that have passed since the General Election enormous improvements have been made in our organisation. Socialist opponents on the morrow of that day said there would never be another Conservative Government, but I have not heard them repeating that prophecy lately. As a matter of fact the growth of the Conservative Party – Tory Party, and I am not ashamed of the word 'Tory', Unionists, Liberal Unionists, National Liberals, Liberals – all are welcomed who care about the reviving life of our country – the growth of that movement has been ceaseless and progressive from day to day and month to month. And now we can safely say to our opponents 'let 'em all come'. We can only say that if the most intense exertions are made. Tireless efforts are required of everyone to make sure that, should the call come, we shall be ready and able to offer to the British nation the means of standing once again erect and proud upon its own feet in the world we have saved. And luckily the progress of the Party has been very considerable. I have today, here, through the exertions of my friends and supporters, 11,000 subscribing members of the Conservative Party. We never had half that number when our constituency was double as big.

Lord Woolton, who has done so much to develop our organisation and recreate it – for we let it fall away during the war as we were busy then – he has done much to recreate that organisation. First of all we had a fund provided in the main by a vast number of small contributions which reached a million pounds. And after that he went for another million, but this was not to be money but men and women. And whereas we had then 750,000 officially subscribing members of the Tory Party a few years ago, we now have half a million gathered in the last few weeks. But if the outlook for our Party is favourable, I wish I could say the same about our national affairs.

During the last week the new Health and Insurance scheme has come into operation. Mr Attlee, the Prime Minister, was quite right in his broadcast last Sunday night not to treat this as a Party matter, and to recognise all that has been done by Conservative and Liberal Governments for the cause of social security in bygone years. I have myself been deeply involved, as you know, in all the schemes for insurance against old age, illness and unemployment which have marked the present century of British political life and which are designed, if I may repeat a phrase I used 20 years ago, 'to bring the magic of averages to the rescue of the millions'.

The actual measure for a National Health Service which is now at work is of course the product of the National Coalition Government of which I was the head, and which rested upon a Conservative majority in the House of Commons of 150 above all other Parties. All the more do I regret that this important reform should have been marred and prejudiced in its initiation by the clumsy and ill-natured hands of the Minister to whom it was confided. Needless antagonisms have been raised, largely by bad manners, with the medical profession, and the whole process of imposing this new contribution

– for all have now to contribute – has been rendered more painful by the spirit of spite and class hatred of which Mr Aneurin Bevan has made himself the embodiment. One would have thought that a man who had been only a burden to our war effort in the years of storm and who had received high office in the days of victory would have tried to turn over a new leaf and redeem his past. Here in inaugurating a National Health Service was a task which to most natures would have brought the balm of healing to the human heart. Instead he has chosen the very moment of bringing the National Health Service into being to speak of at least half of his fellow countrymen as 'lower than vermin', and to give vent to the 'burning hatred' – I quote his words – by which his mind is seared. We speak of the Minister of Health, but ought we not rather to say the Minister of Disease, for is not morbid hatred a form of mental disease, moral disease, and indeed a highly infectious form? Indeed, I can think of no better step to signalize the inauguration of the National Health Service than that a person who so obviously needs psychiatrical attention should be among the first of its patients. And I have no doubt that the highest exponents of the medical profession would concur that a period of prolonged seclusion and relief from any responsible duties would be an equal benefit to Mr Bevan and to the National Health Service.

But meanwhile I regret that the Prime Minister has not had the moral strength to dissociate himself and the Labour Party from this anti-social and undemocratic exhibition on the part of one of his leading colleagues. We can only conclude that he does not feel strong enough as a leader even to rebuke so violent and bitter a colleague. If this be so, his position is pitiful and the odium of the words used by Mr Bevan will lie upon the Socialist Government as a whole. At any rate, we who are gathered here in this great assembly this afternoon, will not easily forget that we have been described as 'lower than vermin', and in common with the 10 millions who voted Tory at the last election, and the 13 or 14 millions who are going to vote Tory at the next election, we will take whatever lawful and constitutional steps are possible to free ourselves from further ill-usage by highly-paid Ministers of the Crown.

I trust however that no one will in any way relax his or her efforts to make a success of the new Health scheme. It may be that there has been great carelessness and lack of foresight in its preparation, and that many disappointments and shortcomings will occur. That is a matter which the electors will take into consideration when the time comes, but no one should allow a great national scheme to suffer through the misbehaviour of the Minister in charge. The remedy will be found at the polls, whenever we are allowed to go to them.

There is another aspect however of Mr Bevan's conduct which requires attention. I have always been a firm supporter of British Trade Unionism. I believe it to be the only foundation upon which the relations of employers and employed can be harmoniously adjusted. I have always advised Conservatives and Liberals to join the Trade Unions. I tried to join the Bricklayers'

Trade Union and it is a complicated legal point whether I have in fact succeeded in doing so. I do so now, even at a time when the influence of Trade Union leaders was never stronger upon the government of the country and was never weaker in the control of their own members. There are certainly millions of Tory Trade Unionists today. We have a right to ask – What is the view of the Trade Union leaders upon the language used by Mr Bevan? Are these millions of Tory Unionists who voted for the Tory Party in the last election, and are going to vote for it in the next, to be rated in the Unions as 'lower than vermin'? It must be remembered that Tory and Liberal Trade Unionists are compelled to pay the political levy used to support the Socialist Party unless they contract out by positive action which exposes their names to be the leaders of the organisation. There is no secrecy of the ballot there. It must also be remembered that Mr Bevan was elected by the largest number of votes to the National Executive Committee of the Labour Party at the recent Scarborough Conference. Are the Conservative, Liberal and Independent members of the Trade Unions still to be forced to take this invidious action of contracting out, or else have their money taken away from them to support a party, one of whose most prominent leaders describes them in words I have never in my long experience heard used in British party controversy about any large body of our fellow countrymen? That is a question which we are certainly entitled to ask.

These are not matters which can be allowed to slide away in all the confusion of the present time. It is the duty of the Prime Minister as Head of the Government and not less of the Trade Union leaders to disavow publicly and unmistakably these utterances of Mr Bevan. If they do not do so they will share with him the censures which the British public will certainly apply to such conduct. There are many reasons in these difficult and anxious days why the ordinary, decent, fair-minded people of all the democratic parties should remember how many precious and vital things they have in common. There are many trenches in which we should all stand together, as we did in the years of mortal peril. The Conservative Opposition in the House of Commons have made it their rule to support the Government, to which on party grounds they are earnestly opposed, in everything which clearly concerns our national and patriotic interest. We support, for instance, Mr Bevin in his foreign policy. Although it is not perhaps very skilful, or in various ways very successful, it is at any rate based on sound lines. I spoke at Fulton in America two and a half years ago about the menace of the Russian Soviet power, and at Zurich I spoke about the need for United Europe, or such parts of Europe as can be rescued from the Soviet yoke. I recognise fully that the British Government like that of the United States has followed a course of action based on combining all forces against Communist intrigue and Russian Imperialism. No abuse or revilings on other questions by individual Cabinet Ministers will deter us from giving our support where our national duty is concerned.

We are met here together this evening in an anxious hour. The free democracies of the West are waiting the reply of the Soviet Government to the joint note which has been sent to them at the Kremlin and is published in today's British newspapers. This note makes it plain that we will not allow ourselves to be blackmailed out of Berlin by the inhuman attempts of the Russian Soviet Government to starve the 2½ million Germans who dwell in the British and American zones. They were our enemies in the war, but we are now responsible that they should not be treated with cruel severity. If we were to yield, we should, in my opinion, destroy the best chance, which is now open to us, of escaping a third world war. It must never be forgotten that with Russia we are dealing not with a great nation that can express its free will but with the 13 men in the Kremlin who have made themselves the masters of the brave Russian people, and who rule them with far more dictatorial authority than has ever been shown by any Russian Czar since the days of Ivan the Terrible.[1] No one can tell what these 13 oligarchs in the Kremlin will do. They do not reason as we do in the western world. They declare openly that they have no moral standards as we understand them. Their prime interest is to preserve their personal power and their party fief and to hold down in subjection the hundreds of millions of peoples of many different races whom they rule with a rod of iron. We cannot tell what internal stresses are at work in this grim oligarchy. It would seem to me that they may be very severe at the present time and that one part of the dictatorship is working separately from, or even contrary to, the other. How else could you explain the Soviet's solemn denunciation and excommunication of Yugoslavia from the ring of satellite states at the same moment when they were bringing the crisis in Berlin to its climax? There is no rational process at work which we can understand. That is an additional element of anxiety. The safest course for us and other western democracies is to pursue as we are doing a plain, fair, straightforward policy based on our undoubted rights and on those instincts of humanity which forbid us either to leave the Germans of Berlin who have courageously stood with us to Soviet vengeance or, alternatively, let them all be starved to death. In all this our Foreign Secretary has the right to speak for a united Britain except of course for the Communist fifth column and those who are connected with them; but these have no power to make us change our national purpose.

[. . .]

---

[1] Ivan IV Vasilyevich, 1530–84. Known as 'Ivan the Terrible' or 'Ivan the Fearsome'. Grand Prince of Moscow, 1533–47. Tsar of All the Russians, 1547–84.

General Dwight D. Eisenhower to Winston S. Churchill
(Churchill papers, 2/148)

12 July 1948

Dear Mr Churchill,

Thank you very much indeed for the copy of your book and for the note that accompanied it.[1]

I am most gratified that you support my decision to attempt to write a war memoir. It was indeed difficult for me to decide to do so – out of a monumental amount of military reading, I long ago formed the conclusion that soldiers rarely ever publish a manuscript except to prove that they themselves are always right and critics wrong.

If my book is finally published I will, of course, do myself the honor of sending you a copy of a planned limited edition, and you would thus have my own account before undertaking the writing of your own narrative of 'Torch' and 'Overlord'.

The Rhodes project occupies only a paragraph in my story, but my comment agrees entirely with yours; namely, that there just wasn't enough strength to do all the things we wanted to do at that moment.

Concerning the 'Anvil' affair, I made the attempt in my narrative to outline every major point that you advanced with respect to it and then gave my own reasons for insisting upon the attack. I made the observation that I always felt that your view could easily have been the correct one provided the Western Allies were at that moment concerned with the post-hostilities situation in Europe. I recall that I suggested to you at the time that if this was an overriding factor in your eyes the matter should instantly be taken up with our President. Considering the matter purely as a military move, aimed at the speediest defeat of the German forces, I still adhere to the opinions I then held.

So far as I could remember them I tried to mention all points of major difference, and briefly discussed them, but in every case, I have used them to point up the obvious truth that over all unity of purpose and of action always prevailed – that even such serious differences of conviction could not destroy what I still consider to be the miracle of Allied cooperation. Quite naturally I realize that this miracle could never have occurred except for the great vision and firm support of the two men principally responsible, yourself and our President.

Turning to things of today, I am not sure that your papers have given you any inkling of the terrific personal struggle through which I have gone during the past twelve months. There was a very great pressure placed upon me to enter the political field in spite of repeated denials and outright refusals.

---

[1] Reproduced above (p. 1098).

Because of my intense belief that no man may limit his own readiness to serve his own country, it was difficult to phrase my successive denials in such a way as to avoid the appearance of violating this basic concept, but I have followed the dictates of my own conscience and have at last – in fact only yesterday – finally succeeded in complete suppression of this ill-advised purpose.

I trust that during the coming months you will find another opportunity to visit our country. I know that you like our Florida climate, and should you at any time be passing through this city to enjoy a winter vacation on the Florida coast, please don't forget that my home is yours.

With lasting personal regards,

Winston S. Churchill: speech
('*Winston S. Churchill, His Complete Speeches*', volume 7, pages 7684–6)

14 July 1948   Kent Agricultural Show
Maidstone

AGRICULTURE

I last visited this beautiful park in November, 1942, in the hard times of war when I inspected the Royal Engineers who were stationed here. Many long months of struggle lay before us but I could feel that the tide had turned and that victory of which we had never doubted was taking a definite shape.

I have a deep affection for Kent. When I received the President's invitation to attend your County Agriculture Show I was prompted to accept because I recognized that it would afford me an opportunity to express my own gratitude to the farmers of my own County and the farm workers, not forgetting that noble band of 4,500 members of the Women's Land Army working in Kent, for the magnificent effort to produce food you all made under the inspiring leadership of your President, Lord Cornwallis,[1] whose service to the Nation as Chairman of the Kent War Agricultural Executive Committee throughout the war years will long be remembered.

Kent was in the British front here. You were indeed beset with many difficulties. Your land and crops were overrun by hordes of contractors obstructing your open fields with poles and wires to act as enemy aircraft deterrents, to hamper airborne attacks. I expect I had something to do with that. Your flocks were evacuated from Romney Marsh where the shadow of invasion lay. The Battle of Britain was fought over your heads as you tilled the fields, and finally the county became the graveyard of flying bombs, which shattered and blasted many of your farmsteads. Under such conditions it would have been

---

[1] Wykeham Stanley Cornwallis, 1892–1982. Educated at Eton and Royal Military College. On active service during WWI (wounded, despatches, MC). JP for Kent, 1926. Chairman, Kent County Council, 1935–6. Baron, 1935. Lord Lieutenant of Kent, 1944–72. KBE, 1945. KCVO, 1968.

natural if food production in Kent had declined. On the contrary, it vastly increased. Kent made her full contribution to the Fighting Services. Nevertheless by 1944 you had doubled the tillage acreage in the County; you increased the wheat acreage from 35 thousand acres in 1939 to 96 thousand acres in 1943; the acreage of other vital food crops and your fruit production also grew, and in spite of all this increase in tillage crops you not only maintained but increased the production of milk. Through your efforts even the pre-war barren grasslands along the top of the cliffs of Dover became waving fields of corn. This was indeed a wonderful achievement. It was accomplished not as a result of detailed direction or orders but by the enthusiasm, energy and tireless devotion of all who worked on the land. It is a grand record, and one which Kentish men and the men of Kent may long celebrate together.[1]

What of the Future? In many ways it is dark and obscure. But in one sphere at least the course is clear and plain. British farmers must produce a much higher proportion than they do at present of the food to sustain, in vigorous health, the 47 million people of this country. This is no temporary emergency programme to tide us over the world food shortages which have followed in the wake of the war. It is a programme of long-term expansion made vitally necessary by lasting economic changes both at home and overseas. The two world wars through which we have fought victoriously have changed our economic position in a most profound degree. We are confronted with an ever-increasing world population without a corresponding increase in the world's acreage of fertile productive lands. We in this island are unable to pay for the foreign food we need by the sale of our manufactures. We must produce all the food we can at home and at the same time maintain the land in a rich and fertile state. A vast population has grown up in Britain; and without our utmost exertions it cannot be kept alive. No longer can we rely upon other countries to the extent that was our custom before the war. Every increase in Home Production of food directly helps to solve our problem of survival. I confess I find it a most astonishing fact that the volume of agricultural production, which was achieved during the war years when the Nation had to face all manner of difficulties and danger has actually diminished under the present baffling conditions of peace. Lately I have taken to farming myself in a modest way, and I try to understand the conditions which are the necessary foundations of an expanding British agriculture. I am told that the main cause for the falling off in production since the peak reached in the war is lack of confidence in the future. I cannot feel that this is justified so far as British agriculture is concerned. The need for home-grown food will be so great in the next 10 to 15 years that no Government, however wanton, will dare to maul or maltreat the agricultural producer.

But, I say with all seriousness, let every word spoken or step taken by any in

---

[1] Kent is traditionally divided into West Kent and East Kent, with those from the west known as Kentish Men and those from the east known as Men of Kent.

authority be directed towards expelling from the minds of all engaged in food production all doubts or suspicious thoughts, and replacing them with a true and lasting sense of confidence. Let every action or decision taken by whatever party may be in office make it abundantly clear that they recognize beyond question that owing to the changed world conditions a healthy and properly balanced British agriculture is today, and will ever remain, a first necessity to our life. Let them encourage the industry and all associated with it in every possible manner. Let our rulers remove as far as possible and as soon as possible needless restrictive regulation. Let them not spread doubt and anxiety by dangling in front of the industry Commodity Commissions as suggested by the Lucas Committee.

Instead I say, tell the agricultural community what is expected of it – tell them in no uncertain terms to produce all you can – give them, the landowner, the tenant farmer, the farm worker, that skilful craftsman, every encouragement, guidance – *not direction*. Let them have the tools and the wherewithal to produce what the Nation needs in order to live. With due encouragement I am confident that the great agricultural industry – the men of the soil – will not fail the Nation but will produce the maximum amount of food and at the same time preserve our own beloved land in a rich and fertile state for the benefit of those who will follow us.

Winston S. Churchill: speech
(Hansard)

15 July 1948　　　　　　　　　　　　　　　　　　　　　　House of Commons

CRIMINAL JUSTICE BILL

The right hon. and learned Gentleman (Sir Hartley Shawcross) has managed to occupy, in a fashion not disagreeable to the House, three-quarters of an hour – (Hon. Members: 'An hour'). Well, it did not seem an hour – in speaking upon this issue. But I feel myself that we cannot consider this new proposal without passing in review the series of events which have led up to it. A great deal of the speech of the Attorney-General – the opening part and the end – might well have been presented by him to the Cabinet before the Criminal Justice Bill was drafted and given to the House. The Criminal Justice Bill as presented to Parliament did not deal with the issue of capital punishment at all. On first thoughts the Government were content with the existing practice, and they advised the House not to disturb the existing practice. So those were their first thoughts. As the cynic has said:

Distrust first thoughts – they are usually honest.

That is what is exemplified by what has happened here.

An Amendment was put down by a number of hon. Members of the party supporting the Government –

Mr Sydney Silverman (Nelson and Colne): Not entirely.

Mr Churchill: Not entirely, no, but the great majority. I do not want to rob them of any credit which may belong to them. An Amendment was put down for the abolition of capital punishment. The Cabinet had to decide how this Amendment should be treated, and they decided, as a result of a sort of bargain, that it should be left to a free vote of the House. This, no doubt, appeared a convenient method of disposing of the differences of opinion which prevailed among Members of the Cabinet and in the Socialist Party.

Mr S. Silverman: And in your party.

Mr Churchill: The Government were considering their own party in this matter. But it was not a proper way of dealing with a matter of this gravity, on which the Cabinet on any given occasion should have a united and collective view. We know from the Home Secretary's speech in the House that this, above all others, was in his opinion not the time to make such a change in the law, and he stated his reasons to the House in the strongest terms. He even said that there might have been an increase in the number of murders but for the enforcement of the death penalty, and added:

> in conclusion . . . the Government, having very carefully considered this matter over a period of months, recommend the House not to pass this new Clause tonight.

Well, then, with what effrontery does the Attorney-General get up and say that when we follow the considered, unbiased opinion and recommendation given by the responsible Minister in this House we are guilty of playing party politics? Such nonsense would hardly earn a fee in the meanest court in this country.

We know that the Home Secretary told us his opinion and we may presume that he imparted that opinion to his colleagues. I have sat in many Cabinets, and I find it astonishing that when his advice was not accepted, or when it was not accepted and while the matter was still in the balance, the right hon, Gentleman should not have tendered his resignation. He could with great propriety have said, as he did later in the House, that he had a special responsibility and that quite apart from the general principle, all the evidence at his disposal showed that this was not the time for such a change. I must say that it was the plain duty of the Home Secretary, if his colleagues would not support him, to safeguard the dignity and character of his office by freeing himself from responsibilities which, on his own showing, he was not able to discharge in accordance with his own view of the public interest.

However, he was no doubt assured that if he made the strongest speech setting forth his views, and was supported by leading members of the Cabinet, it was probable that his views – indeed it was almost certain – would be accepted by the House. On this assurance the right hon. Gentleman – for whom we have the greatest respect and whose fortitude in discharging his functions in times of personal grief we all admire, but we, too, must do our duty – drifted incontinently forward. He committed himself in public to Parliament with all his responsibility to the conviction that it would be detrimental to our country to make this change at the present time. He was supported by the Leader of the House, but all this was of no avail. A gamble on a free vote of the House did not come off. By a chance majority of 25 the Amendment abolishing capital punishment –

Mr S. Silverman: Suspending.

Mr Churchill: – suspending capital punishment was added to the Bill and the long-established custom of our country was suspended against the advice of the Government and especially of the Minister publicly and personally responsible. That in itself was a very grave matter. It was incidentally a gamble with the lives of four convicted murderers, whose executions were imminent, but who were reprieved in consequence of the vote. There was, in fact, an issue of principle, on which it was the duty of the executive Government to make up their minds. Instead it was settled by a casual vote, as a result of which Ministers and no doubt the Whips were stultified, and the Home Secretary himself stripped of authority and responsibility in the discharge of his duties.

Fortunately, in this country we still have a Second Chamber and this lapse from civic and public duty by Ministers was corrected in another place. No one can effectively dispute the fact that in rejecting the abolition of capital punishment at this time the Second Chamber did their duty. They were naturally bound to attach great importance to the arguments which had been used in the House of Commons by the Home Secretary. It was not for them to try to measure the differences of view between individual Ministers, which had led the Cabinet to believe that they would find an easy way out of their difficulties by throwing the burden upon the House by a free vote. They had also to take into consideration the advice tendered them by eminent members of the Judiciary, who spoke for the overwhelming majority of the Judges on the Bench. The Attorney-General, preening his ministerial plumes, spoke in disdainful fashion of the opinion of high legal authorities, and quoted examples from bygone generations where they had proved themselves out of step with the march of events. But I think these matters should be settled not only by professional authorities, but by the weighing of the reasons that are involved. The House of Lords had besides to consider the merits of the case at the moment not only on abstract principles, but in relation to the crime wave which the Home Secretary had reminded us was so violent at the present time. In acting as they did in accordance with their convictions and those of the Government and the Home Secretary, the Second Chamber were only discharging the duties which fell upon him. Scarcely less important than this, they were undoubtedly expressing the views and the wishes of the overwhelming majority of the nation. There was no doubt whatever that they showed themselves far more truly representative of public opinion than did the majority of the House of Commons. I am an old House of Commons man and I was sorry to see the popular Chamber so far out of harmony with the opinion and wishes of those they claim to represent.

Although I entirely agree with the action of the House of Lords in referring the matter back to us for further consideration and am myself opposed to the abolition of capital punishment, I was sorry to see the House of Commons show itself at so great a disadvantage not only in the voting but even more in the Debate. One has only to read the Debates in the two Chambers to feel that the House of Lords on this occasion showed a higher sense of dignity and truer instinct than the House of Commons, deprived, as it was, of its proper leadership from the Government; also I must say that the whole character of the Debate in another place was far superior in seriousness and intellectual quality to that which happened here, excluding, of course –

Mr Benson[1] (Chesterfield): On a point of Order. May I ask whether the right hon. Gentleman is entitled to compare or to give his views on the relative quality of the Debates in the two Houses and whether we also shall be entitled to give reasons and instances?

Mr Deputy-Speaker (Major Milner): We will consider that question when we come to it, but so far I see nothing unparliamentary in what the right hon. Gentleman has already said.

Mr Warbey (Luton): Is it in order for an hon. Member of this House to make comparisons between this House and another House in such a way as to bring disrespect upon this House?

Mr Deputy-Speaker: The rule is that no reflection should be made on either House.

Mr Churchill: With great respect, a natural and healthy emulation between the two Chambers may be conducive to their ultimate efficiency and improvement.

As I was saying, I was sorry that the matter has been put so that the House of Commons is at a disadvantage in the view of the country by the way it has come out of this difficult business. It is no service to the cause of democracy to exhibit the People's Chamber, chosen by universal suffrage, in so inferior a position where they can be criticised, comparatively as well as actually, alike in their standard of duty and in their interpretation of the public will. The burden for this misfortune falls directly upon the Cabinet, particularly upon the Prime Minister, the Leader of the House of Commons, and the Home Secretary, who have shown levity in so sombre an issue and have shown their readiness to sacrifice what they clearly knew was their duty in order to reach

---

[1] George Benson, 1889–1973. Estate agent and valuer. MP (Lab.) for Chesterfield, 1929–31, 1935–64. Knighted, 1958. Author of a *History of English Socialism* (1928).

agreement in the Cabinet and party circles. That is a lamentable transaction, from which the leading Ministers concerned can derive nothing but discredit.

Let me recall what was the original Amendment which this House carried and which the House of Lords has rejected. It was for a five years' experiment without capital punishment. Let us see what happened. I did not agree with that – and I do not – but at least it expressed a principle and a policy. The principle was that a court of law should never pronounce a capital sentence because of the sanctity of human life, the murderer's life, but, still, the sanctity of human life, and the policy was to try this experiment for five years and see what happened. This original Amendment compares favourably with the new proposal now before us, in which no experiment is to be made, and in which there is neither thought nor theme.

The Attorney-General: If the right hon. Gentleman will look at the Clause he will find that the last statement he has made is wholly inaccurate. That is not the only statement he has made that is wholly inaccurate, but I am dealing only with the last one.

Mr Churchill: I have read the Clause, and I do not think I have been inaccurate in any way.

Mr S. Silverman: Withdraw.

Mr Churchill: If the hon. Gentleman will tell me what it is he wants me to withdraw I will repeat it twice over. In my view, this Clause is not an experimental one. (Hon. Members: 'It is.') It has neither thought not theme –

The Attorney-General rose –

Mr Churchill: I am comparing the original Clause which was put down by so many Members and put into the Bill with the one which we have before us now. I am certain –

The Attorney-General rose –

Hon. Members: Give way.

Mr Churchill: The Attorney-General has much more experience of courts of law than he has of the House of Commons, and I will tell him for his own benefit that interruptions which have no purpose but to continue the argument are not a fair use of the right of interruption.

Mr Ede: I am quite sure that no one in the House, least of all the right hon. Gentleman, wishes to go wrong on what is a mere question of fact. If the right hon. Gentleman will look at Subsection (8) he will find that the Clause we are now asking the House to adopt is experimental in exactly the same way as was the original Clause.

Mr Churchill: But experimental in relation to an entirely different set of facts. We all remember how Queen Elizabeth dealt with poetry and blank verse – 'Marry, this is something. This is rhyme! But this' – the blank verse – 'is neither rhyme nor reason.' That is what we have before us now – a mere jumble of points which seem popular at the moment to deal with cases in which, to quote the Attorney-General, public opinion feels that the suspension of the death penalty involves risk – public opinion having been measured in less than a few weeks. It is a mere jumble of points which seem popular at the moment, and which have been suggested by the more recent batch of murders as recorded in the newspapers. It has been put together not with the object of making a better and more humane system of criminal justice but of getting round an awkward Cabinet or Parliamentary difficulty. The Attorney-General said it was a compromise. Confusion is not compromise. A bargain between politicians in difficulties ought not to be the basis of our criminal law. This is an attempt, as the Attorney-General said, to steer a middle course, to steer a course of 'no meaning' between the 'No' of the abolitionists and the 'Yes' of the mass of ordinary folk.

This transaction stands in sorry contrast with the long, majestic evolution across the generations of our Common Law. It is disheartening to see such questions being settled by mere expediency and current party embarrassments. Those who favour the abolition of the death penalty ought to vote against this new proposal which is utterly contrary to their conscientious opinion, or to any opinion about which the plea of conscience can be advanced. Conscience and muddle cannot be reconciled; conscience apart from truth is mere stupidity, regrettable, but by no means respectable.

I come now to a case in which I took some interest myself, and in which an interest was also taken for the hon. Member for Nelson and Colne (Mr S. Silverman), who is so anxious to interrupt, and who, I hope, will be fortunate in being able to catch your eye, Sir, in the Debate. I am unable to understand how Members opposite, who supported the execution of the West Africans a few months ago, after these men had been brought three or four times to the scaffold or to the verge of it, can explain their position, even to themselves. According to the principles I learned at the Home Office, and the feelings I derive from my own heart, it is an act of inhumanity to 'cat and mouse' human beings in this way. This was the most horrible and coldblooded execution which the House of Commons, in my long experience, has ever positively and, to a large extent, directly approved and enforced. I would never have allowed it in any Department or Government of which I was the head. Yet some of those Members, the humanitarians, who approved or acquiesced in this grim deed now tell us that their consciences and sentiments are outraged by the ordinary long-established procedure of British justice. It is not possible to exhibit a more complete lack of consistency or indeed conviction upon these poignant issues.

The same House of Commons, in the same Session, has, by its vote, saved the life of the brutal lascivious murderer[1] who thrust the poor girl[2] he had raped and assaulted through a port-hole of the ship to the sharks and has

---

[1] James Camb, 1916–79. Known as 'The porthole murderer'. Ship's steward, *Durban Castle* liner, 1945–7. Murdered Eileen Isabella Ronnie Gibson, 18 Oct. 1947. Sentenced to death, 23 Mar. 1948. Sentence commuted to life imprisonment.

[2] Eileen Isabella Ronnie Gibson, 1926–47. Stage name 'Gay Gibson'. Actor with a Johannesburg-based theatrical company.

sustained the Colonial Secretary[1] in making these five or six Africans, who were under the spell of a degraded superstition go through the agony of death three or four times over and hanging them in the end. The number of lives taken on this occasion is nearly equal to half the executions in Britain in a whole year. But that is not the point. The point I have in mind is the degree of suffering inflicted. Hanging, under English law, if properly conducted, is, I believe, an absolutely painless death –

Mr Stubbs[2] (Cambridgeshire): Try it.

Mr Churchill: Well, it may come to that. It is in the weeks and days and hours before hanging that the ordeal to which criminals are subjected arises. In this case the men I am speaking of were made to go through this ordeal again and again, without it being considered that they had expiated their crime.

It is impossible to comprehend the mental processes which in a single Session exhibit such devastating contradictions. Although I do not agree with them, I respect those idealists who wish to abolish the capital penalty. In an age which has reduced the value of human life more than any other of which there is good record, and which has multiplied executions in cold blood to an extent which would be amazing to former generations, the abolitionists stand against the storm and hold up their mild Victorian lamp in the blackness of the 20th Century. That is morally and intellectually a respectable and comprehensible position. But there is a consideration I would venture to submit in its proper place now and proportion at this point.

I wonder myself whether, in shrinking from the horror of inflicting a death sentence, hon. Members who are conscientiously in favour of abolition do not underrate the agony of a life sentence. To many temperaments this is a more terrible punishment – to some at least. In any case, the gulf of suffering between the two, death and life, is not so wide as is represented. I found it very distressing nearly 40 years ago to be at the Home Office. There is no post that I have occupied in Governments which I was more glad to leave. It was not so much taking the decisions in capital cases that oppressed me, although that was a painful duty. I used to read the letters of appeal written by convicts undergoing long or life sentences begging to be let out. This was for me an even more harassing task.

I remember one capital case in particular, to which the Attorney-General referred. This was the case of a soldier of about 45 years of age, who in a fit of rage killed his wife or the woman with whom he had long lived. After

[1] Arthur Creech Jones, 1891–1964. National Secretary, Transport and General Workers Union, 1919–29. Married, 1920, Violet May Tidman. Organising Secretary, Workers' Travel Association, 1929–39. MP (Lab.) for Shipley Div., Yorkshire, 1935–50; for Wakefield, 1954–64. Parliamentary Private Secretary to Minister of Labour, 1940–5. Parliamentary Under-Secretary of State, Colonial Office, 1945–6. Secretary of State for the Colonies, 1946–50. UK delegate to UN, 1946; 1947–8. PC, 1946.

[2] Albert Ernest Stubbs, 1877–1962. President, Cambridge Trades Council and Labour Party, 1916. Alderman, Cambridge Borough and County, 1942. MP (Lab.) for Cambridgeshire, 1945–50.

the crime, he walked downstairs where a number of little children to whom he used to give sweets awaited him. He took all his money out of his pocket and gave it to them saying, 'I shall not want this any more.' He then walked to the police station and gave himself up. I was moved by the whole story and by many features in the character of this unhappy man. The judge who tried the case advised that the sentence should be carried out. The officials at the Home Office, with their very great experience, suggested no interference with the course of the law. But I had my own view, and I was unfettered in action in this respect.

One of the great privileges and advantages we have in our present system of procedure is that the Home Secretary is unfettered as to the advice which should be tendered in the use of the Royal prerogative. At every point in our system of criminal justice the benefit of the doubt is given to the accused. At every point in the subsequent consideration of a capital sentence, when it has been passed, the same bias is shown in favour of the convicted person. But when justice and the law have done their best within their limits, when precedents have been searched and weighed, mercy still roams around the prison seeking for some chink by which she can creep in.

In this case I decided to advise a reprieve and commutation to imprisonment for life. This was accordingly done. However, a few weeks afterwards this man committed suicide. He hanged himself in his cell and left behind him on his slate the following letter, which I will read to the House because I am anxious that the whole of this question between capital punishment and life imprisonment shall be seen in its true proportion. While I fully agree that capital punishment is a supreme penalty and that mercy is extended in converting it to a life sentence, yet I do feel that the gulf between them is not nearly so wide as people suppose, at any rate in some cases. I will read the letter:

> I hope you will be as good as to let my sister, Mrs Susan Fenton, 8, Oldfield Road, Oldfield Lane, Wortley; and my brother George William Woodcock, 36, Mickley Street, Tong Road, Armley, bury me in my own grave in Wortley Cemetery, Oldfield Lane. I was pleased at the reprieve for the sake of you; not for myself; because I knew it meant 'for life' in gaol, and there is no pleasure in that. I think I had rather be dead than be in gaol for life. I've been studying ever since how to do away with myself, because I do not intend doing it (i.e. staying in gaol for life). I have kept a cheerful look to keep them off thinking that there was anything going on. But I have been studying this above a week. I think I will be a lot better off in my grave, because if I had to get out with 15 years I should be 61 years old. Where could I find work at that age? So I hope I manage alright, so goodnight and God bless you all.
>
> Your poor unfortunate brother,
> E. Woodcock

I mention this case in order that those who shrink from the horror of inflicting the death penalty may not underrate the gravity and torment of the alternative. Indeed, they must be on their guard lest they be soothing their own personal susceptibilities at the expense of what is in many cases a more severe punishment of the guilty. No one can suppose that if the death penalty were abolished murderers of the most ferocious type could be released after 15 or 20 years. In the United States sentences of 30 years are often imposed, and in some other countries the life sentence is rigidly carried out to the end. There is no official capital punishment in Soviet Russia. Murderers, like political dissentients, are just toiled to death in prison or slave camps, and we are assured that this is a proof of the enlightenment of the Communist ideology. There is a danger that our humanitarians may sleep comfortably in their beds, feeling that they have lifted a burden from the world and from themselves, and never think again of the long years of awful gloom, deprivation and misery of mind and soul which they have inflicted on those they meant to benefit. Personally, I believe that our administration of criminal justice in capital cases reaches a very high standard of justice, compassion and good sense.

I am sure the House would be wise to put the same confidence in our present processes as do the overwhelming majority of the British nation. In my time at the Home Office there were only about a dozen executions a year, and I believe that is not very different from the figures today; that is to say, more than half the convicted murderers are reprieved, and the law is administered in a way which commands the confidence and the approval of the vast majority of our community of 47 million, among whom murder is exceptionally rare compared to many other countries. We may put our trust in the wide and flexible use of the Royal Prerogative.

No reasons have to be given by the Home Secretary, and no limits are put. I am sure that it would be a dangerous mistake to impose, as this Clause does, all kinds of arbitrary rules. Although the full freedom of the Prerogative will no doubt remain under the new proposals of the Government, there is a danger that conventions will grow up in practice which will, in fact, canalise clemency. I am told, and I believe that you might well have just as many executions, if not indeed, more under this proposal as by adhering to the existing system. How then can the abolitionists dwell upon the moral and conscientious issue? How can they invoke that when a very large proportion of the executions which now take place will still continue?

One of the ideas behind the Clause is to prevent the death sentence being passed on certain categories of killing. In many of those, the sentence will never be carried out, and in some it ought to be. The intentional taking of human life for private motives is always a terrible crime against society, and nothing should be done to detract from the awe and solemnity of the death sentence. Even in cases where, in all probability, it will be commuted by the exercise of the prerogative of mercy, its omission may weaken the general reprobation of the crime which has been committed. This affects the community as a whole, but it is worse for the jury, to which I now come.

The ancient Anglo-Saxon foundation of all our system of criminal justice is trial by jury. I say that this new and complicated proposal will weaken the jury's sense of responsibility and by introducing in many cases distinction without difference it will puzzle and baffle juries and make their hard task even more difficult and painful. The inconsistencies and absurdities of the Clause in practice will also prejudice the comprehension by the public of the law of the land and will tend to bring that into disrepute. Innumerable cases can be cited which will expose this present proposal to derision. It is no use hon. Members saying that they can pick holes in the present law. I dare say they can, but nothing like what I am going to cite to the House now can be picked in our present system of law. Innumerable cases will be cited, discussed and debated in every part of the country, and this will impair the high structure of our criminal justice. Let us examine this proposal for a few minutes.

The Government Clause provides that the death penalty will only apply when two conditions are fulfilled. First, there must be, as the Attorney has explained, express malice, which is described as an intent to kill or maim by an act which might reasonably be expected to endanger life. Secondly, the murder must be of a certain type. For example, it must be done in connection with robbery, housebreaking, rape, sodomy, etc., or in connection with avoiding arrest, escape, prison officers, etc., or second murder. Such are the proposals of the Clause. The result is that all the most frequent types of murder, that is to say wounding, stabbing, strangling, drowning, etc., committed for all the most wicked motives, jealousy, greed, revenge, etc., will not carry the death penalty, because that penalty will only apply in such cases if the offence is committed by three or more persons.

Secondly, most of the murders committed in the course of committing a felony with violence, that is to say, robbery, rape, etc., and most of the murders committed in connection with burglary and housebreaking, will also not be punishable with death, because for that it will be necessary to prove an intent at least to maim. Let us take only two examples of the problems to be put before the jury. A housebreaker is disturbed. He fires his gun and kills. His defence at the trial is that he fired only to frighten. How can it be proved beyond reasonable doubt that he intended at least to maim? Again, a ravisher kills a woman he is raping by strangling or throttling her. His defence is accident. How can an intent to maim be proved? Let us now apply more directly the new version of the law which we are asked by the Government to lay down.

I am bound to state the facts, however shocking they may be to our accepted methods of reasoning. The Attorney-General has referred to a case which has been much mentioned in public, the systematic administration of poison. That is punishable by death, but if the crime is committed by a single dose, no death sentence can be passed. A man may deliberately kill his wife with a chopper without being sentenced to death. The Government in fact – this is what we are asked to agree to – say to all and sundry, and ask us to say to all and sundry: 'If you decide to kill your wife because, after cold, calculated and deliberate consideration you come to the conclusion that you will live more agreeably alone or with another woman, or because you will benefit under the terms of her will, you have a variety of methods at your disposal, without risking your life even if found guilty. You can strangle her or hold her head in the gas oven until she expires' – (*Laughter.*) – this is not my language – it is what we are asked to place on the statute book. 'You can stab her. You can cut her throat or dash her brains out, each of which will be quicker. If you can arrange the procedure, you can set her on fire, push her off the station platform in front of an oncoming train or push her through the porthole of a ship. Or, more easily, you can drown her in the bath. There is a reciprocal set of cases which arise on the part of the weaker sex. But whatever you do,' say the Government, 'you must be careful not to invite more than one confederate to help you, otherwise your immunity will be gone.'

These are revolting declarations to be presented to Parliament, and still more to be put in the statute book, by any Government or by any House of Commons that has ever been known in this island. I repeat them with disgust in order to show the folly of trying to categorise murderous brutality and in order to expose the levels of thought and principle to which we are now invited to descend. If the amending Clause now before us becomes law, the murderer will, in all the cases I have mentioned, be able to sleep soundly in the knowledge that, in the event of detection, he cannot be put to death. These cases can be multiplied indefinitely, and will be undoubtedly, as the matter is argued out all over the country among all classes of people. Thus the whole of our system of justice in capital cases will be brought into public contempt. I say that this is a high price to pay for party manoeuvres, to unite a Cabinet, or 'to bring our fellows together in the Lobby'. It is a shameful exhibition that we have been presented with in the whole of this story.

I am told by very high legal authorities that great difficulties will be placed upon the judges in summing up. That is brushed aside by the Attorney-General, for no other reason than that it was necessary to fill in this part of his argument with an assertion resting on his own personal opinion. Practically the whole of this lengthy Clause, which few newspapers have had the space to print in its entirety under present conditions, will have to be explained to juries on many occasions. I am assured that this is so by people whose knowledge, authority and repute in the law are as a pyramid to a molehill compared to that of the Attorney-General. I cannot take his advice against the advice of the people whom I have had the opportunity of consulting. I say that practically the whole of the lengthy Clause will have to be explained to the jury. (*Interruption.*) What did the Attorney-General say?

The Attorney-General: I said 'rubbish'.

Mr Churchill: That may be what the right hon. and learned Gentleman has in his head, but it does not carry conviction. We all know that Law Officers in his position have to be trotted out to cover up the most difficult and unsatisfactory situations into which Governments get. I have often seen it done, but never have I seen it done with such an undue parading of his own particular opinion on a matter upon which a great profession could form its own judgment.

Mr James Hudson[1] (Ealing, West): Who advised the right hon. Gentleman?

Mr Churchill: I take full responsibility for everything I say. The jury will have to be instructed and will have to decide whether a killing was in the course of or in connection with the offences described in Subsection (1,a) of the Clause or whether it was for any of the specified purposes in Subsection (1,b), or whether it was in the case of poisoning by systematic administration under Subsection (1,c).

The Attorney-General: Quite wrong.

Mr Churchill: Well the Government will have an opportunity of speaking. The Home Secretary can say what it is. I am told by people who have studied this and have great professional attainments that what I have just said is correct because the jury will in many cases have to be advised –

The Attorney-General indicated dissent.

Mr Churchill: the right hon. and learned Gentleman may shake his head till he shakes it off, but it does not affect the argument. Intense difficulty will occur in the case of a murder alleged to have happened during a rape. I am advised that the judge would have to direct the jury first as to constructive malice under the law as it is at present – that is to say, the malice that is implied from death resulting from a felony involving violence – and secondly, express malice under the law introduced by the Amendment – that is to say, and intention to kill or maim by an act which might reasonably be expected to endanger life. If that is not correct, when the Home Secretary or any other person of authority winds up, no doubt we shall be told, but it is not much good the Government proclaiming facts which are not correct in regard to the existing interpretation of the law of the land.

Mr Hector Hughes[2] (Aberdeen, North): Would the right hon. Gentleman –

Mr Churchill: The offence –

Mr Hector Hughes rose –

Mr Deputy-Speaker: No hon. Member is entitled to speak unless the right hon. Gentleman or the hon. Member having possession of the House gives way.

---

[1] James Hindle Hudson, 1881–1962. Educated at Manchester University. Married, 1913, Nancy Horsfield (d. 1958). MP (Lab.) for Huddersfield, 1923–31; for Ealing West, 1945; for Ealing North, 1950–5. Parliamentary Private Secretary to Chancellor of the Exchequer, 1924, 1929–31. President of the Board of Trade, 1951.

[2] Hector Hughes, ?–1970. Educated at St Andrew's College and University of Dublin. Called to Irish Bar, King's Inn, 1915; to English Bar, Gray's Inn, 1923. KC, Ireland, 1927; England, 1932. KC, 1932. MP (Lab.) for Aberdeen North, 1945–70. Married, 1966, Elsa Lilian Riley.

Mr Churchill: I really would not say anything more controversial than that the Home Secretary would have the power to answer these points and let us know the view of the Government on them. If I am told that the defence of the ravisher in this case could be that he did not intend to use more force than was necessary to make the unfortunate woman submit to his approaches, is he then to escape the supreme penalty because there is no proved intention to kill or maim? All those points, I am assured, will have to be put to ordinary jurymen and jurywomen who have never before been called upon to split such hairs.

Mr Hector Hughes: It is on that point –

Hon. Members: Sit down.

Mr Churchill: Ordinary jurymen and jurywomen who have never been called upon to split such hairs will now have to do it for the first time with a human life at stake. This Clause will in consequence give rise to endless legal arguments both before the judge and in the Court of Criminal Appeal. The result will be to make it more likely that certain categories of murderers are hanged while other categories, equally heinous, cannot be. Secondly, it must tend in the long run to hamper the Home Secretary or some other Home Secretary in the exercise of his unlimited discretion which is by far the most elastic, sympathetic and comprehending process that can possible be used. But it is the ordeal to which juries will be subjected on which the main weight of the practical case rests.

We do not allow the decision of guilt or innocence to be decided in the first instance by trained legal minds or persons of exceptional education. The prime guarantee of British justice is the honest opinion of the ordinary man or woman. Very striking words are used in the jurymen's oath:

> I swear that I will well and truly try the issue joined between our Sovereign Lord the King and the defendant –

Or prisoner –

> and a true verdict give according to the evidence.

Some systems of society seek to substitute for this the decisions of State stipendiaries or officials acting under the influence of the Government of the day. We regard it as a fundamental safeguard of our democratic liberties and life and a principle which has been woven into the whole history of our judicial system that the supreme question, 'Guilty or Not Guilty?' shall be decided by ordinary folk. At the present time this process of decision by a jury has the merit of simplicity. The jury are asked only one decisive question: 'Have the facts given in evidence proved that the crime was committed?' There is the alternative of manslaughter which was mentioned, but in principle that is the issue required of the ordinary people on whom this stress is cast from time to time. Even now there are disagreements on juries, in which case all the disadvantages of a second trial have to be faced, but now by loading the issues to be decided by a jury with the almost metaphysical subtleties of this Clause the Government will be placing on British juries a task which, however carefully it is defined by the judge, however keenly and lengthily it has been argued by counsel, it will be beyond their compass to fulfil. This will greatly increase the probabilities of disagreement.

I say then that this new Clause constitutes as assault, no doubt not intentional but none the less consequential, upon the system of trial by jury in capital cases and that as such it strikes at the democratic principle inherent in the life of our country that a man is entitled to the judgement of his equals. It seems almost incredible that such a rigmarole of wrong-thinking and right-thinking, of pandering to sectional sentiment and party currents, could have been produced by the collective ability of a British Cabinet. It makes one shudder to feel that this may be only a sample of the processes by which the most overwhelming decisions for this country and for the whole world are now being arrived at.

I would say without hesitation that if I had to choose myself between voting for the original Amendment inserted by the House two months ago or for this new proposal which the Government now thrust before us, I would rather vote for the original proposal and see what happens. Fortunately we are not condemned to a bleak choice between two kinds of error. We are free at this moment, thanks to the moral courage of the Second Chamber, to pass the Bill in the form in which it was first introduced by His Majesty's Government and commended to us so strongly by the Home Secretary and by other leading Ministers. That would be by far the most sensible thing for us to do in the interests of the public, in the interest of this House of Commons, and even in the interests of the Government themselves, for they have no surer way of earning mockery and discredit than by persisting in their present course. I trust that even now good sense and reason will prevail. If not, our duty is clear, and we must not fail to discharge it.

Field Marshal Lord Montgomery to Winston S. Churchill
(Churchill papers, 2/31)

15 July 1948

Notes used by me at a Prime Minister's Conference at 10 Downing Street. I spoke from these notes and it all appears in the minutes of the Conference.[1]

CERTAIN FACTORS AFFECTING THE SITUATION IN THE WEST

1. Do we intend to make it clear to the Russians that our being forced out of Berlin <u>by any means</u> will bring about World War III? Appeasement, or passivity, or 'wobbling', will be fatal.

2. If it is to be war, then Berlin has NO military value; it would be, in fact, a very great military liability.

3. It is unlikely the Russians will start the shooting to get us out.

The action will be a policy of 'squeeze'.

4. How long can we stand up to this squeeze? The British Element in Berlin could stay there for a long time.

But we could not maintain a decent life for the Germans in the British sector.

The Russians will include this German factor as the principal weapon of their 'squeeze' policy.

5. If the Germans in the British sector in Berlin should then turn against us, would it be the policy of HMG that we leave Berlin?

If this happens does this mean World War III, vide para 1.?

FIRM MILITARY FACTORS: ADVERSE

6. The Army is not geared for war.

7. The other nations of the Western Union are definitely not geared for war. Furthermore their spirit is not warlike. For the present they must be regarded as useless.

8. The war would therefore begin with a series of disasters on land in Western Europe.

9. These disasters could not be avoided.

Their effects could be delayed, by taking certain immediate steps such as:
  (a) a proper Command set-up.
  (b) stopping the release scheme.
  (c) returning to the Army many thousands of key men who have been released since World War II ended.

10. In fact, if it is to be war then we must get ready for mobilisation. The examination of any lesser measures will not affect the major issue. We must begin at once.

---

[1] This cover note was handwritten.

July 1948

11. This mobilisation when ordered will involve putting our economic and industrial machine into reverse.

FIRM MILITARY FACTORS: FAVOURABLE

12. We have the atomic bomb, i.e. the USA.

13. We and America possess the industrial potential to ensure our success in a long war.

14. I do not believe that the Russian economy is at present in a fit state to nourish and sustain World War III.

Her leaders must know this, and would shrink from taking the plunge into war.

FINALE

15. The crux of the whole matter is the answer to para 1.
16. You cannot make war without men and materials.

<u>Men</u>. The 4 essential stages will be:
   (a) Stop the Release Scheme and thus halt the run-down of the Army.
   (b) Call up the Army Reserve: about 50,000.
   (c) Embody the TA.
   (d) Recall the 'Z' Reservists. These are all men who served in the late war and who are still liable for service so long as the general emergency has not been concluded. They total 4 million.

These steps must be taken in order, (a) first. (a) must be taken at once.

<u>Material</u>. Certain essential war production must be started up.

For instance khaki cloth; we have only 250,000 suits of battle-dress.

The petrol and oil fuel reserves in the country are practically nil.

Colonel Frank Clarke to Winston S. Churchill
(Churchill papers, 2/161)

16 July 1948 New York

My dear Winston,

It was very thoughtful of Clemmie and you to send me a cable when you heard of my operation. Actually, I have made a remarkable recovery considering that the appendix was ruptured; and while I will be obliged to take it easy for a few weeks I really feel very well indeed and have suffered no ill effects.

I know you must be enjoying Bernie's visit with you and I am sure he has brought you completely up to date on the general situation on this side.

It would appear to me that the political campaign will develop into a knockdown-drag out fight, with no holds barred; and while I believe that our friend in Albany[1] will win, it is by no means a sure thing and the Republicans

---

[1] Thomas Dewey.

cannot afford to be complacent. The Democrats have one strong talking point in their favor which will appeal to the masses, and that is that everyone has a job who wants one and at good wages, and there is a great reluctance to 'kill Santa Claus'.

I am in a position to get both sides of the picture at fairly close range and will continue to keep you informed.

I do hope you are giving thought to coming out to stay with me this winter.
Kindest regards to you all.

Winston S. Churchill: speech
('Winston S. Churchill, His Complete Speeches', volume 7, pages 7697–8)

16 July 1948   Cardiff, Wales

BUILDING A NEW EUROPE

We cannot conceal from ourselves that a shadow rests upon our thoughts, a dark shadow which we had supposed we had banished at any rate for our lifetime and for our children from the world.

It is not my intention to dwell upon the cause or the character of that dark gloom, but this I will say, that there is one simple guide in times of difficulty and that is to do what is right and honourable. It is not only the most proper thing to do but also in most cases the safest course to take. There are many dangers in the modern world from which no country can save itself by flight. A firm, steady, patient honesty will be supported, no matter what government is in power, by the great mass of the British nation.

I cannot think it can be good for the world that we should continue to nurse feelings of hatred against the German people, which, by the follies of its rulers and its own weakness, had been brought so low. I think the time has come when we should turn our faces away from that terrible past and look forward to a time when Germans and Germany, probably in the form of their ancient States, will take their place again in the family of Europe and bring all their gifts and power and all the valour of their race towards undoing the harm they have done and to building up again that great structure of Europe, a continent fallen from its great estate and from its place in the primacy of their world.

That continent must arise again in all its ancient glory. That cannot be done unless all the great elements within its population – our French allies who are ever first in our minds, the German people, the Italians, and the nations with whom we have not fought – are all brought within the majestic structure of a united Europe and become once again the admiration and not the object of pity among all the nations of the world. Let faults be forgotten, let justice be done to all the major criminals, but let us now turn over a new page and look forward.

We must nevertheless recognize that the United States has become the most powerful nation in the world and the greatest force now working for peace and freedom among men. We have need of them and they of us. Let us stand together, confidently pursuing the same ideals, guarding the same sacred treasure and marching forward along the path of duty. We should not hesitate to accept with the greatest cordiality ever closer ties of unity with the United States.

Winston S. Churchill to Field Marshal Lord Montgomery
(Churchill papers, 2/143)

18 July 1948
Private

My dear Monty,

Will this[1] do for the publication of your speeches? If you want it altered let me know.

The gravity of events makes me anxious. I trust we are not approaching another 'Munich'. For such a crime by a British Government there would be no forgiveness.

Winston S. Churchill to Brendan Bracken
(Churchill papers, 2/146)

19 July 1948

My dear Brendan,

I cannot do any more in Palestine.[2] Events must take their course.

Henry Channon: diary
('Chips', page 429)

20 July 1948

I dined with the Palmellas at Claridge's in a private room. People stood up and clapped as Winston and Mrs Churchill passed through. We were about 22, and an agreeable party, but not the one that I should myself have given for Winston. Not sufficiently distinguished. I was between my sister-in-law, Patsy

---

[1] A foreword, enclosed with this letter: 'Whatever Field Marshal Montgomery writes about the structure of our new Army deserves the careful study of all concerned with its welfare and efficiency. His profound knowledge of the art of war and the historic battles in which he played a leading part invest his words with special significance.'

[2] Churchill had been asked by Bracken to intervene again in Parliamentary debate on this subject.

Lennox-Boyd,[1] who was sweet, and Mrs Churchill, who looked most distinguished: beside her Lady Kemsley[2] seemed almost naked. Winston entered like royalty, and bowed a little and made himself charming. . . . at the end of dinner the men remained behind and Gomer Kemsley[3] appointed himself spokesman and tried to draw out Winston (I have long known of their hostility). But the great man needed no prompting: he was gay, he was grave, he was witty, he was provocative, and in the highest spirits, but he admitted, indeed insisted, that never before in our history had the position of England been so precarious. . . . When asked by Gomer if he did not admire Attlee he replied, 'Anyone can respect him, certainly, but admire – no!'

Poor Massigli[4] showed every sign of the French weakening over Berlin (he is without a government, as Schumann's[5] cabinet fell yesterday) and made a slightly defeatist remark to the effect that it would be better to clear out of Berlin and leave it to the Germans – in other words to the Russians, who would, of course, take over. Winston rose in his wrath and snubbed him. At length the Churchills left and everyone rose to say 'Good-night'. I left at 1.30 a.m., just too late to join Bob Menzies for supper at the Orchid Room.

Winston S. Churchill to Clement Attlee
(Churchill papers, 2/67)

21 July 1948
Secret
Urgent

My dear Prime Minister,

I understand that we are to have a statement from the Foreign Secretary tomorrow on the Berlin situation.[6] We have consistently supported the foreign policy of His Majesty's Government on the main issues involved. My colleagues however feel anxiety about the state of our defences and resources, both British and Allied, on which of course we have not been given any

[1] Patricia Guinness, 1918–2001. Married, 1938, Alan Lennox-Boyd.
[2] Helene Candida Hay, 1913–2011. Married, 1933, Lionel Berry, 2nd Viscount Kemsley: four children.
[3] James Gomer Berry, 1883–1968. Newspaper proprietor; brother of Lord Camrose. Bt, 1928. Baron Kemsley, 1936. Viscount, 1945. Chairman, Kemsley Newspapers Ltd, 1937–59. Editor-in-Chief, *Sunday Times*, 1937–59. Trustee, Reuters, 1941; Chairman, 1951–9. One of his six sons was killed in action in Italy in 1944.
[4] René Massigli, 1888–1988. During WWI, served in French Foreign Service. Secretary General, Conference of Ambassadors, 1920–31. Exiled to Turkey, 1938–40, where he served as Ambassador. Commissioner for Foreign Affairs, 1943–4. Ambassador to Great Britain, Sep. 1944 to Jan. 1955. Secretary-General, Quai d'Orsay, 1954–6.
[5] Jean-Baptiste Robert Schuman, 1886–1963. Born in Clausen, Luxembourg. PM of France, 24 Nov. 1947 to 26 July 1948, 5–11 Sep. 1948. First President, European Parliamentary Assembly, 1958–60.
[6] The Soviet Union's blockade of Berlin and the airlift in response by the Western Allies began on 24 July 1948 and lasted until 12 May 1949.

information. I shall therefore ask, after Mr Bevin's statement, whether you will be making any pronouncement before we separate about security and defence, including civil defence. We feel it is the least we can do in all the circumstances. It may be that the Debate on the Appropriation Bill on Wednesday would give you some opportunity of making a statement, necessarily in general terms. We certainly should not consider it desirable to go into detail publicly at this juncture; but we think we ought to know before we go any further that this other aspect of our policy has been the subject of full care and attention.

Winston S. Churchill to Lieutenant-Colonel Bill Deakin
(*Churchill papers, 2/148*)

21 July 1948

My dear Bill,

I leave for Aix-en-Provence on August 22 and propose to stay there for several weeks. I am not touching Volume II till the beginning of September. When you return in the last week of August, will you please get in touch with Kelly and work with him – he has been collecting all the material for the changes in Volume II and will have it in an advanced state of preparation. You should go through it with him, and I should be very glad if you could come out to me on September 4 or 5 bringing out with you Volume II and all the material needed. We could then settle the whole matter once and for all, and you could then take it back with you in a completed form. It is most necessary that you should take over everything from Kelly, who has been most active.

It is quite easy to reach Aix, which is only twenty miles from Marseilles – one night's journey in the Blue Train.

I hope you have a pleasant holiday, and have benefitted from a rest. I have been very hard pressed.

Winston S. Churchill to Clement Attlee
(*Churchill papers, 2/45*)

27 July 1948

My dear Prime Minister,

I understand that it will be possible for us to raise the question of Hyderabad and Kashmir as the first topic on the Agenda on Friday next.

I propose to remind you of your pledges, and indeed of ours, about the rights of these States, and I trust that you will be able to be present on this occasion as the matter is one which affects the good faith of His Majesty's Government past and present.

I am informed that both Hyderabad and Kashmir are willing to have their fate decided by a plebiscite under the auspices of UNO, provided that the basis of election is adult suffrage, without property qualification. This seems to me a solution difficult for any believer in democracy to deny them. I shall appeal to you to say that you will help it forward. Without this much blood will flow and our promises be broken.

Winston S. Churchill to Clement Attlee
(Churchill papers, 2/18)

27 July 1948

My dear Prime Minister,

When you were good enough to receive a deputation composed of members of the British delegation to the Hague Congress, it was agreed that further detailed information should be sent to you about the proposal for the convening of a European Assembly.

The paper which I enclose is a tentative scheme prepared by a group of members of the British delegation drawn from all political parties. The details of the scheme are being worked out by an International Study Committee under the chairmanship of Monsieur Ramadier.

I also enclose a memorandum approved by the International Committee of the Movement for European Unity at its meeting in Paris on July 18 and a draft Resolution to be submitted to each Parliament.

The creation of a European Assembly would represent an important practical step in the advance towards a United Europe, and would greatly help to create a sense of solidarity among the European peoples in the face of the increasing dangers which beset them. In this the lead could be taken by Britain. The encouraging response to the initiative of the Foreign Secretary after the announcement of the Marshall Plan in June 1947 and, more recently, in the negotiations for the Brussels Treaty are proof, if such is necessary, of the influence of British leadership.

I should therefore be most glad if you would consider this memorandum and its enclosures. We should welcome any criticisms or suggestions you make care to make and should, of course, be glad to come and discuss the matter with you further should you desire it.

Winston S. Churchill to General Lord Ismay
(Churchill papers, 4/19)

27 July 1948

About the reinforcement of Crete by tanks.

You will remember how during Operation 'Tiger' I asked that about twelve additional heavy tanks, probably 'I', should be landed in Crete. Some think that had they been there this would have decided the battle. However, the Chiefs of Staff rightly pointed out that bring[1] a ship with nearly a hundred tanks on board to the north of Crete at Suda Bay might endanger the whole cargo. They suggested that Wavell should be asked instead to send about that number to Crete from his Cairo workshops. Being much preoccupied with Gott's fighting in the desert near Sollum he did not like to interrupt the flow from the Cairo workshops to the front of all the damaged tanks in their hands, and I therefore asked that the ship of the Tiger convoy should come to Alexandria and unload there, and that the first twelve tanks unloaded should be sent at once in another ship to Crete. They never got there and it is necessary to know (a) exactly what was the date of the 'Tiger' ship's arrival at Alexandria, and (b) what action was in fact taken upon my decision in which the Chiefs of Staff agreed. My own feeling is that the first Tiger Cubs arrived on the 11th or the 12th of May. It should have been possible to take twelve fully serviceable 'I' tanks from the first ship, and trans-ship them. They could then have reached Crete in 36 hours. The German air blockade was at that time severe, but this would also have affected the movement of any tanks ordered to Crete from Cairo workshops after May 9. Indeed I think they could have arrived from both sources at the same time which was what I had in mind. But let me know exactly what happened as a result of my minute of May 9. We certainly fell between two stools. I should like to know what you think about it.

Winston S. Churchill to General Dwight D. Eisenhower
(Churchill papers, 2/148)

27 July 1948
Private

My dear Ike,

Thank you very much for your letter of July 12.[2] It always gives me great pleasure to hear from you as it recalls the great deeds in which we played our parts. I shall look forward constantly to reading your book, and I think it is your duty to write it.

About the Presidency, my feeling is that you were right not to intervene on this occasion. Because if you had stood as a Democrat, it would have looked like going to the rescue of a party which has so long held office and is now in difficulties. On the other hand if you had stood as a Republican it would have been hard on the party whose President you served. However, luckily there is plenty of time.

I am deeply distressed by what we see now. There can be no stable peace

[1] bringing.
[2] Reproduced above (pp. 1107–8).

in the world while Soviet Imperialism is rampant and Asia on the Elbe. I am strongly of the opinion that waiting upon events to find the line of least resistance will not provide a means of escape for the poor world and the horrors which threaten it. I feel there should be a settlement with Soviet Russia as a result of which they would retire to their own country and dwell there, I trust, in contentment. It is vital to the future that the moment for this settlement should be chosen when they will realise that the United States and its Allies possess overwhelming force. That is the only way of stopping World War Number Three.

Clement Attlee to Winston S. Churchill
(Churchill papers, 2/18)

30 July 1948

My dear Churchill,

On the 27th July you wrote to me[1] on behalf of an all-party group of the members of the British Delegation to the Hague Congress about the proposal for the convening of a European Assembly.

As I told you when we discussed the matter together on July 28th, I am in sympathy with the basic idea behind the movement. I do not, however, see how the Government could support in the United Kingdom Parliament the draft Resolution which the International Committee of the Movement for European Unity has suggested should be moved in the Parliaments of the different participating countries. It seems to me that if an Assembly is to be convened this must, in view of the vital importance of the matter, be done by Governments, and not by independent organisations or by Parliaments. On the other hand I think that this is not the right time for Governments to take this major initiative, when their hands are so full already with urgent and difficult problems.

It seems to me that it would be unfortunate if the chances of action later were to be prejudiced by such a Resolution being raised before the Government feel able to support it, and I cannot therefore but feel that it would be best that the Resolution should not be brought forward at this stage. But of course I see no reason why the independent organizations concerned in the movement should not continue their work of spreading the idea of European Union.

---

[1] Reproduced above (pp. 1129–30).

July 1948

Winston S. Churchill: speech

('Winston S. Churchill, His Complete Speeches', volume 7, pages 7701–6)

30 July 1948　　　　　　　　　　　　　　　　　　　　　House of Commons

HYDERABAD AND KASHMIR

I had intended, in the normal course, to await the statement of the Government before taking part in this Debate, but as I understand the Prime Minister would rather follow me, I defer to his wishes as a matter of courtesy. I will say a few words to emphasise the points which have been so clearly brought out by my hon. and learned Friend the Member for Wirral (Mr Selwyn Lloyd).[1] I feel that they have, by their reasonableness, commended themselves to the House, and, as a matter of fact, the solution I am going to urge on the Government is extremely reasonable and in harmony with modern democratic sentiments and principles.

Let me begin first with the pledges – and I am very glad to see the Chancellor of the Exchequer (Sir Stafford Cripps) in his place. The relations between Hyderabad and the British Crown have been governed by treaties which have been renewed in authority by statements as late as 1943 and 1942, and the Viceroy, during the late Parliament, declared that these treaties were inviolate and inviolable. When the present Chancellor of the Exchequer went out in March, 1942, under the late Government, he told the Hyderabad delegation:

> If you choose to resume your powers and to become even independent, say so and you will have it. The North-Western group of provinces may want to have a union by themselves. You may join either the one or the other or none. We ourselves will not unilaterally revoke our undertaking.

That was what the right hon. and learned Gentleman said when he was a member of the Coalition Government. When he went out again under this Government, it is important that the House should notice the great change in principle introduced by the present Government. We had always insisted that obligations and pledges to the Princes and to the scheduled classes and others must be fully and faithfully carried out as an essential part of any process of transfer of ruling power, but under the present Government this was cast away and the pledges were abandoned. The right hon. and learned Gentleman is reported to have said to Hyderabad representatives in April, 1946, that what he said in 1942 no longer applied about the position of the States –

---

[1] John Selwyn Brooke Selywn-Lloyd, 1904–78. Born in Liverpool. Educated at Cambridge University. Barrister, Gray's Inn, 1930; Master of the Bench, 1951. 2nd Lt., TA, 1939. Capt., 1940. Maj., 1940. Lt.-Col., 1942. Col., 1943. Brig., 1944. OBE, 1943. CBE, 1945. MP (Cons.) for Wirral Div., Cheshire, 1945–76. QC, 1947. PC, 1951. Married, 1951, Elizabeth Marshall (div. 1957). Minister of State, FO, 1951–4.Minister of Supply, 1954–5; of Defence, 1955. Secretary of State for Foreign Affairs, 1955–60. Chancellor of the Exchequer, 1960–2. CH, 1962. Lord Privy Seal and Leader of the House of Commons, 1963–4. Speaker of the House of Commons, 1971–6. Baron, 1976.

It no longer held good since the discussions with the Indian leaders were now on the basis of independence.

Nevertheless, he confirmed that the States themselves would be entitled to their independence on the transfer of power and the lapse of paramountcy. It is important that the House should notice the change which was made by the present Government on coming into power – the abandonment of pledges under which we had acted with them in the previous Parliament and the previous Cripps Mission. When this matter came to be considered in the present Parliament, the Prime Minister used this expression, a sentence of which has been quoted by my hon. and learned Friend, which the House should have in mind. This was at the time when the Indian Independence Bill was going through:

> With the end of the treaties and agreements –

which had been unilaterally repudiated –

> the States regained their independence. . . . It is the hope of His Majesty's Government that all States will, in due course, find their appropriate place within one or other of the New Dominions within the British Commonwealth, but until the constitutions of the Dominions have been framed in such a way as to include the States as willing partners, there must necessarily be a less organic form of relationship between them, and there must be a period before a comprehensive system can be worked out.

That was the Prime Minister, asking the House to assent to the legislation which he proposed. Further, the Secretary of State for India, speaking in another place, said:

> From the date when the new Dominions are set up, the treaties and agreements which gave us suzerainty over the States will become void. From that date the appointments and functions of the Crown Representative and his officers will terminate, and the States will be masters of their own fate. They will then be entirely free to choose whether to associate with one or other of the Dominion Governments, or to stand alone.

This statement was made in Parliament, in conjunction with the passage of the Indian Independence Bill. On this basis, therefore, the treaties with Hyderabad were unilaterally repudiated by Great Britain, and the State of Hyderabad reverted to its original sovereign independence. That is my first point – that it is at present a sovereign independent State. It has a perfect right, as such, to apply for admission to UNO. It has 17 million inhabitants; it has a long history, and a long corporate identity. Of the 54 Member States of the United Nations, 39 have smaller populations, 20 have smaller territory and 15 have smaller revenue.

We are told that Hyderabad is surrounded by Indian territories, that it is completely land-locked, that it has no access to the sea. But such considerations have nothing to do with the right of independence. Switzerland is completely land-locked, and has no access to the sea, but has maintained its independence for hundreds of years. Austria and Czechoslovakia, also, are States which have no access to the sea, but their independence has never been treated lightly by the British House of Commons. Since when are the rights of States to independence to be impugned or compromised by the fact that they are land-locked? I say that Hyderabad has an absolutely indefeasible status of independence, and that it is fully entitled to membership of the United Nations Organisation if accepted by that body and, still more, is entitled to lay its case before that body and appeal for its support and mediation, especially when a breach of the peace may be involved. The first question I wish to have answered by the Government is – will they assist Hyderabad in bringing its case before UNO, and will they instruct our representative there to see that the case of both States is fully and fairly heard and discussed?

What has happened? My hon. and learned Friend has told us a good deal of what has happened, and I do not wish to add much to it, except to say that a very harsh blockade has been imposed on Hyderabad by the Central Government of India, a blockade which, in many aspects, is similar to that which the Soviet Union are now throwing around Berlin, except that the numbers of helpless people are far greater – 17 million compared with 2½ million – and also because several very harsh features have been introduced into it, such as the prevention of the supply of medicines, drugs and hospital equipment. The Prime Minister, as I happen to know from interchanges we have had, contradicts this, but I would suggest that he should search more fully for his facts. There was a letter which appeared in yesterday's *Manchester Guardian*, which I would be glad to place at his disposal, which shows how completely the stoppage of these drugs has been enforced, particularly chlorine.

The process is this, and, here again, it has a Soviet flavour: supplies of drugs are cut off by the Provinces, by Bombay and Madras. The firms that have medicines there are prevented from delivering them. The railways are used in the Provinces to prevent delivery. Before the Prime Minister confines himself to denying this statement on which, as I understand it, he has been misinformed, he had better look into this question. I am prepared to submit to him a number of cases of correspondence which show clearly how medicines and drugs are being blocked by the Provincial Governments, which are also Congress-dominated. Nothing is getting through. It is three months since any chlorine arrived in Hyderabad. The right hon. Gentleman will have a lot to do no doubt, but I was surprised to find that he seemed so confident on this matter. I am sure it will be possible to give him overwhelming evidence on which he can readjust his position.

This letter in the *Manchester Guardian* yesterday, which is confirmed by evidence I have in my possession, was written by Mr Zola, an Indian no doubt, but resident in this country, who gives a full account, with extraordinary elaboration and skill, of how the stoppage has been effected from many points. That is not a very gratifying feature of the present blockade of Hyderabad, because the chlorination of water and chlorine in hospitals are really essential in India to the prevention of very serious pestilences. As I say, I will furnish the right hon. Gentleman with the correspondence. Unless my facts can be contradicted and overthrown, it is an odious incident.

There is another point which I will mention, which was also mentioned by my hon. Friend, and that is that during the war the people and Government of Hyderabad made large contributions to British war loans. The securities for those were deposited in the Bank of India. They have all been frozen. Money was subscribed to help us to win the war and now, in their hour of distress, is frozen by the Government of India, and at the very moment – and this is what I want the Chancellor to pay attention to – when the right hon. and learned Gentleman is making arrangements for releasing large sums from the sterling balances, sustaining and supporting, in fact, the Indian Government by the active diversion of goods from this country. It is impossible for the Government to take that kind of step, and not have some responsibility for the actions which they are taking, in the financial sphere at any rate.

All this, however, is the 'cold' war, but it may be the prelude to actual violence. There was a speech delivered by Mr Nehru since I wrote my letter to the Prime Minister, or at any rate on the same day, and I must read an extract from it, one sentence of which was quoted by my hon. and learned Friend. I am taking it from *The Times*. If it is an incorrect report, it ought to be denied at once. This is what he said, according to *The Times* of 27th July:

> If and when we consider it necessary, we will start military operations against Hyderabad State.

The report in *The Times* went on:

> He said the present régime in the Nizam's State was composed of 'gangsters', and asserted that the only alternatives before Hyderabad were accession to India or disappearance as a State. He ridiculed talk of war, which could only be between independent countries, and said that in the event of action against Hyderabad he would not propose to confer upon it 'that big designation of war'.

It seems to me that this sort of language which really might have been used by Hitler before the devouring of Austria, but I think he was more careful in the choice of his language. It certainly could have been used before the overwhelming of Czechoslovakia. All these matters, these incidents and facts, cannot be brushed aside as of no consequence, merely because they are committed one against another by Indians. I thought we took the principle of the broad equality of the human race, irrespective of colour or creed. If that be so, there is no reason why Indian Ministers and rulers should not be subjected to the same forms of criticism and be assigned the same moral responsibility as would be the case in regard to the Europeans or Americans.

That speech does cause the gravest anxiety, because if an act of aggression were committed by India, or by the Nehru Government of India, upon the independent State of Hyderabad, the British Crown and even the person of His Majesty would be involved, owing to the arrangements which have been made. To say that such a situation should be allowed to arise, while this House were to be unable to discuss it or should drift on while a hideous deadlock of that character arises in the Far East of the Empire, would indeed be an absurd and a wrong contention.

I do not propose to go at any length into the question of Kashmir, except in so far as it is relevant to the Hyderabad situation. Kashmir is, I understand, already engaging the attention of UNO and a commission from UNO is now at work in Kashmir, though not meeting with any great success. Still, there is the fact that UNO is there working in Kashmir. Hyderabad has a far more numerous population than Kashmir, three times, or twice anyhow. If one may have the good offices of UNO, why may not the other? I cannot understand that. Nor can I understand what principle underlies the attitude of the India Government towards these two States. In Kashmir, four-fifths of the people are Muslim and the ruler is a Hindu. His accession to the Dominion of India is accepted without any reference to the vast majority of his people. In regard to Hyderabad, the case, as a communal problem, is the other way round. The ruler is Muslim and the bulk of the people are non-Muslims. The India Government – the Nehru Government – take the line that in one case it is the will of the people and in the other case it is the decision of the ruler. In either case, however we work it, they get them both. I must say that we ought to notice this very curious way of deciding these grave matters.

I would propose that the Government – I mentioned it in my letter, and this is what I hope to obtain – the Government will try to apply the same rules and principles to the settlements of difficulties in both Hyderabad and Kashmir, namely, that both those States should be given access to UNO and that our Government should actively aim at getting access there. Then, we should set up and formulate again the principle for which we have made immense sacrifices in our Colonial Empire, that governments derive their just power from the consent of the governed and that, in difficult and doubtful cases where the fate of communities is to be decided, the United Nations Organisation should be the supreme tribunal to which we should endeavour to appeal, in order to avert war or violence.

I am informed that the people of Hyderabad, like, naturally, those of Kashmir, would be quite willing to have the fate of their State determined by a plebiscite, provided – and I hope that the democrats opposite will take this in – that it is fairly conducted under the auspices and through the organisation of UNO. I should have thought that was a very good way of dealing with the matter. That was what we had in Greece at the beginning of the present Government.

Mr Wyatt:[1] Would the right hon. Gentleman –

Mr Churchill: No. I would not. I cannot do that. I wish to unfold my argument. The hon. Member may have a chance later to unfold what he has to say. I have practically finished my argument, and I cannot see why the hon. Gentleman cannot await his turn when he may catch the eye of Mr Speaker. I am trying to say what I think the Government would be well advised to do. I am saying that both these States are willing to have their case decided by a plebiscite, provided that it is under the auspices of UNO, and – I must make this clear – provided that there is no property qualification. To that, I understand, the Hyderabad Government attach greater importance. They want adult suffrage. That does not seem to me to be a ground on which any objection could be entertained by the party opposite. They want a free plebiscite with adult suffrage, under the auspices of UNO, the result to be accepted by both sides.

That is the question I am putting. I must admit that the reason they want adult suffrage in Hyderabad and not a property qualification is because there are nearly five million Untouchables who, it is believed, would have very little property at all, as in other parts of India. I think it is thought that they would believe that they would get far better treatment on communal grounds in the State of Hyderabad than they would receive under the Government of India as a whole. We cannot look behind it. Any man has the right to say: 'I ask for no more than a plebiscite, on adult suffrage, conducted freely under the auspices of the supreme world instrument for the prevention of war.' I ask the Prime Minister, who is I believe to reply, to deal with that point. I hope earnestly that he will say that he will favour the application to UNO, and that he will consider that a plebiscite of this character so conducted would be a good way of dealing with this problem.

I quite understand that the right hon. Gentleman did not want all this matter to be discussed. If I had his background of pledges in the matter, I should have felt a great deal of compunction in hearing the whole matter put before Parliament and the country. However, we are not yet at the end of this tragic story, and I warn Ministers that, although while they possess a majority in this Parliament they may be totally indifferent to public opinion and to world judgments in many ways, yet they have a personal obligation which affects their honour and good faith not to allow a State which they have assured a declared and sovereign independent status to be strangled, stifled,

---

[1] Woodrow Lyle Wyatt, 1918–97. Dispatch officer in WWII, 1939–45. Maj., 1944. MP (Lab.) for Aston Div., Leicester, 1945–55; for Bosworth Div., Leicester, 1959–70. Contributor to the *Daily Mirror*, 1965–73; to the *Sunday Mirror*, 1973–83. Knighted, 1983. Baron, 1987.

starved out or actually overborne by violence. To sit by after all they have said and to allow that to happen, to shrug their shoulders and say: 'It is not a matter for us; it is a matter for the India Dominion,' would be to commit an act of shame with which their names would be burdened for generations which otherwise might not have paid attention to them.

August 1948

Winston S. Churchill to Admiral Lord Louis Mountbatten
(*Churchill papers, 2/153*)[1]

4 August 1948

My dear Dickie,

Thank you so much for your two letters. I am confronting those who said that the arms had not been fairly divided between Pakistan and Hindustan with the facts presented in your first letter.

As to your letter of July 27, it is most kind of you to remind me of what I said to you in appointing you to be Chief of Combined Operations. I shall certainly publish it in due course, because our American friends all make out that I was the inveterate foe of any descent on the Continent.

I feel that yr decision to go to sea is not only becoming and natural to you, but also in harmony with what is due to yr gt position – hereditary and self-made.

General Lord Ismay to Winston S. Churchill
(*Churchill papers, 4/356*)

6 August 1948

My dear Mr Churchill,

I send you herewith a note on various recent points which you have raised, so that we may discuss them, if you wish, next Wednesday.

1. REINFORCEMENT OF CRETE BY TANKS
(*Reference to Mr Churchill's minute of 27th July*)

It is quite correct to say that you asked for 12 additional heavy tanks to be landed in Crete. Your minute to me of 9th May (Serial No. D. 163/1) reads as follows:

---

[1] This letter was handwritten.

'C-in-C, ME, must not weaken himself now in tanks which will perhaps all be needed for his minor offensives. If it is thought too dangerous to take the *Clan Lamont* into Suda, she should take the twelve tanks or some other ship should take them immediately after she has discharged her cargo at Alexandria. That would still be in time.

Perhaps even the first twelve tanks she unloads at Alexandria could be loaded into a smaller ship for Crete. They would require personnel.'

The attached minute (see Annex I) submitted to you by General Jacob on my behalf, shows that the Chiefs of Staff agreed with your proposal and telegraphed accordingly to General Wavell on the following day (10th May).

General Wavell's telegram to you of 15th May (see No. 107 of Hist. (B) 4) does not deal specifically with the question of the 12 tanks, but reports that he had already put into Crete six 'I' tanks and 16 light tanks.

The Tiger Cubs arrived at Alexandria on 12th May and were unloaded by 17th May. It looks from Tedder's telegram to CAS (see No. 133 of Hist. (3) 4 dated 18th May) that it was the intention to act on your proposal, since he refers to 18 Tiger Cubs 'now standing by for reinforcement of Colorado'. But the German air blockade and attack on Crete intervened.

My own view is that we in this country could see more clearly how to deal with the problem of Crete than the people on the spot. To us it seemed that –

(1) The supreme object was to hold the airfields and thus prevent the arrival, and particularly the departure, of engine-driven transport aircraft. We felt that we could deal with one-way traffic, i.e. parachutists and glider-borne troops, but that once the Germans could use engine-driven transport aircraft, they would be able to build up their forces almost indefinitely; whereas we could not reinforce ourselves because of the air blockade:

(2) The best way of ensuring the safety of the airfields was by a sufficiency of 'I' tanks.

I got the feeling that General Wavell, immersed in a thousand and one other problems, did not see the case quite so clearly, and that he was not convinced of the supreme importance that you and the Chiefs of Staff attached to tank reinforcements.

2. MEETING WITH MR HOPKINS AND US OFFICERS AT CHEQUERS ON 24TH JULY, 1941

General Pownall tells me that you would like to see a copy of the record of the meeting held at Chequers on 24th July, 1941, to which reference is made in Sherwood's[1] book. The record is attached at Annex II.

---

[1] Robert Emmet Sherwood, 1896–1955. A US citizen, he enlisted in the Canadian Army in order to fight in France in WWI; gassed and wounded at Arras, 1917. Editor, *Vanity Fair*, 1919–20. Associate Editor, *Life*, 1920–4; Editor, 1924–8. Pulitzer Prize winning playwright. One of Roosevelt's

I invite particular attention to your own and Sir John Dill's observations at this meeting.

3. IRAQ AND SYRIA

I am preparing a note of the events leading up to our intervention in Iraq and Syria, leaving General Pownall to carry on with the story of operations.

Meanwhile, neither I nor any of us can find any trace of a telegram from the Chiefs of Staff to General Wavell, urging him to be bold and to 'remember Clive[1] and Wolfe[2]'. I have a distinct recollection of this being said, but by whom or where or exactly when I cannot recall.

You yourself told General Wavell (see No. 126 of Hist. (B) 4) that:

'We would both also like to emphasize the vital importance of Habforce acting with the greatest vigour and accepting all risks. General Clark must take a leaf out of the book of our successful leaders in the Indian Mutiny when they were never daunted by superior numbers and struck hard and decisively whatever the cost.'

Meanwhile, I am continuing the search and have not given up hope of tracing the observations about Clive and Wolfe.

Winston S. Churchill to Sir Norman Brook
(*Churchill papers, 4/17*)

12 August 1948

My dear Norman Brook,

I have now been able to study the corrections and suggestions for Volume II which you have sent me. I am deeply indebted to you for the immense pains and care which you have taken. This has been a great help to me in my work. I have met practically every one of the points which you raise, and hope early next

---

speechwriters. In Oct. 1941, appointed head of US Foreign Information Service, charged with co-ordinating anti-Nazi propaganda. In 1948, published the two-volume *The White House Papers of Harry L. Hopkins, an Intimate History*.

[1] Robert Clive, 1725–74. Sent to India as an agent of the East India Trading Co., 1744. Enlisted in the Company army in 1746, fighting in both the First and Second Carnatic Wars. Governor of Bengal, 1755–60. Defeated Sirāj al-Dawlah at Battle of Plassey (1757), securing British control over Bengal. Baron Clive of Plassey, 1762. Knighted in 1764. Reappointed Governor of Bengal, 1764, with orders to re-establish British control over the territory. Reformed the British East India administration in India and consolidated British control over the territory. His governorship ended in 1767 with charges of corruption. Committed suicide, 1774.

[2] James Wolfe, 1727–59. Entered British Army, 1740. Promoted to 2nd Lt, 1741, during War of Austrian Succession. ADC under Gen. Henry Hawley, 1746. Key military figure during Seven Years War (1756–63). Served on the American continent and fought the French in Canada. Col., 1756. Brig.-Gen., 1758. Maj.-Gen., 1759. Defeated French forces at Quebec in 1759; killed at the Battle of the Plains of Abraham. Known as 'The Hero of Quebec' and 'The Conqueror of Canada', he became an icon of British expansionism.

month to send you a corrected copy in its final form. There will still be time for any further changes you may think desirable.

I shall have ready in about a week the Appendices to Volume II which you have not yet seen. It is quite easy to correct these to any extent you consider necessary. In principle I am not allowing anything in my official minutes to reflect sharply upon persons, especially where their opposite statement of the case cannot for reasons of space be given.

I shall also be sending you quite soon the first book of Volume III – Book 5. This is in a very rough preliminary form and does not have to be delivered till May 1, 1949, and even after that there will be another two or three months when corrections will be possible. However, I thought you might be interested to see how this is opening out. I have been very careful not to use the word 'intercept' or indicate the source of our trustworthy information, and I think 'C' will probably be content with it. As there is plenty of time it will not be necessary at this stage to consult Dominion Ministers or Foreign Governments whose letters it is proposed to publish. I have thought it right to move a Chapter from Volume III about the Ribbentrop–Molotov conversations into Book 4 of Volume II, which requires some strengthening. Also, it is chronologically in order. I am sending you a copy herewith as you have not seen it before.

I am sending along an American edition of *The Gathering Storm*. It has been very favourably received in America, and the reviews are most laudatory. The Book of the Month Club has taken it, and also the second Volume when it comes out. Altogether, of Volume I over 600,000 copies will be sold by Christmas. The English edition, by Cassells, comes out on October 4, and they have got the paper for 200,000 copies.

Once more I thank you for all the assistance you have given me. I hope that you are having some holiday. I am going to Aix-en-Provence on the 22nd, and I shall be painting and working on the Book.

Winston S. Churchill to John Colville
(*Churchill papers, 2/161*)[1]

12 August 1948

My dear Jock,

I am delighted to hear yr good news.[2] Few deserve happiness more than you. Let me express the hope that it will belong to you both.

---

[1] This letter was handwritten.
[2] Of his forthcoming marriage. See letter of Aug. 13, reproduced below (p. 1144).

August 1948

James Byrnes to Winston S. Churchill
(Churchill papers, 2/146)

13 August 1948

Dear Mr Churchill,

I am deeply grateful to you for your thoughtfulness in sending me the first volume of your book *Gathering Storm*.

I have been reading instalments as they have appeared in the *New York Times* and share the enthusiasm of the American people about this splendid work. So many inaccurate stories have been printed about important events that it is most fortunate that you have been able to find the time to give the facts to the world. Of course, much of the misinformation circulated in the United States is due to the fact that we have a presidential election this year. I have been greatly irritated at the criticisms of decisions made by you and President Roosevelt, which decisions I know were actually made by the military leaders, whose judgment in such matters you and the President had to consider. Recently I made a speech on the subject, which I take the liberty of sending you.

I sincerely hope that your health is good and that you will be with us for many years to come to lead your people and give comfort to the rest of us who are your friends and admirers.

John Colville to Winston S. Churchill
(Churchill papers, 2/161)[1]

13 August 1948

My dear Mr Churchill,

Thank you very much indeed for your charming letter,[2] which delighted me. I felt it a great honour that you should write in your own hand, which I know you very rarely do, and I shall always keep this letter.

Bridegrooms usually think they are lucky, but I really am. Meg[3] has got the most sterling character and a lively love and distinction, besides a remarkable sense of humour which I am sure is indispensable to a happy marriage! We are being married on October 20th at St Margaret's, and if by chance events allowed you to come to the wedding I should feel I had been properly married.

I hope the sun will shine at Aix and that you will find many agreeable subjects to paint.

---

[1] This letter was handwritten.
[2] Reproduced above (p. 1143).
[3] Margaret Egerton, 1918–2004. Known as 'Meg'. Lady-in-Waiting to Queen Elizabeth, 1945–8. Married, 1948, John Colville.

Alec Spearman[1] to Winston S. Churchill
(Churchill papers, 2/71)

16 August 1948

Dear Mr Churchill,

You will have such a mass of information on the Berlin situation that I am very diffident of bothering you with a letter and only do so because I have been asked by Sir James Hawkey (whom I always obey) to send you a note on a conversation with Mr Eustace Seligman.[2]

Seligman is a prominent New York lawyer, a partner of Foster Dallas[3] and a friend of Governor Dewey. He clearly considers himself more competent to assess the opinion which prevails in Republican quarters than to form an opinion himself; I think he is fully justified in this.

Seligman think that we shall leave Berlin shortly. He gives three reasons:
1. That Congress would not, at this stage, support a war unless a Russian military invasion had taken place. Therefore, as we have mistakenly got into an untenable position, we must cut our losses as soon as possible.
2. That American opinion in general and that of Foster Dallas in particular is very much influenced by France. They sympathise with the French fear of Germany; they believe French leadership to be vital to their cherished plan for a United Western Europe; they think that war, whatever the eventual outcome, would wipe out the France they love.
3. That if war can be prevented during the next two years, then it can be avoided altogether because the military strength of the United States would, by then, be so overpowering that the Soviet would not dare provoke a war.

According to Seligman, it is believed that:

Military aggression will be prevented by drawing a line across Europe beyond which the movement of Russian troops would bring a united and determined America into a war.

Infiltration will be prevented by the Marshall Plan and, perhaps, the organisation of counter underground movements.

His friends think that the loss of prestige caused by a withdrawal from Berlin is exaggerated by General Clay[4] and those who consider that giving

---

[1] Alexander Cadawaller Young Spearman, 1901–82. MP (Cons.) for Scarborough and Whitby, 1941–66. President of the Board of Trade, 1951–2. Knighted, 1956.

[2] Eustace Seligman, 1889–1976. Educated at Amherst College, 1910. Partner, Sullivan & Cromwell law firm, 1914. Married, 1917, Maud Jaretsky. Founder, Voluntary Defenders Committee, 1917. Trustee, Amherst College, 1941–64. Capt., Field Artillery, WWII. President, Legal Aid Society, 1950–65.

[3] Foster Dulles.

[4] Lucius DuBignon Clay, 1897–1978. Married, 1918, Marjorie McKeown. Educated at West Point.

way now would so strengthen the Soviet in Germany, France, Italy and elsewhere that she would inevitably make more and more demands until war became inevitable.

Seligman was surprised and disturbed to find how much we disagreed with these views; he was also much impressed by the unanimity of the Conservative and Socialist view – he met with me two Conservative members and two Socialist Ministers, Frank Pakenham[1] and Jay.[2]

So far as the Marshall Plan is concerned, he believes that the American contribution will be maintained and, if necessary, increased during the whole four years; and that it will not be affected by the nationalisation of steel, much as he and his friends disapprove of that measure.

Peter Thorneycroft, who was present, agrees that this is a fair report of what Seligman said. He also agrees that Dewey, whom we saw together in January, has such a profound admiration for you that he would be much influenced by your views.

Winston S. Churchill: press notice
(*Churchill papers, 1/70*)

19 August 1948

Mr Churchill is about to leave for a private visit to Aix-en-Provence, where he will continue to work on his War Memoirs. During his stay he will be the guest of *Life* and *The New York Times*. He will be accompanied by Mrs Churchill and Captain and Mrs Soames, his daughter and son-in-law.

Mr and Mrs Churchill will not be undertaking any public or official engagements while they are in France.[3]

Instructor, Officers' Training Camp, 1918–19; Engineering School of Application, 1919–20; Dept of Civil Engineering, US Marine Academy, 1924–7. Asst Prof., Military Science and Tactics, Alabama Polytechnic Institute, 1920–1. Director of Material, ASF, 1942–4. CO, Normandy Base, 1944. Deputy Director, War Mobilization and Reconversion, 1945. Deputy Military Governor, Germany, 1945–7; Military Governor, 1947–9. C-in-C, European Command, 1947–9. Chairman, Continental Can Co., 1950–62. Personal Representative of the President in Berlin, 1961–2. Director, Chase International Investment Corp., 1963–72.

[1] Francis Aungier Pakenham, 1905–2001. 2nd son of 5th Earl of Longford (killed in action at Gallipoli in 1915). Educated at Eton and New College, Oxford. Worked in Conservative Party Economic Research Dept, 1930–2. Lecturer in Politics, Oxford University, 1932. Personal Assistant to Sir William Beveridge, 1941–4. Parliamentary Under-Secretary of State, War Office, 1946–7. Chancellor of the Duchy of Lancaster, 1947–8. Minister of Civil Aviation, 1948–51. 1st Lord of the Admiralty, 1951. Succeeded his brother as Earl of Longford, 1961. Lord Privy Seal, 1964–5, 1966–8. Secretary of State for the Colonies, 1965–6. KG, 1971.

[2] Douglas Patrick Thomas Jay, 1907–96. Journalist, *The Times*, 1929–33; *The Economist*, 1933–7; *The Daily Herald*, 1937–41. Fellow, All Souls College, Oxford, 1930–7, 1968–87. Author of *The Socialist Case* (1937). Personal Assistant to the PM, 1945–6. MP (Lab.) for Battersea North, 1946–74. Economic Secretary to the Treasury, 1947–50. President of the Board of Trade, 1964–7. Baron, 1987.

[3] John Snedaker, of *Time–Life International*, wrote to Lettice Marston on Aug. 17: 'Enclosed is a bank draft in the amount of 1,000,000 – (ONE MILLION) French francs, in accordance with the arrangement with which you are familiar.'

Winston S. Churchill to Major-General Sir Stewart Menzies[1]
(Churchill papers, 2/153)

19 August 1948
Private

Dear Mr Menzies,

I am going abroad, to the Hotel Roi Réné, Aix en Provence, twenty miles from Marseilles, on Sunday next and propose staying there or thereabouts until the end of September.

If the situation deteriorated to a point affecting my personal safety I should be very glad if you would send me a message advising me to come home in the following terms: 'ZIP[2] – MENZIES'.

Chiefs of Staff: Higher Defence Policy ('The Cold War')
(Churchill papers, 2/31)

20 August 1948
Top Secret

Higher Defence Policy is well summarized in the following extract from the statement 'Fundamentals of our Defence Policy' contained in paragraph 33 of DO (47) 44:

'The most likely and most formidable threat to our interests comes from Russia, especially from 1956 onwards, and it is against this worst case that we must be prepared, at the same time TAKING EVERY POSSIBLE STEP TO PREVENT IT.'

2. It is towards meeting the threat from 1956 onwards that our long-term defence planning is directed and against it that the ultimate shape and size of our forces are being worked out.

3. Plans for preventing the threat arising are, however, far more vital to the country's well-being than plans for meeting it when it arises because:

(a) Economically we have little chance of surviving war within the next 10–20 years whatever the purely military results.

(b) If weapons of mass destruction are used against us in quantity, the chances of survival, either economically or militarily, are extremely slight.

---

[1] Stewart Graham Menzies, 1890–1968. Nephew of Muriel Wilson, to whom Churchill had proposed marriage in the late 1890s. Educated at Eton. Served in Grenadier Guards, 1909–10; Life Guards, 1910–39. On active service, 1914–18; involved from 1915 in counter-espionage and security duties at GHQ, France (despatches, DSO, MC). Lt-Col., 1919. Chief, War Office Secret Service, 1919 (under Churchill). Military Representative, War Office, Secret Intelligence Service, 1919. Personal Assistant to the Head of the Secret Intelligence Service (Adm. Sinclair), 1923–39. Col., 1932. Brig., 1939. Head, Secret Intelligence Service ('C'), 1939–52. CB, 1942. KCMG, 1943. Maj.-Gen., 1945. KCB, 1951.

[2] ZIP: generic code to indicate commencement of battle – or, in this case, a crisis necessitating immediate action.

4. We are trying to postpone the threat in two ways –
  (a) By giving tangible evidence that we and our allies possess adequate forces and resources and are fully prepared and have the intention and ability to take immediate offensive action.
  (b) By attempting to arrest the spread of Communism particularly to areas where our security would be vitally prejudiced.

5. The first line of prevention, i.e. by showing strength, though essential, will progressively lose its value as Russian preparations advance, particularly as regards the provision of atom bombs, since the UK and Western Europe are more vulnerable to weapons of mass destruction than is Russia.

6. Nor would the prevention of a farther spread of Communism alone significantly reduce the threat, though it would to some extent prevent it becoming more serious.

7. There is therefore an urgent need to find a more positive means of preventing the Russian threat from ever materialising.

COMMUNIST POLICY

8. If we examine Stalin's design for Communism we find that the Communist policy laid down by Lenin, maintained by Stalin and reaffirmed by numerous lending Communists is plain, namely:
  (a) **THE INEVITABILITY OF A STRUGGLE** in order to establish Communism throughout the earth.
  (b) The acceptance of Russian dominated Communism as the only true Communism, all other types of Communism being false and denied by Russia.
  (c) The policy of inciting non-Communist states against each other.
  (d) The conception of peace being merely an armistice during which to prepare for fresh attacks.
  (e) The policy of retreat when necessary with the idea of consolidating and preparing for a later advance.
  (f) The policy of decomposing the enemy from within by Trojan Horse tactics, and finally,
  (g) The policy of using any means, foul or fair, for attaining Communist ends.

Therefore, the only method of preventing the Russian threat from ever materialising is by utterly defeating Russian directed Communism. There can be no parley with Communism. It must be defeated and destroyed.

THE COLD WAR

9. For the first time in our history a totalitarian organisation of states is attempting to impose its will upon us by undiplomatic means other than armed conflict and this has been conveniently described as a 'Cold War'.

10. We are moreover dealing with an organisation whose great strength lies

in a rigid centralisation and power of quick co-ordination and decision and unless we so organise our cold war directive to achieve a similar method of centralisation we shall stand little chance of success.

11. At present we have, however, failed to clarify our thinking concerning this new political concept and we have failed to unify our forces to oppose the Soviet 'Cold War' aggression.

12. We shall not win the 'Cold War' unless we carry our offensive inside Russia and the Satellite States. We must in fact start a world-wide offensive, using every available agency. There must be as complete Allied integration as possible. Planning must take place at the highest level and must be executed in the same way as for a 'Shooting War'.

13. At present we are in danger of losing the 'Cold War'. We have not integrated with our allies, we have not selected our strategic aim, we have not allocated our world resources, we have not designated our 'Cold War' forces. This lack of integration, lack of aim, lack of plan, is brought more forcibly to our attention almost daily. Although in the Defence Committee Mr Bevin stated that it was the agreed policy of HMG and the Western Powers to fight the 'Cold War' on all fronts on the political, economic, and social fronts and if need be on the military front, little has been done to implement this decision.

PRESENT ORGANISATION

14. The only body at present officially charged with the task of conducting the 'Cold War' is a small section of the Foreign Office known as the Information Research Department. The activities of this department are confined by its charter to the collection and dissemination of anti-Communist propaganda. Its primary target is 'to give a lead to and support the truly democratic elements in Western Europe in withstanding the inroads of Communism', whilst its secondary targets include the Middle East and certain countries in the Far East.

15. By its charter the activation of the Information Research Department can include neither the countries behind the Iron Curtain nor the education of the British public concerning the real dangers and meaning of Russian Communism. Moreover, its directive does not seem to be clear to all posts abroad and some seem to be having difficulty in interpreting it.

16. Propaganda however is not the only weapon of 'Cold War'. Every agency and in particular the London Controlling Section and 'C''s organisation[1] must be brought into play.

17. No organisation exists, even within the United Kingdom, for co-ordinating and controlling the activities of all concerned in the conduct of 'Cold War', although total 'Cold War' demands, as does an ordinary war, a

---

[1] i.e. the Secret Intelligence Service.

contribution from practically every form of normal activity – religious, political, economic, cultural, scientific, social and military.

18. Though the main task of the Information Research Department is the support of the western democracies in stemming the tide of Communism, no organisation exists for co-ordinating our efforts with theirs.

19. The scope of the Information Research Department is by its charter far too circumscribed. Its target extends only as far as the line of the Iron Curtain, it has no responsibility for ensuring, through education, that our anti-Communist actions have the full support of our own people and finally its activities are confined to the collection and dissemination of defensive propaganda.

20. There is no integration of our 'Cold War' effort with that of the United States, the British Commonwealth or with Western Union powers.

21. No organisation exists for the planning or the conduct of the 'Cold War'. In consequence, such efforts as we are making are individual and unco-ordinated and the initiative more often than not rests with the Soviet Union. Bogomolov,[1] the Russian Ambassador in Paris, in a conversation with Quaroni[2] the Italian Ambassador in Paris supports this view when he said: 'In the Soviet view the Anglo-Americans have no unified plan of action but adopt the method of countering Soviet actions with ad hoc measures of their own.' 'The Russians,' he added, 'are convinced that in the end their policy of SYSTEMATIC ACTION would prove superior to THE IMPROVISATIONS of their opponents.'

ORGANISATION REQUIRED

22. An organisation is therefore required which is capable of:
    (a) Exercising the higher direction of the 'Cold War'.
    (b) Controlling and co-ordinating all executive action.

23. The existing pattern of the higher direction of war, Defence Committee, Chiefs of Staff, Joint Planners, JIO . . . , etc., suitably reinforced by other bodies concerned with 'Cold War' is appropriate to the higher direction of the 'Cold War'.

24. There is however no organisation charged solely with the responsibility for controlling and co-ordinating executive action. It is a whole time task of great responsibility which we do not consider can be carried out by an existing ministry. Instead we consider that a high level official of Ministerial rank with appropriate staff should be appointed, and that he should report to the

---

[1] Alexander Efremovich Bogomolov, 1900–69. Secretary-General, Collegium of the People's Commissariat for Foreign Affairs, 1939–40. Soviet Ambassador to the Allied Governments in London, 1941–3; to France, 1944–50.

[2] Pietro Quaroni, 1898–1971. Educated at University of Rome, 1919. Italian diplomatic corps, 1920–31. Head, Political Affairs Dept, Ministry of Foreign Affairs, 1932–5. Exiled to Afghanistan for disagreeing with Mussolini's withdrawal from League of Nations, 1936–44. Ambassador to Paris, 1946–58; to Bonn, 1958–61; to London, 1961–4. Order of Merit, Italian Republic, 1952.

Defence Committee or Cabinet, receiving therefrom directives from time to time. We believe that little headway in the 'Cold War' will be made until such an appointment is made.

RECOMMENDATIONS

25. Our aim should be the complete defeat of Russian Communism without resort to war.

26. Our 'Cold War' plans should be made and agreed at the highest level, should have the widest conception and the closest integration with all our democratic allies and should be put into immediate effect.

27. We should take immediate steps to educate our own people and thus ensure that our anti-Communist actions have their full support.

28. A high level official of Ministerial rank with appropriate staff should be appointed whose sole task should be to control and co-ordinate all executive action.

29. Finally we suggest that the Chiefs of Staff may well consider that anything short of total conduct of the 'Cold War', and any 'Cold War' aim less than the 'Total Defeat of Russian Communism without resort to War' will not meet their requirements. If the 'Cold War' leads to no decisive conclusion Russia will assuredly start a 'shooting war' when she is ready to do so. It is then that the Chiefs of Staff will assume the responsibility, as usual with inadequate means.

The successful conduct of the 'Cold War' is therefore of vital interest to the Chiefs of Staff.

Winston S. Churchill to Clement Attlee
(Churchill papers, 2/18)

21 August 1948
Private and Personal

My dear Prime Minister,

It is necessary that the correspondence between us about the creation of the European Assembly should now be published, and I understand that the Foreign Office will take the necessary steps to give it to the Press in the next few days. In view of recent developments in Belgium and France I feel it necessary to add a further letter, which I now enclose. I should be glad to hear from you at your earliest convenience. I am going abroad on Sunday but can be easily reached by telegraph.

1152　　　　　　　　August 1948

Winston S. Churchill to Clement Attlee
(Churchill papers, 2/18)

21 August 1948

My dear Prime Minister,

We were naturally disappointed to receive your letter of July 30[1] because of its negative character. I thought it wise to delay its publication until you had returned from your well-deserved holiday in the hopes that events in Europe might win a more favourable reply.

Now that Monsieur Spaak has made his important pronouncement and that the French Government have not only adopted the policy but officially propose a practical form of action, I venture to hope that His Majesty's Government will find it possible to place themselves more in line with Western European opinion upon an issue which they themselves have already done much to promote.

Clement Attlee to Winston S. Churchill
(Churchill papers, 2/18)

21 August 1948

My dear Churchill,

I have now received your further letter of the 21st August. I note that you now desire that publication should be given to the correspondence which has passed between us about the proposal to convene a European Assembly.

According to press reports, the French Government intend to raise the matter in the first instance with the Brussels Treaty Powers and in that event the issue will probably be placed on the agenda of the Brussels Treaty Permanent Commission very shortly. If you consider that in these circumstances the present is a suitable moment at which to publish our correspondence, I should not wish to dissuade you. I should, however, tell you that when M Bidault raised the question of a European Assembly at the meeting of the Brussels Treaty Consultative Council at the Hague on July 20th, the Foreign Secretary replied that he could not for the time being commit himself and there was general agreement that M Bidault's statement should be given further consideration by the five Governments. In adopting this line the Foreign Secretary took into account the circumstance that the whole question has an important bearing on Commonwealth relations and that in consequence the Government desire to exchange views with the Commonwealth Prime Ministers in October before expressing any definite view. But this consideration need not affect the work of independent organisations

---

[1] Reproduced above (p. 1132).

which, as I suggested in my previous letter, could profitably continue to prepare the ground for European Union.

Winston S. Churchill to Clementine Churchill, Lieutenant-Colonel Bill Deakin and Christopher Soames
(Churchill papers, 1/70)

24 August 1948

Glad if you could ask Bill for Sunday night have much to send to printer Monday.

For Deakin: Could you prepare note, about five hundred words, on my relations with Vichy from armistice to end of year, with any telegrams or minutes of mine including Rougier? Arrive Chartwell Sunday.

For Captain Soames: Am deeply grieved about Tess. All my sympathy.

Winston S. Churchill to General Lord Ismay, Lieutenant-General Sir Henry Pownall, Commodore G. R. G. Allen and Lieutenant-Colonel Bill Deakin
(Churchill papers, 1/70)

24 August 1948

NOTES ON VOLUME II BOOK 3

<u>Chapter I</u>: (Lord Ismay and General Pownall)
Make sure that the Contents Table at the beginning of Chapter I corresponds to the text. See also following notes.
<u>Page 1</u>: I do not gather any tables have been made for the Appendix. If this is so we must amend as I have shown. If there are tables let me see them.
<u>Page 3</u>: Has this statement about 58 millions instead of 47 millions been checked? If possible Lord Cherwell should be asked.

<u>Chapter II</u>: (Mr Deakin) Check Contents Table.
<u>Page 1</u>: You are going to draft a new statement about the Belgian King.[1] This should be sent to me at once, and at the same time you should insert it in the text.
<u>Page 3, para 2</u>: (General P) The disparity between the French and German tanks is not expressed in the present account. To represent it as if the Germans had 3,000 to our 2,300 does not make the point of their overwhelming superiority. I thought that the bulk of the French tanks were not organised in fighting

---

[1] Leopold III.

units. Some comparison should be made of the numbers of heavy tanks on each side. No one reading the present text would realise what trash the French armour was compared to the enemy.

Page 4: 'A million British and French graves in Belgium'. Is this correct? I did not count them.

Page 5: 'She had lost two million men killed'. Is this figure accurate?

Page 6. middle: Who is being quoted for the description of the French Corap's[1] division?

Page 7: The sentence about two or three thousand tanks must be considered in relation to the reference to three thousand on p. 2. Most of the French tanks were little more than armoured cars.

Page 7: (General P) I do not know what you have done about a general map for this part of the book. It should come out on a flap some way forward in the story. It is most necessary that every place mentioned in the text should be printed in one of our maps.

Page 11: (Lord Ismay, Mr Deakin, General P) My French should be checked. There are several accounts of this meeting including a procès verbal, I think in Reynaud's book. There was of course a lot of desultory conversation. Are you satisfied that my account gives the full substance? It would be worth while to compare my account with the Ismay notes and these French stories. I do not want to alter my present text in any way if it can be avoided, but as we may be challenged the matter requires consideration.

Page 13: (Lord Ismay, General P) 'In taking no action'. Surely the 'no' should be deleted, or did I mean 'if they take not action', or 'when they take action'? Please also see at the end of the message, at beginning of p. 14, 'should it be forced to withdraw'. The actual text of the message should be examined.

General: The chapters I am now sending you in a steady stream should be dealt with by you as you think best, and the printer should print 12 copies for our own circulation. This will enable me to make a final check of what you have done on my comments before the 150 are printed.

Chapter III: (Mr Deakin) Check Contents table in relation to text.

Page 2 (first page in print): (Lord Ismay). You say you have no record of a meeting of the Supreme War Council on May 18 or of Reynaud coming over. I know he lunched with me after a long talk at the Cabinet. And this was the same day that I made my broadcast during the battle. I see in 'INTO BATTLE' the date is there given as May 19. All this wants clearing up. I am absolutely sure I lunched with Reynaud and that Lord Halifax came too (at the Admiralty).

'My second broadcast' – there is no record in 'INTO BATTLE' of any but the broadcast of the 19th. I do not remember broadcasting on taking office.

---

[1] André-Georges Corap, 1878–1953. GOC 9th Army, 1939–40.

I think that I must have had in mind the speech in the House of Commons about 'blood, tears, toil and sweat', which was not broadcast. If this is so, 'second' should read 'first' on p. 2.

The reader must have access to a general map with all the places mentioned on it, around this p. 2. 'Petreforce' requires explanation (General P). A footnote would do.

<u>Bottom of Page 7</u>: (Mr Deakin, Mr Kelly) Make sure this goes in correctly.

<u>Page 8</u>, quotation at top: Check third line.

I think a date should come in here. Was it the 21st or 22nd that we were at Vincennes? What time did we fly over? Lord Ismay could help. It may have been all on the 21st. P. 9 shows it was the 22nd.

<u>Page 11</u>: (Mr Deakin) Is the longer message printed in the Appendix? It should be. Ought we not to ask Reynaud about the actual textual quotation of these messages?

Winston S. Churchill to Jo Sturdee
(Churchill papers, 1/70)

24 August 1948   Aix en Provence

I shall want reports on the behaviour of the little dog.[1] Is he very unhappy at being left?

Jo Sturdee to Winston S. Churchill
(Churchill papers, 1/70)

26 August 1948

BULLETIN ON RUFUS

After your departure on Sunday the poor little dog was miserable. He went crying and looking for you all over the house and then, in desperation, came into the office, jumped on our laps, lifted up his head and howled and howled and howled. We all comforted him and loved him and John[2] took him over to the Greenshields' cottage, where he was welcomed and told to be good, happy and comfortable until your return.

I have spoken to Mrs Greenshields[3] on the telephone about him this morning. She says that he has now settled down very well. He seems happy, enjoys playing with Bengie,[4] is out in the garden a lot of the time, and is

---

[1] Rufus II.
[2] Probably John Ogier.
[3] Wife of Churchill's valet.
[4] Another dog.

eating and sleeping well. They were so sorry for him on Sunday afternoon as he seemed lost and unhappy and kept running over to Chartwell. However they took him and Bengie for a long walk on Sunday afternoon, and since then he seems to be in his usual good spirits. They take him for a walk every afternoon and evening, and the other day they took him into Sevenoaks with them. Mrs Greenshields says she will let us know at once if she thinks there is anything wrong with him, and the people at Chartwell are going to keep an eye on him.

Winston S. Churchill to James Byrnes
(Churchill papers, 2/146)

31 August 1948   Aix-en-Provence
Private and Confidential

Thank you for your letter[1] and for the copy of your speech which you have sent me.

It will be quite a time before I reach my account of the closing phase of the war. As you will remember, I was strongly in favour of delaying the American and British withdrawal to the zone agreed with the Russians in 1943 till after there had been a general showdown on the spot and a settlement of all the outstanding problems from Trieste to Corea. I must regard the giving up of the heart of Germany as a terrible event. I think we were quite free to consider the matter in the light of the general situation, after the 'mockery' that was made by the Russians of our agreements at Yalta about Poland.

About Prague; my recollection is that I did my utmost to persuade General Eisenhower to let his two armoured divisions roll into Prague, as they could so easily have done in a few hours. In this also great disasters have followed and none can measure what will happen in the future.[2] We are now confronted with the designs and ambitions of despots as wicked as Hitler and even more absolute. How right you were to stand up firmly to them about Persia in 1945.

---

[1] Of Aug. 13, reproduced above (p. 1144).
[2] Churchill decided to delete the portion from 'As you will remember' in the second paragraph to this point before this letter was sent.

Lieutenant-General Sir Henry Pownall to Winston S. Churchill
(Churchill papers, 4/196)

31 August 1948

I quite see your point that you want to give more emphasis to the Italian attack in the desert in Sept. 1940, just because, after so much anticipation, it was such a flop.

Attached is an expanded narrative of the Italian advance, which I hope will be appropriate. I don't think the operation itself is worth much space. The natural anxiety with which we looked forward to attack by such apparently strong forces is reflected in your Minute to S of S for War and CIGS dated August 16. The subsequent anti-climax is I think straightforward and can be stressed by bringing in Graziani's[1] dismissal. Deakin, with whom I have discussed this, has offered to look for material from the Italian side in Ciano's Diary and elsewhere.

Incidentally the word 'hedgehog', if you want to use it for the Italian formation, ought not to have any critical implication (except for slowness). German tank formations later used a rather similar 'moving square' with guns on front, flanks and rear and thin-skinned vehicles inside. They did well with it.

I hope Christopher will approve my description of his battalion's battle. In poking some fun at the Wops I do not want to imply that his battalion were not up against a considerable problem, which they dealt with most successfully.

---

[1] Rudolfo Graziani, 1882–1955. Active service in Libya, 1911, 1921–31; on the Italian–Austrian front, 1915–18 (twice wounded, decorated for valour). Lt-Col., Macedonian front, 1918. Governor, Cyrenaica, 1931–5. CO, Italian forces, Abyssinia, 1935–6; Axis forces, North Africa, 1940–1. Viceroy of Abyssinia, 1936–7. Created Marquis of Negbelli, 1937. Minister of War, 1943. Led the continuing Fascist armed resistance after the fall of Mussolini, 1943–4. Captured by Italian partisans near Lake Como, 1945. Sentenced to 19 years' imprisonment for collaboration with the Germans, 1950. Freed by Government amnesty, 1950. Hon. President, neo-Fascist Italian Social Movement, 1950–4.

September 1948

Jo Sturdee to Winston S. Churchill
(*Churchill papers, 1/70*)

1 September 1948

Have sent bags and cables every day since your departure. Have you not received them? 'March to Sea' from printer returned to you August 27 'Deliverance of Dunkirk' ditto August 30. 'Back to France Aid to Russia and White House' with Graebner as he will be quicker than mail. 'French Agony and Bordeaux Armistice' returning tonight also every effort for 'Darlan' tonight. Graebner left today with bags 9, 10 and 11 containing above, part of Book 3 checked and settled at meeting yesterday comments from Pownall and Professor Jones.[1] Outstanding points from collaborators and others will be forwarded as soon as they ready. Printer collaborators private office working hard to send you material soonest possible.

Clementine Churchill to Winston S. Churchill
(*Churchill papers, 1/44*)

1 September 1948
Personal

With regard to the future of Chartwell Farm, I herewith make some tentative suggestions:
1. How would it be to leave it to little Winston and for him to come into its possession at the age of 25? (I think 21 is a little too young, don't you, for a farm and its intricate management?) Meanwhile you might direct after your death for the Chartwell Literary Trust to manage it on his behalf and for profits, if any, to be put aside for him.

---

[1] Reginald Victor Jones, 1911–97. Air Ministry Scientific Officer, 1936 (seconded to Admiralty, 1938–9). Asst Director of Intelligence, Air Ministry, 1939–45; Director, 1946. CBE, 1942. CB, 1946. Prof. of Natural Philosophy, University of Aberdeen, 1946–81. Director of Scientific Intelligence, Ministry of Defence, 1952–3. CH, 1994.

2. The Chartwell Literary Trust could then leave Christopher and Mary in possession of the house during this interval unless Christopher became otherwise provided for (Sheffield Park?[1]). Christopher's salary could be paid by the Trust and he would be responsible to them. If Christopher and Mary decided to leave Chartwell Farm in the interval for Sheffield Park or elsewhere, the Trust should have authority to let the farm to a gentleman farmer until little Winston comes of age at 25, and makes his own plans.

3. I am not quite certain what land has been left to the National Trust with the house. I suppose only the pleasure grounds and the vegetable garden? Therefore presumably the lakes and the meadows inside the beech belt go with the farm to which indeed they are necessary for grazing, hay, and growing kale, etc. But do you not think that you should put a clause in your will that no part of the land near the house which would interfere with its amenities and views as a show place should ever be used or sold for building? Or would it be safer and better to leave the valley and Belt to the National Trust with a request that for a peppercorn rent they let it to the occupant of Chartwell Farm?

4. With regard to Randolph, if you consider the above suggestions favourably, you would wish to make up to him for not having the use of Chartwell farm house, and the income, if any, coming from the farm. Could you not in your will direct the Trust to make a payment of, say, twenty or thirty thousand pounds to him in lieu? This could be a direct bequest or could be tied up on little Winston.

Winston S. Churchill to General Lord Ismay
(Churchill papers, 4/19)

3 September 1948

CHAPTER III

I am sure Reynaud paid a visit to London either on May 18 or 19, 1940. Bill is going to see him shortly and will ask him. Apart from this, I am almost certain that Lord Halifax lunched with me and Reynaud downstairs at the Admiralty. He could be asked.

---

[1] Estate purchased by Arthur Gilstrap Soames in 1910 from 3rd Earl of Sheffield. After Soames's death in 1934 his widow, Agnes, cared for the Park until her nephew Arthur Granville Soames, Christopher's father, took over in 1949. He restored the Park after its wartime use but sold it in 1953.

Winston S. Churchill to General Lord Ismay
(Churchill papers, 4/19)

4 September 1948   Aix-en-Provence

My dear Pug,

    VOL. II, BK. 3, CH. II, PAGE 11 OF THE PROOF YOU CORRECTED.

See your note at the bottom, which I enclose. You ought to read the full text of the French procès verbal. See also my minute of 22 February 1948 (attached). Could you compare the French text with the one you have recorded. I have no doubt a great many things were said as we stood and walked about the room, and we endeavoured to adjust ourselves to the information which for the first time the French gave us of their tragic position. I was trying to stop a panic. Naturally my first instinct would be to 'cramponnez-partout' à la Foch and to counter attack from the North and South on the flanks of the bulge. This French account seems to attribute to me the considered opinion that we should hold on in the North and this appears in other books, French and American, whereas it is quite clear that our only chance at this moment was in fact to bolt South to France as fast as possible, and this was my view as soon as I had learned the facts. Unless you see anything in comparing these two accounts with mine which requires serious change, I propose to let mine stand with only one additional paragraph.

The French procès verbal is in Reynaud Vol. II, page 96. Have you got a copy?

Clementine Churchill to Winston S. Churchill
(Churchill papers, 2/73)

5 September 1948

Unless you attach the greatest importance to my presence, I would prefer not to come to the Party Conference at Llandudno in October.

Winston S. Churchill to Field Marshal Lord Montgomery
(Churchill papers, 2/31)

6 September 1948
To be Delivered by Hand

My dear Monty,

    Without of course knowing the facts, I am shocked at the treatment of the German Field Marshals. This has already been severely criticised by the leading newspapers who point out that they have been held for three years and four months as prisoners of war without any charge being brought against them. They are now to be deprived of their military rank, which is a serious procedure affecting the entire military profession throughout the world. They have been given much more rigorous confinement since they were repatriated to Germany than they had during their long stay as prisoners of war in Great Britain. I am quite sure that their treatment is contrary to the whole spirit of the British Army and also strikes the wrong note for our future relations with Germany.

I can assure you that the Conservative Party will press this matter severely in the House of Commons. Unless there are some facts of which we know nothing, I feel, though I have not finally decided, that I shall have to curtail my holiday to come back and challenge this action in the House when it meets on September 14. I must frankly say that I regret very much that you, who have always shown a chivalrous disposition towards the vanquished, should have been involved in all this by the Socialist Government. Perhaps you will write to me about it, being sure that I shall observe the discretion I have always done about your letters.

I see that there has been no slowing-down of the releases and that the armed forces are weaker by about eighty-five thousand men in the last three months.

It is lovely weather and very comfortable here. I paint a good deal and get on with my book.

It pains me very much to see such bad things done.

General Lord Ismay to Winston Churchill
(Churchill papers, 4/19)

8 September 1948

My dear Mr Churchill,
    I have just received:
    (i) Your letter of 4th September on the subject of Book 3, Chapter II, Page 11 (the meeting in Paris on 16th May);[1] and
    (ii) Your minute of 3rd September about Chapter III (Reynaud's visit to London).[2]

As regards (i) – I am getting hold of Reynaud's book and will compare his account of the meeting with yours. I am however as sure as I can be that yours should stand, with the addition of the paragraph that you have recently dictated.

My own memory of the meeting is exactly the same as yours. We did not sit

[1] Reproduced above (p. 1160).
[2] Reproduced above (p. 1159).

round a table and, as you say, much may have been said as we walked about in groups. But I am positive that you did not express any 'considered military opinion' on what should be done. As I see it, the story is this.

When we left London, we considered the break through at Sedan serious, but not mortal. There had been many 'break throughs' in 1914–1918, but they had all been stopped, generally by counter attacks from one or both sides of the salient.

When you realised that the French High Command felt that all was lost, you asked Gamelin[1] a number of questions with, I believe, the dual object first of informing yourself as to what had happened, and what he proposed to do, and secondly of stopping the panic. One of these questions was – 'When and where are you going to counter attack the flanks of the Bulge? From the North or from the South?' But I would be prepared to swear in a Court of Law that you did not press any particular strategical or tactical thought upon the Conference. The burden of your song was: 'Things may be bad, but certainly not incurable.'

Sir Norman Birkett[2] to Winston S. Churchill
(Churchill papers, 2/160)

12 September 1948

Dear Mr Churchill,

I am delivering a lecture on 'The Art of Advocacy' at Liverpool University next month. I am referring to Lincoln and Bright and their speeches. I want to refer to yours; and wondered whether you would have any objection to my saying what you told me when I had the honour of a few words with you at Gray's Inn that the now famous 'Never in the history of human conflict was so much owed by so many to so few' was the result of much thought and care and did not spring unbidden to the mind in the form you have made immortal.[3]

I would not dream of making any reference if you would rather not; but no lecture on 'Advocacy' would be complete without a reference to the form

---

[1] Maurice Gustave Gamelin, 1872–1958. Born in Paris. 2nd Lt, 1893. Lt-Col., 1914. Served on Gen. Joffre's staff, 1911–17; drafted principal directives at Battle of the Marne, 1914. Commanded a brigade during the Battle of the Somme, 1916. Commanded 9th Infantry Div., 1917–8. Military Assistant to Syrian High Commissioner, 1925–8, when he defeated the Druse rebellion. Commanded 20th Army Corps (Nancy), 1929. Army CoS, 1931. Inspector-General of the Army and Vice-President of the War Council, 1935–7. CGS, National Defence, 1938–9. Hon. knighthood, 1938. Generalissimo commanding French land forces, Sep. 1939 to 40, when he was superseded and interned by the Vichy regime. Tried for having 'weakened the spirit of the French armies', 1941. Deported to Buchenwald Concentration Camp, 1943. Liberated by American troops, May 1945.

[2] William Norman Birkett, 1883–1962. Educated at Cambridge University. Practised law. Judge, 1941. Knighted, 1941. PC, 1947. Lord Justice of Appeal, 1950. British representative on the International Tribunal during the Nuremberg Trials. MP for Nottingham in the 1920s. Baron, 1958.

[3] Churchill wrote on this letter: 'It just came into my head while I was preparing the speech.'

and matter of the speeches you made during the war. But I shall, of course, do nothing without your permission.

Winston S. Churchill to Anthony Eden
(*Churchill papers, 2/68*)

12 September 1948   Aix-en-Provence
Private and Confidential
For Immediate Personal Transmission

My dear Anthony,

    I consider Hyderabad is a most grave story and requires the Conservative Party to express decided condemnation of what is taking place. It may lead to very serious consequences if the Nazarkas fight, and this may spread throughout Southern India and affect Pakistan. But whether there is a fight or not, the act is one of villainy. By the stand-still agreement Hyderabad placed its foreign affairs in the hands of the Government of India; but this agreement also provided for the security and immunity of the Hyderabad State. Already the agreement has been broken by the Government of India through the really cruel blockade imposed upon Hyderabad. All that I stated in my speech on the Adjournment before the recess is correct, and Attlee's contradictions are provably untrue. The Hyderabad Mission here can give overwhelming proof of this. Thus Hyderabad is to be denied access to UNO in virtue of agreement which has been already broken, and is now to be destroyed, by the violent measures of the Government of India. At the end of the twelve month period, when the stand-still agreement expires, the Government of Hyderabad will resume its rights, failing any other agreement to which they are a party, to appeal to UNO. But by that time it is the intention of the Government of India that they shall have ceased to exist. This seems to me to be about the most odious of transactions as any in which a British Ministry has ever been implicated. An amendment to the Address might be considered, assuming that fighting is going on. This however is for consideration with our colleagues. I earnestly hope that the strongest possible protest will be made so that the Conservative Party at least is free of the shame.

    2. The question of the German field marshals being brought to trial offends everyone. Some of the most extreme Socialists have signed a letter against it. All decent soldiers and military opinion is shocked. I personally feel so strongly about it that I am considering sending a subscription to the defence of these aged generals. That they should have been kept waiting for three and a half years without any charge formulated and should now be brought to trial is deemed indefensible even by *The Times*. Our improving relations with the mass of the German people have been greatly stimulated by the blockade and our efforts to feed the two and a half million Germans in Berlin, will all be

set back by the continuance of these trials not only of the field marshals but the interminable and indefinite persecution and hunting-down of individuals; after all, the principal criminals have been punished. You perhaps noticed De L'Isle and Dudley's letter to *The Times*. I am sure every honourable solider deplores and resents what is being done.

There is however an explanation which you may be able to elucidate behind the scenes, namely that the Russians are demanding that these men should be handed over to them to try, and that we are acting in order to forestall the Soviet demands. The American attitude must also be borne in mind. I cannot myself believe that Marshall or Eisenhower could approve of such proceedings.

3. We must naturally ask for a full statement about the position in Berlin. It is obvious that the Kremlin have no intention to come to a friendly all-round agreement. If one cause of quarrel is adjusted another will be fomented. If a four-power conference is arranged on the general question of a treaty of peace with Germany or a united Germany, everyone knows that this will only be a pretext for delay resulting in a deadlock. Meanwhile we must be careful not to lose the soul of Germany.

I have felt the misgivings and bewilderment which is latent but general in thoughtful circles about the policy of delaying a real showdown with the Kremlin till we are quite sure they have got the atomic bomb. Once that happens nothing can stop the greatest of all world catastrophes. On the other hand it must be borne in mind that the American Air Force will be nearly double as strong this time next year as today, that the United States will have a third more atomic bombs and better, and far more effective means of delivery both by airplanes and the bases they are developing, the largest of which is in East Anglia. Therefore while we should not surrender to Soviet aggression or quit Berlin, it may well be that we and the Americans will be much stronger this time next year, and it is very improbable, according to my information, that the Soviets should have made the bomb by then. I am not therefore inclined to demand an immediate showdown, though it will certainly have to be made next year. None of this argument is fit for public use.

4. The other remaining point is the extraordinary behaviour of the Government about Western Union and the European Assembly. All the facts about this have been made public. The Government are not carrying their own people with them in their policy, and France, the United States and the Benelux countries are astonished at their obstruction. I enclose you a paper which Max has given me on the state of public opinion on this matter. It seems to me that this might well be a subject for an amendment to the Address. It is quite clear from these figures that we have a large majority of people in all Parties and in the aggregate throughout the country who would not approve of the Government's present attitude. I earnestly hope this matter may be raised and probed, and that strong condemnation should be expressed.

Conceit, jealousy, stupidity are all apparent in the behaviour of Bevin and other Socialist leaders concerned.

5. I do not write about the economic and financial situation because of course you all know more about it than I do at this distance. I hope all these matters may be considered by you and our colleagues at a Shadow Cabinet meeting, and I shall be very glad if you will read this letter to them and comment on it as you think fit.

With all this on my mind I have felt anxious to come home, yet I cannot feel that any of these issues, except Hyderabad, is sufficiently urgent and crucial to make me alter my plans. Moreover Parliament meets again on October 4 when we have another King's Speech, and some of the issues will have developed more clearly by then.

Every good wish to you, my dear Anthony.

Winston S. Churchill to Clementine Churchill
(Baroness Spencer-Churchill papers)[1]

12 September 1948   Cap d'Antibes, Alpes

My Beloved,

I send this token, but how little can it express my gratitude to you for making my life & any work I have done possible, and for giving me so much happiness in a world of accident & storm.

Your ever loving and devoted husband.

[Drawing of a pig]

Field Marshal Lord Montgomery to Winston S. Churchill
(Churchill papers, 2/31)[2]

18 September 1948
Private

Dear Mr Churchill,

I have your letter of 6 Sept.[3] I have seen Anthony Eden and have given him the true facts, in your absence. The facts are that the War Office (Shinwell, myself, and everyone) has always said it is utterly monstrous to deal with the German Fieldmarshals and generals in the war they are doing. It is entirely a Cabinet decision and Bevin is at the bottom of it.

---

[1] This letter was handwritten.
[2] This letter was handwritten.
[3] Reproduced above (pp. 1160–1).

September 1948

Dr Ludwig Noé[1] to Winston S. Churchill
(Churchill papers, 4/390A)

18 September 1948

Dear Sir,

Shortly before the last War you were kind enough to honour me by inviting me to see you in your home, at what occasion we were quite frankly discussing the political situation in Germany and Hitler's policy.

At the last meeting Professor Lindemann was present.

It was your opinion Hitler's policy would lead to war and to Germany's destruction. You charged me with informing Hitler about this view. I did so but this mad man falsely advised by von Ribbentrop, did not hear your warning, but followed the way leading us and with us a great part of the world into dreadful misery.

The situation in Germany is much worse you may think in your country. We are now quite worried the Bolshewists may even come to Western Germany where I am living, preparing us the same fate by which the Germans in the east of our country are struck.

You are today the hope of millions of Germans who feel themselves badly threatened by the Bolshewists.

What dreadful catastrophe your warnings before the War were not heard in Germany. I hope the world will follow your opinion on the great danger by which Bolshewism is menacing us.

By the way it may interest you a young acquaintance of mine at Coburg – Dr jur Heinz Kahle – a lawyer who adores you very much, is lecturing this winter at the Volkshochshule (university extension) at Coburg on the subject.

One World – Scope and ways of the World Federalists.

He intends to publish his lectures in several languages in a book entitled 'Our struggle for the World State'.

He would like you so much to write a foreword to his book. Will you do him this favour?[2] He will then tour the world and lecture anywhere on the subject of the United States of Europe and of the World, founding groups and sections wherever possible.

I remain, dear Mr Winston Churchill, in great veneration most respectfully yours.

---

[1] Ludwig Noé, 1871–1949. German industrialist and politician. Director of Ascherslebener Maschinenfabrik, 1910–19. General director, Gdansk shipyard and railway workshop, 1919–39. Consul of Finland, 1926–39.

[2] Churchill noted in the margin: 'I am afraid I cannot do that.'

General Lord Ismay to Winston S. Churchill
(*Churchill papers, 4/196*)

20 September 1948

My dear Mr Churchill,

Herewith two or three last-minute notes on the latest version of Chapter XIII – Alone.

With reference to your visits to the coast, I am told that Tommy[1] has sent you a full list of these. One or two of the points that I remember, additional to those that you have mentioned, are –

(a) We went down the front at some small sea-side place, where practically every house was a boarding house which relied on the summer visitors for a living. It was a miserable rainy day, but all the old women who owned these boarding houses, and who had temporarily lost their livelihood, turned out and cheered you wildly and called God's blessing upon you.

(b) Your visits were not confined to the Army, but included Air Force stations and dockyards.

Winston S. Churchill to Duke of Windsor
(*Churchill papers, 2/178*)

20 September 1948   Aix-En-Provence
Private

Sir,

I have not till now found an opportunity to thank you and the Duchess for all your gracious hospitality during our charming weekend at Antibes, and for your kindness about our fortieth anniversary of marriage. I am just off, if flying is possible, to stay with Max, and hope we may soon meet. I am eager to resume my Oklahoma battles with the Duchess and am resolved on victory.

About the paragraph in the French papers on the subject of your further memoirs, it occurs to me that you should enquire very carefully how any reference to our private conversation in my bedroom got into the French Press. I never mentioned the subject to anyone. It may be however that you discussed the matter with the Duchess and were perhaps overheard. At any rate it is a very odd coincidence that the French papers should have got to know almost immediately that we even discussed the topic together. I daresay this will have crossed Your Royal Highness's mind, and we might have a word about it when we meet.

---

[1] Charles Ralfe Thompson.

My Cuban friend[1] has sent me another consignment from which I hope you will allow me to cede you a small participation.

Once more my thanks for all your friendship and consideration.

Field Marshal Lord Montgomery to Winston S. Churchill
(Churchill papers, 2/31)

21 September 1948

We the Chiefs of Staff, wish to inform the Government that the state of the Defence Services of Britain today gives cause for the gravest alarm. Unless immediate steps are taken to put the matter right, we can look forward only to great disasters on the outbreak of a war.[2]

STATE OF THE ARMED FORCES.
MEMORANDUM BY THE CHIEFS OF STAFF

21 September 1948
Top Secret

1. Attached to this memorandum are statements on the present condition of the Royal Navy, Army, and Royal Air Force and the principal factors which affect them.

2. There are certain adverse factors which are common to all Services, all of which must be remedied in some degree if the state of the armed forces is to be brought to a position commensurate with all their present and foreseeable commitments. They are:

(a) The lack of regular recruits; particularly to the Army and RAF.
(b) The adverse effect of the length of Service under the National Service Act.
(c) The pay and conditions of servicemen do not under the conditions provide sufficient to meet the present cost of living. They consequently react against the morale of the forces and against improvement in recruiting.
(d) A complete lack of balance and little or no reserves of fighting equipment.

3. The conclusions of each Chief of Staff on the state of his own Service are as follows:

---

[1] Antonio Giraudier. Wealthy Cuban merchant, cigar maker and brewery owner. Giraudier met Churchill on the latter's 1946 visit to Cuba and sent him cigars every three months until Churchill's death in 1965, even after fleeing Cuba in 1961.

[2] This covering note, forwarded to Churchill, was handwritten.

Royal Navy

The Royal Navy is ill prepared for the role expected of it in the event of war. It is insufficiently trained and its fighting efficiency very superficial at present.

The Reserve Fleet is in a poor state of maintenance; there is an inadequacy of reserves of fuel and supplies and a lack of modern equipment. It will moreover be impotent to meet the long term threat unless the manpower requirements are met and unless the phased programme of production requirements is started now and fully implemented.

Army

(a) The Army cannot meet its present commitments with manpower, financial and material resources at present allotted to it.
(b) There is a complete lack of balance in the fighting equipment available.
(c) A minimum of 400,000 men is required by the Army to meet its 1949/50 commitments, and to provide a sound basis on which to meet its role in war.

Royal Air Force

(a) Unless immediate steps are taken to arrest the present trends in the RAF, it will in the near future be impossible to meet even existing peace time commitments, much less any foreseen additional commitments.
(b) In the event of war the strength of the RAF would be quite inadequate to take the first shock, and even so the effort could be sustained only for a very short time.
(c) The existing bomber force is utterly inadequate to carry out even one of the major various tasks which would immediately fall on it.

The RAF Fighter Defence Force is thin and the control and reporting organisation for the defence of the UK would cover only the south east section of England. Coastal Command and the Tactical Air Force are nowhere near sufficient in strength to meet the tasks which would be expected of them.

In the Middle East the total forces available are utterly inadequate to fulfil the tasks which would be imposed on them. The same is true of the Far East.

4. Conclusions.

We conclude –

(a) That the present state of the forces gives the gravest cause for alarm.
(b) The measures recently approved to improve their condition are a step in the right direction but will mean nothing unless the factors in paragraph 2 are remedied energetically.

Tedder
Montgomery of Alamein
Fraser

Clementine Churchill to Winston S. Churchill
(Churchill papers, 1/41)[1]

21 September 1948

My darling Winston,

It was lovely seeing Sarah looking so brown and well; but I am glad you prolonged your holiday and are driving slowly along that coast you love so well. I'm pining to see the pictures but am resisting the temptation of peeping before you arrive. Yesterday 'Charles' and Lady Moran lunched with me and I heard more about you.

Mary has (pending her own release, I hope in February) got a job in London demobilising ATS. She went to it two days ago, but can visit us in the evenings.

Tomorrow Mary Marlborough[2] is giving a little party at the Dorchester to which Mary has been asked. It is for Mary's daughter Caroline and Sunny. I am looking in, so as to have a look at the very young generation.

Winston S. Churchill to Lieutenant-Colonel Bill Deakin
(Churchill papers, 4/19)

24 September 1948

I have sent the Bordeaux Armistice with its new Mandel addition to the Printer for 12 copies. There are however several points to be settled. The following are from the old text.

<u>Page 10</u> Campbell's[3] message at bottom. Who is 'We?' It is not important. It may have been the Counsellor of the Embassy.

<u>Page 11</u>: I pay a considerable tribute to M Charles-Roux.[4] I should like to know a little more about him before letting this go finally.

---

[1] This letter was handwritten.

[2] Alexandra Mary Cadogan, 1900–61. Granddaughter of 5th Earl Cadogan. Married, 1920, Marquess of Blandford (from 1934 10th Duke of Marlborough); Sarah Churchill, then aged six, was one of the bridesmaids. Styled Marchioness of Blandford, 1920; Duchess of Marlborough, 1934. Administered eight Red Cross auxiliary hospitals and convalescent homes, 1939–45. Member, Executive Committee of the Red Cross, from 1944. CBE, 1953. Mayor of Woodstock, 1946–51.

[3] Ronald Hugh Campbell, 1883–1953. Entered FO, 1907. Private Secretary to Lord Carnock, 1913–16; to Lord Hardinge of Penshurst, 1916–19; to Lord Curzon, 1919–20. British Minister in Paris, 1929–35; at Belgrade, 1935–9. Knighted, 1936. Ambassador to France, 1939–40; to Portugal, 1940–5.

[4] François Charles-Roux, 1879–1961. Born in Marseille. Educated at Paris Institute of Political Studies. On diplomatic missions to St Petersburg, Constantinople, Cairo, London and Rome, 1902–16. Minister to Czechoslovakia, 1926–32. Ambassador to the Holy See, 1932–40. Secretary-General, Ministry of Foreign Affairs, May–Oct. 1940. President, Suez Canal Co., 1948–58.

Page 12: What were the actual dates when the First Sea Lord,[1] Alexander and Lord Lloyd[2] went to Bordeaux and what dates did they leave respectively? What date did Mr Campbell, the Ambassador, leave?

Page 12, last para: On the afternoon of June 16 M Monnet[3] and General de Gaulle visited me in the Cabinet Room. Was this the afternoon of the 16th? It seems impossible that we should be talking about transferring French contracts in America to Britain before I knew that Reynaud had fallen. I think this interview must have been later. My impression is that de Gaulle returned to France the night of the 16th. Is this so? What then was the date on pages 11 and 12 when I mentioned to the Cabinet the need for de Gaulle to escape? I think it must have been the 19th. Is it then possible that, having escaped, he still did resist here and came with Monnet to see me? And that it was on the 19th that he came to see me? I do not think so, as he was of course out of office.

Will you kindly clear this up so that the final alterations can be made to the chapter. It should not be difficult to get the dates.

It would be natural to bring in the escape of de Gaulle as I have now done provisionally, so that it immediately precedes the attempted escape of Mendel[4] and Co.[5]

---

[1] Adm. Dudley Pound.

[2] George Ambrose Lloyd, 1879–1941. Educated at Eton and Cambridge University. MP (Cons.) for West Staffordshire, 1910–18; for Eastbourne, 1924–5. On active service in Gallipoli, Mesopotamia and the Hedjaz, WWI; accompanied T. E. Lawrence on one of his desert raids. Present at capture of Gaza, 1917. Knighted, 1918. Governor of Bombay, 1918–23. PC, 1924. Baron, 1925. High Commissioner for Egypt and the Sudan, 1925–9. One of the Vice-Presidents (with Churchill) of the India Defence League, 1933–5. Elected to the Other Club, 1936. Secretary of State for the Colonies, 1940–1.

[3] Jean Monnet, 1888–1979. French representative on Allied Executive Committee for the relocation of common resources, 1916–18. Deputy Secretary-General of League of Nations, 1919. Chairman, Franco-British Economic Co-ordination Committee, 1939. Member, British Supply Council, Washington DC, 1940–3. Commissioner for Armament, Supplies and Reconstruction, French National Committee, Algiers, 1943–4. General Commissioner, Plan for the Modernisation and Equipment of France (Monnet Plan), 1946. Hon. GBE, 1947. President, European Coal and Steel Community, 1952–5. Chairman, Action Committee for the United States of Europe, 1956–75. Hon. CH, 1972.

[4] Georges Mandel (b. Louis Rothschild), 1885–1944. Born near Paris, of Jewish parentage. Journalist; took the name of Georges Mandel. Joined Clemenceau's staff on *L'Aurore*, 1903. Chef de Cabinet to Clemenceau as PM, 1906–9, 1917–19. In charge of the trials dealing with treason and defeatism, 1917–18. Elected to Chamber of Deputies, 1920. Minister of Posts and Telegraphs, 1934–6 (introduced first French television broadcast, Nov. 1935). Minister of Colonies, Apr. 1938 to May 1940. Minister of the Interior, May–June 1940 (when he arrested many Nazi sympathizers). Churchill's choice to lead a Free French movement in Britain, but refused to leave France, June 1940. Imprisoned in France, 1940–2; in Germany, 1943–4. Sent back to France, 4 July 1944. Assassinated by Vichy militia, 7 July 1944.

[5] Twenty-four deputies, one Senator and some refugees.

September 1948

Field Marshal Jan Smuts to Winston S. Churchill
(Churchill papers, 2/176)

27 September 1948

My dear Winston,

I have not troubled you with correspondence, knowing how fully your time is occupied, and how deeply you must be concerned with present world developments. But, as in old times, I wish briefly to unburden myself to you.

War preparations are going on all round and alarming speeches are being made by those in authority. Both Marshall and Bevin speak like men standing in the last ditch for peace. I, myself, have not up to now taken the war situation very seriously. As you will remember in my address at Cambridge I described the real danger before us as the peaceful infiltration which Russia is pursuing through her Fifth Column in all parts of the world. But in view of what is now happening, and openly said in responsible quarters, I do not feel so certain of that view now. Of course I am cut off from all informed official contacts and can only judge by what appears in the Press, and from what is actually happening.

France is so broken by Communist infiltration and lack of leadership and some deeper decay that little can be expected from her, either in a great peace or a war crisis. Britain, our mainstay in the war, remains stricken by war exhaustion and financial dangers, which may come to a head, should America cease to supply her dollar dope. The rest of Europe is ripe for the sickle.

What is to happen if Russia does make up her mind that this is her moment? I have never trusted Russian judgement, which has been clever in small ways but often stupid in big issues. The position now developing in Europe and Asia may appear to her to be her opportunity, and in the near future we may be precipitated, either deliberately, or by blunder, in a war for which we are not ready.

I almost hesitate to have to confess it, but I am beginning to think more and more that the wise course for us is boldly and openly to integrate Western Germany with the West, and, instead of continuing to dismantle and cripple her, to put her on her feet again and make her part of our Eastern Defence Wall, as she has been for centuries. The Slav menace has been so successful and is now becoming so great that a drastic change in European strategy and alignment is called for. With the present weakness of the European situation, I see no way out of the Communist menace short of calling on Germany to play her part. At least that is how I begin to view what is now happening in Europe.

It will mean a rather sharp reversal of the policies we have been pursuing so far. It will come as a shock to public opinion. But the shock will be worse if war breaks out suddenly and soon, and Russia marches practically unopposed to the Atlantic and the Mediterranean. The vacuum created by German elimination from our European system will then appear to have been the greatest blunder of all.

Russia has abused our joint victory to fasten her ideology on much of Europe and to open the way to the complete conquest of the West. And our present policy of continuing the German vacuum is helping her in that sinister game. A reversal of that policy has to be considered very seriously.

Instead of making peace with Germany and saving and securing her as an ally for the future equilibrium of peace, we have continued to break her down and expose her and ourselves and the world to this Communist menace. She should rather be saved, if Europe is to be saved and a halt called to the Communist advance from the East. In this new and quite unforeseen situation now developing, why not call her in to play her part? Why not call her in to play once more in the part she played in the Protestant revolution in the sixteenth century? It is generally recognised that Germany is necessary for the salvaging of Europe.

This may sound explosive stuff. But we live in explosive times, and the question is whether it is not we and our civilisation which will be exploded if our present post-war policy in Central Europe is continued any longer.

Your proposal for European unity is good and sound and making quite fair progress. But present events are outpacing that progress. Some decisive drastic steps may have to be taken to meet the new situation which Russia has herself created by her ruthless exploitation of our joint victory for her own Communist ends.

My suggestion to you is this: now that Marshall is in Paris, will you not raise this matter with him? You may, if you prefer, put it before him, not as our but my suggestion, and put the onus on me if you like. If I were in Europe now I would certainly approach him direct, but I am tied down to my duties here, and am isolated from all inside information about what is really happening. And the position may not be as menacing as it appears to me at this distance. Both of you may consider my alarm exaggerated and unjustified. If so, I shall leave it at that. But if Stalin is going to play the game of Hitler, something far more drastic will have to be done than has hitherto been considered called for, and in that case we should not for a moment hesitate to call in Germany to take her part in the struggle – and prepare for it in time. The hatred for Russia will strengthen the German response, and be the greatest reinforcement we could have in an otherwise very fateful struggle for the West in its present condition.

Yours with every good wish and all my affection.

Winston S. Churchill to Lieutenant-Colonel Bill Deakin
(Churchill papers, 4/19)

29 September 1948

1. I should like your comments on former Ambassador Kennedy's[1] article in the *New York Times* last Sunday.

2. The chapter, Mussolini[2] Attacks Greece, should open or contain very early some account of what led up to it. In your note on Spanish intervention you say, 'the European situation was now modified by the events in the east.' This page requires to be expanded and must be detached from the Spanish story.

On October 28, the day after the ultimatum, Hitler and Mussolini met at Florence. We must have an account of this meeting. So far we have only used it in the Spanish Story as a vehicle of Hitler's account of Hendaye. But here is the place where the facts must be narrated.

Did Hitler know before he arrived in Florence of Mussolini's decision? When was he told? What did he do? Did he agree? Did he expostulate?

I should think as much as 1,000 words might be spent on bringing the eastern political situation, apart from Russia, up to date.

I should be very glad if you could let me have this note awaiting me when I arrive on Saturday, or bring it with you on Sunday night to Chartwell if, as I hope, you can come then.

Winston S. Churchill to Lieutenant-Colonel Bill Deakin and Jo Sturdee
(Churchill papers, 4/201)

29 September 1948

In view of all the piecemeal alterations inserted in Volume II it would be well for Mr Wood[3] to read them through with a fresh eye. I must have a talk with him about commas. I have arranged with Sir Edward Marsh to cut these down as much as possible as they are a nuisance. I have no doubt what principles are correct. I do not want the whole book repunctuated with commas on

---

[1] Joseph Patrick Kennedy, 1888–1969. Born in Boston. Graduated from Harvard University, 1912. Asst General Manager, Fore River Plant, Bethlehem Shipbuilding Corp., 1917–19. Investment banker. Chairman, Securities Exchange Commission, 1934–5; US Maritime Commission, 1937. Ambassador to Great Britain, 1937–41. Of his four sons, Joseph was killed in action, 1944; John (US President) was assassinated in 1963; and Robert (a Senator) was assassinated in 1968.

[2] Benito Amilcare Andrea Mussolini, 1883–1945. On active service, Royal Italian Army, 1915–17. Leader of National Fascist Party in Italy, 1919–45. PM, 1922–43. Deposed by King Victor Emmanuel III, 1943. Leader of Italian Social Republic, 1943–5. Executed near Lake Como by Italian partisans, Apr. 1945.

[3] Charles Carlyle Wood, 1875–1959. Editor and proof-reader for Churchill, first in the 1930s, working on *Marlborough*, and again from 1948 on *The Second World War*. Referred to by Churchill as 'Mr Literary Wood' to distinguish him from the financial consultant 'Mr Accountant Wood'.

each side of the 'however's and 'of courses's. Neither do I want my particular spelling of Tsar, etc., to be altered in accordance with modern malpractice.

On the other hand repetitions are best detected by a fresh eye. This also applies to apparent contradictions of one part of the text by another.

Finally of course he should note all obvious unaccuracies, mistakes and misprints. There is no need however for him to go into merit. Nor does he need to go through the documents on which the book is founded.

If he could lunch with me on Monday at Chartwell I could go through it all with him and give him a clean copy. He would have to read it very quickly as I propose to go into 150 printings on Monday, October 11.

Winston S. Churchill to Lieutenant-General Sir Henry Pownall, Commodore G. R. G. Allen and Lieutenant-Colonel Bill Deakin
(Churchill papers, 4/196)

29 September 1948

DESERT VICTORY

I have not yet used the note by Captain Soames in which the expression occurs 'three or four acres of officers and two square miles of prisoners'. I cannot find this in my boxes at this moment.

2. On page 4 there ought to be some mention of Wavell's use of the 4th Indian Division which had played its part in the opening battle but was very shrewdly sent off to Abyssinia (?) and made Keren possible. This is much acclaimed by Wavell's champions, and it seems to me to deserve mention and tribute here.

October 1948

Field Marshal Lord Montgomery to Winston S. Churchill
(Churchill papers, 2/143)[1]

1 October 1948

Dear Mr Churchill,

I am now settled in my new home: address as above. Will you now give me one of your paintings for my home? I would like to have a talk with you some time. I have much to discuss with you.

Warren Magee[2] to Winston S. Churchill
(Churchill papers, 2/72)

1 October 1948

Dear Mr Churchill,

You will recall I wrote you once before in the matter of the trial of Baron Ernst von Weizsaecker.[3] You replied that you did not personally know the Baron, and, therefore, did not think that you could be of assistance. A new development at the trial at Nurnberg makes it necessary for me to again appeal to you and to your sense of justice for your aid.

Personalities all over the world have rallied to the Baron's defense. Thus

---

[1] This letter was handwritten.

[2] Warren Egbert Magee, 1908–2000. Educated at American University Law School, 1929. Admitted to District of Columbia Bar, 1930. Married, 1930, Sue Mayfield Wrenn (d. 1946): three children; remarried, Leslie Magee. Worked for the Justice Dept, 1935–8. Established private practice and created firm of Magee & Bulow, 1938. Defended Nazi war criminals in the Nuremberg trials, 1946–7. Represented Weizsäcker, 1948. Represented Sen. McCarthy in his libel suit against Sen. Benton, 1953.

[3] Ernst Heinrich Freiherr von Weizsäcker, 1882–1951. Member of prominent German aristocratic family. Born in Stuttgart to Karl Hugo von Weizsäcker (PM of Kingdom of Württemberg, 1897). Joined Kaiserliche Marine, in 1900. Iron Cross, 1917. Korvettenkapitän, 1918. Naval attaché to The Hague, 1919–20. Head of Dept for Disarmament, 1928. Envoy to Oslo (1931) and Bern (1933). Director of Policy Dept at German FO, 1937. Staatssekretär, 1938. German Ambassador to the Holy See, 1943–5. Arrested in Nuremberg in 1947. Sentenced to seven years' imprisonment, 1949. His son, Richard von Weizsäcker, served as President of the Federal Republic of Germany, 1984–94.

OCTOBER 1948   1177

evidence has been produced from His Holiness Pope Pius XII[1] and numerous dignitaries of the Church, Bishop Berggrav,[2] Primate of Norwegian Church, Lord Halifax, Mr Butler,[3] Mr Wille, Ministers Burckhardt and Froelicher[4] of Switzerland, Belgium Ambassador Viscount D'Avignon,[5] Turkish Ambassador Gerede,[6] Swedish Minister Richert,[7] French Ambassador François-Poncet,[8] Countess Attolico of Italy,[9] Counsellor of the American Embassy at Berlin Mayer, Irish Ambassador Kiernan[10] and many other foreign personalities outside of Germany.

The leaders of The Evangelical Church in Germany have also testified for von Weizsaecker, as well as members of The International Red Cross and the World Council of Churches. Almost all members of the old German FO have also testified to his innocence.

In addition, von Weizsaecker played a most important role in the resistance movement in Germany against Hitler. I have prepared this evidence with great care, as I know the tendency of many Germans to make such claims today. Our evidence was obtained from men like Halder,[11] Schlabrendorff,[12]

---

[1] Eugenio Maria Giuseppe Giovanni Pacelli, 1876–1958. Ordained priest, 1899. Appointed to papal secretariat of state, 1901. Secretary of the Congregation for Extraordinary Affairs, 1914. Ambassador to Bavaria, 1917. Pope Pius XII, 1939. In 1949, issued a decree condemning Soviet totalitarianism while excommunicating any and all Catholics who collaborated with the Communists.

[2] Eivind Josef Berggrav, 1884–1959. Born in Stavanger, Norway. Educated at University of Kristiania, Oslo. Bishop for the Diocese of Oslo, 1937. Led Norwegian Bible Society, 1938–55. Earned international attention in WWII for his leading role in the Church of Norway's resistance to Nazi occupation. Arrested and placed in solitary confinement by Vidkun Quisling's Government in 1942 for refusing to comply with Nazi orders to alter liturgical practices. Awarded Medal of Freedom by President Truman.

[3] R. A. Butler.

[4] Hans Froelicher, Swiss minister to Berlin, 1933–45.

[5] Jacques Henri Charles Francois Davignon, 1887–1965. Viscount, 1916. Belgian Ambassador to Germany, 1936–40.

[6] Husreve Gerard, 1884–1962. Served in Ottoman Army, 1903–19; Turkish Army, 1919–28. Held rank of Col. Turkish Ambassador in Tehran, Tokyo, Berlin (1939–42) and Rio de Janeiro. Medal of Independence with Red–Green Ribbon.

[7] Arvid Gustaf Richert, 1887–1981. Swedish Ambassador to Germany, 1937–45. Governor of Alvsborg County, Sweden, 1949–55.

[8] André François-Poncet, 1887–1978. Press Office, French Embassy, Bern, Switzerland 1917–19. Under-Secretary of State and Ambassador to Weimar Republic, 1931. Ambassador to Fascist Italy, 1938–40. French High Commissioner to West Germany, 1949–55. Elected to Académie Française, 1952.

[9] Eleonora Pietromarchi, 1898–1980. Married, 1924, Bernardo Attolico.

[10] Thomas Kiernan, 1897–?. Entered Dept. of External Affairs, Dublin, 1924. Ambassador to US, 1960–4.

[11] Franz Halder, 1884–1972. Joined 3rd Royal Bavarian Field Artillery Rgt, Munich, 1902. Bavarian Staff College, 1911–4. Capt., 1915. Maj., 1926. Maj.-Gen., 1934. CGS of the Army, 1938. Knight's Cross of the Iron Cross, 1939. Meritorious Civilian Service Award, 1961.

[12] Fabian von Schlabrendorff, 1907–90. Adjutant to Col. Henning von Tresckow of the Resistance, 1942–5. Capt., Order of St John, 1957–64. Judge, Constitutional Court of West Germany, 1967–75.

Gisevius,[1] Kessel,[2] The Kordts,[3] Etzdorf[4] and Bussche,[5] all recognized survivors of the 20th of July. In addition, widows and relatives of those who died because of this plot also testified for von Weizsaecker, such as Frau Canaris,[6] Countess Schwerin-Schwanefeld,[7] Frau Goerdeler,[8] Frau von Haeften[9] and numerous others. As a part of this resistance against Hitler, the Kordts brought information and warnings to Lord Halifax in an effort to avert war. On this aspect of the case I enclose copies of Dr Theo Kordt's letter of July 29th to Lord Halifax, and of Lord Halifax's reply of August 9th. Also you will find a copy of a certificate of the State Department of The United States concerning Eric Kordt's being a key figure in the opposition to Hitler. I also enclose a copy of the Gisevius affidavit.

If you are interested in the overall story, I enclose a copy of my opening statement to the Tribunal. I feel I have proven all matters described therein and more. Now at the near end of the case the prosecution seeks to attack von Weizsaecker and the Kordts, two of his most important witnesses, by producing two affidavits of Lord Vansittart, copies of which I enclose. They are self-explanatory. The danger in the situation is that the American judges of our Tribunal may be misled by such 'generalized' affidavits, as they come from 'a Privy Councillor and former Permanent Under-Secretary of State for Foreign Affairs' of the United Kingdom.

[1] Hans Bernd Gisevius, 1904–74. Interior Ministry police officer, 1933–6. Reich Ministry of the Interior, 1936–41.
[2] Albrecht von Kessel, 102–76. Born in Ober-Glauche, Silesia. Joined German Foreign Office, 1927. Stationed in the Vatican, 1930–2, 1843–5; in Katowice, Poland, 1932–5; in Memel (Klaipeda, Lithuania), 1935; in Berne, Germany, 1935–7; in Prague, Czechoslovakia, 1939; in Geneva, Switzerland, 1940–3.
[3] Theodor Kordt, 1893–1962. Born in Düsseldorf. Stationed in Düsseldorf as 1st Lt during WWI. Graduated from University of Bonn in law, 1921. Joined German Foreign Service in 1921, stationed in Nepal and Bern. Assistant to Ambassador in London, 1938. Member of Oster conspiracy to oust Adolf Hitler during the annexation of Czechoslovakia. Joined Nazi party, 1939. Stationed in German Embassy to Bern throughout WWII. Prof. of International of Law, University of Bonn, 1947. Helped defend Nazi Secretary of State for Foreign Affairs at Nuremberg Trials. German Ambassador to Greece, 1953–8.
Eric Kordt, 1903–69. Born in Düsseldorf. Studied at Oxford University (Rhodes Scholar). Minister with German Foreign Office, 1928–44. Joined Nazi party, 1937. Key member of Oster conspiracy. Worked as a spy for the Soviets while stationed in China. Defended Nazi Secretary of State for Foreign Affairs at Nuremberg Trials.
[4] Hasso von Etzdorf, 1900–89. Joined German Foreign Office, 1928; Liaison Officer to Army High Command, 1939–45. Involved in the German Resistance. Joined Foreign Service of Federal Republic of Germany, 1950. Ambassador to Canada, 1956–8; to UK, 1961–5.
[5] Axel von dem Bussche-Streithorst, 1919–93. Born in Brunswick, Germany. Educated at University of Göttingen. Joined Postdam 9th Infantry Rgt, 1937. Iron Cross, 1939. German Cross, 1941. Knight's Cross of the Iron Cross, 1944. Participated in failed attempt to assassinate Adolf Hitler, 1943. Diplomat, West German Embassy, Washington DC, 1954–8.
[6] Erika Waag, 1892–1970. Married, 1919, Wilhelm Franz Canaris: two children.
[7] Marianne Sahm, 1907–88. Married, 1928, Ulrich-Wilhelm Graf von Schwerin von Schwanenfeld: five children.
[8] Anneliese Ulrich, 1888–1961. Married, 1911, Carl Friedrich Goerdeler: five children.
[9] Barbara Curtius, 1908–2006. Married, 1930, Hans von Haeften: five children.

I feel that you have official knowledge of the existence of German resistance movement and of von Weizsaecker's efforts to avoid war and of his opposition to Hitler and Ribbentrop.

In fairness and justice I therefore appeal to you. The actors must strive to be honest and fair and see at this late hour, when the life of a man like von Weizsaecker is in jeopardy, that the Tribunal is informed. I, as an American, took this case in an effort to aid truth and justice, and I fully appreciate how important to these ends a statement from you is.

Could you not furnish me with a statement similar to Lord Halifax's, based on official reports to you, also stating therein that there was a resistance movement in Germany against Hitler? Others were so informed and have come forward and testified. As an example I enclose copies of the affidavits of Lord Halifax, Kirkpatrick,[1] Steel,[2] Minister Burckhardt, Bishop Berggrav and Countess Attolico. If you are disposed to help, I respectfully point out that your statement should be signed before a notary or a commissioner of oaths. My address in Germany is:

> Room 478, Palace of Justice,
> Nurnberg, Germany.
> c/o US Army – APO 696 A – PMNY

Believe me, Sir, I would not have approached you again but for the Vansittart statements [. . .]

Winston S. Churchill to Sir Norman Birkett
(Churchill papers, 2/160)

2 October 1948

My dear Birkett,

Thank you for your letter of September 12[3] which was forwarded to me while I was in France. The passage from one of my wartime speeches about which, you tell me, you had thought of talking in a lecture you are giving

---

[1] Ivone Augustine Kirkpatrick, 1897–1964. On active service, 1914–18 (wounded, despatches twice). Diplomatic Service, 1919. 1st Secretary, Rome, 1930–2. Counsellor, Berlin, 1933–8. Director, Foreign Div., Ministry of Information, 1940. Controller, European Services, BBC, 1941. Joined PWE Policy Committee, Feb. 1942. Deputy Commissioner to Inter-Allied Control Commission in Germany, 1944–5. Asst Under-Secretary of State, FO, 1945; Deputy Under-Secretary, 1948; Permanent Under-Secretary (German Section), 1949. High Commissioner, British Zone, occupied Germany, 1950–3. Permanent Under-Secretary of State, FO, 1953–7. Knighted, 1948. Chairman, Independent Television Authority, 1957–62.

[2] Christopher Eden Steel, 1903–73. Known as 'Kit'. Entered Diplomatic Service, 1927. Asst Private Secretary to Prince of Wales, 1935–6. Served on diplomatic missions to Rio de Janeiro, Paris, The Hague, Berlin and Cairo. Secretary to Minister Resident in the Middle East, 1942–5. British Political Officer, SHAEF, 1945. Political adviser to C-in-C, Germany, 1947. Minister, British Embassy, Washington DC, 1950–3. Knighted, 1951. UK Permanent Representative, North Atlantic Council, 1953–7. Ambassador to West Germany, 1957–63.

[3] Reproduced above (pp. 1162–3).

at Liverpool in October, just came into my head while I was preparing the speech, and it was in the notes from which I delivered the speech. But is it necessary to go into all these details? I would prefer not.

It is good of you to have written to me about this.

Lord Halifax to Winston S. Churchill
(*Churchill papers, 4/19*)

4 October 1948

My dear Winston,

I have just been reading your book, and though I naturally don't agree with all your judgments – and in some comparatively minor points the information at your disposal is not wholly accurate – I think you have laid us all under a very heavy debt of gratitude.

But there is one matter in which you are unwittingly very unjust to Neville, and which stands out in sharp contrast to what is generally your generous expression of judgment in his regard.

You say at the foot of Page 249, 'As his car drove through cheering crowds . . . he said to Halifax . . . "all this will be over in three months;" but from the windows of Downing Street, he waved his piece of paper again, and used these words . . . "I believe it is peace for our time."' The word 'but' plainly suggests that though he did not himself believe in the durability of his so-called settlement with Hitler, he nonetheless proclaimed it from Downing Street to the crowd as 'Peace for our time'.

There was, of course, no connection in thought between the two statements. They referred to two entirely distinct subjects. What he meant in the car was that the kind of immense popularity of which he was the object at the moment would not last more than two or three months, and I remember with complete clearness the context of discussion about a possible immediate election in which he said it. The Downing Street statement made me shiver when I heard it: but not for the reason that your words suggest. And the inevitable implication of these is that Neville was trying to deceive the British public.

This therefore in my view ought in justice to him to be corrected; and I would suggest that either you or I, as I presumably was your informant as to the first statement, – quite obviously it would be much better from you if you so agreed – should write a short letter to *The Times*, making the point clear. I much hope you would do this.

Let me have a line as to how you feel about it.

October 1948

Clementine Churchill to Winston S. Churchill
(Churchill papers, 1/45)

5 October 1948

I would like to discuss with you the plan for the Chartwell Literary Trust to buy Randolph a house.

Randolph and I have seen four houses. The first was extremely suitable and slipped through our fingers because we made too low an offer. They were asking £13,500. I offered £11,000 and this was refused.

Of the three remaining houses only one is good value and therefore a suitable investment for the Trust. At first I thought it too big for Randolph until he explained to me that he intends to marry again, and also that he would like to have room to put up little Winston. If we take Randolph's possible remarriage into consideration we must also suppose that there might be a baby. All this is hypothetical, but Randolph pointed out with a great deal of force and sense that if he were to move from a small house into a big one it would certainly involve him (and therefore, if we mean to help him, the Trust) into greater expenditure than if we buy a big house in the first instance.

The price asked for the house in question is £16,000. I think it would make a sound investment at £14,000. A much smaller house in the same street was £12,500, and in my opinion was not worth more than £5000 or £6000. May I tell the Prof and Brendan that you approve of my negotiation for this house?

Winston S. Churchill: speech
('Winston S. Churchill, His Complete Speeches', volume 7, page 7706)

5 October 1948   Croydon

... At present, the frontier of Asia is upon the Elbe, but we should be very foolish to allow all that is taking place before our eyes and all that is dinned into our ears every morning to have no effect upon our minds.

It would be foolish to repeat again the mistakes of the past and be drawn, under even worse and far less excusable circumstances, into a life-and-death struggle for the mere existence of our country. It is not as if the existence of our country alone were at stake, because the cause of freedom, the resistance to tyranny in all its forms – whatever livery it wears, and whatever slogans it mouths – is a world cause, and a duty which every man and woman owes to the human race in all its circumstances.

When I was appointed commodore of the squadron[1] a year before the war, the auxiliary squadrons were an addition to the country's somewhat straightened air resources. When war began the world 'auxiliary' became not

---

[1] 615 Sqn.

an apologetic or explanatory term but almost an additional title to fame. The auxiliary squadrons fought in every field, and No. 615 shared the experiences to the full; its record was surpassed by none.

The plan now is that there should be 20 auxiliary fighter squadrons – a very considerable contribution. Service in auxiliary squadrons of the RAF is perhaps the most exacting that can be demanded from any voluntary, or even professional, organization. The legal requirements of attendance at parades, on the ground and in the air, bear no relation to what is given – and given freely and blithely by those who dedicate themselves to that most important service.

Winston S. Churchill: speech
('Winston S. Churchill, His Complete Speeches', volume 7, pages 7707–17)

9 October 1948

Llandudno
Wales

PERILS ABROAD AND AT HOME

When we look back across the years that have passed since the disastrous election of 1945 we can all feel satisfaction at the recovery of our Party and the ceaseless progress and expansion of its organisation. Everything that I said to you about this at Brighton last year could be repeated here today in stronger terms and with greater confidence.

In the growing strength of our organization and in the careful study of the by-election figures, we have solid and sober ground for confidence in the result of the next Parliamentary election if only we do not relax our efforts. We have now to make special preparation not only for the General Election but for the local government elections next Spring which will precede it and may well exert an important influence upon it.

We have come to Wales for this Conference. It is very appropriate. The cause of freedom is at stake and have we not often been told, and I have often heard it said by Mr Lloyd George, the former Member of Caernarvon Boroughs, to whose memory you have paid respect, that 'Freedom dwells among the mountains?' We look to Wales to play an increasing part in British affairs. Should we be returned to power we propose, among other steps, to make provision for a Cabinet Minister especially responsible for Wales. There are other proposals which Mr Butler has done splendid work in building our thoughts on an organized structure, which will shortly be published, and I commend them to your approval and to the goodwill of the people of Wales.

On the other hand, when I come to wider spheres, the position of our country in the world has sunk to levels which no one could have predicted. Our minds are oppressed by the accounts of our relations with Soviet Russia, which we read every day in our restricted newspapers and in the speeches of one kind or another of Cabinet Ministers of one kind or another. We are confronted with the deadly enmity and continued aggression of the Russian Communist Government and its imprisoned satellites. No words which I could use could surpass the declarations of the Foreign Secretary, Mr Bevin, or of Mr McNeil, the Minister of State, and their words are only on a par with what is said by the leading responsible statesmen of America, of France, of our Dominions, and of all the smaller States of Europe who have spoken with great eloquence and are still free outside the Iron Curtain. In fact, what should be the majestic centre of world security and later on of world co-operation and finally of world government has been reduced to a mere cockpit in which the representatives of mighty nations and ancient States hurl reproaches, taunts and recrimination at one another, to marshal public opinion and inflame the passions of their people in order to arouse and prepare them for what seems to be a remorselessly approaching third world war. That is a sad disappointment to us. Bolshevik Russia is already heavily armed and her forces in Europe far exceed those of all the western countries put together.

The United States are rearming on a large scale. Efforts are being made to build up a front of resistance in the West by France and the Low Countries, under leadership and with indispensable American support. Our Socialist Government who now call upon us in quavering tones to take all kinds of serious half-measures of preparation and precaution, are the same people who assured the electors in 1945 that they alone possessed the secret of dwelling on good terms with Soviet Russia, and who boasted of the underlying affinities and comprehension subsisting between Left-Wing parties and doctrines all over the globe. The exposure of these pretensions may vex those who were taken in by them at the time – and they were many; but in fairness I must state that the gulf which was opening between Asiatic Communist Russia and the Western Democracies, large and small, was already brutally obvious to the victorious War Cabinet of the National Coalition even before Hitler destroyed himself and the Germans laid down their arms. In fact, as we can all now see, the growing aggressiveness and malignity of the Soviet Government and its complete breaches of good faith at the time should have made both the British and American Governments refrain from dispersing their armies so completely. Nor should they have carried out their great withdrawals in Germany until after there had been a general confrontation along the line upon which the Western and Eastern allied armies had met. It would also have been wiser and prudent to have allowed the British Army to enter Berlin, as it could have done, and as many good judges thought would be done, and for the United States armoured divisions to have entered Prague, which was a matter almost of hours. I and my colleagues of all parties foresaw at that time that the armies of democracy would melt in the sunlight of victory, while the forces of totalitarian despotism could be held together on a gigantic scale for an indefinite time.

Therefore whatever I may think of the unskilful manner in which our foreign affairs have been handled, I do not reproach the British Socialist Government with creating the abyss which now yawns across Europe and the world. This was inevitable once the Russian Communist leaders gave full rein to their instincts of Imperialism and expansion. Indeed I only wondered that it took the British and American peoples, in spite of all the lessons of the past, so long to realize the challenge to their life and freedom which was being opened upon them from the East.

I will not encourage you this afternoon with false hope of a speedy friendly settlement with Soviet Russia. It may be that some formula will be found or some artificial compromise effected which will be hailed as a solution and deliverance. But the fundamental danger and antagonisms will still remain. The 14 men in the Kremlin, who rule nearly 300 million human beings with an arbitrary authority never possessed by any Czar since Ivan the Terrible, and who are now holding down nearly half Europe by Communist methods, these men dread the friendship of the free, civilized world as much as they would its hostility. If the Iron Curtain were lifted, if free intercourse, commercial and cultural, were allowed between the hundreds of millions of good-hearted human beings who dwell on either side, the power of this wicked oligarchy in Moscow would soon be undermined and the spell of their Communist doctrines broken. Therefore, for the sake of their own interest and for their skins, they cannot allow any intercourse or intermingling. Above all they fear and hate the genial influences of free and easy democratic life, such as we have gradually evolved for ourselves in varying forms throughout the Western World. These they know would be fatal, not only to their ideological theories and to their imperialistic appetite for domination but even more to their own dictatorial power. Therefore, while patience should be practised to the utmost limits which our safety allows, we should not delude ourselves with the vain expectation of a change of heart in the ruling forces of Communist Russia.

Neither should we be under any delusion about the foundations of peace. It is my belief, and I say it with deep sorrow, that at the present time the only sure foundation of peace and of the prevention of actual war rests upon strength. If it were not for the stocks of atomic bombs now in the trusteeship of the United States there would be no means of stopping the subjugation of Western Europe by Communist machinations backed by Russian armies and enforced by political police. We have the same example of Czechoslovakia before our eyes, where Stalin has perpetrated exactly the same act of aggression in 1948 as Hitler did when he marched into Prague in 1939 nine years ago. There seems to be no end to the sufferings of the Czechs. They are now writhing under a new degraded bondage as ruthless as and more subtle than any they have previously known. It is part of the established technique of the 'cold war' the Soviets have begun against us all, that in any country which has fallen into their power, people of character and men of heart and personality outstanding in any walk of life, from the manual worker to the university professor, shall be what is called in their savage jargon 'liquidated'. All men, whatever their occupation, are to be reduced to a uniform and mediocre level so as to make it easy to govern them by commissars and masses of officials and police, all well-trained in the Communist colleges and dependent for their very existence upon the satisfaction they give their superiors in the party hierarchy. This is all set forth before our eyes as plainly as Hitler told us about his plans in his book *Mein Kampf*. I hope that the Western nations, and particularly our own country and the United States will not fall into the same kind of deadly trap twice over. Of one thing I am quite sure, that if the United States were to consent in reliance upon any paper agreement to destroy the stocks of atomic bombs which they have accumulated, they would be guilty of murdering human freedom and of committing suicide themselves.

I hope you will give full consideration to my words. I have not always been wrong. Nothing stands between Europe today and complete subjugation to Communist tyranny but the atomic bomb in American possession. If the Soviet Government wish to see atomic energy internationalized and its military use outlawed, it is not only by verbal or written agreements that they must reassure the world but by actions, which speak louder than words. Let them retire to their own country, which is one-sixth of the land surface of the globe. Let them set free the million or more German and Japanese prisoners they now hold as slaves. Let them cease to oppress, torment, and exploit the immense part of Germany and Austria which is now in their hands. We read continually of the blockage of Berlin. The lifting of the blockade at Berlin would be merely the stopping of blackmail. There should be no reward for that. Let them cease to distract Malaya and Indonesia. Let them liberate the Communist-held portion of Korea. Let them cease to foment the hideous protracted civil war in China.

Above all, let them throw open their vast regions on equal terms to the ordinary travel and traffic of mankind. Let them give others the chance to breathe freely, and let them breathe freely themselves. No one wants to take anything they have got that belongs to them away from them. After all, we are asking them to do no more than what the other victorious States have done of their own free will. None of the other allies has tried to add large territories and populations to its domain. Britain indeed has gone to the opposite extreme and cast away her Empire in the East with both her hands. Let the Russians be content to live on their own and cease to darken the world and prevent its recovery by these endless threats, intrigues and propaganda. When they have done this or even some of it and given these proofs of good faith, and given up what they had no right to take, which is all they are being asked, then indeed it will be time to raise the question of putting away the one vast, and I believe sure and overwhelming means of security which remains in the hands of the United States and which guards the progress of mankind.

It was my dream during the war years, when we were all united against the Hitler onslaught that after the war Russia, whatever her ideology, should become one of the three or four supreme factors in preserving peace; that she would receive all the honour which the valour, fortitude and patriotism of her armies had won; that she would help to bring about the Golden Age on which all our hearts are set, which would be possible but for the follies of men, and which President Roosevelt heralded with his declaration of the Four Freedoms. I hoped that Russia after the war would have access to unfrozen waters into every ocean, guaranteed by the world organization of which she would be a leading member; that she would have the freest access – which indeed she has at the present time – to raw materials of every kind, and that the Russians would be everywhere received as brothers in the human family. That still remains our aim and ideal. If it has not been attained, if on the contrary enormous barriers have been erected against it, it is the Soviet Government that has set them up and is fortifying them every day over even-larger areas.

The question is asked: What will happen when they get the atomic bomb themselves and have accumulated a large store? You can judge yourselves what will happen then by what is happening now. If these things are done in the green wood, what will be done in the dry? If they can continue month after month disturbing and tormenting the world, trusting to our Christian and altruistic inhibitions against using this strange new power against them, what will they do when they themselves have large quantities of atomic bombs? What do you suppose would be the position this afternoon if it had been Communist Russia instead of free enterprise America which had created the atomic weapon? Instead of being a sombre guarantee of peace and freedom it would have become an irresistible method of human enslavement. No one in his senses can believe that we have a limitless period of time before us. We ought to bring matters to a head and make a final settlement. We ought not to go jogging along improvident, incompetent, waiting for something to turn up, by which I mean waiting for something bad for us to turn up. The Western Nations will be far more likely to reach a lasting settlement, without bloodshed, if they formulate their just demands while they have the atomic power and before the Russian Communists have got it too. I am therefore of opinion that our Party is bound to support any firm measures which the Government is found capable of taking and that our country with the rest of the British Commonwealth and Empire should be ready to work with the United States and, after consultation, act with them and with the free governments of Europe.

Meanwhile we have, of course, a situation in Berlin which may at any time precipitate a hideous world struggle. Had I been responsible I would not have allowed it to develop in this way. It would have been better to meet, in good time, the blockade of Berlin by counter-measures against Russian shipping, and imports of all kinds, which might be useful for war purposes, than to be driven for the roads, the railways and the canals and left with only the prodigious exertion of what is called the 'Air-Lift' into Berlin, which may at any moment be interrupted by the winter weather or by Soviet action. Thus we should at a much earlier stage have had something practical to bargain with, and not be reduced to bickering and bluster and a very hard task. The blockade of Berlin has now lasted more than three months and we may have several more months before us of effort and anxiety. It is an unequal trial of strength, it is an unfair ordeal, it is like a contest in endurance between two men; one of whom sits quietly grinning in his armchair while the other stands on his head hour after hour in order to show how much he is in earnest.

There is, however, one great benefit which has been reaped from the wonderful and prolonged efforts the American and British Air Forces are making to feed the 2½ million Germans in Berlin to whom we are now in honour bound. This tremendous beneficial and humane effort has demonstrated to the Germans in the Western zones, as no words could have done, that the future of Germany lies with the European family and with the glory and civilization of the West, to which the German race has still a measureless contribution to make. It is not too much to hope that this bitter experience may have finally convinced the Germans of the villainy of totalitarian power and set their feet on the path to true democracy. I am always hoping myself that France and Germany will lay aside their thousand-year quarrel and that France will regain her position in the world by leading back her vanquished enemy into the company and the culture of Christendom and Europe.

It is for this reason that I deplore and condemn the stupidity which, at a time like this above all others, persists, three and a half years after the war, in endless trials of Germans who were connected with the former Nazi regime, and has only lately brought itself under the censure of all Parties in this island except the Communists, by subjecting these aged German Field-Marshals and Generals after this protracted delay without the formulation of any changes, to a new, prolonged ordeal. On every ground soldierly, juridical and humanitarian, it is known to be a wrong and base thing to do. But how foolish, how inane – I might also say insane – it is to make a feature of such squalid long-drawn vengeance when the mind and soul of Germany may once again be hanging in the balance between the right course and the wrong. I trust that even now wiser councils may prevail, and also, on the general question of post-war vengeance, I strongly urge our American friends to let bygones be bygones. After all three years have passed and the principal criminals have suffered the punishments they deserved. When I survey the misfortunes in which Europe is plunged, I admire the wisdom and statecraft which General MacArthur has displayed in his dealing with Japan. He is making it possible for decent Japanese to say 'the future of our country lies with the United States and their sister nation, our old ally, Britain.' That cannot be to the disadvantage of the security of the world.

For all these reasons and with such reservations as I have thought it right to make, we support the foreign policy of His Majesty's Government in labouring for peace, in taking a firm stand against the encroachments and aggressions of Soviet Russia, and in not being bullied, bulldozed, and blackmailed out of Berlin whatever the consequences may be. We support them in developing the closest possible unity with the United States on moral issues and in military measures. We support them also in trying to organize the effective defence of Western Europe and making a faithful effort towards a United Europe by all States who are free to choose their path.

The British Government have gained very little credit in any quarter by their handling of this large issue, and petty and personal jealousies, arising from the fact that I revived this idea of a United Europe two years ago in a speech at Zurich, have clouded the vision of some of them. A wrong-headed desire to reduce United Europe to the United Socialist Europe has misled others. In fact, the Socialist Parties throughout Europe have shown themselves the weakest brethren whenever it has come to making a stand against militant communism and the whole idea of organizing United Europe on a one-Party basis would be destructive of all hopes of taking the greatest step forward founded upon this grand design which is desired by so many. I cannot think, and here I come to the issue which I know is much in your minds, that the policy of a United Europe as we Conservatives conceive it can be the slightest injury to our British Empire and Commonwealth or to the principle of Imperial Preference which I so carefully safe-guarded in all my discussions with President Roosevelt during the war. We in the Conservative Party will vigilantly guard and do all in our power to strengthen the ties which unite this Island and all the sister nations of the British family. The unity of the Empire is the foundation of our Party's political belief to which we shall remain eternally faithful. But there is absolutely no need to choose between a United Empire and United Europe. Both are vitally and urgently necessary to our Commonwealth, to Europe, and to the free world as a whole.

As I look out upon the future of our country in the changing scene of human destiny I feel the existence of three great circles among the free nations and democracies. I almost wish I had a blackboard. I would make a picture for you. I don't suppose it would get hung in the Royal Academy, but it would illustrate the point I am anxious for you to hold in your minds. The first circle for us is naturally the British Commonwealth and Empire, with all that that comprises. Then there is also the English-speaking world in which we, Canada, and the other British Dominions and the United States play so important a part. And finally there is United Europe. These three majestic circles are co-existent and if they are linked together there is no force or combination which could overthrow them or even challenge them. Now if you think of the three inter-linked circles you will see that we are the only country which has a great part in every one of them. We stand, in fact, at the very point of junction, and have the opportunity of joining them all together. If we rise to the occasion in the years that are to come it may be found that once again we hold the key to opening a safe and happy future to humanity, and will gain for ourselves gratitude and fame.

The Government now call upon us to help them in rearmament. The recruiting campaign for the Territorial Army has been set on foot. The release of men from the colours has at last been suspended. We have been urged to take part in this recruiting campaign. The Ministers at the heads of the Service Departments write letters to their Conservative opponents and to many country magnates and prominent men whose aid they need. They appeal for a spirit of national unity. But at the same time another important Cabinet Minister describes us as 'lower than vermin' and the Secretary of State for War, who is specially involved in the recruiting appeal – brave figure to come forward, you would almost think it was a comic turn at a cinema – has explained that, apart from the Trades Unions, he does not care a 'tinker's cuss' for all the rest of us. We must not be put off from doing our duty to our country by the taunts and insults of people like these to whom I have referred. During these last years of national abasement and decline we have always tried, in spite of every political provocation, to set national issues on a higher plane. Thus, we supported the Government in their great embarrassment at the time of the first American Loan. We also supported them in their proposal for compulsory service on an 18 months basis, and even when the Minister of Defence ran away from his convictions and from the expert advice he had received and announced, we still supported his twelve-month proposal.

We have supported the National Savings campaign. We have done our utmost to stimulate and contribute to production. I have already set before you the support we have given and shall give them in their foreign policy, and we have done all this at a time when no word has been spoken by any Minister of the Crown except of insult to the great Party whole leading personalities are gathered in this hall, and who represent today without doubt or question a considerable majority of the British electorate. I know it may be hard and against the grain for some of you to support our Socialist opponents and to stand with them on platforms at recruiting meetings. Things are not always right because they are hard, but if they are right one must not mind if they are also hard. The policy of the Conservative party, which you will allow me to pronounce in your name, will continue to be to sustain the Government of the day in everything that they do in the national interest, and the gibes and slanders which they fling at us must play no part in the decisions which it is our duty to take.

At the same time I must bluntly say – and I am speaking to you this afternoon with considerable plainness – that I have no confidence in the military arrangements and preparations of the Socialist Government or in the men who now come forward to lead a national movement. The Minister of Defence, who was a good man under proper leadership in the war, showed his personal limitations when he abandoned the 18 months' service because he thought that otherwise he might lose his popularity with the extremists of his own Party. It will be very difficult for anyone to build up confidence in him again. As for the Air Ministry and the War Office they have been filled with a series of yearly tenants, many of them absentees for long periods, appointed with no thought of their qualification for the particular task. These fleeting phantoms, lasting a few months each, have given no foundation for any well-wrought plan of national defence to be framed. Here today and gone tomorrow – has been the characteristic of the Service Ministers under the Socialist Government in years of exceptional difficulty, and now of growing danger. We Conservatives therefore cannot take any responsibility for the quality or extent of our military preparations. Nevertheless we must do our best to help even these 'guilty men' to make them better, even though while they make their appeals they also continue to revile us.

The broad and general policy of the Socialist Government upon defence has been a worthy specimen of their handling of our affairs hand to mouth, month to month, week to week. In 1945 and 1946 they held millions of men and many women standing about idle without demobilization, and squandered several hundred millions of money. In November, 1945, namely, three years ago, I was shocked at the needless delay in demobilization and urged that it should be expedited. I even specified the actual figures at which they should aim for the three Services. It was necessary to reduce the great War Establishment and at the same time to build up adequate forces on a different basis for the dangerous interval which follows all great struggles. I therefore proposed a reduction at the utmost speed to 1,500,000 men for the Navy, Army and Air Force. But this was brushed aside when it was both possible and necessary by Socialist incompetence. Thus the Armed Forces could not get properly reorganized on a long-term peace-time basis, and now when the danger looms upon us we are found with only 800,000 men, and those much affected by a tardy method of transition from war to peacetime conditions. When things seemed fairly safe they held all those millions in the Armed Forces; when danger revived they were found in process of casting away our military strength.

Now there is made a loud Socialist cry to build up again towards the minimum which I specified, and to reinstitute the 18 months' service from which Mr Alexander, having proposed it with so much bombast, scuttled with so much alacrity. In spite of all this exhibition of weakness and incapacity, the policy of our Party remains to help all we can on every occasion the Socialist Government to build up our national defences, making it clear at the same time that we can take no responsibility for the state into which they have been allowed to fall.

I must turn to another field. A year ago at Brighton I welcomed the appointment of Sir Stafford Cripps to the control of our economic affairs, and I am sure everyone almost without exception was very glad when a few months later he succeeded Mr Dalton as Chancellor of the Exchequer. I need not labour a point on which all Parties are unanimously agreed. We shall support Sir Stafford Cripps in everything he does for the national interest, but we cannot support him in what he does and says to pay his way with his own foolish Party or give satisfaction to his own doctrinaire obsessions. By his abolition of the Liverpool Cotton Exchange he cost this country two or three millions a year in foreign currency and deprived the cotton trade of its invaluable instrument for making favourable purchases of cotton in all the flexibility of private enterprise. By his capital levy which he introduced in order to keep 'on side' with his Party, and get his first Budget through, he has struck a heavy blow at national savings. And now I am sorry to see that, as I believe against his better judgment and convictions, he has had to advocate the nationalization of steel which no-one knows better than he is deeply detrimental to all the vital work he has in hand, in the doing of which he does not hesitate to appeal to all Parties and all classes.

We are all very glad indeed that there has lately been an improvement over the ruinous record of Dr Dalton. It is all the more creditable that our exports should continue to improve, although they are hampered by the fact that coal, electricity, and transport all cost so much more than before the war, and that the private trader is harassed by so much Government interference and ill-will. It is the duty of the Conservative Party to do all in its power to encourage and contribute to production. Indeed it is a remarkable fact that it is to those very industries which arise most directly from private enterprise and initiative and in which these virtues play their greatest part that the recent improvement is due.

Neither Socialist nationalized industry nor Government planning can claim the slightest credit for it. The improvement is, in fact, mainly due to our invisible exports – banking, broking, insurance, tourist traffic, shipping, and other services in which this island has hitherto been pre-eminent or at least prominent, and in which its brains and contrivance and way of life play a substantial part in earning our national livelihood. The profits made for the nation by private enterprise have thus gone some way to offset the losses of the socialized industries. I must repeat what I said at Brighton, that all our activities are oppressed by the appalling weight of taxation. The Chancellor of the Exchequer has utterly failed to reduce Government expenditure: 3,500 millions, or more than three times the maximum pre-war budget in a period of very considerable rearmament, is being taken for the nation in the current year by the Government. The weight of this falls on every class and weakens the incentives to special exertions. It is too early to judge the effect of the National Health Service, which we supported in principle, but it is already obvious that immense miscalculations have been made about its expense.

There is also the enormous drain upon British manpower caused by the hundreds of thousands of additional civil servants and local government officials who are engaged in managing us all, and are withdrawn from fertile production where they should be found employment with advantage to themselves no less than to the nation. A vast number of controls and regulations which ought never to have survived the war are still in being, or nominally in being; some have fallen into what they call in America innocuous desuetude, and Ministers sing their own praises when any of these are removed, whereas they deserve nothing but censure for having kept them on so long.

The Socialist Government offers no leadership to the industrial effort. Its Ministers continue to preach unity and class-warfare at the same time, and praise of the work of employers and managers alternates with the customary Socialist abuse of these very same people. Although the Conservatives are more than half the nation and contribute more than half of its productive effort, they do so under a steady stream of calumny and abuse. We could afford to treat with disdain the attacks which our Socialist rulers make upon us if they were confined to ill-natured words. It is when they follow these by wrong and spiteful deeds that they strike their heaviest blow at the public welfare and unity of effort. There is no basic industry in the land which is less suited to nationalization than the manufacture of steel in all its intricate refinements and in the full tide of ever more successful producing and exporting power.

There is no moment which could be more wrongfully chosen than this, when the need for national unity is so great, and when we are dependent upon American charity for our bread. Yet nationalization of steel production is, we are assured, to be the culminating act of partisanship to be inflicted upon us regardless of the common weal. It is for the sake of carrying this wanton measure to the Statute Book that Parliament was recently called together for a tick-work session, and an utterly unprovoked attack is being made upon the well-established procedure of the Parliament Act which has served us well for nearly 40 years. The action of the House of Lords, under the wise and distinguished leadership of Lord Salisbury, in rejecting this measure of Socialist aggression, is endorsed by public opinion. It is endorsed as strongly as was the rejection by the Second Chamber of the absurd proposals to deal with capital punishment, from which we have been saved by their sagacious and timely action. At the same time as this attack is made upon them all well-considered proposals for improving the composition of the Second Chamber are blocked and rejected by the Socialist Government. We do not at all shrink from bringing these issues and the nationalization of steel to the test of the approaching General Election. But over and above all special questions there rises before us the dread and solemn issue of the survival of Great Britain and her Empire as a united power in the first rank among the nations. From the day when the news of our landslide into Socialism flashed around the world, we fell in the estimation of every country, friendly or hostile, and this process has continued with every year that has passed. We have recklessly cast away our interests, our duties and our reputation for good faith in many parts of the globe. Our Empire in the East has been squandered with hideous loss of life of innocent and helpless people who have hitherto been protected from internal struggles and from foreign invasion by Britannia's shield. At least 400,000 or more, that is to say a larger number than all our killed in the war, have been butchered in the Punjab alone. We have repudiated all our pledges and obligations to great masses of people who trusted us, princes who had solemn treaties and millions of Untouchables who never had any hope other than British justice. Of all our special obligations the only one which we are punctiliously fulfilling is to pay back the vast sums of money to the new Governments in India for having protected them against the Japanese invasion and conquest.

Sir Stafford Cripps, whose sensitive mind is shocked at the execution of a single murderer for the vilest crimes, treats this frightful holocaust as a mere incident in the process of oriental self-government. The orgy of anarchy and murder which I predicted to you in Burma has already come to pass. Alas that we should have to say it. The Socialists, more than any other Party in the State, have broken their word in Palestine and by indescribable mismanagement have brought us into widespread hatred and disrepute there and in many parts of the world. Southern Ireland, or Eire, is about to cast off the last tenuous association with the Crown, and is apparently expecting Ulster, without whose loyalty we could not have maintained our lifeline into the Mersey and the Clyde during the war, to be driven out by us against her will from the British Empire. You are quite right to record by a special resolution yesterday your inflexible resolve to resist any policy of coercing Ulster to abandon her allegiance to the Crown. These are but some of the misfortunes and tragedies which have befallen us under Socialist misrule on the morrow of our greatest victory and the services we had rendered to all mankind. Once again we have cast away by our folly and inconsequence much that we had gained by our virtue and our valour. It is indeed a strange paradox that after our country had gained its greatest glory, that the British name and even the personal safety of Britons in so many lands, should have fallen so swiftly so low. This process has only to continue, even if peace is preserved, and we trust it will be, to make us more and more incapable of keeping our very large population alive and in maintaining the standards of life and living which have been steadily built up on bygone decades and generations. When the votes are cast at the General Election, or at the local government elections which will be its important prelude, everyone who cares about the life and fame of the dear land we live in, and realizes the tremendous nature of what is at stake, should not fail to act with all the force in his being. We shall be voting not only for freedom and recovery but also for bare survival. Another Socialist Parliament would seal our fate in world history, and close by our own actions amid self-inflicted gloom and squalor the marvellous story of Britain's greatness. Never let us despair; all can be regained if we rouse and rear the mighty energies and the genius of all classes in our land. When the moment of choosing comes we shall make no wild and vain promises of lush and easy times. A new supreme effort is needed and it is our prayer, and we do right to pray, that the underlying solid wisdom and character of our people may bring into being a Parliament which truly represent their strength and virtue. Such a Parliament alone can take without fear or favour every step that is needed to revive the moral health and shining glory of our Commonwealth of our Empire and of our Island home.

Field Marshal Lord Montgomery to Winston S. Churchill
(Churchill papers, 2/143)[1]

10 October 1948

Dear Mr Churchill,

Re the picture you are going to give me. There is one you showed me at Chartwell called The River Loup which I liked immensely. Would you give me that? I thought your speech at Llandudno was magnificent.

Please sign the picture. Some you do are not signed.

Igor Bazovsky[2] to Winston S. Churchill
(Churchill papers, 2/71)

11 October 1948

Slaves to the Bolsheviks by machinations of Benes and Gottwald[3] Czech governments wish to build system of freedom in Danube basin in honest cooperation with other Danube nations. Slovaks will fight for their right to choose freely their own form of government and for a democratic Slovak republic in a free and united Europe. I assure you that the hearts of Slovaks in Bratislava and in all parts of the world beat higher this evening and I beg you to give your kind attention and support to the just case of Slovakia.

---

[1] This letter was handwritten.

[2] Milos Alexander Bazovsky, 1899–1958. Also known as 'Igor'. Slovak painter, considered one of the most prominent Slovaks of the 20th century. Known for his impressionistic landscapes and bringing new insights to the folk genre theme. Resisted socialism both in its artistic influence and personally.

[3] Klement Gottwald, 1896–1953. Born in Moravia, Austria-Hungary. Served in Austro-Hungarian Army during WWI; deserted. Joined Communist Party of Czechoslovakia; edited party newspaper. Became a member of the Czechoslovak Parliament, 1929. President of the Republic, 1948–53. Under Gottwald's presidency, the country was forced to adopt a Soviet model of government and execute 180 party officials.

October 1948

Colonel Frank Clarke to Winston S. Churchill
(Churchill papers, 2/161)

11 October 1948   New York

My dear Winston,

I have just returned from Florida and find that the work on my house will be finished the end of this month and in spite of the two hurricanes that hit Miami very little damage was done to my place.

I am planning to go down there for the winter about the 15th of November and I do hope that you and Clemmie, and anyone else you wish to bring, will come out and visit with me again this winter.

Aside from the importance to your health of getting some sunshine, I believe you could spend some time out here advantageously and getting the opinions on this side as to the possible revisions in the European Recovery Program in the light of recent developments in the Russian situation. Your foresight, as exemplified in your Fulton Speech, is bound to carry weight with the new Administration but it needs your own personal contact.

I believe that Dewey's election will prove to be a landslide. In fact, some of the Southern States may go to him, and I know you can count on a warm welcome from him when you come out.

Won't you please write me a note and let me know whether you can come, and, if so, when it would suit you best to come? Also, whether you would like to see any other parts of the country while you are out here, as I can arrange to get a first class private plane to fly us anywhere we wish to go; or of course if you prefer, there would be no problem in getting a private railroad car.

Please give my love to Clemmie, and also to Sarah and Mary.

PS. Your speech on Saturday has made the headlines in the papers here and comment is most favourable.[1]

Sarah Churchill to Winston S. Churchill
(Churchill papers, 1/45)[2]

11 October 1948

Darling Papa,

Thank you oh so much for the wonderful 'chequelet'. Was darling. I have just burst out into a small flat down on the sea front in Brighton and it will enable me to put in a kitchen and decorate most scrumptiously stable II for Mule. Please forgive my handwriting but I am in the train on the way to visit it.

The reviews of your book are almost all unanimously overwhelmed with

---

[1] Churchill responded: 'Thank you so much for your letter. Am fixed here however for this winter. All good wishes.'
[2] This letter was handwritten.

it – as a literary classic – a personal story – and history. Wow! Hard hardworking wonderful Papa. Only the Communists and the *Times* seem to dislike your speech.

Much much love,
Your loving mule
[Drawing of a mule]

Julian Amery[1] to Editor of The Times[2]
(Churchill papers, 2/145)

12 October 1948

Sir,

Your leading article on Mr Churchill's speech at Llandudno does all that can be done with words to discredit his sombre warning. You seek to dismiss his whole case for firmness backed by the ultimate use of force on the ground that 'no great and proud nation will negotiate under duress'. But are not the blockade of Berlin and the Civil War in Greece, flagrant acts of 'duress' undertaken or instigated by the Russian Government? When and how is that 'duress' to be removed? It is not for me to formulate on Mr Churchill's behalf the precise demands which he would make the test of Western resolution. But seriously, what prospect is there of any demands however reasonable proving acceptable to the Russians, unless backed by overwhelming 'duress'? Was that not the whole sum and substance of Mr Churchill's speech?

I would further venture the following comments on two other aspects of your criticism. You wrote of the speech: 'If there was in it a lighter note, a rather larger use of stress and emphasis, a somewhat slighter recognition of the responsibility of a great, elder statesman and a consequent oversimplification when compared with the famous speeches at Fulton or Zurich or the

---

[1] (Harold) Julian Amery, 1919–96. Son of L. S. Amery. Educated at Eton and Balliol College, Oxford. A war correspondent in the Spanish Civil War, 1938–9. Attaché, British Legation, Belgrade (on special missions in Bulgaria, Turkey, Romania and the Middle East), 1939–40. Sgt, RAF, 1940–1. Commissioned, and transferred to the Army, 1941. On active service in Egypt, Palestine and the Adriatic, 1941–2. Liaison officer (behind German lines) to the Albanian resistance movement, 1944. Churchill's Personal Representative with Generalissimo Chiang Kai-shek, 1945. Unsuccessful Parliamentary candidate (Cons.) for Preston, July 1945. MP (Cons.) for Preston North, 1950–66; for Brighton Pavilion, 1969–92. Married, 1950, Catherine, daughter of Harold Macmillan. Parliamentary Under-Secretary of State, War Office, 1957–8; Colonial Office, 1958–60. PC, 1960. Secretary of State for Air, 1960–2. Minister of Aviation, 1962–4; of Public Building and Works, 1970; for Housing and Construction, 1970–2. Minister of State, Foreign and Commonwealth Office, 1972–4. In 1948, published his Albanian recollections, *Sons of the Eagle*. Biographer of Joseph Chamberlain's career from 1901 to 14 (in succession to J. L. Garvin). Life Peer, 1992.

[2] William Francis Casey, 1884–1957. Journalist and newspaper editor. Educated at Castleknock College and Trinity College, Dublin. Married, 1914, Amy Gertrude Pearson-Gee. Called to Irish Bar, 1909. Joined *The Times* staff, 1913. Correspondent in Washington DC and Paris. Special correspondent in Geneva and Spain. Deputy Editor of *The Times*, 1941–8; Editor, Mar. 1948 to Sep. 1952. Published several plays in the early 1900s and a novel entitled *Private Life of a Successful Man* (1935).

Hague, the explanation must no doubt be found in the air of Llandudno – and in the cheers of the massed Conservatives who welcomed him so movingly.' Was this intended to suggest that Mr Churchill departed from his prepared text in response to the warm welcome he received? If so, I can assure you as one who sat in the audience with the authorised text of the speech in hand, that he departed at no significant point from his typescript.

As to your attribution to Mr Churchill of 'a somewhat slighter recognition of the responsibility of a great elder statesman . . . when compared with the famous speeches at Fulton or Zurich', I do not recall that either of these speeches struck you as particularly statesmanlike at the time. Those of your readers who care to refresh their memories by looking back at your leading articles of March 6, 1946 and September 20, 1946, will find that your comments on those speeches struck much the same note of deprecation and showed the same unwillingness to face an increasingly inescapable issue as did your more recent comments on the speech at Llandudno.

If so much were not at stake it would be interesting to see whether two years hence you will pay the same tribute to the Llandudno speech as you now afford to the Fulton and Zurich speeches two years after their delivery.

Winston S. Churchill to Lieutenant-Colonel John Astor
(Churchill papers, 2/145)

14 October 1948 Chartwell
Private

My dear John,

I send you a letter which Julian Amery, who was and is a candidate for Preston, has written to the *Times* arising from its leading article on my speech at Llandudno. There is no doubt that the two most hostile criticisms of that speech were the *Times* and the *Daily Worker*. It may be that you will wish, however to keep your correspondence columns a free field for discussion.

I was really astonished, when the *Times* leader was shown to me, at the way in which history repeats itself. You will, I daresay, have noticed that the *Daily Herald* has not attacked my speech. This can only be because the Foreign Office have told them that it was helpful to the general position.

Winston S. Churchill to Henry Luce
(*Churchill papers, 4/17*)

14 October 1948

I see Wallace has attacked me personally saying that I am working hand in glove with you for a 'London–Rome–Madrid–Wall St Axis'. I should never intervene in Presidential rivalries between the Republican and Democratic Parties, but I do not feel that the same objections to my answering Wallace can apply. The smaller his vote the better for all. If you like the idea I would consider writing about 2000 words for *Life* before the Poll. On the other hand the mere fact that I reply to him may add to his publicity. Let me know how you feel. Meanwhile I am not committed. Hope you have received my other telegrams.

BBC: monitoring report
(*Churchill papers, 2/69*)

14 October 1948
No. 3139

SOVIET PROPAGANDA THEMES
Mr Churchill as 'Prophet of a New World War'

Abandoning its earlier reserve on the subject, the Soviet radio came out on Tuesday evening with bitter attacks on Mr Churchill's Llandudno speech. In a commentary for the home audience Ermashev[1] recalled past speeches by Mr Churchill 'to the dominant classes' – Fulton exactly two years ago and more recently at Zurich and The Hague. 'Every time,' said Ermashev, 'he prophesies a new world war. At Llandudno he said the same thing. Churchill desires war.' He went on to depict Mr Churchill's past political career as one 'nurtured on war and bloodshed'. It was quite obvious that at the present time he saw his only hope of a return to power in the outbreak of a new war. Mr Churchill, the commentator added, was not just the leader of the Conservative Party but 'one of the most prominent leaders of the imperialist camp and the most experienced adviser of the American expansionists. . . .'

What, asked Ermashev, could have prompted Mr Churchill to 'declare his warlike programme at the present moment?' The basic cause was undoubtedly the confusion in the imperialist camp engendered by the struggle in the UN between 'the two directions of international policy'. The imperialist leaders were alarmed by the growing support of the broad masses for the Soviet disarmament proposals and the Llandudno speech was intended to offset, by

---

[1] I. Ermashev. Soviet historian. Author of *Zakhvat Avstrii* (1938) and *Sun Yat-sen* (1964).

spreading panic and anxiety, the important moral and political defeats they had suffered. Mr Churchill's 'warlike outpourings' were thus a sign of 'the moral and political bankruptcy of the atomists of every shape and kind'.

In the Topic of the Day commentary put out for the general run of Moscow's foreign audiences, Ermashev enlarged upon Mr Churchill's 'confession' of the weakness of the imperialist camp – a weakness which the commentator attributed to the fact that the man in the street the world over had given his wholehearted support to the Soviet policy of strengthening universal peace and security. In his opinion it was indicative of the Soviet 'victory' at UN that the American delegation had 'refrained from speaking out' on important issues and had left the main 'and most unsavoury' tasks to the French, British and other delegations. Another interpretation of this 'silence' advanced by Ermashev was the approach of the Presidential elections and the desire to mislead the US electorate as to what was happening at Paris. This led him to suggest that 'Churchill's speech was nothing but an attempt to bolster US diplomacy. He only said what . . . it is not convenient for the US ruling circles to say themselves at this juncture.'

Mr Churchill's 'Self-Disclosure'

In a further approach to British, French and other Western audiences, Sergeeva took up the question of Mr Churchill's personal motives. In her view the speech was 'an extremely significant self-disclosure. It is shot through with the powerless fury of an imperialist wolf who sees the mighty British colonial Empire crumbling to pieces, who sees the ground shaking under the feet of his class and in his impotence thinks that war against the Soviet Union might wipe out all those social and political advances that have been made, that are being and may be made in the world.' In 1945 the British people had voted for those who promised peace and friendship with the Soviet Union. 'Churchill poisonously reminds the Labour leaders that they haven't lived up to their promise. He entertains hope of again returning to power. He wants to be the first in the camp of the warmongers and promises beforehand no half measures – only force, force and force.' But the thing was that he lacked that force: that was why he 'rattles the US atom bomb', seeing in it a means of restoring the bygone might of the Empire. Yet such machinations were senseless; it was clear that his call for a new war did not strike a responsive chord in the hearts of the British people.

Aubrey Halford-MacLeod[1] to Jo Sturdee
(Churchill papers, 2/72)

15 October 1948

Dear Miss Sturdee,

Thank you for your letter of 4th October about the request made to Mr Churchill by Mr Warren Magee for a statement in favour of Von Weizsaecker.[2] We had some correspondence about this before when I wrote to Miss Gilliatt on the 18th June.

As I said then, Sir Orme Sargent thinks that there is no objection to Mr Churchill's complying with Mr Magee's request to the extent which he feels that he can do so from his own knowledge, but Mr Churchill may well feel that if he cannot speak from personal knowledge, it would be better not to comply.

I should let you know, however, that Mr Magee approached the Foreign Office verbally with a request for a statement that His Majesty's Government had in fact believed that there was a resistance movement to Hitler in Germany. We were not prepared to make such a statement because we did not think it proper that His Majesty's Government should proffer an opinion on this contentious subject.

What Mr Magee appears really to want is a counterblast to Lord Vansittart's two affidavits, expressing his belief that there was little if any resistance movement in Germany and that Weizsaecker certainly did not belong to it. Apparently he fears that the Tribunal will take cognizance of this opinion and is therefore out to obtain a contrary expression of opinion from the most influential sources possible. If on the wider subject Mr Churchill is prepared to express any general or particular views there would be no objection.

I return the enclosures to your letter herewith.

Clementine Churchill to Winston S. Churchill
(Churchill papers, 1/44)

21 October 1948

Before we meet this evening to discuss what you would like to do for Randolph and June,[3] may I point out that you cannot make a settlement out of the Trust upon June because the terms of the Trust do not allow you to make grants out of capital to anybody except your own children.

---

[1] Aubrey Seymour Halford-MacLeod, 1914–2000. Educated at Magdalen College, Oxford. Entered Diplomatic Service, 1937. British Member, Secretariat, Advisory Council for Italy, 1944. Asst Political Adviser to Allied Commission in Italy, 1944; Political Adviser, 1945. Principal Private Secretary to Permanent Under-Secretary at FO, Sir Orme Sargent, 1946. Deputy Secretary-General, Council of Europe, 1949–52. CMG, 1958. CVO, 1965. Ambassador to Iceland, 1966–70.
[2] See Magee to Churchill, 1 Oct. 1948, reproduced above (pp. 1176–9).
[3] Randolph Churchill and June Osborne were married in 1948.

1. Would you like to ask the trust to allow Randolph and June to live rent free? If they paid rent they would have to pay the Trust £435 a year (3% on £14,500), If they live rent free all their lives this would be the equivalent of the trust making a settlement of £14,500, and then eventually the house could become Randolph's share of part of your inheritance. What do you think of this? [. . .]

3. During the past fifteen years I have been steadily saving £200 a year out of my private allowance and putting it in an account called No. 2, or the Children's Account. Out of this I propose to give Randolph and June £500 as a wedding present, which I suppose they will spend on carpets, curtains etc., for their new home.

Jo Sturdee to Winston S. Churchill
(Churchill papers, 2/22)

22 October 1948

Mr Magee, American Counsel for General von Weizsaecker, telephoned from Frankfort to say that they have been informed that they must have collected by October 27 next all the evidence in this case. He quite realizes that this is a difficult matter for you, but he would be grateful to know whether you will or will not be able to send a statement as requested, as soon as possible.[1]

Sir James Grigg to Winston S. Churchill
(Churchill papers, 2/149)

23 October 1948

My dear Winston,

I have just received the gift copy of *The Gathering Storm* and I am immensely pleased and proud to have it. I had already read it because I was asked to do a review of it for one of Kemsley's provincial papers. How good it is especially the first Book!

For the last fortnight I have been wavering whether to send you a copy of my first book,[2] which I have very little doubt will also be my last. My hesitation was not at all because there might be something in it – though I don't think there is – which might displease you, but because I was more than a little afraid to expose my own poor work to the greatest living writer of English. However the moral of the latest work of that same master is that cowardice was ever the worst of sins and so I shall send it, not now in fear and trembling,

---

[1] Churchill wrote on this note: 'No I will not be able to. I don't know enough about it.'

[2] *Prejudice and Judgement* (London, 1948).

but with such humility as I possess. I don't suppose you will have time to read it anyway.

After being somewhat short of income and occupation I now have enough commercial employment to keep me reasonably busy and in very comfortable circumstances. I am glad therefore that I didn't accept your generous offer to crusade for my lost pension rights. I am sure that they couldn't have been revived without my returning to the Civil Service and by standing at the election I had made that impossible. Moreover I hate so much what these people are doing that I couldn't have worked for them anyhow.

I think I hate them most for India and Burma and I should like you to read the enclosed short extract from a letter written by the man who is still the Governor of the West Punjab.[1] It wasn't written to me and I have had no contact with the writer for over 10 years but it fits in with the view I had formed independently that the real danger from Russia is in Asia, and that by abdicating in India and Burma (and also by selling the Dutch in Indonesia by such agents as Killearn and Inverchapel) we have made it all too easy for her.

Once more I send my thanks for your book and my best wishes.

Winston S. Churchill: statement
(*Churchill papers, 2/72*)

25 October 1948
Hold

I have never met Baron Weizsaecker, but from the impressions I derived and from my subsequent study I think it unworthy of the victors that after more than three years he should be brought to trial for performing his functions as an official in the German foreign office.

Winston S. Churchill: speech
(*Hansard*)

28 October 1948   House of Commons

DEBATE ON THE ADDRESS

The Debate on the Address, in reply to the King's Speech, has sometimes been called 'The Grand Inquest of the Nation', and when we consider the Gracious Speech it is our duty to weigh and measure both what it contains and

---

[1] Robert Francis Mudie, 1890–1976. Born in Broughty Ferry, Scotland. Entered Indian Civil Service, 1914. Educated at Fettes College and King's College, Cambridge, graduating with the distinction of Wrangler. Married, 1919, Mary Spencer (d.): one child; 1960, Mary Elizabeth Abercromby. Governor of West Punjab, Pakistan, 1947–9.

what it omits. This is, on the whole, a well-written document which Ministers have submitted to His Majesty, and it comprises a mixture of routine statements, about which there is much agreement, and of controversial assertions which we on this side cannot endorse. I shall endeavour to deal with these, and with the important issues which they affect, to the best of my ability, and mainly in the order in which they are presented to us in the Gracious Speech.

In the first place, we are confronted with various constitutional issues which have been brought before us in language of suitable decorum and marked reserve. The Statute of Westminster decided to sweep away all formal constitutional safeguards, which seemed to cramp the freedom and independence of the great self-governing Dominions, and to rely for the unity and cohesion of the British Empire solely upon the link of the Crown which joined us all. Now we are asked, with some evident hesitation, to consider the abandonment of that sole remaining symbol and legal foundation of the British Empire. For some years the tendency of Socialist and Left-Wing forces has been to gird at the word 'Empire' and to espouse the word 'Commonwealth', because Oliver Cromwell cut off King Charles's[1] head and all that.

Also, I suppose, the word 'Commonwealth' seems to have in it some association with or suggestion of the abolition of private property and the communal ownership of all forms of wealth. This mood is encouraged by the race of degenerate intellectuals of whom our island has produced during several generations an unfailing succession – looked around upon the British inheritance, whatever it was, to see what they could find to demolish, to undermine or to cast away.

It now appears that the word 'Empire' is taboo:

> Oh! no! we never mention it;
> Its name is never heard.[2]

Flushed with electoral success beyond their dreams (*Interruption.*) – enjoy it while you may – the Socialist Government have proceeded further. One must notice in the Gracious Speech, and in other utterances on which Ministers have lately advised the King the calculated omission of three words which have hitherto claimed many loyalties and much agreement. The first word I have mentioned already is the word 'Empire'; the second is 'Dominion', and the third, of course, is 'British'. There are – I do not want to put it too highly – large, long-established and well recognised conceptions associated with all these words. Apparently, the Socialist Government wish to direct us into channels where these words will be heard no more, or as little as possible. The style and title which we are to give to our world-wide associations of States

---

[1] Charles Stuart, 1600–49. Duke of York, 1605. Prince of Wales, 1616. King Charles I of England, 1625–49. In 1642, the English Civil Wars began; in 1648, the last of Charles's supporters were defeated at the Battle of Preston. Charged with high treason and executed, 1649.

[2] The quotation is adapted from a poem by Thomas Haynes Bayley (1797–1839).

and communities must not contain anything that recalls past tradition. It must contain nothing that embodies pride of race or country; it must contain nothing which could be deemed controversial, nothing that could offend the weakest of the weaker brethren in our slowly-formed association throughout the globe.

Indeed, I wonder myself that the word 'Commonwealth' should satisfy the requirements of the Socialist statesmanship. If all these exclusions and inhibitions are to be enforced it would seem only logical to adopt some completely loose and meaningless term such as was suggested some years ago, ironically, by an amusing journalist, Mr Nathaniel Gubbins,[1] when he pictured the world after the war being divided into groups – population group No. 6, population group No. 7. That, at any rate, would achieve what appears to be the ideal of the Socialist Government in respect of the British Empire of committing nobody to anything at any time in any way.

It is argued that no one could be offended by terms so general as to be meaningless, and there is something in that, but, on the other hand, it must be remembered that no one could be powerfully inspired to lay down his life for the common cause in the hour of mortal danger when that common cause and association cannot be expressed in words which carry any intelligible meaning to any human being. The word 'Empire' is to be suppressed. 'Dominion', for some strange reason, is judged peccant and unwholesome, and now, on the morrow of our greatest victory and service to mankind, we come to the elimination of the word 'British', which was so lately held in the highest honour in many lands. Mr St Laurent,[2] the Canadian Acting Prime Minister, is reported to have said – I read newspapers to guide me in these matters – on arrival in Ottawa:

> Britain dropped 'British' in the Commonwealth title of her own free will. It just occurred as a matter of course.

I am sure, Sir, that such grave constitutional changes ought not to be effected in this way, and I do not wonder that this project has excited widespread concern, especially in Australia and New Zealand. The Prime Minister assured us all on Tuesday that no decision had been taken about legislation affecting the King's title. Certainly none is before us in the present Speech. Until such legislation has been introduced and passed through both Houses

---

[1] Edward Spencer Mott (Nathaniel Gubbins), 1844–1910. Journalist. Born near Lichfield. Commissioned in 19th Rgt, 1862. Served in India and Burma until 1867. Joined *Sporting Times*, 1877. Contributed to *Pioneer (India)*, *Pall Mall Gazette*, *Lady's Pictorial*, *Baily's Magazine* and other publications. Gubbins' own published works include *Clear the Course*, *My Hostess*, *Wanted a Wife* (operetta), *Cakes and Ale*, *A Mingled Yarn* and *The King's Racehorses*, among others.

[2] Louis Stephen St Laurent, 1882–1973. Canadian statesman and jurist. Born in Compton, Quebec. Educated at St Charles College and Laval University. MP (Lib.), 1942. Served under PM William Mackenzie King's as Minister of Justice, Attorney-General and Secretary of State for External Affairs. PM of Canada, 1948–57.

of Parliament, Ministers have no right to put into the King's Speech words which are contrary to the facts and to the constitutional position. For instance, in the Gracious Speech the King is made to say: 'The peoples of My Commonwealth'. That is not a constitutional expression, nor is it in accordance with the facts as they exist today. Great Britain is not a Commonwealth but a Kingdom – the United Kingdom of Great Britain and Northern Ireland. Canada has long proudly called herself 'The Dominion of Canada'. But the word 'Dominion', it now appears, is to follow 'Empire' into desuetude. We have not yet heard what will be the reactions of Canada in this suggestion.

The term 'Commonwealth' does not apply to any of the Colonies of the British Empire, all of which, without exception, stood by us so loyally in the darkest days. Therefore, to limit the description of our association to the 'Commonwealth' – 'My Commonwealth' – to do that is to fail to make any correspondence with the actual existing facts, leaving quite apart the impropriety of such changes being introduced in this way. If constitutional titles and names are to be changed let His Majesty's Government make formal and positive proposals to Parliament. We will consider them. I will make it clear, however, that the Conservative Party will resist any attempt to destroy the expression 'British Empire' or to abandon the constitutional term 'Dominion', or to abolish the word 'British' from our collective designation.

In the meanwhile, pending the Government's bringing forward some proposals, there would be no harm in adhering to the comprehensive expression which, though it has no constitutional authority, has become one of common usage, namely, the 'British Empire and Commonwealth of Nations'. I venture to suggest that as a means of carrying on until the Government have made up their minds what we are to be called or to call ourselves. All good Socialists, I understand, however, are expected henceforward to abstain as much as they possibly can from using the words, hitherto held in so much honour, 'Empire', 'Dominion', and 'British'. No penalties I gather – I hope I am right – are at present to be attached to any infraction of this rule. It is not an addition to the thousands of new crimes for which fines and imprisonment may be imposed. Orthodox Socialists will, however, practise, and are urged to practise, this suppression for the sake of enabling Mr Costello[1] and Pandit Nehru to participate to the full, if they choose to, in any benefits and securities of our association, without committing themselves to the slightest obligation or even to any symbolic or sentimental gesture or token in return.

This practice, if developed, may well become an additional distinction between the parties in the State, a distinction between those to whom the word 'British' is distasteful and those among whom it is still held in honour. It

---

[1] John Aloysius Costello, 1891–1976. Born in Dublin. Educated at University College Dublin. Attorney-General, Irish Free State, 1926–32. Member of Dáil Eireann for Co. Dublin, 1933–7; for Dublin Townships, 1937–43, 1944–8; for Dublin South-East, 1948–69. Taoiseach, 1948–51, 1954–7. Leader of the Opposition, 1951–4, 1957–9.

seems to me that the First Lord of the Admiralty, to take a small instance, will be in a difficult position because, as everyone knows, he is invariably saluted on official occasions in the Navy by the tune 'Rule, Britannia', which obviously expresses and arouses all kinds of sentiments which every right-minded Socialist is expected to abhor. For our part I hope we shall still feel free to sing 'Rule, Britannia' at Conservative meetings throughout the country and thus make it simple for people to show how they feel in these matters.

We must not, however, regard the present abject mood as one which will necessarily long dominate all the peoples now within the circle of the Crown. It may well be that in a couple of years another Empire Conference will take an entirely different view. Even this one was not united on the subject. At present there are not many Conservative Prime Ministers in the British Empire but it may be that this proportion will be reversed in the near future and that a more robust spirit will prevail. I leave this question of title and terminology, and come to the march of events which is taking place under this froth and spume.

Some of the important elements which, a few years ago, formed the British Empire are falling away like autumn leaves, over wide areas in many parts of the globe. It is a fashionable mood in these areas to sever connections with the Crown and to retain only such association with this island as carries with it material advantage. Take first the case of Southern Ireland or Eire. I must confess that I was astonished to learn some weeks ago of Mr Costello's decision to sever the last link with the Crown which even Mr De Valera had deemed it necessary to preserve. I have for many years held a consistent view about Ireland. I expressed it nearly a quarter of a century ago, in 1925 or 1926, when I was invited, as Conservative Chancellor of the Exchequer, to address the Ulster Unionists in Belfast. Perhaps I may read for a moment what I then said:

> I have declared again and again that neither by threats, or violence, or by intrigue nor yet by unfair economic pressure shall the people of Ulster be compelled against their wish to sever the ties which bind them to the United Kingdom or be forced, unless by their own free and unfettered choice, to join another system of Government.

I was therefore glad to hear the answer which the Prime Minister has just given to my right hon. Friend[1] and to show that in this matter at any rate there is no difference between us. On that occasion, a quarter of a century ago, in the Ulster Hall, I added the following:

---

[1] Robert William Hugh O'Neill, 1883–1982. Educated at Eton and New College, Oxford. On active service during WWI, 1915–18. MP (Ulster Unionist) for Mid Antrim, 1915–22. PC (Ireland), 1921. MP (Parliament of Northern Ireland) for Co. Antrim, 1921–9; for Antrim, 1922–50; for North Antrim, 1950–2. PC (Northern Ireland), 1922. Speaker of the House of Commons of Northern Ireland, 1921–9. Bt, 1929. PC, 1937. Parliamentary Under-Secretary of State for India and Burma, 1939–40. HM Lt for Co. Antrim, 1949–59. Father of the House of Commons, 1951–2. Baron, 1953.

I may cherish the hope that some day all Ireland will be loyal because it is free, will be united because it is loyal, and will be united within itself and united to the British Empire.

Strange as it may seem, I still cherish that dream.

I shall always hope that some day there will be a united Ireland, but at the same time, that Ulster or the Northern Counties will never be compelled against their wishes to enter a Dublin Parliament. They should be courted. They should not be raped. As the Minister responsible for carrying out the Cabinet decisions embodied in the Irish Treaty of 1921 I have watched with contentment and pleasure the orderly, Christian society, with a grace and culture of its own and a flash of sport thrown in, which this quarter of a century has seen built up in Southern Ireland, in spite of many gloomy predictions. I well know the grievous injury which Southern Irish neutrality and the denial of the Southern Irish ports inflicted upon us in the recent war, but I always adhered to the policy that nothing, save British existence and survival, should lead us to regain those ports by force of arms, because we had already given them up.

In the end we got through without this step. I rejoice that no new blood was shed between the British and Irish peoples. I shall never forget – none of us can ever forget – the superb gallantry of the scores of thousands of Southern Irishmen who fought as volunteers in the British Army, and of the famous Victoria Crosses which eight of them gained by their outstanding valour. If ever I feel a bitter feeling rising in me in my heart about the Irish the hands of heroes like Finucane[1] seem to stretch out to soothe it away. Moreover, since the war, great antagonisms have grown up in this world against Communist tyranny and Soviet aggression. These have made new ties of unity of thought and of sympathy between the Irish and the British peoples, and indeed throughout the British Islands, and they deeply stir Irish feelings. The Catholic Church has ranged itself among the defenders and champions of liberty and the dignity of the individual. It seemed to me that the passage of time might lead to the unity of Ireland itself in the only way in which that unity can be achieved, namely, by a union of Irish hearts.

There can, of course, be no question of coercing Ulster, but if she were wooed and won of her own free will and consent I, personally, would regard such an event as a blessing for the whole of the British Empire and also for the civilised world. It was indeed strange and, if I may say so, characteristically Irish that this moment above all others should be selected by the Dublin Government for breaking that last tenuous connection with the Crown and

---

[1] Brendan Finucane, 1920–42. Known as 'Paddy'. Born in Dublin. A much-decorated fighter pilot (DSO, DFC and two bars). Shot down 32 enemy aircraft, which put him fifth in the British 'league table' of fighter aces. Drowned, 15 July 1942, returning from a sweep over France. His Spitfire was forced to ditch in the sea after being hit by ground fire.

proclaiming themselves a foreign republic. This decision may well prevent for ever that united Ireland, the dream of which is cherished by so many ardent Irish patriots. In this way Mr Costello and his colleagues have constituted themselves the authors of permanent partition. It is they who have digged a gulf between Southern and Northern Ireland deeper than ever before. They have made a gulf which is unbridgeable except by physical force, the use of which I regret to see Mr De Valera in his latest speech does not exclude.

We cannot tell at what point our present decline will stop, but I cannot conceive it within the bounds of possibility that any British Parliament would drive the people of Ulster out of the United Kingdom and force them to become the citizens of a foreign State against their will. So far as we can tell from the newspapers, from the Prime Minister's reply on Tuesday and his answer just given to my right hon. Friend across the Floor of the House, the Socialist Government seem to have acted rightly in bringing home to the Dublin Government the many serious injuries they would inflict upon themselves and upon Irishmen in this country and in many parts of the world by forcing us to regard them legally as foreigners and aliens.

It would be a great mistake, as well as being very wrong, for any British Government to brush aside the natural juridical consequences that must follow such a decision by the Dublin Cabinet. The matter would not stop at Southern Ireland alone. Nothing could be a greater encouragement to Dr Malan[1] to sever all ties between South Africa and Great Britain than to make it clear that, while every form of symbolic association might be destroyed, no practical inconveniences would result. Therefore, I trust His Majesty's Government will act in strict accordance with the policy which they have so far declared.

I now turn to more distant spheres where the same theme differently expressed, must be pursued. In three and a half years of office the Socialist Government have with strange ardour and relish carried the world-famed British Empire in the East from life into history. Burma has swiftly passed as a foreign power into the anarchy of which I warned the House only a year and a half ago. Bloodshed, murder and disintegration ride triumphant over that unhappy land for whose liberation from Japanese conquest we so lately gave so much British blood and treasure. The fate of India, now that British guidance and control have been so suddenly and rapidly withdrawn, hangs heavy over the future of 400 millions of human beings. An awful tragedy has already occurred. At least 400,000 men and women have slaughtered each other in the Punjab alone. Many good judges place the figure far higher. But the massacre by bloody violence of 400,000 human beings is a horror at which, in any other but this stunned and bewildered age, the whole civilised world would have stood aghast.

[1] Daniel Francois Malan, 1874–1959. Born in Riebeek West, Cape Providence. Married Marie Louw: two sons. MP for Calvinia, 1918–38; for Piketberg, 1938–59. PM of Union of South Africa and Minister for External Affairs, 1948–54.

Four hundred thousand human lives – more than the whole loss suffered by the British Empire in nearly six years of world war: 400,000 human lives have been blotted out untimely. Many millions more are fugitives, wanderers, or exiles from their place of birth. It is strange that this Parliament, which so recently was shuddering at the infliction of the death penalty upon one or two of the most atrocious murderers, should be able to watch with so much detachment and cool composure and short memories this frightful holocaust for which the majority of this House and the Ministers in power bear so grave and intimate a responsibility. We can only be thankful that no such catastrophe or anything which approached one-twentieth part of its magnitude, fell upon the helpless Indian people during the long years when they dwelt in peace and safety under the British Raj and the Imperial Crown and, may I say, under the constant, vigilant, and human supervision of the House of Commons.

Mr Scollan (Renfrew, Western): What about the Indian Famine?

Mr Churchill: Famine? I am talking about bloody violence.

Mr Scollan: What about the Indian famine of which the Tory Governments of the past were responsible?

Mr Churchill: We do not know what famines will occur in the future, but certainly during British rule the Indian population in the last 50 years increased by 100 million. It does not seem that the starvation process has at any rate prevented that augmentation. But this is not the end nor even, I fear, the end of the beginning. The Indian subcontinent, as big as Europe, which for almost 100 years had been freer from internal bloodshed and violence than any other equal part of the earth's expanse and population, is facing problems now which are loaded with immeasurable peril and perplexity. Hitherto they have been protected from foreign aggression by the strong shield of our island power. Our policy, our influence among the nations, our modest military Forces, our latent strength and that of the Empire and, of course, the Royal Navy, have protected India from foreign invasion.

Now this protection can no longer be given in any effective form. There is always the United Nations organisation, but it is still struggling for life and torn with dissension. Moreover, in India the causes and signs of a future internal war are already alive, and its portents multiply as the months pass by. Our Imperial mission in India is at an end – we must recognise that. Some day justice will be done by world opinion to our record there, but the chapter is closed and

> 'The moving finger writes; and, having writ,
> Moves on: nor all your Piety nor Wit
> Shall lure it back to cancel half a Line,
> Nor all your Tears blot out a word of it.'[1]

---

[1] From the *Rubáiyát of Omar Khayyám*, a translation of poems by the Persian scholar Omar Khayyám (1048–1131) by Edward Fitzgerald (1859).

We must look forward. It is our duty, whatever part we have taken in the past, to hope and pray for the well-being and happiness of all the peoples of India, of whatever race, religion, social condition or historic character they may be. We must wish them all well and do what we can to help them on their road. Sorrow may lie in our hearts but bitterness and malice must be purged from them, and in our future more remote relations with India we must rise above all prejudice and partiality –

Mr Alpass (Thornbury):[1] Why not practise it?

Mr Churchill: – and not allow our vision to be clouded by memories of glories that are gone for ever. And in this temper we shall find true guidance – and, indeed, our only hope – in strict and faithful adherence to the underlying principles of justice and freedom which are embodied in the United Nations organisation, and for the maintenance of which that instrument of world government was consciously created.

It is those principles, and those principles alone, which must govern our attitude and action towards this vast branch of toiling and suffering humanity. We have long had no interest in India which counted for more with us than the well-being and peace of its peoples. So far as we may be involved in the fortunes of the Indian peoples, and of the Governments of Pakistan and Hindustan, we must judge them, not by race or religion, but impartially, by their future conduct to one another in accordance with the principles of the United Nations organisation under the Charter of human liberties which is being drawn up, and we must use our influence, such as it may be, against aggression, oppression and tyranny, from whatever quarter it comes. These principles alone must rule our actions, must enable us to steer our course in the incalculable tides on which we and our Indian fellow subjects are now embarked.

It is for such reasons and in accordance with such principles, and not for any preference for Moslem or Hindu, that I have deplored and condemned the violent arbitrary act of aggression which, without any plebiscite, has engulfed the ancient state of Hyderabad; and, secondly, I deplored the attempt now being made to incorporate forcibly, against their wishes, the Moslem population of Kashmir in the Hindu regime. Other cases may arise in the future, and in all of them the only path of honour and duty will be for the British people, through the House of Commons, to act in accordance with the principles enshrined in the United Nations organisation, and wherever possible, through its structure and through whatever strength it may gather.

I regard these considerations as on a different plane from any of those questions which arise about the future connections of Pakistan or Hindustan with the Crown. These are, however, of practical importance and may even be upon us very quickly, and on them I must speak for a little. We could not make

---

[1] Joseph Herbert Alpass, 1873–1969. Educated at Merchant Venturers' College, Bristol. MP (Lab.) for Bristol Central, 1929–31; for Thornbury, 1945–50. CBE, 1951.

ourselves responsible for the defence of any part of India against external attack otherwise than as a part of our duty to the United Nations instrument unless a link is preserved with the British Crown and unless they form part of what I shall still call the British Empire and Commonwealth of Nations, or unless treaties of alliance are made, with due balance of advantage of each side, such as we make with other foreign countries for our own security. Furthermore, we ought not to undertake responsibilities towards foreigners as the result of a treaty towards the discharge of which we have not the means of making an effective contribution. And in judging such matters we must have continual regard to our commitments and to the danger in Europe and here at home which involve our national survival as free men.

Above all, and in the first place, in all that we undertake, whether as an individual power or with the United Nations organisation, or in respect of Western Union, we must devote ourselves in all these matters to the preservation of as much as is left to us of the former British Empire or Commonwealth of Nations comprised within the circle of the British Crown. That we rate above all, and all other arrangements which we may make must be subordinate to that. For us to take the responsibility, otherwise than by treaty, carefully considered at the moment, or through the United Nations, for any country not even symbolically or constitutionally associated with us would be to commit ourselves, without return, to obligations beyond our strength to fulfil and to lay burdens upon our people more than they could bear.

I leave the confines of our wide domain and turn to another subject mentioned in the fourth paragraph of the King's Speech. The Speech refers to Germany and the economic revival in the Western Zones which has followed the currency reform. This seems to have been a well-conceived though tardy measure, and we are all glad to learn that it has produced good results, that it has been beneficial in many ways and also that the Germans are working hard to design a democratic constitution for those parts of their country not under the Russian Communist yoke. We on this side cordially approve of every well-considered step that can be taken to associate Germany with the Western civilization, to which German literature, philosophy, art, music and science have made immortal contributions. There is no doubt that the actual spectacle of Soviet rule in the Russian Zone of Germany has had an educational effect throughout all the German States, an effect which no exhortations, appeals or injunctions of the Western Allies could have achieved. But the most important factor lately at work in Germany has been the spectacle of the Western Allies striving to feed the 2½ millions of Germans in the British and American sectors of Berlin by the prodigious achievement of air lift, regardless of cost and difficulty, while the Soviet Government were doing all they could, or all they dared, to starve these helpless people out. My hope is that free, liberal civilization and democratic Parliamentary processes will win the soul of Germany or Europe and that the great underlying harmonies of the European family will predominate over the feuds that have hitherto rent our famous parent Continent and brought upon it miseries and humiliations beyond the power of statistics to measure or language to describe.

We should put no needless obstacles in the way of a reconciliation with Germany. I was surprised that a British Socialist Government should, according to the reports which have been published, have resisted the United States' desire to mitigate and abridge the process of dismantling the plants and factories in Germany which might play an essential part in economic and industrial revival. I am very glad to learn that they have now agreed with the American view. We on this side are strongly opposed to the infliction of needless severities upon the German people and to needless affronts to natural, legitimate German feelings.

It is from this point of view that we deplore the harsh and wrongful procedure which the Foreign Secretary has authorised towards the aged German generals who were taken prisoner and have now for more than three and a half years been in our power, without any change being preferred against them. There has not been any question of this character which I have noticed in the present Parliament upon which there has been such wide and sincere agreement between all parties of the House. We have seen agreement over the whole area, ranging from the very advanced humanitarianism of the hon. Member for Ipswich (Mr Stokes), to the strict themes of military honour and military etiquette which are associated with my hon. and gallant Friend the Member for Petersfield (Sir G. Jeffreys).[1] It is a wide bracket and I am very glad to find it. Conservatives, Socialists and Liberals who spoke in the Debate on the Adjournment vied with one another in condemning from every conceivable angle of approach this act of administrative and political stupidity and of judicial impropriety, equally repugnant to humanitarian and soldierly sentiment. The reply of the Under-Secretary of State for War[2] on Tuesday night to the protests from all quarters was received with almost universal disapprobation. I am amazed that the Foreign Secretary should go out of his way to add to the many burdens he has to bear by picking up and piling so needlessly on his shoulders this lump of folly.

But I go further than this particular case. The time has come to stop these denazification trials which are taking place throughout Germany. We run the risk of creating a veritable vested interest among those who are engaged in conducting the vast number of trials which are in process, or liable to come on. The principal criminals have been executed by their conquerors. There may be some exceptional cases, such as the slaughter of men of the Norfolk

---

[1] George Darell Jeffreys, 1878–1960. Served in British armed forces during the Nile Expedition, South African War and WWI. Gen., 1935. Knight of Norwegian Order of St Olaf. MP (Cons.) for Petersfield, 1941–51.

[2] John Horace Freeman, 1915–2014. MP (Lab.) for Watford, 1945–55. Financial Secretary to the War Office, 1946–7. Under-Secretary of State for War, 1947. Editor, *New Statesman*, 1961–5. High Commissioner to India, 1965–8. British Ambassador to the US, 1969–71.

Regiment, which was the subject of a trial in Hamburg last week. This it was right to pursue, as one would pursue a common case of murder, even after 15 years had passed before it came to light –

Mr Sydney Silverman (Nelson and Colne): So is the other case.

Mr Churchill: – but the general process of denazification has gone on far too long and should be brought to an immediate end. My attention has been drawn to the case of Baron Weizsaecker. I was asked to make some affidavit about him, as many people in this country have been asked. I was not able to do so, because I had never met Weizsaecker; never being brought officially into contact with his work. He was a permanent official in the Foreign Office under Ribbentrop, in a similar capacity as Sir Alexander Cadogan was and now Sir Orme Sargent is, in the Foreign Office here. Now, after three and a half years, he is being tried.

Mr Elwyn Jones[1] (Plaistow): On a point of Order. Is it in Order when the German civilian to whom the right hon. Gentleman is referring is on trial, that this matter, which is *sub judice*, should be brought into discussion?

Mr Churchill: I am not attempting to deal with the merits of the particular case, on which the court will pronounce, and I am not informed upon them. I am using this as an illustration to show the kind of deadly error which, in my opinion, is being committed at this time by the policy –

Mr S. Silverman: On a point of Order. If a man is on trial is it Order for a right hon. Member to say that to put him on trial was a deadly error and to say that in the course of the trial? Is not that out of Order?

Mr Churchill: On that point of Order, may I point out that this is not a matter under the authority of His Majesty's Government?

Mr Silverman: Of course it is.

Mr Churchill: Not at all. It is in the American zone of Occupation and is decided by the United States Government.

Mr Speaker: It appears to me that this person's name has been brought in as a rather hypothetical illustration of what is going on in the American zone, to which the right hon. Gentleman objects. I do not think it is a comment on the innocence or guilt of the individual and I do not think it can affect the actual trial. It is, therefore, not a comment on the trial.

Mr S. Silverman: Further to that point of Order. Is the House to understand that to describe a prosecution as a deadly error is not a comment on the particular case?

Mr Speaker: This particular prosecution is not described as a deadly error, but that was a description of the whole of the proceedings; or so I understood.

Mr Churchill: The hon. Member who tried to differentiate himself from me excites in my heart a great pleasure, but I may point out that, in order to

---

[1] Frederick Elwyn Jones, 1909–89. MP (Lab.) for Plaistow, 1945–50; for West Ham South, 1950–74; for Newham South, 1974. Attorney General for England and Wales, 1964–70. Lord Chancellor, 1974–9. Baron, 1974.

do so, he has to separate himself from the whole line and theme of thought for which he has made himself known in the whole House for a long time, but who cares –

Mr Silverman rose –

Mr Churchill: No, I will not give way.

Mr Silverman: On a point of Order, I should like to ask whether the right hon. Gentleman is entitled, having taken one side in a case, to impute to me that I took the other side. The point of Order I submitted to you was not intended to indicate on my part any agreement, or disagreement, either with the prosecution or the defence in this, or any other case.

Mr Speaker: I hardly think that is a point of Order.

Mr Churchill: The misuse of points of Order is a well known art and device of this House. I have no intention whatever of going into the merits of this matter, although I have just as much right to express any opinion about it as people in England had about the Dreyfus case when for years it was the subject of many comments, and major comment, although it was taking place under foreign jurisdiction. But there are thousands of other cases pending of smaller people of all kinds. Revenge is, of all satisfactions, the most costly and long drawn out; retributive persecution is, of all policies, the most pernicious. Our policy, subject to the exceptional cases I have mentioned should henceforward be to draw the sponge across the crimes and horrors of the past – hard as that may be – and look, for the sake of our salvation, towards the future.

There can be no revival of Europe without the active and loyal aid 'of all the German tribes'. I use the expression because it is not obnoxious to them and, also, because it carries with it the federal conception which, I think, should play an important part. Nothing should stand in the way of enabling them to render to Europe the great services which are in their power. It has been my hope that France, which we see in such political confusion and weakness, will find a way out of her own troubles and a path to true European leadership by stretching out her hand to her enemy of a thousand years and, in the moment of absolute German prostration, bring them back to the circle of Christendom and the family of Europe.

His Majesty's Opposition have supported all the steps which have been taken by the Government to build up the economic strength offered to Western Europe by the Marshall Plan, and very considerable economic progress is being made in many European countries. All this process can only be effected if Europe is shielded from external aggression from the East by the fact that the United States associate themselves morally and physically with the efforts which are being made to create a defensive front for the countries outside the Iron Curtain. We therefore trust that all the military arrangements which are now being made will have the fullest support from the great Republic across the Atlantic, even though what military preparations are made in the West can only be for some years quite subsidiary to the deterrent power of the atomic bomb. This alone at the present time prevents the rebarbarisation and enslavement of Europe by the Communist forces directed from the Kremlin. I am very glad to hear that significant silence from the Government Benches which gives consent. (*Interruption.*)

We have given every support to Western Union. More than that, I may claim that there is an unbroken chain between the speech I made at Zurich in September, 1946, and the Marshall Aid upon which this great and valuable policy of the Government has been founded. I am sorry if personal jealousies, or other motives below the level of events, have led the Socialist Party at first to embark upon the unnatural plan of narrowing United Europe down to United Socialist Europe. I warned them at the very beginning that that was not a hopeful line of advance. I hope that their recent publication, entitled, I think, 'Facing the Facts', or 'Face the Facts' – (Hon. Members: 'Feet on the Ground'.) – 'Feet on the Ground'. If hon. Gentleman opposite were to persist very long in facing the facts they would find their feet on the ground. And they might very soon find the rest of their bodies as well.

Mr Kirkwood (Dumbarton Burghs): The wish is father to the thought.

Mr Churchill: I hope that this recent publication of the Socialist Party means that the Government itself will abandon such an absurd attempt. I am, however, sorry indeed that they should, at the present time, have shown themselves definitely below all the leading statesmen of France and the French Government and below the Netherlands, Belgium and Luxembourg in supporting the project of a European Deliberative Assembly.

Mr Scollan: Who are the French statesmen?

Mr Churchill: Who are the statesmen? Well, many of the vice presidents –

Mr Scollan: They are shooting the miners.

Mr Churchill: The hon. Member asked a question –

Mr Scollan: Yes, I asked, who are the statesmen?

Mr Churchill: Many of the vice presidents of the United Nations movement, which is being carried on and which started at the Hague – M Blum, who deserves to be treated with respect; M Gasperi, the Prime Minister of Italy; M Spaak, a very important statesman who is in charge of Belgian affairs. I believe some of these gentlemen are Socialists. So it certainly does not well beseem the hon. Gentleman to fret and fume himself because their names are mentioned. We should show some respect for the leading figures of the Socialist movement in Europe, even though we shall find it more difficult to do so for those who fill that role over here.

I regret very much the attitude which the Government have taken and I trust it will be amended in the future. I have always considered that our international and unofficial movement for a united Europe should have as its object the creation of an atmosphere in Europe, what Mr Lecky[1] called 'a climate

[1] William Edward Hartpole Lecky (1838–1903). MP (Union.) for Dublin University, 1896–1903. Author of *Leaders of Public Opinion in Ireland* (1861) and *History of England in the Eighteenth Century* (1878).

of opinion', among all its peoples and of the people of this island, and of the British Empire, and of the United States, in favour of the ideal of European unity. If that could be done it would be a very great boon to us all. I believe that this can be achieved without injury to national traditions, sentiments and character of any States, large or small, concerned. In proportion as this succeeds, and as it certainly will succeed unless interrupted by dire violence, our movement will at every stage be a help to the Foreign Secretary in the policy which, if he is not led astray by small motives, may confer upon him a lasting reputation.

I now come back from these wider fields to our domestic affairs and to the paragraph in the Gracious Speech which deals with our defences and the contribution we make to the great causes and projects to which the great majority of the House have earnestly devoted themselves. 'My Ministers' – says the Gracious Speech –

> are taking steps to ensure that My Armed Forces shall be efficient and well equipped, and that the best use shall be made of men called up under the National Service Act.

It is late in the day to make such declarations, however welcome they may be. Three years ago, when the world was peaceful, vast numbers of men and women were kept standing about in military organisations. Then, as the scene darkened, these forces were rapidly diminished to levels which surely should have been considered in good time and in a well-thought-out plan of transition from war to peace defences. When we were safe we were strong. As dangers grew we made ourselves weak. Now, when the risk of war is on the lips of all leading Ministers and the grave words 'a threat to peace' are included, not only in the King's Speech, but in the proceedings of the Security Council of the United Nations, we find ourselves falling between the two stools of previous undue extravagance and later improvident dispersals.

We have received no official information of these military matters, and I have found it necessary to place on record the fact that we as a party can take no responsibility for the present state of our defences. This should certainly be the subject of severe debate, not only on the normal occasions which the Session affords, but perhaps also in Secret Session. I would not be deterred from this expedient by the fear that there may be elements in this House who feel towards Great Britain no sense of comradeship or brotherhood. Even Secret Sessions have their secrets. It is not necessary to say everything. But there are advantages in having a free and unpublished discussion of these vital topics, and it might place the House of Commons in a better position to judge of them correctly without at the same time causing needless untimely public agitation or distress at home or unfavourable reactions among the public of other countries.

For the present all I can say on the subject of defence is that on this, as in all great matters of common interest, we are without official information. Our confidence in the Minister of Defence has been greatly shaken by his grievous lapse from duty to party in the National Service Bill of two years ago. Nevertheless, in fairness, we should acknowledge the courage of a Socialist Government in introducing compulsory military service in time of peace, and that this action of theirs stands forth in favourable contrast with their behaviour about the National Service Bill which was introduced by the Chamberlain Government in the spring of 1939. All I can say this afternoon is that we shall support and aid the Government, irrespective of party politics or interests, in their recruiting campaigns for the Regular and Territorial Forces, and I trust that our manhood throughout the island will not be deterred from coming forward by the record in peace and war or by the frequent utterances of the present occupant of the War Office and several of his principal colleagues. If these Ministers fail in their duty to the nation, the nation must endeavour all the more to fill the gap.

I now come – and let me relieve the House by saying 'finally' – (Hon. Members: 'Hear, hear'.) One has to try to cover the general ground. I now come to our party affairs at home. Two Bills are mentioned in the Gracious Speech – the Parliament Bill and the Measure for nationalisation of steel. It would be out of Order, and I am sure I have no wish, to anticipate on this occasion the Second Reading and other Debates which we shall have upon these proposals. I am content this afternoon to survey the general picture of the legislative programme in which they are the predominant features. The Parliament Bill, as we said some weeks ago, has disturbed a settlement under which we had lived tolerably for 40 years. It has always been described by us as an act of aggression by one half of the nation against what is probably by now the larger half. It was committed at a time when our ears were being wearied by continued Ministerial exhortations to united national effort, both in the military and domestic sphere. It was committed for the purpose of placing up on the Statute Book the Steel Nationalisation Bill before the approaching and now discernible expiry of the life of the present Parliament. I say there has been no justification, if we look back upon the past, for this attack upon the Second Chamber, which had bowed against its better judgment to the decisions of the House of Commons on many issues which a future verdict of the electorate will condemn.

But there is one question generally and of complete detachment from any Measures which we have before us on which I will for a moment dwell. We are told that the attitude of Second Chambers in any country in the world should be absolutely equal as between the two parties. But this argument misunderstands the object for which Second Chambers in so many countries all over the world have been created. That object is to prevent wild and irrevocable decisions being taken, either upon a passing impulse, or in consequence of political intrigue and calculation, and of securing, as did the Parliament Act,

1911, a healthy contact with and recourse to the settled will and wisdom of a democratic Electorate.

The attitude and function of a Second Chamber in any land is essentially one of safeguarding and delaying violent or subversive Measures which may endanger the long-gathered heritage of the whole people, without the gravity and significance of the issues involved being fairly and intelligibly placed before them. From that point of view, it cannot be argued, and has never been argued in any of these countries of which I am speaking, or the Dominions of the Crown in which there are Second Chambers, that a Second Chamber should be absolutely equal as between a party which proceeds by process of gradual and natural evolution on the one hand, and a party that claims, even on an abnormal electoral verdict, that so long as they have mentioned any matter in their party programme, they have an unlimited right to dispose, scatter or destroy the whole structure of tradition and society slowly built up across centuries of trial and error by the genius of the nation. We, therefore, challenge any inroads – and when the time comes we shall discuss the matter – upon the powers possessed by the House of Lords under the Parliament Act, especially when these are unaccompanied by any reform or improvement in the character and influence of the Second Chamber. These are matters pertaining to the general position in which we stand today and, of course, we shall refer to them when the time comes to discuss them in due course.

It is also in this spirit of comprehensive survey appropriate to the general Debate on the Address that I will make one observation upon the further grave step in the nationalisation of industry with which we are threated in the Gracious Speech. I say – I am not dealing with the merits – that this Measure is not brought forward on its merits or to meet a national need, or to help national revival or production. I am certain that it does not command the conscientious convictions of the most responsible Ministers of the Crown or of many Members of the Labour Party. There are, I am sure, many Members on the benches opposite who share the misgivings though not the courage of the hon. Member for Keighley (Mr Ivor Thomas)[1] whose speech produced a deep impression yesterday and very remarkable and encouraging perturbation in the ranks he had just left.

In this further measure of nationalisation we are confronted with an enterprise of faction contrary to the practical and immediate needs and interests of our recovery after the war. I declare that the failure of nationalisation will become more apparent with every month that passes, with every month that

[1] Ivor Bulmer-Thomas, 1905–93. Journalist, author and politician. On staff of *The Times*, 1930–7. Chief Leader Writer, *News Chronicle*, 1937–9. Capt., Royal Norfolk Rgt of Royal Fusiliers, 1941. MP (Lab.) for Keighley, 1942–50. Parliamentary Secretary to Ministry of Civil Aviation, 1945–6. Under-Secretary of State for the Colonies, 1946–7. Deputy Editor of the *Daily Telegraph*, 1953–4. Chairman, Redundant Churches Fund, 1969–76. Chairman, Ancient Monuments Society, 1975–90. Member of the Social Democratic Party, 1981. CBE, 1984.

makes it plain that one basic industry or service after another is being transferred from the credit or profitable side of our economic life to the debit or loss account. It is very wrong, while we are still dependent upon the immense subsidies granted to us by capitalist, free-enterprise America, that any body of Ministers should band themselves together to flourish in the face of the world this flag of party dogma, or national dissension, and of further British impoverishment.

We can discern only too plainly the squalid party motives which lie behind and which have impelled the Government to a further aggravation of our difficulties and burdens. Although many of them see quite clearly what would be best for the country at this time, they are compelled to stand against the light to gratify the party feeling and class hatred of their more extreme followers by this further gratification of the injurious instincts by which they gained office in the past. It is the duty of every one in the industries affected by this new disturbance and oppression to continue to do their utmost, in spite of all antagonisms, to promote the greatest possible productive efforts. It is not anybody's duty to lend assistance to the bringing into operation of party schemes detrimental to British economy in these critical days.

I can only conclude by repeating what was well said on Tuesday by my right hon. Friend the Member for Warwick and Leamington (Mr Eden) – to whom I am under so many great debts for so many years of comradeship – namely, that should we become responsible for the welfare of the nation after the General Election, we should not hesitate to expunge from the Statute Book measures of nationalisation which stand on no better foundation than that of doctrinal fallacy and partisan intrigue.

Winston S. Churchill to Ismet Inönü[1]
(Churchill papers, 2/151)

29 October 1948

My dear President Inönü,

Lord Moran is travelling to Ankara to see his son,[2] to whom you were so kind. I avail myself of this to thank you again for your charming letter of

[1] Ismet Inönü, 1884–1974. Born in Smyrna. Served in Ottoman Army, 1904–18. Active in defence of Gallipoli, 1915. CoS to Mustapha Kemal, 1920; defeated the Greeks near the village of Inönü (1921), from which he took his surname. PM of Turkey, 1924–38, 1961–5; President, 1938–50. Leader of Parliamentary opposition, 1950–61, 1965–72.

[2] Richard John McMoran Wilson, 1924–2014. Ordinary Seaman, HMS *Belfast*, 1943; HMS *Oribi*, 1944–6. Married, 1948, Shirley Rowntree Harris: three children. 3rd Secretary, Ankara, 1948; Tel Aviv, 1950. 2nd Secretary, Rio de Janeiro, 1953. 1st Secretary, FO, 1956; Washington DC, 1959; FO, 1961. Counsellor, British Embassy in South Africa, 1965. Head of West African Dept, 1968–73. British Ambassador to Chad, 1970–3; to Hungary, 1973–6; to Portugal, 1976–81. CMG, 1970. Succeeded his father as 2nd Baron Moran, 1977. British High Commissioner to Canada,1981–4. KCMG, 1981. Elected to House of Lords, 1999.

March 16, in answer to mine, and to send you a copy of *The Gathering Storm*; and also to send you my renewed assurance of my respect and friendship.

As this anxious year unfolds itself I am glad to feel the ties grow stronger which unite the freedom-loving and civilized nations against Bolshevik barbarism. I rejoice that the United States as well as Great Britain are in such close sympathy with Turkey. Our Socialist Government here have put their duty to the cause of world freedom above all party considerations, and from across the Atlantic comes an ever-stronger flow of comradeship and aid. We may therefore face the future together in good heart. I trust you are keeping the gallant Turkish Army in good order to defend, if need be, your native lands.

You will probably have read some of my speeches from time to time and therefore I hardly need to assure you that I march steadily along the same road against aggression and tyranny, whatever garments they wear or language they speak.

In your letter you very kindly invited me to come with my paint box to Turkey, and I shall certainly bear this in mind as a future treat for me. Alas, I have many duties here and they do not look as if they would become lighter in the future. Still, if the chance offers, I shall not hesitate to write you, my valued and honoured friend.

PS. I am sending this letter on to you by Mr John Wilson[1] and also the books.

---

[1] Horace John Wilson, 1882–1972. Entered Civil Service, 1900. Permanent Secretary, Ministry of Labour, 1921–30. Knighted, 1924. Chief Industrial Adviser to the Government, 1930–9. Seconded to Treasury for special service with Stanley Baldwin, 1935–7, and with Neville Chamberlain, 1937–40 (when he had a room at 10 Downing Street). Permanent Secretary to the Treasury and Head of the Civil Service, 1939–42. Succeeded by Sir Richard Hopkins.

November 1948

Duncan Sandys to Winston S. Churchill
(Churchill papers, 2/75)

1 November 1948

I attach a copy of the terms of reference of the new Committee set up at the recent meeting in Paris of the Foreign Ministers of the Brussels Treaty Powers. This document has been given to me in strict confidence by M Schuman.

The primary function of the Committee is to examine the proposal of the French and Belgian Governments for a European deliberative Assembly and the counter-proposal of Mr Bevin for a European Council of ministers.

I have spoken to M Schuman and to M Spaak on this matter and have urged that the Committee should be composed not of officials but of independent persons in public life drawn from the different political parties. Both M Spaak and M Schuman agreed that this was desirable and discussed with me the names of the persons whom they might designate to represent their respective countries. M Spaak has in mind to appoint M Van Zeeland and a leading member of the Belgian Socialist party. M Schuman mentioned the names of M Reynaud, M Bidault and either M Leon Blum or M André Philip.[1] M Spaak has told me that he will get in touch with the Dutch Government and suggest to them that they should nominate persons of the same type.

The British Government may well be considering appointing either a committee of officials or, alternatively, persons who will take detailed instructions from the Government. It is important that this should be avoided. Would you therefore consider speaking to the Prime Minister or to the Foreign Secretary, and suggesting to them that the leaders of the opposition parties should be consulted regarding the composition of this important committee, and should have the opportunity of making proposals.

---

[1] André Philip, 1902–70. French politician, author and academic. Joined French Section of Workers' International, 1920. Interior Minister for the Free French, 1942–5. Member of Consultative Assembly in Algiers, 1943–4. Minister of Finance, 1946 to Jan. 1947; of National Economy, Jan.–Oct. 1947. Taught Economics at University of Saarbrücken, 1951–7; at University of Paris,1957–67. Participated in first meetings of the UN Conference on Trade and Development, 1964, 1968.

Frederick Elwyn Jones to Winston S. Churchill
(Churchill papers, 2/72)

2 November 1948

My dear Winston Churchill,

I took the liberty of calling you to order about your discussion of the Weizsaecker case in the debate last week because I felt that perhaps you were not fully informed of the kind of charges which the Americans are making against this man. I myself have seen some of the documents relating to his case and I am bound to say that they do call for an answer, particularly on the question of Weizsaecker's participation in the Nazi extermination of the Jews. As this matter may again come under discussion before the Nuremberg Court gives its judgment, I hope you will forgive me for bringing to your attention some of the allegations that are being made against Weizsaecker in connection with mass murder.

The plan for the extermination of the Jews was decided at a conference on the 20th January 1942, which was attended by Weizsaecker's subordinate at the Foreign Office, Under-Secretary Luther.[1] The role of the Foreign Office in the plan was to press the often hesitant satellite governments into complicity in the murder programme. For example, a Foreign Office memorandum of August 21st 1942, signed by Under-Secretary Luther, states:

> 'In the conference on 20 January 1942, I demanded that all questions concerned with countries outside Germany must first have the agreement of the Foreign Office, a demand to which Gruppenfuehrer Heydrich[2] agreed and also has faithfully complied with, for the office of the Reichssicherheitshauptamt handling Jewish matters has from the beginning carried out all measures in frictionless cooperation with the Foreign Office.'

The same memorandum gives an excellent illustration of the role of Weizsaecker's office in the extermination:

> '52,000 Jews have been removed from Slovakia. Due to church influence and the corruption of individual officials, 35,000 Jews have received a

---

[1] Martin Franz Julius Luther, 1895–1945. Early member of the Nazi party, 1933. Ran an interior decorating and furniture business. Served as adviser to Foreign Minister Joachim von Ribbentrop. Tried with Franz Rademacher to replace von Ribbentrop as Foreign Minister but failed,1944. Hitler wanted to hang him but he was sent to Sachsenhausen Concentration Camp, 1944. Freed by Soviet troops, 1945. Died of heart failure shortly after his release.

[2] Reinhard Heydrich, 1904–42. Born in Halle, Germany. Entered German Navy, 1922; discharged for misconduct, 1931. Joined SS, 1931. Chief of Political Dept of the Munich police force, 1933; of the SS, 1934; of the SD, the criminal police and the Gestapo, 1936. Ordered the events of Kristallnacht, 9–10 Nov. 1938. Head of the RSHA (security and secret police), 1939. Governor of Bohemia and Moravia, 1941. Chaired Wannsee Conference on the 'final solution', Jan. 1942. On 27 May 1942, two SOE-trained Czech assassins and their lookout attacked Heydrich on his way to Prague Castle; he died from his injuries and resulting infection on 4 June. The town of Lidice was destroyed by the Gestapo in retaliation. See Churchill to Eden, 14 June 1942, in *The Churchill Documents*, vol. 17, *Testing Times, 1942*, p. 788.

special legitimation. However, Minister President Tuka[1] wants the Jewish removal continued, and therefore has asked for support through diplomatic pressure by the Reich. The Ambassador is authorised to give this diplomatic help in that he may state to State President Dr Tiso[2] that the exclusion of the 35,000 Jews is a surprise in Germany, the more so since the cooperation of Slovakia up to now in the Jewish problem has been highly appreciated here. This instruction has been co-signed by the Under-State Secretary in charge of the Political Division and the State Secretary.'

The State Secretary referred to was of course Weizsaecker.

Weizsaecker and his subordinates signed a number of communications to German envoys in foreign countries and to the RSHA, ordering and authorising the departure from country after country of death transports to the East. On March 20th 1942, for example, Weizsaecker and Woermann[3] informed Eichmann,[4] the RSHA official in charge of Jewish extermination, that there was no objection on the part of the German Foreign Office to the deportation of 6,000 French and stateless Jews to Auschwitz.

I won't trouble you with any more examples but I do feel that we shall be rendering little service to democracy or decency if we denigrate the American trial of the men responsible for these abominations.[5]

---

[1] Vojtech Tuka, 1880–1946. Born in Hegybanya, Austria-Hungary. Educated at various universities in Austria-Hungary, Germany and France; later taught Law at Elizabethan University in Austria-Hungary. Worked with Slovak People's Party; was arrested for treason after publishing an article that promoted Slovakia's independence. Named PM of the Slovak Republic 1939–45, and also assumed powers of Minister of Foreign Affairs. He enacted the Ordinance Judenkodex, aimed at the oppression of Jewish citizens. While he was in office, 57,700 Jews were deported to camps where mass executions occurred. Hanged for treason in 1946.

[2] Jozef Tiso, 1887–1947. Catholic priest. Born in Nagybiccse, Austria-Hungary. Enrolled at University of Vienna, 1906; graduated as Doctor of Theology, 1911. Served as a minister to Slovak soldiers during WWI. Member, Slovak Peoples' Party, 1918. Member of Czechoslovak Parliament (SPP), 1925–38. Monsignor, 1921. Secretary to Bishop of Nitra, 1921–3. Negotiated for creation of First Slovak Republic; President, 1939–45. Sentenced to death as a collaborator in post-war Czechoslovakia.

[3] Ernst Woermann, 1888–1979. Born in Dresden, Germany. Educated at Heidelberg, Ludwig Maximilian (Munich), Freiburg and Leipzig Universities. On active service during WWI, 1914–18. Entered German Foreign Office, 1919. Joined Nazi Party, 1937. Under-Secretary, Foreign Office, 1940. Ambassador to China, 1943–5. Tried and found guilty of war crimes, 1949.

[4] Otto Adolph Eichmann, 1906–62. Worked as travelling oil salesman. Joined Nazi party and SS, 1932. SS Lt-Col., 1941. Provided information that led to the Nazis' formal adoption of the doctrine of exterminating the Jews of Europe. Assigned to Hungary, 1944, where he was instrumental in deporting Jews to death camps. Captured in Argentina, 1960, by Mossad, the Israeli secret service. Tried and executed for war crimes, 1962.

[5] On Nov. 9, Jo Sturdee wrote to Miss McCraken: 'Dear Miss McCraken, Mr Churchill wishes Mr Butler to see this letter he has received from Maj. F. E. Jones, Socialist MP for Plaistow, about the case of Baron Weizsaecker. Mr Churchill would be glad if Mr Butler would then forward the letter to Lord Halifax, saying that he (Mr Churchill) thinks Lord Halifax should see it as he also had committed himself' (*Churchill papers, 2/72*).

Marcus Sieff[1] to Winston S. Churchill
(Churchill papers, 2/46)

2 November 1948

Dear Mr Churchill,

Duncan Sandys was kind enough to send you, when you were abroad, a memorandum about Israel, which I prepared following a visit I made there this summer.

I have just returned from a further visit. Many Israeli leaders are anxious to see ties with this country renewed. The present British policy in the UN Assembly vis-à-vis Israel and the Arab States prevents any such rapprochement. Israel could become a bulwark against the spread of Communism in the Middle East. The present Government there has no desire to get tied up with the Eastern Bloc: only a continuation of our present foreign policy can force the new State into the Russian orbit.

I should very much like to see you and ask your advice.

Jo Sturdee to Clementine Churchill
(Churchill papers, 2/46)

3 November 1948

This letter from Mr Sieff arrived this morning. When Mr Churchill was reading it I reminded him that it was the person about whom Mrs James de Rothschild[2] had spoken to you. Mr Churchill said he is very sorry but he cannot see Mr Sieff.

Before telling Mr Sieff this I thought you had better know first in case you want to take action.

---

[1] Marcus Joseph Sieff, 1913–2001. Educated at Corpus Christi College, Cambridge. On active service, WWII, 1939–45. OBE, 1944. Adviser on transportation and supplies to Israeli Defense Ministry, 1948–51. Director, Marks and Spencer, Ltd, 1954; Asst Managing Director, 1963; Vice-Chairman, 1965; Joint Managing Director, 1967–83; Deputy Chairman, 1971; Chairman, 1972–84; President, 1984–5. Baron, 1980.

[2] Dorothy Pinto, 1895–1988. Wife of James de Rothschild of the Rothschild banking family. Known for philanthropy and support for the Zionist movement. Chairwoman of Yad Hanadiv, the Rothschild family charities in Israel. Close friend of Chaim Weizmann. Gifted funds to build Supreme Court of Israel.

Winston S. Churchill: speech
(Churchill papers, 2/336)

4 November 1948								Harrow School

My dear Head Master, Ladies and Gentlemen,

It is quite true, as you have said, Sir, that this is the ninth time that I have been here to hear you sing to me and to cheer me up and inspire me, and I think to cheer us all up. The first time I came, in 1940, most of you present were in your cradles – or at least at your private schools. The Hill was under bombardment; many were advised to leave temporarily, but the bulk stayed and many young gentlemen in their Harrow days had the honour at the time of being under the fire of the enemy. Then there was the long war. This passed and we reached Peace – or at least a cessation of the hot war – into a period not equally dire but in many ways more trying because so much had to be attempted and endured without the supreme stimulus which giving one's whole life and energies to one's country supplied in the days of mortal peril. I have enjoyed all these visits here and they have really covered a long period. When I came here first I thought what a wonderful thing it would be to be a three-yearer; but to be a four-yearer was a very great thing and required no examinations or proficiency in learning or athletics to attain – and I became a four-yearer. But now I am a nine-yearer and I have no need to come and eat ices of various colours and sizes or contract pulmonary phthisis, or give you an opportunity to sing 'Boo hoo'!

Gentlemen, I think the Harrow songs are wonderful things. This Song Book contains indeed a great story, a great theme and a guide. You cannot do better than know it by heart, back and forth. It is an education in itself. Here is something you can carry through life. And let me say that apart from all its pleasure and promptings of morale and memory – it is apart from all this a very great means of giving you command of words. The effect of these Harrow songs is most remarkable. If you look and see how well each word is chosen, how choicely it fits into its place, how varied they are from the point of view of sound and meaning and rhythm, you will be surprised to see what a large addition you would have made to your literary powers both in performance and enjoyment. I commend this to you.

I, in my youth, was not particularly attracted either to Latin or Greek. I got as far as the Greek alphabet and that is all I carried away. With regard to Latin more strenuous measures were taken or put forward on my behalf, but I took a poor view of a classical education. When I was at school I said, I know, let us learn something more practical, something more fitted for the military life for which I was destined. Now in my old age – and I may say that you would be terrified to know how old I am, except Leo Amery, who is a year older still – I take a different view. I am terrified at the idea that our universities should become technical schools, places where every form of material proficiency would be imparted in different grades and so forth, and those great studies of the humanities drop away from our life. It would be a great tragedy if they cast the classics aside. In my period of life I have seen the human race part company from the horse and take to the internal combustion engine. Chauffeurs are very good and I like chauffeurs, but a world of chauffeurs would indeed be a very melancholy state. Those who embark on and have the advantage of enjoying the great privileges of what is called a liberal education should make sure that that education gives them a command of the broader views of life and history and of those who are concerned in the making of history. But I am encroaching on rather serious topics.

Before I go away, before I sit down, I want very much to pay my compliments to Mr Eldridge, who sang Five Hundred Faces. I have never heard it more beautifully sung or a more poignant appeal made by a school-boyish voice to the drama and romance of this Harrow song, and I compliment him very much. It takes a lot of courage to get up and to do that; but courage is not the only quality which he displayed this evening by any means.

I was asked by the Head Master to choose the songs I would like you to sing this evening, but I thought I would ask him to choose them this time as I thought I might always be treading on the same stepping stones. And a very fine selection has been made. But I did say to him 'I wonder if you will dare to sing "Rule Britannia!".' Anything like that is rather shocking to certain forms of modern illumination. 'Rule Commonwealthia . . . citizens of the Commonwealth shall never, never be slaves.' I trust that that will not be substituted this evening.

Here we are on the morrow of our greatest victory yet. What toils still exist abroad on every side! What is needed are effort, perseverance, a firm grip of essentials, a faithful readiness to sacrifice – all the things which make a nation great. That is the lesson you learn at Harrow and that you must carry with you through your lives. There is always the rule that when any great success has been achieved something comes forth to make a greater struggle necessary. There must be an enduring and abiding flame in British hearts that enables them to burn through and sheer through with power and force the ever-marching difficulties and toils and problems and disappointments by which life is haunted. That is the only spirit you must have. Life is precious and especially for the young, whose fine sacrifice made our victory possible, and yet for young and old there must always be a readiness to sacrifice life in order to preserve what makes life worth living for honourable men.

Thank you very much for listening to what I have to say. But do not think that your singing 'Rule Britannia!' will compromise you with the higher intellectual rulings of the modern world. I believe at this moment that that august body, the General Assembly of the United Nations, wherever they sit, will be very glad to know that Britannia rules the waves and that Britons never, never, never will be slaves. There is of course a certain amount of national pride about this song – we must admit that. But pride, instead of being a vice, sometimes becomes one of the most valuable of the virtues and I do not believe that the singing of a song like 'Rule Britannia!' or in France 'The Marseillaise', or in other countries the National Anthem or whatever they sing, is incompatible with the great European world union to which we look with confidence. It seems to me that in the higher synthesis there should be room for the highest expression of every contributory element. By the process of 'Rule Britannia!' we have managed to preserve the life within this island. I shall look forward to joining with you in voice and heart, whatever may be said elsewhere, in singing the famous song 'Rule Britannia!'. It stands for a strength which we can always remember we used to safeguard the freedom of the world.

Winston S. Churchill to Clement Attlee
(*Churchill papers, 2/75*)

4 November 1948

My dear Prime Minister,

I observe from the official communiqué issued last week that the Conference of Foreign Ministers in Paris decided to set up a special committee for the purpose of recommending to Governments measures designed to promote European Unity, including the proposal for a European Assembly.

Since this body is in the nature of an independent commission, I presume that it will be composed of persons drawn from public life, and that the main political parties will be represented. If this is correct I shall be glad to be consulted about the choice of suitable members of the Conservative Party.

I shall like to hear from you before raising the matter in the house.

Field Marshal Jan Smuts to Winston S. Churchill
(*Churchill papers, 2/176*)

6 November 1948

My dear Winston,

I was very glad to receive your cable approving of my suggestion about incorporating Western Germany into Western Union, and in fact, putting it into a position to play its part in the defence of the West against eventual Communist aggression. You have since met Marshall, and I hope you have been able to impress on him the necessity of such a step in view of the increasing threat which Russian policy constitutes for the West.

Meanwhile Marshall has been to Athens, from where I have had reports of his talks with leading personages. As a result I have thought it advisable to send him a letter, putting to him the views I have formed of the Greek position as part of the overall European situation now in process of taking shape. Berlin and Greece are the two focal points on which Russian policy is concentrating for the move against the West, and a break at either of these two points may have very far-reaching consequences.

I do not know whether he has put his views to you in your contacts with him, and at Athens he preserved a more or less non-committal attitude. I thought, however, that what I had written to him should also be communicated to you, for what it is worth.

Russia has not yet finally made up her mind, in view of the atomic bomb and other possibilities, and it would be wise to leave her leader in no doubt of what the consequences will be of continued aggression at either of these two points of attack.

I have much enjoyed your recent grand speeches. Your Fulton policy has been completely justified and has in fact become the policy of the West.

Good luck to you in your leadership of the West.

Clement Attlee to Winston S. Churchill
(Churchill papers, 2/75)

6 November 1948

My dear Churchill,

I have received your letter of 4th November about British representation on the committee for the study of further measures in the direction of European unity. I fear, however, that there is some misunderstanding regarding the scope, composition and functions of this committee.

I enclose the relevant part of the communiqué issued in Paris and from this you will note that the national representatives are to be selected by Governments and that the committee is to report to Governments and therefore to be responsible to Governments. This being the case, it is not our intention to ensure that the British members of the committee should represent the main political parties and the question raised in your letter does not, therefore, arise. On the other hand, you will have noted that the committee is to 'take into consideration all suggestions which have been or may be put forward by Governments or by private organisations' and you may rest assured that full weight will be given to any suggestions which you personally or the Conservative Party may wish to put forward.

EXTRACT FROM COMMUNIQUÉ ISSUED IN PARIS ON 26 OCTOBER

As regards the question of European unity, the Council decided to set up a committee of representatives chosen by the Governments of the five signatory Powers of the Treaty of Brussels, consisting of five French, five United Kingdom, three Belgian, three Netherlands and two Luxembourg members.

The object of this committee, which will meet in Paris, will be to consider and to report to Governments on the steps to be taken towards securing a greater measure of unity between European countries.

To this end the committee will take into consideration all suggestions which have been or may be put forward by Governments or by private organisations. In this connexion it will examine the Franco-Belgian suggestion for the convening of a European assembly and the British suggestion relating to the establishment of a European council appointed by and responsible to Governments for the purpose of dealing with matters of common concern.

This committee will draw up a report for submission to the consultative council at its next meeting.

Winston S. Churchill to President Harry S Truman
(Churchill papers, 2/158)[1]

8 November 1948

My dear Harry,

I sent you a cable of my hearty congratulations on yr gallant fight and tremendous victory. I felt keenly the way you were treated by some of yr party and in particular Wallace who seemed to us over here to be a greater danger than he proved. But all this has now become only the background of yr personal triumph. Of course it is my business as a foreigner or half a foreigner to keep out of American politics, but I am sure I can now say what a relief it has been to me and most of us here to feel that the long continuity and comradeship between us and also with the Democratic Party in peace and war will not be interrupted. This is most necessary and gives the best chance of pursuing Peace.

I wish you the utmost success in yr Administration during this most critical and baffling period in world affairs. If I shd be able to come over I shall not hesitate to pay my respects to you.

Mrs Churchill who predicted yr success sends her compliments and good wishes to yr wife whom she met at Fulton time.

---

[1] This letter was handwritten.

Winston S. Churchill to Christopher Soames
(*Lady Soames papers*)

10 November 1948

I should like to have your narrative of the Battle[1] as you saw it with the Coldstream. I should like you to put this down from your own recollection. I do not want you to try to write the story of the Battle as a whole, because evidently immense compressions would be required. Seven or eight thousand words is all I can give to the tale. Meanwhile I send you a few papers from my own secret file, and Auchinleck's Dispatch. These you might look into as a background and to refresh your memory. I may want them back any day. Meanwhile please keep them under lock and key.

Winston S. Churchill to Clement Attlee
(*Churchill papers, 2/75*)

11 November 1948

My dear Prime Minister,

I am naturally grieved to receive your letter of November 6, which I fear will exercise a depressing effect upon the Movement for European Unity. I understand that the French Government, for their part, have nominated Messieurs Blum, Reynaud, Herriot, Dementhon,[2] and Corbin.[3] I am led to believe that the three Governments of Belgium, Holland and Luxembourg also intend to nominate representatives on an all-Party basis. It will be, in my opinion, a misfortune if His Majesty's Government persist in trying to treat this great cause as a monopoly of the British Socialist Party. In this they would fall below the level both of the event and of the attitude of other members of the Western Union. Moreover I am sure there will be lively disappointment in the United States at the narrow and partisan view which your letter seems to indicate. I am convinced that the Committee should have an independent status like a Royal Commission. Governments can obviously reject its recommendations, but should not regard its members as official delegates acting under instructions. The question of setting up a European deliberative Assembly without executive powers is one of the main issues to be considered by the European Committee, and is of interest to all political Parties. Considering that the Conservative and Liberal Parties in Great Britain represent at least

---

[1] The Battle of Dunkirk. Christopher Soames was one of the Coldstream Guards who helped to reinforce the line at Furnes against the Germans on 31 May 1940.

[2] François de Menthon, 1900–84. Capt. in French Army, 1939. A prominent leader of the French Resistance, starting the first cell of the Liberté Resistance. Left France to follow de Gaulle to London, 1943.

[3] Charles Corbin, 1882–1970. Born in Paris. French diplomat. Ambassador to Spain, 1929–31; to Belgium, 1931–3; to Britain, 1933–40.

half the electorate, it would be quite inappropriate for His Majesty's Government to nominate officials or delegates under instructions to meet all Party groups of leaders nominated by the other countries in the Western Union.

As I understand that the European Committee is to hold its first meeting on Monday next, I suppose to you that this correspondence, copies of which I enclose, should be made available to the Press on Saturday, at such time as may be agreed between us.

Clement Attlee to Winston S. Churchill
(*Churchill papers, 2/75*)

12 November 1948

My dear Churchill,

I have received your further letter of November 11th about the British representation on the Committee for the study of further measures in the direction of European unity.

I fear that you have misconceived the position. I note that, in your opinion, the Committee should have an independent status like a Royal Commission. This, however, was not the decision of the responsible Governments concerned. It was agreed at the Consultative Council that the representatives on the Committee should be appointed by Governments, who would themselves decide whether they should be Parliamentarians or men of administrative or executive experience, professors of constitutional law, or merely private citizens. The task of the Committee would be to study and report to Governments. I am, therefore, surprised at your suggestion that, because the representation of the British Government does not contain representatives of the Opposition, the cause of European unity is being treated as a monopoly of what you term 'the British Socialist Party'. In our Parliamentary system the Government of the day is formed from the majority party; the fact that this is now the Labour Party does not appear to me to affect the general principle. The French Government rests, as you are aware, on a coalition of political parties. It is not, therefore, surprising that some, but not all, of the Government parties should be represented on the delegation. You will not, however, have failed to note that the main Opposition parties are not represented. The British Government have taken the lead in promoting European unity. Our intention is to send a delegation which will be able to assist the Committee in making an effective and realistic study of this complex question.

I may add that the Committee is to hold its first meeting on November 20th, and not November 15th as you surmise. But I have no objection, should you think fit, to your publishing this correspondence on November 13th.

November 1948

General George C. Marshall to Winston S. Churchill
(Churchill papers, 2/144)

12 November 1948
Paris

Dear Churchill,

I am several days behind schedule in my birthday greetings to you, but since being up to date is certainly not standard procedure in the work of the United Nations, I seem to have fallen into the same practice. Belated though this letter is, my wishes are nonetheless sincere, and it is my fervent hope that the world may continue to have the benefit of your wisdom and counsel for many years to come.

Both Mrs Marshall[1] and I were delighted that we were able to see you and Mrs Churchill in London. My talk with you was one of the principal purposes of the trip. It was also a great pleasure to be with you again.

With genuinely affectionate regards and my compliments to Mrs Churchill, believe me, always,

Faithfully yours,

Winston S. Churchill: speech
('Winston S. Churchill, His Complete Speeches', volume 7, pages 7730–1)

12 November 1948
Unveiling of a Memorial Tablet
Westminster Abbey

PRESIDENT ROOSEVELT

I join with the Prime Minister in paying our tribute to the great Statesman with whom we worked in comradeship, trust and goodwill during the years of fearful ordeal through which we have so lately passed.

Macaulay wrote of Westminster Abbey as 'that temple of silence and reconciliation where the enmities of twenty generations lie buried'. But now it is not the ending of the enmities we celebrate. This tablet to the memory of Franklin Roosevelt proclaims the growth of enduring friendship and the rebirth of brotherhood between the two great nations upon whose wisdom, valour and virtue the future of humanity in no small degree depends. Long may it testify upon these ancient walls.

---

[1] Katherine Boyce Tupper, 1882–1978. Educated at American Academy of Dramatic Arts and later the Comédie-Française. Married, 1911, Clifton Stevenson Brown (d. 1928): three children; 1930, George C. Marshall, whose first wife had died in 1927. Published *Together: Annals of an Army Wife* (1946).

Winston S. Churchill to Editor of The Times
(Churchill papers, 2/157)

15 November 1948   Chartwell

Sir,

I do not at all wonder that the uneasy consciences of some ex-ministers and former high officials should be stirred by the account which my book contains of the failure of all three Parties to prevent German rearmament while this was easy, or to take adequate precautions while there was still time. The attempt to throw the blame upon the Ten Years' Rule instituted by Mr Lloyd George from 1919, and amended by Mr Baldwin on my advice in 1928, shows that the search for soothing balm must have been long and bleak. The maintenance of the rule on a day to day basis after 1928 was assented to unanimously by Mr Baldwin's Cabinet, and by the Committee of Imperial Defence, of which both Lord Balfour[1] and Sir Austen Chamberlain were prominent members. When I left office in May 1929 ten-and-a-half years were in fact to run before the outbreak of a major war. The position of the Conservative Cabinet, which quitted office after the General Election of 1929, was therefore in every respect vindicated by events. There are very[2] attempts to forecast the future over so long a period as ten years, which have in fact come true. To try to cast any portion of the burden for the policy or want of policy of those ten-and-a-half years upon me would be a difficult task.

Lord Hankey's personal responsibility as Secretary to the Committee of Imperial Defence no doubt distresses him. With his great record in the First World War no one had more influence than he and no one remained in the centre of full knowledge for so long. I knew him very well. We had thought alike on several of the keenest controversies of the First World War. When I was in office he had access to me, as to the Prime Minister, at any time. I am sure that he never formally or informally raised the slightest protest to the prolongation of the Ten Years' Rule under a day to day scrutiny. Of what he did afterwards during the ten-and-a-half years I was out of office, and the eight years which he continued to serve in his key position, I did not know at the time and have not sought to examine fully. As however the passage of time will reveal the records of the Committee of Imperial Defence to history he would do well to consider whether he is wise to become prominent in this controversy. Certainly in what Sir Thomas Inskip[3] called 'The Locust Years'

---

[1] Arthur James Balfour, 1848–1930. Educated at Eton and Trinity College, Cambridge. MP (Cons.) for Hertford, 1874–85; for Manchester East, 1885–1906; for the City of London, 1906–22. PM, 1902–5. 1st Lord of the Admiralty, 1915–16. Foreign Secretary, 1916–19. Lord President of the Council, 1919–22, 1925–9. Earl, 1922.

[2] Probably an error for 'very few'.

[3] Thomas Walker Hobart Inskip, 1879–1947. Educated at Clifton and King's College, Cambridge. Called to the Bar, 1899. Served in Naval Intelligence Div., Admiralty, 1915–18. MP (Cons.) for Central

few had more influence and none more knowledge.

Lord Stanhope[1] quotes a private letter written to him on June 21, 1939, from the late Sir Oswyn Murray[2], Permanent Secretary of the Admiralty from 1917 to 1936 in which he suggests that I had 'pulled down so much of the building (of naval strength) while in office as Chancellor of the Exchequer that I should find it difficult to shore it up again.' My tenure of the Exchequer lasted from 1924 to 1929. During that time the Naval Expenditure was not reduced. Indeed it rose slightly from £56,505,000 in 1924 to £56,569,000 in 1929. The heavy reductions were made in the more dangerous years after I had left office. To pretend that my administration of the Exchequer ending ten-and-a-half years before the war, produced irreparable damage to our naval strength, again only shows the hard straits to which his Lordship is reduced. It is a somewhat ungracious response to what I have recorded in my book of the state of the Navy when I took over the Admiralty from him on the outbreak of war. 'It would be unjust,' I wrote in my book, p. 322, 'to the Chamberlain Administration and their Service advisors to suggest that the Navy had not been adequately prepared for a war with Germany, or with Germany and Italy.... I therefore felt, when I entered upon my duties that I had at my disposal what was undoubtedly the finest-tempered instrument of naval war in the world, and I was sure that time would be granted to make good the oversights of peace and cope with the equally certain unpleasant surprises of war.'

Bristol, 1918–29; for Fareham, 1931–9. Knighted, 1922. Solicitor-General, Oct. 1922 to Jan. 1924, Nov. 1924 to Mar. 1928, Sep. 1931 to Jan. 1932. Attorney-General, 1928–9, 1932–6. Minister for the Co-ordination of Defence, 1936–9. Secretary of State for Dominion Affairs, Jan.–Sep. 1939, May–Oct. 1940. Lord Chancellor, Sep. 1939 to May 1940. Viscount Caldecote, 1939. Lord Chief Justice, 1940–6. Inskip's appointment as Minister for the Co-ordination of Defence, a new Cabinet-level office for which Churchill had campaigned and which he was widely expected to receive, prompted the critique by 'a famous statesman' that 'there had been no similar appointment since the Roman emperor Caligula made his horse a Consul' ('Cato', *Guilty Men*, London, 1940); Graham Stewart, in *Burying Caesar: Churchill, Chamberlain and the Battle for the Tory Party* (1999), attributes this original comparison to Prof. Lindemann in conversation with Lord Lloyd.

[1] James Richard Stanhope, 1880–1967. Educated at Eton and Magdalen College, Oxford. Grenadier Guards, 1901–8. Succeeded his father as 7th Earl Stanhope, 1905. Served with Grenadier Guards in France, 1914–18 (despatches twice; MC, 1916; DSO, 1917). Parliamentary Secretary, War Office, 1918–19. Civil Lord of Admiralty, 1924–9. PC, 1929. Under-Secretary of State for War, 1931–4. KG, 1934. Parliamentary Under-Secretary of State for Foreign Affairs, 1934–6. 1st Commissioner of Works, 1936–7. President of the Board of Education, 1937–8. 1st Lord of the Admiralty, 1938–9. Leader of the House of Lords, 1938–40. Lord President of the Council, 1939–40. In 1952, succeeded a distant cousin as the last Earl of Chesterfield. He was also the last Earl Stanhope, and bequeathed his country house, Chevening, to the nation.

[2] Oswyn Alexander Ruthven Murray, 1873–1936. Entered Admiralty, 1897; Director of Victualling, 1905–11; Asst Secretary, 1911–17; Permanent Secretary from 1917 until his death. Knighted, 1917.

Winston S. Churchill: speech
(Hansard)

16 November 1948 House of Commons

IRON AND STEEL BILL[1]

When a Measure of first rate importance is presented to the House of Commons it is always necessary for us to ask the question: Is it going to help the country or is it a partisan manoeuvre? Is it progress that is sought or is it faction? This is certainly the time to apply that test, because on the morrow of our greatest victory we are living on subsidies by loan or gift provided by taxes on the hardworking and heavily-burdened people of the United States. I have always thought that we should need their help after the war, but it should be a point of honour with us, irrespective of party nostrums, to regain our full economic independence at the earliest moment, and to do nothing that would put off that event either by hampering our output or wantonly dividing our people.

Does this Bill nationalising the steel industry help us in the right direction or not? That is the question before us this afternoon. I am quite ready myself to look back into the past. I was a member of Mr Lloyd George's Coalition Government after the first world war. I saw at first hand the tremendous effort which he made to avert unemployment. I was very glad that my old Unemployment Insurance plan of 1909 and the labour exchanges which were part of it should become the method and structure upon which a provision from the worst evils of want could be made for the large numbers of unemployed who were thrown upon us. In the first four years from 1919 to 1922 unemployment probably averaged between one million and 1½ million, and the Unemployment Insurance policy without contributions became no more than a dole morally and actually. The dole cost nearly £200 million in those four years alone. Hon. Members opposite need not 'ask your dad' about these things while they have the advantage of asking your grandad.

Certainly, I can assure the House, every endeavour was made to solve the problems of those hard days. Here let me say that Mr Lloyd George's Cabinet stood in about the same relation in brain power and good will compared to the present Administration as does Mr Lloyd George himself in history stand to the latest Welsh product. The present Socialist Government boasts its superior record of achievement compared with 1919 and 1922. There has been full employment since the war stopped, whereas in the similar period after the first world war unemployment was our greatest distress and anxiety. Of course, as time passes and experience is gained more knowledge becomes available. The

---

[1] When the Iron and Steel Act 1949 took effect on 15 Feb. 1951, the government became the sole shareholder of 80 principal iron and steel companies (reduced from the 107 proposed in the first draft of the Bill).

White Paper of the National Government of 1944 shows that the lessons and experiences have been appreciated, but there is a very simple explanation of the improvement which is pointed to so often between the four years after the first great war and the four years after the second.

After the first world war the United States was isolationist. They called for strict accountancy of money that had been loaned and they asked for the repayment of financial debts at the earliest possible moment, both in reparations from the defeated and in repayments from their Allies. We were left to face our problems by ourselves. Now in our present troubles we have no longer, thank God, to face an isolationist United States. They have come to our aid. They gave us a loan which I welcomed, and helped forward to the best of my ability, a loan of £1,000 million. Now, under the Marshall Plan, which had its origin traceably in the movement for a united Europe, they are giving us £300 million a year now and for several years to come. That is what has made the difference in the figures of unemployment. We have not had to do it all ourselves as we did last time. We have had the help of a generous comrade and trusty friend.

The Lord President of the Council (Mr Herbert Morrison) was quite right when he said, in April last in Manchester – this is what he said, and I am quoting him exactly:

> We should be facing big cuts in rations and a million or two people on the dole if our generous and far-sighted friends and allies in America had not come to the rescue.

The Minister of Health himself – I do not see him in his place today, although I think he is the driving power behind this Bill – endorsed the statements of the Lord President of the Council, when he said at Scarborough a month afterwards:

> Without Marshall Aid, unemployment in this country would at once rise by 1,500,000.

Here are plain and candid admissions by leading Ministers in the Government that, but for American Aid there would be as much as, or even more unemployment now, in these days under the Socialist Government, than there was in the similar period after the first world war. I do not think that that fact ought to be overlooked in current party controversy.

It does not therefore seem that the question of American Aid should be ignored in dealing with any comparison between the post-war years of the first war and those which we are now enduring. It should also be remembered that this help comes because the United States, unlike His Majesty's Government where the movement for European unity is concerned, rises above partisan differences in their external policy and does not refuse to help a Socialist Government whose ideology and system are the exact opposite of their own, and are even hostile to its continued existence. We heard a lot of talk about the moral of the recent presidential elections; except in their open hostility to Russia and Communism – in which we support them – His Majesty's Government are far closer to Mr Wallace than to either of the great parties in the United States, and yet the United States continue, in a broadminded spirit, to keep them going.

It is on this footing and by this approach that I come to the Measure which is now before us. (Hon. Members: 'Hear, hear'.) Well, no picture can be painted without due regard to the background. This Measure cannot wholly be judged on its merits or demerits, if such there be, except in relation to the general economic life of Britain and our position in the world, and also in relation to the United States on whom the Socialist Government and Socialist policy are living from month to month and from hand to mouth. Those are facts that ought not to be absent from our minds. They are a condition of our dependence for the time being upon external aid.

When we come to the Bill itself there is surely no need to magnify or multiply the points of difference which divide the Government and the Opposition about the steel industry. They are, in all conscience, grave and numerous enough, and our affairs are becoming increasingly embittered thereby as our dangers grow. This is no case of one side seeking to nationalise an industry and the other side trying to preserve an uncontrolled, unsupervised monopoly or cartel without regard to the public interest. That is not the difference between us. We have heard from my right hon. Friend the Member for Aldershot (Mr Lyttelton) the story of the steel industry since 1932, when it received the much needed protection of a moderate tariff and when a system of control and supervision was set up with the aim of making sure that the powers and opportunities secured to that industry were not abused. In this and similar matters the ideal for which all parties should seek to strive is to combine the maximum thrust, drive, contrivance and ingenuity of private industry under the natural stimulus and correction of profit and loss, and the immense power and economy of a vast co-operative unit of production, with the necessary safeguarding of the rights of the State, and of the interests of the consumers and the smaller producers.

I think it would seem to any dispassionate, fair-minded observer of our affairs that the British steel industry had arrived at a very considerable measure of success in these 16 tremendous years of war and peace. The facts, although undisputed, should be repeated. Steel production rose from 5 million tons in 1932 to 13 million tons in 1939, and now to 15½ million tons. Prices rose over the period before the war, but not more than was justified by the increased cost of manufacture. Continental prices, which had previously been artificially low, rose even more, so that by 1939 British prices were thoroughly competitive in world markets. The industry was enabled by returning prosperity to spend £50 million on new plants between 1934 and 1939. Thereby it increased its capacity by two million tons and thus prepared itself for its magnificent war effort.

Unemployment in the steel industry, which had risen to more than 40 per cent. under the Socialist Government in 1931, was rapidly – (*Laughter.*) Hon. Members laugh. They have no right to laugh at the miseries of the working people. Unemployment is a torment and a nightmare. If any of those hon. Members had worked as hard at the subject as I have, or were responsible for legislation of such far-reaching importance, they would have some right to lay claim to some position of superiority, morality, or sympathy with working-class problems. However, let me get back to the point that unemployment, which in 1931 under the Socialist Government had risen in the steel industry to over 40 per cent, was reduced under the Conservatives to 10 per cent in 1937.

At the present time our steel industry is greatly respected in other countries and the names of its famous firms, the product of free enterprise, are national assets of the greatest importance. Steel is, of course, the main prop of our export trade. Nothing is perfect on the human stage, but one could hardly point to any other instance of an industry which plays so great a part in our productive effort and in world affairs without in any degree embarking on the exploitation of the consumer or harsh or improper practices. Let that assertion stand. During those 16 years there was a strong measure of Government control and supervision which protected the public without hampering the industry. Except for the General Strike, which arose from causes quite unconnected with the steel industry, there has been no serious dispute or stoppage between the employers and the employed during this tumultuous century. It has been one of the few islands of peace and progress in the wrack and ruin of our times. Yet this same steel industry is the one which the Socialist Government have selected for the utmost exercise of its malice, and in complete disregard of national prosperity. When we compare the size of the tasks which confront us and the capacity of the Government to cope with them, it is astounding indeed that they should go out of their way to add to their troubles and to those of their fellow countrymen.

I should like at this point to take off my hat to the steel workers for the fine work they are doing. The Minister[1] pretends that they have only been working much harder because of the hopes of nationalisation. In justice to them, we should believe that they have broader and higher motives. Neither the promise nor the fact of nationalisation has produced such results in the coal trade. Indeed, under nationalisation fining is now being pressed forward because of the increased absenteeism. How, then, can this absurd and insulting allegation against the steel workers be sustained? I believe there was some complaint of statements which were made by the canvassers at a recent by-election of agreeable memory. I trust that the master of political

---

[1] The Minister of Health, Aneurin Bevan.

manoeuvre opposite[1] will carefully expunge from his leaflets and propaganda any suggestion that the steps which the steel workers have taken to help the country in its hour of trouble have been dictated by the gains they hope to make under nationalisation.

In drawing up our line of battle for the grievous and untimely quarrel that is thrust upon us, the Conservative Party in no way abandons the necessary control of the steel industry which has been so long in operation. We certainly consider that the price controls which we ourselves introduced and endorsed, must be taken as an essential and permanent feature of our policy. Neither do we regard the steel industry in its present state as incapable of further reform. I was reading in the *Manchester Guardian* last week a very thoughtful leading article which raised these points. In the Steel Board, which the Government's policy forces out of existence by their plans of nationalisation, we had an instrument at once powerful, flexible and comprehending under which modern needs and emergencies in all their variations, many of them unforeseeable, could be dealt with as they arose.

The right hon. Gentleman the Minister of Supply (Mr Strauss)[2] – I would venture to address him personally for a moment – yesterday pointed to the integration of the Bethlehem Steel Company and dwelt on the virtues of concentrated management. He was asked a pertinent question: Management by whom? Is it to be management by business men under all the inducements of profit and all the penalties of bankruptcy, or is it to be management by politicians interested in their careers or prejudiced by their party doctrines, but otherwise not specially distinguished – or, I should say, who otherwise have their distinction yet to win – who are assisted in their task by officials themselves impartial in the sense that it makes no difference to them whether the industry shows a profit or a loss? For our part we are sure that the future expansion of the steel industry in its relation to our general economic life can be better carried out by the industry itself, and we have no doubt that it could get all the money it wants once the Socialist meddlers and muddlers stand out of the sunlight.

All these questions connected with trusts and monopolies are in our minds today. The laws of capitalist free enterprise America go much further than ours in dealing with trusts and combines. That was because 30 or 40 years ago those great monopolies, protected by an almost prohibitively high tariff, used their advantages in a ruthless way. Thus the antitrust legislation of the United States came into being. Here in this island the same issues have not arisen in a sharp form. Many things in this island are not pushed to extremes in every walk of life and in every relationship. That is one of the peculiar

[1] Probably a reference to Aneurin Bevan.
[2] George Russell Strauss, 1901–93. MP (Lab.) for Lambeth North, 1929–31, 1934–9; for Vauxhall, 1950–79. Parliamentary Secretary to Ministry of Transport, 1945–7. Minister of Supply, 1947–51. Father of the House, 1974–9. Baron, 1979.

characteristics of our way of doing things, of our British way of life. It may well be said that the British – or, perhaps I might even say in this matter, the English – never draw a line without blurring it. That has been a great advantage to us in all sorts of vicissitudes through which we have passed. Therefore, we have not the same laws as have been carried by American democracy to regulate the behaviour of great trusts and cartels. Nevertheless, I have always held the view that where tariff protection is given in any effective form to a particular industry, the State should, if it thinks fit, make sure that the interests of the consumer are safeguarded, and also those of the smaller producers. It is for this reason that we Conservatives are proud to have been the initiators of the policy of the control and price-fixing system which regulates our, at present, buoyant steel trade.

There is another general point which I will mention here. We must not allow ourselves to be misled by any acceptance of the argument that steel is so vital to war that its direct control by the State is needed for military purposes. In the last 40 years I have been from time to time much involved in our military arrangements. Never have I known any occasion when any Government has been hampered in time of peace in taking the military precautions it deemed necessary by any reluctance or refusal of the steel industry to meet those needs. As for wartime, we took complete control.

The Socialists have no right to revile Conservatives as being the sordid defenders of vested interests and private property regardless of our country's welfare. There was that great day – I may remind the Prime Minister of it – in May, 1940, at the time of Dunkirk, when the House of Commons, with a Tory majority of 150 over all the other parties combined, and the House of Lords – 'lower than vermin' as we are now insulted by being called – there was that day when this great Conservative Parliament in both Houses laid on the altar of national safety and victory all private rights, privileges, interests and powers, and confided to the Executive in a single Parliamentary day the entire control and disposition of the lives and property of every family in the land. I wonder the Prime Minister is not ashamed that such insults should be flung –

Sir Richard Acland[1] (Gravesend): Will the right hon. Gentleman allow me –

Hon. Members: Sit down.

Mr Churchill: Go back to Gravesend.

Sir R. Acland rose –

Mr Churchill: It is indeed a base and a melancholy sequel –

Sir R. Acland: It was a completely phoney Act.

Mr Churchill: I have no doubt that the hon. Gentleman wants to make

---

[1] Richard Thomas Dyke Acland, 1906–90. Son of the Liberal politician Sir Francis Acland. MP (Lib.) for Barnstaple, 1935–40; (Lab.) for Gravesend, 1947–55. Founded the Common Wealth Party, 1942. Succeeded his father as 15th Bt, 1939. Senior Lecturer, St Luke's College of Education, 1959–74.

himself as good a footing in the Socialist Party as possible; I will not interrupt the thread of my argument to assist him. It is indeed, a base and melancholy sequel to such an episode as I have described that sacrifices so readily offered and made by a Conservative Parliament should be exploited in peace-time in the sectional interests of Socialist factionaries, anxious to prolong their enjoyment of the sweets of office, and have more patronage to distribute to their backers and friends. I used to say in bygone days, and I repeat it gladly now, 'Socialism attacks Capital, Liberalism attacks Monopoly.'

Mr Shurmer (Sparkbrook): Is that what the right hon. Gentleman used to say about Conservatives?

Mr Churchill: If I were to try to recall at this moment all the utterances I have made during 50 years of public life, I should trespass unduly on the patience of the House. I therefore confine myself to the citation of such statements as I may consider relevant. At any rate this statement – Socialism attacks Capital, Liberalism attacks Monopoly – is one of a very general character. But what sort of monopoly is this which the Government seeks to create? There may be, indeed, a great element of concentration, monopoly and cartel in the present arrangements of the steel trade. That is why we have agreed to the controls, and instituted the controls and the price-fixing. But what sort of monopoly is this that the Government seeks to create? In its presentation to the outer world on whom we depend, and to the United States on whose subsidies we live, it takes the form of national State trading indistinguishable from that of the Russian Communist Government.

I do not dwell at this moment upon the proved incompetence of Socialist officials in State trading, or on the losses we have suffered and are suffering from their further misguided excursions alike into world markets and domestic production. There will be plenty of time to deal with these issues as the facts unfold themselves remorselessly to the electors. But I say that, in principle, the British steel industry now being presented to foreign countries, and particularly to the United States, in the form that this Bill proposes, will arouse against itself equally concentrated and probably more powerful forms of collective bargaining. We must expect to face in our steel exports equally monopolistic organisations, often aided by State subsidies, and the elimination of all beneficial aids which arise from the higgling of the market and the ceaseless process of trial and error from day to day, from which our export trade and, indeed, our international trade as a whole, have hitherto derived so much of their fertility.

I do not know what measures foreign countries will adopt from their own point of view when confronted with the Socialist State monopoly of British steel with whom their producers will have to deal, but I cannot believe that they will be of a helpful or grateful nature. I do not think that the monopoly firm of Strauss Unlimited will have a hearty welcome among the purchasers abroad on whom we depend. It may turn out, however, that agreements will be reached between both the high contracting parties at the expense of the consumers. That often happens.

It is when we turn our eyes to the domestic sphere that the malignity of this Bill becomes most glaring. My right hon. Friend the Member for Aldershot yesterday described to us the difficulties of applying nationalisation to so complex and diverse an industry as steel. The Government have recoiled from drawing a line throughout the whole industry at the basic production of, let us say, steel billets, leaving the higher applications to free enterprise. It is recognised, after much thought, to be plainly impossible to slice this industry horizontally. The picture drawn by my right hon. Friend the Member for Aldershot of the partitions which would have to be erected in some of our greatest steel firms between those parts which would belong to the State and those parts which are still free, and the difficulty of apportioning common services between them; that picture was, I think, conclusive. The Socialist Government, like everyone else, have recoiled from such a solution.

Thus in the Bill we have come to the vertical division. They are picking and choosing, and doing so on no principle but the caprice of a party Minister. No one has explained on what logic or equity Ford's should be spared, while other firms producing steel or pig iron primarily for their own purposes should be devoured. Perhaps the Chancellor of the Exchequer explained this to the American bankers on his recent visit. Perhaps he will explain it to us this evening; it will be most interesting: the picking and choosing, the caprice, and the authority, the decision, of a Minister, himself the representative of a party to whom he is responsible, to decide all these issues, whether they affect the facts or the merits, whether they affect the character of particular firms or a general principle. Of course, no man, however hard he works or however great his capacity, could possibly have control generally over the whole field. He will be at the summit, but he has to devolve a great deal of these decisions to people utterly unknown to Parliament or to the public.

Now, on this principle of vertical – or, if you like, diagonal – division of the steel industry, 107 leading firms are selected for absorption by the State and 2,000 others are for the time being left outside this control. Naturally, the Debate yesterday turned upon the question of what will be the relationship between the State monopoly of the 107 firms comprising, of course, by far the most powerful and largest part of the industry, and the 2,000 who still remain free. There can be no doubt of the power of the State monopoly to ruin them one by one or even in batches. There can be no doubt that that is in the power of the Minister. The State monopoly will be conducted according to the present Socialist plan by the partisan representative of the Government, whose political future in his party depends entirely upon his proving how much better and more prosperous a State monopoly is than any form of private enterprise or trading. That is his target for tonight, his target for the future.

The Minister of Supply yesterday showed clearly that he has already prejudged the issue. 'Do people fear' – he asked –

> that private industry cannot withstand the superior efficiency of public industry.

The text of the Bill and his own words yesterday give the answer to this question themselves. There is Clause 29, which contains a statutory injunction obliging the State monopoly corporations to secure enough revenue

> to meet their combined outgoings properly chargeable to revenue account, taking one year with another.

Let me quote the Minister again, He said, 'they' – the private firms –

> may not extend their production to such a degree as to make the integrated working and efficiency of the major publicly-owned sector impossible.

(Hon. Members: 'Hear, hear'.) There were loud cheers then. Really, he is apparently in fear of a superior effort on the part of private firms and that is why these powers are taken in the Bill to enjoin upon the steel corporation the power to make sure that they are restrained from giving the full effect to all the virtues of production and efficiency which they possess. The big dog has to be fed full first. That is quite clear from Clause 29. If any goes short, it will not be he. However mismanaged it may be, the law we are asked to pass says, 'All is to be made to go well with the State monopoly.'

This is indeed a murderous theme. How will such a Minister as we see opposite, or his successor, mandated by the law we are now called upon to enact, treat these minor industries – or 'spiv' industries, as he will probably soon be calling them in the jargon of Socialism; how will he be treating them if they become inconvenient as rivals? He spoke yesterday in honeyed terms about them, but who is so gullible as to believe that a Socialist industrial commissar – for that is what we are creating – bound by law and also by the need of making a show for his party's policy, will tolerate any competition by an inconvenient rival? He has them at his mercy. By a stroke of the pen he can deprive them of the raw material on which they live. Short of this, he can threaten and coerce them to any extent. Every grade of pressure can be applied or threatened. The kind remarks of yesterday are about as refreshing to the minor firms as the kiss of death.

Today the Socialists boast that they are the opponents of Communism. Socialist parties in every European country have been found altogether inadequate barriers against it. Indeed, as this Bill shows, they are the handmaids and heralds of Communism, and prepare the way at every stage and at every step for its further advance. The Communist text-books are full of this theme; they have been for years. Of the differences between Socialism and Communism, if I may make another quotation from the past, I said a good many years ago:

A strong dose either of Socialism or Communism will kill Britannia stone dead, and at the inquest the only question for the jury will be: Did she fall or was she pushed?

We can now already see that nationalisation and State ownership have been a great and costly failure in all the industries to which they have been applied, and this will become more obvious to the public with every day that passes. I am taking coal first as an illustration. I have always held that miners, working far from the light of the sun, should have special consideration.

Mr Fernyhough[1] (Jarrow): In 1926?

Mr Churchill: Yes, in 1926 particularly. If the hon. Gentleman perused the story of those negotiations he would see how unjust is his interruption. Forty years have passed since I moved the Second Reading of the mines' Eight Hours Bill. In comradeship with Mr Bob Smillie[2] – I do not know if the hon. Member has ever heard of him, he was a much admired leader in those days – I introduced baths at the pitheads. I greatly admired the spirit of the miners in both wars and regretted that I had to deny so many of them the opportunity of winning distinction in the field to which they ardently aspired.

Nationalisation in the mines has already, largely by the creation of its incompetent and top-heavy, over-staffed and over-paid organisation at the top produced an average 20 per cent increase in the cost of coal to the consumers whether it be for the home firesides or for the public services, power, heat, light and transport. That is a heavy handicap to all our production and above all to our export trade. There was a loss of £20 million last year in this nationalised industry, in spite of the increase in price, which affects us so seriously. I see that Lord Balfour, who is, I believe, the head of the Scottish Coal Board, stated the other day that this year the State monopoly of coal would show a profit of £5 million. It is, of course, quite easy for an all-powerful State monopoly of a vital supply to make a profit by raising the price against the general consumer. They only have to know what the loss was to make a provision in price that covers it. It is not so easy to measure the reactions of this price raising upon the main economy of the nation. It must certainly be most injurious.

Let me take another instance, now that we are asked to nationalise another industry; another instance of what is already apparent. There are the State railways which have to compete with modern forms of road transport. We are informed that the railways are to show a heavy loss and such result will reflect upon State monopoly and State management. Can anyone doubt that a Socialist Government, having to brazen out its failures and fallacies, will throw

---

[1] Ernest Fernyhough, 1908–93. MP (Lab.) for Jarrow, 1947–79. Parliamentary Private Secretary to the PM, 1964–7. Parliamentary Under-Secretary of State, Dept of Employment and Productivity, 1967–9. Member of the Council of Europe, 1970–3. Freeman, Borough of Jarrow, 1972.

[2] Robert Smillie, 1857–1940. President of the Miners' Federation of Great Britain, 1912–21. MP (Lab.) for Morpeth, 1923–9. Publications include *My Life for Labour* (1924).

its weight against road transport in all its forms, whether nationalised, or still free? I am speaking of what is going to happen in the minor firms in the steel trade. The machinery is in the hands of the Government. They are taking all power and their machinery is at once simple and overwhelming. They have only to raise the fares on omnibuses and other vehicles under their control until the deficit on the State railways has been wiped out through more passengers and goods being forced to use them. 'We must make a success of our Socialist Railways,' or British Railways – I believe they allow the word British in that connection.

How much greater will be the temptation of the Socialist Minister with a State monopoly of the 107 greatest steel firms in his hands to defend himself and his party from ever-growing criticism and complaint – how much greater will be the temptation for him to knock about these weaker brethren outside the compound and thus to demonstrate the failure of private enterprise and the wisdom and elevation of Socialist methods and ideals?

I say this is not a Bill, it is a plot; not a plan to increase production, but rather, in effect, at any rate, an operation in restraint of trade. It is not a plan to help our patient struggling people, but a burglar's jemmy to crack the capitalist crib – (*Laughter.*) The right hon. Gentleman laughs, but he lives on the exertions of 80 per cent of industries still free and all his hopes are founded on their activities. Those free industries constitute practically the whole of our export trade. They are already hampered by having to bear the weight and extra charges of the nationalised services and the weight of enormous taxation. They are already cramped by a vast network of regulations, interferences and restrictions, but still they are carrying the whole burden of our life and represent our only solvent economic earning power.

By this Bill the 80 per cent of whose exploits in these hard times the Government frequently boast and dilate upon, are to be subjected to the deadly attack of the State steel monopoly, whose tentacles will stretch around, penetrate and ultimately paralyse every form of free national activity. At every turn the Socialist Government and party, whose reputation and survival are engaged in proving the success of their nationalising experiments will have the means of striking down every industrial opponent of their totalitarian or equalitarian – for they come to much the same thing in this case – designs.

I will make only one reference to compensation. We had a very thoughtful and interesting speech last night from my hon. Friend the Member for Central Southwark (Mr Jenkins[1]). I can only speak in general terms about this

[1] Roy Harris Jenkins, 1920–2003. Chairman, Oxford University Democratic Socialist Club, 1941. Capt., RA, 1944–6. MP (Lab.) for Central Southwark, 1948–50; for Birmingham Stetchford, 1950–77; (SDP) for Glasgow Hillhead, 1982–7. Minister of Aviation, 1964–5. Chancellor of the Exchequer, 1967–70. Shadow Chancellor of the Exchequer, 1970–2. Deputy Leader of the Labour Party, 1970–2. Shadow Home Secretary, 1973–4. Home Secretary, 1974–6. President of the European Commission, 1977–81. Leader of the Social Democratic Party, 1982–3. Baron, 1987. Chancellor of the University of Oxford, 1987–2003. Leader of the Liberal Democrats in the House of Lords, 1987–8.

matter. I do not intend to develop it at length, because my right hon. Friend the Member for the Scottish Universities (Sir J. Anderson) will deal with it later on. No one disputes that Parliament has the right to acquire any property which the public interest requires, provided that compensation is paid. The Socialist Government have accepted the principle of compensation and have declared themselves opposed to confiscation; but compensation means fair compensation. Insofar as compensation is unfair, an act of confiscation has been committed. The best method for the compulsory acquisition of property is either agreement or arbitration on certain well designed principles. The system of taking over property compulsorily at its Stock Exchange market value from day to day is not fair to the shareholder –

Professor Savory[1] (Queen's University, Belfast): Sheer robbery.

Mr Churchill: There may only perhaps be 300,000 steel shareholders, but they have their rights and are entitled to justice. The great mass of small investors do not watch the market from day to day and their holdings are not speculative in any sense. They place their money where they think it will be safe and fruitful and thus make provision for old age and darker years. Hardship is inflicted upon them when they are forced, against their wishes, to change their investment. But, in the case of steel, the conduct of the Government in buying compulsorily at the market value is not only unfair, but it seems actually dishonest. We assert, and it is our sincere belief, that by their threats of steel nationalisation they have artificially depressed the value of steel shares.

But there is more than that. By the appeals which the Chancellor of the Exchequer and other Ministers have made to the leading firms not to increase but to 'plough in' their dividends and the co-operation which they have received in consequence, they have definitely affected the market prices. Now they propose to expropriate at this artificially restricted price. What is peculiarly reprehensible about the transaction is that those who hearkened most to the Chancellor's appeals on national grounds – and we all know how heavy are the burdens he carries – will be the ones to suffer most. They will, indeed, suffer in exactly the proportion of the response they made to what was thought to be an appeal in good faith and good will and on grounds of patriotism and national interest. This is indeed a refinement of inverted justice.

It is not only the principle of compensation that is affected, but the personal conduct and political good faith of the Ministers concerned. Such conduct, unless explained or justified, deprives them of the right to speak in the national interest or to be believed if they do. The Bill prescribes the date at which the

---

[1] Douglas Lloyd Savory, 1878–1969. Born in Palgrave, Suffolk. Prof. of French Language and Romance Philology, Queen's University, Belfast, 1909–40. During WWI, attached to Intelligence Div., Admiralty. Secretary to British Minister to Sweden, 1918–19. MP (Ulster Unionist) for Queen's University of Belfast, 1940–50; for South Antrim, 1950–5. Special investigator of the Katyn Wood Massacre; reported Feb. 1944. Secretary, Ulster Unionist Party, 1950–5. Knighted, 1952.

Government are to take over the assets of the companies concerned. There may be some significance about this date. I will venture for a moment to probe. Clause 11 fixes it at 1st May, 1950, or any later date in the 18 months following the passage of the Measure. First May, 1950, is evidently timed, not in relation to the process of taking over the steel companies or anything like that, but to the date of the General Election or to the date of the completion of the legislation under the processes of the Parliament Act.

Thus it serves a double party purpose. It gives the Government the utmost span of office, and at the same time presents the nationalisation of steel as the direct issue at the General Election. Other motives are more a matter of conjecture. To my mind the fixing of this remote date seems to have been the means by which the differences in the Cabinet were adjusted between the extreme nationalisers and the more sober and responsible Ministers. (An Hon. Member: 'Who are they?') The Chancellor was a little belated in his laugh at that. He must not miss the cues which are set for him by the Lord President. It was possible, no doubt, to reach accord in the Cabinet on the basis of, 'If we win the election, the steel Bill will become law, and those of us who choose to go on will be masters of the industrial future of Britain. If we lose the election we shall be out anyway, so there is no need to split among ourselves now.' I suggest to the House that interpretation of otherwise difficult events. A Bill for the nationalisation of iron and steel, which, the Government assume, has to go to and fro between the Houses under the Parliament Act, just ekes out the time. They can explain to their followers, having settled their internal difficulties, 'We must hold on together until we have got it through.' Such are the calculations which have involved the fate and prosperity of this vital key industry in the vortex of party struggles. It is for this purpose that the Government have not hesitated to disrupt the constitutional settlement which was reached 30 years ago in the Parliament Act. I say that this is not an economic Measure conceived in a view, right or wrong, of the national interest, but a party dodge to hold that gang together where they sit until they have run the full length of their term.

None of us have any right, let me say, to assume at this stage what the action of the other House will be, especially in relation to a Measure that cannot come into effective operation until the electors have pronounced upon it. We are evidently in the presence of elaborate political calculations and manœuvres of the Socialist Government, who are primarily concerned with their own party interests. The question of keeping the steel industry in a state of prolonged uncertainty, and any consequent injury to the public interest that may arise therefrom, does not seem to have complicated Ministerial discussions in any way. I read in the newspapers that Mr Lincoln Evans,[1] a trade

---

[1] Lincoln Evans, 1889–1970. General Secretary, Iron and Steel Trades Confederation, 1946–53. Member of Iron and Steel Board, 1946–8. Member of Economic Planning Board, 1949–53. Deputy Chairman, British Productivity Council, 1952–3. Member of BBC General Advisory Council from 1952.

unionist of note, the Secretary of the Iron and Steel Confederation, said three days ago:

> Unfortunately the fixing of 1st May, 1950, as the vesting date means inevitably that steel nationalisation is to be made a major issue at the next General Election, and the industry is therefore to become a focal point of a bitter political conflict. We would have preferred it otherwise.

That is the statement of a man who certainly has the right to be listened by the party opposite when he testifies.

The Government say, 'We are forced by our mandate. We told the electors in our election pamphlet "Let us face the future" that we included the nationalisation of iron and steel. Therefore, we are entitled, nay bound, to use our majority to place a Bill for that purpose on the Statute Book.' It is difficult to believe that this issue bulked largely even in Socialist minds at the General Election of 1945. I do not suppose that many of the electors concerned themselves with it at the time. There had been no election for 10 years. The bulk of the voters believed the promises which were lavished upon them. The victorious armies wanted to come home after all their toils. So, steel was in the programme, but to pretend that it was an issue to which the electorate consciously directed their minds, or upon which they were instructed by political discussion, is humbug. On these lines it would be sufficient for the Socialist Party, at future elections, to put in their programme the word 'etc.' after any catalogue of legislative reforms. I say that the mandate which they derived from the electors at the 1945 election was as soon as possible to put the country on its feet again, to make us independent of foreign charity and to free us from undue war-time restrictions and severities.

I end with the same proposition that I submitted to the House at the beginning. This is not a Measure conceived and brought forward in the interests of the community or the State. It is a feature in party tactics intended to keep the Socialist left wing as far as possible in order, and the Government as long as possible in office. We had another example of this in the Budget. The Chancellor of the Exchequer, who also deals with all our economic policy, and so often calls upon us all to help him, had to pay his way with his supporters for what seemed in many respects a sensible Budget, by putting in something spiteful which would satisfy the Left wing and would convince them of his continued ardour in the class war. Hence the capital levy, with all its unfairness and injury to saving. It is no use the Chancellor pretending that he introduced this on its merits. I rate his intelligence too highly. It was a sop which he had to fling to Cerberus.[1]

Here now, in this Bill, is another instance of the same behaviour on a

---

[1] In Greek mythology, Cerberus, or Kerberos, was the gigantic three-headed hound of Hades who guarded the gates of the underworld. His name roughly translates to 'Death Demon of the Dark' from the Greek words *kēr* and *erebos*.

far larger scale. The Socialist Ministers must have something new to feed the flame of party strife and to prove that they still hate and are trying to maul the other half of their fellow-countrymen. The one thing that fills their minds, the one thing which they fear and shrink from, is the General Election, which is coming upon them, and which will end in obloquy and censure their dismal and evil reign.

Winston S. Churchill: speech
(Hansard)

16 November 1948　　　　　　　　　　　　　　　　House of Commons

THE BIRTHPLACE OF PRINCE CHARLES[1]

It is refreshing to have our party quarrels broken into by so agreeable an interlude, and I am very proud that it falls to my lot, on behalf of the Conservative Party, His Majesty's official Opposition, to express wholehearted support of the Motion which the Prime Minister has moved. I congratulate him upon the appropriate terms and the well-chosen language in which he has commended this Address to us. I am glad that he has invited Privy Councillors on this side and in the Liberal Party, too, to accompany the representatives of the Government to carry this Address, should it be voted by the House, to Buckingham Palace. We shall accept the invitation with pleasure.

The thoughts that are in the minds of the millions to whom the Prime Minister referred are those connected with home and family, which appeal to everyone and especially, if I may say so, to us in this island of ours, so long shielded from foreign invasion and oppression. There is no doubt that it is around the family and in the home that all the greatest virtues, the most dominating virtues of human society, are created, strengthened and maintained. These are feelings which stir the hearts of all parties and classes throughout the land, and give a joy to masses of people which arises only from the finest and most elevating instincts they possess.

Our ancient Monarchy renders inestimable services to our country and to all the British Empire and Commonwealth of Nations. Above the ebb and flow of party strife, the rise and fall of Ministries and individuals, the changes of public opinion or public fortune, the British Monarchy presides, ancient, calm and supreme within its functions, over all the treasures that have been saved from the past and all the glories we write in the annals of our country. Our thoughts go out to the mother and father and, in a special way today, to

---

[1] Charles Philip Arthur George, 1948–. Born in Buckingham Palace, first-born son of Queen Elizabeth II and Prince Philip. Educated at Gordonstoun and Trinity College, Cambridge. Prince of Wales, 1958. Served in RAF, 1971–7. Married, 1981, Diana Spencer (div. 1996); two children; 2005, Camilla Parker Bowles.

the little Prince, now born into this world of strife and storm. I have no doubt he will be brought up, as the Prime Minister has mentioned, in all those traditions of constitutional government which make the British Monarchy at once the most ancient and most secure in the world. I hope that among these principles that will be instilled into him will be the truth that the Sovereign is never so great as when the people are free. There, we meet on common ground, and I have the greatest pleasure in supporting the Motion which the right hon. Gentleman has just presented to the House.

Winston S. Churchill: speech
('Winston S. Churchill, His Complete Speeches', volume 7, pages 7743–4)

17 November 1948   Dorland Hall, London

UNITED EUROPE

There has recently been much public discussion about the constitutional form which a united Europe should take. There are those who advocate the immediate creation of a European customs union and a complete political federation. There are others who consider that close consultation between Governments is the most that can be hoped for, and who regard any form of constitutional or organic union as utterly impracticable. Each of these views is partly right and partly wrong. To imagine that Europe today is ripe for either a political federation or a customs union would be wholly unrealistic. But who can say what may not be possible in the future. Anyone who two years ago had had the audacity to predict that by now Western Europe would have a joint economic planning organisation and a combined military staff would have been taken seriously by nobody. Under the mounting pressure of danger and necessity, conceptions which are impracticable today may quite possibly be thought obvious and inevitable in a few years' time.

My advice is not to attempt at this stage to define too precisely the exact constitutional form which will ultimately emerge. We would do better to concentrate our united efforts on immediately practicable steps. Let us not underrate the process which has already been made in the field of inter-governmental co-operation during the last twelve months. Through the medium of the Marshall Plan and the Brussels Pact, changes amounting to nothing less than a revolution in our international relationships have been brought about. This machinery for joint consultation and planning must be maintained and strengthened and its scope expanded.

But what is good for governments is also good for peoples. They too, through their representatives, must meet together to consult one another upon these great issues which so intimately affect the lives of every European family. Precisely for this purpose the Hague Congress last May recommended the immediate creation of a consultative European Assembly. This proposal has been officially adopted by the French and Belgian Governments, who have rightfully emphasised that the Assembly must be consultative in character and can have no legislative or constitution-making powers.

It may, of course, be argued that a purely deliberative Assembly without Executive power would develop into an irresponsible talking-shop, and that it would be better to leave the work of European unification to be achieved through inter-governmental negotiations. That is not true. The Assembly will perform an essential task and one which cannot be performed by governments; the task of creating a European public opinion and a sense of solidarity among the peoples of Europe.

The creation of a deliberative European Assembly naturally involves no transfer of sovereignty and raises no constitutional problems whatsoever. If the British government decides to give its support to this proposal which has been put forward by the governments of France and Belgium, the European Assembly will assuredly become an accomplished reality. It is therefore to be hoped that our government will not hesitate or become obstructive. Whatever course they take we must and will do our best.

Winston S. Churchill: speech
('*Winston S. Churchill, His Complete Speeches*', volume 7, pages 7744–6)

18 November 1948   University of London

THE ESSENTIAL VERITIES

You have called upon me to return thanks on behalf of all those on whom you have conferred degrees and have given these honours to, and I must say that I am very proud to find myself included in such distinguished company. I share the general regret that we all feel that General Marshall is not with us tonight, with the Archbishop of Canterbury[1], Mr Walter de la Mare,[2] Sir Ernest Pooley[3] and others, and on behalf of all these it is my duty to return thanks.

---

[1] Geoffrey Francis Fisher, 1887–1972. Ordained priest, 1913. Headmaster, Repton School, 1914–32. Bishop of Chester, 1932–9; of London, 1939–44. Archbishop of Canterbury, 1945–61. Knighted, 1953. Baron Fisher of Lambeth, 1961.

[2] Walter John de la Mare, 1873–1956. British poet and novelist. Born in Charlton, Kent,. Educated at Oxford, Cambridge, St Andrews, Bristol and London. Married, 1899, Constance Elfrida Ingpen: four children. CH, 1948. OM, 1953. His many published works include: *Songs of Childhood* (1902); *Poems* (1906); *Collected Stories for Children* (1944); *The Burning Glass* (1945).

[3] Ernest Henry Pooley, 1876–1966. Educated at Winchester College and Pembroke College, Cambridge. Member of the Senate and Court of the University of London, 1929–48. Knighted, 1932. KCVO, 1943. Member of the Goodenough Committee on Medical Education and the Fleming Committee on Public Schools, 1944. Published *The Guilds of the City of London* (1947). Bt, 1953. GCVO, 1956.

We are all, I can assure you, very proud and very grateful to receive a degree from the University of dear old battered London. For myself, as life unfolds, I have been astonished to find how many more degrees I have received than I have passed examinations – I have not been too good at that – and I always feel that even if one never had the advantage of a university education one can still become regarded as remarkably erudite. I think this is a good argument for not being discouraged by the failures or shortcomings of youth but to persevere and go on learning all your life.

The privilege of a university education is a great one; the more widely it is extended the better for any country. It should not be looked upon as something to end with youth but as a key to open many doors of thought and knowledge. The university education is a guide to the reading of a lifetime. We should impress upon those who have its advantages the importance of reading the great books of the world and the literature of one's own country. One who has profited from university education has a wide choice. He need never be idle or bored and have to take refuge in the clack and clatter of the modern age, which requires something new not only every day, but every two or three hours of the day. There is a good saying, which you may have heard before, that when a new book comes out you should read an old one though I perhaps should not recommend too rigid an application!

I would like to say that I have changed my mind about the classics. I had very strong views about them when at Harrow; I have changed my mind about them since. Knowledge of the ancient world and of Greek and Roman literature was a great unifying force in Europe which is now I fear rapidly becoming extinct and I should like to say that university education ought not to be too practical. The duty of the university is to teach wisdom, not a trade; character, not technicalities. We want a lot of engineers in the modern world, but we do not want a world of engineers. We want some scientists, but we must keep them in their proper place. Our generation has seen great changes. We have parted company with the horse; we have an internal combustion engine instead and I wonder whether we have gained by the change.

My old venerable friend, Lord Hugh Cecil as he was (Lord Quickswood), described science recently as 'organised curiosity'. But be careful, perhaps as the Public Orator has said in one of his speeches, we may find out too much and after all some of the things we have found out are not entirely unadulterated gain.

Take all these improvements in locomotion; what do they do but make the world grow smaller, making the heritage of man a far more restricted sphere. It is very convenient of course to flash about, but after all the life of man does not depend upon the external conditions to which he is subjected, provided of course that they are compatible with the maintenance of his existence. I would venture to say here, in the London University, that no amount of technical knowledge can replace the comprehension of the humanities or the study of history, and I have the Vice-Chancellor[1] particularly in my mind. The advantages of the nineteenth century, the literary age, have been largely put away by this terrible twentieth century with all its confusion and exhaustion of mankind.

With all our theoretical values, it is a time when a firm grip on all the essential verities and values of humanity and civilisation should be the central care of the universities of Great Britain. The Greek and Latin philosophers I have spoken about seemed often quite unconscious that their society was based on slavery. At least we have all the finest theories of freedom, but they were not conscious of that fundamentally important fact. At least nowadays we cherish freedom, freedom for all.

The light of Christian ethics remains the most precious guide. Their revival and application is a practical need, whether spiritual or secular in nature, whether to those who find comfort and solace in revealed religion or those who have to face the mystery of human destiny alone. And on this foundation alone will come the grace of life and that reconciliation of the right of the individual with the needs of society from which the happiness, the safety and the glory of mankind may spring. Thank you.

Sir Alan Lascelles to Winston S. Churchill
(Churchill papers, 2/171)[2]

19 November 1948   Buckingham Palace
Top Secret

Dear Mr Churchill,

I should like you to know, for your strictly personal information, that on Tuesday morning next the newspapers will carry an announcement that, on medical advice, The King has been obliged to postpone his trip to Australia and NZ next year; in this advice, the Prime Ministers of UK, Australia and NZ concur.

The announcement will comprise a bulletin signed by three doctors and two surgeons.

The King's left leg has been troubling him for some time past. Recent exhaustive tests of every description reveal a serious condition of the circulation. Unless great care is taken, gangrene, and possibly thrombosis, might appear quite suddenly. In the circumstances, the doctors are unanimous – and emphatic – in saying that HM must cancel all sudden engagements and have

---

[1] Lillian Margery Penson, 1896–1963. Educated first privately, then at Birkbeck College, and later University College, London, 1917. PhD, 1921. Prof. of Modern History, Bedford College, University of London, 1930–62. Member of University of London Senate for 20 years; Member of University Court; Dean, Faculty of Arts; Chairman, Academic Council. First female Vice-Chancellor of the University, 1948. DBE, 1951.

[2] This letter was handwritten.

complete rest (with prolonged and elaborate treatment) for months. This, of course, rules out the projected tour. I have told the GG's and PM's of Australia and New Zealand,[1] who have taken this sad disappointment very well and understandingly. The press-announcement on Tuesday has been carefully scrutinized and will be released simultaneously in the country of Australia – always provided there is no premature leak.

The doctors' bulletin has been, after a great deal of thought, so worded as to bring home to the ordinary citizen the fact that the K is actually unfit to carry out this tour, without giving more alarming details than necessary.

I think it is now framed in such a way as to strike the right note. The doctors told us no hope of the K being able to undertake a trip of this kind any time in 1949; anyhow, their elections are due in the autumn, so it is in effect postponed indefinitely. There can be no question of The Queen going independently; as to P'cess Elizabeth and the Duke of Edinburgh going some day or other, we can only wait and see.

The King takes all this with great calm and good humour. It is an ill wind that blows us good; an enforced rest may do HM a power of good after the unremitting strain of the past 12 years.

I needn't say that he would freely take a line from you after the news has broken next week.

If the Aussies leak, as they are only too fond of doing, I shall instantly release our communiqué at this end.

PS. I've written frankly to you about medical details. Actually, I don't suppose the words 'gangrene' or 'thrombosis' have ever been mentioned this crudely to the K or the Q; but the doctors have used them often enough in talking to me.

---

[1] William John McKell, 1891–1985. Known as 'Bill'. Born in Pambula, NSW, Australia. Joined Australian Labor Party, 1908. Member of the Legislative Assembly for Redfern, Parliament of NSW, 1917–20; for Botany, 1920–7; for Redfern, 1927–47. Minister for Justice, 1920–7. Asst Colonial Treasurer, 1925–7. Minister for Local Government, 1930–1. Minister for Justice, 1931–2. Leader of the Opposition of NSW, 1939–41. Leader of the Australian Labor Party in NSW, 1939–47. Premier of NSW, 1941–7. Colonial Treasurer of NSW, 1941–7. Governor-General of Australia, 1947–53. PC, 1948; GCMG, 1951.

Bernard Freyberg, Governor-General of New Zealand.

Ben Chifley, Prime Minister of Australia.

Peter Fraser, 1884–1950. Born in Scotland. Joined the Independent Labour Party in London, 1908. Migrated to New Zealand, 1910, and became prominent in the labour movement there. Minister of Education, Health, Marine and Police, 1935–40. PM, 1940–9. Minister of External Affairs and Minister of Island Territories, 1943–9. CH, 1945. Minister of Maori Affairs, 1946–9.

Winston S. Churchill to General George C. Marshall
(Churchill papers, 2/144)

20 November 1948

My dear Marshall,

Thank you so much for your letter of November 12[1] and for your very kind birthday greetings. My birthday is not until November 30 but your congratulations are none the less welcome.

Everyone was much disappointed that you were not able to come to the ceremony at the London University the other evening. It was most brilliant and passed off very well except of course that your absence was much regretted.

General Smuts has sent me a copy of the letter he has written to you.

I earnestly hope you are not going to withdraw from your great office at the present critical time, when so many people in so many countries are placing their trust in you.

Mrs Churchill joins me in sending good wishes to you and Mrs Marshall.

Winston S. Churchill to Henry Luce
(Churchill papers, 4/28)

21 November 1948

I know you must have been very busy lately but have you seen my Solicitor's letter to Heiskell[2] of October 26. I don't want to sell the foreign language serial rights and would like to have them handled by Emery Reves who has made a wonderful success abroad of the War Memoirs and who has worked with me since the ante-Hitler days before the War. Although I have made no personal profit by sale of the War Memoirs abroad it is a great pleasure to me to feel that these books are translated into 26 different languages and I am sure no one could have done it except Reves who buzzed around the world for nearly a year making contacts. I had never realized that our arrangement could possibly be understood to extend beyond the serial rights other than English and Eire in the English language. It may well be that this is also your view.

---

[1] Reproduced above (p. 1232).
[2] Andrew Heiskell, 1915–2003. Publisher, *Life* Magazine, 1946–60.

Winston S. Churchill to Sir Alan Lascelles
(Churchill papers, 2/171)[1]

22 November 1948   Chartwell
Private

My dear Alan,

I am grateful to you for yr letter,[2] distressing as is the news it bears. It was kind of you to write to me so fully.

I always dreaded this Australian visit. Few human beings could undergo such an ordeal without an immense loss of vitality.

Now I trust the King will take things easy, and not be worried about the way things are going. All will come right, and I feel sure his reign will see not only Victory but its Reward.

I am sending by yr hand a Volume I have had bound for His Majesty, wh has just come to me from the binders. Will you kindly give it to him when occasion serves.

Let us have a talk in the near future.

Winston S. Churchill to King George VI
(Churchill papers, 2/171)[3]

22 November 1948   Chartwell

Sir,

It is with sorrow that I learn that Yr Majesty has had to abandon Your visit to Australia and New Zealand. I am sure that the decision is a wise one. I had been concerned to think of the intense and prolonged exertions the tour wd have demanded from both Yr Majesty and the Queen. They wd have killed you by kindness! The distances are enormous and everywhere there wd have been delighted and loyal crowds. One must not underrate the strain of such enjoyable contacts with enthusiastic friends.

Sir, I trust that the rest and relief will restore yr health, and enable you to add long years to your reign. It has been a time of intense stress and trial. It may well be that history will regard it as 'our finest hour'. I am proud to have been Yr First Minister in all these great adventures. I ever hope in spite of my age to stand at Yr Majesty's side once again. However this may befall, I remain

                                         Yr Majesty's devoted and grateful servant.

---

[1] This letter was handwritten.
[2] Reproduced above (pp. 1253–4).
[3] This letter was handwritten.

Angus McNeill[1] to Winston S. Churchill
(Churchill papers, 2/99)

23 November 1948   Haifa

My dear Winston,

This may or may not reach you in time for your birthday – it depends on the Censor, and so many other things these days. Anyhow here's wishing you many happy returns – I lead you by exactly 6 months (31 May 1874). You may be surprised at this address. My wife,[2] sad to say, is quite a cripple and can't be moved, so we chanced it and stayed 'put' here all through 'Operation Polly',[3] and this year also in spite of all that has gone on in Western Galilee – and I cannot speak too gratefully of the courtesy, kindness and consideration shewn to us by our Jewish friends and neighbours.

It is of course very lonely here, now that there are so few British in the Country, and I miss the 'Soldiers' very much – we usually had a couple of Battalions in this area plus the OCTU and Battle School – latterly also Howard-Vyse[4] with the 1st Regt RHA to which my son Jock[5] is now on his way as second in command on the Canal. (Now back to Major from the Staff – having run the Air Support Control in SEAC as a full Colonel at 35!)

We are very depressed at the latest news from Paris, a Conciliation Commission for Palestine to report to the 4th meeting of the General Assembly probably not till next September!

This makes at least twenty commissions in Palestine within the last eighteen years to my own knowledge. There may have been more!

One wonders why Partition, according to 29 November, 1947, cannot now be implemented and Israel recognised once and for all. Nothing can stop them, so why not accept the 'fait accompli' and let everyone get down to work once more.

Bevin's policy is making us so unpopular in the Middle East that British

[1] Angus John McNeill, 1874–1950. Contemporary of Churchill at Harrow. On active service in Crete, 1897; at Omdurman, 1898; in South Africa, 1899–1900 (despatches); in Somaliland, 1901; with the Lovat Scouts Yeomanry, 1914–18 (despatches five times; DSO, 1918). Drew sketches for Churchill's book *The River War* (1899).

[2] Lilian Vaughan Barron, 1889–?. Married, 1907, Angus John McNeill.

[3] 'Polly': On 31 Jan. 1947, following escalating political unrest in Palestine, all non-essential British personnel and civilians were ordered to evacuate within 48 hours. 508 men, women and children were taken to Almaza aerodrome in Egypt.

[4] Richard Granville Hylton Howard-Vyse, 1883–1962. Entered Army, 1902. On active service, 1914–18, France (retreat from Mons, 1914) and Palestine (Chief Staff Officer, Desert Mounted Corps, 1917–18). Inspector of Cavalry, 1930–4. Knighted, 1935. Retired from Army, 1935. Recalled, 1939. Head of British Military Mission with French High Command, 1939–40. Chairman, Prisoners-of-War Dept, British Red Cross, 1941–5.

[5] John Malcolm McNeill, 1909–96. 2nd Lt, RA, 1929. Served in north-west Europe and Burma, 1939–45. Deputy Secretary, Chiefs of Staff Committee, Ministry of Defence, 1953–5. Cdr, RA 2nd Div., 1955–8. Commandant, School of Artillery, 1958–60. Cdr, British Army Staff and Military Attaché, Washington DC, 1960–3. Col. Commandant RA, 1964–74. Principal Staff Officer to Secretary of State for Commonwealth Relations, 1964–9. ADC to the Queen, 1958–60.

Prestige may never recover. It is too sad when one looks back only a few years to VE day. I have always held, though many knowledgeable people have disagreed with me, that the Arab States would never combine effectively against the Jews, but I never imagined that they would crack so completely.

There was a lot of bombing, sniping, road blocking, sabotage and sabre-rattling of every description, but when seriously opposed they melted away, leaders first (usually with the cash!) leaving a few of the tougher spirits behind, who were soon either killed or in the bag.

General Riley[1] was absolutely right in his summing up of the Arab Military Situation in my opinion, and if five Arab States with their tails up, couldn't hold their own with the Jews, at that time weak and ill-armed and equipped, they certainly are not going to do it now.

The rank and file of the Arab armies are sick of the War, and their leaders quarrelling amongst themselves. Discontent and desertions are rife, scanty rations and equipment – lack of warm clothing – pay (if any) usually in arrears, and winter just beginning. That is the picture. If only UNO would be realistic they might get somewhere.

Well, old friend, I mustn't bore you any longer if you have read as far? (I hope your Private Secretary will have let you see this!)

All the best for Xmas and 1949.

PS. How is ES[2] getting on as War Minister? And is it true that the Generals like working with him?

Winston S. Churchill: speech
('Winston S. Churchill, His Complete Speeches', volume 7, pages 7746–8)

25 November 1948   House of Commons

IRELAND (RELATIONS WITH THE COMMONWEALTH)*

In the Debate on the Address, we had every reason to suppose that the Government would resist the proposals of Mr Costello's Government to sever the last tenuous link with the Crown, and that the Southern Irish would be confronted with all the difficulties which would arise in respect of the nationality of Irishmen in Great Britain and of the British in Ireland, and also in all matters connected with preference and trade relations. Now it appears from the statement which has just been made –

[1] William E. Riley, 1897–1970. Enlisted in US Marine Corps, 1917. 2nd Lt, 1917. 1st Lt, 1918. Col., 1942. Brig.-Gen., 1943. Platoon leader, 6th Marine Rgt, 1917. Silver Star, 1918. Oak Leaf Cluster, 1918. Fleet Marine Officer, Atlantic Fleet, 1940–2. Navy Commendation Medal, 1942. Cdr, Third Marine Div., 1943. Cdr, UN Truce Supervision Organization in Palestine, 1948. Deputy Director for Management of US Foreign Operations Administration, 1953. Director, US Operations Mission, Turkey, 1955.

[2] Emanuel Shinwell.

Mr Stokes: On a point of Order. Is there any Motion before the House? Are we to proceed to debate this statement, because the Leader of the Opposition is not asking a question? He has come with long prepared notes, and is proposing to make a speech.

Mr Churchill: Further to that point of Order. I submit to you, Mr Speaker, that when a statement of this momentous character is made by the Government, some statement of the position of the Opposition, naturally confined within moderate limits, is permissible and is customary.

Mr Speaker: I think that is so. But it is more convenient under the Rules of the House if the Chief Whip[1] moves 'That this House do now adjourn'. Otherwise, we get into a Debate which I cannot stop, and which is out of Order. From the point of view of the Chair it is more convenient if that can be done.

The Parliamentary Secretary to the Treasury (Mr Whiteley): I beg to move, 'That this House do now adjourn'.

Mr Churchill: I am much obliged to the right hon. Gentleman for his intervention, and, addressing myself with great particularity to the Question whether we should now adjourn, may I be permitted to say that, whereas in the Debate on the Address we had every reason to believe that His Majesty's Government intended to raise all these issues of nationality and preference if the Dublin Government decided to sever this last tenuous link, they have now abandoned that position. They are going to acquiesce in arrangements which leave the Southern Irish in full enjoyment of any advantages there may be in being connected with the British Empire and Commonwealth without having any reciprocal obligations of their own towards it.

I do not wish to exaggerate the significance of the step which the Dublin Government are resolved to take. From the point of view of their relations with this country it is not of a very novel character. Mr de Valera's External Relations Act did not prevent Irish neutrality in war, in mortal war, or the denial to us of the use of the ports on which our life sometimes depended. The External Relations Act did not prevent Mr de Valera's Government from having an Irish Minister in Berlin and in Rome, and German and Italian Ministers in Dublin. I have no doubt whatever that he only retained the use of the symbol of the Crown for matters of domestic and local convenience. Therefore it seems that the severing of this link implies no real or material change – whatever may be the sentimental issues involved – in the position which has been accepted and endured for the last 10 years or more.

We bear no ill-will to the Irish people, and we recognise the fact that world movements and world causes may bring us more closely together in future years, not only for practical purposes in matters of mutual convenience, but also in sentiment and in spirit. It is not the question of the relations between Great Britain and Southern Ireland which is important. The serious matter

---

[1] William Whiteley.

is the attitude of His Majesty's Government towards it and the action – or inaction – which they propose. I should like to make it clear that we on this side in no way associate ourselves with this action. The Government have the power, and they also have the responsibility. Of course, they are taking it in full harmony with the declarations of policy which have been made on their behalf by the Chancellor of the Exchequer. This is only an incident in the melancholy path we are now forced to tread.

But it seems to us of the utmost importance that two things should be made clear. The first is that on account of its geographical position near to Great Britain, and on account of the long, terrible and tragic history of the two countries, it seems clear that Ireland is in an entirely different position from any of the other parts of the world in – I must not say in the British Empire – perhaps I may be allowed to say in which we are still at present interested. No arrangements which may be made by the present Government, or any other Government, in regard to Ireland can afford any rule or precedent for application elsewhere. I think that this is the view of the Government. Each separation from the British Crown will have to be judged in accordance with the circumstances of the time and facts of the case. That is the first point; that this is no precedent. It may be right or wrong, but it is no precedent. No one has the right to say, 'This rule applies without discrimination elsewhere.' It is important we should be agreed upon that.

In the second place, it is quite clear, now that Southern Ireland has separated itself altogether from the Crown, that the maintenance of the position of Northern Ireland becomes all the more obligatory upon us. It is evident that a gulf has been opened, a ditch has been dug, between Northern and Southern Ireland which invests partition with greater permanency and reality than it ever had before. I cannot myself conceive that even the present Socialist Government, in their full tide of destructive success, would coerce the loyal people of Ulster out of their right to choose what shall be their relationship with the British Crown and Commonwealth. It is obvious that the position of the people of Northern Ireland, of Ulster, has been simplified and consolidated by the decisions which the Dublin Government have taken. That is a fact, and I was sorry that some emphasis on that fact found no part in the statement which the Prime Minister has just made to us.

There is only one other observation which I should make. We wish to harbour no ill-will towards the Irish people wherever they may dwell. (Hon Members: 'Oh'.) I have my own mental contacts with that people, whose fortunes I have followed and been connected with in many ways, long before those who make these superficial scoffings were called upon to form, or were capable of forming any intelligent opinion on the subject. I say that we on this side of the House harbour no ill-will towards the Irish people wherever they may dwell, and for my part I shall never allow the hope to die in my heart that, under whatever form may be adopted, our future sentiment and action will be increasingly in harmony. Finally, I must make it clear that in respect of future legislation which may be presented to us we reserve absolute freedom of action.

* This speech arose from the decision of the Government of Ireland to remove itself from the Commonwealth by the repeal of the Eire Executive Authority (External Relations) Act of 1936. The Repeal Bill was entitled 'The Republic of Ireland Bill', but the British Government decided that it would not place 'Eire in the category of foreign countries or Eire citizens in the category of foreigners.' This decision did not please Churchill.

King George VI to Winston S. Churchill
(Churchill papers, 2/171)[1]

25 November 1948

My dear Winston,

I must write & thank you so much for your kind letter[2] & for so kindly giving me the beautifully bound copy of your book *The Second World War* Volume I.

I am very sorry that our tour in Australia & New Zealand has had to be postponed for a while, but I do genuinely feel relief that this malady of mine, which has been aggravated by constant worry & anxiety over the World situation, will keep me at home & will give me a period of rest for a time.

The treatment prescribed by my doctors is already doing me good, & I am benefiting from it to a great degree.

This is really no time for me to go such a long distance from home, as I feel anything may happen in the next 6 months or so.

Thank you again so very much for your letter.

General Sir Reginald Wingate[3] to Winston S. Churchill
(Churchill papers, 2/157)[4]

30 November 1948

My dear Winston

You will be overwhelmed with congratulations on your 74th Birthday & here is another (and a very sincere one!) which requires no answer – it is only the earnest wish that you may long be spared to watch over the destinies of

---

[1] This letter was handwritten.
[2] Reproduced above (p. 1256).
[3] Francis Reginald Wingate, 1861–1953. Lt, RA, 1880. Capt., 1889. Maj., 1898. Gen., 1913. Governor, Red Sea Littoral, 1894. Director, Military Intelligence, 1896–8. ADC to Queen Victoria, 1897. KCMG, 1898. Commanded the operations which resulted in the death of the Khalifa, 1899. C-in-C, Forces of Egypt, 1899–1916. Governor-General, Sudan, 1899–1916. KCB, 1900. High Commissioner, Egypt, 1917–19. Bt, 1920.
[4] This letter was handwritten.

dear old England – coupled with a fervent prayer that the time is not far distant when you will again be elected to the leadership – and be as successful in bringing Peace to the World, as you were in knocking out Hitlerism!

I am so glad you keep fit & well – also Mrs Churchill – to whom all kindest remembrances – I have left Edenbridge & am now comfortably housed in my niece's[1] (_____) little house in Ealing. Ever yours.[2]

---

[1] The name, given here in parentheses, is illegible.

[2] Churchill responded on 12 Dec. 1948: 'It gave me so much pleasure to receive your letter and to think that you have, once again, remembered my birthday. Thank you so much for your good wishes. I never forget our luncheon the day before the Battle of Omdurman began. I am glad you are happily installed with your niece and that all goes well with you.'

December 1948

Winston S. Churchill to Trustees of Chartwell Literary Trust
(Churchill papers, 4/57)

December 1948   Chartwell

Dear Sirs,

Mr Kelly's work is of importance to the completion of my task in writing the book on which the Trust depends. His work comprises both the normal care of the archives, for which £240 a year is paid him, and the special and much heavier task of looking out and extracting from them the papers which I require for the book. He also helps me in a great deal of the spade work. There are two or perhaps three volumes yet to be done, covering the next three years. I suggest to you that a three-year arrangement should be made with Mr Kelly whereby he will receive a consolidated salary of £1200 a year, covering his existing salary from the Trust. In return for this he will give me all his time except that needed for his profession at the Bar. At the end of the three-year period the whole position can be reconsidered. I suggest that the expense should be shared half and half between me and the Trust, and that the arrangement should be retrospective, dating from October 1, 1948.

General Sir Charles Grant[1] to Winston S. Churchill
(Churchill papers, 2/149)

1 December 1948

My dear Winston,

I was over in Paris for an annual dinner of old Foch's[2] Staff which used always to meet on the 11th Nov every year and was revised again this year. It

---

[1] Charles John Cecil Grant, 1877–1950. 2nd Lt, Coldstream Guards, 1897. Served during WWI. Commanded 3rd Battalion Coldstream Guards, 1919–21. Maj.-Gen., 1930. GOC London District, 1932–4. KCVO, 1934. KCB, 1937. Lt-Gen., 1937. GOC-in-C Scottish Command, 1937–40. Governor of Edinburgh Castle, 1937–40. Retired, 1940.

[2] Ferdinand Foch, 1851–1929. Entered French Army, 1871. Director, Ecole de Guerre, 1907–11. Cdr, 9th Army, 1914. CGS, 1917. Supreme Cdr, Allied Forces, and Marshal of France, 1918.

was rather tragic – Weygand[1] at 82 presided and all the members so far as I could make out were elderly Generals. They asked me in a letter which would have charmed a bird from a tree and so I went. There I met Georges whom I had known and always admired as one of the best of them. He spoke a lot of you and was very proud of a book you sent him, and said all sorts of very nice things about you. I thought you would like to know this and so write to you. Weygand made a little speech saying they had all been through des épreuves pénibles which we know.

I did not like to talk much about World War 2, especially to him for I felt bitterly and always did that his efforts in 1940 were terrible. However Georges told me he had been very badly treated by France. I personally was broken-hearted when the French Army chucked it in 1940. There is a book coming or come out called 'Conversations Avec Mons Fils' by Weygand which I have sent for and which is, I suppose, a kind of 'apologia pro vita sua'.

We all went to Foch's tomb before dinner and then to tea with Madame Foch[2] but she was tired and did not appear. The Germans had stripped her house of everything gold but otherwise had not stolen much. Paris was rather dirty; inflation in full swing, a franc worth 1/4 d. and how the rentiers live, I cannot imagine.

PS. Your name stands very high in France, I was told.

Lieutenant-General Sir Henry Pownall to Winston S. Churchill
(Churchill papers, 4/255)

1 December 1948

You asked me to trace the origin of a comment you made in a Minute of December 2, 1941; – 'An attack on the Kra Isthmus would not be helpful to Japan for several months.'

This undoubtedly arose from a telegram despatched by C's in C Far East and China Station on Nov. 28, in which they say:

> 'Attack on the Kra Isthmus if carried out at all at this time of year when it is largely waterlogged is not likely to be an immediate prelude to attack on Malaya', and later:
>
> 'Since ground in Southern Thailand is largely waterlogged at present manoeuvring off roads most difficult and tactical advantage will be with whoever is on the ground first.'

[1] Maxime Weygand, 1867–1965. Hon. British knighthood, 1918. C-in-C, French Army, 1931–5. CGS, National Defence, and C-in-C, from 19 May 1940 until the Armistice a month later. Governor-General of Algeria and Delegate-General of the Vichy Government in French Africa, 1941. A prisoner of the Germans in Germany, 1942–5; a prisoner of the French in France, 1945–6.

[2] Julie Anne Ursule Bienvenüe, 1860–1950. Married Ferdinand Foch, 1878.

I found this statement puzzling, because local commanders for some years had said that the North East Monsoon, though certainly a hindrance to landing operations, was not at all a preventative. This applied especially to Singora and Khota Bharu, where the Japanese did land, because the projecting cape of Southern Indo-China gave there a measure of protection and therefore calmer sea. Nor was it considered that the thickness of the jungle was a bar to infantry movement.

The factor of waterlogged country was a new one to me; I had not, myself come across it before. From the context of the telegrams and the fact that the C in C Far East was pressing for a free hand for 'Matador' (previous seizure of Singora in order to forestall a landing) I have no doubt that the waterlogged country referred to was the lowlying part of the Isthmus North of Singora. Singora is just at the point where the Isthmus starts to bulge out into the Malay Peninsula. He was in fact referring to the difficulties the Japanese would experience in a land advance down the Kra Isthmus Southwards to Singora.

I have talked the whole matter over with General Playfair[1] who was Chief of Staff at Singapore at the time. He agreed with this interpretation, indeed he gave the same opinion without my suggesting it to him.

I should say that whatever the local authorities may previously have thought of the likelihood of Japanese attack in December they were by no means taken by surprise when it occurred and had predicted with accuracy when it would come.

I enclose a copy of the COS Report in which the matter was brought to your notice, appended to which is the telegram from the Far East.

Winston S. Churchill to King George VI
(Churchill papers, 2/171)[2]

2 December 1948

Sir,

I was deeply touched by the most gracious message which I received on my birthday from Yr Majesty and the Queen. I was glad to be able to have a gallop with 'The Old Surrey and Burstowe', and not to be at all tired.

I trust and pray Yr Majesty's progress is good. I think so much of you Sir in these days and of all you have done and have still to do for our country in these dangerous and depressing times.

---

[1] Ian Stanley Ord Playfair, 1894–1972. On active service, 1914–18 (despatches, MC and bar, DSO). GSO, Staff College, Quetta, 1934–7; Imperial Defence College, 1938. Commandant, Army Gas School, 1939. Director of Plans, War Office, 1940–1. Maj.-Gen., General Staff, South-East Asia Command, 1943. CB, 1943. Author of the four-volume official war history, *The Mediterranean and the Middle East, 1939–42*.

[2] This letter was handwritten.

Lord Woolton to Winston S. Churchill
(Churchill papers, 2/64)

6 December 1948
Secret

Discussions have recently taken place between the National Liberals and ourselves on the subject of the party label which candidates sponsored by a combined organisation of the National Liberals and ourselves should adopt at the next election.

Proposals for closer co-operation with the National Liberals were embodied in a memorandum which I sent you on 25th March, 1947, and you subsequently signified your assent at our meeting with Lord Teviot. The agreement is generally referred to as the Woolton–Teviot agreement.

The Woolton–Teviot agreement recognises that local circumstances may give rise to a variety of titles in combined associations, and recommends that candidates adopted under such conditions should assume the label 'Liberal and Unionist'.

Experience has shown that fusion or collaboration in the constituencies has produced considerable variety in nomenclature, as the list attached at A will demonstrate. The titles of associations and committees have little significance outside constituency boundaries, and we do not think it wise to attempt to impose uniformity.

The titles of candidates, however, are a matter of wider interest, and great confusion may be caused in the minds of the public if numerous permutations come into use. Some variations are inevitable owing to the traditional use of 'Conservative' in some places and 'Unionist' in others. There are cases where 'National Liberal' must be used, owing to the presence of a left-wing Liberal candidate, and others where 'Liberal' is more appropriate as the local Liberal association is affiliated to the National Liberal Headquarters.

The use of the word 'and' in the title raises questions of precedence. A generic title such as 'United' or 'Union' has the disadvantage of being less clearly descriptive than one which embodies the component Party titles; 'Union' has Fascist connotations.

The National Liberals and ourselves have therefore come to the conclusion that the advice we should give to candidates who are standing under the aegis of both Parties is to adopt the label 'Liberal-Conservative' or 'Liberal-Unionist', prefixing the word 'National' where local circumstances demand. We do not consider it advisable to issue any advice on this matter until the eve of the general election but merely propose to notify confidentially the Central Office Agents of both Parties so that when their advice is sought (as it may be in the case of new candidatures) they can give it in accordance with this policy.

I shall be glad to know whether these suggestions meet with your approval, in which case I convey it to Lord Teviot.[1]

Winston S. Churchill: note
(Churchill papers, 2/71)

8 December 1948

CONSULTATIVE COMMITTEE

1. It would be wise to form a Committee of businessmen, financiers and technical experts, which we[2] talked about two months ago. Their business would be to discuss among themselves and advise us about the economic and financial situation from a non-political point of view.

Of our own Consultative Committee, Mr Eden, Sir John Anderson, Lord Woolton, Colonel Oliver Stanley, Mr Lyttelton, Mr Bracken and Mr Assheton should keep in close and special contact with them, or even, if thought advisable merge in the Committee. All the names should be kept secret. Lord Leathers and Sir Andrew Duncan should be on the Committee. I thought the number should not exceed a dozen exclusive of any of us. We really must know from sources unbiased by Party feeling how things are going, and where we are. I hope this Committee may be created before Christmas, and that it will hold at least four meetings before the end of January. A Secretary should be provided from the Secretariat.

2. Shortly after Parliament meets we shall require a full-dress Debate on the trade position. The existing financial Committee under Colonel Stanley should study this all-important sphere, and they and their Chairman will have the advantage of being in close contact with the General Technical Advisory Committee. It is most important we should not make mistakes at the present time, and all speak more or less in harmony.

3. Responding to the wish of the Executive of the 1922 Committee, I should like to set up two or possibly three small hybrid Committees consisting or two or three members of the 1922 Executive and four or five technical experts. The first of these Committees should be on Coal, the second on the Export Trade, and the third, I think, on Cotton and Textiles. On the whole I think it would be better that no member of our body should serve on them, but one can see how it works out. The object is that we shall be well informed about

---

[1] Churchill responded on Dec. 12: 'I quite agree with your minute of December 6, for which I thank you. I even wonder whether it should not take the form of correspondence between you and me which could be published. I think the list of Liberals and Conservatives working together under different names is most impressive. However perhaps you will have a word with me.'
[2] The Parliamentary Conservative Party.

where we are and what we can do should we become responsible at some date in the future, and also that we do not adopt wrong positions in the interval.

4. Nothing of the above should be published.

Noël Coward to Winston S. Churchill
(Churchill papers, 2/455)[1]

9 December 1948

Dear Mr Churchill,

I have just, very reluctantly, finished your book and I feel that I really need write to tell you how superb I thought it. Your brilliant and loving use of the English language has been obvious in everything you have ever written but never before have you combined wit and truth and strength so perfectly. Also your magnanimity in dealing with those who were your political enemies during your 'Voice in the Wilderness' years is a moral lesson to anyone who tampers with autobiography. I shall keep it in mind. I love your impeccable sense of theatre which kept bubbling up at unexpected moments. Your 'curtain' line after your description of Ribbentrop that was the last time I saw him before he was hanged was quite wonderful. But there is so much to be grateful to you for in your book, so much wisdom and dreadful truth and sublime use of words, and strangely enough, so little bitterness. I feel self-conscious about saying anymore in case you should think me over effusive. But I do love my country and its traditions and its language and – to hell with self-consciousness – Thank you deeply and sincerely for your immortal contributions to all three.[2]

[...]

Lieutenant-General Sir Henry Pownall to Winston S. Churchill
(Churchill papers, 4/220)

10 December 1948

You have asked Ismay and me to give you some 'general thoughts' on the last few months of Wavell's command.

I have no doubt that Wavell entered into the Greek campaign not just because of its obvious political expediency but because he really thought there was a reasonable chance of its success. Events proved him wrong, but that does not mean that it was bad strategy to try and prevent the Germans from installing themselves on the north shore of the Mediterranean and in the Aegean, where they would, and did, make the whole Middle East position

---
[1] This letter was handwritten.
[2] Churchill replied on Dec. 12: 'Thank you so much for your charming letter' (*Churchill papers, 2/455*).

very insecure. The sine qua non was, however, that the desert flank should be secure. He must have been fully seized of this, but he underrated the enemy and overestimated the value of the troops he left on guard. His very proper effort to succeed in Greece was a primary cause of the failure in the desert. This was a fault of miscalculation, not of intention.

'Battleaxe' was a mess. Wavell has said that a sortie from Tobruk was planned for the second phase of 'Battleaxe'. The reason he did not plan for an earlier sortie was that if the first phase broke down, as indeed it did, the garrison of Tobruk might be so weakened by their effort as to endanger the subsequent defence of the fortress. This is a good argument up to a point, but much can be done by feints and bluff and minor forays to keep the enemy guessing, without engaging on a dangerous commitment. As it turned out the enemy felt free to move their best troops from the Tobruk neighbourhood to deal with 'Battleaxe'. This should have been avoidable.

As you say, Wavell doubtless 'did "Battleaxe" in loyalty to Tiger'. After all the great efforts that had been made, and risks taken, to bring Tiger safely to port, he was almost morally bound to try 'Battleaxe'. Of course he wanted, himself, to attack and relieve Tobruk, if it could be done. But he was doubtful of success and so reported. He did not think he had the necessary superiority in numbers, and he may not have reckoned with the enemy's superiority in quality. It was not a good plan and, such as it was, it was not well carried out. German armoured tactics of those days were much superior to our own. It was not until Montgomery came that we broke away from the habit of fighting in 'penny packets'. Rommel never did; he held to the 'Schwerpunkt' method which paid him handsomely.

I am confident that Jumbo Wilson would have done better. He was a very good tactician and trainer of troops and would soon have put his finger on this weak spot. He had a lot of prestige in the Army and would have stopped the argumentation that sometimes went on. Montgomery did so on his arrival by laying down flatly that he would have 'no belly-aching' about his orders.

It was no surprise to Dill that you decided to replace Wavell, he saw for at least a month before that things were shaping that way. Collins,[1] if I remember rightly, says that Wavell's departure cast a gloom over the Command. On the other hand, de Guingand says:

> 'Many of us working at GHQ Cairo about then felt that the C in C was losing his grip and wanted a rest.' (p. 87)

And also:

> 'Auchinleck's arrival in Cairo was like a breath of fresh air.' (p. 90)

---

[1] Robert John Collins, 1880–1950. Educated at Marlborough College. Commissioned into Royal Berkshire Rgt, 1899. Commandant, Staff College, 1939–41. Author of *Lord Wavell, 1883–1941, a Military Biography* (1948).

Wavell is a very tough man, both physically and morally. I had occasion later to see and admire greatly the way he stood up to disappointment and defeat. But he had had a very bad bucketing in the first six months of 1941.

Wisdom after the event is the easiest form of detraction and in criticising the commanders of that time I appreciate the very severe handicaps under which they laboured. It has recently been said, with great truth:

> 'Our views on generalship may easily become confused because victorious commanders get so much better treatment from History than those who deal brilliantly with Disaster'.

Winston S. Churchill: speech
(Hansard)

10 December 1948   House of Commons

FOREIGN AFFAIRS

Let me begin by joining in the general welcome to the Foreign Secretary on his return to the House after a well deserved and much needed holiday. He and a good many others on the Government Front Bench have had a long spell – eight years or more; they used to work very hard in my day, and no doubt they have been working very hard since. I can assure the right hon. Gentleman that, in welcoming him back from his holiday, we feel that there would be no great harm to the public interest if further and prolonged holidays were taken, not only by himself, but by those of his colleagues who sit with him.

I understand that it will very shortly be in order on Foreign Office Debates to deal with the question of Ireland. I am sure everyone will say that if that should come to pass, it will be an Hibernian corollary to an arrangement between the two countries by which neither of them are to regard themselves as foreigners. I have still some hopes – and I do not intend to go into merits – as far as I can follow the matter, because it requires an effort of mental gymnastics, that the policy of the Dublin Government is that Ireland must be partitioned together and thus excluded into the British Commonwealth. If that were so, any Ruling you might have to give in the near future, Mr Speaker, as to its place in Foreign Office Debates would not only be as wisely considered as all your Rulings are, but would also be thoroughly in harmony with the Irish way of looking at things. For myself, I shall not fret unduly if it all works out in a happy and agreeable manner. There may be larger groupings – in connection with which I shall make some remarks later – then we can see in our present situation, and still less prescribed groupings in which the old feuds of past centuries will find no place. I must, however, warn the Government that there are several serious questions of jurisprudence and international law which are beyond our control, and which may very well hamper the loose and casual arrangements which they have made.

When I come to the Foreign Policy of the Government as a whole, I naturally find myself confronted with some of the same difficulties as those apparent in the Foreign Secretary's speech, namely, that the topics are so varied and wide, and that there are so many different separate countries and theatres to be discussed, that it is very difficult to have a general theme. I see that the right hon. Gentleman has been criticised for a lack of a general theme, though I do not admit that the criticism was justified. At any rate, if he is to be guilty of dealing with matters in compartments on such a Debate, I shall place myself in the dock at his side. In the course of the remarks I wish to make, I should like, if it were possible, to begin by dwelling on matters on which we agree. I must observe, however, that since the Socialist Government came into office, the Opposition have been treated with extreme disdain and altogether excluded from the slightest share in the Government's councils on Foreign Affairs. It is the more remarkable when we remember that we have just emerged from a mortal struggle in which so many of us on both sides were colleagues and comrades for more than five years.

It might have been thought that some sense of continuity, some form of consultation with the Opposition, would have been sought by those who are now in power, especially when they represent less than half the nation and less than half the national effort needed to win the victory. Certainly this aspect of the Socialist conduct of affairs falls very far below the standard set by American democracy. We have seen, for instance, how the bi-partisan principle in foreign policy was respected even throughout the hard-fought clashes of the late Presidential election. We have seen how immediately after the election was over the President invited Mr John Foster Dulles,[1] in the regrettable absence of Mr Marshall through the need of a serious operation, from which we all rejoice to hear he is recovering, to fill temporarily the position of the United States chief representative at the United Nations meeting in Paris, although his name had been mentioned in a manner not to be ignored, as the Republican Secretary of State for Foreign Affairs if Mr Dewey had been successful. That is a remarkable instance of the lengths to which the Americans, who conduct their affairs with so much vigour and tenacity, are able, in determining who are to have the offices in the State to deal with subjects of common interest to the life of the nation as a whole are prepared to go. I think they reach a very high level on these matters in the United States.

But here the Government have used their victory only to ignore and brush aside all political forces not included in their own circle. I should never have

---

[1] John Foster Dulles, 1888–1959. Legal counsel to US delegation to Versailles Peace Conference, 1918. Chief Foreign Policy Adviser for Republican Presidential nominee Thomas Dewey, 1944, 1948. Helped draft the Preamble to the UN Charter, 1945. US delegate to the UN, 1946, 1947, 1950. US Secretary of State, 1953–9.

believed that after the ordeals of the late war had been undergone unitedly, the party which I had the honour to lead, and the Liberal Party, should have been treated in such a high-handed fashion – (*Laughter.*) Hon Members may laugh, but the country does not laugh at this attitude. I hope the day will not come when there are no Liberals in the House of Commons. Certainly during the period of the Conservative Government after the National Coalition, I invited the Prime Minister to come with me to Potsdam, and in letters which I wrote to him I offered the closest consultation and fullest information to him and to the Foreign Secretary in all matters of Foreign Affairs. When I look back, as I can, with my long memory, on the relations in foreign affairs which subsisted between the Liberal Government of 1914 and the Conservative Opposition of those days, relations which were maintained even while party bitterness had almost reached the limits of civil war in Ulster, I cannot but marvel at the gulf which, in their self-sufficiency, arrogance and conceit, our present rulers have opened and maintained between themselves and those who lately led them forward through the years of storm. It is too late now for this Parliament, which is in its closing phase, but I say that should we become responsible at any future time we should not, I hope, follow the bad example which present Ministers have set in matters which are above domestic party politics.

However, we have not allowed this odd and surly treatment to influence or deflect our judgment and actions on the great questions affecting the common cause, which is still under challenge and in jeopardy throughout the world. On the contrary, we have given the Government steady support, not only in foreign affairs, but in questions of Defence, with which foreign policy is inseparably interwoven. We have never hesitated to give them that support. Such, however, is the temper of the Socialist Party that neither the Prime Minister nor the Foreign Secretary has ever dared or deigned to say as much as 'Thank you' for 3½ years of unfailing assistance, both in Debate and in the Lobby, in all these spheres which we regard as above ordinary party politics. But this churlishness, to Conservatives and Liberals, has not shielded the Foreign Secretary, as he might have hoped, from many reproaches from his own Left Wing. There, the Communists and the crypto-Communists, and 'fellow travellers', and the like, maintain their unceasing cacophonous chorus of abuse against the Foreign Secretary.

There is the hon Member for Gateshead (Mr Zilliacus), who spoke last night, and who was reported last week as saying – and I suppose this was the greatest insult he could conceive – that the policy of the Foreign Secretary was only 'Winston and water'. I wish to come to the rescue of the Foreign Secretary. I assure the House that I have not except casually, on social occasions – (*Laughter.*) Yes, social occasions cannot wholly be excluded from the contacts of ordinary daily life – I have not had any conversations with the Foreign Secretary since the early days when he took office. I have managed to keep going without that privilege. But there is an unintentional compliment in the jibes of the hon Member for Gateshead, which I value all the more because it is unconscious and involuntary. What he really means is that the policy of the Foreign Secretary has been to pursue, as far as he could, the major themes for which we all laboured and fought together during the war.

What are these major themes? The first is an ever closer and more effective relationship or, as I like to call it, 'fraternal association', with the United States. We are working with them on all the larger questions all the time all over the world, or almost all over the world. I rejoice in this, because in the ever closer unity of the English-speaking world lies the main hope of human freedom and a great part of the hope of our own survival. Britain, who fought the war from start to finish, was deeply exhausted at its close, and the United States have rightly not hesitated to give vital financial and economic support to a Socialist Government, whose principles they abhor, in order to enable our island to regain its strength and play an effective part among the nations.

Further steps of immense consequence have been taken. The ever-increasing unification of the military forces of both countries; the interchange of officers; the sharing of military knowledge; the standardisation of text books and of weapons, for some of which I pressed at Fulton, have made continuous progress. We gather from what the Foreign Secretary said yesterday that the United States may well now be prepared to do what they have never done before, or dreamed of doing before, namely, to give a guarantee to Western Europe against aggression, coupled with practical measures of military collaboration. It is a tremendous event. As my right hon. Friend the Member for Warwick and Leamington (Mr Eden) said last night, if such an event had occurred in 1940, or in 1939, the whole tragic history of the world might well have been altered, and possibly a catastrophe might have been prevented.

Mr Sydney Silverman (Nelson and Colne): And in 1919 too.

Mr Churchill: Certainly, in maintaining the League of Nations, but we have to bear in mind what one's view would have been had one been an American in those days, America having left Europe to conquer and develop a vast continent, and having, as their main principle, to keep out of European entanglements and quarrels. As I say, I rejoice at what has occurred. The most remarkable of all the measures of collaboration is the stationing of American bomber squadrons in our bases in East Anglia.

Mr Solley[1] (Thurrock): Shame. We do not want them here. They should go back to their own country.

Mr Churchill: The significance of such a step has not been lost on anyone, as the hon. Member's interjection shows, least of all on any potential enemy to the interests of this country. I do not wonder at all that the Communists continually attack this measure, so far as they have any power. I pay my tribute to the Government, and particularly the Prime Minister and Foreign Secretary,

---

[1] Leslie Judah Solley, 1905–68. Born in London. Educated at University of London. MP (Lab.) for Thurrock, 1945–50. Expelled from Labour Party, 1950. Founded Labour Independent Group, 1950.

for having had the wisdom and courage to make such a far-reaching step possible, a step which, so far as I know, is unprecedented in times of peace.

While I am on the subject of Anglo-American amity and brotherhood I should like to refer to General Eisenhower, who laboured so faithfully for that cause throughout the war. I was sorry to read the newspaper attacks which have been made in this country upon his loyalty to the common cause, as evidenced by the book which he has recently published in America, and which will I trust soon be available to British readers. These have been replied to by my old friends the wartime Chiefs of Staff and Lord Ismay, and I should like in the interest of Anglo-American relationship to add my testimonies to theirs. I did not always agree with General Eisenhower on strategic questions, and I shall take the opportunity of expressing my views if my life and the life of the Government are suitably prolonged.

I cannot do better than, with the permission of the House, read a personal telegram which I sent. Words spoken at the moment are always better than words worked up some years after. I like to be judged by the words I spoke at each particular moment. On 9th May, 1945, a few days after the surrender of all the German armies, I sent a telegram to President Truman which I will read to the House, because I know my words will be carried to every part of the American public and facilitate the clearing of the atmosphere in regard to this particularly unfortunate episode. This is what I wrote:

> May 9, 1945. Let me tell you what General Eisenhower has meant to us. In him we have had a man who set the unity of the Allied Armies above all Nationalistic thoughts. In his headquarters unity and strategy were the only reigning spirits. Unity reached such a point that British and American troops could be mixed in the line of battle and large masses could be transferred from one command to the other without the slightest difficulty. At no time has the principle of alliance between noble races been carried and maintained at so high a pitch. In the name of the British Empire and the Commonwealth, I express to you our admiration of the firm, farsighted and illuminating character and qualities of General of the Army Eisenhower.

We on this side of the House are also in agreement with the Government upon the broad outlines, though there are many points of difference in administration, of the policy which the Foreign Secretary and his colleagues have pursued towards defeated Germany. We congratulate them upon the success, surpassing expectation, of the prodigious airlift to feed the people of Berlin. The issues which this famous achievement have raised are far more important than the technical success, magnificent as it has been. It has taught the peoples of Germany on either side of the Iron Curtain, in a way which no speeches, arguments or promises could do, that their future lies in ever-closer association with the Western world.

The recent elections in Berlin have been a proof of the resurrection of the

German spirit, and are a beacon casting its light upon the minds of a mighty race without whose effective aid the glory of Europe cannot be revived. I earnestly hope that nothing will be done by the Government, or so far as we can deter it, by our Allies, to chill or check this vast evolution of German sentiment. It is for these reasons that I look forward to the day when all this hateful process of denazification trials and even the trials of leaders or prominent servants of the Hitler régime may be brought to an end. At any rate, I should like to put this point – surely enough blood has been shed. I would not take another life because of the quarrels, horrors and atrocities of the past.

I trust that the demolition or destruction of German factories and plants, except those which are directly and exclusively concerned with war making – because we must not depart from our resolve to carry out the disarmament of Germany, not only in the military, but in the munitions sphere – will be brought to an end at the earliest possible moment. The right hon. Gentleman has reminded us that it was rather hoped that two years would suffice. I hope we shall continue to use our influence and resources, such as they are, to make the German people or the states and principalities of Germany able to govern themselves and earn a good livelihood as soon as possible. I am hoping that the states of Germany – Bavaria, Saxony, Württemberg, Hanover and others – may regain much of their old individuality and rights. I am sure that it is along that road that both France and Britain will find it easiest to advance, and it is along that road that reconciliation and healing will, in the first instance, be most easily found across the former lines of battle. Individuality should be restored and revived before any degree of structural unity can be achieved. I shall show presently how all this fits in with the European movement.

In all this process of reconciliation with Germany lies the opportunity for France to regain her place in the leadership of Europe. It is time that the thousand-year-old quarrel, which has ruined Europe and almost destroyed world civilisation, should be ended. The accounts can never be squared. Vengeance is the most costly and dissipating of luxuries. Even retributive justice on so vast a scale is beyond the sphere and competence of human emotions. Let France, as the most interested, take the lead in bringing back the Germanic peoples to the European family. In this way alone can they overcome their own failure and regain their place in the world. I feel we have a right to offer this sincere counsel to the French people, at whose side for more than 40 years the British nation has struggled and suffered. When I spoke in this sense at Zurich nearly two and a half years ago, it was not well received in France, although they are always very kind to me. But I find a different mood today. I rejoice to find it. Be careful that the Government do not chill it by any step they take.

This brings me naturally to what is called Western Union, in respect of which the greatest credit will rest upon the right hon. Gentleman and the Cabinet of which he is the Foreign Secretary. It brings me not only to Western

Union but to the wider United Europe movement which has been its herald and will always be its friend, helper and servitor. The swiftest means of bringing Germany back into Western Europe – preferably, as I have said, on a basis of states – may well be found in this European movement in the first instance. It may well be. And when one considers countries like Belgium, Holland, Luxembourg and so on, many German states are much larger and more powerful, much more numerous in population than these, and I cannot see why there should not be a continuous confluence of ideas and goodwill between them all.

Here, when we come to the European movement, I must part company with the Government and the Foreign Secretary. The attitude of the Socialist Party under their guidance has hitherto been far from creditable and below the level of these important world and human events. Petty personal jealousies and party rancour have marred their actions and falsified their principles. We all remember how the Government and their party organisation tried to wreck The Hague conference in May, and how they failed. Last week, at Question Time, I complained about the composition of the delegation which the Government had sent to the Conference on European Unity which is still meeting in Paris. The Government seem to be absolutely and obstinately determined to keep this movement towards the unity of so many people who are divided by such grievous feuds, as a party preserve for the Socialists.

My right hon Friend the Member for Warwick and Leamington yesterday referred to this in scathing terms, and dwelt upon the folly and conceit of such an idea. The movement towards European unity, as he said, cannot be a monopoly of any party; least of all should it at this moment become the monopoly of a party which, in many parts of Europe, has shown in a most lamentable fashion its inherent weakness when exposed to the serious attacks of Communism. The movement towards European unity can only achieve success through the reconciliation and good will of whole peoples, irrespective of their internal political or party bias, divisions or labels.

We are not seeking in the European movement – and I speak as one of the Presidents; I share that honour with M Blum and with the Prime Minister of Italy and the Prime Minister of Belgium, M Spaak – to usurp the functions of Government. I have tried to make this plain again and again to the heads of the Government. We ask for a European assembly without executive power. We hope that sentiment and culture, the forgetting of old feuds, the lowering and melting down of barriers of all kinds between countries, the growing sense of being 'a good European' – we hope that all these will be the final, eventual and irresistible solvents of the difficulties which now condemn Europe to misery. The structure of constitutions, the settlement of economic problems, the military aspects – these belong to governments. We do not trespass upon their sphere. But I am sure there is no government wholeheartedly loyal to the idea of European unity which would not be invigorated and sustained by the creation of a European Assembly such as is now proclaimed and asked for by three, if not four, out of the five Powers which now comprise the Western Union.

For this reason the composition of the British delegation to the Conference which is now proceeding came as a shock. It came as a shock not only to a great body of opinion in both parties in this Island, but to all those powerful elements of European opinion to which we understood so many British Labour men hoped to make their special appeal. Nothing could have been more astonishing than the appointment of the Chancellor of the Duchy of Lancaster as the leader of the delegation after the line he had taken and the speeches, quoted yesterday by my right hon. Friend the Member for Warwick and Leamington, which he had delivered recently. He has been the great opponent of the idea of this European movement –

The Chancellor of the Duchy of Lancaster (Mr Dalton) indicated dissent.

Mr Churchill: except on Socialist party lines. In commenting on this appointment by the Prime Minister, the right hon. Gentleman the Foreign Secretary used some guarded language indicating how it was his duty to take anyone who was put alongside him.

The Secretary of State for Foreign Affairs (Mr Ernest Bevin): I hope I did not convey to the right hon. Gentleman that I was not a party to the appointment of my right hon. Friend, because I have absolute confidence in him in doing the job.

Mr Churchill: The right hon. Gentleman naturally has to express his confidence, but he should read carefully what he said, because a more chilling welcome to a comrade and colleague I have rarely heard expressed. I say that the appointment of the right hon. Gentleman after the speeches he has made – unexplained, unretracted in any way – wore the aspect of nothing less than a resolve to sabotage the whole conception –

Mr Dalton indicated dissent.

Mr Churchill: of European unity except on a Socialist Party basis. I have also criticised on different grounds the appointment of Sir Edward Bridges. There is no man I respect more, but he is the head of the Civil Service and I do not think the Prime Minister should have brought him into this sphere, which is necessarily controversial. The right hon. Gentleman said at Question time that it was quite normal for Governments to employ civil servants when they have Government representatives going to conferences. He said how my right hon. Friend the late Foreign Secretary had often – invariably, in fact – taken his civil servants and advisers from the Foreign Office with him. The right hon. Gentleman completely misses the point. It is an absurd argument to use in this connection. Of course, civil servants may go to conferences to assist Ministers, but to take the head of the Civil Service and make him a delegate to meet the former Prime Ministers of other countries, and so forth, in a matter about which opinions differ in parties and between parties, is an abuse for which there is only one precedent that I know of, and that is not a good one.

Mr S Silverman: I do not know whether the right hon. Gentleman would apply that criticism also to the representation of this country at the United Nations, where the delegation has frequently been led by Sir Alexander Cadogan? I have never heard the right hon. Gentleman object to that.

Mr Churchill: He is the servant of the Foreign Office and is expressing the views of the Foreign Office – a diplomat. I think the head of the Civil Service stands in a special position and that it was a very unfair thing to induce him to act in such a capacity.

We do not know what line the Chancellor of the Duchy is going to take. He is to make a speech and we shall be glad to hear it. Far be it from me to set aside any hopes of his reform or of a modification in the attitude of the Government towards the consultative and deliberative European Assembly. I await his reply. I am willing to judge his attitude by it. It is never too late to mend, or, if I may, on account of his ecclesiastical upbringing, use another similitude:

'Betwixt the stirrup and the ground. He mercy sought, and mercy found.'

If the right hon. Gentleman feels able to make a declaration today in the sense in which I have spoken he will improve the reputation of the Government among the Western Allies and in the United States. If he will not, if he only goes over the old ground of the speeches he delivered to the TUC and at other party meetings, the general condemnation of the Government's attitude, and of the Foreign Secretary's attitude – because it is felt that he has played a leading part in this attempt to hamper and break down the unofficial and private efforts that have been made to build up this public opinion in favour of a united Europe – will be that the Chancellor of the Duchy will have entered another large sphere of activity only to distract, confuse and vitiate it. I hope, however, that we shall hear something encouraging from him today, not only with regard to the salvation of a single human being, but about the larger issues which concern us in Europe.

The subject of Palestine was dealt with yesterday by my right hon. Friend. There is an oft-used quotation of the right hon. Gentleman the Foreign Secretary which I will read. No doubt he has it in mind. On 13th November, 1945, in reply to a question from behind him, he said:

> I give my hon. Friend my personal assurance, as I gave it to one of the Jewish leaders the other day, that I will stake my political future on solving this problem, but –

he added –

> Not in the limited sphere presented to me now.

That was England only, without American aid. I am sure nobody wishes to take the right hon. Gentleman too seriously or too strictly at his word – I do not know who would be his successor – but I must say that no part of the Government's policy has been more marked by misjudgment and mismanagement than Palestine.

It is my belief that in the months immediately following the German capitulation we had the power and the chance to impose and enforce – I must use that word – a partition settlement in Palestine by which the Jews would have secured the National Home which has been the declared object and policy of every British Government for a quarter of a century. Such a scheme would, of course, have taken into account the legitimate rights of the Arabs, who, I may say, had not been ill used in the settlements made in Iraq, in Transjordania and in regard to Syria. I always had in my mind the hope that the whole question of the Middle East might have been settled on the largest scale on the morrow of victory and that an Arab Confederation, comprising three or four Arab States – Saudi-Arabia, Iraq, Transjordania, Syria and the Lebanon – however grouped, possibly united amongst themselves, and one Jewish State, might have been set up, which would have given peace and unity throughout the whole vast scene of the Middle East. As to whether so large a policy could have been carried into being I cannot be sure, but a settlement of the Palestine question on the basis of partition would certainly have been attempted, in the closest possible association with the United States and in personal contact with the President, by any Government of which I had been the head. But all this opportunity was lost.

The Socialist Party gained votes at the election by promising greater concessions and advantages to the Jews than anything to which Britain had formerly been committed. Then, when they came into office, they turned their backs on it all, raising bitter feelings of disappointment and anger. Their whole treatment of the Palestine problem has been a lamentable tale of prejudice and incapacity. When, after a year and a half of growing disorder and detestable murders of British soldiers who were only doing a philanthropic duty, it was evident that nothing could be evolved by the Government, in spite of the very large army maintained at the expense of well over £100 million a year in Palestine, I then suggested to the Government that if they could not make up their minds upon any effective policy or coherent scheme they had better return the Mandate. They took another year, with further terrible episodes and disgraceful murders of our troops, before they acted in accordance with this advice. Then they did. The obvious consequence of the British leaving the country was a trial of strength between the Arabs and the Jews. It seems to me very likely, although I cannot, of course, prove it, that the Foreign Secretary misjudged the relative power of the two sides, and it certainly looked on paper as if the Syrians, Egyptians and Arabs, invading from so many quarters, would win. That was not my view. During the war Lord Wavell was asked by me to express an opinion as to which side was the stronger in Palestine and unhesitatingly he said that if both sides were left to themselves the Jews would win. This is what, in fact, has happened, and it only proves how easy it would have been to have enforced an effective partition after the German defeat.

We now have a new situation. The Palestine problem is not a party question. Both parties are divided upon it. Both parties have their own views about it and it is natural, at any rate while we are in opposition, that there should be a certain latitude of opinion upon it. But whatever party we belong to, and whatever view we take, we must surely face the facts. The Jews have driven the Arabs out of a larger area than was contemplated in our partition schemes. They have established a Government which functions effectively. They have a victorious army at their disposal and they have the support both of Soviet Russia and of the United States. These may be unpleasant facts, but can they be in any way disputed? Not as I have stated them. It seems to me that the Government of Israel which has been set up at Tel Aviv cannot be ignored and treated as if it did not exist.

I entirely support my right hon. Friend the Member for Warwick and Leamington that we should send representatives to Tel Aviv without further delay. The Russians have a very large representation, the Americans are fully represented and other countries are represented – 19 countries altogether have recognised either de facto or de jure this new Government which has been set up and whose setting up is an event in world history. Other countries are represented, and we, who still have many interests, duties and memories in Palestine and the Middle East and who have played the directing part over so many years, would surely be foolish in the last degree to be left maintaining a sort of sulky boycott.

There is a special reason in addition, which was referred to by my right hon. Friend. We have a Treaty with King Abdullah which would pledge us to come to his aid if he were attacked in Transjordania – and Transjordania goes right down, not according to the Jordan, but according to the interpretation, to the Gulf of Akaba. We have a duty to King Abdullah. It is 27 years since I proposed and supported his appointment as Emir of Transjordan. During all that time – and what a time; very few institutions are remaining which stood 27 years ago – he has acted with wisdom to his own people and with fidelity to the Allies, irrespective of the fortunes of war. We cannot remain indifferent to his fate, and treat him as we have treated the Nizam of Hyderabad. But, if Transjordania is attacked and we are drawn in, this might bring us into direct dispute with the United States. After all the good work we did over 20 years in Palestine – and all the progress that was shown there – it would indeed be tragic if the only result we carried away, apart from the hatred and abuse of Jews and Arabs, was a deep divergence on a critical issue between us and the United States. That, indeed, would be a sorry reward for all our efforts. For every reason, therefore, it is our interest to be represented at Tel Aviv as we are at Amman. It is lamentable in my opinion that this should have been so long delayed.

This question of official representation in countries with whom we have difficulties is not confined to Palestine. There is also Spain. My right hon. Friend yesterday made a constructive suggestion of high interest for including Italy in Western Europe and of an arrangement about administering the Italian Colonies, which would be under the Trusteeship of Western Europe, and settling that issue in a manner favourable to Italy. I agree with that, or some of it, but why should the Spaniards be regarded as pariahs? Italy was our foe in the war and many scores of thousands of British lives were lost at Italian hands. Immense labours were expended by us to force Italy out of the war. I am strongly in favour of reviving our traditional friendship with Italy, but what is to be said about Spain? No British or Americans were killed by Spaniards and the indirect aid we received from Spain during the war was of immense service. Trade was precious. The use of the Algeciras anchorage and the use of the neutral ground around Gibraltar were invaluable to us, especially in the crisis preceding the operation known as 'Torch'. Spain refused to facilitate the movement of Germans to take Gibraltar and enter Africa, and the way in which Hitler and Mussolini were treated by General Franco is a monumental example of ingratitude. We cannot say that Spain injured us or the United States at all in the late war. Why, then, should we be told that the Spanish people must be treated as outcasts just because they are governed by General Franco – whose Government, incidentally, have, I believe, prohibited for the time being the publication of my book in Spain, so that we are by no means joining a mutual admiration society?

Mr Francis Noel-Baker[1] (Brentford and Chiswick): Has the right hon. Gentleman quite overlooked the fact that thousands of Spanish troops and airmen fought against our then Allies on the Eastern Front?

Mr Churchill: One division was, indeed, sent to fight in Russia, but, so far as Britain and America were concerned, none of our troops were killed by the Spaniards. As a matter of fact, the sending of a division of Spaniards to fight on the Russian Front, about which Stalin spoke in very contemptuous terms, was a very small thing compared with fobbing off the demands to allow German troops to come down and take Gibraltar. The hon. Member for Brentford and Chiswick (Mr F. Noel-Baker) must have a little sense of proportion on these matters and remember how many facts there are in interplay at the same time.

I say there is certainly far more liberty in Spain under General Franco than in any of the countries behind the Iron Curtain. I do not wish to live in either set of countries and I expect I should get into trouble in both cases, but, at

---

[1] Francis Edward Noel-Baker, 1920–2009. Educated at Westminster School and King's College, Cambridge. MP (Lab.) for Brentford and Chiswick, 1945–50; for Swindon, 1955–69. Married, 1947, Ann Saunders, (div.); 1957, Barbara Sonander: six children.

any rate, we must look at these facts. The great mistake is to allow legitimate objections to Franco and his form of Government to be a barrier between the Spanish people and the Western Powers with whom they have many natural ties, especially with Great Britain, with whom they have the unforgettable association of the War of Independence against Napoleon. There is the folly which, so far from leading to the downfall of Franco, has in fact, consolidated his position at every stage. I was sure it would be so. They are a proud people and rather than be spurned and dictated to by the outside world, they have given allegiance to him, which he never won before, since the Spanish war ended.

I agreed at Potsdam that Spain should not be invited to join the United Nations and I am not going to shirk any of the facts. I did so in the hope of inducing Soviet Russia to give this world instrument generous and friendly aid in support. But time has passed since Potsdam; three and a half years have passed; and I am sorry we have a different relationship with Russia from that for which we all hoped. I certainly see no reason why Spain should be excluded from the United Nations any longer. It is not for us to settle these matters alone, but I see no reason why our vote should not be cast in favour of their inclusion. Still less is it wise to withdraw Ambassadors from Spain, which was done on the authority of the United Nations, and to conduct diplomacy, as I said three years ago, through the back door, a kind of black market diplomacy, because everything has to be dealt with some time or other. I say we should send envoys without delay to Tel-Aviv and, as soon as we can obtain the consent of the United Nations, send them back to Madrid. Ambassadors are not sent as compliments but as necessities for ordinary daily use. The more difficult relations are with any country in question, the more necessary it is to have the very highest form of representation on the spot. I venture to submit to the House that I have tried to argue this with an understanding of the different points of view on this question, but on this latter occasion the key to the problem is to think about Spain and the Spanish people and not allow their welfare to be restricted because of a particular man who is, after all, only a passing incident in the life of the country.

I must beg the indulgence of the House to touch for one moment upon the question of Greece. Here I will venture to address a word of friendly counsel to other countries than our own. The question of intervention by one country in the affairs of another is most anxious, doubtful and debatable, but if a great country intervenes in the affairs of a small country it should make its intervention effective. Of that I am sure. Otherwise all that happens is that it prolongs the agony. If it is thought right to go to all the criticism, opposition, expense and difficulty of intervention, it seems to me that it follows irrefutably that intervention should be on a scale and with a purpose and intent that will make it effective. Certainly when we intervened – I had the courageous support of the Foreign Secretary in those days, and my right hon. Friend was with me

– we did so effectively, and for 40 days we fought the Communists in Athens with three or four divisions, and saved Athens from that hideous domination. I trust that what I have said will not give offence elsewhere.

I have only one more subject to mention. I greatly apologise to the House for having been so lengthy.

While our thoughts are so constantly riveted on Berlin and the delicate day-to-day situation there, we must not forget the enormous events which are taking place in China, where the advance of Communism seems to gain momentum every day. There is also particularly the question of Hong Kong. I see that some reinforcements are to be sent. I hope that it will be made quite clear that British naval, air and military forces will defend Hong Kong from any assault which may be made upon it. I cannot conceive that such an action taken in self-defence, would raise the larger issues on which the balance of European peace depends.

Finally, I wish to say one word – and it shall be only a very brief one – about the greatest topic of all which overhangs our minds, our relations with Soviet Russia. I have frequently advised that we should endeavour to reach a settlement with Russia on fundamental, outstanding questions before they have the atomic bomb as well as the Americans. I believe that in this resides the best hope of avoiding a third world war. I wish to make it clear – and this is the principal reason why I refer to this matter in the Debate – that I have never attempted to suggest the timing of such a solemn and grave negotiation. I have not the official knowledge necessary to form an opinion about that.

I wish also to make it plain, in view of what was said by the hon. Member for Gateshead (Mr Zilliacus), who said that the policy of war with Russia was the policy of the Leader of the Opposition, that that is not at all the policy which I have put forward – far from it. It has always been my earnest desire, which I do not yet abandon, that a peaceful settlement may yet be reached with Soviet Russia if it is within the bounds of possibility. It is not my fault since I left office, nor do I think it is the fault of the Government, that this friendly atmosphere has not been maintained or this happy, amicable settlement reached.

I will only venture to use words, not coined or prepared for the occasion, which express the view which I held about Russia. I will read to the House some passages from a private and personal communication which I made to Mr Stalin on 29th April, 1945. I said this:

> Side by side with our strong sentiment for the rights of Poland, which I believe is shared in at least as strong a degree throughout the United States, there has grown up throughout the English-speaking world a very warm and deep desire to be friends on equal and honourable terms with the mighty Russian Soviet Republic and to work with you, making allowances for our different systems of thought and government, in long and bright

years for all the world which we three Powers alone can make together. I, who in my years of great responsibility have worked faithfully for this unity, will certainly continue to do so by every means in my power and in particular I can assure you that we in Great Britain would not work for or tolerate a Polish Government unfriendly to Russia. Neither could we recognise a Polish Government which did not truly correspond to the description in our joint Declaration at Yalta with proper regard for the rights of the individual as we understand these matters in the Western world.

About Greece I said:

In Greece we seek nothing but her friendship, which is of long duration, and desire only her independence and integrity. But we have no intention to try to decide whether she is to be a monarchy or a republic. Our only policy there is to restore matters to the normal as quickly as possible and to hold fair and free elections, I hope within the next four or five months. These elections will decide the régime and later on the constitution. The will of the people, expressed under conditions of freedom and universal franchise, must prevail; that is our root principle. If the Greeks were to decide for a republic, it would not affect our relations with them. We will use our influence with the Greek Government to invite Russian representatives to come and see freely what is going on in Greece, and at the elections I hope that there will be Russian, American and British commissioners at large in the country to make sure that there is no intimidation or other frustration of the free choice of the people between the different parties who will be contending. After that, our work in Greece may well be done.

I concluded by looking at the other side. I had at that time very good relations personally with Mr Stalin. It was just after Himmler had made overtures to the late Count Bernadotte. I had telegraphed to Russia very promptly the information. Stalin had replied:

You have acted exactly as I thought you would do.

That was the high point of my relationship with him. I finished, therefore, in this way:

There is not much comfort in looking into a future where you and the countries you dominate, plus the Communist parties in many other States are all drawn up on one side and those who rally to the English-speaking nations and their associates or Dominions are on the other. It is quite obvious that their quarrel would tear the world to pieces and that all of us leading men on either side who had anything to do with that would be shamed before history. Even embarking on a long period of suspicions of abuse and counter-abuse and of opposing policies would be a disaster hampering the great developments of world prosperity for the masses which are attainable only by our trinity.

I wrote:

I hope there is no word or phrase in this outpouring of my heart to you which unwittingly gives offence. If so, let me know. But do not I beg of you, my friend Stalin, under-rate the divergencies which are opening about matters which you may think are small, but which are symbolic of the way the English-speaking democracies look at life.[1]

That was my outlook and hope then, in April, 1945. It was my dearest wish. I believe that trinity of co-operation and the efforts of these three Powers would have opened to mankind a golden age of productivity and peace, and moral and intellectual well-being. That was my outlook then. I deeply regret the reasons that exist – and they are known to us all – which make it difficult to share it and express it fully now.

Winston S. Churchill: statement
(Churchill papers, 2/71)

11 December 1948

Mr Churchill has issued the following statement from Chartwell this evening:

'In my references to Spain in my speech in the House of Commons yesterday, I suggested that Spain should be admitted to the United Nations. Russia and her satellites are all members of the United Nations Organization and our differences with them are at least as great as with the present Spanish regime. I have never proposed that Spain should be admitted in present circumstances, either to Western Union or to the proposed European Assembly. This is an entirely different question.

The Under-Secretary of State for Foreign Affairs, Mr Mayhew,[2] when referring to my proposal in his reply substituted, I hope inadvertently, Western Union for UNO. This of course, as Mr Eden pointed out, was a perversion of what I said.'

---

[1] T.675/5, reproduced in *The Churchill Documents*, vol. 21, *The Shadows of Victory, January–July 1945*, pp. 1197–202.
[2] Christopher Paget Mayhew, 1915–97. President, Oxford Union, 1936. Gunner, Surrey Yeomanry RA; BEF, 1939–40. Maj., 1944. MP (Lab.) for South Norfolk, 1945–50; for Woolwich East, 1951–74. Under-Secretary of State, FO, 1946–50. Minister of Defence, 1964–6. Television commentator and party political broadcast presenter for Labour Party, 1951–64. Parliamentary Under-Secretary of State for Defence, 1964. Joined Liberal Party, 1974. Member, Liberal Action Group for Electoral Reform, 1974–80. Baron, 1981. Chairman, National Association for Mental Health, 1992–7.

Clementine Churchill to Winston S. Churchill
(Churchill papers, 1/44)

11 December 1948

The other day I smelt burning coming from your bedroom. I went in and found that the curtains of the window near your bed were scorched brown from heat, and they might have burst into flames. I found that the thermostat above your bed was on and the one on the side of the room was off.

It is important that when there is any heat on in your bedroom, both thermostats must be on, because if one is on at, say, 60 degrees and the other is off, the one that is on endeavours to create the necessary temperature all over the room, and in order to reach the far side of the room a tremendous heat is developed which results in damage to the curtains, and might in an extreme case cause a fire.

Will you be very kind and if you go into your room and find it too hot, will you remember to click off both thermostats. Clicking one does not reduce the temperature in the room, but merely causes the other to work harder. I have asked the servants about this and they positively affirm that they never click one thermostat without the other. I have asked Greenshields to see that this does not happen again, but I thought perhaps I would let you know because even if there is no smell of burning nor danger of fire from having one on, there is always the danger of putting the whole mechanism out of order by overworking one thermostat.

Winston S. Churchill to John Foster Dulles
(Churchill papers, 2/162)

12 December 1948

My dear Mr Dulles,

I am most grateful to you for your letter and for sending me a copy of your speech of November 18, which I have read with the greatest interest.

I was so glad to see the high standard of bi-partisan policy followed by President Truman in appointing you to represent General Marshall during his absence from Paris. It is a great pity that His Majesty's present Government fall so far below American standards in this respect.

Time magazine: article
(Time)

13 December 1948

GREAT BRITAIN
Cassandra Returns

Winston Churchill had a busy week. Three days before his 74th birthday, he donned jodhpurs, fortified himself with rum punch and galloped off to the hounds astride a borrowed horse. Churchill's inevitable, square-crowned Russell hat was jammed well down on his head, his equally inevitable cigar clenched firmly between his teeth.

Later, his birthday and the hunt behind him, Churchill stood up on the floor of the House of Commons and, amid grave silence from his colleagues, demanded from Prime Minister Clement Attlee an account of the Labor government's stewardship over the nation's mouldering defenses.

'I ask the Prime Minister,' Churchill rumbled, 'where are the rifles which, on V-E day, armed 4,600,000 troops and Home Guards of this country alone? Are they in oil? . . . There is no difficulty in keeping rifles. They do not go sour, like milk. . . . What has happened to those latest models of tanks? . . .

'I have long experience in this matter, and I can assure the House that it is most improvident to get rid of the vital weapon you have until you have a better one to put in its place. What has happened to the enormous masses of artillery? . . . What have we . . . in organized and equipped formations that can be sent abroad or brought into action in this country? . . .'

Attlee sat slumped down as far as he could get on the front bench, almost hidden behind a paper on which he doodled continuously. At one point, Churchill asked: 'What have we got to show for it (£305 million voted for the army during 1948)?' Then, looking at Attlee, 'I ask the Prime Minister that question. I see that he is likely to reply.' 'No', said Clement Attlee.

Attlee's silence at the conclusion of Churchill's oratorical barrage was probably the best way out of an embarrassing and messy situation. Since war's end, the Labor government (on the assumption that most existing equipment would be antiquated by the time there was another war) has sold or given away the enormous total of £546 million worth of supplies and equipment. Other material is rotting and rusting in dumps, particularly in Germany. In one case, radio and radar equipment was stuffed down an old mineshaft and sealed with concrete. An energetic farmer dug it out, sold it at a nice profit, and considerably embarrassed the officials who had buried it in the first place.

'Should war come,' concluded Churchill, '– which God forbid; and it does not depend on us whether war comes; less than ever in our history does it depend on us . . . a terrible accountancy will be required from those to whom Parliament has accorded, in time of peace, unparalleled resources and unprecedented power.'

To his hearers, Winston Churchill seemed once more cast in the role of Cassandra; history, apparently, was repeating itself with dire monotony.

General Lord Ismay to Winston S. Churchill
(Churchill papers, 4/220)

13 December 1948

My dear Mr Churchill,

You asked for my recollection of the events leading up to the replacement of Wavell by Auchinleck.

Some pretty rough wires passed between the Chiefs of Staff and Wavell about the Syrian and Iraq affairs. Wavell was inclined to adopt an attitude of non possumus, and to accuse the Chiefs of Staff of putting babies in his lap which he was unable to handle with his existing resources: while the Chiefs of Staff took the line that the babies were none of their choosing, and that the opposition in both places was likely to be so weak that a little would go a long way.

I do not believe, however, that theses tiffs had anything to do with Wavell's subsequent removal. The deciding episode that lives in my mind was that both Eden and Dill thought that Wavell had been tremendously affected by the breach of his desert flank by Rommel. His Intelligence had misinformed him and the thrust came as a complete surprise. I seem to remember Eden saying that Wavell had 'aged ten years in the night'. You yourself said that Rommel had torn the new won laurels from Wavell's brow and thrown them in the sand.

Apart from this particular episode, I think there was a very general impression in Whitehall that Wavell was very tired.

Winston S. Churchill to Anthony Eden
(Churchill papers, 2/99)

13 December 1948

My dear Anthony,

Angus MacNeill is a very old friend. He took over the command of the Montmorency Scouts[1] in the Boer War after Montmorency was killed, and I had a very dangerous ride with him.

It is remarkable how he has held on unmoved in Palestine for twenty-five years. His letter[2] confirms all our views. It comes from an absolutely independent and trustworthy quarter. Please return.

Bernard Baruch to Winston S. Churchill
(Churchill papers, 2/210)

14 December 1948   New York

Dear Winston,

Never give yourself any concern about seeing anybody I send. I want you to know I never send anybody who is not going to be helpful to you. I quite understand how the book and the speeches not alone hunt you but haunt you.

I have in mind starting people to writing and talking about the union of Western Europe, and that there are grave doubts about it because of the by-passing of Winston Churchill. The American people have not the confidence in England run by these people but they had confidence when it was run by you. There is no voice in Europe that can lift the people of those countries as yours can. They do not pay attention to any other speakers. By getting an expression of this throughout the press and into the minds of our legislators, it may have considerable effect. I am interested in seeing it done, but it is not going to be done by those wobbling friends of yours. It looks as if they can out-weather-vane some of my friends here.

I saw the Beaver the other day at luncheon and am going to visit him some time this winter.

As soon as you have any plans about coming here, let me know.

We all are waiting for the President to state what our policy is going to be, nationally and internationally. The two are inextricably twined. He will have to state how much we are going to spend for defense – European, Asiatic and South American relief – health insurance – and education, and then figure

---

[1] Montmorency's Scouts, 1899–1902. Formed by Capt. the Hon. R. de Montmorency, VC, 21st Lancers, in Dec. 1899 to fight in the Anglo-Boer War, 1899–1902. The unit came under the command of Captain McNeill after Montmorency's death in the Battle of Stormberg, and continued fighting until its disbandment upon the cessation of hostilities in 1902.

[2] Reproduced above (pp. 1257–8).

up how we can do all of this and still keep our economy sound. If we overdo it, we shall be prostrate, and the world will go down in ruin around our ears. We can do a lot, but we cannot do it and indulge ourselves at the same time.

They find now that the reduction in taxes and the scuttle-and-run policy, both of which I opposed, were wrong and that they will have to retrace their steps. As you know, that is bitter medicine to swallow.

The President of the United States and Marshal Stalin are the two great figures in the world. They can take the lead.

I think we have to take a stand, even if it is one we might have to take alone. And when we do take a just stand, as we did on atomic energy, we will not be alone as we weren't then.

No one knows better than you, that no matter what you do for some people, whether they are yours or others, the more they will want done and the more they will lean upon you.

I see no voice throughout the world that is your equal, and it has been my concern to encourage that belief. Those I have sent you could help me.

Season's Greetings, and the best to you and yours.

Field Marshal Lord Montgomery to Winston S. Churchill
(*Churchill papers, 2/143*)[1]

27 December 1948

Dear Mr Churchill,

Thank you so very much for the picture. It is superb and it now hangs over the fireplace in my study, for all to see. I seem to recognise the scene, near Marrakesh in Morocco; we all went for a picnic on New Year's Day 1944 and I left by air for England later that night to take over command of 21 Army Group.

What a lot has happened since those days. And what a lot more may happen!

I hope you and Mrs Churchill are well and that you will enjoy some sunshine in the South of France.

All success to you in 1949. A thousand salvos from ten thousand guns.

---

[1] This letter was handwritten.

Jo Sturdee to Winston S. Churchill
(*Churchill papers, 2/46*)

31 December 1948

Miss Gilliatt telephoned the following letter to you from Colonel Walter Elliot, as it appears to need your reply urgently:

'My dear Winston,
    I enclose a letter from Dr Weizmann which it may interest you to see. He asks me to show it to Mr Oliver Stanley which I have done. You will see that he asks me to go out and visit him during the Recess. I have refused for the present on the ground of pressure of work, but I should like to know what your view would be if time permitted. One or two Government supporters have been out – Silverman, and Crossman. I do not quote them as examples. Some touch ought to be kept, though not too obviously.'

This letter from Dr Weizmann is rather long and is being sent out, but it will not reach here until next Monday or Tuesday. It is about the situation in Palestine. He says the British advisers to the Arabs made some serious miscalculations, which he says is a pity. He hints that the British advised the Syrians and the Iraqis to invade Palestine. 'In spite of everything that has happened I believe a world of good could be done if you could come out here at Christmas.' (To Colonel Elliot)

January
1949

Sarah Churchill to Winston S. Churchill
(Churchill papers, 1/46)[1]

January 1949

Darling Papa,

I am so grieved to have upset your holiday by once again intruding one of my friends[2] upon the scene.

Of course I should after Marrakech last year have known better, but 'hope springs eternal in the human breast', and when Mummie told me I could bring someone I was delighted, and thought that perhaps things would go better this year.

If I live a hundred years I shall never understand your point blank rudeness and unkindness.

Am I not a human being? Can you not call me into your room, tell me you do not like him, and for the love that you say you have for me, extend him just the common courtesy that you do to the maître d'Hotel or chef d'orchestre, and trust me to see that the visit is terminated quickly. What kind of a position have you put me into now? It is my mistake, not his, that he is here. Rightly or wrongly, he was invited.

If you think by insulting him you can change one jot, the opinion I hold of him – you are most sorely mistaken. If you think by insulting him you will make him go away – you are certainly right, for he is a young man of considerable dignity and spirit. But except for the love I have for both you and Mama, I should leave at once too, for you have also succeeded in deeply wounding me.

I assure you I shall never again, subject you to any of my friends, nor indeed them, to your contempt.

I do not understand how you can say you love me – when you are so very very unkind.

I love you very much – nothing can ever change that – but I see now how

---

[1] This letter was handwritten.
[2] Antony Beauchamp Entwistle, 1918–57. Official war artist in Burma, 1939–44. Married Sarah Churchill, Oct. 1949.

right I have been to build a life for myself, and arm myself with four good hoofs and a crusty carapace, for the slings and arrows of family life are sharp indeed.

Winston S. Churchill to Sir Alan Lascelles
(Churchill papers, 2/311)

January 1949

My dear Tommy,

I have recently received from the American Air Force a set of pilot's wings. This is a unique honour, held by only three others. I am writing to ask if I may have The King's permission to wear this decoration on appropriate occasions.

Winston S. Churchill to Don Salvador de Madariaga[1]
(Churchill papers, 2/27)

2 January 1949 Monte Carlo
Private

Dear Don Madariaga,

I thank you for your letter of December 17. My position was deliberately misrepresented in Parliament by the Under Secretary of State[2] in the House of Commons. My son does not consult me about what he writes, and I would prefer not to enter into detailed arguments on the points of your draft letter.

It is my belief that Franco would have already disappeared by now but for the fact that foreign countries have so pointedly identified Spain with him. I am sure it is a mistake to punish and insult whole nations. Spain has as much right to be represented on the United Nations Organisation as Russia or Poland, and most civilised people would find it easier to live in Spain than in either of the other two totalitarian countries. I do not propose to live in either.

---

[1] Salvador de Madariaga, 1886–1978. Born in Spain. Member, Press Section, League of Nations Secretariat, 1921–2; Director, Disarmament Section, 1922–7. Prof. of Spanish Studies, Oxford, 1928–31. Spanish Ambassador in Washington DC, 1931; in Paris, 1932–4. Permanent Delegate, League of Nations, 1931–6. Author of *Anarchy or Hierarchy* (1937) and *Theory and Practice in International Relations* (1938). Founder-President, College of Europe (at Bruges). Resident in Oxford, 1939–76. Returned to Spain, 1976, to take his place in the Spanish Royal Academy.

[2] Christopher Mayhew.

Winston S. Churchill to Brigadier Fitzroy Maclean[1]
(Churchill papers, 2/163)

12 January 1949
Private and Confidential

My dear Maclean,

Thank you for letting me see what you wish to write about me in your book. I have only a few casual notes to make.

p. 2. I have never worn pyjamas, heavy silk or otherwise, in my life.

p. 3. I have never addressed anyone as 'my boy'.

p. 5. I was much too feeble to paint during this visit of convalescence to Marrakech.

p. 5. I do not remember the incident about Jajce.

p. 5. The last paragraph of Marrakech Jan. 1944. Why should you dwell on this luxury?

p. 6. We had one dinner, if I remember rightly, at Naples, but certainly not gargantuan banquet. In any case I did not order the food, it was done by Headquarters in Italy.

p. 6. 'his mountain fastness'. Perhaps I am wrong but I thought this was the time when Tito had fled from the mainland and was living under my protection on the island of Viz.

p. 6. 'a full scale invasion of the Balkans was no longer contemplated'. No one ever contemplated at any time a full scale invasion of the Balkans. This is one of the silly stories that the Americans have propagated. I never myself contemplated anything but commando and partisan assistance. A movement through the Lubliana Gap to Vienna was a different story.

I hope all goes well with you.

L. S. Amery to Winston S. Churchill
(Churchill papers, 2/46)

13 January 1949

My dear Winston,

May I venture to make a suggestion to you if you say anything about Palestine? And that is that you should make some direct personal response to the statesmanlike interview by Weizmann to *The Times* correspondent given in this morning's paper, and following up a similar signal of friendship held out in

---

[1] Fitzroy Hew Royle Maclean, 1911–96. Educated at Eton and King's College, Cambridge, 1932. Diplomat in Paris, 1934–7; in Moscow, 1937–9. MP (Cons.) for Lancaster, 1941–59; for Bute and North Ayrshire, 1959–74. Head of British Liaison Mission with Tito, Yugoslavia, 1943–5. CBE, 1944. Married, 1946, Veronica Nell Fraser-Phipps: two children. Maj.-Gen., 1947. Author of *Escape to Adventure* (1950). Financial Secretary, War Office, 1954–7. Bt, 1957. KT, 1993.

his New Year's message to his own people. The old boy is still a great power in Israel and a few words of personal tribute from yourself would not only touch him deeply but greatly strengthen his influence for peace.

As for the rest, could anything be sillier than sending our planes, in company with Egyptian planes, sightseeing in a battle area or than the whole Naval, Military and Air Force excitement which seems to have resulted? One might almost think that Jews were contemplating the invasion of this island.

I hope you have had a really good time on the Riviera. With every good wish for 1949.

L. S. Amery to Winston S. Churchill
(*Churchill papers, 2/46*)

20 January 1949

My dear Winston,

This Palestine reconnaissance business gets curiouser and curiouser. We are now told that, after completely washing our hands of all responsibility for Palestine, we still continued to do high level snooping over the dog-fight, hence the Mosquito shot down some time ago. Since then we have claimed the right of low level snooping down to four hundred feet over a battle field. The plea being that the Jews would not allow the UNO or at any rate inform UNO, and let them warn the Jews, if we were not prepared to tell the Jews ourselves? Also, couldn't we have taken some care to avoid actually accompanying Egyptian Spitfires or flying to the battle field from the same direction as that from which the Egyptians had delivered their air attacks?

There is, however, a more fundamental question which you might well put to Bevin. Does the Government recognize any obligation upon a member of UNO to support, or at any rate not to obstruct or defeat, a UNO decision which it may find unpalatable. He can hardly say 'yes'. But if he says 'no' then he might well be asked what he did to discourage his Egyptian friends from beginning by invading the territory assigned by UNO to Israel, bombing Tel Aviv by sea and from the air, and why, not having done so, he should suddenly regard himself bound as an ally to protect, not any vital position in Egypt, but an imaginary line in the Desert?

Another question that might be worth asking is whether the troops we have sent to Akaba are to interfere with the Jews occupying the little strip of coast next door to Akaba which UNO has assigned to them?

It looks as if the Government are hoping desperately for something to happen at Rhodes or in Washington, to get them out of their difficulty.

JANUARY 1949

Winston S. Churchill to Bernard Baruch
(Churchill papers, 2/210)

24 January 1949

Compton's[1] invitation which he says is favoured by President and your cable have led me to make a tentative plan on the following lines. March 21 sail from Southampton in *Queen Mary*. March 26 Arrive New York. March 27 Luce's banquet Waldorfastoria. Address undergraduates. March 28 in New York. March 29 Dine with *Life Time Fortune*. March 30 In New York see Dewey. March 31 Arrive Boston address Massachusetts Institute of Technology. April 1 President addresses Institute. April 2 Arrive Washington stay until April 5. April 6 Arrive Toronto. April 7 and 8 in Ottawa and so home.

Let us be together throughout especially at Washington where I want to stay at least four days. You know about invitations I have received from Luce. Please talk things over with him and let me know what you advise. It is difficult for me in present political situation to find much time and at my age much strength. I cannot undertake more than three or four speeches altogether and want above all to have time to talk to you and friends. Party would be only me and Christopher[2] with some staff. Every good wish my old and trusted friend.

Brigadier Fitzroy Maclean to Winston S. Churchill
(Churchill papers, 2/163)[3]

25 January 1949

Dear Mr Churchill,

Thank you very much for your letter of 12 January[4] which I found on my return from Italy yesterday.

I am most grateful to you for going through the extracts from my book and I will of course alter the manuscript in accordance with your comments. It was extremely good of you to take so much trouble over it.

[1] Karl Taylor Compton, 1887–1954. Physicist. Born in Wooster, Ohio. Educated at Princeton University. Science attaché, US Embassy in Paris, 1917–18. Prof. at Princeton, 1919–30. President, MIT, 1930–48. National Defense Research Committee, 1940–1. Member, Interim Committee to President regarding atomic bomb, 1945–6.
[2] Soames.
[3] This letter was handwritten.
[4] Reproduced above (p. 1294).

Winston S. Churchill: speech
('Winston S. Churchill, His Complete Speeches', volume 7, pages 7773–83)

26 January 1949   House of Commons

PALESTINE

The right hon. Gentleman (Mr Ernest Bevin) has covered a wide field, both in the extent of the topics with which he has dealt and in the period of history which he has taken into consideration. But I have been asking myself, as I listened to this statement of historical facts and so many arguments which one approves of as such and in their places, what was the conclusion that the Foreign Secretary was asking the House to draw from the statement which he has just made. It seems to me that it would not be doing him any injustice if I said that the conclusion to which he wishes to lead us is that the conduct of this matter and the policy pursued by the Government for the last three and a half years could hardly have been bettered. All is for the best in the best of all possible worlds, and all kinds of arguments can be used with all kinds of varying emphasis at every stage and aspect of the story.

I shall have to tell some of this story, though I trust at not undue length. But before I plunge into it I must make one general remark about the right hon Gentleman and his policy. We have supported the main principles and structure of the foreign policy of the right hon. Gentleman, and everyone is glad that he has had the patriotism and courage to take a firm stand in these last years against the vile and wicked brutalities and manoeuvres of Communism which threaten not only the peace of the world, but even more important, its life and freedom. In this connection I see that one of Mr Ramsay MacDonald's bishops, or perhaps his only bishop,[1] has lately been eulogizing the humanistic virtues of Soviet Communism, while all the time at least 12,000,000 people are being toiled to death as slaves in the Soviet concentration camps. Such an example of mental and moral obliquity on the part of a prelate deserves at least the passing notice of thinking men. As this might be considered to reflect upon a Member of the other House, I shall avoid your rebukes, Mr Speaker, by not pursuing the topic or the prelate any further. We must not forget, and we do not forget, that the Foreign Secretary, supported by the British trade union movement and by the present Socialist Administration and Labour Party, has not hesitated or failed to draw an impassable line between the professional Communist adept and other human beings.

---

[1] Ernest William Barnes, 1874–1953. Mathematician, theologian and pacifist. Educated at Trinity College, Cambridge. Lecturer in Mathematics, Author of 29 mathematical papers between 1897 and 1910. Cambridge University, 1902. Ordained Anglican priest, 1902. Junior Dean of Trinity Hall, Cambridge, 1906–8. FRS, 1909. Appointed Master of the Temple, 1915. Married, 1916, Adelaide Caroline Theresa Ward. Canon of Westminster, 1918–24. Bishop of Birmingham, 1924–52. Published the controversial *Scientific Theory and Religion* (1933) and *Rise of Christianity* (1947).

We are glad of that. We also respect the Foreign Secretary's British outlook. He represents many of the virtues and some of the weaknesses which have enabled our people to make a tolerably collective presentation of their character to the rest of the world in many years of history. There is also, of course, the sense of war comradeship, which although it must not be allowed to interfere with the proper, due discussion of current affairs or with party strife at a time like this, is nevertheless a subsisting element between many of those who sit on the Front Benches of this House.

I wish to say that because I make it perfectly clear that in the general policy which the right hon. Gentleman has pursued – I am not talking about the methods but the spirit of the general policy he has pursued – in resisting the Communist menace and encroachment, and in cultivating ever closer and more friendly relations with the United States, we have given him our support, and we do not withdraw our support at the present time. But it is on this basis and with this background that we are forced this afternoon to consider the right hon. Gentleman's astounding mishandling of the Palestine problem. We feel that this has been so gross and glaring that we should fail in our duty if we did not expose it in the plainest terms. We shall not only do that in Debate; we shall support our criticism in the Lobby. Only in this way can we make an effective protest and lead public opinion to the true conclusions.

The right hon. Gentleman's Palestine plight is indeed melancholy and cannot be covered up with wide generalities. No one ever made such sweeping declarations of confidence in himself on this point as the right hon. Gentleman, and no one has been proved by events to be more consistently wrong on every turning-point and at every moment than he. Every opportunity for obtaining a satisfactory settlement was thrown away. Immediately after the end of the Japanese war, we had the troops in the Middle East and we had the world prestige to impose a settlement on both sides. That chance was missed. Instead, an Anglo-American Committee of Inquiry was set up to examine the problem. It was on that occasion that the right hon. Gentleman staked his political future on solving the Palestine problem. No more rash bet has ever been recorded in the annals of the British turf. Luckily, it is not intended that the wager shall be paid.

Mr Bevin: May I ask whether it was greater than that which the right hon. Gentleman undertook when he went after Denikin[1] and Koltchak?[2] (Editor's

---

[1] Anton Ivanovitch Denikin, 1872–1947. Joined Imperial Russian Army at age 15. Commanded Iron Div., WWI. After revolution of March 1917, CoS to Gen. Alexeyev, supreme C-in-C. By Sep. 1918, sole commander of the White Army. By May 1919, occupied all of Ukraine; Oct. 1918, penetrated as far north as Orel. Early in 1920 the Red forces captured Rostov, the White Army broke up and he fled to Constantinople. Lived in France after 1926; in US after 1945.

[2] Alexander Vasilievich Kolchak, 1870–1920. Crimean Tartar by birth. Served in Russian Imperial Navy. VAdm., 1916. C-in-C, Black Sea Fleet, 1916–17. Minister of War in Siberian 'All Russian Government' (anti-Bolshevik), 1918. Declared himself 'Supreme Ruler', Nov. 1918. Resigned leadership of anti-Bolshevik forces in favour of Gen. Denikin, Dec. 1919. Shot by the Bolsheviks at Irkutsk, 7 Feb. 1920.

JANUARY 1949 1299

Note: A reference to Churchill's statement on the Russian Civil War. General Denikin and Admiral Koltchak were prominent among the leaders of the Anti-Bolshevik forces.)[1]

Mr Churchill: I certainly did not stake my political reputation upon the successes which those generals would have, but I think the day will come when it will be recognized without doubt, not only on one side of the House but throughout the civilized world, that the strangling of Bolshevism at its birth would have been an untold blessing to the human race.

Mr Cocks (Broxtowe): If that had happened we should have lost the last war.

Mr Churchill: No, it would have prevented the last war. Let me return to the more peaceful paths of Palestine and leave these furious controversies of a bygone period. When this Anglo-American Committee reported, its recommendations, although accepted by Mr Truman, were rejected by His Majesty's Government.

Mr Bevin: No.

Mr Churchill: Well, were not effectively accepted.

Mr Bevin: We accepted the ten points. Mr Truman only accepted one – the 100,000. We accepted the lot.

Mr Churchill: If I may quote the right hon Gentleman, 'This is my speech.' No agreement was reached upon this issue. At length, in February 1947, the right hon. Gentleman announced that he had decided to refer the matter to the United Nations. But having done so, what happened? A United Nations Committee was set up to examine the matter. It recommended the termination of the Mandate, and, by a majority vote, it recommended the policy of the partition of Palestine.

This decision was endorsed by the United Nations Assembly on 29 November 1947. Yet, though they had referred the matter to the United Nations for a solution, His Majesty's Government were not prepared to accept their decision. Indeed, they refused to allow the United Nations Palestine Commission to enter the territory of Palestine until a fortnight before the termination of the Mandate. And so it went on. His Majesty's Government were always one, or even two, and sometimes three, steps behind.

The Secretary of State for the Colonies (Mr Creech Jones): I think that, for the sake of accuracy, this rumour, which has been so often repeated, should be denied. The British Government suggested that it would not be wise for the Palestine Commission to go to Palestine more than a fortnight before the Mandate came to an end. (Hon. Members: 'Why?') I met the Palestine Commission on behalf of the Government and discussed their entrance into Palestine, and it was understood that they would come to London at the end of March and discuss with us their entrance into Palestine which would probably

[1] This note was written by Robert Rhodes James, editor of *His Complete Speeches*.

be sometime in the early part of April. That was four or five, possibly six weeks before the Mandate expired.

Mr Churchill: What happened?

Mr Creech Jones: I think this untruth ought to be completely repudiated. What happened was that the Palestine Commission reported to the Security Council that they could not implement the Resolution of 29 November. Subsequently, the Security Council summoned a Special General Assembly in order that the whole Resolution of 29 November should be brought into review.

Mr Churchill: The Foreign Secretary will be grateful for the chivalrous aid which his colleague from the Colonial Office has brought to his notice. In the long interruption which he made, I did not gather from him at what date before the evacuation the United Nations Commission actually began to travel about Palestine.

Mr Creech Jones: The Palestine Commission reported to the Security Council that it was quite unable to implement the Resolution of 29 November and accordingly remained in New York because it could not implement the Resolution which had been passed.

Mr Churchill: It is quite simple. They did not go. And so it went on. I am sorry if hon. Gentlemen do not like the argument I have to unfold. They must not shrink from bearing these strokes. We bear with what fortitude we can summon the heavy blows struck us by the Foreign Secretary, the Prime Minister and others, and similar equanimity and toleration should prevail in the ranks of our opponents. His Majesty's Government, in the whole of this matter, have always been one, or even two, and sometimes three, steps behind the march of events. When the State of Israel was proclaimed, it was recognized at once by the Americans. His Majesty's Government could at least have accepted the principle of partition laid down in the United Nations Resolution. When they finally accepted that principle in the Bernadotte Report of September last, why could they not have faced reality and accorded de facto recognition to Israel?

I have told the tale of different aspects of this story so often that I cannot but mention today the salient features. These have led us, through vast waste of money, to the repeated loss of British lives, to humiliation of every kind, to the fomenting of injurious hatreds, to a position where Britain has given up every interest she possessed and abandoned the task for which all parties in this island had laboured for a quarter of a century, and has quitted – or half quitted, because in some ways we have not; we still manage to get the disadvantages – the scene of so much valuable work and achievement, amid the scorn and hatred of Arab and Jew and the contemptuous disdain of the civilized world. That is what we are asked to believe deserves our general confidence and approbation – the victory of patience and phlegm in the long run.

But with us it is not a case of being wise after the event. It was more than a year before I realized that the Foreign Secretary and the Government had no plan or policy. It took another year after I had urged the Government to quit Palestine, if they had no plan, for them to take the decision to go. They took it a year later when everything was more difficult. Great opportunities were cast away. They took it in such a way as to render themselves unable to bring perfectly legitimate pressure to bear upon the United States to leave the side-lines and come into the arena of helpful action. They lost the opportunities of that year since they were told they had better go. And we paid the bill of £80,000,000 for the troops alone for maintaining order under most trying conditions and facing the horrible murder of many of our brave soldiers.

All that is in the past. We have at length evacuated Palestine. Yet we still find ourselves involved in its problems. This fact has furnished the Foreign Secretary with the opportunity for making further public blunders and committing himself to more painfully obvious misjudgments. There never has been, in my belief, the slightest comprehension of the Palestine problems by the right hon. Gentleman. Every word that he says in his speech is known, by those of us who have lived our lives with this great problem for many years, to be subject to wrong emphasis. Nor will he take advice.

It is six weeks ago that we formally advised the Government to make a de facto recognition of the Israeli Government. The right hon. Gentleman brushed our proposal aside. What is he going to do now? It is difficult to discover, from what he said, what he is going to do. Perhaps he has not yet made up his mind? Perhaps it is a question of how much pressure is brought to bear upon him before he does so? He has lost opportunities and argued for delay and for putting off the action which the great majority of the people know it would have been wise and practicable to take.

I am quite sure that the right hon. Gentleman will have to recognize the Israeli Government, and that cannot be long delayed. I regret that he has not had the manliness to tell us in plain terms tonight, and that he preferred to retire under a cloud of inky water and vapour, like a cuttlefish, to some obscure retreat. De facto recognition has never depended upon an exact definition of territorial frontiers. There are half a dozen countries in Europe which are recognized today whose territorial frontiers are not finally settled. Surely, Poland is one. It is only with the general Peace Treaty that a final settlement can be made. Whoever said, 'How can we recognize a country whose limits and boundaries are not carefully defined?' I am astonished to find the right hon. Gentleman giving any countenance to it. What trouble, what inconvenience, what humbling rebuffs should we have avoided if the Foreign Secretary had taken the sincere advice tendered to him from this side of the House. The only reason, or, certainly, one particular reason, offered by him was irrelevant and incorrect. He talked about the mistakes which some countries have made in hastily recognizing Indonesia. Recognition, or hasty recognition, he thought, would be a bad precedent, but how absurd it is to compare the so-called Republic of Indonesia with the setting-up in Tel Aviv of a Government of the State of Israel, with an effective organization and a victorious army.

Whether the right hon Gentleman likes it or not, and whether we like it or not, the coming into being of a Jewish State in Palestine is an event in world history to be viewed in the perspective, not of a generation or a century, but in the perspective of a thousand, two thousand or even three thousand years. That is a standard of temporal values or time values which seems very much out of accord with the perpetual click-clack of our rapidly-changing moods and of the age in which we live. This is an event in world history. How vain it is to compare it with the recognition, or the claims to recognition, by certain countries, of the Communist banditti which we are resisting in Malaya or of the anarchic forces which the Dutch are trying to restrain in Indonesia.

No one has done more to build up a Jewish National Home in Palestine than the Conservative Party, and many of us have always had in mind that this might some day develop into a Jewish State. (*Interruption.*) I am speaking for myself, anyhow. The hon Gentleman always seems to be faced with the difficulty of knowing which side he is on in any controversy, and of always being faced with the danger of trying to be on both sides at once. I will not discuss the matter any further, but I warn him to be a little more careful. I say that the Conservative Party has done a great task over twenty-five years, with Parliaments which had a Conservative majority, in trying to build a Jewish National Home in Palestine, and now that it has come into being, it is England that refuses to recognize it, and, by our actions, we find ourselves regarded as its most bitter enemies. All this is due, not only to mental inertia or lack of grip on the part of the Ministers concerned, but also, I am afraid, to the very strong and direct streak of bias and prejudice on the part of the Foreign Secretary.

I do not feel any great confidence that he has not got a prejudice against the Jews in Palestine. I am sure that he thought the Arab League was stronger and that it would win if fighting broke out, but I do not suggest for a moment that he wished to provoke war. He was quite right in saying, in effect, that, in that particular quarrel, they needed very little provocation, but the course he took led inevitably and directly to a trial of strength, and the result was opposite to what I believe he expected it to be. I will say no more than that. Everyone has his feelings on this subject, and there is no unanimity of opinion on either side of the House, but, at any rate, the course he took led directly to a trial of strength and it turned out in the opposite way in which he expected, acting on the advice of his military advisers, I have no doubt, and against the recorded opinion of Lord Wavell, as to which side was the stronger.

I certainly felt that the spectacle of the Jewish settlements being invaded from all sides – from Syria, Transjordan and Egypt and with a lot of our tanks and modern tackle was, on the face of it, most formidable, but I believed that that combination would fall to pieces at the first check, and I adhered to the estimate I had formed in the war of the measure of the fighting qualities and the tough fibre of the Zionist community, and the support which it would receive from Zionists all over the world. But the Foreign Secretary was wrong, wrong in his facts, wrong in the mood, wrong in the method and wrong in the result, and we are very sorry about it for his sake and still more sorry about it for our own.

We have so managed our affairs as to find ourselves arrayed in this matter on the opposite side to the United States, to Soviet Russia, to the Palestine settlers and to Zionist supporters all over the world, and without – and I want my hon. Friends on this side to realize this – doing the slightest service to the Arab countries to whom we have very serious obligations. This is not at all a favourable conjunction for British interests, and it should have been the careful aim of the Foreign Office to avoid its being brought into being. It makes our position a very weak one and it predisposes UNO against us on numbers alone. Our influence is therefore at a minimum as a result of our improvident diplomacy.

This is a poor and undeserved result of all that we have created and built up in Palestine by the goodwill and solid work of twenty-five years. We have lost the friendship of the Palestine Jews for the time being. I was glad to read a statement from Dr Weizmann the other day pleading for friendship between the new Israeli State and the Western world. I believe that will be its destiny. He was an old friend of mine for many years. His son was killed in the war fighting with us. I trust his influence may grow and that we shall do what we can, subject to our other obligations – because we cannot forget those other obligations – to add to his influence. I hope that later on a truer comprehension of the Zionist debt to this country will revive. Here I am in agreement with the right hon. Gentleman – I trust it will revive, but for the present we seem to have deprived ourselves of all the fruits of the past. Moreover, as I mentioned just now, the Foreign Secretary's policy has been the worst possible for the Arabs. I am sure we could have agreed immediately after the war upon a partition scheme which would have been more favourable to the Arabs.

The Prime Minister (Mr Attlee): May I ask the right hon Gentleman if he thought that could have been done, why did he not do it after the war? He was in power.

Mr Churchill: No. The world and the nation had the inestimable blessing of the right hon Gentleman's guidance. I am sure that we could have agreed immediately after the war upon a partition scheme which would have been more favourable to the Arabs than that which will now follow their unsuccessful recourse to arms.

Mr Thomas Reid (Swindon):[1] Agreed with whom? Would it not have led to a major war in the Near East if partition had been pursued?

Mr Churchill: I give my opinion. I am sure we could have made better arrangements for the Arabs at that time – I am not talking of the Jews – than will be possible after there has been this unfortunate recourse to arms. Indeed, the scheme of partition proposed by UNO was better than what they will get now, after their defeat. We are evidently in the presence here of prolonged, repeated and serious miscalculations on the part of the Foreign Secretary and his advisers and colleagues.

I do not propose to enter tonight upon the drawing of frontier lines or the details of any partition for which we should use our remaining influence, such as it is. I will, however, say that we ought not to grudge a fair share of the deserts of the Negeb to the Jews. It is nearly thirty years since I came officially and responsibly into this story. I have always felt that the Negeb should afford a means of expansion to the Jewish settlers in Palestine and offer future prospects to Zionist movements. But it is impossible to fly over these regions low down, as I did before the Second Great War, or travel through them to Petra and other places without seeing how fierce and barren these regions of the Negeb are. And yet they once held great cities and nourished important populations. The Jews, by the gift they have and by the means which they do not lack, have a way of making the desert bloom. Those who have seen it can testify. The Arabs, with all their dignity and grace, are primarily the children of the desert, and where they dwell, in this part of the world at least, and for the most part, the desert lands do not become reclaimed while the Arab control is complete over them.

Here let me say a word about how the British have treated the Arabs. I take up the cudgels not for one party or Government; I speak of twenty-five years of British policy and the settlement made after the First World War, supported by a Parliament with a great Conservative majority, in which I was prominently concerned, and which placed Feisal on the throne of Iraq and his dynasty is there today. I myself, with the advice and guidance of (T. E.) Lawrence, took steps to put Emir Abdullah[2] at Amman, where he is still after twenty-five years of shock and strain, always a good friend. We took all pains when we liberated Syria during a difficult moment in the last war to make sure that the Syrian Arabs had their full rights and independence, and although it meant bitter controversy with General de Gaulle we insisted upon that at a moment when, as everyone knows, our margin of control and subsistence was not large.

[1] Thomas Reid, 1881–1963. Educated at Queen's College, Cork, and Royal University, Dublin. Graduated, 1905, as Senior Classical Scholar, Senior Scholar of Jurisprudence, Economics and Modern History, and Ancient History. Mayor and Chairman, Colombo Municipal Council, 1919–24; Member of Ceylon Legislature, 1926–31. Chairman of League of Nations Commission, 1938. MP (Lab.) for Swindon Division of Wilts, 1945–50; for Borough of Swindon, 1950–5.

[2] Abdullah I bin al-Hussein, 1882–1951. Emir of Transjordan, 1921–46. King of Jordan, 1946–51.

I will not have it said that we have not behaved with loyalty to the Arabs or that what has been asked for the Jews, which was supported and sustained by the Conservative Party for so many years, to say nothing of the party opposite, has gone beyond what was just and fair, having regard to the fact that both these races have lived in Palestine for thousands of years side by side. Hon. Gentlemen do not seem to realize that Jew and Arab have always been there. They say, 'How would you like to have a piece of Scotland taken away and to have a lot of other races put in?' The two races have always been there, and I trust always will be there, happily.

In the Negeb there is at least an opportunity and indeed a hope of affording a refuge to the survivors of the Jewish community who have been massacred in so many parts of Europe and letting them try their best – and their efforts are amazing – to bring back into economic usefulness lands which the world cannot afford to leave lying idle. It is obvious that both Jews and Arabs must have access to the Red Sea through the Gulf of Aqaba. This has figured in most of the schemes of partition and it should be possible to reconcile competing claims with justice. The Gulf of Aqaba is in fact to the Red Sea, although on a smaller scale, what Trieste is to the Adriatic. The outlet here should certainly not be monopolized by either of the races who have dwelt together so long in this vast hinterland. It is therefore a place of special significance.

I do not intend today to try to judge whether the Government were right in the prevailing circumstances and in the aftermath of their evacuation of Palestine to send an armed British force to Aqaba. However, in view of our obligation to Abdullah and our treaty with him, I entirely agree that we could not disinterest ourselves in his fate or in that of his country. I should not like to see us repeat in Transjordania the behaviour the Government adopted in respect of our treaty obligations with the Indian Princes, and in particular with the Nizam of Hyderabad. I hope the Emir of Transjordania will have a better tale to tell of us. The act of sending a force to Aqaba did, however, wear an aspect of decision unusual in recent British policy in Palestine. I hope that, having gone there, we shall stay there, and keep an ample margin of force there, until the whole question has been finally decided by the United Nations Organization and until their award has been accepted and obeyed by both Jews and Arabs. We should support any steps taken to that end. We feel bound to make our protests and to dissociate ourselves from a policy of folly, fatuity and futility the like of which it is not easy to find in modern experience, for which the right hon Gentleman and the present Cabinet are responsible. But inside this large parade and presentation of mismanagement and misfortune there is an inset, a cameo, of inconsequence and muddle which cannot, I think, be matched. Here we have wrong thinking and imprudent acting presenting in miniature a working model – a working model of what all persons concerned in public affairs should strive to avoid by all means. A truce had been arranged and a cease fire was to take place at 2 p.m. that afternoon. Yet in the morning the Government – the Prime Minister very properly took full responsibility – sent a reconnaissance into the battle area or the fighting area of Royal Air Force planes which had on preceding days been flying in conjunction with Egyptian planes which were hostile to the other side, the Jewish forces. The pilots were, I am told, to a large extent, trainees – we shall know more about that from the inquiry – and were the product of the Air Ministry in its decline since the war. They were sent out under conditions which exposed them to the maximum danger.

This was no high altitude photographic operation. They were to fly low over areas where they knew hostilities were in progress. No warning had been sent to the Israeli forces, but restrictive orders were given to our pilots about not firing their guns except after having been fired upon effectively by others. The first reconnaissance was sent out on a wholly unnecessary mission, because there was a cease fire that evening. The second reconnaissance was sent out in order to ascertain what had happened to the first, but before the second could have got back the cease fire between Jews and Arabs had already taken place. Why expose our Forces, our young men, to such risks as that? It was in these circumstances that we had to endure the affront and injury for which our two young airmen[1] lost their lives.

When we turn to seek redress from UNO or from the Commissions on the spot, the international bodies, when we look to other nations for sympathy in the matter, we are asked certain questions. For instance, why should we go – this is one question – why should we go out over this area at the very moment of the cease fire? It is said on our behalf in reply that the Jews were invading Egypt and that they had no business to be there. But had not the Egyptians already invaded Palestine some time before? We are told also that the Jews had refused the United Nations observers the right to go to the area to see for themselves. I am told – I may not be correctly informed – but I am told on good information, as far as I can judge it, that the United Nations Palestine Commission has special aeroplanes painted white and known to both sides as entirely neutral and outside the conflict. Is that so? If it is so, why were they not used? Why were our planes used? A British reconnaissance at this moment was very inconsistent with the general purposes of the United Nations and detrimental to a peaceful settlement.

Then it is said the Americans encouraged us to find out what was going on. But is that, if true, a wholly convincing reason? If I criticize His Majesty's Government it is by no means to declare that the action of the United States in all these months has been impeccable. Considering the interests, sentimental and other, which they have in Palestine and Arabia they should have come to our aid two or three years ago, and I believe that if our policy had been wise and wisely conducted, and proper contacts made and developed, we

---

[1] On 7 Jan. 1949, Israeli aircraft attacked and shot down four Spitfire Mk XVIII fighters of RAF 208 Sqn. Two pilots, Ron Sayers and David Crossley Tattersfield, were killed.

should have had their assistance, as an alternative to the evacuation to which we were eventually forced. Curiosity to know what was going on would certainly not justify doing a thing so improvident as this sortie of aircraft at such a moment. I say it was the quintessence of maladresse of which the right hon. Gentleman and the Prime Minister, who takes the responsibility, were guilty. And now poor old Britain – Tories, Socialists, Liberals, Zionists, anti-Zionists, non-Zionists alike, we find ourselves shot down in an air skirmish, snubbed by the Israeli Government, who said, 'We understand you do not recognize us,' and with a marked lack of support from the international bodies upon which we depend so greatly and whose opinions we value so highly.

During all this period the Foreign Secretary has not been able to inform Abdullah, our faithful adherent, where he stood or what he would be wise to do. He has had to wait and guess. I am sure Abdullah would have done everything in his power to work for a peaceful solution with the Jews. I believe that the Government of Transjordan would have been glad to see His Majesty's Government having an effective representative in Tel Aviv during these difficult times. I am sure that Abdullah has done everything to work for a peaceful solution, which is in his interests, and to maintain his loyalty to the British who placed him in his seat at Amman and his brother[1] on the throne of Iraq. No fault can be alleged against him. If any attack were made across the Jordan we should be bound to go to his aid by every obligation of treaty and of honour.

There is this question – I think the last important one to which I wish to refer – of the Arab refugees, on which the right hon. Gentleman dwelt with emphasis and with indignant eloquence. Certainly, it involves much human suffering. The right hon. Gentleman's remark about the policy I put in a memorandum in 1922 shows how very superficial is his knowledge of this question. The whole point of our settlement was that immigration was to be free, but not beyond the limits of economic absorptive power. We could not have had it said that newcomers were coming in, pushing out those who had lived there for centuries. But the newcomers who were coming in brought work and employment with them, and the means of sustaining a much larger population than had lived in Palestine and Transjordan. They brought the hope with them of a far larger population than existed in Palestine at the time of Our Lord. One has only to look up to the hills that once were cultivated and then were defaced by centuries of medieval barbarism, to see what has been accomplished.

In twenty-five years the Jewish population of Palestine doubled or more than doubled, but so did the Arab population of the same areas of Palestine. As the Jews continued to reclaim the country, plant the orange groves, develop the water system, electricity and so forth, employment and means of livelihood were found for ever larger numbers of Arabs – 400,000 or 500,000

---

[1] Faisal I bin Hussein Ali al-Hashemi.

more Arabs found their living there and the relations of the two races in the Jewish areas were tolerable in spite of external distractions and all kinds of disturbances. General prosperity grew. The idea that only a limited number of people can live in a country is a profound illusion; it all depends on their co-operative and inventive power. There are more people today living twenty stories above the ground in New York than were living on the ground in New York 100 years ago. There is no limit to the ingenuity of man if it is properly and vigorously applied under conditions of peace and justice.

When the British Government quitted the scene and the Arab armies from Syria, Transjordania and finally in considerable strength from Egypt rolled forward to extinguish the Jewish National Home, all this Arab population fled in terror to behind the advancing forces of their own religion. Their condition is most grievous, and I agree that it should certainly not be neglected by the Government. The one great remedial measure is peace and a lasting settlement. The Jews need the Arabs. If we can get peace the problem of the refugees will be reduced to one-third, possibly one-quarter, perhaps it will disappear altogether. I do not think we shall find – I make this prediction – that there will be, once fighting stops and some kind of partition is arranged, any difficulty in the great bulk of the present refugees returning to do work essential to the growing prosperity and development of the Jewish settlement in Palestine.

I thank the House very much for allowing me to speak at such length on this topic with which I have been connected for so many years, and on which I feel so very strongly and have always tried to form my own opinions. All this Debate is, of course, on a small scale compared with the sombre march of events throughout the world. But it is a disquieting thought that the mismanagement we notice here in the working model may perhaps be typical of what is proceeding over much wider spheres under the present Government. However that may be, His Majesty's Opposition cannot allow themselves to be involved in this Palestine fiasco and muddle. We must take this opportunity of severing ourselves beyond all doubt or question from these latest acts of mismanagement on the Palestine question. But also we must tonight make our protest against the course of action prolonged over nearly four years which has deprived Britain of the credit she had earned, and of the rights and interests she had acquired, and made her at once the mockery and scapegoat of so many States who have never made any positive contribution of their own.

January 1949

Henry Channon: diary
('Chips', pages 433–4)

27 January 1949

Woke with a violent headache and found that my temperature was 103 degrees. This would happen on the day I was to lunch with Winston. But I was determined to go, and set off for Hyde Park Gate, where I found the street enlivened by the presence of a policeman, and three MPs – all too early, like me. We went in, and I was at once struck by the air of elegance and tidiness that the house had. Mrs Churchill greeted me with 'Hello Chips' as did daughter Mary. . . . Winston soon joined us and was in a rippling mood. He looked small, even diminutive, and his face was pink as a baby's. Clemmie referred to him as 'Winston darling'. She is obviously devoted to him. He greeted me affectionately and put me next to him at luncheon. The dining-room looks onto the garden. Food excellent – and four bottles of champagne – Winston talked of Southend, and suddenly, to my surprise, burst into an old Southend music hall song of the 80s, singing two verses of it lustily. Finally the conversation got into politics and last night's debate: he is immensely pleased with the figures and thinks that we may have deflated Bevin a bit. He then said that he was infinitely bored by the Lynskey Tribunal[1] and its findings; and that the whole thing was a disgrace to our way of life. About 3.30 I rose and party broke up. Very successful – but I still wonder why I was asked?

Pamela Churchill to Clementine Churchill
(Churchill papers, 1/46)

27 January 1949   Royal Hotel Winter Palace
Gstaad

My dear Clemmie,

I cannot tell you how wonderfully well Little Winston is. He has already gained four pounds, and his appetite is enormous and his cheeks bright pink. I only wish you could all see him now. He has completely forgotten his home sickness, and has entered fully into the school life. Today I took him and four friends to tea – needless to say they were all English boys.

I am so relieved that he is so well here, and I finally feel it has been worth all the bother and complications that had to be gone through to get him to Le Rosey. Even the permanent catarrh he always had has disappeared. His knee

---

[1] Tribunal of inquiry convened in 1948 to investigate potential corruption of civil servants and Government ministers, and specifically the activities of the fraudster Sydney Stanley (see p. 1319 n.1 below), who was providing the terrorist group Irgun with secret information. Found several Government ministers to have taken bribes from Stanley. Led to the establishment of the Committee on Intermediaries.

still is not quite right, and I have told the school to get an X-ray done of it. Randolph promised me that he would send the X-ray photos out here – we've waited and waited but they've never arrived.

I had a letter from my lawyer a week ago, reminding me that before long I must do something about that application. I had hoped to hear from you – your views and whether you thought you could persuade Randolph to stop trying to treat me as if I were the governess rather than the mother of his son. It is too humiliating to have to ask Randolph permission for every move Winston makes. Even thinking of the small mindedness of it makes me angry. Randolph hasn't even sent the child a postcard since he's been at school. Forgive this outburst, but it seems foolish and senseless for Randolph and me to quarrel over something on which we are basically in agreement. But if there is no other way we must quarrel, and the one who'll really suffer will be the child.

If you have time I would be so grateful for a letter from you.

As I think you know my flat is rented to Carry Grant[1] for three months, so I do not intend to come home yet and this address will always find me.

I do hope you had a lovely time at Monte Carlo, and that you are feeling well. I think of you often and send you and Winston my affectionate love.

Sir Alexander Cadogan to Winston S. Churchill
(Churchill papers, 4/225)

31 January 1949　　　　　　　　　　　　　　　　　　　　　　　　New York

My dear Winston,

As promised, I have dug my diaries out of the Foreign Office, and I enclose a transcript of what they contain of the Atlantic Meeting.[2]

As I feared, they are of little use. I am afraid my diary is not a historic document. I have generally left the recording of historic events to the historian, who will be plagued by a mass of material which he will be embarrassed to disentangle. My diary is merely jottings of some personal impressions. If ever I had the inclination, or ability, to write of these events, it would serve as a prompter, to me, reminding me of many other things that could be drawn from my memory. To you, these jottings will mean little, but I send them to you in the hope that they may at least remind you, if you read them, of some of the lighter moments which the conscientious historian would be inclined

---

[1] Archibald Alexander Leach, 1904–86. Known as Cary Grant. Actor. Born in Horfield, Bristol, England. Ran away from home aged 13 and participated in a range of small performances on stage in England and America. Contracted by Paramount in 1932. Went on to act in over 20 films, including Hitchcock's *North by Northwest* and von Sternberg's *Blonde Venus* with Marlene Dietrich. Nominated twice for Academy Awards in 1944. Hon. Oscar, 1970.

[2] Meeting of 14 Aug. 1941 between Churchill and Roosevelt, which resulted in the Atlantic Charter.

to disregard. So forgive any apparent flippancy. This record is only the ragged fringe of great events, and is not meant to be more.

I hope you are flourishing. I am much looking forward to Volume II. I can't ask more than that it should provide me with as much interest and give me as much pleasure as Volume I.

Sir Simon Marks[1] to Winston S. Churchill
(Churchill papers, 2/163)

31 January 1949

Dear Mr Churchill,

May I personally, thank you for your powerful intervention in the crucial Debate in the House of Commons,[2] which brought about a change in His Majesty's Government's policy towards Israel.

I know that our mutual friend, Dr Weizmann, will be thrilled at the news, and particularly at your remark that this is a great event in world history.

With my best wishes for your health,

Marcus Sieff to Winston S. Churchill
(Churchill papers, 2/46)[3]

31 January 1949

Dear Mr Churchill,

I heard your magnificent speech[4] in the Palestine Debate in which the emergence of the State of Israel was placed in its true historical perspective.

I know from my experience, not only here but in the Middle East in the early years of the War, how great was the part you played in the last quarter of a century in constructing the bridges between this country and the Jews in Palestine and how high the name of Britain stood in their community.

The Palestine policy which the present government has hitherto pursued, has largely destroyed those bridges. You have again given a lead, which, if sincerely followed by the government, will go a long way to restoring those ties to the advantage of all moderate people, be they gentile, Arab or Jew and for which all moderate people must be grateful.

---

[1] Simon Marks, 1888–1964. Son of joint founder, with Thomas Spencer, of the retail chain Marks & Spencer, which he developed into a leading business institution. Joined RA on outbreak of WWI. Following Balfour Declaration of 1917, seconded to Weizmann to establish and direct Zionist HQ in London. Knighted, 1944. Baron, 1961.
[2] Of Jan. 26, reproduced above (pp. 1297–1308).
[3] This letter was handwritten.
[4] Of Jan. 26, reproduced above (pp. 1297–1308).

February
1949

Winston S. Churchill to General Lord Ismay
(Churchill papers, 4/19)

1 February 1949

My dear Pug,

Thank you so much for all your corrections, which I am incorporating in Volumes III and IV. It would be a help if you could get me the exact dates when Eisenhower and Clark first came to see me at the White House. I think it must have been in the June visit because I do remember handing them, or reading them, my paper about the scale and spirit of a great landing operation, and our having some talk about it.

Also:
1. When exactly did Ike and Mark Clark first come for their ten days' reconnaissance?
2. When did Eisenhower come over here and settle down and actually assume command?
3. When did Mark Clark leave for his secret visit to North Africa?
4. When did Bedell Smith arrive as Chief of the Staff? You say in September, but what date?

With this knowledge I can reconstruct and fit in its proper place the paragraph which now figures on page two of Chapter XVII, and which will be expanded into some account of friendly relations. I am sure these began before I went to Cairo, and were renewed and developed afterwards on my return.

I also want to write a fuller account of my second visit to the White House about June 18, 1942. This was the one when you came with me and the bad news about Tobruk came in. We started from Stranraer in the Catalina (Avalon or Ascalon?) and flew over Gander, where we did not land, arriving in the Potomac in the evening. A long flight. Did we not dine at the Embassy and fly the next morning to Hyde Park? I remember a very bumpy landing on the local airfield. Here at Hyde Park, in the tiny little room the President worked in, we settled the question of the atomic bomb and made the Treaty which lies in the Government archives. Then we returned to New York and heard the bad news about Tobruk. The next night we went with Marshal by train to review the American Army Corps in Carolina. We returned to England by the Catalina. All these details should be checked. You no doubt have a diary of notes. But the point I particularly want is this; what was my main purpose in crossing the Atlantic this time. It must have been a very serious one. My own feeling is that it was about the atomic bomb and that other purposes were subsidiary. Pray let me know at your convenience how matters stand.

I am inserting the tale of the old woman. It comes in later and is not quite as you say. The delinquent went to post some letters and dropped this document out of his pocket by the pillar box. I think the incident should be woven into a considerable passage about our anxieties and efforts to keep secrecy during September and October.

General Lord Ismay to Winston S. Churchill
(*Churchill papers, 4/220*)

2 February 1949

My dear Mr Churchill,

Some time ago you asked me whether I remembered the reasons that impelled you to replace Wavell by Auchinleck, and I replied that you and all of us in London got the feeling that Wavell was a tired man.

Ian Jacob reminded me last night of an episode which confirmed this view, and which I now recollect very vividly. I can see you now, holding out both your hands as though you had a fishing rod in each of them, and you said: 'I feel that I have got a tired fish on this rod, and a very lively one on the other.' You were very pleased with Auchinleck at that time because he had been so forward in the Iraqi affair.

Winston S. Churchill: speech
(*'Winston S. Churchill, His Complete Speeches', volume 7, pages 7783–4*)

3 February 1949   The Guildhall, London

PRESENTATION OF GROTIUS MEDAL[*]

[. . .] I value this presentation as one of the highest honours I have received. I have been deeply touched by the kindness with which I have always been treated by the Dutch people. Queen Juliana is the reigning sovereign of a State which has played so fine a part not only in the history of Europe, but in the cause of freedom. In my view, the Dutch are now striving resolutely to rescue true progress in Indonesia from the twin monstrosities of anarchy and Communism.

Amid many difficulties and grave perils, Britain and the Netherlands, together with their neighbours are striving toward a unity that had never existed in Europe at any time since the fall of the Roman Empire. We are moving forward in goodly company and from far across the Atlantic Ocean there comes a mighty surge of help and strength.

Great progress has been made since the time, more than three years ago, when I ventured to expound the view of a United Europe at the University of Zurich. In the formation of a Western Union a real step toward the establishment of United Europe was recognized.

The structure of the world security should be founded on regional organizations. They are an indispensable part of any world structure worthy of the name. That is what is being striven for in Western Union, which is a stepping stone to United Europe.

. . . At the congress at The Hague last May the creation of a European Assembly was conceived. This month in Brussels a further step will be taken. There must be a European Supreme Court to which breaches of the Declaration of Human Rights, so magnificently proclaimed at Geneva by Powers great and small, can be referred and defended. These aspirations are shared by hundreds of millions of men in Europe and cannot be achieved without the action of Governments. Neither can they be achieved by Governments alone. They must be buoyed up by a rising tide of conscious educated public opinion by which responsible Governments will be aided, stimulated, and sustained. In this way alone can the skeleton structure of world governments be clothed with the fine flesh and blood of a living organism and the acts of State be confirmed by the passionate heart beats of millions of men. In the shadow of the sword it is felt that Grotius and the wisdom of the past have given their blessings to our labours and their guidance to our cause.

* The Grotius Medal was instituted in the Netherlands in 1925 on the tercentenary of the publication of *De Jure Belli et Pacis*, Hugo Grotius' great work on international law.

Winston S. Churchill: speech
(Hansard)

3 February 1949   House of Commons

MINISTERS AND PUBLIC SERVANTS
(OFFICIAL CONDUCT)

I do not feel it necessary this afternoon to trespass long upon the attention of the House. I cannot feel that any party issue is involved. This House of Commons has shown itself vigilant in the protection of its honour, and has realized that it is with its honour that the dignity and strength of democratic

Parliamentary institutions are concerned. The honour of the Labour Party, of the Conservative Party, of the Liberal Party are not the interests of those parties alone but of the British nation, whom all parties try to serve according to their lights – or want of lights. Many odd things happen abroad, but we are all glad today to feel that there is no difference between us and the Socialist Government, between us and the Labour Party, or the great trade union institutions of our country upon the need to keep our public life clean and healthy and to root out corruption in any form.

The course and procedure which the Government adopted when these matters[1] were brought to their notice were not prompted by any party interest. Indeed, it might well be thought that the procedure which they adopted was the least suited to their interests, and also most severe upon the persons concerned. Nevertheless, it is our considered view that the right course was to invoke the 1921 Act and have these matters examined by the statutory Tribunal.

We accept the recommendations and the Reports of the statutory Tribunal. The Tribunal, in its good faith, impartiality, competence and independence cannot be impugned or challenged. There is no need for the House, in my view, to add to what they have had and no need for them to subtract from it. The conduct of the Attorney-General,[2] although a Minister of the Government is involved, has been correct and unbiased. There is, therefore, no difference between the Government and the Opposition upon the steps which were taken by the Prime Minister and his colleagues in dealing with the lamentable matters with which they were contented. Still less is there any suggestion that the Labour Government have not done their best to sustain those standards of decent behaviour and to condemn and punish any departure from those standards of which we have always been proud in this island. I have some other remarks to make, but these are definitely subordinate to the major premises which I have submitted to the House.

I am sorry that I cannot avoid making some comments on the personal issues involved. I am personally acquainted with Mr Gibson,[3] who was recommended to me some time ago on high authority as a most suitable representative of the trade unions to help in the movement with which I and others were concerned for the United Europe. When party trouble came, Mr Gibson did not desert us. I grieve indeed to see him fall into all this trouble. I cannot say, in the face of the Report, that he does not deserve to suffer, but

---

[1] Rumours of fraud and bribery implicating Government ministers and civil servants. See p. 1309 n.1 above.

[2] Sir Hartley Shawcross.

[3] George Gibson, 1885–1953. Member, TUC General Council, 1928–48. Vice-Chairman, National Savings Committee, 1939–49. President, TUC, 1940–1; Chairman, General Council, 1941. Director, Bank of England, 1946–8. Associated with fraudster Sydney Stanley. Found by the Lynskey Tribunal, 1948, to have used his official influence for personal gain. The resulting scandal forced Gibson to resign from all official positions.

we all feel that he has paid a very good service. He has acted with propriety in resigning his directorship of the Bank of England and also his position on the nationalised Electricity Board. This action on his part renders it unnecessary, it seems to me, for such issues to be further discussed in this House.

We accept the Attorney-General's view that a criminal prosecution is not required by the process of law, and one is certainly glad to feel that it is not required for any other purpose. I should also like to make it clear that the Conservative Party will not tolerate any suggestion that the leaders of the great trade unions in this country are susceptible to the temptations of corruption, or that these vital organs in our system of government are not conducted in accordance with British traditions and standards.

I come now to the case of the hon. Member for Sowerby (Mr Belcher),[1] to whose speech we could not listen without pain. He was a Minister of the Crown and a Member of the House. We are all glad that he has chosen himself to resign not only his office but his seat in Parliament. I do not feel that I can do otherwise in this matter than recall to the House the precedents which we followed on the last occasion when the procedure of the special statutory Tribunal was used. This special procedure of law was prescribed to deal, not only with matters where common criminalities and specific charges were involved, but with the special position, obligation and behaviour of Ministers of the Crown.

There is a gulf fixed between private conduct and that of persons in an office, and above all, in a Ministerial position. The abuse or misuse for personal gain of the special powers and privileges which attach to office under the State is rightly deemed most culpable, and, quite apart from any question of prosecution under the law, is decisive in respect of Ministers. I do not think I can do better than quote the words which the Prime Minister himself used when Leader of the Opposition in 1936, 13 years ago, on the J. H. Thomas case[2] – the last occasion, I think, when this particular procedure of the statutory Tribunal was invoked. The right hon Gentleman said:

> The Debate today does not raise in any way at all a party issue. It is a mere House of Commons matter, concerning the honour of Members of this

---

[1] John William Belcher, 1905–64. Began career as a railway clerk. Married, 1927, Louise Moody. Lecturer, Ministry of Information, 1940–5. MP (Lab.), Sowerby Div., West Riding of Yorks, 1945–9. Parliamentary Secretary, Board of Trade, 1946–8. Networked with fraudster and 'contact man' Sidney Stanley. Accepted various gifts from Stanley, leading to an enquiry led by Sir George Lynskey to determine whether he acted unethically. Was found to have been influenced in his conduct as minister. First Labour politician to resign in disgrace over a political scandal. Steward of the Manor of Northestead, 1949. Later returned to work as a railway clerk, becoming an assistant goods agent.

[2] James Henry Thomas, 1874–1949. Began work as an errand boy at the age of nine. Later an engine-cleaner, fireman and engine-driver. Founder member, National Union of Railwaymen; General Secretary, 1918–24, 1925–31. MP (Lab.) for Derby, 1910–31; (Nat. Lab.), 1931–6. PC, 1917. Lord Privy Seal and Minister of Employment, 1929–30. Secretary of State for the Dominions, 1930–5; for the Colonies, 1935–6. Resigned from public life, 1936, having been found to have leaked details of proposed tax changes in the national budget to Stock Exchange speculators.

House ... and the two Members concerned have been found by the Tribunal to have acted in a manner inconsistent with the position which they held in public life. I agree entirely with the Prime Minister that that alone is a very heavy punishment. Other consequences have followed, such as the necessity, which they have rightly realised, that they must vacate their seats, and I do not think that anyone of us would wish, by any word of ours, to add to this punishment. ... We must all sympathise with the families of the Members who necessarily suffer, though entirely innocent, and I think we all have a very natural reluctance to pass judgement on others. We are all conscious of our own faults; at the same time, we must not allow personal sympathy for men who are down to lead us to condone in any way the seriousness of the offences committed. It is our clear duty to vindicate the honour of this House. We owe that duty not only to this House but to democratic government and to the servants of the State. There are many attacks made on democratic government today and any action of the nature of utilization of a public position for private gain cuts at the root of the democratic government. The corruption which accompanies dictatorships is generally hidden; the corruption which enters into a democracy is brought to light and must be dealt with drastically and if there is any suggestion at all, it is that as a democratic assembly we are bound to take action – (Official Report, 11th June, 1936; Vol. 313, c. 420–1.)

That is what the Prime Minister, the then Leader of the Opposition, said thirteen years ago and, I must say that he has certainly lived up to his well-chosen words (Hon Members: 'Hear, hear'.) Holding the position which I do, and which he then held, I cannot find any better words upon this subject, which incidentally, in my opinion, dispose of the question of whether or not the seat of the hon. Member for Sowerby should have been vacated by him. We are ready to accept the Government view that no prosecution is necessary in the case of the hon. Member of Sowerby.

We are glad that the Tribunal has declared that no taint or reproach of corruption lies upon the various other Ministers whose names were mentioned during – to repeat the phrase which the right hon. Gentleman has already quoted from Mr Baldwin –

the unthinkable cruelty of modern publicity. – (Official Report, 11th June, 1936; Vol. 313, c. 419.)

It certainly has been very unpleasant to see our papers clouded by these continuous accounts. It was, perhaps, their duty to report the Tribunal proceedings, but the pain that it must have caused to individuals whose names were mentioned casually and whose characters have been completely cleared, is one which we can most easily comprehend. I am bound to say that whereas the honour of those Ministers has been effectively cleared, the competence of some of them in the discharge of their departmental duties is not free from criticism in all respects and would seem to require at a later stage the attention of the Prime Minister. I must say that I think the head of a Department ought to know pretty well how his immediate Parliamentary subordinates are carrying on.

The right hon. Gentleman at the end of his speech made certain proposals. There is to be a committee to inquire into how guidance can be given to Ministers in various respects, and the right hon. Gentleman then spoke of some conversations which I gather he had had with you Mr Speaker.

The Prime Minister: I think the right hon. Gentleman has confused two things. One thing I said was that I propose to give guidance in a certain matter; the other was a question of an inquiry by a committee.

Mr Churchill: Yes, a committee to inquire into contact men. In addition there was a question of some change in the rules affecting entry of strangers and others into this House, and hospitalities which are shared or given here. We on this side of the House have not noticed the need for such changes, and it is very difficult to change the freedom which has been indulged in by Members of all parties in the House of Commons. If it is abused, this is the kind of occasion which cleanses that abuse and makes it very unlikely that it will continue. If at times persons outside the House have come in as guests and paid for refreshments and so forth, all this will undoubtedly be stiffened up by what has occurred.

I am doubtful myself whether we should do well to take steps which, after all, do imply a reflection on the conduct of the Members of the House of Commons as a whole. I do not like that. I should warn the Prime Minister that a great many more difficulties may be found in dealing with any evils of this kind that exist, than there are in discerning cases when they have occurred. I, therefore, hope, before any decision should be taken with regard to making rules, that there will be some consultation between the leaders of all parties. After all, we are Members of Parliament, and if we cannot manage the conduct of our personal relationships within this building in a decent and reasonable manner, we have smudged ourselves in a manner which no statutory Tribunal has ever done.

I have said all I wish to say upon the Parliamentary and personal aspects of this painful incident which, as I have indicated, has already in my opinion received an amount of publicity beyond what was required for the strict cleanliness of our public life. I trust, however, that the most severe methods open to the law will be used against the disreputable persons who have been concerned in attempts to corrupt our public men or have been concerned in the processes which the Tribunal has censured.

The House will have regretted to hear from the Attorney-General, though I cannot blame him, that he saw grave difficulty in prosecuting some of these figures, particularly the notorious figure, the so-called Stanley.[1] The House will accept the assurance of the right hon. and learned Gentleman that the full rigour of the law, such as it may be, will be applied to any persons who have been found by this Tribunal to be dabbling in corruption. By this I do not mean a measure of deportation but the subjection of the persons involved to whatever prosecution for criminal offences the law renders possible, subject, of course, to the full protection of the rights of the accused. If it is found that nothing can be done, I think it will be a disadvantage of our course of affairs to have people going round trying to suborn and attempting to lead people into evil courses, worming their way into their confidence, and so forth, and offering bribes from motives of corruption. Whether that sort of conduct succeeds or not, it should be visited with the utmost severity that the law allows. If we are told that the law does not allow, I am no judge there.

All this leads me to the last series of comments which I shall venture to offer to the House. We are all Britons and we are all brothers, and we are proud of our decent, tolerant, comprehending life at home. We have been brought up to believe that our standards are certainly not inferior to those of any other long-established or newly-formed system of society in the world, but we must beware of putting too great a strain on British human nature. Some time ago I ventured to remind the House of the French proverb: 'Chase Nature away, and she returns at a gallop.' If you destroy a free market you create a black market. If you make 10,000 regulations you destroy all respect for the law. As Burke said, although I have not been able before this Debate to find his exact words: 'Those who make professions above the ordinary custom of society, will often be found in practice to fall far below them.'

This unpleasant case which has riveted the attention of the public, and which is before us now, warns us of perils to our society which cannot be warded off merely by inflicting severe penalties on those who are found guilty. There is the law of the Land – the ancient common law of England – which still remains to guide the vast English-speaking world. There is the immense force of public opinion in free and civilised countries. There are the honest and honourable conventions of British business life without the observance of which, few men can obtain or maintain any position of responsibility in the commercial world. All these are needed to maintain a healthy, democratic civilisation.

If a whole vast catalogue of new crimes and penalties is suddenly brought into being, and a whole series of actions hitherto free and unchallenged in the

---

[1] Sydney Stanley, 1902–69. Born Solomon Wulkan. Polish immigrant to the UK. Fraudulent businessman. Aliases included Solomon Koszyski, Stanley Rechtand, Schlomo ben Chaim and Blotz. His association with George Gibson, the Director of the Bank of England, and John Belcher, a junior minister in the Labour Party, led to the Lynskey Tribunal in 1948, resulting in both Belcher's and Gibson's resignations.

ordinary play of daily life are to be judged shameful and punishable, Parliament must be careful to carry the public conscience with it. If the permission of State officials has to be sought in innumerable cases for all kinds of trivial but necessary and unavoidable transactions hitherto entirely untrammelled, you will be opening the door to difficulties, stresses and strains to which our social system has not hitherto been exposed. I was in the United States more than once during Prohibition. I saw there, with some complacency a general breakdown and contempt of a law, imposed no doubt from the highest motives, but which did not carry with it the support of public opinion or fit the ordinary needs of the people.

We, on this side of the House, are convinced that the enforcement, or the attempted enforcement, as a peace time policy, of thousands of war-time regulations by scores of thousands of war-time or post-war officials, whatever penalties Parliament may decree, will result in a breaking down of that respect for law, custom, and tradition which has played so large a part in the reputation of our peoples and was so vital a factor in our survival during the period of mortal peril through which we have passed. That is no doubt a theme which will play its part in our future discussions, and its lessons must be impressed upon the nation.

I wish to end where I began, namely, that we approve the course which the Government have taken in appointing the Tribunal; that we accept the measured and carefully limited conclusion to which it has come: that we are glad to see so many public men whose names have been mentioned, as I feared they would be by idle or malicious gossip, cleared from reproach; and above all that we repudiate all slanders upon the general conduct of British public life where questions of tolerating personal corruption and dishonour are concerned.

Winston S. Churchill to Timothy Kerrigan[1]
(*Churchill papers, 2/86*)

7 February 1949

My dear Lord Mayor,

I much regret not having answered your most kind letter earlier. I read with pleasure the newspaper accounts of the debate in the City Council, and of the spirited and effective manner in which you defended my claim to the honour of the 'Churchill Way'.

You send me now a most attractive invitation, which I and my family would gladly accept. I am however so much burdened at the present time that I must beg you to excuse me. I have the most vivid memories of my visit to Cardiff, and of your hospitality and consideration. I have never seen crowds more

---

[1] Timothy James Kerrigan. Former postman; elected Lord Mayor of Cardiff, 1949

friendly or enthusiastic in any of the very numerous cities in which I have been welcome.

I see that one of the Labour men referred to Tonypandy as a great crime I had committed in the past. I am having the facts looked up and will write to you again upon the subject. According to my recollection the action I took at Tonypandy was to stop the troops being sent to control the strikers for fear of shooting, and I was much attacked by the Conservative Opposition for this 'weakness'. Instead I sent Metropolitan Police who charged with their rolled mackintoshes and no one was hurt. The Metropolitan Police played football with the strikers at the weekend. I will let you know the result of my researches.

I hope you will forgive me for being so tardy in replying and also understand why I cannot comply with your gratifying invitation. I am sending you a copy of my book *Painting as a Pastime*, which I have inscribed for you and which I hope you will accept.

Winston S. Churchill to Max Ramsden[1]
(Churchill papers, 2/90)

9 February 1949

My dear Ramsden,

The electors of Batley and Morley have now the opportunity of playing their part in national and world affairs.

After the war there was bound to be a hard call upon the phlegm and endurance of the British nation. Have the Socialist Government helped us make the best of ourselves and of our country in these trying years? Have they lightened our load or, by their own actions, added to it? That is the question to be answered at this important by-election.

Your distinguished record in both the great wars from which we have emerged victoriously, and your social and political work at home, make you in every way qualified to lay the anxious issues of these times before your fellow Yorkshiremen.

I wish you all success. I trust that Liberals will unite with Conservatives and rally to the cause for which you stand, namely: Freedom under just and well-known laws, and Progress by natural and healthy processes. Thus alone can we revive and maintain our island life and fame.

---

[1] Arthur Maxwell Ramsden, 1894–1957. OBE, 1938. Served in TA, RA, during WWII. CB, 1945. Unsuccessful Parliamentary candidate (Cons.) for Leeds South, 1945; for Batley, 1949. Knighted, 1954.

FEBRUARY 1949

Winston S. Churchill to President Chaim Weizmann
(Churchill papers, 2/46)

9 February 1949

My dear Weizmann,

Thank you so much for your telegram. You will no doubt have read my public declaration.

I look back with much pleasure on our long association.

The light grows.

Winston S. Churchill to Winston Churchill
(Churchill papers, 1/46)

9 February 1949

My dear Winston,

Thank you so much for your postcard, with its nice picture of your school. I am delighted to hear that you are happy and also from your Mama that the high air is doing you so much good. It must be great fun skating and skiing in brilliant sunshine. I hope you find your lessons interesting; you should learn all you can about the history of the past, for how else can one even make a guess at what is going to happen in the future?

We have had not bad weather here, and I am making a new pool in my garden so as to have a better waterfall. I expect you have wonderful waterfalls where you are, with which I cannot compete.

Please write to me again as it always gives me great pleasure to hear from you.

Your loving Grandpapa

Winston S. Churchill to Randolph S. Churchill
(Churchill papers, 1/46)

9 February 1949

My dear Randolph,

I have read the letters of Nicholl, Manisty, Few & Co. and Walters & Co., exchanged on December 13, and it seems to me there is very little difference between you and P it would be a great pity if, on such minor points, a friendly settlement should break down. Recourse to the Court of Chancery would not give you very much chance in view of the fact that P has custody of the child.

P has asked me to write to her saying that your Mother and I have confidence in her guardianship of the child as given her by the Court, which letter she could if necessary produce. We do not at this stage wish to engage ourselves like this, but I must tell you that we do not see what better arrangements could be made for the care of the child than those she is carrying out so far in full agreement with you. We therefore strongly recommend a friendly settlement of the minor differences revealed outstanding by the lawyers' letters of December 13. I have no doubt we could help a great deal in the interpretation of any agreement made between you and P, and you could count on our help in this.

I enclose an extract from P's last letter, which is very satisfactory, about little Winston.[1]

Winston S. Churchill to Randolph S. Churchill
(Churchill papers, 1/46)

9 February 1949
Private

My dear Randolph,

I am still waiting for the President's air mail letter, which has already taken five days since its coming was announced. It looks almost certain that Christopher and I will start on March 13. As soon as I hear from the President I will telegraph to Luce confirming the dinner engagement on March 25. You seem to have had an agreeable talk with him. I look forward to seeing you and June,[2] and hope you will not have left before I get there.

We have got some by-elections on here which we hope will show a useful tendency.

I have ___[3] to Belgium on February 24 for four days on our United Europe show. Duncan is doing so well with his tireless persistence and high abilities. The Government are rather puzzled how to make sure I do not become a member of the new Parliament of Europe. What sillies they are!

We have fairly good weather here, and I am just going out to supervise the construction of my new reservoir for the chalk pool. This will give me a respectable cascade for about five hours.

Please see my enclosure. Love to you both.

---

[1] Beginning 'I cannot tell you how wonderfully Little Winston is': letter reproduced above (pp. 1309–10).
[2] June Osborne, 1922–80. Married, 1948, Randolph Churchill, as his second wife: one child, Arabella (b. 1949).
[3] Entirely illegible word on original letter.

Winston S. Churchill to Brigadier-General Sir James E. Edmonds[1]
(Churchill papers, 2/378)

9 February 1949

My dear Edmonds,

I am delighted to receive your signed copy of the latest volume of the 1914–18 history. I am so glad you are able to continue the control and publication of this monumental work. What a shame there should have been another world war before we could finish telling about the first! I wonder if my fate will be the same a lap further on.

You may have seen already Volume I of the book I am writing, *The Second World War*, but I send you herewith a copy which I have inscribed for you.

I hope you find that the eye bandages are useful. I could not get along without them.

Winston S. Churchill to Bernard Baruch
(Churchill papers, 2/210)

10 February 1949

Having received airmail letter from Number One have accepted Compton's invitation Boston March 31 and Henry Luce New York March 25. These are the only formal or public engagements I have made. Propose sailing *QE* arriving 23rd. Looking forward so much to staying quietly with you. It seems to me necessary now to issue Press Communiqué. I have drafted the following for release Saturday noon GMT.

> <u>Begins</u>. Mr Churchill has accepted an invitation from the Massachusetts Institute of Technology to deliver an address in Boston at the Convocation on March 31 on the subject of 'The World in Mid-Century'. He will sail in the *Queen Elizabeth* from Southampton on March 18. He will attend a dinner on March 25 in New York given by Mr Henry R. Luce, Editor-in-Chief of *Time*, *Life* and *Fortune*. He also proposes to visit Washington. Mr Churchill's visit is otherwise of a private character, and he is not making other formal engagements. He will be the guest of Mr Bernard M. Baruch while in the United States. <u>Ends</u>.

Am writing by airmail.

---

[1] James Edward Edmonds, 1861–1956. Educated at King's College School, London. 2nd Lt, Royal Engineers, 1881; Maj., 1899. On active service in South Africa, 1901–2, and on the Western Front, 1914–18. British Delegate to Red Cross Conference, 1907. Col., 1909. Deputy Engineer-in-Chief, BEF, 1918 (despatches six times). Officer in charge, Military Branch, Historical Section, Committee of Imperial Defence, 1919–49. Knighted, 1928. Brig.-Gen., 1936. Author of 12-vol. *Military Operations in France and Belgium* (1922–45); *A Short History of World War I* (1951).

Winston S. Churchill to Julian Sandys
(*Churchill papers, 1/46*)

11 February 1949

My dear Julian,

I was so glad to get your letter, and I hope you will continue to write to me and tell me how you get on. It must have been a very interesting experience going for the first time to a great public school like Eton, where one has so much more liberty and responsibility, than to a private school. I do hope you are enjoying it and getting on well both at work and games. Keep your eye on history because a knowledge of the past is the only way of helping us to make guesses at the future.

Your affectionate Grandfather

Evening Standard: leading article[1]
(*Churchill papers, 1/78*)

11 February 1949

WHERE ARE THE LIBERALS?
LOSING BY DEFAULT

Interest in the political scene quickens at the prospect of four by-elections in the immediate future. On Monday candidates will be nominated at South Hammersmith; on Thursday the voters of Batley go to the poll. At Sowerby, Mr Belcher's former constituency, the Tory candidate is already in the field. Because of the death of Mr George House,[2] a by-election in St Pancras cannot be long delayed.

Great significance is attached to the results of this little General Election. They will provide the first reliable evidence of the political effects of the Lynskey Tribunal. They may indicate whether the perceptible improvement in the country's economic position has checked the gradual swing of votes to the Right. Indeed, they may well have a bearing on the results of the General Election itself.

But where are the Liberals? No Liberal candidate has been nominated at Batley; prominent local Liberals are supporting the Tory, Mr Ramsden. At South Hammersmith the chairman of the local organisation has announced that they are saving themselves for the General Election. There is no news of any Liberal activity at Sowerby. Is it true that Liberal fainthearts are

[1] Written by the editors of the paper.
[2] George House, 1892–1949. Steelworker. Secretary, Constructional Engineering Union, 1924–39. Member of London City Council for Islington South, 1928–31; for St Pancras North, 1937–49. MP (Lab.) for St Pancras North, 1945–9.

counselling the total withdrawal of their party from all by-elections with the aim of conserving their full strength for the General Election?

Such a policy would be absolutely suicidal. The Liberal cause must be kept constantly before the people. If the Liberals refuse to fight for their faith, they will lose their battles by default. Long before the next Election they will have forfeited all hope of increasing their representation in the next Parliament.

No one would suggest that the Liberals should fight every by-election that comes along. Yet in the four by-elections now pending they could surely fight one. It is too late at Batley, too late at Hammersmith, and St Pancras may not appear a promising area.

However, there is a strong Liberal tradition in Sowerby. In 1945 the Liberal candidate polled well over 6000 votes. If the Liberal case were forcibly presented and backed by a first-class fighting organisation, the Liberals would certainly stand a good chance of improving their position.

Will the Liberals let 'I dare not' wait upon 'I would'? The risk of failure must be faced. The Liberals cannot afford many more by-election fiascos. But Sowerby offers a splendid chance to wipe out the memories of lost deposits and feeble candidates. An increased poll would restore the confidence of the Liberal Party in its own future, give fresh heart to Liberals throughout the country.

So the Liberals should make ready for the battle. Let the call for action go forth, and men and women of Liberal beliefs prepare to fight for their noble faith in freedom and the rights of man.

Lord Beaverbrook to Winston S. Churchill
(Churchill papers, 1/78)

12 February 1949   Jamaica

Personally I deplore *Standard* leader[1] and I have asked Robertson[2] for inquiry into circumstances. I can tell you more when I hear result. Surely Conservatives should grasp simple truth that Express Group help their cause more than any other newspapers on account of widespread circulation and independent policy.

---

[1] Reproduced immediately above.
[2] Ewart John Robertson, 1892–1960. Managing Director, Express Newspapers, 1948–55.

Winston S. Churchill to Lord Beaverbrook
(Churchill papers, 1/78)

12 February 1949

Thank you very much for your telegrams. I am most sorry you have to return home and still more because of grindstone. I would never have thought of going to Jamaica except for the fun we have together. Let me know about your health and movements. I am glad to know you do not approve of article in question. My reaction was too impulsive but I felt that all we have worked for all our lives is at stake in the near future.

Winston S. Churchill to Field Marshal Lord Montgomery
(Churchill papers, 2/31)

[13] February 1949
NOT SENT

My dear Monty,

I send you the enclosed[1] as it reached me, personal and private. It was not written for your eyes, and I have taken something of a liberty in sending it to you. The Spanish General's point of view is easily understandable, and he arranges the facts accordingly. As you know, I doubt myself very much whether any defence can be improvised in Europe, apart from altogether devastating effects of the atomic bomb, and the cutting of the 'swath' between the advancing Russian Armies, and the Kremlin and their native land. I am not addressing my mind in this letter to the probabilities of war, or the reverse, and when it would come. I do not think anyone knows. I thought, however, that you might be interested in seeing this viewpoint, and would rate it at its proper importance, which is not negligible, at least from the information side.

---

[1] Notes on a conversation between the Spanish High Commissioner and Mr Hore-Belisha at Tetuan on 13 Jan. 1949.

February 1949

Winston S. Churchill to Lady Londonderry[1]
(Churchill papers, 2/163)[2]

14 February 1949   Chartwell

My dear Edie,

    I was deeply grieved to hear of Charlie's death,[3] and I fear his later years were not happy, and that towards the end life was a heavy burden. Your devotion to him must have been his greatest blessing. I know what all this means to you, and you have my fullest sympathy in your sorrow. These are indeed sad times. How all our old world has crumpled around us! You have the consolation of having done your duty. I have felt for you both so much.

Julian Sandys to Winston S. Churchill
(Churchill papers, 1/46)[4]

15 February 1949

Dear Grandpapa,

    I think your speech[5] was simply wizard, especially the beginning. I hope you like the picture I took of you. I am staying at this chateau with Madam de Witt whom I think you have met. Why weren't you elected President of the Council of Europe? Your foreword in the book was much better than Spaak's. Where are you staying? We have got an E-flag on our car here. I am staying for 3 weeks and then I shall go back to England. It is very nice here but a bit too hot. Please write to me.

PS. Me and the other boy are sleeping out tonight. I enclose a postcard of where I am staying.

---

[1] Edith Helen Chaplin, 1879–1959. Daughter of 1st Viscount Chaplin; granddaughter of 3rd Duke of Sutherland. Married, 1899, Viscount Castlereagh (later Lord Londonderry). Col.-in-Chief, Women's Volunteer Reserve, 1914–15. Founder and Director, Women's Legion, 1915–19. DBE, 1917 (the first woman to be so appointed). Close personal friend of the first Labour PM, Ramsay MacDonald.

[2] This letter was handwritten.

[3] Charles Stewart Henry Vane-Tempest-Stewart, 1878–1949. Churchill's 2nd cousin. Educated at Eton and Sandhurst. Married, 1899, Edith Helen Chaplin. As Viscount Castlereagh, MP (Cons.) for Maidstone, 1906–15. Succeeded his father as 7th Marquess of Londonderry, 1915. Served briefly on the Western Front as Second-in-Command, Royal Horse Guards, 1915. Minister of Education and Leader of the Senate, Government of Northern Ireland, 1921–6. Returned to Westminster as First Commissioner of Works, 1928–9, 1931. Secretary of State for Air and Lord Privy Seal, 1931–5.

[4] This letter was handwritten.

[5] Reproduced above (pp. 1314–20).

Winston S. Churchill: broadcast
('Winston S. Churchill, His Complete Speeches', volume 7, pages 7789–90)

17 February 1949 London

RECRUITING FOR THE FORCES

I come forward tonight to support the Prime Minister, Sir Stafford Cripps, Mr Eden and many others who have spoken on this subject, in the effort His Majesty's Government are making to help recruiting for the Regular Army and the Territorials and indeed for all the Services. The action which the Socialist Government have taken in establishing compulsory national service in this island in time of peace commands the respect of all parties, not least for the reason that it was not particularly popular. But the introduction of compulsory service for the fighting forces makes a very heavy impact upon our pre-war system. It raises many problems, particularly for the Regular Army, and very few of these have so far been solved.

The Regular Army has not only to provide the spearhead of our defence against a sudden attack, but now it must be the training-machine for large numbers of young men who are called up or who may be called up under the National Service Act. This means that our Regular Army must have a very strong professional structure of teachers and leaders in order at once to preserve its glorious traditions and keep abreast of the times. It also means that the Regular Army can provide for the serious-minded, experienced soldier a professional career, which should constitute his life's work and be a guarantee of his later years. When I think of all the youngish men, many in their early prime, that are going around today, men who have dared, endured and learned so much on the field of battle, I cannot doubt that numbers will be willing and will be forthcoming to join on a long-service basis the Regular Army, and make their way and rise in a profession honourable to its members and vital to the State.

The Territorial Army, which succeeded the old volunteers of the nineteenth century, is equally indispensable to any plan made by any Government in these present dangerous times. It is a citizens' army of men who have to earn their livelihood before they do their military work. They will form the structure in time of peace upon which in time of war – and no one wants war; we wish to prevent war – the trained reserves arising from national service will be moulded into many famous regiments which represent to us and remind us of the great deeds of the past. There can be no effective Territorial Army without a strong volunteer element made up of the best kind of men and women we have got – and we have got some good ones still. I earnestly appeal to the young veterans of the late war to come forward and join their Territorial units. People say the times are hard. There are many things we do not like. The Government have compulsory powers. If they want us, why do they not issue their orders? But that is not the way in which the victorious British soldiers of the last war should approach their decision. The volunteer element in our national life, the willingness, nay the urge to do more than is required by law, or required just to keep your head above water is a characteristic of the British spirit without which we should not have survived.

Some have told you of the advantages of joining the Territorials: good comrades, jolly pals, pleasant holiday camps. That is all true, but in my opinion our recruiting campaign for the Territorial Army will only be a success if it makes its appeal to the men who wish to fortify their lives by a special sacrifice for our country, which we love so dearly and which so many of those to whom I now appeal saved from shame and ruin. A suitable man with the right gifts and turn of mind who joins his Territorial battalion or battery now would add to his own stature among his fellow men. It is true that he volunteers to face heavier risks than he otherwise would, but so do the fire brigades and the lifeboat men, and so do lots of people when honour's call rings clear.

The fact of making an extra sacrifice of leisure and life's strength and of undertaking a special obligation to bear a bit of the extra weight gives a man a rightful status of dignity and self-respect. It is a matter which each must settle with his conscience. The more awkward or dreary many things may be in our life, the brighter shine these acts of the spirit. Here is the flame which enabled us, as I firmly believe, to save the freedom of the world and the life of our island in the war. It must not die now or we shall all die with it. A man may well be proud in himself, though he must tell it to none, if, regardless whether things fall well or ill, or whether he likes them or not, he comes forward to do his bit – and a bit more, too.

Lord Beaverbrook to Brendan Bracken
(Beaverbrook papers)

17 February 1949   Jamaica

I have had some tough telegrams from Churchill. He is angry with the *Evening Standard* because of a leader.[1] I have since read it and can't see anything wrong with it. But don't tell him. Before I read it, I said I deplored it. I said that because I (*sic* – ?it) had hurt his feelings.

---

[1] Reproduced above (pp. 1325–6).

February 1949

Bernard Baruch to Winston S. Churchill
(*Churchill papers, 2/210*)

18 February 1949   New York

My dear Winston,

I am pleased at the present setup because now you are coming at the invitation of MIT and the President.

Would you like to have me arrange to have a large private dinner like the last one, and if so, would you want to have it Wednesday the 23rd or Thursday the 24th, or would you prefer to have it after your return from Boston on your way to Washington?

General Eisenhower has said that he would like to entertain you at a small dinner of about twelve people in New York, but that he would only do that which you would like to have him do.

I will let you know later about developments in connection with your Washington visit.

I will arrange to have you travel as comfortably as possible. If the weather is good, do you want to fly to Boston which would take only a little more than an hour, or go by train (and I will provide a private car) which would take about 4½ hours. This also applies to your trip to Washington.

How many secretaries and servants will you have? I would like to know so as to arrange for them to live right around the corner. In my apartment Christopher will have a room and bath, and you will have a room, bath and sitting room and private telephone service. There will be no one at the apartment other than Miss Navarro[1] and myself. Also, be perfectly free to say whether you would rather stay in an hotel.

Will you want to leave New York by steamer to join your family? If so, we ought to make arrangements to get one of the new English liners.

I do not know how the weather will be in the West Indies, but I think it will be getting pretty warm.

My Georgetown home will be the furthest removed from any possible interruption because there is no telephone in the house, and no one can get in to the place for it is five miles from the gate to my house and no sight-seers are ever admitted. There will be a riot of colors to paint. I am bringing this to your attention and you can move according to your desires.

Randolph and June visited me there. She had a little cold so Randolph left her there for a few days while he went on a barnstorming lecture tour in the Carolinas. He is returning there tonight and will stay there until Sunday, February 20th. I shall probably see him on Sunday, for I am flying down.

Have you made up your mind how you propose to return from the West Indies?

---

[1] Elizabeth Navarro was Baruch's nurse. Baruch's wife, Annie Griffin, passed away in 1938, and Navarro was his companion until he died in 1965.

These are matters we ought to be thinking about in order that you and your family are most comfortably taken care of.

I am looking forward with keenest delight to seeing you and Christopher, and I hope I shall see Clemmie and Mary.

Emery Reves to Winston S. Churchill
(Churchill papers, 4/16)

23 February 1949 New York

Dear Mr Churchill,

Many thanks for your cable agreeing that the French publisher should leave out the phrase concerning General Prioux.[1] What a pity that you did not make this decision after receiving my letter of January 21st transmitting this suggestion of the French publisher. After publication in *Figaro* and the violent reaction of General Prioux (I understand many other French Generals have sent protests to *Figaro* which they intend to publish at the same time) this correction in the book now naturally appears as an admission of a mistake.

In view of your tremendous prestige in France, the French publisher was most anxious that no controversy should arise in which you might be accused of having unjustly condemned a popular general. I wonder whether you would not think it advisable to send a short letter either to General Prioux or to *Figaro*, admitting this small mistake.

The protests of Gamelin, Weygand and the son[2] of General Billotte[3] appear to me, on the other hand, quite irrelevant. Gamelin's is even stupid. He actually said in his letter that there were strategic reserves, but they were so far away that they could not be used where they were needed. This puts him in a worse position than your statement does....

It seems that your Memoirs have aroused the aggressive spirit of the French generals which was so sadly lacking in 1939. Perhaps it was a mistake not to publish this second volume at the beginning of the war....

I shall have to return to Europe in a few weeks, and would like to arrange my plans so that I could see you as soon as possible in New York or in London. If the American press is correct, you are due to arrive here on the 23rd March.

---

[1] René Jacques Adolphe Prioux, 1879–1953. Born in Bordeaux. On actives service during WWI (wounded), 1914. Commanded Cavalry Corps, 1939–40. POW, 30 May 1940 to 16 April 1942.

[2] Pierre Billotte, 1906–92. CoS to Gen. de Gaulle, 1942–3. GOC, 10th Infantry Div., 1944–5. Head of French Military Mission, UN, 1946–50.

[3] Gaston Billotte, ?–1940. Cdr, 1st Army Group, 1939, situated on the Belgian border. In a memorandum on 6 Dec. 1939, warned Gens Gamelin and Georges of the German superiority in mechanized divisions, and their ability to sweep through Belgium as they had done through Poland; his warning led to the formation of the first French heavy armoured division ten days later. Advanced into Belgium, to Namur, 10 May 1940. Driven back into France and towards Dunkirk, and cut off from the main French forces. On 19 May 1940, unable to carry out Gamelin's orders to drive southward and link up with the main French armies on the Somme. Died as a result of a car crash, 21 May 1940.

Could you tell me when you expect to leave New York for home? I shall naturally keep any date confidential.

Winston S. Churchill to Bernard Baruch
(Churchill papers, 2/210)

24 February 1949

British Ambassador[1] has now invited me to stay at Embassy during my visit to Washington. I am considering myself your guest there, and we shall be together. Yet I think I ought to go for perhaps a couple of nights to the Embassy otherwise it would be thought there was some affront intended on one side or the other. In my present plan I contemplated being in Washington 3rd to 8th inclusive. Let me know what you advise.

2. Have been bombarded with invitations but have refused all further engagements except United Europe Committee luncheon March 29 in New York, which I must do for Duncan Sandys. I will cable you again in a few more days when I know a little more of the President's programme and movements at Boston. Randolph told me you thought of giving me a considerable dinner in Washington. If so this would be the most agreeable to me, but I am very content to have no plans and am certainly taking your advice about keeping as many days as possible free. Kindest regards.

Winston Churchill to General Lord Ismay and Lieutenant-General Sir Henry Pownall
(Churchill papers, 4/16)

25 February 1949

I should be much obliged if you would consult together about our references to General Prioux's conduct. It is far from my wish to be dragged into a controversy with individual French Generals, and the reference to this point is not in any way necessary to the story. The correction modifying the first version got through and was printed in both the *Life* and *Daily Telegraph* serials and also in *Figaro*. However, the French translation, as you will see from the attached extract, uses the word 'vouloir' whereas we had cut out 'wished' in the revise. There is also the question of General de la Laurencie.[2] Was he

---

[1] Oliver Sherwell Franks, 1905–92. Educated at Oxford University. Married, 1931, Barbara Mary Tanner. Prof., Moral Philosophy, University of Glasgow, 1937–45. Temp. Civil Servant, Ministry of Supply, 1939–46; Permanent Secretary, 1945–6. CBE, 1942. KCB, 1946. Provost, Queen's College, Oxford, 1946–8; Worcester College, Oxford, 1962–76. British Ambassador at Washington DC, 1948–52. PC, 1949. GCMG, 1952. FBA, 1960. Life Peer, 1962. Chancellor, East Anglia University, 1965–84. OM, 1977. Lord Warden of the Stannaries and Keeper of the Privy Seal, Duke of Cornwall, 1983–5. KCVO, 1985.

[2] Benoît-Léon de Fornel de la Laurencie, 1879–1958. Born in Broût-Vernet, France. Educated at

ever under Prioux's orders? It is necessary to look into this matter in detail as it may become the subject of a libel action against me and *Figaro* and I must know whether the words in the modified version are defensible or not. There is also the question of General Billotte, whose son, also a General, has been protesting. Looking at these references I feel they are hard, but they express the feeling that we had at the British HQ about French Commander. Pray let me have your views in a week or so.

Lieutenant-Colonel Bill Deakin to Winston S. Churchill
(Churchill papers, 4/16)

25 February 1949

I have been checking the records of the corrections made to the passage about General Prioux. Your original text was first queried by *Life*, and I passed their comment to General Pownall for a ruling. His reply was:

> 'For "Prioux wished to surrender . . . these orders" read "Prioux seemed prepared to surrender the entire force but General de la Laurencie would not obey."'

And he added as a comment: 'Gort let Prioux off very lightly.'

This modification was correctly embodied in Overtake List No. 7 on January 21.

On the same day (January 21) Mr Reves wrote to you a letter enclosing the comments of the French publisher on the original text. He also drew attention to the original remarks about General Prioux. This was also passed to General Pownall, together with a detailed list of minor points which the French publishers had queried.

On January 25 General Pownall enclosed in a letter to me his list of comments on all these points. Regarding General Prioux he made the following modification of the text:

> 'Delete first sentence "General Prioux . . . obey these orders" and substitute "General Prioux, in command of the First French Army, seemed prepared to surrender the entire force, but eventually he was prevailed upon to change his mind."'

Against this passage in General Pownall's minute I find that I had written 'Done'. All the rulings which he gave, with the exception of this one point, are embodied in Overtake List No. 10 dated January 28.

St-Cyr Military Special School. 2nd Lt of Cavalry, 1901. CoS, Polish Div., 1919. Cdr, French 1st Cavalry Div., 1935–9. Member of tribunal that condemned Charles de Gaulle to death in Aug. 1940 for his attacks on Pétain's Government. In 1941 became member of the National Council in charge of the reorganization of France. Interned by Vichy regime, 1942–4.

On January 29 I drafted a reply to Mr Reves which was shown to you before the despatch. In answer to his remarks about General Prioux I put in this letter the following sentence:

'This has already been the subject of an overtake correction which will by now have reached your office.'

(This can only refer to the correction made on January 21.)

It is clear from the above that I did not issue a further overtake in light of General Pownall's second modification of the text. I can only therefore accept responsibility for this omission and apologise that it has occurred.

Winston S. Churchill: speech
('Winston S. Churchill, His Complete Speeches', volume 7, pages 7791–2)

25 February 1949   Brussels

A UNITED EUROPE

The progress of the European idea has been unceasing because the conception of Europe as a united entity has proved itself to be a living truth, in perfect harmony with the needs of the broad masses of the people in every part of the continent. Less than four years after the cannonade of the most terrible of wars has ended, it has already shown itself superior in many ways to the passions of hatred and revenge which naturally follow the terrible injuries we have inflicted upon one another. Not only do we meet as allies in a common struggle but we welcome to our midst as friends and comrades representatives of the great States and races with whom we have been so lately locked in conflict.

That is indeed an example of the force of an idea triumphing over the fiercest passions of men and nations, to turn our thoughts from the past to the future, and to turn from deeds of hatred to new associations and brotherhoods, which we know are our only hope.

We also receive with warm feelings of sympathy the representatives of the European countries which are at present held in the grip of a tyranny more permanently devastating than that of Hitler, and we will make them free. In the Congress of Europe at The Hague last May we resolved to work for the creation of a deliberative European Assembly. Great Governments and powerful Ministers have passed this plan, or been converted to it, and what was in May last only the expression of an unofficial congress has now become the adopted and concerted policy of almost all the Governments of western Europe.

We must hope, nay, we must make sure, that our present gathering is not less fortunate and fruitful. I will not anticipate the discussions which are to take place, but this is the hour for another positive, forward step towards the structure of united Europe. Thus we may clear the road, open the passage and smooth the path for the ponderous vehicles of executive responsibility and furnish those who drive them alike with a theme and with a plan. We may even, in the form of an active, enlightened and ever more dominant public opinion, give them the fuel they need for their journey and the electric spark to set all in motion. 'Alors ca ira!'

Winston S. Churchill: speech
('In the Balance', pages 26–30)

26 February 1949   Salle des Beaux Arts, Brussels

After each of the fearful wars which have ravaged the lives and homes of mankind, the hopes of humanity have centred upon the creation of an instrument of world government capable, at least, of maintaining peace and law among men. We have all been grieved and alarmed by the fact that the new United Nations Organization should have been so torn and broken. It has made a far less hopeful start in these first four years than its predecessor, the League of Nations.

In spite of the faithful efforts that have been made by the representatives of many countries, great and small, the new organization, to which we had looked for guidance in our problems and guardianship in our dangers, has already been reduced to a brawling cockpit where taunts and insults may be flung back and forth. An institution in this condition cannot have the authority to prevent the approach of a new war and is in danger of losing the confidence and even the respect of those who were most ardent for its creation.

The main cause of this disaster is, of course, the fact that the world is sundered by the aggression of the Communist ideology supported by the armed power of Soviet Russia. But there are also fundamental defects in the structure of the United Nations Organization which must be corrected if any progress is to be made. I had always felt during the war that the structure of world security could only be founded on regional organizations. Regional organizations are encouraged by the constitution of the United Nations, but they have so far played no effective part. In consequence, the supreme body has been cumbered and confused by a mass of questions, great and small, about which only a babel of harsh voices can be heard. Large regional units are the necessary elements in any scheme of world government. It is vain to build the dome of the temple of peace without the pillars on which alone it can stand.

Just as in a great army it is necessary to have army groups; just as in a division it is necessary to have battalions, so there must be these intermediate organizations to make coherent and effective action possible at the supreme summit. What would happen to a military system where there was nothing between the supreme HQ and the commanders of all the different divisions? What plan could emerge from such a concourse? Such a method could only lead through chaos to defeat. Therefore, I believe that the creation of regional organisms is an inseparable part of any structure of world security.

It is the task and duty of the regional bodies to settle a vast number of regional questions among themselves within their own circle and to send representatives of the highest authority from their unit to the supreme world instrument. Unless and until this is done the United Nations Organization will be a failure and even a mockery.

Tonight we meet here, working patiently together, for the building of one and, in some respects, the greatest of the regional organizations. We work here for European Unity and for the creation of the necessary apparatus by which United Europe can become a principal factor in the life and peace of the world, and a worthy member of the world organization. If we are striving to raise Europe from the awful welter of misery and ruin into which we have been plunged, it is not only for the sake of Europe but for the sake of the whole world that we toil. It is not only to the regional organization but to the cause of world government that our loyalties are directed.

We are all encouraged by the progress which the European Movement is making. We feel conscious of the inherent force of the cause we serve and the idea which guides us. It shines like a bright, steady light. In the confusion and exhaustion of our age it shines all the brighter because of the storms which gather. Although we are a regional organism, it is not only geography that unites us. We find our principle of union in the moral sphere. We take our stand on human rights, as set forth in the Charter of Human Rights proclaimed by the United Nations Organization. Any European country that sincerely accepts and adopts the principles set forth will be welcomed by the European Union.

Alas, there are a number of ancient and famous European States which are no longer free to take their stand for those human rights of which they have so great need. The yoke of the Kremlin oligarchy has descended upon them and they are the victims of a tyranny more subtle and merciless than any hitherto known to history. We are glad to see them represented here by men and women who have escaped from the trap that has closed upon their fellow-countrymen. It is this moral bond which first of all unites us.

In the report of the Executive Committee, our principles are set forth with clarity: love of freedom; hostility to totalitarianism of every kind; the humble and conscientious search for truth; respect for the human personality and for the individual as an individual. These moral values, founded alike on Christian faith and charity and on the critical spirit of rationalism, are the message of our 2,000-year-old European civilization and culture. Let us make sure that, enjoying as we do this common inheritance, we take all necessary steps lest it be wasted or cast away.

At The Hague Congress in May, two proposals for practical action were made: the creation of a European Assembly; and the setting up of a European Court for the enforcement of Human Rights. The European Assembly is now on the point of being achieved. The responsible governments of all our countries have reached their agreements. We have now to take the second step forward and to try to establish, as the practical result of our meeting here, the setting up of a European Court of Human Rights. Such a court in no way challenges the authority of a world court, but it may well be that the principles laid down by the United Nations will be better and more effectively interpreted by courts in the more limited and homogeneous area of regional units: Let Europe judge Europe.

We have the Charter of Human Rights, and we must have a European means of defending it and enforcing it. It must not be possible that, within the boundaries of United Europe, such a legal atrocity could be perpetrated as that which has confronted us all in the case of Cardinal Mindszenty.[1] Here you have the crime of religious persecution committed on an innocent man under the direct orders of Moscow, and carried through with all those features of police government with which we are familiar in trials under the Soviets.

There must be means by which such events in any of the countries with which we can consort can be brought to the test of impartial justice. We cannot rest content with the division of Europe into two parts – the free and the unfree. The Europe we seek to unite is *all* Europe; and in our Movement we must strive, by every means in our power, to help bring about conditions in which our fellow-Europeans, now living in the satellite States of Russia, will be united with us.

The task of our Movement is to foster, encourage and develop the sense of being Europeans, a pride in Europe and what she has stood for, and confidence in the greatness of our common mission in the future. These sentiments can only be brought about by Europeans in different countries learning to know each other better. In all this work the new European Assembly can play a vital part. By its discussions, which will be reported in the Press and on the radio, it can create and express a European public opinion, a common European point of view, and the sense of all that we have in common.

We are all agreed that our ultimate aim – the unity and freedom of the whole of Europe – can only be achieved by stages. Our first task is to unite the free countries which are working together under the Marshall Plan. We recognize that individual countries have special problems for which solutions

---

[1] József Pehm, 1892–1975. Born in Esztergom, Hungary. Ordained in 1915. Changed his surname to Mindszenty, 1941. Consecrated Bishop, 1944. Made a Cardinal in 1946 by Pope Pius XII. Arrested in 1946 by Communist authorities for resisting their attempt to take over the Catholic schools. Resisted attempts to make him confess. Was accused of over 40 crimes and found guilty of treason. Sentenced to life imprisonment.

must be found. In Switzerland, in Sweden, in Germany, there are special conditions which must be patiently studied. Great Britain is herself the centre of a free and worldwide commonwealth of States. We are sure in our country that a satisfactory solution can be found whereby we can develop our new association with Europe without in the slightest degree weakening the sacred ties which unite Britain with her daughter States across the oceans.

Europe, which we are striving to revive, must be independent but not isolationist. We desire that our regional structure all be harmoniously fitted into a system of world government, but we stretch our hands out in gratitude and goodwill across the ocean to the other half of the free world, whose generous help has been forthcoming to assist our stricken continent on the path of recovery. We express our admiration of the great United States and of the part they are playing, not only in the restoration of European economy, but also in our security and defence.

The Brussels Pact united the five Western democracies in a scheme of common defence, and we in Britain are glad once again to take our stand with the gallant Belgian Army against the perils of the future. The Atlantic Pact will give us all the guarantee that the cause of freedom in the Old World will not be aggressively assailed without effective aid from the great Republic across the ocean.

This, therefore, is the hour in which we should move forward with confidence, offering to all the men in all the lands the human rights and freedom which we ourselves enjoy and for the preservation of which – if ever it should be necessary – we should be prepared to do our duty whatever the cost might be.

Bernard Baruch to Winston S. Churchill
(Churchill papers, 2/210)

28 February 1949

Most advisable accept Ambassador's invitation for entire Washington visit for reasons stated in your cable. It was Randolph's idea about Washington dinner, but do not agree as not my home ground. Will gladly give your New York dinner as outlined in my last letter to you,[1] to which you have not replied. Will not your Luce, *Times*, Sandys dinners fill your public engagements? We can have a number of small, private dinners and luncheons, but I want everything to be entirely satisfactory to you, as I am quite content to be with you and have you with me, in whatever spare time you have from other engagements which I know you will have to meet.

Both Eisenhower and Marshall want you privately. Newspaper publishers

[1] Of Feb. 18, reproduced above (pp. 1331–2), which did not arrive until Mar. 8 (see Churchill to Baruch, 9 Mar. 1949, reproduced below, p. 1349).

want you April 28th. If you return by way of New York it would be advisable to accept. I think you will have a happy time in America. Returning New York March 3rd.

Winston S. Churchill to Bernard Baruch
(Churchill papers, 2/210)

28 February 1949

Am fixing Washington with Ambassador. Hope you will give me another dinner in New York like last time. What is date of your 'last letter'. Cannot trace anything recent. Am making no more engagements of any kind until I see you which I earnestly desire to do.

Winston S. Churchill to Thomas Dewey
(Churchill papers, 2/263)

28 February 1949
Private

My dear Dewey,

You may have seen in the newspapers that I shall be in New York between 23 and 30 March staying with Bernie Baruch. I hope very much that we shall meet, as I should like to renew our agreeable talks and acquaintance of three years ago. I am writing to Bernie on the subject, and I have no doubt he will get in touch with you.

I cannot write to you without offering my congratulations on the dignity and poise with which you received the heavy political reverse of the Presidential Election. Such experiences are not agreeable, as I know only too well myself.

With kind regards and every good wish to you and Mrs Dewey.

March 1949

Winston S. Churchill to Bernard Baruch
(*Churchill papers, 2/210*)

1 March 1949

1. Please signal me earliest about Connally's[1] resolution. It makes a difference to my work on board. Must be pretty clear when I land.
2. Please settle yourself whether I dine with Laughlin[2] March 30 or lunch April 1 as you suggested. Latter seems best.
All well and happy on board. Millpond so far.

Henry Hopkinson to Elizabeth Gilliatt
(*Churchill papers, 2/86*)

1 March 1949

Dear Miss Gilliatt,
I return the papers which Mr Churchill received about Baron von Weiszacker,[3] and which he asked me to look through. I have taken some time about it, but they are voluminous and to get the true picture it was necessary to read through almost the whole lot.
The impression that I have gained is that Weiszacker was sympathetic towards the persecution of the Jews in Germany from very early days, certainly as early as 1938. The first object of that persecution was the removal

---

[1] Thomas Terry Connally, 1877–1963. Known as 'Tom'. Member, Texas House of Representatives, District 72, 1901–3; District 69, 1903–5. Member, US House of Representatives, Texas's 11th Congressional District, 1917–29. Wrote the Connally Hot Oil Act of 1935. Senator for Texas (Dem.), 1929–53. Chairman, US Senate Committee on Foreign Relations, 1941–7, 1949–53.

[2] Henry Alexander Laughlin, 1892–1977. President of Houghton Mifflin Co., 1939–63. Responsible for the publication of *Mein Kampf* in US. Published Churchill's *The Second World War*. Chairman of Franklin Publications and the 1945 Greater Boston War Fund. President, Princeton University Press. Trustee of Boston Symphony Orchestra, Radcliffe College, Boston Children's Hospital, Concord Public Library and Concord Academy.

[3] Weizsäcker. See Magee to Churchill, 1 Oct. 1948, reproduced above (pp. 1176–9).

of the Jews from Germany itself. When the war led to the occupation of one European country after another, the same policy was extended to other countries. The first intention was to deport all Jews to Madagascar. Later their destination was changed to 'ghettos' or labour camps in Eastern Europe. This policy was certainly carried on with the full knowledge and approval of the German Foreign Office and Weiszacker. The Foreign Office were also aware that during the first German onslaught on Russia in 1941 the Einsatz Gruppen committed the first mass murders of Jews in the Baltic States and Western Russia. Nevertheless, they proceeded with their plan for mass deportations to Eastern Europe. There appears to be no direct evidence that they contemplated the extermination of the Jews thus deported, though at a very early date such mass murders did take place and of course were carried out on an increasingly large scale.

The best that one can say for Weiszacker, I think, is that there is no evidence that he was directly responsible for giving the orders for extermination of Jews which was carried out by the Gestapo. But he certainly must have realised what was going on.

Winston S. Churchill to Charles Wood
(Churchill papers, 4/19)

2 March 1949

Please make all the corrections you see fit in the Index, and let me have it back Saturday or Sunday night next. I am sure from the way you are approaching the subject that your corrections will be of the greatest value. By all means correct the kind of errors that you mention in your Minute to me.

I must regard this as a very special piece of work on your part. It must be very difficult to make an Index. This seems a very long and full one.

Randolph S. Churchill to Winston S. Churchill
(Churchill papers, 1/46)

2 March 1949   Dallas, Texas

My dearest Papa,

Thank you so much for your letter of February 9th.[1]

I am afraid you have misunderstood the point of disagreement between Pamela and myself. I have in no way challenged her custody of Winston, nor have I at any time contemplated recourse to the Court of Chancery. On the contrary, it was she who was contemplating this action. My sole anxiety in

---

[1] Reproduced above (pp. 1322–3).

the matter has been to insure that the principle of Winston's spending the main part of his holidays in England should be assured.

If you want to know more about it, I will explain the whole position when we meet in New York. Meanwhile, I am very glad that you have not written the letter which Pamela asked for.

June and I are sailing for England on April 2nd, in order to get back in time for Winston's holidays.

I have a lecture engagement in North Carolina on March 29th, and shall not be in New York until March 30th. If convenient to you, we should like to come up with you to Boston and hear your speech on the 31st.

Winston S. Churchill to Bernard Baruch
(Churchill papers, 2/210)

3 March 1949

Have heard from British Ambassador that Number One is inviting me to dine Blair House 24th. I shall of course accept when the invitation comes. It was my thought that it was most necessary he and I should be able to talk things over before Boston addresses. Should like to dine with you quietly night of arrival and travel Washington during 24th sleeping Embassy that night and returning in time to do the Luce dinner 25th. I have made no further engagements except those in my last telegrams. Am hoping we may be together quietly. It would be very nice if you would ask Dewey one day and let us be alone together sometimes. If you would like to give me a dinner in New York like last time I wonder whether Wednesday April 27 on my way back from Jamaica the night before I sail for home might not be a good opportunity but there will be plenty of time to talk this over when we are together to which I greatly look forward.

Bernard Baruch to Winston S. Churchill
(Churchill papers, 2/210)

3 March 1949

Agree heartily with your plans. Dewey pleasantly engrossed with State budgetary troubles. Will arrange meeting after your arrival. Expressed great delight. Any arrangements or changes you make will always be most agreeable to me. When travelling between New York and Washington and Boston do you prefer train or plane or will you decide on arrival.[1]

---

[1] Churchill telegraphed Baruch on Mar. 5: 'Thank you so much your cable March 3. Prefer train which I can work in for these short journeys.'

Winston S. Churchill to General Sir Bernard Freyberg
(Churchill papers, 4/19)

3 March 1949

My dear Bernard,

I have now reached the point in my story where the Battle of Crete must be told. I have a good many references to you in my account, which I hope you will not consider unfavourable. Among these I have told about your showing me all your wounds – I think at Breccles. I should be glad if you would allow me to recount this incident and also make sure it is correct.

I should also welcome any comments which you may make upon the two chapters. I have turned down the pages which refer to you.

I am sure you had very nice talks with Eden. He has written to me how splendidly you are doing. New Zealand indeed took the prize in the war. My kindest regards to you both.

Winston S. Churchill to Leslie Charles Graham-Dixon
(Churchill papers, 1/28)

3 March 1949

My dear Graham Dixon,

The news I have received from Moir[1] vindicates the soundness of the advice you have given me, upon which I have acted. Thank you very much indeed for all your help.

Winston S. Churchill to Clement Attlee
(Churchill papers, 2/29)

4 March 1949
Private

My dear Prime Minister,

Do you mind specifying exactly the occasions you had in mind in your reference last night to my request for an interview and to your reply. We have touched upon such matters several times in the last few years, and I should like to know the date and circumstances.

---

[1] Moir told Churchill that the various family Trust arrangements set up over the past three years by Leslie Graham-Dixon were all in order. For the first time, Churchill had been allowed to set his annual literary income aside in a trust fund without it being counted as income as each payment was made by the publishers.

March 1949

Clement Attlee to Winston S. Churchill
(Churchill papers, 2/29)

4 March 1949

My dear Churchill,

The occasion to which I referred was when I saw you and your colleagues on the Indian question before Christmas. The date was in fact December 16. At the end of the meeting you said that you proposed to come and see me on Defence matters. I said that I should, of course, be pleased to see you.

Winston S. Churchill to Clement Attlee
(Churchill papers, 2/29)

4 March 1949

My dear Prime Minister,

I have never doubted that if I asked to come to see you on Defence, or indeed on other matters of public consequence, you would receive me; and the informal interchange which took place between us on December 16 at the close of a meeting on another subject did not to my mind create a new situation. Since then I have not ceased to consider the matter which is not free from difficulty. Once you have given me and any colleagues I may bring with me secret information which we do not already know, then even if that information still leaves us unsatisfied, we should be greatly hampered in discharging our duty of criticizing the Service Estimates. I therefore allowed the matter to rest until after the debates which were expected in the New Year and are taking place.

Now however that you have stated publicly in debate that you invite me to come to see you, our meeting would acquire a greater significance than could attach to informal and private talks. I therefore feel it my duty to accept. In order that the Opposition should not be embarrassed in Defence debates, I must ask you, as I did Mr Baldwin in 1936, that we shall be free to use in public any information of which we are already possessed, with due regard to national interest and safety.

To avoid risk of subsequent misunderstanding I will therefore prepare a Memorandum of the condition of the Armed Forces in relation to our needs as I and my colleagues view them today. This I will send you as soon as it is ready, and after you have considered it we shall be very glad to come to see you, so that the whole subject may be discussed and that we may be placed in possession of information which is now naturally not within our knowledge.

I hope this may be agreeable to you.

1346   March 1949

Clement Attlee to Winston S. Churchill
(Churchill papers, 2/29)

4 March 1949

My dear Churchill,

Thank you for your letter. I may, of course, have been mistaken, but I judged the request which you made to me on December 16 to be rather more than a suggestion that I should offer you normal courtesy. In any case I am ready to accede to the proposal you have now made, and I await the memorandum which you mention.

Winston S. Churchill to Clement Attlee
(Churchill papers, 2/29)

4 March 1949

My dear Prime Minister,

Owing to the many inquiries which are coming from the Press, I feel that this[1] should be published almost immediately, of course with any answer you may wish to send.

May I put our Publicity officer in touch with yours?

Laurence Helsby to Winston S. Churchill
(Churchill papers, 2/29)

4 March 1949
Confidential

Dear Mr Churchill,

The Prime Minister has just left for Germany. Before he went Mr Attlee asked me to tell you that he has no objection to the publication of the attached letter together with yours to which it is the reply. He asked me to add, however, to avoid any risk of misunderstanding, that he assumes that you would not think it necessary to publish his earlier letter of today in which mention was made of consultation 'on the Indian question': you will appreciate that it would be inappropriate to publish a reference to consultation on this subject.

---

[1] The two immediately preceding letters.

Jo Sturdee to Laurence Helsby
(Churchill papers, 2/29)

5 March 1949

This is to confirm the conversation I had with your secretary last evening and to say that Mr Churchill would be glad if you would express his thanks to the Prime Minister for his letter.

Mr Churchill wishes to thank you also for yours. He quite agrees with the suggestion that the previous letter from Mr Attlee mentioning the consultation 'on the Indian question' should not be issued to the Press and that, therefore, only his long letter and the Prime Minister's reply which came at the same time as your letter should be published. As you know arrangements for the release of these two letters to the Press have been made.

Winston S. Churchill to Bernard Baruch
(Churchill papers, 2/210)

5 March 1949

Have had following extract of letter from Laughlin of Houghton Mifflin Company:

'In the hope that you had not anything very concrete planned for your stay in Boston, other than attendance at the various exercises at the Massachusetts Institute of Technology in my telegram I invited you and all those who will be accompanying you to be our guests at the Ritz–Carlton while you are here. Even though you should want to stay at the president's House yourself it might be a convenience for you to have rooms at the Ritz where you could get away and rest and it might make it easier for those who are with you to be housed there. On the chance of that, I have taken the liberty of reserving at the Ritz from Wednesday, March 30 to Tuesday April 5 a number of suites which can readily be given up if you don't want them. I also will have motor cars available.'

And following extract of cable from Burchard[1] of MIT received today:

'Have engaged suite of bedrooms and parlours Wednesday through Saturday for party consisting yourself, Mr Baruch, Mr Soames, a lady secretary and a Yard man. Can increase these or extend time if notified.'

What do you advise. Do you propose to stay there beyond 2nd at latest.[2]

---

[1] John Ely Burchard, 1898–1975. Born in Minnesota. Educated at MIT. Prof. at MIT, 1938–50. Dean, School of Humanities and Social Science, MIT, 1950–69.

[2] Baruch replied: 'Many Boston invitations. Advise stay Ritz as MIT guest and leaving after Truman's departure.'

Clementine Churchill to Winston S. Churchill
(Churchill papers, 1/46)[1]

5 March 1949

My Darling,

I am so unhappy over Jamaica and I must seem to you and I fear to Mary and Christopher as a spoil-sport. But as I said to you in my letter yesterday (which I tore up perhaps before you had time to assimilate it), I feel that for you, at this moment of doubt and discouragement among your followers, to stay with Max will increase that doubt and discouragement. It would seem cynical and an insult to the Party.

You often tease me and call me 'pink' but believe me I feel it very much. I do not mind if you resign the leadership when things are good, but I can't bear you to be accepted murmuringly and uneasily. In my humble way I have tried to help. The political luncheons here, visits to Woodford, attending to your Constituency Correspondence. But now and then I have felt chilled and discouraged by the creeping knowledge that you do only just as much as will keep you in Power. But that much is not enough in these hard anxious times.

My Darling – Please take Mary with you to America. It would give her such joy and I think it's most important for her and Christopher to be together and to share every possible experience while they are young and passionate.

I still hope that you may decide against Jamaica, but I cannot venture to persuade you. I only know, that feeling as I do, it would be wrong for me to go.

Winston S. Churchill to Bernard Baruch
(Churchill papers, 2/210)

7 March 1949

I have at length persuaded Clemmie and Mary to come with me to New York and Boston. I am sure this will be agreeable and I hope not inconvenient to you. Can you receive Clemmie and me at your flat and if necessary the children could go to a hotel. Clemmie will come with me to Boston and return night of April 1 in order to go back with Randolph and June on the *Queen Mary* which sails April 2. Mary and Christopher are coming on with me to Washington and afterwards to Jamaica, if political situation here permits. Do let me know my dear friend whether this fits in with your plans or how you would like it arranged.[2]

---

[1] This letter was handwritten.
[2] Baruch responded on Mar. 8: 'Delighted Clemmie Mary coming. You and Clemmie can stay at my flat. Will arrange hotel Christopher Mary. How many secretaries maids valets your party.'

March 1949

Winston S. Churchill to Bernard Baruch
(Churchill papers, 2/210)

9 March 1949

Thank you so much. Clemmie and I delighted to stay at your flat and children as proposed at hotel. Am telling MIT about the ladies, who do not wish any alteration made in existing plans. Have explained that I cannot make so important a speech without resting before-hand during the day. I have therefore declined their proposal for a large stag dinner on March 31 but of course will attend that on April 1st given to the President before he speaks.

Your letter February 18[1] just received March 8. The twenty days it has taken is not a tribute to the scientific progress of the twentieth century. I should like very much to dine with General Eisenhower in New York. Which of our few nights do you think would suit best? Should prefer go by train to Boston in morning and rest before meeting. Am bringing two lady secretaries and Scotland Yard are sending one or perhaps two men. I have my valet. Neither Clemmie nor Mary are bringing a maid.

I have refused all other engagements or invitations except those mentioned in the following telegram.

Winston S. Churchill to Randolph S. Churchill
(Churchill papers, 1/46)

9 March 1949

Thank you so much for your letter. Have now persuaded your mother and Mary to come with me on *Queen Elizabeth*. They will stay with Bernie in New York and come to Boston. Your mother will then return by *QM* with you both on April 2. This fits in very well. Delighted you can come to Boston where accommodation has been arranged for me and rest of party by MIT at Ritz. I have refused all personal engagements except the discourse March 31 and stag dinner to President before he makes his address on April 1. Your mother will go back by train to New York with you that night. We can arrange all details when I arrive 23rd. Presume you will both stay at Ritz Boston with us. Am telling MIT I will defray but I expect they will wish to do so themselves. Keep in touch with Bernie. Love.

---

[1] Reproduced above (pp. 1331–2).

Winston S. Churchill to Paul Bryan[1]
(Churchill papers, 2/90)

10 March 1949

This bye-election gives an opportunity to the Sowerby Division to take a direct part in British affairs. We live in times of deep anxiety, both about our national safety and our means of earning our independent livelihood in the modern world.

Some facts stand out plainly. Grievous injuries have been suffered by the British Empire and Commonwealth of Nations. Over four hundred thousand of His Majesty's subjects have been killed in India in the last two years that is to say more than all our casualties, military and civilian, in the whole of our victorious war. Burma has become a foreign country and is in anarchy. Although Parliament has given the Government the right to enforce Compulsory Service in the Armed Forces, and although vast sums of money have been voted to equip and maintain them, the condition of our defences is lamentable. Never before was so much manpower and money used for so little result in security.

At home Nationalization has failed wherever it has been enforced. One great industry after another has been transferred from the profit-making to the loss-making side of the account. Now the Socialists, to brazen out their failure, are assaulting our most successful export earner, the Steel Industry. This can only make us a poorer and a weaker country.

I feel sure Yorkshire electors will not be deceived by the inflated pay packets of the wage-earners. What is given with one hand is taken away with the other. Prices are raised upon us by the high costs of State-purchased raw material and of nationalized fuel and power, and wages diminished by heavy taxation.

There is no major step which the Socialist Government have taken in social reform which was not conceived and planned by the war-time Coalition Government, in a Parliament with an overwhelming Conservative majority. The Socialists are making us live in Fool's Purgatory upon the generous grants of free-enterprise capitalist America. They boast they have cured unemployment, and yet at the same time they admit that but for the immense American subsidy there would be between one and two million unemployed today.

Our British Island, with its immense population, will never be able to maintain its pre-war standard of living under a Socialist system of society. If we are to earn our daily bread in the world, it can only be by the strongest possible impulse of individual effort and ingenuity rising from conditions of freedom and fair play.

---

[1] Paul Elmore Oliver Bryan, 1913–2004. Lt-Col., 1943. MP (Cons.) for Howden, East Riding of Yorkshire, 1955–83; for Boothferry, 1983–7. Asst Government Whip, 1956–8. Parliamentary Private Secretary to Minister of Defence, 1956. Vice-Chairman, Conservative Party Organisation, 1961–5; Conservative 1922 Committee, 1977–87. Knighted, 1972.

You are the right man for Sowerby. You live and work in the Constituency. You are well parsed in its local Government. As a war-time soldier, an industrialist, and a sportsman, you have gained distinction. I send you my cordial wishes for success.

Anthony Eden to Winston S. Churchill
(Churchill papers, 2/162)

13 March 1949   Malaya
Personal

My dear Winston,

I enclose copy of a letter which I have received from Ed Stettinius about Yalta. It has been following me around Australia. I propose to reply that I cannot think off-hand of anyone who could do the reviewing but that may be he would like to get into touch with you about it when you are in America. I do not suppose you will want to read it all, but it may be that you could find the time to see him as intentions are clearly very friendly. Alec Cadogan might help.

We have arrived here after two days' delay in Darwin, owing first to bad weather and then to engine trouble, and I have not yet had time to gather any impressions here except that the process of dealing with the bandits here is going to be a long one unless more information is forthcoming, especially from the Chinese. Even then this jungle is terrible country to comb.

I am very sorry to miss you before you go off to the States and I do hope that you have a really good trip there. I am very fit now, but was rather exhausted at the end of the Australian tour which was really strenuous.

My love to Clemmie and very best wishes to yourself. Sorry to read some rather silly writing about Harmsworth.[1] No reason to be dismayed.

Winston S. Churchill to Bernard Baruch
(Churchill papers, 2/210)

14 March 1949

1. Owing to one thing and another have decided to return home with Clemmie by the *QM* leaving New York April 2. This does not alter any of our engagements except that I ought to offer Laughlin to dine with him and Houghton Mifflins on Wednesday March 30 in Boston. We could leave after luncheon 30th and reach Boston in good time. Hope this will be agreeable to you.

---

[1] Vere Harold Esmond Harmsworth, 1925–98. Educated at Eton College. Joined family newspaper business; in 1971, took over all the family newspapers and turned them into a fortune worth US$1.7 billion. Succeeded his father as 3rd Viscount Rothermere, 1978.

2. I have sent following telegram to British Ambassador Washington. I now find it will be necessary for me to return to England with Mrs Churchill by the *Queen Mary* leaving New York April 2. I therefore greatly regret I cannot avail myself of your hospitality from April 3–7. I hope however to have a good talk with you when I come to dine with the President on March 24. This arrangement of course negatives all invitations in Washington including the Cincinnati and the National Press Club about which no engagements have been made. Once more thanking you.

Winston S. Churchill to Bernard Baruch
(*Churchill papers, 2/210*)

15 March 1949

1. Of course if Senate invite me to address them it would alter plans as it would be my duty to express thanks of Britain and Europe to United States for all they are doing for the world. I had better however speak before Bevin arrives as I could make some acknowledgment of his work. What would be hour of address? Could speak Friday, March 25 and return in time for Luce's dinner, flying if necessary. Alternative would be Monday March 28 returning for dinner *New York Times*.

2. Having brought the children to the United States would like them to stay till *Queen Elizabeth* returns April 13. They have some invitations of their own though nothing clinched but it seems a great pity they should not have a longer stay.

3. Have had charming telegram from Ike. Will fix a date as soon as I hear from you about Senate.

4. Our active cable correspondence reminds me of the days when you made me nitrate king and our friendship began.[1]

Henry Hopkinson to Winston S. Churchill
(*Churchill papers, 2/82*)

16 March 1949
Secret

A small informal Committee of Conservative Members of Parliament and members of the Research Department, meeting under the chairmanship of Mr Harold Macmillan, have been considering the question of Greece. We view the situation with great anxiety and feel that there are several issues on

---

[1] Baruch responded: 'What you do is alright. Will cable you from Washington Wednesday definitely about Senate. Agree fully about children. Please advise New York exactly how many your party. Devotedly Bernie.'

which the best hope of a solution lies in your taking the points up direct with President Truman when you see him in America. This is also the personal view of Sir Orme Sargent.

From information at our disposal, including first-hand reports of recent visitors to Greece and conversations with senior officials in the Foreign Office, it seems probable that unless a successful summer campaign can be conducted this year Greek morale will collapse, the present administration will crumble away and we shall find Greece behind the Iron Curtain by the end of the year. Members of the Greek Government with whom we are in contact believe that a successful campaign can be carried out. Their complacency is apparently shared by General Van Fleet,[1] the head of the American Military Mission in Athens. We do not share this confidence, and indeed the Greeks themselves insist on the need for strengthening the Army and Air Force.

It seems to us that the following things require to be done:
1. The Greek Army is at present limited by the Americans to 197,000, but is shortly to be raised by 5,000. Of these 69,000 are engaged in training or ancillary services, and 25,000 are in artillery or armoured units. Of the remaining 100,000 infantrymen, 50,000 form the light infantry battalions and are largely engaged in static defence of towns, communications, etc. The actual mobile infantry force only consists of 50,000 organized into 8 divisions, i.e. 3 Army Corps and 4 Small Commando groups.

    The Rebels engaged in active operations are estimated at between 23,000 and 28,000, with a further 75,000 conscripted civilians and others engaged in supplying and maintaining this force. The result is that the Greek Army has enough superiority to guarantee a victory in any one given place but not in 2 or 3 sectors of the so-called front at the same time. The operations against the Grammos position, which was cleared last summer but which the Guerillas re-occupied while the Greek Army was engaged elsewhere, is a typical example.
2. At present the Greek Air Force disposes only of some 40 Spitfires which are equipped for carrying light bombs, and a few Harvards for reconnaissance. They have been promised 30 Spitfires from Britain but they have not been delivered. This delivery should be carried out at once, and the Greeks should also be proved with a sufficient number of light bombers of the Boston type. If these cannot be made available from Great Britain, the Americans should supply them.

---

[1] James Alward Van Fleet, 1892–1992. Born in Coytesville, Fort Lee, NJ. Attended West Point, 1911. Graduated and commissioned 2nd Lt, 1915. 1st Lt, 1916. Capt., 1917. Maj., 1920. Lt-Col., 1936. Col., 1941. Brig.-Gen., 1946. Maj.-Gen., then Lt-Gen., 1948. Gen., 1951. Served in WWI, WWII and Korean War. Three Silver Stars, two LOMs, three Bronze Stars, three Purple Hearts, three DSCs, four DSMs.

3. The British and American Military Missions exist side by side. They are responsible respectively for training on the one hand and equipment and operational advice on the other. They should be integrated on the AFHQ basis under an American General. I understand that our people would be quite prepared to do this but it has been turned down by the Americans.

4. All of the above measures would greatly contribute to a successful summer campaign. We feel, however, that complete success can only be achieved if the British and Americans take an active part in the running of the country on something along the lines of the Cromer regime in Egypt. We understand that the Greeks would be willing to accept this if suitably camouflaged, and the Foreign Office recently proposed a joint Anglo-American Working Party to examine the matter. This was refused by the Americans, but we feel that the matter should be re-opened.

5. Steps are to be taken to disrupt the Enver Hoxha[1] regime in Albania by propaganda and, understand, dropping of arms and food to his opponents. This should be intensified. On the other hand, the Americans are apparently engaged in dropping Chetnik agents and material in Yugoslavia, which is doing no good and merely irritating Tito. This policy should be abandoned and every effort should be made, by means of commercial assistance, offers of food and coal, etc., to bribe Tito if not to ally himself with the West, at least to seal the Yugoslav–Greek frontier. Bulgarian threats to Yugoslav and Greek Macedonia will be ample justification for such action.

The essence of all this is time. Unless these measures are taken in the next month or two, it will be too late to ensure success for the campaign in the summer, and Greece may be lost to the Western Powers with incalculable repercussions on Turkey and the whole situation in the Eastern Mediterranean.

Bernard Baruch to Winston S. Churchill
(*Churchill papers, 2/210*)

17 March 1949

Connally introducing resolution asking you to speak to Senate noon March 25. Will report as soon as carried. Eisenhower will see you at Luce's and *New York Times*' dinner. Beg you not to discommode yourself or Clemmie about him or his wife. They will gladly hold themselves entirely at your service. He could not be finer. How many and who in your party? Children must surely remain and I will take care of them. Who goes to Boston with you?

[1] Enver Hail Hoxha, 1908–85. Communist Head of State of Albania and C-in-C of armed forces, 1944–85. Chairman, Democratic Front of Albania. PM, 1944–54.

March 1949

Winston S. Churchill to Sir Oliver Franks
(Churchill papers, 2/210)

17 March 1949

Should much like to come to your party at 5.30 leaving me time to dress for dinner. Eugene Meyer[1] occurs to me. I must of course visit General Marshall if he is in Washington. I can perhaps start from New York early 24th. Understand that Senate may invite me to address them March 25. I should consider it my duty to comply as I wish to thank US for all they have done for Europe and our country. Mrs Churchill will now accompany me to Washington so please tell White House. My party in addition will be my son-in-law, one valet, one detective and one lady secretary. I should have to hasten back after the Senate by train to New York for Luce's large private dinner 25th.

Winston S. Churchill to Victor Vincent[2]
(Churchill papers, 2/266)

18 March 1949

1. In my absence you will give directions to Kurn and also to Walter and Hans.[3]
2. First thing. Tidy up round the pool. No more water in new pool. Chalk pool may be filled and overflow till I come back.
3. Gunnerer filter pool. Kurn should make and render, on both sides, the inside up to the circle of brickwork to the level of the overflow. This should be watertight. The pipe and valve has been arranged with Southon's plumber. You should ask Miss Hamblin when you want him. You should always apply to Miss Hamblin in any difficulty.
4. Mrs Churchill wants Kurn to do her kitchen garden orchard steps. He knows about this. You should fit this in. He should also make the steps by the new pool. Four planks have already been laid. He should have some help with this.
5. I told you about buying half a dozen nice rhododendron plants and showed you where to plant them. You may be able to find a bigger one for the angle below the new pool.
6. In case of leakage from the new pool, Walter should re-plug with clay, as he did on Thursday, the possible leaks from the inside.
7. You should watch this carefully; also the goldfish. Try a few roach in

---

[1] Eugene Isaac Meyer, 1875–1959. Financier. Born in Los Angeles. Graduated from Yale University, 1895. Chairman, Federal Reserve, 1930–3. Purchased *Washington Post*, 1933. First President, World Bank Group, June–Dec. 1946.
[2] Head Gardener at Chartwell, 1947–79.
[3] Former German POWs, employed at Chartwell.

the new pool after the first week, and if they die try some more a week later. Report to Miss Hamblin at once any signs of trouble with the goldfish.

8. Capt. Soames wants Kurn to build a small coal locker for the Bothey at French Street. This is urgent. He should have help from either Walter or Hans. It is thought it will only take a day.

9. There is also a door on the farm which Kurn could easily mend, but it may take a couple of days. Capt. Soames attaches importance to this.

10. I am hoping you will turf the surrounding of the new pool. You can of course use all strength for this.

11. Our most serious need is more logs. Capt. Soames tells me that Kurn knows where the fallen beech tree is and certain other trees by French Street. These should be cut up with the motor saw by Walter and Hans together. Kurn will have his own jobs to do. If they need help in the early stages you will have to give it to them. The filling of the wood-shed is most important and must be pushed forward at every possible opportunity.

12. Miss Marston will see that the three pots of lily bulbs are sent down by train to you as soon as possible.

Bernard Baruch to Winston S. Churchill
(Churchill papers, 2/210)

22 March 1949

Owing to shortness of time proposed Washington address for 25th cannot be arranged. In circumstances personally advise you concentrate on Boston speech only. I am authoritatively informed you will have an overwhelming audience present as well as world wide radio coverage and national television. Your dinner with Luce is on the 25th not on the 26th and I have arranged to and from Washington for both private car and plane which ever you decide. Will meet you at pier.

Winston S. Churchill to Lord Camrose
(Churchill papers, 4/63)

23 March 1949
Private

My dear Bill,

I hope we are going to meet at dinner tonight at Bernie's.

There is a serious point which I should like to discuss with you, and on which I send you the enclosed note. Please think it over and give me your opinion.

ENCLOSURE

The third volume which is now finished, subject to further improvement, carries the narrative through 1941 up to my return by Air from Bermuda in January 1942. The fourth volume, on which considerable progress has been made, runs from February 1942 to the final defeat and surrender of the Germans and Italians in Tunis in May 1943. As at present arranged the fifth volume will have to complete the story up to the unconditional surrender of Germany and Japan in May and August 1945. If all this has to be pressed into the fifth volume it is evident that the scale of the narrative will have to be greatly altered and only the salient features presented. In this period we have the invasion of Sicily and Italy, the Cairo and Teheran Conferences, the operations at Anzio, the great cross-channel invasion of France and the tremendous battles there, the capture of Rome by Alexander, the winter fighting in Germany and the passage of the Rhine, von Rundstedt's counter-attack, the Yalta Conference and the serious differences with Russia, the fate of Poland, the final advance into Germany with further tension between the Western Allies and the Soviets, and finally the general victory over Germany with allusion to the General Election, and the surrender of Japan under the Atomic Bomb. To compress all this into a single volume seems a pity. I therefore suggest that you and your friends should consider a sixth volume which the above features would easily fill with matters of the highest interest and importance. It is necessary for me to know whether this would be agreeable to the purchasers, and what terms they will offer, so that I can plan my work accordingly.

Please let me know. I think all the principals are available in New York. I believe Reves is anxious for a sixth volume and probably Luce and the *New York Times* will have the same view. All the three volumes are much longer than the stipulated number of words, but of course I cannot tell how much time will be at my disposal in the future. It seems to me this is an opportunity for testing the opinion of all concerned.

It will talk to you about this when we meet, but thought it would be convenient for you to have this <u>aide memoire</u> to show the others.

Winston S. Churchill: speech
('In the Balance', pages 31–9)

25 March 1949 Ritz-Carlton Hotel, New York

THE COMMUNIST MENACE

I am extremely complimented to be invited here tonight and to find myself your guest amidst a gathering of Americans among whom I can discern many doughty comrades in our common struggle and who, taken together, represent a powerful living element in the future and in the power of the United States. I thank you very much for all the kind things you have said.

You yourself have rendered great services. The wonderful publications which spread so widely through the land and put quality and art and point and pith and so forth in their vanguard, these are in themselves great contributions to the life and strength not only of the United States but of the English-speaking world. This great company, these old friends and comrades, gives me confidence and I am glad to come here and express my profound thanks on behalf of Britain and on behalf of Western Europe, of free Europe, as I have some credentials to do – for all you have done and are doing.

Gentleman – many nations have arrived at the summit of the world but none, before the United States, on this occasion, has chosen that moment of triumph, not for aggrandizement, but for further self-sacrifice – sacrifice for the causes by which the life and strength of mankind is refreshed. The United States has shown itself more worth of trust and honour than any government of men or associations of nations, that has ever reached pre-eminence by their action on the morrow of the common victory won by all. I wish to express the thanks of my own dear island and of its Empire, Commonwealth and also of the many countries in Western Europe who are drawing together on the broad ideals of Anglo-Saxon, British–American, call it what you will, unity, which alone gives an opportunity for the further advance of the human race.

Gentlemen, some time ago, you may possibly remember, I made a speech in Missouri at Fulton – I got into great trouble for that. But now not so much. Now it is thought better of. And I was very glad to see that General Marshall, that great statesman and soldier – I do not know whether you put soldier or statesman first in regard to so eminent a man – General Marshall has created this policy of the Marshall Aid, which shall ever bear his name – not because of what happens in the three or four years of the Aid but because of its effect as a turning point in the history of the world. General Marshall played his part, and then, we have now come to the Atlantic Pact, which when Mr Attlee kindly showed it to me before it became public – but after it was settled – I thought it was one of the most important documents ever signed by large communities of human beings and certainly indicates a very considerable advance in opinion as far as the United States of America are concerned. Well, there you are – you're in it now, because there's no way out, but still if we pool our luck and assure our fortunes I think you will have no reason to regret it.

But what has brought this great change from the time when I was so scolded three years ago for what I said at Fulton? And I do remember Governor Dewey coming down here to back me up at that rather bleak and raw moment when I spoke here in New York. The Governor knows how to take a bump and I've had some of that, too. My father – I remember some words that my father spake when I was an urchin – I remember that he said a man who can't take a knockdown blow isn't worth a damn. Well, I've always tried to live up to that and on the whole it's quite a healthy process. How has this great change from the atmosphere three years ago, when I spoke at Fulton, and now address you here – this distinguished gathering here – how has that great change been accomplished? No one could possibly have done it but Mr Stalin. He is the one. No enemy of Russia, no – and I was never an enemy of Russia – no anti-Communist or no Conservative Republican gathering, missionaries, agitators, propaganda – none of them – if they worked night and day could ever have achieved the extraordinary change of opinion, change of conviction, change of mood, change of attitude and policy which has taken place in the last wo years except the Soviet Government.

And that brings me to a question which we must ask ourselves. What is the explanation of the Soviet policy? Why have they deliberately united the free world against them? I will hazard the answer. These men in the Kremlin are very capable men; they do not act on the spur of the moment; profound deliberations take place in conclaves long welded together and any mistake made by any member of the company may be seriously viewed and punished. Yes – they do not let themselves go like some of us politicians do in the democratic countries. Well, how is it then – that they have deliberately united the free world against them? It is, I am sure, because they feared the friendship of the West more than they do its hostility. They can't afford to allow free and friendly intercourse between their country and those they control and the rest of the world. They daren't see it develop – the coming and going and all the easements and tolerances which come from the agreeable contacts of nations and of individuals. They can't afford it. The Russians must not see what goes on outside and the world must not see what goes on inside the Soviet domain. That is, in my opinion, the explanation. After all if you were one of the fourteen men in the Kremlin – holding down hundreds of millions of people, aiming at the rule of the world – you might well feel that your prime interest was, at all costs, to keep up the barriers. I believe that their motive is self-preservation – not for Russia – but for themselves. Of course going out of office in Russia isn't quite as easy a business as it may be here or over the other side of the ocean. You lose the election, you may lose your life. It's very high stakes they play for – these fourteen men – and I'm sure that self-preservation for themselves lies at the root of this strange, extraordinary, unreasonable policy which has caused them deliberately to alienate all the generous sympathy there was for the brave Russian armies who fought so nobly in the war.

And thus we have come to what is called the cold war, a form of relationship between nations unprecedented in history, unparalleled in history. Never have there been such things that are happening now published all over the world. The insults, the taunts, the affronts, the ultimatums, the holdings up and so forth, and American bombers based in British airports and Soviet plans being pushed in every country to undermine or overthrow the existing state of civilization. All this – never in peace has been possible, but it is going on now and it is called the cold war.

You would like me to examine some of these questions with you tonight because I don't want to trespass upon so important an audience except to put to them points of real vital consequence. And I put this question. Are we winning the cold war?

It's a very important one for all of us, and for our families and our children. We wonder what world they will inherit and come into. Are we winning the cold war? Well this can't be decided, I think, by looking at Europe alone. We must first look to the East. The worst event, I'm sure Mr Luce will agree with me in this – I'm sure the worst event since the fighting stopped has been the subjugation of a large part of China by Communism. There's your most formidable event. Now mind you, I think you have done quite right not to be diverted to make great undue efforts there at this moment, but the American interest in China is enormous. I was very much astonished when I came over here after Pearl Harbour to find the estimate of values which seemed to prevail in high American quarters, even in the highest, about China. Some of them thought that China would make as great a contribution to victory in the war as the whole British Empire together. Well, that astonished me very much. Nothing that I picked up afterwards led me to think that my astonishment was ill-founded. And it was said to me – well, China is an immense factor in the world, an immense population of intelligent, gifted, cultivated people, charming people with so many virtues, and so on. Well, I was thinking what part they would be able to play in our victory. I think on the whole you will not find a large profit item entered on that side of the ledger, but that doesn't alter our regard for the Chinese people. But what has happened now? It's very important, and while I think the decision of the United States is quite right, I am astonished they are not more concerned about it than they appear to be. Here I would like to congratulate you upon, and pay a tribute to, the work of General MacArthur in Japan. (Applause). He has seemed to show a genius in peace equal to the high renown he gained in war.

In my view you don't want to knock a man down except to pick him up in a better frame of mind. That is my view about all these things that happened in the world – and you may pick him up in a better frame of mind. And that is a thing to think about. I say that the Atlantic Pact, in my view, would naturally be followed at no lengthy interval by a Pacific Pact which would deal with that immense portion of the globe.

Well, so much for the East. But a great advance has been made in the West in this cold war. Take the success of the Berlin Airlift, which arose largely from American conviction that it could be done. I will say, quite frankly, without any special knowledge, I wondered really whether it could be done and on the face of it, it seemed rather odd – I mean, carrying coal by air, and so on. But still it has been a great success. Time has been gained for peace. The efficiency of the American and British air forces has been greatly sustained by the enormous practice in almost active service conditions which they have had and are having over all these long months, not without their sacrifices in life. And lastly, and this I care about very much, the airlift into Berlin has won the heart of Germany – gathered the heart of Germany over to us – as nothing else could have done and shown them that their choice should be with the Western Nations and with progress and with freedom and that they should not be drawn into the hideous Communist entanglement which any of them might in their despair otherwise have succumbed to. I think it is a wonderful thing, although when we look at the record of crimes that have been brought out, it seems hard to forget at all the past. I assure you you must forget the past. You must obliterate all parts of the past which are not useful to the future. You must regard the re-entry of Germany into the family of European nations as an event which the Western World must desire and must, if possible, achieve.

Gentlemen – three weeks ago I was in Brussels. I was addressing a meeting of 30,000 people – very friendly, even enthusiastic; 250 Communists were removed or thought it better to be silent – but there were these 30,000 people in this great square at Brussels, and I could feel their anxiety. I could feel, as I spoke, their anxiety – their fear. After all, they haven't got the Atlantic Ocean between them and danger. They haven't even got the Channel and the Channel is pretty good, as we showed you in the last war – and showed others. In ten days – in ten days perhaps the Soviet armour might be in Brussels. Here were these 30,000 people – good, faithful, decent people – naturally they know about it all. The Soviets have a new technique developing for what they do to countries they overrun, and what they will do to the countries they expect to overrun. It is a very elaborate technique – a Swedish professor came and explained it to me at length – he's writing a book about it – it is to liquidate all outstanding personalities in every class and walk of life. To liquidate them so as to have nothing below but a mass of ordinary people whom they can rule like the Communist Party in Russia rules the enormous mass of unfortunate Russian serfs. That is their technique, and they have got lists all made out of the different countries outside the Iron Curtain and of the people and so on. I don't suppose they've troubled to make a list here but they might find quite a lot in this room. But it's a grim thing to have that peril so little away. And while I was talking to these people – in the beautiful surroundings there – I could feel their fear and anxiety, but when I spoke of the United States being with us in this matter of European freedom, I felt a wave of hope in this great concourse and I know you will not let them down in regard to any matter in which you have pledged the word of the great Republic.

Well, gentlemen, it isn't only in Belgium you look at Europe. The hideous process of the subjugation of Czechoslovakia should be studied in the utmost detail. It's a work of art – the methods and so on. Well, the Czechs live on and no nation in bondage should despair, but I was glad to see American veterans tonight displaying a placard on which is written 'Uncle Joe, what happened to Masaryk?' – a friend of ours and fighter in the war, a struggler for freedom. There is terrible danger and peril and if you have not got these great barriers of salt water or short effective barriers, fear must come into their hearts, but that fear is removed because they are relying upon the valour, virtue and the giant strength of the United States.

And France – they have a situation with Thorez, this deserter, saying that this third of the population who vote Communist will fight against their country if the Russians have to invade it or have a chance of invading it. Italy – shattered and ruined in many ways but making a great recovery. In all these countries under direst peril they do look to you to give them the strength, not only to protect them, but to give them the strength to stand up for their own liberties. I don't want to have the whole of the world, of Britain and all that hanging on to the United States to be kept going by them but you must do enough to animate them – that is what you are doing and that is what the Marshall Aid and the Atlantic Pact have done – is to animate these countries and enable them to come forward more and more in their own strength.

If it was not for the aid of the United States and, I will say, of Great Britain (which counts), they would all go down like ninepins before the Communist menace. I tell you – it's no use arguing with a Communist. It's no good trying to convert a Communist, or persuade him. You can only deal with them on the following basis. I have had some experience in direct contact with the highest authorities, under the most favourable conditions, and I can tell you that you can only do it by having superior force on your side on the matter in question – and they must also be convinced that you will use – you will not hesitate to use – these forces, if necessary, in the most ruthless manner. You have not only to convince the Soviet Government that you have superior force – that they are confronted by superior force – but that you are not restrained by any moral consideration if the case arose from using that force with complete material ruthlessness. And that is the greatest chance of peace, it is absolutely necessary that you should be stronger – I say you – we, all of us, we're in it – we should be the stronger and that they should know that we stop at nothing that honour allows. But you will ask – I will press this a little more if you will permit me, and my argument is a whole, is integral – you will ask: Is time on our side and the question whether more decided action should be taken? – Now I have reached a conclusion for the moment upon that. And I do not think any violent or precipitate action should be taken now. I do not regard war as inevitable. I do not think so. I think we still have control to preserve our cause without the world being plunged in another frightful struggle.

Well, now, do not let us however delude ourselves with the idea that we can make armies strong enough in the next year or two which could hold the front of civilization in Europe. I do not think we can. But they're all getting welded together under this pressure. Unities are being formed which would never otherwise have been formed. Give them a little time to knit and set. Let us have it. Our forces are getting stronger, actually and relatively, than they were a year ago. We have probably a year or two before other people are able to make the atomic bomb. And once they are able to make it, then they have to make it, which is another phase, measured by considerable time periods. Well, I heard a lot about that. But – gentlemen, it is sad after all our victory and triumph and all that we hoped for and so on, to find not peace and ease and hope and comfort, but only the summons to further endeavour. But that is life! After our great victory we did hope that the struggle for freedom would be decided in our time, but however long the struggle lasts, British and American people will not weary of it, or if weary of it, they will not desist from it, because victory or defeat are things which happen, but duty is a thing which is compulsory and has to go on irrespective, and carries with it its own rewards whatever the upshot of the struggle may be.

We are now confronted with something which is quite as wicked but much more formidable than Hitler, because Hitler had only the Herrenvolk stuff and anti-Semitism. Well, somebody said about that – a good starter, but a bad stayer. That's all he had. He had no theme. But these fourteen men in the Kremlin have their hierarchy and a church of Communist adepts whose missionaries are in every country as a fifth column, and not only a fifth column, in your country, ours, everywhere, and so on, with a feeling that they may be running a risk, but if their gamble comes off they will be the masters of the whole land in which they are a minority at the present time. They will be the Quislings with power to rule and dominate all the rest of their fellow countrymen. Therefore they have a good prospective advantage. It is certain in my opinion that Europe would have been communized but for the deterrent of the atomic bomb in the hands of the United States. That is my firm belief and that governs the situation today. Sometimes one looks at the terrible alternative. Fancy if they had got it first. Well, I feel that sense that we all should have in our troubled journey – pilgrimage – that Divine protection has shielded those who faithfully sustained the causes of freedom and of justice.

One comfort I've got today is that the democratic nations are not fooled so easily by Stalin as they were by Hitler. You must have noticed that. Whenever Hitler said 'this is the last territorial claim I shall make, I need no more Czechs' and so on – they all used to turn around upon me in those days and say, there are you, now you see how wrong you were! Now you see it's all settled, it's all happy! Look, this is a peace move, it's all friendly, and so on. Well, once bit, twice shy – and I notice now that a very different and far more critical mood about manoeuvring offers by dictators prevails in the most enlightened circles on this side of the Atlantic.

I will say just a word about my own country before I sit down – a word or two about the British scene. Now I'm opposed to the – you might have heard perhaps – I'm opposed to the present Government. But that's our own affair.

Like you, we settle our own affairs in our own way by our own political system. We don't want foreigners interfering any more than you would like any of us to interfere with you. That's all right. And I'm grateful for all the aid you have given to my country, but I say – do not underrate the strength of Britain. And do not ever lose sight of the fact that Britain is an absolutely vital necessity to the strength and future of the United States.

You may be larger and we may be older. You may be the stronger, sometimes we may be the wiser. But let us talk it out like friends and brothers, as we shall, and as we can, because we can understand each other with greater perfection than any two great groupings of the human race have ever been able to before. I said at this speech I made at Fulton, which I got scolded for, I said – don't suppose that half a century from now you will not see 70,000,000 or 80,000,000 of Britons spread about the world and united in defence of our traditions, our way of life and the world causes which you and we espouse. Well, added to all that, you have of power in this world, that fraternal association of the English-speaking world which I plead, far greater than alliances and not so formal, that fraternal association will give the freedom and security that is needed, that we demand for ourselves, and that we together perhaps alone, can bestow on other mortals.

Forward then! Forward, let us go forward, without fear into the future and let us dread naught when duty calls!

Winston S. Churchill: speech
('Winston S. Churchill, His Complete Speeches', volume 7, pages 7801–10)

31 March 1949   Massachusetts Institute of Technology
Boston

THE TWENTIETH CENTURY – ITS PROMISE AND ITS REALIZATION

I am honoured by your wish that I should take part in the discussions of the Massachusetts Institute of Technology. We have suffered in Great Britain by the lack of colleges of University rank in which engineering and the allied subjects are taught. Industrial production depends on technology and it is because the Americans, like the prewar Germans, have realized this and created institutions for the advanced training of large numbers of high-grade engineers to translate the advances of pure science into industrial technique, that their output per head and consequent standard of life are so high. It is surprising that England, which was the first country to be industrialized, has nothing of comparable stature. If tonight I strike other notes than those of material progress, it implies no want of admiration for all the work you have done and are doing. My aim, like yours, is to be guided by balance and proportion.

The outstanding feature of the Twentieth Century has been the enormous expansion in the numbers who are given the opportunity to share in the larger and more varied life which in previous periods was reserved for the few and for the very few. This process must continue at an increasing rate. If we are to bring the broad masses of the people in every land to the table of abundance, it can only be by the tireless improvement of all our means of technical production, and by the diffusion in every form of education of an improved quality to scores of millions of men and women. Even in this darkling hour I have faith that this will go on. I rejoice in Tennyson's lines:

> Men, my brothers, men, the workers, ever reaping something new;
> That which they have done but earnest of the things that they shall do.

I was, however, a little disquieted, I must admit, that you find it necessary to debate the question, to quote Dr Burchard's opening address, 'whether the problem of world production yielding at least a minimum living to the whole population can be solved, and whether man has so destroyed the resources of his world that he may be doomed to die of starvation'. If, with all the resources of modern science, we find ourselves unable to avert world famine, we shall all be to blame, but a peculiar responsibility would rest upon the scientists. I do not believe they will fail, but if they do, or were not allowed to succeed, the consequences would be very unpleasant because it is certain that mankind would not agree to starve equally, and there might be some very sharp disagreements about how the last crust was to be shared. This would simplify our problem, as our greatest intellectual authorities here will readily admit, in an unduly primordial manner.

I frankly confess that I feel somewhat overawed in addressing this vast scientific and learned audience on the subjects which your panels are discussing. I have no technical and no university education, and have just had to pick up a few things as I went along. Therefore I speak with a diffidence, which I hope to overcome as I proceed, on these profound scientific, social and philosophic issues, each of which claims a lifelong study for itself, and are now to be examined, as schoolmen would say, not only in their integrity but in their relationship, meaning thereby not only one by one but all together.

I was so glad that in the first instance you asked me to talk about the past rather than to peer into the future because I know more about the past than I do about the future, and I was well content that the President of the United States, whose gift of prophecy was so remarkably vindicated by recent electoral results, should have accepted that task. We all regret that his heavy State duties prevent him from being here tonight. I shall therefore presently have to do a little of the peering myself.

For us in Britain the Nineteenth Century ended amid the glories of the Victorian era, and we entered upon the dawn of the Twentieth in high hope for our country, our Empire and the world. The latter and larger part of the nineteenth century had been the period of liberal advance (liberal with a small 'l' please). In 1900 a sense of moving hopefully forward to brighter, broader and easier days was predominant. Little did we guess that what has been called the Century of the Common Man would witness as its outstanding feature more common men killing each other with greater facilities than any other five centuries together in the history of the world. But we entered this terrible Twentieth Century with confidence. We thought that with improving transportation nations would get to know each other better. We believed that as they got to know each other better they would like each other more, and that national rivalries would fade in a growing international consciousness. We took it almost for granted that science would confer continual boons and blessings upon us, would give us better meals, better garments and better dwellings for less trouble, and thus steadily shorten the hours of labour and leave more time for play and cultures. In the name of ordered but unceasing progress, we saluted the Age of Democracy expressing itself ever more widely through parliaments freely and fairly elected on a broad or universal franchise. We saw no reason why men and women should not shape their own home life and careers without being cramped by the growing complexity of the State, which was to be their servant and the protector of their rights. You had the famous American maxim 'Governments derive their just powers from the consent of the governed', and we both noticed that the world was divided into peoples that owned the governments and governments that owned the peoples. At least I heard all this around that time and liked some of it very much.

I was a Minister in the British Liberal Government (large 'L' please this time), returned with a great majority in 1906. That new Liberal Government arrived in power with much of its message already delivered and most of its aims already achieved. The days of hereditary aristocratic privilege were ended or numbered. The path was opened for talent in every field of endeavour. Primary education was compulsory, universal and free, or was about to become so. New problems arising, as problems do from former successes, awaited the new administration. The independence of the proletariat from thraldom involved at least a minimum standard of life and labour and security for old age, sickness, and the death of the family breadwinner. It was to these tasks of social reform and insurance that we addressed ourselves. The name of Lloyd George will ever be associated in Great Britain with this new departure, and I am proud to have been his lieutenant in this work and also later, as a Conservative Chancellor of the Exchequer and later, still, as head of the wartime National Coalition to have carried these same themes further forward on a magnified scale.

That is how we began the century. Science presently placed novel and dangerous facilities in the hands of the most powerful countries. Humanity was informed that it could make machines that would fly through the air and vessels which could swim beneath the surface of the seas. The conquest of the air and the perfection of the art of flying fulfilled the dream which for thousands of years had glittered in human imagination. Certainly it was a marvellous and romantic event. Whether the bestowal of this gift upon an immature civilization composed of competing nations whose nationalism grew with every advance of democracy and who were as yet devoid of international organization, whether this gift was a blessing or a curse has yet to be proved. On the whole I remain an optimist. For good or ill Air mastery is today the supreme expression of military power, and fleets and armies, however necessary, must accept a subordinate rank. This is a memorable milestone in the march of man.

The submarine, to do it justice, has never made any claim to be a blessing or even a convenience. I well remember when it became an accomplished military fact of peculiar significance to the British Isles and the British Navy, there was a general belief even in the Admiralty where I presided, that no nation would ever be so wicked as to use these under-water vessels to sink merchantmen at sea. How could a submarine, it was asked, provide for the safety of the crews of the merchant ships it sank? Public opinion was shocked when old Admiral Fisher bluntly declared that this would be no bar to their being used by the new and growing German Navy in a most ruthless manner. His prediction was certainly not stultified by what was soon to happen.

Here then we have these two novel and potent weapons placed in the hands of highly nationalized sovereign States in the early part of the Twentieth Century, and both of them dwell with us today for our future edification. A third unmeasured sphere opened to us as the years passed, which, for the sake of comprehensive brevity, I will describe as Radar. This Radar, with its innumerable variants and possibilities, has so far been the handmaiden of the air, but it has also been the enemy of the submarine and in alliance with the air may well prove its exterminator. Thus we see the changes which were wrought upon our society.

In the first half of the Twentieth Century, fanned by the crimson wings of war, the conquest of the air affected profoundly human affairs. It made the globe seem much bigger to the mind and much smaller to the body. The human biped was able to travel about far more quickly. This greatly reduced the size of his estate, while at the same time creating an even keener sense of its exploitable value. In the nineteenth century Jules Verne wrote *Round the World in Eighty Days*. It seemed a prodigy. Now you can get round it in four; but you do not see much of it on the way. The whole prospect and outlook of mankind grew immeasurably larger, and the multiplication of ideas also proceeded at an incredible rate. This vast expansion was unhappily not accompanied by any noticeable advance in the stature of man, either in his mental faculties, or his moral character. His brain got no better, but it buzzed more. The scale of events around him assumed gigantic proportions while he remained about the same size. By comparison therefore he actually became much smaller. We no longer had great men directing manageable affairs. Our need was to discipline an array of gigantic and turbulent facts. To this task we have certainly so far proved unequal. Science bestowed immense new powers on man and at the same time created conditions which were largely beyond his comprehension and still more beyond his control. While he nursed the illusion of growing mastery and exulted in his new trappings, he became the sport and presently the victim of tides, and currents, of whirlpools and tornadoes amid which he was far more helpless than he had been for a long time.

Hopeful developments in many directions were proceeding in 1914 on both sides of the Atlantic and seemed to point to an age of peace and plenty when suddenly violent events broke in upon them. A spirit of adventure stirred the minds of men and was by no means allayed by the general advance of prosperity and science. On the contrary prosperity meant power, and science offered weapons. We read in the Bible 'Jeshurun waxed fat and kicked.'

For several generations Britannia had ruled the waves – for long periods at less cost annually than that of a single modern battleship. History will say that this great trust was not abused. American testimony about the early period of the Monroe Doctrine is upon record. There was the suppression of the slave trade. During our prolonged period of naval supremacy undeterred by the rise of foreign tariffs, we kept our ports freely open to the commerce of the world. Our Colonial and Oriental Empire, even our coastal trade, was free to the shipping of all the nations on equal terms. We in no way sought to obstruct the rise of other States or navies. For nearly the whole of the nineteenth century the monopoly of sea power in British hands was a trust discharged faithfully in the general interest. But now in the first decade of the twentieth century with new patterns of warships, naval rivalries became acute and fierce. Civilized governments began to think in dreadnoughts. It was in such a setting very difficult to prevent the First World War, far more difficult than it would have been to prevent the second.

There was of course one way to prevent it – one way then as now – the creation of an international instrument, strong enough to adjust the disputes of nations and enforce its decisions against an aggressor. Much wisdom, eloquence and earnest effort was devoted to this theme in which the United States took the lead, but they only got as far as the World Court at The Hague and improvements in the Geneva Convention. The impulses towards a trial of strength in Europe were far stronger at this time. Germany, demanding her 'place in the sun', was faced by a resolute France with her military honour to regain. England, in accordance with her foreign policy of three hundred years, sustained the weaker side. France found an ally in the Russia of the Czars and Germany in the crumbling Empire of the Hapsburgs. The United States, for reasons which were natural and traditional, but no longer so valid as in the past, stood aloof and expected to be able to watch as a spectator, the thrilling, fearful drama unfold from across what was then called 'the broad Atlantic'. These expectations were not borne out by what happened.

After four and a half years of hideous mechanical slaughter, illuminated by infinite sacrifice, but not remarkably relieved by strategy or generalship, high hopes and spacious opportunities awaited the victorious allies when they assembled at Versailles. War, stripped of every pretention of glamour or romance had been brought home to the masses of the peoples in forms never before experienced except by the defeated. To stop another war was the supreme object and duty of the statesmen who met as friends and allies around the Peace Table. They made great errors. The doctrine of self-determination was not the remedy for Europe, which needed above all things, unity and larger groupings. The idea that the vanquished could pay the expenses of the victors was a destructive and crazy delusion. The failure to strangle Bolshevism at its birth and to bring Russia, then prostrate, by one means or another, into the general democratic system lies heavy upon us today. Nevertheless the statesmen at Versailles, largely at the inspiration of President Wilson, an inspiration implemented effectively by British thought, created the League of Nations. This is their defence before history, and had the League been resolutely sustained and used, it would have saved us all.

This was not to be. Another ordeal even more appalling than the first lay before us. Even when so much else had failed we could have obtained a prolonged peace, lasting all our lives at least, simply by keeping Germany disarmed in accordance with the Treaty, and by treating her with justice and magnanimity. This latter condition was very nearly achieved at Locarno in 1928, but the failure to enforce the disarmament clauses and above all to sustain the League of Nations, both of which purposes could easily have been accomplished, brought upon us the Second World War. Once again the English-speaking world gloriously but narrowly emerged, bleeding and breathless, but united as we never were before. This unity is our present salvation, because after all our victories, we are now faced by perils, both grave and near, and by problems more dire than have ever confronted Christian civilization, even in this twentieth century of storm and change.

There remains however a key of deliverance. It is the same key which was searched for by those who laboured to set up the World Court at The Hague in the early years of the century. It is the same conception as animated President Wilson and his colleagues at Versailles, namely the creation of a world instrument capable at least of giving to all its members security against aggression. The United Nations Organization which has been erected under the inspiring leadership of my great wartime friend, President Roosevelt, in place of the former League, has so far been rent and distracted by the antagonism of Soviet Russia and by the fundamental schism which has opened between Communism and the rest of mankind. But we must not despair. We must persevere, and if the gulf continues to widen, we must make sure that the cause of Freedom is defended by all the resources of combined forethought and superior science. Here lies the best hope of averting a third world struggle.

One of the questions which we are debating here is defined as 'the failure of social and political institutions to keep pace with material and technical change'. Scientists should never underrate the deep-seated qualities of human nature and how, repressed in one direction they will certainly break out in another. The *genus homo* – if I may display my Latin – is a tough creature who has travelled here by a very long road. His nature has been shaped and his virtues ingrained by many millions of years of struggle, fear and pain, and his spirit has, from the earliest dawn of history, shown itself upon occasion capable of mounting to the sublime, far above material conditions or mortal terrors. He still remains man – still remains as Pope described him two hundred years ago.

> Placed on this Isthmus of a middle State
> A being darkly wise and rudely great
> Created half to rise and half to fall
> Great Lord of all things, yet a prey to all.
> Sole Judge of truth in endless error hurled,
> The glory, jest and riddle of the world.

In his introductory address, Mr Burchard, the Dean of Humanities, spoke with awe of 'an approaching scientific ability to control men's thoughts with precision'. I shall be very content if my task in this world is done before that happens. Laws just or unjust may govern men's actions. Tyrannies may restrain or regulate their words. The machinery of propaganda may pack their minds with falsehood and deny them truth for many generations of time. But the soul of man thus held in trance or frozen in a long night can be awakened by a spark coming from God knows where and in a moment the whole structure of lies and oppression is on trial for its life. Peoples in bondage should never despair. Let them hope and trust in the genius of mankind. Science no doubt could if sufficiently perverted exterminate us all but it is not in the power of material forces in any period which the youngest here tonight need take into practical account, to alter the main elements in human nature or restrict the infinite variety of forms in which the soul and genius of the human race can and will express itself.

How right you are, Dr Compton, in this great Institution of technical study and achievement, to keep a dean of humanities in the gaining of which philosophy and history walk hand in hand. Our inheritance of well-founded slowly conceived codes of honour, morals and manners, the passionate convictions which so many hundreds of millions share together of the principles of freedom and justice, are far more precious to us than anything which scientific discoveries could bestow. Those whose minds are attracted or compelled to rigid and symmetrical systems of government should remember that logic, like science, must be the servant and not the master of man. Human beings and human societies are not structures that are built or machines that are forged. They are plants that grow and must be tended as such. Life is a test and this world a place of trial. Always the problems or it may be the same problem will be presented to every generation in different forms. The problems of victory may be even more baffling than those of defeat. However much the conditions change, the supreme question is how we live and grow and bloom and die, and how far each life conforms to standards which are not wholly related to space or time.

And here I speak not only to those who enjoy the blessings and consolation of revealed religion but also to those who face the mysteries of human destiny alone. The flame of Christian ethics is still our highest guide. To guard and cherish it is our first interest, both spiritually and materially. The fulfilment of spiritual duty in our daily life is vital to our survival. Only by bringing it into perfect application can we hope to solve for ourselves the problems of this world and not of this world alone.

I cannot speak to you here tonight without expressing to the United States – as I have perhaps some right to do – the thanks of Britain and of Europe for the splendid part America is playing in the world. Many nations have risen to the summit of human affairs, but here is a great example where new-won supremacy has not been used for self-aggrandizement but only for further sacrifice.

Three years ago I made a speech at Fulton under the auspices of President Truman. Many people here and in my own country were startled and even shocked by what I said. But events have vindicated and fulfilled in much detail the warnings which I deemed it my duty to give at that time. Today there is a very different climate of opinion. I am in cordial accord with much that is being done. We have, as dominating facts, the famous Marshall Aid, the new unity in Western Europe and now the Atlantic Pact. Let us inquire into that. The responsible ministers in all the countries concerned deserve high credit. There is credit enough for all. In my own country the Foreign Secretary, Mr Bevin, who has come here to sign the Atlantic Pact, has shown himself indifferent to mere party popularity in dealing with these great national issues. He has shown himself, like many American public men, above mere partisan interest in dealing with these national and world issues. No one could, however, have brought about these immense changes in the feeling of the United States, Great Britain and Europe but for the astounding policy of the Russian Soviet Government. We may well ask: 'Why have they deliberately acted so as to unite the free world against them?' It is certainly not because there are not very able men among them. Why have they done it? It is because they fear the friendship of the West more than its hostility. They cannot afford to allow free and friendly intercourse to grow up between the vast areas they control and the civilized nations of the West. The Russian people must not see what is going on outside, and the world must not see what goes on inside the Soviet domain. Thirteen or fourteen men in the Kremlin, holding down hundreds of millions of people and aiming at the rule of the world, feel that at all costs they must keep up the barriers. Self-preservation, not for Russia but for themselves, lies at the root and is the explanation of their sinister and malignant policy.

In consequence of the Soviet conduct the relations of Communist Russia with the other great powers of the world are without precedent in history. Measures and countermeasures have been taken on many occasions which in any previous period could only have meant or accompanied armed conflict. The situation has been well described by distinguished Americans as the 'cold war'. And the question is asked: 'Are we winning the cold war?' Well, this cannot be decided by looking at Europe alone. We must also look at Asia. The worst disaster since our victory has been the collapse of China under Communist attack and intrigue. China, in which the United States has always taken a high interest, comprises an immense part of the population of the world. The absorption of China and of India into the Kremlin-controlled Communist Empire, would certainly bring measureless bloodshed and misery to 800,000,000 or 900,000,000 people.

On the other hand the position in Europe has so far been successfully maintained. The prodigious effort of the Berlin Airlift has carried us through the winter. Time, though dearly bought, has been gained for peace. The efficiency of the American and British Air Forces has been proved and improved. Most of all, the spectacle of the British and Americans trying to feed the 2,000,000 Germans in Berlin, in their zone in Berlin, while the Soviet Government was trying to starve them out, has been an object lesson to the German people far beyond anything that words could convey. I trust that small and needless provocations of German sentiment may be avoided by the Western Powers. The revival and union of Europe cannot be achieved without the earnest and freely given aid of the German people.

This has certainly been demonstrated by the Berlin Airlift, which has fully justified itself. Nevertheless, fear and its shadows brood over Western Europe today. A month ago in Brussels I spoke to a meeting of 30,000 Belgians. I could feel at once their friendship and anxiety. They have no Atlantic Ocean, no English Channel, between them and the Russian Communist armoured divisions. Yet they bravely and ardently support the cause of United Europe. I was also conscious of the hope and faith which they, like the Greek people, place in the United States. I can see the movement of this vast crowd when I spoke of the hands – strong hands – stretched out across the ocean. You have great responsibilities there for much faith is placed upon you.

We are now confronted with something quite as wicked but in some ways more formidable than Hitler, because Hitler had only the Herrenvolk pride and anti-Semitic hatred to exploit. He had no fundamental theme. But these thirteen men in the Kremlin have their hierarchy and a church of Communist adepts, whose missionaries are in every country as a fifth column, obscure people, but awaiting the day when they hope to be the absolute masters of their fellow countrymen and pay off old scores. They have their anti-God religion and their Communist doctrine of the entire subjugation of the individual to the State and behind this stands the largest army in the world, in the hands of a Government pursuing imperialist expansion, as no Czar or Kaiser has ever done. I must not conceal from you tonight the truth as I see it. It is certain that Europe would have been Communized, like Czechoslovakia, and London under bombardment some time ago but for the deterrent of the atomic bomb in the hands of the United States.

Another question is also asked. Is time on our side? This is not a question that can be answered except within strict limits. We have certainly not an unlimited period of time before a settlement should be achieved. The utmost vigilance should be practised but I do not think myself that violent or precipitate action should be taken now. War is not inevitable. The Germans have a wise saying, 'The trees do not grow up the sky.'

Often something happens to turn or mitigate the course of events. Four or five hundred years ago Europe seemed about to be conquered by the Mongols. Two great battles were fought almost on the same day near Vienna and in Poland. In both of these the chivalry and armed power of Europe were completely shattered by the Asiatic hordes and mounted archers. It seemed that nothing could avert the doom of the famous continent from which modern civilization and culture had spread throughout the world. But at the critical moment the Great Khan died. The succession was vacant and the Mongol armies and their leaders trooped back on their ponies across the 7,000 miles which separated them from their capital in order to choose a successor. They never returned till now.

We need not abandon hope or patience. Many favourable processes are on foot. Under the impact of Communism all the free nations are being welded together as they never have been before and never could be, but for the harsh external pressure to which they are being subjected. We have no hostility to the Russian people and no desire to deny them their legitimate rights and security. I hoped that Russia, after the war, would have access, through unfrozen waters, into every ocean, guaranteed by the world organization of which she would be a leading member; I hoped that she should have the freest access, which indeed she has at the present time, to raw materials of every kind; and that the Russians everywhere would be received as brothers in the human family. That still remains our aim and ideal. We seek nothing from Russia but goodwill and fair play. If, however, there is to be a war of nerves let us make sure our nerves are strong and are fortified by the deepest convictions of our hearts. If we persevere steadfastly together, and allow no appeasement of tyranny and wrongdoing in any form; it may not be our nerve or the structure of our civilization which will break, and peace may yet be preserved.

This is a hard experience in the life of the world. After our great victory, which we believed would decide the struggle for freedom for our time at least, we thought we had deserved better of fortune. But unities and associations are being established by many nations throughout the free world with a speed and reality which would not have been achieved perhaps for generations. Of all these unities the one most precious to me is, to use an expression I used first at Harvard six years ago, and one most precious to me, the fraternal association between the British Commonwealth of Nations and the United States. Do not, my friends, I beg of you, underrate the strength of Britain. As I said at Fulton, 'Do not suppose that half a century from now you will not see 70,000,000 or 80,000,000 of Britons spread about the world and united in defence of our traditions, our way of life, and the world causes which you and we espouse.' United we stand secure. Let us then move forward together in discharge of our mission and our duty, fearing God and nothing else.

April 1949

Frank Fellows[1] to Winston S. Churchill
(Churchill papers, 2/162)

1 April 1949   Washington DC

My dear Mr Churchill,

It was realization that the best of all that is Britain is represented in you which prompted my tearing up and discarding a speech prepared in opposition to the loan, and my vote in favor of it.

In these days when a man suffering from delusions is frequently mistaken for a man of vision, it is some comfort to think that God reigns and Winston Churchill still lives.

Listening to you speak last night, 'fearing God, – and nothing else', I thanked him for you and the things for which you stand.[2]

British Information Services:[3] report
(Churchill papers, 2/265)

1 April 1949   New York

REACTIONS OF THE PRESS TO MR CHURCHILL'S SPEECH
TO MIT ON MARCH 31

Reuters carried the full text. All the chief London papers splashed the speech with banner headlines.

The Times devoted 2½ columns on the main page. Mr J. D. Miller, Washington correspondent, covered the story in person.

---

[1] Frank Fellows, 1889–1951. Educated at University of Maine Law School. Admitted to the Bar, 1911. Clerk, US District Court of Maine, 1917–20. Elected (Rep.) to the 77th (1941) and five succeeding Congresses.

[2] Churchill responded: 'Dear Mr Fellows, I was deeply touched by your letter. Accept, pray, a small token.' This was a copy of Churchill's Fulton speech of 5 Mar. 1946 (reproduced above, pp. 227–35).

[3] British Information Services was a department of the FO based in New York. Its mission was 'to answer the questions most frequently asked in the United States about Britain and provide up-to-date government comment on current events where Britain has a role to play'.

The *Daily Telegraph* led with the speech, with an introduction and descriptive piece. Four columns were devoted to the speech, also a long first leader which said:

> 'It is three years since the Fulton speech in which Mr Churchill warned the non-Communist states that if they did not hang together, they might well be hung separately.'

The paper thinks that in his latest speech he was amply justified in claiming that his warnings have been completely vindicated. It goes on:

> 'Mr Churchill is hopeless of conciliation, but he is hopeful of peace through strength. He considers that time is on our side, provided that the price of liberty is recognized to be still eternal vigilance. And so it is. We can still hope with him that one day mankind will learn better and that all mankind will learn better all together. That is why his recipe for peace is so sound. If time is on our side, we can afford to wait, provided the waiting is not supine.'

The *Daily Mail* thinks the grimmest sentence in Mr Churchill's speech was his statement that London would have been bombed if the United States had not had possession of the atomic bomb. It declares:

> 'Its justification is contained in the words and deeds of the Soviet leaders since 1945. The comparison between what they are doing and what Hitler did is too glaring to be ignored.'

The *Mail* ends by saying:

> 'After Boston the anger of the Russian Communists and the ventriloqual squeaks of their dummies in Britain will descend upon Mr Churchill; let them rant and rage, it will be a measure of their disappointment that, once again, the great Prime Minister has served his country and his generation.'

All the Kemsley morning papers, in London, Manchester, Newcastle, Sheffield, Glasgow, Aberdeen, Cardiff, carried the speech on front pages with introductions and summary.

John Drummond, of Kemsley's New York office, covered the meeting at Boston at Lord Kemsley's special request. The full Reuter text was carried inside by all the Kemsley papers. The *Graphic* also pictures. All Kemsley mornings published leading articles on the speech, and follow-ups were carried in the evenings in all the towns listed above.

The *Manchester Guardian* carried the speech in 5 columns. Its editorial says:

> 'It is hard to be an optimist today, yet Mr Churchill's speech for all its sombreness was not a counsel of despair. The peace of the world lives under perpetual threat, not from a sabre-rattling war lord, but from a creed, backed by the intolerance of a true religion, propagated in the interests

of a powerful state. The challenge is especially directed against the United States which now, through her enormous material power, lies across the forcible advance of Communism.'

The paper thinks Mr Churchill was right to urge on American opinion the dangers of taking violent or precipitate action and says:

'War is not inevitable if the West can show itself strong enough; strong in faith as well as in material preparation.'

The *Daily Express* led with the speech in its third, fourth and fifth editions with 4 columns devoted to the text, two on page 1 and two on page 2.

The *News Chronicle* gave the whole of the speech, with an 8-column banner headline in all editions. The full text occupied 6 columns. Its editorial says:

'Churchill fears the foolishness of Russia, made dangerous by the lust of power.'

Nearly all the London newspapers agree with Churchill that war is not inevitable. The only opposition comes from the *Daily Worker*, which says:

'He is trying to drag this war-shattered world into a new war. . . . senile babblings . . . Churchill is trying to work up the hysteria by which the conditions could be created for a third world war.'

The *Daily Mirror* devotes 7 inches on the back page to the speech.

Many of the papers from behind the Iron Curtain seem to be ignoring the speech.
No reference to it appeared in the Prague or West Berlin papers.
The British-licensed *Social Democrat*, Berlin, says in its headline 'Churchill Unmasks Motives of "Astonishing" Kremlin Policies'.
Russian newspapers carried no comment.

In Paris.
The popular Republican Party newspaper *Laube* described the speech as 'an appeal for goodwill and firmness'.
But the Communist organ *Humanité* denounced it as 'furiously anti-Soviet', and coming 'within the frame of the ideological preparation for war'.
Libération (Independent Left-Wing) declared 'There was nothing original' in the speech. 'The ideas which were new when Churchill made his speech at Fulton three years ago are now stale,' the paper said.
The Gaullist *Ce Matin* said Churchill expressed 'in energetic terms the opinion of free people on the Soviet's policy'.
The Conservative evening paper *Le Monde* said it was a pity Churchill did not offer a solution whereby the world could escape from the present

diplomatic blind alley. In an editorial which otherwise strongly praised the British ex-Premier's speech, the paper said 'Many subscribe to his judgment of the future: He does not rate war as inevitable, but he is not sure that time is on the side of the free nations.' It continued 'It is regrettable that he did not give the solutions whereby he thinks we might escape from the present blind alley. Fortifying one's nerves against the 'cold war' is not enough. One may ask for such steadiness of nerve from peoples but from a Government one has the right to expect more. Resistance only begins to have a meaning if one does something to assure that one day it will be unnecessary.'

Emery Reves to Winston S. Churchill
(Churchill papers, 4/63)

1 April 1949 Boston
Confidential

Dear Mr Churchill,

I understand *Life* and *Time* object to your suggestions regarding a sixth volume. When I arrived in Boston last night, Henry Laughlin told me that Longwell called him up and persuaded him to stick to the 5 volume scheme. I have talked with Laughlin for several hours and believe convinced him to change his mind. I trust that during his meeting with you he accepted to pay another full instalment on a sixth volume.

It is my strongest conviction that you should write your War Memoirs exactly as you think they should be written. Interference in your own judgement seems to me inadmissible.

As I have already told you I am prepared to pay another Ten Thousand Pounds for a sixth volume. I am convinced Lord Camrose, Houghton Mifflin, Cassell and the Dominion papers will want to do the same. This means that you are assured to receive for Volume VI over Fifty Thousand Pounds. This should be sufficient guarantee for you to construct your work the way you think best.

My feeling is that if everybody is paying a sixth instalment and you leave it to Luce and Sulzberger[1] to decide whether they want to be the only ones to publish Volume VI without payment, they might feel ashamed to maintain their present attitude. Perhaps it was premature to raise this question at this time. I strongly feel that this change of plan should not be made public until the fourth volume is published.

---

[1] Arthur Hays Sulzberger, 1891–1968. Nephew of Gershom Mendes Seixas, one of the founders of the New York Stock Exchange. Graduated from Columbia College, NY, 1913. Founder, Columbia's Jewish Advisory Board, 1929. Publisher, *New York Times*, 1935–61. Trustee, Rockefeller Foundation, 1939–57; Columbia University, 1944–59. Fellow, American Academy of Arts and Sciences, 1950. Hundred Year Association of New York's Gold Medal Award, 1954.

I am writing this letter because I am anxious to avoid that the views of a popular picture magazine should influence you in writing this monumental work.

I do hope I can see you before you leave Boston. If not – Bon Voyage! I expect to be on the other side in a few weeks.

Elizabeth Gilliatt to Winston S. Churchill
(Churchill papers, 2/327)

4 April 1949 RMS *Queen Mary*
Confidential

Last year you consented (through Mr Brendan Bracken) to head an appeal for the General Sikorski[1] Historical Institute. Would you therefore like Mr Bracken to convey to Count Racynskiyour regret at your inability either to make a short statement supporting the Appeal, to head the list of Patrons, or to sign an appeal letter in *The Times*?

Alternatively would you consider, if Count Racynski drafted something for you, writing a short statement or a letter, and possibly also sending a small donation?[2]

Winston S. Churchill to Julian Sandys
(Churchill papers, 1/46)

5 April 1949 RMS *Queen Mary*

My dear Julian,

Thank you so much for your letter,[3] which I took with me on my voyage. We had a very interesting time in America, and are now well out in the mid-ocean in this vast ship. It is a floating hotel which rushes along at 33 miles an hour, and is a great credit to our country.

I expect you will by now be home for the Easter holidays, during which I hope to see you. Meanwhile I send you a little present.

---

[1] Władysław Eugeniusz Sikorski, 1881–1943. PM of Poland, 1922–3. Inspector-General of Infantry, 1923–4. Minister of War, 1924–5. GOC VI Corps Area, 1925–8. PM, Polish Government-in-Exile, 1939–43. C-in-C, Polish forces, 1939–43. Killed in air crash at Gibraltar, 1943.

[2] Churchill wrote in response: 'Mr Bracken should say I am afraid I have taken on too much.'

[3] Reproduced above (p. 1328).

Winston S. Churchill to Charles Scribner[1]
(*Churchill papers, 4/311*)

5 April 1949

My dear Charles,

Thank you for your letter and for sending me a copy of the new one volume edition of *The World Crisis*. I should be very glad indeed if you would send me a few more.

I am glad to know that you plan a new edition of *A Roving Commission*. It would be quite wrong to add any parts of *Amid These Storms* to such a volume, as there is no connection whatever between the two.

In view of the increased publicity I now command it astonishes me that the books of which you hold the copyright have not had any sale worth speaking of in the United States during or since the war years.

Thank you for your postscript. Let me know when you come to London.

John Foster Dulles to Winston S. Churchill
(*Churchill papers, 2/162*)

6 April 1949   New York

Dear Mr Churchill,

Permit me to say that I think that your speech as delivered in Boston was a very great speech, which has given us much to ponder about, and you can know that the wisdom expressed in it will, I think, have a very real effect upon our national thinking.

I fear that when I was with you at Bernie's apartment I concentrated so much upon trying to be helpful by way of the criticism you invited, that I did not adequately express my appreciation of the lofty thoughts and pungent expression.

Clementine Churchill to Winston S. Churchill
(*Churchill papers, 2/327*)

6 April 1949

Please forgive me for interfering but do you not think that, as a year ago you gave your consent to head an appeal for the General Sikorski Memorial in London, it would give sorrow and disappointment if you were not able to

---

[1] Charles Scribner, 1890–1952. Joined his father's publishing house, Charles Scribner's Sons Ltd, 1913; Secretary, 1918–26; Vice-President, 1926–32; President, 1932–52. On active service as 1st Lt, France, 1917–18 (US Remount Service). Published Churchill's *Marlborough* in six volumes, but declined to publish *A History of the English-Speaking Peoples*.

fulfil your promises. (Moreover you have headed the Masaryk Memorial Fund in London.)

Will you allow Miss Sturdee to ask the General Sikorski Historical Institute to draft a letter of which you would be the principal signatory?

I would not like a letter in connection with one of the great national figures of the Second World War to be signed by a second-rate figure like Sir John Anderson.

Winston S. Churchill to Duncan Sandys
(Churchill papers, 4/54)

8 April 1949 RMS *Queen Mary*

My dear Duncan,
About the tank story.
It would be a help to me if you would prepare the draft of a Chapter on this, to be included in Volume III, taking the account up to the end of 1941. It should be about four or five thousand words, and must be readable and therefore not too technical or suffer from over-detail. The salient facts are neglect between the wars; failure of the War Office to produce agreed models of medium tanks and to make plans for going into production in the event of war by making jigs and gauges in advance, etc., and briefing firms accordingly, (I complained about this in the House of Commons before the war); the situation at the outbreak – not even one single armoured division ready when the German attack developed in May, 1940; my emergency meeting in June or July 1940 at which measures were taken to order 1,000 Churchill tanks (these were to defend England in the event of invasion in 1941, and everything was sacrificed to having something ready by then – there is a report on this meeting available); the history of the Churchills and the under-gunning; the troubles about making the models desert-worthy, and my efforts in 1941 to overcome these; the episode of my sending the two first Churchills out with their technicians to have them made desert-worthy on the spot under the special care of Auchinleck and Oliver Lyttelton, and how this was almost sabotaged; the real truth about the quality of our tanks in 1941 and 1942; the superiority of the German methods of tank production, and how discreditable to us it was that they, who were strangers to the desert, seemed to have mastered the difficulties of good staff work beforehand. These points occur to me as I speak, but there must be many more, particularly the origin of the Sherman tank which you mentioned although that does not eventuate till the American gift in 1942. The tale can be told here as a prelude to the American gift after Tobruk, in 1942. It is no use going beyond 1942 at this period, but there is no reason why you should not foreshadow what happened in later years, and I can work it in in subsequent Volumes. If you will do this, you should consult with Pownall,

who will be able to get you access to or copies of all the relevant documents at the Cabinet Offices. When you have got your outline ready we could work the story up together.

As we all have to earn our living I hope you will let me pay you a good substantial fee for all your thought and knowledge. We can talk this over. The matter is urgent, as the third Volume will leave my hands finally in the next three or four months, and I should like to have anything you can do for me by the end of June or earlier.

I am also enclosing you a copy of the report of my speech at the United Europe luncheon in New York. I do not at all mind its being reproduced in their literature, but will you kindly cut it down to less than two-thirds of its length, and make it readable and presentable. You will see that Christopher has already made an attempt on it. You need not stick too closely to the text, as I was only speaking from headings. I think the luncheon was a great success, and I am told that as much as $75,000 were collected on the spot. I made it clear that none of this money was to be used for the British movement in England, but for our activities (Conferences, etc.) in Europe.

The Times: article
(Churchill papers, 2/210)

8 April 1949

AMERICA AND THE ATOMIC BOMB
President's Talk to Congressmen

From Our Own Correspondent

The President, in an informal talk to recently elected members of Congress, said last night that he would not hesitate to order the use of the atomic bomb if it were necessary for the welfare of the United States and if the fate of the democracies of the world were at stake. He said that he hoped and prayed it would never be necessary to do so, and added that he considered that the signing of the Atlantic Pact would prevent the United States from having to make such a decision.

President Truman told the Congressmen that whether the United States liked it or not, it had been forced into a position of great responsibility for the welfare of the world by two world wars, both of which could have been avoided if the United States had been willing to assume 'the place which Almighty God intended us to assume back in 1918, instead of having to assume it after two terrible wars'.

April 1949

Bernard Baruch to Winston S. Churchill
(Churchill papers, 2/210)

9 April 1949

Presume you saw president's declaration. He would not hesitate to order bomb dropped again if the welfare of the world's democracies was at stake.

Field Marshal Lord Montgomery to Winston S. Churchill
(Churchill papers, 2/143)[1]

9 April 1949

Dear Mr Churchill

Thank you so very much for the copy of *My Early Life*. I have been reading it with the greatest interest and have now nearly finished it. It is extremely good.

I hope you had a good visit to the USA. I thought your speech was terrific.

L. S. Amery to Winston S. Churchill
(Churchill papers, 2/44)

14 April 1949

My dear Winston,

This Conference on the position of India vis a vis the Crown is going to be a ticklish business. We don't want to be in the position of pushing India out of the Commonwealth because our conception of the Crown does not appeal to her. On the other hand there are great dangers, both from the constitutional and the sentimental point of view, in trying to alter the conception of the Crown as it has grown up hitherto. The practical conclusion from this to my mind is that we should make no attempt to arrive at any general new formula about the position of the Crown in the Commonwealth, but should rather accept in principle the possibility of India's becoming in some sense an associate on some terms which would include a common citizenship, provided she really genuinely wished to be in the Commonwealth and support its causes in the world.

If she goes out altogether it makes the situation much more difficult for Pakistan who would like to stay whereas it will be easier for Pakistan to remain an associate or even a full member if India is still in the picture.

There is another reason which appeals to me. I have always thought it possible that, some day, Norway and Iceland, possibly the whole of Scandinavia

---

[1] This letter was handwritten.

in Europe, and on the other hand in the Far East Burma and Siam, might come within the Commonwealth orbit. That would be much easier on the association basis than on that of full membership. Moreover in course of time association might become closer and differ very little in practice from full membership. The United States were only associates in the First World War but full allies in the second.

Even so, however, I would try and postpone anything in the nature of a definite decision as far as possible. I understand that the Republic of India only comes into existence after an election in 1951[1] and that meanwhile she jogs along as a Dominion under a wise old Governor-General.[2] The longer she has to get accustomed to that position and the more she realizes that it is in fact one of complete independence, the more reasonable she is likely to be about matters of form and substance when they come up for discussion. So I should be inclined, if possible, to let the whole thing be well discussed this time and all decision postponed until after the Indian election. In any case, if India wants something a little more definite, I should confine that to a general agreement that the rest of us will be happy to welcome India as an associate member when the time comes for the new Indian Republic to declare its desire to work with the Commonwealth and to leave the details of such a declaration of adhesion in spirit and in working intention as well as the precise nature of the association, to be discussed when the time comes.

I can quite understand Smuts' attitude. He came back from UNO very much shocked to discover it to be a mainly coloured gathering and one in which South Africa's racial problems were entirely misunderstood, and would no doubt really prefer a white to a piebald Commonwealth. All the same I believe one of the main arguments for the Commonwealth looking to the future is that it does bridge the gulf between races and may in consequence become the natural nucleus round which the ultimate world order will crystallize in due course.

---

[1] Churchill wrote here in the margin: 'Anthony is this true? If so no hurry.'
[2] Chakravarti Rajagopalachari, 1878–1972. Indian politician, lawyer, independence activist and writer. In 1919, joined Gandhi's Indian Independence movement, was elected to Congress Working Committee and served as General Secretary of the party. One of the major leaders of the Tamil Nadu Congress, 1930s. Helped lead the Indian National Congress during the pre-independence era. PM of his home state of Madras, 1937–9. The last (and only Indian) Governor-General of India, 1948–50. Bharat Ratna award for meritorious service to India for his work in politics and literature, 1954. Formed, 1959, the Swatantra Party, an Indian libertarian political party that existed 1959–74.

April 1949

Winston S. Churchill to Count Edward Raczyński
(Churchill papers, 2/327)

14 April 1949

My dear Count Raczyński,

Thank you for your letter about the appeal which is to be launched for the General Sikorski Historical Institute in London.

I am quite agreeable to become a patron of this appeal, and I also have no objection to signing a letter to *The Times* for publication on July 5, if you will send me the suggested draft.[1]

Winston S. Churchill to Bernard Baruch
(Churchill papers, 2/210)

14 April 1949

I certainly saw statement you mentioned[2] and am sure it will help for peace. We have had quite good elections here. We all have most agreeable memories of our stay.

Anthony Eden to Winston S. Churchill
(Churchill papers, 2/210)[3]

19 April 1949

My dear Winston,

Thank you so much for *Their Finest Hour*. I am very proud to have it, with its inscription, for my library.

The Greek chapters have also arrived, but I fear that I shall not be able to give them the time that I should before I come to you at Chartwell. I have to write four articles on my tour and prepare a broadcast all of which have to be completed within the next ten days, and I find it heavy going. The articles are intended to help pay for my travels! What a wonderful Easter. The garden has been a real joy. Nicholas[4] has had some Eton friends to stay and it has all been a very pleasant change.

[. . .]

---

[1] Note by Private Office: 'Mr C doesn't want to be the <u>only</u> signatory – await letter.'
[2] Reproduced above (p. 1382).
[3] This letter was handwritten.
[4] Nicholas Eden, 1930–85. Served in King's Royal Rifle Corps, 1949–51. ADC to Governor-General of Canada, 1952–3. Lt-Col., Royal Green Jackets, 1967–70. Earl of Avon, 1977. Lord in Waiting under Margaret Thatcher, 1980–3. Parliamentary Under-Secretary of State, Dept of Energy, 1983–4; Under-Secretary of State for the Environment, 1984–5.

Winston S. Churchill: speech
('Winston S. Churchill, His Complete Speeches', volume 7, pages 7810–11)

20 April 1949   Economic Conference of the European Movement, London

'THE THREE CIRCLES' (FOREIGN POLICY)

... Europe, which has been and still can be the most comfortable and happy of all the continents, has been brought by crime – and folly – and folly is often the parent of crime – to its present plight. At the Hague, where the European Assembly was born, we declared that there was no hope of recovery if each country simply strove to rebuild itself on the old national lines. We must think, plan, and toil, not only as patriots in our own countries but as Europeans, if we are not to be paupers or slaves. The people of Europe will have to swim or sink together, and we have full faith that the time has come when we will decide to swim.

In this sombre century, mankind, with all its scientific acquirements and proud boastings, has been forced again to think in primordial terms about finding its daily bread to keep alive. Europe, by its united efforts, must expand its own output of food; in addition, it must supply the other world with all kinds of necessary and attractive commodities in return for the additional foodstuffs which our vast population compels us to import from across the oceans.

We in Britain maintain our lives by supplies of wheat, meat, and other foodstuffs from the great Dominions of the Empire. This trade has been built up with mutual advantage, and neither we nor they can afford to relinquish the system. I am certain, however, that it is not impossible for Britain to draw far closer to Europe, and to enter far more forcefully into European life, without abandoning the ties with our Dominions which to us are paramount and sacred, and comprise the ideal of the British Empire and Commonwealth of Nations. ...

I am certain that the special interests of the British Empire and the larger interests of the English-speaking world can both be reconciled with a far more close association with Europe than has ever been possible before. The more Europe is united the more productive and decisive this wide intercourse will be.

There are three circles which are linked together: the circle of the British Empire and Commonwealth, the circle of the English-speaking world, and the circle of united Europe. All these mighty august circles form a common front and bulwark against totalitarian tyranny and aggression in any form. Further, through all their wide ranges over the land, sea and air we can uphold the cause of freedom and, if we remain true and united in that inspiration, none can overcome us.

Linked together in faithful comradeship we can defend ourselves against all enemies, and we may if we persevere rebuild the shattered and bewildered world in all its majesty of ancient nations and in all the happiness of hundreds of millions of humble homes.

(Editor's Note: Appealing that party and personal differences should not be allowed to obstruct the common cause in any of the countries represented at the conference, Churchill stated):[1] . . . I can guarantee, on behalf of the British delegates, that we will help the main policy of Mr Bevin in foreign affairs so far as we are informed of it, and we will help it to the utmost of our ability.

Randolph S. Churchill to Winston S. Churchill
(Randolph Churchill papers)

21 April 1949

DATES

6.10.49 means, to an English reader, 6 October 1949. To an American it means 10 June 1949.

Even if your readers know which system you are using, many of them will still have to do a lot of counting on their fingers. The compromise adopted in Volume 2 of writing '6.X.49.' is far from clear to American readers and encounters an obvious difficulty for all dates in February: thus 2 Feb. 49 would be written under this system 2.II.49, which could easily be mistaken for 2 Nov. 49. The whole difficulty can be overcome and an important lead given to others in this matter if you issue a simple blanket instruction that all dates, at the top of memoranda and minutes, should be printed, '6 Oct. 49.' When more formality is required 6 October 1949 can be used.

The Times always prints dates, 'October 6th, 1949'. Under this system all the numbers come together, instead of being separated by the month, and the 'th' merely wastes space and time, and is an unnecessary tribute by the written word to the spoken. Hansard, I am glad to say, has long printed the date in the style I recommend.[2]

---

[1] This note was written by Robert Rhodes James, editor of *His Complete Speeches*.
[2] Churchill responded on Sep. 22: 'Your note about dates is masterly, and I have given instructions for it to be universally adopted in any works which I may burden the public.'

Lieutenant-General Sir Henry Pownall to Winston S. Churchill
(Churchill papers, 4/16)

21 April 1949

If you decide to add a special note to the French edition of Volume 2, in the light of comments which have appeared in the *Figaro*, I suggest that some of the following points might be made.

1. Attention to be directed to your Preface to Volume 1; such sentences as:

'I do not describe it as history, for that belongs to another generation. . . . it is a contribution to history which will be of service to the future.'

'It has given me pain to record these disagreements with so many men whom I liked or respected; but it would be wrong not to lay the lessons of the past before the future.'

'It must not be supposed that I expect everybody to agree with what I say, still less that I only write what will be popular.'

'Every possible care has been taken to verify the facts; but much that is constantly coming to light from the disclosure of captured documents or other revelations which may present a new aspect to the conclusions I have drawn.'

2. The scope of the work does not admit of detailed description of operations. Consequently there are many gallant actions fought by British, French and Belgian troops which have had to be either greatly compressed or omitted altogether. This applies in particular to the events leading up to the evacuation from Dunkirk.

3. In a book written primarily for British readers it is natural that more space should be devoted to a description of British actions than those of other nations. This applies with particular force to the brief campaign of May 1940 in which the part played by the British services as a whole has not yet received authoritative treatment, and regarding which misconceptions exist even in this country.

4. It is in the light of this that the story of the evacuation from Dunkirk should be read. The story of the gallant defence of the Dunkirk perimeter, in which the French played the greatest part, has still to be told in full. You have but sketched this in, and concentrated on the British contribution during the crisis which was made by the Royal Navy and the Royal Air Force.

5. In the description of past events there are two facets to be presented: a record of what actually occurred, and also a description of the impact of events, as they were believed to exist at the time, on the minds of the principal actors. The latter is especially difficult to recapture with accuracy. In doing so it is possible, however, unwittingly, to offend susceptibilities. It is no desire of yours to do other than full justice to individuals, certainly not to impute unworthy motives, but impressions caused by them on other people's minds,

with perhaps important consequences, are a necessary part of the history of the time.

May I suggest that you should show whatever you propose to say to Ismay?

Lord Beaverbrook to Winston S. Churchill
(Churchill papers, 2/160)

23 April 1949

My dear Winston,

In the spring of 1939 on a cold morning when you came into Stornaway House you asked me to call Anthony Eden on the telephone for you.

I got through to his house and was told that he would come quickly. Hoping to hurry him I said 'Mr Churchill wants to speak to him.'

After a long delay I was informed that 'He was out walking'.

Yesterday after we had finished our telephone conversation you asked me if I would speak to Anthony who was with you. I replied that I would like to. But after some delay you told me 'He was out walking.'

Ten years ago he would rather walk than talk with you. Now he walks but does not talk with me.[1]

Winston S. Churchill to Clement Attlee
(Churchill papers, 2/84)

24 April 1949
Private

My dear Prime Minister,

I have been concerned to see it announced in the newspapers that Princess Margaret[2] is to spend several weeks travelling in Italy as an ordinary British tourist on a £50 currency allowance. I cannot think that it is desirable that the King's daughter should be forced, as would be inevitable in these circumstances, to be dependent upon private hospitality or favours from hotel-keepers and others. Such a situation seems incompatible with the dignity of the Royal Family and of the Crown. I should have thought that however modestly Princess Margaret may travel, there should be no doubt that she should be put in a position where she is clearly independent of foreign or private hospitality. It is certain that her visit to Italy will give occasion for much goodwill between the British and Italian peoples, and that from this point of view it wears a public aspect. In these circumstances I hope you will be able to reassure me, and, if

---

[1] Churchill noted: 'I will speak to him on the telephone.'
[2] Margaret Rose (1930–2002). Sister of Princess Elizabeth, later Queen Elizabeth II. Married, 1960, Antony Armstrong-Jones, created Earl of Snowdon, 1961 (div. 1978).

so, you may count on the support of His Majesty's Opposition in any proposal you may make. When I receive your answer I will put you in a Question on the subject.

Charles Wood to Winston S. Churchill
(*Randolph Churchill papers*)

24 April 1949

DATES

The system of using Arabic figures for the month in short dates, instanced in the first paragraph of Mr Randolph's memorandum,[1] is not followed in the work, so the likelihood of an American reader being misled does not arise.

The method of writing 6.IX.49, with the month in Roman numerals, was not a compromise adopted for Volume II, as far as I am aware. It is used in Volume I. The practice is very familiar among English people, I think, and I cannot imagine its perplexing anybody. It is true that 'II', for February, might be mistaken for 11, meaning November, but not by an attentive reader. February citations are infrequent too.

On the whole, I should not advise any change. The present style is, I find, clear, crisp, saves space and is unobtrusive, and is in agreement with the summary tone of the minutes, etc. A change for Volumes IV and V is inadvisable, because the work must be a unity, and to introduce it in Volumes I, II and III is to invite mistake, large expense, and delay. It is to be remembered that no correction of this kind could be made without its being checked at this end.

So I should say, leave well alone.

Incidentally, some of the dates attached to letters, etc., in Volume I are spelled out, and some of these are in italic and some in roman – see pp. 437, 438 for instance. That, however, is only part of the indifference that went to the preparation of the matter in Volume I, and I can rectify it for the reprint.

Jo Sturdee to Winston S. Churchill
(*Churchill papers, 2/84*)

25 April 1949

Sir Alan Lascelles telephoned with the following message for you. He has heard that you are worried and have written to the Prime Minister about the money which has been put up for Princess Margaret's trip to Italy. Privately he wants you to know that a lot of money has been granted by the Treasury who

---

[1] Reproduced above (p. 1387).

April 1949 1391

has been absolutely ideal in these delicate negotiations, and the last thing they want is for this sleeping dog to be aroused from its slumbers. Sir Alan Lascelles said that if you put a Question in the House, you will not only get a snub, but they do not want the public to know that extra money has been allotted.[1]

Warren G. Magee to Winston S. Churchill
(Churchill papers, 2/36)

25 April 1949   Washington DC

Dear Mr Churchill,

I am taking the privilege of enclosing a copy of some extracts from the final decision of the US Military Tribunal at Nürnberg concerning Baron von Weizsäcker.

I feel that you will be interested in reading this material. The Judgment is over 700 pages long, and we have prepared some of the more important comments from the Dissenting and Majority Opinions.

The Tribunal quoted at length from the affidavits of Lord Halifax and the Bishop of Chichester[2] in finding von Weizsäcker not guilty of the many charges involving crimes against peace, with the exception of the invasion of Czechoslovakia after Munich.

As you probably know, Judge Powers[3] dissented vigorously from these findings of guilt and held that von Weizsäcker used heroic efforts to preserve the peace but nevertheless finds him guilty in the second Czech crisis because he remained silent after the invasion of Czechoslovakia. This finding also ignores the fact that von Weizsäcker was not consulted and did not participate in the planning of this invasion.

Baron von Weizsäcker was also found guilty on one aspect of Count V which involved persecution. This finding to me is clearly erroneous. Judge Powers also dissented from this finding and contends that von Weizsäcker was innocent of this charge and should also be acquitted under it. As in the first finding the majority of the Tribunal ignore the vast amount of evidence establishing von Weizsäcker's humanitarian efforts to aid the persecuted, taken at great personal risk by von Weizsäcker.

---

[1] Churchill replied: 'I will await Mr Attlee's answer. I am very glad to know that it is likely to be favourable and not to require any further publicity.'

[2] George Bell, 1883–1958. Born in Hayling Island. Educated at Christ Church, Oxford; graduated 1905. Published biography of Archbishop Randall Davidson, 1914. Dean of Canterbury, 1925–9. Bishop of Chichester, 1929–58. Sat in House of Lords, 1937–58.

[3] Leon W. Powers, 1888–1959. Member of Iowa State House, 1919–22. Asst Attorney General of Iowa, 1933–4. Judge in Iowa Supreme Court, 1934–6. Judge during the Ministries trial at Nuremberg, 1947–9.

We are now preparing a petition for filing with General Clay for the correction of the judgment.

I thought you might like to receive a report concerning the present status of the trial and that is the reason I am taking the liberty of writing this letter to you.

May I again express to you the sincere thanks of Baron von Weizsäcker and myself for the cooperation and assistance you so courageously furnished us.

Randolph S. Churchill to Winston S. Churchill
(Churchill papers, 1/46)[1]

25 April 1949
Private

My dear Papa,

Thank you for your letter of April 24. I did not realize that there was anything secret about the terms of the Trust and am sorry if I have inquired into matters which you feel do not concern me. I trust you do not think that I was prompted by idle curiosity.

When I became engaged to June the question of a marriage settlement arose and June's father was naturally concerned about it. June wished to settle £10,000 on me and any children of our marriage. Since I had no capital to settle on her I did not encourage this idea; and no settlement was in fact made.

However I explained to June that under the Trust considerable provision had, I understood, been made for your children and grand-children and that therefore, though I was not in a position to make adequate provision for her, the future of any children we might have would be amply safeguarded.

Now that June is going to have a baby I thought it right and proper to inquire as to the terms of the Trust under which I have already been a beneficiary. I had understood that your main object in setting up the Trust had been to provide for the future security of your children and grand-children. It seemed to me that one element in that security would be knowledge, at least in general terms of the provisions of the Trust. It is obviously easier to plan one's life in this uncertain world if one is aware as far as possible of the prospects of oneself and one's children.

Like all your children I am immensely grateful to you for the exertions and generosity by which you have contributed so handsomely to our past, present and future welfare. I hope that this letter will make it plain that my request to my mother to acquaint me with the terms of the Trust was not intended in any way as an intrusion into your private affairs. I had merely thought that I had a duty and responsibility to my wife, my son and any children I may have in the

---

[1] This letter was handwritten.

future to acquaint myself as far as possible with our prospects. For, actually, my plans must to some extent depend upon them. Please forgive if I was at fault.

Winston S. Churchill to Sir Norman Brook
(Churchill papers, 4/17)

26 April 1949

My dear Norman Brook,

I have redrafted Chapter XIV, Book 5 to meet, as far as possible, your wishes about the Staff telegrams. I must say however that they are really essential to the tale and have their bearing upon the eventual change in command. Wavell's reasons for reluctance could not be better set out than in his own words.

The telegrams sent by the Chiefs of Staff to Wavell on page 4. I feel that in their brief setting they are essential, moreover they were the direct result of the decisions reached by the Defence Committee, over which I presided, and were only sent in the name of the Chiefs of Staff because of their formal character following on the Cabinet decision. Wavell's telegram of May 5 is also necessary to show his point of view, I have turned it into indirect narration. If my minute of May 6 appeared out of its context it would not do justice to the view point of the harassed Commander in Chief. I have several other amended and augmented chapters to send you.

Winston S. Churchill to Henry MacCormac[1]
(Churchill papers, 2/173)

26 April 1949

My dear Mr MacCormac,

I have been so grieved to learn of your illness. As I understand you are laid up I thought you might care to read my new volume, *Their Finest Hour*, and I therefore send you a copy of the American edition, which comes out long before the British publication.

You will be glad to know that the various remedies, lotions and ointments which you have prescribed are keeping me free from all annoyance from the facial eczema. I must take this opportunity of thanking you for all the care, kindness and skill with which you have treated me. I hope you will soon be well enough to come and see me again should I need further aid.

---

[1] Henry MacCormac, 1879–1950. Physician and dermatologist. Graduated from University of Edinburgh, MB, ChB, 1903. Lt-Col., RAMC, during WWI. CBE, 1919. Married Marion Broomhall, 1931.

Winston S. Churchill to L. S. Amery
(Churchill papers, 2/44)

27 April 1949

My dear Leo,

Thank you for your letter of April 14.[1] I am afraid the Government have made up their minds to put the matter through now and of course we have no power to stop it. My feeling is that we must save what we can from the wreck. We are, I understand, to have a statement today or tomorrow, in the House.

Clement Attlee to Winston S. Churchill
(Churchill papers, 2/84)

27 April 1949
Private

My dear Churchill,

You wrote to me on April 24[2] about the currency to be made available for Princess Margaret's visit to Italy. I am a little surprised that you have relied on newspaper reports about this, but I can assure you that the facts are not as you feared. I believe Lascelles has already told you that the Treasury have agreed to a currency allowance which the Palace consider entirely adequate, and I hope you will agree with me that public discussion of the exact figure would serve no useful purpose.

Winston S. Churchill to Bernard Baruch
(Churchill papers, 2/210)

28 April 1949

My dear Bernie,

Contrary to the reports which appeared in the newspapers we had a very agreeable and easy passage home, although there was a delay of twenty-four hours at the Cherbourg bar.

I cannot describe to you what a vivid and bright impression my flying visit to you has left in my mind, and in all our minds. It gave us so much pleasure to receive your message saying that you missed us, considering what an invasion we were and how much you set aside your own life to looking after me and my work.

---

[1] Reproduced above (pp. 1383–4).
[2] Reproduced above (pp. 1389–90).

One cannot doubt that the speech was a great success and avoided the many pitfalls that lay open on every side, while at the same time not falling into platitude or pathos & took a lot of trouble & thought.

I was very much struck by Truman's remarks about the Atomic bomb. This was indeed what I urged him to make plain in our short conversation at Washington. It will, I have no doubt, be a help to the cause of peace.

Over here our people have muddled themselves into a sad disaster in the Yangtse. Their conduct is a cameo of 'how not to do it'. It is entirely typical of their administrative quality.

You will have noticed that we did very well in the County Elections, and we expect to do still better in the Boroughs which take place in May. In these local contests the Conservatives have of course larger reserves to bring up of voters who have hitherto never taken the trouble to poll than we have at General or Parliamentary bye-Elections, which have always been fought more strenuously, and on the national party ticket. Nevertheless all my information gives me good expectations that we shall have a much better Parliament in little more than a year than we have now. We shall also, I fear, if we succeed, come into a dismal inheritance and bleak weather. I would not continue but for the fact that I feel it my duty to help the sane and constructive forces in Britain to restore our position in the world.

Sarah is going to Canada in connection with the premiere of her film, *All Over the Town*, and is going to fly over on May 5. She will be in Canada until the 14th and travels overnight to New York, leaving in the *Queen Mary* on the 20th. Expenses and currency are provided for by the Rank Organization, but I am sure you would like her to come and look you up in the four or five days she is in New York, and I shall be grateful if you will cast a paternal eye upon her.

Do let me know if you will come over here at any time, because it would be a great pleasure to me and Clemmie and also to the children. Mary is much better and for the time being we are not at all anxious.

I enclose a separate letter on a matter of which we talked. It does not press for an answer as I do not think in any case any difficulty could arise.

Once more I thank you, dear Bernie, for all the proofs of affection you have shown me.

INDIA (COMMONWEALTH RELATIONS)

The Lord President of the Council (Mr Herbert Morrison): With your permission, Mr Speaker, I should like on behalf of the Prime Minister to make a statement about the meeting of Commonwealth Prime Ministers which has just been concluded. Hon. Members will already have seen the announcement in today's newspapers. It will, of course, be realised that it was necessary to make the results of the Conference known in this way in order to facilitate simultaneous announcements in all the self-governing countries of the Commonwealth. Nevertheless, I think the House would wish to hear the terms of this statement so that a decision which will, I feel sure, be regarded as an historic one in the evolution of the Commonwealth may take its place in the records of the House with the least possible delay. The communiqué is as follows:

Meeting of Prime Ministers

During the past week the Prime Ministers of the United Kingdom, Australia, New Zealand, South Africa, India, Pakistan and Ceylon, and the Canadian Secretary of State for External Affairs have met in London to exchange views upon the important constitutional issues arising from India's decision to adopt a republican form of constitution and her desire to continue her membership of the Commonwealth. The discussions have been concerned with the effects of such a development upon the existing structure of the Commonwealth and the constitutional relations between its members. They have been conducted in an atmosphere of good will and mutual understanding, and have had as their historical background the traditional capacity of the Commonwealth to strengthen its unity of purpose, while adapting its organisation and procedures to changing circumstances.

After full discussion the representatives of the Governments of all the Commonwealth countries have agreed that the conclusions reached should be placed on record in the following declaration: The Governments of the United Kingdom, Canada, Australia, New Zealand, South Africa, India, Pakistan and Ceylon, whose countries are united as Members of the British Commonwealth of Nations and owe a common allegiance to the Crown, which is also the symbol of their free association, have considered the impending constitutional changes in India. The Government of India have informed the other Governments of the Commonwealth of the intention of the Indian people that under the new constitution which is about to be adopted India shall become a sovereign independent republic. The Government of India have however declared and affirmed India's desire to continue her full membership of the Commonwealth of Nations and her acceptance of The King as the symbol of the free association of its independent member nations and as such the Head of the Commonwealth. The Governments of the other countries of the Commonwealth, the basis of whose membership of the Commonwealth is not hereby changed, accept and recognise India's continuing membership in accordance with the terms of this declaration. Accordingly the United Kingdom, Canada, Australia, New Zealand, South Africa, India, Pakistan and Ceylon hereby declare that they remain united as free and equal members of the Commonwealth of Nations, freely co-operating in the pursuit of peace, liberty, and progress.

These constitutional questions have been the sole subject of discussion at the full meetings of Prime Ministers.

That is the statement. I hope the House will bear with me if I venture to suggest that any full discussion of this matter, if it is the wish of the House that this should take place, might more appropriately be deferred until a later occasion. I say this, having regard particularly to the fact that the leaders of delegations from the other countries of the Commonwealth are naturally not yet in a position to report personally to their own Governments or Parliaments.

Mr Churchill: Perhaps I may be allowed to ask whether the Lord President is aware of the deep interest with which we have listened to his statement. I am well aware of the difficulties of clock time and sun time throughout the British Empire and Commonwealth of Nations – and I do not say that they have been satisfactorily solved on this occasion, – which seem to assign to London and Great Britain 2 a.m. as the moment of release for an important declaration. One would think this might be a matter for further consideration on future occasions. But I am all the more glad that His Majesty's Government have met the request which I made to them with the full support of my right hon. and learned Friend the Leader of the Liberal Party, that the joint declaration of the Commonwealth Prime Ministers should be reported formally to the House and thus take its place not merely – or, perhaps, I ought to say, not only – in the newspapers, but in our Parliamentary records. Any other course, I feel, would be derogatory to Parliament and especially to the Mother of Parliaments.

Final judgment on matters of such gravity and far-reaching merit is impossible today. Debates have to take place not only here, but in the Parliaments which are concerned and which are located in the five continents of the globe. There are many questions which arise and which are unanswered, and there are possible consequences, some of them potentially adverse, which cannot yet be measured. Nevertheless, I feel that I should be failing in my duty as

Leader of the Conservative Party if on this occasion I failed to express, under all proper and necessary reserves, a definite view. The test question which, it seems to me, we ought to ask ourselves, and which I have asked myself, is: Do we wish India to remain of her own free will and desire within the Commonwealth or not? I have no doubt whatever that nearly all of us in all parts of the House would answer that question 'Aye'.

I do not in any way retract or regret the views I have expressed over so many years, and I am very glad not to be responsible for much that has been done in the past – (Hon. Members: 'Hear, hear'.) – and in the recent past. But we are all of us governed by events which we cannot control, and by the actions of majorities duly elected to the House of Commons. Six months ago I said in this House in the Debate on the King's Speech: 'We must look forward. It is our duty, whatever part we have taken in the past, to hope and pray for the well being and happiness of all the peoples of India, of whatever race, religion, social condition or historic character they may be. We must wish them all well and do what we can to help them on their road. Sorrow may lie in our hearts but bitterness and malice must be purged from them, and in our future more remote relations with India we must rise above all prejudice and partiality' – (Hon. Members: 'Hear, hear'.) I said this six months ago – 'and not allow our vision to be clouded by memories of glories that are gone for ever'. The present attitude of India seems to me more favourable to continued association than it did when those words were spoken. (Hon. Members: 'Hear, hear'.) It is more favourable. I am unfeignedly glad that an impassable gulf has not opened between the new India and the British Empire and Commonwealth of Nations or between our famous past in India and our anxious present all over the world. I am sure that this will be a help for all in the future. I am well aware of the arguments about equal sacrifices and contributions, belonging to the club and taking the advantages and not contributing to the rules but, as the Bible says, 'It is more blessed to give than to receive'. It is certainly more agreeable to have the power to give rather than the need to receive. We do not always find ourselves in that position in respect to some other countries in the world.

If, on the whole, we most of us feel able to answer the test question in the affirmative and wish to have India associated with us in the future, it is fortunate that the institution of the Monarchy, never more deeply enshrined in the hearts of its proud and willing subjects and citizens all over the world than at the present time, should not have been a barrier to the inclusion of India as a Republic in the Commonwealth.

Some time ago, when, by courtesy of Ministers, I had some indication of what was afoot, I foresaw some danger that the symbol of the Crown, which had hitherto been the circle of unity for the whole British Empire and Commonwealth of Nations, might become an exclusive instrument in respect of India in its new guise. I am sure it has been wise to avoid any chance of that. I cannot feel that either the majesty of the Crown or the personal dignity of the King is impaired by the conditions under which India remains in the Commonwealth. On the contrary, the final significance, the vital significance and value of the Monarchy, seems to be enhanced both by the latest proofs of its enduring importance to the other Dominions, as testified by their responsible Prime Ministers, and to the fact – (Hon. Members 'This is out of Order'.) I take it that it is in the public interest, when an important statement is made in the House by the Government, that the views of other parties should be ascertained, and I have no doubt that the Adjournment could be moved if that were desired by the Government.

It seems to me that the personal dignity of the King is not impaired by the conditions under which India remains in the Commonwealth. The final significance and value of the Monarchy seems to be enhanced by the way in which the King is acknowledged by the Republic of India and by the Commonwealth monarchies alike. (*Interruption.*) It is astonishing how far below the level of events hon. Gentlemen are showing themselves to fall.

Mr Warbey (Luton): On a point of Order, Mr Speaker. May I ask your guidance whether we are to have a series of extensive comments on this statement and, if so, on what Motion those comments are to be made?

Mr Speaker: One knows perfectly well that on these formal occasions it is the right of leaders of political parties to state their party's point of view. Rather than have an Adjournment, I gave my consent to this, and I take full responsibility for it. Realising that the Guillotine has to fall at 5.30 and that, therefore, there is little time for discussion on the Steel Bill, I thought this was the quickest way out: that statements should be made by the responsible leaders of the Opposition parties. It is not for me to tell them how long or how short they should be.

Mr Churchill: I should like to put this point. It seems to me that, far from being any derogation of the Monarchy, the proof of the attachment and importance that all the Dominions gives to it has shown the strength and vitality of that institution.

We cannot, of course, tell how all this will work out in practice, and obviously there are many difficult questions and dangers to be surmounted. There is no doubt however – this I say to all my friends on this side – that it is the duty of us all, wherever we sit, to try our best to make this new expression of the unity of the world-wide association of States and nations a practical and lasting success, and that is the course which we on this side of the House intend to steer. I feel that the tides of the world are favourable to our voyage. The pressure of dangers and duties that are shared in common by all of us in these days may well make new harmonies with India and, indeed, with large parts of Asia. We may also see coming into view an even larger and wider synthesis of States and nations comprising both the United States of America and united Europe which may one day, and perhaps not a distant day, bring to harassed and struggling humanity, real security for peace and freedom and for hearth and home.

Mr Clement Davies: Inasmuch as there is to be further Debate on this at some later stage, may I content myself with merely saying at the moment that I believe there is general satisfaction in every freedom-loving country throughout the world that the Prime Ministers, each one of them with a heavy sense of responsibility for his own country, have nevertheless been able to arrive at this arrangement. I am sure that it is the sincere hope of us all that, using the words of this declaration, there will be even closer cooperation for those causes of liberty, peace and progress which are the desire of all of us.

Let me add this. I think it is only right that we should – and I desire to do so most sincerely – congratulate the Prime Minister on calling these Prime Ministers from the various countries together. I am quite sure that his tact and understanding have played a major part in bringing about this historical agreement and declaration.

Mr H. Morrison: If I may, I would say on behalf of the Prime Minister and of the Secretary of State for Commonwealth Relations that we express our thanks for and appreciation of the generally friendly observations that have been made about this matter by the Leader of the Opposition and the Leader of the Liberal Party. It is a good thing – a very good thing and not a bad thing – that there should be general harmony about this matter between the parties in the House. Therefore I cordially welcome what the Leader of the Opposition has said. He took his time, but I make no complaint about it. I cordially welcome what he said, and thank him for his observations, and no less the Leader of the Liberal Party. In these Commonwealth matters, the more we can march together in this House, the better it is for everybody.

L. S. Amery to Winston S. Churchill
(Churchill papers, 2/44)

29 April 1949

My dear Winston,

You were both magnanimous and wise yesterday in dealing with the new Indian Declaration. We cannot go back on the past and we cannot be certain of the future. But it does look as if, after the terrible low ebb of the last three years, the tides are beginning to flow our way again, and world forces outside the Commonwealth may be helping all the time to keep us together as one of the great world regional groups. If so then the flexibility of our constitution and the fact that we bridge the gulf between East and West may, for all we know, some day make of us a nucleus round which the ultimate world order will crystallise. Anyhow let that be a cheering thought for the closing chapter of our long life's battle.[1]

Winston S. Churchill to Lord Moran
(Churchill papers, 2/163)

29 April 1949
Private and Confidential

My dear Charles,

I hope you will be agreeable to my making two seven-years covenants, operative during my life, so that each of your sons[2] may receive £300 a year, free of income tax. I am sure that these must be years in which this would be a help to them. You have always refused to allow me, even when I was a Minister, to make any return to you for all you have done for me.

I feel that neither you nor Dorothy will mind me expressing my gratitude in this way.

---

[1] Churchill responded on May 8: 'It is our duty to save what we can, and one must not be embittered by the past however much one may regret it.'

[2] Richard and Geoffrey Wilson. Geoffrey Hazlitt Wilson, 1929–. Educated at Eton and King's College, Cambridge. Fellow, Institute of Chartered Accountants, 1955; Chartered Institute of Management, 1959. Director, Blue Circle Industries, 1980–97. Chairman, Delta PLC, 1982–94. CVO, 1989.

May
1949

Winston S. Churchill to General Lord Ismay, Lieutenant-General Sir Henry Pownall, Commodore G. R. G. Allen and Lieutenant-Colonel Bill Deakin
(Churchill papers, 4/19)

May 1949

Volume III is finished for the present so far as I am concerned. I am sending a copy of Book 5 to Field Marshal Wavell, and other parts are being checked by many of the principal people concerned – Eden, General Smuts, Sir Norman Brook and others. I shall not look at it at all until August or September, when my eye will be fresh. Meanwhile will you kindly read it through and mark any errors, omissions, improvements or compressions which commend themselves. I shall be sending round a number of points which have struck me as requiring checking or consideration.

I am now turning to Volume IV. You have already the Provisional Contents Tables of Books 7 and 8. I am not sure where this will end. It may go as far as Cairo and Teheran, but at present I plan to end it before the invasion of Sicily. It would be well to concentrate upon Book 7 which ends with Operation 'Torch'. I shall be glad if you will talk things over, and divide up the help you can give me.

Elizabeth Gilliatt to Winston S. Churchill
(Churchill papers, 2/176)

3 May 1949

Mr Churchill,

In the car yesterday, you started dictating a letter to Field Marshal Smuts, but I do not think you finished it. This is what you have said so far:

'I was sorry not to be able to adopt your position about the Indian settlement. It is absolutely necessary for the Conservative Party to have a policy which is not unfavourable to the new India.'

Winston S. Churchill: speech
(Hansard)

5 May 1949   House of Commons

BERLIN BLOCKADE (REMOVAL)

The announcement which the Foreign Secretary has just made will be received with general rejoicing and relief. It is my duty to offer him and the Government our congratulations upon the successful issue of this difficult and, as at one time it seemed, almost superhuman exercise of the air lift, which has shown a method of solving a deadlock and difficulty far preferable to some others which might have been considered at one time or another. I feel that the firmness which has been shown and the powerful aid and consistent policy of the United States, with whom we have worked hand in hand, have quite appreciably lessened the sense of war tension which has hung over us as each day brought out difficult incidents in Berlin. It is a matter in which we all rejoice, and on this side of the House we are very glad that we never faltered in steady support of the policy of His Majesty's Government and of the Foreign Secretary in the whole of this anxious business. We gladly pay our tribute to them. It only shows how important national unity is in these matters and how desirable it is to exclude party fights as far as possible from these large and important fields.

I shall only venture to add a word or two, not in any way to derogate from what I have said. I am sure that the right hon. Gentleman would be the first to tell us that our difficulties are not yet over. This impediment has been removed from our path but we now approach the problems of the future of Germany. It by no means follows that difficulties may not arise there, even more embarrassing and puzzling than those which we have encountered in the blockade of Berlin. In that case, unity of action by the British nation and by all parties in the British Parliament, in combination with our friends, associates and Allies all over the world, gives by far the best chance of a good solution, and by far the best chance for the maintenance of peace.

Winston S. Churchill to Lieutenant-Colonel Bill Deakin
(Churchill papers, 4/19)

5 May 1949

Mr Deakin,

By sitting up very late several nights, I have finished Volume 3, and the last chapters come back from the Printer tomorrow. You should look through again the Russian chapters and the last five or six of the Book, which I have reshuffled largely in accordance with your suggestions. It is possible that there may be some repetitions, as I have not had the chapter 'Closer Relations with Russia' reprinted yet. I am quite clear it should not run on after the Declaration of War and that the extra matter should be shoved forward. In the last chapter, 'Return to Trouble', there are also a number of telegrams which seem to figure much better in Chapter 1 of Book 7, of which you have a copy, where they already are.

Please look through these closing chapters and let me know of any unintentional omission or duplications on my part. You can bring them down to Chartwell on Sunday.

I am now putting the whole of this Volume 3 away for four or five months. Meanwhile I send you a copy of the minute I have addressed to our group.[1]

Winston S. Churchill to Lord Salisbury
(Churchill papers, 2/85)

7 May 1949

My dear Bobbety,

Thank you for your letter of May 3. Events move so quickly that it is very difficult to keep up with them. I consider that the fatal step towards India was taken when Baldwin supported the Ramsay MacDonald plan in 1930 and enforced it upon the Conservative Party in 1931. I and seventy Conservatives – and your Father – resisted this for four long years, and were systematically voted down by the Baldwin–Ramsay MacDonald combination, supported for this purpose, I need hardly say, by the Socialist Party in opposition. Once the Conservative Party cast aside its duty to resist the weakening of the Imperial strength, the gap could not be filled, and from this point we slid and slithered to the position we have reached today. I could not therefore accept any reproach for the present situation from any Conservative who supported the Baldwin and Chamberlain policies.

I am glad you realize that the clock cannot now be put back. 'The moving finger writes . . . .'[2] All the same I must admit that the latest developments are not so bad as I thought they would be six months ago, when I made a speech in the House which was the result of much sorrowful heart-searching. I thought then that India would become a hostile, as well as an independent, State. But now the door of hope has re-opened in my mind. The world tides are very favourable, and the next ten years may easily see the development and the growth of strong ties. I do not even think it impossible that the Indian people, whose sentimental attachment to the Crown is widespread and deep, may some day accept the full status of Imperial citizenship. Anyhow I am glad no irrevocable gulf has opened.

[1] Reproduced above (p. 1402).
[2] From the *Rubáiyát of Omar Khayyám*. See note on p. 1209 above.

It is possible, even, that Burma may take a second-class ticket back. This I should welcome. Perhaps you will remember the difficulty I had to get the Party to vote against the Burma Independence Bill. But now, in their tragedy and misery, many Burmese must be turning their minds back to the palmy days of Queen Victoria.

These may be but the vain dreams of an aged man. However I cannot despair; still less must you, for whom the future holds so many tasks.

I was so delighted to see you restored yesterday.

Winston S. Churchill to Sir Alfred Munnings
(Churchill papers, 2/163)

8 May 1949

My dear Alfred,

I do not think there is any foundation for the enclosed.[1] All I pressed you to do was to revive the Academy Banquet. I do not remember saying anything about our having 'a good rag'; if I did so, it was at the Other Club and should certainly not have been quoted.

I also heard with surprise your statement that we were 'walking up the street together' when I spoke to you about kicking Picasso[2] if we met him. I do not think we have ever walked up a street together, and anyhow this is not the sort of statement that should be attributed to me.

I know you speak on the impulse of the moment, but I protest none-the-less against these utterances.

Winston S. Churchill to Lord Beaverbrook
(Churchill papers, 4/17)[3]

8 May 1949   Chartwell

My dear Max,

I have studied the American book you sent me and I send you now the resultant revised Chapter. Please let me know if there are any mistakes. I hope you will like it. You certainly, and not for the first or last time, made a 'ferment'. I am so glad to be able to pay my tribute to your services to us all.

---

[1] The reference is to a speech given by Munnings at the Royal Academy of Arts on the occasion of his resignation as President, an event at which Churchill was present. In his speech, Munnings claimed that Churchill had once asked him: 'If you met Picasso coming down the street, would you join me in kicking his something something?', to which Munnings assented.

[2] Pablo Ruiz Picasso, 1881–1973. Spanish artist. Worked in Paris from 1901 until his death. Founder and leader of the Cubist School of painting. Designer for Diaghilev Ballet, 1917–27. Director, Prado Gallery, Madrid, 1936–9. Painted murals for Spanish Pavilion, Paris Exhibition, 1937. Lenin Prize, 1950. Lenin Peace Prize, 1962.

[3] This letter was handwritten.

Winston S. Churchill to Clement Attlee
(Churchill papers, 2/29)

9 May 1949

My dear Prime Minister,

Knowing how much occupied you were with the Imperial Conference and other matters, I have deferred until now sending you my promised note on the state of our Armed Forces.

I should be very glad to come to see you with two or three of my colleagues any time that you may appoint in the near future.

FIRST MEMORANDUM ON DEFENCE
I. Munitions

1. The hostility of Soviet Russia became obvious to the National Coalition in the closing months of the late war. It was made apparent to the public by the first meeting of UNO and other events. No improvement in our relations with the Soviets has occurred since His Majesty's present Government has assumed office.

2. At this time we possessed an immense mass of munitions in rifles, which are the foundation. We must have had at least five millions in the hands of troops and Home Guard. Secondly there was a large reserve, and thirdly the small arms factories were naturally kept working for a good many months after the victory to help the turnover to peace industries. Where then have all these rifles gone? How many have we got now in our control? It must be observed that rifles keep in oil for a quarter of a century or more. We should be glad to know what has happened to them. We are informed they have been largely squandered and that only about two million remain.

3. The same question applies to all other forms of munitions. Is it true that great masses of projectiles, including of course poison gas, with many other munitions, were taken out to sea and sunk in unserviceable ships chartered for the purpose? We are told this is so.

4. It has recently been shown that artillery of all kinds keeps for at least a quarter of a century. What has happened to the enormous numbers of cannons, field, medium, heavy, ack-ack, and especially anti-tank, in our possession at the end of the war? Here again the factories went on working after the surrender. We have a statement of the artillery of all kinds in our possession in Europe and elsewhere on May 10, 1945, and also a statement of what we have now.

5. Cognate to other forms of ack-ack are all kinds of radar. This is a complicated subject by itself. We are led to believe that even for London at the moment the ack-ack batteries, even if they have computers, have not the radar apparatus brought up to date, without which they are useless. What is the truth of this? How many ack-ack batteries (i.e. guns) are there available

for the defence of London and vital sea ports, and to what extent are they equipped? Secondly, to what extent are they manned, or capable of being manned after say a month? We are told there is a complete breakdown.

6. It would seem that anti-tank guns (17-pounders) are the most important artillery feature, not only for ourselves but for our allies. How do we stand with these? There is a new 20-pounder; but very little progress has been made upon it.

7. What has happened to our tanks? We did badly in the last war in this speciality, but in the end we were coming along with very large outputs of superior vehicles. What was our strength on May 10, 1945, and what is it now in serviceable weapons? There is no doubt that though a model of a tank will surely be superseded as the years pass by better types, a good serviceable tank is better than none at all. What was the position at the end of the war, and what is it now? It should again be remembered that the factories were kept working to finish up the existing latest forms of production. We are told that there is a good new model but that production to date is negligible.

8. What has happened to the enormous masses of lorries, armoured cars, Bren-gun carriers, tractors, etc., which existed less than four years ago? We hear tales of immense parks where they have been rusting into ruin. Surely a sufficient proportion should have been preserved in oil and maintenanced? The Americans have a new method of preserving ships, and instead of casting them upon the scrap-heap as the Admiralty have done to so many available vessels, they keep them in a special form of storage which though somewhat costly to apply in the first instance enables them to remain free from deterioration for a good many years. The British have not done this.

9. We hear bitter complaints from the Benelux countries that we cannot give them small parcels of weapons, and their need for them is certainly obvious. We have not got a serviceable fifth of the weapons we had when the German war ended. From every side there are tales of shortages in weapons for our present very small fighting forces, with which our great armies at the end of the war were fully equipped, with reserved and new production coming forward.

II. Manpower

1. We support and admire the decision of HMG to maintain and establish compulsory National Service. We recognize the difficulties of blending conscription with voluntary service. The abandonment of a system of National Service at the present time would be a deadly blow, not only to Western Union but to our claims for sacrifice and support from the United States. Nevertheless we cannot feel that the best method of coping with the difficulties has been adopted. The proposal for eighteen months' service was changed to twelve months and then a year later changed back to eighteen months. All this period was of course covered by the general powers overlapping from

wartime. But nevertheless the changes in policy suggest that there has been no coherent or continuous plan. Although HMG possess what no administration has ever had in time of peace, namely eighteen months' compulsory service, and 305 millions have been voted in the current year for the army alone, and they are relieved of the need to maintain an army in India, hitherto the prime obligation, we are led to believe that the following facts are true. viz. We have two Divisions in Germany only partially equipped. The second of these will not be operational till the end of the current year. We cannot promise to send even a single division to the Continent to reinforce the Western Union in that period. This is explained by the falling off of recruitment in the Regular Army, and the great numbers of recruits cast upon the established units for training purposes, which process destroys their combatant value.

2. The remedy for this would appear to be found not in abandoning the principle of compulsory service, nor in reducing the period of training with the Colours, but rather in taking a smaller number of men in each yearly quota. Other countries who have had great experience of conscription in peace and war have found the ballot on the whole the fairest plan, and less liable to abuse than complicated standards of physical and intellectual quality, which may always be alleged to be unfairly administered.

We draw particular attention to the extraordinary discrepancy between the men and the money voted by Parliament, and the actual fighting power at this present time or in the next year or two, which must certainly be considered anxious years.

We feel that the recruiting for the Regular Army, and especially for the cadres of specialists, NCOs and unit leaders should be stimulated both by increased pay and assurance of permanent careers. Regiments are not buildings or machines but plants which grow and must be tended over periods of time.

We shall be glad to learn the views and policy of HMG on these aspects.

3. It may well be that in the present circumstances emphasis should be laid upon the development of operational combatant units, and high quality of the large reserves accumulated by conscription and thereafter nursed in the Territorial forces. The condition of the Territorial forces themselves causes us all anxiety. All-Party efforts should be made to stimulate and recall any efficient war-experienced elements in the Territorial cadres.

4. Although the resulting fighting power represented by operational units is pitifully small we have heard that the War Office still maintain in peace time a clerical establishment of over ten thousand. Moreover the staffs of every so called combatant unit have been greatly swollen, and even in peace are maintained at wrongful levels. For instance, a Brigade, which was formerly staffed by a brigadier, a brigade major and a staff captain, now requires eleven or it may be thirteen staff officers. The professional urge to create and maintain posts on such a scale should be very searchingly scrutinized by the civilian Ministers.

III

This preliminary memorandum will seem to show the sort of questions which we should like to discuss. We are however preparing a detailed document showing what, from the information we possess, would appear to be the strength and state of readiness of the three services. This we will send to you before the meeting.

We were deeply distressed by the statement of the Secretary of State for Air that the morale of the Royal Air Force had declined, considering that in this sphere quality and ardour are vital, and that the best weapons are useless in the hands of those who lack the personal ascendancy. We trust that the cause of this decline in morale will be dealt with swiftly and drastically by HMG.

We do not attempt at this stage to deal either with the apparition of the latest forms of U-boat now being developed in great numbers by Soviet Russia with German technicians, nor with the subject of latest forms of jet fighters and fast bombers possessed by our Air Force squadrons. We should like to know what the real figures in the Royal Air Force are. Those we have heard mentioned seemed deeply disquieting.

Clement Attlee to Winston S. Churchill
(Churchill papers, 2/29)

10 May 1949

My dear Churchill,

Thank you for sending me, with your letter of the 9th May, your promised note on the state of our Armed Forces. You will realise that I shall need a little time to study this. My Private Secretary will then get in touch with yours to arrange a suitable time for a meeting.

Lord Beaverbrook to Winston S. Churchill
(Churchill papers, 4/17)

10 May 1949

My dear Winston,

It was most kind of you to send me this proof of your revised chapter.

You have made generous use of the American account and, in consequence, I emerge in a more resplendent light than I am entitled to.

This is particularly so, since you quote the briefer but, in my judgment, more telling praise of me occurring in your cable to Attlee.

As a result of your labours as a historian, my defects as a minister will be forgotten as time passes and only my good points will go down to future generations.

For this good fortune I am deeply grateful to you.

Winston S. Churchill to Lord Carton de Wiart[1]
(*Churchill papers, 4/52*)

12 May 1949

My dear Baron,

I am not attempting to write a History of the Second World War but only give the story of events as they appeared to me and to the British Government, and to confine myself to expressions of opinion which I made as its opening tragedy unfolded. In these you will see that I paid the fullest tribute at the time to the Belgian Army. For instance, on May 28 I said, '. . . This army has fought very bravely and has both suffered and inflicted heavy losses. The Belgian Government has dissociated itself from the action of the King, and, declaring itself to be the only legal Government of Belgium, has formally announced its resolve to continue the war at the side of the Allies.'

And on June 4 I said, 'At the last moment when Belgium was already invaded, King Leopold called upon us to come to his aid, and even at the last moment we came. He and his brave, efficient Army, nearly half a million strong, guarded our left flank and thus kept open our only line of retreat to the sea. Suddenly, without prior consultation, with the least possible notice, without the advice of his Ministers and upon his own personal act, he sent a plenipotentiary to the German Command, surrendered his Army and exposed our whole flank and means of retreat.' It might be convenient at this point to read the testimony of General Weygand, at that time Supreme Commander.

Also in my telegram to Lord Gort of May 27 I used the expression which I have since published about the Belgian Army, 'We are asking them to sacrifice themselves for us.'

Moreover I made every effort to prepare to carry away several Belgian divisions with the British and French troops from Dunkirk. There is therefore no justification for anyone to suppose that I have reflected, in any way, upon the valour or the honour of the Belgian Army and its commanders.

With regard to King Leopold, the words which I used at the time in the House of Commons are upon record and after careful consideration I do not see any reason to change them. It is perfectly clear however, from the two telegrams which I now publish, that I concerned myself with the attitude of the King of the Belgians towards his own Government. This was pressed strongly

---

[1] Edmond Carton de Wiart, 1876–1959. Belgian aristocrat. Secretary to King of Belgium. Director, Société Générale de Belgique. Chevalier, 1911. Baron, 1922. Count, 1954.

upon me at the time by that Government and on constitutional grounds it seemed to me and many others that the King should have been guided by the advice of his Ministers and should not have favoured a course which identified the capitulation of the Belgian Army with the submission of the Belgian State to Herr Hitler and consequently taking them out of the war. Happily this was averted, and in the end all came right.

I need scarcely say that nothing I said at the time could be interpreted as a reflection upon the personal courage or honour of King Leopold.

Winston S. Churchill: speech
(Hansard)

12 May 1949   House of Commons

THE NORTH ATLANTIC TREATY

The House will not be surprised if I begin by saying that I find myself in very general agreement with the sombre speech which the Foreign Secretary has just made. I am glad that the lifting by the Soviet Government of the blockade of Berlin has not been taken by him as an occasion for proclaiming that an important peace gesture has been made. Before the last war, I do remember how, every time Herr Hitler made some reassuring statement, such as 'This is my last territorial demand', people came to me and said, 'There, now, you see how wrong you have been; he says it is his last territorial demand'; but the bitter experience we have all gone through in so many countries, on this side and on the other side of the Atlantic, has made us more wary of these premature rejoicings upon mere words and gestures. We give our cordial welcome to the Atlantic Pact. We give our thanks to the United States for the splendid part they are playing in the world. As I said when over there the other day:

> Many nations have risen to the summit of world affairs, but here is a great example where new-won supremacy has not been used for self-aggrandizement, but only further sacrifices.

The sacrifices are very great. In addition to the enormous sums sent to Europe under Marshall Aid, the Atlantic Pact entails further subsidies for military supplies which are estimated at over $1,000,000,000 up to the year 1950. All this has to be raised by taxation from the annual production of the hard-working American people, who are not all Wall Street millionaires, but are living their lives in very different parts of the country than Wall Street. I say that nothing like this process of providing these enormous sums for defence and assistance to Europe – nothing like this has ever been seen in all history. We acknowledge it with gratitude, and we must continue to play our part as we are doing in a worthy manner and to the best of our abilities.

Our differences with the Soviet Government began before the war ended. Their unfriendly attitude to the Western Allies was obvious before the end of 1945, and, at the meeting of the United Nations Organization in London in January 1946, Anglo-Russian relations had already reached a point where the Foreign Secretary had to give the word 'lie' in open conference to Mr Vyshinsky. I was impressed with that indication, which I read in the newspapers, and I was also very much impressed with the statements made at that time by Mr Vandenberg, that great American statesman, as I will not hesitate to call him. His whole career in recent years has been to carry world security and righteous causes far above the level of the fierce and repeated American political contentions and elections.

I have always myself looked forward to the fraternal association of the English-speaking world and also to the union of Europe. It is only in this way, in my view, that the peace and progress of mankind can be maintained. I gave expression to these views at Fulton in March 1946, after the remarks to which I have referred had shown the differences which had arisen with Russia. Although what I said then reads very tamely today, and falls far short of what has actually been done, and far short of what the House actually has to vote at the present time, a Motion of Censure against me was placed on the Order Paper in the name of the hon. Member for Luton (Mr Warbey) in the following terms:

> World Peace and Security. – That this House considers that proposals for a military alliance between the British Commonwealth and the United States of America for the purpose of combating the spread of Communism, such as were put forward in a speech at Fulton, Missouri, USA, by the right hon. Gentleman the Member for Woodford are calculated to do injury to good relations between Great Britain, USA and the USSR, and are inimical to the cause of world peace.

That is the operative part. It is quite unusual, when a Private Member is out of office, that a Motion of that kind should be placed upon the Order Paper with regard to a speech made on his own responsibility, but no fewer than 105 hon. Members of the party opposite put their names to it. I do not see them all here today; some of them are here, but, of course, I feel that there has been a large-scale process of conversion, and, naturally, I welcome converts, and so do His Majesty's Government. They say that there is more joy over one sinner who repenteth than over ninety and nine just persons who need no repentance. Here, we have got about a hundred in a bunch, so far as I can make out, although some of them have emphasized the change of heart which they have gone through by a suitable act of penance by abstaining from attending this Debate.

Mr Sydney Silverman (Nelson and Colne) *rose* –

Mr Churchill: Far be it from me to refuse an opportunity to a penitent.

Mr Silverman: I was only going to say in all humility to the right hon. Gentleman that because a number of people are prepared to support the calling in of the fire brigade, that does not mean that they withdraw one word of censure from those who contributed to the setting of the house on fire.

Mr Churchill: I did not expect that such a condemnation of the Soviet Government's policy would be forthcoming from the hon. Gentlemen. For all these reasons, it is most certainly true that the occasion is not entirely unmingled with joy, for the country sees so many who have changed their courses, but I say that we are now asked to approve this Atlantic Pact, and the only opposition to it is expected from that small band of Communists, crypto-Communists and fellow-travellers whose dimensions have been very accurately ascertained in recent times. In all this matter, the policy of the Foreign Secretary has been wise and prudent. We have given it our fullest support, and we shall continue to do so. There is, of course, a difference between what a private Member of Parliament may say, even if his words carry far, and what a Minister has to do. To perceive a path and to point it out is one thing, but to blaze the trail and labour to construct the path is a harder task, and, personally, I do not grudge the right hon. Gentleman any credit for the contribution which he has made to bringing about the Atlantic Pact. It entitles him, and the Government he represents, to the congratulations of the House which will be formally signified tonight by the passing of this Motion.

We must not, however, lose sight of the fact that the prime agent is the United States. I agree with what the Foreign Secretary said, that if the United States had acted in this way at an earlier period in their history they might well have averted the first world war, and could certainly, by sustaining the League of Nations from its birth, have warded off the second. The hope of mankind is that by their present valiant and self-sacrificing policy they will be the means of preventing a third world war. The future is, however, shrouded in obscurity.

As I have said on former occasions, we are dealing with absolutely incalculable factors in dealing with the present rulers of Russia. No one knows what action they will take, or to what internal pressures they will respond. He would be a bold, and, I think, an imprudent man who embarked upon detailed prophecies about what will be the future course of events. But it is absolutely certain that the strengthening by every means in our power of the growing ties which united the signatories of the Atlantic Pact, of the Brussels Treaty, and the signatories of the Statute of the Council of Europe – on all of which there is overwhelming agreement in this House – is our surest guarantee of peace and safety. Now we must persevere faithfully and resolutely along these courses.

While I like the strong note which was struck by the Foreign Secretary in his speech this afternoon, we must persevere along these courses. It has been said that democracy suffers from the weakness of chopping and changing, that it can never pursue any course for any length of time, especially Parliamentary democracy. But I think that may prove to be a phase from which we are shaking ourselves free. At any rate, persistence at this time and a perseverance which is emphasized in the speech of the Foreign Secretary is, we on this side are quite certain, the safest course for us to follow and also the most right and honourable course for us to follow. It has been said that the Atlantic Pact and the European Union are purely defensive conceptions. The Foreign Secretary has claimed that they are not aggressive in any way. How could they be? When we consider the great disparity of military strength on the continent of Europe, no one can doubt that these measures are of a defensive and non-aggressive character. The military forces of the Soviet Union are at least three or four times as great as those which can be set against them on land. Besides this, they have their fifth column in many countries, waiting eagerly for the moment when they can play the quisling and pay off old scores against the rest of their fellow countrymen. Nothing that can be provided in the Atlantic Pact or the Western Union Agreement on land can make our position and policy other than purely defensive. It remains the first duty of all the signatory Powers to do their utmost to make Europe, and for us here to make Britain, self-supporting and independently secure. For this we must all labour.

I have only a word or two of detail to say upon the subject. It seems that our first duty is to put our own defences in order. I cannot feel – none of us can feel – that any adequate return in actual fighting power is being received for the vast sums of money and the very great numbers of men which Parliament is voting at the request of the Government. There seems, also, to be no close integration of military plans and forces on the Continent. There is no system comparable to that which was created at SHAEF, the Supreme Headquarters of the Allied Expeditionary Force. There, there was great unity under the wise guidance of General Eisenhower. But, according to unofficial reports which we hear, national considerations are playing far too great a part in the present discussions which are taking place.

Thirdly, in view of the inevitable delay in the ratification of the Treaty and the need for speed, I have heard the suggestion that it might be desirable to broaden the activities of the Western Union Military Committee by inviting representatives of the other Atlantic Treaty powers, namely, the Italians, Portuguese, Danes, Norwegians and Icelanders, at any rate occasionally, to attend the Western Union Committee at Fontainebleau as observers. However, I should not wish to impede the precision of their work by the mere addition of numbers. Nevertheless, this might be an advantage.

The absence of Spain from the Atlantic Pact involves, of course, a serious gap in the strategic arrangements for Western Europe. I was glad to hear the right hon. Gentleman, not this afternoon, but the other day, express himself in a favourable sense to the return of ambassadors. I do not ask more than that at the present time. I think it is better to have ambassadors than to carry it all on through the back door, as it all has to be carried on – a sort of black market diplomacy. Also, I do not think it a good thing to appear to insult and to appear to treat with lack of ceremony a people so proud and haughty as the Spaniards, living in their stony peninsula, have always shown themselves to be.

The services rendered by Spain to us in the war were not all negative. First of all, we had a most fertile and serviceable trade with Spain which, in one way or another, the Germans did not dare to interfere with. Products of the greatest value, both to our armaments and to our nourishment, were brought in, but it was at the time of the landing in North Africa – Operation 'Torch' – that the greatest forbearance was shown by Spain in allowing us to use, far beyond any treaty rights, the harbour of Algeciras and the neutral ground between Gibraltar and the mainland for our aeroplanes and for the gathering of our transports. It was a most anxious period for us because the whole of that great operation – the first great Anglo-American joint operation – would have been jeopardized if they had chosen, as they so easily could have done, to plant cannon on the hills overlooking the harbour, and fire them upon the shipping crowded therein.

I cannot feel at all that they did us harm in the war and I personally agree with what Senator Connally said in the American Senate the other day, that he could not see the sense of having relations with Soviet Russia and refusing to have any relations with Spain. As a matter of fact, the conditions under which people live in Spain give far greater freedom to the individual than those under which they live in Russia or, I may say, Bulgaria or Rumania or other countries which have fallen into the grip of – yes, jump up now, if you like.

Mr Skeffington-Lodge (Bedford):[1] The right hon. Gentleman said that he agrees with the expression of opinion of an American Senator. Does he also agree with the expression of opinion which appeared in *The Times* today and which comes from Mr Acheson,[2] the Secretary of State, in which Mr Acheson says that the Franco Government was set up by Hitler and Mussolini and that it is patterned on Germany and Italy, and in which he adds that the judiciary is not independent in Spain today and Habeas Corpus is quite unknown?

Mr Churchill: I should not like to live under the present Spanish regime, but I would rather live there than under the governments of the various countries I have just mentioned, and I imagine that would be the opinion of almost every Member of this House who is not either blinded by fanaticism or sure he would get most favoured treatment in the circumstances which might arise.

As I say, I am not suggesting that we should go further at all at the present

---

[1] Thomas Skeffington-Lodge, 1905–94. Service in Navy as Petty Officer, 1941–4. MP (Lab.) for Bedford, 1945–50.
[2] Dean Acheson, 1893–1971. Born in Middletown, Conn. Educated at Yale College and Harvard Law School. Married, 1917, Alice Stanley: two children. Served in National Guard. Clerk for Supreme Court Justice Louis Brandeis, 1919–21. Under-Secretary, US Treasury, 1933. Asst Secretary of State, 1941–5. Under-Secretary, US Dept of State, 1945–9. Medal for Merit, 1947. Secretary of State, 1949–53.

time than to have the interchange of ambassadors. At the time of Potsdam, I agreed that Spain should not be a member of the United Nations Organization because I felt it was more important to gather together other elements, nor do we include Spain in our United Europe movement, but let us at least take the step of abandoning insult and boycott and exchange formal ambassadors with that country. I am sure that the attitude and policy which has been pursued in the last three years has been a great service to Franco and has enabled him to secure his hold, which might otherwise have been greatly mitigated.

Those are the only points of detail which I venture to mention. This may be an occasion for satisfaction, but it is not an occasion for triumph or for exultation. We are on the eve of the Four-Power Conference out of which we may hope a peace treaty with Germany may come. We must give that conference the best possible chance and be careful not to use language at this juncture which would hamper its discussions or compromise its chances of success. At the same time, I am glad that the Foreign Secretary is not under any illusions and that we shall not be deceived by gestures unaccompanied by action. It is deeds, not words, which are wanted. Any deed done by the Russian Soviet Government which really makes for the peaceful and friendly intercourse of mankind will have its immediate response, but mere manoeuvres must be watched with the utmost vigilance.

Moreover, there can be no assurance of permanent peace in Europe while Asia is on the Elbe or while so many ancient States and famous capitals of Eastern Europe are held in the grip of the thirteen men who form the oligarchy of the Kremlin. The Communist gains in China and the disturbances, all springing from the same source, which are causing so much misery in South-East Asia, all bring home to us the magnitude of the great struggle for freedom which is going on under the conditions of what is called the 'cold war'. We are confronted with a mighty oligarchy disposing not only of vast armies and important armaments by sea and in the air, but which has a theme, almost a religion, in the Communist doctrine and propaganda which claims its devotees in so many countries and makes them, over a large portion of the globe, the enemies of the lands of their birth.

There is this fear which the Soviet dictators have of a friendly intercourse with the Western democracies and their hitherto inflexible resolve to isolate the enormous populations they control. They even fear words on the broadcast. Everyone in this country is free to tune in to the Russian broadcasts at any hour of the day, and I am bound to say I am very glad that they should be free to do so. It would be a terrible thing if we were afraid of anything that might be said about us on the broadcasts. It is a woeful admission of a guilty conscience or a defective political system when you are afraid to let your people listen to what goes on abroad. We soon got used to 'Lord Haw-Haw' during the war, and we never feared what he might have said about us. It is astonishing that there should be this terror in the hearts of these men, wielding such immense material and physical power, merely of words let out by our fairly harmless BBC upon the ether. They must have very poor nerves to get alarmed by that. But the fact remains that there is this fear – fear of friendship and fear of words, and it acts upon men who wield the most terrible agencies of military force.

The situation is, therefore, from many points of view unprecedented and incalculable. Over the whole scene reigns the power of the atomic bomb, ever growing in the hands of the United States. It is this, in my view, and this alone that has given us time to take the measures of self-protection and to develop the units which make those measures possible, one of which is before us this afternoon. I have said that we must rise above that weakness of democratic and Parliamentary Governments, in not being able to pursue a steady policy for a long time, so as to get results. It is surely our plain duty to persevere steadfastly, irrespective of party feelings or national diversities, for only in this way have we good chances of securing that lasting world peace under a sovereign world instrument of security on which our hearts are set. We shall, therefore, support His Majesty's Government in the Motion which the right hon. Gentleman has just commended to us.

Randolph S. Churchill to Winston S. Churchill
(Churchill papers, 1/46)[1]

12 May 1949

My dear Papa,

Thank you so much for your letter. What you have arranged for me is extremely handsome and generous. I am deeply grateful to you and it is a great comfort to me to know that I shall have this security for my lifetime.

As I told you in my previous letter my request to my mother to see a copy of the Trust was not prompted by concern for my own future so much as for that of Winston and any children I may have in the future. I am very glad to hear from you that you are thinking of this.

Thank you again for all you have done and are doing for me and which I appreciate more deeply than I can say.

---

[1] This letter was handwritten.

1418 MAY 1949

Sir Alfred Munnings to Winston S. Churchill
(Churchill papers, 2/163)¹

13 May 1949

My dear Honorary Member,

I received your letter[2] – the only cloud on the horizon – but with no enclosure. After 20 years of dull, heavy banquets your suggestion of a 'rag' was so inspiring that I told it to the RA Council at the next meeting. It stirred us all into action. Instead of resigning at the end of 1948 I offered to carry on for 1949 solely in order that we started the dinner. Seeing a chance of a jolly evening and you with us, the Council decided unanimously to go ahead and get out invitations. So you were really the instigation and I'm glad you were.

I'm more than sorry if I've done anything wrong, but I've not yet gone through the thousands of letters from all over the country – from France – America – even Finland – congratulating and thanking me for what I said. So far, there are four against – one anonymous – telling me I should sign the pledge. Another that I'm not fit to kiss Picasso's boots and that I should look up the dictionary and find out the meaning of the word decorum.

I am enclosing one or two of the many letters coming in for your perusal.

Jo Sturdee to Winston S. Churchill
(Churchill papers, 2/75)

16 May 1949

Mr Sandys says:

1. It would only be for matrimonial and personal reasons that Mr Macmillan and Mr Boothby would not get on.[3] He thinks it would be most unfortunate and unfair if Mr Boothby were not included.[4] He is most keen to be an Opposition representative and has said that he wants to make this United Europe his major interest. Mr Sandys said he talks with much more knowledge about it all than anyone other Conservative MP, and as he has been connected with it from the beginning, he thinks it would be a great pity if he were not to be a delegate to Strassbourg. He hopes therefore you will not decide to exclude him from the Opposition members without consulting him (Mr Sandys) first.

2. Mr Sandys thinks you should protest about the substitutes. He thinks there should be a substitute for every representative, which he understands is happening in other countries. Substitutes are quite useless unless they go to Strassbourg, and they should be free to serve on Committees. A substitute who

---

[1] This letter was handwritten.
[2] Reproduced above (p. 1405).
[3] Boothby had an affair with Dorothy Macmillan which lasted from 1930 until her death in 1966.
[4] In delegation of Conservative MPs to European Assembly. See next item.

appears at the last moment, without having been able to attend the meetings and follow the affairs, would be no good at all.

3. Mr Sandys leaves for Scandinavia on Wednesday morning.

Winston S. Churchill to Herbert Morrison
(Churchill papers, 2/75)

18 May 1949

My dear Lord President,

In response to the communication I have received through your Chief Whip, I hereby propose the following representatives of the Conservative Party to attend the meeting of the European Assembly in August this year:

Mr Churchill.
Mr Harold Macmillan.
Sir David Maxwell Fyfe.
Sir Ronald Ross.[1]
Mr Robert Boothby.
Mr David Eccles.

You will note that I have made provision for Northern Ireland as you desired.

With regard to the substitutes I think it important that there should be six as it is obviously difficult for Members of Parliament to be in two places at once. However I am glad to hear that six will be agreed to by His Majesty's Government. I am informed that it is not necessary for this second list to be with you till next week. I shall have mine ready during the course of Saturday next.

I am very glad that this matter has been settled in an agreeable fashion.

Winston S. Churchill: speech
('Winston S. Churchill, His Complete Speeches', volume 7, pages 7822–3)

20 May 1949   Conservative Rally, Ibrox Park
Glasgow

LABOUR'S NATIONALISATION POLICY: 'CAPRICE AND GREED'

[. . .] I hope we shall continue to call ourselves the British Empire and Commonwealth of Nations. In this title there is room for all and none need be repelled or slighted by its terms.

Lamentable disasters have occurred in India, Burma, and Palestine. The

---

[1] Ronald Deane Ross, 1888–1958. 2nd Baronet, 1919. Served in France during WWI, 1914–18. MP (Union.) for Londonderry, 1929–41. Parliamentary Private Secretary to First Lord of the Admiralty, 1931–5. British Delegate to the Assembly of First Council of Europe, Strasbourg, Aug. 1949; to Second Council of Europe, 1950. Agent in Great Britain for the Government of Northern Ireland, 1951–7.

Conservative Party cannot be held responsible for these disasters, but is bound all the same to face the consequences. We have no choice but to accept what has happened. We must look to the future.

We accept the settlement . . . under which India will come forward as a republic within the circle of our Commonwealth of Nations, and we will do all we can to crown this remarkable adventure with success.

The recent county and borough elections prove the growing distaste of the masses of the people for the Socialist record. The Socialist policy of nationalizing our industries has failed in every case.

Everywhere the State employee is becoming disillusioned. Any general application of nationalization must be fatal to trade unionism as we have known it in this country as a characteristically British, practical, and mitigating force.

The nationalization of steel will be a precise and definite issue at the General Election, and should we obtain a majority we shall immediately repeal, and by every means in our power reverse, this pernicious measure.

Nationalization is specially detrimental and offensive to Scotland, affecting not only its prosperity but its independence. Nationalization schemes have removed your own control over local services like transport. This also is a process which we have every intention of setting in reverse.

Even in industries and undertakings which have been irremediably subjected to the State we mean to re-establish a far greater measure of local control and responsibility. In rail transport there will be a separate Scottish board coordinated with but not subordinate to those in England. There will be a separate Scottish board for electricity for the whole and not just for the north of Scotland.

In these and other matters the Secretary of State for Scotland will ensure that Scottish interests are served. We will not hesitate if necessary to strengthen the establishment of Scottish Under-Secretaries.

The Conservatives are not going back on the national health policy. We have started this idea and we shall save it if we have the time and power from the abuses by which it is at present being overlaid.

The new Labour programmes will open new vistas of jobs for the boys. There is no plan in the selection of industries for nationalization except caprice and greed. The great attraction which lures the Socialist mind and stirs its appetite is the vast system of industrial assurance organizations and collecting societies. . . . The Socialists want to get hold of the funds of the Prudential and the Pearl and many others so that they may use them to buttress their shaky edifice of planning. If this reckless proposal should be carried through the policyholders will find that their moneys, which have until now been managed by men solely concerned with guarding their interest and providing them with the best possible service, will be used by planners to fasten the Socialist yoke upon us.

May 1949

Field Marshal Jan Smuts to Winston S. Churchill
(*Churchill papers, 2/176*)

21 May 1949
South Africa

Cape Town

My dear Winston,

A week or two ago I had a cable from you, asking me in what name you could cable me, and giving your own cable name as 'Colonel Warden'. I cabled 'Henry Cooper' as my cable name. Since then I have heard nothing further from you, and I do not know whether something may have gone wrong, or your plan has been changed. However, I hope to see you soon now, and no cable is asked for.

I have to be at Cambridge on 8th June in my capacity as Chancellor, and shall be there on official business till 11th June (Saturday), and hope to be in London on the following Monday, 12th June, staying at my Hotel (Hyde Park Hotel) till Saturday, 18th June, when I fly home via Rome, Athens and Cairo. During that week (12th–18th June) I hope to see you and make other contacts as widely as possible in order to learn what is going on behind the scenes. The Press is not very helpful when it comes to matters which really matter, and so much is going on at present which one really wants to understand.

As you can appreciate, the London Conference on India is going to have its repercussions in South Africa. One could appreciate the deep concern of the British Government to keep India, in however loose a form, within the Commonwealth. But the arrangement made for India has given the Nationalists here the very opportunity they have been praying for – that is, some halfway house towards complete secession (which is their policy), which might not prove too difficult for South Africans of both races to accept. Now the problem has been solved for them by the republic which still adheres to the Commonwealth. Since Malan's return the Nationalists are jubilant, and their next move may now well be a republic within the Commonwealth, as a stepping stone to full secession in due course. You will appreciate how much more difficult it has become to fight this sort of republic after the London decision. I have done my best to make it appear an exceptional accommodation for India, but they maintain stoutly that it is a complete change of general future application. It has been made easy for South Africa to travel the same way as Ireland. It is a most unfortunate development, but the British Government acquiesced in it with full knowledge, and Malan has welcomed it. As I have expressed it, the Commonwealth may go the way of the Holy Roman Empire and become nothing but a name, and lose all meaning and reality. I know you must deplore this as much as I do, but we have both been put in the most embarrassing position possible. Already many good loyal English people here ask what is the harm of a republic, not knowing that there is so much more behind it than the republic. What has happened in Ireland may not be repeated in South Africa. But these matters we can discuss when we meet again.

And there are others too. Your lead when out of office has been most fruitful, and from this point of view it may yet appear that your defeat in 1945 has been a blessing in disguise. You could scarcely have made either your Fulton or your Lucerne speech when in office; and yet the one has become the basis of our Russian policy, and the other the basis of our European policy. You have been the Elder Statesman of the world and in that way achieved success which would not have been possible to a Prime Minister in office. Western Union and Atlantic Pact are the foundation stones of the future world structure. Of course they are only a beginning, but in great things it is the beginnings that count.

The pendulum appears at last to be swinging in Britain – how much, you would know better. I am not so much concerned with the internal conditions in Britain, as with its world position, where there has been unbelievable decline since 1945. We have lost much of our world position and influence and face. And this is indeed a world calamity, and not to us only. We might not have the physical force, but we have the moral force which counts even more for eventual victory in the world struggle now going on. I hear the Socialist Government has been more concerned over their social programme than over the great issues on which in the end their social aims also depend. In the world revolution now in progress it is essential that the Commonwealth should pull its full weight, instead of creating the impression (perhaps quite mistakingly) of being in retreat and abandoning its world role. I do not know how to put it, but you will understand better what is in my mind. Surely we have not won the war only to appear to lose our proud position and our face before the world? Even America will think less of us as an ally if this were the case.

I long to hear you on these searching matters, which go to the roots of the present mischiefs.

I shall contact you as soon as I am in London.

Winston S. Churchill to Field Marshal Jan Smuts
(Churchill papers, 2/176)

22 May 1949

I was distressed to find myself taking a different line from you about the Republic of India and the Crown. You know well my views and record on this subject. As Conservative Leader I found it my duty to look forward and to have a policy which would not place the Conservative Party in a position of permanent antagonism to the new Indian Government. When I asked myself the question, 'Would I rather have them in, even on these terms, or let them go altogether?', my heart gave the answer, 'I want them in.' Nehru has certainly shown magnanimity after sixteen years imprisonment. The opposition to Communism affords a growing bond of unity.

Para 2. No one can say what will happen in future years. I cannot think that any Soviet invasion of India would occur without involving UNO against the aggressor. Therefore the burden of Indian defence no longer falls on us alone. Finally I felt it would place the Crown in an invidious light if it appeared an exclusive rather than an inclusive symbol. For these reasons among others I took my decision which was accepted without protest by the Party.

Para. 3. I am none the less glad you said what you did and you may be sure I should strongly oppose any attempt by the South African Union to repudiate the Crown. I have not thought however that this was likely because of the rift it would make with Natal and other provinces and the danger of a mortal quarrel among the white minority. Malan now seems not to intend any violent action at the present time. I am earnestly looking forward to your return to power. We are not doing so badly here, though the parties are evenly matched.

Para. 4. Every good wish to you and yours my lifelong friend and comrade. I should welcome a letter.

Winston S. Churchill to Bernard Baruch
(Churchill papers, 2/210)

22 May 1949

My dear Bernie,

Thank you so much for your letters. I was much interested to see the editorials by your friend, James Cox.[1] Yes, as a matter of fact, Major Ormerod[2] of the British Information Services in New York, has been sending me all the press cuttings which dealt with us and our activities.

I am so glad to have also the original of the cartoon by Mergen[3] which you have sent me. I am having it framed for my walls.

Mr Rosenstiel[4] will be here soon and I am asking him to come and lunch with me one day at Chartwell. I remember you and Herbert Swope talking to me about him – and also the letter he wrote to me (or rather his company

---

[1] James Middleton Cox, 1870–1957. Owner of *Dayton Daily News*, 1897–91. US House Representative (Dem.), 1909–13. Governor of Ohio, 1913–15, 1917–21. Presidential candidate (Dem.), 1920. Owner of *Miami Daily News* and *Canton Daily News*, 1923–57.

[2] Berkeley Ormerod, 1897–1983. Royal Rgt of Artillery, 1916–26. British Army Golf Champion, 1924. London Stock Exchange, 1929–39. Director of public relations, British Information Services, New York, 1945–62. Knighted, 1960.

[3] Anne Briardy Mergen, 1906–94. *Miami Daily News* cartoonist, 1933–56. Published in *Atlanta Journal*, *Dayton News* and *Miami Daily News*. Nominee to Florida Women's Hall of Fame, 2011.

[4] Lewis Solon Rosenstiel, 1891–1976. Born in Cincinnati, Ohio. Bought distilleries before the repeal of prohibition in 1933, and in that year started Schenley Distillers Co., which grew rapidly and offered him great success in the bourbon market. Sold most of his stock in 1968 and retired to focus on philanthropy.

wrote to me) some years ago putting forward a dazzling proposition. I look forward to meeting him and hearing what he has to say.

And finally, dear Bernie, I hear you are coming to this country during the summer. Do write and let me know your plans as of course we are all looking forward to seeing you.

I hear that Sarah greatly enjoyed her stay with you. How kind you were to her.

Field Marshal Jan Smuts to Winston S. Churchill
(Churchill papers, 2/176)

23 May 1949 Cape Town

My dear Winston,

I had written to you before your welcome cable arrived, but had not yet posted the letter. I send it forward now, with this additional note.

Be assured that I have no fault to find with your action, and indeed I anticipated you would actually take the line you did. For that reason I had not written you privately, for fear that such a letter would seriously embarrass you in coming to a decision.

The whole issue is indeed a tangled one, presenting different aspects from the Indian and the South African point of view. I was of course bound to take the latter, but in your position I might have been sorely tempted to take the line you did. The total secession of India at this stage would have been a very serious loss of face, for Britain primarily, but also for the Commonwealth as a whole. Our stock has been falling badly, as I point out in my other letter, and the total loss of India would have deepened the impression of decline to the outside world.

But from the South African point of view I was bound to take the anti-republican view. The campaign for the republic is coming, and may be in full spate when I am no longer there to combat it. It will tear up South Africa, as you indicate in your cable, and it may succeed on the Indian model of a republic within the Commonwealth. But it will not stop there, as the fight since the First World War has been for complete secession, and Malan (who is at heart a moderate) will not be able to control his republican extremists, who are very powerful. The danger is therefore very real, and my public statements were meant more as a warning to South Africa about the danger ahead, than a reflection on the Conference Declaration. Of course, as you say, the future overall menace may be Communism, and on that issue even the republicans will stand by the Commonwealth, as I imagine even India is likely to do. But in any case the republican propaganda will influence racial feeling here as no other issue can. We shall be back in the Boer War atmosphere. However, in this rapidly changing world we should not peer too deeply into the future. I think the world is moving into one of the secular crises of history, and no one can forecast the world picture which will ultimately emerge from it. For the sake of the future I am jealous for the coherence and stability of the Commonwealth which, together with American war potential, will save mankind from the rocks as nothing else will. The present tendency to concentrate on social security, without earning it by work, may lead to a fresh outburst of dictatorship, which always follows chaotic economic conditions. If Democracy cannot provide efficient leadership, the road is open for Dictatorship, as recent history has shown. And Dictatorship at once leads to a struggle for world power. The prospect before us is therefore far from bright. You and I shall not see it, but I believe the transition through which we are moving may bring strange developments, from which, one hopes, our Free Western culture should once more emerge, purified and strengthened.

It will be a great joy to discuss these and other issues once more with you, and I hope that during the week I shall be in London (June 13th–17th) this will be possible.

I read your indictment in Scotland of the present indifference to our world position with warm approval. I think that way the long range danger lies. What is lost now can never be retrieved. History does not move backward.

With warm affectionate regards to you and Clemmy.

Winston S. Churchill to Alfred Duff Cooper
(Churchill papers, 4/19)

24 May 1949

My dear Duffie

I had heard from the BBC that you are reviewing *Their Finest Hour* in the European service, as you did in the case of *The Gathering Storm*. I am so glad, and I shall listen with interest.

I am having the points to which you draw my attention looked into by my staff and will see that these particular facts are correct in the second edition. Thank you for writing about them.

I propose to attend the European Assembly, as leader of the Conservative representatives of the British delegation, which is being held in Strasbourg in August.

Every good wish to you and Diana from Clemmie and myself.

Winston S. Churchill to Herbert Morrison
(Churchill papers, 2/75)

27 May 1949
Private

My dear Lord President,

Thank you very much for your letter of May 21. The six names which I propose as substitutes[1] are the following:

> Mr John Foster
> Mr Selwyn Lloyd
> Major Mott-Radclyffe[2]
> Major Peter Roberts[3]
> Major Harden[4]
> Lord Birkenhead

I certainly do not think that they will be needed over there all at once, and I agree with you that careful economy must be maintained. It may be however that some of them will be needed for Committee work even when their companion is absent. This we can however discuss as things develop.

I may say to you that I do not wish myself to be deeply involved in details, and after I have played my part at the opening phase I shall seek relief from regular attendance.

---

[1] For UK delegates to the Consultative Assembly of the Council of Europe.

[2] Charles Edward Mott-Radclyffe, 1911–92. Educated at Eton and Balliol College, Oxford. Served in Diplomatic Service (Athens and Rome), 1936–8. Commissioned, Rifle Bde, 1939. Member, Military Mission to Greece, 1940–1. Liaison Officer, Syria, 1941. MP (Cons.) for Windsor, 1942–70. On active service, Middle East and Italy, 1943–4. Parliamentary Private Secretary to Secretary of State for India (L. S. Amery), Dec. 1944 to May 1945. Junior Lord of the Treasury, May–July 1945. Cons. Whip, 1945–6. Chairman, Conservative Parliamentary Foreign Affairs Committee, 1951–9. Knighted, 1957. Capt., Lords and Commons Cricket, 1952–70.

[3] Peter Geoffrey Roberts, 1912–85. Educated at Harrow School and Trinity College, Cambridge. On active service during WWII. MP (Cons.) for Ecclesall, 1945–50; for Heeley, 1950–66. Bt, 1955.

[4] James Richard Edwards Harden, 1916–2000. Senior liaison officer for Montgomery during WWII. DSO, 1945. MP (Ulster Unionist) for Armagh, 1948–54.

May 1949 1427

Winston S. Churchill to Duke of Devonshire[1]
(*Churchill papers, 2/162*)

27 May 1949

My dear Eddy,

Thank you so much for inviting me to paint my lion at the Zoo myself. As the bars might get in the way and detract from the artistic effect, I suggest you should come inside the cage with me. This is a generous offer on my part considering how much more substantial a repast I can offer!

Anthony Eden to Winston S. Churchill
(*Churchill papers, 2/82*)

27 May 1949

My dear Winston,

I forgot to mention two things when I saw you yesterday.

First, the *New York Times* have asked me to do an article about our Party's aims and policies. I should think there would be no objection to this provided I do not, as I would not, attack Ministers of the Crown or the Government in the process. Our rule is not to attack our own Government when we are abroad, or in foreign papers, but I do not think this should prohibit us from stating our own positive opinions. I hope that you agree.

The second thing was that I have heard from Mayhew, Under-Secretary at the Foreign Office, asking me whether you or I had any recollection of a luncheon party at the Spanish Embassy in October 1941, which, according to General Franco, was attended by yourself, Templewood, and myself, and at which it was allegedly said that Spain could count on Britain's aid in becoming the strongest Mediterranean power.

It seems that the Foreign Office have no record of any such luncheon and Mayhew asked whether we had any recollection, either of us, of it, in order to help them 'assess the value of General Franco's assertions'.

I have no recollection whatever of the luncheon, though it may well have taken place, but I feel quite confident that neither of us ever said that 'Spain could count on Britain's aid in becoming the strongest power in the Mediterranean'.

Would you like me to reply to Mayhew in this sense?

---

[1] Edward William Spencer Cavendish, 1895–1950. On active service in WWI (as Marquess of Hartington), Dardanelles and France (despatches twice). Member of the British Peace Delegation, Paris, 1919. MP (Cons.) for West Derbyshire, 1923–38, before succeeding his father as 10th Duke of Devonshire. Parliamentary Under-Secretary of State for Dominion Affairs, 1936–40; for India and Burma, 1940–2; for the Colonies, 1942–5.

May 1949

Winston S. Churchill to Clement Attlee
(Churchill papers, 2/29)

27 May 1949
Private

My dear Prime Minister,

I enclose to you the second Memorandum on Defence which has been prepared by some of my friends. There has been no time for revision, but I put it forward as a factual statement which I believe to be correct. I do not however regard it as a statement of policy because it obviously takes no account of the financial aspect. I am of the opinion that the provision made by Parliament of 750 million pounds and nearly 750,000 men, if properly applied and administered, should suffice for our needs in the immediate future. I reserve my opinion on this until I have had the advantage of our impending discussions.

As all this question involves so many facts and figures I should be obliged if you would allow me to bring Lord Cherwell with me as a fourth member of our deputation. You will recall how much I depended on his graphs and statistics as well as upon his scientific knowledge during the war.

I may add that, while I cannot claim to have examined the matter with any expert knowledge, it is my personal view at present that the menace of the fast submarine cannot be dealt with by building a comparatively small number of very large ocean-going destroyers, but that the solution of our problem should be sought in a greater improvisation of small aircraft-carriers with detecting apparatus and bombs. I am aware of the difficulty of locating submarines below the surface except at close range on account of the similarity of response given by submerged metallic objects and the salt water which surrounds them. I hope however this may be patiently explored, because once the distinction could be made, the peril could be mastered.

I should like to draw your attention to an error in the text of my first memorandum. On page 2 the last sentence of paragraph 4 should read 'We should like to have a statement of the artillery of all kinds. . . .' etc.

Cecily Gemmell[1] to Winston S. Churchill
(Churchill papers, 2/29)

28 May 1949

Mr Churchill,

I have read your letter to the Prime Minister to Colonel Stanley who suggests that it would be better not to say that the Memorandum has been prepared by the Conservative Secretariat, since, in view of the secrecy of the

---

[1] Cecily Gemmell, 1928–?. Known as 'Chips'. Personal Secretary to Winston Churchill, 1947–53.

matter, this might convey the impression that it had been flung together. He suggests you should say, 'prepared by some of my friends. There has been no time for revision, but I put it forward as a factual statement which I believe to be correct.'

Winston S. Churchill: speech
('Winston S. Churchill, His Complete Speeches', volume 7, pages 7823–4)

28 May 1949 Chigwell

NATIONALISATION

[. . .] This is a fateful year for this island. Before 12 months have passed we shall have another General Election. We must be ready for an autumn election, and if it comes, Conservatives must be mobilized.

A few weeks ago Mr Morrison was uttering threats of using the weapon of labour unrest to prevent a Conservative Government from being duly returned by constitutional means, and from discharging the functions of government. He made indignant denials, which we must accept for what they are worth, but his words remain on record. Now we have one of the leading Socialist thinkers, Mr G. D. H. Cole,[1] chairman of the Fabian Society, expressing the same threat even more crudely and cynically in his recent manifesto.

This is merely an attempt to intimidate the middle-class electors from doing their duty according to their conscience, and if such threats were effective the rights and liberty of the British people would be given over to the one-party system which Socialists and Communists alike have as their final goal, and it would be riveted upon them as securely as upon the people in the Soviet grip.

A Conservative victory at the next General Election is Britain's surest hope. To restore economic confidence one major issue is vital. The Socialist policy of nationalization has failed on every occasion. Everywhere we have seen great industries, which formerly swam on their own and made a profit for shareholders and the Exchequer, transferred from the gaining side to the losing side of the national account. . . .

Here is this Government, which have profoundly injured the economic life of one-fifth of our industry by nationalization, living and keeping their head above water by heavily taxing the profits of the other four-fifths. They are now deliberately saying that it does not matter to the country whether its industries make profits or not, and that all of them might be run in so wasteful or incompetent a manner as to result in loss without injury to the nation. Such arrant nonsense was never put forward even by Mr Dalton in his craziest moments.

---

[1] George Douglas Howard Cole, 1889–1959. Chairman, New Fabian Research Bureau, 1937–9; Fabian Society, 1937–46, 1948–50. First Chichele Prof. of Social and Political Theory at Oxford University, 1944. President, Fabian Society, 1952–9.

Yet the Chancellor of the Exchequer does not hesitate to use the Post Office profits as a means of increasing the revenue by taking more from the public in telephone and other charges. It only illustrates the squalid confusion of the Socialist mentality, and shows plainly that, when a Socialist Government get hold by nationalization of a monopoly with which no private competition is tolerated, they are prepared to use it to increase their profits by utilizing the power of the State to squeeze the individual citizen to the utmost. . . .

It is pathetic to witness the prostitution of a fine intellect to the desire to retain office and power. The most charitable explanation I can suggest is that Sir Stafford Cripps has a mental black-out every quarter. If this is so, he is at least more fortunate than his colleague, Mr Shinwell, whose case is the reverse and shows only periodic interludes of rational illumination.

Walter Graebner: recollection
('My Dear Mr Churchill', pages 27–8)

29 May 1949

One Sunday in 1949 we took five episodes of the March of Time's *Crusade in Europe*, a documentary film on World War II, down to Chartwell. Churchill loved it, as it enabled him to relive his grandest years again, and he watched it with closest attention, tears often rolling down his cheeks and comments on the action continually on his lips. Characteristically he showed no feeling of triumph over his vanquished enemy. 'Poor fellows, poor, poor fellows', he would say with generous pity, as toward the end he watched scenes of German prisoners of war huddling together in their camps. After the hour and forty minutes it took to run off the five reels, Churchill was calling for more, though it was then 11 p.m.

That evening provided a good example of Churchill's extraordinary thoughtfulness. It was the custom at Chartwell to invite everyone who lived or worked on the estate to view the movies. Among the group of twenty or thirty was an ex-German prisoner of war named Walter who did odd jobs like woodcutting and lawnmowing and who, from the way he responded to anything Churchill said, was obviously a devoted servant. The March of Time film was not under way more than a few minutes before it was clear that it would not evoke happy memories for a former member of the Reichswehr. Churchill rose from his seat at once, tapped Walter on the shoulder and motioned him to leave the theatre with him. Later we learned that Churchill's object in going out was to suggest to Walter that perhaps he would prefer not to see the film that evening. Walter, however, returned to the theatre with Churchill and remained till the end.

May 1949

Clement Attlee to Winston S. Churchill
(Churchill papers, 2/29)

29 May 1949
Private

My dear Churchill,

Thank you for sending me, with your letter of the 27th May, your supplementary memorandum on Defence, which reached me on Friday evening and to which I shall give careful consideration with my colleagues. I hope that we shall be ready for you on Wednesday afternoon, but it may be that I shall have to ask you for a little more time.

By all means bring Lord Cherwell, in addition to Lord Winterton and Colonel Stanley. I shall probably be accompanied by the Minister of Defence and the Chancellor of the Exchequer.

Clement Attlee to Winston S. Churchill
(Churchill papers, 2/29)

30 May 1949

My dear Churchill,

I have been considering with my colleagues the two memoranda which you have sent to me. The second memorandum is very long and detailed and I have not yet had time to study it.

It is clear that we may well need more than one meeting. It would, therefore, I think, be a mistake to begin any formal meetings before Whitsun. In any event it is, I think, desirable that we should give some consideration to the basis on which these talks are to take place. I should, therefore, like to meet you alone on Wednesday next for this purpose.

June 1949

Clement Attlee to Winston S. Churchill
(Churchill papers, 2/75)

1 June 1949
Confidential

My dear Churchill,

Further to my letter of 31st May about the composition of the delegation to the Consultative Assembly of the Council of Europe, I now enclose for your advance information a copy of the Statement after Questions which I hope to make to-morrow. I also enclose a copy of a letter which I have sent to the six Members of the Conservative Party whom you have nominated to serve as substitute members of the delegation.

You will notice that in the statement the substitute members are not referred to by name, and I understand that this is in accordance with your own views. I do not think that it will be necessary to make any formal announcement of these names to the House, unless I am pressed to do so at some later date; on the other hand, presumably there can be no question of treating these additional appointments as confidential after tomorrow's announcement has been made.

Winston S. Churchill: speech
('Winston S. Churchill, His Complete Speeches', volume 7, pages 7824–5)

1 June 1949   Royal Borough of Kensington

A TIME WHEN OLD FEUDS MAY DIE

. . . I have always hoped that we shall reach a time when old feuds may die. Terrible things are done in war, but when it is over one must try to clear one's heart of the horrors of the past, and no united Europe can arise without the loyal aid of the German race. I have always appealed to our dear friend and ally, France, to stretch forth the hand of reconciliation in order that we may look forward to the future and enable all the masses of toiling and humble folk who dwell in Europe to regain for themselves the simplest joys and rights of human life, and take a part in rebuilding the glory of their ancient continent.

There was a time, in 1935 and 1936, when I used to hear, in the famous lines, 'ancestral voices prophesying war'; but now, I am thankful to say, I do not hear those voices. I have a growing hope that by the strength of our united civilization, and by our readiness and preparedness to defend our freedom with our lives, we may avert for ever the horrible vision of a third world war. I have a feeling that it is not beyond our power, and certainly the awful experiences through which we have passed should make us resolve not to neglect anything any more which can possibly save us and save the world. That rolling away of those dark oppressions and clouds from the minds of men is the prize – the only prize – which can reward the valiant efforts of our generation; and with unity, vigilance, and unswerving purpose I believe that priceless treasure may still be gained.

(Editor's Note: At the subsequent civic luncheon Churchill repeated an earlier remark.)[1] I do not feel, as I did before the last war, that another terrible war is inevitable. I think the light is broadening, and let honour be given to all those who have done their part to that end. We shall never succeed in evading the perils which surround us by weakness, appeasement, or by cowardness, but by courage, steadfastness, coolness, and, above all, by an unconquerable zeal in the cause of freedom and justice, applied to all races and classes of men wherever they may dwell throughout the world.

General Sir Giffard Le Quesne Martel[2] *to Winston S. Churchill*
(*Churchill papers, 2/84*)

2 June 1949

Dear Mr Winston Churchill,

A great many of your friends and supporters are very concerned because we understand that you remain in favour of conscription. We may of course be misinformed. Some of us have studied this for two years and lectured about it all over the country as well as putting letters in the press.

Among the thoughtful Officers of medium seniority, who are nearly always right, and among many Senior Officers there is only a handful who still believe in conscription. Surely we cannot all be wrong. We do hope that we are

---

[1] This note was written by Robert Rhodes James, editor of *His Complete Speeches*.
[2] Giffard Le Quesne Martel, 1889–1958. On active service, 1914–18 (despatches five times, DSO, MC). Asst Director of Mechanization, War Office, 1936–8; Deputy Director, 1938–9. Cdr, Royal Armoured Corps, 1940–1. Head of British Military Mission to Moscow, Mar. 1943 to Feb. 1944. Knighted, 1943. Chairman, Royal Cancer Hospital, 1945–50. Wrote memoirs, *An Outspoken Soldier* (1949), and several other books, among them *East Versus West* (1952).

misinformed and that you will be in your usual place as leader of the forward view held by so many of us.

I will send you a paper on this subject by the next post, though I fear you may be too busy to read it.

Winston S. Churchill to General Sir Giffard Le Quesne Martel
(Churchill papers, 2/84)

2 June 1949

My dear General,

Thank you for your letter of June 2. I am entirely opposed to the abolition of National Service at the present time. I should consider it a great blow to what is left of British prestige throughout the world. I thank you for the article which you have sent me on the subject.

Sir Alexander Cadogan to Winston S. Churchill
(Churchill papers, 4/51)

5 June 1949   New York

Dear Winston,

I recently received, as a gift from you, your second volume. I have read all of it, including the appendices, and can only give it the highest praise by saying that I think it even better than the first. At any rate it moved me more – as it would any Englishman. Thank you so much for thinking of making this gift to me who contributed nothing to the great events there recorded but an abounding admiration for your leadership in those terrible times. You would say that you only interpreted the feelings and faith of the British people. But 80 or 100 musicians may have all the spirit and the skill and the aspiration (if not the inspiration) in the world, and it still takes the genius of the exceptional leader (with a small l) to weld them together into a perfect instrument.

I am so sorry we missed you on your recent visit to these shores. We only arrived back from California on the morning when you left New York for Boston, and your return passage through this city was so brief that I could not, even if I had been free, have disturbed you in the course of your rapid transference from the Grand Central to the ship.

If, as I hope, you come back here again, I do beg you to let me know some time beforehand, so that I might offer you a day or two in a quiet and quite agreeable house in Long Island, to which I could invite friends whom you might wish to see, or give you the opportunity to – as the Americans have it – relax.

Winston S. Churchill to Anthony Eden
(Churchill papers, 2/82)

7 June 1949

My dear Anthony,

Your letter of May 27.[1] I am sure anything you write will be very good and will be helpful to all our affairs, great and small.

There was undoubtedly a luncheon at the Spanish Embassy in Alva's day when you and I and the other persons mentioned by Franco were present. I should think this was in 1942 when Spanish goodwill was, as you may remember, of the utmost importance to Britain and the United States. It is possible that I used the expression that Spain might well become 'the strongest power in the Mediterranean'. Considering where France and Italy stood in our estimation and indeed in fact at that time, this was no fantastic assertion. That I pledged British aid in any definite or formal manner is of course quite untrue. I had no power to do so. The services rendered to us in this period by Franco Spain were perhaps decisive on the success of 'Torch'. I have no doubt that Alva, who was vehemently pro-British, wrote a despatch making the most of such informal talk as he heard.

I should not hesitate to repeat in public what I have written here, so perhaps it would be well to let Mayhew hew his own way.

PS. You were vy good at Fuley. Nationalization on Monday.

Winston S. Churchill to Clement Attlee
(Churchill papers, 2/29)

9 June 1949

My dear Prime Minister,

I must ask you to include in my Delegation Lord Salisbury, the leader of our Party in the House of Lords. Thus there will be myself, Mr Eden, Colonel Oliver Stanley, Lord Winterton, Lord Salisbury and Lord Cherwell, and Brigadier Head[2] as secretary. This will make us six delegates, all of whom are Privy Councillors. I hope this is not too many.[3]

---

[1] Reproduced above (p. 1427).

[2] Antony Henry Head, 1906–83. Educated at Eton and RMC, Sandhurst. MC, 1940. Brig. Gen. Staff, Combined Operations HQ, 1943. MP (Cons.) for Carshalton, 1945–60. Secretary of State for War, 1951–6. PC, 1951. Minister of Defence, 1956–7. Viscount, 1960. High Commissioner to Nigeria, 1960–3; to Malaysia, 1963–6.

[3] Attlee responded: 'I shall be very glad to receive Lord Salisbury together with the other members of your delegation.'

June 1949

Bernard Baruch to Winston S. Churchill
(Churchill papers, 2/210)

10 June 1949   New York

Dear Winston,
    Here are my plans:
    On June 30th I sail on the *Queen Elizabeth*, arriving in Cherbourg on the 5th. From there I will proceed by automobile either to Paris or down the coast. I shall be in Paris and Vichy for about three weeks. If you are on the Continent anywhere I will go to see you.
    I plan to get to England and be with you the weekend of August 13th and 14th.
    I should like to fly to wherever my daughter is for her birthday on August 16th, and return to London to see you again.
    I propose sailing for home on the *Queen Mary* on August 20th.
    If I change my plans, I will let you know.
    I cannot tell you how pleased I am with the picture. I see that the date on it is '20. I do not think I have seen a better one.
    I just had a look at a bill some of the progressive senators propose introducing for the purpose of stopping the decline in business. If it is put through, it will have the opposite effect. It looks to me as if we are taking the same path you have taken. '*Facilis descensus Averno*'. Nobody has ever gotten to h— and come back to tell us about it, but they do say it is paved with good intentions.
    Some of us here are going to make a fight against this tendency, but it is very hard to fight a man who promises to give you something for nothing. As Al Smith said, 'you cannot shoot Santy Claus.'
    As long as the United States credit is good, these dancing dervishes of finance can make good. The day that savings do not appear for investment in government bonds, the witch dance will end. It seems to me that everybody wants us to try deficit financing. We all will be living on one another's deficits. Woe betide the world when we do that! That might be the opportunity for some other country to get its house in order.
    I think that so far we are on the retreat in the cold war.
    The most terrible thing to contemplate in this country is that we have everything we had yesterday and all the days and years before, and more of it, and yet we are confused and fearful. I see nothing for us to do except to keep our face to the sound of the guns and go on. I shall do that but I feel something like Sir Andrew Barton[1] who said, 'I am wounded but I am not slain. I will lay me down and bleed awhile and then I will rise and fight again.'

---

[1] Andrew Barton, c.1466–1511. High Admiral of the Kingdom of Scotland.

I know I shall see you in the front ranks carrying the banners that free men can follow.

I did not mean to write such a long letter but I feel better now that I have said all this to you, my dear friend.

Jo Sturdee to Editor of the Times
(Churchill papers, 2/86)

16 June 1949
Private

Dear Sir,

I am desired by Mr Churchill to draw your attention to the misquotation of his words which appears in the first paragraph of your leading article of Wednesday, June 15: 'In 1945 he' (Mr Churchill) 'charged them with intentions of establishing a "Gestapo" if they won.' The actual words used by Mr Churchill were: 'A Socialist State once thoroughly completed in all its details and its aspects – and that is what I am speaking of – could not afford to suffer opposition. . . .' And again, 'No Socialist Government conducting the entire life and industry of the country could afford to allow free, sharp or violently-worded expressions of public discontent. They would have to fall back on some form of "Gestapo", no doubt very humanely directed in the first instance. And this would nip opinion in the bud.'[1]

Mr Churchill does not ask for any correction but feels that you may perhaps wish to apprise the writer of the leading article of his words which are frequently distorted.

Winston S. Churchill to Lady Lytton[2]
(Lady Lytton papers)

18 June 1949   Chartwell

Dearest Pamela,

Oddly enough I found this vy picture of Knebworth in my studio some weeks ago & resolved to offer it to you. I have had it framed & varnished & was about to send it to you when yr welcome letter arrived.

I am so glad you will like to have it, and am sending it to you herewith.

---

[1] See broadcast of 4 June 1945, reproduced in *The Churchill Documents* vol. 21, *The Shadows of Victory, January–July 1945*, pp. 1580–5.

[2] Pamela Frances Audrey Plowden, 1874–1971. Daughter of Sir Trevor Chichele-Plowden. On 4 Nov. 1896 Churchill wrote to his mother: 'I must say that she is the most beautiful girl I have ever seen.' Later Churchill proposed to her (at Warwick Castle) but was refused. In 1902 she married Victor Lytton, later 2nd Earl of Lytton. Their elder son, Edward, Viscount Knebworth, died in 1933 as a result of an aeroplane accident; their younger son, Alexander, Viscount Knebworth, was killed in action at El Alamein in 1942.

Winston S. Churchill to Field Marshal Lord Montgomery
(Churchill papers, 2/143)

21 June 1949

My dear Monty,

It will give me great pleasure to come to the Alamein Reunion this year, and I thank you for your invitation. Is it to be at the Albert Hall or is it a dinner?

Winston S. Churchill to Lord Beaverbrook
(Churchill papers, 4/17)

23 June 1949

My dear Max,

I am sending you out by your plane a copy of our Conservative paper on Imperial Policy. I took great pains with it myself bearing in mind what you had written to me at my request. I hope you will find it interesting and not out of harmony with the mission of the Conservative Party. I hope particularly that the title 'British Empire and Commonwealth of Nations' will be adopted universally by our friends. Please ring me up when you have received and read the paper.

Every good wish. We are having lovely weather here.

Christopher Soames to Winston S. Churchill
(Churchill papers, 2/31)

24 June 1949

SUMMARY OF SIR GIFFARD MARTEL'S PAPER ON:
THE PROS AND CONS ABOUT CONSCRIPTION

1. In the immediate future a cold war should be waged by the members of the Atlantic Pact against Russia. The signatory countries should provide twenty regular divisions in Europe which would 'infiltrate' into Eastern Europe and liberate all countries behind the iron curtain, Great Britain did provide four of these twenty divisions. It is considered unlikely that Russia would resist if she were persuaded that resistance would bring down the atomic on her head. They are not in the position to wage a major war.

2. The West must organise an effective propaganda machine to get over to the Russian people the fact that we do not wish them ill. This in order to counteract the Kremlin's story that the 'Capitalist countries' work to conquer Russia.

3. If the above two projects are successful, then is a good chance that the

Communist régime in Russia will collapse. If not they will almost certainly force a war when they are ready for it – say in five years time. If war comes, Great Britain cannot be expected to provide an initial Expeditionary Force of more than four divisions. Our overseas garrisons will have to be strengthened, and defence of this country ensured by the Navy, the Air Force and the Territorial Army.

4. To undertake the commitments laid out in paras 1–3 we need a highly efficient regular army of 200–250 thousand men, which would provide our overseas garrisons, four divisions with attached troops for use in Germany or elsewhere and instructions for the Territorial Army. Even with the present unattractive pay and conditions we already have 174 thousand regulars. But these men, instead of being concentrated in effective units, are being used to train an army of 430 thousand men at an annual cost of £304 million.

This money should be spent:
   (a) In providing pay and conditions for the regular army of 250 thousand men likely to attract the right type of man.
   (b) In building up an efficient Territorial Army. Here it must be remembered that there are in this country some four million men who served in the last war and who would again be available if another war came within five years.

5. The chief disadvantages to conscription are:
   (a) It makes too severe an inroad on our industry.
   (b) The time a man serves is not sufficient to make an effective solider.
   (c) It costs too much money.
   (d) Under the present system there are practically no effective fighting units.
   (e) Valuable equipment is being seriously damaged in the hands of the conscripts.

This is a brief résumé. I think you should read pages 7–11. It is a sound argument.

Harold Macmillan to Winston S. Churchill
(Churchill papers, 2/88)

24 June 1949
Personal

Dear Winston,

Having taken some part with Rab[1] in preparing the policy document, I must tell you how much I admired your handling of our discussions.

We completed the work of revision yesterday and Rab tells me that he

---
[1] R. A. Butler, MP (Cons.) for Saffron Walden.

hopes to have page proofs on Tuesday. There is one point which I would like you to consider.

It should be made clear that this is a document with a quite different degree of authority to those previously published by the Central Office, and even to the 'Charters'. Do you not think you could achieve this by a short preface from your pen? This would serve to make it clear that this document not only had your full endorsement, but was inspired by you.

You will forgive me – but I am so anxious that you should be known to the <u>younger</u> section of the voters (and that means, for this purpose, anyone under 40) not merely as the great war leader, but as the social reformer. Surely with these proposals, the wheel comes full circle? You can appeal to everything which your Father wanted to do and which you helped to accomplish in your Liberal days. Surely this document presents a rallying for all reasonable people, of all political affiliations and of none to oppose Socialism not with a negative but with a positive policy.

Who is so fitted to present this as yourself? In your life these immense social changes have taken place and largely with your support and guidance. The ground won must be consolidated, and then extended; it is in danger of being lost. Make it clear – especially to the young – what has been (in addition to your record as a War Minister) your life-long work.

Winston S. Churchill to Herbert Morrison
(Churchill papers, 2/75)

24 June 1949

My dear Herbert Morrison,

Thank you for your letter. The change of the date upsets my plans but of course I shall be there at the opening.[1] I was not planning to stay there very long as I must have some rest in the holiday season.

I have already inquired of the Prime Minister's private secretary asking for information as to the financial arrangements which the Government may make (a) to meet expenses and (b) to provide currency. I should be quite ready to pay my own expenses, provided sufficient currency were provided. I shall have certain obligations for entertaining. I have not yet heard from the Prime Minister's Private Office. Perhaps you will let me know at your convenience.

About the alternative members, I hope the deputies or substitutes may be allowed to come if they want and if their Parties want them to. I am told that the French and some of the other powers are bringing the whole of their second eleven, and this will make our people seem a much smaller band. There is also a lot of work to do on committees. Perhaps you will let me know.

[1] Of the Consultative Assembly of the Council of Europe.

Winston S. Churchill to Captain Oswald Birley
(Churchill papers, 2/160)

28 June 1949

My dear Oswald,

I am delighted you and your Wife[1] will come and stay with me for a while abroad. I have another plan instead of Gardone, which I think is more attractive. My affairs at the beginning of August are in much uncertainty because of the Council of Europe at Strasbourg. I hope to be clear of this by the middle of the month at the latest, and I am planning to be in Venice, or rather at the Lido which is cooler, for the last ten days in August. Would it be possible for you both to join me there on the 20th? The weather gets much cooler at the end of the month, and Venice with all its wonders should form a fertile field for our oleaginous operations. There are beautiful islands around which we can visit in a launch, and it is but twenty minutes from Venice with all its treasures. If this suits you both I will arrange everything and let you know the details quite soon.

About luncheon here at Chartwell in July, I find we have a lot of children coming on Sunday the 10th, but Saturday the 9th would be splendid. We shall have Mr Baruch staying with us, whom I am sure you will both be interested to meet.

I have been daubing a little today in the heat, but it is not much good. The price paid for 'The Blue Room' is of course all humbug. It was made up with seventy percent notoriety, twenty percent charity and, I hope, ten percent the actual performance.

Arthur Sulzberger to Winston S. Churchill
(Churchill papers, 4/17)

28 June 1949

Dear Mr Churchill,

The other day when I had the pleasure of lunching with you, you were recalling some anecdotes and then said to me that you hated the idea of dying with so many stories and anecdotes untold.

I have been reflecting on that and wondering why you don't tell them. Since you have secretaries available for your major work, wouldn't it be worthwhile, as one of these stories comes into your head, to dictate it, put it aside, and then see if (1) it can't be woven into the major work, or (2) a collection of them wouldn't make a splendid volume.

---

[1] Rhoda Vava Mary Lecky Pike, 1900–81. Married Capt. Oswald Birley, 1921.

Clement Attlee to Winston S. Churchill
(Churchill papers, 2/29)

28 June 1949
Private

My dear Churchill,

I have now had the opportunity of discussing with my colleagues your two memoranda and I am now ready to meet you and your friends. I suggest that we should have the first meeting next week. I should be glad if your Secretary could get into touch with mine in order to find out days and times that will be mutually convenient.

I shall be accompanied by the Minister of Defence, the Service Ministers and the Minister of Supply.

When I saw you, you suggested that Brigadier Head should attend in a secretarial capacity. I was inclined then to agree, but I have since given further consideration to the matter. I have, of course, no doubt whatever as to the reliability of Head, but one has to consider possible repercussions. There might be a demand that I should receive other groups of members, as for instance my own back benchers, and give them also confidential information. The reply would be that these talks are between Privy Councillors who have special obligations. The introduction of Head would destroy this argument. I feel, therefore, that I must ask you to confine those accompanying you to members of the Privy Council. Air Marshal Elliot[1] will be present to take a note.[2]

Winston S. Churchill to Sir Alan Lascelles
(Churchill papers, 2/171)

29 June 1949

My dear Tommy,

I should be so much obliged if you would seek a favourable moment to give the enclosed copy[3] to The King. The bound volume will not alas be ready for some time. The Publishers tell me there has been a record sale, well over a quarter of a million people having bought the book in a single day.

---

[1] William Elliot, 1896–1971. On active service, 1914–18 (despatches, DFC and bar, 1918). Secretary, Night Air Defence Committee, 1940. CBE, 1942. Director of Plans, Air Ministry, 1942–4. CB, 1944. AOC, RAF Gibraltar, 1944; Balkan Air Force, 1944–5. Asst Chief Executive, Ministry of Aircraft Production, 1945–6. Knighted, 1946. C-in-C, Fighter Command, 1947–9. Air Mshl, 1948. Deputy Military Secretary to Cabinet, 1949–51. ADC to King George VI, 1950–2; to the Queen, 1952–4. Air Chf Mshl, 1951. Chairman, British Joint Services Mission, Washington DC, 1951–4. GCVO, 1953.

[2] Churchill wrote on this letter: 'I will speak to Brigadier Head.'

[3] Of *Their Finest Hour*, vol. 2 of *The Second World War*.

Winston S. Churchill to President Harry S Truman
(Churchill papers, 2/158)

29 June 1949
Private

My dear Harry,

I feel I ought to send you the enclosed memorandum which has been written by a very able young member of our Party in the House of Commons, Mr Alec Spearman, as the result of his visit to Greece. I should be grateful to you if you could, among your many preoccupations, find time to read it. I cannot vouch personally for the facts, but you have no doubt full information. In view of the very great responsibility I undertook in 1944–45 to save Athens from falling a prey to the Communists, as it would have done, and in view of the adoption of this policy at great expense by the United States, I venture upon the following comment –

Intervention by a great State in the internal affairs of a small one is always questionable and entails much complicated argument. If the great state thinks it right to intervene surely they should make their intervention effective by using the overwhelming power they have at their disposal. Not to do this is only to prolong the agony at immense expense and possibly to final disastrous conclusion. I hope you will consider this as it affects the future in many ways.

I was deeply impressed by your statement about not fearing to use the atomic bomb if need arose. I am sure this will do more than anything else to ward off the catastrophe of a third world war. I have felt it right to speak, as you may have seen, in terms of reassurance for the immediate future, but of course I remain under the impression of the fearful dangers which impend upon us. Complete unity, superior force and the undoubted readiness to use it, give us the only hopes of escape. Without you nothing can be done.

July
1949

President Harry S Truman to Winston S. Churchill
(Churchill papers, 2/158)

2 July 1949   The White House

Dear Winston,

I appreciated your good letter of the 29th[1] most highly, and read the enclosed note on a visit to Greece by Mr Alec Spearman with a great deal of interest.

I am in agreement with you that Greece must be kept from the hands of the Communists, and we expect to do everything possible to fulfill that objective.

I am not quite so pessimistic as you are about the prospects for a third world war. I rather think that eventually we are going to forget that idea, and get a real world peace. I don't believe even the Russians can stand it to face complete destruction, which certainly would happen to them in the event of another war.

I hope you are in good health and that everything is going well with you. It is always a pleasure to hear from you.

King George VI to Winston S. Churchill
(Churchill papers, 2/171)[2]

4 July 1949   Buckingham Palace

My dear Winston,

Very many thanks for the 2nd Volume of your Book. I have already started reading it and what vivid memories it recalls to mind.

The present situation in the World is not too quieting and I am worried over the outcome of the coming finance talks here and over future financial prospects.

---

[1] Reproduced immediately above.
[2] This letter was handwritten.

I have just received the *White House Papers* of Harry Hopkins. This and your book will be an interesting comparison.

With renewed thanks.

Winston S. Churchill to Clement Attlee
(Churchill papers, 2/29)

5 July 1949

My dear Prime Minister,

Wednesday next at 11.30 at your room in the House of Commons will be very convenient to me and my friends.

I will of course defer to your wishes, which I quite understand, about not bringing Brigadier Head.

Winston S. Churchill to Brigadier Antony Head
(Churchill papers, 2/29)

5 July 1949

My dear Head,

I am so sorry to have to tell you that the Prime Minister, after further consideration, does not want anyone present at our Defence meetings who is not a Privy Counsellor or an official of the Government. Therefore I cannot include you in our delegation as I had wished. I imagine that the reason is that they fear to be confronted with demands from their back benchers as they depart from the line of the Privy Council.

I hope you will continue to help us in our talks by ourselves.

Winston S. Churchill: speech
(Churchill papers, 2/50)

5 July 1949

OPENING OF THE SIKORSKI INSTITUTE

Sir John Anderson, my Lords, Ladies and Gentlemen:

We are met here to invest with structural strength the undying memory of a great and gallant man. In General Sikorski the cause of world freedom found a champion whose activities range far beyond the limits of his own country. He was a great Pole; but he was greater as a citizen of the whole world. He understood, deeply and intensely, the causes which were at stake in the struggle through which we have passed, and for which we are still contending.

I had the pleasure – the honour – of meeting him in the early years of the war when he took me to inspect the magnificent Polish Division we had in Scotland, and often I saw him when we conferred upon the difficult questions which he and I and my friend Mr Eden had to decide and discuss together. And I remember, as if it were yesterday, the shock which came to us both – Mr Eden and I, – when the news of his sudden, tragic, untoward death came in upon us. The aeroplane crash, taking off at that restricted landing-ground at Gibraltar, where many of us had to go several times, and a great factor – a great figure – fell out of the Allied line of battle.

I am so glad this Institute is here being definitely established. I earnestly hope it will receive all the support that is necessary to invest it with permanent strength. The name of Sikorski should be preserved, – I say it in the presence of his gracious widow who is here with us today – should be preserved as an inspiration for all who care about the future of Europe. The future of Europe and the future of the world. I have been speaking about General Sikorski. I knew beforehand that other great Pole, Marshal Pilsudski,[1] who played so fine a part in the years after the late struggle in the first world war was over, and who suffered so much in the period before victory was attained. These are the names which Poland will cherish. I come to a thought, if you will permit me, of Poland itself. In hearts throughout Poland, how long – how many times – are they to suffer. How long, how many times, are they to win their freedom and deliverance, and find it only a mockery. But they must never despair. In all the qualities of the Polish nation, there's none which stands out more strongly than this unconquerable quality of always renewing and refreshing the life strength of the nation from generation to generation; from disaster to disaster; from one tragedy to another. – Always with gleams of triumph and victory. And then, after all that was suffered and all that was endured – and all that was achieved – it was found they had but exchanged one form of oppression for another. But that will pass. The great forces of the world are growing in strength. Recession marks the front of the forces of tyranny in every land, far and wide throughout the world, modern methods and intelligence swift and easy intercourse which, in spite of all their efforts is taking place between human minds all over the world, show that the forces of freedom have formed a broad front, and are advancing steadily. And I am sure the day will come when we shall see that the causes that General Sikorski fought for, and for which he gave his life cheerfully, are causes which will not fall to the ground and perish by the wayside – and perish in the wilderness. No, the day will come undoubtedly, when Poland will enter into the full inheritance which her readiness to endure the sacrifice and martyrdom and her unfailing spirit of revival have entitled her to. And when we shall be able to feel that all of us

---

[1] Jósef Pilsudski, 1867–1935. Polish statesman considered to be the founding father of the Second Polish Republic. Chief of State, 1918–22. 1st Marshal of Poland, 1920–35. Launched successful coup in May 1926 and governed Poland thereafter until his death.

who, in our different ways, have worked for the freedom and independence and the history of the world, and are consolidated by the event. When that day comes there are many names in Polish history which will be honoured, there is none which I feel on which the glint of fame and gratitude will fall more than on that of the famous soldier and statesman, General Sikorski the Institute to whose memory we are here to consecrate tonight. I earnestly hope everyone will try their best to make a great and lasting practical success of our efforts. But all over the world there are thoughts. Far off in America and all over the world, there are thoughts which flow here and find their centre in this room. Let them be made effective and fruitful.

I am very grateful to Sir John Anderson and your Committee for having invited us to share in your proceedings this afternoon.

Field Marshal Lord Montgomery to Winston S. Churchill
(Churchill papers, 4/51)[1]

8 July 1949

Dear Mr Churchill,

Thank you so very much for Vol II: *Their Finest Hour*. It is of course superb, and I am enjoying it immensely.

I have just returned from a sea voyage with the Western Union Fleet. It was most interesting and encouraging. But what times we live in! That such burdens should bear so heavily on us when we have been at peace for over four years, is not good.

I hope you keep well. You will have to take us through the next crisis, as you did the last. So, take care of yourself.

Clement Attlee to Winston S. Churchill
(Churchill papers, 2/75)

8 July 1949

My dear Churchill,

You will recall that, when I announced in the House the names of the delegates to the Consultative Assembly for the Council of Europe, I said that these appointments were for the first Session of the Assembly. Since then it has been brought to my attention that there will probably be advantages in keeping the delegation in being, although, of course, it is unlikely that it will actually function, between one Session of the Assembly and the next. At the same time, it seems improbable, if the Assembly is to meet only once a year, that it will meet

[1] This letter was handwritten.

again before the dissolution of the present Parliament. In these circumstances it seems to us desirable that the appointment of the British representatives on the Assembly should run to the beginning of the second ordinary Session of the Assembly, or until the dissolution of the United Kingdom Parliament, which ever is the earlier.

I hope that this will be agreeable to you, and if so, perhaps you will be good enough to inform those members of your Party who will be on the delegation, and their substitutes, of this adjustment.

L. S. Amery to Winston S. Churchill
(Churchill papers, 2/160)

9 July 1949

My dear Winston,

It is just sixty years this month since you first made an unprovoked and treacherous attack upon me. To show that I bear no malice I suggest that we celebrate the event by your coming to dine with me and I will collect half a dozen old friends to meet you and bear witness to our reconciliation.

Will you suggest a date?[1]

Winston S. Churchill to Herbert Morrison
(Churchill papers, 2/75)

15 July 1949

My dear Lord President,

Thank you for your letter of June 27 concerning the monetary arrangements and accommodation for my stay in Strasbourg. I will have a word with you about this on Wednesday.

I understand that the Municipality of Strasbourg have suggested that I should stay either in the chateau which you mention, or in a house in the town, in Rue Brahms. On the whole, I think it would be more convenient to be in the town. Provided, therefore, there is no objection, I shall accept this latter offer.

We must accept your view for the present about the substitutes. I shall want one on the third or fourth day.

---

[1] Churchill responded on July 20: 'Alas dear Leo I have not a moment before I go abroad. Thank you very much for your invitation.' The 'treacherous attack' was pushing young Amery into 'Ducker', the Harrow School swimming pool. Churchill's account of this episode can be found in chapter 2 of *My Early Life*.

Winston S. Churchill to Bertrand Mather[1]
(Churchill papers, 2/90)

15 July 1949

Dear Mr Mather,

The people of West Leeds should have no difficulty in deciding for whom to vote next Thursday as their Parliamentary representative. You are one of themselves, you were born and bred among them, educated at a Leeds school and the University, and have spent the whole of your business life in their midst. Furthermore, as a Conservative, you stand for the well-founded principles and a free and tolerant way of life which alone can rescue our country and its people from these evil days.

Even Socialist Ministers themselves admit that this is 'a moment of supreme crisis'. Aghast at the results of their own handiwork, they are no longer able to conceal the sombre fact that their much-vaunted 'Planning' has proved a failure. For four feverish years they have stumbled blindly from one crisis into another and now we have to face the imminent prospect of severe cuts in our imports of vital raw materials and food supplies – or, in plain language, short time in the factories and less to eat.

How has all this come about? They cannot blame it on the world conditions, for look at the vast sums they have received from across the Atlantic. The truth is – and it has long been evident – that this Socialist Government, like its Ramsay MacDonald predecessor of twenty years ago, has been squandering the nation's treasure and living far beyond its means. Prodigal expenditure by Government departments, costly losses incurred by the nationalized industries, and centralized buying at inflated prices – these things come home to the public in taxation on an intolerable scale and higher prices all round. Bulkier wage packets are of little avail when, as the housewife knows, it takes something like half-a-crown to buy what used to cost a shilling. On the other hand higher costs of production, swollen by exorbitant Government demands on industry, are making it increasingly difficult to sell our goods for the dollars we urgently need.

To such a pitch has Socialist mismanagement brought us. Nor is this all. The demoralizing influence of the Socialist doctrine has gone far to sap the British people's traditional sense of discipline and national pride. If this nation is to recover its position in the world – and our very survival depends upon it – it must first renew the spirit of unity and patriotic endeavour that got us through the war. Let no one imagine that we shall escape from the dangers that beset us except by our own efforts. Only by the unsparing exertions of our own hands and brains under wise leadership can we raise ourselves again to the height of our destiny.

---

[1] Unsuccessful Parliamentary candidate (Cons.) for West Leeds, 1949.

Winston S. Churchill to Lord Salisbury
(Churchill papers, 2/82)

15 July 1949 — Chartwell

I send my hearty congratulations to your Member[1] on the completion of his first twenty-five years in Parliament. Warwick and Leamington has won national distinction ~~and fidelity~~ by their choice and by their steadfastness.

Anthony and I have been colleagues and comrades, heart and hand, in some of the most formidable events of war and we now work together to win for our country the prosperity and progress which are her due.

Winston S. Churchill to Clement Attlee
(Churchill papers, 2/75)

16 July 1949

My dear Prime Minister,

Thank you for your letter of July 8.[2] Your proposal that the appointment of the British representatives to the Consultative Assembly for the Council of Europe should run to the beginning of the second ordinary Session of the Assembly or until the dissolution of the United Kingdom Parliament, whichever is the earlier, is in every way correct and agreeable.

Winston S. Churchill: speech
(Hansard)

21 July 1949 — House of Commons

FOREIGN AFFAIRS

Mr Churchill (Woodford): I shall venture to trespass for only a very few minutes upon the Committee, but topics have been referred to by the right hon. Gentleman[3] in his speech which, perhaps, require some comment from me. The right hon. Gentleman is, I am sure, uneasy in his mind about the belated, persistent dismantling that is going on in Germany. He is uneasy in his mind – or he should be uneasy in his mind – about the very belated bringing to trial of German generals, and in the mood that he is in, he takes, I think, an altogether exaggerated view of any criticisms that were made by my right hon. Friend the Member for Bromley (Mr H. Macmillan) in his very restrained and carefully phrased speech.

---

[1] Anthony Eden.
[2] Reproduced above (pp. 1447–8).
[3] The Foreign Secretary, Ernest Bevin.

Hon. Members: Oh!

Mr S. Silverman: I wonder what the right hon. Gentleman would say if he abandoned restraint.

Mr Churchill: The hon. Gentleman is always intervening. On this occasion he did not even hop off his perch.

I should not have risen at all had it not been that the right hon. Gentleman felt so uneasy about those criticisms on the two points I have mentioned that he floated back across the years into the history of the war, and touched upon some large and important matters affecting our relations with the United States, with a view to throwing some invidious burden upon me personally; because otherwise there would have been no point in his doing so. (Hon. Members: 'No'.)

I was a person very responsible in these matters, and I must say that the phrase 'unconditional surrender' was not brought before me to agree to in any way before it was uttered by our great friend, our august and powerful ally President Roosevelt. But I did concur with him after he had said it, and I reported the matter to the Cabinet, who accepted the position. Whether if we had all discussed it at home we should have proposed such a settlement is another matter. Still, they did accept the position, as I, in my turn, on the spot, thought it right to do. I cannot feel that there can be any separation of responsibility between us in the matter, having regard to the long years in which we subsequently acted together.

Then the right hon. Gentleman rather used this episode to suggest that the difficulties in Germany were greatly aggravated by the use of this phrase. I am not at all sure that that is true. I am not going to plunge into a lengthy argument, but I am not at all sure that, if Hitler had been murdered by some of the plots which were levelled against him by men whom I do not hesitate to call patriotic Germans, a new situation would have arisen. I believe there was the force and vigour to carry on the fight, as it was carried on, to the very last gasp. He and the band of guilty men around him were in the position that they could not look for any pardon or any safety for their lives and they would certainly have fought to the death.

Mr Zilliacus (Gateshead): rose –

Mr Churchill: I do not wish to give way, if the hon. Gentleman will permit me to continue. I have been rather seriously criticised by the Foreign Secretary trying, as it were, to throw all the discredit for 'unconditional surrender' upon me. (Hon. Members: 'No'.) If he did not mean that, he did not mean anything. He is doing that because he is vexed with what my right hon. Friend said, though I thought my right hon. Friend's statement was very mildly expressed. It cannot be said that the decisions to which the Foreign Secretary has come about the prolongation of dismantling are connected in any way with the use of the phrase 'unconditional surrender' by President Roosevelt, so why bring it in and extend the Debate into other circles, and into matters of really very great gravity?

Another matter to which the Foreign Secretary referred, about which I do not by any means feel so confident in my conscience as to the judgment of my actions, is the Morgenthau Agreement at the second conference – the document published by Mr Morgenthau of the conference. There is an agreement; it was initialled by President Roosevelt and by me, and it undoubtedly proposed treatment of Germany which was a harsh treatment, in respect of largely limiting her to being an agricultural country. But that was not a decision taken over the heads of the Cabinet. It was not one that ever reached the Cabinet. It never reached the Cabinet because it was only ad referendum; it was disapproved by the State Department on the one hand and by my right hon. Friend and the Foreign Office Committee on the other, and it just dropped on one side. I must say that it never required a Cabinet negative; it never had any validity of any sort or kind.

Nevertheless, I must say that I do not agree with this paper, for which I none the less bear a responsibility. I do not agree with it, but I can only say that when fighting for life in a fierce struggle with an enemy I feel quite differently towards him than when that enemy is beaten to the ground and is suing for mercy. Anyhow, if the document is ever brought up to me I shall certainly say, 'I do not agree with that, and I am sorry that I put my initials to it.' I cannot do more than that. Of course, many things happen with great rapidity, but to say it was done over the heads of the Cabinet, or anything like that, is quite untrue, and the Cabinet never agreed to it for a moment.

These two matters of great importance were brought in, in order to justify the right hon. Gentleman in pursuing the policy of dismantling, and some incidents connected with the trial of the German generals. I do not think the right hon. Gentleman need have brought such artillery back from the past to fire at me on such matters. I do not put the case with hostility against him. I consider that in the airlift and the treatment of the Berlin difficulty the Government and the Foreign Office – no one more than he – showed the very greatest determination, skill, good judgment, and tenacity, and their exertions over a long period were crowned by unmistakable success which has been of the greatest advantage to Europe, and very likely played a part in the closer drawing together of Britain and the United States, which has found its manifestation in the Atlantic Pact.

I was very much struck at the way in which all Germany watched the airlift, and how all Germany saw the British and American planes flying to carry food to 2½ million Germans whom the Soviet Government were trying to starve. I thought that was worth all the speeches that could have been made by all the peace leaders of Europe to turn the eyes of Germany to where her true destiny lies: namely, in peaceful and honourable association with the Western democracies and with the future into which they hope to lead the world under the auspices of the United Nations organisation. I indeed thought that was a very great advantage.

I must say that I personally was instinctively disappointed and chilled when I saw the dismantling policy, which has draggled and straggled on for four years, being a cause of upsetting this strong drift and tide of German sentiment which may be of very great value in the future. I could not help feeling that it was untoward. Of course, these things must in some cases be done. They should have been done, or could have been done, two years ago. That would have been all right.

But now, four years after, when Europe is in the midst of all this feeling of hardship and pressure, and of hopes of coming out of it again, to go on tearing down these buildings and solemnly proceeding with methodical routine on some agreement which now no longer has any validity or application to current affairs was, I thought, an error: not an error of major criminality, but a bad touch. I should have hoped that it would have been possible to have let that go. I should have thought it should have been brought to an end. I have said so several times in the last months, and I do not think it is a wrong thing for us to put that view.

Nor do I think that because I was present and supported President Roosevelt when he used the phrase 'unconditional surrender' I am debarred from saying that at any time there should be a little give and take, and a different touch and handling in a sensitive manner of our relations with the German people. I am sure that the munitions which could be made by these factories which still remain to be dismantled would never do half the harm to the cause of peace, or to any future victory of the Allies against aggression, that is done by the great setting back and discouragement, out of all proportion, of the German movement towards Western civilisation and Western ideas. I will not put it at more than that.

As for the generals and so on, that, I think, should have been settled within a year or two of the end of the fighting; but to go on dragging these things out is simply feeding all the forces against peaceful solution and against passing the sponge across the past, with opportunities for making up ill-will and bad feeling. I do not make this a serious case of indictment against the right hon. Gentleman. In the main, we approve of his policy, but he really must not get so very upset and angry when certain notes are struck, even though when they are struck from this side, they awaken a very immediate echo on the benches behind him.

I have only one other thing to say, which I should not have referred to at all had I not felt it right to refer to the important topics which the right hon. Gentleman raised, and that is this question of our future meetings at Strasbourg. There will be a European Assembly at Strasbourg representing 10 nations.

Mr Bevin: More than that.

Mr Churchill: Maybe more. They will not necessarily consider themselves forced to agree with every dictat, ukase or regulation which is made by the Council of Ministers. They may not have any executive powers, but they will not be forced necessarily to accept the directions which come down to them from on high. Maybe, in the course of time, some method of adjusting quarrels, disputes and differences between the European Assembly and the European Council will be devised. Maybe we shall have a sort of Parliament Act and pass it to and fro, to overthrow eventually the veto of the upper chamber. Anyhow, I think this had much better be left until we get there.

What questions we should be allowed to discuss is not a matter on which they must not express an opinion. Personally, I should be very sorry to see military matters discussed, but I am bound to say that a European Assembly meeting together in these conditions should have a wide latitude to discuss matters of general interest not affecting the national safety of their countries and the combination of all the countries that there are. You will have to reckon on the views of the Assembly. You have called it into being reluctantly, and it is a fact, which I hope will not be easily removed from European affairs. I think it would be better for us to wait until we are assembled there and see how the Assembly chooses to act, what its thoughts are and what its political divisions are and may be. I hope and trust that the right hon. Gentleman will make sure that if there is a desire expressed, not only in the Assembly but in the Council of Ministers, that broad views shall be taken and good latitude given to the Assembly, he will not be the principal person to offer resistance, because he may not find himself possessed, either in the Council of Ministers or in the Assembly, of the large majority he commands in this House.

Mr Bevin: Perhaps I may be allowed to make an explanation, because this is very important internationally. In regard to unconditional surrender, I want the House and the right hon. Gentleman to be clear that what I was saying was that the use of that phrase meant that the whole constitution was smashed and that our military governor and the military governors of the Allies have had to build up right from the bottom. Therefore, I do not think the criticism of the right hon. Gentleman the Member for Bromley (Mr H. Macmillan) was justified – he did not take that into account. I do not complain at all of Mr Roosevelt making the statement, and I do not complain at all of the right hon. Gentleman agreeing. I do not complain, because I agreed that in the circumstances the right hon. Gentleman could do nothing else but agree; I stood by that and never said a word in spite of all the criticisms of my own party that followed. I do not think the right hon. Gentleman will accuse me of ever being disloyal to a Cabinet decision in the end.

In regard to the European Assembly, all I shall say is this: That it is an infant institution and that I am not laying down any laws or rules as to what should be discussed or not discussed. What I beg of the right hon. Gentleman is that we should learn to walk in the European Assembly before trying to run. This is really a very delicate instrument which I have nothing to do with except as a member of the Committee of Ministers. It is in a very complicated stage, as we are involved in OEEC and the other things, and all of us, including the right hon. Gentleman in his wise old age and myself in my infancy, I hope may combine together to steer it along the right lines.

Mr Churchill: I did not have this quotation on the subject of unconditional surrender when I first made my speech, but perhaps the House will allow me now to give it. Here is what I said:

> The principle of unconditional surrender was proclaimed by the President of the United States at Casablanca, and I endorsed it there and then on behalf of this country. I am sure it was right at the time it was used, when many things hung in the balance against us which are all decided in our favour now. Should we then modify this declaration which was made in days of comparative weakness and lack of success now that we have reached a period of mastery and power? I am clear that nothing should induce us to abandon the principle of unconditional surrender and enter into any form of negotiation with Germany or Japan, under whatever guise such suggestions may present themselves, until the Act of unconditional surrender has been formally executed. But the President of the United States and I, in your name, have repeatedly declared that the enforcement of unconditional surrender upon the enemy in no way relieves the victorious Powers of their obligations to humanity, or of their duties as civilised and Christian nations. I read somewhere that the ancient Athenians, on one occasion, overpowered a tribe in the Peloponnesus which had wrought them great injury by base, treacherous means, and when they had the hostile army herded on a beach naked for slaughter, they forgave them and set them free, and they said: 'This was not done because they were men; It was done because of the nature of Man.' Similarly, in this temper we may now say to our foes, 'We demand unconditional surrender, but you well know how strict are the moral limits within which our action is confined. We are no extirpators of nations, or butchers of peoples. We make no bargain with you. We accord you nothing as a right. Abandon your resistance unconditionally. We remain bound by our customs and our nature.'

I venture to rest on that.

Winston S. Churchill: speech
('Winston S. Churchill, His Complete Speeches', volume 7, pages 7831–5)

23 July 1949   Wolverhampton

CONSERVATIVE POLICY

[. . .](Editor's Note: Mr Churchill, speaking of the 'momentous choice' the nation would be called upon to make at the General Election, stated):[1] The Socialist Party try to spread two gross and palpable falsehoods. First, that before they got a majority Britain was a backward and miserable country to live in, and, secondly, that they are the authors and originators of social reform.

The truth is that our British system before the war was in advance of any other country in the world in its social services and of any other country in Europe in its standard of living. The vast experiment in social organization and the improvements in the standard of living which have marked the twentieth century in spite of its terrible wars have been the work of the Conservative and Liberal parties, mostly through Parliaments with large Conservative majorities. All that the Socialists have done in their cramping and disastrous rule is to carry out with many partisan distortions the policy devised by a National Government sustained by a Conservative House of Commons. All they have added to this policy are their own biased and sterile measures of restriction and nationalization. From her high and proud position at the end of the war they have brought Great Britain low alike in prosperity and reputation both at home and abroad.

Besides being kept from across the Atlantic, our Socialist spendthrifts and muddlers have dissipated every oversea asset they could lay their hands on, and in addition have exacted and extracted from our people a higher rate of taxation than was required in the very height of the war, from which we victoriously emerged. It will be incredible to those who come afterwards that so much should have been cast away in so short a time, so many sacrifices demanded, so many restrictions and regulations imposed and obeyed, and that at the end we should be where we are now. Never before in the history of human government has such great havoc been wrought by such small men.

We are rapidly approaching a grave and formidable event. The last gold and dollar reserves of the sterling area are running out. These are the last reserves that stand between us and insolvency. If they go we shall not be able – even with the existing American subsidies – to import enough raw material to keep our factories busy and our people at work, or enough food to maintain our health. Widespread unemployment and more privations are inevitable unless this catastrophe is averted.

[1] This note, and the similar note later in this document, were written by Robert Rhodes James, editor of *His Complete Speeches*.

The Government have obviously no effective plan for dealing with this imminent peril. The reckless expenditure in which they have indulged at home and abroad has been the main cause of our country's difficulty. The Chancellor told us only the other day that we had spent £900m in gifts and loans to assist world recovery. What was the sense, or indeed the sanity, of borrowing £1,000m from the United States with one hand to enable us to get on our feet again, and giving it away to foreigners with the other? Be just before you are generous. The greatest help Britain can give to the world is to stand erect in her native strength.

Nationalization is a failure. It is physically impossible to undo the harm that has been done. You cannot thrust the coal mines and the railways back on to their private owners after their property has been commercially impaired. All we can do in these two basic services is to decentralize the management and cut down the enormously swollen staffs of officials. But road transport can still be saved for the interest of the general public. In *The Right Road for Britain* we have set down clearly and precisely what a Conservative Government will do for road transport to save it from the corroding hands of the Socialist State.

Under the Socialist Administration the Post Office, with the telegraph and telephone systems, though it has always been a national service, has been giving a consistently less satisfactory service to the public than in the days before the war, and under the present Chancellor it is being increasingly used as an instrument of taxation. Conservatives would endeavour to improve the Post Office services rendered to the public and reduce the amounts extorted from them by the Exchequer.

The workers in the nationalized industries are far from content with what they have experienced so far. The railwaymen's demand for increased wages is naturally based on the ever increasing cost of living. This is inevitable on account of the frightful over-taxation practised by the Government and their lush and lavish expenditure in so many directions. The establishment of a stable and durable purchasing power for our money in Great Britain, which at least is under our control, is one of the first objectives which a Conservative Chancellor of the Exchequer would have in view.

Conservatives intend to humanize rather than to nationalize industry. In the Workers' Charter we offer security, incentive, and status to the individual. The men who are worst hit by nationalization are the great trade unions and their leaders. The trade unions never had more influence with the Government and never had less control over their own members. That is because, as nationalization proceeds, they lose their position of bargaining in the interests of their members with the private employers and have to play in with the all-powerful State which is being built up.

In the nationalized industries the trade union leaders, for many of whom I have the highest respect, are being more and more drawn into the position of being on the side of the State employer, instead of facing a much more pliable and flexible private owner while the State stands aside to conciliate and mitigate the process of collective bargaining. Can you wonder that we are threatened with a wave of labour unrest manifesting itself in unofficial strikes and go-slow practices, and that the trade union leaders, because they are identified with Government ownership, are unable, for all their courage and good sense, to cope with these new developments? Nationalization spells the doom of trade unionism.

We Conservatives regard the trade union movement, which we have always fostered from its earliest days, as a characteristic feature in British life. We believe in collective bargaining and the right to strike. We believe in the independence of the trade union movement from Government policy. If we should become responsible for the conduct of affairs, it will be our aim to maintain the closest contact with the trusted and able trade union leaders and to discuss with them means of improving working conditions. But we shall not ask them to compromise their position with their members by becoming the agents of Government-owned monopolies.

To maintain the value, responsibility, and independence of the British trade unions is one of the principal aims of Conservatism and Tory democracy. We urge all Conservatives to join the trade unions and take an active part in their organization. At present we are told that more than 40 per cent of trade unionists are Conservatives, Liberals, or non-Socialists. The more this process continues, the more will the trade union movement become truly national and cease to be, to its own cost, invidiously associated with any one political party. . . .

The main aim of all Conservative policy is to restore the greatness of Britain. The first essential step is to regain our . . . independence by earning our own livelihood as other countries have to do and as we have always done before. We mean to set the people free, so far as possible and as soon as possible, from wrong-headed planning and from official interference with our daily life and work.

We shall return to a system which provides incentives for effort, enterprise, self-denial, initiative, and good housekeeping. We cannot uphold the principle that the rewards of society must be equal for those who try and for those who shirk, for those who succeed and for those who fail. But we also must strive to maintain the social services which Conservative and Liberal Governments have called into being and which assure the whole mass of people, whether successful or not, a minimum standard of life and labour below which no one is let fall.

No more wanton act of party malice has been known in our public life than the Government's persistence in nationalizing the steel industry at a time like this. It is a basic and unworthy deed into which no thought of public interest, patriotism, or national unity has been suffered at any stage to enter.

Further blows are being prepared against national solvency and our power to earn our livelihood by the threat to nationalize the highly efficient cement industry, the sugar trade, and our world-famed system of insurance. Here there is no pretence of taking over industries which were faltering or failing under private management. On the contrary, the Socialist object is clearly seen to be the naked pillage for party purposes of great and growing concerns, the prosperity of which can be used to offset the heavy losses they are making in other parts of their nationalization policy.

They cannot bear to see the profit made at low prices by British cement, although over half of those profits already go directly to the Chancellor of the Exchequer in the form of taxation, and thus provide the funds from which the social services alone can be administered. With greedy eyes they gloat on the enormous mass of investments possessed by the industrial assurance companies and societies, although these represent the thrift, foresight, and self-sacrifice of a life-time which millions of policy-holders have made to provide for their old age, or for their loved ones when they themselves die. The Socialists want to get hold of the shares by which these investments are represented, so as to be able to knock about and liquidate every private industry in the country.

I have no difficulty in declaring once again what is the policy of the Conservative Party should we be successful when the appeal to the people is made. We shall immediately repeal the Act for nationalizing steel if it has reached the Statute Book. We shall put a full-stopper on all further nationalization, and we shall restore to the great mass of insurance policy-holders the certainty that they will not be robbed or cheated of the fruits of their thrift.

(Editor's Note: Referring to the 'waste and muddle of bulk purchasing by officials,' Mr Churchill stated): We Conservatives intend to secure for British agriculture even greater opportunities for helping the country. It is our purpose to reserve for the home farmer the first place in the home market. Empire producers come next and must be helped in every way.

We intend to restore a proper balance in our agriculture at home by encouraging the raising of more livestock. For this the farming community will need the feeding-stuffs which the Socialist Government have failed to provide. We will give the farmers clear guarantees in place of the vagueness of the Socialists, and we will give British horticulturists protection from spasmodic foreign dumping which the Socialists seem unable to provide.

Then look at housing. Mr Bevan has lamentably failed to live up to his party's election promises or his own sneers at the plans of the National Coalition. There can be no doubt that the resources devoted to housebuilding in these last four years could have produced more and cheaper houses.

Our object will be to see that men and material are used to the best advantage. To do this we shall give wider scope to the private builder and proceed with the removal of the hindrances and restrictions that lie in his path. We believe it is good for men and women to own the home in which they live, and we mean to do everything we can to spread this blessing.

We intend to set in reverse the centralizing tendencies of Socialism. We shall restore life and vigour to local government. We mean to give proper recognition to the rightful claims and aspirations of both Scotland and Wales. Above all – in agreement, I am glad to say, with the Government – we will never allow the position of Northern Ireland as an integral part of the United Kingdom and of the Empire to suffer any change without the consent of the Northern Ireland Parliament.

I believe a Conservative Government will be able to give not only a less oppressive but also a more efficient administration. The mismanagement and incompetence of the Socialist Ministers would be beyond belief were it not thrust upon us day by day. The vacillation, weakness, and discord in their handling of the dock strike during the last three weeks is typical of the lack of leadership which marks every single part of the vast organization over which they preside and which they are continually trying to enlarge. If you seek the cause of the difficulties and misfortunes under which we are plunged, practical incompetence, not excluding sheer stupidity, must certainly take a high place among them.

The theory of Socialism is contrary to human nature. The more it is enforced on the British people, the worse the results will be. The Socialist Party makes a great parade of its quarrel with the Communists, but there is no real difference between a full application of the Socialist system and Communism.

The difference between Socialism and Communism is not one of principle or theory. It is a difference of method. The Socialists pursue their aim by constitutional methods and sincerely but vainly hope to preserve individual liberty. They are our fellow country-men, however misguided. Even though Mr Bevan calls us 'vermin', we must regard them as brothers with whom, apart from their politics, we have much in common.

The Communists, on the other hand, are the lackeys and tools of a foreign Power seeking the ruin of Britain and its subordination to the decrees of the oligarchy of Moscow, and there is no crime or cruelty they would hesitate to commit if they thought it would give them absolute, despotic power. We have the fate of Czechoslovakia before our eyes.

We are glad that Socialists and Labour men should fight Communism. We are glad it should be a common cause for all of us. But neither Socialism nor Communism will enable or indeed allow the 50m inhabitants of this small island to earn their living in these modern times or hold our position as one of the leading Powers of the world.

Within a year – perhaps much sooner – the British nation will have had to make one of the most momentous choices in its history. The choice is between two ways of life: between individual liberty and State domination;

between concentration of ownership in the hands of the State and the extension of ownership over the widest number of individuals; between the dead hand of monopoly and the stimulus of competition; between a policy of increasing restraint and a policy of liberating energy and ingenuity; between a policy of levelling down and a policy of opportunity for all to rise upwards from a basic standard.

It is not only Britain and her Empire and Commonwealth that will be affected. What we do here on the day of trial will not only determine the future course of British history but will influence the immediate future of the world. Just as we are now at a crisis in our national affairs, so the world, and especially Europe, is at a critical point in the long struggle between western liberal and Parliamentary democracy and the forces of aggressive semi-Asiatic totalitarianism. . . .

Winston S. Churchill to Clement Attlee
(Churchill papers, 2/86)

24 July 1949
Private

My dear Prime Minister,

I dare say you have followed the interchange I had with Bevin in the House last week. He seemed to be laying the blame on me for the use of the phrase, 'unconditional surrender', to which he attributed his difficulties in dealing with Germany after the war.

On the spur of the moment I said that the first time I heard the words, 'unconditional surrender', was when the President used them at our Conference at Casablanca. This was the impression which had rested in my mind and which I had expressed three years ago to Mr Robert Sherwood, when he raised the point with me in the connection with his biography of Harry Hopkins.

However there is great danger in quoting from memory when all these things crop up about the tumultuous past. I have now looked up the telegrams and records of the occasion, and I find that undoubtedly the words, 'unconditional surrender' must have been mentioned in talks between the President and me.

On 19 January 1942 I sent you the following in a long telegram on other matters:[1]

'Para. 6. We propose to draw up a statement of the work of the conference for communication to the press at the proper time. I should be glad to know

---

[1] Reproduced in *The Churchill Documents*, vol. 18, *One Continent Redeemed, January–August 1943*, pp. 162–4.

what the War Cabinet would think of our including in this statement a declaration of the firm intention of the United States and the British Empire to continue the war relentlessly until we have brought about the 'unconditional surrender' of Germany and Japan. The omission of Italy would be to encourage a break up there. The President liked this idea, and it would stimulate our friends in every country.'

To this you and Eden replied on the 21st:[1]

'The Cabinet were unanimously of opinion that balance of advantage lay against excluding Italy because of misgivings which would inevitably be aroused in Turkey, in the Balkans and elsewhere. Nor are we convinced that effect on Italians would be good. Knowledge of rough stuff coming to them is surely more likely to have desired effect on Italian morale.'

It is therefore clear that both Bevin and I were wrong in our recollection. I was wrong in saying that I heard the words, 'unconditional surrender' for the first time when Roosevelt used them.[2] Bevin was wrong in saying that the Cabinet had not been consulted, for they had not only been consulted, but had expressed a very decided opinion. I do not know what happened between the time when your answer to my telegram reached me and the time when the President made his statement. I have the strong feeling that I had cooled off on the point, and that he had too. This is borne out by the agreed communiqué which was settled, with the consent of the Chiefs of the Staff, and which contains no mention of 'unconditional surrender', and also by President Roosevelt's statement to Hopkins (on page 696 of *Roosevelt and Hopkins* by Robert E. Sherwood):[3]

> 'We had so much trouble getting those two French generals together that I thought to myself that this was as difficult as arranging the meeting of Grant and Lee – and then suddenly the press conference was on, and Winston and I had had no time to prepare for it, and the thought popped into my mind that they had called Grant "Old Unconditional Surrender" and the next thing I knew, I had said it.'

You may be asked Questions this week on this topic and I hope you will consult with Eden about the answer which should be given. It is important to do justice to the President.

I suggest that some answer should be given to the effect that 'this matter is not so simple as it appeared from the interchanges in the House last week and a further considered statement would be made when we meet again.'

---

[1] Reproduced in *The Churchill Documents*, vol. 18, *One Continent Redeemed, January–August 1943*, p. 179.
[2] Churchill writes on this episode in *The Second World War*, vol. 4, *The Hinge of Fate*, pp. 614–19.
[3] Robert E. Sherwood, *Roosevelt and Hopkins, An Intimate History* (1948).

Winston S. Churchill to Clement Attlee
(Churchill papers, 2/29)

24 July 1949
Private and Personal

My dear Prime Minister,

Before going abroad I think I ought to tell you how disquieted we all were by the information that was given us on Wednesday.[1]

We cannot reckon upon a 'phoney' war period of seven months next time. The next war, if there is one, will undoubtedly start with violent air attacks designed to cripple our fighting potential. We have not yet been informed about the state of our anti-aircraft defences though I have heard some very depressing tales about them. But even if our anti-aircraft batteries were in first-class condition, we must rely for our main defence against air attack almost entirely upon fighters.

The very small number of our fighters causes us the greatest anxiety. A total of A[2] with only B[3] modern jet-fighters would have very little chance against the C[4] Russian bombers, supported by D[5] fighters once the Russians had reached the Channel, more especially if they can match our E[6] jets with F[7] of their own. Even if it be true that the Russians have only G[8] copies of B29, their H[9] light-bombers and I[10] dive-bombers would be very destructive if they could once achieve mastery of the air over England.

The night-fighter position is even more serious. Apparently the whole defence of these Islands is entrusted to a handful of J[11] obsolescent Mosquitoes. It is now well established that night fighters, even with the beset AI are not very much good unless they can be put on to the enemy bombers by ground Radar stations (GCI) and these it seems are no longer available.

We were assured of course that the Russians were technically very inadequate, but it is unwise to count upon this. They were told many of our secrets during the war and the way they have copied the B29, which fell into their hands and the jet engines which we have sold them, shows that they are capable of profiting by such information.

The weight of our possible counter-offensive is equally disheartening. A

---

[1] Referring to a meeting of July 13 held between Attlee and a small but senior delegation of Conservatives to discuss Soviet military strength and Britain's defence capacity.
[2] 415.
[3] 196.
[4] 4,800.
[5] 8,000.
[6] 196.
[7] 500.
[8] 100.
[9] 4,700.
[10] 3,200.
[11] 48.

mere K¹ heavy bombers could probably scarcely deliver L² tons per month on targets in Russia as against the 50,000 tons per month which we dropped on Germany in the summer of 1944. This would scarcely be a deterrent. Our only hope as usual seems to be the atomic bomb.

What is so distressing and so difficult to understand is the very small result achieved for our present great expense in money and men. We are spending something like ten times as much on the air force as before the war, yet we have fewer fighting aircraft than in 1939. The number of men and women in the RAF is more than one-fifth of the wartime total whilst the front-line strength seems to be about M.³ It is true of course that aircraft become more and more complicated and the fighting technique more and more elaborate, but the increased disproportion between the fighting spearhead and the men and money voted by Parliament seems to be growing greater very fast.

The value of American aid of course depends upon how many of our airfields are suitable for their planes. About this the impression given us was not encouraging; but no doubt we shall hear more next time. I cannot however refrain from commenting on the fact, if I rightly followed the figures, that our of every hundred jet-planes produced only N⁴ flow to our own Air Force, O⁵ to Western Union, whilst P⁶ were sold abroad to countries, some of which will not necessarily be our allies in any forthcoming conflict. Only about 600 jet-planes went to our costly but feeble fighting strength, and over 400 were sold or sent to other countries. This might well turn the scale in Home Defence and our power to carry on the war. The ten million pounds worth of hard currency which we may obtain from these sales may prove a very expensive way of bridging the dollar gap.

In all my long experience I can recall nothing parallel to this giving away of our actual means of life. It compares with the struggle about the twenty-five squadrons which the French demanded in 1940. That we steadfastly refused. I earnestly hope that, from now on, every jet-plane we make will be sent at once to the British fighter squadrons and that the necessary number of airfields will have their run-ways extended to take not only British jet-fighters, but the more exacting American planes.

For greater security I am sending, under separate cover, the actual figures on a separate slip. I am addressing them both personally to you.

I may add that, considering the very large numbers of Russians who are allowed to circulate in our factories – far more, I am assured, than our police

[1] 144.
[2] 5,000.
[3] One-tenth.
[4] 65.
[5] 10.
[6] 25.

and other agents can supervise – it is very likely that the Soviet have already got the bulk of the information about jet-planes which has to be kept secret from Parliament and the nation.

Lettice Marston to Winston S. Churchill
(Churchill papers, 2/67)

26 July 1949

I saw this American journalist[1] and his wife this morning. He has come from Frankfurt specially to see you about the publication of certain information concerning the atomic bomb, which may be detrimental to yourself.

It is apparently alleged that in 1945 a German war leader wrote to you about their having made the bomb, etc., and that on the capitulation of Germany their secrets were allowed to get into the hands of the Russians because you apparently paid no heed to this information. It is not known whether you ever received this letter, and this is obviously what he wants to check. He is also giving you the opportunity of refuting the story before publication.

He will not give the full details of what he knows to anyone but yourself, and asks if you would see him before he returns to Frankfurt. Otherwise International News Service will go ahead and publish something right away, as it is a 'scoop' for them.

He is returning here at 3 p.m. this afternoon to know if and when you will see him. He will not put anything more in writing beyond what he has already said in the attached letter.

Ethel Barrymore[2] to Winston S. Churchill
(Churchill papers, 2/160)

29 July 1949

Dear Winston,

It would be wonderful if you could wish me a happy birthday on August 15 when I shall be all of 70 years, more than 50 of them made proud by having known you.[3]

---

[1] Tom Agoston.

[2] Ethel Mae Blythe, 1879–1959. American actress, known as the 'First Lady of the American Theatre'. Took her father's stage name, Barrymore, as her own. First appeared on stage in New York, 1894; in London, 1897. Began a film career, 1914. Opened Ethel Barrymore Theatre in New York, 1928. Winston Churchill once proposed marriage to her.

[3] On Aug. 15, Churchill telegraphed back: 'Every good wish my dear Ethel and many happy returns of the day.'

August
1949

Winston S. Churchill to Clementine Churchill
(Churchill papers, 1/46)

10 August 1949   Bellagio, Italy

Lovely and cool here beautiful villa charming hostess no mosquitoes expecting you Saturday at latest please wire all your news and address. Love

Winston S. Churchill: speech
('Winston S. Churchill, His Complete Speeches', volume 7, pages 7838–40)

12 August 1949   Strasbourg
Translation[1]

UNITED EUROPE

Take heed! I am going to speak in French.

In this ancient town, still marked by the wounds of war, we have gathered together to form an Assembly which, we hope will be one day the Parliament of Europe. We have taken the first step and it is the first step which counts. This magnificent assemblage of the citizens of Strasbourg has been convened by the European Movement to show the world what force there is in the idea of United Europe, what power, not only in the minds of political thinkers, but in the hearts of the great common masses in European countries where the people are free to express their opinion.

I feel encouraged, but I am astonished also, to see what remarkable results we have obtained in such a short time. It is not much more than a year since, at our Congress of The Hague, we demanded the creation of a European Assembly. We had to mobilize public opinion to persuade powerful governments to transform our requests into realities. We had to overcome serious misgivings.

---

[1] By Ingrid Russell, made for inclusion in the *Complete Speeches*.

But we had also, on our side, with us, many friends of this great cause of United Europe, and among them some friends who held ministerial power. None of these friends had done more for the European Movement than Mr Spaak, who has been the longtime champion of a European Parliament and who, yesterday here in the city, was unanimously elected its first President.

We are reunited here, in this new Assembly, not as representatives of our several countries of various political parties, but as Europeans forging ahead, hand in hand, and if necessary elbow to elbow, to restore the former glories of Europe and to permit this illustrious continent to take its place once more, in a world organization, as an independent member sufficient unto itself.

That primary and sacred loyalty that one owes to one's own country is not difficult to reconcile with this large feeling of European fellowship. On the contrary, we will establish that all legitimate interests are in harmony and that each one of us will best serve the real interests and security of his country if we enlarge at the same time both our sentiment of citizenship and of common sovereignty – if we include in this sentiment the entire continent of the States and of nations who have the same way of life.

These principles which govern us are defined in the Constitution of the United Nations, of which Europe should be a vigorous and guiding element; these principles are also, in general terms, formulated in the Declaration of the Rights of Man proclaimed by the United Nations. Thus, not only will we find the road to the rebirth and to the prosperity of Europe, but at the same time we will protect ourselves against all risk of being trampled, of being crushed by whatever form of totalitarian tyranny, whether it be the hated domination of the Nazis, which we have swept away, or any and all other forms of despotism.

For my part, I am not the enemy of any race or nation in the world. It is not against any race, it is not against any nation whatever that we are gathered. It is against tyranny in all its forms, ancient and modern, that we resolutely rise. Tyranny remains always the same, whatever its false promises, whatever name it adopts, whatever the disguises with which it clothes its servants.

But if we wish to win our supreme reward, we must cast aside all our obstacles and become masters of ourselves. We must elevate ourselves above those passions which have ravaged Europe and put her in ruins. We must have done with our old quarrels; we must renounce territorial ambitions; national rivalries must become a creative rivalry in all spheres where we can give the most genuine service to our common cause.

In addition, we should take all the steps and all the precautions necessary to be very sure that we will have the power and that we will have the time to realize this transformation of Europe in which the European Assembly (now in actual fact assembled at Strasbourg) has such a great role to play. It will only be able to play this role if it shows those qualities of good sense, of tolerance, of independence, and above all of courage, without which nothing great is done in this world.

And to finish, I ask the help of this vast gathering of citizens of Strasbourg; you belong to the tremendous masses of men that we affirm to represent and whose rights and interests we have the duty to defend. There are, in Europe, on both sides of the iron curtain, millions of simple hearths where all hearts are with us. Will they never be able to delight in the simple joys and freedoms that God and Nature have given them? Will the man who works honestly for his bread never be able to reap the fruits of his labour? Will he never be able to raise children in good health, happy, with the hope of better days?

Will he never be free of fear – fear of foreign invasion, fear of the bursting of bombs and shells, fear of the heavy step of the enemy patrol, and above all, and it is this that is the worst fear, of knocks pounded on the door by the political police, who come to abduct a father or a brother outside the normal protection of the Law and of Justice – whereas each day, by a single spontaneous effort of his will, this man, this European could awaken from this nightmare and rise free and virile in the great light of day?

In our long history we have triumphed over the dangers of religious wars and of dynastic wars; after thirty years of strife I am confident that we have come to the end of nationalist wars. After all our victories and all our sufferings, are we now going to sink into a final chaos, into ideological wars launched among us by barbaric and criminal oligarchies, prepared by the agitators of the fifth column who infiltrate and conspire in so many countries?

No, I am certain that it is in our power to pass through the dangers that are still ahead of us, if we so wish. Our hopes and our work are leading to a time of peace, of prosperity, of plentitude, wherein the inexhaustible richness and genius of Europe will make her once more the very source and inspiration of the life of the world. In all of this we are advancing with the support of the powerful Republic beyond the Atlantic and the sovereign states who are members of the Empire and the Commonwealth of British nations.

The dangers which threaten us are great, but great also is our strength and there is no reason to not succeed in realizing the goal and in establishing the structure of this United Europe whose moral concepts will be able to reap the respect and recognition of humanity, and whose physical strength will be such that no one will dare molest her on her tranquil march to the future.

Harold Macmillan: recollection
('Tides of Fortune', pages 174–6)

15 August 1949

Monday 15 August was a holiday. On this day Churchill received the freedom of Strasbourg. I think he was under the impression that the public holiday was in his honour. When it was explained to him that it was for the Feast of the Annunciation, he seemed rather put out.

Finally, on Tuesday and Wednesday, a full-dress debate took place upon the political future of Europe. In the course of it there were some truly remarkable speeches. Both Georges Bidault and Paul Reynaud, who seemed younger than ever, were particularly effective. But when Churchill rose to speak after these preliminary days of skirmishing, the excitement in the hall and in the galleries was intense. I began to realise the tactics that he had been pursuing:

> This extraordinary man, during the early sittings, seemed to come down almost too rapidly to the level of normal political agitation. His intervention in the Layton–Whiteley incident and his several short speeches on the question of the powers of the Assembly to fix its own agenda, were all calculated – perhaps intentionally – to reveal him as a Parliamentarian, rather than as a great international figure. You can imagine that we were all a little alarmed at this. For our pains, we were treated with a firm hand and even harsh refusal to accept our advice. He certainly took more trouble to listen to the debates than I have ever known him do in the House of Commons. He walked about, chatted to each representative, went into the smoking-room, and generally took a lot of trouble to win the sympathetic affection of his new Parliamentary colleagues. This was done with much assiduity. He used his villa for entertaining the more important to luncheon and dinner; and he took much trouble over all this determination to charm them as well as impress them.

Now all these minor manoeuvres seemed to be put aside. He rose to an altogether different plane. Yet this speech, long awaited, must have been to the majority of those present a disappointment, or at least seemed inopportune. Already Western Europe had begun to be darkened by a new shadow, not merely the fear of Russia but the fear of a remilitarized and revived Germany. Some people did not like to think much about this or want to talk about it. Yet perhaps it was the most immediate of European problems. How could it be resolved? Only by making European unity a reality and making it as inclusive as possible. Only so could the danger of a new militarism be avoided or contained. Churchill knew this and was not afraid to speak out. With the wonderful combination of prophetic foresight and moral courage which so often inspired him, he avoided the temptation of making a speech much more to the taste of his audience than that which he delivered. On this occasion he could have been excused for putting popularity before truth; for, after all, the foundation of the Council of Europe was largely the result of his efforts. In a sense, today was his 'benefit'. He could easily have won applause by some well-phrased generalities. Undeterred, he made the question of Germany the main and almost the sole theme of his speech. He shocked some; he almost bullied others. In a dramatic outburst, looking round the hall, he demanded almost fiercely, 'Where are the Germans?' He pressed for an immediate invitation to the West German Government to join our ranks. Time was passing.

There should be no delay. 'We cannot part at the end of this month on the basis that we do nothing more to bring Germany into our circle until a year has passed. That year is too precious to lose. If lost, it might be lost forever. It might not be *a year*. It might be *the* year.'

He was to hold to this position while he remained at Strasbourg, and we were to carry on the struggle in his absence. This speech could not have been delivered by any other man. Although not so long or so closely argued or so copiously developed, it ranked in its effect with those at Fulton and at Zurich.

Winston S. Churchill: speech
('Winston S. Churchill, His Complete Speeches', volume 7, pages 7890–1)

15 August 1949 Strasbourg

A MEETING-PLACE OF THE FUTURE PARLIAMENT OF EUROPE

... I well remember that anxious January afternoon in 1945 when it seemed that Strasbourg might be delivered again into the power and to the vengeance of the Germans, and how grateful I was to General Eisenhower for assuming an additional military burden to prevent that happening. I had had something to do also with making it possible for the Leclerc[1] division to accomplish the liberation of Strasbourg. There were difficulties about its equipment and transport, and I made personal exertions to overcome them, so that the division under its heroic commander would be able to undertake the glorious role it did both at Strasbourg and in Paris.

My last visit to Strasbourg was made almost 10 years ago to the day, when with my friends General Georges[2] and General Gamelin, I visited what soon became the upper Rhine sector of the front. It is most comforting to return and find that all that has happened since has not prevented the rise of France to a great position in Europe again and to economic prosperity. The future is not entirely free from danger, but if we have learned the lesson of these ten years we can steer our course so as to make sure that our lives and liberties will be preserved – by methods, I trust, of peace.

---

[1] Philippe Leclerc de Hauteclocque, 1902–47. Graduated from École Spéciale Militaire de St-Cyr; commissioned into cavalry, 1924. Capt., 4th Infantry Div., 1939. Wounded, June 1940. Escaped to London, serving under de Gaulle and adopting the alias Jacques Philippe Leclerc, 1940. Maj., 1940. Military Cdr of Chad, 1940. GOC French Equatorial Africa, 1941–2; L Force, 1942–3; 2nd Free French Div., 1943; 2nd Armoured Div., 1943–5; III Corps, 1945. C-in-C, French troops, Far East, 1945. Inspector of Land Forces, North Africa, 1947. Killed in a plane crash, 1947. Marshal of France, posthumously, 1952.

[2] Alphonse Joseph Georges, 1875–1951. CoS to Marshal Foch, 1918; to Marshal Pétain, 1925–6. Head of French Military Mission to Yugoslavia, 1918–22. Chef de Cabinet in Maginot Government, 1929. Wounded during the assassination of King Alexander of Yugoslavia in Marseilles, 1934. Cdr, Forces and Operations in the North East, 1939–40. Inspector-General of Land Forces, 1940. Member, French Committee of National Liberation, 1942–5.

Whatever our troubles, if England and France work together a great prospect is open not only to France and Britain but to all Europe. France should take the leading part in the European movement and at Strasbourg find a meeting place of the future Parliament of Europe and the centre from which will be developed the European society embodying the civilization and culture of the great nations of the West.

Winston S. Churchill: speech
('In the Balance', pages 79–83)

17 August 1949   Strasbourg

CONSULTATIVE ASSEMBLY OF THE COUNCIL OF EUROPE

Mr President, and colleagues:

I must congratulate the Assembly upon the high level maintained during this Debate. Not only have the speeches been full of thoughts which have their own particular value because they have been contributed from so many angles, but also there have been successful attempts at oratory which have triumphed over the acoustic conditions which, I must tell you, are none too good and which will, I trust be subject to development, like all the rest of our proceedings. We are engaged in the process of creating a European unit in the world organization of the United Nations. I hope that we shall become one of several continental units which will form the pillars of the world instrument for maintaining security, and be the best guarantee of maintaining peace. I hope that in due course these continental units will be represented in the world organization collectively, rather than by individual States as in the present system, and that we shall be able to settle a great mass of our problems among ourselves in Europe before they are brought, or instead of them being brought, to the world council for decisions.

We are not in any way the rival of the world organization. We are a subordinate but essential element in its ultimate structure. The progress of our first meeting has so far been encouraging. Our relations with the Committee of Ministers show a desire on both sides to reach a working harmony. That should not be difficult if we recognize clearly what our respective functions are. We are a deliberative Assembly, and we must have full freedom of discussion on all questions except defence. We must assert our right to this freedom and we must have our own Parliamentary officers to assist us in our debates. I trust that the necessary Amendments to the Statute will be made by the Committee of Ministers on this point as the result of our first session here at Strasbourg.

But while I feel that we should insist upon full freedom of debate and choice of subjects, we do not possess executive power, and at this stage in our development we could not possibly claim it. Our foundation by selection by the Government of the day from the various parliaments is not such as to give us authority at this stage to take decisions. We claim, however, to make proposals. It is not for us to make decisions which would require executive authority. We may discuss European problems and try to bring about a sense of unity. We must feel our way forward and by our good sense, build up an increasing strength and reputation. But we must not attempt on our present electoral basis to change the powers which belong to the duly constituted national parliaments founded directly upon universal suffrage. Such a course would be premature. It would be detrimental to our long-term interests. We should, however, do our utmost to ensure that these parliaments examine and let us know their views upon any recommendations on European problems that we may make. That, I think, we may require of them. Each of us, in our respective parliaments, should take the opportunity to raise points according to the procedure which prevails.

I touch upon some of the points which are upon our agenda. I am not myself committed to a federal or any other particular solution at this stage. We must thoroughly explore all the various possibilities and a committee, working coolly and without haste, should, in a few months, be able to show the practical steps which would be most helpful to us. I will not prejudge the work of the committee, but I hope they will remember Napoleon's saying: 'A constitution must be short and obscure.' Until that committee reports, I think we should be well advised to reserve our judgment. I am in accord with what Mr Morrison has said on this subject. I share his view that we would be wise to see what are the recommendations of our committee which, I hope will sit permanently and not be broken up by our departure. To take a homely and familiar test, we may just as well see what the girl looks like before we marry her. It is to our advantage to have an opportunity of making a detailed examination of these problems.

Then there is the question of human rights, which is the second subject set down on our agenda. We attach great importance to this, Mr President, and are glad that the obstacles to discussion by the Assembly have now been removed by the Committee of Ministers. A European Assembly forbidden to discuss human rights would indeed have been a ludicrous proposition to put to the world. Again, I should like to see the report of the committee on this subject before we put forward our proposals to the Committee of Ministers. There is an urgency about this because once the foundation of human rights is agreed on the lines of the decisions of the United Nations at Geneva – but I trust in much shorter form – we hope that a European Court might be set up, before which cases of violation of these rights in our own body of twelve nations might be brought to the judgment of the civilized world. Such a court, of course, would have no sanctions and would depend for the enforcement of its judgments on the individual decisions of the States now banded together in this Council of Europe. But these States would have subscribed beforehand to the process, and I have no doubt that the great body of public opinion in all these countries would press for action in accordance with the freely given decision.

I now come to the question of the empty seats, which was put before us by M André Philip. Ten ancient capitals of Europe are behind the Iron Curtain. A large part of this continent is held in bondage. They have escaped Nazism only to fall into the other extreme of Communism. It is like making a long and agonizing journey to leave the North Pole only to find out that, as a result, you have woken up in the South Pole. All around are only ice and snow and bitter piercing winds. We should certainly make some provisions for association with representatives of these countries, who are deprived of ordinary democratic freedom but who will surely regain it in the long march of time. This is a matter which should be carefully considered by the Assembly, and I agree with all those, and there are many, who have spoken in favour of setting aside some seats in the Assembly as a symbol of proof of our intention that the Assembly shall someday represent all Europe, or all Europe west of the Curzon Line.

I now come sir, to the greatest and most important of all the questions that are before us. A united Europe cannot live without the help and strength of Germany. This has always been foreseen by the European Movement to whose exertions our presence here is due. At The Hague fourteen months ago, where we resolved to press for the formation of this Assembly, a German delegation was present and was welcomed by all, especially by the representatives of France. One of the most practical reasons for pressing forward with the creation of a European Assembly was that it provided an effective means, and possibly the only effective means, of associating a democratic and free Germany and the Western democracies.

It is too early to judge the results of the German election; but so far as we can yet appreciate the results, many of us, apart from party considerations, may have felt encouraged by the evident size and validity of the poll and by the general results. We cannot part at the end of this month on the basis that we do nothing more to bring Germany into our circle until a year has passed. That year is too precious to lose. If lost, it might be lost forever. It might not be a year, but it might be the year.

On the other hand, I am assured – and here I must break the rule which Mr Harold Macmillan laid down this morning, that the word 'impossible' must never be used again – that it is physically impossible for any German Government that may emerge in the next few weeks to be represented here before we separate. I need scarcely say that I should be very glad if a way could be found. If, however, this cannot be found, then we must draw the attention of the Committee of Ministers to Article 34 of the Statute, which says: 'The Committee of Ministers may convoke an Extraordinary Session of the Consultative Assembly at such time and place as the Committee with the concurrence of the President of the Assembly, shall decide.' I think we must ask that an assurance shall be given to us before we separate that the Committee of Ministers will convoke an Extraordinary Session of the Consultative Assembly at the earliest suitable date. If we could be told that we should meet again for an extraordinary session under this Article 34 in December or in January, I personally should be content to leave the matter in the hands of the Committee of Ministers, and even to forgo our claim for a debate upon this subject at this juncture.

I would ask that we should receive an assurance that an Extraordinary Session will be convened and I appeal to you, Mr Vice-President,[1] personally to place yourself in communication with M Spaak and urge him to confer with the Committee of Ministers upon this subject, so that we may have an answer and know what course we should take in the limited number of days and weeks which are at our disposal. When we meet in the Extraordinary Session – if one is granted – in December or January next, it is my hope that we shall find ourselves already joined by a German delegation similar to that of the other Member States; but if this cannot be done, then it will be the time for us to debate the issue in full freedom.

Mr Vice-President, I earnestly hope that an agreement on this matter may be reached along these lines, and that we may be informed of it as soon as possible. It would enable us to avoid serious difficulties at the present moment and would, I think, give the best chance for the further future development of the European Assembly, and the best chance of making sure that the peace of Europe will be given every opportunity to consolidate itself. Such an event as the arrival in our midst of a German delegation as a result of our work here this month would certainly crown our first Session with a solid and memorable achievement and would have a highly beneficial result in the cause of world peace and European security.

I have only ventured to deal with these particularly important practical points, and I have not attempted to speak of the sentimental and moral aspects of our work. I hope that we shall not put our trust in formulae or in machinery. There are plenty of formulae – 'slogans' I think Mr Morrison called them – and in spite of all the misfortunes which occurred, there is still plenty of machinery in the political field. It is by the spirit that we shall establish our force, and it is by the growth and gathering of the united sentiment of Europeanism, vocal here and listened to all over the world, that we shall succeed in taking not executive decisions, but in taking a leading and active part in the revival of the greatest of continents which has fallen into the worst of misery.

---

[1] Lord Layton.

Harold Macmillan to Winston S. Churchill
(Churchill papers, 2/75)

19 August 1949

Yesterday's meeting of the Assembly dealt entirely with the procedure for electing committees. Nothing very startling happened. Once again Mr Morrison's interventions showed complete lack of mastery of the subject or sympathy with the audience.

He will report later on the German question.

Winston S. Churchill to Herbert Morrison
(Churchill papers, 2/75)

19 August 1949

Dear Lord President of the Council,

Thank you for your letter of August 13. I used the word 'accost' in my letter because you did not approach me 'quietly for a private word' but addressed me familiarly in the presence and the hearing of at least twenty-five people, many of whom were foreigners, on the question how long I should stay in Strasbourg, and when I said I did not know you proceeded to state that you would deprive Mr Foster of his £2.10.0 per diem allowance. It would have been quite easy for you to have written me on this subject, or indeed to Mr Foster.

I regret for your own sake that you should have brought such small and petty matters forward in public at an international gathering of this kind. However if you are content with the general reception of this incident I have no more to say.

Private Office: note
(Churchill papers, 2/75)

23 August 1949

1. In the Assembly this morning Mr Dalton so misrepresented a statement made by Mr Churchill as to indicate that Mr Churchill was opposed to British assistance of European countries. Whereas in fact speaking at Wolverhampton on 23rd July, Mr Churchill supported his criticism of the reckless expenditure and ineffective planning of the Socialist Government by saying that there was clearly no sense in our borrowing £1,000 million from the USA if we intended to give £900 thousand of it to other countries. Here, quite clearly Mr Churchill was opposed to the method of assisting foreign countries rather than the principle.

2. The actual statement made by Mr Churchill was as follows:

'The Government have obviously no effective plan for dealing with this imminent peril. The reckless expenditure in which they have indulged at home and abroad has been the main cause of our country's difficulty. The Chancellor told us only the other day that we had spent £900 million in gifts and loans to assist world recovery. What was the sense or indeed the sanity of borrowing £1,000 million from the USA on the one hand to enable us to get on our feet again and giving it away to foreigners with the other.'[1]

It may be seen that by omitting the first sentence of Mr Churchill's statement Mr Dalton has so mis-quoted him as to give an impression of opposition to assisting Europe that was never intended by Mr Churchill.

Michael Wardell:[2] recollection
('Churchill's Dagger', Atlantic Advocate, February 1965)

[24–25] August 1949

Churchill planned to spend a week with his old friend of forty years[3] and return to Strasbourg. From the moment he arrived at the villa, it was clear that he was in a holiday mood. He insisted immediately on putting on a pair of blue bathing drawers and walking down to the sea, down a hundred steps through Beaverbrook's enchanted garden of bougainvilleas and orange trees and roses. Arriving at length where the Mediterranean laps the rocks at the foot of the garden, Churchill literally plunged into his holiday. He wallowed like a porpoise; he blew spouts of water like a whale, and he swam round and round like a schoolboy. He turned and he twisted, and he lost his baggy blue bathing drawers. It didn't matter, for there was no one there to see him but Beaverbrook and me and his own male retinue.

[. . .]

The pace increased each day as Churchill's enjoyment seemed to spur him on, as though time were short and not one hour to be missed. Every morning he dictated new passages of his book and corrected proofs. 'I lay my egg every morning,' he said. 'Every day I send it to the printer. In a day or two proofs come back. I must finish four volumes by May. I may be called to another sphere (chuckle).' He referred to the likelihood of winning an election.

---

[1] See speech of 23 July 1949, reproduced above (pp. 1456–61).
[2] Michael Wardell, 1895–1973. Journalist. Joined Beaverbrook Newspapers, 1926. Rejoined the Army, 1930. Retired with rank of Brig., 1946. Vice-Chairman of the Beaverbrook organization, 1947–50. Moved to Fredericton, New Brunswick, and bought the *Daily Gleaner*, 1950. Later established University Press of New Brunswick Ltd and launched the *Atlantic Advocate*. Lord Beaverbrook's representative in New Brunswick.
[3] Lord Beaverbrook.

[. . .]

As he played his cards that night,[1] he talked of his father, of his own young days as a war correspondent and officer in the Fourth Hussars.

[. . .]

At one o'clock in the morning we stopped for soup and cigars. Presently we resumed playing.

At about two o'clock he complained of cramp in his right hand, the hand from which he had removed the ring. He went on playing, giving his attention to the game. At the end of it he said he had a most peculiar sensation and must go to bed. He added up the score, and wrote in a clear hand an 'IOU' which I still have.

We walked up the stairs. I carried his cigars. As he slowly mounted the steps he paused, turning to me who followed him. He said: 'The dagger is pointing at me. I pray it may not strike. I want so much to be spared, at least to fight the election. I must lead the Conservatives back to victory. I know I am worth a million votes to them,' and, taking another step on to the landing at his bedroom door, he stopped, turned again, and said: 'Perhaps two million!' He entered his room.

Those might have been his last words. And none could have been more typical.

I entirely missed the significance of his words. I did not sense he was in mortal danger. I thought he was suffering from a chill. I asked if I should give him a rub. He said no, his valet was next door if he wanted him. 'I still have cramp,' he said, and described the numbness, swept his right hand up and carefully felt his hand, arm, shoulder and chest. He said: 'I've a strange sensation I have never had before.' He was in full possession of all his faculties. I was not alarmed.

He took a pill. 'My sleeper,' he said with a smile. 'I'll give you one, if you like.'

I declined, said I never touched the things. He undressed and I left him. I went downstairs to lock the door and turn out the light. As I came up, he was closing his door, standing naked. He waved his hand and said: 'Goodnight.'

I myself felt very tired, from a series of late nights and unwonted action during the days. I was many years younger than Churchill, and strong as an ox. 'It would be impossible,' I thought, 'if he did not feel a reaction from what he has been through in the past five days.' I went to sleep.

In the morning, when I woke, I found the local doctor was with Churchill, and Lord Moran, his own physician, was on his way by air. Beaverbrook had telephoned to his son, Max Aitken, during the night, and he had made the arrangements.

Lord Moran's diagnosis confirmed that Churchill had suffered his first stroke.

[1] 23 Aug. 1949.

It was to be a secret to the grave. Later in the day came the news that his horse Colonist had won his race at Salisbury. By the following day the press was alerted, but not suspicious. Reporters gathered at the gate of La Capponcina[1] and asked for news. This was to be one of the very few occasions in his life that Lord Beaverbrook decided to mislead them. A bulletin was prepared, and I was to deliver it at the gate. It stated the truth, but not the whole truth. It read: MR CHURCHILL CONTRACTED A CHILL WHILE BATHING. LORD MORAN WAS SENT FOR AND HE SAYS THAT MR CHURCHILL IS MUCH BETTER THIS MORNING BUT THAT HE WILL REQUIRE A FEW DAYS OF REST AND QUIET.

[. . .]

The padding of feet along the stone passage caused us to raise our eyes, and to our astonishment we saw the figure of Churchill himself, risen from his bed, advancing in his white towelled dressing gown. He could not bear to lie in bed and think that we were interfering in his press relations. He had decided to direct them himself.

The bulletin was issued and now Churchill, back in bed again, wanted the newspapers. 'Where are they?' he asked. 'I want to see what they have to say about my horse.' Colonist II had celebrated that previous ill-fated day, 24 August, by winning his race at 6 to 4 on. Now the proud owner read the newspaper accounts with delight. 'Max,' he said, as Beaverbrook came into the room, 'you see that Christopher did me well after all. The horse is going to run again. There must have been a lot of money on him yesterday for him to have started at 6 to 4 on. I must warn the public not to bet on him next time.'

Beaverbrook: 'But if he wins after that they will grumble more than ever.'

Churchill: 'Yes. That's the trouble. I don't know how to get over that.'

'Let's play some rummy,' he said, but he could not pay attention either to cards or cigar. He showed all too plainly the marks of his seizure.

'I've quite lost my equilibrium,' he said. 'It's a distressing, uncomfortable sensation.'

The next day his condition had greatly improved.

'I feel much better today,' he said. 'Quite different from yesterday. I am really very hopeful that I shall escape the consequences. The dagger struck, but this time it was not plunged in to the hilt. At least, I think not. But the warning is there, and I shall have to pay marked respect to it. [. . .] I am a very different man to the one who was sitting playing cards with you only three nights ago. The dagger struck. I am left without energy or initiative or enterprise. I don't ever remember spending so idle a day as this, with nothing accomplished and nothing attempted. I am changed.'

---

[1] Beaverbrook's villa, where Churchill was staying.

August 1949

Lord Moran: diary
('The Struggle for Survival', pages 355–6)

[25] August 1949

Dr Gibson[1] telephoned from Monte Carlo this morning: 'I think Mr Churchill has had a stroke. I would like you to see him as soon as you can.'

When I arrived at the airfield at Nice, Max told me what had happened:

'He was playing cards at two o'clock this morning when he got up and, steadying himself with his hands on the table, bent his right leg several times as if it had gone to sleep. 'I've got a cramp in my arm and my leg,' was all he said. He kept closing and opening his right fist. Then he went on playing, but when he woke this morning – it would be seven o' clock – the cramp was still present. A little later he found he could not write as well as usual. Dr Gibson was called, and he got on to you. It's a true bill, I am afraid,' Max added after a pause. 'But let's go and see him.'

With that he took me to his bedroom. When Max left us Winston said: 'I am glad you've come; I'm worried.' I could find no loss of power when I examined him; his grip was strong. Later, when he squeezed paints out of their tubes, he could not do it as well as usual. Max had told me that he was not sure whether his speech was affected. Winston was certain that it was not, and there was nothing I could detect. I asked him about his writing. Reaching for his pen, and steadying a bit of paper against a book, he wrote very slowly and carefully:

'I am trying to do my best to make it legible. It is better than it was this morning. W. Churchill.'

He handed me the paper, which shivered as he held it out – I felt he was watching my face as I read.

'What has gone wrong, Charles? Have I had a stroke?'

'Most people,' I explained, 'when they speak of a stroke mean that an artery has burst and there has been a haemorrhage into the brain. You've not had that. A very small clot has blocked a very small artery.'

'Will I have another?' he demanded at once. 'There may be an election soon. An election in November is now more a probability than a possibility. I might have to take over again.' He grinned. 'It feels like being balanced between the Treasury Bench and death. But I don't worry. Fate must take its course.'

His memory did not seem to be impaired. He was quite calm, though perhaps a little fearful.

Moran: 'Do you notice anything different?'

Winston: 'There seems to be a veil between me and things. And there's a sensation in my arm that was not there before.'

---

[1] Herbert Robert Burnett Gibson, 1885–1967. Churchill's doctor when he was in the French Riviera.

Moran: 'What kind of sensation?'
Winston: 'Oh, it's like a tight feeling across my shoulder-blade.'

I told him he had done enough talking and that I would come back later. When Max heard the verdict he at once said:

'Oh, he must go on with things; he wouldn't agree to rust out.'

It hardly seemed the time to make decisions of that kind. The Press, Max said, were waiting at the gate.

'You must say something to them. It is no use,' he insisted, 'trying to fool them. You were seen at the aerodrome. They are all agog.'

He handed me a message which he had concocted. It was ingenious, but I was sure it would only excite their suspicions.

'Why say anything at all? Tell them that I am your guest for a few days, that I've brought my golf clubs. We'll produce him in a day or two, and that will convince them there is nothing wrong.'

Max wasn't persuaded, but when he saw my mind was made up he said no more.

Bernard Baruch to Winston S. Churchill
(Churchill papers, 2/210)

31 August 1949　　　　　　　　　　　　　　　　　　　　　　　　　　New York

My dear Winston,

I was so pleased to receive your cable saying that you were improved.

I have a set of your racing colors which one of my friends made for you. I should like to send it to you, but will have to wait for an opportunity as I presume there would be a difficulty in getting through the Customs.

Yesterday, one of the top men in the Readers' Digest organization came to me and said that the Editor, Mr Wallace, had suggested that you and I do a piece – along the lines of a conversation at Chartwell – regarding the world outlook and particularly the relationship between England and America.

This might be a good thing for the magazine, but I do not see where that would leave us, or, and this is more important, whether it would be beneficial. The whole thing is in the hands of the politicos and your elections are looming near and we will have Congressional and Senatorial elections next year and it will be well along some settlement soon.

I haven't any definite thoughts about this, except that I do not like to work unless some real results could come from it.

I am sending it along to you to wrestle with. Perhaps you will send back some idea.

August 1949

Jo Sturdee to Winston S. Churchill
(Churchill papers, 2/86)

31 August 1949

This is a request from the publishers of an illustrated edition of Dr Weizmann's autobiography for a Foreword from you.

I have ascertained from the Israeli Embassy in London that this book has the blessings and approval of Dr Weizmann and that of course it would be much appreciated if you did accede.

I know you will not write a Foreword, but would you think of allowing them to use the words about Dr Weizmann you used in a speech in the House of Commons in August 1946[1] (marked in red pencil on second page of attached letter)?

If you agree to allow this, Hamish Hamilton, Ltd who published the original (unillustrated) edition of this autobiography would like to include it in their new edition.[2]

---

[1] Reproduced above (pp. 427–36).
[2] Churchill wrote on this note: 'Yes, certainly'.

September
1949

Winston S. Churchill to King Abdullah of Jordan
(Churchill papers, 2/80)

1 September 1949

Sir,

I deeply regret that we did not meet during your visit to this country, and I thank you warmly for your Majesty's gracious letter. It is a long time since you and Colonel Lawrence rode into Jerusalem to meet me at Government House, but the work we did has survived the shocks of these fearful decades.

With every good wish for the future,
Believe me,
Your Majesty's obedient servant and friend,

Winston S. Churchill to Pamela Churchill
(Churchill papers, 1/46)

1 September 1949   Cap d'Ail

Dearest Pamela,

Alas, I shall not see you again before going home. I found it too hot here, especially at nights, but I may be back presently. Moreover, the Birleys could not come out in time to paint with me.

Thank you so much for sending me the cards in their nice leather case. I will give you your revenge the first time we meet.

I am not taking the picture of Winston with me because you said you wished to talk to the artist about it. Will you pick it up from the Villa as and when convenient?

It was so nice to see you again.

Let me know when you come to England.

Sarah Churchill to Winston S. Churchill
(Churchill papers, 1/46)[1]

3 September 1949

My Darling Papa,
    I was so terribly relieved to hear that it was only a cold, and that you are now alright again. Darling – I was thrilled by your Strassbourg speech – so was everyone here. I cannot tell you how wonderful it is to move around the world and have people come up to me to wring my hand because of what they know you have done for the world. I wish I could convey to you – all the simple, sincere, heart-warming things people say – Everyone here stayed up half a night because you had a cold! You really must take more care!
    This tour – my peregrinations through the straw hat circuit has been all and more than I could have ever hoped.
    They come because of you of course – but I feel they like me – more some places – less others of course – but the play goes wonderfully well – and they do have a good evening – I hear them as they go out. They pass by my dressing room window quite often – laughing and talking gaily – and I do feel happy about that.
    The theatre guild (equivalent to our Old Vic) want to sponsor a road tour of it to all the major cities of America also possibly Toronto and Montreal.
    This is considered a definite feather in my cap – for it is unusual – if not the first time that they have thought of sending out a show as a result of a Summer Stock Season. They usually only take on Broadway successes.
    I would have to ask Korda again – also American Equity would have to give us permission. If both these are granted I shall definitely do it. All this should be decided within a fortnight – and I will let you know.
    Antony Beauchamp will shortly be coming over here. You know that for a year I have been thinking seriously about marrying him. I am almost certain that I shall – but again – I shall make my decision when I see him in about three weeks time. I will let you know. Till then please do not think about it – and then when I tell you my decision – be with me on it. I should need you in either case.
    My love to you.
    I don't think you have any idea how much I love you. I love you very dearly. You and mama are not only the source of my life – but together and individually – you are the inspiration of every effort.

---

[1] This letter was handwritten.

Jo Sturdee to Hamish Hamilton
(Churchill papers, 2/86)

5 September 1949

Dear Sir,

Upon his return to this country Mr Churchill has now had an opportunity of seeing your letter to him of August 26, for which he thanks you.

Mr Churchill asks me to explain that he could not undertake to write a Foreword for the special edition of Dr Weizmann's autobiography, *Trial and Error*, which you are publishing. If it would suit your purpose, however, Mr Churchill has no objection to your using the words, quoted by you in your letter, from his speech in the House of Commons in August 1946, provided of course that you made it clear where and when he made these remarks.

This particular speech is included in a volume of Mr Churchill's speeches, *The Sinews of Peace*, published in this country by Messrs. Cassell & Co, Ltd, and, should you wish to use this quotation, their permission should, I think, be obtained.

Jo Sturdee to Hamish Hamilton
(Churchill papers, 2/86)

5 September 1949

Dear Mr Hamilton,

We spoke the other day on the telephone about the request Mr Churchill has received from Dr Horovitz[1] for a foreword for his illustrated edition of Dr Weizmann's autobiography, *Trial and Error*.

I enclose herewith copies of Dr Horovitz's letter and of my reply. You will see that Mr Churchill has no objection to the words he used about Dr Weizmann in a speech in the House of Commons in August, 1946, being used, subject to certain provisions.

Mr Churchill wishes you also to be given the opportunity of using this quotation in your edition of *Trial and Error*, in the same way as Dr Horovitz.

---

[1] Béla Horovitz, 1898–1955. Hungarian-born British publisher. Co-founder with Ludwig Goldscheider of Phaidon Press, 1923. In 1938, transferred his publishing company from Vienna to London. Edited the illustrated edition of *Trial and Error: The Autobiography of Chaim Weizmann* (1949). A dedicated Jew, he worked for the preservation of Jewish cultural heritage by publishing Jewish classical works. Founded the East and West Library, which published books of Jewish interest. Married Lotte Beller: at least three children. Their youngest child, Hannah Horovitz (1936–2010) was a classical music promoter and their son, Joseph Horovitz (b. 1926) a composer and conductor.

Clement Attlee to Winston S. Churchill
(*Churchill papers, 2/29*)

6 September 1949
Private and Personal

My dear Churchill,

Now that you are back in this country I am writing more fully in reply to your letter of 24th July[1] giving your thoughts on the subject we discussed at our last meeting on defence than it was possible to do at the time.

The detailed points as to the exact allocation of aircraft we can discuss at our next meeting.

The question in its broader aspect does not lend itself to discussion by letter but, as I see it, involves a major matter of policy.

Your line is, as I see it, short term and, so to speak, isolationist.

We consider that the defence of Britain and the Commonwealth depends on building up what you used to call 'The Grand Alliance'.

Western Union and the Atlantic Pact are the foundation on which we are building.

The United States of America now recognize that the defence of America and Western Civilization involves support by her of the Western European Group. The Arms Bill will, I hope, be an important step forward. The administration has, of course, to contend with those who say 'Arm America first.'

Obviously we want the United States of America's active cooperation now. How, then, can we say that we cannot help our Continental Allies to arm, until we are complete in every way? We are seeking to build Western Union as an integrated force, not a bundle of disintegrated forces. Therefore planes directed there form part of the common Defence of Western Union.

Similarly a number of planes have gone to Commonwealth countries that are cooperating with us in defence.

I am puzzled by your last paragraph. My information is that no Russians are circulating in our aircraft factories. There has been a complete ban for a long time. I should be glad to have any instance that has been brought to your notice investigated.

---

[1] Reproduced above (pp. 1463–5).

Hamish Hamilton to Jo Sturdee
(Churchill papers, 2/86)

7 September 1949

Dear Miss Sturdee,

Thank you very much for your letter about *Trial and Error*.[1] I shall be obliged if you will tell Mr Churchill how grateful we are for his permission to quote the passage. I only wish we had thought of it when the book first appeared, as there was at that time considerable prejudice against the author, which Mr Churchill's words would have helped to dispel.

General Lord Ismay to Winston S. Churchill
(Churchill papers, 4/362)

7 September 1949

My dear Mr Churchill,

Very many thanks for letting me see the enclosed papers. I had completely forgotten that Ike's Planners had got cold feet about 'Husky',[2] and that they had infected Ike himself with their fears. But I now recall your horror and the stinging telegram that the Chiefs of Staff sent to Washington. I also remember our relief when the American Chiefs of Staff told us that they entirely shared our views and that Ike had been informed accordingly.

At the same time, I am sure that the main motive of our visit to Washington in May 1943, and thence to Algiers, was not to argue about 'Husky', because there was no more jittering about that particular operation after the telegrams printed in DO (43) 7: but that you were determined that, after 'Husky', we should go on to the mainland and knock the Italians out of the war. In other words, it was not 'Husky', but post-'Husky', that you were chiefly worried about. The views which you held before 'Trident',[3] and which you expressed at 'Trident', are clearly written in Cunningham's villa at Algiers. This paper is reproduced in the minutes of the Algiers Conference and really settled the issue.

I am just completing my story of the voyage to 'Trident', the 'Trident' Conference, the air trip to Algiers, and the meetings in Ike's villa at Algiers. I hope to let you have this before the weekend.

---

[1] Reproduced above (p. 1484).
[2] 'Husky': operation to capture Sicily.
[3] 'Trident': Third Washington Conference between Churchill and Roosevelt, 12–27 May 1943.

Lady Phillips[1] to Winston S. Churchill
(Churchill papers, 4/51)[2]

8 September 1949

Dear Mr Churchill,

The Navy have been so very good to me, and allowed me a portage from and return to Malta in their store ship, with only my messing to pay and so after nearly four years, I have been dashing around seeing as many friends and relatives as possible, I don't know when I'll be able to visit the UK again.

This address, my son's,[3] is my headquarters and I return here between visits. I have just returned again and found waiting for me, your second volume, which had been redirected to me from Malta. I was overjoyed, it is very good of you and very generous. I had already read most of it, borrowed from a friend, but am so proud to possess it myself and in future dip into it or refer to it.

I return to Malta about the end of October, in RFA *Bacchus*.

I do hope you are really better, the whole world I think and we at home were very concerned when we read in the papers you had caught a chill – for all our sakes, in this grim world of today, please take care of yourself.

Again thank you so very much for your precious gift.

Antony Beauchamp to Clementine Churchill
(Churchill papers, 1/46)

11 September 1949

Dear Mrs Churchill,

Here is the income tax demand. I do not like having to worry you with this, and I am sure it must have come as a shock to you, just when Sarah is really doing so well for herself.

I am afraid she will be very angry with me, and very humiliated. But the matter is now far too serious to allow it to drift any longer, whatever her reactions may be.

Her secretary, Miss Norman, has been dealing with it so far, but she is not experienced enough to be able to deal effectively with matters of this nature so I have taken it upon myself to write to you.

Whatever Sarah's reactions are, it is essential that this matter is settled

---

[1] Widow of Adm. Sir Thomas Spencer Vaughan Phillips (1888–1941). Adm. Phillips, also known as Tom Thumb, is best known for commanding Force Z during the Japanese invasion of Malaya during WWII. He went down with the battleship HMS *The Prince of Wales* and was the highest-ranking Allied officer to be killed in battle during the war. Lady Phillips archived her husband's papers and was in charge of them until her death in the 1970s.

[2] This letter was handwritten.

[3] Gerald Phillips. Served in the British Navy. Inherited his father's papers upon the death of his mother.

quietly, without the deprecating publicity for her that would accompany legal proceedings.

I have now decided to tell her straight away of the action I have taken, as I feel it is better that way.

Now that I am writing to you, it would be better to let you know all the facts, as it would not be possible for you to deal with the matter otherwise. I know she has only not told you herself because she has a great desire to stand firmly on her own feet, and be no bother to anyone. As you know, this is necessary to Sarah to gain her own self-respect. At last she has done that but the past threatens to destroy everything she has gained. I have often asked her to go to you and seek your guidance and help so that she can start afresh. But she could never bring herself to bother you. I wrote a letter the other day suggesting this course <u>again.</u> But if she can't help herself she will have to be helped <u>in spite</u> of herself.

The position (as far as I have been able to get it out of her) is this:

She was paid quite a considerable sum for her earnings 1946/7 for her Italian films. However what with flights to London (in the middle of the film) to see Mary married, when she had to pay the entire production costs of the film for every day it was held up – and charity to friends, she made nothing out of it and had nothing left to pay the taxes. Knowing her I don't suppose she spent a fraction of it on herself.

The Income Tax people have asked her for about £2000. The first instalment is the £450 I told you about which has to be paid immediately. Although a good accountant could probably have reduced this figure, it is now too late to do much about that.

She has now learnt her lesson and has her taxes deducted at source, so that this can never occur again. But with income tax at its present rate she will never be able to save enough to pay off her past taxes.

Did you know, I wonder, that by touring in a British Standard car when she was in Canada recently she was responsible for sales which amounted to nearly <u>one and a half million dollars</u>? Not bad! But of course they would hardly be likely to weigh that against her income tax. Not even a letter of thanks from either Standards or Treasury for that unexpected windfall of dollars!

She feels her Father is already over-generous in making her an allowance which he is in no way bound to do and cannot bring herself to ask any further help of him. This is an attitude which shows great integrity, but it would be quite disastrous to carry it to the lengths of having law-suits brought against her, and the scandal that would follow. It seems she would almost rather <u>go to prison</u> than ask any further help of her Father! During the past 18 months I have seen the effect it has had upon her – the constant worry of how and where to find the money. It is beginning to show in her face and manner and if it goes on much longer it will rob her of the fruits of the really great success she has at last made of her life. At 35, though still lovely, she has not a long time to go as a leading lady in stage or films. That does not matter really however. The main thing is that she can at last say 'Look! I have done it!' Once she has reached the goal she has striven for, she could give it up when the time came without worrying too much. It is much easier to give something up when you have gone to the top of the tree. It is impossible to do if you have never got there. I don't think she will <u>ever</u> want to give it up, but if she does it will be easier for her. But it would be a tragedy to see her robbed of the few years she seems to have ahead of her, which she deserves so greatly and has worked for so hard. She lost the most vital years in a woman's (and particularly an actress's) life during the war when she was almost the only actress to give up her career and join the forces.

Now she has suddenly really got to the top. It won't last for ever but I feel a few years of success are due to her. I, as much as you would, would like to see her really happy and at peace, and to be able to reap all the rewards that are at hand. Not the money, she does not care much about that. She just wants to feel that she has really done something with her life and made people respect her.

I am afraid I am rambling on rather expansively but it is difficult to control my pen when talking about my favourite subject.

When she hears of this letter it is going to be a very big blow to her. Try not to scold her. She has suffered a great deal because of this already. She knows only too well <u>how</u> bad it is, and she has had quite enough scoldings from me in any case! I cannot help her yet to pay this off myself as I would like to. The American trip is going to absorb all my spare cash.

I do hope I have done the right thing writing to you. I have felt very unsure about what course to take, and have delayed writing to you for the past three days. But I have been able to think of no other course to take.

I am not insensitive to the fact that it is difficult for you to be approached by someone you really know very little concerning your daughter's affairs, but there is no one else to do it for her. If she won't do it herself, then I, as the next closest person to her must do it.

I am writing a letter to Mr Churchill (as yet unfinished) which will clarify my relationship, intentions and regard for Sarah before I leave for New York.

Winston S. Churchill to James Stuart
(Churchill papers, 2/93)

14 September 1949

My dear James,

I have since my return from abroad been considering your Memorandum of August 13, 1949, with which you sent me the draft statement of policy for Scotland, together with three appendices, upon which your Committee asked me to give a decision.

First – to deal with the appendices –

A. CONSULTATIVE COMMITTEE

I understand from your covering Memorandum that 'the Committee was equally divided on this subject', and that the responsibility for giving a decision was therefore referred to me. In my view, any movement for setting up such a Council (or Committee) should have had the support of a considerable majority, before it reached the field of practical action.

Further I am of the opinion that a Secretary of State for Scotland is already perfectly competent to seek advice from the various bodies individually, which would compose this Council, as they are already in being. Each one – or all – of them can therefore be consulted at any time on any subject upon which they are competent to give advice.

B. FINANCIAL AND ECONOMIC RELATIONSHIP BETWEEN SCOTLAND AND ENGLAND

I have always believed that Scotland has not, in the past, been unfairly treated in this respect and, as you know, I have experienced some years of office as Chancellor of the Exchequer. It was certainly never the wish of Parliament that Scotland should not receive, at least, the full share to which she is justly entitled.

However, in the event of our obtaining power after the coming General Election, if a genuine desire should be expressed in the new Parliament for a Royal Commission on the ground that Scotland is not receiving a fair and square deal financially, there could be no objection to the setting-up of a Royal Commission.

C. THE HIGHLANDS AND ISLANDS

No one will dissent from the view that this question deserves our full attention, but it is a matter which can be dealt with more appropriately in a Scottish edition of *The Right Road for Britain*.

The proposal to publish such an edition is one which should be brought before the Party's Policy Committee immediately after the special Conference in Scotland has considered the main statement of your Committee.

With regard to the draft statement of policy, I am most grateful to the Committee for the valuable and useful work which they have carried through. As Leader of the Party, I accept this as a carefully-considered statement of the views of the Party in Scotland which will act as a most helpful guide in handling these matters of high policy in the event of our being returned to power as a result of the next General Election. At the same time, while not dissenting from the advice tendered by your Committee on the strengthening of the Office of the Secretary of State and the establishment of an additional Under-Secretary (see paragraphs 8–11 inclusive), I feel it my duty to state that all questions of Ministerial appointments must remain the prerogative of His Majesty, acting on the advice of His First Minister. I must therefore make it clear that no Leader of any Party could permit himself to be committed in advance on such questions.

Before proceeding further it is my intention to consult one or two of my colleagues about the proposals relating to nationalized industries and other matters, and I will write to you again when I have done so.

Clementine Churchill to Winston S. Churchill
(Churchill papers, 1/46)[1]

14 September 1949

My Darling,

Please read this letter[2] from Antony Beauchamp.

The total Sarah owes is £2000 and £450 must be paid at once. I enclose the final notice which expired on August 31st. I am making a cheque out for the smaller sum to be signed by 'Prof', Brendan and myself.

I am seeing Antony Beauchamp this afternoon.

I will be with you darling before dinner.

Sarah has not had a penny yet from the Chartwell Literary Trust and I am sure you will argue that the trust should pay the whole sum.

Winston S. Churchill to Lord Moran
(Churchill papers, 2/163)

16 September 1949

My dear Charles,

I have been thinking over our talk the other night and have come to the conclusion that the best way in which I can express my gratitude to you in the present circumstances is to execute another seven-years Deed of Covenant in favour of Dorothy for £500 a year, free of tax.

I hope you will not forbid me to do this, and I have taken the necessary steps with the Bank.

---

[1] This letter was handwritten.
[2] Reproduced above (pp. 1487–9).

Field Marshal Lord Montgomery to Winston S. Churchill
(Churchill papers, 2/143)[1]

17 September 1949

Dear Mr Churchill,

I would like to come and see you some time about the Alamein Reunion on Friday 21 October. I want to tell you the general arrangements, what I shall say in my speech, and suggest what I hope you will say in your speech.

The BBC are reporting the speeches from 7.30 to 8.15. I hope you will speak for at least 25 minutes. I hope your general theme will be a review of the post war years and discuss the sorry plight in which we find ourselves today after nearly 5 years of peace; then look into the future.

I could come on Sunday 9th October. Would that suit you? I am going to America in November and would like your advice on certain matters.

Winston S. Churchill to Clement Attlee
(Churchill papers, 2/82)

19 September 1949

My dear Prime Minister,

Anthony and I, who are here together, both feel that Parliament ought to be called together to consider the new financial situation in all its bearings, and that is certainly the wish of our Party. I therefore make the formal request which I understand is necessary, and having regard to the interchanges which took place in the House before the Recess I have no doubt you will feel able to meet our wish. I am making a communication to this effect to the Press this afternoon.

I suggest that Tuesday of next week would be a convenient day for Parliament to reassemble.

Clement Attlee to Winston S. Churchill
(Churchill papers, 2/82)

19 September 1949

My dear Churchill,

I have your letter in which you make a formal request for the calling together of Parliament.

As was stated in the House by the Lord President any such request will be given full consideration.

---

[1] This letter was handwritten.

As soon as I have had the opportunity of considering the matter with my colleagues I will communicate with you.

Bernard Baruch to Winston S. Churchill
(Churchill papers, 2/210)

20 September 1949   New York

My dear Winston,

This is a quick answer to your cable.[1]

The adjustment of the Pound to what the market had already valued it, will not be of much avail and the influence of this action will gradually be dissipated unless it is accompanied by all the following:

1. Some neutralization or adjustment, and a very drastic one, of the 3½ billions frozen Sterling.
2. Sterling should be multilateral and not unilateral, that is, transferable. If Denmark has accumulated Sterling in its sale of products to England and trades with Holland, Denmark ought to be able to use that Sterling with Holland.
3. England must increase its production in order that it can meet competition in the rest of the world.

I never could understand why England has not taken advantage of the elimination of Germany and Japan from the world marketplace. Has she not been devoting too much of her thoughts and energies to nationalization instead of modernization of her plants? I do not think Socialism has caused England's troubles. I think she adopted Socialism to cure the troubles which started, I think, at the time of the Boer War and increased after each war, because Germany, Japan and the United States had gradually been taking up her markets; and many of the countries, even her own commonwealths, were developing productions to take care of some of the things they had formerly imported.

Another thing – England suffered severely when she gave up her colonies East of the Suez. It posed the question as to whether England using her present methods can take care of her present population.

I think Cripps made a very grave error when he said that he did not think the cost of living would go up and at the same time said bread would go from 4½ to sixpence. Everything will go up. I do not believe you can cut the value of the Pound and put the lid on prices at the same time. Prices must go up.

I also believe that the demands for increased wages and social services will keep the English cost up so that she cannot compete with the rest of the world.

---

[1] Asking to have Baruch's view, by airmail, on the devaluation of sterling. On 19 Sep. 1949, the Labour Government devalued the pound by 30.5% to $2.80. Its dollar value had been fixed at $4.03 since 1940 following an agreement with the US.

We have the same thing here but our plants are modernized to a greater extent than England's.

England will have to develop her colonies. She cannot do so with the present handicaps under which foreigners have to compete.

When all is said and done, whether it be there or here, unless we have incentive or hope of reward instead of fear of punishment or a sullen satisfaction because no one can have much more than another, there will not be much increased production at lower costs or any investment which is indispensable.

I think Cripps' position among thoughtful people has been injured as they do not look upon him as being so logical and such an errant champion of the truth. If, as I think will happen, the cost of living goes up over there, he will be discredited.

In getting rid of the frozen Sterling, you have the problem of what to do with Indian purchasers. If India cannot use the frozen Sterling she will have to get some credit.

I am wondering whether any promises have been made through the Export–Import Bank, the International Monetary Fund or through some promised Congressional aid.

PS. – Since signing the letter, I have thought I would give you an additional thought as the fourth necessity to buttress the action on the devaluation of the Pound.

A sound basis for investment, domestic and international, must be re-established. This requires permitting the earning of an adequate return to induce men and women to venture their earnings and savings commensurate with the risks involved.

I want to say further, you cannot consider any one segment, for the military, the economic, political and social, nationally and internationally, all intertwine. This devaluation, or as I prefer to call it, revaluation, is only a part and unless the sufferings the British have been through are justified by a long time as well as a short time program, they and we also will suffer much.

I am also including a memo made for me by [. . .] an associate of mine made the day after the Washington announcement.

Winston S. Churchill to Charles Wood
(Randolph Churchill papers)

20 September 1949

I have decided to adopt Mr Randolph's proposal about dates and have sent the following instruction to the printer. There is no doubt in my mind that he is right. The discrepancy between the American and English methods of thinking about these things is decisive for an author like me who writes for both publics. February is an incidental reinforcement. I am sorry for these reasons to disagree with you.

'All dates at the top of memoranda and minutes should be printed "6 Oct. 49". When more formality is required "6 October 1949" can be used, but this will be specified.'

Lady Moran to Winston S. Churchill
(*Churchill papers, 2/163*)[1]

21 September 1949

Very dear Mr Churchill,

Charles has just taken away all my breath and left me very overwhelmed and a little trembly by telling me of the truly magnificent gift that you have made to us. I don't really know how to say thank you properly, especially when this has come on the top of your wonderful generosity to our children. What can I say except thank you with all my heart and to tell you, what you must know already, of the deep devotion which Charles and I feel to you and to dear Mrs Churchill.

Winston S. Churchill to Clement Attlee
(*Churchill papers, 2/29*)

22 September 1949

My dear Prime Minister,

Thank you for your letter of September 6.[2] As I see it, the question is not between short-term and long-term policies, or between isolation and a Grand Alliance. It concerns the physical life of Britain as a unit. A defenceless Britain can play no part in the defence of Europe. Her power to help in the past has arisen from an integral, insular security. If this falls, all falls. If it endures, all may be defended or regained. Mere contributions, however generous, to European schemes of defence will be useless to Europe if Britain is herself no longer a living military entity. It is certainly not isolationism to set this first objective first. On the contrary it is the only foundation upon which effective help can be given to Europe and to other parts of the Empire.

An illustration of this will, I am sure, appeal to you. In 1940 we did everything in human power and ran great risks to help France, sending almost our last divisions abroad, but the one thing we did not ever give way upon was sending the twenty-five fighter air squadrons. This is always considered

[1] This letter was handwritten.
[2] Reproduced above (p. 1485).

to have been a cause of our salvation. Distributing 'jets' to Allied European countries or to our Dominions or still more selling them to strangers, while they are so scarce and precious, is in my opinion exactly on a footing with distributing the twenty-five last fighter squadrons in 1940. There would be no objection to a few for training, but to cripple our Air Force and reduce its strength below the safety margin, as has, I am grieved to say, been done, seems to me a terrible event.

The principles set forth in my first paragraph are of course of permanent and general application, but they never were more relevant and practical than in relation to the actual facts of today.

I do not feel myself that war is imminent, but nothing is more likely to bring about a Soviet attack on Western Europe than the knowledge that they could not only reach the coast with their ground forces, but could overwhelm, by mass attacks, the air defence of Britain, which would otherwise, in the long run, be fatal to them as it was to Hitler.

With regard to the question of Russian agents in our midst, I was informed some time ago that there were 150 members of the Russian Embassy here, excluding the Trade Delegation and its affiliates. The corresponding figure for our representation in Moscow is 85, but varying in ones and twos from day to day. The Russian Trade Delegation here numbers at least 70. In addition to the Russian Trade Delegation there are always up to 20 Russian representatives with firms. These also enjoy diplomatic privileges and are considered attached to the Trade Delegation. These privileges mean in practice unrestricted travel. I am informed that there is no effective watch on persons attached to the Embassy or to the Trade Delegation, either by the police or by MI5. They have not got the necessary numbers for such a task.

I am also informed that in May the Russian figures, including minor attachments, were 236 as against 113 of ours in Russia, and that these figures hold good today. I am sure that if these facts are true there must be a vast number of details about our aircraft and munitions production which are reported to the Soviet, about which the House of Commons is denied all information.

I am obliged to you for promising to look into this yourself.

Clement Attlee to Winston S. Churchill
(*Churchill papers, 2/82*)

22 September 1949

My dear Churchill,

As you have already been informed by telephone, the Government have decided to ask Mr Speaker to summon the House of Commons to meet next Tuesday, 27th September. What we have in mind is that there should be a three day debate on a Government motion, the terms of which have not yet been fixed, but which I think I can promise you will make possible a wide debate. We propose that the House should adjourn, at the close of business on Thursday, 29th September, until 18th October. I trust these arrangements will be agreeable to you.

The Lord Chancellor is being asked to recall the House of Lords also on the 27th September, but it is suggested that, in this case, a debate of one, or at the most two, days' duration will be sufficient.

Winston S. Churchill to Henry Luce
(Churchill papers, 4/25)

23 September 1949
Confidential

My dear Luce,

I have made great progress with Volume IV and it is at this moment as far advanced as Volume III. That is to say it only requires final polishing and three laggard chapters to be completed or curtailed. Considering that we have about fourteen months in hand before it need finally leave my hands for serial publication in January, 1951, we are certainly well ahead with the work. I think you will like Volume IV. Reves, who was with me at Monte Carlo, read it through and called it 'superb', but it will be better before I hand it in. It is about two hundred and fifty thousand words and carries the tale down to the end of June, 1943, just before the attack on Italy, that is to say up to the invasion of Sicily. I hope to send you and Longwell each a provisional copy before October is out.

I am now working hard at Volume III which I hope to have ready for you by November 15, 1949. As I have already told you, I cannot extend its scope. There is no good stopping-place between 'My Return to Trouble' at the end of Volume III and the eve of the Battle of Alamein and 'Torch'. This would not only make an inordinately long book but leave me entirely in the air as far as Volume IV is concerned.

There thus remains a great mass of material for the last two years of the war, including much vital correspondence with the President and Stalin, and the illumination of many current controversies and legends of Tehran, Quebec and Yalta.

I must at this point remind you of the astonishing uncertainties which overhang us during the next nine months. The chances of a General Election before Christmas or in the early spring have increased. It is thought that the Socialist Government have got enough to tide them over the next few months, so that they will be able to go to the country without having to take unpopular and drastic steps which our situation will impose on any British Government. If they win they will have a new lease of power. If they lose they will leave a baleful inheritance to their successors, who may not have a large majority with which to face their heavy task.

In the case of an Election before Christmas it will be all I can do to deliver Volume III in good order. Once the Election is announced my whole time and remaining strength will be absorbed, and should I have to take office, there will be nothing else.

Volume IV however, in its present condition, is already a complete entity. It will not have to be published till June, 1951. A margin is provided in our agreement of eighteen months, which I presume would date from May 1, 1950, in which we can decide what it is best to do.

There is therefore no hurry in coming to a decision about whether there should be a sixth volume, or whether the last two years of the war should be wound up in one volume by my hand or the hands of others.

On the other hand the Conservative Party may not obtain a majority in November, 1949, or March or June, 1950. Then I shall be able to see my own course more clearly, and I think it very likely in that event that I should offer the leadership to someone else and retire from active public life. In this case I should almost certainly wish to deliver the remaining tale in two volumes of which it is well worthy, making six in all. I fully recognize that you have bought the entire work, whether it be five or six volumes. *The Daily Telegraph*, Cassells, Houghton Mifflin, Canada, Reves and foreign translations are all anxious to take a sixth volume and have already offered over £50,000 for it. There is however no obligation on you to pay anything more for the additional volume, which you could use in its regular succession. Our relations have been so pleasant and on such a high level that you would not receive any complaints from me.

Besides and beyond the political uncertainties, which I have set forth, there lie the hazards of life and health in an author nearly seventy-five years old. I think I have now set out how the matter stands, and it seems clear that no immediate decision is required from any of us. In a few months we shall know much more than we do now. We can but await the unfolding of time, life and fortune.

I greatly enjoyed my short spell on Lake Garda, though it was rather hot, and at Strasbourg (not much of a holiday), and at Monte Carlo; but I caught a chill which had some unpleasant symptoms, which forced me to cut my stay there short. Thank you very much for your hospitality which alone enabled me to overcome the exchange problems which restrict Englishmen in these gloomy and baffling years.

I am repeating the substance of this to Daniel Longwell and Arthur Sulzberger.

President Harry S Truman to Winston S. Churchill
(Churchill papers, 2/158)[1]

27 September 1949

Dear Winston,

Yesterday evening, Mrs Truman,[2] a couple of guests and I drove out to Olney in Maryland to see *The Philadelphia Story* by Philip Barry.[3] Your lovely daughter Sarah had the leading part.

I know you must be as proud of her as I am of Margaret.[4] We enjoyed the presentation very much. I went behind the scenes and had my picture taken by a large number of news photographers with Miss Sarah Churchill. This happened immediately after the first act.

After the show was over Mrs Truman and our guests accompanied me to an informal reception where we met all the members of the cast and had a most pleasant visit with Sarah.

I hope all goes well with you and that Old England is on the road to happiness and prosperity.

PS. Miss Sarah is a wonderful actress!

Winston S. Churchill: speech
('Winston S. Churchill, His Complete Speeches', volume 7, pages 7844–57)

28 September 1949   House of Commons

DEVALUATION OF THE POUND

Order read for resuming Adjourned Debate on Question (27 September 1949):

That this House approves the action taken by His Majesty's Government in relation to the exchange value of the pound sterling, supports the measures agreed upon at Washington by the Ministers of the United States, Canada and the United Kingdom which are designed to assist in restor-

---

[1] This letter was handwritten.
[2] Elizabeth Virginia Wallace, 1885–1982. Known as 'Bess'. Married, 1919, Harry S Truman. Often served as an adviser and aide to her husband in both official and unofficial capacities.
[3] Philip James Quinn Barry, 1896–1949. American playwright. Rejected for military service during WWI because of bad eyesight. Deciphered cables at the US Embassy in London, 1918. Wrote and directed several plays while studying at Yale and Harvard Universities, 1919–22. Married Ellen Semple, 1922. Wrote almost two dozen Broadway plays. Best remembered for *Holiday* (1928) and *The Philadelphia Story* (1939).
[4] Mary Margaret Truman, 1924–2008. Educated at George Washington University, 1946. Made her debut as a professional vocalist, 1947. Married Clifton Daniel, 1956. Wrote 23 novels and nine books of non-fiction.

ing equilibrium in the sterling–dollar balance of trade for the purpose of enabling the economy of the sterling area to maintain stability independent of external aid; and calls upon the people for their full co-operation with the Government in achieving this aim, whilst maintaining full employment and safeguarding the social services. – (Sir S. Cripps).

Question again proposed.
Mr Churchill (Woodford): I beg to move, in line 1, to leave out from 'House', to the end of the Question, and to add

welcomes the measures agreed upon in Washington but regrets that His Majesty's Government, as a result of four years' financial mismanagement, should now be brought to a drastic devaluation of the pound sterling, contrary to all the assurances given by the Chancellor of the Exchequer, and considers that a return to national prosperity, the maintenance of full employment and the safeguarding of the social services can never be assured under the present Administration, which, instead of proposing fundamental cures for our economic ills, resorts to one temporary expedient after another.

We have reached a point in our post-war story and fortunes which is both serious and strange. We have before us this afternoon the financial measures which have to be taken as a result of four years' government by the Socialist Party. It is our common interest and our first duty in the pass to which we have come, to decide what it is best to do and to help it to be done in the most effective manner.

There also lies before us a General Election, the date of which will be settled in accordance with what the party opposite consider to be in their tactical interest. All political thought and party machinery is affected by this. We are, I think, most of us agreed that it is high time for another Parliament and that all our difficulties will have a better chance of being solved in a new House of Commons. We are a Parliamentary democracy – (Hon. Members: 'Hear, hear'.) – created before the Labour Party was born, or thought of. We are organized on a two-party basis – (An Hon. Member: 'Two?') – in the main, and an appeal to the nation is due and overdue. There can be no doubt that this Election overlays all our domestic affairs and also, I am sorry to say, it looks as if it will be fought out with more fundamental divergences at every grade and in every part of our society than have been known in our lifetime.

Finally, over all there looms and broods the atomic bomb which the Russian Soviet, for reasons not yet explained, have got before the British, though happily not before the Americans. If you take these three factors together, the financial crisis, the party conflict and the atom bomb, it will, I think, be generally agreed that the hour is grave.

The Socialist Government ask for a vote of confidence in their financial and economic policy during the last four years and in the measures they have adopted in the present crisis and they call upon the people for their full co-operation with the Government. This is a considerable demand, this vote of confidence, and it forces us to look back on the past conduct and record of the Socialist Party who, with almost absolute power, have ruled us during this difficult and harassing period. No one must underrate the task which fell upon these Labour Ministers as the consequence of the Election of 1945. Britain and her Empire were in the war from the start and ran at full gallop, keeping nothing back, aiming only at victory till the finish. Britain had great claims on the respect of the world and on the good will of the United States. At the end there was an inevitable phase of national exhaustion, physical and psychical, which required time to repair. There was also the tremendous transition from war to peace to be accomplished.

Under the unchallenged working of our Constitution a new Parliament was brought into being by the free choice of our people. Of course the circumstances were exceptional. There had not been a General Election for ten years; 3,000,000 or 4,000,000 of our men were with our Armies abroad. The present Government were the result. They were the heirs not only of the problems of that grievous but triumphant hour, but also of all the slowly gathered treasures, customs, qualities and traditions of the ancient and famous British State.

How have they done? That is the question which by their Motion they ask us to consider this afternoon, and that is the question upon which the electors will have to pronounce at no distant date. I think it will be generally admitted that we are not in a very good position as a result of all we have done and put up with since the fighting stopped. In these last four lavish years the Socialist Government have exacted upwards of £16,000,000,000 and spent them – over four times as much every year as was the cost of running the country in our richer days before the war. They have used up every national asset or reserve upon which they could lay their hands; they have taken 40 per cent of the national income for the purposes of Governmental administration. Our taxation has been the highest in the world. It oppresses every effort and transaction of daily life.

Large incomes are virtually confiscated. The exertions and rewards of the most active class of wage-earners and craftsmen have been burdened in times of peace by the harsh direct taxation which in war, when we are fighting for life, may be a matter of pride to bear, but which in victory is at least a disappointment, and I believe has been a definite deterrent to production. Every capital reserve we had has been gobbled up. As has been well said, we ate the Argentine railways – £110,000,000 – last year as a mere side dish. Our reserves of gold and hard currency which at the end of 1946 were £650,000,000 have been draining away until we are brought together here and brought up against the fact that only £300,000,000 at the old rate are left and that this would hardly last for a few months. It is because we are now brought to the verge of national and international bankruptcy after the dissipation of all this wealth that this emergency Session has been called.

Mr Shurmer (Birmingham, Sparkbrook): Let the right hon. Gentleman sell his horse.

Mr Churchill: I could sell him fur a great deal more than I bought him for but I am trying to rise above the profit motive. Let us see how great is the help we have received from the productive efforts and generosity of countries outside this small crowded island which has been led so far astray. We have been given or loaned – and have spent – about £1,750,000,000 sterling by the United States. We have been helped to the extent of over £300,000,000 by Canada, Australia and New Zealand. In addition, at the end of the war, Australia owed us £220,000,000 and we now owe them £10,000,000, a turnover of about £230,000,000; and there are other very considerable items which could be mentioned.

In all history no community has ever been helped and kept by gratuitous overseas aid, that is to say, by the labour of other hard-working peoples, to anything approaching the degree which we have been under the present Socialist Government. And where are we at the end of it all? That is the emergency which we have been called together here to face.

After these preliminary observations I come to the actual Motion and Amendment which are before us, and the measure which has given rise to them, namely, the devaluation of the pound sterling from 4.03 down to 2.80 of the American dollar. The Government declare that this was all they could do in the extremity to which we have come or to which we have been brought by them. Nay more – they even try to represent it as a benefit and a fine shrewd stroke of timely policy. Here again in this matter I will venture to recur to first principles and seek for realities. One must be careful not to be baffled and bewildered by technical jargon. There is no sphere of human thought in which it is easier for a man to show superficial cleverness and the appearance of superior wisdom than in discussing questions of currency and exchange. I saw a very good cartoon in a newspaper the other day of a hospital ward filled with patients who had become demented through trying to explain the devaluation problem to their wives.

But I will submit to the House some simple propositions which they may deem worthy of consideration and which are at any rate easy to understand. The reduction of the rate of dollar exchange from 4.03 to 2.80 means, subject to certain minor abatements, that we may have to pay up to nearly half as much again, some say 35 per cent, some 40 per cent, for what we buy – much of it necessaries without which we cannot live – from the dollar area. We may have to pay up to nearly half as much again over an area of almost one-fifth of our imports – actually 17 per cent.

That cannot be good for us. It can only mean that we are forced to give much more of our life energy, that is to say toil, sweat, physical fatigue, craftsmanship, ingenuity, enterprise and good management, to buy the same quantity of indispensable products outside this country as we had before. We have to do more work and draw more upon our spirits and our carcasses to win back the same amount of food, raw materials and other goods without which we cannot carry on. That is bad for us; it is a new blow to our economic health and a new burden which we have to bear.

Now, the life thrust of the British nation, if not impeded, is magnificent, but we have been, as I said at the beginning, exhausted by our glorious efforts in the war. Great exertions are made by the people, but we can ill afford to make a new drain upon our latent strength and remaining motive power. We are not in a state of health to become a blood donor on a large scale at the present time. We are already a blood donor on a tremendous scale through our unrequited exports to India, Egypt and other countries to whom we became indebted for local supplies while we were defending them from being conquered by the Italians, the Germans or the Japanese. The *Manchester Guardian*, perhaps at this moment a better guide on economics than on ethics, has estimated these unrequited exports at nearly one-fifth of our total exports. That is a lot.

Many hundreds of thousands of our skilled or semi-skilled wage earners are toiling today to make desirable things for those countries which are paid for simply by somebody scratching something off with his pen from what is described by the misleading term 'sterling balances', which really means British debts. Nothing comes back in return to nourish the productive energies of the island. Trade is exchange, but here is neither trade nor exchange. An intense effort goes out and nothing comes back. I am not at this moment arguing the rights and wrongs, though I am quite willing to do so on a suitable occasion. I think that an amount for our expenses for the defence of those countries should have been set against the local supplies, but it would be a long argument and much could be said. I am not arguing it at the moment; I am only setting forth the brutal fact.

On the top of all this, the devaluation of the pound sterling draws a further draft in life blood and initial energy not only from the wage-earning masses but from all that constitutes the productive fertility of Britain. We are to give anything up to 45 per cent more products of our own toil for the same amount of dollar imports. That cannot be a good thing, it cannot be something to rejoice about, it cannot be something to parade as a triumph or to boast over as some new benefit bestowed by the Socialist Government upon our struggling community. It is a hard and heavy blow. However necessary it may be at the point to which we have been led, even if it be the best step open to us to take in the plight into which we have fallen – and all that is arguable – the hard, blunt, simple conclusion remains; it cannot be a good thing. We have suffered a serious disaster. In all this my mind would have marched step by step with that of the Chancellor of the Exchequer until a fortnight ago. Now, he probably finds these notions revolting and reactionary. So much for the first of the realities of devaluation. I must not again make the joke about revaluation. The delicacy of the point will I am sure be fully respected.

Now I come to the second reality which is more complicated. Anybody can understand that it is not good for a man in a weak state of health with an overstrained vitality to be tapped month by month for his life blood for the good of others across the oceans, be they stronger or weaker, in order to win his daily bread and that of his wife and children. But this second point concerns the whole sterling area of which the British Empire and Commonwealth is the foundation; and also it concerns all the mighty regions of Europe outside the Iron Curtain.

I see it said that the effect of our devaluation of the pound and its consequences on European and on sterling currencies is to erect something like a 40 per cent tariff wall against the United States. I am myself a supporter of Imperial Preference, of European Unity and of the sterling area and I am glad to see all these vast regions and forces becoming conscious of a common identity. I cannot regret in itself the drawing of a girdle or *zollverein*[1] around themselves. But here it is a question of degree. Up to a certain point it would be a help. It would help world recovery. But beyond that point it may well be a hindrance.

I think of course as a free trader. I may have adopted some variations and modifications, as we all have in the course of years, but still that is the basis on which my thought was formed many years ago. If we pierce down to the economic roots of world production and human material and creative power, the erection of a new barrier in addition to the political and economic barrier of the Iron Curtain in the modern world of today cannot be deemed a stimulus. Restriction is never a stimulus in itself. It may in a crisis make for order, but it is not a stimulus. It may on a long-term view promote a wider harmony and more equal bargaining power, but in so far as world trade is restricted this is a contrary force to the ideal of plenty. Abundance or plenty is the aim of mankind. Plenty is within its power. Plenty should be its inheritance. Plenty is hope for all. Restriction is inevitably the enemy of plenty.

It has been stated that the United States Government have pressed us to devaluate the pound. The Chancellor need not even shake his head. I was not going to omit the point. The Chancellor told us yesterday that he did it of his own free will when the time came. I do not suppose that the United States, this gigantic capitalist organisation, with its vast and super-abundant productive power – millions of people animated by the profit motive – I do not suppose that it will be seriously injured by a moderate wire fence being placed around the British Empire, the sterling area and United Europe. But I cannot believe

---

[1] Customs union (German).

that American manufacturers will see in such a development any immediate inducement to reduce their own highly protective tariff behind which they have built up their unrivalled economic power and which tariff is backed – as all tariffs are – by potent political interests.

I should be very glad to be contradicted by events. I have always hoped for a large reduction in American tariffs, but this is no time to nurse illusions or delusions. We must seek the truth even if we cannot give full effect to it at this particular moment, and we must face it when found however ugly it may be. I cannot feel that what has taken place – namely, the erection of a 40 per cent tariff around the European area and the sterling area – is likely to promote in itself the probability of an important United States change from her present protective policy. I hope, however, that they will rise above the considerations which obviously present themselves at this stage.

I come to my third point, my third reality, upon this issue of devaluation and it centres upon the word 'truth'. Whatever the currency experts may say – and they say all sorts of things and with learned grimaces change their views very frequently – but whatever they may say, the true exchange value between pound and dollar, or between all other currencies and the dollar or the pound, the true one is the right one; and the one at which we ought to aim. In the present circumstances if the Chancellor of the Exchequer felt it necessary to devaluate the pound to a fixed figure, I think it was right to go the whole hog; and that it was better to cut down the rate of exchange to this level in the hopes of a later revival than to take half measures which would soon have been overtaken and overwhelmed by the true and real forces which are relentlessly at work.

Now the matter is done, and when we have had to give up our exchange position which we had maintained so long, I feel entitled to take a fresh view. I am all for a free market and a true market. As I told the House two or three years ago, it is only a false and untrue market officially supported that breeds a black market. A sham market can no more escape a black market than a man can escape from his own shadow. Therefore I should myself have been more inclined, had I been in any way responsible, to set the pound free under regular and necessary safeguards and control – (*Laughter*) – certainly, and accept the results, than to the present rigid method of pegging the exchange at the very lowest rate which anyone could possibly conceive.

The Chancellor of the Exchequer argued at some length against this yesterday, and it is obvious that anything that is free or largely unregulated is obnoxious to the Socialist mentality. But this was what we did in 1931 – the last time we had to clear up the Socialist financial mess – (*Interruption*) – Oh, I remember it well. Quite soon we had a natural exchange rate of 3.30 which through the actions of both countries rested fairly stable until the war came. I do not think that the idea of the liberation of the pound should be ruled out by any Government which can command confidence abroad. That may be the decisive reason for the Chancellor of the Exchequer rejecting it at the present time.

I believe that great strength still resides in the sterling area of which Britain is the centre. That has to some extent been proved by the many countries which, roughly as they were used, and little though they were consulted, have had to conform to our action. I believe that this strength, working freely and backed by the intense productive effort of all the communities concerned, would in a short while achieve a far better rate of exchange against the dollar than the present figure of 2.80 to which we have been condemned. I believe further that in its intrinsic strength under favourable circumstances a free pound might establish itself at a rate which, while far more beneficial for us than the present position, would nevertheless promote and express a natural but conscious affinity throughout the sterling and associated currencies of the world.

To sum up this part of my argument which I am submitting to the House, the devaluation of the pound sterling is a new and serious drain upon the life strength of Britain. We always supported, my right hon. Friend in particular, the Chancellor of the Exchequer in resisting it. It might have been better in my view, and may still be better when confidence is restored, to let the pound go free under proper safeguards – (Hon. Members: 'What are they?') – control of the sending of large sums of money from this country – all this applied in 1931 – (*Laughter*) – what are hon. Members laughing at? They had very little to laugh at in 1931. It might have been better, I say, and may well be better when confidence is restored to let the pound go free under proper safeguards and reach its natural level. A free pound would impose a less severe drain upon our conditions of life and labour, and nevertheless, in reaching its true level would afford a girdle to the European and sterling area which, without being unduly restrictive, would afford an effective means of economic as well as political association.

Now I turn from discussing the policy of devaluation to the timing of the act and the sequence of events in which it lies. Judged by the results, the management of our finances has been deplorable. If as a result of that mismanagement the devaluation or liberation of the pound sterling had become inevitable, ought it not to have been taken as part of a general policy of setting our finances in order? A reduction in expenditure –

The Minister of National Insurance (Mr James Griffiths):[1] On what?

Mr Churchill: a substantial relief in taxation – (Hon. Members: 'On what?') – The Chancellor of the Exchequer does not say there should never be any

---

[1] James Griffiths, 1890–1975. Marxist Central Labour College, 1919–21. MP (Lab.) for Llanelli, 1936–70. Chairman, National Executive Committee of the Labour Party, 1939. Secretary to Welsh Parliamentary Party, 1942. Minister of National Insurance, 1945. Hon. degree, University of Wales, 1946. Chairman, Labour Party, 1948–9. Secretary of State for the Colonies, 1950. Deputy Leader, Labour Party, 1955–9.

reduction in expenditure. Hon. Members should ask him on what. He has the power to answer the question, and the duty to answer the question – (An Hon. Member: 'It is your duty too.') – I am as good a judge of my duty as the hon. Member is of his.

I say that a reduction in expenditure, a substantial relief in taxation applied to increase incentives to production and earnings, especially among the wage-earners liable to direct taxation, widespread relaxation of needless and vexatious controls and interferences with the flexibility of private enterprise, the definite lifting of the shadow of further nationalization from our most active and prosperous industries and, above all, the return to power of a Government commanding national and international confidence – all these would have created and may still create conditions in which the liberation of the pound sterling would have a good chance of opening wide doors of prosperity into the future.

But by one means or another devaluation or liberation, if this step were inevitable, should have been taken as part of a general scheme of financial reform instead of being plunged into as an isolated act forced upon us at the last moment. Again and again the Chancellor was warned from this side of the House and by financial authorities outside that he was living in a fool's paradise. But all these warnings were in vain. I think he made some remark about 'Dismal Desmonds'. Was that his phrase or did one of his colleagues achieve this alliterative gem?

Therefore, whatever may be thought of the relative advantages or disadvantages of devaluing or liberating the pound sterling, the timing of the step was obviously wrong. A drastic alteration in the exchange rate, if proved necessary, should not have been left till the crisis broke upon us but should have been taken in anticipation of it. It is not easy to palliate the right hon. and learned Gentleman's blunder. We all know the abilities of the Chancellor of the Exchequer. In his position he had more and better information on the subject at his disposal than anyone else in the world. He ought, surely, to have exercised foresight and decision in good time before our remaining gold reserves had been drained away and he was forced higgledy-piggledy into action which we know he loathed, under the worst possible circumstances.

I am sorry not to see the Lord President of the Council (Mr Hebert Morrison) in his place because I wish to quote with great approval some remarks which he has made on this subject:

> The real problem of statesmanship (said the Lord President of the Council in June 1946), in the field of industry and economics is to see trouble coming and to prevent ourselves getting into the smash. We are determined that we are not going to be caught unawares by blind economic forces under this Administration.

But that is exactly what has happened to his colleague the Chancellor of the

Exchequer. He could not possibly have described it in more precise or harmonious language. In fact, it has almost a prophetic aspect about it.

I come to another point. The question is much discussed in the country of the Chancellor's political honesty. Ordinary people find it difficult to understand how a Minister, with all his knowledge and reputation for integrity, should have felt it right to turn completely round, like a squirrel in its cage, abandon his former convictions and do what he repeatedly said he would never do, and moreover, enforce upon his party and his most faithful followers the humiliating tergiversation which we have witnessed. I am surprised, I must say, that the Chancellor's own self-respect did not make him feel that, however honest and necessary was his change of view, his was not the hand that should carry forward the opposite policy. Certainly he stands woefully weakened in reputation, first by his lack of foresight, and secondly, by having had completely to reverse the reasoned convictions with which he made us familiar. Of course, we know that changes in currency cannot be announced beforehand. The secret had to be kept. It was certainly very well kept, perhaps too well kept considering the position of some of our friendly countries like France. But we congratulate the Chancellor – and he will agree with this – and the Foreign Secretary on the high art which they displayed in the necessary process of deception. The histrionic quality of their performance was indeed remarkable.

But I am not speaking of the last month but of the position three and four months ago. I have been shown nine quotations from the Chancellor's speeches declaring himself the inveterate opponent of devaluation. It is very important that our Chancellor of the Exchequer should have foresight. It is also desirable that he should have consistency, as far as possible. It is important that Parliament and the country should believe that when he speaks at that Box opposite he means what he says. Otherwise, how can people attach the weight to his declarations and pledges without which a Chancellor of the Exchequer is grievously crippled? How he of all men could adopt the policy, 'What I tell you nine times is untrue,' is most astonishing.

Although his personal honour and private character are in no wise to be impugned, it will be impossible in the future for anyone to believe or accept with confidence any statements which he may make as Chancellor of the Exchequer from that Box. He stands convicted of lamentable lack of foresight. His usefulness, for all his abilities in the great office he holds, has been definitely impaired, and I find it most difficult to believe that he would have been content to stay in office if he had thought the ordeal was likely to be a long one.

It is odd that the Chancellor of the Exchequer in his present weak and vulnerable position should feel entitled to judge his predecessors with so much severity and to impute wrong and unworthy motives to them. The right hon. and learned Gentleman referred yesterday to my action in returning to the

Gold Standard a quarter of a century ago. He said that his policy today was a substitution for the alternative policy of severe deflation.

> That policy − (I quote his words from *Hansard*) − was pursued at one time under the aegis of the right hon. Gentleman the Leader of the Opposition and depended for its efficacy upon a massive extension of unemployment, with the accompanying lowering of wage rates and so the impoverishment of the employed and unemployed.

There were loud cheers from hon. Gentlemen opposite.

This was a very aggressive and I may even say offensive reference to past history. To suggest that people would like to see other people unemployed is I think deserving − (*Interruption*). I will pick my epithets with care, and I have a large collection of them − is I think deserving of the word 'offensive'. I think that the whole passage in which he referred to me is singularly out of keeping with the governess and sermon-like passages of some other parts of his discourse. I must say that I am obliged to him for making his accusations here, where they can be answered, instead of circulating them, as is no doubt being done far and wide at this present moment by his party propaganda machine.

The House must pardon me if I make a short digression −

Mr George Thomas (Cardiff, Central):[1] This whole speech has been a digression.

Mr Churchill: The hon. Gentleman is very talkative. One of the strongest claims that the party opposite have is that with their great majority they have never hampered free speech, however detrimental they might find it to themselves.

I will cite only one quotation in answer to the Chancellor. It is by Mr Snowden, Chancellor of the Exchequer in the first Socialist Government of 1924, and Chancellor again in 1929. In the interval he led the Socialist Opposition in all financial matters. He was one of their most respected and influential founder members.

On the Second Reading of the Gold Standard Bill he said that while the Government had acted with undue precipitancy, he and his Socialist colleagues were in favour of a return to the Gold Standard at the earliest possible moment. The Socialist Opposition thereupon refrained from voting against what, in the right hon. and learned Gentleman's words of yesterday, was a policy which:

---

[1] George Thomas, 1909–97. Born in Port Talbot, South Wales. Educated at University College, Southampton; trained as a teacher. MP (Lab.) for Cardiff Central, 1945–50; for Cardiff West, 1950–83. Under-Secretary of State for the Home Department, 1964–6. Minister of State for Wales, 1966–7. Minister of State for Commonwealth Affairs, 1967–8. Secretary of State for Wales, 1968–70. Chairman of Ways and Means, 1974–6. Speaker of the House of Commons, 1976–83. Viscount Tonypandy, 1983.

... depended for its efficacy upon a massive extension of unemployment with the accompanying lowering of wage rates.

Later on, in December of 1926, Mr Snowden wrote an article in the *Financial Times* in which he said:

> All the facts do not support the impression that the return to gold has been detrimental to industry. The bank rate has not been raised; unemployment has not risen; real wages have not fallen; and the price level has been fairly well maintained.

I am rather astonished that the right hon. and learned Gentleman, before he went out of his way to attack me about transactions long buried in the past, should not have acquainted himself with these declarations of Mr Snowden's in the heyday of his power and influence with the Labour Party. I must also state, since the matter has been raised, that during my four and a half years' tenure of the Chancellorship, the cost of living declined by at least 18 points, while money wages remained stable. That certainly compares very favourably with what has occurred in the last four years, what is occurring now, and what is going to recur in a harder degree.

Secondly, I may remind the House when I am charged with seeking a massive extension of unemployment, that it was not until I left the Exchequer in 1929 that, under the Socialist administration, the rate of unemployment doubled and overtopped the 2,000,000 figure. It really is remarkable that the accusation of being callous about unemployment or the welfare of the people should be launched against me, the author of the labour exchanges and of the first Unemployment Insurance Act, and, as Conservative Chancellor of the Exchequer, of the Old Age Pensions age being lowered from 70 to 65 and the institution of the Widows' and Orphans' Act.

When the right hon. and learned Gentleman or anybody on those benches can show services rendered to the working classes equal to those I have mentioned they will be more free to throw stones at others. All the benevolent and beneficial aspects of this Parliament – apart, that is to say, from sterile controversial party measures – were actually planned in great detail by the National Coalition Government. (*Interruption.*) The right hon. Gentleman the Minister of Health was not a member of that Government; he was otherwise occupied in those days. That legislation was actually planned by the National Coalition Government of which I was the head and which rested on an over-all Conservative majority in the House of Commons of 150.

I noticed by the way – the right hon. and learned Gentleman in his difficult position is showing himself not unruffled – that the Chancellor yesterday used a new term of prejudice and opprobrium. He spoke with disdain of doing anything which would start a period of freedom for the profit earners. What is this prejudice against profit earners? 'Profiteer' is the word which all may abhor, but the stigma in that term is not 'profit earner' but unfair exploitation. How can a country like this live without its profit earners? How could the Chancellor of the Exchequer collect his revenues without taking, as he admits, 50 or 60 per cent of the profits that they earn? How can anything stand without the profit earners? How wrong it is for a statesman in his position to cast his censures upon them, and, presumably, reserve his tributes for the disinterested loss-makers who manage our nationalized industries?

In the closing sentence of our Amendment, which I am now moving, we have given prominence to the Chancellor of the Exchequer's own words. He has certainly been candid in his confession. He has admitted that the financial policy of the Government he is supposed to be defending has been 'the resort to one temporary expedient after another'. That is certainly a frank confession, and it is, to a large extent, an explanation of our continued drift and slide downhill. I can only say confession is good for the soul, but after confession comes penance, not power.

His Majesty's Government in their Motion appeal for the co-operation of the whole people. It is certainly the duty of everyone to help in every way to increase our production and improve its efficiency. But surely it is not for the present Government to appeal to us on the grounds of national interest. Of our own accord, in spite of many provocations and insults, we have helped them throughout their long four years of power in all that we believed was necessary in the public interest.

First, there was the American Loan of £1,000,000,000. Not without some doubts and differences, and some criticism in our own party, I and my colleagues on this bench helped them all we could, both here and in the United States, to obtain the loan, little though we liked its terms. Secondly, the Marshall Aid Plan on which the Government are now living was stated by General Marshall to have arisen in his mind out of the movement for United Europe which he directly associated with my name. This, he said, had led him to what we all acclaim as his wise and generous policy without which, according to the Lord President of the Council at Manchester on 17th April, 1948, 'we should be facing cuts in rations and a million or two people on the dole.' And the Minister of Health on 18th May, 1948, in a momentary lapse, which he has no doubt greatly regretted since, said: 'But for Marshall Aid, unemployment in this country would at once rise by 1,500,000.' That the Socialist Government have been spared the distress, nay the agony, of an immense rise in unemployment which would have been fatal to them and for many years to their party, has been directly due, and provedly due, to the aid which the Conservative Opposition have given, irrespective of party interests.

I think that some acknowledgment of these facts by Ministers in this Debate would have been becoming. We cannot, of course, forgo our right or neglect our duty to criticize the maladministration of our affairs or fail to warn the people of what lies before them if they allow themselves again to be misled by promises and fallacies. At one moment we were told – it now appears, from the account given by the Chancellor of the Exchequer, none too accurately – that the mission which the Chancellor and the Foreign Secretary were carrying out in the United States was concerned with matters vital to our financial interests, and that it all hung in the balance. From that moment we used all our influence to silence all criticism, and we only resume it now that these matters have been settled and because a new policy has been declared.

At every moment throughout this Parliament we have urged all those with whom we have influence – probably the majority of the workers and producers of the nation, employers and employees alike – to do their utmost to stimulate production. We have supported, at the request of the Prime Minister, on the public platform the Savings campaign and the recruiting campaign, and we shall continue to do so. We have done this because though we are party men, we feel bound to put country before party.

But how does His Majesty's Government behave in this field? I will admit that they have done many unpopular things, some of which were in the public interest. But, on the whole, they have played the party game with national stakes in a manner which no other Government I can remember in my long life or read about in modern history have ever done. They perpetuated a mass of wartime controls to give them that power of interference in the daily life of the country which is a characteristic of Socialism. They reasserted by regulation the wartime control of the severest form of direction of labour. They have the power today to take anyone and send them anywhere they will. Though they took these powers, they have not dared to enforce them, but the insult to national and personal liberty remains unreduced. As a mere act of party spite the Chancellor of the Exchequer abolished, at substantial annual loss, the Liverpool Cotton Exchange. The Government thrust upon the nation struggling out of its wartime exhaustion the evils of nationalization and their party doctrines.

It is some consolation, I must admit, that the miners and the railwaymen should have learned, and learned by practical experience, what the nationalization of great industries means in practice to the workers in them and to the public at large. The whole policy of nationalization is being proved every day more clearly to be a costly failure and a further drain upon our life blood. Now at this moment when we are brought to this melancholy pass, and now that we are in this position of grave difficulty, the Government still proclaim their intention to nationalize the steel industry, and, should they be returned to power, they proclaim their resolve to nationalize insurance, cement and sugar. Never have a Government or a party more completely divested themselves of the title deeds to speak in the name of the nation.

But all this ill-usage in no way relieves us of our duty to encourage everyone to do his or her utmost to improve the national effort in these days of crisis, and thus to preserve to the British nation the power to regain in the future the great position in the world which it has held in the past. Nor must we allow the insults which have been hurled at us to provoke us into similar taunts. (*Laughter.*) Hon. Members opposite laugh. Personally, I do not think that a large part of the British people are lower than vermin. I think that the British nation is good all through.

More than forty years ago I sat myself in a Left-wing Government with a majority even greater than that of the present one, and I was one of their most prominent and controversial figures. The House returned in 1906 represented, in my view, more or less the same slice of the population, the people who elected it coming very largely from the same homes and from the same areas, as does this majority today. I found them very good people to work with, and I renewed this comradeship in the long and terrible years of the war. But there was a great difference between those days of forty years ago and these in which we are now living. The Liberal Government of 1906 was built around and upon those great principles of Liberalism which have since passed into the possession of every party except the Communists, and are still spreading with irresistible appeal throughout the world. But now those who sit opposite to us are not ranged around the great truths of Liberalism; they are ranged around the fallacy of Socialism, which is in principle contrary to human nature and which I believe can only be enforced upon nations in its entirety in the wholesale fashion of Communism.

At present only 20 per cent of our industries are nationalized, and we have been living upon the other 80 per cent, which the Government eye with so much disfavour and malice. There is indeed a great gulf of thought and conviction between us. 'All men are born equal,' says the American Constitution. 'They must be kept equal,' say the British Socialist party. Here is the deadly stroke at the mainspring of life and progress. I grieve that in these perilous years we should be so harshly and needlessly divided. Only an appeal to the people and a new Parliament can relieve the increasing tension.

And let me say this. If at this moment the Government were to drop steel nationalization and their other extreme plans, it would certainly enable the approaching General Election to be conducted in an atmosphere much less dangerous to the underlying national unities on which 50,000,000 in this island depend for their survival. (*Laughter.*) The Chancellor of the Exchequer may lead the cackles opposite at those sentiments if he believes it worthy of his position and of the serious part he has played and is playing in our affairs. It is my duty and that of those whom I lead to warn the country in good time of its dangers. But I thank God that in my old age I preserve an invincible faith that we shall overcome them.

What has been the great characteristic of our age? As I have seen it during my lifetime, it has been the arrival at an ever more bountiful table of millions and tens of millions and scores of millions of people. There is no reason why this march should not continue. There is no reason why the struggle of the masses for a more spacious life, for shorter hours, for constantly improving conditions of labour, should not be crowned with increasing success. Otherwise, what would be the use of all the machinery and improved methods of modern times? There is no reason, I say, why the forward march should not continue, provided that mistaken guides do not enforce the rule that all must come to the table at once or none at all. That indeed would bar the door to that continuous progress and expansion which has been maintained even during the convulsions of our lifetime, and which it is ours to enjoy if we do not wantonly cast it away.

Clement Attlee to Winston S. Churchill
(*Churchill papers, 2/81*)

30 September 1949
Personal and Private

My dear Churchill,

You probably saw in the Press yesterday a report from Washington that the Combined Chiefs of Staff Organisation has been abolished. You may like to know the background to this.

Ever since the end of the war the French have been pressing the United States Chiefs of Staff to admit them to the Councils of the Combined Chiefs of Staff Organisation.

When the United States Chiefs of Staff met our Chiefs in London early in August this year, this was the first problem they raised. With the creation of the Atlantic Pact defence machinery we knew this issue would have to be faced and our Chiefs of Staff, after listening to the arguments put forward by the Americans, reluctantly agreed that there was no alternative but to agree to the formal dissolution of the Combined Chiefs. The Americans made it quite clear at that meeting that this would make no difference to the continued close co-operation between the Military Staffs of the two countries – a state of affairs to which they attached the greatest importance. This was endorsed by Mr Acheson himself in a recent discussion with Mr Bevin on the Atlantic Pact Organisation. When handing Mr Bevin a written statement regarding US participation in the European Regional Planning Groups, Mr Acheson said 'this statement will not in any way limit the ultra-secret global planning arrangements which now exist between the United States and the United Kingdom'.

Although we may be losing something in form by the dissolution of the Combined Chiefs of Staff as a peace time organisation, we are, I think, in no real danger of losing the substance of this well developed organisation.

It was agreed at the August meeting that the Americans, on their return to Washington, would put forward proposals for continuing the work of the various sub-committees of the Combined Chiefs Organisation when they were disbanded. We have received these proposals which appear quite satisfactory to us.

The question of publicity was also discussed at the August meeting and Tedder, speaking for the British Chiefs of Staff, expressed the view that there was no need to make a formal announcement of the dissolution of the Combined Chiefs but, if questions were asked, it should be explained that the Combined Chiefs of Staff had ceased to exist soon after the end of the war except for dealing with Trieste and certain other residual problems. It was agreed however, at this meeting that our staffs in Washington would have to move out of the Pentagon Building where their especially privileged position could hardly be justified in the eyes of the other signatories of the Atlantic Pact, especially the French. Our Joint Staffs are now well housed by the Americans in what used to be a Navy Department building on Constitution Avenue.

It appears however, that with the creation of the Atlantic Pact Defence Organisation and the impending meeting of Defence Ministers on October 5th, the Americans have been under pressure to make some definite statement. This may explain the recent references in the press, about which we were not consulted.

We do not propose to issue any statement ourselves but if we are asked a question at any time we shall take the above line, which was agreed between the Chiefs of Staff in August.

We shall, of course, do our utmost to keep alive the spirit underlying the Combined Chiefs Organisation and we know it is the Americans' intention to revert to this type of High Command in the event of hostilities.

October
1949

Clementine Churchill to President Harry S Truman
(Churchill papers, 2/158)

2 October 1949   Chartwell

Dear Mr President,
   Winston has shewn me your letter.[1]
   I had seen in the newspapers that you and Mrs Truman had done Sarah the honour of witnessing her performance and also how kind you had been in visiting her personally behind the scenes and afterwards entertaining her and her fellow actors and actresses.
   Winston and I are so glad and touched and we much value the letter you wrote him.
   Please present my warm respects to Mrs Truman and to your daughter Margaret and believe me to be yours very sincerely.

Randolph S. Churchill to Editor of the Times
(Churchill papers, 1/46)

3 October 1949

THE FINANCIAL DEBATE

Sir,
   In your leading article of September 29 entitled 'Mr Churchill's challenge' I was shocked to read that Mr Churchill 'roamed, in his own fashion, from the atom bomb to some unworthy words about Sir Stafford Cripps' political honesty'.
   I do not know where you derived the information on which your editorial writer based this stricture, but admirers of the accurate and objective reporting of your Parliamentary staff must have been happy to notice that it cannot

---
[1] Reproduced above (p. 1499).

have been from them. For on the same date in your Parliamentary Sketch I read 'He (Mr Churchill) was careful not to impugn the Minister's honesty.'

Winston S. Churchill to King George VI
(Churchill papers, 2/171)

3 October 1949

Sir,

I have at last received from the binders the copy of my last Volume on the War which your Majesty said you would accept. I shall look forward in due course to sending the third and fourth Volumes – both of which are virtually done. It is a serious task to tell this tale amid gathering political cares, and I am very glad to have got well ahead with it.

I do trust your Majesty is continually improving in health. All will be needed in the anxious days that lie ahead. We may hope they will not be so perilous as those we went through together.

Winston S. Churchill to Princess Wilhelmina
(Churchill papers, 2/174)[1]

3 October 1949

Madam,

I venture to send your Majesty the last Volume of my book on the war which has now at last come back from the binders. It gives me great pleasure to be able to present it to one for whom I have so deep a respect.

I trust in Your Majesty's retirement that Painting has come into the highest ranks of Your Majesty's favourites. I have had a lot of fun out of it lately, but now politics thrusts its unattractive head round the corner of the studio and I have to scrape my palette for the time being.

I always look back to all the kindness and gracious hospitality I received from the people of the Netherlands and their Queen.

---

[1] This letter was handwritten.

Donald Tyerman[1] to Randolph S. Churchill
(Churchill papers, 1/46)

3 October 1949

Dear Mr Churchill,
 I am sorry that you feel that our editorial comments on Mr Churchill's references to the Chancellor of the Exchequer were less than just. I have consulted the full text of what Mr Churchill said, and I am still unconvinced that the phrase in our leader was a misleading interpretation.
 You quote our Parliamentary Sketch as saying that 'He was careful not to impugn the Minister's honesty.' Mr Churchill actually said 'although his <u>personal</u> honour and private character are in no wise to be impugned, it would be impossible in the future for anyone to believe or accept with confidence any statements which he may make as Chancellor of the Exchequer from that Box.' You will notice the stress on the word 'personal', in contrast to the phrase 'political honesty', which we used in our editorial comment and which Mr Churchill used in introducing a passage very plainly, to the ordinary eye, 'impugning' the Chancellor. In other words the distinction between 'political' and 'personal' honesty was Mr Churchill's own, and it was the Chancellor's 'personal' honesty, not his 'political' honesty, which he did not wish to impugn. To me this still seems to be the plain English of it.

Winston S. Churchill to Sir Stafford Cripps
(Churchill papers, 2/161)

3 October 1949

Dear Stafford,
 I am sorry indeed that you feel my criticism of your political conduct should prevent you from accepting the degree from Bristol University, which it would have given me much pleasure to confer upon you.
 If you will read the Official Report of what I said, you will see that your personal honour and private character were in no way impugned at any time by me. At the same time it is quite true that I consider your policy at the Exchequer in this crisis is open to criticism on public grounds. This would certainly not, in my view make it embarrassing for us to meet together on an entirely non-Party occasion. We have done so frequently before, although our differences of outlook were extreme. If you feel that the darkening political scene in Britain renders it impossible for opponents to meet on non-Party occasions, I should regret it for many reasons.

[1] Donald Tyerman, 1908–81. Educated at Brasenose College, Oxford. Asst Editor of *The Times*, 1944–55. Chairman, Executive Board, International Press Institute, 1961–2. Member, Press Council, 1963–9. Governor, London School of Economics, 1951–75.

October 1949

Randolph S. Churchill to Donald Tyerman
(Churchill papers, 1/46)

4 October 1949

Dear Mr Tyerman,

Thank you for your letter of October 3. I am obliged to you for the attention you have given to this matter. I must admit, however, that I find your explanation somewhat unsatisfactory.

To justify your use of the phrase 'unworthy words' you quote the sentence from Mr Churchill's speech beginning 'Although his personal honour and private character . . .'. To sustain a charge of either personal or political dishonesty in utterance it would be necessary to show that the statements concerned were deliberately untruthful. Mr Churchill nowhere did this. On the contrary, in his very next sentence he gives an explanation of why he thinks it is 'impossible for people in the future to believe statements by the Chancellor'. 'He stands convicted' said Mr Churchill, 'of a lamentable lack of foresight.' The 'plain English' of it, therefore, is that it was lack of foresight and not personal or political dishonesty with which Mr Churchill charged the Chancellor, and it is these words which you have stigmatised as 'unworthy'.

Moreover, I do not think that there is much substance in the contrast you try to draw between Mr Churchill's reference to 'political honesty' and to 'personal honour'. The second phrase occurs several hundred words after the first and all he said about the Chancellor's 'political honesty' was that it had been much discussed – a plain reference to the recent correspondence in the *Manchester Guardian*. So far from one phrase being used as a contrast to the other, it is very clear that the first was merely introductory to the other.

Since writing to you yesterday I have re-read the speech not only in Hansard but in *The Times* to try to discover which of Mr Churchill's words might legitimately be considered 'unworthy'. In *The Times* report I came across a paragraph beginning 'Referring to the Chancellor's "political dishonesty", the Rt. Hon. Gentleman said that ordinary people found it difficult to understand. . . .' etc. It occurred to me that these words which you specifically put in inverted commas in a passage which was reported in indirect speech might have been the foundation for your charge; but on comparing your report with Hansard I find that the passage reads: 'The question is much discussed in the country of the Chancellor's political honesty.'

Since you did not make use of these words in your letter to me, I take it that you will agree that Hansard was right and that *The Times* was wrong, and that it is desirable in the interests of historical accuracy that the matter should be rectified. In this belief I enclose another letter for publication in the place of the one I sent you yesterday.

PS. When your leader writer wrote the article he cannot have seen the official report and he was presumably relying for his information upon the *Times* report with its inaccurate phrase about 'political dishonesty'. If this is in fact what occurred, I am sure you will welcome an opportunity of withdrawing the accusation of 'unworthy words'.

Randolph S. Churchill to Editor of The Times
(Churchill papers, 1/46)

4 October 1949

Sir,

May I call your attention to a serious discrepancy between *The Times* report in your issue of September 29 of Mr Churchill's speech in the House of Commons, and the official text as published in Hansard?

The Times says: 'Referring to the Chancellor's "political dishonesty", the Rt. Hon. Gentleman said that ordinary people found it difficult to understand how a Minister . . . should have felt it right to turn completely round like a squirrel in its cage. . . .' Hansard, on the other hand, quotes this passage as beginning: 'The question is much discussed in the country of the Chancellor's political honesty.'

There have been occasions in the past when *The Times* has been right and Hansard has been wrong, but I submit to you, Sir, that this is not one of them. For though, in your leading article of September 29 you thought fit to refer to 'some unworthy words about Sir Stafford Cripps's political honesty' your own Parliamentary Sketch of the same day said 'He Mr Churchill was careful not to impugn the Minister's honesty.'

Randolph S. Churchill to Winston S. Churchill
(Churchill papers, 1/46)

4 October 1949

My dearest Papa,

I gather from Christopher that, like myself, you have been irked by *The Times*'s outrageous reference to your 'unworthy words'; so I thought you might be interested in the enclosed correspondence. If they do not print my second letter I think they will, at any rate, be compelled to print my third which will confine itself to exposure of their factual error.

When one reflects on how *The Times* have been wrong on nearly every major issue in the last thirty years, it makes one very angry that they should presume to sit in an ivory tower and pass judgment upon someone without whose exertions *The Times* might now be printed in German.

Winston S. Churchill: note
(Churchill papers, 4/351A)

5 October 1949

What would have happened if the Germans had not attacked Russia?
? The air war over Germany in such circumstances.
US + GB against Germany.
Bomb in Canada.
I still believe that we (US + GB) could have won single-handed.

The great contrast between the war as presented to the Russian mind of great masses of men moved and manoeuvred overland and the problem of the Allies which was all sea, amphibious, and air.

Clementine Churchill to Winston S. Churchill
(Churchill papers, 2/178)

5 October 1949

Brendan lunched with me today in connection with the Chartwell Literary Trust.

He is disturbed because Mr Murphy, who is either editing or publishing the Duke of Windsor's Memoirs, showed him (Brendan) a letter which you had written to the Duke while he was still King at the time of the Abdication. It is apparently the intention of the Duke to publish this letter, and Brendan thought it unsuitable for publication.

He asked me if the Duke had asked your permission to publish this letter or indeed any other letters and if you had gone over them carefully. Brendan asked Mr Murphy if your permission had been sought and he said he did not know. Brendan seemed very anxious that you should know of this and be on the look-out, as of course *Life*, who are publishing the Duke's Memoirs would like to have any intimate letters from you to the Duke and would not worry as to whether their publication might be harmful.

Sir Stafford Cripps to Winston S. Churchill
(Churchill papers, 2/61)[1]

5 October 1949

Dear Winston,

I have read through Hansard again and cannot agree with your version of your speech – nor is it consistent with a large number of letters that I have had from Conservatives and others upon the matter.

---

[1] This letter was handwritten.

The sentence starting at the bottom of Col. 167 and running on to the top of 168 is an accusation of lack of 'integrity'.

The last sentence of the following paragraph accuses me of 'deception'. I am afraid I cannot personally separate what an individual says 'as Chancellor of the Exchequer' and as himself. If therefore I am called a liar it is of no consequence that it is hedged about by some fine distinctions!

This is not a question of political opponents meeting on non-Party occasions – I do continually meet my opponents most pleasantly and shall certainly not draw distinctions because of political views.

Had you been in my own party it would not have made the slightest difference to my action.

It is merely the case that I do not wish to receive a degree or any other gift from a person who has publicly accused me of being 'void of integrity', 'a deceiver' and a liar.

Winston S. Churchill to Sir Stafford Cripps
(Churchill papers, 2/161)

6 October 1949

Dear Stafford,

I have received your letter of October 5.[1] The sentence starting at the bottom of Column 167 and running on to the top of Column 168 is not an accusation of lack of integrity but of inconsistency. This is apparent from the next sentence, which contains the words '. . . however honest and necessary was his change of view . . .'.

The word 'deception' is part of the phrase 'the necessary process of deception', and is preceded a few lines earlier by 'Of course we know that changes in currency cannot be announced beforehand. The secret had to be kept.' This is no more dishonest than what we all did so often in the war to guard the secrecy of military operations.

I have never accused you of being 'void of integrity', 'a deceiver' and 'a liar', as your last sentence states, and no such words were uttered or implied by me. In fact if anyone applied such terms to you I should be among the first to repudiate them.

I can only hope that you will reflect upon these matters in a calmer frame of mind.

Of course the charges which I made and adhere to against your financial administration and lack of foresight and lack of consistency, and the suggestion that your change of view might well have been accompanied by your resignation are serious. So also was your accusation against me, namely that I

---

[1] Reproduced above (pp. 1521–2).

had pursued a policy 'which depended for its efficacy upon the massive extension of unemployment with the accompanying lowering of wage rates and so the impoverishment of the employed and of the unemployed'. This seemed to me to be a very harsh statement, but as I was able to prove in the House that it was quite untrue, I did not let it rankle in my mind; nor should I have referred to it again but for this correspondence.

Since however, in view of my speech, you have taken the attitude you have chosen to do, you are quite right not to attend our function at Bristol University, much though we shall all regret your absence.

Sir Stafford Cripps to Winston S. Churchill
(Churchill papers, 2/161)[1]

7 October 1949

Dear Winston,

Thank you for your letter with its further explanation. I will not prolong the argument. I can only judge the public interpretation put upon your statement (which is the important matter) by the reactions of the Press and the very numerous people who have spoken to me and written to me.

I am glad at any rate that we agree as to my action as regards the Bristol degree.

King George VI to Winston S. Churchill
(Churchill papers, 2/171)[2]

8 October 1949   Balmoral Castle

My dear Winston,

Thank you so very much for giving me the beautiful bound copy of the 2nd volume of your book. You must be glad that your stupendous task of writing the 4 volumes is at last finished. I am very worried about the country's present condition though those who should know do not appear to be in the least perturbed, at least outwardly. I am very much better & my stay here has done us worlds of good. Hoping we should meet some time on my return to London.

---

[1] This letter was handwritten.
[2] This letter was handwritten.

OCTOBER 1949

Winston S. Churchill to President Harry S Truman
(*Churchill papers, 2/158*)[1]

10 October 1949   Chartwell

Dear Harry,

I was touched by yr kindness to Sarah and by the charming letter wh you wrote me.[2] This letter will certainly be kept as one of my and Sarah's most treasured possessions. I thank you also for the signed programme which I am having framed to hang in my room beside a letter from FDR which I greatly value. It is pleasant to receive these gestures of friendship at a time when so much is uncertain and when – as I see it – the sky darkens for us all.

                                             Believe me, Yours vy sincerely,

I enclose a note from my wife,[3] who like me was delighted and moved.

Winston S. Churchill: speech
('*Winston S. Churchill, His Complete Speeches*', volume 7, pages 7857–8)

11 October 1949   Conservative and Unionist Associations Conference

LOCAL GOVERNMENT

... During the perverse and ill-starred reign of the Socialists during the last few years much has been done to injure and even, in some cases, to destroy local government. The Socialists have transferred many important duties from the local authorities to boards not elected by the people but amenable – I think that is the right word – to government patronage. They have taken away from the smaller boroughs and district councils many of their most cherished functions. They have destroyed the machinery devised by the wartime Coalition Government, resting upon its large Conservative majority in the House of Commons, to effect with safety and economy the adjustment of local authority boundaries.

What then have the Socialists in store for English and Welsh local government? Let the Socialists say now whether they intend to carry out their threat to replace our well-timed systems of local government by an alien regionalism, easily manipulated from Whitehall. This is a large issue which may lie before us in every part of the country in the near future. I doubt whether the Socialists will dare to answer the question, or dare to tell you at this moment, when not only the local elections but the national election must be considered. The local authorities have a right to receive the information. We shall

---
[1] This letter was handwritten.
[2] Reproduced above (p. 1499).
[3] Reproduced above (p. 1516).

press for the fullest disclosure of every means we can, and at the earliest possible moment.

I can only declare to you the policy and aim of the Conservative Party. As I said some months ago at Wolverhampton,[1] we intend to set in reverse the centralizing tendencies of Socialism. Should we become responsible, we should consult with all local authorities in the overhaul of their areas, functions, and financial arrangements. Nothing is fixed or permanent: all must move steadily forward along the lines of progress. We shall strive to invest local government with renewed confidence in itself and with full responsibility.

We shall offer to local authorities the return of all transport undertakings nationalized at the time of the forthcoming General Election – should they be in such a condition as to be desirable. Personal health services may in many cases be better administered by councils elected directly in the districts where they work.

Our guiding aim will be to stimulate rather than to strangle, to liberate rather than to hobble, all the energies of local government – and to raise instead of diminishing the dignity and importance of the immense mass of voluntary service now given to our local institutions.

Above all, Conservatives will take care that local government remains local – and remains a true reflection of the communities which it exists to serve, rather than become a mere appendage, or even utensil, of any government that rules in Westminster.

(Editor's Note: Mr Churchill referred to)[2] a matter on which the Conservative conference, when it meets tomorrow, should know my opinion. I have read the election programme put forth by Lord Beaverbrook in the *Daily Express* – with a proposal for an all-round minimum wage of £6 a week. Lord Beaverbrook is a friend of mine. I was glad to give him his opportunity during the war of rendering distinguished and invaluable service on more than one critical occasion.

Lord Beaverbrook's opinions are his own, but it is my duty to say that they must not be taken as representing the considered policy of the Conservative Party. It is certainly not our intention to try to win votes by wholesale promises of higher wages at the present grave time. On the contrary, I personally am inclined to the view upon a minimum wage attributed to Mr Deakin, who is a responsible trade union leader and has spoken with great clarity on this subject.

Just because the Socialist Party got into office last time by making all kinds of promises, it ought not to be supposed that is the way to gain or hold the confidence of the British nation. Anyhow, that is not the course I am going to advise you or the Conservative Party to follow in the immediate future.

---

[1] See speech of 23 July 1949, reproduced above (pp. 1456–61).
[2] This note was written by Robert Rhodes James, editor of *His Complete Speeches*.

1526 OCTOBER 1949

Clement Attlee to Winston S. Churchill
(Churchill papers, 2/29)

11 October 1949
Top Secret

My dear Churchill,

During our discussion about Defence on 20th July, I promised to let you have particulars of the present rate of production of jet fighter aircraft, showing how the machines were being allocated as between the Services and overseas buyers.

I now attach two copies of a memorandum giving this information. I shall be obliged if you will return them when we meet on 20th October for our next discussion.

Although your enquiries were mainly about jet fighters, I thought you might like to have some general information about other types of service aircraft. Total figures of the production and sales for all types, including jets, are therefore shown in paragraph 1 of the memorandum.

The build-up of Fighter Command strengths and reserves to the figures shown in paragraph 5 of the memorandum will, of course, be dependent on the provision to be made in Estimates for future years.

Winston S. Churchill to Clement Attlee
(Churchill papers, 2/81)

11 October 1949
Confidential

My dear Prime Minister,

Thank you for your letter.[1] I am very sorry that the Anglo-American Combined Chiefs of Staff Organisation has been abolished. It would have been much better to have preserved it and created an additional and larger organization to cover the Atlantic Pact Powers. France, without a French army, is a liability and not an asset to Great Britain, and there is no reason why our ties with the United States should have been weakened, in form at any rate, to please her. I can fully understand the reluctance of our Chiefs of Staff to assent to those proposals, and I wonder why they did so.

I note what you say about the verbal assurances which have been given, including Mr Acheson's remarks, and I thank you for making me acquainted with them.

---

[1] Of Sep. 30, reproduced above (pp. 1514–15).

Winston S. Churchill: speech
('Winston S. Churchill, His Complete Speeches', volume 7, pages 7858–60)

13 October 1949   Londonderry House

CONSERVATIVE TRADES UNION CONGRESS

I am very glad to see you here in Londonderry House. In the bygone aristocratic days it was associated with the glories of the Napoleonic era, in which our island defended not, as it proved, for the last time, the liberties of Europe against tyranny. It is appropriate that Conservative trade unionists should meet here, because the private enterprise of the Londonderry family drove out the great shaft to the coalbeds under the sea, which has been a source of enduring employment and a permanent enrichment to the coal supplies of Britain. The Government have told us today that there is to be no General Election before Christmas. In their announcement they say that this is because of the disturbing effect on trade and industry and on the national effort, which has been caused by the continuance of speculation about the date. There has indeed been disturbance of trade and industry, but whose fault is it? It is the fault of one man, the Prime Minister – Mr Attlee – who could at any time in the last month by a nod or a gesture have dispersed the rumours that he intended to spring a snap election. He need not even have spoken himself; he could have told his party organ, the *Daily Mirror*. Instead of this, he has held everything in the balance and in suspense until the last moment, and has in fact arranged all kinds of discussion and all kinds of party bargaining while they made up their minds what it would pay them best to do. Any loss there has been, and it may be heavy, has been entirely due to Mr Attlee and to his failure to make up his mind what was the proper course to take. Some say he was waiting for Mr Bevin's return from America; but I did not know that the Labour Party had abolished the electric telegraph. Others will wonder whether he was not awaiting reports from the Party machine as to how the effects produced by devaluation, with its certain rise in the cost of living, had gone down in the constituencies. Perhaps they will come in now that undoubtedly, in the words of the Government communiqué, 'grave disturbance has been caused to business and to industry at this critical time'.

So far as the Conservative Party is concerned, looking at the matter on purely party grounds, we are quite indifferent as to the date of the election. The only thing we are concerned with, as party men, is that we should be ready whenever it comes, so that we are not taken by surprise and are ready for it in every way – we are pretty sure that Lord Woolton will look after that. But this is not to be judged as a matter of Party advantage or disadvantage. From a national point of view the sooner a new Parliament, the better. A continuance of the present uncertainty and friction can only be an impediment to national revival. I said two years ago there ought to be a new Parliament; had there been one, we should be much better off now in many ways. There is only one course open to the Socialists if they wish to redeem their record. They should do their duty in the intervening months by carrying out the financial reforms that are necessary, however unpopular they may be. But whatever the Government propose that is for the national good will be supported by the Opposition, whether it is popular or not. But above all it is the duty of the Government, if they care for the country, to call an immediate stop to all schemes of nationalization and to concentrate their energies upon the grievous task of saving us from bankruptcy. If they were to do this, great improvements in every direction might be possible. But if they merely continue to falter and show themselves, on this occasion, incapable of decision, and at the same time continue their vague attacks upon the foundations of our national prosperity they will only make things worse for all and, you may be sure, for themselves.

The Conservative position towards trade unions is well known. We support the principle of collective bargaining between recognized and responsible trade unions and employers, and we include in collective bargaining the right to strike. They have a great part to play in the life of the country and we think they should keep clear of Party politics. We hope that Conservative wage-earners in industry will join the trade unions and will take effective part in their work not as Party men, but as good trade unionists. I consider myself a trade unionist. When, in the beginning of 1945 there was a great national meeting of the trade union leaders at which I was to be presented by Lord Citrine himself with my trade union ticket, my public duty forced me to go to Yalta, to the talks there, and I am not quite sure when the engagement is postponed to.

I am told about 32 per cent of the trade unionists are Conservatives; the more the better. If we should become responsible for the conduct of affairs it will be our aim, as I said at Wolverhampton,[1] to maintain the closest contact with the trusted and able trade union leaders and to discuss with them all means of improving continually working conditions, and to further those principles of co-operation and profit-sharing which are set out at length in our short book, *The Right Road for Britain*. But we do not wish to compromise their position with their members by trying to make them become the agent of Government-owned monopolies – partisans of any particular political group. I hope trade union leaders will realize that as nationalization proceeds, they lose their position of bargaining on behalf of their members with private employers. I trust they will consider this. In the nationalized industries the trade union leaders, for many of whom I have much respect, are being more and more drawn into the position of being on the side of the State employer, instead of facing a much more flexible private owner while the State stands aside ready to conciliate and mitigate the process of collective bargaining.

---

[1] Speech of 23 July, reproduced above (pp. 1456–61).

Now I am pretty sure in the near future the Conservative Party will become responsible for the government of this country. We were 10,000,000 in the last election; it is more likely to be between 12,000,000 and 14,000,000 in the forthcoming election. We have every intention, if we have to accept responsibility of government, of exercising those responsibilities in no class or party spirit and to do the best for all. In order to do that it will be necessary for the great trade union bodies to play their part in the Councils of State and take their part in bringing forward improvement in new industries and bringing prosperity to our industrial life.

The British nation is one all the world over. No one party has the right to use insulting terms about the other. Like a great family we go forward to more glorious service to our fellow men.

Randolph S. Churchill to Winston S. Churchill
(*Churchill papers, 2/85*)

13 October 1949

My dearest Papa,

I do not know if it is too late to make a suggestion about your speech for tomorrow night. It arises from my having just re-read all your speeches of the last two years. All of those delivered at Party meetings are powerful stuff, but they suffer by comparison with those made in the House of Commons and still more with those made on international occasions. They will not live so long and they do not seem to have affected the course of events very much even at the time. This, of course, is to a certain extent inevitable; but I think the reason for the contrast is very plain, namely, that they were 'party' speeches.

The speeches in which you have most influenced public opinion and the course of events have been those in which you have appeared as the leader not only of Britain but of the civilized world. I fully see that you cannot make a speech of quite the same character as Fulton or Zurich, but I am sure that the nearer you can approach it the more effective electioneering it will be. This suggestion applies not so much to the actual arguments you use as to the mood and frame of the speech.

If you could speak tomorrow night as if you were addressing an international gathering on 'The condition and prospects of Britain in the World', I am sure you would have a success which would rally not only the whole Conservative Party but millions of peoples beyond its bounds.

I trust you will not think it impertinent of me to make this suggestion but I do it as perhaps the closest student and most ardent fan of your magnificent oratorical powers.

Winston S. Churchill: speech
('*Winston S. Churchill, His Complete Speeches*', volume 7, pages 7860–71)

14 October 1949   Empress Hall, Earls Court

CONSERVATIVE ANNUAL CONFERENCE

We have all been kept on tenterhooks about whether there would be a General Election before Christmas and about when we should be graciously told. The Prime Minister spoke yesterday about the grave disturbance he had caused to trade and industry by his inability to decide. That is quite true.

All over the country, in every form of productive and business activity, people have been kept in needless uncertainty, waiting about from day to day. At the very moment when we should all be driving full steam ahead, we all had to wait until the Cabinet could agree among themselves what would pay their Party best. Now at last they have made up their minds.

What part have we in all these twittering calculations? How glad we are that we have nothing to do with them at all. We are indifferent as to when the election comes. Whenever it comes we are ready. On Party grounds alone we can certainly afford to wait. But on natural grounds, a very grave, practical question arises. Can Britain, in the pass to which she has been led, or has been brought, afford to spend three or four, or five months' manoeuvring about Party tactics and electioneering, with a Parliament which is not only dead but decomposing, with divisions growing ever deeper and passions rising ever higher in the bosom of our hard-pressed people by whose actions in this crisis the fortunes of our world-wide empire and of many other lands are affected?

I said two years ago that we ought to have a new Parliament in view of the unrepresentative character of the House of Commons resulting from the last election, the first for ten years, with many of our men abroad and so on. It is certain now that if we had had a new Parliament two years ago we should be in a very much better position in the world tonight than we are at this moment. All our reserves and resources would not have been used up. We should be a stronger, a richer, and it might well be a more united nation in the deepening crisis of our own and world affairs.

We have now before us a period of several months more Socialist rule, at the end of which an election must come. It would be in the public interest that Ministers should make up their minds and announce to the public at least the month in which they intend to appeal to the country; that would be in the public interest, and I have just put in a plea for that. If they do not do so, it is inevitable that all our affairs, especially our trade, will be hampered every week and every day by the unrest of an impending election, at which so much is at stake, and which may pounce upon us at some moment tactically selected by the Socialist Party. We have got to live through these months on the alert for any blow that may be struck; but what a way to treat the serious situation in this country! If the Socialists repeat in the New Year the uncertainty, which Mr Attlee told us yesterday had already done harm in this year, theirs will be the responsibility, and on them will fall the censure of the nation.

What then should be our attitude in the intervening period? We shall support the Government in all measures which we consider necessary to restore the national finances and economy, however unpopular they may be. We shall not grudge them any advantages which they may gain by doing their duty to the country. But we, too, are bound to discharge our duty as an Opposition and to labour ceaselessly to explain to the nation the evils that have been brought upon us and to convince the electors that these are only a foretaste of what full Socialism would bring upon the British people.

In Parliament, for instance, we have now to meet two of the most controversial measures – the mutilation of the Parliament Act and the crowning stroke at British trade recovery, the steel nationalization Bill; these are coming upon us – they are being thrust upon us. We shall make our most earnest protest and resistance against these acts of party spite and economic sabotage. They completely strip the Socialist Ministers of the slightest right to appeal for national unity. If these two Bills are driven through Parliament in this economic crisis, the gulf between the two parties will become wider and deeper than ever before. And here again the blame will fall on the heads of those who give this renewed provocation.

But let me say this. We are here a Party straining at the leash to drive from power the men who we think have done our country so much harm and robbed it in a large measure of the fruits of our hard-won victory. I know Conservatives will never allow our Party feelings and natural righteous desires to lead us into welcoming bad news or hoping that the misfortunes of our country will help our return to power. We are Party men, but we shall be all the stronger if in every action we show ourselves capable, even in this period of stress and provocation, of maintaining the division where there is a division – between national and Party interests. And it is in this way that we shall prove to our fellow countrymen that Conservative interests are identical with national interests, that we stand for the nation and its fortunes as a whole, and that if we fight as partisans it is only because we deserve and desire to serve not one class or one party but the whole of our dear island.

We are often asked what we should do ourselves if we had the power. Today the Conservative Party has neither the power nor the responsibility to decide the policy and shape the fortunes of the State. All the instruments of Government and much of the machinery of propaganda are in Socialist hands. At this moment we can only utter words, but the national safety requires deeds. It is not propaganda but action which is required and for action we must have both responsibility and power. The advantage and significance of deeds is that they bring consequences. A number of well-considered actions might each one of them be unpopular or even painful in itself, but if all were taken at the same moment as part of a general design might quite soon bring about a widespread improvement which would more than compensate for what we have had to endure or give up.

A programme of words can be pulled to pieces bit by bit without there being any compensating results to show in the general welfare of the State. That is why I have advised you consistently during these last four years not to commit yourselves to detailed rigid programmes, but to let the nation learn as it is learning from its own experience – the hard teaching of facts. That is what we have done. Two years ago at our Conference at Brighton I ventured to give the Government some advice. I said then:

> The wasteful and needless expenditure which we see on all sides must be reduced by several hundred million pounds a year, and this must, when saved, be immediately given in relief of taxation in such a way as to increase the incentives to diligence, to thrift, to ingenuity and profit-making.[1]

Well, I say the same tonight. Of course, the Socialists answer: 'Show us in detail what economies you intend.' But how could we do this without knowledge and without control of the great departments and machinery of State? Of course the Socialists only ask the question with the sole object of enabling their canvassers to go around from house to house appealing to individual and personal local self-interest of the narrowest kind. Now, two years too late, they have to start to cut expenditure themselves. It will be interesting to see what their plans are, but whatever they are we may already say that there is nothing they can do now which would not have been much better done two years ago, when they were advised to do it by us.

In our statement on Tory outlook and aspiration, which we have called *The Right Road for Britain*, we have set forth in much detail the mood and temper in which our half of the nation, and it may well be the better half – and it may well prove to be the larger half – approach the future. *The Right Road for Britain* shows where we want to go. It offers a broad, tolerant, progressive and hopeful prospect to the British people. I am very glad that this little book, for which Mr Butler deserves much credit, should already have gone into 2,000,000 British homes. It constitutes an overwhelming repudiation of the taunt that we are a class Party seeking to defend abuses or willing to tolerate the exploitation of the mass of the people by vested interests, by monopolies or by bygone ideas. Here then is the right road for Britain, that is the road we shall strive to tread.

But there is one thing which I want to make clear tonight above all else and that is the position of the Conservative Party whenever the election comes. We are not going to try to get into office by offering bribes and promises of immediate material benefits to our people. The Socialists did that in 1945. We offer no smooth or easy path to the British nation now fighting for its life

---

[1] Speech reproduced above (pp. 793–803).

almost as it did in the war. We do not know what will be the facts with which we shall be confronted should we be returned to power. Certainly they have gravely worsened in the last few months and we have found out much more about them only in the last few weeks. Nothing will induce me as your leader at this election to bid for office by competing with the Socialists in promises of Utopias around the corner or of easy escape from the hard facts by which we are surrounded. It would be far better for us to lose the election than to win it on false pretences.

All I will promise to the British electorate in your name and the only pledge that I will give on behalf of the Conservative Party is that if the Government of Britain is entrusted to us at this crisis in her fate we will do our best for all, without fear or favour, without class or party bias, without rancour or spite, but with the clear and faithful simplicity that we showed in the days of Dunkirk. We did not think then about party scores. We did not divide the men we rescued from the beaches into those we cared about and those for whom, to quote a Ministerial utterance, we did not care a tinker's curse. The rescuing ships that set out from Britain did not regard a large part of the wearied and hard-pressed army we were bringing back to safety, and as it proved in the end to victory – we did not regard them as 'lower than vermin'.

However the voting may go in this part or that, in this district or the other, in the town or the country, our sole aim will be to act for all our fellow countrymen and bring them out of the perils and privations by which they are now oppressed and surrounded. Above all we shall go forward without fear and with unconquerable hope that our ancient and mighty people which, as I believe and declare, saved the world in the early stages of the war, are not confronted with any problem they cannot solve, or with any difficulty or danger they cannot overcome.

The Socialists claim that they have cured unemployment and they seek to make this a prime issue. Devaluation is defended by Sir Stafford Cripps as a means of stopping unemployment and he makes the cruel charge against the Conservative Party and against me of all men, who am, after all, responsible for more anti-unemployment legislation than anyone alive, of seeking to use mass unemployment as a means of spurring on the efforts of those who are employed. Well, he is very touchy himself, this Chancellor of the Exchequer – nervous about his reputation for political integrity. He has given up all hope of having one for political consistency.

But let us see how this matter stands. In 1944 when I was Prime Minister of a National Government, resting upon a Conservative House of Commons with a majority over all Parties of 150, I set up a committee to inquire into the ways of preventing unemployment after the war. The principal members of the present Socialist Government and the principal members of the present Conservative Opposition were upon it; the chairman was Lord Woolton. This document gives a most fresh, strong and ingenious view of what should be done on all occasions when a world slump threatens to affect the daily life of our island. It is published and can be read – and should be read; it expresses our policy today. The foreword to their report begins:

> The Government accept as one of their primary aims and responsibilities the maintenance of a high and stable level of employment after the war.

It goes on:

> There will, however, be no problem of general unemployment in the years immediately after the end of the war in Europe. The total manpower available will be insufficient to satisfy the total demands for goods and services.

This was the joint declaration of the Socialist and Conservative Ministers and of Sir Archibald Sinclair representing the Liberals, all serving side by side in a national administration, and with no conceivable motive except to find and tell the truth. They foresaw with remarkable accuracy that fact that in the years immediately after the war there would be no problem of general unemployment and they all declared jointly that one of the primary aims and responsibilities of the Government was the maintenance of a high and stable level of employment. This historic document, for the preparation of which no one was more responsible than the chairman of the committee, Lord Woolton, was approved by the War Cabinet and was presented to Parliament in May 1944.

Now it is not hard to believe that men like Mr Attlee, Mr Bevin, Mr Herbert Morrison and Sir Stafford Cripps, can have the face to go about propagating the double falsehood, first, that it is they who have prevented unemployment after the war, and secondly, that their Conservative colleagues – now their opponents – would deliberately use mass unemployment as an economic weapon. Yet all these four high Ministers now holding power appear ready to spread the exact opposite of what they know to be the truth and what they are on record as having said they knew would be the truth – in order to gain votes in the hope of securing their return to office in the next few months. I hope these statements which I have read to you, and the names of those who approved them in all three Parties, I hope they will be placarded throughout the length and breadth of the country, in order that the Socialist charges about the Conservative attitude towards unemployment may be refuted and Socialist claims to have cured it with what they did in the last few years may be disproved out of their own mouths.

There is another legend which the Socialist leaders have invented and are spreading. It is that between the wars, unemployment was worse under Conservative Government than under Socialist Government. Why it was under the disastrous Socialist administration of 1931, which lasted from 1929–1931, that unemployment bounded upwards to the figure never before reached of nearly 3,000,000. The National Government, which succeeded the Socialists and was sustained by the enormous Conservative majority gained in 1931, grappled with the evil. At the beginning of 1939, before the outbreak, the number of unemployed was less than half the total recorded at the date the Socialists ended their lamentable term of office.

Here again these facts should be placed before the nation in every constituency and on every platform, not just to those who are here who have special duties and responsibilities for making sure the people know the truth. Those who have the special duties and responsibilities will make it their business to see that the people in the constituencies where they live are acquainted with the facts and are not swept away with the lie. It is part of the Communist–Socialist theory that the repetition of an untruth long enough makes it a truth. Let us be very careful not to be subjugated by such base methods.

When Mr Attlee and his present principal colleagues subscribed to and helped compose our joint statement that there would be no problem of general unemployment in the years immediately after the war, none of us knew of the generous American aid that was to be forthcoming in these four years. This up to date, I mean up to the end of the current Marshall Aid year, amounts to £1,750,000,000 sterling. All this vast sum of money which has been pouring into this island from the United States was a makeweight, which should have made employment still more secure. They are not all Wall Street millionaires in the United States; they are as hard-working people as are found anywhere in the world. But after we had had nearly three years of Socialist Government, Mr Herbert Morrison in fact confessed at Manchester in April 1948, that but for the American aid 'we should be faced with a million or two people on the dole'. Yet it is with these facts proving the case, staring them in the face, that the Socialist leaders whose names I have mentioned have the effrontery to try to dupe the people into believing that it is they and their policy which has prevented unemployment, and to spread the falsehood – I refrain from using any other word – that the Conservatives would have used unemployment as a means of spurring the exertions of labour. Now, I think this is some proof of the ill-treatment in public behaviour that we are receiving from the leading Socialist Ministers.

For what then, we are asked, will be the employment policy of a Conservative Government, if returned to power in the present crisis now everything has become or has been made much more difficult, and the years immediately after the war when the whole world wanted to buy all kinds of things – what they call a sellers' market – have come to an end. Our policy is exactly the same as we laid before the nation and laid before a Conservative House of Commons in 1944. Any Conservative Government would accept 'as one of their primary aims and responsibilities the maintenance of a high and stable level of employment'. Of course, I cannot tell what the future will bring forth. It is not now possible after four years of Socialist rule, to speak with the same confidence about the future as Conservative and Socialist Ministers were able together to do in 1944. But our purpose and intention remains unchanged. And the first of all conditions that will help us is a restoration of confidence and enterprise, impossible under Socialist Government.

One thing I will say now. We shall not rely upon the compulsory direction of labour in time of peace. The regulations which the Socialist Government reintroduced two years ago for the compulsory direction of labour, which in my opinion are an insult to the rights and liberties of the British people, will be abolished and the present insurance benefits will stand, as a powerful aid and help to every man and woman entitled to draw them.

The four years of this Government have been, from beginning to end, a rake's progress of unbridled expenditure. In these four years the Socialist Government have begged, borrowed – or exacted – and have spent £16,000,000,000 or nearly as much as was spent in the twenty years between the two wars. That is a fact which takes some thinking about. They have used up almost every national asset or reserve upon which they could lay their hands. They have taken 40 per cent of the national income for the purposes of government administration. Our taxation has been the highest in the world. It oppresses every transaction of daily life. Besides the £1,750,000,000 from the United States, they have had over £300,000,000 advanced by Canada, and £50,000,000 of gifts from the Dominions. They have eaten up our Argentine Railways, and many other foreign investments, and £350,000,000, or more than half our gold and hard currency reserves, the last reserves, our sacred treasure, have all gone down the drain. Whilst all this riot of spending has been going on, the spendthrifts themselves have exhorted us to save more, to work harder, and to endure austerities. Great efforts have been made by the British people and their loyalty, but at the end all we have is devaluation – that is all we have come to at the end of all these years and all these efforts. The £ sterling, which Lord Woolton well called 'Our financial Union Jack', has been hauled down to half-mast, or almost. It is not only our money which has been devaluated. Our prestige and reputation abroad have been devaluated. What is thought about us in Germany? I am going to quote you what the Socialists say themselves about that:

> There is no doubt it is said that whereas in 1945–46 British prestige in Germany was higher than that of the Americans and French, the position is now reversed.

Whose words do you think I am quoting? These are the words of two of the leading intellectuals of the Socialist Party, Sir Richard Acland and Mr Richard Crossman, who have been travelling in Germany this year, and this is what they wrote to *The Times* newspaper. What is the position in France? Anyone can see what must be the effect in France of Sir Stafford Cripps' devaluation, giving them hardly a moment to prepare, as the result of which an exceptionally stable Government has been overthrown.

But I could multiply these examples of our loss of prestige, influence and esteem we had won abroad by our conduct in the war, which never stood so high as when the Socialists rollicked into power in 1945. But there is one bit of devaluation which is a comfort. The false theories of Socialism and the mischievous policy of nationalizing our industries have been, like those industries themselves, devaluated too.

And, when they, our opponents, ask us will the Conservatives cut the social services or the food subsidies, why they have already been cut by the Socialist Government and are being cut more every day. Every increase in the cost of living is a direct reduction in the social services. Every step to devaluate the money we spend and every increase in the cost of living is a slashing cut to the social services of all kinds. Now we are to have more – that is the work which lies immediately before us – how much more our people will find out in the months that lie ahead.

I said at Wolverhampton[1] that nationalization had already been exposed as a failure. Every major industry which the Socialists have nationalized without exception has passed from the profit-earning or self-supporting side of our national balance sheet to the loss-making or debit side. The Government speakers denied this. The Economic Secretary to the Treasury, Mr Jay, said that the Bank of England and the Cables and Wireless Company were not making losses. Who has ever suggested that the Bank of England and Cables and Wireless Company were major British industries. I was of course speaking about the great branches of our industrial life – coal, railways, road transport, gas and electricity and, on a smaller scale, air transport. The Prime Minister, Mr Attlee, himself has challenged me on this. As usual, I cannot feel he has been right. We must not look only at the balance-sheets presented by the uneasy boards of officials and Party nominees who now manage these industries. It is easy when you have a State monopoly and can charge the public what you like and what you dare to show a paper profit. The Coal Board boast that they have made the enormous profit of nearly £2,000,000 last year, but Mr Attlee must take into consideration the great cost to the public. Since coal has been nationalized the price has gone up by 6s 6d a ton. On an annual output of about 200,000,000 tons that has meant nearly £100,000,000 more has been paid by the consumer directly or indirectly, and forms a definite part of that higher cost of living and manufacture expressed in a devaluated currency.

I must, however, say this, that the great part of the increase has gone in the higher wages of the coal miners, and I have always drawn a distinction between the work of men underground and those who work in the light of the sun. There is no question of our going back on that. What we hope is that a proportionate increase of production will follow from this heavy addition to the public burden.

[1] Speech of 23 July, reproduced above (pp. 1456–61).

About the railways, I said the paper deficit might be over £20,000,000. We now know the figures. It is £13,000,000. Not £20,000,000, only £13,000,000 deficit. What a triumph! Something to celebrate! But this takes no account of what the report of the Transport Commission calls 'that marked deterioration in 1949'; nor of the fact that fares were raised very substantially immediately before the nationalization began. I cannot refer to the railways without paying my tribute to the restraint of that splendid body of railway workers who, in spite of the disappointments and disillusionments they have sustained by nationalization, which they have been urged to ask for year after year, have nevertheless shown their earnest desire not to add to our many difficulties at this time.

Then there are gas and electricity about which no financial statement has yet been presented. Prices have, however, been heavily marked up against the housewife and the general consumer, and they only have to compare their electricity bills for this last Easter with those of the year before to see what happens when an industry of this kind is run from Whitehall. The State-run airlines have now declared, with an air of pride and glee, that they have only lost £9,000,000 this year, compared with £11,000,000 last year. Here is another triumph for the Socialist nationalizers to parade. Despite Mr Attlee, I repeat my carefully measured assertion that all major nationalized industries have ceased to be assets to the public, and have become instead burdens upon it, and that the losses they make will be paid for either by the taxpayer, through the Exchequer, or by the consumer in higher prices or by both. You are both.

We are asked what a Conservative Government would do with these nationalized industries. It is physically impossible to undo much that has been done. You cannot thrust the coal mines and the railways back upon the private owners. They would not take them. All that can be done in these two basic services is to decentralize and cut down the enormously swollen costs of management. We have already stated in detail in *The Right Road for Britain* what a Conservative Government will do for road transport. We are now threatened, besides the nationalization of steel, with that of insurance, sugar and cement. All of these thriving industries are to be disturbed, mauled and finally chilled and largely paralysed by the clumsy and costly grip of State bureaucracy, infected by Party patronage and manipulation.

Ministers call, and they are going to call, for further sacrifices from all classes. Why do they not set the example themselves? Why do they not sacrifice to the general welfare some of these wrong-headed partisan indulgences of Socialist theory, and concentrate their efforts upon their plain duty to save our country from approaching bankruptcy? They talk of economy. Why do not they try to save themselves? Perhaps they are to make some suggestions on that subject; at any rate we shall have some few suggestions of our own. There is no doubt what the policy of the Conservative Party will be. It will be to put a full-stop – here and now – to all further nationalization. This, of course, will be one of the major issues on which the electors will have to pronounce.

Now I turn to another aspect of the same problem and must ask your indulgence if I unfold these matters to you as this is an occasion of great importance. The question is asked: 'Are Conservatives opposed to planning?' There is nothing new in planning. Every Government, ancient or modern, must look ahead and plan. Did not Joseph advise Pharaoh to build granaries and fill them for the lean years when the Nile waters failed? He followed the opposite course to the present Government, which is to waste the favourable period of getting the country on to its feet and meanwhile squander all the accumulated resources. But of course we are in favour of planning. But planning what for?

We hold that in these modern times planning, with all the resources of science at its disposal, should aim at giving the individual citizen as many choices as possible of what to do in all the ups and downs of daily life. The more a man's choice is free, the more likely it is to be wise and fruitful, not only to the chooser but to the community in which he dwells. Now there is an important distinction between the quality and kind of planning. This kind of planning differs fundamentally from the collectivist theme of grinding them all up in a vast State mill which must certainly destroy in the process the freedom and independence which are the foundation of our way of life and the famous characteristic of our race.

The Socialist policy and aim is to flatten out all those differentials – to use an important trade union expression – which result from the efforts and qualities of individuals and at all costs to establish a dead level above which no one but Socialist lackeys and politicians shall be allowed to rise. Of course they can only bring this about gradually, but that is the goal they seek, and that is the only goal that the political philosophy can reach.

I am glad to see that responsible trade union leaders, Socialists though they may call themselves, who are in daily contact with the realities of industry and labour, do not hesitate to resist this ironing-out process. That process would be fatal to all those forces which make for more abundant and progressive production, and would deny to every man that right to make the best of himself and his abilities for the benefit not only of his family but of his fellow countrymen, within the limits set by the old broad and well-known laws upon which our way of life in this island has been built.

We should certainly plan for the future. And let me tell you what we should plan first of all. We should plan first of all how to keep alive in the next ten years 50,000,000 of people in Britain. In my life-time our population has nearly doubled. Under cheap imported food given us in return for the sale of our manufactures, we brought nearly 25,000,000 more people into being. Without that we should not have been a great power. Without that we might not have turned the balance in the world struggle against tyranny when we were all alone. But now we cannot be sure that foreign countries will wish to buy our manufactures to the same extent, nor as in Victorian times that the food they have to sell us will be cheap. There is no possibility of emigrating such great numbers of our population in the next ten years or in the next twenty. The first thing we must do to establish our national independence is to increase our production of home-grown food.

In *The Right Road for Britain* we have set out clearly how we propose to set about this task. I wish to repeat this evening our cardinal principle, that first place in the home market must be reserved for the home farmer. Next to him must come the Empire producer.

If long-term plans for the production of food and raw materials are made now in our Empire and Commonwealth of Nations there is no reason why our main supplies should not, after a period of years, flow in steadily from these widespread, trusty sources under the British flag.

We can, I am sure, depend upon our farming community to do all that lies in their power to increase production if the Government provides them with the necessary means. They need clear guarantees on which they can rely. In particular the horticulturists who have suffered so much recently from destructive foreign imports of a temporary and freak kind must in future receive the fair treatment they deserve. The livestock population of the country can be greatly increased. To do this we shall provide the farmers with the feeding-stuffs which the Socialist Government have so lamentably failed to procure. We shall extend the Hill Farming Act to provide for the reclamation of marginal land.

No less urgent is the need for improvement in the conditions of life in our countryside. The Socialists have delayed or obstructed the reconditioning of rural houses and the extension of rural water supplies. We shall see that proper priority is given to these and other essential rural requirements. The machinery of the County Agricultural Committees must be overhauled. The recent report of the Select Committee on Estimates shows that losses on the trading services operated by these committees alone have amounted to over £17,000,000. There is a great need for team-work and leadership in the countryside and an example could well be set at the top, by more team-work between the Ministries of Food and Agriculture. But in all matters of good housekeeping the Socialists have proved themselves an effective substitute for some of the evils we overcame in the war. I expect there is many a housewife who looks back to those hard days with reflection, as she only wishes old Woolton had it in his hands again. I was, of course, only quoting the housewife, because as a matter of fact he is quite a young fellow compared to me. But going back from food and agriculture to general topics, freedom of choice and variety of method are also the main solutions of the urgent problem of housing our people. In this Mr Bevan has been his own and our worst enemy. Our Conservative policy is to give greater freedom to the private builder. We shall sweep away the hindrances and restrictions that at present impede private enterprise in creating the vast number of dwellings needed, which hindrances have kept the building of houses in these years of frustration so much below the level quite naturally and normally maintained in the days of Mr Chamberlain's Conservative Government before the war.

Mr Bevan insists that for every one house built for sale four must be built to be let by the local authorities at rents subsidized out of the pockets of taxpayers and ratepayers. There is still a great need for council houses, but surely it is nonsense that four out of every five families who are going into new houses should be subsidized by their fellow citizens. Building costs are now so high that the rents of some council houses, despite the subsidy, are too high for those to whom they are offered and many of the poorest families have to stay where they are, mocked by the fact that, through their rates and taxes, they provide subsidies for others who are richer. Planning is indeed needed in our housing sphere, but it is planning to remove the burdens and restrictions that cramp and hobble the building industry today.

And I sum up the picture at home, control, devaluate and flatten out. That is the message of the Socialist Government and to it we oppose our Conservative policy. Liberate the genius and initiative of our race. Revive and stabilize the value of the money on which wages, pensions and social services are based. Build with enterprise and courage the forward and everchanging structure of our industrial and agricultural life without which this island cannot live, or its population be sustained. There is the contrast between the two policies which lie before you.

It is a relief to turn from the hard and, I fear, darkening scene at home to the inspiring spheres into which this conference soared yesterday. The Empire: that is the word we use, nor are we ashamed of the word 'British'. The British Empire: its unity, its development, and its consolidated strength. I hope all Conservatives will call it the British Empire and Commonwealth of Nations, and let other Parties imitate us as they learn. But there is our first thought and dream and aim. Then there is our fraternal association with the United States in what is called the English-speaking world. And thirdly, there is this grand design of a free and United Europe in which we are resolved to play our part. I rejoice at the wisdom of this conference which did not allow itself to be led astray by arguments that these were divergent or contradictory objectives, and declared almost unanimously in favour of pursuing them all at once. As I see it there are these three circles in each of which we have a vital share. And these may all be linked together by Britain, if we in this island prove ourselves worthy of it.

Great progress is being made in all these directions, and we shall move forward earnestly and resolutely upon all of them. The unity of the Empire is no longer a Party question. Friendship with the United States grows in spite of the abuse of the Communist Party and their fellow travellers in the House of Commons. The policy of United Europe, out of which Marshall

1542   October 1949

Aid originated, has made steady headway in spite of jealousies and prejudices in high Socialist quarters.

All is moving forward. When we are asked: 'What is your policy abroad and overseas?' we can answer: 'It has already been adopted, largely upon our initiative, impulsion and guidance.' We shall carry it forward with all our might and main. Yes, and at home as well as throughout the world, we shall strive to carry forward the great social evolution which has covered the lifetime of the oldest of us here, namely the bringing forward of ever larger numbers of mankind to an ever more bountiful table of moral and material rewards. To this process of unceasing, untiring expansion and advance, the Conservative Party devotes itself and, linking as we do the past with the present, we shall gain for all the mastery of the future.

Lieutenant-General Sir Henry Pownall to Winston S. Churchill
(Churchill papers, 4/218)[1]

16 October 1949

Mr Churchill,

Mr Davin,[2] the NZ war Historian, has returned the two Crete chapters with a few comments. He had none overall on 'Crete the Advent'. On 'Crete the Battle' there are half a dozen small ones of operational details.

I will arrange with Kelly for these to be inserted, with one or two of my own, on your Master Copy.

I asked Davin particularly to overhaul the figures of evacuation and casualties. He says that the former correspond with his own. As to casualties, no really firm official figures exist and he cannot better those that appear in his text.

Lord Cherwell to Winston S. Churchill
(Churchill papers, 2/36)

17 October 1949   Oxford

My dear Winston,

I am afraid this is a very inadequate draft, but it seemed difficult to say anything quantitative which was very relevant concerning the broad figures which

[1] This letter was handwritten.
[2] Daniel Marcus Davin, 1913–90. Born in Invercargill, New Zealand. Educated at University of Otago and Balliol College, Oxford. Joined British Army during WWII. 2nd Lt, 1940. Wounded in action in Crete; evacuated to Egypt, where he became an intelligence officer. Left military service at the end of the war, with rank of Major. Worked at Oxford University Press as an academic publisher. Published *Crete* in the New Zealand official war history series, as well as many novels, short stories, and poems.

they have given us. I do not know whether you want to send it off before our meeting on Thursday, but I am forwarding it in case it may be of use.

As I told you, I propose to ask Attlee to give me an opportunity to talk over with him our own atomic energy project. Unless something is done quickly there is a serious risk of the staff disintegrating and our bargaining power with the United States vanishing.

I trust you will have a pleasant time at Bristol and remain,

as ever,
Yours

In view of the threat of the Russian Air Force, now much accentuated by their early achievement of the atomic bomb, it does seem to me most unfortunate that so many of our jet-aircraft should have been sent abroad. It seems to me very unsatisfactory that our Fighter Command Squadrons should only be fully equipped by the end of 1951 and the auxiliary squadrons six months later. Surely they should be our prime consideration. It is true that there may be some financial advantage in selling 100 of these invaluable aircraft to the Argentine, but they can have no strategic use unless it be against the United States. Having regard to the enormous wastage which occurs in wartime, it would certainly have seemed better to keep them to add to our meagre reserves at this critical period.

Jo Sturdee to Winston S. Churchill
(Churchill papers, 4/52)

17 October 1949

The Press are ringing through to ask for your comments on parts of a statement issued this evening by King Leopold. What he says contradicts what you and M Reynaud have already made public, and makes you both appear not to be telling the truth. The following are extracts from King Leopold's statement –

1. 'Great Britain's decision in 1940 to abandon the fight and to evacuate the British Army from Dunkirk was taken without the slightest knowledge of the Belgian Command.'

2. 'The Belgians advised the British and French of the possibility of capitulation on May 20, eight days before the actual surrender. The French were informed that the Front was giving way. An emissary was sent, on the evening of May 27, to the Germans to ask the terms for Belgium of a "Cease Fire". The French and British Missions had been duly warned of this. Then the King gave instructions for Belgium to lay down arms on May 28 at 4 p.m. On May 27, the day before the capitulation, Mr Churchill

sent a message with his officers to the Belgians to tell King Leopold personally, "We are asking them to sacrifice themselves." But this message was never delivered in the confusion.'

Winston S. Churchill: speech
('Winston S. Churchill, His Complete Speeches', volume 7, pages 7871–2)

19 October 1949   Bristol University

CHANCELLOR'S ADDRESS

... I recall the last occasion on which I conferred an honorary degree upon an Ambassador of the United States. That honour was Mr Winant's, on a day in 1941 when the roof timbers were smouldering and academic robes were worn by many over the drenched clothing in which they had been fighting fires.

Many distinguished men are sent from the United States. In Mr Lewis Douglas (United States Ambassador) we have one who was a great worker in the business of war, and is a great friend of our country and of the unity and brotherhood of the English-speaking world. Every opportunity is welcome to show our gratitude and appreciation to the great country which he represents so ably at the Court of St James'. Of all the countries that have risen to world power none has ever shown itself so devoid of selfish ambition, or so animated by whole-hearted resolve to further the great causes of mankind, as the United States. I am glad to hear from Sir Philip Morris,[1] the Vice-Chancellor, that the numbers in the university have more than doubled since before the war and that quality has been maintained. In the United States university graduates are numbered by millions. If we are to survive we must make sure that an ever increasing number of men and women go into the world with the advantages of a university education and with the chance to have the broad and tolerant outlook that could be gained at our universities and academic institutions. We see ever larger numbers invited to an ever more bountiful table, laden with not only material comforts and indulgences. I know that Bristol University will not forget the study of the humanities, without which man would not be worthy of the weapons placed in his hands or of the secrets he has wrested.

In the study of history and philosophy will be found the means to give men and women the knowledge and wisdom of the ancients and a clear idea what their work and struggle here before are for.

---

[1] Sir Philip Morris, 1901–79. Educated at Trinity College, Oxford, 1923. Teachers' Diploma, London University, 1924. Director, Kent Education Committee, 1938–43. Director-General, Army Education, 1944–6. Vice-Chancellor, Bristol University, 1946–66. Vice-Chairman, BBC, 1954–60. Member, Governing Board, National Institute for Research in Nuclear Science, 1957–8. Honorary Fellow, Bristol University, 1966. Wrote *Christianity and the World of Today* (1961).

The University must not fail to inculcate clear-cut thought about the themes of government and society. All kinds of formulas are mouthed and labels are bandied about. Let there be clear investigation and thought on these subjects, and let our young men and women go forth to face the problems of the young generation, having in their mind, I will not say rigid opinions, but instructed and informed light to play on their future paths.

It is perhaps a somewhat depressing period, following as it does a great victory. During the war one put up with much to have the gleam and sunrise of victory; but when it came one was exhausted by all one had done, and the sunshine does not seem so genial or refreshing as one had hoped. Victory is less pleasing when possessed, though without it one does not have the chance to turn further pages of history.

We have seen the failure of the great world instrument – for the present – which we hoped to create to obviate all danger of war and enable mankind to move steadily and safely forward upon his path. We find ourselves in an armed and divided world. We hoped to get rid of religious wars, dynastic wars, mere territorially aggressive wars, and nationalistic wars. We hoped we had grown out of them. Now there comes along the ideological wars which gather together a great many of those violent tendencies which we hoped the world instrument would be able to surmount.

The great desire and the need of harassed humanity is to have a period of repose, of rest and peace in which culture and arts might flourish, wealth and prosperity be regained, ruins be rebuilt, and science, which had caused them, be turned to the enrichment of the multitudes of every country of the globe.

We still hope and pray that the period of rest and repose may not be denied us. Two terrible wars and the ideological quarrel which has rent the world in twain are too much to thrust upon a generation or two of struggling human beings. I earnestly hope we may be spared further calamities and may be permitted to rebuild our world and create our life in such a manner that all that has been discovered will not be thrown aside but enriched by its union with all that science and progress have given us.

Field Marshal Lord Montgomery to Winston S. Churchill
(Churchill papers, 9/27)[1]

20 October 1949

Dear Mr Churchill

I enclose herewith a copy of my speech tomorrow night, Friday, at the Alamein reunion.

We shall expect you and Mrs Churchill at the Empress Hall at 7 p.m.

---

[1] This letter was handwritten.

Your speech will follow mine. I hope you will take up my theme and speak very plainly about the situation in which we find ourselves today: after nearly 5 years of peace. Many of the nations that were defeated by the Germans in 1940, or that we ourselves defeated later on, are better off than we are. The situation in Britain today is very similar to the situation in the Eighth Army when I took over command in August 1942: Bad leadership, no plan, low morale.

You will get a great reception.

Bernard Baruch to Winston S. Churchill
(Churchill papers, 2/210)

20 October 1949   New York

Dear Winston

Clare Luce has gone to Rome and on her way back will stop off at London. She will be at Claridge's from November 15th to 20th. You might want to see her.

I received a telegram from Sarah telling me of her marriage and how happy she is and how pleased the family is. I telegraphed her and told her to bring the young man in so I could give them both my blessing. I will, if they want me to, give them some kind of party or reception.

I see that the Labor Party has postponed the election. Unless something, which I cannot yet see, occurs, I think they will probably be worse off than they are now. We are having a few rows of our own over here.

By the time this reaches you, you will have heard the testimony of practically all our Chiefs of Staff, including Marshall, and men like Hoover and others.

I presume you have read that Jimmie Byrnes will probably run for governor of South Carolina.

I sent W. S. Robinson his colors and he cabled that he had won the big race and his horse ran to the right.

Thank you for Hansard. I read the debate with much interest.

Winston S. Churchill: speech
(Churchill papers, 9/27)

21 October 1949   Empress Hall, Earls Court

FOURTH ALAMEIN REUNION

I am glad to come to the fourth, as I came to the first, Reunion of the Eighth Army to celebrate the victory of El Alamein. How right you are to keep together and to preserve that spirit of devotion to duty, of self-sacrifice and daring and of comradeship, that only burns the brighter for all the storms that blow. The toils and trials of war are hard and cruel, but when they are crowned with victory veterans who have shared them together have a common inheritance of brotherhood and of memories which is a treasure to them when they meet in after-years.

By a blessed dispensation, human beings forget physical pain much more quickly than they do their joyous emotions and experiences. A merciful Providence passes the sponge of oblivion across much that is suffered and enables us to cherish the great moments of life and honour which come to us in our march through life. Such meetings as these not only give expression to the deep feelings of those who fought and won, they also are a salute to the memory of those who fell. I hope you will long continue to preserve the fame and the spirit of the Eighth Army.

The story of the Eighth Army does not begin with Alamein. We must not forget the long months of fierce fighting with many surprising turns of fortune which were its record, and that of the Desert Army before it, or that Rommel's advance was brought to a standstill by General Auchinleck before the changes in command were made. When I arrived in Cairo at the beginning of August 1942, I found a grave and critical, but by no means hopeless, situation. I found also a British and Imperial Army that did not know why it had been forced to retreat 400 miles with a loss of 80,000 men. It was an Army in no wise daunted, but an Army bewildered and enraged. My visit came at the same time as the arrival of powerful reinforcements, including the very latest weapons and tanks which we had set in motion around the Cape a good many months before.

As the result of the decisions for which I am proud to be responsible, General Alexander became Commander-in-Chief in the Middle East, with a definite directive to concentrate all his efforts against Rommel, and, after the death of General Gort, who was killed the next day, the illustrious Field-Marshal, who has just spoken to us so movingly, took the command of the Eighth Army into his strong and skilful hands. The appointment of these two great officers, whose names, at the time, were little known outside professional circles, will be acclaimed by history. Neither of these men was ever defeated or long checked in the intense and bloody fighting in so many different lands in the thirty-three months which still lay between us and our goal. 'Alex' and 'Monty' are now household words. They are beloved by the peoples of the Empire as they were by their soldiers, and their fame will long be cherished by their fellow-countrymen and honoured by the free nations of the world.

And it is to Monty (as he has long allowed me to call him), that we pay our tribute tonight. The advance of the Eighth Army under his command will ever be a glittering episode in the martial annals of Britain, and not only of Britain, but of the mighty array of Empire and Commonwealth which gathered around our island in the days of its mortal peril and found its expression in all the desert battles.

Field-Marshal Montgomery is one of the greatest living masters of the art of war. It has been my fortune and great pleasure often to be with him at important moments in the long march from Alamein to the Rhine. He has always shown himself equal, and more than equal, to the largest operation, and the true and comprehending leader of every unit of the mighty armies in his grip. The Battle of Alamein ranks among the most famous victories in British history. It was the turning-point in our military fortunes during the World War.

Up till then my own experience had been none too agreeable. I had had to face nearly three years of unbroken defeat and disappointment on land. Indeed, it was astonishing that Parliament and the nation put up with me for so long. (They made up for it afterwards.) But now, at Alamein, was the turning of the tide for which we had so carefully prepared in secret. Alamein was the herald of the great Anglo-American invasion of North-West Africa and, from that time forth, although there were ups and downs, we were borne forward irresistibly to complete and final victory. Up till Alamein we survived. After Alamein we conquered.

I do not wonder that those who played a personal part in this ever-famous event rejoice together when they look back upon it; or that, as the Field-Marshal has told us, they should find in it a source of further inspiration to help our dear country to their utmost strength and at every moment in their lives.

Monty has reminded us of all that Britons have in common and how much more precious is this heritage than the differences which are so prominent today. He will excuse me if I say that, from whatever angle you measure them, they are not small – they are in some respects fundamental. It is impossible that public opinion should not remain deeply divided at a time when a General Election is approaching. It is only in countries where tyrants rule and from which freedom is banished that a sham uniformity is imposed and that strong and sharp differences are not expressed. If they were not, the voting would be a mere pretence, as in Soviet Russia and other Communist satellite countries. My own hope is that this period of unavoidable Party strife will be as short as possible. For it is certainly a great and growing hindrance to our national welfare, and a danger to the preservation of all we have to defend in common. Nothing can be more harmful to national unity than a prolonged period of electioneering.

There is one thing I will tell you tonight which I feel is most appropriate to this gathering of men and women of all Parties. You have seen discussions reported in the newspapers which show that there is in all Parties a strong movement for the abolition of national service. No doubt, from many points of view, that would be a popular policy. But it is my conviction that to make such a change at this time would be deeply injurious to the strength of Britain and would reduce our chances of maintaining what we all desire – peace of the world.

The Field-Marshal holds a position of far-reaching responsibility in Western Europe, and I am sure that no one will agree more when I say that for Britain to abandon the principle of national service at this present anxious time would strike a deadly blow at the great defence combination which has come into being under the Atlantic Pact, and is ever growing stronger – a combination not only of Britain and her Empire and Commonwealth, but of the free nations of Western Europe and of our great Ally across the Atlantic Ocean.

I have therefore assured the Prime Minister, in the name of the Party which I lead, that we shall give His Majesty's Government full support in maintaining national service and, so far as it is in our power, will not allow it to be made a partisan election issue. I feel sure this step will win the approval of the men who fought and conquered in the Battle of Alamein.

Winston S. Churchill to L. S. Amery
(Churchill papers, 2/160)

25 October 1949

My dear Leo,

Thank you so much for your letter of October 17. I am glad you thought the Conference was a success.

Alas, much as I should like to be able to speak to the Empire Industries Association on February 28 as you suggest, I feel that my commitments will be so numerous by then that I ought not to add to them. I am sure you will understand.

PS. I have suggested December 8 for our Harrow Song reunion. Can I give you a lift, if they agree.

Sir Norman Brook to Clement Attlee
(Premier papers, 8/1321)

26 October 1949

In Volume III of his book, which covers 1941, Mr Churchill has to describe the difficulties which arose with the Australian Government in that year – first over the withdrawal of the Australian forces from Tobruk and later over their fears of a Japanese invasion. In the first drafts of this Volume he expressed himself somewhat trenchantly, and included some rather rancorous telegrams, on these matters. But in view of representations by me and others he has now toned down these references considerably, and in the final version I think it is fair to say that he deals with these difficult episodes with moderation and restraint. The relevant passages are in Chapter II, pages 10 to 15, and Chapter XV page 4. I attach the text of Chapter II and the relevant extract from Chapter XV.

I submit that, as these passages now stand, the United Kingdom Government need raise no objection to them. We have still, however, to verify that the Australian Government have no objection to the publication of the telegrams which Mr Churchill wishes to reproduce. (We have not undertaken to consult them on Mr Churchill's text, which is his responsibility, and I should think it better not to do so.) As you know, we deliberately refrained from referring to them earlier, as we hoped that Mr Churchill would delete (as he has in fact done) some of the messages which he had included in his earlier drafts, and it seemed unwise to provoke difficulties about telegrams which he might not in the end desire to reproduce. This delay meant, however, that there would be little time for consultation on the final draft; and I therefore sent out to our High Commissioner in Canberra by air mail in the summer numbered copies of all the messages which Mr Churchill <u>might</u> wish to publish, so that we should be able to carry out the consultation, when the time came, by telegram. This accounts for the form of the attached message[1] which, I suggest, should now be sent to our High Commissioner.[2]

Winston S. Churchill: speech
('Winston S. Churchill, His Complete Speeches', volume 7, page 7875)

26 October 1949   Aldersbrook, Wanstead

LABOUR'S DISASTROUS RULE

... Britain's position today is the direct result of four and half years of gross misgovernment. The Socialist Party has not failed to make extreme claims upon the country's confidence. They have spread throughout the land two gross and palpable falsehoods. The first is that before they got a majority Britain was a backward, miserable country to live in, and secondly, that they are the authors and originators of social reform.

All they have done in their cramping and disastrous rule is to carry out with partisan distortion a policy devised by a National Government sustained by a Conservative House of Commons. I believe our recovery would have been very much less hampered if it had not been for the vast network of regulations, prescriptions, and incompetent planning by Whitehall officials which has proved to be such a disastrously costly experiment.

---

[1] Attlee responded: 'Could you not suggest to Mr Churchill the substitution of "apprehension" for "fear" [. . .] fear suggests cold fear.'

[2] Edward John Williams, 1890–1963. Known as 'Ted'. Agent, Garw District, South Wales Miners' Federation, 1919–31. MP (Lab.) for Ogmore, 1931–46. High Commissioner to Australia, 1946–52.

The Conservative Party is not a class party. We will try to act for all with malice to none and try our utmost, should we be given power, to find the best way out of the very difficult situation.

Winston S. Churchill: speech
(Hansard)

27 October 1949   House of Commons

THE ECONOMIC SITUATION

[...]

Parties differ on a great many matters of principle. I was brought up to believe that taxation was a bad thing but the consuming power of the people was a good thing. The Chancellor of the Exchequer please note – the consuming power of the people is a good thing. Many of his predecessors have opened their Budgets with the statement, 'The consuming power of the people is well maintained,' but he adopts a different tone. I was brought up to believe that trade should be regulated mainly by the laws of supply and demand and that, apart from basic necessaries in great emergencies, the price mechanism should adjust and correct undue spending at home, as it does, apart from gifts and subsidies, control spending abroad.

I was also taught that it was one of the first duties of Government to promote that confidence on which credit and thrift, and especially foreign credit, can alone stand and grow. I was taught to believe that those processes, working freely within the limits of well-known laws for correcting monopoly, exploitation and other measures in restraint of trade, as the old phrase had it – that those principles would produce a lively and continuous improvement in prosperity. I still hold to those general principles.

However, between the terrible wars which have rent the world, we were subjected to violent convulsions in world trade. To guard against their coming upon us again when the Second World War was at an end the National Government – my colleagues, in large numbers, are on the Bench opposite – at my suggestion or by our common instinct, set up a formidable inquiry into the means of preventing and forestalling the effect of world fluctuations upon our employment. There is the White Paper of 1944 which was presented to Parliament. The Lord President was a party to it, not in the vague way of being connected with the Government; he followed these things with great perspicacity and attention – he will surely not deny that – and the Chancellor of the Exchequer and the Prime Minister and others of great importance in those days.

This White Paper was praised by the Foreign Secretary only three years ago. It is a modern and enlightened statement of the ways of meeting world wide fluctuations and preventing the kind of terrible surge of unemployment which wrecked the Socialist Government of 1929–31. I believe that all those ideas and methods, for what they are worth, are an essential part of a wise and up-to-date outlook and policy in economics. I may say that this White Paper said that there would be no problem of general unemployment in the years immediately after the war in Europe, and that the difficulty would be to find the labour to do the jobs. The right hon. Gentleman today, finding fault with this, said that his prophecy as well as mine – he is as much involved in it – referred to a statement that we were at the time contemplating a normal rate of 8 per cent unemployment whereas we had had only 2 per cent. That is really not so. It is in the Appendix and is not on the authority of those who prepared the Report. It was in fact a statement by Sir William Beveridge on his plan and on what would be the cost of meeting unemployment if its proportions reached such a point. We must have a little accuracy in these discussions.

But all the principles which I have unfolded on taxation being an evil and consuming power being good, etc., are all violated and repudiated by the policy and outlook of the present Government. Socialists regard taxation as good in itself and as tending to level our society. Come on, give a cheer to that. What a pity the Minister of Health is consistently absenting himself from our Debates. This would have been the point where he might have come in and gathered some followers behind him on the great theme for commercial and hard pressed Britain of having a redistributed taxation based upon retribution – a great contribution to all the work which the Chancellor of the Exchequer has been left to do.

The Socialists rejoice in Government expenditure on a vast scale, and they believe it is a sure method of preventing unemployment, which it may be for a short time. Apparently increased consuming power, except by the Government, even in the home market is an evil which must be curbed by every form of Government intervention. The laws of supply and demand, regulation of consumption by price mechanism, apart from the basic essentials, are ruled out as part of the devices of outworn capitalism; while exhortations to thrift and saving are reiterated until they have become almost continuous – I mean unceasing. Everything possible is done to discourage and stigmatise the inventor. The Chancellor speaks in slighting terms of profit earners. What a lot of contempt he put into it – 'profit earners!' When I pressed him upon the subject he received it with one of his mirthless smiles which is the common form in which his personal philosophy has to express itself.

There was the old Gladstonian expression, 'Let the money fructify in the pockets of the people.' That is regarded as a monstrous device of a decadent capitalist system. As for maintaining confidence and credit what is to be thought when one of the most powerful Ministers, to whom I have already referred, is able to speak about redistribution of wealth in a spirit of retribution, at this junction of all others? And when the Prime Minister under whom he is serving does not feel strong enough – (*Interruption*) – strong enough to disavow it?

The Prime Minister has not dared to contradict his Minister of Health. But even the Prime Minister's submissive demeanour and docility – unbecoming in one holding such great power and bearing such responsibility – has not, so far as I can see induced this future leader of the Socialist Party and its highly acclaimed spokesman at the present time, to come within the precincts. I want to ask, how are the Government going to restore confidence and credit when they show themselves in every mood and action the enemy of wealth gathered, accumulated or inherited in private hands; when they penalise enterprise and deny thrift and good housekeeping their due reward?

Thus we have been led for four years of unprecedented and unbridled expenditure, of ceaseless interference in every form of private enterprise and activity to taxation unparalleled in times of peace and unequalled throughout the whole world today – (Hon. Members: 'We have heard that before.') Hon. Members say they have heard that before; they will hear it again, and over and over again. We see the Government taking 40 per cent of the entire national income into their far from competent hands. We have spent – I have said this before and I will say it again whenever I speak in the country – in the four years since the war we have spent £16,000,000,000; nearly as much as was spent in the whole 20 years between the wars. Are not these among the more important explanations of the plight to which we have been brought?

It must be remembered as we sit here tonight that Britain is a capitalist society, and that 80 per cent of its whole industry is in private hands. It is this part alone which earns the profits which the Chancellor of the Exchequer censures but on which he lives, taking over 60 per cent of them by taxation, and on which the 20 per cent loss-making nationalised industries are at present carried.

Under the Communist system all capital is sequestrated, all capital-owners are liquidated, and society is reduced to a strong hierarchy and army of officials and politicians by whom the proletariat are ruled under a one-party system with absolute tyranny, and a very considerable measure of ease. However abhorrent this conception may be to our spiritual outlook, and our physical resolves, on both sides of the House no one can say that it is not a system which has a hideous and logical symmetry about it.

Luckily, that is not an issue in our country today. But what we have here now is a capitalist society on which we are dependent for our daily life and survival, and a Socialist Government which views it with the utmost hostility and is trying continually to gain credit with its own extremists by casting a baleful net over its activities, by denouncing and threatening it all the time and stabbing it with gusto whenever a chance offers.

No one can possibly devise an economic theory that can fit or can even explain such a process. In a progressive and ever-broadening society, many corrections of emphasis can be made and are made as the years pass by. But a deliberate attack on the capitalist system by a Socialist Government, responsible and in power, a Socialist Government which has, I am glad to say, neither the hardihood nor the wickedness to embark on Communism, cannot be reconciled with any theory based on principle or any policy which can be accompanied in peacetime by a wide measure of prosperity and social well-being. Sir, the violent assault of Socialism upon the intricate and artificial economy of Britain at the moment when it was exhausted and quivering from the ordeal of total war has so far been fatal to our recovery.

Two or three years ago on several occasions I asked for a large reduction in Government expenditure. I named the figure of £500,000,000. I will not read out the quotation, because time is short and I have to consider the Prime Minister. We are all waiting to hear from him his views upon the present situation. I named the figure of £500,000,000. What was the reply of the Government? It was the same as they are so anxious to use today, namely, 'Please say exactly what your economies would be.' They do not ask this in order to gain good advice but in order that their canvassers at by-elections, or at a General Election, can go from door to door and endeavour to accuse the Conservative and the Liberal Parties of being the enemies of social welfare and improvement. That has certainly been the atmosphere in this Debate.

[. . .]

One of the main foundations upon which our standard of living can be maintained is a stable value of money. In theory, though not always in practice, Socialists view money with great disdain. It is, however, the sole means by which the innumerable millions of ordinary transactions of daily life, the exchange of goods and services, all the thought and provision that can be made for the future, all our social services and the like, can be maintained. Surely, the maintenance of this stable rate should be one of the first duties of any civilised and democratic Government?

The Communist Party take a different line. They say, 'Give us control of the currency, and we can overthrow any capitalist country in the world.' We can see in every direction the fall in the value of our money, not only at home, but abroad, and we are now to face a new crop of depression as a result of devaluation. The devaluation of money, arising mainly from the astounding extravagance in Government expenditure, causes anxiety even in those most responsible for it. The word 'disinflation' has been coined in order to avoid the unpopular term 'deflation'.

The Socialist Party are very mealy mouthed today, and the Chancellor of the Exchequer is very delicate in his language. One must not say 'deflation', but only 'disinflation'. In a similar manner, one must not say 'devaluation', but only 'revaluation', and, finally, there is the farce of saying that there must be no increase in personal incomes when what is meant is no increase in wages. However, the Chancellor felt that a certain broad prejudice attaches to the word 'income' and that consequently no one would mind saying that shall not increase – but wages, no. However, it is wages that he means. I am sure that the British electors will not be taken in by such humbug. I suppose that presently when 'disinflation' also wins its bad name, the Chancellor will call it 'non-undisinflation' and will start again.

Whatever name one cares to use, the maintenance of a stable medium of exchange for the ordinary transactions of daily life is one of the first tasks of Government – (*Interruption*). I was only anxious to consult my colleague in order to make sure that I shall not violate the time at my disposal. I am going through the experience, which no doubt many hon. Members have had, of wondering what on earth I can find to say, and then, when I had started to assemble it, of finding I had about three times as much as I should be able to get out. It is not only the value of money that we are interested in – the purchasing power of money – but the steady and grievous fall in Government securities which is a direct result of financial mismanagement and the attempt to bring about 'Socialism in our Time'.

In this affair, the two Chancellors of the Exchequer whom we have known in late years, and whom I see before me and under whom we have suffered, have shared a responsibility which I think I may say is gradually becoming more equal. If I may use a sporting term, it looks as if there will be a 'pretty close finish'. For the Consols called 'Daltons', in compliment to the right hon. Member for Bishop Auckland (Mr Dalton), which were issued at £100 three years ago, only £66 can be realised today. What an encouragement to saving; what a sinister advertisement of the financial insecurity and depression which have been brought upon us. It cannot even be claimed as part of the policy of the Minister of Health of retributive redistribution. The loss is not redistributed; the value has vanished into thin air. This is a serious matter for the whole country and particularly for the many thousands of people whose savings have been slashed by this fall.

The latest statement of the National Insurance Reserve Fund shows that on 31st March this year the Fund held £201 million worth of these securities. The current value of their stock is now £133 million, representing a loss, unless they have been realised, of some £68 million. All that is taken out of the subscriptions of the wage-earning population of this country. The Government are continually exhorting the people to save, and we for our part have always lent our support to the National Savings Movement, but how can people be expected to save and invest their savings in Government securities when they see what is happening? The fact is that the public at large have lost all confidence in this Government's financial administration, and they are pretty clear on what the financial intentions of the party behind the Government are.

I had meant to deal with the cuts proposed by the Government. I have just one word to say on them. I am strongly of the belief that if the great policy and decision of national military service had been used properly and a smaller number called up for a longer time, great economies might have been made and might still be made in the Military Services. I have no time to elaborate that, although I am not in the least bit afraid to do so. The Government have failed in their duty to the nation and they will be severely judged by it. That is no reason why we for our part should fail. We shall do our utmost to encourage everybody in the country to work as hard as they can in order to get things ready for the day when there will be a Government capable of aiding their efforts.

Anyone who has been in this Debate must feel that the main issue that is before us tonight is the need of a new Parliament. We are indifferent to the date of the election. We do not mind if the Government put it off. Many experts think that the longer the drop the surer the execution, but nothing could be worse for the country than a very long period of electioneering uncertainty. We have before us two malignant Bills, relating to steel and the alteration of the Parliament Act, which are bound to divide this House more than ever and bring fierce party fighting. We have apparently to live for three, four or five months in the present state of increasing domestic strife and uncertainty. It is not giving the country a chance not at least to curtail this period and to impart an element of certainty into it.

I say to the Government: you have the fortunes of this great country in your hands. For four years you have had power and wealth such as no Government have ever possessed. It is not only devaluation but bankruptcy which confronts us now. Here we are concerned only with party manoeuvres and calculations. The Government have devalued the pound and devalued the British nation, but most of all they have devalued themselves and brought us to bankruptcy. They have shown themselves not only financially but mentally and morally bankrupt, and the sooner they appeal to their fellow countrymen the better it will be for all who wish to see this country rise again in its own strength.

Clement Attlee to Winston S. Churchill
(*Churchill papers, 2/29*)

27 October 1949
Top Secret

My dear Churchill,

I enclose two copies of the record of the meeting on Defence which was held in my room in the House of Commons in Thursday, October 20.

When you have had time to study this I should be glad if you would let me know if you think that the records are a fair presentation of the proceedings which have taken place at the three meetings we have had on Defence.

You might also care to consider the suggestion I put to you at our first meeting that you should in due course return all the copies to the Secretary of the Cabinet. They would, of course, still be your copies and available if you ever wish to refer to them.

L. S. Amery to Winston S. Churchill
(*Churchill papers, 2/160*)

28 October 1949

My dear Winston,

I quite understand the necessity for limiting your commitments and must regretfully accept your decision not to address the Empire Industries Association on February 28th.

I was down at Harrow last night giving a lantern slide lecture to the boys on mountaineering in which I mentioned your gallant perseverance in getting to the top of Monte Rosa. The Head Master told me that you had provisionally suggested December 8th for the School Concert. I am happily free that day and shall be delighted to take a lift from you.

November 1949

Winston S. Churchill: speech[1]
('Winston S. Churchill, His Complete Speeches', volume 7, pages 7883-4)

2 November 1949   Grosvenor House, London

RICHES OF ENGLISH LITERATURE

... As an author, I can speak about the difficulties and dangers of writing a book. I have written a great many, and when I was 25 years old, I had, I believe, written as many books as Moses. I have almost kept up that pace since. Writing a book is an adventure. To begin with it is a toy, an amusement; then it becomes a mistress, and then a master, and then a tyrant, and then the last phase is that, just as one is about to be reconciled to one's servitude, one kills the monster.

It is of the utmost importance that every one should strive to devote some portion of every week to reading. We must refresh our minds. My advice to English people is to make sure they read the great books of the English language, and my advice to the young is not to begin to read them too soon. It is a great pity to read works of classical value hurriedly or at an immature period in one's development. Above all, schoolmasters should be careful not to set the reading of famous books as holiday tasks for their pupils. But everyone reaching manhood ought to master the great literature of his own country and, if possible, of another country too. It is a great advantage to be able to read in two languages. But some school curricula try to teach four or five languages at once, which means that one gets a smattering of all and profit from none. The object of learning another language is to gain access to another literature.

English literature is a glorious inheritance which is open to all – there are no barriers, no coupons, and no restrictions. In the English language and in its great writers there are great riches and treasures, of which, of course, the Bible and Shakespeare stand on the highest platform. English literature is one of our greatest sources of inspiration and strength. The English language is

---

[1] To the National Book Exhibition on receiving the *Times* Literary Award.

the language of the English-speaking peoples, and no country, or combination or power so fertile and so vivid exists anywhere else on the surface of the globe. We must see that it is not damaged by modern slang, adaptions, or intrusions. We must endeavour to popularize and strengthen our language in every way. Broadly speaking, short words are best, and the old words, when short, are the best of all. Thus, being lovers of English, we will not only improve and preserve our literature, but also make ourselves a more intimate and effective member of the great English-speaking world, on which, if wisely guided, the future of mankind will largely rest.

Commodore G. R. G. Allen to Winston S. Churchill
(Churchill papers, 4/215)

2 November 1949

VOL III. AND BOOK I. CHAPTER XIII.
Tripoli and Tiger

p. 2. Footnote regarding blockships.

I am sure that Admiral Cunningham would disagree with this. I do not see how the skeleton crew required could have been less than some hundreds of men. The ship had to steam at operational speed with the fleet for a thousand miles which would necessitate a large engine room complement besides the upper deck navigating party. She would also have required at least her own AA defence.

Nothing less than destroyers would have been needed to bring off this crew under the greatest hazards and the C-in-C's statement seems to me fully justified.

It does not seem right to compare this affair with cross-channel blocking operations, nor with the case of the ships used to form the Mulberry harbour, where very large resources were available and much time could be given to preparation.

Winston S. Churchill to Commodore G. R. G. Allen
(Churchill papers, 4/215)

3 November 1949

I am not convinced by this. The AA defence could have been provided by the destroyers and other large ships close by. The personnel not needed to pilot the ship to the point where it should be sunk to block the channel could all have got off on to a destroyer alongside five miles away by the ships simply slowing down. This could have been calculated before-hand too. I should think twenty people would have been quite enough to do the final handling and thinking. Anyhow the batteries did not open fire for twenty minutes.

I have a great regard for Andrew Cunningham but I think he was absolutely wrong on the facts, and at any rate was proved so in this case.

Randolph S. Churchill to Winston S. Churchill
(Churchill papers, 4/52)

7 November 1949

My dearest Papa,

I return to you herewith Chapters I to XI, less V and VI which I have not yet received. They make most fascinating reading and are fully up to the level of the previous volumes.

I have noticed a number of mistakes and have made a number of suggestions. They are mostly of a minor character and could be dealt with by Bill Deakin. I have marked such mistakes as I have noticed in the text, but have made my comments separately so as to avoid defacing your proofs.[1]

DENNIS KELLY TO WINSTON S. CHURCHILL[2]

1) Much has already been connected by Mr Wood. This is deleted in blue on the attached comments.
2) New points are starred red here & noted on Master Copy, both on relevant page & at front of each chapter.
3) A complete page of Randolph's comments has gone to Deakin for settling.

Winston S. Churchill to General Lord Ismay, Lieutenant-General Sir Henry Pownall, Commodore G. R. G. Allen, Colonel Bill Deakin and Denis Kelly
(Churchill papers, 4/19)

8 November 1949

I hope your meeting will be fruitful. It seems to me there should be several. I am counting on you to let me have this book free from serious errors of fact. It is already very far advanced in this direction.

I shall be very glad also to have general views about shortenings and transferences from chapter to chapter. As soon as I get these chapters back from you I shall start reading Book 6 straight through. I am keeping the last three chapters, as I hope to work on them tonight and tomorrow morning.

---

[1] Churchill wrote on the top of the letter: 'Mr K, go through these with me.'
[2] This three-point note was handwritten by Kelly at the bottom of Randolph's letter.

Bernard Baruch to Winston S. Churchill
(Churchill papers, 2/210)

10 November 1949
New York

My dear Winston,

I understand your people are going to recognize Communist China. I was told by a man who saw Bevin when he was here that if he had his way, he would recognize China as that might save Hong Kong. Of course that is a lot of nonsense.

I expect Brother Nehru to pull a rope trick on us. I would not give him a quarter, if I had my way.

My congratulations to you and Clemmie on the two new granddaughters[1] and also my best to them.

What are your plans for the winter?

Commodore G. R. G. Allen to Winston S. Churchill
(Churchill papers, 4/215)

10 November 1949

BK 5 CHAP 13

I am sorry to be difficult about this. I still believe that this footnote as drafted gives a wrong impression. Would it meet your case to substitute for it the sense of the three lines at the end of your minute to me?

This is your personal view which cannot be challenged but if you insert definite reasons for your belief, they will certainly be challenged by professional sailors. I should add that one of the most potent reasons in Cunningham's mind against the project was the need for concealing the intention up to the last moment. Thus it would have been very difficult, if not impossible, to make the necessary and elaborate preparations for scuttling a great ship like this in the short time available before sailing from Alexandria and without the crew being aware of the intention.[2]

---

[1] Arabella Spencer-Churchill, daughter of Randolph Churchill and June Osborne, born 30 Oct. 1949; Emma Mary Soames, daughter of Mary Churchill and Christopher Soames, born 6 Sep. 1949.
[2] A member of the Private Office wrote at the bottom of this note: 'Not accepted by WSC'.

Winston S. Churchill to Bernard Baruch
(Churchill papers, 2/210)

15 November 1949

Many thanks for your letter.[1] Diplomatic relations are not a compliment but a convenience. If we recognize the bear why should we not recognize the cub? Every good wish.

Bernard Baruch to Winston S. Churchill
(Churchill papers, 2/210)

16 November 1949

I would not recognize the bear if we had it to do over again nor would I recognize the cub who may grow up to be an ever greater bear.

Winston S. Churchill: speech
(Hansard)

17 November 1949   House of Commons

FOREIGN AFFAIRS

Before I come to the matter of the speech of the right hon. Gentleman the Foreign Secretary, it is my duty to clear up a matter upon which I was misinformed at our last foreign affairs Debate in July. The right hon. Gentleman introduced into the Debate as a controversial issue the question of responsibility for the introduction for the term 'unconditional surrender' into our policy in the war-time conference at Casablanca. It seemed to me that he cast some of the responsibility on me for the use of that phrase. He seemed to complain that the Cabinet had not been consulted, and he asserted his inveterate opposition to the idea. I had left him, he said, with nothing but a shambles to deal with in Germany – the House will remember the occasion – and from this arose many of the difficulties of his task. This was, of course, the exact opposite of what he had said 18 months before when – and I entirely agree with him – he said that he did not think unconditional surrender had played an important part in the conditions in which the war was brought to an end.

The right hon. Gentleman raised this matter without giving me any notice, and on the spur of the moment I said that the first time I heard the words 'unconditional surrender' – in regard, of course, to the late war – was when

---

[1] Reproduced above (p. 1561).

the President used them in his speech to the Press Conference at Casablanca.[1] This was the impression which had been left in my mind and which I had expressed to Mr Robert Sherwood three years before when he raised the point with me in connection with his biography of Mr Harry Hopkins. This impression was confirmed in my mind by what President Roosevelt said himself on the point, which is quoted in the Hopkins biography. This is the quotation:

> Suddenly the Press Conference was on, and Winston and I had no time to prepare for it, and the thought popped into my mind that they had called Grant 'Old Unconditional Surrender', and the next thing I knew, I had said it. However, there is a great danger in quoting, from memory when all these things crop up about the tumultuous past. We all remember the advice which the aged tutor gave to his disciples and followers on his deathbed when they came to him – 'Verify your quotations.'

At any rate, I have now looked up the telegrams and records of the occasion, and I find that undoubtedly the words 'unconditional surrender' were mentioned, probably in informal talks, I think at meal times, between the President and me. At any rate, on 19th January, 1942, five days before the end of the Conference, I sent the present Prime Minister, then the Deputy Prime Minister, the following message as part of a long telegram on other matters:

> We propose to draw up a statement of the work of the conference for communication to the Press at the proper time. I should be glad to know what the War Cabinet would think of our including in this statement a declaration of the firm intention of the United States and the British Empire to continue the war relentlessly until we have brought about the 'unconditional surrender' of Germany and Japan. The omission of Italy would be to encourage a break-up there.

The President liked this idea, and it would stimulate our friends in every country. To which the Prime Minister and my right hon. Friend and Member for Warwick and Leamington (Mr Eden) – he is not here today; he is absent in his constituency, as many hon. Members have to be in present circumstances – replied on the 21st:

> The Cabinet were unanimously of opinion that balance of advantage lay against excluding Italy because of misgivings which would inevitably be aroused in Turkey, in the Balkans and elsewhere. Nor are we convinced that effect on Italians would be good. Knowledge of rough stuff coming to them is surely more likely to have desired effect on Italian morale.

It is clear, therefore, that the right hon. Gentleman was mistaken, I have no doubt quite innocently –and I was in my own way, though not in such an

---

[1] See speech of 21 July 1949, reproduced above (pp. 1450–5).

important aspect – in saying that the Cabinet had not been consulted. They not only had been consulted but had expressed a very decided opinion. Also, I think he was mistaken in saying that he was not a party to that opinion before President Roosevelt's speech was given to the Press.

It will be seen that the opinion of the Cabinet was not against the policy of unconditional surrender. They only disapproved of it not being applied to Italy as well. I did not want this, because I hoped – and the hope has not been unfulfilled – that Italy, freed from Mussolini's dictatorship, might fight on our side, which she did for several years of the war, with lasting beneficial results to the state of Europe. I have the strong feeling that I cooled off on the point because I did not want to bring Italy into this sphere; and I thought that that would influence the President, too. This is borne out by the agreed communiqué which was drafted by the Combined Chiefs of Staff and approved by both of us, and which contains no mention of unconditional surrender.

As the issue was raised in debate by the right hon. Gentleman in his very responsible position, and as my own memory was at fault on the subject, I felt it my duty to place the true facts on record in the journals of the House if only in justice to the memory of President Roosevelt. I apologise for this digression which I think was necessitated by what had already occurred in the House.[1]

I now come to the review of the spacious European scene which the right hon. Gentleman has given us in, I might almost say, dulcet tones – at any rate, in a manner which seems to leave it free from all atmosphere of urgency or danger. I will begin with this question of Germany and German dismantlement. We all admire the work which has been done since the war in the British zone in Germany. It has been a great achievement into which, as in the American zone, an immense fund of personal devotion has gone. We have also spent large quantities of British money which we could not properly afford, in enabling our enemies of yesterday to recover after the shattering conditions of defeat, and they have made a very remarkable recovery in many ways. The success of the Air Lift into Berlin, where the Allies were trying to feed the German people, and the Soviet Government were trying to starve them –

Mr Gallacher: That is not true.

Mr Churchill: – was a famous event.

What a pity it is that the right hon. Gentleman should mar, as I think he has to come extent marred, these sacrifices and achievements by errors which arise from smaller facts and lesser considerations. I cannot speak, of course, now about the trial of German generals four and a half years after the Armistice, because that is at present sub judice, but on this side of the House for two years past we have steadily drawn attention to the unwisdom of belated dismantlement. Yet this is what the Foreign Secretary has pursued with astonishing perseverance. It is impossible to reconcile his insistence upon belated

---

[1] See also Churchill to Attlee, 24 July 1949, reproduced above (pp. 1461–2).

dismantlement with the policy which he also supported of free elections in Western Germany.

To bring on the elections and then feed the fires which burn at such times with all this fuel of dismantlement, is an act which cannot be explained by any wise or rational processes. To persist in belated dismantlement – after all, the great bulk of it has already been completed – and at the same time to give the German people full freedom to say what they thought about it as an election issue, was to authorise and stimulate every force in Germany hostile to the Western democracies to give full vent to their passions. There was something to be said for finishing up dismantlement; there were serious arguments, certainly. Security against future perils must always be on our minds, and I can assure the right hon. Gentleman that it is not excluded from my mind by mere sentiment.

There was something to be said for finishing up dismantlement. There was much also to be said for German self-government, but no human being can find anything in reason to say for the combination and the exact timing of the two processes. It was, I say, a grotesque piece of mismanagement. Now that the harm is largely done, we are to have a new set of proposals probably going half way or a third of the way, and these are soon to be put before us. There is not an argument for stopping or mitigating dismantlement now which was not valid or even clamant six months, 12 months or even 18 months ago.

In this matter, as in the Palestine policy, the Foreign Secretary, I regret to say, has succeeded with astonishing precision in securing for our country the worst of both worlds at the same time. It is, indeed, melancholy to find that the fine work of British administration in Germany is blurred over in this way, and needless misunderstandings are created between peoples who, for good or ill, have to live together if the world is to revive. It is really like someone painting, with art and labour, a magnificent picture and then, at the moment when it is about to be exhibited, throwing handfuls of mud all over it. Happily, perhaps the mud can be washed off by other hands.

I say that the right hon. Gentleman has made serious mistakes in this. Some of these mistakes have had beneficial reactions. We are, I think, largely indebted to the right hon. Gentleman for the present Right wing complexion of the Government of Western Germany. The House will remember how three years ago His Majesty's Government declared that they would enforce nationalisation of German industries throughout the British zone, and specially the Ruhr. Then the United States used its influence –

Mr Gallacher: Hear, hear.

Mr Churchill: – and asked them whether it would not be better to allow the Germans to express their own opinion upon a matter of that kind. The right hon. Gentleman had to give way, or gave way, and so it was decided that this matter should be left to the first elected Government of Western Germany.

It is said that the speech about dismantling made here by the right hon.

Gentleman in July when the German elections were about to take place turned a million votes over against the Socialists of Germany. I should not at all mind if any oration which the right hon. Gentleman delivered has a similar effect here. At any rate, the Parliament chosen by the German people and the Government based upon it have rejected the policy of nationalisation and support that of private enterprise under customary modern controls. Here is a case, and not the only one, when the right hon. Gentleman has shot at a pigeon and hit a crow. Which is the pigeon and which is the crow I shall not at this moment attempt to define. I am sure it is a wise decision of the German electorate and the Government resting upon them not to take all these industries into the direct control of the German State but to allow others to exist in their country besides the State itself.

This is not the only case of these difficulties. We have in the main throughout this Parliament supported the foreign policy of the right hon. Gentleman –

Mr Gallacher: It is Tory policy.

Mr Churchill: – but I must say quite plainly, after fully considering the French position as well as that of the United States, that it seems to me that no Government in this country after the present one is likely to carry the official Socialist policy of dismantling, as it has been pursued up to the present time, very much further.

Mr Bellenger (Bassetlaw) rose –

Mrs Leah Manning (Epping): What about the French?

Mr Churchill: The greatest part of dismantling is in our own British Zone. Therefore, we have for a very long time been in the extremely unfortunate position of getting all the unpopularity with the Germans while our friends the French were largely immune from it. (*Interruption.*) I have my opinion, which I have expressed.

Now I come to Strasbourg and United Europe. The right hon. Gentleman told us in a previous Session that United Europe was his idea, that he had thought of it 20, or even 30, years ago. But the unlucky thing was that the right hon. Gentleman forgot to take out a patent for it at the time. If he had only done that, how much smoother the course would have been; and he could have had all the credit to himself, and he might have been much more helpful and friendly to the development of this great idea. Instead, the right hon. Gentleman has been forced, as everyone knows, by deep tides of public opinion in Europe and in his own party, to make great concessions to the idea of a United Europe, but he has always done it, it seems to me, in the least possible degree, at the latest moment and in a grudging manner.

This process reached its climax at Strasbourg, where the right hon. Gentleman was so ably assisted by the Lord President of the Council and the Chancellor of the Duchy of Lancaster. It was remarkable to me to witness how quickly they lost all effective contact with their own Socialist comrades in Europe. These three Ministers together completely threw away what the

British Socialist Party had long greatly desired – namely, the leadership of Social democracy in Europe.

The party opposite, under the control of the right hon. Gentleman, have completely lost their influence as a party in Europe and they are regarded with bewilderment by their own best friends. The right hon. Gentleman referred to M Leon Blum. He is a friend of both of us and certainly must be considered one of the most eminent of all the Socialist statesmen of Europe. I was reading in the *Manchester Guardian* yesterday what he had written in *Le Populaire*. Hon. Members opposite should take notice of these words by M Leon Blum, a man of very high elevation in intellect and spirit, who says: "On various occasions doubt has arisen as to whether our comrades of the (British) Labour movement were not opposing the European movement. Although they declare that these impressions were false a great deal of damage has been done by them already. We have the right to turn to our English comrades and to insist that they should spare no effort to dissipate such an impression. That should be weighed by members of the Socialist Party throughout the country." If I were a Socialist – which I am not – I certainly would be rather pained to see, on a great matter like this European Movement, the most prominent European Socialist expressing himself in terms like that, which are all the more powerful because they are so moderately expressed.

Steady progress has, however, been made in this field. At Strasbourg in August I pointed out that the admission of Germany to membership of both the Consultative Assembly and the Council of Europe was a matter of urgent necessity for the future of Europe. This has indeed been my theme since I spoke at Zurich in 1946, when I appealed to France to take Germany by the hand and lead her back into the European family and forget the age-long quarrel which has rent Europe and the world.

Everyone present at Strasbourg this summer agreed that the matter was one of primary importance and deserved the gravest consideration, but there were some who thought that it was being raised at too early a date. Since then opinion has advanced by long strides. Two months later nobody considered the matter premature. At the beginning of November the Committee of Foreign Ministers, to which the right hon. Gentleman referred, met and gave out to the Press a statement that they were unanimously in favour of the principle of the admission of the Federal Republic of Western Germany as an Associate Member.

The Foreign Ministers did not themselves decide to admit Germany. They decided, very wisely I consider and very courteously, to take the opinion of the Standing Committee of the Consultative Assembly. That committee met and considered the matter and on 9th November, the week before last, it was announced that this committee were also unanimously in favour of the admission of Germany provided that the new German Government indicated its wish and ability to comply with the democratic conditions of membership.

Mr Harold Davies (Leek):[1] May I interrupt the right hon. Gentleman? This is of vital importance. I put this question in no partisan spirit whatever. (*Laughter*.) Hon. Members opposite need not smile – this is vital to the destiny and peace of the world. Is the right hon. Gentleman prepared to take the risk of completely rearming Germany at this juncture, because that is what his proposal really ultimately means?

Hon. Members: Nonsense.

Mr Churchill: I must leave the House to judge of the total lack of connection between what the hon. Member has said and any language being used by me or anything in the immediate circumstances before us in Europe.

It was a very remarkable decision of the Consultative Assembly Standing Committee, and I hope that it may become a milestone on our journey. The Standing Committee contained representatives of nations, including France, which the Germans did over-run and occupy for long hard years. The representatives of those countries, especially of France, deserve the thanks of every lover of peace and of every good European for their sagacious and tolerant view. There could be no stronger proof of the advance which European opinion has made towards greater unity and, as we know, it is in this greater unity that the best chance and hope resides of the future salvation of the world.

Nevertheless, we must remember that the formal admission has not yet taken effect. I urge His Majesty's Government to make every effort to ensure that no time is lost. Nineteen hundred and fifty may well prove a critical year as to how the minds of Germans will turn; I mean Germans free to express a conviction, outside the Iron Curtain. I am troubled by the thought that even if the admission becomes a fact at once, it may not be until next August, or September, that the Germans will take their seats. I am sure it will be of great benefit if the meeting of the next Assembly could be brought forward, so that the introduction of German representatives to this infant, but vital, democratic body could at the earliest moment become an accomplished fact.

I wish to turn to a kindred, but different topic in the great field that lies before us. There is, I think, some obscurity of thought about the recognition of different countries and diplomatic representation which should be sought with them. I spoke some time ago about Spain. Fancy having an ambassador in Moscow, but not having one in Madrid. The individual Spaniard has a much happier and freer life than the individual Russian – (Hon. Members: 'Oh'.) – or Pole, or Czechoslovak. I do not suppose that there are ten hon. Members in this House who, if it was actually put before them as a decision which they must take tomorrow morning, whether they would rather live the next five years in Franco Spain or in Soviet Russia, would not book their ticket for the south.

---

[1] Harold Davies, 1904–85. MP (Lab.) for Leek, 1945–70. Parliamentary Secretary, Ministry of Pensions, 1946–66; to Minister of Social Security, 1966–7. Parliamentary Private Secretary to PM, 1967–70. Baron, 1970.

Mrs Manning: I can assure the right hon. Gentleman that I should not have a chance of living for five years in Spain – nor for five minutes.

Mr Churchill: Happily the hard choice is not thrust before the hon. Lady. Other difficulties and interests will confront her over here. She will still have full liberty to remain in this country and to discharge her duties. But the question remains, which I leave for reasonable people to consider, if we have an ambassador to Moscow, why should we not have one in Spain?

Now the question has arisen also of what our attitude should be towards the Chinese Communists who have gained control over so large a part of China. Ought we to recognise them or not? Recognising a person is not necessarily an act of approval. I will not be personal, or give instances. One has to recognise lots of things and people in this world of sin and woe that one does not like. The reason for having diplomatic relations is not to confer a compliment, but to secure a convenience. When a large and powerful mass of people are organised together and are masters of an immense area and of great populations, it may be necessary to have relations with them. One may even say that when relations are most difficult that is the time when diplomacy is most needed.

We ought certainly to have suitable contacts with this large part of the world's surface and population under the control of the Chinese Communists. We ought to have them on general grounds, quite apart from all the arguments – and they are very important arguments – about the protection of specific British interests. Again I would say it seems difficult to justify having full diplomatic relations with the Soviet Government in Moscow and remaining without even de facto contacts with its enormous offshoots into China. On this side of the House, however, I am speaking of the general principles, the general line of approach to these topics – we agree with the Foreign Secretary in the answers he gave yesterday that no such step should be taken by us, except in consultation with the whole of our Commonwealth and also, of course, with the United States.

Mr Gallacher: Why the United States?

Mr Churchill: We should certainly not be in favour of isolated action in this respect, although, if it could be brought about as a joint policy, as the right hon. Gentleman foreshadowed, it would seem to be well worthy of consideration.

A very different issue arises when His Majesty's Government deliberately select a country which is held in Russian bondage, which is not free to express its own opinions and whose Government is a mere Quisling tool of Soviet policy. His Majesty's Government deliberately select such a country to be placed on the Security Council of the United Nations. We all have deep memories about Czechoslovakia and much British blood was shed to save her from German tyranny. As things have turned out, the unhappy people of Czechoslovakia have only exchanged one tyranny for another. Everyone knows that they have been to a large extent robbed of their civic liberties and national independence –

Mr Gallacher: Nonsense.

Mr Churchill: – and that they have become a mere pawn in the Kremlin game.

Mr Ronald Chamberlain (Norwood):[1] Rubbish.

Mr Churchill: Who said 'rubbish'?

Mr Chamberlain: May I ask the right hon. Gentleman –

Mr Churchill: No.

Mr Gallacher: The hon. Member has just come back from Czechoslovakia.

Mr Churchill: I think the Communist Members and fellow travellers have a pretty good run in this House.

Mr Gallacher: On a point of Order. A direct reference has been made to the Communist Members getting 'a good run in this House', by the right hon. Gentleman, who never comes to this House except when he is going to make a speech.

Mr Deputy-Speaker (Major Milner): Order. I hope that all hon. Members in this House get 'a good run'.

Mr Churchill: I have been wondering of late years and months whether indeed representation ought not to be made to the Chair on the abuse of raising questions on points of Order which have nothing whatever to do with Order. It is no doubt a fault which is not confined to any one party. That I can well believe, but I certainly think that some more precise definition would be a help to hon. Members in the discharge of their duties.

I say that not one of the present representatives of Czechoslovakia has the slightest right to speak in the name of the brave Czechoslovak people, whose love of democracy is as strong as ever.

Mr Chamberlain: Rubbish.

Mr Churchill: The right hon. Gentleman seems to have nothing in his head but rubbish.

Mr Chamberlain: On a point of Order.

Mr Deputy-Speaker: No point of Order can arise. The hon. Gentleman has made persistent efforts to interrupt the right hon. Gentleman who has possession of the House. He is not entitled to do that.

Mr Chamberlain: My point of Order has nothing to do with rubbish. I wish to know if it is in Order for the right hon. Gentleman to classify me along with himself by referring to me as 'the right hon. Gentleman'?

Mr Churchill: I quite agree that my profound apologies are due to the House.

I wish to say a few words about the Czechoslovak people. It has been their fate to live under outside rule for many generations, but in all this time they

---

[1] Ronald Arthur Chamberlain, 1901–87. Educated at Gonville and Caius College, Cambridge. MP (Lab.) for Norwood, 1945–50.

have learned how to preserve a very great deal of their own national life. They have by their own means of internal and passive resistance presented a kind of subdued but constant opposition to all those who have sought to rule them in the past 300 years. At the present moment they are under extraordinary stress. The Communist form of tyranny is far more efficient than any that has ever been devised in bygone centuries. Many things are happening in Czechoslovakia which must be the cause of anxiety to their foreign overlords and to those persons whom those overlords employ in ministerial offices.

There have been cruel executions, in some cases of men who fought valiantly for the Allied cause during the war. Purges have taken place in every grade of society. There is a tense if partly concealed reign of terror. Large numbers of refugees of every class are making their escape from this Soviet prison camp. We read in the newspapers only yesterday how the whole Czechoslovakian Reparations Commission in Western Germany were seeking asylum and British protection for themselves and their wives and children rather than go back to their native land in the plight into which it has fallen. What a symbol this is of what is actually going on inside Czechoslovakia.

I cannot feel that there is any Government in Europe less deserving of being chosen to be on the Security Council of the United Nations. I cannot think of any step more likely to discourage all the forces in Czechoslovakia who are working so patiently and steadfastly to free their country from the Soviet yoke. The fact that Great Britain, which has always been looked upon with so much regard by the Czechs, should give its vote for placing on the Security Council a Government which at the dictation of the Kremlin is trying to torment them into Communism will be a heavy blow to all those in Czechoslovakia with whom, on both sides of the House, there is a great measure of sympathy.

Yet that is what the right hon. Gentleman has done, and that is what he asks the party who sit on the benches opposite to become responsible for. We are told that there was a 'gentlemen's agreement' to the effect that representatives of the Eastern bloc behind the Iron Curtain should in practice be chosen for the Security Council in accordance with the wishes of the majority of those States. But the 'gentlemen's agreement' was in 1946, and since then the revolution in Czechoslovakia has taken place. We have an entirely new situation. Was the fate of Masaryk and Benes covered by the 'gentlemen's agreement'? Was the execution and purging of some of the finest Czechoslovak patriots part of the 'gentlemen's agreement'?

The United States at any rate did not consider themselves bound in this way. They voted for Yugoslavia which has to a large extent freed itself from Kremlin oppression though not from Kremlin menace. (An Hon. Member: 'It is still Communist.') I think that the way in which they manage their internal affairs is for them to decide but I certainly do not think that they should be held down under foreign pressure from outside. Even if they be Communist, which I largely question because they are a very free, rough and ready mountain people, the product of centuries of war in the struggles with Turkey – I doubt very much whether they are – I say that it was in those circumstances an extraordinary thing for Great Britain to vote for the election of the present Czechoslovak Government to membership of the Security Council.

I have also heard, although I cannot vouch for it, and I am quite ready to be corrected if I am contradicted, that there was some kind of deal – that if we voted for the Soviet-managed Government in Czechoslovakia the votes of the bloc of satellite States would be given to one of the British Dominions for a seat on the Security Council. If this is true – and I shall be very glad to hear that it is not true – it would seem to be an unworthy transaction reflecting not only upon those concerned, but affecting the dignity of the United Nations institution itself. Be this as it may, we are astonished that the right hon. Gentleman has lent himself to supporting the controlled, satellite Government of Czechoslovakia rather than the free and independent – in the national sense – Government of Yugoslavia. I am sure that the majority of the party opposite, if they dared express their minds, would condemn such a decision.

It is the sort of behaviour which makes people in many friendly countries in Europe and America feel that they do not know where Britain stands on some of the large issues for which in the past we have fought so hard. It robs the foreign policy of His Majesty's Government of all distinction, and indeed to a very large extent of rational explanation. On both sides of the House, I think, we are glad that Yugoslavia and not Czechoslovakia was elected to the vacancy on the Council of the United Nations in spite of the British vote to the contrary.

The threatened position of Yugoslavia raises directly that of Albania. It is known that the Soviet 'Diplomatic Mission' includes some thousands of military and scientific personnel and that the Russians are in physical possession of the former Italian submarine base at Sassano opposite Valona. The internal development schemes, including oil exploration, which formerly were being carried out with Yugoslav help, are now directly in Russian hands. On the other hand, the land communications with Albania are in the hands of Tito. This certainly seems to be a danger point at the present time. We have no reason to trust the Government of Albania. The regime of Enver Hodja, like other Kremlin-controlled institutions, commands no real national support. Last June, Hodja's Deputy-Premier Xoxe,[1] who also held the position of Minister of the Interior – a very important position – and was also General Secretary of the Communist Party was executed after charges of collaboration with Tito had been made against him.

It is clear that fierce political stresses rack Albania, and I must remind the House before leaving Albania that it is now three years since the mining of

---

[1] Koci Xoxe, 1911–49. Leading figure in Albanian Communist Party; rival of Enver Hoxha. Minister of Defence and Minister of the Interior, 1945–9. Deputy PM, 1946–8. Hanged in 1949 on a charge of conspiracy with the British.

the British destroyers in the Corfu Channel proved Albania's complete disregard of international law. Forty British lives were lost for which compensation, adjudged by the International Arbitration Court to which the matter was referred, was accorded and, of course, has not been paid.

Mr Bevin: The point is that compensation has not been assessed. The Court have given the verdict but they have not assessed the compensation and in this case I have to wait for the lawyers.

Mr Churchill: I certainly cannot blame the right hon. Gentleman for that. The fact remains that we have not yet received any compensation, after three years, for the murder, in defiance of international law, of 40 British sailors.

Mr Bevin: I must ask the right hon. Gentleman to appreciate that we are in the hands of the International Court –

Mr Churchill: Certainly.

Mr Bevin: – and if he is blaming anybody, he is blaming the International Court.

Mr Churchill: I was not so much – (Hon. Member: 'You were.') Hon. Gentlemen opposite do not know what I am going to say. I was not so much blaming anybody as deploring what is an undoubted fact.

Albania is, of course, the principal base from which the Communist rebellion in Greece has been sustained, and it has also been the refuge of the Greek Communist forces whenever they have been in difficulties. We must all rejoice that the fortunes of Greece have so greatly improved. High credit is due to the Americans for the strong aid they have given to Greek freedom. They took over, adopted, and made their own the policy which Great Britain under the National Coalition – the right hon. Gentleman and I were associated in that – initiated in Greece during the war – not without much criticism here and much criticism in the United States.

We are glad that a British Brigade has been kept in Greece all this time. I had myself thought that it would be withdrawn after the General Election in Greece held under inter-Allied supervision in 1946, but I readily agree that circumstances have changed and that the Soviet-sponsored Greek Communist rebellion made it desirable for us to continue to associate ourselves with the Greek policy of the American Government in every way. I hope that the date of the withdrawal of the British Brigade, however desirable on other grounds, will not be determined purely on the grounds of expense, but only in due relation to the whole situation in the Balkans and, I may add, generally throughout the world.

The latest attitude of the Soviet Government is curious. They have now asked for a free election in Greece under international supervision. But this was the very proposal which we made – which the right hon. Gentleman made – to the Russians three years ago, and we strongly urged them to join us in seeing that the election was fairly and freely conducted, but they refused. Now they have asked for it. They have also asked for an amnesty for the defeated Greek rebels, but this also was offered by the Greek Government two years ago and spurned. It seems to me that, after all that has happened, the question of holding another supervised election in Greece and also that of extending an amnesty, are measures about the timing of which the Greek Government, after all it has gone through, is entitled to be the prime judge.

I apologise to the House for having kept them so long but even if one deals only selectively with this vast field there is much to be said. I now reach the end. I have had to make some serious criticisms of the right hon. Gentleman, most of which I imagine will have their echo in the breasts of Members of the Socialist Party because in this matter I think he has put a needless strain upon their feelings.

I wish to end on a different note. I have on former occasions paid my tribute to the many characteristic British qualities which the right hon. Gentleman possesses and to the courage with which he has faced misunderstanding and unpopularity among his own supporters. We all trust that his public life and personal health may long be preserved. It may be, however, that this is the last Parliamentary Debate on foreign affairs we shall see in the present House of Commons, and it may be that so far as the tenure of the Foreign Office by the right hon. Gentleman is concerned, we have listened this afternoon to his swan song.

The right hon. Gentleman certainly had a great opportunity. When he took up his important office we were the most respected country in Europe and not surpassed by any other country in the world in the esteem in which we were held. Under this Administration we have fallen back in many spheres and from this we cannot exclude the foreign sphere. The policy of the right hon. Gentleman has not represented the coherent outlook of Socialists or of Liberals or of Conservatives. It cannot be reconciled with any integral theme of thought. It has been swayed, and even at times dominated, by his personal likes and dislikes, strengthened by pride and enforced by obstinacy.

We on this side have done our best to support him. We have sustained him in all aspects of his policy which are a logical and harmonious part of the great causes which Britain has at heart. His manly resistance to Communism, his preservation of good relations with the United States, the Brussels agreement about Western Europe –

Mr Bevin: Good.

Mr Churchill: – the Atlantic Pact –

Mr Bevin: Good.

Mr Churchill: – the air-lift into Berlin –

Mr Bevin: Good.

Mr Churchill: – the policy pursued in Greece, the reinforcement of Hong Kong – are all events of the first magnitude in which the right hon. Gentleman has played a prominent part. We are sorry indeed that those achievements do not stand by themselves unclouded by other and lesser actions, but still they stand, and on that note I will take the opportunity of bringing my remarks to a close.

Winston S. Churchill: speech
('In the Balance', pages 151–4)

28 November 1949　　　　　　　　　　　　　　　　Kingsway Hall, London

EUROPEAN MOVEMENT

Monsieur Spaak, as Prime Minister of Belgium, made the first governmental declaration in support of The Hague Congress demand for a European Assembly, and has throughout, with the French Government, sustained the idea. As one of the Presidents of Honour of the European Movement he has led public opinion in favour of European Union. Now, as President of the European Assembly, he has become the guide and champion of the new Parliament of Europe. We salute him as a great Belgian and, at the same time, as a great European.

You, my Lord Archbishop, have referred to the progress made by the European Movement since you presided at our Albert Hall meeting in May 1947. That progress has indeed been remarkable. Exactly a year later, in May 1948, the Hague Congress demanded the creation of a European Assembly. Exactly a year after that, in May 1949, ten governments signed the Statutes of Europe.

In Strasbourg last August delegates to the European Assembly, representing widely differing political tendencies, declared themselves convinced of the urgent necessity for creating a United Europe and the dire consequences of hesitation or delay. The recommendations sent by the Assembly to the Committee of Ministers were bold and challenging. But they cannot be said to have been unrealistic. Whilst people may disagree with a point here and there, these recommendations represent broadly the requirements of the situation which confronts us. The policy enunciated at Strasbourg offers to Europe the only possible means of preserving her peace and freedom and of maintaining and developing the living standards of her peoples.

We all recognize, of course, that the policy of European Union raises many serious and practical difficulties which will require solution. But the difficulties are not a reason for inaction. They are rather a justification for the redoubling of our efforts. As we advance we shall hear more and more about these difficulties, but we have no choice but to go on. The alternative is to face the certainty of wholesale economic collapse as soon as American Aid ceases, accompanied by the spread of misery and Communism.

The French Foreign Minister, M Schuman, declared in the French Parliament this week that 'Without Britain there can be no Europe.' This is entirely true. But our friends on the Continent need have no misgivings. Britain is an integral part of Europe, and we mean to play our part in the revival of her prosperity and greatness. But Britain cannot be thought of as a single State in isolation. She is the founder and centre of a world-wide Empire and Commonwealth. We shall never do anything to weaken the ties of blood, of sentiment and tradition and common interest which unite us with the other members of the British family of nations. But nobody is asking us to make such desertion. For Britain to enter a European Union from which the Empire and Commonwealth would be excluded would not only be impossible but would, in the eyes of Europe, enormously reduce the value of our participation. The Strasbourg recommendations urged the creation of an economic system which will embrace not only the European States, but all those other States and territories elsewhere which are associated with them.

The British Government have rightly stated that they cannot commit this country to entering any European Union without the agreement of the other members of the British Commonwealth. We all agree with that statement. But no time must be lost in discussing the question with the Dominions and seeking to convince them that their interests as well as ours lie in a United Europe. An opportunity for these consultations offers itself at the Conference of Commonwealth Foreign Ministers at Colombo early next year which Mr Bevin is going to attend – we hope to be a help. We ask that the issue of European Union be placed upon the agenda of this conference. Then when the European Assembly next meets at Strasbourg, the representatives of Britain in the Committee of Ministers and in the Assembly will no longer be restrained as they are now by uncertainty about the opinions and wishes of their partners overseas.

At The Hague, and now this summer at Strasbourg, the importance of admitting the new German Federal Republic as an associate member of the Council of Europe appeared, and we rejoice that this step has now been decided in principle. Understanding and cooperation must be established between Germany and the rest of free Europe. Therefore, although belated, we welcome the recent decision in favour of the partial abandonment of the provocative and, at the same time, ineffective policy of dismantling. Western Germany, overcrowded as she is, with millions of German refugees from the East, cannot hope to restore lasting prosperity except within the framework of a wider unity in which her peoples could find a peaceful outlet for their energies and abilities. Europe needs Germany, but Germany still more needs Europe.

At Zurich I said France has a special responsibility for taking Germany by the hand and leading her back into the European family. I congratulate the French Parliament upon its decision to approve the admission of Germany into the Council of Europe. At The Hague I said: 'For us the German problem is to restore the economic life of Germany and revive the ancient fame of the

German race without thereby exposing their neighbours and ourselves to any reassertion of their military power of which we still bear the scars. United Europe provides the only solution to this two-sided problem. It is a solution which can be implemented without delay.'[1]

The basic idea underlying the conception of European Union is the desire to preserve and develop the free way of life of the participating nations. This implies the acceptance of collective responsibility for the defence of liberty and the dignity of man. That was the purpose of the proposal put forward by the European Movement and adopted by the Assembly for the conclusion of a European Convention on Human Rights. We understand that the Government may require to consider carefully the details of such a convention but we ask them, without further delay, to make it clear that they accept the principle of joint responsibility for the maintenance of freedom and that they intend not merely to issue pious declarations but to set up judicial and executive machinery to make this a reality.

We trust that the Government will be in a position to announce the signing of this Convention on Human Rights and the setting-up of the machinery to implement it before the next session of the Assembly. Nothing could give to the Assembly more confidence in the Government's sincerity. Nothing could give greater inspiration to the European peoples than this step. The European Movement must campaign for the Convention on Human Rights as it campaigned so successfully for the creation of the Assembly.

We are at present forced by circumstances to confine our action to the democratic nations of Europe who are free. But let us never for a moment forget that behind the Iron Curtain there are peoples who share our culture and our traditions and who have no greater desire than to be united with us. All our plans for the new Europe must be based on the firm assumption that our fellow Europeans now living under totalitarian domination will, as soon as they are free, come and take their places with us in the Council of Europe.

The European Assembly at Strasbourg, under Monsieur Spaak's leadership, has proved that it is capable of bold initiative. But the decisions rest with governments. The ability of the Assembly to persuade governments to act will depend upon the backing which exists for this idea among the broad masses of the people in every country. To create this body of public interest and public support is one of the main tasks of the European Movement. The union of Europe must be a union not only of governments but of peoples.

The European Movement, an international all-party organization, was the inspiration and motive force which brought the European Assembly into being. It must now build up a vast body of popular support behind the Assembly so that the Assembly's recommendations may be translated by the governments into action. Many of you here are no doubt already supporters

[1] See speech of 7 May 1948, reproduced above (pp. 1037–42).

of the European Movement. Those of you who are not will have an opportunity during the meeting to enrol tonight. I hope that you will join us and work with us in this historic campaign, the triumph of which will be decisive for the peace and well-being of Europe and the world for generations that are to come.

Randolph S. Churchill to Winston S. Churchill
(Churchill papers, 4/57)

29 November 1949

My dearest Papa,

I do not know if you are aware of the following facts. In case not, I pass them on to you:

(1) Money invested in agricultural land in Britain pays death duties at a rate of 40% lower than if it is invested in any other way.

This applies (and has been tested in the courts) even in settlements made *inter vivos*.

(2) Money invested in real estate or agricultural land outside the United Kingdom (the possibilities of doing this are now restricted to the Sterling area) is liable for death duties at the local rate which, in many cases, is almost non-existent. No tax is payable in Britain. If the money is invested in a number of different countries not only does the advantage arise of paying a much lower rate, but each particular investment falls into a lower bracket on the already reduced local scale, since the assessment is based only on the money invested in that country and takes no account of investment in other parts of the world.

I understand that this second device, in so far as it affects *inter vivos*, has not yet been tested in the courts, but that the best legal opinion is that the principle would be unaffected by the fact that an *inter vivos* settlement was involved.

December 1949

Winston S. Churchill to Sir Stafford Cripps
(*Churchill papers, 2/161*)

1 December 1949

My dear Chancellor of the Exchequer,

I readily admit that any further weakness of sterling would be a national disaster, and its maintenance must be the main preoccupation of His Majesty's Government whatever Party is in power.

My colleagues and I feel very strongly that the level of sterling is determined not by words but by deeds, or the lack of them. We believe that the weakness of sterling in the past and any threat to it in the future are largely caused by the policies and political character of the present Socialist Government. It is our sincere conviction that nothing can avoid a further fall in sterling if the present Government, pledged to pursue its declared courses, is once again returned to power, and therefore that the best way to help sterling is to defeat the Government at the polls. This is a position which we cannot abandon.

Subject to this being understood beyond any possibility of future reproaches, I should, of course, feel it my duty to accept your invitation and hear anything you wish to put before me and my colleagues.

I should suggest that any such meeting should be on the same basis as those with the Prime Minister on Defence, viz., that we on our side should make no use of any confidential and exclusive information you give us, but that we should continue at liberty to use any information which has already come to us or may come in the future through other channels.

Finally, I must point out that these difficulties would never have arisen had the Election been held in the autumn, as I believe was in the national interest, and they must reign with increasing force the longer this decision is withheld.

1580   December 1949

Winston S. Churchill: speech
(Churchill papers, 2/336)

1 December 1949   Harrow School

Dr Moore, Ladies and Gentlemen, Harrow School,

You have reminded me how the years pass, for I must say that it does not seem credible to me personally that this is the tenth time running that I have come here to listen to your singing the Harrow Songs I love so much. The tenth year, and nine years have passed; and when I first came it was very rough weather. As I said at the time, many of the Harrow boys, while still quite young, had the honour to serve under the fire of the enemy and to behave with effective serviceability and simplicity when under the various stresses of air-raids and alarms. This was nine years ago. Now I have been coming here all this time regularly to sing these songs. But years are perhaps not the right form I think in which to compute such a lapse of time. There are two generations, by school reckoning, in nine years. I suppose you have plenty of three-yearers and some four-yearers – I got to be that; but still it is something to have stayed so long. I do not think you have had any five-yearers, but if I am wrong perhaps anyone aspiring to this rank would correct me. Two generations of Harrow boys have passed and it seems to me quite a brief interval. Yet I always look forward very much to coming down. I do not look forward to this part of the entertainment; but it was said by me and desired by me that I might come to hear you sing and not that you might hear me speak; I have to do so much of that elsewhere. But the songs are agreeable to hear and the speech somewhat toilsome to make. This is the tenth occasion, and if you look back over so many occasions – and you can count them on your fingers and thumbs – you will see that it is a very serious thing to have to make ten speeches about the same things in the same settings, with the same associations, and yet never to repeat yourself – I hope I have lived up to that – and never to run short of something to say. You will find how serious it is, I can assure you, if you live on, as I trust you will, to the advanced age which I have attained (and Mr Amery is one up on me; he was a Monitor and at one time he was by no means certain that he was not going to whop me; but his better sense of justice prevailed and he did not whop me). On all these occasions but one he has been down here and therefore he is in a position to be a critic and to catch me out if I should fall back upon some of the jokes or truisms with which I have endeavoured to acquit myself or former times.

I am always very glad indeed to come because I do love the Harrow songs. I hope you all realize, I hope that everyone in the School realizes what a wonderful inheritance the Harrow School Song Book is. Eton has a very fine song, but no Song Book, and I do not know what songs Winchester has. Perhaps I must ask Sir Stafford Cripps about that. We have to ask him about so many things nowadays. But in the Harrow School Song Book you have a treasure, you have a treasure-house of learning and inspiration, and literature. For the words which are written in these songs, if properly understood in their full pregnant meaning, these words which are used here form a vocabulary which would give a man a good start on a literary career, as I know. More than lines are here. This song that we have just sung has always struck Mr Amery and me in our sixty-five years' acquaintance, this one which goes,

> 'While thought to wisdom wins the gay,
> While strength upholds the free.'

They are beautiful, compact, alive. These two great writers whose songs are here – I knew them both, Mr Bowen[1] and Mr Howson[2] – they both have written most famous and charming lines. Bowen always seemed to me to have many of the qualities of the great English poets, and Howson's poems and songs are also splendid. But the tunes stay with you all your lives and come back to you and return when you are dropping off to sleep, return when you wake and I personally have found it the greatest pleasure to find my old memories stirred by these famous songs. You ought to try to learn them off by heart. It is extremely important. I do hope, Dr Moore that you will inculcate the importance of cultivating memory. Memory is not improved by reading things over and over again, but it is improved by reading a thing once and recalling it again and again until it becomes perfect. Memory is the art of recalling; memory in itself is very often defective. It is the art of recalling that is really memory and this can be trained. I always thought there was a lot to be said for the ancient Druids who made everybody learn everything by heart and always transmitted outside their inner circle by word of mouth. Undoubtedly what you learn by heart sinks in and becomes a part of your life; and also to learn good poetry by heart gives you a real storehouse on which you can draw for all the occasions in which you have to find the right word at the right time. I strongly recommend the closest knowledge of the Harrow Songs and their study, not only as a means of enjoyment here but as a guide and a help through the life you must lead. And I must say that it seems to me that it is a great bond of union between Harrow boys, as they grow up and move about in the world, that they have this in common. This Song Book plays in Harrow the same sort of part that Shakespeare plays in the English-speaking world.

Now I must thank you most warmly and cordially for letting me come. I hope that is not the last time that I shall have the opportunity of coming. On one of these nine occasions I was even allowed to play the kettle-drum – one of the cherished ambitions of my life.

---

[1] Edward Ernest Bowen, 1836–1901. Asst master, Marlborough College, 1858. Master, Harrow School, 1859–1901. Wrote the Harrow school song 'Forty Years On (1872) and *Harrow Songs and Other Verses* (1886).
[2] Edmund Whytehead Howson, 1855–1905. Poet and master at Harrow School.

I am so glad to hear about the steady progress of the school, so glad to hear that it is emerging stronger and more powerful after the ups and downs through which we have passed.

Hard times lie ahead; no easy resting-place is open to us now. We have to march on, not indeed under the enemy's bombardment; but we have to march on under other trials and stresses and toil on up the hill. But if there is any nation which is capable of unbroken effort it is our British race, and if there is any place which Harrow boys would seek to occupy in that race, in that march, it should be in the forefront of the battle and the van of the marching columns.

I thank you very much. We are now going to sing Forty Years On. That is not much good to Mr Amery and me. Fifty years on is no good to us. It is very nearly to me 60 years on. Well, what about it? At any rate I wish you all good fortune in the future which lies before you. And may you march along the path with the Harrow Songs in your hearts and the future of your school and your country ever as your highest endeavour.

Clement Attlee to Winston S. Churchill
(Churchill papers, 2/29)

7 December 1949
Top Secret

My dear Churchill,

I am sending to you for your own private and personal information two papers which have been submitted to the Defence Committee by the Minister of Defence giving an account of the Meetings of the North Atlantic Defence Committee. I think that you will be interested to learn how this matter is proceeding.

You will, I know, realise that the amount of information that can be made public depends on the agreement of other Powers and on considerations of public policy, but I should desire to keep you as fully informed as possible.

Should there be any points requiring elucidation, Alexander would be ready to see you. I should be obliged if you would return these documents after perusal.

Winston S. Churchill to Bernard Baruch
(Churchill papers, 2/210)

8 December 1949

My dear Bernie,

I put this short note* down on paper the other night out of my head. It is of course only a goal and an ideal to work for, like the United States of Europe which I suggested at Zürich in 1946.

Of course the basis would have to be arranged by treaty between you and us. I know your convictions about the gold standard, but that is plainly impossible. On the other hand, among the twenty or more commodities which would be takes[1] as the basis for the new sterling dollar, gold would be the leading commodity and could be put at twenty or thirty per cent of the whole, or even more if it dropped off one point per annum. The great thing is to have some kind of standard of tears, toil and sweat – and wit – by which goods and services can be exchanged over the dominant area of the world.

Please keep this entirely to yourself, as it is only my own poor personal venture of thought. But I am getting rather keen on it.

* Enclosing Note on sterling–dollar situation.

Winston S. Churchill to Christopher Soames
(Churchill papers, 1/46)

15 December 1949

Should the Lakes become frozen over during my absence it will be necessary in good time to collect the ten black swans as quickly as possible and keep them in the little yard below the woodshed until there is water again. They must be kept in their present three separate batches, and will have to be specially fed as they will not be able to graze in the field or from the weeds in the Lake. Will you look after this personally for me?

[1] taken.

Anthony Eden to Winston S. Churchill
(Churchill papers, 2/82)

16 December 1949

My dear Winston,

The High Commissioner for India[1] has asked me to attend a ceremony on January 26th in connection with the coming into force of the new Indian Constitution. The Prime Minister is attending. The occasion is under the auspices of the India League.

I find the situation slightly embarrassing, but as you will remember you did in the House bless the new constitutional arrangements by which India remains in the Commonwealth while being a Republic, and I am rather at a loss to find an excuse for not going. On balance therefore I should be inclined to accept. This is also Rab Butler's view. I shall be grateful to know if you concur.

Bernard Baruch to Winston S. Churchill
(Churchill papers, 2/92)

22 December 1949   New York
Private

My dear Winston,

You are entirely right about the importance of establishing a basis of genuine convertibility between the dollar and the pound – and all other currencies. That will not be accomplished until there is good money – a good money being one which people will voluntarily and with confidence take for their goods or services in any part of the world.

You say, 'I know your convictions about the gold standard but that is plainly impossible'. It is quite impossible to return to a gold standard now, or at any time, and keep there when governments are dealing in such nonsense as is yours, mine and everyone else's. So much for that.

As regards the commodity dollar that is something that has been talked about over and over again. I will send you a couple books written about it – one by Irving Fisher,[2] who had a brilliant mind, explored a good many

---

[1] Archibald Edward Nye, 1895–1967. Enlisted as a private soldier. On active service, 1914–18. Lt, 1916. Maj.-Gen., 1940. Director of Staff Duties, War Office, 1940. Lt-Gen., 1941. VCIGS, 1941–6. Knighted, 1944. Governor of Madras, 1946–8. High Commissioner for UK in India, 1948–52; in Canada, 1952–6.

[2] Irving Fisher, 1867–1947. American economist, statistician, inventor and Progressive social campaigner. Born in Saugerties, NY. First to receive a PhD in economics, Yale University, 1891. Editor, *Yale Review*, 1896–1910. Prof. of Political Economy, Yale, 1898–1935; later Prof. Emeritus. President, American Economics Association, 1918. Gibbs Lecturer, American Mathematical Society, 1929. Co-founder and president of Econometric Society, 1930. Advocate of vegetarianism, prohibition and eugenics.

subjects, entered into many fields, and finally ended up broke. Also, a book by a young man named Benjamin Graham,[1] who is a far cleverer man.

I agree with you completely that, 'Production is wealth. Trade is exchange. Both are ruled by the laws of supply and demand. Money is the token by which they are measured. The need of the world is for a true and stable measure of value. The slower it changes the better for most. The wider it ranges the better for all.'

And indeed it would be a good thing 'to have some kind of standard of tears, toil and sweat – and wit – by which goods and services can be exchanged over the dominant area of the world'. But as long as governments have the power to issue money (whether directly or indirectly through national banks) and exercise no more morality or competency about it than do our present governments, you will never have the standard you seek. Until England balances her budget and people believe that she will continue to do so, her money will always be suspect. Ours only *looks* better because we still are an export and not yet an import nation, as you are.

In my report of April 20, 1945, which was intended for President Roosevelt but was delivered to President Truman instead, I stated:

'The matters chiefly troubling English officials are about in this order:
1 – Russia.
2 – The continuance of their food supply.
3 – How to export enough to pay for these food imports and their debts. They continually feel for some kind of peace lend-lease.
4 – How to struggle away from the necessity of sound money.'

That No. 4 is what you are trying to do, and indeed, what the whole world is trying to do. Suppose we had a dollar–sterling money based upon commodities and the United States government should have deficit spending of $5 billions or $10 billons next year. We would sell bonds and make the Federal Reserve take them and issue currency. Every other country does that in some form.

The value of gold is that people have confidence in it and have had confidence in it over the ages. It is indestructible. The labor of producing it has shown a very close relationship to the labor in producing the things for which it can be exchanged. But by far its principal value has been that of restraining influence upon sovereigns and sovereignty, upon the over-issuance of money or credit. No 'planner', no breast-beater, no bootstrap-lifter will ever willingly accept a standard which will restrain him in his self-defeating activity of

---

[1] Benjamin Graham, 1894–1976. Investor and economist. Born Benjamin Grossbaum, in London. Moved to New York aged 1. Graduated salutatorian from Columbia University, 1914. Partner at Newburger, Henderson & Loeb, 1920. Co-founded the Graham–Newman partnership, 1926. Lectured at Columbia, Anderson School of Management, and UCLA until his retirement in 1956. Considered the 'father of value investing'. Wrote *Security Analysis* (1934, with David Dodd) and *The Intelligent Investor*, 1949.

professing to do 'more' for everybody by passing out more money – of lessening purchasing power The Russians did their devaluation of savings, of past sweat and past tears, more honestly – and more brutally.

Until some restraining influence against the over-issuance of money is restored, the currency of the British Empire, of the United States and of other nations must remain suspect. The gold standard is the one effective restraining influence we have known over the ages.

It has grown fashionable among some economists to blame our 'monetary ills' upon gold. Perhaps a 'case against gold' might have been made out when the gold standard was operating. It can hardly be blamed for current conditions, King Gold being definitely a refugee. I rather think that the weakness in our present currencies lies in their being all too accurate a reflector of the lack of morality and character on the part of governments.

You will never be able to select any commodity, or group of commodities which can maintain an equitable balance with government by political expediency.

Rest assured I will keep your letter entirely to myself, and I would advise that you keep it to yourself, as well, until you have considered it much more carefully.

I'll bet the Prof does not agree with you.

Winston S. Churchill to Clement Attlee
(*Churchill papers, 2/29*)

22 December 1949

My dear Prime Minister,

I think you ought to see the enclosed extract from a letter which I have received in my capacity as Honorary Air Commodore of 615 (County of Surrey) Squadron, RAAF.[1] I have not yet raised in public the serious question of the jet fighters, about which we have had some correspondence, but I thought I ought to send you this letter which shows how the sale of one hundred jets to the Argentine and other countries of that character affects the Auxiliary Air Force. Will you kindly treat this letter as confidential as it is for your personal information only.

---

[1] The letter of Nov. 21 from Peter DeVitt notified Churchill that 615 Squadron had not received its Vampire Mk II jet fighters but had instead been given a single Vampire Mk I.

December 1949   1587

John Peck to Winston S. Churchill
(*Churchill papers, 2/82*)

22 December 1949

Mr Eden telephoned to say that he has now been invited to an Australian dinner on the same night as the ceremony mentioned in his letter.[1] He is going to accept for the Australian dinner, and make that the excuse for not going to the Indian one, but before he does this he would like your approval.[2]

Winston S. Churchill to Clement Attlee
(*Churchill papers, 2/29*)

23 December 1949

My dear Prime Minister,
Thank you for sending me the papers about the North Atlantic Defence Committee meetings at Washington and at Paris.[3] I have read these with attention and hope they may prove beneficial to our security.
I now return them to you.

Winston S. Churchill to Christopher Soames
(*Lady Soames papers*)

24 December 1949

From now on till I return in January, Kurn and the two Germans should complete the clearance work they are doing for Mrs Churchill beyond the water garden, and the new rhododendrons should be planted at the earliest suitable moment. Vincent will take general charge of this. Wood-cutting and filling the woodshed is an important job for rainy days.

2. As soon as Mrs Churchill's work has been finished, the most urgent work is to improve the fox-proof fence as far as possible. For this purpose we must buy as much wire netting as we can get. There are also a number of iron standards with hooks at the end of them, which I saved from the water-garden fence, which could be worked in where necessary. All three men should work on this and do the best they can. What are the possibilities of getting the wire netting? Southon should be asked about this.

3. Mrs Churchill wants the path from the stepping-stones across the mill pond (after the leafy arch) to the ground she has cleared to be of ashes or gravel, wide enough for two to walk side by side, and this should be completed

[1] Reproduced above (p. 1584).
[2] Churchill wrote on this note: 'I think that is much better.'
[3] See Attlee to Churchill of Oct. 27, reproduced above (p. 1557).

as convenient. The stones should be stacked in a handy position, as there are various small jobs to be done in the garden with them.

4. The first of these is the making of the steps down the bank from the house to the new reservoir, which are to be done exactly as Kurn did the others.

5. Vincent should tell Kurn and the Germans to fill in the holes near the waterfall next week.

Winston S. Churchill to Lord Camrose
(Churchill papers, 2/161)

29 December 1949

My dear Bill,

I send you at last your picture. I had hoped it would reach you for Christmas, but it now strikes the New Year. I hope you will approve of it in its final form. The picture should be varnished in about a year, and if you let me know I will arrange to have this done.

We are off today – a fortnight's sunshine in our hopes, and some weeks or months, or other things in our minds.

Every good wish for 1950.

January
1950

Lady Killearn[1] to Winston S. Churchill
(Churchill papers, 2/171)[2]

5 January 1950

My dear Winston,

Once before a great battle, I gave you a lucky Egyptian cat (Bubastes!).

Now, before a battle just as great, I send you a British black cat (Tiger Tim!) with my warmest good wishes.

Forgive the chip on his paw, he is much travelled! It is no chip on his shoulder despite his non success in bringing us luck lately! However, they say a change of ownership brings back the luck!

Miles is off to Batavia so won't be here for the Great Day. We must leave Chilham and so far have found no roof we can afford. I shall have to continue the dreary search.

Might you want a tried proconsul for Washington? (Don't they dearly love half American lords there?) or a g.g. somewhere? Pray think of your good and faithful servants who chew the sour cud of inactivity and only long to work beneath your shining leadership once again.

All good luck and fortune, with affectionate admiration.[3]

Winston S. Churchill: speech
('Winston S. Churchill, His Complete Speeches', volume 8, page 7903)

12 January 1950   Southampton

I heard there was going to be a General Election. So I thought I had better come back in case I was wanted. I think it is high time we had a new Parliament. I think the Government have been quite right in giving six weeks' notice. It is just what I did last time. I hope it will be an equally good result

---

[1] Née Jacqueline Castellani: see biographical note on p. 779 above.
[2] This letter was handwritten.
[3] Churchill wrote to Lady Killearn on Feb. 16: 'It is very kind of you to send me the little black cat. Thank you so much for your thought.'

– the other way round. We have great need for a new surge of impulse to put our country back into its proper and true place in the world, and at the head of an Empire on which the sun never sets.

Winston S. Churchill to Clementine Churchill[1]
(*Churchill papers, 1/47*)

13 January 1950

Am alone children shooting with Bendor.[2] Babies thriving. Your steps and path beautifully completed. Anthony lunched with me today. Rab Butler comes tonight and Woolton tomorrow. All going well.
Love.

General George Kenney[3] *to Winston S. Churchill*
(*Churchill papers, 2/171*)

13 January 1950   Maxwell Field, Alabama

Dear Mr Churchill,

I have just returned from a visit with a mutual friend of ours – Bernard Baruch. Your name came up several times during the conversation and if expressions of admiration and good wishes mean anything, events during the immediate future should be eminently satisfactory to you.

I want to express my sincere thanks for the two autographed books which you sent me. They are among my most prized possessions. I have long admired the author, but in addition, the style and the graphic presentation of events during those interesting and critical days of the world's history, make them fascinating recitals that I find myself reading and rereading at rather frequent intervals.

If our paths should cross at any time, I want to tell you personally how much I am enjoying them and to satisfy my own curiosity, I will ask for your own opinions and criticisms of the story of my own American and Australian youngsters in the South West Pacific, especially during the dark days of 1942 and 1943. That was their finest hour.

[1] The Churchills were holidaying in Madeira when, on 11 Jan. 1950, Parliament was dissolved and a general election called for Feb. 23. Churchill, as Leader of the Opposition, returned to England immediately; Clementine remained abroad until Jan. 20.

[2] Hugh 'Bendor' Grosvenor, Duke of Westminster.

[3] George Churchill Kenney, 1889–1977. Asst Military Attaché for Air to France, 1940. Technical Executive, Air Corps Material Div., 1940–1. Maj.-Gen., 1941. Commanding Gen., Air Corps Experimental Depot and Engineering School, 1941–2; 4th Air Force, 1942; Allied Air Forces SW Pacific, 1942–5; 5th Air Force (Australia), 1942–4; Far East Air Forces, 1944–5; Pacific Air Command, US Army, 1945; Strategic Air Command, 1946–8; Air University, 1948–51. Senior US Representative to UN Military Staff Committee, 1946.

In the meantime, please accept my very best wishes for your success this year and for the many years ahead.

Winston S. Churchill to Clementine Churchill
(Churchill papers, 1/47)

16 January 1950

Hope all has been pleasant. Here nothing but toil and moil. Longing to see you.

Winston S. Churchill to Lady Violet Bonham Carter
(Churchill papers, 2/111)

17 January 1950

My dear Violet,

I see that you are not included among the four Liberal Party speakers chosen to broadcast between now and polling-day.

I regret that your voice should not be heard in this serious crisis in our history. I therefore offer you one of the occasions allotted to us, namely February 9.

I need not say that no conditions of any kind are attached to this proposal which is made by me only in the name of fair play and free speech for those whose voices should not be absent from the national debate.

Winston S. Churchill to Clementine Churchill
(Baroness Spencer-Churchill papers)

19 January 1950   Chartwell

My Darling,

Welcome home! And what a pack of toil and trouble awaits you! I have not thought of anything in the week since I returned except politics, particularly the Tory manifesto on which we have had prolonged discussions. One day we were nine hours in the dining room of No. 28.

The Socialists are forcing the Election on to the most materialist lines. All bold treatment of topics in the public interest is very dangerous. The Liberals are running over four hundred candidates, of which at the outside seven will be elected, apart from the sixty others who are working with us.

The Gallup Polls I showed you on the diagram have taken a big dip. Instead of being nine points ahead we are only three. This I think is due to Christmas and the fact that none of the evils of Devaluation have really manifested themselves yet and are only on the way. How many seats the Liberal 'splits' will cause us cannot be measured. All is in the unknown. However there would be no fun in life if we knew the end at the beginning.

Hawkey is in much better health. I think you will find things locally getting into good order. My Liberal opponent has withdrawn and gone to fight Herbert Morrison at Lewisham. He must be a very pugnacious fellow. We have a new one, but I do not recall his name.

I have an immense programme but not more than I can carry. The broadcast speech is finished. I am planning to open my speaking campaign in the constituency with an address to the same lot of Headquarters staff and workers that we met the other night, last month. This will enable me to make a nationwide speech on Saturday, January 28.

You will like to see Randolph's admirable opening speech. They now say that Foot[1] is going to bolt to a safer seat. Randolph is coming for the weekend. June is staying in the constituency to electioneer with Arabella.[2]

I was grieved to learn this morning from Christopher that he has a duodenal ulcer. Until he is photographed next week we cannot tell how serious it is. The doctor hopes he will be able to fight. If not, Mary will have to fill the gap.

I am so glad your voyage home was comfortable, but it would have been disastrous if I had not been on the spot here during this difficult week when so many grave decisions had to be taken, not of what to <u>do</u> – that would be easy – but of what to <u>say</u> to our poor and puzzled people. I am much depressed about the country because for whoever wins there will be nothing but bitterness and strife, like men fighting savagely on a small raft which is breaking up. 'May God save you all' is my prayer.

Come home & kiss me

Your ever loving
[Drawing of a pig preceded by word 'Tusks']

Lord Simon to Winston S. Churchill
(*Churchill papers, 2/65*)[3]

19 January 1950

Dear Winston,

Every good wish for your Broadcast on Saturday. If you can include a word of appeal and commendation addressed to the 'National Liberals', you will put them in good heart.

---

[1] Michael Foot, MP (Lab.) for Plymouth Devonport.
[2] Arabella Spencer-Churchill, 1949–2007. Daughter of Randolph Churchill and June Osborne. Educated at Fritham School for Girls and Ladymede School. Co-founder, Glastonbury Festival, 1970. Started Children's World International, 1999.
[3] This letter was handwritten.

Winston S. Churchill: broadcast
('In the Balance', pages 155–60)

21 January 1950 London

THE CONSERVATIVE POINT OF VIEW

All the world is wondering what is going to happen here at this election. In every country – friend, ally, foe; victor, rescued or vanquished – inquiring or anxious minds are turned to Britain. What is she going to do? That is the question on every lip. The Empire, the English speaking world, all Europe outside the Iron Curtain are once again looking to us in curiosity and anxiety. For what it is worth, this is a compliment. We need not shrink at all from this attention. Under our British Constitution, slowly and painfully built but solidly established, and not yet overturned, all can vote and none need fear to discharge their civic duty. Not to vote on what is now at stake for our country – or to vote in a way which wastes the vote – would be a failure to rise to the level of events. The ballot is secret. The votes can be freely recorded and will be fairly counted, and the results will govern our fortunes – it may be for a long time to come.

At this moment everyone ought to consider very carefully what is his duty towards his country, towards the causes he believes in, towards his home and family and to his own personal rights and responsibilities. What then is the supreme and fundamental question which we have to answer and have to answer now? As I see it, the choice before us is whether we should take another plunge into Socialist regimentation, or by a strong effort regain the freedom, initiative and opportunity of British life. I believe that on this decision depends not only our future as a leading nation in world thought and progress, but also our physical ability to maintain our vast population upon decent standards without foreign charity. Let us therefore examine the matter without being confused by the hum and throb of events.

Socialism is based on the idea of an all-powerful State which owns everything, which plans everything, which distributes everything, and thus through its politicians and officials decides the daily life of the individual citizen. We have not of course got this – or anything like it – in Britain at the present time. The process of establishing the Socialist State has only begun. The practical question which we have to settle now is whether we shall take another deep plunge into State ownership and State control, or whether we shall restore a greater measure of freedom of choice and action to our people, and of productive fertility and variety to our industry and trade.

Before deciding upon this, it is well to look around. Except in Scandinavia, Socialism and Socialist parties are on the decline throughout Europe everywhere outside the Iron Curtain. Socialism has been found in all European countries, bond or free, to have been the weakest defence against

Communism. In taking another lurch into Socialism at this juncture we should be moving contrary to the general trend and tide of reviving European society. Still more should we be out of harmony with the States and nations of the English-speaking world, the British Dominions and the United States. Mr Attlee at this moment is the head of the only Socialist government to be found anywhere in the whole English-speaking world, the birthplace and the home of parliamentary democracy – the only one.

New Zealand and Australia, which have given a prolonged trial to Socialist governments, though not of course to Socialism in its complete form, have recently shaken themselves free. A young nation, like Australia, dwelling in a continent growing ample food for itself and for export may try experiments in Socialism without the risk of fatal injury, but the 50,000,000 gathered together in this small island are in a very different position. We are a highly artificial community, balanced precariously at a level of well-being which before the war was superior to anything in Europe, but whose means of existence have been seriously, though not yet irreparably, undermined by changes in the surrounding world, and also by the actions of our own Government during these last critical and difficult years.

No nation of equal size, no society of equal civilization, has ever been in time of peace in the economic peril in which we stand. We do not grow enough food at home to keep ourselves alive, nor have we many of the raw materials which we need to earn our living. I am sure that if we act wisely we can make our way through our dangers as we have done before. But if, through political thoughtlessness or wrong guidance, we make grave mistakes and consume our strength in domestic quarrels and class war, consequences may descend upon us the like of which we have never yet suffered or even imagined.

The main reason why we are not able to earn our living and make our way in the world is because we are not allowed to do so. The whole enterprise, contrivance and genius of the British nation is being increasingly paralysed by the wartime restrictions from which all other free nations have shaken themselves clear, but these are still imposed upon our people here in the name of a mistaken political philosophy and a largely obsolete mode of thought. Our Government is the only one glorying in controls for controls' sake. I am sure that a parliament resolved to set the nation free would soon enable it to earn its own living in the world. I am sure on the other hand that the Socialist policy of equalizing misery and organizing scarcity instead of allowing diligence, self-reliance and ingenuity to produce abundance, has only to be prolonged to be fatal to our British island home.

The scheme of society for which Conservatives and National Liberals stand is the establishment and maintenance of a basic standard of life and labour below which a man or a woman, however old or weak, shall not be allowed to fall. The food they receive, the prices they have to pay for basic necessities, the homes they live in, their employment, must be the first care of the State, and must have priority over all other peace-time needs. Once we have made that standard secure we propose to set the nation free as quickly as possible from the controls and restrictions which now beset our daily life. Above the basic standard there will be free opportunity to rise. Everyone will be allowed to make the best of himself, without jealousy or spite, by all the means that honour and the long respected laws of our country allow.

One of the main pillars of any modern society is a stable value for money. 'Honest money', as it is called, is the only means by which goods and services can be fairly interchanged for mutual benefit between fellow citizens. The Socialist Government has spent every penny which it could lay its hands on, or which it could beg or borrow. They have spent in their term of office over £17,000,000,000 including the enormous sums given or loaned to us from abroad. They have exacted from us the heaviest taxation in the world. We are now paying £500,000,000 more a year even than in the height of the war.

At the same time they have cut down the buying power of every pound we earn in wages, salaries or in trading with one another. The British pound has fallen since the war stopped by no less than 3*s*. 8*d*. This has struck a heavy blow at the social services, at pensions of every kind, at every form of national insurance and at all savings. Thus what is given with the one hand is taken away with the other, and Socialist claims about safeguarding or extending the social services are vitiated by the fraud of giving only 16*s*. 4*d*. and calling it a pound. This is one of the gravest evils which we have to face and, remember, we still have the consequences of devaluation coming upon us to make it worse. I hope, my friends, you will think carefully about this and what it means to all of us. As head of the wartime Government I proclaimed the Four-Years' Plan of social reform – Education, Family Allowances and the National Health Scheme. Although mauled and twisted a bit by ministerial ineptitude, this programme has now largely been carried through. At that time I summed it up in three words: Food, Work and Homes.

Without food, work is impossible and homes a mockery. I am sorry indeed that Lord Woolton is not looking after our food as he did in the war. We should have a better diet now if he were and at about half the administrative cost. Cheap and abundant food is the foundation of our strength. It will be the foundation of our policy. But this can only come in the long run from the workings of a free market. There is, however, a larger aspect of the food problem. We must grow more food at home. We must set to work forthwith to raise our home-grown food supply. We must also make long-term arrangements inside the Empire for the mutual trade, whereby our brothers in their spacious food lands will feel that they have an assured market in the Mother Country and can plan ahead to supply it.

Now I come to work. All parties are agreed that the prevention of unemployment ranks next to food in the duties of any government. The policy on unemployment which all parties will follow was set forth in the commanding scheme of the National Government to which the leading men of all parties bound themselves in 1944. The scheme has not had to be put into operation for two reasons. First, because all the world is still at work and engaged in repairing the damage of the war, and replacing all kinds of things that were not made while it was going on. And, secondly, there has been very little unemployment because the Americans and our own Dominions have lent or given us over £400,000,000 a year ever since the war stopped.

The Government calculate, and their leading members have declared, that but for the large subsidies which the United States have so generously supplied, but which the Socialists somewhat ungratefully do not even mention in their manifesto, there would have been between 1,500,000 and 2,000,000 unemployed in this island during these years. I am not prepared myself to challenge these calculations, though I think perhaps we could have done better than that. But that is what Mr Morrison and Mr Bevan say, and we must agree with our opponents on facts whenever we can.

Thus on the question of unemployment there is no real difference between the two political parties. Why then in this election should all kinds of wrongful charges and false claims of party achievements be bandied about, when we are all agreed that American aid has prevented the kind of unemployment which appeared after the last war and rose again to hideous heights under the Socialist Government of twenty years ago, and when we are also agreed on the kind of remedies we should use to cope with it should it occur? The Conservative and National Liberal Parties regard the prevention of mass unemployment as the most solemn duty of government. Great difficulties lie ahead when the consequences of devaluation come home to us and when American aid ends. If human brains and will-power can conquer these dangers, we shall, with God's blessing, succeed. It is not the first time we have been through a life and death struggle together.

Lastly our homes. It is the homes that I wish to end in tonight. Three years ago we were promised that by the time of this election there would be no housing shortage as far as the mass of the British people were concerned. But the council waiting-lists are longer than ever. Before the war under a Conservative Government we were building by the normal process of supply and demand 1,000 houses a day. With all this need, and the same labour force, we are building only half as many now, and every house costs three times as much. Surely something must have gone wrong – and very wrong.

What then will you do about all these problems? Will you simply go on melting down the treasures of the past, and shrug your shoulders at the perils of the future? If so, a terrible awakening lies not so far ahead. It will not only be worldly fame and power which will pass from Britain, but the long treasured theme of British history and British greatness will be broken. I am sure it is not too late for our nation to lift itself above its troubles and resume, amid world-wide thanksgiving, its share in guiding the upward march of man. But if we should sink into mere materialism, and petty calculations of immediate personal advantage and fleeting gain, it will not be our reputation only which will perish, but our power to keep ourselves independent and even alive.

Class quarrels, endless party strife, on a background of apathy, indifference and bewilderment, will lead us all to ruin. Only a new surge of impulse can win us back the glorious ascendancy which we gained in the struggle for right and freedom, and for which our forebears had nerved our hearts down the long aisles of time. Let us make a supreme effort to surmount our dangers. Let faith, not appetite, guide our steps. There still remain forces in our island that can bring back all our true glories and range our people once again in the vanguard of Christian civilization to revive and save the world.

Clement Davies to Winston S. Churchill
(Churchill papers, 2/64)

23 January 1950

My dear Churchill,

I have been studying the statement put out under your name and that of Lord Rosebery yesterday, and the reply of the Liberal Headquarters, and I cannot help wondering if you have been fully informed of the circumstances in which a number of so-called Liberal-Conservative bodies have come into being.

Having studied the facts, there is no doubt in my mind that Liberal Party Headquarters is quite right in claiming that these bodies are 100% Conservative-controlled, and in no way connected with the Liberal Party, of which you yourself were once so distinguished a member.

I ask you in the interests of fair play to investigate personally such examples as the following:

(i) In November of last year a meeting was held in Dunstable in private, with only invited persons present. The Prospective Liberal candidate and some members of the local Liberal and Unionist Association were refused admittance to a meeting which set up the 'United Liberal and Conservative Association'.

(ii) In December last a meeting was held in Kirriemuir to consider a merger between the local Liberal and Unionist Associations. A handful of Unionists attended; no Liberals were present. The merger was approved by no single Liberal.

(iii) In February last a meeting was held in North Angus, attended by some 400 Conservatives and three Liberals, steps having been taken deliberately to exclude Liberals in general. The three present were asked to leave when they voiced their objection. The formation of a Liberal-Unionist Association was approved – but by no single Liberal.

(iv) In March last all Liberals and Conservatives 'interested' were invited to attend a meeting of the 'Torrington Division United Liberal and Conservative Association (Bideford area)'. The chairman, secretary and some members of the Bideford and District Liberal Association were 'interested' enough to attend, but too interested to be allowed to remain. They were informed in reply to a question that 'Liberal' had been incorporated in the title of the conveners as a result of a decision taken at an earlier meeting which was attended by no Liberals. On rising to protest, the secretary of the Liberal Association was told that she could remain silent or leave the hall. She left with some 20 other Liberals.

These appear to me to be devices for attempting to regularise the use of the world 'Liberal', with which, once you know the facts, I feel certain you would not wish to be associated.

I believe it is of paramount importance that the public should know exactly for whom they are voting this time and which Party's Whip a member of Parliament will take when he is elected.

Is it too much to ask that the Conservative Party should fight under its own name, or at least under a name which does not clash with that of another party which is recognized throughout the world?

PS. Inasmuch as so much publicity has attended yesterday's statement over your name and that of Lord Rosebery, copies of this letter are being given to the Press.

Field Marshal Lord Alexander to Winston S. Churchill
(Churchill papers, 2/30)

23 January 1950
Confidential

My dear Churchill,

The United States Mutual Defence Assistance Act of 1949 requires amongst other things that a series of Bilateral Treaties should be negotiated before the President can authorise the expenditure of the monies voted by Congress for military aid.

As you are probably aware, discussions between the United States and ourselves have been going on in Washington of recent weeks. The main object of the Treaties is to determine the conditions which will govern the furnishing of military assistance by one contracting government to the others, and we have now reached the position in which there is reasonable hope that an agreement will be ready for signature in the course of the next few days.

As you are aware, there is a rule of practice (not of law) which has, for a long period, been followed by successive governments under which international agreements, which do not come into force immediately on signature but require ratification or some similar formal step, are laid before both Houses of Parliament for twenty one working days before they are brought into force by the deposit of an instrument of ratification, or whatever the subsequent formal step may be. This gives an opportunity for any Member of Parliament to raise the matter in the appropriate way before His Majesty's Government become committed to the obligations of the Agreement in question. The practice is inapplicable to agreements which come into force immediately on signature, and a number of quite important agreements concluded by successive governments have come into force on signature. Further, this practice, even in the cases where it applies, has always been subject to a discretion vested in the Government of the day to dispense with the twenty one days' rule in any case where the Government thought that it was necessary and appropriate to do so, having regard in particular to the urgency of the matter.

As I said earlier, we are now, I hope, on the point of being ready to sign an agreement with the United States under which the United States will, under certain conditions, furnish the United Kingdom with military assistance in the material form of aircraft (B.29's) and possibly certain raw materials and the like. In return, the United Kingdom agrees to make available to the United States such equipment, materials, services or other military assistance as we authorise in accordance with detailed arrangements to be made from time to time. The Agreement does not commit us as to the amount or form of such reciprocal facilities except as regards the cost of the US Government's administrative expenditure in this country in connection with assistance furnished to the United Kingdom and on this point, as explained in a later paragraph of this letter, we have safeguarded the need for securing Parliamentary authority.

A copy of the Agreement in draft is attached and it will not come into force immediately on signature but only when His Majesty's Government formally notify the United States of its acceptance. In principle, therefore, it falls under the twenty one days' rule, but the Government consider that there are good reasons for making this one the Agreement does require expenditure of money by His Majesty's Government, you will observe that Article VII (1) safeguards this point because the obligation itself is conditional on the Government of the United Kingdom obtaining from Parliament the provision of the necessary appropriations.

In the circumstances, having regard to the undoubted importance of the matter, the Government have thought it right to consult the Leaders of the Opposition Parties before dispensing with the twenty one days' rule, although in less important cases it has been the practice to dispense with it without consulting the Members of the Opposition.

The Americans very much want to sign the series of treaties by the end of this week and I should, therefore, be greatly obliged if you could let me have your views very quickly.

I should perhaps add that, as you will see from the text, there are two technical points, one relating to customs arrangements and the other to diplomatic immunity, on which full agreement has not yet been reached. Neither issue is fundamental to the main object of the Treaty and I hope that the Americans will be prepared ultimately to accept something on the lines of our proposals.

I am sending a similar letter to Clem Davies.

Lady Violet Bonham Carter to Winston S. Churchill
(Churchill papers, 2/111)[1]

23 January 1950

Dearest dear Winston,

I know that B[2] has written to you to tell you of the infinite sorrow and disappointment I felt in refusing the opportunity you offered me so generously.[3]

I still don't know whether what I did – or rather what I didn't do – was right or wrong.

I think that it was probably politically right, but possibly morally wrong.

It was not my colleagues' judgement (or their screams!) which influenced me (though Walter Layton's opinion had some weight.)

It was the fear that all the humble, loyal, rank-and-file Liberals in the country who trust me and believe in me, would feel that on the eve of battle I had stabbed them in the back.

As you know, I am no more sanguine about the outcome of this battle for us than you are.

If the general result is indecision there may well be another before long, but it may also well be too late for us to play a decisive part.

Dearest Winston – apart from all moral-political considerations what I minded most was not to do anything in the world you asked of me. Please believe this.

Your drooping, moulting and bedraggled 'Bloody Duck'[4]

PS. So much did I mean this that after reading you my draft letter of acceptance on the telephone that night I started straightaway to write my broadcast.

[1] This letter was handwritten.
[2] Maurice Bonham Carter, 1880–1960. Known as 'Bongie'. Educated at Winchester and Balliol College, Oxford. Barrister, Lincoln's Inn, 1909. Private Secretary to H. H. Asquith, 1910–16. Married, 1915, Helen Violet Asquith. KCB, 1916. KCVO, 1917.
[3] See Churchill to Lady Violet Bonham Carter, 17 Jan. 1950, reproduced above (p. 1591).
[4] The 'bloody duck' refers to Churchill's tongue-in-cheek reminiscence of PM Stanley Baldwin's offer of the office of Chancellor of the Exchequer in 1924. He 'should have liked to have answered, "Will the bloody duck swim?"'. See Martin Gilbert, *Winston S. Churchill*, vol. 5, *The Prophet of Truth: 1922–1939* (Hillsdale, MI, 2009), p. 59.

I think I could have done a reasonably good one (better than Priestley's anyway!) Yours was magnificent I thought – so does Gilbert Murray,[1] who has written to me today about it.

Winston S. Churchill to General Lord Ismay
(*Churchill papers, 4/299*)

24 January 1950

I should be very much obliged if you would get the story of 'tube alloys' in their order, so far as it goes in Book 7. The subject might be introduced in the chapter WAR IN THE AETHER, which might then be called AETHER AND THE ATOM, or something like it. The first part should describe the progress we had made before we went to Washington, and the contacts established with the Americans and the French. 'The Prof'[2] and Sir John Anderson have all the details and would, I am sure, help.

Now we come to our Tobruk visit to Washington. Am I right in thinking that the discussions about the atomic bomb took place then? I have described the talks in Chapter XVIII, but I am not absolutely sure if the date of the Agreement was drawn up between the President and me. I think I wrote it out myself, and it is I believe in the Government Archives. When and where was this settled? Only after we got back to the White House I am sure. It may be however that it was not settled in this formal manner till some months later. It was arranged at a visit which I paid to the White House. An accurate description is required of these negotiations. At least a thousand words will be needed. However there was one occasion when we fetched Sir John Anderson over for that purpose. I am not sure that this was not immediately after the talks at Hyde Park on the 19th. My general impression is that our scientists were a little ahead of the Americans and at any rate more confident that results could be achieved during the war. What evidence is there of this and who were the men principally concerned? This matter is of the highest interest and importance. I do not think we have had the information I expected from the United States about information being interchanged. We have not now either got any bombs or the way of making them or, so far as I know, have made any arrangements to have them brought over. The whole subject requires most careful statement. We must get the dates and facts right first.

Here on we shall require a brief account of the gigantic measures taken by the United States. Our difficulties about exchanging information did not

---

[1] George Gilbert Aime Murray, 1866–1957. Classical scholar. Regius Prof. of Greek, Oxford University, 1908–36. Chairman, League of Nations Union, 1928–40. President, United Nations Association, 1947–9.
[2] Lord Cherwell.

begin until the matter was taken over by the American War Department, who wished to keep the secret wholly to themselves. It is an interesting story about how this enormous expenditure was passed through Congress, and even the object to which it was to be devoted being mentioned. And there is the enormous number of American university graduates employed as well as the leading scientists. I need to tell the whole of this, but certainly not at this point or in this volume. A general picture should be given of the part Canada played. This is very important and must be featured at every stage.

There is of course no hurry, but I should like to know the main dates as soon as possible.

Winston S. Churchill to Bernard Baruch
(Churchill papers, 2/175)

24 January 1950

My dear Bernie,

I do not know if you have yet met Sir Leslie Rowan who last November took up his new position as Economic Minister at the British Embassy in Washington. If you have not I think you would find it worthwhile for you to do so. He ranks in seniority second only to the Ambassador.

During the war he was one of my Principal Private Secretaries at Number 10, and in those years I formed a great liking for his personality and a high regard for his ability and character. He remained at Number 10 for some time after I left and then went to the Treasury as a senior and responsible official. I like him very much and have made him one of my executors.

It would be most helpful I am sure, from our point of view, if you could find the time to see him. Sir Leslie is a highly intelligent and most agreeable person and I know you would find him interesting and well-informed. He has a charming wife.

Winston S. Churchill to Clement Davies
(Churchill papers, 2/64)

25 January 1950

My dear Davies,

I thank you for you kindness in writing to me amid your many cares.[1] As you were yourself for eleven years a National Liberal and in that capacity supported the Governments of Mr Baldwin and Mr Neville Chamberlain, I should not presume to correct your knowledge of the moral, intellectual and

---

[1] Letter reproduced above (pp. 1597–8).

legal aspects of adding a prefix or a suffix to the honoured name of Liberal. It has certainly often been done before by honourable and distinguished men. There has also been a general custom that at Elections people are free to call themselves – and to some extent their opponents – what they like, and that it is for the electors in each Constituency to judge for themselves about it all. The local Associations in the Conservative Party enjoy a measure of freedom and independence unrivalled in modern political life, and I should certainly not attempt to limit their rights. Indeed, it is natural and proper that Conservatives and Liberals who conscientiously are opposed to Socialism should join together in this crisis in whatever seems to be the most effective way in order to resist the common danger to our country, and to defend so much that is dear to us in our way of life. Thus alone can they give effect to their most sincere convictions. But you have been through all this yourself, and I do not need to dwell upon it further.

Since, however, you have been good enough to address me, I will venture to draw your attention to the fact that you and your friends do not seem to have any difficulty on the question of nomenclature with the Socialist Party. I have not heard, for instance, of any candidate who is standing as a Liberal-Socialist. The reason is, no doubt, that the two terms are fundamentally incompatible. No one can be at once a Socialist and a Liberal. The establishment of a Socialist State controlling all the means of production, distribution and exchange, is the most complete contradiction of Liberal principles that now exists. I do not therefore expect that you will have to write any letter to Mr Attlee on this point.

It is not the Conservatives who have ousted the Liberals from their position as a great Party. The Liberal Government that entered the war in 1914 had 263 Members in the House of Commons. Making such allowances as are possible for Redistribution, it is not I think inaccurate to state that four out of every five Liberal seats have been devoured by the Socialists. I saw a cartoon the other day of a lion with its mouth wide open confronting the Liberal Party. On the lion's stomach was inscribed the word 'Toryism'. This was evidently a mistake on the part of the gifted cartoonist. The true word would have been 'Socialism'. They have not only devoured the bulk of the Liberal Party; they have digested it. Not a trace of their meal remains. Not even a label is hanging out of the Socialist lion's mouth.

Why then should you and your friends and your four hundred candidates always blame the Conservative Party, and do all in your power to help the Socialists? It seems to me that as patriotic men you are taking a grave responsibility by a policy of vote-splitting on a fantastic scale. It is strange political conduct to scheme for the return of minority candidates with whom you disagree, be they Tories or Socialists, at the risk of bringing about a stalemate or deadlock at this anxious juncture. We hope that responsible and serious minded Liberals will not waste their votes on this occasion, and that the solid strength of the Conservatives and National-Liberals will save the country from this danger. But if such a misfortune were to happen the six or seven members you may have in the new Parliament, even if they agreed, would be quite unable to cope with the consequences.

There is a real measure of agreement between modern Tory democracy and the mass of Liberals who see in Socialism all that their most famous thinkers and leaders have fought against in the past. An intense passion of duty unites us in this fateful hour in an honourable freedom in which the undying flame of Liberalism burns.

I hope you and your friends will ponder carefully upon what I have set down, and do not hesitate to write to me again if you think I can be of further service.

Clement Davies to Winston S. Churchill
(Churchill papers, 2/64)

26 January 1950

My dear Churchill,

I have received your reply. I am sorry that, on a matter of such public importance, it should appear to be, and is evidently intended to be, facetious and evasive. In my letter I set out the facts in four specific instances where so-called Liberal-Conservative Associations were set up without the participation of a single member of the Liberal Party and asked whether, when those facts were brought to your attention, you would still be prepared to lend your great name and the high prestige of your position to the perpetuation of a calculated deception. I gather that, knowing those facts, you are, nevertheless prepared to support and approve of what we Liberals rightly regard as an unworthy subterfuge.[1]

Anthony Eden to Winston S. Churchill
(Churchill papers, 2/36)

26 January 1950

My dear Winston,

Thank you so much for letting me see the enclosed.[2] It is true, as Alexander says, that laying documents for twenty-one days before Parliament is not a law, but it is a long-established practice and we have always observed it. It is unfortunate that these important agreements should not have reached us a little earlier so that we could all have discussed them in the House. I

---

[1] Churchill wrote to his staff: 'No further answer.'
[2] Letter of Jan. 23 from FM Lord Alexander to Churchill, reproduced above (pp. 1598–1600).

have only hurriedly looked through them, but it is clear that they do give very far-reaching powers. Some people will not like them (e.g., Max,[1] I suppose.) It would have been much better if they could all have been properly discussed in the open when the strong arguments in their favour could have been fully deployed.

Alexander says that the Americans want to sign the series of Treaties by the end of this week, which again seems a remarkable hustle, since the North Atlantic Treaty to which they give effect was signed nearly a year ago. The two technical points on which he mentions agreement has not been reached are both important ones, particularly diplomatic immunity. The privileges we gave to Americans and other foreigners during the war were not liked, although they were accepted, and I remember as Leader of the House I had a pretty difficult time with them.

It appears that the urgency is to ensure that the flow of equipment should be made available by the 30th of June. I should have thought myself that this could quite well have been ensured by early ratification as soon as Parliament meets in March.

I am most anxious, as you are, to give effect to the Atlantic Treaty, but at the same time I cannot feel that the reasoning here is sufficiently strong to compel an agreement of this importance to be dealt with in this way, without the public having any knowledge of it or an opportunity to debate it. This is a very difficult question and you may think the risk of war is so imminent that we ought not to insist upon even a few weeks' delay, but personally I do not think so, and I fear if agreements are come to in this way they may not be as well received by the British public as they would have if the whole matter had been carried through by our ordinary constitutional practices.

Later. Jebb,[2] of the Foreign Office, has just telephoned to say our Ambassador in W'ton[3] has telegraphed urging immediate signature and that other European powers are doing so. I still resent this hustle, but you may feel that you can tell gov't, that responsibility is theirs and they must decide.

---

[1] Lord Beaverbrook.

[2] Hubert Miles Gladwyn Jebb, 1900–96. Graduated in History, Oxford University, 1922. Entered Diplomatic Service, 1924. Served in Teheran, Rome, and FO. Married, 1929, Cynthia Nobel (d. 1990). Private Secretary to Parliamentary Under-Secretary of State, FO, 1929–31; to Permanent Under-Secretary of State, 1937–40. Asst Under-Secretary, Ministry of Economic Warfare, 1940–5. Executive Secretary, Preparatory Commission of the UN, Aug. 1945. Deputy Under-Secretary, FO, 1949–50. Permanent UK Representative to UN, 1950–4. Ambassador to France, 1954–60. Member, European Parliament, 1973–6.

[3] Sir Oliver Franks.

1606　　　　　　　　　　January 1950

Winston S. Churchill to Field Marshal Lord Alexander
(Churchill papers, 2/36)

26 January 1950

My dear Minister of Defence,

I have to acknowledge your letter of January 23.[1] The subject is complicated and of the highest importance. We are now brought into it for the first time and are told that a decision is a matter of extreme urgency. In these circumstances we feel that the responsibility must rest with the Government of the day, and that it would not be right for us at this stage to seek to share it with you. This does not of course imply that we are opposed to the general line of policy which you are pursuing of which we have publicly expressed approval from time to time so far as we have become aware of it.

Winston S. Churchill: speech
('Winston S. Churchill, His Complete Speeches', volume 7, pages 7907–14)

28 January 1950　　　　　　　　　　　　　Woodford County School for Girls

WOODFORD ADOPTION MEETING

I thank you sincerely for the honour you have done me in choosing me for the sixth time to be your candidate for Parliament.[2] It is more than a quarter of a century since you first elected me, and it is indeed a pleasure to me and to my wife, the President of the Association, to feel that we still preserve your confidence and goodwill. Here in Woodford we have three opponents, Socialist, Liberal and Communist. On purely local grounds we are very content that they should all come and divide the hostile vote, among themselves. During the last fortnight the Liberal candidate has been changed. The one who has left us must have been a combative politician. He came out to fight me, but he has now gone to Lewisham to do his best to try to help Mr Morrison get in by fighting him. This somewhat curious procedure arises out of the decision of a very small and select group of Liberal leaders who conceive themselves the sole heirs of the principles and traditions of Liberalism, and believe themselves to have the exclusive copyright of the word 'Liberal'. I was very much amused to read a letter in the *Daily Telegraph* from the son of my old friend and colleague Mr George Lambert,[3] who served with me at the Admiralty in Mr Asquith's Government before the First World War. Mr Lambert quoted

---

[1] Reproduced above (pp. 1598–1600).
[2] Churchill won his constituency in the Feb. election with 60% of the vote.
[3] George Lambert, 1866–1958. MP (Lib.) for South Molton, 1891–1924, 1929–31; (Nat. Lib.) 1931–45. Civil Lord of the Admiralty, 1905–15. PC, 1912. Chairman, Parliamentary Liberal Party, 1919–21. Viscount, 1945.

some lines attributed to Dean Swift which he considered applicable to Mr Clement Davies and his associates.

> We are the chosen few
> All others will be damned
> There is no place in Heaven for you,
> We can't have Heaven crammed.

I have never read these lines before, but I think they deserve a wide circulation at the present time. This super select attitude finds an example in the exclusion of Lady Violet Bonham Carter and I may add of Sir Archibald Sinclair from the four broadcasts the Liberals are making between now and the poll. In Lady Violet Bonham Carter we have not only a Liberal of unimpeachable loyalty to the party but one of the finest speakers in the country. Her speech against Socialism which was so widely read two months ago recalled the style of old and famous days. But her voice must not be heard on the air on this occasion. 'We can't have heaven crammed.' Perhaps there may be more room after the votes have been counted in this particular celestial parlour. It is fifteen years since we have had a Liberal opponent in Woodford and we certainly have had very good and agreeable relations with our Liberal friends and have worked together in many ways. I earnestly hope that they will set an example to Liberal voters throughout the country by voting according to their consciences and convictions, and according to the long established principles of their party and world Liberalism against the establishment of the Socialist State.

When Mr Attlee's Government came into power nearly five years ago we did not underrate the difficulties with which they would have to contend. These difficulties would have strained to the utmost all the resources of a National Government and a united nation. We did not grudge the new Ministers their offices, nor envy them their responsibilities. We have steadfastly supported them in every step they have taken sincerely in the public interest. I always felt that we should need American aid to enable us to get on our feet again. We therefore supported the Government policy of seeking an American loan, and used what influence we possessed in the United States for that purpose. We hoped this would tide us over the transition from war to peace and help us to re-equip our industries, our agriculture and our mines. We also supported the policy of Marshall Aid. Indeed, General Marshall directly connected this broadminded and generous American action with the speeches which I had made about the need for European unity. If such help, or anything like it, had been forthcoming from across the Atlantic after the First World War almost measureless advantages might have been reaped by both Europe and America, and our own fortunes here at home in those hard days would have been far brighter. But this time we had a real chance. The object of the American Loan and of Marshall Aid, and the only possible justification for this being given or accepted, was to enable us to get our industry and agriculture working with the fullest activity, and to bring in the necessary food and raw materials to keep us going till conditions of world trade were restored. It was thought that this would take between three and four years of good administration, strict economy and united effort by all parties and classes under conditions of growing freedom from wartime restrictions.

Alas, these hopes were falsified. The Socialist Government, instead of devoting themselves to the supreme national task which the people had confided to them, put their party politics and the advancement of the doctrines of Socialism above all other considerations. Owing to their follies and wrongful action, a great part of all the loans and gifts we have received from abroad has been spent not upon the re-equipment of our industry, nor upon the import of basic foodstuffs: instead much of this precious aid was lavishly frittered away in American films and tobacco and in large quantities of foods and fruits which, however desirable as indulgences, were not indispensable to our recovery. When you have to borrow money from another country for the sacred purpose of national rehabilitation it is wrong to squander it upon indulgences. It was also wrong to send vast sums in unrequited exports to India and Egypt, both of which countries owed their safety from Japanese or German conquest to the exertions of our fleets and armies. We had every right to demand from those we had saved fair consideration for the immense expense to which we had been put in shielding them from the horrors of foreign invasion. It was also most improvident for our Government to make loans, advances and gifts to foreign countries on a scale out of all proportion to our means. We could not afford this lavishness ourselves but had to pay for it all out of borrowed money. There is an old saying, 'Be just before you are generous.'

The truest service we could render other countries in these years after the war was won was to get Britain on her feet again erect, strong and self-supporting. Thus we should have become again a world safeguard not a world problem. But Mr Attlee's Government seemed to have no thought of the grim realities of our position. They embarked upon the most profuse expenditure in all directions. As you know, in their four and a half years they have spent nearly £17,000,000,000. They have raised our taxation until it is the highest in the world, and even stands higher today than in the worst years of the war. With the immense aid given us by the US and our Dominions from overseas and the unparalleled sacrifices exacted from the taxpayers here, there was no reason why we should not have got back by now to solvency, security and independence. This has been denied us not only by the incompetence and maladministration of the Socialist Government and their wild extravagance, but even more by the spirit of class hatred which they have spread throughout the land, and by the costly and wasteful nationalization of a fifth part of our industries.

We now approach the crisis to which every spendthrift comes when he has used up everything he can lay his hands on, and everything he can beg or borrow and must face the hard reckoning of facts. That is no doubt the reason why they have fixed the election now instead of June, and hope to take advantage of the brief lull before the consequences of extravagance and devaluation come down upon us with their full inexorable force.

Our national campaign has opened well. The Conservative statement of policy *This is the Road* not only gives the detailed answers to many of the disputed and difficult questions of this momentous election, but also constitutes a broad, humane and progressive policy in which all Conservatives, Unionists and Liberal-minded men may find a wide sphere of common action. I have never seen any declaration of this character which has been received with so wide a measure of acclamation and approval.

A few months ago the Socialists hoped to win the election on the issue of unemployment. The Tories, they said, would like to have unemployment which they could use as a spur to compel greater exertions from the wage-earners. This was an outrageous charge. But although the British Socialist Party profess great hostility to Communism, they seem to have learned the Soviet doctrine, which was also Hitler's, that if you repeat a falsehood often enough it counts just as much as the truth. They claimed for themselves the credit of having provided full employment, and drew contrasts with what happened after the last war. Is it not surprising that in their official manifesto they should not even mention the aid they have received from the United States? There is not one word from the beginning to the end of this document, either of thanks to a generous and friendly nation, for the help on which they have lived politically or of recognition that, but for the American subsidies, mass unemployment would have fallen upon us, with all its sorrow and suffering. Yet Mr Morrison and Mr Bevan have both declared in public that, but for American aid there would have been between 1,500,000 and 2,000,000 unemployed during these years. However, the truth has become so widely known and realized that it is difficult for the Socialists either to make good their claims to have cured unemployment since the war, or their unfair charge that the Conservatives are not as resolute as they are to do everything in human power to prevent it.

Let me repeat, however, that we regard the maintenance of full employment as the first aim and duty of a Conservative Government. We do not underrate the difficulties which will follow the stopping of American aid under the Marshall Plan. We realize the efforts that will be required from the whole nation – all classes, all parties – if we are to regain our economic and moral independence. We believe, however, that nothing will help us more than that revival of world confidence and credit which would attend the return to power of a Conservative and National-Liberal Government pledged to a sound administration of the finances, and the simultaneous dismissal from power of a Socialist administration whose aid and object is to destroy wealth by class warfare and to stifle enterprise by nationalization.

It is worth while looking further in the Socialist election manifesto. We are told that it is Mr Herbert Morrison's plan for catching the middle-class vote. The word 'Socialism' is only mentioned twice. It is called *Let Us Win Through Together.* Mr Aneurin Bevan, the most popular figure in the Socialist Party, their potential Prime Minister, has been kept off the air. As he has described millions of his fellow-countrymen as 'lower than vermin' it no doubt was felt that his appeals through the broadcast might not fit with the theme, 'Let us win through together'. There might seem to be some incongruity. So he has been muzzled. Hitherto he has been neither muzzled nor led. The Prime Minister did not feel able to disavow his insults, but now –

> The Trumpet's silver voice is still
> The warder silent on the hill.[1]

Nevertheless we should look searchingly at this latest Socialist manifesto. It must be remembered that if they were returned to office, even though upon only a minority vote, the Socialists would feel themselves entitled to carry into law, or by regulation or executive action enforce every point that is mentioned in their declaration, however modestly it is tucked away.

They will of course nationalize the steel industry. Quite apart from the injury to this magnificent feature in our domestic life and export trade, this will give them the power to dominate for their party interests a large group of other industries for whom steel in one or other of its thousand forms is the foundation. They will have immense political power over all these industries and can make or mar them by expediting or delaying vital supplies, about which a tangle of formalities will be created in triplicate. Here, in itself, would be a long step forward to the establishment of the Socialist State. All this is rendered possible by the harmless looking words, 'The steel industry will be responsible to the nation'. It has certainly rendered our country incomparable and irreplaceable service, under the system which has been in practice for so many years of free enterprise, subject to Government supervision on prices and development as in Conservative days.

All this is to be thrown into disorder not because the Government want more *steel* but because they want more *power.* Should we be sustained by the electorate we shall repeal the Steel Nationalization Act before it comes into operation. The House of Lords has secured you the opportunity of deciding this question by a direct vote. Let us not forget that if the steel industry falls into Socialist Party hands it can be used as an instrument and weapon of party warfare to create the full Socialist State. There is another paragraph which has a deep and formidable significance. 'The Government will be empowered', says their manifesto, 'to start new competitive public enterprises in appropriate circumstances'. That means that a Socialist government can use the

[1] The quotation is from *Marmion* (1808) by Sir Walter Scott (1774–1832), taken from a passage on the death of the British PM William Pitt the Younger in 1806.

resources of the taxpayer to compete in trade rivalry with any private business they dislike or which, apart from any law, does not obey their wishes. They would in fact have the power to ruin any private undertaking in the country. They would be the sole judges of how, when and where to strike at it, and if they waste public money in this form of trade warfare, they have only to send in the bill to the Exchequer. No more deadly or far-reaching threat at private business and companies of all kinds – and it is on these that we depend for four-fifths of our whole industry, including more than nine-tenths of our export trade – has ever been levelled at the free productive life of Britain.

Other prosperous and well-managed industries, like cement and sugar and chemicals, are to be nationalized so that the consumer will have to pay more for their products, as he does for coal and electricity and transport, and so that a new horde of officials can be set up over them with new vistas of patronage opening out to Socialist politicians. Having made a failure of everything they have so far touched, our Socialist planners now feel it necessary to get hold of a few at present prospering industries so as to improve the general picture and the general results. There appears to be no plan or principle in the selection of these industries, except caprice and appetite. It does not matter how well they are now managed, how well they are serving the public, how much they sustain our export trade, how good are the relations between employers and employed. The Socialists just like the look of them, and so they think they will have them. But here you have your vote and your responsibility.

There is one more organization which is mentioned, and because it is mentioned made liable to nationalization. I refer of course to the vast business of life insurance, for which we are renowned all over the world and by which we earn over £30,000,000 a year in foreign exchange. The only anxiety which the Socialists have about nationalizing life insurance is whether it will lose them support among the very large number of insurance agents who have done so much to popularize thrift in the homes of people. They are most anxious to reassure these agents for the time being, and until they have got them properly in their grip. What they now seek is the control of the vast sum of money which represents the savings over many years of millions of people to provide by self-denial and forethought, for their widows, their orphans and their own old age or infirmity. The control over this great mass of investments would be another most powerful means of bringing the whole financial, economic and industrial life of Britain into Socialist hands.

I have no hesitation in saying that the new Socialist manifesto contains, under much smooth language, an effective design or plot – for that is a truer term – to obtain a power over their fellow-countrymen such as no British Government has ever sought before, and that this would be fatal alike to their freedom and prosperity. Here I must point out that there is no dispute between parties on this important point. 'The important fact', says the *Tribune* weekly newspaper which is the voice of Mr Aneurin Bevan, 'The important fact about the manifesto is that it will give a new Labour Government the mandate to go forward with the construction of a Socialist society in Britain.' This is indeed a clear case of 'You have been warned.' Before I leave the Socialist manifesto there is a point I noticed in the paragraph dealing with children's welfare. The admission is all the more revealing because it is unconscious. Here it is:

> The policy of putting the children at the head of the queue will be continued.

We are all agreed that the children should come first in our thoughts and in our resources. But why should they be at the head of the queue? Why should queues become a permanent, continuous feature of our life? Here you see clearly what is in their minds. The Socialist dream is no longer *Utopia* but *Queuetopia*. And if they have the power this part of their dream will certainly come true. Our earnest hope is that it may be granted to us to proclaim not the continuance but the doom of the queues and restore the normal relations between the shopkeepers and public.

But beware! For we may be at the parting of the ways. The wisdom of our forebears for more than 300 years has sought the division of power in the Constitution. Crown, Lords and Commons have been checks and restraints upon one another. The limitation of the power of absolute monarchy was the cause for which as Liberals used to say, 'Hampden died in the field and Sidney on the scaffold.' The concentration of all power over the daily lives of ordinary men and women in what is called 'the State', exercised by what is virtually single-chamber government, is a reactionary step contrary to the whole trend of British history and to the message we have given to the world. The British race have always abhorred arbitrary and absolute government in every form. The great men who founded the American Constitution expressed this same separation of authority in the strongest and most durable form. Not only did they divide executive, legislative and judicial functions, but also by instituting a federal system they preserved immense and sovereign rights to local communities and by all these means they have maintained – often at some inconvenience – a system of law and liberty under which they thrived and reached the physical and, at this moment, the moral leadership of the world. The Socialist conception of the all-powerful State entering into the smallest detail of the life and conduct of the individual and claiming to plan and shape his work and its rewards is odious and repellent to every friend of freedom. These absolute powers would make the group of politicians who obtained a majority of seats in Parliament, the masters and not the servants of the people and centralize all government in Whitehall.

So far we are only at the first stage in this evil journey. But already enterprise, daring and initiative are crippled. Property is destroyed by the heaviest taxation in the world. Regulations increasingly take the place of statutes passed by Parliament. These are contained in twenty-eight volumes, which can be purchased by all and sundry for £65. In these you may find that there are thousands of new crimes unknown before the war, now punishable by fine or imprisonment. The right is claimed in full peace by the executive Government to direct a man or woman to labour at any work or in any place a Minister or the officials under him may choose. Here are the words which Mr Isaacs, the Minister of Labour, used in the House of Commons on 3 December 1947, nearly three years after the war had stopped; when defending the Order giving him absolute power over the livelihood and employment of all men and women between the ages of 18–50 and 18–40 respectively:

> If any specific case is brought to our notice of a person claiming conscientious objection to a particular job we will give it our consideration; but we are not prepared to recognize that anyone has a right to conscientious objection to going to work unless that person is prepared at the same time to say that he will not eat.

This is the old and shameful doctrine of 'Work or starve', which no Government in Britain has ever dared to utter in time of peace for more than a hundred years. It is the greatest affront offered in modern times to the dignity of labour which rests upon a man's right to choose or change his job. I made my protest at the time, but in vain. The Regulation was imposed. It is still imposed. The Socialists have not dared to use it on any large scale, as yet. They are waiting for a renewal of their mandate. Conservatives and National Liberals on the other hand are resolved to expunge this blot from our industrial life.

In the face of moral issues like these, cutting right down to the roots of civilized society, it astounds me that liberal-minded men of any party can doubt where their duty lies. Picture to yourselves upon this background the small group of Left-Wing Liberals gathered in London and planning to run four hundred candidates, of whom not one in fifty and perhaps not one in a hundred will be returned to Parliament, in the hopes that by splitting votes they may frustrate the will of the majority of the nation and so show how important they are. I am sure that British Liberalism will recoil from and rise superior to such sorry and wanton machinations.

The British nation now has to make one of the most momentous choices in its history. That choice is between two ways of life; between individual liberty and State domination; between concentration of ownership in the hands of the State and the extension of a property-owning democracy; between a policy of increasing restraint and a policy of liberating energy and ingenuity; between a policy of levelling down and a policy of finding opportunity for all to rise upwards from a basic standard. It is no exaggeration to say that what we do here on the day of electoral trial will not only determine the course of British history, but will profoundly influence the immediate future of the world. Grapple with your duties and your perils while you still have your ancient strength.

Lord Swinton to Winston S. Churchill
(*Churchill papers, 2/101*)

31 January 1950

My dear Winston,

Our Questionnaire Committee is working very well; and we are enormously helped by the Research Department being able to answer all our questions and give us the facts we want on any subject at a moment's notice. I knew by experience they were very good, but I did not think it possible for this Department on a great variety of subjects to supply the information we have been able to get on other occasions from all the Government Departments; but we have not been able to fault them once. There is, however, one subject on which we need an authoritative statement to give to candidates. There is an insidious rumour that a Conservative Government would lengthen the period of National Service. We are told in some cases the figure has been given as three years. We all feel that this whispering campaign should be quickly and definitely scotched. It would be a very great help if you could do this in your speech at Leeds.

February 1950

Winston S. Churchill: statement
(Churchill papers, 2/64)

1 February 1950

Mr Churchill issued the following statement from Chartwell this evening, February 1st:

> Mr Byers' statement about my attitude toward Liberal Election broadcasts is both incomplete and incorrect. I was not present at the confidential meetings between the representatives of the three Parties, which Mr Byers has improperly disclosed and misreported. It has been the portion of the Government and the Official Opposition to have the same number of political broadcasts during the Election. On this basis five Socialist, five Conservative and one Liberal broadcast were agreed upon by the Socialist and Conservative Parties.
>
> Nevertheless the suggestion was made by Mr Eden, who represented me, that the Liberals should have two broadcasts of ten minutes each after the six o'clock news, as well as an evening broadcast. I entirely agreed with this proposal. Later on when I saw how the Liberal group had distributed their broadcasts, I offered, with the full consent of my colleagues, one of the Conservative twenty-minute broadcasts to Lady Violet Bonham Carter. This offer was made of course without any conditions whatever. Lady Violet was perfectly free to say whatever she pleased. She was dissuaded from accepting this not ungenerous offer by the Clement Davies group.[1]
>
> The public will not therefore hear on the broadcast any clear exposition of the views held by the majority of Liberals who, while remaining loyal to the Liberal Party, are strongly opposed to Socialism.
>
> This account of what took place shows that Mr Byers' statement that I tried to prevent a full expression of Liberal opinion is contrary to the truth.

---

[1] When asked for her comment, Lady Bonham Carter stated to the press: 'Mr Churchill's account of his very generous offer was completely accurate. I have no further comment to make.'

1616   February 1950

Winston S. Churchill to Lord Swinton
(*Churchill papers, 2/101*)

1 February 1950

My dear Philip,

I cannot give a pledge that the period of National Service would not be lengthened. I do not believe any real economy can be made in the Army unless much fewer men are taken by compulsion, and kept somewhat longer. What I am saying at Leeds on the subject of National Service is that we should endeavour to reduce the burden which it places upon the country while maintaining the principle, on the establishment of which I compliment the Labour Party.

You will have seen the statement which I made in my speech at Leeds. I hope everything is going well on your most important Committee.

Winston S. Churchill: speech
(*'In the Balance', pages 170–80*)

4 February 1950   Town Hall, Leeds

ELECTION ADDRESS

I must admit that my earlier political life was more concerned with Lancashire than Yorkshire, but I have learnt enough about Yorkshire folk to know that they despise flattery. So I will not waste any time upon it this afternoon. You know well enough your importance and responsibility in Britain, and through Britain, in world affairs. I trust indeed that Yorkshire may be rightly guided at this fateful hour and point the way to others. Whatever side you may take in the election battle which has now begun, no one who looks at things with a steady and truth-seeking eye can fail to take a serious view about the immediate future of our country. We have a population of 50,000,000 for whom we can grow here at home only half the food they need to keep them alive. Our finances are in sad disorder. During their $4\frac{1}{2}$ years of office the Government have spent every penny they could lay their hands on. Every asset they could realize has been spent in lavish profusion. Every reserve has been cut down below the safety level. We have been living upon the generous aid, loaned or given by the US or by our Dominions. The buying power of the British pound has been steadily dwindling. The Government have now been forced to devaluate our money so that we have to give a third more hours of labour to buy the same amount of what we need from dollar countries.

The election has been held at a date carefully chosen by Mr Attlee in the hopes of obtaining a new lease of office before the further inevitable rise in the cost of living comes down upon us. He has not dared to produce a

Budget which, if it had been honest, would certainly have been unpopular. The trade unions have been persuaded to maintain the wage-freeze until after the votes have been counted. Supplementary estimates, even above the immense expenditure of £3,300,000,000 budgeted for last year, have been kept in the background. Probably £100,000,000 or more must be added to the bill. The Government have made no plan to fill the dollar gap. The American subsidies which, according to Mr Morrison and Mr Bevan, have alone saved us from having nearly 2,000,000 unemployed, will come to an end at the latest in 1952. German and Japanese competition in all the export markets on which we depend to make the wheels of British industry turn, has already begun and will grow more severe with every month that passes. Even if all our strength were united we should be confronted with the hardest task and problem we have ever faced in time of peace. But we are a deeply divided nation. Class warfare has rent the unities and comradeship which brought us through the war. Party politics dominate the scene. A great gulf of principle and doctrine is open in our midst. But even while this remains vital it is obscured by appeals to envious self-interest.

There is another element of instability in our British life which does not exist in most of the other free countries of the world. There is no written constitution. The safeguards provided by the Parliament Act have been almost entirely swept away. We have virtually single-chamber Government. If after this election the Socialists have a majority in the House of Commons, even though they only have a minority vote in the country, there is nothing they cannot carry into law. We see that they have taken power in their manifesto to make a very large increase of nationalization of industry and also to start up rival businesses with public money to knock out any existing firms whom they do not like or who do not comply with their wishes, apart altogether from any law. There is therefore no limit upon the action they may take to overturn and sweep away the entire structure of our society and industry as these now exist and by which we earn our daily bread. According to the interview which Mr Attlee is reported to have given to an American journalist, his own intentions are to set up an absolute Socialist State at the earliest moment. Let me read you what he is reported to have said, which he has not contradicted: When asked, 'when does Socialism stop in England?' he replied, 'It does not. It goes right on. Nothing can stand between a nation and its goal. No one has any cause to misunderstand. Twelve years ago, long before our party came to power, I gave a specific warning.' So here we are at a moment of extreme financial and economic instability also confronted with a declaration by the Prime Minister in favour of the most overwhelming changes in our slowly-built up British way of life which have ever been proposed. There is at this moment no foothold where anyone in Britain or those who watch us from outside can say, 'This is solid ground.'

[. . .] I rest my hopes on a new Parliament. It cannot be more unequal to the nation's needs nor more unworthy of its destiny than the one which has been just been dissolved. I hope that the Government arising from the new Parliament will represent the will of the people as expressed by a majority of the votes cast. It will be an additional misfortune if another administration comes into power which only represents a minority of the electors. That section of the Liberal Party which is led by Mr Clement Davies has openly avowed its desire to bring about a deadlock or stalemate, so that the handful of members who follow his guidance may hold the balance and dominate the scene. As they cannot exceed seven or eight, this is a vain expectation, however gratifying to the self-importance of a few individuals. In order to realize it they are running 400 candidates, procured by dozens and scores, and insuring with Lloyd's against the forfeit of 250 deposits. In nearly every case the votes cast for these candidates will be thrown away; that is to say they will play no part in deciding the tremendous issues which are at stake. It is hoped, however, by the authors of this reckless demonstration that they may so queer the pitch that the result of the great electoral struggle may be meaningless. They take a great responsibility upon themselves for which they may afterwards be held accountable to public opinion. The return of a number of minority candidates through split votes cannot be of any help to the British nation in its present difficulties and dangers. Moreover, it is essentially undemocratic for a party or section of a party to work for the return of minority candidates, and thus frustrate or pervert the true expression of the national will.

I do not believe that these tactics will be successful. But I am very sorry that such a state of things should have come about. It certainly is not my fault. Nothing would have given me greater comfort two or three years ago than to have made an honourable and friendly arrangement with all who hold to the Liberal faith, which would have enabled all true Liberals and Conservatives to work together as separate and independent parties for the main interest of the nation and in resistance to the establishment of a Socialist State to which both are equally opposed. But when overtures were made they were repeatedly spurned, and we were mocked for our efforts. Thus the years passed. Conservative candidates came forward and every constituency was filled. It is not possible at the last minute to ask men who have built up their position in the different constituencies to stand down. Nor would the local associations agree to their doing so. Here and there a sensible arrangement may be made; but in the main the die is cast. We have therefore at this grave and critical moment in our history an element of confusion which, however understandable because of the hardships which the present electoral system inflicts upon minorities, is a serious aggravation of the public dangers.

A main cause of our present plight has been the waste, disorder and uncertainty arising from the Socialist policy of nationalization. Instead of bending all their strength to recovery after the war, and to carrying through our Four Years' Plan, which surely was enough for any Government, they have divided the nation by a series of ill thought-out measures to make the State the owner and employer in about one-fifth of our industries and services. In every case this has already been proved an injury to the common weal. [. . .]

But even more injurious to the national economy is the second dose of nationalization with which we are menaced. The prosperous and active steel industry will at once pass into the hands of State officials and Government favourites, and this Act is so framed that it will give Socialist Ministers the power to interfere with and hamper the great number of other trades which use steel in all sorts of ways. But for the service which the House of Lords has rendered under the Parliament Act, the electors would have been denied the opportunity which was surely their right of pronouncing upon steel nationalization before it had become law.

There is also another series of prosperous key industries, rendering services of the highest efficiency to the public, upon all of which the clammy grip of Socialist politics is to be laid. Our cement, the cheapest in the world; sugar, water supplies, meat, perhaps chemicals, are to pass from the skilled and successful management by which they have been developed, into the dull and uncomprehending control of official boards. Over 60 per cent of the profits of these industries now go to the Revenue and provide for the social services. These profits will soon be converted into losses borne by the taxpayer, or higher prices paid by the consumer.

There is one more which is threatened, namely, industrial life insurance. But now, on the eve of the election, the Socialists have had second thoughts. Their doubts do not arise from any lack of zeal or appetite, but only because they are afraid they may lose votes by offending the numerous and influential bands of agents who have done so much to popularize thrift. This, and this alone, has led to a modification of the Socialist plan for industrial life insurance. Here is a good example of how British interests are handled by Socialist doctrinaires and fanatics. These matters are not dealt with on their merits, or even in accordance with Socialist theory. Conviction is lacking. Plan and design even for a mistaken policy, do not rule once it is a question of votes. You can in no country, least of all our own, least of all at this moment, make a way forward under such principles of public conduct.

[. . .] Here again Conservative policy is clear. We shall restore the safeguards of the Parliament Act and repeal the nationalization of steel before it can come into law, and we shall free all other industries from the cloud of oppression and uncertainty under which they lie at the present time by forbidding all further nationalization. No single broad decision will do more to prevent unemployment, to improve our credit, and to lighten and simplify our problems both at home and abroad than the stopping of nationalization.

During the war when every sacrifice had to be made to preserve the life of the nation all kinds of controls and taxes were imposed and everyone was proud to give life, liberty, and worldly possessions in the cause of freedom. All the democracies of the Western world were equally desirous of getting rid of wartime controls when the peril had passed away. The United States led the way and in 1946 by a most daring decision of policy they swept away practically all the wartime controls, prices, rationing and regulations of all kinds which they regarded as a great evil likely to hamper their recovery.

As I said in Parliament more than two years ago, 'They threw the reins on the horse's neck and trusted him to pull their wagon up the hill.' Although a Presidential Election has taken place meanwhile, none of these controls have been reimposed. The strong horse still has the reins on his neck and is still pulling the wagon up the hill, and letting us hitch-hike behind him. Our Dominions have followed the same course, though step by step. Every country in Western Europe has moved in the same direction, including the nations who were actually defeated and marched through and occupied. Our friends in France, Belgium, Holland and Denmark have all freed themselves as fast as possible to the utmost extent, and all have made remarkable recoveries from the conditions of war. Rationing has been abolished in all these countries, which like ourselves depend on democratic institutions and universal suffrage. We see in all them that controls are regarded as a wartime evil to be dispensed with at the earliest moment. Our former foes have done the same, as far as they could. In particular Germany, fortified by an appeal to the people on a democratic franchise, has shaken itself free in a manner remarkable in a people so often criticized for their love of regulations and discipline. Thus some people learn wisdom in defeat while others are led into folly by victory.

Of course conditions vary in different countries. With so little home-grown food we in Britain must move with more caution. We must first ensure that the prime necessities of life are within the reach of every family and each individual. But there is no doubt of the direction in which we ought to move as quickly and as strongly as we possibly can. The point to notice in all these examples I have given you is that rationing and price controls are everywhere in the world, outside the Soviet sphere, regarded as evils and an impediment to be got rid of at the earliest moment. But here in Britain the only Socialist Government now existing outside Scandinavia and the Iron Curtain saw in wartime controls not an evil to be got rid of but a means of getting everybody's daily life into the Socialist clutches. They saw the opportunity of creating 'Socialism in our time', by prolonging the evils which were necessary in war. British Socialism in indeed a prolongation of wartime conditions in time of peace. In Soviet Russia and its satellite States the withdrawal of the ration book is the most normal and most lenient method of enforcing direction of labour or political discipline. By this mechanism British Socialists hope to get everyone into their power, and make them stand in queues for the favours which an all-wise and all-powerful governing machine chooses to bestow. To have power over their fellow-countrymen and be able to order them about is the natural characteristic of any Socialist. He loves controls for controls' sake

– 'Rationing is permanent,' says Mr Bottomley,[1] the Parliamentary Secretary for Overseas Trade. 'We are the masters now,' says the Attorney-General.[2] I must say this rouses indignation in my heart.

Mr Attlee's Socialist Government in time of peace decreed, though they have not yet ventured to enforce, the direction of all labour, demanding the right to take any man from his job and his home and move him under threats of imprisonment to any form of work in any part of the country they may choose. No greater affront to the dignity of British labour has ever been perpetrated. The right to choose or change his employment is one of the fundamental distinctions of a free Briton. British labour has now been deprived of this ancient right. A Conservative Government will immediately restore it.

I must now speak about conscription or national service. The Labour Party have enforced conscription in time of peace. Everyone must serve in the Armed Forces for eighteen months. While we cannot approve industrial conscription, we have felt it our duty to support the Socialist policy of compulsory national service in the Armed Forces. We think it is necessary in order to preserve peace. If Britain were to repudiate national service at this election, as the Liberals ask you to do, it would mean, in my opinion, the downfall of the whole great structure embodied in the Brussels Treaty, in the Atlantic Pact, in Western Union, in the whole idea of the English-speaking world, and of course of the united British Empire and Commonwealth of Nations. If Britain were to pull out now, all this vast defensive structure that has been raised by both the Labour and Conservative Parties in this country, might crash to the ground, and then you would be once again in danger of the most horrible of all fates – a third world war. That is what we are determined to avoid. Now nothing would have been more easy than for the Tory Party to gain votes at the expense of our political opponents by finding many good reasons to abandon conscription. If we had come out against compulsory service in the Armed Forces, we should have gained many votes in the General Election. But I and my colleagues would be ashamed to gain a party advantage on terms which would weaken the whole structure of the free democracies of Europe and America, through whose increasing cohesion world peace can alone become continually more secure.

But this does not mean that I do not think that great improvements cannot be made in our military system. It may well be that much better value in fighting power can be obtained for the money we are spending. The Conservative Party do not intend to take compulsory powers to lengthen the term of

---

[1] Arthur George Bottomley, 1907–95. OBE, 1941. MP (Lab.) for Chatham Div. of Rochester, 1945–50; for Rochester and Chatham, 1950–9; for Middlesbrough East, 1962–74; for Teesside, Middlesbrough, 1974–83. Parliamentary Under-Secretary of State for Dominions, 1946–7. Secretary for Overseas Trade, Board of Trade, 1947–51. Secretary of State for Commonwealth Affairs, 1964–6. Delegate to UN, New York, 1946, 1947, 1949. UK Delegate to Commonwealth Conference, Delhi, 1949. PC, 1951. Member, Consultative Assembly, Council of Europe, 1952, 1953, 1954. Baron, 1984.

[2] Sir Hartley Shawcross.

national service. On the contrary it is our view that too many men are being called up each year, either for the staff to train or for the units to absorb, and that the burden of national service can be sensibly reduced. I have a feeling, having handled these things before, that unless the foreign situation gets worse, which I do not think it will (but of course I may be wrong), a considerable reduction in the expense and burden of our defences might be combined with an actually stronger fighting power and better conditions for the troops. Let us leave it at that.

I do not join with those who suggest that our people are not working as they ought to. Most people do a good day's work in Britain, and after the intense effort of the war a sense of psychic and physical fatigue was natural. Sir Stafford Cripps has said that we have increased our output since 1939 by nearly a third – 30 per cent. If this is confirmed it will be good. It may be good and yet it may not be good enough. The Americans in the same period have increased their output by 80 per cent. But our people have also put up with severe austerity. They have submitted to thousands of regulations. They have not had the houses they were promised, nor the meals which a free market could have brought. They have shown both fortitude and discipline. Properly handled by a National Government such as won the war, their ordeal need not have been so hard and its results would have been far more fruitful. The property of the rich has been largely confiscated by taxation; but every class has borne very heavy exactions in PAYE, purchase tax and in enormous taxation of tobacco, beer and skittles. More nourishing and stimulating food would mean better work. More eating would mean less drinking. Less spent outside the home would mean more spent inside it. It would all be good. I am not sure we cannot get it if we pull together in a sensible way.

[...]

Let me look abroad. There is a lot of dispute about what is going on abroad. Those who come back tell opposite tales, many in accordance with what they think their parties wish. The Germans have rapidly built themselves up with Allied aid, rightly given, from almost nothing to a very active community, working like demons, and eating well amid ruins. When Socialists say there are 1,700,000 unemployed in Western Germany they ought not to forget that 8,000,000 people have fled as refugees from the old Eastern food-lands of Germany, and have had to be absorbed in the liberated part of the Reich. What would have happened here if 7,000,000 or 8,000,000 extra people of our own stock had suddenly been dumped on us? Do not underrate the recovery of Germany. I am glad of it. I want to work with them and the French. We three, together, with our cherished friends in the 'Benelux' countries, Belgium, the Netherlands and Luxembourg, and several other countries outside the 'Iron Curtain', all constitute a vast and solid organization of free, civilized, democratic peoples which once forged and riveted together is not likely to be molested.

I spoke of France just now. I have worked in peace and war on the side of France for more than forty years. I rejoice in the undoubted growing recovery of France; but I want to warn you that the kind of political whirligig under which France lives, which is such great fun for the politicians and for all the little ardent parties into which they are divided, would be fatal to Britain. We cannot afford to have a period of French politics in Westminster. It is not in accordance with the British character, but still more it is not in accordance with the grim facts of our life. France is a self-supporting country. If the French woke up tomorrow morning and found that all the rest of the world had sunk under the sea, and that they were alone, they could make a pretty good living for themselves from their fertile soil. But if Britain woke up tomorrow morning and found nothing else but salt water on the rest of the globe, about one-third of our people would disappear.

What distresses me about our plight and our mood is that so many of our people take everything for granted and feel quite sure everything will work out all right whatever they do. Certainly I can give them the assurance that all the world outside Britain is not going to disappear under the waves of the sea. But they really must understand that we are not a self-supporting country, that we are an artificial country precariously poised at a splendid height. Above all things we must make sure that our foundations are not undermined. We cannot afford to play the pranks which French parties and French politicians play. We have not got, thank God, the cruel spur of defeat which animates the Germans. If ever there was a moment, when after all our victories and service to the cause of human freedom every patriotic man and woman ought to be thinking about the country and taking a long view, that moment is now.

Whatever happens at this General Election it will be a pretty rough show for those who win as well as for those who lose. There are some who say, 'Let the Socialist Government reap where they have sown.' A stronger dose is needed to put our people back on the right line. Nothing, they say, will convince the British people but suffering and disaster. They always insist on buying their experience over again each time. But I do not say this to you. I do not think we need plunge into the pit of torment to rise again like the Phoenix from her ashes. I cannot feel sure that in this vast and swiftly-changing modern world that has grown up around us in the twentieth century, if we fell, we should ever emerge again as a great power, and we certainly cannot go on living on Dominion charity and American subsidies, even if they were going to continue. No – we have got to rise now to the occasion, and overcome all perils to our life and independence as we have always done before.

Mr Herbert Morrison said the other day, there must be no Coalition. There certainly seems no likelihood of that. I am quite sure that a Coalition between men and parties as the result of a lot of petty bargains and deals and compromises would be no use at all. There must be some great common bond of union, like we had in 1940, to lead to that melting of hearts where sacrifice seems to be an indulgence and pain becomes a joy, and when life rises to its highest level because death has no terrors.

If we got into that state of mind, which most of us have been through no doubt we could all come together, and then I do not doubt that Britain would rise again in her unconquerable strength. Do not fail in your effort. Do not despair of your native land. No one can tell what the future will bring forth. But I believe that if we act wisely and deal faithfully with one another and set our country, its history, glorious and inspiring, and its future, unlimited except by our own shortcomings, before our eyes, we should come through. Not only can the dangers of the present be overcome and its problems solved, but, having saved the world in war, we should save ourselves in peace.

Randolph S. Churchill to Winston S. Churchill
(Churchill papers, 2/272)

5 February 1950

My dearest Papa,

As you will see from the enclosed copy of last night's paper, the news of your visit[1] has been extremely well received. It has put great heart into all our workers and, subject to limitations of space, I am sure we can guarantee you a very fine meeting.

The Forum Cinema where you will be speaking holds 1,800 and, if the weather is fine, we ought to have six or seven thousand people outside who will be encouraged, after the meeting, to follow the procession of cars down to the station and give you a great send off at 4.10.

I think the most helpful line for you to take here would be to deal with the issue of unemployment. Perhaps you might tell the story of the National Government's White Paper as you did at Earls Court.

The other note I would like you to strike would be about your Liberal past. Both Plymouth and the West Country as a whole still have a strong Liberal tradition. Your teasing of Clement Davies and the Liberals has been well received here; but I suggest that on Thursday you woo them by talking to them of the great days of the Liberal Party in which you and Lloyd George played the leading roles. You could explain how with Ll.G. and Asquith you layed the foundations of what is today called the Welfare State, and how proud you are of your actions as a Liberal and how they are entirely reconciled in your heart and mind with your present role as leader of the Conservative Party. If you were to speak along these lines it would in no way offend the Conservative Party who have long forgotten and forgiven the controversies of the 1910 and 1911 elections; and it would give immense pleasure to the very large body of

[1] To Plymouth Devonport, where Randolph was standing as the Conservative Parliamentary candidate in the general election. Churchill's speech on Feb. 9 is reproduced below (pp. 1635–41).

Liberals who mean to vote for Conservative candidates in the West Country. It would also rally others who are thinking of voting for the Clement Davies Liberals but feel it would be more effective to come our way.

I think it would also be very helpful if you could make a re-statement of traditional Liberal philosophy and show how most of the principles for which Gladstone, John Morley and, to some extent, Lloyd George stood have today been incorporated in Conservative thought. Here you could reiterate your excellent point about the impossibility of anyone being a Liberal-Socialist.

When you suggested Thursday to me I did not realise that Bevan was speaking here that night. It is a very happy coincidence. I hope you will utterly ignore him. He will no doubt try to hit the headlines by attacking you in the evening; but he will be entirely blanketed by the much greater demonstration which we will have achieved in the afternoon. The Exmouth Hall where he is speaking only holds 600 and you may be quite sure that the local Press, as well as the National Press, will give you two or three columns and that there will be a quarter of a column at the end to say that Mr Bevan also spoke. Foot was counting on Bevan's visit to be the high point of the campaign. Your visit on the same day will prick this cherished bubble.

June and I are both delighted that you are coming and we are taking every step to see that your visit will involve you in the least effort while assuring us the maximum advantage.

Duncan Sandys to Winston S. Churchill
(*Churchill papers, 1/48*)

6 February 1950

Urgent

For what they are worth these are my impressions of the progress of the Election Campaign up to date:

1. The Conservative Party organization at the centre and in most of the constituencies is in a high state of efficiency.

2. The Party's Election Manifesto has been well received by the Press and by the public, and has gone a long way towards killing the story that the 'Tories have no policy'. On the other hand the Manifesto, in guarded phrases, skates over many ticklish points upon which candidates all over the country are being tackled and which are being taken up in broadcasts and articles by Socialist leaders. It is essential that criticisms and misrepresentations of our policy should be answered authoritatively over the name of a prominent Conservative leader within a few hours. If it has not already been done it is suggested that the Party's Policy Committee should have a small day and night organization for drafting and issuing these stop-press replies.

3. The Labour Party has so far made infinitely better use of radio and platform opportunities than the Conservatives.

4. There are many uncertain voters who are sympathetic to free enterprise but who are seriously troubled by the Labour arguments to which they have not yet received sufficiently precise replies.

5. The electors, even Labour supporters, are prepared to accept that the Socialist Government have been incompetent and wasteful and that nationalization has produced disappointing results. Too much time should not therefore be devoted to making this point, which has already largely been accepted, except in the course of explaining how the Conservatives would do better.

6. The electors are not interested in liberty. They are not aware that they have lost any. Nothing that can be said in the next fortnight will make them seriously believe that there is any fear of freedom being suppressed by such moderate men as Attlee, Morrison and Cripps. If on the other hand it were thought that Aneurin Bevan would be Prime Minister many of the present voters would be frightened over to our side.

7. Whilst there are many grumbles about variety, people are, by and large, satisfied with the amount of food they are getting except in the case of meat. The hope of getting more food interests them less than the fear of dearer food. In consequence there are few votes to be won and many to be lost on food.

8. Above all the electors are interested in employment, the cost of living, fair distribution of food.

9. The Conservative speeches and propaganda should therefore concentrate on saying positively how a Conservative Government would benefit the country, and should deal, in particular, with the following points:

   (a) Continuation of present Socialist policy will mean mass unemployment in 1952, whereas free enterprise will stimulate extension of production of goods at prices at which foreigners will buy, and so will help close the dollar gap.

   (b) Conservatives will reduce the cost of living and protect the value of the pound by eliminating waste and lowering taxation.

   (c) A Conservative Government will maintain the system of 'fair shares' by rationing and price control so long as the shortage continues, but we intend by better organization and increased exports to abolish the shortage, and with it rationing, as soon as possible. (The Labour Party are undoubtedly winning votes on the allegation that Conservatives will abolish food subsidies. Anything that can be done to reassure people on this point will be valuable.)

   (d) A Conservative Government will re-establish British influence in international affairs and will in particular make a renewed effort to secure the establishment of a world authority to control Atomic Energy and stop the Arms Race. If successful this would not only assure peace but release enormous sums of money to improve the standard of living of the people. (This point may be worth a lot of Liberal votes.)

10. The one most popular and most constructive point in domestic policy is reduction of taxation, including of course indirect taxation, and in particular the unpopular purchase tax. We should say again and again in different ways and in every way, 'The Conservatives will reduce taxation and cut out waste.' This will reduce the cost of living and raise the purchasing value of earnings and savings. It will stimulate production and so assure employment.

Winston S. Churchill to John Maclay[1]
(Churchill papers, 2/65)

6 February 1950

My dear Maclay,

I was most pleased to receive the letter signed by you and Herbert Butcher,[2] and I thank you warmly for the kindness of this. It is a great encouragement to me to be able to count on the support of the National Liberal Party, and to know of their loyalty to the Party I have the honour to lead; and also to know that they are content with the relations between this Party and those who sustain the Liberal faith.

Winston S. Churchill: speech
('In the Balance', pages 181–9)

8 February 1950   Ninian Park Football Ground
Cardiff, Wales

ELECTION ADDRESS

It gave me great pleasure to drive along the splendid road you have so kindly named after me. I greatly value this honour which you have conferred on me, and it will last long after party differences have passed away. Perhaps you will allow me to tell you about an incident which, though it happened long ago, was a cause of controversy when the naming of this road was under discussion. I am told that the Socialists and Communists continually spread the story that I used the troops to shoot down the Welsh miners and that the

---

[1] John Scott Maclay, 1905–92. Educated at Winchester College and Trinity College, Cambridge. Married, 1930, Betty L'Estrange Astley. MP (Nat. Lib.) for Montrose, 1940–50; for Renfrew West, 1950–64. Secretary of State for Scotland, 1957–62. 1st Viscount Muirshiel, 1964. KT, 1973.

[2] Herbert Walter Butcher, 1901–66. MP (Nat. Lib.) for Holland with Boston, 1937–66. Parliamentary Private Secretary, Ministries of Health and Transport, 1938–40. Chief Whip, Nat. Lib. Party, 1945–51. Deputy Chief Whip for the Government, 1951–3. Knighted, 1953. Bt, 1960.

story of Tonypandy will never be forgotten. I am quite content that it should be remembered, provided that the truth is told.

When I was Home Secretary in 1910 I had a great horror and fear of having to become responsible for the military firing upon a crowd of rioters or strikers. Also I have had sympathy for the miners and think they are entitled to better treatment because they work far from the light of day. At that time there were many disputes and much violence in the Cambrian Coal Trust Collieries and the Rhondda Valley. Shops were looted and property destroyed. The Chief Constable of Glamorgan[1] sent a request for the assistance of the military and troops were put in motion in the usual way. But here I made an unprecedented intervention. I stopped the movement of the troops and I sent instead 850 Metropolitan Police from London with the sole object of preventing bloodshed. I was much criticized for this so-called weakness in the House of Commons. But I carried my point. The troops were kept in the background and all contact with the rioters was made by our trusted and unarmed London police who charged, not with rifles and bayonets, but with their rolled-up mackintoshes. Thus all bloodshed, except perhaps some from the nose, was averted and all loss of life prevented. That is the true story of Tonypandy, and I hope it may replace in Welsh villages the cruel lie with which they have been fed all these long years.

Today we are facing a turning-point in our British way of life, and I come here to ask for your support. The Conservative Party of our day is the heir and apostle of those great traditions and principles of Tory democracy enunciated by Benjamin Disraeli and after him by my father, Lord Randolph Churchill. One of those principles, whose truth is borne out again and again upon the pages of history is Disraeli's oft-cited maxim, 'Centralization is the death-blow of public freedom.' The truth of these words was never more apparent than it is today, nor more relevant to the thought and resolve of those who would have men not only live, but live freely. Welsh traditions and culture go back to the dawn of our island history. The Education Act passed by the wartime Government of which I was the head safeguarded the position of the Welsh language with all its expression and poetic force.

Your great university, now deprived of its Parliamentary representation, and the National Museum here in Cardiff abide as monuments of Welsh fame and culture. Forty years ago as Home Secretary I read a Proclamation creating a Prince of Wales to an august assembly at Caernarvon Castle. It would be a shocking loss if all this pride of nationality were to be merged and engulfed in some centralized Socialist State where the rich variety of British life would be replaced by drab uniformity. How natural it is that the Welsh people should resent the increased control of their affairs from Whitehall which comes inevitably with Socialism. The Welsh people must be careful that

---

[1] Lionel Lindsay, 1861–1941. Chief Constable, Glamorgan, 1891–1937. Oversaw police action during the Tonypandy Riots, 1910–11.

the handcuffs of centralization are not slipped on them by a Socialist Government at Westminster.

The Liberal Party say that there ought to be a Parliament in Wales. It is easy, though not very dignified, to make promises when you are quite sure you will never be called upon to fulfil them. If I thought a Welsh Parliament at the present time would be in the best interests of the Welsh people I would not hesitate to recommend it to you. But Wales and England though two nations are a single, economic whole. A Welsh Parliament which could not consider the main economic issues, or could only consider them in isolation from England would not be good for you, or for us.

Should the Conservative Party be called upon to assume responsibility of government and I were connected with it I should at once assign to a member of the Cabinet the special responsibility for Welsh affairs. Advised and assisted by a Council of Wales, broadly representative of all aspects of Welsh life, he would ensure that Wales obtained steady and effective representation at the highest level in every aspect of national life, and that the machinery of government would work more speedily, more effectively and with full comprehension where Wales is concerned. The road would thus be open for the building up, not by the hands of Government, but with all the aid that Government can give of a strong, wide range of industries founded upon Welsh mining, and iron and steel. We shall do our utmost to assure to rural Wales a better provision of water and electricity and vigorous development of hill farming, and the strengthening of rural life which dominates her character. 'Freedom dwells in the mountains,' but there is no reason why Wales should not have abundance, too. Freedom and abundance are our watchwords.

An extraordinary propaganda of falsehood has been spread in all directions by the Socialist Government about the lamentable conditions in Great Britain mainly under Conservative Parliaments between the wars, and a lot of young people are being taught to believe that this was a sad period of stagnation in our national and social life. In Mr Herbert Morrison's flowery language the period between the wars 'was paradise for the profiteers and hell for everyone else'. He seems to have got through it all right himself. But the Socialist Party hope that by creating this impression they will find some excuse for their own failure, which has brought such needless hardship on the masses of our people at the present time. In fact, however, the years between the two wars, although scarred by a general strike and a prolonged coal stoppage, which I did my best to avert, and although scarred by the economic and financial collapse of Mr Ramsay MacDonald's Second Socialist administration in 1931 – these years were a period of almost unequalled expansion, and progress in the life of the wage-earning masses throughout the island.

Let me give you a few facts to support that statement. Between 1919 and 1939 4,000,000 new houses were built in England and Wales alone, or half as many houses as already existed before the First World War. Before the First

Great War the average week in the majority of industries was 54 hours. But before the Second World War in 1939 under Parliaments resting on Conservative majorities the normal hours of work had come down to 47 or 48. The Socialists claim for themselves all the improvements which modern medical science has brought within our reach. They did it all themselves – so they did. To hear them talk one would think that no one had ever thought of children's welfare before that unlucky day when, much to their surprise, they found themselves in office four and half years ago.

But you would like to know the truth. I will tell it to you. Immense improvements in the care of children were made in these terrible Tory days when Mr Morrison was what he calls 'in hell'. This I may remark is a somewhat disparaging description of the London County Council in which he was a prominent figure. I hope it will give him no additional twinge if I remind him that children's school meals and free milk were instituted by the pre-war Conservative Government and later extended by the wartime Government over which I presided.

In this period of 'hell for all except the profiteers' the expectation of life for all babies who had the courage to be born rose by nine years. That was an important fact to be borne in mind not only by the parents but by the baby. When these survivors of five years of hell went to the elementary schools in London it was found that they had gained an average of two inches in height and five pounds in weight compared with the standards before the First World War. How very surprising! The warm climate must have suited them. There was also a steady improvement in the food of the people, and a marked increase in the consumption of milk, cheese, butter and eggs, and of fruit and vegetables. But I do not wish to make your mouths water.

In the fifteen years from the formation of Mr Baldwin's Second Administration in 1924 in which I had the honour to be Chancellor of the Exchequer, down to the outbreak of war in 1939, in these fifteen years, a period during which for more than twelve years there were controlling Tory majorities in the House of Commons, wage rates increased by nearly 6 per cent and the cost of living fell by nineteen points. In this Tory 'hell' there was no wage freeze. I suppose it was too hot. And all the time the £ rose in value instead of falling, as it had done in the Socialist paradise, to 16*s* 3*d*. So much for the Socialist planners and their boasting. So much for Mr Herbert Morrison and his sojourn in the infernal regions.

Both Nazis and Communists have held the common principle that if an untruth is told often enough and widely enough it becomes as good as the truth. Their doctrine is that the difference between truth and untruth is whether it is good for the party or not. Now of course the British Socialist Party are as much opposed as we are to these wicked totalitarians. But they sometimes take a leaf out of their book. And there is another example of this evil practice which I must bring to your notice. It is more serious because it has only just happened, and because the falsehood is not merely part of a whispering campaign but the official declaration of the Socialist Party, prepared with deliberation and in cold blood. I mean the 'empty bellies' story which appears in the Labour Manifesto. This is their official statement: 'Empty bellies,' one Tory has said, 'are the one thing that will make Britons work.' Fancy a great party, governing the land and asking for a further lease of office, picking out the foolish remark of one unnamed irresponsible person among all the millions of Conservatives, and trying to defame the whole Conservative Party by fastening on them the monstrous charge that they wish to inflict empty bellies upon the people to make them work harder. We have, however, made inquiries. Apparently a Mr Higgs,[1] formerly a Conservative member, made this statement three years ago when visiting New Zealand. He had no right whatever to speak for the Conservative Party. His words were, however, noted by our vigilant central office and they were promptly, at the time, officially repudiated. Here is what was said and published in the Conservative Weekly News Letter of 19 April 1947: 'Mr Higgs is not at all representative of the Conservative Party. He would never be adopted as a candidate on that sort of speech, for it is the most arrant nonsense.' They added the following comment, which I can't help reading: 'If Mr Higgs' theory were right our national output would be very high today, for thanks to Mr Strachey's efforts, our bellies are getting emptier and emptier.' I did not know that the Socialist Government were so hard-pressed, even at the outset of this campaign, that they have to sink to such methods. It gives you a measure of the kind of propaganda by which the Socialist Party hope to win the votes of the British nation. I invite Mr Attlee, or Mr Morrison, when they next address you either to maintain or repudiate this 'empty bellies' story, for which they are at present nominally and formally responsible.

The British people have worked hard since the war and the great qualities of perseverance and endurance which they showed in the struggle have not been found wanting in the years that followed its close. The Conservative Party has done its utmost to aid the Government and the people as a whole in every step which has been taken with a sincere desire to regain our prosperity and to re-establish our peacetime life. The post-war effort of the British nation has been made not through the help of the Government but to a very large extent in spite of it. The greatest burden which the people have had to carry has been the practical incompetence and misguided mentality of the Socialist Party. At a time when every scrap of our life and strength should have been devoted to reviving our prosperity they have added to our difficulties and burdens for the sake of the party doctrinal fads.

The greatest mismanagement has been in finance. Dr Dalton and Sir Stafford Cripps have each squandered the public treasure at a pace unknown before. It is a photo finish between them. Not only have they spent all the

---

[1] Walter Frank Higgs, 1886–1961. Member, Birmingham City Council, 1934–7. MP (Union.) for West Birmingham, 1937–45. Member, Select Committee on National Expenditure, 1939–43.

prodigious wartime taxes we imposed upon ourselves in the supreme hour of trial, but they have even added to them. Our taxation today is heavier than it was even in the most intense climax of the war. The Government of today is spending 40 per cent of the entire national income through the hands of its officials. The taxes in Britain are higher than in any other country in the civilized world. Waste and extravagance are presented on every hand. £18 5s a night for every Government guest entertained at what is called the Cripps Austerity Arms off Park Lane. £16,000,000 for information services to blow the Government's trumpet when the Ministers get tired. £31,000,000 for Mr Strachey's groundnut excursion. £80,000,000 lost to date on nationalization. These are but instances which leap to the mind. The Socialists attempt to escape the public censure to the profusion in the following way: they tell their supporters, 'Never mind, it is all taken from the rich.' This is a stupid error and one which is effectively exposing itself. If everything were taken from every man and woman whose income is above a thousand pounds a year, earned or unearned, it would not meet a quarter of the expenditure in which the Socialists are indulging. We are brought up against the hackneyed saying, 'Making the rich poor will not make the poor rich.' It is only the first part of this policy in which the Socialists are having any success.

The Socialist housing policy has turned out even worse than we feared. Under the much abused Tory rule before the war, we were able to build 1,000 permanent houses a day in the island, two-thirds by private enterprise. In the 4½ years of the Socialist new-world impulse and revelation, vast, profound State planning, we have built barely 400 permanent houses a day. The Minister of Health declared: 'I confidently expect that before the next election every family in Great Britain will have a separate house.' In this city of Cardiff alone there are no fewer than 15,000 families on the waiting list for houses. This tragic fiasco, causing severe and needless distress to hundreds of thousands of overcrowded people, is mainly due to the pedantic, irrational enforcement of Socialist prejudice. In a spiteful desire to wipe out the private builder by ordering that only one house in four should be built by private enterprise the Minister responsible has thrust a burden upon the local authorities which in many cases they were quite unable to bear. The Socialist Government have failed in almost everything they have touched. Houses are built of bricks, mortar and goodwill, not of politics, prejudices and spite.

I always like to come to Wales. I was the friend and comrade of the most famous Welshman of our time, David Lloyd George. Most people are unconscious of how much their lives have been shaped by the laws for which Lloyd George was responsible. He it was who launched the Liberal forces of this country effectively into the broad stream of social betterment and social security along which all modern parties now steer. Nowadays this is called 'the Welfare State'. We did not christen it but it was our political child. I hope the Liberal Party whose aid we need so much will not forget all this now. When

I first became his friend and active lieutenant nearly fifty years ago his deep love of the people, his profound knowledge of their lives and of the undue and needless pressures under which they lived made a deep impression on my mind. Nearly two generations have passed since those great days. I also served under his leadership in the First World War when he rendered lasting service to the British Empire and to the cause of freedom and brought world-wide honour upon the name of Wales. I must turn aside for a moment to make one observation. There can be no greater insult to his memory than to suggest that today Wales has a second Lloyd George. Oh, I think it much better not to mention names.

Mr Lloyd George was a democrat if ever there was one, but he recoiled, like all those who are ready to fight for freedom must recoil, from the fallacy and folly of Socialism. This is what he said about it almost a quarter of a century ago. His words are vivid: they are also prophetic:

> You cannot trust the battle of freedom to Socialism. Socialism has no interest in liberty. Socialism is the very negation of liberty. Socialism means the community in bonds. If you establish a Socialist community it means the most comprehensive universal and pervasive tyranny that this country has ever seen. It is like the sand of the desert. It gets into your food, your clothes, your machinery, the very air you breathe. They are all gritty with regulations, orders, decrees, rules. That is what Socialism means.

These are the words of Lloyd George. See how they live and ring through the years. He might have said this yesterday. He knew what it would feel like long before it came upon us.

I hope you have all mastered the official Socialist jargon which our masters, as they call themselves, wish us to learn. You must not use the word 'poor'; they are described as the 'lower income group'. When it comes to a question of freezing a workman's wages the Chancellor of the Exchequer speaks of 'arresting increases in personal income'. The idea is that formerly income taxpayers used to be the well-to-do, and that therefore it will be popular and safe to hit at them. Sir Stafford Cripps does not like to mention the word 'wages', but that is what he means. There is a lovely one about houses and homes. They are in future to be called 'accommodation units'. I don't know how we are to sing our old song 'Home Sweet Home'. 'Accommodation Unit, Sweet Accommodation Unit, there's no place like our Accommodation Unit.' I hope to live to see the British democracy spit all this rubbish from their lips. Mr Herbert Morrison made a complaint the other day. 'Socialized industries,' he said, 'are the subject of the most persistent misrepresentation, whereas the difficulties and deficiencies of private industries are glossed over.' How does he mean, 'glossed over'? If private enterprise fails the owners may find themselves in the bankruptcy court. Is that being glossed over?

It makes no material difference to the official bulk buyer or Government nominee on some Board of Control whether the business is solvent or sends in its bill to the Exchequer. So long as he does his duty in an honest way, attends punctually to his work and is respectful to the Socialist politicians who employ him, he is safe and secure. Whereas a private businessman may have everything to lose if his judgment is wrong or his administration wasteful. Thus you maintain the most searching process of natural selection, out of which the public gets increasingly good service and value for their money. Nationalized industries are monopolies in the worst sense of the word. If a private business should become a monopoly and abuse its position there is no difficulty in dealing with it. But a Government monopoly has behind it the whole strength of the Government and, under a Socialist Government, the Ministers themselves have a political interest in trying to bolster it up so as to justify their own policy and conduct. In this remark which I have quoted, Mr Herbert Morrison shows how little he realizes the actual facts and processes which are at work in modern life. We have seen lately the extraordinary case of Lord Pakenham repudiating the report on a terrible aeroplane accident by an impartial committee which he himself had picked and set up, thus weakening confidence in the safety of British landing grounds among all other countries.

I remember in Victorian days anxious talks about 'the submerged tenth' (that part of our people who had not shared in the progress of the age) and then later on in the old Liberal period (the grand old Liberal period) we spoke of going back to bring the rearguard in. The main army we said had reached the camping ground in all its strength and victory, and we should now, in duty and compassion, go back to pick up the stragglers and those who had fallen by the way and bring them in.

That was the Liberal solution then. It is the policy of the Conservative and National Liberal parties now. But now, under the Socialists, it is no longer a question of bringing the rearguard in, but of bringing the whole army back. It is no longer the plan of helping the submerged tenth, but of submerging the other nine-tenths down to their level. This is what in fact is taking place day by day, as you can see in your own lives and homes as you look around you.

Mr Morrison (I am so sorry to keep mentioning him. Perhaps we'll hear from Mr Attlee. He is the Prime Minister, you know) said at Leeds the other day, 'We are leading the world.' So far as social services are concerned we have always led it. But as for leading the world in any other sense what nation is following the British Socialist Party? The Russian Soviet Government and its satellites claim to be going on ahead. They claim to lead. They call upon Socialists to come quicker. The rest of the world has turned decisively away from the Socialist theory. As a Socialist Prime Minister working for the establishment of a Socialist State, Mr Attlee and his party are alone among the English-speaking peoples. The United States, at the head of the world today, vehemently repudiate the Socialist doctrine. Canada repudiates it. Australia and New Zealand, after a considerable trial of it in a very incomplete form, have just shaken themselves free. Remember also there is no Socialist Government in Europe outside the Iron Curtain and Scandinavia. It seems to me a very perilous path that we are asked to tread, and to tread alone among the free democracies of the West.

Winston S. Churchill: speech
('In the Balance', pages 190–6)

9 February 1950   Forum Cinema, Devonport

ELECTION ADDRESS[1]

I last visited Devonport when I was First Lord of the Admiralty to welcome home the *Exeter* after her glorious victory in the Battle of the Plate. Alas, the gallant *Exeter*, after all her victories, was to sink in action under the fire of overwhelming numbers of the Japanese fleet, but her name will live for ever, and the memory of those who died for their country and the cause of freedom will long be cherished in Britain and throughout the West Country.

The next time I came to you was on the morrow of one of your worst bombing raids; my wife was with me when we drove through your streets, and I was inspired to see the high morale which everyone in the city and in the dockyards maintained. We went through a lot in those days together. Let us make sure we do not throw away, by the follies of peace, what we have gained in the agonies of war. Let us make sure that in the exhaustion which follows fighting for the freedom of others we do not cast away the freedom which has made us what we are.

I would like to say a word or two in favour of my son. Randolph is a mature, formidable and experienced politician. He has done his part in the struggles through which this country has passed, and I was glad – very glad – that he escaped from any terrors in the war, and I have a feeling he is going to come into his own. We have here also Mr J. J. Astor. I trust they may carry on the torch. We want them both. We want them both now. We rely on you by your exertions to gain two distinguished Members and send two valuable supporters to what, I trust, will be a Conservative Government.

I should like to make it clear, at the outset, not only here at home but to foreign countries, that at this General Election full political liberty is being maintained and that the voting will be conducted in a correct and fair manner. All votes may be freely recorded. All will be fairly counted: and let me add that the ballot is secret. No one living in council houses need have the slightest fear that their rents will be put up if they vote Conservative. It is necessary to make

---

[1] This speech was made on behalf of Randolph Churchill, who was on the podium with his father.

this statement as there is a good deal of anxiety about it in the new estates which are coming into being.

I wish I could say the same about the propaganda with which we are assailed. In the election we have had to face several grotesque untruths the kind of thing that could not be maintained in Parliament or before any fair-minded audience, but which can be mouthed from door to door by the Socialist canvassers.

The first colossal misrepresentation of facts – 'terminological inexactitude', if you like the expression (there are shorter variants, but we have to be very careful now at this election, which we are told must be kept thoroughly genteel) – well, the first of these misrepresentations of fact was a statement that the Conservative Party meant to create unemployment in order that the need for finding a job should add a greater spur to labour. There is no truth in this. It is a monstrous suggestion. There was reference to this last night on the wireless by a Government spokesman (Mr James Griffiths).

The Socialist boast that they cured unemployment has been exploded out of their own mouths by the statements of Mr Morrison and Sir Stafford Cripps. All of them have said there would be anything up to 2,000,000 unemployed if it had not been for the American Loan. Fancy the Socialist Government in England keeping itself alive, economically and politically, by these large annual dollops of dollars from capitalist America! They seek the dollars; they beg the dollars; they bluster for the dollars; they gobble the dollars. But in the whole of their 8,000-word manifesto they cannot say 'Thank you' for the dollars.

It has also been proved that we had a joint plan in the days of the wartime Government for dealing with unemployment should it occur after the war. To this plan all the leading Socialist Ministers were party. That plan still holds good. So it is no longer a matter of dispute. We are all agreed upon it. They admit unemployment has been avoided by American dollars; and we are broadly agreed what we should do to prevent it or mitigate it should it recur. Everyone knows that any Government that comes into power as a result of this election will do its utmost to prevent unemployment. How far they will be successful will depend upon the methods they employ and the plight we are found to be in. I assure you there can be no greater safeguard against unemployment in the coming years than the return of a Government which will revive confidence in our country all over the world.

And now there is the tale of food subsidies. Sir Stafford Cripps told us on the broadcast that the Conservative Party had decided to abolish food subsidies. £406,000,000 is being spent in food subsidies, which is represented as a kindly gift by the kindly Government to the whole nation. It is not a gift. A great deal more is taken in tax by the kindly Government. Mr Morrison, evidently in collusion, repeated this whatever-you-care-to-call-it on a separate night. It is utterly untrue. We have no intention of abolishing food subsidies until and unless we are absolutely sure that the basic necessaries of life are available at prices all the people can pay down to the poorest in the land.

More than a fortnight ago Dr Edith Summerskill said at Kettering: 'The British Government could abolish rationing tomorrow if it were prepared to let the lowest income groups do without while the wealthiest bought up all available supplies. But it was not prepared to do so.' This is a very good example of the cumbrous and costly working of Socialist methods and machinery. The question immediately arises whether there is not some better way of helping the lower income groups to obtain their food at cheap prices than to keep in being for their sake the whole vast, complex, costly apparatus of rationing.

In our view the strong should help the weak. In the Socialist view the strong should be kept down to the level of the weak in order to have equal shares for all. How small the share is does not matter so much, in their opinion, so long as it is equal. They would much rather that everyone should have half rations than that anybody should get a second helping. What are called 'the lowest income groups' before the war when there were no rations in fact consumed under the 'wicked Tories' one and a half times as much meat and more than twice as much sugar as Dr Summerskill doles out to all of us today.

In the years before the war the dietary of London workhouses was in every way superior in meat, fats, sugar and also in variety to that which can be bought by a fully-employed wage-earner today. Yet to hear the Socialists talk on the broadcast, especially Mr Herbert Morrison and Sir Stafford Cripps, you would believe that we were living in a perfect paradise of plenty and good management. To apply the Socialist principle of equality at all costs is, in fact, to lay down the law that the pace of our advancing social army must be the pace of the slowest and the weakest man. Such a principle is, of course, destructive of all hopes of victory in social and philanthropic advance. It would undoubtedly condemn our island, with its enormous population, to a lower and more restricted standard of living than prevails anywhere else in the civilized world.

We are told: 'See what happened when sweets were derationed.' I am not at all sure that that was not a put-up job done with the hope of failure, so as to be an example. Certainly it was done in the most clumsy manner by those who had every interest to prevent its being a success. We certainly look forward to the day when we shall cease to be the only country in the civilized and free world where wartime rationing prevails. But I pledge any Conservative Government with which I am concerned not to take off rationing on any basic commodity until we are certain it will not only confer benefits upon the great mass of the people, but will protect the lower income groups from hardship.

You know, ladies and gentlemen, our Socialist masters think they know everything. They even try to teach the housewife how to buy her food. Mr Douglas Jay has said: 'Housewives as a whole cannot be trusted to buy all the right things, where nutrition and health are concerned. This is really no more than an extension of the principle according to which the housewife herself would not trust a child of four to select the week's purchases. For in the case of nutrition and health, just as in the case of education, the gentleman in Whitehall really does know better what is good for people than the people know themselves.'

That is what Mr Jay has said. Was there ever a period in the history of this island when such a piece of impertinence could have been spread about by a Minister? Let us call upon this Government to account for more of their own failures. Let us take them first on all the promises they made about housing. Before the war, under the 'wicked' Tory Government, with Mr Neville Chamberlain in charge, we were running to a thousand homes a day. There was no fuss about it. A certain amount of aid was given to local authorities, but no subsidizing of private industry. They just let things work naturally. A thousand houses a day!

Now what has happened? They cannot build half what the Tories under Mr Neville Chamberlain were building without mentioning it; without it being a political question at all. The 'wicked Tories' – a thousand; the 'noble Socialists' – five hundred, each of them costing three times as much as they did before the war. Here in Plymouth I am told you have a waiting list of 11,000 houses. Randolph tells me that there are in Devonport houses which were built by private enterprise before the war in 1938 for which people paid £685. These houses sell for £2,000 today. What a sign of Socialist efficiency. What a sign of getting value for money. What a sign in the fall of the purchasing power of money, on which depends for everyone the innumerable transactions we have to carry out between man and man in any community.

If the Government had been trying to give you houses instead of playing politics; if they had been thinking in terms of bricks and mortar instead of in spite and venom, many a family in this city and many a score of thousand families in this island would today have a roof and front door and a hearth of their own. I think the Socialists should be called to account by the electors after their sorry and discreditable performance. Boasts, promises, pledges on the one hand, and the shameful underproduction of the other. No Government but this Socialist Government could have fallen so far short of public duty and of solemn obligation.

I should like to say a few words to the numerous owners of motor-cars and motor-bicycles in this country. People are not necessarily 'lower than vermin' because by their skill and thrift they have earned and saved enough money to buy a car or a motor-bicycle. We realize the deprivation and often hardship involved in the strict rationing of petrol which the Socialist Government have enforced, and we are determined to put an end to it at the earliest possible moment.

We cannot, and do not, make any definite promises at this stage. We have been kept in the dark to such an extent that it is impossible for us to measure the difficulties and repercussions which freeing the sale of petrol at this moment might involve. But when we remember the enormous amount of petrol produced in the sterling area, it does seem strange that this country should be almost the only one in which petrol is rationed. We believe that by skilful management and readjustment of exports of sterling petrol, even if it may not be possible to abolish petrol rationing altogether, it may soon be possible for a Government concerned with the interests of owners of motor-cars and motor-cycles at any rate to increase greatly the basic ration.

Sir Stafford Cripps is reported to have said: 'You must have controls so that people cannot do just as they like.' There speaks the true voice of the Socialist. People must not do what they like. They must do what their Socialist masters (to use the word of the Attorney-General) think is good for them and tell them what to do. Thus the Socialist Party and Dr Summerskill have other reasons for wishing to keep the whole business of food rationing in full operation, besides their sympathy for the lower income groups and ignorance of the best way to help them. Mr Bottomley, the Under-Secretary for Overseas Trade, said eighteen months ago in Copenhagen: 'As long as a Socialist Government remains in office in Britain it can be expected that a rationing system will be maintained.' Thus we have not only rationing for rationing's sake, but the Food Ministry for the Food Ministry's sake. And under Socialist administration these sorts of organizations grow in cost with every month that passes.

In wartime, rationing is the alternative to famine. In peace it may well become the alternative to abundance. There is now one Food Ministry official for every 250 families in the country. There are more than 42,000 officials in all. But Dr Summerskill and her chief (I will not say her superior), Mr Strachey, exult in the feeling that they have so large an army to command. Their difficult and anxious problem is to make sure that it has enough to do to justify its existence, and give them this great mass of patronage and innumerable opportunities of interfering with other people's lives.

In the crisis of the war in 1940, when Lord Woolton was Food Minister, when the U-boats were sinking our ships and the air raids destroying our ports, the salaries paid to the Ministry of Food officials were less than £4,500,000 and the total administrative costs of the whole department were less than £8,000,000. However, the costs of all these departments tend to grow. The Socialists try to make them grow because it is part of their policy to have this vast machinery in existence. Also, they like to have as many ordinary people as possible in their power and dependent upon them as often as possible every day. In 1949 the salaries paid by the Socialists to the Ministry of Food officials had gone up from £4,500,000 in 1940 to nearly £14,000,000. The total administrative cost of running the department and working the rationing scheme had gone up from £8,000,000 to £21,000,000. It has well been said, 'The costs go up, but not the rations.'

Who do you suppose pays for all these 42,000 officials and lavish administrative expense? Every family in the country pays for it on the food they get. The food they get comes to their table weighted with this heavy charge, for which you pay as well as for the food subsidies which are given regardless of expense to millions of well-to-do people who do not need them at all. In order to pay for this and similar Socialist institutions, oppressive taxes are exacted from all, and beer and tobacco are taxed as they have never been taxed before. The purchase tax inflicts real hardships on the housewife, and particularly on those who have households and families to keep.

Income tax levied upon overtime and the highest forms of skilled craftsmanship discourages the extra effort and superior skill without which our industries cannot hold their own and compete in the modern world. Socialists pretend they give the lower income groups, and all others in the country, cheaper food through their system of rationing and food subsidies. To do it they have to take the money from their pockets first and circulate it back to them after heavy charges for great numbers of officials administering the system of rationing – which Mr Strachey and Dr Edith Summerskill are determined to keep in being whether it is needed or not – have been deducted. Little gifts have been given and came in handy for the election. We are all expected to change our political convictions and give our votes to the Government because a little extra tea and sugar had been saved up and given out. It is an insult to the intelligence of the British nation.

Sir Stafford Cripps now boasts, having first denied it, that the Socialist Government had given away to countries abroad £1,500,000,000 since they came into power to help the reconstruction of the world. They had to borrow it first from the United States or be given it by them. It was only lent or given to help Britain get on her legs again. Now it is gone. One-hundredth part of this £1,500,000,000 would have been enough to give every private motorist a reasonable ration of petrol. Conservatives are as keen as the Socialists to help revive the other countries of the world; but we believe we should be just before we are generous. It will take very strong arguments to convince me that our people should be deprived of the use of their motor vehicles, while other countries enjoy abundant supplies of petrol, largely bought with the money which we have presented to them, and for a large part of which we still remain debtors to America.

Socialism is contrary to human nature. Commerce and trade have always been a great power in this country. If difficulties have come upon them these last four and a half years it is because they have been hampered. The black patch confronting us now is due to the men at the head of the Government who have led and managed us. We must plunge into this pit of torment to rise again and overcome all perils to our life and independence as we have always done before.

The reason I ask for a strong majority is not that one party might ride roughshod, or that special favours might be granted to one class, or to vested interests. I ask for a strong majority towards that broad national unity in which our salvation will be found. Do not fail in your effort. Do not despair of your native land. No one can tell what the future will bring forth, but I believe that if we act wisely and deal faithfully with one another, and set our country, its history, glorious and inspiring, and its future – unlimited except by our own shortcomings – before our eyes, we should come through. Not only can the dangers of the present be overcome and its problems solved, but, having saved the world in war, we should save ourselves in peace.

Winston S. Churchill: speech
('Winston S. Churchill, His Complete Speeches', volume 8, page 7935)

10 February 1950 Woodford

ELECTION ADDRESS

... The British people face a momentous decision. Never was a community in such a precarious position. We are not like the vast areas of Russia or Australia, or other great food-producing areas. We are an artificial product – we more resemble Venice amid its lagoons, or Holland protected by its dykes from the ocean, or Egypt, which has lived so long upon the fluctuating chances of the Nile flood.

Trade union leaders in nationalized industry cannot really serve their members' interests. They are, in a way, the servants of the State, and trade unionism has disappeared in almost every country where Socialism or Communism has gained its control. The State is all, the all-powerful State. I am dead against it. For hundreds and hundreds of years the British people have tried to prevent themselves from being ruled by an absolute power.

Lord Swinton to Winston S. Churchill
(Churchill papers, 2/101)

11 February 1950

Thank you for your letter.[1] Your statement at Leeds was just what was wanted.

I have not bothered you about our Committee as it is working very well. We are keeping well up to date, and candidates are very well satisfied with the answers we give them.

As I told the Dominion Press yesterday, the strongest impression I have got

---

[1] Reproduced above (p. 1616).

of the Election to date is that we have taken and hold the initiative everywhere. This has been made possible by your initial broadcast and the Manifesto.

It was good of you to speak for Henry[1] at Taunton; I hear you had a tremendous reception. I hope you have made Randolph safe.

Winston S. Churchill: speech
('In the Balance', pages 197–207)

14 February 1950   Usher Hall, Edinburgh

ELECTION ADDRESS

I have spoken several times in the Usher Hall during this twentieth century so filled with tumult, but I am sure that there was no occasion, not even in the height of the war, when the issues which it was in our power to settle were so serious for the whole world, for Great Britain and for Scotland. The Prime Minister, Mr Attlee, has made it clear that his intention is to establish a Socialist State in this island at the earliest moment. He intends to create a society in which the State will control and own all the means of production, distribution and exchange. We have had one instalment of this during the last four and half years, and now we are asked to vote whether we want to take a second plunge into this immense social and economic revolution. The Socialists have issued a manifesto which, in a vague and general manner, prescribes the limits within which they will feel themselves entitled to act in the Parliament about to be elected. They involve already a profound change in our national life and one which, having been adopted, will be irrevocable.

The Socialists propose at once to nationalise steel, for which the Bill is already passed, and in addition they mention cement, sugar, chemicals, meat and industrial life insurance. They also claim the right to set up with the taxpayers' money rival State businesses wherewith to knock out any private enterprises which they dislike or which do not, apart from the law of land, obey their wishes. If they ruin those businesses it will be bad. If they fail in their ventures they have only to send in a bill for the loss to the Exchequer and you will pay it in your taxes. This is what they call their programme and what they would feel themselves entitled to do if they got a majority in the country, or even if they have a majority in Parliament resting upon a minority of votes in the country.

There is, however, no guarantee that they will keep themselves within these limits. If the more violent element in their party get control there are no lengths to which they cannot go. The Minister who might well be Mr Attlee's successor in leading the Socialist Party has not hesitated to speak of revolution, civil

[1] Hopkinson.

war and a blood bath. You have every need to use your votes to protect our country from such hateful threats. This attempt to establish a Socialist State in Great Britain affects the relations of England and Scotland in a direct and serious manner. The principle of centralization of government in Whitehall and Westminster is emphasized in a manner not hitherto experienced or contemplated in the Act of Union. The Supervision, interference and control in the ordinary details of Scottish life and business by the Parliament at Westminster has not hitherto been foreseen, and I frankly admit that it raises new issues between our two nations.

If England became an absolute Socialist State, owning all the means of production, distribution and exchange, ruled only by politicians and their officials in the London offices, I personally cannot feel that Scotland would be bound to accept such a dispensation. I do not therefore wonder that the question of Scottish home rule and all this movement of Scottish nationalism has gained in strength with the growth of Socialist authority and ambitions in England. I would never adopt the view that Scotland should be forced into the serfdom of Socialism as the result of a vote in the House of Commons. It is an alteration so fundamental in our way of life that it would require a searching review of our historical relations.

But here I speak to the Scottish Nationalists in words, as diplomatic language puts it, of great truth and respect, and I say this position has not yet been reached. If we act together with our united strength it may never arise. I do not believe that the British nation or the English people will accept the Socialist State. There is a deep fund of common sense in the English race and they have all sorts of ways, as has been shown in the past, of resisting and limiting the imposition of State autocracy. It would be a great mistake for Scotsmen to suppose that Mr Attlee's policy can be effectively imposed upon us at the present time. And here in this election, so momentous in its character and consequences, we all have the opportunity of inflicting a shattering defeat upon this menace to our individual liberties, and to the well understood and hitherto widely-admired British way of life. I most strongly urge all Scotsmen to fight one battle at a time. We have every hope that the Socialist schemes for netting us up and tying us down will be torn in pieces by the votes of the British people. We shall know more about it after February 23rd. It may indeed be a turning-point in our island story. Scotsmen would make a wrong decision if they tried to separate their fortunes from ours at a moment when together we may lift them all to a higher plane of freedom and security. It would indeed be foolish to cast splitting votes or support splitting candidates, the result of which might be to bring about that evil Whitehall tyranny and centralization, when by one broad heave of the British national shoulders the whole gimcrack structure of Socialist jargon and malice may be cast in splinters to the ground.

We of the Conservative and Unionist Party hold firmly to the principles of union and freedom, and we hold equally to those who[1] principles. We have every reason to believe that we shall win, and that the strength of the Socialist forces will be so broken that they will not be able to impose their restive tyranny upon us. Let Scotsmen therefore take one step at a time, and not take extreme decisions carrying with them grievous misfortunes both to England and Scotland, before no other choice is open. Besides all this, as we know from many a hard fought fight, the Scots do not quit their comrades in the hour of peril.

The Socialist centralization menace has however advanced so far as to entitle Scotland to further guarantees of national security and internal independence. These can be provided effectively by new additional representation at the centre and at the summit which, if the Conservatives and Unionists are returned to power, will be accorded to Scotland by a Unionist Cabinet. Besides strengthening the establishment of Under-Secretaries of State, we shall advise the creation of a new office of Minister of State for Scotland. He would be a Minister of Cabinet rank and would be deputy to the Secretary of State. Such an appointment would enable a senior member of the Cabinet to be constantly in Scotland. Because of the large changes in economic and financial affairs which have come about in recent years, we shall appoint a Royal Commission to review the whole situation between Scotland and England, and we shall take good care that this does not become an instrument of delay upon practical action.

During the first fortnight of this election battle, we have had to combat a number of falsehoods launched upon us by our opponents. I can but mention them. First there was the unemployment falsehood. This took the form of party propaganda claiming that they had cured unemployment by their planning, whereas they had already repeatedly admitted that there would be 2,000,000 unemployed but for the subsidies from capitalist America, on which the British Socialist Government have lived financially and even more politically.

Even worse, there has been the vile and shameful charge that the Conservative Party would deliberately create unemployment in order to make the rest of the people work harder. This has been refuted overwhelmingly by the White Paper presented to Parliament in 1944, for which all the leading Members on both Front Benches are responsible. This proclaimed our joint resolve to ward off unemployment and also prescribes the methods which should be adopted should it come upon us. Here was a policy to which all parties had pledged their faith, and it still remains the policy to which all Conservatives adhere. Therefore, the unemployment falsehood has been repelled from all forms of open and public discussion, though it may still be whispered in lies and slanders from doorstep to doorstep.

The next main falsehood by which we are assailed is found in the official

---

[1] two.

manifesto of the Socialist Party. It charges the Conservative and Unionist Party with seeking to make people work harder by cutting down their food supplies. I must read you the actual phrase, 'empty bellies'. 'Empty bellies are the one thing that will make Britons work.' This was attributed to an unnamed person and used as a means of vilifying the whole of our great party, representing, as will presently be shown, the majority of the nation. The Socialist leaders have printed this irresponsible utterance without mentioning that it was repudiated at the time and described as 'arrant nonsense' by the official authority of the Conservative organization. I invited Mr Morrison and Mr Attlee to cleanse themselves from this unfair and untruthful behaviour. I am surprised that they have not chosen even to acknowledge the repudiation which we immediately gave to such a cruel and unworthy accusation.

Then there are the family allowances. Everywhere the Socialists have been spreading the double falsehood that they initiated the family allowances and that we, the Unionist Party, intend to cut them down. The reverse is the truth. It was the Conservative Caretaker Government over which I presided which established the family allowances and if, in the reform and reorganization of our finances which are so urgently needed, family allowances are altered in any way, it will be not to diminish them but to augment and improve them.

All these three sets of falsehoods have been voiced by the leading Socialist Ministers and all, I am glad to say, have been beaten down in public controversy before we are halfway through our election campaign. We are therefore entitled to turn over the counter-attack. [. . .]

Mr Attlee, the Prime Minister, has been making play with the expression 'property-owning democracy', which constitutes an essential part of Conservative policy. He said:

> The nation was much more a property-owning democracy than when Labour came into power. They own the railways, the Bank of England and the coal mines, and there are a lot more things the nation will own presently.

I doubt if it gives very much pleasure to the average Socialist when he wakes up in the morning to say to himself, 'Oho, I own the Bank of England, I own the railways, I own the coal mines.' But if it does give him any actual pleasure, he is certainly paying dearly for it. It may gratify his pride, but it makes a nasty hole in his pocket. In order that these Socialist enthusiasts may enjoy this little thrill in the morning, very large sums are being taken from them and their wives and families in taxes, or in prices, or in both.

His thrill of pride has cost him and the rest of us dear. I am quite sure that when the railwaymen, who have behaved in a public-spirited manner in not pressing their wage claims at this critical juncture, wake up in the morning they do not get much fun out of saying to themselves, 'We own the railways.' In fact there is a great deal of evidence to the contrary, as will be proved when the votes are counted. Railway workers had a far better bargaining position when they were dealing with the railway companies and could have had the full help of their trade unions than when they have to bargain with an all-powerful State monopoly whom the union leaders are in with and do not like to offend.

Mr Attlee's remark about a property-owning democracy reminds me of a story told me at one of the naval stations a few years ago. A portly gentleman demanded to go on board a battleship as she lay alongside the quay. 'Who are you?' said the sentry. 'I am one of the proprietors' was the reply. But he did not see much of the battleship. The truth is that Mr Attlee and his friends feel the force of our Conservative theme, a property-owning democracy, and are trying to avoid it by talking nonsense about it. They know perfectly well that what we mean is a *personal* property-owning democracy. Households which have possessions which they prize and cherish because they are their own, or even a house and garden of their own, the Savings Certificates that their thrift has bought, a little money put by for a rainy day, or an insurance policy, the result of forethought and self-denial which will be a help in old age or infirmity, or after their death for those they love and leave behind – that is what the Conservatives mean by a property-owning democracy. And the more widely it is distributed and the more millions there are to share in it, the more will the British democracy continue to have the spirit of individual independence, and the more they will turn their backs on the Socialist delusion that one ought to be proud of being totally dependent on the State.

Mr Attlee also referred to my statement about the need for increasing the petrol ration. He described it as 'window dressing', and said I had not given a minute's thought to it. I give a great deal of thought to what I say and to what I do. My task at this election has not been the dressing of windows so much as the dressing of humbugs. It is curious that almost at the very moment when Mr Attlee was deriding the idea of an increase in the basic patrol ration at Liverpool, his own Minister of Fuel, Mr Gaitskell, at Harrogate was saying that the prospects of an increased petrol ration were 'not bad'. Talks, he said, were now going on in Washington to see if we could get extra petrol without spending dollars. This is important news, and I am very glad to have extorted it from the Government by the demand which I made for a review of the petrol ration. I have never suggested we should use dollars to buy petrol. We have vast masses of petroleum in the sterling area, and if the Socialist Ministers had not shown their usual ineptitude and incompetence the refineries would be in existence and at work today which would secure us ample supplies.

Everything they touch turns to muddle, whether it be Mr Bevin's mismanagement and loss of influence in the Middle East, which has led to the closing of the Haifa refinery, or whether it be the Socialist department red tape and restrictions which have hitherto paralysed the construction of the great refinery at Southampton, the cause is the same; a thoroughly inefficient administration absorbed in playing party politics, and a Prime Minister who has failed to give the necessary guidance and leadership, which no one else but a Prime Minister can provide. Mr Attlee spoke of the importance of controls. He took as an example the lorry from which he was speaking. He said that without controls the lorry would run into the ditch. That is just what is happening to the Government, of whose lorry he was supposed to be the driver. What we need is fewer *controls* throughout the country and more *control* at the head the Government.

The vote-catching election cry 'Fair shares for all' should not deceive keen-minded men and women. It is meaningless unless it is also stated who is to be the judge of what is fair. The Socialist appeal is to envy and hatred. These can be no foundation for a civilized or prosperous society. But what the average Socialist really means when he speaks of 'Fair shares for all' is *equal* shares for all. Equal shares for those who toil and those who shirk. Equal shares for those who save and those who squander. No reward offered to the skilled craftsman. No incentive to the industrious and experienced piece-worker. No extra payment for overtime that is not taken back from him in PAYE. No reward for enterprise, ingenuity, thrift and good-housekeeping. 'Equal shares for all', that is what the Socialist Government really mean.

Even in Soviet Russia such ideas are not applied. If carried into force they would bring the whole community down to a dead level with the weakest, the idlest and the most wasteful. But that is what they mean. It would bring ruin to any but the most primitive society. Yet these are the ideas which are put forward not only by the wilder members of the Socialist Party but by the Chancellor of the Exchequer himself. Sir Stafford Cripps has a brilliant intellect, but it is so precariously poised that his public life has been disfigured by lamentable and spasmodic utterances to which he falls a victim in moods of excitement or moments of strain. I can quite understand the stresses through which he is passing now when his clear mind sees so plainly the harm he has wrought his country and when his career and ambitions prompt him to try to outbid Mr Aneurin Bevan. Nevertheless, I was astounded to read what he said at Bristol on Saturday. I quote the report in the London *Times*. These are his words:

> We are sharing out more fairly the national resources that exist. We have not shared them out all equally *yet*. It takes a bit of time to do these things.

Here you have the gospel of equal shares for all proclaimed as the aim and policy of the Chancellor of the Exchequer responsible for the finances of this vast and complicated, but now seriously endangered, British society. It is not 'Fair shares for all', whatever that may mean, but a levelling down to a uniform standard governed by the contribution of the weakest elements in our national life. In the whole English-speaking world, in the whole of Europe outside the Iron Curtain, there is no government today that would tolerate such language from its finance minister. In the whole world Great Britain is the country which can least well afford to suffer the injury which such frantic outbursts will do.

In the first place the Chancellor obviously struck a mortal blow at the Savings Movement, which all parties have been urged to support and have supported, and in favour of which he himself has made so many speeches. What right has he to appeal for thrift and saving, forethought and self-denial when at the same time in his heart he is aiming at the confiscation of all property down to the level of equality for all (except of course members of the Government and those who enjoy their favour). Nothing could be more likely than this declaration to weaken the impulse to production at home, or still further impair our credit abroad. Nothing could be more likely to bring unemployment upon our people. My hope is that the British electorate will by a strong and ample majority repudiate these reckless and frenzied exhibitions by the Chancellor of the Exchequer. We have an Administration intent upon the class war and hostile to every form of wealth and property. Sweeping them out of power will do more to prevent unemployment, revive the purchasing power of the money we earn, and regain for us the confidence and credit of the civilized world than any other step that could be taken. You have the opportunity of taking that step on February 23rd.

I have waited till I reached this imperial and ancient capital of Scotland to say a few words about world politics. We are all absorbed naturally during the election in domestic disputes. But outside this island a vast and formidable world has come into being dwarfing our calm and Victorian days. It laps us about on every side, and we no longer have controlling power or even it seems to me a sufficient influence upon what happens. When the war stopped the United States, Great Britain and Russia were what was called 'The Big Three'. But with the decision taken by the British electorate in one day of voting in 1945, we lost for the time being our place and rank in world affairs which we had gained and held throughout the terrible days of struggle. We became a nation absorbed in its own class and party warfare. All the countries of the free and civilized world were conscious of a sense of loss. Then we fell into our economic difficulties which would in any case have been severe, and very soon instead of being one of the world's leaders, our famous island became one of the world's problems.

I recognize fully that Mr Bevin, steadfastly sustained by Mr Attlee, has followed in main essentials the right course in foreign policy. The execution of that policy has been marred by many pitiful blunders. Mr Bevin has managed to make British foreign policy equally disliked by France and Germany, by Jew and Arab, and by Communist and by anti-Communist forces. He has done this through some great and many minor errors. Still, he has not failed to uphold the main principles on which our life and safety depends. He has followed with steadfastness the line I marked out at Fulton of fraternal association with the United States, and the closest unification of our military arrangements. In the Atlantic Pact we have a great instrument making for world peace. In the Brussels Treaty and the building up of Western European Union he has, albeit somewhat sheepishly, given effect to the theme of United Europe. But for his personal feelings it might all have been a great deal easier. Nevertheless he has come along more or less quietly, and Western Union has taken its place with the British Empire and the English-speaking fraternity in that vast amalgamation of free democracy upon whose unity and strength world peace depends. These supreme objectives have not been lost. We have given our Conservative support to the main principles of the Government's foreign policy while we have deplored the astonishing errors which have hampered its application. In the end it is the larger issues that will count.

While we are all so busy with our internal party controversies we must not forget the gravity of our position or indeed that of the whole world. Soviet Russia – the immensely powerful band of men gathered together in the Kremlin – has ranged itself against the Western democracies. They have added to their dominion the satellite States of Europe; the Baltic States, Poland, Czechoslovakia, Hungary, Bulgaria, Rumania. Tito of Yugoslavia has broken away. Greece has been rescued by the United States, carrying on the task which we began. At the other side of the world the 500,000,000 of China have fallen into the Communist sphere. But Communism is novel and China is old. I do not regard China as having finally accepted Soviet servitude.

Still, when you look at the picture as a whole you see two worlds ranged against one another more profoundly and on a larger scale than history has ever seen before. The Soviet Communist world has by far the greatest military force, but the United States have the atom bomb; and now, we are told that they have a thousandfold more terrible manifestation of this awful power. When all is said and done it is my belief that the superiority in the atom bomb, if not indeed almost the monopoly of this frightful weapon, in American hands is the surest guarantee of world peace tonight. But for that we should not be talking about all these burning domestic questions that fill our minds, our mouths and our newspapers today. It is my earnest hope that we may find our way to some more exalted and august foundation for our safety than this grim and sombre balancing power of the bomb. We must not, however, cast away our only shield of safety unless we can find something better and surer and more likely to last. When I say 'we' I must not let you forget that 'we' means the United States and that it is their power which protects not only Britain but Europe. I really do not know why it is that when we were so far advanced into this new, mysterious region of atomic war, we should have fallen so completely behind in these last four years. When we are spending such enormous sums upon our army, navy, and air force, it is very odd that we should not have been able to make the atomic bomb for ourselves by now.

It seems to me one of the most extraordinary administrative lapses that have ever taken place. It is like the unwisdom of selling a hundred of our very few jet aircraft to the Argentine for a couple of million pounds or so. It would be incredible if it had not happened.

But I must not be drawn from the larger theme. I look back to 1945 when I was last in relation with Mr Stalin and his colleagues. I read to the House of Commons a year ago one of the telegrams I sent him then, and I am glad to repeat these words because they express what is in my heart today. Here is what I wrote in April 1945:

> There is not much comfort in looking into a future where you and the countries you dominate, plus the Communist parties in many other States are all drawn up on one side, and those who rally to the English-speaking nations and their associates or Dominions are on the other. It is quite obvious that their quarrel would tear the world to pieces and that all of us leading men on either side who had anything to do with that would be shamed before history. Even embarking on a long period of suspicions, of abuse and counter-abuse and of opposing policies would be a disaster hampering the great developments of world prosperity for the masses which are attainable only by our trinity.

That was written nearly five years ago. Alas, it was only too true. All came to pass with horrible exactitude. But I do not blame Mr Bevin for that. All the talk at the 1945 General Election about Left speaking to Left has been proved to be foolish, but on the main issue he has done his best. I have not of course access to the secret information of the Government, nor am I fully informed about the attitude of the United States. Still I cannot help coming back to this idea of another talk with Soviet Russia upon the highest level. The idea appeals to me of supreme effort to bridge the gulf between the two hatreds of the cold war. You must be careful to mark my words in these matters because I have not always been proved wrong. It is not easy to see how things could be worsened by a parley at the summit, if such a thing were possible. But that I cannot tell.

At least I feel that Christian men should not close the door upon any hope of finding a new foundation for the life of the self-tormented human race. What prizes lie before us; peace, food, happiness, leisure, wealth for the masses never known or dreamed of; the glorious advance into a period of rest and safety for all the hundreds of millions of homes where little children play by the fire and girls grow up in all their beauty and young men march to fruitful labour in all their strength and valour. Let us not shut out the hope that the burden of fear and want may be lifted for a glorious era from the bruised and weary shoulders of mankind.

FEBRUARY 1950

Joyce C. Hall[1] to Winston S. Churchill
(Churchill papers, 1/26)

15 February 1950

We are happy to welcome the world's most famous artist to the company of Hallmark Painters for 1950 Christmas Cards. Your work will now be seen and appreciated by thousands of Americans who hold you in highest esteem.[2]

Winston S. Churchill: press notice
(Churchill papers, 2/116)

16 February 1950

Mr Churchill issued the following statement from Chartwell this morning: 'I am informed from many quarters that a rumour has been put about that I died this morning. This is quite untrue. It is however a good sample of the whispering campaign which has been set on foot. It would have been more artistic to keep this one for Polling Day.'

Winston S. Churchill: broadcast
('In the Balance', pages 208-19)

17 February 1950   London

Nearly three weeks have passed, my friends, since I last spoke to you all,[3] and we now approach the end of this momentous election which all the world has watched with anxious eyes. The moment of decision draws near, and all can vote freely. They can vote with the certainty that the ballot is secret, and that if they live in council houses, or are on the long waiting-lists to get a house, or even if they are State employees, they cannot be called to account for the way in which they use their vote any more than they can by the landlord or private employer. This we owe to the respect still shown to our slowly built up British constitution and British way of life. Long may it be preserved.

All the same, everyone is accountable to his or her conscience, and everyone has an honourable responsibility to vote according to what they believe will be best for our country at this difficult moment in its history. We are in fact at a turning point in our fortunes, and the result of your action on Thursday may well shape the famous occasion: 'Think well, think wisely, think not for

[1] Joyce Clyde Hall, 1891-1982. Purchased engraving firm leading to the first Hallmark card designs, 1915. Founded Hall Brothers, Inc., 1923. Started marketing his cards under the Hallmark brand name, 1928.
[2] Churchill telegraphed back: 'I am delighted at the opportunity of having my paintings exhibited in America through the medium of Christmas Cards.'
[3] Broadcast of Jan. 21, reproduced above (pp. 1593-7).

the moment, but for the years that are to come, before you make your choice.'[1] Above all, do not abstain; do not stand out of the fight through indolence of hesitation or throw your votes away on candidates who have no chance of becoming Members of Parliament.

Since the election fight began, the issues at stake have become more serious. This is due to the statements about ultimate aims in Socialism by the Prime Minister and the Chancellor of the Exchequer, with all their high authority. Mr Attlee has made it clear that he does not regard the Socialist election manifesto – except, I presume, in the coming Parliament – as setting any limit to his aims. 'Socialism does not stop,' he said. 'It goes on. Nothing can stand between a nation and its goal – no one.' Here then is the proclamation by the Prime Minister of his resolve to create the complete Socialist State as soon as he can, by the nationalization of all the means of production, distribution and exchange – that is to say, the creation of a monster State monopoly, owing everything and employing everybody. Here is the goal towards which Mr Attlee seeks to lead the British nation. In fact, however, I doubt very much whether even a fifth part of our people are convinced Socialists, or that they realize the sacrifice of personal liberty, both economic and political, which must inexorably follow from the concentration of all industry and the direction of labour in the hands of the State.

The Chancellor of the Exchequer has not lagged behind his chief; for at Bristol on Saturday last he used words which reveal his mind and purpose. This what he said, and when challenged he has not withdrawn, about sharing out the national resources: 'We have not shared them out equally yet. It takes a bit of time to do these things.' That is what he said. These are indeed grave words. They imply a levelling down of British society to a degree not hitherto presented by any responsible person. There would of course be the governmental and political and official class lifted, as in Soviet Russia, into a privileged position above the mass of the people whose lives they direct and plan. But on the basis of 'equal shares for all' there would it seems to me be little consideration for what Mr Arthur Deakin,[2] the General Secretary of our largest trade union, has aptly called the 'differentials' in industry, and for all the infinite variation in the human contribution. This confession of the Exchequer's inner purpose spells the death-blow, so long as he remains at the Treasury, to the great savings movement which at his request we have all supported. He is of course angry with me for giving world-wide publicity to his own imprudent

---

[1] William Gladstone, House of Commons, June 1886.
[2] Arthur Deakin, 1890–1955. National Secretary of General Workers, Transport and General Workers' Union, 1932–5; Asst General Secretary, 1935–45 (Acting, 1940–5); General Secretary, 1945–55. President, World Federation of Trade Unions, 1946–8. Co-Founder, International Confederation of Trade Unions, 1948. President, TUC, 1952. President, International Transport Workers' Federation, 1954–5.

and baleful words. His rival, Mr Aneurin Bevan, during this election has at least given us this reassurance: 'It is not part of our programme,' he said, 'this time that all private enterprise should be destroyed.' Thank you so much.

I do not mind what names they call me. The grave point for us all is what will happen to the credit and well-being of this country if men who hold the doctrines and pursue the aims of Mr Attlee and Sir Stafford Cripps and their associates were to be given a mandate at this critical juncture in our national affairs to carry Britain another long stage towards their disastrous goal. Nothing would be more likely to bring upon us the mass unemployment which all parties are pledged to do their utmost to avert, but which all parties know threatens us when Marshall Aid is withdrawn.

In taking another plunge into Socialism we should be absolutely alone in the free and civilized world. The United States, on whose bounty Mr Attlee's Government have been living, produces its vast wealth and high wages upon the capitalist, free enterprise system. Canada that mighty land of the future, is anti-Socialist. New Zealand and Australia have at their recent elections cast Socialism off. Although they have only taken the dose in a modified form, they cast it off. In Europe, there is not a single country outside the Iron Curtain, except in Scandinavia, where there is a Socialist government, and even in Scandinavia they have called a halt. The first declaration of the Socialist Prime Minister in Norway after winning the election was: 'No further nationalization for the next four years.' The British Socialist Government now ask us to go forward under their guidance alone. Alone we are to make this dire experiment. We are the only one to try it now. Mr Morrison says we are leading the world – but the world is not following. On the contrary, all free and civilized States are in recoil from Socialist rule and Socialist doctrines. One of the chief reasons which has turned the tide in Europe against Socialism is the utter failure of Socialist governments to make any effective resistance to Communist aggression and permeation.

Now you will have to say on Thursday whether we are to plunge deeper into the thickets and briars of Socialist regulations and controls, or whether, by a resolute effort, we shall rejoin our friends and comrade nations on the high-road of ordered freedom and progress. By one heave of her shoulders Britain can shake herself free. Do not miss this opportunity. It may not return. I am reminded of the tale of the prisoner in the Spanish dungeon. For years he longed to escape from his bondage. He tried this, he tried that – all in vain. One day he pushed the door of his cell – it was open. It had always been open. He walked out free into the broad light of day. You can do that now on this very Thursday, and what a throng there will be to welcome us back in the forefront of the nations who now regard us with bewilderment and pity, but for whom only a few years ago we kept the flag of freedom flying amid all the winds that blew.

The Socialists have tried to confuse the main issue by a number of false statements with which I must deal. The Conservatives, they say, would like there to be some unemployment because it would make men work harder. This is an unworthy accusation. Our policy is of course the exact reverse. Our aim is full employment and abundant food. We have no intention of abolishing food subsidies until and unless we are absolutely sure that the basic necessities of life are available at price all the people can pay, down to the poorest in the land.

It is also said that the Conservative Government would cut the family allowances which the Labour Government has given you. But what is the truth? The Family Allowances Act was passed by the Conservative and National Liberal Government over which I had the honour to preside – the Caretakers, you remember, they were called – I suppose because they took good care. The Family Allowances Act was passed in June 1945. We have no intention of altering family allowances except to improve them or extend them as part of some larger beneficial scheme.

All parties are equally desirous to maintain the social services and where necessary improve them. The question is whether Socialism or free enterprise would best be able to find the money to pay for them. This money has in the main to be found from the earnings of industry. If the Socialists go on nationalizing one great industry after another, turning their profits into losses or into rises in cost to the public, the revenue from taxation will shrink until the country can no longer pay and the social services will in consequence collapse. Only by liberating the creative forces in British industry can we earn the revenue to maintain that edifice of social security, of the building of which the Conservative and the Liberal Parties had the right to be proud before the Socialist Party ever figured in national affairs.

Our opponents are also telling old-age and ex-service pensioners, as they go from door to door: 'The Tories will cut your pensions'. But it is they who have already cut them by 3s 9d in the pound through the rise in prices, and the full results of devaluation, when they fall upon us, will cut them still more. We, on the other hand, by reviving national credit and the buying power of our money will restore to the pensioners and those who live on fixed incomes at least – I say, at least – what has been taken away. I have felt obliged to present to you these outstanding falsehoods because no matter how often they are contradicted the whispering campaign goes on.

The oppressive burden of taxation is the first problem to which a Conservative Government will turn its attention. Ours is the most over-taxed country in the world. Our people are prevented from putting forth their full effort. The initiative of industry is being stifled; the incentive of overtime and piece rates is diminished. Those who would like to save for marriage or old age are discouraged. We intend to revise and reduce the rates of both direct and indirect taxation, including especially PAYE and purchase tax. By reducing taxation we shall stimulate increased industrial activity, increased output, and in consequence we shall increase earnings. By this means we shall make good a large part of the revenue which would otherwise be lost by reducing taxation. The rest we shall save by purging lavish Government expenditure, by abolishing the wasteful system of bulk buying in food and materials, and by stopping the unbridled extravagance in Government departments and nationalized industries. During this election the Government have made it plain that they do not mean to make any reductions in taxation. In fact, Sir Stafford Cripps has threatened increases. He said in his broadcast that no substantial economies were possible. We are now spending at the rate of £3,300,000,000 a year and if the Labour Government cannot, or will not, even try to cut out waste, it is high time someone else comes in who will.

Another matter in which the Socialist Government have failed the British people is housing. The Minister of Health, after he had had a year to survey the situation, promised that every family in the land would have a separate home before this election. Everybody knows from the waiting-lists of their local councils that today we are further from that objective than we were five years ago. The Socialist Government are building at the rate of only 500 houses a day, whereas with the same building force under a Conservative Government before the war, 1,000 a day were built. We intend to use to the full all the resources of the building industry, building houses both to let and for sale, and make an intense effort to recover the leeway and all the time that has been lost, and all the energy that has been spent in bitter politics.

You must not blind yourselves to the fact that many grievous difficulties lie ahead. The election has been held in February instead of June in order to get it over before the consequences of devaluation came home to roost in higher prices, and before a Budget had to be produced which if it were honest would be unpopular. A new outlook, a more efficient administration and a new impulse with less faction, hate and spite will, I believe, be given to our people. And if so it may bring to them the power to realize many hopes and desires which are dear to their hearts.

I have now dealt with the great choice we have to make in our domestic affairs. I have once again contradicted the falsehoods by which we are assailed. But I cannot end my message and appeal to you (as you sit in your homes searching your hearts and minds, I hope, and wondering who is telling you the truth, I daresay, and what it is best to do for our dear land) – I cannot end my message without looking beyond our island coasts to the terrible and tremendous world that has grown up around us in the twentieth century of shock and strife. At Edinburgh the other night I said: 'I cannot help coming back to this idea of another talk with Soviet Russia upon the highest level. The ideal appeals to me of a supreme effort to bridge the gulf between the two worlds so that each can live their lives, if not in friendship at least without the hatreds of the cold war. At least I feel', I said, 'that Christian men and women should not close the door upon any hope of finding a new foundation for life of the self-tormented human race.'

Mr Bevin, the Secretary of State for Foreign Affairs, dismissed all this by the scornful word 'stunt'. By this he only showed how far his mind dwells below the true level of events. Why should it be wrong for the British nation to think about these supreme questions of life and death, perhaps for the whole world, at a time when there is a general election? Is not that the one time of all others when they should think about them? What a reflection it would be upon our national dignity and moral elevation, and indeed upon the whole status of British democracy, if at this time of choice, this turning point in world history, we found nothing to talk about but material issues and nice calculations about personal gain or loss! What a humiliation it would be if proud Britain, in this fateful hour, were found completely absorbed in party and domestic strife! I am glad I put a stop to all that.

Even on this material basis a continuance of the present arms race can only cause increasing danger, increasing military expense and diminishing supplies to the homes. The only time when the people really have a chance to influence and in fact decide events is at a general election. Why should they be restricted to the vote-catching or vote-snatching game? Why should they be told that it is a 'stunt or 'soapbox diplomacy' to speak to them of the great world issues upon which our survival and salvation may well depend?

Mr Bevin says that everything must be reserved to the United Nations. We all support the great ideal of world government; but the United Nations cannot function while it is rent asunder by the conflicting forces of the two worlds which are ranged against each other. It is only by the agreement of the greatest Powers that security can be given to ordinary folk against an annihilating war with atomic hydrogen bombs or bacteriological horrors. I cannot find it in my heart and conscience to close the door upon that hope. By its fruition alone can the United Nations discharge their supreme function.

My friends, I ask for a strong majority, for one capable of giving both guidance and design and securing the necessary time to make great purposes effective. We do not seek the power to enable one party to ride rough-shod over the other, we do not seek the power in order that special interests or classes should have privileges or unearned increment and profit. This will be the supreme opportunity for the Conservative and National Liberal Parties to prove that they stand high above the level of mere sectional appetites. Should we become responsible we shall govern on behalf of the entire British people no matter to what party or class or part of the country they belong. We shall respect the sentiments of minorities in what is just and fair no matter whether they vote for us or against us. This is the true essence of democracy. It is only by inspiring the nation with unity and common purpose, by taking without fear or favour the necessary measures to restore our solvency and independence that we shall overcome the dangers and solve the problems that confront us.

Of course, I am – as I am reminded – an old man. It is true that all the day-dreams of my youth have been accomplished. I have no personal advantage to gain by undertaking once more the hard and grim duty of leading Britain and her Empire through and out of her new and formidable crisis. But while God gives me the strength, and the people show me their good will, it is my duty to try, and try I will. I do not know tonight the full extent of the harm which has been done to our finances, to our defences and to our standing in the world. I am grieved at what I see and hear but it may well be there are worse facts, not made public, and perhaps not even understood by our present rulers. Therefore we are not going to promise you smooth and easy times. What we promise is, that, laying aside every impediment, we will faithfully and resolutely carry forward the policy we have proclaimed, we will do our best for all, and build on a sure foundation the structures of British greatness and world peace. Goodnight to you all. Think – and act!

Lord Swinton to Winston S. Churchill
(Churchill papers, 2/101)[1]

18 February 1950

My dear Winston,

We are through on the Committee; & I am going off to do a round of speaking in Yorkshire.

You gave us a great wind up last night. I find everywhere devout thankfulness that you have given a lead on Russia. And I believe where you come in, you will get Fort Knox behind sterling.[2]

Winston S. Churchill to Douglas Clifton Brown
(Churchill papers, 2/101)

21 February 1950

Dear Mr Speaker,

I have been shocked to hear that an Independent candidate has put himself forward for election in the constituency you have so long represented.

The high office which you hold lifts you above the cockpit of Party politics, and I am sure that, whatever their political allegiance, the electors of Hexham will give their undivided support.

---

[1] This letter was handwritten.
[2] Churchill replied: 'Thank you so much.'

1658 February 1950

Jo Sturdee to Winston S. Churchill
(Churchill papers, 1/47)

24 February 1950

Mrs Oliver asked to be kept informed. Last night we sent the following cable:

'Duncan in with eleven thousand majority. Randolph lost by three thousand. Other results not out yet'. Do you wish to send anything further?

Jo Sturdee to Sarah Churchill
(Churchill papers, 1/47)

24 February 1950

Mr Churchill elected in his constituency with 18 thousand majority. Captain Soames in by 2 thousand. At present Socialists lead by 15 seats with about 100 results to come in.

Lord Salisbury to Winston S. Churchill
(Churchill papers, 2/101)[1]

25 February 1950

My dear Winston,

This is just to thank you most gratefully for asking us to come in on Thursday night. We did appreciate it so much, and it was intensely interesting, if a little anxious, in view of the earlier return. However, that is all right now. Indeed, if we could not get a whacking great majority, this is, I suppose, the best thing that could have happened, except for the fact that it is those miseries, and not you, who are in office.[2] I wish that you were at the helm. But you would have had an almost impossible job, with a majority of 20–30, and no doubt the Labour Party and Trades unions would have made it as difficult as possible, whereas we shall no doubt behave in a more decent and orderly manner. So, from the point of view of the country, and especially of its position abroad, it may be that this is the best solution, for the time being, at any rate, so long as the parliamentary machine can be made to work at all under these conditions. I gather from the papers that the Gov are going to try to carry on, and I imagine, from our point of view, that this is all to the good. For they will have to take the responsibility, under what I am afraid are likely to be steadily deteriorating circumstances, and what we have said at the election will prove to have been true. But it will mean that we shall, if we are to give them

---

[1] This letter was handwritten.
[2] Labour lost 78 seats (total 315); Conservatives won 90 seats (total 298); Liberals lost 3 seats (total 9).

rope to hang themselves, have to exercise a great deal of restraint. Indeed, it rather looks as if the Conservative Party will have to adopt, in the House of Commons, the same sort of attitude as we have had to adopt in the Lords in the last five years. However, I imagine that you & Anthony and Oliver S.[1] are thinking all this out. I shall be intensely interested to learn the conclusions to which you have come.

So far as the Liberals are concerned, they have of course behaved as badly and as foolishly as possible, and no doubt the Party will be very angry with them. But I hope that we shall be able to avoid recriminations. They have had an appalling debacle, and are no doubt feeling very sore. But as soon as this has worn off, we may get the psychological moment to bring them into a really enduring partnership with us. The Moynihans,[2] Mcfadyeans[3] and Fothergills will be utterly disorientated, and the moderates like Violet Bonham Carter, Reading[4] and Rennell[5] will, I hope, resume control. I shall personally like to enter in a negotiation with them for a permanent merger between the two parties, under a new name and with an agreed manifesto. This should not be impossible to achieve. So far as I know, there are no fundamental issues that separate us. Pure unadulterated Free Trade is pretty dead, and though I know that Herbert Samuel is passionately keen to do away with the hereditary system in the House of Lords altogether, I think that that is his non particular idiosyncrasy & we are ready to go quite a long way in the way of reform. I do not personally like idea of an alliance between the two parties, both keeping their own individuality. That would only lead to continual squabbles as to who gets what. Moreover, it perpetuates the existence of those main parties in the state, which always breeds uncertainty. I feel that if we are to do anything effective and enduring it must be on the basis of a complete merger, which would after all be only a recognition of the undoubted fact that the dividing line between left and right has moved to the left. To get an agreement of this kind seems to me the most important thing at the present time, and the most urgent, as we may clearly be faced with another election before long. I do hope that Tory intransigence will not stand in the way.

Please forgive this long screed but I wanted you to know what is in my mind. If you think I can be of any use in talking to Liberals, I hope you will let me know. I have had a certain amount of conversation with Francis Rennell in the House of Lords during the last parliament – purely of course on a personal

[1] Stanley.
[2] Patrick Berkeley Moynihan, 1906–65. Baron, 1936. Served in RA, 1939–45.
[3] Andrew McFadyean, 1887–1974. President, Liberal Party, 1949–50; Vice-President, 1950–60.
[4] Gerald Isaacs, 1889–1960. Served in WWI (MC, 1918). Unsuccessful Parliamentary candidate (Lib.) for Blackburn, 1929. Succeeded as 2nd Marquess of Reading, 1935. Joined Churchill's Conservative administration in 1951 as Joint Parliamentary Under-Secretary of State for Foreign Affairs. Minister of State, 1953. PC, 1953.
[5] Francis Rodd, 1895–1978. Intelligence Officer, WWI. Married, 1928, Hon. Mary Constance Vivian Smith. Chief of Civil Affairs, AMG, Sicily, 1939. Succeeded his father as 2nd Baron Rennell, 1941. President, National Geographic Society, 1945–8.

basis – and I am pretty sure that he and probably Reading would be helpful. And the atmosphere of the Lords is so detached that it is perhaps easier to get in touch with one's political opponents there than in the Commons, or any rate to supplement other conversations.

We <u>were</u> so sorry about Randolph. He seems to have made a splendid fight, and it would have been grand if he could have thrown out that odious Foot.

I go to Hatfield on Monday, and am of course at your disposal at any time, if ever you want to come see me about House of Lords affairs or anything else.

Winston S. Churchill to Sir Alan Lascelles
(Churchill papers, 2/171)

27 February 1950

My dear Tommy,

Oliver[1] gave me an account of your telephone talks with him. I certainly think that the occasion has not come for a conference of the character mentioned,[2] though of course I should obey if summoned. The Government have a majority and must meet the new Parliament, whose temper cannot be prejudged. Whatever happens, I think that another General Election in the next few months is inevitable. I cannot suppose that any Party would attempt to withhold supplies, as this would expose them to the charge of wishing to break down the whole organization of the country, including the social services and pensions. I do not feel that such a point need be the subject of such assurances at the present time.

The rift in the Nation is very deep, for both the Socialists and the Conservatives have greatly strengthened in their position in the areas where they are the strongest. I doubt whether the Government will seek any parley with us, and we certainly seek none with them. I see no reason why matters should not clear themselves by the normal Constitutional processes. If any conference were held as suggested, it would seem to me that if the Leader of the Liberal Party were invited a similar invitation should be extended to the Leader of the National Liberal Party, whose representation in the House of Commons is more numerous.

While I am writing to you I venture to put on record my view about a dissolution. If the present Prime Minister were to ask for a dissolution in the near future, I am of opinion that Constitutional practice and tradition, including a fairly recent Canadian precedent, would seem to indicate that the Crown should be satisfied that the new Parliament has already outlived its usefulness and that no alternative arrangements or combinations are possible, before granting such a request. The principle that a new House of Commons has a

[1] Stanley.
[2] A meeting of party leaders under the auspices of the Palace.

right to live if it can and should not be destroyed until some fresh issue or situation has arisen to place before the electors, is, I believe, sound.

There is one other minor point which I must mention to you. I received before the Election a letter from the Lord Chamberlain saying that The King wished me, as Lord Warden of the Cinque Ports, to be present at Dover on March 7 to receive the President of the French Republic.[1] Naturally I should greatly like to do this. I cannot however leave the House of Commons on that day. The debate on the Gracious Speech will have opened the day before, and it will be my duty as Leader of His Majesty's Opposition to reply to Mr Attlee when the debate reopens on the 7th. I have therefore written in this sense to Clarendon,[2] but perhaps you would say a word to The King, explaining that I have duties at Westminster as well as at Dover and, not being a bird, I cannot be in two places at once.

Winston S. Churchill to Lord Salisbury
(Churchill papers, 2/101)

28 February 1950

My dear Bobbety,

I marvel at your beautiful handwriting and that you can write so many pages without a single correction.[3]

Our vigil the other night was a case of 'the evening red, the morning blue'.

I have thought carefully over all you say. We may not have the power to turn these people out unless they want to be turned out, and if they want to be it will be very difficult to bar their exit. Among other unpleasant prospects there is a period of six or seven months when the Socialists, with full control of the executive, will be trying to make a good case for the electors, and the Conservatives will be counting on things going wrong with the country and having great difficulty in hiding their feelings. An executive Government in a desperate situation has great and unexpected powers of action. I do not know enough about the financial situation to judge whether they could produce a popular budget with heavy increases of death duties or capital levy coupled with considerable remissions which we have suggested in our Election speech.

I hope you will consider this as well as other points of view.

---

[1] Vincent Auriol, 1884–1966. Graduated in Law, Collège de Revel, 1904. Co-founded socialist newspaper *Le Midi Socialiste*, 1908. Entered Chamber of Deputies as a Socialist Deputy, 1914. France's first representative, UN Security Council, 1946. First President, French Fourth Republic, 1947–54.

[2] George Herbert Hyde Villiers, 1877–1955. Succeeded his father as 6th Earl of Clarendon, 1914. Capt., Hon. Corps of Gentlemen-at-Arms, 1922–4, 1924–5. PC, 1931. Governor General of the Union of South Africa, 1931–7. Chief Scout of South Africa, 1931–7. KG, 1937. Lord Chamberlain of the Household, 1938–52.

[3] Letter of Feb. 25, reproduced above (pp. 1658–60).

Lord Cecil to Winston S. Churchill
(Churchill papers, 2/95)

28 February 1950

My dear Winston,

I hope you will forgive me for sending you my warmest congratulations on the Conservative success in the Election and the very great part you played in it.

Your intervention about Russia was more than justified. Indeed, I cannot help feeling that the desire to keep foreign affairs out of Party politics has perhaps been carried too far. I may be prejudiced, but I cannot think that Bevin's policy has been successful. No doubt the Russians are intolerable. But mere recrimination does no good. Certainly a fresh effort should be made.

In the Harry Hopkins book, his report of his dealings with Stalin seems to show that one can sometimes get the Kremlin to be reasonable. After all, the insistency of the Americans as well as the Russians on the Veto was the immediate cause of the breakdown of the United Nations. But the mistake went further back than that. It was curious, after all our experience, that anyone should believe that it was feasible to set up what was, in effect, a super State, acting through the Security Council. It was obvious that at present none of the important Powers would give to an international body the right to order national troops to take belligerent action in a cause disapproved by the national Government. The Veto was introduced to prevent that happening, but of course it made nonsense of the super-State proposals.

When America and other Powers insisted on this safeguard, it should have been clear that the super State idea was impracticable and that the proper remedy was to recast the Charter sufficiently to make it an enabling and not a coercive document. This has partly been done under the Atlantic Pact. But I see that Bevin still praises it as giving, for the first time, a direct mutual obligation to defend its signatories. That was an obligation which existed under the Covenant. The difficulty was to make Members of the League act up to their duties.

Possibly the Atomic Bomb will remove this difficulty by making war still more devastating than it was. But I doubt it. The only way to save us from destruction is to get rid of war and for that purpose the Atlantic Pact is very faulty. It does not enable joint action by the signatories to intervene to stop preparations for war – or even threats of war. There must be actual armed attack. And it does not give any right to maintain peace in a broad sense but only to protect its signatories from the consequences of war. At present its only result has been to invigorate the arms race, an increase and not a diminution of danger.

Then I cannot think that the clause prohibiting any fresh adhesion to the Pact unless approved by all the existing signatories was wise. It looks like a

Veto on the adhesion of Russia and I believe it has been so construed in the States. What is the good of Bevin professing to want Russia to come in and help when he makes no effort to facilitate it and retains the right to bar her out. I cannot help thinking that a properly phrased offer to make the United Nations an enabling body might meet Russian difficulties. If we only had a Harry Hopkins available!!

Sir Alan Lascelles to Winston S. Churchill
(Churchill papers, 2/171)[1]

28 February 1950   Buckingham Palace

Dear Mr Churchill,

Thank you for your letter of yesterday, & for its wise advice. I have shown it to the King, who is glad to know that you can come here at 6.15 p.m. tomorrow (Wednesday) & have a talk with him.

The King readily understood that factors of space & time would make it impossible for you to go to Dover on March 7th.

Anthony Barber[2] to Winston S. Churchill
(Churchill papers, 2/97)

28 February 1950

Dear Mr Churchill,

Thank you for your kind telegram of congratulations for the effort which we made here in Doncaster.

Although I was naturally somewhat disappointed with the result, I had never considered that we had more than an even chance of succeeding and the very narrow majority achieved by the Socialist candidate only bears out that view.

At the next election, which it seems must come before very long, I have not the slightest doubt that we can win here in Doncaster.

To most of the young candidates like myself, it was a great inspiration to have a man of your personality and experience at the helm and I hope that you will not consider it either impertinent or common place when I say that your leadership since the end of the war has been one of the most vital factors which has brought our Party back to its present position.

---

[1] This letter was handwritten.
[2] Anthony Perrinott Lysberg Barber, 1920–2005. RAF pilot, 1940–5. Barrister-at-law, Inner Temple, 1948. Married, 1950, Jean Patricia Asquith (d. 1983); 1989, Rosemary Youiens (d. 2003). MP (Cons.) for Doncaster, 1951–64; for Altrincham and Sale, 1965–74. Minister of Health and member of the Cabinet, 1963–4. Chancellor of the Exchequer, 1970–4.

March 1950

Julius Holmes[1] to Winston S. Churchill
(Churchill papers, 2/98)

2 March 1950

Dear Mr Churchill,

I am most grateful for your kindness in receiving me yesterday morning and for your great assistance in permitting me better to understand the parliamentary position which has developed as a result of the general election.

In compliance with your request, I am enclosing herewith a memorandum which I asked our Press Officer[2] to prepare and which explains fully the discrepancies between the testimony John Kenney[3] actually gave before the Foreign Relations Committee of the Senate on Thursday, February 24,[4] and the versions of that testimony published in the press.

I am also enclosing a paraphrase of the confidential message which I have sent to the Secretary of State following our conversation. I hope that you will find this note accurately reports the substance of your remarks to me.

CONFIDENTIAL

Yesterday I sought Mr Churchill's advice with respect to the parliamentary situation which has resulted from the general election. He was good enough to make some general observations, the principal of which were as follows:

1) The Conservative Party when in opposition has constantly supported the

---

[1] Julius Cecil Holmes, 1899–1968. Educated at University of Kansas, 1922. Executive Officer for JCS, 1942–4. Asst Secretary of State for Administration, 1944–5. Minister, US Embassy in London, 1953–5. US Consul-General in Morocco, 1955–6; in Hong Kong, 1959–61. Ambassador to Iran, 1961–5.

[2] Edward Ware Barrett, 1910–89. Educated at Princeton University, 1932. Chief, Overseas News Div., Office of War Information, 1942–5. Asst Secretary of State for Public Affairs, 1950–2. Dean, Columbia University Graduate School of Journalism, 1956–68. Founder, *Columbia Journalism Review*, 1961.

[3] William John Kenney, 1904–92. Educated at Stanford University and Harvard Law School. General Counsel for the Navy, 1945. Asst Secretary of the Navy, 1946–7. Under-Secretary of the Navy, 1947–9. Operating Chief, Marshall Plan, 1950–2.

[4] Feb. 24 actually fell on a Friday in 1950.

Government in any measure in the national interest and will continue to do so. This is particularly true in the realm of foreign affairs where in the last Parliament the Government had only been opposed in foreign affairs by its own back benches and Communists. Mr Churchill observed with satisfaction that this element had been eliminated from the new Parliament. Mr Churchill was in agreement with the objectives of the foreign policy of the present government but was critical of the manner in which these affairs had been handled.

2) Mr Churchill was of the opinion that Mr Attlee could not seek an early dissolution but was bound to attempt to govern even with his reduced majority. While stating that he did not know the Government's plan, he expressed doubt that controversial legislation would be introduced. He felt that the ideological differences between the party had been drawn out in the election, particularly nationalization, and that sooner or later this question, possibly in connection with the steel bill, would again become an issue. Mr Churchill felt that the new Parliament must have an opportunity to live but that this newborn infant might suffer either from 'infant mortality or infantile paralysis', and it was not impossible that there would be another government formed before a subsequent general election.

3) Mr Churchill will receive on Sunday afternoon on a confidential basis the text of the speech from the Throne and will discuss it with his colleagues at a dinner he is giving them Sunday night when a position for the following day in the House will be taken.

4) The incorrect version of Kenney's testimony before the Foreign Relations Committee on February 24 was raised with special reference to the alleged statement concerning another devaluation of the pound. Mr Churchill told me that this matter had been discussed in the Executive Committee meeting of his party on Tuesday with great interest and some concern. I assured him that Kenney had been misquoted, and I am furnishing him with the correct text of Kenney's testimony.

5) Mr Churchill voluntarily brought up the question of his Edinburgh speech and relations with the Soviet Union. He pointed out that he had been consistent in his attitude with respect to the Soviets and cited his Fulton and MIT speeches. He was prompted by the conviction that no thoughtful man, no Christian man could in the face of the grave situation which threatens the world leave any door closed or fail to employ any honourable opportunity to bring a settlement. He had wanted known that remarks that he was a war monger had no validity and that should he come into power there would be no hardening of attitude which would make the settlement with the Soviets more difficult.

Winston S. Churchill to Lord Kemsley
(Churchill papers, 2/171)

2 March 1950

My dear Kemsley,

Thank you very much for your letter.

I would gladly serve you as you suggest but I am so hard pressed with political work, and the book which absorbs all my spare time that I cannot undertake the task. Please forgive me.

I take this occasion to thank you for the invaluable support which your newspapers gave during the Election. One more heave before the year is out and we may have a stable Government in Britain.

John Profumo[1] to Winston S. Churchill
(Churchill papers, 2/97)[2]

4 March 1950   Warwickshire

Dear Mr Churchill,

I've only just found your telegram of congratulations. It had been forwarded here to my cottage where I've not yet been able to arrange for a caretaker in my absence.

I hasten to send you my thanks and to take the opportunity of telling you how happy I am to be back in the House once more.

I assure you of my loyal support and I look forward to contributing in any possible way towards the election, which, under your inspiring leadership, must be carried out by our party in the months which lie ahead.

May you yourself enjoy good health and strength.

---

[1] John Profumo, 1915–2006. Known as 'Jack'. Commissioned as 2nd Lt, RAC, 1939. MP (Cons.) for Kettering, 1940–5; for Stratford-upon-Avon, 1950–63. OBE, 1944. Parliamentary Secretary, Ministry of Civil Aviation, 1952. Married, 1954, Valerie Hobson. Parliamentary Under-Secretary of State for the Colonies, 1957. Under-Secretary of State at the FO, 1958. Minister of State for Foreign Affairs, 1959. Secretary of State for War, 1960–3. CBE, 1975.

[2] This letter was handwritten.

Winston S. Churchill to Lord Salisbury
(Churchill papers, 2/101)

4 March 1950
Private

My dear Bobbety,

I am very sorry to receive your letter[1] because I take the opposite view. It seems to me – but we shall know more about it in a week or so – that the Government are very anxious to remain in office with the power to choose the moment for an election and conduct it with authority. I hope therefore you will keep an open mind upon the subject, and judge the situation if and when it arises. It is one of course on which our House of Commons colleagues are very directly concerned.

[. . .]

Winston S. Churchill to Lord Cecil
(Churchill papers, 2/95)

5 March 1950
Private

My dear Bob,

Thank you very much for your letter of February 28,[2] which I will show to Anthony.

During the Election I was most anxious that the return of a Conservative Government to power, which was a possibility, should not be taken as involving an exacerbation of the already tense situation that exists. I also feel that we owe it to our consciences that no door should be closed which may lead to better prospects. I do not of course take a sanguine view of the position, whatever efforts are made. It is our Christian duty to try our best.

This is unhappily not a situation which Time and Patience, those great solvents, can cure.

---

[1] In his letter to Churchill, Lord Salisbury had expressed his concern about the Conservatives entering into an alliance with the Liberals, fearing that such an alliance would alienate Conservative voters and that the Liberals would break rank when the timing suited them. He preferred the Conservatives wait to assume power until they had a clear majority in Parliament.

[2] Reproduced above (pp. 1662–3).

MARCH 1950

Winston S. Churchill: speech
(Hansard)

7 March 1950   House of Commons

DEBATE ON THE ADDRESS

I must frankly confess, as I look around, that I like the appearance of these Benches better than what we had to look at during the last 4½ years. It is certainly refreshing to feel, at any rate, that this is a Parliament where half the nation will not be able to ride roughshod over the other half, or to sweep away in a Session what has been carefully and skilfully constructed by generations of thought, toil and thrift. I do not see the Attorney-General in his place, but no one will be able to boast 'We are the masters now.' On the contrary, if it be not presumptuous for me to say so, we are equals. So far as the Conservative and Socialist parties are concerned, we seem to have reached in the electoral field that position – if I may listen to the echoes of the election – of equal shares for both. I will not say equal shares for all, for we certainly have not achieved even fair shares for all.

Here, I must guard myself carefully against any suggestion of uttering what are called blandishments to the nine representatives of the Liberal Party,[1] most of whom we see in their places under the guidance so generously provided by the Principality of Wales. I do not often quote from *The Times*, but I must say that I found myself in some agreement with their leading article of 27th February, that the Liberal leaders who are here, and others out of doors, have performed 'a national disservice' – these are not my words: I am only quoting, having read them with some relish in *The Times* – 'by the irresponsible

[1] Megan Lloyd George, 1902–66. Younger daughter of David Lloyd George. MP (Lib.) for Anglesey, 1929–51; for Carmarthenshire, 1957–66. President, Women's Liberal Federation, 1936, 1945. Chairman, Welsh Parliamentary Party, 1944–5. Deputy Leader of the Liberal Party, 1949–51. Joined Labour Party, 1957. CH, 1966.
Roderic Bowen, 1913–2001. Army Capt., Judge Advocate General's Office, 1939–44. MP (Lib.) for Cardiganshire, 1945–66. National Insurance Commissioner for Wales, 1967–86. President, St David's University College, Lampeter, 1977–92.
Sir Rhys Hopkin Morris.
Edgar Granville.
Donald Baron Wade, 1904–88. Educated at Mill Hill and Trinity Hall, Cambridge. MP (Lib) for Huddersfield West, 1950–64. Liberal Whip, 1956–62. Deputy Leader, Liberal Parliamentary Party, 1962–4. Deputy Liberal Whip, House of Lords, 1965–7. President, Liberal Party, 1967–8.
Emrys Owen Roberts. 1910–90. Educated at Caernarfon Grammar School and at University College of Wales, Aberystwyth. Served MP (Lib.) for Merionethshire, 1945–51.
Clement Davies.
Joseph Grimond, 1913–93. Known as 'Jo'. Educated at Balliol College, Oxford. Married, 1938, Laura Bonham Carter. Director of Personnel, European Office, UNRRA, 1945–7. Secretary, National Trust for Scotland, 1947–9. MP (Lib.) for Orkney and Shetland, 1950–83. Baron, 1983. Author of *The Liberal Future* (1959), *The Liberal Challenge* (1963) and *Memoirs* (1979).
Archibald James Florence Macdonald, 1904–83. Known as 'Archie'. Joint Chief Executive, Management Research Groups, 1937–40. Secretary, Paint Industry Export Group, 1940–7. MP (Lib.) for Roxburgh and Selkirk, 1950–1. Director, Joseph Freeman Sons & Co. Ltd, 1962–6.

spattering of the electoral map with hundreds of candidatures for which there was never the remotest chance of substantial support, but which might just deprive the Members elected of certainty that they represented the majority of their constituents. The legislature, by requiring the £150 deposit, has expressed its disapproval of frivolous candidature; but it was never foreseen that a great and historic party would use its considerable financial resources to evade the spirit of the rule.' The object of the Liberal leaders was nakedly stated by Lord Samuel in his broadcast of 7 February, when he said:

> It may be that no party will have a working majority in the new House of Commons In such an event the Liberals might be called upon to form a Government.

It is quite true that one of the objectives mentioned by Lord Samuel has been gained. No party has a working majority. A stalemate or deadlock has undoubtedly been produced in the effective government of the country and the certainty of a prolonged electioneering atmosphere at a time when the situations both at home and abroad are grave and crucial.

Lord Samuel's second objective – the formation of a Liberal Government – still remains in a sphere so speculative as to be outside even the bounds of Lloyd's insurance. It has, perhaps, been too readily assumed that the nine gentlemen below the Gangway on this side will have in this Parliament a position of exceptional and undue influence. I hope that the House of Commons is not going to allow itself to be dominated or let its fate and future to be decided by any small body of hon. Members. We do not wish to emulate some foreign Parliaments where small parliamentary parties are able, by putting themselves and their favours in the balance, to sway the course of considerable events. Indeed, it seems to me that this would be an undignified attitude for the Mother of Parliaments, especially in a time so serious as this.

I have lived nearly all my life in the House of Commons and I believe it to be the enduring guarantee of British liberties and democratic progress. I do not think we ought to assume that this new House of Commons, elected by the greatest vote ever recorded in our history, and with earnestness and heart-searching by tens of millions of our people, should fall into petty bargaining almost before it had breathed. The House of Commons is founded on the party system, and, in the main, very much in preponderance upon the two-party system. But, personally, I have the feeling – as I ventured to say the other day when offering you, Sir, my congratulations on your election as Speaker – that this assembly, fresh from contact with the people, is a more potent body than the mere numerical aggregate of its parties suggests, and I hope that this feeling will play its full part in our Debates, whether its life is destined to be long or short.

Whatever view we may take of particularist manoeuvres to frustrate the will of democracy as expressed through majorities, and thus creating the present grave embarrassment to the country, we must not be blind to the anomaly which has brought to this House of Commons 186 representatives who are returned only by a minority of those who voted in their constituencies. Nor can we, to whatever party we belong, overlook the constitutional injustice done to 2,600,000 voters who, voting upon a strong tradition, have been able to return only nine Members to Parliament. My experience of life, becoming a long one, has led me to the belief that ill-conduct often results from ill-treatment. I do not think this is a matter which we can brush aside or allow to lie unheeded.

I therefore make the following proposal to His Majesty's Government – namely, that we should set up a Select Committee to inquire into the whole question of electoral reform. A Select Committee of the House of Commons would not be likely to lose its way amid the endless arguments and details with which this question bristles. I am well aware that it has several times been examined before, but we have never examined it in the light of a practical situation of major importance such as has now been brought about. I believe a House of Commons Committee would take a practical view and give us advice which would be a guide to future Governments in this Parliament or in another Parliament. As to the composition of the Committee, I would suggest that it should be based not on the numbers of the Members here, but upon the numbers of votes recorded by the electorate for the three parties which are represented in the House, as, otherwise, I do not see how the Liberals would obtain any representation at all on a matter which is certainly of keen and special interest to them.

I ask the Government – I ask the right hon. Gentleman the Lord President who, I understand, is going to follow me – in the course of this Debate to say whether they will allow such a Committee to be set up or not. We have certainly reached a parliamentary deadlock or stalemate differing in its character from any in living experience. It is not true that the Liberal Party here or, what is of far more importance, the Liberal Party in the country, can, by simply throwing its weight on to one side or the other determine the issue. Any step that was taken as a mere bargain or deal might not only be difficult to implement, but might well produce unfavourable reactions for those concerned. The nation might deeply resent the feeling that its fortunes had been bartered about without regard to principle by a handful of politicians, no matter what party they come from, and that its vital interests were but a piece in a jigsaw puzzle. In such a situation candour, sincerity, simplicity, firm adherence to well-known and publicly asserted principles, combined with a dominating regard for national rather than party interests, will be found to be the surest guides.

We have of course, on this side of the House, to discharge our duties as a Parliamentary Opposition, and the period before us will be very difficult. Moreover, it is by no means certain that another election, held in a few months under conditions which no one can foresee and arising from occasions which perhaps no one can select, would remove the conditions of deadlock which now prevail. I am one of the very few who lived in high office through the year 1910. I was Home Secretary then – (*Interruption*) – well it is a very important office and very well discharged by its present occupant.

There was an election in January, 1910, and another election in December. There was virtually no difference between the two results. The people remembered how they had voted last time and they meant to vote the same way again. Unless some entirely new facts can be found to place before the people there is no certainty that the electors will alter their opinion, however much we might plead with them in the interval covered by the compass of a year. There will, therefore, be an indefinite period of uncertainty, extremely detrimental to our country at this critical time. Every action of the Government will be taken, no doubt, in regard to the impending election. We all have to be careful of every word we say or fact we cite.

The Lord President of the Council (Mr Herbert Morrison): You especially.

Mr Churchill: I thought the Chancellor of the Exchequer interrupted.

The Chancellor of the Exchequer (Sir Stafford Cripps) *indicated dissent*.

Mr Churchill: I do not think I am the only one who needs to be careful.

Every word we say may be pounced upon and made the peg for some monstrous misrepresentations – (Hon Members: 'Hear, hear'). I am quite willing to carry the whole House with me on that. The reasoned Amendment which was moved to the Health and Insurance Bill – which we originated in the Government over which I presided, and which I did my utmost to help forward – was recently misrepresented to the electors as Tory hostility to the principle of the Measure. Certainly it will be very difficult to find good solutions in the national interest for the grievous, dark and difficult problems which press upon us. Yet there never was a time when good solutions and drastic remedies in our financial and economic life were more needed and more overdue. We must do the best we can.

I am coming now to the text of the Gracious Speech to which we listened yesterday. A friend of mine has suggested that it might have been stated more shortly. This was his suggestion: 'My Lords and Members of the House of Commons: My Government will not introduce legislation in fulfilment of their Election programme because the only Mandate they have received from the country is not to do it.' There is however one paragraph in the Gracious Speech about the need for a renewed effort to expand the production of food from our own soil, which will, I am sure, be welcomed by all sides. It conforms very closely to the statements contained in our Agricultural Charter and in the Conservative election manifesto. And I said myself, at Luton Hoo in June, 1948:[1]

---

[1] See speech reproduced above (pp. 1086–96).

Anyone can see that the vigorous production of food on the largest possible scale in this island holds the first place. Let us be under no error in this matter. The prosperity of agriculture and food production depends on larger supplies of labour, and to have the labour we must have the rural houses in which they can dwell and rear their families. These the Socialists have refused. It also depends upon a full supply of the agricultural machinery which the Government has so recklessly exported to foreign countries. This was indeed devouring the seed-corn. In our Agricultural Charter, published this morning, we have declared that the proper level of agricultural production in this country must be half as much again as pre-war. This is our aim.

I see I also said at Luton Hoo:

The State is entitled to give guidance and, if necessary, to see this is enforced, to ensure that farmers and landowners do not flout the rules of good husbandry and good estate management.

(Hon Members: 'Hear, hear'.) I thought you would like that. This speech was at the time dismissed by the Prime Minister somewhat curtly as 'Luton Hooey'.

Well, we have a more helpful response in the Gracious Speech. I assume of course that it is not intended to use compulsory powers to nationalize marginal land, or to nationalize water supplies in rural areas, unless it is proved to the satisfaction of the House as a whole, that no other method is available in certain exceptional cases. If this be so, I see no reason why this important paragraph, which I admit was not contained in my abridged edition of the Gracious Speech, should not provide some common ground between us during these next few months I cannot leave this agricultural topic without referring to the Bill announced in the Gracious Speech for the placing and maintaining of cattle grids on the highways. I see the Patronage Secretary[1] is in his place. We are always glad to see him in his place. Surely he should study with special attention in times like these any measure to keep the herd from straying.

Much was said upon the hustings about mass unemployment. There is no real difference between the parties on this subject. All the leading men on both sides agreed to the White Paper laid before Parliament in 1944 by the Government over which I presided. We adhere to that Paper, though happily the conditions with which it was intended to deal have not yet arisen. Moreover, the principal Ministers concerned have frankly told us that there would have been between 1,500,000 and two million unemployed but for the American aid which we have been receiving. That was an altogether unwonted slip on

---

[1] William Whiteley.

their part, I am sure, for which I must say they have had to endure a good deal of punishment in the discussions which have taken place. But we have not challenged them upon that point. There is, therefore, a broad measure of general agreement between us, although of course Socialist Ministers naturally claim all the credit, past, present and prospective, for everything good that has been done in this field.

There is, however, another aspect which the House should bear in mind, especially as it presents itself as an addition to the statements about the help of the American subsidies to which I have already referred. I state these points simply as facts, but serious facts. If we compare the present situation with that under the Chamberlain Government in 1939, the year before the war, there are four important differences on the point I am making. There are many other differences, but these four are relevant to this problem of employment or unemployment.

First, there are 750,000 more national and local government officials than existed then. Secondly, there are 250,000 more men in the Armed Forces – I do not say whether rightly or wrongly; I merely mention it. Thirdly, about 400,000 young people are withheld from the labour market by the extension of the school age. I am not arguing this afternoon whether that is good or bad, though personally I am not greatly attracted by overcrowded schools and underpaid teachers. However, that makes a total of 1,400,000. Fourthly, it has been estimated that there are 500,000 people employed in making unrequited exports, in the main to India and Egypt – that is to say, exports in return for which nothing comes back into this island from this heavy expenditure of our life energy expressed in sweat and skill. Again I do not attempt to argue this afternoon the merits of the so-called sterling balances or repayment of unfair British war-time debts as they are in fact, though I should be quite prepared to do so on a suitable occasion.

Nor do I say that the Government are wrong not to make a violent change in this method of preventing further unemployment in the circumstances that prevail. Nevertheless we should not shut our eyes to the realities. We should not go on without being conscious of the fact that we are getting nothing back in return. Trade is exchange, or, at the simplest, barter. It would be much better, for instance, if some of this work could find its reward in the spread of goods to the public convenience at home, or in their sale to other countries in the sterling area, which would repay us to some extent in nourishing imports for this immense outward stream of valuable commodities.

There are the four differences. There is one more. Finally, there are the 350,000 persons who are actually unemployed at the moment, many of whom no doubt are changing from one job to another. This makes a total of 2,250,000 persons altogether not now employed in productive industry, comparable with the 1,100,000 unemployed at the time of the Chamberlain Government in the year before the war. (*Laughter.*) The hon Member for Sparkbrook

(Mr Shurmer) is not a new Member: he should not show himself so conspicuously needing Parliamentary education as he does this afternoon. This is, of course, without taking into consideration at all the fruits of the American subsidies. I am quite sure that there is now more real unemployment in the sense of people not being employed in requited or productive work than in the years immediately before the war – not that I in any way under-rate the valuable services rendered by those very numerous categories which I have mentioned. I think the party opposite might address their minds to this topic because it plays an important part in the understanding of our affairs.

There is another whole series of difficult questions connected with the Ministry of Food. The discussions on food subsidies and rationing are, of course, hampered by the fact that an election cannot be far off, and we may, no doubt, be again exposed to the slander that the Conservative Party wish to make food dear so that the rich can live in luxury while the wage earners are impelled by 'empty bellies', to quote the official document of the party opposite, to work harder.

I see that experienced politician the Lord President of the Council opposite me: he is, I believe, the supreme author of the manifesto in which this incident was mentioned, and it does astonish me. He and his friends must have very strange opinions about their fellow countrymen if they think that 12,500,000 of them would support such a cruel and wicked policy as that. I do not believe a word they say on the subject. Where they go wrong is that they assume that the mass of the people are taken in by arguments of manifest unfairness and untruth. But for that there would not be this thoughtful, pensive air upon the Government Front Bench. No doubt, every word spoken in our Debates on food subsidies and other aspects of the food problems will be liable to be wrested from its context, carefully scanned and pulled out if there is anything worth having in it, in order to provide material for electioneering of this disreputable kind.

Our policy is, in fact, aimed at full and better meals for the nation and we are quite sure that the more food manual workers can get to eat, the better will be our output. I do not think we should be deterred from discussing these grave problems by the peculiar and, I admit, unpleasant conditions which prevail in this precariously balanced Parliament. I do not hesitate to say that it is foolish to prevent production through oppressive taxation by paying food subsidies to enormous numbers of people who do not need them, and that it is our duty to search for more sensible solutions of the problem, while maintaining a basic standard for all. I was glad to read the statement of the new Minister of Food[1] – I do not think he is in his place – that he would think in terms of food

---

[1] Maurice Webb, 1904–56. Educated at Christ Church School, Lancaster. Married, 1931, Mabel Hughes Lancaster. Writer, *Daily Herald*, 1935–44; *Sunday Express*, 1944–5. MP (Lab.) for Central Bradford, 1945–55. Chairman, Parliamentary Labour Party, 1946–50. PC, 1950. Minister of Food, 28 Feb. 1950 to 1951.

and not of calories. This seemed to me the most helpful contribution we have had on this subject from the Minister of Food so far. We wish the right hon. Gentleman success in the arduous office which he has undertaken.

The food question is, however, not one which can be judged apart from the state of our national finances. The need to reduce the heavy burden of taxation and arrest the continued fall in the purchasing power of wages, pensions and allowances of all kinds is urgent and, as we believe, vital. The House was, I am sure, impressed with the figures given yesterday by my right hon. Friend the Member for Warwick and Leamington (Mr Eden) about the ever-increasing drain of the sterling balances upon us. On the top of all this comes devaluation which, apart from its effects at home, so far as they have yet been manifested, also means that British labour – and I would be most grateful to the Chancellor of the Exchequer if he could attend just to this one point: I know he has to prompt his colleague, for it would be lamentable if a different theme were developed: devaluation means that British labour has to work one-third longer hours to earn the same quantity of dollar imports as before. It is a terrible fact – one-third longer hours and what you get back is no more than it was before. You call yourselves the Labour Party, and yet it does not even rouse you and strike a note in your breasts. It is a shocking and odious thing that we should so handle our affairs as to have to work 12 hours instead of eight to obtain the same return.

There is also the danger that further devaluation may become necessary. From this crowded island our life blood is draining away in an ever more copious flow without compensating nourishment. That is my very deep fear. We are a hard-pressed blood-donor whose general health has already been weakened by his war service. This deadly process is to some extent, no doubt, veiled by the American subsidies under Marshall Aid, but they are coming to an end. Indeed, they may soon be offset by the obligation to repay the first £1,000 million loan so blithely dispersed as soon as it was received. They are now coming to an end, it is said.

The restoration of the £ sterling at home and abroad and the re-establishment of confidence and credit will not take place as long as there is a Government in office which, even though held in check in this Parliament by lack of voting strength, is known to be animated by bitter hostility to accumulated wealth and is the declared enemy of the capitalist system to which all the rest of the free democracies of the world outside Scandinavia, and with some exceptions there, constantly affirm their adherence on a basis of universal suffrage.

It would be vain to touch in the Debate upon the vast sphere of finance and economics. I ask that an opportunity for a full Debate upon it may be accorded to us in the next fortnight or so.

Mr H. Morrison *indicated dissent.*

Mr Churchill: It will take more than the oscillation of the Lord President's head in this Parliament necessarily to convince us that our desires must be put aside; I ask for a full Debate. So much has been concealed from us and distorted by the speeches of the Ministers concerned during and before the Election that we really do not know where we are. (*Laughter.*) The hon. Member opposite should not think it is funny or be delighted that half the House of Commons has not been properly informed. I am sure he is no better informed than we are.

I ask that the true facts should be laid before the House as soon as possible. If they are good we shall rejoice. If they are bad we must all face them, if not together at any rate at the same time. I find encouragement from the fact that the Government evidently wish to continue in office. There is something real about that. It gives one a certain assurance that the prospects in the next few months are not too bad. I trust my intuition has not misled me on this point. The Government would, I am sure, be well advised in the interests of the country as well as in their own interest, which they are not prone to overlook, to make a full and candid statement before we separate for Easter.

We have certain Supply days at our disposal if no facilities are given. We shall expect a statement from the Chancellor of the Exchequer. If he refuses to give one, we shall certainly not hesitate to draw any inference we choose, but we are quite sure that if he had a favourable statement to make he would be the first to put it out either in the House or over the broadcast. I see the Prime Minister arriving: he has been away on duty and I should like to put him in touch. I was asking for a Debate on the financial situation so that we may have a general statement made on the position before we separate for the Easter Recess. We shall try to press that by every means open to us, which are more numerous than they were.

We have thought it our duty, in accordance with our political convictions, and those of the constituents who returned us here, to place two Amendments to the Address upon the Order Paper.

> (But humbly regret that the Gracious Speech contains no reference to the future of the Iron and Steel Industry and that in a time of rising world competition this vital industry will be kept in a state of anxiety and suspense.)
>
> (But humbly regret that the Gracious Speech makes no reference to the grievous and growing distress in town and country arising out of the continuing decline in the number of new houses built each year and contains no indication that the Government intend to take more effective measures to deal with the situation.)

The first deals with the nationalization of iron and steel. Owing to the action of the House of Lords under the now mutilated Parliament Act, the people were given the right to say whether they wanted this Measure or not. The electors, by a large majority in votes, have pronounced against it, but it will come into action automatically, perhaps in the lifetime of this Parliament, unless parliamentary action is taken either to repeal the Measure, or, at least, to alter the date, so that the electors will certainly have a further chance of affirming their repudiation of it.

It is obvious that the Government have not the power to nationalize cement, sugar, chemicals, or to mutualize industrial assurance. But steel is different. It happens unless it is stopped. Had we obtained a majority we should have repealed the Act: and that is, of course, our policy. Nevertheless, we should be willing not to press our Amendment to a Division if the Government will give the assurance that the position of the steel industry will not be worsened because of the present deadlock, or by its indefinite prolongation. We ask for a declaration that the vesting date shall be not less than nine months after the next General Election, and that all necessary measures shall be taken to that end.

I think it is a very modest demand. There was an enormous vote of the people against this Measure, and with a Parliament which admittedly has no right to bring it into law – (Hon Members: 'Oh'.) No right. I thought it was understood that that was not asserted. So I ask for something which would put us into exactly the same relation, after another Dissolution, to the time factor as we were in on the last occasion. We could not make a more reasonable request than that.

This will have the double advantage of making sure that the people are duly consulted before their decision is reversed, and that the industry will be given a breathing space, of probably at least a year, to get on with their vital work. If we can receive those assurances today it would, I think, be convenient to the House as a whole. If not, we feel ourselves bound by our convictions, and by the mandate we have received from the electors, to vote for the Amendment in our full strength.

We also feel compelled to invite the House to express itself upon the lamentable state of our housing. No material issue affecting the daily lives of the people has stirred them more than the housing shortage, which strikes at the very root of family life. No one underrates the many difficulties which constitute the housing problem at the present moment, and we no doubt shall hear more about them in due course from the Minister who bears a direct and peculiar responsibility for the failure.

I will only venture to mention a suggestion – a constructive suggestion – which I made to my colleagues in our war-time Government, and which seems to me still to have relevance. It occurred to me as a member of the bricklayers' trade union, of which I still hold a membership card signed by Mr George Hicks, whom we miss as the former Member for Woolwich, although he has had adequate replacement. The bricklayer or builder's operative is always asking himself, 'What happens when this job is done?' He is really like a man on a raft in mid-ocean who has to burn a bit of his raft every day to cook his dinner. With all this vast mass of building that is needed, it ought to be possible to give the building operatives, bricklayers and others, effective security. It seemed to me that this was so in 1944, and I, therefore, made the following proposal to my colleagues in what was called a 'directive':

> The whole of the emergency housing scheme must be viewed in relation to a ten years' plan for the steady full-time employment of a considerably enlarged building trade for permanent houses. Instead of a fever for three or four years and then a falling off, the building trade should have a broad, steady flow giving all its members a good assurance of employment, and thus encouraging piece-work.

I venture to keep that particular suggestion alive at the present time, although it is only one small contribution to a mass of improvements which could be made in the whole process of our winning houses for our people to live in.

The two sides of the House face each other deeply divided by ideological differences. I have lived through many of the fierce quarrels of the past, about Irish Home Rule, about Church or chapel, about Free Trade and Protection, which all seemed to be very important at the time. They were, however, none of them, fundamental to our whole system of life and society. Those who believe in the creation of a Socialist State controlling all the means of production and distribution and exchange, and are working towards such a goal, are separated from those who seek to exalt the individual and allow freedom of enterprise under well-known laws and safeguards – they are separated by a wider and deeper gulf than I have ever seen before in our island.

This was, in my view, the moral and intellectual issue which was at stake in the election, and which a substantial Socialist majority, if obtained, would in four or five years have carried, in all probability, to irrevocable depths. It is a significant and serious fact which should not escape the attention of thoughtful men that the differences which separate us have become more pronounced by the voting, because each of the main parties has very often increased its strength in those very parts of the country where it was already the stronger. We shall certainly not survive by splitting into two nations. Yet that is the road we are travelling now, and there is no sign of our reaching or even approaching our journey's end.

The basic fact before us is that the electors by a majority of 1,750,000 have voted against the advance to a Socialist State, and, in particular, against the nationalization of steel and other industries which were threatened. The Government, therefore, have no mandate, as is recognized in the Gracious Speech, to proceed in this Parliament with their main policy. The Prime Minister is the only Socialist prime minister in the English-speaking world – the only one: and he has behind him a majority of only seven – or it soon may be only six. Nevertheless, he continues not only to persevere upon his path, but to state the differences which separate him and his followers from the rest of us all over the world, in the most extreme terms.

The right hon. gentleman complained during the election that I quoted his interview with an American journalist, which he had not disavowed for some time after it was published and which was much commented on. In fact I saw only the comments and then searched for the actual text. I will meet the right hon. Gentleman. I promise him that I will quote that interview no more. I do not need to quote it anymore because in his letter to his candidate at Moss Side[1] he has proclaimed his faith and policy beyond the slightest doubt and in the most sweeping terms. He wrote on 2nd March:

> Labour stands for the policy of equal shares, and for the ordered and progressive realisation of a society based on social justice.

The last part covers both sides of the House. But this 'equal shares' declaration goes even further than the speeches of the Chancellor of the Exchequer in his election campaign at Bristol, when he spoke of 'fair shares for all' being only a preliminary step to 'equal shares for all'. It is at least an advantage that the differences between us should be stated so plainly, because there can be no excuse for anyone making a mistake about them afterwards.

The *Tribune*, which is believed to express the views of the Minister of Health, fully supports the Prime Minister's pronouncement. I quote from its latest issue of 3rd March:

> It is the faith of Socialism carried across this land with a new crusading zeal which can win the second election in 1950. And once that fact is securely grasped, how futile becomes the talk of compromise and manoeuvre in the House of Commons, which must continue until the new appeal to the country takes place.

The Prime Minister has accepted the burden of government in virtue of his majority of seven; and no one doubts that it was his right and his duty to do so. But we on this side feel that he, and those whom he leads or with whom he goes, have inflicted deep injury upon our country in years when our task of recovery was heavy enough, and we are sure that the course he now proclaims has only to be followed far enough to lead to our economic ruin, and to our inability to maintain 50,000,000 people in this island, still less to maintain them on their present standards of living, such as they are. We are therefore bound to confront him and those who follow him with our united and resolute resistance, and we believe that this is the first duty which we owe to our country, to the British Commonwealth of Nations, to Western Europe and to the English-speaking world.

---

[1] Roland William Casasola, 1893–1971. Unsuccessful Parliamentary candidate (Lab.) for Stalybridge and Hyde, 1935; for Stockport, 1945; for Manchester Moss Side, 1950; for Blackburn West, 1951. Member, Executive, Amalgamated Union of Foundry Workers, 1946–54; Chairman, 1954–8. Member, National Executive Committee, Labour Party, 1956–8. Joined Communist Party, 1961.

1680 MARCH 1950

J. G. Crowther[1] to Winston S. Churchill
(Churchill papers, 2/94)

7 March 1950

Sir,

I have the honour to inform you that an International Delegation including His Grace The Archbishop Jannos Peter,[2] Senator Mario Palermo,[3] M Charles Serre,[4] French Deputé, M Grunais, General Secretary of the International Maritime Union and Madame Elizabeth Poisson, Conseil National des Femmes de France, will be in Great Britain on Tuesday, March 14th.

Similar delegations have been visiting the Parliaments of the world in recent weeks and have been received by, among others, the leaders of the French and Italian Parliaments.

The World Peace Movement desires to present a most earnest appeal for Peace to the elected assemblies of the nations.

I write to ask you to receive the International Delegation and a supporting British Delegation, led by Professor J. D. Bernal,[5] FRS, and myself, in order to hear their appeal on this subject of such profound importance.

The two Delegations will call at the House of Commons at 4.15 p.m. on Tuesday March 14th, and trust that they may have the great honour of being received by you.

The Delegations will also call on the leaders of the other political Parties.[6]

---

[1] James Gerald Crowther, 1889–1983. Technical books representative for Oxford University Press from 1924. Science correspondent for the *Manchester Guardian*, 1927–49. Regular contributor to BBC broadcasts, 1940–7. Director of Science Committee, British Council, 1941–6.

[2] János Péter, 1910–99. Calvinist Bishop in Hungarian Reformed Church. Hungarian Minister of Foreign Affairs, 1961–73.

[3] Mario Palermo, 1898–1985. Councillor, Naples, 1946–60. Senator, Legislature of Italy, 1948–68.

[4] Charles Serre, 1901–54. Member, French National Assembly, 1946–51.

[5] John Desmond Bernal, 1901–71. Known as 'Sage'. X-ray crystallographer and molecular biologist. Educated at Emmanuel College, Cambridge, 1919–23. Joined Communist Party of Great Britain, 1923; maintained lifelong allegiance to the Soviet Union. FRS, 1937. Prof. of Physics at Birkbeck College, University of London, 1937. Scientific adviser to Lord Mountbatten, 1942. Provided detailed maps of Normandy beaches for Operation 'Overlord', 1944. Author of *The World, the Flesh and the Devil* (1929), *The Social Function of Science* (1939), *Science in History* (1954) and *The Origin of Life* (1967).

[6] Churchill instructed his Private Office: 'Do not answer it. Let it be mislaid.'

Cabinet: record
(Churchill papers, 128/21)

9 March 1950
Top Secret
No Circulation
9.30 a.m.
Cabinet Meeting No. 9, Minute 1, of 1950

The Prime Minister said that the two Conservative amendments to the Address, both that on the Iron and Steel Act and that on Housing, would be pressed to a division; and he had been considering what advice he should tender to His Majesty if the Government were defeated in either of these divisions. He did not think it would be right to ask for a Dissolution so soon after the General Election, and he was inclined to think that his proper course would be to advise the King to send for Mr Churchill. The resulting Parliamentary situation would be very unsatisfactory, for the Conservatives, being in a minority, would find it even more difficult to carry on the essential business of Government; but this situation would have been created by the Conservatives and he thought that they should be forced to assume the responsibility for handling it.

In discussion emphasis was laid upon the embarrassments which the Labour Party would face if they went into Opposition in the present Parliament. The Conservatives, if they assumed office, would have to present some kind of programme to the House, and the Labour Party would find it difficult to avoid challenging at least some of the features of that programme. But the Labour Party would be in greater difficulty than the Conservatives were at present for, with their majority, they would be in a position to defeat the Government at any time and any challenge which they found it necessary to make was likely to lead to a Government defeat. They would thus be faced with the unpleasant dilemma of assuming responsibility for turning the Government out and forcing a Dissolution or, alternatively, refraining from challenging policies which were distasteful to their supporters. At the present time the country's greatest need was a period of political stability; and, as the strength of the two main Parties in the House of Commons was so evenly balanced, it was the duty of both to practise moderation and avoid unnecessary controversy for the time being – at any rate until the essential financial business of the spring and summer had been completed. There was some reason to believe that Mr Churchill's action in making an immediate challenge to the Government in the debate on the Address might be regarded as irresponsible by a substantial section of public opinion, which recognised that the Labour administration were right in deciding that, despite their narrow majority, it was their duty to carry on the King's Government. It might therefore be expedient for the Prime Minister to give a warning, during the debate on the Address, that if the Labour Party were prevented, by factitious and irresponsible action on the part of the Opposition, from discharging their duty of carrying on the King's Government, a further appeal to the people might have to be made. This would have the effect of bringing home to the House the serious risks that were being run.

While the sentiment underlying this view commanded general support, it was pointed out that an early Dissolution was hardly practicable, in view of the necessity for passing the Budget and making the other financial provisions without which the ordinary business of administration could not be carried on.

The Prime Minister, in conclusion, said that he was grateful to his colleagues for this expression of their views, which he would bear in mind. At the moment this question was only hypothetical, for he has no reason to fear that the Government would in fact be defeated in the divisions in the debate on the Address. And the issues involved were so grave that he would wish to have an opportunity of considering them again, and possibly holding further discussions with some of his colleagues, before he finally made up his mind what advice he would tender to His Majesty if the Government should in the event be defeated.

Winston S. Churchill to General Dwight D. Eisenhower
(Churchill papers, 2/175)

9 March 1950

My dear Ike,

I am anxious, if you happen to have an opportunity that you should meet Sir Leslie Rowan who last November took up the responsible position of Economic Minister at the British Embassy in Washington.

In the War he was one of my Principal Private Secretaries at Number 10, and perhaps you remember meeting him. He remained there for some time after I left until he was given a senior post in the Treasury.

During those years he worked in close contact with me and I formed a high regard for his capabilities as well as a particular liking for his personality. I know it would give him great pleasure to meet you again, and also I feel that from our point of view it would be most beneficial. I think you would find him very agreeable, intelligent and well-informed.

I hope everything goes well with you. We are still in the midst of political upheavals and the last month, as you can imagine, has been very strenuous.

Winston S. Churchill to Lord Salisbury
(Churchill papers, 2/107)

March 1950
NOT SENT

My dear Bobbety,

Thank you for your letter of the 7th. It seems to me that the immediate problem has been successfully handled. There is very little chance of the Government being defeated on our own two Amendments to the Address. Thus we can testify to our convictions, our Party in the House and the country have a fighting policy, and no change in the situation need be expected in the near future.

I now send you a note of the 'Byng' case,[1] which Lascelles kindly gave me. This is of course extremely confidential at the present time, and I should be glad to have it back. Anthony is probably the only other person to whom I shall show it. In acknowledging its receipt, I said to Lascelles that in my view, if Meighen,[2] though unable to command a majority in Parliament, had been able to present a new situation or combination, or if anything exceptional happened, Byng might well have acceded to his request. Naturally, I would not expect any answer to this.

I think myself that the present Government will probably continue till June, or it may be October, and will pounce at the moment they think best. It may well be however that later in the Session they will be defeated on some important issue in the Commons, because we must carry on the effective opposition and there will certainly be many Divisions. The future therefore is as usual veiled in obscurity. What a bore life would be if it were not. I am personally convinced that we should gain greatly from forming a Government, possibly on a wider basis than is now open, and then appealing to the people. I hope you will bear these possibilities in your mind, and I must repeat my quotation of Abe Lincoln: 'Never cross the Fox river till you get to it.'

---

[1] Julian Hedworth George Byng, 1862–1935. Entered Army, 1883. On active service in the Sudan, 1884; in South Africa, 1899–1902. Maj.-Gen., 1909. CO, Troops in Egypt, 1912–14; 3rd Cavalry Div., 1914–15; Cavalry Corps, 1915; 9th Army Corps, 1915–16; 17th Army Corps, 1916; Canadian Corps, 1916–17; 3rd Army, 1917–19. Knighted, 1915. Gen., 1917. Baron, 1919. Governor-General of Canada, 1921–6. Viscount, 1926. Commissioner, Metropolitan Police, 1928–31. FM, 1932. The 'Byng' case refers to his 1926 refusal to sign the writ for a general election in Canada.

[2] Arthur Meighen, 1874–1960. Educated at University of Toronto, 1896. Married, 1904, Isabel J. Cox. Canadian MP, 1908–26. Leader, Canadian Conservative Party, 1920–6, 1941–2. PM, 1920–1, 1926. Senator, 1932–41. Retired, 1942, after losing a by-election.

Winston S. Churchill to Stephen Pierssené[1]
(Churchill papers, 2/130)

13 March 1950

Dear Mr Pierssené,

I should be much obliged if you would have a calculation made showing what would happen if a Second Ballot were applied to the results of the last General Election. How many seats would be affected, and how are they now held? You should assume that the Liberal vote would give one third to the Labour and two thirds to the Conservatives. Also if there were an arrangement between the Liberal and Conservative Parties and the Liberal vote was directed to support the Conservatives what would be the result?

What would be the result if the big cities of England and Scotland were formed into PR units and the same disposition of the Liberal vote was made as above?

Winston S. Churchill to Field Marshal Jan Smuts
(Churchill papers, 2/101)

15 March 1950

Should be grateful for full information about your views Seretse[2] by swiftest airmail. Feeling here very strong against Government muddle.

Betsy Gore to Clementine Churchill
(Churchill papers, 2/101)

16 March 1950

Dear Mrs Churchill,

It is so long since we have met that I feel I must begin by explaining who I am, for you will never remember me: I am Betsy Gore, Alice Salisbury's half-sister.

At the present moment I am looking after the Colonial Student work at the Conservative Overseas Bureau, and, in the course of this work, I have

---

[1] Stephen Herbert Pierssené, 1899–1966. Lt, Queen's Rgt, 1922. Knighted, 1953. General Director, Conservative and Unionist Central Office, 1945–57.

[2] Seretse Khama, 1921–80. Son of Chief Sekgoma and Queen Tebogo Khama. Succeed his father as King of Bechuanaland, 1925. Educated at Fort Hare University, South Africa, 1944; Balliol College, Oxford. Barrister, Inner Temple, 1946. Married, 1948, Ruth Williams. Exiled from the British Protectorate of Bechuanaland for his interracial marriage, 1951; returned on condition of abdication, 1956. Elected to the Tribal Council, 1957. Founder, Bechuanaland Democratic Party, 1961. PM, Bechuanaland, 1965–6. First President, Republic of Botswana, 1966–80. Grand Comrade, Order of the Lion of Malawi, 1967. Hon. PhD, Fordham University, NY, 1967. Royal Order of Sobhuza II Grand Counsellor, Swaziland, 1978.

received the attached letter from a young Sierra Leone Student over here, Mr Tejan-Sie,[1] who is Librarian of the West African Students' Union: a Union which includes all the Unions of Students of the separate West African Colonies.

As the letter contains a great tribute to Mr Churchill in connection with the Seretse Khama affair, I just thought that he might like to see it, as I am sure that the tribute is one which would be made by every young West African in this country.

I think that the tribute also has an added interest in that most Colonial Students in this country have heretofore inclined to the Labour Party. You will note what a salutary effect has been made by Mr Churchill's intervention in the Khama debate, and what excellent repercussions it is likiely to have for the Conservative Party. Of course if you feel that it is not worth while to show this letter to Mr Churchill – when he has so very much to occupy him – I shall well understand.

ATTACHMENT

'The Seretse Khama affair and the decision of the Government has rebounded unfavourably on the Labour Party, as all those students who hitherto were Labour-minded are now recoiling to the string, which Mr Churchill so ably described as a 'disreputable transaction'. Mr Churchill incidentally stands high today in the estimation of Colonial Students, and I think this is a change for the Conservative Party to instil a feeling of confidence in these students. Indeed such a move would have its effects not only in this country but all over the African Continent. I believe the action of the Government has damaged British prestige, and some of us with moderate opinions who have always held as sacrosanct the British regard for justice, fairplay and humanism, now rightly or wrongly question the genuineness of such conclusions.

Quite apart from the Colour Bar, it is the question of principle that we are anxious to uphold. The fact that a political nit-wit like Gordon Walker, who only became known as a public man because of this rather complicating issue, can talk of kicking out a Chief who is virtually a spiritual leader of his peoples hurts our pride. I think you will agree with me that the attitude of the Government is dastardly.'

---

[1] Banja Tejan-Sie, 1917–2000. Born in Moyamba, Sierra Leone. Educated at Prince of Wales School, Freetown, London School of Economics and Lincoln's Inn. Married, 1946, Admira Stapleton: three children. Member, West African Students' Union, 1948–51. Called to the the Bar, 1951. National Vice-President, Sierra Leone People's Party, 1953–6. Police Magistrate, Eastern Province, 1955; Northern Province, 1958. Senior Police Magistrate, 1961. Speaker, Sierra Leone House of Representatives, 1962–7. CMG, 1967. Chief Justice of Sierra Leone, 1967–70. Acting Governor-General, 1968–70. GCMG, 1970. Governor-General, 1970–1.

Winston S. Churchill: speech
(Hansard)

16 March 1950   House of Commons

DEFENCE

No one will accuse the Minister of Defence (Mr Shinwell) of plunging the House into vehement controversy by the speech he has just made. He seems to have been guided throughout by a strong spirit of self-restraint and of moderation of statement rendered even more remarkable by the regular forms of official verbiage in which it was so happily expressed. So far as adding to the knowledge of the House upon this vast and grave topic, I can only say that I found his remarks about the atomic bomb a model of non-informatory eloquence. This is what the Minister told us about the atomic bomb, which is after all, a topic of some lively interest: 'The chiefs of staff have given full weight to this new factor.' There we may leave it for the moment. Let us hope it will be content with that position.

As the House knows, I, and some of my colleagues, at the Government's invitation, have had several conferences with the Prime Minister and Service Ministers in the last Parliament at which disclosures of matters not known to the House, or not fully known, were made. In my published correspondence with the Prime Minister I made the following stipulation:

> In order that the Opposition should not be embarrassed in Defence Debates, I must ask you, as I did Mr Baldwin in 1936, that we should be free to use in public any information of which we are already possessed, with due regard to the national interest and safety.

The Prime Minister agreed to that. Last year, we moved a reasoned Amendment on defence and we had thought of repeating it in the same terms this year.

I was not myself particularly anxious to have a Division on this issue at this time, if it could be avoided. I found it, however, impossible to commit myself and my colleagues even tacitly to the word 'approve' which was announced to be a part of the Motion to approve the White Paper on Defence which is now before us. Such a step on our part might well be regarded hereafter, in view of the conferences that have taken place, as to some extent committing us to sharing, albeit indirectly, in the Government's responsibility. While recognizing the efforts which have been made we could not take any responsibility for the present state of affairs in the Armed Forces. I am, therefore obliged to the Prime Minister for being willing to substitute for the word 'approve' the words 'take note of' in the Government's Motion. I am sure that, in all the circumstances that prevail, this is a right decision on his part. Therefore there is no need to divide the House tonight.

MARCH 1950 1687

I must now refer briefly to the disagreeable topic of the recent Ministerial appointments in the military sphere. I do not wish to dwell upon them unduly, but they cannot be omitted from any review of our defence position. I said in December 1948 in this House:

> We all understand the difficulties of a party leader in these times when he has not only to conduct government but to preserve general good feeling among all his supporters. In these appointments I must say it seemed to me that the Prime Minister put party first, party second and party third. . . . I thought the appointment of the present Secretary of War was surprising. . . . I believe that the Army would be better entrusted to men who are not engaged in the most bitter strife of politics. Nor should the War Office be regarded as a receptacle for Ministerial failures.

Mr Shinwell: Would the right hon. Gentleman prefer to appoint his son-in-law (Mr Duncan Sandys) to a post?

Mr Churchill: I was not aware that he had been appointed to a high military post.

The Parliamentary Secretary to the Admiralty (Mr James Callaghan):[1] Anyway, the right hon. Gentleman is the biggest politician there is.

Mr Churchill: I am merely reading what I said a year and a quarter ago. No doubt it has stung the right hon. Gentleman, but it is really not so much an attack upon him as a criticism of the method of these appointments. We now have a different situation. We have a new Parliament. We have other personalities,[2] yet I cannot feel that my complaint of December 1948 is not as valid and true as when I uttered it. Indeed, it seems to have had renewed confirmation. Under the Atlantic Pact we have much military business to do with the United States and other Powers, and I cannot feel that that business, or other aspects of our military organization, will be facilitated by the Prime Minister's choice.

Coming to a more general question, it seems to me that more information should be given to the House about all the three Services. The guiding rule should be to tell Parliament everything that is certainly and obviously known to those foreign governments with whom we do not have confidential relationships in defence matters. That is a good working guide. It is not right, for instance, that the House of Commons should be so much worse informed about our defences than the Soviet Government. What is well known abroad should also, in most cases, be imparted to the House of Commons which, after

---

[1] (Leonard) James Callaghan, 1912–2005. MP (Lab.) for Cardiff South and Penarth, 1945–87. Parliamentary Secretary, Ministry of Transport, 1947–50; Admiralty, 1950–1. Shadow Chancellor of the Exchequer, 1961–4; Home Secretary, 1970–1; Secretary of State for Employment, 1971–2; Foreign Secretary, 1972–4. Chancellor of the Exchequer, 1964–7. Home Secretary, 1967–70. Foreign Secretary, 1974–6. Leader of the Labour Party, 1976–80. PM, 1976–9. Leader of the Opposition, 1979–80. Father of the House, 1983–7. KG, 1987. Baron, 1987.

[2] Shinwell was replaced as Secretary of State for War by John Strachey in Feb. 1950.

all, has the responsibility of providing the money now required on an unprecedented scale in time of peace.

I am sure it would be a great advantage if we could have a Debate in secret session on defence. We might then go into the atomic bomb question and see whether more information can be elicited than that 'the chiefs of staff have given full weight to this new factor'. I do not mean that the Government should impart all their secret information to the House. Even if no further disclosure of military secrets were made, it would be much easier to discuss the whole question of defence without having every word reported and read all over the world.

It is sometimes one's duty to say things in public which give rise to anxiety and alarm. This may give satisfaction in some foreign countries and cause distress and want of confidence in us in others. I had to do this on several occasions before the late war when I was dealing with a Government and with Ministers at least as capable as those with whom we are now concerned.

Mr Shinwell: Does the right hon. Gentleman's observation apply to the late Sir Thomas Inskip?

Mr Churchill: Yes, sir. I certainly think he had a far greater command of the large sphere of thought and action over which he presided as Minister for the Coordination of Defence than – since the right hon. Gentleman puts the point – the right hon. Gentleman himself is ever likely to acquire. I carefully refrain from pressing the points against the right hon. Gentleman because, although he has many faults, I still believe his heart is in the right place. But he should not show himself so frightfully sensitive. We are only at the beginning of an ordeal which will be prolonged during this Parliament whatever duration it may be, and we earnestly trust the right hon. Gentleman will reserve some of his retorts and indignation for later phases in the criticism he will have to undergo. I was on the question of importance of having a Debate on defence in secret Session. I think it would be an advantage to have one in the next few months. I have never yet, in my experience, seen a secret Session from which the Government of the day did not derive advantages. I think there are a good many points which ought to be rammed home with more force than one would like to do on these topics in public hearing.

I therefore ask the Prime Minister to consider whether, in view of the balance of parties in the House and in view of the fact that the new House of Commons has been purged by the electors of certain untrustworthy elements, and that we are all united in our opposition to Communism, we should not have the advantage of the candour and freedom of speech together with any fuller information possible in a Session at which only the Members of both Houses can be present. If this request were refused one would have to consider whether more would not have to be said in public upon matters already known to foreign governments in order that our own people should be more truly informed. This afternoon, however, I shall say nothing that is not public knowledge to the newspapers in this or other countries, or that I do not derive from my own knowledge and do not mention on my own responsibility.

I will begin with the Army. In the forefront of Army policy comes the question of National Service. The Labour Government have enforced conscription in time of peace. Everyone is liable to serve in the Armed Forces for eighteen months. We could not approve industrial conscription in peacetime, and I am very glad that it has been withdrawn, but we have felt it our duty to support, and we still support, the Government in maintaining the principle of compulsory National Service. It would have been very easy for us to gain popularity and votes at the recent election by denouncing it, as did the Liberal Party, but we felt bound to help the Government carry this burden. We think National Service is necessary not only to maintain the structure of the Army but to preserve peace. If Britain were to repudiate National Service at this time, as the Liberals propose, it would mean, in my opinion, the downfall of the whole defensive structure embodied in the Brussels Treaty and in the Atlantic Pact, and now being very slowly brought into being. We therefore made our position clear during the last Parliament, and we adhere to it now.

I think we were somewhat ungratefully treated on this subject in the election. I was surprised to learn that an active whispering campaign was on foot, especially in garrisons abroad, in Germany and the Mediterranean fortresses, in Singapore and Hong Kong, that the length of compulsory service would be increased if the Conservatives were returned to power. (Hon. Members: 'We never heard of it.') We received numerous communications of that character. The troops were upset by the suggestion that they would be kept abroad for a longer time. We contradicted this false rumour as best we could, but it only shows how difficult it is to develop a true and wise national policy in a period when prolonged and vicious electioneering is the order of the day.

I still adhere to what I said last year:

> I am strongly of the belief that if the great policy and decision of national military service had been used properly and a smaller number called up for a longer time, great economies might have been made and might still be made in the Military Services.[1]

The right hon. Gentleman in one of his references did not challenge that. He said there were other considerations. Of course, that statement in no way affected men who were already serving, and I was much shocked to hear, for instance, that widespread rumour was being put about at Malta and everywhere that if the Conservatives were returned the men would all have their service increased.

The Prime Minister: The right hon. Gentleman is constantly talking about whispering campaigns. There was a ridiculous one which he suggested had

---

[1] Speech of 27 Oct. 1949, reproduced above (pp. 1551–6).

been put about that he was dead. No one has heard of these whispering campaigns except the right hon. Gentleman. (Hon. Members: 'Oh') Perhaps the hon. Members on the second opposition bench will allow me to address their Leader. Unless the right hon. Gentleman can give us some evidence of where these whispering campaigns came from, he should not make charges of this kind. No one here has heard of any of these reports. I am unaware that anyone out in Malta has. It is extraordinary to have these constant suggestions by the right hon. Gentleman about these whispering campaigns being put about.

Mr Churchill: I certainly do not withdraw what I have said. Hundreds of messages and letters were received. Of course, I have not suggested that the Prime Minister himself went about whispering, but that other statements –

Mr Paget (Northampton): On a point of Order. The right hon. Gentleman has referred to certain documents. Ought not those documents to be available to the House?

Mr Churchill: The hon. and learned Gentleman should learn a little more about our Rules of Order before he raises points of Order. All I can say is that I was very glad to be in a position myself to deny the rumour that I was dead, and I only regret it was not as easy to get upon the track of and kill a great many other falsehoods to which we were subjected. Personally I think it was very shabby for hon. Members and others, if they were engaged in the campaign at all – (Hon. Members: 'If'.) – considering the help that we have given them in supporting National Service, to have taken every advantage that they could as occasion offered. Hon. Members do not disturb me at all by their indignation. I am only sorry that the topics I have to deal with this afternoon are of a laborious and technical character and do not enable me to stimulate them more vigorously than I shall be able.

I am now coming to the question of the structure of the Regular Army. Here I must say that I do not agree with the Government's view, expressed in the last sentence of the White Paper on Defence, which reads:

> The idea that the present principle of universality of national service should be abandoned in favour of a scheme under which a smaller number of men, selected by ballot or otherwise, would be required to serve for a period of eighteen months or more is, in the Government's view, impractical.

Nearly 300,000 men come within the scope of National Service every year. Of these the intake for 1950–1 is to be 168,000. I am quoting from the Paper. I do not suggest that this number should be increased. On the contrary, I think that by wise administration it might well be somewhat diminished. But I believe that the method of choosing those who are required could be greatly improved, and I do not exclude the principle of selective service by ballot from a proper application of our National Service law. I think it is a matter which should not be too lightly brushed aside.

I believe that if, by various inducements of a voluntary or optional character, men called up could be persuaded to serve for a somewhat long period, important economies, easements and improvements would be possible in our whole military system. I am satisfied that conscription could be applied with less burden and with less expense, combined with greater efficiency, having regard especially to our peculiar needs; and I do not think the Minister of Defence disagrees with that. I do not propose, however, to go into details, but I renew the assurance, which I gave during the election, that the Conservative Party do not intend to use compulsory powers to lengthen the terms of National Service above the eighteen months which now prevail.

One aspect of the evils of the present application of the compulsory Service Acts is shown in our lamentable inability to produce, even with the present severe measures of compulsion, any adequate reinforcement or expeditionary force even for the minor contingencies which arise in the world, and that for a nation whose responsibilities, as the Minister of Defence reminded us, are still so widely spread as ours. We have, of course, the German garrisons to maintain and more troops are needed in the Far East; but to set against this there is the relief of what used to be our prime burden of maintaining a great long-service army in India.

Even with all the compulsory powers which the Government have taken, with 380,000 men in uniform, I do not believe there are a couple of well-formed brigade groups which could be sent abroad at short notice; I should be quite ready to be contradicted on that point and be very glad. That would compare with the six divisions produced under the Haldane scheme, without compulsion, before the First World War, or with the four or five divisions which stood ready at the outbreak of the Second World War. Of course, things are not exactly on all fours, I quite agree. There have been many changes, but such great contrasts should not be ignored and, with facts like these staring us in the face, it is hard to believe that we are presented with a successful solution of the military problem by those who have had unprecedented control for the last $4\frac{1}{2}$ years. We have an enormous mass of men in uniform, and here we are reduced to this pitiful shortage of the means to send small reinforcements, modest reinforcements, abroad at short notice. It is not a thing to laugh at; it is a thing to puzzle at, and to try to find a way to do it. We shall not get through our difficulties by this attempt at geniality when under examination.

Time does not permit me this afternoon to recur to the extraordinary disappearance and dispersal of immense masses of war materials which were at our disposal when the present Government came into office. The right hon. Gentleman said something about it, and of course some weapons become obsolete in a few years but others, properly taken care of, especially artillery and rifles, of which we had enormous masses, can be kept in good order for a whole generation. Now I return to the recruiting for the Regular Army and for the Territorial Forces. How seriously this has fallen off is shown by the figures on page six of the White Paper. There has been a fall in the Regular

Army recruiting from 33,900 in 1948 to 23,800 in 1949 – that is to say, a drop of nearly one-third. Yet it is on this Regular Army, so heavily burdened by the need of training the National Service recruits, and losing them as soon as they begin to be most useful, that there falls the task of providing not only our garrisons overseas with units of real fighting quality, but also the supply of effective reinforcements available at short notice, which all admit are needed.

I come to the wider aspects of our military affairs. The decision to form a front in Europe against possible further invasion by Soviet Russia and its satellite States was at once grave for us and also imperative. There was a school of thought in the United States which held that Western Europe was indefensible and that the only lines where a Soviet-Satellite advance could be held were the Channel and Pyrenees. I am very glad that this view has been decisively rejected by the United States, by ourselves and by all the Powers concerned in the Brussels Treaty and the Atlantic Pact. I find it necessary to say, however, speaking personally, giving my own opinion, that this long front cannot be successfully defended without the active aid of Western Germany. For more than forty years – and what years! – I have worked with France. Britain and France must stand together primarily united in Europe. United they will be strong enough to extend their hands to Germany. Germany is at present disarmed and forbidden to keep any military force. Just beyond her eastern frontier lies the enormous military array of the Soviet and its satellite States, far exceeding in troops, in armour and in air power all that the other Allies have got. We are unable to offer any assurance to the Germans that they may not be overrun by a Soviet and satellite invasion.

Seven or eight millions of refugees from the East have already been received and succoured in Western Germany. In all the circumstances this is a marvellous feat. Another 250,000 are now being or about to be driven across the Polish and Czech frontiers. This mighty mass of the Russian armies and their satellites lie, like a fearful cloud, upon the German people. The Allies cannot give them any direct protection. Their homes, their villages, their cities might be overrun by an Eastern deluge and, no doubt, all Germans who have been prominent in resisting Communism or are working for reconciliation with the Western democracies would pay the final forfeit. We have no guarantee to give except to engage in a general war which, after wrecking what is left of European civilization, would no doubt end ultimately in the defeat of the Soviets, but which might begin by the Communist enslavement of Western Germany, and not only of Western Germany. If the Germans are to have neither a guarantee of defence nor to be allowed to make a contribution to the general framework of defence they must console themselves, as they are doing, by the fact that they have no military expense to bear – nothing like the £800,000,000 we are now voting or the contributions of the French and other treaty Powers, or the far greater sums provided by the United States. They are free from all that.

The Germans may also comfort themselves with the important advantages which this relief from taxation gives to German commercial competition in all the markets of the world, growing and spreading with every month that passes. I cannot feel that this is a good way to do things, or that we should let them drift on their course. I say without hesitation that the effective defence of the European frontiers cannot be achieved if the German contribution is excluded from the thoughts of those who are responsible.

The Minister of Defence does not admit to deal with this issue, although it and others are the foundation of the responsibilities confided in him; but I hope that the Prime Minister will be able to speak to us about them tonight. The decision, of course, does not rest with this country alone, but we must have a policy, and the House ought to know what is our policy. To remain as we are now for a long period of time is certainly not the best way of preventing the measureless horrors of a third world war. It is painful to witness the present indecision, and also the petty annoyances, by which the reconciliation of France and Great Britain with the German people is hindered, by the belated dismantlement of a few remaining German factories and the still more belated trials of aged German generals. All this plays into the hands of the Communist fifth column in Western Germany and the reviving Nazism, or neo-Nazism, which is only another variant of the same evil. All this squanders the precious years that still remain in which war can be averted and peace established on a lasting foundation. I felt it my duty to raise this subject today, and I think it would be altogether wrong that these Debates should proceed upon a basis of guarded platitudes and the avoidance of any real statement of the issues upon which our lives and fortunes depend.

Now I come to the Navy. Estimates of £193,000,000 are put forward for the Navy, and a reduction is proposed in the manpower under Vote A from 144,000 at 1 April 1949 to 127,000 in April 1951. I do not quarrel with this. I have urged in successive years the combing of the tail and the numbers employed ashore in non-combatant jobs and in clerical duties at the Admiralty. I am glad to see that the Minister of Defence is a convert to this process. I am glad to see it has been going forward, albeit slowly and tardily. I was sorry, however, to read in the Admiralty paper that 'for reasons of economy there will be no increase in the strength of the Royal Fleet Reserve during 1950 to 1951'. The maintenance of the Royal Fleet Reserve is not expensive in proportion to the security which it gives and the service that it renders. I have also studied the tables given in the Admiralty paper of the strength of the Fleet, both active and reserve, and such information as is vouchsafed us about new construction, modernization and conversion. I do not propose to make any comments in detail upon this, but rather to deal generally with the great change that has come over the naval position, and to try to focus for the House, so far as is possible, the new Admiralty problem. This is not like the period before the First World War when all was thought to culminate in a decisive engagement between the battle fleets at sea, and we maintained the ratio of 16 to 10 over the German capital ships. There is no surface fleet potentially hostile to us in the world today. The only other surface fleet of consequence is that of the United States, nearly all of which – or a great part of which – has, with much wisdom, been placed in material reserve, protected from decay by costly but well worth while systems of preservation. In the Navy the war in the air and the war on the sea have become so closely interwoven as to be indistinguishable and inseparable.

It is obvious and imperative that the Navy should manage its own air service. Nevertheless, in the sea war of the future it is the air which will decide the fate and fortunes of ships of war. Therefore, the aircraft carrier with proper naval protection must increasingly replace the battleships of former times. But what kind of aircraft carrier, and how many of the large or small types? To decide this you must look at the actual problem which lies before us. The combat of gunfire between lines of battle is utterly extinct. What we have to face in the next few years is the Germanized Soviet U-boat. The nation does not seem to know much about this, and the right hon. Gentleman did not mention it in his statement, but the salient facts are public property and govern the thoughts of all the staffs in many countries. I am not going to attempt to compute the Soviet U-boat force. According to Brassey's[1] Naval Annual, the strength given out by Soviet propaganda is 250, and Brassey's Naval Annual regards this as a reliable figure. Between 75 and 100 of these, according to this authority, are of war-time or post-war construction.

It may not be wise to publish what we ourselves have in anti-U-boat craft and forces, but there really cannot be any reason for the Government not stating broadly what we might have to face. At the end of the war the Soviets became possessors of a great part of Germany and of several of its Easter Baltic ports. They engaged, by persuasion or pressure, a large number of German scientific personnel. They have made a great U-boat fleet, in the designing and building and even handling of which a considerable proportion of Germans are involved, by seduction or duress. Certainly an immense advance has been made in the character and quality of the U-boat menace to the ocean life lines without whose maintenance we cannot live. An entirely new type of U-boat has been developed. Instead of a ship going eight or nine knots under the water and having to come up to breathe at comparatively short intervals, we have a type of U-boat which can manoeuvre below the surface at upwards of twenty knots or thereabouts. By the use of the breathing tube or snorkel – or 'snort' as we call it – it can make passages

---

[1] Thomas Brassey, 1836–1918. Educated at Rugby School and University College, Oxford. Married, 1860, Anna Allnutt; 1890, Lady Sybil de Vere Capell. Barrister-at-law, Lincoln's Inn, 1864. MP (Lib.) for Devenport, 1865; for Hastings, 1868–86. President, Statistical Society, 1879–80. KCB, 1881. Lord of the Admiralty, 1884–5; as such he published the first *Naval Annual Report*, of which his son was a long-time editor. Baron, 1886. GCB, 1906. Viscount Hythe, 1911; Earl Brassey, 1911. Lord-in-Waiting, 1893–5. Governor of Victoria, 1895–1901. President, London Chamber of Commerce, 1901–4.

of thousands of miles without appearing on the surface where it might be detected.

The flotillas and anti-U-boat vessels which, in enormous numbers, broke the U-boat peril and saved our lives in the last war are now largely obsolete for this purpose. In those days we used to employ 12-knot or 14-knot ships to hunt the U-boats, and it was comparatively easy to multiply those; but now, with U-boats capable of moving, for a short time at any rate, at 20 knots submerged, all this great anti-U-boat fleet which we created would be useless. We should have to have much faster vessels going at 30 knots or more merely to do the same hunting as we did in the last war.

Here also is a sphere in which numbers are imperative, but to create vessels of 30 knots in the numbers required involves impossible expense. We have to have many scores of them and each one costs four or five times as much as the old kind and takes two or three times as long to build or adapt. The problem of mastering the new German-designed and Soviet-owned U-boat cannot be solved along the lines of multiplying flotillas of larger and faster vessels. If the story stopped here, I should feel gloomy about it. Happily, however, as is often forgotten, all things are on the move together, and here the naval air and longer-range land-based aircraft come to the aid of the Navy.

The light type of aircraft carrier, if provided in sufficient numbers, can search immense areas of sea. There are also, no doubt, improvements in the methods of destroying U-boats. We have to find them, however, before we can destroy them, and only the air can do this. I submit to the House that the main emphasis of our naval effort at the present time should be to create the largest numbers of light fleet aircraft carriers and auxiliary carriers capable of carrying the necessary modern types of aircraft.

This is a time to concentrate upon essentials. It does not at all follow that this means a vast augmentation of expenditure. It is necessary to concentrate upon essentials and beware, of all things, of frittering strength away on remedies against dangers which have passed away in time. An intense effort should be made to improve the methods of detecting submerged U-boats from the air. Great advances have already been made. I heard no reference to this by the right hon. Gentleman, but I have seldom seen a precise demand made upon science by the military which has not been met. Perhaps the solution has already been found. At any rate, it may be possessed by others. On 23 February – a date when some of us were preoccupied with other matters – the United States authorities published an official statement on new measures designed to combat the snorkel submarine. They said:

> The Navy has accepted delivery of a new model of the long-range Neptune, which will be the first aircraft specifically designed to meet the threat of snorkel type enemy submarines. This plane holds the world's non-refuelling distance record of 11,236 miles. Built by the Lockheed Aircraft Corporation, the twin-engined Neptune carries the latest electronic and ordinance

equipment. Its sensitive search radar permits detection of smaller targets, such as a snorkel tube, over a much greater distance than heretofore possible with long-range patrol planes.

That shows that the information that other countries find it possible to give has all been made public; it is a contrast to the limits to which the House of Commons is confined.

To locate submerged submarines accurately, the P2V will utilize magnetic detection gear and sonobuoys. These small radio buoys are dropped in a specific pattern over the area where a submarine is suspected. Floating on the surface the buoy lowers a small hydroplane to the proper depth, where the noise of the submarine's propellers is detected by the hydrophone and transmitted. Receivers in the aircraft permit the operators to plot the submarine's position by interpreting the relative noise level transmitted by the sonobuoys.

I have not read anything so encouraging or hopeful for many a long day. I am bound to say I am astonished that more information should not have been volunteered by the Minister of Defence in the statement which he has made. If this should come true, the menace of modern U-boats may finally be overcome under the attack of modern aircraft launched from a sufficient number of small aircraft carriers. I think that the House ought to know and reflect upon these important facts in a debate of this character, and that they should play a real part in our consideration of these questions of defence policy.

Now I come to the general air problem – not the one connected with the Navy, but the general air problem. Here again, I shall only mention to the House what is already well-known to those who study such matters. In the forefront stands the enormous numerical strength of the Soviet air force. There never has been an air force of the size that the Soviet have built and are building in time of peace. In the air quantity is best defeated by quality. That is how we got through in 1940 when all hung in the balance. But now we have a far greater disproportion of numbers to face, though happily of a lower relative quality. Still no one can say that a sufficient quantity cannot overwhelm superior quality. If we wish to have that strength which will deter war, or if the worst comes to the worst, enable us to win through, we require far larger numbers of the highest class aircraft than we now possess. Every sacrifice should be made on other branches of defence to make sure that that is not neglected. The highest priority should be accorded to it. Fortunately and providentially there is the American Air Force, far stronger than ours and of equal quality. We have allowed them to establish in East Anglia a base for their bombing aircraft, the significance of which cannot be lost on the Soviets.

We on this side supported His Majesty's Government in the steps they have taken. If any other party had taken such steps I do not know whether the Socialists in Opposition would have sustained them. Certainly they have not been put to that test. It was certainly a step which in any other period but this strange time in which we live might have led to war. What has distressed and disquieted me is that those who took it should appear not to be fully conscious of its importance. Our defensive forces in fighter aircraft should be raised and our radar precautions should be raised by our utmost exertions to the highest possible level.

We have the jet fighter. This is the product of British genius. There is nothing to surpass it in the world and it is continually improving. I was glad to read in the White Paper, page 5, paragraph 15, the plan for doubling the jet fighter strength of Fighter Command would be completed. I hope that means really 'doubling' and not merely filling up existing squadrons and bringing them up to strength. I was glad to read it for what it was worth. But I cannot understand why a British Government which has established an American base in East Anglia should have allowed anything to diminish the supply of jet fighter aircraft upon which our deterrent against war and our survival should it come might alike depend.

Here again I base myself only upon what has been made public in the newspapers and is common property. The right hon. Gentleman made a reference to jet fighters. British jet fighters have hitherto been for many good but insufficient reasons – and a good reason if insufficient in a matter like this is a bad reason – dispersed and distributed in various quarters. I am content to deal only with those which have been sold to the Argentine, or written off against what are called 'sterling balances' to Egypt. I do not know how many have been sent or given – for that is what it comes to – to Egypt; but it is already public knowledge that 100 jet fighter aircraft have been sold to the Argentine for little more than £2,000,000.

There is a sense of disproportion about an act like this which passes the frontiers of reason. The Air Force lays before us Estimates for £223,000,000, and yet to gain perhaps little more than £2,000,000 in foreign exchange – which the Liverpool Cotton Exchange could have earned for us in a year; a trifle compared to the vast scale of our expenditure – 100 of these vital instruments have been sent away.

Even upon the basis of the facts known to the public I am prepared to argue this matter in a little further detail. A wise use of our jet aircraft would have enabled the whole of our Auxiliary Air Force squadrons to be at this moment effectively re-armed. I do not think that those who conduct the Government of the country, although animated I am sure by a sincere purpose, have comprehended this aspect of their problem. As far as I could understand him this afternoon, the Minister of Defence gave a most extraordinary reason. He said that the Air Force could not afford to buy them; and when I asked why they could not afford to, it was because apparently they had overrun the Estimate agreed with the Chancellor of the Exchequer. But all this is in the same sphere of ministerial responsibility, and money should be saved elsewhere rather than that a vital need of this kind should be denied to the Air Force.

I will try to put this problem in the simplest terms for the benefit of the right hon. Gentleman. Here we have an Air Force at an overall cost of £223,000,000, and to get £2,000,000 of dollar exchange we deprive ourselves of this part of an element vital to our security. Let me take a really simple example derived from the days which some of us have lived in, in the early years of the century, of old-fashioned war. Suppose we had a regiment of Lancers 500 strong. It might have cost £100,000 a year. There were the overheads; there were the fine uniforms, there were the horses, the barracks, the band and all that. What would have been thought of an Administration which cut off the steel spear-points of 100 of the lances and sold them to the local ironmonger at half-a-crown apiece to reduce expense? I have put it simply to the right hon. Gentleman, and I hope he has managed to take that in anyhow. But that is exactly what this particular transaction of selling 100 jet fighter aircraft to the Argentine, published in all the newspapers and common knowledge all over the world has amounted to.

We shall hear all sorts of excuses about the time it takes to lengthen runways on the airfields, the collection of skilled mechanics, the importance of building up, as the right hon. Gentleman told us, a future clientele of customers abroad, and the like. We have only to think of the total cost of the Air Estimates of £223,000,000 to see what such arguments are worth. We have only to think of the time that has passed since we allowed the Americans to establish their bombing base in East Anglia to see how vain are these excuses for not having taken all the concomitant measures at the same time. If we had strictly safeguarded our jet fighter aircraft of the waste of which I have given only one example – and that because it is public – the whole of our Auxiliary Air Force could have been re-armed by now, and even further aircraft might have been made.

In putting this point before the House I must repeat that I am citing no fact which is not known to the world, or was not known to me apart from any information I have derived from discussions with the Government. I do not know how much of this sort of thing has been vitiating our enormous expenditure upon armaments, but I am sure that far greater value for the money we voted could have been achieved, and that far better use could now be made of our British resources. If we wish to prevent the fearful tensions which exist in the modern world we must not only be cool and patient, but also firm and strong. Here is one of the reasons why I could not possibly accept the word 'approve' when errors of this kind have been committed in the open light of day.

Do not, I beg the House, nurse foolish delusions that we have any other effective overall shield at the present time from mortal danger than the atomic bomb in the possession, thank God, of the United States. But for that there would be no hope that Europe could preserve its freedom, or that our island could escape an ordeal incomparably more severe than those we have already endured. Our whole position in this atomic sphere has been worsened since the war by the fact that the Russians, unexpectedly as the Minister admitted, have acquired the secrets of the atomic bomb, and are said to have begun its manufacture. Let us therefore labour for peace, not only by gathering our defensive strength, but also by making sure that no door is closed upon any hope of reaching a settlement which will end this tragic period when two worlds face one another in increasing strain and anxiety.

Field Marshal Jan Smuts to Winston S. Churchill
(Churchill papers, 2/101)

16 March 1950

My dear Winston,

In reply to your cable[1] for my views on the Seretse affair, I send you the following note.

The matter has various aspects. In the first place, as regards the way in which Seretse has been treated, there is much to be said for his view that he has been tricked into the London visit, and that once having been inveigled to London, he has then been forbidden to return. He should at least have been warned in advance of this possibility. I imagine this is appreciated, and it is possible that the Government may now allow him to return, and thereafter banishing him from the Territory.

As regards the non-recognition of Seretse, I do not see how the Government can change their announced decision without very grave damage from the South African point of view. A form of passive resistance, or boycott, has already been started by the tribe against the Government, and any change now by the Government will be looked upon as a capitulation, which might seriously damage British authority, and indeed, all Government authority in South Africa. Our Native situation is already a troubled one, and it would be an inducement to Natives in the Union to do likewise, with far-reaching consequences. We have repeatedly had cases where we had to refuse to acknowledge claimants for chieftainship, and it has generally been accepted. Natives traditionally believe in authority, and our whole Native system will collapse if weakness is shown in this regard.

This argument would apply in any case of an unsuitable candidate, but it is here aggravated by the undesirable marriage of Seretse. People, both in South Africa and Rhodesia, are as a whole united in their opinion against

---

[1] Reproduced above (p. 1684).

Seretse's marriage to a white woman. Indeed, in both countries miscegenation of this kind is legally criminal and would certainly be fatal to any claim to the chieftainship.

Should the British Government ignore this sentiment in South Africa, public opinion here would harden behind Malan's claim for the annexation of the Protectorates to the Union, and in case this claim were refused, the extreme course of declaring South Africa a republic would at once become a live issue. This is already the declared policy of the Nationalist Party, and any surrender of the British Government on the Seretse issue would at once give the Nationalists a very strong argument in favour of annexation, and if refused, of adopting the extreme course of attempting to realise their public propaganda.

I think this, from a South African point of view, the most serious aspect of the Seretse case. Its gravity for the whole Commonwealth must be evident. South African public opinion might be mobilised in favour of a republic because of the Seretse affair and the refusal of annexation of the Territory thereafter.

I believe the feud between Tshekedi[1] and the Seretse factions is another plausible excuse which the British Government may have for banishing both from the Territory. Whether they will make use of this I cannot at present say. But from all this you will see that the Seretse case in its full implications is full of dynamite, and I think it would be a mistake to exploit British feeling in favour of Seretse to an extent which may damage the relations of South Africa to the Commonwealth and the Commonwealth itself.

I would therefore counsel caution in this matter, as it may raise an issue between South Africa and Britain which I am naturally most anxious to avoid. I assume this is an expression of my opinion which you want to have.[2]

Winston S. Churchill to Lieutenant-General Sir Henry Pownall
(Churchill papers, 4/281)

20 March 1950

THE STORY OF THE DIEPPE RAID

I agree that it is much better in the Return to Cairo chapter on account of chronology, and I am having it reprinted in its present form to come in for the May 1 delivery. There is a lot more to be said about it than you have included in your military accounts, and some very large questions are involved. There is

---

[1] Tshekedi Khama, 1905–59. Uncle of Seretse Khama. In 1926, became Regent of Bechuanaland because his nephew, the king, was only 4 years old. Educated at Fort Hare University, South Africa, 1923–5. Opposed his nephew's marriage to Ruth Williams.
[2] Churchill responded: 'Thank you so much.'

both interest and controversy in Canada on the subject, and Mountbatten has taken a strong line, claiming all the responsibility, which surely is more than he need bear. We have two or three months in which to complete the tale, and I shall be very glad if you will assemble all the material for me.

According to my recollection we had prepared this large descent as a specimen raid on a great scale. Please see my remarks at Moscow. 'It was to be like putting your hand into a bath and seeing how hot it was.' But there is a lot more of great interest in it. There was first of all the plan Jubilee.[1] It was to have been launched in July, or at the beginning of August. Montgomery was charged with the military preparations, and played an important part while holding the Southern Command (?). All was ready. The troops were put on board ship under sealed orders. Then, owing to weather or some misgivings, the operation was cancelled after all the ten thousand men embarked had been told about it. I was not consulted about the resumption. I am sure I should have been very much worried by the ten thousand men knowing all about it and being dispersed through the southern ports with their deadly knowledge. You cannot help people talking, especially after they think the show is off. I think I had already started for Cairo and Moscow when the decision to renew the operation was taken. Certainly I heard about it and did not oppose it. There is no doubt Mountbatten pressed most strongly for it, and I expect you will find that the War Cabinet gave their assent in my absence.

Montgomery has strong views about this and declares that he never accepted the slightest responsibility for the military side of the operation after the first attempt was cancelled. His part in the affair requires careful elucidation. He has very strong views on the subject, which he expressed to me with great vigour a year or so ago. All this must be carefully explored.

It seems to me almost certain that surprise was destroyed by leakages, and that the Germans knew we were going to attempt a big descent at Dieppe. How big of course they could not tell. The Dieppe harbour lay out had not been well studied. There were all those caves on the side of the harbour in which people have lived for hundreds of years, but which made splendid machine gun and AT gun posts. A deadly fire came from these. One night when I was talking about this business to Mrs Churchill (who spent several years of her youth at Dieppe), she spoke about these caves and said what a help they would be to the enemy. I have seen them myself when landing at Dieppe. The whole cliff is pock-marked. Was there any mention of these in the plans of the second attempt, or the first attempt?

It will be necessary for the whole story to be told. It cannot merely be a narrative of the actual military events. How it happened. Why it was done. Who was responsible? Was there a leakage? What part did Mountbatten and Montgomery play? All these are the matters which people want to know about.

---

[1] 'Jubilee' (formerly Rutter): British and Canadian landing at Dieppe, planned Apr. 1942 for implementation at the end of June 1942, eventually carried out on 19 Aug. 1942.

Where different bodies of attacking troops landed and how they fared is only secondary in importance. This is a great controversial issue and may conceivably need a chapter by itself. However please get all the material together and study it yourself. Meanwhile I am printing your account at the end of the chapter Return to Cairo, and we will hand it in in this form in the May 1 delivery. It could never come in the middle of my picnic in the Desert as proposed. It is a very grave matter.

It may be possible perhaps to bind the Dieppe Raid and the final Rommel attack into a chapter by themselves. They have certainly got to be described and cannot be omitted. But they are both pretty big stuff. Please let me know what you think of all this.

General Lord Ismay to Winston S. Churchill
(*Churchill papers, 4/281*)

22 March 1950

Many thanks for letting me see the minute which you have sent to Pownall about the Dieppe raid. I agree with every word of it, and I am writing to Pownall to say that I will gladly co-operate in producing the material for it.

Meanwhile, my recollection is that you had approved the raid in principle before you left for Cairo, but that the decision to launch the operation was taken after you had left. Mountbatten certainly pressed hard for it, but he did not have the deciding voice; nor should he claim, or be saddled with the sole responsibility.

My general impression is that it was not one of our most creditable ventures, because the underlying object was never sufficiently clearly defined; nor, so far as I can remember, was the chain of responsibility. I do not, in fact, believe that we deserved success: though I would not go so far as to say that the results achieved were in the long run not worth the sacrifice. There was the experience gained, there was a considerable air battle in our favour, and the psychological effect of our taking the offensive on a fairly large scale was probably good.

Winston S. Churchill: speech
(*Hansard*)

28 March 1950   House of Commons

EUROPEAN UNITY

I notice, Mr Speaker, that you looked to the other side of the House, and I certainly fully comprehend the motives which led you to look in that direction. I am sorry that the Foreign Secretary was not willing to open this Debate

— (Hon Members: 'Where is he?') — by making a general statement on foreign affairs to the new House of Commons. I should have thought that when a new Parliament assembled, the chief representatives of His Majesty's Government, either the Foreign Secretary or the Prime Minister, would welcome the opportunity of laying before us a full statement of their policy and theme. Nor can I recall any situation in which such guidance was more imperatively demanded, not only by the Opposition, but still more by the movement of events.

However, our request has been rejected. The object, I suppose, was a manoeuvre or tactics to draw whoever spoke for the Opposition into a statement of their views and then to pick out such odd points as emerged for debating purposes — and this on the subject of foreign affairs, which surely should be and can be lifted above the untimely and costly party struggles to which we are now condemned. In all the main issues of foreign policy the opposition in the late Parliament supported, sustained and even pointed the course which the Foreign Secretary has pursued.

Then we were weak; now we are equals — almost. But our intention is to give the same help to His Majesty's Government in foreign affairs as we did in the years when we were helplessly outnumbered. In fact, it will be stronger help numerically. The Foreign Secretary need not, therefore — I trust that he is not in any way indisposed — (Hon Members: 'Where is he?') — but it does seem to me that as he is going to reply to the Debate one would have had the opportunity of his attention at this moment.

The right hon. Gentlemen need not be afraid — perhaps someone will tell him when they see him — that any decision which he makes in the national interest will be obstructed or baffled by the votes of those over whom he has a majority numbered only by digits. On the contrary, he may feel assured that so long as he marches forward on the broad lines of policy on which we have been agreed, he has overwhelming Parliamentary support. The fact that the Government have a precarious existence need in no way hamper him. The fact that we lie between General Elections need not induce him, or whoever is to take his place, to take weak courses or play for small party gains. We do not intend that the national interest at a time so anxious and critical as this shall suffer from the equipoise of political parties. But let us make sure where our national interest lies and how our part in shaping world affairs can best be played.

I do not intend this afternoon to occupy too much time in the Debate in which so many Members wish to take part. I shall, therefore, not refer to a great many topics and episodes which are in our minds or attempt to deal myself with the Far Eastern problems, which, although they may be touched upon in this Debate, are so urgent and serious as to require a separate Debate as soon as opportunity can be found. I shall now only attempt to deal with the crucial and cardinal aspects of the Western scene. I select the key problems, namely, the relations between Britain and France, acting together, and Germany, and of the bearing of all this upon Western Europe, its life, its hopes and its self-defence. The whole of this discussion, of course, and the whole of my argument are sustained by the decisive strength of the United States as expressed by the Atlantic Pact. Thereafter it is my duty to refer to the relations of the Western democratic world with Soviet Russia. I am most anxious that the tremendous issues with which we are now confronted should be presented in a simple form.

The Prime Minister accused me last week of 'irresponsibility' in raising the question of Germany – by which I mean liberated Germany – taking any part in Western defence. My feeling is, and I hope the Prime Minister will allow me to say so, that I am as good a judge of these matters as he is. Certainly I should not like to be responsible for not stating my true and faithful belief and counsel to the House, as I have done several times in the past when it was not particularly popular to do so. I remember that during the last Parliament, not to go too far back, I made a speech at Fulton which became the object of a Motion of Censure signed, I think, by more than 100 Members of the Socialist Party. But shortly afterwards, the policy I had advocated was adopted on both sides of the Atlantic and by all parties in this House. So I shall not feel myself utterly extinguished by the Prime Minister's censure.

The Prime Minister also complained that such a question as that of Germany aiding in Western defence should have been 'injected' – that is the word he used, 'injected' – into a Debate on defence, but that was surely its natural and obvious place in the first instance. Other hon. Members, notably the hon. Member for Coventry East (Mr Crossman), whom I see in his place, misquoted what I said and then criticized the distorted version. I picked my words very carefully and I do not wish to modify them in any way today. I said nothing about the rearmament of Germany or about recreating the German Army, but I see no reason why the Germans should not aid in the defence of their own country and of Western Europe, or why British, American, French and German soldiers should not stand in the line together on honourable terms of comradeship as part of a combined system of defence.

I try to pursue, as it seems to me, a steady theme and my thought as far as I can grasp it, is all of one piece. It is the building up of effective forces of resistance to tyranny and aggression in any form, or from any quarter. The House of Commons is the foe of tyrants, whatever uniform they wear, whatever formulas they use. We must discern their character in good time and labour to resist their force with all our strength. But I am not concerned today only, or even mainly, with the military aspect. We are nearly all of us now agreed in seeking the unity and restoration of Europe as a great hope for the future. We cannot do this without the aid of the Germans. The strong German race, which, during the last forty years, we and our Allies twice fought and defeated, have now the opportunity of rendering an immense service to mankind. Having submitted to internal tyranny and brought measureless suffering upon us all, and especially themselves, they now have a chance of redeeming the German name by helping to repair what has happened in the past and by playing their part – and it might be a great one – in lifting the civilization of Europe to a level where its old glories may revive and where the various forms of tolerant freedom and resulting happiness and culture may be restored. There can be no hope for a United Europe without Germany, and there is no hope for Germany except within a free and United Europe. How can these vital conditions be achieved? Here is a problem in which you may wander around all sorts of tangled labyrinths of thought, but you will come back to the overpowering fact that Europe cannot be restored without the active aid of Germany and that without a restored Europe world peace cannot be established on sure foundations.

When I spoke at Zurich nearly four years ago, I said it would be the proud duty of France to stretch forth her hand and lead Germany back into the European family. I said at the time that this statement would create astonishment, and it certainly did. But since then we have made great progress. The whole structure of Western Union has developed. We thank the Foreign Secretary for the part he has played in it. We are presently to have a meeting at Strasbourg of the Council of Europe and the Assembly where, we trust, in spite of all that has happened, French and German hands will be clasped in concord. I recommend to the House that we should do all in our power to encourage and promote Franco-German reconciliation as an approach to unity, or even perhaps some form, in some aspects, of union. Let anyone who can take a point on this beware how he mocks at such themes. But France, after her tribulations and in her present disturbed condition, may not be strong enough to accomplish single-handed her mission. That is why the intimate and inseparable relationship between Britain and France and between the British Empire and Commonwealth of Nations and France must be affirmed and asserted continually in the most effective manner. France and Britain, both sorely distressed, can combine together and, thus joined, have the superior power to raise Germany, even more shattered, to an equal rank and to lasting association with them.

Then these three countries, helping each other, conscious of their future united greatness, forgetting ancient feuds and the horrible deeds and tragedies of the past, can make the core or the nucleus upon which all the other civilized democracies of Europe, bond or free, can one day rally and combine. Woe be it to anyone in the free world, who, by lack of understanding, or by lack of goodwill, or by lack of world hope, or any more flagrant fault or blunder, obstructs or delays this essential combination. There was a time when men thought that the conception of a United States of Europe would be resented by the United States of America, but now we have the American people, with their own heavy burdens to bear, sacrificing themselves and using all their power and authority to bring about this very system. In this lies the hope of the Western world and its power to promote beneficial solutions, perhaps, of what happens in Asia.

I do not wish to fall into vague generalities. Let me, therefore, express our policy as I see it in a single sentence. Britain and France united should stretch forth hands of friendship to Germany, and thus, if successful, enable Europe to live again. I am distressed when I read in the newspapers, for I have no other information on these matters except my own knowledge, about petty obstructive vexations which hamper this grand design. We read of the belated blowing up of the tail-end of the German munition factories; and of the trial of aged and decrepit German field-marshals. We read on the other hand of an impudent Goebbels film improperly released in the American zone at which Germans cheer anti-British propaganda. How easy it is to mar large unities, how hard to make them. We in this House and in these islands must rise above these pettinesses. It may well be that our safety depends on our proving ourselves capable of doing so. Follies on one side lead to misbehaviour on the other. Europe, at this moment of resurgence, cannot afford to make silly mistakes, or, if they are made, allow them to darken her thought or divert her aim. We here have all been busy in a General Election, and over us hangs another with all its preoccupations for our divided and harassed land. But meanwhile many things are happening abroad which should not pass unnoticed or unmeasured.

Almost the same time that I spoke in the defence Debate a statement was being made by General de Gaulle on Franco-German relations. As the House knows, I have not always seen eye to eye with that patriotic Frenchman, who represented in the war more than any other man the will to live of France. Certainly there is no one in France who could have opposed with more vigour and injurious effect the reconciliation between French and German people. He represents the most powerful forces which could have been arrayed on the wrong side. But what did he say? He spoke of the proposal which Dr Adenauer[1] had just made for an economic union between France and Germany. I shall read his words. He said:

> I have followed for thirty years the ideas of the German Chancellor. In what this good German has said I have found the echo of the call of Europe.

Relations between the two countries must be viewed against a European

---

[1] Konrad Adenauer, 1876–1967. Studied Law at Universities of Freiburg, Munich and Bonn. Practised law, Cologne, from 1900. Deputy Mayor, Cologne, 1906; Senior Deputy Mayor, 1909; Lord Mayor, 1917–33, 1945. Member, Provincial Diet of Rhine Province, 1917–18. Member, Executive Committee of Centre Party, 1917–33. Member, Prussian Herrenhaus, 1917–18. Member, Prussian State Council, 1918–33; President, 1926–33. Dismissed from all offices by Goering, 1933. Imprisoned for political reasons, 1933, 1944. Member and President, Parliamentary Council of Bonn, 1948–9. Member, German Council of European Movement, 1949. Chancellor, Federal Republic of Germany, 1949–63; President, 1950–66; Foreign Minister, 1951–5.

background. In short the Grand Design of Charlemagne must be readapted to modern conditions. General de Gaulle went on:

> Why would not the Rhine become a street where Europeans meet, rather than a ditch dividing hostile camps?

I must say that when I read this statement in the newspapers I hoped that it might be received throughout Europe, as it has been here in the House, to quote the lines of Rupert Brooke,[1] 'with the silence followed great words of peace'.

It certainly was treated with the utmost respect throughout the Continent. Some will call Dr Adenauer's proposal for an economic union between Germany and France premature, unsure, only partly thought out. Surely, however, it lies near the root of the matter. What we want is far more than that, but these two speeches by General de Gaulle and Dr Adenauer together constitute a memorable event.

Here is the forward path along which we must march if the thousand-year feud between Gaul and Teuton is to pass from its fierce destructive life into the fading romance of history. Here are two men who have fought and struggled on opposite sides through the utmost stresses of our times and both see clearly the guidance they should give. Do not let all this be cast away for small thoughts and wasteful recriminations and memories which, if they are not to be buried, may ruin the lives of our children and our children's children. It may be that this year, 1950, on which we have entered in so much perplexity and dispute, can be made the occasion for launching Europe on its voyage to peace with honour. Let us make sure that we play our part in turning thought into action and action into fame.

I am very glad to see the right hon. Gentleman the Secretary of State for Foreign Affairs. I can assure him that he has a great fund of goodwill among all parties. We know what a burden he has had to bear. Some of us had to bear that burden for five years; he has borne it at the same tenseness for ten. We speak of him always with great feelings of personal regard although it is our duty to criticize errors in the conduct of foreign policy rather than in its inspiration which come to our notice. I hope to hear from the Foreign Secretary tonight that no British party will fall behind in its duty in the European cause. People say that all these are visionary and sentimental ideas which ignore the practical realities. They say that they blot out the lessons of the past and the difficulties of the present and thus will have no real application for the future. But it is a great mistake to suppose that nations are not led by sentiment. It takes too poor a view of man's mission here on earth to suppose that he is not capable of rising, to his material detriment far above his day-to-day

---

[1] Rupert Chawner Brooke, 1887–1915. President, Cambridge University Fabian Society, 1907. 2nd Lt, Royal Naval Div., Sep. 1914; served at Antwerp. Died of blood poisoning on his way to the Dardanelles, 23 Apr. 1915. Churchill's obituary of Brooke was published in *The Times*, 26 Apr. 1915.

surroundings. The dominant forces in human history have come from the perception of great truths and the faithful pursuance of great causes.

I have always held that the cause of united Europe would not be helped, and might well be injured, by attempts to draw up precise and rigid constitutions and agreements too soon or in a hurry. The first stage is to create a friendly atmosphere and feeling of mutual confidence and respect. Even a day's delay in working hard for this is a matter for regret. Once the foundation of common interest and solidarity of sentiment has been laid it may well be that formal agreements would take the form, not of hard bargains or weak compromises, but of setting down on paper the living basic truths and thoughts which were in all minds. Then difficulties at present insuperable might well become irrelevant.

In this field it is a practical and immediate step that can be taken, namely the arrival at Strasbourg this summer of a German delegation to the European Assembly of the Council of Europe. More than two years have passed since the Germans came to The Hague on the invitation of our unofficial European movement. I had an agreeable and, to me, a memorable interview with them. It was there I met Dr Adenauer, little knowing how soon he would be the German Chancellor at the head of a German Government. Since then great forward steps have been taken. The Council of Europe and the European Assembly are institutions formally and permanently established; young, but august; sustained by many freely elected Parliaments. The presence of Germany in our midst will be an event from which nothing but good can come. It would be a great pity if doubts and further delays were caused by boggling and haggling, or the drawing up of conditions. I was sorry to see that the Germans had written out a number of conditions on which they would be prepared to join the Council of Europe. That is falling below the level of events.

Many voices are raised of provocation and false counsel on every side. I sincerely hope that Dr Adenauer will show that the new Germany can rise superior to such distractions, no matter how or whence they come. I am glad to see that there is better news about this today, but I would say to the Germans, 'Let it all happen naturally and easily, and you will find that very soon Germany will take her proper place, and that all questions of legalistic status will cease to be of any importance.'

I have one more observation to make about the European Assembly. Substantial results flowed from that Assembly at Strasbourg last year. But the contrast between the activities of the Assembly and the apparent inaction of the Committee of Ministers has created the impression that the Ministers are not whole-hearted in their intention to promote the Union of Europe. Whether this impression is correct or incorrect it is gaining ground, and I say to the right hon. Gentleman, who is off on a journey there tonight, that only some positive unequivocal pronouncement by the Committee of Ministers when it meets next week can undo it. The situation is especially serious because our own position is called in question. It is widely thought on the Continent and in America that the British Government are lacking in zeal for the whole plan – 'dragging their feet' is, I believe, the American expression. It is said that on the Committee of Ministers the Foreign Secretary is always amongst those who wish to advance less far and less fast. This is what is widely believed and it tends to weaken our general influence in Europe. I hope that the right hon gentleman will clear away these misgivings when he speaks this afternoon.

It would certainly be ungracious on my part if I left the subject without acknowledging the services rendered by the recent Colombo Conference in proclaiming that there is no incompatibility or inconsistency between Britain's part in a United Europe and her position as the centre and pivot of the British Empire. Now I come to the last aspect of what I wish to say.

I come to our relations with Soviet Russia. I will begin by stating the reason why I do not believe that another war is imminent or inevitable, and why I believe that we have the time, if we use it wisely, and the hope of warding off that frightful catastrophe from our struggling, ill-informed and almost helpless human race. Here is the reason. There never was a time when the deterrents against war were so strong. If penalties of the most drastic kind can prevent in our civil life crime or folly, then we certainly have them here on a gigantic scale in the affairs of nations. It is extraordinary. The penalties have grown to an extent undreamed of; and at the same time many of the old incentives which were the cause of the beginnings of so many wars, or featured in their beginning, have lost their significance. The desire for glory, booty, territory, dynastic or national aggrandisement; hopes of a speedy and splendid victory with all its excitement – and they are all temptations from which even those who only fight for righteous causes are not always exempt – are now superseded by a preliminary stage of measureless agony from which neither side could at present protect itself.

Another world war would begin by both sides suffering as the first step what they dread most. Western Europe would be overrun and Communized, with all that liquidation of the outstanding non-Communist personnel of all classes, of which I understand in respect of several countries elaborate lists have already been prepared – and which are, no doubt, kept up to date in those countries by the Communist groups and parties in their midst. That is one side. On the other hand, at the same time, Soviet cities, air-fields, oil-fields and railway junctions would be annihilated; with possible complete disruption of Kremlin control over the enormous populations who are ruled from Moscow. These fearful cataclysms would be simultaneous, and neither side could at present, or for several years to come, prevent them. Moralists may find it a melancholy thought that peace can find no nobler foundations than mutual terror. But for my part I shall be content if these foundations are solid, because they will give us the extra time and the new breathing space for the supreme effort which has to be made for a world settlement.

No one need delude himself by underrating the difficulties which stand in the way of a settlement or by closing his eyes to the gulf which yawns between the two worlds, now facing each other, armed and arming, reaching out for agencies which might eventually destroy the human race. As I said at Boston last year, I think it probable that the Soviet Government fear the friendship of the West even more than they do our hostility. The Soviet regime and the lives of its rulers might be imperilled by allowing free, easy and friendly intermingling with the outer world. An endless series of quarrels, a vehement and violent antagonism, the consciousness of an outside enemy in the minds of the masses, may be regarded by the Soviet as a necessary precautionary element in maintaining the existence of the Communist power. There indeed is a gloomy thought. There indeed is a reason for fear. But fear must never be allowed to cast out hope.

During the election I was most anxious that the return of a Conservative Government to power, which was a possibility, should not be taken as involving an exacerbation of the already tense situation that exists, and that we should make it clear above all things that we should strive faithfully for peace. I also felt, and feel, that we owe it to our consciences, all of us, that no door should be closed which may lead to better prospects. I do not, of course, take an over-sanguine view of the position whatever efforts are made, but it is our Christian duty to try our best. Moreover, the democracies of the West must be constantly convinced that those who lead them do not despair of peace if they are to take even the measures which self-preservation demands in case the worst should come to the worst.

Let me repeat what I said at Edinburgh[1] – only a few lines:

> I cannot help coming back to this idea of another talk with Soviet Russia upon the highest level. The idea appeals to me of a supreme effort to bridge the gulf between the two worlds so that each can live their life, if not in friendship at least without the hatreds of the cold war.

I was answered by the Foreign Secretary that all this was a 'stunt'. Whatever this American college slang, as I find it is described in the dictionary, may have implied, it did not seem to me completely to dispose of the subject which had been raised. He also said that through the United Nations must be found our only process and resource. But three days later, on 17 February, at a Press conference at Lake Success, Mr Trygve Lie,[2] the Secretary

---

[1] Speech reproduced above (pp. 1642–50).
[2] Trygve Halvdan Lie, 1896–1968. Educated at Oslo University, 1919. Asst Secretary, Norwegian Labour party, 1919–22. Legal Adviser to Trade Union Federation, 1922–35. Member, Norwegian Parliament, 1935. Minister of Trade, Industry, Shipping and Fishing, 1939–40. Acting Foreign Minister, 1940. Foreign Minister, 1941. Norwegian delegation, UN General Assembly in London, 1946. UN Secretary-General, 1946–53. Governor of Oslo and Akershus, 1955.

General of UNO, said he was in favour of great Power negotiations:

> All the time and on all levels – top level, middle level and lower level – inside and outside the United Nations. This world would be a lot better today if there had been more real negotiations among the great Powers during the past three years.

He added, what we shall all agree:

> The only people who can rightly judge the timing and form of negotiations and meetings are those who are responsible for conducting the foreign affairs of the countries concerned.

We are all agreed, but those who are responsible, as the right hon. Gentleman and his principal colleagues are, must not fail to seize any opportunities. We cannot go on with a policy of hesitation and drift. Every day is precious if the chance occurs.

I have explained this afternoon the arguments on which I base my belief that a further spell of time will be granted to us. Even at the risk of afterwards being reproached for being wrong, I have not hesitated to state my view that it may well be that several years may pass before a war breaks out. I will take the chance of making that remark although I have no special information at my disposal. Certainly we must seek to negotiate from strength and not from weakness. We all agree on that. Certainly we must move hand in hand with our Allies, and above all with the United States, as the right hon. Gentleman has so far done. We should do well to study the recent and most important announcements on foreign policy by the American Secretary of State, Mr Acheson, whose gifts and services are so widely recognized. And here let me say how warmly we welcome in this House the news that that great American statesman, Senator Vandenberg, has recovered from his grievous operation and is able to exert again his clarifying and elevating influence on world events. The American people are fortunate in finding so many outstanding figures at the time when they hold the leading place among the nations.

But if there is a breathing space, if there is more time, as I feel and do not hesitate to say, it would be a grave mistake of a different order, perhaps a fatal mistake, to suppose that, even if we have this interlude, it will last for ever, or even last more than a few years. Time and patience, those powerful though not infallible solvents of human difficulties, are not necessarily on our side. When the last Parliament met, I mentioned four years as the period before any other Power but the United States would possess the atomic bomb. That period has already gone by, and our position is definitely worse than it was in this matter both as regards our own safety and as to the conditions which are, I believe, effectively preserving the peace of the world.

There is no doubt now that the passage of time will place these fearful agencies of destruction effectively in Soviet hands, that is to say, where there is no customary, traditional, moral or religious restraint. Of course, there is an interlude between the discovery of the secret and the effective large-scale production of the article, and that also has to be borne in mind. Of course, the United States have their 'stockpile', as it is called, and it will be only by a gradual process that anything similar can be built up in Soviet Russia. The atomic bomb, though preponderating, is only one of the factors in the military situation before us, but it is the dominant factor. If, for instance, the United States had a 'stockpile' of 1,000 atomic bombs – I take the figure as an illustration merely; I have no knowledge of any sort or kind of what they have – and Russia had fifty, and we got those fifty, fearful experiences, far beyond anything we have ever endured, would be our lot. Therefore, while I believe there is time for a further effort for a lasting and peaceful settlement, I cannot feel that it is necessarily a long time or that its passage will progressively improve our own security. Above all things, we must not fritter it away. For every reason, therefore, I earnestly hope that we shall hear from the Foreign Secretary a clear exposition of the facts and policy of His Majesty's Government upon matters graver than anything which human history records.

Man in this moment of his history has emerged in greater supremacy over the forces of nature than has ever been dreamed of before. He has it in his power to solve quite easily the problems of material existence. He has conquered the wild beasts, and he has even conquered the insects and the microbes. There lies before him, as he wishes, a golden age of peace and progress. All is in his hand. He has only to conquer his last and worst enemy – himself. With vision, faith and courage, it may still be within our power to win a crowning victory for all.

Winston S. Churchill to Patrick Buchan-Hepburn
(Churchill papers, 2/64)

29 March 1950

I propose to set up a committee of the Consultative Committee to go into all the questions open between Conservatives and Liberals and to see what can be done to secure greater unity among the forces opposed to Socialism.

This Committee would be under the Chairmanship of Mr Butler, and have as members Mr Harold Macmillan, Mr Duncan Sandys and Mr James Stuart. They would work in the closest concert with Lord Woolton who would come whenever he desired.

We must have the whole of this position studied with close attention from the House of Commons' angle.

Winston S. Churchill to Duke of Marlborough[1]
(Churchill papers, 1/48)

30 March 1950

My dear Bert,

I have found another version of the Blenheim Tapestry picture, but it requires some re-touching, including particularly the hind-legs of Cadogan's[2] horse as he gallops away, before it is fit to be seen. I cannot do this till the Easter holidays, after which I will send it to you, if it is not ruined in the process.

Meanwhile I send you another picture which I think was done in Blenheim Lake. Perhaps this will do till the other one is ready. It will reach you by Friday.

---

[1] John Albert Edward William Spencer-Churchill, 1897–1972. Elder son of Churchill's cousin the 9th Duke of Marlborough and Consuelo Vanderbilt (Balsan). Marquess of Blandford. Capt., 1st Life Guards, 1916; retired, 1927. Succeeded his father as 10th Duke of Marlborough, 1934. Mayor of Woodstock, 1937–42. Military Liaison Officer to the Regional Commander, Southern Region, 1942. Lt-Col., Liaison Officer, US Forces in Britain, 1942–5. In 1972, shortly before his death, he married, as his second wife, Mrs Laura Canfield, formerly Countess of Dudley and Viscountess Long.

[2] William Cadogan, 1671–1726. Educated at Westminster College and Trinity College Dublin. Maj., Inniskilling Dragoons, 1701. QMG to Earl of Marlborough, 1701. Duke of Marlborough's CoS, 1704. Lt-Gen., 1709. KT, 1716. Earl, 1718. Governor of the Isle of Wight, 1715–26. Master-General of the Ordinance, 1722–5.

April 1950

Winston S. Churchill to Lord Camrose
(*Churchill papers, 4/13*)

3 April 1950

My dear Bill,

I shall be able to deliver Volume IV to you before May 1 for the fourth instalment. It will be in a condition which is far more advanced than Volume III was this time last year. It will be capable of improvement in the three or four following months. These improvements would not be noticed by the public or affect the serialization, but they would add to the merit of the work and thus please the author and perhaps the readers. I gather that *Life* want the serials of Volume IV to begin in October. I have not been told when, in this case, the volume publication would begin. Houghton Mifflin are publishing Volume III at the end of April, 1950, and Cassells not until July. The early date of Houghton Mifflin is, I suppose, dictated by the 'Book of the Month' arrangements. I am anxious that Volume IV should also be the 'Book of the Month'. Most of us think that Volume IV is better than Volume III. Will not this be prejudiced by trying to have two Books of the Month in one calendar year? Although I can probably work to a middle of August delivery of Volume IV, I do not know why there is all this hurry. However if there are special reasons for the serials of Volume IV beginning in October I expect I could cut the improvements down so as to be ready at that date. The above is still influenced by the political uncertainty.

It is certain now that if I live and have my liberty, the book will be six volumes. I was glad to learn the other night that full payment will be made for the fifth Volume. For the sixth volume I understand that the *Daily Telegraph*, Cassells, Houghton Mifflin and Reves will pay £50,000. Out of this I shall take my £35,000 for the expenses of my book production staff, etc., and £15,000 loan will go to the Trust or be used to pay off the £15,000 loan to the *Daily Telegraph*. However all this is becoming highly speculative. We must not try to look too far ahead.

I enclose you a copy of a letter I have had from Reves and my answer to it. Please note that he advises that a definite statement should be made at the time of the publication of Volume IV that the total work will be six volumes. It is also interesting to see what Adler said (para. 6) to him at luncheon, so perhaps after all they will do something. Pray let me know whether there are any points which are not clear between us.

Winston S. Churchill to Commander Robert Allan[1]
(Churchill papers, 2/90)

5 April 1950

Dear Commander Allan,

Twice you have come within an ace of winning over West Dumbartonshire to the Unionist cause. As a gifted son of the County, with your grand record in the war, you are the man to represent the Division in Parliament in the critical days that lie before us.

Our country is reaping the consequences of five years of Socialist misgovernment. The ever rising cost of living that hits no one more hardly than the harassed housewife; the Government's failure to build sufficient houses or to let others build them; the steadily diminishing value of the Social Services; the restraints imposed by taxation on personal saving and industrial expansion; the daily frustrations to which we are all subjected; all these evils spring from the spendthrift and incompetent administration and the attempt to apply the fallacious doctrines of Socialism to our complex island life.

The glaring failure of Nationalization and the condemnation of the Electors stare the Socialist Government in the face. But even now they persist in trying to nationalize steel and add it to the debit side of British industry centralized at Whitehall.

The Unionist policy for recovery is plain and practical. We shall reduce Government expenditure and lighten taxation so as to increase incentives all round especially to the most skilled and industrious wage-earners. We believe that this can be done without hardship to those who need the help that subsidies and the Social Services afford; and that by stopping the fall in the buying power of our money we can help all.

As a Unionist you stand for the fruitful policies to which we have committed ourselves in our Election Manifesto 'This is the Road'. The electors of West Dumbartonshire must know by now that no good can come from prolonging

[1] Robert Alexander Allan, 1914–79. Educated at Harrow and Clare College, Cambridge. Lt, RNVR, July 1939. Cdr, 1943; Senior Officer, Inshore Sqn, 1944–5. Deputy Chief of Naval Information, Washington DC, 1945–6. During WWII, posted to HMS *Mosquito* at Alexandria in Egypt; commanded 10th Flotilla of motor torpedo boats. Parliamentary candidate (Union.) for Dunbartonshire, 1945; for West Dumbartonshire, 1950. Married, 1947, Maureen Catherine Stuart-Clark: two children. MP (Cons.) for South Paddington, 1951–66. Asst Whip, 1953–5. Parliamentary Private Secretary to PM, 1955–8. Life Peer, 1973.

from day to day the impotent and precarious life of a discredited Government. By returning you to the House of Commons they will bring nearer the day when a Unionist Government will take firm charge of the nation's affairs at home and abroad and lead Britain back to greatness.

Jo Sturdee to Winston S. Churchill
(Churchill papers, 2/90)

12 April 1950

The Central Office telephoned this morning with particulars of the Dumbarton Bye-Election campaign.

The Conservative candidate, Commander Allan, is still hors de combat with appendicitis, but they think he will be in action again in six or seven days. Mrs Allan[1] is taking meetings for him. Our candidate is receiving help from Mr Eden, Sir David Maxwell Fyfe, Sir William Darling, Mr Walter Elliot, Mr Lennox-Boyd and Dr Charles Hill.[2] There is no shortage of local speakers also.

Generally speaking it is difficult to get the interest going and the campaign is very cool. There may be a much-reduced poll. Commander Allan's Election Address is being printed together with a Broadsheet and a large distribution of leaflets and posters is going ahead. Canvassing has already started and it is hoped there will be a full canvass of the constituency as time goes on. They hope to let you have some figures in a day or two.

The candidate has received a questionnaire from the Liberals and has returned a satisfactory reply. He hopes to get most of the Liberal support.

<u>Prospects</u>. At the last Election there was a Socialist majority of 600 votes over us. Now the Communist candidate, who polled 1,500 votes last time, is almost certainly not standing – so we start with 2,000 votes against us. There is apathy and lack of interest. And of course we are handicapped by the candidate's illness. It is a much bigger hurdle than the figures show. Polling Day is April 25.

---

[1] Maureen Catherine Stuart-Clark. Married, 1947, Robert Allan: two children. Her son, Sir Alex Allan, became Chairman of the Joint Intelligence Committee.

[2] Charles Hill, 1904–89. Born in Islington, London. Educated at St Olave's Grammar School and Trinity College, Cambridge. MP (Cons. and Nat. Lib.) for Luton, 1950–63. Postmaster General, 1955–7. Chancellor of the Duchy of Lancaster, 1957–61. Baron, 1963. Chairman, Independent Television Authority, 1963–7; BBC Board of Governors, 1967–72.

Winston S. Churchill to President Harry S Truman
(Churchill papers, 4/55)[1]

16 April 1950   Chartwell

My dear Harry,

Only our friendship entitles me to send you one of the earliest copies of my new Volume III on the War, and to warn you that you may have to face in future years IV, V and even possibly six. Forgive me.

Winston S. Churchill to Bernard Baruch
(Churchill papers, 4/55)[2]

16 April 1950   Chartwell

My dear Bernie,

Herewith another Volume is inflicted on yr good nature. There are more to come in future years, if the world goes on – for me, or for itself. It well may.

Winston S. Churchill to Clementine Churchill
(Baroness Spencer-Churchill papers)[3]

18 April 1950

My darling one,

Randolph, June & little W came for the night. All passed off well, but there is evident tension. She never looked prettier, but is on the verge of tears. R I thought seemed 'masterful'. However I think they mean to have another try.

I am so sorry that you have had disappointing weather.[4] I do hope you have enjoyed the change of scene & the relief of household cares, & that you will come back refreshed. I have passed a peaceful ten days at the Chart, & plunged deeply into my task of finishing Vol IV. One page leads to another & three new chapters have come to life. I never had a chance to squeeze a tube to any purpose. Mary & Christopher were a blessing and often came to meals. The days flashed away & now here I am back in 28 w the Budget opening upon us, and crisis prowling around the corner, and the Primrose League & Reading Dinner hanging like vultures overhead.

I have thought much about you my sweet darling, and it will be a joy to have you back. Your flowers are growing beautifully on the Chartwell balcony & here the cherry tree is a mass of blossom. All yr arrangements

---
[1] This letter was handwritten.
[2] This letter was handwritten.
[3] This letter was handwritten.
[4] Clementine, accompanied by her secretary Penelope Hampden-Wall, was on a tour of Italy.

have worked perfectly in yr absence, and no one cd have been more comfortable than yr P.

PS. The Chartwell Bulletin is attd. & will give you more news. I hope to see you before the week is out. x x x

CHARTWELL BULLETIN

Before he went to Cannes Anthony Eden said that the hawthorn had come out early and that this was a sure sign of cold weather. This was the only thing he knew about the weather. Certainly it turned out true. We have had sunshine and showers but the temperature is very low.

The waterfalls and filters are all running in good order. As coke is off the ration it would be possible to heat the swimming pool this year, but this would mean erecting the chimney again, or at least half of it – eight feet. As the old tree has been cut down there is no cover for it, and I am sure it would offend everyone's eye. Moreover I myself cannot bathe, so I have not done anything about it. Although the pool has not been cleaned out, the water is very clear.

All the fish, big and small, and the ten black swans are well and send their compliments. The father swan has fallen in love with one of his daughters, and I think they mean to make a nest on the island. We are watching this most carefully. The other three (outside the Iron Curtain) are friendly with each other, and Papa only comes to be fed. Four of the ten now eat readily from the hand and also pinch my fingers.

On Saturday week I went round the farms with Christopher. I was very much impressed by the improvements made and the tidiness. The overhanging branches have been cut almost everywhere and a large part of the Bardogs and Chartwell Farms have been ditched and hedged. A good plan of cultivation is on foot, approved by Mr Cox who is most helpful. Bardogs, especially the farthest part of it, is immensely improved. The land one turns down to the right after leaving Bardogs has been completely stripped of its overhanging branches and trees and is now quite open country – a great improvement. There is still a good deal more to be done.

Even greater improvement is taking place in the quality of the two milking herds. At Bardogs there are forty-five calves from a month to eighteen months old. All are pedigree and will be worth far more than their predecessors. There are twelve jerseys in milk, looking very well and pretty. Altogether it is a very fine show up there and works much better now there is a man in charge. Doris[1] and her husband are looking forward to moving into their new cottage. This will be better for all. The shorthorn herd is also steadily improving, and practically all the rubbish has been got rid of. I am considering

---

[1] Doris Edelson, daughter of the gardener at Chartwell. She had married the under-gardener.

getting rid of the belties,[1] but have not yet heard from Mr _____?,[2] to whom Christopher has written about them. I am sorry to let them go as they are most ornamental and characteristic. But there is no doubt that six or seven milch cows of good quality would save three or four hundred pounds a year of loss. The little grey pony which is with them comes now when called, at a gallop, three or four hundred yards, to eat a piece of bread – a new feature in my daily peregrinations.

The two filly foals are growing well and strong and will have to be broken in very soon. The brood mare Poetic went to Lord Derby's to have her foal, which is a colt with three white anklets and a white star, said to be very good looking. He is by King Legend and might well be a valuable animal. Poetic will be married this week to Lord Derby's Borealis, and it is thought that this progeny will also be valuable. I may buy another brood mare with a colt foal in order to keep company with the new foal by Poetic.

April 29 will be a big day for us. Colonist II runs in the 'Winston Churchill' Stakes at Hurst Park, and the same day Cyberine, his sister, runs for the first time there too.[3] I hope you will come with me to see these two horses running. So far all this shows a quite substantial profit, and the whole outfit could be sold for two or three times or more what we gave for it. In addition there are twelve hundred pounds of winnings with Wetherby's. Of course I do not expect Colonist II to win the 'Winston Churchill' Stakes. He will meet the best horses in the world there.

Sir Gerald Kelly[4] and the RA Committee picked out of the seven sent them to choose from, the following four which you may remember: your Carezza sketch (No. 1); the snow scene out of the studio window; a very old one of the Calanque at Cassis, and, to my surprise, Mont Ste Victoire, which was one of our Christmas cards. I think it was better to send in four and not six. The Academy opens on the 27th and I have to speak at the dinner. The pairing difficulty has been arranged.

I have completely turned off politics these last ten days in a struggle to deliver Volume IV in good condition on May 1. This will certainly be achieved. Indeed I am almost at the end of it now. Another two or three mornings and it can go. It is a great relief. If there is no General Election till October I shall

---

[1] Black cattle of Dutch origin with a broad band of white round the middle.
[2] Churchill left a blank and inserted a question mark at this point.
[3] Five days earlier, Christopher Soames had written, about Colonist II, to Churchill: 'This will be a very difficult race to win, as he will be competing with the best horses in the world, but bearing in mind the good which the race at Salisbury will have done him, and the fact that he has another fortnight to improve, I am quite sure that he will not be disgraced. He is in my opinion quite good enough to run in such a race, though I do not think it will be a race to bet on him' (*Baroness Spencer-Churchill papers*).
[4] Gerald Festus Kelly, 1879–1972. Educated at Eton and Trinity Hall, Cambridge. Member, Royal Fine Arts Commission, 1938–43. Painted State Portraits of the King and Queen, 1945. Commander of Legion of Honour, 1950. Membre correspondant de la section de peinture de l'Académie des Beaux Arts de l'Institut de France, 1953. Academico Correspondiente de la Réal Academia de Bellas Artes de San Fernando, Madrid, 1953. Commander of Order of Oranje Nassau, 1953.

hope to have Volume V far enough advanced to earn the fifth instalment. But no one can tell what will happen. Cripps opens his Budget tomorrow and we may get some indication from it about Government tactics.

Various visitors came to lunch or dinner: Lord Woolton, with whom I had a very good talk; Camrose, with whom much was settled, and Randolph, June and little Winston stayed the night. Pamela L.[1] came for the weekend which was very agreeable and peaceful. Mary did the honours. Pamela brought with her her little white Pekinese, called Puff, who was very sweet and made tremendous friends with Rufus, although both are boys.

I am now on my way to the Duchess of Kent's[2] luncheon and am going up to London thereafter as it is only forty minutes. I shall be alone working with Mr Kelly at the book tonight.

All this week is the Parl. And I shall be back at Chartwell Thursday night late.

After talking things over with Christopher I have abandoned the idea of making any further enquiries about that nearby property, and no expense has been incurred. It would be better to buy land which is already let, without reference to how near it is to Chartwell. We shall know more about what to do after the Budget tomorrow. It is quite possible Cripps will have something spiteful in it in order to placate his followers.

I send you a cutting from the *Manchester Guardian* which I thought very interesting about Germany. It is incredible what follies Bevin has committed. No one but he could have managed to quarrel at the same time with Germans and French, with Russians and Americans, with Arabs and Jews. I do not think the poor old creature can last long in office, whatever happens.

Lord Reading and Rennell having joined the Conservatives was a heavy blow to Violet, who was counting on them in her fight with the Party Committee. On the whole I think the foreign situation is darkening somewhat, and it is thought that this year will see Soviet intensification at the least of the 'cold war'. There is nothing we can do about it.

---

[1] Lytton.
[2] Princess Marina, 1906–68. Born in Athens to Prince Nicholas of Greece and Denmark and Grand Duchess Elena Vladimirovna of Russia. Married, 1932, Prince George, Duke of Kent: three children. First Chancellor, University of Kent at Canterbury, 1963–8.

Winston S. Churchill: speech
(Hansard)

24 April 1950   House of Commons

THE BUDGET

During the last five years the Socialist Government have spent or are spending more than £19,000,000,000. The Estimates for the year now before us amount to nearly £4,000,000,000. No one can say, therefore, that a 5 days' Debate and a 2½ hours' speech from the Chancellor of the Exchequer are disproportionate to these colossal figures which mark the most amazing dissipation of national resources on record in any civilized community of our size. Not only is our taxation the highest in the world, not only have we used up every available resource and asset on which the Government could lay their hands, not only has the future been mortgaged in every possible way, but we have enjoyed during this period of extravagance, upwards of £1,700,000,000 of financial aid from the United States and from our Dominions.

There is the first formidable set of facts which glare upon us today. However, I wish to state the case with sobriety and accuracy. We must not judge by the figures alone. The £4,000,000,000 we are to find this year are, owing to the depreciation of our money, really worth not much more than £3,000,000,000 compared with the goods and services they would have represented five years ago. The purchasing power of the £ sterling at home has fallen during this period by nearly 4s. We hear a lot of talk about the word 'inflation', with its refinements of 'disinflation', and so on, but that word carries little meaning to the average man. What is meant to him by the word 'inflation' is the fall in the buying power of the wages he earns or of the pension on which he lives. This is a serious and homely point both to himself and in many ways even more so to his wife. We see in our national Budget that Income Tax and Surtax provide 42 per cent of our tax revenue, but it must not be overlooked that the continued fall in the purchasing power of our money – of the £ sterling – is a tax on the wage earners of the utmost severity, and that it falls upon pensioners and those living on fixed incomes with cruel and devastating force. It finds no place in the balance of the Budget, but it ought to hang heavy on all our minds. If we take the wages earned and the pensions drawn in Britain in the last financial year and deduct 4s. in the £ from them – that is a little more than it actually is, but I take a simple figure – we shall see how much these five years of Socialist Government have taken from the wage earners.

I have had a calculation made on the basis of the official figures of wages, pensions and Government grants for social services which shows that all these classes and masses were deprived of £1,500,000,000 last year alone, which they would have had in goods and services if only the money values of 1945 could have been preserved. And what right have the Socialist orators to talk to us of the exploitation of the toiling masses when the Socialist Government themselves have deprived the wage earners on a gigantic scale by this devaluation or depreciation of the money they work so hard to earn? Even more has the power of our money to buy goods across the dollar exchange been reduced. As the result of devaluation, British industry and workers have now to do twelve hours' work to buy the same quantities of necessary goods and raw materials as nine hours would have produced before the devaluation of the £.

It is quite true that we have not spent all this money that I mentioned just now upon ourselves or upon the revival of British industry. The Chancellor boasted in the election that he had given away over £1,300,000,000 in loans or in repayment of so-called sterling balances – otherwise British debts incurred during the war from the countries we had defended from invasion. Indeed, he and his predecessor begged and borrowed immense sums from the United States with the one hand in order to transfer the treasure thus obtained to foreigners or overseas wartime creditors with the other.

It is common ground between all parties, and it was the main theme of the speech of the Chancellor, that we have now entered upon a period of the utmost difficulty and anxiety. The Chancellor made it clear that greater stresses lie ahead. Expenditure in his opinion, will increase irresistibly; Marshall Aid will stop in the near future; German, Japanese and other competition will rapidly and steadily increase; taxation, direct and indirect, has reached its limit. At home the cupboard is bare. Here, then, is the background, the unchallengeable background, upon which the present Budget must be examined and judged.

What, then, is the upshot of the Budget speech? Let me quote from the *Economist*, a well-informed and independent organ which each side is always ready to quote when its observations are in harmony with their political views. This is what the *Economist* says of the Budget:

> It is a recipe for ever-increasing Government expenditure, and for a permanent structure of high taxes with no hope of relief – a guarantee, in sum, of ultimate economic decay.

The speech of the Chancellor showed that there was no prospect for years to come of any improvement in the cost of living or in the rate of taxation. So, in a certain sense, we have reached finality. Utopia is no longer a dream of the future. This is it. Here we are. It is here now on top of us, and here to stay if only it does not get worse. The one thing, the Government say, is to know when you are well off and rejoice while good things last. What we are going through now is the result of five years of Socialist management and control with far more power and vastly larger financial resources than any other peace-time Government in history.

Now I come to some of the specific proposals of the Budget. None of them affects in any appreciable way the general depressing picture which the Chancellor has painted. We on this side of the House are naturally pleased that the Government have adopted the policy of lessening the discouragement of PAYE to overtime and highly efficient piecework. This is one of the points on which we fought the General Election, and we are very glad to have gained this limited concession for the most active and industrious class of wage earners. I was particularly gratified myself to hear the Chancellor announce the doubling of the petrol ration. As has been pointed out in this Debate, when I raised this matter during the election I was assailed with a storm of abuse for irresponsibility, for asking for the impossible in order to gain votes. How wicked, it was said, to squander the dollars needed to buy food and raw materials without which full employment cannot be maintained, in order to indulge the luxuries of pleasure motorists. The storm was severe but I survived it.

Now, the Government are themselves forced to do the very thing that was urged upon them and which they sought to discredit by mockery and misstatement. All this talk of dollar spending was, as I was advised at the time, and as the Government knew well at the time, quite unfounded. Only a few weeks later they have done themselves what they had so vehemently denounced. I gladly forgive them their abuse, the only result of which has been to deprive them of any claim upon the good will of the motoring community.

The continuing reductions of control and release of articles of food from 'points' are, of course, all welcomed by us. There is no reason why they should not have been done in still greater numbers two or three years ago, just as there is no reason why extravagances now detected and purged, should not have been corrected three or four years ago so that we should have had the advantage of the savings. We have suffered loss and inconvenience in the interval, for no good reason except that in those days the party opposite had more hope of carrying us irrevocably into Socialism than they have now.

We are also glad, in reference to the Amendment which we moved to the Address, that the reduction of the housing target from 200,000 to 175,000, against which we voted, has been repaired and that 200,000 for this year has been restored. Why should we have to kick the party opposite into doing these things? It is not the need for giving houses to the people that has enforced this change in the last three weeks upon the Government, but only the fear that they might lose votes by refusing to alter their policy. Obviously, if it can be done now, it need never have been brought into question. Even so, we do not accept 200,000 as the target for three years to come.

I have nearly finished that passage of approbation and commendation which I felt it my duty to make upon the proposals contained in the Budget. I have nothing to say against the Chancellor's proposal to exempt the high-class motor cars from Purchase Tax. I remember five years ago pointing out how a thriving and fertile export trade could only maintain its continuous perennial quality by being based upon a strong domestic industry, and how I was rebuked by the Chancellor of the Exchequer, then President of the Board of Trade, for such reactionary ideas.

I am glad to see that the right hon. and learned Gentleman's education in finance, for which we have to pay so much, is not wholly devoid of some signs of progress. He is not a star pupil but it would be too soon to say that he is completely unteachable. Of course, however, in this and some other aspects of finance he may have to encounter the criticism that he is, to use an American expression, 'taking the poor man's money away from the millionaire to give it to the plain rich'.

This brings me to the attitude of the Government towards wealth and large fortunes. Four years ago I travelled back from America with Lord Keynes, who had been on a Government mission and was working at the Treasury. I asked him why the then Chancellor of the Exchequer, when reducing the Income Tax by a shilling, should have made sure that the Surtax on these largest incomes was retained at the confiscatory rate of 19s 6d in the £. I shall never forget the look of contempt which came over his expressive features, on which already lay the shadow of approaching death, when he replied in a single word 'Hate'. Hate is not a good guide in public or in private life. I am sure that class hatred and class warfare like national revenge, are the most costly luxuries in which anyone can indulge. The present Chancellor has boasted of the number of persons who have net incomes of £5,000 or over a year. He has boasted that it has been reduced from 11,000 before the war to 250 at the present time, and that the number of those over £6,000 has been reduced from 7,000 to 70. Those are great achievements. However necessary this extreme taxation was in the war – I was responsible, as Prime Minister, for its imposition – it certainly is not a process which increases the long-term revenue of the nation or its savings.

I will take a simple illustration. I always find these financial matters better explained by simple illustrations. I will take that which occurred to me the other day when I was looking at a cow. Late in life I have begun to keep a herd of cows, and I find that quite a different principle prevails in dealing with cows from that which is so applauded below the Gangway opposite in dealing with rich men. It is a great advantage in a dairy to have cows with large udders because one gets more milk out of them than from the others. These exceptionally fertile milch cows are greatly valued in any well conducted dairy, and anyone would be thought very foolish who boasted he had got rid of all the best milkers, just as he would be thought very foolish if he did not milk them to the utmost limit of capacity, compatible with the maintenance of their numbers.

I am quite sure that the Minister of Agriculture would look in a very different way upon the reduction of all these thousands of his best milkers from that in which the Chancellor of the Exchequer looks upon the destruction of the most fertile and the most profitable resources of taxation. I must say the cows do not feel the same way about it as do the Socialists. The cows have not got the same equalitarian notions and dairy farmers are so unimaginative that they think mainly of getting as much milk as possible; they want a lot of political education. The Lord President of the Council is turning his attention to the agricultural sphere and, no doubt, this will stimulate his fancy as to some suggestions he may make to the farmers.

I will pursue this point, I hope not unduly. Rich men, although valuable to the Revenue, are not vital to a healthy state of society, but a society in which rich men are got rid of, from motives of jealousy, is not in a healthy state. This brings me to the applause from his own side – a comparatively remarkable event – which the Chancellor gained last Tuesday when he announced that retroactive taxation would be imposed on two individuals who had received large gifts from the shareholders of the companies for which they worked. It is not a case of sympathizing with these gentlemen, or with the action of the firms concerned. Indeed, I shared the general feeling that such a transaction was unworthy of a time when the trade unions were loyally endeavouring, in the national interest, to prevent wage increases, justified by the ever-increasing cost of living.

I have no doubt that the promise that the Chancellor made to introduce retroactive legislation to hit these two men was worth many votes to him in the election, and it certainly gave him his loudest cheer when he opened his Budget. It is true also that there are precedents, especially in the war, for retroactive legislation in such matters. Nevertheless, I found myself in full agreement with the statement of the leader of the Liberal Party last week in condemnation of the principle of retroactive legislation and of the idea that a warning by a Minister which had no force of law should be accepted as a justification. After all, the law, as pronounced by the highest courts in the land, was clear. It was not new; the judgment was seven years old. The Government could easily in their five years of office, have introduced into any of their Finance Bills the Clause which they now propose to deal with this matter. The transaction was open – more than open, it was blatant. It was effected and made in full confidence of the validity of the law. It would have been more in accordance with the broad principles which guide our way of life to alter the law for the future than to use retroactive legislation, however popular it may be to penalize a couple of wealthy individuals.

The Chancellor's new proposals are on a comparatively miniature scale and affect only £80,000,000 or £90,000,000 of money one way or the other in the immense bill of nearly £4,000 million we have to meet. They do not appreciably affect the finance of the year; 1 per cent, or 2 per cent, is the most involved in all of it. It cannot be said that they affect the life and effectiveness of the Budget which is before us. But the gravamen of the case against them is to be found in the new taxes which are now to be levied. The increase of the tax on petrol is a new burden to the travelling public and has already led to a rise in cab fares. Bus fares, I am told, will inevitably follow. The imposition of a heavy purchase tax on vans and lorries is a direct attack upon the economy and efficiency of our production and distribution, entirely out of harmony, indeed absolutely contrary, to the exhortations and lectures which we hear so often from the Chancellor's lips. Both the raising of the fares and the deterrent now placed on the sale and use of commercial vehicles and the tax on their fuel are, as everyone can see, designed to force the travelling public and our industry to use nationalized railways and thus offset by a countervailing evil the impending rise in railway freights and passenger fares. The Government bought the railways by compulsion, of their own free will, at a singularly odd moment in railway history and they feel they owe it to the cause of nationalization to make them into a paying proposition, no matter what that may cost.

Moreover, I submit that it is intolerable that any new taxes should be imposed at a time like this. Remissions are welcome, but they should be made by economies in Government expenditure and not by additions to taxation. We shall feel it our duty to vote against both these new taxes when the Resolutions concerning them are reported to the House on Wednesday next. Not to do so would be to abrogate the rights of Parliament out of fear of precipitating an appeal to the people. The Government have raised these provocative issues themselves, and we have no choice but to express our sincere conviction that both the new taxes are wrong in principle and will be harmful in practice.

I always try, especially in a new House of Commons, to study the opinions of those to whom I am opposed, their expressions and moods, so far as I can. I confess I am surprised that hon. Members opposite who hold Socialist conceptions – there are, I believe, some of them – were not shocked at this rise in the bus and taxi fares. Is this not a case of rationing by the purse? Ought they not to ask themselves, on their theories, whether this is not allowing mere money to decide who can ride in a bus or taxi and who has to walk? And what about the pleasure motorist and so forth? Is it really fair that some poor man who voted Socialist at the last election, who spends his increased bus fare by lingering too long on the Chancellor's stronger beer in the public house, should have to walk home?

We on this side of the House stand for the policy of reducing both expenditure and taxation. I am repeatedly asked, 'How would you cut down expenditure?' The object of the question may indeed be to procure guidance, but it could also be used for election misrepresentations. We have not the detailed information which alone would allow a precise and detailed statement to be made. We do not know what we should find if we gained access to the secrets of Whitehall. I do not accept the statements of Ministers as giving a complete or even perhaps a correct picture. We are assured that they wish to hold on to office until after the next appeal to the country is made because they fear exposure at the hands of any incoming Administration.

Be that as it may, it is not possible for an Opposition to make a detailed plan without full knowledge of the true situation and the aid of the Government Departments. But I have no doubt, after a long experience of affairs, even longer than that of the Father of the House, if I may say so, that substantial economies could be made which could be passed on to the taxpayer in a manner which would be highly beneficial to production and to savings, and that they could be made in such a way as would effectually safeguard the weak and poor. (*Laughter.*) Do not laugh at the weak and poor. I know that in Socialist jargon they are described as 'lower income groups'. These concessions, secured by a reduction of taxes, might even restore to the weak and poor a portion of what they have lost through the depreciation of the wages they earn or the pensions they receive.

I will, however, say that our Defence Services, now costing nearly £800,000,000, require searching attention, and that I am sure there never was a time when we got less value in fighting power from the immense sums which Parliament has voted. Our foreign dangers, which seem to be sharpening, will not be warded off by the wasteful and ineffectual expenditure of money but rather by concentration upon the modern forms of war power in the light of our knowledge. The spending of vast sums of money in ill-conceived ways may salve people's consciences and make them feel that it is all right, but that in itself affords no guarantee for our safety although, of course, it may be described as a most full and generous provision for defence.

I turn to another point. If the National Health Service is to yield, over a long-term period, the results we hoped for when the policy was adopted by the war-time National Government, it will undoubtedly be necessary to purge abuses and waste and prevent the exploitation of State benefits by thoughtless or unworthy methods or habits.

In regard to food subsidies, now fixed at £410 million – the 'floor' and the 'ceiling' have come together – I say without hesitation that they should be recast in such a way as to concentrate the relief upon those who really need it, and not to squander enormous sums on the majority who could well afford to pay for their own food at prices which would soon be established in a free market, and which might easily fall to the level or below the level of the existing subsidized price. I am sure that a scheme can be rapidly evolved which would achieve a substantial reduction of Government expenditure without causing hardship to the lower income groups; and that this present time, when there is a glut of food in the markets of the world, affords the opportunity of regaining the economies, flexibility and conveniences of a free market such as has been successfully re-established in so many European countries, some of which were defeated in the war or long occupied by hostile garrisons.

There is also the general field of Government expenditure – travelling, advertising, wasteful State trading, mistaken investments in enterprises such as we have heard of before, hosts of officials, enormous hosts of officials, never needed to manage our affairs before. All these provide a fertile field for additional economy. I was asked the other day 'What would you do to economize?' I have, within the limits which are open to anyone who has not access to official information, offered a full and considerable statement of the field upon which I am bound to say I think we might hopefully advance with our blue pencils.

I have referred to the advantages of a free market, subject to proper safeguards, and provision for the lower income groups. We are all agreed that we are not going to make our great reforms and advances at the expense of the poorest of the poor. On this question of a free market, I am much interested in this experiment in regard to fish, which has been liberated after nine years of control. The Minister of Health – I do not think I see him in his place – said, in one of his more exalted moments, that we were an island of coal surrounded by fish. Perhaps it was later that he added that it was mainly populated by 'vermin'. I think it was a different occasion. But what about the fish? I believe that in this and in similar matters the higgling of the market will, under healthy and improving world conditions, after a month or two, give the people a far better diet than all the planning of all the planners. No doubt the markets would jump about, as we saw the fish market do, for a month or two, but in the end, and probably soon, they would come down to the true and natural level where the customer – not the 'gentlemen in Whitehall' – and the consumer, know best. This is of course an old-fashioned idea, but it does not follow for that reason that it is necessarily wrong.

I have now surveyed the details of the Budget; those that I have felt it my duty to pay my tribute to, and those which I am bound to say it is equally our duty on this side of the House to resist by every means in our power. The Chancellor of the Exchequer stands before us at that Box when he speaks, uplifted, austere, almost ecclesiastical, pronouncing sombre judgments. A different aspect of his personality and outlook was presented to us at the General Election. At Bristol on 11 February he said:

> We are sharing out more fairly the national resources that exist. We have not shared them all out equally yet. It takes a bit of time to do these things.

These were deplorable words. Never has a Chancellor of the Exchequer, with all his influence upon domestic and international credit, spoken in such a way. How the right hon. and learned Gentleman could reconcile language of that kind with the appeals in which we are asked to join to save money and invest in Savings Certificates, it is difficult to explain. What he said, in the words I have quoted, is not even fair shares for all, whatever that may mean, and undoubtedly to have any meaning it depends on who is the judge of what is fair – it is equal shares for all, a condition which is contrary to nature and to every form of progress and civilization.

But in his Budget speech last Tuesday the right hon. and learned Gentleman fell into heresies of the opposite character, and extremes of the opposite character. This is what he said: 'The real difficulty is that there are still' – he was explaining why he could do nothing for the lowest paid workers – 'some cases of low earnings which are very difficult to correct without upsetting the relative wage levels that have been established within each industry for the different grades and classes of workpeople employed in it.' I fully agree that respect must be shown for what that robust trade union leader, Mr Arthur Deakin, has described as 'differentials' in industry. But to draw from this the principle that the lowest paid workers cannot have their position improved without all the classes above them receiving simultaneous and similar advances falls into an error which is antisocial. That error is to feel aggrieved because someone less fortunate than you gains an advantage which does you no harm. The principle of levelling up is right, and is free from the hate and envy which accompanies the process of levelling down.

I am astonished that the fine intellect of the Chancellor of the Exchequer, even if all else failed him, has not guarded him from self-contradiction and erroneous doctrines of the character I have described. I trust that the right hon. and learned Gentleman will search his conscience in the matter, because, in my opinion, it is absolutely wrong to say that the lowest paid worker is not to have his wages brought up unless or until similar advances can be made to others. One of the very first Measures I had the honour to pass through this House was the 'sweated trades' Bill, for the very purpose of 'bringing the rear-guard in', as we used to say in those old days; and I am not at all prepared to admit that there is any excuse for the exclusion of the poorest paid workers from all help and assistance in a Budget drawn up by a Chancellor who had a few weeks before given expression to the wildest levelling and equalitarian and totalitarian views upon equal shares for all.

I hope to detain the Committee very little longer. I have tried as well as I can to present the case as we feel it; an Opposition aggrieved at the maltreatment and mismanagement of our finances. But I think it also right to say that in my long life I have never seen the nation divided quite as it is today. It is not so much divided in enmity as in opinion. The question forces itself upon us – how long can we afford to be dominated by this ideological conflict which, as it paralyses our national judgment and action, must be deeply detrimental to an island like ours, with its 50,000,000 growing only half their food? I must confess that I cannot get these 50,000,000 out of my head. They keep recurring in one's mind – 50,000,000 crowded in this small island, growing only half their food.

The floor which separates the two sides of the House, so evenly balanced now, is not a gulf of class; nor does it mark a breach in fundamental brotherhood. It is one of theme and doctrine. The Conservative and Liberal Parties stand for a way of life which at every stage multiplies the choices open to the individual. The Socialist devotees – I will not say the Party opposite, for many would repudiate it – stand for the multiplication of rules. There is planning on both sides, but the aim and emphasis are different. We plan for choices, they plan for rules, and in this lies one of the aspects of our melancholy domestic quarrel.

Let us look, if possible without party bias, at the effects of the present political tension as it governs our actions and our fortunes. Everyone knows that free elections, such as we have in this country, are the foundation of democracy. But no community like ours can thrive permanently in an electioneering atmosphere. It is not giving the people a fair chance, with all their hard work and other preoccupations, to ask them to live for prolonged periods under such conditions. Every word in this Debate, and others, which hon. Members opposite or we on this side speak, will be considered by large party machines with regard to the forthcoming trials of strength in the constituencies.

I listened to several of the maiden speeches which were made and which have won approval from every part of the Committee. I sympathize particularly with these maiden speakers, because I felt that perhaps you, Major Milner, from the Chair might have said – this is not a criticism – 'I have to warn you,' as the police formula runs, 'that anything you say may be used in evidence against you.' Here we are, in the supreme economic crisis of our whole history, watching each other like cat and mouse. And who shall say who is the cat and who is the mouse?

I was relieved when the Prime Minister announced in the beginning of the year that there would be an election in February. I thought that at any rate this would give us a solution one way or the other of our deep-seated domestic quarrels. The election was held, and I suppose everybody did his best according to his lights. But, far from ending the electioneering period, the results of the voting have been only to prolong it. We are split half and half as I have never seen this country split before, and the question arises: How long have we got to go on with neither one side nor the other having the power to do anything to grapple effectively on its merits with the national needs?

The fortunes of other countries are no guide in these matters. Party names do not mean the same things, nor is their parliamentary government in any way the same as ours. In Belgium, for instance, which we rescued in the war, they are not worried apparently about material things and are entirely absorbed in a question affecting their monarchy. In France, whatever else happens, the fertile soil gives abundant food for all its people. In Germany, everyone has the natural resolve to recover from defeat. They want to have free petrol. They want to reduce their income tax below ours. Oh, how shocking! They even want to sing their National Anthem. But none of those countries is in the same position as our island, with our 50,000,000 people, brought here in the great Victorian age by a vast expansion of manufactures and now left in a perilous plight.

I was thinking when I was preparing this speech about the whales who come ashore and are caught by the tide, but I remembered that I had used that before. However, when I woke up yesterday morning I found that the poor whales have come ashore again, and I must say it does seem to me that we run very great risks of finding ourselves stranded, with our immense population, on a shore which leaves very little hope of escape. To change the metaphor, suppose we were 50,000,000 of us on the fifth or sixth floor of one of these steel-structure buildings the foundations of which were being undermined and the major girders sawn through. Many societies have vanished in the past and found no recorded or recognizable place in history. But never has this hideous fate presented itself more brutally to so numerous, complex and powerful a community as we are, and never has it presented itself to a victorious nation on the morrow of its triumph in saving the freedom of the world.

Of course, there are politicians who say that it is only by suffering that the people learn, and that the English people, above all others, insist on buying their experience fresh and new every time. Things, we are told, must get worse before they are better. I am not comforted by this. We may easily get so far downhill that we have not strength left to climb back. In the modern world everything moves very quickly. Tendencies which, 200 or 300 years ago worked out over several generations, may now reach definite decisions in a twelve-month. I hate to feel the lowered opinion of British strength, will-power and life-thrust, which now prevails alike in countries we have defeated and in those we have rescued. But, of course, if we go on year after year absorbed in our internal party and class fights, there may never be any chance for the might and glory of Britain to show itself again. Somehow or other we must reach firm ground again and have a Government that is not afraid or unable to do things if they are in the national interest.

I was pondering the other day upon what a difference it would have made to our fortunes if what happened in the 1950 election had happened in the election of 1945. Undoubtedly there would have been a national coalition. The old ties that had bound us together through the perils of the war had not been severed by the rough talk of the election as they have now been severed by all that has since occurred. The task before us was the completion of all we had worked for. We had won the war. We could have won the peace. An equipoise of parties would have been a national mandate for the continuance of the united action which had saved us from destruction. We had a common programme and a far-reaching four years' plan. But darker fortunes and more harassing ordeals were reserved for our exhausted people. The conditions of 1945 have passed away. It is 1950 now. Great disasters have come upon Britain, both in the economic sphere and in her standing among the nations. With them have grown antagonisms felt on each side by millions of men and women here at home. I do not believe in coalitions that are formed only as the result of party bargainings. It is vain to suppose that anything but a blinding emergency, internal or external, would revive the comradeship of the war-time years, or that an artificial arrangement between party leaders would meet our needs.

Therefore, it is with deep anxiety, into which my personal feelings do not enter at all, that I try to read the mysteries of our immediate future. How deep shall we have to descend the dark stairway which lies before us no one can tell. This should be an awe-striking thought for this new Parliament, so rich in earnestness and quality, so baffled and so bewildered, and so near, apparently, to its latter end. All the more should it be an awe-striking thought when we remember that we are responsible for all the millions of our people who fought so well, who endured so much and who try so hard.

Harold Macmillan to Winston S. Churchill
(Churchill papers, 2/76)

25 April 1950

Dear Winston,

You must have been delighted with the reception of the speech yesterday and still more pleased with the tremendous press today. It was a privilege to have been present on Sunday during part of its composition.

I am sending you herewith a short Note about Strasbourg. I am seeing Duncan tomorrow and I think we can get out a short memorandum on what we think should be the policy.

STRASBOURG

After our return from the Consultative Assembly in the autumn, there was a certain amount of anxiety expressed in the Party about the implications of United Europe.

We carried our Resolution at the Party Conference without difficulty, partly by linking Imperial unity with the European theme, and partly by the powerful aid of Leo Amery.

My only thought about the persons whom you might choose as our representatives was that if you could have put in somebody of importance, who had not played any role in the United Europe Movement hitherto, it would help.

I do not know whether you have been asked to nominate eight substitutes in addition to eight principals. If there are to be substitutes, it might be possible to include in their number one or two such figures. Our Party 'Inter-Group' Committee – which consists of representatives of the Foreign Affairs, Imperial and Finance Committees, sitting with representatives of the Strasbourg delegation – is doing useful educative work.

So far as I am concerned, I shall be glad to accept your nomination, for which I thank you. Naturally, it will be a great help to have Duncan Sandys with us, especially as I am working with him all the time on United Europe and on the Executive Committee of the European Movement.

As regards policy, I will try to let you have a note on some of the major issues which I think will arise. I will prepare this with Duncan's help. I can, to some extent, guide the findings of my Committee of the Assembly – on General Affairs – which has to report on the feasibility of creating 'A European authority with limited functions but real powers'. It is much better, if possible, to get the report to our taste, than to get into an embarrassing position in full assembly.

No doubt David Maxwell Fyfe can do something of the kind on his Committee which meets next in London in May. I am only anxious to make sure that our colleagues are agreed and that we can avoid the Socialists saying that our Party is divided on this European question. Actually, the more progressive we can be, the more it helps to carry the Liberals with us in this country.

I am indeed sorry that Lord Salisbury cannot go with us to Strasbourg. It would be a great help if you could persuade him to associate himself with our United Europe Movement.

Lord Salisbury to Winston S. Churchill
(Churchill papers, 2/101)

26 April 1950
Private and Personal

My dear Winston,

It was very good of you to let me know that you had tried out the idea of a manifesto on Clem Davies and that he seemed to like it. But I gather that, in your discussions with him, it formed part of a plan by which the Liberals were to be built up into a more effective party, with a view to their joining us as allies in a Government to be formed in the event of Attlee throwing in his hand. You will, I am sure, understand if I am worried lest he should get the impression that I favour such a plan or would in any circumstances be a party to it. I do not believe in rebuilding the Liberal Party as a party. Rightly or wrongly, I do not think that there is any place for it in this Country, where the political system is based on the conception of two and not three or more parties. My idea of the manifesto was to register a merger not to cement an alliance. Possibly I am wrong about this. I certainly would not wish to claim infallibility of judgement. But, rightly or wrongly, that is the view I hold, and I do not want Clem Davies, now that my name has been mentioned in connection with the manifesto, to be in any doubt about it. Moreover, I am quite sure that the Conservative Party would not accept the idea of an alliance with a strengthened Liberal Party. The only effect of trying to force it through would be to split us from top to bottom. I hope therefore that you will agree to my seeing Clem Davies and having a talk with him, so that I can explain to him where I stand. I feel that I am in honour bound to do this, and am sure that, on reconsideration, you will see no objection to such action on my part.

Winston S. Churchill to Lord Salisbury
(Churchill papers, 2/101)

26 April 1950

My dear Bobbety,

I am sorry indeed to receive your letter. It is largely based on misconception. I in no way committed you to any course beyond that of the joint manifesto and at the same time I made it clear that many Conservatives held a different opinion from me about the future of the Liberal Party.

It is not for me to assign any limits to whom you see or what you say to them. If however you think it necessary to explain to Clement Davies that you are convinced that the Liberal Party should be extinguished as a Party at the present time or in the near future and that this is the policy you are pursuing, I hope you will also at the same time make it clear that I take a different view. Otherwise you may affect in a very diverse manner the course of events in the House of Commons on which so much depends at the present time.

Winston S. Churchill: speech
('Winston S. Churchill, His Complete Speeches', volume 8, pages 7997–8)

27 April 1950

LORD KEYES[1] AND HIS SON[2]

Three years have passed since the Dean and Chapter of St Paul's Cathedral reserved a place for a memorial to Roger Keyes and his son, Geoffrey. And now we are gathered here today to unveil the tablet which preserves and proclaims the admiration of our war-worn generation for these two heroic Englishmen – the one a great naval commander, the other a young colonel awarded, after his death, with the Victoria Cross. The tablet also expresses the enduring affection with which their memory is cherished by their many friends and, most of all, by those who knew them best.

For more than thirty years I was one of the closest of the Admiral's friends.

---

[1] Roger John Brownlow Keyes, 1872–1945. Entered RN, 1885. Commodore in charge of submarines, North Sea and adjacent waters, Aug. 1914 to Feb. 1915. CoS, Eastern Mediterranean Squadron (Dardanelles), 1915. Director of Plans, Admiralty, 1917. VAdm. in command of Dover Patrol (and Zeebrugge raid), 1918. Knighted, 1918. Bt, 1919. Deputy CNS, 1921–5. C-in-C, Mediterranean, 1925–8; Portsmouth, 1929–31. Adm. of the Fleet, 1930. MP (Nat. Cons.) for North Portsmouth, 1934–43. Director of Combined Operations, 1940–1. Baron, 1943. Churchill wrote the foreword to Keyes' memoirs, *Adventures Ashore and Afloat* (1939).

[2] Geoffrey Charles Tasker Keyes, 1917–41. Royal Armoured Corps; Royal Scots Greys (2nd Dragoons). Killed 18 Nov. 1941, while serving as a Lt-Col. in the Commandos, leading a raid on Rommel's headquarters in the Western Desert, 250 miles behind enemy lines. Buried in the Commonwealth War Graves Commission Cemetery in Benghazi. For his part in the raid he was posthumously awarded the VC.

When I was at the Admiralty in 1911 he was already an officer of high distinction and in charge of our submarine flotillas at the time when this new and terrible weapon began to break upon the naval world and cast its menace upon the life and safety of Britain.

But we have to go back to the beginning of the century for the first occasion when the light of martial distinction shone upon the young lieutenant who, acting on his own initiative, stormed with thirty men the Chinese fort on the Pei Ho river, for which 4,000 Allied troops had been considered insufficient to attack, and thus opened the channel to the relief of the European garrisons besieged in Tientsin. From then, down to the last period of his life, Admiral Keyes sought glory in the face of danger, and his intense impulse for action was always armed with the highest degree of naval skill and technical efficiency.

He was always in the van of naval progress, and stimulated the tactical development of the destroyer flotillas, of our submarines and, most of all, of the Fleet Air Arm. His exploits afloat and ashore will always excite the enthusiasm of the youth of Britain, and are also full of guidance for the leaders of the Royal Navy.

The splendid feat of arms conceived and executed by him – that the canal entrance to the German submarine base of Zeebrugge, from which the U-boats sallied forth to attack our life-lines, was blocked and rendered useless – will long be famous. This outstanding example of audacity and organization is matched at every period in the sixty years of devoted service which Roger Keyes gave to the Navy and to the nation he loved so well.

In the late war, as Chief of Combined Operations, he lent a most important impulse to amphibious warfare. There radiated from him the Commando spirit to which we owe so many glorious episodes. He animated and impelled from his earliest days all the vast design and construction of landing-craft of all kinds, without the timely preparation of which the great victories of the West Allies could never have been gained. In many ways his spirit and example seemed to revive in our own stern and tragic age the vivid personality and unconquerable and dauntless soul of Nelson himself.

The tablet which I am to unveil adorns the walls of our famous cathedral. The light of honour and of duty which springs from it will, as the years go by, serve as an inspiration and beacon to our island race.

House of Commons: Oral Answers
(Hansard)

27 April 1950

JORDAN AND ISRAEL (GOVERNMENT DECISION)

Mr De Chair[1] (by Private Notice): asked the Secretary of State for Foreign Affairs, in view of our military commitments to defend the frontiers of the Kingdom of Jordan, whether His Majesty's Government were consulted by our ally, King Abdullah of Jordan, before he annexed the Arab-held parts of Palestine and whether he will make a statement.

The Minister of State (Mr Younger): His Majesty's Government in the United Kingdom have been officially informed by the Government of the Hashemite Kingdom of Jordan of the union of the Kingdom of Jordan and of that part of Palestine under Jordan occupation and control. The Jordan Government, in this communication, have stated that an Act providing for this union was unanimously adopted on 24th April by the Jordan Assembly, which is composed of representatives of both these territories, and received the Royal Assent on the same day. His Majesty's Government have decided to accord formal recognition to this union. They take this opportunity of declaring that they regard the provisions of the Anglo-Jordan Treaty of Alliance of 1948 as applicable to all the territory included in the union.

This action is subject to explanation on two points. The first of these points relates to the frontier between this territory and Israel. This frontier has not yet been finally determined. The existing boundary is the line laid down in the Armistice Agreement signed between Israel and Jordan on 3rd April, 1949, and is subject to any modification which may be agreed upon by the two States under the terms of that Agreement, or of any final settlement which may replace it. Until, therefore, the frontier between Israel and Jordan is determined by a final settlement between them His Majesty's Government regard the territory to which the Anglo-Jordan Treaty is applicable as being bounded by the Armistice Line, or any modification of it which may be agreed upon by the two parties.

The second point relates to Jerusalem. The part of Palestine which is now united to the Kingdom of Jordan includes a portion of the area defined in the Resolution on the internationalization of Jerusalem adopted by the General Assembly of the United Nations on 9th December, 1949. His Majesty's Government wish to state that, pending a final determination of the

---

[1] Somerset Struben de Chair, 1911–95. MP (Cons.) for South-West Norfolk, 1935–45; for South Paddington, 1950–1. On active service, Iraq and Syria, 1941 (wounded). Parliamentary Private Secretary to Minister of Production, 1942–4. Member, Executive Committee, UN Association, 1947–50. Novelist and historian; also wrote two volumes of autobiography, *Buried Pleasure* (1985) and *Morning Glory* (1988).

status of this area, they are unable to recognise Jordan sovereignty over any part of it. They do, however, recognise that Jordan exercises de facto authority in the part occupied by her. They consider, therefore, that the Anglo-Jordan Treaty applies to this part, unless or until the United Nations shall have established effective authority there. His Majesty's Government's obligations under the Treaty are, of course, subject always to their overriding obligations under the United Nations Charter.

His Majesty's Government wish to add that they have no intention of requesting the establishment of military bases in peace time within the area of Palestine now united to the Kingdom of Jordan.

His Majesty's Government have also decided to accord de jure recognition to the State of Israel, subject to explanations on two points corresponding to those described above in regard to the case of Jordan. These points are as follows. First, that His Majesty's Government are unable to recognise the sovereignty of Israel over that part of Jerusalem which she occupies, though, pending a final determination of the status of the area, they recognise that Israel exercises de facto authority in it. Secondly, that His Majesty's Government cannot regard the present boundaries between Israel, and Egypt, Jordan, Syria and the Lebanon as constituting the definitive frontiers of Israel, as these boundaries were laid down in the Armistice Agreements concluded severally between Israel and each of these States, and are subject to any modifications which may be agreed upon under the terms of those Agreements, or of any final settlements which may replace them.

In announcing these two acts of recognition, His Majesty's Government wish to reaffirm their conviction that the problem of Palestine is capable of solution by peaceful means, given good will and understanding on the part of all the parties concerned. It is their earnest hope that the steps they have now taken will help to create stability in the areas concerned, and will, therefore, make a contribution towards the peace of the Middle East as a whole.

Mr Churchill: Does not the hon. Gentleman realize that Dr Weizmann and King Abdullah have both, over the vicissitudes of 20 or 30 years, shown themselves always staunch friends to this country, and will he avail himself to the full of the possibilities of bringing these two eminent men into the closest harmonious contact? Am I right in assuming that that is the general path upon which the Government are embarked and which is expressed in the statement to which we have just listened?

Mr Younger: Yes, Sir, the right hon. Gentleman is quite correct, and I am glad to associate myself with the remarks he made about His Majesty King Abdullah and Dr Weizmann.

Mr De Chair: May I thank the hon. Gentleman for his very full and interesting reply, and ask if he would consider offering the services of the Government to call a conference of all the Middle East countries involved in an attempt to try to get a workable settlement of outstanding problems which he has mentioned, such as the future of Jerusalem and the closing of the canal and the pipe line, as no two of these Middle East countries seem to be agreed; and thereby make a positive contribution, as he has suggested, to the solidarity of the area, which is essential to resisting the spread of Communism in the Middle East?

Mr Younger: We hope the action we are announcing today will help towards reaching agreement over some of the many problems in the Middle East, but I do not think I can commit myself to the view that a conference at the present moment is necessarily the best way of settling the outstanding difficulties we know to exist.

Mr Churchill: In view of the statement which has been made, will the hon. Gentleman and the Government reconsider the decision to give or sell 110 jet aircraft to the Egyptian Government?

Mr Younger: I think the right hon. Gentleman will appreciate that the whole question of the supply of arms in the Middle East is one which is under constant consideration. I do not think I have got anything to add in that connection to the statement I have just made.

Mr Churchill: Perhaps the hon. Gentleman will bring it to the notice of the Prime Minister, who may possibly have heard the question? It is a very important one. Might he not discuss with the Egyptian Government the stoppage of tankers passing through the Canal, which are deeply needed to get the Haifa refinery into working order?

Mr Younger: These are, of course, among the more important of the numerous difficulties to which I have referred, and which are still outstanding, and which are under consideration.

Mr Sydney Silverman: While congratulating my hon. Friend on the positive and constructive step forward in the announcement he has made, may I ask if he does not consider that the whole question of the supply of arms under our treaties with the surrounding Arab States might be reconsidered, and, indeed, suspended, until, at any rate, such time as they are prepared to negotiate treaties of peace with the State of Israel, to which we have now afforded de jure recognition?

Mr Younger: I take note of my hon. Friend's views, but I do not think that any comment from me is called for in connection with the statement.

Earl Winterton: Is the hon. Gentleman aware that some of us who have had many intimate connections with these parts in the past, welcome his announcement, and are entirely in agreement with the point, which is an entirely non-party one, put by the Leader of the Opposition, and believe that the State of Israel and the State of Jordan are by far the most stable States in the Middle East, and that first things should come first, and that a treaty between them should be the object of His Majesty's Government as far as His Majesty's Government are able to influence it?

Major Legge-Bourke:[1] Speaking strictly for myself, may I say to the hon. Gentleman that I consider the de jure recognition of Israel to be the most hideous betrayal of all those men who fought in Palestine in the past?

Earl Winterton: With regard to my question, does the hon. Gentleman agree that that should be the object of His Majesty's Government?

Mr Younger: Of course His Majesty's Government wish to see an agreement between Israel and all the neighbouring States.

Several Hon. Members: rose –

Mr Speaker: I hope that we may finish with this now without sounding any more discordant notes.

---

[1] Edward Alexander Henry Legge-Bourke, 1914–73. Born in Windsor. Educated at Eton College and RMC, Sandhurst. Married, 1938, Catherine Jean Grant: three children. Entered Royal Horse Guards, 1934. Served in 7th Armoured Div. at El Alamein. MP (Cons.) for Isle of Ely, 1945–73. Chairman, 1922 Committee of Conservative backbenchers, 1970–2.

May
1950

Winston S. Churchill to Robert Menzies
(Churchill papers, 2/94)

4 May 1950
Private and Personal

Difficult for me to support the six million Burma loan debated next Tuesday. Neither past history nor our present financial burden justify this new burden which falls on us through sterling balances apart from your share. Am also concerned about the Karens[1] who fought so well for us in the war but now in their stress have had to mix up with the Communists. Feel it would be better to concentrate on Malaya and make a success of that. Burma Government have treated us with great ingratitude and harshness in all matters of British property. How much does this all matter to you? Loan will probably be carried anyway by small Socialist majority. Kind regards.

Lord Cherwell to Winston S. Churchill
(Churchill papers, 2/168)

7 May 1950

My dear Winston,

I have been thinking over what you said the other day about the large numbers attending your Consultative Committee and the desirability of refreshing it with new blood. As I entirely agree with this view it occurs to me that it may be opportune for me to resign from it. I am probably the oldest member and almost certainly the only one who would not be able to take office in any Government you might form. In the circumstances you may well consider that the time has come for me to make way for someone more useful,

---

[1] The Karen, or Yang, people of south-eastern Burma (now Myanmar) comprise about 7% of Burma's population. The Karen National Union began waging war against the central Government in 1949. A ceasefire with the military government was signed in 2012.

though of course I would always remain at your service unofficially if you thought I could be of any help.

I am sure you realise how grateful I am to you for having given me an opportunity to contribute what little I could to the prosecution of the war and how much I enjoyed having the honour to serve you during those momentous days.

I am looking forward to seeing you on Thursday.[1]

Clement Attlee to Winston S. Churchill
(Churchill papers, 2/29)

7 May 1950
Top Secret

My dear Churchill,

I sent you last December two papers about the North Atlantic Defence Committee. I now enclose, once more for your private and personal information, a paper giving an account of the meeting of the North Atlantic Defence Committee at The Hague on 1st April and the meeting of the Brussels Treaty Consultative Council in Brussels on the 16th and 17th April.

I should be obliged if you would return the paper after you have read it.

President Chaim Weizmann to Winston S. Churchill
(Churchill papers, 2/102)

7 May 1950

Dear Mr Churchill,

It was with real gratification that I learned of His Majesty's Government's decision to extend de jure recognition to Israel. Your kind words about my own long standing association with Britain touched me deeply.

I feel I ought to tell you how impressed I was by your understanding of an aspect of the situation borne out by your reference to arms supplied to Egypt. There is no doubt that the man in the street, as well as the Government here, are anxious and apprehensive. The accumulation of arms in one country only breeds counterpreparations and tends to plunge the nations of this area into a costly armaments race which they can ill afford and only deflects their limited resources from real constructive work.

As regards Israel's tasks of reconstruction, they are so great as to require

---

[1] Churchill responded on May 14: 'Thank you for your letter of May 7. I certainly do not wish you to resign from the Consultative Committee and shall expect to see you there as usual.'

all our efforts and application. The great ingathering of the remnants of once large Jewish communities from Europe, Asia and North Africa, continues unabated. These new settlers have to be fully integrated into the national life. There is within our borders, and especially in the Negev, ample development work for generations to come.

Yet for this work to fructify we need peace and goodwill around us. Throughout my life I have striven for peace and goodwill between my people and their neighbours and never ceased to believe that one day we shall be able, Jew and Arab, to join forces in building up a happy prosperous belt of countries extending from the Mediterranean to the Indian Ocean.

It is my sincere hope that Britain will use its best endeavours to smooth the path to peace and stability in the Middle East. May we, once again, witness a close relationship between the peoples of Britain and Israel.

I look forward to continuing our long association and to the pleasure of seeing you one day, perhaps in Israel. I hope you are well. My own health leaves much to be desired.

Jo Sturdee to Winston S. Churchill
(Churchill papers, 4/390A)

11 May 1950

Mr Saunders,[1] the House of Commons Librarian, has written a History of the Royal Air Force during the late war. It is now being revised and there is one important point about which he wishes to consult you. It is the following:

In February 1945 there was a bomber attack on Dresden. Not less than 100,000 persons were killed. It was the most severe single blow against Germany by Bomber Command. He must have a reason why it was ordered, as there is a great deal of controversy on this point. The official excuse – and he has been in touch with all authorities on the point – is that the Russians asked for it to be laid on. Unfortunately there is no proof that this is true; there is nothing in writing. The Chief of the Air Staff during the war, Lord Portal, has been asked but he cannot remember. Mr Saunders would like to know, please, whether it was referred to you at the time and if you had any hand in ordering the attack, and if so what the reasons were. He feels that it is important that the reason he gives in the official history should be correct, as otherwise the Russians will accuse this country of propaganda against them, etc.

---

[1] Hilary Aidan Saint George Saunders, 1898–1951. Author. Known also by the pseudonyms Francis Beeding, Barum Browne, Cornelius Cofyn, David Pilgrim and John Somers. Entered Welsh Guards during WWI (MC). Biographer of Robert Baden-Powell. Wrote *The Battle of Britain, Bomber Command, Coastal Command, Pioneers! O Pioneers!, The Sleeping Bacchus* and *The Left Handshake.* Librarian of House of Commons, 1946–50.

If necessary Mr Saunders says he would come and see you on the subject. He expects you will refer to the matter in your own Memoirs and he feels the reason for the attack should be the same in both books. He is so sorry to have to worry you but he thinks the point is important.

He would like to settle it soon.[1]

Winston S. Churchill: speech notes
(Churchill papers, 2/99)

16 May 1950

1922 COMMITTEE LUNCHEON

Faithful discharge of our national duty will give Conservative Party a chance of rendering true service to Britain and its Empire such as the centuries seldom bring.

From the beginning we have pursued the right policy, both during the election and since the session began.

I do not see where we have made a serious mistake. We have not pulled our punches. We have done the natural honest simple things from day to day in accordance with our mandate from the constituencies and with the principles we all believe in. Do not let us be upset by the violent squealings and squallings this has aroused from the Socialists, or by the timid shiverings of the 9 Liberals. Whether there is an election in June or November does not depend on us. We have no control over it at all. It depends on what the Socialist Government thinks would pay them best. I am sorry this should be so. I wish we had the initiative. We have not got it. As far as one can see, what the Government want is holidays with full pay. That is not so bad, provided we do not in any way weaken our fighting spirit or that of our supporters by the failure to fulfil our constitutional duty. A Party which shows by its behaviour that it is afraid of an appeal to the people would be hardly likely to win their confidence. I agree that nothing is certain. I agree we cannot tell what they will do. I am quite sure that what we have done so far has been right and wise, and advantageous. I strongly recommend continuing in the same mood and method.

(Tribute to the Whips and to you all for your attendances.)

I should prefer that the election should be delayed till the end of October. That is perhaps one of the reasons why it may not be so long delayed. No one can tell. It is always better to find out what the enemy really wants and take your course accordingly, because it is very rarely that the enemy wants the same thing as you do. Nevertheless I believe that October or November will be the chosen date. No one can say for certain, but the probabilities point to the

---

[1] Churchill replied on May 12: 'I cannot recall anything about it. I thought the Americans did it. Air Vice Marshal Harris would be the person to contact.'

autumn. We must be ready, but above all we must be ready then. Whenever the moment comes, be it sooner or later, the Conservative Party will get their chance of saving the country. I am sure we had to act in that spirit and in that faith. We must be united. We must stand fearlessly by our principles. I hope in the time which may be given us we shall do our best to form the strongest anti-Socialist front possible.

We must obtain Liberal aid both as individuals and if possible as a Party, not by any political deal or bargain, but by proclaiming the fundamental principles on which all those who voted against Socialism agree.

(Notes in margin in Mr Churchill's handwriting):

1. State servant not master.
2. Individual right freedom.
3. No more nationalization. No steel.
4. The right road. United Europe.

As Lord Woolton pointed out there is a great overlap of common doctrine. Those who sincerely agree upon this common doctrine should try their best to help each other as much as they can and to hurt each other as little as they must. I am sure that if we can create this friendly atmosphere very great advantages might be gained and not only for our Party but for our country, and a great responsibility rests upon every one of us during the critical weeks and months that lie before us.

(Great responsibility on me as Leader.)

I do not propose today on this festive occasion when I am your guest to be drawn into detail of policy some of which might be controversial, but I will offer you a broad principle of action which has its place in policy as well as strategy. You should try not to quarrel with two at a time. I did not want Mr Bevin to quarrel with Germany and with Russia at the same time. I am very content with the influence we have exerted in the last 5 years upon foreign policy. Applied to the domestic sphere, I would rather not, unless, we are forced to do so, fight Liberal and Labour at the same time. The little parlour of interested individuals who control what is left of the Liberal Party gives us endless provocation and were guilty, through their partisanship, of a great national disservice at the late election, but it is always better to look forward than to look back. The word 'appeasement' is not popular, but appeasement has its place in all policy. Make sure you put it in the right place. Appease the weak, defy the strong. It is a terrible thing for a famous nation like Britain to do it the wrong way round. It would be a mistake for a Party as strong as ours and with our dominant responsibility to be provoked into doing anything to antagonise weaker elements from joining in the common struggle with Socialism, provided of course we do not sacrifice the principles or the cause to which we are in honour bound. I hope you will give me as your Leader the confidence and the sympathy which I require. Your welcome here today has removed the barrier which had risen in my mind, and I hope to come more frequently to the 1922 Committee in the future, and also to see your executive at regular intervals. I want a Liberal Party as a witness, not one as a makeweight.

Hugh Astor[1] to Winston S. Churchill
(Churchill papers, 2/173)

17 May 1950

Dear Mr Churchill,

During the course of a recent visit to Tokyo, I was fortunate enough to meet General MacArthur, who asked particularly that I should convey his good wishes and warmest regards to you.

He spoke at considerable length about the aftermath of war and the spread of Communism in Eastern Europe, which he insisted could have been avoided had the main invasion taken place through the Balkans. He stated repeatedly, 'tell Mr Churchill that he was right. He will know what I mean.'

I hope you will forgive me for writing to you in this way, but General MacArthur spoke with such evident enthusiasm and admiration that I felt obliged to pass on his message.[2]

Winston S. Churchill to Oliver Stanley
(Churchill papers, 2/101)[3]

18 May 1950

My dear Oliver,

I was grieved to get your letter and to feel that you are suffering pain and discomfort, as well as from uncertainty about the remedy. I would not in your place hesitate to take more than one opinion – but perhaps you have already done this. You are greatly missed by all of us and Clemmie sends her love. Do not however come back till you are really well again. I do not expect any serious political storm over the Finance Bill, and I think the chances are at least three to one against an election before the autumn. (Excuse my racing lingo.) You must give yourself every chance. That is the most important of all. Do let me know if I can be of any service.

Always your sincere friend.

PS. I am just off to Edinburgh instead of Hurst Park, alack!

---

[1] Hugh Waldorf Astor, 1920–99. Lt-Col., 1939. Served in Europe and Southeast Asia, 1939–45. Asst Middle East Correspondent for the *The Times*, 1947. Married Emily Lucy Kinlock, 1950: five children. JP, Berkshire, 1953. Elected to Board of *The Times*, 1956. Director, The Times Publishing Co., 1956–66; Deputy Chairman, 1959–67. Chairman, Times Trust, 1967–82.

[2] Churchill responded on June 2: 'I was very pleased to receive General MacArthur's good wishes, and I read his message with interest. I am most obliged to you for passing these on to me.'

[3] This letter was handwritten.

May 1950

Winston S. Churchill: speech
('In the Balance', pages 271–80)

18 May 1950   Usher Hall, Edinburgh

SCOTTISH UNIONIST MEETING

I think I must regard this as a red-letter day. This afternoon I am victor in the Paradise Stakes.[1] This evening I have the honour once again to address a great audience in the Usher Hall. When I was here last we had good hopes of bringing about an immediate and decisive change in the politics of our country and of establishing in effective power a Unionist and Conservative Government which would prove itself worthy of its trust and equal to these difficult and dangerous times. Now we see that in spite of the substantial advantages we gained, a second intense effort will be necessary. It is certain that another General Election must come soon. How soon we cannot tell. The initiative does not at present rest with us. It depends upon what the Socialist Government think will pay them best. Meanwhile we lie in the lull between two storms. The only Socialist Government in Europe outside the Iron Curtain continues its control of our affairs, although in a minority of more than 1,500,000 votes in the country and with a majority of only seven in the House of Commons. In estimating this majority of seven it must be remembered that if the Speaker and the Deputy Chairman of Committees, who both sit for Conservative seats, were members of the Government party, as frequently happens, and if the Unionist seat held by Mr Macmanaway[2] in Belfast were not temporarily disfranchised, the Government majority would be only two.

It is certainly satisfactory that such a Government with such credentials and with such a record is virtually deprived of all power of legislation. They have had to abandon for the time being their whole scheme for nationalizing another set of prosperous key industries, sugar, cement, insurance and the like, with which they threatened us at the General Election. Steel alone hangs in the balance, and it would indeed be an outrage if its nationalization were to be brought into force by the present Government, after its decisive rejection by the electorate. With this exception the Socialist plans for revolutionizing British industry have been brought to a full stop, and the Socialist Ministers and Members of Parliament have now to limit their immediate

---

[1] A race at Hurst Park, won in May 1950 by Churchill's horse Colonist II.
[2] James Godfrey Macmanaway, 1898–1951. Educated at Campbell College, Belfast, and Trinity College, Dublin. Ordained Priest, Church of Ireland, 1925. Married, 1926, Catherine Anne Swetenham Trench. Elected to Northern Irish Parliament, June 1947, as Member (Union.) for the City of Londonderry; to House of Commons, 1950, as Member for Belfast West. On 19 Oct. 1950 the Judicial Committee of the Privy Council determined that Macmanaway was disqualified from sitting in the House of Commons by the House of Commons (Clergy Disqualification) Act of 1801, which debarred any person ordained to the office of priest or deacon from sitting or voting in the House of Commons.

programme to the personal satisfaction of prolonged summer holidays on full pay. It must not be forgotten, however, that although the Government cannot pass any more mischievous laws, their power to squander our national resources remains unbridled. In their five years of office Socialism has consumed £19,000,000,000, and now in the new Budget they propose to spend nearly £4,000,000,000, and even to add to our taxation, already the highest in the world. Under devaluation, or *re*valuation as they were so anxious to have it called, we are still forced to give twelve hours' work for goods purchased across the dollar exchange, for what nine hours would have sufficed before that disastrous measure. The rise in the cost of living, or in other words the fall in the purchasing power of the money we earn, continues steadily. Hardly a day passes without some new increase in prices, in the cost of production, in fares and freights, in petrol, fuel and transport. Much of this adds to the burden upon every home and family, and to the difficulties of our country winning its livelihood in the increasing competition of the world. It is evident therefore that the longer this evil Socialist rule continues the worse our position will get, and the more grievous will be the problems we shall have to face. I need not appeal to you gathered here to make every exertion in your power in order to secure an effective majority for Unionism, at the impending election, because I know how earnest are your resolves and how tireless are your activities. But the need to secure a strong Government, opposed to the fallacies and frauds of Socialism, is not merely a party objective but a national aim.

We have every reason to be encouraged by the trend shown in the three by-elections that have taken place since this Parliament began, and still more with the decided victories which have been gained, especially in Scotland, during the municipal contests. But it seems to me that while we put forth every scrap of strength we can command, we should also endeavour to gather the support of all men and women of goodwill outside our own party limits. We should endeavour to unite in the common front against Socialism, not only Liberals, but the large floating vote, which played such a hesitating part last time in the trial of strength. For this purpose I should like to see an honourable understanding reached with the Liberals as a party, or where that is not possible, with individuals. This is a moment when we have a right to appeal to all patriotic and broadminded men and women who are in agreement on the main issues to do their utmost to secure the establishment of a strong, broadly-based, and stable Government capable of dealing in a courageous and progressive spirit with the ever-darkening problems that confront us. You read in the newspapers about negotiations. There are no negotiations. You read about party deals in seats. There are no party deals in seats. The Conservative and Unionist Parties have not the power to override and do not seek the power to override the decided will of constituency associations. Still, I feel this is the time when those who agree on fundamental issues should stand together. Let me mention to you some of the great issues on which Unionists and Liberals are agreed, and which constitute the elements of the common cause vital to our national welfare.

First, we proclaim that the State is the servant and not the master of the people. We reject altogether the Socialist conception of a division of society between officials and the common mass. We repudiate their policy of levelling down to a minimum uniformity, above which only politicians and their agents may rise. We stand for the increasingly higher expression of individual independence. We hold most strongly to the Declaration of Human Rights, as set forth by the United Nations at Geneva. It is worth noting that among all these United Nations we are the only great Power under Socialist rule. That is why Socialist policy has been in these past years increasingly out of step and out of harmony with, or lagging behind, the movement of thought among the democracies of the modern world.

Then we declare ourselves inveterately opposed to any further nationalization of industry, including, of course, and especially, the nationalization of steel. Further, we come to those large bodies of practical, domestic reforms set forth in *This is the Road*, and, from a very slightly different angle, and with several interesting features, set forth in the Liberal manifesto. No doubt there are other points upon which Liberals and Unionists do not agree. But how small they are in scale and importance compared to the great body of fundamental principles and practical schemes of application on which both anti-Socialist Parties are in accord and which are supported by a large majority of electors all over the country.

There is a great overlap of agreement, both in doctrine and in action, between those who have hitherto been brought up to regard themselves as political opponents. But now the times are very grave, and it is the duty of every man and woman who agrees upon so large a proportion of the main principles and practical steps, to make sure that these are not overwhelmed by the ignorant and obsolete fallacy of Socialism, against which the British nation stands today in marked recoil. All I ask, and as your leader I have a right to ask, and it is a modest demand, is that those who agree upon the fundamentals shall, in our party conflicts, try to help each other as much as they can, and to harm each other as little as they must. Let that climate of opinion and theme of conduct prevail, and we shall have cleared the path of progress of many of its pitfalls and barriers, and perhaps gain the power to rescue our native land from some of the perils and forms of degeneration to which it is exposed.

There is no doubt that nationalization, so far as it has gone, has proved an utter failure financially, economically and morally. But there is now an argument against it which undoubtedly makes an impression upon the Socialist leaders – it is evidently politically unpopular. Therefore there is to be a conference this weekend at Dorking to see whether they can think of something else. They do not know whether to bury Socialism and nationalization, which they have been preaching for fifty years and practising for five, and look for some other method of carrying on the class war. In any case, we are confronted with a party which has lost its convictions and has no longer a theme and plan and which, instead of proclaiming an ideological design for the reconstruction of human society, is now hungrily looking around for a new election cry.

I see that some of the newspapers say the whole seventy of them at Dorking are to be *locked up* together. That I think would be going too far. After all we are still a free country. Besides Dorking is much too close to my home at Chartwell. I might have to go and feed them through the bars. If they ran short of coupons I might be put in among them. Then I should be told I was trying to form a coalition by backstage methods. It would never do.

Meanwhile we must do our duty in the new Parliament in such a way as to limit on every possible occasion the mismanagement of our affairs by the Socialist Government and so far as possible to mitigate the evils which it brings upon our people. I assert that from the beginning we have pursued the right policy, both during the election and since the session began. We have not pulled our punches, we have done the natural, honest, simple thing from day to day on serious issues in accordance with our mandate from the constituencies and with the principles and cause we all believe in. I do not know whether any of the violent squealings and squallings which this policy has aroused from the Socialists have reached you here in Scotland. It is natural that the Government do not like being opposed. Their argument is that the smaller their Parliamentary majority the less they should be opposed, and they even make the remarkable claim that the Opposition should never vote against them without being sure beforehand that there are enough Socialists in their places doing the work for which they are paid, to give the Government a majority. Any failure of their members to be in their places on a critical occasion they represent a 'snap decision'. This is a novel constitutional doctrine utterly inconsistent with British Parliamentary life, and it has that totalitarian flavour about it which we notice in some of the dummy parliaments which have been erected in the satellite countries of Europe. These Socialist complaints leave us unmoved. The course we have adopted has already procured several notable advantages for the country as a whole. We have forced the Socialist Government to make many concessions to the public interest which they harshly refused in the days when they had an automatic majority to vote down any opposition and ride roughshod over us all. The first of these has been the abolition of the compulsory conscription of labour in time of peace. That has been swept away. They have been forced to arrest all nationalization except steel. You will remember what an outcry they made when I said that the petrol ration should be increased, what a shocking thing, they cried, to cast away the precious dollars on which we depend for the food of our people, merely for the luxury of pleasurable motoring. How irresponsible to make such a suggestion, but now they have themselves doubled the petrol ration, proving, as I said, that it was always possible, or has been for a long time possible, and exposing the untruthful character of their electioneering arguments and propaganda. There have also been minor concessions in controls in the building industry. The private builder is to be given more scope in England and Wales at any rate, and it is to be easier for the citizen – fancy that, easier for him – to enlarge his house or his farm buildings. PAYE has been modified, as we urged in the *Right Road for Britain*, so as to be less penal in its discouragement of overtime and effect. We are even to be allowed stronger beer. I should certainly take Sir Stafford Cripps some of that. It might do him good. It could hardly do him harm.

I must, however, draw your attention to the characteristic remark by Dr Dalton, the new Minister of Town and Country Planning. In announcing one of his minor concessions he said, 'This is an experiment in freedom. I hope it will not be abused.' Could you have anything more characteristic of the Socialist rulers' outlook towards the public? Freedom is a favour; it is an experiment which the governing class of Socialist politicians will immediately curtail if they are displeased with our behaviour. This is language which the head of a Borstal Institution might suitably use to the inmates when announcing some modification of a disciplinary system. What an example of smug and insolent conceit! What a way to talk to the British people! As a race we have been experimenting in freedom, not entirely without success, for several centuries, and have spread the ideas of freedom throughout the world. And yet, here is this Minister, who speaks to us as if it lay with him to dole out our liberties like giving biscuits to a dog who will sit up and beg prettily. This characteristic of the official Socialist temperament and attitude in office should not pass uncensured by the British people who expect Ministers of the Crown to behave as the servants and not as the masters of the nation.

Finally we have made them replace the 25,000 houses they had cut from the building programme, and raise the total from 175,000 back to 200,000 a year. I am very glad they have been forced to do this; of course it in no way meets the housing problem which continues to hold the first place in our domestic needs. Nevertheless all these concessions we have wrung and wrested from the Socialists show how right in fact, and how fruitful to the public has been the severe pressure which we have applied in the House of Commons and shall continue to apply. It would indeed be an ill day if an Opposition virtually as strong as the Government numerically were to be deterred from doing its duty in Parliament out of fear of causing an appeal to the electors. I must dwell for a moment on the housing problem – or on the housing scandal as it may be more justly described.

The Government now tell us that 200,000 houses a year is the most we are to expect for the next three years. Such a programme in no way meets the needs of the people or the capacity of the people to meet those needs; 200,000 houses a year is less than the number the Socialist Government themselves managed to produce in 1948. It is less than two-thirds of the number built each year under the Conservatives before the war, at less than half the price; 200,000 houses according to Mr Aneurin Bevan, was the number we needed merely to replace the houses which got worn out each year. It makes no attempt to reduce the melancholy and growing waiting lists kept at every Town Hall throughout the country. It offers no hope at all of resuming the slum clearance campaign, which was well on the move under the wicked Tories in the years before the war.

But if things are bad in England I assert that the Scottish housing programme is even worse. To tell the Scottish people, as the Socialist Government do, that it will take another three years to bring the Scottish building rate up to 27,500 houses a year, is a confession of administrative failure of the most shameful kind. Why, the waiting lists at Edinburgh and Glasgow alone amount to 110,000 families. Surely it is a time for a new deal, a new hand. Surely this is a time when the people of this country may say to the Socialist Government: 'We have had enough of you. Get out and let someone else have a go!'

The increased petrol tax, the new purchase tax on lorries, and the increases in rail charges, will place an additional burden of more than £100,000,000 a year on the cost of transport. In Scotland, where long distances often separate manufacturers and customers from their markets and sources of supply, the burden will be especially severe. In this as in so many other matters, Scottish needs and difficulties have received scant attention from Socialist-ridden Whitehall. The Unionist Party is pledged to give fresh consideration to the whole question of Scotland's place in our economic and political life, and to relieve her from the present over-centralization in Whitehall. In particular we have put forward proposals for the establishment of separate Scottish boards, in no way subordinate to the English boards, for the railways and other industries remaining under public ownership.

The increased railway charges are in effect a new tax of £27,000,000. Yet the Government were extremely reluctant to allow Parliament an opportunity of debating it. We insisted on a debate, but there was no opportunity of putting forward amendments. Increases in the price of nationalized coal, gas and electricity have never been laid before Parliament for approval. This in my view constitutes a marked abrogation of Parliamentary liberties and of the prime duty of the House of Commons to deal with taxation.

Control over taxation and the revenues of the State has always been the foundation on which Parliamentary Government has rested, and indeed there is no other foundation upon which it can rest. Once the State acquires sources of revenue independent of Parliament, then the power of Parliament to curb and check the maladministration is seriously diminished. The whole system of controls rests on the Supplies and Services Act, 1945, which expires at the end of this year. Mr Morrison at the 1949 Socialist Conference announced that it would then be replaced by a permanent measure. I take this occasion of announcing that we shall oppose the permanent extension of the Act and insist on continuation only on a year-to-year basis, in order to retain full Parliamentary control. Well, after what I have said, they will not be able to call that division a snap division.

Our attitude as an Opposition today remains precisely what it has been ever since the Socialists took office in 1945. Every measure based on their party doctrine or prejudice meets with our resistance. Every measure conceived in the national interest, even if it is unpopular, receives our support. Thus we have supported conscription – in time of peace – when it would have been to our electoral advantage to have denounced it. We are entitled to justice and respect in these matters. We have supported every step Mr Bevin has taken in foreign policy, however belated or ill-combined. We have frequently sustained the Government against the attack of their own followers. What a contrast is all this to the behaviour of the pre-war Socialist Party, when they were in Opposition and when they opposed every defence estimate, did their best to hamper the recruiting campaign, and, led by Mr Attlee, voted against National Service only four months before war broke out.

I ask this great meeting of the Unionists of Scotland for a firm and decided endorsement of the work we have already done in this connection. Since we have been able to achieve these results while in a minority, it may well be that if the tables were turned the British nation could speedily be relieved of an immense network and oppression of needless controls by a new administration seeking the public welfare with whole-hearted security.

It is with relief that I turn to wider fields. You will remember the last time I was here how I spoke of the world situation. There has just been a conference in London of the Foreign Ministers of all the countries associated with the Atlantic Pact and with Western Union, and above all with our common defence against aggression. As you know I have in Parliament formally disclaimed any responsibility for the actual military preparations nor can I be accused for the delays which have occurred, but naturally I am glad to see so much of what I and my friends have urged and worked for making progress, even if it is mainly in words and sentiments. Mr Eden pointed out at the beginning of the Parliament that although the Government had a small majority and were weak politically at home, there was no reason why they should not pursue a strong and imaginative foreign policy. In all these five years we have supported the Government on the broad lines of foreign policy. It was, and still is, easy for us to do so, because that policy has followed, although tardily, the path we have pointed and prescribed. For more than forty years I have worked with France. At Zurich I appealed to her to regain the leadership of Europe by extending her hand to bring Germany back into the European family. We have now the proposal which M Schuman, the French Foreign Minister, has made for the integration of French and German coal and steel industries. This would be an important and effective step in preventing another war between France and Germany and lay at last to rest that quarrel of 1,000 years between Gaul and Teuton. Now France has taken the initiative in a manner beyond my hopes. But that by itself would not be enough. In order to make France able to deal on proper terms with Germany, we must be with France. The prime condition for the recovery of Europe is Britain and France standing together with all their strength and with all their wounds; and then these two nations offering their hands to Germany on honourable terms and with a great and merciful desire to look forward rather than back. For centuries France and England, and latterly Germany and France, have rent the world by their struggles. They have only to be united together to constitute the dominant force in the Old World and to become the centre of United Europe around which all other countries could rally. But added to this you have all the mighty approval of the great world power which has arisen across the Atlantic, and has shown itself in its hour of supremacy anxious only to make further sacrifices for the cause of freedom.

While therefore this Schuman proposal is right in principle we must consider with proper attention the way in which Great Britain can participate most effectively in such a larger grouping of European industry. We must be careful that it does not carry with it a lowering of British wages and standards of life and labour. We must I feel assert the principle of levelling up and not of levelling down. We are all surely proud of the British steel industry which plays so large a part in our export trade. The terms on which we could combine with Continental nations must be carefully and searchingly studied. If we were to destroy or even to impair the efficiency of our steel industry by nationalization, we might find ourselves at a serious disadvantage compared to Continental countries which are free from Socialist abuses. We must be reassured on these and other points while welcoming cordially the whole principle and spirit of what is proposed. At present no detailed information has been published and the Government themselves were taken by surprise. I have therefore assented to Mr Attlee's request that the debate upon this matter should be postponed until after the Whitsuntide holidays, by which time we should all know more than we do now. Great events are happening. They happen from day to day, and headlines are never lacking. But we must not allow the ceaseless clack and clatter which is the characteristic of our age to turn our minds from these great events. I still hope that the unities now being established among all the Western democracies and Atlantic Powers will ward off from us the terrors and unspeakable miseries of a third world war. I wish also that every effort should be made on the highest level to bring home to the Russian Soviet Government the gravity of the facts which confront us all. I do not give up the hope which I expressed to you here on this very spot three months ago, of 'a supreme effort to bridge the gulf between the two worlds, if not in friendship, at least without the hatreds and manoeuvres of the cold war.'[1] I have not abandoned that hope. But of this I am sure: that the best hopes will be founded upon the strength of the Western democracies and upon their unwavering willpower to defend the causes for which they stand. To work from weakness and fear is ruin. To work from wisdom and power may be salvation. These simple but tremendous facts are I feel being understood by the free nations better than they have ever been before.

I believe that the faithful discharge of our national duty by everyone of us laying aside all impediments, all prejudices, all temptation, will give the Unionist Party a chance of rendering true service to Britain, its Empire and the world.

Winston S. Churchill: speech
('Winston S. Churchill, His Complete Speeches', volume 8, pages 8007–8)

20 May 1950   Astley, Worcestershire

LORD BALDWIN

I am honoured by being asked to perform the ceremony of handing over to the Trustees this Memorial to my old chief, Stanley Baldwin, under whom I served as Chancellor of the Exchequer for nearly five years.

I was very glad when his son,[2] who is here today, asked me to do this, because although I had several deep political differences with his father, we were always good friends, and I never remember a time when I could not discuss with him any matter, public or private, frankly and freely, as man to man.

Here was a statesman who, over a long period of years, exercised a remarkable personal influence upon British politics and British fortunes. He was three times Prime Minister. He led the Conservative Party in five elections, in three of which he won the solid and considered support of the majority of his fellow countrymen. In domestic politics he was one of the most capable leaders you could have found for many generations. There was a strong sentiment of comradeship and kinship between him and the English people, and here near Bewdley, where he was born, and at Astley Hall, where he lived – here, in Worcestershire, which he cherished and revered, lay the centre of his strong patriotism. He loved England, and in every part of our country he

---

[1] Speech reproduced above (pp. 1651–7).
[2] Oliver Ridsdale Baldwin, 1899–1958. Educated at Eton. Active service in WWI, 1914–18. Acting Vice-Consul at Boulogne, 1919. Fought in Turkish–Armenian War, 1920, and in Russian–Armenian War, 1921. Wrote *Six Prisons and Two Revolutions* (1925) and *Socialism and the Bible* (1928). MP (Lab.) for Dudley, 1929–31; for Paisley, 1945–7. Maj., Intelligence Corps, 1939. Active service in WWII, 1940–5. Succeeded as 2nd Viscount Corvedale and 2nd Earl Baldwin of Bewdley, 1947. Governor and C-in-C, Leeward Islands, 1948–50.

found men and women who recognized in him moods and qualities which they admired.

He was the controlling power in two long and notable administrations. He was the most formidable politician I have ever known in our public life. He had profound knowledge of the workings of the mind of the average man, and a sincere desire to be helpful to them. If he shared some of their weaknesses he shared much of their calm, patient strength. He won and kept over nearly twenty years a steady measure of their confidence and good will. While pursuing by gradual and continuous steps his general theme of an ever-broadening democratic way of life, he was always ready to stand in the background himself and let others have the publicity and spectacular prominence. In private life we must not forget how, after the First World War, he presented anonymously a fifth of his private fortune – £120,000 – to the nation, seeking no thanks or political advantage.

In his administration from 1924 to 1929, in which I served as one of his most intimate colleagues, living in the house next door to No. 10, he achieved two enduring triumphs. The first was the Pact of Locarno, in the making of which he earnestly sustained Sir Austen Chamberlain. This marked the highest point reached in the peaceful settlement of Europe between the two world wars. The second was a five years' steady improvement, judged by every test, in the standards of life, labour and employment of the British people. There was nothing in our domestic life at the end of that period which, in spite of the harsh interruption of the General Strike, was not markedly better at the end than at the beginning.

I had parted political companionship with him before he began his second long term of power. My difference arose about India. I hold to the views I then expressed today, but I am content to leave history to judge as it unfolds over the years that are to come. But the British nation, all parties in the State, have endorsed Mr Baldwin's views and the consequences that follow from them. No one who accepted his guidance then has a right to reproach his memory now.

In his second administration, for the greater part of which he was not officially Prime Minister but actually wielded the controlling power, he undoubtedly presided over a great recovery from the financial and economic collapse of 1931, and brought us back into steady, stable and constantly improving conditions of national life. A whole series of foreign and military events with which he was not specially fitted to deal then broke in upon his conduct of home affairs. As I was his chief critic upon these issues, and my words are upon record, I have a right to declare here and now, by this sandstone memorial, that his courage and patriotism did not fail, although the tragic course of events belied his judgment.

When, at length, in 1937, oppressed by the infirmities of age, he retired from public office into private life, it was amid the almost universal plaudits and tributes of his fellow countrymen. Presently there broke upon us all those fearful catastrophes which have wrecked, though we are sure not irretrievably, the progress and prosperity of mankind. Not all who now claim superior wisdom foresaw what was approaching.

Here, then, there is erected this simple monument to the virtues and services of a good Englishman, who loved his country and faithfully sought the advance in the well-being of those whom it is now the fashion to call 'the common people', but who were always dear to his heart.

Of all parts of England, Worcestershire stood in his mind honoured and pre-eminent, and, of all parts of Worcestershire, the soil in which he lies and the ground on which we now stand was his most sacred spot. Let me now discharge my task by presenting this Memorial of Stanley Baldwin to the Trustees. As the years roll by and the perspective of history lengthens and reduces so many of our disputes to their due proportion, there will be few who will pass this place without giving their respectful salute.

Winston S. Churchill to Randolph S. Churchill
(Churchill papers, 1/48)

21 May 1950

My dear Randolph,

Did you receive my letter with the cheque for £50? Was that the right sum, and have you settled up with the bookmaker accordingly? We were very pleased to win this race. I am glad to hear from Christopher that you had a modest bet.

With regard to the wireless set that I now have with me, I understood that the one you have left belonged to June, and that you had lent it to me only temporarily. What I wish is to return you this set, and that you should send me a new one, and of course the bill as well. How does this matter stand now?

I hope you are happy down there, and are making progress. I am still not absolutely certain in my own mind that they may not make a pounce in June, but I think the odds are 3 or 4 to 1 in favour of October or early November. Anyhow it will soon be too late for June. I have had a strenuous patch – 3 speeches and two nights in the train.

Winston S. Churchill to Clement Attlee
(Churchill papers, 2/29)

24 May 1950

My dear Prime Minister,

I return you the paper you have been good enough to send me enclosed in your letter of May 7.[1] I hope you will not mind me saying that it is not very informative. I have known for a long time that something between seventy and a hundred divisions, with proportionate armour and air force, would be required to resist a Russian attack upon the Western front. My own opinion is that the Western forces have barely ten divisions, a proportion of which are dependent on German services for their transport. We are very much outnumbered in the air after making every allowance for quality. It seems that nearly a whole year has been spent by the Atlantic Powers in talk. I cannot imagine that a European Army of ninety divisions could possibly be created under three or four years of intensive effort, and expenditure beyond what anyone has dreamed of.

Without the strong aid of a German contingent beginning with five and running up, as American, British and French armies grew, perhaps to twenty divisions, there are no means of offering any effective defence for Western Europe. At present the only Germans who are allowed to be trained are the Communists, whom the Russians have been for a long time organizing into an Army on a large scale both inside and outside the Eastern Zone.

The only thing that keeps the peace is the American possession of the atomic bomb. I see however that General Omar Bradley[2] said that 'in three or four years the Soviets would have sufficient supply of these to cause a major catastrophe at any time they so decided', or words to that effect. They may not be affected by the same moral restraints as have governed the United States during their phase of unquestioned superiority. At any rate they will have in three or four years both overwhelming military superiority in Europe and a formidable supply of atomic bombs. We have quite rightly given the Americans a base in East Anglia for the obvious purpose of using the atomic bomb on Moscow and other Russian cities. We are therefore a prime target for attack. Our defence against such an attack has been greatly weakened by our sale of jetfighter airplanes to the Argentine and Egypt as we have read in

[1] Reproduced above (p. 1741).
[2] Omar Nelson Bradley, 1893–1981. Married, 1916, Mary Elizabeth Quayle (d. 1965); 1966, Esther 'Kitty' Buhler. Instructor at US Military Academy, West Point, 1934–8. Chief of Operations Section, G-1, War Dept General Staff, 1938–40. Asst Secretary of General Staff, Office of CoS, War Dept, 1940–1. Commandant, Infantry School, 1941–2. Commanding Gen., 82nd Div., Feb.–June 1942; 28th Div., June 1942 to Feb. 1943. Personal Representative in the Field for C-in-C US North African Theater of Operations, Feb.–March 1943. Deputy Commanding Gen., II Corps, Mar.–Apr. 1943; Commanding Gen., Apr.–Sep. 1943. C-in-C, 1st Army Group (UK), Oct. 1943 to July 1944. Commanding Gen., 1st Army, 1943–4. C-in-C, 12th Army Group, Aug. 1944 to July 1945. Administrator for Veteran Affairs, 1945–7. CoS, US Army, Feb. 1947 to Aug. 1949. Chairman of JCS, 1949–53.

the newspapers, and no doubt elsewhere to an even larger extent. In my long experience I have never seen a situation so perilous and strange.

We lie between two elections and of course your people would be very glad to be able to use my warnings to found a charge of 'warmongering'. Nevertheless I am sure the House of Commons ought to have some realization of the position. I shall ask after Whitsun for a Secret Session. This is not because any secrets not already known to the potential enemy need be disclosed, but so that the position can be fairly put before the House of Commons. I think you will be bearing a very exceptional load of responsibility if you deny this knowledge to Parliament. I hope you will very carefully consider this letter which I write in all truth and respect, and which you are at liberty to show to anyone in your confidential circle.[1]

Winston S. Churchill: broadcast
('Winston S. Churchill, His Complete Speeches', volume 8, pages 8008-10)

24 May 1950

FIELD MARSHAL SMUTS'S EIGHTIETH BIRTHDAY

It is with feelings not only of honour but of the keenest pleasure that I propose on his eightieth birthday the health of Jan Smuts. It is just over fifty years ago that I first met him. It was not an agreeable occasion. I was a wet and weary prisoner-of-war, and he was questioning me on my status as a war correspondent and the part I had played in the fighting for the armoured train in Natal. Since then our relationship has steadily improved, and tonight I can say that I have no more respected and cherished friend in the world. Warrior, statesman, strategist, philosopher, the illustrious Field Marshal has indeed claims to the admiration and gratitude of lovers of freedom and of civilization in every land.

[. . .]

And now here we have him in our midst, an august octogenarian. Here is the man who raised the name of South Africa in peace and war to the highest rank of respect among the freedom-loving nations of the world. Let us pray that this may not be smirched or cast away in the demoralization which so often follows the greatest human triumphs.

Such a melancholy stroke will certainly not fall on South Africa if Smuts's life and strength are prolonged, and that is why we rejoice in his presence here tonight, and why I call upon this distinguished company to rise and drink to his health, and wish him from the bottom of our hearts many, many happy returns of the day.

[1] Attlee responded the next day: 'Thank you for your letter of the 24th May with which you returned the paper on the North Atlantic and Brussels Treaty Councils. I will consider the points you raise with my colleagues during the Whitsun Recess.'

May 1950

Lord Moran: diary
('The Struggle for Survival', pages 359–60)

25 May 1950

Winston is quite sure that the tightness over his shoulders has increased. He can't get the stroke out of his mind. To reassure him I called in Russell Brain.[1]

'The cells in your brain,' he explained, 'which receive sensory messages from your shoulder are dead. That's all. It's a bit of luck that sensation only is affected.'

He seemed relieved by Brain's air of finality, and began talking about his dyspepsia. For ten years he had been 'tortured' by it, then he heard of Mac-Mahon's[2] name.

'He cured me by his breathing exercises. Why, after his third visit there was an enormous difference in the whole structure of the body.'

Winston S. Churchill to Cyril Garbett[3]
(Churchill papers, 2/102)

28 May 1950

My dear Archbishop,

I have read a report in the newspapers of your observations on 'Snap' divisions in the House of Commons. As I am anxious to profit to the full by your guidance in these matters I enclose a list of all the divisions that have taken place in the present Parliament. I should be much obliged if you would mark whose which you consider deserving of censure on account of being 'Snap' divisions, and I will then address myself to the facts about them in detail.

---

[1] Walter Russell Brain, 1895–1966. Neurologist and physician to Winston Churchill. Educated at Mill Hill School and New College, Oxford. Friends Ambulance Unit, 1914–18. Fellow, Royal College of Physicians, 1931; President, 1950–6. Knighted, 1952. Baron, 1952.

[2] Cortlandt MacMahon, 1875–1954. Instructor for Speech Defects and Breathing Exercises at St Bartholomew's Hospital, London, 1911–39. Treated many cases of gunshot wounds in the chest, and cases of speech damage due to the war, on behalf of the Ministry of Pensions, 1918–26. Author of several papers on stammering, published in medical journals.

[3] Cyril Forster Garbett, 1875–1955. Born in Tongham, Surrey. Educated at Keble College, Oxford, and Cuddesdon Theological College. Curate of St Mary, Portsea, 1900–9; Vicar, 1909–19. Bishop of Southwark, 1919–32. Bishop of Winchester, 1932–42. Clerk of the Closet to the King, 1937–42. PC, 1942. Archbishop of York, 1942–55. GCVO, 1955.

Cyril Garbett to Winston S. Churchill
(Churchill papers, 2/102)

30 May 1950

Dear Mr Churchill,

Hearty thanks for your letter and for your kindness in sending me a list of the divisions which have taken place in the present Parliament. I had not any intention of reflecting on the Opposition by my remark on 'snap divisions'. I was congratulating the members of our new Convocation on the fact that their attendance would not be under such compulsion as that of the members of the House of Commons. I then went on to say that democracy 'will emerge triumphant if common sense and self-restraint are shown by both the great parties' – I am afraid I forgot the Liberal Party – 'and no advantage will come to the nation through snap divisions and the consequent tension, which are exhausting to the physique and trying to the temper'. I added that though coalition was out of the question at the present time, there were many uncontroversial matters of national importance on which fruitful co-operation should be possible in a short lived Parliament, and though our Convocation might in the future be known as 'the short Convocation', I hoped it would also be remembered for useful work. It had not occurred to me that what I was saying was in any way controversial, though I feared it might be somewhat platitudinous. The rest of the charge was devoted to ecclesiastical problems. I am very sorry there should have been any misunderstanding.

June 1950

Winston S. Churchill to President Chaim Weizmann
(Churchill papers, 2/102)

2 June 1950

My dear Weizmann,

It was with very great pleasure that I received, through Sir Simon Marks, your kind letter of May 7.[1] I am so much interested to know your views on these terrific events which are taking place in your country. I am told by people who have recently visited Israel of the many signs of hard work, courage and foresight on the part of your fellow-countrymen, and of the great progress which is being made in the agricultural and industrial life there.

As always I follow your fortunes with keen interest, and I take this opportunity of sending you my warmest regards and my good wishes for your continued health and strength. I feel that it is under your leadership and guidance that Israel will enjoy prosperity and happiness.

Winston S. Churchill to Clement Attlee
(Churchill papers, 2/76)

4 June 1950

My dear Prime Minister,

I am disappointed by your letter of May 23 about substitutes for Strasbourg. You have, I think, been misled into saying that it was 'the unanimous decision of last year's Assembly that substitutes should be abolished'. This was only half the story. The resolution which was carried was that the number of full delegates should be doubled. This would, of course, have made substitutes superfluous. I should be much obliged if you could look into these facts again.

We are however in your hands. I am willing to accept the nine substitutes which you have offered (four Labour, four Conservatives and one Liberal): but

[1] Reproduced above (pp. 1741–2).

I hope and request that these nine substitutes shall be entitled to remain at Strasbourg throughout the Session so that they can be fully conversant with the work. I do not think this would add greatly to the expense. If so, we shall be content with currency facilities within the limits assigned.

Winston S. Churchill to Sir Alexander Korda[1]
(Churchill papers, 2/171)

4 June 1950

My dear Korda,

Thank you so much for your letter of May 26. I am very glad you heard good reports of the reception of my third volume in the United States. My feeling is that the fourth will be better. I am indeed grateful to you for writing to me such encouraging accounts.

I am sure you will forgive me for not attending the premiere of *Odette*, to which the King and Queen are going. My burdens are heavy and holidays are short. I should be most grateful if you would let me have this film for a show at Chartwell, when that is convenient.

Winston S. Churchill to R. A. Butler
(Churchill papers, 2/99)

4 June 1950

A NOTE

It looks as if the Socialists, having failed in nationalization, would try a popularity electioneering stunt upon the Middlemen's profits and alleged exploitation by the public. We need to know the facts about this. It would be a misfortune if the Conservative Party got lumbered-up with anything like what might be called 'a ramp' in this field. We must see how the matter stands before we take any decision. There is no doubt that the difference between, for instance, the price paid to the trawlers for fish and the prices charged by retail trade in London, and probably elsewhere, is very large. In the same way one feels that vegetables etc., have a large burden laid upon them between the grower and the retail seller. This may be an excessive burden which we should certainly not share as a Party.

---

[1] Alexander Korda, 1893–1956. Born in Hungary. Educated at Budapest University. Film producer in Budapest, Vienna, Berlin, Hollywood and Paris. Founder and Chairman of London Film Productions Ltd, 1932. Became a British subject, 1936. Founded Alexander Korda Productions, 1939. Made 112 films, including *The Scarlet Pimpernel* (1934), *The Third Man* (1949) and *Richard III* (1956). Knighted 1942.

Will you suggest to me the form of inquiry which would be most convenient and fruitful. Once we have the broad facts it will be possible to take action. We could, for instance, invite the key figures among the Middlemen to a conference, in the first case secret. I should be willing to preside myself. At a suitable moment we should let them know that we shall not support them unless they make good their case. The lack of our support would certainly be fatal to their schemes, because the other side have only the interest of destroying them, and also the mood. After having explored the ground together, and seeing where we all stand, we might even be able to declare a programme of action by voluntary agreement, which would supersede and avoid the inefficiency of government controls.

<p align="center">Winston S. Churchill to Hugh Astor
(<i>Churchill papers, 2/173</i>)</p>

8 June 1950

My dear Astor,

I write with further reference to my letter to you of June 2.[1] I was very glad to receive the message from General MacArthur, of whom I have always been a great admirer.

I wonder what he means by the expression, 'the Balkans'. I never had any idea of sending an Army there. He is probably referring to the proposed advance by Istria and through the Lubliana Gap, of which I was of course strongly in favour.

<p align="center">Winston S. Churchill to Cyril Garbett
(<i>Churchill papers, 2/102</i>)</p>

9 June 1950

My dear Archbishop,

I am glad to learn from your letter of May 30[2] that you had 'no intention of reflecting on the Opposition' by your remark on 'snap' divisions. As however the matter is extremely controversial and a subject of current Party disputes, your observations caused regret and concern to some of my advisors. I thought it therefore right to send you a full statement of the divisions which have taken place so far. In the only case when the Government were defeated it was at the close of an important debate on the quality of coal supplies, and no few[3] than five hundred and forty Members were present in the House. It

[1] Reproduced above (p. 1745 n. 2).
[2] Reproduced above (p. 1760).
[3] fewer.

would not therefore have been in any way proper to describe this as a 'snap' division.

The expression 'snap division' has not been defined with any precision, nor has it ever been considered improper or unfair in my long Parliamentary experience, but certainly it implies the three elements of surprise to the Government of the day, paucity of numbers in the House and unimportance of the issue. It is the duty of the Government of the day to maintain a majority in all circumstances. But if a division were characterized by the three features I have mentioned above, it would of course be natural for the Government to set the vote up again and make it a vote of confidence. This would also apply in quite a large range of divisions.

We Conservatives consider it our duty to vote against the Government with our full strength on every occasion upon issues where our convictions are involved and about which we have received a mandate from our constituencies. There would be very great complaints from those who had returned us to Parliament if we neglected these duties.

Walter Graebner: recollection
('My Dear Mr Churchill', pages 33–4)

10 June 1950

One day in 1950 I went down to visit him at Chartwell, and found him busily at work on a manuscript in his study.

'I've done a lot of work,' he told me happily. 'Volume Five is in good shape. It can be called a Property. And I'm getting along with Six, too.' He then jumped and marched to the long wooden counter along the wall where a complete set of proofs was always kept. 'See', he said. 'Eighty thousand words in the first book of Volume Five and ninety thousand in the second. If I should fall down dead tomorrow this book could carry my name.'

'But you're in the best of health,' I declared. 'You've not looked better in years.'

'I know,' he answered. 'The important thing is that I live until July 1. By that time the trust will be five years old, and after that I can die without the government taking most of it away in taxes. I must be careful about flying until then because I want to be sure the kids are looked after. But after July ... hmmm ... then I can fly like hell. I'm getting thirty-five thousand pounds out of Volume Five. That's plenty for me, but nothing of that will be left for the trust. Still the trust has had five whacks at the book already. Not so bad.'

In many ways Churchill was one of the most extravagant of men. Several years after the war he spent £5,000 to build a small new reservoir at Chartwell because he was not satisfied with the water flow; less than a month later he came to the conclusion that the reservoir was not necessary at all.

At other times he could be extremely cautious. When a storm struck Kent and caused havoc among his trees Churchill spent a morning negotiating a fee of £50 to be paid a local tree doctor for patching up some of the worst damage near the house. In the few weeks that followed, Churchill himself spent many mornings sawing up limbs that had been blown down.

Randolph S. Churchill to Winston S. Churchill
(Churchill papers, 1/51)[1]

11 June 1950

My dearest Papa,

Thank you so much for your cheque.[2] It was very generous of you to give me a share in your win on Canyon Kid.[3]

When I decided to fight Devonport again you very kindly said that you would try to help me financially. I fear I am urgently in need of said help. I have virtually earned no money at all since the end of last year, and as a result have been running into debt.

I should hate to be a burden to you in this matter as I know how many calls there are on you; I was wondering if the Trust could give me some extra help this year in view of the special circumstances? I will be most grateful if something can be arranged.

[. . .]

Hugh Astor to Winston S. Churchill
(Churchill papers, 2/173)

13 June 1950

Dear Mr Churchill,

Thank you very much for your letters of 2nd and 8th June.[4] I think there is no doubt that General MacArthur was referring to the proposed plan to advance by way of Istria and through the Lubliana Gap.

Unfortunately, General MacArthur's reference to Eastern Europe came at the end of a lengthy account of developments in Japan since the end of the war, and of the spread of Communism in China and South East Asia. To the best of my recollection, however, General MacArthur said that you had been strongly in support of the plan, but that it had finally been abandoned, largely at the insistence of General Marshall.

[1] This letter was handwritten.
[2] See letter of May 21, reproduced above (p. 1756).
[3] One of Churchill's racehorses. Acquired 1948. He won the Speedy Stakes at Windsor, but died shortly thereafter, having broken a blood vessel at exercise.
[4] Reproduced above (pp. 1745 n. 2 and 1763).

General MacArthur seemed to be of the opinion that events had proved your own policy correct, and that much of the trouble in Eastern Europe might have been averted if the plan had been adopted. He was anxious that his message should be transmitted to you, and seemed confident that it would convey some meaning.

Clement Attlee to Winston S. Churchill
(Churchill papers, 2/29)

13 June 1950

My dear Churchill,

I write in reply to your letter of the 24th May,[1] in which you told me that you had it in mind to ask, when Parliament reassembled, that the House of Commons should meet in Secret Session to discuss the defence of Western Europe.

I have considered very carefully all that you say in your letter, and I have consulted some of my senior Cabinet colleagues on the point – I was glad that you gave me leave to show your letter to them. I have, however, come to the conclusion that it would be inexpedient for Parliament to debate these matters in Secret Session. My reasons are the same as those which led me to deprecate a similar suggestion which you made in the autumn of 1948; and, as I explained them to you fully at that time, I need not perhaps elaborate them again now. Briefly, I believe that the holding of a Secret Session would give rise to serious public alarm, and a crop of irresponsible rumours, which neither the Government nor the Opposition would be able to control. I cannot imagine that such a situation could do any service to the countries which are friendly to us; and I feel confident that those which are unfriendly would not fail to exploit it to our disadvantage. I fully recognize that the Government is responsible to Parliament: but Parliament itself has responsibilities towards the public and, if the holding of a Secret Session in time of peace gave rise to the widespread public anxiety which I fear, I for my part should find it difficult to resist the pressure which, I feel sure, the Press would bring to bear for some public debate or statement which would enable the public to put matters in their true perspective. So far as I am aware, Parliament has never met in Secret Session in time of peace – and this, doubtless, is due to considerations of the kind to which I have drawn attention.

This does not mean, however, that I do not share much of your anxiety about the defence problems of Western Europe. There are many features in the present situation which are disquieting. We are not here concerned only, or even mainly, with the acts or omissions of His Majesty's Government – indeed,

[1] Reproduced above (pp. 1757–8).

I believe that more has been done to maintain the country's defences during the past five years than has ever been done by any previous Administration in a comparable post-war period. We are more concerned with the weaknesses of our Allies in Western Europe, and the means of remedying these and welding the total resources of the Atlantic Treaty Powers into an effective system for the defence of Western Europe. I should hope that these problems, including our own deficiencies, need not become issues of Party controversy. They are matters on which I should be glad to have the advantage of your help and advice. The suggestion which I put forward – and I ask you to give it your most earnest consideration – is that, instead of expressing your views and your anxieties in debate, even in Secret Session, you should bring some of your friends who share your confidence in these matters to discuss them with me and some of my Cabinet colleagues.

In the course of last year we had several confidential discussions of this kind on the strength of our Armed Forces. At the last of these meetings on 20th October, you said that you would revise the memorandum which you had presented to us in the light of the information which you had obtained from Ministers in the course of these talks. May I suggest that those confidential discussions should now be resumed, and that their scope should be widened to cover the more general questions relating to the defence of Western Europe which you raised in your letter of the 24th May?

L. S. Amery to Winston S. Churchill
(*Churchill papers, 2/166*)[1]

19 June 1950

My dear Winston,

Julian and I returned a week ago after an immensely interesting visit to Israel and Jordan. Weizmann asked me to send you a most cordial invitation to come out some time soon and see things for yourself. I would endorse that, for the place is an amazing eye-opener and incidentally also full of natural beauty worth painting, while Weizmann could make you most comfortable at his place and there are good modern hotels in Jerusalem, Haifa, Tiberias and above Safed in Galilee. However there are likely to be one or two things engaging your attention here in the autumn!

I have not been in Israel since 1925 and the transformation is amazing. The whole place pulsates with the creative energy of a nation which has found its feet, fought its way to victory against overwhelming odds, and now means to make the utmost of the heritage which it has secured. They mean to make the most of every acre of land from Dan to Beersheba and beyond and are

---

[1] Churchill wrote to his Private Office on this letter: 'Put away now.'

actually going to pipe the Jordan from its source at Dan round to Beersheba to irrigate the upper Negeb. They are laying themselves out for industrial development on a really big scale, as well as to create a merchant navy. Their plans for Haifa and Tel Aviv will presently make them ports of the first importance. They have all sorts of almost incredible balance of trade difficulties, but with American and British financial aid and their own ability and resolution they are confident of worrying through.

I found the attitude towards us much better than I had expected. Bevin they class, not unnaturally, with Haman[1] and Hitler, as one who meant their utter destruction – which an Arab victory would undoubtedly have involved. But they regard him as an abhoration and are only too anxious to get back to the perspective of the Balfour Declaration, realizing that nobody but ourselves would ever have given them their chance. They are almost pathetically anxious for any sort of friendly gesture on our part, and I found that particularly strong among their service people. A few places at our staff colleges and other technical service establishments would make all the difference in the world.

The one thing they need is peace. That is equally true of Jordan. Abdullah and the Jews would have come to terms long ago but for his fear of the Arab League and our misguided advice to him not to make peace except with the League's consent. Why the Foreign Office should have attached such importance to a League which is militarily impotent, apart from the Arab Legion, and dominated by Farouk[2] who is only concerned with his own power and animated by hatred of us, I cannot conceive. The sooner the League breaks up and is replaced by one excluding Egypt, and the sooner we are tough with Egypt and tell her that we are staying for good on the Suez Canal the better.

I enclose a copy of a hastily dictated memorandum on the whole Middle Eastern defence position giving my conclusions somewhat more fully. I am sending a copy to Shinwell, with whom I had a talk the other day and who is pretty sound in his general attitude; and will send others to Anthony and Harold Macmillan and Bobbety. If you would like a talk about all these matters I could come round any time. Or you could get hold of Julian in the smoking room and make him tell you further details of what we saw both in Israel and Jordan.

---

[1] Haman, c.520–475 bc. As second-in-command of the Medo-Persian empire, attempted to exterminate the entire Jewish race. He was confronted by Esther, the Jewish Queen of Persia, and subsequently hanged by order of King Xerxes.

[2] Farouk, 1920–65. Born in Cairo. King of Egypt, 1936–52. Overthrown after displaying for many years a politically fatal combination of corruption and incompetence. Died in exile in Rome.

June 1950

Randolph S. Churchill to Winston S. Churchill
(Churchill papers, 1/51)

19 June 1950

My dearest Papa,

Thank you so much for your letter of June 14. I am sorry to say that my debts amount to no less than £3,324 and an unsecured overdraft at Lloyds of £980, making a total of £4,304. About £520 of this is owed to bookmakers.

It is with a deep sense of shame that I set these figures down, but in view of your letter I felt that I should let you know the worst.

Clement Attlee to Winston S. Churchill
(Churchill papers, 2/76)

20 June 1950

My dear Churchill,

I have been considering your letter of June 4th about Substitutes for Strasbourg.[1]

I agree that the nine Substitutes (four Labour, four Conservative and one Liberal), shall be entitled to remain at Strasbourg throughout the Session. It seems right that such Substitutes as go to Strasbourg should receive payment for their board and lodging and also allowances on the approved scale during the days that they remain in Strasbourg, together with one return fare from the United Kingdom to Strasbourg.

I trust that this arrangement will be agreeable to you.

If you will let me have the names of those of your colleagues whom you wish to act as Substitutes, I will make the necessary announcement as soon as possible.

House of Commons: Oral Answers
(Hansard)

26 June 1950

KOREAN REPUBLIC (INVASION)

Mr Churchill: asked the Prime Minister whether he has any statement to make on the situation in Korea.

The Prime Minister: Yes, Sir. Reports were received yesterday indicating that forces from North Korea had crossed the 38th Parallel at a number of

---

[1] Reproduced above (pp. 1761–2).

points, in the course of the invasion of the Korean Republic. At the request of the Government of the United States of America an emergency meeting of the Security Council was held, at which a resolution was passed to the effect that the action of the forces of North Korea constituted a breach of the peace. The resolution called for the immediate cessation of hostilities, and called upon the authorities of North Korea to withdraw forthwith their armed forces to the 38th Parallel. The resolution further called upon all members to render every assistance to the United Nations in the execution of this resolution and to refrain from giving assistance to the North Korean authorities. The delegate of the Soviet Union did not attend.

His Majesty's Government are deeply concerned that this breach of the peace should have occurred in a country which is the special responsibility of the United Nations, and where a United Nations' Commission is actually functioning. His Majesty's Government welcome the resolution adopted by the Security Council, and it is their earnest hope that all concerned will duly comply with it.

Mr Churchill: We shall be grateful if the Prime Minister will keep us informed from day to day in the next day or two on this matter.

The Prime Minister: Certainly, Sir.

Mr A. Fenner Brockway[1]: In view of the momentous gravity of a possible situation and the absence of the Russian delegate from the Security Council owing to the Chinese representation upon it, will the Prime Minister take steps through the Secretary-General of the United Nations to try to find some other means of opening discussions with the Russians on this matter?

The Prime Minister: This is a matter which is before the Security Council. It is not a matter of opening discussions with the Russians. The situation has arisen between North Korea and South Korea.

Mr Keeling: Can the Prime Minister say whether contact is being maintained with His Majesty's Minister in Seoul?

The Prime Minister: No, Sir. We only have a Consul, I think, in Seoul. We are keeping in contact.

Mr Keeling: He is a Minister.

Mr Bellenger: Did my right hon. Friend understand from the question put by the Leader of the Opposition that he was asking that the House should be kept fully informed within the next few days?

The Prime Minister: Yes, that is what I said.

Mr Peter Roberts: In view of the very grave situation, if the North Korean Government refuse to consider this resolution will the Prime Minister advise his representative in the United Nations to ask for the use of the atomic bomb

---

[1] Archibald Fenner Brockway, 1888–1988. MP (Lab.) for East Leyton, 1929–31; for Eton and Slough, 1950–64. Chairman, Independent Labour Party, 1931–3. Took part in last public socialist campaign against Hitler in Germany, 1932. Committee of Socialist Movement for United Europe, 1947–52. Baron, 1964.

– (Hon. Members: 'Oh!') – Certainly – upon the capital of North Korea?

Mr Speaker: A question which asks 'if' is bound to be hypothetical, and, therefore, out of order.

Major-General Arthur Chater[1] to Winston S. Churchill
(Baroness Spencer-Churchill papers)

27 June 1950 High Croft

Dear Mr Churchill,

I have met you only twice, and the first time was on the outskirts of Antwerp on 4 October 1914, so I hope that you will pardon me addressing you like this. My reason for writing is that I have been prevailed upon by some of those who were my subordinates in British Somaliland in 1940 'to do something' about a certain passage in Volume II of *The Second World War*.

We feel that the statement on page 383:

'I am far from satisfied with the tactical conduct "of this affair", which remains on record as our only "defeat at Italian hands"'

is very unfair on those who strove hard to defend the Protectorate, and is not wholly true.

Before going to British Somaliland in 1937, I was told at the War Office that their policy was not to defend the Protectorate against an Italian attack. I then gave as my opinion that British territory could not be surrendered without fighting, and I continued to push this idea up to the end. In March 1938 I conducted the first exercise on the very ground on which we fought the five day battle in August 1940. In April 1938 I submitted a defence plan involving £100,000 expenditure. This was not approved. Despite lack of support or encouragement, I and my subordinates – a small team of enthusiastic young Officers – continued to make all the defence preparations we could with the very little we had.

Our defeat was due, not to 'the tactical conduct of the affair', but to:

(a) The collapse of the French forces in French Somaliland. Our defence plan was based on their co-operation. The British force was under command of the French General.

(b) The failure of the War Office and the Colonial Office to give approval to the proposals for defence, which had to be submitted to them, until it was too late.

[1] Arthur Reginald Chater, 1896–1979. 2nd Lt, Royal Marines, 1913. Served with Sudan Defence Forces, 1925–31. CB, January 1941. Senior Royal Marines Officer, East Indies Station, 1931–3. Senior Royal Marines Officer, 1935–6. Commanded Somaliland Camel Corps, 1937–40; defence of British Somaliland, 1941–3; Portsmouth Div. Royal Marines, 1943–4. Director, Combined Operations, India and SE Asia, 1944–5. Commanded Chatham Group, Royal Marines, 1946–8. Retired, 1948. Col. Commandant, Somaliland Scouts, 1948–58.

Although 'the CIGS declared' (in December 1939) 'for the defence of the territory' (page 383), no action to give effect to this was permitted until mid-May, and the action then approved was inadequate. The result was that we found ourselves with an unbalanced force, <u>lacking the artillery stated to be essential</u> and almost all recognized means of maintenance. Reinforcements, when sent, arrived piecemeal. The two African battalions arrived minus the COs who had trained them; and you will know that the African soldier loses much of his value when deprived of the leader whom he knows. The Black Watch arrived after battle had been joined.

An enquiry would show that this defeat was caused by dilatory action in the offices of Whitehall rather than to the tactical conduct of the operations by the leaders in the field, who did a great deal with very little against heavy odds. Typical examples of delay were (a) the Colonial Office took 7 months to approve the enlistment of 50 more Somalis. Approval came too late for them to be properly trained. (b) in January 1940 the supply of badly needed wireless equipment was with-held by the Colonial Office 'since the relaxation of defence measures was under consideration'. The lack of this effected our communications during the battle.

As events turned-out the decision to fight in Somaliland and then to withdraw proved to be right strategically (page 379). By fighting we drew a large proportion of the Italian forces away from the ill-defended frontiers of the Sudan and Kenya at a critical period. Withdrawal released our force for employment on other fronts at a time when every unit counted. In our own good time we re-occupied Berbera and used it as our base for the advance on Addis Ababa. From the military angle our withdrawal from Somaliland was no more a 'defeat' than were our withdrawals from Gadaref or Sidi Barrani, where our forces were, in fact, far better equipped and supported than we were in Somaliland.

That I have not written before to bring this to your notice is due to my reluctance to approach you about it. I now feel that it is perhaps right that you, Sir, should know how bitterly discouraged some of your greatest admirers have been by what they regard as the injustice of this passage, and we do hope that you may be able either to amend it or to omit it from future editions of the book.

June 1950

Winston S. Churchill: speech
('*Winston S. Churchill, His Complete Speeches*', volume 8, pages 8026–7)

28 June 1950

KOREA

This speech was in reply to the toast of 'Her Majesty's Opposition' at the annual dinner of the 1900 Club.[1]

. . . In 1945 we had advanced from weakness and terror to a great position of world victories and alliance. Our enemies had everywhere surrendered unconditionally.

Then suddenly the continuity was broken. Entirely new views, entirely opposite interests and considerations in many aspects of our life supervened. We have had the pleasure of five years of Socialist administration which, even if one wished to avoid anything in the nature of party politics, one could not help feeling has not carried our country forward at the level which it had achieved when the war came to an end. . . .

(Editor's Note: Referring to the expenditure of public money and the need now to live from year to year upon the good will of 'our cherished friends' across the Atlantic, he stated): I feel that the sooner we regain our full economic independence the sooner we shall be able to resume our place in the world, which we held through the greatest storms that ever blew and which we need to hold if the whole development of our destiny, and world destiny, are to be fulfilled.

(Editor's Note: Stating that when the 1900 Club was founded he was having 'a temporary disagreement with the Conservative Party' and could not therefore claim to be a founder of the Club, he continued): In the years since then I have found myself getting a great measure of support from the 1900 Club in the struggle to keep India effectively within the British Empire. That has been decided by events, but I have nothing but good will towards the new Indian Republic, which is at least associated with the British Commonwealth of Nations. I am utterly impenitent for the effort we have made to give a greater future to the British association with India.

What a terrible century this twentieth century has been. Two frightful world wars have shattered almost every institution. We have managed to come through because of the strength and vitality of the British people and the way in which they have been able to adapt themselves to the new situations which arose around them.

We have come through an awful struggle. In the period covered by the history of this club there has been a revolution as great as any which ever took

---

[1] This commentary, and the Editor's notes within the extract, were inserted by Robert Rhodes James, editor of *His Complete Speeches*.

place in France or Russia; nevertheless, not a drop of English blood has been shed in it, and there are no hatreds which divide the British people and no revenges which turn one section against another.

(Editor's Note: Referring to Korea, he said that something had occurred which transcended all their domestic quarrels): The United States, seeing a country which has been definitely given its own right to self-government invaded – on whose prompting we cannot tell – (*laughter*) – has decided to aid the South Koreans in defending themselves from one of the most obvious and brutal attacks of aggression. They have obtained that authority and mandate from the United Nations organization, which we have all pledged ourselves in the most solemn manner to sustain and to serve.

What hope can there be for the future of the world unless there is some form of world government which can make its effort to prevent the renewal of the awful struggles through which we have passed?

We have found this issue thrust upon us unexpectedly at a moment when we were occupied with our own fierce, sharp domestic party politics, and I for my part am very glad that the Conservative Party is represented in such strength in the House of Commons that it is able to assure the Government that they will be supported in any steps they take to maintain the honourable obligations of the country and for the defence of the free development of the life of the world.

It may well be that the action which the United States has taken, with which we have associated ourselves today, placing a fleet equal to the Americans' at their side, and showing the fraternal association of the English-speaking race all over the world, may in the end be found to be effective in warding off from us the infinite horrors of a third world war.

The hour is anxious, but I am satisfied that the course which is proposed by the Government is correct and wise and that there was no other open to them in honour. We shall give them our full support in the necessary measures which they have taken.

(Editor's Note: Referring to the next election, he stated): We must work our hardest to secure full representation in the new Parliament. The present situation is not good for the country. It is not a good thing that people should have to discuss all kinds of difficult matters with always the election atmosphere poisoning their talk and necessarily governing the kind of argument they are prepared to use. We must try to get a definite majority at the next poll.

Winston S. Churchill to Clement Attlee
(Churchill papers, 2/29)

29 June 1950

My dear Prime Minister,

I do not feel that it would be useful for me to reply to your letter of June 13[1] until the present crisis has passed its immediate climax. I still feel that a Secret Session is desirable and necessary, and that if it is refused by His Majesty's Government it will be necessary to have a debate in public. I do not think this course is open to us while the present tension lasts.

I also feel that the renewal of inter-Party conversations such as we had last year had better await the developments. I am of course always at your service if any special point arises, and I hope you will not hesitate to call on me if you wish to do so.

Clement Attlee to Winston S. Churchill
(Churchill papers, 2/29)

29 June 1950

My dear Churchill,

Thank you for your letter. I am sure at the present juncture a Secret Session would not be useful.

I understand that for the present the matter is in abeyance without prejudice to your raising it at some other time. I shall be glad to call on you should some special point arise.

---

[1] Reproduced above (pp. 1766–7).

June 1950

Randolph S. Churchill to Winston S. Churchill
(Churchill papers, 1/51)[1]

30 June 1950

My dearest Papa,

Thank you so much for your very kind and personal letter. I value your help and advice more than I can say.

I send you herewith the list of bills and debts.

The money you sent to pay for your bets has been sent to the bookmakers. I have had no card loans this year of more than a few pounds.

I have thought very seriously about your suggestion of my reading for the Bar. I will start doing this as soon as the Plymouth Fair is over.

It is indeed good of you and the trustees to treat me with such generosity and I assure you I shall make a resolute effort to arrange my life more prudently from now on.

---

[1] This letter was handwritten.

July 1950

Winston S. Churchill: speech[1]
('In the Balance', pages 309–12)

4 July 1950   Dorchester Hotel
London

THE ANGLO-AMERICAN ALLIANCE

I was glad when you asked me to join you tonight in celebrating Independence Day. Among Englishmen I have a special qualification for such an occasion, I am directly descended through my mother from an officer who served in Washington's Army. And as such I have been made a member of your strictly selected Society of the Cincinnati. I have my pedigree supported by affidavits at every stage if it is challenged. So what? Well, Ladies and Gentlemen, it is a long time since the War of Independence and quite a lot of things have happened, and keep on happening. There is no doubt that I was on both sides then and it gives me a comfortable feeling of simplification as the years have passed to feel that we're all on the same side now. The drawing together in fraternal association of the British and American peoples, and of all the peoples of the English-speaking world may well be regarded as the best of the few good things that have happened to us and to the world in this century of tragedy and storm.

It was Bismarck who said in the closing years of his life that the most potent factor in human society at the end of the nineteenth century was the fact that the British and American peoples spoke the same language. He might well have added, what was already then apparent, that we had in common a very wide measure of purpose and ideals arising from our institutions, our literature and our common law. Since then, on the anvil of war, we have become so welded together that what might have remained for generations an interesting historical coincidence has become the living and vital force which preserved Christian civilization and the rights and freedom of mankind. Nearly two

---

[1] To the American Society in London (founded 1895).

months have passed since the Ambassador talked over with me the invitation with which you have honoured me. Mr Lew Douglas is an intimate war comrade of mine, and one of the best friends from across the Atlantic which our country had in the struggle; and that is saying a lot. He is esteemed throughout this island and we all have felt the utmost sympathy for him in his accident,[1] and admiration for the courage with which he has surmounted so much physical pain. No one I am sure can do more to prevent misunderstandings – diplomatic or otherwise – between our two countries than His Excellency the American Ambassador.

When I accepted your invitation I could not foresee that when the date arrived we should once again be brothers in arms, engaged in fighting for exactly the same cause that we thought we had carried to victory five years ago. The British and Americans do not war with races or governments as such. Tyranny, external or internal, is our foe whatever trappings or disguises it wears, whatever language it speaks, or perverts. We must forever be on our guard, and always vigilant against it – in all this we march together. Not only, if need be, under the fire of the enemy but also in those realms of thought which are consecrated to the rights and the dignity of man, and which are so amazingly laid down in the Declaration of Independence, which has become a common creed on both sides of the Atlantic Ocean.

The inheritance of the English-speaking world, vast and majestic though it is in territory and resources, derives its glory as a moral unity from thought and vision widely spread in the minds of our people and cherished by all of those who understand our destiny. As you may have heard (I don't want to give away any secrets) we had a General Election here a few months ago by which a Parliament was returned very evenly balanced but still more sharply divided; but divided not by small matters but by issues which cut deep into our national life. We have not developed to any extent over here the bipartisan conduct of external policy by both great parties like that which has in these later years so greatly helped the United States. Nevertheless, once the deep gong of comradeship between kindred nations strikes, resounds and reverberates, and when our obligations of the United Nations are staring us in the face, we shall allow no domestic party quarrels – grievous though they may be – to mar the unity of our national or international action. You can count on Britain, and not only Britain. Four years ago, when President Truman, whom we salute tonight, took me to Westminster College at Fulton in Missouri I ventured to offer the American people my counsel, and I said, 'Let no man underrate the abiding power of the British Empire and Commonwealth. Do not suppose that we shall not come through these dark years of privation as we came through the glorious years of agony, or that half a century from now will not see 70,000,000 or 80,000,000 Britons spread throughout the world and

[1] In Apr. 1949, Douglas had suffered an injury to his left eye while fly fishing. His recovery was slow and incomplete recovery, and he had to wear an eyepatch for the rest of his life.

united in defence of our traditions, our way of life, and the world causes which you and we espouse.' In the increasing unity of the Anglo-American thought and action resides the main foundations of the freedom and progress of all men in all the lands. Let us not weary, let us not lose confidence in our mission, let us not fail in our duty in times of stress, let us not flinch if danger comes.

We must ask ourselves whether danger – I mean the danger of a third world war, has come nearer because of what has happened in the last week and is happening now. I do not think, myself that the danger has grown greater. But then, I thought it very serious before. It all depends where you start thinking in these matters. I must say that we – Britons and Americans – and the many States and nations associated with us have had hard luck. The Russian Communists have built up an empire far beyond the dreams of the Tsars out of a war in which they might have been conquered or driven beyond the Ural mountains in spite of the bravery with which the Russian Army fought for its native soil. They would have been conquered or driven out but for the immense diversionary aid of Britain and the United States on land and sea and, above all, in the air. And also the vital supplies which had cost so much self-denial, and peril – and the Ambassador knows a lot about all that because the shipping on which everything depended was throughout influenced in the most effective manner by his personal care and courage. Not only do the Soviets hold at the present time all the famous capitals of Europe east of the line – which I call 'the Iron Curtain' drawn from Stettin to Trieste, not only are they endeavouring with great cruelties to compel these many States and countries to adopt the Communist system and become incorporated in the Soviet mass, but they have gained also vast populations in Asia, including practically the whole of China. And they are pressing forward in insatiable, imperialist ambition wherever any weakness on the part of the free world gives them an opportunity.

Thus, I say we have had hard luck, just when we thought we had finished with Hitler and Mussolini, with Nazism and Fascism, we have Stalin and Communism lumping up against us representing the former Hitler tyranny in barbaric form and Asiatic guise. We had hoped that the task of this hard-pressed generation was done. Your poet Walt Whitman said: 'Now understand me well, it is provided in the essence of things that from any fruition of success, no matter what, shall come forth something to make a greater struggle necessary.' We pray this may not be so. These hard decrees may be the lot of the human race in its unending struggle for existence, but the question which we have to consider tonight, and in regard to which the Ambassador laid before you in a cogently related argument many essential facts, is whether our dangers have been increased by the Communist act of aggression in Korea. I agree with the British Government speakers that they have not been increased. How does this new menace differ in principle from the Berlin blockade, two years ago, which together we faced with composure and overcame by the Allied airlift, mainly carried by American planes but in which we bore an important share? It differs in one major fact. We are told that the Kremlin oligarchy now know how to make the atomic bomb. That is the one new fact. To that extent there is a change to our disadvantage. It certainly seems to me that there is a better hope of a general settlement with Soviet Russia following on the defeat of aggression in Korea on a localized scale, than that we should drift on while large quantities of these devastating weapons are accumulated. Indeed I feel that there is nothing more likely to bring on a third world war than drift.

It is always difficult for free democracies, governed in the main by public opinion from day to day, to cope with the designs of dictator States and totalitarian systems. But hitherto we have held our own, or we should not be here tonight. We have only to be morally united and fearless, to give mankind the best hope of avoiding another supreme catastrophe. But I must say one thing before I sit down. It is of vital consequence to these hopes of world peace that what the Communists have begun in Korea should not end in their triumph. If that were to happen a third world war, under conditions even more deadly than now exist, would certainly be forced upon us, or hurled upon us before long. It is fortunate that the path of duty, and of safety, is so plainly marked out before our eyes, and so widely recognized by both our nations and governments, and by the large majority, the overwhelming majority of the member States comprised in the United Nations Organization.

We owe it not only to ourselves, but to our faith in an institution, if not a world government at least a world protection from aggressive war, not to fail in our duty now. Thus we shall find the best hopes of peace and surest proof of honour. The League of Nations failed not because of its noble conceptions, but because these were abandoned by its members. We must not ask to be taught this hard lesson twice. Looking around this obscure, tumultuous scene, with all its uncertainties as it presents itself to us tonight, I am sure we shall not be guilty of such incurable folly; we shall go forward; we shall do our duty; we shall save the world from a third world war. And should it come in spite of all our efforts, we shall not be trampled down into serfdom and ruin.

Winston S. Churchill: speech
(Hansard)

5 July 1950   House of Commons

KOREA

On a Motion moved by the Prime Minister that this house fully supports the action taken by HM Government, in conformity with their obligations under the UN Charter, in helping to resist the unprovoked aggression against the Republic of Korea.

I feel that the whole House is indebted to the Prime Minister for the cogent and lucid account which he gave of the events in Korea leading up to the present situation, and also for the full disquisition which he gave on the legal aspects of the decision of the Security Council, on which some questions have been raised by the Soviet Government. I found myself in very general agreement with the Prime Minister in the closing part of his address, and am fully able to associate myself with him, for reasons which I will presently venture to dwell upon, in his broad conclusion that the action which has been taken by the United States and endorsed, supported and aided by His Majesty's Government gives, on the whole, the best chance of maintaining the peace of the world.

We consider that the Government were right to place a Motion on the Order Paper asking for approval in general terms of the course which they have adopted since the invasion of South Korea began. There are grave reasons, as we learned in the war, that false impressions may be created abroad by a Debate prominently occupied by a handful of dissentients. It is better to have a Division so that everyone can know how the House of Commons stands and in what proportion. Should such a Division occur, we on this side will vote with the Government. I do not propose to embark upon a detailed argument about the merits of questions which have been raised by events in Korea, nor upon the decision reached by the Security Council and the United Nations. They have been ventilated in the Press and have just now been clearly explained to us by the Prime Minister. I do not believe that Soviet and Communist propaganda, with its perverted facts and inverted terminology, has made the slightest impression upon the well-tried common sense of the British people. No one outside the small Communist circles in this island or their fellow-travellers believes for an instant that it is South Korea which is the aggressor and North Korea which is the victim of a well and deliberately-planned and organized attack. On the contrary, the very unpreparedness and inefficiency of South Korea is the proof of their innocence, though, not, perhaps of their wisdom.

Few, I think, will believe that Seoul, Suwon and other places which have been captured by the North Korean armies have been liberated from tyranny by Communist rescuers. Even the charge that the United States has attempted to create a diversion in Europe by scattering Colorado beetles from their aircraft throughout Saxony and elsewhere – although it has actually formed the subject of a formal and official protest by the Soviet Government to the United States – has not, so far as I can gather, made any deep or permanent impression upon the British public. On this side of the House we hold, in full agreement with the Government, that President Truman's action in South Korea was right and that His Majesty's Government, accompanied as their action has been by the action of other members of the Commonwealth, were also right in acting as they have done under the mandate of the Security

Council by giving armed support to the intervention of the United States. The Conservative Party give their full support to the Government in these matters. We understand that the Liberal Party take a similar view of their duty and that their position will presently be put before the House (*interruption*). Do not despise help and friendship when it is offered. Neither of us see what else the Government could have done in these circumstances.

I must for a moment step aside from my general theme to express the hope that the action of the Government and their supporters will be upon this same level. I cannot overlook the fact that in giving our support we run some party and political risks. I was reading *Reynolds' Newspaper* at the weekend and in it there was an article called 'Tom Driberg's Column', though whether that has any direct relationship with the hon. Member for Maldon (Mr Driberg).

Mr Driberg (Maldon) *indicated assent.*

Mr Churchill: 'Tories bay for war' — that is the headline, but — (*interruption*)

Mr Harold Macmillan (Bromley): Did the hon. Member for Ayrshire, South (Mr Emrys Hughes) say 'It is true'? That is shameful.

Mr Churchill: Perhaps the hon. Member for Maldon will say that he is not responsible for the headlines but only for the text?

Mr Driberg *indicated assent.*

Mr Churchill: I understand that the hon. Member accepts the responsibility.

Mr Driberg: Certainly, for both.

Mr Churchill: And also these words? Let me just read them, because the House ought to see how all this is working out:

> There is quite a substantial number of the back-bench Tories who, true to their jungle philosophy, cannot help baying their delight at the smell of blood in the air.

Hon. Members: Shame.

Mr Driberg: I am grateful to the right hon. Gentleman the Member for Woodford (Mr Churchill) —

Mr Osborne[1] (Louth): Judas.

Mr Driberg: — for his courtesy in giving way. May I just say here and now that I consider that a perfectly accurate description of a scene in this House last week, and that I only wish that the right hon. Gentleman could have seen it before the editor toned it down and modified it.

Mr Churchill: I know it is the hon. Member's pride that he can be neither muzzled nor led, and no doubt what we have seen in the columns of *Reynolds' Newspaper* is only a bowdlerized version of the total and utter untruths which he was scattering to the world.

Mr Osborne: Did the hon. Member for Maldon (Mr Driberg) get thirty pieces of silver for it?

---

[1] Cyril Osborne, 1898–1969. MP (Cons.) for Louth, Lincolnshire, 1945–69. Hon. Treasurer, Inter-Parliamentary Union, 1964–7.

Mr Churchill: The cheers from the Conservative benches were for the Prime Minister when he made his declaration, while some of the benches behind him were curiously silent.

Mr Driberg: That was not what I was describing.

Mr Churchill: We are also told that it is being put about in many constituencies that if the Tories had been in office there would have been war now. That is not true. If we had been in office when the news of President Truman's action arrived we should have acted in very much the same way as His Majesty's Government have done. I am not at all sure that we should have received from all the Members opposite and from all their followers the same measure of goodwill and support that we are giving them on this occasion. We shall not, however, allow our action to be deflected in great matters by behaviour of this kind. We believe that the electorate, in judging these matters for themselves, will be influenced by the ordinary British standards of fair play, and it is on that that we rest ourselves.

I must say one word here about the Secretary of State for War (Mr Strachey), whose speech at the weekend was the subject of question and answer just now. As to the merits of his comments on the Schuman Plan, I shall not attempt to pronounce, except to say that they are very different from the formal Amendment placed on the Order Paper by the Government that they welcomed the French Plan, but I really wonder that the right hon. Gentleman cannot a little cast his past behind him and rise to the occasion of the great responsibilities which he has the honour to bear as the head of a Fighting Service at this critical time. I really wonder that he should find it necessary to hamper his work in a great Service and reduce his influence in the country by plunging into these bitter political controversies. Surely he has enough responsibilities to bear and enough work to do, and surely he has been treated with a great deal of forbearance by the House of Commons?

I was commenting on the article of the hon. Member for Maldon just now, but I must confess that in some ways I prefer his outspoken diatribes to the comments of the hon. Member for Coventry who really has laid down a principle – (Hon. Members: 'Which one?') The hon. Member for Coventry East (Mr Crossman). Certainly I would not like to saddle any other constituency with the responsibility of the hon. Member. But this is to my mind one of those little sayings which should always be placed on record. This is what the hon. Member wrote in the *Sunday Pictorial*:

> But there is one lesson we can and must learn from recent history – the time to start thinking about peace is the beginning and not the end of the fighting.

All I can say is that it has usually been thought, and I hope will not be overlooked on the present occasion, that between the beginning of fighting and the end of fighting, between the beginning of a war or a military operation and peace, there is an intervening stage called victory. It seems that the hon. Member for Coventry East in trying – curiously and even characteristically – to have it both ways has really excelled himself in this particular statement, which has only to be followed by any Government carrying on military operations to lead to certain military disaster. We naturally cannot accept the responsibility for creating the present situation, nor do I suggest that this falls primarily upon Great Britain. Still less, as I have already stated to the House, can we accept any responsibility for the military position of our country or of Europe, or for the use that has been made of the unprecedented sums of money which have been voted by the House for the Defence Services, or for the resources of manpower placed with our full support on this side at the disposal of His Majesty's Government.

Some time in May, before this crisis occurred, I asked the Prime Minister for a Secret Session of Debate on our military position in order that this new Parliament might have some idea of where we stood in Europe and of the state of our own defences. The Prime Minister did not grant my request and we had therefore intended on this side of the House to have a public Debate on Defence before we separated for the Recess. Now that this crisis has arisen I do not feel that it would be helpful at this stage if we had a general Debate on Defence in public, even though all responsible Members taking part in it were to confine themselves strictly to facts which they were sure the Soviet Government already knew. But even within this limitation there is a vast amount of matter which is public knowledge, which has appeared in British newspapers, and, far more, which has appeared in the United States either in the Press or in the continuous proceedings of the Congress and its varied committees.

There never has been a period that I can remember covering the present century in which the British public and the British Parliament were so totally ignorant of the conditions which exist. I must, therefore, renew my request here and now across the Floor of the House for a Debate in Secret Session upon this matter before we separate. I do not ask that even in Secret Session we should be told any secrets of a special or technical character. On the contrary, I should be quite content if the Government limit themselves in their statements to what they are sure is already known abroad. I do not pretend myself to have anything like the detailed and precise information on which I based my warnings before the last war. Nevertheless, I am sure I could tell the House a lot of things which they ought to bear in mind, and these the Government could amplify or correct at their discretion, and other hon. Members would make their fruitful contributions.

If a Secret Session is refused and we do not ourselves, even within the limits I have prescribed, have a public Debate, the House will go forward into this deepening crisis with less information about it than any previous Parliament at any similar time. It seems to me that the Prime Minister and his colleagues will be taking an invidious and unprecedented responsibility upon themselves if they refuse us the Secret Session for which we ask. It is a responsibility which we on this side can in no wise share. Our responsibility is limited to supporting them in what they are doing in the international sphere since last Tuesday week, and does not extend to the military field or to what has happened since 1945 or to the methods which have been adopted or to the Ministers chosen to deal with our defences.

I will, therefore, confine myself today to a few general observations which are necessary to justify the support we are giving to His Majesty's Government. It might be asked of us: 'How can you judge without the fullest information whether the United Nations, the United States and Great Britain are strong enough to resist Communist aggression in the Far East when that resistance may conceivably bring about a major crisis in Europe? Might it not be that the rulers in the Kremlin are drawing us all into the Far East as a preliminary to striking in the West?' I answer these questions to myself, as one's mind asks questions at these times, as follows. The forces required for the defence of South Korea, or even its recapture should that become necessary, would not make any decisive or even appreciable difference to the situation in Europe. The immunity of Western Europe from attack depends overwhelmingly on the vastly superior stockpile of atomic bombs possessed by the United States. There is the deterrent, and the sole decisive deterrent, which exists or can be brought into being in the near future. Therefore I do not feel that a major issue of security is raised by the necessary measures which have to be taken in Korea.

Secondly, I have for a long time felt deeply concerned at the discovery by the Soviet Government of the secret of the atomic bomb, and the probability that it is already in production. I saw that General Omar Bradley, who occupies one of the most responsible executive positions in the United States defence system, said recently that in three or four years the Soviets will have a sufficient supply of these bombs to cause a major catastrophe at any time they so decided, or words to that effect. It is for this reason that I think it very much better that we should make a resolute effort to come to a settlement with them by peaceful means, but on the basis of strength and not of weakness, on the basis of success and not on fatuous incapacity of resistance to aggression. We should endeavour to come to a settlement with them before they become possessed of this devastating power in addition to all the military and air superiority and armour superiority which they undoubtedly possess at this present time in Europe and Asia.

I can quite understand the Communist propaganda about banning the atomic bomb, for such a decision would leave the civilization of the world entirely at their mercy even before they had accumulated the necessary stockpile themselves. Since this new aggression in Korea and the spirited reaction of the United States, I feel that we ought to bring the policy of drift to an end, and I believe that no better prelude to the opening of major discussions with the Soviet Government could be found than the successful repulse of the Communist forces that are now invading Korea. I believe that if this is achieved, conditions may be created less unfavourable to a general settlement than any others I can conceive before the Soviet power is freed from the deterrent of the immense American superiority in atomic resources. That hope may fail, but it is the best hope that now exists of averting from Europe and America perils and suffering utterly beyond anything we have hitherto experienced. It is my belief that the American superiority in atomic warfare is, for the time being, an effective deterrent against a general Communist onslaught. Of course, I may be wrong – no one can tell; no one can give a guarantee.

Still, if it be true that there are at present no signs of exceptional preparations or concentrations behind the Iron Curtain in Europe, it would at least give a temporary indication that the supreme events of misfortune are not immediately imminent. Indeed, it may well be that the Soviet Government have been taken aback by the resolute action of President Truman, supported as it has been by His Majesty's Government and by so many other States and members of the United Nations. This is no time to despair of world peace being achieved upon tolerable foundations. Certainly, we must not despair. To do so is to despair of the life of the world. But one thing is essential now, and I cannot think that the Government will differ from me when I say that it is of vital consequence alike to our hope of world peace and to our own safety here at home, namely, that what the Communists have begun in Korea should not end in their triumph. If that were to happen, as I said last night to an American gathering, a third world war under conditions more deadly than now exist might be forced upon us – would be forced upon us – before long.

There could be no more certain way of bringing about the destruction of civilization than that we should drift on helplessly until the Soviets are fully equipped with the atomic bomb. Neither, meanwhile, must we accept defeat and humiliations in one place after another wherever the Communists thrust and gnaw their way forward, and in this process of continued misfortune lose the faith in us of everyone else in the world, and lose our own confidence in ourselves. There could be no greater disaster than that; there could be no more certain road to what it is our first duty to avoid than that; and it is because of my confidence that those men of His Majesty's Government with whom I worked so long and with whom I have gone through so much are resolved to prevent by every means in their power anything like that, that I shall follow the Prime Minister tonight should the need come to give him a vote.

July 1950

Winston S. Churchill to Randolph S. Churchill
(*Churchill papers, 1/51*)

6 July 1950

My dear Randolph,

I understand that the Trust are paying off your overdraft at the Bank today and that, in addition, they are paying into your account approximately £325.0.0. to pay your Plymouth bills. This is considered most urgent as it might otherwise prove most injurious to your candidature. I hope you will pay these off tomorrow by your own cheques, and send the receipts to Mr Moir. The Trust will also want to ask you various questions about your accounts as presented, in the course of the next few days.

I am very glad that you have decided to read for the Bar as soon as the Plymouth Fair is over next week. Your acceptance of our suggestion of course implies that when you are called to the Bar you will practise and do your best to make a success of this profession. It would be quite possible to combine this, as many do, especially in the early stages, with House of Commons work should you become a Member. I should like to have your assurance that this is so.

I propose to fly down from Biggin Hill to Plymouth on Saturday and hope to be with you for luncheon. Do not please book me up for anything, as it is a great exertion for me to prepare and deliver a speech of this character, especially at this anxious time. I shall return immediately after the meeting unless prevented by weather.

Winston S. Churchill to Major-General Arthur Chater
(*Chater papers*)

9 July 1950
Private

Dear General Chater,

Thank you for your letter of June 27,[1] which I have studied carefully. In view of what you say I propose to amend the passage about British Somaliland to read as follows in future editions of *Their Finest Hour*:

'I was very much disappointed with this affair, which remains on record as our only defeat at Italian hands. This in no way reflects upon the officers or men of the British and Somali troops in the Protectorate, who had to do their best with what equipment they were allotted, and obey the orders they received.'

I hope this will remove any bad feeling from you and your friends.

---

[1] Reproduced above (pp. 1771–2).

July 1950

Winston S. Churchill to Clement Attlee
(Churchill papers, 2/29)

12 July 1950

My dear Prime Minister,

I feel that it will be necessary for us to have a debate on Defence before we separate. I should prefer that it should take place in Secret Session, but if you cannot agree to this my colleagues feel we have no choice but to ask for the necessary facilities on the Appropriation Bill. This will be done through the usual channels.

Brigadier Anthony Head, J. P. L. Thomas[1] and Arthur Harvey to Winston S. Churchill
(Churchill papers, 2/36)

13 July 1950

The three Service Committees met yesterday, 12th July and discussed the present condition of the Defences of this country with special reference to our commitments in the Far East and within the Atlantic Pact. In reviewing the present condition of the Army and the Royal Air Force, we felt most concerned that not only was there no sign of improvement either in preparedness or recruiting, but that the present trend indicated an increase in wastage of the Regular element and, consequently, increased difficulties in maintaining the necessary number of instructors to train the National Service men and technicians to look after the increasingly complex modern equipment.

We know of no steps which have been taken, or are proposed by the Government, to improve the situation. Future prospects, if the present trend continues, are most discouraging, and it is our opinion that unless something is done, and done quickly, we may drift into a position which can only be rectified by more drastic and difficult steps than would now be necessary.

Very briefly and at the risk of over-simplification we believe that in the case of both the Army and the Royal Air Force, the main problem can only be solved by stimulating and improving the number of voluntary long term recruits combined with a proportionate adjustment of the present system of National Service in terms of numbers and/or length of service. We believe that this must be done at an early date as such steps are unlikely to become effective before at least two or even three years have elapsed.

As far as the Royal Navy is concerned, their ability to recruit sufficient long

---

[1] James Purdon Lewes Thomas, 1903–60. Educated at Rugby and Oriel College, Oxford. MP (Cons.) for Hereford, 1931–55. Asst Private Secretary to Stanley Baldwin, 1931. Parliamentary Private Secretary to Anthony Eden, 1932–8; 1940 (when Eden was Secretary of State for War). Lord Commissioner of the Treasury, 1940–3. Financial Secretary, Admiralty, 1943–5. Vice-Chairman, Conservative Party, 1945–51. PC, 1951. 1st Lord of the Admiralty, 1951–6. Viscount Cilcennin, 1955.

term recruits puts them in a more favourable position and although there are many points which we believe could well be ventilated, their difficulties and problems are not so deep-seated, nor do they need such immediate and drastic remedies.

You may recall that in May, 1949, we sent you a Memorandum on the present condition of the three Services so far as we knew it. Since then, you have had talks with the Prime Minister and are, no doubt, in a better position than ourselves to judge whether the fears we expressed at that time were justified. Nevertheless, our anxiety has increased since then and the purpose of this Minute, is to state our disquiet and to suggest that a Debate on the general subject of Defence should be initiated before Parliament adjourns for the Summer Recess.

Clement Attlee to Winston S. Churchill
(Churchill papers, 2/29)

14 July 1950
Private

My dear Churchill,

I have with my colleagues given very careful consideration to your request for a debate on Defence before the House rises.

You have informed me that you would prefer a secret Session, but that, if that is not conceded, you will feel it your duty to raise the question of Defence in open session in the Appropriation Bill.

While fully understanding your position, I am bound to say that I do not think that a debate on Defence would be in the public interest at the present time. If, however, you decide that it is necessary, it is the view of my colleagues and myself that an open debate is preferable to one in secret.

I think a debate on Defence at the present time is inopportune for the following reasons.

Firstly because, although we have set up the machinery of the Atlantic Pact and Western Union, the development of the necessary forces has proceeded far more slowly than we wished. In particular it has been difficult to get successive French Governments to act with any vigour. The new Government under Pleven[1] is likely to be more satisfactory than its predecessors as Pleven is

---

[1] René Pleven, 1901–93. Banker and businessman. In June 1940 he was in England on a purchasing mission for the French Government. One of the first Frenchmen to join de Gaulle in London, he was placed in charge of the finances of the fledgling Free French movement. Sent by de Gaulle to Chad, he won over the rest of French Equatorial Africa to the Free French. Negotiated first Franco-American lend-lease agreement, and the withdrawal of British forces from Madagascar. Minister of Colonies, 1943–4. Minister of Finance, 1944–6. PM of France, July 1950 to March 1951, Aug. 1951 to Jan. 1952. Minister of Defence, 1952–4. Author of the 'Pleven Plan' for a European Army including full German participation (rejected by the French Assembly, 1954). Foreign Minister, 13–30 May 1958.

far more conscious of the needs of defence than the other French statesmen. I fear that criticism of the French contribution to Western Defence, which is almost certain to arise in debate, would not help Pleven in his task.

Secondly, the set back to the American Forces in Korea, which we hope will soon be recovered, might lead to unhelpful speeches. I should add, for your personal information, that although in deference to the susceptibilities of the Powers the Joint Chiefs of Staff Committee was abolished, the Joint Staff Mission under the leadership of Tedder in effect carries on the work of cooperation in much the same way as before.

Thirdly, I do not think that a debate in which there would inevitably be a good deal of criticism of the preparedness of democracies would be helpful at this critical time, in which the authority of the United Nations is being challenged. I do not think that these disadvantages would be obviated by a secret session, indeed others would be added.

I do not think that it is likely that a public discussion would add much to the knowledge possessed by the USSR, although it is always useful for a Government to have the conclusions of its intelligence services confirmed authoritatively. There is not, therefore, much advantage on this score.

On the other hand, I think that the general public might be disturbed by the fact of a secret session and while no doubt privilege would prevent any actual disclosure rumours of criticism might well cause exaggerated anxiety, not only among our own people, but among our Western Allies.

But more serious, I think, would be the effect in the United States. There would be a demand from the Americans for us to state what occurred in secret session. We could not tell them without breach of privilege. I am advised that this could cause difficulties with Congress when it is voting Appropriations for Arms Bills, etc.

For these reasons, I have come to the conclusion that the disadvantages of a secret session outweigh the advantages.

On the general question I would say that we have never pretended that the present defence position of the democracies is satisfactory, although progress is being made. Nor do I feel complacent over our own position. I need not enlarge on the difficulties which we have to face owing to our bearing the brunt of the cold war, nor need I stress the limitation imposed on us by the economic circumstances of the time. None the less, good progress is being made and I am not running away from a debate. I am at all times ready to give to you and your colleagues full information on all aspects of defence and to consider any suggestions.

If you should feel disposed to discuss the question of the debate with me further I am at your disposal.

Should you decide that a debate must take place, I suggest that it should not be taken until the week after next as very important meetings of the Western Union Powers are taking place next week at Fontainebleau.

Winston S. Churchill to Clement Attlee
(*Churchill papers, 2/29*)

15 July 1950
Private

My dear Prime Minister,

I am sorry that you have refused my request for a debate on Defence in Secret Session. I do not think that your statement about the effect on the United States is correct. They are quite familiar with Secret or Executive Sessions in the case of their Congress Committees.

According to the views expressed in your letter, the House ought to have no information on the subject of Defence, either in Secret or in Public Session, before it separates for its prolonged holiday. I will consult my colleagues upon the situation thus created, but I cannot doubt that they will share my view that we must warn Parliament of the dangers which are gathering.

If there is any hope that further discussion between us might change you decision, I would gladly come to see you on Tuesday or Wednesday next.[1]

Winston S. Churchill: speech
(*'In the Balance', pages 320–9*)

15 July 1950   Saltram Park, Plymouth

NATIONAL AND INTERNATIONAL POLITICS

Five months have passed since I came to Plymouth to address a West Country audience. Then we had good hopes of bringing about an immediate and decisive change in the politics of our country, and of establishing in effective power a broad based Conservative Government which would prove itself worthy of its trust and equal to these difficult and dangerous times. Now we see that in spite of the substantial advantages we gained, a second intense effort will be necessary. [. . .]

I need not appeal to you gathered here to make every exertion in your power in order to secure an effective majority for the Conservative Party at the impending election, because I know how earnest are your resolves and how tireless are your activities. The need to secure a strong Government, opposed to the fallacies and frauds of Socialism, is not merely a party objective but a national aim, on which the future of our country depends. But it seems to me that while we put forth every scrap of strength we can command, we should also endeavour to gather the support of all men and women of

---

[1] Attlee responded on July 17: 'I shall of course be very glad to see you on Tuesday or Wednesday if you wish, but I do not see very much likelihood of an alteration of our views on the subject of a Secret Session.'

goodwill outside our own party limits, and unite in the common front against Socialism, not only Liberals, but that large floating vote, which played such a hesitating part last time in the trial of strength. This is a moment when we have a right to appeal to all patriotic and broadminded men and women who are in agreement on the main issues, to do their utmost to secure the establishment of a strong, broadly based and stable Government, capable of dealing in a courageous and progressive spirit with the ever darkening problems that confront us.

I feel this is the time when those who agree on fundamental issues should stand together. Let me mention to you some of the great issues on which Unionists and Liberals are agreed, and which constitute the elements of the common cause vital to our national welfare. First, we proclaim that the state is the servant and not the master of the people, and that freedom under the law is not what Dr Dalton calls 'an experiment' but our *right*. We reject altogether the Socialist conception of a division of society between officials and the common mass. We repudiate their policy of levelling down to a minimum uniformity above which only politicians and their agents may rise. We stand for the increasingly higher expression of individual independence. We hold most strongly to the Declaration of Human Rights, as set forth by the United Nations at Geneva. While placing first in our thoughts the British Empire and Commonwealth of Nations, we welcome the growing movement towards European unity, and the ending of the old Continental feuds that have brought so much misery upon us all. We intend to help this movement forward all we can within the limits of our main obligations. We do not believe in the organization of Europe in the name of any single party. Socialist policy has been in these past years increasingly out of step and out of harmony with, or lagging behind, the movement of thought among the free democracies of the modern world and especially in Europe.

Far from being in the van of international progress, they have become a brake and an obstruction. We have seen a painful example of this in the abuse lavished on the Schuman Plan by a Minister and many of the rank and file in the last week. This is a plan to bring Germany and France together by a union of their basic industries, beginning with coal and steel. Every argument of prejudice and isolationism has been used against not only the plan but against our merely taking part in these discussions, while remaining effectively safeguarded from any commitments if in the end we do not feel the scheme is practical. Mr Strachey, so oddly Secretary of State for War in this critical period, has given his word of honour that he did not call the Schuman Plan a 'Plot'. If that is true it is almost the only term of abuse he did not apply to it. His views might have been taken almost verbatim from his old friend the *Daily Worker*, and are in this matter in full accord with the guidance given from Moscow to the Communist world. I trust they will not prevail against the decent and responsible elements in the Socialist Party.

Then we declare ourselves inveterately opposed to any future nationalization of industry, including, of course, and especially, the nationalization of steel. There is thus a large overlap of agreement, both in doctrine and in action, between those who have hitherto been brought up to regard themselves as political opponents. But now the times are very grave, and it is the duty of every man and woman who agrees upon so large a proportion of the main principles and practical steps, to make sure that these are not overwhelmed by the ignorant, partisan and obsolete fallacy of Socialism, against which the British nation stands today in marked recoil. All I ask, and it is a modest demand, is that those who agree upon the fundamentals shall, in our party conflicts, try to help each other as much as they can, and harm each other as little as they must. Let that theme of conduct prevail, and we shall have cleared the path of progress of many of its pitfalls and barriers, and perhaps have the power to rescue our native land from some of the perils and forms of degeneration by which it is oppressed. But I must make it clear that I do not contemplate merely the absorption of Liberals in the Conservative Party as individuals (that will certainly go on) but an honourable agreement and alliance between the Liberal and Conservative Parties as integral institutions. This will give the best chance of bringing into power a stable and progressive Government capable of dealing with our practical needs and in harmony with the movement of thought throughout the free world.

[. . .]

I ask from this great meeting, representing six constituencies in the West Country, a firm and decided endorsement of the work we have already done. Since we have been able to achieve these results while in a minority, it may well be that if the tables were turned the British nation could speedily be relieved of an immense network and oppression of needless controls, hardships and interferences with their daily lives by a new administration seeking the public welfare with wholehearted sincerity. It is our duty to fight hard as a party against Socialist wrong thinking and mismanagement. Everyone can see what a change has taken place in our position at home and in the eyes of other countries since that thoughtless vote of the electorate in 1945. When I laid down my commission the British nation, Empire and Commonwealth was victorious, respected and safe. There was perhaps no country in the world so much honoured, not only by friends, but even by vanquished enemies, as this island. It is painful to contrast our position and opportunities five years ago with what they are today. We had been united in our struggle to preserve the freedom of the world. Now when our dangers have revived and gathered again we lie in an unfortunate position. The indecisive vote of last February leaves us in the unpleasant atmosphere between two elections. Parliamentary democracy can only express itself by regular and not infrequent appeals to the electorate, but no one has ever suggested that prolonged electioneering is capable of settling our problems at home, or warding off our dangers from abroad. On can hardly imagine anything more unfortunate in Britain than that we should find ourselves at the present juncture split in half on domestic politics, with both parties gathering and arranging their forces for another trial of strength. That this should continue for many months without remedy can only be disastrous to our prosperity, and may well endanger both our life and even our survival as a great power.

Who is it that has brought about this deep gulf in our national life? No doubt each side will blame the other. Certainly many hard and bitter words are being spoken, by both sides. There are always words in partisan warfare, and the British people have always been free spoken in their party fights. But deeds are stronger than words, and it is the deeds, or misdeeds, of the Socialist Government, who alone wield executive power, which have brought about the present violent internal antagonism in the midst of renewed and increasing national peril.

Armed conflict has broken out between the United Nations, comprising almost all the free people of the world, and the Russian organized and well-equipped Communists of Northern Korea. The United States are bearing with courage and resolution in a noble way the burden of this clash which is in all essentials a renewal of our fight for human freedom against Hitler. I do not say that what has happened and is happening in Korea has made the dangers of a third world war greater. They were already grave. It has brought them nearer, and they are more apparent and I trust indeed that it has made the great masses of people throughout the free world more aware, awake and alive to where they stand.

I have myself for some time past believed that the worst chance for the life of the free world was to continue a policy of drift. At least three precious years of the United Nations have been wasted in floating along from day to day hoping, in spite of ceaseless disappointments and warnings, that all would come out right if we hoped for the best and let things take their course. But meanwhile the Communist menace and aggression continues to spread throughout the world. The fourteen men in the Kremlin are not drifting with events. They work on calculation and design. They have a policy the aim of which we can see; but the execution and timing of their ambition for Communist world government we cannot predict. They infiltrate in all countries with adepts and agents. Their adherents have no loyalty to any home. They care nothing for their native lands. They owe allegiance solely to Moscow. Communism is a religion with all its discipline and some of its fervour – a religion not only without God, but anti-God. It is a philosophy of base materialism in the name of which the world is to be reduced to the Soviet-Socialist pattern just as Hitler wanted it reduced to the Nazi-Socialist pattern. They have condemned Christian ethics and civilization, as we have known them, to a formidable struggle.

But behind all this doctrinal and ideological movement of thought which might well be defeated, and is indeed being defeated by the free play of Parliamentary democracy in countries where this is allowed, lies the mighty Russian armed power. The Communists pay lip-service to the doctrine of peace, but by peace they mean submission to their will and system. They preach the reduction of armaments, but they have more men organized and trained under arms than all the rest of the world put together. They urge the banning of the atomic bomb which in the hands of the United States is at this moment the only physical shield and protection of the free world, while they themselves have rejected any bona fide international control and inspection, and are trying to make bombs as fast as they can. Meanwhile around all the vast frontiers of Soviet Russia and her satellite or conquered countries they maintain a policy of unending aggression or menace. Since the war nearly all China with its hundreds of millions of people has been incorporated in the Soviet system. They are massing troops against Tibet. They threaten Persia. They are seeking to overawe and quell Yugoslavia. They cause deep fear in Finland and Sweden.

President Truman, under the full sanction and authority of the United Nations, and with the overwhelming support of the American people, and of the British Empire, and of its Commonwealth, has confronted aggression in Korea. I have not the knowledge to enable me to predict how this Korean fighting will end. But let me here express our admiration for the daring and skill with which the handful of American soldiers, three or four battalions at most, who have as yet been brought into action in Korea have fought their delaying action against overwhelming odds. I rejoice to learn that so far they have suffered only a few hundred causalities. Now, however, a more serious collision impends, or has begun. But whatever happens in Korea is only a part, and a small part of the pressures under which our free civilization lies, and which it must face or perish.

What is the position in Western Europe? Nearly half of Europe has already been subjugated by the Kremlin since the war. Large areas of Germany, occupied by the liberating armies of Britain and the United States, were handed over at the end of the war to the Russian rule, in virtue of wartime agreements which in so many other respects the Stalin domination had already completely broken in the case of Poland and Yugoslavia. I see that General de Gaulle declared a few days ago that Europe was in mortal peril. I have often disagreed with General de Gaulle, but I cannot feel that what he has said at this time is untrue. We are none of us free from peril even here in this island, where at least we have the waves, winds and tides of the Channel between us and the unhappy Continent. Even here in this beautiful and famous Devonshire so long and so valiantly defended in bygone generations we do not know what our fortunes will be. We live our ordinary lives, we go about our business and work hard as we must and ought to earn our livelihood and that of our country. But I tell you with the utmost earnestness that my own anxieties about the safety not only of the free world, but of our own hearths and homes, often remind me of the summer of 1940 ten tragic years ago. By this I do not mean that war is imminent. But I must not lead you to suppose that time is on our side; that we have only got to go on with our party quarrels and close our eyes and stop our ears to the facts of the situation to find that all will work out all right in the long run. This might be a fatal delusion. We have not been able ourselves since the war to make an atomic bomb. I don't know why.

We are dependent in this and in so much else upon the United States. But the oligarchy of the wicked men at the head of the Communist world have had the secreted betrayed to them, and have found out also from other sources, how to make this fearful weapon for themselves. At present, so far as I have been able to learn, they have very few atomic bombs. But I do not see how the passage of two or three years, during which they will be building up a large stock of them, is going to make our problems simpler or our dangers less. It is time that the British people should know more about the facts upon which the causes they defended and championed, and their very lives, may well depend.

You may have noticed that I have formally asked for a Secret Session in order that Parliament may be given some fuller information on the state of our defences at home and in Europe, and that Mr Attlee has so far refused. But I hold that Members of the House of Commons are responsible to their constituencies for making themselves generally acquainted with matters which concern the lives and safety of those who sent them to Westminster. At present the Socialist majority are content to remain in ignorance even of the main facts, and are prepared to vote down any proposal to give more information. We may not even talk things over among ourselves in Parliament. I take a high view of the duties of the elected representatives of the people. They should be kept at least as well informed as their predecessors before the war about the main foundations of our national safety. This Parliament is more uninformed about these matters than any I have ever seen. We do not want to be told deadly and technical secrets, but we ought to know broadly and truly where we are and how we stand. I should certainly not expect that even in Secret Session anything should be told us that the Soviet Government do not already know. But Members representing large masses of electors ought to have a sense of responsibility for their survival. It would be much better for Parliament to have a free discussion within the limits I have mentioned instead of going on blindfold like this.

It is argued that there would be leakage from a Secret Session. The disclosure of matters which pass in a Secret Session is a breach of privilege, and this has always proved a good check, even on indiscretion. Moreover, at the General Election we got rid of the Communist Members and the most noticeable of their fellow-travellers; and I cannot believe this present House could not be trusted with what His Majesty's Government would think fit to tell them, none of which would tell the Russians what they do not already know. Of course we have the right and the power to raise these matters in Public Debate, and if a Secret Session is refused this may be forced upon us by our duty to the country. It would indeed be wrong if the new Parliament were to disperse for two-and-a-half months' holiday without its Members receiving from the Ministers of the Crown any assurance that the frontiers of Western Europe, and indeed our own national security, can be maintained in the face of a Russian Communist onslaught. I did not fail to give my warnings before the war although things were at least as dangerous as they are today.

I still hope that the unities now being established among all the Western Democracies and Atlantic Powers will ward off from us the terrors and unspeakable miseries of a third world war. I wish also that every effort could be made on the highest level to bring home to the Russian Soviet Government the gravity of the facts which confront us all, them as well as us. I do not give up the hope which I expressed to you five months ago, of a supreme effort to bridge the gulf between the two worlds, if not in friendship, at least without the hatreds and manoeuvres of the cold war. But of this I am sure: that the best hope will be founded upon the strength of the Western Democracies and upon their unwavering will-power to defend the causes for which they stand.

To work from weakness and fear is ruin. To work from wisdom and power may be salvation. These simple but tremendous facts are, I feel, being understood by the free nations better than they have ever been before. I believe, moreover, that the faithful discharge of our national duty by every one of us laying aside all impediments will give the Conservative Party a chance of rendering true service to Britain, its Empire and the world. In this there lies before us an opportunity such as the centuries do not often bring.

Winston S. Churchill to Duke of Westminster
(Churchill papers, 1/47)

19 July 1950
Private

My dear Benny,

I want as a wedding present or settlement for Sarah to give her and her Husband a house.

Some time ago I formed a Trust to administer my literary earnings in favour of my Children – I myself and Clemmie cannot benefit by it. This Trust is administered by Lord Cherwell and Brendan Bracken, with Clemmie as Chairman.

They found the ideal house – 186, Ebury Street – and were deep in negotiations for its purchase when it was found that the house could not be used for professional purposes.

Sarah, as I expect you know, is on the stage, and her Husband, Antony Beauchamp, is a photographer. Permission for a studio on the ground floor has been obtained for seven years from the Town Planning Department of the London County Council; but the Trust solicitors, Fladgate and Co., have now received a letter from Mr Barty-King[1] from your office in Davies Street, saying that your Estate advisers cannot give this permission.

There would be no plate on the front door, and no indication that the house was not used entirely for residential purposes. In fact, in the evening Sarah would be using the 'studio' as her drawing room.

She and her Husband are very anxious for the studio to be in the house where they live. Antony Beauchamp certainly takes very beautiful photographs, but he may not have many sitters, not as many, I fear, as a successful portrait painter. The house would be used just as the Laverys[2] used 5, Cromwell Palace, and as the Birleys now use their house in St John's Wood.

If Sarah continues on the stage she may be obliged to go every year to the United States – but I earnestly want her to live in England and not to settle in America. I would like her to live in a pretty house with enough room for a nursery, and this can be afforded only if the studio is allowed to be part of it. Her Husband is a hard-working intelligent young man, and I am anxious to do all I can to make them happy and to enable him to make a success of his profession.

Clemmie and I want Sarah so much to settle down here this autumn, and 186, Ebury Street, needs no alterations whatever. When they come home they could just step into it.

Since writing this, I have had an agreeable talk with Mr Barty-King, and he explained to me the difficulties of granting an official licence, no matter how unobjectionable in practice was the use made of it. I suggested to him that we might have an informal agreement, without an official licence, for say seven years, and see how things went on. I do not think there would be any complaints or trouble, and in any case the literary Trustees, who would be the owners of the house, would have the power to regulate this. Mr Barty-King seemed to think this might be a solution; at any rate he will discuss it with you when you return.

I am so sorry to bother you with all this. Let me know when you get home.

---

[1] George Ingram Barty-King, 1907–81. Married Barbara Baxter: two children. Solicitor at Boodle Hatfield and Co.

[2] John Lavery, 1856–1931. Painter. Born in Belfast. A Roman Catholic. Exhibited his first oil painting at Glasgow, 1879. Vice-President, International Society of Sculptors, Painters and Gravers, 1897. Married, 1910, as his second wife, Hazel Trudeau Martyn (c.1887–1935). Knighted, 1918. President of the Royal Society of Portrait Painters from 1932 until his death. Some of Churchill's earliest paintings had been done in Lavery's London studio. The Laverys lived at 5 Cromwell Place, a few yards from the house at 41 Cromwell Road which in 1915–16 Winston and Clementine had co-owned and shared with Jack and Goonie Churchill.

JULY 1950 1799

Air Chief Marshal Sir Arthur Harris to Winston S. Churchill
(Churchill papers, 4/390A)

20 July 1950
Personal and Confidential

My dear Great Man,
 You asked me to let you know more about Dresden.
 It is hard at this distance of time to recall every factor that weighed in the selection of any individual target amongst the thousands selected during the 365 days and nights of that year. But as I recall it, the following factors applied to Dresden:
   1. Dresden, amongst other centres in that locality, was explicitly and newly placed on the target list at that time by the Air Ministry.
   2. Intelligence information, and military talk generally then, stressed the Nazis' probable intention to withdraw what they could of their failing forces to their so called 'Southern Fortress' where, it was surmised – and said – the Nazis intended a final fight to the death. It would have done them no good – except for their own personal satisfaction – but, had it materialised, it would certainly have caused the Allies additional and perhaps large casualties.
   3. Dresden and the area round it formed about the only remaining operationally intact centre of rail and road communications available to the Nazis in a comparatively intact Zone between the converging Allied fronts, and that lent colour to the assumption that that centre would be used, and was probably then being used, for the collection, marshalling and despatch of picked Nazi troops towards the 'Southern Fortress area'. I recall that it was said at the time to be packed with troops, transports, guns and AFVs etc.
   4. I also seem to recall that the Russians had indicated Dresden amongst other places as a desirable target to assist them in getting forward and – on our side – Patton was making that way, as usual far in advance of support and supply. (If the Russians in fact made any request that resulted in Dresden being put on the target list by the Air Ministry, it would be all in line with the normal methods of their propaganda – and that of their stooges here and in the USA – to now celebrate the anniversaries of the attack on Dresden, which is in their Zone, by holding it up as an example of Anglo-America ferocity.)
   5. Weather and tactical factors weighed heavily on every target selection and no doubt on this one. Chemnitz, another such target, had already 'had it' and by that time might have been in our hands, or too nearly so.
 Such would be the factors that weighed but, without all the available details

to refresh my memory, I could not say that they all weighed, or which were the most important, or not others. So far as I recall the RAF Bomber Command Force had its usual bomb loading, with a high proportion of incendiaries. The Boche[1] had learnt his lesson at Hamburg and as a rule, after Hamburg, such bomb loads did not cause high casualties, but enormous material destruction. Either once or twice or more, during the ensuing days, the USAAF attacked Dresden heavily with HE and, while I am not trying in any way to hand the baby to them, it may well be that the peculiarly high casualty rate claimed (if it indeed occurred) was caused mainly by these HE attacks.

Apart from the above, my answer to the 'Why Dresden?' critics is, in brief: 'Why not?'

If Hamburg, Berlin, the Ruhr towns, Hanover, Kassel, London, Coventry or Canterbury and half a hundred others – why not Dresden? It was, at least potentially, amongst the last few remaining probable centres of resistance and I personally never thought even the last intact brick in Germany worth the life of one Allied soldier. Neither do I now. Frankly, I consider the outcry – if there is any beyond the long haired gentry and Communist stooges – is largely due to the association of Dresden with china shepherdesses, tin musical boxes and mechanical toys – all of which industries lent themselves admirably to a rapid war time switch to V1 and V2 mechanisms, insulations, bomb and shell time-fuses and all the other devilries of Hitler's war.

As for the casualties, if they were as bad as claimed, all Germany had had ample warning from you yourself, and from experience over the War years, to get out of all such places and keep out.

I offer no apologia for Dresden and never will. I hope and feel sure that you won't. The Boche was played and outplayed at his own games; we won and he doesn't like it. If Dresden saved the life of one Allied soldier, it was well worth it. If it did not, then I regret, not Dresden, but wasted military effort.

My Deputy –
  Air Marshal Sir Robert Saundby,[2]
    Oxleas,
     Burghclere,
      Newbury.

will, I am sure, be pleased to discuss, or further investigate or elucidate. I shall be sailing on Saturday, 29th.

My very warmest regards and wishes. I am sending you shortly the framed photograph for your rogues gallery.

---

[1] Boche: derogatory word for a German soldier, used frequently during WWII. Derived from the French word *alboche*, a combination of the words *allemand* (German) and *caboche* (cabbage).

[2] Robert Henry Magnus Spencer Saundby, 1896–1946. On active service during WWI (MC). Wg Cdr, 1933. Directing Staff, RAF Staff College, 1934. Deputy Director of Operations, 1937. Gp Capt., 1937. Deputy Director of Operational Requirements, 1938; Director, 1938–40. AVM, 1940. Asst CAS, Operational Requirements and Tactics, 1940. Senior Air Staff Officer, HQ Bomber Command, 1940. Deputy AOC-in-C, Bomber Command, 1943. KBE, 1944. Air Mshl, 1944. KCB, 1956.

Winston S. Churchill to Clement Attlee
(Churchill papers, 2/29)

25 July 1950

My dear Prime Minister,

We are asking through the usual channels for the continuance of the Defence Debate till dinner time on Thursday. I shall move at the beginning of that day that we go into Secret Session. I shall appeal to you not to force us to divide against you on a matter of this kind when the issues are so grave for us all.

Winston S. Churchill: speech
(Hansard)

26 July 1950   House of Commons

DEFENCE

We gladly yielded our right to open this Debate to the Minister of Defence when he asked for this facility. It was certainly necessary that a statement should be made to the House before we separate. One of our reasons for asking for a Debate in public, after a Secret Session, or a Debate in private, had been refused, was to give the Government an opportunity of explaining their position and, to some extent our position, and it was very fortunate, I think, that we did so. Otherwise, the House would have had no opportunity, according to the Government's plan, of debating the statement which has just been made to us. It is entirely due to our request that this difficulty has been surmounted. I do not intend myself to discuss in detail this afternoon the proposals which the Minister of Defence has announced, though they appeared few and far between, or the general tenor and character of his statement. I will reserve what I have to say until we come to the Third Reading of this Bill tomorrow, either in public or in private session, as the House may decide.

Let me say at once that we shall give our support to any measures proposed by the Government which seem right or necessary in the public interest, whether they are popular or not. We may even feel it our duty to support measures which are not only belated but may be judged inadequate, while criticising them in these respects. I could not help feeling, while I listened to the right hon. Gentleman, that he gave no decided or clear answer on the question of lengthening the period of service, which clearly lies at the root of the economy of our Army. I ventured to say in the last Parliament that we should take fewer men for a longer period. I quite see the complications of that, but that is a great matter. I can only say that should the Government decide to embark upon that course, in some way or other – undoubtedly one which would not be popular to the country or in any part of the House – we shall give them our support, as we have done throughout the whole story of national compulsory military service in time of peace.

I must say in passing that one would have thought, to hear the right hon. Gentleman's speech about these great dangers, which were brought home to us by his candid statement of the vast strength of Russia in Europe, that he and his colleagues of the Socialist Government had only just come into power and that all this situation had developed overnight, as it were, whereas it has been building up for at least three years during which the Allied Forces were falling while the Russian power was steadily maintained and strengthened in every way. These are matters which we shall have to examine. But, Sir, as we shall give the Government our support should it be needed at any time, they have no excuse for not asking for whatever they require, nor have they in the past had any difficulty because of the immense sums of money which Parliament has accorded them during these five years. During this period they have spent, I think, over £5,000,000,000 in maintaining the Armed Forces. It is remarkable that by far the vastest proportion of this was spent during the period when, according to the right hon. Gentleman's argument, the danger was the least, and the amounts fell off steadily as the danger, by contrast, grew.

They also had the great advantage of starting with an enormous mass of munitions, much of which was quite new and some of which was even produced after the war had ended, because the factories were allowed to run to complete weapons on which they had begun – I do not say wrongly. Many of the rifles, which are the great foundation of the armaments of any nation, have been frittered away and squandered, but still there was a vast amount left. The artillery, in the main, is something which will last. A large portion of the munitions available at the end of the war could have been, if they had not been improvidently used, available for expanding the defensive Forces that we had, and developing them. It seems to me that all this requires fairly careful detailed examination. After all, even weapons that were new five years ago are better than no weapons at all. This also touches the question of arming the forces of other countries, and I trust it will be looked into and examined.

I do not intend to be drawn into any personal controversy with the right hon. Gentleman if I can help it. He stated at the weekend that I had no confidence in him. As I have said before, I have confidence that his heart is in the right place, and any reservations I might have to make would be in regard to other aspects of his suitability for discharging the tremendous tasks entrusted to him.

There is, however, one point which occurred in the House last week to which I must refer. The right hon. Gentleman, when speaking at Question Time, about the possibilities of a Debate on defence said that he quite understood my 'natural curiosity'. If curiosity were my motive, I might easily have satisfied it, because the Prime Minister and the right hon. Gentleman himself have several times, even since this new Parliament was formed, offered to give me and any colleagues I might bring with me the fullest information in their possession. I have not availed myself of this latest offer up to the present, for the following reasons. I did not find that the conversations we had last year, although conducted in a friendly manner on both sides, were fruitful in results. On the other hand, the fact that we had these conversations, which were in progress from June to October at intervals, undoubtedly made it difficult for the Opposition to examine in public the state of our defences and to make those criticisms which are usual every few months, or at any rate every year, in Parliament. In fact, the subject of our defence was not dealt with in a searching or controversial manner at all in the House last year by the Opposition.

The difficulty of the leaders of the Opposition parties receiving confidential information from the Government – the chief difficulty – is of course that their lips are thereby sealed in respect of everything they did not know before, and that these two fields of information – what they knew before and what they are told – overlap and affect one another in a manner which is certainly embarrassing to any public discussion which may follow. I therefore contented myself with saying, at the beginning of this new Parliament, that I accepted no responsibility for the present state of our defences, and, at my request, the Prime Minister altered the Government Motion on presenting the White Paper by substituting the words 'That this House takes note of' for the original words 'That this House approves'. Our position is therefore perfectly clear. We cannot take any course which may hamper us in the discharge of our duty as we conceive it, or prevent us giving any warnings to the House and also, in due course, to the country, which may be required as the situation develops.

I greatly regret that the Prime Minister and the Socialist Government persist in refusing a Debate in Secret or private Session. It might, I think, have been quite natural and in the public interest that after hearing a public statement by the Minister of Defence and after some public discussion upon it, we should have gone into private Session and talked things over among ourselves as Members of the House of Commons. The point has been raised, that, if we were to hold a Secret Session, it would be resented by the United States Government, who would want to know what had happened, but could not be told. I can assure the House that there is no validity in this suggestion. The Americans are very familiar with the procedure of secret sessions. The Congressional Committees often hold them; they are called Executive Sessions. These Congressional Committees, especially those of the House of Representatives, have enormous powers of obtaining information for their members. They can summon generals, admirals, air marshals and other experts before them subject only to the veto of the Minister in charge of the Department, very rarely exercised, and can examine them to any extent, either in public or in secret. There is no doubt whatever that the American House of Representatives exercises its responsibilities towards its constituents in a far more vigilant and rigorous manner than anything we have adopted over here. We are a very ill-informed body on defence questions compared with them, and the idea that they would object to our having a Secret Session is utterly absurd, and, indeed would constitute an interference with our domestic affairs of which, I am sure, the United States would never be guilty.

It was also said by the Lord President of the Council that there was no precedent for a Secret Session except in time of war, but we are now at war technically. As a mandatory of the United Nations, we are technically at war with the Republic of Northern Korea, so that that argument, for whatever it was ever worth, is effectively disposed of. I still hope that a Secret or private Session will be claimed by the House tomorrow. I do not understand why the Government do not wish to take the House into their full confidence, so far as that may be possible without revealing secrets not already known to the Soviet Government and to the General Staffs of Europe and of the United States. The discussion can be easier and freer when every word we say is not carried immediately all over the world. I believe that such a Debate might have the effect of bringing us more together and promoting a better understanding between us in the facts of our grave common danger. I feel that Members of Parliament have a deep obligation to seek the fullest information possible about matters which affect the lives and safety of their constituents, and that they might well be held accountable to those constituents if, by their votes tomorrow, they put their veto upon such a discussion.

Considering how evenly the parties are balanced in this Parliament, and that the Prime Minister's party is in a minority in the country of nearly 2,000,000 voters, it is much to be regretted that he should adopt such an authoritarian attitude. I cannot think that his decision will be helpful, either to his party, or, what is of far greater importance, to the welfare of the country.

With regard to the Debate tomorrow, I must make the reservation that I may have to make certain changes in what I think it is possible to say to the House, in accordance with the decision to which we have come. With regard to the Debate in public this afternoon, there is a great deal that can be said, especially on the administrative aspects, and much can be said on the general issue, without trenching on facts which are not already public property and well-known to those who follow these matters with attention in every country. I am sure that my hon. and right hon. Friends on this side of the House will be able to throw much light on our problems within the wide limits that are open to us.

Winston S. Churchill to Clement Attlee
(*Churchill papers, 2/29*)

26 July 1950

Dear Prime Minister,

In view of your refusal to my repeated appeals that you should allow the defence debate to take place in secret or private session, my colleagues and I feel bound, owing to the daily increasing gravity of the situation, to press this issue to a division at the beginning of business on Thursday.

We have been willing to yield to Mr Shinwell the opening of the public debate today, and the fact that he has asked for this shows how necessary was the public debate which you have deprecated in your correspondence with me. I wonder you do not acknowledge this courtesy.

I cannot understand why you should seek to make the grave differences between us as public as possible. Considering how narrowly parties are balanced in the House I should have thought that you would have shown some consideration to those whose aid you will surely need in carrying here and bringing into operation in the country the various measures which may be found necessary at this time of public danger. It seems to me that you are taking a grave additional responsibility upon yourself by the course of action you have chosen. This will however make no difference to the support which we shall give here or out-of-doors to any measures which you may propose for the strengthening of our defences.

Clement Attlee to Winston S. Churchill
(*Churchill papers, 2/29*)

26 July 1950

My dear Churchill,

I have your letter of yesterday's date[1] in which you ask for a continuance of the Defence Debate till dinner time on Thursday and state that you propose to move for a secret session on Thursday.

I am surprised that this proposal for an extended debate is only raised at this late stage.

The business of the week was accepted without comment on Thursday last and no suggestion of a change was made on Monday or Tuesday at Question time. This seems to me to be treating the House of Commons with very scant courtesy. It is, of course, the right of the Opposition to choose the subject of debate on the Appropriation Bill but it is usual to give the House some prior notice of intentions.

---

[1] Reproduced above (p. 1801).

I cannot think that your suggestion that the Debate on Defence should be partly conducted in public and partly in secret session is a wise one.

The fact of the secret session will obviously detract from the value of the public debate and will tend to cause the greatest amount of suspicion and uneasiness both to home and abroad.

I hope you will reconsider this proposal which the Government will be bound to oppose.

Charles de Gaulle to Winston S. Churchill
(Churchill papers, 2/169)

26 July 1950
Translation

Dear Mr Churchill,

I am about to write my Memoirs of the last war. Although I do not foresee any definite date for publication, I would like to forward to you the attached text of what I say about yourself on the occasion of our first meeting on 8 June 1940 in your study at Downing Street. This communication is needless to say only destined for yourself.

I would like you to be the witness of my personal feelings of fidelity both in relation to the past and in confidence for the future.

ENCLOSURE

Mr Churchill received me at Downing Street. It was my first contact with him. The impression he gave me confirmed me in my conviction that Great Britain, led by such a fighter, would certainly not flinch. Mr Churchill seemed to me to be equal to the rudest task, provided it had also grandeur. The assurance of his judgment, his great culture, the knowledge he had of most of the subjects, countries and men involved, and finally his passion for the problems proper to war, found in war their full scope. On top of everything, he was fitted by his character to act, take risk, play the part out-and-out and without scruple. In short, I found him well in the saddle as guide and chief. Such were my first impressions.

What followed only confirmed them and revealed to me, in addition, the eloquence that was Mr Churchill's own and how well he knew how to use it. Whatever his audience – crowd, assembly, council, even a single interlocutor, whether he was before a microphone, on the floor of the House, at table or behind a desk, the original, poetic, stirring flow of his ideas, arguments and feelings brought him an almost infallible ascendancy in the tragic atmosphere in which the poor world was gasping. Well tried in politics, he played upon that angelic and diabolic gift to stir up the heavy dough of the English as well as to impress the minds of foreigners. The humour, too, with which he seasoned his acts and words, and the way in which he made use now of graciousness, now of anger, contributed to make one feel what a mastery he had of the terrible game in which he was engaged.

The harsh and painful incidents that often rose between us, because of the friction of our two characters, or the opposition of some of the interests of our two countries, and of the unfair advantage taken by England of wounded France, have influenced my attitude towards the Prime Minister, but not my judgment. Winston Churchill appeared to me, from one end of the drama to the other, as the great champion of a great enterprise and the great artist of a great History.

Winston S. Churchill: speech
(Hansard)

27 July 1950   House of Commons

DEFENCE

It has been decided by the House that our Debate must be in public, and I shall confine myself to stating facts which are certainly well-known to the Soviet Government and to the General Staffs of Europe and the United States. The most important things that I shall say I have already said in public before. I shall base myself on matter which has already appeared in the newspapers or been disclosed by various authorities in Europe or the United States. I shall ask the Government a number of questions, but if they do not wish to answer them now that they have escaped into public Session, I shall not press them. I have little doubt that they could have been answered in private Session, as they are already within the limits I have prescribed of being certainly known to foreign Powers.

I had intended to open today with a statement of the strength of the Armed Forces of the Soviet Government. This would obviously give them no information which they do not already possess. But yesterday, in what seemed to me the most impressive part of his speech, the Minister of Defence gave us the figures on which the Government rely. There were, he said, 175 active divisions. This I presume is a part of the much larger number, nearly double, which could be produced in a few months. Even if only half of the 175 were used against us in Western Europe, they could, therefore, launch over 80 divisions upon us without any further mobilisation. The Minister of Defence also stated that one-third of these 175 divisions are mechanised or armoured. Sir, that is a tremendous statement. I see that Mr Vinson,[1] the chairman of the

---

[1] Carl Vinson, 1883–1981. Educated at Georgia Military College and Mercer University School of Law. Member (Dem.) for Georgia, US House of Representatives, 1908–12, 1914–65. Chairman, House Armed Services Committee, 1955–65. 38th Dean, US House of Representatives, 1961–5.

Armed Services Committee of the House of Representatives at Washington, whom I mentioned yesterday, quoted the total Russian tank strength as 40,000, or seven times that of the United States. Our figure of 6,000 British, given yesterday by the Minister of Defence, is comparable, I take it, to this estimate of 40,000.

But even more important than the reserve or general stock of tanks is the number organised in formations. Could we be told, since so much has been disclosed, of the number of Soviet tanks now assembled on or near the Western Front in formations? Would 4,000 or 5,000 tanks in organised formations be an excessive estimate? In Korea we have seen how formidable even a few score of tanks can be, and how tough the heavy Russian tanks are. Any development and improvement in the bazooka and other anti-tank weapons would be greatly welcomed. I do not know how well the Western Union Forces are equipped with the latest and largest patterns, but I cannot think that the threat of the enormous mass of the Soviet armour is in any way mastered, or that there is anything in use and service at the present time which could cope with the array of armoured avalanches we must expect on the outbreak of war, should war occur.

Now let us see what the Western Union could put against all this. The former war-time French Prime Minister, M Reynaud, recently again a Minister, made some precise statements on this point last week, which have been published in the newspapers and which I do not think should escape the attention of the House. M Reynaud said that we and our European Allies have in Western Germany two British Divisions, two American and three French. For the rest, he said the French have four divisions in Europe and, I think, the Belgians one, a total of 12. I should think that M Reynaud is tolerably well informed on these matters. The French and the Belgian divisions must inevitably be hampered in their tactical efficiency by having to train the annual intake of conscripts. The two British divisions are of course largely composed of men completing their eighteen months' service, and are almost entirely dependent upon a numerous German civilian contingent for their transport, without which of course they cannot move. One of the two American divisions, I believe, is armoured, but I ask if the British have one full armoured division.

On this assumption, Western Union would have 12 divisions, against more than 80, and of these less than two are armoured, against anything from 25 to 30. The Russians know their own strength, but it is certain that they also know with great precision the Allied weakness and condition. Apart from agents, there are Communists all over Germany who see the troops living among them day after day, and we here in the House of Commons are entitled to ask the Government – are these figures, which I have just quoted, and their proportions, broadly speaking, true? Are the odds in ground troops on the Western Front eight or nine to one against us, or are they four, five, or six, or seven to one? Or is there no truth in this figure at all and are things much better? I hope the Prime Minister, if he is going to reply – or is it the Minister of Defence?

The Minister of Defence (Mr Shinwell) indicated assent.

Mr Churchill: I hope the Minister of Defence, when he replies, will tell us. There is really no reason why we should not know what the Soviets and all the General Staffs of Europe know, and what the Prime Minister and the Minister of Defence must themselves have known for a long time. In a Secret Session, there would I think, have been no difficulty in giving the broad facts.

When, in March, in the Debate on the White Paper, I said in the House that it would be necessary and right to enable the Germans of Western Germany to take part in the defence of their hearths and homes from the hideous menace under which they lie, the Prime Minister dismissed my advice as irresponsible. However, it is the advice which I understand the military commanders of the United States, at any rate, would give. At present, we have followed the principle that the only Germans who may be re-armed are the Communist Germans in the Eastern zone, who have been formed by the Soviets into a highly effective police army with powerful weapons and numbering 45,000 or 50,000 men – it may be more – and with considerable offshoots in the Communist cells and caches of arms known to exist in Western Germany. I do not wonder that something like panic prevails along the Eastern frontiers of Western Germany. Every true German friend of reconciliation with the Western democratic world, and the redemption of their past by faithful service, knows that the lurking Communist in the neighbourhood has marked him down for early liquidation. How can there be any foundation for a helpful German policy under such conditions?

In all that I have said so far, I have only spoken of the Soviet forces with which we are confronted – eight or nine to one against us in infantry and artillery, and probably much more than that in tank formations. I have not mentioned the satellite Powers. Poland, under strict Russian control, with a Russian marshal at the head of her forces, has a powerful party army. Czechoslovakia has another army, though less trustworthy, and the arsenals of Skoda, possibly the largest arms plant now in Europe, are steadily pouring out their weapons. If the facts that I have stated cannot be contradicted by His Majesty's Government, the preparations of the Western Union to defend itself certainly stand on a far lower level than those of the South Koreans. I notice that the right hon. Gentleman said yesterday with candour:

> I will not conceal from the House that the Forces at present available, or in sight, fall a long way short of requirements estimated even on the most conservative basis. There is nothing to be gained by failing to recognise this fact.

It is always, I think, true to say that one of the main foundations of the British sense of humour is under-statement, and this appears to be a very excellent example of that fact.

We may, no doubt, throw much of the blame on France and the Benelux countries, weakened by the disasters of the war, but do not let us imagine that we are not in danger ourselves. If, as M Reynaud says, and I have no reason to dispute him, the Soviet armies, with their armoured columns, could be at Calais and reach the Channel – or the Atlantic, that is to say – before any substantial reinforcements from the United States could arrive upon the scene – if that is true, then we ourselves, although protected from an immediate incursion by the anti-tank obstacle of the Channel, with its waves, tides and storms, will be subjected to a bombardment by rocket-propelled and guided missiles – I am not speaking of atomic bombs – incomparably more severe than anything we have endured or imagined. The Soviet Government picked up and developed all the Germans knew about this form of war. Peenemünde fell into their hands, and all the German secrets of this new phase of warfare, on which Hitler had set his final hopes, but the development of which was cut short by our advance – all this new phase of warfare has been developed in five years of intensive study and production.

The Russians do not need to come to the coast to plant their batteries. Very long ranges are within the compass of these weapons, and they can pick and choose their places. If we were alone, I might give some indication of the inconvenience which might be caused thereby. All this is true, and may be near – how near no one knows for certain, except the dictator oligarchy in the Kremlin, who accept no moral principles as known to us, but who are able to pursue, year after year, their calculated plans for world conquest without being concerned with public opinion or elections or any of the scruples which rule the Western and the Christian world.

Here I leave the first part of my subject – the relative strength of the armies and of the tanks upon the Western Front. Let us now look to the air. Immense figures have been published in America and in this country about the Soviet air forces – 25,000 military aircraft produced yearly was one figure. The Minister of Defence said yesterday that the Russian forces – he was speaking of their total military forces – are backed by 19,000 military aircraft, including jet aircraft of the latest design, both bombers and fighters. But, on the Western front, which is the matter which I have most in point at the moment, in fighter and bomber aircraft, how many have they got in full commission? Would 4,000 or 5,000 or 6,000 be too large an estimate? I should be greatly relieved if the Government were able to answer this question in a reassuring manner. But, considering all we have been told of the Russian strength, I can see no reason why, even under the conditions of a public Session, it should not be answered. But, even if we take it as only 4,000, how many have we got? We and the Americans and the Western Allies, how many have we got on the Continent – I am not speaking of home forces – to sustain our Armies of perhaps 12 divisions, as stated by M Reynaud, against 80 or 90? Here, again, even if we were in Secret Session, I would not ask the Government to state the exact figure, but could they say, for instance, that we have a half, a third, a fourth, a fifth, a sixth, or a seventh of what we know we have to face? I do not press them for a reply unless they wish to give one.

Upon the question of quality, no doubt we may hope to have superiority in machines and pilots, but this is by no means certain. The right hon. Gentleman has told us that a large proportion of the Russian aircraft are of the highest quality. They have certainly made great improvements on the jet aeroplanes in regard to which we so lightheartedly furnished them with our specimen engines a few years ago. There are other aspects of the Russian air menace not concerned with the mainland of Europe with which I must now deal. If the Russian Armies reached or approached the coast of France and held the airfields there from which we were attacked by the Germans 10 years ago, they could, I fear, outnumber us in the air by a far larger number of machines than Hitler ever had. Anything that the Government choose to say upon the fighter forces available for the defence of London and our vital feeding seaports which would reassure the House would give the deepest satisfaction to us all.

But there is another aspect of the air defence of Britain which is even more grave and intense. Two years ago, the Government agreed that the Americans should establish a bombing base in East Anglia from which they could use the atom bomb upon the Russian cities and keypoints. The Americans have other bases, but this is one of the most important. We on this side of the House do not criticise the Government for taking this very serious step for which, in any case, they had the large Socialist majority of the last Parliament at their disposal.

Mr Sydney Silverman (Nelson and Colne): Would the right hon. Gentleman give way for a moment?

Mr Churchill: Not at this point. All this has been in the newspapers for a long time. I would not have asked the Government, even in Secret Session, for the exact numbers of the American offensive forces for using the atomic bomb on Soviet Russia which are located here in this island. However, the Prime Minister stated them on Monday as 10,000 men and 180 planes in three bomber groups. To this, the Minister of Defence added last night that there were fighter squadrons also, so we may be sure that the Russians know the main facts pretty well. It is on this foundation that the Communists base their oft-repeated charge that Britain is an aircraft carrier moored to attack the Soviet Union. It is also, this base in East Anglia, our major defence against the consequences which would follow or accompany a Russian onslaught in Europe, and it is a vital part of the atomic bomb deterrent, which is what we are living on now.

More than two years have passed since this base was established and became public. It was obvious, whatever else was done or not done, that from that moment the utmost endeavours should have been used to make the base secure by every form of anti-aircraft artillery and by the most perfect and elaborate development of radar, and, above all, by the largest number of the latest fighter aircraft which we could produce ourselves or get from the United States. I hope this has been done. I naturally do not ask for a detailed reply, but one fact makes me anxious – it has been mentioned before, and I must refer to it now for it may be typical of much else in our present administrative policy. I simply cannot comprehend a policy which while, on the one hand, taking this extraordinary risk of establishing this base, can disperse or distribute so large a proportion of the jet aircraft in the production of which British genius has held the lead.

We wonder how many jet aeroplane engines we have distributed to our friends or sold to foreign countries. I do not ask for a reply in detail; I will content myself with reminding the House, as my right hon. Friend did yesterday, of what has been published in the newspapers and admitted by Ministers, namely, that 100 of these jets were sold to the Argentine, which lays its claims to the Falkland Islands and is at this moment in wrongful occupation of British territory in the Antarctic. It has also been stated, and not denied when raised in the House, that 110 were sold, traded, or given to Egypt – written off against sterling balances, or the like – to Egypt of all countries at the present time, which was actually blocking the Canal in violation of the treaty, and no doubt given to them in order to enable them to face the new State of Israel. Here at any rate are 210 machines, only, of course, a proportion of what have been dispersed or disposed of, out of the total of these invaluable jets, and of these 210 we have been deprived by an act of improvidence beyond description or compare.

We have the Auxiliary Air Force, which is an important element in our home defence – about 20 squadrons – and is manned by very high quality volunteers really worthy of the finest weapons which our factories can make. This Auxiliary Air Force could all have been re-armed by now with the jets we have distributed to these foreign countries. I simply cannot understand it. In the 50 years since I entered this House, I have never seen anything quite like it. I made my protests and appeals to the Prime Minister more than a year ago. Perhaps he or the Minister of Defence will tell us tonight that at least the sale of our jets to neutrals has now been stopped.

But this particular illustration of the manner in which the policy of the Government has been incoherent or uncoordinated, ugly though it be, must not draw our minds from the general picture which I am presenting to the House. I have dealt with the relative strengths of the armies and the armoured forces on both sides in Europe. I have spoken of the Air Force, though I have not attempted to go into actual or relative strengths, except to state that we are, I believe, outnumbered as we have never been before.

Now I come, thirdly, to the naval sphere and the Soviet U-boats. Reliable naval reference books estimate the present Russian U-boat fleet at 360 divided, no doubt, between the Pacific and the West, of which between 100 and 200 are ocean-going and capable of high speeds. These seem to me very large figures, and I am not at all accepting them as final figures, but what is the truth about them? I do not see why the Minister of Defence should not give us his best estimate, considering the information which has been given about other portions of the Russian forces. Many of these boats, we are told, are of 20 knots. A modern 20-knot submerged U-boat would, it is calculated, be able to search five times the area of water that was covered by the last war U-boats with their maximum submerged speed of nine knots. What is the truth of this? There can be no harm in giving this information to the public. All German technical discoveries and, no doubt, some German technical aid have been at the command of the Soviets since the war.

Considering that we and the world have been told the deadly details of the American atomic force in East Anglia, surely the facts about the Russian U-boat construction can be given on the best estimate that is available. When I went to the Admiralty at the beginning of the last war the Germans had 30 ocean-going U-boats with a maximum underwater speed of nine knots. Only 30. And now the figure of 300 is mentioned; but it may be much less and yet be most grave. I am not committing myself to any precise figure, but they only had 30 then. I hope it may be possible to reassure us on the present position.

I do not know, nor do I ask, what resources we have in up-to-date anti-U-boat craft, but I doubt very much whether they are in number equal actually, or still less proportionately, to what those who are called the 'guilty men' of the last war had prepared. I believe it is probably true to say that the Russian-Soviet U-boat menace to our trans-ocean Atlantic life-line and world communications, which also comprise all American reinforcements for Europe, would be far more severe than was the German U-boat force in their attacks of 1939 and 1940; and this seemed quite enough then.

We have, however, the Air Force Coastal Command, and in this and in multiplication of aircraft carriers and antisubmarine vessels lies our hope, and, I trust, our policy. But it was said yesterday that the Coastal Command is below its approved strength, both in aircraft and in their personnel. I hope this may be contradicted, and if it cannot be contradicted I trust it will be made good. I do not feel I should be exaggerating if I said that the Soviet attack by modernised German U-boats in Russian hands upon our ocean life-line would, for a year at least, perhaps for more, be far more severe than was the Hitler attack in 1939 and 1940. I ask specifically if the Minister of Defence will deal with this in his speech, because it is fundamental and vital.

Summing up the scene, it looks as if there is at present no effective defence in Western Europe beyond the Channel, and that the Russian advance to the

Channel or towards it will bring us under air bombardment, apart from the atomic bomb, far worse than we have ever endured. Secondly, it would be very bad for us if the Russians were to gain the command of the air over the Channel and over this island by an overpowering use of numbers. On the sea we are also at a serious disadvantage, as I have just described, compared with the last war. It is, perhaps, worth while for the House and the country to weigh these facts attentively. If they can be substantially corrected, no one will be more fervently thankful than I.

If the comparison of British and Western Union forces ended at this point, with a survey of land, sea and air, our position might well be judged forlorn. We might feel the need of the striking phrase used the other night by my hon. Friend the Member for Carlton (Mr Pickthorn)[1] when he said, 'While there is death there is hope.' Fortunately, there is a fourth vast sphere of defence in which the United States have enormous and measureless superiority. Two years ago I said in the country, at Llandudno:[2]

> If it were not for the stocks of atomic bombs now in the trusteeship of the United States, there would be no means of stopping the subjugation of Western Europe by Communist machinations backed by Russian armies and enforced by political police.

Again, I said on the same occasion:

> Nothing stands between Europe today and complete subjugation to Communist tyranny but the atomic bomb in American possession.

It is to this aspect that I must now recur. I understand that we have no atom bombs of our own. Considering how far we were forward in this matter during the war – we could not ourselves undertake it because we were under fire, that was the only reason why we did not – and that we earnestly pressed the Americans into it, as my conversations with President Roosevelt in 1942, which are on record, will show, it is remarkable, considering all this, how quickly we were denied the confidence of the United States after the war was over, and how we have never been able in five years with all our own gathered knowledge to make the atom bomb ourselves.

I also said in 1948:

> What will happen when the Russians get the atomic bomb themselves and have accumulated a large store? You can judge for yourselves what will happen then by what is happening now. If these things are done in the

---

[1] Kenneth William Murray Pickthorn, 1892–1975. Constitutional historian. Fellow of Corpus Christi College, Cambridge, from 1914. On active service in France and Macedonia, 1915–19. Dean, Tutor and subsequently President of Corpus Christi College, 1919–44. MP (Cons.) for Cambridge, 1935–50; for Carlton (Nottinghamshire), 1950–66. Parliamentary Secretary, Ministry of Education, 1951–4. Bt, 1959.

[2] Speech reproduced above (pp. 1182–94).

> green wood, what will be done in the dry? If they can continue month after month disturbing and tormenting the world, trusting to our Christian and altruistic inhibitions against using this strange new power against them, what will they do when they themselves have large quantities of atomic bombs?

And further:

> The Western nations will be far more likely to reach a lasting settlement, without bloodshed, if they formulate their just demands while they have the atomic power and before the Russian Communists have got it too.

No attention was paid to this. I fully realise the difficulties and the dangers of such a policy and it did not rest entirely with us.

But now things have definitely worsened. It is painful in every respect to be told, as we were officially told some months ago, that the Russians have been able to gain the secret of the atom bomb through Communist traitors in the American and also notably in the British service. But between having the secret and making any large number of bombs, there is undoubtedly a considerable interval. It is this interval which we must not waste. We must endeavour to make up the melancholy leeway in military preparations which oppresses us today, and we must never abandon the hope that a peaceful settlement may be reached with the Soviet Government if a resolute effort is made on the basis not of our present weakness but of American atomic strength. This is the policy which gives the best chance of preventing a fearful war and of securing our survival should it break upon us.

I do not expect that any of the Allies know how many atomic bombs the Soviet Government have yet been able to make, but – here I am only stating my personal opinion – I do not think that they have made many yet, or that their rate of production is at present rapid. As I say, I only candidly state my own personal view to the House. It would be very wrong that the House should attach any undue importance to it, but it is one of the stepping stones upon which my thought advances. I see, however, that I said to the House earlier in this Session, two months ago, that if the Americans had a stock-pile of, say, 1,000, and the Russians had only 50, and we got those 50, it would not be pleasant.[1] I was surprised that this crude remark did not affect opinion. But then, only two months ago there was a different atmosphere. All these matters, quite wrongly, seemed outside the range of ordinary politics and daily life. Now they dominate the minds of all thinking and patriotic men, and will increasingly do so as the months pass by.

It was stated officially at some Lobby conference with, I think, the Home Office, according to the *Daily Telegraph* of Tuesday, that each bomb costs as

---

[1] Speech reproduced above (pp. 1702–12).

much as a battleship. This, of course, is ludicrous nonsense. It might be that the first two or three would cost that amount or more if they were saddled with the whole expense of research and production up to date, but once they were in production the cost would certainly be less than one-twentieth or even one-fiftieth of a modern battleship. Nevertheless I still adhere to my feeling – I am quite ready to be instructed by those who have the advantages of official information – that so far, very few have been produced, and the extraordinary efforts which the Soviet Government are making to obtain even small quantities of uranium seem – I only say 'seem' – to justify a hopeful view.

If this should happily be true, there can be no doubt that the United States possesses at this moment a superiority so vast that a major act of Russian aggression is still subject to an effective and even perhaps decisive deterrent. It is for this reason I have ventured on several occasions to express the opinion that a third world war is not imminent, and I cherish the hope that it may still be averted. I noticed in the Debate on Civil Defence on Monday, at which I regret I was not present, that there was a considerable tendency, not confined to any one part of the House, to minimise the effects of the atomic bomb, and the Government have issued a carefully thought out booklet on this subject. No doubt, it is right nearly always to take a robust and cheerful view, but I expect this booklet, from what I have been able to learn of it, looking through it – I have not had time to read it with the attention it deserves – will be more cheering to the Russians than to us, because the atomic bomb is the only weapon on land, sea and air in which the Americans – that is to say the Allies – can possibly have overwhelming superiority during the next two or three years.

I should have thought, therefore, that it was a mistake in propaganda to weaken or discount the deterrents upon those who are already so much stronger in every other sphere except this. We shall need the whole weight of these deterrents to gain us the time which remains while this great advantage of ours endures. We are, of course, dependent upon the United States both for the supply of the bomb and largely for the means of using it. Without it, we are more defenceless than we have ever been. I find this a terrible thought. In 1940 I had good hopes that we should win the battle in the air even at heavy odds and that if we won, the Navy could stave off and repel invasion until eventually vast air power was developed here which would bring us out of our troubles, even if left alone. But now I cannot feel the same sense of concrete assurance.

We must never despair. We must never give in. We have over 5 million men and women who had service in the Armed Forces in the last war. We have three-quarters of a million who have been trained since, and there are nearly 700,000 now in the Armed Forces, and many thousands in our Volunteer and Auxiliary Forces. Our industrial capacity and that of the free world is gigantic. Our scientific and technical ability is unsurpassed. We may well have time to reorganise and develop the mighty latent strength of Britain surrounded by her Commonwealth. But I warn the House that we have as great dangers to face in 1950 and 1951 as we had 10 years ago. Here we are with deep and continuing differences between us in our whole domestic sphere, and faced with dangers and problems which all our united strength can scarcely overcome. It was this that led me to hope that in Private Session the sense of the corporate life of the House of Commons might have asserted itself. But that has been forbidden by the Prime Minister. (Hon. Members: 'By the House'.) It has been forbidden by the Prime Minister, and at his request the House has prevented our meeting together and talking things over among ourselves in secret.

It is with deep grief that I have to say these things to the House, and to reflect that it is only five years ago almost to a month when we were victorious, respected and safe. The whole burden does not rest upon this country, nor upon the Government of this country. They have done several important things, like establishing compulsory National Service and the East Anglian American base. They have fostered the closest relations with the United States and our European friends, and they have maintained active resistance to Communism in its various forms. Nevertheless, I say they bear a fearful accountability. The Prime Minister and his party have had power, men, and money never enjoyed before by any Government in time of peace. If they had asked for more, Parliament would have granted it to them and we would have given it our full support. It was with a sense of relief that I felt entitled to say in March that we could accept no responsibility for the present state of our defences. That does not mean that we will not strive to help the Government, in spite of their total lack of consideration for our wishes and point of view, in every measure, however unpopular, which they may propose and which we recognise is aimed solely at securing national survival.

Winston S. Churchill to General Douglas MacArthur
(Churchill papers, 2/173)[1]

28 July 1950

My dear General MacArthur,

I send these few lines of introduction for my son who starts tomorrow for the Korean front as one of the correspondents of the *Daily Telegraph.*

Randolph has a considerable political experience in England and was for five years in the House of Commons. He did not see much of it as he served

---

[1] This letter was handwritten.

in the Commandos most of the time, and was an officer in my own regiment, the 4th Hussars (of which he is a reserve member). He has lectured all over the United States, and is fully versed in all forms of public discussion. He was with me at Casablanca and Teheran and heard many very confidential things. I found his discretion impeccable on all these serious matters. His outlook is broadly mine; and I therefore feel I may trespass upon you in these days of growing stress by commending him to you as a comprehending admirer of all the work you have done and are doing.

August 1950

Winston S. Churchill to Brendan Bracken
(*Churchill papers, 2/178*)

1 August 1950
Private and Personal

My dear Brendan,

I have now read the extracts and enclosed from the Duke of Windsor's Memoirs over which the publication in book form is impending.

I am sure it would not be in accordance with HRH's character or reputation for him to publish reports of private conversations which he had with me, and still less to impute to me political motives, and I request and hope that these may be cut out. I responded to his appeal to come to see him and to give him my aid solely out of loyalty and friendship and also in accordance with my Constitutional views.

The story about my advising HRH to retire to Windsor Castle is inaccurately told. When I arrived at Fort Belvedere I formed the impression that the King was physically and mentally overstrained and that what he needed was rest. The reference to his retiring to Windsor Castle for a fortnight would not be complete without adding that I said that Sir Thomas Horder[1] should guard one gate and Lord Dawson of Penn[2] the other. This advice was given because I hoped that if delay was obtained, Mrs Simpson could be persuaded to renounce all ideas of marrying him. Thus the crisis would have ended without an abdication.

---

[1] Thomas Jeeves Horder, 1871–1955. Born in Shaftesbury. Tutored in Biology by H. G. Wells. Educated at St Bartholomew's Hospital, London. Knighted, 1918. KCVO, 1925. Baron, 1933. Physician to King George VI, 1936–52. GCVO, 1938. Chairman of the Committee on the Use of Public Air-Raid Shelters, 1939–45. Member of the Representative Body in the British Medical Association, 1945–51; of the Committee which negotiated the acceptance of the National Health Service, 1947–8; of the BMA Council, 1948–51.

[2] Bertrand Dawson, 1864–1945. Born in Croydon, London. FRCP, 1903. Physician-Extraordinary to King Edward VII, 1907–10. Physician-in-Ordinary to King George V, 1910–14. KCVO, 1911. KStJ, 1916. CB, 1916. GCVO, 1918. KCMG, 1919. Baron, 1920. President, of Royal Society of Medicine, 1928–30; Royal College of Physicians, 1931–7.

I return the copy of the manuscript which you sent with the passages marked which I think should be excised.

PS. I find I dictated <u>at the time</u> a full account of my action. This will interest you later. I am not going to Biarritz.

ENCLOSURE

Note – page 13.

This statement is founded on fact and some years after I believe I mentioned it to the Duke of Windsor myself. It did not however occur on this occasion but only at the close of Mr Baldwin's speech announcing the Abdication nearly a week later. In any case it is purely private and should not be published now. It is not at all true that I left the House 'shaken and dismayed' though naturally I was conscious of the overwhelming opinion of its members. In fact that afternoon I addressed a very large gathering of the Conservative Committee on military defence, speaking I think for nearly an hour and was listened to with the utmost attention.

Lord Cherwell to Winston S. Churchill
(Churchill papers, 2/28)

1 August 1950

My dear Winston,

I am sorry to have to tell you that the Government apparently last Thursday decided against the action everyone concerned with atomic energy has been pressing for so long, namely, to take the project out of the Ministry of Supply's hands and to make it into an independent body like the Medical Research Council or like one of the nationalised boards as in America. I am very much afraid that this may lead to the resignation of several leading men and the disintegration of the staff, who have been hoping for a change for a long time now.

Of course, if war breaks out we shall have other things to worry about. But if we remain at peace it is surely vital, unless we are to become a second-class nation armed with inferior weapons, that we should be in a position to make our own bombs. Furthermore, the possibility of achieving full collaboration concerning plutonium and hydrogen bombs with the US will vanish unless we have something of our own to show.

I think it would be lamentable if all the work and effort that has been put into this project were wasted – hampered and delayed though it has been by being under the Ministry of Supply. But I am afraid production and even research will gradually atrophy if the Government insists as apparently was decided last Thursday, on maintaining the present unsatisfactory organisation.

Winston S. Churchill to Lord Woolton
(*Churchill papers, 2/102*)

2 August 1950

My dear Fred,

Thank you for your minute of July 31. I will carefully read Pierssené's report. I agree with you that matters are not necessarily so urgent as they were. On the other hand I was gratified to find the 1922 Committee, when I saw them last week, much more conscious of the necessity for an arrangement with the Liberal Party. I am quite sure there is no possibility of a Conservative majority without not only an arrangement about seats but active cooperation.

I am sorry you have formed so adverse an opinion about Mr Davies. I do not think he imagines his Party will be returned to power at the next Election. He and his followers in the House have been most helpful lately and you have no doubt noticed the natural drawing together of the actions and opinions of Liberals and Conservatives. I understood from you that you would see Mr Davies and have a talk to him, and I mentioned this to him and he told me he had heard nothing from you. I am sorry for this.

About Mr Byers, I have always disliked him but he is [. . .] too clever, I think, to imagine he is going to be Prime Minister immediately. There is a great difference between the positions of Davies and Byers.

I hope you are having a good holiday. I have decided to spend the better half of August here.[1] I hope we may meet.

PS. Let me thank you also for your letter of July 25.

Winston S. Churchill to General Lord Ismay
(*Churchill papers, 4/25*)

2 August 1950

THE DIEPPE RAID

I can see nothing in the papers I now have from you and Allen and my own records which explains who took the decision to revive the attack after it had been abandoned and Montgomery had cleared out. This is the crux of the story. Surely this decision could not have been taken without the Chiefs of Staff being informed. If so, why did they not bring it to my attention, observing I did not leave England till July 30 or 31? It was a major decision of policy to renew it after the men had been put on board the ships, and dispersed with the secret. If the decision was taken after I left the country, was the Defence

---

[1] In Strasbourg.

Committee or the War Cabinet informed? How did this all go? It is left a blank in these accounts.

2. Another important point is what addition did the Germans make to the garrison and defences of Dieppe between the time of their raid on the shipping gathering for the first proposed attempt and the date when we actually attacked? What we say about this is a matter for subsequent consideration, but we must at least know ourselves exactly what the factors were – namely; did the Chiefs of Staff, or the Defence Committee or the War Cabinet ever consider the matter of the revival of the operation (a) when I was in England, (b) when I was out of England, or was it all pushed through by Dickie on his own without reference to higher authority?

3. I must say that I have very little recollection of this matter. I was in favour as my minutes show, of largescale raids up to 10,000 on the French coast, but I expected to be consulted on timing and details. Of course if I was out of the country at the time it is a different story. Is there anything on record on this point? I cannot write the tale without being informed on all this.

4. Of course Dickie would be the authority to consult. He has taken all responsibility upon himself in his speech in Canada, but I cannot believe that he was allowed to do this without higher authority becoming responsible. The question is at what stage was this matter cut off from the supreme war direction, or how and when was it put up to them?

John Colville to Winston S. Churchill
(Churchill papers, 2/168)

3 August 1950
Private and Personal

British Embassy, Lisbon

Dear Mr Churchill,

I was furious when I read Mr Michael Foot's review of 'The Grand Alliance' in the 'Tribune' of the 28th July, although I am sure that his aspersions, if indeed you troubled to read them, left you cold.

In his review Foot wrote:

> 'Throughout I took a more sanguine view than my military advisers of the Russian powers of resistance', he (Mr Churchill) says on page 351. That is what he writes today. But if he possessed one scrap of evidence to prove it from his writings at the time, he might have been depended upon to assist us with a quotation. It may be, of course, that Mr Churchill was slightly more optimistic than some of his advisers who were utterly pessimistic on the point. But the suggestion that Mr Churchill was anything other than convinced of the Russian inability to withstand the German attack amounts to a downright falsehood. It is clear from quotations cited

for other purposes that he along with many others grossly underestimated the Russian powers of resistance, and that the main strategy of the war as directed from Downing Street was not altered at all for several months by Hitler's huge plunge eastwards.

If, which I doubt, Foot is right in saying there is no evidence to prove that you took a more sanguine view of the Russian powers of resistance than did your military advisers, I can at least provide oral testimony. On that Sunday in June 1941 when Hitler invaded Russia, I remember a discussion on this very point at Chequers. Sir John Dill and Mr Winant both thought the Russians could not last six weeks. After everybody had expressed their views, including Mr Eden, Sir Stafford Cripps and Lord Salisbury, I remember your closing the discussion with the following words: 'I will bet anybody here a Monkey to a Mousetrap that the Russians are still fighting, victoriously, two years from now.' I recorded your words in writing at the time because I thought they were such a daring prophecy, and because it was such an entirely different point of view from that which anybody else had expressed. So much for Michael Foot.

I have taken the liberty of recounting this privately in writing to the Librarian at the Foreign Office in order that he may make a note of the fact at some appropriate point in the archives. I have done this not because your policy in 1941 will ever require defending from the theories future historians may produce, but because legends easily grow and Michael Foot, as witness his book 'Guilty Men', has a gift for disseminating them. I hope you won't mind my having done this.

Winston S. Churchill to Sir Alan Lascelles
(Churchill papers, 2/175)

4 August 1950
Private

My dear Tommy,

Yesterday Prince Frederick of Prussia[1] and his wife came to luncheon with us. He wished to see me on the question of his name and title. You no doubt are aware of the hard time he had in the war as an internee, or 'refugee' of undefined status. I did all I could to mitigate his mood when the facts came to my notice in 1942. During the war period and up till the present he has used the name of George Mansfelt. Mansfelt is one of his titles. He has been for three years a British subject.

He and his wife are going in about three weeks to the United States and

[1] Friedrich Georg Wilhelm Christoph von Preußen, 1911–56. Known as 'Friedrich von Preussen'. Born in Berlin. Married, 1945, Brigid Katherine Rachel Guinness: five children. Naturalized as British citizen, 1947.

they had thought of resuming their proper names of Prince and Princess of Prussia, as his American hosts are urging him to do. My advice, which he asked, was to defer a decision on this matter until he returns to England in two or three months' time. He will, I think, act accordingly. He is most anxious to act in accordance with the King's wishes, but he desires that his case may be considered, and he be allowed to call himself by some suitable name and title from among those he bears by hereditary right. On these points I advised him to have a talk with you, when he can tell his own story fully. I hope you will be willing to get into touch with him, and make an appointment. He lives fairly close to Sandringham so perhaps an early meeting could be arranged in the neighbourhood.

I think very highly of this young man, and it is conceivable that he might have a helpful part to play in any struggle in which the German people are ranged with us against the Russian Communist menace. Eventually, it seems to me, the advice of Ministers should be sought, but the first thing is for you to know the facts and thus be able to present them to The King.

Anthony Eden to Winston S. Churchill
(Churchill papers, 2/28)[1]

4 August 1950

My dear Winston,

Thank you so much for your letter and for showing me what you had written to Attlee.

I didn't telephone you this morning because I had really nothing to add to what I had said in The House. I am convinced that the most urgent need for the RAF and the Army, particularly the army, is for more regulars. I would urge increase of pay and improvement of conditions to obtain these. At the moment we have many training battalions in this country but no fighting formations. What is required is to free these regular battalions from a part of their training duties so that they can be formed into Brigades and divisions and provide us with the tactical personnel we so urgently need.

I consider this to be more important than lengthening the period of service, which, unless we have more regulars, will still not provide us with the mobile striking power we need.

At the moment, virtually all the combat units we have are overseas. The first need is surely to create a reserve which will be available to meet any new emergency.

If you want to pass on any part of these arguments, or the whole of them, to the Prime Minister, I have, of course, no objection.

---

[1] This letter was handwritten.

But I remain convinced that our most urgent need, short term and long term, is for more regulars, and if we are to get them, we shall have to pay for them.

Winston S. Churchill to Henry Laughlin
(Churchill papers, 4/24)

4 August 1950

I find it extremely difficult to settle all the corrections, overtakes and cuts to be made in Volume 4 in time for a December publication by Book of the Month. You must realize how heavily the public affairs in the international crises are pressing upon me. I have postponed my holiday at Biarritz and am returning here as soon as I can leave Strasbourg. I cannot see why the Book of the Month can only publish in December. Would not February be quite good? Surely this can be arranged? I must ask for consideration in view of international events. Meanwhile you set up in galley proofs. Please telegraph.

How is Volume 3 going? Here the reception and reviews have been very good. Nearly 300,000 were sold on the first day. Kind regards.

Winston S. Churchill to Clement Attlee
(Churchill papers, 2/28)

6 August 1950
Private

My dear Prime Minister,

I am obliged to you for informing me last Wednesday of the measures which you are taking in concert with the United States.

I [. . .] enclose a Note from Lord Cherwell,[1] with which I am in agreement, upon the organization of Atomic Research.

We shall give our support to all measures proposed by the Government which we ourselves deem necessary for national defence. This cannot however limit in any way the right and duty of the Opposition to criticize, either in public or secret debate, the existing state of our defences, or the rate and methods with which the necessary increases are to be effected. We do not of course know anything about the Government's new plan except what has now been published. It is certain that we are in a condition of great danger and that surprisingly little practical results have followed from the immense outlay of money and control of manpower used by the Government during recent years.

---

[1] Reproduced above (p. 1820).

I understand that the American Congress will have taken its decisions about aid to Britain by the middle of this month. It seems to me, and to those of my colleagues I have been able to consult, that Parliament should be called together if possible before the end of August.

I propose to hold a meeting of my colleagues on or about August 15, and it is probable that we shall then make a formal request for the recall of Parliament.

Winston S. Churchill to Anthony Eden
(Churchill papers, 2/28)

8 August 1950

My dear Anthony,

Thank you very much for your letter of August 4. I send you a note on the military points you make.

Everything went all right yesterday at the Opening Session. There was considerable feeling that Spaak had blotted his copybook as a good European. I see no harm in Harold launching a 'Schuman sans larmes' or 'Schuman sans dents', and when I speak I will make a friendly reference to it as a constructive contribution, but I will not formally identify myself with it.

I am hoping to fly back on Saturday from Nancy.

PS. I liked your speech.

NOTE ON ARMY PROBLEMS

I do not see how it is possible to acquire any substantial number of Regulars quickly. First they have to be attracted by conditions which will be enormously expensive, many of which, like married quarters, cannot be supplied for a long time. They then have to be trained for at least two years. After that they have to mature in units which are themselves free from training duties. If they enlist for say seven years with the colours and five with the reserve they will secrete no reserves for seven years. The Regular Army and the units that compose it are plants of slow growth, and though it would be no doubt electorally safe and proper to concentrate upon increases of pay and improvement of conditions, this will by itself in no way meet our urgent need.

The only practical measure is to retain by compulsion the services of those who are already under arms, whether they be Regular or conscripts. Great numbers have had a year, others eighteen months. Every month added to this makes a man into a soldier. It might well be that in order to free the units from congestion of new recruits a smaller number should be taken by conscription. The only way of obtaining any substantial force in the next year is by prolonging the service of all men now serving and freeing as many units as possible from the duty of training the annual influx of recruits.

It might be possible to strengthen the cadres of the Regular Army by inducing individuals to re-engage. This is in time of peace a slow and limited process, highly selective.

In your last paragraph, when you speak about creating a reserve which will be available to meet any new emergency, you mean I presume a Reserve Army and not a Reserve in the ordinary sense of men who have passed through the colour service and await call-up by proclamation. The two are of course quite different. The only way to form a Reserve Army rapidly in England is to keep all men now serving there with the colours, clear the largest number of units from training duties and let them ripen under tactical instruction. Once the re-organization is made, every month these men remain together in their battalions the units will improve.

Winston S. Churchill: speech
('In the Balance', pages 347–52)

11 August 1950   Strasbourg

EUROPEAN UNITY AND A EUROPEAN ARMY

I am sure we can all agree with the Committee of Ministers that definite progress has been made in the last year in building up the European conception represented by this Assembly. There are, however, several important points which lie open between us. We regret that these should have been somewhat inconsiderately set aside by the Committee of Ministers until October 1. I think the Assembly should press its points and its opinions on the question at issue. There really is, for instance, no reason why a Resolution passed here by a two-thirds majority should not be formally made known to and laid before our respective parliaments, it being, of course, obvious that nothing can prevent either the Government or the parliament concerned from taking its own decision upon the questions raised after whatever debate they may think desirable.

It is important to the future of this Assembly that it should be brought continually into closer contact not only with the executive Governments but with all the representative intuitions upon which, in all true democracies, executive Governments can alone be founded. For Great Britain I can, however, guarantee that all Resolutions of the Assembly will be brought before the House of Commons for discussion on their merits, whether we agree with them or not. For this purpose we shall use the facilities at the disposal of the British official Opposition, and I do not doubt that the House of Lords will take corresponding action. I suggest to my colleagues of other countries here that they use the liberties of procedure which their own Parliaments possess in abundance for the same purpose, and that this become our general practice unless or until the obstructive influences on the Committee of Ministers have been overcome or have disappeared.

There are other points of difference which may well be readjusted as a result of our discussion. I have always thought that the process of building up a European Parliament must be gradual, and that it should roll forward on a tide of facts, events and impulses rather than by elaborate constitution-making. Either we shall prove our worth and weight and value to Europe or we shall fail. We are not making a machine. We are growing a living plant. It certainly is a forward step that Mr MacBride,[1] the representative of the Committee of Ministers, should be here among us to express their collective mind – if they have one – directly to the Assembly, and to deal by word of mouth with matters which we may raise. Indeed, when we look back over the past twelve months – and not only over the past twelve months but to The Hague two years ago – it is marvellous to see how great is the progress which has been made in this time. From an unofficial gathering of enthusiasts, pleading the cause of reconciliation and revival of this shattered Continent, we have reached the scene today when we sit as a body, with ever-growing influence and respect, in our own House of Europe, under the flags of fifteen historic States and nations. In all that we do and say here, we must not belie the hopes and faith of millions and scores of millions of men and women not only in the free countries of Europe but in those which still lie in bondage.

The message which we have received from the 'composite throne', if such I may term it, has directed our attention to the Schuman Plan of associating in an effective manner the basic industries of the Western nations, and has invited us to express our opinion about it. Sir, we as an Assembly are very ready to do so and it may well be that it is in our power to smooth away some of the misunderstandings which have arisen or the prejudices which have been stirred. We may handle this large and hopeful scheme in a manner which will be favourable to the general principle which it embodies.

Some of my British colleagues have offered a constructive contribution on this subject to the Debates of the Assembly, and I trust their views will receive careful and friendly consideration not only from other Governments and Parliaments but from their own. It will be a memorable achievement if this Assembly is able to offer practical guidance to uncertain Governments and competing parties in regard to a scheme which seeks to build around the tomb of Franco-German wars and quarrels the structure of a more productive, a more stable industrial life for the vast numbers of our peoples who are concerned. We express our thanks to M Schuman for his bold initiative and also for his courtesy in coming here to tell us all about it.

But, sir, the message we have received from the Committee of Ministers

---

[1] Seán MacBride, 1904–88. Born in Paris. Joined IRA, 1919; Director of Intelligence, 1927; CoS, 1936–7. Founded Saor Éire ('Free Ireland') movement, 1931. Founder and leader of Clann na Poblachta, 1946–65. MP, Dáil Eireann, 1947–58. Minister for External Affairs of Ireland in Inter-Party Government, 1948–51. President, Committee of Ministers of Council of Europe, 1950. Secretary-General, International Commission of Jurists, 1963–71.

directs our attention in its final paragraphs to the gravest matters which now impend upon world affairs. We are invited to approve the action of the United Nations in Korea and to proclaim our 'complete solidarity' with the resistance to aggression the burden of which is now being borne by the United States, but which involves us all. No one can sustain the cause of freedom and the rule of law in the face of a most grievous and violent challenge. But what is our position here in these smiling lands and war-scarred cities, their peoples so rich in tradition, virtue and glory, striving to rise again from the consequences of the tragedies of the past.

Sir, the Committee of Ministers has, by its message, virtually invited us to consider in the broader aspects the military aspects of our position. Certainly it would be futile and absurd to attempt to discuss the future of Europe and its relation to world affairs and to the United Nations Organization if this dominating military aspect were arbitrarily excluded. Nearly all the speakers who have addressed us, including our two British Socialist colleagues, have trespassed upon this hitherto forbidden territory, and its effective occupation by the Assembly has now become a *fait accompli*.

I am very glad that the Germans, amid their own problems, have come here to share our perils and augment our strength. They ought to have been here a year ago. A year has been wasted, but still it is not too late. There is no revival of Europe, no safety or freedom for any of us, except in standing together, united and unflinching. I ask this Assembly to assure our German friends that, if they throw in their lot with us, we shall hold their safety and freedom as sacred as our own.

I have heard it said that if any German – I think the argument was raised yesterday – except Communists were to be armed, this might be the pretext for a preventive war by Russia. Believe me, Mr President,[1] the long calculated designs of the Soviet Government will not be turned or deflected by events of this order. There is no doubt that we are all of us in great danger. The freedom and civilization of Western Europe lie under the shadow of Russian Communist aggression, supported by enormous armaments. The Soviet forces in Europe, measured in active divisions, in Air Force and in armoured vehicles, outnumber the forces of Western Union by at least six or seven to one. These are terrible facts, and it is a wonder that we are sitting here in our new House of Europe, calmly discussing our plans for the future happiness and concord of our peoples and their moral and cultural ideals. It is a wonder, but at least it is better than getting into a panic. The danger is, of course, not new. It was inherent in the fact that the free democracies of the West disarmed and dissolved their forces after the war, while the dictatorship in the Kremlin maintained gigantic armies and laboured tirelessly by every means to re-equip them.

[1] Paul-Henri Spaak.

Two years ago the Western Union Pact was signed and a number of committees were set up which, as M Reynaud and others say, have been talking ever since. Imposing conferences have been held between military chiefs and experts, assisted by statesmen, and the pretentious façade of a Western front has been displayed by the Governments responsible for our safety. In fact, however, apart from the establishment of the American bomber base in England, nothing has been done to give effective protection to our peoples from being subjugated or destroyed by the Russian Communist armies with their masses of armour and aircraft. I and others have given what warnings we could, but as in the past, they fell on unheeding ears or were used to sustain the false accusations of 'warmongering'.

Now, however, suddenly the lightning-flash in Korea, and the spreading conflagration which has followed it, has roused the whole of the free world to a keen and vehement realization of its dangers, and many measures are now proposed which, if they had been taken two years ago, would at least have yielded fruit by now. Indeed, what is now proposed and on the move, if inaugurated two years ago, might well have gone half-way to meet our needs.

I do not doubt that, as the realization of our mortal danger deepens, it will awaken that sense of self-preservation which is the foundation of human existence, and this process is now going forward. Our British Socialist colleague, Mr Edelman, reminded us of the immense superiority in steel, in oil, in aluminium and other materials on which the defence potential of the free nations rests. But much of this might be the prize of aggressors if we were struck down. M André Philip said on Tuesday that France did not wish to be liberated again. After a period of Russian Communist occupation there would not, as M Reynaud pointed out, be much to liberate. The systematic liquidation of all elements hostile to Communism would leave little which would be recognized by the rescue of the survivors.

We in this assembly have no responsibility or executive power, but we are bound to give our warnings and our counsel. There must be created and in the shortest possible time, a real defensive front in Europe. Great Britain and the United States must send large forces to the Continent. France must again revive her famous army. We welcome our Italian comrades. All – Greece, Turkey, Holland, Belgium, Luxembourg, the Scandinavian States – must bear their share and do their best. Courage and unity must not consider what they can get but what they can give. Let that be our rivalry in these years that lie before us.

The question which challenges us is: Shall we have the time? No one can answer that question for certain but to assume that we were too late would be the very madness of despair. We are still under the shield of the atomic bomb, possessed in formidable quantities by the United States alone. The use of this weapon would shake the foundation of the Soviet regime throughout the vast area of Russia, and the breakdown of all communications and centralized control might well enable the brave Russian peoples to free themselves from a tyranny far worse than that of the Czars. It seems very likely that such possibilities will constitute an effective deterrent upon Soviet aggression, at least until they have by a lengthy process built up an adequate supply of atomic bombs of their own.

There is another reason why the general armed assault by Communism against the Western democracies may be delayed. The Soviet dictators have no reason to be discontented with the way things have gone so far, and are going. Since the world war stopped in 1945 they have obtained control of half Europe and of all of China without losing a single Russian soldier, thus adding upwards of 500,000,000 people to their own immense population. They have a wealth of opportunities for creating trouble and tempting us to disperse our forces unduly through the action of their satellites. It seems that Tibet is to be the next victim. Engaged in these diversions they are able to preach peace while planning aggressive war and improving their atomic stockpile. But in my judgment, which I present with all diffidence, we have a breathing space, and if we use this wisely and well, and do not waste it as we have already wasted so many, we may still greatly increase the deterrents against a major Russian Communist aggression. It is by closing the yawning gap in the defences of the Western Powers in Europe that we shall find the surest means, not only of saving our lives and liberties, but of preventing a third world war.

If in the next two years or so we can create a trustworthy system of defence against Communist invasion, we shall at least have removed the most obvious temptation to those who seek to impose their will by force upon the free democracies. This system of defence in the West will alone give the best chance of a final settlement by negotiation with the Soviets on the basis of our strength and not of our weakness. But there is not a day to be lost nor a scrap of available strength to be denied.

As I have already said, this Assembly has no power to act, nor do we seek to relieve the responsible executive Governments of their duties. We ought, however, to make our united convictions known. We should now send a message of confidence and courage from the House of Europe to the whole world. Not only should we reaffirm as we have been asked to do, our allegiance to the United Nations, but we should make a gesture of practical and constructive guidance by declaring ourselves in favour of the immediate creation of a European Army under a unified command, and in which we should all bear a worthy and honourable part.

Therefore, Mr President, I propose to you a Motion which, after some previous consultation in various quarters, I have ventured to place upon the Order Paper. I trust that this Motion will, by an open and formal vote, receive the overwhelming, if not indeed the unanimous, support of this Assembly. This would be the greatest contribution that it is in our power to make to the safety and peace of the world. We can thus go forward together sure at least that we have done our duty. I beg to move that:

> The Assembly, in order to express its devotion to the maintenance of peace and its resolve to sustain the action of the Security Council of the United Nations in defence of peaceful peoples against aggression, calls for the immediate creation of a unified European Army subject to proper European democratic control and acting in full co-operation with the United States and Canada.

Winston S. Churchill to Clement Attlee
(Churchill papers, 2/29)

13 August 1950

My dear Prime Minister,

I thank you for the intimation I received from you about the recall of Parliament. I feel however that the date you propose, September 12, is altogether too remote, and bears no relation to the crisis and the new facts which are before us. I have therefore to ask you on behalf of the Conservative Party to be so kind as to consider the recall of Parliament in a week or ten days at the latest. I have also consulted Mr Clement Davies, the Leader of the Liberal Party, who informs me that he is writing to you in the same sense.

I hope that our representations may be favourably regarded by you in view of the assurances that were given to the House by Mr Herbert Morrison on the subject of recall.

Clement Attlee to Winston S. Churchill
(Churchill papers, 2/29)

13 August 1950

My dear Churchill,

Thank you for your letter about the recall of Parliament. As we stated before the Adjournment, the Government would give full consideration to any request by the Opposition for the recall of Parliament, and that if necessary the Government would itself take the initiative. You will not of course expect an immediate reply.

The decision to recall Parliament on September 12 was of course taken after full consideration of the relevant facts.

Your letter does not disclose any particular reason why an earlier date should be chosen. If you would care to come to see me to explain why you think this is necessary, I should of course be glad to see you and to consider what you have to tell me with my colleagues.

Winston S. Churchill to President Harry S Truman
(*Churchill papers, 2/32*)

13 August 1950

My dear Harry,

I dare say and certainly hope that you read my speech at the Strasbourg assembly and I trust you will have an account presented to you of the deeply interesting debate which led up to the great majority by which the Resolution for a European Army was carried. This is of course to me the fruition of what I have laboured for ever since my speech at Zurich four years ago. I enclose a marked copy of what I said at that time.

The ending of the quarrel between France and Germany by what is really a sublime act on the part of the French leaders, and a fine manifestation of the confidence which Western Germany have in our and your good faith and goodwill, is I feel an immense step forward towards the kind of world for which you and I are striving. It is also the best hope of avoiding a third World War.

The only alternative to a European Army with a front against Russian aggression in Europe, is of course, a kind of neutrality arrangement by Germany, France and the smaller countries with the Soviets. This is what the Communists are striving for, and it could only mean the speedy absorption of the neutral European countries by the methods which have subjugated Czechoslovakia, as they would be in a sort of no-man's-land between Britain, with its American air-bombing base, and the Soviet armies. They and their cities and junctions might all become involved, especially if these countries were used for the rocket bombardment of Britain.

Although none of us can tell what the Soviet intentions are, I have no doubt that we ought, at this stage, to reject the strategy of holding the Channel and the Pyrenees and strive for the larger hope.

The point however on which I wish particularly to address you is, what will happen to the Germans if they send a substantial contingent – say five or six divisions – to the European Army, in which British and, I trust, Americans will be strongly represented, and the Soviet retaliate by invading Western Germany? Would the United States treat a major aggression of this kind into Western Germany in the same way as it would treat a Soviet attack on France, the Benelux or Britain, or should we let these German people, whom we have disarmed and for whose safety we have accepted responsibility, be attacked without the shield of the atomic deterrent? I should indeed be grateful if I could have your views on this.

You will note that I said at Strasbourg that if the Germans threw in their lot with us, we should hold their safety and freedom as sacred as our own. Of course I have no official right to speak to anyone, yet after the firm stand you have successfully made about Berlin, I think that the deterrent should be made to apply to all countries represented in the European Army. I do not see how this would risk or cost any more than what is now morally guaranteed by the United States.

Perhaps you will consider whether you can give any indication of your view. A public indication would be of the utmost value and is, in my opinion, indispensable to the conception of a European front against Communism. Perhaps it may be the case that Mr Acheson, or your representative in Germany, has already given an assurance in this respect.

You may perhaps have noted the unexpected and fortunate fact that the view of the German Delegation, who represent all parties in the German Government, is that Germany should send a contingent to the European Army (say of five or six divisions), but should not have a National Army of her own. I had feared they might take the opposite view, namely, 'let us have a National Army with its own munitions, supplies, and the right to re-arm, and we will then give a contingent to the European Army'. I need not say what an enormous difference this had made to the French view. They and we can get it both ways.

Lewis Douglas to Winston S. Churchill
(Churchill papers, 2/32)

14 August 1950
Top Secret

My dear Winston,

I am enclosing herewith a copy of the cable which I sent posthaste this morning after talking with you on the telephone. Your letter with the enclosure goes by pouch this afternoon. It should be in the President's hands Wednesday morning.

You told me you were coming to London tomorrow. Could I drop in to see you for just a few minutes as I think it may be of some importance for us to exchange views on the matter in which we both are so interested.

Winston S. Churchill: article[1]
(Churchill papers, 2/95)

14 August 1950

THIS IS FREEDOM

There stretches between Socialists on the one hand and Conservatives and Liberals on the other a deep gulf of principle. They believe that the people belong to the State. We believe that the State belongs to the people. They believe that Ministers are the masters of the people. We say they are their servants. They put their faith in the organization. We put ours in individual men and women. They believe in the maximum control of daily life. We believe in the maximum of freedom of choice.

The very essence of Socialism has been revealingly expressed in an observation let slip by a junior Minister of the present Government. 'The gentleman in Whitehall,' he told the housewives of Britain, 'really does know better what is good for people than the people know themselves.'

This unwarrantable assumption lies at the root of all Socialist thinking and policy-making. It takes too poor a view of the commonsense and ingenuity of ordinary men and women in living their daily lives. It assumes a degree of what they call 'supra' wisdom in our rules which is certainly in bitter contrast with their proved incompetence. British freedom is no abstract conception. It involves the essential quality of self-respect, on which our island way of life has been built up. This can be the only foundation for a healthy, buoyant and progressive society.

The liberties that Britons have been proud to regard as their birthright and have been tenacious to defend did not fall into our laps as a gift from the gods. Freedom of conscience, freedom of worship, freedom of the written and the spoken word, freedom of assembly, freedom of association, <u>habeas corpus</u>, trial by jury, the maxim that 'an Englishman's home is his castle' (now threatened by a horde of officials) – such liberties as these were painfully won over the centuries. Not one of them is enjoyed today by the serf-like citizens of the countries under collectivist control. In all the modern societies around us we can see the difference between those where the Government owns the people and those where the people own the Government. The British Socialists imagine that they can preserve individual political freedom and, at the same time, hold us all in economic bondage.

In wartime all kinds of controls and sacrifices of freedom are necessary. That is why we hate war and seek to establish peace on the sure foundation of strong defences. A proud and patriotic nation will make every sacrifice in order to defend its life and survival against all foreign aggressors. But the

[1] Written for the first edition of a magazine intended for publication by the Conservative Party, Sep. 1950, but never in fact published.

Socialists take advantage of wartime controls in order to establish their narrow and bigoted doctrines.

We are not yet a Socialist country. The people of Britain, like those of New Zealand and Australia, all called a halt to further Socialist measures at their last General Elections. Grandiose schemes of nationalization have been put into cold storage. Under unremitting Conservative pressure, the Government consented to take petrol off the ration. A few niggling restrictions on building were condescendingly removed by a Minister who advertised his magnanimous action as 'an experiment in freedom'. The five-shillings restriction on restaurant meals, which had long become meaningless, was reluctantly abolished, not for our sakes of course, but in the hopes of gaining dollars by lessening the irritation to visitors from free-enterprise America.

But we must not be deceived by such incidents. Nationalization is not dead but only dormant. If the electorate can be persuaded for the brief period of an Election campaign to vote them back into power, the full programme of 'Socialism in our Time' will at once be brought out of the shallow grave in which it is buried. And when the icy hand of State Monopoly grips our major industries, State Domination of all our major trade unions will inevitably follow. For the Trade Union has no function within a State Monopoly except to carry out the orders of the State bosses.

Conservatives have no affection for systems of government which concentrate excessive power over the lives and activities of their fellow-citizens in the hands of a clique of Party doctrinaires who think they are supermen.

The ordinary Briton wants nothing so much as to be left to go his own way, to get on with his job in life, to enjoy himself according to his own lights, to spend his own money as he thinks fit, to give his children a good home and a rather better start in life than he had himself, and to do his duty as a citizen to the community. This is the sort of life that our people seek. This is what they mean by freedom. This is what Conservatives and Liberals mean by freedom, and it is the basis of all our policies. It is commonsense. How far removed from this is the Socialists' regimented Utopia of which we have had a foretaste during these past five years!

However we may rely on the good judgment and commonsense of the British people. Slowly, with great determination, they veer back into the natural way they want to go. It is only those societies in which the free way of life is predominant that have the will and the power to make sacrifices for the nation in the hour of danger, and they make these because of their unwearying resolve to return to the true path at the earliest moment when foreign menace is past.

General Lord Ismay to Winston S. Churchill
(Churchill papers, 4/281)

14 August 1950

THE DIEPPE RAID

I am so sorry for being so inadequate about the Dieppe Raid, but I have searched through all the records and there is nothing therein which throws any light on the particular questions posed in your minute of 2nd August.[1]

2. It would appear, from the extract of the minutes of a meeting of the Chiefs of Staff held five months later that, in the vital interests of secrecy, nothing was put on paper. Indeed, I can now recall the fury of General Nye, then VCIGS, who had no idea that the operation was on until reports started to flow in from the scene of the action.

3. I have now got in touch with Dickie Mountbatten who has promised to look through any personal papers he may have and to consult those who were nearest to him at the time.

4. Meanwhile, there is one point in your minute which I feel can be answered at once. You yourself must have approved the operation in principle before you left England for the Middle East on 2nd August. Otherwise how could you have known of the operation's new code name ('Jubilee' vice 'Rutter') when you telegraphed to me two days before it took place, on 17th August: 'Please report if and when "Jubilee" takes place.'

5. I will let you have Dickie Mountbatten's comments immediately I receive them.

Winston S. Churchill: note
(Churchill papers, 2/32)

15 August 1950

ON THE EUROPEAN ARMY

1. The countries at present included in the Brussels and Atlantic Pacts should assign, as most of them have done already, divisional formations from their own armies to a European Defence Force, on which the nucleus staff already exists at Fontainebleau. This Army should consist of a number of divisions from the various countries which should be stationed in Western Europe within eighteen months. Germany has no National Army and does not wish to have one. She would therefore raise and contribute her quota of divisions directly.

---

[1] Reproduced above (pp. 1821–2).

2. The divisional formation would be the unit. The existing nationalities would not be mixed up within the divisional unit, but a high degree of interchangeability of divisions would be sought. All troops taking part in the European Army would be of equal status and equally armed and equipped. The conditions of service would be determined, as at present, by each contributing power. The model for relationships to be followed as a general guide would be that which existed between British, American and other Allied forced in SHAEF.

3. If the strength of the Army to be formed immediately is fixed at sixty divisions, the respective contributions might be:

    Great Britain – 10
    America – 10
    France – 15
    Germany – 10
    Italy – 7
    Benelux – 4
    Scandinavian – 4
    Total – 60

4. The contracting powers would also agree to hold in their own National Armies, for the defence of Europe, a further forty divisions from the ninetieth day after general mobilization. As the Germans will not have a National Army their contribution would be limited to the ten aforesaid.

5. There would be a unified command as at SHAEF in which all the contingents would bear their proper parts.

Winston S. Churchill: note
(*Churchill papers, 2/29*)

15 August 1950

ON MEETING WITH MR ATTLEE

Mr Attlee asks why a date earlier than September 12 should be chosen for the recall of Parliament. We should first of all ask him why he is recalling Parliament on September 12 instead of October 17, and what relation September 12 has to our and world affairs. If it is necessary to have an emergency recall of Parliament surely a whole month should not intervene?

However if he should continue to request our reasons, they are as follows:

1. The Government proposals for large military increases. When we separated they said one hundred million would suffice for this year. Within a few days they made a far larger proposal. Why? What happened in the interval to make this great change?

2. What has been decided about increasing the length of compulsory

military service? Surely every variant of the length of service has been explored during the last five years and no delay is necessary from that cause?

3. What has happened to the expeditionary force which is to be sent to Korea? How long is it going to be before it leaves the country? Is it true that it will be more than two months from the date of the announcement before this handful of men – less than a brigade group; of all arms – can be found from our military resources, in spite of all their calls for money and manpower?

4. Is it true that the anti-aircraft artillery of this group had to be taken from the batteries protecting the American bomber base in East Anglia? A statement about the delay in sending the expeditionary force is urgently needed.

5. What is the Government's policy about Formosa?[1] On this we need to have at the earliest notice a statement from the Foreign Office.

6. Finally, there is the resolution of the Consultative Assembly of the Council of Europe about a European Army, which gives us the welcome news that the Germans are willing to contribute a contingent to the European Army though they do not want a national army of their own. This is surely a great advance.

All the above issues require urgent Parliamentary attention, and it would not be in accordance with the undertakings given by the Leader of the House, when Parliament rose, that this should be denied.

Winston S. Churchill to Duncan Sandys
(*Churchill papers, 2/32*)

15 August 1950

About the European Army, each country would of course supply divisional units, tactically interchangeable and the military organization would follow the model of SHAEF. It would seem that about sixty divisions should be formed at once and stationed in Europe with another forty ear-marked as reinforcements for the ninetieth day after general mobilization. However these figures are of course only illustrative. A unified military command, in which all contributors take their proper part, and a civilian Defence Chief responsible to the existing national Governments, acting together and/or through the United Nations, is of course indispensable.

I think the best plan would be for you to let me have any draft scheme which is being prepared and also to give me a list of questions in which you think I can help. This would be better than my putting forward a cut and dried plan, even in general outline.

---

[1] On 5 Jan. 1950 President Truman had announced that the US would not intervene in the Taiwan (Formosa) Straits dispute between the People's Republic of China and the Republic of China. However, following the outbreak of the Korean War on 25 June 1950, US forces seized Taiwan for strategic purposes.

I should very much deprecate our getting involved in detail, for we have not the military knowledge or any kind of authority to make a plan.

Winston S. Churchill to Harold Macmillan
(Churchill papers, 2/32)

17 August 1950

Ask Duncan to show you the message I sent him early on the 15th. I am sure it would be a mistake to get involved in details. The Council of Europe can never at this stage in affairs deal with problems which belong to executive governments. It may point the way and give inspiration. It would be better to wind up in an easy fashion without any serious issue being raised. Certainly avoid any formal debate in the Assembly. We cannot possibly do better than by our Resolution.

President Harry S Truman to Winston S. Churchill
(Churchill papers, 2/32)

18 August 1950

Dear Winston,

I certainly appreciate your good letter of August thirteenth.[1] I read it with deep interest as I had already read your Strasbourg speech and the copy of the speech which you had made four years ago.

We are living in a tumultuous and uncertain age and I am sincerely hoping that the right decisions may be made by our Government to create a condition that will lead to general world peace.

I hope that everything is going well with you and that sometime in the not too far distant future it will be possible for us to see each other again.

Please remember me to Mrs Churchill.

General Sir Giffard Le Quesne Martel to Winston S. Churchill
(Churchill papers, 2/173)

21 August 1950

Dear Mr Winston Churchill

I feel sure that you must realise that it is a universal desire that you yourself should be given supra-national powers to band together the forces of the Western Nations and the USA without delay and to save the Western World.

---

[1] Reproduced above (pp. 1833–4).

The only point that has been raised in doubt, among your numerous friends and supporters, is whether you quite agree that what we need in the Army is highly trained forces making full use of mobility and armour, more than hastily trained man power forces, to meet the threat from the Russian masses. We respectfully suggest that this is a vital matter.

Field Marshal Montgomery is probably the greatest solider that we have ever seen in position warfare and his magnificent victories at Alamein and in Normandy will never be forgotten. Unfortunately however he was carried away with the idea of fighting similar battles against quite a different enemy by holding a linear defence on the Elbe or the Rhine and he carried the Western Nations with him. This was against the main lesson of the war which was that mobility must be used when fighting an enemy with superior numbers, vide Hitler's great victories in the early stages of the war. Monty never really understood mobility. He could have put Rommel in the bag after Alamein and when we broke out from Normandy no plans were made to maintain the mobility of the armoured divisions. The German front would have collapsed if the necessary plans had been made to keep them mobile. It is true that Monty wanted to advance in this way with considerable infantry forces, but this was a misunderstanding of the use of mobility. Real mobility can only be maintained with comparatively small forces. Mobility replaces numerical strength.

Many of us pressed at the end of the war that we should concentrate on raising well trained forces that used mobility and armour. If this policy had been adopted the present crisis would never have arisen. As it is we must now raise these forces and the Western World needs your prestige and drive to enable us to do so in the limited time that is left to us. Of course some Territorial divisions are needed as a follow up and to defend our bases etc., but the vital necessity is the highly trained mobile and armoured forces. A return to large numbers of hastily trained forces would be fatal for use in the main theatre which is still in Europe or the Middle East.

The Russian Army is still mainly dependent on horse transport and very vulnerable to armoured attack in spite of the protection of Stalin tanks. The latter can easily be evaded by our mobile forces.[1]

---

[1] Churchill responded on Aug. 27: 'Thank you so much for your letter of August 21 which I read with much interest. I am not a candidate for the position you mention, although I am glad to know that you would favour such a step. Pray keep me informed of anything you think I should know.'

August 1950

Winston S. Churchill to General Charles de Gaulle
(Churchill papers, 2/169)

22 August 1950
Private

My dear de Gaulle,

I had the pleasure of receiving the Comte d'Harcourt[1] at luncheon down here last week on my return from Strasbourg.

I must indeed most cordially thank you for the very generous tribute[2] you have paid to me in your Memoirs. It is remarkable that in spite of all the hard contretemps of War through which we lived we should both have gained so much understanding of each other's position, and preserved everything that matters in fundamental goodwill. I often look with pleasure on the gallic cock which you presented to my wife and am reminded of the historic events in which we were comrades through trying to serve our own countries and the common cause of freedom and tradition which united us and stands above all.

How terrible it is to feel that all that we were able to achieve is now plunged in the greatest peril I have ever known, and that is saying a good deal.

Winston S. Churchill to Captain Sir Oswald Birley
(Churchill papers, 2/167)

22 August 1950

My dear Oswald,

Thank you so much for your charming letter. I have had to give up all my holiday and cannot even squeeze a tube. Volume IV is a worse tyrant than Attlee. I hope things will be better after the broadcast.

Winston S. Churchill to Sir Norman Brook
(Churchill papers, 4/24)

22 August 1950

My dear Norman Brook,
[...]
I am most profoundly grateful to you for all the help you have given me in my seemingly unending toil. The reconstruction of the 'Suspense and Strain' chapter was a masterpiece. I do not know how you can find the time and energy to help me so much with all the other exacting work you have to do.

I am continually oppressed by the sense of the perils which surround us

---

[1] Charles Jean Marie, duc d'Harcourt, 1902–97. Married Antoinette Gérard, 1927.
[2] See De Gaulle to Churchill of July 26, reproduced above (pp. 1806–7).

now. I am glad you are in a position where you can do much to ward them off. Old or young one can only do ones best.

Malcolm Muggeridge[1] to Winston S. Churchill
(Churchill papers, 2/173)

24 August 1950

My dear Mr Churchill,

I must tell you what a great pleasure it was to come down and see you yesterday. It is a thing I shan't easily forget. Talking about Yalta and related matters was, to me, particularly interesting, and if ever you had another hour or two to spare, I should like more than I can say to come and continue the discussion.

I was extremely sorry to hear this morning about Randolph's injury,[2] but relieved to learn that it was not serious.

Winston S. Churchill: broadcast
('In the Balance', pages 353–7)

26 August 1950

THE PERIL IN EUROPE

When Parliament separated a month ago, the Government had just placed before us their £100,000,000 plan for strengthening our defences. Five days later the Prime Minister asked me to go to see him at Downing Street and there read to me the announcement of an entirely new and much larger plan, costing £300,000,000 or £400,000,000 a year for three years, and requiring far-reaching changes in our whole national industry and economy. Obviously, this was a matter on which the House of Commons should be consulted at the earliest moment. Indeed, we are all entitled to be told why there should have been this immense change between the policy of 26 July and that of 2 August.

After our talk I wrote to Mr Attlee that we should give our support to all measures proposed by the Government which were necessary for national

---

[1] Thomas Malcolm Muggeridge, 1903–1990. Educated at Selhurst Grammar School and Selwyn College, Cambridge. Lecturer at Egyptian University, Cairo, 1927–30. Editorial Staff, *Manchester Guardian*, 1930–2. *Manchester Guardian* correspondent, Moscow, 1932–3. Asst Editor, *Calcutta Statesman*, 1934–5. Editorial staff, *Evening Standard*, 1935–6. Served in WWII in Intelligence Corps (East Africa, North Africa, Italy and France). Maj., 1939. Legion of Honour, Croix de Guerre with Palm, Médaille de la Reconnaissance Française. *Daily Telegraph* Washington Correspondent, 1946–7; Deputy Editor, 1950–2. Editor of *Punch*, Jan. 1953 to 1957. Rector, Edinburgh University, 1967–8.

[2] Randolph Churchill was wounded in the lower right leg by a friendly mortar shell while in South Korea as a newspaper correspondent with 1st Cavalry Div.

defence. 'It is certain,' I said, 'that we are in a condition of great danger and that surprisingly little practical results have followed from the immense outlay of money and control of man-power used by the Government during recent years.' I added that our urgent need is to form efficient combatant units, of which we have hardly any at the present time, and that if the Government could bring forward well-conceived plans of this kind, even if they involved increasing the length of compulsory service, I should recommend the Conservative Party to support such measures both in Parliament and the country. We hold that national safety should rise above party differences, deep and wide as they have become in recent years.

I thought this offer was fair and friendly, and I hoped it would be treated in the same spirit. There was not, however, even the usual consultation with the official Opposition before the summoning of Parliament for 12 September was announced. A month's interval for an emergency recall of Parliament seemed much too long. I thought that either the date should be earlier or its announcement have been put off. Mr Eden and I, with the Liberal Leader, Mr Clement Davies, were invited by Mr Attlee to visit him at Downing Street, and after a lengthy, and none too pleasant, discussion, he arbitrarily refused our request for an earlier recall. I do not think it is a wise or right course for a Prime Minister in a minority of nearly 2,000,000 votes at the recent division – I do not think it is a wise course for him to treat with so little consideration the views of those political opponents who offer to support him on all the things that matter most and on whose help he is counting to carry through the measures necessary for public security. It is a bad thing that His Majesty's Prime Minister should show himself so sullenly resolved to lead only one-half of the nation.

We see from day to day many instances of the improvidence and want of foresight with which our affairs are conducted. Take this case of sending the expeditionary force to Korea: on 27 June, the United Nations called upon their members to defend South Korea against violent aggression from the north. It took the Socialist Government a month to make up their minds whether or not to send an expeditionary force to comply with this request of the United Nations Organization. There was no new fact in the interval. Another month has passed since the decision to send the small force from here was announced, and more than a third month will pass before it can embark on its six weeks' voyage. I should myself have thought it better to have sent even a smaller force in good time from Hong Kong and to replace it from home later on. I was told this was impossible, but now it has been done.

There are graver cases of lack of prevision, of hesitancy and changes of plan which are at work throughout our whole system of defence, adding to its heavy cost and diminishing its already inadequate strength. Some of these are more suited to a Secret Session of Parliament than to a public broadcast. I have already mentioned in Parliament the astonishing episode of selling hundreds of our jet fighters to Egypt and the Argentine, and actually sending some to Russia at an earlier period when all the time our own Auxiliary Air Force so urgently needed them, and this at the moment when by establishing the American bomber base in East Anglia – a policy which the Opposition supported on national grounds – we have placed ourselves in the front line of targets in the event of war.

I heard a few days ago of a case which shows the same kind of infirmity and disconnection of thought and action, though in a different sphere. The head of the Craven Brothers machine tools works at Stockport – the largest but one for producing these vital and very slowly made instruments – informed me that he had for more than two years been asking the Ministry of Supply whether he should go on doing this when so many of our own Royal Ordnance factories are in sore need of renovation for this very purpose. He could not get any clear guidance. He told me that his highly skilled craftsmen were seriously disturbed at doing work of this kind for Soviet Russia and for her satellite Poland. They feared it would weaken our country and strengthen our most likely assailant. They also did not like the presence of Russian Government inspectors, under present conditions, inside their workshops, where a lot of confidential production is also being done for His Majesty's Government. Surely, orders should be given now to stop the export by any firm of machine tools, diesel engines and the like to Soviet Russia and other countries behind the Iron Curtain, and thus release these firms from the contracts, by which they are otherwise bound. I understand the Prime Minister is going to speak on this subject next week; I trust that he will be able to tell us that this, at any rate, has been done.

But fancy going on in this sort of way, and from day to day, with this lack of control and management of great matters, while everything is getting worse, and when we are literally begging the United States for aid in every form. It is a glaring example of the lack of grip, conception and design by our present ministerial planners. What is the use of appealing to the country for unity, exertions and further sacrifices when such feebleness of purpose vitiates our action? The question we must ask ourselves is how much more of this is going on all over the place? Another example of the Government's lack of foresight is shown in their treatment of the question of inviting German aid for the defence of Western Europe and of their own hearths and homes. Five months have passed since I raised this matter in Parliament, and Mr Attlee then described what I said as 'irresponsible' (this was the same word that I think he used about abolishing petrol rationing). Now his Government are making plans with the representatives of America and Europe for doing this very thing, for bringing Germany into the system of defence. Perhaps it is better to be irresponsible and right than to be responsible and wrong. I am certainly thankful not to be responsible for what has happened to our country and its empire during the last five years. At Strasbourg, where we had the meeting the other day of the Council of Europe, two very remarkable things happened. The Germans declared that they did not want to create a German national army, but were willing to serve in a European defence force; and, soldiers standing side by side in defence of freedom. This is a great event in the history of Europe, and I am proud to have had something to do with it.

Alas, it also marks the sense of common peril which oppresses us all. Dr Adenauer, the German Prime Minister, points to the very large, heavily armed Communist German forces which have been raised in the Russian zone which, he says, may amount to several hundred thousand men. They are disguised as police, but they are really an army. Is this not exactly the same technique which the Kremlin oligarchy carried out in Northern Korea before the recent attack? Except, of course, that the danger in Europe is nearer and on an incomparably larger scale. Mr Shinwell has made public what those who study these matters had long known, namely that the Brussels Treaty and Atlantic Pact Powers in Western Europe are already out-numbered six, seven or eight to one – it may be more – by the Russian armies, to say nothing of their satellites and Communist pawns. That is a terrible fact.

We have not been able ourselves to make an atomic bomb, although we played so great a part in its discovery during the war. But the Russian Soviets have had the secret betrayed to them by their spies and fanatics and we have been officially informed by our own Government that they have begun to make it. It is indeed a melancholy thought that nothing preserves Europe from an overwhelming military attack except the devastating resources of the United States in this awful weapon. This is at the present time the sole deterrent against an aggressive Communist invasion. No wonder the Communists would like to ban it in the name of peace. They would then have Europe naked and at their mercy.

European and British weakness endangers peace, for which we must all patiently strive. We are in grave danger. It is not a new danger. I have warned you about it for several years, but it is only since the war broke out in Korea that people have begun to realize how we all stand. I have several times said that I do not believe that a major war is imminent. No one can be sure, but I believe myself we still have a breathing space, and that if we use it wisely we may still ward off this horror from the world. I am sorry that an effort was not made to have a personal talk on the highest level with the leaders of the Soviet Government. I urged this at Edinburgh in February last,[1] but nothing was done and all sorts of things have happened since.

My eyes are not fixed upon Korea, though I admire the American action there, and am glad our men are going to help. There may soon be Communist

---

[1] Speech reproduced above (pp. 1642–50).

attacks upon Tibet and Persia. But the supreme peril is in Europe. We must try to close the hideous gap on the European front. If, in two or three years – should that be granted us – we can make a reasonable defence for the free countries outside the Iron Curtain, while at the same time the United States maintains and increases its superiority in the atomic bomb, the best hope will be given for reaching a final peace settlement. The only way to deal with Communist Russia is by having superior strength in one form or another, and then acting with reason and fairness. This is the plan for the battle of peace and the only plan which has a chance of success. Here at home the Socialist policy since the war has divided our own people in a needless and painful manner. We lie between two general elections. We have to make our case against each other. But we must never forget that, whatever our party differences may be, we all share the same dangers, and we all, when we wake up, mean to defend the same great causes. I pray we may wake up in time.

I have used the few minutes in which I may speak to you – I wish I had an hour – but now I can only say: let us not cast away the remaining chances, or the chances of all the great democracies, of averting a new world war, and of not being wiped out in it if it comes. If the Ministers – many of them at heart well-meaning and patriotic men – who have had all this power and control for the last five years are proved to be incapable of meeting our dire need, it is for Parliament and, above all, for the nation to say whether they should not be replaced by others before it is too late.

Winston S. Churchill to James Chuter-Ede
(Churchill papers, 2/102)

26 August 1950

My dear Ede,

I think I ought to let you know that as a former Home Secretary I feel that the execution of the three British soldiers for the murder of one person goes beyond that I believe to be the usual practice. Perhaps you would consult recent precedents at the Home Office. It must be very rare that as many as three should suffer when only one pulled the trigger. Justice is usually, though not always, satisfied with a life for a life, but three seems to me most severe.

I write to you in the hopes that you will bring this point to the notice of the War Office and because it may well be raised in Parliament.

James Chuter-Ede to Winston S. Churchill
(Churchill papers, 2/102)[1]

27 August 1950

My dear Churchill,

Your letter of 26th about three British soldiers now under sentence of death reached me last night in the country. I am giving instructions that your letter shall be brought to the notice of the Secretary of State for War.

Away from the office I cannot give a full list of recent precedents but I recall that during my term of office three men associated in an armed raid on a shop were all found guilty of murder although only one shot was fired. Two were executed; the third was a few months under the minimum age below which a murderer may not be hanged. More recently two men engaged in an armed raid on a bank were both executed for the murder of a man who attempted to stop their flight although only one shot was fired.

Of course the details of the cases you mention are not known to me but I have no doubt Strachey will consider your views in any decision he has to make.

Lieutenant-Colonel Bill Deakin to Winston S. Churchill
(Churchill papers, 4/281)

29 August 1950

I have spoken to Lord Ismay about Dieppe. His frank opinion is that you will get little of value out of Lord Mountbatten who is at the moment playing polo and visiting Naval establishments.

Mountbatten took the responsibility for the operation and Ismay says that this is the only occasion in the whole War when nothing was put in writing by the Chiefs of Staff about a final operational decision. Six months later there is a minute of a Chiefs of Staff meeting at which Mountbatten stated that he had taken this responsibility himself.

Ismay's opinion is that the Dieppe story does not logically belong to your narrative in 'Return to Cairo'. Your minute to him is the only relevant document and he thinks that it might well, if you see fit, go into the Appendix. The story of Dieppe as produced by Allen is a bare summary of the operation, in the launching of which you had no direct part, although you knew of the early planning and the ultimate change of code names.

If anyone wishes to read the story of Dieppe there is a detailed account in the Canadian Official History.

---

[1] This letter was handwritten.

September 1950

Admiral Lord Louis Mountbatten to Winston S. Churchill
(Churchill papers, 4/17)

4 September 1950

My dear Churchill,

Thank you for your letter of 1st September which reached me this morning. It is very kind of you to give me this opportunity of making suggestions on the Dieppe Raid.

I apologise for the delay in answering the questions which Pug put to me on your behalf about it, but I was most anxious to be quite certain that the replies should be thoroughly substantiated and therefore consulted Major General Wildman Lushington[1] (the present CCO) who was my Chief of Staff, Rear Admiral J. Hughes-Hallett,[2] who was my Senior Naval Planner and the Naval Force Commander of the operation, and others, in a position to know.

I enclose my file copy of the answers which I sent to Pug on Friday, but I gather he was away with you.

From these you will see –

(1) That you were (as ever) the moving spirit behind carrying out another operation that summer, as Dieppe had been cancelled.

(2) That the only way we could devise to meet your wishes was to carry out the Dieppe operation under a different name and in extraordinary secrecy.

(3) You and the Chief of Staffs went into the revived plans carefully (which were hardly changed except in respect of substituting Commandos for airborne forces to silence the flank batteries) and gave

---

[1] Godfrey Edward Wildman-Lushington, 1897–1970. Educated at Wellington College. Served in WWI, 1914–19. CoS to Chief of Combined Operations, 1942–3. Asst CoS to Supreme Allied Cdr, 1944. Maj.-Gen., 1946. Chief of Combined Operations, 1947–50. Officer Légion d'Honneur, Croix de Guerre (France).

[2] John Hughes-Hallett, 1901–72. Naval Cdr for Dieppe Raid, 1942. CB, 1945. MP (Cons.) for Croydon East, 1954–5; for Croydon North-East, 1955–64. British Representative at the Council of Europe, 1958–60.

your approval. You decided to tell the Foreign Secretary but not the Defence Committee.

(4) The reason why no written records were kept was that you and the Chiefs of Staff agreed to this on account of the extraordinary secrecy. Thanks, perhaps, to this there was not the slightest leakage.

I sincerely appreciate the spirit in which you stated that my assumption of the whole responsibility both for planning and execution went beyond what is called for.

Following your great example I have never tried to evade responsibility, but it would have been improper for me to have claimed powers which were not mine, since the Force Commanders, with General Montgomery for 'Rutter' and General Crerar for 'Jubilee', made the detailed plan and in doing so, changed the original plan to suit their views. It was this plan which you and the Chiefs of Staff approved. The execution was in the hands of the Naval Commander-in-Chief at Portsmouth and the AOC of the Fighter Group at Uxbridge, whilst forward operational control was in the hands of the Force Commanders.

I remember you tackling me at Buckingham Palace with having assumed the responsibility for the Dieppe Raid in a speech which I had made in Canada. You will remember that I assured you that I had been misrepresented in the Press and that the idea behind the speech was to help the Canadians appreciate what great value the Dieppe Raid had proved to be, and that I had not wished to take more than my share of responsibility.

Hughes-Hallett drew my attention to the fact that the CIGS had given his firm conviction to you that until an operation on the scale of Dieppe was undertaken no responsible General would take the responsibility of planning for the main invasion. I am sure you will remember this important remark as distinctly as I do myself.

On the advice of Pug Ismay I have taken the liberty of amending your draft to meet these points and I am sending you the original draft together with a retyped version and will post a copy to Pug.

I have read my letter and my redraft out to Pug on the telephone. He cannot remember the incidents but is clear that they must represent the facts. I submit that if you accept my redraft the printing of your minute to General Ismay and his reply is rendered unnecessary, the more so as Colonel Stacey's[1] book deals with the important points very fully, and with more recent knowledge.

I need hardly tell you how honoured and pleased I was to be called on to be of some service to you.

---

[1] Charles Perry Stacey, 1906–89. Canadian Army's historical officer in London, 1940–5. Chief Army Historian, 1945–59. Prof., University of Toronto, 1959–76.

Togo Sheba[1] to Winston S. Churchill
(*Churchill papers, 1/48*)

4 September 1950

Dear Mr Churchill,

This is just to inform you that your son is recovering rapidly from his leg wound. I had the opportunity of meeting your son on the fourth floor room of the Tokyo Army Hospital this morning. He shares his small room with another soldier.

When I entered he was resting comfortably, his wounded leg above the covers, and was reading a novel. Rather a brusque man, but kind hearted when I began talking to him.

The Tokyo Army Hospital is the best institution of its kind in Japan. Before the war it was known as St Luke's Hospital and was founded by an American, Rudolph Bolling Teusler,[2] with funds raised in the United States. The hospital is located about a mile east of the SCAP headquarters in quiet surroundings at the intersection of two canals.

You had a narrow escape in the Boer War. So had your son recently. God be with you both.

Arthur G. Marshall:[3] note
(*Churchill papers, 2/110*)

5 September 1950

ANGLO-RUSSIAN SHORT TERM TRADE AGREEMENT 1947

The principle of this Agreement, arranged by Mr Harold Wilson, was that we should pay for our purchases of grain, timber, etc., by selling Russia Locomotives and British machinery of various kinds.

Russia had inserted a clause to the effect that if she was unable to agree terms and conditions of contract with British Manufacturers she should have the right of spending the proceeds of the sale of Russian goods in Colonial markets.

Russia insisted on prices, terms and conditions from British Manufacturers in this country to which we on our side could not agree, and took advantage

---

[1] Editor, Rengo Press, Tokyo.
[2] Rudolf Bolling Teusler, 1876–1934. Founded St Luke's International Hospital, Tokyo, 1902. Lt-Col. and Commissioner of the Red Cross with Allied Forces in Siberia, 1918–21.
[3] Arthur Gregory George Marshall, 1903–2007. British engineer. Born in Cambridge, England. Educated at Jesus College, Cambridge. Married, 1931, Rosemary Dimsdale: three children. Founded Marshall Aerospace, 1935. OBE, 1948. Knighted, 1974.

of the provision above to purchase rubber, tin, wool etc., from Commonwealth markets, all of these goods being direct munitions of war. She is still continuing this practice.

I was personally interested in the Locomotive negotiations and we did everything we could to meet the Russian requirements. The firm in whose name the negotiations were carried on was the North British Locomotive Co., Ltd.

If Mr Churchill wants further particulars I should be only too pleased to supply them or to discuss the matter with him when I return from Finland.

Winston S. Churchill to Admiral Lord Louis Mountbatten
(Churchill papers, 4/17)

7 September 1950

My dear Dickie,

I am very much obliged to you for the pains you have taken, and I have accepted practically verbatim your redraft. I must confess that I cannot remember all the details you mention, which is not surprising considering that no written records were kept, and how much was going on. Certainly I wanted a large scale raid in the summer of 1942.[1] Also I was abroad for a fortnight before Zero.[2] And of course the overall responsibility is mine. In these circumstances I am omitting my minute of questions written four months later and the replies thereto.

I am in touch with Pug.

Winston S. Churchill: speech
(Hansard)

12 September 1950   House of Commons

DEFENCE (GOVERNMENT PROPOSALS)

On a Motion moved by the Prime Minister

that this House approves the proposals contained in the White Papers Command No. 8026 and 8027, designed by HM Government to meet the growing dangers to world peace of which the war in Korea is an example; and is of opinion that the necessary legislation to amend the National Service Acts should be brought in forthwith.

[1] After '1942' Churchill wrote, in the first draft of this letter: 'and I said to Stalin at Moscow: "It will be like putting one's hand in a bath before getting in to feel how hot the water is", or words to that effect'.

[2] Zero hour.

We shall on this side, of course, support the Motion which you have just read, sir. We shall vote for it and we shall help to resist any Amendment which may be moved to it. We shall also support the Bill to extend the length of military service which is to be introduced. Several points may well arise upon that Bill for discussion in Committee, but I should hope that it can be passed through this House, certainly without any hindrance if not, indeed, in a single day.

I shall not on this occasion ask that any of our Debates should be in Secret Session. I just mention this to relieve any anxiety that may prevail on the benches opposite. Looking around, I cannot on this occasion spy any strangers participating in our debates. I must, however, make it clear that our approval of the Prime Minister's Motion is not a vote of confidence in the Government. We could not, on this side of the House, give a vote of confidence in the present Administration, least of all in its handling of military affairs. Although in all questions where the safety of the country is concerned we continue to give our support to His Majesty's Government, it must not be supposed that we are in any way ready to share their responsibility, such as it is, for the present condition of our affairs. We recognize that Ministers are by no means wholly responsible for the situation in which we all now lie. They have made many needless mistakes, but much that has happened has been outside their control.

Both Governments and Oppositions have responsibilities to discharge, but they are of a different order. The Government, with their whole control over our executive power, have the burden and the duty – and we can all see that it is a very heavy one – to make sure that the safety of the country is provided for; the shape, formation and direction of policy is in their hands alone. The responsibilities of the Opposition are limited to aiding the Government in the measures which are required, which we agree are required, for national safety and also to criticizing and correcting, so far as they can, any errors and shortcomings which may be apparent; but the Opposition are not responsible for proposing integrated and complicated measures of policy. Sometimes we do, but it is not our obligation. In voting for what the Government propose, which we are going to do on this occasion, we in no way limit our right and duty to comment with the fullest freedom upon their policy and the course of events.

The Prime Minister has appealed to us for national unity on Defence. That does not mean national unity on mismanagement of Defence. In our view, which I shall endeavour to sustain, the present Government, although right-minded on essentials, have shown themselves conspicuously lacking in forethought, conviction and design. It was never in their power, as I have most frankly declared, to prevent the sombre deterioration of our affairs which has resulted from the Russian-Communist aggression upon so many countries and poisoning or infection of so many more. We are in full accord with the Labour Party, as I call them on occasions when I am in a good humour with them, in their resistance to Communism in all its manifestations. We can hardly compete with the Prime Minister in the language he uses on this subject, but we rejoice with them that the Trades Union Congress should have so decisively ranged itself, as was only to be expected by those who understand the solid qualities of British trade unionism, with the unfaltering and unflinching defence of the free way of life of the Western parliamentary democracies. A vote was given last week at Brighton – I think trade unionists with His Majesty's Government and also with the Conservative and Liberal Parties – (*interruption*) – these last two, for all the jeers and mockery of hon. Members, comprising a majority of nearly 2,000,000 of our people, according to the recent election. In giving faithful and fearless support to the United Nations Organization in confronting totalitarian tyranny, whether it wears the garb of Communism, Nazism, Fascism, or Russian Imperialism – on these supreme issues Britain can indeed present a united front, not only for this island but for our sister nations throughout the British Empire and Commonwealth. However grave our differences are in domestic matters or however sharp must be our criticisms of ministerial handling of affairs, that is the message of unity which we are resolved to send at this juncture from the House of Commons to the world.

Having made this clear, I will give the House a short narrative of what has happened, so far as I am aware, since we separated six weeks ago. We had then received from the Minister of Defence a most serious statement of the immense preponderance – seven or eight to one – of the Soviet Forces in active divisions, in organized armour and in air power over the Western allies in Europe. The Government proposed that we should spend £100,000,000 on additional preparations for defence and this was, of course, accepted, so far as it went. However, five days after we parted, the Prime Minister asked me to come and see him and read to me the text of the statement which was to be published the next morning of an entirely new and greatly enlarged defence policy, namely, the three years' plan involving an additional expenditure of £1,100,000,000. Quick work, it seemed to me.

After this interview I wrote him a letter dated 6 August – before I had to go to Strasbourg – thanking him for informing me of the measures which he was now taking in concert with the United States, and saying:

> We shall give our support to all measures proposed by the Government which we ourselves deem necessary for national defence. This cannot, however, limit in any way the right and duty of the Opposition to criticize, either in public or secret Debate, the existing state of our defences, or the rate and methods with which the necessary increases are to be effected. However, we do not, of course know anything about the Government's new plan, except what has now been published. It is certain that we are in a condition of great danger, and that surprisingly little practical results have

followed from the immense outlay of money and control of manpower used by the Government during recent years. It seems to me and to those of my colleagues I have been able to consult that Parliament should be called together if possible before the end of August. I propose to hold a meeting of my colleagues on or about 15 August, and it is probable that we shall then make a formal request for the recall of Parliament.

We were impelled to think of the steps made possible by the very full assurances given by the Lord President of the Council before we separated.

In the note which I enclosed to the Prime Minister on the military position – and it is that military aspect with which we are dealing today – I said:

> I do not myself see how the British contribution can be achieved without holding existing men with the Colours and increasing the length of service. The urgent need is to form efficient combatant units, of which we have hardly any at the present time. Should the Government bring forward well-conceived measures of this kind, I should recommend the Opposition to support them both in Parliament and in the country.

That is what I wrote before I knew of the decision that the length of service was to be extended. That is what we now propose to do, and I hope the assurance given was of assistance to the Government in the extremely difficult problems which they are called upon now to face, and about which, of course, they have to agree among themselves.

I must say that it looks as if a meeting of Parliament in the last week of August would have given the Prime Minister a very appropriate and convenient opportunity for presenting not only his new proposals for the increase of our military expenditure to £1,100,000,000 under the three years' plan but also for telling Parliament of the Government's decision to prolong compulsory National Service from eighteen months to two years, as well as the welcome statement, so long pressed for on this side of the House, of the increase in the pay of the Regular Forces. However, the Prime Minister, without any further contact, even through the usual channels, announced the recall of Parliament for today, 12 September. So here we are.

This is an emergency recall, and it seemed odd to announce it nearly a month before, and with such timing as to make it necessary that the important declaration of the lengthening of the period of National Service should be given over broadcast rather than presented, according to normal constitutional practice, to the House of Commons. But these are not large matters. (*Interruption.*) Still, after all, Parliamentary usage is something which is quite important to consider. I repeat, these are not large matters compared with the vast and glowering facts by which we are encircled. I put them to the House only to illustrate the sudden and inconsequent changes in Government policy which are now before us.

Why was it that, when we were last gathered here, we were offered the £100,000,000 plan whereas a few days later this was suspended by the three years' £1,100,000,000 plan? What happened in the interval to make such a sweeping change desirable? I gather from the Prime Minister's speech that the Americans appealed to us to take some further action. But surely all these matters should have been well known and familiar to a Government that have been for over five years in office? Surely we do not need the prompting of a foreign country, however friendly, to show us where our duty lies? What happened, I say? Why was it that only, perhaps, a fortnight elapsed after Parliament rose before the new, formidable decision was taken, namely, to prolong the period of National Service?

When we were last together the Minister of Defence told how completely undecided the Government were, when he said:

> In present circumstances, we are not satisfied that an increase in the period of the whole-time National Service would solve our problem. But this is a matter we intend to keep under constant review.

That was only a fortnight before this tremendous change was proposed and put forward and given to the nation. All we were told at that time was that we must keep the matter under continuous review. I may refer to that phrase about keeping things 'under continuous review' a little later. What happened, I ask, to make so complete a change of plan in the military structure of our country necessary?

This is the kind of quick, impulsive change in the dominating issues of our Defence policy which makes it difficult to have confidence that our vital affairs are being conducted in accordance with any clear and persistent theme. What new facts, I ask again, had arisen between our separation for the Recess and the £1,100,000,000 plan? All right: it is said America appealed to us. What new facts had arisen between the declaration of this plan and the declaration of the lengthened service and the other proposals which form the subject of the Prime Minister's Motion today? Surely, these are fair and, indeed, unavoidable questions? I do not feel that the Prime Minister has given any adequate answer to them in his speech today.

But this is not merely a matter of the last few weeks. I do not know of any great change in the balance of world power or the imminence of world danger that has occurred since the dark day when the Government informed us that the Russian Communist Government had gained possession of the secret of the atomic bomb and led us to believe they had produced it. But this was a year ago. It is quite true that the Soviet-impelled aggression in Korea, and the vehement and valiant action of the United States in pursuance of the United Nations mandate, and the fierce and enlarging war now proceeding in Korea, had made everyone realize and pay attention to dangers which were quite well known to those who follow these matters, and were certainly well known to His Majesty's Government.

The dread balance has not been changed. It is only that the flare of actual war in one distant theatre – out of several that may be opened – has broken upon the public. But the Government must have had the whole picture before them for two years past or three years past. As I have said, it is for five years they have been studying all these matters – with responsibility and power. If the Motion before us this afternoon had been made two years ago how much better off we should be at this moment. The facts disclosed by the Minister of Defence, before we adjourned, about the position in Europe did not spring into existence overnight; they must have been known to the Prime Minister and his principal colleagues long ago. The war in Korea has only made the ordinary people in many lands understand what must have been plainly visible, nay, obvious, to those who were entrusted with the sacred duty of guarding their safety and who had all the knowledge that was available.

Why, then, were the necessary measures not proposed in good time? That is another question to which I cannot feel that the Prime Minister has given us any answer this afternoon or in his broadcast; but then, no doubt, he was occupied with more important topics. It is quite true that, unhappily, in this country we are deeply divided about internal politics and that first-class issues affecting the whole character of our country and its economic life are raised thereby. But the Socialist Government have been in a position of great advantage compared with other British Governments we have experienced. Compare their position, for instance, to that of the Baldwin and Chamberlain Governments before the war – (*Interruption.*) Hon. Members opposite had better listen to what I have to say, then they will know which side to cheer.

The present Socialist Government have known that they could rely upon the whole-hearted support of His Majesty's Opposition, comprising both the other parties in the State, in any steps they might think it necessary to take for national defence, and international duty. At any time they could propose, with the certainty of our support, unpopular steps. They knew quite well that the Conservative Party in the last Parliament, as in this, would vote with them if, for instance, they demanded a prolongation of National Service, and would not vote against them, as the Prime Minister led the Socialist Party into doing on the same issue four months before the outbreak of the Second World War. I hope they will not indulge further in that propaganda of 'Guilty Men' which has played so large a part in their platform talks in recent years. Such discrepancies of conduct – I can hardly use a milder term – will not affect our action or the course we are bound now to take in the national interest. But they cannot be, and ought not be, excluded from our minds in judging the record and character of the present Administration. This indecision and these sudden changes, without any new material facts, in what ought to be long-term policies and, shall I say, 'supra-party issues' – I am always willing to endeavour to throw myself into the mood of those who, at any rate, we shall be supporting on this question – this indecision and these sudden changes have aggravated the inevitable perils and burdens of the position to which, with the nation's eyes at last opened, we have now come. That is why, in supporting the Motion now before us, we do not in any way absolve the Government from the just censure which lies upon them for their conduct of affairs.

Let me turn to another and more precise aspect of this indecision and hesitancy in regard to fateful but also simple issues. On 27 June, the United Nations organization declared the Soviet-impelled invasion of South Korea to be an act of aggression and called upon all its members to render support to the United States in resisting it. Accordingly, British warships and some local air squadrons were very rightly ordered to participate. But when, after nearly a month, the Government made up their minds to send a military force from this country to stand in line with the Americans, the questions arises: Why have they not been able to send it out before? It certainly was what is called an 'eye-opener' to the vast majority of our people that, after all the money and control of manpower and control of administrative arrangements that the Government have enjoyed for five years, it should take months to organize even a strong brigade group from this country. It is not ready yet.

I thought myself that a token force should have been provided much earlier from Hong Kong and replaced by reinforcements of troops from this country, who need not be capable of going immediately into battle, but who would rapidly mature and fill the gap in the Hong Kong garrison. But the Government decided otherwise. Let me ask the Prime Minister a question: What was the date when he changed his mind and decided to send a force from Hong Kong to Korea? What was the date?

The Prime Minister: I am afraid that I have not that date with me. I did explain in a broadcast that the original request was that we should send a balanced force, and stress was not laid on sending them immediately; but, subsequently, we had an urgent request to which we at once responded by sending a force from Hong Kong.

Mr Churchill: It certainly was a great surprise to me, and I am sure also to my right hon. Friend the Member for Warwick and Leamington (Mr Eden) and to the Leader of the Liberal Party. (*Interruption.*) I hope that members of the Liberal Party all over the country will take note of that cry of derision. No one counts at all except those who are managed by the Labour caucus; no one else counts at all. Yet they come forward appealing for national support and unity. It was a great surprise to us after our interview with the Prime Minister on 16 August to learn on 20 August that a force was to be sent from Hong Kong. The Prime Minister does not remember what was the date of the decision, but, at any rate, I have given him fairly limited brackets in which he will be able to make his further investigations.

The Prime Minister: I cannot quite make out what is the right hon. Gentleman's special point about this date. What is he hanging on the date that is so important? I have told him the facts.

Mr Churchill: I am hanging on the fact that these great matters which are continually before us and before the nation appear to swing about between one day and another, almost upon caprice, at the hands of the Government.

The Prime Minister: The right hon. Gentleman has more experience in conducting military affairs than anyone else in this House. He has been accustomed, no doubt, to receiving advice from those who are responsible for running a campaign. The campaign in Korea is being run by the Americans. We respond to their requests, and if the request changes from what is was before it is not the fault of His Majesty's Government. We have responded to the request made to us.

Mr Churchill: No, sir. I do not feel that this is so. (Hon. Members: 'Oh'.) I think the Americans are bitterly disappointed. (*Interruption.*) Why is the Prime Minister's colleague shouting? He does not know anything about it. That is my personal view. I do not mind noise in the least. Please go on, although we gave the Prime Minister a very silent and patient hearing.

It is my personal view that the Government and their military advisers, having rejected this project for many weeks, suddenly made a right-about turn and did what they had hitherto declared to be impossible. There was really nothing new in the situation, except perhaps the growing disappointment of the United States that we were so long in sending them anything from anywhere. (Hon Members: 'Shame'.) The tangled story of sending and delaying sending, and changing of plans in the method of sending, what could only be a token force, and rightly could only be a token force, to Korea, is a culminating example of the incapacity to take decisions and of living from day to day, which casts its shadow on all our military affairs at a time when small-scale issues are sharp and urgent, and when potentially mortal perils gather their clouds around.

Now let me speak of another aspect. I do not think it will be any more agreeable to hon. Members opposite. Let me speak of another aspect, not so much of indecision as of disconnection in policy – I mean the continued exportation of machine tools and other appliances to Soviet Russia and Poland. Our British industries are very short of machine tools. Diesel engines, electrical plant and many other kindred high-grade manufactures have been pumped out of this country in the last few years although they are greatly needed at home. This was done in the name of dollar balances or in unrequited exports. The sending away of machine tools which are needed here at a time like this is like selling the seed corn in the lean years, which in bygone days was regarded as an unwise thing to do.

We see the same kind of want of foresight, the same defective sense of values and proportion, which I have already mentioned in the military sphere, the same system and habit of indecision in this question of the export of machine tools as we have seen in the military sphere. Of course, the crowning example is the sale of hundreds of jet aeroplanes which were needed so imperatively for our own self-defence and security. The Prime Minister has referred to it today, and perhaps the party opposite will allow me to comment on his remarks. He said out of doors, that this is an 'old story'. But there has never been a satisfactory answer to it. One hundred and ten jet aeroplanes were sold or given to Egypt, and what we read in the papers seems to show that is has not at all improved their good feeling towards us. Fancy sending them away. Then, 100 to the Argentine. These are sent away at a time when our auxiliary air forces are hopelessly lacking and eagerly longing for these machines. The right hon. Gentleman said that it would have upset all our financial and economic arrangements, or words to that effect. What nonsense! The aeroplanes that were sold to the Argentine were, I believe, credited for about £2,000,000 or £3,000,000. We are dealing with a Budget for which we voted £700,000,000 to £800,000,000, and now we come forward into these colossal figures. This £2,000,000 or £3,000,000 for an absolutely vital asset which we require, is brought up as a reason for this very gross neglect.

The Government have now, according to the broadcast of the Prime Minister, definitely decided that any machine tools, no matter how vital their war potential, which have been ordered by Soviet Russia or its satellites before the British restrictive regulations of eighteen months ago, must, when made, be delivered to Soviet Russia. I have heard a lot of vague language from the Prime Minister, but I could not see anything which countered or contradicted that quite definite assertion he made in his broadcast.

The Prime Minister: The right hon. Gentleman has not got it quite right.

Mr Churchill: No doubt what I have said is quite true.

The Prime Minister: What I said was that the machinery and tools were being delivered in respect of contracts already entered into, and the statement made in 1949 – I think in February – by the President of the Board of Trade to this House was that that was the practice we were following. I did not say that if at the present time we required these we should not step in and take them over. I was referring to what the practice was then. As a matter of fact, a whole lot of trading goes on which is outside the control of the Government.

Mr Churchill: It is very extraordinary that the right hon. Gentleman should take the tremendous step of proposing a £1,100,000,000 three-year plan, announcing to the country the lengthening of service from eighteen months to two years, and no one in the Government should have seen that at some time a stoppage should have been put on vital military materials leaving this country. No, sir, what I gathered from what the right hon. Gentleman said led me to preserve this particular phrase: 'The matter is to be kept under continuous review.'

Surely, if the Government's view is maintained this altogether ignores the position. These tools take a long time to make, and the British machine tool industry has for years been pressed with orders which it can only fulfil in sequence. There is an endless queue of orders for machine tools, and only comparatively few firms and craftsmen can make them. We have now reached the point where vital war-making materials are to be sent in an increasing flow for some time from this country to Soviet Russia. We think that this is wrong and ought to be stopped. It is surprising that the Government, in other directions so prone to retrospective legislation, should find themselves puristically and pedantically hampered in the matter of war materials when an entirely new situation has arisen and become acute.

The right hon. Gentleman said that he was endeavouring to stop certain materials being actually sent to North Korea which would help the North Koreans to shoot down our soldiers. We should all approve of a step of that character. The Prime Minister can commit himself to it without any fear that he would be severely criticized in the House. It is intolerable to think that our troops today should be sent into action at one end of the world while we are supplying, or are about to supply, if not actual weapons of war, the means to make weapons of war to those who are trying to kill them or get them killed. I was astonished when I was told what was going on. I was astounded by the attitude that the Prime Minister has taken. I should think that the feeling of the great majority of those in this House would be that no more machine tools of war-making purposes should be sent from this country to Soviet Russia or the Soviet satellite nations while the present tension continues. I do not intend to go into details this afternoon, though they are all available and can be produced if there is any challenge. I do not suggest that this is done out of any ill-will on the part of the Government, but is only another example of the disconnection between the various Departments arising from lack of grip and control.

I will return to the purely military aspect of this Motion, for which we intend to vote. The arguments for it are very strong. The imposition in time of peace of eighteen months' compulsory service was a severe departure from our past customs, and a heavy burden on our people. The Government deserve credit for having discharged their duty in this respect. However, as has now been realized on both sides of the House, a period of eighteen months was singularly awkward for our affairs. It gave us a very heavy burden for a very small result in combatant units. It is true that a great reserve of well-trained men for the Territorial Army is being built up, and I wonder that the Prime Minister did not emphasize that a little more, because certainly, it will be a very different kind of Territorial Army filled with men who have served eighteen months in the ranks. It is being built up, and if the other elements are provided this gives a strong foundation for military defensive power after a considerable interval.

But the need of producing a number of effective combat units speedily, and maintaining them abroad or on the continent of Europe – not quite the same thing in my opinion – is most unhandily met by a period of eighteen months' service. Our Regular formations are drained and also burdened by the need of training the large flow of recruits coming throughout the year. I presume the Minister of Defence will look into the question of whether they are called fortnightly throughout the year or at longer intervals. I am not sufficiently informed to make up my mind. We lose our men just at the period when they really are useful for foreign service and for fighting formations. Our considerable sacrifice has given us the worst of both worlds. Clear thinking and clear policy on this question has, no doubt, been hampered by the harsh conditions of political and party strife which, however regrettable, now exist between us. There is no doubt that the proposal of this Motion for two years' compulsory service and a well-paid Regular Army will, if properly applied, bring a swift, solid and substantial increase in our defensive power. It ought to be possible under this system rapidly to build up a very good army if the weapons are found for them.

There will be a marked improvement even in the next six months if, instead of reaching a discord at a great cost, we reach a harmony for a somewhat heavier period. There can be no doubt that this is a wise measure, and also that in spite of all its difficulties it ought to have been taken before. All of us hate the idea of another war. Is there anyone in this island who can think of any country that we wish to attack or invade? But we must make ourselves capable of serving the great cause to which we have pledged our faith, and in which our own survival is also directly involved. There can, therefore, be no question, so far as we here on this side of the House are concerned, that this measure should go through, and if the Government gain credit for it – however belated it may be – so much the better for them. We need not at this time grudge anybody the credit of doing anything, anywhere, anyhow for anyone. That is the position to which we have got today. The military chiefs should in my opinion be held strictly responsible for making the best use of the extraordinary, unprecedented measures of State which are being taken to help them in their task.

The Prime Minister has spoken, not today but out-of-doors, scornfully about a European army – apparently, it would have been all right if I had said 'a European defence force' – and about the Germans being included in our Western defence system. Are they being discussed? No, they are being kept under continuous review. Where does he stand about these matters? Is he still opposed to Germans being armed as a part of the Western defence forces or as part of an armed German police force; or does he still think the only Germans to be armed are the Communist Germans, whom the Soviets have formed into a powerful army in the Russian zone? Again, I think the right hon. Gentleman was very guarded and very obscure when he said he was keeping the matter under review, and what he said about the Germans was so very vague that one could hardly understand it. Still I must say that I was encouraged on both these points, and I feel that the normal process of belated conversion to the obvious is still steadily going forward.

Let me here say, again, that the fact that the liberated German representatives voted at Strasbourg for sending a quota to a European army, while not seeking to raise a national army of their own is a most helpful fact, and has been so regarded throughout Europe and the United States. This has rendered it far easier for the French to welcome them and for the closing of a thousand-year quarrel in this historic gesture of French and German soldiers standing in the line together against the Russian-Communist aggression and menace. I feel sure that all this process of bringing the Germans back into the family of united Europe and enabling them to take a part in a European army or European defence force for the defence of freedom and civilization – for which some of us on this side of the House have worked so hard for several years – has been helpful not only to the free world but even to the British Socialist Government. The Prime Minister should welcome it instead of discouraging or even disparaging it. But whatever his feelings may be he would be wise to accept it, because a European army with a strong German quota is going to be formed quite quickly – that is to say, if we are given the time. That is a fact that none can challenge or deny.

I have never seen an occasion when what is going on in Europe generally is more uncertain and what we ought to do is more clear. Never was the future more inscrutable and never was our policy and duty more plain. We have to form, as fast as possible, a European Army of at least sixty or seventy divisions to make some sort of front in Europe to close what I have called 'the hideous gap' in the protection of Western Europe from a Russian-Communist onrush to the sea. For this purpose every nation still enjoying freedom from totalitarian tyranny should make extreme exertions. Each of the countries ruled by parliamentary democracies must dedicate their quota of divisions. Since these matters were last debated in this House, in March, the French have resolved to contribute twenty divisions, I understand, but it may be fifteen divisions. I rejoice to see the famous French Army lift itself again into the vanguard of freedom.

There should certainly be ten divisions from the United States, two or three from Canada and six or eight from this island. I must say that the suggestion of three from Germany and one and a half or two available here does not seem to me to be a proportionate contribution, even in making allowance for the fact that although we have got rid of India we have still important obligations to meet in tropical countries. I do not think that that should be accepted as a full and complete contribution on our part. Germany and Italy should also contribute eight or ten divisions apiece and the Benelux countries, comprising ancient and characteristic States, at least four more. Then there is Scandinavia. So here are sixty or seventy divisions which can be produced and organized.

If such an army can be deployed on our gaping Eastern front, the greatest danger of a third world war in the next three or four years will be substantially diminished, if not indeed removed. We shall become free from the present horrible plight in which the American possession of measureless superiority in the atomic bomb is our only safeguard against what might well be the ruin of the world. This will undoubtedly give the Western democracies the best chance of securing the return to the normal relationships of States and nations. Whether we shall have time or not no one can tell. There are two factors which we cannot measure, let alone control, either of which may prove decisive. They are the following: first, the calculations and designs of the Soviet autocracy in the Kremlin, and, secondly, the anger of the people in the United States at the treatment they are receiving and the burden they have to bear. Neither of these is within our control.

It is my firm conviction that while there is a real, solid hope of building up an effective European army the United States will forbear, and that while American superiority in atomic warfare casts its strange but merciful shield over the free peoples the Soviet oligarchy will be deterred from launching out upon the most frightful of world wars yet waged in this unhappy and distraught world. It may well be that the vast masses of human beings, who ask for so little, but only to be let alone to enjoy the fruits of peaceful toil and raise their children in the hope of a decent and improving future, can still be rescued from the melancholy and frightful fate which has seemed to be, and now seems to be, closing in upon them. We cannot control, and no one nation can control, the march of destiny, but we can at least do our part. It is because the Motion now before us offers a minor but none the less considerable make-weight to the peaceful settlement of world affairs that we on this side of the House, Conservatives and Liberals alike, will give it our united and resolute support.

Winston S. Churchill: speech
(Hansard)

13 September 1950   House of Commons

FIELD MARSHAL SMUTS[1]

I earnestly join with the Prime Minister in the tribute he has paid to the life and work of Jan Smuts; and also in the sympathy he has expressed with that gracious and remarkable woman[2] who has sustained his long march through life, and with his son[3] who carries on an honoured name. Personally I mourn

---

[1] Jan Smuts died of a heart attack at his family farm in South Africa on 11 Sep. 1950.

[2] Sybella 'Isie' Margaretha Krige, 1870–1954. Known as 'Ouma', meaning grandmother. Educated at Victoria College, Stellenbosch, 1887. Married Jan Smuts, 1897. Active in South African Women's Federation and Women's United Party. Founded Gifts and Comforts Fund for South African soldiers serving in WWII, 1940.

[3] Jan Christian Smuts Jr, 1912–95. Known as 'Klein Jannie'. Son of FM Jan Smuts. Married, 1938, Daphne Webster. In 1952, published a biography of his father, *Jan Christian Smuts*.

the loss of a cherished friend with whom I had worked intimately in many kinds of anxious and stirring events. It is just over fifty years since I first met him in somewhat unpropitious circumstances. I was a cold tired-out prisoner of war and he was questioning me as to my status as a war correspondent and the part I had been said to have played in the fighting. I always followed with great interest after that the accounts of his long and dauntless fight as a guerrilla leader for the independence of the Transvaal Republic, of which he had already been State Attorney.

My memories of him are, however, most enriched by the two main periods of our work together. The first was the framing and bringing into force of the Transvaal Constitution. It is only a few months since I referred to this on the occasion of his eightieth birthday. The Transvaal Constitution was an act of generous statecraft which will always be associated in Great Britain with the name of Campbell-Bannerman,[1] and in South Africa, and to the comradeship and brotherhood in arms between South Africa and the old country and between Boer and Briton which stood the hardest strains which lay before us and which was crowned in the end with so much honour.

No act of reconciliation after a bitter struggle has ever produced so rich a harvest in goodwill or effects that lasted so long upon affairs. Magnanimity in victory is rare, and this is an instance and almost unique example of its reward, because rare though it be it is by no means always rewarded. This was because we in Britain found great South Africans to deal with. In Louis Botha and Jan Smuts we found those qualities of unswerving fidelity to honourable engagements, the power to see each other's point of view and above all – and this was the point I made on his eightieth birthday – that resolve not to be outdone in generosity which ranks among the noblest and most helpful impulses in the human breast.

But it was, of course, during the last five years of the recent war that we came most closely together. Here I speak not only for myself but for my colleagues in the then War Cabinet, whom I think I shall carry with me when I say that in all our largest decisions and our best thoughts we found ourselves fortified by the spontaneous accord of the South African Prime Minister. In his farm near Pretoria or at Groote Schuur, no doubt receiving all the telegrams but without any of the whole process of consultation which we went through among ourselves and with the Chiefs of Staff, thousands of miles away, dealing with these matters practically alone, again and again he sent us conclusions and advice at which we had arrived here simultaneously by a much more elaborate and entirely separate process of thought. It was a comfort to all of us, and above all to me, to feel by this quite independent

---

[1] Henry Campbell-Bannerman, 1836–1908. MP (Lib.) for Stirling Burghs, 1868–1908. Leader of the Opposition, 1899–1905. PM, 1905–8. Father of the House, 1907–8. Under his leadership, the British Government granted the Boer states of Transvaal and Orange River Colony self-government in 1906 and 1907, respectively.

cross-check that we might have confidence in what we were going to do and that we were on the right course. I must say that I can hardly recall any occasion where we did not reach the same conclusions by these entirely different roads of mental travail.

Jan Smuts was a shining example of the Latin saying: *Mens sana in corpore sano*. His mental and physical efficiency seemed to undergo no change with the passage of years. Up to his eightieth birthday he could not only concentrate his mind for many hours a day, but could march with a brisk and alert step to the top of Table Mountain, and if he chose back again down the descent. Perhaps he did it once too often. This prolonged harmony of mind and body was the foundation of a luminous, normal, healthy, practical common sense, which guided him in daily action but in no way limited the depth of his vision or his far-ranging outlook over the world scene.

I agree with the Prime Minister in enumerating all the various fields in which he shone. Warrior, statesman, philosopher, philanthropist, Jan Smuts commands in his majestic career the admiration of us all. There is no personal tragedy in the close of so long, full, and complete a life. But those of his friends who are left behind to face the unending problems and perils of human existence feel an overpowering sense of impoverishment and of irreparable loss. This is in itself also the measure of the gratitude with which we and lovers of freedom and civilization in every land salute his memory.

Winston S. Churchill to General Dwight D. Eisenhower
(Churchill papers, 2/168)

14 September 1950

My dear Ike

Lord Camrose is now leaving for the United States. As you know, he is a very great friend of mine, and plays a most important part in our British affairs. It would I am sure be valuable if you could meet him. He knows my views on every aspect of this continually darkening scene.

Winston S. Churchill to Captain Arthur Granville Soames
(Churchill papers, 2/177)

15 September 1950

My dear Arthur,

I must apologise for being so long in answering your letter and invitation of September 1. As you may have seen in the papers I have been very hard pressed by politics lately. It would give me great pleasure to come and help you shoot your pheasants if I felt equal to it. I think it would be beyond my strength and so beg you to forgive me if I do not accept. I spend a great deal of my time resting in bed and would not be able to get through all my trials if I were to attempt to renew the sports of former days.

PS. I hope you sometimes back Colonist II wh Christopher found me.

Eliahu Elath[1] to David Ben-Gurion[2]
(Government of Israel Archives)

15 September 1950

Had hours conversation Churchill his home. Welcomed me warmly said Israel's creation great event all time human history. Proud his contribution our cause was Zionist all his life. Had feared Bevin would overshadow Balfour and what Britain did for Nat Home be forgotten but fortunately conditions improved and no reason why Israel Britain shouldn't cultivate friendship. Israel has no better friend than Britains. British romantic realists deeply respect admire determination courage wherewith our independence achieved also great historical significance restoration free Jewish nation after centuries persecution. Israel must preserve close association Bible embody spiritual moral heritage restored Jewish people.

Churchill emphasized need Israel be strong political military factor Mideast for her own and democracies sake. View gravity international situation every moment precious should be used increase our potential all fields. Glad we beat Egypt. Cares for no Arab States except Jordan. Abdulla whom he 'put on throne' only reliable stable ruler. Greatly respects our army. Said when documents published one day will reveal extent he favoured Jewish force during world war believing our moral physical ability became best soldiers Mediterranean.

Discussing world situation he stressed decisive importance for preservation peace of Americas ownership 'large stock pile'. How close our relations Truman his government shown interest composition functioning our government's. Asked extent communist danger Israel.

Churchill enquired our plans agricultural industrial development particularly Negev. Suggested we use scientific resources make up for deficiencies other respects. Remarking 'God blessed Israel with Weizmann' whose statesmanship scientific attainments made him one of great men our time, eminently fitted leader guide Jewish people decisive hour their destiny.

[1] Eliahu Elath, 1903–90. First Israeli Ambassador to US, 1948–50. Ambassador to UK, 1950–9. President of Hebrew University, 1962–8.

[2] David Ben-Gurion, 1886–1973. Recognized as founder of the State of Israel. Attended University of Warsaw, 1905. Studied Law, Istanbul University, 1912. General Secretary, Zionist Labour Federation in Palestine, 1921–35. Declared establishment of State of Israel, 14 May 1948. Leader of Israel in Arab–Israeli War, 1948. Served as first Israeli PM and Minister of Defence, 1949–63.

Though doing most of talking Churchill heard me attentively showing genuine interest our problems. Was at his best speaking Jewish plight in world both as persecuted people and guardians Bible heritage. Reference to Bevin spiced by uncomplimentary adjectives an latters Palestine policy called 'disgusting outrageous'. Offered help us whenever possible.

Winston S. Churchill: speech
(Hansard)

19 September 1950   House of Commons

IRON AND STEEL

I beg to move, 'That this House regrets the decision of His Majesty's Government to bring the Steel Nationalisation Act into immediate operation during this period of tension and danger thus needlessly dividing the nation on Party political issues and disturbing the smooth and efficient working of an industry vital to our defence programme.' Last week, the Conservative and Liberal Parties gave their support in all the Measures which were deemed necessary for national defence. In spite of the very serious criticisms that could be made of the mismanagement of our defence problems and the inadequacy of the remedies, the Government Motion was passed without Division or Amendment. Furthermore, the Bill prolonging the period of compulsory Service from 18 to 24 months, imposing a very heavy sacrifice on British homes and families, was carried through the House of Commons in a single day, and has now received the Royal Assent.

This was done because everyone realised the grave and growing danger in which we stand, and we have all agreed that an immediate strengthening of our Forces, in conjunction with those of our Allies, gives the best hope of averting a third world war and of escaping ruin should it break upon us. The speed and unanimity with which these far-reaching decisions were taken by Parliament sent a message forth to the world, of British national unity, rising above internal quarrels, and in spite of the virtual equipoise in this House between parties, grievously divided as they are. Only the magnitude and imminence of possible mortal dangers could have enabled us to present this encouraging example to the friends of peace and law all over the world.

While, however, this beneficial process was going forward in Parliament, the Government were secretly preparing a new and deadly blow at national unity and co-operation by an act of party aggression which was bound to plunge us, and evidently has plunged us, and all our affairs into violent controversy. The action of the Prime Minister in taking such a step at such a time and in such circumstances will, I believe, be sternly judged by the nation and by history. (*Laughter.*) Laughter will not carry it off.

Objection is always taken on the other side of the House to the argument that, judged by the votes cast at the recent election, here is a Government resting on a minority of 1,800,000 votes, and that this applies particularly to the nationalisation of iron and steel, which was a definite, direct and leading issue at the polls. The Prime Minister argues, if I understand him aright, that seats alone must count, and that the adverse votes of the people, however numerous, are irrelevant and should not influence Government policy. This theme does not do justice to the spirit of democratic institutions, nor is it at all in accordance with the way in which things have long been done in British public life.

The theory that a mandate has been granted by the election for any change, however sweeping, which has been mentioned only as an afterthought in the party manifesto, goes far beyond the bounds of reason. To claim that a majority of two, three, four, five, or whatever it is, gives the Government a title to impose on the other half of the nation, and in this case the larger half, any law they may choose to propose is carrying meticulous logic to dangerous extremes. It is liable to make the fortunes and fate of any country that is so circumstanced dependent entirely upon accident and hazard. Very few democratic and parliamentary constitutions in the world are so devoid of safeguards as our own. Half of the nation ought not, in such circumstances, to claim the right on so slender a margin to knock the other half about and ride rough-shod over it.

His Majesty's Government, in making far-reaching changes, should strive to act in harmony with a substantial preponderance of the mass of the people, and to interpret their general wish. That has always been the British way of working our constitution – there have been some lamentable exceptions, such as we see now – and it is only in this manner, I venture to think, that our affairs can be handled in the public interest and our unwritten constitution made to work. Parliament can, of course, only decide by voting, but Ministers of the Crown who force the House to take decisions which rend the nation upon the vote of an individual Member or a handful of Members one way or the other, are abusing their trusteeship. I am quite sure that the underlying common sense of British democracy will endorse these general propositions. If all this be true in tranquil times, how much more is it true in these days of common peril and common action in so many spheres?

The British steel industry is a prime feature in our exports and the foundation for a thousand secondary trades and productive processes. It has served us well in the dollar struggle, which was certainly serious enough, but now in addition we are urged by the Government to support and aid in a re-armament effort, which is almost unanimously regarded in this House to be urgent and vital. This armament effort cannot possibly proceed, except with the smooth, efficient working of the steel industry at its highest. To disturb and damage the steel industry at this juncture is to disturb and damage the whole effort which occupied our attention last week.

The record of the steel industry in recent years has been magnificent. The output of the industry has expanded from its low point of five million tons a year in 1931, when hon. Gentlemen opposite were largely in office – I mean their party was largely in office. As I say, it has expanded from five million tons a year in 1931 to 16 million tons at the present time. (An Hon. Member: 'Under a Labour Government'.) Yes, certainly, and why spoil it now? Each year when the present Government have set a production target, now vital to our re-armament, the steel industry has surpassed the target. Steel prices have risen by considerably less than the general rise in industrial prices, and are below the general level both in Europe and in the United States. The Government are, in fact, picking out for fundamental disturbance the one great basic industry which, of all others, deserves the prize for its efficiency and its smooth working expansion.

Nothing is more remarkable in the history of the British steel industry than the good relations that have prevailed between the employers, management and the employees. I have known in my time a succession of leaders in the iron and steel trade union. I served in the Government in the First World War with Mr John Hodge,[1] who became an important Minister. Then there was Arthur Pugh,[2] who fought a splendid fight on my behalf for a 12½ per cent increase which, as Minister of Munitions in 1917, I wished to give to what I may call the non-commissioned officers of war-time production, the men who teach the dilutees and have taught them. I am sure that on both sides of the House there is a general respect for Mr Pugh. I did not know Mr John Brown,[3] and I have only once, some time ago, met Mr Lincoln Evans, the present General Secretary of the Iron and Steel Trades Confederation.

These remarkable men have played their part over the last half century in the Labour movement, and in the relations of ownership and labour in the key and basic industry of iron and steel. It is a fact that, apart from the General Strike of 1926, there has never been, for more than 50 years, a dispute in the steel industry which was not settled by the well-known machinery without a major stoppage of work. Why this industry of all others should be selected for the malevolence of Socialist politicians is impossible to understand.

There was the argument that industries which were failures and could not give good service to the public should be nationalised, but here, especially since the war, there has been the finest service. There was the argument that better service would be given by the employees if they were under the direct control of the State. But there is really not much margin now for further effort on the part of the steel workers. They have outstripped all demands made

[1] John Hodge, 1855–1937. Helped form British Steel Smelters' Association, 1885. MP (Lab.) for Gorton Div., Lancs, 1906–23. Minister of Labour, 1916–17. President, British Iron Steel and Kindred Trades Association, 1916–31.

[2] Arthur Pugh, 1870–1955. General Secretary, Iron and Steel Trades Confederation and British Iron Steel and Kindred Trades Association, 1917–36. Chairman, General Council, TUC, 1925.

[3] John Wesley Brown, 1873–1944. MP (Cons.) for East Middlesbrough, 1922–3.

upon them. There is the argument that monopolies should not be in private hands and that so great an organisation as the steel trade should not be free from public control. But this is all met, and more than met, by the excellent arrangements which have been in force under the Iron and Steel Board, and which have proved and vindicated themselves by results.

This new stroke of party faction by a Government already confronted with a vast superiority of potentially hostile forces in Europe, and also by the challenge of the Communist fifth column here at home – this new stroke, I say, took all of us and our friends abroad by surprise. (*Interruption.*) There was no need for the Prime Minister to take this hazardous course at the present moment. (*Interruption.*) I am sorry that the facts that I am unfolding give so much pain and cause so much confusion, but it only shows the guilty consciences and lack of conviction which prevail on the benches opposite.

There was no need for the Prime Minister to take this hazardous course at the present moment. The Iron and Steel Act gives 12 months' latitude for fixing the vesting date. The reason given by the Minister of Supply on 28th April last year, nearly 18 months ago, for taking this flexibility was plainly stated by him: 'There may be industrial or political developments which would make it harmful for the iron and steel industry to be transferred on that date.' – (Official Report, 28 April 1949; Vol. 464, c. 430.) The date he was then speaking of was May, 1950. But all his reasons for safeguarding flexibility are stronger than ever today, and the provision which he made in the Act leaves the whole of 1951 open.

Now, however, the Government have decided to appoint a Corporation on 2nd October, in order to facilitate vesting at the earliest possible date at the beginning of 1951. Surely there have been both industrial and political developments which would make it harmful for the iron and steel industry to be transferred now, which would fully have justified using this provision of the Act to see whether, in the face of common danger and on the basis of common action in defence, this Parliament might not have had a better chance of life and honour.

Let us look at the industrial developments to which the Minister referred. There has been one which is of the first importance. A new proposal has been put forward by the economic committee of the Trades Union Congress, in their report to their Brighton congress, as an alternative to more nationalisation. The report, which was approved by the congress without any dissenting vote, states in paragraph 14 that if further extensions of nationalisation are to be justified and acceptable to the community the existing schemes must be shown to be successful. Some judgment is then attempted in the report upon the existing schemes, which are specifically referred to as 'coal, transport, electricity, gas and aviation'.

The report leads to the conclusion that it is only when these existing schemes can be shown to be generally successful that further schemes should be undertaken. The Trades Union Congress report says that no clear judgment can yet be reached on this. There is a significant paragraph in the report which reads: 'It may further be that in important cases a more practicable means of public control, alternative to both public ownership and development councils, would be the Statutory Board of Control on the lines of the tripartite body described in paragraphs 38 and 39' – that is to say, on the lines of the Iron and Steel Board. In order that there may be no mistake I will read the bulk of paragraphs 38 and 39, the relevant parts of which are as follows. First, paragraph 38: 'Development councils are not an appropriate form of organisation for all private industries, and particularly for those which are already highly integrated. Consequently, an alternative method of public control over private industry which deserves further consideration is the statutory Board of Control. This method has already been used by the Government, for a short period, in the iron and steel industry with the intention of securing a measure of control pending the transfer of the industry to public ownership.' (*Laughter.*) I am not quoting unfairly. Here is paragraph 39: 'The Iron and Steel Board was composed of representatives of employers and workpeople with independent members, one of whom was Chairman. Its functions were to review and supervise the industry's development schemes; to supervise the industry generally and to administer such direct controls over production, distribution and imports as were needed; and to advise on price policy. What the Board lacked, however, was power to compel private firms to undertake schemes when and where they were considered necessary in the public interest, and it had no authority to undertake such schemes on its own initiative. If this form of control were to be used in appropriate cases it might be possible to extend the functions of such Boards to include the power to set up their own undertakings, either to promote development which would otherwise not take place or to act as a yardstick of efficiency for the rest of the industry.' This report was presented to the Congress by Mr Lincoln Evans, the General Secretary of the Iron and Steel Trades Confederation, in a speech which contained a significant sentence. I did wish to quote a great part of the speech because I admired its thought and structure so much, but this particular sentence is a relevant one: 'If the community can exercise sufficient control over industry without accepting the risks and liabilities of ownership, that is a matter which should have the serious concern of everybody.' We on this side of the House are opposed to a general application of the principle of competitive public ownership which might, if clumsily or malevolently applied, lead to the ruin of slowly-built-up private businesses, or which, if unsuccessful, would only cause a further burden on the taxpayer. I stated the objections to this method in the strongest terms in the election, and I do not in any way recede from them.

I am informed that the Iron and Steel Federation do not by any means close the door upon such an extension of the powers of the late Iron and Steel Board, within the limits of their own industry, and that they would welcome a discussion of the subject. If that were so, and an agreement were reached, the steel question would be settled, at any rate for the present years of crisis – matters could always be renewed and revived – in a manner agreeable to both sides in the industry.

It would be a serious matter for Parliament to reject such a solution in a strictly limited sphere on the single ground of objecting in principle to competitive public ownership. Certainly both the grave and thoughtful report, which represents responsible conclusions of the Trades Union Congress, and the speech in which it was presented, are in refreshing contrast to the partisanship of His Majesty's Government. The Trades Union Congress report seems to seek practical solutions by agreement and good will. The Government are athirst with campaigning zeal and long for party triumph.

These pronouncements by the responsible trade union leaders, taken in conjunction with the dangers that surround us and draw near, might well have been made the subject of careful consideration not only by the Government but by the House. The flexibility of the Act gives the necessary time, and the general situation the natural impulse. I am told that the Iron and Steel Federation are agreed, not only in principle but in a great measure of detail, with the recommendations of the trade union report. Why, then, should the Government not take advantage of this wide area of agreement in the interval provided by the Act, in order to see if a better solution might not be offered to us than can be made by party warfare?

The decision of the Government to precipitate this internal crisis by immediately bringing the Iron and Steel Act into operation, setting up their Corporation, and fixing the vesting date at the earliest moment, has prevented a settlement which might well have led us into a very different atmosphere than is now, I fear, to be our fate. It might have given this House of Commons not only a longer life but an opportunity of rendering memorable service to the nation as a whole; but all that has been brushed aside by the Prime Minister, acting for the party doctrinaires on the political side of the Socialist movement. Instead of our being led into fairer fields, the Prime Minister has chosen to aggravate and inflame political and party strife, not by words only – we all use words in party politics – but by deeds. Actions speak louder than words and they cut deeper.

The initiative throughout has rested with the Government. The power of action is in their hands only. The choice was theirs, and the responsibility for what is going to happen falls on them and on them alone. The Opposition have neither the power to act nor the choice of methods which are open to the Government. It is our duty on grounds far wider than party to protest to the utmost of our strength against this sudden and untimely decision, arrived at in the midst of our perils and common action.

Why then should the Prime Minister, in the same week in which he had asked for and received the support of the whole House on the hard measures which he thought it his duty to propose for national safety, strike a blow at this vast and complicated sphere of our productive activities at the very moment when their smooth-working efficiency is more imperative than it ever was before? He is not only fomenting national discord for party purposes but, by disturbing the whole steel organisation, he is placing an obstacle, which may be very serious, in the way of the swift re-equipment of our Defence Services. This will, I am sure, be condemned all over the country and all over the free and friendly world as both reckless and unworthy.

The right hon. Gentleman the other day accused me of being party-minded. Everyone would naturally be shocked if a party leader were party-minded! But we are all party-minded in the baffling and unhappy period between election decisions and between parties so sharply divided and evenly balanced. However, the nation may be assured that, whatever the conduct of the present Government and dominant party may be, the Conservative and, I believe, the Liberal Oppositions will not, I am told, withdraw in any way the aid they have offered and given to all measures for the national defence. We shall do our utmost to encourage recruiting, and we shall be prepared to accept additional burdens wherever they are shown to be unavoidable.

I trust that all Conservatives and Liberals throughout the country will not be deterred by this vicious by-blow from doing their utmost to stimulate production in all its spheres. After all, there are millions of Conservative and Liberal trade unionists throughout the land, and I say to them from here – and my voice carries some distance – that they must not let themselves be discouraged in their national efforts by the political and party manoeuvres of a fanatical intelligentsia – the Home Secretary is laughing; I did not mean to include him in the intelligentsia.

(The Secretary of State for the Home Department Mr Ede: 'I was quite sure the right hon. Gentleman did not. That was why I laughed.')

The right hon. Gentleman could surely find other things in life to laugh at besides those which do not include himself. Otherwise life might be rather gloomy for him. I was saying – a fanatical intelligentsia obsessed by economic fallacies.

Let us look for a moment at the new Corporation which has been set up to be the agent and instrument of the Government in nationalising a curiously hand-picked but nonetheless dominant portion of the iron and steel industry, with far-reaching reactions throughout a far wider field. At its head is a millionaire Socialist,[1] a recent recruit, who, I am informed, enjoys the reputation of being one of the strictest and sternest monopolists in the country. Hardly any of the Corporation members have the slightest knowledge of the steel industry. One has already resigned.

How can this Corporation compare with the tripartite Iron and Steel Board which commends itself to the Trades Union Congress and is even held

---

[1] Steven Hardie, 1885–1969. Served in WWI, 1914–19 (despatches thrice, DSO). Chairman, Jute Working Party, 1946–7. Chairman, Iron and Steel Corporation of Great Britain, 1950–2.

up as an alternative model and has proved itself in every respect by its notable success? This change can only mean an immense impoverishment of the brain-power and experience which we never required more than we do now and profound disturbance of the life of the whole industry and of its innumerable ramifications.

Leaders of the steel industry, both employers' and workers' representatives, have declined to become members of the new Corporation. Can we blame them for refusing to identify themselves with a policy which they consider – and I think rightly – wrong and prejudicial to the work to which they have given their lives and a policy which they claim was disapproved by the nation at the General Election? They will, I am sure, continue to manage their particular firms, in so far as they are allowed to, in a faithful and loyal effort to limit the harm which is being so wantonly done, but no man can be blamed for refusing to take personal responsibility for an experiment of which he wholly disapproves and which he is sure will be harmful and for which, in his opinion, no decisive mandate has been given by the electors.

No doubt in the conflict so gratuitously forced upon us, these men will be covered with abuse and slime by the party opposite. If they are attacked, let me read what the Minister of Supply said in the House of Commons on 16th November, 1949. It has been quoted before but it is very necessary that it should receive the widest publicity at this moment. He said: 'In an atmosphere of political tension and uncertainty it would plainly be unwise to proceed now with the selection of individuals to serve on the Corporation. Men who may well be best suited for this responsible task might understandably be reluctant to commit themselves to accepting such a position, and throw up their present jobs, as long as they think there is a possibility, however remote, that the Corporation may not, after all, be established. . . . I think that right hon. and hon. Members on both sides of the House will agree that the success of the nationalised industry will depend to a considerable extent on the calibre of the men serving on the Corporation, and that it would be folly – a word we have heard in other quarters – to rush our selection of these people unnecessarily.' – (Official Report, 16th November, 1949; Vol. 469, c. 2042–3.) I have a long past of speeches to look back upon, but it always refreshes me to look back on something which I said a year or two or even 10 years ago and to find out that it exactly fits the circumstances of the moment. I therefore offer my congratulations to the Minister of Supply who, nearly a year before the event, forecast this picture of the situation with astonishing accuracy and not entirely without happy colouring.

The word 'folly' is mentioned. I take that word and also the mood from *The Times* and *The Manchester Guardian* – those eminent symbols of wise, measured, superior judgment and responsibility. We are bound to proclaim the 'folly' of the proposals for immediate action which are now thrust upon us.

We believe that the Iron and Steel Act now to be brought into immediate force will seriously damage the efficiency of production through the centralisation of responsibility which the new Corporation will involve. We believe that added risks and burdens will be thrown on to the taxpayer. We believe that the position of consumers who are also manufacturers in relation to prices and other matters will be further weakened by vesting control in a public ownership Corporation in the place of an impartial non-ownership public board.

We believe that the position of labour in the industries affected will be weakened by concentrating control in a Corporation identified with ownership in the place of an impartial public board on which an active and responsible labour interest was jointly represented together with the management. We believe that the trade unions in their report, and the Iron and Steel industry in particular, have offered a solution which, from every angle, offers superior advantage both to the employees and to the safety and progress of our country.

The Government supporters place some hopes upon being able to darken counsel by spreading the allegation that the Conservative and Liberal Parties were willing, under the Schuman Plan – get ready to cheer now; a long breath – to hand over British iron and steel to the control of a supra-national European cartel which would have the power to close any mine or factory in Britain by a majority vote.

I do not think hon. Gentlemen – and I gather that from their rather quiescent mood today – will get very far with this falsehood in any prolonged national discussion. (An Hon. Member: 'Wait and see.')

We thought, and we still think, that the representatives of the Government could perfectly well have gone to Paris and taken part in the discussions, it being clearly understood by all parties that they could break them off at any moment. (*Laughter.*) I have often gone to discussions which I could break off at any moment. (*Laughter.*) Do not be too sure that there may not be other discussions which can be broken off at any moment. There may be discussions in this House which the House may decide to break off at a suitable moment. As I have just said, the representatives of the Government could perfectly well have gone to Paris and taken part in the discussions, it being clearly understood that they could be broken off, and that in any case all the results were to be submitted for ratification to the House of Commons and all the other national Parliaments concerned.

It would have been an advantage not only to Europe but to our own steel industry for British representatives to have been present at meetings upon a project which carried with it many hopes for the ending of the Franco-German quarrels which have wrecked Europe in our lifetime and, by removing them, thus to strengthen the foundations of peace. We might have helped others and helped ourselves, and we should have run no risk at being committed to anything in the slightest degree – (Hon. Members: 'Oh'.) – which affected the full control of the House of Commons.

We may, indeed, be encouraged by the adoption of this argument as an electioneering tactic, because it shows how weak is the Government case upon the main issues that lie before us.

(Mr Harrison:[1] 'This is one of your weakest efforts.')

The hon. Member may set himself up as a judge, but I must ask him to take his place in the general assembly of the House and not to assume that his will be the casting vote upon a decision of such moment.

There is another point I must mention before I close. On Friday last, the Minister of Labour made a serious statement to us about the Communist conspiracy to disturb and cripple our industrial life. He told us of the steps which were being taken, and of the possibility that legislation would be required. We are entirely at one with the Government in grappling with the Communist menace in our midst, and we shall no doubt support any legislation brought before the House, provided that the normal foundations of British liberty are not affected and that the right to strike, upon which British trade unionism is founded, is not in any way impaired when it is used by responsible official trade unionists.

(Mr Harrison: 'What did you do to the railwaymen in 1911?')

We must also preserve our sense of proportion. It seems difficult to believe that the activities of the small number of Communists in our midst could at the present time inflict upon our defensive effort, or upon our national unity, anything like the injury that will be done to us all by this Act of party sabotage.

Now let me say what would be the policy of the Conservative Party – (*Laughter.*) Why should hon. Members opposite laugh? I have never seen that side of the House behave so disreputably. It does not affect me with 50 years' experience. I have seen many awkward situations. Hon. Members opposite only reveal the deep, internal, mental and moral malaise which distresses and disturbs their consciences.

Now let me say what is the policy of the Conservative Party, and, judging from the public declarations, of the Liberal Party also, on iron and steel. (*Laughter.*) I like hon. Members to laugh. It may be undeserved but it may not be unrequited. What is now, and what will be the policy of the Conservative Party should the burden of public affairs be entrusted to us?

(Mr Shurmer: 'Never!')

We shall, if we should obtain the responsibility and the power in any future which is possible to foresee, repeal the existing Iron and Steel Act, irrespective of whether the vesting date has occurred or not. We shall then proceed to revive the solution which has been set forth in the Trades Union Congress Report and which is accepted by the Iron and Steel Federation, and we shall set up again the tripartite Board, which has been proved to have worked so well. This would be the policy if we had the power, either before or after another General Election.

[1] James Harrison, 1899–1959. MP (Lab.) for Nottingham East, 1945–55; for Nottingham North, 1955–9.

The Prime Minister seemed vexed the other day because I had described him as 'sullenly resolved to lead only half the nation'. Certainly he has provided us with an illustration of my words this afternoon. It is, however, a compliment to anyone that they should be considered to have a chance of leading the nation. It is that hope which lends the highest honour to public life. Is he not, I ask him, throwing away a golden opportunity of serving the whole nation at a crisis in its fate? Take the famous words of Mr Gladstone: Think well, think wisely, think not for the moment but for the days which are to come. Let me, however, state the position in clear and unmistakable terms. If the Government were even now, even at this moment, to allow an effort to be made to settle the steel question on the lines suggested by the Trades Union Congress report, which are accepted by the employers, and to agree to use the latitude they have fortunately reserved to postpone the operation of the Act, we might well reach an all-party agreement within the lifetime of the present House of Commons. If the right hon. Gentleman says now that he will postpone the operation of the Act within its approved compass with a view to pursuing with common sense and good will a settlement on lines that apparently have the approval of the trade unions and the Steel Federation, I will, of course, at once withdraw this Motion. On the other hand, if he remains set upon his wrongful course, we have no choice but to resist him to the utmost of our strength. And let there be no doubt that the responsibility rests upon him for consequences which no one can foretell.

General Dwight D. Eisenhower to Winston S. Churchill
(Churchill papers, 4/52)

21 September 1950

Dear Winston,

I shall leave word for Lord Camrose at appropriate places to the effect that I shall be delighted to see him. I like him for himself but, beyond this, I am eager to hear from a friend of yours an intimate discussion of your current views.

Just recently the *New York Times* asked me whether I had any objection to your use, in your new book, of my 1942 views as expressed in the recorded minutes of a meeting at Algiers. I replied that I had no objection whatsoever to your using the minutes because – while I do not recall the exact details of the presentation I made at those meetings – the minutes certainly expressed what everybody else understood that I meant. Consequently, they were part of history.

I have had a lot of fun since I took up, in my somewhat miserable way, your hobby of painting. I have had no instruction, have no talent and certainly no justification for covering nice white canvas with the kind of daubs that seem constantly to spring from my brushes. Nevertheless, I like it tremendously and, in fact, have produced two or three little things that I like well enough to keep. This last paragraph was inspired by the fact that, only recently, I saw in one of our magazines some prints of certain of your pictures and I liked them very much indeed, particularly one of a mill by a small lake.

Eliahu Elath to Justice Felix Frankfurter[1]
(Government of Israel Archives)

24 September 1950

My dear Mr Justice,

We have recently returned from Israel, where we spent an absorbing month-and-a-half, exhilarated by the tremendous strides forward which the country is making and the faith and determination of the people, and yet seriously concerned at the grave economic situation. Israel's population has readily accepted a regime of austerity more severe than was that of many countries involved in World War II, and shrinks from no sacrifice in the dogged resolve that the doors of the Jewish state shall remain open for Jewish immigrants; but it stands to reason that it cannot alone provide for 18,000 new arrivals every month, most of them destitute. Funds from abroad fall seriously short of requirements, and powerful financial aid is needed.

On our way back we visited President Weizmann in Berne. He was then getting over a bout of illness and appeared almost well and in excellent spirits. I learned from his physicians, however, that in reality his health did give rise to concern, and that fears had been entertained that he might not recover from the pneumonia which he had contracted while staying at the Bürgenstock. When I saw him he conversed with animation and complete clarity of mind, but I did notice occasional lapses of memory; these, it is hoped, may disappear with the improvement of his physical condition.

I have dispatched to Professor Goodhart[2] the letter which you so kindly gave me, and hope for an early opportunity of meeting him.

I think you may be interested to hear that I have met Mr Winston Churchill. He was good enough to invite me to call on him on September 14th, after I had sent to him on September 11th a letter of introduction from Mr Bernard Baruch. Accordingly I went to his flat in Hyde Park Gate, where I found him in bed; the hour was 12.30 p.m., and he had evidently been at work for books and papers were all about him. Mr Churchill, who was smoking his customary

---

[1] Felix Frankfurter, 1882–1965. Graduated from Harvard Law School. Later taught administrative and occasionally criminal law at Harvard. Justice of US Supreme Court, 1939–62.

[2] Arthur Lehman Goodhart, 1891–1978. American-born academic jurist and lawyer. Educated at Hotchkiss School, Yale University and Trinity College, Cambridge. Fellow and Prof. of Jurisprudence, University of Oxford, 1931–51.

large cigar, received me with the utmost cordiality, saying that he always saw his friends in bed; he offered me a whisky and himself drank to the success of Israel. He kept me for an hour, himself doing most of the talking, but also listening with attention to my answers to questions.

Mr Churchill spoke with great admiration of our President, saying that Providence had blessed Israel by giving us one of the few great men of our time as leader and guide, a role for which he was eminently fitted by his statesmanship and scientific attainments.

The setting-up of our State, he said, ranked as a great event in the history of mankind, and he was proud of his own contribution towards it. He had himself been a Zionist all his life. He had been afraid at a certain time that all Britain had done for the National Home would be forgotten, but now there was no reason why Israel should not recognize that Britain was her best friend, and act accordingly. Romantic realists that they were, the British admired the determination and courage which gained Israel her independence, and fully understood the historical significance of the Jewish nation's rebirth.

Mr Churchill was movingly eloquent on the sufferings of the Jews throughout history, as a persecuted people and the faithful guardians of the Biblical heritage. The free Jewish nation, he declared, must preserve close association with the Book; Israel must guard the people's spiritual and moral inheritance.

He then made a lightning survey of the world situation, and dwelling on the Middle East, said that, for her own sake and that of the democracies, Israel must lose no time in developing her potential; she must hasten to become a strong political and military factor.

Expressing his pleasure at the fact that we had beaten the Egyptians, Churchill remarked that he did not care for any of the Arab States, with the sole exception of Jordan. Abdullah, whom he had 'placed on the throne', had proved the only reliable and stable ruler in that region.

The Israel Army was accorded great praise. He said he admired and respected it; but then he had always believed that the Jews had the moral and physical qualities to become the best soldiers of the Mediterranean and the Middle East. Once all his documents were published, we should see how he had supported the setting-up of a Jewish force during the Second World War.

He then put a number of questions to me. He showed interest in the composition of our Government and the way it works; in the extent of Communist danger in Israel; and in our schemes for agricultural and industrial development, especially in the Negev. He suggested that we make up for natural deficiencies by the use of scientific resources.

I have given you an extensive account of the interview, but cannot hope to convey any idea of his felicity of phrase.

In conclusion, he said that he would always be ready to give us any help he could.

Please forgive the length of this letter, but I felt that I wanted you to know of this interview.

My wife joins me in sending you and Mrs Frankfurter[1] cordial good wishes for the year just begun and kindest regards.

Winston S. Churchill to Prince Charles, Count of Flanders
(Churchill papers, 2/167)

30 September 1950

I venture to send you a copy of my new Volume on the War, which I hope will be of interest to you.

I have not thought it right to intrude upon Your Royal Highness in these last anxious months, but I should like now to express my feelings of admiration for the constitutional and selfless part which you have played in the revival of Belgium in the five difficult years after the war. Students of history will effectively recognise what a faithful servant you were to the unity of Belgium, to the maintenance of its Parliamentary and democratic institutions, and to the preservation of the monarchy itself. It is this certain verdict of posterity which will be your reward, and I am sure that it is the one which you would value the most.

Let me also thank you for your many gracious courtesies to me in recent years. I have the most pleasant memories of my visits to Brussels, and of painting excursions, and of the kindness with which I have been treated. But most of all I value our long talks together into the small hours of the morning. They have given me an enduring picture of a Prince whose resolve was to do his duty.

Pray convey my warm regards to Monsieur de Staercke,[2] and accept from my Wife and me the tribute of our highest respect.

---

[1] Marion A. Denman, 1891–1975. Married, 1919, Felix Frankfurter. Co-editor of *The Letters of Sacco and Vanzetti* (1928).

[2] André de Staercke, 1913–2001. Belgian politician and diplomat. CoS to Hubert Pierlot, 1942–5. Secretary of the Regent, 1945–50. Dutch representative at NATO, 1950–76.

October 1950

Lord Cherwell to Winston S. Churchill
(Churchill papers, 2/36)

2 October 1950

My dear Winston,

I return herewith the papers received from Major Clarke,[1] who used to work under Jefferis[2] at the little establishment we had at Whitchurch called MDI.

Whether it would do any good to forward it to DCIGS (weapons) I do not know, but I am quite sure that the proposals are sound and ought to have been put into effect long ago. We had very nearly perfected these weapons, which seem likely to be greatly superior to any existing mortar bombs as Major Clarke says. But despite urgent entreaties all this work was stopped, Jefferis and his colleagues were not allowed to finish off their developments and MDI was closed down. This applies not only to mortar bombs but to several other anti-tank inventions and the like.

As a result of this, I understand that the weapons which are issued to the troops are just the same today as those with which we ended the war and that there have been scarcely any improvements and practically no new developments since 1945. From what I hear much the same could be said about rockets. Indeed it is difficult to see what useful results have been obtained in return for the tens of millions of pounds which have been spent on service research and development – quite apart from atomic energy.

I hope you will have a pleasant time in Denmark. The Camroses who

---

[1] Cecil Vandepeer Clarke, 1897–1961. British engineer and soldier. 2nd Lt, WWI. Worked as a special weapons designer during WWII.

[2] Millis Rowland Jefferis, 1899–1963. Joined Royal Engineers, 1918. Maj., 1937. Commanded 1st Field Sqn, Royal Engineers, 1937–9. Served in Norway, 1940 (despatches). Designer of bombs, mines, mortars and anti-tank rockets, working directly under Churchill (as Minister of Defence) at an experimental establishment at Whitchurch near Chequers, 1940–5. CBE, 1942. Brig., 1942. Knighted, 1945. Maj.-Gen., 1945. Deputy Engineer-in-Chief, India, 1946. Engineer-in-Chief, Pakistan, 1947–50. Chief Superintendent, Military Engineering Experimental Establishment, 1950–3.

visited Copenhagen said the whole country was looking forward with great excitement to your coming.

PS. I was sorry they did not adopt Harrod here. The other man will probably be a very good candidate, but I doubt whether he will be very distinguished member if elected.

Winston S. Churchill to Major-General Sir Stewart Menzies
(Churchill papers, 2/101)

3 October 1950
Private

My dear Menzies,

I have received the following information from a most trustworthy man I know well and have measured. SS General Walter Schellenberg[1] was the assistant to Himmler. It is claimed on his behalf that he prevented many horrible things. The Swiss believe that on two occasions he dissuaded Hitler from invading Switzerland, and in one way and another he saved thousands of peoples' lives. However this may be, I am assured he is now living in seclusion under Government protection in Switzerland. As things have got easier he has I suppose come out of his hole. He has written, or is writing, a book about the German Secret Service from the inside. If the above assumptions are true it should be of great interest to many people, but to none more than you. It might be well worth your while to make enquiries.

Anyhow please let me know whether you have heard about this, and what you think should or can be done to clear up the facts.

---

[1] Walter Friedrich Schellenberg, 1910–52. Born in Saarbrücken, Germany. Educated at Bonn, 1929–33. Joined NSDAP and SS, 1933. Married, 1938, Käthe Kortekamp (div.); 1940, Irene Grosse-Schönepauk: three children. Himmler's personal aide and special plenipotentiary, 1939–42. Deputy Director of *Reichssicherheitshauptamt*, 1942. Intelligence Chief, 1944. Arrested, June 1945; testified against other Nazis at Nuremberg Trials, 1945–6; Ministries Trials, 1949. Sentenced to six years' imprisonment. Released on grounds of poor health, 1951. During his imprisonment, wrote his memoirs, *The Labyrinth, Memoirs of Walter Schellenberg, Hitler's Chief of Counterintelligence* (1956).

October 1950

Isie Smuts to Winston S. Churchill
(Churchill papers, 2/176)

4 October 1950

Dear Winston Churchill,

That is what we always call you, so I hope you won't mind my addressing you like this. You and I have never met, but you and the Oubaas[1] were always great friends and you also know my two sons, Japie[2] and Jannie, and Jannie esp often speaks of you and Auntie Clem and of the pleasant times he spent with you at Chequers during the war.

Tonight I am just writing to thank you for all the love and friendship you showed the Oubaas and for all the good things you said about him on several occasions. Particularly on his 80th birthday when you made that speech at the birthday dinner in Johannesburg. It was a very fine speech and he appreciated it very much indeed. I have often wanted to write to you to express my gratitude for all you have been to him and all you have done for him, but I did not like to bother a busy man like you. And when you lost that big election we all felt dreadfully sorry and we could not understand how your own people could let down a man who had done so much for them. We little knew then that the same fate was waiting for your friend in South Africa and that very sad, dark days were ahead for him too. But now he is gone and his place is empty – just at a time when he is needed so badly and there is no one to take his place.

He was ill a long time and suffered much and we passed many anxious days, hoping and praying for his recovery, but not knowing what the morrow would bring. But on that last day he had been particularly bright and happy; we had gone for two long motor drives over the veld which he loved so well and he had taken dinner with us all and been very cheerful and full of fun – And then he had gone to his bedroom and collapsed suddenly, so suddenly indeed that all was over before we even realised it. He was then dressed in his Field Marshal's uniform with red tabs and war ribbons and looked very peaceful and beautiful as he lay there. And after a big military funeral and services in the church and crematorium his ashes have been put on a hilltop on the farm where he often walked and where he now rests with Japie and three other little ones. You were very dear to the Oubaas and he thought very highly of you and I thought you might like to know this. He was looking forward to seeing you in England on his way to Cambridge, but it was not to be and he was called Home instead.

I am an old woman now, nearly 80 myself, but I want you to know how I thank you for your loving sympathy and how I share your sorrow at present. God bless you, Winston, and keep you strong!

---

[1] Nickname meaning 'senior', in years and/or rank.

[2] Jakob Daniel Smuts, 1906–48. Known as 'Japie'. Elder son of FM Jan Smuts. Educated at Cambridge. Served with British Army, 1939–45. Temp. Capt., 1944. Manager of Welgedacht mine near Springs, South Africa, 1947–8.

Eliahu Elath to Winston S. Churchill
(Churchill papers, 2/96)

6 October 1950

Dear Mr Churchill,

It gives me the utmost pleasure to convey to you congratulations from my Government and the Israel Knesset, to which I add my personal good wishes, on the occasion of your Parliamentary jubilee.[1]

The people of Israel, for whom democracy is the only conceivable way of life, cherish their own young Parliament, and deeply admire the British House of Commons which has been its model. They look up to you as an illustrious representative of all that is best in British Parliamentary tradition, and wish that you may long continue to adorn the British political scene.

I take this opportunity to thank you again for sparing me so much of your time when I had the privilege of calling on you. I was greatly encouraged by your very kind reception and your friendly interest in my country.

Winston S. Churchill: speech
('In the Balance', pages 386–9)

10 October 1950   Copenhagen University

HONORARY DEGREE CONFERMENT

I must express my thanks to the Rector and to the Prorector for what they have said in their far too complimentary speeches – much that no man should hear till dead. I am most grateful for what Professor Hansen[2] has said about England, or Britain. I was only the servant of my country and had I, at any moment, failed to express her unflinching resolve to fight and conquer, I should at once have been rightly cast aside.

Here I may mention a debt which Britain owes to the ancient Danes. We did not regard it as such at the time. The Danish sailors from the 'long ships' who fought ashore as soldiers brought with them into England a new principle represented by a class, the peasant-yeoman-proprietor. The sailors became soldiers. The soldiers became farmers. The whole of the East of England thus received a class of cultivators who, except for the purposes of common defence, owed allegiance to none. Particularly in East Anglia did this sturdy, upstanding stock take root. As time passed they forgot the sea; they forgot the army; and thought only of the land – their own land, as it became. They merged with the English.

---

[1] Churchill was elected MP for the first time on 1 Oct. 1900, representing Oldham, Manchester. He took his seat in 1901.
[2] Hans Marinus Hansen, Rector of Copenhagen University, 1948–56.

The Danish settlement differed entirely from the Saxon settlement 400 years earlier. There was no idea of exterminating the older population. The gulf between the Danes and Saxons in no way resembled that which divided the Saxons from the Britons. Human and natural relations were established. The bloodstream of these vigorous individualists, proud and successful men of the sword, mingled henceforward in our island race. A vivifying, potent, lasting and resurgent quality was added to the breed. As modern steel is hardened by the alloy of special metals in comparatively small quantities, this strong strain of individualism, based upon land ownership, was afterwards to play a persistent part, not only in the blood but in the politics of England. The centuries did not destroy their original firmness of character nor their deep attachment to the soil. All through English history this strain continued to play its part, and to this day the peculiar esteem in which law and freedom are held by the English-speaking peoples in every quarter of the globe may be shrewdly and justly referred to a Viking source.

I am very proud and very grateful to receive a Degree of Philosophy from the famous University of Copenhagen. As life unfolds I have been astonished to find how many more degrees I have received than I have passed examinations. I was never very good at those. But now I am treated as if I were quite a learned man. This is a good argument for not being discouraged by the failures or shortcomings of youth but to persevere and go on trying to learn all your life.

I never had the advantage of a university education. But it is a great privilege and the more widely extended, the better for any country. It should not be looked upon as something to end with youth but as a key to open many doors of thought and knowledge. A university education ought to be a guide to the reading of a lifetime. We should impress upon those who have its advantages the importance of reading the great books of the world and the literature of one's own country. One who has profited from university education has a wide choice. He need never be idle or bored. He is free from that vice of the modern age which requires something new not only every day but every two or three hours of the day. There is a good saying, which you may have heard before, that when a new book comes out you should read an old one, though I perhaps should not recommend too rigid an application!

The University of Copenhagen is justly renowned for its advance in the scientific sphere. I feel sure also that the humanities play their living and vital part in your curriculum. The first duty of a university is to teach wisdom, not a trade; character, not technicalities. We want a lot of engineers in the modern world, but we do not want a world of engineers. We want some scientists, but we must make sure that science is our servant and not our master. It may well be that the human race has already found out more than its imperfect and incomplete stature will enable it to bear. My old venerable friend, Lord Hugh Cecil as he was (Lord Quickswood), described science recently as 'organized curiosity'.

Take all these improvements in locomotion; what do they do but make the world grow smaller, making the heritage of man a far more restricted sphere. It is very convenient, of course, to flash about but, after all, the life of man does not depend upon the external conditions to which he is subjected, provided, of course, that they are compatible with the maintenance of his existence. No amount of technical knowledge can replace the comprehension of the humanities or the study of history and philosophy. The advantages of the nineteenth century, the literary age, have been largely put aside by this terrible twentieth century with all its confusion and exhaustion of mankind.

This is a time when a firm grip on all the essential verities and values of humanity and civilization should be the central care of the universities of Europe. The Greek and Latin philosophers seemed quite unconscious that their society was based on slavery. They propounded all the finest theories of freedom, but they were not conscious of the false foundations on which they all lived.

At least nowadays we cherish freedom, freedom for all. The light of Christian ethics remains the most precious guide. Their revival and application is a practical need, whether spiritual or secular in nature; whether to those who find comfort and solace in revealed religion or those who have to face the mystery of human destiny alone. And on this foundation only will come the grace of life and that reconciliation of the right of the individual with the needs of society from which the happiness, the safety and the glory of mankind may spring.

Winston S. Churchill to J. R. Greenwood[1]
(*Churchill papers, 2/110*)

10 October 1950

Dear Mr Greenwood,

I have much pleasure in returning you the books you sent me signed. ~~May I at the same time express my compliments to you on having been forbidden by the Socialist Government to export your machines to Russia. I am sure you will bear this intervention in your Company with the fortitude and patriotism you have already shown.~~[2] There is no doubt your letter to me[3] had its effect on policy and perhaps on history.

---

[1] Chairman and Managing Director of Craven Brothers Ltd, Manchester.
[2] Churchill struck out these two sentences before sending the letter.
[3] The letter included evidence that several firms in Britain, including Craven Brothers Ltd of Manchester, were making machine tools for Russia.

Winston S. Churchill: speech notes
(Churchill papers, 2/102)

11 October 1950
Students' Association
Danish–British Society
Copenhagen

All the greatest things are simple,
    and many can be expressed in a single word:
    Freedom; Justice; Honour; Duty;
        Mercy; Hope.

We who hv come together there tonight,
    we also can express our purpose
        in a single word –
            'Europe'.

At school we learned from the maps hung on the walls,
    and the advice of our teachers
        tt there is a continent called Europe.

I remember quite well being taught this as a child,
    and after living a long time,
        I still believe it is true.

However professional geographers now tell us
    tt the Continent of Europe
        is really only the peninsula
            of the Asiatic land mass.

I must tell you in all faith
    tt that I feel tt this wd be
        an arid and uninspiring conclusion,

and, for myself, I distinctly prefer
    what I was taught when I was a boy.

=

A young English writer has said
    tt the real demarcation betw Europe & Asia
        is no chain of mountains,
            no natural frontier,

               but a system of beliefs and ideas
                         wh
               we call Western Civilization.

'In the rich pattern of this culture
         there are many strands;

               the Hebrew belief in God;
                    the Christian message of compassion
                              and redemption;

               the Greek love of truth,
                    beauty and goodness;

         the Roman genius for law.

Europe is a spiritual conception.

But if men cease to hold that conception
         in their minds,
         cease to feel its worth in their hearts,
         it will die.'

=

These words express my faith.

We should proclaim our resolve
         tt the spiritual conception of Europe
                    shall not die.

We declare, on the contrary,
         tt it shall live and shine,

               and cast a redeeming illumination
                    upon a world of confusion and woe.

That is what has brought us all together
         here this evening,
                    and tt is what is going to keep us
                         all together

       until our goal is reached
       and our hopes are realized.

=

In our task of reviving the glories
       and happiness of Europe,
              and her prosperity,

       it can certainly be said
              tt we start at the bottom of her fortunes.

Here is the fairest, most temperate,
       most fertile area of the globe.

The influence end the power of Europe
       and of Christendom hv for centuries
              shaped and dominated the course of
                                                history.

The sons and daughters of Europe
       hv gone forth and carried their message
              to every part of the world.

Religion, law, learning, art, science,
       industry, throughout the world

       all bear, in so many lands,
              under every sky and in every clime,

       the stamp of European origin,
              or the trace of European influence.

=

But what is Europe now?

It is a rubble-heap, a charnel-house,
       a breeding-ground of pestilence and hate.

Ancient nationalistic feuds and modern
       ideological factions

    distract and infuriate
        the unhappy, hungry populations.

Evil teachers urge the paying-off old scores
    w mathematical precision,

    and false guides point to unsparing
            retribution
    as the pathway to prosperity.

Is there then to be no respite?

Has Europe's mission come to an end?

Has she nothing to give to the world
    but the contagion of the Black Death?

Are her peoples to go on harrying & tormenting
    one another by war and vengeance

    until all tt invests human life
        w dignity and comfort
            has bn obliterated?

Are the States of Europe to continue for ever
    to squander the first fruits of their toil
        upon the erection of new barriers,

    military fortifications and tariff walls
        and passport networds
            against one another?

Are we Europeans to become incapable,
    w all our tropical and colonial dependencies,

    w all our long-created trading connections,

    w all tt modern production
        and transportation can do,

    of even averting famine
        fm the mass of our peoples?

Are we all through our poverty
    and our quarrels,

      for ever to be a burden and a danger
        to the rest of the world?

Do we imagine tt we can be carried forward
    indefinitely upon the shoulders
        – broad though they be –
        of the USA?

=

If the people of Europe resolve
    to come together and work together
      for mutual advantage,

    to exchange blessings instead of curses,

    they still hv it in their power
      to sweep away the horrors and miseries
        wh surround them,

and to allow the streams of freedom,
    happiness and abundance
      to begin again their healing flow.

=

After each of the fearful wars
    wh hv ravaged the lives and homes
      of mankind,

    the hopes of humanity hv centred
      upon the creation of an instrument
        of world govt.

    capable at least of maintaining peace & law
      among men.

We accept without question the world supremacy
    of the UNO.

In the Constitution agreed at San Francisco
    direct provision was made
        for regional organizations to be formed.

United Europe will form one major Regional
                                entity.

There is the United States w all its dependencies
    there is the Soviet Union;
        there is the Brit. Empire & Commonwealth;

    and there is Europe,
        w wh Gt. Brit. Is profoundly blended.

Here are the four main pillars of the world
    Temple of Peace.

Let us make sure tt they will all bear
    the weight wh will be imposed
        and reposed upon them.

=

We hope to reach again a Europe
    purged of the slavery of ancient days

        in wh men will be as proud to say,
            'I am a European,'

        as once they were to say
            'Civis Romanus sum'.

We hope to see a Europe
    where men of every country
        will think as much of being a European

as of belonging to their native land,

and wherever they go in this wide domain
    will truly feel,
        'Here I am at home.'

How simple it would all be,
    and how crowned w glory,
        if that should ever arise.

=

When I first began writing
    about the United States of Europe
some 15 years ago,

      I wondered whether the USA would regard
        such a development as antagonistic
          to their interest,
            or even contrary to their safety.

But all that has passed away.

The whole movement of American opinion
    is favourable to the revival
      and re-creation of Europe.

This is surely not unnatural
    when we remember how the manhood of the USA
      has twice in a lifetime bn forced
        to re-cross the Atlantic Ocean

    and give their lives and shed their blood
      and pour out their treasure

    as the results of wars
      originating fm ancient European feuds.

One cannot be surprised
    tt they wd like to see
      a peaceful and united Europe
        taking its place among
          the foundations of the World
            Organization
          to wh they are devoted.

Far fm encountering any opposition
    or prejudice fm the Gt. Republic
      of the New World,

October 1950

   our Movement has had their blessing
       and their aid.

=

We see before our eyes
    hundreds of millions of humble homes
        in Europe
            and in lands outside

   wh hv bn affected by war.

Are they never to hv a chance to thrive
   and flourish?

Is the honest, faithful, breadwinner
   never to be able to reap fruits of his
            labour?

Can he never bring up his children
   in health and joy
       and w the hopes of better days?

Can he never be free fm the fear
   of foreign invasion,

     the crash of the bomb or the shell,
       the tramp of the hostile patrol,

     or what is even worse,
       the knock upon his door
         of the political police
           to take the loved one
              far fm the protection
                of law and justice,

     when all the time
       by one spontaneous effort of his will
         he could wake fm all these nightmare
               horrors

     and stand forth in his manhood,
       free in the broad light of day?

We do not of course pretend tt United Europe
    provides the final and complete solution
        to all the problems
            of international relationships.

The creation of an authoritative,
    all-powerful world order

    is the ultimate aim towards wh
        we must strive.

Unless some effective World Super-Government
    can be set up
        and brought quickly into action,

    the prospects for peace
        and human progress
            are dark and doubtful.

=

Without a United Europe
    there is no sure prospect of world govt.

It is the urgent and indispensable step
    towards the realization of that ideal.

After the First Gt. War
    the League of Nations tried to build,

    without the aid of the USA,
    an international order
        upon a weak, divided Europe.

Its failure cost us dear.

4 years hv passed since, at Zürich,
    I sought to revive the conception
        of European unity.

There was nothing new in the idea.

We may go back to Charlemagne
    and Henry IV

    but never was the application of the principle
        more necessary.

Since I spoke at Zürich
    progress has bn unceasing.

What was then but an aspiration
    is today becoming one
        of the dominant facts in world affairs.

The progress we hv made towards our goal
    in these 4 years
        has far outstripped
            all tt we dared to hope for.

Before attempting to unite Europe,
    we had to unite ourselves.

At the Hague Congress in 1948
    we brought together
        nearly a thousand leading men and women
            in Europe
                of all Parties and all countries.

There we proclaimed our resolve
    to work together
        to achieve the broad unity of Europe.

=

Out of the Hague Congress
    there emerged the demand
        for the creation of a European Parlt.

The campaign launched at The Hague
    was rapidly crowned w success.

Exactly a year later
    the Govts. of 10 nations of W Europe

signed a treaty setting up
   the Council of Europe at Strasbourg.

The European Movement has had distinguished
   support fm Denmark.

Mr Frode Jakobsen,[1]
   leader of the Underground Organization,
      is a delegate at Strasbourg.

He has shown the same independence
   and resolution in this wide European field

      as for the cause of Danish freedom
         during the German occupation.

He is a Socialist by political allegiance.

Then we hv Prof. Thorkil Kristensen,[2]
   former Finance Minister,
      who is a Liberal,

   and Mr Kraft,[3]
      former Defence Minister,
         who is a Conservative.

Thus Denmark has bn fully represented
   in all the work we hv bn doing.

We are all encouraged by the progress
   wh the European Movement is making.

We feel conscious of the inherent force
   of the cause we serve
      and the idea wh guides us.

---

[1] Frode Jakobsen, 1906–97. Danish writer and politician best known for his contribution to the Danish resistance during WWII. Formed a secret resistance organization in 1941 called 'Ring' or 'Ringen'.

[2] Thorkill Kristensen, 1899–1989. Born in Fløjstrup, Denmark. Member, Presidency of Labour and Conciliation Board, 1940–5. Member, Danish Parliament (Left), 1945–60. Finance Minister, 1945–7, 1950–3. Prof., Copenhagen Business School, 1947–60.

[3] Ole Bjørn Kraft, 1893–1980. Born in Copenhagen, Denmark. Member, Danish Parliament (Cons.), 1926–64. Delegate to League of Nations, 1933–7. Member, Council of Europe, 1949–50. Minister of Foreign Affairs, 1950–3. Member, Nordic Council, 1953–64; Chairman of its Economic Committee, 1958.

It shines like a bright steady light.

In the confusion and exhaustion of our age
> it shines all the brighter
>> because of the storms wh gather around us.

=

We find our principle of union
> in the moral sphere.

We take our stand on human rights,
> as set forth in the Charter of Human Rights
>> proclaimed by the UNO.

Any European country
> tt sincerely accepts and adopts
>> the principles there set forth

> will be welcomed to the European Union.

=

Our principles are set forth w clarity:
> love of freedom;
> hostility to totalitarianism of every kind;
> the humble and conscientious search for truth;
> respect for the human personality
>> and for the individual as an individual.

These moral values,
> founded alike on Christian faith and charity
>> and on the critical spirit of rationalism,

>> are the message of our 2,000-year-old
>>> European civilization and culture.

Let us make sure tt,
> enjoying as we do
>> this common inheritance,

>> we take all necessary steps
>>> lest it be wasted or cast away.

October 1950

The Europe we seek to unite is <u>all</u> Europe,
    and in our Movement we must strive
        by every means in our power

    to help bring about conditions
        in wh our fellow-Europeans
            now living in the satellite States
                of Russia
        will be united w us.

=

The task of our Movement is to foster,
    encourage and develop
        the sense of being Europeans;

    a pride in Europe
        and what she has stood for,

    and of confidence in the greatness
        of our common mission in the future.

These sentiments can only be brought about
    by Europeans in different countries
        learning to know each other better.

In all this work
    the new European Assembly
        can play a vital part.

It can create and express
    a European public opinion,
    a common European point of view,
    and the sense of all tt we hv in common.

We are all agreed tt our ultimate aim
    – the unity and freedom of the whole of
                    Europe –
    can only be achieved by stages.

Our first task is to unite the free countries.

OCTOBER 1950

We stretch our hands out
    in gratitude and goodwill
        across the ocean
             to the other half of the free world,

    whose generous help has bn forthcoming
        to assist our stricken Continent
            on the path of recovery.

We express our admiration of the gt US
    and of the part they are playing
        not only in the restoration
            of European economy

but also in our security and defence.

Marshall Aid achieved European recovery.

The Brussels Pact was the beginning
    of the European Army.

The Atlantic Pact will give us all
    and especially the Scandinavian nations

    the guarantee tt the cause of freedom
        in the Old World
            will not be aggressively assailed

    without effective help
        fm the gt Republic across the ocean.

Every step tt we hv made
    towards closer European unity

    has encountered the vehement hostility
        of the Communist Party in every country;

    and the more we hv progressed
        the more bitter has become
            the Communist campaign of vilification.

This is certainly no surprise.

The tyranny upon wh Communism is founded,
	the hatred fm wh it draws its strength,
		and the poverty on wh it thrives

	wd all of them be directly threatened
		by the establishment
			of a united, peaceful and prosperous
				Europe.

The tide of Communism in Europe
	wh only 2 years ago engulfed Czechoslovakia,

	has for the moment bn halted
		and its parliamentary strength
			has bn greatly reduced
				by the good sense of the electors
					in all our countries.

This is due to a large extent
	to the economic integration
		of the peoples of Europe

	wh has bn so powerfully aided and encouraged
		by the USA.

There is no doubt tt Communism as an ideology
	is losing ground in all countries
		where free speech is allowed
			and parliamentary institutions thrive;

	but behind the sub-human chatter
		of Communist doctrinaires
			stands the armed might
				of the Kremlin oligarchy

	wh while frothing words of peace
		has since the war maintained
			larger armed forces,
				trained and organized

	than almost all the countries in the world
		put together.

October 1950

For some time now Western Europe has bn living
    under the stress and pressure
        of the Communist 'cold' war.

But it is in the Far East and not in Europe
    tt the first blow in the 'hot' war
        has fallen.

It may be tt the growing unity and solidarity
    of the Nations of the West
        has influenced the Soviet aggressors.

The free peoples of Europe
    hv certainly not added to their dangers,
        however gt they may be,
            by proclaiming as they hv
                through the Council of Europe
                      and through the Atlantic Pact
                              their resolve to fight together,

    and if need be to die together,
        in defence of the freedom
            wh is their joint treasure.

But the world problem at the present moment
    is indivisible.

The cause of Europe is the cause
    of world progress and freedom.

The battle wh the US wi our support
    are fighting in Korea
        under the authority of the UN

    is as much the battle of Europe
        as if it were being fought out here
            in our own towns and countryside.

=

A United Europe is one of the indispensable
    pillars of world peace.

By itself Europe is not enough.

But unless a strong, united and valiant Europe
    can be created,

        there is little hope of peace,
            freedom or civilization
                for the rest of mankind.

=

Those who are best informed among us
    will not be those who underrate our dangers.

They are grave.

If they have not broken upon us
    it is only because our adversaries
        are content to let them grow.

We should certainly not ward them off
    or reduce them
        by showing any failure
            in unity, conviction or will-power.

It is the exact opposite wh is true.

We Europeans shd best preserve world peace
    and our own survival by standing together

        and bringing all the force
            of a steadily and swiftly uniting
                continent
                    to aid of the world organization

        in the perils and problems
            w wh it is confronted.

Once again the path of duty
    is the path alike of safety and of honour.

Winston S. Churchill: speech
('In the Balance', pages 389–402)

14 October 1950   Conservative Annual Conference
Blackpool

SITUATION AT HOME AND ABROAD

I thank you all for your kindness which constitutes the bright flash in the serious times in which we live. We may all rejoice at the favourable turn the war has taken in Korea. The United States under Mr Truman's leadership, and with the formal and moral sanction and support of the United Nations Organization, acted with courage and promptness in resisting aggression by Communists inspired by Moscow. We are glad that British forces have been represented with those of other Commonwealth countries, and several other members of the world instrument, to preserve peace. We admire the skilful conduct of the campaign by that great soldier, General MacArthur, and we all hope that it may be brought to a speedy conclusion so that the people of Korea may be liberated and, if I may quote Mr Stalin's message on the subject, free to shape the future life of their country in accordance with democratic institutions.

We must also hope that the forces of the free peoples of the world will not become too deeply involved in the Far East, because the dangers there are upon a very small scale compared to those which, as the Government have told us, tower up against us on the Continent of Europe. The Soviet onslaught upon South Korea has made many people realize the perils which menace us, and all that is left of European civilization. The success which has been gained by firm action in Korea must not lull us into a sense of false security. None the less I believe that what has happened in Korea has set world peace for the time being on stronger foundations, and that there may be time though no one can guarantee it to build up a European Army, with strong aid from Britain, the United States and Canada, for the defence of the famous and ancient States and races who have no thought or aim but to dwell in peace, and who at present are protected from Soviet Communist ambitions only by the vast American superiority in the atomic bomb. I do not believe that war is inevitable. On the contrary, I believe that the hopes of reaching a peaceful settlement with Russia have been improved by what has happened in Korea. I need scarcely say, speaking in the name of the Conservative Party, that we shall continue to give our help to the Government in any wise measures, either of defence or diplomacy, which they may ask or take to establish that peace and freedom arising from moral and material strength, which is our heart's desire.

It is a year to a day since it was my duty to address the Conference of the National Union. At that time we lay under the burden of uncertainty in our political life. A socialist Government held the levers of power. At any moment selected by them they could advise a dissolution of Parliament, and all that that brings with it in more than 600 constituencies. We had no means of knowing what their intentions were, and everyone felt that the marshalling-up of the two sides of the nation, if prolonged for an indefinite period, would be harmful to our common interests at home and abroad.

Well, a year has passed and I could describe the situation in more accurate terms than those I have used. There can be no doubt that it is bad for our country, I dare say for any country, to dwell for a long time in an electioneering atmosphere. His Majesty's Government should be thinking all the time for all the people, and for the long-term welfare and safety of our country over whose fortunes they have the honour, and it is a great honour, to preside. Any party Government has, every four or five years, to think about winning an election by gaining a party majority. Even His Majesty's Opposition cannot shut its eyes to that aspect. This is one of the ways, part of the process by which we make sure that the people own the Government and not the Government the people. But it is not good for our society, or for our survival as a leading power, that we should continue for long periods to be dominated by party politics, and that the two halves of the nation, who have to sink or swim together, whatever they may say or do, should have to face each other all the time like pugilists in the boxing ring.

Therefore I thought when we last met that the undue prolongation of a period of partisan conflict would hurt us all and weaken our influence in the world. But now when everyone can see that everything has become far more grave, we find ourselves in the same condition of party strife, impending elections and uncertainty as to when polling day will be fixed, as we did a year ago. Nothing could put a greater strain upon our island or hamper it more in making its gift of long-experienced guidance to the counsels and actions of the civilized world. We are a nation vehemently divided on domestic issues, but profoundly united as an island race, who have so long given guidance to the world on the progress of democracy, and who, in the greatest crisis of human affairs, kept the flag flying of British freedom, and not of British freedom only. How can Britain do herself justice or play her rightful part whilst this suspense continues? Yet it is Mr Attlee's policy to aggravate the uncertainty and prolong the strain. That is a responsibility which is a grave one for him and one which he bears in a personal sense.

Great harm was done to national interests at the General Election by the policy of the Liberal Party in running hopeless or vote-splitting candidatures in hundreds of constituencies. Nevertheless when the new Parliament met I thought it right to look forward and not to look back, and to do my best to help come together in the House of Commons and the country all those forces which are united in opposition to Socialism, and to the nationalization of the means of production, distribution and exchange. This process of union, of merging, has been making progress in many ways and in many constituencies.

The Liberals themselves have, of course, declared at their Party Conference that they are very strongly opposed to agreements or pacts to limit or in any way reduce the number of candidates at Parliamentary Elections. No offer has been made by us to them. Still it is my hope that in view of the great body of doctrine and principle which the opponents of Socialism hold in common an increasingly friendly mood will result in spite of minor provocations and churlishness, and that we shall, as I put it at Edinburgh in May,[1] so conduct our affairs at the next election as to help each other as much as we can, and harm as little as we must.

It is also the duty of constituency associations to think not only of their own local position but also of the part which they have to play in our national struggle against the aggressive and unscrupulous forces which endanger the future greatness of Britain, and I trust that the constituencies will also consider carefully, especially those who can make the return of a candidate to Parliament almost a certainty, the selection of genuine active trade unionists and others representing the view of our brothers and sisters in the working classes of the nation with whom Tory democracy is for ever profoundly associated. I hope they will consider facilitating the return of such representatives to Parliament when the opportunities occur.

I invite you to compliment our party representatives upon their work in the House. We have already forced the Government to adopt five measures which we urged and they derided at the election. We have made them abolish the whole system of direction of labour in time of peace. We have made them abandon Mr Morrison's slimy plan of making permanent the Supplies and Services Act. This was the foundation of the means of interfering with our normal peacetime lives and will require to be sanctioned by Parliament only from year to year instead of being made permanent as the Socialists would have wished. We have made them abolish petrol rationing, which they said was impossible. They have raised the pay of the Services, as we had advocated for three years past. They have restored the cut of 25,000 houses which they had inflicted upon the housing programme. These are all proofs that our members in the House of Commons are able to make their efforts felt and that what we told the country at the last election, although we have not had the direction of affairs, has in many ways already been fulfilled.

[. . .]

I have been impressed and encouraged by what I was told of the gust of passion which swept through our body yesterday about the shameful failure of the Socialist housing policy. Without the struggles imposed by extreme need, without the spur of seeing bomb-shattered sites, the Tory Government before

---

[1] Speech reproduced above (pp. 1746–54).

the war was building 350,000 houses a year. We were doing this mainly by private enterprise and with comparatively few subsidies. Moreover, under the slum clearance campaign begun in 1933, 1,500,000 slum dwellers have been rehoused in England and Wales. In the last year before the war slum dwellers were moving into better houses at a rate of 1,000 people a day. If the war had not brought the Conservatives' programme to a stop, England would today be free from slumdom. The Socialist Government have been found utterly incapable of resuming slum clearance. Now the Minister, who has called us all 'vermin', you can remember his name for yourself and the name he called you after five years of power in time of peace, can only build us 200,000 houses at triple the expense and with enormous subsidies. I do not wonder at your anger. We share it with you. I agree with you that housing comes first in the whole field of social progress.

Well was it said of old: 'The foxes have holes; the birds of the air have nests, but the Son of Man hath nowhere to lay his head.' It is strange that this task of housing should have been deemed and found insuperable by those who have the handling of our affairs. For there is no object except self-preservation which could enlist behind it a greater drive of British ingenuity and effort.

You have demanded that the target that we should put in our programme should be 300,000 a year. I accept it as our first priority in time of peace. I and the Government of which I was head are the authors of all that is real and effective in the Health Act. We took all the decisions and had the plans worked out in great detail, but it seems to me that houses and homes come even before the reform of the health system, etc. Houses and homes come before health, because overcrowding and slum dwellings are fatal to the family life and breed more illnesses than the doctors can cure. It may well be that hard times lie before us, and that the opportunities for making a better Britain, which these foolish Ministers have squandered for party purposes, will not be open to those who take their places when the nation records its final verdict. No one can tell how the rearmament burden may strike our industry and finances, but this I am sure, that homes for people to live in and rear their families in decent independence come ever in front of wigs, spectacles and false teeth, however desirable all these may be and however urgent it is to press forward with meeting the public requirements in every respect. However our fortunes may go and from whatever angle the pressures of life may come, the Tory Party puts homes for the people in the very forefront of all schemes of our development.

We are ready for an election whenever it may come. Thanks to Lord Woolton's energy and inspiration, we now have a national organization second to none. It has achieved results far above the expectations which any of us had when the National Union last met in conference at Blackpool four years ago. Also I have the aid of colleagues whose ability has been proved in war and peace. In Mr Eden I have a friend and helper upon whom any office of the

State, however great, could be devolved with the assurance that he has both given the proof and acquired the experience to do full justice to it.

In February's election we added nearly 3,000,000 to our poll, and 100 members to our Parliamentary representation. Now we need just one more heave. If all of us make the best use of whatever time and strength we may have, we may well fling this Socialist Government out of power and replace it by a broad, progressive and tolerant administration, the slave neither of class nor of dogma but putting national need first and determined to make Britain and the British Empire once again both great and free.

Winston S. Churchill to Jock Colville
(Churchill papers, 2/168)

15 October 1950

My dear Jock,

I was very much obliged to you for your letter,[1] and I am sorry that pressure of work has prevented me from replying to it before now. As you surmise, Foot's review 'left me cold', but I am nevertheless grateful to you for taking the trouble of putting the facts as you remember them in writing to the Foreign Office Librarian.

I hope all goes well with you both.

Winston S. Churchill to Eliahu Elath
(Churchill papers, 2/168)

15 October 1950

My dear Minister,

I was very pleased to receive your letter of October 6,[2] and I thank you for it. It was indeed kind of you to write, and I appreciate very much the good wishes you sent me. Pray convey to your Government and the Parliament of your country, and accept yourself, my warm thanks.

---

[1] Of Aug. 3, reproduced above (pp. 1822–3).
[2] Reproduced above (p. 1885).

Winston S. Churchill to George Bernard Shaw[1]
(Churchill papers, 2/176)

18 October 1950

My dear Bernard Shaw,

Thank you so much for your letter and self sketches. It was a great pleasure to receive them from you and still more to learn of your recovery.

Let me retaliate as only an author can by sending you these few self sketches of a different character.

Perhaps they will persuade you to take up Painting as a Pastime.

Winston S. Churchill: speech
('In the Balance', pages 403–5)

20 October 1950   Empress Hall, Earls Court, London

FIFTH ALAMEIN REUNION

I always regard it as a great compliment and as a real pleasure to be invited to your Alamein reunions. May they long continue. I feel that comrades and veterans by this kind of meeting, year after year, realize the treasures of memory which they have acquired during rough and hard times in the field, but afterwards there's always something for a few pals to talk together about, and certainly they have managed to get a few pals here tonight.

General Montgomery has now great and important functions to discharge. But when all his toil and labour of life is over, and when he has finished entertaining any persons who nourish evil designs upon our country as they should be entertained, I earnestly hope that his great gifts of organizing public entertainment will be at the service of the English-speaking peoples all over the world. For certainly he puts as much thought and taste and skill and quality into an annual show like this as might easily have gained a great battle.

Ladies and gentlemen, Alamein was indeed a milestone and more than that, a turning-point in the war. You know I write books nowadays. I'm calling my fourth volume *The Hinge of Fate*. Certainly Alamein was where the hinge turned. Till then we'd survived; after that we conquered. Till then we had nothing but misfortune to record, but also we were alive and kicking. But after Alamein, the long months of strife lay before us, but we never suffered – or hardly ever suffered – any failure in the field. And thus we came to our triumphant end of that terrible war. How hard it is that destiny compels us after all our victories, to face new, strange, gathering dangers. But I agree with the Field-Marshal, that we face them united; we face them united in

---

[1] Inscribed in a gift copy of *Painting as a Pastime*.

spite of certain difficulties which I should not attempt to dwell upon here.

Well, it is impossible, as I said to you last year, that we should not remain deeply divided at a time when a General Election is approaching. It is only in countries where tyrants rule and from which freedom is banished, that a sham uniformity is imposed, and that strong, sharp differences are concealed or forbidden expression. If they were not, if there were not to be full and free discussion here, then voting would be a mere pretence as in Soviet Russia or in the other Communist satellite countries.

My own hope – and this is what I said a year ago – is that this period of unavoidable party strife will be as short as possible. A year has passed, and still these evil conditions afflict us. But in all matters affecting national safety and honour we must act together. We have done so. The House of Commons passed in a single day the new National Service Act and thus sent a message to the world that Britain on the greatest issues is still a united nation. She kept the flag of freedom flying in the war and for a long time – or it seemed a long time – she kept it flying alone. She could never have done that had she not been united. We are united now; more than that, we are not alone. All the might of the United States and all the authority of the United Nations is with us, and I agree with the Field-Marshal that here is the true hope of peace.

The danger in Europe is serious. Montgomery – Monty, as we are allowed to call him, at any rate tonight – Monty has a great office and great responsibilities to bear. There must be created a European Army with the aid of the Atlantic Powers which can make a front in Europe, and thus enable the nations on both sides of the Iron Curtain to return to normal relations instead of war being held off only by the terrible, sinister weapon of the atomic bomb in which the United States, thank God, have overwhelming superiority.

How to build this Western Front, this front towards the East, how to build it is now a main preoccupation not of this country alone but of all those who are working with us. For more than forty years I have been the friend of France in peace and in war, in all the ups and downs of fortune, and never lost my faith in the French people and the French spirit. But where is the French Army today? Alas, it has still to be re-created. There are no means of making a defensive front for the West without the aid of the German nation in defending at least the soil they live on from Russian Communist aggression and subjugation. I trust that France will not become an obstacle to this idea of common defence. I feel sure that she will rise to the occasion, and I do not believe that the United States would make the great efforts and sacrifices which are required from her in Europe if narrow and unwise views prevailed.

I say now, these words of serious import to you. We wish the Field-Marshal all good fortune in his work; in its success lies one of our surest hopes in averting the horrors of another way. We must all try our utmost to sustain the authority of the United Nations and thus lay broad and solid foundations for a world where law and freedom reign.

Winston S. Churchill: speech
(Hansard)

24 October 1950   House of Commons

MOTION FOR ADDRESS IN REPLY[1]

Mr Churchill (Woodford): I beg to second the Motion. We are all indebted to the Prime Minister for his speech. We join with him in all that he has said. His speech was full of memories and showed how comprehending he is of the background to our daily political life. We associate ourselves with the tributes he has paid to the work of the Select Committee and my right hon. Friend the Member for Horsham (Earl Winterton), to the designers, architects and engineers, and also to the craftsmen to whom the rebuilding of the House of Commons, was, I am sure, a labour of love. Also we support him in expressing our thanks to the Government of the British Empire and Commonwealth of Nations, whose representatives we welcome and whose gifts we cherish.

I must thank the Prime Minister for his personal reference to me. I am a child of the House of Commons and have been here – or there, I am not quite sure which it is – I believe longer than anyone. I was much upset when I was violently thrown out of my collective cradle. I certainly wanted to get back to it as soon as possible. Now the day has dawned, the hour almost come, and I am grateful to His Majesty's Government for the persistence and vigour and efficiency which they have shown in the task of rebuilding in so short a time and amidst many other competitive pre-occupations.

It excites world wonder in the Parliamentary countries that we should build a Chamber, starting afresh, which can only seat two-thirds of its Members. It is difficult to explain this to those who do not know our ways. They cannot easily be made to understand why we consider that the intensity, passion, intimacy, informality and spontaneity of our Debates constitute the personality of the House of Commons and endow it at once with its focus and its strength.

It is likely, Mr Speaker – I must warn you of this beforehand – that there will be differences of opinion even among ourselves when we meet again in our old Chamber with so many Members who have only known this spacious abode.[2] However, I believe that in ten or twenty years everyone will be thoroughly used to it. Anyhow, even if they do not, I do not see what they are going to do about it. For good or for ill the old gangs of all parties are united. They are a pretty tough lot when they stand together like that. That is not to say that

---

[1] In reply to His Majesty's Gracious Message: 'Your former place of sitting has now been rebuilt. Adorned and equipped with the generous gifts received from other countries of the British Commonwealth of Nations it is ready for your use as a new House of Commons. It is my pleasure that you do occupy the new Chamber on Thursday, the 26th day of October.'

[2] The House of Lords, where the Commons had been meeting since the Commons Chamber had been destroyed by a German bomb on 10 May 1941. See Churchill's speech of 28 Oct. 1943, reproduced in *The Churchill Documents*, vol. 19, *Fateful Questions, September 1943 to April 1944*, pp. 685–90.

minor changes may not be necessary, and we can quite easily, without raising structural issues, work our way into the most convenient arrangements for our lighting, heating, hearing, overhearing and ventilation technicalities.

I have been astonished to look what lies behind what I may call the presentation of Government policy in this matter. I trust that all their subterranean designs are not of such a highly elaborate and, on the whole, effective character. An hon. Member who was wounded by being deprived of the pomp and perquisite of a special seat and special desk for himself in the Chamber might find himself fully consoled by the material comforts and conveniences which he can derive from his life underground.

The Prime Minister said – and said quite truly – that the House of Commons was the workshop of democracy. But it has other claims too. It is the champion of the people against executive oppression. I am not making a party point; that is quite unfitting on such an occasion. But the House of Commons has ever been the controller and, if need be, the changer of the rulers of the day and of the Ministers appointed by the Crown. It stands forever against oligarchy and one-man power. All these traditions, which have brought us into being over hundreds of years, carrying a large portion of the commanding thought of the human race with us, all these traditions received new draughts of life as the franchise was extended until it became universal. The House of Commons stands for freedom and law, and this is the message which the Mother of Parliaments has proved itself capable of proclaiming to the world at large.

I have the honour to second the Motion.

Winston S. Churchill to Lieutenant-Colonel Bill Deakin
(Churchill papers, 4/24)

24 October 1950

My dear Bill,

I send you herewith some rough notes I have put down about the Greek mutiny in April, 1944. I should be much obliged if you could find time to correct, strengthen and improve this account, which I have no doubt is incorrect in many places.

I also send you the record I had printed at the time. More is needed about ELAS and EAM, and how the Communist aggression developed in Greece. The whole story is important because it leads up in Volume VI (to come), to my flight with Anthony to Athens on Christmas Eve, 1944, and to all that business there, which was much condemned in England and America at the time, but was afterwards carried through by the British Socialist and American Governments. The theme thus runs on.

Please see what you can do therefore to improve this chapter. The printers are still on strike, so we may as well give them a fairly finished copy when they are open again. Please make the best contribution which you can, and let me have the text back, together with the documents, as soon as possible. If you are unable to find any time to attend to this, I should be glad to have it back at once. It is the only copy.

Winston S. Churchill: speech
(Hansard)

26 October 1950 House of Commons

THE NEW CHAMBER OF THE HOUSE OF COMMONS

On a Motion moved by the Prime Minister that this House welcomes the Speakers, Presiding Officers and other representatives of the countries of the British Commonwealth and Empire who have come from overseas to join in the ceremonies on the occasion of the opening of the new Chamber; expresses its thanks to their Legislatures and peoples for the generous gifts with which the Chamber is adorned; and assures them that their presence on this day will be a source of inspiration in the years to come.

In rising today at a somewhat mature time in my life to make my maiden speech in this House, I feel, Mr Speaker, that I ought not to conceal from you that I have a past. I have many memories of the air space in which we sit, now enclosed afresh in its traditional garments; in fact, I think I was the last person to speak here until today, and I have a lively recollection of the support and stern enthusiasm with which my remarks were then received.

There has, no doubt, been some change in the seating arrangements, for, so far as my recollection serves, I sat on the other side of the House. The Prime Minister and his principal colleagues sat beside me there. It seemed to me a very good and satisfactory way of carrying on our affairs. But then came a loud explosion, or perhaps that explosion was later on. So many things happened at the time that it was a little difficult to keep track of them, and my recollection may well be at fault. Anyhow, here we all are again, and, if everything is not entirely to our liking, we have, at any rate, much to be thankful for. The Prime Minister spoke of the parliamentary systems shared in common by so many of us represented here, and how they combine the effective Government of the majority with full respect for the views of the minority. That certainly is the high ideal towards which we should all perseveringly strive.

I can also congratulate His Majesty's Government upon many features of the new Chamber which they have erected. When I think of all that lies above us, around us and beneath us, it seems to me that, so far as accommodation is concerned, His Majesty's Ministers have managed to combine in a singularly harmonious manner the greatest need of the greatest number with a reasonable preservation of the privileges of the deserving few.

It gives me great pleasure to support the Motion which the Prime Minister has commended to us in his admirable and eloquent speech. We are proud today to have with us the Speakers and representatives of so many famous States and Governments of the British Empire and Commonwealth of nations. We rejoice that they are with us to see our phoenix rising again from its ashes, and we wish them all the same good luck should they at any time be exposed to similar vicissitudes.

There is no doubt that the assembly of the Speakers of so many free and fairly elected Parliaments on this historic occasion shows a new link of unity and mutual comprehension which has sprung into being in our world-wide society and family. It is our hope, sir, which perhaps we may be pardoned for expressing upon an occasion for rejoicing such as this, that the tolerant, flexible, yet enduring relationship which binds us all together by ties which none could put on paper but are dear to all, may some day be expanded to cover all the peoples and races of the world in a sensible, friendly and unbreakable association, and so give mankind, for the first time, their chance of enjoying the personal freedom which is their right and the material well-being which science and peace can so easily place at their disposal.

Lord Camrose: note
(Camrose papers)

26 October 1950

When W drove down to see the House of Commons after the bombing his chauffeur followed him in to see the ruins. W said – 'I shall never live to sit in the Commons Chamber again.'

The chauffeur wrote to him recently reminding him of this remark.

Today he took his seat in the House. He says Colonist II must have made up his mind to make it a double event by winning at Newmarket.

When he bought Colonist II, Clemmie expressed grave doubts and Miss Sturdee felt so strongly about it that she sent him a note expressing her fear that it would affect his great reputation.

He stayed in bed the whole of 13th October resting 'and not to chance bad luck'.

Perhaps, he said quizzically, Providence had given him Colonist as a comfort for his old age and to console him for disappointments.

Attlee has been very nice in naming the Arch in the House of Commons after him. He had expressed the opinion that he thought it ought to be preserved but had no idea that it should be given his name.

Thinks the King's Speech will indicate what the intentions of the Government are in regard to an Election. Feels the tide is now running against the Government; that the leaders realise that they have got to go slow in social measures and that the official Party would like to take on the role of the Liberal Party of thirty or forty years ago.

Winston S. Churchill to Lord Cherwell
(Churchill papers, 2/36)

27 October 1950

My dear Prof,

Thank you for your letter of October 2,[1] returning the papers from Major Clarke. I have noted what you say, and shall keep the material by me.

Our visit to Denmark was enjoyable, but very strenuous. We had a tremendous reception.

Henry Spalding[2] to Winston S. Churchill
(Churchill papers, 2/117)

28 October 1950

Dear Mr Churchill,

On 3rd April last you wrote asking me to keep you 'fully informed' as to the possibilities of a conference with Mr Stalin with a view to reaching a general settlement. I am not sure from your secretary's letter of 16th May whether you wish me to write again.

Sir S. Radhakrishnan,[3] the Indian Ambassador to Moscow, has recently returned to Oxford (where he remains Professor of Eastern Religions and Ethics). He tells me he has had frank, unofficial talks with Gromyko (the Acting Foreign Minister) and other members of the Soviet Foreign Office. Since his return he has discussed the situation with the Prime Minister and other statesmen.

If you should wish to see him, he would be glad to call on you any day between 7th and 30th November (except on Wednesdays and Fridays) or next term. In the Christmas vacation he will go to India and in March return to Moscow till the Autumn.

---

[1] Reproduced above (pp. 1882–3).
[2] Henry Norman Spalding, 1877–1953. British philanthropist. Educated at Oxford University. Barrister-at-law, Lincoln's Inn, 1906. Married, 1909, Nellie Maud Emma Cayford. Deputy Director, Welfare Dept, Ministry of Munitions, 1915–18. Founded Spalding Chair of Eastern Religions and Ethics at Oxford, 1936. Aided Oxford University's gifts of books to universities in China, 1939; to universities in devastated areas of Europe and Asia, 1947.
[3] Sarvepalli Radhakrishnan, 1888–1975. Prof. of Philosophy, University of Mysore, 1918–21. King George V Prof. of Philosophy, University of Calcutta, 1921–32. Knighted, 1931. Vice-Chancellor of Andhra University, 1931–6. Spalding Prof. of Eastern Religions and Ethics, Oxford University, 1936–52. Indian Representative to UNESCO, 1946–52. Ambassador to Soviet Union, 1949–52. Vice-President of India, 1952–62. President of India, 1962–7. Nominated 15 times for Nobel Prize in Literature and 11 times for Nobel Peace Prize.

October 1950

Winston S. Churchill: speech
(Hansard)

31 October 1950   House of Commons

DEBATE ON THE ADDRESS[1]

[. . .]
    This is the point I wish to make. It is treated as a most extraordinary thing that we should ask that the rate of building should be raised from 200,000 to 300,000 houses a year. That is the view. We are denounced for having suggested it. It seems to show a great lack of proportion. It shows the want of a sense of proportion to suppose that such a measure as building at the rate of 100,000 houses a year more, is an impossible task for this powerful, well-equipped country. Why should it be thought to be impossible? One hundred thousand houses at £1,500 apiece would cost £150 million a year. That ought not to be beyond our capacity if the priorities are properly arranged (Hon Members: 'Ah!') I repeat, if the priorities are properly arranged and a reasonable time is given to collect the materials. (Hon Members: 'Ah!') Certainly, it should not be impossible for a country to find this rearrangement of the expenditure of £150 million. It should not be impossible to find a method of doing that, when we consider that our national income is around £10,000 million a year. It is a very small re-adjustment and re-arrangement of priorities that is required. Do not let the House be put off by all this, what I should have thought was to hon. Members opposite, most injurious outcry and clamour that to try to get 300,000 houses a year built for the people was a wrong and shameful thing for anyone to advocate. We shall ask the House next week to inflict its censure upon the Government for this grave mismanagement of the housing problem.
    I have only one word more to say, because interruptions have rather lengthened what I had thought of saying. Uncertainty – I address myself very much to the Prime Minister – about the election date is harmful. Prolongation of the electioneering atmosphere is not good for the country. A year has passed already in which we have lived in that atmosphere, which can be felt here; even already it has infected our new House. The House is not at its best when parties are so evenly balanced and on the verge of another appeal. The increasing rigidity of party discipline deprives debate of much of its value as a means of influencing opinion except out of doors. All kinds of uncertainties are created in every direction; all kinds of animosities and rancours are fed and worked up, on both sides, I fully admit – (Hon Members: 'Oh'.) Certainly; and I cannot think it good for the country that this should continue. The Prime Minister deliberately tries to increase and prolong this uncertainty. He says, 'The election will come at the moment when I judge fit.'

---

[1] The King's Speech to the new Parliament.

Mrs Braddock (Liverpool, Exchange):[1] What did the right hon. Gentleman do in 1945?

Mr Shurmer: What would the right hon. Gentleman do?

Mr Churchill: The hon. Gentleman asked what I would do. I say deliberately that I think that if I were with the responsibilities of the Prime Minister at this juncture, having regard to all that is going on, I would try to limit the uncertainty as much as possible. I would carefully consider whether I could not say, provided we had the control of events, that we should not have an election until a certain date. I think it is well worthy of consideration whether that might not be of general interest. (*Interruption.*) I have finished. Of course, it is very natural that anyone should like to feel that he can keep the rest of his countrymen on tenterhooks and that we are always awaiting the moment when he shall give the signal. All I can say is that I am quite satisfied that the right hon. Gentleman is indulging his personal power in these matters in a manner most costly to the community and harmful to all large enduring interests of the State.

---

[1] Elizabeth Margaret Braddock, 1899–1970. Member, Liverpool County Borough Council, 1930–61. President, Liverpool Trades and Labour Council, 1944. MP (Lab.) for Liverpool Exchange, 1945–70. Royal Commissioner for Mental Health, 1953–7.

November 1950

Lieutenant-General Sir Henry Pownall to Winston S. Churchill
(Churchill papers, 4/333)[1]

1 November 1950

Mr Churchill,

I send you herewith a copy of the record of the meeting on Jan 24 1944 at which time Mulberry Harbour was discussed; and also two papers which were considered at that meeting.

There was a further meeting on Jan 31 on the same subject, of which also I enclose the record.

I will send you a more general paper on the development of Mulberry in a few days' time.

Prince Charles, Count of Flanders to Winston S. Churchill
(Churchill papers, 2/167)

2 November 1950

Cher Monsieur Churchill,

I feel very penitent at the great delay in my answer to your kind message.[2]

I'm sure, however, you will understand the reason and thus excuse me.

I have been asked and very forcibly at that to leave the Palace both by my family and by the Prime Minister. This has caused me great work and a lot more trouble.

Today, thank God, my packing is almost over and the sadness which might have resulted from having to leave a house where I have lived 40 years has been replaced by anger and disgust.

Nevertheless your letter has been like a ray of sunshine in the middle of the storm of hostility which has been shown me by my predecessor and his followers since his return.

[1] This letter was handwritten.
[2] Of Sep. 30, reproduced above (p. 1881).

It is for me a very great compensation and a real encouragement for the future, that a man like you should approve my 5 years in office and I thank you with all my heart.

I received your book with much pleasure as your works have always greatly interested me.

I hope to see you again one day when I have had time to settle down again and in a home of my own.

Veuillez presenter mes hommages à Madame Churchill et accepter pour vous même l'expression, de mes sentiments, bien dévoués.[1]

Lady Phillips to Winston S. Churchill
(Churchill papers, 2/171)

4 November 1950

Dear Mr Churchill,

A friend whose Army son is serving with the British occupation in Germany has just returned from a visit to him.

I am most distressed by all she has told me, and I felt I must write to you, who is so understanding and ask if anything can be done.

She tells me there is no co-operation between the Allies and the Germans, no attempt is being made to foster any feeling, but hate between us. Even the British children if they meet German children say 'Get away you dirty Germans we hate you' and words to that effect, will this attitude help for the future of our own security with the Germans if the young grow up hating each other? It is no good dwelling on the past, we all fully realize what Germany has done in the last two wars, but this attitude will only widen the gap of any hope of understanding between us, it all seems to be breeding more hatred and bitterness for the future. Of course a firm hand over them is needed and never must they have the power again to bring all the misery and devastation they have caused in the last two wars. But can't we achieve something by trying to stop horrible hatred and ill will that seems so prevalent between us.

I express myself so badly – but I do want to know can nothing be done and is it impossible to train them in the right way of thinking and feeling and make them like us a little better.

Also can nothing be done to let the Army of occupation have say their own cows and livestock without having to have the dreadful NAAFI meat and Tin milk etc. lovely food, milk meat in the German shops, but all for the Germans – (who won this war?) – and if we are to keep off their food etc: why can't we send farmers or land girls over to feed and nourish our men and families of the occupation Army. (I believe land girls have been disbanded, a great pity.)

---

[1] 'Please present my respects to Mrs Churchill and accept for yourself the same expression of my most devoted sentiments.'

Please forgive me. I get rather wrought up by things I hear, and feel that you are the one who can do something about it if anyone can.

Winston S. Churchill: speech
(Hansard)

6 November 1950

HOUSING

The hon. Member for Blackley (Mr Diamond)[1] seemed, so far as I was able to follow his argument, to be somewhat diverging from the party lead in addressing himself to the merits of the subject. I am bound to say that it seemed to me that he raised many interesting points in the course of his speech. Of course, one quite realised the strength of feeling behind his condemnation of vote-catching in any form. That is certainly greatly to be deplored. On the other hand, we must not forget what votes are. Votes are the means by which the poorest people in the country and all people in the country can make sure that they get their vital needs attended to. (Hon. Members: 'Hear, hear'.)

I am very glad to begin upon a note which receives such universal approbation because I had, after all, been led to expect that I was to undergo very unpleasant ordeals on this day. The Prime Minister – he is not here at the moment – expressed his confidence that the Minister of Health would 'wipe the floor' with me. As I have only just taken the floor and he has already exhausted his right of speaking, I naturally feel a sensation of liberation and relief. But I cannot feel that this prospect, or the language of the Prime Minister, did justice to the grave issue open between the two parties and still less to the housing problem.

The suffering caused to millions of people by the want of houses throughout the island is a tragedy, and this is on quite a different level to any clashes that may occur across the Table, or across the Floor, between individual Members of the House. I think this Debate should end, as it has largely been maintained, upon a serious note, and I was very glad that my hon. Friends on this side of the House did not allow themselves to be provoked by taunts or abuse from an embarrassed party or a guilty Minister.

During the whole of the last Parliament the need for houses and the failure to supply them was constantly debated, and the outlines of the controversy are familiar to us all. It is necessary, however, to restate the salient points on the verge of an important Division. They may be summed up as follows: First, the expectations aroused by the Government's assurances and pledges in 1945;

[1] John Diamond, 1907–2004. Known as 'Jack'. MP (Lab.) for Blackley Div. of Manchester, 1945–51; for Gloucester, 1957–70. Chief Secretary to the Treasury, 1964–70. Private Secretary to Ministry of Works, 1946–7. Baron, 1970. Leader of Social Democratic Party in the House of Lords, 1982–8.

secondly, the extraordinary shortfall in their fulfilment; thirdly, the gravity of the position and prospects now before us; and, finally, the need and the hope of a new constructive effort. It is on these points I shall venture to dwell tonight.

The House knows only too well the catalogue of pledges and promises which were made to the people by the Socialist Party during the Election of 1945. All were renewed on many occasions by the responsible Ministers after they had obtained power and were fully acquainted with official facts and figures. A few examples will suffice – I do not wish to burden the House with them. The former Minister, Mr Charles Key,[1] said on 12th October, 1946: Six million houses are needed in the next 10 years. To get that figure we shall have to build 600,000 a year, but I believe that by temporary prefabs and things of that sort we shall be able to do it. The present Minister of Health said on 24th May, 1946: I confidently expect that before the next election every family in Great Britain will have a separate house. Again, two years later, on 24th April, 1948, he said: By the next General Election the back of the housing programme will have been broken. Contrast all this – and it could be multiplied to any extent; whole budgets of quotations are available – with the actual performances of the Socialist Government. In 1948 they had reached a total of 227,000 permanent houses. Since then, instead of getting better, things have got worse, and in 1949 the total of permanent houses was only 198,000. These results are indeed deplorable when we consider the crying need, the vehement demand and the immense subsidies now being paid, and when we compare the results with what was being done with hardly any subsidies, on a very small scale, before the late war broke upon us.

The Prime Minister said in the Debate last week: We consider that the 200,000 houses a year is an actual programme, a programme which is being carried out, and it is as nearly as possible the number of good houses which can be built with the available resources of labour and materials – (Official Report, 31st October, 1950; Vol. 480, c. 41). I must say that I think that statement cast a chill on the party opposite. On the other hand, it has certainly been endorsed today by the Minister of Health. He has confirmed it and in every way associated himself with it. That is his duty, and any exhibition of loyalty on his part to his chief might well excite approbation even beyond the limits of the Government Bench.

What a strange position we find ourselves in tonight. The Conservative Party ask for the house building to be raised to a rate of 300,000 a year at the earliest moment. The Prime Minister, the head of the Labour Party, supported by his most ardent champion, declares that 200,000 is the most that can be done. Our demand, which represents the wish and the will of the

---

[1] Charles William Key, 1883–1964. Cpl, Royal Garrison Artillery, 1914–19. Headmaster of schools in Hoxton and Poplar, 1919–22. MP (Lab.) for Bow and Bromley division of Poplar, 1940–50; for Poplar, 1950–64. Parliamentary Secretary to Ministry of Health, 1945–7. Minister of Works, 1947–50. Freedom of the Borough of Poplar, 1953.

nation, is dismissed in contemptuous terms and brushed aside with all sorts of aspersions on our motives. One would have thought it would have been welcome, and it might even have afforded a basis for common action.

The prime basic fact which stares us in the face tonight is that building at the rate of 200,000 a year in no way solves the problem. We do not make any progress with rehousing the people. We only keep level with houses which are already falling or have fallen into decay. The social evils affecting every aspect of our life, which are connected with the present housing shortage, are now presented to us by the Government as bound to continue, so far as can be seen, indefinitely. Sir, that situation is obviously intolerable.

Take the argument about comparing what was done in the five years after the First World War. There is this great difference between them. The first is that after the First World War there was no American aid. (Hon. Members: 'Cheap'.) On the contrary, a hard demand was pressed upon us for the repayment of war debts. The second is that there was practically no destruction by bombing in the First World War. Thirdly, the local authorities were virtually without experience of building in 1918. This time they had all the practical experience gained by the pre-war slum clearance and other municipal housing schemes. And finally, far more preparations were made by the war-time Government on this at the end of this war than were ever thought of in 1917 or 1918 – (*Interruption.*) I am talking of the National Coalition Government and, on this occasion, there are still one or two representatives of it on the Front Bench.

What stood out dramatically at the end of this war was the need to rehouse the people after the devastation of the bombing. We all recognised it in the National Coalition. I will read to the House what I wrote at the time to some of my colleagues – on 5th April, 1944:

> The whole of this emergency housing scheme must be viewed in relation to a 10 years' plan for the steady, full-time employment of a considerably enlarged building trade for permanent houses instead of a fever for three or four years and then a falling off. The building trade should have a broad and steady flow giving all its members a good assurance of employment and thus encouraging piece work.

Everyone realizes, of course, that what is given for one purpose may, to some extent, have to be taken from others. The Government supporters naturally seek to obtain from us a list of reductions or economies which we would make in order to use these for electioneering purposes. That is quite natural in the unhappy conditions in which we have lived for a year and which seem likely to continue. I have no intention of making any piece-meal propositions. (*Laughter.*) I have a feeling, listening to the debates and watching hon. Members opposite, that their anxious consciences find relief in laughter. No one would grudge them any solace they can get from giggling.

Naturally, I have no intention of making piecemeal propositions. There is no obligation on a party in opposition, without access to Government machinery, to produce a detailed scheme. That can only be done where they have the power to act. But it is on such a definite, general design alone that changes of a large character of this kind can be judged. It may well be that a general design for an increase in housing would contain some features unpopular in themselves, but when presented in its entirety and harmony it would be greatly in the interests of the nation and would be generally welcomed.

In this matter of housing there are two questions: first to get the houses, and second to allot them. Do not let us quarrel too much about the second point. Do not let us quarrel so much about it as to prevent us from achieving the first, without which the second would not arise. Mrs Beeton[1] and, I believe, her predecessors in the cookery book, begins the recipe for jugged hare, 'First catch your hare.' One of the reasons for the Minister of Health's failure is that he mixes up these two processes. In order to make sure that nobody who was well-to-do could get a house, he has in fact prevented large numbers of houses being built for the ordinary wage-earners.

I listened to the speech of the right hon. Gentleman tonight with sorrow, because – here I make an admission – I do not believe he is as bad as he makes himself out to be. But I will say this to him. Hate is a bad guide. (*Interruption.*) I have never considered myself at all a good hater – though I recognise that from moment to moment it has added stimulus to pugnacity. People who have been denied an opportunity in life are deeply embittered, but the Minister of Health does not belong to that class. No man's services in the war were accorded such a wonderful reward as he received.

With the mood, and the need, and the ruins in the country glaring at us all from day to day, and with the piling up of arrears of house building, could there have been a task so plain and so inspiring as that which was offered to him? It was one which any man of vitality and vigour, in the prime of life, and gifted with abilities of a high order and Parliamentary gifts, would have embraced with joy, and gratitude to the land in which he lived. With the immense powers at his disposal under war-time regulations and with the long five years which have been granted to him, he might have left a mark upon the social life of the British people, and rendered them a service which would have made his name at once famous and beloved. I cannot understand how this did not appeal to him, and how it did not drive out all hampering passions and prejudices, the indulgence of which have led to the present unhappy plight that he is in.

It is not only a question of building houses, not only a question of numbers but the cost has risen to a point which, despite subsidies on an enormous scale, involves rents which many of those in most need of houses cannot afford.

---

[1] Isabella Mary Beeton, 1836–65. Author of *The Englishwoman's Domestic Magazine* (1857) and *Mrs Beeton's Book of Household Management* (1861–5).

The rents charged to the tenants have risen remorselessly. Before the war the average rent of a local council house was 7s a week. (Hon. Members: 'No'.) In many places now £1 a week rent is charged. In some cases, 25s is charged by councils.

Mr Bevan rose –

Mr Churchill: No, I really cannot give way. (Hon. Members: 'Give way.') I do not want to be – (Hon. Members: 'Give way.') We can always shout each other down. I do not want to be involved in a personal altercation.

Mr Shurmer: Tell the truth.

Mr Churchill: We gave the right hon. Gentleman a patient and courteous hearing. There is no use in having a state of rowdiness, as if rowdiness paid any party. I do not want to be involved in an altercation with the right hon. Gentleman. However, if there is a point on which I am in error and upon which I am open to correction, I will gladly give way.

Mr Bevan: I am very much obliged to the right hon. Gentleman for giving way. I am not anxious to engage in a personal altercation. I only want to get the facts correct. The right hon. Gentleman has compared the net rent of a pre-war house with the gross rent of a post-war house.

Mr Churchill: No.

Mr Bevan: Yes. As representatives of local authorities who saw me the other day will confirm – and there are hon. Members now sitting on both sides of the House who were present with the deputation – the average rentals in Great Britain upon which the subsidies are based are rents of between 14s and 15s, including the repair allowances, as against the net – (*Interruption.*) Perhaps hon. Members will just listen. The rents upon which subsidies are paid are net rents, and the 7s compares with the 14s to 15s post-war rents.

Mr Churchill: The other day the Chancellor of the Exchequer showed us how all the rise in the cost of living was a delusion. The Minister of Health now proceeds to show us that there is no appreciable rise in rents. I am told that in some cases they have gone up to 25s and 27s a week, and that is clearly a level which ordinary working people cannot pay out of their wages. So much for the cost, which has certainly greatly increased in housing.

When we complain that houses have not been supplied in the necessary quantities it is said: 'Half a loaf is better than no bread.' But half a house is not a good plan. We could usefully use more two-bedroomed houses, and more small flats for old people enabling them to move out of their large houses to make room for families. Any habitable house is better than no house at all, or a house so dear that the poorest class, for which it is built, cannot afford to pay the rent which the local authority is bound to charge. There are many cases of that of which we know, and the richer class of people take the houses because those for whose needs they were specially designed and intended are unable to reach the level of rent. It is no service to the lower income group to offer them prizes which are beyond their reach; indeed it is a mockery.

Before the war, the size of a house was 800 square feet. The Government raised it to 1,050 square feet. That is more than the figure that rules in the United States, whose economic position is vastly more powerful than our own, and from whom we have received such immense assistance. The amount of space is less important than how it is used. I am assured that there may well be scope for improved design within the existing compass of housing.

It is necessary also, I think, for the Government to understand the peculiar position of house-building labour. I said some time ago how a bricklayer and his mates engaged in building a house were like people living on a raft of which they had every day to burn a plank or two to cook their dinner. That is the feeling which is in their minds. They ask themselves what is going to happen to them when it is finished. In the present circumstances there is a field of employment for the house builders unlimited for many years except by Government decision. As I said earlier, I thought that we should give them an assurance of a 10-years' guaranteed programme. Free from the anxiety that their work may end with the job, they could go ahead with piece work without fear or stint and all the incentives, including the bonus system, could apply.

Here alone might be a 20 or 25 per cent increase in the building effort. There is really no reason why the output per man in the building trade should be lower than pre-war or so much lower than in the United States. Make them a fair and attractive proposition and we will get surprising results, but this policy of the Prime Minister that 200,000 is the limit, endorsed by the Minister of Health – I dare say to his regret – is bad for the rate of output – even within that limit.

There is no trade in the country which can more readily adapt itself to a static condition than the building trade. They would like a progressive condition but they are quite ready, after the rough time which they have had in the last generation – I have seen it: the first to be called up for mobilisation and so on and the first to be turned off when building slackens and so on – (*Interruption.*) I am the author of the labour exchanges and the first Unemployment Insurance Act. I was in these matters years before many hon. Gentlemen opposite were able to take an adult interest in them. I say that the building workers are quite ready, after their experiences, to settle down into a static condition.

The Government limit of 200,000 houses – it was only 175,000, as the Minister reminded us, until this new Parliament forced the restoration of the cut – undoubtedly has most evil and discouraging effects. How long it is to last, we cannot tell. The late Chancellor of the Exchequer, whose absence from our councils we deeply regret and still more the reason for it, told us in the Budget that this limit would last for three years. Such a limit, or anything like it, must reproduce the deterrence of efforts, enterprise and piece work which ruled in the days when the building trade had always an unabsorbed tail of unemployment.

Therefore, when I endorsed as a resolute aim of the Conservative Party the raising of the rate of building to 300,000 a year, I did not mean that to be the static limit. We shall thrust towards it with all our life, strength and wit, but once this figure gleams upon our horizon – 'forward again' must be the policy and the order. So much for the Government's policy and the Prime Minister's statement. I am sure that the Prime Minister's statement represents the rigid attitude of planners who understand only about half of what is really going on.

Now I come to the question whether the proposal we make is possible and practicable, or whether it is all moonshine. (Hon. Members: 'Hear, hear'.) I am glad to carry Members opposite with me. I said that 100,000 houses would cost £150 million a year from an annual income of over £10,000 million. The Prime Minister's reply is that houses are not built with money. Money, of course, is only a fairly well known method of expressing effort and resources. I am surprised it has not occurred to the Prime Minister, because it has been known in quite a lot of countries for quite a long time.

Let us look at the additional effort and resources required. Judgment on this kind of enterprise depends on two conditions: are they so big that they are beyond our power, and, secondly, if they are within our scope, are there bottlenecks which prevent them? Several constructive speeches have been made today. We have also made, in our own research department, a considerable examination. My personal experience of Government machinery is considerable, and I must say that I have never seen a major task which I was more sure of as being within practical limits. I would not fear to take responsibility for this achievement. I offer my assurance that it is a reasonable objective, and that, should we be called upon to exercise power, it would receive the highest priority and the most vehement effort jointly with national defence.

That is what I have to say on the proportion, but let us now look at the bottlenecks. My hon. Friend the Member for Wallasey (Mr Marples),[1] in his admirable speech today, dealt with these details. I was very glad that with his technical knowledge he was able to put this subject before the House as a practical matter of detail and on its merits, instead of trying to reduce it to the ordinary bang and slam on one side and the other of party politics. I was sorry that my hon. Friend, a private Member speaking from a back bench, should have been made the victim for so prolonged a personal attack by the Minister of Health. I really thought that the Minister would have done himself much more good – though he is the judge of that – if he had devoted himself to the merits of the question, and tried to give the House the feeling that his heart was burning to conquer in this struggle to find homes for the British people.

---

[1] Alfred Ernest Marples, 1907–78. Married, 1937, Edna Harwood (div. 1945); 1956, Ruth Dobson. Capt., RA, 1941–4. MP (Cons.) for Wallasey, 1945. Parliamentary Secretary, Ministry of Housing and Local Government, 1951–4. Joint Parliamentary Secretary, Ministry of Pensions and National Insurance, 1954–5. Postmaster-General, 1957–9. Minister of Transport, 1959–64. Baron, 1974.

I shall not attempt to go into details. (Hon. Members: 'Go on.') If I did so, I would trespass on the reply to this Debate.

The Secretary of State for Scotland (Mr McNeil): If another five minutes would furnish the House with any details, I should be delighted to give up that time.

Mr Churchill: Eight billion bricks were made before the war, but we are now making a little over six billion. Of this six billion a little more than three billion are used for the construction of the traditional brick dwelling house. Out of them are built about 160,000 houses. To build another 100,000 houses would need about two billion more bricks. That is well within the range of the pre-war brick fields. If these had not been restricted and jogged about by changes of policy, there would be plenty of bricks. But the brickfields are already running at 80 per cent of their pre-war capacity, and there should be no great difficulty or delay in restoring them to their pre-war normal output. So much for bricks.

More cement will also be needed to achieve our target, but this need present no great problem. An extra 900,000 tons would produce 100,000 houses. The industry already produces 10 million tons, and it would be producing more if it had been allowed to go ahead with the expansion plans it had in 1945. Next year this industry plans to produce 10½ million tons. As a temporary measure, we could, if necessary, reduce for a time the exports, which are running at a rate of 1,600,000 tons. Certainly by the end of next year the cement industry if not nationalised, will have caught up with all our demands, including rearmament.

Then there is timber. We have been told that if no timber can be got from sterling area countries like Norway, it will affect the dollar position. But here again I am sure that the quantities and proportion would have their say. I am assured that about £9¾ million worth of dollars or less than half of our last year's tobacco bill, would give all the dollars necessary to buy from Canada the extra timber. I do not believe it would be necessary to go so far, because I am sure a good deal can be got within the sterling area. Far greater elasticity will come from the abolition of bulk buying by officials. Anyhow, the whole timber transaction is one well within our compass. The improvement in the dollar exchange would more than justify such a step. We lose at home by the higher prices for raw materials, but in the exchange we gain, especially by the sale of tin and rubber. It may well be that we could find a partial compensation for Britain at home in using our improved dollar position to buy more timber, and thus help to solve the housing question.

I am asked, 'Are you for or against controls?' But what a crude and absurd way to state the issue. Government speakers talk as if there were no middle course between the universal regulation of a Socialist State administering all the means of production, distribution and exchange, and what they call the anarchy of the jungle. But the vast majority of the human race dwell in the temperate zones which lie between the burning heat of the Equator and the freezing cold of the Polar regions. Our belief is that the fewer the controls the better; that the more freedom and enterprise can play their part the more chance there is of a fertile, prosperous and progressive community.

We also think that private management is far more economical and resourceful than management by State officials. We are sure that the completion of the Socialist aim of substituting State industry for every form of private industry would reduce our standard of life and would reduce the present number of our population. In the United States, where a capitalist competitive system prevails and where war-time regulations were practically swept away until recently – (Hon. Members: 'Ah'.) Well, there is a war in Korea. What about that 'Ah' now? The United States have three times our population, so, according to Government standards, they ought to be building 600,000 houses a year. They are actually building more than a million.

Now, when rearmament casts its shadow upon the world and upon our country, there must evidently be a maintenance or even a renewal of some war-time regulations. We have agreed that the Supplies and Services Act should be renewed on an annual basis, but our hope of establishing full freedom under the well-known and long-established laws of our country remains our goal. The difference between the two sides of the House is that the Socialists aim at the maximum of controls and the Conservatives aim at the minimum. Both seek to progress in those opposite directions for different reasons as fast as they possibly can. Can we now accept that as a summary of the differences between us?

If we apply that mood of thought to the position of the building industry at the present time it means that we should, of course, use the local authorities as well as the private builders, and that we should only alter the system of licences step by step. The Minister of Health has suggested that under a Conservative Government a great number of houses would be built for sale to the well-to-do, by speculative builders and that few houses would be built to let for the ordinary man. It is our intention that, under a Conservative Government, the priority given to houses built by local authorities will be maintained. This obligation will be scrupulously honoured in our housebuilding programme.

Mr Bevan: In what proportion?

Mr Churchill: We want the local authorities to be able to reduce their waiting lists and to resume the process of slum clearance which was interrupted by the war.

Mr Bevan: The right hon. Gentleman has made a very important statement. In what proportion would the right hon. Gentleman maintain local authority housebuilding?

Mr Churchill: I said that I had no intention of stating exact details. Give me the power and I will give you the figures. We have to indicate our principles, and I am indicating some very clear principles. Over and above that commitment, to which we are all pledged, we should expand output so as to make it possible for free enterprise and renewed impulse to build large numbers of additional houses, both for sale and to let. So long as the housing shortage continues, the Government must restrict the ceiling on price or size of houses built for sale, and this must be dependent upon the prevailing, and sometimes upon the local, conditions. We shall take steps to prevent the diversion to any kind of luxury building, whether public or private, of the resources of men and materials – (*Interruption*) – a great deal is being taken for public building – which could be devoted to the housing of the people.

I listened to the speech of the noble Lady the Member for Anglesey (Lady Megan Lloyd George). (Hon. Members: 'Hear, hear'.) I hope that the applause from the other side of the House will assure her of any immunities which she may be seeking. I need not say that I speak as a life-long friend of her father and her family, but I feel that she should have verified the facts before making the statement about the Carlton Club claiming a licence to rebuild the bomb-damaged premises. We have given up all hope of ever rebuilding the Carlton Club and no application for a licence has ever been made. The site is being disposed of. Speaking as one who lived in her father's generation, I do not consider that prefixing the words 'I am informed that' relieves one of all responsibility.

Lady Megan Lloyd George: I am sorry to interrupt the right hon. Gentleman, but when I was informed that that was not the case, I withdrew the statement. (Hon. Members: 'No'.) Certainly I did so.

Mr Churchill: I was here at the time but I suffer a little from deafness and did not realise that the charge had been withdrawn.

Lady Megan Lloyd George: I said that I was very glad that it was so and that no licence had been granted.

Mr Churchill: Honour is completely satisfied on both sides.

We say that the emphasis should be placed upon new houses. In 1935 new housing absorbed 48 per cent of the building industry's output. In 1947 the figure was only 34 per cent, and in 1948 31 per cent. We have no later figures, but I am informed – (*Laughter*) – I must be careful – that it might well be only 30 per cent today.

I think that the Government have been at once ambitious and ineffectual in their building plans. They have dispersed, instead of concentrating, their resources. They have been very loose in their application of principles of selection in regard to their objectives. The need above all is to establish in this sphere, as in many others, the right priorities. They ask, for instance, whether we would cut the new power stations. The answer is 'No'. Without power we cannot build houses, carry out our defence programme or expand our industrial output. But the question of whether the necessary electrical supply could not be obtained with fewer bricks subtracted from the housing programme is still open, and my hon. Friend the Member for Wallasey drew our attention to American practice on this subject, which certainly seems to deserve study.

I am grateful for the five minutes extra which the right hon. Gentleman has granted me, and I shall draw to a conclusion the remarks I have ventured to offer to the House.

We must not let this 'wiping the floor' mood of the Prime Minister and the Minister of Health blot out from our minds the pathos and the tragedy of the shortage of houses. The life of the nation and the happiness and virtue of the human race are founded upon the family and upon the home. Empire, ideologies, party struggles, class warfare, all present their attractive temptations to the active mind, but the foundations of all our health and honour lie in the home and the family.

It was John Bright who spoke of his supreme pleasure in seeing little children playing upon the hearth. I cannot understand why this result should not be won. Let us have less chatter and planning and scheming for future Utopias. Let us get on with this imperative job of housing the millions who ask so little and get so little for all their efforts. The family requires a home and the home requires a house or, if you like it, an 'accommodation unit' – something, at any rate, where a man has his own front door.

Outside is the great, bewildering, tumultuous world; inside, the family can plan what is best for themselves, what it is best to aim for, what it is wisest to give up. And in so deciding they create at once the foundation and the motive power without which all the super planners are only chasing shadows. Where does the family start? It starts with a young man falling in love with a girl – (*Interruption.*) No superior alternative has yet been found! Look at the number of couples who, as the statistics show, either cannot get married because they cannot get a house to live in, or have to live with their parents, or jam up in the sort of collectivist squalor of Communist lands. I see that a judge in Plymouth said the housing shortage was the principal cause of divorces. Then what of health? There is no doubt that tuberculosis thrives on bad housing conditions. In Scotland it has actually gone up since the war. Then comes the sharp issue of children not having a home they love, or a family circle which commands their loyalty, and of the many forms of consequential juvenile misconduct of which we read.

The Minister of Health cannot brush all this aside and escape from this Debate without incurring blame and condemnation outside for not having offered us a constructive statement and words of encouragement. All his critics will not be on one side of the House. I have a number of quotations, some very moving, from speeches made last week from the Benches opposite, one particularly from the hon. Member for Kirkdale (Mr Keenan)[1] who said:

---

[1] William Keenan, 1899–1955. MP (Lab.) for Liverpool Kirkdale, 1945–55.

What is the good of having fine schools or even fine hospitals if there is no home in which the children can rest? . . . I believe in bedrooms before schoolrooms. . . . It is certainly a fact that not all building trade workers who are capable of house-building are engaged on house-building. – (Official Report, 1st November, 1950; Vol. 480. c. 200 and 201.) It astounds me that the House has not rallied to this proposal which we make and resolved that it shall be carried into effect by every priority to other issues except self-preservation.

But, Sir, you may be sure that the nation will not endure this mismanagement and misdirection much longer. They will not agree to a system of British life and society which means that no progress is being made to overtake the housing arrears, that as many houses are falling into decay every year as are being built, that slum clearance is static like all the rest of it, that all the personal stresses now endured by hard-working couples are to continue, and that even to raise these issues in the House of Commons is to incur the insulting charge of vote-catching and partisanship.

Early last week there came across my mind some lines about our island life which Charles Masterman[1] used to repeat to me. Oddly enough, while I was seeking to verify the quotation it was used in the House by the hon. Member for Oldham, West (Mr Leslie Hale).[2] The poet and the teacher, as he was – William Watson[3] – speaking of the hard social conditions of the life of the people, asked: Is there no room for victories here, No fields for deeds of fame? But I have found another verse of William Watson, which I remembered at the same time: The England of my heart is she, Long hoped, and long deferred, That ever promises to be, And ever breaks her word. Why should she always break her word to those who love her so well and defend her safety and honour with their lives? Now is the time, here is the occasion, and this housing issue is the deed to sweep that hard reproach away.

---

[1] Charles Frederick Gurney Masterman, 1874–1927. Educated at Christ's College, Cambridge. Married, 1908, Lucy Blanche Lyttelton. MP (Lib.) for West Ham North, 1906–14. Under-Secretary to Churchill, Home Office, 1909–12. Financial Secretary to the Treasury, 1912–14. Chancellor of the Duchy of Lancaster, 1914–15. Forced to leave the Government after nine months of being unable to find a Parliamentary constituency after being defeated at a by-election, Feb. 1914. MP (Lib.) for Manchester Rusholme, 1923–4.

[2] Charles Leslie Hale, 1902–85. Educated at Ashby-de-la-Zouch Boys' Grammar School. Member, Leicestershire County Council, 1925–50. Married, 1926, Dorothy Ann Latham. Unsuccessful Parliamentary candidate (Lab.) for South Nottingham, 1929. MP (Lab.) for Oldham Div. of Lancs., 1945–50; for West Div. of Oldham, 1950–68. Freedom of Oldham, 1969. Baron (Life Peer), 1972.

[3] William Watson, 1858–1935. Published *Odes and other Poems*, 1894. Knighted, 1917.

Winston S. Churchill to Sir Alan Lascelles
(*Churchill papers, 2/171*)

7 November 1950

My dear Alan,
During my recent visit to Denmark I received from the hands of King Frederik[1] the Order of the Elephant. I am writing to ask if I may have the King's permission to wear this Order on appropriate occasions.

Sir Alan Lascelles to Winston S. Churchill
(*Churchill papers, 2/171*)

8 November 1950

My dear Mr Churchill,
The King gladly gives permission for you to wear the Order of the Elephant given you by King Frederik on appropriate occasions, as requested in your letter to me of November 7th.

Lieutenant-General Sir Henry Pownall to Winston S. Churchill
(*Churchill papers, 2/32*)

[November 1950]

This is an interesting and logical paper by General Mast[2] on the defence forces needed to resist Russian attack on Western Europe. He sends it to you because you dealt with the subject at the Albert Hall and spoke of the need to raise a German Army. With this he fully agrees. I attach a summary of the paper.
I suggest that you thank him for his paper, recall your meeting him at Carthage and, perhaps, congratulate him on his subsequent distinguished career.[3]

SUMMARY OF GENERAL MAST'S PAPER

The forces at present available are ludicrously insufficient to meet Russian attack, at present security is given us only by the atom bomb. We must develop land and air forces to check and throw back invasion from the East.

---

[1] Christian Frederik Franz Michael Carl Valdemar Georg, 1899–1972. Educated at Royal Danish Naval Academy. King of Denmark, 1947–72.
[2] Charles Emmanuel Mast, 1889–1977. French Military Attaché to Tokyo, 1932–7. CO, 137th Infantry Rgt, 1938. GOC, 3rd North African Infantry Division, 1940. Imprisoned after Battle of France, 1940–1. Released and made GOC March Division Algeria, 1941; Casablanca, 1942. Head of French Military Mission to Syria and Egypt, 1943. Resident-General of Tunisia, 1943–7. Director of Institut des Hautes Etudes de Défense Nationale, 1947–50. Retired, 1950.
[3] Churchill instructed his staff: 'Thank. Keep Handy in Defence Box.'

Russia keeps 175 divisions and 15,000 aircraft on her peace establishment; on mobilization these would grow to 250 divisions, 20–30,000 aircraft and 300 submarines. In three months there would be 350 divisions; after a year 500 divisions. Her strategic aims would be:
    (i)   Alaska, Spitzbergen, Iceland
    (ii) Middle East, especially the oil producing areas
    (iii) Western Europe and NW Africa
    (iv) Harassing action in the Far East
    (v) Submarine warfare on the oceans

The estimate of forces available on mobilization for Task (iii), Western Europe, is 170 divisions and 12,500 aircraft.

The proposed Allied Army of 50–60 divisions might hold the Russians on the Pyrenees, but then nearly all Europe would have been over-run. To hold them on the line of Jutland – half of them ready for immediate action, together with 15,000 aircraft. As the USA and Britain would have to deal principally with the wider theatres they could find more than 10 British and 10 US divisions for Europe. It would be a year before any greater forces could be expected of them. Allowing for 10 divisions comes to 50 divisions and 5000 air craft, the German to 30 divisions and (?) 3000 aircraft.

As she had 100 divisions and 2500 aircraft in 1940, this requirement from France is not beyond her present capacity but in order to meet it help from the USA is essential. It must be met because the alternative is slavery. Speed is essential, but in the best circumstances the programme cannot be fulfilled till 1954 or 1955. Whether so much time will be given us is doubtful, that is no argument, however, against launching it. Old quarrels must be forgotten; the choice lies between constructive effort to get security, and destruction.

Winston S. Churchill to Sir Edward Boyle[1]
(Churchill papers, 2/90)

10 November 1950

My dear Edward Boyle,

I am glad to know that the Unionist cause is represented in the Handsworth contest by a young man of promise like you. I look forward to your return to Parliament by a majority that will proclaim the growing desire of the electorate to have the nation's affairs entrusted once again to our Party.

You have rightly placed Peace and Security in the forefront of your Election

---

[1] Edward Boyle, 1923–81. Bt, 1945. MP (Cons.) for Handsworth, 1950–70. Parliamentary Private Secretary to Parliamentary Under-Secretary of Air, 1951–2; to Minister of Defence, 1952. Parliamentary Secretary of Education, 1957–9. Financial Secretary to the Treasury, 1959–62. PC, 1962. Minister of State, Education and Science, 1964. Trustee, British Museum, 1970–81. Baron, 1970. CH, 1981.

programme. The Socialist Government have been brought, however reluctantly and half-heartedly to realize that if the free nations of the world are to escape the calamity of another world war, they must unite to defend themselves against the treacherous, aggressive tyranny which threatens them today from without and from within.

You wisely lay stress on the need to develop thrift and initiative. Our present Government are discouraging these virtues by oppressive taxation, high prices, and by controls that hobble, harass, and frustrate individual enterprise. Under the guise of 'defending full employment' and controlling prices, they propose to perpetuate the Emergency Powers which were endured as a wartime necessity. With such powers their caucus machine and its rigidly disciplined members could control the daily life of the people and the activities of every industry. They could destroy the independence both of Parliament and the Local Authorities, and make the Trade Union leaders their tools.

The financial and economic planning of the last five years has, by its incompetence, raised the cost of living to an oppressive level. This will be worsened by every step to blight and chill individual effort and enterprise and to concentrate power in the hands of a clique of doctrinaire politicians.

The Prime Minister and Mr Bevan have made it plain that the Socialist Government have no plan to end the Housing shortage and all the miseries this inflicts on millions of people, old and young alike. They have brought Housing to a dead end where the new houses only just equal those that are falling into decay each year. Indeed the present Housing scandal can only get worse because the rents of Council houses have risen, and are rising so high that the poorer people for whom they were mainly built cannot afford to pay the weekly sums demanded. A fresh supreme, intense effort is needed to lift the whole process of Housing out of this dismal quagmire. The Unionist, or Tory, Party will make this their first aim, jointly with National Defence. Handsworth should give them the chance now that the Socialists, in spite of their boasts and promises, have cravenly thrown up the sponge. Let us go forward together without fear or favour. We have done lots of bigger things than this, and none is more needful now.

Your admirable Address brings these truths home to the citizens of the Handsworth Division and their vote will surely confirm the condemnation of our Socialist rulers recently recorded by the electors in Glasgow and in Oxford City.

Lord Salisbury to Winston S. Churchill
(*Churchill papers, 2/101*)

17 November 1950
Private and Confidential

My dear Winston

I have been distressed to see that the *Manchester Guardian*, in referring to the speech which I made in the Lords on Wednesday, says that as I did not indicate that I was speaking only for myself I must be regarded as giving the official views of my Party with regard to policy towards Russia. This seems to imply that in the opinion of the Paper I was saying something entirely new. Had that been the case I should of course have taken steps to consult you before speaking. But I was under the impression – indeed I still am – that I was merely repeating what you had already said with so much force in your speech at Edinburgh during the General Election. The only reason why I did not specifically mention the Edinburgh speech was that that seemed likely to give a Party slant to something which I meant as a general appeal. I only hope that I did not in any way embarrass you.

I had particular reason for saying what I did at the present juncture. It seems to me – and I know you think the same – that the next two years are likely to be ones of especial delicacy. We and the Americans have announced loudly that we propose to re-arm, and the Americans in particular have rather unwisely emphasized that they will not be ready for two or three years. I cannot help feeling that this is simply asking the Russians to press matters to a crisis during that period, and I feel very strongly that our policy ought to be, during this time of especial danger, to prevent things coming to the boil. If we could get into some negotiations with the Russians which we could keep going over the next summer, we should have gained more valuable time. That clearly was something which I could not say publicly, but I feel I ought to let you know what was in my mind.

I was further influenced in the same direction by a conversation which I had with Lew Douglas just before he left. He mentioned the difficulties with which Dean Acheson was now being faced in taking a moderate line owing to the reputation which he had unfortunately got of being somewhat leftist. This made it necessary for him to take a more rigid attitude than we would otherwise wish. Lew indicated that anything that could be said on this side of the Atlantic on the side of moderation would be very helpful to Dean. I told him that I would do what I could to help, and this seemed to be a good opportunity.

Please do not bother to answer this letter. I only write it because I feel that it is due to you to know what was behind my speech. As a matter of fact I was quite astonished that it attracted any special attention. It seemed to me that I was merely repeating what you as Leader of the Party had said with far more authority and power than I should find it possible to do.

November 1950

Winston S. Churchill to Lord Salisbury
(*Churchill papers, 2/101*)

19 November 1950
Private and Confidential

My dear Bobbety,

Thank you for your letter. I have in no way departed from what I said at Edinburgh in the General Election, but a great deal has happened since then, for instance, Korea and the valiant lead taken by the United States. What you said of course splits the Socialist Party, as you have no doubt seen. I do not think however we could march with them, and I am sure you would not want to.

Before I got your letter I had a word with Anthony on the telephone today, and he said that he thought that the Soviets ought to be asked to settle up about Austria before we embark on the far greater questions connected with Germany. I agree with this, and I expect you do too.

I thought you and I and Anthony might have a talk together next week. Would 4 o' clock on Tuesday in my room at the House of Commons suit you? Let my people know if this is agreeable.

Winston S. Churchill to Sir Ivone Kirkpatrick
(*Churchill papers, 2/171*)

19 November 1950

My dear Ivone Kirkpatrick,

I have received the enclosed letter[1] from the widow of the late Admiral Sir Thomas Phillips, who you probably heard of during the War. I thought you might be interested to read it.

I have not forgotten about the picture I promised you, but I hope you will understand that the long delay in selecting a suitable one is due to the tremendous pressure of work and events that I am subjected to at the moment. However I hope it will not be long before it reaches you.

---

[1] Reproduced above (pp. 1920–1).

Winston S. Churchill to Lady Phillips
(Churchill papers, 2/171)

19 November 1950

Dear Lady Phillips

Thank you for your letter of November 11.[1] I fully agree with you that the situation in Germany at the present time is most worrying and what you describe is indeed distressing. I am sending your letter to Sir Ivone Kirkpatrick the High Commissioner for the British Zone as I think it will interest him. I am glad you thought of writing to me.

Winston S. Churchill to Isie Smuts
(Churchill papers, 2/176)[2]

19 November 1950   Chartwell

My dear Mrs Smuts,

I have just read again your moving letter of October 4.[3] I value this letter so much because it preserves and recalls the splendid memories I have of the great man whose friendship and comradeship in action I treasured for so many years. I value it also because it admits me to your family circle and enables me to see for myself what you must have been for him in his long full reign of wisdom and power. Please accept my deepest sympathy in your sorrow and deprivation. I know how vain are words in such sadness, and how much worse it is for those who stay than for those who go. But there must be comfort in the proofs of admiration and gratitude which have been evoked all over the world for a warrior-statesman and philosopher who was probably more fitted to guide struggling and blundering humanity through its sufferings and perils towards a better day, than anyone who lived in any country during his epoch.

His name and fame will shine the brighter as the generations pass – not only in South Africa but in all the lands where Freedom and Truth are cherished. I pray that this conviction will cheer your heart and inspire your children. I had a beautiful but melancholy letter from Jannie telling me how frail his Father's hold on life had become in those last weeks before the end. Please give him my affectionate regards and wishes and accept them also yourself from the bottom of my heart. In all this Clemmie joins with deep emotion.

---

[1] Of Nov. 4, reproduced above (pp. 1920–1).
[2] This letter was handwritten.
[3] Reproduced above (p. 1884).

Clement Attlee to Winston S. Churchill
(Churchill papers, 2/95)

21 November 1950
Confidential

My dear Churchill,
　I enclose a copy of a statement[1] after Questions which I shall be making tomorrow. This is, I think, self-explanatory, and I have little doubt that you will agree that it is appropriate there should be consultation at this time between Prime Ministers of these countries.
　I should like to add that the Prime Minister of Ceylon[2] has expressed a particular wish to announce the holding of this conference before his House rises tomorrow evening which will be by our time about two hours before I make my announcement. I know that you will understand that it is very difficult to resist a request of this sort, although consequently there is some risk that there may be something in the evening papers here before I am able to make my own announcement. This of course implies no lack of respect for our own House of Commons; with the differences in the time of day in various parts of the world it is always extremely difficult to arrange these things at exactly the same moment.

Winston S. Churchill to Duncan Sandys
(Churchill papers, 2/32)

22 November 1950

My dear Duncan,
　I send you herewith the note about which we spoke on the telephone.

A NOTE

　The European Army should consist of the Brussels Treaty Powers and other free nations who have joined them, and should be an enclave in, or core of, the Atlantic Pact Powers, and under the Supreme Commander appointed by them. All countries concerned should dedicate from their National Armies the approved and agreed quota. Whether this should be expressed in 'Divisions' or in 'Combat Groups' of the three arms (infantry, armoured vehicles and artillery) should be no obstacle so long as numbers are sufficient and proportions right. The Germans who have no National Army and do not seek

---

[1] Announcement of Commonwealth Prime Ministers' Conference scheduled for Jan. 1951.
[2] Don Stephen Senanayake, 1883–1952. Educated at St Thomas' College, Mutwal. Elected unopposed to Legislative Council of Ceylon from Negombo, 1924. Elected to State Council of Ceylon, 1931. Minister of Agriculture and Lands, 1942–7. Leader of the House and Vice-Chairman, Board of Ministers, State Council, 1942–7. Ceylon's first PM, 1947. Member of Ceylon Parliament, 1947–52.

one, should be invited to make their due contribution. All troops of every country in the European Army, as in the Atlantic Pact Super-Army, should have equal status, and be equipped with equal weapons. Their supplies and munitions should be drawn from the common pool. At present this would be an Atlantic Pact pool, and later a European pool may develop subject of course to the great importance of uniformity or at least similarity of weapons. The question remains whether the British should dedicate their contribution to the European Army or to the Atlantic Pact Army. I am in favour of the former, namely the European Army, but the issue is not fundamental or final, and should not prevent general agreement.

Clementine Churchill to Winston S. Churchill
(Churchill papers, 1/47)[1]

22 November 1950

My darling,

I am sad that Queen Juliana should have felt hurt in her personal feelings and offended in her National Pride by your absence at Dover. (The Lord Warden of the Cinque Ports is the first person to greet a foreign Sovereign visiting these shores.)

I must also take some blame for having too easily agreed (or was it even perhaps my suggestion!) that we should not go to the Guildhall today and join in the City Welcome. I fear that this smaller defection will be noticed now. It will grieve me if we should lose the affection of Queen Juliana and particularly of her Mother who flew here specially to honour you and to give you the precious casket of Marlborough letters. And you are the God Father of the little half-blind daughter whom they cherish most of all.

Do you think, Darling, you need wait upon the Queen or if that is impossible, write to her in your own 'paw' and say you are sorry.

Don't say you are too old! because you are as young as a game cock and the whole world knows about the flight from Copenhagen to London and on to Newmarket and Blackpool.

It was just a slip, because you <u>are</u> Monarchical No 1 and value tradition, form and Ceremony.

Your Clemmie but with ears [drawing of a cat] and tail drooping.

[1] This letter was handwritten.

General Lord Ismay to Winston S. Churchill
(*Churchill papers, 4/335*)

23 November 1950

My dear Mr Churchill,

I have already sent you some notes on my recollection of the events of the two or three days before the Normandy D-Day.

I think that you might wish to mention the important Conference that took place almost three weeks before D-Day at St Paul's School, and to debunk the story told by Alan Moorehead in his life of Montgomery.[1] Accordingly, the attached notes are submitted.

NOTES ON PRE-D-DAY EVENTS

On 7th April you attended an exercise (Code name 'Thunderclap') at St Paul's School. This conference is mentioned in Eisenhower's book, but he does not make any reference to your presence. I do not know what transpired as you did not take me with you: nor, so far as I can remember, did you ever mention it to me. I doubt whether you would wish to mention it in your book.

The final conference, however, which was held at St Paul's School, on 15th May, is, I submit worthy of inclusion. The King, Field Marshal Smuts, the British Chiefs of Staff and you were present, in addition to the whole of the SHAEF staff and Commanders.

The whole stage was a map of the Normandy beaches and the immediate hinterland, set at a slope so that the audience could see it clearly – the high officers explaining the plan walked about on the map pointing out the landmarks involved.

At the outset the King made a short speech and you followed. In the course of this speech (which I fear was not recorded anywhere), you said: 'I am hardening on this enterprise'. (This has been taken to mean that you were always against it (see Eisenhower Page 269), but you had often used this expression to me and I had taken it to mean that the more you thought about it, the more certain you were of success.)

You were followed on the stage by General Eisenhower, who gave a general dissertation, and then by Montgomery, who was quite first class. His line was: 'We have a sufficiency of troops, we have all the necessary tackle. We have an excellent plan. This is perfectly normal operation which is certain of success. If anyone has any doubts in his mind, let him stay behind.' I think that he must have been reading Henry V before Agincourt –

> He that hath no stomach for this fight
> Let him depart.
> His passport shall be made
> And crowns for convoys put in to his purse.

[1] See Alan Moorehead, *Montgomery, A Biography* (London, 1946), pp. 158, 194–6.

Montgomery was followed by the administrative staff officers, including General Sir Humfrey Gale who (rather tactlessly, I thought) dwelt upon the elaborate preparations that had been made for the administration of the force when ashore. The amount of paraphernalia sounded staggering, and reminded you of Andrew Cunningham's story of the dental chairs being landed at Algiers in the first flight.

Anyway, on 17th May you instructed me to write to Montgomery and say that you were concerned about the excessive administrative arrangements and that you would like to discuss it with him on 19th May when you were dining together. Your talk with him was grossly misreported in Alan Moorehead's book entitled *Montgomery*, and when the extracts appeared in the *Sunday Express*, you told me to take it up with Montgomery himself. The rest of the story of this episode is told in the attached correspondence.

Private Office to Winston S. Churchill
(Churchill papers, 2/32)

23 November 1950

MESSAGE FROM MR MACMILLAN AT STRASBOURG

The situation here is getting rather critical about the Germans and the German cooperation in the European Army. The election results in Germany[1] have intensified this.

Would you authorize me to make the following statement on Friday? Would you send me your decision in the course of today and the final draft? I would not make the statement without consultation with some reliable French friends. Duncan agrees. Of course both in my speech and Duncan's we would make some fairly stiff observations to the Germans to keep the balance.

I have spoken to Anthony to give him the general sense of this message and have asked him to get into touch with you –

> 'I have consulted Mr Churchill and he has authorized me to make the following statement. The German people feel that it is illogical and impossible to maintain two systems which are morally opposed.
>
> Germany cannot be, even formally, at the same time an occupied country and a partner in European Defence.
>
> I fully understand that Germany does not want a National Army. We are not suggesting that. We ask her to join a European Army on some such basis as has been proposed and was voted by the Assembly last August.

[1] The West German federal election of 1949 was the first contested election in Germany since 1933. The Christian Democratic Union–Free Democratic Party coalition won a plurality of votes in the new Bundestag. CDU leader Konrad Adenauer became the first Chancellor of the new Federal Republic of Germany.

But the only basis on which men can be comrades in defence – or, if the worst should come, in war – is a basis of equality.

Membership of a European system of Defence demands equality of status among the members of the Council of Europe.

The period of occupation must end. The period of partnership must begin.

But such an act of faith from Germany's former enemies deserves – and I am sure will receive – an attitude of sincerity in return. There must be genuine cooperation over the whole European field.

The early adherence of the German Government to the Schuman Coal/Steel Pact would do more than anything else to create that confidence.'

Winston S. Churchill to Harold Macmillan
(Churchill papers, 2/32)

23 November 1950

I have consulted Anthony and we are sure that no such far reaching statement should be made by you at Strasbourg at this juncture. The most you could say is that if the Germans joined a European Army they would be received as comrades with equally honourable military status.

Sir Ivone Kirkpatrick to Winston S. Churchill
(Churchill papers, 2/171)

23 November 1950
Confidential

Dear Mr Churchill,

Thank you for your letter[1] of November 19th enclosing one in which Lady Phillips expresses her anxiety about the state of Anglo-German relations.

There is of course no truth in the allegation that there is no cooperation between the Allies and the Germans and no attempt to foster any feeling but hate. But since I know that you are particularly interested in the German situation, I should like to tell you in a few words how matters stand.

Our relations with the Germans since the war have fluctuated. First we were greeted as liberators and when we declined to play that role our popularity sank. In a subsequent phase we made a substantial and costly effort to put Germany on her legs. This was widely realised and our relations correspondingly improved. Last year they deteriorated again because of dismantling and

---

[1] Reproduced above (p. 1937).

of the belief that restrictions on German industry were being maintained by British influence in order to throttle German competition.

Since then things have taken a turn for the better. The Foreign Secretary instructed me when I came out in June to do all I could to improve the atmosphere and I have done my best to gain the confidence of the Chancellor, the Leader of the Opposition,[1] and the many Germans I meet in every walk of life. In all this I have been actively supported by the senior officials in Germany and by the three Service Commanders. But it would of course have been impossible to make any impression if we had not been able to demonstrate that British policy was adjusting itself to events. The termination of disarmament (explosions of all kinds) in the British Zone, the New York Conference at which we were known to have sponsored a liberal policy towards Germany, the removal of all restrictions on shipbuilding for export, our efforts to have other restrictions removed, have all combined to create a better feeling towards us.

So much for the general picture. The relationship of individual Germans and Britons is a more difficult matter. The Army and Air Force live in cantonments far removed from the towns. They rarely come in contact with Germans and the tradition of non-fraternisation dies hard. But even here we are making progress, principally through sporting contests, football, hockey, horse shows and race meetings at which British and Germans take part together. There is also a certain amount of joint shooting. I hope with the assistance of the Commanders-in-Chief gradually to extend these contacts. This should not be difficult since the Germans have a high regard for our troops and I get very few complaints of bad behaviour. The requisitioning of houses is, and always will be, a sore point.

The personal relations of our Control Commission with the Germans are on the whole excellent. Almost all our executive officials speak German, live in the towns and meet a lot of Germans. When they have to leave Germany they are often the object of touching manifestations of affection and regard. I know this because I am sometimes asked by German Ministers to intervene to prevent a transfer. We have British Centres in many German towns and there are a large number of Anglo-German clubs and enterprises designed to promote a better understanding. I will not bother you with details of all these, but I should like to mention Wilton Park where we have a series of courses for selected Germans. When we thought of closing it not long ago on grounds of economy the government of North Rhine/Westphalia at once put up a substantial sum of money to enable it to continue.

All this sounds very complacent. I know, however, that we have a long way to go before Anglo-German relations are put on a sound footing and that a

---

[1] Kurt Schumacher, 1895–1952. Private, German Army, 1914–15. Joined SPD, 1918. Member, Württemberg Landtag, 1924–30; Reichstag, 1930–3. Arrested by Nazis, 1933. Imprisoned, 1933–43, 1944–5. Leader, SPD, 1946–52.

sustained effort is required, particularly since the Germans are clumsy, tactless and difficult partners.

I will not comment on Lady Phillips' misgivings about our rations except to say that whilst it is now permissible for everyone to buy food in the German shops within the limits set to our mark expenditure, I find it much cheaper and not deleterious to health to live as much as possible on British rations.

Finally may I thank you for your promise about the picture. It was with an eye to Anglo-German relations that I ventured originally to make the request.

Winston S. Churchill: speech
(Churchill papers, 2/336)

23 November 1950   Harrow School

Dr Moore, Ladies and Gentlemen,

The years slip by with extraordinary rapidity, or they seem to do so I suppose when you have to count so many, and it is most surprising to me that twelve months – not unmarked by events and ups and downs and a certain amount of ups – have passed since we were last gathered together here.

I must thank you Dr Moore for all the things you have so kindly said about me. I have had on other occasions to make this remark about some of the things I listen to nowadays that they are things which no man should hear until his death; but nevertheless, though I feel unworthy of hearing such praise I nonetheless feel very grateful for it and for the apparent unanimity with which it has been received. But I can assure you that it is not always so; if you had been in the House of Commons a couple of hours ago you would have found a far from unanimous audience.

I always enjoy listening to these Songs and I feel about them that, although the tunes are so splendid and link them into your minds year after year to make the inheritance you have, yet the words also deserve great attentive study. I think I have said before that anyone who knows the Harrow Song Book by heart is possessed of a vocabulary, a very good vocabulary, and a guide to a far better vocabulary, of our great English language.

I asked the Head Master whether we might disinter for today a very old song which I remember. I have not heard it sung for fifty years, but I remember it. I could not find it in my book and I dictated three or four verses from memory in a letter to the Head Master and on this they were able to identify the song in question. I hope you do not mind. It is a pretty good song, especially that verse about 'Buzz was the word on the island'. When I first came here in the War that was the situation through which we all lived. Nearly two generations of Harrow have passed since I had the pleasure of coming to you then. But there is only one part of this Song to which I have to suggest an amendment. It is the part about 'Hold a bit there, let 'em fire and air'. I think that should be 'Hold a bit there, we must have the air; and we'll have the sea and the island'.

Another thing came across my mind the other day which I wanted to congratulate you about and that is the Harrow hat. It really is a very fine head-dress. It is more than equal to keeping out any excessive sunshine we may have in this country, and its texture on the whole stands up to our rainy weather – on the whole. But just look at our friends at Eton. They haven't been able to think of a hat. The top hat they are unable to make. I wonder some Old Etonian does not endow them with a factory to make their top hats. At present they walk about like shock-headed Peters in tail coats. In all this formality I must say I feel great sympathy for them. On the other hand in the last few years we do not seem to have beaten them at Cricket as often as we used to do; so to some extent they can boast the advantage there. But we have got the hat trick – a remark which I venture to hope will not lead to any undue partisanship when you may be brought into contact with each other later on. I was going to say a word about Winchester, but I must be careful not to be drawn into Party politics.

Now ladies and gentlemen and Harrow boys, I again thank you most heartily for singing to me this evening, and I do beg you to regard these precious songs and words and ideas and themes as a great inspiration in later years and as a bond of contact and unity between you when you meet far away across the world and join together and to keep alive in your hearts the great themes of duty and honour for which this School has ever stood and for which its sons have been willing to make every sacrifice in life at any time they were called upon. These songs are an inspiration; they are a companion; they are a comfort. The more you sing them and the better you know them by heart and remember them, the more glad you will be to have them with you in the browner evenings in life.

I thank you very much indeed. I am so glad to see some of my old friends here: Mr Amery and, I think, the wife[1] of Bishop Nugent Hicks, by whom I had the pleasure to be whopped. But he was very kind. Even in the most stern part of his duty his kind heart got the better of him; that is an occasion on which we value the good sense and geniality of one who is set in authority over us.

Thank you very much indeed. I hope I will be able to come on some future occasion. I am sure that if you go forward with the spirit of the Harrow Song Book, you will find yourself more able to conquer, more able to secure all those things worth winning either for yourself or for the land which brought you forth.

---

[1] Ethel Katherine Hicks.

Anthony Marlowe to Winston S. Churchill
(Churchill papers, 2/99)

24 November 1950

My dear Churchill,

At yesterday's meeting of the '22 Committee I raised a point which I cannot claim met with any great enthusiasm and which I therefore wish to bring to your notice because I believe it provides a possibility of defeating the Government. I would be grateful for your consideration of it.

On the Order Paper there is a motion by some twenty Socialist members. This says, in effect, that the recent Russian approach should not be rejected out of hand but that we should take the initiative in calling a Conference to consider counter proposals. There is no difference whatever between this motion and the substance of Salisbury's speech in the Lords last week, nor is it very far removed from your own proposals during the General Election.

This is therefore a motion that could easily have come from our side of the House. My proposal is that the party should to a man, yourself included, put their names to this motion. A majority of the House would then have their names to it; a debate could not be refused. In such a debate the twenty members must either vote with us or abstain. Either way means defeat for the Government.

The objection, of course, is that it is beneath our dignity to put our names after these people who are without doubt the scum of the Left. On the other hand, if we had put the motion down (as well we might have done) we could not have prevented them putting their names to it after ours. Therefore there is no issue as to whether all these names could or could not appear on the same motion; the only question is who came first. I hope that if an opportunity presents itself to defeat the Government we are not going to lose it merely on a question of priorities or on the dignity of precedence.

This Government will not be defeated until some of their side come into our lobby. When that day comes, are we going to say that we cannot go into the same lobby as they? Obviously not. Therefore if we are prepared to go into the same lobby with them, why should we cavil at having our names on the same piece of paper?

Nobody likes the idea of joining with these dirty fellows to bring the Government down, but in a war one is often justified in accepting the most uncongenial ally and I feel this is no time for over-refinement in the matter. I am also convinced that we can have no better battle ground for the next election than Foreign Policy. The other side are waiting till they can make a Lords v. Commons issue. At the moment the people are scared stiff and if we can beat the Government to it by precipitating an election on the issue as to whether they would prefer our Foreign Affairs at this point to be in your hands or Bevin's I have no doubt of the answer.

November 1950

Winston S. Churchill to King George VI
(Churchill papers, 2/171)[1]

24 November 1950

Sir,

It gives me very great pleasure to send to Your Majesty this copy of the Third Volume of my War Memoirs which has at last reached me from the binders. I earnestly hope Your Majesty will accept it, and should regard that as a high honour.

I also send an early copy of the American edition of Volume IV. This will not be published here till the summer by Cassell's. I hope then I may send this also when it has been bound.

And with my humble duty remain Your Majesty's faithful and devoted servant and subject.

Winston S. Churchill to James Lindsay[2]
(Churchill papers, 2/90)

25 November 1950

My dear Lindsay,

The electors of South-East Bristol have an opportunity to confirm the lesson lately taught at Glasgow, Oxford and Birmingham, that the Conservative cause is gaining strength throughout the country and that this Socialist Government has not long to live.

The State monopolies which the Socialists have set up under their policy of Nationalization have already shown their vices. Their cost has played its part in reducing the buying power of our money. Month by month the pound buys fewer goods, and our social services and pensions are cut. The workers in the nationalized industries find State rule powerful, obstinate and clumsy. Trade Unions cannot play their proper part when the State combines the duties of umpire and employer.

This Socialist Government admits that it is powerless to halt the rise in the cost of living. They have now to buy coal abroad instead of selling it. They are spending four thousand million pounds a year, and our taxation, already the heaviest in the world – heavier than at the height of the war – is now to be increased. The prejudices which keep our building industry in shackles have led to such a failure, that the Socialist Party have abandoned hope of mending the housing shortage. 'Mark time' is the best they can do. This helpless attitude

---

[1] This letter was handwritten.
[2] James Lindsay, 1906–97. Youngest son of David Lindsay, Earl of Crawford. Served as Maj. in King's Royal Rifle Corps during WWII. Parliamentary candidate (Cons.) for the vacant seat of Bristol South-East, formerly held by Stafford Cripps, in by-election, 1950. MP (Cons.) for North Devon, 1955–9.

ought not to be accepted by a nation which in the war again and again did what faint hearts deemed impossible.

To the housing scandal is added the state of our defences. In spite of the vast sums voted by Parliament since the war was won, these are inadequate. A Conservative Government would turn on energy, contrivance and coherence not to be found in the present dispirited and worn-out Administration.

I am confident that the poll in South East Bristol will show that thoughtful men and women can now see that Socialist theories have brought us to a dead end. The only escape is by a speedy and decisive change of men and methods.

Your electors can be sure that in voting they support a man imbued with the spirit of disinterested public service, and possessed of a practical knowledge of British agriculture, on which our cities depend for food and life.

Winston S. Churchill to Anthony Marlowe
(Churchill papers, 2/99)

26 November 1950
Private

Dear Mr Marlowe,

I have no doubt whatever that it is our duty to vote against the amendments placed on the Order Paper by the Socialist dissentients, and this is the advice I shall give the Party. It would be fatal to our reputation and deeply injurious to the public interest to take a Party advantage in such a case.

Thank you indeed for writing.

King George VI to Winston S. Churchill
(Churchill papers 2/171)[1]

26 November 1950

My dear Winston,

Thank you so very much for giving me the bound copy of your 3rd Volume of your War Memoirs, and an early copy of the 4th Volume.

When I am reading them I always find that my heart beats faster. They remind me so vividly of the days through which we lived, and when we were so much together.

I was glad of our few minutes talk on Wednesday, but I hope you will come and see me one evening before Christmas when you do not have to attend the House of Commons, as there is much which I would like to discuss with you.

Thanking you again for the books.

---

[1] This letter was handwritten.

Sarah Churchill to Winston S. Churchill
(Churchill papers, 1/47)[1]

27 November 1950

Darling Papa,

The other night I saw a friend off on the *Queen Mary*. We had booked our passage back on her, and then had to cancel. As I arrived at the pier I saw the whole beauty and majesty of the ship, and a great nostalgia overwhelmed me. I had to remind myself that where she spelled 'home' for me she meant 'parting' for other people, otherwise I should have dissolved in tears! We so want to come home, but cannot yet, but all of our thoughts are homeward bound, but we still have things to do and problems to meet here. I am alone in a strange house, this was the only notepaper I could find! Anthony is still in Hollywood – I have told Mummie all his news and my daily doings. This is my birthday letter to you. I wonder if you know how much I think of you. I read in the *New York Times* the excerpts of *The Hinge of Fate*. It is so so brilliant – vivid, purposeful, thrilling. Generally I resent the way they chop it up, but this time it seems they have really done it well. I rushed to my paper every morning to find the next instalment!

It had a great effect here. They loved the wise, measured, truthful account, and I loved your wonderful warm generosity in your unstinted praise of them, giving always credit where credit was due, yet always holding us, and our own, proudly and firmly.

Reading it plunges me back not 6 or 7 years but into another lifetime. What must it be like when you look back through your life?

I am homesick for you all. Yet all is well here, and things look bright for Anthony, and we are a going concern so please believe in us, and if we are absent a little longer, it is not because we are not deeply rooted with you all, but because of the demands of the life we have chosen.

Happy happy birthday darling darling Papa.

Winston S. Churchill: speech
(Hansard)

30 November 1950   House of Commons

FOREIGN AFFAIRS

I hope that the level calm of yesterday's debate will be regarded as an example of our composure in times of danger and not as an instance of any failure on our part to realise its gravity. Perhaps the calm in all its aspects

---

[1] This letter was handwritten.

represents various characteristics in our national character. Certainly we are in danger, but the danger is not new. It was visible in all its terrible potential from the moment when the armies of democracy dispersed and melted away in the hour of victory while the armies of the Soviet oligarchy were maintained at an enormous strength and were re-equipped to a very high degree and when, on top of this, Russian imperialism, clothed in a new garb, advanced to carry the creed of Communism and the authority of the Kremlin forth in every direction until some solid obstacle was reached.

This danger became apparent to some of us before the war ended and was recognised widely throughout our confidential circles. It began to be realised by much larger numbers of people in Britain and the United States when the first conference of the Council of the United Nations took place at the beginning of 1946. Up till then for the great masses of the people all had been softened and shrouded in the Western democracies by the comradeship of the great struggle, by their relief in hard-won victory and by their admiration of the valour and sacrifices of the Russian armies. However, I must remind the House that already at the beginning of 1946 the Foreign Secretary felt himself forced to describe, to his face and in public, Mr Vyshinsky's statements as lies. I am not blaming the Foreign Secretary, but it showed how rapidly, in the course of a year, we had been disillusioned, or the outer world had been disillusioned. Since then, the increasing realisation by the Western democracies of the danger in which they stood and stand has been continuous.

There were two major differences between the state of the world after the First and after the Second World Wars. The sour aftermath of triumph in arms, however complete, brought with it in both cases many troubles, but here are the two differences. After the First War, when the victors had disarmed the Germans and their allies, no powerful organised army remained upon the scene except the French Army. After this war the armed might of Russia has emerged steadily year by year, almost month by month, as a rock shows more and more above an ebbing tide.

The second difference, which arose out of the realisation of the first, was that the United States, instead of retiring into isolation, instead of demanding full and prompt repayment of debts and disinteresting herself in Europe and even in the League of Nations, of which she had been one of the founders, has come forward step by step as the knowledge of the situation has dawned upon her and has made the great counterpoise upon which the freedom and the future of our civilisation depends. This fundamental change in the policy of the United States constitutes, in my view, the best hope for the salvation of Christian civilisation and democracy from Communist and Russian conquest and control. I hope, therefore, that we shall regard it as our first objective not to separate ourselves in action or in understanding or in sympathy in any degree, however slight, that can be avoided from the United States.

But the favourable policy of the United States after this last war, which has been so helpful to us in so many ways, did not affect the military disparity caused by the maintenance of immense Russian armies year after year and the development of their armoured forces, their air power and their submarines. We did not come to terms with them at the moment of German surrender while we, too, had the weapons in our hands. The Western Allies abandoned the whole of Eastern Germany, including an immense area of which they stood in occupation, to Soviet control, and Russia remained the overwhelming armed power, towering up in Europe and in Asia, avid for the expansion of their creed and their rule. The war had liberated Russia from her two pre-occupations – Germany and Japan. Both these warlike nations have inflicted terrible defeats and injuries upon Russia in this present twentieth century. Now both have ceased to be military factors and the years that have followed our victory have brought enormous increases of power and territory to Soviet Russia. In one form or another they have gained control of half Europe and all China without losing a single Russian soldier. They have every right to be encouraged by the progress they have made, but they show no signs of being in any way satiated or satisfied or even contented with it, and we can perceive no limits at present to their aims.

So much for the past. Let me now, in the very few minutes I shall detain the House, look to the present and the future. I hoped myself – and my view was shared by my colleagues at that time – that a lasting settlement might be reached with Russia before we evacuated our portion of central and eastern Germany, and before the United States' armies were demobilised and dispersed. Later, in 1948, I hoped that we might come to terms with them before they gained the secret of the atomic bomb. Now I hope that we may come to terms with them before they have so large a stockpile of these fearful agencies, in addition to vast superiority in other weapons, as to be able to terrorise the free world, if not, indeed, to destroy it.

Let us look at the time factor. In some aspects it is in our favour; in some it is adverse. The Soviets, under the restraint of the immense United States superiority in the atomic sphere, and also by the consolation of the rapid and immense gains which they have made and are still making in many directions without incurring any direct risk – under these two opposite forces – have hitherto been under restraint and control.

They have repeatedly been assured that the United States would not fight what is called a 'preventive' war. The United States have expressed the general opinion of the civilised world upon that aspect. On this basis the war, if ever it comes – which God forbid – will come at the moment of their choice. It, however, should be noted that the two restraining or consoling arguments which I have mentioned are both diminishing. The Soviet stockpile of atomic bombs is growing. How fast, I have no idea. I do not know whether the Government have knowledge. At any rate, we have none. And the Soviets must expect, while this stockpile is growing in their favour behind them, more resistance to their further expansion, and they will not find their progress so easy as it has been in the past. It is impossible to prophesy what they will do, or when, or how they will do it. One can only judge these matters by estimating what is their interest. The great Duke of Marlborough quoted as saying in his day: 'Interest never lies'; and there is no doubt that trying to put oneself in the position of the other party to see how things look to him is one way, and perhaps the best way, of being able to feel and peer dimly into the unknowable future. It is, at any rate, the only guide – and it does not include accident, passion, folly or madness, madness which may arise from some error, some blunder, or from the results of some internal convulsion. All that can be said is that it certainly does not seem to be in the Russian interest to begin a major struggle now.

We are told that it is provocative to organise an Atlantic army, with, as I see it, a European army inside of it and a German contingent, on honourable terms, inside that. We are told that that is provocative. It does not seem likely, however, that anything that we can do in the next two years in Europe will reverse the balance of military power. We may be stronger, but not strong enough in that time to deter, still less to prevail. There is plenty of room for us to get much stronger without altering the situation in Europe decisively. Therefore, while it is right to build up our forces as fast as we can, nothing in this process, in the period I have mentioned, will deprive Russia of effective superiority in what are called now the conventional arms. All that it will do is to give us increasing unity in Europe and magnify the deterrents against aggression, and, perhaps, give us the means of gradually approaching the situation when relations between world Powers may express themselves in normal terms and not only be measured in the strange and novel methods of the atomic age.

Dangerous as it may be to make such a prediction – I make it in all good faith, and without official knowledge – I would venture to express the opinion that a major attack by Russia in Europe is unlikely in the near future, and that it will not be provoked or produced by the modest measures of defence now being so slowly, so tardily and ineffectively developed up to the present by the Atlantic and Western Powers. Even if our preparations developed more rapidly, a long period must elapse before they could offset the Russian superiority, even if the Russian strength itself were not increased meanwhile. It is upon this that I found my hope that we still have time, that there is still a breathing space for us to pursue the policy of seeking an understanding, and for us to also pursue the essential counterpart and foundation of any such hope, namely, the building up of a more reasonable measure of defensive strength. This may be a vain hope. I may live, perhaps, to be mocked at if proved wrong by events. It is, at any rate, the working hypothesis of my thought in these anxious and agonising times.

Therefore I am in favour of efforts to reach a settlement with Soviet Russia as soon as a suitable opportunity presents itself, and of making those efforts while the immense and measureless superiority of the United States atomic bomb organisation offsets the Soviet predominance in every other military respect and gives us the means to talk together in a friendly and dignified manner and, at least as equals. I think that we are all agreed with what my right hon. Friend the Member for Warwick and Leamington (Mr Eden) said yesterday about the kind of answer we should make to the Russian proposals for a Four-Power conference. I was very glad to hear the Foreign Secretary fully endorse the suggestion which he made for drawing up an agenda, which should no doubt be done in the first instance by competent officials.

I hope, however, that at the right and best time, especially after matters are stabilised in the Far East, a conference will arise which will not merely be like those of which we have had too many in the past, of two sides arguing against each other in the glare of publicity, but that the decisive conversations will take place in confidence, in privacy and even in secrecy, and will be conducted at the highest levels. It is what I asked for at Edinburgh six months ago.[1] I agree that much has happened since then, particularly these great developments in the Far East and also the immense and active leadership now assumed by the United States, with whom we must march, or walk, hand in hand and to whom we must give all the help and good will which our power and experience allow. Much has happened since then but I do not think we should exclude from any of the discussions which may take place, perhaps after the present unhelpful crisis has passed away, the personal touch between those who have the right and the power to speak for the great States involved. That is only what I said at Edinburgh. I fully agree that time and the new circumstances which have come into view must influence, and even perhaps govern, our action.

This brings me to the crisis in Korea and China. We all find much that is disquieting in it, but I do not see that what is happening in the Far East should make the Soviets in a hurry to depart from their present policy of expansion by means of the cold war and of using others to advance their aims. The Foreign Secretary asked yesterday: Is this move of the Chinese into Korea part of a grand strategy for a definite purpose?

'Is there a Russo-Chinese conspiracy on a world-wide scale?' They were very proper questions for the right hon. Gentleman to ask, and to ask himself out loud. He said that he did not know the answers. I do not know who does. If it were true, that certainly would not suggest that the Russians contemplated an immediate violent action in Europe. We can only use the facts as they are known to us and endeavour to deduce conclusions from them.

On the contrary, the plan would evidently be to get the United States and the United Nations, so far as they contribute, involved as deeply as possible in China, and thus prevent the reinforcement of Europe and the building up of

---

[1] Speech reproduced above (pp. 1746–54).

our defensive strength there to a point where it would be an effectual deterrent. It is one of the most well-known – almost hackneyed – strategical and tactical methods, to draw your opponent's resources to one part of the field and then, at the right moment, to strike in another. Military history shows countless examples of this and of variants of it. Surely, however, the United Nations should avoid by every means in their power becoming entangled inextricably in a war with China. For this reason I had hoped that General MacArthur's advance in Korea – and I paid my tribute to him the other day, and to the extraordinary skill with which the operations had been handled, up to the point which we had then reached – would stop at the neck or wasp waist of the peninsula and would leave the country between the neck and the Yalu River and the Chinese frontier as a kind of No-man's-land which Allied air power would dominate. Under this cover there might have been constructed an ever-stronger fortified line, across the neck, wherever it might be found suitable. Of course, to hold such a line it is essential that the approaches to it should also be commanded, and therefore such a line cannot be exactly along the imaginary lines which are drawn on the maps to indicate the parallels. To take a practical guide, the shortest space might be chosen and the strongest defence made there, with a hinterland or neutral space before it – or if not neutral, a No-man's-land, a disputed No-man's-land – which would give the necessary facilities to the defence.

Whether this will be possible now depends upon the result of the great battle which is at this moment raging. I suppose we shall know in a few days what the results are. I am sure, however, that the whole House feels that the sooner the Far Eastern diversion – because, vast as it is, it is but a diversion – can be brought into something like a static condition and stabilised, the better it will be for all those hopes which the United Nations have in hand. For it is in Europe that the world cause will be decided. As my right hon. Friend the Member for Warwick and Leamington said yesterday, it is there that the mortal danger lies. I am sure that we all agree with that. Perhaps we are biased by the fact that we live there or thereabouts. But none the less, one cannot conceive that our natural bias has in any way distorted the actual facts.

There is another reason why we should be very careful not to indulge in criticisms of the United States or their commanders, or do anything which could weaken, even by gusts of opinion, the vital ties that bind our fates together. We fight in the name of the United Nations. That gives a great moral sanction to our action, but in Korea and the Far East the burden falls almost entirely on the United States. It is important to get the proportions right. The Minister for Defence read us out yesterday, or circulated, the British casualties before the recent fighting. I fear that they may have been increased since then. The killed were 51, wounded 175 and missing 5. We have not been told what are the American casualties, but I have heard on good authority that they have lost at least 7,000 or 8,000 men killed and between 20,000 and 30,000 wounded. It may be accurate or inaccurate, but that was before this recent fighting. And therefore I say that we must realise the enormous weight of the burden that rests upon them and of the noble sacrifices they are making in the common cause.

Casualties are no doubt not the only measure of war effort, but they are the supreme and truest measure of the sacrifice and exertion of the brave troops made by any army. Our contribution and that of the other United Nations countries, however precious to us, cannot in any way be compared with that of the United States. Our thoughts are with our own gallant soldiers. We watch their fortunes with the deepest sympathy and confidence that they will do their duty with distinction. But their presence there must be taken as a symbol of our loyalty to the common cause and our main responsibility lies here at home in Europe.

I thought that it was a great pity when at the American suggestion and under American pressure the Combined Chiefs of Staff Committee was allowed to lapse. Contacts have, I fear, been lost which cannot be wholly regained by larger bodies speaking different languages. The Combined Chiefs of Staff Committee was the keystone of our arch of victory. Formally or informally, in one way or another, it should, I am sure, be reconstituted at the earliest moment. It is quite true that when we have so few troops engaged in the existing theatre of war, we cannot expect to exert influence except by reasoned argument. But let us make sure we have full opportunity for that, especially taking place as it would between officers who have been through the great struggle together and who know each others' minds and have confidence in each others' characters. I entirely agree with what my right hon. Friend said yesterday that the strongest British representation possible should be available – I mean Ministerial representation – in Washington and if necessary at Lake Success. It should be there in these present anxious and formative weeks. No one must underrate the latent strength of our country or the contribution we are capable of making directly or indirectly to the common cause of the United Nations.

When your friend and ally is bearing almost the whole weight, it is natural that he will have the control. War is little more than a catalogue of mistakes and misfortunes. It is when misfortune comes, however, that allies must hold more firmly together than ever before. Here in Britain, and I doubt not throughout the British Empire and Commonwealth of Nations, we always follow a very simple rule, which has helped us in maintaining the safety of this country: 'The worse things get, the more we stand together.' Let it also be seen that the English-speaking world follows the same plan. Nothing will be more helpful in rousing the nations of Europe to coherent measures of self-defence than the feeling that the unity of the English-speaking world and of the free nations of Western Europe is unbreakable, and that the stresses and perils of our position only weld us more solidly together and call forth whatever exertions are necessary for self-preservation.

This also applies in a smaller sphere to our party affairs at home. Had some of the Amendments, or one of the Amendments, on the Paper been moved, we should, of course, have voted with His Majesty's Government. But even if there is no Division – and I understand that a Division is unlikely – the House of Commons has here today, by its temper and its attitude, an opportunity of making our fundamental unities apparent to the world, and we may be sure that all this process gives the best hope of avoiding a third world war, not by appeasement of opponents from weakness, but by wise measures, fair play from strength and the proof of unconquerable resolve.

December
1950

Clement Attlee to Winston S. Churchill
(Churchill papers, 2/28)

3 December 1950

Top Secret

My dear Churchill,
 I promised to send you a note about the circumstances in which the clause in the Quebec Agreement was allowed to lapse which provided that neither the Americans nor ourselves would use the bomb against third parties without each other's consent. I enclose a copy of a note setting out the facts.
 The salient points are, I think, the following:
 1. In negotiations after the war the Americans showed themselves most anxious to get rid of this clause and, indeed, of what might be called the political as opposed to the technical provisions of the Quebec Agreement. This was not so much because they wished to escape the obligation of the Agreement, but because its existence put them in a very embarrassing position with Congress. It was, as you know, a secret agreement of which Congress has not been told and it obviously went much further than the normal scope of an Executive Agreement such as the President has power to conclude, nor did they think it practicable to get a treaty embodying its terms ratified by the Senate. The best solution for them therefore was that it should be allowed to lapse with the exception of those technical provisions providing for interchange of information and sharing of raw materials which were continued under an informal agreement known as the *modus vivendi* concluded in January 1948.
 2. We for our part were equally anxious to get rid of the fourth clause which prevented us from making use of atomic energy for industrial purposes except on terms to be specified by the President.
 3. Moreover we had been working ever since the end of the war to restore the war-time co-operation with the Americans which they

had broken off with the coming of peace and the passing of the MacMahon Act.[1] The dropping of the second and fourth clauses seemed likely to smooth the way.

4. Finally, and most important, we realised that harmony of action in such a vital matter as the use of the weapon must in the last resort depend upon the degree of friendship and understanding prevailing between our two countries and not on any written agreement, one of the original authors of which was no longer alive.

I do not of course for a moment wish to detract from the very great importance to us of the Quebec Agreement during the war. You will remember very well the difficulty you had in getting the Americans to conclude it, and it was a great achievement. But I think you may also agree that in the quite different circumstances of peace the secret war-time agreement no longer had the same character as a binding understanding between the two countries.

ATOMIC ENEGRY
The Quebec Agreement of 1943

The (Anglo-American) Quebec Agreement of August, 1943, is no longer in force.

2. The arrangements which were made in Washington in 1945 for a fresh agreement on cooperation between the United States, United Kingdom and Canada in the whole field of atomic energy were nullified by the passage of the McMahon Act and cooperation virtually ceased. In 1948 cooperation on a tripartite basis, with the Canadians coming in as equal partners, was resumed on a limited basis under the *modus vivendi* concluded in January, 1948.

3. This *modus vivendi* abrogated the previous agreements to which the three governments, or any two of them, were a party in the atomic energy field with certain named exceptions.

4. Specifically, the *modus vivendi* did not reproduce the second and fourth clauses of the Quebec Agreement which were political in character, namely that

'we will not use it (the bomb) against third parties without each others' consent'

and

'in view of the heavy burden of production falling upon the United States as the result of a wise division of war effort, the British Government recognise that any post-war advantages of an industrial or commercial character shall be dealt with as between the United States and Great Britain on terms

---

[1] The McMahon Act, passed in 1946, set guidelines for US management of nuclear technology developed with the UK and Canada. The Act further called for civilian, not military, management of nuclear weapon development, and to that end the Atomic Energy Commission was formed.

to be specified by the President of the United States to the Prime Minister of Great Britain. The Prime Minister expressly disclaims any interest in these industrial and commercial aspects beyond what may be considered by the President of the United States to be fair and just and in harmony with the economic welfare of the world.'

5. The limited inter-change of technical information under the *modus vivendi* still continues and an interim agreement has been made covering raw materials allocation pending the conclusion of negotiations, which are still proceeding, with the United States and Canadian Governments for complete technical cooperation in the atomic energy field. On this we are awaiting some fresh American proposals which are in the course of preparation.

Randolph S. Churchill to Winston S. Churchill
(Churchill papers, 1/48)[1]

4 December 1950

My dearest Papa,

I have just heard of a suggestion which it seems to me might afford us a way out of other difficulties without running the risk of 'extending the war' or getting bogged down in China. It is to use the atom bomb tactically <u>south</u> of the Yalu river so as to seal off the enemy's supply lines.

If four or five of the main roads and essential passes were atomised the effect might be decisive. Yet it could be done with a negligible loss of human life. At the same time it would be the best possible way of showing our enemies – declared and undeclared – that we are in earnest. If we are never going to use the bomb we had better stop making it and divert the immense effort involved to making some weapons we are not too squeamish to use, perhaps bows and arrows.

It may be that this use of the bomb is already in your mind. In which case I am sorry for taking up your time. But I thought it right to pass it on. Your loving son.

---

[1] This letter was handwritten.

Lord Cherwell to Winston S. Churchill
(Churchill papers, 2/28)

6 December 1950

My dear Winston,

Thank you for your letter with enclosures handed to me by Deakin.

Frankly I had never thought of your agreement with the President[1] as binding in perpetuity. It was, I thought, a provisional arrangement which would be replaced by a more detailed treaty when we knew more about how things were likely to develop after the war.

The President could scarcely by a secret agreement bind America for ever, either constitutionally or in fact, to accept our having a veto on the use of the bomb. Nor I imagine would you have consented to leave us completely and permanently at the mercy of whatever administration happened to be in office at Washington as regards the commercial and industrial exploitation of atomic energy, however this might develop in the centuries ahead.

At the time, as you will remember, the Americans had very exaggerated ideas about this industrial aspect and attached great importance to it. I always believed it would take a generation to develop atomic energy for civilian use and therefore saw no objection to the 4th Clause. And so far at any rate, the assessment has proved right for there seems little probability of any great developments in industrial uses for several more years at the very least.

But these clauses, which were entirely reasonable in wartime when we had the same enemies and allies and when we were sharing all our inventions and ideas and when we expected to obtain and profit by all the knowledge collected in the course of the immense American effort (at least twenty times as great as ours), were clearly bound to be unsuitable if the two countries each went their separate ways. And I think we all expected some new agreement would have to be negotiated if and when this happened.

After the war of course, Congress intervened and passed the MacMahon Act, which strictly speaking would have stopped all collaboration. Presumably if the President had tried to oppose it, praying in aid Roosevelt's agreement with you, the agreement would have been declared unconstitutional and ultra vires.

So far as I know, by stretching the Act a bit we have been co-operating in some slight degree in technical matters to which we attached great importance and this collaboration we hoped to expand. But the Americans always said the MacMahon Act stood in the way of doing this and that it would require legislation. And when we hoped we had brought them up to the point of facing

---

[1] The Quebec Agreement of August 1943 on the joint Anglo-American development of nuclear technology, in particular weaponry.

this the Fuchs[1] case came to a head and they said there was no hope of getting Congressional approval for extending collaboration.

I do not, of course, know any of the details of all these negotiations, but I think this is the broad outline of what happened. Portal must of course be completely informed.

Broadly, therefore I do not think the Government can be blamed for negotiating a new agreement after the war. Whether they could have got better terms is another matter. But I am sure America would not have allowed us to assert a veto in perpetuity on her use of the bomb on the strength of the secret agreement between you and Roosevelt.

Please excuse this hasty note and believe me as ever.

Winston S. Churchill: speech
('Winston S. Churchill, His Complete Speeches', volume 8, pages 8135–7)

6 December 1950   House of Commons

THE EARL OF OXFORD AND ASQUITH

I am grateful for being asked to unveil this monument to my old chief, Herbert Henry Asquith. I served with him and under him for ten convulsive, formative and momentous years. After having been Home Secretary for three years, and Chancellor of the Exchequer for two, he was Prime Minister for eight.

[. . .] At fifty he was Prime Minister. He made his way by his distinction in House of Commons debate. Hard, clear-cut, lucid argument, expressed in happy terms with many a glint of humour and flash of repartee, brevity, as well as clarity – these were his weapons in those days of lengthy, sonorous harangues. He was no ebullient orator pouring forth his sentimental or passionate appeal. But few there were who could face him in the tense debating of issues, large or small. Here was a man who dealt in reasoned processes, who placed things in their proper scale and relation, who saw the root of the matter and simplified the tale.

You must not think of him, however, as the embodiment in public affairs only of common sense and goodwill. These were his foundation, but in action he showed himself as hard and as stern as the times required. Henry Asquith was not only a Liberal, he was a Radical. He had made his own way by his talents and driving power. He was determined to broaden the road and break

---

[1] Emil Julius Klaus Fuchs, 1911–88. Born in Germany. Recruited by Rudolf Peierls to work on Tube Alloys project, 1941. Granted British nationality, 1942. Head of Theoretical Physics Div., Atomic Energy Research Establishment, Harwell, UK, 1946–50. Convicted of supplying Manhattan Project information to Soviet Union, 1950. Deputy Director, Institute for Nuclear Research, Rossendorf, East Germany, 1979. Patriotic Order of Merit, 1980. Order of Karl Marx, 1980.

down the remaining barriers so as to enable ever larger numbers of ordinary people to win their place in an expanding society and have a fair share of the show. In this way he was in basic harmony with an age which has brought, and is bringing, ever more millions of men and women to a table which might but for human folly and wickedness be ever more bountifully laden for the whole human race.

He was not in essence an organizer, or administrator, nor was he a revolutionary impulse. As I saw him he was a *Ruler* who, as I have written,

> knew where he stood on every question of life affairs in an altogether unusual degree. Scholarship, politics, philosophy, law and religion were all spheres in which, at the time when I knew him best, he seemed to have arrived at definite opinions. On all, when the need required, his mind opened and shut smoothly and exactly, like the breech of a gun.
>
> He always gave me the impression of measuring all the changing, baffling situations of public and parliamentary life according to settled standards and sure convictions. There was also the sense of a scorn, lightly and not always completely veiled, for arguments, for personalities, and even for events, which did not conform to the patter he had with so much profound knowledge and reflection adopted. (*Great Contemporaries*)

I wrote these words nearly twenty years ago, and I am content to repeat them now, because the statue which we shall presently see should express the character of a strong man, not drifting with the tide, or trimming his sails to the gusts of popularity, but making his impact on the society in which he lived by pursuing purposes – far above party – which served the causes he had made his own.

Henry Asquith was a patriot, who at all times sought, according to the broad light by which he marched, the welfare of the British people, and the enduring splendour of the British Empire. At no time, in power or out of power, did the clatter and anger of political struggles in a free democracy prevent him from responding to those deep undertones of national honour and of national safety for the country and the people, whom he served or led.

Although I was in a subordinate station – one of his lieutenants – and nearly a generation behind him, I saw him often and knew him well. He had a full and joyous life. His blood bit deep, and he transmitted to his children the untiring courage and far-ranging intellect by which he had himself been upborne. Some of them are here today to see their father's memory proclaimed, and enshrined amid universal respect in the House of Commons, where he shone and which he loved. All his sons of military age fought in the forefront of the First World War. Raymond[1] was killed with the

---

[1] Raymond Asquith, 1878–1916. Admitted to Inner Temple, 1904. Married, 1907, Katharine Frances Horner. Killed in action, 15 Sep. 1916.

Grenadiers on the Somme. 'Ock'[1] died before his time as the result of wounds received in battle, rising through four years of repeated deeds of prowess from sub-lieutenant to brigadier-general. Brilliant figures stand here with us today who carry on Henry Asquith's lineage and his fame.

Before their eyes, while all salute, I now unveil the statue of their sire.

General Dwight D. Eisenhower to Winston S. Churchill
(Churchill papers, 2/169)

6 December 1950

Dear Winston,

Thank you very much for sending me a copy of *The Hinge of Fate*. I have, of course, read in my daily paper some of its selected passages, but I am starting now to give it thorough study. A single glance shows it to be as full of meat as are its predecessors in the series.

Your book describes the arrangements that were made at Casablanca for setting up an Allied Headquarters. There is related, a bit later, Brendan Bracken's attitude with respect to the probable public reaction in Britain to any overplaying of the Supreme Commander's role. In these passages more than history is involved – there are valuable hints on human behaviour, and there are lessons for the future.

If I were pushed to place a tag on the one lesson on which I feel able to comment with some confidence, I would call it 'The Gradual Approach' in developing efficiency in Allied Command machinery. Only tolerance, patience, readiness to conciliate and an ability to look at the other side of the coin can make a success of such ventures. Since these are the qualities that soldiers traditionally abhor (there is no D'Artagnan flavour to them), there is plenty of room for error and failure, after the headquarters has been theoretically established.

If future war-time Statesmen should become dogmatic in the assumption that through written documents, chock-full of provisos, whereases and conditions, they can assure the success of an Allied Command or of the military operations that are to be directed by that Command, then we shall have nothing but sterile, uninspired and totally unsatisfactory performance. Likewise, if any military individual, designated for a high position in such a headquarters, becomes obsessed with the need for glorifying his particular position (and this they sometimes do in the name of their country's prestige), a similar failure will result. This applies – and I hope that this does not make me appear immodest – with particular force to the Supreme Commander.

[1] Arthur Melland Asquith, 1883–1939. Known as 'Ock'. On active service during WWI (wounded four times, despatches, DSO thrice). Married, 1918, Betty Constance Manners: four children. Member of the Council of the Ministry of Labour, 1918–20.

I am particularly confident that any man named to Supreme Commander must approach it <u>studiously</u> and <u>gradually</u> and imbued with an idea to 'earn' his way rather than to take the attitude that most of us in the military do when we encounter a routine change of assignment. In the normal case, the size and composition of our commands are specified exactly and the scope and extent of our authority defined accurately by regulation and custom. Consequently, we waste no time in getting on with whatever chore may be given us; we demonstrate without delay 'who is boss'. That whole attitude must be left behind when an Allied Command is brought into being.

Historically, the peak of mutual confidence and trust – which must exist not only between these governments and their commanders in the field and among these commanders as individuals – was reached in the war in Europe when you and the CIGS informed me in no uncertain terms that, if ever I had any dissatisfaction with any British commander, no matter what his rank or his position, he would be relieved instantly upon my request. Incidentally, on that day I saw you with new eyes – in a light that has never since left you, so far as I'm concerned.

When such a situation as this has been brought about through mutual tolerance, understanding and application to duty, the problem has become easy; only disaster clearly traceable to the stupidity of the top man could possibly unhorse him. But the real job is to bring everyone forward to this cooperative attitude.

Forgive me if I have seemed to write to you about this point at excessive length. But I cannot forget that events march fast in the world. Much of what we did in World War II has no application whatsoever to any future conflict into which we might be forced. But these experiences and lessons that deal with human beings – and particularly when these human beings are placed into positions of such responsibility that they involve capacity to damage the coalition as well as to rivet it tightly together – should, if remembered and heeded, do much to smooth out future difficulty and to expedite the true business of soldiers, which is merely to win victories and then to retire to the rear of the stage.

My present personal plans (if not interrupted by a call to duty) will bring me to the United Kingdom in the late spring. I shall then, of course, hope to call upon you to pay my respects. If you should have any interest in the matters I have so haltingly spoken of in this letter, we could talk about them then.

Again, my warm thanks for your magnificent volume. Please extend my greetings to your charming wife and to your nice family.[1]

---

[1] Churchill responded: 'Deeply grateful for your letter.'

December 1950

Winston S. Churchill: speech
('Winston S. Churchill, His Complete Speeches', volume 8, pages 8138–9)

13 December 1950   House of Commons

OLIVER STANLEY

On this side of the House we are greatly obliged to the Prime Minister for the kindly tribute which he has paid to our late colleague. We are all also very glad that the Government in this matter have not been bound by a narrow view of the precedents for such a tribute. There have been exceptions, and they have been made in accordance with the general feeling of the House, which, in such matters, is probably the safest of guides. The Prime Minister has mentioned two outstanding cases where the exact forms were not observed, but where the feelings of the House desired an opportunity of corporate expression. Oliver Stanley may well be another of these exceptions.

The appreciations published in the newspapers of every hue show how widely understood and admired were his exceptional and outstanding gifts and qualities. Reading them must have been a comfort to his many friends in the House of Commons and throughout the land. He served at the front in the line as a regimental officer through many of the severities of the First World War. He filled great offices of State in peace and war. I regretted very much that I could not persuade him to accept the Dominions Office at the time of the formation of the National Government. He preferred to rejoin his regiment. It was not until two years later that I was able to persuade him to allow me to submit his name as Secretary of State for the Colonies. This delay was not due to any breach in our personal friendship or in our political relations.

Oliver Stanley always set the interests of his country, as he conceived them, far above his personal fortunes or career. In the year before the war he wrote to Mr Chamberlain advising him that the Government should be widened and strengthened in composition, and placing his own office at the Prime Minister's disposal in order to help such a process. I did not know about this for several years afterwards, but it is a remarkable example of his bearing and relationship to public life, and a proof of the high level upon which his actions proceeded.

He was indeed, as so many of us know, a delightful companion. His conversation never lost its dignity, even in casual talk, and he always preserved in it the spark of the unexpected. His memory will long be cherished, and cherished most dearly by those who knew him best. Our keen sympathy, as the Prime Minister has said, goes out to his family and the children he has left behind him.

Oliver Stanley's career has been cut short in its prime. Nonetheless, it is not lacking in the sense of completeness, because we have the presentation in an integral and matured form of his personality, of his gifts, and of his record that endures with us. On this side we have suffered a heavy party loss, and, many of us, a keen personal loss; but, as the Prime Minister has said, the House of Commons as a whole is conscious that Parliament is definitely and seriously the poorer by the untimely removal of this capable, experienced and attractive figure, who adorned our debates with a happy combination of wit and wisdom, and enriched our public life by high character, by disinterested public service, and by a commanding view of wide horizons.

Winston S. Churchill: speech
(Hansard)

14 December 1950   House of Commons

THE INTERNATIONAL SITUATION

I hasten to associate myself wholeheartedly with the tribute which the Prime Minister has paid to Mr Peter Fraser. His part in the war was in every way worthy of the country he represented and of the magnificent New Zealand Divisions which served with honour in every field.

We are all very glad to see that the military situation for the time being in Korea has somewhat improved. I hope also that there is truth in the reports that a measure of censorship is being established over the despatches from the front or from Tokyo by the war correspondents of all the United Nations. I should think most of us agree with General Robertson's[1] protest upon this point. When one sees set forth day after day the exact position, numbers, condition and intentions of the United Nations troops, very often unit by unit, one cannot but feel that it is hardly fair to the soldiers who are fighting that the enemy should be presented with such complete intelligence, whereas so little seems to be known by us about the other side, and such a large measure of ignorance prevails, among the general public at least, about the enemy's dispositions, strength and movements. Indeed, the wildest estimates are given on high authority only to be contradicted and reversed a few days later.

One instance, a small one, but not without significance, particularly struck me. A Centurion tank was damaged and left behind. This was immediately

---

[1] Brian Hubert Robertson, 1896–1974. On active service, WWI, 1914–18. MC, DSO, 1919. Managing Director, Dunlop South Africa Ltd, 1935–40. Asst Quartermaster, General East African Command, 1940–1; Gen. 8th Army, North Africa, 1941–2. CBE, 1942. Deputy Adjutant and Quartermaster, Gen. 8th Army, North Africa, 1942–3. Commandant, Tripoli, 1942. Chief Administration Officer, 15th Army Group, Italy, 1943–4; Allied Armies, Italy, 1944. KCVO, 1944. Chief Administration Officer, 15th Army Group, Italy, 1944–5. Chief, Central Commission, Germany, 1945–7. Deputy Military Governor, British Zone, Germany, 1945–7. KCMG, 1947. Military Governor, British Zone, Germany, 1947–9. British High Commissioner, Allied High Commission, Germany, 1949–50. GBE, 1949. ADC General to the King, 1949–52. C-in-C, Middle East Land Forces, 1950–3. ADC General to the Queen, 1952. GCB, 1952. Retired, 1953. Chairman, British Transport Commission, 1953–61. Baron, 1961. Director, Dunlop PLC, 1961–9.

published and its importance emphasised. All the secrets were published of the latest British tank. Thus this vehicle, left behind among great numbers of no doubt other broken down vehicles, and in all the litter of retreat amid the snow, acquired instantly, in the enemy's eyes, an exceptional significance. I was very glad to read – I hope it is true – that it had been successfully destroyed from the air. That would have been a very good tale to tell if true, after it had happened, but why was it necessary to attract the enemy's attention to this vehicle beforehand. That seems to me a particular illustration. We really must have tighter control over what is published. We all seek to prevent and limit aggression, and one of the additional deterrents which we might impose upon the enemy's aggression would be to tell them that if it goes on much longer we shall cut them off from these invaluable supplies of information.

The Prime Minister's visit to Washington has done nothing but good. The question we all have to consider this afternoon in the House of Commons is, how much good. The Prime Minister spoke of the importance of renewing the series of meetings between the President and the Prime Minister which had taken place during the war and since the war. We all agree with that. We all agree with the advantages of direct discussion to which the Prime Minister has just referred.

I must say it seems to me that five years is rather a long interval, and the decision when it came, was very suddenly taken. My right hon. Friend the Member for Warwick and Leamington (Mr Eden) spoke on 29th November and urged that we should have stronger representation at Washington at the highest level. I endorsed this when I spoke the next day. I did not wish to appear to reflect any more than he did, in the slightest degree, upon our excellent Ambassador in Washington,[1] and I used the particular phrase, Ministerial representation. That very evening we were told that the Prime Minister was going. During the afternoon there was some excitement caused in the House by the accounts of Mr Truman's interview with the Press which appeared on the tape. But I understand that this was not the reason that led to the Prime Minister's decision to go and that this was taken earlier in the day. Certainly the decision was very hastily arrived at, after an interval of five years.

Many will think that earlier meetings might have been held. Several recent occasions occur to one. When the Soviet-inspired aggression by the North Korean Government across the 38th Parallel took place, and when the United States intervened vigorously and actively with the approval of the United Nations Assembly and we joined with them at the end of June, that was certainly an occasion which the Prime Minister might have considered for talking matters over with our great Ally and friend.

Again, after General MacArthur's brilliant counter-stroke, which gave us back Seoul and changed the whole aspect of the fighting up to that point in

---

[1] Sir Oliver Franks.

Korea, would have been, it seems to me, a good moment to talk over the next steps. At that moment many issues were open, which would have gained by having that direct discussion face to face between the heads of Government assisted by their military advisers. It is always easy to be wise after the event, but there were many people in this country who were wise before the event. I am by no means sure that His Majesty's Government and their expert advisers are excluded from that large number.

Those who had this view felt that it would be wiser to fortify a line, if not at the 38th Parallel, at the waist or at the best military position in advance of it, thus leaving a broad no-man's-land in which we could reconnoitre and into which we could go with mobile columns and, of course, with the all-powerful air forces available while building up all the time a strong fortified line which we could hold while, perhaps, conversations went on.

There is much to be said for strong fortified lines. If properly organised in depth, if protected in front by ever-expanding minefields and wire entanglements, and if developed week after week by concreted structures and excavations and firmly held with modern fire power, they would prove a terrific obstacle to the advance of infantry. All this becomes greater when both flanks rest upon the sea and the sea is in Allied command and when we have unquestioned mastery of the air. Such a position, once established, as it would have been possible to do, about 100 miles long, presents a very different obstacle to the advance and infiltration of masses of enemy infantry, from a moving front in hilly, rocky, scrub-covered country, then broadened to about 300 miles.

I am speaking only of what has happened in the past. I do not attempt to say anything about what may happen in the future. (Hon. Members: 'Why not?') It would be very unwise and unnecessary to do so in military operations. To pierce a properly fortified line not only would masses of artillery have to be accumulated, but there would also have to be very heavy concentrations of armour. These would present admirable targets to overwhelming air power. It certainly seems that the Chinese armies, if they had attacked such a line, might well have renewed on an even larger scale the painful experiences which we ourselves so often suffered on the Somme and at Passchendaele and in other bloody battlefields of the First World War. I cannot help feeling that it would have been well if all these matters had been talked over at the right moment and in good time in Washington by the highest authorities in both our countries.

We immediately approved the Prime Minister's decision to go when he did, and I feel sure that no one regrets it now. We welcome and wholeheartedly support the Prime Minister's statement about British and American unity and how their two flags will fly together however the winds may blow. That is, indeed, the foundation, as he said in his closing words, of our safety and the best hope for the peace of the world and for the survival of free civilisation. It is a great comfort in the darkening scene to feel that there are no party differences, or very limited party differences, in this country on this supreme issue, and that the task of trying to drive a wedge between us and the United States is left to the Communists and their fellow-travellers, aided perhaps, no doubt through folly rather than malice, by the usual Ministerial indiscretions.

Another advantage which has come from the Prime Minister's journey has been the renewed explicit declarations by the United States emphasising the priority of the defence of Europe. We are glad indeed that General Eisenhower is to be appointed to the Supreme Command of the army – however it may be denominated – which is being constituted there. We were led to believe that this appointment would be made many weeks ago. Progress in European defence, which was tardily begun, continues to be lamentably slow. It is more than nine months since I pointed out that no effective defence of Europe was possible without the armed strength of Germany. The movement of opinion in that direction has been continual, but nothing has been done. No agreement has been reached, and meanwhile Germany lies even more undefended than do other European countries under the menace of Communist and Russian aggression.

The months slip quickly away all the time. Several years have already been wasted, frittered away. The overwhelming Russian military power towers up against us, committees are multiplied, papers are written, words are outpoured and one declaration succeeds another, but nothing in the slightest degree in proportion to the scale of events or to their urgency has been done. When we return after our anxious Recess we shall require a full and prolonged debate upon defence, and we shall demand that a portion of it shall be in secret.

It was with the danger of Europe in my mind that I said some weeks ago that I hoped that we should not get entangled in China. In order to protect myself from the charge of being wise after the event, I venture to remind the House that on 16th November, before these recent reverses in Korea had taken place, I asked the Minister of Defence a supplementary question, which I do not think he resented in any way:

> '... whether he and the Foreign Secretary will constantly bear in mind the great importance of our not becoming, and of our Allies so far as we can influence their actions not becoming, too much pinned down in China or in the approaches to China at a time when the danger in Europe is ... occupying all our minds?' – (Official Report, 16th November, 1950; Vol. 480, c. 1910.)

I need scarcely say that I hold to that conviction still.

In view, however, of what has happened since then in Korea and in the United Nations Assembly, I feel it requires to be stated with more precision and refinement. We must not at any time be drawn into urging a policy which would inflict dishonour or humiliation upon the United States or upon the United Nations. Such a course would be at least as full of danger as any other now open to us. We learn from the newspapers that the proposals for a truce or cease fire which were proposed by the 13 Asiatic and Arab states, have been opposed by the Soviet delegation. They certainly seemed to be very far-reaching proposals from our point of view.

I will not say more about them, but, while the fullest priority should be given to the defence of Western Europe, it would be a great mistake to lose our sense of proportion and cast everything to the winds elsewhere. The only prudent course open to the United States and ourselves is to stabilise the local military position and, if the opportunity then occurs, to negotiate with the aggressors and at least make sure that we negotiate from strength and not from weakness.

We shall no doubt hear from the Foreign Secretary tonight how the question of further conversations with Soviet Russia stands. There was, I think, fairly complete agreement in the House that no abrupt negative or merely dilatory action would be appropriate to the Russian request, and from what we have read in the newspapers, it does not seem likely that there will be any serious disagreement between us upon the procedure eventually to be adopted.

I am strongly in favour of every effort being made by every means, to secure a fair and reasonable settlement with Russia. I should, however, be failing in frankness to the House, and to some of those who agree with me upon this matter, to whom I am much opposed in many ways, if I did not make it clear at this stage that we must not place undue hopes upon the success of any negotiations which may be undertaken. It is our duty – and a duty which we owe to the cause of peace and to our own consciences – to leave no effort unmade that wisdom and fair play can suggest, and that patience can bring forward. But on this side of the House we have never contemplated that if negotiations failed, we should abandon any of the great causes for which we have stood in the past, and for which the United Nations organisation stands today.

The declaration of the Prime Minister that there will be no appeasement also commands almost universal support. It is a good slogan for the country. It seems to me, however, that in this House it requires to be more precisely defined. What we really mean, I think, is no appeasement through weakness or fear. Appeasement in itself may be good or bad according to the circumstances. Appeasement from weakness and fear is alike futile and fatal. Appeasement from strength is magnanimous and noble and might be the surest and perhaps the only path to world peace.

When nations or individuals get strong they are often truculent and bullying, but when they are weak they become better mannered. But this is the reverse of what is healthy and wise. I have always been astonished, having seen the end of these two wars, how difficult it is to make people understand the Roman wisdom, 'Spare the conquered and confront the proud'. I think I will go so far as to say it in the original: *Parcere subjectis, et debellare superbos*. The modern practice has too often been 'punish the defeated and grovel to the strong'.

Unhappily, except as regards the atomic bomb – about which I shall have a word to say before I sit down – we are in a very weak position and likely to remain so for several years. As I have repeatedly said, it is only the vast superiority of the United States in this awful weapon that gives us any chance of survival. The argument is now put forward that we must never use the atomic bomb until, or unless, it has been used against us first. In other words, you must never fire until you have been shot dead. That seems to me undoubtedly a silly thing to say and a still more imprudent position to adopt.

Moreover, such a resolve would certainly bring war nearer. The deterrent effect of the atomic bomb is at the present time almost our sole defence. Its potential use is the only lever by which we can hope to obtain reasonable consideration in an attempt to make a peaceful settlement with Soviet Russia. If they had superiority, or even something like equality in this weapon with the United States, I cannot feel any assurance that they would be restrained by the conscientious scruples or moral inhibitions which are often so vocal in this country. It would certainly be a poor service to the cause of peace to free them from all cause of apprehension until they were in every respect ready to strike.

The Soviet power could not be confronted, or even placated, with any hope of success if we were in these years of tension through which we are passing to deprive ourselves of the atomic bomb, or to prevent its use by announcing gratuitously self-imposed restrictions. Of course, when we say 'we', we must not forget that we have been unable to make the atomic bomb ourselves. Our failure during five years of peace has astonished me very much when I remember how far we were advanced, not only in knowledge but in initiative, in 1942 and 1943.

In the communiqué published last week by the President and the Prime Minister, President Truman stated that it was his 'hope that world conditions would never call for the use of the atomic bomb', and he undertook to keep His Majesty's Government informed of developments 'which might bring about a change in the situation'. This assurance by the President contained in the joint communiqué is in very general terms. There is no guarantee in that assurance even of consultation. But in war-time we were on equal terms with the United States in the whole business of atomic research. Today the Prime Minister used a new phrase when he said that full weight will be given to any representations we may make. In 1943 I made an agreement with the President. Since then I understand other arrangements have been made. The Prime Minister tells us today that the same spirit and the same background are there in the present understanding, but he and one or two of my friends and former colleagues on both sides are the only ones in the House to know exactly what this means. I am sure that the Government would be wise to make a fuller statement upon this subject than we have yet heard.

Mr Sydney Silverman (Nelson and Colne): Would the right hon. Gentleman allow me –

Mr Churchill: No, I would rather not, thank you very much. One can always take examples from what happens. The President of the United States the other day let himself be cross-examined freely during a Press conference on this very topic. In my opinion, one ought not to say anything upon the subject one has not very carefully considered beforehand. I certainly do not intend to be cross-examined by the hon. Gentleman, because I have considered carefully what I should say. I am strongly of opinion that the Government should make a fuller statement upon this subject, and that this would be beneficial both to our own position and to our relationship with the United States. After all, this matter has become one of very real and vital consequence to us since the decision of the Government to afford the United States the bomber base in East Anglia, which makes it all the more necessary that the position in which we stand should be clearly defined.

We are debating this afternoon matters of supreme importance to ourselves and to the whole Empire and Commonwealth of Nations. We do so at a time when, on domestic questions, parties are evenly balanced and deeply divided. A continuance of these conditions is harmful to our national strength. The responsibility lies in the first instance upon the Government and in a special degree, of course, upon the Prime Minister. They decide the movement of our affairs. We respond to the action which they take in these matters.

The Prime Minister has taken marked steps to increase the differences in home politics. I ask him, even now, if he will not reconsider – (*Interruption.*) Hon. Members opposite can get ready to howl. They have not had much at which to cheer during the speech to which they listened earlier; now, perhaps, they will have their chance. I ask the Prime Minister, even now, whether he will not reconsider his decision to force the steel nationalisation Act upon us in the midst of all these storms and dangers. Not only should he consider that an abatement of domestic quarrels would be advantageous –

Mr S. Silverman: So that they can get the profits.

Mr Churchill: – but he should also consider the injury that will be done to our rearmament programme by taking this industry from the competent hands in which it now rests and placing it under the imperfect and inexperienced State management by which it is threatened. It really is not a matter for mere hilarity for uneasy minds and unsettled consciences below the Gangway.

Mr Emrys Hughes (South Ayrshire): Profits!

Mr Churchill: The Prime Minister spoke about raw materials and the arrangements which were being made for them, but steel is the mainspring of all effective rearmament measures. We wished the right hon. Gentleman well upon his Transatlantic mission, and we have recognised the advantages which it has secured, but I will say now that if he persists in his present attitude on steel nationalisation, he will fail in his duties to the country as a whole. Although we approved of the visit of the Prime Minister to the United States, although we lent him full support on his mission, although the results have been helpful so far as they go, we cannot in these circumstances feel confidence in the loyalty of the Government to the people of this country. The Prime Minister is counting on our support, which will – (Hon. Members: 'No'.) – which will not be withheld on issues of national importance abroad, while at the same time he is seeking to placate his political tail by acts of party faction at home.

Mr Frederick Elwyn Jones (West Ham, South) *rose* –

Mr Churchill: It is very doubtful whether these –

Hon. Members: Point of order.

Mr Speaker: Does the hon. Member wish to raise a point of order?

Mr Frederick Elwyn Jones: Is it in order for the Leader of the Opposition to question the loyalty of His Majesty's Government?

Mr Speaker: That is a matter for the right hon. Gentleman and not for me. That is not a point of order.

Mr Churchill: As my voice was drowned by hon. Members opposite, I might repeat the sentence on which I closed – namely, that we think it is very doubtful whether –

Mr S. Silverman *rose* –

Mr Churchill: If there is any one man in this House who should hang his head in shame – (*Interruption*) – it is the hon. Gentleman, who won cheers by abusing the United States as shabby moneylenders.

Mr Silverman *rose* –

Hon. Members: Sit down.

Mr Speaker: Is this another point of order?

Mr Churchill: – and now has to applaud with all his strength the tributes paid by the leader –

Mr Silverman: Mr Speaker –

Mr Speaker: Does the hon. Member rise to a point of order?

Mr Silverman: Yes, Sir.

Mr Speaker: Then will the hon. Member put it?

Mr Silverman: I want to ask you, Sir, whether it is in order for the Leader of the Opposition to use his great opportunity on an historic occasion to accuse everybody in the world except himself of disloyalty.

Mr Speaker: That is not a point of order. Hon. Members must not waste the time of the House by these mere party accusations.

Mr Churchill: As the hon. Gentleman went out of his way to interrupt me in what I was hoping would be the closing sentence that I should have to utter, I thought it right to point out what he had said in the past and to draw his attention –

Mrs Braddock (Liverpool, Exchange): What has the right hon. Gentleman said in the past?

Mr Churchill: – to draw his attention to the very different sentiments which have been put forward today. I regret very much that the Prime Minister

– (*Interruption.*) – I beg hon. Gentlemen opposite not to interrupt any expression of their feelings which they may desire to make, because it does not trouble or worry me in the slightest. It only prevents my getting on with what I have to say.

Mrs Braddock: If your gang had been in control, we would have been at war by now.

Mr Churchill: I am quite determined to utter my last sentence if I have to stand here half an hour. What I say is that I very much regret that the Prime Minister has not risen to the heights of his national responsibility, and I predict that he will encounter misfortunes and reproach on the discordant course to which he has devoted himself. (*Interruption.*)

Lord Beaverbrook to Brendan Bracken
(*Beaverbrook papers*)

15 December 1950

Will you[1] ask Mr Bracken to tell Mr Churchill that I have been reading his thirty-sixth article in the *Daily Telegraph*, in which he gives an account of the journey to Shangri La. He says that Mrs Roosevelt was in the wagon. That is not correct. I sat with my seat (*sic*) to the engine along with Harry Hopkins and I took part in the quotations of Barbara Flashetty. The fact was that the President asked me to go and spend that weekend at Shangri La. Churchill was not on good terms with me because of attacks being made on him in the British House of Commons in connection with my appearance on the journey to New York which Churchill had invited me to take. Also when were at the White House I – when I was at the White House I suggested to the President by letter that I didn't think that Churchill would want me at this Shangri La Sunday outing, but I got a letter back from the President saying the President selected his own guests and therefore I resolutely took my place in the carriage and also spent the weekend at Shangri La and Mr Churchill gave me a dusting on Saturday night after the President had gone to bed. No doubt he will remember the circumstances. I am telling it to Mr Bracken and again to Mr Churchill merely as a piece of interest to him and I don't care at all, of course, otherwise.

Furthermore, I once made a speech in Fredericton in praise of Mr Churchill in which I told an account of that very same journey, without quite so much credit to Mr Churchill but a good bit. The other day I was in New York and one of our University of New Brunswick honorary doctors, who is a professor at Columbia, told me that she (a woman) had read Mr Churchill's account and it didn't quite agree with mine.

[1] Bracken's secretary.

December 1950

Winston S. Churchill to Clementine Churchill
(Baroness Spencer-Churchill papers)

19 December 1950   Marrakech

We arrived after a perfect flight, almost to the minute – seven hours. Everything in the hotel is excellent and I have begun two daubs – one from the hotel tower and the other today from our old picnic spot at a slightly different angle. The river is entirely changed. It flows a hundred yards away from where it did, and the dam has been replaced by a bridge which they are still building.

We have six of those rooms on the verandah and everybody, I think, is comfortable. General Juin[1] has come here and is calling upon me this evening as I come back (so punctually) before 4 o'clock from painting by the river. We had a picnic under the olive trees which you will remember.

After General Juin, the Glaoui is coming. He has sent some beautiful honey and other presents.

We have so far made no plans. Monday's papers arrived this morning, Tuesday, so we are up to date. The sun is lovely and warm, but all the time one is aware that the wind is cooler than it ought to be. I wrap up assiduously.

I asked Dr Diot to come to see me in order to see how he was getting on. He has been frightfully ill and, after twenty-five years hard service in Morocco, he has been removed to take charge of the laboratory. He says he has a highly competent successor, to whom he is going to introduce me in case I need him at any time.

The aeroplane and its crew and its two hostesses are settling down, and the crew are in the other hotel. They seemed to be looking forward to their month here so much.

Alas Timbuktoo is 1,500 miles, so it cannot be considered. However the British Consul, a young man, who met me at the airfield here and came to dinner afterwards, says there is a far better trip the other way – left-handed instead of right. When you go through the mountains you come to two lovely native cities with extraordinary springs of blue water and rocky gorges, which seem by all accounts to be most paintacious. It is six hours motoring, and then next day six hours more, but there is a good hotel with central heating at each place run by the same management as the Mamounia; so it may be that later on I shall make a dart in that direction. At present I am settling myself down to the idea that time does not count and that Marrakech is the centre of the still existing universe. (Poor Beast). It looks as if a similar stabilization is developing in Korea.

[1] Alphonse Pierre Juin, 1888–1967. GOC, 15th Motorized Infantry Div., 1939–40. POW, 1940–1. Appointed Cdr of French troops in Morocco by Pétain, 1941. C-in-C, North Africa, 1942–3; Allied Forces, Central Europe, 1953–6. Urged Adm. Darlan to negotiate a ceasefire with the Allies, 1942. Gen., 1942. Resident-General of Tunisia, 1943; of Morocco, 1947–51. GOC Corps Expéditionnaire Français, Italy, 1943–4. Chief of National Defence Staff, 1944–7. Member, Supreme War Council, 1948–54. Inspector-General of the Army, 1951–3. CoS, Combined Armed Forces, 1951–3. President, CoS Committee, 1951–3. Marshal of France, 1952.

I try to put the world out of my thoughts as much as possible, but somehow indeed, it intrudes its ugly face from time to time. Somehow, when one detaches oneself, and has a new scene around, the salient points stand out more clearly.

I am asking Diana, and Duncan if he or she or they can come about the 4th or 5th, when the Prof has to go home for the Oxford term. The change has done him good. He had the best night last night for months.

I find it is possible to telephone from here and I have got a call booked through to you tonight between 8 and 9 o'clock – three minutes for 27/-d. (Done – it was worth it.)

The book Randolph gave me, *The God that Failed*, is an impressive study of Communist mentality by those who have recovered from the disease.

I shall be delighted to hear your news and also how Rufus is bearing up. I am sure he will soon make friends with Hedy.

All my best love my darling Clemmie from your ever loving husband.

Randolph S. Churchill to Winston S. Churchill
(Churchill papers, 1/48)

21 December 1950

My dearest Papa,

This brings you all my deepest love and good wishes for Christmas: also my thanks for your very kind and generous cheque.

My present to you, *Keesing's Contemporary Archives*, is, I fear, dull though practical and will be of more service to your literary assistants and secretaries than it will be of immediate pleasure to yourself. Kelly took it out in the aeroplane and I hope it will be of some use.

Alanbrooke's speech at the unveiling of your portrait at the Junior Carlton Club was an astonishing tour de force. He spoke in the lobby of the Junior Carlton Club for over 40 minutes to a gathering of about 150 swells all in white ties and decorations and including the Pug, Andrew B. Cunningham, Peter Portal and Anthony Eden. It was against all the normal rules to speak for so long, but I think he felt that this was his first opportunity of paying a measured and considered tribute to you. He had obviously taken immense pains about the preparation of his speech and though everybody was standing, no one was restive or uncomfortable or seemed to note the passage of time. His magnificent appearance, his fine speaking voice and his most unusual approach to the topic delighted and indeed amazed all who were there. I told him afterwards that I was glad you were not present as if you had been you would have heard 'words which no man should hear while he is still alive'.

The accounts in the papers did much less than justice to what was an agreeable and moving performance. It was very thrilling to see all your Chiefs of Staff there, all looking as young and active as yourself and all ready to get back into harness the moment the signal is given.

I was sad, though, that Portal, whom I admire the most, seemed the least keen for a tough policy. I fear the Air Marshals neglected our defences to a shameful extent and are anxious to postpone any exposure of their neglect as long as possible.

Earlier the same day I spoke at the Constitutional Club. There were about 400 tough city gents present and it was apparently the largest attendance they had had for a long time. I gave them pretty strong meat about Korea. The younger ones lapped it up, but the older ones were saddened. I enclose a paragraph from Peterborough[1] about it, also an extract from Sam Hoare's speech on 11 September 1935 with which I teased them but which seems to me to contain the best statement of principle on which we can stand today.

Thomas Dewey to Winston S. Churchill
(Churchill papers, 2/168)

22 December 1950

I have hesitated for a long time about burdening you with this but since you were kind enough to send it in the first place and since it would mean so much to John,[2] I am taking the liberty of imposing upon you for it.

Last week I made a speech which caused considerable comment here and of which I enclose a copy in the event you should have any interest in reading it.

Mr Hoover[3] made a speech night before last,[4] the implications of which are appalling to me. The press reports today it has had wide and unhappy repercussions in Great Britain and on the Continent.

I am still not quite sure why I ran again but in any event, having no ambitions or expectations of having any other office I am free to proselyte to the limit of my capacity for the point of view expressed in my speech and intend to do so.

If you find any spot on the horizon more cheerful than I do, I should appreciate hearing of it. The world is filled with gloom and almost in extremis.

With warm regards and every good wish for a very much Happier New Year than now seems likely.

---

[1] The *Daily Telegraph*'s diary column (since 2003 named 'London Spy').
[2] John Martin Dewey, son of Thomas Dewey.
[3] Herbert Hoover, former US President.
[4] On Dec. 20, Hoover gave a speech advocating a 'Gibraltar' geopolitical strategy, building up America's air and naval forces but not its army, focused on defending the Western hemisphere and the free island nations on the Pacific and Atlantic rims, such as Taiwan and the UK 'if she wishes to cooperate'. Hoover also proposed refusing to send 'another man or dollar' to continental Europe for its defence until the non-Communist nations there strengthened their own military forces. His advice (denounced by his critics as isolationist) differed from President Truman's plan, announced just the day before, to send more US troops to western Europe to assist in NATO's defence preparations.

DECEMBER 1950

Jo Sturdee to Clementine Churchill
(Churchill papers, 1/47)

22 December 1950

Dear Mrs Churchill,
Such a lot seems to have happened since we have been here, and it seems weeks since we left home. We often think and talk about you all battling your way through snow and slush, and presents and Christmas trees and things like that. Here the sunshine is brilliant and the sky bright blue — not a bit like Christmas.

Mr Churchill settled in at once and seems quite happy. He seems conscious all the time that the climate here can be colder than it looks, and so fortunately there has been no trouble so far about getting him to wrap up well and be home early.

We landed in perfect weather — Mr Churchill was met at the airfield by General D'Hauteville[1] (he has apparently been promoted from Colonel since we were last here), by the Glaoui's son and by Mr Pullar,[2] the British Consul at Casablanca, who looks just like David Niven.[3] Mr Pullar had reserved himself accommodation at this hotel for that first night in case there were any details with which he could help us, so he had dinner with Mr Churchill and told him about some lovely places over the mountains.

Denis[4] has been busying around leaving cards on General Juin, General D'Hauteville and the Glaoui. General Pownall and Denis went to luncheon with Mr and Mme Lyautey[5] the other day. And then the evening before last everyone went to dine with the Glaoui. We are now trying to get a day fixed for him and for the D'Hautevilles to come and lunch or dine with Mr Churchill.

We all had a lovely day at Ourika and picnicked in the same spot. Today is so brilliant and warm again that it has been decided that, after an early luncheon at 12 sharp in the hotel, Mr Churchill should go there again and work on his picture. Sergeant Murray[6] and Norman are going on ahead to set up

[1] Roger Marie Antoine Benoit d'Hauteville, 1895–1970. Married, 1929, Kathleen MacCarthy. Commanded territory of Agadir. Director, Military Cabinet of Resident General Gabriel Puaux, Rabat. Chief of the Marrakech region, 1944–54. Survived attempted assassination, 20 June 1954.

[2] Hubert Norman Pullar, 1914–88. Entered HM Consular Service, 1938; served in Turkey, 1938–42; US, 1943–6; Persia, 1946–8; Morocco, 1949–52; FO, 1952–4; Finland, 1954–6; Syria, 1956; Iraq, 1957–9. Coronation Medal, 1953. Consul-General, Antwerp, 1960–4; Jerusalem, 1964–7; Durban, 1967–71.

[3] (James) David Graham Niven, 1910–83. Entered Army, 1929. Resigned Commission, 1932. Actor in films including *Wuthering Heights, Around the World in 80 Days, The Birds and The Bees, The Best of Enemies, 55 Days at Peking, The Pink Panther, Casino Royale* and *Death on the Nile*. On active service, 1939–45.

[4] Denis Kelly.

[5] Louis Hubert Gonzalve Lyautey, 1854–1934. Born in Nancy, France. Resident General of Morocco, 1912–25. Member of the French Academy, 1912–34. Minister of War, 1916–17. Marshal, 1921.
Ines de Bourgoing, 1862–1953. Established French Red Cross in Morocco. Married, 1909, Hubert Lyautey. Hospital administrator in France, WWI and WWII. Vice-President, Central Committee of the Ladies of the French Red Cross, 1940.

[6] Edmund Murray, ?–1996. Metropolitan Police Special Branch Officer. Churchill's bodyguard, 1950–65. Special detective to Churchill, 1955–65. Frequently painted with Churchill.

the apparatus, and General Pownall is going to see that the operation for today is ended in good time.

Lord Cherwell is taking care and says he seems to be better. Alas he is having to make plans to return about the 7th as he is needed then in Oxford. He takes endless photographs. Miss Gemmell and I feel frightfully simple when we come out with our Brownie cameras, but he takes a keen interest in what we take and how we take it, and goes into long scientific explanations about the speed of the film, the focus, the light. We try to understand but I must confess I usually go 'click' and hope for the best.

A lot of the staff here in the hotel is the same. M Singla, the Director, and M Simon, the Manager, are still here. Also the tall concierge and practically all the little Arab porters are the same. Practically every time I see M Simon he says he hopes you will come out later on. It really is a friendly place, and Miss Gemmell and I enjoy having our breakfast on our balcony and feeding the birds. They really are rather greedy and come right in to our room and hop all over our pillows.

We are told that General and Lady Anderson,[1] the Governor of Gibraltar, are coming here for Christmas. Also Mr and Mrs Bolson, who were at Madeira at the same time as you, arrived yesterday. I must confess I do not remember them at all, but General Powell remembers them well – he says they stayed at his hotel and are very nice.

Sir Cyril Cane,[2] the British Consul at Rabat, and his daughter are coming here with friends also for Christmas – so we shall have to keep an eye open for them. There are the usual queer specimens staying here, but we at our table say that they no doubt think we are even queerer! At any rate so far, touch wood, they are not being tiresome!

I expect Mr Churchill has told you all his news. He was so much pleased to be able to talk to you on such a clear line to London the other evening. The most important thing to report really is that Mr Churchill is in good health and happy. He is making quite good progress with the book and is pleased with the two paintings he has started. I think he wishes you were here; but perhaps you will be able to get away later on.

We all think about you all at No. 28 so often. Our thoughts will be with you at home especially on Christmas Day.

---

[1] Kenneth Arthur Noel Anderson, 1891–1959. Educated at Charterhouse and RMC, Sandhurst. Lt, 1913. Capt., 1915. MC, 1916. Married, 1918, Kathleen Gamble. Lt-Col., 1930. Col., 1934. Maj.-Gen., 1940. CB, 1940. GOC, VIII Corps, 1941; II Corps, 1941–2; 1st Army, 1942–3; 2nd Army, 1943–4. GOC-in-C, Eastern Command, 1942, 1944. Lt-Gen., 1943. KCB, 1943. C-in-C, East Africa Command, 1944–6. Governor-General and C-in-C, Gibraltar, 1946–52. Gen., 1949.

Kathleen Lorna May Gamble, 1894–1983. Only daughter of Sir Reginald Arthur Gamble. Married, 1918, Kenneth Anderson.

[2] Cyril Hubert Cane, 1891–1959. Served at Consulate-General, Antwerp, 1908–14. Vice-Consul at Addis Ababa, 1919–22. Consul at San Francisco, 1929–39; at Detroit, 1939–43. Consul-General, Rabat, Morocco, 1948–51.

Winston S. Churchill to Clementine Churchill
(Churchill papers, 1/47)

25 December 1950   Marrakech

My darling Clemmie,
    How would you like to meet me in Paris about the 15th for three or four days? We could go to Bennie's quiet hotel (? Hotel Maurice). There are several people I ought to get into touch with. Besides there are shops, theatres, galleries and restaurants. We would be independent of the Embassy but no doubt they would wish us to lunch and dine there to see some political notabilities. Send me a telegram whether you like this idea or not, so that I can make plans.
    I really do not think it would be worth your while to come here. Kelly leaves here on the 3rd or 4th. Diana arrives on the 5th. The Prof wishes to go home on the 8th. Pownall will stay till, say, the 14th, and if the Paris plan comes off will fly back in the big plane with me to Paris. You and I could both go back together in it on the 18th, 19th, or 20th from Paris. Bill Deakin will probably come here with his wife somewhere around the 4th or 5th. Also the Graebners but that is their affair with *Life* and the *NY Times*.
    We had a great dinner with the Glaoui. The D'Hautevilles came and both Miss Sturdee and Miss Gemmell. Everybody liked shoving their paws into the dish and remembered with pleasure that fingers were made before forks. The Glaoui is as old as I am but quite lively. He pretends to know neither French nor English, but I believe he understands everything that is said at least in French. After dinner there were dances – three troupes of five each with tomtoms, the first Berber females, the second Arab females and the third Berber males. I never saw dancing, music, or the human form presented in such unattractive guise – the woman with sullen expressions on their faces, stamping their feet on the floor, the men in the same vogue but more repellent. All were dressed up in quilts and blankets – they looked like bundles of cotton waste. However no one could say it was not highly respectable. The music brays and squawks and tomtoms, and the singing, which was maintained throughout, was a masterly compendium of discords.
    I have a great regard for the Glaoui who no doubt has endured all this and many other afflictions in his journey through this vale of sin and even more woe.
    I have been painting for a few hours every day. We went to Ourika where the river comes out of the mountains, and the pebbles – you know. It is entirely different but I found a good place. On the whole a better landscape than any I have tried of this scene. I went back again three days later, but though the sun shone brilliantly at Marrakech, the clouds round the mountains cut it off just before my effect came. I am hoping to go tomorrow or the next day. Meanwhile I have advanced the picture by working from photographs in the studio. I have one other picture on the stocks. There has been quite a lot of cloud in the air. Today has been grey with hardly a gleam.

Everybody enjoyed themselves very much last night at the Christmas celebrations. I turned up at the hour appointed – a quarter to 12 – and was introduced to the company, who loudly applauded to the strains of Lillie Marlene. (I am terrified of this getting into my mind again. I have several antidotes ready.)

The Governor of Gibraltar and his wife are here and they came to luncheon this Christmas Day. Also the British Consul-General at Rabat, Sir Cyril Cane, and his daughter. The Governor, General Anderson, invited me to go Gibraltar on my way back. I suppose I have seen it ten times, so I did not commit myself. His wife is a magnificent Tory and helped Randolph to oppose Malcolm MacDonald[1] when he stood for the Scottish Islands in the far north after we came back from Marrakech fifteen years ago. (This is my fifth visit here.)

My day is most tranquil and I do absolutely nothing that I do not want to. The food is the best you can get. I have discovered Marennes oysters – excellent. I get at least eight or nine hours sleep. The weather is sharply cool and there are too many clouds. However I hope for a sunshine spell not only in the garden but in the foothills of the Atlas.

We are developing our plan to go to Wowowow, which they are going to call it in future – namely the left-handed excursion over the mountains. But I shall probably wait till Diana arrives as she would like the adventure.

The one thing that has gone best of all is the one thing that is most needful – namely the book. I have been here tonight eight days, and eight chapters of Volume VI, Book 12, have been sent to the Printer. These are largely, in their present stage, stringing together of telegrams, minutes and other documents with their introductions and tail pieces. However Volume VI, though not yet a 'literary masterpiece', at which we must always aim, is nevertheless an important commercial property. Nobody could sort these telegrams but me, who alone know the sequence and the value. I have worked as much as eight hours a day in my bed, which is very comfortable.

I have received two letters from you. I am so glad you have got a new secretary.[2] She certainly seems magnificent, and we shall have two historians in the house. I am very sorry Pennylope[3] is going. I suppose by the time you get this Maria and Christopher will be back in the bunny. I earnestly hope that all is well at Chartwell. The little fish, the Black Mollies, the golden orfes in the

---

[1] Malcolm John MacDonald, 1901–81. Son of Ramsay MacDonald. Educated at Bedales and Queen's College, Oxford. MP (Lab.) for Bassetlaw, 1929–31, (Nat. Lab.) 1931–5; for Ross and Cromarty, 1936–45. Parliamentary Under-Secretary, Dominions Office, 1931–5. PC, 1935. Secretary of State for Dominion Affairs, 1935–8, 1938–9; for the Colonies, 1935, 1938–40. Minister of Health, 1940–1. High Commissioner, Canada, 1941–6. Governor-General of Malaya, Singapore and British Borneo, 1946–8. Commissioner-General for South-East Asia, 1948–55. High Commissioner, India, 1955–60. Governor-General of Kenya, 1963–4; High Commissioner, 1964–5. British Special Representative in East and Central Africa, 1965–6; in Africa, 1966–9. OM, 1969.
[2] Heather Mason.
[3] Penelope Hampden-Wall.

pools (but they do not eat now), the black swans (I hope the lakes are unfrozen and they can go back to their various domains). All these I think of, and then there is the sulky, illmannered cat and poor, dear Rufus. I hope he had a good howl but I expect he is reconciled by now to my absence.

Much depends for us all upon the impending battle in Korea. I hope they have made a proper defensive line across the peninsula, with mine-fields and barbed wire and machine guns, well posted with a good artillery organized in the rear. They have had three weeks to do this and if they have behaved in a sensible way they should be able to teach the Chinese the sort of lessons we learned upon the Somme and at Passchendaele. I have bet General Pownall ten shillings to one that, if the Chinese attack, they will be repulsed with heavy slaughter. After all they need not go unless they want to, and we are never likely to run short of Chinese.

I hope the tale will please you. I came here to play, but so far it has only been *work* under physically agreeable conditions.

You have my fondest love. I do pray that all is well with all of you. I am looking forward to come home again. But here I have no distraction & can make extensive progress with my mainstay,

Give my love to all & believe me your devoted & ever loving husband.

PS. My eyes are closing – good night.

Winston S. Churchill to General Douglas MacArthur
(Churchill papers, 2/173)

27 December 1950

All good wishes for the New year. Remembering the Somme and Passchendaele I have many hopes. Thank you for receiving Randolph so kindly some months ago. His wound is healed.

Winston S. Churchill to Randolph S. Churchill
(Churchill papers, 1/48)

27 December 1950

Am delighted with *Keesings Contemporary Archives*. Thank you so much for your most interesting letter.

January
1951

Winston S. Churchill to Clementine Churchill
(Churchill papers, 1/47)

1 January 1951

We have leapt the mountains and found a sunlight painting paradise at Tinerhir. You shall come here too.

Love.

Winston S. Churchill: article[1]
(Churchill papers, 2/102)

1 January 1951

Once again we enter upon the New Year with the prospect of a General Election in the not very distant future. Twelve months ago I called upon Conservative workers, young and old, everywhere to make an earnest effort to rid the country of a Government whose unfitness to govern was producing such disastrous consequences. Their response to my appeal, though it fell just short of complete success, was magnificent. Thanks in large measure to their zeal and enthusiasm in the constituencies the Conservative and allied poll was increased by 2½ million in 1950. The Socialists' majority in the House of Commons dwindled to a handful, and their power for further mischief, while not destroyed, was markedly reduced.

Yet even in the face of the electorate's decisive repudiation of their experiments the Socialists have not refrained from putting party above country and, by the misuse of their slender and unrepresentative Parliamentary majority, have pressed on with their half-worked-out and wholly unworkable scheme for the nationalization of the iron and steel industry, now so vital to the fulfilment of their own belated rearmament programme. The Conservative Party's well-considered policies for national revival stand out in shining contrast with

---
[1] Written by Churchill for the New Year edition of *Tory Challenge*.

the muddled meddling of the Government. The task of all Conservatives and Unionists is to spread the broad principles of our Party, and to bring into the glare of public opinion the record of the Socialists. No one must forget their costly failure to maintain and equip the nation's defensive forces, the breakdown of their housing policy, the mismanagement of extravagance that have sent prices, fares, taxation and charges of all kinds to heights inhuman in peace time. Since the last General Election it is obvious to all that the Socialist Party have lost their faith in Nationalization, and have found no new policy or programme. In our domestic affairs the rising cost of living and the shortage of houses are matters of great concern to all of us. The Conservatives will do their utmost to stop the rising cost of living, and we set ourselves with good confidence the target of building 300,000 houses a year.

In these dangerous days it is right that all parties should give united support to any effort to safeguard national security. This does not mean that we approve or endorse administrative mismanagement. The safety and continuance in peace and prosperity of the British Empire and Commonwealth stands first in our minds. One more united heave by our Party and its friends may give us the opportunity of turning our words into actions, and our wishes into facts.

General George C. Marshall to Winston S. Churchill
(Churchill papers, 2/173)

3 January 1951

My dear Mr Churchill,

I have waited until I had finished reading your last volume, which you were good enough to send me, before thanking you, which I do now. (That's a pretty long sentence and not after your pure English style, but expresses the idea), and now Mrs Marshall and I also have to thank Mrs Churchill and you for that very handsome Christmas card.

I would like an opportunity to see you these days and talk over things with the frankness of the past, but reactions, criticisms and pressures seem very much a repetition of those war years. I can only pray that we will have a repetition of the success of those same days.

I was called back into service at a rather difficult time and fortunately was able to obtain the services of my old first assistant in the State Department and former Pentagon companion, Bob Lovett. We have very complete coordination these days in contrast with some of our struggles in other years and, of course, in one sense we are far better prepared. However, in another, particularly as to the time element and the over-all development of the communist threat with its hordes of people, its knowledge of the organization and leadership of great armies and its industrial set-up, the situation is, I fear, far more serious.

This was to be a pleasant New Year's note, or to pun a little bit, it was to carry a pleasant note, but I can't escape the urge to make a few comments to you.

With warm regards to both Mrs Churchill and yourself, and with great respect and affection.[1]

Winston S. Churchill to Clementine Churchill
(Churchill papers, 1/47)

3 January 1951

Returned safely over mountains last night after really lovely two days. You will have to see that place which is in French military occupation. Officers most attentive and look forward much to your visit which I promised them. I got two interesting pictures there. Hope all well with you. Tender love.

Winston S. Churchill to Anthony Eden
(Churchill papers, 2/112)

8 January 1951   Hotel de la Mamounia
Marrakech

My dear Anthony,

The Prof is leaving for home this morning. I think his rest out here has been good for his health. I send this letter by his hand.

Naturally I have followed everything in the newspapers, and am as gravely concerned as you must be about our national perils and party puzzles. I do not understand why the Americans could not form a defensive line in Korea after nearly three weeks' breathing space to fortify it. I cannot get the Somme and Passchendaele out of my head, and I thought that the Chinese might well renew our experiences of those days with the added effect of vastly increased modern fire power. It now looks like a retirement on the former perimeter around Pusan. There must be something very wrong in the whole lay-out. I shall look forward to talking all this and other matters over with you.

The only point which it seems urgent for me to make now is that we should on no account approve any separation between our policy and that of the United States on the measures to be taken against China. I see they are bringing a resolution before the United Nations on the point. We should act with them irrespective of anything that Nehru, who is neutral, may do or say. This would involve not only severing diplomatic relations and withdrawing recognition, but also sharing in any blockade measure which may be proposed. Hong

[1] Churchill responded on Jan. 11: 'Thank you so much for your letter. I wish indeed we could have a talk.'

Kong no doubt would suffer gravely, but that must be accepted. It is possible that the Americans might find such face-saving measures a means of getting out of Korea altogether. They can hardly be more humiliated than they are already. Possibly the best solution is, without declaring war on China, to cut her off for the time being from the comity of the United Nations and in this posture await further developments.

I only send this in case the matter may be raised with you by the Government. If you think well of it and are in agreement, it might be right to inform the Government of our position.

On all other aspects I should deprecate any overtures at this time to them. They have no right to ask for sacrifices from others while being unwilling to give up at this crisis their Party Nationalization of Steel. I have no doubt they will do so eventually under the growing pressure of events.

I feel increasing doubts about the Festival of Britain now that the United States have declared and are taking vast emergency measures.

I am going to Paris on the 20th, and shall stop there for two or three days at the Loti to renew my French contacts. I expect to be with you on the 23rd. I have not burdened you with other matters, though I am thinking continually about the very grave situation closing in upon us.

All good wishes, dear Anthony. I hope you are having a rest. I toil night and day at the book and painting. The lack of sunshine hampers the painting, but the book, both Volumes V and VI, are leaping ahead.

PS. I send you the following telegram I had from Stassen, and the answer I have sent him. Now that Taft and Hoover have come out against us[1] I may find an opportunity of speaking to the United States, either on a flying visit or by broadcast. Pray send these enclosures back to No. 28.

Anthony Eden to Winston S. Churchill
(Churchill papers, 2/112)

11 January 1951

My dear Winston,

Thank you so much for your letter which I was very happy to get. I also had a talk with the Prof on the telephone. He seems to have enjoyed himself. I must confess that I envy you the sunshine. It has been very cold and grim here, with Flu and Fibrositis attacking all and sundry, but I have been well.

The Korean campaign is completely inexplicable. Apparently the Americans had intended to defend Seoul. They later changed their minds and thought they could hold a line further south. This again they failed to do.

---

[1] Robert Taft (son of President William Howard Taft) and Herbert Hoover both took a strong public stance against Truman's interventionist policy in Asia.

One hears rumours that the fighting value of most of the divisions is not very high, the Marines and our troops excepted. Certainly MacArthur's communiqués do not seem calculated to inspire his men. He talks all the time of 'large Chinese armies'.

I have heard nothing official about all this from Ministers, excepting that Attlee last night at a Reception to the Commonwealth Prime Ministers was clearly distressed at the military failure. I told him I thought that we must at least hold Pusan and try to fight back, for there has been some defeatist talk about leaving Korea. But as some things are now they would surely be much worse if we had been pushed off the whole peninsula. Attlee appeared to share this view.

I have only made one speech of any importance since you went away, and that was at the Pilgrims' dinner. I expect that you saw it in *The Times*, but on the chance that you did not I inflict a copy on you.

I have had no conversation of any kind with the Government about the situation, nor have they asked me to see them. I have therefore made no move. There are rumours in the Press, notably in *The People* of last Sunday, about the possibility of a Coalition. I take this to be mainly a measure of the Government's anxiety.

I go to Germany next week for a few days, and shall not be back until the 24th. Patrick BH[1] knows all about this, and I could of course return any moment in a few hours if required. Kirkpatrick has asked me to stay and General Keightly[2] also. It seemed to me a good chance to have a look round.

All good wishes. I feel quite sure myself that international events will have their domestic political impact before long. I wish I could see as clearly how to handle this Far Eastern business.

I cannot share the optimism of American Republicans that Chiang Kai-Shek is of any military value.

Love to your Clementine.

PS. I hear that Ike comes here soon. I will try to see him and report.

---

[1] Buchan-Hepburn.

[2] Charles Frederic Keightley, 1901–74. Cdr, 30th Armoured Bde, 1941. GOC, 11th Armoured Div., Tunisia, 1942; 6th Armoured Div., Tunisia, 1942–3; 78th Infantry Div., 1943–4. CB, 1943. DSO, 1944. Cdr, V Corps, 1944–5. KBE, 1945. KCB, 1950. C-in-C Far East Land Forces, 1951. GCB, 1953. GBE, 1957.

Lord Cherwell to Winston S. Churchill
(*Churchill papers, 4/52*)

11 January 1951

My dear Winston,
  In the first place I should like to thank you for the wonderful holiday I had in Morocco which I hope really put me on the road to recovery. It was more than kind of you to let me come and I only fear that I did very little to work my passage.
  As I did not put anything in writing perhaps I might recall my suggestion that in the chapter recounting the talks at Teheran about the future of Germany it might be well to insert a few hundred words calculated to reduce the painful impression that might be created in that country on reading these discussions. Of course you might omit some parts, but if you did no doubt the Russians would publish them so that matters would not be improved.
  The other point which occurred to me was that the telegrams about de Gaulle might require elisions. If he came to power again in France cooperation with him might be even more difficult if he had read some of the comments.
  I happened to have a long talk to a very highly placed civil servant yesterday, who seemed to think a February election was quite probable. He said that he used to think the Government would hold on until October, so that Morrison could enjoy the Festival, but that the shocking situation now anticipated owing to coal shortage might induce them to go to the country earlier. I myself should not have thought it possible to get the election over before the coal crisis becomes acute.
  There is, of course, a good deal of talk about a coalition here. But there seems to be an idea in some Government circles that it would be well to get Bevan and the other violent Left-Wingers, who would go into opposition, thoroughly committed to the unpleasant measures rearmament will entail before making any move so that they should not be able to escape responsibility afterwards and attack any coalition which might be formed for having imposed them.
  Owing to engine trouble and fog we did not take off on Tuesday till after 8 a.m., but we arrived about 6 p.m. after a pleasant flight and Anthony got his letter the next morning.
  Please give my love to Clemmie and Diana and believe me, once more with many thanks,

January 1951

Winston S. Churchill to General Lord Ismay
(Churchill papers, 1/83)

11 January 1951
Marrakech
Hotel de la Mamounia

Life is very pleasant out here, and I have been working hard both on the book and at my painting. The weather however is somewhat capricious, and we have not had our full share of sunshine.

Marcus Sieff: note
(Churchill papers, 2/46)

18 January 1951

OIL SUPPLIES

1. The Government of Iraq, since the Arab–Israel War, have stopped the supply of crude oil to Haifa and the Iraq Petroleum Company's Southern Pipeline system remains closed. Israel receives her crude oil requirements by tanker from overseas and the Refineries work to approximately one-third capacity and meet only local Israeli needs.

2. The main losers today from the continued idleness of this Pipeline and only partial operation of the Refineries, are Great Britain, certain Allied Nations in Western Europe and the Mediterranean Basin and Iraq. The capacity of the old twelve-inch pipeline is now four million tons of crude oil annually as the new pumping stations created for the sixteen-inch pipeline can be connected with the twelve-inch pipeline. It would take only a few months to complete the sixteen-inch pipeline, which would increase the throughput of crude oil to Haifa to six and a half to seven million tons annually. Iraq production of crude is sufficient to make full use of both the pipelines to Tripoli in Syria as well as Haifa.

3. To lift six and a half million tons of crude oil from the Persian Gulf area to the Mediterranean, entails the continuous employment of at least thirty tankers of fifteen thousand tons deadweight. In addition, the fact that Haifa refines only for Israel's needs means that considerable cross-freighting to such countries as Turkey, Greece, etc., is necessary as crude has to be brought from the Middle Eastern, Persian Gulf or other areas, by tankers to such countries as Italy and France, where there is refining capacity, and after refining is shipped to the consuming countries. It is probable that the full utilisation of Haifa, even if none of the Iraqi crude went to meet Israel's needs, would free thirty-five tankers.

4. Tanker rates have risen by over two hundred per cent since 1949. The release of over thirty tankers would not only materially improve the tanker

supply situation, but as freight rates are sensitive, would probably have a material effect on general tanker rates. In addition, the release of some thirty-five tankers would ease the position in British Shipyards, which are becoming heavily engaged on work connected with the Defence Programmes of the Western Powers.

5. The addition of three million tons of refining capacity is still a bottleneck in the supply of fuel.

6. Even if the Oil Companies continue to bring in Israel's crude requirements by tanker and thus, Iraqi crude would not go to meet Israel's needs, Iraq would benefit greatly from the increased royalties and employment which would result from the re-opening of the pipeline to Haifa and Great Britain and the Western Powers would get the benefit of what is a very valuable asset, particularly at this present time of International tension.[1]

Winston S. Churchill to Willy Sax
(Churchill papers, 2/176)

24 January 1951
Private

Dear Mr Sax,

I spent a day at Marrakech looking at M Majorelle's pictures. He has lived there for thirty years and is a highly accomplished painter. I was much impressed with his work. He has turned entirely to tempera, which he generally uses in the powder form. He certainly has produced remarkably vivid colour effects, which I have never seen surpassed. I have not used tempera lately. There is no doubt that, for skies in Morocco, it is far superior to oils. Pray let me know the recipe which you recommend for making it possible to paint with tempera over oil. I think you told me about it. There is rather a severe chemical wash which, after it has been applied to the oil-painted surface, renders it fit for tempera. Have you got any of this? If so please send me a bottle urgently.

M Majorelle also showed me a sky of wonderful blue, the intensity of which I had never before seen. I asked him how he got it and he gave me the enclosed description. I got him to come round to my studio at the Mamounia Hotel and he showed me how it worked. He paints the surface in tempera from tempera powder with as much white as is desired. Thereafter he takes natural cobalt powder (such as is the foundation I think of cobalt oil paint) and blows the powder on with a little bulb spray. The result is to leave a number of fresh particles of great brilliance on the surface and really the colour was wonderful to one's eyes. Do you know anything about

---

[1] Elizabeth Gilliatt wrote to Sieff on Jan. 30: 'About the Oil, Mr Churchill feels that the question is how to persuade the Arabs to allow the pipeline to be used.'

this? It would seem to me that you might be very well advised to look at M Majorelle's paintings which are a manifestation of the power of tempera, the like of which I have never seen.

Will you please send me another outfit of tempera in tubes like the one you did last time; and please let me have the bill as I have a few francs available.

I had rather a sad account from his brother about Charles Montag. Please let me know how he is and also whether there is anything I can do. Would £50 be of any use?

Every good wish and pray let me know when you come over to England.

Bernard Van Leer[1] to Winston S. Churchill
(Churchill papers, 2/177)

26 January 1951

Dear Mr Churchill,

Trusting that I am not disturbing you too soon after your well-earned holiday, I would be honoured and very happy if you could find time to visit the Exhibition of our Mobile Drum Factory in Empire Hall, Olympia. The exhibition takes place from 30th January to 9th February inclusive.

I will be in London during the whole period of the exhibition and will be pleased to have the opportunity of meeting you to show you an engineering unit which, I am sure will interest you and you will agree is fast becoming an essential to modern commercial and military operations. I am wondering if it would be possible for you to visit the exhibition either on the 3rd, 4th, or 5th of February.

This Mobile Factory was designed and built by engineers of our Group and I think can be considered the first of its kind in the world.

I am sending you a booklet, illustrating the factory in operation in Paris last year.

I would like to mention that we have taken the entire Empire Hall for our own exhibition and your visit would be planned entirely for your convenience.

---

[1] Bernard Van Leer, 1883–1958. Dutch businessman and international industrialist. Married, 1912, Polly Rubens. Started his own private circus during the 1930s. Exiled during German occupation of the Netherlands, 1940–5. Established Bernard Van Leer Foundation, 1949.

Winston S. Churchill to Sir Alan Lascelles
(Churchill papers, 2/171)

30 January 1951

My dear Tommy,

The King and Queen sent me a lovely signed Christmas card, for which I have for the first time, owing to my absence abroad, today been able to express my thanks.

I wonder if it would amuse The King to see these reproductions of some of my paintings which have been made in the United States, not altogether to my disadvantage. They have had an enormous success over there, more than two million being sold in the first year. What is remarkable about them is that whereas the ordinary English colour reproduction has four or five colours, these have nine or ten. In consequence a far greater refinement is possible; in fact they are very much better than the originals. Perhaps you will take an opportunity of telling The King and Queen about these when there is nothing of importance going on.

Winston S. Churchill to Thomas Dewey
(Churchill papers, 2/168)

30 January 1951
Private

My dear Dewey,

I am sending you a couple of books which I trust are correctly inscribed for your two boys. I am so glad that they feel this is of importance to them, and very sorry I made the original mistake.

I have thought a great deal about your letter[1] in the month that has passed since it was written. It is a comfort to me that you felt Hoover's speech was 'appalling'. I think that your own declarations are of far more consequence. You may be quite sure that whatever misunderstandings may arise from the petty by-play now going on between Mr Attlee's Government and the United States, the 'fraternal' association is unbreakable, and in this respect at least things have only to get worse to get better.

---

[1] Reproduced above (p. 1978).

JANUARY 1951

Winston S. Churchill to Lord Camrose
(Camrose papers)

30 January 1951
Private

My dear Bill,

I received in confidence information dated January 6 about a Gallup Poll taken in December, the results of which were more favourable to the Conservatives even than those of the *Daily Express* Poll announced about a fortnight ago. The *News Chronicle* hold the copyright of the Gallup Polls, but they have suppressed all mention of this last important result. I have now received confirmatory information from the Central Office of the favourable character of this poll, and it seems to me that the *News Chronicle* should be pressed to disclose it.

I hope that the *Daily Telegraph* will raise this matter in an interrogative form. I should think this alone would lead to the publication by the *News Chronicle*. If not I hope the matter should be pursued.

PS. Volumes V and VI herewith.

Yugoslav Ambassador[1] to Edvard Kardelj[2]
(Churchill papers, 2/114)

31 January 1951

Djilas, Dedijer[3] and myself paid a visit today to Churchill, as he expressed through his secretary the wish to see Djilas. The conversation was confidential, informal and friendly.

1. In the conversation Churchill has mentioned Anglo-Yugoslav relations during the war and their deterioration immediately after the war.

---

[1] Vladimir Popović, 1914–72. Educated at University of Belgrade, School of Medicine, 1937. Capt., Spanish Republican Army, Spanish Civil War, 1937. Maj.-Gen., Partisan 3rd Army Corps, Bosnia, 1944. Yugoslavia's first Communist Ambassador to UN, 1945. First Deputy Minister of Foreign Affairs of Yugoslavia, 1948. Ambassador to US, 1950; to China and Vietnam, 1955–8.

[2] Edvard Kardelj, 1910–79. Imprisoned for Communist activities, 1930–2. Worked for Comintern in Moscow and became close friends with Tito, 1934–7. Founded Slovene Communist Party, 1937. Helped Tito rebuild Yugoslav Communist Party. Member of Communist Party's Central Committee and Politburo, 1940–79. Vice-President, Provisional Government, 1943. Secretary, Central Committee, League of Communists of Yugoslavia, 1952. Foreign Minister of Yugoslavia, 1948–53. Secretary, Central Committee, Yugoslav Communist Party, and Vice-President, Yugoslav Government, 1952–79.

[3] Vladimir Dedijer, 1914–90. Journalist and foreign correspondent, *Politika*, in Poland, Denmark, Norway, 1935; in England, 1935–6; in Spain, 1936. Lt-Col., Tito's HQ, 1941. Col., 1943. Member, UN General Assembly, 1945–52; Yugoslav Delegation, Paris Peace Conference, 1946. Member, Communist Party Central Committee, 1952; of Federal Assembly, 1953. Prof. of History, University of Belgrade, 1954–5. Vice-President, Bertrand Russell International Tribunal on War Crimes, 1967 (twice), 1977.

2. He has mentioned also the agreement with Stalin on Balkans, among other matters, the agreement 50:50 on Yugoslavia, pointing out that it was not on territorial basis, but the division of influence.

3. Speaking about world situation, Churchill has expressed the opinion that it is possible to achieve an agreement with Stalin but only under the condition that the West is strong enough. He considers that Soviet Union is not yet ready for a war.

Minister Djilas will inform you in details about the contents of the conversation after his return.

Sir Alan Lascelles to Winston S. Churchill
(Churchill papers, 2/171)

31 January 1951

My dear Mr Churchill,

I am sending the cards down to Sandringham, where I know The King and Queen will be delighted with them.

If I may say so, they are the cat's whiskers. I have never seen more agreeable reproductions of good pictures, and whatever the process they now use in the USA, it is obviously a long way ahead of anything we have got in this country.

I take a quasi-professional interest in all this, because years ago, just before I took the hard and stony road of Courtiership, I worked for a while with the Medici people.

Winston S. Churchill to Bernard Van Leer
(Churchill papers, 2/177)

31 January 1951

Dear Mr Van Leer,

Thank you for your letter of January 26[1] and booklet about the Exhibition of your Mobile Drum Factory which I was interested to see. I am afraid that I am pressed for the next few weeks, and I am therefore unable to accept your invitation to visit the Exhibition at Olympia, which nevertheless I much appreciate having received.

I hope your beautiful horse, Salve, continues to give you pleasure. I well remember my ride at Chartwell.

---

[1] Reproduced above (p. 1992).

February 1951

Winston S. Churchill to Francis Brown[1]
(Churchill papers, 2/169)

February 1951

My dear Francis,

I thought I would like to send General Georges some of my cigars to smoke. I wonder if you would be good enough to take them round to him in hospital with my letter, on my behalf.

It was so nice to see you again at the Embassy the other day. I hope all is well with you.

Jo Sturdee to Winston S. Churchill
(Churchill papers, 2/114)

1 February 1951

The Private Secretary at the Foreign Office telephoned to say they wonder whether you would mind and would be good enough to let him know what happened when you saw Mr Djilas.[2] They say they think it would be most helpful for them to know.[3]

---

[1] Francis David Wynyard Brown, 1915–67. 3rd Secretary, FO, 1938–40. Capt., Coldstream Guards, 1940–1. Asst Private Secretary to PM, 1941–4. Asst British Political Adviser, SHAEF, 1945. Political Div., Central Commission for Germany, 1945–6. 1st Secretary, British Embassy, Paris, 1949–52. Delegate to NATO, Paris, 1952–4. Minister at Ankara, 1959–62. Deputy Minister, Mission to the UN, 1965.

[2] Milovan Djilas, 1911–95. Born in Podbišće (Mojkovac), Kingdom of Montenegro. Educated at University of Belgrade. Joined Communist Party of Yugoslavia, 1932. Political prisoner, 1933–6. Central Committee of the Communist Party, 1940. Helped form Yugoslav Partisan resistance, 1941.

[3] The meeting took place on 31 Jan. 1951. Churchill wrote on this note: 'I can't remember what he or I said.'

Winston S. Churchill to A. J. White
(*Churchill papers, 2/168*)

1 February 1951
Private

Dear Mr White,
Thank you so much for communicating with me about General Mark Clark's book, *Calculated Risk*. I have looked at the passages which refer to me. I am sure the General wishes to be friendly in what he writes. Of course to English readers much of his tales about his visits to Chequers will be considered vulgar: They are certainly vitiated by inaccuracy. I cannot accept many of the statements which he attributes to me, let alone the form in which they are expressed. I always say 'aren't' instead of 'ain't'. The bulk of these passages constitutes an abuse of hospitality and intimacy in conversation and will, I am sure, do no good to the General or his publication over here. It in no way represents the manner in which Americans I received were accustomed to behave. I doubt very much whether the style in which this book is written is palatable in the United States. I am sure it will not be here. Once more thanking you for your courtesy.

Winston S. Churchill to Colonel J. B. Whitehead[1]
(*Churchill papers, 2/111*)

2 February 1951
Confidential

Dear Colonel Whitehead,
I learn from Lord Woolton that the Liberals in the Colne Valley Division have now agreed to adopt Lady Violet Bonham Carter as their candidate. I write this letter to you in the earnest hope that you and our Conservative friends in the Division will support her candidature with enthusiasm. She is a remarkable figure, and I should think probably on the whole the best woman speaker we have alive today. All her life has been spent in a political atmosphere. She has been the strongest fighter in several elections for her Father. She has a high, broad, enlightened view of the needs and duties of this country, both in war and peace.

As Leader of the Conservative Party I can assure you that the Colne Valley Association would be making an invaluable, and in some ways decisive, contribution to the cause of our country in these perilous times if they carried her into Parliament as a Liberal Member.

Pray let me know if any difficulties arise, because I take the keenest personal interest in this matter, having regard to questions which are above Party.

[1] Joshua Baxter Whitehead, 1865–?. CO, 41st (Oldham) Royal Tank Rgt, 1942.

February 1951

Winston S. Churchill to Winston Churchill
(Churchill papers, 1/48)

5 February 1951

My dearest Winston,

I was so glad to get your letter of January 27 in which you tell me so much of your news. I was so sorry not to be at Chartwell when you were there, for it is always a great pleasure to me to see you, and I hope we shall get to know each other better as we both grow older.

I showed your letter to Grandma and she was delighted you were pleased with the stamps you sent her from Marrakech. I did not know you were collecting stamps and I will see if I can find a few as they come in on my large correspondence.

I hope you will not lose your early interest in painting because that is a great amusement in after-life, and you seem to me to have a real liking for it.

Please write me other letters and you will always get an answer from your loving Grandpapa.

David Butler[1] to Winston S. Churchill
(Churchill papers, 2/109)

5 February 1951

Dear Mr Churchill,

The Gallup poll figures suggest a Conservative majority of 250 seats. That is the briefest answer to the question which you put to me on the telephone today. But perhaps you would like me to expand it and to make some reservations.

If 51 per cent of the votes at the last General Election had been given to the Conservatives and 38 per cent to Labour – a swing of 7½ per cent from the actual result – the Conservatives would have won about 430 seats and Labour about 180. The Conservatives would have had a clear majority of almost 240 over all parties. Since today there would be many fewer Liberal candidates in the field, it seems probable that such a division of the popular vote would produce a Conservative majority of more than 250 votes.

However I should hesitate to predict that an election now would lead to so large a majority. For four reasons the figures in today's *News Chronicle* must be accepted with some reserve.

    1. <u>Technical accuracy.</u> Owing to various factors – mainly sampling

---

[1] David Butler, 1924–. Psephologist. Educated at St Paul's School and New College, Oxford. Published annual *Nuffield Election Studies*, 1945–2010. Summoned by Churchill to Chartwell to discuss election numbers, 1950. On-screen expert for Great Britain's election nights on BBC TV, 1950–79. Co-inventor of 'swingometer', 1955. CBE, 1991. Knighted, 2011.

- the public opinion polls must be allowed a 2 per cent margin of error. Such an error might mean that the Conservative lead is only 9 per cent and not 13 per cent. A 9 per cent lead would produce a majority of about 200 in the House of Commons. It is notable that the Gallup poll has tended to err on the side of the Conservative Party. In both 1945 and 1950 Labour strength was underestimated by between 1 per cent and 2 per cent.
2. Undecided Voters. According to the current poll, 14 per cent of the electorate are uncertain how they would vote. This is a considerable increase on recent months when only 10 per cent have been undecided. These waverers are drawn most heavily from the poorer sections of the community and past experience suggests that the majority of them will come down on the Labour side of the fence,
3. The Fickleness of the Electorate. A study of past answers to the question 'How would you vote?' reveals considerable and sudden fluctuations. In November 1947 the Conservatives led by 51 per cent to 38 per cent – exactly as they do today; two months later by their lead was only 1 per cent. Again, in November 1949 the Conservatives led by 48 per cent to 38 per cent; by January 1950 that lead had disappeared. A study of past trends suggests that the Government's stock falls heavily for the period just after a major crisis – the Convertibility crisis and Devaluation provide the most outstanding examples – and then gradually recovers. In the absence of some new shock, comparable to the combination of the Chinese intervention in Korea and the threat of a new fuel crisis, I should expect the Government to recover some of its support as the spring advances.
4. The Effect of an Election Campaign. On the whole the Labour Party gained in strength during the campaign last February. Over the past thirty years there is considerable evidence to suggest that usually an election campaign helps the party in power. There is no reason why it should always do so but it seems wise to make allowance for this possibility.

Bearing in mind all these factors, I should be surprised if an election in the near future would give the Conservatives quite as overwhelming a victory as today's poll would suggest. But, even if all these factors told heavily against them, I should be still more surprised if the Conservatives failed to win an appreciable majority of the votes. A lead of only 2 per cent, I am certain, would be sufficient to give the Conservatives a Parliamentary majority of over 50 seats. A lead of 5 per cent would give them a majority of well over 100 seats.

In short, although the poll results should not be taken as too literal an indication of the precise outcome, they give very strong reason to suppose that an early appeal to the country would return the Conservatives with a very comfortable majority.

PS. This is a copy of the letter which I have sent off to Chartwell by the same post.

Lettice Marston to Winston S. Churchill
(Churchill papers, 2/28)

7 February 1951

Mr Kelly has not been able to find the document about the Atomic Bomb Agreement, as he says it is not contained in the archives.

Winston S. Churchill to Clement Attlee
(Churchill papers, 2/28)

8 February 1951

My dear Prime Minister,

I have been thinking over our conversation of last week and am still convinced that our national interest requires the publication of the original document governing the use of the Atomic Bomb signed by Mr Roosevelt and me at Quebec in 1943, and since revoked and superseded. The question becomes all the more important because of the arrangement subsequently made by which the United States has an important air base in East Anglia. I therefore propose to bring the matter before Parliament in due course.

Winston S. Churchill to Sir Walter Monckton
(Churchill papers, 2/90)

9 February 1951

My dear Walter Monckton,

By the untimely death of Oliver Stanley, our Party and the country have suffered an irreparable loss. His Parliamentary experience, his skill in debate, the integrity of his intellect, his lovable personality, and above all his statesmanlike breadth of view were qualities of high distinction. I am glad indeed that in you we have a candidate who discharged functions of major importance during the war, including acting Minister of State at a critical time in Cairo, and who has also served as Solicitor-General in the Conservative Government which I formed. Your arrival in Parliament will be a valuable reinforcement.

The issues at the bye-election which you are fighting in the West Bristol

Division stand out only too plainly. The costly and dilatory mishandling of our defences by the Government over the past five years leaves the country in grave danger. The Socialist Party has not got the capacity to give the people the leadership needed to preserve peace through strength. In the seven anxious months since the Communist aggression in Korea began, the record of the Socialist Government has been marred by hesitation and timidity. This reflects the deep division in their ranks, which you can see for yourselves in West Bristol. Thus they have confused our relations with the United States, without whose powerful aid our safety and freedom cannot be preserved. It is not by drifting that we shall find the harbour of world peace.

At home we gaze upon a panorama of ineptitude. The Health Service as planned by the National Government is in danger of breaking down. The houses they promised to build, and even the will to build them, are lacking. There is a perpetual shortage of fuel and power. The cost of living rises steadily. Eight-pennyworth of low grade meat, or a third of the Workhouse ratio pre-war, is the result of five years of Socialist planning and buying. The nationalized industries and services, to which Iron and Steel are now to be added, not only fail to deliver the goods but throw heavy cost on the taxpayer. When Ministers fail they are only transferred to other posts to which they are even more unsuited. The time has come when there should be a change.

I appeal to all the electors of West Bristol to turn out in full force on February 15, and I look forward to welcoming to Parliament a wartime colleague of exceptional experience and ability.

Clement Attlee to Winston S. Churchill
(Churchill papers, 2/28)

9 February 1951
Top Secret

My dear Churchill,

Thank you for your letter of the 8th February telling me that you are still convinced that the national interest requires the publication of the original document governing the use of the atomic bomb, signed by Mr Roosevelt and yourself at Quebec in 1943.

You will remember that when we discussed this matter last week I made it clear that I did not share this opinion, but said that I would be quite willing to obtain the views of the United States Government on the publication of the agreement.

I subsequently arranged for our Ambassador in Washington to be instructed to put this point to the United States Government. I have not yet had a reply but as soon as I do I shall of course get in touch with you.

FEBRUARY 1951

Winston S. Churchill to President Harry S Truman
(Churchill papers, 2/28)

10 February 1951

I have asked that you should assent to the publication of a certain document of which you will by now have heard through our diplomatic channels. I hope you will await the letter I am sending you before agreeing, refusing or agreeing to refuse publication. The matter may become a serious political issue over here and as co-signatory of the agreement I feel I have a right to express my views to you.

Winston S. Churchill to Clement Attlee
(Churchill papers, 2/28)

12 February 1951

My dear Prime Minister,

Thank you for your reply of February 9 to my letter of the 8th. I do not of course know the terms of your communication to President Truman.

I note you mark your letter of February 9 'Top Secret'. I cannot myself see in what essential particular it goes beyond our public exchanges in Parliament, but of course I should not publish your letter without your permission.

I may add that, as co-signatory of the original Agreement, I have thought it right to communicate myself with the President of the United States, and I trust that he will at least agree that the atomic weapon shall not be used from British bases without prior consent.

Winston S. Churchill to Walter Gifford[1]
(Churchill papers, 2/169)

12 February 1951

My dear Ambassador,

Let me thank you for your courtesy in transmitting my message to your President. In the days of your predecessor I was always accorded these facilities by your Embassy, as sometimes they touch important matters.

I regret very much that owing to my absence from this country I have not met you at any of the public dinners at which you were welcomed on taking up your mission over here. I wonder whether you and Mrs Gifford would

---

[1] Walter Sherman Gifford, 1885–1966. Educated at Harvard University. US Official Adviser to Council of Defense, 1916–18. Controller, AT&T, 1918–19; Vice-President of Finance, 1919–23; Executive Vice-President, 1925–48. US Official Director on Unemployment Relief, 1931–2. Ambassador to UK, 1950–3.

come and lunch with us one day? Only my Wife and I would be present, so that we could have a good talk about things, which are by no means all that one would wish them to be. Would February 27 be convenient, or should I find another date? Mrs Churchill is writing to Mrs Gifford.

Winston S. Churchill to President Harry S Truman
(Churchill papers, 2/28)

12 February 1951

Dear Mr President,

I venture to address you on the question of the publication of the Agreement which I signed with President Roosevelt about the atomic bomb in Quebec in 1943. I have lately learned that this has been superseded by other agreements made by you with Mr Attlee's Government in 1945 and later. Nothing was said to the British Parliament at the time about this very important change, and I feel it my duty to press for a disclosure of the original document and Agreement. As this has been revoked, and has no longer any binding force, I feel it belongs to the past and to history. Parliament however has a right to know what the British position was at the end of the war, and I cannot believe that the facts can be indefinitely withheld. The Agreement, although made in wartime, was, as its references to the use of atomic power for commercial purposes show, intended to cover more than the wartime period.

The original Agreement, now superseded, has acquired a new and practical significance from the fact that His Majesty's Government have, with my full support, accorded the United States a most important bombing base in East Anglia, and I have little doubt that Parliament would consider that this base should not be used for the atomic bomb without the consent of His Majesty's Government.

I believe that the publication of the original document would place us in a position where this guarantee would willingly be conceded by the United States. This would I am sure strengthen the ties which bind our two Countries together in 'fraternal association' and effective alliance. This remains as always the prime object of any policy which I should support.

I congratulate you on the more favourable turn which events in Korea have lately taken. I have always hoped that the United States, while maintaining her necessary rights in the Far East, would not become too heavily involved there, for it is in Europe that the mortal challenge to world freedom must be confronted. I express my gratitude to you and to you Country, which I love so well, for the Eisenhower Mission and the far-reaching measures which it implies. In this I see the best hope of world peace, if time is given to us.

Clement Attlee to Winston S. Churchill
(Churchill papers, 2/28)

14 February 1951
Top Secret

My dear Churchill,

Thank you for your letter. I am still awaiting a reply from the Government of the United States to the communication which I sent to them after our exchange of views.

I do not understand the basis of your communication to the President. While the Quebec Agreement was made between Roosevelt and yourself, it was, of course, in your capacities as President and Prime Minister. I do not see that a personal communication of the kind which you have made will advance a matter which is at present under discussion between Governments.

President Harry S Truman to Winston S. Churchill
(Churchill papers, 2/28)[1]

16 February 1951

Dear Winston,

Your personal note, attached to your request for the release of the Quebec Agreement of 1943, is highly appreciated.[2]

I am making a sincere effort to carry out the Atlantic Treaty with my position in the Congress, which might be termed vicious and unfair under present emergency conditions.

I hope you won't press me in this matter. It will cause unfortunate repercussions both here and in your country, as well as embarrassment to you and to your government.

The reopening of this discussion may ruin my whole defense program both here at home and abroad. Your country's welfare and mine are at stake in that program.

I hope you are in good health and enjoying life as much as one can enjoy it in these troubled times.

---

[1] This letter was handwritten.

[2] Churchill's covering note, in his own hand, read: 'My dear Harry, Forgive me for burdening you with the enclosed, but I feel it my duty to my country to send it to you' (letter of 12 Feb. 1951, *Churchill papers, 2/28*).

Winston S. Churchill: press notice
(Churchill papers, 2/116)

16 February 1951

BACKGROUND INFORMATION FOR THE PRESS
To be given if they inquire

A little girl ran across the road in front of the car in which Mr Churchill was travelling from London to Westerham this morning. The car was not travelling fast but she was knocked down. After making sure that she was not badly hurt Mr Churchill left her in the care of her mother who was there, having just fetched her from school. It was not necessary for the girl to be taken to hospital as her injuries were so slight.

John Peck to Winston S. Churchill
(Churchill papers, 2/28)

18 February 1951

The following is Lord Cherwell's note on your draft statement to the Press. 'Making atom bombs falls into two parts requiring equal effort.
1. Making the stuff and extracting it.
2. Preparing the bomb so that it will be possible to detonate it.

It would not be reasonable to make only one prototype, for a quite definite amount of stuff is needed for each weapon. If one builds small piles it might take ten years or more to make enough. In large piles enough can be made in a very much shorter time, from a day to a month according to size and number of piles. I think the piles on which we decided (one of which has now come into operation) are about the right size. But once built they will go on producing the stuff and it would be foolish not to go on extracting it and preparing to use it as required.

Thus I do not think we should say that we object to mass production. Incidentally mass production scarcely seems the right word for an output in single figures per week or even per month.'

Winston S. Churchill: press notice
(Churchill papers, 2/28)

19 February 1951

Mr Churchill issued the following statement from Chartwell this afternoon:
There seems to be some misunderstanding in the newspapers about the interchanges which Mr Churchill had with the Prime Minister on the subject

of the Atomic Bomb during the Rearmament Debate. The policy of the present Government has been to pursue the experiments and research necessary to give them the power to make the bomb. Mr Churchill did not disagree with that policy. He considered it however a matter of complaint that after five and a half years with all the knowledge we possessed at the end of the War we had not yet succeeded in making even one single specimen although the Soviet Government have not only solved the initial difficulties but have also entered into regular production. The cause of this in Mr Churchill's opinion is largely due to the whole process being kept in the hands of the Ministry of Supply instead of being entrusted to a special sub-department under the direct control of the Prime Minister. Mr Churchill pressed this upon the Prime Minister some time ago with a very great measure of scientific support. However nothing was done and the post-war story of the British attempts to make an atomic bomb affords another instance of administrative failure about which it is right that the public should be informed.

The matter has no strategic significance on account of the overwhelming superiority of the United States in this weapon.

Geoffrey Shakespeare[1] to Winston S. Churchill
(Churchill papers, 2/65)

21 February 1951

Dear Mr Churchill,

After consultation with Jack Maclay, I enclose a telegram I propose to send you on Friday evening from the National Liberal Executive at Hastings, and I also enclose suggested reply from yourself, in the form of a telegram.

We should like the maximum publicity for these messages, and I should be grateful if you would ask your Secretary to return the draft, amended, of course, as you would wish, to myself at 30, Marsham Court, SW1 (Tel: Victoria 8181) not later than noon on Friday next, the 23rd February. This will enable us to give full publicity.

We are most grateful for your help in this respect.

---

[1] Geoffrey Hithersay Shakespeare, 1893–1980. Educated at Emmanuel College, Cambridge. Served in WWI. Private Secretary to David Lloyd George, 1921–3. MP (Lib.) for Wellingborough, 1922–3; for Norwich, 1929–45. Parliamentary Secretary to Ministry of Health, 1932–6; to Board of Education, 1936–7; to Dept of Overseas Trade, 1940. Parliamentary and Financial Secretary to the Admiralty, 1937–40. Parliamentary Under-Secretary of State for Dominions Affairs, 1940–2. Bt, 1942. PC, 1945.

Lieutenant-General Sir Henry Pownall to Winston S. Churchill
(Churchill papers, 4/333)

22 February 1951

This is my draft of the chapter 'Preparations for Overlord'.

I think it is probably also Overlong, especially as part of Garrod's[1] paper should come into it. The pages of that paper for transfer are 29, 30, 31, 32, 32a, 32b, 32c, and 33 (first two paragraphs down to '. . . in the last of these volumes').

However, certain easements are possible, pages 14A, B and C of my paper dealing with the Service plans and the joint fire plan can well go into the last chapter 'On the Eve', where you describe Montgomery's exposition of the plans on May 15. Also the last page (18), dealing with the choice of D-day and H-hour, could go into that chapter. Eisenhower's postponement of D-day, which presumably will come into that chapter, could hook on to it.

Partly because of space and partly because I think it is more closely related to the later stages of the Anvil argument, I have not included anything about 'Caliph' (Bay of Biscay attack). Otherwise I have used the more important material in the existing print of 'Preparations for Overlord'.

I do not doubt that there is room for improvement in this story, especially on the naval side, but you may think it worth printing before attempting serious revision.

Clement Attlee to Winston S. Churchill
(Churchill papers, 2/28)

22 February 1951
Top Secret

My dear Churchill,

I promised to let you know the outcome of the consultation with the United States Government on the proposal that the Agreement governing the use of the atomic bomb signed by Mr Roosevelt and yourself in Quebec in 1943 should be published.

I have now been officially informed that the United States Government could not agree to the publication of the Quebec Agreement at the present time.

Although Mr Mackenzie King was not a signatory of the Quebec Agreement, Canada is an interested party in view of its membership of the

---

[1] Guy Garrod, 1891–1965. Chief Instructor, Oxford University Air Sqn, 1928–30. Deputy Director of Organization, Air Ministry, 1934–6. Deputy Allied Air C-in-C SE Asia, 1943–5. Air Mshl, 1945. Permanent RAF Representative, Military Staff Committee, UN, 1945–8. Air Chf Mshl, 1946. Head, RAF Delegation, Washington DC, 1946–8.

Combined Policy Committee referred to in the Agreement. I therefore thought it well to inform the Canadian Government of the proposal for publication. In reply the Canadian Government have expressed the opinion that publication of the Agreement is not a good idea at the present time. The Canadian Government apprehends that publication could only lead to further unwelcome questioning.

Winston S. Churchill to Geoffrey Shakespeare
(Churchill papers, 2/65)

23 February 1951

My warmest thanks for your telegram.[1] I am glad to have the assurance of the continued goodwill and support of my National–Liberal friends. The Liberal and Conservative parties have had their historic differences, but they have also in times of danger united together to the advantage of our Country.

Today, perhaps more than ever before, our sacred rights and liberties, indeed our very existence as a Nation of free people are in jeopardy. It is more than ever necessary that Liberals and Conservatives and many of those without definite party attachment should cooperate to face the growing danger to everything that our two Parties hold dear.

The Liberal–Unionist Group in the House of Commons, and the combined associations in the Country, provide a most effective channel for the pooling of constructive Liberal and Conservative thought.

I hope that this form of cooperation will grow and I send you best wishes for the success of your Conference.

Jo Sturdee to Winston S. Churchill
(Churchill papers, 2/104)

23 February 1951

Sir James Hawkey telephoned to say he has just heard that Mr Nigel Davies[2] will not be standing at the next Election as candidate.

He says it has occurred to him that it would be suitable and nice if Mr Randolph were adopted, if he is not committed to Devonport. He says he has still a certain amount of influence in the district and he is sure it could be arranged if you would like it. In view of the historic association you have with the Epping Division, he thinks it would be most suitable that your son should be the candidate. He has no doubt that the seat can be held.[3]

---

[1] Reproduced above (p. 2006).
[2] Claude Nigel Byam Davies. Served in Middle East, Italy and Balkans, 1942–6. MP (Cons.) for Epping Div. of Essex, 1950–1.
[3] Churchill wrote back: 'I think it would be better not to have too much family in a locality.'

Winston S. Churchill to Sir Stafford Cripps
(Churchill papers, 2/168)

26 February 1951

My dear Stafford,

Clemmie and I have followed with close attention in the newspapers the reports of your progress. These encourage me to send you a copy of the American edition of my fourth volume, *The Hinge of Fate*, which may be of interest to you. I do hope however you will not burden yourself with reading it if you find it tiring or boring. Still, we have a great story in common of those days we went through together.

Please do not bother to answer this but give my warmest regards to your Wife.

With every good wish for your speedy recovery and return.

Ian Colvin[1] to Winston S. Churchill
(Churchill papers, 2/168)

28 February 1951

Dear Mr Churchill,

I thought you might like to know that people here are giving me short leave to follow up enquiries with C's people, and I hope to be able to report something very soon.

My book about Admiral Canaris,[2] entitled *Chief of Intelligence* will be published shortly. As you are mentioned in it, perhaps I should say that there is nothing else than you already saw in the submitted manuscript on Kleist[3] last year.

There is, however, one important fact which I wish I had been able to tell you sooner. I have it on the authority of General Erwin Lahousen,[4] Deputy

---

[1] Ian Goodhope Colvin, 1913–75. Reporter, *Morning Post*, 1932; Reuters, 1933. Correspondent in Berlin, *News Chronicle*, 1938–9. News Dept, FO, 1939–40. Served in Royal Marines, Combined Operations HQ, 1940–4. Flotilla Cdr, 1944–5. On the staff of Kemsley newspapers, 1946–52. Foreign Editor, *Sunday Express*, 1953–5. Leader writer and foreign correspondent, *Daily Telegraph*, 1955–75.

[2] Wilhelm Franz Canaris, 1887–1945. Born in Aplerbeck, Westphalia. Married, 1919, Erika Waag: two children. Entered Imperial Navy, 1905. Graduated from Submarine School, 1917. Head, Abwehr, 1933–44. Plotted coup against Hitler and the Nazi Party. Arrested on suspicion of disloyalty to Nazi regime, July 1943. Dismissed by Hitler, Feb. 1944. Under house arrest, March–June 1944. Head, Special Staff for Mercantile Warfare and Economic Measures, June–July 1944. Executed by hanging, Flossenburg concentration camp, Apr. 1945.

[3] Ewald von Kleist-Schmenzin, 1890–1945. Knight of Honour, Order of St John, 1922. Knight of Justice, 1935. Secret Emissary to Admiral Wilhelm Canaris and Col.-Gen. Ludwig Beck, 1938. Organized and supported an attempt to overthrow and assassinate Hitler, 1944. Sentenced to death for his part in the plot, 1945.

[4] Erwin von Lahousen, 1897–1955. Born in Austria. Served in Austro-Hungarian Army during WWI. Entered Abwehr, 1938. Responsible for sabotage plots during invasion of Poland, 1939. Voluntarily testified at Nuremberg War Crimes Trials, 1945–6.

Chief of German Intelligence, that Hitler gave orders for an attempt to be made on your life while you were at Casablanca. Arab agents from Spanish Morocco were thought to be able to carry out these orders. Admiral Canaris did not pass them on.

I am also told that a reconnaissance squadron of the Luftwaffe, attached to the German Intelligence Service, had instructions to watch the Biscay and Spanish coasts for your aircraft. I hope to be in touch with the Squadron Leader soon.

March 1951

Private Office: press notice
(Churchill papers, 1/47)

1 March 1951

Mr Churchill has been suffering from a localised staphylococcal infection, and has been having treatment for it. On the advice of Lord Moran and Sir Thomas Dunhill[1] he must rest for a few days and will be unable to attend to his duties. Mr Churchill has therefore had to cancel his engagements at Sheffield on Monday and Tuesday.

Winston S. Churchill to Lady Lytton
(Lady Lytton papers)

1 March 1951

Dearest Pamela,

I send you some of the American Christmas cards of this year. They had a two million sale over there. As they reproduce in over a dozen colours, instead of our three or four, they get very good results.

It was lovely your coming down for the weekend. Rufus and Puff were also very happy together.

I am laid up with an unexpectedly violent reaction to a penicillin injection which I took. I had a dreadful night with pain and a swollen face. I have, alas, had to cancel the Freedom and the Cutlers' Feast at Sheffield next Monday and Tuesday.

---

[1] Thomas Peel Dunhill, 1876–1957. Born near Kerang, Australia. Educated at Clinical School, Melbourne Hospital, 1903. Married, 1914, Edith Florence Affleck McKellar (d. 1942). On active service in WWI (despatches thrice). CVO, 1919. CMG, 1919. Asst to Dr George Gask, St Vincent's Hospital, London, 1920. Surgeon to the Royal Household, 1928. Hon. Surgeon to George VI, 1930. KCVO, 1933. Hon. Fellow, Royal College of Surgeons, 1939. Dunhill had seen Churchill at Chequers on 1 Dec. 1940; Churchill later (1941) sent Dunhill a copy of *Marlborough: His Life and Times*. On 11 June 1947, Dunhill operated on Churchill's hernia. GCVO, 1949.

March 1951

Winston S. Churchill to Ian Colvin
(Churchill papers, 2/168)

3 March 1951

My dear Ian Colvin,

Thank you for your letter of February 28.[1]

I had not previously heard about the alleged plan by the Germans to assassinate me at Casablanca. Let me know if you glean any more information.

I am glad that your plans are working out.

Winston S. Churchill to Lord Trenchard[2]
(Churchill papers, 2/117)

5 March 1951
Private

My dear Trenchard,

I have read with great interest and attention your speech in the House of Lords which you kindly sent me. With much of it, especially in 'cutting down the tail', I agree. I think however our first need in the air at the moment is fighters. I would not embark on the bomber programme, at their expense, until we have at least enough to give us the essential protection.

I am very glad the Americans should develop a long-range bomber, but when you think of our present plight in this country and how easily we could be overwhelmed by mass attack: by bombing, we ought surely to have enough fighters to take so heavy a toll of the enemy that he would be deterred from continuing, as he was last time. After this requirement is met, we could throw our efforts into bombers. What would have happened in the last war if we had had twenty per cent more long-range bombers and fifty per cent less fighters? Not only our daily life but our whole fighting power could have been destroyed. I am also concerned at large-scale paratroop raids – twenty thousand or so – in our present defenceless condition, where our troops are out of the country, or to be sent away, and we have no Home Guard. I do not admit that giving the highest priority to fighters in 'defence'. It is counter-attack of a very high order.

---

[1] Reproduced above (pp. 2009–10).
[2] Hugh Montague Trenchard, 1873–1956. Entered Army, 1893. On active service in South Africa, 1899–1902 (dangerously wounded). Maj., 1902. Asst Commandant, Central Flying School, 1913–14. GOC RFC in the Field, 1915–17. Maj.-Gen., 1916. Knighted, 1918. CAS, 1918–29. Air Mshl, 1919. Bt, 1919. Air Chf Mshl, 1922. Mshl of the RAF, 1927. Baron, 1930. Commissioner, Metropolitan Police, 1931–5. Viscount, 1936. His elder son, and both his stepsons, were killed in action in WWII.

March 1951

Princess Margaret to Winston S. Churchill
(Churchill papers, 2/173)[1]

6 March 1951   Buckingham Palace

My dear Mr Churchill,

I am writing to thank you most sincerely for giving me your new book. It was such a kind thought on your part, and I shall always treasure it. It will be a charming reminder of a lovely visit to your house. Thank you so very much for showing me all your lovely pictures and all your fascinating treasures of the war. I shall always remember it as being one of the pleasantest afternoons I have ever spent anywhere.

Thank you again so much.

Admiral Lord Fraser to Winston S. Churchill
(Churchill papers, 2/35)[2]

14 March 1951
Personal

Dear Mr Churchill,

Listening at question time today, it did not seem to me that the facts were quite clear.

I went out to the Fleets to see the exercises and talk to the sailors and many questions were asked about the Command set-up.

I could only speak to the small ships some 25 of them and 3,000 officers and men by mustering them on shore by their ships and using loud speakers which the Gibraltar press overheard. An admiral must of course talk to his officers and never as he thinks and I am glad to say that the morale and efficiency which I observed was as good as ever.

This letter is not to make excuses or to avoid closure but just to say how sorry I am that I have offended you, as you know so well how much you command my respect.

The path of duty in this case does not seem to have led to the path of glory!

---

[1] This letter was handwritten.
[2] This letter was handwritten.

Winston S. Churchill: broadcast
('Winston S. Churchill, His Complete Speeches', volume 8, pages 8169–73)

17 March 1951

CONSERVATIVE CASE FOR AN ELECTION

We have suffered a serious loss in the departure of Mr Bevin from the Foreign Office. After nearly eleven years of continuous service of the most arduous character it was felt that for some time past he was breaking under the strain. Although I differed from him in his handling of many questions, I feel bound to put on record that he takes his place among the great Foreign Secretaries of our country, and that, in his steadfast resistance to Communist aggression, in his strengthening of our ties with the United States and his share of building up the Atlantic Pact, he has rendered services to Britain and to the cause of peace which will long be remembered. As his war-time leader I take this opportunity to pay my tribute to him and to his devoted wife.

My friends, our country is in a position of danger and perplexity. Abroad, things are bad, and we are becoming ever more divided at home. At a time when it would take our whole genius and united strength to cope with our troubles and ward off our perils, we are more sharply and evenly separated than I can remember in a long life. In 1940, you remember that, at the time of the Battle of Britain, everyone could see our danger was very great. In my opinion the dangers which many of us cannot see are even greater now. But then we were a united people – now we are absorbed in party strife. I am not going to pretend that all the faults are on one side. It takes two to make a quarrel. But I submit to you that the prime responsibility must rest with the Government of the day. They have the initiative and power. They create the situations and present the issues, and the Opposition parties react to them as best they can.

When Parliament was recalled last September, there was, I think, a chance of this House of Commons having a longer and more useful life than will now be its fate. The Prime Minister proposed to us the first version of the great rearmament schemes – £3,600 million in three years – and he asked for the institution of two years' compulsory military service. In spite of our party differences, I asked the House to pass the measures almost in a day, and thus send a message of national unity on defence and foreign policy around the world. This was done, and if the Prime Minister had met us in a similar spirit our home politics might well have taken a better turning. However, within a week of receiving our support in this effective manner, Mr Attlee astonished us by the announcement that he was proceeding at once to carry out the Steel Nationalization Act. This was playing at party politics with a vengeance. There was a perfectly good working compromise put forward by the Trades Union Congress under which owners, employers and men in the steel industry could have worked happily together. But the Prime Minister brushed this aside and used the nationalization of steel as a means of increasing antagonism by which his party live and thus placated his own extremists. By this act of partisanship he destroyed whatever chance there was of friendly co-operation in the present Parliament. I have no wish to be too hard upon Mr Attlee. He certainly has a lot to bear. I sincerely trust his health will stand the strain. I resented Mr Stalin calling him a warmonger. I thought this was quite untrue. It was also unfair, because this word 'warmonger' was, as you have no doubt heard, the one that many of Mr Attlee's friends and followers were hoping to fasten on me whenever the election comes – they were keeping that for my especial benefit. Stalin has therefore been guilty, not only of an untruth, but of infringement of copyright. I think Mr Stalin had better be careful or else Mr Silverman will have him up for breach of privilege, or something like that.

Obviously we approach an election. Parliamentary democracy rests upon elections. But prolonged electioneering is not good for Britain. We have already had fifteen months of election fever. That would try the strongest constitution. It was hoped that the election a year ago would give a decision one way or the other, but instead it produced almost exact equality. Since then we have had a Government representing a minority of the electors trying to conduct all our grave and critical affairs without a normal working majority in the House of Commons. All their work is cut out in keeping their heads above water from day to day: indeed, I might say from night to night.

Parliamentary debate has become largely meaningless. All the time the two great party machines are grinding up against each other with the utmost energy, dividing every village, every street, every town and city into busy party camps. Each party argues that it is the fault of the other. What is certain is that to prolong the process indefinitely is the loss of all. After all, no nation possesses in common such long gathered moral and social treasures. No nation is more accustomed to practical methods of give and take from day to day, and few countries have at the present time – let me remind you – to look mortal dangers more directly in the face. Naturally, we all ask the question, are we really to go on all through the spring, summer and autumn with this struggle in Parliament and strife in the constituencies? Democracy does not express itself in clever manoeuvres by which a handful of men survive from day to day, or another handful of men try to overthrow them. Once it can be seen that a great new situation or great new issues lie before us, an appeal should be made to the people to create some governing force which can deal with our affairs in the name and in the interest of the large majority of the nation.

An entirely new situation is now before the country – there is the tremendous policy of rearmament. Why was this not mentioned by the Government at the General Election? All essential facts were known to Mr Attlee and his colleagues. The outbreak in Korea six months later merely showed the public what was well known to the Government. The Government knew as well as they do now the menacing strength of the Soviet armies and air force and U-boats. They knew what had happened to Poland and Czechoslovakia and in the Russian zone of Germany. They knew perfectly well that to make an efficient army for Britain with its numerous overseas requirements two years' service was needed. Why did they not propose it? Why did they not even mention it? The operative responsibility was theirs. They were seeking a new mandate. It is for them to answer that question. Why did they not do it? Mr Baldwin, as you may remember, was censured for not having warned the country as Prime Minister in 1935 that rearmament was necessary. Mr Baldwin knew that, had he done so, he would have been violently attacked by the other side. But Mr Attlee had not even that excuse, because he knew that the Conservative Party would support him if he asked for their support, not only upon rearmament but on the increase of the military service to two years. He did not do so. Thus, the present Parliament was elected on a basis quite different from that which now exists. Here, apart from all other arguments, is a plain case for consulting the people on the new issues.

Should there be an immense rearmament? We say 'Yes' – but if so, are the Ministers, who now have it in hand, having regard to their proved incapacity, the men to be trusted with it? The most disturbing and harmful condition in our domestic politics is the uncertainty about when an election will come. This keeps party strife at its keenest point. The Prime Minister has deliberately aggravated this evil. 'The election will come,' he says, 'at the right time,' meaning, of course, the right time for him and his party. Of this he is to be the sole judge. Any day, therefore, we may be plunged into all this tumult of electioneering. Both sides must be continually prepared. All our problems at home and abroad are made more difficult by this uncertainty. Yet Mr Attlee's policy seems to be to prolong it to the utmost limit in his power.

This magnifies party interests and organization out of all proportion to national affairs. It keeps everything on edge. Every word spoken has to be tested by the controversial use that might be made of it. It cannot be good for our public life. It cannot strengthen our position in the world. It harms the whole of our business. No one can compute the loss in money and prosperity, yet we are led to believe that the Government intend to go on until the last possible minute, prolonging all these strains and stresses. It is more than plain that they have lost the confidence of the nation, but the plainer it becomes the more obstinately and desperately they cling to their offices on the chance that something will turn up. They seek to prolong this hateful and costly uncertainty. We seek to bring it to an end. It is in the national interest that it should come to an end and that a broad-based Government resting on a clear and strong majority should come into power. We need a Government unhampered by narrow doctrinal party dogma or by the interests of any particular class. We need a Government able to address itself with a fresh eye and calm resolution to all our problems and deal with them on their merits. Certainly it is not an inviting prospect for any new Government to have to face. The more the consequences of devaluation make themselves remorselessly felt, the harder will be our lot. There are some who argue that we should leave the burden in the hands of those who have so largely brought it into being. 'Let them reap where they have sown': that is what is said. I hold, on the contrary, that it would be unpatriotic to allow the present degeneration to continue.

Look at the dangers to world peace which come from a weak, divided and largely disregarded Britain. Look at the way we are treated by so many countries whom we have helped in days not long gone by. The Conservative and Unionist Party have therefore made up their minds on national rather than on party grounds to do their utmost to bring about an appeal to the nation at the earliest moment, and to use to the full our parliamentary and constitutional rights for that purpose. What happens at home, my friends, is in our hands. We cannot control what happens abroad. We have an influence – we might have a much greater influence. But the supreme decisions are outside our power. It is, however, within our power to reach a solid, stable, coherent settlement at home. If we did, we should not only be much stronger and therefore much safer, but we should have far more power to shape and lever the movement of events towards our goal.

What is our goal? What is our hearts' wish? It is very plain, it is very simple. It is only the hearts' desire of all the millions of ordinary men and women with their hard workaday lives, all the peoples still outside the totalitarian curtain all over the world – only their hearts' desire: freedom and peace. The right to be let alone to lead our own lives in our own way, under our own laws, and give our children a fair chance to make the best of themselves. It is not wrong for anyone to ask for that. It is not much for Britain to ask. We did our best to fight for it, in the late war; for a whole year we fought alone. When at last all our enemies surrendered we thought we had won it – won it at least for a lifetime. But now it seems that we are again in jeopardy. We are in a sad, sombre period of world history where no good-hearted, valiant Russian soldier, worker or peasant; no hard-pressed, disillusioned German family; no home in the war-scarred democracies of Western Europe or in our own islands we have guarded so long, so well, or far across the Atlantic in mighty America – no household can have the feeling after a long day's faithful toil that they can go to sleep without the fear that something awful is moving towards them; and this is what has come to us after all our efforts and sacrifices, and come upon us at a time when, but for the thoughtlessness of the free democracies and the organized designs of the Kremlin oligarchy, expanding science, like a fairy godmother, could have opened the gates of the Golden Age to all.

I do not suggest that any one country or any party in any country has the power or the virtue to sweep away this nightmare which darkens ever more in our deep confusion and unrest. But there are a great many nations who are trying very hard and it ought to be our earnest resolve that Britain should play her part, and her full part, in saving mankind from the two hideous alternatives thrust before us – Communist tyranny or annihilating war.

My friends, I have traced for you in these few minutes tonight the outlines of this strange and awe-inspiring world picture, and everyone around every table or fireside who is listening to me here in our island and beyond it – because many are listening – will, I feel, be asking themselves: what ought we to do to make Britain strong and splendid so that we can play our true and real parts once again in the defence of human rights and dignity, founded as they can only be upon justice and peace? Surely our duty shines clear and plain before us. Surely we ought not to let the inevitable difficulties of our party strife prevent our rising to our full majesty and becoming once again one of the foremost champions and guides of the free world.

I have a long experience and this has come into my mind. In critical and baffling situations it is always best to recur to first principles and simple action. Trust the people, go to the people, let the people have their say. Let there be a General Election where they can express their will – where they can express their will through a Parliament worthy of what is strongest and best in our race. It is for this that we are resolved to strive. Goodnight!

Winston S. Churchill to Admiral Lord Fraser
(Churchill papers, 2/35)

19 March 1951

My dear Fraser,

I am very glad to have heard from you[1] that you did not intend to make any public pronouncement on the Command arrangements, and to have had your explanation of how the leakage occurred. It is most important that Ministers, who can be criticized, should deal with these controversial matters, and that the Service chiefs should not be involved.

Thank you very much for what you say at the end of your letter. I look back with pleasure on our work together during so many years.

Somerset de Chair to Winston S. Churchill
(Churchill papers, 4/44)

20 March 1951

Dear Mr Churchill,

Here are the page proofs of Caesar's *Commentaries*, which you asked to see in connection with the idea of my dedicating the book to you. If by any chance,

---

[1] Letter reproduced above (p. 2013).

you felt like giving Caesar a pat on the back before he goes into battle, there is a page standing invitingly blank for a Foreword, facing the Introduction.

The first sixteen pages are on the paper on which the book will finally be printed and the publishers have set up the form of dedication which I suggested but this is, of course, only on the proof and entirely subject to your permission.

I very much hope you will allow me to pay you this tribute and need hardly add that a Foreword from you would give Caesar's *Commentaries*, in this edition, a great deal of added interest.

Winston S. Churchill: speech
(Hansard)

21 March 1951　　　　　　　　　　　　　　　　　　　House of Commons

COMPLAINT OF PRIVILEGE

Mr Churchill (Woodford): No one can complain of any violence in the temper or tone of the speeches in which this Motion has been introduced to the House. The hon. Member for Nuneaton (Mr Bowles), who seconded it, referred to my great and unique age in this House, and that was also a subject of interest on the Ministerial Front Bench a little while ago. I remember well that my father – if we are to go back into the past – called Mr Gladstone 'an old man in a hurry'. That was in the year 1885, and 16 years later Mr Gladstone was engaged in forming another Administration. I do not, however, want to suggest that such a precedent will be repeated, in order not to dishearten hon. Members opposite.

I have listened to a great deal that the hon. Member for Nelson and Colne (Mr S. Silverman) has said, with a great deal of sympathy for his general principles, but I am bound to say that I do not think that he dealt with the actual issue which is before us. There is this question that Mr Speaker, on 13th March, ruled that there was no *prima facie* case to refer to the Committee of Privileges.

Mr S. Silverman: He did not say that.

Mr Churchill: He said that there was not a *prima facie* case. (*Interruption.*) I cannot be interrupted. The House has a perfect right to reverse Mr Speaker's Ruling, but the step is a serious one, and I do not remember it happening in my time – an immense period, far longer even than that of the Father of the House. It is quite open to a Member to put down a Motion on the Order Paper such as we have tonight, but I contend that it could not be carried without implying stultification of Mr Speaker's Ruling. I do not mean it is any censure on Mr Speaker, but it implies a different view taken by the House from the view taken by Mr Speaker in the very brief time accorded to him when a

Motion of this kind is made. My submission to the House is that Mr Speaker's Ruling was right. There was no *prima facie* case then, there is not now a prima facie case; still less is there a case, not *prima facie* but, as it were, to a certain extent, pre-judged by the decision of the House.

Let us look into this question of Privilege. Privilege means Parliamentary Privilege. It is a privilege which protects Parliament, its Members, its officers, its witnesses, counsel, people who appear before it or its Committees, and also petitioners. It is a Parliamentary Privilege protecting this House and those who take part in it. It does not protect or refer to the electors or the general public. The hon. Member for Nelson and Colne may shake his head. He had better be careful not to shake it too much. That is a fact. Privilege is not instituted to protect the universal suffrage electorate. They can protect themselves if they get a chance. It is to protect the House and Members of Parliament.

The electorate and the general public have their rights under the ordinary law, and they have their votes – quite an important thing. The Motion by the hon. Member for Nelson and Colne is based upon the assumption that the House should use its Privilege to protect a correspondent, who wrote to my hon. Friend the Member for Sevenoaks (Mr John Rodgers[1]), from some real or supposed injury. I say that Privilege was never instituted or intended for such a purpose. It is to protect us and those who have to deal with us, and not to protect the vast mass of the nation outside.

The correspondence of a Member with his constituents or other persons is regulated by the existing law of libel, blackmail and that sort of thing. That is the law. The correspondence of a Member is also governed by good taste, good faith, and respect for private and confidential matters. If these aspects come before the public or the electors in any constituency it is for them to judge, and unless the conduct of some Member of the House, in the course of his Parliamentary duties, or the conduct of the Chair, or other matters directly connected with Parliamentary proceedings, are involved, no question of Privilege arises. It is no good not liking it, because I am quite certain that it is a solid, established fact, upon which this matter rests and stands.

It is true that the Court of Criminal Appeal, in the case of *Rex* v. *Rule*, in 1937, held that a Member of Parliament – I use this case because it is a good illustration of how the matter stands – to whom a written communication was addressed by one of his constituents, asking for his assistance in bringing to the notice of the appropriate Minister a complaint of improper conduct on the part of some public official acting in that constituency in relation to his office, had sufficient interest in the subject matter of the complaint to render the occasion of such a publication a privileged occasion. But, here, the word 'Privilege' refers to privilege under the common law. It has nothing whatever

---

[1] John Charles Rodgers, 1906–93. Educated at St Peter's School and Oxford University. Married, 1930, Betsy Aikin-Sneath. MP (Cons.) for Sevenoaks, 1950–79. Private Parliamentary Secretary to David Eccles, 1951–7.

to do with Parliamentary Privilege, which is the only thing with which we are concerned on this Motion. How could the Court of Criminal Appeal pronounce on a question of Parliamentary Privilege?

There is, therefore, I submit, no case, *prima facie* or otherwise, on this issue that is before us. It is ordinary privilege and does not come under Parliamentary Privilege at all. Nor is any ruling by any court relevant in the slightest degree to our affairs.

Mr S. Silverman: I quite appreciate the point the right hon. Gentleman is making, but does he remember that in the last Parliament the House of Commons, with his consent, treated as cases of Privilege those of Mr Garry Allighan and Mr Evelyn Walkden[1] where the only breach of Privilege alleged was that they communicated, without authority, to a third party, information which had come to them only because they were Members of Parliament?

Mr Churchill: I cannot pretend to argue the merits and details of this extremely complicated case, but what I do stand on is that Parliamentary Privilege is to protect Parliament and its Members and not to protect the general public.

For 250 years the House has conformed to the Resolution, passed in 1704, that it would not extend its privileges. It is very remarkable how strong and rigidly that principle has been carried out. There is, however, a wide right of interpretation. Now we are asked by the hon. Gentleman, not in one case only but in another case which he raised, and we may be asked in many others, greatly to widen the interpretation of Privilege and to bring the ordinary correspondence of any Member of Parliament within the ambit of Privilege. I am sure that that would be a grave and most unwise departure from our proceedings. It would appear to entitle constituents to write libellous statements to their Member, and plead immunity on the grounds that their communication was privileged in the Parliamentary sense, which overrode the ordinary sense of the common law.

Apart from this it would involve Parliament in almost endless embarrassment and work, and the raising of so-called 'Privilege cases' arising out of a Member's correspondence might become a fertile cause of obstruction, and would certainly cast an undue burden not only upon the Chair but upon the Table. I cannot conceive anything that would be more inconvenient or more unworkable in practice than the fact that any issue, of anybody, at any time in this House arising from the ordinary correspondence which we have to discharge in such great volume, might be raised as a matter of Privilege, and then referred to the Committee of Privileges to decide or examine in the utmost

---

[1] Evelyn Walkden, 1893–1970. Educated at Lancashire Evening Institutes and through Workers' Educational Association. Joined Lancashire Hussars, 1914. On active service, Salonika, 1916–19. Organizer, National Union of Distributive and Allied Workers, 1928–41. MP (Lab.) for Doncaster, 1941–50. Parliamentary Private Secretary to Minister of National Insurance (Sir William Jowett), 1944–5; to Minister of Food (Sir Ben Smith), 1945–6. Member of All-Party Parliamentary Mission to Greece, 1946.

detail. We would ruin a valuable and vitally important protection, on which the dignity, power and freedom of the House rests if we cast upon it these cataracts of irrelevant and absurd issues.

No difficulty about the correspondence of Members has been experienced in our present practice in the 50 years that I can recall. The right of a Member at his discretion to send a letter or show a letter from a constituent to any other person cannot be a matter of Privilege. If it were, we would be imposing a special and invidious responsibility and disability upon them not open to others. I must be careful how I deal with this matter. At any moment my conduct might be called in question, and I might be called before the Committee of Privileges. Someone might write a most improper or demanding letter. Is that to be within the Privilege of Parliament? If it is, it is putting a curb and a burden upon Members.

If the House accepts the view that Mr Speaker's Ruling was correct and that there was no *prima facie* case, the question of the injury, if any, to the Vicar of Crockham Hill[1] does not arise. It has gone. It was no breach of Privilege and there is no *prima facie* case. We are not concerned with the matter, no Parliamentary Privilege being involved. The bishop is not involved, and my hon. Friend the Member for Sevenoaks, who has left the Chamber, is not involved. I would not, in ordinary circumstances, have attempted – because I do not wish to take up the time of the House unnecessarily – to discuss the local and special aspects of this case, but the circumstances are somewhat peculiar. I dwell in the diocese of the Bishop of Rochester,[2] I am a parishioner of the Vicar of Crockham Hill and I am a constituent of the hon. Member for Sevenoaks. Therefore, it makes for me what is called, in racing parlance, a triple event.

Naturally, I know something about the local position. I should be very sorry if it were to be thought that, with all his extravagances and improprieties, as I hold them, the Vicar of Crockham Hill does not try to do his work and to make a contribution. I agree with what has been said about the dangers of irony and sarcasm, but I am certain that there are many phrases in the letter which, taken from their context, would be very injurious but which, read in the general scope of the letter, merely indicate an extravagant mood and a desire to use words and language beyond the power of words and language to carry. This led him into saying things which were very painful and which, for people less instructed than we are in this House, including the hon. Member who moved the Motion, might very well darken their counsel and cause them pain and distress.

I turn to the hon. Member for Sevenoaks. I take a special interest, as his

---

[1] Oliver Fielding Clarke, 1899–?. Vicar of Crockham Hill, 1941–51, where Churchill attended church. Open Communist sympathizer. Published his autobiography *The Unfinished Conflict* (1970).

[2] Christopher Chavasse, 1884–1962. Competed in London Summer Olympics, 1908. Chaplain, Royal Army, 1916–18. Bishop of Rochester, 1940–60.

constituent, in how he conducts his correspondence. I may say that the idea that all constituents, that is to say universal suffrage constituents, should be protected from any consequences that might conceivably arise out of any letter that they write to their Members is, on any interpretation of the Privilege rule in respect of correspondence, an absurd idea. If everything that was written down were to impose a great question of Parliamentary Privilege upon us, it is quite possible that a call upon the telephone or a personal interview might result in all kinds of things. After all, we know the kind of world in which we are living, and it is very dangerous to put undue pressure upon normal actions because we might easily create abuses that otherwise would not have occurred.

One thing is important – I am not admitting the relevance of this point to the main argument – and it is that Members of Parliament should be careful, in dealing with a letter from a constituent, not to get that constituent into trouble which might cost him his livelihood, unless criminal or libellous considerations are involved. What did my hon. Friend the Member for Sevenoaks do? He wrote to the bishop, and he sent this extraordinary document, which, evidently, was not written to be published. It has seen the light of day far beyond the hopes of its author. What did my hon. Friend do? He wrote to the bishop. The Church of England differs from most of the important religious institutions in having no power to discipline its priests or ministers in their opinions and doctrines. Jews, Presbyterians, Baptists, Methodists, all have the power, exerted by the authority of the religious community or by the congregation, to discipline or change their ministers, but the Church of England has not that power. A bishop is without power to remove from his living a clergyman of whose views or doctrines he disapproves. The highest authority in the Church has no power. That is why persons like the Dean of Canterbury[1] can do a great deal of harm with impunity. I am not at all inflicting any sort of stigma upon the Vicar of Crockham Hill by comparing him in the slightest degree with the Dean of Canterbury. Neither have the parishioners the right or power to relieve themselves of a priest whose character, opinions or doctrines they resent. I am not sure that it might not in the long run turn out that freedom in a healthy community will be found to be the best solution of all difficulties; but still, there is no comparison. The only way in which parishioners can express their feelings is by not attending the religious services in the church of the priest concerned. Crockham Hill church is nearly always empty. There is no doubt about that, although the vicar makes special efforts by special classes, and so forth. I am in no way impugning his character or the efforts he makes, but there is no doubt of what the action of the parishioners would be if they had the same power as is possessed by many other communities and congregations.

This bishop who was appealed to in this case has no power to do anything,

---

[1] Hewlett Johnson, 1874–1966. Deacon, 1905. Priest, 1906. Vicar of St Margaret's, Altrincham, 1908. Examining Chaplain to Bishops of Chester, 1913–24. Dean of Manchester, 1924–31.

except one thing. He has the right, and I think he has the duty, to wrestle spiritually with the Minister. That is the worst sanction that can be invoked in the proceedings between my hon. Friend and the bishop, who has the power to apply all the resources of reason and persuasion, moral and spiritual. Why should they not be turned on? We all have the right to wrestle spiritually with one another when the proper time comes. I may even make myself the agent, in the short time left to me, of converting the hon. Member for Nelson and Colne to a proper outlook on the way of life. Nothing was done that could possibly injure this vicar in his worldly affairs, in his office, or his pitifully small stipend.

My hon. Friend was quite right to write to the bishop and send the letter to the bishop. (Hon. Members: 'Oh.') I will tell the House why, because it is one of the things we might vote about tonight. My hon. Friend had a duty to his constituents, who are the parishioners of this priest and who suffer the inconvenience – some of them – through the lack of religious administration and through their dislike of his opinions, of having to go to some other church which may be much further off. Perhaps that has not occurred to the hon. Member for Nelson and Colne. That has not troubled him.

The hon. Member for Sevenoaks was only discharging his duty to his constituents in endeavouring to induce the bishop to use his moral and spiritual authority to remove the evil. How illogical and absurd it is for all the supporters of the Motion to work themselves into a state of indignation and fury at the alleged ill-usage of the Vicar of Crockham Hill as a correspondent writing to his Member when they have heard nothing about the suffering of hundreds of constituents – 200 families are involved – who are deprived to a large extent of the religious comfort and services to which they are entitled.

I will not keep the House much longer. I could say a great deal, but I think I have made the point very clearly. But I will say one thing. We were all much impressed by the declaration of the Leader of the House[1] the other day about his position as Leader of the House, his not being identified with any party, his responsibility to the House as a whole, and so forth. Now we have passed out of the realm of words into the realm of action, and I should like to know what he is going to do tonight. I think he should tell us.

We have heard that the Government are not putting their Whips on in the ordinary way in favour of the Motion. I should have thought that it was their duty to vote against the Motion, as we shall certainly do, but if they are going to leave it to their followers to vote exactly as they please, how are they going to vote themselves? Is the Leader of the House going to vote for something which he knows is incorrect in procedure, or is he going to vote against it? How is he going to deal with his colleagues on the subject? I do not want to add to the many complications that he has at the present time, but, at any rate, I think it is his duty to tell the House exactly how he proposes to vote upon this Motion.

[1] James Chuter Ede.

As far as we are concerned, we shall not, in these circumstances, put on the party Whips. On the merits, in perfect freedom and after full consideration of the arguments, some of which I have ventured to bring before the House tonight, we shall, I think, vote against the Motion on the grounds that no case of Privilege arises and also because we think that it is the duty of the Member to act for all his constituents – not only for those who write to him – and to be guided as a general rule in so doing by the greatest good of the greatest number.

President Harry S Truman to Winston S. Churchill
(Churchill papers, 2/28)

24 March 1951

Dear Mr Churchill,

I have given most careful consideration to the request contained in your letter to me of February twelfth, 1951,[1] for publication of the Quebec Agreement. While I appreciate and have given full weight to the considerations prompting your request, I am forced to the conclusion that the Agreement should not be made public at this time.

It is true, as you say, that the Agreement recognized certain problems of cooperation in this field after the termination of hostilities. The resolution of these problems has been, and continues to be, a matter of discussion and arrangement between the Governments of the United Kingdom and the United States. Publication of the Agreement would be misleading unless it were also decided to make public the current status of cooperation and collaboration among the United Kingdom, Canada, and the United States in the field of atomic energy. Indeed, it would be exceedingly difficult, if not impossible, to resist pressures to make known this information once the Agreement were made public. I feel strongly that in present circumstances such a development would be seriously prejudicial to the interests of the United Kingdom and the United States as well to our Allies under the North Atlantic Treaty.

I wish to express the appreciation of the United States and my own personal gratification for your far seeing and generous support for the granting of air base rights in East Anglia to the United States. I have been informed that the understandings that have been arrived at concerning these air base rights are mutually satisfactory to the political and military authorities of the two Governments.

I am moved by the sentiments you express concerning the turn of events in Korea and your gratitude for the Eisenhower appointment, developments of great significance to our common cause.

---

[1] Reproduced above (p. 2003).

Winston S. Churchill to Clementine Churchill
(Baroness Spencer-Churchill papers)

25 March 1951

My darling,

I had a harrying ten days after you left,[1] what with the broadcast, the Privilege case and other trouble in Parliament, and it is pleasant to have ten days at Chartwell. I send you some cuttings about the broadcast, which was generally considered all right. I also send you the speech I made about Crockham Hill Vicar's Privilege case. It was considered very successful.

Attlee has gone to hospital with a duodenal ulcer, so I sent some flowers from us both, and I thought you would like to see his letter. Also one from Pamela about little Winston. You see he is to go to Ludgrove in May. He is very nice and well-behaved down here now and has a very good pony so that June can take him out riding.

The sun has shone a little in the mornings but it soon clouds over. There has been a frightful lot of rain. Luckily I have plenty to amuse myself with. So far I have not found time to paint. The Book is a gt standby.

Stassen came over here on purpose to press me to go to Philadelphia for the Bi-centenary of Pennsylvania University. Principal leaders of both Democrat and Republican Parties would be there, and there is no doubt that I could make a helpful speech. It would be an advantage with all this Party fighting in the House of Commons to have this outside engagement lying ahead. If I went at all I should fly both ways in one of the best BOAC special airplanes which is offered. The date of the meeting would be May 8, and I should be away altogether for about a week. My decision turns on what precisely is the President's attitude. At present he has sent a message through Stassen that he would like me to dine with him either the night before or the night after the Philadelphia speech. I require more direct evidence of his wishes as I do not want to embarrass him or myself. I send you Bernie's letter which speaks for itself. I should of course only make one address. It is a week of one's life, but might be a week well spent.

The whole place here is just sodden, and we have not been able to do any ploughing. Everything is behind-hand. Everyone else is in a similar plight.

I have fixed it up all right for Violet in Colne Valley, but the voting of the Conservative Association (secret) was very close: 33 to 26. However no conditions were attached and she is going to accept. Once she gets down there and begins making her good speeches against the Socialists I expect all will be well.

---

[1] for Seville.

Winston S. Churchill to Somerset de Chair
(*Churchill papers, 4/44*)

28 March 1951

My dear de Chair,

Thank you so much for sending me the beautifully-produced page proofs of Caesar's *Commentaries*. I am reading them as fast as I can in these difficult times. I am deeply impressed by what I have read so far. It would be a great achievement to rescue Caesar from the Class-room.

I am much honoured by your dedication.

Winston S. Churchill to Sir William Haley[1]
(*Churchill papers, 2/38*)

30 March 1951

My dear Sir William,

I have been told that you have started a new series of *Argument* following on the Driberg–Randolph Churchill series, in which politics are discussed between Mr Dingle Foot, Liberal, and Mr Percy Cudlipp, the Editor of the *Daily Herald*.

Considering that, as I am told, a very large audience listens in to these discussions, it is wrong that for four weeks no Conservative representative should speak, and that the common ground between the two selected speakers is hostility to Conservatism. It seems to me that if an undue bias is to be avoided a third person representing Conservative opinion should be introduced into the discussion.

Perhaps you will let me know what are the facts.

---

[1] Director-General of the BBC.

April 1951

Eliahu Elath to Winston S. Churchill
(Churchill papers, 2/170)

2 April 1951

It gives me great pleasure to convey to you an invitation from the Jewish National Fund, extended at the personal request of the President of Israel, to attend the ceremonial opening of the Weizmann Forest in Israel on April 13th, 1951.

This Forest has been planted with funds raised for the purpose by Jewish communities in all parts of the world as a tribute to the President on the occasion of his 75th birthday. It is intended to make the opening ceremony expressive of the deep admiration and regard in which Dr Weizmann personally is held, and of the Jewish people's gratitude for his services to the cause of Jewish statehood and independence.

The President feels that on this occasion he would like to have as his guests some of those whose vision and sympathy have been of such powerful aid to him. It is very much hoped therefore that it may be possible for you to spare the time to be present at the ceremony.

Should you feel able to accept this invitation, the Legation will make all necessary arrangements for your visit.

Clementine Churchill to Winston S. Churchill
(Churchill papers, 1/65)

5 April 1951

I have been reflecting upon the conversation we had about Mr Wood, and I would like to bring forward the following points for your consideration.

There are a great many people who call here[1] in connection with your

---

[1] The Churchills' house at No. 28 Hyde Park Gate.

work; for example Brigadier Blunt,[1] Mr Bremridge, Mr Christ,[2] as well as Lord Ismay, General Pownall, Commodore Allen, Mr Deakin and Mr Kelly, all of whom are sometimes here for hours on end. In addition there are odd callers from time to time, who come without notice with matters for the attention of you or your secretaries – e.g. various Town Clerks, the Chief Rabbi (who came the other day) and representatives of organizations of all descriptions. Consequently, as there is no other room available, they are received and interviewed, and work, in either the Library or the Morning Room, sometimes both. This means that when I go downstairs to use these rooms I often find complete strangers there. If the studio were free, all these people could be accommodated there. I do not think it would be suitable for them to use the front room of No. 27 as it is full of your confidential Trust files. It would not be practicable to ask Mr Wood to vacate the studio when necessary, as this would be every few minutes.

You did ask if Mr Wood could remain there for another two months, until Volume V is finished; but then there will be Volume VI and the revises of the previous volumes.

Would you approve of the following letter[3] now being written to Mr Wood?

Clementine Churchill to Winston S. Churchill
(Churchill papers, 1/65)

5 April 1951

With regard to Mr Wood, when I suggested that he should use the front room, I had alas quite forgotten the detectives. They now have nowhere to sit. Do you not really think that with a little politeness and pressure Mr Wood could be asked to do his work in his own house, and come two or three times a week to Hyde Park Gate to hand it over? We are really horribly short of room. The Studio is used every day by a succession of people; and as I said, having offered the Front Room to Mr Wood which I regret to say he spurns, we now have nowhere for the detectives. Sergeant Murray was seen sitting outside the Servants' Hall on a laundry basket. It is impossible for the detectives to sit in

---

[1] Gerald Charles Gordon Blunt, 1883–1967. Educated at RMC, Sandhurst. Married, 1921, Kate Fox. Asst Director, Supplies and Transportation, War Office, 1932–36; Aldershot Command, 1938–9. Deputy Director, Aldershot, 1939; Western Command, 1940–3. Commandant, RASC Training Centre, Aldershot, 1936–38. ADC to the King, 1938–9. Director of Supplies, GHQ, BEF, 1939–40 (despatches). GSO I, Civil Affairs, War Office, 1943. Director of Supply, Civil Affairs, SHAEF, 1943–4. Head of Relief Supplies branch, Ministry of Supply, 1945–9.

[2] George Elgie Christ, 1904–72. Educated at King's College London. Married, 1938, Marianne Evans. Political Correspondent, *Daily Telegraph*, 1940–5. Parliamentary Liaison Office, Conservative Party, 1945–65. CBE, 1955.

[3] Reproduced below, after Clementine's second letter of Apr. 5.

the Servants' Hall. They would not like it. It is very small; and the Servants would not like it either.[1]

Clementine Churchill to Charles Wood
(Churchill papers, 1/65)

5 April 1951

NOT SENT

Dear Mr Wood,

I am so very sorry that you find the front room uncomfortable, and while I was away in Spain you mentioned the matter to my Husband who, I think, arranged for you to continue using the studio room until he was able to discuss the subject with me on my return home.

The reasons which I explained to you are, I fear, still valid. We should so much like to be able to find room for all those who do such important work for my Husband, but the numbers are increasing day by day.

It has occurred to me that, if you find the front room rather sunless and oppressive, perhaps you would prefer to work at home. I am sure this could be arranged if that is what you would like best.

Sir Norman Brook to Winston S. Churchill
(Churchill papers, 2/176)

6 April 1951

Mr Attlee has now written to Dr Malan asking him to confirm that the South African Government have no objection to your publication of the messages to and from General Smuts which you wish to include in Volume V of your book. In view of what you told me in your letter of the 5th March, he has added that, in view of the personal nature of these exchanges, you are also proposing to communicate directly with Mrs Smuts regarding your proposed publication of the messages from her husband.

I am writing, as you asked, to let you know that Mr Attlee's letter has now been sent and that the way is clear for you to write to Mrs Smuts, as you proposed to do.

I enclose copies of the messages to and from General Smuts which are included in the present text of this volume. I send these in the hope that they may save you trouble in identifying the messages and having them copied

---

[1] Churchill wrote: 'I will not have him turned out now. We are at the crisis of the book – I use him on the book every hour of the day.'

— though it may be that these copies may not be in a form which you would care to send on the Mrs Smuts.

Winston S. Churchill to Eliahu Elath
(Churchill papers, 2/170)

9 April 1951

As a Zionist since the days of the Balfour Declaration I am much complimented to receive this invitation[1] from so great a world statesman as Doctor Weizmann, whose son fell in the cause of freedom, which we now all labour to defend. It is with much regret therefore that I do not find it possible to come to the ceremony which signifies another stage in reclaiming the desert of so many centuries into a fertile home for the Jewish people.

Please convey my warm thanks to the President and express my great regrets.

Winston S. Churchill to Isie Smuts
(Churchill papers, 2/176)

9 April 1951

Mr Attlee has written to Dr Malan asking him to confirm that the South African Government have no objection to the publication of the messages to and from your Husband which I wish to incorporate in Volume V of my War Memoirs. Previously Jan had always given his permission, both as head of the Government and personally. I should be very glad if you would give your consent to the publication of these, apart from anything which the South African Government may say. I do not doubt they will agree, but I should like to know that you are in accord.

I enclose for you a copy of the letters and telegrams from your Husband which I now desire to publish. They are an essential part of the story I have to tell and reflect nothing but honour upon his name, and are an additional proof of his wisdom and of our friendship.

I trust that all goes well with you and yours.

---

[1] See letter of Apr. 2, reproduced above (p. 2028).

Winston S. Churchill: speech
(Hansard)

10 April 1951   House of Commons

BUDGET PROPOSALS AND ECONOMIC SURVEY

I think I shall be expressing the opinion of the whole House if I pay our compliments to the Chancellor of the Exchequer[1] upon the lucid, comprehensive statement which he has made to us this afternoon, and upon the evident lack of hatred or malice which I felt was apparent while he was unfolding his proposals. We have had what is, upon the whole, an objective statement, and the proposals which have been made, for all the difficulty which attaches to many of them, have been designed as he himself claimed, as an honest attempt to solve the problems which lie before him. I have listened to many Budgets in this House, and have even contributed five myself. I am bound to say that I feel the right hon. Gentleman has placed himself, by his opening statement this afternoon, in a good position to conduct the long and severe debates we shall no doubt have on many aspects of the policy.

I would not like to turn to criticisms without saying that again I feel sure that the whole House would wish to send a message of goodwill and encouragement to Sir Stafford Cripps. (Hon. Members: 'Hear, hear'.) If he is heavily burdened by affliction at the present time, it is largely because of the devoted manner in which he has endeavoured to serve the public. As one who has differed from him fundamentally in many ways, and worked with him as a trusted comrade in many others, I feel that the few words I have spoken might well carry the message of the House across the seas to him.

The speech to which we have just listened can, of course, only be considered in relation to the sombre background against which it stands. Here I cannot expect any longer to carry with me approving glances from those who sit opposite. After all, this is the seventh Budget which has been opened since the Socialist Party have become masters of our affairs.

The Secretary of State for Foreign Affairs (Mr Herbert Morrison): Oh!

Mr Churchill: I was quoting the Attorney-General. We dwell in the aftermath of devaluation. I cannot help feeling that that dark shadow hangs over us now. It has increased by nearly a third the working and productive effort needed from Britain to make the exports out of which our vital supplies and raw materials have to be bought. The Chancellor referred to this. I have not his actual words, but they certainly stressed the fact that this 30 per cent devaluation of our national products, relative to what we get in return, was a very heavy burden, and that weighs upon us all the time. There are, no doubt, other causes at work, but it is this hard, dominant fact of the aftermath of

---
[1] Hugh Gaitskell.

devaluation which impinges upon us at the present time. Much of the life energy of our island, already over-strained when the war ended, drained away from this cause, and also from unrequited exports and from lavish expenditure.

Those who hold that taxation is an evil must recognise that it falls upon this country in a most grievous manner at the present time, continually burdening the mass of the nation and continually clogging – I do not know why that word came into my mind – or, at any rate, hampering our efforts. There is to be an increase of taxation. I am not at all concerned today to examine even cursorily the detailed proposals which the Chancellor has made, but taxation is to be increased; it is to be heavier still. Naturally, many people will feel that the issue should be argued out very tensely as to whether other economies in Government expenditure might not have relieved us from the need of applying new burdens and new taxation.

Of course, we know the times are difficult. The Prime Minister told us the other day that the price rises were due to world causes, but almost in the same breath he claimed the whole credit for full employment for his own party. Everything that is bad is due to world events; everything that is good is due to the Socialist Party. That may be a very comforting theory, but I feel bound to warn the Chancellor of the Exchequer that it is not one which we can adopt as the basis upon which our debates on the Budget and the Finance Bill will be conducted.

If we take the whole period of the rule of the Socialist Party, I think it is fair to say that the mismanagement of our finances over the whole period tells the same tale, or almost the same tale in different terms, as the mismanagement of our defences. We must not be led by the agreeable presentation which the right hon. Gentleman has given us of these proposals into any weakening in our conviction of the grave financial position in which this country stands and of the very heavy drains which have been made, not only upon its accumulated wealth made since the war, but also upon the incentives and resourcefulness by which our future daily bread can be earned.

Of course, it is quite true to say that there has been a great increase in production, a steady annual increase, but compared to capitalist, free enterprise United States, the increase has not been on anything like the same level. If we take the whole period of Socialist rule, we must see that during this costly period we have fallen from the position which we held at the end of the war in almost every sphere of our activities and reputation at home and abroad. The Chancellor of the Exchequer is not primarily responsible for this; he bears his share of collective responsibility.

We shall, of course, study and consider with great attention the proposals which are now put before us. I should not attempt – I would not try even cursorily – to examine in these few remarks the proposals in detail or to judge them on the spur of the moment. It is our duty, however, to subject, not only the Budget, but the whole of our financial and economic position, to severe and searching examination, and we shall not fail to do it in the weeks and months which lie ahead. One thing, however, is clear, and that is that the necessary money for rearmament has got to be provided and that the House of Commons is the sole authority which should do its best to find it in the least harmful manner.

I shall certainly conclude, as I began, by thanking the Chancellor for what I think everyone will recognise was a remarkable Parliamentary performance which will, I trust, make the foundation upon which a high reputation as a Chancellor of the Exchequer – we are all in the club together – may be expected to rest.

Winston S. Churchill to President Harry S Truman
(Churchill papers, 2/28)

11 April 1951
Private

Many thanks for your official answer[1] to my letter of February 12, and still more for your very kind personal answer[2] which preceded it. I am not pressing the question any more at present.

I have accepted with pleasure the invitation with which you have honoured me for May 10. I look forward very much to a talk with you. May I also assure you that your action in asserting the authority of the civil power over military commanders, however able or distinguished, will receive universal approval in England.[3]

Winston S. Churchill to Sir William Haley
(Churchill papers, 2/38)

12 April 1951

My dear Sir William,

Thank you for your letter of April 3.

I am surprised that you should think that twelve out of thirty-two speakers is fair representation for the Conservative Party. Out of the sixteen broadcasts in this series there is none in which Labour will not be represented.

I am sending this correspondence to Lord Woolton, and I shall also raise the matter at the approaching meeting between the Party Leaders and the Governors of the BBC. Meanwhile I record my protest.

[1] Reproduced above (p. 2025).
[2] Reproduced above (p. 2004).
[3] On 11 Apr. 1951, President Truman dismissed Gen. MacArthur from his commands in Korea after MacArthur made public statements contradictory to the administration's war policy.

Winston S. Churchill to Sir Albert Braithwaite[1]
(Churchill papers, 2/90)

14 April 1951

My dear Braithwaite,

The Socialist Government, elected in 1945, went to the country last year commanding a Parliamentary majority of 157 over all other Parties. It crawled back with a majority of seven. That was the measure of its fall in public esteem. Since then the verdict of the bye-elections has made it ever more certain that the people have had enough of Socialist misrule. It is the Government's duty to appeal to the country for a fresh mandate to meet the changed circumstances of today. Yet they cling ignominiously to office.

The need for a strong Britain, if the world is to be preserved from the horrors of another war, has been manifest for at least three years. But the Socialist Government, obsessed with the desire to transform Britain into a Marxist Utopia, turned a deaf ear to all warnings. Even after the Communist aggression in Korea, they neglected with total lack of foresight the obvious duty to lay in special stores. Now the country finds itself faced with a heavy programme of rearmament in the teeth of rising prices and shrinking supplies.

But the cost of rearmament is far from being the only or even the main cause of the enduring expenditures demanded in the Budget. The highest taxation in the world already imposed upon our people is part of the price we pay for Socialism and its gambling experiments and mismanagement. The vultures of devaluation are now coming home to roost, seeking a higher perch each night. Nationalization has proved a costly failure in every case. Trying to buy our food and other needs through the agency of State officials has created friction and shortage which private enterprise and trade experience would have avoided. The tale of misguided policies and clumsy administration must be brought to an end.

The Conservative Party hold that in these times of grave peril the affairs of the nation should not remain in the hands of a tottering Government without moral purpose, practical efficiency or national confidence.

The electors of the Harrow West Division have the chance, coveted by the whole country, of giving a patriotic signal to all. They should return you to Parliament with a resounding majority. I look forward to welcoming back to the House of Commons an old colleague and a Parliamentarian of proven worth.

---

[1] Albert Braithwaite, 1859–1959. Educated at University of Leeds. Served with Yorkshire Hussars, WWI. DSO, 1918. MP (Cons.) for Buckrose, 1926–45; for Harrow West, 1951–9. Knighted, 1945.

April 1951

Winston S. Churchill to General Sir Gifford Le Quesne Martel
(*Churchill papers, 2/115*)

14 April 1951

My dear General,

Thank you for writing to me. I am entirely opposed to departing from compulsory national service. Quite apart from the practical aspect, on which I disagree with you, such a step would be profoundly injurious to our moral position in the world and to our country's safety.

I am sorry to see you pressing such views, which only darken Counsel.

Winston S. Churchill: speech
(*'Winston S. Churchill, His Complete Speeches', volume 8, pages 8180–1*)

16 April 1951 Sheffield

GRAVER DANGERS LOOM IN EUROPE (KOREAN WAR)

... (Mr Bevin was)[1] a great friend and countryman whose loss we all deplore. He was a man who represented with unchallengeable right the characteristics of trade unionists and also those English characteristics which we regard as virtues of our race and of which we are justly proud. He showed how it is possible to make your way in this free democracy of ours from the humblest situation to the greatest and most responsible employments in the State.

In 1943, the Sheffield City Council, with a Socialist majority, unanimously decided to offer me the freedom. I valued that highly. Although my political opponents on the council far outnumber the other members, it was again a unanimous decision which has brought me to Sheffield. Such actions carry a message to foreign countries who may not understand, when they read of Britain's fierce party contentions, that underneath is a deep unity.

(Editor's Note: Commenting on reports from Lake Success that North Korea had sent a message to the United Nations, Mr Churchill said): Tonight we have good news from Korea. It may be only a report, but if it is true that North Korea has asked for peace terms, it would be a relief and satisfactory to every one of us. Neither we nor the United Nations have the slightest wish to become involved in Korea or China. Far graver dangers loom in Europe.

---

[1] This parenthetical interpolation, and the 'Editor's Note' below, were inserted by Robert Rhodes James, editor of *His Complete Speeches*.

Winston S. Churchill: speech
('Stemming the Tide', pages 45–7)

17 April 1951   Sheffield

CUTLERS' FEAST

It is nearly forty years since I last spoke at a Cutlers' Feast. I was at the Admiralty and I said: 'I am proud to come to Sheffield which, though a considerable distance from the sea, nevertheless contributes an essential part to the naval security of our country. I wish I could add to that by saying that we were as secure in the air tonight as we were on the sea forty years ago. Here again I may quote: 'But we must be prepared. We must be ready for all eventualities. It is good to be patient; it is good to be circumspect; it is good to be peace-loving. But that is not enough. We must be strong. We must be self-reliant, and, in the end for all our party politics, we must be united.' I could say all that tonight, for here we are again 'forty years on'.

The continued vitality and progress of your ancient and famous city springs from craftsmanship and new ideas applied to the production of steel. There is a long story in the past about craftsmanship and how much you and we all owe to the Trade Guilds. There is hardly any direction in which craftsmanship counts for more than in the field of alloys and special steels. But craftsmanship alone might have stagnated. Sheffield has had the fortune and genius to nourish a succession of pioneers and leaders whose names are household words in industry. [. . .]

What is the characteristic that all these craftsmen, pioneers and industrialists have had in common? Surely it is the individual effort of hand and brain and the development of free and independent enterprise. It would be hard to find a city to whose life these qualities have made so great a contribution as Sheffield, which I am told, today produces 14 percent of our total steel production and 70 percent of our alloy steel. If these qualities were lost all would be lost. Those who seek to plan the future should not forget the inheritance they have received from the past, for it is only by studying the past as well as dreaming of the future that the story of man's struggle can be understood.

As the new rearmament programme develops the country once again will look increasingly to Sheffield to satisfy its special requirements. They must look not only to the large firms among you but also to the small. The small are no less a permanent and essential part of the structure of any industry than the large. Many people are misled nowadays by the cult of bigness for bigness' sake. One of the efforts of nationalization is to make the big more powerful. But the life of Sheffield has grown from the efforts and triumphs of individuals and all the inexhaustible variety of human initiative. To lose this would be fatal.

Often when the conditions which have made possible the growth of a city have passed away there is decline. The world is full of these examples. But it is not so with Sheffield. You have shown yourselves for generations supremely adaptable to new uses and to technical changes. That is the secret of your success and survival: adaptability, contrivance, inventiveness, dependence on freedom to initiate, a chance to push out for the prizes of the future and take the risk of losing without sending in your bill to the Chancellor of the Exchequer. Everything that restricts this vital freedom is a deadly threat to Sheffield and to our islands.

We live in an age of mass production. But mass production can only be kept healthy and vital by the continued refreshment of new processes. At present, although you are nationalized by law the authors of this policy have not chosen to take the practical, working management out of the skilled, experienced hands of the Iron and Steel Federation. The Steel Corporation vulture hovers in the sky with its two grasping claws, Uniformity and Monopoly. It has not dared to swoop and its life may be short. Meanwhile, Sheffield must have good courage and, adhering faithfully to its tradition of craftsmanship and progress, drive ahead in tireless resilience. The old Guilds were founded on a slow-achieved combination and compromise between friendly rivalry among their members on the one hand and on the other the sense of solidarity arising from members of a common trade. There has been unending argument. Some have stressed the need for solidarity. Others, swinging to the other extreme, have questioned the need for competition. Through your remarkable institution you have kept to a very large extent the proper balance and have not only maintained Sheffield in a healthy expansion, but may claim to be a model for every other industry and city in our island.

I do not wish to talk party politics tonight, but at a Cutlers' Feast it is quite impossible to avoid some occasional references to steel, and alas, steel has been plunged into the very centre of party strife. But there is one cardinal rule for the British nation (and the English, we may mention them sometimes), 'Never despair'. That word is forbidden. Our fortunes and our fate are in our hands. I end where I began forty years ago. Standing here tonight, I hope I shall express our true conviction that although perfect solutions of our difficulties are not to be looked for in an imperfect world, and although persistent disagreement as to methods is inevitable, and not necessarily unhealthy, yet in our own British fashion, which no one else understands, we shall in our lifetime make a notable advance and hold our ground at every point. To that work all parties in their turn can and ought to contribute. If they do so simply and sincerely according to their lights, then the nation, which is far greater than all the parties put together, will have no reason to doubt or fear its future.

Leland Ford[1] to Winston S. Churchill
(Churchill papers, 2/114)

18 April 1951

My dear Mr Churchill,

You, no doubt, will not remember me as one of the Congressmen you met in Washington on your several visits to our country during World War II, but I remember you.

For your information I was the only Republican in Congress who voted 100% with the Roosevelt Administration on their foreign policy for the several years prior to the War and during the time I was there. Although I never voted for Mr Roosevelt, for President of the United States, and belonged to the party who opposed him, I always thought it my duty to vote for the party I thought was right. This, I did.

My past actions, however, have placed me in a very peculiar light with my fellow Republicans, inasmuch as they question my sound judgment in my statements wherein I said that England was a friend and an ally of America whom we could always count on. I say this in light of the recent events which have transcribed in connection with the removal of Douglas MacArthur and the <u>claimed</u> British participation in his removal.

I am quite sure that I bespeak the sentiments of the greater majority of Americans when I say we had full confidence in the Government which you had, prior to and during the War. Many of us do not have that confidence in the present Government which many question, 'Where does Socialism end and Communism begin?' Whether it is right or wrong I cannot say. However, many of our people feel that this country has been double-crossed by the present Government of England.

I say this with regret but I have heard it on too many recent occasions. The things that bring about these ideas of our people are as follows: While we are fighting the Reds and the Communists in Korea, and the British are fighting with us as soldiers, (it is thought that these Red Communists are Chinese Communists and, without fooling ourselves, many of us believe that they are) many of us believe that Russia is fomenting as much trouble in Korea as she possibly can. Therefore, they cannot reconcile the following facts:

1. The interference of the English State Department or the meddling of that same Department to the extent of having our ablest General, Douglas MacArthur, discharged.
2. That while the British and the Americans are fighting back-to-back, as soldiers, against a common foe, namely the Reds, the present English Government requests that these same Reds, who certainly

---

[1] Leland Merritt Ford, 1893–1965. Born in Eureka, Nev. Educated at University of Arizona. Member, Los Angeles County Board of Supervisors, 1936–8. US Representative (Rep.) for California's 16th Congressional District, 1939–43.

are the aggressors, be given a seat in the United Nations on equal terms with the British and Americans.

3. That this present British Government would have the same Chinese Reds, or the Russian Reds, participate in making a peace treaty with Japan or Korea.
4. While we are fighting back-to-back as allies this present British Government would give Formosa to the Chinese Reds with whom we are now at war, although it is not declared, though some 60,000 American casualties are now the record in Korea.
5. This same British Government has recommended these Reds diplomatically on one hand and, on the other hand, have sent their soldiers to Korea to fight these same Reds.
6. We note with interest that Mr Morrison had stated that it is a 'terrible' thing that five or six English soldiers have been killed in Iran – primarily through Communism. Yet, we have had 60,000 casualties in Korea.

I say this with all the kindness and respect for you that I can muster and I reaffirm my confidence in you. That is the reason, very frankly, why I am writing to you. I think the majority of the American people would like to see good relations continue between the British and Americans who are natural allies, and this alliance promises the only hope, as far as I can see, of a permanent, reasonable peace.

There is a tremendous undercurrent in this country, among our people, that we are being played with and that some of the cards are being dealt under the table for diplomatic reasons. I think I can very definitely say that if the American people find that they have ever been 'sold down the river' or that the British diplomatic handling of their affairs with this country are not in accordance with the highest ethical standards this country will drop any alliance they may have or any thought of further alliance.

I have discussed this with many of my friends and decided to write you this letter and ask you if it is not time, to save the good relations between these two countries that the present British Government come out in plain English and tell which side of the picture they are on and, if they are on our side, to say so and put their actions in accordance therewith and quit suggesting that these Red Communists be treated as equals in the United Nations.

I expect to be in Europe for some five or six months. I am sailing on the *Queen Elizabeth* on May 8. I hope to be able to see you and discuss this with you.

Winston S. Churchill: speech
(Hansard)

19 April 1951   House of Commons

NORTH ATLANTIC (SUPREME COMMANDER)

Churchill: As this matter concerns both our country and the United States, I hope I may have your indulgence, Mr Speaker, if I say, I think on behalf of all parties and every hon. Member, with what deep regret we have received the news this morning of the death of Senator Vandenberg, a great American statesman whose sure balance of mind and lofty disinterested pursuance of large purposes won him the respect of all parties in his own country and of all parties in our island here.

Now I come to the business of the afternoon, and I hope the House will permit me to range rather widely over this extensive topic. In the event of war with Soviet Russia, two dangers would menace the defence of free Europe and our own life here. The first is the large number of U-boats, far more than the Germans had at the beginning of the late war, of an improved German type and of vastly increased underwater speed and endurance. The second is, of course, the mining peril at all our ports and all free European ports.

This mining attack required from us in the late war nearly 60,000 men and more than 1,000 vessels, sweeping and watching ceaselessly under hard conditions. Every kind of device was tried, and, in the main, mastered by us, but now we must expect ever more subtle scientific inventions to prevent detection and clearance by sweeping or explosives. There is no doubt that the whole of this process is being studied and developed by the Soviet Government, aided by German science and German brains. Our means of keeping alive, and the power of the United States and of ourselves to send armies to Europe, depend on our mastering these two problems.

I am sure that no one knows so much about dealing with U-boats in the Atlantic and the mine menace around our shores and harbours of any kind as the British Admiralty, not because we are cleverer or braver than others, but because, in two wars, our existence has depended upon overcoming these perils. When you live for years on end with mortal danger at your throat, you learn in a hard school. 'Depend upon it,' said Dr Johnson, 'if a man is going to be hanged in a month, it concentrates his mind wonderfully.'

During these two recent wars, as First Lord of the Admiralty or as Minister of Defence, I studied from week to week the hopeful or sinister curves upon the charts, and nothing ever counted more with me than their movements. It is the kind of experience, prolonged as it was, which eats its way into you. The late U-boat war lasted nearly six years. I say that to take the control of this process out of Admiralty hands would, I am sure, be a grave and perhaps a fatal injury, not only to ourselves, but to the common cause.

I would begin by asking where, in fact, did this idea of a Supreme Commander for the Atlantic originate. What were the reasons for the acceptance and enforcement of so radical a change from the system which had proved itself in the recent long years of war to work effectively? What would be the powers, apart from the imposing title, of the American Supreme Commander of the Atlantic? Our coastal waters and the English Channel are not under him. It is in the White Paper. He could not move warships and flotillas from the Eastern Atlantic Zone without disrupting or changing all the intricate business of receiving convoys and keeping the ports open.

Then, what about merchant ships? The Prime Minister told us the other day: 'That is really another matter altogether. The allocation of our merchant fleet is, of course, under the Government of this country.' – (Official Report, Feb. 26, 1951; Vol. 484, c. 1767.) Well, the merchant fleet can no more be considered apart from the escorts than the escorts can be considered apart from the merchant fleet. What powers will the Supreme Commander have over the American Navy Department? Can he transfer ships from the Pacific to the Atlantic? Surely not? He might make representations, but they would be settled by the American naval authorities, no doubt after consultation with the British Admiralty. Could he move naval forces from the North Atlantic to the South Atlantic? Is, in fact, the South Atlantic under his command at all? Could he take ships from the South Atlantic or from the Mediterranean and bring them into the Eastern or the Western Atlantic Zones?

It would be quite impossible for him to settle any of these matters, even if he had the authority on paper, except after consulting the United States Navy Department and the British Admiralty. We are told that his appointment is necessary to avoid the ocean war being conducted by a committee composed of twelve Powers, such as the Committee set up under the Atlantic Pact. But who ever imagined that the intricate handling of the U-boat and mining war could be entrusted to a committee of twelve Powers, most of whom have contributed little or nothing to the common stock?

It would not be fair to a distinguished and capable officer, like Admiral Fechteler[1] to cast all the nominal responsibility upon him when, in actual practice, he could not have real power. There is no doubt whatever that the business of bringing in the convoys safely to Europe can only be settled by an officer, whatever his nationality, seated at the Admiralty, and having immediately under his orders the executive Officer Commanding the Western Approaches and the merchant shipping which is the object of the enemy's attack, and whose safety is the whole object of the operation.

Reading the White Paper, which I had the time to do, one finds that

[1] William Morrow Fechteler, 1896–1967. Educated at US Naval Academy, 1916. Served aboard USS *Pennsylvania* during WWI. Bureau of Navigation, 1942–3. Cdr, Amphibious Group 8, 1944–5. Asst Chief of Naval Personnel, 1945. Deputy Chief of Naval Operations, 1947–50. Chief of Naval Operations, 1951.

Paragraph 25 is strange reading. It says: 'The Atlantic command will include an Eastern and a Western area. The Eastern area, which is obviously the more vital so far as this country is concerned, will be under the command of a British Admiral in association with Coastal Command of the Royal Air Force. This British Admiral will be the Commander-in-Chief, Home Fleet,' an appointment at present held by Admiral Sir Philip Vian.[1] But what has the Home Fleet got to do with the U-boat and mining menace? It has very little to do with them. Of course, when it comes out from its harbours into the ocean it has to look after the convoys and protect them against U-boat attack, and, of course, when it stays in, sometimes it lends the flotillas of the Western Approaches some flotillas of its own. But the Home Fleet, in war-time, dwells mainly at Scapa Flow, and only comes out to deal with enemy surface raiders.

In this imaginary war, to which I am addressing myself, we have, of course, to look at the facts with which one is confronted. The Russians have some modern cruisers, but they have no fast capital ships like the *Scharnhorst*, the *Gneisenau*, the *Bismarck* and the *Tirpitz*, and they can have none in the next two or three years – two, anyhow. How is it then proposed that the Commander-in-Chief of our Home Fleet is to control the movement of convoys in the Western Approaches? The routes to be followed by convoys entering or leaving Britain must be arranged from the British Admiralty. Are the merchant ships sailing from British ports to be given their orders from America, and, if so, how can the American Commander be informed of all that is going on from hour to hour? Fancy presenting us with a plan whereby an American admiral, seated in Norfolk, Virginia, has the supreme command of the Atlantic, although the business of the reception of the convoys and bringing them in through the U-boat and mining attack, must be mainly over here and is vital to us all. I repeat that the Supreme Commander of the Atlantic, if there is one, whatever his nationality, should be situated here.

Of course, since the war stopped, changes in military science have been continued. The power of the air grows ceaselessly. Even at the end of the war, it was at least equal to that of the naval forces at sea. But the movement of convoys on the sea is a matter for naval directions, and in Great Britain the air forces allotted to their defence must conform to a comprehensive plan prepared, in the first place, by the Admiralty. This important fact was recognised when, from the outbreak of the last war, the operational control of the Coastal Command of the Royal Air Force was vested in the Admiralty.

It is not clear from the White Paper whether this policy is intended to be applied in the future. Paragraph 25 of the White Paper says: 'The Eastern

---

[1] Philip Vian, 1894–1968. Cadet, RN, 1907. DSO, 1940; and bar, 1940; and second bar, 1941. Commanded 15th Cruiser Sqn, Mediterranean, 1941–2. KBE, 1942. Commanded Eastern (British) Task Force, Normandy invasion, 1944. CB, 1944. KCB, 1944. VAdm. commanding Carrier Force, British Pacific Fleet, taking part in the assault on Okinawa, 1945. 5th Sea Lord, 1946. C-in-C, Home Fleet, 1950–2. GCB, 1952. Author of *Action this Day* (1959).

area . . . will be under the command of a British Admiral in association with Coastal Command of the Royal Air Force.' Is there then to be no American air contribution to this Eastern Zone? Surely, information of this might have been given to us. It is a serious omission on the part of those who drew up this document.

Let me return to the first point I am making, that there is no need for a Supreme Commander of the Atlantic. That is the point which I submit to the House, and, not only to the House, but to the Committee. The overwhelming weight of British naval opinion supports the view that there is no need to appoint a Supreme Commander of the Atlantic.

Commander Pursey[1] (Hull, East): Nonsense.

Mr Churchill: I will affirm and sustain my statement. Admiral Andrew Cunningham, a very great sailor –

Commander Pursey: A bath chair warrior now.

Mr Churchill: I think the hon. and gallant Gentleman might, at any rate, lay off his sneering snarls when naval officers of great distinction have their names mentioned in the House. Admiral Andrew Cunningham used the expression that it would be 'a fifth wheel on the coach'. Admiral Tovey,[2] who commanded the Home Fleet for a long time, and had a very important action at sea, and Lord Cork and Orrery[3] have spoken in the same sense. I have here a letter, which I am authorised to read, from Sir Percy Noble,[4] who has not hitherto expressed himself in public, but who has unequalled credentials, because he managed the business himself with success last time. It says:

> My dear Mr Churchill, from experience in the last war – first in command of the Western Approaches and then as one of the Combined Chiefs of Staff – it is my opinion that there is no need for a Supreme Commander in the Atlantic at all. In 1942, when I was at Liverpool, Admiral of the Fleet Sir Dudley Pound discussed this very question with me, and we agreed that such a form of command was not only unnecessary, but might (and probably would) impose an undue strain on the already very complex system of

---

[1] Harry Pursey, 1891–1980. Served in RN during WWI. National Speaker, Ministry of Information, 1940–1. MP (Lab.) for Hull East, 1945–70.

[2] John Cronyn Tovey, 1885–1971. On active service as destroyer capt., 1914–18 (despatches, DSO). Appointed Cdr after Battle of Jutland, 1916, for 'the persistent and determined manner in which he attacked enemy ships'. RAdm., Destroyers, Mediterranean, 1938–40. VAdm., Second-in-Command, Mediterranean Fleet, 1940. C-in-C, Home Fleet, 1940–3 (including responsibility for Murmansk and Archangel convoys). Knighted, 1941. Adm. of the Fleet, 1943. C-in-C, the Nore, 1943–6. Baron, 1946.

[3] William Henry Dudley Boyle, 1873–1967. Adm. 1932. President of Royal Naval College, Greenwich, and Adm. commanding Royal Naval War College, 1929–32. Succeeded as 12th Earl of Cork and Orrery, 1934.

[4] Percy Lockhart Harnam Noble, 1880–1955. Cadet, RN, 1894. Served in Grand Fleet, 1914–18. Knighted, 1936. C-in-C, China Station, 1938–40. Adm., 1939. OC-in-C Western Approaches, 1941–2. Head, British Naval Delegation, Washington DC, 1942–4. First and Principal ADC to the King, 1943–5.

wireless and other communications. When I was in Washington in 1943 the whole of our machinery for controlling the North Atlantic convoys was again re-examined by Admiral King and myself with Admiral Sir Henry Moore,[1] who was at that time the Vice-Chief of the Naval Staff in London. Had it then been considered wise to introduce a change in the system, it is probable that a British officer would have been selected for this Supreme Command as Britain and Canada were providing almost the whole of the escorting forces in that area. However, we decided that no change was necessary. Great Britain is the 'receiving end' of the Atlantic life-line and the jumping-off place for forces entering Europe. In view of certain statements to the contrary which have appeared in the Press, I feel it is worth mentioning that in my experience no serious confusion ever arose in regard to the exercise of control by the methods we employed in the last war.

That is not an opinion which should be dismissed in contemptuous terms. It is not an opinion which should be ignored, and I am sure our American friends with whom Admiral Noble worked so intimately will give it full weight in considering this matter now under discussion between us. My first submission, therefore, to the Committee is that there is no need for the appointment of a Supreme Commander in the Atlantic.

Let me now approach the question from another angle. We all rejoiced when General Eisenhower was appointed Supreme Commander of the Armies of the Atlantic Powers. There is no man in the world who can do that job so well. Although the American troops under his command will only be a fraction of the whole of the European Forces which are needed – and far less than the French Army which, if France and Europe are to live, must be reborn – yet everyone was contented, and have been more contented every day since his appointment. It was a great shock however to most of the 50 millions in our island when they learned that a United States admiral was also to be put in command of the Atlantic and of a large proportion of our Fleet employed there.

During the war the life-lines across the Atlantic fell in an overwhelming degree to the care of the Admiralty. We were always most anxious for the Americans to extend their zone eastwards towards us, even during the first two years of the struggle when we were alone and they gave us magnificent help. But in 1942, after they had come into the war, their major theatre in that war – I say that war – was, inevitably and rightly, in the Pacific. They suffered terrible losses in the massacre of shipping through their own inexperience of

[1] Henry Ruthven Moore, 1886–1978. Cadet, RN, 1902. Served in Grand Fleet, 1914–18 (DSO, 1916). Royal Naval Staff College, 1920–1. Imperial Defence College, 1927. RAdm. Commanding 3rd Cruiser Sqn, 1939–40. VAdm., 1941. VCNS, 1941–3. Knighted, 1942. Second-in-Command, Home Fleet, 1943–4. C-in-C, Home Fleet, 1944–5. Adm., 1945. Head of British Naval Mission, Washington DC, 1945–8.

dealing with the U-boat. The 'U-boat paradise' – the Germans called it – took a terrible toll of their own Eastern coast in 1942, and hard pressed though we were ourselves, we were very glad to send them all the help we could in creating their convoy and escort system. They did not suffer to any serious extent from the mining danger.

But the climax of the U-boat war was reached in 1943, and during this struggle nearly the whole business was managed and the burden borne by Britain and Canada. In fact it was by agreements reached between the British and American Governments, the Joint Chiefs of Staff Committee, and between the Admiralties, that Britain and Canada assumed full responsibility for the protection of all trade convoys, apart from American troop convoys, in the North Atlantic, and the American naval contribution fell by agreement to a little more than two percent of the total. This was the period when the U-boat attack was decisively broken by all the means that were available.

We have become relatively, I regretfully admit, a weaker Power since those days – not only on the seas. Nevertheless, we have the experience, we have the art. Our latent resources in trained sea-faring personnel are out of all proportion to what we have presented in recent years. We need, of course, American aid. So does the whole world. We need aid particularly in the air at the reception end, but I can find no valid reason for subordinating Great Britain in the Atlantic Command. The responsibility should be shared on equal terms and with equal status between the two chief naval Powers. That is my submission.

We are told we are to have the sole command of British coastal waters and the English Channel. We are not told what 'coastal waters' mean. The First Lord of the Admiralty in another place spoke of the Americans 'commanding in deep waters'. What does that mean? Does that mean up to the 100-fathom line, or what? I had better give way if the right hon. Gentleman the Minister of Defence wishes to answer.

The Minister of Defence (Mr Shinwell): I am very anxious not to interrupt the right hon. Gentleman because I am intensely interested in what he is saying, but he must take into account what appears in the White Paper about the control of the Eastern Atlantic.

Mr Churchill: I was coming to all that, but I was talking of the coastal waters. I ask what that means because the Eastern Atlantic like the Western is under Supreme American command. It is the coastal waters alone that are reserved for Great Britain and I am asking if they end at the 100-fathom line. (Hon Members: 'The Minister does not know.') In any case the area is severely restricted round our own coast, and the line that is drawn, be it the 100-fathom line or not, like the line that will be drawn across the Atlantic in no way corresponds to any boundary which applies to U-boat attack. The English Channel is reserved to us. It is surely not more vital to the integrity of the reception of convoys than the Bay of Biscay or the waters between Iceland

and Ireland, or the North Sea, or the Arctic approaches to and from North Russia. It is all one story, and one story that can only be intelligently told from one place.

Let me turn now to another aspect – sentiment. Sentiment should not rule in war, but neither should it be forgotten or overlooked. I am sorry that the Prime Minister is not here and still more sorry for the cause of his absence,[1] but I must state the case. He plays too important a part in it to be omitted from any coherent discussion. He certainly does not understand British sentiment about the Navy. Going back a long time, I admit, to 27th March, 1936 – it was on the same subject and in the same discussion – the Prime Minister said, according to the *Daily Herald* – from which I take the report: 'We shall have to give up certain of our toys – one is "Britannia rules the Waves".' This was certainly a misquotation. As has been often pointed out, it is, 'Britannia rule the Waves' – an invocation not a declaration of fact. But if the idea 'Rule Britannia' was a toy, it is certainly one for which many good men from time to time have been ready to die.

No one can doubt that it was a great shock and even an affront – quite unintended by the United States – to the whole nation when, following on an American general's supreme command in Europe, which we all welcome, we were told that an American admiral would have the supreme command of the Atlantic. It was also a shock to see that our Prime Minister had so little knowledge and even less feeling in the matter. However, the United States themselves should consider the sentiments of others in executing their great mission of leading the resistance of the free world against Communist aggression and infiltration. It should not be possible for their enemies to say that they are grasping the supreme command everywhere – on the land, in the air, on the sea. Moreover, it is not true; that is not their wish or their desire.

To create this superfluous supreme command of the Atlantic would be a psychological mistake, making things harder than they are already. Of course, it plays right into the hands of the Communist propagandists and their fellow travellers who declare, in their lying fashion, that we have all been bought up by Wall Street and the almighty dollar. Why make them this present in the discussion when the matter is not, as I have said, of real and fundamental importance? It would, I think, have been a natural thing in sentiment, and also on practical and technical arguments, to have shared the Atlantic Command with equal status between the Admiralty and the United States Navy Department.

I am quite sure it was not the wish of the American people or their government to treat us roughly in this matter, or to make an issue of it at all. When I made my protest I received most active and sincere and widespread

---

[1] Attlee was suffering from an ulcer that required hospital treatment.

American support. It is a trouble into which they have been brought, not at all by their own decision or desire but through other reasons which I will presently indicate.

I have heard the argument used – and it is even suggested in the last sentence of paragraph 28 in the White Paper – that we shall get much more out of the Americans by letting them have the command, even though it is mainly nominal. That, I think, is a train of thought unworthy of the dignity of both our countries. It implies that the Americans are willing to be fooled by being flattered and that the British have no pride if they can get more help. We should dismiss such arguments from our thoughts. But still we can see the traces of them on the last page of the White Paper. The issue, I think, should be settled between comrades and brothers in common danger and on a self-respecting moral basis, and with the sole desire and resolve to find the best way of winning victory and salvation from our dangers.

It is true, no doubt, that the United States has a larger fleet than we have – double, we are told – in ships in commission, and a great preponderance in the air. Also, they have wisely and carefully kept in 'mothball' many scores of war vessels which we have improvidently scrapped, sold or given away. Thus, they have a larger material reserve. Broadly speaking, it can be said that the Supreme Command in war goes naturally with the size of the forces involved, and I accepted and affirmed that rule in the late struggle.

The Parliamentary and Financial Secretary to the Admiralty (Mr James Callaghan): It may be quite true that the Americans have a much larger material reserve, but I suggest to the right hon. Gentleman that they do not possess a proportionately larger material reserve than we have, compared with their active fleet.

Mr Churchill: It is rather difficult to work out these rule-of-three sums. (Laughter.) Hon. Members opposite laugh at that; that is all they are fit for. Why should they laugh because I am not prepared to argue that question of whether it is a proportionately larger reserve? It is a grave and foolish thing to cast away valuable ships at the end of a war. It is much better to keep them, even if you do not want them, in care and maintenance, and then you can never tell when they will turn out to be useful. I have not worked it out in proportion, but at any rate the Americans have a far larger material reserve than we have.

I was saying that, broadly speaking, the supreme command in war goes naturally with the larger forces. I think that may be taken as the rule. Nevertheless, in the campaign of Tunis we did not hesitate to allow our armies to remain under General Eisenhower's command, although we had eleven divisions in action to the Americans' four. On the other hand when, later in that year, the United States asked for an American supreme commander to have control both of the 'Overlord' campaign in France and also of the Mediterranean, I refused to agree, and although there were tense arguments the matter was settled agreeably, as so many other matters were settled between us, and it was settled without any ill-feeling.

How was this accomplished? It was accomplished by the personal relations between the Heads of Governments and, of course, based upon the continued comradeship and intercourse of our Combined Chiefs of Staff Committee. I shall come back to this institution before I sit down, but the conclusion I now draw is that commands in particular operations and in various theatres are not necessarily regulated merely by the size of the forces locally involved.

In estimating the size of these forces one must not only consider the relative naval strengths of the fleets and flotillas and aircraft squadrons as they now stand. I know we are in a temporary eclipse, but we are capable of a far greater and more rapid development of strength in the naval sphere than almost any other country. Besides the warships of all kinds, there is the Mercantile Marine. We must not forget them, or the sacrifices the merchant seamen made in the struggle – many of them sunk three or four times with their ships, but always going back. We may have let our Navy down, but it can be revived. We have not let our Mercantile Marine diminish. On the contrary –

Mr Callaghan *rose* –

Mr Churchill: The Parliamentary Secretary is a subordinate Minister of the Government and he should not interrupt from the Front Bench. We have not let our Mercantile Marine diminish. On the contrary, here are the figures. (*Interruption.*) I think I have the right to put forward the case for the potential contribution which Britain can make to war and transport on the seas. The United States have 12,400,000 tons of merchant shipping in use and 14 million tons in reserve. They have 250,000 tons under construction. Great Britain has 16,600,000 tons in use, or 19,600,000 tons if the Commonwealth and Empire are added, and two million tons under construction, some of it for foreign account. Moreover, we have far larger reserves of merchant –

Mr Snow (Lichfield and Tamworth):[1] Damned old fool.

Colonel Gomme-Duncan (Perth and East Perthshire):[2] On a point of order. Is it in order for an hon. Member to refer to the right hon. Gentleman as 'a damned old fool'?

The Chairman: It is certainly not in order.

Mr Snow: I beg to withdraw that statement and to apologise but, of course, the right hon. Gentleman has been extremely provocative.

Hon. Members: Get out.

Mr Churchill: I always accept an apology here.

Mr Snow: Will not the right hon. Gentleman follow my example and apologise to my hon. Friend?

---

[1] Julian Snow, 1910–82. Served with RA, 1939–45. MP (Lab.) for Portsmouth Central, 1945–50; for Lichfield and Tamworth Div. of Staffordhisre, 1950–70. Baron, 1970.

[2] Alan Gomme-Duncan, 1893–1963. Served in WWI; with the Black Watch in India, 1919–27, 1933–7. HM Inspector of Prisons for Scotland, 1938–9. MP (Cons.) for Perth and Kinross, 1945–59.

Mr Ivor Owen Thomas (The Wrekin):[1] May I call attention to the fact that this whole incident arose from –

The Chairman: It was within the hearing of all Members of the Committee, and there is no point in calling attention to it now.

Mr Thomas: On a point of order. Is it in order for the right hon. Gentleman to refer to an hon. Member of the Committee as somewhat subordinate to another – (*Laughter.*) Let hon. Members wait for the whole of it – and, therefore, not entitled to the same consideration as a Member of the Government? Are not the rights of every Member on the Floor of the Committee equal?

The Chairman: I do not think any procedural objection can be taken to the right hon. Gentleman's reference to the Parliamentary Secretary to the Admiralty. (Hon Members: 'Oh'.) But it is, of course, true that the hon. Gentleman is the chief Minister of the Admiralty in the House.

Mr Churchill: Well, I understood that the Minister of Defence was going to take responsibility for the case today; and everything is relative in importance, and consequently, compared with the Minister of Defence, the hon. Gentleman must accept the position of being subordinate; although let me make it quite clear that this is the first time that I have ever heard the word 'subordinate' regarded as un-Parliamentary or even as almost an obscene expression. However, the 'damned old fool' has accepted the apology.

I was saying that, moreover, we have far larger reserves of merchant seamen than the United States; we have a much larger merchant fleet; and I say that that is not a negligible contribution to the solution of the problems we have to settle between our two great, friendly countries.

This very serious mistake arises from the fault of planning from the bottom instead of planning from the top. When the top are incompetent to plan or give guidance, the process naturally begins from the bottom. We suffer from the fallacy, *deus ex machina*, which, for the benefit of any Wykehamists who may be present, is 'A god out of the machine'. There are layers of committees and super committees, and the business is passed upwards stage by stage to a decision. When all the process has been gone through, the machine speaks, but what one gets at the end is not truth or wisdom or common sense: it is a White Paper. All that comes out of the machine is unreal and meaningless formulae expressed in official jargon and accompanied by fatuous grimaces.

Now let me tell the Committee, so far as I know the facts, the procedure by which an American admiral was appointed to the Supreme Command of the Atlantic. I have been looking into the workings of the machine, which, I hope, will interest the right hon. Gentleman. Here let me say and let me emphasise that I have no doubt that Admiral Fechteler is a most capable and competent officer. Although he has no special experience of the Atlantic theatre, he is, I am sure, a naval officer of the highest quality. But so far as I have been able to ascertain, this is how the decision was taken by planning from the bottom.

---

[1] Ivor Owen Thomas, 1898–1982. MP (Lab.) for Wrekin Div. of Shropshire, 1945–55.

The original proposal came at a meeting in Washington some time last year, and was made by the Canadian representative. So I ask the Minister of Defence, when he replies, to tell the Committee whether this was agreed or was, at least, a matter of consultation beforehand between the British and the Canadian Governments. If it was not, it would seem it ought to have been. All the other Powers present supported the proposal. The British representative, Vice-Admiral Schofield,[1] who has been very vocal in the recent discussions, felt that the best he could do was to ask that the Supreme Commander's deputy should be British. Now I ask the Minister of Defence, did he have instructions to take this course? Surely on a matter of such high importance of this character, he should have had definite instructions from above. If he had none, he should, in my opinion, have said that the matter was too important to be decided without reference to higher authority, and asked for an adjournment. But all passed off very pleasantly with unanimous agreement. The matter then slumbered for several months while the machine was grinding away from day to day, until the decision leaked out from Copenhagen.

Mr Driberg (Maldon): Washington first.

Mr Churchill: Let us look at some of these countries whose subordinate officers – I beg the pardon of the Committee for using that word – settled the matter. I may say that they are all countries for whom I have the strongest regard and from whom I have received many compliments and honours. But let me take four of them – Norway, Denmark, Belgium, Holland. Though we accept the statement that the American Navy is double as strong as the British, the British Navy, even in its present phase, is more than twelve times as strong as all these four put together. Even if France be included, their combined strength is less than a quarter of ours.

These four Powers I am speaking of have between them one aircraft carrier, acquired from Britain since the war, and 15 destroyers and 16 frigates, many of which have been purchased from Great Britain. Yet the voting strength of each round the table was equal to ours, and also, of course, to the United States, whose Navy is larger than everyone's. Everything went off smoothly, and the American representative, no doubt with a becoming blush, accepted the supreme command for his country.

All this is happening far below the cognisance of statesmen, premiers, presidents, and leading people – even, perhaps, Ministers of Defence – who manage our affairs. But it went on steadily up to the higher levels – the committees of greater status – until we reached the present situation.

Since the disclosure was made to Parliament, the Government have become conscious that the policy to which they had been bound by the workings of the machine was neither sensible nor – what is, perhaps, for the moment more

---

[1] Brian Betham Schofield, 1895–1984. Educated at Royal Naval Colleges Osborne and Dartmouth. Midshipman, 1913. Lt-Cdr, 1925. Cdr, 1931. Capt., 1938. CBE, 1943. Commanded HMS *George V*, 1945–6. RAdm., 1947. CB, 1949. Retired with rank of VAdm., 1950. Author of *British Seapower* (1967), *The Loss of the Bismarck* (1972), *Operation Neptune* (1974).

relevant to their preoccupations – popular. Why have we been waiting so long for the White Paper, and now have only an interim incomplete document? It is because His Majesty's Government suddenly became aware of what was going on and that it was bringing them into discredit, and they have tried to find some counterpoise to restore the balance and help them out of their scrape. Then the happy thought came: 'If we have given up the command of the Atlantic, let us try, as a sop to placate our people to keep or gain the commander-in-chiefship of the Mediterranean. That would make things more even.'

Though I have no definite information, I presume that most active discussions have been proceeding on the basis that as Britain has given up the Atlantic she must at least have the Mediterranean. But here again there is a great difficulty. This is the cause of the delay in our getting the full White Paper. The Mediterranean Powers, whose Governments have now been brought into the matter – not a mere committee of medium officials sitting round a table – want to have the Americans in command of the Mediterranean. There are almost as many powerful arguments in favour of the United States having the command in the Mediterranean as there are against them having the over-riding command in the Atlantic.

Mr Shinwell: At this stage I want to be quite clear about the statement the right hon. Gentleman has just made. Do I understand him to say that Governments who are concerned in the Mediterranean zone have decided that there should be an American commander, or have suggested that there should be an American commander? If so, will the right hon. Gentleman be good enough to let me have the evidence on this?

Mr Churchill: I will say what I have said and what I am going to say. I say that, since all this matter became public in discussions on the American command of the Atlantic, there has been a very great deal more attention paid to the discussions about the command in the Mediterranean; very much more.

Mr Shinwell *rose* –

Mr Churchill: The right hon. Gentleman ought to keep something for his speech.

Mr Shinwell: The right hon. Gentleman need be under no illusions. He will be surprised, and probably disagreeably surprised, at how much I have to say in replying to him. I want to put him right about the facts, because I think that is very desirable, and all I say to him now is that the discussions about the Mediterranean and the discussions about the whole command have been taking place simultaneously.

Mr Churchill: They may have been taking place simultaneously, but one ended before the other. That sometimes happens in horse racing. I am certainly not seeking to gain personal popularity by what I am going to say. On the contrary, I am saying only what I think is right and true, and should be considered and weighed by the Committee and the Government. I say that there are almost as many powerful arguments in favour of the United States having the command in the Mediterranean as there are against them having the over-riding command in the Atlantic.

Personally, if I had to choose I should prefer, on nigh military and national grounds, the United States having command in the Mediterranean. I am sorry to have to trouble the Committee with details, but it is better that the matter should be understood. A powerful fleet – and this will interest hon. Gentlemen opposite below the Gangway – of American carriers can be and is being placed in the Mediterranean which, working in conjunction with the air bases America has obtained from France and in Tripoli, would bring a tremendous potential attack with the atomic bomb upon the most vulnerable parts of Russia, including the oil fields, in the event of war, and this fact constitutes an immense and precious deterrent against another war.

The United States can, if it chooses, have by far the most powerful fleet in the Mediterranean, and a fleet suited to the actual task which might have to be performed if the worst came to the worst. I think we should be ready and proud to be the hosts of our American allies and comrades at our famous and vital Mediterranean bases at Gibraltar, Malta and, presumably, Cyprus. I would much rather the British offensive atomic base in East Anglia were not the only major deterrent of this kind upon Communist aggression.

Mr Emrys Hughes (South Ayrshire): Who is being aggressive now?

Mr Churchill: This is rather up the hon. Gentleman's street. It is right to spread the risk of reprisals. We at home should be safer, and the United Nations and Atlantic Powers would be stronger.

Therefore, I do not oppose the United States taking the command, if that is their wish, of the Mediterranean on the practical and strategic merits. Moreover, there are far-reaching political arguments. We are no longer strong enough ourselves to bear the whole political burden we have hitherto borne in the Mediterranean, or even to take the leading part in the diplomatic control of that theatre. But the United States and Britain together, aided by France – which in the Mediterranean makes a very different contribution to the common strength than it is possible for her to do in the Atlantic, with her bases and her ships – we three together would be in a most powerful position to deal with, say, the Egyptian problem and the whole question of the defence of the Suez Canal. We and the United States ought to act together there and in these matters.

I am always looking out for something to give the Government a good mark for, and I read the papers vigilantly every day, and I was very glad to see that about the Persian oil, the Government are already working with the United States. That is right and wise. The same combination will enormously relieve our difficulties in Egypt, the Levant and throughout the Middle East. After all, the United States are now looking after Turkey, and have taken over from us the salvation of Greece. These countries would welcome the United States in the Mediterranean, and would gladly accord them the supreme command there.

What are the Government trying to do? Having let the question of the Atlantic command go largely by default, they hope to put themselves right with the public – this is my guess – by claiming the Mediterranean. It is as if a man had put the wrong shoe on his right foot should say: 'I will put the other shoe on my left foot, and that will be a compromise which will make it all right.' Such absurdities have no part in the grim realities of warding off war or of war itself.

I ask that this matter should be reconsidered from the beginning. I ask that the command of the Atlantic shall be agreeably divided between Great Britain and the United States on equal terms. In the war the line was eventually drawn at the 26th Meridian – quite a different thing from the 38th Parallel. But wherever the line is to be drawn, it would be easy to arrange for the taking over of the convoys and for their air defence; and the adjustments, sometimes almost daily, can be made quite easily, and can only be made, between the Admiralty and the Canadian and United States Navy Departments. If it is a question of large transfers of forces from one side to the other, that is really a matter first for a Combined Chiefs of Staff Committee, if they exist still, and in the ultimate issue for settlement between the Prime Minister and the President, who together control 90 percent of all the effective air and naval forces involved in this whole business.

Now I come to the existing organisation for the Atlantic Pact. The costly error was made when the Combined British and American Chiefs of Staff Committee was dissolved, of sweeping this away, of breaking up this organisation. It was a disaster. We speak the same language; we have many other ties. What a pity it was to let go that organisation which served us so well, and which carried the direction of war between allies to the highest and most smooth-working efficiency ever reached in history.

The Prime Minister told us that he regretted the abolition of the Combined Chiefs of Staffs Committee. But why did he not put up a fight about it? Surely this was an occasion when he might have crossed the Atlantic and had a personal talk with the President on the top level. Keeping the Combined Chiefs of Staffs Committee in existence need not have prevented a co-existent instrument with other powers on it for the purpose of executing the Atlantic Pact. Half the misunderstandings which have been so dangerous to Anglo-American relations during the Korean War would, I believe, have been avoided had there been a regular and constant meeting, as there were in the bygone years, between our two Chiefs of Staffs Committees. We cannot afford, in the dangers in which we now stand, to make mistakes like this. By mismanaging these affairs the responsible Ministers may bring untold miseries upon the hard-working, helpless millions whose fate lies in their hands.

What organisation have we got now to replace the contact between the

President and the Prime Minister and the continued daily intercourse of the Combined Chiefs of Staffs Committee? We are told of a standing group of Powers under the Atlantic Pact. This group which deals with the forces deployed under that Pact consists of three men – a French general, a British airman and an American vice-admiral. There is not a British sailor on it at all; not at the head of the Fleets not in this higher organisation. But surely the carrying of food and supplies from which Britain lives, carrying the armies of the New World to Europe, and maintaining them there across the broad oceans and through the narrow seas – surely that is a business in which sailors and merchant seamen and ships of all kinds, and naval skill and knowledge have their part.

I hope that the House will carefully consider many of the arguments that I have ventured to put before them, and I hope that we shall not allow this matter to rest as a thing definitely settled. I hope myself that the mistakes that have been made will be recovered.

This White Paper, so long withheld, is mainly a repetition of the one we got over a year ago. It has the addition of the names of various officers appointed by General Eisenhower in his Continental Command. But it gives us no real information. It is only a painful exposure of the paralysis of Cabinet mentality. If the Minister of Defence is not able tonight to make a genuine contribution to our knowledge, I shall feel it my duty to move a nominal reduction of his salary as a protest against the manner in which these grave matters have, so far, been handled by him and by the Government as a whole.

Richard Greville[1] to Captain Alfred M. Granum[2]
(Hillsdale College Archives)

25 April 1951

Dear Captain Granum,

I am writing on behalf of Mr Churchill to thank you for your letter of April 11.[3]

Mr Churchill appreciates the compliment you pay him in choosing his book *The Hinge of Fate* for this year's award of your NROTC Unit and in

---

[1] A secretary at the House of Commons.

[2] Alfred Marcellus Granum, 1899–1997. Born in Albuquerque, NM. Commissioned, 1921. Lt junior grade, USS *Canopus*, 1924; USS *Paul Jones*, 1925. Educated at US Naval Academy, 1926–7; Harvard University, 1927–8. Lt Cdr, Bureau of Engineers, 1938. Cdr, USS *Raleigh*, 1938. Sea Frontier Operations officer, Philippine Sea Frontier, c.1941. Capt., 1942. Prof. of Naval Science, University of New Mexico (NM), 1948–51. Skipper, University of NM's Naval Reserver Officers' Training Corps, 1948–51. RAdm., 1951.

[3] The NROTC Unit of the University of NM presented an annual award to a midshipman demonstrating outstanding leadership and citizenship. In 1949, the award was Eisenhower's *Crusade in Europe*. In 1950, it was Admiral Leahy's *I Was There*. In 1951, Churchill's *Hinge of Fate* was selected to be presented to Midshipman James. V. Neely.

asking that he should send his personal congratulations to the winner.[1] Whilst thanking you for this honour, however, Mr Churchill feels it would be inappropriate for him to mingle in this way in a purely USA ceremony of which he has no special knowledge.[2]

Winston S. Churchill: speech
('Winston S. Churchill, His Complete Speeches', volume 8, pages 8195–7)

27 April 1951
Albert Hall, London

Grand Habitation of the Primrose League

OUR RACE AND DESTINY

We meet for our Annual Meeting this year in a grave hour for our country. I cannot recall any period in my long life when mismanagement and incompetence have brought us into greater danger. At home prices and taxes go up and up, abroad the influence of Britain goes down and down. In every quarter of the world we are regarded by our friends with anxiety, with wonder and pity: and by our enemies, including some of those countries we have helped most in the past, like Egypt and Persia, we are regarded or treated with hostility or even contempt. Not one of them is so weak that they cannot spare a kick or a taunt for Britain. It is hard to believe that we are the same nation that emerged from the last war respected and admired throughout the grand alliance for all the part we played, for a long time alone, in the defence of the cause of freedom. Six years of Socialist rule have brought us low.

Nevertheless we must not lose faith in our race and in our destiny. We are the same people, in the same islands, as we were in the great days we can all remember. Our spirit is unconquerable, our ingenuity and craftsmanship unsurpassed. Our latent resources are unmeasured. Our underlying unities are enduring. We have but to cast away by an effort of will the enfeebling tendencies and fallacies of Socialism and to free ourselves from restrictive Socialist rule to stand erect once more and take our place among the great Powers of the world. Never must we lose our faith and our courage, never must we fail in exertion and resolve.

We are all glad that the Prime Minister has left the hospital and can turn from the jigsaw-puzzles of Cabinet shuffling to the urgent tasks which confront him. It is hard on any country when no one is looking after it.

[1] James V. Neely, 1930– . Born in West Virginia. Son of a locomotive engineer and an elementary school teacher. Educated at West Virginia University and University of New Mexico. Served with US Navy in Korea and Camp Lejeune, 1952–4. Made his career in nuclear research, working for Sandia Nuclear Laboratories and then for his own engineering firm Nuclear Power Consultants Inc. Published *Beauty is My God* (2017).

[2] Churchill reconsidered this decision. See Sturdee to Granum of May 24, reproduced below (p. 2090).

Mr Attlee combines a limited outlook with strong qualities of resistance. He now resumes the direction and leadership of that cluster of lion-hearted limpets – a new phenomenon in our natural history, almost a suggestion I could offer Mr Herbert Morrison for his fun fair – who are united by their desire to hold on to office at all costs to their own reputations and their country's fortunes, and to put off by every means in their power to the last possible moment any contact with our democratic electorate. This they do in the name not of principle or policy but of party loyalty enforced by party discipline carried to lengths not previously witnessed in our system of representative and Parliamentary Government.

But in the last week three Ministers[1] resigned from this Government which itself stands on a minority in the country and hangs from day to day and night to night upon a thread in the House of Commons. I shall not occupy your time this afternoon in lengthy eulogies of these Ministers or explanations of their motives. The first might be deemed insincere; the second would certainly be laborious. But at any rate they have rendered a public service by exposing to Parliament the scandalous want of foresight in buying the raw materials upon which our vital rearmament programme depends. Frantic, belated efforts are now, we are assured, being made to repair the evil which resembles, though on a larger scale, and in a more dangerous sphere, the meat, the nuts, the eggs and other muddles with which we are already only too familiar. But for the resignation of these Ministers we should not have known about it until too late. We should have known no more about the raw material shortages than the Prime Minister knew about the appointment of the American admiral to the supreme command of the Atlantic. What is happening now in raw material is typical of the way our affairs drift and bump and flop. Next week we shall bring the disclosure of the resigning Ministers to the full rigours of debate in the House of Commons.

Nowhere in the darkening scene has more harm been done during Mr Attlee's tenure than in the loss of those intimate contacts between the British Prime Minister and the President of the United States which were so helpful and fruitful in the war. A wave of irritation is passing across the United States and the Isolationist forces there are glad to turn it upon Great Britain. The reproaches against General MacArthur – that great soldier and great statesman as his settlement of difficulties with Japan after the war have proven – in which Mr Shinwell, and even so staid a Minister as Mr Chuter Ede have indulged, enable those who do not like us in the United States to suggest that His Majesty's Government have had something to do with General MacArthur's dismissal. I cannot believe there is the slightest right to interfere between him and his officers. This great meeting here this afternoon should take the opportunity to pay their full tribute to our American

---

[1] Aneurin Bevan (Minister of Labour and National Service), John Freeman (Parliamentary Secretary to the Ministry of Supply) and Harold Wilson (President of the Board of Trade).

friends and allies, for the sacrifices and exertions they have made, and are making and are going to make, to save the world from Communist tyranny, and we should all of us bear in mind the well-known maxim 'United we stand, Divided we fall.'

And that applies with equal force to what is going on in our own island now. We are rent by party struggles which are inevitably and deliberately provoked when a Government, which has no claim to rest upon the will and confidence of the people, continues to keep us month after month on the brink of an election and whose fear of the judgment of their own fellow-countrymen is their only bond of union. I can assure you we shall do all in our power, by every constitutional means open to us, to bring this harmful suspense and uncertainty to a speedy end. Be sure you are ready for the call when it comes. Be sure that you lay aside every impediment and allow no class or privilege or vested interest to stand between you and your duty to the nation, and then all will be well and in the end all will be well for all.

Harold Wilson: recollection
('A Prime Minister on Prime Ministers', pages 267–8)

[April 1951]

Winston Churchill was, above all things, a Parliamentarian. He loved the House, he had dominated it over the years. In its most degenerate days it had refused to listen to his warnings and had treated him with disdain and hostility. His loyalty to Parliament, and his obeisance to the courtesies of an almost forgotten age, caused him to take personal initiatives which the world of today might find it hard to understand. When Aneurin Bevan and I resigned from the Attlee Government in April 1951, because we could not accept the unrealistic arms policy forced on the Government – and in Bevan's case its consequences for the National Health Service – Winston came up to us. He expressed sympathy with us: we were facing a situation which had been much familiar to him, though, as he pointed out, we would never be obsecrated as he had been. We had gone out with honour, but, he added with a twinkle in his eye, he and his party would make the most of the situation which resulted.

That evening Brendan Bracken sought me out. He had been charged, he said, 'by the greatest living statesman, for that is what Mr Churchill is' to give me a message to convey to my wife. First, Mr Churchill wanted me to know, he had been 'presented' to my wife, otherwise he would not presume to send her a message. The message was that whereas I, as an experienced politician, had taken a step of which he felt free to take such party advantage as was appropriate, his concern was with my wife, an innocent party in these affairs, who would undoubtedly suffer in consequence; he recalled the number of occasions his wife had suffered as a result of his own political decisions. Would I therefore convey to her his personal sympathy and understanding?

Thanking Bracken, I went home about 1 a.m., we had a narrow majority – and conveyed the message, which was greeted with gratitude and tears. I was enjoined to express her personal thanks. On leaving home the next morning I was again enjoined to see 'the old boy' and make sure I delivered the message.

In the early evening I saw Winston in the smoke-room and went up to him and told him I had a message from my wife. He interrupted me to point out that he had on one occasion been presented to her, otherwise he would not have presumed, etc. I acknowledged this undoubted fact, and expressed her thanks. Immediately – and with Winston this was not a rare event – tears flooded down his face, as he expatiated on the way that wives had to suffer for their husbands' political actions, going on to recall a number of instances over a long life.

When I reached home it was 2 a.m., but she was awake – I was asked if I had seen the old boy and thanked him. I had, and recounted the interview. She burst into tears, and I was moved to say that whereas two days earlier I had been a minister of the Crown, red box and all, now I was reduced to the position of a messenger between her and Winston Churchill, each of whom burst into tears on receipt of a message from the other. Of such is the essence of Parliament, or at least of bygone Parliaments, but this was the essential Winston Churchill.

May 1951

Winston S. Churchill to General Lord Ismay, Lieutenant-General Sir Henry Pownall, Commodore G. R. G. Allen, Colonel Bill Deakin and Dennis Kelly
(Churchill papers, 4/392)

1 May 1951

VOLUME VI. BK I. PROVISIONAL NOTE

1. I regard Volume V as finished except for overtakes, American corrections and final reading by me (by about the beginning of July). Mr Kelly should deal with everything connected with Volume V. If there are any overtakes or alterations, please send them to him. Sixty copies will have been printed by the end of this week.

2. From now on we turn to Volume VI. Copies of what is already done in outline are being forwarded to you all. Mr Kelly should look out and make dockets of the material for me. This can remain at Chartwell for the moment.

3. I should be glad if General Pownall would take up the story from the end of Chapter I 'The Struggle in Normandy', and describe the salient military events in France and Normandy covering the liberation of France and Belgium. A third chapter, No. XIV, 'The Rundstedt Offensive', would be about 5,000 words. These three chapters should take us to the end of 1944. It would be best in the first instance to assemble the material, books, etc., and let me have a synopsis and a report, rather than attempt at present the writing of the chapter. I recognize that each of these involves a great deal of work. It will only be possible to narrate the main military events, incorporating any of my personal material.

4. I should be glad if Mr Deakin will bring 'Balkan Policy' along.

5. I should be glad if Commodore Allen could survey the assembled material that will come in this Volume for 'Burma and the Pacific'. We only want skeletons to begin with.

6. Perhaps Lord Ismay could look after 'The Second Quebec Conference'.

7. I am asking Mr Sandys to do me a note on the 'Pilotless Bombardment'

which I will then send to Sir Guy Garrod. I think we have already got some material of Mr Sandys on this.

8. I do not think it wise to begin Book 12 at the present time, and we will break the Volume at the arrival of Yalta.

9. It would I am sure be most helpful if the Syndicate could meet early next week after all the circulations have been made, and could discuss this note, which is of course only my first thoughts on approaching our new text. I thought it would be a help if I put this forward as a sort of guide. I welcome all suggestions.

Lord Simon to Winston S. Churchill
(Churchill papers, 2/126)

2 May 1951

My dear Winston,

PERSIAN OIL

The weak and hesitating action taken by Morrison in this matter ought, I think, to be contrasted with the vigour and promptness of the Government in 1932, when the Persian Government announced that it cancelled the oil Concession under which the Anglo-Persian Oil Company was operating. Vansittart and I called attention to this precedent in the House of Lords on 21st March this year, but the contrast in method is striking.

In 1932, we at once took the matter to Geneva and I claimed that it should be dealt with immediately, under Article 15 of the Covenant, by the Council of the League of Nations itself. The case was heard by the members of the Council sitting round the table at Geneva. I presented the British case, with documents and argument, on behalf of the Company, and the Persian case was presented by a distinguished French advocate, whom Persia briefed for the purpose. Beneš acted as <u>rapporteur</u> and in the short time the dispute was amicably settled by the Agreement of 1933, under which the Company is now operating and which included an Article that the position of the Company under the Concession should not be modified, <u>even by Persian legislation</u>, save by agreement between the Persian Government and the Company.

Observe the contrast. In spite of this precedent, Her Majesty's Government has taken no prompt action to bring the threat before the United Nations, or to claim to raise the breach of contract before the Hague Court. Morrison's statement is merely an appeal that Persia will be injured if expropriation is carried through. All that has been done is to instruct our Ambassador at Teheran to put forward 'unofficially' the lines on which we thought a satisfactory agreement between the Persian Government and the Company could be worked out. He expresses his anxiety to settle this matter by negotiation, 'but we cannot negotiate under duress'. He acknowledges the right of Persia 'to acquire property in her own country', but does not emphasise the crucial fact that the Agreement of 1933 was an Agreement not to legislate to the disadvantage of the Company except by agreement. It is the special character of this Agreement which is our best point. No doubt a foreign country can, in ordinary circumstances, nationalise property in its own country, but it cannot lawfully do so <u>if it has contracted that it will not do so during the period of Concession.</u>

It has to be remembered that the British Government is the major shareholder in the Company. No wonder flouting by Persia is followed by flouting by Egypt.

Might it not be well to ask for a White Paper setting out what happened in 1932–33? It is all in the records of the League of Nations, but these are difficult to get at.

Perhaps, when the Shadow Cabinet considers Persia, you would ask me to your counsel.[1]

Lord Beaverbrook to Dr Stanley Morison[2]
(*Beaverbrook papers*)

4 May 1951

You say that 'Churchill, having disagreed over India, was excluded' from the 1931 Government. This is wrong. The National Government of 1931 contained men of many opinions. It was a Government of All Talents. The facts are that after the election of 1929 Churchill visited Baldwin in his room at the House of Commons. They talked about Davidson,[3] the party manager. There was a strong movement against him, and Churchill told Baldwin that Davidson would have to be abandoned – he had become a focus of unpopularity. Baldwin told Churchill there was nobody more unpopular than himself. The difficulty of carrying Churchill, said Baldwin, was one of the main reasons for losing the election.

That conversation ended their association until after Churchill had himself become Prime Minister. Then, with that magnanimity of his, Churchill met

---

[1] Churchill responded in a handwritten note on this document: 'Thank you for your letter which I am studying.'

[2] Stanley Morison, 1889–1967. Editor, *The Fleuron*, 1926–30; *Times Literary Supplement*, 1945–7. Senior Fellow, Royal College of Art, 1950.

[3] John Colin Campbell Davidson, 1889–1970. Called to the Bar, Middle Temple, 1913. MP (Union.) for Hemel Hempstead Div. of Hertfordshire, 1920–3, 1924–37. Parliamentary Private Secretary to Leader of House of Commons, 1920–1; to President of the Board of Trade, 1921–2; to Mr Bonar Law, 1922–3. Chancellor of the Duchy of Lancaster, 1923–4, 1931–7. Parliamentary Secretary to the Admiralty, 1924–7. Chairman, Conservative Party, 1927–30. PC, 1928.

Baldwin again and established friendly relations with him. They lunched and dined together. And, when nearly everybody else was ready to forget Baldwin, Churchill unveiled a memorial to him. He was almost alone.

Walter Fletcher[1] to Winston S. Churchill
(Churchill papers, 2/114)

8 May 1951

Dear Mr Churchill,

I am venturing to send you the attached notes in connection with Thursday's debate, which unfortunately I shall not be able to attend. I also attach an extract from a letter from Washington, which shows that MacArthur has been fostering, even to the extent of subsidy, the export of vital war material, including manufactured goods, to China, which makes American reflections on us, somewhat hollow.

The American Consul-General's[2] denial this morning of MacArthur's quotation about oil from Hongkong to China, should also be noted.

The shipment of rubber from Malaya has been known to the Government for a long time, and I can see no reason why shipments to China should not be prohibited altogether. There is little difference between that and the 2,500 tons a month, and in any case, China can import freely from Indonesia and Ceylon if she wants to, until the Anti-Communist powers are willing to institute a real blockade by active intervention in the stopping of all ships. As long as Indonesia, Ceylon and part of India are willing – and they have stated so at recent War Material Conferences – to sell and ship to China, Russia and satellite states, no effective action from sources of origin of raw materials can take place, but this is not necessarily a reason for our continuing on the same course.

India as a supplier of manufactured goods is far more dangerous. Shipments from Europe – Holland and Belgium in particular – will also continue and trans-shipments of goods from this country can also not be dealt with by a simple Government prohibition of direct export to China or Hongkong.

The position of Hongkong is precarious and has only been left free from Communist attention from the mainland as long as China was getting what she wanted from or through Hongkong. *The Times* today is quite right in pointing out that Hongkong cannot blockade China, but China can blockade Hongkong. It is equally true that Japan cannot maintain her population and

---

[1] Walter Fletcher, 1892–1956. In business in East Africa, 1918–24. Travelled extensively in Far East, East Indies, Europe and US, 1924–39. MP (Cons.) for Bury, 1945–50; for Bury and Radcliffe, 1950–5.
[2] Walter Patrick McConaughy, Jr, 1908–2000. US Consul-General, Hong Kong, 1950–2. US Ambassador to Burma, 1957–9; to South Korea, 1959–61; to Pakistan, 1961–6; to the Republic of China, 1966–74.

her industries without commerce with China. The problem therefore seems to be – how far one can go in stopping vital munitions going through Hongkong, while allowing sufficient flow to render improbable either an open attack from the mainland or a Communist disrupted movement from within. If the supplies of food, water, etc, from the mainland are denied over-populated Hongkong, there must inevitably be serious trouble, the exact conditions which the Communists will seize upon.

The probable opening retaliatory move by China will be the arresting of British or American shipping. There have already been instances of this and it would only want one or two such cases, for the Marine – which can find plenty of freight elsewhere – to avoid this area, and this isolation of Hongkong would almost certainly lead to the maximum of trouble.

It is worth pointing out that both through Hongkong and Japan, America is obtaining large quantities of two important items for her munition programme; bristles for certain types of paint brushes, for which there is no substitute, and wood oil, and America continues to be a daily large-scale buyer of these articles in spite of her attacks on us.

Any serious trouble in Hongkong, and the ultimate disaster of its fall, will be felt at once in Malaya, Indo-China, etc, and would have a far greater effect than could ever be balanced by denying a not very great flow of essential war materials to China. The amount of rubber used, or likely to be used in the Korean campaign, is relatively low, fully 80% of the rubber going to China is being used for boots and shoes, as it is now the correct insignia of a 'comrade', to wear 'sneakers' or rubber-soled shoes. That is no reason for continuing the shipment of rubber, but is an explanation of why its consumption has gone up.

I am not pleading on behalf of traders or the commercial community, who can well look after themselves and in many cases have an unenviable record. Their interest, in any case, is quite secondary in times like this. As we have frequently asked the Government if they are going to hold Hongkong, and have received an affirmatory reply, we may be opening a flank if we ask for measures that would really jeopardise it.

Communism is a world movement and is organised as such. Quite recently Czecho-slovakian arms were being supplied to China against bristles and wood oil which were offered from Prague. Sales of munitions to neutral and satellite states, and to Russia itself, are therefore just as probably an aid to the Chinese war movement in Korea, as supplies in Hongkong, where the potential of manufacture is still very low. I believe, therefore, that the things to press for are:

1. Something like clear plan of operation, with all Departments participating, which from Attlee's and Shinwell's statements certainly has not existed up till now,
2. Co-ordination with America on both import and export programmes, including Japan, and covering also the indirect export to neutrals and other countries.

3. The utmost pressure by the Atlantic powers on countries which can wreck our plans, such as Indonesia, Ceylon and India.
4. A carefully calculated and controlled amount of entrepot trade, sufficient to keep Hongkong on its feet and counter-balance by valuable imports from China.

1. The Builders (about Mr Churchill)
2. The Man Who Called (Labour canvasser)
3. Think of Scotland.
4. Tax facts – 8½d. on beer
   2/9½ on cigarettes
   3/11¾d on toilet things
   4/8d on kitchen things
5. Queer quotes – 'A little of what you fancy' (Webb)
   Mr Strachey – so proud of the groundnuts scheme
   'We do not intend to take everything away from everybody – not immediately, that is' (Shinwell).[1]

Anthony Eden to Winston S. Churchill
(*Churchill papers, 2/126*)

9 May 1951

My dear Winston,

PERSIAN OIL

Thank you so much for sending me Simon's letter,[2] at which I must confess I was considerably amused. The decision to take the issue to the League was made in Simon's absence and nobody complained more loudly than he did when he returned. However, it must be admitted that having made every kind of difficulty he advocated the case brilliantly at Geneva. No doubt poor Simon has forgotten all this, and anyway it does not matter very much.

I do not really think that there is much to be gained by making comparisons with that period, for the Russians of course would block any United Nations action and use the discussions for their own purposes.

---

[1] Churchill responded on May 12: 'Thank you for your letter and enclosures of May 8. They were of considerable assistance to me in preparing my speech, and I am so much obliged to you for the trouble you took.'
[2] Reproduced above (pp. 2061–2).

Winston S. Churchill: speech
(Hansard)

10 May 1951   House of Commons

EXPORTS TO CHINA

I hope the Committee will forgive me if I try to look at this topic in its general setting. I am quite sure that justice cannot be done to it in any other way. In November 1949 I was in favour of the recognition of Communist China, provided that it was *de facto* and not *de jure*, or as it would probably be called among the old-school-tie-brigade of the party opposite, '*day yuri*', and provided that it could be brought about as a joint policy with the United States and the Dominions.

The United States had largely disinterested themselves in the civil war in China, and Chiang Kai-shek, who used to be paraded to me in those bygone days of the war as the champion of the new Asia, was being driven off the mainland. I could see no reason why, if we had diplomatic relations with Communist Russia, Communist Poland and other countries inside the Iron Curtain, we could not have them with China. Recognition does not mean approval. One has to recognize and deal with all sorts of things in this world as they come along. After all, vaccination is undoubtedly a definite recognition of smallpox. Certainly I think that it would be very foolish, in ordinary circumstances, not to keep necessary contacts with countries with whom one is not at war.

However, a little later, the Government recognized Communist China, not only *de facto* but *de jure*, and they recognized it as an isolated act, without agreement with the United States or joint action with the Dominions. The date was oddly chosen. I am told that it was three days before the Colombo Conference of Commonwealth Foreign Secretaries. One would have thought that it was a matter that might have been talked over there. The response of the Chinese Communists was very surly. They took all they could get from our recognition and gave nothing in return. They did not even recognize us. The United States were much offended by our isolated action, and that is how that part of the story ends.

Presently, the situation in the Far East was transformed and every thing was sharpened by the Communist aggression in Korea, and was presently brought to a much more serious and intense position by the Chinese intervention. When the United Nations definitely passed the resolution, to which His Majesty's Government assented, branding China as an aggressor, we were left in an uncomfortable and illogical position of having diplomatic relations with a Chinese Government formally censured by the United Nations, and which was engaged in attacking United States soldiers – United Nations soldiers – and also our own small contingent in Korea.

There is no doubt that the maintenance of our relationship with Red China had been and has been totally devoid of advantages to us or to the United Nations, and that it became a reproach against us in wide circles in America. This made a bad foundation between us for discussion with the United States about all the vexing questions of trading with the enemy – as the Chinese Communists had undoubtedly become. Of course, it is the first interest of Britain and of Europe, and also, I believe, of the United States, to make some kind of defence front against the at present overwhelming Soviet power on the European Continent, and all of us on both sides of the House saw good and cogent arguments for our not getting too deeply involved in Korea, still less in China.

We on this side, without taking academic views about the 38th Parallel, were most anxious that the United Nations forces should not go beyond the waist or narrow part of the peninsula and should keep a broad no-man's-land between their own front and the Yalu River. It did not seem wise to broaden the front by another 200 or 300 miles by emerging from the narrow part of the Korean Peninsula into this much expanded area. As it was the policy of the United Nations and of the United States not to enter Chinese territory nor even to bomb beyond the frontier line, it seemed especially dangerous to advance close up to that frontier line. It is always dangerous in war to march or walk close up to a wall without being allowed to look over the other side and see what is going on there, and act against it if necessary.

Therefore, personally, not having an opportunity of obtaining any technical information, I wanted to stop at the waist and have a no-man's-land. I think that there was pretty general agreement on that in the House. However, General MacArthur's forces became heavily involved on a much wider front far beyond the waist, and a series of heavy Chinese counter-attacks were delivered. War was in fact begun on a considerable scale between the United Nations and China without any formal declaration of war on either side; and that is the position that exists today with ever-intensifying gravity.

There is no doubt that the Chinese Communist Government is waging war at Russian instigation and with powerful Soviet aid in weapons and supplies against the troops of the United Nations. Our recognition and maintenance of diplomatic relations with China has undoubtedly been a cause of misunderstanding with the United States, and has made more difficult the discussion of our other joint problems with them in the Far East. I cannot believe that a policy of appeasement to Chinese Communist aggression will bring about peace with Red China. On the contrary, any form of weakness or indecision or division among the anti-Communist forces will only prolong the fighting and increase its scale. I have ventured to deal with these rather wider aspects this afternoon in order to place the matter objectively before the Committee.

I now wish to consider the position of the United States. I always watch the hon. Gentlemen below the Gangway opposite, as that is where the weather comes from. I have an advantage over the Foreign Secretary in being able to keep them directly under my view, whereas if he were to keep his head turned it might well be thought that he was paying them undue attention. We cannot watch and listen to them without deriving the impression that their sympathies are, on the whole, more with Red China than with the United States. But Red China has been branded as an aggressor by the United Nations with the full assent of the present Socialist Government.

Mr Sydney Silverman (Nelson and Colne): Not with their full assent.

Mr Churchill: Even those Ministers who have resigned were members of the Government at the time that decision was taken.

We now know that the Communists are killing United Nations soldiers, and our soldiers. We know that they have established a reign of terror in China, with horrible executions and mob butcheries and a merciless purge characteristic of Communist tyranny wherever it is applied, especially in the transitional stages, all over the world. We ought not, I say, to have any sympathies with Red China, and the more they are expressed and manifested in this House the more harm is done to our relations with the United States. After all, the United States are doing nineteen-twentieths of the work and suffering losses of fifty and sixty to one compared to us. We must try to understand their position.

We really cannot get through life either as individuals or as a State, without trying to put ourselves in the position of others with whom we come in contact and have to deal. The United States have lost nearly 70,000 men, killed, wounded and missing. We know how we feel about the Gloucesters,[1] and that should enable us to measure the feelings of people in the United States, in many cities, towns and villages there, when the news comes in of some one who has lost a dear one in the fighting overseas. Feelings are tense, very dangerous to distress or to disturb. We can measure these American feelings by our own. They also know that they are bearing virtually the whole weight of the Korean war.

Look also at all the money they have given to Europe. Look at the money they have lent or given to our country during the period of Socialist rule. I doubt whether we should have had the Utopia which we enjoy without their aid. Where should we all be without their assistance in Europe? Free Europe is quite incapable of defending itself, and must remain so for several years whatever we do. These considerations must be kept in our minds when we discuss these matters of trade which I consider minor matters, and the different points of friction between us and the United States. What would be our position in this island if Western Europe were overrun as it would be –

---

[1] On 22 Apr. 1951, during the Battle of Imjin River in Korea, 1st Battalion the Gloucestershire Rgt was attacked by overwhelmingly superior Chinese forces. Though cut off, suffering heavy casualties and running short of ammunition, water and supplies, the battalion held out for four days and nights before making a final stand. Only 46 officers and men out of a total of 750 managed to fight their way back to the British lines; the remainder were killed or captured.

Mr Harold Davies (Leek): If we went to war with China.

Mr Churchill: The hon. Member really must learn to cultivate a sense of proportion in the matter. It is not a matter of whether there is a war with China or not but whether there is a rift between Britain and the United States or not. That is the thought that haunts me, and I hope and trust that it will be considered everywhere else. What would be our position, I say, if Europe were overrun, as it would be but for the immense American ascendency in the atomic bomb, and the deterrent effect, not necessarily upon the Russians but upon the Communist Kremlin regime, of this tremendous weapon? The fact that we are bitterly divided and absorbed in party strife, and kept month after month –

Mr Ellis Smith[1] (Stoke-on-Trent, South): So is America.

Mr Churchill: Quite true, but they have at any rate a fixed date for their elections. To exist month by month in such an electioneering atmosphere as this may provide many topics to fill the public mind and what is left of the newspapers, but our external dangers do not diminish meanwhile; they grow continually. It is said that we are getting stronger, but to get stronger does not necessarily mean that we are getting safer. It is only when we are strong enough that safety is achieved; and the period of the most acute danger might well arise just before we were strong enough. I hope that may be pondered upon because it is a very potent and relevant factor.

Our great danger now is in pursuing a policy of girding at the United States and giving them the impression that they are left to do all the work, while we pull at their coat tails and read them moral lessons in statecraft and about the love we all ought to have for China. I would plead in the very short time I beg leave to keep the House this afternoon – because our time is very limited – for the sense of proportion – (Hon. Members: 'Hear, hear'.) – yes, on the grounds of national safety and even of survival.

I say that we must think not only of ourselves; we must think of our friends in Europe; of the Norwegians, the Danes, the Dutch, the Belgians, the French and others who lie still nearer to the Soviet Power with its mighty armies and satellite States. Their plight is even worse than ours. We, at least, have the Channel, although even that as a means of safety would, without air superiority, soon depart; and air superiority cannot be obtained by us without the fullest aid from the United States. Therefore I say that on every ground, national, European and international, we should allow no minor matters – even if we feel keenly about them – to stand in the way of the fullest, closest intimacy, accord and association of the United States.

I felt bound to raise these matters, these broader considerations, because we really cannot discuss the intimate and complicated matters which have brought about this debate without holding foremost in our minds all the time

---

[1] Ellis Smith, 1896–1969. Engineer's pattern maker. On active service, 1914–18 (Machine Gun Corps, Tank Corps). MP (Lab.) for Stoke-on-Trent, 1935–66. Parliamentary Secretary, Board of Trade, 1945–6. General President, United Pattern Makers Association, 1946–50, 1958–64.

the overwhelming issues. If the Government so conducts our affairs that we become a cause of diminishing American help for Britain and for Europe, and stimulate the sentiment for isolation which has powerful exponents in the United States, they might well become primarily responsible, not only for our ruin, but for that of the whole of the free world. It is on this basis, and only on this basis, that I venture to examine the details, or some of the details, or some of the aspects of the exports to Communist China which are the cause of the debate – (Hon. Members: 'Hear, hear'.) That is not, I hope, a reproach against me for having placed the matter in its proper setting.

These questions of raw materials and of trading with the enemy were brought prominently before us by the resignation of the three Ministers a fortnight ago. When the resigning Ministers threw the blame for raw material shortages in Britain upon the United States, the Americans immediately were greatly stimulated in making their counter-charge that we, while still recognizing the enemy and killing them by the thousand in the battles that were taking place, were making profits directly or indirectly out of commerce with them. This tangled question of the supplies of what are called strategic materials to Red China from Great Britain and the Commonwealth and our tropical Colonies is of course only part of the subject, much of which lies in spheres and forms, which are beyond our control. Red China is not the only place and Hong Kong is not the only channel.

Some months ago I complained of the export of high-grade war manufactures, and even machines and machine-tools, to Russia or to its satellites. The Government denied the charge, but took steps to stop it. Whether those steps have been successful I cannot pronounce, nor could we even in a much longer debate reach any definite conclusions here. But even on the direct point of strategic materials being sent by us to China, through Hong Kong or by other routes, it would be difficult this afternoon to reach plain and final conclusions. The statements made by the Minister of Defence, and after him by the Prime Minister, created, I am sure I am right in saying, general astonishment that these Ministers, whose responsibility in the matter is outstanding, were not better informed. It seemed typical of the way in which our affairs are conducted. It was refreshing on Monday to listen to what seemed at first to be a much more precise statement form the new President of the Board of Trade (Sir Hartley Shawcross). Here at least there seemed to be evidence of the workings of a clear-cut mind which had been, in the last week or so, turned upon the problem, or upon his brief of the subject.

So far as the regions covered by the figures given by the right hon. and learned Gentleman are concerned the general impression was that the scale of these transactions from the United Kingdom was small, and that there could be no ground for saying that the Chinese have received important assistance from the United Kingdom with the approval of His Majesty's Government. The exports from the United Kingdom are indeed petty, and the right hon.

and learned Gentleman the President of the Board of Trade was right in saying that it is wrong to suppose that they have been a factor of any significance in the Korean campaign.

We were surprised, however, that he confined his lengthy, well-drafted statement to the exports from the United Kingdom and only mentioned, by reference to the previous answer by the Under-Secretary of State for the Colonies,[1] the exports of rubber from Malaya. This is the gravamen of the whole dispute. 'Exports of rubber from the Federated States of Malaya and Singapore to China', said the Under-Secretary on 12 April, 'amounted in all to 77,000 tons in 1950, and are estimated to amount to 46,000 tons' – I am speaking in round numbers – 'in the first quarter of 1951.' Up till 9 April therefore the Government have taken no effective action in this matter and the exports in the first quarter of the present year show an immense and significant increase on what took place last year; 46,000 tons a quarter – (Hon Members: 'That is right.') – Is that right? Thank you very much. That is to say two-an-a-half times the annual rate of 1950. That is a very remarkable, substantial, significant advance at this time when matters are becoming more and more tense, serious and critical.

The right hon. and learned Gentleman – I shall have to ascertain the right hon. Gentleman's wish as to whether I continue to insert the complimentary and formal token 'learned', it will be just as he likes, but I am doing it for today, anyhow – the right hon. and learned Gentleman ended his statement by saying that the Government had from 9 April announced their intention, and that of the Governments of the Federation of Malaya and Singapore, to control exports of rubber down to the estimated civilian requirements of China, namely, about 2,500 tons a month.

I raised the point of how the Government could be sure that these 2,500 tons a month would be solely devoted to civilian purposes, considering that in time of war any Government can commandeer for military purposes all civilian supplies. The right hon. and learned Gentleman admitted that it was 'quite difficult' – that was his expression – to ensure that these limited rubber supplies were not being misapplied. Anyhow, on the Government's own figures, China has already had in the first quarter of this year, imports, approved formally and officially by us, of 45,000 tons; or half as much again as would be the full civilian Chinese ration, as calculated by the Government, for the whole year.

Mr Blackburn (Birmingham, Northfield): Would the right hon. Gentleman forgive me for one moment?

Mr Churchill: I thought we were on the same side of the line.

Mr Blackburn: The position is a little worse than that, because these figures, as I have been informed by the Colonial Office this morning, are exclusive of

---

[1] Thomas Fotheringham Cook, 1908–52. MP (Lab.) for Dundee, 1945–50; for East Dundee, 1950–2. Parliamentary Under-Secretary of State, Colonial Office, 1950–1.

exports to Hong Kong, which in effect go to China, and therefore, the figure may be approximately double.

Mr Churchill: That is a new and very valuable fact of which I was not aware and I trust that it will be dealt with by the right hon. and learned Gentleman when he speaks in this debate.

Mr Harold Davies *rose* –

Mr Churchill: No –

Mr Ellis Smith: He is not on the right hon. Gentleman's side.

Mr Churchill: The hon. Member for Leek (Mr Harold Davies) will have a chance later.

If that is so, that will have altered my argument, because we were, in fact, no doubt unwittingly, misled by the President of the Board of Trade the other day. At any rate, my argument may be doubled in strength by the figures, if they are right, but it is not in any way vitiated by the figures I have quoted which show that the Chinese have already had half as much again of what the Government consider is their full civilian ration for the whole year.

The question we have to consider today in this sphere, is whether it is worth while to go on nagging, and haggling, and higgling with the United States over a lot of details, and extremely complex details, and making little progress and creating ill-will out of all proportion to any advantages gained by us. The United States have a valid complaint on the admitted fact that rubber is an indisputable strategic material. We ought not to be exporting any rubber to China at all, and we suggest on this side of the Committee to the Government, and to the Foreign Secretary, who has a direct responsibility in this matter, that as far as they have it in their power they should stop at once and completely all further export of rubber to China. If there is smuggling, we should do our best to prevent it, and we ought not ourselves to be in the position of agreeing that any rubber should be sent at the present time to Red China.

Surely this would be a simple and straightforward course? It is not so much for the actual facts that I am concerned, but for the consequences. To stop it abruptly and firmly and decisively would clear the air and it would make possible, and perhaps fruitful, the far more complicated discussions about the further steps that are necessary to control any trade which we and the Americans may have with China. It would be a step that everybody could understand, and it might well be the prelude to a whole-hearted agreement with the United States in this sphere, which causes offence and anger far beyond its actual military importance.

I hope we are not going to have another back-biting controversy with the United States about whether any goods are going from Japan into China with their consent.

Hon. Members Oh.

Mr Harold Davies *rose* –

Mr Churchill: Perhaps I am going to use the very argument of which the hon. Gentleman is thinking. Anyhow, it is my show at the moment. It might be a very good debating point, if there were really no division between the two sides of the Committee on the matter, here this afternoon, or on some other occasion – a very good debating point – and it is a point which might well be used between Governments if we were bearing an equal burden with the United States – (Hon. Members: 'Oh'.) – an equal burden in the war. But, in the present circumstances, is it really sensible –

Mr Poole (Birmingham, Perry Barr):[1] Do not write down your own country all the time.

Mr Churchill: Will the hon. Member yell it out again?

Mr Poole: I suggested that the right hon. Gentleman should not so continuously write down his own country.

Mr Churchill: There is no better way of writing down your own country than to make boastful and untruthful statements about facts which are known to all. There is no doubt or question of the proportions of the troops who are involved or of the losses which are being suffered in the Korean War. The hon. Member should not put out his hand like that; does he accept what I say? Really, the idea that we can uphold the prestige and standard of our country by adopting positions which are entirely divorced from actual and well-known facts is one of those which I think hon. Members above the Gangway opposite should endeavour to rise above.

I say it would be a great pity to get drawn into this discussion with the United States in detail at the present time and in the present atmosphere, irritating them about minor things, making ineffective repartees. That is not what we should do now when our life and future depend upon their aiding the Atlantic Powers in Europe. Neither let us be baffled by the local difficulties about Hong Kong. I have no doubt they can be solved by measures agreed upon with the United States. Together we have the command of the sea and of the air.

As to a direct attack by the Chinese upon Hong Kong, it must, of course, be resisted by force of arms. We have every sympathy with our fellow-subjects in Hong Kong, but the greatest disservice that we could do them would be to allow a rift to open between us and the United States as a result of our bowing to Communist threats and blackmail.

Let me make this passing observation. Of course, it is always very dangerous, and never more so than at the present time, to predict anything that may happen in the future. But in my view, a Soviet attack will not arise because of an incident. An incident may be a pretext, but the moment will be fixed by the result of long, cold calculations, or miscalculations, and among the factors which will play a potent part of the season of the year, including harvest time, will be extremely important. I do not, therefore, consider that the question of

---

[1] Cecil Charles Poole, 1902–56. MP (Lab.) for Lichfield Div. of Staffordshire, 1938–50; for Perry Barr Div. of Birmingham, 1950–5.

our doing our duty by Hong Kong should be overclouded by all the statements that may be made that this will bring on a general war. Nobody knows what will bring on a general war except those who have the supreme power in the Kremlin.

Our advice to the Government is to stop rubber entirely now and to reach an agreement with the United States on the general question of trade with China in a spirit which will make the United States feel that their cause is our cause, and that we mean at all costs to be good friends and allies. I read with emotion the testimony of General Marshall before the Senate Committee – (*Interruption.*) The right hon. Gentleman had better take a back seat; well, he has done so.

The Minister of Defence (Mr Shinwell) *rose* –

Mr Churchill: It is quite right that the right hon. Gentleman should take a back seat. He made a statement the other day about no appeasement and so on. I was glad to read it, but he had spoiled it all beforehand by the remark he made at a most disturbing moment in the United States, that now, perhaps, things will go better in Korea, once General MacArthur had been dismissed. If anything –

Mr Shinwell *rose* –

Hon. Members: Withdraw.

Mr Churchill: Hon Members will not frighten me by their yelling. If anything could at that time have got about 50 million Americans furious with him, and with the Government for whom he spoke, it would have been to use language like that. I am very glad that he tried to undo the harm he did by making his speech against appeasement.

Mr Shinwell: The right hon. Gentleman has just asserted that I declared that the dismissal of General MacArthur should be brought about because it would be of advantage to us. (Hon Members: 'No'.) Let me tell the right hon. Gentleman that the statement which he has just made, in which he alleges that I made that statement about General MacArthur, is utterly false, and I challenge the right hon. Gentleman to produce the written evidence or withdraw. I challenge him in this House to produce the written evidence that I made a statement similar to what he has just said.

Mr Churchill: I understood, from what was reported in the Press –

Mr Shinwell: Which Press?

Mr Churchill: – that the right hon. Gentleman said that perhaps things will now go better in Korea since General MacArthur had been removed.

Mr Shinwell: Let me tell the right hon. Gentleman that I never made any such statement. I challenge him to produce that statement.

Hon Members: Withdraw.

Mr Churchill: No, I would not think of withdrawing. I will produce the newspaper report on which I base myself. I have not got it in my notes at the moment, but I will get it. I thought it a most unfortunate statement.

Mr Shinwell: I never made that statement.

Mr Churchill: We shall be very glad to hear what was the statement which the right hon. Gentleman actually made. It is always part of the tactics to throw the blame on to the Press, and so on. However, I will produce the Press reports which I read on the subject, and I think they were pretty widely noted. Of course, nobody wishes to accuse the Minister of Defence of crimes which he has not committed.

Mr Shinwell *rose* –

Hon Members: Sit down.

Mr Shinwell: I shall not sit down. May I tell the right hon. Gentleman that he has made a most false statement about me in this House, and that he has no right to make such statements about Ministers?

Mr Churchill: Do not be so nervous about it.

Mr Shinwell: I am not nervous about it. (*Laughter.*) You should be ashamed of yourself. The right hon. Gentleman has done more harm to this country than anyone.

Mr Churchill: Very helpful, but it is not the right hon. Gentleman who would have any right to teach me my conduct. However, I am sorry to see him so infuriated. The French have a saying that it is only the truth that wounds. I hope that is not the case, because no one would be more pleased than I to find him not guilty on this occasion.

May I now return to the few words I have still to say to the House. Our advice to the Government is to stop the export of rubber to China entirely now, and to reach a general agreement in the favourable atmosphere which this step would create in the United States. I read with emotion the testimony of General Marshall before the Senate Committee. This great world statesman has proved himself to be one of the leading figures in our life since the Great War. He has spoken with the utmost consideration for our point of view. In him, in General Omar Bradley, and in General Eisenhower here in Europe are men in whose judgment on the world scene we may safely repose the fullest confidence. They are the members or instruments –

An Hon. Member: What about the Admiral?

Mr Paton (Norwich, North): What about Admiral Fechteler?

Mr Churchill: I try to give consideration to interruptions however irrelevant, and, sometimes, however foolish, but I really cannot be asked such a question as that. I have a great respect for Admiral Fechteler, but I do not think he was put in the right place, and it may be that my view on that, will eventually prevail.

These men are the members or instruments of President Truman's administration who have enabled him to take the valiant stand he has against the Communist menace, and to lead the great Republic to the rescue of the free world from mortal peril. It is the duty of His Majesty's Government so to act as to prove, beyond all doubt or question, that we are good and faithful comrades of the American democracy, and will stand with them, whatever may happen, as brothers in arms.

Jo Sturdee to Winston S. Churchill
(Churchill papers, 4/362)

10 May 1951

YALTA CONFERENCE

The following are some details which have occurred to me, which may or may not be of use. I have told Mr Kelly about some of them, and others occur to me now:

1. The story about the plane crashing is not quite right as it stands at the moment. You took with you in your own plane to Malta Mr Martin, Commander Thompson, two young ladies and one detective of your own staff. You had of course other VIPs with you in the plane. Mr Rowan and the rest of your personal staff were to fly with other people going to the Yalta Conference straight to Saki, via Naples, in two planes. It was one of these planes that crashed. Three of the crew and two passengers I think survived.

2. About Saki. Do you wish to mention the fact that about 2 months (I think) beforehand a contingent of RAF men under Group Captain S . . . (?) had gone out to make everything ready to handle the large number of planes and people who would be arriving. The airfield was under deep snow. Runways and tents and accommodation had to be prepared and erected. . . . I can remember after a long and cold flight from Naples how welcome it was to go into one of these large long tents, all spick and span with a table down the centre with white tablecloths and laden with food – Duckboards on the ground. We had a good meal – all American tinned food as far as I can remember. You will remember that after you and the President had inspected the Guard of Honour you all went into an elaborate marquee for a drink and refreshments.

3. About the drive from Saki to your villa at Yalta, do you wish to mention about the soldiers, some of them women, who lined the whole route, shoulder to shoulder in villages and over bridges and mountain passes and wider apart elsewhere. I think Lord Moran drove with you in the car, (? and Mr Martin?) but I am not sure. You will remember it was all bleak and cold until you got to the other side of the mountains, then it became brilliant, warmer and almost sub-tropical. I do not think the journey lasted more than seven hours altogether.

4. About the accommodation at Yalta. With you in the Vorontsov chateau at Alupka were Mrs Oliver, Mr Eden, Sir Alexander Cadogan, the Chiefs of Staff (Lord Alanbrooke, Sir Andrew Cunningham and Lord Portal), Lord Ismay, Lord Moran, Sir Archibald Clark Kerr and others. Apart from your

bathroom there was one bathroom between the rest and one 'washroom' with three sinks and cold water – there was always a long queue! The sleeping accommodation for the others was separated from your private rooms by the many large reception rooms.

Those not accommodated in the Vorontsov Villa slept in two sanatoria, both about 20 minutes drive away. Five or size had to sleep in each room, and the sanitary arrangements were primitive. Some quite high-ranking officers lived like this, but nobody minded.

You will remember that somebody happened to remark that there was no lemon-peel for the cocktails at your villa. The next day a lemon tree, in a large tub and laden with lemons, appeared.

The range of mountains just behind the villa was called I think the Yaila mountains, and I was told that the peak nearest the villa was the highest in the Crimea. The villa was built in 1837 for Prince Vorontsov for 3 million rubles (1½ million dollars), from the plans of the English architect, Blore,[1] who adopted a combination of the Gothic and Moorish styles. You will remember the carved white lions and the beautiful park containing many rare subtropical plants and cypresses, including two in the courtyard planted by Potemkin. Vorontsov was at various times Governor of Odessa, Viceroy of the Caucasus and Russian Ambassador to the Court of St James. The area had only been evacuated by the Germans ten months previously, and the buildings used to accommodate the delegations were a complete shambles a month before your arrival. 1,500 men had been hurriedly getting things ready – putting in windows and installing the furniture and stores from Moscow. You will remember Mr Ershov was in charge of your villa and your comforts, as he had been in Moscow. I think you also had the same Russian bodyguard as you had had before in Moscow – that enormous man. We were warned that the area had not been completely cleared of mines, but the grounds of your villa were of course made quite safe. Russian guards of course patrolled all the time.

4. You mention Pavlov,[2] but not your own interpreters – Major Birse[3] and

---

[1] Edward Blore, 1787–1879. Surveyor of Fabric of Westminster Abbey, 1826. Completed Buckingham Palace, taking over from John Nash, 1847–50. FRS, 1841.

[2] Vladimir Pavlov, 1921–93. Ukrainian Soviet diplomat and translator. Skilled in German, English, Spanish and French. Chief Interpreter, Soviet Foreign Ministry, 1939. First Counsellor with rank of Ambassador to Soviet representative in Berlin, 1939, 1940. In Aug. 1939, participated as translator in negotiation between Soviet Foreign Minister Molotov and German Foreign Minister Joachim von Ribbentrop that resulted in the so-called German–Soviet Non-Aggression Agreement (Ribbentrop–Molotov Pact). Official translator for negotiations between Molotov and Hitler in Berlin, Nov. 1940. Interpreter and Director, Central European Div., Soviet Foreign Ministry in Moscow, in charge of ministerial analysis and evaluation of Anglo-Soviet relations, from Dec. 1940. Took part in most inter-Allied war conferences, 1942–5, translating in talks between Stalin, Churchill and Roosevelt at Teheran (1943), Yalta (1945) and Potsdam (1945) conferences. Soviet delegate to founding conference of UN in San Francisco, 1945. After the war, employed as one of the Soviet representatives in London and in the late 1940s as a Counsellor at the Soviet Embassy in Paris. Soviet delegate to Four Power Conference of Foreign Ministers in Paris, 1949.

[3] Arthur Herbert Birse, 1889–1967. A British subject, born in St Petersburg and raised in Russia.

Major Theakstone.[1]

5. President Roosevelt and the American delegation were accommodated at Alushta, the former in the villa Livadia which had formerly belonged to Tsar Nicolas II.

6. Averell Harriman and Admiral Healy were also with the President.

7. Your two private secretaries, Mr Martin and Mr Rowan (now Sir Leslie) were at Yalta. Also you had your Map Room, under Captain Pim,[2] there. The Map Room had gone in the *Franconia* beforehand. Also, in the FO delegation was Mr Jebb, now Sir Gladwyn, and Mr Pierson Dixon.[3]

8. About Ibn Saud, you might like to see the attached list of the people who accompanied him.

9. Another detail. The British had sent four or five (I think) Humber limousines, by the *Franconia*, to help with the transport between the various villas and sanatoria. They were left behind for the Russians – anyway they were battered after the rough roads there.

10. I remember that when President Roosevelt and Marshal Stalin came to dine with you at the Vorontsov Villa the members of the British delegation assembled in the hall to watch the arrivals and departures. When they left I remember you called for 'Three Cheers for Marshal Stalin', to which we all responded. Several hours before Marshal Stalin was due to arrive a squad of Russian soldiers came to the villa. They locked the doors each side of the rooms which were going to be used for dinner and reception and would let no one enter. They then made a most thorough search of the rooms, under tables and behind walls, etc. Guards were then placed on all the doors to make sure that no one went in. This meant that everyone had to go outside to get from your rooms and office to their own rooms.

After the Revolution of 1917, left Russia and became a banker in Amsterdam and London. Registered with Officers' Reserve, 1939. Transferred from Cairo to Moscow, 1941; when the FO interpreter on whom Churchill normally relied fell ill, Birse was asked to take his place at Churchill's first meeting with Stalin. After the war, Birse went back to banking.

[1] Louis Marguarde Theakstone. British interpreter to the secretariat, CCS.

[2] Richard Pike Pim, 1900–87. Served in RNVR, 1914–18. Cdr, RNVR Ulster Div., 1929. Joined Royal Irish Constabulary, 1921. Asst Secretary, Ministry of Home Affairs, Northern Ireland, 1935. In charge of Churchill's War Room at the Admiralty, 1939–40, at Downing Street, No. 10 Annexe, and on Churchill's wartime travels from Newfoundland in 1941 to Potsdam in 1945. Knighted, 1945. Inspector-General, Royal Ulster Constabulary, 1945–61. Council Member, Winston Churchill Memorial Trust, 1965–9.

[3] Pierson John Dixon, 1904–65. Principal Private Secretary to Foreign Secretary, 1943–8. CB, 1948. Ambassador to Czechoslovakia, 1948–50. KCMG, 1950. Deputy Under-Secretary of State, FO, 1950–4. Permanent Representative to UN, 1954–60. GCMG, 1957. Ambassador to France, 1960–4.

May 1951

Winston S. Churchill to Lord Simon
(*Churchill papers, 2/126*)

13 May 1951

My dear John,

I have now had an opportunity of studying your interesting notes[1] on the Persian Oil question and fully agree that prompt actions in 1932 are in marked contrast to the hesitancy of Mr Morrison. I have shown your letter to some of my colleagues and we shall certainly keep this aspect of the matter in mind as the situation develops and is debated.

There is however one important distinction to be drawn, I think, between an Appeal to the old League of Nations and one to the United Nations of today. Soviet Russia would almost certainly prevent any effective action, if not indeed any discussion, and she would undoubtedly use the machinery of Lake Success in every possible way that might be to her own advantage.

Winston S. Churchill to Sir Arthur Salter
(*Churchill papers, 2/117*)

14 May 1951

My dear Salter,

Thank you for the very valuable notes you gave me last week for my speech on the exports to China. They were of great assistance, and I am so much obliged to you.

Somerset de Chair to Winston S. Churchill
(*Churchill papers, 2/168*)

16 May 1951

Dear Mr Churchill,

I hope it will save you a little trouble if I send you my copy of John Buchan's[2] *Caesar* which you wanted to read. It is very sketchy by comparison with the Commentaries but fills in the period you were enquiring about, after Pompey's death, notably Caesar's defeat of Cato at Utica. You will see on Page 162 what Buchan says about the books on the Alexandrine, African and Spanish wars.

---

[1] Reproduced above (pp. 2061–2).

[2] John Buchan, 1875–1940. Educated at University of Glasgow. Director of Information for Lord Beaverbrook, 1917–18. MP (Union.) for the Scottish Universities, 1927–35. Lord High Commissioner of the Church of Scotland, 1933–4. Baron Tweedsmuir of Elsfield, 1935. Governor-General of Canada, 1935–40. Wrote over 80 books of non-fiction and fiction; considered one of Scotland's finest novelists.

I also enclose a copy of Napoleon's Memoirs in which you expressed an interest; and it will show you the sort of maps which will be provided for Caesar; a point which you raised. In practice, 'rescuing Caesar from the classroom' was a less complex operation than rescuing Napoleon from St Helens.

Lord Simon to Winston S. Churchill
(*Churchill papers, 2/126*)[1]

17 May 1951

My dear Winston,

PERSIAN OIL

Thank you for your letter. I agree that appeal to the United Nations would not avail; what I had in mind was appeal to the <u>International Court at The Hague</u>. The prompt threat of this might have brought out the legal point, which has nothing to do with the abstract right of Persia to nationalize. It arises from Persia's contract with the Oil Company that <u>she would not attempt to interfere</u> with the current concession. If the FO had taken this stand clearly and at once, he might have got the strong support of American lawyers and statesmen. As it is, with Russia so close and claiming a sphere of influence in Northern Persia the oil may end in a blaze.

Winston S. Churchill: speech
('*Winston S. Churchill, His Complete Speeches*', *volume 8, pages 8207–14*)

18 May 1951　　　　　　　Scottish Unionist Association Annual Conference
　　　　　　　　　　　　　　　　　　　　　　　　　　　　　Glasgow

THE CONSERVATIVE CASE

It is a year almost to a day since we met at Edinburgh, and I wish indeed that I could tell you that our affairs have improved since either at home or abroad. The Communist aggression in Korea was promptly and valiantly resisted by President Truman and the United States acting with the United Nations, of whom we are part, and under their authority fighting has been going on for nearly a year. It would not have been right for us to send more than a small force to Korea, but we may all be proud of the manner in which it has distinguished itself. The United States have borne nineteen-twentieths of the burden, and have suffered nearly 70,000 casualties. When we feel grief at our own losses, we ought to understand the keen feelings of the American

---

[1] This letter was handwritten.

people if they feel they are being reproached or hampered by weaker or less engaged allies.

The Americans are not only bearing the burden in the Far East but also are making heavy contributions in men, arms and money to the defence of Western Europe. Without their help there would be no hope of preventing the conquest and subjugation of all the free peoples of Europe by the immense Russian Communist armies and those of their satellite States which stand ready for action at any moment the order is given from Moscow. The presence of General Eisenhower in Europe at the head of such forces as the free peoples have so far been able to organize is a living pledge and symbol of the resolve of the American nation to use its measureless resources and its rapidly growing fleets and armies for the defence of civilization. Behind all this lies the dread and incalculable power which the United States possesses in the atomic bomb and it is this factor, fearful though it be, which alone gives us the hope of being able to form a front in Europe capable of deterring the Kremlin tyrants from further aggression there. Dark and tragic indeed is the picture which stares us in the face whenever we look up from our daily toil. The key to our safety and survival is of course our alliance and friendship with the United States.

I was shocked last week in the House of Commons to see how much anti-American feeling there was among the Left-wing Government supporters below the Gangway. They showed themselves definitely pro-Chinese, although it is the Chinese who are killing our men and the Americans who are helping us. This unhappy Government which itself rests on a minority vote at the last election and clings to office from day to day by a handful of votes, is hampered in dealing with our problems, even where it sees the light, by having at every stage to placate a section of its own followers and persuade or compel them by party discipline to come along with them in taking the necessary steps for the public safety. During all this last anxious and critical year abroad Mr Attlee's tactics have deliberately kept us in a state of party tension and protracted uncertainty at home. The General Election, he declares, will come at the moment which he chooses. Thus we are all compelled to be prepared from month to month and even week to week. Prolonged electioneering is not good for Britain. We have already had fifteen months of election fever. We have this Government without confidence in the country, trying to conduct all our grave and critical affairs, without a normal working majority in the House of Commons.

Parliamentary debate has become largely meaningless. The two great party machines grind up against each other in every village, every street, every town and city. Party strife is kept at its keenest point. This is a heavy cost to the ordinary life and daily business of the nation. Party interest and organization are magnified out of all proportion to national affairs. Everyone knows that the healthy, honest, clean thing to do would be for the Government to announce an early date for an appeal to the electorate. But the more it is plain that the Socialists have lost the confidence of the nation, the more tenaciously they cling to their offices. Mr Attlee bears an exceptional and by no means honourable responsibility for prolonging this hateful, costly uncertainty, and his party machine puts pressure upon the members of his party to toe the line, which has not been seen in modern British political history. Instead of trying to bring about or work towards a united nation, he does all he can to keep it bitterly divided by exploiting the narrow voting margin on which he lives, and placating his disreputable tail by acts of partisanship like steel nationalization, against which so large a majority was recorded at the General Election. I have borne a great deal of responsibility at one time or another in my life, but I am very glad never to have tried to lead this great country through its growing perils against the will of the British people in fear of their verdict.

The performance of the administration is incompetent in an unprecedented degree. 'We are witnessing,' I said a few weeks ago in the House of Commons, 'a process of the gradual education of those who ought to know best and have the power, but who have to reach agreement by an endless series of compromises among themselves and with their military advisers.' Since then we have had striking proof of the divisions made inside the Cabinet, and three Ministers – Mr Bevan, Mr Wilson and Mr Freeman – have resigned after stating their objections of one kind or another to the Government's defence programme and health policy. But while these Ministers have left the Government Mr Attlee still has to rely upon their votes and those of their friends to keep himself in office. What kind of defence policy and programme are we to expect if the Prime Minister has to carry with him at every step, men whose hearts are not convinced of the need for strong defence, and who have a deep-seated mistrust and jealousy of the United States, which they regard reproachfully as a successful exponent of the capitalist theory?

Sir Hartley Shawcross five years ago boasted: 'We are the masters now.' He has lately shown some signs of reformation and even talks about going back to the Bar. We shall place no obstacle in his path. A lesser figure, Mr Maurice Webb, the Minister of Food, has taken up his dictatorial style. We had a speech from him at Bradford on 6 May, in which he said: 'The Labour Party has got to understand that it is no longer a street-corner mob. It is a governing class of this country, and it has got to conduct itself like a ruling class. It has got to have the poise and self-assurance of the ruling class.'

I thought this was a revealing declaration. While I have always challenged the ridiculous claim that the Socialist Party have the credit for everything that has been done in Britain for the social progress of the British nation, I have never gone so far as to consider that they were until recently only a 'street-corner mob'. On the contrary I consider that the trade unionists, who are the backbone of all that commands respect in Socialist ranks, have, since their position was finally established by the Conservative Party seventy-five years ago, played an honourable and indeed indispensable part in the life of our country, and it is only Mr Webb's ignorance of our political history which leads him to use such an expression as 'street-corner mob' about the Labour Party. But the phrase to which I direct your attention is his claim that they are the governing class of this country and have to conduct themselves like 'a ruling class'.

We Unionists do not believe in class government or that any section of the community should set themselves up as a ruling class. We hold that everyone should have a fair chance to make the best of himself or herself under just laws and with representative government and parliamentary institutions should secure – to quote a definition of democracy I was taught many years ago – 'the association of us all through the leadership of the best'. The idea of setting up again in this country a ruling class, based on a political machine or rigorous party discipline or any other sectional device, is at once odious and obsolete. The Liberalism and the Tory democracy of the nineteenth century swept away these restrictive ideas. The French Revolution established, I trust for ever, the conception of 'la carrière ouverte aux talents' – the career open to talents.

It is indeed astonishing in the twentieth century to find a Socialist Minister, never heard of until he began to mismanage our food, claiming for a minority Government afraid to face their fellow-countrymen, that they are the ruling class. If this is their mood, the sooner they are subjected to the judgement of a free democracy the better.

We are often asked: 'Tell us exactly what you would do if you came into power. Please give us at once your whole constructive programme and the remedies which you would apply to all the evils which prey upon us at home and abroad.' I have no intention of attempting to solve the problems of Government without the power to act by deeds and not by words. We have no intention of bribing our way into office by all kinds of promises like the Socialists spouted forth in the 1945 election. A hard and difficult time lies before us, requiring not only patience and self-restraint, but a new effort and a broader theme.

Our first aim must be to preserve peace by helping the United States to marshal effectively the whole strength of the free and law-respecting nations. The core and life thrust of the world alliance of free peoples is of course the English-speaking world united by language, literature, history and tradition. The Empire and Commonwealth of Nations joined to the United States in fraternal association form a mass so vast and powerful that none would dare molest it, and with this central force we should have the power to sustain and build up a united Europe lifted for ever above the worn-out quarrels which have laid it in ruins. All this process is moving slowly but irresistibly forward, and in it lies the highest hope for the general reconciliation of self-tormented mankind. For our part we must do our best to revive and liberate the native energies and genius of the British race and to preserve and reassert the strength of our Empire and Commonwealth of Nations. We shall not seek to re-establish, like Mr Webb, a ruling class operating through a party caucus, but we shall try our utmost to undo the needless harm that has been done and to restore to all our fellow-countrymen the sense of pride and honour in our ancient land.

None of all the problems which faced Britain at home on the morrow of her victory six years ago compared in urgency with that of housing the people. None called for a more resolute effort by the Government of the day. House-building had perforce come to a standstill for six years of war; many homes had been destroyed by the enemy, and thousands which stood had been condemned as slums before the war started. Meanwhile the population had increased. That was the problem. In the wartime Coalition, of which I was the head, we estimated in 1943 that our long-term need after the war, if we were to give every family a separate home and replace slums and other unsuitable houses, would be at least 3,000,000 houses.

To have contrived the building of homes on such a scale would have been an achievement of which any Minister might have been proud. If the Government had given housing the proper priority they could have secured such a response from local authorities, the building industry and the public, that the problem could have been largely surmounted by now. Good housing is the first of the social services. Bad housing makes more disease than the best health service can cure. It undermines the efforts of our schools to produce worthy citizens. It prevents our people doing their best work in the factory, field and office. That is why Conservative and Unionist Governments in the years before the war put slum-clearance at the head and centre of their drive to improve the social conditions of our country. Today those achievements are too often forgotten, but in the six years before 1939 we rehoused over 1,500,000 people who had lived in slums. But for the war the last of our slums would have disappeared seven or eight years ago.

Before the 1945 election the Socialist Party produced their statement of post-war policy, and called for 4,000,000 houses in the first ten years after the war – 400,000 a year. Today, after nearly six years, they have built under 900,000 permanent houses, an average of only 150,000 a year. They are not even keeping pace with the growing waiting-lists. In Glasgow last month there were 100,000 on the waiting-list, and the Ministry allocation for 1951 was only 5,000 houses.

At Blackpool last October a gust of passion swept the annual conference of the National Union of Conservative and Unionist Associations when they debated the Government's housing failure. I said that I accepted their demand that the target should be 300,000 and added: 'No one can tell how the rearmament burden may strike our industry and finances, but however our fortunes may go and from whatever angle the pressures of life may come, the Tory

Party puts homes for the people in the very forefront of all schemes for our development.' I repeat that now. 300,000 houses a year remains our aim. It is second only to national safety. We still believe that by giving builders freer initiative the rate of building can be increased and the rise in costs halted, even during the period of rearmament. No one can foresee the march of events. But we should try our best to reach again the rate of housebuilding achieved by the Chamberlain Government before the late war.

But now I come to the root of all our troubles at home – the ever-rising cost of living. The pound sterling buys only three-quarters of what it did when the Socialists took office after the war and is falling ever faster. Five shillings in the pound is now taken out of every wage-packet; out of every housewife's purse; it is cut off all family allowances and all the cash payments under the social security schemes, which all parties combined to bring forward during the war years. The increase which the Chancellor of the Exchequer boasts he is making in his Budget for the more elderly old-age pensioners will barely restore the cut which the financial policy of his predecessors took from them.

Socialist canvassers go from door to door saying that the Tories will reduce the social services. There is no threat to the social services today like the fate which threatens them if the fall in the value of money is not halted. It will not be a planned economy to fall less heavily on those who most need help, but a blind indiscriminate lopping off, and the worst victims will be the very poorest sections of our people. In the face of this danger the Socialist Government have no policy, only excuses. Their chief excuse is that the rise in the cost of living is the result of world rearmament since the fighting started in Korea. This is not true. We are only just beginning to experience in the shops the effects of the increases in the price of raw materials since last summer. The biggest cause of the rise in prices during the last eighteen months has been the devaluation of the pound in September 1949.

Four previous years of Socialist extravagance and mismanagement made devaluation inevitable. It raised the price of our dollar imports and cut the price of our exports by one-third. That means that we have as a nation to do twelve hours' work instead of eight to buy what we need from overseas, while we get paid only eight hours' reward for what we produce in twelve hours' work. No politician of any party could claim today that he has the formula to restore our money to what it was worth in 1945 when the Socialists took charge. Things have gone too far for that. It will take all our efforts to hold the value of the pound at whatever level the Socialists reduce it to before the country is able to dismiss them. In their six years of office they have spent some £23,000 million – £11 million a day. This year they are planning to spend an additional £1,300 million on defence without making any compensating economies in their other expenditure. I am quite sure that in the field of administration alone scores of millions of pounds a year could be saved by wise management. No economies would be popular, but they would be less hurtful than the calamity of unchecked inflation, which is what we face.

The Socialist Government are taking in taxation £1,000 million a year more than was deemed prudent at the height of the war. That is nearly 10s a week more from every man, woman and child in the country. In addition there is the growing burden of the local rates, and the concealed taxation levied in the form of higher postal and telephone charges. In addition there are the increases imposed by our nationalized industries in their pretence of reducing and avoiding heavy losses, and the high and increasing charges for nationalized road and rail transport which fall with special severity on Scotland, where such long distances have to be covered.

You have rightly been discussing the rehabilitation and development of the Highlands and Islands. A question you may ask yourselves is – how much might not have been done in this direction, and in the improvement of our hill and marginal lands, if the Socialist Government had devoted to this purpose only a fraction of that £36½ million they frittered away on their Groundnuts Scheme in East Africa.

A Conservative Government would aim at keeping State expenditure within bounds. We believe that a healthy economy depends, as Mr Gladstone used to say, on money being allowed to fructify in the pockets of the people. For the production we need for the defence programme, for the export trade, and to maintain decent living standards at home, we look to the impulse of individual effort as well as the well-conceived State policy. We would encourage work and thrift. We shall call a halt to all further nationalization, and rely for increased production on the experience, skill and enterprise of our great industries. Wherever we can we shall restore freedom to those industries which the State has taken over. Iron and steel will become again a great free-enterprise industry, strengthened and aided as the TUC proposed, by a board representing workers, management and the Government. Where industries cannot be restored to the full freedom of competition we intend to do everything possible to lessen the unhealthy grip of Whitehall and revive local initiative and responsibility.

And here is where I come to Scotland. I have nothing new to say about the ancient and sacred relationship which joins us together in the United Kingdom. I predicted last year at Edinburgh that Scotland would not desert a friend in need. The fact that England, for the time being, is in eclipse and seems to foreign eyes to be declining, makes it all the more certain that Scotland will stand at her side. My faith in the free peoples of the British Isles and in Northern Ireland is strong. I do not believe that we are at the end of all our glories, and it is in the struggle to prevent such a catastrophe that all the sanity, wisdom and steadfast tenacity of the Scottish race must be engaged. We believe that together we can break this attempt to manage everything from Whitehall.

We are sure that Socialism has already proved its failure and that, as soon as the people have a chance to express their opinion, this foolish fallacy and aberration of a minority of our countrymen will receive a resounding rebuke at the hands of the electors. It would be wrong to attribute all the difficulties and dangers which are closing in upon us abroad to the Government. They would certainly have been very grave whatever party was in power. It is true and just, however, to say that they have comprehension shown by a weak-minded and tottering administration absorbed in its party affairs and setting their own retention of office; whether they have the confidence of the nation or not, above everything else. Let me give you a few examples.

Take the latest. On Monday of last week, when we saw how excited the Americans were getting about our trading with China – though it was no more than what they were doing themselves – we Conservatives asked that we should reach an agreement with them about an embargo on what are called 'strategic materials' going into China, and I requested that above all the import of rubber into China from Hong Kong and other British colonies should be stopped. On the Thursday the Government announced that they had done both these things. That was good, but why should it be left to the Opposition to point out the step, the need for which had been obvious for many months and which, if our affairs were conducted with ordinary foresight would have prevented a great deal of misunderstanding between us and our vital ally.

Another foolish blunder was made when an American admiral was given the supreme command of the Atlantic, although the bringing in of convoys to Europe and the feeding of this island can only be dealt with, as it was so successfully dealt with, from this side of the ocean and from this island with all its knowledge and experience during the two world wars. While the public outcry was going on about this, the Government have been seeking to gain the supreme command in the Mediterranean, to offset what they had given away in the Atlantic. But it would be in our interests that the United States should command in the Mediterranean. The closer they are associated with us and with France in the Mediterranean the better it will be for all our fortunes, there and in the Middle East. Two wrongs do not make a right, but that is exactly what the Government are trying to do. The best arrangement would I am sure be to have the passage of the convoys and of the trade across the Atlantic arranged as it was in the war, between the British and American Admiralties, and to welcome the Americans with their powerful fleets of aircraft carriers in the Mediterranean, as the leading Allied Power there. I have no doubt that if there were any guidance of our affairs from the top, and if intimate relations like we had in the war had been maintained between the Prime Minister and the President, all this could have been quite easily settled to the general advantage and satisfaction.

Since the Socialists obtained power in 1945, the prestige of Britain has fallen steadily. We have cast away our Oriental Empire with both our hands and at the cost of hundreds of thousands of Indian and Burmese lives. We have gained the hatred both of the Arabs and of the Jews. The Egyptians, in violation of all law and treaty, have closed the Suez Canal to the passage of oil-tankers. We have not only put up with this, but have continued to send arms, ships, aeroplanes, destroyers and all kinds of supplies to Egypt, although that Government is thoroughly unfriendly and demands our immediate evacuation of the Canal Zone. The Egyptian Government does not even have to pay for those weapons. All they do is to mark off the money involved on what are called the sterling balance accounts, which means the debt we are supposed to owe them for the supplies we bought in Egypt while we were defending them from being conquered by Germany and Italy.

The impression has got about the world that we have only to be kicked or threatened to clear out of any place. The Persians like the idea of nationalization of other people's property and, under the pressure of the terrorists in Teheran, they now propose to seize the Anglo-Persian oilfields, which have been discovered and developed by fifty years of British brains and capital. Iraq threatens the same policy of spoliation. Wherever you look you see our rights and interests disregarded. Albania murdered forty-four of our sailors by laying a mine trap for them, and refuses to pay the compensation awarded to us as the result of the arbitration at The Hague, and the Argentine has planted her flag on British territory in the Antarctic as a prelude to their demand for the Falkland Islands.

All this and much else is happening within six years of the world war, in which for more than a year we sustained the cause of freedom alone and from which we emerged with complete victory and world-wide respect. Six years of Socialist rule have brought us low. Nevertheless, we must not lose faith in our destiny. We are the same people in the same island as we were in the great days we can all remember. Our spirit is unconquerable, our ingenuity and craftsmanship are unsurpassed, our latent resources are unmeasured, our underlying unities are enduring. We have but to cast away by an effort of the will the enfeebling tendencies and fetters of Socialist rule, and then we can stand erect once more and take our place among the Great Powers of the world. Never must we lose our faith and courage. Never must we fail in exertion and resolve.

Be sure you are ready for the call when it comes. Be sure you lay aside every impediment and allow no class or privilege or vested interest to stand between you and your duty to the nation.

May 1951

Winston S. Churchill to Somerset de Chair
(Churchill papers, 2/168)

23 May 1951

My dear de Chair,

Thank you so much for your letter and for sending me a copy of John Buchan's *Caesar* and of Napoleon's Memoirs. I had already got hold of *Caesar*, so I return your copy to you herewith. I look forward to reading Napoleon, which from a quick glance, looks most interesting.

I much enjoyed your masterly *Julius Caesar*.

Jo Sturdee to Margaret Nairn
(Churchill papers, 2/174)

24 May 1951

Dear Mrs Nairn,

Mrs Churchill unfortunately had to go into hospital the other day for an operation,[1] and as she is not yet well enough to write letters, she asks me to say how much pleasure it gave her to hear from you again and to thank you for your letter. The doctors say she is making good progress, but I do not think she will be home for another week or two, and then she has been told she must take things very quietly for at least three months.

First of all, about the proposal that some of Mr Churchill's paintings should be exhibited in the United States. This suggestion has been made on many occasions by all kinds of people and organizations, but this is the first time that Mr and Mrs Churchill have felt any inclination to agree, because they have so much confidence in your judgement and opinion. Mr Churchill has carefully considered all you say, but he still feels that he does not want to hold an exhibition of his paintings in America, or anywhere else. He seems shy of the idea, and he hopes you will understand.

Mr and Mrs Churchill are so glad you are liking your new life in the United States. You will have seen that their plans for going to Philadelphia at the beginning of this month had to be postponed. Although Mr Churchill was careful not to admit it publicly, this was because of the MacArthur controversy which has been sweeping and splitting the country. He felt that the speech he will deliver at the University of Pennsylvania will be better received when these domestic Party political issues are over. Is Philadelphia too far away from you? I see it is half a continent away.

Mr and Mrs Churchill so much enjoyed their visit to Marrakech last winter. They had many painting expeditions into the Ourika valley; and they flew over

[1] Referred to by Mary Soames as a 'major "repair" operation which kept her in St Mary's Hospital, Paddington, for three weeks' (*Clementine Churchill*, p. 467).

the Atlas mountains to a place called Tinerhir, where Mr Churchill stayed for about a week and painted five or six bright and brilliant pictures, two of which are in this year's Royal Academy Exhibition – with the Surrealists! It was a heavenly place and an absolute paradise for Mr Churchill. You would have been amused at all the visits and exchanges with the old Glaoui, who is still going strong, and his sons. They missed you both so much.

Mrs Churchill is so glad you have seen Sarah and to know that you think she is looking well and happy. There are many reports in the papers here of her plays and of the reception she receives. At the moment Diana Sandys is staying with her in New York.

Mrs Churchill sends you her love and was really so glad to learn all your interesting news. She says she hopes it will not be too long before you all meet together again.

Winston S. Churchill to Lord Simon
(Churchill papers, 2/126)

24 May 1951

My dear John,

Thank you for your letter of May 17.[1] Are you quite sure that our case is good in international law for an appeal to The Hague?

Jo Sturdee to Captain Alfred M. Granum
(Hillsdale College Archives)

24 May 1951   Chartwell

Dear Captain Granum,

Mr Churchill has given further consideration to your letter of April 11, to which Mr Greville sent a reply on behalf of Mr Churchill on April 25.[2]

Upon reflection Mr Churchill has been glad to write a plain inscription on a sheet of paper, which if you think suitable and acceptable, could be inserted in the copy of *The Hinge of Fate* which has been awarded to Midshipman James V. Neely.[3]

Mr Churchill sends Midshipman Neely his congratulations and good wishes.

---

[1] Reproduced above (p. 2080).
[2] Reproduced above (pp. 2055–6).
[3] The inscribed book is held at the Hillsdale College Mossey Library.

Lord Simon to Winston S. Churchill
(*Churchill papers, 2/126*)

26 May 1951

PERSIAN OIL

In reply to your letter of May 24, there is no doubt –
  (1) that Persia's action in internationalizing oil at Abadan is a breach of her contract of 1933 with the British Company, which was negotiated through the League of Nations;
  (2) that this is a breach of International Law, especially as HMG are the principal shareholders;
  (3) that HMG are entitled to complain of this breach and take it up on behalf of the Company.

HMG can therefore apply to The Hague Court for a decision that Persia's action is a breach of International Law and for such relief as the Court can give.

(Morrison should have done so long ago, and may be expected to do this when he finds time to study this matter properly).

The only difficulty is that Persia may claim that she has never submitted to the jurisdiction of The Hague Court in such a case. That depends on the terms in which Persia has signed 'the optional clause'. My present impression is that it should be found that she *has* agreed to be bound by the decision of The Hague Court in such a case, for she has a treaty with us to give our nationals most-favoured-nation treatment, and that should be treatment in accordance with International Law. This is a highly technical point which is likely to involve argument. But that does not alter the fact that HMG have been slow and hesitating. A prompt and definite challenge would have done much to bring American opinion to our side earlier, for they have continuous interests in oil in the Persian Gulf.

Winston S. Churchill to Duke of Windsor
(*Churchill papers, 2/178*)

28 May 1951

Sir,

I thank your Royal Highness most sincerely for the kindness of sending me a copy under your own signature of the Memoirs[1] you have published of your life and marriage and of the Abdication which have their lasting place in history.

---
[1] *A King's Story* (1951).

It was very good of you to meet my suggestions about myself and I am most grateful. I am glad the book has had so marked a success here and in America.

I hope indeed I may have the privilege of meeting you and the Duchess of Windsor in the not too distant future, and meanwhile send my message of friendship and respect.

Your Royal Highness's faithful servant

Winston S. Churchill to Captain Arthur Granville Soames
(Churchill papers, 2/171)

29 May 1951

My dear Arthur,

Alas I cannot come to see your beautiful gardens on Sunday, June 3. Miss Margaret Truman, the President's daughter, who will only be here for a day or two is coming to luncheon at Chartwell, and the Ambassador and his wife are bringing her down. As Clemmie is ill I am hoping that Mary and Christopher will help me entertain these unexpected but very welcome guests.

Colonist really seems to have a good chance now for the Gold Cup, which will be a wonderful event in my life.

Winston S. Churchill to Somerset de Chair
(Churchill papers, 2/168)

30 May 1951

My dear de Chair,

As I have spent so much of my life reading proofs I cannot help marking points as they occur to me. I send you a few suggestions on your account of Julius Caesar. It is beautifully printed. May I keep the proof sheets you have sent me?

<u>Page 16</u>, [. . .]

I do not like the last four lines, particularly the use of the word 'bounder'. Napoleon was not an ~~aristocrat~~ parvenue but a country gentleman. Have you not seen the charming little house in Corsica which belonged to his family? He was certainly never a bounder, nor did he ever become an aristocrat; he became a sovereign. These four lines would harm the whole introduction.[1]

---

[1] Somerset de Chair responded to Churchill on June 9: 'I have had no difficulty in persuading the publishers to reset the type to incorporate your suggestions and you will be pleased to know that I am removing the offending paragraph from the introduction altogether so that no words of mine will, or indeed could, dim "the glow of the Emperor's personality".'

June 1951

Winston S. Churchill to Sir Stafford Cripps
(*Churchill papers, 2/168*)

4 June 1951

My dear Stafford

Mr Stockwood[1] tells me he is paying you a visit and so I take the opportunity to send you a few flowers from me and Clemmie. We are so glad to hear of your progress and of the gallant fight you are making.

Every good wish to you both.

Your sincere friend and comrade

Winston S. Churchill: speech
(*'Winston S. Churchill, His Complete Speeches', volume 8, pages 8214–15*)

7 June 1951   House of Commons

FIELD MARSHAL SMUTS
(WESTMINSTER MEMORIAL STATUE)

I am very glad indeed to have the opportunity of offering the Prime Minister our cordial support for the proposal which he has just made. It was a matter which required careful consideration. One has to have a just sense of proportion in all these matters and, of course, one cannot judge the proportion of the individual except in relation to the background of world affairs, all of which has to be considered in its entirety. The first 50 years of the 20th century have been among the most terrible that the human race has ever lived through, with two frightful world wars and immense disturbance and destruction of human life. On the other hand, they have contained the greatest promise for the future in the advance of science, knowledge and the broadening assembly of peoples in every way.

---

[1] Arthur Mervyn Stockwood, 1913–95. Vicar, St Matthew's, Moorfields, 1941–55; Great St Mary's, Cambridge, 1955–9. Bishop of Southwark, 1959–80. Sat in House of Lords, 1963–80.

All that hangs in the balance now. No one can judge. Posterity alone can judge whether this has been a great age or one which preceded some vast disaster. But no one can, I think, doubt that on our present knowledge and view of the proportions of these matters, Jan Smuts played a great part and was a noble and outstanding figure in his faithful and courageous support of his own countrymen when they seemed to be opposed by overwhelming forces, and in his response to magnanimity which carried us forward along the road, and in all the work which he did and the play of his thoughts upon the movements of nations and peoples. In every way he seemed to be one of the most enlightened, courageous and noble minded men that we have known in these the first 50 years of the 20th century in which he played so prominent a part.

I am grateful that the Prime Minister should have taken this action. I am sure he will gather the full support of the House of Commons for what is done, and that this national tribute will be well supported and sustained by the arrangements which are being made to have a private subscription opened for a system of Commonwealth scholarships at Cambridge University, of which Jan Smuts was an undergraduate and a graduate, and of which, when he died, he was Chancellor.

John Foster Dulles to Winston S. Churchill
(Churchill papers, 2/114)

8 June 1951

My dear Mr Churchill,

I greatly appreciate the opportunity to have lunch with you today and to have had this good chance to exchange views. What you say always reflects the ripeness of experience and vigor of a dynamic faith.

I enclose, as you suggested, a copy of my talk last night before the English-Speaking Union.

Winston S. Churchill to Lieutenant-General Sir Henry Pownall
(Churchill papers, 4/25)

9 June 1951

My dear Henry,

I send you a few rough notes which I have put down on my two visits to Montgomery in March 1945. It does not follow that I shall use them in their present form, but perhaps you could make them fit into your account of the battle. We do not want to give a detailed description, but only the results of each day's fighting.

About the general campaign, it seems to me that you might deal with some of Omar Bradley's points. I do not think he does justice to Montgomery's case in his book. There is no doubt however of the tremendous achievement of the Americans in encircling the Ruhr and forcing all the fortifications on their own front. We did well also on our front. In the whole of Book 12 I do not think I could give more than five or six thousand words to the actual account of the military operations. It is only in their larger aspects that they should be portrayed.

I hope you have had a good holiday in Ireland.

Winston S. Churchill: speech
('Winston S. Churchill, His Complete Speeches', volume 8, pages 8219–21)

21 June 1951   House of Commons

FINANCE BILL AMENDMENTS (CHAIRMAN'S SELECTION)

The Leader of the House[1] has spoken in that usual strain of temperate, reasonable moderation which endeavours, by carefully selected stepping-stones, to reach a conclusion which suits his own side. (Hon. Members: 'Cheap'.) Far from complaining of that, hon. Gentlemen opposite ought to treat it as a compliment to one of their leading Parliamentarians. I do not intend to take up much of the time of the House – although, of course, if I am interrupted I shall go on for much longer – because of the other matters which press upon our attention, but I must say a few words in reply to the statement which the Leader of the House has just made to us.

We were enormously relieved to hear his declaration, or assertion, that there was no collusion between the Chancellor of the Exchequer, for instance, or the Government Whips, or himself, and the occupant of the Chair.[2]

Mr Bowles (Nuneaton): Did the right hon. Gentleman think that there was?

Mr Churchill: That he should have dwelt at such length upon that, and made it one of the foundations of his entire argument, certainly gave me a feeling of surprise, because I should have thought everyone knew that it would be grossly improper for any Minister to try to get at the Chairman of Committees, who, though a party man and appointed by the Government of the day, and charged with certain, I will not say overriding but underlying responsibilities for advancing Government business – that is so, and has long been understood – is, nevertheless, certainly to be kept free from all appeals and

[1] James Chuter-Ede.
[2] Charles Glen MacAndrew, 1888–1979. Born in Ayrshire, Scotland. Educated at Trinity College, Cambridge. Married Lilian Cathleen Curran, 1918: three children (div. 1938); 1941, Marion Eleanor Bonthron Mitchell: one child. MP (Cons.) for Kilmarnock, 1924–9; for Partick, 1931–5; for North Ayrshire, 1935–59. JP, 1929. Lt-Col., Ayrshire Yeomanry, 1932–6. Knighted, 1935. Chairman of Ways and Means, 1951–9. PC, 1952. Baron, 1959.

addresses made to him, publicly or privately, by the Ministers of the Crown. I was astonished that the right hon. Gentleman should devote so much time to relieving our minds of a suspicion which has certainly never entered them.

Mr Ede: The right hon. Gentleman will recollect that in response to an interruption he made I made it quite clear that I did not think the suspicions resided in the House, but that it was as well to take the opportunity of relieving the suspicions of certain people outside the House.

Mr Churchill: I was astonished, nonetheless, that the right hon. Gentleman should have devoted so much of his speech to that subject. In these matters we are primarily concerned with the opinion of the House, and we cannot always provide against ideas which may arise or may be floating about through the public who take an interest in political affairs. At any rate, we did not suggest at any time that there was collusion, and I am very glad to reach a point on which we can have general agreement between the two sides of the House.

The right hon. and learned Gentleman the Member for Montgomery (Mr C. Davies) the Leader of the Liberal Party, who gave me the impression that he was very much surprised at the Ruling given by the Chairman of Ways and Means, seemed to disapprove very much of the course that has been taken in putting this Motion upon the Order Paper. The right hon. and learned Gentleman must be careful not always to want to have everything both ways.

The fact is that he was surprised, as most people were, as experienced Members were, and as the Home Secretary himself has told us he was, to find that all the Amendments to Clause 1 had been swept away by a decision of the Chair and that immediately we came to deal with the Motion, 'That the Clause stand part of the Bill.' That is a criticism upon the decision of the Chair. (Hon. Members: 'No'.) Yes, of course it is. It is not the final stage of a criticism, but it is surprise at an action or a decision, and is the first foundation upon which one gradually builds and which eventually leads up to the Motion we have put upon the Order Paper.

There was general surprise at the decision, a surprise in which the Leader of the Liberal Party joins. There was the right hon. Gentleman the Home Secretary sitting in his room. I will not say that he was staggered; I will keep to the words he has used – he was surprised. We on this side of the House have a duty to carry out. Not only was there surprise on the part of my hon. Friends, but there was indignation because all these Amendments of a different character were swept on one side, and immediately we came to a general debate upon the Motion, 'That the Clause stand part of the Bill.'

I am bound to say that I thought it was a wrong decision on the part of the Chairman of Ways and Means to sweep them out of the way in that method. As I have said, I do not doubt that he wished to do what was right, and that he sought the best method of correctly interpreting his difficult, discretionary duties.

I make no imputation upon his *bona fides*, a word which was dragged in by the Leader of the Liberal Party, nor his good faith. Nothing in the speech of my right hon. and gallant Friend, in moving the Motion, suggested that, but we think we were unfairly treated. One may be unfairly treated – (*Interruption.*) I hope the right hon. Gentleman the Member for Bassetlaw (Mr Bellenger) is not going to get very indignant. One may be unfairly treated just as much by an error of judgment as by want of good faith or malice. We do not impute malice. There was an error of judgment, which resulted, in practice, in what we consider unfair treatment of the Opposition in regard to important Amendments on Clause 1. That is what has brought us to this point today.

What is the point of the argument – which has been brought forward in a letter which was read to the House – that the Amendments were the same old Amendments that were put forward last year? Each year is different. We live on the principle of annual finance. That is the foundation of this House and its whole existence, which has been fought for over the centuries. What is the use of saying that because these Amendments were moved last year, they should not be moved the next year or the year after? There is nothing in that. The circumstances of every year are entirely different, as are the circumstances of every day if we can measure them accurately.

Each year taxes are being altered, and, therefore, each tax is altered in its general incidence and bearing. It is suggested that because an Amendment was moved last year it should be improper, out of order or unnecessary to raise it again in the succeeding year. That is a most injurious objection to put forward. Taxes may continue the same year as last year, or they may be increased owing to other events which have occurred. I am astonished that such a false argument should be cherished.

It does not depend on whether a tax is increased. That aggravates the case, but the mere fact that it should be suggested that the House should not have the fullest right to raise the same question on our finances year after year, if it wants to, is one which betokens a lack of appreciation of the general principles and sense of the House. One might as well ask why should we have the Army and Air Force (Annual) Bill, which comes on every year. These matters must be judged and considered in relation to Parliamentary custom and experience.

In our view, on this side of the House, the Chairman of Ways and Means, while in no way being guilty of any moral fault, did commit an error of judgment, which came as a surprise to those who are experienced in the procedure of this House. This error of judgment reflected hardship upon individuals and affected or marred our discussion on an important part of the Finance Bill. Those are the reasons that led us – and still lead us – to present this Motion to the House. I am very glad it is to be disposed of today. I do not think I have said anything which would inject a note of personal bitterness into our debate. We are dealing with a constitutional issue, and it is our duty to deal expressly with any constitutional issues.

There can be no question whatever of our responding to the suggestion of the Leader of the House that we should withdraw this Motion. If it is to be negatived let it be done by the House. We have placed it on the Order Paper. It is a record of the feelings and actions of the Opposition at a particular phase in the present Finance Bill. Let us hope that the moral will be drawn, and that the general principle on which the House of Commons has been conducted will be carefully observed in the future, the stricter because on this question they have been brought to sharp, precise and even meticulous attention.

Winston S. Churchill to Lord Woolton
(Churchill papers, 2/118)

25 June 1951

I am not happy about the West Houghton contest.[1] Twenty thousand votes, or two-thirds of the whole electorate were uncanvassed. When I spoke to the Area Agent he said it was thought better not to disturb the mining areas which comprised between ten and twelve thousand electors, but only to concentrate on the districts favourable to us. This is the essence of defeatism. Surely there was plenty of time for the area to have organised a strong campaign in these districts? They could not anyhow have done worse. But the idea that the Conservatives were afraid to show their noses in these areas must have had a thoroughly bad effect not only on them but throughout a constituency. Considering how important bye-elections are at the moment it would surely have been worthwhile for the area to force the local people into accepting the outside help which you no doubt could readily have afforded. I hope you will go into this matter searchingly with the area organization and with the local people.

Turning to another topic. I think the Gallup Poll in the *News Chronicle* this morning is open to serious suspicion. I doubt very much whether the Liberals have gained 2 percent of the national vote. Of course the *News Chronicle* aim at a deadlock between Liberals and Conservatives with the Liberals holding the balance. I do not trust their bona fides and certainly they have presented the matter in the most depressing way.

[1] Held on 21 June 1951, after the resignation in April of Rhys Davies (Lab.) owing to poor health. Tom Price (Lab.) defeated Frank J. Land (Cons,).

Winston S. Churchill: speech
(Hansard)

26 June 1951   House of Commons

TSHEKEDI KHAMA (BANISHMENT)

I shall not stand for more than a very few minutes between the House and the Prime Minister. We have had a deeply interesting debate and I think I may say that I have rarely listened to a debate which has caused more heart searchings on both sides of the House than this. The problems are difficult, they are undefined and we all of us want to give a right, honest, sincere, truthful opinion upon the issues which are before us.

The hon. and learned Member for Camarthen (Mr Hopkin Morris) has unfolded with a considerable sweep the broad conceptions of human liberty which we cherish in our hearts and which, whatever the divisions, party divisions, between us, we should in the ultimate issue all stand and die together to preserve. Then there was the right hon. and learned Gentleman the Leader of the Liberal Party. It was not without very careful consideration that I and my colleagues on this Bench came to the conclusion that we ought to associate ourselves with the Motion, or with a version of the Motion, which the right hon. and learned Gentleman had placed on the Order Paper and ought to use our facilities for securing an opportunity of it being debated by the House. We considered the matter very carefully and I must say it seemed absolutely right to make the affirmation of the opinion of Parliament which is expressed by the Motion upon the Order Paper.[1]

A Motion of the House on a subject like this is not an executive act, although it is a strong act of guidance, a signal to the Executive Government, and leaves many solutions open to them, but it does give an opportunity for a true and fair expression of the opinion of the House upon the issues involved. I came down to the House with the intention of voting for this Motion and I am bound to say that what has occurred this afternoon in the speech of the Secretary of State for Commonwealth Relations[2] only makes me feel that I have no choice whatever but to carry out that purpose.

Everyone recognizes the ability of the right hon. Gentleman and his courage and the frankness, candour and mastery of the subject which he presented to the House was admired in all quarters. But I did not like this last minute, alarmist telegram, the authority for which had not been fully presented to the

---

[1] Put forward by Clement Davies: 'That this House deplores the decision to continue the banishment of Tshekedi Khama from the Bamangwato Territory without hearing or inquiring into the grounds for such banishment; and calls upon His Majesty's Government to rescind the order of banishment and allow him to dwell freely within the territory of his tribe.'
[2] Patrick Gordon Walker, 1907–80. MP (Lab.) for Smethwick, 1945–64; for Leyton, 1966–74. Secretary of State for Commonwealth Relations, 1947–66; for Education and Science, 1967–8.

House. I did not like that; one does not know how much that really represents and I do not think that after all these weeks and months of discussion the House ought to let itself be stampeded by a message of that kind and scattered by a message of that kind, read out at the last moment.

I did not like the alarmist telegram, but much worse than the alarmist telegram were the new proposals. How anyone with a clear conscience could possibly vote for the new proposals, put forward as a sort of sop and way out of difficulties to those on the other side of the House who have difficulties, I cannot imagine. A special Kgotla[1] is to be set up, and two or maybe three Members of Parliament are to go out there beforehand. Undoubtedly the Kgotla would, by its decision, have the absolute power to decree what would be the perpetual banishment of Tshekedi.

Tshekedi is undoubtedly a distinguished African and whatever may be the inconveniences of his continuing to live in this world, like so many of us have to do, the fact remains that while he is here he has his rights and is perfectly entitled to due and proper consideration. But the proposal is that he should be invited to go out – dared to go out – and present himself to this gathering of 10,000 or 12,000 people, which is to be assembled by the Secretary of State for Commonwealth Relations and all his undoubtedly most impartial aides-de-camp on the spot and his assistants, and that this body is to pronounce whether this man is to be banished without his having committed any crime. For Parliament to commit itself to accepting a proposition of that kind is far worse than anything that we have been asked to consider today.

All of us here agree in loathing methods of Communism and Communist terrorism. I am told that in Communist China people are tried by a howling mob of many thousands and are then led off to be shot. Naturally, no one who has the decency to be a Member of the House of Commons would be responsible for that, but, nevertheless, there is something in the idea of a mob decision, of a violent decision, which is to inflict immense injury upon an individual without an appeal of any kind, which makes the whole of the proposal abhorrent and places the policy of the Government in a much sharper position of contrariety to our views than anything which we saw before.

For this reason, I and my colleagues on this side of the House see no reason to change the opinion with which we came down to the House, namely, to vote for the Motion which has been so ably supported by speakers on this side of the House from both the Conservative and the Liberal Parties. We see no reason whatever to change our view on the subject. On the contrary, we propose to record it in the Division Lobbies.

We cannot compel the Government to take any particular executive action, but we hope that the fact that the Motion is placed in and recorded upon the

---

[1] In the democratic tradition of the Tswana of Botswana, a kgotla is a large assembly held by the chief and local villagers.

Journal of the House of Commons as a decision of Parliament and as an expression of the modern view of the House of Common will have the effect of stimulating the Government into finding some far better means of coping with the difficulties of the situation than that which the Secretary of State for Commonwealth Relations has placed before us this evening.

Winston S. Churchill to Robert Menzies, Sidney Holland[1] and Louis St Laurent
(Churchill papers, 2/77)

26 June 1951

You will no doubt have received through formal channels invitation of Consultative Assembly at Strasbourg to send representatives from your parliament as official observers to September session expected to last twenty-fourth September to twelfth October. Invitation originally sent out in response to an initiative of British members in August 1950 but owing to many preoccupations it may have escaped your notice. As a result of further resolution of Consultative Assembly it has now been formally repeated by President Spaak to speakers of your parliament. May I urge you to make every effort to see that representatives are sent for September since I think it is of the greatest importance to British leadership in Europe and to ensure that developments towards European unity should be in fullest harmony with broad Commonwealth interests. I appeal to you with confidence because I know your deep interest in these vital questions and appreciate the encouragement you have shewn towards our efforts during the last few years. If you want further information do not hesitate to ask me.

Winston S. Churchill to Field Marshal Lord Alexander
(Churchill papers, 4/52)

28 June 1951

My dear Alex,

I have not hitherto troubled you with my proofs because Pownall, whom you know and trust, keeps careful check of them. However in this Volume V there is so much that affects your conduct of our war that I hope you will not mind if I burden you with these chapters which Pownall has selected. If there is anything of error or omission which you feel should be corrected or anything you do not like, please let me know.

---

[1] Sidney George Holland, 1893–1961. Born in New Zealand. Entered father's engineering business, 1912. Joined NZEF, 1915. Married, 1920, Florence Beatrice Dayton. New Zealand MP (Nat.) for Christchurch North, 1935–46; for Fendalton, 1946–57. Leader of Opposition, 1940–9. PM of New Zealand, 1949–57. Minister of Finance, 1949–54. PC, 1950. Minister of Police, 1954–6.

How I have grieved that all these years have passed by without my being able to come and spend a week with you in Canada. I never would have hesitated to propose myself if there was an opportunity, knowing your lasting kindness to me.

I am very hard-pressed here and everything is plunged in grotesque uncertainty. I shall not however visit the United States again without asking for your hospitality in Canada.

Winston S. Churchill to President Harry S Truman
(Churchill papers, 2/126)

29 June 1951
Private and Personal

I feel it my duty to add to the representations His Majesty's Government are making to you about Persia my own strong appeal for your help. The question of commercial oil is minor compared to the strategic and moral interests of our two countries and the United Nations. Short of an invasion of Western Europe I cannot think of any Soviet aggression more dangerous to our common cause than for the region between the Caspian Sea and the Persian Gulf to fall under Russian-stimulated Tudeh[1] Communist control. If this area fell behind the Iron Curtain it would be a serious blow to Turkey, for whom you have made great exertions. Iraq would inevitably follow suit (forgive the metaphor) and the whole Middle East, both towards Egypt and India, would degenerate. Limitless supplies of oil would remove the greatest deterrent upon a major Russian aggression. I see that the Soviets have just paid up eleven tons of gold to Persia, which shows what they think about it all, and may well enable the tottering Mossadeq to carry on for a while.

Now that he has appealed to you I beg you to reply by word and action so as to lighten the burdens which press upon us all.

[1] Iranian Communist Party, formed in 1941.

July
1951

Henry Channon: diary
('Chips', page 461)

2 July 1951

I watched Winston today, with his hand to his ear, listening to a fellow MP in the Division Lobby. He has this trick of pretending to be deafer than he is, when he wants to shed a bore, or protect himself from importunities.

Herbert Morrison to Winston S. Churchill
(Churchill papers, 2/126)

3 July 1951
Private

Dear Winston,

Thank you very much for your letter of the 2nd July, enclosing a copy of the Private and Personal telegram which you have sent to President Truman about Persia.[1] I think this message might be very helpful, and I am glad that you sent it. I am also grateful to you for letting me have a copy.

I shall be very glad to arrange for Fitzroy Maclean, Amery and Soames to see Bowker,[2] who is the Under-Secretary in charge of Middle Eastern questions, and I shall be interested to hear what they have to report about the present position of the Persian Government.

---

[1] Of June 29, reproduced above (p. 2102).
[2] Reginald James Bowker, 1901–83. CMG, 1945. British Minister in Cairo, 1945–7. High Commissioner in Burma, 1947–8. Asst Under-Secretary of State, FO, 1950–3. KCMG, 1952. Ambassador to Turkey, 1954–8; to Austria, 1958–61. GBE, 1961.

3 July 1951   London

THE CHALLENGE OF OUR TIME:
HAND OF AGGRESSOR IS STAYED BY STRENGTH ALONE

One hundred seventy-five years ago, the founding fathers of the American Republic declared their independence of the British Crown. Little could they have known – in the heat and bitterness of the hour – that the severance, accomplished in passion, would through the years flower into an alliance of such fitness and worth that it was never recorded on legal parchment, but in the hearts of our two peoples. The bond that joins us – stronger than blood lines, than common tongue and common law – is the fundamental conviction that man was created to be free, that he can be trusted with freedom, that governments have as a primary function the protection of his freedom.

In the scale of values of the English-speaking people, freedom is the first and most precious right. Without it, no other right can be exercised, and human existence loses all significance. This unity of ours in fundamentals is an international fact. Yet on more than one occasion, it has been obscured in Britain and in my own country by concern with trifles and small disputes, fanned into flames of senseless antagonisms.

Serious differences in conviction must be beaten out on the anvil of logic and justice. But scarcely need they be dragged into the public forum, in the petty hope of capturing a fleeting local acclaim, at the expense of an absent partner. There are men in this room with whom, in World War II, I had arguments, hotly sustained and of long duration. Had all these been headlined in the press of our two countries, they could have created public bitterness, confusing our peoples in the midst of our joint effort. Decisions were reached without such calamitous results, because those at odds did not find it necessary to seek justification for their personal views in a public hue and cry. Incidentally, a more personal reason for this expression of satisfaction is a later conclusion that my own position in the arguments were not always right. In any case, may we never forget that our common devotion to deep human values and our mutual trust are the bedrock of our joint strength.

In that spirit of our countries are joined with the peoples of Western Europe and the North Atlantic to defend the freedoms of western civilization. Opposed to us – cold and forbidding – is an ideological front that marshals every weapon in the arsenal of dictatorship. Subversion, propaganda, deceit and the threat of naked force are daily hurled against us and our friends in a globe-encircling, relentless campaign.

We earnestly hope that the call for a truce in Korea marks a change in attitude. If such a welcome development does occur, the brave men on the

United Nations forces did much to bring it about. We entered the conflict one year ago, resolved that aggression against free and friendly South Korea would not be tolerated. Certain of the nations furnishing forces had heavy demands elsewhere, including postwar reconstruction at home. Nevertheless, every contingent added evidence of the solidarity and firmness of the free nations in giving an object lesson to aggression. Our success in this difficult and distant operation reflects the fortitude of the Allied troops and the leadership that guided them.

The stand in Korea should serve notice in this area, as well as in the Far East, that we will resist naked aggression with all the force at our command. Our effort to provide security against the possibility of another and even greater emergency which will never be of our making – must go forward with the same resolution and courage that has characterized our Korean forces. The member nations in the North Atlantic Treaty Organization need not fear the future or any Communistic threat – if we are alert, realistic and resolute. Our community possesses a potential might that far surpasses the sinister forces of slave camp and chained millions. But to achieve the serenity and confidence that our potential can provide, we must press forward with the mobilization of our spiritual and intellectual strength; we must develop promptly the material force that will assure the safety of our friends upon the continent and the security of the free world.

This is the challenge of our times that, until satisfactorily met, establishes priorities in all our thoughts, our works, our sacrifices. The hand of the aggressor is stayed by strength – and strength alone.

Although the security of each of us is bound up in the safety of all of us, the immediate threat is most keenly felt by our partners in Europe. Half the continent is already within the monolithic mass of totalitarianism. The drawn and haunted faces in the docks of the purge courts are grim evidence of what Communistic domination means. It is clearly necessary that we quickly develop maximum strength within free Europe itself. Our own interests demand it.

It is a truism that where, among partners, strength is demanded in its fullness, unity is the first requisite. Without unity, the effort becomes less powerful in application, less decisive in result. This fact has special application in Europe. It would be difficult indeed to overstate the benefits, in these years of stress and tension, that would accrue to NATO if the free nations of Europe were truly a unit.

But in the vital region, history, custom, language, and prejudice have combined to hamper integration. Progress has been and is hobbled by a web of customs barriers interlaced with bilateral agreements, multilateral cartels, local shortages, and economic monstrosities. How tragic. Free men, facing the specter of political bondage, are crippled by artificial bonds that they themselves have forged, and they alone can loosen. Here is a task to challenge the efforts of the wisest statesmen, the best economists, the most brilliant diplomats.

European leaders, seeking a sound and wise solution, are spurred by the vision of a man at this table – a man of inspiring courage in dark hours, of wise counsel in grave decisions. Winston Churchill's plea for a united Europe can yet bear such greatness of fruit that it may well be remembered as the most notable achievement of a career marked by achievement.

The difficulties of integrating Western Europe, of course, appear staggering to those who live by ritual. But great majorities in Europe earnestly want liberty, peace, and the opportunity to pass on to their children the fair lands and the culture of Western Europe. They deserve, at the very least, a fair chance to work together for the common purpose; freed of the costly encumbrances they are now compelled to carry.

Europe cannot attain the towering material stature possible to its people's skills and spirit so long as it is divided by patchwork territorial fences. They foster localized instead of common interest. They pyramid every cost with middlemen, tariffs, taxes, and overheads. Barred, absolutely, are the efficient division of labor and resources and the easy flow of trade. In the political field, these barriers promote distrust and suspicion. They serve vested interests at the expense of peoples and prevent truly concerted action for Europe's own and obvious good.

This is not to say that, as a commander, I have found anything but ready cooperation among the governments of Western Europe. Time and again, I have saluted from my heart the spirit of their armed services – of officers and men alike – from the mountains of Italy to the fjords of Norway, from Normandy to the curtain. Within political circles, I have found statesmen eager to assure the success of their current defense programs. I have no doubt as to the capacity of NATO to surmount even the formidable obstacles imposed upon us by the political facts of present-day Europe.

Yet with the handicaps of enforced division, it is clear that even the minimum essential security effort will seriously strain the resources of Europe. We ignore this danger at our peril since the effects of economic failure would be disastrous upon spiritual and material strength alike. True security never rests upon the shoulders of men denied a decent present and the hope of a better future.

But with unity achieved, Europe could build adequate security and, at the same time continue the march of human betterment that has characterized western civilization. Once united, the farms and factories of France and Belgium, the foundries of Germany, the rich farmlands of Holland and Denmark, the skilled labor of Italy, will produce miracles for the common good. In such unity is a secure future for these peoples. It would mean early independence of aid from America and other Atlantic countries. The coffers, mines and factories of that continent are not inexhaustible. Dependence upon them must be minimized by the maximum in cooperative effort. The establishment of a workable European federation would go far to create confidence among people everywhere that Europe was doing its full and vital share in giving this cooperation.

Any soldier contemplating this problem would be moved to express an opinion that it cannot be attacked successfully by slow infiltration, but only by direct and decisive assault, with all available means.

The project faces the deadly danger of procrastination, timid measures, slow steps and cautious stages. Granted that the bars of tradition and habit are numerous and stout, the greatest bars to this, as to any human enterprise, lie in the minds of men themselves. The negative is always the easy side, since it holds that nothing should be done. The negative is happy in lethargy; contemplating almost with complacent satisfaction, the difficulties of any other course. But difficulties are often of such slight substance that they fade into nothing at the first sign of success. If obstacles are of greater consequence, they can always be overcome when they must be overcome. And which of these obstacles could be so important as peace, security and prosperity for Europe's population? Could we not help? We, the peoples of the British Commonwealth and of the United States, have profited by unity at home. If, with our moral and material assistance, the free European nations could attain a similar integration, our friends would be strengthened, our own economies improved, and the laborious NATO machinery of mutual defense vastly simplified.

A solid, healthy, confident Europe would be the greatest possible boon to the functioning and objectives of the Atlantic Pact.

But granting that we cannot reach maximum security without a united Europe, let us by no means neglect what is within our immediate grasp or deprecate the achievements already attained.

Look back, I ask you, over a space of 2 years only. Consider the dangerous level to which morale and defensive strength had descended, the despairing counsel of neutralism, appeasement and defeatism that then existed. Against such a backdrop, the accomplishments of the North Atlantic Treaty Organization are magnificently manifest. We are joined together in purpose and growing determination; we know the danger, we have defined our goals. Each day we make headway. The basic economies of European nations are on the upswing; the chaos and floundering of the postwar years are definitely behind. The international forces for Atlantic defense are no longer merely figures on paper; the international organization is no longer a headquarters without troops. The forces – ground, naval and air – are assembling. They are training together and the spirit of mutual respect and cooperation that marks their joint maneuvers is heartening and encouraging. Still far too few in numbers and short of equipment, their ranks are filling; machines and weapons reach them in a steady stream.

The military and political leaders of the participating nations no longer slowly feel their way forward in an endeavor without guiding precedent.

Caution that is inescapable in a new and unique enterprise has been replaced by confidence born out of obstacles overcome. The Allied Powers in Europe are constituting a team for defense; one capable of assuring a lasting and secure peace.

The winning of freedom is not to be compared to the winning of a game – with the victory recorded forever in history. Freedom has its life in the hearts, the actions, the spirit of men and so it must be daily earned and refreshed – else like a flower cut from its life-giving roots, it will wither and die.

All of us have pledged our word, one to the other, that this shall not be. We have cut the pattern for our effort – we are devoting to it available resources for its realization. We fight not only our own battle – we are defending for all mankind those things that allow personal dignity to the least of us – those things that permit each to believe himself important in the eyes of God. We are preserving opportunity for men to lift up their hearts and minds to the highest places – there must be no stragglers in such a conflict.

The road ahead may be long – it is certain to be marked by critical and difficult passages. But if we march together, endure together, share together, we shall succeed – we shall gloriously succeed together.

Winston S. Churchill to Stephen Pierssené
(Churchill papers, 2/114)

5 July 1951
Urgent

Mr Piersenné,

Pray make a hundred copies of the enclosed speech of General Eisenhower. This should be completed by noon tomorrow at the latest. Then send some copies to Lord Woolton with the enclosed letter from me. I do not know whether he is in London or not. Make sure it reaches him without an hour's delay.

Please also send one of the earliest copies to Mr Sandys who will make his own circulation of it to the United Europe Organization for whose work it is so powerful a stimulant. Pray also send me twenty copies and send one to every member of the Shadow Cabinet by my directions. I should like you to report as soon as possible tomorrow that all this is in train.

Winston S. Churchill to General Dwight D. Eisenhower
(Churchill papers, 2/114)

5 July 1951
Private

My dear Ike,

As I am getting rather deaf I could not hear or follow your speech[1] when you delivered it. I have now procured a copy for which I am arranging the widest circulation in my power.

Let me say that I am sure this is one of the greatest speeches delivered by any American in my life time, – which is a long one, – and that it carries with it on strong wings the hope of the salvation of the world from its present perils and confusions.

What a great conclave we had last night! I had not comprehended the splendour of your speech until I read the text this evening, which I procured only with some difficulty. But I feel that we were close enough together anyhow. I think we ought now to be able to see the way forward fairly clearly, and I believe that events in the next two years are going to be our servants and we their masters.

You will no doubt have seen the interim judgement[2] of the Hague Court on the Persian tangle. I am sure it would be a great help if in accordance with the view you expressed last night when I read you my telegram to the President, you sent something home on the timelines in support from your angle.

I look forward to seeing you again before many weeks have passed.

Meanwhile with all my heart believe me your comrade and friend.

Winston S. Churchill to Lord Woolton
(Churchill papers, 2/114)

5 July 1951

My dear Fred,

This is one of the greatest speeches that has been made by an American for many years. It was scarcely reported at all in the British Press and Ike had to read it so fast on account of the time limit that it was difficult to follow at the moment. It seems to me that it expresses the policy of our Party, and I trust of our country, in the most complete and perfect manner.

I ask you to give directions for the immediate circulation of this speech in every constituency and through every form of organization that you control. I wish that several millions of copies shall be printed, and that it shall become

[1] Reproduced above (pp. 2104–8).
[2] The Hague Court ruled in favour of BP, which owned a lease on an oilfield recently nationalized by the Iranian Government. Iran ignored the ruling.

apparent that this is *our* policy, purpose and plan. Please telephone me tomorrow at Chartwell on receipt of this letter.

Pray also consider any other measures which will help.

Lord Salisbury to Winston S. Churchill
(Churchill papers, 2/126)[1]

6 July 1951
Private and Personal

My dear Winston,

Anthony has just rung me up. I am so distressed that you and he should think that I embarrassed you yesterday. I needn't say that that was the last thing that was in my mind. On the contrary, what I said seemed to me entirely in harmony with one of the main points we discussed after our last rather unhappy meeting with the PM, the necessity of maintaining the morale of our people in Persia. From this point of view, the Govt statement seemed absolutely deplorable. That was no suggestion that HMG meant to support them in any way. The situation was intolerable; the Persian Govt seemed bent on pushing them out; and that was all. I am afraid that I blew up, and said what I thought. It is, of course, a thing which is always liable to happen under our system, under which simultaneous statements are made in both Houses. I can't know what you or Anthony are going to say; you can't know what I am going to say. There is no opportunity for consultation. So far as I know, he might have been going to say exactly this same thing. However, all this does not alter the fact that I am very sorry to have put you in a position of embarrassment. Anthony asked whether I could do anything to put it right. I don't see what I can do. I can't and won't eat my words. They represent my sincere views. I could of course absent myself from any future meetings with the Govt. You may well think that wise, and I should entirely understand this. Or, further, if you wished it, I could retire from the leadership of the House of Lords and make way for someone in whom you had more confidence. I should be very happy to do this, if you thought it right. I sometimes wonder whether I am very suited to politics. Actually, I imagine that the march of events will make any remarks, especially by anyone so unimportant as myself, run of date in a very few days. The Hague Court decision itself entails a new situation, in which the Govt may well find it possible to take a finer line. At any rate, I have not involved you and Anthony with them. I told the Lord Chancellor last night, before I left the House, that I had spoken entirely for myself and not as the result of any consultations with you. I am entirely in your hands. Please say whatever you think right.[2]

[1] This letter was handwritten.
[2] Churchill responded: 'Thank you so much for your letter. Our friendship and alliance are far superior to all incidental slight discrepancies.'

Winston S. Churchill to Clement Attlee
(*Churchill papers, 2/126*)

9 July 1951

My dear Prime Minister,

In our three conversations with you and some of your colleagues about Persia, we have tried to make certain points clear.

1. That the Anglo-Iranian personnel should be encouraged to remain at their posts in Abadan, although we cannot judge of the position in the mountainous oilfield. We understood that this was your policy, but that in addition, should it be decided to withdraw the personnel, they would be kept concentrated and intact at Sheiba and upon a liner. We think it would be a disaster if our personnel were hustled and bullied out of Abadan. It would be an aggravation of this if the personnel were dispersed and scattered. We should like to be reassured about the Government's policy upon this point.

2. We noted your repeated declarations that all necessary force would be provided and used to secure the withdrawal of the personnel if at any time they were exposed to peril of life and bloodshed. We were also led to hope in our first conversation that military movements would be continuous so as to secure ample forces, naval, air, and army, on the spot to meet any emergency.

3. We also asked that if the worst came to the worst the Government should not exclude the possibility of a forcible occupation of Abadan, and we were told that plans for this contingency were in preparation. We have made it clear that should such regrettable measures be forced upon you, you could count on our support. As it seems to us, the judgement of the Hague Court greatly strengthens our world position should such action become necessary.

4. We earnestly hope that there has been no interruption of the military movements described to us.

5. We have urged that the strongest representations should be made to the United States to take positive action in supporting the common interests of the Atlantic Powers, which would be deeply endangered by the Sovietization of the vital area between the Caspian Sea and the Persian Gulf, and we are glad to know that there is no question of our asking for mediation.

PS. I am sending a copy of this to the Foreign Secretary.

July 1951

Winston S. Churchill: speech
('Winston S. Churchill, His Complete Speeches', volume 8, pages 8223–5)

10 July 1951   The Royal College of Physicians

LORD MORAN

First of all I must thank you for according me an Honorary Fellowship of the Royal College of Physicians. I also had the honour to be made a surgeon eight years ago, and now I can practise, in an honorary fashion, the arts of surgery and medicine. Unless there is a very marked shortage of capable men in both these professions, I shall not press myself upon you. No doubt in these difficult times it will be a comfort not only to the profession but to the nation at large that you have me in reserve.

I have not yet taken any final decision as to which of these beneficent branches I should give priority to (in case an emergency arises). Being temperamentally inclined to precision and a sharp edge, it might be thought that I should choose the surgeon's role. At any rate you can be sure of having something to show, and I have been told that this was the view of many young medical students. However, all comes out even at the end of the day, and I am assured that latterly an entirely new phase has come over the art of medicine. It has become much less a process of emphasizing or mitigating, or correcting tendencies, and making grave and luminous pronouncements upon them, than of taking hard and quick decisions. Science, progged on by the urge of the age, has presented to us in the last decade a wonderful bevy of new and highly attractive medicinal personalities. We have M and B, penicillin, tetramycin, aureomycin and several others that I will not hazard my professional reputation in mentioning, still less in trying to place in order. And medical science has presented to you an ever-increasing growth of decisions as rapid and as refined as ever presented to the surgeon.

It is arguable whether the human race have been gainers by the march of science beyond the steam engine. Electricity opens a field of infinite conveniences to ever greater numbers, but they may well have to pay dearly for them. But anyhow in my thought I stop short of the internal combustion engine which has made the world so much smaller. Still more must we fear the consequences of entrusting to a human race so little different from their predecessors of the so-called barbarous ages such awful agencies as the atomic bomb. Give me the horse.

But in all this advance of science which we can no more resist or delay than we can stop the tides of destiny, there is one grand outstanding exception, the healing arts. All that cures or banishes disease, all that quenches human pain, and mitigates bodily infirmity, all those splendid names, the new arrivals which I have just mentioned to you, all these are welcome whatever view you may take of religion, philosophy or politics. Of course it may be said these discoveries only lengthen the span of human life, and then arises the delicate and difficult question, is that a good thing or not? It is a question which presents itself in a blunt form to the rising generation.

For my part I shall not attempt to pronounce because my impartiality might be doubted. I might be thought an interested party, and this brings me to my main and most agreeable task this evening, because, but for Lord Moran's wisdom and decision, I should probably not be here this evening discoursing jauntily to you all.

It is my duty to pay your tribute to Lord Moran and, when the time comes, to present him with the portrait which has been painted by Professor Pietro Annigoni.[1] Well, I know Charles Moran I would say almost as well as he knows me. He was for nine years President of your illustrious College. His war record is magnificent. In the First World War he won the MC and was mentioned in many dispatches and has Italian decorations – all gained under the hard fire caused by the mistakes of our military experts in the first great struggle with which our generation has been afflicted. In the last war, Charles came with me wherever I went. That puts me in the position of the man who said one night, 'I think my companion here ought to have the VC because he has been everywhere I have been.' At any rate, we went for a good many long journeys by air at a time when the comforts of air travel had not been developed to the almost perfect state they have now. I do not think a great deal about travelling by air so long as you get there, and he will remember some awkward moments. I am deeply indebted to him. He was for twenty-five years Dean of St Mary's Hospital. He is a great figure in your life, for nine years head of the College, a man deeply versed in his profession and in all its most profound characteristics, a man who apart from his profession stands out as a leading figure in the public life of Britain. I must now mention Lady Moran, who sustained him as only a wife can, and I know all about that.

In the National Health Service, which you all enjoy so much, Lord Moran in my view did his duty in recognizing that he should lead the College in a policy of co-operation with the Government, with constructive criticism from time to time, and in spite of opposition from outside the College, and even perhaps sometimes within, he moved forward with this great body in dignified array. He left the College in your hands, Mr President – than whom no more worthy successor could be conceived – in a position of greater influence than it had held at any time in recent history. I am indebted to you for the kindness and receptiveness with which you have treated me tonight, and if I have digressed into the sphere of levity, I trust that you will consider that one of those minor symptoms, dwelling upon which would only complicate the ultimate diagnosis.

---

[1] Pietro Annigoni, 1910–88. Born in Milan, Italy. Gained international renown for his portrait of Queen Elizabeth II, 1955.

General Dwight D. Eisenhower to Winston S. Churchill
(Churchill papers, 2/126)

11 July 1951

Dear Winston,
    It would be quite impossible for me to tell you how flattered I was by the nice things you had to say about my talk. While I have no great hope that the timorous leadership of Europe will, under the spell of Eisenhower eloquence, suddenly begin with head up and chest out to march sturdily forward along the rocky road to unification, yet the making of the talk did me the personal good of putting into public words something that I believe very deeply.
    With respect to the Persian matter, I have already informed Washington with what seriousness I regard it and of my hope that our Government will find it possible to support some reasonable solution. I am, of course, particularly anxious that the technicians and the professional people now on the job should stay there, and an interim agreement should be reached that would allow the oil to keep flowing.
    Should you by any happy chance be traveling in this region, be sure to let me know so that we can arrange a long meeting. My evening with you and our old comrades of the wartime days was a high spot.

President Harry S Truman to Winston S. Churchill
(Churchill papers, 2/126)

12 July 1951

Dear Winston,
    I appreciate your personal message of June twenty-ninth regarding the situation in Iran,[1] and fully share your views as to the dangers involved. This matter is being given constant and most careful attention by this Government and we are, as you know, in touch with the Government of the United Kingdom concerning all developments. I earnestly hope that counsels of moderation will yet prevail and that a satisfactory solution can be found. I will do everything possible to assist in bringing this about.

---

[1] Reproduced above (p. 2102).

Clement Attlee to Winston S. Churchill
(*Churchill papers, 2/126*)

12 July 1951

My dear Churchill,

Thank you very much for your letter of 9th July about Persia.[1]

I have taken careful note of the points you make and with much of your letter I am in substantial agreement. In particular, we are keeping up strong pressure on the United States Government and are urging them to give us their full support. Some of the other points you raise could perhaps with advantage be pursued in oral discussions, and I would be very glad to have another meeting with you on this subject early next week, if you would like it.

Harold Macmillan: diary
(*'Tides of Fortune', page 322*)

16 July 1951

Conscious that many people feel that he is too old to form a Government and that this will probably be used as a cry against him at the election, he has used these days to give a demonstration of energy and vitality. He has voted in every division; made a series of brilliant little speeches; shown all his qualities of humour and sarcasm; and crowned all by a remarkable breakfast (at 7.30 a.m.) of eggs, bacon, sausages and coffee, followed by a large whisky and soda and a huge cigar. This latter feat commanded general admiration. He has been praised every day for all this by Lord Beaverbrook's newspapers; he has driven in and out of Palace Yard among groups of admiring and cheering sight-seers, and altogether nothing remains except for Colonist II to win the Ascot Gold Cup this afternoon.[2]

Winston S. Churchill to Sir Alexander Korda
(*Churchill papers, 2/171*)

19 July 1951
Private and Confidential

My dear Korda,

The Conservative and Unionist Films Association have sent me this script on which they are at work. I have not taken any part in it but it would be impossible for me to hamper them in this Party matter. I do not see that it

---

[1] Reproduced above (p. 2111).
[2] The horse finished second.

would get in the way of the project you and I have been considering,[1] as it would be purely of temporary electioneering interest. I think however you ought to know about it at this stage.

Pray let me have the text back as soon as you have read it.

Winston S. Churchill: speech
('Winston S. Churchill, His Complete Speeches', volume 8, pages 8225–9)

21 July 1951   Royal Wanstead School, Woodford

SOCIALIST BLUNDERS

It is six years almost to a week since the Socialist Government came into office and we entered upon that melancholy period of eclipse and frustration which if it continues will lead to our decline and fall. What a contrast between our position at the end of the war and that to which we have been already reduced today. Not only were we victorious after all the hard toils and struggles but we were more honoured, respected and admired by friend and foe alike than we had ever been before.

And where do we stand today in the eyes of the world? For the time being we have lost our rank among the nations. There is hardly any country in the world where it is not believed that you have only to kick an Englishman hard enough to make him evacuate, bolt or clear out. Countries we have defended from Nazi and Fascist violence, countries we have rescued after they had been subjugated, countries which had found us strong and steadfast comrades and allies, are watching with astonishment a Britain which they think is in retreat or in decline. Egypt, Persia, Albania, the Argentine and Chile compete with each other in the insults and the humiliations they inflict upon us – and what is the cause? It is the attempt to impose a doctrinaire Socialism upon an island which has grown great and famous by free enterprise and valour and which six years ago stood in honour though not in size at the summit of the world. I say 'though not in size' because a vast larger world is growing up around us. But never forget that fifty millions have come into being in Great Britain under the impulse and inspiration of former generations and now if our native genius is cribbed, cabined and confined these fifty millions will be left physically stranded and gasping, like whales which swum upon the high tide into a bay from which the waters have receded.

Almost every year we have some new crisis. Now this year we are heading for another. The gap between our imports and exports during the first six months of this year was £550 million. The position is worsening and for the month of June alone the gap was nearly £150 million. The pound sterling

---

[1] Korda wished to show in cinemas a film in which Churchill appeared briefly on behalf of the RAF Benevolent Fund.

which, when we came out of the Second World War, was worth 20*s*, has now in these six years fallen to 14*s* 10*d*. What does that mean? Everybody's salaries, pensions, wages and savings have been reduced by more than a quarter. Think of all the thousands of millions that that means when translated into the life of a great people. Surely this is a tremendous fact. All the boastings of the welfare State have to be set against the fact that more than what they have given with one hand has been filched back by the other. More than what they have given by benefits and improvements has been taken back by the reduction in the value of the money we use.

'Oh!' they say, 'all this is due to Korea. If it had not been for Korea we should never have fallen into our present position.' This is an utter untruth. The main reason for the fall in the buying power of our money at home and still more abroad is not Korea but devaluation. But devaluation did not come by itself. It forced itself upon our Socialist 'Masters' as they call themselves by four years of grotesque, reckless squandering of our treasures and resources. They had got the control of the Government for their own party. No Government in our history has spent money to the vast extent and reckless manner as our present rulers. Apart from £2,000 million they have begged or borrowed from the United States and received from the Dominions, they have spent more than £11 million a day or £24,000 million in their six years. No community living in a world of nationalism and competition can possibly afford such frantic extravagances.

All this happened long before Korea or what is called 'rearmament'. Devaluation was the child of wild profuse expenditure, and the evils which we suffer today from what I have called 'the money cheat' are the inevitable progeny of that wanton way of living. The greatest national misfortune which we are now entering is the ever falling value of our money, or to put it the other way round, the ever increasing cost measured by work and thrift of everything we buy. Taxation is higher than in any country outside the Communist world. There they take all. There no one has anything except the salaries paid them by the privileged Communist aristocracy. British taxation is higher now than it was in the height of the late war – even when we stood alone and defied all comers.

Is not that an astonishing fact? Six years of Socialist Government have hit us harder in our finance and economics than Hitler was able to do. Look at the effects you face of devaluation abroad. We are an island with a population of fifty millions living on imports of food and raw materials, which we have to buy by our exertion, ingenuity and craftsmanship. We have to pay across the dollar exchange twelve hours of work, with hand or brain, to buy what we could before have got with eight hours. We are a hard-working people. We are second to none in ability or enterprise so far as we are allowed to use these gifts. We now have to give a third more of our life strength, energy and output of every kind and quality to get the same revivifying intake as we had before devaluation two years ago. 'Korea', they say, but this is a shoddy excuse, utterly divorced from fact or truth.

'Rearmament', they say, but it has hardly begun. No Government has ever had such generous provision for our national defence as has been made by Parliament with the full support of the Conservative Party during the Socialist reign. But when the Minister who called us 'vermin' and the Minister who said no one else but the organized workers of his party 'were worth a tinker's cuss' woke up to the fact that we were again in gravest peril, it was found that we were almost defenceless. So then there was a panic programme a year ago of £3,600 million of military expenditure in three years. And then the revised programme nine months ago – because they seem to have added up their figures wrong – by which £4,700 million are to be spent over these current three years. We have supported the steps that they took and done our utmost to meet the demands that they have made, but that does not mean that we condone the grievous social, political and administrative blunders they have committed or that we bear the responsibility for the plight into which we are now plunged.

The whole social programme of which the Government boast was devised in conception and detail by a National Government resting upon a House of Commons with a Conservative majority of one hundred over all parties. Only one single new idea has been contributed by the false guides who have led us far astray, who have robbed us of the fruits of our victory and mauled our daily life. Only one. You know the one I have in mind. Nationalization. What an awful flop! Show me the nationalized industry which has not become a burden on the public either as taxpayers or consumers or both. There is hardly an industry in which the employees are contented with changing the private employers with whom they could negotiate on equal terms through the trade unions for the hordes of all-powerful officials in Whitehall. And now our Socialist Utopians are getting fed back with their own tail in Persia and other countries, where we have in the past gathered or created valuable possessions. Others can play at that game too. It must be with many a prick of conscience that Mr Attlee and Mr Morrison and the band of misguided careerist intellectuals they have collected around them regard the meagre and mouldy harvest of nationalization which they have bought for us so dearly both at home and abroad.

But they are incorrigible. Obstinacy at the national expense seems to them a virtue. Even at this moment of all others when they are confronted with failure, fallacy and exposure – as they well know – of their scheme of thought, they try to brazen it out by nationalizing, of all others, the steel industry which in enterprise, planning, organization and efficiency has raised itself, in spite of all deterrents, to a pinnacle in British production. Not one of them believes that the nationalizing of steel is good for our country at this moment. In fact in spite of their boasting they have been forced to admit that they cannot possibly manage the business themselves. They have recoiled from the consequences of their own arguments and at this moment the two Socialist millionaires, Mr Strauss, Minister of Supply, and Mr Hardie, head of the Socialist Steel Corporation, have had to confess by actions which speak louder than words, their utter inability to manage the business or deliver the goods. They have had to leave the whole working and conduct of the steel industry in the skilful, experienced hands of the Steel Federation from whom they tried to take it. They have learnt the lessons here at home which at present they are trying to teach Persia, that it is one thing to nationalize a vast industry and quite another to manage it so that it works and pays and provides the livelihood for all its wage-earners and a decent service for the community which depends upon it.

And now I come to the worst thing of all. We had a speech the other day from the Communist Horner in which he said: 'If a Tory Government is returned it is certain that there will be a national strike of the miners. . . . It is only responsibility and loyalty to the Labour Government that has caused the miners to pull their punches.' This speech, which is, of course, only a part of the Communist conspiracy to bring Britain under the whole of the Kremlin, would not have counted if it had only been the mouthings of a Moscow lackey. But there, sitting at his side, was a Minister of the Crown – Mr Griffiths. I give the Government credit for their hostility to Communism, though they are bringing it nearer by all they do. But fancy this Minister sitting there beside this Communist agent and not daring to open his mouth in protest or contradiction. And fancy that a week has elapsed without the Prime Minister or any other member of the Government disowning and denouncing the declaration which Mr Horner made. Let us see exactly what this declaration means. If the people of Britain should at any time be allowed to have a General Election, and if the will of the people expressed through the universal suffrage electorate should return a Conservative Government to power, Mr Horner says it is certain that there will be a national strike of the miners. This of course, if it happened, would paralyse the whole life and industry of our country.

Now I have always been a friend of the miners. Just over forty years ago I moved the Second Reading of the Mines Eight Hours Bill. I set up the system of mines inspectors drawn from the miners themselves which exists today as one of the main measures to ward off the perils of coal-mining. In 1925 as Chancellor of the Exchequer I provided £20 million to give a year for further negotiations to solve the difficulty in the mining industry and thus avoid a national or general strike. The only quarrel I have ever had with the miners was in the war when I had to forbid them from pouring out of the mines to join our armies in the field. Let them dismiss from their minds these malicious tales that a Conservative Government would be hostile to the mining community. I have always affirmed that those who work in these hard and dangerous conditions far from the light of the sun have the right to receive exceptional benefits from the nation which they serve.

But now the Communist Horner has stepped outside the sphere of industrial disputes, and threatens the whole British democracy, thirty million voters, with a national strike to bring the country down if they dare express their opinion and wishes at the polls. This is an insult to the will of the people which no free democracy could endure. The idea that one section, however worthy, in our island should claim the right to deny political liberties and rights to all the rest of us, is one which would never be tolerated and one which, in my belief, the miners themselves would be the first to repudiate.

But while these shameful menaces are uttered, the Socialist Government, intent on electioneering – and false electioneering as it will turn out to be – remains 'mum'. Attlee doodles, Morrison gapes and only Mr Bevan grins. Well, anyhow, we are going to have a General Election as soon as we can force these office-clingers to present themselves before their fellow countrymen. Then the people will have a chance to express their will. Great as are the difficulties of the time, ugly as the inheritance is which the Socialists will leave behind them, long as is the period of stable progressive government which will be required to remedy our misfortunes, and to rebuild our national power and fame, I have no doubt that it is the duty of all those who are here this evening and of every man and woman in the land, to prepare themselves fearlessly and faithfully for the splendid opportunity they will have of reviving the strength and renewing the glory of our island home.

Randolph S. Churchill to Winston S. Churchill
(Churchill papers, 2/126)

22 July 1951

ARAMCO

Though it is true that the Anglo-Persian Oil Company were more forward than HMG in detecting the trouble in Persia, the Company itself acted much too slowly. The key event was the new agreement negotiated by ARAMCO (Arabian American Oil Company) in December 1950.

This agreement shared the profits 50–50 between the Americans and the Saudi-Arabians and also gave the Saudi-Arabians representation upon the Board. The US Government, in order to sweeten the negotiations, waived all claims to income tax over the Saudi-Arabian 50 per cent, while still taxing the American share-holding.

ARAMCO was originally incorporated in 1933 in the state of Delaware as the California, Arabian Standard Oil Company. In 1944 it changed its name to Arabian–American Oil Company – a useful example of how American big business has come of age in the diplomatic field.

American industrial diplomacy and free enterprise aided by an intelligent government, have naturally scored over Socialist sloth and Socialist monopolistic greed.

Winston S. Churchill: speech
(Hansard)

23 July 1951 — House of Commons

ASSASSINATION OF KING ABDULLAH OF JORDAN

All quarters of the House will share the sorrow and concern with which we learnt of the news of the murder of King Abdullah of Transjordan. I was myself responsible for taking the direct steps which led to his appointment or creation as Emir of Transjordan in 1922.

Of the institutions which have survived the shock of the Second World War, he continued, up till this murder, to be an example of the character and quality of his administration, a man of the greatest fidelity and a vehement Arab patriot if ever there was one, who left Mecca to endeavour to expel the French from Syria by force of arms.

When I was on the spot, having the great advantage of Colonel Lawrence's advice, we persuaded him not to take this disruptive step, on which he was prepared to sacrifice his life, and he became, instead, a skilled and consistent worker for the peace and prosperity of that part of the world and for the interests and the honour of Arab peoples wherever they may be.

It is a great source of regret that he should have been struck down. In the war, as the Prime Minister has said, whenever things went wrong Abdullah was at his very best. He ran every risk to keep good faith with those with whom he had worked. Not only was he a champion of Arab rights, but he always sought that reconciliation between the Arabs and the Jews, the Arabs and the Israelites, which is the foundation of all future hopes in Palestine.

I am very glad that a Motion will be moved by the Prime Minister tomorrow. It will certainly win the support of the whole House, I am sure, no matter what may be the deviations of thought on these subjects, because we know that the Arabs have lost a great champion, that the Jews have lost a friend and one who might have reconciled difficulties, and that we have lost a faithful comrade and ally.

Winston S. Churchill: speech
('Winston S. Churchill, His Complete Speeches', volume 8, pages 8230–2)

23 July 1951

Mansion House, London

UNITED EUROPE

In his memorable speech in London the other day, General Eisenhower made it clear that his task as Commander-in-Chief was made infinitely more difficult by the divergencies in Europe and the tangle of authorities with which he has to deal. Let us try to smooth his path and strengthen his hand.

How much we owe to the great Republic which has arrived at the summit of the world, only with the ambition to render service to others. We have here tonight, as a piece of good fortune, an outstanding American statesman, Mr Bernard M. Baruch. In the alliance of free peoples the USA provide the driving power and a large part of the resources. After helping to restore Europe's economy by the Marshall Plan, America has now created the North Atlantic defence system. We are particularly indebted to President Truman for sending to Europe to command our combined forces that great Commander and trusted friend of Europe – General Eisenhower. He has indeed undertaken an heroic mission. He has become deeply convinced of the need for closer European union. This was urged at Strasbourg in May. Now the British Government have at last accepted this view. Better late than never. But one ought not to be late in measures which, if taken promptly and unitedly, give the world its best chance of escaping another hideous catastrophe.

How clever the Soviets have been in preventing for so many months all progress with the German part of the plan by prolonging the futile discussions in Paris about the Agenda for the Conference of Foreign Ministers for which they asked. How foolish we have been in letting these many important months slip away. In the end no doubt the advice given at Strasbourg will be followed. But meanwhile one of the great deterrents on Communist aggression has been retarded. Take again the question of including Turkey and Greece in the European defence system. By staying out of the conference, we have had no say in its decisions. It may well be that, as in the case of the Schuman Plan, the scheme which will emerge will contain features unpalatable to us. Still, without a European Army it will be almost impossible to get agreement upon German rearmament; and without a substantial German contribution there can be no effective system of Western Defence.

But look at the hideous delays which have occurred. It is more than a year since we passed our resolution at Strasbourg expressing the idea of a European Army in which France and Germany would play their parts. The main criticism has been that the European Army would cut across the organization of the Atlantic Force. This was, I think, the first reaction of the American Government, but there have lately been signs that they are looking upon the proposal for a European Army with increasing favour. They now see that it is the only basis on which France is willing to agree to German rearmament. And there also are disadvantages and even dangers to us in standing aloof. I trust, therefore, that a renewed attempt will be made to find some basis on which Britain can be associated in one form or another with the Schuman organization.

Then there is the proposal for a European Army. This has two aims. First, to create in Europe a permanent system of joint defence against outside aggression. The second is to make it as difficult as possible for the European nations at any time in the future to fight against one another. In the course of the negotiations the earlier proposals have been considerably modified, but the scheme still contains features which we do not like. I very much regret that the British Government did not accept the invitation to take part in these talks. I believe that if a British representative had been there, we might very likely have secured further modifications which would have made it possible for Britain to join in this scheme, either on the same footing as the others or as some kind of associate member. From the Continental standpoint the Schuman Plan is greatly weakened by the absence of Britain – the largest steel and coal-producing nation in Europe. The re-establishment of Franco-German relations has become something much more than a return to normality. There is being developed between them a close and active partnership such as was never dreamed of before. The most remarkable manifestation of this new spirit is the Schuman Plan, which, apart from its economic benefits, will make war between Frenchman and German more than ever difficult and improbable. However, we in this country could not accept the supra-national federal institutions envisaged originally in the Schuman Plan.

It was with a sense of deep comfort that I saw the representatives of the German Parliament take their seats in the European Assembly at Strasbourg. Our European Movement and the European idea for which it stands have undoubtedly played a large part in bringing nearer the reconciliation of these two foes whose quarrels through the centuries have wrought both them and all of us grievous injuries. The first notable forward step was the invitation to Germans to attend The Hague Congress convened by the European Movement in 1948. I well remember, at this unofficial but now historic conference, welcoming a distinguished delegation of Germans headed by Dr Adenauer, now the first Chancellor of the new German Republic.

The mainspring of all our efforts is the assembly at Strasbourg, where we sit together with the representatives of other European Parliaments under the vigilant eye of our President, M Spaak. It is right that the seat of the Council of Europe should be situated in France. France is the keystone in the arch of European understanding which we seek to build. But the leadership required to unify Europe cannot be provided by one country alone. There can be no Europe unless it be based upon a solid foundation of trust and comradeship between the French and German peoples. Within the wider framework of the UNO a Council of Europe has been set up. A European Army is beginning to take shape, and a European Court of Human Rights is shortly to be established. In the economic field practical measures are being taken to reduce barriers and stimulate the flow of European trade. These are important and much-needed gains because the international situation has deteriorated, and the need for uniting and strengthening Europe has become ever more urgent.

I have long believed in the idea of a United Europe. In the turbulent year 1943 I said:

> Under a world institution representing the United Nations there should come into being a Council of Europe. We must try to make this Council of Europe into a really effective league with a High Court to adjust disputes and with armed forces, national or international or both, held ready to enforce its decisions and to prevent renewed aggression. This Council must eventually embrace the whole of Europe.

Much of what I then hoped for is already beginning to come to pass. The cause of United Europe is growing in strength and resolve with every day that passes; there are forces at work in Britain which will enable our island and our Empire and Commonwealth to play their full part – and a leading part – in building the temple of peace and freedom upon foundations which none will dare assail.

Winston S. Churchill to Bernard Baruch
(Churchill papers, 2/169)

27 July 1951

My dear Bernie,

I think Mr Godfrey[1] must have given you a wrong account of his visit. He was with me for about fifteen minutes. I understood that he was to bring me messages from the President and from General Marshall. When I asked him what the messages were, he said they were 'just messages'. He did not seem to have anything particular to discuss, but expressed a keen desire to go and visit the Arab Breeding Stud at Crabbet Park. Randolph had arranged with Lady Wentworth[2] for him to go on the following Monday, but now Mr Godfrey said that it must be that afternoon, Thursday, or not at all. I therefore got my secretaries to see if the appointment could be altered, and for half an hour they

---

[1] Arthur Morton Godfrey, 1903–83. American radio and television entertainer. Also known as 'The Old Redhead'. Entered US Navy, 1920. Radio operator on naval destroyers, 1920–4, 1927–30. Radio announcer for Baltimore station WFBR, 1930. Staff announcer for WRC, 1930–4. Hosted *Professor Quiz*, 1937; *Arthur Godfrey Time*, 1945–72; *Arthur Godfrey's Talent Scouts*, 1946–56.

[2] Judith Anne Dorothea Blunt, 1873–1957. Horse breeder. Married, 1899, Neville Stephen Lytton (div. 1923): three children. Baroness Wentworth, 1917.

were on the telephone; but alas, it was impossible. I enclose Lady Wentworth's letter explaining why, and also my reply to her. I also send you a copy of the letter I wrote to Mr Godfrey.

In these circumstances I cannot feel he has any reason to be offended with me.

Winston S. Churchill: speech
(Hansard)

30 July 1951　　　　　　　　　　　　　　　　　　　　　　House of Commons

FOREIGN AFFAIRS (MIDDLE EAST)

When the right hon. Gentleman the Foreign Secretary (Mr Herbert Morrison) asked me to forgo the opportunity of opening this debate, I was encouraged to hope that he would have something to tell us. I thought that he would be able to cast a light on some of these anxious and serious problems which in more than one quarter press upon our minds this afternoon. Instead, he has treated us to an able and agreeable parade of bland truisms and platitudes which I fear must, in these busy times, have caused him many long hours of toil and study.

I, also, shall indulge in a somewhat general survey, though I shall not go back so far as the collapse of the Ottoman Empire, which, after all, took place at the end of the First and not of the Second World War. The decline of our influence and power throughout the Middle East is due to several causes. First, the loss of our Oriental Empire and of the well-placed and formidable resources of the Imperial armies in India. Second, it is due to the impression which has become widespread throughout the Middle East that Great Britain has only to be pressed sufficiently by one method or another to abandon her rights and interests in that, or indeed any other, part of the world. A third cause is the mistakes and miscalculations in policy which led to the winding-up of our affairs in Palestine in such a way as to earn almost in equal degree the hatred of the Arabs and the Jews. I was struck by the fact that the right hon. Gentleman should have confessed mistakes which have been made in this matter. One failure, he said, we admit. It has long been evident how disastrous was the course we followed there, and all these put together, the loss of our power in the world, and in that part of the world, the diminution of our resources, the mistakes which we have made, and the feeling that we are incapable of putting up an effective resistance – most unjust assumptions I would certainly say – all these have brought us to the melancholy and anxious position in which we stand this afternoon.

The position is not necessarily irretrievable in its long-term aspects, but we certainly cannot restore it by ourselves alone. It can only be retrieved in any case at a lower level than before the Second World War, and it can only be retrieved, in my opinion, by the joint co-operative action of Britain and the United States, and, in the Mediterranean sphere, of France. (An Hon. Member: 'And Turkey'.) And Turkey, I entirely agree with that.

It is for this reason that I have been most anxious to encourage the United States Navy to take a leading part in the Mediterranean and that I welcome so strongly the support which they have given both to Greece and Turkey, and the keen attention they are at length – I might almost say, at last – giving to Persian and Iraqi affairs. The oil supplies from this part of the world have a value far above their commercial or financial importance, great though this be. The strategic aspect of the destination of the oil supplies and the immediate future of the Middle East countries is of immense importance, not only to Britain, but to the United States. It plays a part in their whole plan of creating ever-increasing deterrents, direct or indirect, to the spread of Communism, and thus to preserving the peace of the world by reaching conditions on which a lasting and friendly settlement may be made with Soviet Russia on the basis not of weakness and divided policy, but of strength, unity and well-conceived measures.

We may, indeed, truly say that the events which are taking place in Egypt and Persia play an integral and, possibly, vital part in the whole purpose of the vast alliance, under the supreme authority of the United Nations Organisation, to which we have all bound ourselves. The consequences of this alliance now present themselves to us in this country in a manner which dominates our domestic life, with our immense expenditure on rearmament and the reactions which that entails on the standards of life of all classes throughout Great Britain. The issues at stake in the Middle East are of capital importance to us at home and abroad, and to all our Allies.

Since the war stopped, I have always been anxious that the United States should become more interested in what is taking place in Persia and in Egypt. We admire and support the sacrifice and exertions they have made to resist aggression in Korea. Mortal injury would have fallen upon us all, upon the free democratic world, if we had been unable to serve, or unwilling to serve, the United Nations Organisation in resisting armed aggression at any point. But in a material and geographical sense, Korea, after all, is a promontory jutting out into salt water, ruled by American sea-power under an air canopy controlled by, in the main, American air-forces. It is not a place from which things can spread in a physical way against the main interests of the United Nations. The moral and strategic importance of Persia and Egypt, on the other hand, and the relation of those countries to the Atlantic Pact system, profoundly affect American interests and the success of their world policy, in which Great Britain and the Dominions of the Commonwealth are all joined.

If, for instance, the Persian situation arising out of the oil dispute, and the wrongful treatment meted out to us by Persia, with the consequent prolonged paralysis of the Persian oilfields, were to lead to the regions from the Caspian Sea to the Persian Gulf being included in the satellite countries which are Kremlin-controlled today, the consequences would be far more deadly, not only to us, but to the United States than anything that could have arisen in Korea. Therefore I have done, speaking as an individual, whatever was in my power to impress upon leading American statesmen and citizens whom I have met and with whom I am in contact that their main interests are engaged in the Middle East at least as much as they are in any other part of the world outside their own country.

General Eisenhower's sphere of responsibility is also deeply affected by what happens in Persia and Iraq. Turkey is the right flank of any front that can be formed in Europe against Soviet aggression – should that occur, which I do not pre-judge – and the position of Turkey would be greatly endangered if the Soviet control covered all the regions immediately south of the Caspian Sea. The European situation is, therefore, directly involved in what takes place in Persia and Iraq. In surveying the general scene in the Middle East, our relations with Egypt, to which the right hon. Gentleman devoted some of the closing passages in his speech, are of the first importance. During the war we preserved Egypt from the injury and pillage of Nazi–Fascist subjugation. I shall not speak of our loss of life, for that cannot be computed in material terms, but we spent vast sums of money in Egypt maintaining a local wartime prosperity there beyond that which any other country was enjoying in the whole world. Unhappily, that prosperity was shared almost exclusively by the rich and well-to-do classes, while the peasantry seemed to remain in very much the condition in which I saw them when I first went to Egypt as a young officer towards the end of the last century.

This point of view was confirmed and, indeed, emphasised by the Foreign Secretary in his speech. These rich, well-to-do classes who have so much control in Egypt are the very ones who are trying to keep a popularity with the masses of the people by ungratefully assailing us today. It was calculated at the end of the war that we owed more than £400 million to Egypt. Most of it was for the local services and supplies we had purchased to maintain the armies which protected them. These are the notorious wartime sterling balances – I said wartime sterling balances, because more complicated forms of sterling balances have come into existence at later dates, but I am speaking of the wartime sterling balances, which are presented to us as British debts. The War Cabinet of the National Government had always reserved the right to present counter-claims against these debts for the services we rendered in saving Egypt from the horrors of war and conquest.

When, some weeks ago, I was referring to our immense volume of unrequited exports under the heading of sterling balances, the Chancellor of the Exchequer used extravagant language condemning anyone who could so violate, or talk of violating, contractual obligations as to refuse to pay or put in a counter-claim against these wartime debts. But his predecessor, the Minister of Local Government and Planning (Dr Dalton), used very different language, which I shall venture to quote to the House. This is what he said – it is a lengthy quotation, but I think hon Members ought to have it in their minds as it was spoken by so high an authority at the beginning of the Socialist reign:

> 'That vast accumulation of debt represents an unreal, unjust and unsupportable burden. If Lend-Lease and mutual aid had been applied among all the members of the Grand Alliance, as they were applied between the United States and the British Commonwealth, by far the greater part of these debts would never have been charged up against us. Sooner or later – and it would be better sooner than later – this mass must be very substantially scaled down. Britain is strong, but one side of her strength must be refusal to take on fantastic commitments, which are beyond her strength and beyond all limits of good sense and fair play. Nor could I, as the British Chancellor of the Exchequer, support financial arrangements which would mean that for years and generations to come this little island, which led the fight for freedom, would, through this peculiar wartime accountancy, carry a crushing load which even the defeated enemies of freedom – Germans, Japanese and the rest – would escape.'

Pretty good stuff, that. The Chancellor is not here – no doubt he has some other preoccupations – but I trust that this quotation may be brought to his attention by some of his colleagues on the Front Bench. It is of special importance because the Prime Minister – who, I understand, is to wind up the debate tonight – was asked on 12th May, 1947, whether the Chancellor of the Exchequer's speech represented the views of the Government. The right hon. Gentleman replied, with his usual laconic precision, 'Yes, sir'. Surely the Chancellor of the Exchequer should moderate his denunciations of a policy which his predecessor declared in such illuminating terms and which his chief endorsed without a qualification of any kind.

I hold that we should have presented counter-claims and that such a policy would have been supported by the United States. At the same time as we were being so strict, pedantic, meticulous, and punctilious in paying Egypt, we were borrowing or accepting from the United States far larger sums of money which I doubt if we shall ever be able to pay back. It must be an odd state of mind in which the Chancellor of the Exchequer can go on begging and borrowing from one country in order to pride himself and preen himself and plume himself in cutting such a fine example of financial probity, dignity and decorum with another. It is said that one should be just before one is generous. In this case we ask the Americans to be generous in order that we might be just to the Egyptians and indeed, as I hold, unjust to our own people. I say that because it was known at the time that the United States' object in lending to us, giving us these very large sums, by which the

Government have maintained themselves so remarkably – which, as I think the right hon. Gentleman said, have prevented unemployment rising to levels of millions in this country – the United States' motive in doing this was in order that the British people should be able to rebuild their own strength and stand securely on their own feet.

However, the payments of sterling balances continue on a large scale, and only the other day – I believe it was the day when the *Empire Roach* was attacked; but that was a mere coincidence, a pure accident, I am not making any serious point out of it – almost on that day another agreement for heavy payments was announced to the House. What form do these payments take? There is a destroyer of the Hunt class. HMS *Cottesmore* was her name. She, I understand, has been traded to the Egyptian Government, and her name has now been changed to the *Ibrahim el Awal*. (*Laughter.*)

Mr H. Morrison: They are laughing at the right hon. Gentleman behind him.

Mr Churchill: I expect that the right hon. Gentleman wishes that he had such cordial relations with his own back benchers. It would have been strange for the Government to have sold a destroyer to any Power outside the Atlantic Pact at this time, when anti-submarine vessels are regarded as top priority in our shipbuilding programme. But to have given one to Egypt in the circumstances, and at this moment is, I think – I appeal to the ordinary unprejudiced common sense of the House – quite inexcusable.

And how will Egypt pay for it? They will not send us anything which will help our standard of life in this country; they will not send anything to us which will help us in our production of goods for export; not at all. All they will do is simply to scratch a few figures off their sterling balances account. I ask: Is this destroyer still in our shipyards or has she already been delivered? I am told that she is at present at Cowes – I may be misinformed. The Hunt class is a very valuable class of destroyer. Apparently we have not been able to afford to develop them for anti-U-boat purposes because of the money difficulties in which we are plunged. Here was one which we could have had for nothing. If it is not too late I say without any hesitation that she ought not to be handed over unless or until there has been a settlement of other matters.

There is another aspect which should be examined. After the brief war in which Israel, contrary to the expectations of His Majesty's Government –

Mr Crossman (Coventry, East): And of the Opposition.

Mr Churchill: Not at all. The hon. Gentleman has been on all sides in this particular question. After the brief war in which Israel so conclusively demonstrated its fighting superiority over the much better armed Egyptian troops – perhaps the hon. Gentleman would agree with that?

Mr Crossman: Armed by us.

Mr Churchill: All right. I think that was a very foolish thing to do, but it was done in the period of the war when, naturally, arms got loose in different directions.

But this is a question of this destroyer; it is a question of going on arming Egypt now, long after the war. I quarrel with the hon. Gentleman on a great many things. I do not want to quarrel with him on any one of those points with regard to the innumerable facets of which we might occasionally get a gleam of agreement. After this war with Israel an armistice was arranged. In breach of this armistice the Egyptians have closed the Suez Canal. The Foreign Secretary – let me put hon. Gentlemen at their ease – is entirely against the Egyptian closing of the Suez Canal, is he not?

Mr H. Morrison: Yes, Sir, I am. But, unlike the right hon. Gentleman, if I could come to an overall friendly agreement of good relations with Egypt, I would do so.

Mr Churchill: The question is whether the right hon. Gentleman is adopting the right course or not. At any rate, the course which he has adopted, as I shall presently show and have to some extent shown, has certainly not led to the conclusion which the right hon. Gentleman desires, and the closing phrases of his speech were instinct with an atmosphere of disappointment on this point. But an armistice was arranged after this war. In breach of the armistice the Suez Canal was closed to all passage of tankers to the Haifa refinery. Here was a property in which we had an important interest and which could have made our petrol position easier here at home. We have been putting up with this complete breach of the armistice, and utterly illegal blockade, as I contend – I do not think that the right hon. Gentleman will challenge me – under the Suez Canal Convention – for more than two years.

And all through this time we have been releasing money – I am not talking about payments with Egypt; they were going on all the time – to Israel to buy oil that has to be brought all the way from South America. If one takes those things together – our treatment of Egypt, the misbehaviour of Egypt, our indemnifying of Israel; which I do not particularly quarrel with because it was our weakness that let them suffer through the Canal being blockaded – there one really has an example of British submissiveness to find an equal to which one would have to search the world very far. All the time we were sending valuable exports to Egypt for no return, including ships of war, aeroplanes and other munitions, while all they had to do, for their part, was to go on breaking the Suez Canal Convention, insulting us ever more bitterly every day, clamouring for the Sudan and extorting further sterling balance concessions from us in the various agreements which were made.

The extraordinary thing is to see the Foreign Secretary carrying out this policy and the Chancellor of the Exchequer carrying out what looks to be an entirely separate policy. It is not departmentalism, it is compartmentalism of a kind quite extraordinary. I have not seen its like before. I contend that no payments of sterling balances should, on any account, have been made to

Egypt while they persisted in their illegal action in the Suez Canal. Fancy not bringing this strong point and leverage into the argument. There is the Prime Minister. I think it is a question to which he should address himself because he is not at the Foreign Office or the Exchequer; he sits over both. Fancy, I say, not bringing this into the general argument. Let the right hon. Gentleman give us his reasons when he winds up the debate tonight.

Here is another fact. I do not know why we should have waited all this time for Israel to bring the breach of the armistice before the United Nations. Why could we not have done this two years ago, or supported Israel in doing it two years ago? Why could we not have refused all military exports and all payments on the ground of sterling balances until the matter was satisfactorily settled? That is an argument which I honestly think requires the attention of the Government. Although much can be brushed aside in our present course, nevertheless there are verities and sequences of causation which should be in the minds of hon. Members of the House of Commons.

The right hon. Gentleman is not directly responsible for much of this mistaken Egyptian policy. For more than a year we all watched with sorrow Mr Bevin's illness. It was evident that we were virtually without a Foreign Secretary —

The Prime Minister (Mr Attlee): That is quite untrue.

Mr Churchill: — for a very long period. The Prime Minister is responsible for whatever happens, but I think it will be found that we were virtually without a Foreign Secretary during the whole of that period.

(The Prime Minister indicated dissent.)

Mr Churchill: The Prime Minister may hold a very different view, but he cannot dismiss an argument or even an assertion by muttering, 'Quite untrue, quite untrue'.

The Prime Minister: I was trying to correct the right hon Gentleman on a point of fact. It is quite true that my right hon. Friend was ill, but he was an effective Foreign Minister throughout. It may well have shortened his life, but it is quite untrue to say that Mr Bevin ever let his hand go off the Foreign Office. Anybody in close contact with him knows that that is not in accordance with the facts.

Mr Churchill: That, of course, is a matter of opinion, but I adhere strongly to my statement. I fully admit that the Prime Minister had opportunities of closer study of what was actually taking place, but, anyhow, he is directly and personally responsible for allowing the Foreign Office to be without effective guidance during all this critical and, as it may well prove, costly time. We have now got a new deal. The curtain has risen on a new star. The right hon. Gentleman is now at the Foreign Office. I have here a report of the speech delivered by him to the Durham miners a few days ago. I do not intend to inflame our debate or, indeed, to detain the House by reading it.

Mr Ellis Smith (Stoke-on-Trent, South): Why not?

Mr Churchill: Because I do not wish to inflame or detain the House. I have already given those two reasons, and it did not require any 'why not' from the hon. Gentleman. This, however, I must say. Viewed against the sombre background of the world scene it must be considered as one of the most lamentable utterances which a British Foreign Secretary or, indeed, the Foreign Minister of any important Power has ever made in recent times. It shows how far the right hon. Gentleman dwells below the level of events, and how little he understands their proportion in the discharge of the great office to which he has been appointed. It will certainly be viewed abroad as a measure of the contribution he is capable of making to foreign affairs, and of the spirit in which he approaches this grave and solemn task.

Mr Morrison: Will the right hon. Gentleman be good enough, after condemning me so strongly and so sweepingly, to quote what is objected to?

Mr Churchill: It will certainly not make for the tranquillity of the House if I read it out. (Hon. Members: 'Read the lot.') It will add considerably to the length of the proceedings. If the right hon. Gentleman really wants it I will read it.

Mr Morrison: That is the sort of churlishness we are accustomed to. All I can say is that there is presumably in the speech something to which the right hon. Gentleman takes strong exception. Will he read those parts of it to which he does take exception?

Mr Churchill: I really have no choice, but it will certainly add to the length of our proceedings and I expect it will give opportunities for cheering by partisans on both sides. I was hoping that we could keep this Foreign Office debate if not in uncontroversial at any rate in calm channels. Let me say this in advance. In judging what I am now about to read, the House, I am sure, will feel how much better it would have been if the right hon. Gentleman had got Foreign Office officials to write for him his speeches to be delivered in the country and he had devoted some of the leisure made possible thereby to learning something about the great task he has undertaken. Here is what he said:

> 'But Mr Churchill had shown a sensible restraint, which, however, had not restrained the warlike fever of the Conservative back-benchers. A substantial body of Tory back-bench MPs and a number of Conservative newspapers are playing quite a vigorous party game in foreign affairs. It started way back in the days of Ernest Bevin and has, if anything, intensified in recent weeks. I make no personal complaint. I can take it.'

The right hon. Gentleman must not be so touchy today.

> 'Indeed, I have naturally been a target of Tory attacks all my public life. And if some of the less distinguished chat paragraphists or London letter writers find their work easier by accepting cantankerous and untruthful

copy from Tory quarters, well, have a heart! The weather has been warm and some folks find it tiring. Nevertheless, we have seen signs of dangerous Tory irresponsibility in Foreign Affairs. It is one of my duties as Foreign Secretary to stand up for the proper interests of our country. In doing so I rule out nothing that is legitimate.'

That is a very far reaching assertion.

'But what I will not do is needlessly, precipitately and irresponsibly to take warlike courses.'

The Parliamentary and Financial Secretary to the Admiralty (Mr James Callaghan): What is wrong with all that? It is very small beer.
Mr Churchill: The right hon. Gentleman asked me to read it.
Mr Callaghan *rose* –
Mr Churchill: I expect the Foreign Secretary can look after himself, but will, no doubt, express his thanks to the hon. Member for his chivalry in coming to his rescue.

'If you had seen and heard the semi-hysteria of back-bench Tory MPs in the last fortnight, if you have read the more excitable of the Conservative newspapers, then you will find it difficult not to come to the conclusion that, if they had had their way, we should have been involved in two wars in the last ten days.'

I say that was a falsehood, all the more shameful because all the facts were known to the right hon. Gentleman. I could read more, but I have taken up enough time. I have been forced to take up the time of the House with it. Let me press this point. Here is the new Foreign Secretary, who shows to all the world that his main thought in life is to be a caucus boss and a bitter party electioneer. It is tragic indeed that at this time his distorted, twisted and malevolent mind should be the one to which our Foreign Affairs are confided.

Now I turn to Persia. The right hon. Gentleman told us nothing new about Persia. (An Hon. Member: 'Neither have you'.) The newspapers seem well informed, and I base myself on them. It is necessary for those on either side of the House to make their position clear. Judged by every standard, the conduct of the Persian Government has been outrageous, but this must not lead us to ignore what is fair and equitable in the Persian case. In February, 1948, Sir Stafford Cripps appealed for dividend restraint – we seem to go round that circle still – the Anglo-Iranian Oil Company was earning about 150 per cent and paying 30 per cent. As payments by the company to Persia were in part proportional to the distributed profits, this had the effect of keeping down the amount received by the Persian Government, not on commercial merits, but because of the domestic policy of the British Government. All this was put before the House in June by my right hon. Friend the Member for Warwick and Leamington (Mr Eden). I must repeat what he said then:

> 'As they' – the Persian Government – 'saw it, the company was earning 150 per cent or thereabouts but they were still paying 30 per cent. His Majesty's Government were getting a good rake-off, not as a shareholder but from taxation.'

It was quite clear from the moment this situation developed, and indeed before it, that new proposals must be made to the Persian Government. In 1949, negotiations between the Anglo-Iranian Oil Company and the Persian Government ended in a Supplemental Agreement, which was signed in 1949. Meanwhile, an agreement had been made in Saudi Arabia on a 50–50 basis by the American company which has been tactfully renamed 'Aramco'. Just watch that a little. It is as if we had changed the name of our company to 'Persanglo'. There is nothing like studying the customer.

The Supplemental Agreement of 1949 – to quote the Foreign Secretary a few days ago – offered a

> 'more advantageous return for a ton of oil than was now enjoyed by any Middle Eastern Government'.

Nevertheless the agreement was not ratified by the Persian Government for eighteen months, and General Razmara,[1] the Persian Prime Minister, who favoured it, was murdered on March 17. The fall of British prestige in the Near and Middle East, particularly as a result of Anglo-Egyptian relations, must be considered as the main reason why this beneficial measure was not accepted, as it deserved to be. It is also a reflection on the British Government that they were not more active or more effective in pressing this matter from here, during the long interval of eighteen months in 1950 and even before the end of 1949. Then was the time to send a British Minister of the Crown to the spot. Then was the time to try to form with the United States a properly-conceived joint or harmoniously co-ordinated policy; but the Foreign Office had fallen into the disarray to which I have referred, and which I believe was caused by the illness of Mr Bevin. It had not the acumen, at any rate, or the ability to enable the Department to benefit from the accumulated experience of the old Foreign and Political Department of the Government of India, whose personnel they had absorbed.

As usual, no foresight was shown and nothing constructive or effective was done. It may be said, 'How easy to be wise after the event', but surely it is the business of the British Government to be wise before the event. In this case, the facts were obvious. The loss of India as a factor in these regions had effects plainly visible, not only on our prestige but on our power, which could only,

---

[1] Haj Ali Razmara, 1901–51. Studied at Military Academy of St-Cyr in France. Appointed PM of Iran by the Shah, 1950. Assassinated, 17 March 1951.

and can only, be compensated by a closer association of British policy in Persia with that of the United States. The issue was of such great importance as to be well worth a visit by the Prime Minister to the United States at a time when the two countries were acting so closely together in matters like the Atlantic Pact and its development. This matter might well have been incidental to the important topics discussed; but, as we know, an interval of five years passed between his visit after taking office in 1945 and the hastily-resolved mission on which he went eight months ago. The truth is that the Government are so unequal to the enormous and complicated task and so oppressed by their own political preoccupations that they only live from hand to mouth and week to week, and seem to derive no benefit from the invaluable resources of special information and the opportunities of guiding and shaping events which, as an Executive, they enjoy.

I have before pointed out to the House the different characters of the responsibility borne by the Executive Government and the Parliamentary Opposition. This presents itself in the sharpest form where military operations are in question. It is not the duty of the Opposition to suggest or demand specific military operations. They do not know what are the forces available, nor what course of action the Government are pursuing. It has well been said – I think, by Lord Lansdowne,[1] although I have not been able to verify this – that an Opposition may properly urge restraint upon a Government where military action is concerned, but ought to be very chary in demanding military action. (Hon Members: 'Hear, hear'.) That is the course which I have followed. (Hon Members: 'Oh!')

I say that if military action were to be taken, it would usually be unwise for the Executive Government themselves to describe it or to discuss it beforehand. For that reason, I and my colleagues thought that some private interchanges would be useful, and might help the Government and the general policy of the country, by avoiding undue Parliamentary interrogation and debate which otherwise was inevitable on a matter about which we would feel very strongly and which rouses so much justifiable anxiety. I may say here that there has been no question of any agreement between the representatives of the Opposition and those of His Majesty's Government at these private discussions. We have expressed our opinion. We have offered some suggestions. We have endeavoured to make the Government feel that a policy of firmness, exercised with prudence, would in this matter, as in other matters, be treated in a non-party spirit. On the other hand, there is one point, which I shall come to later, which we have made absolutely clear.

Our general attitude on this side of the House is not the same as that of the Prime Minister when he led his party into the Lobby against National Service

---

[1] George John Charles Mercer Nairne Petty-Fitzmaurice, 1912–99. Marquis of Lansdowne, 1944. JP for Perthshire, 1950. Lord-in-Waiting, 1957–8. Joint Parliamentary Under-Secretary of State, FO, 1958–62. Minister of State, Commonwealth and Colonial Affairs, 1962–4. PC, 1964.

less than four months before the late war. Then he was only asked to give the support of his party to measures which no one knew better than he were necessary and, indeed, overdue. If there is any urgent need which the Government feel for stronger military preparation, I can only remind them that they have always received our support in all major things that concern the national safety. But the giving and promising of our support to such measures of security and preparation is quite different from, and has no relation to, the urging upon the Executive of definite military operations. For these, the initiative and sole responsibility fall upon the Government of the day.

The situation in Persia is indeterminate. It follows from what I have already said that I attached great importance to the announcement that the President was sending Mr Averell Harriman to Persia. He is a man who has a complete grasp of the whole world scene and a man of the highest personal capacity. Naturally, he was not, in our view, going as a mediator, still less as an arbitrator. We rightly take our stand upon the judgment of The Hague Court. That was the attitude of His Majesty's Government. It is the prima facie duty of those who believe in the rule of law to sustain in every way they can judgments of this character and not to make compromises between them and some other solution. Mr Harriman does not necessarily represent British views. Nevertheless, I believe that the Harriman mission has been helpful and that it has improved, and not lessened, the hopes of eventual agreement. Mr Harriman's exertions have, at any rate, brought the prospects of a resumption of civilised conversations much nearer than they were before. We have been told nothing about this today, but at any rate I hope that what I have said will be found to be true.

If I may digress for a moment, it would seem that the Government have an advantage in their task in Persia in having so much in common with the Persian Government. They, like them, are holding on to office by the skin of their teeth and, like them, they are persevering in a policy of nationalisation without the slightest regard for national interests. This can certainly form a basis for mutual sympathy and future understanding. We are now embarked upon a period of negotiations which may conceivably be protracted. The Government have been quite right to insist that the persecution and maltreatment of our personnel shall stop before sending a special envoy to Teheran. It does not follow that time is necessarily against us. The position in which the Persian Government have placed themselves so needlessly, and, as we all see, so heedlessly, has brought the whole process of producing and refining oil to a standstill. The tankers are dispersed on other business and cannot be replaced except as the result of an agreement. The markets to which Anglo-Persian oil was sent are almost entirely closed against them by agreements between the various oil companies. Finally, the Abadan refinery has been shut down. We, both British and Persians alike, suffer from the delay, but the Persians suffer more and run greater risks with each week it continues; and meanwhile their

Government is standing between their people and the immense new benefits embodied in the Supplemental Agreement, or variants of it, and the further welcome and important promises of American aid in arms and money. This seems to me to be a situation calling, in an exceptional degree, for patience on the basis of firmness.

Obviously, if the House were not rising this week, we should have postponed this debate. As it is, we have no choice but to set forth our position upon essentials in plain terms. We do not mind if the Government consider it necessary to withdraw our oil personnel from the mountain oilfields into Abadan. It may be necessary or it may not, but it may well be that we could not easily protect them there from violence and murder in their scattered positions in the oilfields. If they are withdrawn – it is said in the papers that there are 300 or 400; it may be true or not, I do not know – to Abadan, they may quite well be the ones who would not be needed there and would be surplus to the essential staff. The matter is not one, in my opinion, which raises any important issue. We have, however, in all our discussions with the Government made it clear that the Conservative Party will oppose and censure by every means in their power the total evacuation of Abadan. (Hon Members: 'Hear, hear'.) The refinery must continue to be occupied by a sufficient number of British Anglo-Persian personnel to make it possible for the installations to be maintained in an effective fashion and for the business to be progressively re-started whenever a settlement is reached. Every effort should be made to rally this nucleus of British personnel to the high opportunity they have of rendering distinguished service to their country. They must stay, and we must never agree to their being withdrawn. If violence is offered to them, we must not hesitate to intervene, if necessary by force, and give all the necessary protection to our fellow subjects. But this I must say in conclusion. If the Government so manage this affair as to lead in the end to the total evacuation of the British oil personnel from the Abadan refinery, it will be our duty to challenge them here and in the country by every means in our power. The issue between us – which I trust may not arise – is the total evacuation, in any circumstances which are at present foreseeable, of the Abadan refinery by the nucleus of British personnel.

We request that if this decision is taken, and if possible before it is taken, Parliament should be recalled in order that a clear issue may be presented. All the power lies in the hands of the Government. If they use their precarious and divided majority to cast away one of the major interests of the nation, and indeed injure, as I think and I have sought to show, the world cause, if they are found to have been guilty of such a course of action now that they are asking of all of us so many sacrifices to carry out the policy of rearmament, then I say the responsibility will lie upon them for this shameful disaster, and we are quite certain that in the long run justice will be done to them by the British people.

July 1951

Winston S. Churchill to Clementine Churchill
(*Churchill papers, 1/49*)

31 July 1951

Darling the telephone is dreadful. Hope all is well. Telegraph please tonight about weather, accommodation and general news.[1] Much love from all.

---

[1] Mrs Churchill had gone to France to continue her convalescence at Hendaye, near Biarritz.

August 1951

Lieutenant-General Sir Henry Pownall to Winston S. Churchill
(Churchill papers, 4/334)

3 August 1951

Mr Churchill,

You may like to see this letter from Alex,[1] which came with his returned proofs. His various amendments have been 'taken care of' on the master copy. They are few.

I haven't done anything about a special pat of butter for the Poles and the French. The trouble is that if one does too much of that sort of thing the poor b—— English feel out in the cold. I don't think 8 Ind. Division need it anyway.

1 August 1951

My dear Henry,

Herewith the galley proof copies of Winston's book. I have made a few comments in pencil on the pages of the chapters I have read. The chapters I have read I have initialled – I am sorry I have been so long, but I have been very busy.

I don't know of someone WSC would like to pay a special tribute to the Polish Corps and the French Corps – They were both excellent, also say something about the 3 Indian Divisions. These latter got on very well with the Italian people [. . .]

I leave for Canada this evening by air.

---

[1] FM Lord Alexander.

August 1951

Henry Ford[1] to Winston S. Churchill
(Churchill papers, 2/169)

2 August 1951

Dear Mr Churchill,

I wanted to write to tell you how much I appreciated the opportunity of having lunch with you during my recent visit to London. You were certainly generous to include me in your very heavy schedule, and it was most interesting to me to hear your views on the many subjects which we discussed during the luncheon.

Needless to say, the City of Detroit and I are very sorry that you do not feel that you can visit us this year during the 250th Anniversary of the city. However, I certainly appreciate your problem and can well understand why you cannot accept.

Again, many thanks for your kindnesses.

Winston S. Churchill to Clementine Churchill
(Churchill papers, 1/49)

2 August 1951

Colonist and Why Tell both ran last of all at Goodwood but with satisfactory excuses. Camrose dined at Chartwell last night to celebrate the five-year jubilee. Randolph and Winston leave today. They enjoyed themselves here at Goodwood. Birleys come tomorrow. Weather bright and warm. I do hope all is going well with you. Fondest love to both. Twenty pounds is my limit for your adventures.

Winston S. Churchill to Clementine Churchill
(Churchill papers, 1/49)

3 August 1951

My Darling,

We had a rotten day at Goodwood. Nightingall[2] should not have proposed running Colonist only ten days after his effort in the Festival Stakes. He was undoubtedly an overworked horse. Also he lost a shoe early in the race and hurt himself, though not seriously. There is no reproach on him, but

---

[1] Henry Ford II, 1917–87. Attended Yale University without graduating. Married, 1940, Anne McDonnell. Served in US Navy, 1941–3. President, Ford Motor Co., 1945–60; Chairman of the Board and CEO, 1960–87. Presidential Medal of Freedom, 1969.

[2] Walter Nightingall, 1895–1968. Racehorse trainer. Trained to be a jockey, but retired at age 14 after fracturing his skull at Windsor racecourse. Trained horses for Churchill, including Welsh Abbott, Tudor Monarch and Colonist.

August 1951 2141

undoubtedly his immediate sale value has been reduced. Why Tell, who was only being trained to the racecourse, did not have an experienced jockey put upon her by Nightingall, and when the gate went up, the poor lamb turned the other way and started fifty lengths behind everybody. However both these misfortunes were understood sufficiently for everybody to make polite explanations to me. The Duke and Duchess of Richmond[1] were most affable. I had not seen him before – he seems a very nice fellow. He was an airman in the war, and has several extremely presentable young boys and girls. Princess Margaret was there, very piano, but she assured me that she had recovered from the German measles.

The Session has ended, thank God, but no one knows what is going to happen next. The uncertainty is a bore, as one cannot make clear-cut plans about the farm, etc.

I am plunged in Volume V, which I am trying to deliver in time for the Book-of-the-Month-Club in America, which sells 350,000, to take it for November. They have taken the whole five volumes, and this is a record when you think of the enormous figures involved. The British edition of Volume IV comes out today, or rather tomorrow, August 4, and is reviewed in all the papers today. I thought you would like to see *The Times* leading article, *The Times Literary Supplement* review, and *The Manchester Guardian* review, which are now enclosed. I am sending a hundred copies of the book to our friends. I am virtually re-writing the early chapters of Volume V as I deal with them. They take four or five hours apiece, and there are twenty in each book. You may imagine I have little time for my other cares – the fish, indoors and out-of-doors, the farm, the robin (who has absconded). Still, I am sleeping a great deal, averaging about nine hours in the twenty-four.

Camrose came here the other night to celebrate the five-years consummation of our Literary Trust gift. Randolph and Christopher were there too, and all passed off jubilantly. (Camrose has a similar anniversary of his own, though on a smaller scale.) This of course is the most important thing that could happen to our affairs, and relieves me of much anxiety on your account.

I am dead set on taking the Freedoms of Deal and of Dover in the morning and afternoon of August 15, leaving with Christopher by the ferry after midnight, and expecting to meet you and Maria at the Lotti Hotel in Paris (unless you can make better plans) on the 16th. Then the night train to Annecy. I am sure it would not be well to chop and change now, unless you have some altogether new plans for staying longer at Hendaye.

Here I must mention that Massigli arrived yesterday. He is coming with

---

[1] Frederick Gordon-Lennox, 1904–89. Educated at Eton College and Christ Church, Oxford. Married, 1927, Elizabeth Grace Hudson: two children. Racing driver: 1st place, Brooklands 500 Miles, 1930; founded MG Migets racing team, 1931. Duke of Richmond, 1935. Joined RAF, 1939. Vice-President, Royal Automobile Club, 1948–89.

Elizabeth Grace Hudson, 1900–92. Born in Oxford. Married, 1927, Frederick Gordon-Lennox: two children.

his wife to Hendaye on August 12, and I think you should offer them some salutation. They are staying at your hotel. Perhaps you would send him a telegram. How clever the French are to get on without a Government, or Prime Minister, or Parliament. All these follies cancel themselves out. The civil servants run the show, and the happy land rejoices in the sunshine and complete contempt of politics.

I send you the Hansard of the Debate on Persia, in which I spoke, with this letter and other stuff which I have mentioned, by Randolph who goes forth tomorrow. His visit passed off all right and I think Winston enjoyed himself all right riding at Sam Marsh's[1] and swimming and petting Nicko. He enjoyed going to the races and spotted a winner which no one else had thought of. The reason was because it belonged to the Aga Khan, whose sons were with him in the school at Switzerland. This is as good a reason as any other.

Give my best love to Maria,[2] and please don't get drowned by the billows of the Bay of Biscay.

The Birleys are arriving at 5 o'clock, and I shall have to sit up in a chair for two hours a day.

Clementine Churchill to Winston S. Churchill
(Churchill papers, 1/49)[3]

5 August 1951

My darling Winston,

How proud and happy you must be of the warm and glowing reception of 'The H of F'.[4] The *Continental Daily Mail* was the first read, followed by *The Times* proper and its 'Literary Supplement'. And I have the Book with me to read, as a Book, and not in fragments. Mary and I are happy here; and we are at this instant basking in the sun (not a very hot sun, but oh! So welcome after six days of lowering clouds which emptied themselves from time to time violently but alas not completely).

Randolph is at Biarritz and is coming over presently to lunch with us at a 'Bistro' we have found in the town. There the food is <u>delicious</u> which cannot be said of the food at our hotel. But the bedrooms are spacious and there is nothing between my bed and America except the Atlantic Ocean which sometimes lulls me to sleep and sometimes thunders and roars like great guns. Randolph sent your letter last night; and I am sad about your racing disappointment. Miaow – yesterday we lunched in Spain with my friend The

---

[1] A racehorse trainer.
[2] Mary Soames.
[3] This letter was handwritten.
[4] *The Hinge of Fate*, vol. 4 of *The Second World War*.

AUGUST 1951 2143

Marchesa of Casa Valdés.[1] She has a seaside house in a lovely village beyond San Sebastian which was hung with flags for Franco's arrival.

Tender Love from Clem the Bird

PS. Our Ambassador (Sir John Balfour)[2] and his wife were there.

Winston S. Churchill to Lord Camrose
(Churchill papers, 4/13)

6 August 1951

My dear Bill,

I have revised the first seven chapters of Book 9, and hope to complete final revision before I leave on August 15. The improvements and rearrangements are considerable. I am having twenty revised copies printed as I go along. How many did you send out in May? I think you gave Reves only ten or a dozen, and not more than fifty were printed altogether. This time however you will require to make a full distribution. If so I will mark all the Finals as I return them to the printer with the number you require. Please let me know by Tuesday night. The first seven chapters will then be ready to return to the printer. Unless I hear to the contrary I will make them a hundred.

Reves has sent a long list of suggestions and amendments, most of which, as usual, are extremely good. I wish he had sent them earlier. I have asked him to come to London on Wednesday next, and I will have a good bunch of Finals for him to read. I am very glad that all is progressing so well. I am myself feeding Houghton Mifflin on account of urgency of the Book-of-the-Month Club. Otherwise I should leave the distribution to you.

You may I think count on Book 9 by the 15th, when I leave, and Book 10 by the end of the month.

Clementine Churchill to Winston S. Churchill
(Churchill papers, 1/49)[3]

6 August 1951

My darling,

Mary has had news from Christopher of all your doings at Chartwell. The Cocktail Party must have been a Wow! I heard 32 bottles of

---

[1] Beatriz Valdés y Ozores, 1926–. 4th Marquesa de Casa Valdés.
[2] John Balfour, 1894–1983. British diplomat. Educated at Oxford and Freiberg, Germany. Married, 1933, Frances van Milligan. POW in Germany, 1914–19. Served in Portugal, Spain (1951–4), Argentina, the Soviet Union and the US. Author of *Not Too Correct an Aureole, Recollections of a Diplomat* (1983).
[3] This letter was handwritten.

Champagne were consumed among 32 people. I hope the tasty tit-bits made by Mrs Landemare[1] were also appreciated.

Christopher says that you both are in love with Vivien Leigh[2] but that he hasn't a look-in! Am longing to see you. Christopher Holland Martin[3] and his charming wife Anne[4] (she is a sister of Eddie Devonshire) have arrived and we are by way of going for an expedition with them today but the weather is atrocious.

Nevertheless we plunge into the breakers. The sea is warm.

We are seeing a lot of Randolph. His little Arabella is staying at a small hotel not far from him. My friend the Duke of Sanlúcar[5] lunched with us yesterday and we pop over to lunch with him at the Café de Paris in Biarritz now and then.

John Colville to Winston S. Churchill
(Churchill papers, 4/59)[6]

6 August 1951

My Dear Mr Churchill

Your unfailing kindness in sending me volume after volume of *The Second World War* as they appear in print is one of the brightest things in this depressing age, and I am indeed grateful. I should prize them in any case, but coming as a gift from you they are beyond price and will remain so to me as long as I live.

---

[1] Georgina Landemare, 1882–1978. Trained as a cook and worked in the kitchen of a French chef, whom she later married. After his death (Grace Hamblin writes), 'she used her quite remarkable skills by cooking for weekend parties in various large country houses. Thus it was she was introduced to Mrs Churchill, and during the thirties she was often called upon to go to Chartwell in this capacity. She was both physically and by temperament a "large" person, and not only her cooking, but her very delightful personality, gave pleasure to the whole household. She was a truly wonderful cook, and even with wartime restrictions, she never failed to produce delicious meals' (letter to Sir Martin Gilbert, 8 Dec. 1992). During the war Mrs Landemare went to Downing Street on a more permanent basis, and then stayed on with Mrs Churchill until her retirement in 1953, at the age of 70. She later wrote a book, *Recipes from No. 10*, for which Mrs Churchill wrote a foreword.

[2] Vivien Mary Hartley, 1913–67. Stage name, 'Vivien Leigh'. Educated at Royal Academy of Dramatic Art, London. Acted in films including *Gone With the Wind* (1939), *Waterloo Bridge* (1940), *That Hamilton Woman* (1941), which was Churchill's favourite, and *A Streetcar Named Desire* (1951).

[3] Christopher John Holland-Martin, 1910–60. Educated at Eton and Balliol College, Oxford. Military Secretary to Governor-General of New Zealand, 1942–4; to Governor of Kenya, 1945. Joint Hon. Treasurer, Conservative and Unionist Party, 1947. Married, 1949, Lady Anne Cavendish. MP (Cons.) for Ludlow, 1951–5.

[4] Anne Cavendish, 1909–81. Daugher of 9th Duke of Devonshire. Married, 1929, Lt-Col. Henry Philip Hunloke (div. 1945); 1949, Christopher John Holland-Martin (d. 1960); 1962, Alexander Victor Edward Paulet Montagu (annul. 1965). OBE, 1952.

[5] Joaquín Álvarez de Toledo y Caro, 1894–1955. 20th Duke of Medina Sidonia (encompassing Sanlúcar). 16th Marquis of Villafranca del Bierzo. 24th Count of Niebla. 17th Marquis of Los Vélez. Married, 1931, María del Carmen Maura y Herrera: one daughter, Luisa Isabel (1936–2008), who came to be known as *La Duquesa Roja* (the Red Duchess).

[6] This letter was handwritten.

I am glad to see you are having a holiday in France before returning to the rigours of the political battle and, very soon I am sure, of No. 10.

Give my love to Mrs Churchill and again so many thanks.

Clementine Churchill to Winston S. Churchill
(Churchill papers, 1/49)

11 August 1951

Delighted to hear we shall all meet in Paris. Longing to see you. Here it is pouring with rain.

Winston Churchill to Winston S. Churchill
(Churchill papers, 1/49)[1]

13 August 1951

Dear Grandpa,

Thank you very much for having me to stay at Chartwell. I enjoyed it a lot especially shooting and riding, and I hope you are enjoying your holiday. I am having lots of fun in the South of France and I have learnt to water-ski and I think it is great fun. I hope you are well. Lots of love to Grandma and you.

Winston S. Churchill to Lady Lytton
(Lady Lytton papers)[2]

14 August 1951   Chartwell

Dearest Pamela,

It is always a gleam of sunshine to get a letter from you. For Annecy all depends on sunshine, for I hope to paint as well as toil at the Book. Volume V now going into final print!

[. . .]

We must meet when I get back in September. I trust indeed all is well with you. I am sure you are happy at Knebworth, but the world is grim, & I am glad we had our lives when we did. I should be very doubtful about beginning all over again.

Poor India – a hard fate lies before her. Not yr fault or mine anyhow!

With my love,

---

[1] This letter was handwritten.
[2] This letter was handwritten.

Winston S. Churchill to Lord Moran
(*Churchill papers, 2/173*)

22 August 1951

My dear Charles,

I have sent the enclosed letter to Dr Russell to avoid delay as I thought perhaps you were in the North. I think it would do me good to have a little swim, and also the salt water would be good for the skin. Your doctors here have been most helpful. I have greatly simplified the remedies, using practically only powder, with the black at one threatening point. I have had a little trouble with the left ear, inside, but a very good young aurist here has practically cleared it up.

It would be good if you would give me your advice about a general practitioner in Venice. I shall be at the Excelsior Hotel, Lido, Venice, from Thursday.

Winston S. Churchill to Dr Russell Brain
(*Churchill papers, 2/167*)

22 August 1951

My dear Dr Russell Brain,

I am going to Venice for a fortnight and there will be beautiful bathing at the Lido. I think it would do me good provided that first, the water is well over 70° and secondly, that I do not plunge in but change the temperature gradually, taking two minutes or more in the process. This is after all only what I do in my bath.

Will you kindly telegraph your advice to me at The Excelsior Hotel, Lido, Venice, after you have had a word with Charles.

Winston S. Churchill to Denis Kelly
(*Churchill papers, 4/342A*)

27 August 1951

Have this printed straight away and then send a copy to Air Marshal Sir Guy Garrod, one to Lord Cherwell, Lord Ismay and General Pownall. Try to collect their comments and corrections, if any, as quickly as possible. Meanwhile send me proofs without waiting for comments. This is one of the chapters which may well delay our deliveries.

September 1951

Winston S. Churchill to Dennis Kelly
(Churchill papers, 4/342A)

1 September 1951

1. I now send you herewith 'Rome'. It was not possible to describe the entry from Clark's extracts. Please send more and varied material. I would like perhaps 500 words. I must see 'Rome' again.

2. Map references. Reves has advised their omission and I have deleted them in Book 10. I agree to Reves omitting them in his foreign translations. I feel however that the American and British editions should contain them. It is important to draw attention to the maps at the point where the uninstructed reader should look at them. These maps, if not inset in the text, should be at the end of the chapter to which they refer, with a slip which enables them to be pulled out for reference during reading. You should consult with Pownall and Allen and report what references you will make in the text. This applies to the whole of Book 10.

3. In my Revise of Book 10 I have frequently substituted 'United States Corps' for 'US Corps', etc. Printer should be told to print 'US Corps', etc., throughout. I may make a few exceptions on final reading.

4. Your corrections and suggestions are most valuable and I find it hard to improve upon them.

Winston S. Churchill to Denis Kelly
(Churchill papers, 4/342A)

3 September 1951

1. I send you herewith the first five pages of your improvements to Chapter XIII. I am awaiting any others in the rest of this chapter.

2. *Preliminary Matter.* I telegraphed to you that I could not release this for final printing by Mifflin or the 150. I have sent you the revised version. I should like to see it in print before final release. If the matter is very urgent

please telegraph. Note please that I did not know that there was only one 'facsimile' so the word 'facsimile' can be singular.

3. The Air chapter must remain provisional until I get your material and the comments of Garrod and Pownall.

4. I have nothing more to say about Chapter VI and see no reason why it should not go into 150. The only provisionals are the Air chapter, Burma and Beyond and the new chapter Strategy Against Japan.

I presume all the chapters are being given a final proof read for clerical errors. I am not reading any of them again.

Winston S. Churchill to Lord Woolton
(*Churchill papers, 2/117*)

3 September 1951

My dear Fred,

I send you herewith the draft of the Party statement which I have carefully read. I have made a few notes, which may be taken as a guide though not as a rule. Personally I like 'Empire and Commonwealth' rather than the other way round. Still I would not press my opinion. I am a little doubtful of the phrase 'thinking imperially' as it has been hard-worked in former times.

I like the statement very much and think it full of good sense, moderately and lucidly stated. I do not think it can do anything but good, and may do a great deal of good. It affects great credit on you and Rab and all who have been engaged in preparing it. Pray let him see this letter of mine.

When do you propose to publish? I shall be home on the 12th, and we might have a meeting of some of us to decide the date of publication.

Winston S. Churchill to David Eccles
(*Churchill papers, 2/113*)

4 September 1951

My dear Eccles,

Thank you very much for sending me your speech which I have read with much interest. I am very glad you mentioned the basic standard below which we should not allow conditions to fall and above which there would be free competition, subject of course to the correctives against monopolistic exploitation. In my Liberal days I coined the phrase 'bring the rear guard in'. The socialists now seem to have chosen 'keep the vanguard back'.

It is not so much a programme we require as a theme. We are concerned with the lighthouse not a shop window. It looks as if the chances of an election are somewhat increased. I shall be back by the 12th and we must have a talk.

Sir Oliver Harvey: record of a conversation
(*Churchill papers, 2/221*)

10 September 1951   Embassy in Paris
Secret

On the subject of the United States, Mr Churchill said he did not believe that the USA could be counted upon to continue indefinitely with their present scale of rearmament and aid to Europe. In two or three years they would insist on having a show-down, and Russia would then have to withdraw from her present forward positions in Poland and Czechoslovakia, or there would be war. Mr Churchill admitted that it was seven years since he had seen Stalin, and they might have brought a change. Nevertheless, if he were again Prime Minister he would certainly seek a personal meeting in order to see whether some arrangement could not be reached. 'You can't argue with Communists but you can bargain with them.' As an instance of this, Mr Churchill cited the agreement reached in Moscow in 1944 about zones of influence in the Balkans. He suggested that there were concessions we could make. For instance, he would give the Russians access to warm waters by instituting international control of the exits of the Baltic and the Dardanelles. He believed the Russians might gain assurance and be more willing to co-operate with the outside world.

Sir Oliver Harvey: record of a conversation
(*Churchill papers, 2/221*)

11 September 1951   Embassy in Paris

Mr Churchill referred to his conversation on the previous night with his French friends on the European Army and he repeated his view that he believed the European Army which did not preserve national contingents would have no fighting spirit.

General Eisenhower reacted strongly and said that it was necessary in life sometimes to attempt to do things which appear impossible. From every point of view it was possible to pick holes in the European Army Plan. Nonetheless he believed that with sufficient determination it could be made to work. He had taxed the French with using the Plan as a means of evading their own burden for self defence, but they had convinced him that they were genuinely in favour of a European Army for genuine motives. He explained that in his view the unit, whatever it was called, should be about 13,000 men and be a combatant unit without any tail of its own, the tail or army service troops being provided by the corps which would be an integrated force. In this way the division would be lighter and more combative and at the same time it could not of itself, without its own services, be a menace. He told the French that he would be prepared to take a leading part in the formation of this Army – and indeed would consent to become its Commissioner provided it was clearly understood that the Governments concerned would confine themselves to settling the general principles which should cover the formation of the European Army and not attempt to settle the details of uniforms, formations, pay, ranks etc. Those were details of a military character for which he must himself be responsible, as otherwise he would be unable to work it and would not undertake it.

Mr Churchill had a long and rather technical discussion with General Eisenhower about French manpower and what in effect happened to the call-up if, as the French maintained, they only produced ten or fifteen divisions. He pressed strongly the need for a call-up of three years service in limited numbers of one in three of those military age, the selection being made by lot. He mentioned that it was more important now to train cadres capable of using the highly complicated weapons of the day rather than embody vast numbers of peasant boys with a year or 18 months' service only. Nonetheless, he and General Eisenhower agreed that the French should adopt training camps to undertake the training of troops from their first call-up, rather than push them straight into the division which would thus be bogged down and quite incapable of combativity owing to having to train their own men.

Mr Churchill observed that he believed Montgomery was cooperating better than in the past. General Eisenhower said that he had mellowed a great deal and they got on extremely well together and indeed their views on the military problems coincided. Montgomery was one who saw everything clearly in simple military terms, completely ignoring the political complications of a situation. This however was a very valuable point of view.

General Eisenhower said it was not possible for the French to build up their metropolitan army and to continue the war in Indo-China and at the same time maintain financial solvency. He had told them therefore that they should clear up with the United States and ourselves the importance to be attached to the Indo-China campaign (with a view presumably to requiring much more assistance if the answer was that Indo-China was an essential part of the common front, although the General did not say so).

Mr Churchill said in reference to the German contribution to Western defence that we should certainly not allow ourselves to be blackmailed by the Germans. He would put the position quite squarely to them, either they would participate in the common defence of the West as everybody else or the West would decide to do without them, which would simply mean withdrawing their effective frontier to the Rhine and leaving Germany as No-Man's Land to be bombed and fought over. The Germans should not think we were asking favours of them. We were in fact merely giving them the opportunity of joining in the common defence with the rest of us. He was strongly in favour of letting all the German Generals and Admirals out of prison now, as a gesture before we were forced to do it.

Sir Oliver Harvey: record of a conversation
(Churchill papers, 2/221)

11 September 1951   Embassy in Paris

My French guests were Monsieur Pleven, Monsieur Bidault and Monsieur Maurice Schumann[1] (now the equivalent of Parliamentary Under-Secretary at the Quai[2]). The two former seemed very tired, and Monsieur Bidault in particular was difficult to follow. Lord Hood[3] was also present.

Mr Churchill developed his theme about the European Army, deploring the disappearance of the French army and urging that French military strength should be rebuilt. He asked once again the question how the annual intake of 220,000 troops could be usefully employed if there were only 10 divisions to which they could be sent, and he suggested that the French would do much better to take fewer recruits (calling up only one in three by ballot) and give them longer training.

The French Ministers were unanimous in rejecting this idea. The system of military service by ballot had been applied in France from 1870 to 1905 and, because priests had been exempted, the system had become identified with clericalism. It would be quite impossible to restore it now. Monsieur Bidault, in an attempt to counter Mr Churchill's criticism of the lack of training cadres, quoted two surprising figures:

(a) that France at this moment had in service 15,000 more regular troops than in 1914, and

(b) that France at this moment had in service more regular troops than ever before in peace time.

The war in Indo-China was of course a deadly drain in the sense not only of casualties but because it tied up such a high proportion of experienced troops. Nevertheless the figure of 10 divisions quoted by Mr Churchill was the figure of the units which would be available by the end of this year. It was in no sense a ceiling and would be increased progressively up to an eventual total of 28 divisions. Monsieur Pleven maintained that the French system of training with the unit gave better results than the British system of training camps. He knew this was a matter of opinion, and Field-Marshal Montgomery held the opposite view. The latter was due to attend a practical demonstration of the mobilisation of a division quite soon and perhaps he

---

[1] Maurice Schumann, 1911–98. Married, 1944, Lucie Daniel. Political Editor, *L'Aube*, 1944–51. Deputy, Nord Dept, 1945–58. French Deputy Minister of Foreign Affairs, 1951–4. Minister of Foreign Affairs, 1969–73.

[2] The Quai d'Orsay, the French foreign office.

[3] Samuel Hood, 1910–81. Educated at Eton and Trinity College, Cambridge. Succeeded his uncle as 6th Viscount Hood of Whitley and 6th Baron Hood of Catherington, 1933. Asst Private Secretary to Secretary of State for India, 1936–9. Private Secretary to Minister of Information, 1939–41. FO, 1942–69: Council of Foreign Ministers, 1945–7; Deputy to Foreign Secretary Ernest Bevin, 1947–8; Head of Western Organisation Department, 1951–6; Deputy Ambassador to US, 1957–62; Deputy Under-Secretary for Western European affairs, 1963–9. CMG, 1953. KCMG, 1960. GCMG, 1969.

might be converted. The French Ministers praised the spirit of the French troops and invited Mr Churchill to visit them in the French zone in Germany.

In the course of the evening Mr Churchill repeated his belief that the United States would wish for a show-down in the next two or three years. He stressed in particular the pressure which could be brought to bear upon the USSR by threats of atomic attack upon

(a) 60 selected cities, of which in the event it would be necessary at most to bomb two or three;
(b) centres of communication which would immediately bring life and administration to a standstill;
(c) the oil wells.

He believed himself that the men in the Kremlin were frightened and were conscious of the growing strength of the West and the ever-increasing superiority of the USA in the field of atomic warfare. He believed that it was possible to do business with them. They would have to retire from the countries in Eastern Europe which they had wrongfully over-run, but we could guarantee the gains both in Europe and Far East which we had recognised during the war and we should give them access to more ports by instituting international control of the Baltic entrances and the Dardanelles. He was against surrendering control of the atomic bomb until the Russians had proved their good intentions.

Much of this conversation took place after the French Ministers had left and, when saying that he himself favoured a meeting between President Truman, Stalin and himself, he made it quite clear that he would exclude France from such a meeting.

Winston S. Churchill: broadcast
('*Winston S. Churchill, His Complete Speeches*', volume 8, pages 8243–4)

16 September 1951

RAF BENEVOLENT FUND

'Never in the field of human conflict was so much owed by so many to so few.' With those words in 1940 – our darkest and yet our finest hour – I reported to the House of Commons on the progress of the Battle of Britain, whose eleventh anniversary we now celebrate. I repeat my words tonight with pride and gratitude. They spring from our hearts as keenly at this moment as on the day I uttered them.

Time dims our memories of many events which, while they are happening, seem tremendous. But the fame of the pilots – a thin blue line indeed – who broke the aerial might of the enemy and saved their native land shines ever more brightly. Our debt is now not only to the few. As the Royal Air Force grew larger and larger and the hard years of war unrolled, many thousands of their comrades died so that our island might live, free and inviolate. By 1945, alas, as our casualty lists told the tale, the few had become the many. Had it not been for those young men whose daring and devotion cast a glittering shield between us and our foe, we should none of us be sitting at rest in our homes this Sunday evening, as members of an unconquered – and, as we believe, unconquerable – nation.

Let us all welcome this chance to pay a small measure of the debt we owe to the paladins of the Royal Air Force. And I will tell you one thing we can do, and do now. I am appealing to you tonight on behalf of the Royal Air Force Benevolent Fund. This fund exists solely to help members of the Royal Air Force – men and women – in time of need, and their families or dependants when they are in trouble. More than £2 million has been spent in this cause during the last three years. But the demands upon the fund are great. The rising cost of living presses heavily upon all, especially pensioners. During the last three years alone, the money which has had to be spent by the Royal Air Force Benevolent Fund has gone beyond the fund's ordinary income by nearly £600,000. A renewed effort must be made if the future is not to be over-clouded.

My friends, I am certain that we are all together upon this and that we are all agreed upon our purposes. We all rejoice that there is a Royal Air Force Benevolent Fund to give help to the dependants of those undaunted men who lost their lives in the war or have died since, leaving their record behind them. This fine organization for which I now appeal, has fortunately up to the present always been able to give at least a measure of aid. It is our duty now to make sure that the fund will be able to go on helping, and will not fail as the survivors of the war grow old and feeble. Only thus can the fund maintain its claim and reputation that no genuine case of distress is ever turned away.

The Royal Air Force Benevolent Fund is part of the conscience of the British nation. A nation without a conscience is a nation without a soul. A nation without a soul is a nation that cannot live.

Please send whatever you can to: Winston Churchill, Royal Air Force Benevolent Fund, 1 Sloane Street, London, SW1.

I thank you all for listening to me. Good night.

Clement Attlee to Winston S. Churchill
(Churchill papers, 2/128)

20 September 1951

My dear Churchill,
    I have decided to have a General Election in October.
    I am announcing it tonight after the nine o' clock news.

John Peck to Winston S. Churchill
(Churchill papers, 2/171)

23 September 1951

The Prime Minister would be glad of your approval of the following message of sympathy to The Queen.

'Madam,

At this time of anxiety we wish, with our humble duty, to assure Your Majesty that our thoughts are with You and The Princesses. It is our earnest prayer that His Majesty The King may soon be fully restored to health.[1]

Your Majesty's humble and obedient servants,
C. R. Attlee
Winston S. Churchill
Clement Davies'

Lettice Marston to Winston S. Churchill
(Churchill papers, 2/171)

23 September 1951

The Prime Minister has received a reply from The Queen to your joint message of sympathy. It reads as follows:

'My daughters and I are so grateful to you, to Mr Churchill and to Mr Davies for the kind message that you have sent us, and for your prayers for The King's restoration to health. We are deeply touched by your thought of us at this moment of anxiety.

Elizabeth R.'

The Prime Minister proposes to release your joint message and The Queen's reply at once, and it will be broadcast on the 9 o'clock news tonight.

---

[1] On this date the King's left lung was removed after a malignant tumour was found.

Lettice Marston to Winston S. Churchill
(*Churchill papers, 2/171*)

23 September 1951

The following medical bulletin was issued from Buckingham Palace just before 4.30 this afternoon:

'The King underwent an operation for lung resection this morning. Whilst anxiety must remain for some days, His Majesty's immediate post-operative condition is satisfactory.'

Signed by eight doctors.

Winston S. Churchill to Clement Attlee
(*Churchill papers, 2/114*)

23 September 1951
Secret

My dear Prime Minister,

I think I ought to let you know that in the present circumstances it would be, in my opinion, wrong for The Princess Elizabeth to fly the Atlantic. This seems to be more important than any of the inconveniences which may be caused by changing plans and programmes in Canada.

I talked to Alan Lascelles on this subject and authorised him to tell you what I said. However he preferred that I should write to you direct. This I now do.

Thank God the operation this morning has so far been successful, but a period of grave anxiety evidently lies before us.

Winston S. Churchill to Clement Attlee
(*Churchill papers, 2/126*)

26 September 1951

My dear Prime Minister,

In view of the latest reports in the newspapers about the demand that the remaining three hundred Britons will be ordered to leave Abadan, and of the undertaking which you gave in the House of Commons, Eden and I think that we ought to have a private talk with you to learn what is the present position.

If you agree, perhaps you will telephone and suggest a time suitable to you.

Lettice Marston to Winston S. Churchill
(Churchill papers, 2/126)

26 September 1951

The Prime Minister has received your letter about the Persian situation. He would like to see you and Mr Eden, and suggests a meeting at No. 10 tomorrow, Thursday, at 3 p.m., if you agree.

Foreign Office: record of a meeting
(Churchill papers, 2/126)

27 September 1951
Secret

Mr Churchill began by saying that the purpose of his visit was to assure the Government that in the event of a decision by them to defend our position in Abadan, if need be, by force, His Majesty's Government would receive our support. He had wished to make this plain in view of the new Persian threats of expropriation by force.

The Prime Minister thanked Mr Churchill for the assurance and said that he expected that this would be the purpose of the visit. He then said he wished to give us an account of recent developments. He read the text of a telegram which was a personal message from himself to the President. The gist of it was to explain the far reaching dangers of failure to take a firm stand in Persia now, and to ask for American support. In particular, a request was made that the President should at once make representations to the Shah,[1] urging him to bring about a change of government in Persia.

The Prime Minister next read to us the text of the President's reply, which was brief. This indicated that further views would follow but that in the meanwhile he wished to make it plain that the United States government was strongly opposed to any military measures on our part in Persia. The tone and text of this telegram, which had arrived at 5 a.m. this morning, was most discouraging. In reply to questions it appeared that His Majesty's Government had not so far sent any reply to the President's message but were awaiting the further communication. As regards the representations, the President's reply merely stated that the United States government would point out to the

---

[1] Mohammad Reza Pahlavi, 1919–80. Shah (Emperor) of Iran from Sep. 1941 until his overthrow by the Iranian Revolution on Feb. 1979. The second and last monarch of Iran from the House of Pahlavi. Educated at Institute Le Rosey, Switzerland, until 1935. Came to power after forced abdication of his father, Reza Shah, by Anglo-Soviet invasion. After his succession as Shah, Iran became a major conduit for wartime British and, later, American aid to the USSR. This massive supply effort became known as the Persian Corridor and marked the first large-scale Western involvement in Iran, which would continue to grow until the revolution against the Iranian monarchy in 1979.

Persian government the grave consequences that might result from the use of force by them. There was no mention of appealing to the Shah.

The Prime Minister went on to explain, in response to our questions, that in view of the attitude of the United States government, His Majesty's Government did not propose to use force in Abadan. When his attention was drawn to the statements that he and the Lord Chancellor made before Parliament rose, his argument was that his position had always been that he did not intend to withdraw but that he had never said that he would resist withdrawal by force.

Mr Churchill remarked that on his knowledge of the Prime Minister's character he would never have expected the decision which had been conveyed to us that day. It was one on which he could clearly make no public comment at the present time.

In the course of discussion it had earlier emerged that the necessary military forces were available to enable His Majesty's Government to take action within twelve hours, should they so decide.

Winston S. Churchill: dictated note
(Churchill papers, 2/126)

[27 September 1951]

I told the Prime Minister that we had asked to come because we thought our presence might show the Persians that the Election did not weaken national unity on any measures which might be necessary to deal with the Persian crisis.

He then explained what had taken place and read the telegrams which had passed between him and Truman.

I informed him that if he chose to resist the expulsion of our personnel by force, he would have our support in this matter, which would be treated as entirely outside election politics.

When the Prime Minister said that he did not interpret his declaration in the House of Commons about refusing to evacuate the nucleus oil personnel as including being pushed out by *force majeure*, I said that knowing him as I did I was very much surprised.

I said that we should of course treat the information he had given us as strictly secret until the events had occurred. It may be indeed that any publication by us of the true position would destroy what slender chance remains of the British and American pressure upon the Shah being effective.

We then departed.

Winston S. Churchill to General Douglas MacArthur
(Churchill papers, 2/173)

27 September 1951

My dear General MacArthur,

I have to thank you for your kindness in sending me, through Lord Beaverbrook, an inscribed copy of your Address to Congress, which I shall always preserve as a historic document in my library.

I watched with much admiration your far-seeing, broad-minded policy towards Japan, out of which the present Peace Treaty, so necessary in these critical times, has arisen.

We are here in the midst of an election which may be of great consequence to the future. I earnestly hope it may bring all of us on both sides of the Atlantic into the fraternal association for which I have so long worked.

Winston S. Churchill to Lord Kemsley
(Churchill papers, 2/171)

27 September 1951

My dear Kemsley,

Let me thank you very much for the powerful and capable support which all your newspapers are giving to us in this very grave and critical Election.

I read your article in the *Sunday Times* with the greatest interest and agreement, and also the most helpful article by Lincoln Evans last Sunday.

I think the prospects are very favourable so long as we do not indulge in over-confidence.

Lord Kemsley to Winston S. Churchill
(Churchill papers, 2/171)

28 September 1951

My dear Churchill,

Thank you for your letter.

As I told you on the telephone, I am naturally determined to go full out, using the resources of all the papers under my control. As you know, our morning and evening papers circulate in the main industrial areas and I am giving the whole matter my personal attention.

It was good of you to refer in such kind terms to my recent article in *The Sunday Times*. We are having two further articles on the subject this week, by Sir

Charles Renold[1] and Arthur Horner. From what I hear, and to judge from the articles published and the large correspondence which has reached us, there can be no question that many leaders on both sides are anxious to meet round a table in the right spirit. On account of the Election it will, of course, be impossible for us to continue the campaign, and we shall announce on Sunday that the matter is, for that reason, being held over until a later date.

I was very interested to receive the early copy of the Manifesto and only sorry, for the reason I stated on the telephone, that it was not possible to adhere to your original intention of releasing it for first publication on Sunday.

Winston Churchill to Winston S. Churchill
(Churchill papers, 1/49)[2]

30 September 1951

Dear Grandpa,

Thank you very much for having me to stay. I enjoyed it a lot. I am looking forward to going to Plymouth with you. Father took me to luncheon yesterday. We play football this term. I am reading your book called *My Early Life*, it is very interesting. I hope you win the 'ELECTION'. I hope you are well.

---

[1] Charles Garonne Renold, 1883–1967. Educated at Abbotsholme School and Cornell University. Director, Renold Chains Ltd, 1906–43; Chairman, 1943–67; Hon. President, 1967. Married, 1909, Margaret Hilda Hunter (d. 1958); 1960, Noel Garry Dunne (d. 1966). Knighted, 1948.
[2] This letter was handwritten.

October 1951

Winston S. Churchill: manifesto
(Churchill papers, 2/122)

[undated]

THE MANIFESTO OF THE CONSERVATIVE AND UNIONIST PARTY
GENERAL ELECTION, 1951

We are confronted with a critical Election which may well be the turning point in the fortunes and even the life of Britain. We cannot go on with this evenly balanced Party strife and hold our own in the world, or even earn our living. The prime need is for a stable government with several years before it, during which time national interests must be faithfully held far above party feuds or tactics. We need a new Government not biased by privilege or interest or cramped by doctrinal prejudices or inflamed by the passions of class warfare. Such a Government only the Conservative and Unionist Party can today provide.

There must be no illusions about our difficulties and dangers. It is better to face them squarely as we did in 1940. The Conservative Party, who since victory have had no responsibility for the events which have led us to where we are now, offers no bribes to the electors. We will do our best to serve them and to make things better all round, but we do not blind ourselves to the difficulties that have to be overcome, or the time that will be required to bring us back to our rightful position in the world, and to revive the vigour of our national life and impulse.

We all seek and pray for peace. A mighty union of nations tread that path together, but we all know that peace can only come through their united strength and faithful brotherhood.

Contrast our position today with what it was six years ago. Then all our foes had yielded. We all had a right to believe and hope that the fear of war would not afflict our generation nor our children. We were respected, honoured and admired throughout the world. We were a united people at home, and it was only by being united that we had survived the deadly perils through which we had come and had kept the flag of freedom flying through the fateful year when we were alone. There, at any rate, is a great foundation and inspiration. Everyone knows how the aftermath of war brings extraordinary difficulties. With national unity we could have overcome them. But what has happened since those days?

The attempt to impose a doctrinaire Socialism upon an Island which has grown great and famous by free enterprise has inflicted serious injury upon our strength and prosperity. Nationalisation has proved itself a failure which has resulted in heavy losses to the taxpayer or the consumer, or both. It has not given general satisfaction to the wage-earners are ill-content with the change from the private employers, with whom they could negotiate on equal terms through the Trade Unions, to the all-powerful and remote officials in Whitehall.

Our finances have been brought into grave disorder. No British Government in peace-time has ever had the power or spent the money in the vast extent and reckless manner of our present rulers. Apart from the two thousand millions they have borrowed or obtained from the United States and the Dominions, they have spent more than 10 million pounds a day, or 22 thousand millions in their six years. No community living in a world of competing nations can possibly afford such frantic extravagances. Devaluation was the offspring of wild, profuse expenditure, and the evils which we suffer today are the inevitable progeny of that wanton way of living.

A Conservative Government will cut out all unnecessary Government expenditure, simplify the administrative machine, and prune waste and extravagance in every department.

The greatest national misfortune which we now endure is the ever falling value of our money, or, to put it in other words, the ever-increasing cost, measured in work and skill, of everything we buy. British taxation is higher than in any country outside the Communist world. It is higher by eight hundred millions a year than it was in the height of the war. We have a population of fifty millions depending on imports of food and raw materials which we have to win by our exertions, ingenuity, and craftsmanship. Since Devaluation it takes nearly twelve hours of work with hands or brains to buy across the dollar exchange what we could have got before for eight hours. We have now to give from one-quarter to one-third more of our life's strength, skill and output of every kind and quality to get the same intake as we did before Devaluation two years ago. We pay more for what we buy from abroad; we get less for what we sell. That is what Socialist Devaluation has meant. This costly expedient has not prevented a new financial crisis.

We are a hard working people. We are second to none in ability or enterprise so far as we are allowed to use these gifts. We now have the only Socialist Government in the Empire and Commonwealth. Of all the countries in the world Britain is the one least capable of bearing the Socialist system.

The Nation now has the chance of rebuilding its life at home and of strengthening its position abroad. We must free ourselves from our impediments. Of all impediments the class war is the worst. At the time when a growing measure of national unity is more than ever necessary, the Socialist Party hope to gain another lease of power by fomenting class hatred and appealing to moods of greed and envy.

Within the limits of a statement of this kind, it is only possible to deal with some of the main questions now before us. We wish to be judged by deeds and their results and not by words and their applause. We seek to proclaim a theme, rather than write a prospectus. Many years ago I used the phrase, 'Bring the rearguard in.' This meant basic standards of life and labour, the duty of the strong to help the weak, and of the successful to establish tolerable conditions for the less fortunate. That policy is adopted by all Parties today. But now we have the new Socialist doctrine. It is no longer, 'Bring the rearguard in,' but 'Keep the vanguard back.' There is no means by which this Island can support its present population except by allowing its native genius to flourish and fructify. We cannot possibly keep ourselves alive without the individual effort, invention, contrivance, thrift and good housekeeping of our people.

In 1945 I said:

'What we desire is freedom; what we need is abundance. Freedom and abundance – these must be our aims. The production of new wealth is far more beneficial than class and Party fights about the liquidation of old wealth. We must try to share blessings and not miseries. The production of new wealth must precede common wealth, otherwise there will only be common poverty.'

It is because these simple truths have been denied and our people duped by idle hopes and false doctrine that the value of our money has fallen so grievously and the confidence of the world in Britain has been impaired. Confidence and currency are interdependent and restoring confidence by sound finance is one of the ways in which the value of our money may be sustained and the rising cost of living checked.

The Conservative aim is to increase our national output. Here is the surest way to keep our people fully employed, to halt the rising cost of living, and to preserve our social services. Hard work, good management, thrift – all must receive their due incentive and reward.

In the wider world outside this Island we put first the safety, progress and cohesion of the British Empire and Commonwealth of Nations. We must all stand together and help each other with all our strength both in Defence and Trade. To foster commerce within the Empire we shall maintain Imperial Preference. In our home market the Empire producer will have a place second only to the home producer.

Next, there is the unity of the English-speaking peoples who together number hundreds of millions. They have only to act in harmony to preserve their own freedom and the general peace.

On these solid foundations we should all continue to labour for a United Europe, including in the course of time those unhappy countries still behind the Iron Curtain.

These are the three pillars of the United Nations Organisation which, if Soviet Russia becomes the fourth, would open to all the toiling millions of the world an era of moral and material advance undreamed of hitherto among men. There was a time in our hour of victory when this object seemed to be within our reach. Even now, in spite of the clouds and confusion into which we have since fallen, we must not abandon the supreme hope and design.

For all these purposes we support the Rearmament programme on which the Socialist Government have embarked. We believe however that far better value could be got for the immense manpower and sums of money which are involved. Special sacrifices are required from us all for the sake of our survival as free democratic communities and the prevention of war.

Our theme is that in normal times there should be the freest competition and that good wages and profits fairly earned under the law are a public gain both to the Nation and to all in industry – management and wage-earner alike. But the vast Rearmament policy of spending five thousand millions in three years on Defence inevitably distorts the ordinary working of supply and demand, therefore justice requires special arrangements for the emergency. We shall set our face against the fortuitous rise in company profits because of the abnormal process of Rearmament. We shall accordingly impose a form of Excess Profits Tax to operate only during this exceptional period.

At the same time a revision of the existing system of taxation on commercial and industrial profits is required. Relief will be given in cases where profits are ploughed back and used for the renewal of plant and equipment.

We believe in the necessity for reducing to the minimum possible all restrictive practices on both sides of industry, and we shall rely on a greatly strengthened Monopolies Commission to seek, and enable Parliament to correct, any operations in restraint of trade, including of course in the nationalised industries.

I will now mention some other practical steps we shall take.

We shall stop all further nationalisation.

The Iron and Steel Act will be repealed and the Steel industry allowed to resume its achievements of the war and post-war years. To supervise prices and development we shall revive, if necessary with added powers, the former Iron and Steel Board representing the State, the management, labour, and consumers.

Publicly-owned rail and road transport will be reorganised into regional groups of workable size. Private road hauliers will be given the chance to return to business, and private lorries will no longer be crippled by the twenty-five mile limit.

Coal will remain nationalised. There will be more decentralisation and stimulation of local initiative and loyalties, but wage negotiations will remain on a national basis.

All industries remaining nationalised will come within the purview of the Monopolies' Commission and there will also be strict Parliamentary review of their activities.

We seek to create an industrial system that is not only efficient but human. The Conservative Workers' Charter for Industry will be brought into being as early as possible, and extended to agriculture wherever practicable. The scheme will be worked out with trade unions and employers, and then laid before Parliament.

There you have a clear plan of action in this field.

Housing is the first of the social services. It is also one of the keys to increased productivity. Work, family life, health and education are all undermined by overcrowded homes. Therefore a Conservative and Unionist Government will give housing a priority second only to national defence. Our target remains 300,000 houses a year. There should be no reduction in the number of houses and flats built to let but more freedom must be given to the private builder. In a property-owning democracy, the more people who own their homes the better.

In Education and in Health some of the most crying needs are not being met. For the money now being spent we will provide better services and so fulfil the high hopes we all held when we planned the improvements during the war.

The whole system of town planning and development charges needs drastic overhaul.

We shall review the position of pensioners, including war pensioners, and see that the hardest needs are met first. The care and comfort of the elderly is a sacred trust. Some of them prefer to remain at work and there must be encouragement for them to do so.

To obtain more food practical knowledge and business experience must be released to comb the world for greater supplies.

We shall maintain our system of guaranteed agricultural prices and markets and protect British horticulture from foreign dumpers. We have untilled acres and much marginal land. Farmers and merchants should work together to improve distribution in the interests of the public.

Subject to the needs of Rearmament, the utmost will be done to provide better housing, water supplies, and drainage, electricity and transport in rural areas.

The fishing industry will be protected from unrestricted foreign dumping. Every effort will be made by international agreement to prevent over-fishing.

Food subsidies cannot be radically changed in present circumstances, but later we hope to simplify the system and by increases in family allowances, taxation changes and other methods, to ensure that public money is spent on those who need help and not, as at present, upon all classes indiscriminately.

Apart from proposals to help Britain to stand on her own feet by increasing productivity, we must guard the British way of life, hallowed by centuries of tradition. We have fought tyrants at home and abroad to win and preserve the institutions of constitutional Monarchy and Parliamentary government. From Britain across the generations our message has gone forth to all parts of the globe. However well-meaning many of the present Socialist leaders may be, there is no doubt that in its complete development a Socialist State, monopolising production, distribution and exchange, would be fatal to individual freedom. We look on the Government as the servant and not as the masters of the people. Multiplying orders and rules should be reduced, and the whole system kept under more rigorous Parliamentary scrutiny. We shall call an all-Party conference to consider proposals for the reform of the House of Lords.

We shall restore the University constituencies, which have been disfranchised contrary to the agreement reached by all three Parties during the war.

The United Kingdom cannot be kept in a Whitehall straitjacket. The Unionist policy for Scotland, including the practical steps proposed for effective Scottish control of Scottish affairs, will be vigorously pressed forward.

There will be a Cabinet Minister charged with the care of Welsh affairs.

We shall seek to restore to Local Government the confidence and responsibility it has lost under Socialism.

All these and other issues of the day can only be stated briefly in our Party Manifesto. A much fuller account will be given of them in *Britain Strong and Free* which will be published in a few days.

I close with a simple declaration of our faith. The Conservative and Unionist Party stands not for any section of the people but for all. In this spirit, we will do our utmost to grapple with the increasing difficulties into which our country has been plunged.

Lord Beaverbrook to Sir Archibald Sinclair
(Beaverbrook papers)

2 October 1951

I hear from Winston now every morning. It is always just about 9 o'clock. It is always a question. I have given him so much bad advice in life that I should have thought he would be afraid to take any more by this time. But he does persist.

He is speaking tonight at Liverpool. His material on Abadan gives him cause for some anxiety. But I think he is on the right lines.

Winston S. Churchill: speech
('Stemming the Tide', pages 118–27)

2 October 1951   Liverpool Stadium

ELECTION ADDRESS

I come tonight to make my appeal to this great City of Liverpool in the most momentous election that I have ever seen. I have been many times on Merseyside, I was brought up politically in Lancashire and I have spoken in many other Lancashire cities, when party passions ran high at home or dangers threatened our country from abroad. It was all very vivid and exciting, but somehow or other I never had the same feeling – no, not even in the war – that I have now that the whole future of our country is hanging in the balance. Passions run deep rather than high. There are no spirited interchanges between political figures. The problems which surround us and are presented to us every day that passes are in so numerous an array, and so complicated, that they do not lend themselves to the ordinary bickerings and clatter of lively electioneering. A mood of deep anxiety, mingled with bewilderment, oppresses the nation. They have tried so hard and they have done so well, and yet at the end of it all there is a widespread sense that we have lost much of our strength and greatness, and that unless we are careful and resolute, and to a large extent united, we may lose more still. We have indeed reached a milestone in our national history, when everyone who cares about the life of Britain, with its fifty millions of people crowded in our small island, far more than we can win a living for, except by expression of our genius, must seek faithfully the path of duty and try to find the best way through, not for this party or that, but for us all.

In the main lines of foreign policy the Socialists have followed the course suggested to them by the Conservative Party. But they have done this so clumsily and tardily that much of what we might have gained, has been thrown away in the execution. They have joined the US in its effort to maintain the peace of the free world, but they have coupled this with so much ill-natured criticism of the Americans that they have lost a lot of the goodwill we had gained during the war years. On the Continent, outside the Iron Curtain, they have set back the cause of United Europe by making it only too clear that what they meant was a United Socialist Europe. Thus they and the other Socialist parties on the Continent have lost a great deal of their influence. The Government, after long delays, have adopted a more conciliatory policy to Western Germany, and now they seek German military assistance against the Soviet menace. But they kept up their demolitions of factories and trials of German generals so long after the war as to rob their present attitude of any sign of magnanimity; and magnanimity may be priceless in the advantages it may sometimes win for the victors. Thus they have lost in these six disastrous years much that Britain had gained and more that she might have gained for herself and for the Empire and Commonwealth by all our efforts and sacrifices during the war and after.

I did not intend to speak to you tonight about Persia. I understood until twenty-four hours ago that no final decision would be taken by the Government, pending the result of the belated appeal which they had made to the Security Council of the United Nations. But now they have given orders and made arrangements to withdraw and evacuate all the remaining British and Indian staffs from Abadan, and this is to happen tomorrow. This decision convicts Mr Attlee and the Lord Chancellor (Lord Jowitt)[1] of breaking the solemn undertakings they gave to Parliament before it rose early in August. Let me read them to you. In the House of Commons the Prime Minister said: 'There may have to be a withdrawal from the oil wells and there may have to be a withdrawal from some parts of Abadan, but our intention is not to evacuate entirely.'

In the House of Lords the next day the Lord Chancellor repeated the Prime Minister's assurance, and added that the Government 'accept all the implications that follow from that decision'. I do not remember any case where public men have broken their word so abruptly and without even an attempt at explanation. But the immediate issue is now settled. We have been ejected from the immense economic structure and organization built up over fifty years by British enterprise and management. We are markedly impoverished thereby. All this has been done in defiance of the ruling in our favour of The Hague Court. Mr Morrison, the Foreign Secretary, and his party associates no doubt hope to cover up their failure by saying that the Tories want war, while they are for peace at any price.

But this question of war or peace is not now a living issue. There is no question of using force. We have fled from the field even before the parleys were completed. Dr Mossadeq[2] can hardly follow us over here. I don't know what would happen if he got loose in Downing Street, but that cannot happen, so the question of whether force should or should not be used to defend our rights or protect our people is settled. Dr Mossadeq has won a triumph, although at a heavy cost to his own people. He has penetrated the minds and measured accurately the will-power of the men he had to deal with in Whitehall. He knew that with all their cruisers, frigates, destroyers, tank-landing craft, troops and paratroops, sent at such great expense, and all their bold confident

---

[1] William Allen Jowitt, 1885–1957. Educated at Marlborough College and New College, Oxford. MP (Lib.) for the Hartlepools, 1922–4; for Preston, 1929–31; (Lab.) for Ashton-under-Lyne, 1939–45. Attorney-General, 1929–32. Solicitor-General, 1940–2; Paymaster-General, 1942; First Minister of National Insurance, 1944–5. Baron, 1945. High Lord Chancellor of Great Britain, 1945–51. Trustee of National Gallery, 1946–53; Trustee of the Tate Gallery, 1947–53; Chairman of Trustees, 1951–3.

[2] Mohammed Mossadeq (or Mosaddegh), 1882–1957. Iranian PM, 1951–3. Nationalized Iranian oil industry, 1951. Overthrown by a coup directed by the CIA at the request of MI6 known as Operation Ajax, 1953.

statements, they were only bluffing. They were only doing what the Prime Minister calls, 'rattling the sabre'. And the Persian Prime Minister shrewdly chose the moment of the election, knowing what they would be thinking about then. And so this chapter is finished. The Conservative Party accepts no responsibility for what has happened. Presently it will be my duty and that of my trusted friend and deputy, Mr Anthony Eden, to unfold and expose the melancholy story of inadvertence, incompetence, indecision and final collapse, which has for six months marked the policy of our Socialist rulers.

Had foresight, alertness and reasonable common sense been shown there need have been no danger of any serious conflict. But all this belongs to the past. We have now only to bear the loss and suffer the consequences. I now turn to our fortunes at home.

We have suffered seriously from six years of partisan rule and party strife. An attempt has been made to fasten upon the British people a doctrinaire system of society which is certainly foreign to our nature, and a form of economic life which is most injurious to our power to win our livelihood in the modern world. Whatever may be thought of the merits or demerits of the Socialist theory, there never was a time like these six years when the attempt to put it into force could produce more harm. We only survived the war because we were united. After the victory was won we had no less need of unity and comradeship than in the deadly days of the struggle, but the Socialist Party, who were returned in overwhelming strength at the Election of 1945, allowed themselves to use their power to force upon our varied society their straitjacket system of State management and State control, although many of them did not believe in it and many more did not understand it. We hoped that the last Election eighteen months ago would put an end to these harassing and distressing conditions. Instead of that it only brought about a Parliamentary stalemate which resulted in futility of Government and harsh strife of factions.

Parliamentary democracy rests upon elections, but prolonged electioneering is not good for any country, least of all is it good for Britain in these years of world change and turmoil. For nearly two years we have suffered from electioneering fever. No doubt it takes two parties to make a quarrel and we certainly have done our duty in the Opposition, but I am dealing with facts which none will deny. A Government supported only by a minority of the electors, and split to the core from what we now see at Scarborough,[1] dependent from day to day and night to night upon half-a-dozen members, a Government which, weak though it was, pursued its party aims with scrupulous and gigantic rigidity, could not possibly sustain our reputation or defend our rights amid all the new difficulties and perils which have fallen upon the free nations of the world. The result of these lamentable eighteen months of Socialist

---

[1] Where the Labour Party Conference was held on 1–3 Oct. 1951. It resulted in a party split, with the more radical segment following Aneurin Bevan.

minority rule has been growing disunity at home and a continuous diminution of the respect in which Britain is held abroad. Our friends have been baffled and downcast by the way we seem to have fallen from the high rank we had won. Our enemies rejoice to see what they call 'the decline and fall of the British Empire'. You will have your opportunity in this fateful month to show that our enemies are wrong. But do not fail. The chance may not come again.

There is a conviction not confined to any one party that we cannot go on like this. What we need is a period of steady, stable administration by a broadly-based Government, wielding the national power and content to serve the nation's interest rather than give party satisfaction. What is required is a Government with the power to carry on a tolerant, non-partisan, non-doctrinaire system of policy for a considerable time. We need four or five years of calm, resolute policy and administration to enable us, after all we have been through, to regather our inherent strength and allow our native qualities and genius to shine forth and earn their reward.

This will be no vindictive triumph for Tories over Socialists, no dull exclusion of Liberal and independent forces, but rather a period of healing and revival. If this purpose is to be achieved there must be no subservience to class or privilege at home and no deflection from our known and agreed policy of acting with the other free democracies, with strength, patience and firmness; and we must do this in order to prevent a renewal in catastrophic form of the horrors of war. The only foundation is a Parliament, an enduring Parliament, which will cast its broad shield over our island and win it safety for itself and help it to get well after all it has gone through. I ask therefore for a substantial and solid majority to bring to an end this period of unavoidable but mischievous party strife, to let the nation get on with its work with the least possible political interference, and to promote the greatest measure of agreement among ourselves that is possible. So far as the Conservative Party is concerned, our whole effort will be directed towards national recovery, both at home and abroad, and we recognize that that cannot be done without a very considerable measure of goodwill from the great majority of the people.

At this point I must turn aside from my main argument to a question regarding the armed forces. Unlike Mr Attlee, who led his party into the Lobby four months before the late war to vote against Mr Chamberlain's modest scheme of compulsory service, the Conservative Opposition have always supported the Socialist Government in all their changing plans of conscription. Nothing would have been more easy than for the Tory Party to gain votes at the expense of our political opponents by finding many good reasons to abandon compulsory service. We should have been ashamed to gain party advantage on terms which would weaken the whole structure of the free democracies of Europe and America. This did not prevent the Socialist Party agents at the last Election from spreading the rumour through all the garrisons at home and abroad, and especially in Malta from which I had scores of telegrams, that we intended to lengthen the period of National Service beyond eighteen months. I therefore gave this assurance at Leeds in February 1950: 'The Conservative Party do not intend to take compulsory powers to lengthen the terms of National Service.' However, our Socialist opponents, having got what they could by spreading the rumour, proceeded themselves to raise the period from eighteen months to two years, and that is what it is at present. It is in fact now higher than in France. In this Election, the one we are in now, they are trying to spread the same rumours by their whispering campaign. I can only repeat, and I am asked to do so for general information, the same statement which I made at Leeds in 1950, namely: 'The Conservative Party do not intend to take compulsory powers to lengthen the term of National Service.'

I have thought it necessary to diverge from my general argument, to make this position clear, because serving soldiers and their parents ought not to be left in doubt about it, and also the story is a good measure of the kind of tactics to which we are exposed, even on issues on which the Socialists depend on our support.

Let me make it clear that we do not intend to enter upon this electoral contest on the basis of Utopian promises. We shall not follow the bad example of the Socialist Party at the Election of 1945. It is evident that this Election has come upon us largely because the Prime Minister foresaw how dark and bleak were the winter months that lie ahead, and felt it good political tactics to cast the burden on to his opponents. It would be very unwise and also wrong for us who have no special or official knowledge of the exact state of affairs to make all kinds of promises for the immediate future. How can anyone suppose that the results of six years' government, warped by faction and class prejudice and hampered by quite unusual incompetence can be repaired by magic? Evils can be created much quicker than they can be cured. How easy to slide downhill! How toilsome to climb back uphill. Not only have we to face the present conditions, but the tide is still running and may even continue to run against us. Please remember that, and, this is important, bear witness: I have tonight, at the opening of our campaign, not concealed the hard and grim facts, and that we do not in any way underrate the difficulties with which a new Government will be faced. I do not promise or predict easy times. On the contrary, a new period of effort lies before us, and this effort will require the whole weight and drive of Britain behind it.

We must clear the obstacles from our path. The Socialist system of State trading has fostered recriminations between nations without ensuring delivery of the goods. State buying has provoked State selling. It has brought national feelings into what ought to be ordinary commercial dealings. Governments flourish their national flag at each other before they can even buy or sell a pig or a cow. State trading has given us bad quality in our imports of raw materials. The closing of commodity markets has lost us valuable foreign exchange.

It has caused dislocation and uneconomic use of shipping. It has resulted in the housewife having to spend a lot more money on very little more meat. The 'invisible' international trade handled by British commodity merchants before the war amounted on the average to about £500 million a year. This represented control over the movement of a vast quantity of goods and the consequent use of British freight, of insurance on our market and financing through our banks. An expert merchant buying from abroad risks his own money on the experience of a lifetime. If he makes a mistake he suffers. If he makes too many mistakes he disappears. But a State official or employee has only to keep his office hours punctually and do his best and if anything goes wrong he can send in the bill to the Chancellor of the Exchequer. He is truly what is called 'disinterested' in the sense that he gains no advantage from wisdom and suffers no penalty for error. It is we who pay the penalty. In 1950 the Government agents did not buy because they hoped for a fall in prices, but this never happened. In consequence in 1951 stocks had to be increased in the middle of a startling boom. Also in 1951 the Socialist Food Minister[1] agreed to buy Argentine meat for £128 a ton, when he could have got it for £120 a ton a month or two earlier. No penalty for him. It was only Britain that had to pay more for raw materials and meat than she need have done.

But look at cotton. When in 1946 the Socialists introduced the Centralized Buying Act, we were promised that their proposals would result in cheaper cotton, more stable prices, the end of speculation and more efficient buying. But what happened? In recent months the Raw Cotton Commission's prices to the spinner have more often been above the world price than below it. Lancashire has experienced severe fluctuations in the prices of most varieties of cotton. In the bad old days in the pre-war free market, the movement of a penny was regarded as being a considerable event. But now the mills of Lancashire have to face sudden jumps up or down of 6d or 1s a pound. An even worse fault in the State buying of cotton has been the failure to give to the spinner the same selection of the exact quality he requires that he used to get. This strikes a deadly blow at the Lancashire cotton industry, which cannot hold its pre-eminence except by quality. In addition to these hard facts – this is all the more true in view of what we must face in Japan – we have improvidently cast away the advantage of being the cotton market of the world. Our policy is to re-establish and reopen the Liverpool Cotton Exchange. But here again it is much easier to destroy than to rebuild. The resources of the market in men and capital have been scattered. They cannot be reassembled by a gesture. The Liverpool market was a world market, and once it was abolished by the Socialists other countries stepped in and many new arrangements were made. We should do everything in our power, if we become responsible, to retrieve the Liverpool Cotton Exchange and bring it back to life. But time will

[1] Maurice Webb.

be needed in this as in many other directions to undo the harm so wantonly done. There are few instances in this or any other country of a Government going out of its way to deprive one of its leading and key industries, at once of an invaluable piece of commercial mechanism and of a symbol of its primacy in world trade.

Let me give you another example of Socialist mentality and tactics. All parties know that it is of the highest importance to avoid what is called the wage-and-prices spiral. The present Chancellor of the Exchequer[1] two months ago sought to freeze wage increases. To win the extreme section of the trade union leaders to this policy, he proposed that dividends should also be frozen. Observe that this was not done on the merits, but because much of the driving power of the Socialist movement is derived from jealousy and envy of others whom they think are more fortunate than themselves. Mr Gaitskell's declaration about the freezing of dividends caused a collapse of values on the London Stock Exchange. At least two hundred millions of our capital values vanished in an afternoon. So he was entitled to pride himself upon this example of soaking the rich, although it is a fact that the shareholders upon whom the bulk of the losses fell are not a handful of wealthy men, but masses of ordinary folk upon whose thrift or readiness to venture or invest their money our buoyancy and strength as a commercial country depends. His colleague Dr Dalton, a former Chancellor of the Exchequer, hastened to add insult to injury. 'My friend Gaitskell has thrown the Stock Exchange into complete disorder,' he said, 'that is good fun anyhow,' he said with one of those inevitable smiles which are only to be seen to be believed.

Six weeks later the Prime Minister obtained a Dissolution of Parliament from the Crown. October 25, a day which we must make memorable in our history, was fixed. Can you think it extraordinary that the investing public and those who handle their affairs in the Stock Exchange were encouraged by the hope and belief, which may not prove to be ill-founded, that Socialist rule may be ended? Values on the Stock Exchange recovered in a day about half what they had lost six weeks before. Instantly the Socialist Party managers rushed forward to proclaim that this partial recovery proved that the Conservative and Unionist Party were the tools of the speculators and gamblers in the City of London and to make the issue of the Election a vote between the working classes on the one hand, and the Stock Exchange on the other. Even the Prime Minister himself has lent support to this slander, by talking about 'A high old time, and high prices on the Stock Exchange' as being the result of a Conservative victory. But the day we are responsible we intend to form a Government which will be the servant of no vested interest any more than it will be the slave of party dogma. On the contrary we shall strive faithfully to administer the national trust without fear, favour or affection for the lasting benefit of all.

---

[1] Hugh Gaitskell.

The present Chancellor of the Exchequer, Mr Gaitskell, speaking the other day about our decision to impose an Excess Profits Tax during the period of rearmament, which I announced in my manifesto on behalf of the party last week, called it a 'somersault'; he thus showed that he does not see the difference between taxation imposed for social justice and taxation imposed for party spite. His dividend limitations, as I said just now, had the avowed purpose to console the more bitter and violent elements in his party for the wage-freeze which is the Socialist policy by assuring them that he was hitting shareholders as well. It is a strange and un-Christian habit of mind which makes it easier to endure misfortunes because one sees that others are having them inflicted on them too. Between this ill-natured exhibition and the measure we have proposed there is this serious ethical gulf.

We seek a free enterprise society with minimum basic standards and competition above that. Subject to the well-established laws and customs, competition should be free. But if abnormal conditions are forced upon us by world events, and £5,000 million have to be devoted to armament production in all its complex aspects; if one set of producers are to be benefited by every kind of priority in materials and manpower, then surely it is right to consider special temporary arrangements to equate, or at least to mitigate, what is an unnatural element and phase in our affairs. Hence excess profits tax during this period is in accordance with social justice and would appeal to all true democracies. It has another aspect which is important. Considering the abuse to which we are subjected the fact that it has been accepted almost without a murmur by the Conservative Party shows how false is the tale that we are the servant of wealth or the Stock Exchange. We defend the rights of property. We recognize the many high qualities of our Stock Exchange which have often been considered a model to other countries, but a Conservative Government will view all institutions with a fair and level eye and do the best for the whole community, independent of any special interests.

The Chancellor of the Exchequer says, 'don't put the clock back.' But the danger that faces us today is not putting the clock back. The clock is running down. Everyone can feel it in their bones when they look at our position whether at home or abroad. No, what we need is a new impulse to wind up the clock and regulate it in an orderly and accurate manner so that it will tell the hours of a long day of recovery. To hear the Socialists talk you would suppose that there was nothing here before they came into office. Nothing was ever done by all the generations of which we are the heirs. All that we have that is worth having is due to the agitators and apostles of class warfare who came in to office in 1945 and have lived upon, exploited and squandered the hard-won, long-stored treasures and glories of British history.

It was a fine legacy that they inherited when they took over in 1945. All our enemies had surrendered or were about to surrender. We stood at the pinnacle of worldly renown. All over the world our friends saluted us as the one solid, enduring champion of freedom, ready to stand alone, starting from the first day, and ending in full strength, on the last. But our vanquished foes, they also regarded us with a strange admiration. We alone had never hesitated to stake our life on freedom. We had never faltered in the year of darkest peril. We had given all we had freely and without stint from first to last.

Very different will be the inheritance which it may be our duty to take over from Mr Attlee and his friends in a few weeks' time. But we do not fear it. We have not lost faith in our race and in our destiny. We are the same people, in the same island, as we were in the great days we can all remember. Never shall we lose our faith and courage, and never shall we fail in exertion and resolve.

Winston S. Churchill to Sir John Anderson
(Churchill papers, 2/113)

4 October 1951

re 'general lines' of a proposed speech.

You are not a Party politician, for which you may thank God, but nevertheless it is most necessary we should keep in step.

Sir Archibald Sinclair to Lord Beaverbrook
(Beaverbrook papers)

5 October 1951

Winston's habits are improving! It used to be 3 a.m. when he sought your advice. Now he lets you sleep till 9.

He is speaking splendidly – after Winston's speeches, press criticism, Abadan and the fiasco of the Scarborough conference, it seems odd that the Socialists are catching up on the Polls.

Winston S. Churchill: speech
('Winston S. Churchill, His Complete Speeches', volume 8, pages 8252–3)

6 October 1951   Loughton County High School

PERSIAN CRISIS

Mr Morrison has asked me whether in my judgment we should have gone to war with Persia or not. He had no right to ask this question. The responsibility is entirely that of the Socialist Government who alone had the power and should have had the knowledge. He is only asking the question in order to gain acceptance for the falsehood he and his associates – I can hardly call them his friends – are spreading about that the Conservative Party want another world war. I am quite sure that if a strong Conservative Government had been in power the Persian crisis would never have arisen in the way it did. It is only when the British Government is known to be weak and hesitant that these outrages are inflicted upon us and upon our rights and interests. I cannot believe there would have been any need for a war with Persia.

The Prime Minister has now explained that when he said he would not evacuate our oil staff from Abadan he meant he would not do so unless he was forced. His policy was that nothing would induce him to go unless he were pushed. If he were pushed nothing would induce him to stay. But this was not the interpretation which Parliament and indeed the whole world placed upon his words. And I am bound to say that after the private meetings I and my colleagues have had with him it was certainly not the impression I sustained.

When he saw he was being misunderstood by the whole country, Mr Attlee could easily have set the matter right. On the contrary, he allowed his Lord Chancellor, the next day, to repeat in the House of Lords what he had said, and to add the remarkable and decisive phrase: 'We accept all the implications that follow from that decision.' Of course he was hoping to deceive Dr Mossadeq. But Dr Mossadeq saw through his bluff. It was only the British people and the world in general who were taken in.

I repeat, no satisfactory explanation has been given by Mr Attlee of his and the Lord Chancellor's statements to Parliament when we separated in early August. I cannot recall any large matter of policy which has been so mishandled as this dispute with Persia. It arose out of the great decline of British prestige and authority in the Middle East which followed inevitably from the loss of India. But foresight would have enabled us to be much better informed than we were at the outset. For a long time we were virtually without a Foreign Secretary owing to Mr Bevin's ill-health. When the Persian Government decreed the nationalization of our oil industry we were quite right to go to The Hague Court. When The Hague Court had given its decision in our favour then was the time, nearly three months ago, to lay our case before the United Nations. But Mr Attlee and Mr Morrison have simply drifted until after every kind of humiliation, we have been ignominiously ejected a week before our appeal to UNO could even be considered.

Even at the last moment, after the mission of Mr Stokes, the Persian Government offered new discussions, and the answer from the Foreign Office was that they would not negotiate with Dr Mossadeq any more. How can this be reconciled with a definite resolve not in any circumstances to resist physical pressure of any kind? What we have been witnessing is not a policy either of resistance to violence or of negotiation. It is simply a case of Ministers drifting from day to day and week to week, unable to make up their minds, until now we have been confronted with a major loss and disaster.

The lamentable story shows that our influence in the United States, in spite of our close association with them and the great causes we have undertaken together to defend, has fallen to a very low ebb. I cannot believe this would have happened with any other Government than this one. Of course, now it is known that we will not in any circumstances offer physical resistance to violence and aggression on a small scale in these Middle East countries, we must expect that Egypt will treat us more roughly still and many other evils will come upon us in the near future unless the Ministers who have shown themselves to be utterly incapable are dismissed from power by the electors. Anyhow, the financial loss is most grave and affects the whole of our position in the present dollar crisis. Now that the Abadan refinery has passed out of our hands we have to buy oil in dollars instead of in sterling. This means that at least 300 million dollars have to be found every year by other forms of export and services. That is to say, that the working people of this country must make and export at a rate of one million dollars more, for every working day in a year. This is a dead loss, which will directly affect our purchasing power abroad and the cost of living at home.

Mr Bartholomew's[1] newspaper, the *Daily Mirror*, coined a phrase the other day which is being used by the Socialist Party whom he supports. 'Whose finger', they asked, 'do you want on the trigger, Attlee's or Churchill's?' I am sure we do not want any fingers upon any trigger. Least of all do we want a fumbling finger. I do not believe that a Third World War is inevitable. I even think that the danger of it is less than it was before the immense rearmament of the United States. But I must now tell you that in any case it will not be a British finger that will pull the trigger of a Third World War. It may be a Russian finger, or an American finger, or a United Nations Organization finger, but it cannot be a British finger. Although we should certainly be involved in a struggle between the Soviet Empire and the free world, the control and decision and the timing of that terrible event would not rest with us. Our influence in the world is not what it was in bygone days. I could wish indeed that it was greater because I am sure it would be used as it always has been used to the utmost to prevent a life-and-death struggle between the great nations.

---

[1] Harry Guy Bartholomew, 1884–1962. Known as 'Bart'. Office boy, *Daily Mail*, 1899–1904. Educated at Slade School of Art, London. Asst Art Director, *Daily Mirror*, 1904; Art Editor and Director, 1913; Editorial Director, 1934; Chairman, 1944. Retired, 1951

Winston S. Churchill: broadcast
('Winston S. Churchill, His Complete Speeches', volume 8, pages 8254–8)

8 October 1951

OUR POLITICAL FUTURE

We have reached a moment when it is the duty of the British people to take a decision one way or the other about our political future. Nothing could be worse than no decision at all. We have lost a lot in the last two years by the party strife which belongs to electioneering times. We cannot go on like this with two party machines baying at each other in Parliament and grinding away all over the country in order to gain votes for one side or the other. We could not afford it for long even if the world were calm and quiet and if we were a self-supporting nation safer and more independent than we ever were before.

The uncertainty has got to come to an end at home if we are to play our part in the world and receive due consideration for our British point of view and, still more, if we are to keep a decent standard of life for our people and even keep them alive. Remember, we have brought into being through the progress of Victorian times fifty million people in an island which only grows the food for thirty million and that all the rest has to be provided for by the goods and services we can render to other countries. There never was a community of fifty million people, standing at our high level of civilization, on such an insecure foundation. We have maintained ourselves there by the qualities of our race, by the soundness of our institutions, by the peaceful progress of our democracy, and by the very great lead which we had gained in former generations.

Thus we have been able to withstand and surmount all the shocks and strains of this terrible twentieth century with its two awful wars. We shall endanger our very existence if we go on consuming our strength in bitter party or class conflicts. We need a period of several years of solid stable administration by a Government not seeking to rub party dogmas into everybody else. It will take us all we can do to keep going at home and play our part, which is a great one, in maintaining the freedom and peace of the world.

Of course, everyone wants to win his own election fight and after the bitter wrangling of the last two years there is no prospect of a coalition except under actual mortal danger. Nevertheless, we need not magnify our differences. We have to make them more clear and not make them more wide. After all, the whole policy of social reform, the Welfare State as it is now called, was the policy of the National wartime Government of which I was the head and which rested upon a Conservative and National Liberal majority in the House of Commons of 160.

At the height of the war, in the spring of 1943 – in a broadcast longer even than I am making to you tonight, with the full agreement of the Cabinet of all parties, I unfolded what we called the Four Years Plan. This covered the Beveridge scheme of national compulsory contributory insurance for old age, accident, ill health and unemployment. It included what is called the Butler Education Act, the Hudson Agricultural Policy, the National Health Service, Family Allowances and other important schemes. But all of this was common policy. It was British policy, not party policy.

One of the chief boasts which the Socialists make is that they have cured unemployment. But in the National Government, before the end of the war, the principal leaders of the Socialist Party agreed with their Conservative colleagues in a report which was published and can be read today. It says:

> There will be no problem of general unemployment in the years immediately after the end of the war in Europe. The total manpower available will be insufficient to satisfy the total demands for goods and services.

There was indeed no shortage of demand. There was, however, the danger of a shortage of materials. That difficulty was removed by the £2,000 million worth of gifts or loans from America and the Dominions which the Socialists have received. Mr Herbert Morrison admitted this fact when he said in Manchester in April:

> We should be facing big cuts in rations and a million or two people on the dole if our friends and allies in American had not come to our rescue.

How, then, can these public men in high positions reconcile it with their reputation to claim the credit of full employment since the war as the monopoly of their party?

We were able to carry out some of our four years' plan during the war and what could not be done while it lasted occupied the Parliament which followed the victory. Our joint plans were mauled and marred by the plastering upon them of Socialist Party politics which added far more to the cost than was gained in benefits to the public. Fancy, for instance, knocking out the voluntary hospitals, excluding the friendly societies or showing spiteful and pedantic prejudice against the private builder! Nevertheless, it is true today that four-fifths of the social legislation since the war was the agreed policy of all parties when I was Prime Minister with a large Conservative majority. What has happened is that we have been mishandled for several years by a spendthrift and partisan administration obsessed by a false theory of life and economics. To continue like this would lead to ruin. But the British electors hold the remedy in the hollow of their hand. October 25! Just make a note of that date. While on this point let me remind and assure everyone that British elections are free. Everyone can vote as they choose with the certainty that the ballot is secret, and if they live in council houses or are on the long waiting lists to get houses, or even if they are State employees, they cannot be called to account for the way in which they use their vote any more than they can by the landlord or private employer.

There are of course two new features which have been introduced into our life by our masters of the last six years. First, the nationalization, subject to compensation, of a number of our leading industries and services, the whole amounting to about one-fifth of our production; and secondly, the maintenance of as many wartime controls and restrictions as possible in order to prepare for general Socialist state control.

Nationalization is now admitted to have been a failure. It has been very costly to the public. It has given a poorer service to the user or consumer and, except perhaps in the coalmines, it is not popular among the employees. This ill-starred experiment has caused immense injury both to our harassed finances and our creative energy. The Socialist Party, in their Election programme, do not even use the word 'nationalization'. They have a vague sentence which would enable them, if they got a majority, to strike at any industry or any firm which they did not like, and just to say it 'could fail', and either to take it over or make it bankrupt by starting a State-subsidized rival which could dump any of its losses on the taxpayer. That is what they now say. Such is the undignified exit of nationalization.

Now I come to their second contribution to our affairs, namely, the keeping on of wartime controls and restrictions. This has hampered our recovery, fettered our enterprise and enormously added to the cost and apparatus of government. Here the difference between the two parties may thus be summed up. Our opponents say: 'The more controls and restrictions we have the nearer we approach the Socialist ideal.' The Conservatives say: 'The fewer we have the better for a vigorous and expanding Britain.'

The difference between our outlook and the Socialist outlook on life is the difference between the ladder and the queue. We are for the ladder. Let all try their best to climb. They are for the queue. Let each wait in his place till his turn comes. But, we ask: 'What happens if anyone slips out of his place in the queue?' 'Ah!' say the Socialists, 'our officials – and we have plenty of them – come and put him back in it, or perhaps put him lower down to teach the others.' And when they come back to us and say: 'We have told you what happens if anyone slips out of the queue, but what is your answer to what happens if anyone slips off the ladder?' Our reply is: 'We shall have a good net and the finest social ambulance service in the world.' This is of course only a snapshot of a large controversy.

But now, since the General Election of 1950, an additional heavy burden has come upon us. The Soviet aggression in Korea led to a fierce war on a considerable scale. This has started an immense additional process of rearmament against Communist Russia by all the free democracies of the world, with the United States doing and paying the bulk. We have supported the Socialist Government's proposals. At first we were told they amounted to

£3,600 million, but later on, when they added the bill up again, they told us that it is nearly £5,000 million in military expenditure spread over three years. This is a very heavy load for our island to bear. A Conservative Government would have the full right to examine in severe detail the way in which the money is being spent and what is the fighting power and defensive security resulting from it. If anything like the groundnuts and Gambia egg muddles are being repeated in this vast field heavy sacrifices will be exacted from our hard-pressed people without enabling them to take their proper share in the world defence of freedom.

What are we rearming for? It is to prevent Communist Russia, its reluctant satellites and its ardent votaries spread about in many countries – some of them even here – from beating us all down to their dead level as they have done as much as they can to the people of every country they have occupied during and since the war. But rearmament is only half a policy. Unless you are armed and strong you cannot expect any mercy from the Communists; but if you are armed and strong you may make a bargain with them which might rid the world of the terror in which it now lies and relieve us all from much of the impoverishment and privations into which we shall otherwise certainly sink.

The Conservative and Liberal Parties and part of the Socialist Party support the policy of rearmament and the effective binding together of all the nations all over the world outside the Iron Curtain, not because we are seeking war, but because we believe it is the only method by which a reasonable and lasting settlement might be reached. I believe that if the British Empire and Commonwealth joined together in fraternal association with the United States and the growing power of Western Europe – including a reconciled France and Germany – worked together steadfastly, then the time will come, and may come sooner than is now expected, when a settlement may be reached which will give us peace for a long time. That is our hearts' desire.

I do not hold that we should rearm in order to fight. I hold that we should rearm in order to parley. I hope and believe that there may be a parley. You will remember how, at Edinburgh in the 1950 election, I said that there should be a meeting with Soviet Russia, not of subordinates but of heads of Governments in order to enable us at least to live peacefully together.[1] You will remember, also, that this gesture, which I did not make without some knowledge of the personalities and forces involved, was curtly dismissed by the Socialist Government as an electioneering stunt. It might be that if such a meeting as I urged had taken place at that time the violent dangers of the Korean War and all that might spring out of it would not have come upon us.

But now we have a different situation. In a way it is more tense. We are actually at war. Blood is being shed and cannons fire. The murder on Saturday

---

[1] Speech of 14 Feb. 1950, reproduced above (pp. 1642–50).

of our High Commissioner in Malaya, Sir Henry Gurney,[1] reminds us how fiercely the struggle there burns on. On the other hand, the gigantic rearmament of the United States, their development of the atom bomb, the growth of British and of European defence and the unities which have sprung into being among the free democracies, including our old enemies in the war, give a foundation, ever growing in strength and solidarity, upon which a fruitful and durable peace settlement might be made.

Britain has a great part to play in this if only she can regain the influence and the power she wielded during the war. She injures and weakens herself by her Parliamentary stalemate. She strikes herself cruel blows when she accepts humiliations such as we have suffered in the Persian Gulf. We have to face a great lowering of our reputation. The Persian outrage, in disregard of the decision of The Hague Court, has weakened the cause of peace all over the world. It is a grievous injury to the whole of the Western Allies in Europe or in the Atlantic Pact when Britain falls flat on her face as if she were a booby and a coward. But this is not the real Britain, it is only the grimace of an exhausted and divided administration, upon whose conduct the nation will soon be able to pronounce.

I have explained from time to time the Tory outlook upon our ever-changing British society. We feel that process of bringing larger numbers to an ever wider table ever more bountifully provided with moral and material satisfactions of life is the true way to measure our national progress. Give everyone a better chance to rise and let the successful help to pick up and bring along those who do not succeed. We are resolved that this evolution shall be tireless and perennial.

If the electors choose to entrust to the Conservatives an effective measure of power for a considerable period I pledge my word that the party I have led so long through such historic years will not be the partisans of any hidebound doctrine but will try its best to make things good and continually improving for the nation as a whole. We stand for freedom and unceasing progress and this can only be achieved by valiant perseverance. On the other hand we make no promises of easier conditions in the immediate future. Too much harm has been done in these last six years for it to be repaired in a few months. Too much money has been spent for us to be able to avoid another financial crisis. It will take all our national strength to stop the downhill slide and get us back on the level, and after that we shall have to work up.

We ask to be judged by our performances and not by our promises. We do not promise to create a paradise – and certainly not a fool's paradise. We are

---

[1] Henry Gurney, 1898–1951. King's Royal Rifle Corps, 1917–20. Entered British Colonial Service, 1921. Asst District Commissioner, Kenya, 1921–35. Chief Secretary to Conference of East Asia Governors, 1938–44. Colonial Secretary, Gold Coast, 1944–6. Chief Secretary to Palestine, 1946–8. KCMG, 1947. High Commissioner to Malaya, 1948–51. KStJ, 1949. Killed in ambush by Malayan Communist Party guerrillas, 1951.

seeking to build a lighthouse rather than to dress a shop window. All I will say is that we will do our best for all our fellow countrymen without distinction of class or party. I cannot offer you any immediate relaxation of effort. On the contrary, we have not yet got through the danger zone at home or abroad. We must do our duty with courage and resolution. But there is a wise saying 'the trees do not grow up to the sky'.

If we can stave off a war for even five or ten years all sorts of things may happen. A new breeze may blow upon the troubled world. I repudiate the idea that a Third World War is inevitable. The main reason I remain in public life is my hope to ward it off and prevent it. The desire of mankind in this tragic twentieth century can be seen and felt. The human race is going through tormenting convulsions and there is a profound longing for some breathing space, for some pause in the frenzy. Why not make a change in this harassed island and get a steady stable Government, sure of its strength, fostering the expansion of our society, making sure of our defences, being faithful to our allies and to the common cause of law and freedom, but seeking as its final and supreme aim that all classes, all nations, friends and enemies alike can dwell in peace within their habitations?

Winston S. Churchill: speech
('Winston S. Churchill, His Complete Speeches', volume 8, pages 8258–61)

9 October 1951   Woodford

ELECTION ADDRESS

Obviously at this anxious time our first interest is to maintain the best and closest relations with the United States. Apart from the world-wide causes of freedom and peace in which the whole English-speaking world is solemnly engaged, what is happening in the Middle East and in the Mediterranean makes it all the more necessary for us to work in harmony and consultation. It is six months since I said in the House of Commons:[1]

> We are no longer strong enough ourselves to bear the whole political burden we have hitherto borne in the Mediterranean, or even to take the leading part in the diplomatic control of that theatre. But the United States and Britain together, aided by France – we three together would be in a most powerful position to deal with, say, the Egyptian problem and the whole question of the defence of the Suez Canal.

One gets quite tired of saying things which are first mocked at and then adopted, sometimes, alas, too late. I urged the Government to try to bring

---

[1] Speech of 19 Apr. 1951, reproduced above (pp. 2041–55).

about a threefold combination of our diplomatic and other forces. On this basis I believe that much of the harm that has been done in Persia can still be recovered, and the evil developments with which the free world is threatened by disorder, aggression and the one-sided breaking of treaties, might well be solved in a peaceful but firm and honourable manner. This is only a part of the great world problem, but it is an important and crucial element in its solution. I was concerned to see that our influence with the United States has not so far brought us the support in the Persian dispute which it is their interest to give, as well as ours to gain.

The Prime Minister has been emphasizing in his election speeches the importance which he attaches to Anglo-American relations, and I daresay he has done his best. There is no doubt, however, that he has been hampered by the highly critical mood of his supporters below the Gangway in the House of Commons. Their prejudice against the United States has been painfully evident on numerous occasions. The result of the voting at Scarborough for the Executive Committee of the Labour Party has, however, placed Mr Bevan and his supporters and lieutenants at the head of the poll. This shows that the critical attitude of British Socialism towards the United States is not by any means limited to the group of members who have made themselves obnoxious in the House. On the contrary they have received support in the Labour Conference which shows only too clearly the anti-American current which is flowing among the Left-wing masses. If the Socialists should be successful in this Election, Mr Bevan and his views would dominate or at least sway the Labour Government even if Mr Attlee or Mr Morrison succeeded in holding the nominal leadership. This is indeed a dangerous development.

It is vital to world peace and especially to our own safety that our relations with the United States should be continually growing stronger and that our influence with their Government, which wields such enormous power in the world today, should be restored and improved. The return of the Socialists to office, with Mr Bevan's following now proved to be so large, would increase not only British difficulties but also the dangers of a general war. A Conservative Government would, I am sure, be able to rebuild those relations of cordial and intimate comradeship and understanding with America which played so important a part in the war. Even I might be some help in this. For I have many friends in the great Republic and they have often listened to me, and I believe they would say that on the whole, the advice I have given during the last fifteen years has not always been wrong. But I have never accepted a position of subservience to the United States. They have welcomed me as the champion of the British point of view. They are fair-minded people. They know a friend when they see one; and they have never resented the very blunt and plain things I found it necessary to say to them from time to time.

There can be no greater danger to world peace than for the Bevan movement and the momentum which it has in the Labour Party to become representative of Britain and American minds. The United States are in a very different position from our British island. They are a continent lapped by oceans. They are self-supporting, and far more than self-supporting. They are rapidly becoming the strongest military Power in the world. Some of the Socialists say: 'Well, let them go and fight Russia by themselves.' But Mr Attlee's Government, apart from binding us by solemn treaties like the Atlantic Pact, have given the United States in East Anglia their main atomic bombing base on this side of the Atlantic. This was a formidable step for any British Government to take. We supported it on our broad principle of sustaining national policy in defence and foreign affairs. If we were to lose our moral unity and contact with the United States and they felt themselves free to judge the world situation in isolation it might well be that we should run the gravest of perils without having our proper say in the course of events and without having the consideration which is our right.

A Bevan-coloured Government or even a Bevan-tinted Government, or tainted (to change the metaphor excusably), might well lead to our still being left in the front-line of danger without our fair share of influence upon the course of events. I warn you solemnly that the mass growth of the Bevan movement inside the Socialist Party, which the Scarborough Conference revealed, may make the return of a Socialist Government a real blow to our hopes of escaping a Third World War. It would indeed be the irony of fate if the peace-at-any-price voters became the means of destroying our prospects of getting safely through the next two or three years of anxiety. It is certain that a vote for Bevanite Socialism is in fact, whatever its intention, a vote which increases the hazard of a world catastrophe. Let us make October 25 a day of liberation from fears, as well as from follies.

Mr Deakin, the trade union leader, has asked whether the Conservative Party contemplate legislation affecting the trade unions. He is a man for whom I have much respect because he holds the leadership of the largest trade union which exists and does not fear to take unpopular courses. I was much interested in his statement some months ago about the importance of preserving the 'differentials' in our complex industry. We certainly could never earn our living by world trade or even exist in this island without full recognition of all forms of exceptional individual contribution, whether by genius, contrivance, skill, industry or thrift. After compliments, as they say, let me now set Mr Deakin's mind at rest. The Conservative Party have no intention of initiating any legislation affecting trade unions, should we become responsible in the new Parliament. We hope to work with the trade unions in a loyal and friendly spirit, and if this is disturbed by party politics the fault will not be on our side.

There is of course the question of the political levy being exacted from Conservative and Liberal trade unionists, putting the onus on them to contract out. We do not think that this is fair. But the Conservative and Liberal membership of the trade unions obtained their charter and lawful foundation from the Conservative Party many years ago. We regard them as an essential factor, working for the stability and progress of the country. The trade unions will, I am sure, respect the verdict of the people as expressed constitutionally in a General Election. If we should be returned we shall consult with them and work with them on a non-party basis in a frank and friendly manner.

Take, for instance, the repeal of the nationalization of steel which we shall certainly carry out forthwith. There we shall adopt the kind of scheme which was recommended for many industries in the Trades Union Congress Report which owed so much of its wisdom to Mr Lincoln Evans. Of course, the trade union leaders and the Conservatives have recently gained another link. Both are insulted by Mr Bevan and his movement. We are vermin, they are stooges.

Fortified by this, let us try to get on with the job together. There is only one question which has to be considered at the present time, namely the closed shop. This has raised a legal issue between the present Socialist Government and the local authorities in Durham. In our view the Durham County Council was wrong to insist upon the closed shop principle for all its employees, and the Socialist Government were right in the attitude which they adopted with the assent of the trade union leaders themselves. Like other matters in this field, it may well be left to the working of commonsense and public opinion. There is, therefore, no issue open between us and the trade unions. Indeed we consider that by bringing to an end the policy of further nationalization we shall be leaving them free to exercise their long-established right and duty of collective bargaining between employers and labour without the State being involved except as a neutral mediator. I hope Mr Deakin will find that I have answered his question in a manner which is satisfactory.

Oliver Lyttelton to Winston S. Churchill
(<i>Churchill papers, 2/51</i>)</center>

10 October 1951

My dear Winston,

I am exceedingly sorry to have to bother you about a comparatively trivial matter at this moment.

You may or may not remember that during these last six years I have handled film matters on behalf of the Opposition. It is for this reason that Sir Wilfrid Eady[1] of the Treasury has now written me a letter.

The Film Finance Corporation have exhausted their present statutory powers and are not in a position to finance any further films. The Chancellor of the Exchequer and the President of the Board of Trade informed

---

[1] Wilfred Griffin Eady, 1890–1962. KBE, 1939. KCB, 1942. Joint 2nd Secretary to the Treasury, 1942–52. British delegate to the Bretton Woods Conference, July 1944. GCMG, 1948.

Parliament before the Recess that the Government would introduce legislation to increase the funds at the disposal of the Film Finance Corporation from £6,000,000 to £8,000,000.

The Ministers also agreed that this should be the final instalment, and that the advances to the Corporation should not exceed £8,000,000.

The Accounting Officer of the Board of Trade, Sir Frank Lee,[1] does not feel justified, upon a mere statement to Parliament, in authorising the Corporation to incur further commitments, but he would do so if the Opposition agreed that if they came into power a one-clause Bill would be introduced authorising the increase in the capital from £6,000,000 to £8,000,000. He asked me to write and agree.

I have replied by telephone that of course I cannot commit the Opposition to any such course, but that I would refer it to you. I can give you very much more information about the proposal, but I hesitate to do so. Perhaps it would be enough if I were to say that I don't think the risk of loss is very great and that on the whole the proposal is a reasonable one, to which I think we should agree. My main reason for making this statement is because a levy of a 1/4d per seat for the benefit of the producers has been agreed by the industry for three years. It will produce substantial sums.

If you would ask one of your young ladies to telephone, I will send a suitable reply to the Treasury.[2]

Winston S. Churchill: speech
('Stemming the Tide', page 141)

11 October 1951

I am grateful for this opportunity of sending a personal message to the people of loyal Ulster, for I recall with pride and thankfulness the great and essential part which they played in winning the last war. I have followed with interest your progress in recent years and your trading success in world markets, which have been a most valuable contribution to the economy of the United Kingdom.

In this General Election the Unionist Party is the only one which mentions that it is concerned with the constitutional position of Northern Ireland, and in our Policy Statement, *Britain – Strong and Free*, we reaffirm our determination that the present relationship of Ulster to the United Kingdom and the Empire

---

[1] Frank Godbould Lee, 1903–71. Colonial Office, 1926–40; in Nyasaland, 1931–3. Married, 1937, Kathleen Mary Harris. Imperial Defence College, 1938. Treasury, 1940. Treasury Delegation, Washington DC, 1944–6. Ministry of Supply, 1946. Deputy Secretary, 1947. Minister at Washington DC, 1948. Knighted, 1950. Permanent Secretary, Board of Trade, 1951–9. Permanent Secretary, Ministry of Food, 1959–62. Treasury, 1960–2. PC, 1962.

[2] Churchill telephoned the next day: 'We must not commit ourselves in any way before we are responsible' (*Churchill papers, 2/51*).

shall never in the slightest degree be altered without the consent of the Parliament of Northern Ireland. This has ever been a fundamental principle of Unionist policy, this must continue, for your destiny is forever bound up with Britain and the British Commonwealth.

The people of Ulster can play a great part in the improvement of our standards of life at home and in the preservation of peace throughout the world by supporting all Unionist candidates at the polls on October 25. Make sure that that becomes a famous date in our history.

Arthur Waters[1] to Winston S. Churchill
(Churchill papers, 2/129)

12 October 1951

Dear Mr Churchill,

May I remind you of your kind promise to write a 1,200 word article for the October 21st issue of the *News of the World*, summing up the Conservative Party's case in the Election.

I realise, of course, that your time is very fully occupied, but it would be a great convenience if we could have the article in this office by Thursday, October 18th.

Winston S. Churchill: speech
('Winston S. Churchill, His Complete Speeches', volume 8, pages 8262–4)

12 October 1951   Constituency Meeting, Woodford

'ABADAN, SUDAN, AND BEVAN – A TRIO OF MISFORTUNE'
(ELECTION ADDRESS)

Abadan, Sudan and Bevan are a trio of misfortune.

The Prime Minister has been enlivening his tour throughout our land by making many attacks on me. I have not wished to be in personal controversy with him, especially when he is having such a bad time, but there is one statement in his speech at Leicester which I cannot overlook, and which is so remarkable that the general panorama of this Election would not be complete without it. Mr Attlee, speaking of the achievements of his Government, said that he was not satisfied with what had been done. Here are his words: 'How can we clear up in six years the mess of centuries?' 'The mess of centuries!' This is what the Prime Minister considers Britain and her Empire represented when in 1945 she emerged honoured and respected from one end of the world

---

[1] Arthur George Waters, 1888–1953. Joined *News of the World*, 1914. Married, 1919, Priscilla Maude Evans. Editor, *News of the World* from 1947 to his death.

to the other by friend and foe alike after her most glorious victory for freedom. 'The mess of centuries' – that was all we were.

The remark is instructive because it reveals with painful clarity the Socialist point of view and sense of proportion. Nothing happened that was any good until they came into office. We may leave out the great struggles and achievements of the past – Magna Charta, the Bill of Rights, Parliamentary institutions, Constitutional Monarchy, the building of our Empire – all these were part of 'the mess of centuries'. Alas, he cries, he has only six years to do it in. Naturally he was not able to accomplish his full mission. We have endured these six years. They have marked the greatest fall in the rank and stature of Britain in the world, which has occurred since the loss of the American colonies nearly two hundred years ago. Our Oriental Empire has been liquidated, our resources have been squandered, the pound sterling is only worth three-quarters of what it was when Mr Attlee took over from me, our influence among the nations is now less than it has ever been in any period since I remember. Now the Titan wants another term of office!

I have not replied to Mr Attlee before, but it would hardly be respectful of me to ignore all that he says about me. He charges me with putting party before the nation. This is ungrateful considering that the Conservative Party has supported him in every important measure that he has taken for national defence and safety. Last year when he proposed the great scheme of spending £4,700 million in three years upon rearmament, we immediately gave him our full support, although if we had suggested that such steps were necessary he and his friends would no doubt have called us warmongers. We also supported him in increasing the compulsory military service from eighteen months to two years, although at the Election of 1950 his party had tried to gain votes by accusing the Tories of this very intention. But what was the return we received from the Prime Minister for our aid in his rearmament scheme? Within a week of our giving him our full support he announced the intention to complete the nationalization of steel. This was a harsh act of partisanship which was bound to make the gulf between the parties wider. Now that we know what forces the Prime Minister had to contend with in his own Cabinet and party, and how he was being continually harried from behind and from inside by Mr Bevan and his crowd, we see the explanation of his conduct. In order to do what he knew was his duty to his country, he had to pay his way with these evil elements by creating fresh antagonism with the Tory Party, without whose support he would have fallen.

After all I suppose that it is a very complicated business to clear up 'the mess of centuries' and to have only six years to do it in. Let us look at our Conservative record on the charge of 'putting our party before our country'. Speaking in the House of Commons a year ago, I said:[1]

---

[1] Speech of 19 Sep. 1950, reproduced above (pp. 1868–78).

The Prime Minister the other day accused me of being party minded. . . . We are all party minded in the baffling and unhappy period between election decisions and between parties so sharply divided and evenly balanced. However, the nation may be assured that, whatever the conduct of the present Government and dominant party may be, the Conservative and, I believe, the Liberal Opposition will not, I am told, withdraw in any way the aid they have offered and given to all measures for the national defence. We shall do our utmost to encourage recruiting, and we shall be prepared to accept additional burdens wherever they are shown to be unavoidable.

But let us look back on the conduct of Mr Attlee and his own friends in the years before the war. The Labour Party denounced the Baldwin Government for 'planning a vast and expensive rearmament programme which will only stimulate similar programmes elsewhere'. Mr Attlee said on 10 November 1935: 'The National Government is preparing a great programme of rearmament which will endanger the peace of the world.' Mr Morrison in the same month said: 'The Government leaders are all urging a policy of rearmament, and Mr Chamberlain is ready and anxious to spend millions of pounds on machines of destruction.' And again: 'Every vote for the Unionists would be a vote for an international race in arms and a vote for that was a vote for war.' Such was the language of the Socialist leaders in the years while Hitler's Germany was rearming night and day. But after all, actions speak louder than words, and the most remarkable event in the Prime Minister's conduct was his leading his party into the Lobby to vote against conscription on 27 April 1939, although this was four weeks after he and his party had welcomed the British guarantee to Poland against German aggression. And yet later on, when the war was raging, and after it was won, the Labour Party gained great credit by denouncing the Chamberlain Government as guilty men for not having made larger and more timely preparations. But that Mr Attlee, bearing this load upon his shoulders, should accuse the Conservative Party, on whose support as we now know he has lived in all matters of national importance of setting party before country, deserves a prize for political impudence.

In their six years of office the Socialists have reduced the purchasing power of the pound by 5s 6d. This is a consequence of vast and reckless expenditure and extravagance. It is the result of economic policies which have changed like the changing tints of autumn and of promises as thick as falling leaves. We must get back to honest money. Sound financial policies must restore confidence in the pound at home and abroad. This decline in the value of money represents a cut which falls most heavily on the shoulders least able to bear it – the elderly, and all in every class who live on fixed incomes; those who saved and who wish to save, those who draw benefits under our social insurance schemes. Take the one example of family allowances. Parliament fixed these at 5s. Today that 5s is worth only 3s 8d. Already the stream of small savings is fast drying up. This must not continue. Unless we can encourage thrift in all sections of the community our industries will never be able to obtain the capital and resources they require for new equipment to keep them abreast of our world competitors. If our industries are not kept modern and efficient, we cannot look for that increase in productivity on which our ability both to defend ourselves and keep ourselves alive depends. Socialist speakers are telling us that the rise of prices in this country is the result of Korea, rearmament and other world causes outside their control. This is not so. The chief cause of the rise of prices here has been the devaluation of the pound which four years of Socialist extravagance forced upon the Government in 1949. By that single act we had to pay more for the things we bought, and we got paid less for the things we sold. In the nine months between the devaluation of the pound and the outbreak of the Korean War, the wholesale price index rose by eleven per cent. It is that single fact which explains the increases in prices we found in the shops up to the middle of the summer of this year.

The second argument which Socialists put forward is that things are a lot better here than they are anywhere else. This again is a distortion of facts. If you compare today with 1947, when the worst of the wartime effects on economic life had been largely overcome, you will find that the cost-of-living has risen less in Norway, Denmark, Belgium, Italy, the United States and Switzerland than it has in Socialist Britain. One of the main contributions a Conservative Government will make to tackling the cost-of-living is to cut out extravagance where it is found. Some forms of Government expenditure are unnecessary. They must go. We must simplify the whole machine of administration. We will cut out all elements of waste and extravagance in every department, including the defence programme and the nationalized industries.

Winston S. Churchill: press statement
(*Churchill papers, 2/131*)

13 October 1951

Mr Herbert Morrison on October 12 is reported to have said, 'The Tories are threatening . . . to revive the old controversy about trade union law. . . . Surely it would be the most reckless unwisdom thus to rouse the resistance of the whole trade union movement at a time when continued industrial peace and maximum productive effort are absolutely vital to the solution of all our pressing problems at home and abroad.'

On the same date Mr Gordon Walker said he doubted 'whether any political party has ever before gone into an election proclaiming that, if it becomes the Government, it would stage a head-on collision with the trade union movement'.

Both the above statements were made by these Ministers three days after

I had on October 9, as Leader of the Conservative Party made the following statement, 'Mr Deakin, the Trade Union leader, has asked whether the Conservative Party contemplate legislation affecting the Trade Unions. . . . The Conservative Party have no intention of initiating any legislation affecting Trade Unions, should we become responsible in the new Parliament. We hope to work with the Trade Unions in a loyal and friendly spirit, and if this is disturbed by Party politics the fault will not be on our side.'[1]

My statement was fully reported in all the leading newspapers throughout the country. It is remarkable that both Mr Morrison and Mr Gordon Walker should have misrepresented the declared policy of the Conservative Party on an important issue of this kind, and that they should both do so simultaneously. Perhaps however they neither of them had read my statement when they spoke. This would be a coincidence, but it would at least explain their conduct.

R. A. Butler to Winston S. Churchill
(*Churchill papers, 2/130*)

13 October 1951

Dear Mr Churchill,

I have attached the Government statement on legislation affecting Voluntary Schools in England and Wales. The points in this statement have been discussed behind the scenes by officials of the Ministry of Education with the Roman Catholics and the Anglicans. I have been aware that such discussions were going on, though I have had to obtain my information from officials, whose names I cannot disclose. I have also obtained some information from the Church of England and a certain amount from Bishop Beck.[2]

The Conservative Education Committee, with Miss Horsbrugh[3] as Chairman and Christopher Hollis[4] (a Roman Catholic) as Secretary, had been intending to call on the Minister of Education[5] to discuss points similar to these. The Minister has unfortunately been ill for some time. It is presumed

---

[1] Speech reproduced above (pp. 00–00).

[2] George Andrew Beck, 1902–78. Educated at Clapham College and Assumptionist College of St Michael. Ordained priest in the Roman Catholic Church, 1927. Catholic Bishop of Brentwood, 1951–5; of Salford, 1955–64; Catholic Archbishop of Liverpool, 1964–76.

[3] Florence Gertrude Horsbrugh, 1889–1969. MBE, 1920. MP (Cons.) for Dundee, 1931–45; for Manchester Moss Side, 1950–9. Minister of Education, 1951–4. CBE, 1939; GBE, 1954.

[4] Maurice Christopher Hollis, 1902–77. Educated at Eton and Balliol College, Oxford. Prof. of History, Stonyhurst College, 1925–35. Visiting Professor, University of Notre Dame, Indiana, 1935–9. RAF intelligence officer during WWII. MP (Cons.) for Devizes, 1945–55. Parliamentary commentator for *Punch*, 1955.

[5] George Tomlinson, 1890–1952. MP (Lab.) for Farnworth, 1938–52. Joint Parliamentary Secretary, Ministry of Labour and National Service, 1941–5. Minister of Works, 1945–7. Minister of Education, 1947–51.

that this Government statement has been hastily issued as a result of pressure by Dick Stokes (a Roman Catholic), Morrison and presumably Chuter Ede. The weakness of this statement, from the Government point of view, is that it does not mention the need for obtaining agreement of the Free Churches, the teachers and the local Education authorities. This, I should have thought, in the long run was rash, since the major section of our population feels that the Voluntary Schools have had a very good deal.

Now I come to our attitude. We have issued a statement with the help of Lord Swinton and his Committee, which I also attach. This indicates quite clearly enough to Anglicans and Roman Catholics alike that we intend to try to help them with their outstanding difficulties. The difference so far between our statement and that of the Government is that, not being in Office, we do not go into specific details, and secondly that we refer to the need for agreement. I think it important to adhere to both these aspects of our statement, since in the complexities of this subject, it would be a bold man who could say exactly what detailed points a Bill would contain.

As regards agreement, I think it important at any rate that we should retain the right to consult the other partners before we act. We should certainly get much more public support if we did this.

It will be interesting to hear Bishop Beck's reaction to our statement. Being an expert negotiator, he will press for more. I consider that it will be perfectly legitimate to say to him we have in mind the need to redefine 'displaced pupils' so as to cover the children of those parents who have moved into new housing estates or built-up areas since the war. Thus we are in general agreement upon the first point of the Government statement.

On the second point of the Government statement, I should be perfectly ready to agree with the Minister to pay grants and make loans for re-housing aided schools in existing premises.

I think there is no objection, in principle, to the third point that the Authority should build a controlled school to take the place of two or more existing Voluntary Schools, because this, in fact, has the effect of lessening the number of aided Schools.

The fourth point is a small point and need not be discussed at present.

The less we go into detail the better, but by mentioning the above, I am simply indicating to you that, in principle, there is not a lot to worry about. But we should warn the Bishop that we cannot do anything that creates an exceptional burden on the Exchequer or the rates in view of the country's financial and economic position.

Second, we should say that what is done for one Denomination must be done for all.

Third, we must work within the framework of the 1944 Act settlement (witness the Free Church letter to which I have drafted an answer).

Finally, I don't think the Hierarchy will give instructions that their supporters should vote Labour. I think they will be influenced by the report they will receive of your interview with Bishop Beck.

I think there are positive advantages in your seeing him alone; but I have only to be rung at home in Essex in order to be present, if you so desire.

Lord Simon to Winston S. Churchill
(*Churchill papers, 2/130*)

13 October 1951

NOTE FOR MEETING WITH BISHOP BECK

We are in full sympathy with the Voluntary Schools and are determined to do everything possible to meet their present difficulties.

The 1944 settlement made in my Government was the result of agreement between all the interests. Because the question was lifted above Party Politics and agreement was reached, the reforms were lasting.

The only way to get a lasting settlement of the present difficulties is by getting agreement in the same way.

No Government could guarantee to get a Bill through Parliament, unless there was general agreement.

Moreover, the prospects of such a Bill would be gravely prejudiced, if the Ministers responsible had committed themselves to specific measures in advance, without consultation with the other parties.

That was why in the Conservative Statement of Policy issued on the 10th October, while affirming our intention to deal with the new difficulties of the Voluntary Schools, we said we should undertake the negotiations which are the only way to get agreement, and to get, as in 1944, a lasting settlement.

Nothing could be more harmful to the Voluntary Schools than to plunge them into Party controversy. Conservatives will do all they can to prevent that injury to these schools.

Our sympathy is proved by what we did in 1944.

It was Butler's handling of the negotiations which got for the Voluntary Schools all the benefits of that settlement.

A Conservative Government will almost certainly be returned and have to deal with this. They must follow the only line which will make it possible to do what they and the Voluntary Schools both want to see done.

Very grave issues at this election, which touch many matters Catholics all over the world hold dear.

What kind of Government does the Bishop think is most likely to further the cause of the Catholic Schools and all the other causes for which the Catholic Church stands in the world today?

Winston S. Churchill to The Right Reverend George Beck
(Churchill papers, 2/130)

13 October 1951
Private

My dear Lord Bishop,

By a strange series of mishaps it is only this afternoon that I have received your letter of the 8th. It has received careful consideration from Mr Butler, Lord Woolton, Lord Swinton, and others of my friends. They naturally thought I had it in my possession all the time.

My colleagues have now given me their advice and I send you my enclosed reply. It seems to me important that we should meet, and I suggest, if it is convenient to you, 11 o'clock on Monday morning next, the 15th, at my house in London – 28, Hyde Park Gate, SW7. I have to leave for a speaking tour of a very laborious character in the north at 1 o'clock, but if you could come to me at 11 I should welcome a talk. I propose that Mr Butler should be there too. If Monday is not convenient to you let us find a suitable time on Thursday, the 18th when I return from the north.

Perhaps you will send me a telephone message tonight which date you prefer.

13 October 1951

My dear Lord Bishop,

I am much obliged to you for the courtesy of your letter and for the frank explanation you give of the difficulty that has been created by the Government statement on the Voluntary Schools. I have of course studied with great care the Government pronouncement and the statements of the Hierarchy and of the Archbishop of Canterbury.

The Conservative Party yields to none in its desire to help the Voluntary Schools of all denominations to make their irreplaceable contribution to the life and character of English education, and I feel that our record in the past both in Government and in Opposition is sufficient warrant of this. We share devoutly your hope that this question may be kept out of the arena of party politics and that any solution to the very real difficulties that the churches have been experiencing, especially over the question of the displaced pupils, may be an agreed solution. It is precisely because we share that hope that we thought it unfortunate that proposals of which we have no knowledge and whose details may or may not have the assent of all parties to the 1944 agreement should have been issued on the eve of an Election campaign.

I shall certainly have no hesitation at all in advising my friends and supporters to associate themselves with your wish that relief should be given to the Voluntary Schools within the framework of the present Education Acts. This indeed was the sense and substance both of our general Conservative statement of policy 'Britain – Strong and Free' and of the later statement published in the Press on October 10, of which you now have a copy. Our views and our purpose are in harmony. But I do not think, nor frankly do I feel that any other Party thinks, that a lasting settlement can be achieved without general accord, and I beg your Lordship not to underestimate the consequences to our national life if these problems were to become matters of public controversy instead of agreement.

I welcome an opportunity to talk these matters over with you.

Jo Sturdee to Winston S. Churchill
(Churchill papers, 2/115)

14 October 1951

Mr Macmillan telephoned the following message to you this morning:

'I have just completed a week mostly in Lancashire and the Midlands, and feel much encouraged. Your broadcast had a profound effect – it was perfect. The people seem in a serious mood and prefer to listen to serious arguments. This is especially important since the Liberal vote is open to persuasion in so many seats. With these I have found the fact of Conservative and Liberal Cooperation in the European Movement, and the Socialist boycotting of it, quite a useful point. All good wishes.'

Lord Killearn to Winston S. Churchill
(Churchill papers, 2/171)

15 October 1951

Dear Winston,

We are all delighted you are trouncing them as they deserve.

Here the local result is a certainty (Deedes):[1] at Faversham Young Bossom[2] had a hard fight for it.

Persia is a marvel of mishandling. So I suspect is Egypt! And the worm has been forced to turn. Morrison is a natural disaster.

This letter is however solely to put before you, in case of any use, that when

---

[1] William Francis Deedes, 1913–2007. On active service during WWII (MC, 1944). MP (Cons.) for Ashford Div. of Kent, 1950–74. PC, 1962. Baron, 1986. KBE, 1999.
[2] Clive Bossom, 1918–2017. Educated at Eton. Served in Far East (Maj.) and Europe (Royal East Kent Rgt), 1939–48. City Councillor, Kent, 1949–51. Unsuccessful Parliamentary candidate, Faversham, 1951. Married, 1951, Barbara Joan North: four children. MP (Cons.) for Leominster, 1959–74. Succeeded as 2nd Bt Bossom, 1965.

you are back in office and you most certainly will and must be, my services will be at your entire disposal, Sir, if you should so desire.

And may I add that nothing would afford us both such pleasure as to serve you again.[1]

Winston S. Churchill: speech
('*Winston S. Churchill, His Complete Speeches*', volume 8, pages 8265–9)

15 October 1951   Town Hall, Huddersfield

ELECTION ADDRESS

The Conservatives in the Colne Valley have made a party sacrifice in not running a candidate of their own and in giving all their support to the Liberal candidate. Considering that nearly 16,000 electors voted Conservative at the last election, and about 10,000 Liberal, this must be considered a remarkable decision. It shows how deeply anxious the Conservatives in the Colne Valley are about the state of our country, and that they have come to the conclusion after much heart-searching that our safety, honour and progress as a nation depend upon the defeat of the Socialist Government. I admired this course of action because the crisis we have now reached is sharp enough to override the ordinary party differences which are a healthy part of our free constitutional political life. Indeed I was so much attracted by the far-reaching mental and moral vigour of the decision of the Conservative Association that I wished to come here myself to share in it.

My long experience of life has shown me that when any step is taken by a large body of people on national and patriotic grounds the great thing is not to do it grudgingly or half-heartedly. I said to my friends of the Conservative Association when they visited me in London:

> If you are going to make a sacrifice of your party claims, make sure you do it in style. That is the only way in which any advantage will be gained for the common cause.

The Conservative Association have accordingly decided to do their utmost to return the Liberal candidate to Parliament without asking for any promises or for any conditions in return. The Liberal candidate for Colne Valley will have, I am sure, the fervent and ardent support of every true Tory patriot, not as the result of a political bargain or compromise, but because they feel that to rid the nation of its Socialist incubus is a public duty at a moment so grave as this in our national and international affairs.

I have been given a list of a dozen constituencies in which a Liberal

---

[1] Churchill responded: 'Thank you so much.'

candidate, without the faintest chance of getting elected himself, is doing what is most likely to get the Socialist in. Naturally, I am told this will make it very difficult to persuade all the Conservatives in the Colne Valley to vote for a Liberal candidate, and there are some who think that I ought not to have come here at all. I do so because the true guide of life is to do what is right. Both the Liberals and Conservatives who are unanimously opposed to Socialism and regard the return of the Socialists at this juncture as a very serious evil to our country, would be in the wrong if they fell away on the party grounds from the main objective. I am sure that if the spirit which is running in this Constituency were to prevail, it could have nothing but advantage to the permanent good, both of the Liberal and Conservative Parties, and above all of our country.

Of course you cannot consider public and party questions apart from personalities. It happened that there descended upon the Colne Valley a bright figure in our public life. She came 'out of the blue'. In Mr Asquith's famous daughter you have one of the very best speakers, male or female, in this island at this time. She is also an absolutely unswerving exponent of the Liberal theme. She has never varied from her fidelity to her party, and there is no Liberal in the whole of Great Britain who can impugn or rival her record. Therefore there is no question of any Conservative or any Liberal in this Constituency departing by a jot from his principles or convictions. There is only that larger and higher feeling that in the anxious days through which we are passing, our respective party sentiments may find their fullest and most resolute expression by returning Lady Violet Bonham Carter to Parliament by a resounding majority. As one who has lived his life in the House of Commons I feel interested in seeing fine speakers and strong personalities elected. The representation of Colne Valley will certainly not lack distinction if you return Lady Violet Bonham Carter to Parliament.

That is all I have to say this evening about the party and political issues which come to so intense a focus in the Colne Valley. All over the country in this buoyant election, people are looking to the Colne Valley. I am sure the more the spirit which has prevailed here spreads, the fewer Liberal votes through the country will be wasted and the more surely a coherent and decisive verdict of the electors will be obtained against Socialism.

Let me mention to you some of the great issues on which Conservatives and Liberals are agreed, and which constitute the elements of the common cause vital to our national welfare. First, we proclaim that the State is the servant and not the master of the people. We reject altogether the Socialist conception of a division of society between officials and the common mass. We repudiate their policy of levelling down to a minimum uniformity, above which only politicians and their agents may rise. We stand for the increasingly higher expression of individual independence. We hold most strongly to the Declaration of Human Rights, as set forth by the United Nations at Geneva.

It is worth noting that among all these United Nations we are the only great Power under Socialist rule. That is why Socialist policy has been in these past years increasingly out of step and out of harmony with, or lagging behind, the movement of thought among the free democracies of Europe and the modern world.

We then declare ourselves inveterately opposed to any further nationalization of industry. We intend to repeal the nationalization of steel. Further, we come to those large bodies of practical domestic reforms set forth in our booklet, *Britain – Strong and Free*, and from a very slightly different angle, in Liberal election literature. No doubt there are other points upon which Liberals and Conservatives do not agree. But how small they are in scale and importance compared to the great body of fundamental principles and practical schemes of application on which both anti-Socialist parties are in accord, and which are now supported by a large majority of electors all over the country.

There is in fact a wide overlap of agreement, both in doctrine and in action, between those that have hitherto been brought up to regard themselves as political opponents. But now the times are very grave, and it is the duty of every man and woman who agrees upon so large a proportion of the main principles and practical steps, to make sure that these are not overwhelmed by the ignorant and obsolete doctrine of Socialism against which the British nation stands today in marked recoil. All I ask, and it is a modest demand, is that those who agree upon the fundamentals shall in our party conflicts try to help each other as much as they can and harm each other as little as they must. Let that climate of opinion and theme of conduct prevail and we should have cleared the path of progress of many of its pitfalls and barriers and perhaps have the power to rescue our native land from some of the perils and forms of degeneration by which is it oppressed.

More than forty years ago I sat myself in a Left-wing Government with a great majority, and I was one of their most prominent and controversial figures. The House of Commons returned in 1906 represented, in my view, more or less the same slice of the population, the people who elected it coming very largely from the same homes and from the same areas as does the Socialist majority today. But there was a great difference between those days of forty years ago and these days in which we are now living. The Liberal Government of 1906 was built around and upon those great principles of Liberalism which have since passed into the possession of every party except the Communists and are still spreading with irresistible appeal throughout the world. But now our opponents are not ranged around the great truths of Liberalism; they are ranged around the fallacy of Socialism, which is in principle contrary to human nature and which I believe can only be enforced upon the nations in its entirety in the wholesale fashion of Communism.

We are now only at the beginning of the Socialist imposition. At present only 20 per cent of our industries are nationalized, and we have been living upon the other 80 per cent which the Government eye with so much disfavour and malice. The complete nationalization of all the means of production, distribution and exchange would make it impossible for this small island to support a large part of its population. There is indeed a great gulf of thought and conviction between us. It is more than a matter of thought; our actual survival is at stake. I look back with pride to the great measures of social reform – Unemployment Insurance, Labour Exchanges, Safety in Coalmines, bringing Old Age Pensions down from seventy to sixty-five years of age, the Widow's and Orphans' Pensions – for which I have been responsible both as a Liberal and a Conservative Minister. I find comfort in the broad harmony of thought which prevails between the modern Tory democracy and the doctrines of the famous Liberal leaders of the past. I am sure that in accord with their speeches and writings, men like Asquith, Morley, and Grey, whom I knew so well in my youth, would have regarded the establishment of a Socialist State and the enforcement of the collectivist theory as one of the worst evils that could befall Britain and her slowly-evolved, long cherished way of life. All those who are resolved to strive for the restoration of Britain's greatness, for its tolerances and liberties and for its true progress, have this underlying sense of unity, which petty partisanship or outworn prejudices must never destroy.

You will have seen in the Conservative statement of policy, *Britain – Strong and Free*, the detailed answers to many of the disputed and difficult questions of this anxious election. I hope, however, that you will keep foremost and paramount in your mind the intellectual and moral issue now to be decided for their future by the British electors. The supreme question is, are we after our experience of the last six years to take another deep plunge into Socialism or regain the high road which all the rest of the English-speaking world are now treading, of free enterprise and opportunity for all, and of the strong helping the weak? It is better for the strong to help the weak than for the weak to hinder the strong. Basic standards of life and labour must be secured in our society and civilization, and on this foundation everyone should be free to use his or her gifts and qualities to the full. In this way alone can our fifty millions safeguard their food, their work and their homes.

But Beware! For we may be at the parting of the ways. The wisdom of our ancestors for more than 300 years has sought the division of power in the Constitution. Crown, Lords and Commons have been checks and restraints upon one another. The limitation of the power of the Monarchy was the cause for which, as Liberals used to say, 'Hampden died in the field and Sidney on the scaffold'. The concentration of all power over the daily lives of ordinary men and women in what is called 'the State', exercised by what is virtually single-chamber government, is a reactionary step contrary to the whole trend of British history and to the message we have given to the world. The British race have always abhorred arbitrary and absolute government in every form. The great men who founded the American Constitution embodied this separation of authority in the strongest and most durable form. Not only did they divide executive, legislative and judicial functions, but also by instituting a federal system they preserved immense and sovereign rights to local communities, and by all these means they have preserved – often at some inconvenience – a system of law and liberty under which they have thrived and reached the leadership of the world. The Socialist conception of the all-powerful State entering into the smallest detail of the life and conduct of the individual and claiming to plan and shape his work and its rewards is odious and repellent to every friend of freedom. These absolute powers would make the group of politicians who obtained a majority of seats in Parliament the masters and not the servants of the people and would centralize all government in Whitehall. So far we are only at the first stage of this evil journey. But already enterprise, daring and initiative are crippled. Thrift is penalized by the heaviest taxation in the world. Regulations increasingly take the place of statutes passed by Parliament. There are many hundreds of new crimes unknown before the war, punishable by fines or imprisonment. And all this is avowedly only a step to complete Socialization.

'All men are created equal,' says the American Declaration of Independence. 'All men shall be kept equal,' say the British Socialist Party. The only exceptions are no doubt to be the Ministers and the members of the Government and their associates. If this is already taking place before our eyes, when only one-fifth of our industries have been nationalized, and while we still retain our political rights and freedom, we can judge what will happen when the whole process is complete. The worship of an all-powerful State, beneath which the ordinary mass of citizens lie prostrate, is one of the most deadly and insidious delusions by which a free people as we still are can cast away rights and liberties, which for their own sake and the sake of their children, they ought to hold dearer than life itself.

The British nation now has to make one of the most momentous choices in its history. That choice is between two ways of life; between individual liberty and State domination; between the concentration of ownership in the hands of the State and the extension of a property-owning democracy; between a policy of increasing control and restriction, and a policy of liberating energy and ingenuity; between a policy of levelling down and a policy of finding opportunity for all to rise upwards from a basic standard. There is not a field in which the Socialists have acted during these six years in which they have not failed. In the domestic fields we can see the cost-of-living; the disorder of our finances; the vast increases in the cost of Government. All that is apparent.

Abroad they have been false to the cause of the United Europe by proclaiming that there should be no United Europe unless it is a Socialist United Europe. They have lost all their influence on the Continent. It was a wonderful thing, which really ought to be preserved as a model of what not to do, how they managed to excite equally the animosity of the Israelites and the Arabs in the Middle East. Towards the United States their attitude has been to take everything they can. Indeed they have been maintained upon the bounty of capitalist America, whilst at the same time trying to become the moral superior over them. Now is the time to break with these follies.

Winston S. Churchill: speech
('Winston S. Churchill, His Complete Speeches', volume 8, pages 8269–74)

16 October 1951   St James's Boxing Hall, Newcastle upon Tyne

ELECTION ADDRESS

I cannot recall any period in my long life when mismanagement and incompetence have brought us into greater danger. At home prices and taxes go up and up, abroad the influence of Britain goes down and down. In every quarter of the world we are regarded by our friends with anxiety and pity, by others, including some of those countries we have helped in the past, like Egypt and Persia, with hostility and contempt. Not one of them is so weak that they cannot spare a kick or a taunt for Britain. It is hard to believe that we are the same nation that emerged from the last War, respected and admired throughout the Grand Alliance for the part we played (for a long time, alone), in the defence of the cause of freedom. Six years of Socialist rule have not been good for us.

The Socialists started this Election on the basis that the party who could grovel best abroad would win most votes at home. We have yet to see whether that is true, whether it fully expresses the convictions of the British nation or whether it is the surest way to secure a lasting world peace. I do not myself believe that the British electors are thinking only of their material interests, seriously though these are affected. There is a deep-seated sense of pride in the greatness of Britain, and a widespread desire that our power shall be maintained and our reputation restored.

Of all the countries in the world, none has given up more worldly and Imperial power and position than we have under Socialist rule. All our Oriental Empire has been given away, with the frightful slaughter of innocent and helpless people amounting to two or three times the total loss of lives suffered by the whole British Empire in the Second World War. Has that won us more respect in other parts of the East? For three years we have put up with the Egyptians, contrary to International Law, blocking the Suez Canal to the oil supplies for Israel and Europe. Did that pacify or placate them? No. On the contrary. When a great structure or organism like the British Empire seems to fail, for the time being, prostrate, every concession that is made is only an incitement to others to come and press upon it more. How is it that we who have given away and sacrificed more than any other country to this cry of anti-Imperialism, should also be the most hated? The French are holding on to their Empire and fighting for it against the Communists as we indeed are doing in Malaya. The Belgians hold firmly to the Congo, in the administration of which great reforms have been made. The Portuguese are holding on to Goa in India. But Britain, the greatest donor, who under Socialism has given everything away in all directions (except in Malaya), is the one who is denounced as the arch-tyrant and reactionary. It is an astonishing episode in world history. But after all it is only what you see in ordinary daily life, that if people are known to be ready to cast aside their rights and to give in and clear out, if their Government tries to undermine every argument by which their position may be maintained, to make a feature of it and glory in it, they will find lots of hungry wolves to come and eat up an easily-gotten prey.

In Egypt the Government in their latest proposals offer to hand over our historic position of defending the Suez Canal to a Five-Power combination of which Egypt would be one. Naturally I regret that this should be necessary, but having regard to our altered position in the world, I cannot say that it is wrong. It is six months since I said in the House of Commons:[1]

> We are no longer strong enough ourselves to bear the whole political burden we have hitherto borne in the Mediterranean, or even to take the leading part in the diplomatic control of that theatre. But the United States and Britain together, aided by France – we three together would be in a most powerful position to deal with, say, the Egyptian problem and the whole question of the defence of the Suez Canal.

I am very glad that Turkey has been added to the other Powers I mentioned. We now learn that Egypt has refused to accept this generous offer which would advance her sovereignty and which would at the same time secure her safety. We must all hope that the Socialist Government will adhere firmly to the position which they have taken up in conjunction with these important Allies and not let brave words be followed by ignominious deeds.

There is one other comment that may be made. Why have these proposals to bring America and France into the defence of the vital interests of the free world, in the Middle East, not been taken earlier? If at the time I offered my advice to Parliament the Government had accepted it a different reception might have been obtained from Egypt and it may well be that the Persian disaster would never have occurred. Owing, however, to the late Mr Bevin's ill-health there was practically no Foreign Secretary during the most critical months in the Middle East and when Mr Morrison succeeded him his mind was much distracted by the Festival of Britain and preparations for a General Election which were his specialities. The conduct of foreign

---

[1] Speech of 19 Apr. 1951, reproduced above (pp. 2041–55).

affairs has therefore suffered all the evil consequences of delay and lack of attention. What is needed now is a period of stable and steady Government able to look ahead and foresee difficulties before they arise, and with time and authority at command to deal with them in the true national interest. In this way the greatest guarantee for the maintenance of world peace, so far as it rests with Britain to give it, will be secured.

Let me now come to our affairs at home and in Newcastle. This city of much renown both in peace and war has proved itself one of the key points in our national life. I remember my visits to you in war and long before it. It is ten years since I last came to Newcastle and fifty years since I first came. I am very sorry that differences have broken out in the Conservative Association for North Newcastle. Naturally as Leader of the party I was kept informed of all that occurred and, while we do not interfere from the centre in constituency matters more than we can help, it was evident that this dispute should be examined by an impartial Committee of the National Union of Conservative Associations. This was done, and no one judging from a detached position could doubt that the report of the Committee should be our guide. Mr Gwilym Lloyd George is therefore the official and accepted candidate of the Conservative Party and he carries with him my warmest wishes not only for his own qualities but because he revives a name famous in the social history of Britain and also in our victory in the First World War. It is surprising that he should be opposed by an Independent Conservative candidate[1] and I wish to make it plain that any Conservative who at this critical juncture in our history of our country allows personal or sectional motives to lead him to cast a vote which could only have the consequence of handing this famous seat over to the Socialists will have cause to reproach himself for having failed in his duty not only to his party but to his country.

I wonder if you have been following Mr Attlee's electioneering tours. I see that he complains that the Conservative Opposition have shown themselves party minded. But remember what happened when he proposed that £4,700 million rearmament programme. We gave him full support. We also supported him in his extension of compulsory service to two years, when he and his friends had tried to gain votes at the last Election by accusing us of wishing to do so. But what was the reception of our patriotic aid? Within forty-eight hours of the Conservative and Liberal Parties agreeing to support the Government's rearmament proposals just over a year ago, the Government announced that it was their intention to proceed at once with the nationalization of the steel industry. This was a double blow to the country. First it destroyed the prospects of national unity at a time of national danger and difficulty. Second, it struck at the smooth working of an industry whose position in the rearmament drive was fundamental. Here was an industry

---

[1] Colin Gray, formerly Chairman of the Wallsend Young Conservatives. He received 12.1% of the vote to Lloyd George's 51.1%.

which has moved with the times and often led the way, one which for more than forty years had had no internal dispute between capital and labour, whose wage differences had been continually adjusted by the normal processes of collective bargaining, conducted by responsible trade unions, whose relations with the State and the users were agreeably regulated by the Steel Board. Here was an industry whose trade unions may be proud to have had at their head men like Mr Arthur Pugh, Mr John Brown, and a worthy successor, Mr Lincoln Evans. Let me, at this point, compliment you on all your candidates for Newcastle and Wallsend. They are all on our platform tonight. I do not wonder at all that Mr Alfred Edwards,[1] your very able and distinguished candidate for Newcastle East, should, with his knowledge of the steel industry, have thought it his duty to leave the Socialist Party upon a major issue of this character.

Steel was an industry for whom the Trades Union Congress Report furnished an admirable guide for a working arrangement between employers and employed which, I understand, would give an acceptable basis for both sides. When you look out upon this troubled world and our anxious, embarrassed, bewildered country, you might easily say this was the brightest spot. Why should this then be chosen of all others for restrictive, hampering, convulsive regulation and change? When you think of all the evils that are rife and the muddles that are rampant, surely there were other reforms which might have claimed priority from the destructive zeal of Socialist doctrinaires and millionaires. Mr Attlee had long been reluctant to proceed with steel nationalization. Discussion of it has disturbed the Cabinet for two or three years. We may wonder whether it was the price he had to pay to keep Mr Bevan in his Cabinet, and to retain his support by the Left-wing of his party in Parliament and the country. It was a classic example of appeasement, and it obtained only the result of appeasement from weakness. Within six months Mr Bevan had left the Cabinet and the Left-wing was in revolt. Fortunately for the country there is now the chance to reverse this fateful and foolish decision about steel before it is too late. The organization of the industry and its individual firms still remain intact. The Socialists have not yet been able to go far enough or fast enough to undermine it. If we are returned to power we shall at once repeal the Iron and Steel Act. It is not too late for us to enable British steel to resume once again, under free enterprise, its high achievements of the past. We shall appoint a board representative of Government, management, labour and consumers, if need be with new powers, to supervise prices and development in the industry, as it did so successfully during the war and until it was wrecked by the Nationalization Act.

Steel leads me naturally to coal. The Conservative Party always had grave

---

[1] Alfred Edwards, 1888–1958. Married, 1917, Anne Raines Hoskison. MP (Lab.) for Middlesbrough East, 1935–48; (Ind.) for Middlesbrough East, 1948–9; (Cons.) for Middlesbrough East, 1949–50. Expelled from the Labour Party in 1948 when he opposed nationalization of the steel industry.

misgivings about the results of placing detailed responsibility for this basic industry on a national board located in London. Remote control of this kind is not the way in which to make the best use of our widespread coal resources. As the result of Conservative pressure on this point during the last five years the National Coal Board has recently been reconstituted so that it can concentrate more on questions of broad policy and general financial control. We welcome this development; but we must make sure that it is extended. If we are elected we shall propose the regrouping of collieries into districts of manageable size. Our aim is to see district boards which, while they would have to conform to national standards, would be free from day-to-day interference from the centre. Such boards would be able to inspire local enthusiasm and local loyalties. We intend to discuss all these matters with the miners. We do not want to have any discrimination against those areas where the pits are less modern or the coal is less easily won. But we do want to restore to the districts the sense of local pride they seem to have lost under Whitehall control. I believe that by giving the miners themselves more say in the working of the pits we should find an improvement in output. Let me make it clear that our proposals for reorganizing the industry will in no way affect the present machinery for wage fixing. A national minimum wage is now guaranteed for the industry and that system of negotiation must and will remain on a national basis.

Nationalization has disappeared from the Socialist election manifesto. In 1950, they were going to nationalize cement, sugar, water and the wholesale meat trade, semi nationalize insurance, and possibly the chemical industry as well, besides proceeding with steel nationalization. The present manifesto is silent on these matters. This is not only because the Socialist Party has found out that the nationalization is costly, but they see that it is unpopular. We should beware. Nationalization has been taken out of the shop window, but it is still under the counter. Their Scarborough manifesto says:

> We shall take over concerns which fail the nation and start new public enterprises wherever this will serve the national interest.

This is asking for a blank cheque to enable them to nationalize anything they like, or dislike, if they get a majority. They would be able to strike at any industry or firm which they chose to say has 'failed'. They could either take it over, or make it bankrupt, by starting a State-subsidized rival, which would of course dump any of its losses on the taxpayer. We must not assume that the Socialists have abandoned their belief that the gentlemen in Whitehall know best – better than the housewife, better than the mother about what should be ordered for food and how the family should be brought up, and that we can prosper only if the bureaucrats plan our lives in minute detail. They have discovered that their theories are unpopular. The creation of the Socialist State has not been abandoned; it is only deferred until such time as their party can achieve a Parliamentary majority. Our aim and object is to get rid of the whole system of controls and restrictions as soon as possible. We recognize, of course, that while shortages persist some controls are inevitable, but we regard wartime controls in time of peace as a regrettable necessity. While they remain we should insist upon the closest scrutiny and review by Parliament. Post-war shortages must not be made the excuse for clamping a permanent system of control upon the free life of this great British community.

We are not going to try to get into office by offering bribes and promises of immediate material benefits to our people. The Socialists did that in 1945. We offer no smooth or easy path to the British nation now fighting for its life almost as it did in the war. We do not know what will be the facts with which we shall be confronted should we be returned to power. Certainly they have very gravely worsened in the last few months and we have found out much more about them only in the last few weeks. Nothing will induce me as your Leader at this Election to bid for office by competing with the Socialists in promises of Utopias round the corner, or of easy escape from the hard facts by which we are surrounded. It would be far better for us to lose the Election than to win it on false pretences. All I will promise the British electorate in your name, and the only pledge that I will give on behalf of the Conservative Party is that if the Government of Britain is entrusted to us at this crisis in her fate, we will do our best for all without fear or favour, without class or party bias, without rancour or spite but with the clear and faithful simplicity that we showed in the days of Dunkirk. We did not think then about party scores. We did not divide the men we rescued from the beaches into those we cared about and those for whom, to quote a Ministerial utterance, we did not 'care a tinker's cuss'. The rescuing ships that set out from Britain did not regard a large part of the wearied and hard-pressed army we were bringing back to safety, and as it proved in the end to the victory – we did not regard them as 'lower than vermin' – we were all one then. However the voting may go in this part or that, in this district or the other, in the town or the country, our sole aim will be to act for all our fellow-countrymen and bring them out of the perils and privations by which they are now oppressed and surrounded. Above all, we shall go forward without fear and with unconquerable hope that our ancient and mighty people, who, as I believe and declare, saved the freedom of the world in the early stages of the war, are not confronted with any problem they cannot solve, or with any difficulty or danger they cannot overcome, if only they act with wisdom and courage and above all – if they act now.

Lady Violet Bonham Carter to Winston S. Churchill
(Churchill papers, 2/111)

18 October 1951

Beloved Winston,

The Valley is still aglow with your presence and the echoes of your speech are still ringing through it. What I owe you cannot be expressed – but you know it. I am proud and happy to be 'in the line' with you.

It is wonderful to think that a week today you may be leading the country again and that this crazy crew on their leaking craft may be sunk 'full fathom five'. No one will hail the result with greater joy than you.

Grateful,
– Bloody Duck
V –

PS. Samuel was here last night and made an excellent speech in the Town Hall in which he gave his whole-hearted blessing to your visit and said that though you two had been apart in many things, in this common aim – victory in Colne Valley – you were together. He also said, quite unequivocally, that he wanted a change of Government. This is important.

PPS. I spoke to Ronald Walker,[1] President of our Yorkshire Federation about Shipley. Alas, it is too late to do anything after nomination day. If only I had known before something might, (I do not say would), have been possible, but one cannot ask a young man to lose £150 and break off a campaign in medias res. Do remember however that Liberals are not fighting in 500 seats this time.

L. S. Amery to Winston S. Churchill
(Churchill papers, 2/166)

18 October 1951

My dear Winston,

This is just to say that if you want to make use of my services as from next week, they are willingly at your disposal. I know I have still plenty of useful work left in me and I believe my name still goes for something in the Dominions as well as with the Party at home.

I would, in that case, prefer to stand for Oxford University where I used to be chairman of the Conservative Association and where I have kept in touch with successive undergraduate generations. But if it suited you better to have me in the 'other place', I would go there readily on the assumption that you

---

[1] Ronald Fitz-John Walker, 1880–1971. President, Yorkshire Liberal Party, 1947–60. President, Liberal Party, 1952–3.

really do mean to reform it, so that Julian should not be suddenly evicted from the House of Commons on my demise.

He is doing well up here and will, I think, hold the seat. I have had some very good meetings up here in Lancashire.

Ian Colvin to Winston S. Churchill
(Churchill papers, 2/117)

18 October 1951

Dear Mr Churchill,

I am sending in these questions which I hoped to ask you during your Northern tour, which I want very much to embody as an interview in the *Sunday Times* this week when we shall be publishing your photograph in our Portrait Gallery.

1. What is the main issue at this general election?

2. ~~Mr Morrison repeated in his wireless speech his past insinuations that the Tories, and you particularly, had been war mongering. What is your answer to this in the situation that has developed abroad?~~[1]

3. What does the Conservative Party offer to the youth of Great Britain?

I hope that it will be possible for you to give these answers for use in the form of an interview, which I could come and receive.

I am writing a report of your Northern tour for the *Sunday Times*.

Arthur Waters to Winston S. Churchill
(Churchill papers, 2/129)

19 October 1951

Dear Mr Churchill,

I have pleasure in enclosing a proof of the article you have written for Sunday's *News of the World*. Unless we hear to the contrary on Saturday morning, may we take it, please, that everything is in order?[2]

SUNDAY'S *NEWS OF THE WORLD*

By the Rt Hon Winston Churchill OM

On Thursday 34,000,000 people in this free democracy will have the right to decide – and decide by secret ballot – how their affairs are to be conducted

---

[1] Churchill struck through this proposed interview question.
[2] Churchill sent Waters the following addition: 'It is six months ago that I urged the gov't to act with America and France in settling these problems in the Middle East. I am glad they have now done that; but it would have been better if they had acted sooner. It might well have averted bloodshed and the serious dangers which now loom ahead.' This addition was incorporated by Waters into the final version of the article.

for the next five years. Of all the elections in which I have taken part over the long span of my public life, I can recall none in which the issues at stake were more momentous.

Upon the deep, instinctive political wisdom of the ordinary men and women of Britain depends the destiny of the nation, maybe for generations to come.

For make no mistake, however much the Socialists try to obscure the gravity of recent and present events in the Middle East and of our growing difficulties at home, the fact remains – and none knows it better than the present Ministers – that in a world beset by the menace of war, our economic situation is precarious.

The 50,000,000 people of this island would not be able to exist without raw materials and food obtained from overseas. These have to be won, in a world of increasingly acute competition, by the exertions, ingenuity and craftsmanship of those engaged in the exporting industries.

Another great factor in keeping our population employed, fed and clothed is the money earned by our banking, insurance and shipping services, and by enterprise overseas – the oil wells of Persia, the rubber and tin mines of Malaya and the cotton fields of Egypt and the Sudan. I affirm with a firm sense of responsibility that what is happening in the Middle East may affect the living standards of the humblest person in this country. By the closing down of the Abadan refinery we have lost millions of dollars that must be earned elsewhere.

The new situation in Egypt and the Sudan raises even more dangerous possibilities of interference with our supplies of raw cotton. Mr Harvey Rhodes,[1] the Socialist Parliamentary Secretary to the Board of Trade, has been courageous enough to recognise this and point it out to Mr Morrison.

We all ought to ponder what the late Mr Ernest Bevin once told the House of Commons: 'The British interests in the Mid-East contribute substantially, not only to the prosperity of the people there, but also to the wage packets of the workers of this country.'

I must say a word about the other aspect of these disputes with Persia and Egypt. We have watched the contest in Persia and its lamentable end. We have since seen Egypt, at the moment of our abasement, demand our evacuation of the Suez Canal and the breaking of our pledges to the Sudanese. Thus one act of weakness leads to another.

The situation, as I write, is as yet unresolved, but I am certain that at this anxious time one of our first aims must be to cement the closest relations with the United States.

---

[1] Harvey Rhodes, 1895–1987. Served in King's Own Lancashire Rgt, Yorkshire Rgt, RFC, 1914–18. DFC, 1918. Lt-Col., 1918. CO, 36th Battalion, Duke of Wellington's Rgt, 1940–5. MP (Lab.) for Ashton-under-Lyne, 1945–64. Parliamentary Private Secretary to Paymaster-General and Minister of Pensions, 1945–50. Parliamentary Secretary to the Board of Trade, 1950–1, 1964–7. Baron, 1964. Lord Lt of Lancashire, 1968. PC, 1969. KG, 1972. Deputy Lord Lt of Greater Lancashire, 1974–87.

Clearly, if Britain is to play her proper part in these and other international affairs, we must secure a Government which has a clear majority, a Government which the world will realise is stable and can plan ahead with assurance.

Our relations with the United States, upon which so much depends, would be seriously weakened by the return of a Socialist Government in which inevitably Mr Bevan would be a dominating figure. He and his bitter faction are opposed to the Government's rearmament programme and never cease to vilify the United States. What confidence can anyone feel when leading Ministers appear on the platforms of Socialist candidates who have been sabotaging their own Government's proposals?

Our Socialist opponents are saying in what appears to be a drilled chorus that the Conservative Party would land the country in a war. Such an insinuation is mean and contemptible, and also the reverse of the truth. We all hate the idea of another war.

Socialist Ministers proclaim their belief in a policy of peace through strength. But their party is not behind them. The Conservative Party, on the other hand, is united in knowing that nothing is more likely to comfort and encourage a potential aggressor than the sight of Britain weak and wanting in self-confidence, or a Britain estranged from America.

Peace will be safe in the hands of a strong Conservative Government, which would offer the hand of a good neighbour to all, but accept the dictate of none. You should understand that this story of 'war-mongering' is just an evil-smelling red herring introduced by the Socialists to distract the minds of the people from their Government's own shortcomings and failures.

These shortcomings are legion. The parade of improvidence, incompetence, and lack of elementary foresight has been continuous. We are all appalled by the steady and continuous fall in the purchasing power of our money. Our food supplies are scanty, monotonous and often of inferior quality. Hundreds of thousands of young couples and young families are waiting hopelessly for homes.

Our social services have been established by successive Governments over many years. The Wartime Government, of which I was the head and which rested on a solid Conservative majority, planned all the advances made since the war. But their value has been whittled down as the purchasing value of the pound has dropped. For instance, Family Allowances, fixed at 5s. by Parliament, are today worth only 3s. 8d. The Socialists have no remedy except bigger and deeper draughts of Socialism.

All these evils cannot be cured at a stroke. I make no easy promises that a Conservative Government will bring about rapid transformation. One of the reasons which led Mr Attlee to go to the country was that he knew what bad times lay ahead. He knew that both a fuel crisis and a financial crisis approached. We have first to stem the tide.

I am convinced that a Conservative Government, resting on a national decision, will get fair play from the great trade unions, and that they will not be backward in working with us to create an industrial system that is not only efficient but humane as well. A Conservative Government will not initiate any legislation affecting the unions. If our relationships with them are disturbed by party politics, the fault will not be on our side.

A Conservative Government will be the servant and not the master of the nation. It will be the tool of no vested interest, but will single-mindedly seek the good of all.

On these lines Britain can steadily win back her rightful place in the world. If we all work together we can face the coming years with confidence. The alternative is a steady decline in our ability even to survive. We have an ever-falling pound and a widening overseas trade gap. We have had two financial crises in the last four years, and a third is nearly upon us. We cannot go on like this.

A broad-based Conservative Government, which trusts the people, and in turn is trusted by them, is the only Government that can grapple energetically with these urgent matters. We shall try our best.

George Christ to Jo Sturdee
(Churchill papers, 2/117)

19 October 1951

Dear Miss Sturdee,
I attach –
1. Some answers to the *Sunday Times* questions, about which Mr Ian Colvin will be ringing you.[1] If it is to be of any use it must, of course, be dealt with tomorrow for this Sunday's issue.
2. Some notes for the Plymouth speech, which Mr Churchill might like to look at during the weekend.

FOR *SUNDAY TIMES*

What is the main issue at this general election?

What the country has got to decide at this election is whether Britain is going to be able to pay her way, and play a proper part as a great Power in maintaining the peace of the world. These two issues are linked. We shall certainly never be able to make the effort necessary to carry through the rearmament programme and overhaul our defences unless we are able to increase our productivity. Without an increase in productivity the demands of rearmament and of the export industries upon whom we rely for our essential raw materials and foods, would reduce our living standards at home

---
[1] See letter reproduced above (p. 2208).

to an impossible level. Six years of Socialist Government have led to a steady rise in the cost of living, shortages of every kind, and a succession of crises of one sort of another. A Conservative Government with a strong and solid majority, will seek to restore British repute abroad and liberate the native genius of the British people at home.

What does the Conservative Party offer to the youth of Great Britain?

Nobody who has gone round the country during this election can have failed to be impressed by the number of young men and women fighting this campaign for the Conservative Party. More than one-third of our Parliamentary candidates are forty or under. The Young Conservative movement which has grown up in the past five years is the largest free political youth organization in the world. The reason for all this is that the Conservative Party offers youth opportunity. As I said in my broadcast, we believe in the principle of ladders rather than that of queues. Most young people have a natural and proper desire to get on in the world, and we want to see them given a chance to rise. '"All men are created equal," says the American Declaration of Independence. "All men must be kept equal," adds the Socialist Party.' We Conservatives take our stand on basic minimum standards below which nobody should be allowed to fall, but above which everybody should have the fullest opportunity to rise.

Winston S. Churchill: speech
('*Winston S. Churchill, His Complete Speeches*', volume 8, pages 8281–6)

23 October 1951   Home Park Football Ground, Plymouth

ELECTION ADDRESS

I am always glad to come to the West Country and here we have the candidates for Totnes, Tavistock, Bodmin, Sutton and, as you will understand, last but not least to me, Devonport. The House of Commons will be the richer for the return or arrival of these capable, earnest and patriotic members. Let us ram them all home with a run. We can do it if we try.

The Prime Minister in his broadcast dilated upon the increase of industrial production and improvements in national health that have taken place in the six years since the war. 'The health of the nation is better', he says, 'than ever before. People are living longer. Many fewer babies are dying than ever before.' He claims that the credit for this is due to the action of his Government. But this is not true. The advance in productivity and in physical conditions is not due to Socialism; it is science not Socialism that has the honour of whatever has been achieved. Every day science is bestowing in an ever widening flow upon mankind more material benefits than in any other period ever known. All the machinery and electric power and improved methods of production that are at work, are not the results of politics. It was not the Socialist Party that discovered penicillin. M and B – that marvellous healer – does not stand for Morrison and Bevan. It was not the Socialists who made possible the tireless advance in medicine and surgery. On the contrary it would be more true to say that the dose we have had of Socialism has hampered and restricted the progress of science, and reduced the benefits which the whole nation might have gained from the tremendous conquest of natural forces which is now being made all over the world, and which, if world peace can be maintained, and I believe it can be, may open to the whole human race an age of prosperity beyond their brightest hopes. One-fifth of our industries have been nationalized. This is the part which is lagging behind. Our export trade by which we live, and the vast mass of our production which pays its way, is made by the other four-fifths on which Socialism has not yet laid its clumsy, partisan and rigid grip. The free enterprise four-fifths pays for the Socialists' errors and yet earns enough so far to keep us going by a narrow margin. The Socialists have no more right to claim the credit for the technical advance of this age of science than they have for maintaining employment. Both are the result of world causes, and £2,000 million in gifts and loans from the capitalist United States. A far richer harvest would have been reaped by our hardworking people if they had not been hampered by doctrinaire experiments, misguided planning and astonishing financial mismanagement and waste.

Of course everyone can say, especially at Election time, how much better we should have done it than the other chaps. But if the electors take a calm and sober view of how and where we stand this afternoon at home and in the world, surely there would be very few who would not feel that things would be much better in Persia and Egypt if Mr Eden had been at the Foreign Office for the last few years; and I think the housewives and the old age pensioners and others living on fixed incomes, might well feel the pressure upon them was a good deal less if Lord Woolton had been looking after our food supplies and if some check had been imposed upon the wild extravagances with which our limited finances have been dispersed.

The Conservatives and National Liberals come before the electors as a united party. In fact we are at once the least formally disciplined and the only united party. We seek to preserve the old dignity of a Member of the House of Commons which Edmund Burke asserted in his famous speech. For sixteen years my friend, Mr Eden, and I, whether in or out of office, have worked together in close accord and on all the great and changing issues of the foreign situation, whether before, during or since the war. We have measured the British position in relation alike to our allies and other countries with the same sense of values and the same guiding purpose. As I said at the Albert Hall a year ago: 'Mr Eden will carry on the torch of Tory democracy when other and older hands have let it fall.'

Mr Eden's recent visit to the United States was most helpful to our country.

It did a lot to repair the damage to Anglo-American harmony which had been caused and is being caused by the constant attacks and criticisms of Mr Bevan and Mr Harold Wilson, the Dribergs, the Silvermans and the Foots – I hope that is grammar! Nothing could be worse for our country and nothing could be more injurious to the cause of world peace than for Mr Attlee to be returned, dependent upon a sham reconciliation between the main body of the Socialist Party and the powerful and turbulent Left-wing forces whom Mr Bevan represents, and who, as he says, are looking forward to the 'luxury of a quarrel'. The whole process of growing unity and confidence between us and the great Republic across the Atlantic Ocean would be weakened and our power to influence the course of American policy might be seriously impaired. I do not hesitate to say that such a situation would be prejudicial to the growing hopes of reaching a good working arrangement with Soviet Russia, by negotiation based upon the patient growing strength and living concord of the free world. This is not the time when we can afford either to weaken American comradeship or to lose our influence upon American thought based upon confidence and goodwill.

I must now refer to a personal issue. The Socialists somewhat shamefacedly, and the Communists brazenly, make the charge that I am a 'warmonger'. This is a cruel and ungrateful accusation. It is the opposite of the truth. If I remain in public life at this juncture it is because, rightly or wrongly, but sincerely, I believe that I may be able to make an important contribution to the prevention of a Third World War and to bringing nearer that lasting peace settlement which the masses of the people of every race and in every land fervently desire. I pray indeed that I may have this opportunity. It is the last prize I seek to win. I have been blessed with so much good fortune throughout my long life, and I am treated with so much kindness by my fellow countrymen far outside the ranks of party, and indeed also in the United States and in Europe, that all the daydreams of my youth have been surpassed. It is therefore with a single purpose and a strong sense of duty that I remain at my post as Leader of the Conservative Party through these baffling and anxious years. I applied the word 'ungrateful' a moment ago to the slander by which some of our opponents hope to gain advantage. I think it is the right word to use. It is quite true that at a very dark moment in our history I was called upon to take the lead for more than five years of awful war and that I did my best until victory was won. But that that should be made the ground, as Mr Shinwell suggests, for saying that I want to have a Third World War to show off my talents is mean and shabby. Trusting as I do to the sense of justice and fair play which inspires the British race, I am sure that these taunts and insults will recoil upon the heads of those who make them. We shall not have very much longer to wait before we shall see what the British answer is to all that.

Now I leave the personal question and am only sorry to have had to burden you with it. But the charge is also made that the expected return of a

Conservative Government on Thursday next will increase the likelihood of a world war. This is also false and also ungrateful. Mr Attlee's Government in their six years of power, have taken many grave steps for national and international defence. They have introduced conscription in time of peace. They have taken part in a whole system of alliances to resist a possible aggression by Soviet Russia. They now call upon us to spend nearly £5,000 million in three years, on rearmament upon a vast scale. In all this the Conservative Party have given them their effective support. We now know what were the adverse forces at work inside the Socialist Party. They came into the light of day when Mr Bevan and his colleagues resigned and received such prominence by the election of Mr Bevan and his supporters to the head of the Socialist Executive at the Scarborough Conference. Is it not ungrateful as well as untruthful to turn on those upon whose aid the Government have depended, and accuse them of wishing to bring about another war?

But there is one particular instance to which I must draw your attention. Mr Attlee's Government agreed to the establishment of an enormous American air base in our Eastern Counties, which could have no other purpose than to bring home the threat of atomic war as a deterrent to Russian aggression. Again we supported them. I must, however, say that no more formidable step has been taken in time of peace by any Government that I can remember, nor one that would be more certain to put us in the front line should war come. Is it not disgraceful that they should accuse us of being war-minded because we have supported them in this as in other measures of defence on patriotic grounds? We can easily see what they would have done had the positions been reversed and we had been responsible for proposing such measures. We have only to look at Mr Attlee's and Mr Morrison's conduct before the last war in resisting every measure of rearmament and even in voting against conscription a few months before the outbreak. And then they spoke of Mr Chamberlain's Government as Guilty Men! We ought to be proud that our party record bears no such stain. But the fact that because we have acted fairly by them in these great matters of national safety and that they should now seek to make shameful capital out of our support reaches a lower level than anything so far recorded in the public life of modern times.

There is one subject with which I must deal though it is not in any way an issue at this Election. Several Socialist speakers have suggested that if I had been returned at the 1945 Election we should have been involved in war with the people of India. This is quite untrue. I and my Conservative colleagues were all pledged to the granting to India of Dominion status carrying with it the right to secede from the British Empire and Commonwealth. The only question open was how this transference of power was to be made. Mr Attlee so conducted the process that five hundred thousand innocent human beings were slaughtered in the Punjab alone and at least two or three hundred thousand more in other parts of the vast Indian peninsula. That is to say, three or four times as many lives were destroyed by violent and avoidable butchery in India as were lost by the whole British Empire in the Second World War. I am astonished that this should be treated as a mere incident in the progress of Oriental liberation and self-government. I am sure that it would have been possible to maintain law and order in India as we did in the face of the armed revolt of the Congress Party at the time of the attempted Japanese invasion without any serious difficulty or bloodshed; and that a Constituent Assembly far more representative of all the real forces of Indian life than the Congress Party could have shaped an Indian constitution and transferred the power to the new rulers of India in an orderly manner. This, of course, is arguable, but statements to the contrary are mere assertions. The vast human tragedy which occurred in the process of handing over is a fact for which I thank God I had no responsibility. I cannot leave this question without saying that what has been done in India is irrevocable. It can no more be reversed than we can bring back from the grave the myriads who have perished. The Conservative Party wishes the new India, Pakistan and Ceylon all success in their future. We shall show them all friendship and goodwill. But the burden which rests upon the Socialist Government for the frightful catastrophe of slaughter is one which only history can measure. As I said in the House of Commons some years ago, the Socialist Government's responsibility is not that of a criminal who throws a train off the line by sabotage, but rather that of a signalman who has pulled the levers in the wrong way or in the wrong order and thus caused the disaster.[1]

While we demonstrate and argue among ourselves here at home events are moving all over the world. One must not suppose that resistance to lawless outrages contrary to treaty or other obligations by Powers morally and physically not in the first rank raises the issues of a world war. A Third World War could only come if the Soviet Government calculated or miscalculated their chances of an ultimate victory and fell upon us all in ferocious aggression. That is why I am hopeful about the future. If I were a Soviet Commissar in the Kremlin tonight looking at the scene from their point of view I think I should be inclined to have a friendly talk with the leaders of the free world and see if something could not be arranged which enabled us all to live together quietly for another generation. Who can look beyond that? However, I have not yet been chosen as a Soviet Commissar – nor for any other office that I can think of – there or here. But what I cannot understand is how any of the leaders of Soviet Russia or the United States or here in Britain or France or in United Europe or anywhere else, could possibly imagine that their interests could be bettered by having an unlimited series of frightful immeasurable explosions. For another world war would not be like the Crusades or the romantic struggles in former centuries we have read about. It would be nothing less than

---

[1] See speech of 5 Nov. 1947, reproduced above (pp. 846–9).

a massacre of human beings whether in uniform or out of uniform by the hideous forces of perverted science. Science, which now offers us a Golden Age with one hand, offers at the same time with the other hand the doom of all that we have built up inch by inch since the Stone Age.

My faith is in the high progressive destiny of man. I do not believe we are to be flung back into abysmal darkness by those fearsome discoveries which human genius has made. Let us make sure that they are our servants but not our masters. Let us hold fast to the three supreme purposes. The freedom of the individual man in an ordered society; a world organization to prevent bloody quarrels between nations by the rule of law; and for ourselves who have played so great a part in what I have called 'our finest hour', to keep our own fifty millions alive in a small island at the high level of progressive civilization which they have attained. Those are the three goals. To reach them we have first to regain our independence financially, economically and morally. If we are to play our part in the greater affairs of the free world, we have to gather around us our Empire and the States of the British Commonwealth, and bind them ever more closely together. We have to give our hand generously, wholeheartedly, to our Allies across the Atlantic Ocean, upon whose strength and wisdom the salvation of the world at this moment may well depend. Joined with them in fraternal association, drawn and held together by our common language and our joint inheritance of literature and custom, we may save ourselves and save the world.

We support the Government's belated policy of firearms in Egypt. If we become responsible we should go on with it firmly and resolutely. But if even six months ago they had taken the advice I gave in Parliament, and approached the problems of the Middle East on the three-Power or four-Power basis, as they have now at least done, how differently might all the Persian and Egyptian situations have been unravelled. We are no longer strong enough ourselves alone to protect the rule of law in these important regions. That was the reason why I thought we should much earlier have tried to bring the United States into our Middle Eastern problems. I have used every channel open to me to impress upon our American friends how much more important what is happening in the Middle East is to the cause of world peace even than the stern struggle which is still open on the promontory of Korea. I am sure that if even six months ago Britain, the United States and France, with Turkey by all means, had developed a united policy in regard to Persia, Iraq, Egypt, Palestine and Syria, none of the present unsolved embarrassments would have arisen. Without any question of world war for the free nations no needless loss and humiliation would have been inflicted upon John Bull. We recognize the difficulties and tangles of the Middle Eastern scene. No doubt the murder of the Persian Prime Minister was a disastrous surprise for the British Government, but a wider and more far-seeing view would have brought into action at an earlier stage these larger groupings which now all are working for and through which much better solutions for all, including the Persians and the Egyptians, might have been, and may still be, achieved.

We are now at the final stage in this fateful election. Whatever happens on Thursday, we must all hope that we get a stable, solid Government and get out of this exhausting and distracting electioneering atmosphere, where all the forces of two great party machines have to go on working in every street and in every village week after week, to try to range the British people in opposing ranks. This is indeed a crisis in our island story. Never before in peacetime did we have so much need to judge policy on the merits and act in the true interests of our country, and of its Empire and Commonwealth of Nations. To go on like we have for the last twenty months with a Government struggling to keep its head above water from day to day and thinking of its party chances and of an election at any moment, is to give all that is strong and noble and resurgent in Britain the heaviest load to carry and the hardest battle to win.

It is not my fault, nor indeed is it Mr Attlee's entirely, that we have had this prolonged period of uncertainty. He had a majority of seven at the last Election. The burden fell on him and on his party. It is indeed remarkable that under the conditions we have not fallen more. But we have only to go on indefinitely absorbed in our party quarrels to use up so much of our vitality and to be written down so much in the world repute that our influence upon events may well become almost negligible. Terrible decisions that would immediately affect our whole lives may be taken by others at a time when we seem to count little more than many of the smaller states of Europe whom we liberated after the great struggle. We cannot afford to go on like this.

Here now is the main point I make to you, and indeed to all parties. Bear in mind that we ought to have a strong and stable Government resting on a majority that can uphold the responsibilities and burdens of Britain in the world for three or four years at least. The other point which I submit to you for your judgment and your vote is whether it is not time for a change? Ought there not to be an approach to world problems and home problems from a new angle, a new point of view? The Government is wearied and worn out. Its leading Ministers have borne nearly twelve years of stress. They have no message to give. Their principal figures, the late Mr Bevin and Sir Stafford Cripps, are no longer in the scene. Let me say how glad I am to see the recovery of health that Sir Stafford Cripps is making. And in this mood let me tell you how much I look forward to the time when this loud clatter and turmoil of party strife dies down for a spell and gives us a good, long, steady period in which the opposing parties may be able to see some of each other's virtues instead of harping on each other's faults. The British people are good all through. We face the same toils and perils. We share many of the same desires and anxieties. We are in many ways more truly one nation than can be found the wide world o'er. Let us rise to our full height above class and party interests, and guard with growing comradeship and brotherhood the land of hope and glory we all love so well.

The general election of 25 October 1951 resulted in the Conservative Party winning twenty-three additional seats, giving them a total of 321 and a majority in Parliament. Labour took a slightly higher proportion of the popular vote but lost twenty seats, their total falling to 295. The Liberals won six seats.

Court Circular
(Churchill papers, 6/4)

26 October 1951

The Right Honourable C. R. Attlee had an audience of The King this evening, and tendered his resignation as Prime Minister and First Lord of the Treasury, which His Majesty was graciously pleased to accept.

The King subsequently received in audience the Right Honourable Winston Spencer-Churchill, and requested him to form a new Administration. The Right Honourable Winston Spencer-Churchill accepted His Majesty's offer, and kissed hands upon his appointment as Prime Minister and First Lord of the Treasury.

General Lord Ismay: recollection
('The Memoirs of General the Lord Ismay', pages 425–8)

26 October 1951

Throughout the Festival year, the Labour Party had held office with an infinitesimal majority in the House of Commons, and although they had managed to keep their heads above the water, the situation was thoroughly unsatisfactory. Early in October, the King granted Mr Attlee's request for a dissolution, and polling for the General Election took place on 25 October. By the next afternoon it was clear that the Conservatives would have a majority of sixteen or seventeen. Mr Attlee resigned, and Mr Churchill once again received the King's mandate to form a Government. I went to bed very early that night and was fast asleep when the telephone bell rang – the same bell which had awakened me to hear of the invasion of Norway, the assault on the Low Countries, the death of President Roosevelt, and the signature of the German surrender at Rheims. I was told that Mr Churchill wanted to speak to me. There were many people sitting by their telephone that night, hoping, and perhaps praying, that the new Prime Minister might have something to offer them, but these were problems which were no concern of mine. The conservation was brief. 'Is that you, Pug?' 'Yes, Prime Minister. It's grand to be able to call you Prime Minister again.' 'I want to see you at once. You aren't in bed, are you?' 'I've been asleep for over an hour.' 'Well, I only want to see you for five minutes.'

I put my head under a cold tap, dressed in record time, and was at 28, Hyde Park Gate, within a quarter of an hour of being wakened. Mr Churchill was alone in his drawing-room, and told me, without any preliminaries, that he wanted me to be Secretary of State for Commonwealth Relations. I thought that the cold tap had failed to do its work and that I was still dreaming; but Mr Churchill brushed aside my doubts and hustled me into the dining-room, where I found Mr Eden, Lord Salisbury, Sir Norman Brook, and a bevy of secretaries working away on a variety of drafts. The years rolled back. It was like old times. Officials do not usually make good Cabinet Ministers, and there was no reason why I should be an exception to the rule. But I was overjoyed at the prospect of serving under Churchill again.

Field Marshal Lord Montgomery to Winston S. Churchill
(Churchill papers, 2/463)

26 October 1951

Dear Mr Churchill,

Thank God. At last we have you back again and in charge of the ship. May you stay there for five years and more.

Firoz Khan Noon to Winston S. Churchill
(Premier papers, 11/227)

27 October 1951 East Pakistan
Secret, Private and Personal

Dear Mr Churchill,

Your return to power has come as a great relief to Asia – a drifting Asia – which I am confident having found a reliable anchor in you, will stabilise. A strong Turkey and a strong Pakistan may be the two firm pillars on which can be built an arch which will secure the peace in the Middle-East and SE Asia also.

2. The balance of power in this sub-continent was upset when even <u>our</u> share of the undivided India armaments – including 25 armament factories – was handed over to India. Out of the 160 thousand tons of Army stores we received not more than 30 thousand tons and a good part of this were

useless land mines. Even the rifles of the Muslim soldiers who returned to Pakistan were taken away from them when they left Indian Cantonments. A train-load of technicians, signallers, electricians, etc. were all murdered on the way between Delhi and Karachi. Wagon-loads of our files were also destroyed before they could reach Karachi. However, we have by God's grace and our unity and effort built up a strong Pakistan.

3. In this province of East Pakistan, apart from our regular forces, we have 280 thousand Ansars. These are volunteers like your Home Guards during the war and have been fully trained to shoot and are armed. But since India threatened to invade our country, during the past five months we have increased this strength to a million men already and they are all under training. The Indians have concentrated a large number of their troops on all three sides of our border: they are entrenched and they are building up their ammunition dumps, tank stores etc.

4. It is now for your consideration if you can quickly restore the balance of power in this Indo-Pakistan sub-continent by ordering immediate supply of armaments and aeroplanes which we wish to buy from England. If this is done and Pakistan defences are made strong, I am confident that India also will have some respect and need for the friendship of Britain. The policy of neutrality in case of an attack on Pakistan – a full Dominion – by India – a symbolic Dominion – is responsible for the unsettled condition of this part of the world. A policy on your part of coming to the succour of whoever is attacked will immediately give relief to all those who are for peace. It will also restore mental equilibrium of those who are dreaming of assuming leadership of Asia through aggression and thus building up an anti-West Asia. Unfortunately, owing to the great problem of meeting Communist aggression in the world, the whole attention of America and England had been concentrated on Communist aggression. Meanwhile – ever since the partition of India – a new and powerful aggression has been stealing a march on everyone. Six hundred Indian States have been forcibly occupied by India Government. Hyderabad, which had the right to remain independent, was actually invaded by Indian troops and conquered. The States of Junagarh and Manwadar – which had acceded to Pakistan – were also invaded by Indian troops and conquered and annexed, and the same process was adopted in the case of Kashmir. But worse still is the example of the independent Kingdom of Nepal against which Patel – before he died – arranged a plot sitting in Calcutta. Certain rebellious elements were created inside Nepal and Indian troops marched into that State in plain clothes and later in uniforms for the succour of these elements, and there is a puppet pro-Hindu Government established in Nepal – the proud Gurkha Kingdom.

The next country in this process on the Indian programme is Pakistan, and if Pakistan goes under there is nothing to stop India in the whole of

Asia. I came here as Governor of this province in April, 1950. Our late Prime Minister – Liaquat Ali Khan[1] – had originally asked me to go to Paris as our Ambassador, but he suddenly changed his mind and on three days' notice he sent me here because India was going to invade this province: she needed the jute. However, that moment passed over and now this threat of war against the whole of Pakistan has become constant.

5. We have a wonderful man-power. Five million fighting soldiers can easily be raised in both wings of Pakistan and you know it better than anyone else what fighting qualities the Western Pakistan Muslim soldier has.

6. I have taken the liberty of writing this letter being encouraged by the personal confidence that you have always reposed in me. My Government have nothing to do with this letter which may please be treated as strictly private and personal meant for yourself.

Your sitting in the Downing Street alone will make a wonderful difference in giving stability and peace to the world and I wish you all success, and may you be spared many more years of good health and vigour to serve the cause of peace.[2]

Harold Macmillan: recollection
('Tides of Fortune', pages 363–6)

28 October 1951

On the morning of 28 October I received a message summoning me to Chartwell.

On arrival, at 3 p.m., I found (Churchill) in a most pleasant, and rather tearful mood. He asked me to 'build the houses for the people'. What an assignment!

I was rather taken aback by this proposal. I knew nothing whatever about the housing problem except that we had pledged ourselves to an enormously high figure, generally regarded by the experts as unattainable. I asked what was the present housing 'set-up'. He said he had no idea, but the 'boys' would know.

So the boys (Sir Edward Bridges, Head of the Civil Service, and Sir Norman Brook, Secretary to the Cabinet) were sent for – also some whiskey. It seems

---

[1] Nawabzada Liaquat Ali Khan, 1895–1951. Educated at Muhammadan Anglo-Oriental College and Exeter College, Oxford. Married, 1918, Jehangira Begum: one son (div.); 1945, Sheila Irene Pant: two sons. Minister of Finance, 1946–51. Minister of Foreign Affairs, 1947–9. First PM of Pakistan, 1947–51; also Minister for Kashmir and Frontier Affairs and Minister of Defence. Assassinated, 1951.

[2] Churchill wrote to Lord Ismay on Nov. 11: 'All of this is very serious. He is of course a friend of mine. Please note what he says about the privacy of his letter, but let me have a draft of a non-committal reply' (M.21c/51, *Premier papers, 11/227*).

that there is much confusion in all this business. Broadly speaking, the old Ministry of Town and Country Planning retains these functions, but is now called Ministry of Local Government and Planning. All the functions of supervising Local Government in general remain with it. It also has to administer the ill-fated Town and Country Planning Act. It is also responsible for Housing. But the actual agent which controls all building, whether for Housing or other purposes, is the Ministry of Works. (This also does the work of the old Office of Works.) The building priorities or allocations are made by the Cabinet. It was at once clear that the Ministry must be rechristened, in order to pin the Housing flag firmly to the masthead.

Of course, the Minister would be in the Cabinet and the Minister of Works would not. Churchill went on to say that to build 300,000 houses, which we were pledged to do, was a great adventure. If I did not want it I could have the Board of Trade. But that was a mere matter of routine.

We then discussed who should be Minister of Works, and I wondered whether Lord Swinton could be persuaded to take such a post, although after so long an experience in the Cabinet it would not be easy. (Later he accepted the Duchy of Lancaster, and in that capacity was of invaluable help to me because raw materials, including steel, came under his control.) Who should be my Parliamentary Secretary? I proposed Ernest Marples. Yes, he would accept Marples. He knew a great deal about housing and indeed about many other things. He was a clever man. At the end of this conversation Churchill solemnly said to me:

> 'It is a gamble – (it will) make or mar your political career. But every humble home will bless your name, if you succeed.' More tears. I said I would think about it.

My wife[1] had driven me over and was walking in the garden with Mrs Churchill. I joined her and asked for her advice, which from a long experience I knew to be generally sound. She was in no doubt at all that I ought to accept. I had always agreed to do anything that I had been asked by Churchill, and it had up to now succeeded. When I went to Algiers nobody could have thought that the appointment would turn out as it did. It had for the first time earned me real status in the political world. She also reminded me of my experience at the Ministry of Supply and the many friends with whom I had kept up from those days. Surely we could build the houses in the same way that we built the tanks and the guns.

So I went back to the PM's room and told him that I would do as he wished. Much goodwill and many blessings followed. Being now, as it were, readmitted to the official family, I was made to stay. It was fun to join again in the

---

[1] Dorothy Evelyn Cavendish, 1900–66. Daughter of the 9th Duke and Duchess of Devonshire. Married, 1920, Harold Macmillan: four children.

old scenes which reminded me of the war-time Churchill. Children, friends, Ministers, private secretaries, typists, all in a great flurry but all thoroughly enjoying the return to the centre of the stage. I was reminded of the signal that went round the Fleet in 1939 – 'Winston is back'.

Meanwhile,

> The usual . . . 'va et vient'. Lord Leathers arrives. He is to be Secretary of State for co-ordination of Transport, Fuel and Power. But where is Sir John Anderson? He is to be a viscount and co-ordinate Raw Materials, Supply, etc. Has he been told this? No, not yet. Let's ring him up. So this is done. Meanwhile Clem Davies has come and gone. Will he be Minister of Education? He would love this, but what about the Liberal party? He will try to persuade them, but Megan L. George and Lord Samuel will resist. He leave for the meeting. (We hear later – on the wireless – that the Liberals will not play.) Then much talk about junior office. Harry (Crookshank) and Patrick Buchan-Hepburn (who have arrived) are very strong on this. Churchill hardly knows the names – except that Eccles must have a job. And then Ralph Assheton. (Then there are other posts to be filled) not in the Cabinet, like Postmaster-General, Minister for National Insurance, etc. But what about the Service ministers? And then the Speaker? Shall it be WS Morrison[1] or Hopkins Morris – both good men? And so on.

Out of all this confusion some kind of a plan did at last emerge. In these long discussions, which continued during the afternoon and evening, it was clear that whatever the future had in store for us, at any rate

> we are certainly buying this business at the bottom of the market. There is a financial crisis, a foreign crisis, a defence crisis. Everything is in a state of muddle and confusion. It is 1940, without bombing and casualties – but without also the sense of national unity. Can this be somehow created? All these – and many other – questions are posed, discussed, turned away from, returned to from 3 to 7.

At last my wife and I left for home. When I got back I began to realize what a burden I had undertaken. I knew that Churchill was grateful to me and would back me; but I had not any real clue of how to set about the job. This exciting day ended on a lighter note. The telephone was ringing from Chartwell and from No. 10 for me urgently. I expected some new turn of the wheel.

---

[1] William Shepherd Morrison, 1893–1961. Known as 'Shakes'. Served in Royal Field Artillery, France, 1914–18 (wounded, MC, despatches three times). Capt., 1919. President, Edinburgh University Union, 1920. Called to the Bar, 1923. Married, 1924, Catherine Allison Swan: four children. MP (Cons.) for Cirencester and Tewkesbury, 1929–59. KC, 1934. Financial Secretary, Treasury, 1935–6. PC, 1936. A member of the Other Club from 1936. Minister of Agriculture and Fisheries, 1936–9. Chancellor of the Duchy of Lancaster and Minister of Food, 1939–40. Postmaster-General, 1940–3. Minister of Town and Country Planning, 1943–5. Speaker of the House of Commons, 1951–9.

But it was only that James Stuart, Dorothy's brother-in-law, who was believed to be in Scotland, had disappeared.

But he is wanted, to be Secretary of State for Scotland. Nobody can say the Tories stand about waiting for office. It is a job to get hold of them.

Two days later, on 30 October, with a number of other Ministers, I kissed hands on my appointment. I thought the King looked worn but somewhat better than I expected after his recent illness. Alas, it was to prove only an illusory convalescence.

Cyril Garbett to Winston S. Churchill
(Churchill papers, 2/462)

28 October 1951

May you have health and strength and wisdom to do something to restore Great Britain to the place she once had among the nations. This seems at the moment to be the task of supreme importance for the nation and the world.

Winston S. Churchill to Anthony Eden
Prime Minister's Personal Minute M.1c/51
(Premier papers, 11/92)

29 October 1951

It seems to me that this verbose disquisition[1] is intended to be an argument for 2(b), marked in red.[2] I expect you agree with this and so do I. I do not think we ought to have anything sharp or sudden and only kick back when we are maltreated. But we should maintain the full legal freedom of the Canal and make sure that the ships of all nations can pass through it, including those carrying oil to Haifa. The American telegrams on this subject seem to show the American State Department in a very puzzled mood.

(Later.) I am so glad to find that we are in agreement about 2(b).

---

[1] Referring to the lengthy confidential report from Stevenson to Morrison (No. 347, 16 Oct. 1951) entitled 'Events Leading Up to the Egyptian Government's Arrogation of the 1936 Treaty and 1899 Condominium Agreement'.

[2] Churchill refers to the following paragraph in Sir Ralph Stevenson's No. 838 to the Foreign Office:
'2. We seem therefore to be faced with two alternatives:
(a) By the ruthless use of all sanctions at our disposal to have an immediate showdown with Egypt and to force the Government out of power.
(b) To run the Canal Zone more or less independently of Egypt, overcoming obstruction by force, where local arrangements do not suffice, and being faced with an increasing drain away from us of Egyptian labour.'

Winston S. Churchill to Lord Swinton
(Churchill papers, 6/1)

29 October 1951

My dear Philip,

I have thought it well to make some changes in the structure of the Government Offices. Harold Macmillan has accepted the Ministry of Housing and Local Government, with a seat in the Cabinet. You know how much we are committed to a supreme effort to face this problem, and I am much obliged to Harold for risking his reputation upon it. The Ministry of Works has now a double function. It discharges all the former duties of the First Commissioner of Works in regard to the Palaces and Public Offices. But in addition, it is the agency through which the resources of the building industry are distributed in accordance with the Cabinet policy. I should be very glad if you would undertake this task, which is essential to the success of our housing programme. Much would depend upon your personal relations with Harold, but you have worked easily together before.

I hope that the holding of this Office would enable you also to act as Deputy Leader of the House of Lords, which I know would be agreeable to Salisbury.

I am sending this letter to you by Sir Norman Brook, who will be able to explain to you the articulation of the Ministry of Works with the other Departments. If you would like to come and talk about things with me, pray come down after luncheon tomorrow any time between 3 and 6 o'clock.

Winston S. Churchill to Sir John Anderson
(Churchill papers, 6/1)

29 October 1951

Several Departments are concerned with defence production – notably the Ministry of Supply, the Controller's side of the Admiralty, and the new Ministry of Materials. None of the Ministers in charge of these Departments will be in the Cabinet, and it is right that there should be a senior Minister to knit together the work of these Departments and speak in the Cabinet on behalf of defence production as a whole.

This allocation of physical resources to rearmament must also be related to the other calls on our financial and economic strength. I hope that you may be able to assist the Chancellor of the Exchequer in this task.

October 1951

Oliver Lyttelton to Winston S. Churchill
(Premier papers, 11/122)

30 October 1951
PM(51)1

The Malayan problem appears to me to be the first priority here. A new High Commissioner for the Federation has to be appointed and partly for reasons of health a suitable man will be difficult to find from the Colonial Service. Sir Rob Lockhart,[1] the newly appointed Director of Operations, is leaving to succeed Harold Briggs[2] on the 6th November. The Governor of Singapore[3] retires in April, and MacDonald's term of office is due to end in May, 1952.

It therefore seems to me important that I should visit Malaya as soon as possible and I would propose to leave for Singapore about the 25th November for a short visit in order to see and judge for myself. I should thus be present at a time when new arrangements, both civil and tactical, are first under discussion by the men newly appointed and should be able to make recommendations more surely to you and my colleagues. It so happens that there is to be about that time a meeting of all the Governors of the area and the British representatives in other South East Asian and Far Eastern territories, including India. It would clearly be most valuable for me to meet them and I have hopes that this could be arranged.

I would also hope to take this opportunity to go to Hong Kong for a few days which is particularly desirable because my predecessor[4] was unable to visit Hong Kong when he went to Malaya in May, 1950, and this caused a good deal of feeling in Hong Kong.

---

[1] Robert Hamilton Bruce Lockhart, 1887–1970. Head of Special Mission to Soviet Government, Petrograd, Jan. 1918. Political Intelligence Dept, Foreign Office, 1939–40. British Representative with Provisional Government of Czechoslovakia, London, 1940–1. Director-General, PWE, 1941–5. Lt-Gen., 1944. Gen., 1947. Acting Governor, North West Frontier Province, British India, 1947. C-in-C, Indian Army, 1947. Director of Operations during Malaya Emergency, 1951–2. Author of *Memoirs of a British Agent* (1932); *My Europe* (1952); *Giants Cast Long Shadows* (1960).

[2] Harold Rawdon Briggs, 1894–1952. Educated at Bedford School and Sandhurst. On active duty in France, 1915. Capt., 1917. Maj., 1932. Lt-Col., 1937. Col., 1940. DSO and bar, 1941, 1944. Acting Maj.-Gen., 1942. Maj.-Gen., 1945. KBE, 1945. Lt-Gen., 1946. GOC-in-C, Burma Command, 1946–8. GCIE, 1948. Director of Operations, Burma, 1950–1.

[3] Franklin Charles Gimson, 1890–1975. Entered British Ceylon Civil Service, 1914. Additional Asst Colonial Secretary, British Ceylon, 1919. Asst Colonial Secretary, 1920–2. Acting Asst Government Agent, 1922–4. Landing Surveyor, 1924–8. Asst Government Agent, 1935–7. Controller of Labour, 1937–41. Colonial Secretary, Hong Kong, 1941. Japanese POW, 1941–5. Governor of Hong Kong, 1945. Knighted, 1945. Governor of Singapore, 1946–52.

[4] James Griffiths.

2228　　　　　　　　　October 1951

Cabinet: conclusions
(Cabinet papers, 128/23)

30 October 1951
Secret
3 p.m.
Cabinet Meeting No. 1 of 1951

1. The Prime Minister welcomed his Cabinet colleagues[1] at their first meeting. He said that later in the day he would be making a formal submission to the King recommending the appointment of Lord Simonds[2] as Lord Chancellor, Mr Peter Thorneycroft as President of the Board of Trade and Lord Cherwell as Paymaster-General. This would complete the composition of the Cabinet. The King had already been consulted informally, and it was with his knowledge and approval that Lord Simonds and Mr Thorneycroft were attending the present meeting as Ministers designate. Lord Cherwell was expected to join the Cabinet at their next meeting.

2. The Cabinet were informed that the Opposition had been consulted through the usual channels about the choice of a Speaker. It had been suggested to them that Mr W. S. Morrison might be elected Speaker, and that one of the Chairmen of Committees might be a member of the Labour Party. They had at first shown readiness to fall in with this proposal; but they had subsequently indicated that they would propose Major J. Milner as Speaker and would not be willing to provide, from among their supporters, one of the Chairmen of Committees. The Cabinet agreed that, when Parliament met on the following day, the Government should propose that Mr W. S. Morrison be elected Speaker, and that Sir Charles MacAndrew should be Chairman of Ways and Means and Mr R. Hopkin Morris Deputy Chairman. The Prime Minister undertook to consult the Leader of the Liberal Party in order to enlist his support for these proposals.

3. The Cabinet had a general discussion on the content of the King's Speech on the Opening of Parliament on 6th November. They agreed that it should include references to the repeal of the Iron and Steel Act, 1949, the restoration of the University franchise and the amendment of the law relating to private road hauliers. It was suggested that the Speech might also include some promise of social legislation – for example, measures affecting the elderly or regulating conditions of employment in factories.

The Cabinet agreed that it should be made clear in the King's Speech

---

[1] For details of the Cabinet's composition, please see Appendix A below.
[2] Gavin Turnbull Simonds, 1881–1971. Educated at New College, Oxford. Called to the Bar, 1906. Married, 1912, Mary Hope Mellor: three sons. KC, 1924. Judge, Chancery Division, High Court of Justice, 1937–44. Chairman, National Arbitration Tribunal, 1940–4. Lord of Appeal in Ordinary 1944–51, 1954–62. PC, 1944. Baron, 1944. Lord High Chancellor of Great Britain, 1951–4. High Steward, Winchester, 1951; Oxford, 1954–67. Viscount, 1954.

that the Bill restoring the University franchise would not become effective until elections were held for a new Parliament and, further, that it would not perpetuate the old system of dual voting – a person qualified to vote for a University candidate would in future have to choose between exercising that right and voting in the constituency in which he resided. It was suggested that, as the University constituencies would be so much smaller than the ordinary constituencies, there was much to be said for limiting University representation in the Commons to one member for each University. It was agreed that this was a point which might be considered when the time came to draft the legislation.

The Prime Minister said that he hoped it might be possible for Parliament to complete by the end of November all the essential legislative and financial business which must be disposed of before the end of the year. Parliament might then be adjourned for a long recess until the middle of February.

The Cabinet –

Appointed a Committee consisting of the Minister of Health[1] (in the Chair), the Lord Privy Seal[2] and the Minister of Housing and Local Government[3] to prepare a draft of the King's Speech and to submit it for the Cabinet's approval by the end of the week.

4. The Prime Minister said that urgent consideration must be given to the means of implementing the Government's pledge to repeal the Iron and Steel Act, 1949, and to restore the industry to free enterprise. If a short and simple Bill would suffice for this purpose, it might be passed into law before Parliament was adjourned for the Christmas Recess. If, however, complicated legislation was necessary, its introduction would have to be postponed until after Christmas.

In discussion it was suggested that the restoration of the industry to private ownership was likely to involve complex questions which it would take some time to resolve. The most urgent need, therefore, was to appoint a new Board to control the industry in conformity with the policy of the new Government, while those questions were being considered.

The Cabinet –

Appointed a Committee consisting of the Minister of Health (in the Chair), the Chancellor of the Duchy of Lancaster,[4] the Minister of Supply[5] and the Attorney-General,[6] to consider and report to the Cabinet what action was required to implement the Government's pledge to restore the iron and

[1] Harry Crookshank.
[2] Lord Salisbury.
[3] Harold Macmillan.
[4] Lord Swinton.
[5] Duncan Sandys.
[6] Lionel Frederick Heald, 1897–1981. Educated at Christ Church, Oxford. Married, 1923, Flavia Forbes: two children (div., 1928); 1929, Daphne Constance Price: three children. Called to the Bar, Middle Temple, 1923. Junior Counsel, Board of Trade, 1931–7. RAF, 1939–45. Governor, Middlesex Hospital, 1946–53. MP (Cons.) for Chertsey, 1950–70. Knighted, 1951. Attorney-General, 1951–4. PC, 1954. Retired, 1970.

steel industry to free enterprise and, in particular, whether legislation for this purpose could be passed before Parliament adjourned for the Christmas Recess.

5. The Chancellor of the Exchequer[1] handed to the Cabinet a note by the Permanent Secretary to the Treasury[2] analysing the current economic situation and the prospects for 1952. The Chancellor stressed the gravity of the situation disclosed by this note. It was clear that there had been a progressive deterioration for some weeks past and that the previous Government had taken no steps to arrest this while the General Election was pending. The Government must lose no time in making the facts of the situation known to Parliament, and a full statement on this subject would have to be made in the course of the Debate on the Address. If, however, confidence was to be restored, the Government must at the same time state what remedies they proposed to apply. The Chancellor outlined to the Cabinet the remedies which he thought would be necessary.

The Prime Minister suggested that, before the Cabinet considered this matter more fully, the Chancellor of the Exchequer should discuss with a small group of Ministers his detailed proposals for remedying the situation. This group could meet at once, and the Chancellor should be in a position to lay his recommendations before the Cabinet at their next meeting. Meanwhile, a copy of the note by the Permanent Secretary to the Treasury should be sent to the Leader of the Opposition; he should at once be made aware of the factual position as it had been made known to the Government when they first took office.

The Cabinet –
  (1) Appointed a Committee consisting of the Chancellor of the Exchequer (in the Chair), the Lord President,[3] the Lord Privy Seal, the Secretary of State for the Colonies,[4] the Minister of Housing and Local Government, and the President of the Board of Trade to consider the current economic situation and the measures necessary to remedy it.
  (2) Invited the Chancellor of the Exchequer to report further to the Cabinet at their meeting on 1st November, in the light of his consultations with this Committee.
  (3) Took note that the Prime Minister would send to the Leader of the Opposition a copy of the note by the Permanent Secretary to the Treasury analysing the current economic situation and the prospects for 1952.

6. The Prime Minister said that it was his wish that during the period of

[1] R. A. Butler.
[2] Sir Edward Bridges.
[3] Lord Woolton.
[4] Oliver Lyttelton.

rearmament or for three years, whichever ended first, Ministers entitled by statute to a salary of £5,000 a year should draw £4,000 a year. He himself proposed to draw during that period £7,000 a year, instead of his statutory salary of £10,000.

The Prime Minister said that substantial reductions must be made in the use of official cars by Ministers. Detailed proposals to this end should be worked out without delay.

The Cabinet –

Approved the Prime Minister's proposals regarding Ministers' salaries and the use of official cars by Ministers, and took note that a public statement on both points would be issued by the Prime Minister that evening.

7. The Foreign Secretary[1] said that since assuming office he had been in consultation with the Chiefs of Staff about the military situation in Egypt. The local commanders had now been given discretion to arrest any persons who constituted a threat to military security in the Canal Zone; but they had been instructed that any persons so arrested should, where possible, be deported from the Zone rather than detained in it.

The Foreign Secretary said that, at the Prime Minister's request, he had considered a proposal by the Chiefs of Staff that the balance of the 3rd Infantry Division should be sent to Cyprus in order to strengthen the forces available in the Middle East generally. So far as he was concerned there was no objection to this proposal. The Prime Minister said that the despatch of these reinforcements to the Middle East would mean that, apart from the 6th Armoured Division which was due to go to Germany in the near future, there would be no strategic reserve in the United Kingdom. It might be necessary to postpone the despatch of the 6th Armoured Division to Germany; but, before taking any final decision on this point, he would consult with General Eisenhower. It would certainly be necessary to consider means of strengthening the defences of the United Kingdom, e.g., by pressing on with the organisation of a Home Guard and by calling up Territorial Army divisions in rotation.

On the political aspects of the situation in Egypt, the Prime Minister said that he endorsed the policy followed by the previous Government regarding the Sudan. For the rest, he suggested that policy should now be based on the principle that it was the duty of the United Kingdom Government to keep the Suez Canal open to the shipping of the world, using such force as might be necessary for that purpose. It would be consistent with that principle that oil tankers bound for the refinery at Haifa should be allowed to pass through the Canal. The Foreign Secretary said that, while he fully endorsed the principle suggested by the Prime Minister, he doubted whether it would be expedient to apply it at the moment to the passage of oil tankers bound for Haifa. This

[1] Anthony Eden.

was a matter of timing. Our immediate aim should be to prevent the other Arab States from supporting the attitude taken by the Egyptian Government in abrogating the Anglo/Egyptian Treaty of 1936; and precipitate action on our part regarding the passage of tankers through the Canal would be likely to arouse resentment in some of the other Arab States.

The Foreign Secretary said that His Majesty's Ambassador in Tehran[1] had been recalled to London for consultations. Mr Harriman would also be in London at the end of the present week. This would provide him with a valuable opportunity for consultations on the future handling of the Persian oil dispute.

The Foreign Secretary said that complicated negotiations were now proceeding between the three Occupying Powers regarding the future status of Western Germany. The objective was to give Western Germany a greater measure of independence, while preserving safeguards against any resurgence of German militarism. The Foreign Secretary said that he need not trouble the Cabinet at this stage with the detail of the proposals. Broadly speaking, the present position was that we and the Americans were in agreement about the concessions which we considered reasonable, but the French were still reluctant to go so far. He had now instructed our representative in these discussions to join with the Americans in pressing the French to accept our proposals.

The Cabinet were reminded that the visit which the Chancellor of the German Federal Republic[2] had intended to make to this country in October had been postponed on account of the General Election. It would be appropriate that arrangements should now be made for Dr Adenauer to visit this country at the end of November.

The Cabinet –

Took note of the Foreign Secretary's statements.

8. The Secretary of State for the Colonies said that he was concerned about the situation in Malaya, and would like to take an early opportunity of visiting the territory in order to confer with the authorities on the spot. A Conference of Governors was due to be held in Singapore towards the end of November. If the Parliamentary situation permitted, he proposed to go out to Malaya then. He hoped to be able to pay a visit to Hong Kong at the same time.

---

[1] Francis Michie Shepherd, 1893–1962. Special Reserve, 1915–20. Consular Service, San Francisco, Buenos Aires, Lima, Antwerp, Hamburg, Haiti, 1920–32. MBE, 1932. Minister Resident and Counsel, Haiti, 1935–7. Acting Consul-General, Barcelona, 1938; Danzig, 1939. Counsellor of Legation and Consul-General, Reykjavik, 1940–2; Leopoldville, Belgian Congo, 1942. OBE, 1941. British Political Representative in Finland, 1944–7. CMG, 1946. British Counsel-General, Netherlands East Indies, 1947–9. KBE, 1948. British Ambassador to Persia, 1950–2; to Poland, 1952–4. Grand Officer, Order of Hamayoun, 1951.

[2] Konrad Adenauer.

Appendices

Appendix A: Ministerial Appointments, October 1951

THE CABINET, OCTOBER 1951

The following appointments were made between 26 and 31 October 1951

Prime Minister, First Lord of the Treasury and Minister for Defence
  Winston S. Churchill
Lord Chancellor
  Lord Simonds
Lord President of the Council
  Lord Woolton
Lord Privy Seal and Leader of the House of Lords
  Marquess of Salisbury
Chancellor of the Exchequer
  R. A. Butler
Secretary of State for Foreign Affairs
  Anthony Eden
Secretary of State for Home Affairs
  Sir David Maxwell Fyfe
Chancellor of the Duchy of Lancaster
  Lord Woolton
Minister of Agriculture and Fisheries
  Sir Thomas Dugdale
Minister for the Co-ordination of Transport, Fuel and Power
  Lord Leathers
Minister for Economic Affairs
  Arthur Salter
Minister of Education
  Florence Horsbrugh
Minister of Food
  Gwilym Lloyd George

Minister of Health and Leader of the House of Commons
    Harry Crookshank
Minister for Housing and Local Government
    Harold Macmillan
Minister of Labour and National Service
    Sir Walter Monckton
Paymaster-General
    Lord Cherwell
President of the Board of Trade
    Peter Thorneycroft
Secretary of State for the Colonies
    Oliver Lyttelton
Secretary of State for Commonwealth Relations
    Lord Ismay
Secretary of State for Scotland
    James Stuart
Secretary of State for War

OTHER MINISTERIAL APPOINTMENTS

First Lord of the Admiralty
    James Thomas
Minister of Fuel and Power
    Geoffrey Lloyd
Minister of Materials
    Lord Swinton
Minister of National Insurance
    Osbert Peake
Minister of Pensions
    Derick Heathcoat-Amory (from 5 Nov. 1951)
Minister of Supply
    Duncan Sandys
Minister of Transport
    John Maclay
Minister of Works
    Sir David Eccles
Postmaster-General
    Lord De La Warr (from 5 Nov. 1951)
Secretary of State for Air
    Lord De L'Isle and Dudley
Secretary of State for War
    Antony Head

Appendix B: Code Names

Anvil: Allied operation against the South of France, originally planned to take place simultaneously with 'Overlord', the Allied invasion across the English Channel.

Battleaxe: failed Allied invasion of Cyrenaica, 16–18 June 1941.

Dedip: heading designating material for named individual officers

Deyou: heading designating sensitive material about a fellow officer or operation

Hammer: planned assault on Trondheim.

Husky: operation to capture Sicily.

HW: catalogue code referring to records created or inherited by Government Communications Headquarters.

Jubilee (formerly Rutter): raid on the German-held port of Dieppe by a force of some 6,000 troops (mainly Canadian, with RAF and RN support), 19 Aug. 1942

Mulberry: artificial harbours used by the Allies off the beaches of Normandy during Operation 'Overlord'

Overlord: Allied invasion of Western Europe across the English Channel, June 1944

Polly: operation to evacuate all non-essential British personnel and civilians from Palestine to Egypt, 31 Jan. 1947.

Rutter *see* Jubilee.

Sextant: Cairo Conference, attended by Churchill, Roosevelt and Chiang Kai-shek, 22–26 November 1943

TA: *see* Tube Alloys

Thunderclap: proposal to bomb the easternmost cities of Germany to disrupt the transport infrastructure behind the Eastern Front

Tiger: British merchant convoy carrying tanks and aircraft from Gibraltar to Egypt, 5–12 May 1941

Torch: Allied invasion of French North Africa, November 1942

Trident: Third Washington Conference between Churchill and Roosevelt, 12–27 May 1943.

Tube Alloys: British work on what would become the atomic bomb, which from late 1941 had involved British and Canadian scientists working in collaboration with counterparts in the United States

ZIP: generic code for 'action begun'.

Appendix C: Abbreviations

AA: anti-aircraft
ABDACOM: American–British–Dutch–Australian Command
ACAS: Assistant Chief of the Air Staff
ADC: aide-de-camp
Adm.: Admiral
ACNS: Assistant Chief of the Naval Staff
AFC: Air Force Cross
AFV: Armoured Fighting Vehicle
AFHQ: Allied Force Headquarters
AI: Airborne Interception (radar)
Air Chf Mshl: Air Chief Marshal
Air Mshl: Air Marshal
AMG: Allied Military Government
AOC: Air Officer Commanding
AOC-in-C: Air Officer Commanding-in-Chief
ARW: Air Raid Warden
ASF: Army Service Forces
Asst: Assistant
AT: anti-tank
ATS: Auxiliary Territorial Service
Aus.: Australia
AVM: Air Vice-Marshal

b.: born
BAOR: British Army of Occupation on the Rhine
BBC: British Broadcasting Corporation
Bde: Brigade
BEF: British Expeditionary Force
BMA: British Medical Association
Brig.: Brigadier
Brig.-Gen.: Brigadier-General
BSAA: British South American Airways
Bt: Baronet

Capt.: Captain
CAS: Chief of the Air Staff
CB: Companion of the Order of the Bath
CBE: Commander of the Order of the British Empire
CCF: Cooperative Commonwealth Federation
CCS: Combined Chiefs of Staff

Cdr: Commander
CDS: Chief of the Defence Staff
CEO: Chief Executive Officer
CGM: Conspicuous Gallantry Medal
CGS: Chief of the General Staff
CH: Companion of Honour
ChB: Bachelor of Surgery
CHL: Chain Stations Home Service Low Cover
CI: Imperial Order of the Crown of India
CIA: Central Intelligence Agency
CIE: Companion of the Order of the Indian Empire
CIGS: Chief of the Imperial General Staff
C-in-C: Commander-in-Chief
CIO: Congress of Industrial Organizations (US)
CMG: Companion of the Order of St Michael and St George
CNAS: Chief of Naval Air Services
CNS: Chief of the Naval Staff
CO: Commanding Officer
Co.: Company
Col.: Colonel
Cons.: Conservative [Party]
Co-op.: Co-operative [Movement]
Corp.: Corporation
CoS: Chief of Staff
COS: Chiefs of Staff
Cpl: Corporal
CSO: Chief Staff Officer
CVO: Commander of the Royal Victorian Order

d.: died
DBE: Dame Commander of the Order of the British Empire
DC: District of Columbia
DCAS: Deputy Chief of the Air Staff
DCI: Director of Central Intelligence
DCIGS: Deputy Chief of the Imperial General Staff
DCL: Doctor of Civil Laws
DCNS: Deputy Chief of the Naval Staff
Dem.: Democrat (US)
Dept: Department
DFC: Distinguished Flying Cross
diss.: [marriage] dissolved
div.: divorced
Div.: Division

DSC: Distinguished Service Cross
DSM: Distinguished Service Medal
DSO: Distinguished Service Order

FBA: Fellow of the British Academy
FDR: Franklin Delano Roosevelt
Flt Lt: Flight Lieutenant
FM: Field Marshal
FO: Foreign Office
FRCP: Fellow of the Royal College of Physicians
FRCS: Fellow of the Royal College of Surgeons
FRS: Fellow of the Royal Society

GAF: German Air Force
GB: Great Britain
GBE: Knight Grand Cross of the Order of the British Empire
GCB: Knight Grand Cross of the Order of the Bath
GCI: Ground-Controlled Interception
GCIE: Knight Grand Cross of the Order of the Indian Empire
GCMG: Knight Grand Cross of the Order of St Michael and St George
GCSI: Knight Grand Commander of the Order of the Star of India
GCVO: Knight Grand Cross of the Royal Victorian Order
Gen.: General
GG, g.g.: Governor-General
GHQ: General Headquarters
GOC: General Officer Commanding
GOC-in-C: General Officer Commanding-in-Chief
Gp Capt.: Group Captain
GSO: General Staff Officer

HE: high explosive
HM: His/Her Majesty('s)
HMG: His/Her Majesty's Government
HMS: His/Her Majesty's Ship
Hon.: Honorary
HQ: headquarters
HRH: His/Her Royal Highness

Inc.: Incorporated
Ind.: Independent
IFF: Identification Friend or Foe
IKP: [Dutch] Indies Catholic Party
IRA: Irish Republican Army

Appendices

JCS: Joint Chiefs of Staff
JP: Justice of the Peace
Jr: Junior
JSM: (British) Joint Staff Mission in Washington DC

KBE: Knight Commander of the Order of the British Empire
KC: King's Counsel
KCB: Knight Commander of the Order of the Bath
KG: Knight of the Garter
KCMG: Knight Commander of the Order of St Michael and St George
KCVO: Knight Commander of the Royal Victorian Order
KKE: Communist Party of Greece
KRRC: King's Royal Rifle Corps
KStJ: Knight of Grace in the Venerable Order of St John
KT: Knight of the Thistle
KVP: [Dutch] Catholic People's Party

Lab.: Labour [Party]
Lib.: Liberal [Party]
LL.D: Doctor of Laws
LOM: Legion of Merit
LRCP: Licentiate of the Royal College of Physicians
LST: landing ship, tank
Lt: Lieutenant
Lt-Col.: Lieutenant-Colonel
Ltd: Limited [Company]
Lt-Gen.: Lieutenant-General

Maj.: Major
Maj.-Gen.: Major-General
MB: Bachelor of Medicine
MBE: Member of the Order of the British Empire
MC: Military Cross
MDI: Ministry of Defence 1 (secret weapons research establishment)
Mena: Middle East and North Africa
MIT: Massachusetts Institute of Technology
MP: Member of Parliament
MRCS: Member of the Royal College of Surgeons
MSc: Master of Science
Mshl of the RAF: Marshal of the Royal Air Force
MVO: Member of the Royal Victorian Order

NAAFI: Navy, Army and Air Force Institutes, the official trading organization of the British Armed Forces

Narkom: *Soviet narodnykh kommissarov* (councillor on the Soviet Government's Council of People's Commissars)
Nat.: National
Nat. Gov.: National Government
Nat. Dem.: National Democrat (Poland)
NATO: North Atlantic Treaty Organization
NCO: non-commissioned officer
NEP: New Economic Policy (Soviet)
NKVD: Narodnyy Komissariat Vnutrennikh Del, the Soviet People's Commissariat for Internal Affairs (security service)
NROTC: Naval Reserve Officers' Training Corps
NSDAP: Nationalsozialistische Deutsche Arbeiterpartei (Nazi Party)
NSW: New South Wales
NZEF: New Zealand Expeditionary Force

OBE: Office of the Order of the British Empire
OC: Officer Commanding
OC-in-C: Officer Commanding-in-Chief
OCTU: Officer Cadet Training Unit
OEEC: Organization for European Economic Co-operation
OM: Order of Merit

PAYE: Pay As You Earn (income taxation)
PC: Privy Councillor
PhD: Doctor of Philosophy
PM: Prime Minister
POW: prisoner of war
Prof.: Professor
PSL: Polish Peasants' Party
PWE: Political Warfare Executive

QC: Queen's Counsel
QMG: Quartermaster-General

RA: Royal Artillery
RAAF: Royal Auxiliary Air Force
RAC: Royal Armoured Corps
RAdm.: Rear-Admiral
RAF: Royal Air Force
RAFVR: Royal Air Force Volunteer Reserve
RAMC: Royal Army Medical Corps
RASC: Royal Army Service Corps
Rep.: Republican (US)

RFA: Royal Fleet Auxiliary
RFC: Royal Flying Corps
Rgt: Regiment
RHA: Royal Horse Artillery
RHAF: Royal Hellenic Air Force
RMC: Royal Military College
RN: Royal Navy
RNAS: Royal Naval Air Service
RNVR: Royal Naval Volunteer Reserve
RSHA: Reichssicherheitshauptamt

SACSEA: Supreme Allied Commander, South East Asia
SCAP: Supreme Commander for the Allied Powers
SD: Sicherheitsdienst
SDP: Social Democratic Party
SE: South-east
Sgt: Sergeant
SHAEF: Supreme Headquarters, Allied Expeditionary Force
SHAPE: Supreme Headquarters, Allied Powers Europe
SOE: Special Operations Executive
S of S: Secretary of State
SPD: Sozialdemokratische Partei Deutschlands
Sqn: Squadron
SS: Schutzstaffel
SW: South-west

TA: Territorial Army; Tube Alloys
Temp.: temporary
T/B: tuberculosis
TUC: Trades Union Congress

UCLA: University of California at Los Angeles
UDC: Urban District Council
UJ: Uncle Joe, i.e. Stalin
UK: United Kingdom
UNA: United Nations Association
Union.: Unionist
UN(O): United Nations (Organisation)
UNRRA: United Nations Relief and Rehabilitation Administration
US, USA: United States of America
USAAF: United States Army Air Forces
USN: United States Navy
USS: United States Ship

VAdm.: Vice-Admiral
VC: Victoria Cross
VCIGS: Vice-Chief of the Imperial General Staff
VCNS: Vice-Chief of the Naval Staff
VCS: Vice-Chief of Staff
VE: Victory in Europe
VJ: Victory over Japan
VRD: Volunteer Reserve Decoration

WAAF: Women's Auxiliary Air Force
Wg Cdr: Wing Commander
WRNS: Women's Royal Naval Service
WVS: Women's Voluntary Service
WWI: First World War
WWII: Second World War

YWCA: Young Women's Christian Association

Appendix D: Churchill's Travels, September 1945 to October 1951

Date	Destination	Description
1945		
2 Sep.	Lake Como	Holiday to visit FM Alexander, accompanied by Lord Moran and Sarah Churchill.
19 Sep.	Villa Pirelli	Holiday continued on Mediterranean coast 18 miles east of Genoa.
	Monte Carlo	Holiday continued at Hôtel de Paris.
24 Sep.	Villa Sous le Vent, Antibes	Holiday continued at villa of Gen. Eisenhower.
12 Nov.	Paris	Diplomatic visit. Stayed at British Embassy. Speech at French Institute
15 Nov.	Brussels	Received hon. degree from Brussels University. Speeches also at British Embassy and Joint Meeting of the Belgian Senate and Chamber.
1946		
9 Jan.	New York	Embarked at Southampton on RMS *Queen Elizabeth*.
15 Jan.	Miami	Holiday at Miami Beach with Clementine and Sarah.
1 Feb.	Havana	Holiday continued
9 Feb.	Miami	Holiday continued. Received hon. degree from University of Miami.
3 Mar.	Washington DC	Holiday continued. Stayed at British Embassy.
4 Mar.	Fulton, Missouri	Travelled with Truman in his private train car.
5 Mar.	Fulton, Missouri	'The Sinews of Peace' speech at Westminster College.

7 Mar.	Washington DC	Returned to British Embassy by train from Missouri.
8 Mar.	Richmond, Virginia	Speech to General Assembly of Virginia, on invitation by joint resolution.
9 Mar.	Washington DC	Speech at Pentagon, on invitation by Secretary of War and Gen. Eisenhower.
14 Mar.	New York	Holiday ending. Dinner at Union Club with Henry Luce. Speeches at Waldorf Astoria Hotel and Columbia University defending Fulton speech.
20 Mar.	London	Set sail for Britain, arriving Mar. 26.
27 Apr.	Aberdeen	Received hon. degree from University of Aberdeen.
29 Apr.	Edinburgh	Speech on socialism at Scottish Unionist Rally.
9 May	The Hague	Speech to States-General of the Netherlands. Received hon. degree from University of Leyden.
14 July	Luxembourg	Visit to Grand Duchess Charlotte.
15 July	Metz	At invitation from Mayor of Metz, speech on France, Europe, and United Nations.
23 Aug.	Villa Choisi, Switzerland	Painting and writing holiday accompanied by Clementine and Mary. Worked on war memoirs and prepared University of Zurich address.
16 Sep.	Geneva	Lunch with President and Committee of International Red Cross.
17 Sep.	Berne	Luncheons with Swiss Federal Council and French Ambassador. Speech at Berne Town Hall.
19 Sep.	Zurich	University of Zurich speech appealing for a United States of Europe.
25 Sep.	Brussels and Paris	Trip with Clementine and Mary.
5 Oct.	Blackpool	Speech to Conservative Party Conference.

1947

9 May	Paris	Received Médaille Militaire at ceremony at Cour des Invalides. Dined with French PM Georges Bidault. Dined with President of the Republic Vincent Auriol at Elysée Palace.
16 May	Ayr	Speech to Unionist Associations of Scotland.
5 Dec.	Manchester	Received Freedom of the City. Conservative Party speech to North-Western Area Meeting, Belle Vue.
10 Dec.	Marrakech	Painting and writing holiday accompanied by Sarah and Col. F. W. Deakin. Worked on war memoirs.

1948

7 May	The Hague	Speech to Hague Conference on European unity.
9 May	Amsterdam	Speech on Europe in public square.
11 May	Oslo	With Clementine, guest of King of Norway at Royal Palace. Received hon. degree from University of Oslo.
28 May	Perth, Scotland	Speech to Scottish Unionist Party Conference.
16 July	Cardiff	Speech on Europe.
23 Aug.	Aix-en-Provence	Writing holiday accompanied by Clementine, Sarah, Mary and Christopher Soames. Worked on war memoirs.
10 Sep.	Cap d'Antibes	Holiday continued at villa of Duke and Duchess of Windsor. Celebrated 40th wedding anniversary with Clementine on Sep. 12.
13 Sep.	Aix-en-Provence	Holiday continued.
20 Sep.	La Capponcina, Côte d'Azur	Holiday continued at Lord Beaverbrook's villa.
25 Sep.	Monte Carlo	Holiday continued at Hôtel de Paris.

8 Oct.	Llandudno	Speech to Conservative Party rally at Pier Pavilion.
28 Dec.	Paris	Dinner with Duke and Duchess of Windsor.
29 Dec.	Monte Carlo	Holiday at Hôtel de Paris accompanied by Clementine, Sarah and Antony Beauchamp.

1949

12 Jan.	Paris	Visit to British Embassy.
26 Feb.	Brussels	Speech to Congress of International Council of European Movement.
18 Mar.	New York	Embarked at Southampton on RMS *Queen Elizabeth* with Clementine, Mary and Christopher Soames.
25 Mar.	New York	Speech on communism at dinner given by Henry R. Luce at Ritz-Carlton Hotel.
27 Mar.	Washington DC	Visit to White House.
31 Mar.	Boston	Speech at Massachusetts Institute of Technology.
4 Apr.	London	Departed aboard RMS *Queen Mary* for Southampton, arriving in London 20 Apr.
19 May	Liverpool	Received hon. degree from Liverpool University.
20 May	Glasgow	Speech to Conservative rally, Ibrox Park.
23 July	Wolverhampton	Speech on Conservative Party policy.
10 Aug.	Bellagio	Holiday accompanied by Clementine.
12 Aug.	Strasbourg	Speech on Europe (in French) at open-air meeting, Place Keebler. Speech at Freedom of the City ceremony. Speech at European Assembly.
19 Aug.	La Capponicina, Côte d'Azur	Holiday continued at Lord Beaverbrook's villa. Suffered a stroke while there. Returned to London, Aug. 31.

APPENDICES

19 Oct.	Bristol	Address as Chancellor of Bristol University.
29 Dec.	Madeira	Writing trip (cut short by announcement of impending general election).

1950

4 Feb.	Leeds	Election address at Town Hall.
8 Feb.	Cardiff	Election address at Ninian Park Football Ground.
9 Feb.	Devonport	Election address at Forum Cinema.
10 Feb.	Buckhurst Hill (London)	Election address at Woodford.
14 Feb.	Edinburgh	Election address at Usher Hall.
20 Feb.	Manchester	Election address.
18 May	Edinburgh	Speech to Scottish Unionist Meeting at Usher Hall.
20 May	Worcestershire	Presentation of Memorial of Stanley Baldwin to the Trustees at Astley.
15 July	Plymouth	Conservative Party speech at Saltram Park.
20 July	Bath	Speech on United Nations.
6 Aug.	Strasbourg	Speech to Consultative Assembly of the Council of Europe.
10 Oct.	Copenhagen	Received hon. degree from Copenhagen University
14 Oct.	Blackpool	Speech to Conservative Party Conference.
17 Dec.	Marrakech	Painting and writing holiday with various guests visiting.

1951

1 Jan.	Tinerhir, Morocco	Painting holiday continued.
3 Jan.	Marrakech	Holiday continued.

20 Jan.	Paris	Visit to British Embassy.
16 Apr.	Sheffield	Speech at Cutlers' Feast.
18 May	Glasgow	Speech to Scottish Unionist Association Annual Conference.
15 Aug.	Annecy, France	Writing and painting holiday with Clementine. Worked on war memoirs.
22 Aug.	Venice	Holiday continued at Excelsior Hotel, Lido.
10 Sep.	Paris	Diplomatic visit to British Embassy.
2 Oct.	Liverpool	Election address at Liverpool Stadium.
15 Oct.	Huddersfield	Election address at Town Hall.
16 Oct.	Newcastle upon Tyne	Election address at St James's Boxing Hall.
17 Oct.	Glasgow	Election address at St. Andrew's Hall.
23 Oct.	Plymouth	Election address at Home Park Football Ground.

Index

CSC = Clementine Spencer-Churchill
FDR = Franklin D. Roosevelt
RSC = Randolph S. Churchill
WSC = Winston S. Churchill

Abd al-Ilāh (Abdullah), 430, 430 n.2, 951, 1280
Abdullah I bin al-Hussein (King of Jordan)
   biographical information, 1304 n.2
   Anglo-Arab relations, 1304, 1305, 1307
   Assassination of King Abdullah of Jordan (July 1951 WSC speech), 2121
   Jordan and Israel, Government Decision (Oral Answers), 1737
   WSC praises, 1880
   WSC recalls meeting with, 1482
Acheson, Dean
   biographical information, 1415 n.2
   Anglo-American policy towards Russia, 1936
   comments on Franco Government, 1415
   dissolution of Combined Chiefs of Staff, 1514, 1526
   European Army proposals, 1834
   WSC praises US foreign policy, 1711
Acland, Richard Thomas Dyke, 1240, 1240 n.1, 1536–7
Adams, Samuel Vyvyan Trerice, 1003, 1003 n.1
Addison, Christopher, 96, 96 n.1, 362, 399, 656, 928
Adenauer, Konrad
   biographical information, 1706 n.1
   economic union of France and Germany, 1706, 1707
   Federal Republic of Germany election (1949), 1942 n.1
   first Chancellor of Federal Republic of Germany, 2123
   Hague Conference, 1708
   Soviet rearmament of Eastern Germany, 1846
   visit to England postponed (1951), 2232
agriculture
   Agriculture (July 1948 WSC speech), 1108–10
   Conservative Party policies, 801–2, 1070, 1078, 1095, 1459, 1540, 1620
   WSC criticises Labour Government policies, 475–6, 889
   see also food
air defence
   Air Force Coastal Command, 1813
   Air Ministry Pamphlet 156, 555, 557
   American bomber squadrons stationed in East Anglia, 1273–4, 1811–12, 1839, 1845, 2003, 2025, 2053, 2215
   Auxiliary Air Defence, 1697, 1812
   British jet fighter production rates, 1526, 1542–3, 1586, 1586 n.1, 2012
   Defence (March 1950 WSC speech), 1696–8
   effect of warfare on, 1367
   Ground-Controlled Interception (GCI), 613, 613 n.2
   Russian presence in British aircraft factories, 1464–5, 1485, 1496
   sale of British jets to Argentina and Egypt, 1859–60
   Soviet air force, 1696, 1810–11
   Soviet military strength and British defence capacity, 1463–5
Aitken, John William Maxwell ('Max'), 520–1, 520 n.1, 548
Aitken, William Maxwell: *see* Beaverbrook, Lord ('Max')
Ajax, HMS, 1090–1
Akers, Wallace, 18–19, 18 n.1
Alanbrooke, Lord (Alan Francis Brooke)
   biographical information, 5 n.1
   Alamein Reunion Dinner, 106–7
   and Attlee: Alanbrooke stays on as CIGS under Attlee, 14, 15, 22; Attlee plans national broadcast upon surrender of Japan, 6; WSC suggests COS appointments to Attlee, 14, 15, 22
   Egypt, 320–1
   Resolutions for Thanks to Commanders, 162

Alanbrooke, Lord (Alan Francis Brooke) *(continued)*
  The Second World War: war-time Supreme Command decisions, 297–9, 299–300, 599; WSC asks for notes on first battle in France prior to Dunkirk, 457, 517, 517 n.2
  unveiling of WSC's portrait at the Junior Carlton Club, 1977–8
  WSC proposes Peerage for, 5
Albania, 931, 931 n.1, 1090, 1354, 1572–3, 1573
Alexander, Albert Victor
  biographical information, 6 n.2
  Attlee plans national broadcast upon surrender of Japan, 6
  conversion of Czechoslovak railways to Russian gauge, 527–8
  criticises Conservative Party, 648, 658, 670
  Kesselring's death sentence, 695
  National Service Bill, 670, 671, 672–3, 677, 678, 683, 695–6, 696–9
  Navy Estimates: manpower, 538, 659; National Service Bill, 673, 674; WSC criticises Labour Government policies, 831, 987, 988, 989, 990, 991, 993
  North Atlantic Defence Committee meeting minutes, 1582
  WSC congratulates on being named Minister of Defence, 537
Alexander, Sir Harold
  biographical information, 14 n.1
  Fourth Alamein Reunion (October 1949 WSC speech), 1547
  Governor-General of Canada appointment, 14
  Lake Como villa, 54, 55, 58, 74
  Resolutions for Thanks to Commanders, 162
  XIII Corps meeting in Trieste, 47, 55
  United States Mutual Defence Assistance Act, 1598–600, 1604–5, 1606
  and WSC: Alexander admires WSC's Academy painting exhibits, 1101; thanks WSC for copy of *The Gathering Storm*, 1101; war-time Supreme Command decisions, 297–9, 601–2; WSC asks for feedback on proofs for Volume Five of *The Second World War*, 2101, 2139; WSC hopes to visit in Canada, 2102; WSC sends paints and holiday greetings to, 171; WSC visits and paints with in Lake Como, 56, 66, 67, 68, 69, 70, 76–7, 81, 1101
Alexander, Lady Margaret Diana Bingham, 81, 81 n.3
Ali, Syed Waris Ameer, 470–1, 470 n.1, 471 n.1
Allan, Maureen Catherine Stuart-Clark, 1716, 1716 n.1

Allan, Robert Alexander, 1715–16, 1715 n.1, 1716
Allen, George Rolland Gordon ('Peter')
  biographical information, 711 n.2
  The Second World War: feedback and suggested edits for, 978–9, 1057, 1153–5, 1175, 1402, 1559, 1559–60, 1560, 1561, 1561 n.2, 2060–1, 2147; 'Jubilee' (Dieppe raid), 711, 1821, 1848
Allighan, Ernest George ('Garry'), 837–9, 837 n.3, 2021
Alpass, Joseph Herbert, 1210, 1210 n.1
Álvarez de Toledo y Caro, Joaquín, 2144, 2144 n.5
Ambedkar, Bhimrao Ramji
  biographical information, 332 n.1
  appeals to WSC regarding future of Untouchables in India, 332, 342, 395, 518
  provides brief on Untouchables to WSC, 562
  seeks independence from Hindus, 562, 574–5
  Wavell asks Nehru to form Interim Congress Government, 450
Amery, Florence Greenwood ('Brydde'), 32, 32 n.1
Amery, (Harold) Julian, 1196–7, 1196 n.1, 1197, 1767, 1768, 2208
Amery, Leopold ('Leo')
  biographical information, 31 n.1
  declines GCB honour, 31
  describes Conservative criticisms to Beaverbrook, 97–8
  economics: Empire Preferences policy, 803; opposes US loan to England, 381–2
  Europe: Pan-European Council proposals, 423, 424; reaction to WSC's United States of Europe proposal, 461–2
  India: Amery hopes for interim Indian government, 382; Commonwealth relations, 1383–4, 1394, 1401, 1401 n.1; offer of Commonwealth status for, 330–1; Statute of Westminster 1931 on legality of secession, 633; WSC reviews text of Cripps proposals, 633
  Israel, 1767–8
  Pakistan, 1383
  Palestine: Amery suggests WSC respond to Weizmann's *Times* interview, 1294–5; British policy towards, 393, 402, 949–52; King David Hotel bombing, 423
  Persian oil, 2103
  and WSC: Amery suggests Zermatt visit to WSC, 423, 424; congratulates WSC on Foreign Affairs speech, 381–2, 382 n.1; Harrow School concert, 1549, 1557; Harrow School swimming pool, 1448, 1448 n.1; offers services to WSC pending

INDEX

1951 General Election results, 2207–8; pledges to work with WSC in HofC, 31; WSC declines Empire Industries Association speaking engagement, 1549, 1557; WSC mentions Amery in Harrow School speeches, 1225, 1946; WSC thanks for letter, 101

Anderson, Lady Ava Bodley Wigram, 63, 63 n.3, 730

Anderson, Sir John
biographical information, 10 n.3
atom bomb: Atomic Bomb Committee members, 40, 49, 63; Attlee asks WSC to comment on letter to Truman, 74; information for *The Second World War* chapter, 1601; Parliamentary Questions on raw materials for, 89, 92; WSC's Atomic Bomb statement, 17–18
Coal Bill Debate, 201
CSC's opinion of, 1381
economics: Consultative Committee for economic and financial issues, 1267; Finance Bill (June 1946 WSC speech), 388; taxation comments, 79; wartime budget for 1945–1946, 153
India: Dominion status for proposed as interim stage before independence, 726; effect of partition on Imperial Services, 641–2
Iron and Steel Bill, 1246
National Insurance Bill, 201
National Service Bill, 688–9, 692
Opening of the Sikorski Institute (July 1949 WSC speech), 1445–7
politics: General Election polling percentage for Labour Party, 647; WSC asks Attlee to invite Conservative colleagues to meeting with George VI, 29, 30; WSC co-ordinates on proposed speech content with, 2174; WSC forms new Government (1951), 2224, 2226

Anderson, Kathleen Lorna May Gamble, 1980, 1980 n.1, 1982

Anderson, Kenneth Arthur Noel, 1980, 1980 n.1, 1982

Anders, Władysław, 258, 258 n.2

Anglo-American relations
American bomber squadrons stationed in East Anglia, 1273–4
British policy towards Greece, 932–3
dissolution of Combined Chiefs of Staff, 1514–15
Eden's US visit (1951), 2213–14
Eisenhower hopes to discuss 'History of the War' accounts with WSC, 187
Friedman writes to WSC about British and American political systems, 269–70
Hoover's 'Gibraltar' speech, 1993
Imperial Preference, 803
joint policy towards Yugoslavia, 501–2
King discusses with WSC, 112–13
Marshall and war-time Supreme Command decisions, 599–600
military alliance proposals, 133–4, 143, 236–7, 239, 310
and relations with Soviet Russia, 133–4
speeches (WSC): The Anglo-American Alliance (July 1950), 1777–80; Exports to China (May 1951), 2068–9; Foreign Affairs (July 1949), 1451–5; Foreign Affairs, Middle East (July 1951), 2126; Foreign Policy, President Truman's Declaration (November 1945), 119–27; The Future of Europe (November 1945), 141; North Atlantic Supreme Commander (April 1951), 2047–8; Our Race and Destiny (April 1951), 2057–8; The Sinews of Peace (March 1946), 230–5, 236–7, 238–9, 253–5; Woodford Election Address (October 1951), 2182–4
Truman's opinion of Bevin, 11–12
world policy regarding atom bomb, 84–7
WSC advocates unity and fraternal association of English-speaking peoples, 245–6, 266, 267, 273, 316, 326, 372, 757–8, 1273, 1364, 1374, 1412, 1541, 1956–7, 2083–4, 2217
WSC criticises use of terms 'bloc' and 'ganging up' to describe, 372
WSC disagrees with Halifax proposal for UN Trusteeship, 133
WSC emphasises need for unity and co-operation, 270–1, 684, 2209–10
WSC promotes anti-Communist solidarity and importance of UN, 809–11
WSC proposes Anglo-American alliance against Russia, 254
WSC reports to Attlee and Bevin on his visit with Truman, 241–2
WSC's tribute to Baruch, 482–3

Anglo-Arab relations, 430, 951, 1280, 1304, 1305, 1307

Anglo-French relations, 394, 398, 404–7

Anglo-Jordan Treaty of 1948, 1736–7

Anglo-Persian Oil Company, 2061–2, 2062 n.1, 2065, 2079, 2080, 2088, 2090, 2091

Anglo-Russian relations, 120

Anglo-Russian Short Term Trade Agreement (1947), 1851–2

Anne, (Queen of Denmark), 764, 764 n.5

Annigoni, Pietro, 2113, 2113 n.1

'Anvil', 401, 401 n.2, 1098

Appleton, Edward Victor, 18, 18 n.4

Argentina, 194, 195, 1812, 1845, 1859–60
al Armanazi, Najeeb, 296–7, 296 n.3, 300–1, 309
Arnold, Henry Harley, 162, 162 n.3
Ashley, Maurice Percy, 43, 43 n.1
Asquith, Arthur Melland ('Ock'), 1964, 1964 n.1
Asquith, Cyril, 102 n.3, 348
Asquith, Helen (Lady Violet Bonham Carter)
  biographical information, 102 n.2
  Liberal candidate for Colne Valley Division, 1997, 2016, 2196–7, 2207
  Liberal Party election broadcasts, 1591, 1600–1, 1607, 1615, 1615 n.1
  praises A New Parliament broadcast, 968
  praises The Sinews of Peace speech, 275
  sends WSC well wishes, 927
  thanks WSC for meeting, 874
  WSC criticises Liberal Party, 132–3
  WSC declines to attend 'Focus' (Freedom and Peace) luncheon, 102–3, 103, 128–9
  WSC seeks solidarity with Liberals against Labour Government, 1659, 1720
  WSC's political support for, 1997
Asquith, Herbert Henry (Earl of Oxford and Asquith), 138, 138 n.1, 661, 715, 754, 769, 832, 862, 1624, 1962–4, 2199
Asquith, Raymond, 1963–4, 1963 n.1
Assheton, Ralph
  biographical information, 108 n.1
  cleaning of defaced and dirty election posters, 386–7
  Conservative Party Chairman, 109, 286, 288
  Consultative Committee for economic and financial issues, 1267
  Control of Investment Bill, 200
  thanks WSC for encouraging unified Party vote for upcoming by-election, 190
  WSC congratulates on City of London election, 108
  WSC forms new Government (1951), 2224
Astor, Hugh Waldorf, 1745, 1745 n.1, 1763, 1765–6
Astor, John Jacob
  biographical information, 385 n.1
  The Times article on Perils Abroad and at Home (October 1948 WSC speech), 1197
  WSC compliments Astor's painting skills, 1074
  WSC's Devenport Election Address (February 1950), 1635
  WSC urges Astor to control content of *The Times* leading articles, 385–6, 390–1, 404
Astor, Violet Mary Elliot, 1075, 1075 n.1
Atkins, John Black, 761, 761 n.1
Atlantic Charter, 370, 437, 460

atom bomb
  American production methods (1945), 123–5
  Anglo-American policy regarding, 74, 83–4, 84–7, 91, 122–3, 125–7, 126–7
  Atomic Bomb Committee, 40, 49, 63, 269, 1820, 1825
  Baruch discusses with WSC, 745
  British atomic energy project, 1543
  British Civil Defence booklet on minimisation of effects of, 1816
  British lack of production of, 1649–50, 1796, 1814, 1846, 1972
  Cherwell derides Darnley's anxiety regarding, 95
  Cold War arms race, 1656, 1712, 1757, 1780, 1785–6, 1795, 1796, 1814–16, 1846–7, 1952–3, 2179–81
  dangers of, 122, 461
  development of peace-time use of, 114–15
  Korean Republic Invasion (Oral Answers), 1770–1
  McMahon Act, 1959, 1959 n.1, 1961
  Parliamentary Questions on raw materials for, 89, 92, 93, 99
  prospects for American bombing of Russia, 877–8
  Quebec Agreement of 1943, 114, 125–6, 1601, 1958–60, 1961–2, 1972–3, 2000, 2000, 2001, 2002, 2003, 2004, 2007–8
  RSC suggests use of on Korea, 1960
  Russian knowledge of (1945), 1465
  Russian possession of, 1186, 1543, 1711–12, 1785–6, 1796, 1814–16, 1846, 1856
  speeches (WSC): Foreign Policy, President Truman's Declaration (November 1945), 122, 123–7, 128; The Sinews of Peace (March 1946), 229, 239; Defence (March 1950), 1686, 1688
  Truman's declaration to Congress about willingness to use, 1382, 1383, 1385, 1395
  Tube Alloys research, 7 n.1, 23
  world policy regarding, 84–7, 91, 95–6
  WSC cites importance of as leverage against Russia, 591, 1185–6, 1373, 1814
  WSC comments on at Cuban press conference, 196, 197
  WSC discusses possibility of war with Russia, 2152
  WSC discusses in *The Second World War*, 1312–13
  WSC discusses with Shaw, 453
  WSC's Atomic Bomb statement, 7, 10, 14, 16, 17–21
  WSC's opinion of leverage afforded to US Government by, 23, 490

INDEX

WSC's press statement on making atom bombs, 2005, 2005–6
WSC's tribute to Baruch, 482–3
WSC's war-time correspondence with Attlee regarding, 482, 486
Attlee, Clement Richard
biographical information, 3 n.5
Anglo-American relations, 2183
British Commonwealth Prime Ministers' Conference (1951), 1939
Burma, 580–2, 846–9
China, 2064, 2070
domestic affairs: coal industry, 617, 651, 655, 1537; Criminal Justice Bill, 1113–14; demobilisation, 130, 486, 489–90; employment, 1534–5; food, 418, 1671–2; Government Hospitality Fund, 388; housing, 1921, 1922–3, 1927, 1931; Imperial Defence College, 282; National Health Service proposals, 1103–4; nationalisation of British iron and steel industries, 1753, 1868, 1871, 1873–4, 1878, 1973–4, 2014–15, 2203–4; Political Gerrymandering (June 1948 WSC speech), 1079, 1081–2; Representation of the People Bill (February 1948 WSC speech), 974, 975, 976
Europe: Attlee's opinion on need for federation of, 710; British arms for the Netherlands, 1073; Council of Europe, British delegation to, 1130, 1132, 1151, 1152, 1152–3, 1221, 1227, 1228–9, 1230–1, 1231, 1432, 1447–8, 1450, 1761–2, 1769; European Army proposals, 1862–3; Hague Conference, 947, 952, 953–4, 960, 964; United States of Europe proposals, 556, 565, 589, 935; WSC's visit to Metz, 394, 398
foreign affairs: Attlee's US visit, 1968, 1969–70; Foreign Affairs, Middle East (July 1951 WSC speech), 2131; Foreign Policy, President Truman's Declaration (November 1945 WSC speech), 119–27; Mansion House address, 531
General Election (1950): Debate on the Address (March 1950 WSC speech), 1676, 1678–9; Labour Government discusses post-election Parliamentary strategy, 1681–2; Labour Party maintains slim majority, 1665; petrol rationing, 1646–7; timing of, 1527, 1530; WSC criticises Attlee's leadership, 1647; WSC criticises Attlee's silence, 1634; WSC criticises Attlee's Socialist platform, 1642–3, 1652, 1653; WSC criticises nationalisation of British industries, 1645–6; WSC criticises 'Work or Starve' policy, 1631, 1645
General Election (1951): Abadan, Sudan and Bevan – A Trio of Misfortune (October 1951 WSC speech), 2187–90; Attlee resigns as PM, 2219; Attlee sets October date for, 2153; timing of, 2081–2; WSC criticises Attlee in Plymouth Election Address (October 1951), 2212–13, 2218
Germany: Allied Unconditional Surrender Policy, 1461–2; Kesselring's death sentence, 704, 734; 'Morgenthau Plan' for Germany, 36; Russian blockade of Berlin, 1128–9; WSC cites need for Western Germany to aid in defence of Europe from Russia, 1704–5, 1809, 1845
honours and awards: Campaign Star qualifications, 97, 100–1, 274; Defence Medal qualifications, 100, 274–5; 14th Army War Medal Clasps proposal, 97, 101; India Service Medal proposal, 274; sends Committee on the Grant of Honours, Decorations and Medals report to WSC, 96–7, 100–1; War Medal qualifications, 274
India: Attlee calls meeting with Liberals and Conservatives regarding, 399, 399 n.4; Constituent Assembly procedures, 574, 575; dismissal of Wavell as Viceroy of, 640; Dominion status for proposed as interim stage before independence, 725, 726, 728–30; HofC resolution of appreciation for Indian Civil and Military Services, 748, 748 n.1; Hyderabad and Kashmir, 1129–30; India Cabinet Mission (July 1946 WSC speech), 411–12; India Cabinet Mission, Statement on the Adjournment (May 1946 WSC speech), 329, 331; India Independence Bill, 736, 737, 738–9; Jinnah criticises British Government and Indian Congress negotiations, 400; WSC criticises 14-month time limit for achieving Indian independence, 641; WSC criticises Labour Government policy towards, 829; WSC defends Conservative Party stance towards partition of, 2215–16; WSC discusses British policy towards with Attlee, 622; WSC opposes independence for, 328; WSC questions name of India Independence Bill, 736, 740
Ireland, 1206, 1208
Japan: Attlee invites WSC to meeting with George VI upon surrender of, 29, 30,

Attlee, Clement Richard *(continued)*
   Japan *(continued)*
      30 n.1; Attlee plans national broadcast upon surrender of, 6; Attlee plans National Service of Thanksgiving, 28–9; Attlee updates WSC on expected surrender of, 25; Japanese surrender (V-J Day), 31, 34–5, 35
   Korea: British forces in, 1858–9, 1988; Korea (July 1950 WSC speech), 1780–6; Korean Republic Invasion (Oral Answers), 1769–71; quadripartite occupation of Korea without an Allied Control Commission, 46
   Middle East: Anglo-Iranian personnel in Abadan, 2111, 2115, 2155, 2156, 2156–7, 2157, 2167–8; Assassination of King Abdullah of Jordan (July 1951 WSC speech), 2121; British policy towards Palestine, 393, 394, 398–9, 1303; motor car presented by WSC and British Government to Ibn Saud, 404 n.2; Persian Crisis (October 1951 WSC speech), 2174–6; proposed removal of British troops from Egypt, 311–12, 349, 351, 367; transfer of British Mandate in Palestine to UN, 646
   Parliament: Committee of Privileges, 693, 695; Commons Chamber reopening, 1912–13, 1914–15; Lynskey Tribunal, 1318; Parliament Act of 1911, 832–4; Parliament Bill, 863, 889; PM's salary and expenses, 596–7; Preserving Continuity (May 1948 WSC speech), 1060–1; WSC notifies Attlee of his intent to formally request the recall of Parliament, 1825–6, 1832, 1838–9, 1844, 1854–5
   personal life: granddaughter's birth, 56; Marian Holmes's opinion of working for Attlee, 3–4; ulcer, 2026, 2047, 2047 n.1, 2056
   Royal Family: Address of Congratulations to Their Majesties and Princess Elizabeth on the Forthcoming Royal Marriage (October 1947 WSC speech), 816–17; Princess Elizabeth's annuities, 852–3; Princess Margaret's travel allowance for Italy trip, 1389–90, 1390–1, 1391 n.1, 1394; proposed job for Duke of Windsor at British Embassy in America, 310, 337; sympathy message for Queen Elizabeth during King George's surgery and recovery, 2154; WSC recommends that Princess Elizabeth not fly to Canada during King George's illness, 2155
   Russia: Attlee warns of Soviet Communist imperialism, 937; British policy towards, 1971; Russian espionage in Canada, 551; Russian forces in Eastern Europe, 504, 565, 567, 569, 583; Stalin refers to Attlee as 'warmonger', 2015
   Second World War: commemoration of war-time Dinners with the King at No. 10 Downing Street, 737; Marshall and war-time Supreme Command decisions, 602–3, 604; memorial statue and tablet for FDR, 387–8; Potsdam Conference conclusions, 6–7, 8, 10, 14; Resolutions for Thanks to Commanders, 162–3, 166; Victory celebrations, 334, 339; WSC recalls inviting Attlee to Potsdam Conference, 682
   tributes: Field Marshal Smuts Westminster Memorial Statue (June 1951 WSC speech), 2093–4; Roosevelt Memorial Bill, 489, 490–1; Roosevelt Memorial Fund, 550–1
   Truman's opinion of, 11–12
   and WSC: Attlee criticises WSC as worst Chancellor Exchequer of the century, 689, 689–90, 690–2, 714–15, 716; Attlee disputes WSC's claims about whispering campaigns, 1689–90; Attlee does not recommend Peerage for Harris, 178, 213; Attlee sends book and well wishes after WSC's hernia operation, 733; exchange of Christmas greetings, 583; invites WSC to National Service of Thanksgiving, 28–9; photograph of WSC for 10 Downing Street staircase, 103; WSC criticises Attlee, 796–7, 799, 1087, 1091, 1272, 1594, 1679, 1844, 1906, 2120; WSC pledges to work with Attlee toward common goals, 10; WSC proposes Peerages for Brooke, Cunningham and Portal, 5; WSC reports on visit with Truman, 241–2, 263; WSC's earnings from *The Second World War*, 945, 958–9; WSC's opinion of Attlee, 222–3, 1128, 1842
   see also atom bomb; communications; defence; economics; Labour Government
Attlee, Violet Helen Millar, 56, 56 n.2
Attolico, Countess (Eleonara Pietromarchi), 1177, 1177 n.9, 1179
Attorney-General: *see* Shawcross, Hartley William
Auchinleck, Sir Claude John Eyre ('The Auk'), 1100, 1100 n.2, 1230, 1269, 1288, 1313, 1381
Auriol, Vincent, 1661, 1661 n.1

INDEX

Australia
  Australian opinion of British Labour Government, 778
  George VI cancels tour of, 1254, 1256, 1261
  loan repayments to England, 660
  publication of war-time telegrams to Australian Government, 1549–50
  RSC's press conference statements on, 783, 783 n.3
  socialism in, 1594, 1653
  zinc mines, 779
Austria and South Tyrol, 93–4, 102, 370–1, 436, 451–2, 456–7, 464

Baillie, Hugh, 508–12, 508 n.2
Baillieu, Clive Latham, 742–3, 742 n.3
Baldwin, Lord (Stanley)
  biographical information, 354 n.2
  announces abdication of Edward VIII, 1820
  death of, 900, 900 n.5
  East Fulham by-election (1933), 919
  eightieth birthday, 741
  India, 1404
  Labour Party denunciation of (1935), 2189
  Lord Baldwin (May 1950 WSC speech), 1754–6
  National Government of 1931, 2062–3
  publication of Administration papers, minutes and personal correspondence, 354–5
  rearmament of British forces between the wars, 2016
  social legislation, 754
  Thomas case (1936), 1316–17
  WSC criticises in *The Second World War*, 913, 914, 1233
  WSC recalls serving as Chancellor of the Exchequer for, 756, 1600 n.4
  WSC's opinion of, 741
Baldwin, Oliver Ridsdale, 1754, 1754 n.2
Balfour, Arthur James, 1233, 1233 n.1
Balfour, John, 2143, 2143 n.2
Balinski, Ignacy, 437–9, 439 n.1
Balkan nations
  Bulgaria, 786
  Russian sphere-of-interest arrangement with the British, 1995
  Sovietisation of Eastern Europe, 437–9, 1745, 1745 n.2, 1763, 1765–6
Ballard, Frank H., 583–4, 583 n.1
Baltic States
  Lithuania, 265, 268, 280, 295
  reincorporation of into Russia, 265, 268, 376
  Sovietisation of Eastern Europe, 437–9
  WSC asks Sargent for advice on how to respond to Zadeikis, 280, 295
Bancroft School, 104, 104 n.2

Barber, Anthony Perrinott Lysberg, 1663, 1663 n.2
Baring, Evelyn (Earl Cromer), 314, 314 n.1
Barker, Evelyn Hugh, 607, 607 n.1
Barne, Anthony Miles, 58, 58 n.1
Barnes, Ernest William, 1297, 1297 n.1
Barnes, Lady Gunilla, 582, 582 n.1
Barnes, Reginald Walter Ralph, 185, 185 n.1, 582
Barnes, Thomas James, 961, 961 n.1
Barrett, Edward Ware, 1664, 1664 n.2
Barr, George M., 184, 184 n.2, 208, 209, 210
Barrington-Ward, Robert McGowan, 385, 385 n.3, 391
Barrymore, Ethel Mae Blythe, 1465, 1465 n.2, 1465 n.3
Barry, Philip James Quinn, 1499, 1499 n.3
Bartholomew, Harry Guy ('Bart'), 2176, 2176 n.1
Bartley, Reginald James, 777, 777 n.3
Barton, Sir Andrew, 1436, 1436 n.2
Barty-King, George Ingram, 1798, 1798 n.1
Baruch, Bernard Mannes
  biographical information, 211 n.1
  British recognition of Communist China, 1561, 1562
  carving tools for Clare Sheridan, 296, 311
  economics: Baruch discusses with WSC, 744–5, 840–2, 857, 871; economic controls in the US and England, 840–2, 857; Pound Sterling devaluation, 1493–4, 1493 n.1, 1583, 1584–6; US loan to England, 211–12, 213, 269
  Europe: Baruch's Europe visit (1948), 1046, 1125; Baruch's Europe visit (1949), 1424, 1436–7, 1441; United Europe (July 1951 WSC speech), 2122; Western Europe Union proposals, 1289
  at The Other Club, 666
  Sarah Churchill's marriage, 1546
  Truman's national and international policy, 1289–90
  Truman's willingness to use atom bomb, 1383, 1385
  UN Atomic Committee, 269
  world affairs and Anglo-American relations, 1480
  and WSC: discusses the war and the future of the world with WSC, 742–7; friendship with WSC, 1590; WSC asks Baruch to establish close relations with Portal, 320; WSC introduces Rowan to, 1602; WSC plans US visit (1948), 908, 978, 1002–3; WSC sends volume three of *The Second World War* to, 1717; WSC's meeting with Godfrey, 2124–5; WSC's tribute to, 482–3, 486; WSC's US visit (1949),

Baruch, Bernard Mannes *(continued)*
and WSC *(continued)*
1296, 1324, 1331–2, 1333, 1339–40, 1340, 1341, 1343, 1343 n.1, 1347, 1347 n.2, 1348, 1348 n.2, 1349, 1351–2, 1352, 1352 n.1, 1356, 1394–5; WSC thanks for letter and Mergen cartoon, 1423–4
Battenberg, Prince Louis Alexander, 875, 875 n.2
Battle of Alamein, 106–8, 1548, 1910
'Battleaxe', 1099, 1099 n.2, 1269
Battle of Britain, 61
Battle of Stalingrad (film), 724, 726–7, 731–2, 731 n.5, 733
Baxter, Arthur Beverly, 520, 520 n.7, 870
Bazovsky, Milos Alexander ('Igor'), 1194, 1194 n.2
Beaconsfield, Lord (Benjamin Disraeli), 447, 447 n.1, 516, 797, 872, 1628
Beauchamp, Antony: *see* Entwistle, Antony Beauchamp
Beaverbrook, Lord ('Max')
biographical information, 97 n.1
Conservative Party: Aitken reports on HofC and 1922 Committee debates, 520–1; criticisms of Beaverbrook, 97–8; Imperial Policy paper, 1438; minimum wage proposals, 1525; WSC seeks Beaverbrook's advice, 2165, 2174; WSC's Opposition leadership, 493
Daily Express anti-American tone, 999, 999 n.3
Evening Standard by-elections articles, 960, 1326, 1327, 1330
Evening Standard political cartoon of Marshall, 580, 664
Finance Bill (June 1946 WSC speech), 388
National Government of 1931, 2062–3
observes that Eden no longer wishes to speak with him, 1389, 1389 n.1
Sunday Express articles and book on WSC and Montgomery, 528, 528 n.2, 541–2
United States Mutual Defence Assistance Act, 1605
and WSC: Chartwell chickens, 60, 64; congratulates WSC on Order of Merit, 175; CSC advises WSC to not visit Beaverbrook in Jamaica, 1348, 1351–2; feedback and edits for *The Second World War,* 1405, 1409–10, 1975; invites WSC and CSC to Monte Carlo, 783, 835; Morrison publicly withdraws statements about WSC's income, 1077; stroke suffered by WSC, 1476–8, 1479–80
Beck, George Andrew, 2191–3, 2191 n.2, 2193, 2194–5

Bedell Smith, Walter ('Beetle'), 189, 189 n.1, 469
Beel, Louis, 1009, 1009 n.2
Beeton, Isabella Mary, 1924, 1924 n.1
Belcher, John William, 1316, 1316 n.1
Belgium
British policy towards, 1622
European Youth Rally, 1036
Leopold III's statement on 1940 British surrender and evacuation from Dunkirk, 1543–4
Parliamentary Questions on raw materials for atom bomb, 89
post-war restoration and rebuilding of, 371
speeches (WSC): The Foundations of Freedom (November 1945 WSC speech), 136–7; Honorary Degree Conferment (November 1945 WSC speech), 137–9; The Future of Europe (November 1945 WSC speech), 139–41, 158
WSC recalls 21 March 1918 German offensive, 185
WSC's depiction of Belgian Army and King Leopold in *The Second World War,* 1410–11
WSC visits Brussels (November 1945), 142, 145
Bellenger, Frederick John
biographical information, 538 n.2
Finance Bill Amendments, Chairman's Selection (June 1951 WSC speech), 2097
Foreign Affairs (November 1949 WSC speech), 1566
Korean Republic Invasion (Oral Answers), 1770
WSC criticises British Army spending practices in Germany, 660
WSC praises, 538
Bell, George (Bishop of Chichester), 1391, 1391 n.2
Beneš, Edvard, 376, 376 n.1, 967–8, 2061
Ben-Gurion, David, 1867–8, 1867 n.2
Benn, William Wedgwood (Lord Stansgate), 343 n.1, 538, 830
Benson, George, 1113, 1113 n.1
Berggrav, Eivind Josef, 1177, 1177 n.2, 1179
Berlin, Isaiah
biographical information, 909 n.1
feedback for WSC on *The Second World War,* 909, 911, 914, 921, 921 n.1, 966–8, 999
Bernal, John Desmond, 1680, 1680 n.5
Bernhard, Prince (Bernhard Graf von Biesterfeld), 1009, 1009 n.4
Berry, William Ewart: *see* Camrose, Lord (William Ewart Berry)
Bevan, Aneurin ('Nye')
biographical information, 151 n.1

INDEX

Devonport election address (1950), 1625
Greece, 932
Labour Party split (1951), 2168 n.1, 2183–4, 2204, 2215
resigns as Minister of Labour and National Service (April 1951), 2057, 2058, 2070, 2082
WSC comments on improving health of, 656
WSC criticises Bevan: housing rebuilding and repair efforts, 151–2, 306–7, 474–5, 540, 656–7, 719, 747, 1540–1, 1655, 1751; in letter to CSC, 764; in Socialist Blunders speech (July 1951), 2120; in Abadan, Sudan and Bevan – A Trio of Misfortune speech (October 1951), 2187–90; WSC notes Bevan's absence from HofC debates, 1552
WSC criticises Labour Government: coal policies, 752; health insurance proposals, 1017, 1092, 1104; Housing (November 1950 WSC speech), 1921, 1922, 1924–5, 1926, 1927, 1929–30, 1931–2; *Let Us Win Through Together* statement, 1610, 1611–12; 'socialist' policies, 1653, 2210, 2214; steel industry nationalisation, 1236, 1238–9, 2204; Trade Union policies, 1104–5

Beveridge, William Henry, 452, 452 n.2, 1552

Bevin, Ernest
biographical information, 2 n.1
Anglo-American relations: American bomber squadrons stationed in East Anglia, 1273–4; dissolution of Combined Chiefs of Staff, 1514; military alliance proposals, 133–4, 143; and relations with Soviet Russia, 133–4; Truman's opinion of Bevin, 11–12; WSC disagrees with Halifax proposal for UN Trusteeship, 133
Europe: Atlantic Pact, 1371; Bevin warns of Soviet expansion in Eastern Europe and calls for European Union, 930, 930 n.1, 933; Council of Europe, 1152, 1164–5, 1221, 1277; Czechoslovakia, 1028, 1028 n.1; European Unity (March 1950 WSC speech), 1702–3, 1707–8; Four Power Conference (1949), 1416; France, 280–1, 290–1, 398; Hague Conference, 1037; Italy, 371; Marshall Plan conference, 758; The North Atlantic Treaty (May 1949 WSC speech), 1411, 1413–14; Paris peace conference, 379–80; Potsdam Conference, 7; Switzerland, 467–8; United States of Europe proposals, 757, 933–5, 947; Western European Union policy, 1004–5, 1013; WSC suggests French–German partnership, 1705–7
foreign affairs: Albania, 1573; anti-Communist foreign policy, 682, 724, 1063–4; Bevin serves as Foreign Secretary for Labour Government, 2, 113; Bevin steps down as Foreign Secretary, 2014; China, 1970; Conference of Commonwealth Foreign Ministers (1950), 1576; Conservative Party support for Bevin, 1752; Egypt Treaty Negotiations (May 1946 WSC speech), 343; Foreign Affairs (December 1948 WSC speech), 1271, 1272–3; Foreign Affairs (July 1949 WSC speech), 1450–4; Foreign Affairs (November 1949 WSC speech), 1574; Greece, 147–8, 281, 368, 499–500, 932; Laski's criticism of Bevin published in *The Times*, 385; Poland, 781, 788, 788 n.1, 789–90, 805; The Three Circles, Foreign Policy (April 1949 WSC speech), 1387; United States Mission and visit, 497–8; WSC criticises Labour Government foreign policy, 1648–50, 1655–6, 1744; WSC reports on visit with Truman, 241–2, 263; Yugoslavia, 287, 290, 295–6
Labour Government: Attlee plans national broadcast upon surrender of Japan, 6; Cooper's political future, 65–6; demobilisation efforts, 151; employment policies, 1534–5; Employment White Paper, 795, 1551–2; Halifax plans to leave Washington post in May 1946, 160; Middle East oil supplies, 1646; national spending policies, 886; Navy Estimates, 831; proposed jobs for Duke and Duchess of Windsor at British Embassy in America, 168, 310, 337; publication of WSC's war-time Administration papers, 941; WSC's Opposition leadership, 485
personal life: poor health of, 913; death of, 2036, 2131, 2202
WSC praises: in A Civic and Patriotic Duty speech (September 1947), 785; in Conservative Party Annual Conference Address (October 1947), 794; in Foreign Affairs speeches, 365, 366, 497, 505, 531–2, 935–6; in A New Parliament broadcast (February 1948), 963; in A New Parliament speech (July 1948), 1105; in *News of the World* article, 2209
see also Germany; Palestine; Russia

Bidault, Georges-Augustin
biographical information, 383 n.1
Council of Europe, 1152, 1221, 1469
French election results (1946), 383, 560
Hague Conference, 1037

Bidault, Georges-Augustin *(continued)*
  Marshall Plan conference, 758
  WSC meets with in Paris, 2151–2
Billotte, Gaston, 1332, 1332 n.3, 1334
Billotte, Pierre, 1332, 1332 n.2, 1334
Birkenhead, Earl (Frederick Winston Furneaux Smith), 899–900, 899 n.2, 1426
Birkenhead, Lady (Sheila Berry Smith), 899–900, 899 n.2
Birkett, William Norman, 1162–3, 1162 n.2, 1162 n.3, 1179–80
Birla, Ghanshyam Das, 335, 335 n.3
Birley, Oswald Hornby Joseph
  biographical information, 101 n.1
  in Europe with WSC, 1441
  portrait of WSC, 101, 395
  WSC thanks Birley for his interest in WSC's paintings, 1060
  WSC thanks for letter, 1842
Birley, Rhoda Vava Mary Lecky Pike, 1441, 1441 n.1
Birmingham Post, 690–2
Birse, Arthur Herbert, 2077, 2077 n.3
Bisco, Jack, 273, 273 n.2
Bismarck, Otto Eduard Leopold von, 938, 938 n.1
Blackburn, Albert Raymond, 125–6, 125 n.2, 762, 764, 2071–2
Blackett, Patrick Maynard Stuart, 40, 40 n.1, 49, 63
Blair, Patrick James, 596, 596 n.1
Blake, Helen, 741, 741 n.2
Blake, William, 1040, 1040 n.1
Blamey, Thomas Albert, 163, 163 n.2
Bland, (George) Nevile Maltby, 338, 338 n.1
Bland, Portia Ottely, 338, 338 n.3
Blenheim Tapestry, 1713
Blomberg, Werner von, 844, 844 n.3
Blore, Edward, 2077, 2077 n.1
Blum, Léon
  biographical information, 65 n.1
  Council of Europe, 1221, 1230, 1276, 1567
  European Parliamentary Union proposals, 759
  French Foreign Minister in England, 65
  Hague Conference planning, 1005, 1035
  United States of Europe proposals, 600, 1004–6, 1215
  WSC suggests CSC invite Blum to lunch, 78
Blunt, Gerald Charles Gordon, 2029, 2029 n.1
Blunt, Judith Anne Dorothea (Lady Wentworth), 2124, 2124 n.2
Blyton, William Reid, 821, 821 n.1
Boggs, Thomas Hale, Sr, 725–6, 725 n.1
Bogomolov, Alexander Efremovich, 1150, 1150 n.1
Bonaparte, Napoléon, 272, 272 n.3

Bonham Carter, Lady Violet: *see* Asquith, Helen (Lady Violet Bonham Carter)
Bonham Carter, Maurice ('Bongie'), 1600, 1600 n.2
Boothby, Robert John Graham
  biographical information, 451 n.1
  Conservative MP delegates to Council of Europe, 1418, 1419
  Dorothy Macmillan, 1418 n.3
  South Tyrol, 451–2, 452, 456–7, 464
Bossom, Clive, 2195, 2195 n.2
Botha, Louis, 1062, 1062 n.2
Bottomley, Arthur George, 1621, 1621 n.1, 1639
Bowen, Edward Ernest, 1581, 1581 n.2
Bowen, Roderick, 1668–9, 1668 n.1
Bowker, Reginald James, 2103, 2103 n.2
Bowles, Francis George, 294, 294 n.1, 360, 2019, 2095
Boyle, Arthur Brian, 81, 81 n.2
Boyle, Edward, 1934–5, 1934 n.1
Boyle, William Henry Dudley, 2044, 2044 n.3
Bracken, Brendan
  biographical information, 48 n.2
  Baruch discusses British Government with WSC, 746
  Chartwell Literary Trust, 1797
  Conservative Party: Consultative Committee for economic and financial issues, 1267; MP for Bournemouth, 66; WSC's Opposition leadership, 493; WSC's political message of support for Bracken, 117–18
  Control of Investment Bill, 200
  criticises nationalisation of gas industry, 1016
  letter from WSC in Duke of Windsor's memoirs, 1521, 1819–20
  Moorehead's *Montgomery* book, 549
  Morrison publicly withdraws statements about WSC's income, 1077
  Navy Estimates, 992
  The Other Club, 666
  Palestine, 1127, 1127 n.2
  political broadcasting, 979, 1024
  RSC's opinion of, 48
  The Second World War: appointment of Eisenhower as Supreme Commander of Normandy invasion, 1964; references to Poland in, 1099, 1099 n.1; WSC visits Shangri-La with FDR, 1975
  Sikorski Historical Institute appeal, 1379, 1379 n.2
  Wilson recollects WSC's essence as Parliamentarian, 2058–9
  WSC criticises *The Economist*, 397
  WSC criticises *Evening Standard* by-elections article, 1330

INDEX

Braddock, Elizabeth Margaret, 1918, 1918 n.1, 1974–5
Bradley, Omar Nelson, 1757, 1757 n.2, 2075, 2095
Brain, Walter Russell, 1759, 1759 n.1, 2146
Braithwaite, Albert, 2035, 2035 n.1
Brandeis, Louis Dembitz, 270, 270 n.5
Brand, Robert Henry, 212, 212 n.1
Brassey, Thomas, 1694, 1694 n.1
Brazil, 89
Briand, Aristide, 384, 384 n.4, 459
Bridges, Sir Edward
   biographical information, 6 n.3
   Attlee plans national broadcast upon surrender of Japan, 6
   deed for safeguarding Lady Lloyd George's papers, 354
   The Second World War: Anzio operations, 401–2; publication of WSC's wartime papers, minutes and personal correspondence, 465–6, 488, 488–9, 492; publication of WSC's war-time Parliamentary Secret Session speeches, 174–5; WSC's earnings from, 942–3, 958–9
   WSC forms new Government (1951), 2222–3, 2230
   WSC inquires about foreign travel regulations for MPs, 815, 819–20
   WSC inquires about Grigg's pension rates, 130
   WSC plans paper on Russian espionage in Canada, 551
   WSC's salary as Opposition Leader and pension as former PM, 611
Briggs, Harold Rawdon, 2227, 2227 n.2
Bright, John, 473, 473 n.2, 661, 825, 1931
British Armed Forces
   British Commonwealth, 315–19, 1258–61, 2186–7
   compulsory service in, 597 n.2, 1433–4, 1434, 1556, 2036, 2135–6
   Le Quesne Martel's paper on conscription, 1438–9
   manpower: allocations (November 1945), 130; Defence Memorandum (May 1949), 1407–8; estimates (March 1950), 1673
   National Expenditure Committee (proposed), 677
   rearmament of, 1189–90, 1691, 2014, 2015–16, 2035, 2037, 2203–4, 2226
   recruitment: recruiting efforts (1948), 1189–90; Recruiting for the Forces broadcast (February 1949), 1329–30; recruiting efforts (1950), 1691–2, 1788–9, 1824–5, 1826–7, 1838–9, 1843–4, 1855; voluntary recruitment for, 597
   Resolutions for Thanks to Commanders, 162–3, 166
   Russian forces in Eastern Europe, 511
   shipping requirements, 130
   speeches (WSC): Alamein Reunion Dinner (October 1945), 106–8; Fourth Alamein Reunion (October 1949), 1546–9; Fifth Alamein Reunion (October 1950), 1910–11; National Service Bill (March 1947), 670–7; National Service (April 1947), 687–8; National Service (May 1947), 696–702; Navy Estimates (March 1948), 986–97; Unveiling of the Commando Memorial (May 1948), 1058–9, 1060; Recruiting for the Forces broadcast (February 1949), 1329–30; RAF Benevolent Fund (September 1951), 2152–3
   Time article on WSC as Cassandra, 1287–8
   troops' opinion of WSC after election loss, 61–2, 75
   WSC criticises Labour Government policies, 830–1, 1287–8, 1689–99
   WSC and Montgomery discuss readiness of, 1072–3, 1073, 1074, 1168–9
   see also British Army; defence; demobilisation; national service; Royal Air Force (RAF); Royal Navy
British Army
   4th Hussars, 58–9, 77–8, 184–5, 597
   Eighth Army, 106–8, 178, 1546–9
   13th Paratroop Battalion, 539, 539 n.1
   XIII Corps meeting in Trieste, 47, 55
   14th British Imperial Army, 25, 97, 101, 470, 847
   51st Highland Division, 301–2
   National Service, 1689–91
   Queen's Own Oxfordshire Hussars, 445
   State of the Armed Forces Memorandum, 1168–9
   WSC criticises Labour Government policies, 1689–92
   WSC criticises merging of Calvary Regiments with Royal Armoured Corps in Army Estimates, 597, 613
   WSC disagrees with suspension of Territorial Army units, 445
British Broadcasting Corporation (BBC)
   Communism and BBC broadcasts, 980–1
   political broadcasts on, 398, 522, 523, 525, 980–1, 1025, 2027, 2034
   Soviet propaganda themes monitoring report, 1198–9
   WSC suggests BBC broadcast for Czechs who escaped from Czechoslovakia, 1023, 1027, 1027 n.2

British Commonwealth and Empire
  Anglo-American military alliance (proposed), 133–4, 236–7, 239
  Baruch discusses with WSC, 840
  Conference of Commonwealth Foreign Ministers (1950), 1576
  Conservative Party policies, 683, 1438
  emigration of English citizens to, 768–9
  Imperial Preference, 533–4, 2162
  Labour Government use of 'Commonwealth' as alternative to 'Empire', 1203–6
  Prime Ministers' Conference (1951), 1939
  'Rule Brittania!' song, 1226–7
  speeches (WSC): The Future of Europe (November 1945), 141; The Sinews of Peace (March 1946), 231, 236–7, 239; The Needs of a Sick World (April 1946), 303–4; The British Commonwealth (May 1946), 315–19; Burma (December 1946), 580–2; Burma Independence Bill (November 1947), 846–9; Britain in Peril (December 1947), 883–4, 890; Perils Abroad and at Home (October 1948), 1188, 1199; Ireland, Relations with the Commonwealth (November 1948), 1258–61; The Three Circles, Foreign Policy (April 1949), 1386–7; The Anglo-American Alliance (July 1950), 1778–9; Ulster (October 1951), 2186–7
  WSC cites importance of British naval power to, 986, 992–3
  WSC praises devotion of members to England, 802
  WSC promotes unity and preservation of, 680, 802, 1541
  see also Dominion Governments; India
British Information Services, 1375–8, 1375 n.3, 1423
British Mercantile Marine, 2049
British Somaliland, 1771–2, 1787
Broadhurst, Harry ('Broady'), 447, 447 n.4
Brockway, Archibald Fenner, 1770, 1770 n.1
Brogan, Denis William, 179–80, 179 n.1, 392
Brook, Norman Craven
  biographical information, 921 n.2
  Crown copyright on WSC's personal minutes written while WSC was in office, 959, 961–2
  publication of WSC's war-time Administration papers, minutes and personal correspondence, 940–3, 943, 943 n.2, 983–4, 984 n.1, 2030–1
  The Second World War: feedback and suggested edits for, 921, 955–6, 956, 1142–3, 1393, 1402, 1842–3; publication of war-time telegrams to Australian Government, 1549–50, 1550 n.1; publication of WSC's war-time correspondence with Smuts, 2030–1; WSC's earnings from, 942–3, 958–9
  WSC forms new Government (1951), 2222–3, 2226
Brooke, Sir Alan: *see* Alanbrooke, Lord (Alan Francis Brooke)
Brooke, Rupert Chawner, 1707, 1707 n.1
Brooke-Popham, Henry Robert Moore, 555, 555 n.1
Brown, Douglas Clifton
  biographical information, 3 n.3
  Complaint of Privilege, 2019–20, 2022
  elected Speaker of the House of Commons, 3
  Independent candidate rivals Brown for Hexham seat, 1657
  India, Commonwealth Relations (Oral Answers), 1399
  India Transfer of Power, 728
  Ireland, Relations with the Commonwealth, 1259
  Parliamentary Questions on raw materials for atom bomb, 89, 92, 99
  Representation of the People Bill, 970–1, 972, 974, 975, 976
  Table Office and Clerks, 955, 957
  Town and Country Planning Bill and Parliamentary Democracy, 632
  treatment of German Field Marshals, 1213–14
  WSC criticises British Communist Party, 366
Brown, Ernest, 584, 584 n.1
Brown, Francis David Wynyard, 1996, 1996 n.1
Browning, Frederick, 597, 597, 597 n.1, 613
Brown, John Wesley, 1870, 1870 n.3, 2204
Brown, William John, 520, 520 n.3, 541
Bruce, Ethel Dunlop, 91, 91 n.3, 92
Bruce, Pamela Alice (Lady Digby), 176–7, 176 n.1
Bruce, Stanley Melbourne, 91, 91 n.3, 92
Brugmans, Hendrik, 1036, 1036 n.3
Brundrit, Reginald Grange, 1101, 1101 n.4
Brussels University, The Foundations of Freedom (November 1945 WSC speech), 136–7
Bryan, Paul Elmore Oliver, 1350–1, 1350 n.1
Buchan-Hepburn, Patrick George Thomas, 1098–9, 1098 n.1, 1713
Buchan, John, 2079, 2079 n.2, 2089
Buckle, George Earle, 872, 872 n.2
Bulgaria, 786
Bullitt, William Christian, 167, 167 n.3
Bulmer-Thomas, Ivor, 1218, 1218 n.1
Burchard, John Ely, 1347, 1347 n.1, 1365, 1370
Burckhardt, Carl Jacob, 467, 467 n.3, 1179
Burke, Edmund, 377, 377 n.1, 615, 699, 2213

INDEX

Burma
  British Army in, 675
  British loan to, 1740
  Karen people, 1740 n.1
  massacres in, 829, 1208
  speeches (WSC): Burma (December 1946), 580–2; Burma Independence Bill (November 1947), 846–9
  WSC discusses with Salisbury, 1405
  WSC warns of civil war in, 849, 1090
Burns, Robert, 937, 937 n.1
Bussche-Streithorst, Axel von dem, 1178, 1178 n.5
Butcher, Harry C., 189, 189 n.2, 191
Butcher, Herbert Walter, 1627, 1627 n.2
Butler, Chas, 892, 892 n.1
Butler, David, 1998–2000, 1998 n.1
Butler, Richard Austin ('Rab')
  biographical information, 201 n.1
  at Chartwell, 1590
  Conservative Party: Consultative Committee, 1713; Industrial Policy Committee, 723, 799; Party statement (1951), 2148; policy document proofs, 1439; WSC forms new Government (1951), 2230
  Education Act, 1017, 1092
  Germany, 498
  India: Ambedkar appeals to WSC regarding future of Untouchables, 518; Attlee calls meeting with Liberals and Conservatives regarding, 399; India Committee, 726; India Independence Bill, 738–9; new Indian Constitution ceremony (1950), 1584; offer of Commonwealth status for, 330; Resolution regarding fate of minorities and Indian States, 450
  Middlemen's profits, 1762–3
  National Insurance Bill, 201
  Voluntary Schools in England and Wales, 2191–2, 2193, 2194
  von Weizsäcker's trial, 1177, 1223 n.5
Byers, Charles Frank, 702, 702 n.1, 1615, 1821
Byng, Julian Hedworth George, 1683, 1683 n.1
Byrnes, James Francis
  biographical information, 11 n.3
  Byrnes comments on growing tension between the US and Russia, 508–9
  Far East Yalta Agreement, 202, 202 n.1
  opinion of Attlee and Bevin, 11, 11 n.3
  Russian forces in Eastern Europe, 569
  sends WSC speech about war-time decisions made by WSC, FDR and military leaders, 1144, 1156
  South Carolina governor's election campaign, 1546
  thanks WSC for copy of *The Gathering Storm*, 1144
  US loan to England, 211–12
  WSC meets with, 469
  WSC plans The Sinews of Peace speech, 212–13, 242
  WSC thanks for letter, 68

Cabinet minutes
  publication of WSC's war-time papers, minutes and personal correspondence, 487, 492, 940–2, 944–5, 955–6
  WSC forms new Government (1951), 2228–32, 2233–4
Cadogan, Sir Alexander
  biographical information, 16 n.1
  Atlantic Meeting notes for WSC, 1310–11
  British representative to the UN, 1278
  Franckenstein appeals to WSC regarding South Tyrol, 93–4
  Stettinius's letter about Yalta Conference, 1351
  thanks WSC for second volume of *The Second World War*, 1434
  WSC thanks for letter and encourages future work, 16
Cadogan, William, 1713, 1713 n.2
Caesar, Julius, 844, 844 n.2
Cairo Conference, 579
Calculated Risk (Clark), 1997
Callaghan, (Leonard) James, 1687, 1687 n.1, 2048–9, 2133
Camacho, Manuel Ávila, 127, 127 n.1, 157
Camb, James, 1115, 1115 n.1
Campbell-Bannerman, Henry, 1865, 1865 n.1
Campbell, Craig D., 80, 80 n.3
Campbell-Johnson, Alan, 738–40, 738 n.4
Campbell, Ronald Hugh, 1170, 1170 n.3
Campbell, Ronald Ian, 226, 226 n.2
Campion, Gilbert Francis Montriou, 38–9, 38 n.1
Camrose, Lady (Mary Agnes Corns Berry), 900, 900 n.1
Camrose, Lord (William Ewart Berry)
  biographical information, 23 n.1
  at Chartwell, 2140, 2141
  Commons Chamber reopening, 1915
  Conservative Party: post-election strategy (1950), 1720; General Election (1951) Gallup Polls, 1994; Woolton suggested for Conservative Party Chairman, 396–7; WSC's political future, 24
  CSC dines with, 899–900
  The Second World War: feedback and edits for, 911, 921, 921 n.1, 954, 1714–15, 2143; offers for serialization book rights to, 554, 556–7, 595; radio rights for, 1061; sixth volume proposed for, 1356–7, 1378, 1714–15; WSC negotiates contract for,

Camrose, Lord (William Ewart Berry) *(continued)*
  The Second World War (continued)
    594, 761; WSC plans multi-volume account, 491–3, 492 n.1; WSC's earnings from, 1030
  WSC asks Eisenhower to meet with, 1866, 1878
  WSC discusses atom bomb with, 23
  WSC establishes trust for personal and war papers, 396
  WSC's drinking habits, 397
  WSC sends painting and New Year's greetings to, 1588
Canada
  British Labour Government use of 'Commonwealth' as alternative to 'Empire', 1204
  Empire Preferences policy, 803
  European Army proposals, 1863
  Sir Harold Alexander appointed Governor-General of, 14
  Permanent Defence Agreement with the US, 231
  Post-War Higher Defence Organisation, 281–2
  Quebec Agreement of 1943, 2007–8
  socialism in, 1653
  Soviet espionage in, 374, 551
  WSC praises King's leadership of, 113–14, 375
  WSC's Atomic Bomb statement, 20
Canaris, Erika Waag, 1178, 1178 n.6
Canaris, Wilhelm Franz, 2009, 2009 n.2
Canby, Henry Seidel, 923, 923 n.1
Cane, Cyril Hubert, 1980, 1980 n.2, 1982
Canning, George, 317, 317 n.2
Carr, Edward Hallett, 391, 391 n.1
Carton de Wiart, Adrian, 26–7, 26 n.3, 73, 1410–11
Carton de Wiart, Edmond, 1410, 1410 n.1
Casasola, Roland William, 1679, 1679 n.1
Casey, Richard Gardiner, 777, 777 n.2, 778
Casey, William Francis, 1196, 1196 n.2
Catholic University of Louvain, Honorary Degree Conferment (November 1945 WSC speech), 137–9
Cavendish, Spencer Compton (Lord Hartington), 276, 276 n.1
Cecil, Lord (Edgar Algernon Robert, 'Bob'), 384–5, 384 n.2, 392, 436, 451–2, 1662–3, 1667
Cerberus, 1248, 1248 n.1
Ceylon, 1939
Chadwick, James, 19, 19 n.1, 21
Chain Stations Home Service Low Cover (CHL), 613, 613 n.1
Chamberlain, (Arthur) Neville
  biographical information, 82 n.1
  conscription policies, 671
  Conservative Party in 1931, 1404
  Eden's 1938 resignation as Foreign Secretary, 948, 953, 956, 977
  Halifax disagrees with WSC's characterization of Chamberlain's settlement with Hitler, 1180
  housing policies, 1638
  Labour Party criticism of, 2215
  Palestine White Paper, 82, 428
  Stanley serves in Government of, 1966
  timing of WSC's control over wartime COS directives, 352
  WSC's depiction of in *The Second World War*, 913, 914, 1234
Chamberlain, (Joseph) Austen, 522, 522 n.2, 1233, 1755
Chamberlain, Ronald Arthur, 1570, 1570 n.1
Chancellor of the Duchy of Lancaster: *see* Dalton, Edward Hugh John Neale
Chancellor of the Exchequer: *see* Cripps, Sir Stafford; Dalton, Edward Hugh John Neale; Gaitskell, Hugh
Chandor, Douglas, 98, 98 n.2, 128
Channon, Henry ('Chips')
  biographical information, 3 n.1
  attends new Parliament assembly after Conservative election loss, 3
  Debate on the Address (October 1947 WSC speech), 837
  dines with WSC and CSC, 1127–8
  lunches with WSC and CSC, 1309
  WSC addresses 1922 Committee, 37
  WSC predicts election win (1948), 1072
  WSC pretends deafness in Parliament Lobby, 2103
Channon, Henry Paul Guinness, 837, 837 n.2
Charles II (King of Sweden), 180, 180 n.6
Charles I, King, 1203, 1203 n.1
Charles, Prince (Count of Flanders)
  biographical information, 468 n.2
  WSC declines theatre outing, 871
  WSC sends volume of *The Second World War* to, 1881, 1919–20, 1920 n.1
  WSC thanks for visit and sends well wishes, 468–9
Charles, Prince of Wales (Charles Philip Arthur George), 1249–50, 1249 n.1
Charles-Roux, François, 1170, 1170 n.4
Chartwell
  butterflies for grounds, 387
  cottage, 51, 64, 72–3
  Crusade in Europe (film) showing, 1430
  CSC at, 1076, 1982–3
  CSC proposes leaving to grandson Winston, 1158–9
  farming: chickens, 60, 64; dairy cows, 1724–5; garden, 765; salary increase for

INDEX

Soames serving as Farm Manager, 947–8, 949; Soames reports on economic conditions to WSC, 1011–12; WSC thanks Marnham for cutting corn, 451
Marnham sells farm to WSC, 496–7
Maryott Whyte ('Cousin Moppett', 'Nana') cooks for WSC and CSC, 12, 28, 43–4
Montgomery and WSC lunch at, 1073, 1073 n.2, 1074
National Trust purchases from WSC (November 1946), 561
protection of black swans from freezing lakes, 1583
renovations: Fish Pool instructions, 131–2; German prisoners work on landscape restoration, 50, 60, 131, 181, 685, 816, 845, 846, 892, 906; new water reservoir, 1764; progress of, 64, 67, 78, 916, 1590; roof repairs, 63; WSC's instructions for restoration of landscape and grounds, 50–1, 181, 685, 815–16, 845–6, 892–4, 905–6, 912, 1355–6, 1587–8
secretarial and accounts staff, 28, 37–8
WSC asks CSC for news of while in Marrakech, 902, 912
WSC at: bathing, 764; 'Chartwell Bulletin' for CSC, 1718–20; and CSC move back to after WSC's election loss, 12–13, 27–8, 28 n.2, 43–4; hunting, 762; painting, 1033, 1060
Chartwell Literary Trust, 1158–9, 1181, 1344, 1344 n.1, 1521, 1764, 1797–8
Chater, Arthur Reginald, 1771–2, 1771 n.1, 1787
Chatfield, Alfred Ernle Montacute, 321, 321 n.1
Chavasse, Christopher, 2022, 2022 n.2
Chenery, William Ludlow, 483, 483 n.1, 483 n.2, 554
Cherwell, Lord (Frederick Lindemann, 'the Prof')
biographical information, 17 n.2
atom bomb: exclusion from Atomic Bomb Committee under Attlee's government, 40, 49, 63; Quebec Agreement of 1943, 1961–2; retention of Atomic Bomb Committee within Ministry of Supply, 1820, 1825; talking points for Parliamentary Debate on world policy for, 95–6; WSC's Atomic Bomb statement, 17–18; WSC's press statement on making atom bombs, 2005
Chartwell Literary Trust, 1797
Conservative Party: WSC invites Cherwell to join Shadow Cabinet (1945), 42; Consultative Committee, 1740–1, 1741 n.1; economic planning and policies, 779–80; WSC discusses election strategy with Cherwell (1951), 1989; WSC forms new Government (1951), 2228
defence: British jet fighter production rates, 1542–3; weaponry report, 1882–3, 1916; WSC's Defence Memorandums (May 1949), 1428, 1431
food: bread rationing in England, 408; world food shortages, 362; WSC comments on draft statement on global food shortages, 337–8
in Marrakech with WSC, 1980, 1981, 1986, 1987, 1989
The Second World War: atom bomb chapter, 1601; feedback and suggested edits for, 1989, 2146; Foot's review of *The Grand Alliance*, 1822–3
WSC declines visit to English Speaking Union, 337
Chiang Kai-shek, 26–7, 26 n.2, 73, 203–4, 2066
Chichester, Arthur (Lord Templemore), 66, 66 n.2
Chichester, Desmond Clive, 66, 66 n.1
Chiefs of Staff (British)
Campaign Star qualifications, 100
Cold War Higher Defence Policy, 1147–51
Japan: Ismay and COS congratulate WSC on V-J Day, 33; WSC's Atomic Bomb statement, 18
National Service Bill, 689, 695, 696–9
proposed removal of British troops from Egypt, 313, 314, 345
Second World War: final months of Wavell's command, 1288, 1393; Ismay agrees to destroy COS minute with WSC's criticism of Tedder, 172; Ismay's recollections on despatch of tanks to the Middle East, 529–30; 'Jubilee' (Dieppe raid), 711, 1821–2, 1848, 1849–50; Marshall and war-time Supreme Command decisions, 601–2, 603; publication of WSC's war-time Administration papers, minutes and personal correspondence, 955–6, 983–4, 984 n.1; 'Tiger' and Crete operations', 1131
State of the Armed Forces Memorandum, 1168–9
unveiling of WSC's portrait at the Junior Carlton Club, 1977–8
WSC suggests COS appointments to Attlee, 14, 15, 22
Chiefs of Staff (Combined)
dissolution of, 1514–15, 1526, 1956, 2054–5
Marshall and war-time Supreme Command decisions, 601–2, 603
WSC recommends continuation of CCS Committee (November 1945), 134
Chifley, Joseph Benedict, 563, 563 n.1, 1254

China
- Anglo-American policy towards, 1986–7
- British defence of Hong Kong, 1283, 2073–4
- British policy towards, 1970, 2087
- British recognition of Communist China, 1561, 1562, 1569, 2066
- Exports to China (May 1951 WSC speech), 2066–76, 2079
- Far East Yalta Agreement, 203–4
- Fletcher provides Far East trade overview to WSC, 2063–5 n.1
- Malayan rubber shipments to, 2063, 2064, 2071
- Soviet expansion into, 1831, 1954–5
- WSC advises against English entanglement in, 1970

Cholmondeley, Lord, 75, 75 n.1, 78
Cholmondeley, Sybil Sassoon, 75, 75 n.2
Christ, George Elgie, 2029, 2029 n.2, 2211
Christmas
- in London (1945), 157
- in Marrakech (1947), 909–10

Churchill, Clarissa, 625, 625 n.5
Churchill, Clementine Hozier (CSC; later Baroness Spencer-Churchill)
- biographical information, 12 n.2
- Aix-en-Provence visit, 1146, 1170
- Brittany visit, 762–3, 763
- charitable work, 56, 67
- Chartwell Literary Trust, 1521, 1797
- Chartwell renovations, 50, 63, 1355, 1587, 1590
- Clarke invites to Florida, 39
- daughter Mary, 42–3, 48–9, 568, 579, 621–2
- daughter Sarah, 53–5, 56, 60, 63, 67, 68, 69, 72, 76–7, 78, 147, 164, 165, 170, 173, 894–5, 898–9, 902–4, 909–10, 915, 917, 1487–9, 1491, 1516, 1524
- death of Jack Spencer-Churchill, 625–7
- dines with the Attlees and the Bruces, 91, 92
- dines with Mackenzie King, 109–10
- Eisenhower plans visit with, 203
- Eisenhower sends regards to, 129
- health, 467, 880, 895, 1076, 2089, 2089 n.1
- lunches with Channon and WSC, 1309
- Morton sends regards to, 815
- Netherlands visit, 334, 338
- Paris visit, 2141, 2145
- Westminster Gardens, 12–13, 27–8, 47
- and WSC: advises WSC to not visit Beaverbrook in Jamaica, 1348, 1351–2; Biarritz correspondence, 2138, 2140, 2140–2, 2142–3, 2143–4, 2145; Brittany correspondence, 762–3, 763, 764–5; Christmas in London (1945), 157; CSC declines to accompany WSC to Conservative Party conference, 1160; feedback and suggested edits for *The Second World War*, 1553; Florida visit planning (1946), 146–7, 164, 165; General Election (1950), 1591–2; instructs Rogers to prevent WSC from gambling in Monte Carlo, 78–9; Italy correspondence, 1717–20; Lake Como correspondence, 55, 56, 58–60, 63, 65, 66–8, 72–3, 76–8; Lake Geneva visit, 392; Madeira correspondence, 1590, 1591; Marrakech correspondence, 896–7, 897, 899–900, 901–2, 906–8, 911–12, 1976–7, 1979–80, 1981–3, 1984, 1986; Marrakech visit planning, 815, 820–1, 854, 880; Oslo visit, 1056; Provence correspondence, 1170; Seretse Khama affair, 1684–5; Seville correspondence, 2026; Sieff asks to meet with WSC, 1224; 'Sous les Vents' villa correspondence, 80–2, 83; space constraints at Hyde Park home, 2028, 2029–30, 2030 n.1; thermostats and fire danger in WSC's bedroom, 1286; in US with WSC (1949), 1348, 1349; WSC appears at new Parliament assembly, 35–6; WSC cries over effects of his political career on CSC, 2059; WSC fails to meet Queen Juliana at Dover, 1940; WSC recalls CSC singing 'In the Gloaming' to him, 67; WSC recovers from hernia operation, 739; WSC suggests inviting Alexander to lunch, 81; WSC thanks CSC for giving him happiness, 1165; WSC writes to CSC from Council of Europe meeting, 1466

Churchill, John (1st Duke of Marlborough), 118, 118 n.2, 180, 322, 333, 340, 352, 396, 1043, 1940, 1953
Churchill, June Osborne
- biographical information, 1323 n.2
- Churchill family trust arrangements, 1392
- General Election (1950), 1592, 1625
- marriage to RSC, 1717, 1720, 1756
- in US with RSC, 1331

Churchill, Mary: *see* Soames, Lady (Mary Churchill)
Churchill, Pamela: *see* Digby, Pamela
Churchill, Randolph Henry Spencer, 261, 261 n.1, 276, 277, 279, 354, 516, 572, 581, 680, 1097, 1628
Churchill, Randolph Spencer (RSC)
- biographical information, 9 n.3
- agricultural land investment death duties, 1578
- American speaking tour, 183, 519, 519 n.2, 614–15
- Australia and New Zealand speaking tour and

INDEX

Far East travel, 777–9, 779 n.3, 812–13
Australia press conference statements, 783, 783 n.3
Baruch meets with, 486, 841, 1331
in Biarritz, 2142, 2144
Bisco praises in letter to WSC, 273
Canyon Kid (racehorse), 1756, 1765
Chartwell, 614, 1159, 2140, 2141, 2142
Churchill family trust arrangements, 1392–3, 1417
CSC purchases home for, 1181
CSC and WSC discuss money and rent situation for RSC and June, 1200–1
dates format, 1387, 1387 n.2, 1390, 1494–5
debts owed by, 1765, 1769, 1776, 1787
divorce settlement with Pamela Digby, 1322–3
Economist article on Palestine, 1057, 1057 n.1
Flandin's trial, 443
friendship with Flandin, 135
friendship with Mordaunt, 59
General Election (1950): RSC loses election bid, 1658, 1660; RSC's opening speech for, 1592; RSC suggests WSC focus on his Liberal past, 1624–5; WSC's Devenport Election Address (February 1950), 1624–5, 1635, 1638, 1642
in Ireland with Lord Fitzwilliam, 88
Korea: RSC in Korea as correspondent for *Daily Telegraph*, 1817–18, 1843, 1851; RSC meets with MacArthur, 1983; RSC speaks at Constitutional Club regarding, 1978; RSC suggests use of atom bomb on, 1960
in London, 109
marriage to June Osborne, 1200–1, 1200 n.3, 1323, 1717, 1720, 1756
Persian oil and ARAMCO, 2120–1
political career, 614–15, 1765, 1787, 1817, 1982, 2008, 2008 n.3
son Winston's health and care, 1309–10, 1342–3
and WSC: drinks champagne with WSC at Chequers, 9; encourages Nicolson to relay comments about RSC to WSC, 61, 62, 78; feedback and suggested edits for *The Second World War*, 1560; RSC apologises to WSC for argument, 48; RSC sends corrected proofs of *The Sinews of Peace* to WSC, 777, 777 n.1; RSC suggests tone of international gathering for WSC's annual Conservative Conference speech (1949), 1529; *The Times* coverage of WSC's criticism of Cripps, 1516–17, 1518, 1519–20, 1520; unveiling of WSC's portrait at the Junior Carlton Club, 1977–8; WSC comments on RSC's land ownership article, 446; WSC criticises proofs of Leslie's book, 1001, 1009; WSC's US visit (1949), 1323, 1333, 1339, 1343, 1349; WSC thanks for copy of *Keesing's Contemporary Archives*, 1977, 1983

Churchill, Sarah Millicent Hermione Spencer (WSC's daughter)
biographical information, 47 n.3
American theatre tour, 1483, 1499
Canada premiere of *All Over the Town*, 1395
Christmas in London (1945), 157
Cooper's Paris farewell party, 880, 896
death of Jack Spencer-Churchill, 626–7
income tax issues, 1487–9, 1491
marriage to Antony Beauchamp Entwistle, 1483, 1546, 1797–8, 1950
meets Truman, 1499, 1516, 1524
in New York, 2090
use of house as photo studio, 1797–8
in Williamsburg, Virginia, 203
and WSC: complains to WSC about his rudeness to Entwistle, 1292–3; describes film shoots to WSC, 627, 627 n.1, 804; in Florida with WSC and CSC, 147, 164, 165, 170, 173; in Lake Como with WSC, 53–5, 56, 60, 63, 67, 68, 69, 72, 76–7, 78; in Marrakech with WSC, 894, 894–5, 896, 897, 901, 902–4, 908, 909–10, 915, 917, 927–8; sends WSC birthday greetings and praises *The Hinge of Fate*, 1950; sends WSC well wishes, 1483; thanks WSC for cheque, 1195; thanks WSC for pictures, 456, 456 n.2; thanks WSC for US visit, 278; writes to WSC and CSC from Rome, 804–5

Churchill, Winston Spencer (WSC)
animals: Canyon Kid (racehorse), 1756, 1765, 1765 n.3; Colonist II (racehorse), 1478, 1719, 1719 n.3, 1746, 1867, 1915, 2092, 2140–1; Rufus II (family dog), 954, 954 n.1, 1155, 1155–6, 1977, 2011
bathing, 56, 58, 392, 764, 828, 1476, 2146
brother Jack, 47, 47 n.2, 157, 625–8, 664–5
car accident involving schoolgirl, 2005
caught in fog walking home, 580
Churchill family trust arrangements, 1344, 1344 n.1, 1392–3
CSC describes WSC's unhappiness to Mary Churchill, 43–4
food and drink: breakfast in bed and alone, 284; dines on caviar at the Union Club, 261; drinking habits, 9, 79, 224, 284, 338, 397, 899, 1880, 2143–4, 2222
friendship with FDR, 550–1
friendship with Tim Rogers, 77–8, 78–9
health: avoidance of long air journeys, 563;

Churchill, Winston Spencer (WSC) *(continued)*
   health *(continued)*
      colds and sore throats, 101, 104, 157, 896, 899, 915, 916, 917, 922; dizziness, 286; dyspepsia, 1759; hernia operation, 730, 730 n.3, 733, 739, 741–2, 879; staph infection, 2011; stroke suffered while attending Council of Europe meeting in Strasbourg, 1476–8, 1479–80, 1759; visits to warm climates, 163, 169, 946
   Lake Como visit, 46
   Lake Geneva visit, 392
   Marrakech visits, 821, 835, 894, 946, 1976–7
   napping, 82, 283–4
   Provence visit, 1129, 1146, 1146 n.3, 1147
   reflects on election loss, 1–2
   reflects on life, 2145
   Riviera visit accommodations, 44–5, 74, 80–1, 83
   smoking habits, 284, 954, 1000, 1168, 1477, 1879–80, 1996
   speaking style, 111, 837
   spending habits, 1764–5
   Sulzberger suggests dictation of stories and anecdotes, 1441
   travels, September 1945–October 1951, 2243–8
   Westminster Gardens, 12–13, 27–8, 47
   WSC and CSC move to Chartwell after WSC's election loss, 12–13, 27–8, 43–4
   WSC discusses his political future with Camrose, 24
   WSC'S letter to Bourke during Second Boer War, 186, 208
   see also Conservative Party; honours and awards; painting (WSC); *The Second World War* (Churchill); speeches (WSC)
Church of Pompey restoration, 563–4, 564 n.1
Chuter-Ede, James Chuter
   biographical information, 631 n.1
   Committee on Privileges Report (October 1947 WSC speech), 838
   Complaint of Privilege (March 1951 WSC speech), 2024
   Criminal Justice Bill, 1111–12, 1113–14, 1117, 1118, 1121–3
   Finance Bill Amendments, Chairman's Selection (June 1951 WSC speech), 2095–8
   Iron and Steel (September 1950 WSC speech), 1874
   Political Gerrymandering (June 1948), 1079–80, 1083–4
   Representation of the People Bill (February 1948 WSC speech), 968–9, 974–5
   Town and Country Planning Bill and Parliamentary Democracy (March 1947 WSC speech), 631
   Voluntary Schools in England and Wales, 2192
   WSC inquires about death sentence for three British soldiers, 1847, 1848
Ciano, Gian Galeazzo, 1052, 1052 n.1, 1157
Citrine, Walter McLennan, 368, 368 n.1, 447, 556
Civil Aviation Debate, 198, 199
civil service expansion and expenditures, 658, 681, 692, 713, 721, 754, 966, 1093–4, 1673
Clarendon, Earl (George Herbert Hyde Villiers), 1661, 1661 n.2
Clarke, Cecil Vandepeer, 1882, 1882 n.1
Clarke, Frank William
   biographical information, 39 n.1
   CSC thanks for letter and invitation to Florida, 39
   WSC plans visit to Florida (1945), 127–8, 146–7, 163–4, 165, 169–70, 173
   invites WSC to Florida (1948), 1195, 1195 n.1
   praises WSC's Congress of Europe speech (May 1948), 1045–6
   thanks WSC and CSC for well wishes and describes US presidential campaign, 1125–6
   train journey to Missouri with Truman and WSC, 226
   WSC keeps late hours during US visit, 189
   WSC plans US visit (1948), 978
   WSC sends Christmas wishes and books to, 567–8
   WSC thanks for cigars, 1000
Clarke, Oliver Fielding, 2022, 2022 n.1, 2023–4
Clarke, Rufus, 895, 895 n.1
Clark, Mark (Wayne)
   biographical information, 299 n.2
   references to WSC in Clark's war memoir *Calculated Risk*, 1997
   The Second World War, 1312–13
   WSC's statement on war-time Supreme Command decisions, 299
Clay, Lucius DuBignon, 1145, 1145 n.4
Clayton, William Lockhart, 211–12, 211 n.2, 355, 363, 533
Clemenceau, Georges, 379, 379 n.1
Clements, John Selby, 13, 13 n.2
Cleveringa, Rudolph Pabus, 327, 327 n.1
Clifford, Clark McAdams, 222–4, 222 n.1
Clive, Robert, 1142, 1142 n.1
coal industry
   Baruch discusses with WSC, 840
   Coal Bill Debate, 199–200, 200–1
   coal production and employment projections, 653
   coal shortages in England, 475, 1989

INDEX

Conservative Party policies, 2164, 2204–5
Dalton criticises coalowners in Gateshead speech, 619–20
domestic coal and electricity consumption, 656
Fuel and Power Crisis (February 1947 WSC speech), 615–20
Horner warns of mining strikes if Conservatives win General Election (1951), 2119–20
WSC criticises Labour Government policies, 649, 652–6, 752, 887–8, 1537
WSC relates Tonypandy story, 1627–8

Coalition Government
Attlee congratulates WSC on V-J Day victory, 35
Coalition Government medallion for George VI, 423
Eden thanks WSC for Coalition Government medallion, 403
housing programme, 719
Labour Government claims of credit for legislation drafted and approved by, 716, 723, 755–6
Political Gerrymandering (June 1948 WSC speech), 1079–84
WSC asks Attlee to invite Conservative colleagues to meeting with George VI, 29, 30

Cobden, Richard, 447–8, 447 n.6
Cockcroft, John Douglas, 19, 19 n.7
Cockran, Anna Louisa Ide, 186, 186 n.2
Cockran, William Bourke, 186, 186 n.3, 230
Cocks, Frederick Seymour, 932, 932 n.3, 1299

Cold War
arms race, 1656, 1712, 1757, 1780, 1785–6, 1795, 1796, 1814–16, 1846–7, 1952–3, 2179–81
Attlee declines to hold Secret Session debate on defence, 1789–90, 1791, 1791 n.1
Baruch discusses Russia with WSC, 745–6
British COS Higher Defence Policy, 1147–51
Council of Europe stance toward European capitals behind the Iron Curtain, 1473
Information Research Department, 1149–50
Le Quesne Martel's paper on conscription, 1438–9
prospects for American bombing of Russia, 877–8
Russian demands at Foreign Ministers conference (September 1945), 82
Soviet propaganda themes BBC monitoring report, 1198–9
speeches (WSC): Perils Abroad and at Home (October 1948), 1182–7, 1198–9; The Communist Menace (March 1949), 1359–63; The Anglo-American Alliance (July 1950), 1779–80; University of Copenhagen Danish–British Society speech notes (October 1950), 1903; Foreign Affairs (November 1950), 1950–7
WSC describes Russian techniques of, 1184–5, 1371–2
WSC predicts intensification of (1950), 1720
WSC promotes idea of summit with Russia, 1650, 1655–6, 1665, 1710–11, 1753–4
WSC refers to Iron Curtain, 233–4, 758, 933
WSC sees US as guarantor of world peace, 1649, 1864, 1951–2, 1972, 2176
WSC speaks out against policy of 'drift', 1794
WSC states that a Third World War is not inevitable, 2176, 2182, 2216–17

Cole, George Douglas Howard, 1429, 1429 n.1
Collins, Robert John, 1269, 1269 n.1
Colville, John Rupert ('Jock')
biographical information, 16 n.2
at Chartwell, 1033
CSC lunches with, 622
death of Jack Spencer-Churchill, 627–8
Foot's review of *The Grand Alliance*, 1822–3, 1909
Japanese surrender (V-J Day), 31
'Morgenthau Plan' for Germany, 33, 36
Potsdam Conference, 731, 731 n.2
thanks WSC for volumes of *The Second World War*, 2144–5
WSC congratulates on upcoming marriage, 1143, 1144
WSC criticises demobilisation efforts (August 1945), 47
WSC's Atomic Bomb statement, 16

Colville, Margaret Egerton ('Meg'), 1144, 1144 n.3
Colvin, Ian Goodhope, 2009–10, 2009 n.1, 2012, 2208

communications
Budget Proposals, Newspaper Publication (Oral Answers), 869–70, 870
categorisation of and responses to post-war letters sent to WSC, 70–1, 94–5
correction of Dalton's selective quotation of WSC's statement on British assistance to European countries, 1475–6
Crown copyright on WSC's personal minutes written while WSC was in office, 959, 961–2
dates format, 1387, 1387 n.2, 1390, 1494–5
Eden's 1938 resignation as Foreign Secretary, 665–6, 948–9, 952–3, 956, 967, 977
Journals of the HofC, War Sessions (1939–1945), 38–9, 39 n.1
Labour Government use of 'Commonwealth' as alternative to 'Empire', 1203–6

2267

communications *(continued)*
  Marshall's statement on enemy tapping of WSC's telephone calls with Truman, 164
  political broadcasting: on the BBC, 386, 397–8, 402–3, 980; Communist views on the BBC, 980–1, 1021–2, 1022–3; controversial political broadcasts, 522–4; current legislation broadcasts, 1023–5; meeting minutes, 424–6, 522–6, 979–82; ministerial broadcasts, 525; note of proposals Annex, 525–6; The Week in Westminster, 981, 1025
  Publication of Teheran and Yalta Decisions (Oral Answers), 204–5
  publication of WSC's war-time Administration papers, minutes and personal correspondence, 354–5, 481–2, 484–6, 487, 488–9, 940–3, 943 n.2, 944–5, 955–6, 983–4, 984 n.1, 985, 1450 n.1, 1549–50, 2030–1, 2031
  statements justifying the resignations of Ministers, 357–9, 363, 640
  Teheran Agreement, 668
  WSC criticises weekly papers as anti-Conservative, 397
  WSC declines lunch with Jinnah and suggests use of different names for their correspondence, 569
  Yalta Conference papers and telegrams, 668–9
Communism
  anti-Communist sentiment in America, 519
  BBC broadcasts, 980–1
  British Communist Party, 365–6, 1541
  British recognition of Communist China, 1561, 1562, 1569, 2066
  Burma, 1740
  China, 1283, 1360, 1416, 2063–5
  Communists within the BBC, 980–1, 1021–3
  election practices in Communist countries, 1084
  Europe: Council of Europe stance toward European capitals behind the Iron Curtain, 1473; Italy, 233, 804–5, 1014; Soviet influence on Western Germany, 774; spread of Communism in Eastern Europe, 1745, 1745 n.2, 1763, 1765–6; United States of Europe proposals, 590; WSC cites need for Western Germany to aid in defence of Europe from Russia, 1692–3; Yugoslavia, 501
  French Communist Party, 285, 316
  French election results (1946), 383
  Greece: British policy towards, 932–3, 1282–3; Conservative Party concerns with Communist threat to, 1443, 1444; Greek election results (1946), 368; resurgence of EAM and Communism in, 105–6; Salonica executions, 855–7; WSC discusses Greek political situation with Bevin, 147–8; WSC warns of Communism in, 500
  Korea, 1794, 1808, 2066–8
  Labour Government foreign policy, 682, 724, 1063–4, 2039–40
  Labour Party refuses affiliation with, 285
  Russia: Attlee warns of Soviet Communist imperialism, 937; British COS Higher Defence Policy, 1148–51; Russian espionage in Canada, 112–13; WSC criticises Soviet concentration camps, 1297; WSC discusses possibility of war with, 937–40; WSC warns against Soviet expansion in Central and Eastern Europe, 232–3, 237
  Shaw discusses English politics with WSC, 447–8, 453
  speeches (WSC): The Sinews of Peace (March 1946), 232–4, 237–8, 239, 253–4, 261–2; 'Every Dog His Day' (October 1946), 472–3, 479; Communism (October 1946), 505; A Civic and Patriotic Duty (September 1947), 785–6; Conservative Party Annual Conference Address (October 1947), 796; Al Smith Memorial (October 1947), 809–11; The Communist Menace (March 1949), 1357–64; University of Copenhagen Danish–British Society speech notes (October 1950), 1901–3; North Atlantic Supreme Commander (April 1951), 2047, 2053; Exports to China (May 1951), 2066–76
  Wallace's Oslo speech, 682, 724
  WSC compares Labour Government to, 1243–4, 1460, 1609
  WSC criticises Labour Government as poor defence against, 1593–4
  WSC criticises as threat to Christian civilization, 233–4, 590, 1373, 1794
  WSC praises common Government and Opposition resistance to, 963, 1031, 1063–4
  WSC reiterates opposition to, 272–3
Compton, Karl Taylor, 1296, 1296 n.1, 1370
Connally, Thomas Terry ('Tom'), 1341, 1341 n.1, 1354, 1415
Connell, Charles Gibson, 1070, 1070 n.1
Connelley, Matthew J., 226, 226 n.2
Conolly, Richard Lansing, 1002, 1002 n.4
conscription: *see* national service
Conservative Party
  A.V. Alexander criticises, 648, 658, 670
  by-elections: Dumbarton, 1716; Preston of

INDEX

1946, 199; results and candidates, 553, 596; Sowerby, 1350–1; West Houghton, 2098, 2098 n.1; West Leeds, 1449; WSC encourages unified Party vote, 188, 190; WSC sends Mullan well wishes for upcoming election, 339–40
Chief Whip, 1098–9
Conservative Association for North Newcastle, 2203
Consultative Committee, 1267–8, 1713
criticisms of Beaverbrook and WSC, 97–8
CSC advises WSC to not stay with Beaverbrook during Jamaica visit, 1348
Eden's twenty-fifth year in Parliament, 1450
Europe, 461–2, 679, 2195
Fighting Fund, 1020–1
National Liberal Party collaboration with, 440, 761, 811, 812, 817–19, 819 n.2, 1713, 1821
New York Times article on, 1427, 1435
1922 Committee: Luncheon speech notes (May 1950), 1743–5; meetings, 37, 37 n.1, 520–1, 679, 686, 687, 692; stance on policy towards Russia, 1947, 1949; WSC seeks solidarity with Liberals against Labour Government, 1821
Parliament Bill, 928–9, 929 n.1
Party Chairman, 109, 286, 288, 289, 396–7
policies: agriculture, 801–2, 1070, 1078, 1095, 1459, 1540, 1620; *Britain Strong and Free*, 2165, 2186, 2198–9; British policy towards Scotland, 1489–91; budget planning and spending, 1539–41; coal, 2164, 2204–5; economics, 800–1, 802–3, 1070, 1267–8; education, 2164; Election Manifesto, 1625–7; employment, 1535–6, 1609, 1644, 1654; food, 2164; food subsidies, 1636–7, 2165; foreign and world policy principles, 683–5; Four Years' Plan, 155, 723, 2178; Freedom and Empire policy, 521; health, 2164; housing, 1540–1, 1908, 1929–30, 2084–5, 2164; human rights, 1748, 1792, 2197–8; Imperial Policy paper, 1438; Industrial Policy Committee, 723, 799; industry nationalisation, 1538–9, 2163–4; iron and steel industries, 1877, 2163; The Manifesto of the Conservative and Unionist Party, General Election 1951, 2160–5; minimum wage proposals, 1525; National Service, 670–7, 678–9, 686, 686–7, 689, 692, 701, 1616, 1621–2, 2169–70; Party statement (1951), 2148; pensions, 2164; personal property-ownership, 1645–6; policy document proofs, 1439–40; publication of, 341–2, 353; railways and road transport, 2163–4; *The Right Road for Britain*, 1528, 1532, 1538, 1540; taxation, 648–9, 1627, 2173; This is Freedom (August 1950 WSC article), 1835–6; *This is the Road* statement, 1609, 1715–16, 1748; Trade Unions policy ('The Industrial Charter'), 721–3, 754–5, 799, 800, 890, 1016, 1069–70, 1094, 1458, 1528, 2184–5, 2190–1, 2211; WSC article on (January 1951), 1984–5; WSC describes Tory task to rouse British people to sense of greatness, 892; WSC summarises, 479–81, 769–70, 798–9, 824–5, 890–1, 1984–5
political broadcasting, 424–6, 2034
Potsdam Conference, 532
proposed name change for, 440, 442, 444, 449, 479
Seretse Khama affair, 1685
Shadow Cabinet: by-election candidates, 596; Macmillan's managing committee proposal, 957, 957 n.1, 959; National Service Bill, 686, 692; Opposition managing committee proposal, 957, 957 n.1, 959; stance on US loan to England, 168; Stuart reports on effective Opposition debates to WSC, 199; weekly meetings, 286; WSC invites colleagues to join, 42, 76, 81; WSC sends copies of Eisenhower's speech to, 2108; WSC sets up (1945), 42, 76, 81; WSC writes to Eden about critical issues, 1165
speeches (WSC): 'Every Dog His Day' (October 1946), 472–81; Conservative Policy on Home Affairs (March 1947), 663–4; Empire and Freedom (April 1947), 680–5; Trust the People (May 1947), 712–23; A 'Doctor's Mandate' (August 1947), 749–58; A Civic and Patriotic Duty (September 1947), 784–8; Conservative Party Annual Conference Address (October 1947), 793–803; Central Council of the Women's Advisory Committee of the Conservative Party (April 1948), 1013–21; WSC asks Maudling for speech material for upcoming Conservative Fete (June 1948), 1078; Conservative Policy (July 1949), 1456–61; Local Government (October 1949), 1524–5; Conservative Trades Union Congress (October 1949), 1527–9; Conservative Annual Conference (October 1949), 1530–42; The Conservative Point of View (January 1950), 1593–7; 1922 Committee Luncheon speech notes (May 1950), 1743–5; Scottish Unionist

Conservative Party *(continued)*
  speeches (WSC) *(continued)*
    Meeting (May 1950), 1746–54; National and International Politics (July 1950), 1791–7; Conservative Case for an Election (March 1951), 2014–18; The Conservative Case (May 1951), 2080–8; Situation at Home and Abroad (October 1950), 1905–9
  Woolton–Teviot agreement, 1266–7, 1267 n.1
  and WSC: Loraine criticises WSC's absence from England, 190; Macmillan asks WSC to meet with Swainston, 773, 773 n.1; Macmillan requests political message of support from WSC, 114, 116; WSC asks Attlee to invite Conservative colleagues to meeting with George VI, 29, 30; WSC forms new Government (1951), 2219–20, 2220, 2222–5, 2226, 2228–32, 2233–4; WSC plans Primrose League address, 516; WSC praises Eden, 1908–9; WSC praises Woolton, 793, 1103, 1533–4; WSC proposes anti-Labour Government propaganda, 442; WSC's Munich criticisms and pro-Zionism, 1072
  see also General Election (1950); General Election (1951); Labour Government
Control of Investment Bill, 200
Cook, Thomas Fotheringham, 2071, 2071 n.1
Cooper, Alfred Duff
  biographical information, 60 n.1
  Europe: attitudes toward Communism in, 278–9, 285–6; French election results, 383; Paris farewell party, 845, 854, 880, 891, 895, 896
  Foreign Ministers conference in London (September 1945), 65
  political career and future of, 65–6, 88, 820, 844–5
  reviews *Their Finest Hour* on the BBC, 1425
  and WSC: discusses Conservative Party loss and future of English politics with WSC, 64, 75–6; invites WSC to Paris, 60, 72, 76; WSC describes writing of *The Second World War* to, 820–1, 844; WSC invites to join Shadow Cabinet, 76; WSC plans trip to France, 383–4; WSC plans trip to Switzerland, 443
Cooper, Diana Manners, 60, 60 n.2, 64–5, 72, 76, 895
Coote, Colin Reith, 913, 913 n.1
Corbin, Charles, 1230, 1230 n.3
Cornwallis, Wykeham Stanley, 1108, 1108 n.1
Costello, John Aloysius, 1205, 1205 n.1, 1206, 1208, 1258

cotton, Liverpool Cotton Exchange, 651–2, 720, 797, 1191, 1512, 2171
Coudenhove-Kalergi, Richard Nikolaus ('Ejiro')
  biographical information, 384 n.3
  European Parliamentary Union proposals, 758–9
  Pan-European Council proposals, 384, 392, 423, 424, 459, 465
Council of Europe
  August 1950 meeting, 1826
  Bidault attends and speaks at, 1469
  British delegation to, 1130, 1132, 1151, 1152, 1152–3, 1215–16, 1221, 1227, 1228–9, 1230–1, 1231, 1276–8, 1418–19, 1419, 1426, 1432, 1447–8, 1450, 1761–2, 1769, 2101
  Brussels Treaty Powers Foreign Ministers Committee, 1221
  Committee of Ministers, 1708–9
  Conservative Party policy on United Europe, 1732–3
  defence of Western Europe, 1829–32
  German representatives to, 2123
  Human Rights Convention, 1577
  Macmillan criticises Morrison's participation in, 1475
  meeting dates and expenses, 1440, 1448, 1475
  proposals for, 384–5, 392, 423, 424, 459, 465, 1152, 1221
  Spaak's leadership of, 1467, 2123
  speeches (WSC): United Europe (November 1948), 1250–1; Foreign Affairs (July 1949), 1453–5; United Europe (August 1949), 1466–8; A Consultative Assembly of the Council of Europe (August 1949), 1471–4; European Unity and a European Army (August 1950), 1827–32; Foreign Affairs (November 1949), 1566–8
  stance toward European capitals behind the Iron Curtain, 1473
  stance on UN military actions, 1829–32
  WSC attends Strasbourg meeting (1949), 1425, 1440, 1441, 1466
  WSC calls for German inclusion, 1468–70, 1473–4, 1474, 1567–8, 1576–7, 1708
  WSC speaks in support of, 2123–4
Cove, William George, 409, 409 n.1, 575, 674
Coward, Noël Pierce, 13, 13 n.1, 1268, 1268 n.2
Cox, Jacques, 136, 136 n.1
Cox, James Middleton, 1423, 1423 n.1
Cox, Percy, 181, 181 n.1, 451, 496–7
Cox, P. W., 50, 50 n.1
Cranborne, Lord: *see* Salisbury, Lord (Robert Gascoyne-Cecil, 'Bobbety')
Crerar, Henry Duncan Graham, 163, 163 n.1, 1850

Index

Criminal Justice Bill, 1110–23
Cripps, Sir Stafford
  biographical information, 110 n.4
  domestic affairs: coal and electricity consumption, 656; Debate on the Address, 1671, 1675, 1676; electric generating production industry, 660; employment, 1622, 1636; food, 886, 1636–7; Housing, 1925; Iron and Steel Bill, 1246–7, 1248; Liverpool Cotton Exchange, 651–2, 720, 797, 1191, 1512; Nationalisation, 1430; National Service Bill, 687; A New Parliament, 962, 964, 965; Parliament Bill, 889; political broadcasts on the BBC, 980; Recruiting for the Forces, 1329
  economics: The Budget (April 1950 WSC speech), 1721–32; Economic Situation (March 1947 WSC speech), 647; National Savings Campaign, 1648; Pound Sterling devaluation, 1493–4, 1499–500, 1503–14, 1516–17, 1533, 1579
  Hitler's invasion of Russia, 1823
  India: Ambedkar appeals to WSC regarding future of Untouchables, 518; British policy towards, 569–70, 1193; Constituent Assembly procedures, 576; Cripps Mission (1942), 408–9, 411, 633, 634–8; Interim Government (1946), 414; Hyderabad and Kashmir (July 1948 WSC speech), 1133
  Middle East: Anglo-Persian Oil Company, 2133; Palestine (August 1946 WSC speech), 427, 428, 431–2
  and WSC: Cripps sends Christmas and New Year greetings to WSC, 146; *The Times* coverage of WSC's criticism of Cripps, 1516–17, 1518, 1519–20, 1520; WSC apologises for his criticism of Cripps, 1518, 1521–2, 1522–3, 1523; WSC sends well wishes, 2009, 2032, 2093, 2218; WSC's opinion of, 907, 1580; WSC thanks for diary extracts, 925; WSC thanks for letter regarding disposition of gifts, 1030
Croft, Henry Page, 7–8, 7 n.2, 24
Cromer, Earl (Evelyn Baring), 314, 314 n.1
Cromwell, Oliver, 150, 150 n.1
Crookshank, Harry Frederick Comfort, 200, 200 n.3, 732, 2229
Crossman, Richard Howard Stafford, 701, 701 n.1, 1536–7, 1783–4, 2129–30
Crosthwaite-Eyre, Oliver, 452, 452 n.3
Crowder, Frederick Petre, 161, 161 n.1
Crowley, Leo Thomas, 41, 41 n.3
Crowther, Geoffrey, 397, 397 n.1

Crowther, James Gerald, 1680, 1680 n.1, 1680 n.6
Cuba, 189, 193–7
Cunliffe-Lister, Philip: *see* Swinton, Lord (Philip Cunliffe-Lister)
Cunningham, Sir Andrew Browne
  biographical information, 5 n.1
  Attlee plans national broadcast upon surrender of Japan, 6
  blockships information for *The Second World War*, 1559, 1559–60, 1561, 1561 n.2
  North Atlantic Supreme Commander (April 1951 WSC speech), 2044
  Resolutions for Thanks to Commanders, 162
  with WSC in Lake Como, 53
  WSC proposes Peerage for, 5, 24–5
Cunningham, John Henry Dacres, 53 n.1, 401
currency
  Devaluation of the Pound (September 1949 WSC speech), 1499–514
  Debate on the Address (March 1950 WSC speech), 1675
  Imperial Preference, 533–4, 800–1, 803, 1188, 1504
  Pound Sterling devaluation, 1492, 1492–3, 1493–4, 1493 n.1, 1496–7, 1536, 1554–5, 1579, 1583, 1584–6, 1595, 1665, 1721–2, 1747, 2035, 2085, 2116–18, 2161, 2189–90
Curtis, Lionel George, 384, 384 n.5, 436
Cyrankiewicz, Józef, 789, 789 n.2
Czechoslovakia
  arms trade with China, 2064
  Bazovsky appeals to WSC regarding Slovak independence, 1194
  British policy towards, 376
  conversion of Czechoslovak railways to Russian gauge, 527–8
  Masaryk's death, 998, 998 n.1, 1014, 1362
  Sovietisation of, 1014, 1184, 1361–2, 1373, 1569–72, 1902
  stance towards Russia and Western Europe, 376, 967–8
  WSC disagrees with UN Security Council membership of, 1571–2
  WSC suggests all-Party HofC meeting for Czechs who escaped from, 1028, 1028 n.1
  WSC suggests BBC broadcast for Czechs who escaped from, 1023, 1027

Daily Express, 97–8, 999, 999 n.3, 1994
Daladier, Edouard, 65, 65 n.6
Dale, Henry Hallett, 18, 18 n.2
Dalton, Edward Hugh John Neale
  biographical information, 113 n.2
  Council of Europe, 1277–8

2272 INDEX

Dalton, Edward Hugh John Neale *(continued)*
  domestic affairs: Coal Bill Debate, 199, 617; Dalton criticises coalowners in Gateshead speech, 619–20; Nationalisation (May 1949 WSC speech), 1429; Princess Elizabeth's annuities, 851–2, 852–3, 858; Shaw discusses English politics with WSC, 448
  economics: British wartime debt, 2128; Budget Debate, 294; Budget Proposals, Newspaper Publication (Oral Answers), 869–70; Finance Bill, 388–90; Fuel and Power Crisis, 616, 617, 619–20; US loan to England, 213, 269; wage increase freeze and Stock Exchange collapse, 2172
  Germany, 498, 532
  Labour Party: declines role on United Europe Committee, 1063; WSC criticises budget planning and spending, 681–2, 687, 713, 752–3, 965, 1092–3; WSC criticises industry nationalisation, 1066; WSC questions cost of civil service expansion and expenditures, 658
  and WSC: Private Office correction of Dalton's selective quotation of WSC's statement on British assistance to European countries, 1475–6; WSC attempts to contribute to Church of Pompey restoration, 563–4, 564 n.1; WSC criticises Dalton, 305–6, 720, 800, 885, 1017, 1191, 1632–3, 1792; WSC's salary and expenses, 596–7; WSC's salary as Opposition Leader and pension as former PM, 611
Darlan, Jean Louis, 174–5, 174 n.3
Darling, William Young, 185, 185 n.6, 209, 1716
Darnley, Earl (Esme Ivo Bligh), 95, 95 n.1
Darwin, Sir Charles Galton, 19, 19 n.6
Davenport, John, 262, 262 n.1
Davidson, John Colin Campbell, 2062, 2062 n.3
Davies, Claude Nigel Byam, 2008, 2008 n.2
Davies, Clement
  biographical information, 399 n.2
  Finance Bill Amendments, Chairman's Selection, 2096–7
  General Election (1950): Davies questions exclusion of Liberals from National Liberal-Conservative meetings, 1597–8, 1602–4, 1604, 1604 n.1; Lambert praises Davies, 1607; RSC suggests WSC focus on his Liberal past, 1624–5; WSC criticises Liberal Party electoral deadlock plans, 1618, 1668–9
  India: Attlee calls meeting with Liberals and Conservatives regarding, 399; India, Commonwealth Relations (Oral Answers), 1400; India Independence Bill, 738–9
  Liberal Party: WSC criticises Liberals during Blackpool Conservative Party Conference, 473; WSC seeks solidarity with against Labour Government, 1733, 1734
  National Service Bill, 672
  Palestine, 428–9
  Tshekedi Khana Banishment, 2099
  Woolton's opinion of, 1821
  and WSC: WSC criticises Labour Government economic planning policies, 661; WSC forms new Government (1951), 2224; WSC notifies Attlee of his intent to formally request the recall of Parliament, 1832; WSC's opinion of, 1821
Davies, Cyril Noel, 78, 78 n.2
Davies, Harold, 1568, 1568 n.1, 2069, 2072
Davignon, Jacques Henri Charles Francois, 1177, 1177 n.5
Davin, Daniel Marcus, 1542, 1542 n.2
Dawson, Bertrand, 1819, 1819 n.2
D Day: *see* Normandy invasion
Deakin, Arthur, 1652, 1652 n.2, 1729
Deakin, Frederick William Dampier ('Bill')
  biographical information, 762 n.2
  Conservative Party trade unions policy, 2184–5, 2190–1
  Cooper's Paris farewell party, 880, 891
  in Marrakech with WSC, 894, 896, 898, 901, 902, 907, 908, 909, 911, 927
  at Oxford, 966
  Sarah Churchill sends regards to, 925
  The Second World War: feedback and suggested edits for, 762, 880, 978–9, 1057, 1153–5, 1157, 1159, 1170–1, 1174, 1174–5, 1175, 1402, 1403–4, 1560, 2060–1; French language version references to General Prioux, 1334–5; Greek mutiny, 1913–14; 'Jubilee' (Dieppe raid), 1848
  WSC visits Aix-en-Provence, 1129
Deakin, Livia Stela Nasta ('Pussy'), 898, 898 n.1, 901, 907, 910, 915
de Chair, Somerset Struben
  biographical information, 1736 n.1
  Buchan's *Caesar* and Napoleon's memoirs, 2079–80, 2089
  Caesar's *Commentaries* page proofs, 2018–19, 2027, 2089, 2092, 2092 n.1
  Jordan and Israel, Government Decision (Oral Answers), 1736–8
Dedijer, Vladimir, 1994, 1994 n.3
Deedes, William Francis, 2195, 2195 n.1
defence
  Attlee's COS appointments, 14, 15, 22

Index

British Armed Forces preparedness and recruiting efforts (1950), 1824–5, 1843–4, 2014
British merchant fleet, 2042
Central Organisation for Defence white paper, 482, 486
defence budget planning and spending, 1843–4, 1854–7, 2082
Defence Memorandum discussions with Attlee, 1344, 1345, 1346, 1431, 1435, 1435 n.2, 1442, 1445, 1463–5, 1485, 1495–6, 1526, 1557, 1767, 1802–3
dissolution of Combined Chiefs of Staff, 1514–15, 1526
export of British machine tools and diesel engines to Russia, 1860–1
Morrison warns of need for armed forces readiness, 937
National Service Bill, 671, 678, 700, 1689–90, 1852–3, 2135–6
North Atlantic Defence Committee meeting minutes, 1582, 1587, 1741, 1757–8, 1757 n.1, 2054–5
Post-War Higher Defence Organisation, 274, 275–7, 279, 281–2
rearmament, 2188–9, 2203–4, 2215
Soviet military strength and British defence capacity, 1463–5
speeches (WSC): Defence (March 1950), 1686–99; Defence (July 1950), 1801–4, 1807–17; Defence, Government Proposals (September 1950), 1852–64; North Atlantic Supreme Commander (April 1951), 2047; Recruiting for the Forces (February 1949), 1329
United States Mutual Defence Assistance Act, 1598–600, 1604–5, 1606
Western Europe, 1757–8, 1766–7, 1775, 1784
WSC asks for Secret Session debate on, 1757–8, 1766–7, 1775, 1784–5, 1788, 1789–90, 1791, 1791 n.1, 1796–7, 1801, 1803–4, 1805, 1805–6, 1817
WSC criticises Labour Government policies, 1287–8, 1727
WSC's Defence Memorandums (May 1949), 1406–9, 1409, 1428, 1428–9, 1431
see also air defence
demobilisation
manpower allocations (November 1945), 130
pace of, 63, 66, 117–18, 305, 486, 489–90, 536
Russian forces in Eastern Europe, 511
shipping requirements, 130
WSC anticipates HofC debate on, 82
WSC criticises demobilisation efforts, 47, 151, 537–8, 1190
WSC revises views on desired pace of, 502–4

Demosthenes, 507
Denikin, Anton Ivanovitch, 1298–9, 1298 n.1
Denmark
Honorary Degree Conferment, Copenhagen University (October 1950 WSC speech), 1885–7
Order of the Elephant awarded to WSC, 1933
University of Copenhagen Danish–British Society speech notes (October 1950 WSC speech), 1888–904
Deputy Speaker of the House of Commons: *see* Milner, James
Derby, Lord (Edward George Villiers Stanley), 190, 190 n.1
de Valera, Eamon, 345, 345 n.1, 446, 448
de Valera, Juan Vivion, 448, 448 n.3
Devers, Jacob Loucks, 299, 299 n.1
Devonshire, Duke of (Edward William Spencer Cavendish), 1427, 1427 n.1
Dewey, Frances Eileen Hutt, 566, 566 n.2
Dewey, Thomas Edmund
biographical information, 566 n.1
Hoover's 'Gibraltar' speech, 1978, 1978 n.4, 1993
Seligman assesses possible US response to Russian blockade of Berlin, 1145
US Presidential election (1948), 1125, 1340
WSC's US visit (1949), 1340, 1343, 1358
WSC thanks for letter and for hospitality during WSC's US visit, 566
DeWitt Wallace, William Roy, 578–9, 578 n.1, 595
Diamond, John ('Jack'), 1921, 1921 n.1
Digby, Edward Kenelm, 177 n.2, 177
Digby, Lady (Pamela Alice Bruce), 176–7, 176 n.1
Digby, Pamela
biographical information, 176 n.4
CSC lunches with, 900
divorce settlement with RSC, 1322–3
son Winston's health and care, 1309–10, 1342–3
WSC unable to meet with in Europe, 1482
Dill, John Greer, 542, 542 n.1, 601, 1269, 1288, 1823
Disraeli, Benjamin (Lord Beaconsfield), 447, 447 n.1, 516, 797, 872, 1628
Dixon, Pierson John, 2078, 2078 n.3
Djilas, Milovan, 1994–5, 1996, 1996 n.2, 1996 n.3
domestic affairs
cars and petrol for WSC, 32, 44
Civil Aviation Debate, 198, 199
civil service expansion and expenditures, 658, 681, 692, 713, 721, 754, 966, 1093–4, 1673

domestic affairs *(continued)*
   Control of Investment Bill, 200
   Criminal Justice Bill, 1110–23
   death penalty abolishment proposals, 1003
   Fuel and Power Crisis, 615–20
   Government Hospitality Fund, 388
   Imperial Defence College, 282
   Liverpool Cotton Exchange, 651–2, 720, 797, 1191, 1512, 2171
   Ministers and Public Servants, Official Conduct, 1314–20
   National Insurance Bill, 200–1
   Petrol Rationing, 836
   rationing: WSC criticises Labour Government policies, 152–6
   Redistribution Bill, 1078–86, 1088
   Special Powers Bill, 762, 764
   speeches (WSC): Fuel and Power Crisis (February 1947), 615–20; Petrol Rationing (October 1947), 836; Criminal Justice Bill (July 1948), 1110–23; Iron and Steel Bill (November 1948), 1235–49, 1235 n.1; Nationalisation (May 1949), 1429–30; Iron and Steel (September 1950), 1868–78; Housing (November 1950), 1921–32
   Town and Country Planning Bill and Parliamentary Democracy, 629–33
   Trade Disputes Bill, 201
   Transitional Powers Bill, Supplies and Services, 759–60
   Transport Bill, 663–4
   working class reception of WSC's Fuel and Power Crisis speech, 620–1
   see also coal industry; economics; education; employment; food; housing; industry; social legislation
Dominion Governments
   independent status of, 737, 740
   New Zealand, 660, 812–13, 1594, 1653
   Post-War Higher Defence Organisation, 275, 281–2
   proposed removal of British troops from Egypt, 313–14, 350, 351
   publication of WSC's war-time papers, minutes and personal correspondence, 465, 487
   Resolutions for Thanks to Commanders, 163, 166
   speeches (WSC): Burma (December 1946), 580–2; United Europe (May 1947), 709; Burma Independence Bill (November 1947), 846–9
   see also Australia; Canada; South Africa
Douglas, Lewis Williams
   biographical information, 666 n.1
   asks to meet with WSC, 1834
   Bristol University honorary degree, 1544
   Douglas and Smuts reflect on WSC's election loss, 1077–8
   eye injury, 1778, 1778 n.1
   radio rights for *The Second World War*, 1061
   Russia: Anglo-American policy towards, 1936; WSC discusses possibility of war with, 1012–13
   thanks WSC for draft copy of paper, 669
   WSC invites to dine at The Other Club, 666, 669
   WSC suggests meeting with Czechs who escaped from Czechoslovakia, 1028, 1028 n.2
Douglas, William Sholto, 100, 100 n.2
Dowding, Hugh Caswall Tremenheere, 162, 162 n.6
Driberg, Thomas Edward Neil
   biographical information, 73 n.2
   Korea (July 1950 WSC speech), 1782–3
   motion of censure against WSC, 251–2
   North Atlantic Supreme Commander (April 1951 WSC speech), 2051
   sculpting of Roosevelt statue, 562
   WSC's Parliamentary Secret Session remarks about de Gaulle, 174
Druids, 1581
Dudley, Lord (William Humble Eric Ward), 893, 893 n.1
Duff, Juliet, 765, 765 n.1
Dugdale, Arthur, 986, 986 n.1
Dugdale, John, 931, 931 n.2, 986
Dulles, John Foster
   biographical information, 1271 n.1
   lunches with WSC, 2094
   praises WSC's Twentieth Century speech (March 1949), 1380
   Seligman assesses possible US response to Russian blockade of Berlin, 1145–6
   UN meeting in Paris, 1271, 1286
   WSC thanks for copy of speech, 1286
Duncan, Sir Andrew Rae, 108 n.3, 201, 1267
Dunhill, Thomas Peel, 2011, 2011 n.1

Eady, Wilfred Griffin, 2185, 2185 n.1
EAM (Ethniko Apeleftherotiko Metopo, National Liberation Front), 105–6, 1913
Eccles, David McAdam, 200, 200 n.2, 1419, 2148, 2224
economics
   Attlee criticises WSC as worst Chancellor Exchequer of the century, 689, 689–90, 690–2, 714–15, 716
   Baruch discusses with WSC, 744–5, 840–2, 857, 871
   British debt, 841, 2128
   British policy towards Scotland, 1490

British taxation of large incomes, 1724
China: British exports to, 1087, 2066–76, 2070, 2079; Fletcher provides Far East trade overview to WSC, 2063–5
Conservative Party policies, 800–1, 802–3, 1070, 1267–8; taxation, 648–9, 1627, 2173
Control of Investment Bill, 200
currency: Devaluation of the Pound (September 1949 WSC speech), 1499–514; Debate on the Address (March 1950 WSC speech), 1675; Imperial Preference, 533–4, 800–1, 803, 1188, 1504; Pound Sterling devaluation, 1492, 1492–3, 1493–4, 1493 n.1, 1496–7, 1536, 1554–5, 1579, 1583, 1584–6, 1595, 1665, 1721–2, 1747, 2035, 2085, 2116–18, 2161, 2189–90
economic controls in the US and England, 840–2, 857
economic union of France and Germany, 1706, 1707
electric generating production industry, 660
Family Allowances, 801, 1017, 1092, 1645, 1654
Halifax updates WSC on financial and trade negotiations with the US, 159, 165
Labour Government policies: austerity measures, 152, 153–4, 821–2, 828–9, 883–4, 891, 965, 1619–21, 1622, 1637–8, 1639, 2179, 2205–6; budget planning and spending, 657–8, 661–3, 663, 681–2, 687, 713, 752–3, 886–7, 965, 1018–19, 1067–8, 1092–3, 1190–1, 1536, 1539, 1551–3, 1595, 1608–9, 1640, 1720, 1727–8, 1747, 1843–4, 2161; export trade, 152–4, 659–61, 720, 797, 822–4, 835, 887, 1673, 1723–4, 2116, 2170–1; industry nationalisation, 152, 305, 476, 480, 540–1, 718, 797–8, 822, 1016–17, 1192, 1457–8, 1537–8, 1618–19, 1633–4, 2035, 2118; taxation, 796, 1631–3, 1640, 1642, 1645, 1654–5, 1675, 1721–7, 1747, 1750–2, 2033, 2035, 2086, 2097, 2117, 2161, 2163, 2173; WSC criticises post-war expenses and lack of savings, 153; WSC promotes free trade over State control, 823–4, 827; WSC questions cost of civil service expansion and expenditures, 658
Lend-Lease Programme, 40–1, 551
Middlemen's profits, 1762–3
national savings, 648, 1555
speeches (WSC): Finance Bill (June 1946), 388–90; Economic Situation (March 1947), 646–63; A 'Doctor's Mandate' (August 1947), 750–2, 757; No Easy Passage (August 1947), 766–8; A New Parliament (February 1948), 962–3, 964–6; Devaluation of the Pound (September 1949), 1499–514; The Economic Situation (October 1949), 1551–6; The Budget (April 1950), 1721–32, 1732; Budget Proposals and Economic Survey (April 1951), 2032–4; Exports to China (May 1951), 2066–76, 2079; Finance Bill Amendments, Chairman's Selection (June 1951), 2095–8
Stock Exchange collapse, 2172
in a united Europe, 464, 706
US economic policies, 825–7
US investment in British industries, 1078
US loan to England: Amery opposes, 381–2; repayment of, 1722, 2128–9; WSC criticises allocation and spending of, 658, 680–1, 717, 750–4, 888, 889, 965, 988, 1017–18, 1068, 1092–3, 1511, 1607–8; WSC criticises Labour Government plans to borrow money from the US, 154, 306, 648; WSC discusses with Attlee, 211–12, 213, 263, 269
The Economist, 397
Eden, Beatrice Helen Beckett, 207, 207 n.1
Eden, Nicholas, 1385, 1385 n.4
Eden, (Robert) Anthony
 biographical information, 29 n.2
 Anglo-American relations, 1968
 atom bomb, 91
 at Chartwell, 1718
 communications: Beaverbrook observes that Eden no longer wishes to speak with him, 1389, 1389 n.1; controversial political broadcasts, 523; Eden's 1938 resignation as Foreign Secretary, 665–6, 948–9, 952–3, 956, 967, 977; publication of Yalta Conference telegrams, 668, 668–9, 669
 defence: British Armed Forces preparedness and recruiting efforts (1950), 1824–5, 1826–7; Recruiting for the Forces (February 1949 WSC speech), 1329; United States Mutual Defence Assistance Act, 1604–5
 domestic affairs: Coal Bill Debate, 199; food shortages in England, 206–7; industry nationalisation, 1219; Princess Elizabeth's annuities, 852; statements justifying the resignations of Ministers, 640; Town and Country Planning Bill, 629
 economics: Baruch discusses economic controls in the US and England with

Eden, (Robert) Anthony *(continued)*
  economics *(continued)*
    WSC, 871; Lend-Lease Programme cancelation, 41; Pound Sterling devaluation, 1492, 1675; Shadow Cabinet stance on US loan to England, 168
  Europe: Council of Europe, 1164–5, 1276, 1277; Hague Conference planning, 1009; US involvement in Western European security, 1273
  General Election (1950), 1615
  General Election (1951), 1986–7, 1988, 2213–14
  Germany: Allied Unconditional Surrender Policy, 1462, 1563; participation in European Army, 1943; Russian blockade of Berlin, 1164; WSC criticises treatment of German Field Marshals, 1163–4, 1165
  India: Attlee calls meeting with Liberals and Conservatives regarding, 399; Dominion status, 726, 1384, 1384 n.1; food situation in, 360; HofC resolution of appreciation for Indian Civil and Military Services, 748, 748 n.1; Hyderabad, 1163, 1165; India Independence Bill, 739; new Indian Constitution ceremony (1950), 1584, 1587, 1587 n.2
  meets with Freyberg in New Zealand, 1344
  Poland: exiled Polish senators criticise Sovietisation of eastern Europe, 442, 449; Mikołajczyk's status and safety in, 781, 805; Opening of the Sikorski Institute (July 1949 WSC speech), 1446
  Russia: Anglo-American policy towards, 1937; British estimates of Russian forces in eastern Europe, 565, 567; Four Power Conference proposals (1950), 1954
  The Second World War: feedback and suggested edits for, 944, 952–3, 956, 977, 1002, 1385, 1402; final months of Wavell's command, 1288; Hitler's invasion of Russia, 1823
  and WSC: Eden sends WSC New Years greetings, 912; Eden thanks WSC for Coalition Government medallion, 403; Eden thanks WSC for copy of *Their Finest Hour*, 1385; lunches with WSC at Chartwell, 1590; WSC reports on visit with Truman, 263; WSC seeks British Government support for fair trial for Mihailović, 287, 290
  see also Conservative Party; Middle East; Second World War
Edmonds, James Edward, 1324, 1324 n.1

education
  Conservative Party policies, 2164
  Education Act, 1017, 1092
  school age extension, 1673
  Voluntary Schools in England and Wales, 2191–3, 2193, 2194–5
Edward the Confessor, 179, 179 n.3
Edwards, Alfred, 2204, 2204 n.1
Edwards, Harold Clifford, 119, 119 n.1
Edward VII, King, 1076, 1076 n.3
Edward VIII, King: *see* Windsor, Duke of
Egypt
  British arms and jets for, 1738, 1741, 1812, 1845, 1859–60, 2088, 2129–30
  British demobilisation and shipping requirements, 130
  British destroyer traded to, 2129
  British policy towards, 499, 2217, 2231–2
  British trusteeship of Cyrenaica (proposed), 347–9
  exclusion of Egypt from Arab League suggested by Amery, 1768
  removal of British troops from (proposed), 313, 320–1, 328, 329, 344, 349, 350, 367, 499, 535
  speeches (WSC): British Troops in Egypt (May 1946), 311–15; Egypt Treaty Negotiations (May 1946), 343–52; Foreign Affairs, Middle East (July 1951), 2127; Palestine (January 1947), 609
  Suez Canal closure, 2088, 2130–1, 2201–2, 2209
  Suez Canal and Isthmus, 346, 348, 402, 435, 436, 2225, 2225 n.2, 2231–2
  WSC criticises Labour Government export trade policies, 1673
Eichmann, Otto Adolph, 1223, 1223 n.4
Eighth Army, 106–8, 178, 1546–9
Eisenhower, Dwight David
  biographical information, 44 n.2
  Europe: The Challenge of Our Time: Hand of Aggressor Is Stayed By Strength Alone speech (July 1951), 2104–8, 2109, 2114, 2122; European Army Command, 1970, 2025, 2081, 2149–50; North Atlantic Supreme Commander (April 1951 WSC speech), 2042, 2044, 2045, 2047, 2055
  Middle East: Foreign Affairs, Middle East (July 1951 WSC speech), 2127; Persian oil, 2109, 2109 n.2, 2114
  political career, 1107–8, 1131
  Resolutions for Thanks to Commanders, 162
  The Second World War: Algiers meeting minutes, 1878; Anzio operation despatches, 401; appointment of Eisenhower as Supreme Commander of Normandy invasion,

Index

598, 1964–5; Eisenhower thanks WSC for copy of *The Hinge of Fate*, 1964–5, 1965 n.1; Ismay assists WSC with research and notes for, 1312–13; pre-D-Day events, 1941–2
  sends regards to CSC, 129
  and WSC: Eisenhower plans UK visit (1951), 1965; Eisenhower praises in Pentagon introduction, 248; Eisenhower's painting hobby, 1878–9; invites WSC to meet during WSC's US trip, 171–2, 186–7, 188–9, 191–2, 203; meets with in Williamsburg, 210, 243; publication of WSC's war-time Parliamentary Secret Session speeches, 174–5; Riviera visit accommodations, 44–5, 74, 80–1, 83; war-time decisions regarding troop deployments in Alsace, 129; war-time Supreme Command decisions, 297–9, 300, 599, 601, 603; WSC asks Eisenhower to meet with Camrose, 1866, 1878; WSC asks Eisenhower to meet with Rowan, 1682; WSC criticises Butcher's wartime accounts, 189, 191; WSC praises, 1274, 2075; WSC praises 'Challenge of Our Time' speech, 2109, 2114; WSC praises war-time joint staff cooperation, 249; WSC speaks to US Army and Navy officers at the Pentagon, 247–51; WSC's US visit (1949), 1331, 1339, 1349, 1352, 1354; WSC thanks for letter and looks forward to reading Eisenhower's war-time memoirs, 1098, 1107–8, 1131–2; WSC voices concerns about Soviet imperialism, 1131–2

Eisenhower, Mamie Geneva Doud, 187, 187 n.1
ELAS (Ellinikós Laïkós Apeleftherotikós Stratós, Greek People's Liberation Army), 1913
Elath, Eliahu, 1867–8, 1867 n.1, 1885, 1885 n.1, 1909, 2028, 2031
El Glaoui, Thami, 898, 898 n.3, 901, 902–4, 908, 1976, 1981
Elizabeth, Princess (later Queen Elizabeth II)
  biographical information, 738 n.2
  Address of Congratulations to Their Majesties and Princess Elizabeth on the Forthcoming Royal Marriage (October 1947 WSC speech), 816–17
  annuities, 851–2, 852–3, 858
  The Birthplace of Prince Charles (November 1948 WSC speech), 1249–50
  engagement to Philip Mountbatten, 738, 739–40, 740, 741
  thanks WSC for book volumes, 807
  WSC recommends that Princess Elizabeth not fly to Canada during King George's illness, 2155

Elizabeth, Queen (later Queen Mother)
  biographical information, 29 n.1
  Address of Congratulations to Their Majesties and Princess Elizabeth on the Forthcoming Royal Marriage (October 1947 WSC speech), 816–17
  His Majesty's Return From South Africa (May 1947 WSC speech), 703
  Japanese surrender (VJ Day), 31
  Motion of Congratulations to Their Majesties on their Silver Wedding (April 1948 WSC speech), 1029
  Princess Elizabeth's engagement to Philip Mountbatten, 739
  Reader's Digest subscription for, 578–9
  refuses to receive or recognize Duchess of Windsor, 143
  sympathy message for during King George's surgery and recovery, 2154
  WSC thanks George VI for signed 'balcony scene' photograph, 171
Elliot, Walter, 448, 448 n.1, 1291, 1716
Elliot, William, 1442, 1442 n.1
Elmes, Cecil Frederick, 186, 186 n.1, 208
Elmhirst, Thomas Walker, 546–7, 547 n.3
employment
  average work week lengths, 1630
  British national output, 1622
  Conservative Party policies, 799–800, 1533–4, 1595–6, 1644
  Employment White Paper, 795, 1551–2, 1644, 1672
  steel industry unemployment, 1238
  Unemployment Insurance, 480, 1235
  unemployment rates: in 1947, 713–14; post-war, 1068–9, 1596, 1609, 1636, 1644, 1673–4; between the wars, 715, 885–6
  wages, 1630, 2172
  WSC criticises Labour Government claiming credit for full employment, 2178
  WSC criticises Labour Government policies, 796, 1534–5, 1672–4
English, Crisp, 877, 877 n.1, 879
English politics
  Batley by-elections, 1325
  conclusion of Parliament (1947), 912–13
  Cooper discusses future of with WSC, 64, 75–6
  County elections (1949), 1395
  Dumbarton by-election, 1715–16, 1716
  East Fulham by-election (1933), 76, 76 n.2, 918–20
  Friedman writes to WSC about British and American political systems, 269–70
  Jarrow by-election (1947), 712
  Lynskey Tribunal, 1309, 1309 n.1, 1314–20, 1325

English politics *(continued)*
  Municipal Elections, 722
  Preston by-election (1946), 199
  Shaw discusses with WSC, 446–9, 453
  Smuts discusses with WSC, 1422
  Sowerby by-elections, 1350–1
  speeches (WSC): Tasks Ahead (October 1945), 105; Failures of the Government's 'Doctrinaire Socialism' (April 1946), 304–7; Representation of the People Bill (February 1948), 968–9; Political Gerrymandering (June 1948), 1078–86; Britain 'Floundering and Sinking' (June 1948), 1086–96; Ministers and Public Servants, Official Conduct (February 1949), 1314–20; Nationalisation (May 1949), 1429–30
  Stalin criticises single-party control of British Government, 258, 265–6
  West Leeds by-election, 1449
  Westminster by-election (1923), 315–16
  Where are the Liberals? Losing by Default (February 1949 *Evening Standard* article), 1325–6, 1326, 1327, 1330
  Woolton–Teviot agreement, 1266–7, 1267 n.1
  WSC cites by-election results in calling for new Parliament (December 1947), 890
  WSC confides depression about future of to CSC, 896–7, 902
  WSC criticises *Evening Standard* by-elections article, 960
  WSC encourages unified Party vote for upcoming by-election, 188, 190
  WSC lunches with Unionist Party members, 949
  WSC thanks Kemsley for election support, 1666, 2158, 2158–9
  see also Coalition Government; Conservative Party; General Election (1945); General Election (1950); General Election (1951); Labour Government
Entwistle, Antony Beauchamp
  biographical information, 1292 n.2
  marriage to Sarah Churchill, 1483, 1546, 1797–8, 1950
  Sarah Churchill complains to WSC about his rudeness to, 1292–3
  Sarah Churchill's income tax issues, 1487–9, 1491
  use of house as photo studio, 1797–8
Ermashev, I., 1198–9, 1198 n.1
Erroll, Frederick James, 520, 520 n.6
Ertegun, Munir, 241, 241 n.1
Etzdorf, Hasso von, 1178, 1178 n.4
Europe
  Austria and South Tyrol, 93–4, 102, 370–1, 436, 451–2, 456–7, 464

  Baruch's Europe visit (1948), 1046, 1125
  Baruch's Europe visit (1949), 1424, 1436–7, 1441
  economic integration of, 464, 706
  Eisenhower's Challenge of Our Time speech (July 1951), 2104–8
  Foreign Secretaries' Conference, 370
  Luxembourg, 142, 1622
  Portugal, 231, 338
  post-war restoration and rebuilding of, 324–5
  publication of WSC's war-time correspondence with Attlee, 481–2
  Russian forces in Eastern Europe, 511, 519
  Sovietisation of, 375–7, 531, 591, 1649
  speeches (WSC): A New Europe (November 1945), 132; The Foundations of Freedom (November 1945), 136–7; The Future of Europe (November 1945), 139–41, 158; The United States of Europe (May 1946), 321–6; France and Europe (July 1946), 404–7; The Tragedy of Europe (September 1946), 458–61; United Europe (May 1947), 704–11; The Congress of Europe (May 1948), 1037–42, 1045, 1045–6; United Europe (May 1948), 1042–4; Building a New Europe (July 1948), 1126–7; United Europe (November 1948), 1250–1; A United Europe (February 1949), 1335–6; Europe and regional United Nations organisations (February 1949), 1336–9; Berlin Blockade Removal (May 1949), 1403; The North Atlantic Treaty (May 1949), 1411–17; United Europe (August 1949), 1466–8; A Meeting-Place of the Future Parliament of Europe (August 1949), 1470–1; Consultative Assembly of the Council of Europe (August 1949), 1471–4; European Movement (November 1949), 1575–8; European Unity (March 1950), 1702–12; European Unity and a European Army (August 1950), 1827–32; University of Copenhagen Danish–British Society speech notes (October 1950), 1888–904; The Peril in Europe (August 1950), 1843–7; Graver Dangers Loom in Europe (Korean War) (April 1951), 2036; North Atlantic Supreme Commander (April 1951), 2041–55; United Europe (July 1951), 2122–4
  see also Council of Europe; Czechoslovakia; France; Germany; Hague Conference; Italy; Marshall Plan; North Atlantic Treaty; Poland; United States of Europe; Western Union (European Army)

Index

Evans, Lincoln, 1247–8, 1247 n.1, 1870, 1872, 2185, 2204
Evatt, Herbert Vere, 778, 778 n.1
Evening Standard
   by-elections articles, 960, 1326, 1327, 1330
   CSC convinces to desist from publishing article about Chartwell renovations, 63
   political cartoon of Marshall, 580, 664
ibn Ezra, Abraham, 186, 186 n.7

Fadiman, Clifton Paul, 923, 923 n.5
Faisal I, King of Syria, 430, 430 n.1
Falls, Cyril Bentham, 1026, 1026 n.2
Family Allowances, 801, 1017, 1092, 1645, 1654
Farouk (King of Egypt), 1768, 1768 n.2
Feather, Norman, 19, 19 n.9
Fechteler, William Morrow, 2042, 2042 n.1, 2050, 2075
Fellows, Frank, 1375, 1375 n.1, 1375 n.2
Ferdinand Magellan (Truman's railcar), 222, 222 n.2
Fernyhough, Ernest, 1244, 1244 n.1
Field, Marshal III, 224, 224 n.2, 240
51st Highland Division, 301–2
Film Finance Corporation, 2185–6
Finland, 511
Finucane, Brendan ('Paddy'), 1207, 1207 n.1
First World War, 1368–9
Firt, Julius, 1023, 1023 n.1, 1027
Fisher, Dorothy Frances Canfield, 923, 923 n.2
Fisher, Geoffrey Francis (Archbishop of Canterbury), 1251, 1251 n.1
Fisher, Irving, 1584–5, 1584 n.2
Fisher, John Arbuthnot ('Jackie'), 663, 663 n.2
Fitzwilliam, Lord (William Henry Lawrence Peter Wentworth-Fitzwilliam), 88, 88 n.3
Flanders, Count of: *see* Charles, Prince (Count of Flanders)
Flandin, Pierre-Étienne, 134–6, 134 n.1, 443
Fletcher, I. C., 146, 146 n.1
Fletcher, Walter, 2063–5, 2063 n.1, 2065 n.1
Foch, Ferdinand, 1263–4, 1263 n.2
Foch, Julie Anne Ursule Bienvenüe, 1264, 1264 n.2
food
   bread rationing, 649–52
   British fish market, 1728
   British imports of Argentinian meat, 2171
   calorie allowances, 886
   calories required for maintenance of human health, 650–1
   Conservative Party policies, 1595, 1626, 1671–2, 1674
   dried eggs, 658
   food shortages in England, 474
   food subsidies, 1636–7, 1727
   home-grown food planning, 659, 1671–2, 1729
   Labour Government rationing policies, 1637, 1639, 1640
   Labour Government 'Work or Starve' policy, 886, 1613, 1631, 1645, 1674–5
   Ministry of Food administrative costs, 1639–40
   'points' policy, 1723
   post-war austerity measures, 152, 153–4, 821–2, 828–9, 883–4, 891, 1637–8, 1674
   potato shortage, 885
   speeches (WSC): World Food Situation (May 1946), 355–63; Rationing of Bread (May 1946), 363–4; Bread Rationing (July 1946), 415–22; Agriculture (July 1948), 1108–10
   world food shortages, 356–7, 362, 364
Foot, Michael Mackintosh, 174, 174 n.2, 1592, 1660, 1822–3, 1909
Ford, Henry II, 2140, 2140 n.1
Ford, Leland Merritt, 2039–40, 2039 n.1
foreign affairs
   Albania, 1573
   Attlee's US visit, 1968, 1969–70
   Foreign Ministers conference in London (September 1945), 65, 68, 72, 82, 88
   Labour Government policies, 931, 935–6, 1271–85, 1648–50, 1752, 2039–40, 2166–7, 2200–1, 2201–3, 2209
   Poland, 781, 788, 788 n.1, 789–90, 805
   speeches (WSC): The Atomic Bomb (August 1945), 17–21; Foreign Policy, President Truman's Declaration (November 1945), 119–27; The Sinews of Peace (March 1946), 227–35; The English Speaking Peoples (March 1946), 242–6; WSC speaks to US Army and Navy officers at the Pentagon (March 1946), 247–51; The Darkening International Scene (March 1946), 263–6; A Broader and Fairer World (March 1946), 267; The Needs of a Sick World (April 1946), 301–4; Foreign Affairs (June 1946), 365–80; Foreign Affairs (October 1946), 497–504; Communism (October 1946), 505; Past Mistakes in Foreign Affairs (October 1946), 506–7; Peacetime Difficulties (September 1947), 791–3; Foreign Affairs (January 1948), 929–40; Royal Dinner Address, Oslo (May 1948), 1046–7, 1047 n.2; Why Must We Always Fight? (May 1948), 1052–4; Suspicion Between Nations (October 1946), 517; Foreign Affairs (December 1948), 1270–85; The Communist Menace (March 1949), 1357–64; The Twentieth Century–Its

foreign affairs *(continued)*
  speeches (WSC) *(continued)*
    Promise and Its Realization (March 1949), 1364–74, 1375, 1375–8, 1395; The Three Circles, Foreign Policy (April 1949), 1386–7; A Time When Old Feuds May Die (June 1949), 1432–3; Foreign Affairs (July 1949), 1450–5; Chancellor's Address (October 1949), 1544–5; Foreign Affairs (November 1949), 1562–75; The Anglo-American Alliance (July 1950), 1777–80; Foreign Affairs (November 1950), 1950–7; The International Situation (December 1950), 1967–75; Our Race and Destiny (April 1951), 2056–8; The Anglo-American Alliance (July 1950), 1777–80
  World Peace Movement delegation visit to England, 1680, 1680 n.6
  WSC praises US foreign policy, 1711
  WSC warns against totalitarianism, 796, 965
  Yugoslavia, 287, 290, 295–6
  see also Anglo-American relations; Cold War; Communism; Europe; India; Israel; Japan; Korea; Middle East; North Atlantic Treaty; Palestine; Russia
Foreign Office
  Bevin serves as Foreign Secretary under Attlee's new Labour Government, 2
  Cold War: Information Research Department, 1149–50; Perils Abroad and at Home (October 1948 WSC speech), 1197
  Lascelles asks WSC to review draft of George VI's speech to UN delegates, 176, 177
  Magee asks WSC for statement for von Weizsäcker's trial, 1200
  Marshall and war-time Supreme Command decisions, 599–600, 601–2, 602–3, 603
  Parliamentary Questions on raw materials for atom bomb, 89
  publication of WSC's war-time papers, minutes and personal correspondence, 488–9
  Quebec Agreement of 1943, 33, 36, 41–2
  WSC seeks British Government support for fair trial for Mihailović, 287, 295–6
  WSC's meeting with Djilas, 1996, 1996 n.3
  WSC suggests unpaid official positions for Duke and Duchess of Windsor at British Embassy in America, 168
Foreign Secretary: *see* Bevin, Ernest; Morrison, Herbert Stanley
Forrestal, James V., 247, 247 n.1
Foster, John Galway, 199, 199 n.4, 1426, 1475
Fothergill, Charles Philip, 819, 819 n.1, 1659
4th Hussars, 58–9, 77–8, 184–5, 597

Four Power Conference (1949), 1416
Four Power Conference proposals (1950), 1954, 1971
Four Power Treaty, 373
Four Years' Plan, 155, 723, 2178
14th British Imperial Army, 25, 97, 101, 470, 847
France
  Anglo-French relations, 394, 398, 404–7
  British policy towards, 280–1, 285, 290–1, 1622–3
  Communism in, 1362
  Cooper describes political climate of to WSC (September 1945), 65
  Council of Europe proposals, 1152, 1152–3
  dissolution of Combined Chiefs of Staff, 1514, 1526
  election results (1946), 383
  French actions toward Franco, 285
  French and German coal and steel industries, 1752–3, 1783, 1792, 1828, 1876, 2123
  French participation in Western Union (European Army), 2149–50
  Indo-China war, 2150, 2151
  National Assembly of the Fourth Republic, 519, 519 n.1
  Paris Peace Conference, 443, 456–7, 497
  Pleven Government, 1789–90
  post-war restoration and rebuilding of, 371–2
  speeches (WSC): A New Europe (November 1945), 132; France and Europe (July 1946), 404–7; United Europe (May 1947), 707–8; The Twentieth Century–Its Promise and Its Realization (March 1949), 1377–8
  UN role, 319
  Vichy Government, 135
  WSC suggests French–German partnership, 460, 461, 464, 466, 555, 560–1, 934, 1039, 1275, 1432–3, 1576–7, 1705–7
France, Anatole (Jacques-Anatole-François Thibault), 180, 180 n.3, 453
Franckenstein, Sir George, 93–4, 93 n.2, 102
Franco Bahamonde, Francisco, 272 n.1, 285, 316, 368–9
Franco Government, 1415
François-Poncet, André, 1177, 1177 n.8
Frankfurter, Felix, 1879, 1879–81, 1879 n.1
Frankfurter, Marion Denman, 1881, 1881 n.1
Franks, Oliver Sherwell
  biographical information, 1333 n.1
  Attlee's US visit, 1968
  Quebec Agreement of 1943, 2001
  United States Mutual Defence Assistance Act, 1605
  WSC's US visit (1949), 1333, 1339–40, 1340, 1343, 1355

Index

Fraser, Bruce Austin
  biographical information, 57 n.1
  describes Japanese surrender ceremony and tour to WSC, 57, 99
  First Sea Lord appointment, 881, 982–3
  fleet review in Gibraltar, 2013, 2018
  Resolutions for Thanks to Commanders, 162
Fraser, Peter, 1254, 1254 n.1, 1967
Fraser, Thomas, 1080–1, 1080 n.1
Frederik (King of Denmark), 1933, 1933 n.1
Freeman, Douglas Southall, 244, 244 n.3
Freeman, John Horace, 1212, 1212 n.2
Frewen, Clara Jerome, 1001, 1001 n.3
Freyberg, Bernard Cyril, 163, 163 n.4, 813, 1254, 1344
Friedman, Elisha Michael, 269–70, 269 n.1, 270–1
Froelicher, Hans, 1177, 1177 n.4
Fuchs, Emil Julius Klaus, 1962, 1962 n.1
Fuel and Power Crisis (February 1947 WSC speech), 615–20
Fulbright, James William, 725–6, 725 n.2
Fuller, John Frederick Charles ('Boney'), 1101, 1101 n.1
Furness, George Abbot, 593, 593 n.1
Fyfe, David Patrick Maxwell, 732, 732 n.2, 859, 1419, 1716, 1733

Gairdner, Charles Henry, 634, 634 n.1
Gaitskell, Hugh Todd Naylor
  biographical information, 828 n.1
  Excess Profits Tax, 2173
  export trade policies, 2127–8, 2130, 2171
  Film Finance Corporation, 2185–6
  Finance Bill Amendments, Chairman's Selection (June 1951 WSC speech), 2095
  old age pensions, 2085
  petrol rationing easements, 1646
  wage increase freeze and Stock Exchange collapse, 2172
  WSC criticises Labour Government post-war austerity measures, 828–9
  WSC praises in Budget Proposals and Economic Survey speech (April 1951), 2032, 2034
Galbraith, John Kenneth, 178, 179 n.3
Galbraith, Thomas Dunlop, 199, 199 n.1
Gale, Humfrey Myddleton, 528, 528 n.3, 1942
Gallacher, William
  biographical information, 366 n.1
  Baldwin's death, 900
  criticises WSC, 933
  Foreign Affairs (November 1949 WSC speech), 1564, 1565, 1566, 1569–70
  India Transfer of Power (June 1947 WSC speech), 729
  Parliament Bill, 860
  political broadcasts on the BBC, 981
  United States of Europe proposals, 933
  WSC criticises British Communist Party, 366
Gamelin, Maurice Gustave, 1162, 1162 n.1, 1470
Gandhi, Mohandas Karamchand
  biographical information, 330 n.1
  Ambedkar appeals to WSC regarding future of Untouchables in India, 518
  India Cabinet Mission (July 1946 WSC speech), 408
  meets with RSC, 779
  rejection of Commonwealth status offer for India, 330
  war-time National Coalition Government's arrest of Indian Congress leaders, 636
  WSC criticises, 643
Garbett, Cyril Forster, 1759, 1759 n.3, 1760, 1763–4, 2225
Garibaldi, Giuseppe, 805, 805 n.1
Garnock, Lord (William Tuckder Lindesay-Bethune), 341–2, 341 n.1, 353
Garrod, Guy, 2007, 2007 n.1, 2061, 2146, 2148
Gascoyne-Cecil, Cicely Alice Gore, 22, 22 n.4
Gascoyne-Cecil, Hugh, 'Linky' (Lord Quickswood), 664–5, 664 n.1, 1252, 1886
Gascoyne-Cecil, James Edward Hubert, 22, 22 n.2
Gascoyne-Cecil, Robert Arthur James: see Salisbury, Lord (Robert Gascoyne-Cecil, 'Bobbety')
Gasperi, Alcide de, 457, 457 n.1, 1215
Gaulle, Charles de
  biographical information, 65 n.2
  Cooper describes political climate of France to WSC (September 1945), 65
  defence of Western Europe, 1795
  Eisenhower's wartime decision regarding troop deployments in Alsace, 129
  Franco–German relations, 1706–7
  French interests in Syria, 561
  French politics and General Election results, 560
  opinion of WSC, 1806–7, 1842
  Russian forces and intentions in Eastern Europe, 519, 555, 559–60
  United States of Europe proposals, 555, 560–1
  WSC confides pessimism about the future to, 1842
  WSC's Parliamentary Secret Session remarks about, 174
  WSC's visit to Metz, 406
Gault, Andrew Hamilton, 44–5, 44 n.3
Geddes, Eric Campbell, 541, 541 n.1
Geikie-Cobb, Ivo, 341–2, 341 n.2

2282　Index

Gemmell, Cecily ('Chips'), 1428–9, 1428 n.1, 1980, 1981
General Election (1945)
　cleaning of defaced and dirty election posters, 386–7
　Douglas and Smuts reflect on WSC's election loss, 1077–8
　Halifax reflects on WSC's election loss, 1–2
　popular vote, 474, 474 n.1
　Tasks Ahead (October 1945 WSC speech), 104–5
　WSC describes unique conditions preceding, 794–5, 868
　WSC reflects on election loss, 104–5, 110, 184, 209
General Election (1950)
　Conservative Party: election results, 1658, 1664–5; post-election strategy, 1658–60, 1683, 1720, 1743–7, 1793–4, 1908; Sandys reports on election campaign progress to WSC, 1625–7; WSC describes campaign plans to CSC, 1591–2
　election results, 1658, 1658 n.2, 1663
　Gallup Polls, 1591–2
　Labour Government: 'Fair shares for all' slogan, 1647–8; *Let Us Win Through Together* statement, 1610, 1611–12; maintains slim majority, 1658, 1658 n.2, 1665; post-election Parliamentary strategy, 1681–2; Woodford Adoption Meeting (January 1950 WSC speech), 1607–9
　Liberal Party: broadcasts, 1591, 1600–1, 1615; Conservative Party alliance with National Liberal Party, 1591, 1592, 1594–5; Davies questions exclusion of Liberals from National Liberal-Conservative meetings, 1597–8, 1602–4, 1604, 1604 n.1; Lambert praises Davies, 1607; WSC criticises electoral deadlock plans, 1618, 1668–9
　speeches (WSC): General Election (January 1950), 1589–90; The Conservative Point of View (January 1950), 1593–7; Woodford Adoption Meeting (January 1950), 1606–14; Leeds Election Address (February 1950), 1616–24; Devonport Election Address (February 1950), 1624–5, 1635–41; Cardiff Election Address (February 1950), 1627–35; Woodford Election Address (February 1950), 1641; Edinburgh Election Address (February 1950), 1642–50; London broadcast (February 1950), 1651–7
　timing of, 795, 817, 889–90, 966, 1071, 1497–8, 1500, 1527, 1527–8, 1530, 1546, 1556, 1590 n.1, 1616

and WSC: RSC suggests WSC focus on his Liberal past, 1624–5; rumoured death of, 1651; WSC asks Pierssené for Second Ballot analysis of results, 1684; WSC emphasises free and fair nature of voting for, 1635; WSC reacts to results of, 1664–5, 1667, 1668–70, 1678–9, 1730–2; WSC suggests forming Select Committee on electoral reform, 1669–71; WSC vows to continue serving England, 1657
General Election (1951)
　Conservative Party: Conservative and Unionist Films Association film script for WSC, 2115–16; The Manifesto of the Conservative and Unionist Party, General Election 1951, 2160–5; Party statement (1951), 2148; trade unions policy, 2190–1, 2211; WSC article for *News of the World*, 2187, 2208–11, 2208 n.2; WSC article on policies of, 1984–5; WSC discusses strategy with Cherwell, 1989; WSC discusses strategy with Eden, 1986–7, 1988; WSC forms new Government, 2219–20, 2222–5, 2233–4
　election results, 2195–6, 2196 n.1, 2219
　Gallup Polls, 1994, 1998–2000, 2098
　Labour Government: Liverpool Election Address (October 1951 WSC speech), 2166–74; resignation of Attlee as PM, 2219; Socialist Blunders (July 1951 WSC speech), 2116–20
　speeches (WSC): Conservative Case for an Election (March 1951), 2014–18; Socialist Blunders (July 1951), 2116–20; Liverpool Election Address (October 1951), 2166–74; Our Political Future (October 1951), 2177–82; Woodford Election Address (October 1951), 2182–5; Ulster (October 1951), 2186–7; Abadan, Sudan and Bevan – A Trio of Misfortune (October 1951), 2187–90; Huddersfield Election Address (October 1951), 2196–201; Newcastle upon Tyne Election Address (October 1951), 2201–6; Plymouth Election Address (October 1951), 2212–19
　timing of, 1917–18, 1989, 2015, 2081–2, 2153
　Voluntary Schools in England and Wales, 2191–3
　and WSC: Macmillan notes WSC's demonstrations of energy and vitality, 2115; Montgomery congratulates WSC on election win, 2220; *Sunday Times* interview questions for WSC, 2208, 2208 n.1, 2211–12; WSC discusses strategy with Eden, 1986–7, 1988;

Index

WSC emphasises free and fair nature of voting for, 2178–9; WSC responds to Communist and Labour 'warmonger' accusations, 2210, 2214; WSC seeks Beaverbrook's advice, 2165, 2174; WSC thanks Kemsley for election support, 2158, 2158–9

Geoffrey-Lloyd, Geoffrey William, 620–1, 620 n.1

Georges, Alphonse Joseph, 1470, 1470 n.2, 1996

George V, King, 680, 806–7, 812, 812 n.1, 1076 n.2

George VI, King
  biographical information, 4 n.2
  Auriol's visit to England, 1661
  Australia and New Zealand tour cancelation, 1254, 1256, 1261
  Civil List Act, 920, 926
  commemoration of war-time Dinners with the King at No. 10 Downing Street, 737
  Debate on the Address (October 1948 WSC speech), 1202–6, 1216–17
  health: circulatory issues, 1253–4, 1256, 1261; lung surgery, 2154, 2154 n.1, 2155, 2225; sympathy message for Queen Elizabeth during King George's surgery and recovery, 2154; WSC sends well wishes, 1517, 1523
  honours and awards: Campaign Star qualifications, 97; Coalition Government medallion from WSC, 423, 527; Order of Merit for WSC, 208; WSC asks permission to wear American Air Force pilot's wings, 1293; WSC asks permission to wear Grand Cross and Chain of the Royal Order of St Olav, 1075, 1076; WSC asks permission to wear Order of the Elephant, 1933
  Japanese surrender, 6, 31
  Labour Government: Attlee resigns as PM (1951), 2219; post-election Parliamentary strategy, 1681–2; WSC asks Attlee to invite Conservative colleagues to meeting with George VI, 29, 30
  meeting with Truman, 10
  Prince Frederick of Prussia, 1823–4
  Princess Elizabeth's annuities, 851–2, 852–3, 858
  Princess Elizabeth's engagement to Philip Mountbatten, 738, 739–40, 741
  proposed jobs for Duke and Duchess of Windsor at British Embassy in America, 143–5, 310, 337
  renounces title as Emperor of India, 1089
  The Second World War: WSC sends copies of Volumes Three and Four to, 1948, 1949; WSC sends copy of *Their Finest Hour* to, 1442, 1444–5, 1517, 1523

South Africa: His Majesty's Return From South Africa (May 1947 WSC speech), 702–3; meets with WSC before departing for, 603–4

Transitional Powers Bill, Supplies and Services (August 1947 WSC speech), 759–60

Trooping of the Colours cancelation, 1075, 1076, 1077

Victory celebrations, 334

and WSC: Address of Congratulations to Their Majesties and Princess Elizabeth on the Forthcoming Royal Marriage (October 1947 WSC speech), 816–17; asks WSC to review speech for unveiling of King George V statue, 680, 806–7, 812, 812 n.1; discusses 1950 General Election results with WSC, 1660–1, 1663; Lascelles asks WSC to review draft of George VI's speech to UNO delegates, 176, 177; Motion of Congratulations to Their Majesties on their Silver Wedding (April 1948 WSC speech), 1029; WSC forms new Government (1951), 2219, 2228; WSC praises the constitutional monarchy, 920; WSC's Hallmark Christmas cards, 1993, 1995; WSC steps down as Lord Warden of the Cinque Ports, 4–5; WSC thanks for birthday wishes, 1265; WSC thanks for Christmas card, 920, 926; WSC thanks for farewell letter and friendship, 11; WSC thanks for signed 'balcony scene' photograph and sends Christmas and New Year greetings, 171

Gerard, Husreve, 1177, 1177 n.6

Gerard, James Watson, 279–80, 279 n.2, 280 n.1

Gerbrandy, Pieter Sjoerds, 323, 323 n.1

Germany
  Allied dismantlement of, 1452–3, 1564–6
  Allied Unconditional Surrender Policy, 1451, 1453, 1454–5, 1461–2, 1562–4
  British policy towards, 498, 532–3, 1622, 1720
  Council of Europe, 1469–70, 1473–4, 1567–8, 1576–7
  Dresden bombing, 1742–3, 1743 n.1, 1799–800
  food production regions, 377, 930
  food shortages in, 360, 364, 532
  Four Power Conference (1949), 1416
  French and German coal and steel industries, 1752–3, 1783, 1792, 1828, 1876, 2123
  German Fleet disposition, 7
  Goering's trial, 287
  industry, 377, 1275
  Labour Government aid to, 657, 800–1

Germany *(continued)*
  loss of British prestige in, 1536–7
  'Morgenthau Plan' for Germany, 24, 24 n.3, 33, 36, 41–2, 1010–11
  Noé describes German situation to WSC, 1166
  Nuremberg trials, 193, 194, 195, 377–8, 510, 533
  Occupied Germany: Berlin airlift, 1187, 1211–12, 1274, 1360–1, 1372, 1452, 1564; Berlin Blockade Removal (May 1949 WSC speech), 1403; Berlin elections (1948), 1274–5; British Zone, 753, 774–5, 1920–1, 1938, 1943–5; Russian actions in, 232–3, 376–8, 1012–13; Russian blockade of Berlin, 1088–9, 1105–6, 1145–6, 1185, 1186–7, 1411; Stalin's views on future of, 509–10
  rearmament between the wars, 1233–4
  reparations, 6–7, 10, 36
  rise of neo-Nazism in, 1693
  Soviet rearmament of Eastern Germany, 1809, 1846, 1862, 1952
  speeches (WSC): Foreign Policy, President Truman's Declaration (November 1945), 121–2; The Sinews of Peace (March 1946), 232–3, 235, 257; Past Mistakes in Foreign Affairs (October 1946), 506–7; United Europe (May 1947), 707; Building a New Europe (July 1948), 1126–7; Berlin Blockade Removal (May 1949), 1403; A Time When Old Feuds May Die (June 1949), 1432–3; Foreign Affairs (July 1949), 1450–5
  United States of Europe proposals, 460
  Western Union (European Army) proposals, 1692–3, 1704–5, 1809, 1829, 1833–4, 1845, 1862–3, 1939–40, 1942–3, 1943, 2150
  West German federal election (1949), 1942 n.1
  WSC calls for British reconciliation with, 1212, 1275
  WSC criticises treatment of German Field Marshals, 1165, 1212–13
  WSC recalls 21 March 1918 German offensive, 185
  WSC recalls Rhineland invasion (1936), 134–5
  WSC's Atomic Bomb statement, 21
  WSC seeks rapid achievement of peace with, 377–9
  WSC suggests French–German partnership, 460, 461, 464, 466, 555, 560–1, 934, 1039, 1275, 1576–7, 1705–7
Gfroerer, Fannie Palmer, 283, 283 n.2

Gfroerer, Herbert, 283, 283 n.1
Gibson, Charles William, 556, 556 n.1
Gibson, Eileen Isabella Ronnie, 1115, 1115 n.2
Gibson, George, 1315–16, 1315 n.3
Gibson, Herbert Robert Burnett, 1479, 1479 n.1
Gifford, Walter Sherman, 2002–3, 2002 n.1
Gilliatt, Elizabeth
  biographical information, 563 n.2
  Committee of Privileges, 732, 732 n.3
  in Marrakech with WSC, 899, 903, 910
  Marshall and war-time Supreme Command decisions, 599–600, 601–2
  Sikorski Historical Institute appeal, 1379, 1379 n.2
  Stalin's request for base on the Aegean Sea, 731, 731 n.2
  unfinished letter to Smuts regarding Indian settlement, 1402
  von Weizsäcker's role in Nazi extermination of Jews, 1341–2
  WSC attempts to contribute to Church of Pompey restoration, 563–4, 564 n.1
  WSC lunches with Unionist Party members, 949
  Yalta Conference proceedings, 667
Gimson, Franklin Charles, 2227, 2227 n.3
Giraud, Henri-Honoré, 394, 394 n.1, 406
Giraudier, Antonio, 1168, 1168 n.1
Gisevius, Hans Bernd, 1178, 1178 n.1
Gladstone, William Ewart, 61, 125, 125 n.1, 220, 323, 460, 473, 784, 992, 1625, 1651–2
Glanville, James Edward, 989, 989 n.2
Gluckstein, Louis Halle, 97, 97 n.3
Godfrey, Arthur Morton, 2124–5, 2124 n.1
Godlewski, Józef, 437–9, 439 n.4
Goerdeler, Annaliese Ulrich, 1178, 1178 n.8
Goering, Hermann, 287, 287 n.1
Goethe, Johann Wolfgang von, 1059, 1059 n.1
The Golden Fleece (Graves), 69
Gollancz, Victor, 573, 573 n.1, 584, 764, 1003
Gomme-Duncan, Alan, 2049, 2049 n.2
Goodhart, Arthur Lehman, 1879, 1879 n.2
Goodwin, Albert, 555, 555 n.2, 557, 612–13
Gordon, Adam Lindsay, 1008, 1008 n.1
Gordon, John Rutherford, 541–2, 541 n.2
Gordon-Lennox, Elizabeth Grace Hudson (Duchess of Richmond), 2141, 2141 n.1
Gordon-Lennox, Frederick (Duke of Richmond), 2141, 2141 n.1
Gort, Lord (John Vereker), 457, 457 n.2, 1410, 1547
Gottwald, Klement, 1194, 1194 n.3
Gott, William Henry Ewart ('Strafer'), 107, 107 n.2
Gouin, Félix, 290–1, 290 n.5
Gouzenko, Igor, 112, 112 n.1

Index

Government Hospitality Fund, 388
Grabski, Stanisław, 449, 449 n.3
Graebner, Walter
  biographical information, 282 n.1
  Crusade in Europe (film) showing at Chartwell, 1430
  The Second World War: proofs and photographs for, 761, 911, 1158, WSC describes progress on, 623, 954, 1764; WSC dislikes text of blurb announcing *Life* serialization of, 694 n.2
  SoundScriber recording of Gfroerer's conversation with WSC, 282–4
  WSC plans US visit (1948), 978
  WSC requests Cuban cigars, 954
  WSC sends news of Rufus the Second, 954, 954 n.1, 954 n.2
  WSC's Marrakech trip costs, 881, 908
Graham, Benjamin, 1585, 1585 n.1
Graham-Dixon, Dorothy Rivett, 565, 565 n.2, 1344, 1344 n.1
Graham-Dixon, Leslie Charles, 565, 565 n.1
Graham-Harrison, Francis Laurence Theodore, 667, 667 n.1
Graham, Miles William Arthur Peel, 528, 528 n.4, 529
Grandi, Dino, 623–4, 623 n.2, 623 n.3, 624 n.1
Grant, Cary (Archibald Alexander Leach), 1310, 1310 n.1
Grant, Charles John Cecil, 1263–4, 1263 n.1
Granum, Alfred Marcellus, 2055–6, 2055 n.2, 2090
Granville, Edgar Louis, 38–9, 38 n.2, 1668–9
Graves, Robert von Ranke, 69, 69 n.1
Gray, Colin, 2203, 2203 n.1
Graziani, Rudolfo, 1157, 1157 n.1
Greece
  British policy towards, 367–8, 499–500, 564, 931–3, 1282–3, 1573–4
  British troops in, 194, 197, 500, 511, 564
  Communism in, 105–6, 1352–4
  EAM (Ethniko Apeleftherotiko Metopo, National Liberation Front), 105–6, 1913
  ELAS (Ellinikós Laïkós Apeleftherotikós Stratós, Greek People's Liberation Army), 1913
  Greek election results (1946), 368
  OPLA organisation, 855
  Russian policy towards, 1227–8
  Salonica executions, 839, 839 n.2, 854–7
  Spearman's memorandum on, 1443, 1444
  WSC asks Ismay for war-time notes on British actions in, 1025–6, 1026–7
  WSC discusses Greek political situation with Bevin, 147–8, 281
  WSC disputes veracity of Moorehead's *Montgomery* book, 542–3
  WSC praises election process in, 232, 238, 499–500, 564
  WSC thanks Graves for copy of *The Golden Fleece* book, 69
  WSC views election results as vindication of British policy toward, 281
Green, Eleanor Essie, 90, 90 n.2
Green Foundation
  itinerary for WSC's Missouri visit, 225
  McCluer invites WSC to deliver Green Lectures, 90–1, 128
  WSC plans speech at Westminster College, 170, 189–90, 210
  see also The Sinews of Peace (March 1946 WSC speech)
Green, John Findley, 90, 90 n.4
Green, John Raeburn, 170, 170 n.1
Greenwood, Arthur, 6, 6 n.1, 719, 801
Greenwood, J.R., 1887, 1887 n.1
Grenville, Richard, 243, 243 n.1
Grey, Sir Edward, 348, 348 n.1, 775, 2199
Gridley, Arnold Babb, 520–1, 520 n.4
Griffiths, James, 1506, 1506 n.1, 2119, 2227
Grigg, Edward William Macleay ('Ned'), 771, 771 n.1, 789
Grigg, Gertrude Charlotte Hough, 130, 130 n.3
Grigg, Sir James
  biographical information, 15 n.1
  criticises Labour Government, 1202
  manpower allocations (November 1945), 130
  thanks WSC for copy of *The Gathering Storm*, 1201
  WSC inquires about Grigg's pension rates, 15, 130, 1202
  WSC thanks for War Office service, 15
Grimond, Joseph ('Jo'), 1668–9, 1668 n.1
Gromyko, Andrei Andreyevich ('Mr No'), 374, 374 n.1, 1916
Groot, Huig de, ('Grotius'), 324, 324 n.1
Grosvenor, Anne Winifred Sullivan (Duchess of Westminster), 764, 764 n.3
Grosvenor, Hugh Richard Arthur ('Bendor'), (Duke of Westminster), 92 n.2, 764, 1590, 1797–8
Ground-Controlled Interception (GCI), 613, 613 n.2
Grüner, Dov Bela, 606, 606 n.1, 607–8
Guingand, Francis Wilfred de ('Freddie'), 1026, 1026 n.1, 1269
Guinness, Walter Edward (Baron Moyne), 494, 494 n.1
Guisan, Henri, 467, 467 n.1
Gurney, Henry, 2181, 2181 n.1

Haakon VII (King of Norway), 1046–7, 1046 n.1, 1052–3, 1056
Haeften, Barbara Curtius von, 1178, 1178 n.9

Hague Conference
  attendees, 1035–6
  Council of Europe, 1130, 1338
  German delegation to, 1039
  Human Rights Charter and Court, 1038–9, 1338
  Labour Party declines role on United Europe Committee, 958, 960, 968, 1004, 1063
  organising committee, 1036
  planning, 1005, 1008–9, 1033–6
  speeches (WSC): The Congress of Europe (May 1948 WSC speech), 1037–42, 1045, 1045–6; United Europe (May 1948 WSC speech), 1042–4; University of Copenhagen Danish–British Society speech notes (October 1950 WSC speech), 1897
  WSC criticises Socialist Party monopoly of United Europe efforts, 963–4
  WSC describes to Attlee and invites Labour Party representatives to, 947, 952, 953–4, 960, 964
  WSC praises Bevin and Bidault at, 1037
  WSC praises Marshall at, 1037
  WSC praises Spaak at, 1037
  WSC promotes apolitical British approach to, 1004–6, 1013–14, 1030, 1063
Halban, Hans Heinrich von, 19, 19 n.3
Halder, Franz, 1177, 1177 n.11
Hale, Charles Leslie, 1932, 1932 n.2
Haley, William John
  biographical information, 398 n.3
  political broadcasts on the BBC, 398, 523, 980–1, 2027, 2034
  WSC suggests BBC broadcast for Czechs who escaped from Czechoslovakia, 1023, 1027
Halford-MacLeod, Aubrey Seymour, 1200, 1200 n.1
Halifax, Lady (Dorothy Evelyn Augusta Onslow Wood), 160, 160 n.2, 247, 292
Halifax, Lord (Edward Frederick Lindley Wood)
  biographical information, 1 n.1
  economics: Halifax updates WSC on financial and trade negotiations with the US, 159, 165; Lend-Lease Programme cancelation, 40–1; US loan to England, 211–12, 213
  political career, 66, 160
  poor health of Hopkins, 160
  sends well wishes to CSC, 160
  The Sinews of Peace (March 1946 WSC speech): WSC plans speech, 165; Halifax reacts to, 247; Stalin's criticism of, 308
  Sumner Welles praises WSC's world affairs speeches (1946), 309
  Truman's opinion of Attlee and Bevin, 11–12
  UN Trusteeship proposal, 133
  von Weizsäcker's trial, 1177, 1178, 1179, 1223 n.5, 1391
  and WSC: Halifax reflects on WSC's election loss (1945), 1–2; Shadow Cabinet, 291, 292; WSC addresses the Virginia Legislature, 210; WSC's characterization of Chamberlain's settlement with Hitler, 1180; WSC's Florida visit (1946), 159, 165, 169, 173; WSC updates Halifax on Labour Government, 291–2
Hall, George Henry, 881, 881 n.1
Hall, Joyce Clyde, 1651, 1651 n.1, 1651 n.2
Haman, 1768, 1768 n.1
Hamblin, Grace Ellen ('Hambone'), 28, 28 n.1, 37–8, 689, 1355, 1356
Hamilton, James Hamish, 944, 944 n.1, 1481, 1484, 1486
Hamish Hamilton publishing house, 549, 549 n.1
'Hammer', 955–6, 955 n.2
Hampden, John, 797, 797 n.1
Hankey, Maurice Pascal Alers, 18, 18 n.3, 953, 977, 1233–4
Hansen, Hans Marinus, 1885, 1885 n.2
Harald Hardrada (King of Norway), 1053, 1053 n.1
d'Harcourt, Comte (Charles Jean Marie), 1842, 1842 n.1
Harden, James Richard Edwards, 1426, 1426 n.4
Hardie, Steven, 1874, 1874 n.1, 2119
Harding, Allan Francis ('John'), 734, 734 n.3
Hardinge, Alexander Henry Louis, 851, 851 n.1, 858
Hare, William Francis, 398, 398 n.2
Harmsworth, Esmond Cecil (Lord Rothermere), 81, 81 n.1
Harmsworth, Vere Harold Esmond, 1351, 1351 n.1
Harriman, William Averell, 247 n.2, 603, 604, 2136
Harris, Sir Arthur Travers ('Bomber Harris')
  biographical information, 100 n.1
  Attlee does not recommend Peerage for, 178, 213
  Campaign Star qualifications, 100
  Dresden bombing, 1743 n.1, 1799–800
  WSC reviews extracts on Allied war-time bombing actions, 441
Harris, E. G., 226, 226 n.2
Harris, Henry Wilson, 520, 520 n.2
Harrison, James, 1877, 1877 n.1
Harrod, (Henry) Roy Forbes, 811, 811 n.1, 812, 1883
Harrow School speeches (WSC)
  November 1946, 557–9

Index

November 1947, 842–4
November 1948, 1225–7
December 1949, 1580–2
November 1950, 1945–6
Hartington, Lord (Spencer Compton Cavendish), 276, 276 n.1
Hartley, Vivien Mary (Vivien Leigh), 2144, 2144 n.2
Harvey, Arthur Vere
  biographical information, 199 n.2
  British Armed Forces preparedness and recruiting efforts (1950), 1788–9
  Civil Aviation Debate, 199
  European Army, 2149–50, 2151
  Palestine (January 1947 WSC speech), 604
  WSC discusses possibility of war with Russia, 2149
Harvey, Oliver Charles, 665, 665 n.2
Hassell, Ulrich von, 944, 944 n.2
d'Hauteville, Roger Marie Antoine Benoît, 898, 898 n.2, 901, 1979, 1981
Hawkey, Alfred James
  biographical information, 104 n.1
  Freedom of the City of Bancroft School awarded to WSC, 104, 104 n.2
  health, 1592
  Seligman assesses possible US response to Russian blockade of Berlin, 1145–6
  Woolton suggested as successor to Assheton for Conservative Party Chairman, 289
  WSC thanks for friendship, 1102
Head, Antony Henry, 1435, 1435 n.2, 1442, 1442 n.2, 1445, 1788–9
Heald, Lionel Frederick, 2229, 2229 n.6
Health Insurance, 1017, 1092, 1104
Hearst, William Randolph, 396, 396 n.1
Heinsius, Anthonie, 118, 118 n.3
Heiskell, Andrew, 1255, 1255 n.2
Helsby, Laurence Norman, 943, 943 n.1, 943 n.2, 1346, 1347
Henderson, Arthur, 359–60, 359 n.1, 830
Henderson, George Francis Robert, 244, 244 n.4
Henderson, John Nicholas, 599–600, 599 n.1, 601–2
Henley, Sylvia Laura Stanley, 763, 763 n.2
Henry III, King (Henry of Bourbon, Henry IV of France), 1037–8, 1037 n.1
Henry, Patrick, 243, 243 n.3
Henry VII, King (Henry Tudor), 180, 180 n.1
Herriot, Édouard, 65, 65 n.3, 383, 1230
Heydeman, Cecil Albert, 59, 59 n.1
Heydrich, Reinhard, 1222, 1222 n.2
Hicks, Ernest George, 526–7, 526 n.1, 545–6, 556
Higgs, Walter Frank, 1631, 1631 n.1
Hill, Charles, 1716, 1716 n.2

Hillman, Sydney, 742, 742 n.1
Hill, Rose Ethel Kathleen
  biographical information, 33 n.2
  categorisation of letters to WSC, 70–1
  'Morgenthau Plan' for Germany, 33, 36
  responses to letters to WSC, 71
  WSC requests larger table for Opposition committee, 131, 146
  WSC's secretaries and work schedules, 37–8
Himmler, Heinrich Luitpold, 844, 844 n.4, 1883
Hinchingbrooke, Lord (Alexander Victor Edward Paulet Montagu, 'Hinch'), 520, 520 n.5
Hiroshima, 16, 21
A History of the English Speaking Peoples (Churchill), 178, 179–80, 392
Hitler, Adolf
  Allied Unconditional Surrender Policy, 1451
  Chamberlain's settlement with, 1180
  death of, 792
  Franco Government, 1415
  German re-armament and territorial encroachments prior to Second World War, 139
  German resistance movement against, 1177–8, 1179
  invasion of Poland, 317
  invasion of Russia, 1823
  Israelis compare Bevin to, 1768
  Munich Agreement, 135
  non-aggression pacts of, 809
  orders for assassination attempt on WSC, 2009–10, 2012
  Stalin compares WSC to, 255–6
  Swiss belief that Schellenburg persuaded Hitler to not invade Switzerland, 1883
  Truman's opinion of, 807
  WSC compares Soviet–Socialists to Nazi–Socialists, 1794
  WSC compares Stalin to, 1184–5, 1779
  WSC criticises Hitler and the Nazis, 136–7
  WSC declares Kremlin and Communism greater threats than, 503, 938, 1335, 1363, 1372
  WSC discusses Russia with Baruch, 746
  WSC discusses in *The Second World War*, 914, 1174
  WSC praises role of Netherlands in defeat of, 323
Hoare, Reginald, 185, 185 n.2
Hoare, Samuel John Gurney, 635, 635 n.1
Hocquard, Gabriel, 384, 384 n.1
Hodge, John, 1870, 1870 n.1
Hofer, Andreas, 370, 370 n.1
Holland-Martin, Anne Cavendish, 2144, 2144 n.4

2288 INDEX

Holland-Martin, Christopher John, 2144, 2144 n.3
Holland, Sidney George, 2101, 2101 n.1
Hollis, Leslie Chasemore ('Jo'), 401–2, 401 n.1, 983–4
Hollis, Maurice Christopher, 2191, 2191 n.4
Holmes, Julius Cecil, 1664–5, 1664 n.1
Holmes, Marian, 3–4, 3 n.4
Home Secretary: *see* Chuter-Ede, James Chuter
Hong Kong, 1283, 2063–5, 2073–4
honorary degrees and awards (WSC speeches)
   Honorary Degree Conferment, Brussels University (November 1945), 137–9
   University of Miami speech notes (February 1946), 213–21
   Let Freedom Reign (May 1946), 327
   The Flame of Christian Ethics (May 1948), 1048–50
   To End Bitterness (May 1948), 1050–2
   The Essential Verities (November 1948), 1251–3
   Presentation of Grotius Medal (February 1949), 1313–14
   Honorary Degree Conferment, Copenhagen University (October 1950), 1885–7
honours and awards
   Amery declines GCB honour, 31
   Campaign Star qualifications, 97, 100–1, 274
   Coalition Government medallions, 423, 527, 578
   Committee on the Grant of Honours, Decorations and Medals report, 96–7, 100–1
   Defence Medal qualifications, 100, 274–5
   14th Army War Medal Clasps proposal, 97, 101
   India Service Medal proposal, 274
   shoulder badges for Calvary regiments, 613
   War Medal qualifications, 274
   WSC: American Air Force pilot's wings, 1293; Catholic University of Louvain, Honorary Degree Conferment (November 1945 WSC speech), 137–9; Danish Order of the Elephant awarded to WSC, 1933; Freedom of the City of Bancroft School, 104, 104 n.2; Grand Cross and Chain of the Royal Order of St Olav, 1075, 1076; Honorary Degree Conferment, Copenhagen University (October 1950 WSC speech), 1885–7; Lord Warden of the Cinque Ports, 4–5, 1940; Order of the Elephant, 1933; Order of Merit, 175, 208; WSC declines Order of the Garter, 4
Hood, Samuel, 2151, 2151 n.3
Hoover, Herbert, 270, 270 n.6, 362, 1978, 1978 n.4, 1987, 1993

Hope, James Fitzalan (Lord Rankeillour), 42, 42 n.1
Hope, Victor Alexander John ('Hopie'), 635, 635 n.2
Hopkins, Harry
   biographical information, 160 n.1
   Allied Unconditional Surrender Policy, 1461, 1462, 1563
   Baruch asks WSC how he will discuss Hopkins in war-time memoirs, 742–3
   death of, 191–2, 198
   poor health of, 160, 173, 190
   White House Papers, 1445, 1662
   WSC visits Shangri-La with FDR, 1975
Hopkins, Louise Gill Macy, 160, 160 n.3, 190
Hopkinson, Henry Lennox D'Aubigne, 514, 514 n.1, 1341–2, 1352–4, 1642
Horder, Thomas Jeeves, 1819, 1819 n.1
Hore-Belisha, Leslie ('Horeb Elisha'), 671, 671 n.1, 1327
Horner, Arthur Lewis, 653, 653 n.1, 980, 2119–20, 2159
Horovitz, Béla, 1484, 1484 n.1
Horsbrugh, Florence Gertrude, 2191, 2191 n.3
House of Commons (HofC)
   Burma: Burma (December 1946 WSC speech), 580–2; Burma Independence Bill (November 1947 WSC speech), 846–9
   Committee of Privileges: Committee on Privileges Report (October 1947), 837–9; Complaint of Privilege (March 1951), 2019–25; WSC withdraws from, 693, 695, 732, 732 n.3
   Commons Chamber: Brown elected Speaker of the House, 3; HofC Convening Time, 292–5, 292 n.1; Motion for Address in Reply, 1912–13, 1912 n.1, 1912 n.2; The New Chamber of the House of Commons, 1914–15; Table Office and Clerks, 955, 955 n.1, 957
   communications: Budget Proposals, Newspaper Publication (Oral Answers), 869–70, 870; publication of the Journals of the HofC, War Sessions (1939–1945), 38–9, 39 n.1; Publication of Teheran and Yalta Decisions (Oral Answers), 204–5; statements justifying the resignations of Ministers, 357–9, 358, 363, 640
   Debate on the Address speeches (WSC): November 1946, 530–41; October 1947, 821–35; October 1948, 1202–19; March 1950, 1668–79; October 1950, 1917–18
   defence speeches (WSC): March 1950, 1686–99; 26 July 1950, 1801–4; 27

INDEX

July 1950, 1807–17; September 1950, 1852–64, 1868
domestic affairs: Budget Debate, 294; Civil Aviation Debate, 198, 199; Coal Bill Debate, 199–200, 201; Control of Investment Bill, 200; Criminal Justice Bill, 1110–23; Fuel and Power Crisis, 615–20; Housing, 1921–32; Iron and Steel, 1235–49, 1235 n.1, 1868–78; Liberal Government of 1906, 2198; Ministers and Public Servants, Official Conduct, 1314–20; National Insurance Bill, 200–1; National Service Bill, 670–7, 678–9, 696–702; Navy Estimates, 986–97; Petrol Rationing, 836; Redistribution Bill, 1078–86, 1088; Representation of the People Bill, 968–77; Special Powers Bill, 762, 764; Town and Country Planning Bill and Parliamentary Democracy, 629–33; Trade Disputes Bill, 201; Transitional Powers Bill, Supplies and Services, 759–60; Transport Bill, 663–4; WSC suggests forming Select Committee on electoral reform, 1669–71
economics speeches (WSC): Finance Bill (June 1946), 388–90; Economic Situation (March 1947), 646–63; Devaluation of the Pound (September 1949), 1499–514; The Economic Situation (October 1949), 1551–6; The Budget (April 1950), 1721–32; Budget Proposals and Economic Survey (April 1951), 2032–4; Exports to China (May 1951), 2066–76; Finance Bill Amendments, Chairman's Selection (June 1951), 2095–8
Europe speeches (WSC): The North Atlantic Treaty (May 1949), 1411–17; European Unity (March 1950), 1702–12; North Atlantic Supreme Commander (April 1951), 2041–55
food speeches (WSC): World Food Situation (May 1946), 355–63; Rationing of Bread (May 1946), 363–4; Bread Rationing (July 1946), 415–22
foreign affairs speeches (WSC): Foreign Policy, President Truman's Declaration (November 1945), 119–27; Foreign Affairs (June 1946), 365–80; Foreign Affairs (October 1946), 497–504; Foreign Affairs (January 1948), 929–40; Foreign Affairs (December 1948), 1270–85; Foreign Affairs (July 1949), 1450–5; Foreign Affairs (November 1949), 1562–75; Foreign Affairs (November 1950), 1950–7; The

International Situation (December 1950), 1967–75; Tshekedi Khama Banishment (June 1951), 2099–101, 2099 n.1
India: India (December 1946 WSC speech), 569–78; India Government Policy (March 1947 WSC speech), 634–46; India Transfer of Power (June 1947 WSC speech), 728–30; HofC resolution of appreciation for Indian Civil and Military Services, 748, 748 n.1; Hyderabad and Kashmir (July 1948 WSC speech), 1133–9; India, Commonwealth Relations (Oral Answers), 1396–400
Ireland, Relations with the Commonwealth (November 1948 WSC speech), 1258–61
Korea: Korea (July 1950 WSC speech), 1780–6; Korean Republic Invasion (Oral Answers), 1769–71
Middle East: British Troops in Egypt (May 1946 WSC speech), 311–15; Palestine (August 1946 WSC speech), 427–36; Palestine (January 1947 WSC speech), 604–10; Palestine (January 1949 WSC speech), 1297–308; Jordan and Israel, Government Decision (April 1950 Oral Answers), 1736–9; Assassination of King Abdullah of Jordan (July 1951 WSC speech), 2121; Foreign Affairs, Middle East (July 1951 WSC speech), 2125–37
tributes: Attlee congratulates WSC on V-J Day victory, 34–5, 35; Baldwin's death, 900; The Earl of Oxford and Asquith, 1962–4; Field Marshal Smuts Westminster Memorial Statue, 2093–4; His Majesty's Return From South Africa, 702–3; Motion of Congratulations to Their Majesties on their Silver Wedding, 1029; Oliver Stanley, 1966–7; Roosevelt Memorial Fund, 550
and WSC: Salter praises WSC's demeanor toward new MPs in new HofC, 62; WSC asks Garbett about 'snap divisions' observations, 1759, 1760, 1763–4; WSC as elder statesman of, 62; WSC praises Nicolson after election loss, 2; WSC requests larger table for Opposition committee, 131, 146
see also Parliament
House, George, 1325, 1325 n.2
housing
built between the wars, 714, 1629
Conservative Party policies, 1070–1, 1596
Housing Rural Workers Act, 476

housing *(continued)*
  speeches (WSC): Tasks Ahead (October 1945), 105; Housing (November 1950), 1921–32
  WSC criticises Labour Government rebuilding and repair efforts, 151–2, 306–7, 474–5, 539–40, 656–7, 718–20, 747, 827–8, 1540–1, 1632, 1633, 1638, 1655, 1677–8, 1723, 1750–1
Howard, Greville Reginald, 315, 315 n.1
Howard-Vyse, Richard Granville Hylton, 1257, 1257 n.4
How Bill Adams won the Battle of Waterloo (comic monologue), 616, 616 n.1
Howson, Edmund Whytehead, 1581, 1581 n.2
Hoxha, Enver Hail, 1354, 1354 n.1
Hoy, James Hutchison, 530–1, 531, 531 n.1
Hudson, James Hindle, 1121, 1121 n.1
Hudson, Robert Spear
  biographical information, 357 n.1
  food: Bread Rationing (July 1946 WSC speech), 418; Indian food situation, 360; long-term agricultural programme, 476, 801; world food shortages, 357
  National Service Bill, 686
Hughes, Emrys, 1025, 1025 n.1, 1782, 1973, 2053
Hughes-Hallett, John, 1849, 1849 n.2, 1850
Hughes, Hector, 1121–2, 1121 n.2
Hughes, William Morris, 777, 777 n.4
Hugo, Victor, 586–7
Hull, Cordell, 372, 372 n.1
'Husky', 1486, 1486 n.2
Hynd, John Burns, 447, 447 n.5, 650

Ibn Saud, 209 n.1, 404, 404 n.2, 430
Iceland, 1383–4
Identification Friend or Foe (IFF), 612, 612 n.2
Imperial Chemical Industries Limited, 18
Imperial Defence College, 282
India
  Amery hopes for interim Indian government, 382
  Attlee calls meeting with Liberals and Conservatives regarding, 399
  British Army in, 675
  British indebtedness to, 624–5
  Commonwealth relations: Amery discusses with WSC, 1383–4, 1394, 1401, 1401 n.1; Commonwealth status offer, 330–1; Dominion status proposal, 635, 666–7, 725, 726, 728–30; India, Commonwealth Relations (Oral Answers), 1396–400; India States relations with British Government, 332, 412–13; Smuts discusses with WSC, 1402, 1421–2, 1422–3, 1424–5; WSC comments on, 1420, 1773
  Cripps mission (1942), 328, 329–31, 408–11, 572, 633, 634–8, 728
  famines in, 359–60, 364, 1209
  George VI renounces title as Emperor of, 1089
  Hyderabad and Kashmir, 1090, 1129–30, 1163, 1165, 1210–11
  independence and partition: Conservative Party Resolution regarding fate of minorities and Indian states, 443, 476–7; effect on Imperial Services, 641–2; India Independence Bill, 738–9; loss of India as part of British Empire, 477, 688, 690; post-Imperial British policy towards, 1209–11; religious massacres, 573, 786–7, 786 n.2, 793–4, 829, 885, 1089, 1193, 1208–9, 2215–16; Statute of Westminster 1931 on legality of secession, 633; WSC appeals for peaceful British transfer of power to, 571–2, 577–8; WSC criticises 14-month time limit for achieving Indian independence, 640–6; WSC criticises Nehru's Government, 1089–90; WSC defends Conservative Party stance towards, 2215–16; WSC opposes Indian independence, 328, 410, 435, 536; WSC warns of civil war, 435, 455, 477, 534–5, 571–4, 642–3
  Indian Comforts Fund, 32
  Interim Congress Government: Ali criticises, 470–1, 471 n.1; Constituent Assembly procedures, 574–7, 581; Jinnah criticises British Government and Indian Congress Party negotiations, 400, 440–1, 454, 455; Monckton describes representatives to WSC, 335–6; Muslim League dissatisfaction with, 413–14; Wavell asks Nehru to form, 450; WSC cites massacres of Indians as evidence of lack of Indian unity under Nehru's Interim Administration, 572–4; WSC criticises establishment of and lack of Indian unity under, 572–4; WSC criticises Nehru, 639
  Muslims' status and future, 331, 412, 440–1, 574–8, 638–9, 641, 642–3
  speeches (WSC): The British Commonwealth (May 1946), 318; India Cabinet Mission, Statement on the Adjournment (May 1946), 329–32; India Cabinet Mission (July 1946), 408–14; India (December 1946), 569–78; India Government Policy (March 1947), 634–46; India Transfer of Power (June 1947), 728–30; Hyderabad and Kashmir (July 1948), 1133–9

Index 2291

Untouchables' status and future, 331–2, 332, 342, 395, 411–12, 413, 440, 518, 562, 574–8, 1193
WSC criticises Labour Government policy towards, 570, 885, 1015, 1673
WSC declines lunch with Jinnah and suggests use of different names for their correspondence, 569
WSC receives Indo-Pakistan affairs assessment from Noon (1951), 2220–2, 2222 n.1
industry
Baruch describes industry trade scheme to WSC, 744
Baruch discusses modernisation of British industry with WSC, 841
Conservative Party policies, 2163–4
export of British machine tools and diesel engines to Russia, 1845, 1859–61, 1887
French and German coal and steel industries, 1752–3, 1783, 1792, 1828, 1876, 2123
iron and steel: Iron and Steel Bill, 1239, 1243; steel industry expansion, 1870; WSC criticises nationalisation of, 822, 832, 834, 1016–17, 1093, 1192, 1217–19, 1420, 1531, 1610–11, 1619, 1642, 1676–7, 1746, 1753, 1793, 1973–4, 1987, 2014–15, 2118–19, 2119, 2203–4; WSC plans repeal of Iron and Steel Act of 1949, 2228–30
life insurance, 1611, 1619
railways, 540–1, 1244–5, 1538, 1645–6, 1751
speeches (WSC): Iron and Steel Bill (November 1948), 1235–49, 1235 n.1; Labour's Nationalisation Policy: 'Caprice and Greed' (May 1949), 1419–20; Nationalisation (May 1949), 1429–30; Iron and Steel (September 1950), 1868–78; Cutlers' Feast, Sheffield (April 1951), 2037–8
transition to peace-time production, 105
US investment in British industries, 1078
Van Leer's mobile drum factory exhibit, 1992, 1995
worker wages, 1728–9, 1753
WSC criticises nationalisation of, 152, 305, 476, 480, 540–1, 718, 821–2, 888, 1016–17, 1065–8, 1512–13, 1537–9, 1611, 1618–19, 1633–4, 1641, 1645, 1654, 1746, 1748–9, 1793, 2118, 2161, 2179, 2198–9, 2205
see also coal industry
Ingersoll, Ralph, 355, 355 n.1
Ingr, Sergej, 1023, 1023 n.1, 1027
Inönü, Ismet, 1219–20, 1219 n.1
Inskip, Thomas Walker Hobart, 1233, 1233 n.3, 1688

Inverchapel, Lord: see Kerr, Archibald Clark
Iran: see Persia
Iraq, 1990–1, 1991 n.1, 2127
Ireland
British policy towards, 1193, 1460
Dublin Cabinet, 1206, 1208
Irish neutrality policy, 345
loss of British ports in southern Ireland, 313, 321, 329, 345
speeches (WSC): Debate on the Address (October 1948), 1206–8; Ireland, Relations with the Commonwealth (November 1948), 1258–61; Foreign Affairs (December 1948), 1270–1; Ulster (October 1951), 2186–7
WSC discusses settlement of the Irish Question with Shaw, 453
Ironside, William Edmund, 738, 783 n.2
Isaacs, George Alfred
biographical information, 47 n.4
Iron and Steel, 1877
National Service Bill, 670, 696
WSC criticises demobilisation efforts (August 1945), 47
WSC criticises 'Work or Starve' policy, 886, 1613
Isaacs, Gerald, 1659, 1659 n.4, 1660
Ismay, Sir Hastings ('Pug')
biographical information, 5 n.2
communications: Ismay agrees to destroy COS minute with WSC's criticism of Tedder, 172; publication of WSC's wartime Administration papers, minutes and personal correspondence, 956
Companion of Honour award, 5, 30
India: India Independence Bill, 738–9; Noon sends Indo-Pakistan affairs assessment to WSC (1951), 2222 n.1
Japan: Attlee plans national broadcast upon surrender of Japan, 6; Ismay and COS congratulate WSC on VJ Day, 33
Moorehead's *Sunday Express* articles and book on WSC and Montgomery, 528–9, 544–5, 547, 549
The Second World War: 'Air Ministry Pamphlet 156', 552, 554–5, 557; despatch of tanks to the Middle East, 529–30; feedback and suggested edits for, 978–9, 1057, 1153–5, 1159, 1160, 1161–2, 1402, 1560, 2060–1, 2146; final months of Wavell's command, 1288, 1313; French language version introductory note, 1389; French language version references to General Prioux, 1333–4; 'Husky' and 'Trident' operations, 1486; Iraq and Syria, 1142; 'Jubilee' (Dieppe raid), 711, 711 n.1, 1702, 1821–2, 1837, 1848,

Ismay, Sir Hastings ('Pug') *(continued)*
  The Second World War *(continued)*
    1849–50, 1852; 'Overlord' preparations, 544–5, 1941–2; Paris conversations (1940), 978; research and notes for, 1167, 1312–13, 1486; 'Sledgehammer', 516, 521; 'Tiger' and Crete operations, 1130–1, 1140–1; Tours speech (1944), 977; tube alloys research and atom bomb, 1601–2; war-time Supreme Command decisions, 297–9, 299–300, 339, 598, 601; WSC asks for feedback on draft chapters on 1940 French battle, 469; WSC asks for war-time notes and documents, 521, 529–30, 551–2, 598, 1025–6; WSC reviews timing of his control over COS directives, 352–3; WSC works on in Marrakech, 1990
  WSC forms new Government (1951), 2219–20
Israel
  Amery reports on Israel and Jordan visit to WSC, 1767–8
  British policy towards, 1224, 1311
  British recognition of, 1301–2, 1741–2, 1761
  Elath meets with WSC, 1867–8, 1879–81
  Elath visits, 1879
  Israeli attitude towards Bevin, 1768
  Israeli territory and frontiers, 1304, 1305
  Jordan and Israel, Government Decision (Oral Answers), 1736–9
  McNeill discusses British policy with WSC, 1257–8
  Middle Eastern oil supplies, 1990–1, 1991 n.1
  reconstruction of, 1741–2
Italy
  Allied Unconditional Surrender Policy, 1563–4
  Austria and South Tyrol, 93–4, 102, 370–1, 436, 451–2, 456–7, 464
  Communism in, 233, 804–5, 1014
  Italian fleet disposition, 930–1
  Sarah Churchill and WSC describe Italian people and Lake Como region to CSC, 54–5, 59, 72
  Trieste and Venezia Giulia, 370, 371, 501–2
  United Europe (May 1947 WSC speech), 708
  UN role, 319
  WSC criticises Tito's claims to former Italian territory, 233, 501–2
  WSC's 1939 letter to Grandi, 623–4, 623 n.3, 624 n.1
  WSC seeks rapid achievement of peace with, 378–9
  WSC's message to the Italian people (August 1944), 117, 117 n.1

Yugoslavia refuses to sign peace treaty with, 509
Ivan the Terrible (Ivan IV Vasilyevich), 1106, 1106 n.1

Jackson, Francis Stanley, 558, 558 n.1, 559
Jackson, Thomas ('Stonewall'), 107, 107 n.3
Jacob, Edward Ian Claud, 1027, 1027 n.1, 1027 n.2
Jakobsen, Frode, 1898, 1898 n.1
James, Frederick (Lord Leathers), 130, 130 n.2, 1267, 2224
Japan
  administration of without an Allied Control Commission, 46
  Astor meets with MacArthur in, 1745, 1763, 1765–6
  atom bomb dropped on Hiroshima, 16, 21
  Attlee congratulates WSC on V-J Day victory, 34–5, 35
  Attlee plans National Service of Thanksgiving after surrender of, 28–9
  Attlee updates WSC on expected surrender of, 25
  Furness serves as defence counsel for Shigemitsu, 593
  Japanese surrender (V-J Day), 6, 31, 33, 34, 35, 57, 99
  WSC praises MacArthur's administration of, 771–2, 1187, 1360
  WSC's Atomic Bomb statement, 21
  Yalta Agreement, 203–4
Jastrzebowski, Wojciech, 437–9, 439 n.2
Java, 194
Jay, Douglas Patrick Thomas, 1146, 1146 n.2, 1537, 1637–8
Jeanne d'Arc ('Maid of Orleans'), 180, 180 n.2
Jebb, Hubert Miles Gladwyn, 1605, 1605 n.2
Jefferis, Millis Rowland, 1882, 1882 n.2
Jefferson, Thomas, 243, 243 n.3
Jeffreys, George Darell, 1212, 1212 n.1
Jenkins, Roy Harris, 1032, 1245, 1245 n.1
Jerome, Jeanette ('Jennie'), 448, 448 n.2
Jerome, Leonard Walter, 245, 245 n.1
Jews
  Friedman thanks WSC for support of Zionism, 270
  Ibn Saud's views on potential Jewish National Home in Palestine, 209
  von Weizsäcker's role in Nazi extermination of, 1222–3, 1223 n.5, 1341–2
  see also Israel; Palestine
Jinnah, Mohammed Ali
  biographical information, 335 n.1
  Ambedkar appeals to WSC regarding future of Untouchables, 518
  India Independence Bill, 738–9

INDEX

Jinnah criticises British Government and Indian Congress Party negotiations, 400, 440–1, 454, 455
   Muslims' status and future, 335
   WSC declines lunch with and suggests use of different names for their correspondence, 569
John 'Lackland', King, 179, 179 n.5
Johnson, Hewlett, 2023, 2023 n.1
Joint Intelligence Committee, 546–7
Joint Intelligence Staff, 527–8
Jones, Arthur Creech, 1116, 1116 n.1, 1299–300
Jones, Frederick Elwyn, 1213, 1213 n.1, 1222–3, 1223 n.5, 1974
Jones, Reginald Victor, 1158, 1158 n.1
Jordan, 1736–9, 1767–8
Jouhaux, Léon, 1035, 1035 n.1
Jowitt, William Allen, 2167–8, 2167 n.1
'Jubilee' (Dieppe raid), 1701, 1701 n.1, 1702
Juin, Alphonse Pierre, 1976, 1976 n.1
Juliana, Queen (Juliana Louise Emma Marie Wilhelmina), 1009, 1009 n.3, 1313, 1940

Kardelj, Edvard, 1994, 1994 n.2
Katelbach, Tadeusz, 437–9, 439 n.5
Keeling, Edward, 850, 850 n.2, 1770
Keenan, William, 1931–2, 1931 n.1
Keightley, Charles Frederic, 1988, 1988 n.2
Keith, Arthur Berridale, 633, 633 n.2
Kelly, Gerald Festus, 1719, 1719 n.4
Kelly, Richard Denis Lucien
   biographical information, 735 n.1
   document cataloguing and indexing for WSC, 735–6
   in Marrakech with WSC, 1979, 1981
   Press extracts on the East Fulham by-election (1933), 918–20
   Quebec Agreement of 1943, 2000
   salary, 1263
   The Second World War: feedback and suggested edits for, 1129, 1263, 1560, 2060, 2146, 2147, 2147–8; Yalta Conference, 2076
Kemsley, Lady (Helene Candida Hay Berry), 1128, 1128 n.2
Kemsley, Lord (James Gomer Berry), 1128, 1128 n.3, 1666, 2158, 2158–9
Kennedy, Joseph Patrick, 1174, 1174 n.1
Kenney, George Churchill, 1590–1, 1590 n.3
Kenney, William John, 1664, 1664 n.3, 1665
Kent, Duchess of (Princess Marina), 1720, 1720 n.2
Kerr, Archibald Clark (Lord Inverchapel)
   biographical information, 194 n.1
   Marshall and war-time Supreme Command decisions, 599–600, 601–2, 602–3, 603, 604
   WSC expresses confidence in Kerr's ability to handle situation in Java, 194
Kerr, Charles Iain (Lord Teviot), 1087, 1087 n.1, 1266–7, 1267 n.1
Kerrigan, Timothy James, 1320–1, 1320 n.1
Kerstens, Pieter Adriaan, 1008–9, 1008 n.3
Kessel, Albrecht von, 1178, 1178 n.2
Kesselring, Albert, 695, 695 n.2, 704, 734
Key, Charles William, 1922, 1922 n.1
Keyes, Eva Mary Salvin Bowlby, 901, 901 n.2
Keyes, Geoffrey Charles Tasker, 1734–5, 1734 n.2
Keyes, Roger John Brownlow, 1734–5, 1734 n.1
Keynes, John Maynard, 40–1, 41 n.1, 211, 1724
Khama, Seretse, 1684, 1684–5, 1684 n.2, 1699–700, 1700 n.2
Khama, Tshekedi, 1700, 1700 n.1, 2099–101, 2099 n.1
Khan, Hamidullah, 336, 336 n.1
Khan, Osman Ali, 335 n.2, 336, 336 n.2
Kiernan, Thomas, 1177, 1177 n.10
Killearn, Baron (Miles Wedderburn Lampson), 779, 779 n.1, 2195–6, 2196 n.1
Killearn, Lady (Jacqueline Aldine Leslie Castellani Lampson), 779, 779 n.1, 1589, 1589 n.3
King David Hotel bombing, 423, 423 n.2
King, Ernest Joseph, 162, 162 n.2
King-Hall, William Stephen Richard, 600, 600 n.1
King, William Mackenzie
   biographical information, 109 n.1
   lunches with WSC and CSC in London, 109–14
   publication of WSC's war-time papers, minutes and personal correspondence, 985
   Quebec Agreement of 1943, 2007–8
   Russia: prospects for American bombing of, 877–8; Russian espionage in Canada, 112–13
   WSC praises King's leadership of Canada, 113–14
Kinna, Patrick Francis, 579, 579 n.2
Kinsky, Charles, 1001, 1001 n.2
Kirkpatrick, Ivone Augustine, 1179, 1179 n.1, 1937, 1938, 1943–5
Kirkwood, David, 342, 342 n.3, 644, 863, 868, 1215
Kleist-Schmenzin, Ewald von, 2009, 2009 n.3
Kluang court martial, 539, 539 n.1
Knatchbull-Hugessen, Hughe Montgomery ('Snatch')
   biographical information, 116 n.1
   sends well wishes to CSC, 158

Knatchbull-Hugessen, Hughe Montgomery ('Snatch') *(continued)*
   speaking programme for WSC's visits to Paris and Belgium, 116–17, 145, 158
   WSC visits Brussels, 142, 145, 158
Knatchbull-Hugessen, Mary Gilmour Wolrige Gordon, 145, 145 n.2, 158
Koc, Adam, 437–9, 439 n.3
Kofitsas, Dimitrios, 856, 856 n.1
Kolchak, Alexander Vasilievich, 1298–9, 1298 n.2
Korda, Alexander, 1762, 1762 n.1, 2115–16, 2116 n.1
Kordt, Eric, 1178, 1178 n.3
Kordt, Theodor, 1178, 1178 n.3
Korea
   Anglo-American military response to invasion of, 1774, 1781–2, 1785, 1955–6, 1968–9, 1983, 2075–6
   British forces in, 1839, 1844, 1846, 1858–9, 1905, 2068, 2068 n.1, 2073, 2080
   Chinese Communist aggression in, 2066–8
   Council of Europe stance on UN action in, 1829
   Korean Republic Invasion (Oral Answers), 1769–71
   Labour Government blames fall in buying power on Korean War, 2117–18
   North Korean invasion of Korea Republic, 1779–80
   quadripartite occupation of without an Allied Control Commission, 46
   RSC in as correspondent for *Daily Telegraph*, 1817–18
   RSC speaks at Constitutional Club regarding, 1978
   RSC suggests use of atom bomb on, 1960
   Russian encroachment into, 242
   Soviet backing of Korean Republic invasion, 1794, 1808
   speeches (WSC): Korea (June 1950), 1773–4; Korea (July 1950), 1780–6
   truce negotiations, 2036, 2104–5
   UN forces in, 1967–8
   US forces in, 1790, 1794, 1795, 1846, 1905, 1986, 1987–8, 2003, 2025, 2068, 2073, 2080, 2126–7
   worldwide implications of conflict in, 1830, 1846, 1856–7, 1903, 1905
Kraft, Ole Bjørn, 1898, 1898 n.3
Krajina, Vladimir Josef, 1023, 1023 n.1, 1027
Kristensen, Thorkil, 1898, 1898 n.2
Kruger, Stephanus Johannes Paulus, 186, 186 n.6
Kurile Islands, 203–4

Labour Government
   anti-Communist stance, 285, 365, 505, 555, 1853–4
   Bevan resigns as Minister of Labour and National Service (April 1951), 2057, 2058, 2070, 2082
   communications: correction of Dalton's selective quotation of WSC's statement on British assistance to European countries, 1475–6; use of 'Commonwealth' as alternative to 'Empire', 1203–6
   Council of Europe, 1227, 1228–9, 1230–1, 1231
   'Fair shares for all' slogan, 1647–8, 1652–3
   India, 570, 638–45, 794, 829, 1202
   Pakistan, 850
   Palestine, 949–52
   Parliament: new Parliament assembly after Conservative election loss (1945), 3, 35; Towards a New Parliament (April 1948 WSC speech), 1031–2; A New Parliament (July 1948 WSC speech), 1103–6; Parliament Act of 1911, 832–4; Parliament Bill, 859–69, 888–9, 928–9, 929 n.1, 1612
   policies: austerity measures, 152, 153–4, 821–2, 828–9, 883–4, 891, 965, 1619–21, 1622, 1637–8, 1639, 2179, 2205–6; budget planning and spending, 657–8, 661–3, 681–2, 687, 1018–19, 1190–1, 1456–7, 1500–2, 1511–14, 1536, 1539, 1551, 1552–4, 1595, 1608–9, 1640, 1720, 1727–8, 1747, 1843–4, 2161; civil service expansion and expenditures, 658, 681, 692, 966; coal industry, 200, 649, 652–6; cotton industry, 476, 2171; death penalty abolishment, 1015; employment, 796, 1534–5; export trade, 152, 660, 720, 797, 822–4, 835, 1673, 1723–4, 2116, 2170–1; foreign affairs, 931, 935–6, 1271–85, 1648–50, 1752, 2039–40, 2166–7, 2200–1, 2201–3, 2209; fuel and energy, 618–20, 720; housing, 151–2, 306–7, 474–5, 539–40, 656–7, 718–20, 747, 827–8, 1540–1, 1632, 1633, 1638, 1655, 1677–8, 1723, 1750–1, 1907–8, 1917, 1921–32, 2084–5; income equalization, 110; industry nationalisation, 152, 305, 476, 480, 540–1, 718, 797–8, 1016–17, 1192, 1457–8, 1618–19, 1633–4, 2035, 2118; Iron and Steel Bill (November 1948 WSC speech), 1235–49; petrol rationing, 1638–9, 1640, 1646–7, 1723, 1749–50; rearmament, 2035, 2117–18, 2163, 2179–81, 2188–9, 2215; social legislation, 716, 723, 755–6, 795, 1017, 1092–3, 1629–30; taxation, 1631–2, 1633, 1640, 1642, 1645, 1654–5, 1675, 1721, 1722–3, 1724–7, 1747, 1750,

1751–2, 2033, 2035, 2086, 2097, 2117, 2161, 2163, 2173; WSC criticises 'socialist' Labour Government policies, 117, 340, 472, 473, 476, 480, 618–20, 691–2, 1350, 1449, 1553–4, 1678–9, 1715, 1726–7, 1729–30, 1747–8, 1791–4, 1835–6, 1847, 2033, 2035, 2056–7, 2082–3, 2116–18, 2161–2, 2212–13; WSC criticises 'Work or Starve' policy, 886, 1613, 1631, 1645
political broadcasting: Communist views on the BBC, 980–1, 1021–2, 1022–3; controversial political broadcasts, 522–4; current legislation broadcasts, 1023–5; meeting minutes, 424–6, 522–6, 979–82; ministerial broadcasts, 525; note of proposals Annex, 525–6; number of broadcasts, 525; The Week in Westminster, 981, 1025
Russia, 193–6, 1183–4, 1188
Shaw discusses English politics with WSC, 447–8
Smuts discusses with WSC, 1422
speeches (WSC): The Perils of Socialist Control (November 1945), 148–56; Failures of the Government's 'Doctrinaire Socialism' (April 1946), 304–7; Debate on the Address (November 1946), 530–41; No Easy Passage (August 1947), 766–70; Municipal Elections press statement (October 1947), 819; Debate on the Address (October 1947), 821–35; Local Election Victories (November 1947), 842; Britain in Peril speech notes (December 1947), 882; Britain in Peril (December 1947), 883–91; Britain in Peril press statement (December 1947), 891; The Evils of Socialist Government, Scottish Unionist meeting (May 1948), 1062–71; Britain 'Floundering and Sinking' (June 1948), 1086–96; Perils Abroad and at Home (October 1948), 1182–94, 1196–7, 1197, 1198–9; Debate on the Address (October 1948), 1202–19; Labour's Nationalisation Policy: 'Caprice and Greed' (May 1949), 1419–20; Labour's Disastrous Rule (October 1949), 1550–1; Debate on the Address (March 1950), 1668–79; Debate on the Address (October 1950), 1917–18
wage increase freeze and Stock Exchange collapse, 2172
War Office, 538–9, 830
WSC accuses of spreading propaganda about Great Britain between the wars, 714–15
WSC describes to CSC, 764–5

WSC's Opposition leadership, 24, 117–18, 127, 168, 173, 285–6, 287–8, 289, 290, 337, 356, 367, 396, 478–9, 482, 485–6, 506, 508, 563, 682–3, 796–7, 834, 870, 888, 957, 1075, 1531, 1663, 1681–2, 1752, 1803, 1853, 1857–8, 1873–4, 1905–7, 2135
see also defence; General Election (1950); General Election (1951)
Labour Party
Europe: Labour Party declines role on Hague Conference United Europe Committee, 958, 960, 963, 968; United States of Europe proposals, 545; WSC criticises monopoly of United Europe efforts, 963–4
General Election landslide win (1945), 1–2
Liberal and Labour support for Conservative Opposition, 764
motion of censure against WSC, 251–2, 1412
new Parliament assembly after Conservative election loss, 3, 35, 481
Sandys reports on Conservative election campaign progress to WSC, 1625
Seretse Khama affair, 1685
Shaw discusses English politics with WSC, 447–8
speeches (WSC): Failures of the Government's 'Doctrinaire Socialism' (April 1946), 304–7; Palestine (August 1946), 431; Representation of the People Bill (February 1948), 969–71, 973, 976–7
split (1951), 2168, 2168 n.1, 2183–4, 2204, 2215
West Houghton by-election, 2098, 2098 n.1
Lafayette, Gilbert du Motier, Marquis de, 279, 279 n.1
La Guardia, Fiorello Henry, 173, 173 n.1
Lahousen, Erwin von, 2009–10, 2009 n.4
la Malfa, Ugo, 1035, 1035 n.2
Lamartine, Alphonse de, 804, 804 n.2
Lambert, George, 1606–7, 1606 n.3
Lambert, Guy Williams, 445, 445 n.1
Lampson, Miles Wedderburn (Baron Killearn), 779, 779 n.1, 2195–6, 2196 n.1
Landemare, Georgina, 2144, 2144 n.1
Lang, Gordon, 759, 759 n.1
Lansbury, George, 485, 485 n.1
Lansdowne, Lord (George John Charles Mercer Nairne Petty-Fitzmaurice), 2135, 2135 n.1
Lascelles, Sir Alan Frederick ('Tommy')
biographical information, 4 n.1
Auriol's visit to England, 1661, 1663
Byng case, 1683
Duke of Windsor: WSC disapproves of Duke of Windsor's plan to go to Ireland and study Anglo-American relations, 156, 156 n.1; WSC suggests unpaid official

Lascelles, Sir Alan Frederick ('Tommy') *(continued)*
  Duke of Windsor *(continued)*
    positions for Duke and Duchess of Windsor at British Embassy in America, 144
  George VI: asks WSC to review speech for unveiling of King George V statue, 780, 806–7, 812, 812 n.1; Coalition Government medallion for, 423; health, 1253–4, 1256; Lascelles asks WSC to review draft of George VI's speech to UNO delegates, 176, 177; wishes to see WSC before departing for South Africa, 603–4; WSC sends copy of *Their Finest Hour* to, 1442; WSC's Hallmark Christmas cards, 1993, 1995; WSC steps down as Lord Warden of the Cinque Ports, 4–5
  honours and awards: WSC asks permission to wear American Air Force pilot's wings, 1293; WSC asks permission to wear Grand Cross and Chain of the Royal Order of St Olav, 1075, 1076; WSC asks permission to wear Order of the Elephant, 1933
  Labour Government retains slim majority after 1950 General Election, 1660, 1663
  Prince Frederick of Prussia, 1823–4
  Princess Elizabeth: annuities, 851–2, 852–3, 858; engagement to Philip Mountbatten, 738; WSC recommends that Princess Elizabeth not fly to Canada during King George's illness, 2155
  Princess Margaret's travel allowance for Italy trip, 1390–1, 1394
  publication of WSC's war-time Administration papers, 942
  Trooping of the Colours cancelation, 1075, 1076, 1077
Laski, Harold Joseph, 385, 385 n.2
Laughlin, Henry Alexander, 1341, 1341 n.2, 1347, 1351, 1378, 1825
Laurencie, Benoît-Léon de Fornel de la, 1333–4, 1333 n.2, 1334
Lavery, John, 1798, 1798 n.2
Lawford, Valentine G. ('Nicholas'), 912, 912 n.2
Lawrence, Thomas Edward, 430, 430 n.3, 1304, 1482, 2121
Lawrence, W. A. J., 441, 441 n.1
Law, Richard Kidston, 201, 201 n.2, 950
Lawson, John James ('Jack'), 10 n.4, 15, 22
Laycock, Angela Clare Louise Ward, 900, 900 n.3
Laycock, Robert Edward, 900, 900 n.2, 1060
Layton, Elizabeth
  biographical information, 32 n.2
  cars and petrol for WSC, 32
  engagement and marriage to Frans Nel, 67–8, 289
  in Lake Como with WSC, 72
  'Morgenthau Plan' for Germany, 33, 36
  WSC's secretaries and work schedules, 37–8
Layton, Walter Thomas, 817–18, 817 n.1
Leader of the House of Commons (HofC): *see* Morrison, Herbert Stanley
League of Nations, 121–2, 139, 234, 253, 324, 378, 405–6, 427–8, 459, 506, 876
Leahy, William D., 226, 226 n.2, 241, 242, 248
Leathers, Lord (Frederick James), 130, 130 n.2, 1267, 2224
Lecky, William Edward Hartpole, 1215, 1215 n.1
Leclerc de Hauteclocque, Philippe, 1470, 1470 n.1
Lee, Frank Godbould, 2186, 2186 n.1
Lee, Richard Henry, 243–4, 244 n.1
Lee, Robert E., 244, 244 n.5, 245
Leese, Oliver William Hargreaves, 704, 704 n.1, 704 n.2
Legge-Bourke, Edward Alexander Henry, 1739, 1739 n.1
Leigh, Vivien (Vivien Mary Hartley), 2144, 2144 n.2
Lend-Lease Programme, 40–1, 551
Lennox-Boyd, Alan Tindal, 1072, 1072 n.1, 1716
Lennox-Boyd, Patricia Guinness, 1127–8, 1128 n.1
Leopold III (King of Belgium), 469, 469 n.1, 1410–11, 1543–4
Le Quesne Martel, Giffard
  biographical information, 1433 n.2
  European Army proposals, 1840–1, 1841 n.1
  paper on conscription, 1438–9
  WSC's views on conscription, 1433–4, 1434, 2036
Leslie, John Randolph Shane, 156, 156 n.1, 156 n.2, 1001, 1006, 1006 n.2, 1097
Leslie, Marjorie Ide, 186, 186 n.4
Le Tonnelier, Suydam Gaston (Marquis de Breteuil), 896, 896 n.2
Lever, Harold, 974, 974 n.1
Leveson, Arthur Edmund, 167, 167 n.2
Liaquat Ali Khan, Nawabzada, 2222, 2222 n.1
Liberal Government of 1906, 2198
Liberal Party
  Davies questions exclusion of Liberals from Liberal-Conservative meetings, 1597–8, 1602–4, 1604, 1604 n.1
  election broadcasts, 1615
  election results (1950), 1659
  electoral deadlock and vote-splitting tactics, 1618, 1668–9, 1906–7
  National Service Bill, 671–2, 678, 702

INDEX

Palestine (August 1946 WSC speech), 428–9
Representation of the People Bill (February 1948 WSC speech), 969–71
support for Conservative Opposition, 764
Where are the Liberals? Losing by Default (February 1949 *Evening Standard* article), 1325–6, 1326, 1327, 1330
WSC criticises: during Blackpool Conservative Party Conference, 473–4, 479; in letter to Lady Violet, 132–3; in letter to Lord Woolton, 444
WSC discusses by-elections results and candidates with Woolton, 553
WSC seeks solidarity with against Labour Government, 827, 1618, 1659–60, 1713, 1733, 1734, 1744–5, 1747, 1791–4, 1821, 1906–7, 2196–9
see also National Liberal Party
Lie, Trygve Halvdan, 1701–11, 1710 n.2
Lincoln, Abraham, 270, 270 n.1, 491, 1683
Lindemann, Frederick: *see* Cherwell, Lord (Frederick Lindemann, 'the Prof')
Lindsay, James, 1948–9, 1948 n.2
Lindsay, Lionel, 1628, 1628 n.1
Lippmann, Walter, 254, 254 n.1
Lithuania, 265, 268, 280, 295
Liverpool Cotton Exchange, 651–2, 720, 797, 1191, 1512, 2171
The Lives of Winston Churchill (Davenport and Murphy), 262
Lloyd, George Ambrose, 1171, 1171 n.2
Lloyd George, David, 379, 379 n.1, 657, 672, 860, 883, 913, 1182, 1233, 1235, 1366, 1624, 1632–3
Lloyd George, Gwilym, 201, 201 n.3, 522, 2203
Lloyd George, Lady (Frances Louis Stevenson), 354, 354 n.1
Lloyd George, Megan, 1668–9, 1668 n.1, 1930
Lockhart, Robert Hamilton Bruce, 2227, 2227 n.1
Logan, David Gilbert, 124, 124 n.1
Londonderry, Lady (Edith Helen Chaplin), 1328, 1328 n.1
Londonderry, Marquess (Charles Stewart Henry Vane-Tempest-Stewart), 1328, 1328 n.3
Longwell, Daniel, 761, 761 n.3, 1378, 1498
Loraine, Sir Percy Lyham, 190, 190 n.2
Lord President of the Council: *see* Morrison, Herbert Stanley
Lord Warden of the Cinque Ports (Keeper of the Coast), 4–5, 4 n.3
Louis XIV, King of France, 118 n.4, 322, 322 n.3
Lovett, Robert Abercrombie, 1012–13, 1012 n.1
Low, David, 98, 98 n.1, 664
Luce, (Anne) Clare Boothe, 623, 623 n.1

Luce, Henry Robinson
biographical information, 260 n.2
Communism in China, 1360
dines with WSC, 260–2
The Second World War: feedback on draft of first volume of, 871–4, 875, 875–7; foreign language serial rights, 1255; *Life* serialization of, 694, 694 n.2, 872, 874; proofs of, 911, 1497–8; serialization book rights to, 554, 556–7; sixth volume proposed for, 1357, 1378; WSC describes progress on, 622–3
US Presidential election campaign (1948), 1198
WSC's US visit (1949), 1323, 1324, 1339, 1343, 1354, 1355, 1356
Lumsden, Herbert, 771–2, 771 n.3
Luther, Martin Franz Julius, 1222, 1222 n.1
Luxembourg, 142, 1622
Lyautey, Ines de Bourgoing, 1979, 1979 n.5
Lyautey, Louis Hubert Gonzalve, 1979, 1979 n.5
Lynskey Tribunal, 1309, 1309 n.1, 1314–20, 1325
Lyttelton, Oliver
biographical information, 29 n.3
Consultative Committee for economic and financial issues, 1267
Film Finance Corporation, 2185–6, 2186 n.2
Iron and Steel Bill, 1237
Malaya and Hong Kong, 2227, 2232
prepares iron and steel remarks for WSC, 289
The Second World War, 507, 1381
Trade and Industry Committee, 201
WSC asks Attlee to invite Conservative colleagues to meeting with George VI, 29, 30
WSC forms new Government (1951), 2230
Lytton, Lady (Pamela Frances Audrey Plowden), 1437, 1437 n.2, 1720, 2011, 2145

MacAndrew, Charles Glen, 2095, 2095 n.2, 2228
MacArthur, Douglas
biographical information, 46 n.2
administration of Japan without an Allied Control Commission, 46
Astor meets with in Japan, 1745, 1763, 1765–6
Fraser meets with in Japan, 57
Korean War, 1905, 1955, 1968–9, 1988, 2034, 2034 n.3, 2039, 2057, 2067, 2074, 2089
Resolutions for Thanks to Commanders, 162
RSC cancels visit with, 813
RSC in Korea as correspondent for *Daily Telegraph*, 1817–18

MacArthur, Douglas *(continued)*
  sends regards to WSC, 634
  spread of Communism in Eastern Europe, 1745, 1745 n.2, 1763, 1765–6
  US exports to China, 2063
  and WSC: WSC praises at Cuban press conference, 194, 197; WSC praises MacArthur's administration of Japan, 771–2, 1187, 1360; WSC sends letter of introduction for RSC, 771, 1817–18, 1983; WSC sends New Year's greetings to, 1983; WSC thanks for inscribed copy of Address to Congress, 2158
Macaulay, Thomas Babington, 333, 333 n.3, 352
MacBride, Seán, 1828, 1828 n.1
MacCormac, Henry, 1393, 1393 n.1
Macdonald, Archibald James Florence ('Archie'), 1668–9, 1668 n.1
MacDonald, (James) Ramsay, 446–7, 446 n.2, 714, 715, 717, 755, 756, 918, 1297, 1404, 1629
MacDonald, Malcolm John, 1982, 1982 n.1
MacGeagh, Henry Davies Foster, 734, 734 n.2
Mackay, Ronald William Gordon, 864, 864 n.1
Mackensen, Friedrich August Eberhard von, 734, 734 n.4
Mackinder, Halford John, 381, 381 n.2
Maclay, John Scott, 1627, 1627 n.1, 2006
Maclean, Fitzroy Hew Royle, 1294, 1294 n.1, 1296, 2103
MacMahon, Cortlandt, 1759, 1759 n.2
Macmanaway, James Godfrey, 1746, 1746 n.2
Macmillan, Dorothy Evelyn Cavendish, 2223, 2223 n.1
Macmillan, (Maurice) Harold
  biographical information, 114 n.1
  The Budget (April 1950 WSC speech), 1732
  Civil Aviation Debate, 199
  Coal Bill Debate, 200
  Conservative Party: Conservative and Liberal co-operation in the European Movement, 2195; Macmillan asks WSC to meet with Swainston, 773, 773 n.1; Macmillan notes WSC's demonstrations of energy and vitality, 2115; Macmillan requests political message of support from WSC, 114, 116; Opposition managing committee proposal, 957, 957 n.1, 959; policy document proofs, 1439–40; Preston by-election of 1946, 199; WSC forms new Government (1951), 2222–5, 2226, 2229; WSC proposes that Macmillan replace Assheton as Conservative Party Chairman, 286; WSC seeks solidarity with Liberals against Labour Government, 1713
  Council of Europe: Conservative MP delegates to, 1418, 1419; Macmillan criticises Morrison's participation in, 1475; WSC calls for German inclusion, 1468–70, 1473–4
  death of Jack Spencer-Churchill, 629
  European Army (Western Union), 1840, 1942–3, 1943
  Foreign Affairs (July 1949 WSC speech), 1450–1, 1454
  Greece, 564, 1352–4
  India, 726, 738–9
  Korea (July 1950 WSC speech), 1782
  Middle East, 1768
  National Service Bill, 686
Madariaga, Salvador de, 1293, 1293 n.1
Maeterlinck, Maurice, 453, 453 n.2
Magee, Warren Egbert, 1176–9, 1176 n.2, 1200, 1201, 1391–2
Magna Carta, 179
Majorelle, Jacques, 901, 901 n.3, 1991–2
Malan, Daniel Francois, 1208, 1208 n.1, 1421, 1423, 1424, 1700, 2030, 2031
Malaya, 539, 539 n.1, 2063, 2064, 2071
Malaya, HMS, 993
Mallon, James Joseph, 102–3, 102 n.4
Malzer, Kurt, 734, 734 n.5
Manchuria, 242
Mandel, Georges, 1171, 1171 n.4
Manning, Elizabeth Leah Perrett, 929–30, 929 n.2, 1566, 1569
manpower: *see* British Armed Forces
Mare, Walter John de la, 1251, 1251 n.2
Margaret, Princess (Countess of Snowdon), 1389–90, 1389 n.2, 1394, 2013
Margesson, Henry David Reginald, 970, 970 n.1
Marks, Simon, 1311, 1311 n.1, 1761
Marlborough, Duchess of (Alexandra Mary Cadogan), 1170, 1170 n.2
Marlborough, 1st Duke of (John Churchill), 118, 118 n.2, 180, 322, 333, 340, 352, 396, 1043, 1940, 1953
Marlborough, Duke of (John Albert Edward William Spencer-Churchill), 1713, 1713 n.1
Marlowe, Anthony, 198–9, 198 n.1, 1947, 1949
Marnham, Reginald John, 50, 50 n.2, 451, 496–7, 1056, 1056 n.3
Marples, Alfred Ernest, 1927, 1927 n.1, 1931, 2223
Marquand, John P., 923, 923 n.4
Marquis, Frederick James: *see* Woolton, Lord (Frederick James Marquis)
Marriott, John Charles Oaks, 1057, 1057 n.2
Marshall, Arthur Gregory George, 1851–2, 1851 n.3

INDEX

Marshall, George Catlett
  biographical information, 34 n.1
  CSC dines and meets with, 899–900, 907
  Evening Standard cartoon of, 580
  Hague Conference, 1037
  Low's political cartoon of, 664
  Marshall's statement on enemy tapping of WSC's telephone calls with Truman, 164, 167–8
  Palestine, 646
  relations with and opinion of Truman, 900
  Russia: Russian policy towards Greece, 1227–8; Smuts discusses British policy towards with WSC, 1172–3
  war-time Supreme Command decisions, 298, 599–600, 601–2, 602–3, 603, 604
  and WSC: congratulates WSC on V-J Day, 34; sends birthday greetings to WSC, 1232, 1255; sends WSC birthday greetings, 854, 854 n.3; thanks WSC for book, 1985, 1986 n.1; WSC asks Marshall to meet with Gollancz, 1003; WSC praises, 250, 2075; WSC's US visit (1949), 1339, 1355
Marshall, Katherine Boyce Tupper, 1232, 1232 n.1, 1985
Marshall Plan
  aid to England, 1236, 1535, 1607–8
  Baruch describes as another version of the United States of Europe, 744
  British repayment of American subsidies, 1675
  British support for, 1130, 1214–15
  proposed revisions to, 1195
  Seligman assesses possible US response to Russian blockade of Berlin, 1145–6
  WSC praises, 757–8, 803, 934, 1005, 1013, 1037, 1358
Marsh, Edward Howard, 625, 625 n.1, 667
Marston, Lettice, 689, 689 n.1, 911, 1356, 1465, 2000, 2155
Martell, Edward Drewett, 553, 553 n.6
Martin, John Miller, 626, 626 n.1
Marx, Karl Heinrich, 619, 619 n.1
Mary, Queen (Mary of Teck), 143, 143 n.4
Masaryk, Jan Garrigue, 998, 998 n.1, 1014, 1362, 1381
Massigli, René, 1128, 1128 n.4, 2141–2
Mast, Charles Emmanuel, 1933–4, 1933 n.2, 1933 n.1
Masterman, Charles Frederick Gurney, 1932, 1932 n.1
Mather, Bertrand, 1449, 1449 n.1
Maudling, Reginald, 782, 782 n.1, 1078
Maugham, Robert Cecil Romer ('Robin'), 2, 2 n.3
Maxton, James, 342, 342 n.1, 447

Maxwell, Charles E., 288, 288 n.1
May, Alan Nunn, 763, 763 n.7
Mayhew, Christopher Paget, 1285, 1285 n.2, 1293, 1427, 1435
McCluer, Frank Lewis, 90–1, 90 n.1, 128, 170, 191, 225
McConaughy, Walter Patrick, Jr, 2063, 2063 n.2
McCormick, Robert Rutherford ('Col'), 240, 240 n.1
McCorquodale, Malcolm Stewart, 1020, 1020 n.1
McFadyean, Andrew, 1659, 1659 n.3
McKell, William John ('Bill'), 1254, 1254 n.1
McKinlay, Adam Storey, 942, 942 n.1, 958–9
McNeil, Hector, 504, 504 n.1, 1183, 1928
McNeill, Angus John, 1257–8, 1257 n.1, 1289
McNeill, John Malcolm, 1257, 1257 n.5
McNeill, Lilian Vaughan Barron, 1257, 1257 n.2
Meighen, Arthur, 1683, 1683 n.2
Melchett, Baron (Henry Ludwig Mond), 9, 9 n.2
Menthon, François de, 1230, 1230 n.2
Menzies, Robert Gordon
  biographical information, 612 n.3
  Australian political career, 778
  Bristol degree recipient, 612
  British loan to Burma, 1740
  Council of Europe meeting (September 1951), 2101
  Schellenburg's location in Switzerland, 1883
Menzies, Sir Stewart Graham, 1147, 1147 n.1
Mergen, Anne Briardy, 1423, 1423 n.3
Messervy, Frank Walter, 1100, 1100 n.1
Mexico, 127, 157
Meyer, Eugene Isaac, 1355, 1355 n.1
Middle East
  Anglo-Arab relations, 430–1, 951, 1280, 1304–5, 1305, 1307
  British policy towards, 1257–8, 1768
  Iraq, 1990–1, 1991 n.1, 2127
  Jordan, 1736–9, 1767–8
  King David Hotel bombing, 423, 423 n.2
  oil supplies, 1990–1, 1991 n.1, 2053–4, 2061–2, 2065
  removal of British troops from (proposed), 313, 344, 349, 350, 367
  speeches (WSC): British Troops in Egypt (May 1946), 311–15; Egypt Treaty Negotiations (May 1946), 343–52; Palestine (August 1946), 427–36; Palestine (January 1947), 604–10; Palestine (January 1949), 1297–308, 1311; Assassination of King Abdullah of Jordan (July 1951), 2121; Foreign Affairs, Middle East (July 1951), 2125–37; Persian Crisis (October 1951), 2174–6

Middle East *(continued)*
  Syria, 296–7, 300–1, 309, 561
  see also Egypt; Israel; Palestine; Persia
Mihailović, Draža
  biographical information, 258 n.3
  Stalin criticises, 258
  WSC requests note from Sargent on his statements about Tito and Mihailović, 280, 295
  WSC seeks British Government support for fair trial for, 287, 290, 295–6
  Yugoslav Government refuses US request to provide statements in support of, 295–6
Mikardo, Ian, 701, 701 n.2
Mikołajczyk, Stanisław
  biographical information, 438 n.1
  exiled Polish senators criticise Sovietisation of eastern Europe, 438, 449
  status and safety of in Poland, 781, 788, 788 n.1, 789–90, 805
Mill, John Stuart, 473, 473 n.1, 661
Mills, Charles, 747, 747 n.1
Mills, George Holroyd, 552–3, 553 n.3
Milner, James, 618, 618 n.1, 973, 1113, 1730, 2228
Minister of Agriculture and Fisheries: *see* Hudson, Robert Spear
Minister of Defence: *see* Alexander, Albert Victor; Shinwell, Emanuel
Minister of Food: *see* Strachey, John; Webb, Maurice
Minister for Fuel and Power: *see* Gaitskell, Hugh Todd Naylor; Shinwell, Emanuel
Minister of Health: *see* Bevan, Aneurin ('Nye')
Ministerial offices and titles, 274, 275–7, 282
Minister of Labour and National Service: *see* Isaacs, George Alfred
Minister of Supply: *see* Strauss, George Russell
Ministry of Aircraft Production, 17
Ministry of Food, 1639–40
Ministry of Supply, 1845, 1859–61, 1887, 2006
Missouri, USS, 241
Mohr, Otto Lous, 1048, 1048 n.1
Moir, Anthony Forbes, 595 n.4, 1344, 1344 n.1, 1787
Molotov, Madame (Polina Semyonovna Zhemchuzhina), 110, 110 n.3
Molotov (Vyacheslav Mikhailovich Scriabin), 88, 110 n.2, 503, 878
Monckton, Walter Turner
  biographical information, 144 n.1
  India: Monckton describes Indian Congress representatives to WSC, 335–6; Monckton's role as Constitutional Advisor to Osman Ali Khan, 335 n.2, 336; Muslims' status and future, 335–6
  proposed job for Duke of Windsor at British Embassy in America, 144

West Bristol by-election, 2000–1
  WSC's political support for, 2000–1
Mond, Amy Gwen Wilson, 9, 9 n.4
Mond, Henry Ludwig (Baron Melchett), 9, 9 n.2
Mongolia, 203–4
Monnet, Jean, 1171, 1171 n.3
Monroe Doctrine, 317, 317 n.1, 1368
Montag, Charles
  biographical information, 46 n.3
  recommends Switzerland visit to WSC, 382, 467
  WSC asks Saxe about, 1992
  WSC plans visit with, 1074
  WSC's Lake Como painting visit, 46, 69, 72, 77, 171
Montagu, Beatrice Venetia Stanley, 763, 763 n.3
Montgomery, Sir Bernard Law
  biographical information, 14 n.2
  British Armed Forces: pace of demobilisation, 130; proposed removal of from Egypt, 328, 329; WSC and Montgomery discuss readiness of, 1072–3, 1073, 1074, 1168–9
  earnings on *Normandy to the Baltic*, 943
  Europe: defences against possible Russian aggression, 1327; European Army, 1911, 2150; Russian blockade of Berlin, 1124–5
  honours and awards: Coalition Government medallion from WSC, 578; shoulder badges for Calvary regiments, 613
  leadership style, 1269
  Le Quesne Martel's opinion of, 1841
  Moorehead's *Montgomery* book, 528, 528–9, 541–2, 542–5, 547–8, 549
  National Service Bill, 688–9, 692
  Resolutions for Thanks to Commanders, 162
  The Second World War: 'Jubilee' (Dieppe raid), 711, 1701, 1821, 1850; 'Overlord' preparations, 1941–2, 2007; war-time Supreme Command decisions, 297–9; WSC asks Brooke for notes on first battle in France prior to Dunkirk, 457; WSC visits with Montgomery (March 1945), 2094–5
  and WSC: Alamein Reunion Dinner (1949), 1438, 1492, 1545–6, 1547–9; asks Mary Churchill about WSC after election loss, 13; asks to meet with WSC about upcoming Alamein Dinner, 93; in Brussels with WSC, 142; Fifth Alamein Reunion, 1910–11; Montgomery asks WSC for one of his paintings, 1176, 1194, 1290; Montgomery congratulates WSC on election win (1951), 2220; Montgomery praises WSC's No Easy Passage broadcast, 770; Montgomery relays greetings from Stalin to WSC,

598, 613; Montgomery thanks WSC for copy of *My Early Life*, 1383; Montgomery thanks WSC for copy of *Their Finest Hour*, 1447; paints and canvasses for WSC's Zurich visit, 422; presents WSC with map of Tactical HQ sites, 94, 99; sends WSC well wishes and photographs from Alamein Reunion Dinner, 159; WSC agrees to write foreword to *Forward from Victory*, 1072, 1073, 1074, 1127, 1127 n.1; WSC criticises treatment of German Field Marshals, 1160–1, 1165; WSC praises, 107–8, 792; WSC suggests COS appointments to Attlee, 14, 22; WSC thanks for copy of *Ten Chapters* book, 177–8, 329; WSC thanks for letters, 119, 598

Montmorency's Scouts, 1289, 1289 n.1
Monypenny, William Flavelle, 872, 872 n.1
Moore-Brabazon, John Theodore Cuthbert, 18, 18 n.5
Moorehead, Alan McCrae, 528–9, 528 n.1, 541–2, 542–5, 547, 548, 549
Moore, Henry Ruthven, 2045, 2045 n.1
Moore, Ralph Westwood, 557, 557 n.2, 558, 842–3, 1580, 1581, 1945
Moorman, Daniel J., 226, 226 n.2
Moran, Lady (Dorothy Dufton Wilson), 917, 917 n.3, 1491, 1495
Moran, Lord (formerly Sir Charles Wilson)
  biographical information, 52 n.1
  Sarah Churchill's health, 456 n.2
  visits son John in Turkey, 1219
  and WSC: International Congress of Physicians (September 1947 WSC speech), 777; in Lake Como with WSC, 53, 54, 60, 61, 63, 67, 72, 76–7; Lord Moran (July 1951 WSC speech), 2112–13; WSC asks Moran to join him in Marrakech, 917, 921, 922, 946; WSC reviews his COS and War Cabinet meeting minutes, 52–3, 61; WSC sets up annual monetary gift for Moran's sons, 1401; WSC sets up monetary gift for Moran's wife Dorothy, 1491, 1495
  WSC's health: Moran recommends against open-air reception in New York, 169–70; Moran recommends month in warmth and sunshine, 157, 163; stroke suffered by WSC, 1477–8, 1479–80, 1759; treats WSC for dizziness, 286; treats WSC for staph infection, 2011; WSC asks for referral to doctor in Venice, 2146
Mordaunt, Nigel John, 59, 59 n.3
Morgenthau, Henry, Jr
  biographical information, 24 n.1
  'Morgenthau Plan' for Germany, 24, 24 n.3, 33, 36, 41–2, 1010–11, 1452

Morison, Stanley, 2062–3, 2062 n.2
Morley, Christopher, 923, 923 n.3, 2199
Morley, John, 473, 473 n.3, 775, 829, 862, 1625
Morrison, Herbert Stanley
  biographical information, 3 n.2
  Coal Bill Debate, 200
  Council of Europe: accommodations at, 1448; Conservative MP delegates to, 1419; Macmillan criticises Morrison's participation in, 1475; meeting dates and expenses, 1440, 1475; UK substitute delegates to, 1426; WSC calls for German inclusion at, 1474
  Criminal Justice Bill, 1113–14
  defence: Navy Estimates (March 1948 WSC speech), 991; Defence (26 July 1950 WSC speech), 1804; Morrison warns of need for armed forces readiness, 937
  employment: unemployment rates, 1018, 1068–9, 1093, 1236, 1596, 1609, 1636; WSC criticises Labour Government claiming credit for full employment, 2178; WSC criticises Labour Government policies, 1534–5
  food: Bread Rationing, 416, 417; food subsidies, 1636; post-war wheat allocations, 649–50; potato shortage, 885; World Food Situation, 355–6, 363
  General Election (1950): *Let Us Win Through Together* statement, 1610; Liberal opponent to Morrison, 1592, 1606; Morrison sees Coalition as undesirable result of, 1623; WSC criticises industry nationalisation, 1633–4; WSC criticises Morrison's statements on the period between the wars, 1629, 1630; WSC criticises 'Work or Starve' policy, 1631, 1645; WSC disagrees with Morrison's statement on Britain leading the world, 1634; WSC suggests forming Select Committee on electoral reform, 1670, 1671
  General Election (1951): Conservative Party trade unions policy, 2190–1; Morrison accuses Conservatives of war-mongering, 2188, 2208; WSC criticises Morrison in Socialist Blunders speech (July 1951), 2120; WSC forms new Government (1951), 2228
  India, Commonwealth Relations (Oral Answers), 1396–7, 1400
  Labour Government: Budget Proposals and Economic Survey (April 1951 WSC speech), 2032; Ford criticises Labour Government foreign policy, 2040; WSC criticises for claiming credit for full employment, 2178; WSC criticises demobilisation efforts, 47; WSC criticises

Morrison, Herbert Stanley *(continued)*
  Labour Government *(continued)*
    employment policies, 1534–5; WSC criticises industry nationalisation, 1429, 2118
    Marlowe refers to as a totalitarian gentleman, 198–9
    Middle East: Foreign Affairs, Middle East (July 1951 WSC speech), 2125, 2129, 2130; Palestine, 427, 428, 950; Persian oil, 2061, 2079, 2103, 2134, 2167, 2174–6; proposed removal of British troops from Egypt, 349; WSC criticises Labour Government foreign policy, 2202–3, 2209
    Parliament: Committee on Privileges Report (October 1947 WSC speech), 839; Debate on the Address (March 1950 WSC speech), 1675–6; HofC convening time, 292 n.1; new Parliament assembly after Conservative election loss (1945), 3; Parliament Act of 1911, 832; Parliament Bill, 859–63, 864, 868–9; Political Gerrymandering (June 1948 WSC speech), 1079, 1082; recall of, 1832; Representation of the People Bill (February 1948 WSC speech), 971–3, 974, 975; Supplies and Services Act, 1751–2, 1907; Transitional Powers Bill, Supplies and Services (August 1947 WSC speech), 759–60
    political broadcasting: on the BBC, 398, 403; meeting minutes (July 1946), 424–6; meeting minutes (November 1946), 522–3, 524, 525; meeting minutes (February 1948), 979–80, 981
    and WSC: Morrison publicly withdraws statements about WSC's income, 1075, 1077; Morrison's criticisms of Conservative Party foreign policy, 936, 2132–3; WSC criticises, 799, 1507, 2057; WSC's interactions with in HofC, 557, 837
Morrison, William Shepherd ('Shakes'), 2224, 2224 n.1
Morris, Sir Philip, 1544, 1544 n.1
Morris, Rhys Hopkin, 630, 630 n.1, 1668–9, 2099, 2228
Morton, Desmond John Falkiner, 813–14, 813 n.1, 814–15
Mossadeq, Mohammed, 2102, 2167–8, 2167 n.2, 2175
Mott, Edward Spencer (Nathaniel Gubbins), 1204, 1204 n.1
Mott-Radclyffe, Charles Edward, 1426, 1426 n.2
Motz, Roger Jean Henri, 1035, 1035 n.3

Mountbatten, Lord Louis ('Dickie')
  biographical information, 167 n.1
  India: Dominion status for proposed as interim stage before independence, 666–7, 725, 726, 729–30; India Independence Bill, 736, 737, 738–9; Mountbatten appointed Viceroy of (March 1947), 640, 640 n.1; WSC criticises 14-month time limit for achieving Indian independence, 640–6; WSC praises Mountbatten's achievements, 875
  Pakistan, 875, 1140
  Park recalls serving with, 494
  Second World War: 'Jubilee' (Dieppe raid), 1701, 1722, 1837, 1848, 1849–50, 1852, 1852 n.1; war-time Command decisions, 1140
  sends Christmas and New Year greetings to WSC, 167
  sends samurai sword to WSC, 167
Mountbatten, Philip
  biographical information, 738 n.3
  The Birthplace of Prince Charles (November 1948 WSC speech), 1249–50
  engagement to Princess Elizabeth, 738, 739–40, 740, 741
  Princess Elizabeth's annuities, 851–2
Moyne, Baron (Walter Edward Guinness), 494, 494 n.1
Moynihan, Patrick Berkeley, 1659, 1659 n.2
Mudie, Robert Francis, 1202, 1202 n.1
Muggeridge, Thomas Malcolm, 1843, 1843 n.1
'Mulberry', 1919
Mullan, Charles Heron, 339–40, 339 n.1
Munnings, Alfred James, 1101, 1101 n.3, 1405, 1405 n.1, 1418
Murdoch, Keith Arthur, 595, 595 n.3
Murphy, Charles J. V., 260–2, 260 n.1, 1521
Murray, Edmund, 1979, 1979 n.6
Murray, George Gilbert Aime, 1601, 1601 n.1
Murray, Oswyn Alexander Ruthven, 1234, 1234 n.2
Mussolini, Benito, 54, 343, 624 n.1, 1174, 1174 n.2, 1415
Myers, Henry Tift ('Hank'), 189, 189 n.3

Narayan, Jayaprakash, 335, 335 n.4
Nares, Eric Paytherus, 73, 73 n.1
National Government of 1931, 2062–3
National Health Act, 448
National Health Service, 1103–4, 1727
National Insurance, 201, 480–1, 1017, 1092
National Liberal Party
  alliance with Conservative Party, 811, 812, 817–19, 819 n.2, 1656, 1659, 1660, 2008

INDEX

Coal Bill Debate, 201
Davies questions exclusion of Liberals from National Liberal-Conservative meetings, 1597–8, 1602–4
publicity for National Liberal Executive telegram to WSC, 2006, 2008
Salisbury seeks merger of with the Conservative Party, 1733, 1734
Woolton–Teviot agreement, 1266–7, 1267 n.1
WSC seeks solidarity with against Labour Government, 827, 1602–4, 1618, 1720, 1744–5, 1747, 2196–9
WSC thanks Maclay for Butcher's letter of support, 1627
National Savings campaign, 1189, 1648
national service
British Armed Forces preparedness and recruiting efforts (1950), 1824–5, 1855
compulsory national service in British Armed Forces, 536–7
Conservative Party policies, 1616, 1621–2, 1689, 2169–70
Defence (July 1950 WSC speech), 1801–2
Le Quesne Martel's paper on conscription, 1438–9
WSC's views on conscription, 1433–4, 1434, 2036
National Service Bill
alteration of terms for, 683, 686, 686–7, 687–8, 695–6, 700
amendments to (September 1950), 1852–3, 1861–2, 1868, 1911
Labour Government policies, 1216–17, 1689–91
Montgomery urges passage of, 688–9, 692
speeches (WSC): National Service Bill (March 1947), 670–7; National Service (April 1947), 687–8; National Service (May 1947), 696–702; Trust the People (May 1947), 721
WSC press notice regarding, 678–9
National Union of Conservative and Unionist Associations, 444, 449
Navarro, Elizabeth, 1331, 1331 n.1
Neame, Philip, 1026, 1026 n.5
Neely, James V., 2056, 2056 n.1, 2090
Neguebauer, Wanda Norwid, 437–9, 439 n.6
Nehru, Jawaharlal
biographical information, 408 n.3
Baruch criticises, 1561
Dominion status for India proposed as interim stage before independence, 666–7
Hyderabad, 1136
India Cabinet Mission (July 1946 WSC speech), 408
India, Commonwealth Relations, 1422–3

Indian policy towards China, 1986
war-time National Coalition Government's arrest of Indian Congress leaders, 636
Wavell asks Nehru to form Interim Congress Government, 450
WSC criticises establishment of Nehru's Interim Administration, 572–4
Nel, Frans, 67–8, 67 n.2
Nelson, HMS, 993, 995
Nelson, Horatio, 1091, 1091 n.1
Netherlands
British arms for, 1073
British policy towards, 1622
Hague Conference planning, 1034
Parliamentary Questions on raw materials for atom bomb, 89
post-war restoration and rebuilding of, 371
Queen Juliana, 1009, 1009 n.3, 1313, 1940
speeches (WSC): Let Freedom Reign (May 1946), 327; United Europe (May 1948), 1042–4; Presentation of Grotius Medal (February 1949), 1313–14
WSC fails to meet Queen Juliana at Dover, 1940
WSC praises, 321–6
WSC thanks Bland for successful visit to, 338
Newman, George, 387, 387 n.1
New York Times, 554, 1427, 1435
New Zealand, 660, 812–13, 1594, 1653
Nicholls, George Heaton, 595, 595 n.1
Nicholson, Godfrey, 726, 726 n.2
Nicolson, Harold George
biographical information, 2 n.2
Salter's opinion of WSC in new HofC, 62, 75
troops' opinion of WSC after election loss, 61–2, 75
WSC praises after election loss, 2
WSC thanks for letter, 75, 78
Niemöller, Friedrich Gustav Emil Martin, 533, 533 n.1
Niezabytowski, Karol, 437–9, 439 n.7
Nightingall, Walter, 2140–1, 2140 n.6
Nimitz, Chester William, 162, 162 n.1, 248
1922 Committee: *see* Conservative Party
Niven, (James) David Graham, 1979, 1979 n.3
Noble, Percy Lockhart Harnam, 2044–5, 2044 n.4
Noel-Baker, Francis Edward, 1281, 1281 n.1
Noel-Baker, Philip John, 538, 538 n.1, 830
Noé, Ludwig, 1166, 1166 n.1
Noon, Firoz Khan, 850, 850 n.1, 875, 2220–2, 2222 n.1
Normandy invasion
Eisenhower plans to write war-time memoirs, 1107
'Overlord' preparations, 2007
vehicle and loading priorities, 528–9, 543–5

Normandy invasion *(continued)*
  war-time Supreme Command decisions, 297–8, 299–300, 598, 599–600, 601–2, 602–3, 603
  WSC comments on at Cuban press conference, 195
North Atlantic Treaty
  absence of Spain from, 1414–16
  British Armed Forces preparedness and recruiting efforts (1950), 1788–9
  Cecil discusses with WSC, 1662–3
  The Challenge of Our Time: Hand of Aggressor Is Stayed By Strength Alone speech (July 1951 Eisenhower speech), 2104–8
  dissolution of Combined Chiefs of Staff, 1514–15, 1526
  Eisenhower's European Army Command, 1970, 2025, 2081
  Foreign Ministers conference in London, 1752
  Le Quesne Martel's paper on conscription, 1438–9
  North Atlantic Defence Committee meeting minutes, 1582, 1587, 1741, 1757–8, 1758 n.1
  North Atlantic Supreme Commander, 2041–55, 2087
  Smuts sees as foundation stone of future world structure, 1422
  speeches (WSC): The North Atlantic Treaty (May 1949), 1411–17; United Europe (July 1951), 2122
  United States Mutual Defence Assistance Act, 1605–6
  WSC criticises organisation of, 2054–5
  WSC voices support for, 1371, 1649, 1752, 1753
Northern Ireland, 537, 2186–7
Norton, Clifford John, 857, 857 n.1
Norway
  Amery proposes Commonwealth association for, 1383–4
  Harald Hardrada (King of Norway), 1053, 1053 n.1
  Russian relations with, 511
  single-Chamber government, 864–5, 1055
  socialism in, 1653
Nuremberg trials, 193, 194, 195, 377–8, 510, 533
Nye, Archibald Edward, 1584, 1584 n.1, 1837
Nygaardsvold, Johan, 1047, 1047 n.1

Obrenović, Milan, 1001, 1001 n.1
O'Connor, Richard Nugent, 1026, 1026 n.4
Ogier, John, 53, 54, 54 n.1, 55, 58–9, 72, 73, 80, 81, 83, 88

Old Age Pensions, 480, 714–15, 756, 1654, 2164
Oliphant, Marcus Laurence Elwin, 19, 19 n.8
O'Neill, Ann Charteris, 895, 895 n.2
O'Neill, Robert William Hugh, 1206, 1206 n.1
Ormerod, Berkeley, 1423, 1423 n.2
Osborne, Cyril, 1782, 1782 n.1
The Other Club, 666, 669
'Overlord': *see* Normandy invasion

Paget, Reginald Thomas, 700, 700 n.1, 1690
Pahlavi, Mohammed Reza (Shah of Iran), 2156–7, 2156 n.1, 2157
painting (WSC)
  Alexander admires WSC's Academy painting exhibits, 1101
  at Chartwell, 1033, 1060
  during US visit (1949), 1331
  Hallmark uses WSC's paintings for Christmas Cards, 1651, 1651 n.2, 1993, 2011
  in Lake Como, 46, 54, 55, 56, 58, 60, 63, 65, 66, 67, 68, 69, 70, 72, 74, 77, 101
  lion at zoo, 1427
  in Marrakech, 821, 835, 876, 896, 897, 898, 901, 906, 922, 927, 1294, 1976, 1979–80, 1981, 1984, 1986, 1987, 1990, 2089–90
  Montgomery asks WSC for one of his paintings, 1176, 1194, 1290
  Painting as a Pastime (Churchill), 1321, 1910, 1910 n.1
  in Provence, 1161
  at 'Sous les Vents' villa, 81, 101
  in Switzerland, 382, 457, 467
  in Veracruz, 189, 198
  WSC declines US exhibit of his paintings, 2089
  WSC describes Majorelle's paintings and tempera techniques, 1991–2
  WSC recommends as hobby to Queen Wilhelmina, 1517
  WSC sends paints and brushes to grandson Winston, 593–4
  WSC thanks Birley for his interest in WSC's paintings, 1060
  WSC thanks Sax for paints, 493
  WSC values times spent on, 184
  WSC visits Majorelle in Marrakech, 1991–2
Pakenham, Francis Aungier, 1146, 1146 n.1, 1634
Pakistan
  arms for, 850, 875
  British policy towards, 1210–11
  Conference on Commonwealth status of, 1383
  Noon sends Indo-Pakistan affairs assessment to WSC (1951), 2220–2, 2222 n.1

INDEX

Palermo, Mario, 1680, 1680 n.3
Palestine
  American troops and aid in (proposed), 320–1, 346–7
  Amery suggests WSC respond to Weizmann's *Times* interview, 1294–5
  Anglo-American Commission report, 318, 328, 346–7, 433–4, 1299
  Anglo-Arab relations, 430–1
  Anglo-Jew relations, 431–2, 434
  Arab-Jew relations, 429–30, 431, 1307–8
  Arab–Israeli war: British policy towards, 1061, 1064–5; *Economist* article on, 1057, 1057 n.1; RAF reconnaissance flights during, 1295, 1305–7, 1306 n.1
  British forces in Aqaba, 1305
  British policy towards, 393, 394, 402, 604–10, 949–52, 1257–8, 1278–81, 1280, 1291, 1297–308, 1311
  British troops and aid in (proposed), 346–7, 348–9, 367
  evacuation of non-essential British personnel and civilians from (1947), 1257, 1257 n.3
  Jewish National Home in, 209, 270, 346, 394, 399, 431–6, 432–5, 535–6, 1302–3
  Jordan and Israel, Government Decision (Oral Answers), 1736–9
  King David Hotel bombing, 423, 423 n.2
  transfer of British mandate to UN, 434–5, 436, 499, 536, 609–10, 644–5, 646, 753, 787–8, 800, 829–30, 885, 950–2, 1016, 1299–300
  White Paper regarding, 428–9
  WSC criticises Bevin in conversation with Elath, 1868
  WSC criticises Labour Government policy towards, 477–8, 535–6, 643–5, 657–8, 688, 713, 753, 787–8, 1015–16, 1064–5, 1090, 1193, 1278–81
  WSC refuses to intervene in Parliamentary debates regarding, 1127, 1127 n.2
  WSC shares McNeill's letter regarding with Eden, 1289
  see also Israel
Papageorgiou, Andreas, 856, 856 n.2
Papandreou, Damaskinos (Archbishop of Athens), 105–6, 105 n.1
Paris Peace Conference, 443, 456–7, 497
Park, Keith Rodney, 61, 61 n.1, 494, 494 n.2
Parliament
  Commons Chamber reopening, 1912–13, 1912 n.1, 1912 n.2, 1914–15, 1915
  Conservative Party post-election strategy (1950), 1749–54
  General Election (1950) results, 1664–5, 1681–2

House of Lords Criminal Justice Bill (July 1948), 1112–13
Parliament Act of 1911 Constitutional settlement, 832–4
Parliament Bill, 864, 928–9, 929 n.1, 1217–18, 1531, 1612, 1617, 1619, 1676, 2199–200
Pound Sterling devaluation, 1492, 1492–3, 1496–7
speeches (WSC): inspiration for WSC's phrase 'Never in the history of human conflict was so much owed by so many to so few', 1162–3, 1162 n.3, 1179–80, 2152; publication of WSC's war-time Parliamentary Secret Session speeches (1945), 174–5; HofC Convening Time (April 1946), 292–5, 292 n.1; Town and Country Planning Bill and Parliamentary Democracy (March 1947), 629–33; Transitional Powers Bill, Supplies and Services (August 1947), 759–60; Committee on Privileges Report (October 1947), 837–9; Parliament Bill (November 1947), 859–69; A New Parliament (February 1948), 962–6; Representation of the People Bill (February 1948), 968–77; Towards a New Parliament (April 1948), 1031–2; Parliamentary Democracy (May 1948), 1054–5; Preserving Continuity (May 1948), 1060–1; Political Gerrymandering (June 1948), 1078–86; A New Parliament (July 1948), 1102–6; Ministers and Public Servants, Official Conduct (February 1949), 1314–20, 1328; Motion for Address in Reply (October 1950), 1912–13, 1912 n.1, 1912 n.2; The New Chamber of the House of Commons (October 1950), 1914–15; Complaint of Privilege (March 1951), 2019–25
United States Mutual Defence Assistance Act, 1598–600, 1604–5
Wilson recollects WSC's essence as Parliamentarian, 2058–9
WSC appears at new Parliament assembly, 3, 35–6, 111
WSC notifies Attlee of his intent to formally request the recall of Parliament (August 1950), 1825–6, 1832, 1838–9, 1844, 1854–5
WSC's Parliamentary jubilee, 1885, 1885 n.1, 1909
Parry, William Edward, 546–7, 547 n.1
Paton, John, 452, 452 n.3, 2075
Patterson, Robert Porter, 247, 247 n.4
Patton, George Smith, Jr, 88, 88 n.2
Pavelich, Ante, 258, 258 n.4

Pavlov, Vladimir, 2077, 2077 n.2
Peck, John Howard
  biographical information, 46 n.1
  Eden declines to attend new Indian Constitution ceremony (1950), 1587, 1587 n.2
  Jo Sturdee thanks for letter, 288–9
  occupation of Korea and administration of Japan without an Allied Control Commission, 46
  sympathy message for Queen Elizabeth, 2154
  WSC's press statement on making atom bombs, 2005
Pehm, József, 1338, 1338 n.1
Peierls, Rudolph Ernst, 19, 19 n.2
Penson, Lillian Margery, 1253, 1253 n.1
Persia
  Anglo-Iranian personnel in Abadan, 2111, 2115, 2136–7, 2155, 2156, 2156–7, 2157, 2167–8
  Anglo-Persian Oil Company, 2061–2, 2062 n.1, 2065, 2079, 2080, 2088, 2090, 2091, 2133–5
  ARAMCO, 2120–1, 2134
  British citizens in, 2110
  British policy towards, 2217–18
  Eden in Persia and Arabia with Lawford, 912
  oil supplies, 2053–4, 2061–2, 2065, 2102, 2103, 2109, 2109 n.2, 2114, 2134, 2136–7
  Russian encroachment into, 233, 242, 264–5, 271, 1847
  speeches (WSC): Foreign Affairs, Middle East (July 1951 WSC speech), 2126–7; Persian Crisis (October 1951 WSC speech), 2174–6; Abadan, Sudan and Bevan – A Trio of Misfortune (October 1951 WSC speech), 2187–90
Petacci, Clara, 54, 54 n.2
Pétain, Henri Philippe, 65 n.5, 484, 945
Peter I, Tsar ('Peter the Great', Pyotr Alekseyevich), 180, 180 n.5
Péter, János, 1680, 1680 n.2
Peterson, Maurice Drummond, 727, 727 n.1, 731–2, 731 n.5, 733
Pethick-Lawrence, Frederick William, 359–60, 360 n.1
Petkov, Nikola, 786, 786 n.1, 789
Philip, André, 1221, 1221 n.1, 1473
Phillips, Gerald, 1487, 1487 n.3
Phillips, Lady, 1487, 1487 n.1, 1920–1, 1937, 1938, 1943, 1945
Phillips, Sir Thomas Spencer Vaughan, 1487 n.1, 1937
Picasso, Pablo Ruiz, 1405, 1405 n.1, 1405 n.2, 1418
Pickersgill, John ('Jack'), 109, 109 n.2

Pickthorn, Kenneth William Murray, 1814, 1814 n.1
Pierssené, Stephen Herbert, 1684, 1684 n.1, 2108
Pilgrims' Dinner to Mrs Roosevelt (April 1948 WSC speech), 1006–8
Pilsudski, Jósef, 1446, 1446 n.1
Pim, Richard Pike, 2078, 2078 n.2
Piratin, Philip, 931, 931 n.3, 981
Pirelli, Giovanni Battista, 80, 80 n.1
Pitt-Rivers, George Anthony Lane-Fox, 763, 763 n.6
Pitt-Rivers, George Henry Lane, 763, 763 n.5
Pitt-Rivers, Rosalind Venetia Henley, 763, 763 n.4
Pitt, William (the Elder), 302, 302 n.1, 340, 407
Pitt, William (the Younger), 4, 4 n.4, 1610, 1610 n.1
Pius XII, Pope (Eugenio Maria Giuseppe Giovanni Pacelli), 1177, 1177 n.1
Playfair, Ian Stanley Ord, 1265, 1265 n.1
Pleven, René, 1789–90, 1789 n.1, 2151–2
Pleydell-Bouverie, Audrey James, 13, 13 n.3
Poett, Joseph Howard Nigel, 552–3, 553 n.2
Poland
  eastern frontier with Russia, 929
  exiled Polish senators criticise Sovietisation of eastern Europe, 437–9, 442, 449
  Mikołajczyk's status and safety in, 781, 788, 788 n.1, 789–90, 805
  western frontier of, 6–7, 10, 258, 360, 375, 511, 929–30
  WSC criticises Sovietisation of, 232, 257–9, 375, 376, 500–1
  WSC's references to in *The Second World War*, 998–9, 998 n.2, 998 n.3, 1099, 1099 n.1
Polish Army, 376, 658
Pollitt, Harry, 980, 980 n.1, 1021
'Polly', 1257, 1257 n.3
Poole, Cecil Charles, 2073, 2073 n.1
Poole, William Henry Evered, 163, 163 n.3
Pooley, Ernest Henry, 1251, 1251 n.3
Popović, Vladimir, 1994, 1994 n.1
Portal, Sir Charles Frederick Algernon ('Peter')
  biographical information, 5 n.1
  Attlee plans national broadcast upon surrender of Japan, 6
  Dresden bombing, 1742
  Resolutions for Thanks to Commanders, 162
  unveiling of WSC's portrait at the Junior Carlton Club, 1977–8
  WSC asks Baruch to establish close relations with, 320
  WSC proposes Peerage for, 5
Portugal, 231, 338
Potsdam Conference
  Attlee reports on conclusions of to WSC, 6–7, 8, 10, 14

INDEX 2307

Halifax reports on to WSC, 11–12
'Morgenthau Plan' for Germany, 36, 41–2
Stalin's demeanor at, 7, 11
Stalin's opinion on adherence to, 510
Stalin's request for base on the Aegean Sea, 731, 731 n.2
WSC asserts Conservative Party not responsible for results of, 532, 584
WSC recalls inviting Attlee to, 682
Pound, Alfred Dudley Pickman Rogers, 162, 162 n.4, 1171, 2044
Pound Sterling devaluation, 1492, 1492–3, 1493–4, 1493 n.1, 1496–7, 1536, 1554–5, 1579, 1583, 1584–6, 1595, 1665, 1721–2, 1747, 2035, 2085, 2116–18, 2161, 2189–90
Powell, Allan, 522, 522 n.1, 525
Powell, Anthony George, 853, 853–4, 853 n.1, 904–5, 946
Powell, John Enoch, 633, 633 n.1
Power, Arthur John, 402, 402 n.1
Powers, Leon W., 1391, 1391 n.3
Pownall, Henry Royds
  biographical information, 911 n.1
  in Marrakech with WSC, 1979–80
  Mast's paper on defence needs for Western Europe, 1933–4, 1933 n.3
  The Second World War: Dieppe Raid story, 1700–2; feedback and suggested edits for, 978–9, 1057, 1153–5, 1157, 1175, 1402, 1560, 2094–5, 2101, 2139, 2146, 2147, 2148; final months of Wavell's command, 1268–70; French language version introductory note, 1388–9; French language version references to General Prioux, 1333–4, 1334–5; military aspects of, 911, 953, 1099–100, 1101, 1141–2, 1264–5, 1381–2, 1542; 'Mulberry', 1919; 'Overlord' preparations, 2007; *Triumph and Tragedy* (Volume 6), 2060–1
Pravda, 255–60
President of the Board of Trade: *see* Cripps, Sir Stafford; Shawcross, Hartley William; Wilson, (James) Harold
Preussen, Friedrich von, 1823–4, 1823 n.1
Price, C. S., 854, 854 n.1
Price, Morgan Philips, 205, 205 n.1
Priestley, John Boynton, 810, 810 n.1
Primrose, Archibald Philip (Lord Rosebery), 260, 260 n.4, 1597, 1598
Primrose League, 516, 680
Prioux, René Jacques Adolphe, 1332, 1332 n.1, 1333–4, 1334–5
Prisoners of War (POWs)
  calories in daily rations, 651
  condition of freed British POWs in Japan, 57

Crusade in Europe (film) showing at Chartwell, 1430
German prisoners help with English harvest, 475–6
German prisoners work on landscape restoration at Chartwell, 50, 60, 131, 181, 685
WSC criticises treatment of German Field Marshals, 1160–1, 1163–4, 1165, 1187, 1212–13, 1450, 1453
Profumo, John ('Jack'), 1666, 1666 n.1
propaganda
  Battle of Stalingrad (film), 724, 726–7, 731–2, 731 n.5, 733
  Soviet propaganda regarding Korea Republic invasion, 1781
  Soviet propaganda themes monitoring report, 1198–9
  WSC criticises Soviet propaganda and espionage, 373–5
  WSC proposes anti-Labour Government propaganda, 442
Pugh, Arthur, 1870, 1870 n.2, 2204
Pullar, Hubert Norman, 1979, 1979 n.2
Pursey, Harry, 2044, 2044 n.1
Purvis, Arthur Blaikie, 742, 742 n.2

Quarles, Francis, 250, 250 n.1
Quaroni, Pietro, 1150, 1150 n.2
Queen Elizabeth class ships, 993
Queen Elizabeth, HMS, 993, 995
Queen's Own Oxfordshire Hussars, 445
Quibell, David John Kinsley, 657, 657 n.1
Quickswood, Lord (Hugh Gascoyne-Cecil, 'Linky'), 664–5, 664 n.1, 1252, 1886

Raczyński, Edward Bernard André Maria
  biographical information, 449 n.4
  exiled Polish senators criticise Sovietisation of eastern Europe, 449
  Poles offended by WSC's references to Poland in *The Second World War*, 1099, 1099 n.1
  Sikorski Historical Institute appeal, 1379, 1379 n.2, 1385, 1385 n.1
radar technology, 612, 612 n.2, 613, 613 n.1, 613 n.2, 1367
Radek, Karl Bernhardovich, 967, 967 n.1
Radescu, Nicolae, 259, 259 n.2
Radhakrishnan, Sarvepalli, 1916, 1916 n.3
Raikes, Henry Victor Alpin, 200 n.1, 200, 869–70
Rajagopalachari, Chakravarti, 1384, 1384 n.1
Raleigh, Walter, 243, 243 n.1
Ralli, Eustratio Lucas (Strati Ralli), 380–1, 380 n.1
Ramadier, Paul, 1009, 1009 n.1
Ramillies, HMS, 993

Ramsden, Arthur Maxwell, 1321, 1321 n.1, 1325
Rankeillour, Lord (James Fitzalan Hope), 42, 42 n.1
Rapp, Thomas Cecil, 854–5, 855 n.1
Rattigan, Terence, 837, 837 n.1
Razmara, Haj Ali, 2134, 2134 n.1
Rdultowski, Konstanty, 437–9, 439 n.8
Reader's Digest subscriptions for Smuts and the Queen, 578–9, 595
Redistribution Bill, 1078–86, 1088
Reid, James Scott Cumberland, 199, 199 n.6, 200, 732, 1068
Reid, Thomas, 1304, 1304 n.1
Renold, Charles Garonne, 2159, 2159 n.1
Renown, HMS, 993
Replogle, Jacob Leonard, 840, 840 n.1
Reves, Emery
 biographical information, 554 n.1
 The Second World War: feedback and edits for, 922, 922–4, 924, 925, 926, 926–7, 1497, 2143, 2147; foreign language serial rights, 1255; French language version references to General Prioux, 1332–3, 1334–5; offers for serialization book rights to, 554; Sarah Churchill reassures WSC regarding feedback and suggested edits for, 897–8; sixth volume proposed for, 1357, 1378–9, 1714–15
Rex v. Rule, 2020
Reynaud, Paul
 biographical information, 65 n.4
 Europe: Cooper describes political climate of France to WSC (September 1945), 65; Council of Europe, 1221, 1230, 1469; Hague Conference, 1035; Western Union manpower estimates and preparedness, 1808, 1810; Western Union Pact, 1830
 The Second World War: events in Bordeaux in June 1940, 791, 806, 806 n.1; Leopold III's statement on 1940 British surrender and evacuation from Dunkirk, 1543–4; research and notes for, 1159, 1160, 1161–2
Rhodes, Harvey, 2209, 2209 n.1
Rhys-Williams, Lady (Juliet Glyn), 553, 553 n.5, 811, 812, 817–19, 819 n.2
Richards, Arthur Harold, 103, 103 n.1
Richert, Arvid Gustaf, 1177, 1177 n.7
Richmond, Duchess of (Elizabeth Grace Hudson Gordon-Lennox), 2141, 2141 n.1
Richmond, Duke of (Frederick Gordon-Lennox), 2141, 2141 n.1
Riley, William E., 1258, 1258 n.1
Rivet, Paul, 1035, 1035 n.4
Roberts, Edward V., 508, 508 n.1

Roberts, Emrys Owen, 1668–9, 1668 n.1
Robertson, Brian Hubert, 1967, 1967 n.1
Robertson, Ewart John, 1326, 1326 n.2
Roberts, Peter Geoffrey, 1426, 1426 n.3, 1770–1
Robinson, George Geoffrey, 391, 391 n.2
Robinson, William Sydney, 779, 779 n.2, 853
Rodd, Francis, 1659–60, 1659 n.5
Rodgers, John Charles, 2020, 2020 n.1, 2022–4
Rodney, Charles Christian Simon, 424, 424 n.1
Rodney, Gladys Greenwood ('Sadie'), 424, 424 n.2
Rodney, HMS, 995
Rogers, A. D. D. ('Tim'), 77–8, 77 n.1, 78–9, 80–1
Romania, 513, 514, 515–16, 953
Romer, Tadeusz
 biographical information, 449 n.2
 exiled Polish senators criticise Sovietisation of eastern Europe, 449
 Mikołajczyk's status and safety in Poland, 781, 788, 788 n.1, 789–90
Romilly, Nellie Hozier, 157, 157 n.1
Rommel, Erwin, 107, 107 n.1, 1547
Roosevelt, Anna Eleanor, 24, 24 n.2, 1006–8
Roosevelt, Franklin Delano (FDR)
 biographical information, 20 n.1
 Ford's political support for, 2039
 Four Freedoms, 322, 460, 586, 1041, 1186
 tributes to: memorial statue and tablet in England, 387–8, 1232; Pilgrims' Dinner to Mrs Roosevelt (April 1948 WSC speech), 1006–8; Roosevelt Memorial Bill, 489, 490–1; Roosevelt Memorial Fund, 550–1; sculpting of Roosevelt statue, 562
 and WSC: Atlantic Meeting, 1310 n.2; WSC recalls FDR'S comment on America as a land of unending challenge, 245; WSC visits Shangri-La with FDR, 1975; WSC visits White House (1942), 1312–13
 see also atom bomb; Second World War
Rootes, William Edward, 32, 32 n.3, 52
Rosada, Stefan, 437–9, 439 n.9
Rosebery, Lord (Archibald Philip Primrose), 260, 260 n.4, 1597, 1598
Rosenstiel, Lewis Solon, 1423–4, 1423 n.4
Ross, Charles Griffith, 223–4, 223 n.1
Ross, Ronald, 1419, 1419 n.1
Rothermere, Lady (Ann Charteris), 895, 895 n.2
Rothermere, Lord (Esmond Cecil Harmsworth), 81, 81 n.1
Rothschild, Dorothy Pinto de, 1224, 1224 n.2
Rothstein, Andrew, 180, 180 n.4
Rougier, Louis Auguste Paul, 945, 945 n.2
Rowan, Thomas Leslie
 biographical information, 10 n.2
 Baldwin's eightieth birthday, 741

Index

Marshall's statement on enemy tapping of WSC's telephone calls with Truman, 164
Marshall and war-time Supreme Command decisions, 602–3, 603
motor car presented by WSC and British Government to Ibn Saud, 404, 404 n.2
serves as Attlee's private secretary, 128
thanks WSC for honour of serving, 27
WSC asks Eisenhower to meet with, 1682
WSC asks for War Cabinet papers on India, 624–5
WSC introduces to Baruch, 1602
Royal Air Force (RAF)
  Air Estimates: National Service Bill, 673–4
  auxiliary fighter squadrons (October 1948 WSC speech), 1181
  Dresden bombing, 1742–3, 1743 n.1, 1799–800
  morale, 1409
  preparedness and recruiting efforts (1950), 1788–9
  RAF Benevolent Fund (September 1951 WSC speech), 2152–3
  State of the Armed Forces Memorandum, 1168–9
  WSC criticises Labour Government policies, 1696–8
  see also air defence
Royal Family speeches (WSC)
  His Majesty's Return From South Africa (May 1947), 702–3
  Address of Congratulations to Their Majesties and Princess Elizabeth on the Forthcoming Royal Marriage (October 1947), 816–17
  Motion of Congratulations to Their Majesties on their Silver Wedding (April 1948), 1029
  The Birthplace of Prince Charles (November 1948), 1249–50
Royal Navy
  British destroyers damaged in Corfu Channel, 931, 931 n.1, 1090, 1572–3
  British Home Fleet, 2043
  Fleet Air Arm manpower, 995–6
  historic British dominance of the seas, 1368
  preparedness and recruiting efforts (1950), 1778–9
  speeches (WSC): The British Commonwealth (May 1946), 317; National Service Bill (March 1947), 673, 674; Debate on the Address (October 1947), 830–1; Navy Estimates (March 1948), 986–97; North Atlantic Supreme Commander (April 1951), 2042–5, 2047
  State of the Armed Forces Memorandum, 1168–9

submarine technology, 1367
WSC criticises Labour Government policies, 830–1, 982–3, 986–99, 1090–1, 1693–6
WSC recommends against scrapping of older ships, 993–4
Royal Sovereign, HMS, 993
Ruini, Bartolomeo, 1035, 1035 n.5
Rundstedt, Karl Rudolf Gerd von, 654, 654 n.1
Russell, Bertrand Arthur William, 584, 584 n.2
Russia
  Anglo-American policy towards, 254, 1936
  Anglo-Russian Short Term Trade Agreement (1947), 1851–2
  Anglo-Soviet relations, 373, 375, 1662–3, 1709–12
  atom bomb: leverage afforded to US Government against Russia, 23, 1376; Russian knowledge of (1945), 1465; Russian possession of, 1186, 1543, 1711–12, 1785–6, 1796, 1814–16, 1846, 1856
  Baruch discusses post-war world with WSC, 745–6
  BBC monitoring report: Soviet propaganda themes, 1198–9
  Berlin blockade, 1105
  British policy towards, 193–6, 1183, 1283–5, 1947, 1949, 1971
  control of Balkan nations, 111
  conversion of Czechoslovak railways to Russian gauge, 527–8
  Czechoslovakian stance towards Russia and Western Europe, 376, 967–8
  Europe: Bevin warns of Soviet expansion in Eastern Europe, 930, 930 n.1, 933, 939–40; exiled Polish senators criticise Sovietisation of eastern Europe, 437–9, 449; Mast's paper on defence needs for Western Europe, 1933–4, 1933 n.3; Soviet influence on Western Germany, 774; United Europe (May 1947 WSC speech), 709; United States of Europe proposals, 463, 590–2; WSC cites need for Western Germany to aid in defence of Europe from Russia, 1692–3; WSC refers to reports of Russian mistreatment of Vienna, 102; WSC warns against Soviet expansion in Central and Eastern Europe, 232–3, 236–7, 238–9, 256–60, 265–6
  export of British machine tools and diesel engines to, 1845, 1859–61, 1887, 2070
  Four Power Conference proposals (1950), 1954, 1971
  Hitler's invasion of, 1823
  Italian fleet disposition, 930–1
  Korea, 1781, 1794, 1808

Russia *(continued)*
  Palestine, 536
  Potsdam Conference, 6–7, 10
  prospects for American bombing of, 877–8
  Russian Air Force, 1543, 1696, 1810–11
  Russian demands at Foreign Ministers conference (September 1945), 82
  Russian entry into Pacific theatre of war, 262
  Russian establishment of naval base at Tripoli, 241
  Russian Navy U-boat fleet estimates, 1813, 2041
  Smuts discusses British policy towards with WSC, 1172–3
  Soviet propaganda film, 724, 726–7, 727, 731–2, 731 n.5, 733
  speeches (WSC): Foreign Policy, President Truman's Declaration (November 1945), 120; The Sinews of Peace (March 1946), 232–5, 236–7, 238–9, 938–9; The Darkening International Scene (March 1946), 263–4; The British Commonwealth (May 1946), 319; Al Smith Memorial speech (October 1947), 809–11; Foreign Affairs (October 1946), 502–4; Foreign Affairs (January 1948), 932–3, 937–40; Perils Abroad and at Home (October 1948), 1182–8; The North Atlantic Treaty (May 1949), 1411–17
  Treaty of Collaboration and Mutual Assistance with England, 231, 256
  Truman discusses possibility of war with, 1444
  Twenty Years' Treaty, 134, 326, 373
  UN meeting in London, 1412
  US relations with, 1415
  WSC criticises Soviet propaganda and espionage, 373–5
  WSC discusses possibility of war with, 1012–13, 1362, 1373, 1376–7, 1433, 1796, 1816, 1952–3, 1995, 2041, 2149, 2152
  WSC discusses Russian regime with Mackenzie King, 111
  WSC predicts Russian demands for air bases in Eastern Mediterranean, 347
  WSC promotes idea of discussions with, 1650, 1655–6, 1665, 1710–11, 1753–4, 1797, 1953–4, 2149
  WSC scorns Russian propaganda broadcasts, 1416–17
  Yalta Agreement, 203–6
Russian Army
  Baruch discusses prospect for Russian Army desertions with WSC, 745
  Directors of Plans report on estimates of Russian strengths and intentions, 552–3
  Joint Intelligence Committee estimate of Russian forces in the Far East, 547
  Joint Intelligence Committee report on Soviet Army re-organisation and re-equipment, 546–7
  Russian forces between the Baltic and the Black Sea, 504
  Russian forces in eastern Europe, 504, 513, 514, 515–16, 559–60, 565, 567, 569
  Voroshilov's command role, 546

Sahm, Marianne (Countess Schwerin-Schwanefeld), 1178, 1178 n.7
Sakhalin Island, 203–4
Salisbury, Lord (Robert Gascoyne-Cecil, 'Bobbety')
  biographical information, 22 n.3
  Anglo-American policy towards Russia, 1936, 1937
  Conservative Party: Eden's 1938 resignation as Foreign Secretary, 665; Eden's twenty-fifth year in Parliament, 1450; government co-partnership proposals, 353; post-election strategy (1950), 1658–60, 1661, 1683, 1733, 1734; WSC forms new Government (1951), 2220, 2226, 2229; WSC invites to join Shadow Cabinet, 42; WSC seeks solidarity with Liberals against Labour Government, 1659–60, 1667, 1667 n.1
  domestic affairs: death penalty abolishment proposals, 1093; Defence Memorandum discussions with Attlee, 1435, 1435 n.2; Parliament Bill, 928–9
  Europe: South Tyrol, 452; United Europe movement, 1733; WSC discusses United States of Europe proposals with, 494–5
  Hitler's invasion of Russia, 1823
  India: British policy towards, 624; Commonwealth relations, 1404–5; India Independence Bill, 738–9
  Middle East: British citizens in Persia, 2110, 2110 n.1; British policy towards, 1768; Palestine, 624; Persian oil, 2110
  WSC praises, 22
Salter, James Arthur, 62, 62 n.1, 2079
Samson, Odette, 895, 895 n.4
Samuel, Herbert Louis
  biographical information, 399 n.3
  House of Lords hereditary system, 1659
  India: Attlee calls meeting with Liberals and Conservatives regarding, 399; India Independence Bill, 738–9
  Liberal Party collaboration with the Conservative Party, 818
  WSC criticises Liberal Party electoral deadlock plans, 1669

Index

Sandys, Diana Churchill
  biographical information, 12 n.3
  at Chartwell, 912
  Christmas in London (1945), 157
  move to new flat, 12, 27
  visits CSC in London, 621
  WSC invites to Marrakech, 1977
  with WSC in Switzerland, 458
Sandys, Edwina, 900, 900 n.6, 912
Sandys, Edwin Duncan
  biographical information, 12 n.4
  Brussels Treaty Powers, 1221
  Christmas in London (1945), 157
  Consultative Committee, 1713
  Eisenhower's 'Challenge of Our Time' speech, 2108
  Europe: Council of Europe, 1418–19, 1732–3; French politics and General Election results, 560; Hague Conference planning, 1008–9; Pan-European Council proposals, 392, 424; Russian forces and intentions in Eastern Europe, 519, 559–60; United Europe Committee luncheon, 1333, 1339; United States of Europe proposals, 560–1, 566–7, 679; Western Union (European Army), 1839–40, 1939–40, 1942–3, 1943
  'Focus' Freedom and Peace luncheon, 102–3
  General Election (1950), 1625–7, 1658
  Israel, 1224
  moves to new flat, 12, 27
  The Second World War, 1381–2, 2060–1
  and WSC: WSC forms new Government (1951), 2229; WSC invites to Marrakech, 1977; WSC proposes Sandys as candidate for next General Election, 747; with WSC in Switzerland, 392, 458
Sandys, Julian George Winston, 764, 764 n.1, 912, 1325, 1328, 1379
Sankey, John, 961, 961 n.3
Sargent, Sir Orme ('Moley')
  biographical information, 280 n.2
  Communist threat to Greece, 1352–4
  Magee asks WSC for statement for von Weizsäcker's trial, 1200
  'Morgenthau Plan' for Germany, 1010–11, 1011 n.1
  publication of WSC's war-time Administration papers, 942
  Salonica executions, 839, 839 n.2, 854–7
  Soviet propaganda film, 724, 726–7, 731–2
  WSC asks for advice on how to respond to Zadeikis, 280
  WSC requests note on his statements about Tito and Mihailović, 280, 295

WSC thanks for letter and information, 782
Saundby, Robert Henry Magnus Spencer, 1800, 1800 n.2
Saunders, Hilary Aidan Saint George, 1742–3, 1742 n.1, 1743 n.1
Sausmarez, Cecil Havilland de, 145, 145 n.1, 158
Savory, Albert, 185, 185 n.3
Savory, Douglas Lloyd, 1246, 1246 n.1
Sawyers, Frank, 78, 78 n.1, 226, 380–1
Sax, Willy, 493, 493 n.1, 1991–2
Schaik, Josef van, 321, 321 n.2
Schellenberg, Walter Friedrich, 1883, 1883 n.1
Schlabrendorff, Fabian von, 1177, 1177 n.12
Schofield, Brian Betham, 2051, 2051 n.1
Schumacher, Kurt, 1944, 1944 n.1
Schuman, Jean-Baptiste Robert, 1128 n.5, 1221, 1575, 1752–3, 1783, 1792, 1826, 1828, 1876
Schumann, Maurice, 2151–2, 2151 n.1
Schuster, Max Lincoln, 224, 224 n.1
Schwerin-Schwanefeld, Countess (Marianne Sahm), 1178, 1178 n.7
Scollan, Thomas, 935, 935 n.1, 1215
Scorgie, Norman Gibb, 961, 961 n.2
Scotland
  British policy towards, 1489–91
  Conservative Party in, 712–13
  Conservative Party support for Unionist Party, 722–3, 2165
  rebuilding of housing in, 718, 719
  Scottish nationalism and home rule movement, 1643–4
  Scottish Unionist Meeting (May 1950 WSC speech), 1746–54
  speeches (WSC): The Conservative Case (May 1951), 2086; The Needs of a Sick World (April 1946), 301–4
  tribute to war-time efforts of, 531
  WSC proposes new Scottish Cabinet Minister position, 1644
Scriabin, Vyacheslav Mikhailovich (Molotov), 88, 110 n.2, 503, 878
Scribner, Charles, 1380, 1380 n.1
Seal, Eric Arthur, 1045, 1045 n.1
Second World War
  Allied Unconditional Surrender Policy, 1451, 1453, 1454–5, 1461–2, 1562–4
  Baruch describes Hopkins's effect on progress of, 742–3
  German re-armament and territorial encroachments prior to, 139
  Marshall's statement on enemy tapping of telephone calls, 167–8
  Mediterranean command, 2052–4, 2087, 2126
  Moorehead's *Montgomery* book, 542–3

Second World War *(continued)*
   Normandy invasion: Eisenhower plans to write war-time memoirs, 1107; preparations, 2007; war-time Supreme Command decisions, 297–9, 299–300, 598, 599–600, 601–2, 602–3, 603
   operations, code names for, 2235
   painting of WSC, FDR and Stalin, 98, 128
   Potsdam Conference: Attlee reports on conclusions of to WSC, 6–7, 8, 10, 14; Halifax reports on to WSC, 11–12; 'Morgenthau Plan' for Germany, 36, 41–2; Stalin's demeanor at, 7, 11; Stalin's opinion on adherence to, 510; Stalin's request for base on the Aegean Sea, 731, 731 n.2; WSC asserts Conservative Party not responsible for results of, 532, 584; WSC recalls inviting Attlee to, 682
   Prisoners of War (POWs): calories in daily rations, 651; condition of freed British POWs in Japan, 57; *Crusade in Europe* (film) showing at Chartwell, 1430; German prisoners help with English harvest, 475–6; German prisoners work on landscape restoration at Chartwell, 50, 60, 131, 181, 685; WSC criticises treatment of German Field Marshals, 1160–1, 1163–4, 1165, 1187, 1212–13, 1450, 1453
   publication of WSC's war-time papers, minutes and personal correspondence, 465, 487, 488
   publication of WSC's war-time Parliamentary Secret Session speeches, 174–5
   Quebec Agreement of 1943, 36, 42, 1010–11, 1452
   Russian entry into Pacific theatre of war, 262
   Spanish Embassy luncheon (1941), 1427, 1435
   speeches (WSC): The Future of Europe (November 1945 WSC speech), 139; France and Europe (July 1946 WSC speech), 406
   Three Great Powers, 41–2, 193–4, 195, 197, 203–4
   Yalta Agreement, 202, 202–6, 207, 234
   Yalta Conference, 667, 1351, 2076–8
The Second World War (Churchill)
   The Gathering Storm (Volume 1), 1101, 1102
   Their Finest Hour (Volume 2), 1425, 1442, 1444–5, 1517, 1523
   The Grand Alliance (Volume 3), 1010, 1717, 1822–3, 1909
   The Hinge of Fate (Volume 4), 1825, 1910, 1964–5, 1965 n.1, 2055–6, 2056 n.2, 2090, 2090 n.3, 2141, 2142
   Closing the Ring (Volume 5), 2141, 2143, 2145
   Triumph and Tragedy (Volume 6), 2060–1
   research and notes for: 'Air Ministry Pamphlet 156', 552, 554–5, 557; Algiers meeting minutes, 1878; Anzio operations, 401–2; atom bomb information, 1601; Blitz and Battle of Britain, 612–13; blockships information, 1559, 1559–60, 1561, 1561 n.2; Crete operations, 1130–1, 1140–1, 1344, 1542; defence of British Somaliland, 1771–2, 1787; despatch of tanks to the Middle East, 529–30; EAM, 1913; Eden's 1938 resignation as Foreign Secretary, 944, 948–9, 952–3, 956; events in Bordeaux in June 1940, 791, 806, 806 n.1; final months of Wavell's command, 1268–70, 1288, 1313; German attack on Russia, 1521; Greek mutiny, 1913–14; 'Husky' and 'Trident' operations, 1486; Iraq and Syria, 1142; 'Jubilee' (Dieppe raid), 711, 711 n.1, 1700–2, 1702, 1821–2, 1837, 1848, 1849–50, 1852; Leopold III's statement on 1940 British surrender and evacuation from Dunkirk, 1543–4; Lyttelton's bombing notes, 507; 'Mulberry', 1919; 'Overlord' preparations, 528, 529, 544–5, 1941–2, 1942, 2007; Paris conversations (1940), 978; 'Sledgehammer', 516, 521; tank production, 1381–2; 'Tiger' and Crete operations, 1130–1, 1140–1; Tours speech (1944), 977; tube alloys research and atom bomb, 1601–2; war-time Supreme Command decisions, 297–9, 299–300, 339, 598, 601; WSC's depiction of Belgian Army and King Leopold in, 1410–11; WSC's references to Poland in, 998–9, 998 n.2, 998 n.3, 1099, 1099 n.1; WSC visits with Montgomery (March 1945), 2094–5; WSC visits Shangri-La with FDR, 1975
   reviews: Cooper reviews *Their Finest Hour* on the BBC, 1425; Coote describes draft text to Watson, 913; Coward praises, 1268, 1268 n.2; Foot's review of *The Grand Alliance*, 1822–3, 1909; positive reviews of, 1195–6; reception of third volume in the US, 1762; Sarah Churchill reassures WSC regarding critiques and editing of, 897–8
   rights: foreign language serial rights, 1255; radio rights for, 1061; serialization book rights to, 554, 556–7, 595
   writing and editing of: Allen assists WSC with, 1559, 1559–60, 1561, 1561 n.2; Beaverbrook assists WSC with,

INDEX

1405, 1409–10, 1975; Berlin provides feedback to WSC, 909, 911, 914, 921, 921 n.1, 966–8, 999; Brook assists WSC with, 955–6, 1142–3, 1393, 1842–3; Crown copyright on WSC's personal minutes written while WSC was in office, 959, 961–2; dates format, 1390, 1494–5; Deakin assists WSC with, 762, 880, 911, 978–9, 1057, 1153–5, 1157, 1159, 1170–1, 1174, 1174–5, 1175, 1402, 1403–4, 1560, 2060–1; French language version introductory note, 1388–9; French language version references to General Prioux, 1333–4, 1334–5; Halifax disagrees with WSC's characterization of Chamberlain's settlement with Hitler, 1180; index corrections, 1342; Industrial Intelligence Centre, 813–14; Ismay assists WSC with, 521, 529–30, 551–2, 598, 978–9, 1025–6, 1057, 1141–2, 1153–5, 1159, 1160, 1161–2, 1167, 1312–13, 1402, 1560, 2060–1, 2146; Pownall assists WSC with, 911, 953, 978–9, 1057, 1099–100, 1101, 1153–5, 1157, 1175, 1264–5, 1402, 1542, 1560, 2094–5, 2101, 2139, 2146, 2147, 2148; production schedule, 954, 1714–15, 2143; proofs and photographs for, 761, 1498; publication of war-time telegrams to Australian Government, 1549–50, 1550, 1550 n.1; publication of WSC's war-time Administration papers, minutes and personal correspondence, 487, 492, 940–3, 943, 943 n.2, 944–5, 983–4, 984 n.1, 2030–1; publication of WSC's war-time Parliamentary Secret Session speeches, 174–5; Reves suggests titles for first volume of, 925; Reynaud assists WSC with, 1159, 1160, 1161–2; RSC assists WSC with, 1560; sixth volume proposed for, 1356–7, 1357, 1378–9, 1378, 1714–15; Wood's work space at WSC's Hyde Park home, 2028–9, 2029–30, 2030, 2030 n.1; WSC describes colossal scope of to Attlee, 583; WSC describes to CSC, 762; WSC discusses suggested edits with Reves, 922–4, 924, 926, 926–7; WSC negotiates contract for, 594, 761; WSC plans multi-volume account, 491–3, 492 n.1; WSC's earnings from, 942–3, 958–9, 1030; WSC sends Volume 3 instructions to Cassell & Co., 1010; WSC works on at Chartwell, 1719–20, 1764, 2141, 2143, 2145; WSC works on in Marrakech, 897, 898, 901, 907, 908, 911, 922, 925, 1982, 1987, 1990

Secretary of State for Air: *see* Noel-Baker, Philip John
Secretary of State for Dominion Affairs: *see* Addison, Christopher
Secretary of State for Foreign Affairs: *see* Morrison, Herbert
Secretary of State for War: *see* Shinwell, Emanuel; Strachey, John
Seiler, Joseph, 423, 423 n.1
Seligman, Eustace, 1145–6, 1145 n.2
Selywn-Lloyd, John Selwyn Brooke, 1133, 1133 n.1, 1426
Senanayake, Don Stephen, 1939, 1939 n.2
Serre, Charles, 1680, 1680 n.4
Sewell, Gordon, 705, 705 n.1
'Sextant', 579
Seymour, Horatia, 51, 51 n.2, 64, 72–3
Sforza, Carlo, 1035, 1035 n.6
Shakespeare, Geoffrey Hithersay, 2006, 2006 n.1, 2008
Shawcross, Hartley William
  biographical information, 618 n.2
  Criminal Justice Bill, 1110, 1111, 1112, 1114, 1115, 1119–21
  Exports to China (May 1951 WSC speech), 2070–1
  Fuel and Power Crisis (February 1947 WSC speech), 618–19
  Lynskey Tribunal, 1315, 1316, 1318–19
  WSC criticises, 2082
  WSC criticises Labour Government rationing policies, 1621
Shaw, George Bernard, 446–9, 446 n.1, 453, 1910
Shepherd, Francis Michie, 2232, 2232 n.1
Sheridan, Clare Consuelo, 296, 296 n.1, 311, 395
Sherman, William Tecumseh, 768, 768 n.1
Sherwood, Lady (Molly Patricia Berry), 900, 900 n.4
Sherwood, Robert Emmet, 1141, 1141 n.1, 1461, 1462
Shigemitsu, Mamoru, 57, 57 n.2, 593
Shinwell, Emanuel
  biographical information, 199 n.5
  China: British policy towards, 1970; Exports to China (May 1951 WSC speech), 2074–5; Fletcher provides Far East trade overview to WSC, 2064–5
  coal industry: Coal Bill Debate, 199, 615–16, 617; WSC criticises Labour Government policies, 475, 539, 615–16, 652, 653, 720, 752, 889, 1189–90, 1430
  defence: American bomber squadrons stationed in East Anglia, 111; Defence (26 July 1950 WSC speech), 1801–3; Defence (March 1950 WSC speech),

2314 INDEX

Shinwell, Emanuel *(continued)*
  defence *(continued)*
    1686–7, 1688, 1693, 1696, 1697–8; HofC public debate on, 1805; National Service periods, 1856, 1862; North Atlantic Supreme Commander (April 1951 WSC speech), 2046, 2050–1, 2052; Russian Armed Forces manpower estimates, 1807–8, 1809, 1846, 1854; Russian U-boat fleet estimates, 1813
  Germany, 1165
  Greece, 932
  Hague Conference, 958, 960, 1004
  Korean War, 1955
  McNeill asks WSC about, 1258
  Middle East, 1768
  political broadcasting, 979, 980, 1025
Shurmer, Percy Lionel Edward
  biographical information, 539 n.3
  criticises WSC during HofC debates, 539, 540, 1502, 1877, 1918, 1925
  Iron and Steel Bill, 1241
  post-war unemployment rates, 1673–4
Sieff, Marcus Joseph, 1224, 1224, 1224 n.1, 1311, 1990–1, 1991 n.1
Sikorski, Władysław Eugeniusz
  biographical information, 1379 n.1
  Opening of the Sikorski Institute (July 1949 WSC spech), 1445–7
  Sikorski Historical Institute appeal, 1379, 1379 n.2, 1380–1, 1385, 1385 n.1
Silone, Ignazio, 1035, 1036 n.7
Silverman, Samuel Sydney
  biographical information, 358 n.1
  domestic affairs: Defence (27 July 1950 WSC speech), 1811; Complaint of Privilege (March 1951 WSC speech), 2019–21; Criminal Justice Bill, 1111, 1112, 1114, 1115; nationalisation of British iron and steel industries, 1973, 1974; Parliament Bill, 865
  foreign affairs: Foreign Affairs (December 1948 WSC speech), 1273, 1278; The North Atlantic Treaty (May 1949 WSC speech), 1412–13; Foreign Affairs (July 1949 WSC speech), 1451; The International Situation (December 1950 WSC speech), 1972; Exports to China (May 1951 WSC speech), 2068; British support for Jewish National Home in Palestine, 432; criticises US as 'shabby moneylenders', 825; Jordan and Israel, Government Decision (Oral Answers), 1738; treatment of German Field Marshals, 1213–14
  WSC criticises, 358, 2015
Simonds, Gavin Turnbull, 2228, 2228 n.2

Simon, Franz Eugen Francis, 19, 19 n.4
Simon, John Allsebrook
  biographical information, 507 n.1
  Anglo-Persian Oil Company, 2061–2, 2062 n.1, 2065, 2079, 2080, 2090, 2091
  India, 399, 666–7, 726
  political broadcasts on the BBC, 981, 1021–5
  thanks WSC for copy of 'secret session speeches', 507
  Voluntary Schools in England and Wales, 2193
  wishes WSC good luck for election broadcast, 1592
Sinclair, Sir Archibald
  biographical information, 41 n.2
  death of Jack Spencer-Churchill, 625–6
  Lend-Lease Programme cancelation, 40–1
  Liberal Party broadcasts, 1607
  National Service Bill, 671
  Palestine, 950
  South Tyrol, 452
  WSC does not wish Blair to run against Sinclair in Caithness, 596
  WSC seeks Beaverbrook's advice, 2165, 2174
Sinclair, Marigold Forbes, 625, 625 n.4
The Sinews of Peace (March 1946 WSC speech)
  Conservative reaction to, 278
  Duke of Windsor praises, 309–10
  Gallacher criticises, 933
  Halifax reacts to, 247
  Labour Party members repudiate with motion of censure against WSC, 251–2, 1412
  Lady Asquith praises, 275
  Press articles on: *Chicago Sun*, 238–9, 240; *The Times*, 236–8; *Washington Post*, 253–5
  published as part of WSC's first volume of post-war speeches, 240 n.3
  Stalin criticises, 255–60, 261–2, 308
  text of, 227–35
  Truman refers to as prophetic, 807
  Truman's reaction to, 252
  WSC assesses long-term reactions to, 566, 1358–9, 1371, 1376, 1412
  WSC plans and writes, 156–7, 160, 163–4, 165, 170, 189–90, 191, 210, 210–11, 212–13, 241–2
  WSC press release on reception of, 271
  WSC suggests Anglo-American military alliance, 133–4, 143, 236–7, 239, 310
Skeffington-Lodge, Thomas, 1415, 1415 n.1
Slade, Roland Edgar, 19, 19 n.5
'Sledgehammer', 516
Sloggett, Arthur Thomas, 814, 814 n.1
Smillie, Robert, 1244, 1244 n.2
Smith, Adam, 608, 608 n.1, 661
Smith, Alfred Emanuel, 808, 808 n.1, 1436, 1436 n.1

Index

Smith, Ben
  biographical information, 206 n.2
  food shortages in England, 206–7
  post-war wheat allocations, 649
  US loan to England, 263
  WSC questions abrupt resignation and lack of statement from, 357–9, 363, 640
Smith, Bracewell, 775, 775 n.2
Smith, Ellis, 2069, 2069 n.1, 2072, 2131
Smith, Frederick Edwin ('F.E.'), 521, 521 n.1
Smuts, Jakob Daniel ('Japie'), 1884, 1884 n.2
Smuts, Jan Christian
  biographical information, 31 n.2
  Companion of Honour award, 31
  death of, 1864–6, 1884
  Douglas and Smuts reflect on WSC's election loss, 1077–8
  electoral defeat of (1948), 1062
  Europe, 589, 1227–8
  Greece, 1227–8
  India, Commonwealth relations, 1402, 1421–2, 1422–3, 1424–5
  Navy Estimates, 992–3
  resistance to multi-racial composition of the UN, 1384
  Russia, 877–8, 1172–3
  Seretse Khama affair, 1684, 1699–700, 1700 n.2
  and WSC: Alamein Reunion Dinner (October 1945 WSC speech), 106–7; Field Marshal Smuts's Eightieth Birthday (May 1950 WSC speech), 1758; Field Marshal Smuts Westminster Memorial Statue (June 1951 WSC speech), 2093–4; publication of WSC's war-time correspondence with, 2030–1, 2031; Smuts provides feedback on *The Second World War*, 1402; WSC meets with, 469; WSC orders *Reader's Digest* subscription for, 578–9, 595; WSC praises political career of, 1062; WSC praises Smuts's remarks on Germany, 377; WSC thanks for defence of England, 477
Smuts, Jan Christian, Jr ('Klein Jannie'), 1864, 1864 n.3, 1884, 1938
Smuts, Sybella 'Isie' Margaretha Krige ('Ouma'), 1864, 1864 n.2, 1884, 1938, 2030–1, 2031
Snavely, Guy Everett, 215, 215 n.1, 219
Snowden, Philip, 447, 447 n.3, 691, 715, 1509–10
Snow, Julian, 2049, 2049 n.1
Snow, Phyllis Annette Malcomson, 468, 468 n.1
Snow, Thomas Maitland, 382–3, 382 n.2, 467–8
Snyder, John Wesley, 888, 888 n.1
Soames, Arthur Christopher John
  biographical information, 548 n.3

Aix-en-Provence visit, 1146
Battle of Dunkirk, 1230
Canyon Kid (racehorse), 1756, 1765
Chartwell: Christmas at, 900, 911–12, 916; cocktail party at, 2143–4; Colville at, 1033; farming at, 1011–12, 1159, 1718–19; garden at, 765; Margaret Truman at, 2092; meals at, 1717; nearby properties, 1720; protection of black swans from freezing lakes at, 1583; salary increase for Soames serving as Farm Manager of, 947–8, 949; WSC goes bathing at, 764; WSC hunts rabbit at, 762; WSC's instructions for restoration of landscape and grounds at, 685, 815–16, 845–6, 892–4, 905–6, 1356, 1587–8
Colonist II (racehorse), 1719 n.3, 1867
feedback and suggested edits for *The Second World War*, 998–9, 998 n.2, 998 n.3, 999 n.1
Germany, 774–5
health, 1592
Persian oil, 2103
political career, 765, 1658
summarises Le Quesne Martel's paper on conscription, 1438–9
and WSC: thanks WSC for gift of whisky, 916; thanks WSC for lunch at Chartwell, 548–9; *The Times* coverage of WSC's criticism of Cripps, 1520; WSC sends sympathy to, 1153; WSC's US visit (1949), 1296, 1323, 1331, 1348, 1355
Soames, Arthur Granville, 568, 568 n.1, 1866–7, 2092
Soames, Emma Mary, 1561, 1561 n.1
Soames, Lady (Mary Churchill)
  biographical information, 12 n.1
  birthday: CSC reminds WSC of Mary's upcoming birthday, 56, 67, 73; WSC sends birthday greetings to, 68–9
  birth of son Nicholas, 871, 871 n.3
  career: Army of Occupation duties in Germany, 12, 39, 43, 44; ATS demobilisation in London, 1170; War Office Holding Unit posting in London, 48–9, 63, 68
  at Chartwell, 764, 900, 911–12, 1033, 1159, 1717, 1720
  Christmas in London (1945), 157
  CSC writes to while Mary is on her honeymoon, 621–2
  health, 911–12, 916
  lunches with CSC, 88
  marriage to Christopher Soames, 568, 579–80, 598, 621, 621 n.1, 625, 627
  travel: Aix-en-Provence visit, 1146; Biarritz

Soames, Lady (Mary Churchill) *(continued)*
  travel *(continued)*
    visit, 2142; in Brussels with WSC, 142; in Lake Geneva with WSC, 392; in the Netherlands, 334, 338; in Switzerland with WSC, 392, 467–8
  and WSC: WSC appears at new Parliament assembly, 35–6; WSC and CSC move back to Chartwell, 12–13, 27–8, 28 n.2, 43–4; WSC's US visit (1949), 1348, 1349
Socialist Party: *see* Labour Government; Labour Party
social legislation
  children's welfare, 1630
  Family Allowances, 801, 1017, 1092, 1645, 1654
  Health Insurance, 1017, 1092, 1104
  Labour Government policies, 716, 723, 755–6, 795, 1017, 1092–3, 1629–30
  National Insurance Bill, 201
  Old Age Pensions, 480, 714–15, 756, 1654, 2164
  Unemployment Insurance, 480, 1235
  WSC criticises Labour Government budget (April 1950), 1721–2
  WSC criticises Labour Government claims of credit for legislation drafted and approved by Coalition Government, 716, 723, 755–6, 795, 1017, 1092–3, 1629–30
  WSC describes helping 'the submerged tenth', 754, 1634
  WSC describes success of Conservative Governments in enacting social legislation between the wars, 714–15, 1629–30
Solley, Leslie Judah, 1273, 1273 n.1
Sorensen, Reginald, 576, 576 n.1
Sosnkowski, Kazimierz, 258, 258 n.1
'Sous les Vents' villa, 45, 80
South Africa
  death of Smuts, 1864–6, 1884
  India Commonwealth relations with England, 1421–2, 1423, 1424–5
  Seretse Khama affair, 1684, 1684–5, 1684 n.2, 1699–700, 1700 n.2
South America, 768–9
Southon, Robert, 78, 78 n.6, 815, 845, 906, 1587
Soviet Government: *see* Russia
Spaak, Paul-Henri
  biographical information, 1036 n.1
  Council of Europe: August 1950 meeting, 1826; defence of Western Europe, 1829–32; proposals, 215, 1152, 1221, 1276; Spaak's leadership of, 1467, 2123;

WSC calls for German inclusion at, 1474
European Movement (November 1949 WSC speech), 1575, 1577
Hague Conference, 1036, 1037
Spaatz, Carl, 248, 248 n.1
Spain
  British policy towards, 368–70
  British relations with, 1281–2, 1568–9
  Franco asserts that Britain promised aid to (1941), 1427, 1435
  Franco Government, 1415
  UN member nations relations with, 369
  UN membership, 1282, 1285, 1293, 1416
  US relations with, 1415
  WSC comments on at Cuban press conference, 193, 194, 196, 197
  WSC press release on Franco and Spanish Government, 272
Spalding, Henry Norman, 1916, 1916 n.2
Speaker of the House of Commons: *see* Brown, Douglas Clifton
Spearman, Alexander Cadawaller Young, 1145–6, 1145 n.1, 1443, 1444
Spears, Edward Louis, 484, 484 n.1
Special Powers Bill, 762, 764
speeches (WSC)
  British Armed Forces: Alamein Reunion Dinner (October 1945), 106–8; Fourth Alamein Reunion (October 1949), 1546–9; Fifth Alamein Reunion (October 1950), 1910–11; National Service Bill (March 1947), 670–7; National Service (April 1947), 687–8; National Service (May 1947), 696–702; Navy Estimates (March 1948), 986–97; Unveiling of the Commando Memorial (May 1948), 1058–9, 1060; Recruiting for the Forces broadcast (February 1949), 1329–30; RAF Benevolent Fund (September 1951), 2152–3
  British Commonwealth: The British Commonwealth (May 1946), 315–19; Ireland, Relations with the Commonwealth (November 1948), 1258–61; Ulster (October 1951), 2186–7
  Burma: Burma (December 1946), 580–2; Burma Independence Bill (November 1947), 846–9
  Conservative Party: 'Every Dog His Day' (October 1946), 472–81; Conservative Policy on Home Affairs (March 1947), 663–4; Empire and Freedom (April 1947), 680–5; Trust the People (May 1947), 712–23; A 'Doctor's Mandate' (August 1947), 749–58; A Civic and Patriotic Duty (September 1947),

INDEX

784–8; Conservative Party Annual Conference Address (October 1947), 793–803; Central Council of the Women's Advisory Committee of the Conservative Party (April 1948), 1013–21; WSC asks Maudling for speech material for upcoming Conservative Fete (June 1948), 1078; Conservative Policy (July 1949), 1456–61; Local Government (October 1949), 1524–5; Conservative Trades Union Congress (October 1949), 1527–9; Conservative Annual Conference (October 1949), 1530–42; The Conservative Point of View (January 1950), 1593–7; 1922 Committee Luncheon speech notes (May 1950), 1743–5; Scottish Unionist Meeting (May 1950), 1746–54; National and International Politics (July 1950), 1791–7; Conservative Case for an Election (March 1951), 2014–18; The Conservative Case (May 1951), 2080–8; Situation at Home and Abroad (October 1950), 1905–9

defence: Recruiting for the Forces broadcast (February 1949), 1329–30; Defence (March 1950), 1686–99; Defence (July 1950), 1801–4, 1807–17; Defence, Government Proposals (September 1950), 1852–64

domestic affairs: Fuel and Power Crisis (February 1947), 615–20; Petrol Rationing (October 1947), 836; Criminal Justice Bill (July 1948), 1110–23; Iron and Steel Bill (November 1948), 1235–49, 1235 n.1; Nationalisation (May 1949), 1429–30; Iron and Steel (September 1950), 1868–78; Housing (November 1950), 1921–32

economics: Finance Bill (June 1946), 388–90; Economic Situation (March 1947), 646–63; A 'Doctor's Mandate' (August 1947), 750–2, 757; No Easy Passage (August 1947), 766–8; A New Parliament (February 1948), 962–3, 964–6; Devaluation of the Pound (September 1949), 1499–514; The Economic Situation (October 1949), 1551–6; The Budget (April 1950), 1721–32, 1732; Budget Proposals and Economic Survey (April 1951), 2032–4; Exports to China (May 1951), 2066–76, 2079; Finance Bill Amendments, Chairman's Selection (June 1951), 2095–8

Europe: A New Europe (November 1945), 132; The Foundations of Freedom (November 1945), 136–7; The Future of Europe (November 1945), 139–41, 158; The United States of Europe (May 1946), 321–6; France and Europe (July 1946), 404–7; The Tragedy of Europe (September 1946), 458–61; United Europe (May 1947), 704–11; The Congress of Europe (May 1948), 1037–42, 1045, 1045–6; United Europe (May 1948), 1042–4; Building a New Europe (July 1948), 1126–7; United Europe (November 1948), 1250–1; A United Europe (February 1949), 1335–6; Europe and regional United Nations organisations (February 1949), 1336–9; Berlin Blockade Removal (May 1949), 1403; The North Atlantic Treaty (May 1949), 1411–17; United Europe (August 1949), 1466–8; A Meeting-Place of the Future Parliament of Europe (August 1949), 1470–1; Consultative Assembly of the Council of Europe (August 1949), 1471–4; European Movement (November 1949), 1575–8; European Unity (March 1950), 1702–12; European Unity and a European Army (August 1950), 1827–32; University of Copenhagen Danish-British Society speech notes (October 1950), 1888–904; The Peril in Europe (August 1950), 1843–7; Graver Dangers Loom in Europe (Korean War) (April 1951), 2036; North Atlantic Supreme Commander (April 1951), 2041–55; United Europe (July 1951), 2122–4

food: World Food Situation (May 1946), 355–63; Rationing of Bread (May 1946), 363–4; Bread Rationing (July 1946), 415–22; Agriculture (July 1948), 1108–10

foreign affairs: The Atomic Bomb (August 1945), 17–21; Foreign Policy, President Truman's Declaration (November 1945), 119–27; The Sinews of Peace (March 1946), 227–35; The English Speaking Peoples (March 1946), 242–6; WSC speaks to US Army and Navy officers at the Pentagon (March 1946), 247–51; The Darkening International Scene (March 1946), 263–6; A Broader and Fairer World (March 1946), 267; The Needs of a Sick World (April 1946), 301–4; Foreign Affairs (June 1946), 365–80; Foreign Affairs (October 1946), 497–504; Communism (October 1946), 505; Past Mistakes in Foreign Affairs (October 1946), 506–7; Peacetime Difficulties (September 1947), 791–3;

speeches (WSC) *(continued)*
  foreign affairs *(continued)*
    Foreign Affairs (January 1948), 929–40; Royal Dinner Address, Oslo (May 1948), 1046–7, 1047 n.2; Why Must We Always Fight? (May 1948), 1052–4; Suspicion Between Nations (October 1946), 517; Foreign Affairs (December 1948), 1270–85; The Communist Menace (March 1949), 1357–64; The Twentieth Century–Its Promise and Its Realization (March 1949), 1364–74, 1375, 1375–8, 1395; The Three Circles, Foreign Policy (April 1949), 1386–7; A Time When Old Feuds May Die (June 1949), 1432–3; Foreign Affairs (July 1949), 1450–5; Chancellor's Address (October 1949), 1544–5; Foreign Affairs (November 1949), 1562–75; The Anglo-American Alliance (July 1950), 1777–80; Foreign Affairs (November 1950), 1950–7; The International Situation (December 1950), 1967–75; Our Race and Destiny (April 1951), 2056–8; Tshekedi Khama Banishment (June 1951), 2099–101, 2099 n.1
  General Election (1945): Tasks Ahead (October 1945), 104–5
  General Election (1950): General Election (January 1950), 1589–90; The Conservative Point of View (January 1950), 1593–7; Woodford Adoption Meeting (January 1950), 1606–14; Leeds Election Address (February 1950), 1616–24; Devonport Election Address (February 1950), 1624–5, 1635–41; Cardiff Election Address (February 1950), 1627–35; Woodford Election Address (February 1950), 1641; Edinburgh Election Address (February 1950), 1642–50; London broadcast (February 1950), 1651–7
  General Election (1951): Conservative Case for an Election (March 1951), 2014–18; Socialist Blunders (July 1951), 2116–20; Liverpool Election Address (October 1951), 2166–74; Our Political Future (October 1951), 2177–82; Woodford Election Address (October 1951), 2182–5; Ulster (October 1951), 2186–7; Abadan, Sudan and Bevan – A Trio of Misfortune (October 1951), 2187–90; Huddersfield Election Address (October 1951), 2196–201; Newcastle upon Tyne Election Address (October 1951), 2201–6; Plymouth Election Address (October 1951), 2212–19

Harrow School: November 1946, 557–9; November 1947, 842–4; November 1948, 1225–7; December 1949, 1580–2; November 1950, 1945–6
honorary degrees and awards: Honorary Degree Conferment, Brussels University (November 1945), 137–9; University of Miami speech notes (February 1946), 213–21; Let Freedom Reign (May 1946), 327; The Flame of Christian Ethics (May 1948), 1048–50; To End Bitterness (May 1948), 1050–2; The Essential Verities (November 1948), 1251–3; Presentation of Grotius Medal (February 1949), 1313–14; Honorary Degree Conferment, Copenhagen University (October 1950), 1885–7
India: The British Commonwealth (May 1946), 318; India Cabinet Mission, Statement on the Adjournment (May 1946), 329–32; India Cabinet Mission (July 1946), 408–14; India (December 1946), 569–78; India Government Policy (March 1947), 634–46; India Transfer of Power (June 1947), 728–30; Hyderabad and Kashmir (July 1948), 1133–9
Korea: Korea (June 1950), 1773–4; Korea (July 1950), 1780–6
Labour Government: The Perils of Socialist Control (November 1945), 148–56; Failures of the Government's 'Doctrinaire Socialism' (April 1946), 304–7; Debate on the Address (November 1946), 530–41; No Easy Passage (August 1947), 766–70; Municipal Elections press statement (October 1947), 819; Debate on the Address (October 1947), 821–35; Local Election Victories (November 1947), 842; Britain in Peril speech notes (December 1947), 882; Britain in Peril (December 1947), 883–91; Britain in Peril press statement (December 1947), 891; The Evils of Socialist Government, Scottish Unionist meeting (May 1948), 1062–71; Britain 'Floundering and Sinking' (June 1948), 1086–96; Perils Abroad and at Home (October 1948), 1182–94, 1196–7, 1197, 1198–9; Debate on the Address (October 1948), 1202–19; Labour's Nationalisation Policy: 'Caprice and Greed' (May 1949), 1419–20; Labour's Disastrous Rule (October 1949), 1550–1; Debate on the Address (March 1950), 1668–79; Debate on the Address (October 1950), 1917–18

INDEX

Middle East: British Troops in Egypt (May 1946), 311–15; Egypt Treaty Negotiations (May 1946), 343–52; Palestine (August 1946), 427–36; Palestine (January 1947), 604–10; Palestine (January 1949), 1297–308, 1311; Assassination of King Abdullah of Jordan (July 1951), 2121; Foreign Affairs, Middle East (July 1951), 2125–37; Persian Crisis (October 1951), 2174–6

Parliament: inspiration for WSC's phrase 'Never in the history of human conflict was so much owed by so many to so few', 1162–3, 1162 n.3, 1179–80, 2152; publication of WSC's war-time Parliamentary Secret Session speeches (1945), 174–5; HofC Convening Time (April 1946), 292–5, 292 n.1; Town and Country Planning Bill and Parliamentary Democracy (March 1947), 629–33; Transitional Powers Bill, Supplies and Services (August 1947), 759–60; Committee on Privileges Report (October 1947), 837–9; Parliament Bill (November 1947), 859–69; A New Parliament (February 1948), 962–6; Representation of the People Bill (February 1948), 968–77; Towards a New Parliament (April 1948), 1031–2; Parliamentary Democracy (May 1948), 1054–5; Preserving Continuity (May 1948), 1060–1; Political Gerrymandering (June 1948), 1078–86; A New Parliament (July 1948), 1102–6; Ministers and Public Servants, Official Conduct (February 1949), 1314–20, 1328; Motion for Address in Reply (October 1950), 1912–13, 1912 n.1, 1912 n.2; The New Chamber of the House of Commons (October 1950), 1914–15; Complaint of Privilege (March 1951), 2019–25

Royal Family: His Majesty's Return From South Africa (May 1947), 702–3; Address of Congratulations to Their Majesties and Princess Elizabeth on the Forthcoming Royal Marriage (October 1947), 816–17; Motion of Congratulations to Their Majesties on their Silver Wedding (April 1948), 1029; The Birthplace of Prince Charles (November 1948), 1249–50

tributes: Roosevelt Memorial Bill (October 1946), 490–1; International Congress of Physicians (September 1947), 775–7; The Al Smith Memorial (October 1947), 808–11; Pilgrims' Dinner to Mrs Roosevelt (April 1948), 1006–8; Unveiling of the Commando Memorial (May 1948), 1058–9, 1060; Croydon speech on auxiliary fighter squadrons (October 1948), 1181; President Roosevelt (November 1948), 1232; Opening of the Sikorski Institute (July 1949), 1445–7; Riches of English Literature (November 1949), 1558–9; Lord Keyes and His Son (April 1950), 1734–5; Lord Baldwin (May 1950), 1754–6; Field Marshal Smuts's Eightieth Birthday broadcast (May 1950), 1758; Field Marshal Smuts (September 1950), 1864–6; The Earl of Oxford and Asquith (December 1950), 1962–4; Oliver Stanley (December 1950), 1966–7; Cutlers' Feast, Sheffield (April 1951), 2037–8; Field Marshal Smuts Westminster Memorial Statue (June 1951), 2093–4; Lord Moran (July 1951), 2112–13; Assassination of King Abdullah of Jordan (July 1951), 2121; RAF Benevolent Fund (September 1951), 2152–3

see also The Sinews of Peace (March 1946 WSC speech)

Spencer-Churchill, Arabella, 1561, 1592 n.2, 2144

Spencer-Churchill, John Strange ('Jack'), 47, 47 n.2, 157, 625–8, 664–5

Spencer-Churchill, Winston (WSC's grandson)
biographical information, 177 n.1
at Chartwell, 2140, 2142, 2145
CSC lunches with, 900
CSC proposes leaving Chartwell to, 1158–9
health and care of, 1309–10, 1342–3
hopes WSC wins the General Election (1951), 2159
thanks WSC and CSC for visit, 774, 774 n.2
WSC sends paints and brushes to, 593–4, 679
WSC thanks for letter, 1998
WSC thanks for postcard, 1322

Spencer, Dorothy, 70–1, 70 n.1, 71, 94–5

Stacey, Charles Perry, 1850, 1850 n.1

Staercke, André de, 1811, 1881 n.2

Stalin, Josef Vissarionovich Djugashvili
biographical information, 23 n.2
atom bomb, 7, 23, 512
Battle of Stalingrad (film), 731–2, 731 n.5, 733
British policy towards Russia, 1173, 1283–5, 1650, 2149, 2152
commercial aviation, 512
CSC describes Russia visit to WSC and King, 110
Finland, 511
Greece, 511, 932
Japan, 512

Stalin, Josef Vissarionovich Djugashvili *(continued)*
　Norway, 511
　Poland: Mikołajczyk's status and safety in, 781; Stalin criticises Anders and Sosnkowski, 258; western frontier of, 511
　Potsdam Conference: Stalin's demeanor at, 7, 11; Stalin's opinion on adherence to, 510; Stalin's request for base on the Aegean Sea, 731, 731 n.2
　refers to Attlee as 'warmonger', 2015
　Russian forces in Eastern Europe, 511, 513–14
　Sovietisation of Eastern Europe, 111
　Sovietisation of Poland, 500–1
　Soviet propaganda and espionage, 373
　Stalin's United Press interview, 508–12, 513–14
　Sweden, 511
　Truman's opinion of, 807
　US-Russian relations, 508–9, 878
　war-time Supreme Command decisions, 601
　and WSC: Foreign Policy, President Truman's Declaration (November 1945 WSC speech), 120; Foreign Affairs (October 1946 WSC speech), 503; The Sinews of Peace (March 1946 WSC speech), 232, 255–60, 261–2, 308; The Communist Menace (March 1949 WSC speech), 1359, 1363; Montgomery relays greetings from Stalin to WSC, 598, 613; painting of WSC, FDR and Stalin, 98, 128; Stalin criticises WSC as instigator of new war, 509; thanks WSC for birthday greetings, 172; WSC thanks for message and sends well wishes, 613
　Yalta Agreement, 202, 203–4
　Yalta Conference, 2078
　Yugoslavia refuses to sign peace treaty with Italy, 509
Stalin, Nadezhda Sergeevna Alliluyeva, 110, 110 n.1
Stamp, Josiah Charles, 270, 277 n.3
Stanhope, James Richard, 1234, 1234 n.1
Stanley, Oliver Frederick George
　biographical information, 289 n.2
　British estimates of Russian forces in eastern Europe, 565, 567
　Budget Debate, 294
　Consultative Committee for economic and financial issues, 1267
　CSC dines with, 900
　death of, 2000
　Defence Memorandum discussions with Attlee, 1431
　Eden's 1938 resignation as Foreign Secretary, 948–9, 952
　Palestine: British policy towards, 394, 399, 605–6, 1291; British troops and aid in (proposed), 367; Palestine (August 1946 WSC speech), 427
　proposed removal of British troops from Egypt, 367
　provides feedback to WSC on proofs of *The Second World War*, 948–9
　WSC asks to monitor HofC proceedings on iron and steel, 289
　WSC sends well wishes, 1745
　WSC's tribute to (December 1950), 1966–7
Stanley, Sydney, 1309 n.1, 1319, 1319 n.1
Stansgate, Lord (William Wedgwood Benn), 343 n.1, 538, 830
Stark, Harold Raynsford, 25, 25 n.2
Stassen, Harold, 1045, 1045 n.2, 1987, 2026
Steel, Christopher Eden ('Kit'), 1179, 1179 n.2
Stelling, C. David, 1078, 1078 n.1
Stepinac, Aloysius, 501, 501 n.1, 789
Stettinius, Edward Reilly, Jr, 743, 743 n.1, 1351
Stevens, John Felgate, 552–3, 553 n.1
Stimson, Henry Lewis, 20, 20 n.2
Stirbey, Barbu Alexandru, 259, 259 n.1
St Laurent, Louis Stephen, 1204, 1204 n.2, 2101
Stockwood, Arthur Mervyn, 2093, 2093 n.1
Stokes, Richard Rapier
　biographical information, 202 n.2
　India Transfer of Power, 728
　Ireland, Relations with the Commonwealth, 1259
　Persian Crisis, 2175
　treatment of German Field Marshals, 1212
　Voluntary Schools in England and Wales, 2192
　Yalta Agreement, 202, 204–6
Stone, Earl Everett, 1002–3, 1002 n.2
Strachey, John
　biographical information, 357 n.2
　Conservative Party criticises, 1631
　food: Bread Rationing (July 1946 WSC speech), 415, 416–18, 419, 421; world food shortages, 357, 362–3; WSC criticises bread rationing, 650; WSC criticises Labour Government rationing policies, 1639, 1640
　French and German coal and steel industries, 1783, 1792
　WSC inquires about death sentence for three British soldiers, 1848
　WSC praises, 363–4
　WSC thanks for copy of speech and reminisces about Nairobi, 1096
Stransky, Jaroslav, 1023, 1023 n.1, 1027
Strauss, George Russell, 1239, 1239 n.2, 1243, 1871, 1875, 2119
Strauss, Henry George, 520–1, 520 n.8

INDEX

Street, Margery ('Streetie'), 778, 778 n.2
Streit, Clarence Kirshman, 253–5, 253 n.1
Stuart, James Gray
  biographical information, 79 n.1
  Anderson's taxation comments, 79
  British policy towards Scotland, 1489–91
  Committee of Privileges, 732
  Consultative Committee, 1713
  1922 Committee meeting, 521
  potential loss of Conservatives because of coal-mining industry nationalisation, 175
  reports on Parliament to WSC, 198–201
  Woolton suggested as successor to Assheton for Conservative Party Chairman, 289
  WSC notes lengthy delay in receipt of Shadow Cabinet telegram, 291
  WSC requests larger table for Opposition committee, 146
  WSC's Opposition leadership and salary, 286
Stubbs, Albert Ernest, 1116, 1116 n.2
Sturdee, Nina Edith ('Jo')
  biographical information, 37 n.3
  in America with WSC, 173, 278, 288–9
  butterflies for grounds at Chartwell, 387
  Council of Europe Conservative MP delegates, 1418–19
  foreword for Weizmann's autobiography, 1481, 1481 n.2, 1484, 1486
  General Election (1950) results, 1658
  George VI wishes to see WSC before departing for South Africa, 603–4
  list of WSC's speeches made in 1945 and since the General Election, 450, 450 n.2
  Magee asks WSC for statement for von Weizsäcker's trial, 1200, 1201, 1223 n.5
  Marrakech trip costs and logistics (1947), 858, 881, 908
  in Marrakech with WSC, 899, 904, 910, 1979–80, 1981, 2089–90
  Palestine, 1291
  Press relations: *Daily Mirror* asks WSC to comment on RSC's statements on Australia, 783, 783 n.3; public notice of Attlee's meetings with WSC on Defence matters, 1347; *Sunday Times* interview questions for WSC, 2211–12; WSC misquoted in *The Times*, 1437
  Princess Margaret's travel allowance, 1390 n.1, 1391 n.1
  RSC's political career, 2008
  Rufus II updates for WSC, 1155, 1155–6
  Russian forces in Romania, 514
  The Second World War: feedback and suggested edits for, 1174–5; proofs and edits for sent to WSC in Provence, 1158; serialization book rights to, 595; Yalta Conference, 2076–8

Secret Session Speeches for Furness, 593
Sieff asks to meet with WSC, 1224
  updates Thompson on CSC and WSC, 579–80
  WSC declines US exhibit of his paintings, 2089
  WSC's secretaries and work schedules, 37–8
Suez Canal: *see* Egypt
Sully, Duke of (Maximilien de Béthune), 1037–8, 1037 n.2
Sulzberger, Arthur Hays, 1378, 1378 n.1, 1498
Summers, Gerard Spencer, 97, 97 n.2, 309
Summerskill, Edith Clara, 418, 418 n.1, 651, 1637, 1639, 1640
Sumner Welles, Benjamin, 309, 309 n.2
Sunday Express, 528–9, 541–2, 542–5, 547–8, 549
Supplies and Services Act, 1751–2
Swainston, H. I., 773, 773 n.1
Sweden, 511
Swinton, Lord (Philip Cunliffe-Lister)
  biographical information, 286 n.1
  General Election (1950): Conservative campaign, 1641–2, 1657, 1657 n.2; Questionnaire Committee, 1614, 1641, 1657
  National Service periods, 1616
  Voluntary Schools in England and Wales, 2192, 2194
  WSC forms new Government (1951), 2223, 2226, 2229
  WSC invites to Shadow Cabinet meeting, 286
Swope, Herbert Bayard, 482–3, 482 n.1, 486, 1423
Sydney, Algernon, 797, 797 n.2
Sydney, William Philip, 765, 765 n.2
Syria, 296–7, 300–1, 309, 561

Taft, Robert, 1987, 1987 n.1
Taiwan, 1839, 1839 n.1
taxation
  Conservative Party policies, 648–9, 1627, 2173
  Labour Government policies, 796, 1631–2, 1633, 1640, 1642, 1645, 1654–5, 1675, 1721, 1722–3, 1724–7, 1747, 1750, 1751–2, 2033, 2035, 2086, 2097, 2117, 2161, 2163, 2173
Taylor, Edith Bishop, 896, 896 n.1
Tedder, Arthur William
  biographical information, 162 n.5
  dissolution of Combined Chiefs of Staff, 1515
  Ismay agrees to destroy COS minute with WSC's criticism of Tedder, 172
  JSM leadership, 1790
  WSC's statement on war-time Supreme Command decisions, 299
  WSC suggests Resolutions for Thanks to Commanders, 162

2322 INDEX

Teheran Agreement, 204–5, 668
Teitgen, Pierre-Henri, 1036, 1036 n.2
Tejan-Sie, Banja, 1685, 1685 n.1
Templemore, Lord (Arthur Chichester), 66, 66 n.2
Templer, Gerald Walter Robert, 546–7, 547 n.2
Tennyson, Alfred
  WSC quotes in article on United States of Europe, 585, 585 n.2
  WSC quotes during Parliament Bill debate, 862, 868
  WSC quotes in The Twentieth Century–Its Promise and Its Realization speech (March 1949), 1365
Teusler, Rudolf Bolling, 1851, 1851 n.2
Teviot, Lord (Charles Iain Kerr), 1087, 1087 n.1, 1266–7, 1267 n.1
Theakstone, Louis Marguarde, 2078, 2078 n.1
Thibault, Jacques-Anatole-François ('Anatole France'), 180, 180 n.3, 453
13th Paratroop Battalion, 539, 539 n.1
XIII Corps meeting in Trieste, 47, 55
Thomas, George, 1509, 1509 n.1
Thomas, Ivor Owen, 2050, 2050 n.1
Thomas, James Henry, 1316, 1316 n.2
Thomas, James Purdon Lewes, 1788–9, 1788 n.1
Thompson, Charles Ralfe ('Tommy'), 579–80, 579 n.1, 1167
Thomson, Catharine, 791, 791 n.1
Thomson, Charlotte, 791, 791 n.1
Thomson, George Paget, 17, 17 n.1
Thorez, Maurice, 272, 272 n.1
Thorneycroft, Peter, 201, 201 n.4, 520, 596, 1146, 2228
'Thunderclap', 529, 1941
Tibet, 1831, 1847
'Tiger', 530, 530 n.1, 1033, 1099, 1099 n.3, 1130–1, 1140–1
The Times
  America and the Atomic Bomb article, 1382
  Attlee criticises WSC as worst Chancellor Exchequer of the century, 689–90
  coverage of WSC's criticism of Cripps, 1516–17, 1518, 1519–20, 1520
  German rearmament between the wars, 1233–4
  speeches (WSC): The Tragedy of Europe (September 1946), 461, 462–4; Perils Abroad and at Home (October 1948), 1196–7, 1197; The Twentieth Century–Its Promise and Its Realization (March 1949), 1375
  WSC misquoted in, 1437
  WSC urges Astor to control content of leading articles, 385–6, 390–1, 404
Tiso, Jozef, 1223, 1223 n.2

Tito, Josip Broz
  biographical information, 280 n.3
  Alexander comments on Tito's leadership of Yugoslavia, 1101
  Anglo-American policy towards, 1354
  Sargent's statements about Tito and Mihailović, 280, 295
  WSC criticises Tito's claims to former Italian territory, 501–2
  WSC seeks British Government support for fair trial for Mihailović, 287
Tomlinson, George, 2191–2, 2191 n.5
'Torch', 394, 394 n.2, 1098, 1107, 1415
Tovey, John Cronyn, 2044, 2044 n.2
trade unions
  Conservative Party Trade Unions policy ('The Industrial Charter'), 721–3, 754–5, 799, 800, 890, 1016, 1069–70, 1094, 1458, 1528, 2184–5, 2190–1, 2211
  A New Parliament (July 1948 WSC speech), 1104–5
  Shaw discusses English politics with WSC, 447, 448
  Trade Unions Conference, 147–8, 1871–3, 1877–8
  WSC praises anti-Communist stance of, 1854
Trenchard, Hugh Montague, 2012, 2012 n.2
Trend, Burke Frederick St John, 563–4, 563 n.3, 564 n.1
Trevelyan, George Macaulay, 333, 333 n.1, 340, 352
tributes (WSC speeches)
  Roosevelt Memorial Bill (October 1946), 490–1
  International Congress of Physicians (September 1947), 775–7
  The Al Smith Memorial (October 1947), 808–11
  Pilgrims' Dinner to Mrs Roosevelt (April 1948), 1006–8
  Unveiling of the Commando Memorial (May 1948), 1058–9, 1060
  Croydon speech on auxiliary fighter squadrons (October 1948), 1181
  Opening of the Sikorski Institute (July 1949), 1445–7
  Riches of English Literature (November 1949), 1558–9
  Lord Keyes and His Son (April 1950), 1734–5
  Lord Baldwin (May 1950), 1754–6
  Field Marshal Smuts's Eightieth Birthday broadcast (May 1950), 1758
  Field Marshal Smuts (September 1950), 1864–6
  The Earl of Oxford and Asquith (December 1950), 1962–4
  Oliver Stanley (December 1950), 1966–7

INDEX

Cutlers' Feast, Sheffield (April 1951), 2037–8
Field Marshal Smuts Westminster Memorial Statue (June 1951), 2093–4
Lord Moran (July 1951), 2112–13
Assassination of King Abdullah of Jordan (July 1951), 2121
RAF Benevolent Fund (September 1951), 2152–3
'Trident', 1486, 1486 n.3
Truman, Elizabeth Virginia Wallace ('Bess'), 1499, 1499 n.2, 1516
Truman, Harry S
  biographical information, 114 n.2
  atom bomb: Attlee asks WSC to comment on draft letter to Truman, 74, 83–4, 91; Attlee writes to Truman about need for world policy regarding, 84–7; Foreign Policy, President Truman's Declaration (November 1945 WSC speech), 119–27, 128; Quebec Agreement of 1943, 1972–3, 2002, 2003, 2004, 2004 n.2, 2025, 2034; Truman asserts equal partnership among US, Canada and Great Britain on development of peacetime use of atom bomb, 114–15, 126; Truman's declaration to Congress about willingness to use, 1382, 1383, 1385, 1395; Tube Alloys discussed with Stalin at Potsdam Conference, 23; WSC's Atomic Bomb statement, 7
  Attlee's US visit, 1968
  CSC sends compliments to, 1229
  Europe: European Army proposals, 1833–4, 1840; WSC praises Marshall Plan proposals, 757–8; WSC proposes United States of Europe, 459
  Greece, 1352–4, 1443, 1444
  Korea, 1781–2, 1786, 1795, 1905, 2075–6, 2080
  meets with George VI, 11
  meets with Sarah Churchill, 1499, 1516, 1524
  Middle East: Anglo-Iranian personnel in Abadan, 2156–7; Palestine, 346, 399, 1299; Persian oil, 2102, 2103, 2109, 2114, 2136
  Pound Sterling devaluation, 1585
  Presidential primary elections, 1046
  proposed jobs for Duke and Duchess of Windsor at British Embassy in America, 337
  sends USS *Missouri* to Turkey, 241
  The Sinews of Peace (March 1946 WSC speech), 156–7, 160, 163–4, 165, 191, 210–11, 212–13, 227, 241–2, 252, 308
  Taiwan, 1839 n.1
  and WSC: encourages WSC to present Green Lectures at Westminster College, 113, 128; Marshall's statement on enemy tapping of WSC's telephone calls with Truman, 164, 167–8; painting of WSC, FDR and Stalin, 98, 128; plays poker with, 223–4; resolution inviting WSC to address the General Assembly of Virginia, 203; thanks WSC for copy of *The Gathering Storm*, 1102; thanks WSC for pen and photograph, 9; train journey to Missouri, 222–4, 225, 226; Truman hopes he and WSC can solve Communism problem, 1102; Truman thanks and sends well wishes, 688; WSC admires Truman's policies and sends well wishes, 781, 807–8; WSC congratulates on Presidential election win, 1229; WSC sends set of his war-time books to, 240–1, 252; WSC sends volume three of *The Second World War* to, 1717; WSC sends well wishes, 703; WSC's opinion of Attlee, 222–3; WSC visits US (1946), 127–8, 147, 156–7, 160, 169, 189–90, 195, 197, 198; WSC visits US (1949), 1323, 1331, 1343, 1352; WSC visits US (May 1951), 2026, 2034
Truman, Mary Margaret, 1499, 1499 n.4, 1516, 2092
Tube Alloys
  research, 7 n.1, 23
  see also atom bomb
Tudor, Sir Henry Hugh, 184–5, 184 n.1, 208–10
Tuka, Vojtech, 1223, 1223 n.1
Turkey
  Foreign Affairs, Middle East (July 1951 WSC speech), 2126, 2127
  WSC criticises Soviet pressure on, 233, 242, 265
  WSC reiterates British and US support for in letter to Inönü, 1219–20
Twenty Years' Treaty, 134, 326, 373
Tyerman, Donald, 1518, 1518 n.1, 1519–20

U-boats
  Defence (March 1950 WSC speech), 1694–6
  German Fleet disposition, 7
  North Atlantic Supreme Commander (April 1951 WSC speech), 2041, 2045–6
  Russian Navy U-boat fleet estimates, 1813, 2041
Ulster, 537, 2186–7
Unemployment Insurance, 480, 1235
unemployment rates
  in 1947, 713–14
  post-war, 1068–9, 1596, 1609, 1636, 1644, 1673–4
  between the wars, 715, 885–6

Unionist Party
  Scottish Unionist Meeting (May 1950 WSC speech), 1746–54
  WSC congratulates Allan on election campaign, 1715–16
  WSC pledges Conservative Party support for, 722–3
  WSC praises Boyle's election programme and address, 1934–5
  WSC seeks solidarity with against Labour Government, 827
United Nations (UN)
  atom bomb, 96
  Austria, 370–1
  British National Service Bill, 695–6
  British support of, 531, 2163
  China, 1954–5, 1986–7
  Conservative Party foreign and world policy principles, 683–5
  Declaration of Human Rights, 1467, 1748, 1792, 1899, 2197–8
  Egypt, 349
  Europe: Council of Europe stance on UN military actions, 1829–32; Hague Conference, 1040; WSC proposes United States of Europe, 326, 407, 459, 461, 565, 587; WSC seeks rapid achievement of peace with Germany and Italy, 379; WSC's Statement of Aims memorandum, 496
  Greece, 500
  Halifax's UN Trusteeship proposal, 133, 143
  India: Hyderabad and Kashmir, 1129–30, 1134–5, 1137–8, 1163; post-Imperial British policy towards, 1210–11
  Korea: Chinese Communist aggression in, 2066–8; Korea (July 1950 WSC speech), 1780–2; Korean Republic Invasion (Oral Answers), 1770; North Korean invasion of Korean Republic, 1794; peace negotiations, 2036; US troops in, 1905
  Morton describes Brussels duties to WSC, 814–15
  Palestine: Arab–Israeli war, 1057, 1057 n.1, 1295; Jerusalem internationalisation, 1736–7; transfer of British Mandate to United Nations, 434–5, 436, 499, 536, 609–10, 644–5, 646, 753, 787–8, 800, 829–30, 885, 950–2, 1016, 1299–300
  Russia: Stalin's view of UN guarantee of small States' integrity, 509; use of veto power, 497, 510, 1662; WSC press release on Soviet troop movements in Persia, 271; WSC promotes idea of summit with England, 1656
  Spain, 369
  speeches (WSC): Foreign Policy, President Truman's Declaration (November 1945), 121–2; The Future of Europe (November 1945), 141; The Sinews of Peace (March 1946), 212–13, 228–35, 238–9, 253; The Darkening International Scene (March 1946), 263–4, 265; The British Commonwealth (May 1946), 318–19; Suspicion Between Nations (October 1946), 517; United Europe speech (May 1947), 706, 709; Al Smith Memorial speech (October 1947), 809–11; Europe and regional UN organisations (February 1949), 1336–9; University of Copenhagen Danish–British Society speech notes (October 1950), 1892–3
  WSC cites Communism as threat to, 1336, 1545
  WSC comments on rights of small States, 193, 196, 323–4
  WSC praises establishment of, 1369
  WSC proposes regional military groups as part of, 587–8
  WSC stresses Anglo-American unity as necessary to success of, 266
United States
  economic policies, 823, 825–7, 1653
  emigration of English citizens to, 768–9
  The English Speaking Peoples (March 1946 WSC speech), 242–6
  US Army, 162–3, 166, 248, 249–51
  US Presidential election (1948), 1198, 1229, 1237
  Western Union (European Army) proposals, 1863
  WSC invited to address the General Assembly of Virginia, 182, 203, 210
  WSC visits (1949), 1323, 1331, 1343, 1352
  WSC visits (1951), 2026
  WSC visits Williamsburg with Eisenhower, 210, 243
United States of Europe
  articles (WSC): The Grand Design of a United Europe, 589–92, 592 n.1; One Way to Stop a New War, 585–8, 585 n.1; WSC plans United States of Europe article, 483, 483 n.2
  Committee for a United Europe, 933–5
  Handling Group, 526–7, 545–6, 556
  proposals for, 461–2, 494–5, 555, 560–1, 566–7, 583–4
  Smuts discusses with WSC, 1173
  speeches (WSC): The United States of Europe (May 1946), 321–6; The Tragedy of Europe (September 1946), 459–61; Empire and Freedom (April 1947),

683; A 'Doctor's Mandate' (August 1947), 757–8; Conservative Party Annual Conference Address (October 1947), 803; Perils Abroad and at Home (October 1948), 1183–5, 1188
The Times article on WSC's proposal for, 461, 462–4
United Europe Committee, 133, 958
Usborne speaks in favour of, 530–1
US Congressional resolution regarding, 725–6
WSC asks Marshall to meet with Gollancz, 1003
WSC promotes apolitical British approach to, 1004–6, 1013–14, 1030, 1063, 2195
WSC's Statement of Aims memorandum, 495–6
WSC writes to Blum regarding, 1004–6
United States Government
  American bomber squadrons stationed in East Anglia, 1273–4, 1811–12, 1839, 1845, 2003, 2025, 2053, 2215
  Congressional Committee Executive Sessions, 1803–4
  Korean Republic Invasion (Oral Answers), 1770
  Lend-Lease Programme cancelation, 40–1
  'Morgenthau Plan' for Germany, 41–2
  Palestine, 536
  Pound Sterling devaluation, 1504–5
  Quebec Agreement of 1943, 1958–60, 2007–8
  speeches (WSC): A Civic and Patriotic Duty speech (September 1947), 785–6; The Congress of Europe (May 1948), 1039–40; United Europe (May 1947), 708–9
  United States of Europe: proposals, 587, 1894; US Congressional resolution regarding, 725–6
  United States Mutual Defence Assistance Act, 1598–600, 1604–5, 1606
  US policy towards Russia, 1145–6, 1183
  US Presidential election (1948), 1237, 1271
  WSC to address US Senate (proposed), 1352, 1354, 1356
  WSC praises bipartisan nature of, 1087
  WSC praises US foreign policy, 1711
  WSC's Atomic Bomb statement, 20–1
  Yalta Agreement, 206
Usborne, Henry Charles, 530–1, 530 n.4

Valdés y Ozores, Beatriz, 2143, 2143 n.1
Valiant, HMS, 993, 995
Vandenberg, Arthur Hendrick, 239, 239 n.1, 1412, 1711, 2041
Van Fleet, James Alward, 1353, 1353 n.1

Van Leer, Bernard, 1992, 1992 n.1, 1995
Vansittart, Robert Gilbert, 452, 452 n.1, 1178, 1179, 1200, 2061–2
Van Waeyenbergh, Honoré Marie Louis, 137, 137 n.1
van Zeeland, Paul, 706, 706 n.1, 1036, 1221
Vaughan, Harry Briggs, 226, 226 n.2
Vian, Philip, 2043, 2043 n.1
Viant, Samuel, 292–3, 292 n.2, 294
Vichy Government, 135
Victoria, Queen (Alexandrina Victoria), 920, 920 n.3
Villiers, David, 915, 915 n.1
Vincent, Victor, 1355–6, 1355 n.2
Vinson, Carl, 1807–8, 1807 n.1
Visser, Willem, 1008, 1008 n.2
Voluntary Schools in England and Wales, 2191–3, 2193, 2194–5
Voroshilov, Klimenti Yefremovitch, 546, 546 n.1
Vyshinsky, Andrei Yanuarevich, 291, 291 n.1, 1412, 1951

Wade, Donald Baron, 1668–9, 1668 n.1
Waldron, William James, 918, 918 n.2
Wales
  Welsh Parliament proposals, 1628–9
  WSC praises David Lloyd George in Cardiff Election Address (February 1950), 1632–3
  WSC proposes Welsh Cabinet member and Council of Wales, 1629, 2165
  WSC relates Tonypandy story, 1627–8
Walkden, Evelyn, 2021, 2021 n.1
Walker, Patrick Gordon, 2099, 2099 n.2, 2190–1
Walker, Ronald Fitz-John, 2207, 2207 n.1
Wallace, Henry Agard
  biographical information, 183 n.2
  proposals for division of Europe into Eastern and Western blocs, 495
  US Presidential election (1948), 1198, 1229, 1237
  WSC criticises Oslo speech, 682, 724
Warbey, William Noble
  biographical information, 251 n.1
  Criminal Justice Bill, 1113
  India, Commonwealth Relations (Oral Answers), 1399
  motion of censure against WSC, 251–2, 1412
  Parliament Bill, 864–5
Wardell, Michael, 1476–8, 1476 n.2
Ward, George Reginald, 199, 199 n.3
Ward, Kenneth Langhorne Stanley, 911–12, 911 n.3
Ward, William Humble Eric (Lord Dudley), 893, 893 n.1
Warfield, Wallis (Duchess of Windsor), 143–5, 143 n.3, 337, 1819

Washington, George, 244, 244 n.2, 491
Washington Post, 253–5
Waters, Arthur George, 2187, 2187 n.1, 2208, 2208 n.2
Watson, Arthur E., 913, 913 n.2
Watson, William, 1932, 1932 n.3
Wavell, Lord (Archibald)
  biographical information, 37 n.2
  India: Ali criticises Indian Congress Party, 471; Ambedkar appeals to WSC regarding future of Untouchables, 518; Interim Congress Government, 450, 454, 455; offer of Commonwealth status for, 331; WSC criticises Labour Government policy towards, 639–40
  Moorehead's *Montgomery* book, 542–3
  opinion of Arab–Israeli war, 1057
  returns to England (August 1945), 37
  The Second World War: final months of Wavell's command, 1268–70, 1288, 1313, 1393, 1402; 'Tiger' and Crete operations, 1131, 1141; WSC asks Ismay for wartime notes on British actions in Greece, 1026–7
  WSC criticises 'dull' biography of, 1026
Webb, Maurice, 1674–5, 1674 n.1, 2082–3, 2084, 2171
Webb, Sidney James, 447, 447 n.2, 797
Weizmann, Chaim
  biographical information, 433 n.1
  Elath meets with, 1879
  foreword for Weizmann's autobiography, 1481, 1481 n.2, 1484, 1486
  Israel: British policy towards, 1311; British recognition of, 1741–2, 1761; British support for Jewish National Home in Palestine, 951; Israeli relations with the Western world, 1303; Jordan and Israel, Government Decision (Oral Answers), 1737; Weizmann invites WSC to visit, 1767
  Palestine: Amery suggests WSC respond to Weizmann's *Times* interview, 1294–5; British policy towards, 1291; Palestine and Anglo-American relations, 436–7
  Weizmann Forest in Israel, 2028, 2031
  WSC praises, 433, 436, 437 n.1, 1867
  WSC thanks for telegram, 1322
Weizsäcker, Ernst Heinrich Freiherr von
  biographical information, 1176 n.3
  Magee asks WSC for statement for von Weizsäcker's trial, 1176–9, 1200, 1201, 1213
  role in Nazi extermination of Jews, 1222–3, 1223 n.5, 1341–2
  trial verdict, 1391–2
  WSC's statement regarding, 1202

Wellesley, Arthur (Duke of Wellington), 446, 446 n.3, 1056, 1056 n.3
Wentworth, Lady (Judith Anne Dorothea Blunt), 2124, 2124 n.2
Werth, Alexander, 512, 512 n.1
Western Union (European Army)
  composition of, 1939–40, 2149–50, 2151
  defence of Western Europe, 1757–8, 1758 n.1, 1766–7, 1775, 1784–5, 1795–6, 1829–32, 1863–4, 1911, 1933–4, 1933 n.1, 1971, 2041–3
  Eisenhower's Command of, 1970, 2122, 2149–50
  German participation in, 1275–6, 1942–3, 1953, 2122–3
  manpower estimates and preparedness, 1808–9, 1810–17
  Military Committee, 1414
  proposals for, 1829–32, 1833–4, 1837–8, 1839, 1839–40, 1840, 1840–1, 1841 n.1, 1845–6, 1862–4, 1911
  Smuts sees as foundation stone of future world structure, 1422
  US involvement in, 1273, 1361–3, 2081
  WSC voices support for, 1649, 1752, 2106, 2163
Westminster College, Missouri
  McCluer invites WSC to deliver Green Lectures, 90–1, 128
  Truman encourages WSC to speak at, 113
  WSC plans speech at, 156–7, 160, 163–4, 165, 212–13, 213
Westminster, Duchess of (Anne Winifred Sullivan Grosvenor), 764, 764 n.3
Westminster, Duke of (Hugh Richard Arthur Grosvenor), ('Bendor'), 92 n.2, 764, 1590, 1797–8
Westminster Gardens, 12–13, 27–8, 47
Weygand, Maxime, 1264, 1264 n.1, 1332, 1410
Wheeler, John Neville, 554, 554 n.2
Whitaker, Robert Frederick Edward, 764, 764 n.4
Whitbread, Henry
  biographical information, 51 n.1
  Chartwell farm wages, 1011–12
  Chartwell renovations: Fish Pool instructions, 131–2; painting instructions, 816; restoration of landscape and grounds, 51, 51 n.1, 181, 685, 845, 846, 892–4, 905–6, 912, 916
Whitehead, Joshua Baxter, 1997, 1997 n.1
Whiteley, William, 25, 25 n.1, 1259, 1672
Whitman, Walter, 558, 558 n.2, 1779
Whyte, Maryott ('Cousin Moppett', 'Nana'), 12, 12 n.5, 28, 43–4, 181
Wigram, Ralph Follett, 730, 730 n.4
Wilde, Oscar, 1082, 1082 n.1

Index

Wildman-Lushington, Godfrey Edward, 1849, 1849 n.1
Wilhelm (Emperor of Germany), 121, 121 n.1
Wilhelmina (Queen of the Netherlands)
  biographical information, 118 n.1
  Hague Conference, 1009
  WSC recommends painting as hobby, 1517
  WSC sends copy of *Their Finest Hour* to, 1517
  WSC thanks for gift of casket of letters written by John Churchill (1st Duke of Marlborough), 118, 322
  WSC thanks for hospitality and kindness, 334, 338
William de Zwijger, 322, 322 n.1
William III, King, 322, 322 n.2, 1043
William IV, King, 260, 260 n.3
Williams, Edward John ('Ted'), 1550, 1550 n.2
Williams, Sir Herbert Geraint, 444, 444 n.1
Williams, Michael Sanigear, 731, 731 n.1
Williams, Thomas, 47 n.1, 475–6
Willkie, Wendell Lewis, 1007, 1007 n.1
Wilmot, John, 918–20, 918 n.1
Wilson, Charles McMoran: *see* Moran, Lord (formerly Sir Charles Wilson)
Wilson, Geoffrey, 1401, 1401 n.2
Wilson, Sir Henry Maitland ('Jumbo'), 298–9, 298 n.1, 401–2, 1269
Wilson, Horace John, 1220, 1220 n.1
Wilson, (James) Harold
  biographical information, 131 n.1
  recollects WSC's essence as Parliamentarian, 2058–9
  resigns as President of the Board of Trade (April 1951), 2057, 2058, 2070, 2082
  WSC requests larger table for Opposition Consultative Committee, 131
Wilson, Richard John McMoran, 1219, 1219 n.2, 1220, 1401
Wilson, Thomas Woodrow, 270, 270 n.2, 379
Winant, John Gilbert ('Gil'), 128 n.1, 157, 160, 1544, 1823
Windsor, Duchess of (Wallis Warfield), 143–5, 143 n.3, 337, 1819
Windsor, Duke of
  biographical information, 143 n.2
  letter from WSC in memoirs of, 1521, 1819–20
  plans to study Anglo-American relations, 156, 156 n.1
  praises The Sinews of Peace (March 1946 WSC speech), 309–10
  proposed British Embassy job in America, 143–5, 168, 310, 337
  WSC describes Shadow Cabinet stance on US loan to England, 168
  WSC thanks for copy of memoirs, 2091–2
  WSC thanks for hospitality and friendship, 1167–8
Wingate, Francis Reginald, 1261–2, 1261 n.3, 1262 n.2
Winterton, Lady (Cecilia Monica Wilson), 450, 450 n.1
Winterton, Lord (Edward Turnour)
  biographical information, 430 n.4
  Commons Chamber reopening, 1912
  Defence Memorandum discussions with Attlee, 1431
  in the desert with Lawrence, 430
  India Resolution regarding fate of minorities and Indian States, 443, 450
  Jordan and Israel, Government Decision (Oral Answers), 1738–9
  United States of Europe proposals, 803
Wise, Alfred Roy, 774, 774 n.3
Woermann, Ernst, 1223, 1223 n.3
Wolfe, James, 1142, 1142 n.2
women
  Central Council of the Women's Advisory Committee of the Conservative Party (April 1948 WSC speech), 1013–21
  Government proposals to alleviate hardships and inconveniences of housewives, 540
  Widow's Pensions, 480
  women's labour issues, 1020
  Women's Land Army ('Land Girls'), 43, 43 n.3
  working class reception of WSC's Fuel and Power Crisis speech, 621
Woodburn, Arthur, 973, 973 n.1, 1082–3, 1420, 1490
Wood, Charles Carlyle
  biographical information, 1174 n.3
  The Second World War: dates format, 1390, 1494–5; feedback and suggested edits for, 1174–5; index corrections, 1342; work space at WSC's Hyde Park home, 2028–9, 2029–30, 2030, 2030 n.1
Wood, Edward Frederick Lindley: *see* Halifax, Lord (Edward Frederick Lindley Wood)
Wood, James, 947–8, 947 n.1
Wood, Kingsley, 108, 108 n.2
Woolton, Lord (Frederick James Marquis)
  biographical information, 42 n.2
  at Chartwell, 1590
  Conservative Party: by-elections results and candidates, 553, 596; Consultative Committee, 1267, 1713; economic policies, 1070; Party statement (1951), 2148; political broadcasts on the BBC, 2034; post-election strategy (1950), 1720, 1744, 1908; West Houghton by-election, 2098, 2098 n.1; Woolton suggested as Conservative Party Chairman, 288, 289, 396–7; Woolton–Teviot agreement, 1266–7, 1267 n.1; WSC forms new

Woolton, Lord (Frederick James Marquis) *(continued)*
  Conservative Party *(continued)*
    Government (1951), 2230; WSC invites to join Shadow Cabinet, 42; WSC plans Primrose League address, 516; WSC praises Woolton, 793, 1103, 1533–4; WSC proposes anti-Labour Government propaganda, 442; WSC seeks good Conservative relations with National Liberal Party, 440, 761, 1821; WSC suggests new Union Party, 440, 444
  Eisenhower's 'Challenge of Our Time' speech, 2108, 2109–10
  employment, 795, 1018
  food: Conservative Party policies, 1595; food shortages in England, 206–7; war-time food administration in England, 361; welfare foods, 1017
  Pound Sterling devaluation, 1536
  Voluntary Schools in England and Wales, 2194
Wootton-Davies, James Henry, 188, 188 n.1, 190, 208
Wyatt, Woodrow Lyle, 1138, 1138 n.1

Xoxe, Koci, 1572, 1572 n.1

Yalta Agreement, 202, 202–6, 207, 234
Yalta Conference, 667, 1351, 2076–8
Young, Arthur Stewart Leslie, 596, 596 n.2
Younger, Kenneth Gilmour, 604, 604 n.1, 1736–9
Yugoslavia
  British policy towards, 501–2
  refuses to sign peace treaty with Italy, 509
  refuses US request to provide statements in support of Mihailović, 295–6
  Russian delivery of winter clothing to Yugoslav Army, 546
  Tito's leadership of, 1101
  UN Security Council membership, 1571–2
  WSC meets with Popović and Djilas, 1994–5, 1996, 1996 n.3
  WSC seeks British Government support for fair trial for Mihailović, 287, 290, 295–6

Zachariadis, Nikos, 855, 855 n.2
Zadeikis, Povilas, 265, 268, 268 n.1, 280, 295
Zarubin, Georgiy Nikolaevich, 731–2, 731 n.4, 731 n.5, 733
Zilliacus, Konni, 644, 644 n.1, 645, 1272–3, 1283, 1451